CHI 2014
One of a CHInd

Conference Proceedings

Toronto, Canada | April 26 – May 1, 2014

Association for Computing Machinery

SIGCHI

The 32nd Annual ACM Conference on Human Factors in Computing Systems

Association for
Computing Machinery

Advancing Computing as a Science & Profession

The Association for Computing Machinery
2 Penn Plaza, Suite 701
New York, New York 10121-0701

ISBN: 978-1-4503-2473-1 (Digital)

ISBN: 978-1-4503-3290 -3 (Print)

Additional copies may be ordered prepaid from:

ACM Order Department
PO Box 30777
New York, NY 10087-0777, USA

Phone: 1-800-342-6626 (USA and Canada)
+1-212-626-0500 (Global)
Fax: +1-212-944-1318
E-mail: acmhelp@acm.org
Hours of Operation: 8:30 am – 4:30 pm ET

Printed in the USA

Welcome to CHI 2014!

CHI is more than a conference, it is an international community of researchers and practitioners who want to make a difference. Everything we do is focused on uncovering, critiquing and celebrating radically new ways for people and technology to evolve together. People in their everyday contexts, in diverse regions of the world, from very different backgrounds, with alternative outlooks on life drive this innovation. As you take part in the conference sessions we really hope you will experience how powerful this people-centred approach to technological transformation can be. CHI as a conference is now in its 32nd year and has grown to become the premier international forum on human-computer interaction, gathering us all to share innovative interactive insights that shape people's lives. CHI draws together a multidisciplinary community from around the globe.

Our great strength is our ability to bring together students and experts, researchers and practitioners, scientists, designers and engineers, drawing from their rich perspectives to create new visions of humancomputer interaction. This year's conference theme is One of a CHInd. We chose this nearly two years ago as we began planning for this event. It has helped us focus our efforts and we hope you will use it to keep your eyes open to the bigger picture amongst all the excitement, range of presentations and activities at the conference.

CHI 2014 is One of CHInd because it is a celebration of the conference's one of a kind diversity; from the broad range of backgrounds of its attendees, to the diverse spectrum of communities and fields that the conference and its research have an impact on. CHI 2014 will take place at the Metro Toronto Convention Centre in Toronto, Canada, a city itself known for its one of a kind cultural diversity. But, CHI 2014 is more than a celebration of the diversity of our community and conference setting.

We hope that this year's event, more than anything, reminds you that the "people," "participants," "users" or "humans" that you hear described throughout this week are actually uniquely wonderful individuals full of hopes, concerns, joys and frustrations. CHI is here to serve all of these one of a kinds.

CHI 2014 features two outstanding keynote speakers: Booker prize winning author, Margaret Atwood and leading UX designer, Scott Jenson.

New for CHI 2014, we have Provoke! Wisdom! Impact! plenary talks first thing each morning on Tuesday, Wednesday and Thursday. Come along, join the crowd and be energised by our speakers who will each bring in their experience of the Big Picture to inspire us. The talks will be short - twenty minutes - and then the rest of the day's programme will begin.

We are also delighted to host a timely retrospective exhibition on wearable technology curated by Thad Starner and Clint Zeagler. CHI 2014 also includes two days of focused workshops and four days of technical content, including CHI's prestigious technical program, with 16 parallel sessions of rigorously reviewed research Papers, engaging Panels, Case Studies and Special Interest Groups (SIGs), an extensive Course program and invited talks from SIGCHI's award winners: Steve Whittaker, Gillian Grampton Smith and Richard Ladner.

We also host student research, design, and game competitions, provocative alt.chi presentations and last-minute SIGs for discussing current topics. Interactivity hands-on demonstrations showcase the best of interactive technology. We also highlight over 241 Work-In-Progress posters: this year we have added some features to these sessions to better help you get the most out of the exciting, early stage work on show; do go along and engage with the authors about their work. Evening events include the CHI 2014 conference reception, Sponsors and University events, local performances and the Job Fair.

We received over 3200 submissions and accepted nearly 1000 that will appear in the ACM Digital Library. To help you navigate through this immense program, there are a number of online and digital resources from the conference website to our mobile apps. You can also browse the videos, papers and extended abstracts on the CHI 2014 USB Key. But, CHI 2014 is about being in Toronto so perhaps the best way to select from and experience the event is by asking for pointers and chatting with your fellow attendees, our wonderful student volunteers, the information desk helpers or any of this year's committee.

We are all here to make your experience as useful and enjoyable as possible. We are deeply indebted to our vast number of volunteers, without whom CHI 2014 would not be possible, including over 3800 reviewers, over 180 senior members of the program committee, nearly 100 members of the CHI 2014 conference committee and, of course, the more than 180 student volunteers. We thank you all! We are honored and excited by the opportunity to host CHI 2014 and wish you a productive and enjoyable stay in Toronto!

Matt Jones,
Swansea University, Wales, UK
CHI 2014 General Conference Co-Chair

Philippe Palanque
Université Paul Sabatier
CHI 2014 General Conference Co-Chair

Albrecht Schmidt
University of Stuttgart, Germany
CHI 2014 Technical Program Co-Chair

Tovi Grossman
Autodesk Research, Canada
CHI 2014 Technical Program Co-Chair

From ACM SIGCHI's President and Vice President for Conferences

SIGCHI is proud to sponsor the premier annual conference in the field of human-computer interaction. We are extremely grateful to the CHI 2014 Conference Chairs Matt Jones and Philippe Palanque , to Technical Program Chairs Albrecht Schmidt and Tovi Grossman, and to their wonderful crew, who succeeded to build an impressive program and experience.

CHI 2014 is back in Toronto, Canada, returning to the same location of CHI 1987, 5 years after the first conference, on Human Factors in Computer Systems, in Gaithersburg, MD, March 1982. That first conference in Gaithersburg drew over 900 attendees, and since then CHI, with the official name: "ACM Conference on Human Factors in Computing Systems", has continued to grow and broaden its range of topics and contributing disciplines: the founding psychologists and software engineers began to meet new visions from ethnography, sociology, communication sciences and arts, among others. Relevant industries, as well as research institutes and academia, showed an increasing - and often long-lasting - interest and involvement (through volunteers and through sponsorship for conference expenses).

CHI is an ideal forum for people to meet formally as well as informally, to exchange knowledge and views, to share experiences, and to learn. The CHI conference brings together professionals from research and practice; people from industry, academia, and from government; long-term veterans of HCI, young professionals and students; all in an environment designed to encourage interaction. We invite you to actively participate in that interaction: introduce yourself to people, interact with presenters and speakers, renew old friendships and make new ones.

CHI is organized on behalf of ACM's Special Interest Group on Computer-Human Interaction (SIGCHI), an international community of professionals who share an interest in the many diverse facets of HCI. SIGCHI is committed both to advancing the field of HCI, to facilitate exchange of information within the SIGCHI community, and to support students to enter the domain.

The CHI conference is arguably the single most visible activity of SIGCHI, but we also sponsor and support a wide range of specialized conferences and workshops in areas ranging from interactive systems design to user interface technology to computer-supported cooperative work to "intelligent" user interfaces. Visit the SIGCHI website at **http://www.sigchi.org** to find our conference schedule, listing upcoming as well as past conferences.

SIGCHI and ACM produce some of the most respected publications in the field. All members receive interactions, a highly-acclaimed magazine covering the broad field of HCI and user interface design. ACM Transactions on Computer-Human Interactions (ToCHI), now in its 21st year, is our flagship journal - a quarterly publication with the top-quality archival research aimed at researchers and those translating research into practice.

SIGCHI is truly an international organization, with over 30 local chapters and 3 student chapters in 25 countries on 6 continents. We encourage all SIGCHI members to join their local chapter - or if there isn't one in your area, we would love to help you create one. And don't forget virtual communities! SIGCHI hosts dozens of electronic mailing lists on topics ranging from HCI and the Web, to HCI educations, to public policy and beyond. Those lists range from dozens of subscribers to thousands, and are an excellent way to keep up with the field and with friends and colleagues.

Finally, on behalf of ACM SGICHI, we again want to thank the conference committee and all of the hundreds of volunteers who make this conference possible. Their work makes this a rewarding experience for all of us.

Gerrit C. van der Veer
SIGCHI President

John "Scooter" Morris
SIGCHI Vice-President for Conferences

CHI 2014 Papers and Notes Chairs' Welcome

The CHI Papers and Notes programme is continuing to grow and this year we received more than 2000 submissions for the first time. We are pleased that CHI is still the leading conference for research in humancomputer interaction.

CHI 2014 continued the use of subcommittees to manage the review process. Authors selected the subcommittee they believed was best qualified to review their work: Due to the changing pattern of submissions we split some subcommittees into more manageable sizes and coalesced others. We are pleased with the subcommittee process: By dividing the work, each paper received much more careful discussion than would otherwise have been possible.

This year we considered 2036 submissions, including 1428 papers and 608 notes, representing a 4% growth over last year. We accepted 465 submissions (23%): 382 papers and 83 notes.

The CHI review process demands a tremendous amount of work from all areas of the human computer interaction community. As co-chairs of the process, we are amazed at the ability of the community to organize itself to accomplish this task. We would like to thank the 2866 individual reviewers for their careful consideration of these papers. We also deeply appreciate the huge amount of time donated to this process by the 205-member program committee, who paid their own way to attend the face-to-face program committee meeting, an event larger than the average ACM conference.

We are proud of the work of the CHI 2014 program committee and hope that you enjoy these papers and notes, which represent the best research in human-computer interaction.

Stephen Brewster,
Glasgow University
CHI 2014 Papers and Notes Chairs

Andy Cockburn,
University of Canterbury
CHI 2014 Papers and Notes Chairs

Table of Contents

Image and Animation Authoring

Session Chair: Tomer Moscovich, *Lab126*

Studying and Designing Gameplay

Session Chair: Carl Gutwin, *University of Saskatchewan*

Force Input and Haptic Feedback

Session Chair: Ian Oakley, *Ulsan National Institute of Science and Technology*

Hackerspaces, Making and Breaking

Session Chair: Manfred Tscheligi, *University of Salzburg & AIT Austrian Institute of Technology*

April 29th, 2014 – Volume 2a

Interactive Visualization and Visual Elements

Session Chair: Eytan Adar , *University of Michigan*

Understanding and Designing Games

Session Chair: Lennart Nacke , *University of Ontario Institute of Technology*

Personal Values and Preferences

Session Chair: Katharina Reinecke , *University of Michigan*

April 29th, 2014 – Volume 2b

Learning and Education

Session Chair: Deborah Tatar , *Virginia Polytechnic Institute and State University*

April 30th, 2014 – Volume 3a

Telepresence and Connecting over Video

Session Chair: Kori Inkpen , *Microsoft Research*

Exergame Design

Session Chair: Sean Munson , *University of Washington*

April 30th, 2014 – Volume 3b

Learning and Games

Session Chair: Amy Ogan , *Carnegie Mellon University*

Persuasive Technologies and Applications

Session Chair: Erin Cherry , *University of Rochester*

Whole Body Sensing and Interaction

Session Chair: Otmar Hilliges , *ETH Zurich*

Novel Mobile Displays and Devices

Session Chair: Clifton Forlines , *Draper Laboratory*

HCI Paradigms: Past, Present and Future

Session Chair: Jeffrey Bardzell , *Indiana University Bloomington*

CHI 2014 Conference Organization

General Chair: Matt Jones, *Swansea University, Wales, UK*
Philippe Palanque, *Université Paul Sabatier, France*

Technical Program

Technical Program Co-Chairs: Albrecht Schmidt, *University of Stuttgart , Germany*
Tovi Grossman, *Autodesk Research, Canada*

Technical Program Chair Assistant: Michael Glueck, *Autodesk Research, Canada*

Papers and Notes: Stephen Brewster, *University of Glasgow, UK*
Andy Cockburn, *University of Canterbrury, New Zealand*

Panels: Gillian Hayes, *University of California, Irvine, USA*
Khai Truong, *University of Toronto, Canada*

Case Studies: Jonathan Arnowitz, *Google, USA*
DJ Hoets, *SAP, USA*
Michael Arent, *Rivendel Consulting, USA*
KAIST, Republic of Korea in Henderson, *Flipside, The Netherlands*

Courses: Regina Bernhaupt, *Ruwido, France*
Elizabeth Churchill, *eBay Research Labs, USA*

Interactivity: Steven Benford, *University of Nottingham, UK*
Julie Rico Williamson, *University of Glasgow, Scotland, UK*

Video Showcase: Jinwook Seo, *Seoul National University, Korea*
Nicolas Roussel, *INRIA, France*

SIGs: Enrico Rukzio, *Ulm University, Germany*
Henry Duh, *University of Tasmania, Australia*

Doctoral Consortium: Manfred Tscheligi, *University of Salzburg, Austria*
Katherine Isbister, *New York University, USA*

Workshops: Nadir Weibel, *University of California, San Diego, USA*
Juergen Steimle, *Max Planck Institute, Germany*

Works in Progress: Shelly Farnham, *Microsoft, USA*
Shamsi Iqbal, *Microsoft, USA*
Shaun Lawson, *University of Lincoln, USA*

Student Research Competition: Celine Latulipe, *UNC Charlotte, USA*
Floyd Muller, *University in Melbourne, Australia*

Student Design Competition: Thecla Schiphorst, *Simon Fraser University, Canada*
Youn-Kyung Lim, *KAIST, Korea*

Student Game Competition:	Seth Cooper, *University of Washington, USA* Alessandro Canossa, *Northeastern University, USA*
alt.chi:	Daniela Rosner, *University of Washington, USA* Lilly Irani, *UC San Diego, USA*
TOCHI Papers:	Jeffrey Nichols, *IBM Research, USA*
Best of CHI Awards:	Daniel Wigdor, *University of Toronto, Canada* Karyn Moffatt, *McGill School of Information, Canada*

Spotlights

Spotlights Chairs:	Kristina Höök, *Royal Institute of Technology, Sweden* Ed Chi, *Google Research, USA*
Games & Entertainment:	Magy Seif El-Nasr, *Northeastern University, USA* Heather Desurvire, *Behavioristics, Inc, USA* Lennart Nacke, *University of Ontario, Canada*
HCI For Development (HCI4D):	Melissa Densmore, *Microsoft Research, USA* Matthew Kam, *Carnegie Mellon University, USA* Ban Al-Ani, *University of California, Irvine, USA*
Interaction Science:	Andrew Howes, *University of Birmingham, UK* Benjamin R. Cowan, *University of Birmingham, UK* Stephen J. Payne, *University of Oxford, UK* Paul Cairns, *University of York, UK* Christian P. Janssen, *The Smith-Kettlewell Eye Research Institute, USA* Anna L Cox, *University College London, UK* Anthony J. Hornof, *University of Oregon, USA* Peter Pirolli, *Palo Alto Research Center (PARC), USA*
Making Cultures:	Jeffrey Bardzell, *University Bloomington, USA* Shaowen Bardzell, *Shaowen Bardzell, USA* Carl DiSalvo, *Georgia Institute of Technology, USA* Ann Light, *Northumbria University, UK* Daniela Rosner, *University of Washington, USA*
Art and Interaction:	David England, *John Moores University, UK* Joceyn Spence, *University of Surrey, UK*

Operations

Student Volunteer Coordinators:	Lindsay Reynolds, *Cornell University, USA* Jon Haber, *University of Calgary, Canada*
Technology Liaisons:	Scooter Morris, *University of California, San Francisco, USA* Sara Drenner, *University of Minnesota-Twin Cities, USA*
Webmaster:	Liam Betsworth, *Swansea University, Wales, UK*

Social Media: Max Wilson, *Nottingham University, UK*
Katie Panciera, *University of Minnesota, USA*

Proceedings: Marco Winckler, *Université Paul Sabatier, France*
Yann Riche, *Microsoft, USA*
Stéphane Conversy, *ENAC, France*

Infrastructure Accessibility Chair: Jennifer Rode, *Drexel University, USA*

Digital Accessibility Chair: Jonathan Lazar, *Towson University, USA*

Community Sourcing & Scheduling: Paul André, *Facebook, USA*
Anant Bhardwaj, *MIT, USA*
Lydia Chilton, *University of Washington, USA*
Juho Kim, *MIT, USA*
Steven Dow, *Carnegie Mellon University, USA*
Rob Miller, *MIT, USA*
Haoqi Zhang, *Northwestern University, USA*

Mobile Apps: Stephen Oney, *Carnegie Mellon University, USA*
Eiji Hayashi, *Carnegie Mellon University, USA*
Jason Wiese, *Carnegie Mellon University, USA*
Célia Martinie, *Université Paul Sabatier, France*

Video Previews: Gene Golovchinsky *[in memory]*
Gonzalo Ramos, *University of Toronto, Canada*
Fanny Chevalier, *INRIA, France*

Conference Management: Janeé Pelletier, *Conference & Logistics Consultants, USA*
Allison Perrelli, *Conference & Logistics Consultants, USA*

Sponsors, Exhibits & Recruitment: Carol Klyver, *Foundations of Excellence, USA*

Registration: Yvonne Lopez, *Executive Events, Inc. USA*
Brooke Daley, *Executive Events, Inc. USA*

PCS Liaisons: Max van Kleek, *University of Southampton, UK*
Carol Klyver, *Foundations of Excellence, USA*
Scooter Morris, *University of California, San Francisco, USA*

Women's Breakfast Event: Allison Druin, *University of Maryland, USA*

CHI 2014 Papers and Notes Subcommittee & Associate Chairs

Subcommittee Chairs:

Mark Ackerman, *University of Michigan, USA*
Victoria Bellotti, *Xerox PARC, USA*
Laura Dabbish, *Carnegie Mellon University, USA*
Stephen Fairclough, *Liverpool John Moores University, UK*
Steven Feiner, *Columbia University, USA*
Jon Froelich, *University of Maryland, USA*
Vicki Hanson, *IBM Research, USA*
Jettie Hoonhout, *Philips Research, The Netherlands*
Hilary Hutchinson, *Google Research, USA*
Shahram Izadi, *Microsoft Research, UK*
David Kirk, *Newcastle University, UK*
Antonio Krueger, *DFKI, Germany*
Myriam Lewkowicz, *Université de Technologie de Troyes, France*
Youn-Kyung Lim, *KAIST, South Korea*
Joanna McGrenere, *University of British Columbia, Canada*
Bilge Mutlu, *University of Wisconsin-Madison, USA*
Fabio Paterno, *CNR ISTI, Italy*
Wanda Pratt, *University of Washington, USA*
mc schraefel, *University of Southampton, UK*
Sriram Subramanian, *University of Bristol, UK*
Bill Thies, *Microsoft Research, India*
Manfred Tscheligi, *CURE, Austria*
Ron Wakkary, *Simon Fraser University, Canada*
John Zimmerman, *Carnegie Mellon University, USA*

Associate Chairs: Eytan Adar, *University of Michigan, USA*
Jason Alexander, *Lancaster University, UK*
Paul André, *Carnegie Mellon University, USA*
Judd Antin, *Yahoo! Research, USA*
Alissa Antle, *Simon Fraser University, Canada*
Paul Aoki, *Intel Labs, USA*
Daniel Ashbrook, *Nokia Research Center Hollywood, USA*
Gabriela Avram, *University of Limerick, Ireland*
Brian Bailey, *University of Illinois, USA*
Lynne Baillie, *Glasgow Caledonian University, UK*
Ravin Balakrishnan, *University of Toronto, Canada*
Jeffrey Bardzell, *Indiana University Bloomington, USA*
Richard Beckwith, *Intel Research, USA*
Hrvoje Benko, *Microsoft Research, USA*
Timothy Bickmore, *Northeastern University, USA*
Jeffrey Bigham, *Carnegie Mellon University, USA*
Mark Blythe, *Northumbria University, UK*
Alexander Boden, *University of Siegen, Germany*
Sebastian Boring, *University of Copenhagen, Denmark*
Duncan Brumby, *University College London, UK*
A.j. Brush, *Microsoft Research, USA*
Andreas Bulling, *Max-Planck Institut Für Informatik, Germany*
Daniela Busse, *Samsung Research America (SRA), USA*
Andreas Butz, *Ludwig-Maximilians-Universität München, Germany*
John Canny, *UC Berkley, USA*
Xiang Cao, *Lenovo Research & Technology, China*
Erin Carroll, *University of Rochester, USA*
Nicholas Chen, *University of Maryland, UK*
Yunan Chen, *University of California, USA*
Coye Cheshire, *UC Berkeley, USA*
Fanny Chevalier, *University of Toronto, Canada*
Keith Cheverst, *Lancaster University, England, UK*
Luigina Ciolfi, *Sheffield Hallam University, UK*
Rob Comber, *Newcastle University, UK*
Lorrie Cranor, *Carnegie Mellon University, USA*
Scott Davidoff, *Jet Propulsion Laboratory, USA*
Antonella de Angeli, *University of Trento, Italy*
Alexander de Luca, *University of Munich, Germany*
Rogerio de Paula, *IBM Research, Brazil*
Marco de Sá, *Facebook, USA*
Morgan Dixon, *University of Washington, USA*
Steven Dow, *Carnegie Mellon University, USA*
Pierre Dragicevic, *INRIA, France*
Mark Dunlop, *University of Strathclyde, Scotland, UK*
Darren Edge, *Microsoft Research Asia, China*
Serge Egelman, *University of California, USA*
Niklas Elmqvist, *Purdue University, USA*
Ylva Fernaeus, *KTH, Sweden*
Clifton Forlines, *Draper Laboratory, USA*
Jodi Forlizzi, *Carnegie Mellon University, USA*
Zhiyong Fu, *Information Art and Design Department, China*
Dominic Furniss, *University College London, UK*
Susan Fussell, *Cornell University, USA*

Associate Chairs:

Krzysztof Gajos, *Harvard University, USA*
Luciano Gamberini, *University of Padova, Italy*
David Geerts, *KU Leuven, Belgium*
Darren Gergle, *Northwestern University, USA*
Jennifer Golbeck, *University of Maryland, USA*
Judith Good, *University of Sussex, UK*
Ning Gu, *Fudan University, China*
Tiago Guerreiro, *University of Lisbon, Portugal*
Mona Leigh Guha, *University of Maryland, USA*
Carl Gutwin, *University of Saskatchewan, Canada*
Mark Hancock, *University of Waterloo, Canada*
Beverly Harrison, *Yahoo! Labs, USA*
Steve Harrison, *Virginia Tech, USA*
Mike Hazas, *Lancaster University, UK*
Otmar Hilliges, *ETH Zurich, Switzerland*
Eve Hoggan, *Aalto University, Finland*
Jonathan Hook, *Newcastle University, UK*
Kasper Hornbæk, *University of Copenhagen, Denmark*
Eva Hornecker, *Bauhaus Universität Weimar, Germany*
Gary Hsieh, *University of Washington, USA*
Elaine Huang, *Georgia Institute of Technology, USA*
Jina Huh, *Information Studies, USA*
Faustina Hwang, *The University of Reading, UK*
Kori Inkpen, *Microsoft Research, USA*
Lilly Irani, *University of California, USA*
Pourang Irani, *University of Manitoba, Canada*
Petra Isenberg, *INRIA, France*
Michal Jacovi, *IBM Research Lab In Haifa, Israel*
Giulio Jacucci, *Aalto University, Finland*
Wendy Ju, *California College of the Arts, USA*
Evangelos Karapanos, *Madeira Interactive Technologies Institute, Portugal*
Abhijit Karnik, *University of Bristol, UK*
Judy Kay, *University of Sydney, Australia*
Patrick Gage Kelley, *Carnegie Mellon University, USA*
Aisling Kelliher, *Carnegie Mellon University, USA*
Julie Kientz, *University of Washington, USA*
David Kim, *Newcastle University, UK*
Jesper Kjeldskov, *Aalborg University, Denmark*
Predrag Klasnja, *University of Michigan, USA*
Per Ola Kristensson, *University of St Andrews, UK*
Effie Law, *ETH Zurich, UK*
Christopher Le Dantec, *Georgia Institute of Technology, USA*
Joonhwan Lee, *Seoul National University, South Korea*
Yang Li, *Google Research, USA*
Silvia Lindtner, *University of California, USA*
Kris Luyten, *Hasselt University - Tul - Iminds, Belgium*
Kent Lyons, *Yahoo, USA*
Nicolai Marquardt, *University College London, UK*
Paul Marshall, *University College London, UK*
Michael Massimi, *Microsoft Research, UK*
Marilyn Mcgee-Lennon, *University of Glasgow, UK*
David Mcgookin, *Heriot-Watt University, Scotland, UK*
Helena Mentis, *University of Maryland, USA*

Associate Chairs: Natasa Milic-Frayling, *Microsoft Research Ltd, UK*
Robert Miller, *The Pennsylvania State University, USA*
Karyn Moffatt, *McGill University, Canada*
Tom Moher, *University of Illinois at Chicago, USA*
Wendy Moncur, *University of Dundee, Scotland,*
Dan Morris, *Microsoft Research, USA*
Tomer Moscovich, *INRIA, France*
Ingrid Mulder, *Delft University of Technology, The Netherlands*
Michael Muller, *Alexander Von Humboldt Institute for Internet and Society, USA*
Jörg Müller, *University of Arts, Berlin, Germany*
Sean Munson, *University of Washington, USA*
Lennart Nacke, *University of Ontario Institute of Technology, Canada*
Michael Nebeling, *ETH Zurich, Switzerland*
Carman Neustaedter, *Simon Fraser University, Canada*
Jeffrey Nichols, *IBM Research, USA*
Ian Oakley, *Ulsan National Institute of Science and Technology, South Korea*
Marianna Obrist, *Newcastle University, UK*
William Odom, *Carnegie Mellon University, USA*
Amy Ogan, *Carnegie Mellon University, USA*
Patrick Olivier, *Newcastle University, UK*
Alex Olwal, *Royal Institute of Technology (KTH), USA*
Claire O'malley, *University of Nottingham, UK*
Antti Oulasvirta, *Max-Planck Institut Für Informatik, Germany*
Andrea Parker, *Northeastern University, USA*
Sameer Patil, *Aalto University, Finland*
Mark Perry, *Brunel University, UK*
Christopher Power, *University of York, UK*
Aaron Quigley, *University of St. Andrews, UK*
Chris Quintana, *University of Michigan, USA*
Emilee Rader, *Michigan State University, USA*
David Randall, *University of Siegen, UK*
Pei-Luen Patrick Rau, *Tsinghua University, China*
Stuart Reeves, *University of Nottingham, England*
Katharina Reinecke, *Harvard University, USA*
Anne Roudaut, *University of Bristol, Germany*
Mark Rouncefield, *Lancaster University, UK*
Daniel Russell, *Google, USA*
Nithya Sambasivan, *University of California, USA*
Corina Sas, *Lancaster University, UK*
Martina Angela Sasse, *University College London (UCL), UK*
Christina Satchell, *The University of Melbourne, Australia*
James Scott, *Microsoft Research, UK*
Andrew Sears, *Rochester Institute of Technology, USA*
Abigail Sellen, *Microsoft Research, UK*
N. Sadat Shami, *IBM Research, USA*
Rajinder Sodhi, *University of Illinois at Urbana-Champaign, USA*
Erin Solovey, *Drexel University, USA*
Danae Stanton Fraser, *University of Bath, UK*
Jürgen Steimle, *Massachusetts Institute of Technology, USA*
Wolfgang Stuerzlinger, *York University, Canada*
Hironobu Takagi, *IBM Research, Japan*
Yuichiro Takeuchi, *Sony Computer Science Laboratories, Japan*
Deborah Tatar, *Virginia Tech,*

Associate Chairs:

Jaime Teevan, *Microsoft Research, USA*
John Thomas, *IBM T.J. Watson Research Center, USA*
Melanie Tory, *University of Victoria, Canada*
Zachary Toups, *New Mexico State University, USA*Deborah Tatar, *Virginia Tech*
Elise Van Den Hoven, *University of Technology Sydney, Australia*
John Vines, *Newcastle University, UK*
Daniel Vogel, *University of Waterloo, Canada*
Amy Voida, *Indiana University, USA*
Annalu Waller, *University of Dundee, Scotland, UK*
Hao-Chuan Wang, *National Tsing Hua University, Taiwan*
Nadir Weibel, *University of California San Diego, USA*
Daniel Wigdor, *University of Toronto, Canada*
Lauren Wilcox, *Georgia Institute of Technology, USA*
Maria Wolters, *University of Edinburgh, UK*
Volker Wulf, *University of Siegen and Fraunhofer FIT, Germany*
Sarita Yardi Schoenebeck, *University of Michigan, USA*
Svetlana Yarosh, *AT&T Research Labs, USA*
Thorsten Zander, *TU Berlin, Germany*
Shengdong Zhao, *National University of Singapore, Singapore*
Michelle Zhou, *IBM Research - Almaden, USA*
Xiaomu Zhou, *Rutgers University, USA*

CHI 2014 Papers and Notes Reviewers

Konstantin Aal, *University of Siegen, Germany*
Parham Aarabi, *University of Toronto, Canada*
Francisco Abad, *Universitat Politècnica de València, Spain*
Julio Abascal, *University of the Basque Country, Spain*
Evgeniy Abdulin, *Texas State University, USA*
Saeed Abdullah, *Cornell University, USA*
Troy Abel, *Virginia Tech, USA*
Gregory Abowd, *Georgia Institute of Technology, USA*
Alessandro Acquisti, *Carnegie Mellon University, USA*
Lada Adamic, *University of Michigan, USA*
Anne Adams, *UCL Interaction Centre, USA*
Anne Adams, *Simplec, UK*
Dustin Adams, *University of California, USA*
Kim Adams, *University of Alberta, Canada*
Phil Adams, *Cornell University, USA*
Idris Adjerid, *Carnegie Mellon University, USA*
Rachel Adler, *Northeastern Illinois University, USA*
Tamara Adlin, *USA*
Daniel Afergan, *Tufts University, USA*
Ana Afonso, *Universidade de Lisboa, Portugal*
Stefan Agamanolis, *Akron Children's Hospital, USA*
Maneesh Agrawala, *University of California, USA*
David Ahlström, *Alpen-Adria Universität Klagenfurt, Austria*
Salman Ahmad, *Stanford University, USA*
Teemu Ahmaniemi, *Nokia Research Center, Finland*
June Ahn, *University of Maryland, USA*
Aino Ahtinen, *VTT Technical Research Centre, Finland*
David Akers, *Stanford University, USA*
Devdatta Akhawe, *UC Berkeley, USA*
Abdullah Al Mahmud, *Delft University of Technology, Netherlands*
Vicent Alabau, *Universidad Politécnica de Valencia (UPV), Spain*
Amro Al-Akkad, *Fraunhofer Institute for Applied Information Technology (FIT), Germany*
Gazihan Alankus, *Washington University In St. Louis, USA*
Turadg Aleahmad, *Coursera, USA*
Saleem Alhabash, *Michigan State University, USA*
Abir Al-Hajri, *UBC, Canada*
Dzmitry Aliakseyeu, *Philips Research, The Netherlands*
Doris Allhutter, *Institute of Technology Assessment, Austria*
Sonya Allin, *University of Toronto, Canada*
Norman Alm, *University of Dundee, UK*
Abdullah Al-Mahmud, *Delft University of Technology, The Netherlands*
Omar Alonso, *Microsoft, USA*
Basak Alper, *University of California Santa Barbara, USA*
Mohammad Al-Smadi, *Tallinn University, Estonia*
Florian Alt, *University of Munich, Germany*
Bashar Altakrouri, *University of Luebeck, Germany*
Reem Alzahabi, *Michigan State University, USA*
Saleema Amershi, *Microsoft Research, USA*

Morgan Ames, *Stanford University, USA*
Oliver Amft, *TU Eindhoven, Netherlands*
Farshid Amirabdollahian, *University of Hertfordshire, UK*
Swamy Ananthanarayan, *University of Colorado, USA*
Margarita Anastassova, *CEA, France*
Nazanin Andalibi, *Drexel University, USA*
Erik Andersen, *University of Washington, USA*
Fraser Anderson, *University of Alberta, Canada*
Ken Anderson, *Intel Corporation, USA*
Nazareno Andrade, *Universidade Federal de Campina Grande, Brazil*
Adrienne Andrew, *University of Washington, USA*
Christopher Andrews, *Virginia Polytechnic Institute and State University, USA*
Sean Andrist, *University of Wisconsin--Madison, USA*
Marvin Andujar, *Clemson University, USA*
Leonardo Angelini, *University of Applied Sciences Western Switzerland, Svizzera*
Michelle Annett, *University of Alberta, Canada*
Craig Anslow, *Victoria University of Wellington, New Zealand*
Lisa Anthony, *University of Florida, USA*
Thomas Apperley, *The University of New South Wales, Australia*
Caroline Appert, *Université Paris-Sud, France*
Bruno Araujo, *INESC-ID, Portugal*
Daniel Archambault, *Swansea University, UK*
Carmelo Ardito, *University of Bari, Italy*
Ahmed Arif, *Ryerson University, Canada*
John Arnott, *University of Dundee, UK*
Rosa Arriaga, *Georgia Institute of Technology, USA*
Kate Arrington, *Lehigh University, USA*
Thierry Artieres, *Université Pierre Et Marie Curie, France*
Mariam Asad, *Georgia Institute of Technology, USA*
Chieko Asakawa, *IBM Research - Tokyo, Japan*
Felix-Robinson Aschoff, *University of Zurich, Switzerland*
Debi Ashenden, *Cranfield University, UK*
Maryam Ashoori, *IBM, Canada*
Ilhan Aslan, *Universität Salzburg, Austria*
Zeina Atrash, *Northwestern University, USA*
Alan Au, *University of Washington, USA*
Anne Aula, *Google, USA*
Hane Aung, *University College London, UK*
Nikolaos Avouris, *University of Patras, Greece*
Daniel Avrahami, *Intel, USA*
Katerina Avramides, *London Knowledge Lab, UK*
Yuji Ayatsuka, *Koozyt, Japan*
Matthew Aylett, *Cereproc Ltd., UK*
Ruth Aylett, *Heriot-Watt University, UK*
Mobolaji Ayoade, *Glasgow Caledonian University, UK*
Phillip Ayoub, *Pennsylvania State University, USA*
Yadid Ayzenberg, *MIT, USA*
Shiri Azenkot, *University of Washington, USA*
Maryam Azh, *National University of Singapore, Singapore*
Tamara Babaian, *Bentley College, USA*
Chris Baber, *The University of Birmingham, UK*

Benjamin Bach, *INRIA, France*
Paula Bach, *The Pennsylvania State University, USA*
Myroslav Bachynskyi, *Max-Planck Institut Für Informatik, Germany*
Jonathan Back, *University College London, UK*
Maribeth Back, *FX Palo Alto Laboratory, USA*
Norm Badler, *University of Pennsylvania, USA*
Sangwon Bae, *Yonsei University, Seoul*
Seok-Hyung Bae, *KAIST, Republic of Korea*
Ronald Baecker, *University of Toronto, Canada*
Naveen Bagalkot, *IT University of Copenhagen, Denmark*
Zhen Bai, *University of Cambridge, UK*
Gilles Bailly, *CNRS, France*
Ryan Baker, *Teachers College, USA*
Suzanne Bakken, *Columbia University, USA*
Saskia Bakker, *Eindhoven University of Technology, The Netherlands*
Eytan Bakshy, *Facebook, USA*
Madeline Balaam, *Newcastle University, UK*
Aruna Balakrishnan, *Google, USA*
Guha Balakrishnan, *MIT, USA*
Matthias Baldauf, *FTW Telecommunications Research Center, Austria*
Rebecca Balebako, *Carnegie Mellon University, USA*
Elizabeth Bales, *University of Washington, USA*
Robert Ball, *Stephen F. KAIST, Republic of Korea in State University, USA*
Stinne Ballegaard, *KORA, Denmark*
Till Ballendat, *University of Munich, Germany*
Liam Bannon, *University of Limerick, Ireland*
Nikola Banovic, *Carnegie Mellon University, USA*
Francesco Banterle, *ISTI-CNR, Italy*
Xuan Bao, *Duke University, USA*
Evan Barba, *Georgetown University, USA*
Simone Barbosa, *Pontifical Catholic University of Rio de Janeiro (PUC-Rio), Brasil*
Jakob Bardram, *IT University of Copenhagen, Denmark*
Shaowen Bardzell, *Indiana University Bloomington, USA*
Javier Bargas-Avila, *Google, Switzerland*
Louise Barkhuus, *Stockholm University, Sweden*
Connelly Barnes, *Princeton University, USA*
Douglas Barnes
Pippin Barr, *University of Malta, Malta*
Barbara Barricelli, *University of West London, UK*
Barbara Barry, *MIT Media Lab, USA*
Tom Bartindale, *Newcastle University, UK*
Christoph Bartneck, *University of Canterbury, New Zealand*
Thomas Bartoschek, *University of Münster, Germany*
Lyn Bartram, *Simon Fraser University, Canada*
Santosh Basapur, *Illinois Institute of Technology, USA*
Rahul Basole, *Georgia Institute of Technology, USA*
Arianna Bassoli, *London School of Economics, UK*
Archer Batcheller, *University of Michigan, USA*
Scott Bateman, *University of Prince Edward Island, Canada*
Oliver Bates, *Lancaster University, UK*
Agathe Battestini, *Nokia, USA*
Olivier Bau, *Samsung Research America, USA*
Patrick Baudisch, *Hasso Plattner Institute, Germany*

Christine Bauer, *Vienna University of Economics and Business, Austria*
Jared Bauer, *University of Washington, USA*
Lujo Bauer, *Carnegie Mellon University, USA*
Eric Baumer, *Cornell University, USA*
Gordon Baxter, *University of St Andrews, UK*
Philip Beaman, *University of Reading, UK*
David Beattie, *Glasgow Caledonian University, Scotland, Uk*
Michel Beaudouin-Lafon, *Université Paris-Sud, France*
Elke Beck, *University of Salzburg, Austria*
S. Ann Becker, *Florida Tech, USA*
Benjamin Bederson, *University of Maryland, USA*
Roman Bednarik, *University of Eastern Finland, Finland*
Jenay Beer, *University of South Carolina, USA*
Andrew Begel, *Microsoft Research, USA*
Marios Belk, *University of Cyprus, Cyprus*
Rachel Bellamy, *IBM Research, USA*
Francesco Bellotti, *University of Genoa, Italy*
Raquel Benbunan-Fich, *Baruch College, USA*
Peter Benda, *The University of Melbourne, Australia*
Zinaida Benenson, *University of Erlangen-Nuremberg, Germany*
Steve Benford, *University of Nottingham, UK*
Mike Bennett, *Microsoft, USA*
Peter Bennett, *University of Bristol, UK*
Frank Bentley, *Motorola Mobility Inc., USA*
David Benyon, *Edinburgh Napier University, UK*
François Bérard, *CLIPS-IMAG, France*
Bettina Berendt, *KU Leuven, Belgium*
Alistair Beresford, *University of Cambridge, England*
Ofer Bergman, *Bar-Ilan University, Israel*
Kirsten Bergmann, *Bielefeld University, Germany*
Shane Bergsma, *Johns Hopkins University, USA*
Joanna Bergstrom-Lehtovirta, *Helsinki Institute for Information Technology HIIT, Finland*
Shlomo Berkovsky, *NICTA, Australia*
Gunilla Berndtsson, *Ericsson AB, Sweden*
Regina Bernhaupt, *IRIT, France*
Olav Bertelsen, *Aarhus University, Denmark*
Florent Berthaut, *INRIA, France*
Andrew Besmer, *UNC Charlotte, USA*
Michael Best, *Georgia Institute of Technology, USA*
Katrien Beuls, *Vrije Universiteit Brussel, Belgium*
Chris Bevan, *University of Bath, UK*
Nigel Bevan, *Professional Usability Services, UK*
Anastasia Bezerianos, *Université de Paris-Sud, France*
Konstantin Beznosov, *University of British Columbia, Canada*
Anant Bhardwaj, *Massachusetts Institute of Technology, USA*
Samit Bhattacharya, *IIT Guwahati, India*
Xiaojun Bi, *Google, USA*
Andrea Bianchi, *KAIST, Republic of Korea*
Nadia Bianchi-Berthouze, *University College London, UK*
Peter Bibby, *University of Nottingham, UK*
Nicola Bidwell, *CSIR-Meraka, South Africa*
Gerald Bieber, *Fraunhofer IGD, Germany*

Ralf Biedert, *German Research Center for Artificial Intelligence (DFKI), Germany*
Jacob Biehl, *FX Palo Alto Laboratory, USA*
Matthew Bietz, *University of California, USA*
Lukas Biewald, *CrowdFlower, USA*
Ali Bigdelou, *Technical University of Munich, Germany*
Dania Bilal, *University of Tennessee, USA*
Mark Billinghurst, *University of Canterbury, New Zealand*
Dorrit Billman, *NASA Ames, USA*
Jens Binder, *University of Manchester, UK*
Jon Bird, *City University London, UK*
Max Birk, *University of Saskatchewan, Canada*
Jeremy Birnholtz, *Northwestern University, USA*
Walter Bischof, *University of Alberta, Canada*
Pradipta Biswas, *University of Cambridge, England*
Staffan Björk, *University of Gothenburg, Sweden*
Pernille Bjorn, *IT University of Copenhagen, Denmark*
Alan Blackwell, *University of Cambridge, UK*
Rachel Blagojevic, *University of Auckland, New Zealand*
Renaud Blanch, *Université Grenoble I, France*
Ann Blandford, *University College London, UK*
Benjamin Blankertz, *Berlin Institute of Technology, Germany*
Eli Blevis, *The Hong Kong Polytechnic University, USA*
Brett Bligh, *Lancaster University, UK*
Jan Blom, *Nokia Research Center, Switzerland*
Katherine Blondon, *University of Washington, USA*
Marco Blumendorf, *Yetu AG, Germany*
Susanne Bødker, *Aarhus University, Denmark*
Mads Boedker, *Copenhagen Business School, Denmark*
Kirsten Boehner, *Cornell University, USA*
Cristian Bogdan, *KTH, Sweden*
Matthias Böhmer, *German Research Center for Artificial Intelligence (DFKI), Germany*
Susanne Boll, *University of Oldenburg, Germany*
Albertus Bongers, *University Technology Sydney, Australia*
Joe Bonneau, *USA*
Matthew Bonner, *Georgia Institute of Technology, USA*
David Bonnet, *Université Paris-Sud & CNRS, France*
Elizabeth Bonsignore, *University of Maryland, USA*
Kellogg Booth, *University of British Columbia, Canada*
Jan Borchers, *RWTH Aachen University, Germany*
Silvia Bordin, *TrentoRise, Italy*
Marcela Borge, *Penn State, USA*
Michelle Borkin, *Harvard University, USA*
Alan Borning, *University of Washington, USA*
Nis Bornoe, *Aalborg University, Denmark*
Gaetano Borriello, *University of Washington, USA*
Brennon Bortz, *Virginia Polytechnic Institute and State University, USA*
Nathan Bos, *University of Michigan, USA*
Claus Bossen, *University of Aarhus, Denmark*
Paolo Bottoni, *University of Rome - 'la Sapienza', Italy*
Matt-Mouley Bouamrane, *University of Glasgow, UK*
Stephane Bouchard, *Université Du Quebec En Outaouais, Canada*
Andy Boucher, *Goldsmiths College, UK*

Nadia Boukhelifa, *INRIA Saclay, France*
Anders Bouwer, *University of Amsterdam, Netherlands*
Judy Bowen, *The University of Waikato, New Zealand*
Chris Bowers, *University of Birmingham, UK*
John Bowers, *Newcastle University, UK*
Geoffrey Bowker, *UC Irvine, USA*
Doug Bowman, *Virginia Polytechnic Institute and State University, USA*
John Boyd, *Google, Na*
Erin Bradner, *Autodesk, USA*
Erin Brady, *University of Rochester, USA*
Andrew Bragdon, *Microsoft, USA*
Jonathan Bragg, *University of Washington, USA*
Giorgio Brajnik, *University of Udine, Italy*
Pedro Branco, *University of Minho, Portugal*
Joel Brandt, *Adobe Research, USA*
Stacy Branham, *Virginia Tech, USA*
Tone Bratteteig, *University of Oslo, Norway*
Cristian Bravo-Lillo, *Carnegie Mellon University, USA*
Matthew Brehmer, *University of British Columbia, Canada*
Margot Brereton, *Queensland University of Technology, Australia*
Robert Brewer, *University of Hawaii at Manoa, USA*
Jo Briggs, *Northumbria University, UK*
Pam Briggs, *Northumbria University, UK*
Willem-Paul Brinkman, *Delft University of Technology, The Netherlands*
Katie Brittain, *Newcastle University, UK*
Juliana Brixey, *UT Health Science Center at Houston, USA*
Anke Brock, *IRIT, France*
Eric Brockmeyer, *Disney Research, USA*
Gregor Broll, *DOCOMO Euro-Labs, Germany*
Geert Brone, *University of Leuven - Campus Antwerp, Belgium*
Jonas Brönstrup, *Technical University of Berlin, Germany*
Andy Brooks, *University of California, USA*
Mark Brosnan, *University of Bath, UK*
Ryan Brotman, *Intel Corporation, USA*
Anne-Marie Brouwer, *TNO Human Factors, Netherlands*
Barry Brown, *University of California San Diego, USA*
Deana Brown, *Georgia Institute of Technology, USA*
Michael Brown, *The University of Nottingham, UK*
Jed Brubaker, *University of California, USA*
Amy Bruckman, *Georgia Institute of Technology, USA*
Gerd Bruder, *University of Würzburg, Germany*
Pascal Bruegger, *University of Applied Sciences, Switzerland*
Clemens Brunner, *Graz University of Technology, Austria*
Miguel Bruns Alonso, *Eindhoven University of Technology, The Netherlands*
Anders Bruun, *Aalborg University, Denmark*
Nick Bryan-Kinns, *Queen Mary, UK*
Martin Brynskov, *Aarhus University, Denmark*
Michael Brzozowski, *Google, USA*
George Buchanan, *City University London, UK*
Sarah Buchanan, *University of Central Florida, USA*
Karolina Buchner, *Yahoo! Labs, USA*
Elizabeth Buie, *Northumbria University, UK*
Andrea Bunt, *University of Manitoba, Canada*

Cody Buntain, *University of Maryland, USA*
Judee Burgoon, *University of Arizona, USA*
Stefano Burigat, *University of Udine, Italy*
Moira Burke, *Facebook, USA*
Gary Burnett, *University of Nottingham, UK*
Margaret Burnett, *Oregon State University, USA*
Jesse Burstyn, *Queen's University, Canada*
Chris Burton, *University of Edinburgh, UK*
Jerry Busby, *Lancaster University, UK*
Marc Busch, *CURE - Center for Usability Research & Engineering, Austria*
Georg Buscher, *Microsoft, USA*
Monika Buscher, *Lancaster University, UK*
Stefano Bussolon, *Università di Trento, Italy*
Brian Butler, *UMD, USA*
D. Alex Butler, *Microsoft Research, UK*
Fabio Buttussi, *University of Udine, Italy*
Ayse Buyuktur, *University of Michigan, USA*
Daragh Byrne, *Arizona State University, USA*
Michael Byrne, *Rice University, USA*
Béatrice Cahour, *CNRS Télécom Paristech, France*
Kelly Caine, *Clemson University, USA*
Paul Cairns, *University of York, UK*
Maya Cakmak, *University of Washington, USA*
Jeffrey Calcaterra, *IBM Corporation, USA*
Roberto Calderon, *University of British Columbia, Canada*
André Calero Valdez, *RWTH Aachen University, Germany*
Janko Calic, *CVSS, UK*
Chris Callison-Burch, *Johns Hopkins University, USA*
Gaelle Calvary, *Grenoble Institute of Technology, France*
Licia Calvi, *NHTV Breda University of Applied Sciences, The Netherlands*
L Jean Camp, *Indiana University, USA*
Jose Campos, *Universidade do Minho, Portugal*
Heloisa Candello, *University of Brighton, UK*
Angelo Cangelosi, *Plymouth University, UK*
Cristina Cannone, *Università degli Studi di Milano, Italy*
Robert Capra, *University of North Carolina at Chapel Hill, USA*
Baptiste Caramiaux, *Goldsmiths College, London*
Giuseppe Carenini, *University of British Columbia, Canada*
Stefan Carmien, *University of Colorado, Spain*
Davide Carneiro, *University of Minho, Portugal*
Sheelagh Carpendale, *University of Calgary, Canada*
Luis Carriço, *University of Lisbon, Portugal*
John Carroll, *The Pennsylvania State University, USA*
Scott Carter, *FX Palo Alto Laboratory, USA*
Thomas Carter, *University of Bristol, UK*
Samuel Carton, *Northwestern University, USA*
Mark Cartwright, *Northwestern University, USA*
Géry Casiez, *University of Lille & INRIA Lille, France*
Alvaro Cassinelli, *University of Tokyo (todai), Japan*
Steven Castellucci, *York University, Canada*
Marcelo Cataldo, *Carnegie Mellon University, USA*
Grevet Catherine, *GVU Center, USA*
Abigail Cauchi, *Swansea University, UK*

Marc Cavazza, *University of Tesside, UK*
James Caverlee, *Texas A&M University, USA*
Melissa Cefkin, *IBM Research, USA*
Robert Cercos, *RMIT University, Australia*
Daniel Cernea, *University of Kaiserslautern, Germany*
Matteo Cesana, *Politecnico di Milano, Italy*
Pablo Cesar, *CWI, The Netherlands*
Ruy Cevantes, *UC Irvine, USA*
Elizabeth Cha, *Personal Robotics Lab, USA*
Samidh Chakrabarti, *Google, USA*
Matthew Chalmers, *University of Glasgow, UK*
Teresa Chambel, *University of Lisbon, Portugal*
Alan Chamberlain, *The University of Nottingham, UK*
Erik Champion, *Curtin University, Australia*
Deborah Chan, *University Health Network, Canada*
Joel Chan, *University of Pittsburgh, USA*
Liwei Chan, *Academia Sinica, Taiwan*
Angela Chang, *MIT Media Lab, USA*
Keng-Hao Chang, *University of California, Berkeley*
Remco Chang, *Tufts University, USA*
Peter Chapman, *University of Nottingham, UK*
Olivier Chapuis, *Université Paris-Sud, France*
Catherine Chase, *Carnegie Mellon University, USA*
Duen Horng (polo) Chau, *Georgia Institute of Technology, USA*
Beenish Chaudry, *Indiana University, USA*
Fang Chen, *Tsinghua University, Spain*
Gaowei Chen, *Pittsburg University,*
Hsiang-Ting Chen, *University of Tokyo, Taiwan*
Jay Chen, *New York University, USA*
Jilin Chen, *IBM Research, USA*
Judy Chen, *University of California, USA*
Liming Chen, *University of Ulster, UK*
Monchu Chen, *University of Madeira, Portugal*
Xiang 'Anthony' Chen, *Carnegie Mellon University, USA*
Yi-Shin Chen, *National Tsing Hua University, Taiwan*
Britte Cheng, *SRI International, USA*
Kai-Yin Cheng, *Microsoft Research Asia, Taiwan*
Lung-Pan Cheng, *National Taiwan University, Germany*
Shiwei Cheng, *Zhejiang University of Technology, China*
Mauro Cherubini, *Telefonica Research, Italy*
Marshini Chetty, *University of Maryland, USA*
Gifford Cheung, *University of Washington, USA*
Ed Chi, *Google, USA*
Pei-Yu Chi, *University of California, USA*
Sonia Chiasson, *Carleton University, Canada*
Mark Chignell, *University of Toronto, Canada*
Parmit Chilana, *University of Waterloo, USA*
Lydia Chilton, *MIT CSAIL, USA*
Alvin Chin, *Nokia Research Center, China*
George Chin, *Pacific Northwest National Laboratory, USA*
Clark Chinn, *Rutgers University,*
Winyu Chinthammit, *University of Tasmania, KAIST, Republic of Korea*
Eun Kyoung Choe, *University of Washington, USA*
Erik Choi, *Rutgers University, USA*

Ming Ki Chong, *Lancaster University, UK*
Wen Huei Chou, *Yunline University of Science and Technology, Taiwan*
Tanzeem Choudhury, *Dartmouth College, USA*
Ellen Christiansen, *Mads Clausen Institute, Denmark*
Georgios Christou, *Cyprus College, Cyprus*
Hao-Hua Chu, *National Taiwan University, Taiwan*
Jason Chuang, *University of Washington, USA*
Tyng-Ruey Chuang, *Academia Sinica, Taiwan*
Chia-Fang Chung, *University of Washington, USA*
Eunki Chung, *Carnegie Mellon University, USA*
Karen Church, *Telefonica Research, Spain*
Elizabeth Churchill, *eBay Research Lab, USA*
Marcelo Cicconet, *New York University, USA*
Jesse Cirimele, *Stanford University, USA*
Gabriel Cirio
Adrian Clark, *University of Canterbury, New Zealand*
Alan Clark, *Northwestern University, USA*
Lillian Clark, *University of Portsmouth, UK*
Rachel Clarke, *Newcastle University, UK*
James Clawson, *Georgia Institute of Technology, USA*
Adrian Clear, *Lancaster University, UK*
Tamara Clegg, *University of Maryland, USA*
Torkil Clemmensen, *Copenhagen Business School, Denmark*
Sue Cobb, *University of Nottingham, UK*
Michael Coburn, *RMIT University, Australia*
Gilbert Cockton, *Northumbria University, UK*
Gabe Cohn, *University of Washington, USA*
Marisa Cohn, *University of California Irvine, USA*
Michael Cohn, *Compukol Communications LLC, USA*
Jared Cole, *Carnegie Mellon University, USA*
Heather Cole-Lewis, *Columbia University, USA*
Lizzie Coles-Kemp, *Royal Holloway, UK*
Christopher Collins, *University of Ontario Institute of Technology, Canada*
Kevyn Collins-Thompson, *University of Michigan, USA*
Sébastien Combéfis, *Université Catholique de Louvain, Belgium*
Cristina Conati, *University of British Columbia, Canada*
Karin Coninx, *Hasselt University, Belgium*
Kay Connelly, *Indiana University Bloomington, USA*
Sunny Consolvo, *Google, USA*
Stéphane Conversy, *ENAC, France*
Gregorio Convertino, *Xerox Research Center Europe, Italy*
Perry Cook, *Princeton Computer Science, USA*
Michael Cooke, *Trinity College Dublin, Ireland*
Kovila Coopamootoo, *Newcastle University, UK*
Seth Cooper, *University of Washington, USA*
Andrew Cordar, *University of Florida, USA*
Raymundo Cornejo, *CICESE, Mexico*
Nicola Corradi, *Università di Padova, Italy*
Dan Cosley, *Cornell University, USA*
Joao Costa, *University of Ontario Institute of Technology, Canada*
Marc Cavazza, *University of Tesside, UK*
Gennaro Costagliola, *University of Salerno, Italy*
Enrico Costanza, *University of Southampton, UK*
James Coughlan, *Smith-Kettlewell Eye Research Institute, USA*

Tim Coughlan, *The University of Nottingham, UK*
Paul Coulton, *Lancaster University, UK*
Scott Counts, *Microsoft Research, USA*
Céline Coutrix, *Université Joseph Fourier, France*
Lynne Coventry, *University of Northumbria, UK*
Benjamin Cowan, *University of Birmingham, UK*
Anna Cox, *University College London, UK*
David Coyle, *University of Bristol, UK*
Michael Crabb, *University of Dundee, Scotland, UK*
Claire Craig, *Sheffield Hallam University, UK*
Scotty Craig, *Arizona State University,*
Henriette Cramer, *Yahoo! Labs, USA*
Meg Cramer, *UC Irvine, USA*
Angela Crandall, *iHub, Kenya*
Justin Cranshaw, *Carnegie Mellon University, USA*
Charles Crook, *University of Nottingham, UK*
Andrew Crossan, *University of Glasgow, UK*
R. Jordan Crouser, *Tufts University, USA*
Kevin Crowston, *Syracuse University, USA*
David Crundall, *University of Nottingham, UK*
Weiwei Cui, *Microsoft Research Asia, China*
Yanqing Cui, *Nokia Research Center, Finland*
Franco Curmi, *Lancaster University, UK*
Simone Cutini, *Università di Padova, Italy*
Edward Cutrell, *Microsoft Research India, India*
Chandrika Cycil, *Brunel University, UK*
Allen Cypher, *IBM Research - Almaden, USA*
Mary Czerwinski, *Microsoft Research, USA*
Alexei Czeskis, *Google, USA*
Raimund Dachselt, *Technische Universität Dresden, Germany*
Palle Dahlstedt, *Chalmers,*
Peng Dai, *Google, USA*
Florian Daiber, *DFKI German Research Center for AI, Germany*
Peter Dalsgaard, *Aarhus University, Denmark*
Ruth Dalton, *Northumbria University, UK*
Sashikanth Damaraju, *Texas A&M University, USA*
Chi Tai Dang, *University of Augsburg, Germany*
Andreea Danielescu, *Arizona State University, USA*
Darcy Dapra, *Google, USA*
Sauvik Das, *Carnegie Mellon University, USA*
Jennifer Davidson, *Oregon State University, USA*
Nigel Davies, *Lancaster University, UK*
James Davis, *UC Santa Cruz, USA*
Janet Davis, *Grinnell College, USA*
Katie Davis, *University of Washington,*
Richard Davis, *Singapore Management University, Singapore*
Rahmad Dawood, *Universitas Syiah Kuala, Indonesia*
Munmun de Choudhury, *Microsoft Research, USA*
Tjerk de Greef, *Delft University of Technology, The Netherlands*
Edward de Guzman, *Autodesk, USA*
Martin de Jode, *University College London, UK*
Daniele de Massari, *Fondazione Ospedale San Camillo, Italy*
Clarisse de Souza, *PUC-Rio, Brazil*

Cleidson de Souza, *Universidade Federal do Pará, Brazil*
David Dearman, *Twitter, USA*
Rob Deline, *Microsoft Research, USA*
Nicola Dell, *University of Washington, USA*
Robert Deloatch, *University of Illinois at Urbana-Champaign, USA*
Cagatay Demiralp, *Stanford University, USA*
Carrie Demmans Epp, *University of Toronto, Canada*
Nick Depalma, *Massachusetts Institute of Technology, USA*
Jan Derboven, *IBBT-KU Leuven, Belgium*
Katie Derthick, *University of Washington, USA*
Parag Deshpande, *Umeå Institute of Design, Sweden*
Audrey Desjardins, *Simon Fraser University, Canada*
Heather Desurvire, *Behavioristics, USA*
Sebastian Deterding, *Hans Bredow Institute for Media Research, Germany*
Laura Devendorf, *UC Berkeley, USA*
Guy Dewsbury, *Gdewsbury, UK*
Anind Dey, *Carnegie Mellon University, USA*
Barbara di Eugenio, *University of Illinois, USA*
Nicholas Diakopoulos, *Rutgers University, USA*
E.ilana Diamant, *University of Pittsburgh, USA*
Michael Dickard, *Ohio University, USA*
Margaret Dickey-Kurdziolek, *Virginia Tech, USA*
Sarah Diefenbach, *Folkwang University of the Arts, Germany*
Paul Dietz, *Microsoft, USA*
Tawanna Dillahunt, *Carnegie Mellon University, USA*
Jill Dimond, *Sassafras Tech Collective, USA*
Christian Dindler, *Aarhus University, Denmark*
Xianghua Ding, *Fudan University, China*
Abdigani Diriye, *Carnegie Mellon University, USA*
Betsy Disalvo, *Georgia Institute of Technology, USA*
Carl Disalvo, *Georgia Institute of Technology, USA*
Anke Dittmar, *University of Rostock, Germany*
Stephen Diverdi, *Adobe Systems Inc, USA*
Alan Dix, *Lancaster University, UK*
Sidney D'mello, *University of Notre Dame, USA*
Chuong do, *Coursera,*
Gavin Doherty, *Trinity College Dublin, Ireland*
Lynn Dombrowski, *University of California Irvine, USA*
Judith Donath, *MIT, USA*
Tao Dong, *University of Michigan, USA*
Birsen Donmez, *University of Toronto, Canada*
Marco Donnarumma, *Goldsmiths College, UK*
Jonathan Donner, *Microsoft Research India, USA*
Mira Dontcheva, *Adobe Research, USA*
James Doodson, *University of Leicester, England, UK*
Tanja Döring, *University of Bremen, Germany*
Marian Dörk, *Newcastle University, UK*
Brian Dorn, *University of Nebraska at Omaha, USA*
Michael Dorsch, *University of Michigan, USA*
Afsaneh Doryab, *Carnegie Mellon University, USA*
Jakub Dostal, *University of St Andrews, UK*
Wenwen Dou, *University of North Carolina at Charlotte, USA*
Andre Doucette, *University of Saskatchewan, Canada*

Audubon Dougherty, *MIT, USA*
Mark Doughty, *University of Lincoln, UK*
Paul Dourish, *University of California, USA*
John Downs, *The University of Melbourne, Australia*
Julie Downs, *Carnegie Mellon University, USA*
Toby Dragon, *Ithaca College, USA*
Christoph Draxler, *LMU München, Germany*
Martha Driessnack, *Oregon Health & Science University, USA*
Laurie Dringus, *Nova Southeastern University, USA*
Milena Droumeva, *Simon Fraser University, Canada*
Steven Drucker, *Microsoft Research, USA*
Allison Druin, *University of Maryland, USA*
Honglu Du, *Palo Alto Research Center, USA*
Ruofei Du, *Microsoft Research Asia, China*
Tina Du, *University of South KAIST, Republic of Korea ralia, Australia*
Carlos Duarte, *Universidade de Lisboa, Portugal*
Luís Duarte, *University of Lisbon, Portugal*
Emmanuel Dubois, *University of Toulouse, France*
Nicolas Ducheneaut, *Palo Alto Research Center, USA*
Andrew Duchowski, *Clemson University, USA*
Tobias Duckworth, *University of Salford, UK*
Casey Dugan, *IBM, USA*
Geoffrey Duggan, *University of Exeter, UK*
Susan Dumais, *Microsoft Research, USA*
Bruno Dumas, *Vrije Universiteit Brussel, Belgium*
Sean Duncan, *Indiana University, USA*
Lucy Dunne, *University College Dublin, Ireland*
Paul Dunphy, *Newcastle University, UK*
Andreas Dünser, *CSIRO - CCI, Australia*
Sophie Dupuy-Chessa, *University of Grenoble, France*
Shree Durga, *University of Wisconsin, USA*
Abigail Durrant, *Newcastle University, UK*
Erik Duval, *KU Leuven, Belgium*
Tim Dwyer, *Monash University, Australia*
Jason Dykes, *City University London, UK*
James Eagan, *Télécom-Paristech, France*
Sarah Eagle, *University of Bristol, UK*
David Ebert, *Purdue University, USA*
Florian Echtler, *Siemens Corporate Technology, Germany*
Dean Eckles, *Stanford University, USA*
Ernest Edmonds, *De Montfort University, UK*
Alistair Edwards, *University of York, UK*
Keith Edwards, *Georgia Institute of Technology, USA*
Kate Ehrlich, *IBM, USA*
Michael Eisenberg, *University of Colorado, USA*
Inger Ekman, *Aalto School of Economics, Finland*
Rana El Kaliouby, *University of Cambridge, UK*
Irene Eleta, *University of Maryland, USA*
Gunnar Ellingsen, *University of Tromsø, Norway*
Dan Ellis, *Columbia University, USA*
Geoff Ellis, *Lancaster University, UK*
Nicole Ellison, *University of Michigan, USA*
Lia Emanuel, *University of Bath,*
Bernadette Emsenhuber, *Johannes Kepler University of Linz, Austria*

Alex Endert, *Pacific Northwest National Laboratory, USA*
Klaus-Peter Engelbrecht, *Telekom Innovation Laboratories, Germany*
David England, *Liverpool John Moores University, UK*
Arvid Engström, *Mobile Life @ Stockholm University, Sweden*
Johan Engström, *Volvo Group Trucks Technology, Sweden*
Barrett Ens, *University of Manitoba, Canada*
Clayton Epp, *University of Saskatchewan, Canada*
Daniel Epstein, *University of Washington, USA*
Sheena Erete, *Northwestern University, USA*
Ingrid Erickson, *Rutgers University, USA*
Thomas Erickson, *IBM Research - T. J. Watson, USA*
Elina Eriksson, *KTH, Sweden*
Eva Eriksson, *Chalmers University of Technology, Sweden*
Lizbeth Escobedo, *Universidad Autonoma de Baja California, Mexico*
Parisa Eslambolchilar, *Future Interaction Technologies Lab, UK*
Sergio Espana, *Universitat Politecnica de Valencia, Spain*
Augusto Esteves, *University of Madeira, Portugal*
Michael Evans, *British Broadcasting Corporation, UK*
Vanessa Evers, *University of Twente, The Netherlands*
Marc Fabri, *Leeds Metropolitan University, UK*
Jerry Fails, *Montclair State University, USA*
Shamal Faily, *University of Oxford, UK*
Anthony Faiola, *Indiana University (IUPUI), USA*
Fiona Fairlie, *Glasgow Caledonian University, UK*
Majdi Faleh
Josef Faller, *Graz University of Technology, Austria*
Daniel Fallman, *Umeå University, Sweden*
Min Fan, *Simon Fraser University Surrey, Canada*
Xianyong Fang, *Anhui University, China*
Jill Fantauzza, *Georgia Institute of Technology, USA*
Jan Erik Farbrot, *Institute for Energy Technology / OECD Halden Reactor Project, Norway*
Elisabetta Farella, *DEIS - University of Bologna, Italy*
Shelly Farnham, *Microsoft Research, USA*
Umer Farooq, *The Pennsylvania State University, USA*
Karen Farris, *University of Michigan, USA*
Michael Farrugia, *UCD Dublin, Luxembourg*
Rosta Farzan, *University of Pittsburgh, USA*
Haakon Faste, *California College of the Arts, USA*
Andrew Faulring, *Carnegie Mellon University, USA*
Stu Favilla, *Swinburne University of Technology, Australia*
Melanie Feinberg, *University of Texas at KAIST, Republic of Korea in, USA*
Jean-Daniel Fekete, *INRIA, France*
Niels Feldmann, *Karlsruhe Institute of Technology (KIT), Germany*
Karla Felix Navarro, *University of Technology Sydney, Australia*
Deborah Fels, *Ryerson University, Canada*
Sidney Fels, *University of British Columbia, Canada*
Adrienne Felt, *Google, USA*
Jinjuan Feng, *University of Maryland, USA*
Robert Ferguson, *McGill University, Canada*
Jennifer Fernquist, *Google,*
Denzil Ferreira, *University of Oulu, Finland*
Pedro Ferreira, *Mobile Life @ KTH, Sweden*

Gabriele Ferri, *Indiana University, USA*
Brian Ferris, *University of Washington, USA*
Francesco Ferrise, *Politecnico di Milano, Italy*
Bruce Ferwerda, *Johannes Kepler University, Austria*
Mirko Fetter, *University of Bamberg, Germany*
Stephen Few, *Perceptual Edge, USA*
Christos Fidas, *University of Cyprus, Cyprus*
Rebecca Fiebrink, *Princeton University, UK*
Daniel Filonik, *Queensland University of Technology, Germany*
Leah Findlater, *University of Maryland, USA*
Thomas Finholt, *University of Michigan, USA*
Julia Fink, *Ecole Polytechnique Fédérale de Lausanne (EPFL), Switzerland*
Janet Finlay, *Leeds Metropolitan University, UK*
Andrew Fiore, *Facebook, USA*
Joel Fischer, *The University of Nottingham, UK*
Brian Fisher, *Simon Fraser University, Canada*
Danyel Fisher, *Microsoft Research, USA*
Stephen Fitchett, *University of Canterbury, New Zealand*
Daniel Fitton, *University of Central Lancashire, UK*
Elizabeth Fitzgerald, *The Open University, UK*
George Fitzmaurice, *Autodesk, Canada*
Geraldine Fitzpatrick, *Vienna University of Technology, Austria*
Zachary Fitz-Walter, *Queensland University of Technology, Australia*
Steve Flaherty, *Northeaster University, USA*
David Flatla, *University of Dundee, UK*
Ivan Flechais, *University of Oxford, England, UK*
Rowanne Fleck, *University College London, UK*
Scott Fleming, *University of Memphis, USA*
Martin Flintham, *The University of Nottingham, UK*
John Flowers, *University of Nebraska -- Lincoln, USA*
Allen Flynn, *University of Michigan, USA*
Brynn Flynn, *Carnegie Mellon University, USA*
James Fogarty, *University of Washington, USA*
Bj Fogg, *Stanford University, USA*
Sean Follmer, *MIT, USA*
Eelke Folmer, *University of Nevada, USA*
Peter Forbrig, *University of Rostock, Germany*
Alain Forget, *Carleton University, Canada*
Azadeh Forghani, *Simon Fraser University, Canada*
Laura Forlano, *Parsons The New School for Design, USA*
David Forsyth, *University of Illinois at Urbana-Champaign, USA*
Andrea Forte, *Drexel University, USA*
Jutta Fortmann, *University of Oldenburg, Germany*
Lesley Fosh, *The University of Nottingham, UK*
Elizabeth Foss, *University of Maryland, USA*
Derek Foster, *University of Lincoln, UK*
Stephen Foster, *UC San Diego, USA*
Marcus Foth, *Queensland University of Technology, Australia*
Brooke Foucault, *Northwestern University, USA*
Adam Fourney, *University of Waterloo, Canada*
Adam Fouse, *University of California, USA*
Allan Fowler, *Waiariki Institute of Technology, New Zealand*
Sarah Fox, *University of Washington, USA*

Suely Fragoso, *Federal University of Rio Grande do Sul (UFRGS), Brazil*
Anders Frank, *Swedish National Defence College, Sweden*
Mario Frank, *UC Berkeley, Germany*
Mike Fraser, *University of Bristol, UK*
Christopher Frauenberger, *University of Sussex, UK*
Dustin Freeman, *University of Toronto, Canada*
Euan Freeman, *University of Glasgow, Scotland, UK*
Andre Freire, *Universidade de Lisboa, Brazil*
Luanne Freund, *University of British Columbia, Canada*
Jill Freyne, *CSIRO, Australia*
Sarah-Christin Freytag, *Berlin Institute of Technology, Germany*
Enrique Frias-Martinez, *Telefonica Research, Spain*
Adrian Friday, *Lancaster University, UK*
Doron Friedman, *The Interdisciplinary Center, Israel*
Mathias Frisch, *MID Gmbh, Germany*
Chris Frisina, *Virginia Tech, USA*
Jonas Fritsch, *Aarhus University, Denmark*
Mario Fritz, *MPI Informatik, Germany*
Thomas Fritz, *University of Zurich, Switzerland*
Bernd Froehlich, *Bauhaus Universität Weimar, Germany*
Jon Froehlich, *University of Maryland, USA*
David Frohlich, *University of Surrey, UK*
Peter Fröhlich, *FTW Telecommunications Research Center, Austria*
Erik Frøkjær, *Københavns Universitet, Denmark*
Mads Frost, *IT University of Copenhagen, Denmark*
Wai-Tat Fu, *University of Illinois at Urbana-Champaign, USA*
Georg Fuchs, *Fraunhofer Institute Intelligent Analysis and Information Systems IAIS, Germany*
Johannes Fuchs, *University, Germany*
Verena Fuchsberger, *ICT&S Center, Austria*
Kaori Fujinami, *Tokyo University of Agriculture and Technology, Japan*
Kentarou Fukuda, *IBM Research - Tokyo, Japan*
Benjamin Fung, *McGill University, Canada*
Mathias Funk, *Eindhoven University of Technology, The Netherlands*
Silvia Gabrielli, *Create-Net, Italy*
Hind Gacem, *Télécom-Paristech, France*
Martin Gaedke, *Technische Universität Chemnitz, Germany*
Andrea Gaggioli, *Catholic University of Milan, Italy*
Sarah Gallacher, *UCL, UK*
Teresa Galvão, *Universidade do Porto, Portugal*
Maribeth Gandy, *Georgia Institute of Technology, USA*
Eva Ganglbauer, *Vienna University of Technology, Austria*
Ge Gao, *Cornell University, USA*
Ruth García-Gavilanes, *Universitat Pompeu Fabra, Spain*
Simson Garfinkel, *MIT, USA*
R. Kelly Garrett, *Ohio State University, USA*
Daniel Gartenberg, *George Mason University, USA*
Franca Garzotto, *HOC-Politecnico di Milano, Italy*
Nadia Gauducheau, *ICD-CNRS, France*
Steffen Gauglitz, *University of California, USA*
Paul Gault, *University of Dundee, UK*
William Gaver, *Goldsmiths College, UK*
Tom Gedeon, *KAIST, Republic of Korea ralian National University, Australia*

Nils Gehlenborg, *Harvard Medical School, USA*
Sven Gehring, *German Research Center for Artificial Intelligence (DFKI), Germany*
Johanna Gelderblom, *University of Pretoria, South Africa*
Hans Gellersen, *Lancaster University, UK*
Aaron Genest, *University of Saskatchewan, Canada*
Kallirroi Georgila, *University of Southern California, USA*
Elizabeth Gerber, *Northwestern University, USA*
Peter Gerjets, *Knowledge Media Research Center*
Jens Gerken, *ICT Innovative Communication Technologies AG, Germany*
Kathrin Gerling, *University of Lincoln, UK*
David Gerritsen, *Carnegie Mellon University, USA*
Paul Gestwicki, *Ball State University, USA*
Luc Geurts, *KU Leuven, Belgium*
Werner Geyer, *IBM Research - T. J. Watson, USA*
Giuseppe Ghiani, *ISTI-CNR, Italy*
George Ghinea, *Brunel University, UK*
Emilien Ghomi, *Université Paris-Sud, France*
Maysam Ghovanloo, *Georgia Institute of Technology, USA*
Alicia Gibb, *Nycresistor, USA*
Lorna Gibson, *University of Dundee, UK*
Eric Gilbert, *Georgia Institute of Technology, USA*
Kathleen Gilbert, *Indiana University, USA*
Alastair Gill, *University of Surrey, UK*
Kiel Gilleade, *Liverpool John Moores University, UK*
Nicholas Gillian, *MIT Media Lab, USA*
Stephen Gilroy, *Teesside University, UK*
Shuli Gilutz, *Interdisciplinary Center (IDC) Herzliya, Israel*
Shiry Ginosar, *University of California, USA*
Jeffrey Girard, *University of Pittsburgh, USA*
Audrey Girouard, *Carleton University, Canada*
Voula Gkatzidou, *Brunel University, UK*
Dylan Glas, *ATR, Japan*
Marie Glasemann, *Aalborg University, Denmark*
Michael Glueck, *University of Toronto, Canada*
Janet Go, *Autodesk, USA*
Kentaro Go, *University of Yamanashi, Japan*
Fernand Gobet, *University of Liverpool, UK*
Mayank Goel, *University of Washington, USA*
Anja Goeritz, *University of Freiburg, Germany*
Sean Goggins, *University of Missouri, USA*
Wooi Boon Goh, *Nanyang Technological University, Singapore*
Sergio Goldenberg, *Georgia Institute of Technology, USA*
Scott Golder, *Cornell University, USA*
Ilya Goldin, *Carnegie Mellon University, USA*
Dan Goldman, *Adobe, USA*
David Golightly, *Experian UK, UK*
Connie Golsteijn, *Eindhoven University of Technology, Netherlands*
Evan Golub, *University of Maryland, USA*
Richard Gomer, *University of Southampton, UK*
Antonio Gomes, *Queen's University, Canada*
Rafael Gomez, *Queensland University of Technology, Australia*
Steven Gomez, *Brown University, USA*

Jorge Goncalves, *Instituto Superior Técnico, Finland*
Daniel Gonçalves, *University of Oulu, Portugal*
Tiago Gonçalves, *FCUL, Portugal*
Nan-Wei Gong, *Massachusetts Institute of Technology, USA*
Amy Gonzales, *Indiana University, USA*
Berto Gonzalez, *University of North Carolina at Charlotte, USA*
Victor Gonzalez, *University of Manchester, UK*
Walkyria Goode, *SPARK Experience, USA*
Elizabeth Goodman, *UC Berkeley, USA*
Paul Gorman, *Oregon Health & Science University, USA*
Sandy Gould, *University College London, UK*
Rúben Gouveia, *University of Madeira, Portugal*
Nitesh Goyal, *Cornell University, USA*
Kazjon Grace, *UNC Charlotte, USA*
Michele Graffeo, *University of Trento, Italy*
Connor Graham, *National University of Singapore, Singapore*
Martin Graham, *Napier University, UK*
Nicholas Graham, *Queen's University, Canada*
Klaus Gramann, *Berlin Institute of Technology, Germany*
Dimitris Grammenos, *Foundation for Research and Technology - Hellas, Greece*
Sukeshini Grandhi, *Eastern Connecticut State University, USA*
Laura Granka, *Google, USA*
Raphael Grasset, *Graz University of Technology, Austria*
Colin Gray, *Indiana University, USA*
Rebecca Gray, *Michigan State University, USA*
David Green, *Newcastle University, UK*
Keith Green, *Clemson University, USA*
Michael Greenberg, *Northwestern University, USA*
Saul Greenberg, *University of Calgary, Canada*
Chris Greenhalgh, *The University of Nottingham, UK*
Peggy Gregory, *University of Central Lancashire, UK*
Catherine Grevet, *Georgia Institute of Technology, USA*
Harry Griffin, *University College London, UK*
Erin Griffiths, *University of Virginia, USA*
Thomas Grill, *University of Salzburg, Austria*
Rebecca Grinter, *Georgia Institute of Technology, USA*
Laurent Grisoni, *University Lille, France*
Alex Groce, *Oregon State University, USA*
Georg Groh, *TU Muenchen, Germany*
Diane Gromala, *Simon Fraser University, Canada*
Kaj Grønbæk, *University of Aarhus, Denmark*
Erik Grönvall, *IT University of Copenhagen, Denmark*
Mark Gross, *Carnegie Mellon University, USA*
Shad Gross, *Indiana University Bloomington, USA*
Tom Gross, *University of Bamberg, Germany*
Jens Grossklags, *The Pennsylvania State University, USA*
Jens Grubert, *University of Technology Graz, Austria*
Shion Guha, *Cornell University, USA*
Yves Guiard, *Télécom-Paristech CNRS, France*
François Guimbretière, *Cornell University, USA*
Rebecca Gulotta, *Carnegie Mellon University, USA*
Hatice Gunes, *University of Technology, Australia*
Philip Guo, *Stanford University, USA*

Ankit Gupta, *University of Washington, USA*
Sidhant Gupta, *University of Washington, USA*
David Gurzick, *Hood College, USA*
Sean Gustafson, *Hasso Plattner Institute, Germany*
Mattia Gustarini, *University of Geneva, Switzerland*
Francisco Luis Gutiérrez Vela, *University of Granada, España*
Ricardo Gutierrez-Osuna, *Texas A&M University, USA*
Mark Guzdial, *Georgia Institute of Technology, USA*
Tajin Ha, *KAIST, S. Korea*
Joerg Haake, *Fernuniversitaet Hagen, Germany*
Eija Haapalainen Ferreira, *University of Oulu, Finland*
Eben Haber, *IBM Research - Almaden, USA*
Jonathan Haber, *University of Calgary, Canada*
Martin Hachet, *Labri-INRIA University of Bordeaux, France*
Mieke Haesen, *Hasselt University - Tul - Iminds, Belgium*
Joshua Hailpern, *Hewlett Packard, USA*
Oliver Haimson, *University of California, USA*
Julia Haines, *University of California, USA*
Maria Håkansson, *Chalmers University of Technology, Sweden*
David Hakken, *Indiana University Bloomongton, USA*
Jonna Hakkila, *University of Oulu, Finland*
Jonna Häkkilä, *Soul4design, Finland*
Jukka Häkkinen, *Aalto University School of Science and Technology, Finland*
Timothy Hale, *Partners Healthcare Inc., USA*
Aaron Halfaker, *University of Minnesota, USA*
Joseph Hall, *The Center for Democracy & Technology, USA*
Michael Haller, *University of Applied Sciences Upper KAIST, Republic of Korea ria, Austria*
Lars Hallnäs, *Chalmers University of Technology, Sweden*
John Halloran, *Coventry University, UK*
Kim Halskov, *Aarhus University, Denmark*
Christine Halverson, *IBM Research - T. J. Watson, USA*
Tim Halverson, *Air Force Research Laboratory, USA*
Martin Halvey, *Glasgow Caledonian University, UK*
Perttu Hämäläinen, *Aalto University, Finland*
William Hamilton, *Texas A&M University, USA*
Jessica Hammer, *Carnegie Mellon University, USA*
Nils Hammerla, *Newcastle University, UK*
Tracy Hammond, *Texas A&M University, USA*
Jaehyun Han, *KAIST, Republic of Korea*
Jeonghye Han, *Computer Education, Republic of Korea*
Kyungsik (keith) Han, *The Pennsylvania State University, USA*
Teng Han, *University of Bristol, China*
Jeff Hancock, *Cornell University, USA*
Mark Handel, *The Boeing Company, USA*
Alina Hang, *University of Munich, Germany*
Benjamin Hanrahan, *Virginia Polytechnic Institute and State University, France*
Derek Hansen, *Brigham Young University, USA*
John Paulin Hansen, *IT University of Copenhagen, Denmark*
Kotaro Hara, *University of Maryland, USA*
Mona Haraty, *University of British Columbia, Canada*
Marian Harbach, *Leibniz University Hannover, Germany*

Gunnar Harboe, *University of Zurich, Switzerland*
Ellie Harmon, *UC Irvine, USA*
Morten Harning, *Dialogical ApS, Denmark*
Franklin Harper, *University of Minnesota, USA*
Richard Harper, *Microsoft Research, UK*
Simon Harper, *University of Manchester, UK*
Erik Harpstead, *Carnegie Mellon University, USA*
Rikard Harr, *Umeå University, Sweden*
Chris Harrison, *Carnegie Mellon University, USA*
Daniel Harrison, *University College London, UK*
Lane Harrison, *University of North Carolina at Charlotte, USA*
Jennefer Hart, *Lancaster University, UK*
Casper Harteveld, *Northeastern University, USA*
Björn Hartmann, *University of California, USA*
Mark Hartswood, *University of Edinburgh, UK*
Andrea Hartzler, *University of Washington, USA*
Catherine Harvey, *University of Nottingham, UK*
Khalad Hasan, *University of Manitoba, Canada*
Chelsea Hash, *Polytechnic Institute of NYU, USA*
Mitsuyo Hashida, *Soai Uiversity, Japan*
Marc Hassenzahl, *Folkwang University of the Arts, Germany*
Doris Hausen, *University of Munich, Germany*
Sabrina Hauser, *Simon Fraser University, Canada*
Kirstie Hawkey, *Dalhousie University, Canada*
Eiji Hayashi, *Carnegie Mellon University, USA*
Gillian Hayes, *University of California, USA*
Helen He, *University of Calgary, Canada*
Marti Hearst, *UC Berkeley, USA*
Brent Hecht, *University of Minnesota, USA*
Per-Olof Hedvall, *Lund University, Sweden*
Jaimee Heffner, *Fred Hutchinson Cancer Research Center, USA*
Tomi Heimonen, *University of Tampere, Finland*
Eric Hekler, *Arizona State University, USA*
Robert Held, *University of California, USA*
Bradley Hemminger, *University of North Carolina, USA*
Niels Hendriks, *University of Leuven, Belgium*
David Hendry, *University of Washington, USA*
Fabian Hennecke, *University of Munich, Germany*
Nathalie Henry Riche, *Microsoft Research, USA*
Niels Henze, *University of Stuttgart, Germany*
Cormac Herley, *Microsoft Research, Ghjhj*
Hamilton Hernandez, *Queen's University, Canada*
Davinia Hernandez-Leo, *Universitat Pompeu Fabra, Spain*
Marc Herrlich, *University of Bremen, Germany*
Morten Hertzum, *University of Copenhagen, Denmark*
Philipp Herzig, *SAP Research CEC Dresden, Germany*
Phil Heslop, *Newcastle University, UK*
Luke Hespanhol, *University of Sydney, Australia*
Jan Hess, *University of Siegen, Germany*
Susan Hessey, *Brithish Telecom, UK*
Wilko Heuten, *OFFIS - Institute for Information Technology, Germany*
Clint Heyer, *IT University of Copenhagen, Denmark*
Nadja Heym, *University of Nottingham, UK*

Jutta Hild, *Fraunhofer IOSB, Germany*
Benjamin Mako Hill, *University of Washington, USA*
Serena Hillman, *Simon Fraser University, Canada*
Juan David Hincapié-Ramos, *IT University of Copenhagen, Canada*
Ken Hinckley, *Microsoft Research, USA*
Jon Hindmarsh, *King's College London, UK*
Uta Hinrichs, *University of St Andrews, UK*
Sen Hirano, *University of California, USA*
Matthew Hirsch, *MIT Media Lab, USA*
Tad Hirsch, *University of Washington, USA*
Leanne Hirshfield, *Hamilton College, USA*
Chaya Hiruncharoenvate, *Georgia Institute of Technology, USA*
Christina Hochleitner, *CURE - Center for Usability Research & Engineering, Austria*
Nadia Hocine, *Montpellier 2 University, France*
Duncan Hodges, *University of Oxford, UK*
Gray Hodgkinson, *Massey University, New Zealand*
Orland Hoeber, *University of Regina, Canada*
Jesse Hoey, *University of Waterloo, Canada*
Guy Hoffman, *IDC Herzliya, Israel*
Bernie Hogan, *University of Toronto, Canada*
Trevor Hogan, *Cork Institute of Technology, Ireland*
Andrew Hogue, *University of Ontario Institute of Technology, Canada*
James Hollan, *UCSD, USA*
Simon Holland, *The Open University, UK*
Tobias Hollerer, *University of California, USA*
Nic Hollinworth, *University of Reading, UK*
Caitlin Holman, *University of Michigan, USA*
David Holman, *Queen's University, Canada*
Hrönn Holmer, *Cornell University, USA*
Stefan Holmlid, *Linköpings universitet, Sweden*
Lars Erik Holmquist, *Indep. Consultant, USA*
Kenneth Holmqvist, *Lund University, Sweden*
Bree Holtz, *Information Studies and Media, USA*
Christian Holz, *Yahoo! Labs, USA*
Andreas Holzinger, *Graz Medical University, Austria*
Hwajung Hong, *Georgia Institute of Technology, USA*
Jason Hong, *Carnegie Mellon University, USA*
Jin-Hyuk Hong, *Carnegie Mellon University, USA*
Lichan Hong, *Google, USA*
Kristina Höök, *KTH, Sweden*
Mohammed Hoque, *University of Rochester, USA*
Michael Horn, *Northwestern University, USA*
John Horton, *Harvard University, USA*
Matthew Horton, *Child Computer Interaction Group, UK*
Simo Hosio, *University of Oulu, Finland*
Steven Houben, *IT University of Copenhagen, Denmark*
Kirralie Houghton, *Queensland University of Technology, Australia*
Robert Houghton, *The University of Nottingham, UK*
Juan Pablo Hourcade, *University of Iowa, USA*
Rachid Hourizi, *University of Bath, UK*
Aaron Houssian, *Philips Research, The Netherlands*
Andrew Howes, *University of Manchester, UK*

James Howison, *Carnegie Mellon University, USA*
Kate Howland, *University of Sussex, UK*
Iris Howley, *Carnegie Mellon University, USA*
Idris Hsi, *Microsoft, USA*
Yi-Ta Hsieh, *University of Helsinki, Finland*
Chang Hu, *Microsoft, USA*
Jun Hu, *Eindhoven University of Technology, Netherlands*
Mengdie Hu, *Georgia Institute of Technology, USA*
Y. Charlie Hu, *Purdue University, USA*
Yuheng Hu, *Arizona State University, USA*
Chung-Ching Huang, *Indiana University, USA*
Haosheng Huang, *Research Group Cartography, Austria*
Jeff Huang, *University of Washington, USA*
Kevin Huang, *Georgia Institute of Technology, USA*
Shih-Wen Huang, *University of Washington, USA*
Jochen Huber, *MIT Media Lab, USA*
Bernardo Huberman, *HP Labs, USA*
Matthew Hudson, *The University of York, UK*
Scott Hudson, *Carnegie Mellon University, USA*
David Huffaker, *Google, USA*
Amanda Hughes, *Utah State University, USA*
Julie Hui, *Northwestern University, USA*
Alina Huldtgren, *Delft University of Technology, Germany*
Jessica Hullman, *University of Michigan, USA*
Shah Rukh Humayoun, *University of Kaiserslautern, Germany*
Seth Hunter, *MIT Media Lab, USA*
Stephane Huot, *Université Paris-Sud, France*
Annika Hupfeld, *University of Nottingham, UK*
Amy Hurst, *Carnegie Mellon University, USA*
Wolfgang Hürst, *Utrecht University, The Netherlands*
Christophe Hurter, *University of Toulouse, France*
Heinrich Hussmann, *Ludwig-Maximilians-Universität München, Germany*
Dugald Hutchings, *Elon University, USA*
John Hutchinson, *Lancaster University, UK*
C.j. Hutto, *Georgia Institute of Technology, USA*
Luke Hutton, *University of St Andrews, UK*
Ebba Thora Hvannberg, *University of Iceland, Iceland*
Inseok Hwang, *KAIST, South Korea*
Sungjae Hwang, *KAIST, South Korea*
Aulikki Hyrskykari, *University of Tampere, Finland*
Ioanna Iacovides, *UCL, UK*
Djilali Idoughi, *University A. Mira of Bejaia, Algeria*
Takeo Igarashi, *The University of Tokyo, Japan*
Klas Ihme, *University of Leipzig, Germany*
Masahiko Inami, *KMD, Japan*
Todd Ingalls, *Arizona State University, USA*
Stephen Intille, *Northeastern University, USA*
Alexandra Ion, *University of Applied Sciences Upper KAIST, Republic of Korea ria, Austria*
Iulia Ion, *Google, USA*
Panos Ipeirotis, *New York University, New York*
Shamsi Iqbal, *Microsoft Research, USA*
Ellen Isaacs, *PARC, USA*

Katherine Isbister, *Polytechnic Institute of New York University, USA*
Tobias Isenberg, *INRIA, France*
Kentaro Ishii, *The University of Tokyo, Japan*
Poika Isokoski, *University of Tampere, Finland*
Ali Israr, *Disney Research, USA*
Howell Istance, *De Montfort University, UK*
Yuichi Itoh, *Osaka University, Japan*
Bret Jackson, *University of New Mexico, USA*
Daniel Jackson, *Newcastle University, UK*
Steven Jackson, *Cornell University, USA*
Tanner Jackson, *Princeton, USA*
Robert Jacob, *Tufts University, USA*
Mattias Jacobsson, *Mobile Life @ SICS, Sweden*
Nassim Jafarinaimi, *Georgia Institute of Technology, USA*
Nils Jäger, *University of Nottingham, UK*
Mohit Jain, *University of Toronto, Canada*
Sharad Jaiswal, *Bell Labs India, India*
Timo Jakobi, *University of Siegen, Germany*
Mikkel Jakobsen, *University of Copenhagen, Denmark*
Hamid R. Jamali, *Kharazmi University, Iran*
Anthony Jameson, *German Research Center for Artificial Intelligence (DFKI), Germany*
Jacek Jankowski, *Digital Enterprise Research Institute, France*
Maddy Janse, *Philips Research, The Netherlands*
Bernard Jansen, *The Pennsylvania State University, USA*
Yvonne Jansen, *Université Paris-Sud, France*
Christian Janssen, *Smith-Kettlewell Eye Research Institute, USA*
Joris Janssen, *Eindhoven University of Technology, The Netherlands*
Ryan Janzen, *University of Toronto, Canada*
Tim Jay, *University of Bristol, UK*
K. Neil Jenkings, *Newcastle University, UK*
Tom Jenkins, *Georgia Institute of Technology, USA*
Carlos Jensen, *Oregon State University, USA*
Jennifer Jenson, *York University, Canada*
Seokhee Jeon, *ETH Zurich, Switzerland*
Jin-Woo Jeong, *Hanyang University, Republic of Korea*
Hans-Christian Jetter, *University of Konstanz, UK*
Jiepu Jiang, *University of Massachusetts Amherst, USA*
Nan Jiang, *Bournemouth University, UK*
Marina Jirotka, *University of Oxford, UK*
Kazuhiro Jo, *IAMAS, Japan*
Bonnie John, *IBM Research, USA*
Andrew Johnson, *University of Illinois at Chicago, USA*
Gabe Johnson, *Blank Slate Systems, USA*
Jeff Johnson, *UI Wizards, USA*
Kimberly Johnson, *Google, USA*
Maritza Johnson, *University of California, USA*
Mikael Johnson, *Helsinki University of Technology, Finland*
Steven Johnson, *Temple U., USA*
Aditya Johri, *Virginia Tech, USA*
Tero Jokela, *Nokia Research Center, Finland*
Brett Jones, *University of Illinois at Urbana-Champaign, USA*
J. Adam Jones, *University of Southern California, USA*

Malcolm Jones, *Northumbria University, UK*
Matt Jones, *Swansea University, Wales, UK*
Steve Jones, *University of Waikato, New Zealand*
William Jones, *University of Washington, USA*
Martin Jonsson, *Södertörn University, Sweden*
Sergi Jorda, *Universitat Pompeu Fabra, Spain*
Joaquim Jorge, *INESC-ID, Portugal*
Rui Jose, *Universidade do Minho, Portugal*
Anirudha Joshi, *Indian Institute of Technology, India*
Neel Joshi, *Microsoft, USA*
Ricardo Jota, *University of Toronto, Portugal*
M.-Carmen Juan, *UPV, Spain*
Oskar Juhlin, *Mobile Life @ Stockholm University, Sweden*
Satu Jumisko-Pyykkö, *Tampere University of Technology, Finland*
Heekyoung Jung, *University of Cincinnati, USA*
Malte Jung, *Cornell University, USA*
Tzyy-Ping Jung, *UCSD, USA*
Yumi Jung, *Michigan State University, USA*
Beyerer Jürgen, *Karlsruhe Institute of Technology (KIT), Germany*
Marko Jurmu, *University of Oulu, Finland*
Mike Just, *Glasgow Caledonian University, UK*
Antti Jylhä, *University of Helsinki, Finland*
Dennis Kafura, *Virginia Tech, USA*
Anne Kaikkonen, *Nokia Corporation, Finland*
Sanjay Kairam, *Stanford University, USA*
Yasuaki Kakehi, *Keio University, Japan*
Matthew Kam, *American Institutes for Research, USA*
Noreen Kamal, *University of British Columbia, Canada*
Alexander Kan, *The University of Melbourne, Australia*
Sean Kandel, *Stanford University, USA*
Eser Kandogan, *IBM, USA*
Bridget Kane, *Trinity College Dublin, Ireland*
Shaun Kane, *University of Maryland Baltimore County, USA*
Ruogu Kang, *Carnegie Mellon University, USA*
Marije Kanis, *Brunel University, UK*
Gopinaath Kannabiran, *Indiana University, USA*
Anne Marie Kanstrup, *Aalborg University, Denmark*
Ashish Kapoor, *Microsoft Research, USA*
Dennis Kappen, *University of Ontario Institute of Technology, Canada*
Evangelos Kapros, *Trinity College Dublin, Ireland*
Maurits Kaptein, *Eindhoven University of Technology, The Netherlands*
Victor Kaptelinin, *Umeå University, Sweden*
Mustafa Karagozler, *Disney Research, USA*
Karrie Karahalios, *University of Illinois, USA*
Amela Karahasanovic, *SINTEF ICT, Norway*
John Karat, *IBM Research - T. J. Watson, USA*
David Karger, *MIT, USA*
Thorsten Karrer, *RWTH Aachen University, Germany*
Christos Katsanos, *Hellenic Open University, Greece*
Brian Katz, *LIMSI-CNRS, France*
Larry Katz, *University of Calgary, Canada*
Andrea Kavanaugh, *Virginia Tech, USA*
Fahim Kawsar, *Phd Candidate, Japan*

Matthew Kay, *University of Waterloo, Canada*
Joseph 'jofish' Kaye, *Nokia, USA*
Gabriella Kazai, *Microsoft Research, UK*
Konstantinos Kazakos, *Newcastle University, UK*
Rubaiat Habib Kazi, *National University of Singapore, Canada*
Elizabeth Kaziunas, *University of Michigan, USA*
Wendy Keay-Bright, *University of Wales Institute, Wales, UK*
Daniel Keefe, *University of Minnesota, USA*
Brian Keegan, *Northeastern University, USA*
Flavius Kehr, *University of Koblenz-Landau, Germany*
Caitlin Kelleher, *Washington University, USA*
Wendy Kellogg, *IBM Research - T. J. Watson, USA*
Diane Kelly, *University of North Carolina, USA*
Ryan Kelly, *University of Bath, UK*
Logan Kendall, *University of Washington, USA*
Denisa Kera, *National University of Singapore, Singapore*
Dagmar Kern, *Bertrandt Ingenieurbüro Gmbh, Germany*
Andruid Kerne, *Texas A&M University, USA*
Andreas Kerren, *Linnaeus University, Sweden*
Karina Kervin, *University of Michigan, USA*
Cem Keskin, *Microsoft Research, UK*
Rilla Khaled, *University of Malta, Malta*
Mohammadreza Khalilbeigi, *Darmstadt University of Technology, Germany*
Vassilis-Javed Khan, *NHTV Breda University of Applied Sciences, The Netherlands*
Ahmed Kharrufa, *Newcastle University, UK*
Rohit Khot, *RMIT University, Australia*
Vera Khovanskaya, *Cornell University, USA*
Emre Kiciman, *Microsoft Research, USA*
Wolf Kienzle, *Microsoft Research, USA*
Johan Kildal, *Nokia, Finland*
Dongwhan Kim, *Seoul National University, Republic of Korea*
Hyang-Sook Kim, *St. Norbert's College, USA*
Hyung Nam Kim, *Northwestern University, USA*
Joy Kim, *Stanford University, USA*
Juho Kim, *Massachusetts Institute of Technology, USA*
Ju-Whan Kim, *KAIST, Republic of Korea*
Kibum Kim, *Kochi University of Technology, Japan*
Seung Wook Kim, *Samsung R&D Center Silicon Valley, USA*
Seungjun Kim, *Carnegie Mellon University, USA*
Si Jung Kim, *University of Central Florida, USA*
Sung-Hee Kim, *Purdue University, USA*
Sunyoung Kim, *Carnegie Mellon University, USA*
Taemie Kim, *Sociometric Solutions, USA*
Kenrick Kin, *University of California, USA*
Jennifer King, *University of California, USA*
Michael Kipp, *Augsburg University of Applied Sciences, Germany*
Reuben Kirkham, *Nottingham University, England*
Iacovos Kirlappos, *University College London, UK*
Alex Kirlik, *University of Illinois at Urbana, USA*
Ben Kirman, *University of Lincoln, UK*
Paul Kirschner, *Open Universiteit, Nederland*
David Kirsh, *University of California, USA*

Christopher Kirwan, *Parsons The New School for Design, USA*
Yoshifumi Kitamura, *Tohoku University, Japan*
Kris Kitani, *Carnegie Mellon University, USA*
Aniket Kittur, *Carnegie Mellon University, USA*
Funda Kivran-Swaine, *Rutgers University, USA*
René Kizilcec, *Stanford University, USA*
Scott Klemmer, *UC San Diego, USA*
Jayne Klenner, *King's College, USA*
Clemens Klokmose, *Aarhus University, Denmark*
Eric Klopfer, *MIT, USA*
Jarrod Knibbe, *University of Bristol, UK*
Bart Knijnenburg, *University of California, The Netherlands*
Cory Knobel, *University of California, USA*
Hendrik Knoche, *EPFL, Switzerland*
Bran Knowles, *Lancaster University, UK*
Masatomo Kobayashi, *IBM Research - Tokyo, Japan*
Michael Koch, *Bundeswehr University Munich, Germany*
Kenneth Koedinger, *Carnegie Mellon University, USA*
Lone Koefoed Hansen, *Aarhus University, Denmark*
Christian Koehler, *Carnegie Mellon University, USA*
Hyunseung Koh, *Indiana University, USA*
Kyle Koh, *Seoul National University, South Korea*
Hideki Koike, *University of Electro-Communications, Japan*
Mario Kolberg, *University of Stirling, UK*
Boriana Koleva, *The University of Nottingham, UK*
Beth Kolko, *University of Washington, USA*
Jon Kolko, *Frog Design, USA*
Thomas Költringer, *Ventum Consulting, Austria*
Steven Komarov, *Harvard University, USA*
Anita Komlodi, *University of Maryland, USA*
Andreas Komninos, *University of Strathclyde, UK*
Joseph Konstan, *University of Minnesota, USA*
Matthias Korn, *Aarhus University, Denmark*
Oliver Korn, *University of Applied Sciences Esslingen, Germany*
Gerd Kortuem, *The Open University, UK*
Robert Kosara, *Tableau Software, USA*
Timothy Koschmann, *Southern Illinois University, USA*
Ilpo Koskinen, *University of Art and Design Helsinki, Finland*
Vassilis Kostakos, *University of Oulu, Finland*
Ilkka Kosunen, *University of Helsinki, Finland*
Theodora Koulouri, *Brunel University,*
Matthias Kovatsch, *ETH Zurich, Switzerland*
Yong Ming Kow, *University of California Irvine, Hong Kong Sar*
Nicole Kraemer, *University of Duisburg-Essen,*
Adam Kramer, *Facebook, USA*
Jan-Peter Krämer, *RWTH Aachen University, Germany*
Matthias Kranz, *University of Passau, Germany*
Sven Kratz, *University of Munich, Germany*
Robert Kraut, *Carnegie Mellon University, USA*
Christian Kray, *University of Münster, Germany*
Shivsubramani Krishnamoorthy, *Amrita University, USA*
Ernst Kruijff, *Graz University of Technology, Austria*
John Krumm, *Microsoft Research, USA*
Erin Krupka, *University of Michigan, USA*

Ravi Kuber, *UMBC, USA*
Sebastien Kubicki, *CERV - Centre Européen de Réalité Virtuelle, France*
Alex Kuhn, *University of Michigan, USA*
Kai Kuikkaniemi, *Helsinki Institute for Information Technology HIIT, Finland*
Sari Kujala, *Aalto University, Finland*
Tuomo Kujala, *University of Jyväskylä, Finland*
Hannu Kukka, *University of Oulu, Finland*
Anand Kulkarni, *University of California, USA*
Chinmay Kulkarni, *Stanford University, USA*
Anuj Kumar, *Carnegie Mellon University, USA*
Arun Kumar, *IBM Research, India*
Neha Kumar, *University of California, USA*
Ranjitha Kumar, *Stanford University, USA*
Santosh Kumar, *University of Memphis, USA*
Ponnurangam Kumaraguru, *IIIT-Delhi, India*
Andrew Kun, *University of New Hampshire, USA*
Andreas Kunz, *Swiss Federal Institute of Technology Zurich, Switzerland*
Kai Kunze, *Osaka Prefecture University, Japan*
Liisa Kuparinen, *University of Jyväskylä, Finland*
Sri Kurniawan, *University of California, USA*
Gordon Kurtenbach, *Autodesk, Canada*
Arma an Kuru, *Middle East Technical University, Turkey*
Raja Kushalnagar, *Rochester Institute of Technology, USA*
Diana Kusunoki, *Drexel University, USA*
Kari Kuutti, *University of Oulu, Finland*
Stacey Kuznetsov, *Carnegie Mellon University, USA*
Youngshin Kwak, *Ulsan National Institute of Science and Technology, South Korea*
Bum Chul Kwon, *University of Konstanz, Germany*
Gyu Hyun Kwon, *Virginia Polytechnic Institute and State University, USA*
Jarmo Laaksolahti, *Swedish Institute of Computer Science, Sweden*
Richard Ladner, *University of Washington, USA*
Ben Lafreniere, *University of Waterloo, Canada*
Carl Lagoze, *University of Michigan, USA*
Susan Lai, *San Jose Gateway, Canada*
Denis Lalanne, *University of Fribourg, Switzerland*
Mary Lalomia, *Philips Medical, USA*
Shyong Lam, *Google, USA*
Anthony Lamarca, *Intel Research Seattle, USA*
Kristin Lamberty, *University of Minnesota, USA*
Cliff Lampe, *University of Michigan, USA*
Airi Lampinen, *Helsinki Institute for Information Technology HIIT, Finland*
James Landay, *University of Washington, USA*
Richard Landers, *Old Dominion University, USA*
Monica Landoni, *University of Lugano, Switzerland*
Pascal Landry, *Universitat Pompeu Fabra, Spain*
Steven Landry, *Purdue University, USA*
Peter Landwehr, *Carnegie Mellon University, USA*
Nicholas Lane, *Microsoft, China*
Patrick Langdon, *University of Cambridge, UK*
Marc Langheinrich, *Università Della Svizzera Italiana, Switzerland*
Joel Lanir, *University of Haifa, Israel*

Edward Lank, *University of Waterloo, Canada*
Rosa Lanzillotti, *Università di Bari, Italy*
Astrid Larssen, *Ashesi University College, Ghana*
Walter Lasecki, *University of Rochester Computer Science, USA*
Nancy Latham, *Boston University School of Public Health, USA*
Thomas Latoza, *UC Irvine, USA*
Celine Latulipe, *University of North Carolina at Charlotte, USA*
Manfred Lau, *Lancaster University, UK*
Felix Lauber, *University of Munich, Germany*
Carolyn Lauckner, *Michigan State University, USA*
Gael Laurans, *Delft University of Technology, The Netherlands*
Eric Laurier, *University of Edinburgh, UK*
Yann Laurillau, *University of Grenoble, France*
Debra Lauterbach, *Google, USA*
Joseph Laviola Jr., *University of Central Florida, USA*
Joseph Lawrance, *Oregon State University, USA*
Shaun Lawson, *University of Lincoln, UK*
Shawn Lawson, *Rensselaer Polytechnic Institute, USA*
Amanda Lazar, *University of Washington, USA*
Jonathan Lazar, *Towson University, USA*
Marco Lazzari, *University of Bergamo, Italy*
Lucian Leahu, *SICS, Sweden*
Alex Leavitt, *University of Southern California, USA*
Eric Lecolinet, *Télécom-Paristech, France*
Kerstin Leder Mackley, *Loughborough University, UK*
David Ledo, *University of Calgary, Canada*
Bongshin Lee, *Microsoft Research, USA*
Charlotte Lee, *University of Washington, USA*
Geehyuk Lee, *KAIST, Korea*
Joon Suk Lee, *Virginia Tech, USA*
Joyce Lee, *University of Michigan, USA*
Matthew Lee, *Philips Research, USA*
Michael Lee, *University of Washington, USA*
Min Kyung Lee, *Carnegie Mellon University, USA*
Stephanie Lee, *University of Washington, USA*
Uichin Lee, *KAIST, South Korea*
Young Lee, *Motorola Research, USA*
Colby Leider, *University of Miami, USA*
Darren Leigh, *USA*
Iolanda Leite, *Instituto Superior Técnico, Portugal*
Daniel Leithinger, *Massachusetts Institute of Technology, USA*
Luis A. Leiva, *Universitat Politècnica de València, Spain*
Eva Lenz, *Folkwang University of the Arts, Germany*
Pedro Leon, *Carnegie Mellon University, USA*
Chiara Leonardi, *Fondazione Bruno Kessler, Italy*
Stefania Leone, *University of South Carolina, USA*
Tuck Leong, *University of Technology, Australia*
George Lepouras, *University of Peloponnese, Greece*
Gilly Leshed, *Cornell University, USA*
Catherine Letondal, *ENAC, France*
Rock Leung, *University of British Columbia, Canada*
Vincent Levesque, *Immersion, Canada*
Peter Levin, *Intel Corporation, USA*

Vincent Lewandowski, *KTH, Sweden*
Clayton Lewis, *University of Colorado, USA*
Caroline Leygue, *University of Nottingham, UK*
Ian Li, *Carnegie Mellon University, USA*
Karen Li
Na Li, *Pennsylvania State University, USA*
Nan Li, *EPFL, Switzerland*
Wei Li, *Autodesk Research, Canada*
Hai-Ning Liang, *Xi'an Jiaotong-Liverpool University, China*
Rung-Huei Liang, *National Taiwan University of Science and Technology, Taiwan (r.o.c.)*
Fotis Liarokapis, *Coventry University, UK*
Ilaria Liccardi, *INRIA Paris, France*
Henry Lieberman, *Massachusetts Institute of Technology, USA*
Michael Liegl, *Lancaster University, UK*
Ann Light, *Northumbria University, UK*
Lassi Liikkanen, *Helsinki Institute for Information Technology HIIT, Finland*
Brian Lim, *Fraunhofer Center for Sustainable Energy Systems, USA*
Sohye Lim, *Ewha Womans University, Republic of Korea*
James Lin, *Google, USA*
Jialiu Lin, *Carnegie Mellon University, USA*
Min Lin, *Samsung Electronics, P. R. China*
Per Linde, *Malmö University,*
Robert Lindeman, *Worcester Polytechnic Institute, USA*
Rhema Linder, *Texas A&M University, USA*
Gitte Lindgaard, *Carleton University, Canada*
Siân Lindley, *Microsoft Research, UK*
Janne Lindqvist, *Rutgers University, USA*
Stephen Lindsay, *Swansea University, Wales, UK*
Conor Linehan, *University of Lincoln, UK*
Jessica Lingel, *Microsoft Research, USA*
Heather Lipford, *University of North Carolina at Charlotte, USA*
Roman Lissermann, *Technische Universität Darmstadt, Germany*
Eden Litt, *Northwestern University, USA*
Greg Little, *Massachusetts Institute of Technology, USA*
Linda Little, *Northumbria University, UK*
Jin Liu, *Cornell University, USA*
Leslie Liu, *University of Washington, USA*
Tracy Liu, *University of Michigan, USA*
Wei Liu, *Delft University of Technology, Netherlands*
Yefeng Liu, *Waseda University, Japan*
Ying Liu, *Charles Sturt University, Australia*
Ying Hsang Liu, *Intel, China*
Yun-En Liu, *University of Washington, USA*
Zhicheng Liu, *Georgia Institute of Technology, USA*
Zhicheng Liu, *Georgia Institute of Technology, USA*
Mark Livingston, *Naval Research Laboratory, USA*
Avishay Livne, *The University of Michigan, USA*
Sara Ljungblad, *LOTS Design AB, Sweden*
Markus Löchtefeld, *German Research Center for Artificial Intelligence (DFKI), Germany*
Dan Lockton, *University of Warwick, UK*

Thomas Lodato, *Georgia Institute of Technology, USA*
Courtney Loder, *UC Irvine, USA*
Sebastian Loehmann, *University of Munich, Germany*
Steffen Lohmann, *University of Stuttgart, Germany*
Benjamin Lok, *University of Florida, USA*
Lian Loke, *University of Sydney, Australia*
Derek Lomas, *Carnegie Mellon University, USA*
Benjamin Long, *Bristol University, UK*
Kiel Long, *Lancaster University, England, UK*
Chee Kit Looi, *NTU, Singapore*
Jack Loomis, *UCSB, USA*
Arminda Lopes, *Instituto Politecnico de Castelo Branco, Portugal*
Pedro Lopes, *Hasso Plattner Institute, Germany*
Fabien Lotte, *INRIA Bordeaux Sud-Ouest, France*
Danielle Lottridge, *San Francisco State University, USA*
Sandy Louchart, *Heriot-Watt University, Scotland, UK*
Oriana J Love, *Pacific Northwest National Laboratory, USA*
Hao Lu, *Intel, USA*
Hong Lu, *IBM Research, USA*
Jie Lu, *Samsung, USA*
Mei Lu, *CUNY Graduate Center, USA*
Pengfei Lu, *Fudan University, USA*
Tun Lu, *University of Washington, China*
Hao Lü, *Google, USA*
Andrés Lucero, *Nokia Research Center, Finland*
Bernd Ludwig, *University of Regensburg, Germany*
Patrick Lühne, *Hasso Plattner Institute, Germany*
Rowena Luk, *AMITA Telemedicine, Canada*
Kristian Lukander, *Finnish Institute of Occupational Health, Finland*
Jonathan Lukens, *University of Tennessee, USA*
Stephan Lukosch, *Delft University of Technology, The Netherlands*
Jay Lundell, *Intel Research, USA*
Kurt Luther, *Carnegie Mellon University, USA*
Wayne Lutters, *UMBC, USA*
Marianne Lykke, *Aalborg University, Denmark*
Peter Lyle, *Queensland University of Technology, Australia*
Leilah Lyons, *University of Illinois at Chicago, USA*
Michael Lyons, *Ritsumeikan University, Japan*
Heikki Lyytinen, *University of Jyväskylä, Finland*
Xiaojuan Ma, *Noah's Ark Lab, Hong Kong, China*
Catriona Macaulay, *University of Dundee, UK*
Craig Macdonald, *Pratt Institute, USA*
Carolyn Macgregor, *University of Waterloo, Canada*
Cristiano Maciel, *Universidade Federal de Mato Grosso, Brazil*
Giuliano Maciocci, *Qualcomm Research Cambridge, UK*
Wendy Mackay, *INRIA, France*
Scott Mackenzie, *York University, Canada*
Allan Maclean, *Image Semantics Ltd, UK*
Karon Maclean, *University of British Columbia, Canada*
Christopher Maclellan, *Carnegie Mellon University, USA*
Andrew Macvean, *Heriot-Watt University, Edinburgh*
Rui Madeira, *ESTSetúbal/IPS, Portugal*
Pattie Maes, *Massachusetts Institute of Technology, USA*

Rachel Magee, *Drexel University, USA*
Charlotte Magnusson, *Lund University, Sweden*
Mary Lou Maher, *University of Sydney, Australia*
Jalal Mahmud, *IBM Research - Almaden, USA*
Nasim Mahmud, *Hasselt University - Tul - IBBT, Belgium*
Angela Mahr, *German Research Center for Artificial Intelligence (DFKI), Germany*
Scott Mainwaring, *Intel Research, USA*
Julie Maitland, *Populus Global Solutions Inc., Canada*
Päivi Majaranta, *University of Tampere, Finland*
Yasutoshi Makino, *Keio University, Japan*
Sylvain Malacria, *University of Canterbury, France*
Miguel Malheiros, *University College London, UK*
Alessio Malizia, *University 'la Sapienza' of Rome, Italy*
Lone Malmborg, *IT University of Copenhagen, Denmark*
Lena Mamykina, *Columbia University, USA*
Hiroyuki Manabe, *NTT DOCOMO, Japan*
Clara Mancini, *The Open University, UK*
Regan Mandryk, *University of Saskatchewan, Canada*
Jennifer Mankoff, *Carnegie Mellon University, USA*
Daniela Mapelli, *Università di Padoa,*
Valérie Maquil, *Public Research Center Henri Tudor, Luxembourg*
Gabriela Marcu, *Carnegie Mellon University, USA*
Adam Marcus, *MIT CSAIL, USA*
Georgios Marentakis, *Institute for Electronic Music and Acoustics - Graz, Austria*
Gloria Mark, *University of California, USA*
Anders Markussen, *University of Copenhagen, Denmark*
Thomas Markussen, *Kolding School of Design, Denmark*
Jennifer Marlow, *Carnegie Mellon University, USA*
Elena Márquez Segura, *Uppsala University, Sweden*
Gary Marsden, *University of Cape Town, South Africa*
Andrea Marshall, *Drexel University Ischool, USA*
Catherine Marshall, *Microsoft, USA*
Joe Marshall, *University of Nottingham, UK*
Mark Marshall, *Sheffield Hallam University, UK*
Stuart Marshall, *Victoria University of Wellington, New Zealand*
Jean-Bernard Martens, *Eindhoven University of Technology, The Netherlands*
Stefan Marti, *Harman International, USA*
Anna Lisa Martin, *Zurich University of the Arts, Switzerland*
Aqueasha Martin, *Clemson University, USA*
Benoît Martin, *Université de Lorraine, France*
David Martin, *Xerox Research Center Europe, France*
Taylor Martin, *USU, USA*
Sarah Martindale, *The University of Nottingham, UK*
Diego Martinez Plasencia, *University of Bristol, UK*
Célia Martinie, *University Toulouse 3, France*
Misa Maruyama, *University of Hawaii at Manoa, USA*
Sergio Mascetti, *University of Milan, Italy*
Afra Mashhadi, *Alcatel-Lucent, Ireland*
Mikhil Masli, *Grouplens Research, USA*
Winter Mason, *Stevens Institute of Technology, USA*
Justin Matejka, *Autodesk, Canada*

Anijo Mathew, *Illinois Institute of Technology, USA*
Akhil Mathur, *University of Toronto, Canada*
Ben Matthews, *The University of Queensland, Australia*
Mark Matthews, *Cornell University, USA*
Tara Matthews, *IBM Research - Almaden, USA*
Denys Matthies, *University of Munich, Germany*
Frank Maurer, *University of Calgary, Canada*
Max-Emanuel Maurer, *University of Munich, Germany*
Deborah Maxwell, *University of Edinburgh, UK*
Aaron May, *Simon Fraser University, Canada*
Simon Mayer, *ETH Zurich, Switzerland*
Christopher Mayhorn, *North Carolina State University, USA*
Walterio Mayol-Cuevas, *University of Bristol, UK*
Oscar Mayora, *ITESM Cuernavaca, Mexico*
Rene Mayrhofer, *Lancaster University, UK*
Ali Mazalek, *Georgia Institute of Technology, USA*
Melissa Mazmanian, *University of California, USA*
Michelle Mazurek, *Carnegie Mellon University, USA*
Emanuela Mazzone, *University of Central Lancashire, Spain*
Victoria Mcarthur, *York University, Canada*
Simon Mccallum, *Gjøvik University College, Norway*
John Mccarthy, *University College Cork, Ireland*
Scott Mccrickard, *Virginia Tech, USA*
Sean Mcdirmid, *Microsoft Advanced Technology Center, Peoples Republic of China*
David Mcdonald, *University of Washington, USA*
Nora Mcdonald, *Drexel University, USA*
Mary F Mcdonough
Daniel Mcduff, *MIT Media Lab, USA*
Gregor Mcewan, *University of Saskatchewan, Canada*
Daniel Mcfarlane, *Lockheed Martin Advanced Technology Laboratories, USA*
Kevin Mcgee, *National University of Singapore, Singapore*
Mark Mcgill, *University of Glasgow, UK*
William Mcgrath, *Stanford University, USA*
Joanna Mcgrenere, *University of British Columbia, Canada*
Michael Mcguffin, *École de Technologie Supérieure, Canada*
Ross Mclachlan, *University of Glasgow, Scotland, UK*
Ryan Mcmahan, *University of Texas at Dallas, USA*
Donald Mcmillan, *SICS, Sweden*
Indrani Medhi-Thies, *Microsoft Research, India*
Richard Medland, *Queensland University of Technology, Australia*
Ben Medler, *EA, USA*
Elisa Mekler, *University of Basel, Switzerland*
Volkamer Melanie, *TU Darmstadt, Germany*
David Mellis, *Massachusetts Institute of Technology, USA*
Gustavo Mello Machado, *University of Stuttgart, Germany*
Nemanja Memarovic, *Universita Della Svizzera Italiana, Switzerland*
Maria Menendez, *University of Trento, Italy*
Sarah Mennicken, *University of Zurich, Switzerland*
Rachel Menzies, *University of Dundee, UK*
Emma Mercier, *University of Illinois at Urbana-Champaign, USA*
David Merrill, *Massachusetts Institute of Technology, USA*
Ronald Metoyer, *Oregon State University, USA*

Johanna Meurer, *University, Germany*
Jochen Meyer, *OFFIS - Institute for Information Technology, Germany*
Miriah Meyer, *University of Utah, USA*
Haipeng Mi, *Tsinghua University, China*
Nicholas Micallef, *Glasgow Caledonian University, UK*
Martin Mihajlov, *Ss. Cyril and Methodius University, Macedonia*
Silvia Miksch, *Vienna University of Technology, Austria*
David Millen, *IBM Research, USA*
Andrew Miller, *University of British Columbia, USA*
Gregor Miller, *Massachusetts Institute of Technology, Canada*
Scarlett Miller (herring), *Georgia Institute of Technology, USA*
Michael Minge, *Berlin University of Technology, Germany*
Aliaksei Miniukovich, *University of Trento, Italy*
Andrea Minuto, *University of Twente, The Netherlands*
Pejman Mirza-Babaei, *University of Ontario Institute of Technology, Canada*
Sonali Mishra, *University of Michigan, USA*
Taniya Mishra, *AT&T, USA*
Alex Mitchell, *National University of Singapore, Singapore*
Tanushree Mitra, *Georgia Institute of Technology, USA*
Tracy Mitzner, *Georgia Institute of Technology, USA*
Takahiro Miura, *The University of Tokyo, Japan*
Takashi Miyaki, *Inria, France*
Bart Moens, *Ghent University, Belgium*
Andrew Molineux, *Lancaster University, England*
Andreas Möller, *Technische Universität München, Germany*
Max Möllers, *RWTH Aachen University, Germany*
David Molyneaux, *Microsoft Research, England, UK*
Arthur Money, *Brunel University, UK*
Andrew Monk, *University of York, UK*
Andres Monroy-Hernandez, *Massachusetts Institute of Technology, USA*
Toni-Jan Keith Monserrat, *National University of Singapore, Philippines*
Kyle Montague, *University of Dundee, Scotland, UK*
Bob Moore, *PARC, USA*
Simone Mora, *Norwegian University of Science and Technology, Norway*
Stuart Moran, *University of Nottingham, UK*
Neema Moraveji, *Microsoft Research Asia, China*
Guillaume Moreau, *Ecole Centrale de Nantes, France*
Lourdes Moreno, *Universidad Carlos III de Madrid, Spain*
Jonathan Morgan, *University of Washington, USA*
Giulio Mori, *ISTI-CNR, Italy*
Joji Mori, *The University of Melbourne, Australia*
Carlos Morimoto, *University of Sao Paulo, Brazil*
Janine Morley, *Lancaster University, UK*
Fabio Morreale, *University of Trento, Italy*
Patricia Morreale, *Kean University, USA*
Margaret Morris, *Intel Corporation, USA*
Meredith Morris, *Microsoft Research, USA*
Ann Morrison, *Aalborg University, Denmark*
Cecily Morrison, *Microsoft Research, UK*
Richard Mortier, *The University of Nottingham, UK*
Lee Morton, *Glasgow Caledonian University, UK*
Christiane Moser, *ICT&S Center, Austria*
Vicki Moulder, *Simon Fraser University, Canada*

Christos Mousas, *University of Sussex, England, UK*
Mu Mu, *Lancaster University, UK*
Omar Mubin, *University of Western Sydney, Australia*
Christian Muehl, *Inria Bordeaux, France*
Florian "Floyd" Mueller, *Exertion Games Lab, Australia*
Stefanie Mueller, *Hasso Plattner Institute, Germany*
Christian Mueller-Tomfelde, *CSIRO ICT Centre, Australia*
Max Mühlhäuser, *TU Darmstadt, Germany*
Adiyan Mujibiya, *The University of Tokyo, Japan*
Heiko Müller, *IBM Research, Germany*
Gernot Müller-Putz, *Graz University of Technology, Austria*
Alessandro Mulloni, *Qualcomm Research KAIST, Republic of Korea ria, Austria*
Cosmin Munteanu, *National Research Council Canada, Canada*
Helmut Munz, *RMIT University, Austria*
Martin Murer, *University of Salzburg, Austria*
Dianne Murray, *Indep. Consultant, UK*
Ildar Muslukhov, *University of British Columbia, Canada*
Mirco Musolesi, *University of Birmingham, UK*
Brad Myers, *Carnegie Mellon University, USA*
Elizabeth Mynatt, *Georgia Institute of Technology, USA*
Mor Naaman, *Cornell University, USA*
Miguel Nacenta, *University of St Andrews, UK*
Frank Nack, *University of Amsterdam (uva), The Netherlands*
Till Nagel, *University of Applied Sciences Potsdam, Germany*
Tobias Nägeli, *ETH Zurich, Switzerland*
Hideyuki Nakanishi, *Osaka University, Japan*
Kevin Nam, *University of Michigan, USA*
Suranga Nanayakkara, *Singapore University of Technology and Design, USA*
Mathieu Nancel, *University of Canterbury, France*
Nitya Narasimhan, *edupreneur, USA*
Bonnie Nardi, *University of California, USA*
Amani Naseem, *RMIT University, Australia*
Chris Nash, *University of Cambridge, UK*
Meena Natarajan, *UC Berkeley, USA*
Lisa Nathan, *University of British Columbia, Canada*
David Navarre, *IRIT, France*
Elena Nazzi, *IT University of Copenhagen, Denmark*
Mark Neerincx, *TNO Human Factors, Netherlands*
Michael Neff, *UC Davis, USA*
Paolo Negri
Matei Negulescu, *University of Waterloo, Canada*
Matti Nelimarkka, *Helsinki Institute for Information Technology HIIT, Finland*
Les Nelson, *PARC, USA*
Cornelius Neufeldt, *University of Siegen, Germany*
Alena Neviarouskaya, *University of Tokyo, Japan*
Alan Newell, *Dundee University, Scotland, UK*
Mark Newman, *University of Michigan, USA*
Victor Ng-Thow-Hing, *Honda Research Institute USA, USA*
David Nguyen, *Nokia Research Center, USA*
Duyen Nguyen, *Cornell University, USA*
James Nicholson, *Northumbria University, England, UK*

Hugo Nicolau, *University of Dundee, UK*
Lene Nielsen, *IT University of Copenhagen, Denmark*
Gerrit Niezen, *Swansea University, UK*
Femke Nijboer, *University of Twente, The Netherlands*
Valentina Nisi, *University of Madeira, Portugal*
Xi Niu, *Indiana University, USA*
Sylvie Noël, *Universita di Trento, Italy*
Pedro Nogueira, *LIACC - Artificial Intelligence and Computer Science Laboratory, Portugal*
A. Imran Nordin, *University of York, UK*
Mie Nørgaard, *Aarhus School of Architecture, Denmark*
Francesco Nori
Maria Normark, *Södertörn University, Sweden*
Lauren Norrie, *University of Glasgow, Scotland, UK*
Chris North, *Virginia Polytechnic Institute and State University, USA*
Oded Nov, *Polytechnic Institute of New York University, USA*
Laurie Novak, *Vanderbilt University, USA*
Francisco Nunes, *Vienna University of Technology, Austria*
Petteri Nurmi, *Helsinki Institute for Information Technology HIIT, Finland*
Andreas Nürnberger, *Otto-Von-Guericke-University Magdeburg, Germany*
Stina Nylander, *Swedish Institute of Computer Science, Sweden*
Heather O'brien, *University of British Columbia, Canada*
Marita O'brien, *University of Alabama-Huntsville, USA*
Brendan O'connor, *Carnegie Mellon University, USA*
Lora Oehlberg, *INRIA, USA*
Anne Oeldorf-Hirsch, *University of Connecticut, USA*
Eyal Ofek, *Microsoft Research, USA*
Corinna Ogonowski, *University of Siegen, Germany*
Alice Oh, *KAIST, Republic of Korea*
Jonghwan Oh, *Seoul National University, Republic of Korea*
Kenton O'hara, *Microsoft Research, UK*
Harri Oinas-Kukkonen, *University of Oulu, Finland*
Aisling O'kane, *University College London, UK*
Bugra Oktay, *University of Nevada, USA*
Patrick Oladimeji, *Swansea University, UK*
Halla Olafsdottir, *Université Paris-Sud, France*
Erica Olmsted-Hawala, *U.S. Census Bureau, USA*
Dan Olsen, *Brigham Young University, USA*
Gary Olson, *University of California, USA*
Judith Olson, *U of Michigan, USA*
Katherine Olson, *Georgia Institute of Technology, USA*
Thomas Olsson, *Tampere University of Technology, Finland*
Sile O'modhrain, *University of Michigan, USA*
Jacki O'neill, *XRCE, France*
Stephen Oney, *Carnegie Mellon University, USA*
Wei Tsang Ooi, *National University of Singapore, Singapore*
Elisa Oreglia, *University of California Berkeley, USA*
Tihomir Orehovacki, *University of Zagreb, Croatia*
Eleanor O'rourke, *University of Washington, USA*
Valeria Orso, *University of Padova, Italy*
Martin Ortlieb, *Google, Switzerland*
Keith Ostfeld, *Children's Museum of Houston, USA*
Nuno Otero, *Linnæus University, Sweden*
Tom Ouyang, *MIT, USA*

Derya Özçelik, *Eindhoven University of Technology, The Netherlands*
Jeni Paay, *Aalborg University, Denmark*
Tyler Pace, *Indiana University Bloomington, USA*
Tim Paek, *Microsoft Research, USA*
Michel Pahud, *Microsoft Research, USA*
Helen Pain, *University of Edinburgh, UK*
Drew Paine, *University of Washington, USA*
Aditya Pal, *IBM Research - Almaden, USA*
Philippe Palanque, *ICS-IRIT, France*
Leysia Palen, *University of Colorado, USA*
Henri Palleis, *Ludwig-Maximilians-Universität München, Germany*
Susan Palmiter, *Design Technologies, USA*
Viktoria Pammer, *Know-Center, Austria*
Yingxin Pan, *IBM Research - China, China*
Yue Pan, *Indiana University Bloomington, USA*
Zhengzheng Pan, *Facebook, USA*
Katherine Panciera, *University of Minnesota, USA*
Sabrina Panëels, *McGill University, France*
Carolyn Pang, *Simon Fraser University, Canada*
Saurabh Panjwani, *Microsoft Research India, India*
Katrina Panovich, *MIT, USA*
Nadia Pantidi, *The University of Nottingham, UK*
Caroline Pantofaru, *Willow Garage, USA*
Eleftherios Papachristos, *University of Patras, Greece*
Savvas Papaioannou, *University of Oxford, UK*
Joseph Paradiso, *MIT Media Laboratory, USA*
Aditya Parameswaran, *Stanford University, USA*
Zachary Pardos, *UC Berkeley, USA*
Pablo Paredes, *University of Berkeley, USA*
Narcis Pares, *Universitat Pompeu Fabra, Spain*
Tapan Parikh, *UC Berkeley, USA*
Minsu Park, *KAIST, South Korea*
Souneil Park, *Univ. of Michigan, USA*
Sun Young Park, *University of California, USA*
Taiwoo Park, *KAIST, South Korea*
Young-Woo Park, *KAIST, South Korea*
Chris Parnin, *Georgia Institute of Technology, USA*
Kurt Partridge, *Google, USA*
Gaurav Paruthi, *University of Michigan, USA*
Marco Pasch, *University of Lugano, Switzerland*
Gert Pasman, *Delft University of Technology, The Netherlands*
Jerome Pasquero, *Research In Motion Limited, Canada*
Kayur Patel, *University of Washington, USA*
Nirmal Patel, *Georgia Institute of Technology, USA*
Rupa Patel, *University of Washington, USA*
Rupal Patel, *Northeastern University, USA*
Shwetak Patel, *University of Washington, USA*
Jessica Pater, *Georgia Institute of Technology, USA*
Andrew Patrick, *Carleton University, Canada*
Donald Patterson, *University of California Irvine, USA*
Sharoda Paul, *GE Global Research, USA*
Eric Paulos, *University of California, USA*
Dana Pavel, *University of Essex, UK*

Ioannis Pavlidis, *University of Houston, USA*
Andriy Pavlovych, *York University, Canada*
Stephen Payne, *University of Bath, UK*
Jennifer Pearson, *Swansea University, UK*
Fabrizio Pece, *University College London, UK*
Evan Peck, *Tufts University, USA*
Sonja Pedell, *Swinburne University of Technology, Australia*
Sonjs Pedell, *Swinburne University of Technology, Australia*
Esben Pedersen, *University of Copenhagen, Danmark*
Thomas Pederson, *IT University of Copenhagen, Denmark*
Peter Peltonen, *University of Helsinki, Finland*
Jorge Peña, *University of California, USA*
Wei Peng, *Information Studies, USA*
Gerald Penn, *University of Toronto, Canada*
Kylie Peppler, *Indiana University, USA*
Lucas Pereira, *Madeira Interactive Technologies Institute, Portugal*
Adam Perer, *IBM Research, USA*
Manuel Perez-Quinones, *Virginia Tech, USA*
Charles Perin, *INRIA Saclay, France*
Trevor Pering, *Intel Research, USA*
Ken Perlin, *New York University, USA*
Simon Perrault, *National University of Singapore, Singapore*
Daniel Perry, *University of Washington, USA*
Florian Perteneder, *University of Applied Sciences Upper KAIST, Republic of Korea ria, Austria*
Marianne Graves Petersen, *Aarhus University, Denmark*
Daniela Petrelli, *Sheffield Hallam University, UK*
Helen Petrie, *University of York, UK*
Tamara Peyton, *Penn State University, USA*
Laura Pfeifer Vardoulakis, *Google, USA*
Max Pfeiffer, *Leibniz Universität Hannover, Germany*
Thies Pfeiffer, *Bielefeld University, Germany*
Bastian Pfleging, *University of Stuttgart, Germany*
Martin Pielot, *Telefonica Research, Spain*
James Pierce, *Carnegie Mellon University, USA*
Jeffrey Pierce, *Samsung UX Innovations Lab, USA*
Emmanuel Pietriga, *INRIA, France*
Mary Pietrowicz, *National Center for Supercomputing Applications, USA*
Thomas Pietrzak, *University of Lille, France*
Hannah Pileggi, *Georgia Institute of Technology, USA*
Clément Pillias, *CNAM, France*
Laura Pina, *'UCSD' As In University of California at San Diego, USA*
Fabiano Pinatti, *Institute of Design and Assessment of Technology, Austria*
Kathleen Pine, *University of California, USA*
Claudio Pinhanez, *IBM Brazil, Brazil*
Volkmar Pipek, *University of Siegen, Germany*
Anne Marie Piper, *Northwestern University, USA*
Michael Pirker, *Ruwido KAIST, Republic of Korea ria Gmbh, Austria*
Peter Pirolli, *PARC, USA*
Catherine Plaisant, *University of Maryland, USA*
Andreas Pleuss, *University of Limerick, Ireland*
Bernd Ploderer, *The University of Melbourne, Australia*
Thomas Ploetz, *Newcastle University, UK*

Barry Po, *HSBC, Canada*
Henning Pohl, *University of Hannover, Germany*
Margit Pohl, *Vienna University of Technology, Austria*
Anna Pohlmeyer, *Delft University of Technology, Netherlands*
Ioannis Politis, *Eindhoven University of Technology, Netherlands*
John Pollak, *Cornell University, USA*
Marc Pomplun, *University of Massachusetts Boston, USA*
Heather Pon-Barry, *Informatics, USA*
Suporn Pongnumkul, *University of Washington, USA*
Erika Poole, *Penn State University, USA*
Alan Pope, *NASA Langley Research Center, USA*
Ana-Maria Popescu, *Pinterest, USA*
Leslie Poppe, *University of Washington, USA*
Kristi Potter, *University of Oregon, USA*
Tania Pouli, *Technicolor, France*
Ivan Poupyrev, *Disney Research, USA*
Sören Preibusch, *Microsoft Research, UK*
Chris Preist, *University of Bristol, UK*
Nora Presson, *University of Pittsburgh, USA*
Mike Preuss, *WWU Münster, Germany*
Blaine Price, *The Open University, UK*
Sara Price, *Institute of Education, UK*
Reid Priedhorsky, *Los Alamos National Laboratory, USA*
Rafael Prikladnicki, *Pucrs, Brazil*
Michael Prilla, *University of Bochum, Germany*
Suzanne Prior, *Media and Computer Games, UK*
Kathrin Probst, *University of Applied Sciences Upper KAIST, Republic of Korea ria, Austria*
Jason Procyk, *Simon Fraser University, Canada*
Halley Profita, *University of Colorado, USA*
Sebastian Prost, *CURE - Center for Usability Research & Engineering, Austria*
Janna Protzak, *Berlin Institute of Technology, Germany*
Emily Provost, *University of Michigan, USA*
John Pruitt, *Microsoft, USA*
Larissa Pschetz, *Microsoft Research Asia, Midlothian*
Deborah Ptak, *University of Toronto, Canada*
Pearl Pu, *EPFL, Switzerland*
Andreas Pusch, *Julius-Maximilians-Universität, Germany*
Cynthia Putnam, *Depaul University, USA*
Pardha Pyla, *Virginia Tech, India*
Huamin Qu, *HKUST, Hong Kong*
Novi Quadrianto, *University of Cambridge, UK*
Daniele Quercia, *Yahoo! Research, UK*
Whitney Quesenbery, *Whitney Interactcive Design, USA*
Alexander Quinn, *University of Maryland, USA*
Philip Quinn, *University of Canterbury, New Zealand*
Pablo-Alejandro Quinones, *University of Michigan, USA*
Andrew Quitmeyer, *Georgia Institute of Technology, USA*
Pernilla Qvarfordt, *FX Palo Alto Laboratory, USA*
Daphne Raban, *University of Haifa, Israel*
Mashfiqui Rabbi, *Cornell University, USA*
Robert Racadio, *University of Washington, USA*
Irene Rae, *University of Wisconsin, USA*

Matthew Rafalow, *University of California Irvine, USA*
Nikunj Raghuvanshi, *Microsoft Research, USA*
Tauhidur Rahman, *Cornell University, USA*
Kari-Jouko Räihä, *University of Tampere, Finland*
Andrew Raij, *University of South Florida, USA*
Roope Raisamo, *University of Tampere, Finland*
Eeva Raita, *Helsinki Institute for Information Technology HIIT, Finland*
Mikko Rajanen, *University of Oulu, Finland*
Thusha Rajendran, *UK*
Nitendra Rajput, *IBM Research, India*
Ismo Rakkolainen, *University of Tampere, Finland*
Raf Ramakers, *Hasselt University - Tul - Iminds, Belgium*
Ernesto Ramirez, *University of California, USA*
Gonzalo Ramos, *Microsoft, USA*
Adriane Randolph, *Kennesaw State University, USA*
Nimmi Rangaswamy, *Microsoft Research India, India*
Juhi Ranjan, *University of Virginia, USA*
Dimitrios Raptis, *Aalborg University, Denmark*
Umar Rashid, *University of Kent, UK*
Kirsten Rassmus-Gröhn, *Lund University, Sweden*
Rabindra Ratan, *Information Studies, USA*
Matt Ratto, *University of Toronto, Toronto*
Martina Rau, *University of Wisconsin, USA*
Janet Read, *University of Central Lancashire, England*
Kyle Rector, *University of Washington, USA*
Madhu Reddy, *Penn State University, USA*
Fiona Redhead, *Queensland University of Technology, Australia*
Johan Redström, *Umeå Institute of Design, Sweden*
Darren Reed, *University of York, UK*
Robert Reeder, *Google, USA*
Sarah Reeder, *Indiana University, USA*
Tim Regan, *Microsoft, UK*
Holger Regenbrecht, *University of Otago, New Zealand*
Derek Reilly, *Dalhousie University, Canada*
Peter Reimann, *University of Sydney, Australia*
Bryan Reimer, *MIT, USA*
Sofia Reis, *Universidade Nova de Lisboa, Portugal*
Wolfgang Reitberger, *Vienna University of Technology, Austria*
Harald Reiterer, *University, Germany*
Thomas Reitmaier, *UCT Centre In ICT4D, South Africa*
Jun Rekimoto, *University of Tokyo / Sony CSL, Japan*
Christian Remy, *University of Zurich, Switzerland*
Gang Ren, *University of Bath, UK*
Xiangshi Ren, *Kochi University of Technology, Japan*
Yuqing Ren, *Carnegie Mellon University, USA*
Karen Renaud, *University of Glasgow, UK*
Christian Rendl, *University of Applied Sciences Upper KAIST, Republic of Korea ria, Austria*
Stefan Rennick-Egglestone, *The University of Nottingham, UK*
Ronald Rensink, *University of British Columbia, Canada*
Paul Resnick, *University of Michigan, USA*
Glenda Revelle, *University of Arkansas, USA*
Gabriel Reyes, *Georgia Institute of Technology, USA*
Lindsay Reynolds, *Cornell University, USA*

Mark Rice, *Institute of Infocomm Research, Singapore*
Alex Richardson, *The KAIST, Republic of Korea ralian National University, Australia*
Alexander Richter, *Unibwm, Germany*
Jochen Rick, *Saarland University, Germany*
Angela Riechers, *School of Visual Arts, USA*
Jens Riegelsberger, *University College London, UK*
Soo Young Rieh, *University of Michigan, USA*
Andreas Riener, *Johannes Kepler University, Austria*
Alexander Rind, *Vienna University of Technology, Austria*
Lazlo Ring, *Northeastern University, USA*
Mikko Rissanen, *Move Correctly, Singapore*
Tobias Ritschel, *MPI Informatik, Germany*
Giuseppe Riva, *Università Cattolica Del Sacro Cuore, Italy*
Christopher Roast, *Sheffield Hallam University, UK*
Lionel Robert, *University of Michigan, USA*
Jonathan Roberts, *Bangor University, UK*
Judy Robertson, *Heriot-Watt University, UK*
Scott Robertson, *University of Hawaii at Manoa, USA*
Toni Robertson, *University of Technology, Australia*
Jeffrey Robins, *Google, USA*
Simon Robinson, *Swansea University, UK*
Carsten Röcker, *RWTH Aachen University, Germany*
Tom Rodden, *University of Nottingham, UK*
Edgar Rodriguez, *Wellington, New Zealand*
David Roedl, *Indiana University, USA*
Yvonne Rogers, *University College London, UK*
Daniel Roggen, *Newcastle University, UK*
Markus Rohde, *International Institute for Socio-Informatics, Germany*
Michael Rohs, *University of Hannover, Germany*
Daniel Romero, *Northwestern University, USA*
Mario Romero, *Delft University of Technology, Sweden*
Natalia Romero Herrera, *KTH, The Netherlands*
John Rooksby, *University of St Andrews, UK*
Chris Rooney, *Middlesex University, UK*
Carolyn Rose, *Carnegie Mellon University, USA*
Asta Roseway, *Microsoft Research, USA*
Joel Ross, *University of California, USA*
Chiara Rossitto, *Stockholm University, Sweden*
Mattias Rost, *Mobile Life @ SICS, Sweden*
Robert Roth, *University of Wisconsin-Madison, USA*
Virpi Roto, *University of Helsinki, Finland*
Nicolas Roussel, *Inria, France*
Maria Roussou, *Makebelieve Design & Consulting, Greece*
Debjani Roy, *IIT Bombay, India*
Quentin Roy, *CNRS LTCI UMR 5141, France*
Agata Rozga, *Georgia Institute of Technology, USA*
Elisa Rubegni, *Universita Della Svizzera Italiana, Switzerland*
Steve Rubin, *University of California, USA*
Michael Rubinstein, *MIT, USA*
Stefan Rüger, *The Open University, UK*
Jaime Ruiz, *Colorado State University, USA*
Enrico Rukzio, *Lancaster University, Germany*

Sonja Rümelin, *University of Munich, Germany*
Tuukka Ruotsalo, *Aalto University, Finland*
Derek Ruths, *McGill University, Canada*
Kimiko Ryokai, *MIT Media Laboratory, USA*
Jeffrey Rzeszotarski, *Carnegie Mellon University, USA*
Daniel Saakes, *Delft University of Technology, The Netherlands*
Selma Sabanovic, *Indiana University, USA*
Andreas Sackl, *FTW Telecommunications Research Center, Austria*
Ramik Sadana, *Georgia Institute of Technology, USA*
Alireza Sahami Shirazi, *University of Stuttgart, Germany*
Arnaud Sahuguet, *Google, USA*
Alan Said, *CWI, The Netherlands*
Daisuke Sakamoto, *The University of Tokyo, Japan*
Mona Sakr, *Institute of Education, UK*
Ben Salem, *Northumbria University, UK*
Pascal Salembier, *University of Technology of Troyes, France*
Mariana Salgado, *Laurea University of Applied Sciences, Finland*
Guarionex Salivia, *Minnesota State University, USA*
Eva Lotta Sallnäs Pysander, *Royal Institute of Technology, Sweden*
Katri Salminen, *University of Tampere, Finland*
Antti Salovaara, *Aalto University, Finland*
Anastasia Salter, *University of Baltimore, USA*
Frode Sandnes, *Oslo University College, Norway*
Aditya Sankar, *University of Washington, India*
Vagner Santana, *State University of Campinas, Brazil*
Pedro Santana-Mancilla, *University of Colima, Mexico*
Carmen Santoro, *ISTI-CNR, Italy*
T. Saponas, *Microsoft Research, USA*
Aleksandra Sarcevic, *Drexel University, USA*
Makoto Sasaki, *Iwate University, Japan*
Daisuke Sato, *IBM Research - Tokyo, Japan*
Munehiko Sato, *Disney Research, USA*
Yoichi Sato, *The University of Tokyo, Japan*
Debra Satterfield, *Iowa State University, USA*
Allison Sauppé, *University of Wisconsin-Madison, USA*
Valkyrie Savage, *University of California, USA*
Nadav Savio, *Google.org, USA*
Pete Sawyer, *Lancaster University, UK*
Walt Scacchi, *University of California, USA*
Christopher Scaffidi, *Carnegie Mellon University, USA*
Joey Scarr, *University of Canterbury, New Zealand*
Christopher Schaefbauer, *University of Colorado, USA*
Patricia Schank, *SRI International, USA*
Raimund Schatz, *Forschungszentrum Telekommunikation Wien (ftw.), Austria*
Florian Schaub, *Carnegie Mellon University, USA*
Benjamin Scheibehenne, *University of Basel, Switzerland*
Jesse Schell, *Carnegie Mellon University, USA*
Ansgar Scherp, *Business Informatics and Business Mathematics, Germany*
Gianluca Schiavo, *University of Trento & FBK, Italy*
Markus Schilling, *Simon Fraser University, Canada*
Thecla Schiphorst, *Simon Fraser University, Canada*
Steven Schirra, *Massachusetts Institute of Technology, USA*
Chris Schmandt, *Massachusetts Institute of Technology, USA*

Dominik Schmidt, *Hasso Plattner Institute, Germany*
Holger Schnädelbach, *University of Nottingham, UK*
Jodi Schneider, *National University of Ireland, Ireland*
Guy Schofield, *Newcastle University, UK*
Jean Scholtz, *Pacific Northwest Laboratory, USA*
Johannes Schöning, *Hasselt University - Tul - Iminds, Belgium*
Marén Schorch, *University of Siegen, Germany*
Falk Schreiber
Ronald Schroeter, *Queensland University of Technology, Australia*
Kai Schubert, *University of Siegen, Germany*
Daniel Schultheiss, *Ilmenau University of Technology, Germany*
Timothy Schultz, *Drexel University, USA*
Victoria Schwanda Sosik, *Cornell University, USA*
Tobias Schwartz, *Fraunhofer FIT, Germany*
Julia Schwarz, *University of Washington, USA*
Lauren Scissors, *Northwestern University, USA*
Stacey Scott, *University of Waterloo, Canada*
Peter Scupelli, *Carnegie Mellon University, USA*
Sue Ann Seah, *University of Bristol, UK*
A. Fleming Seay, *Carnegie Mellon University, USA*
Michael Sedlmair, *University of Vienna, Austria*
Magy Seif El-Nasr, *Northeastern University, USA*
Julian Seifert, *Ulm University, Germany*
Susanne Seitinger, *MIT Media Lab, USA*
James Self, *UNIST, South Korea*
Kate Sellen, *OCAD University, Canada*
Katherine Sellen, *University of Toronto, Canada*
Bryan Semaan, *University of Hawaii at Manoa, USA*
Shilad Sen, *University of Minnesota, USA*
Phoebe Sengers, *Cornell University, USA*
Sepandar Sepehr, *McMaster University, Canada*
Marcos Serrano, *IRIT, France*
Lauren Sessions Goulet, *Facebook, USA*
Leslie Setlock, *Cornell University, USA*
Burr Settles, *Carnegie Mellon University, USA*
Teddy Seyed, *University of Calgary, Canada*
Aviv Shachak, *University of Toronto, Canada*
Orit Shaer, *Tufts University, USA*
David Shaffer, *University of Wisconsin, USA*
Chirag Shah, *Rutgers University, USA*
Priti Shah, *University of Michigan, USA*
Qonita Shahab, *Eindhoven University of Technology, The Netherlands*
Noor Shaker, *IT University of Copenhagen, Denmark*
David Shamma, *Yahoo!, USA*
Ben Shapiro, *Tufts,*
Ehud Sharlin, *University of Calgary, Canada*
Moushumi Sharmin, *University of Memphis, USA*
Sarah Sharples, *University of Nottingham, UK*
Wes Sharrock, *Manchester University, UK*
Aaron Shaw, *Northwestern University, USA*
Richard Shay, *Carnegie Mellon University, USA*
John Shearer, *Newcastle University, UK*
Mohamed Sheik-Nainar, *Synaptics Inc, USA*
Chia Shen, *Harvard University, USA*

Dawei Shen, *Massachusetts Institute of Technology, USA*
S. Andrew Sheppard, *University of Minnesota, USA*
Yuanchun Shi, *Tsinghua University, China*
Patrick Shih, *The Pennsylvania State University, USA*
Choonsung Shin, *Carnegie Mellon University, USA*
Hiroyuki Shinoda, *The University of Tokyo, Japan*
Frank Shipman, *Texas A&M University, USA*
Sajad Shirali-Shahreza, *University of Toronto, Canada*
Mariya Shiyko, *Northeastern University, USA*
Buntarou Shizuki, *University of Tsukuba, Japan*
Irina Shklovski, *IT University of Copenhagen, Denmark*
Garth Shoemaker, *Google, USA*
Milad Shokouhi, *Microsoft Research, UK*
Jamie Shotton, *Microsoft Research Cambridge, UK*
Mark Shovman, *Yahoo! Inc., Israel*
George Siemens, *Athabasca University, Canada*
Beat Signer, *Vrije Universiteit Brussel, Belgium*
Six Silberman, *Bureau of Economic Interpretation, USA*
Elizabeth Sillence, *Northumbria University, UK*
Liz Sillence, *Northumbria University, UK*
Paula Alexandra Silva, *University of Hawaii at Manoa, Portugal*
Johanna Silvennoinen, *University of Jyväskylä, Finland*
Adalberto Simeone, *Lancaster University, UK*
David Simmons, *University of Glasgow, UK*
Ian Simon, *University of Washington, USA*
Judge Simon, *RAT Group, UK*
Laurent Simon, *University of Cambridge, UK*
Jolynna Sinanan, *The University of Melbourne, Australia*
Leif Singer, *University of Victoria, Canada*
Karan Singh, *University of Toronto, Canada*
Supriya Singh, *Royal Melbourne Institute of Technology, Australia*
Vikash Singh, *University of North Carolina at Charlotte, USA*
Valentina Sintsova, *EPFL, Switzerland*
Behzod Sirjani, *Northwestern University, USA*
David Sirkin, *Stanford University, USA*
Daniel Sjölie, *Umeå University, Sweden*
Mikael B. Skov, *Aalborg University, Denmark*
Marjorie Skubic, *University of Missouri, USA*
Roger Slack, *Bangor University, Wales, UK*
Bernhard Slawik, *University of Munich, Germany*
Manya Sleeper, *Carnegie Mellon University, USA*
Karin Slegers, *KU Leuven, Belgium*
James D. Slotta, *University of Toronto, Canada*
Petr Slovák, *Vienna University of Technology, Austria*
Jan Smeddinck, *University of Bremen, Germany*
Joshua Smith, *University of Washington, USA*
Madeline Smith, *Cornell University, USA*
Matthew Smith, *Leibniz Universität Hannover, Germany*
Ross Smith, *University of South KAIST, Republic of Korea ralia, Australia*
Thomas Smith, *Newcastle University, UK*
Michael Smyth, *Edinburgh Napier University, UK*
Jaime Snyder, *Syracuse University, USA*
Timothy Sohn, *Google, USA*
Tomas Sokoler, *IT University of Copenhagen, Denmark*

Jacob Solomon, *Michigan State University, USA*
Andreas Sonderegger, *University of Fribourg, Switzerland*
Hyunyoung Song, *University of Maryland, USA*
Junehwa Song, *KAIST, Korea*
Yale Song, *MIT CSAIL, USA*
Diane Sonnenwald, *UCD, Ireland*
Daniel Sonntag, *DFKI German Research Center for AI, Germany*
Vladimir Soroka, *IBM Haifa Research Lab, Israel*
Alexander Sorokin, *CrowdFlower, USA*
Iris Soute, *Eindhoven University of Technology, The Netherlands*
Caleb Southern, *Georgia Institute of Technology, USA*
Michiel Sovijärvi-Spape, *Aalto University, Finland*
Anna Spagnolli, *University of Padova, Italy*
Oleg Spakov, *University of Tampere, Finland*
Lucio Davide Spano, *University of Cagliari, Italy*
Mirjana Spasojevic, *Nokia, USA*
Chris Speed, *Edinburgh College of Art, UK*
Tess Speelpenning, *Philips Research, The Netherlands*
Wolfgang Spiessl, *BMW Research and Technology, Germany*
Tasos Spiliotopoulos, *Madeira Interactive Technologies Institute, Portugal*
Martin Spindler, *University of Magdeburg, Germany*
Adam Sporka, *Czech Technical University In Prague, Czech Republic*
Mary Ann Sprague, *Xerox, USA*
Srinath Sridhar, *Max-Planck Institut Für Informatik, Germany*
Saurabh Srivastava, *IBM India Research Laboratory, India*
Robert St. Amant, *North Carolina State University, USA*
Tad Stach, *Queen's University, Canada*
Frank Stajano, *University of Cambridge, UK*
Jeannie Stamberger, *Carnegie Mellon University, USA*
Brodie Stanfield, *University of Ontario Institute of Technology, Canada*
Kevin Stanley, *University of Saskatchewan, Canada*
Pieter Jan Stappers, *Delft University of Technology, The Netherlands*
Kate Starbird, *University of Washington, USA*
Thad Starner, *Georgia Institute of Technology, USA*
John Stasko, *Georgia Institute of Technology, USA*
Bogdan State, *Stanford University, USA*
Ian Stavness, *University of Saskatchewan, Canada*
Anthony Steed, *University College London, UK*
Ann Steele, *The University of Texas at KAIST, Republic of Korea in, USA*
Daniel Steffen, *German Research Center for Artificial Intelligence (DFKI), Germany*
Ben Steichen, *University of British Columbia, Canada*
Martin Stein, *University of Siegen, Germany*
Sebastian Stein, *University of Dundee, Scotland, UK*
Fabius Steinberger, *University of Technology, Australia*
Thomas Steiner, *Hamburg, Germany*
Aaron Steinfeld, *Carnegie Mellon University, USA*
Frank Steinicke, *University of Würzburg, Germany*
Sophie Stellmach, *Technische Universität Dresden, Germany*
Amanda Stent, *Yahoo! Labs, USA*
William Steptoe, *UCL, UK*
Sarah Stevenage
Gunnar Stevens, *University of Siegen, Germany*
Craig Stewart, *University of Glasgow, Scotland, UK*

Michael Stewart, *Virginia Polytechnic Institute and State University, USA*
Rainer Stiefelhagen, *Universität Karlsruhe (TH), Germany*
Jeremiah Still, *Missouri Western State University, USA*
David Stillwell, *University of Nottingham, UK*
Greg Stoddard, *Northwestern, USA*
Erik Stolterman, *Indiana University Bloomington, USA*
Margaret-Anne Storey, *University of Victoria,*
Cristiano Storni, *University of Limerick, Ireland*
Steven Strachan, *CEA, France*
Daniel Strazzulla, *INRIA, France*
Yolande Strengers, *AHURI-RMIT Research Centre, Australia*
Dagny Stuedahl, *University of Oslo, Norway*
Simone Stumpf, *City University London, UK*
Christian Sturm, *Hamm-Lippstadt University of Applied Sciences, Germany*
Norman Su, *University College Dublin, Ireland*
Ozge Subasi, *Vienna University of Technology, Austria*
Sriram Subramanian, *University of Bristol, UK*
Yusuke Sugano, *The University of Tokyo, Japan*
Masanori Sugimoto, *Hokkaido University, Japan*
Bongwon Suh, *Seoul National University, Republic of Korea*
Hyeon-Jeong Suk, *KAIST, South Korea*
Piyawadee Sukaviriya, *IBM Research - T. J. Watson, USA*
Gita Sukthankar, *University of Central Florida, USA*
Evan Suma, *University of Southern California, USA*
Chengzheng Sun, *Nanyang Technological University, Singapore*
David Sun, *UC Berkeley, USA*
Huatong Sun, *University of Washington Tacoma, USA*
Xiao Hua Sun, *IBM Research China, China*
Hari Sundaram, *Arizona State University, USA*
Petra Sundström, *Mobile Life @ SICS, Sweden*
Ja-Young Sung, *Georgia Institute of Technology, USA*
Siddharth Suri, *Microsoft Research, USA*
Alistair Sutcliffe, *The University of Manchester, UK*
Dag Svænes, *NTNU, Norway*
David Swallow, *University of York, UK*
Colin Swindells, *University of Victoria, Canada*
Cristina Sylla, *University of Minho, Portugal*
Anna-Liisa Syrjänen, *University of Oulu, Finland*
Daniel Szafir, *University of Wisconsin, USA*
Agnieszka (aga) Szostek, *Warsaw School of Social Psychology, Poland*
Gerd Szwillus, *Universität Paderborn, Germany*
Aurélien Tabard, *University of Munich, Germany*
Leila Takayama, *Willow Garage, USA*
Justin Talbot, *Stanford University, USA*
Chek Tien Tan, *University of Technology, Australia*
Hong Tan, *Microsoft Research Asia, China*
Kumiko Tanaka-Ishii, *University of Tokyo, Japan*
Joshua Tanenbaum, *Simon Fraser University, Canada*
Karen Tanenbaum, *Simon Fraser University, USA*
Anthony Tang, *University of Calgary, Canada*
Charlotte Tang, *University of British Columbia, Canada*
John Tang, *Microsoft Research, USA*
Stefano Targher, *University of Trento, Italy*
Andrea Tartaro, *Furman University, USA*

Craig Tashman, *Georgia Institute of Technology, USA*
Dan Tasse, *Carnegie Mellon University, USA*
Sarah Tausch, *University of Munich, Germany*
Alex Taylor, *Microsoft Research, UK*
Nick Taylor, *University of Dundee, UK*
Robyn Taylor, *Newcastle University, UK*
Stuart Taylor, *Microsoft Research, UK*
Robert Teather, *McMaster University, Canada*
Kimberly Tee, *SMART Technologies, USA*
Daniel Teibel, *Cassia, USA*
Paul Tennent, *The University of Nottingham, UK*
Monica Tentori, *UABC, Mexico*
Leong-Hwee Teo, *Carnegie Mellon University, Singapore*
Lucia Terrenghi, *Google, Switzerland*
Michael Terry, *University of Waterloo, Canada*
Loren Terveen, *University of Minnesota, USA*
Ambuj Tewari, *University of Michigan, USA*
Anuj Tewari, *UC Berkeley, USA*
Anja Thieme, *Newcastle University, UK*
Harold Thimbleby, *University of Swansea, Wales, UK*
Elizabeth Thiry, *Pennsylvania State University, USA*
Jennifer Thom, *Amazon, USA*
Katherine Thomas, *University of North Texas, USA*
Edison Thomaz, *Georgia Institute of Technology, USA*
Bart Thomee, *Yahoo Labs, Spain*
Robin Thompson, *Newcastle University, UK*
Feng Tian, *Chinese Academy of Sciences, P.r. China*
Lorenza Tiberio, *National Research Council of Italy (CNR), Italia*
Rob Tieben, *Eindhoven University of Technology, Netherlands*
Janko Timmermann, *OFFIS - Institute for Information Technology, Germany*
Nava Tintarev, *University of Aberdeen, Scotland, UK*
Mike Tissenbaum, *University of Toronto, Canada*
Hiroaki Tobita, *Sony CSL Paris, Tokyo*
Eran Toch, *Tel Aviv University, Israel*
Lisa Tolentino, *Arizona State University, USA*
Konrad Tollmar, *KTH, Sweden*
Peter Tolmie, *University of Nottingham, UK*
Catalina Toma, *University of Wisconsin-Madison, USA*
Christian Tominski, *University of Rostock, Germany*
Martin Tomitsch, *Vienna University of Technology, Australia*
Bill Tomlinson, *University of California, USA*
James Tompkin, *MPI Informatik, Germany*
KAIST, Republic of Korea in Toombs, *Indiana University Bloomington, USA*
Mercan Topkara, *IBM Research, USA*
Tammy Toscos, *Indiana University-Purdue University, USA*
Chad Tossell, *Rice University, USA*
W. Ben Towne, *Carnegie Mellon University, USA*
Cuong Tran, *University of California, USA*
Minh-Triet Tran, *University of Science, Vietnam*
Matthias Treder, *Technische Universität Berlin, Germany*
Jeffrey Treem, *Northwestern University, USA*
Shari Trewin, *IBM Research - T. J. Watson, USA*

Ha Trinh, *University of Dundee, UK*
Giovanni Maria Troiano, *Universitat Pompeu Fabra, Spain*
Khai Truong, *University of Toronto, Canada*
Janice Tsai, *Microsoft Research, USA*
Theophanis Tsandilas, *Inria, France*
Jason Tsay, *Carnegie Mellon University, USA*
Edward Tse, *SMART Technologies, Canada*
Nikolaos Tselios, *University of Patras, Greece*
Yuan-Chi Tseng, *National Cheng Kung University, Taiwan*
Jessica Tsimeris, *KAIST, Republic of Korea ralian National University, Australia*
Gill Tsouri, *Rochester Institute of Technology, USA*
Katherine Tsui, *University of Massachusetts Lowell, USA*
Oren Tsur, *Harvard University, USA*
Huawei Tu, *Swansea University, UK*
Alexandre Tuch, *University of Basel, Switzerland*
Zeynep Tufekci, *University of North Carolina, USA*
Kathleen Tuite, *University of Washington, USA*
Marcello Turconi, *University of Trieste, Italy*
Jayson Turner, *Lancaster University, UK*
Thea Turner, *USA*
Lisa Tweedie, *Tweedie Consulting, UK*
Michael Twidale, *University of Illinois at Urbana-Champaign, USA*
George Tzanetakis, *University of Victoria, Canada*
Brygg Ullmer, *Louisiana State University, USA*
Kent Unruh, *University of Washington, USA*
Connor Upton, *Intel Labs Europe, Ireland*
Blase Ur, *Carnegie Mellon University, USA*
Dina Utami
Stephen Uzor, *Glasgow Caledonian University, UK*
Kaisa Väänänen-Vainio-Mattila, *Tampere University of Technology, Finland*
Heli Väätäjä, *Tampere University of Technology, Finland*
Philip Vahey, *SRI International, USA*
Rajan Vaish, *University of California, USA*
Consuelo Valdes, *Wellesley College, USA*
Dimitar Valkov, *University of Muenster, Germany*
Anna Vallgårda, *IT University of Copenhagen, Denmark*
Philip Van Allen, *Art Center College of Design, USA*
Bram Van de Laar, *University of Twente,*
Robin Van Den Akker, *Belgium*
Jan Van Den Bergh, *Hasselt University - Tul - Iminds, Belgium*
Bart Van Den Hooff, *VU University Amsterdam, The Netherlands*
Janet Van Der Linden, *The Open University, UK*
Jelle Van Dijk, *Eindhoven University of Technology, Netherlands*
Aart Van Halteren, *Philips Research, Netherlands*
Frank Van Ham, *IBM Research, USA*
Nancy Van House, *University of California, USA*
Max Van Kleek, *MIT, UK*
Kristof Van Laerhoven, *TU Darmstadt, Germany*
Jos Van Leeuwen, *University of Madeira, Portugal*
Christof Van Nimwegen, *Utrecht University, The Netherlands*
Paul Van Schaik, *Teesside University, UK*

Peter Van Waart, *Rotterdam University of Applied Sciences, The Netherlands*
Davy Vanacken, *Hasselt University - Tul - Iminds, Belgium*
Jeroen Vanattenhoven, *KU Leuven, Belgium*
Andrew Vande Moere, *KU Leuven, Belgium*
Jean Vanderdonckt, *Université Catholique de Louvain (UCL), Belgium*
Kami Vaniea, *Carnegie Mellon University, USA*
Elina Vartiainen, *Nokia Research Center, Sweden*
Asimina Vasalou, *University of Birmingham, UK*
Radu-Daniel Vatavu, *University Stefan Cel Mare of Suceava, Romania*
Yolanda Vazquez-Alvarez, *University of Glasgow, UK*
Eduardo Veas, *Graz University of Technology, Austria*
Rajesh Veeraraghavan, *UC Berkeley, USA*
Laurian Vega, *Virginia Tech, USA*
Tiffany Veinot, *University of Michigan, USA*
Eduardo Velloso, *Lancaster University, UK*
Gina Venolia, *Microsoft Research, USA*
Colin Venters, *University of Huddersfield, UK*
Nervo Verdezoto, *Aarhus University, Denmark*
Arnold Vermeeren, *Delft University of Technology, The Netherlands*
Amber Vermeesch, *Michigan State University, USA*
Jo Vermeulen, *Hasselt University - Tul - Iminds, Belgium*
Frederic Vernier, *Université Paris XI, France*
Keith Vertanen, *Montana Tech, USA*
Roel Vertegaal, *Queen's University, Canada*
Janet Vertesi, *Princeton University, USA*
Carla Verwijs, *In Transition, Canada*
Chi Vi, *University of Bristol, UK*
Melodie Vidal, *Lancaster University, UK*
Timothy Vidas, *Carnegie Mellon University, USA*
Sarah Vieweg, *Qatar Computing Research Institute, Qatar*
Markel Vigo, *University of Manchester, UK*
Nicolas Villar, *Microsoft Research, UK*
Vinayak, *Purdue University, USA*
Jussi Virkkala
Jessica Vitak, *University of Maryland, USA*
Lisa Vizer, *University of Maryland, USA*
Vasillis Vlachokyriakos, *Newcastle University, UK*
Simon Voelker, *RWTH-Aachen University, Germany*
Christian Vogler, *Gallaudet University, USA*
Stephen Voida, *Indiana University, USA*
Martin Voigt, *TU Dresden, Germany*
Dirk Vom Lehn, *King's College London, Great Britain*
Ulrich Von Zadow, *Archimedes Exhibitions Gmbh, Germany*
Emanuel Von Zezschwitz, *University of Munich, Germany*
Mihaela Vorvoreanu, *Purdue University, USA*
Hana Vrzakova, *University of Eastern Finland, Finland*
Romain Vuillemot, *Harvard University, USA*
Dhaval Vyas, *University of Twente, The Netherlands*
Katarzyna Wac, *Carnegie Mellon University, USA*
Chat Wacharamanotham, *RWTH Aachen University, Germany*
Juan P. Wachs, *Purdue University, USA*
Greg Wadley, *The University of Melbourne, Australia*

Johanna Wagner, *Graz University of Technology, Austria*
Julie Wagner, *INRIA, Germany*
Patrick Wagstrom, *Carnegie Mellon University, USA*
Shahtab Wahid, *Virginia Tech, USA*
Brendan Walker, *The University of Nottingham, England, UK*
Bruce Walker, *Georgia Institute of Technology, USA*
Erin Walker, *Arizona State University, USA*
I Walker, *University of Bath, UK*
Lorna Wall, *UCL, UK*
Steven Wall, *System Concepts Ltd, UK*
James Wallace, *University of Waterloo, Canada*
Jayne Wallace, *University of Dundee, UK*
Guenter Wallner, *University of Applied Arts Vienna, Austria*
Jagoda Walny, *University of Calgary, Canada*
Greg Walsh, *University of Maryland, USA*
Tanja Walsh, *Tampere University of Technology, Finland*
Robert Walter, *Telekom Innovation Laboratories, Germany*
Lin Wan, *University of Siegen, Germany*
Chaoli Wang, *Michigan Technological University, USA*
Fei Wang, *IBM Research - Almaden, USA*
Jing Wang, *The Pennsylvania State University, USA*
Jingtao Wang, *University of Pittsburgh, USA*
Liang Wang, *Microsoft, USA*
Robert Wang, *Massachusetts Institute of Technology, USA*
Rongrong Wang, *Samsung Research America, USA*
Xiaoyu Wang, *University of North Carolina at Charlotte, USA*
Yang Wang, *Syracuse University, USA*
Yi-Chia Wang, *Carnegie Mellon University, USA*
Yuchen Wang, *University of Alberta, Canada*
Colin Ware, *University of New Hampshire, USA*
Andrew Warr, *Google, USA*
Rick Wash, *Michigan State University, USA*
Gloria Washington, *Clemson University, USA*
Takayuki Watanabe, *Tokyo Woman's Christian University, Japan*
Kari Watkins, *Georgia Institute of Technology, USA*
Diane Watson, *University of Waterloo, Canada*
Martin Wattenberg, *IBM Research, USA*
Leon Watts, *University of Bath, UK*
Jenny Waycott, *The University of Melbourne, Australia*
Kimberly Weaver, *Georgia Institute of Technology, USA*
Gerhard Weber, *Technische Universität Dresden, Germany*
Michael Weber, *University of Ulm, Germany*
Ina Wechsung, *TU Berlin, Germany*
Rina Wehbe, *University of Ontario Institute of Technology, Canada*
Xuetao Wei, *University of Cincinnati, USA*
Anne Weibert, *University of Siegen, Germany*
Christian Weichel, *Lancaster University, UK*
Karl-Heinz Weidmann, *Fachhochschule Vorarlberg, KAIST, Republic of Korea ria/Europe*
Alexandra Weilenmann, *IT-University of Göteborg, Sweden*
Tino Weinkauf, *Max-Planck Institut Für Informatik, Germany*
Astrid Weiss, *Vienna University of Technology, Austria*
Stephan Wensveen, *Eindhoven University of Technology, The Netherlands*

Elizabeth Wenzel, *NASA Ames Research Center, USA*
Wayne Westerman, *Apple, USA*
Adam Westerski, *Universidad Politecnica de Madrid, Spain*
Tara Whalen, *Dalhousie University, Canada*
Joseph Wherton, *Barts and The London School of Medicine and Dentistry, UK*
Brandyn White, *University of Maryland: College Park, USA*
Kevin White, *University of Maryland Baltimore County, USA*
Sean White, *Nokia, USA*
Anthony Whitehead, *Carleton University, Canada*
Michael Whitney, *University of North Carolina at Charlotte, USA*
Steve Whittaker, *University of California Santa Cruz, USA*
Jon Whittle, *Infolab21, UK*
Mikael Wiberg, *Umeå University, Sweden*
Hadley Wickham, *Rstudio, USA*
Josef Wiemeyer, *Sport Science, Germany*
Jason Wiese, *Carnegie Mellon University, USA*
Alexander Wiethoff, *University of Munich, Germany*
Andrea Wiggins, *University of New Mexico, USA*
Danielle Wilde, *Rmit University, Australia*
Erik Wilde, *UC Berkeley, USA*
Oliver Wilder-Smith, *Northeastern University, USA*
David Wilfinger, *University of Salzburg, Austria*
Wesley Willett, *INRIA, France*
Amanda Williams, *Wyld Collective Ltd., Canada*
Amanda Marisa Williams, *University of California, Canada*
Joseph Williams, *Stanford University, USA*
Kaiton Williams, *Cornell University, USA*
John Williamson, *University of Glasgow, UK*
Julie Williamson, *University of Glasgow, UK*
Andrew Wilson, *Microsoft Research, USA*
Graham Wilson, *University of Glasgow, Scotland, UK*
Mathew Wilson, *Swansea University, UK*
Max Wilson, *Swansea University, UK*
Raphael Wimmer, *University of Munich, Germany*
Marco Winckler, *ICS-IRIT, France*
Christian Winkler, *Ulm University, Germany*
Sarah Wiseman, *University College London, UK*
Pamela Wisniewski, *The Pennsylvania State University, USA*
Jason Wither, *Microsoft, USA*
Jens Witkowski, *Albert-Ludwigs-Universität Freiburg, Germany*
Dan Witzner Hansen, *IT University of Copenhagen, Denmark*
Jacob Wobbrock, *University of Washington, USA*
Jill Woelfer, *University of Washington, USA*
Donghee Yvette Wohn, *Northwestern University, USA*
Katrin Wolf, *Deutsche Telekom Laboratories, Germany*
Peter Wolkerstorfer, *CURE - Center for Usability Research & Engineering, Austria*
B.l. William Wong, *Middlesex University, UK*
Nelson Wong, *University of Saskatchewan, Canada*
Krist Wongsuphasawat, *University of Maryland, USA*
Gavin Wood, *Newcastle University, UK*
Simon Wood, *ABC, Australia*
Emma Woodberry, *Addenbrooke's Hospital, UK*

Rob Woodbury, *Simon Fraser University, Canada*
Allison Woodruff, *Intel Research, USA*
Kirk Woolford, *University of Surrey, UK*
Marcel Worring, *University of Amsterdam, The Netherlands*
Rita Wouhaybi, *Intel Corporation, USA*
Julie Wright, *Umass Boston, USA*
Michael Wright, *University of Bath, UK*
Peter Wright, *Newcastle University, UK*
Andy Wu, *Georgia Institute of Technology, USA*
Anna Wu, *Pennsylvania State University, USA*
Jiayu Wu, *Tsinghua University, China*
Mike Wu, *The University of Toronto, Canada*
Shaomei Wu, *Information Science, USA*
Yu Wu, *The Pennsylvania State University, USA*
Daniela Wurhofer, *University of Salzburg, Austria*
Susan Wyche, *Michigan State University, USA*
Peta Wyeth, *Queensland University of Technology, Australia*
Ruth Wylie, *Arizona State University, USA*
Lonce Wyse, *National University of Singapore, Singapore*
Robert Xiao, *Carnegie Mellon University, USA*
Xiao Xiao, *Massachusetts Institute of Technology, USA*
Xing Xie, *Microsoft Research Asia, China*
Anbang Xu, *University of Illinois at Urbana-Champaign, USA*
Heng Xu, *The Pennsylvania State University, USA*
Yan Xu, *Intel Labs, USA*
Kota Yamaguchi, *University of Tokyo, Japan*
Katsu Yamane, *Disney Research, USA*
Naomi Yamashita, *NTT Communication Science Laboratories, Japan*
Hirotake Yamazoe, *Osaka University, Japan*
de-Nian Yang, *Academia Sinica, Taipei*
Huahai Yang, *IBM Research - Almaden, USA*
Jiang Yang, *University of Michigan, USA*
Rayoung Yang, *University of Michigan, USA*
Rui Yang
Stephen Yang, *SUNY Cortland, USA*
Xing-Dong Yang, *University of Alberta, Canada*
Koji Yatani, *Microsoft Research Asia, China*
Yina Ye, *Helsinki Institute for Information Technology HIIT, Finland*
Nick Yee, *PARC, USA*
Tom Yeh, *University of Colorado, USA*
Yeliz Yesilada, *University of Manchester, UK*
Jude Yew, *National University of Singapore, Singapore*
Samantha Yglesias, *Virginia Tech, Montgomery*
Ji Soo Yi, *Purdue University, USA*
Emine Yilmaz, *University College London, UK*
Langxuan Yin, *Northeastern University, USA*
Ming Yin, *Harvard University, USA*
Jason Yip, *University of Maryland, USA*
Salu Ylirisku, *Aalto University, Finland*
Christian Yoder, *University of California, USA*
Daisy Yoo, *Carnegie Mellon University, USA*
Hyoseok Yoon, *KAIST, Korea*
Chuang-Wen You, *Academia Sinica, Taiwan*

Alyson Young, *UMBC, USA*
James Young, *University of Manitoba, Canada*
Chun Yu, *Tsinghua University, China*
Lixiu Yu, *Carnegie Mellon University, USA*
Michael Yu, *Carnegie Mellon University, USA*
Neng-Hao Yu, *National Taiwan University, Taiwan*
Zhiwen Yu, *School of Computer Science Xi'an, China*
Chien Wen Yuan, *Cornell University, USA*
Nicholas Yuan, *Microsoft Research Asia, China*
Beste Yuksel, *Tufts University, USA*
Stanislaw Zabramski, *Uppsala University, Sweden*
Lisl Zach, *Drexel University, USA*
Jose Zagal, *Georgia Institute of Technology, USA*
Panagiotis Zaharias, *Athens University of Economics and Business, Greece*
Bieke Zaman, *IBBT-KU Leuven, Belgium*
Massimo Zancanaro, *FBK-Irst, Italy*
Richard Zanibbi, *Rochester Institute of Technology, USA*
Michael Zarro, *Drexel University, USA*
Polle Zellweger, *Maczell Consulting, USA*
Shumin Zhai, *Research @ Google, USA*
Cheng Zhang, *Georgia Institute of Technology, USA*
Haimo Zhang, *National University of Singapore, Singapore*
Haoqi Zhang, *Harvard University, USA*
Pei Zhang, *Carnegie Mellon University, USA*
Tao Zhang, *North Carolina State University, USA*
Yan Zhang, *University of Texas at KAIST, Republic of Korea in, USA*
Yanxia Zhang, *Lancaster University, UK*
Chen Zhao, *Alibaba International UED, USA*
Dejin Zhao, *PSU, USA*
Jian Zhao, *University of Toronto, Canada*
Xuan Zhao, *University of Michigan, USA*
Bin Zheng, *University of Alberta, Canada*
Yangshuo Zheng, *Tsinghua University, China*
Jia Zhou, *Chongqing, China*
Lina Zhou, *University of Maryland, USA*
Yajin Zhou, *Raleigh, USA*
Bin Zhu, *Microsoft Research Asia, China*
Haiyi Zhu, *Carnegie Mellon University, USA*
Mengxiao Zhu, *Rutgers University, USA*
Zhigang Zhu, *The City College of New York, USA*
Martina Ziefle, *Rwth Aachen University, Germany*
Juergen Ziegler, *University of Duisburg-Essen, Germany*
Caroline Ziemkiewicz, *Brown University, USA*
Roshanak Zilouchian Moghaddam, *University of Illinois at Urbana-Champaign, USA*
Ryder Ziola, *University of Washington, USA*
Miriam Zisook, *Northeastern University, USA*
Hadar Ziv, *University of California, USA*
Goranka Zoric, *Stockholm University, Sweden*
Jo Zucco, *University of South KAIST, Republic of Korea ralia, Australia*
Sacha Zyto, *MIT, USA*

Special thanks for the financial support provided by the following sponsors:

CHI Champion Sponsors

AUTODESK.

Bloomberg

Google

Graphisme, animation et nouveaux médias
GRAND
Graphics, Animation and New Media

Microsoft

NAVER

Computer Science
UNIVERSITY OF TORONTO

CHI Contributing Sponsors

facebook.

NSF

YAHOO! LABS

Friends of CHI

Disney Research   Newcastle University

Printed on Rolland Enviro 100
100% post-consumer fiber
Certified EcoLogo
Processed chlorine free
Manufactured using biogas energy
Printed using soy-based inks

Social Epistemic Cognition in Online Interactions

Rosanna Yuen-Yan Chan
Department of Information Engineering
The Chinese University of Hong Kong
yychan@ie.cuhk.edu.hk

Silu Li
Centre for the Advancement of IT in Education
The Chinese University of Hong Kong
siluli@cuhk.edu.hk

Diane Hui
Department of English
Lingnan University
diane.hui@ln.edu.hk

ABSTRACT
Social media and online social networks dramatically change the way in which knowledge is acquired and disseminated. How do we re-understand about human knowledge and knowing? This work aims at extending the current understanding of human epistemic cognition in online social environments, where epistemic cognition refers to cognitions and cognitive processes related to epistemic matters such as knowledge and beliefs justification. We approach our inquiry with mixed methods: (1) quantitative study to test whether epistemic cognition might differ in individual and social contexts, and whether online interactions might mediate the later; and (2) social cognitive task analysis with interviews to manifest the intricate interplay of dynamics between social epistemic cognition and online interactions. We introduce the new construct of social epistemic cognition and contribute to the field of HCI with an evolved theory which states that epistemic cognition can be promoted in online social environments as mediated by online interactions.

Author Keywords
Social epistemic cognition; social epistemology; social cognitive task analysis; CSCL; Interaction Science.

ACM Classification Keywords
H.1.2. User/Machine systems: Human factors, human information processing. H.5.m. Information interfaces and presentation (e.g., HCI): Miscellaneous.

INTRODUCTION
Perspectives from multiple disciplines acknowledge the critical role of social interactions in human knowledge advancement [7, 14, 22, 38, 46]. For thousands of years, philosophers and epistemologists have been studying about beliefs, knowledge, and desirable ways of attempting to find the truth (see [6, 49]). Undoubtedly, social media and online social networks (OSNs) have changed the ways in which people acquire and disseminate knowledge in essential ways. Web 2.0 and Internet technologies enable new forms of knowledge-based activities such as mass collaboration in Wikipedia and argumentations in virtual knowledge communities such as Quora.com. To the HCI community, it is important to understand the extent to which *epistemic* (i.e. concerning or involving knowledge [36]) and cognitive processes may be involved when human individuals (as well as collective individuals) are engaged in online social activities that aim at knowledge and knowing. Such understanding of people can inform about the design and implementation of computing systems that will potentially enhance human's capabilities in achieving various epistemic goods including true-belief formation, scientific knowledge discoveries, and ultimately the co-attainment (or at least the approximation) to truth, which is the highest human activity and value according to Aristotle [49, p.150].

The HCI community has been investigating human users' knowledge-related beliefs and behaviors in online social environments, as well as how to enhance existing design, such as user interfaces, for collaboration and knowledge-based purposes. For example, schraefel [40] suggested a number of approaches to improve existing search mechanisms to facilitate knowledge building. Antin [1, 2] studied the beliefs and behaviors of Wikipedia readers, and argued for a legitimate peripheral participation (see [30]) of the reader-participants. In one of the pioneer works by Scardamalia and Bereiter in the 1980s, networked computers were used to support intentional learning and the co-construction of group knowledge among students. Their Computer-Supported Intentional Learning Environment (CSILE) had evolved into the knowledge building enterprise nowadays that aims at the creation of public knowledge through dynamic social processes [38, 45]. Together with CSILE, various early works including the Electronic Networks for Interaction (ENFI) and the Fifth Dimension (both reviewed in [45]) later emerged in the field of computer-supported collaborative learning (CSCL), one of the major areas of focus within CSCW that mainly concerns about how people learn together through social interactions with the help of computers [44].

CHI 2014, April 26 - May 01 2014, Toronto, ON, Canada
Copyright 2014 ACM 978-1-4503-2473-1/14/04...$15.00.
http://dx.doi.org/10.1145/2556288.2556977.

Relating closely to CSCL [38, 44, 45] and taking also into consideration the interdisciplinary perspective of the Learning Sciences [7, 9] that aims at the scientific investigation of human learning in real-world settings, this work continues the above endeavors by inquiring into *why* online interactions can lead to community epistemic co-advancements; and attempt to extend the current understanding of the social and epistemic dimensions of human cognition. In this paper, we introduce the new construct of **social epistemic cognition (SEC)** which concerns about human cognitions and cognitive processes directed by epistemic aims and in social settings. To the HCI community, the current work offers a new understanding of human cognition in socio-technical environments and contributes an evolved theory which states that human cognitions related to epistemic matters can be promoted through social interactions mediated by scaffolds achievable by proper HCI designs.

PERSPECTIVES AND THEORETICAL FOUNDATION

Social Interactions in the Online World

Social interactions have been at the core of human mental functioning and communication since ancient times as hunters and gatherers stayed connected and lived together by interacting with each other [24, 42]. Social interactions play a critical role in the advancement of human knowledge in the society. Effective communication enables individuals to receive and interpret messages that might lead them to form new beliefs or revise the existing ones [22], which is one of the fundamental mechanisms that sustain scientific revolution and paradigm shifts [28].

Nowadays, there is a dramatic increase in the use of social media to support various social interactions. Figure 1a-c (derived from Barnatt's framework [4]) depict the new paradigm of interactions (human-to-human, machine-to-machine, and human-to-machine) over online social environments that include three key components: (1) online social networks, (2) social multimedia, and (3) cloud computing technologies and various access devices. These elements interconnect with hyperlinks and result into an extensive, worldwide online environment.

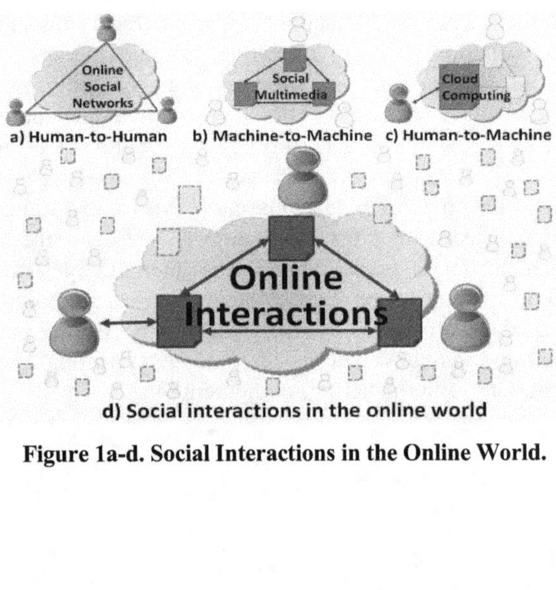

Figure 1a-d. Social Interactions in the Online World.

Three Levels of Human Cognitive Processing

Cognition and human information processing are within the fundamental interests of HCI [8, 35]. According to Kitchener [25], three levels of cognitive processing can be distinguished when human perceivers encounter ill-structured problems:

(1) **cognition** - at which individuals perceive through reading, writing, listening, and memorizing
(2) **metacognition** - at which individuals monitor and regulate their own progress while engaging in the first level activities, such as highlighting important words when reading an article; and
(3) **epistemic cognition** - the highest level among the three at which individuals reflect on epistemic matters such as the limits of their knowing, and the certainty and criteria of knowing.

A higher level of cognition can enclose a lower level but not vice versa. The second and third levels correspond to macrocognition according to Klein *et al.*'s perspective [27]. More specifically, epistemic cognition (EC) at the third level is an essential condition for solving real world open-problems (which are very often ill-defined and unsolved, in contrast to puzzles with defined solutions) [25] which can lead to new knowledge formation.

Epistemology and Cognition

Epistemology, which is also known as the "theory of knowledge", is a central field in Philosophy and has a long history dated back to Plato and Aristotle [6, 49]. Philosophical epistemology concerns about knowledge and related concepts including truth, objectivity, trust, belief, and perception, and the ways of believing, knowing, understanding, and the attempting to find the truth [6, 21, 49]. Contemporary philosophers also investigate about the relationship between cognition and epistemology [21], and the relevance of the social dimension of knowledge [14, 22, 23]. In recent decades, a number of works in psychology and human development also studied personal epistemology or *epistemic beliefs*, such as those by Perry [33], Schommer [39], Hofer and Printrich [15, 16]. Concerning about people's beliefs related to knowledge and knowing, these works provided various empirical evidences to conclude that epistemic beliefs predict human learning (see [17]). Chinn *et al.*'s recently re-examined various efforts and findings in psychology and human development, and proposed a framework for epistemic cognition (the *EC framework*) grounded in philosophical epistemology [10]. Chinn *et al.*'s framework includes five interconnected components that describe human cognition related to epistemic matters:

(1) **Epistemic aims and values** – concerns about what aims (e.g. true beliefs, understanding, or explanations that fit the data [9]) one may adopt in conducting cognitive processes and the expected worth (value) of the resulting achievements.

(2) **Structure of knowledge** – concerns with one's view about the representation and the structural forms of knowledge which can be multifaceted and highly multidimensional (e.g. probabilistic vs. deterministic, simple vs. complex etc. [10]). This component also intertwines with the one's ontological beliefs about the structure of the world (p.150).

(3) **Source, justification, and epistemic stances** – corresponds to the epistemic attitudes that one may take with respect to information, e.g. believing it or doubting it. Also they include one's beliefs about the sources (i.e. the origin) of the knowledge claims and the reasoning about their beliefs [15].

(4) **Epistemic virtues and vices** – concerns about the kinds of intellectual virtues one may exhibit (e.g. intellectual courage and intellectual carefulness [43, 49] versus epistemic vices), and how one might response to dilemmas related to intellectual virtues and obligations in social situations.

(5) **Processes of achieving epistemic aims** – concerns about the processes (e.g. data analyses and methods of inquiries) one may conduct to achieve the epistemic aims, and the reliability of such processes.

EC distinguishes itself from other perspectives of cognition by its underlying epistemic aims (i.e. goals related to beliefs, knowledge, and understanding, etc.) [10]. Chinn *et al.* examined human EC mostly within an individual dimension, while confirming the potential of a social dimension of EC as "a very promising area for future EC research" (p.163). In fact, the social aspects of human knowledge and knowing, as well as the impact of information technologies on the social dimension of knowledge are within the common core interests of contemporary philosophers (e.g. [13, 22, 23]) as well as the HCI community.

Social Epistemic Cognition: The Current Research

The current research investigates the social dimension of human EC in online social environments through a new construct called **social epistemic cognition (SEC)** which we define as follow:

Definition. Social Epistemic Cognition (SEC). Social epistemic cognition is a human individual's cognition and cognitive processes related to epistemic matters when situated in a social context.

As implied in Bandura's Social Cognitive Theory [3], an individual's SEC is influenced by and continuously influencing the SEC of other individuals during social interactions. To the HCI community, it is methodologically critical to study SEC with the collective individuals at a group level in order to manifest the important role played by technology in shaping human SEC through group processes and collaboration. We extend Chinn *et al.*'s EC framework to include some critical elements involving social cognition [3, 12] and social epistemology (SE) [22], namely Goldman's first variety of SE based on the mainstream epistemology (p.14). We ground our SEC construct from philosophical epistemology perspectives that acknowledge the existence of truth and human knowledge. In particular, we adopt the perspectives from [21, 34, 43, 49] that *knowledge is true belief formed in epistemically conscientious ways* (see [49, p.127]) such as reasoning, argumentation, and reliable processes. SEC inherits the disposition from EC with its underlying *epistemic aims* and *values* [49, Ch. 1] that motivate a human individual (or a community of collective human individuals) to participate in *social interactions* - which are nowadays largely mediated [47] by technologies and social media.

Research Questions and Hypotheses

Our research questions in the current work include:

1. (RQ1a-c): Is there any promotion of EC when people are situated in social contexts? Does such promotion vary across levels of online interactions? Do online interactions mediate SEC?
2. (RQ2a-b): How do we contextualize SEC in the online environments? What are the dynamics relationship between SEC and online interactions?
3. (RQ3): What empirical evidences on SEC do we have that provides insights to effective HCI design that can promote human epistemic cognition?

This research is guided by the following principal hypothesis:

Principal hypothesis: Human epistemic cognition can be promoted through social interactions, and can be mediated in the online environments.

Social interactions in the online environments are essentially *online interactions* involving human actors, and are sustained by the underlying machine-to-machine interactions (Figure 1). Our principal hypothesis can be further decomposed into the following five hypotheses:

Hypothesis 1: Human individuals' epistemic aims can be promoted through online interactions.

The epistemic aims as discussed in the philosophy literature include minimally justified belief, propositional knowledge, understanding, knowledge construction, and ultimately the attainment (or at least the approximation) to truth (see [6, 14, 21, 28, 29, 49]). Hypothesis 1 holds that individuals who originally enter the online interactions with lower level epistemic aims such as minimally justify beliefs (e.g. information seeking) can be promoted to higher level epistemic aims such as knowledge co-construction (or *knowledge building* [38, 40]) through online interactions.

Hypothesis 2: Human individuals' beliefs about the structure of knowledge can be enhanced through online interactions.

Hypothesis 2 holds that an individual can shift from a more generic belief about the structure of knowledge (e.g. simple one-to-one matching between his or her beliefs to knowledge in a domain) to a more specific, fine-grained view [10] (e.g. the awareness and attention to the details of cases, and the realization of causal accounts of explanations [37] with knowledge within or beyond the domain) through interacting with other individuals online.

Hypothesis 3: Online interactions can enhance human individuals' justification on knowledge and knowledge source, and their stances towards various knowledge claims as offered by other individuals.

Hypothesis 3 suggests that individuals can be promoted into enhanced justificatory beliefs about the knowledge claims and their sources through interacting with the others online, such as recognizing the opinions and ideas provided by other individuals online as *testimony* (see [22]), and the realization of the connection between various testimonial knowledge. They will also adopt a more sophisticated justificatory standard (see [30]) in their *reasoning* and *justification* of testimony-based knowledge [22, p.126] available online.

Hypothesis 4: Epistemic virtues withheld by human individuals can be promoted through online interactions.

The construct of epistemic virtues is grounded in virtue epistemology [43], which refers to the stable disposition that direct an individual in his or her pursuit of various epistemic goods such as knowledge, understanding, and reasonableness. Hypothesis 4 suggests that through online interactions, an individual will move away from epistemic vices (e.g. close-mindedness, dogmatism and other dispositions that might impede the achievement of epistemic aims [10, p.158]) towards epistemic virtues (e.g. the willingness to share knowledge with others [38] online with conscious and intellectual carefulness).

Hypothesis 5: Online interactions can enhance human individuals' awareness about the processes of achieving epistemic aims and the reliability of these processes.

Processes of achieving epistemic aims can include the procedures and activities that can result in epistemic goods e.g. scientific knowledge [28]. According to the reliabilists' perspectives, a true belief is justified only if it is resulted from reliable formation processes [43]. Hypothesis 5 suggests that individuals' awareness about the reliability of their own processes of inquires will be fostered through online interactions. It is also likely that such awareness will encourage individuals to adopt more reliable possesses in the pursuit of both individual and community knowledge in online social environments.

STUDY ONE

Study One is a belief-behavior user study which measures users' EC in individual and social contexts, compare their difference across levels of online interactions, and test whether online interactions might mediate users' SEC.

Method

Participants

Participants are convenient samples solicited from two universities in Hong Kong including 205 students and staffs (65 females, 140 males) from disciplines including engineering and humanities, who need to be competent in using a wide range of social networking platforms to undergo online interactions. Participants were explicitly assigned into groups with low, middle, and high level of online interactions according to their availability for online participation for a sustained period of about 4 months. Accordingly, 86, 83, and 36 of the participants were respectively assigned into the low, middle, and high level groups.

Design and Measures

The study adopts a two-way design with one within-subjects factor (*context* with conditions *individual* and *social*) and one between-subject factor (*online interactions* with levels *low*, *middle*, *high*) as the independent variables. The task aims to engage participants in social epistemic activities such as knowledge co-construction through online interactions. There are eight dependent variables: five belief variables which respectively measures participants' belief associated to the five EC components (*epistemic aim*, *structure of knowledge*, *justification*, *epistemic virtues*, and *processes and reliability*); and three behavior variables which respectively quantify participants' online interactions behavior in terms of the number of online communities participated (*online communities*), online discourses produced (*online discourses*), and blog posts published (*blog posts*).

Specifically, the five EC belief variables are measured by the **Epistemic Cognition Instrument (ECI)** that we developed based on [6, 10, 21, 22, 49]. The ECI contains 32 5 points Likert-scale response items which are grouped into five scales correspond to the five belief variables. We have examined the ECI for reliability and validity by Cronbach's alpha and confirmatory factor analysis (CFA) [27] on a separated population with a sample size of N = 563, which is an appreciable sample size for a structure model with 5 factors and 32 items [48]. Table 1 shows the questionnaire scales, items, factor loadings, reliability, and CFA indexes.

Task and Procedures

The task was to learn about a theme within the participants' own knowledge domain (e.g. information security for participants from the engineering discipline) by means of individual learning (e.g. reading books and browsing web materials alone) and/or social interactions (e.g. participating in online or offline discussions) for the experimental period of about 4 months. Three types of online communities, including the wikis (over Moodle Wikis and PBWorks), blogger communities (over Tumblr and Blogger.com), and discussion forums (over Moodle and PBWorks) were established to facilitate participants' social interactions.

	Factor loading	α
Epistemic Aims		.83
1. I want to know more about things because I care.	.73	
2. I like to find new things out and understand them.	.73	
3. To me, it is more important to understand things than just to know a list of information.	.67	
4. I like to explore the connection between items of information.	.81	
5. I like to see how information fits together.	.77	
6. I like to weight different justifications against each other to find out the truth.	.69	
Structure of Knowledge		.70
7. Knowledge is true belief resulted from reliable processes.	.59	
8. Reality in the world is structured in integrated, complex, and sometime ambiguous concepts.	.64	
9. While there exist some universal principles in the real world, knowledge can be highly particular, specific, and context sensitive.	.67	
10. The real world is full of uncertainty and randomness.	.68	
11. Explanations are important for understanding things because they provide causal accounts showing what causes a phenomenon.	.63	
12. The causal relationships between things are often reciprocal and non-directional.	.58	
Justification		.70
13. Logical reasoning can produce new knowledge.	.57	
14. Information and knowledge shared by the other people can be a valuable source of knowledge.	.50	
15. We must rely on experts for knowledge outside our own spheres of experience.	.57	
16. When I need to reasoning over multiple statements, I like to refer to knowledge comes from authority (e.g. experts and or scholars).	.61	
17. My knowledge is derived from multiple sources simultaneously, such as reading books, personal experience, as well as other people's information.	.57	
18. I like to evaluate explanations provided by the others according to objective standards.	.62	
19. The more the claim is justified, the more certain it is.	.70	
Epistemic Virtues		.82
20. During inquiry, I process information very carefully.	.73	
21. I am willing to gather information and reach conclusions for achieving true beliefs.	.63	
22. I stand up for an unpopular but correct belief.	.60	
23. I have an open mind to learn from other people.	.66	
24. I am always conscientious during inquiry.	.76	
25. I maintain my perseverance during inquiry.	.76	
26. I maintain my humility during inquiry.	.73	
Processes and Reliability		.72
27. We need to consider alternative viewpoints, reasons, and evidence during the inquiry process.	.64	
28. A knowledge source is credible if it has been reviewed by many people.	.54	
29. Whether the experimental results are reliable or not depends on the conditions under which they are generated.	.60	
30. Interpersonal processes such as argumentation and group decision making can influence knowledge formation.	.71	
31. For argumentation to be effective, everyone in the group needs to participate actively and democratically.	.75	
32. It is very important to evaluate the messages delivered by the media according to their reliability of their practices.	.65	

Overall Cronbach's alpha = .92. Confirmatory factor analysis (CFA) indexes: $\chi^2/df = 1.90$, CFI = .93, SRMR = .05.

Table 1. Epistemic Cognition Instrument (ECI) with scales, items and factor loadings, reliability, and confirmatory factor analysis (CFA) indexes (N = 563).

Participants in the high level group were required to participate in three online communities, one of each type, throughout the entire experiment period. Participants in the middle level group were required to participate in at least one of the online communities of any type. Participants in the low level group (the control) were not required to participate in the specified online communities. It is noted that participants of the three groups had equal chance to engage in online as well as offline social interactions outside the specified online communities, thus contributing to the unexplained variances. Participants' interactions were recorded from the online communities' activity logs. At the end of the experiment period, we invited the participants to complete the ECI by asking them to provide two responses to each of the 32 items, which respectively correspond to the participants' beliefs when they learn about things (i) individually (the *individual context* condition) and (ii) socially through interacting with other individuals (the *social context* condition).

Results

Descriptive Statistics and EC Scales in Individual and Social Contexts

Table 2a and 2b provide descriptive statistics for the beliefs variables across conditions and the behavior variables across group levels, respectively. ANOVAs were performed to determine if EC differ in individual and social context (RQ1a). Significant main effects for the within-subject factor (individual vs. social condition) are obtained in all scales, all favoring social context over individual context.

	Epistemic aims	Structure of knowledge	Justification	Epistemic virtues	Processes reliability
Individual	3.75 (0.78)	2.82 (0.70)	3.76 (0.60)	3.85 (0.61)	3.83 (0.64)
Social	4.15 (0.63)	4.07 (0.59)	3.94 (0.64)	3.98 (0.64)	4.07 (0.64)
F	32.84***	15.14***	9.73**	4.16*	14.90***

Notes: N = 205. ***p < .001, **p < .01, *p < .05.

Table 2a. Descriptive statistics of belief variables across individual context and social context.

Group	Online communities	Online discourses	Blog posts
High	3.00 (0.00)	15.08 (9.16)	12.56 (6.47)
Middle	1.22 (0.88)	10.36 (10.05)	2.07 (2.01)
Low (Control)	0.00 (0.00)	0.00 (0.00)	0.00 (0.00)

Note: N = 205.

Table 2b. Descriptive statistics of behavior variables across levels of online interaction.

Effect of Online Interactions on EC Promotion

In order to determine if the promotion of EC varies across levels of online interactions (RQ1b), a two-way ANOVA was performed to compare the overall EC (obtained by aggregating the scores of the 5 EC scales) with one between-subjects factor, *online interactions* (high, middle, and low levels), and one within-subject factor, *contexts* (individual versus social conditions). Significant interaction effect (online interactions×context) on EC exists ($F[1, 202] = 10.83$, $p < .001$), showing the promotion of EC in social context over EC in individual context differ between groups with manipulated levels of online interactions.

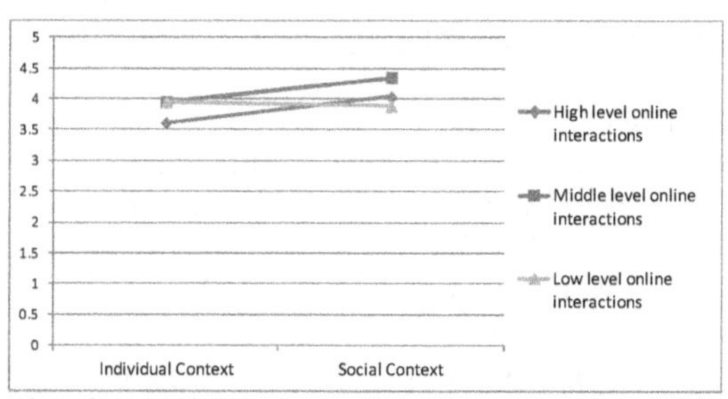

Figure 2. EC in individual and social context across groups with low, middle, and high level of online interactions.

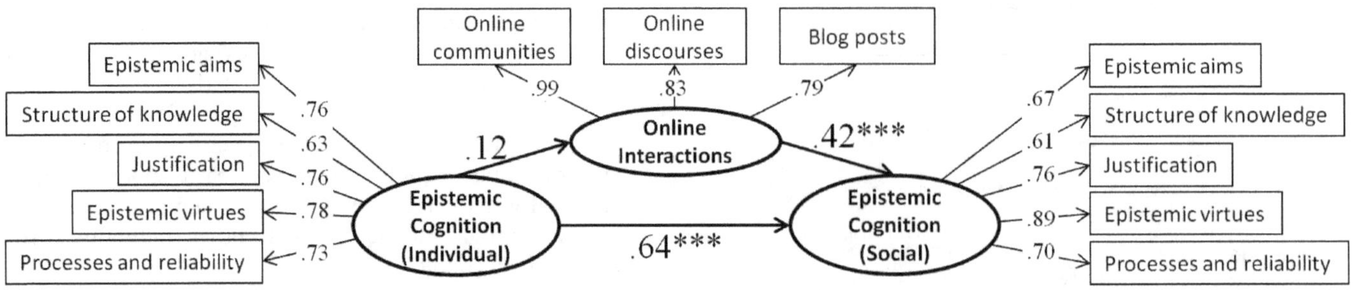

Note: ***$p < .001$. Model fit indexes: $\chi^2/df = 1.62$, CFI = .98, SRMR = .05.

Figure 3. Structural equation model (SEM) analysis on online interactions as a mediator.

Mediation of Online Interactions on SEC

In order to examine any mediation effect of online interactions on SEC (R1c), a structural equation model (SEM) with three latent variables corresponded to EC in individual context, EC in social context, and online interactions is constructed (Figure 3). Path weights are analyzed for the mediation of online interactions on EC in the social context condition (i.e. SEC). A significant mediation effect is detected ($z = 1.78, p < .05$).

Discussion

Our results show that human EC differs significantly in individual and social environment settings, and indicate that participants' levels of online interactions have a significant effect on the promotion of epistemic cognition in social context over individual context. Furthermore, the promotion of epistemic cognition in social context is mediated by online interactions. These results together support our Principle Hypothesis. In particular, participants indicate a significantly more positive belief associated to epistemic aims (Hypothesis 1), structure of knowledge (Hypothesis 2), justification (Hypothesis 3), epistemic virtues (Hypothesis 4) and reliability of processes (Hypothesis 5) when socially interacting with the others. However, it is also worthy to note that Hypothesis 4 is only weakly supported with the least significant difference exists in *epistemic virtues* between individual and social contexts; which implies epistemic virtues is the least varied EC components across conditions. Two possible interpretations can be that epistemic virtues are human innate cognitive faculties which are stable and reliable [43], or depositions such as intellectual carefulness and honesty may be either enhanced or impeded by system factors such as user anonymity and system integrity.

STUDY TWO

Study Two aims at contextualizing SEC in online environments (R2a) and investigates the dynamics between SEC and online interactions (R2b) using social cognitive task analysis (SCTA), which is a systematic approach we evolved from existing cognitive task analysis (CTA) techniques [11, 19] to reveal the cognitive processes associated with the participants' social interactions.

Method

Participants

Participants are 44 postgraduate students in the first study with background in the information engineering discipline (12 females, 32 males).

Task and Procedures

Participants are formed into 8 groups and are engaged in collaborative project works with the support of cloud-based collaboration platforms (such as Google Docs and PBWorks) (Figure 4). The groups conducted their project works via online interactions over a period of 4 months. The groups were allowed to meet face-to-face during the project period, but the online platforms were their primary channel of communication for most of the time.

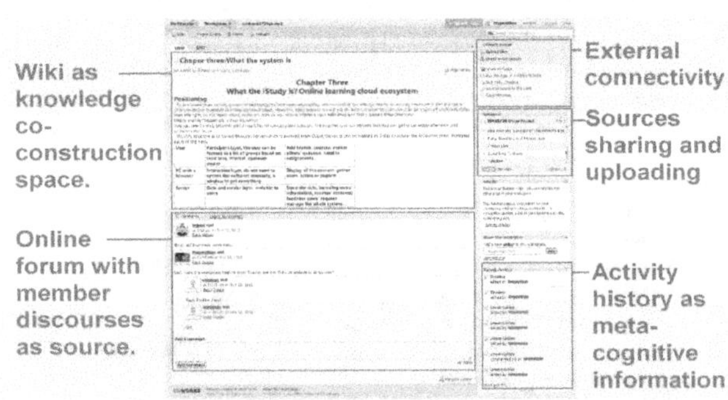

Figure 4. Online project workspaces and online interactions among group members.

Social Cognitive Task Analyses and Representation

CTA interviews were conducted on a whole group basis to investigate participants' epistemic experiences in online interactions when they performed the task in Study One. Our interview objectives and probes are designed according to Hypotheses 1 to 5. We also performed field observations on the participating groups' online workspaces (e.g. Figure 4) by examining the discourses and artifacts produced by the participating group members and associating the analyses to the interview transcripts. Critical Decision Method (CDM) [18] approaches were used to guide the participants to recall and elaborate on their group project experiences and online interactions, including the people and online objects with which they have socially interacted, and the

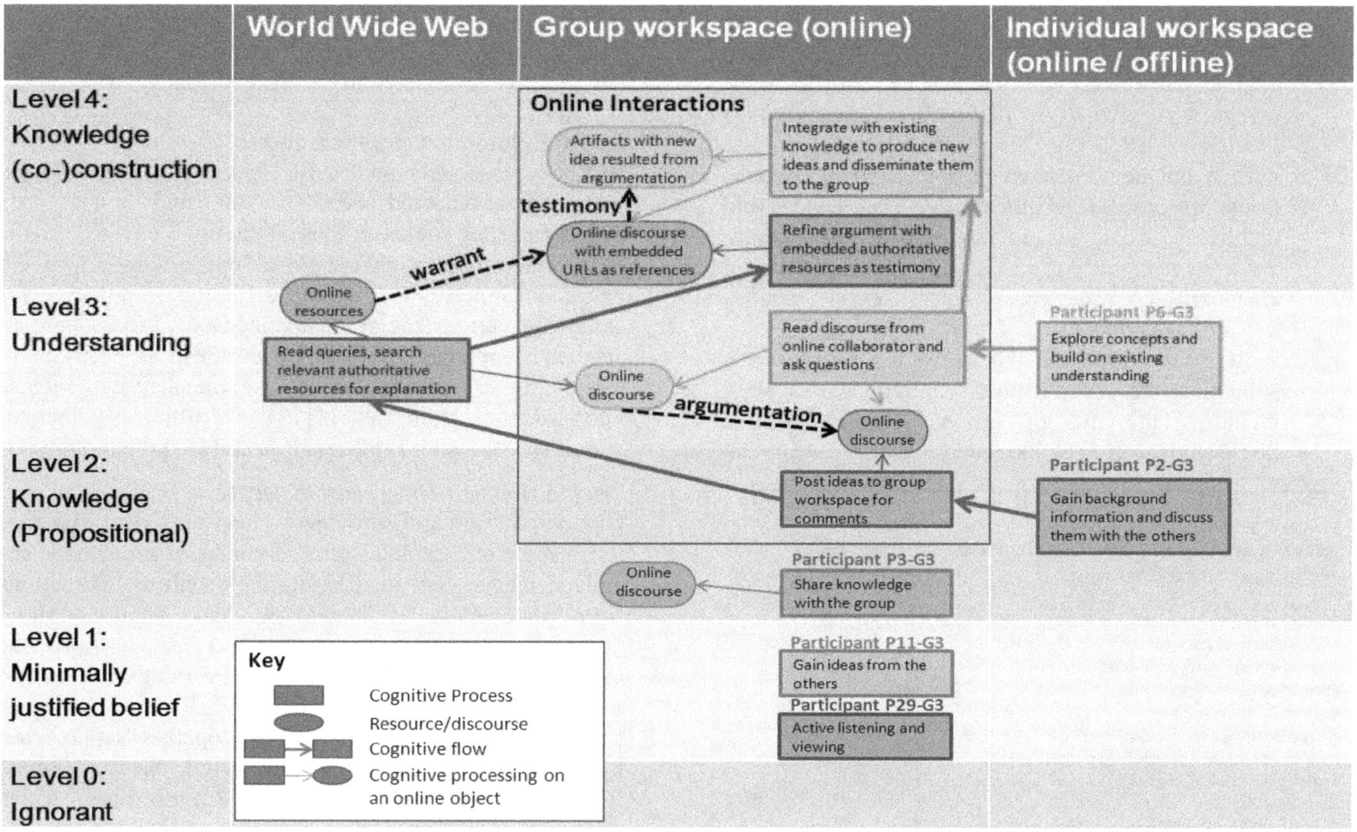

Figure 5. Abstraction-Decomposition matrix of online interactions.

conditions in which their social interactions occurred. An Abstraction-Decomposition (A-D) matrix (see [18, 19]) is developed to capture participants' progression of epistemic aims during online social interactions. The levels of abstraction correspond to the hierarchical epistemic aims [21, 28, 29, 49] that guide the participants' cognitive processes. And the work domain decomposition corresponds to the logical online workspaces (individual, group, and public) in which the participants and objects in concern were situated or located.

Results and Discussion

Figure 5 shows the A-D matrix of a fragment of cognitive activities as demonstrated by one of the participating groups (Group 3) which illustrates the dynamics of collective SEC in online collaboration. Online interactions took place when two or more participants cognitively processed on a same online object. Interactions associated with social epistemology, e.g. argumentation and the adoption of testimonial knowledge, can also be identified (e.g. P2-G3 and P6-G3 respectively produces and responds to an online discourse which represents certain knowledge, and P2-G3 embeds an online object produced by other individuals into new discourses). The underlying online social environments (i.e. the group workspaces in our SCTA) further sustain the interactions via the connectivity between objects. Epistemic activities that took place outside the group workspace were also observed, e.g. the citation of (or embedding) authoritative resources from the Internet as epistemic warrant (see [22]) for justification. As indicated along the vertical scale in the A-D matrix, participants' epistemic aims have been jointly promoted to a higher level through online interactions. E.g., participants who originally entered the online group workspace with a lower level epistemic aim (e.g. propositional knowledge of P2-G3) were prompted to adopt a higher level epistemic aim such as understanding through the online argumentation with another participant (e.g. P6-G3 who was unsatisfied with P2-G3's claims). High level social epistemic aims such as knowledge co-construction were also reported from other participants during the CTA interviews (see Table 4).

Table 4 provides excerpts of interview transcripts that reflect the dynamics of participants' SEC during online interactions. The results below are of particular interest:

1. Some participants reflected that an enhancement in beliefs associated with the structure of knowledge took place through online social interactions, e.g. a participant mentioned that *"in the group workspace, members share their own knowledge and we can get information from various aspects"* (P20-G8).
2. As indicated in the A-D matrix, participants were prompted to justify their knowledge claims with online resources. A participant expressed that *"it's*

difficult for an individual alone to justify the correctness of a new belief" (P21-G6), while another participant reported that he "*can examine others' view and try to justify [his views] against the others*'" (P35-G1).

3. Participants demonstrated epistemic virtues because of the presence of the others. E.g., a participant told that he "*was careful... so that [his] comments were more convincing*" (P35-G1). Another participant also expected "*the group help[s] every member avoid false beliefs*" (e.g. P5-G8).
4. In terms of processes, participants used diverse strategies in the groups' online workspaces, including the use of group wiki and online discussions to convey ideas and solicit explanations.

Interview transcript chucks	EC components
"I just quickly go through the document and try to find the answers…" (P24-G1)	Epistemic aim (minimally justified belief)
"I tried to verify whether the cliams are correct and explore more about the concept." (P39-G6)	Epistemic aims (propositional knowledge and attempt of understanding)
"I search for more resources online and discuss with the others. Through sharing information, conveying ideas, and discussions, some new knowledge may be generated." (P2-G3)	Epistemic aim (knowledge co-construction); justification; reliable processes
All of our group members satisfied [on a point] except *(a member's name)*, who provided additional information by searching the Internet. And all of us agreed and adopted his ideas. (P6-G3)	Justification (and testimonial-based knowledge)
"I was careful and I quoted sources, so that my comments were more convincing. Moreover, I examined others' view and try to justify the views of mine against the others'." (P35-G1)	Epistemic virtues; justification; processes and reliability
"When someone voiced out his [or her] opinion, he [or she] should explain it in order to make others agree. The group can help every member avoiding false beliefs." (P5-G8)	Epistemic aim (explanation for group understanding); justification
"We use the Google Doc together to collaborate. Each of us highlighted words and sentences on the document that we thought were important. We save those that we all thought as useful and neglected some less important ones…" (P27-G5)	Structure of knowledge; processes and reliability

Table 4. Excerpts of interview transcripts.

DISCUSSION

Social Epistemic Cognition in Online Interactions

Various theories and practices in fields closely related to HCI including CSCW and CSCL (such as [38, 44, 45]) suggest that knowledge can be co-constructed through social interactions among members within a community. Epistemologically speaking, the World Wide Web is a social *epistemic system* [23] that sustains a variety of processes and interpersonal influences which in turn affect the knowledge outcomes of its members. An Internet user's cognition, from a Vygotskian perspective [46], is a product of a complex and dynamic process involving the social interaction between the user and the immediate UGC object(s) hosted in the Internet cloud. Human-to-human online interactions are essentially mediated by the UGCs (as depicted in Figure 1d) which represent the symbolic variables to be integrated into the users' mental models. Our results provide scientific evidence to show that the outcome of such online interactions is the promotion of EC, and in particular, the SEC (Study One). This novel interpretation of HCI has been further manifested in our SCTA (Study Two).

Social Epistemic Cognition and HCI

We conceptualize human SEC in the current work and have operationalized SEC in our two studies. By connecting our robust empirical findings on SEC to the extant literature in philosophical epistemology, we are better informed about the scaffolding conditions for achieving various social epistemic goods, virtues, and an aesthetic appreciation of HCI designs, as well as to sustain higher levels of human epistemic activities such as knowledge creation [38, p.113] and ultimately the co-attainment to truth [49] through future HCI technologies.

Contribution and Theoretical Implications

Our current research provides robust empirical evidence to illustrate and explain some reasons *why* knowledge co-advancements can happen through online interactions from philosophical epistemology and social cognition perspectives. Such empirical findings confirm the important role played by social media in amplifying and extending human epistemic capabilities. Overall, results from Study One and Study Two together support our hypotheses, leading to a new HCI theory (**Social Epistemic Cognition in Online Interactions**) which states that *human social epistemic cognition can be mediated through online interactions*.

Design Implications

Our fine-grained examination of online interactions with the lens of SEC helps informing HCI designers about the possible human-computer interface to facilitate human knowledge and knowing in online social environments. For example, epistemic scaffolds can be those that address the social epistemic cognitive processes identified in our SCTA (Study Two), e.g. search mechanisms that design for efficient access of disperse online resources outside the group workspace for epistemic *warrant*; and the facilitation of reliable processes among members in their co-construction of epistemic artifacts (e.g. the wikis being co-edited among collaborating members) through online *argumentations* and constructive use of *testimony* knowledge. Having a new understand of human knowledge and knowing in contemporary online world with the lens of SEC, various human epistemic activities (e.g. search for epistemic objects such as a professional blog post written by a certain philosopher to learn about a particular topic such as the mind-body problem, and mass collaboration in Wikipedia through wikis co-editing and asynchronous remote argumentations via Wikipedia Talk) will hope to be sustained by *epistemic scaffolds* for online interactions achievable by careful HCI design.

Limitations and Necessary Works

The ECI constructed in the current study measures an individual's EC mostly using items presented in an individual context. Having conceptualized SEC with empirical evidences, the ECI needs to be further revised and be administered to measure individuals' beliefs associated with the social dynamics of epistemic matters.

CONCLUSION

Contemporary HCI researchers have called for a reflection on human values in HCI design, and advocate the need to keep human values as one of the core missions of HCI [41]. For thousands of years, philosophers have been inquiring into the truth and the core of human values including moral, ethics, trust, and virtue. SEC, having a theoretical root in philosophical epistemology, is an important attribute associated to people's knowledge-related beliefs and behaviors in HCI contexts. Various endeavours in the HCI community have been made to understand people's knowledge-related beliefs and behaviors in online environments (e.g. [1, 2]), as well as to enhance existing HCI design for social epistemic purposes (e.g. [40]). Our work provides exciting opportunities to connect the HCI literature to philosophical epistemology, covering many important concepts such as Goldman's Systems-Oriented Social Epistemology [23, p. 18], social epistemic networks, and the Internet as an epistemic engine [22, 23]. In the current work, we have introduced a new and groundbreaking construct of SEC, and examined SEC in various online social environments. We have obtained robust empirical evidence on SEC, and have affirmed the mediational role of online interactions in SEC. Our findings will provide important insights to the HCI community in the proper design of scaffolding aids to sustain human epistemic activities; and the connection between the HCI design and the foundations of philosophical epistemology which emphasizes the epistemic conscientious ways in the pursuit of the truth as well as the core human values including moral, ethics, and virtue. All in all, HCI technologies for SEC should aim at supporting human users in the co-attainment towards true beliefs as well as various epistemic goods in the presences of other members in the online social world.

REFERENCES

1. Autin, J. My kind of people? Perceptions about Wikipedia contributors and their motivations. In *Proceedings of the 2011 SIGCHI Conference on Human Factors in Computing Systems*, ACM, New York, NY, USA, 2011, pp. 3411-3420.
2. Antin, J. and Cheshire, C. Readers are not free-riders: Reading as a form of participation on Wikipedia. In *Proceedings of the 2010 ACM Conference on Computer Supported Cooperative Work*, ACM, New York, NY, USA, 2010, pp. 127-130.
3. Bandura, A. *Social Foundations of Thought and Action: A Social Cognitive Theory*. Prentice-Hall, Englewood Cliffs, NJ, USA, 1986.
4. Barnatt, C. *A Brief Guide to Cloud Computing*. Robinson, London, 2010.
5. Bereiter, C. Principled practical knowledge: Not a bridge but a ladder, to appear in *Journal of the Learning Sciences*, 2013.
6. Bernecker, S. and Pritchard, D. Eds. *Routledge Companion to Epistemology*. Routledge, London, UK, 2010.
7. Bransford, J.D., Brown, A.L. and Cocking, R.R. Eds. *How People Learn: Brain, Mind, Experience, and School*. National Academy Press, Washington DC, USA, 2000.
8. Card, S.K., Moran, T.P., and Newell, A. *The Psychology of Human-Computer Interaction*. Erlbaum, Hillsdale, NJ, USA, 1983.
9. Chinn, C. A., Buckland, L. A., and Samarapungavan, S. C. B. Integrating philosophy into learning sciences research on epistemic cognition. In *Proceedings of the 9th International Conference of the Learning Sciences (ICLS 2010), 2*, 2010, 37-44.
10. Chinn, C., Buckland, L. and Samarapungavan, A. Expanding the dimensions of epistemic cognition: arguments from philosophy and psychology. *Educational Psychologist, 46*, 3 (2011), 141-167.
11. Crandall, B., Klein, G. and Hoffman, R.R. *Working Minds: A Practitioner's Guide to Cognitive Task Analysis*. The MIT Press, Cambridge, MA, USA, 2006.
12. Fiske, S.T. and Taylor, S.E. *Social Cognition* (2nd Ed.). McGraw-Hill, New York, NY, USA, 1991.
13. Floridi, L. Information ethics: Its nature and scope. In *Information Technology and Moral Philosophy*, van den Hoven, J. and Weckert, J. Eds. Cambridge University Press Cambridge, NY, USA, 2008.
14. Fuller, S. *Social Epistemology*. Indiana University Press, Bloomington, IN, USA, 2002.
15. Hofer, B.K. Dimensionality and disciplinary differences in personal epistemology. *Contemporary Educational Psychology, 25*, 4(2000), 378-405.
16. Hofer, B.K. and Pintrich, P.R. The development of epistemological theories: Beliefs about knowledge and knowing and their relation to learning. *Review of Educational Research, 67,* (1997), 88-140.
17. Hofer, B.K. and Pintrich, P.R. *Personal Epistemology: The Psychology of Beliefs about Knowledge and Knowing*. Erlbaum, Mahwah, NJ, USA, 2002.
18. Hoffman R. R. and Lintern, G. Eliciting and representing the knowledge of experts. In *Cambridge Handbook of Expertise and Expert Performance*, Ericsson, K. A. *et al.* Eds. Cambridge University Press, New York, NY, USA, 2006, 203-222.

19. Hoffman R.R. and Militello L.G. *Perspectives on Cognitive Task Analysis: Historical Origins and Modern Communities of Practice*. Taylor & Francis Press, New York, NY, USA, 2009.

20. Hu, L. and Bentler, P.M. Cutoff criteria for fit indexes in covariance structure analysis: Conventional criteria versus new alternatives. *Structural Equation Modeling, 6*, 1 (1999), 1-55.

21. Goldman, A. I. *Epistemology and Cognition*. Harvard University Press, Cambridge, MA, USA, 1986.

22. Goldman, A.I. *Knowledge in a Social World*. Oxford University Press, New York, NY, USA, 1999.

23. Goldman, A.I. A guide to social epistemology. In Goldman, A.I. and Whitcomb, D. Eds. *Social Epistemology: Essential Readings*. New York, NY, USA, Oxford University Press, 2011.

24. Kadushin, C. *Understanding Online Social Networks: Theories, Concepts, and Findings*. Oxford University Press, New York, NY, USA, 2012.

25. Kitchener, K.S. Cognition, metacognition, and epistemic cognition. *Human Development, 26*, 4 (1983), 222-232.

26. Klein, G., Ross, K.G., Boom, B.M. and Klein, D.E. Macrocognition. *IEEE Intelligent Systems, 18*, 3 (2003), 81-85.

27. Kline, P. *The Handbook of Psychological Testing* (2nd Ed.). Routledge, London, UK, 1999.

28. Kuhn, T.S. *The Structure of Scientific Revolutions*. University of Chicago Press, Chicago, IL, USA, 1962.

29. Kvanvig, J.L. *The Value of Knowledge and the Pursuit of Understanding*. Cambridge University Press,Cambridge, UK, 2003.

30. Laudan, L. *Science and Values*. University of California Press, Berkeley, CA, USA, 1984.

31. Lave, J. and Wenger, E. *Situated Learning: Legitimate Peripheral Participation*. Cambridge University Press, Cambridge, UK, 1991.

32. McDonald, R.P. and Ho, M.H.R. Principles and practice in reporting structural equation analyses, *Psychological Methods, 7*, 1 (2002), 64–82.

33. Perry, W.G., *Forms of Intellectual and Ethical Development in the College Years: A Scheme*. San Francisco, CA, Jossey-Bass, 1968.

34. Pritchard, D., Millar, A. and Haddock, A. *The Nature and Value of Knowledge: Three Investigations*, New York, NY, USA, Oxford University Press, 2010.

35. Proctor, R.W. and Vu, K.P.L. Human information processing: An overview for human-computer interaction. In *The Human-Computer Interaction Handbook: Fundamentals, Evolving Technologies, and Emerging Application* (3rd ed), Jacko, J.A. Ed. Taylor and Francis, Boca Raton, FL, USA, 2012.

36. Proudfoot, M. and Lacey, A.R. *The Routhedge Dictionary of Philosophy*, 4th Ed. Routledge, New York, NY, USA, 2010.

37. Salmon, W.C. *Four Decades of Scientific Explanation*. University of Minnesota Press, Minneapolis, MN, USA, 1989.

38. Scardamalia, M. and Bereiter, C. Knowledge building: Theory, pedagogy, and technology. In *Cambridge Handbook of the Learning Sciences*, Sawyer, K. Ed. Cambridge University Press, New York, NT, USA, 2006, 97-118.

39. Schommer, M. Effects of beliefs about the nature of knowledge on comprehension. *Journal of Educational Psychology, 82*, 3 (1990) 498-504.

40. schraefel, mc. Building Knowledge: What's beyond Keyword Search? *IEEE Computer, 42*, 3 (2009), 52-59.

41. Sellen, A., Rogers, Y., Harper, R. and Rodden, T. Reflecting human values in the digital 21st-century sociotechnical environments. *Communications of the ACM 52*, 3 (2009), 58-66.

42. Sharp, H., Preece, J., and Rogers, Y. *Interaction Design: Beyond Human-Computer Interaction* (3rd Ed.). John Wiley & Son, West Sussex, UK, 2011.

43. Sosa, E. Reliabilism and intellectual virtue. In *Epistemology: Internalism and Externalism*, Kornblith Ed. Blackwell, Malden, MA, USA, 2001, 147-162.

44. Stahl, G. Contributions to a theoretical framework for CSCL. In *Proceedings of Computer-Supported Collaborative Learning (CSCL 2002)*, 2002, 62-71.

45. Stahl, G., Koschmann, T., and Suthers, D.D. Computer-supported colla*borative learning. In Cambridge Handbook of the Learning Sciences, Sa*wyer, K. Ed. Cambridge University Press, New York, NT, USA, 2006, 409-425.

46. Vygotsky, L. S. *Mind in Society: The Development of Higher Psychological Processes*. M. Cole, *et al*. Eds. Cambridge, MA, USA, Harvard University Press, 1978.

47. Wertsch, J.V. *Voices of the Mind: A Sociocultural Approach to Mediated Action*. Cambridge, MA, USA, Harvard University Press, 1991.

48. Westland, J.C. Lower bounds on sample size in structural equation modeling. *Electronic Commerce Research and Applications, 9*, 6 (2010), 476-487.

49. Zagzebski, L. *On Epistemology*. Wadsworth, Cengage Learning, Belmont, CA, USA, 2009.

Share your View: Impact of Co-Navigation Support and Status Composition in Collaborative Online Shopping

Yanzhen Yue[1*], Xiaojuan Ma[2*], Zhenhui Jiang[1*]
[1]Information Systems, National University of Singapore, Singapore; [2]Noah's Ark Lab, Hong Kong
[1]{yanzhen, jiang}@comp.nus.edu.sg; [2]xiaojuan.c.ma@gmail.com
* All authors have equal contribution to this paper

ABSTRACT

Collaborative online shopping, an emerging paradigm in e-commerce, allows remote shoppers to extend purchase-oriented social interactions into the digital environment. Online vendors have been experimenting ways to facilitate this activity. However, more research needs to be done on identifying what feature can create a pleasing shopping experience and ultimately encourage spending. In this paper, we present an exploration of the impact of co-navigation supports, including location cue, split screen, and shared view, on the experiences and performance of 60 co-shopper dyads. We also studied if status composition of shopping companions played a role in this process. By analyzing about 1800 minutes of eye-tracking data, video footages, and web logs, we found that split screen encouraged more diverse product search, shared view enabled better coordination, and location cue was the least distracting. Co-buyers achieved better factual and inference understanding, though buyer-advisor dyads were more likely to stay together.

Author Keywords

Collaborative Online Shopping; co-navigation; location cue; split screen; shared view; status composition; co-buyers; buyer-advisor; eye-tracking.

ACM Classification Keywords

H.5.m. Information interfaces and presentation (e.g., HCI): Miscellaneous.

INTRODUCTION

With increasing popularity over the decade, shopping over the Internet has revealed its benefits of being convenient, time-saving, and universally available in comparison to the traditional shopping in physical stores. For example, the US expects online sales in 2013 to reach $248.7 billion - a 13% rise from the previous year [16]. E-Business professionals have been investigating ways to maintain such revenue growth in online retail. Inability to remotely shop with friends and families has been listed among the top inhibitors of buying online, together with factors like high shipping cost and disruptive customer service [15].

CHI 2014, April 26 - May 01 2014, Toronto, ON, Canada
Copyright 2014 ACM 978-1-4503-2473-1/14/04...$15.00.
http://dx.doi.org/10.1145/2556288.2557143

Recently, more and more attention is paid to tackle one of the primary motivations for people to shop, i.e. social interaction that accompanies the shopping behavior [32, 33]. *Collaborative Online Shopping (COS)*, defined as "the activity in which a customer shops at an online store concurrently with one or more remotely located shopping partners" [35], is considered the "next wave in e-commerce," as the Internet itself is becoming a big social platform [11].

Online retailers and e-commerce technology companies, e.g. BevyUp [3], and DecisionStep [13], experiment with various COS mechanisms that drive the shared shopping process in a more or less synchronized manner. On one hand, this benefits customers as online shopping is no longer a lonely experience with constraints such as geographic location and time of day removed. On the other hand, businesses that exploit COS are likely to gain an increase in profit as people tend to respond more positively towards both the e-shop website and the products in a social-supportive environment [26, 35]. In an empirical study with a German cosmetics brand Hautbalance Naturkosmetik, a COS tool called ShopTogether brought in a 15% growth in sales and 50% growth in average order value since deployment [13].

E-Commerce researchers try to gain an understanding of how different collaborative mechanisms support or hinder customers' online shopping experiences, but mostly from a social, relational, or emotional perspective. A body of literature has looked into various approaches, e.g. product display format, recommendation agent, and chatting tool, to enhance remote shoppers' sense of co-presence, shared understanding, conflict resolution, and intention to return [22, 23, 34, 35]. However, little in-depth investigation has been done on co-shoppers' actual browsing and searching behavior.

As Cuevas, the CEO of BevyUp, pointed out, one of the potential business advantages that COS technology can introduce is better engagement with the e-retail website, which can be measured by time on site and number of viewing (page, product, review, etc.). Online businesses have devoted a significant amount of monetary resources in

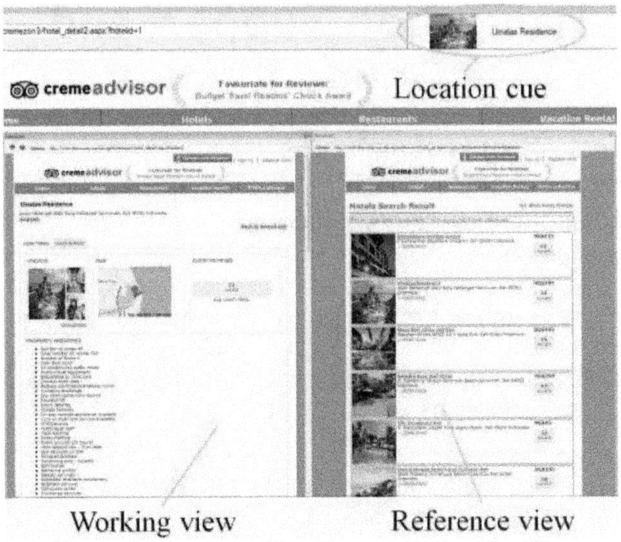

Figure 1. Interface of location cue (top) and split screen (bottom) co-navigation support.

designing and testing the appearance and navigation features of their websites for the same purpose. While companies that promote collaborative e-commerce constantly adjust their COS services according to user feedback, guidelines to direct the development of appropriate mechanism are largely missing. There is a lack of research effort on how COS features and the social interaction they evoke may influence people's attention, browsing pattern, and information processing as well as decision making schema from a theoretical point of view.

To make up for the deficiency, this paper presents a large scale empirical eye-tracking study that explored how various COS co-navigation support impact the behavior of 60 pairs of separated shopper companions during a hotel booking task. More specifically, we compared coordination, concentration, and comprehension of two types of shopper dyads, i.e. co-buyers and buyer-advisor, given three types of co-navigation mechanisms, namely location cue, split screen, and shared view (Figure 1). We chose navigation support for investigation because it is one of the features that have been employed in all commercially available COS tools. Different from prior e-commerce research that largely counted on participants' subjective feedback, this study also utilized eye-tracking technology to help identify people's actual browsing behavior. We analyzed participants' gaze data, video footage, web logs, and survey responses. Results suggest that different co-navigation mechanisms had advantages in different aspects. Groups of different status composition behaved rather differently in collaborative online shopping activities.

We organize the rest of the paper as follows. We first review existing COS technologies and computer-medicated collaboration support in a larger scope. Then we derive a set of hypotheses from theories on psychology and information systems. Following that, we describe the setup of our study and present the data.

RELATED WORK

Shopping, the activity of searching for or buying goods or services, is often driven by psychosocial motivations [33]. Shopping companions may actively interact with one another when splitting social responsibilities or financial commitment [9], seeking information, opinions, and assurance of a product, or merely socializing [1]. Traditional e-commerce stores are designed for solitary browsing. It is cumbersome for shopping companions who are not co-located to build sufficient common ground for effective collaboration [10, 12]. Collaborative online shopping tools aim to make this process frictionless by adding a collaborative social layer to the online retail sites.

Collaborative Social Support for Online Shopping

Existing COS tools provide assorted supports on co-navigation, communication, and information annotation. For example, Plurchase implemented a sidebar extension to Amazon and Zappos where users could check the product URL currently viewed by their shopping companion, jump to the page via a click, or participate in text chat at any time [30]. Similar functions could also be found in ShopTogether [13]. These two applications could be classified as location cue support, which allows co-shoppers to separately browse the web page in their own browsers and meanwhile get aware of the shopping partner's location on the website (i.e. which web page the partner is viewing), or even navigate to the same web page being viewed by partners via clicking on the location cue indicator.

Split screen navigation support, such as the function enabled by BuddyShopping, divides the browser into two equal-sized screens [5]. A shopper could easily control the personal screen and navigate on the website on his own while being aware of how the partner navigates on the web page in the shared screen.

BevyUp, one of the most active COS technical companies, creates a platform that enables multiple shoppers to interact in real time on the same webpage via emotion stickers, comment notes, drawing tools, and video chat [3]. The navigation support provided by BevyUp could be termed as shared view, since co-shoppers with this function will bind together on a same single browser. They synchronously navigate on the website at exactly the same pace and the same view of the web page is instantly shared among them.

These tools have similar communication features, but they adopt rather different mechanisms to support collaborative navigation. Location cue deployed by Plurchase and ShopTogether allows users to navigate separately in their own browsers with a small clickable visual location indicator, providing high autonomy in browsing but low synchronicity in awareness of each other's actions; whereas shared view used by BevyUp keeps collaborators on the same page all the time but sacrifices the ability to act on their own, leading to high synchronicity but low autonomy. Split screen applied by BuddyShopping is somewhat in the middle along both dimensions. It provides a personal screen and a reference screen to monitor the partners' behaviors, which leads to higher synchronicity than location cue but lower synchronicity and higher autonomy than shared view.

Workspace Sharedness Affects Cost of Grounding

Common ground, which refers to the knowledge held in common by the collaborators combined with their awareness of what they have in common, has long been considered as an indispensible element for collaborative activities [6]. Prior research suggested that a strong common ground leads to less uncoupling, greater satisfaction, and a better task performance [6].

Given that people have the tendency to discuss and base their judgment mainly on shared information in collaborative work [29, 31], common ground should be kept up-to-date. Grounding is not merely about placing and absorbing the messages in a common space which everybody can access. It involves formulating the information to share as well as obtaining a joint focus on it. The time and effort consumed on these steps are all costs of grounding. The principle of least collaborative effort proposed by Clark and Wilkes-Gibbs states that "in conversation, the participants try to minimize their collaborative effort" [8]. In other words, collaborators tend to reduce the cost to present and accept information.

Prior research on collaboration has found that a shared workspace reduces the transmission cost of grounding by improving mutual awareness, coordination, and initiation of communication among distributed group members (e.g. the tools for shared visualization, co-browsing, collaborative search, etc.) [2, 6, 27, 28]. To be more specific, through viewing and/or synchronously manipulating objects in a visually shared virtual environment, group members can build joint references to the entities to discuss, achieve up-to-the-moment awareness of all other members' actions, and interpret collaborators' thoughts more easily [2, 19].

However, increased workspace sharedness may introduce competition in attention and resources. For example, people may get distracted or even interrupted from the task at hand by the behavior of the collaborators [20], and may fight for the control of task object or for conversation turns. This results in a persistent negative influence on collaboration outcomes, as group and individual efforts are wasted on resolving the conflict [18]. In other words, the interaction cost of grounding goes up.

In this paper, we compared the level of workspace sharedness among three co-navigation mechanisms, and presented a thorough cost-benefit assessment.

Information and Group Characteristics Affect Collective Knowledge

Collaborative online shopping, fundamentally speaking, is a practice of Collective Information Processing (CIP). CIP is defined as the degree to which information, ideas, or cognitive processes is shared and being shared among the group members, and how this sharing of information affects individual- and group-level outcomes [21]. CIP contains three sub-processes, i.e. information search, information exchange, and weighting and use of information for decision making [31]. Information search happens mostly in the individual knowledge base stage of the CIP model. Activities in this stage are affected by information characteristics, e.g. access to information and the knowledge load created by the sum total of information ready to be shared in the group. Information exchange contributes to the establishment of a group knowledge base, which instead is shaped by group-level characteristics, e.g. group size, status composition, and preference structure [31]. In the end, a group distills the collective knowledge and renders a judgment or choice.

In this paper, we are particularly interested in the influence of the status composition of a group. People with different status in a co-shopping group would have different decision responsibilities and commitment. Literature suggested that in a status-heterogeneous group, members with a higher status are likely to provide more information for discussion and their words are more influential in the final decision [31]. To avoid other confounding factors, we studied the smallest group – dyads – and focused on two most typical status compositions, i.e. co-buyers and buyer-advisor. In a co-buyers dyad, the two individuals have equal commitment and thus equal power in decision making; while only the buyer in a buyer-advisor dyad is the owner of the shopping task, with the advisor merely providing suggestions for the buyers' consideration. We controlled other group characteristics in the study, such as co-shoppers' familiarity with each other.

HYPOTHESES

Seeking insights from theories in psychology, information systems, and collaborative work, we developed a set of hypotheses on how co-navigation mechanisms and status composition of dyads may influence co-shoppers' behaviors and performance in two dimensions. The first dimension, including product views, time on site, and search scope, indicate shoppers' purchase intent. The second dimension, consisting of three metrics (coordination, concentration, and comprehension), reflects to what extent a technology may facilitate grounding in collaboration [7].

Products Viewed, Time on Site, and Search Scope

Time on site and number of products viewed are two of the leading metrics for e-commerce sales, and as a whole could provide a general view of how users behave while shopping together. Conventionally online retailors use page views to estimate product views. Eye-tracking data enables us to conduct a finer evaluation. More specifically, by coding the gaze and conversation video footage, we counted the total number of unique hotels examined by a dyad, the number of overlapping candidates between the two persons in the same dyad, and the number of hotels being concurrently viewed by both members. In addition, we recorded the task completion time and obtained a subjective measure "satisfactory with search scope" in the post-study questionnaire.

As discussed in the previous section, searching for candidate hotels corresponds to the individual knowledge base stage in CIP, and is mainly influenced by the characteristics of information. In particular, different co-navigation methods vary in their ability to access information and in the size of knowledge load produced by the difficulty to share and utilize all information collected by individual members.

Among the three types of co-navigation support examined in our study, both location cue and split screen allow shopping companions to search hotels concurrently, while shared view only enables one person at a time to control the search path. In terms of readiness for information sharing, co-shoppers can see what their partner is browsing at a glance via split screen and shared view. On the contrary, people in the location cue condition have to click on the link and give up on their current view to go to the other party's page. In a word, with split screen, co-shoppers can search candidates separately, and have less trouble exchanging a large amount of information. Location cue enables individual search but the output is constrained by its inability to support efficient information sharing. Although shared view makes it easy for co-shoppers to achieve readiness for information sharing, the constraint of only one person can control the web page as a time decreases the search efficiency, as users usually have to spend time and effort to coordinate the search path that both parties could agree on. Therefore, we hypothesize that there is a significant main effect of co-navigation support:

> H1. Under the split screen condition, co-shoppers examine significantly more items (H1a), with significantly fewer overlaps (H1b) than when location cue is in use; both significantly outperform the shared view mechanism (H1c, H1d respectively).
>
> Under the split screen condition, as they tend to conduct more independent search, co-shoppers spend significantly more time on the COS site than when location cue is in use (H1e); both significantly outperform the shared view mechanism (H1f).

Coordination

Coordination is critical in collaborative work [6]. When conducting co-shopping online, people usually focus on a particular piece of information within the session of a webpage, and thus coordination in COS means identifying the page under viewing and further pinpointing the area of interests. As Zhu et al. pointed out, having participants report failure in coordination upon its occurrence destroys their natural behavior [35]. Therefore, we combined co-shoppers' gaze data and their communication log and used the number of "conversation-gaze alignment" to measure their coordination performance.

Clark and Brennan [7] found that increased sharedness of a workplace enhances the visibility of information and consequently reduces the cost of presenting and receiving information. In the worst case scenario, a shopper needs to first jump to the corresponding page and then scroll to the right place for coordination in the location cue condition. On a split screen, users need to move their eyes to the reference view and then locate the content their companion is referring to, which requires one more step than on a shared view. Therefore, we hypothesize a main effect of co-navigation mechanisms:

> H2. Co-shoppers have significantly better conversation-gaze alignment using shared view than split screen (H2a), and both are better than location cue (H2b).

Concentration

As a shared space expands, group members' actions that take place in it, e.g. scrolling, movement of mouse cursor, manipulation on artifacts, become more and more visible to all. As a result, group members may often step into one another's way, driving shopping partners' attention away from tasks related to their primary goal (e.g. information processing), causing distractions and even interruptions [19]. Visual awareness enabled by different co-navigation systems may cause distraction. Particularly, when forced visual exposures of one's partners' actions interfere with one's own task at hand, "distraction by action" occurs. To measure how well co-shoppers can concentrate on their own task at hand in a given co-navigation mode, we counted the number of "distraction by action" by analyzing the eye-tracking data.

In the location cue condition, the shared space is only the small area next to the address bar (Figure 1, top), and distraction may be mainly caused by the flash of the cue when the other party navigates to a new page. In comparison, half of the window is occupied by the other party when using split screen. People may be easily interrupted by the scrolling and page switch in the reference view. The interference in shared view is even more severe, as people may lose their focus of attention each time the other party performs some action that leads to change in the window. Therefore, we hypothesize that:

> H3. Users of location cue encounter significantly less distraction by action than those of split screen (H3a); and both are better than shared view (H3b).

Comprehension

During a CIP process, individual knowledge bases seldom remain the same, since knowledge is accumulated and transformed as the search for information goes on. Hence, effective collaboration requires collaborators to establish a mutual understanding of the work, the situation, and the information shared among them, i.e. creating a group knowledge base [7]. In our study, we divided such mutual understanding into two categories: factual understanding that refers to the comprehension of information available on the website, and inference understanding which is defined as an informed guess or prediction of the other party's opinion based on available facts and observations. We used the average similarity between each shopper's preference and his/her partner's prediction to estimate the level of inference understanding. In addition, we asked participants to rate their perceived factual understanding as it was hard to compute objectively.

According to Propp, forming a collective knowledge potentially available to all group members is largely the characteristics of the group. Shopping dyads with distinct status composition differ in knowledge contribution and information distribution. For example, prior research showed that in a status-heterogeneous group (buyer/advisor), information contribution and knowledge influence are not equal (see [31] for a summary of literature). While for group with equal status (co-buyers), both parties share the responsibility to establish the knowledge base for further information provision and discussion. This may result in discrepancy between the levels of mutual understanding achieved by members of different status. Thus, we hypothesize that

> H4. Co-buyers dyads reach significantly higher levels of factual understanding (H4a) and inference understanding (H4b) than buyer-advisor dyads.

As suggested by Brennan, computer-mediated shared workspace enables dynamic maintenance of common ground, a process of communicating, testing, updating, tailoring, and repairing mutual understanding [4]. This is particularly important for a group whose members are equal contributors. However, in a status-heterogeneous group, the shared space is more likely to be controlled by higher status members. Those with lower status may not get involved in the discussion as much. In this study, we considered a buyer-advisor dyad is heterogeneous in status, whereas co-buyers have equal status. Therefore, we hypothesize that there is an interaction effect in comprehension between group status composition and co-navigation mechanisms:

> H5. Co-buyers dyads will reach higher level of factual understanding (H5a) and inference understanding (H5b) as the sharedness of co-navigation support increases; whereas the factual (H5c) and inference understanding (H5d) of buyer-advisor dyads will drop when the sharedness of co-navigation support goes up.

RESEARCH METHOD AND STUDY DESIGN

To test the hypotheses, we conducted a 3×2 between-subject experiment, i.e. three types of co-navigation support × two types of dyad status composition. We did not include separate navigation with no collaboration support in this study, because results from our pilot studies showed that participants' performance were significantly worse without co-navigation support than with all the other three methods. People tended to value the three conditions similarly when no navigation support was the control condition; in other words ceiling effects occurred.

Task Design

We chose hotel booking as the COS task, because it is considered as one of the most common services that people would purchase online, e.g. more than 80% of the travelers would research online to make their decisions [14]. Traveler shoppers may benefit more from COS technologies than average shoppers, since hotel availability/pricing tend to change frequently and exchanging information/opinions via traditional methods such as email is inefficient [11].

We designed a scenario, i.e. reserving a hotel room for a vocation on the Bali Island in Indonesia, a popular travel destination. We told the co-buyer dyads that the two persons were going to share the room, while only the buyer in the buyer-advisor dyads were going to stay in the room. We did not specify any other criteria, such as budget or location preference, to resemble a real-world situation.

To simulate an online hotel booking service, we created a website that inherited the style of TripAdvisor, a popular travel site, and the hotels used in the study are real hotels extracted from it. On the experiment website with corresponding co-navigation support, participants were asked to browse and search in the hotel inventory, and make a reservation collaboratively. Shopping dyads are expected to vary in the number of hotels viewed with different co-navigation support.

Co-navigation Support Interface Development

We developed a program called cremeAdvisor using ASP .NET and MySQL on Windows server 2008 that overlaid three types of co-navigation support on top of the experiment website to create an experience of shopping side-by-side for remote customers. The location cue mechanism offers a clickable area near the address bar, displaying the instantly updated page title and thumbnail image of the product currently being examined by the shopping companion (Figure 1, top). Whenever necessary, co-shoppers could navigate to the same webpage by clicking on the hyperlink embedded in the thumbnail image or page title in the location cue.

Split screen divides the browser view into a working view and a reference view. The working view (on the left) is fully controlled by users for web browsing. The reference view (on the right) is read-only and provides a synchronous replica of their remote shopping partner's working view, including the scrolling action (Figure 1, bottom).

Shared view binds co-shoppers on a single shared browsing window. In other words, co-shoppers use the same single browser. Any manipulations on this shared view by one of the co-shoppers, such as pointing, scrolling, clicking, and

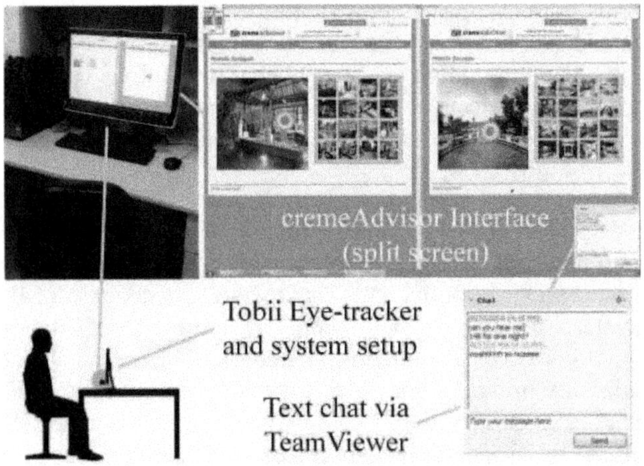

Figure 2. Interface design and experiment setup; the red dots on the screenshots indicate eye fixations.

typing, are all reflected simultaneously in the companion's window. Each party can control the shared view without explicitly shifting handler. The synchronization is backed up by TeamViewer[1] software running in the background.

Experiment Setup

To accommodate non-co-located shoppers in the same dyad, we prepared two rooms with identical settings. Each room was equipped with a Tobii TX60 eye-tracker which consists of a flat-panel 51cm x 32cm computer monitor to display intended information and a copy of Tobii Studio software that can process gaze data and video footage in real-time. The eye-tracker was connected to and operated by a desktop computer sitting by the side. We had one experimenter in charge of each room. They were responsible for setting up the machines, welcoming the participants, obtaining consent, providing instructions and training, calibrating the eye-tracker, monitoring and recording task progress, collecting questionnaire responses, and debriefing.

Same communication tools, including both text chat and voice chat, were provided to all participants for them to talk with their shopping partners (Figure 2).

Participants

We posted recruitment flyers in a local university. Each person who signed up for the study was asked to invite "a close friend who you would love to travel with" to take part in the experiment as his/her co-shopping partner. A total of 60 pairs of participants (120 people, 78 females) enrolled; 21 were mixed-gender dyads. Participants' ages ranged from 19 to 28 (AVG = 21.65, SD = 1.77); 111 of them were undergraduate students and the rest were graduate students, coming from nine different departments. They were all experienced Internet users (ranging from five to 18 years, AVG = 10.98 years, SD = 2.60). 88.3% of the shopper dyads had known each other for more than six months. We randomly assigned the dyads to the six conditions, and there was no significant difference in terms of demographic distribution among different conditions. 83.3% of the participants had never been to Bali. We also asked participants to rate their familiarity with hotels in Bali on a 7-point Likert scale, with 1 as not familiar at all and 7 as very familiar. The average rating was 1.72 (SD = 1.15). In the post-study questionnaire, all participants indicated that they had never known of any of the hotels listed in cremeAdvisor before.

Study Procedure

When pairs of participants came in, they provided consent to take part in the study and be video recorded. Experimenters primed them with the scenario. Then each pair was randomly assigned to one of the status composition conditions. Between two persons in the buyer-advisor dyad, the one who signed up for the study became the main buyer, while his/her friend invited to the study took the role of an opinion-giver to resemble real-world scenarios. The task for shopping dyads is to book a hotel room online collaboratively for a coming overseas trip. Specifically, for co-buyers, participants were asked to book a hotel room as if they were going to share the accommodation (equal status). On the contrary, buyer/advisor dyads acted as if only the buyer would stay in the room, and the advisor only provided suggestions for the buyer to consider (heterogeneous status).

After explaining the scenario and task, we put the two participants in the same dyad in two different rooms. We then gave them a detailed training towards the particular co-navigation support assigned to them. We monitored the process to ensure that dyads had used all the functions, and orally confirmed that they had familiarized themselves with the interface. After that the eye trackers were calibrated for the participants to start the task.

When a dyad submitted their choice, we asked each dyad member to provide two ranked lists of hotels names separately: 1) "the top five hotels that you would prefer to choose (for buyer) or suggest (for advisor)," and 2) "the top five hotels that you think your partner would like to choose or suggest." Similarity between one person's first list and the partner's second list (and vice versa) was an indicator of the dyad's mutual understanding. We adapted Jiang and Klein's discrepancy analysis to calculate the distance between two lists [24].

At the end of the study, participants filled out a questionnaire which aimed to capture information that may be hard to measure objectively. In particular, we asked participants to rate their level of agreement with two statements regarding "perceived search scope (S1)" and "factual understanding (S2)" during the hotel booking task on a 5-point Likert scale (1 meaning strongly disagree and 5 meaning strongly agree).

[1] www.teamviewer.com

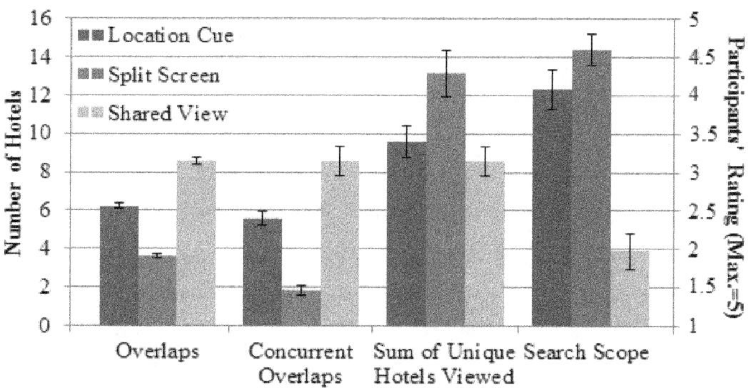

Figure 3. Comparison of product views and perceived search scope given three co-navigations; with std. error.

S1. My partner and I have performed a thorough hotel search on the website, and compared sufficient potential hotel alternatives to make an informed decision.

S2. My partner and I have formed a collective understanding of the quality, merits, and drawbacks of hotels on the website.

Each participant received a payment in cash equivalent to $10 on the way out. Dyads that successfully completed the study automatically entered a lucky draw of three $120 worth of hotel vouchers.

DATA COLLECTION, ANALYSIS AND RESULTS

Over the course of the study, we collected over 1800 minutes of eye-tracking gaze video footage and conversation transcripts. We were able to compute a set of objective measures of co-shoppers behaviors, in addition to the subjective feedback gathered from the questionnaires.

Split Screen Encourages More Separate Product Search

We acquired information on product views and time on site of each dyad from gaze videos and web logs. We counted the total number of unique hotels viewed by a dyad, the number of hotels considered by both shoppers in the same dyad, and the number of ones being examined concurrently. At individual level, ANOVA analysis showed that there were no significant differences between the number of items searched by each shopper in a dyad or on their perceived search scope, regardless of the status composition and the co-navigation support employed.

At group level, split screen encouraged co-shoppers to conduct significantly more independent search of candidate hotels than the other two co-navigation mechanisms according to ANOVA results (total number of unique hotels searched: $F(2,54)=6.66$, $p<0.05$, $\eta^2=0.20$, H1a accepted; number of overlaps: $F(2,54)=16.27$, $p<0.05$, $\eta^2=0.38$; number of concurrent overlaps: $F(2,54)=40.78$, $p<0.05$, $\eta^2=0.60$, H1b accepted). According to post-hoc Scheffe's test, the overlaps in the list of hotels viewed given location cue was significantly smaller than given shared view ($p<0.05$, H1d accepted), but no significant difference was found in terms of the total number of hotel views (H1c rejected) (Figure 3, left).

However, the time on site in the split screen condition (AVG=14.17mins, SD=3.36) was only marginally longer than that in the shared view condition (AVG=12.15mins, SD=1.81) ($p=0.08$, H1e rejected). No significant difference in time was found between location cue (AVG=13.50mins, SD=2.72) and the other two methods (H1f rejected). Different types of dyads demonstrated similar information search performances, and there was no interaction effect.

We conducted further analysis on shoppers' perception in comparison with their actual practice. According to responses in the questionnaire, co-shoppers considered that they had reached a significantly wider search scope when location cue or split screen was in use (ANOVA: $F(2,114)=37.03$, $p<0.05$, $\eta^2=0.39$), but no significant difference was found between these two conditions (Figure 3, right).

In summary, the *actual* search scope with location cue, compared to that with split screen, was constrained by the decreased readiness to exchange individual search results. However, the *subjective* results show no difference between these two conditions. It suggests that co-shoppers appreciated the search autonomy provided by location cue and split screen, and thus "perceived" that both methods enabled wider search. In other words, the effect of "illusion of control" [25] may make users overestimate their search performance. From the e-retailors' perspective, split screen has more potential to encourage spending in COS.

Shared View has the Best Coordination Performance

We took a different approach from the conversation analysis method used in Zhu et al. [35] to identify failure in coordination. We used eye-tracking technology to synchronously compare the browsing activity of all parties in the same dyad. We used conversation-gaze alignment to measure co-shoppers' coordination performance. More specifically, an incident of alignment is counted if participants in the same dyad both gaze on the target area when they want to discuss some specific information.

To assess dyads' coordination performance, we first counted the number of utterance exchange during the hotel booking task. ANOVA results suggested that co-shoppers did similar amount of talking regardless of their status composition and the co-navigation method in use (number of conversational turns: AVG=211.85, SD=43.87).

We then analyzed the number of alignments associated with these conversational turns. Results showed that what co-shoppers said and what they saw were significantly more aligned in shared view than in the other two conditions ($F(2,54)=11.14$, $p<0.05$, $\eta^2=0.29$; H2a accepted). But the difference between location cue and split screen was not significant. Since only shared view, but not split screen,

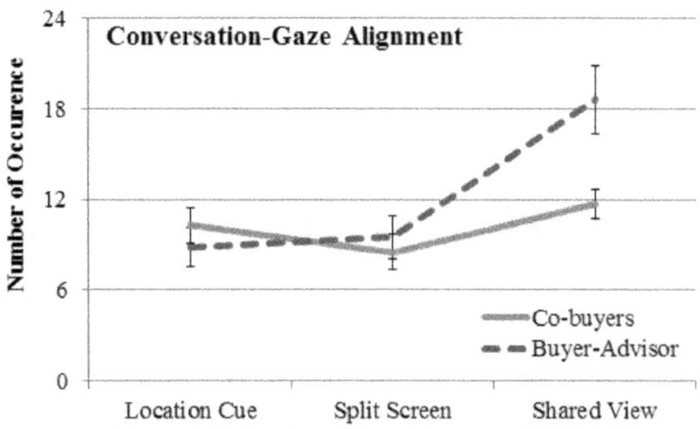

Figure 4. Comparison of conversation-gaze alignment with std. err.

leads to more gaze-alignment than location cue, H2b was partially accepted.

Further investigation showed that marginally more instances of conversation-gaze alignments were found in buyer-advisor dyads ($F(2,54)=3.28$, $p=0.08$, $\eta^2=0.06$). Additionally, we found interaction effect (Figure 4) in coordination performance ($F(2,54)=4.47$, $p<0.05$, $\eta^2=0.14$).

To get a better insight, we conducted follow-up analysis on different dyad's coordination pattern using eye-tracking data. When location cue was present, buyer-advisor dyads have marginally more fixations and mouse clicks on the location cue than co-buyers dyads (ANOVA: $F(1,19)=3.75$, $p=0.07$). More specifically, advisors gazed and clicked more on the location cue than the buyers in their group (an average of 18.40 clicks for advisors vs. 2.80 clicks for buyers; $F(1,19)=13.23$, $p<0.05$), and also more than the shoppers in co-buyers dyads ($F(1,19)=6.07$, $p<0.05$).

In the split screen condition, though not significantly different, buyer-advisor dyads generally had more (167.50 times vs. 158.50 times) and longer (419.48 sec vs. 382.93 sec) visit to the reference view than co-buyers dyads. Similarly, advisors spent marginally longer time on the reference view than the buyers they supported ($F(1,19)=4.10$, $p=0.06$). Although not significant, advisors had more visit count (86.8 times vs. 76 times) and longer (271.15 sec vs. 183.53 sec) visits to the reference screen than those in co-buyers dyads.

This implied that advisors tend to be more aware of their decision makers' focus of attention, and thus may benefit more from collaborative workspace with high sharedness.

Location Cue Allows Better Concentration on Task

To gain an idea of how severe a co-navigation support may distract users from their work flow, we employed a metric extracted from the eye-tracking data, i.e. distraction by action. As suggested by its name, it refers to any gaze movement caused by actions displayed in the window that were conducted by the other party, e.g. page switch, scrolling, mouse movement, typing, etc. (Figure 5).

ANOVA and post-hoc Scheffe's test showed that co-shoppers encountered significantly fewer distractions by

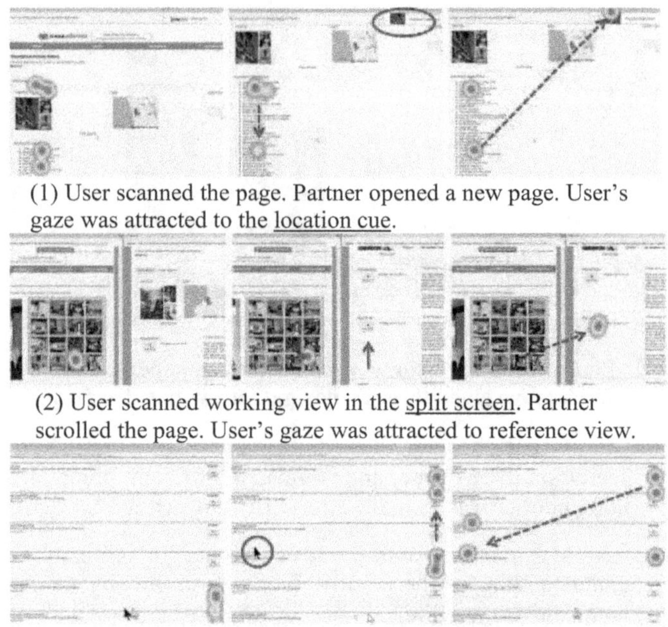

(1) User scanned the page. Partner opened a new page. User's gaze was attracted to the location cue.

(2) User scanned working view in the split screen. Partner scrolled the page. User's gaze was attracted to reference view.

(3) User scanned the page. Partner moved the cursor in the shared view. User's gaze was attracted by the moving cursor.

Figure 5. Gaze path (red dashed arrows) examples of distraction by action with different co-navigation support.

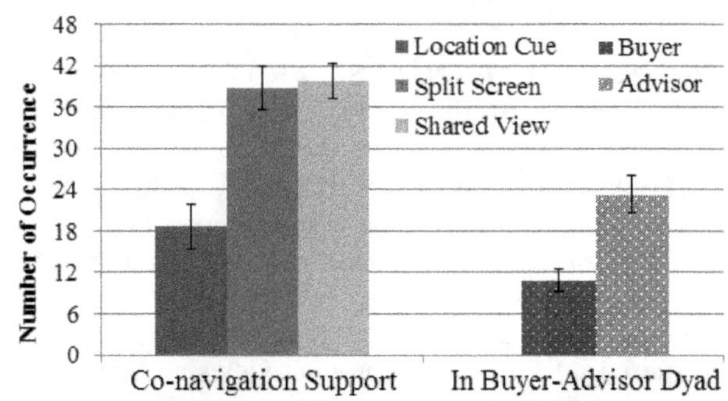

Figure 6. Comparison of distraction by action with std. err.

action with location cue than with split screen and shared view ($F(2,54)=15.51$, $p<0.05$, $\eta^2=0.37$, H3a accepted). There was no significant difference between split screen and shared view. Since only location cue, but not split screen, leads to fewer distractions by action than shared view, H3b was partially accepted. This confirmed the argument that increased sharedness in a workspace makes both information and actions more visible to the group (Figure 6, left). Results did not show any significant main effect in status composition. However, advisors were distracted by their partners' action significantly more than vice versa ($F(1,59)=11.78$, $p<0.05$) (Figure 6, right).

Co-buyers Achieve Deeper Comprehension

We used participants' self-assessment on the extent to which their dyads had achieved a collective understanding of the hotel information on the booking site, to measure their level of factual understanding. Results showed that co-buyers' perceived level of factual understanding was marginally higher than that of buyer-advisor dyads

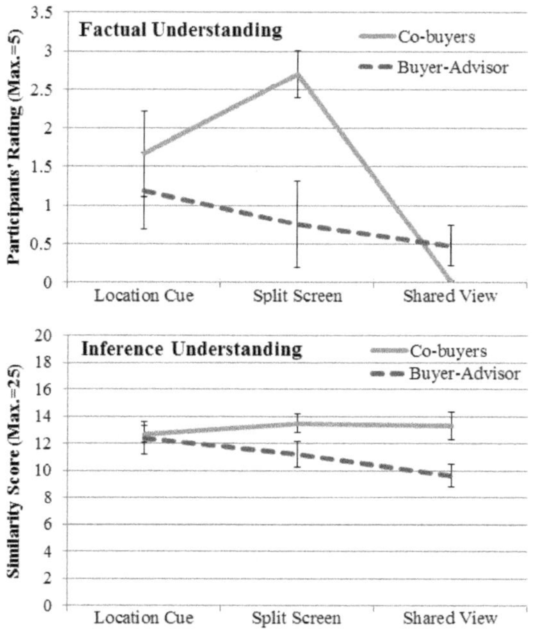

Figure 7. Comparison of factual (top) and inference (bottom) understanding with std. err.

(ANOVA: $F(1,114)=3.77$, $p=0.055$, $\eta^2=0.03$; H4a marginally accepted). However, ANOVA and post-hoc Scheffe's test suggested that location cue and split screen were significantly more effective for factual understanding ($F(2,114)=7.10$, $p<0.05$, $\eta^2=0.11$). This suggested that the ability to search more diverse information may be more important for establishing factual understanding.

Furthermore, there was a significant interaction effect ($F(2,114)=4.27$, $p<0.05$, $\eta^2=0.07$). To be more specific, co-buyers who had equal responsibility in decision making benefited more from a co-navigation support that has higher sharedness but still allows independent product search by each individual (H5a rejected). On the contrary, the increase in sharedness impairs buyer-advisor dyads' understanding of factual information (H5c accepted) (Figure 7, top).

To measure co-shoppers' inference understanding, we conducted discrepancy analysis on the extent to which participants in the same dyad understood each other's opinions. We computed the similarity between one member's prediction and his/her partner's actual preference as the individual-level of inference understand. We then took the average to obtain a measure of the dyad-level inference understanding.

ANOVA results showed that co-buyer dyads achieved significantly higher inference understanding than buyer-advisor dyads ($F(1,114)=7.95$, $p<0.05$, $\eta^2=0.07$; H4b accepted). There was no significant difference in terms of the co-navigation mechanism. Although the interaction effect is small but not significant ($F(2,114)=1.75$, $p=0.18$, $\eta^2=0.03$), one can still see some trend (Figure 7, bottom). Overall, higher sharedness in co-navigation support led to better inference understanding in co-buyers dyads (H5b accepted) but the effect was opposite in buyer-advisor dyads (H5d accepted).

Products Viewed, Time on Site, and Search Scope			
H1a	Accepted	H1d	Accepted
H1b	Accepted	H1e	Rejected
H1c	Rejected	H1f	Rejected
Coordination			
H2a	Accepted	H2b	Partially Accepted
Concentration			
H3a	Accepted	H3b	Partially Accepted
Comprehension			
H4a	Marginally Accepted	H5b	Accepted
H4b	Accepted	H5c	Accepted
H5a	Rejected	H5d	Accepted

Table 1. Summary of Hypotheses and Results.

In summary, for co-buyers, split screen is the most helpful for establishing deeper factual and inference understanding. A rise in workspace sharedness enhanced their inference understanding but impairs their factual understanding. For buyer-advisor dyads, location cue worked better.

CONCLUSION AND FUTURE WORK

In this paper, we presented an eye-tracking study that explored the influence of various co-navigation supports on the process of collaborative online shopping conducted by different types of co-shopper dyads. We conducted detailed analysis on metrics that are of interest to the e-commerce community as well as researchers on collaboration. In general, split screen encouraged more diverse product search, shared view enabled better coordination, and location cue was the least distracting. Co-buyers had better factual and inference understanding, though buyer-advisor dyads were more likely to stay together during the shopping process. The results were summarized in Table 1.

Our study has some limitations. First, we only explored COS with two co-shoppers. Although dyad is the most common case in daily life, people also shop in bigger groups. A group with more members may use and perceive the co-navigation tools rather differently. Second, we investigated three typical navigation support designs, but there may be more designs alternatives that can reduce the distractions as in the split screen condition but still maintain enough autonomy and awareness for people to collaborate. Third, we used hotel in the study which is an experience (or service) product. People's COS behaviors may be different when they are looking for a utilitarian product e.g. camera.

In the future, we plan to conduct further studies comparing other factors that may affect the practice of collaborative online shopping, such as other group characteristics like size, product characteristics, and interface characteristics. In addition, we plan to take a closer look at co-shoppers' information processing performance, e.g. reading objective product details vs. subjective user reviews, with the help of eye-tracking technology.

ACKNOWLEDGMENTS

We thank the Ministry of Education of Singapore [Grant: MOE2009-T2-1-062] for its financial support.

REFERENCES

1. Arnold, M.J. and Reynolds, K.E. Hedonic Shopping Motivations. *Journal of Retailing*. 79, (2003).77-95.
2. Balakrishnan, A.D., Fussell, S.R. and Kiesler, S. Do Visualizations Improve Synchronous Remote Collaboration? In *Proc. CHI'08*, (2008). 1227-1236.
3. BevyUp. www.bevyup.com. (accessed in 2013).
4. Brennan, S. E. The Grounding Problem in Conversations with and through Computers. In S. R. Fussell & R. J. Kreuz (Eds.) *Social and Cognitive Approaches to Interpersonal Communication*. Mahwal, NJ: Erlbaum, (1998). 201-225.
5. BuddyShopping. http://www.ecommerce-guide.com/article.php/3648641/Whos-Your-Buddy-A-New-Social-Shopping-Site.htm. (2006).
6. Carroll, J. M., Neale, D. C., Isenhour, P. L., Rosson, M. B., and McCrickard, D. S. Notification and Awareness: Synchronizing Task-Oriented Collaborative Activity," *Internation Journal of Human-Computer Studies* 58(5). (2003). 605–632.
7. Clark, H. H., & Brennan, S. E. Grounding in communication. In L. B. Resnick, J. M. Levine & S. D. Teasley (Eds.), *Perspectives on socially shared cognition*. American Psychological Association. (1991).
8. Clark, H.H. & Wilkes-Gibbs, D. Referring as a collaborative process. *Cognition*, 22 (1986): 1-39.
9. Corfman, K. P., and Lehmann, D. R. Models of Cooperative Group Decision-Making and Relative Influence: An Experimental Investigation of Family Purchase Decisions. *Journal of Consumer Research*. 14(1987): 1-13.
10. Cramton, C. The Mutual Knowledge Problem and Its Consequences for Distributed Collaboration. *Organization Science* 12(3), (2001). 346-371.
11. Cuevas, M. Collaborative Online Shopping: The Next Wave in E-Commerce. *E-Commerce Times*. (2013).
12. Dabbish, L., and Kraut, R. Awareness Displays and Social Motivation for Coordinating Communication. *Information Systems Research* 19(2), (2008). 221-238.
13. DecisionStep. http://socialcommercetoday.com/social-shopping-test-15-sales-50-average-order-value/. (2010).
14. European Travel Commission. Consumer Trends. http://etc-digital.org/digital-trends/consumer-behaviour/consumer-trends/. (2013).
15. Evans, P.F, Carini, A., Simposon, M., and Zeidler, B. *What Stops Consumers from Buying Online: Inhibitors of Online Shopping Behavior in Europe*. Forrester Research, Inc. (2010).
16. Forrester Research, Inc. *US Online Retail Forecast, 2012 To 2017*. (2013).
17. Gibson, C.B. From knowledge accumulation to accommodation: Cycles of collective cognition in work groups. *J. of Org. Behavior*, 22(2001). 121-134.
18. Greer, L. L., & Jehn, K. A. The pivotal role of negative affect in understanding the effects of process conflict on group performance. In E. A. Mannix,M. A. Neale, & C. Anderson (Eds.), *Research on managing groups and teams*. 10: 23-45. Stanford, CT: JAI. (2007).
19. Gutwin, C., and Greenberg, S. Workspace Awareness for Groupware Companion. In *Proc. CHI'96*, ACM Press, (1996). 208-209.
20. Hill J. and Gutwin, C. The MAUI Toolkit: Groupware Widgets for Group Awareness. *Proc.CSCW'04*. (2004).
21. Hinsz, V.B., Tindale, R.S., and Vollrath, D.A. The Emerging Conceptualization of Groups as information Processor. *Psychological Bulletin*, 121(1997): 43-64.
22. Jiang, Z. and Benbasat, I. Investigating the Influence of the Functional Mechanisms of Online Product Presentations. *Information Systems Research,* 18(4), (2007). 454-470.
23. Jiang, Z., Chan, J., Tan, B.C.Y., and Chua, W.S. Effects of Interactivity on Website Involvement and Purchase Intention. *Journal of the Association for Information Systems*, 11(1), (2010). 34-59.
24. Jiang, J. and Klein, G. A Discrepancy Model of Information Systems Personnel Turnover. *Journal of Management Information Systems*, 19(2002):249-272.
25. Kottemann, J.E., Davis, F.D., and Remus, W.E. Computer-Assisted Decision Making: Performance, Beliefs, and the Illusion of Control. *Org. Behavior and Human Decision Processes* 57, (1994). 26-37.
26. Limayem, M., Khalifa, M., and Frini, A. What Makes Consumers Buy from Internet? A Longitudinal Study of Online Shopping. *IEEE Trans. on Sys., Man, and Cyber., Part A: Systems and Humans*. 30(4). (2000).
27. Lowet, D. and Goergen, D. Co-Browsing Dynamic Web Pages. In *Proc. WWW'09*, ACM Press, (2009). 941-950.
28. Morris, M.R., Teevan, J. and Bush, S. Enhancing Collaborative Web Search with Personalization: Groupization, Smart Splitting, and Group Hit-Highlighting. *Proc.CSCW'08*. (2008).
29. Paul, S.A. and Morris, M.R. CoSense: Enhancing Sensemaking for Collaborative Web Search. In *Proc. CHI'09*, ACM Press, (2009). 1771-1780.
30. plurchase. http://mashable.com/2009/10/13/plurchase/.
31. Propp, K.M. Collective information processing in groups. In L. Frey, D. Gouran, & MS Poole (Eds.), *Handbook of group communication theory and research* Thousand Oaks, CA: Sage. (1999). 225–250.
32. Puglia, S., Carter, R., and Jain, R. MultECommerce: A Distributed Architecture for Collaborative Shopping on the WWW. In *Proc. EC'00*, (2000).
33. Tauber, E. M. Why Do People Shop? *Journal of Marketing* (36). (1972). 46-49.
34. Yue, Y & Jiang, Z. Enhancing Shared Understanding in Collaborative Online Shopping.In *Proc. ICIS'13*.(2013).
35. Zhu, L., I. Benbasat, and Z. Jiang. Let's shop online together: An empirical investigation of collaborative online shopping support. *Information Systems Research*, 21(4), (2010). 872-89

Nutriflect: Reflecting Collective Shopping Behavior and Nutrition

Wolfgang Reitberger, Wolfgang Spreicer, Geraldine Fitzpatrick
Institute for Design & Assessment of Technology, Vienna University of Technology
Argentinierstraße 8, 1040 Vienna, Austria
{wolfgang.reitberger, wolfgang.spreicer, geraldine.fitzpatrick}@tuwien.ac.at

ABSTRACT
A poor nutritional state, as is the case for many people today, can increase risks for cancer, cardiovascular disease and obesity. Technology supported approaches could potentially be used to positively influence food consumption. We present the Nutriflect system, which utilizes users' shopping data to inform them about their long term shopping behavior. In an initial study we conducted structured interviews in grocery stores. Based on the results we implemented a system that visualized a household's collective shopping information via situated displays. The aim was to raise awareness about shopping habits and to enable reflection about nutrition without burdening the users with the manual entry of their eating habits. We evaluated the system in a 4 week field study in 8 households with 21 users. The results indicate that contextually situated displays, showing shopping patterns against personal nutrition goals, can foster a reflective and respectful approach towards better shopping and nutrition.

Author Keywords
Nutrition; shopping; awareness; behavior change; reflection; situated displays; field study

ACM Classification Keywords
H.5.m. Information interfaces and presentation (e.g., HCI): Miscellaneous.

INTRODUCTION
In Austria as well as across the European Union, people's food consumption and nutrition still leaves considerable room for improvement [2, 9]. On average we still eat too much fat and salt, and too little fruit and vegetables [9]. Nutrition has been associated with a number of health issues, e.g., the regular consumption of fruit has been linked with a lower risk of asthma in children [8], whereas unhealthy diets are seen as one of the major risk factors (besides physical inactivity) for cardiovascular disease and cancer by the WHO [3]. Furthermore, obesity is another pressing nutrition and health related issue, with 34% of adults being overweight globally (body mass index > 25) [18], and one fifth of the population either overweight or obese in Austria [9]. This provides an opportunity for HCI to design technology-enabled solutions in support of good nutritional choices but the challenge is to do so in a way that respects the autonomy and unique contexts of people, and to provide support without undue effort on their part.

CHI 2014, April 26 - May 01 2014, Toronto, ON, Canada

ACM 978-1-4503-2473-1/14/04...$15.00.
http://dx.doi.org/10.1145/2556288.2557384

The Nutriflect system presented in this paper addresses this challenge and aims to empower people to make use of their own grocery shopping data as a source of awareness about their household's consumption patterns[1]. By providing the possibility of continuous reflection about nutrition through situated displays, it potentially nudges users towards healthier shopping behaviors.

This paper starts with a presentation of related work and continues with a description of an initial exploratory study in the domain of food shopping. After this our Nutriflect approach is presented, followed by a description of the actual prototype used in the field study. Subsequently, the study setup is introduced and the results are outlined. This is complemented by a discussion and some concluding remarks. The main contribution of this paper, arising from the exploratory study and the field study with a deployed prototype, is showing that contextually situated displays can foster a reflective and respectful approach towards behavior change regarding shopping behavior and nutrition. The Nutriflect system serves as a research vehicle to explore ubiquitous computing technologies that provide feedback about food consumption patterns.

RELATED WORK
In this section we present an overview of related work in the areas of ubiquitous computing and situated displays as enabling technologies for Nutriflect. Furthermore we look into the area of behavior change and persuasive technology, in which this research is theoretically grounded. We end

[1] In this paper, *consumption patterns* refers to the groceries bought over time and not to the actual act of consuming, i.e. eating the food.

with a brief overview of related current approaches in HCI regarding food and nutrition related issues.

Ubiquitous computing and situated displays

The utilization of ubicomp technology for influencing behavior enables the presentation of persuasive cues in a contextually adequate way [31], raising the potential for successful behavior change by utilizing the principle of *kairos*, which states that "a computing technology will have greater persuasive power if it offers suggestions at opportune moments." [11]. While there are several potential opportunities where consumption decisions take place, e.g., while shopping in a supermarket etc., in this paper we focus on people's homes as a place for continuous reflection on their household's consumption, and not so much on providing immediate in-store feedback.

The home context has also been subject to numerous behavior change interventions, mostly in the area of sustainable energy consumption. Systems in this area typically consist of a situated display that gives feedback about electricity [17] [19], or water consumption [10] with the goal of raising users' awareness about their related behaviors and ultimately influencing them towards a reduction in energy use. The input for the system is derived automatically based on people's consumption patterns.

However, in the area of food and nutrition the input is usually performed manually by the users [32, 34]. As this can be time consuming and burdensome for the people who utilize such systems in the long term, Andrew et al. propose the use of a simplified mobile food diary [4]. There are also approaches to make food logging easier, based on the use of mobile photography [20], and Noronha et al. use crowdsourcing to analyze nutrition information about photographed meals [25]. Furthermore, Pässler et al. propose the utilization of wearable sensors for food intake recognition [28]. The Nutriflect system explores a different novel approach to generate awareness about nutrition without burdening the user with manual data entry by using existing grocery shopping data to provide feedback about food consumption patterns.

Behavior change and persuasion

The use of computers to change peoples attitudes and/or behaviors has been denoted as persuasive technology by Fogg [11]. He states several principles that can be used to facilitate behavior change, among them recognition, self-monitoring and social facilitation. Based on Fogg's work, Oinas-Kukkonen et al. [26] developed the concept of behavior change support systems that informs the design of systems and applications in this area. According to Fogg [12], the principle of social facilitation, which refers to technology allowing user to compare themselves and their behaviors, is one of the most powerful persuasion strategies. Yet, the excessive and unelected use of strong persuasive mechanisms in interactive systems has been the subject of critical discussion within HCI [29, 30]. Taking this critique seriously, the Nutriflect does not follow a strict persuasion paradigm but rather provides resources and opportunities for awareness and reflection, aiming to empower users to make more informed choices. Nutriflect also respects the users privacy and does not force social competition on them by sharing their data via social media but rather aims to engage them in a collective dialogue about their nutrition.

Our work is also informed by research in the area of behavioral economics and in particular by the concept of nudging, where people's free choice is preserved while they are provided with a choice architecture to enable them to make better decisions [33]. Key strategies in this domain are the default option strategy, the planning strategy, and the asymmetric choice strategy, which have been applied already in HCI by Lee et al. [21]. For our prototype design we employed the default option strategy by using the settings of the food pyramid, which is a beneficial and healthy choice for most users, as default setting in which the shopping behavior was framed.

Food and Nutrition

There is also a growing body of HCI research on how to use ICTs to promote healthy nutrition. Grimes et al. [16] present a game, which is based on the Transtheoretical Model. It is targeted at adults and aims at fostering healthful eating. Mankoff et al. [24] describe a system based on optical character recognition of shopping receipts, which offers healthier alternatives based on the previous purchase. The approach of collecting the shopping data by using receipts is also part of the Nutriflect System. As outlined in their future work, Nutriflect explores the use of ambient displays to give feedback. Whereas the Mankoff et al. [24] system provides users with particular healthy alternatives, Nutriflect enables reflection about health aspects of nutrition but leaves the decision about which specific foods to buy with the users. As Maitland et al. [22] suggest, system designers should not force behaviors onto users but rather help them make their personal changes. They also propose that systems should enable realistic goals, which Nutriflect supports through its configurability.

Mamykina et al. showed in a study that collaborative tagging of food pictures enhances the ability of individuals to remember the meals [23]. This underlines the importance of social aspects of nutrition, as stated also by Comber et al. Food consumption and preparation are complex and situated within the broader social practices of a household [6]. While Grimes et al. [15] focus on the community level in systems for nutritional change, Nutriflect emphasizes the household as context for food practices, where social interaction is not only mediated but takes place face to face. Ganglbauer et al. point out the significance of visibility for everyday food practices in the household, in particular food waste [13]. In Nutriflect, we build upon these findings and employ the principle of visibility to shed a light on a household's food shopping practices. We acknowledge the social nature of food related practices by focusing not on individuals but rather on the entire household as a collective and complex entity.

EXPLORATORY STUDY

To get a sense of the technology use and the attitude of people towards new ICT based approaches in shopping, we conducted 125 structured in-situ interviews with shoppers in different retail stores in the Vienna metropolitan area, including shops from the major national supermarket chains. The interviews were documented on paper forms by the researchers. In particular we were interested in the topics of CO2 footprint, healthy nutrition and costs/pricing information. The interviews focused on whether these topics were in fact interesting and relevant for shoppers and whether they would like to use a potential system in these areas. The questions were coded according to our research themes and subsequently analyzed descriptively using a pragmatic taxonomy developed for this study. Conducting the interviews in actual shops lead to a heterogeneous sample of people already in an everyday shopping routine. The participants' average age was 37 (SD=14; Min=14; Max=75), 54% were female, 39% with bachelor degree or higher. We asked about general technology and usage, smartphone usage, Near Field Communication (NFC) awareness (as an example of a fairly new technology), and interest in in-situ and long-term information of purchased products.

Analysis of the data showed that 88% of the participants use a PC on a regular basis (2-3 times a week), 30% a DVD-player, 37% a MP3-player, 100% a mobile phone, 16% a tablet PC and 56% a stereo. 71% of the participants have already shopped over the Internet. 64% own a smartphone, but only 29% of them had already heard of NFC. Another 10% of those have already used it. Regarding shopping behavior, 52% of the participants, who almost always or often care about the carbon footprint of products they buy, would appreciate support through PC or mobile phone. Moreover, 45% of those who just sometimes, seldom or never care about the carbon footprint would more likely care about it when having support through PC or mobile phone. 48% were interested in a long-term overview of their purchased products, 80% of them strongly agreed or agreed to a long-term overview regarding carbon footprint, and 80% were interested in health and nutritional aspects and 83% in costs (see Figure 1). This shows that, just like the topic of sustainable shopping, healthy nutrition and a technologically supported long-term overview of purchased products are very promising areas in which to focus further research efforts.

IMPLICATIONS

These results serve as a first indication that an ICT based approach would enable us to reach a large portion of average shoppers, as indicated by the high percentages of participants who use PCs, mobile phones and other devices

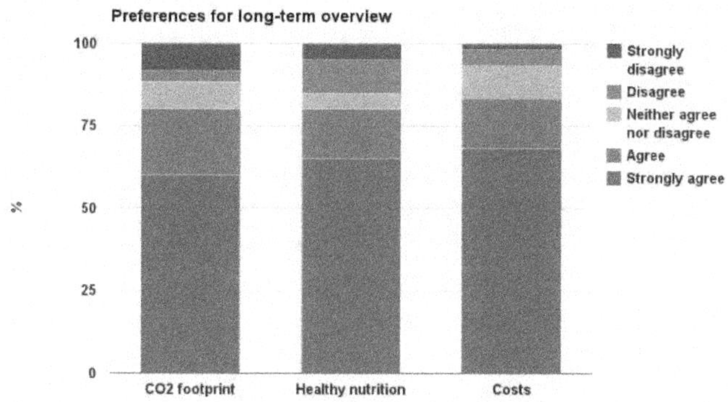

Figure 1. Preferences for long-term overview

regularly. Using a smartphone and shopping over the internet are not the exclusive domain of particularly tech-savvy sub-groups anymore, and systems designed to reach the average shopper can thus build on these experiences without excluding large user populations. The key finding of the exploratory study was that roughly half (48%) of the participants were interested in a technologically supported long-term overview of purchased products. Thus, we looked further into the promising areas of sustainable shopping (CO2 footprint) and healthy nutrition. We discovered that while data about the CO2 footprint of selected products is available, there is a lack of reliable information about the CO2 footprint for a considerable number of products included in everyday grocery shopping (cf. [14]). Therefore it would be difficult to provide accurate and comprehensive feedback to the users based on their actual real world consumption patterns. We thus decided to focus on nutrition, where data for a large number of products is available and where we could develop a prototype that enables a long-term overview of shopping behavior with a particular focus on nutritional aspects.

NUTRIFLECT APPROACH

With Nutriflect, we want to address an important sociopolitical challenge that faces many developed countries. According to the Austrian nutrition report 2012 [9], a major part of the population eats too much fat and too much salt and too few fruits and vegetables. This is confirmed by the fact, that one in five Austrians is deemed to be obese. Nutriflect provides users the possibility to continuously reflect on their consumption patterns. To keep the additional effort for users to a minimum and reduce the need for manually recording nutrition behavior, the consumption data should come from existing sources. Currently, customers more or less voluntarily leave their data to the shopping retail chains where they buy their products. A large number of companies use data analytics for personalized and highly tailored advertising [7]. Nutriflect aims at developing possibilities that also enable the customers themselves to benefit from the collected data. Therefore, we propose to make use of these data to provide a long-term overview of a household's shopping habits in terms of their nutritional composition. Thus, the purchased

Figure 2. The Austrian food pyramid (by Österreichisches Bundesministerium für Gesundheit [Austrian Ministry for Health]) [27]

products are analyzed and classified according to the current Austrian food pyramid (see Figure 2)

The categories of this food pyramid are as follows [1]:

- Fatty food, sweets and savory products: Food with high amounts of fat, sugar and salt. Sweets, pastries, fast food, snacks, lemonades.
- Fats and oils: High quality vegetable oils as olive oil, rapeseed oil, other oils (walnut, soya, linseed, corn, sunflower, pumpkin seed and grape seed), nuts, seeds, butter, margarine, whipped cream, sour cream.
- Fish, meat, sausage and eggs: sea fish with high fat content or domestic cold water fish, low-fat meat, low-fat sausage products, red meat, eggs.
- Milk and milk products: milk, yoghurt, curd cheese, cottage cheese, cheese.
- Cereals and potatoes: cereals, bread, pasta, rice, potatoes, bread/whole-grain bread, pastries, bread rolls.
- Vegetable, pulses and fruits: cooked vegetables, raw fruit and vegetables, salad, pulses, fruit, fruit juice.
- Non-alcoholic beverages: water, mineral water, unsweetened fruit or herbal teas, watered down fruit and vegetable juice.

We use these categories to group the shopping data of the users according to the recommendations of the food pyramid. To make the products comparable, we used the calorific value (Kcal/100g or Kcal/100ml). To ensure a clear understanding for the user, the processed shopping data is presented as a graphical visualization that can be accessed via a situated display, for example in the user's kitchen. Through the constant awareness of the food composition, the hope is that users can continuously reflect on their purchases and are motivated to adapt them to reach the goals of the food pyramid. Households are also able to set their own goals as an alternative to the defaults of the food pyramid to adapt the system according to their specific needs and preferences. To gather the relevant data about purchased products, we propose a cloud-based system, where billing data can be synchronized during the payment process. In the next section we present the Nutriflect prototype which is used to explore this approach. The prototype encompasses the key elements of our approach except the fully automated data retrieval, which is approximated via wizard of oz.

PROTOTYPE

Based on the Nutriflect approach, we iteratively developed an interactive prototype to evaluate our approach. The prototype served as the basis for our study, conducted in realistic settings in several households. To reach highest possible compatibility with a variety of devices and platforms, we chose to base our implementation on a web service. This allowed us the usage of different devices to display the graphical feedback of Nutriflect. Furthermore, we were able to keep track of the process of the study (once the system was deployed) at all times by logging in to the web service. The backend of the web service was implemented on a server located at our University, using PHP and a MySQL database. For the user frontend we used different types of tablet PCs, 5 Nexus 10, 2 iPads and 1 Galaxy Tab. As we implemented the user interface as a web service, Internet access was required for the devices. Therefore, we provided mobile broadband SIM-cards for participating households without Internet access.

For the visualization of the nutrition data, we needed to store all the products bought by the participants, including the EAN-code as primary identification number, the name of the product, the number of calories per 100g or 100ml and the appropriate food pyramid category. As none of the major retail companies agreed to provide the shopping data of their customers, we had to enter all the products including the details by hand. Through this wizard of oz approach we could almost keep with the desired principle of no manual entry for users, who only had to submit their shopping receipts. Although not very scalable, this was adequate for our initial study to explore proof of concept. The manual data collection led to a minor delay between the time of shopping and the entry of the receipt into the Nutriflect system. However, we tried to minimize this delay by distributing the necessary data entry of the receipts between the members of the research team, which was augmented with an additional person for this task.

The data entry was quite challenging, as the receipts only showed the name and the price of the product and not all the retailers provide the necessary product information (see above) online. For some receipts we even had to check the calories and the package size directly in the store. To support this, we designed an easy-to-use web interface for

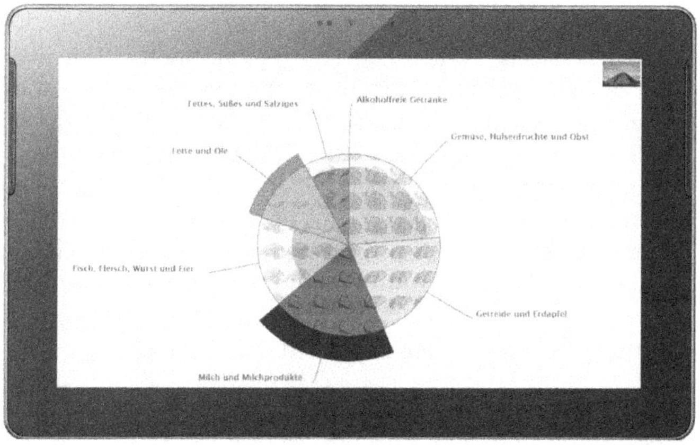

Figure 3. Nutrition Circle visualization showing a comparison between goals and actual consumption

Figure 4. Rising Smiley visualization indicating the overall status of a household regarding its goals

both building up the product database as well as entering the user receipts. To support the workflow of the food data entry, we connected our Nutriflect system with an existing food database called "FDDB". Through a developer API provided by "fddb.info" we were able to automatically retrieve the necessary product information, at least for a large number of products. After all products of a receipt were entered, the Nutriflect system calculated a delta value indicating the difference between the optimal ratios of food types based on the food pyramid and the actual ratios for the household. This delta value was the basis of the two information modes provided for the users in the households.

Information Modes

We provided two different types of visualization for the Nutriflect user interface. The first visualization showed the analysis of the shopping data in an adapted pie chart, which we called the "Nutrition Circle"; the second represented a more ambient approach to visualize the data.

Nutrition Circle

The Nutrition Circle showed the delta between the optimal food composition according to the food pyramid and the actual shopping data of the household (see Figure 3). It was implemented as an overlay of multiple interactive JavaScript charts, using the highcharts.com API. The Nutrition Circle consisted of a basic pie chart, showing the optimal composition. Each sector represented a category of the food pyramid, which was illustrated through a colored and slightly opaque background image. The actual ratios for the purchased food were shown as overlays on the sectors of the basic chart. These overlays used a more saturated color to be clearly silhouetted against the ground circle.

Additionally, each sector had a textual description. Each sector of the Nutrition Circle showed the difference between the recommendation of the food pyramid for the particular category and the actually purchased products by the distance between the arc of the basic sector and the arc of the overlay. If the purchased products met the recommendations, the overlay exactly filled the basic sector. To change to the other visualization, a button was placed in the top right corner of the screen, showing a small preview of the next screen.

Rising Smiley

The second ambient visualization showed a smiley icon climbing a pyramid (see Figure 4). The position of the smiley was determined by the overall delta value between optimal food composition according to the food pyramid and the actual shopping behavior. If the delta was very high, the smiley had to stay on the very bottom of the pyramid. If the shopping behavior met the recommendations very well, the smiley reached the top of the pyramid. Thus, the positioning of the smiley mapped the summed up distances between the arcs of the basic pie and those of the overlays in the Nutrition Circle view.

However, the Rising Smiley view had a very important additional type of feedback for the user: The mood of the Smiley indicates the impact of the last receipt of the particular household against the overall food composition. If the last receipt caused an improvement in the overall composition, the smiley was happy. If the last receipt had a negative impact, the smiley was sad. Twelve hours after the last receipt was stored in the Nutriflect system, the Smiley changed back to a neutral mood. This was implemented to provide the users immediate feedback, also for smaller changes in the delta value. Again, to change back to the other visualization, an image button was placed in the corner of the screen.

STUDY SETUP

To explore the use of the Nutriflect system in the wild and to assess potential behavior change effects, we conducted a 4 week situated field study in 8 households with a total of 21 inhabitants. Out of these, 4 younger children aged 7 or below were present in two of the households but did not actively participate in the study. The households were recruited from pre-study participants who indicated their interest in participation and via neighborhood and university announcements. They were not financially remunerated. The study participants were a diverse group, with ages ranging from 13 – 73 years and different migration backgrounds and technological skills, which should enable a multifaceted perspective on our prototype.

In the pre-study phase participants were asked to collect their shopping receipts for 2 weeks. These were entered in the system to provide a baseline for the respective households. The study started with an initial semi-structured interview, which included an introduction to the prototype. The researcher explained the different functions and helped the participants to customize the prototype according to their specific nutritional goals and needs, if these differed from the default settings that were based on the standard food pyramid guidelines. The displays were deployed in the kitchen (see Figure 3), where a suitable location for the displays was selected based on the preferences of the household members. The main considerations were visibility and reachability, and that the displays should not obstruct or interfere with any activities taking place in this space.

The participants were given a diary in the form of a calendar where they could enter whether they looked at the prototype on a particular day, if they had talked about it and any other observations or comments that they wanted to share. The prototype also logged any interaction with the system in order to get further insights into the interaction with the system over time. Furthermore, they were asked to keep any grocery receipts and scan them either with their smartphone or at home with their PCs and send them to the researchers for entering the shopping data into the system. With each new receipt we recorded the changes in the household's delta value, so we were able to analyze the progress of the consumption patterns over time.

At the end of the study, another semi-structured interview was conducted. The interview included questions about the usage and usefulness of the prototype as well as open-ended questions based on the diary and logging information. The interviews were audio recorded and the researchers took detailed notes, using the audio records to fill in missing details after interview. The data of the interview recordings, notes and from the diary were analyzed qualitatively to get an understanding of use of the prototype and to identify emerging themes. This was complemented with the quantitative data derived from logging the system usage and shopping behavior. As the interviews were conducted in German, the quotes were translated into English.

IDs of inhabitants	No. of inhabitants	Age and Gender
A1, A2	2	59(f), 73(m)
B1, B2	2	42(m), 39(f)
C1, C2	2	30(f), 32(m)
D1, D2	4	37(m), 35(f), + children
E1, E2	2	73(m), 63(f)
F1, F2, F3	5	37(f), 38(m), 12(f) +children
G1, G2, G3	3	47(f), 17(f), 9(m)
H1	1	29(f)

Table 1. Summary of households and participants in the study.

RESULTS

We collected a considerable amount of data from the above mentioned sources during our study. To feed the Nutriflect system with the necessary shopping data, we entered a total of 505 different products to our product database as well as 177 receipts consisting of a subset of one or more of these products. In the following we describe the various themes that emerged from the analysis of the collected data.

Situated Displays

The diaries and the corresponding log data show the continuous use of the system in all households throughout the time of the study. In the final interviews, users conveyed their observation that the Nutriflect display in their kitchen acted as a situated reminder of the system. In the words of D2,

"The display was in the kitchen, so I looked at it when I was doing food related things like cooking there. This was different from nutrition related smartphone apps I have used previously. I only used them a couple of times and then forgot about them as they were buried among all the other apps on my phone."

In a similar observation, E1 confirms the usefulness of a situated display:

"Having a display in the kitchen was clearly more convenient than a website, as it was there all the time and I did not need to do anything to see the information". For him, use of the system was also triggered after his grocery store trips:

"I had a look at the prototype at least once a day, in particular after I went shopping to see how it changed."

For F1 the central location of the displays served as a reminder; she stated that :

"I could hardly go to the refrigerator or cook something without having a look at the display."

Figure 3: Nutriflect Displays situated prominently in user's kitchens

Catalyzing Conversations

In the multi-person households, the Nutriflect prototype fostered conversations among the household members about food, grocery shopping and nutrition. Since the system did not display individual information about a single person's grocery shopping behavior but rather collective information based on the shopping data of the entire household, it was up to the members of the household to make sense of the results and understand their possible individual contributions and their implications for the entire household. As D2 stated:

"I thought we were doing pretty well already in terms of what we eat, until I saw that our sweets bar was still quite high. I asked my husband how this was possible and found out that he bought more sweets than I thought."

A similar sentiment echoing the collective responsibility for the results was voiced by C1: *"I always have the receipts with positive impact and you are always destroying our ratio!"* to which C2 responded: *"Yes, but you are only buying vegetables and fruits on the weekend, I have to buy the other stuff during the week!"*

The capability of the system to support collective awareness and collective action based on a reflection of the current status quo in a particular family could also be witnessed in household F. In the initial interview, they were surprised and even shocked by how poorly their current shopping habits looked in comparison to the food pyramid, especially in the sweets category. In F1's words: *"After we saw this we got together and decided as a family to try to drastically cut back on buying sweets."* Accordingly, their daughter F3 mentioned in the final interview: *"Whenever I got back home from school I would have a look at the display to see how we were doing."* This was seconded by her mother F1: *"F3 would talk almost everyday about the system to discuss if we were doing well."* Designing for the household as a collective also led to social facilitation and motivation of individual household members by their co-inhabitants, as exemplified in this statement by G1:

"In the beginning of the study, I looked quite often at the display. But after a few days, I stopped, you know, I don't really think that technologies like this are useful. But my son (G3) kept playing with it and always wanted to talk about the circle on the screen. Sometimes he forced me to look at the display and to discuss with him how we can further improve our circle."

Goals and Categories – Customization and Adaptation

The possibility to customize the system in terms of nutritional goals enabled the adaptation to specific user preferences. While the settings of the food pyramid were thought to be a good default and thus not changed by the majority of users, we also observed some minor and major changes initiated by the users. Some users reduced the size of the non-alcoholic beverage category to account for the fact that they mostly consumed tap water, which would not show up on their shopping bills. A bigger adaptation was carried out by participant H1, who stated in the initial interview: *"The standard food pyramid is no use to me because I'm on a low carb diet, so the default settings don't work for me."* The researcher then went on to show her the customization possibility and H1 used this to lower the goal for grains and potatoes, according to her dietary goals.

Furthermore, users could also customize the display by choosing between the two different visualizations. When asked about their preference in the initial and final interviews, all users consistently favored the Nutrition Circle visualization. While they saw that the Rising Smiley could give an approximate overview about a household's standing with respect to its goals, the detailed information about the consumption in the distinct categories was considered more useful. This is exemplified by a statement from A1: *"The circle visualization has a clear categorization, is more accurate and shows more detail"*.

Awareness, Reflection and Behavior Change

To assess the change in the users' food shopping behavior, Nutriflect compared the difference between a household's goals and what the members of this household were actually buying based on the information we received from the household's shopping receipts. The differences were calculated for each of the nutrition categories given by the food pyramid and then summed up to have an overall delta value for the household. The smaller this value was, the closer the household was to the nutritional goals of its members. Over the time of the study, we saw a very significant change in the delta for all households ($t(7)=3.86$, $p < 0.01$, paired t-test) indicating a change in the users' shopping behavior towards their nutritional goals.

The quantitative findings are in line with the results from the interviews, where e.g., B1 remarked: *"During shopping, I had the system in the back of my mind."* He also suggested that: *"It would have been useful to have even finer grained feedback, e.g. how buying one can of cola would affect how I'm doing with respect to my goals."*

E2 and A1 made similar remarks: *"When we were in the shop together and were about to buy chocolate, I would ask E1 whether it was still ok to get it or if it would destroy our circle." [E2]*

"I was standing in front of the ice cream shelf and hesitated about whether I should buy chocolate ice cream or not. In the end I decided against it because this would have meant a further increase in my sweets-sector." [A1]

This shows that users were consciously aware of the system during shopping and that the circle metaphor used by the system, where a perfect circle was the sign of a match between one's goals and actual shopping behavior, was a powerful and memorable visual heuristic. It was easy for users to latch onto and understand and it had power to persuade even though not actually present.

Completeness of the Representation

To seamlessly integrate the system with the household's existing practices, the Nutriflect prototype was designed to capture the shopping data almost automatically, with minimal need for manual data entry by the users. The small delay caused by entering the receipts into the system was either not noticed by most users or not considered relevant for the general reflection, as they used the system to get a big picture overview of their consumption patterns. Only G1 expressed her interest in having "*the timestamp of the most recent receipt on the screen*" to clarify the last purchase added to the system. The low effort regarding data entry afforded by the system was well received by the users, as many of them made clear that it would be either impractical or impossible for them to find the time for recording their food consumption over an extended period of time due to their already busy schedules. B1 mentioned:

"I can eat all kinds of bad things like fried food for lunch and a kebab on my way home without the system knowing it. This [lack of accuracy] is a small trade-off for the fact that the shopping is recorded automatically, which is key for someone to use this system in the long run."

Big purchases, with oil purchases as an example, were also a topic related to representation in one household (B). First, they were unhappy about the big impact of an oil purchase on their nutrition circle, but in the long term, the effect was seen as less problematic as it became smaller due to the influence of other purchases. Since the study was taking place in the summer, some participants supplemented their shopping with fruit and vegetables from their own gardens or farmers markets. E2 for example pointed out:

"We could have done even better in the system if it accounted for all the fruit and vegetables we ate from our own garden. Anyway, we mostly focused on reducing bad things like pork and sweets, as they were represented in the system, even though it didn't include all the good things we ate."

Users understood that the representation in the system only included foods from grocery stores and found meaningful ways to utilize Nutriflect despite this lack of completeness.

DISCUSSION

The design of Nutriflect is based on an understanding of households as complex and interrelated systems, in which the everyday practices of their members unfold. Higher-level phenomena such as healthy nutrition emerge from these practices and are influenced through ongoing individual and collective negotiation by the people that inhabit a household. Long-term food consumption patterns are an elusive factor and objective information about them is typically not available to these household members. By using Nutriflect to make these patterns visible we enabled individual and collective reflection about them and fostered a dialog about nutrition among household members.

Emergent Social Practices

The complexity of nutrition related practices could be seen in the range of social interactions catalyzed by Nutriflect. They included: constructive conversations, e.g., finding out about the individual contributions to the current position of the Rising Smiley; playful taunting, e.g., accusing other people of "destroying" the Nutrition Circle; and downright coercion, e.g., forcing others to look at the display and discuss possible further improvements. This kind of social facilitation was not prescribed or designed into the system, e.g., through explicit social comparison features, but rather emerged dynamically as people interacted with the system over time and within their specific social/cultural contexts.

Respectful Persuasion

In the design of the Nutriflect system we aimed to strike a balance between nudging people towards a more balanced nutrition and still preserving their freedom of choice. Following the 'default option' strategy from the domain of behavioral economics, we decided to use the food pyramid recommendations as the default option on which the comparison with a household's actual food shopping behavior was based. Adaptation was possible to accommodate for different user preferences. As expected, most users stayed with the default option or only made minor adaptations, highlighting the fundamental importance of making well-informed design decision regarding validity and user benefit of the built in defaults, as well as the benefits of a personalization option.

Despite the automated tracking of people's shopping behavior by the prototype, we were careful not to create a total surveillance system that would leave no wiggle room for its users. As users observed during the study, they could e.g., easily eat unhealthy snacks on the way home from work without the system noticing it. Rather than employing precision, coercion and control to persuade people, we aimed to raise their awareness and help them to improve their decisions about nutrition while respecting their personal autonomy.

Good Enough is Enough

The Nutriflect system is based on a minimalist design approach, both regarding the amount of data collected and regarding the effort for people to use the system. We consciously decided to trade off completeness of the represented data for ease of use by abstaining from integrating manual food data entry. As our study showed, this worked out well regarding our goal of enabling reflection about nutrition and improving users' food consumption patterns. This could be termed as Pareto efficient [5] design, building on the idea of designing systems that utilize only the necessary minimum of data and users' resources to achieve the desired outcome.

Limitations

While our study showed that there was a significant change in people's shopping behavior over 4 weeks after the deployment of the Nutriflect system, we cannot rule out the role of other factors, such as the novelty effect of the system regarding this result. Thus, longer-term studies are needed to confirm our findings and to determine the optimal duration of deployment. Furthermore, the manual entry of grocery receipts into the system prototype led to minor delays in the feedback and the update of the presented information. However, this delay was not relevant for the long term reflection on a households nutrition patterns in our study. Yet, the manual data entry limits the scalability of the system, so a future version could fully automate the data retrieval, e.g., through a direct connection to a retailer's database. This would further reduce the effort for the user and allow a larger scale implementation.

CONCLUSION

In this paper we contribute to HCI research with a novel approach towards making use of food shopping data generated by a household. We conducted 125 in-situ interviews to better understand supermarket customers and their needs. We designed and implemented the Nutriflect system that makes use of the already existing information about a household's shopping behavior and visualizes this information on a situated display in the kitchen. Nutriflect allows the comparison of a household's food consumption patterns with the food pyramid or with people's own nutritional goals. The collective approach taken by Nutriflect showed the potential to foster reflection, catalyze conversations among household members and positively influence their shopping behavior. We hope that the results from the field study will encourage and inform further research in this area.

ACKNOWLEDGMENTS

We thank Matthias Karan and Hansjörg Hofer for implementation support and Okiemute Akpuma for support during the studies. Authors 1, 2 gratefully acknowledge the Internet Foundation Austria grant 'Die Netidee 2012'

REFERENCES

1. *Die Ernährungspyramide im Detail - 7 Stufen zur Gesundheit*. Bundesministerium für Gesundheit. http://bmg.gv.at/home/Schwerpunkte/Ernaehrung/Empfehlungen/
2. *White Paper on a Strategy for Europe on Nutrition, Overweight and Obesity related health issues*. European Commission, Brussels, 2007.

3. *WHO Global Strategy on Diet, Physical Activity and Health*. WHO, Geneva, 2004.
4. Andrew, A. H., Borriello, G. and Fogarty, J. Simplifying Mobile Phone Food Diaries. In *PervasiveHealth 2013* (2013), 260-263.
5. Cirillo, R. *The economics of Vilfredo Pareto*. Cass, London ; Totowa, N.J., 1979.
6. Comber, R., Hoonhout, J., Halteren, A. v., Moynihan, P. and Olivier, P. Food practices as situated action: exploring and designing for everyday food practices with households. In *Proc. CHI13*, ACM (2013), 2457-2466.
7. Duhigg, C. *How Companies Learn Your Secrets*. City, 2012.
8. Ellwood, P., Innes Asher, M., García-Marcos, L., Williams, H., Keil, U., Robertson, C., and Nagel, G. Do fast foods cause asthma, rhinoconjunctivitis and eczema? Global findings from the International Study of Asthma and Allergies in Childhood (ISAAC) Phase Three. *Thorax*(2013).
9. Elmadfa, I. *Österreichischer Ernährungsbericht 2012*. 9783901861970, Vienna, Austria, 2012.
10. Erickson, T., Podlaseck, M., Sahu, S., Dai, J. D., Chao, T. and Naphade, M. The dubuque water portal: evaluation of the uptake, use and impact of residential water consumption feedback. In *Proc. CHI12*, ACM (2012), 675-684.
11. Fogg, B. J. *Persuasive Technology: Using Computers to Change What We Think and Do*. Morgan Kaufmann Publishers Inc., 2003.
12. Fogg, B. J. *The Six Most Powerful Persuasion Strategies*. Springer, City, 2006.
13. Ganglbauer, E., Fitzpatrick, G. and Molzer, G. Creating visibility: understanding the design space for food waste. In *Proc. MUM12*, ACM (2012), 1-10.
14. Grießhammer, R. and Hochfeld, C. *Memorandum Product Carbon Footprint* BMU, UBA, Öko-Institut e.V., Freiburg, 2009.
15. Grimes, A., Bednar, M., Bolter, J. D. and Grinter, R. E. EatWell: sharing nutrition-related memories in a low-income community. In *Proc CSCW08*, ACM (2008), 87-96.
16. Grimes, A., Kantroo, V. and Grinter, R. E. Let's play!: mobile health games for adults. In *Proc. Ubicomp10*, ACM (2010), 241-250.
17. Gustafsson, A. and Gyllenswärd, M. *The power-aware cord: energy awareness through ambient information display*. ACM, N.Y., 2005.
18. Kimokoti, R. and Millen, B. E. Diet, the Global Obesity Epidemic, and Prevention. *Journal of the American Dietetic Association*, 111, 8 (2011), 1137-1140.
19. Kjeldskov, J., Skov, M. B., Paay, J. and Pathmanathan, R. Using mobile phones to support sustainability: a field study of residential electricity consumption. In *Proc. CHI12*, ACM (2012), 2347-2356.
20. Kong, F. and Tan, J. DietCam: Automatic dietary assessment with mobile camera phones. *Pervasive and Mobile Computing*, 8, 1 (2012), 147-163.
21. Lee, M. K., Kiesler, S. and Forlizzi, J. Mining behavioral economics to design persuasive technology for healthy choices. In *Proc. CHI11*, ACM (2011), 325-334.
22. Maitland, J., Chalmers, M. and Siek, K. A. Persuasion not required Improving our understanding of the sociotechnical context of dietary behavioural change. In *Proc. PervasiveHealth 2009. IEEE* (2009), 1-8.
23. Mamykina, L., Miller, A. D., Grevet, C., Medynskiy, Y., Terry, M. A., Mynatt, E. D. and Davidson, P. R. Examining the impact of collaborative tagging on sensemaking in nutrition management. In *Proc. CHI11*, ACM (2011), 657-666.
24. Mankoff, J., Hsieh, G., Hung, H. C., Lee, S. and Nitao, E. Using Low-Cost Sensing to Support Nutritional Awareness. In *Proc. Ubicomp02,* Springer-Verlag (2002), 371-376.
25. Noronha, J., Hysen, E., Zhang, H. and Gajos, K. Z. Platemate: crowdsourcing nutritional analysis from food photographs. In *Proc. UIST*, ACM (2011), 1-12.
26. Oinas-Kukkonen, H. and Harjumaa, M. Persuasive Systems Design: Key Issues, Process Model, and System Features. *Communications of the Association for Information Systems*, 24, 28 (2009).
27. Österreichisches Bundesministerium für Gesundheit, *Österreichische Ernährungspyramide*, 2010.
28. Pässler, S., Wolff, M. and Fischer, W.-J. Food intake recognition conception for wearable devices. In *Proc. ACM MobiHoc*, ACM (2011), 1-4.
29. Purpura, S., Schwanda, V., Williams, K., Stubler, W. and Sengers, P. Fit4life: the design of a persuasive technology promoting healthy behavior and ideal weight. In *Proc. CHI11*, ACM (2011), 423-432.
30. Reitberger, W., Güldenpfennig, F. and Fitzpatrick, G. *Persuasive Technology Considered Harmful? An Exploration of Design Concerns through the TV Companion*. In *Proc. Persuasive12*. Springer, 2012.
31. Reitberger, W., Ploderer, B., Obermair, C. and Tscheligi, M. The perCues Framework and its Application for Sustainable Mobility. In *PERSUASIVE 2007*, Springer (2007), 92-95.
32. Siek, K. A., Connelly, K. H., Rogers, Y., Rohwer, P., Lambert, D. and Welch, J. L. *When Do We Eat? An Evaluation of Food Items Input into an Electronic Food Monitoring Application*. 2006.
33. Thaler, R. H. and Sunstein, C. R. *Nudge : improving decisions about health, wealth, and happiness*. Yale University Press, New Haven, 2008.
34. Tsai, C. C., Lee, G., Raab, F., Norman, G. J., Sohn, T., Griswold, W. G. and Patrick, K. Usability and feasibility of PmEB: a mobile phone application for monitoring real time caloric balance. *Mob. Netw. Appl.*, 12, 2-3 (2007), 173-184.

Didn't You See My Message? Predicting Attentiveness to Mobile Instant Messages

Martin Pielot, Rodrigo de Oliveira*, Haewoon Kwak, Nuria Oliver
Telefonica Research, Barcelona, Spain
*The author is currently affiliated with Google Inc., USA.
pielot/haewoon/nuriao@tid.es — oliveirar@google.com

ABSTRACT
Mobile instant messaging (*e.g.*, via SMS or WhatsApp) often goes along with an expectation of high *attentiveness*, *i.e.*, that the receiver will notice and read the message within a few minutes. Hence, existing instant messaging services for mobile phones share indicators of availability, such as the last time the user has been online. However, in this paper we not only provide evidence that these cues create social pressure, but that they are also weak predictors of attentiveness. As remedy, we propose to share a machine-computed prediction of whether the user will view a message within the next few minutes or not. For two weeks, we collected behavioral data from 24 users of mobile instant messaging services. By the means of machine-learning techniques, we identified that simple features extracted from the phone, such as the user's interaction with the notification center, the screen activity, the proximity sensor, and the ringer mode, are strong predictors of how quickly the user will attend to the messages. With seven automatically selected features our model predicts whether a phone user will view a message within a few minutes with 70.6% accuracy and a precision for fast attendance of 81.2%.

Author Keywords
Prediction; Attentiveness; Messaging; Asynchronous Communication; Availability; Mobile Devices

ACM Classification Keywords
H.5.2 Information interfaces and presentation: Miscellaneous; H.4.3 Communications Applications: Other.

General Terms
Human Factors

CHI'14, April 26–May 1, 2014, Toronto, Canada.
Copyright © 2014 ACM ISBN/14/04...$15.00.
http://dx.doi.org/10.1145/2556288.2556973

Figure 1. "Last seen" shows the time that the user had last opened WhatsApp.

INTRODUCTION
In the past few years, SMS flat rates and pervasive mobile Internet access combined with Internet-based mobile messaging applications, such as WhatsApp[1], have reduced the cost of a message to zero. These applications are used increasingly as mobile instant messengers (MIM) and users tend to expect responses to their messages within a few minutes [6, 18].

This expectation of immediacy in the communication is problematic for both the sender and the receiver of the message. For the sender his/her messages will not always be addressed within the expected time frame for a variety of reasons, including the lack of availability of the receiver. The receiver, on the other hand, increasingly feels the pressure of having to deal with dozens of notifications per day [20] and constantly checking for new messages to comply with this expectation [17].

Many instant messengers thus share cues about the user's availability. Traditionally this status is set manually, but users typically do not keep their status updated [4], and hence it becomes meaningless or creates false expectations. To tackle this issue, WhatsApp introduced what we will refer to as *last-seen time*, *i.e.* the time that the user had last opened the application, serving as an automatic approximation of availability (see Fig. 1).

This approach has two drawbacks. First, knowing when a person is online has raised privacy concerns, as it creates strong expectations: *"if you're online, it sort of means that it's in front of you and you are doing other stuff and you are ignoring me..."* [6]. Second, neither a manual availability status nor sharing the last time a person accessed a messenger are good predictors of whether the receiver will actually attend to a message soon or not. For example, the message recipient might

[1] `http://www.whatsapp.com/`

have just read messages before engaging in a distracting task (*e.g.*, driving, answering emails, etc.).

In this paper, we explore the value and the feasibility of answering the question: "*Will my instant message be seen within the next few minutes?*" Rather than displaying last-seen time or relying on manually-set status updates, we envision a service that automatically predicts and updates a receiver's availability to attend to instant messages (*attentiveness*).

In this paper, we define user *attentiveness* as the degree to which (s)he is paying attention to incoming instant messages. On the Android platform, attending to a message can be done in two ways: first, by opening the application that received the message, and second, by opening the notification drawer, which typically shows sender and significant portions – typically all content – of the message. At this time, the receiver gets a first idea about topic, sender, and the message's urgency. Potential social pressure, *e.g.*, the need to respond fast, begins to manifest. Further, if the message is unimportant or not urgent, the message can be discarded here.

In a survey with 84 participants, we learned that people dislike sharing WhatsApp's last-seen time, because it creates social pressure, but that they see great value in sharing at tentativeness. Thus, we developed a monitoring tool and recorded actual attentiveness and contextual factors from 24 volunteers over a period of 2 weeks. We found that seven easily-computed features can predict attentiveness with an accuracy of 70.6% and achieve a precision of 81.2% when predicting a fast reaction. In contrast, the prediction power of WhatsApp's *last-seen* status turned out to be close to random.

RELATED WORK

Instant messaging, availability for communication, and interruptibility have been extensively studied in the literature, in particular in the context of information workers and desktop computers. One of the main challenges with asynchronous communication is that when starting a conversation, time and topic are convenient for the initiator, but not necessarily for the recipient [16, 18]. In the work context, emails and instant messages have been found to interrupt workers from current tasks and make it difficult to resume it after the interruptions [1, 7].

People often **expect fast responses** when initiating instant messaging conversations: "*If I started a conversation and it's something urgent, then I expect them to respond immediately*" [6]. There is also a very fine sense towards how fast others respond: "*People do adjust their responsiveness [...] Because I try to be very responsive to people, and I expect that same responsiveness. So if they do not match up, then I am going to change my responsiveness level*" [23]. Therefore, not being able to respond fast to a message may violate the expectations of the sender and lead to tensions in the relationship. This pressure may explain why people frequently check their phones for new messages and updates [17, 21].

Sharing availability, in particular *unavailability* [18], is a way to potentially lower this pressure, as senders can adjust their expectations if they knew that the other person is busy. One of the solutions that can be found in many instant messengers is manually setting and sharing one's availability. However, the reality is that many users do not update this status reliably [4, 22].

In addition, even if people set their status to *unavailable*, it does not mean that they will not respond to inquiries. According to a recent study by Teevan *et al.* [22], people seem to even be more receptive to communication attempts received while their status shows that they are unavailable. The rationale for this unintuitive behavior is the receiver's belief that if they receive messages while being "unavailable", then the messages must be important or urgent if people contact them in spite.

Hence, relying on manually setting one's availability does not seem to be a reliable way to help users manage expectations about how fast they attend to messages.

Sharing the users' online activity is being used as an alternative. WhatsApp, for example, displays when users have last accessed the application. The idea is that this *last-seen time* would allow the sender to make an estimate of how long it will take each of their contacts to attend to their message. If a receiver has been active in the last few minutes, it may be plausible that s/he is next to the phone and hence will notice an incoming message quickly. If the person hasn't used the application for hours, s/he might be away from the phone and therefore not read a message any time soon. The study presented in this paper, however, will provide evidence that *last-seen time* is a weak predictor for attentiveness.

Further, sharing this kind of information turns out to raise privacy concerns in WhatsApp users [6]: "*people read too much into when you're online and [...] why you didn't reply and they try to guess why, and sometimes this is annoying [...] It seems like an invasion of privacy or something on the other person.*"

An alternative –not necessarily privacy-preserving– approach proposed in the literature is to provide the sender of a message with a cue of the receiver's activity. For example, Harper and Taylor [13] describe an approach which allows callers to "glance" at the recipient through their mobile phone's camera before a call, in order to see whether the person is available, which of course represents quite an intrusion into the recipient's privacy.

Predicting the reaction of the sender by the means of machine-learning techniques has been studied in the context of desktop environments.

Dabbish *et al.* [8] conducted a survey with 124 respondents from Carnegie Mellon University to investigate the features which make it more likely to reply to an email. The results show that the importance of an email is a weak predictor. Instead, people were most likely to respond to information requests and social emails.

In a diary study with 13 participants, De Guzman *et al.* [9] found that callers often desire to know more details about the potential call receiver, such as the location, or her/his physical or social availability. They suggest to share details on the receivers context prior to the call. However, as shown in [13], such approaches have privacy issues since many details about the receiver are shared.

Fogarty, Hudson *et al.* [10, 15] recorded data from four information workers to learn cues that would allow to predict when they could be interrupted in their offices. They conclude that a single microphone, the time of the day, the use of the phone, and the interaction with mouse and keyboard can estimate an office worker's interruptibility with an accuracy of 76.3%. On the basis of these findings, Begole *et al.* [4] implemented a prototype called *Lilsys*. It senses sounds, motion, use of the phone, and use of the door to predict whether an office worker is potentially available to face-to-face interruptions. Lilsys was tested with 4 colleagues and was found to help better frame their interruption, *i.e.* instead of avoiding interruptions, co-workers would start a conversation with "*I see that you are busy, but ...*"

BusyBody [14] by Horvitz *et al.* creates personalized models of interruptibility for desktop computer users, by a service running in the background and constantly monitoring computer activity, meeting status, location, time of day, and whether a conversation is detected. Tested with 4 participants, it achieved an accuracy between 70% and 87% with 470 to 2365 training cases.

Rosenthal *et al.* [19] presented a personalized method to predict when a phone should be put to silent mode. They used experience sampling to learn user preferences for different situations. The considered features include time and location, reason for the alert, and details about the alert (*e.g.*, whether it is a caller listed in the user's favorites). After two weeks of learning, thirteen out of nineteen participants reported being satisfied with the accuracy of the automatic muting.

Finally, Avrahami *et al.* [3, 2] studied the feasibility of predicting how fast a user will respond to an instant message in a desktop computer environment. In a study with 16 co-workers at Microsoft, they collected over 90,000 messages. From this data, they built models that were able to predict with an accuracy of 90.1%, whether a message sent to initiate a new session would get a response within 30 seconds, 1, 2, 5, and 10 minutes. The features included in their model were events from the instant messaging client, such as whether the message was sent or received, and events from the desktop environment, such as keyboard/mouse activities or window events. Features that were strong predictors of responsiveness included the amount of user interaction with the system, the time since the last outgoing message, and the duration of the current online-status.

Most previous work has focused on personal computers in the work environment. However, the use of these systems is typically associated with a stable context of use (e.g. work) and provides natural ways to opt-out (e.g. by not starting the messenger or by walking away from the PC). Conversely, we carry our mobile phones with us most of the day. Hence, Mobile IMs are used in very diverse contexts and are typically 'always on', keeping users engaged by means of push notifications. Hence, MIM users have greater expectations towards responsiveness, even when users are clearly unavailable, e.g. driving, in the movies, before going to bed. Thus, corpus of related work cannot necessarily be applied directly to instant messaging on mobile phones. What is missing is an extension of previous work, in particularly that by Avrahami *et al.*, [3, 2] from desktop instant messengers to mobile instant messengers (MIMs).

In view of this gap in the literature, the **main contributions** of this paper are:

1. a user survey with 84 participants to understand the perceived value and concerns of sharing predictions of availability and attentiveness,
2. a privacy-preserving machine-learning algorithm to automatically classify the user's level of attentiveness, *i.e.* whether the user will view an incoming message notification within the next few minutes or not, and
3. an extensive discussion of the importance of the tested features and the implications for the design of automatic means to share attentiveness in MIMs.

SURVEY

In order to acquire insights into people's perception about sharing availability/attentiveness in MIMs, we carried out an online survey. In particular, we were interested in feedback about three main aspects:

- How much value do people see in sharing their availability and what are their concerns?
- Could sharing a prediction of their expected attentiveness(*i.e.* "likely to read in a few minutes") be a well-accepted alternative to the state-of-the-art availability sharing, such as *last seen* used in WhatsApp?
- What should designers have in mind when incorporating such a prediction into mobile messaging solutions?

To address these questions, the survey described both approaches, *last-seen time* and a prediction of attentiveness, and asked about the subjective value and concerns regarding both of them. The survey was created with Survey Monkey and advertised via mailing lists and social networks: 102 people responded, of which 84 (19 female, 65 male) completed the whole survey, and were considered in the analysis.

Results - Quantitative

Knowing friends' availability/attentiveness

The respondents agreed to see value in knowing when a friend was last seen online ($Mdn = 4$, where 1 ='*strongly diagree*' and 5 ='*strongly agree*') as well as a prediction of the friends' expected attentiveness ($Mdn = 4$). We did not find a statistically significant difference between the ratings ($W = 304.5, p = 0.65$).

Table 1 summarizes our participants' preferences: both types of information are considered valuable.

Preference	#	%
Prediction of attentiveness	16	19 %
Last-seen time	18	21 %
Both	35	42 %
None	15	18 %

Table 1. What would you prefer to know?

Sharing own availability/attentiveness

Regarding concerns about sharing their own availability with friends, the participants tended to be comfortable with sharing when they were last seen online ($Mdn = 3.5$) and a prediction of their expected attentiveness ($Mdn = 4$). We did not find a statistically significant difference between the ratings ($W = 466, p = 0.86$).

Table 2 shows that many respondents are comfortable with sharing information about their availability/attentiveness.

Preference	#	%
Prediction of attentiveness	23	27 %
Last-seen time	18	21 %
Both	17	20 %
None	26	31 %

Table 2. What would you prefer to share?

Results - Pros and Cons

In order to obtain strong opinions, we took a closer look at the feedback given by strong supporters of their approach, *i.e.* the respondents who had provided a clear preference for only one of the methods. In the following, we explain each of the points and illustrate it with a comment from a respondent.

Cons Sharing a Prediction of Attentiveness

Respondents preferring to share the *last-seen time* ($n = 18$) were concerned about sharing their attentiveness prediction because of

(1) being afraid to create **false expectations** ($n = 6$): *"It could be confusing and make someone not very tech-savvy misunderstand the 'probability' for a 'certainty'"*,

(2) **not believing** that the method works ($n = 4$): *"I wouldn't trust 'magic figures' unless I know how they are calculated"*,

(3) thinking that it's **not useful** ($n = 4$): *"won't really need that detail at all, either do or do not read but 'likely to read'?"*,

or (4) having **privacy concerns** ($n = 2$): *"Depending on the source used for calculating the probability, it might reveal personal information about my future actions"*.

Cons Sharing Last-Seen Time

Respondents preferring to share a prediction of attentiveness ($n = 23$) were concerned about *last-seen time* because of

(1) feeling **observed and patronized** ($n = 9$) : *"Easy prey for stalkers if you cant differ between friend and 'friend'. Too much information for certain people"*,

(2) creating **social pressure** ($n = 8$): *"I might not always want to answer immediately to all messages. If this information is available [...] that puts pressure in answering or has the risk that other people thinking you're ignoring their messages"*,

and (3) being the **wrong metric** ($n = 3$): *"You don't know if they have really read the unread messages"*.

Pros Sharing Last-Seen Time

Respondents indicating preference to share the *last-seen time* ($n = 18$) preferred it, because of

(1) being **valuable information as message sender** ($n = 6$): *"it gives me a timeframe and allows me to estimate when my message will be read"*,

(2) **communicating** to potential senders **when the user is online** ($n = 5$): e.g. *"That they can notice if I am active"*,

(3) being an implicit way of **acknowledging** that a message was read ($n = 3$): *"For people I trust [...] providing a hint of their messages reaching me is relevant"*,

but (4) respondents also were expressing the **wish for an option to deactivate this function** ($n = 2$): *"It would be a good idea if you can choose when to activate or deactivate it."*.

Pros Sharing a Prediction of Attentiveness

Respondents preferring to share a prediction of their attentiveness ($n = 23$) preferred this approach because of

(1) allowing to **manage expectations** ($n = 7$) *"I can spend several hours without reaching the phone. Messages are asynchronous in nature, and people should realise that. I prefer to water down expectations."*,

(2) being **curious** towards the solution ($n = 7$) *"I find it interesting to know this"*,

(3) considering it **less privacy invading** ($n = 5$) *"It is less privacy-invading than knowing exact dates and times. It feels more human"*,

and (4) considering it helpful to **initiate chat sessions in suitable moments** ($n = 3$) *"May help my contacts know when its better to contact me if they expect a reply"*.

Implications

The quantitative responses did not reveal a clear tendency towards either of the methods. In general, our respondents had a positive attitude towards knowing their friends' attentiveness and a neutral-to-positive attitude towards sharing their own level of attentiveness.

WhatApp's model of sharing *last-seen time* was valued, because, as a sender, the respondents assumed that they could estimate when they would be receiving a response. As a receiver, it was appreciated for being an easy, implicit way of showing that one is active and reads messages. The biggest concerns were that it creates social pressure and that people feel observed and patronized. This indicates that there is a need for more privacy-preserving methods of conveying availability.

Sharing an estimate of the user's level of attentiveness was appreciated for being less privacy invading and allowing to manage expectations at the same time. The biggest concerns were that the respondents did not believe that the method would work and hence create wrong expectations. Therefore, this method would only be considered valuable –from a user-centric perspective– if it works well, and at the same time, communicates clearly that it provides an estimate and is fallible.

In summary, the survey reveals that phone users have concerns about sharing their own availability, in particular if it creates false expectations and social pressure. At the same time, over 25% of the respondents see value in sharing an estimate of how fast they are likely to view message notifications. In other words, their *attentiveness* to incoming message notifications. However, their major concerns are about whether it is feasible to accurately predict attentiveness. Hence, we investigate attentiveness prediction with state-of-the-art machine learning methods and data available on today's smartphones.

DATA COLLECTION

In order to study the feasibility of predicting attentiveness to incoming mobile messages and to explore what features could be strong predictors, we set up a study to collect ground truth data. We developed logging application and installed it on the phones of 24 Android phone users. For two weeks, we recorded both contextual data and actual attentiveness information.

Participants

We recruited participants via announcements on social networks and community forums. 24 participants (8 female, 16 male) aged 22-43 ($M = 28.7$, $SD = 5.37$) living in Europe and North America volunteered to take part in our study. Due to technical constraints (using Android accessibility APIs to intercept notifications), they had to own an Android phone with OS 4.0 or higher.

On average, participants estimated that they were receiving between 10 and 30 messages per day. *WhatsApp* was the most frequently-used mobile instant messenger, followed by *Google Hangout*, and SMS.

Asked to judge how fast they typically respond to messages, half of the participants reported to respond within a few minutes, while the other half reported to typically respond within an hour. Participants estimated that others expect them to respond within similar time frames: half within a few minutes, half within an hour.

Collected Measures

For the data collection, we developed *Message Monitor*, a background mobile service that records contextual information and message notification data on the user's phone, namely: application and time of arrival for each message, elapsed time between the time of arrival and the time of reading the message, opening and closing times of each messaging application, time when the phone's screen was turned on or off, time when the phone's screen was (un)covered (via proximity sensor), and the phone's ringer mode (silent, vibration, sound).

To learn when a message is received, Message Monitor registers as an accessibility service and intercepts notification events. If a notification belongs to a messaging app, such as SMS, WhatsApp, or Google Talk, the service logs the application and the time when the notification arrived. Note that we logged all types of notifications, and then created a whitelist-filter, containing all messaging applications that were present in the logs.

When a message arrives on Android, the phone, depending on its mode, creates a buzz and an audible notification sound. At the same time, a little icon appears on the top left part of the phone screen, the so-called *Notification Area* (see Fig. 2).

Figure 2. The Notification Area in the top left corner of the screen shows unseen notifications as little icons. The icons depict the applications, WhatsApp and SMS in this case.

No notification is generated if the messaging application is already opened. In this case, the our Message Monitor ignores the message.

In the Introduction Section we have introduced the concept of user *attentiveness* to messages, defined as the degree to which (s)he is paying attention to incoming instant messages. Ideally, we would predict *responsiveness* as done in previous work [3], but we did not do this because the act of responding is unmeasurable without instrumenting all messaging apps or the phone. Further, as confirmed by our data and previous work [8], not all messages provoke an immediate response.

To *attend* to a message the user can pull down this area and extend it into the *Notification Drawer*[2], shown in Figure 3. In the view that opens, users are provided with more details about the notifications. For short messages, the whole message can be read there. For longer messages, the user can read the subject line. Alternatively, users can *attend* to a message by directly opening the application, which has received an unread message.

When opening the Notification Drawer, we consider all unread messages as *attended* by the participant. If the user opens an application which has unread messages,

[2]See `http://developer.android.com/guide/topics/ui/notifiers/notifications.html` for detailed description

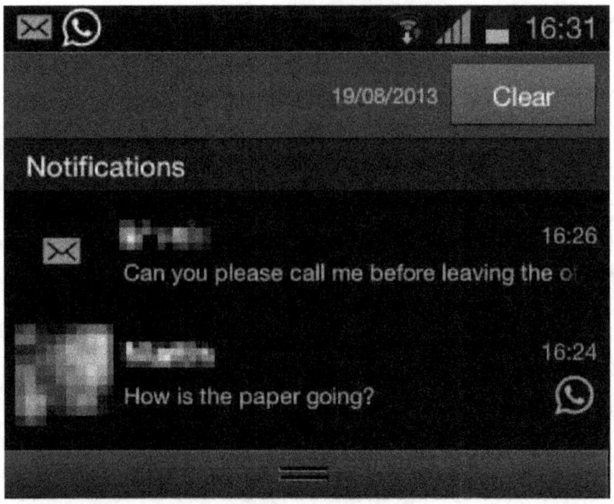

Figure 3. The Notification Drawer can be accessed by pulling down the Notification Area. This view shows details about the messages, which can include the sender and content of the message.

we consider that all messages sent to this app have been *attended*.

The status of the phone's screen and ringer were collected by registering to internal events. These events are internally fired when the respective status changes. We used the device's proximity sensor, which is located on the top of the screen next to the camera, to collect events of whether the screen was covered or uncovered.

Procedure

The study was conducted in Spring 2013. The participants installed Message Monitor and left it running for two weeks. They received 40 EUR as compensation.

Results and Feature Extraction

We collected a total of 6,423 message notifications. In average, a participant attended to a message within a median delay time of 6.15 minutes. In 74.2% of the cases, the participants first viewed a new message in the notification drawer. From within the notification drawer, they launched the messaging app in 69.1% of those cases. Thus, 22.9% of the messages were attended via the notification drawer, 77.1% via the app.

On the basis of previous work and available data, we extracted 17 potential features for the prediction of the user's attentiveness (see Table 3). The list includes features regarding, (1) the *user's activity*, such as interaction with the screen or with the phone itself, (2) *recent notification activity*, such as the number of pending notifications, (3) *the phone's state*, such as the ringer mode or whether the phone is in the pocket, and (4) the *context*, such as the hour of the day or the day of the week.

Note that we did not include any features related to the application used to exchange the message for two reasons: First, we aim at providing feedback for all messaging channels independent from the application. Second, the receiver's phone, which will estimate its user's attentiveness, does not know *a priory*, for which application to carry out this estimation, and hence would need to generate multiple statuses, one for each of the sender's messaging applications, which neither easily scales nor seems to be a usable solution.

Also note that we did not log the user's location for privacy reasons. Our focus is on capturing high-level features related to the phone's activity and its status that would preserve the user's privacy within reason. Hence, we opted against recording such privacy-sensitive data.

TOWARDS A MODEL OF USER ATTENTIVENESS

Attentiveness Classification: High or Low?

In our data collection, the median delay between receiving and attending to a message is 6.15 minutes. This is in line with the results from the recruitment survey indicating that many phone users expect responses to messages within a few minutes. Therefore, we opted to build a classifier of the user's attentiveness with two classes: *high* and *low*, with the median attending delay as pivot threshold. Hence, the problem of modeling user attentiveness turns into a class-prediction problem. Class-prediction problems have been well studied in the machine-learning community. There are many publicly available machine-learning tools to apply well established methods to specific observational records of a given problem. We have used Weka [12] for the machine-learning tasks in this work.

Classifier Selection

To solve the classification task, we tested and empirically compared the performance of a wide range of well-known classifiers, including naive Bayes, logistic regression, support vector machines (SVM), random decision trees, and random forests. We obtained the best performance with random forests, and thus used them as classifiers throughout the remaining analysis. Random forests train an ensemble of random decision trees and return the class that is the mode of the classes from the individual trees [5]. We built our random forests by using 10 decision trees.

For all tests, we randomly split the data and used 80% of the data as training data and 20% as test data. Thus, our results show how well the model can predict previously unseen data. Building a model from all features and testing it with this setup achieved an accuracy of 68.71%.

Asymmetric Error Penalization

Given that our classifier is meant to be part of a mobile intelligent user interface, it is critical to incorporate human-centric considerations when building the classifier. In the particular case of our classifier, we observe that not all misclassifications are equally *bad* from the user's perspective. In fact, as previously described in the Introduction of this paper and supported by previous work [6, 18], high expectations in terms of quick reaction times generate stress in the users of MIMs. Hence, from

No	Feature	Levels	Explanation
01	TimeSinceLastNotSec	Time (s)	Time since the last notification was received
02	LastNotifViewed	Boolean	Flag whether last notification has already been viewed
03	PendingNotCount	#	Number of unveiled notifications
04	TimeSinceLastViewed	Time (s)	Time since the user last viewed any notification
05	IsScreenOn	Boolean	Flag whether screen is on or off
06	TimeSinceLastScreenOnOff	Time (s)	Time since the screen was last turned on OR off
07	TimeSinceLastScreenOn	Time (s)	Time since the screen was last turned on
08	TimeSinceLastScreenOff	Time (s)	Time since the screen was last turned off
09	IsScreenCovered	Boolean	Flag whether screen is covered (using proximity sensor)
10	TimeSinceCoverChangedEvent	Time (s)	Time since the status of the proximity sensor last changed
11	TimeSinceLastScreenCovered	Time (s)	Time since the screen was last covered
12	TimeSinceLastScreenUnCovered	Time (s)	Time since the screen was last uncovered
13	IsInPocket	Boolean	Flag whether device is in pocket
14	RingerMode	Status	Ringer mode: unknown, silent, vibration, or sound
15	HourOfTheDay	Number	Hour of the day, e.g. '16' for 16:32
16	DayOfTheWeek	Number	Day of the week, e.g. '1' for Monday
17	IsWeekend	Boolean	Flag whether it is Saturday or Sunday

Table 3. List of features extracted from the collected sensor data.

the perspective of reducing expectations and stress, it would be better to falsely predict a slow reaction and surprise the sender with a fast response, than falsely predicting a fast reaction and keep the sender waiting, possibly leading to disappointment. In the model used above, the precision for predicting high attentiveness, *i.e.* correctly recognizing that the receiver is going to see a message within a few minutes, is 74.5%. To investigate whether we can improve this value, we explored configurations where misclassifications are not treated equally. Both for training and testing the classifier, we assigned a higher penalty cost when the *low* class is misclassified as *high* than when the *high* class is misclassified as *low*.

Such a different misclassification cost implies a trade-off between the overall classification accuracy and the accuracy for the *high* class. The higher the difference in cost between the two classes (*high* and *low*), the higher the accuracy for the fast class prediction and the lower overall accuracy. We tested the classifier by changing the relative cost of the misclassification of high from 1.0 (*i.e.* the same as that of *low*) to 2.0 (*i.e.* two times larger than that of *low*) with a regular interval of 0.1 increments. We found a significant change when the relative cost reached 1.5. Hence, the final misclassification penalty factor for the *high* attentiveness class is 1.5.

Feature Ranking for Resource Efficiency

In order to make the algorithm resource-efficient for use on mobile phones, we performed feature ranking to understand which features are the strongest predictors and to filter out redundant or irrelevant features. Using a stepwise feature-selection method, we ranked the 17 features described in Table 3. As ranking measure, we used the number of instances that are no longer classified correctly when removing a features from the full set (see Table 4, first column). Large numbers indicate high predictive power, while numbers close to 0 show that the feature has almost no predictive power. For example, when removing *TimeSinceLastScreenOn*, 8.8% less of the instances are classified correctly when compared to using all features.

Merit	Name	Acc.	Prec.
-0.088	TimeSinceLastScreenOn	0.524	0.529
-0.053	TimeSinceLastViewed	0.603	0.649
-0.042	HourOfTheDay	0.635	0.718
-0.038	TimeSinceLastNotifSec	0.622	0.701
-0.038	TimeSinceLastScreenCovered	0.672	0.75
-0.037	LastNotifViewed	0.628	0.694
-0.037	TimeSinceLastScreenOnOff	0.672	0.757
-0.036	InPocket	0.672	0.748
-0.036	RingerMode	0.689	0.763
-0.036	PendingNotifCount	0.65	0.724
-0.035	TimeSinceCoverChangedEvent	0.656	0.73
-0.034	TimeSinceLastScreenOff	0.693	0.788
-0.034	DayOfTheWeek	0.696	0.783
-0.034	ScreenOn	0.706	0.812
-0.034	Weekend	0.695	0.792
-0.033	ScreenCovered	0.684	0.759
-0.032	TimeSinceLastScreenUnCovered	0.663	0.741

Figure 4. Model performance (Overall accuracy and Precision for "High" are computed with cumulative top features)

To select an ideal subset of features for an implementation, we created a model from the feature with highest predictive power: *TimeSinceLastScreenOn*, and then subsequently added features. We added features from strongest to weakest –in terms of predictive capability– and computed accuracy and precision when classifying *high* attentiveness. If by adding the feature we improved accuracy and precision, we kept the feature, otherwise we discarded it. Table 4 shows the features that ultimately were kept in green color, the ones that were discarded are highlighted in orange color.

The selected features comprise (1) the time since the screen was last turned on, (2) the time since the user last viewed a notification, (3) the hour of the day, (4) the time since the proximity sensor last reported that the screen was covered, (5) the ringer mode, (6) the time since the screen was last turned off, and (7) a boolean value indicating whether the screen is on or off. Using these seven features, our model achieves 70.60% overall accuracy and 81.20% *precision* for correctly classifying *high* attentiveness.

Introducing a 'very high' class

To see whether the approach could predict more classes, we tested a third *very high* attentiveness class for notifications that were viewed in less than 60 seconds – the lower quartile. This reduced overall accuracy to 61.6%, which might be too low to ensure trust in the prediction and be usable.

Comparison with Last Seen

In order to compare the achieved accuracy with cues that we find in today's mobile instant messengers, we built a *last-seen* model. It predicts the user's attentiveness on the basis of a *LastSeen* feature, which mimics the information that WhatsApp provides to its users: the time since the user last opened the messaging app. If the user is currently running the application, *LastSeen* is set to 0 in our model.

Using only WhatsApp messages and *LastSeen* as the only feature, we trained a random-forest model as described above. The resulting model achieves 58.8% overall accuracy and 53.7% of precision for the *high* attentiveness class prediction. As such, using WhatsApp's last-seen time to predict whether a user will read a message within a few minutes is almost a random guess, since by using the median response time to split the data into *high* and *low*, a random guess has an accuracy of 50%.

From the perspective of the overall accuracy & the precision for predicting the *high* class, our model with the selected features is considerably better than relying on *last seen* or random guesses. This shows that our model is a significant improvement over existing strategies.

Reflection on the Selected Features

Next, we shall discuss the selected features, which capture aspects of the user's activity, context, and habits.

Activity is approximated by *TimeSinceLastViewed*, *ScreenOn*, *TimeSinceLastScreenOn*, *TimeSinceLastScreenOff*, and *TimeSinceLastScreenCovered*. The first feature approximates whether the user has recently been viewing notifications. The screen-activity-related features are an indicator for the general use of the phone, independent from notifications or messaging services. The time since the screen was last covered is an indicator of whether there was a physical interaction around the device recently, *i.e.* has the user moved her hand in front of the screen or taken it out of the bag.

Context is approximated by the *RingerMode* and by the proximity sensor. For example, if the phone is in silent mode and in the user's pocket, new notifications will most likely go unnoticed and hence be seen with a delay.

Habits are approximated by *HourOfTheDay*. We are creatures of habit and our daily behavioral patterns are somewhat predictable [11], that is, we typically commute, work, eat, relax and sleep at around the time every day, at least during the working week. Hence, this factor captures a rough approximation of activity and attentiveness due to habits.

DISCUSSION

In sum, we have found that a data-driven model with 7 high-level features can successfully estimate a user's level of *attentiveness* to mobile messages, *i.e.* predict whether the user will attend to an incoming message within the next 6.15 minutes or not. Our model achieves 70.6% overall accuracy and 81.2% precision when predicting high attentiveness, *i.e.* the message will be seen within a few minutes. This result offers great opportunities to better manage expectations in mobile messengers.

In the following, we discuss the advantages of our proposed approach when compared to a *last-seen time* model and propose four implications for the design of mobile instant messaging applications.

Last-Seen Time versus Attentiveness Prediction

There are three dimensions where, from a human-centric perspective, there is a significant difference between currently used approaches, particularly *last-seen time*, and our proposed approach of predicting attentiveness.

Expectation Management: Previous work has argued that conveying the *last-seen time*, *i.e.* the time a messaging application had last been opened, has severe disadvantages [6], such as people reading too much into this information. Our dataset confirms that predicting whether a message notification is likely to be viewed within the next few minutes on the basis of when the user was last-seen using the application has an accuracy of only 58.8%, which indicates that expectations will be frequently violated.

Conversely, the accuracy of the proposed model represents a step forward in designing tools that help MIM users manage expectations. Unlike manual status updates, which are often forgotten to update [4], or sharing the *last-seen time*, which is a less accurate predictor, the level of accuracy that our algorithm achieves might be sufficient to make senders trust it. We plan to deploy an in-the-wild user study to shed light on the trust and value that users attribute to the proposed prediction of attentiveness. We also plan to study if this approach has a positive impact on managing expectations in MIMs.

Social Pressure: Our survey further revealed concerns of towards the *last-seen* approach, since it easily creates social pressure. For example, people cannot postpone answers in a polite manner: "*I might not always want to answer immediately to all messages. [Sharing last-seen time] puts pressure in answering or has the risk that other people thinking you are ignoring their messages.*"

We believe that it is not only positive, but crucial that the proposed model is not perfect, because it allows for plausible deniability [3] and *Butler Lies*, such as "*Sorry! I just saw your message*" [18]. Since the system will indicate that its prediction may be wrong, receivers can always blame it to an estimation error if they don't want to react in the way that the system predicted. At the same time, knowing that expected attentiveness is being shared with the sender may alleviate some of the pressure on the receiver, since the receiver won't have to explicitly explain that s/he is busy.

Privacy: Finally, *last-seen time* has raised important privacy concerns, both in our survey and previous work [6]. This is underlined by the fact that popular mobile applications have been designed to hide this *last-seen* status[3]. The features required for the computation of the proposed model, in contrast, do not require accessing personal information, and do not have to be shared with a third-party. The solution can be implemented by running a local background service on the user's phone, which monitors the phone usage and updates the prediction accordingly. If the prediction changes, it pushes a binary value (high/low) to a server, which then can be accessed by potential senders.

Despite privacy concerns, there is a certain level of desirability in users for novel solutions that help them make their receptiveness visible to others, as collected in the survey previously described: "*I can spend several hours without reaching the phone. Messages are asynchronous in nature, and people should realise that. I prefer to water down expectations.*" Predicting attentiveness may serve this desire in a privacy-preserving way.

Design Implications

Nevertheless, the survey responses suggest that a simple implementation of attentiveness prediction will not automatically be successful. User acceptance to any particular solution will depend on a number of factors.

First, it is essential to clearly communicate that the algorithm only predicts the level of user *attentiveness*, that is, if the receiver of the message will *see* the message notification within a few minutes or not. This neither means that the receiver will thoroughly read the message nor that s/he will reply. Since we found that at least 22.9% of the message did not receive an immediate reply, any implementation that fails to transparently communicate this will create false expectations.

[3]Hide-whatsapp-status `https://play.google.com/store/apps/details?id=com.hidewhatsappstatus`, last visited on Jan 5, 2014, has 500,000 - 1,000,000 downloads

Second, the service must communicate that it provides an estimate, which will be wrong in roughly $20-30\%$ of the cases. Only if this is done well, it can mitigate concerns voiced in the survey saying that senders might mistake "*'probability' for a 'certainty'*". In addition, it still needs to be empirically validated if this level of accuracy is sufficient to help users of MIMs manage expectations in their communication.

Third, the algorithm should not be perfect to allow *plausible deniability* [3]. Plausible deniability refers to a situation where the system predicts the receiver's attentiveness correctly, but the receiver decides to act the opposite way. This is particularly crucial if the system correctly predicts high attentiveness, but that the user for some reason decides to delay to respond to it. In order to take social pressure from the shoulder of the receivers, users should be able to blame false predictions to the imperfection of the system.

Finally, it might be worthwhile to investigate whether the service benefits from the user knowing the internal mechanisms of the prediction. It mitigate concerns, such as "*I wouldn't trust 'magic figures' unless I know how they are calculated*". On the other hand, it might invite to *game* the prediction. Nevertheless, there is a trend in intelligent user interfaces to allow users understand the rationale behind the intelligence, *e.g.* recommender systems explaining the reasons for their recommendations. As such, disclosing the underlying mechanism seems preferable and –thanks to the simplicity of the features– will be sufficiently easy to communicate.

CONCLUSIONS

In this paper, we have proposed a novel machine-learning approach for predicting and informing whether a person will see a phone message notification within the next few minutes (fast) or not (slow). We refer to this as the level of *attentiveness* of the user.

In a survey deployed with 84 users of MIMs, we learned that this approach is likely to be well received, given that respondents considered it to provide valuable information to both message sender and receiver in order to better manage expectations. They reported being comfortable to share a prediction of their expected attentiveness (*i.e.* "likely to read in a few minutes").

In order to verify the technical feasibility of this approach, we collected 2-week data from 24 phone users and found that not only they expect fast responses, but also that they react to message notifications with a median time of 6.15 minutes after arrival. Using the collected data and state-of-the-art machine learning algorithms, we determined that 7 easily-computed, privacy-preserving features can predict a user's attentiveness with an accuracy of 70.6% and a precision for high attentiveness (fast message viewing) of 81.2%. The selected features capture aspects of user activity, context, and user habits.

When compared to WhatsApp's *last seen* status, which turned out allow predictions not much better than random guesses, the presented approach not only offers higher accuracy, but also was commended for being less privacy invading and reducing social pressure, as informed by our survey. If designed carefully, it may strike the right balance between managing expectations and providing plausible deniability, allowing new forms of shaping communication while taking pressure off of phone users to regularly check their phones.

Longitudinal studies will be necessary to investigate if the accuracy of the system offers the right balance between trust and plausible deniability, and whether it may help to reduce impolite social behavior.

ACKNOWLEDGMENTS
We thank the people who participated in this study.

REFERENCES

1. Adamczyk, P. D., and Bailey, B. P. If not now, when?: the effects of interruption at different moments within task execution. In *Proc. CHI '04*, ACM (2004).
2. Avrahami, D., Fussell, S. R., and Hudson, S. E. IM waiting: timing and responsiveness in semi-synchronous communication. In *Proc. CSCW '08*, ACM (2008).
3. Avrahami, D., and Hudson, S. E. Responsiveness in instant messaging: predictive models supporting inter-personal communication. In *Proc. CHI '06*, ACM (2006).
4. Begole, J. B., Matsakis, N. E., and Tang, J. C. Lilsys: Sensing unavailability. In *Proc. CSCW '04*, ACM (2004).
5. Breiman, L. Random forests. *Machine Learning 45*, 1 (2001), 5–32.
6. Church, K., and de Oliveira, R. What's up with whatsapp? comparing mobile instant messaging behaviors with traditional sms. In *Proc. MobileHCI '13*, ACM (2013).
7. Czerwinski, M., Horvitz, E., and Wilhite, S. A diary study of task switching and interruptions. In *Proc. CHI '04*, ACM (2004).
8. Dabbish, L. A., Kraut, R. E., Fussell, S., and Kiesler, S. Understanding email use: Predicting action on a message. In *Proc. CHI '05*, ACM (2005).
9. De Guzman, E. S., Sharmin, M., and Bailey, B. P. Should i call now? understanding what context is considered when deciding whether to initiate remote communication via mobile devices. In *Proc GI '07*, ACM (2007).
10. Fogarty, J., Hudson, S. E., Atkeson, C. G., Avrahami, D., Forlizzi, J., Kiesler, S., Lee, J. C., and Yang, J. Predicting human interruptibility with sensors. *ACM Trans. Comput.-Hum. Interact. 12*, 1 (Mar 2005), 119–146.
11. Gonzalez, M. C., Hidalgo, C. A., and Barabasi, A.-L. Understanding individual human mobility patterns. *Nature 453* (2008), 779 – 782.
12. Hall, M., Frank, E., Holmes, G., Pfahringer, B., Reutemann, P., and Witten, I. H. The weka data mining software: an update. *ACM SIGKDD Explorations Newsletter 11*, 1 (2009), 10–18.
13. Harper, R., and Taylor, S. Glancephone: an exploration of human expression. In *Proc. MobileHCI '09*, ACM (2009).
14. Horvitz, E., Koch, P., and Apacible, J. Busybody: creating and fielding personalized models of the cost of interruption. In *Proc. CSCW '04*, ACM (2004).
15. Hudson, S., Fogarty, J., Atkeson, C., Avrahami, D., Forlizzi, J., Kiesler, S., Lee, J., and Yang, J. Predicting human interruptibility with sensors: a wizard of oz feasibility study. In *Proc. CHI '03*, ACM (2003).
16. Nardi, B. A., Whittaker, S., and Bradner, E. Interaction and outeraction: instant messaging in action. In *CSCW '00*, ACM (2000).
17. Oulasvirta, A., Rattenbury, T., Ma, L., and Raita, E. Habits make smartphone use more pervasive. *Personal Ubiquitous Comput. 16*, 1 (Jan 2012), 105–114.
18. Reynolds, L., Smith, M. E., Birnholtz, J. P., and Hancock, J. T. Butler lies from both sides: actions and perceptions of unavailability management in texting. In *Proc. CSCW '13*, ACM (2013).
19. Rosenthal, S., Dey, A. K., and Veloso, M. Using decision-theoretic experience sampling to build personalized mobile phone interruption models. In *Proc. Pervasive '11*, Springer-Verlag (2011).
20. Sahami Shirazi, A., Henze, N., Pielot, M., Weber, D., and Schmidt, A. Large-scale assessment of mobile notifications. In *Proc. CHI '14*, ACM (2014).
21. Shin, C., and Dey, A. K. Automatically detecting problematic use of smartphones. In *Proc. UbiComp '13*, ACM (2013).
22. Teevan, J., and Hehmeyer, A. Understanding how the projection of availability state impacts the reception incoming communication. In *Proc. CSCW '13*, ACM (2013).
23. Tyler, J. R., and Tang, J. C. When can i expect an email response? a study of rhythms in email usage. In *Proc. ECSCW '03*, Kluwer Academic Publishers (2003).

Using Extracted Features to Inform Alignment-Driven Design Ideas in an Educational Game

Erik Harpstead, Christopher J. MacLellan, Vincent Aleven, Brad A. Myers
Human-Computer Interaction Institute
Carnegie Mellon University
Pittsburgh, PA 15213
{eharpste, cmaclell,aleven,bam}@cs.cmu.edu

ABSTRACT
As educational games have become a larger field of study, there has been a growing need for analytic methods that can be used to assess game design and inform iteration. While much previous work has focused on the measurement of student engagement or learning at a gross level, we argue that new methods are necessary for measuring the alignment of a game to its target learning goals at an appropriate level of detail to inform design decisions. We present a novel technique that we have employed to examine alignment in an open-ended educational game. The approach is based on examining how the game reacts to representative student solutions that do and do not obey target principles. We demonstrate this method using real student data and discuss how redesign might be informed by these techniques.

Author Keywords
Educational Games; Alignment; Analytics; Game User Research

ACM Classification Keywords
H.5.2 User Interfaces: Evaluation/methodology; K.3.1 Computer Uses in Education: Computer-assisted instruction (CAI); K.8.0 Personal Computing: Games.

INTRODUCTION
The idea that well-designed games can possess powerful affordances for education has become well accepted by researchers and practitioners alike [1,7,11,19]. The original question of whether or not games are good for learning has given way to new questions of what particular aspects of effective games lead to good learning and out-of-game transfer, and how new games can be better designed to improve learning [6]. This change in orientation toward design issues requires a new suite of methods that can be applied within the design process of an educational game. Having rich analytics data earlier in the process can facilitate discussions around what does and does not work in a particular educational game's design.

CHI 2014, April 26 - May 01 2014, Toronto, ON, Canada

ACM 978-1-4503-2473-1/14/04...$15.00.
http://dx.doi.org/10.1145/2556288.2557393

Designing educational experiences is difficult because there are a number of different perspectives and concerns that need to be balanced [13,30]. Taking an educational design in one direction may cause some other aspect to swing out of balance. This issue is particularly salient when talking about educational games, which must balance the concerns of being an engaging experience, so students actually play them, and an educational experience, so students actually learn something that they can apply outside of the game. One important aspect of games as educational experiences is alignment, which is the idea that game success and educational success go hand-in-hand, meaning that the game rewards actions that are likely to be educationally effective.

To assist educational game designers in balancing these concerns, a number of researchers have put forth theoretical frameworks and patterns for good educational game design [1,11,19,21]. These frameworks are based on existing work in the learning sciences and input from practicing game designers. Having a theoretical grounding while designing can provide a context for discussing design issues and how they might impact the numerous components of an educational game's design; however, a theoretical framework alone will not guarantee that a game achieves its ultimate goals. Throughout the design process, factors inherent in normal design iteration can impinge upon the design and cause conflicts between different components [13]. While having a design framework can inform what redesign options educational game designers might have for addressing a given design conflict, it may not easily inform them which option is most valuable to explore.

Design decisions made within an iterative design loop are often based on intuitions. However, the notion that design intuitions can fail when subjected to empirical scrutiny is a well-documented phenomenon in HCI and game user research [4,16,17]. A better approach is to guide design by using theoretical frameworks, but even this approach may lead to undesirable outcomes when there are no clear methods for assessing design outcomes. Bringing analytical methods into the design process to assess the design of a game can help inform discussions by providing objective measures to compare alternatives.

We believe that combining theory based design thinking with early-stage analytic techniques can help designers to reason through the nuances of their game designs in an empirically informed way. In this paper, we demonstrate a specific technique which we have found useful for addressing alignment related design issues in the educational game *RumbleBlocks* [5]. The technique employs a clustering method that we have described previously [8] and situates it within an educational game design framework of our own design [1]. We believe these elements to be modular and in demonstrating this process we make two contributions to the educational game design and HCI literature:

- A novel analytical technique that uses log data from actual students to assess the alignment of an educational game's mechanics to its stated educational goals.
- A demonstration of how the EDGE educational game design framework [1] can be applied within the design process of a game, where prior work has only demonstrated the summative capacity of the framework.

ANALYTICS IN GAMES

Analytics has become one of the principal research thrusts in game user research. Analytics research proposes a number of methods for understanding players' behavior within games [4,12,25,31]. All of these methods are driven by a desire to understand players' experiences and use that knowledge to reason about game iterations and redesigns. The vast majority of existing work on game analytics is concerned with measuring player *engagement.* A primary reason for this is the simple principle that players will not actually play a game if it is not fun. While this work is certainly important, within the realm of educational games, engagement cannot be the only measure applied. We argue that how closely a game *aligns* with the educational goals is an important metric that should also be considered.

ALIGNMENT

Alignment is not something traditionally tested for as part of educational game design. In practice, alignment issues are normally caught during the course of standard efficacy testing, where students would take pre- and posttests to measure learning after playing a game, or during an A/B manipulation to test the impact of a particular game feature. Such experimental designs tend toward making conclusions about a game as a whole, making it hard to consider the impact of particular features of a game's design, unless a large number of experimental conditions are employed [20].

Evaluating alignment is important because there are a number of ways that an educational experience can be misaligned with its educational goals. One of the more common ways a game can be misaligned lies in how it provides feedback to a learner. If the feedback is inconsistent or poorly timed, then it makes it difficult for the learner to associate their actions with correct understanding. This focus on feedback differentiates our work from the related psychometric concept of construct irrelevant variance [18] which concerns itself with how well a test is measuring what it should be measuring.

One situation where feedback might be inconsistent occurs when the instructional task requires knowledge that the designer did not anticipate [15]. These unexpected demands can result in inconsistent feedback in situations where a learner is performing some task that requires some desired knowledge as well as some unanticipated knowledge. In these situations, learners may be told they are wrong even if they possess the desired knowledge simply because they are lacking the unanticipated knowledge. This results in the learner receiving negative feedback even when they may be correctly applying the desired knowledge. A classic example of such unanticipated knowledge comes from the work of Koedinger and Nathan when examining the student performance on different types of algebra problems [15]. The common wisdom among teachers was that algebraic word problems were more difficult than formal symbolic problems, such as $5x + 3 = 6$, because students had to intuit the underlying mathematical equation the story represented. Contrary to this common wisdom, Koedinger and Nathan found that students actually have more difficulty with the formal symbolic problems because there was a barrier in understanding what the mathematical symbols meant. As there was no feedback for how well a student understood the original problem, they could not learn to correct their understanding and improve on formal symbolic problems.

A different situation where feedback tends to become inconsistent is when feedback is delayed from student actions that express understanding of the concept or when students must infer the nature of the feedback from the complex state of the world. In educational technology literature this phenomenon is commonly referred to as situational feedback [24,26], where learners execute one or more actions and must then infer from the system's response whether or not they were correct in their thinking. These situations arise most prominently when learners must exercise multiple skills at once. If a learner applies one skill correctly and one incorrectly they would receive a single piece of negative feedback and be left to intuit which skill they failed to apply correctly. These situations make it difficult for learners to determine which of their actions are correct. This issue is especially common to games which fall into the "configure and run" design pattern [21], where players build up some complex structure as a potential solution to an in-game puzzle and finally ask the system to evaluate it by running a simulation and seeing if it achieves the desired result. While such puzzles can be engaging, their feedback leaves the learner having to reason about what exactly lead to their success or failure.

The issue of misaligned feedback is particularly important in educational games because they are feedback-rich environments that can provide many, often subtle, cues about player status. Players can take this feedback as guidance

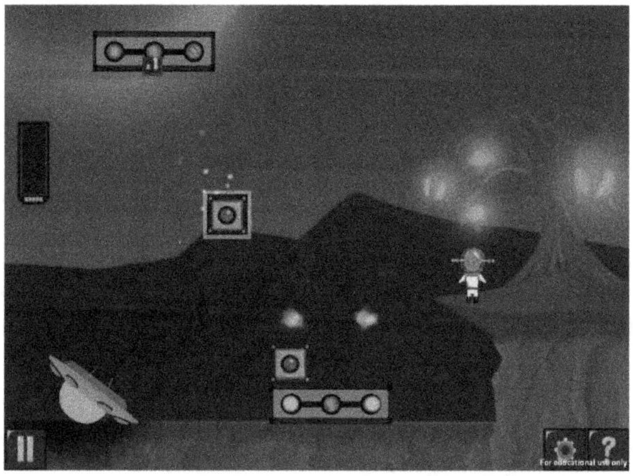

Figure 1. A screenshot from *RumbleBlocks*. Players must build a tower that is tall enough to reach the alien on the cliff, while also covering the blue energy balls.

and adjust their behavior accordingly. When a game is being designed to convey an instructional message, it is important that the game provides feedback that aligns with the instructional goals of the system.

THE EDGE FRAMEWORK

Issues of alignment represent complex problems that exist in the interactions between multiple game design elements; so solving them is not a simple task. Employing a theoretical educational game design framework can assist in thinking across the elements of a design. The framework that we employ in our own work is called the EDGE framework [1]. EDGE, which stands for *Engaging Design of Games for Education*, employs three main components in looking at educational game design: educational objects, game design theories, and learning science principles.

The framework starts with advocating for rigorous educational objectives, drawing on inspiration from the educational theory of "backwards design" [32]. Backwards Design calls for starting from a set of goals, determining how you will assess students based on those goals, then considering how you will design an intervention, which "moves the needle" on those assessments.

The EDGE framework conceptualizes game mechanics mainly through the lens of the Mechanics, Dynamics, and Aesthetics (MDA) framework [10]. MDA is particularly applicable to the educational setting because of its bi-directional perspective on game design, considering both the designer's and the player's views. A game designer primarily has control over the mechanics of a game, or the base rules of the game's system. The player, on the other hand, interacts with a game as an aesthetic experience, which can only ever be indirectly perceived by the designer. In between these two perspectives are the dynamics of the game's system, which can be hard to anticipate and control from a design perspective. Instructional design can be seen through a similar set of perspectives: a teacher, or instructional designer, has control over the base mechanics of an educational experience while the student's learning of intended content takes place as indirectly perceivable events [14], with many messy dynamic factors in between complicating the process.

The learning principles covered in the EDGE framework are left intentionally modular, to allow for changes in theoretical perspective and context of use. The principles used in the framework can be taken from a number of sources that exist in the learning sciences literature [14,22,28]. Each collection of principles represents a summation of many years of research in the learning sciences, not unlike the usability heuristics commonly employed in the HCI community [27]. The specific collection of principles used will change based on the goals, context, and demographics of the game.

In general, the EDGE framework could be seen as trying to combine the three wisdoms of instructional design practitioners, game design practitioners, and learning science researchers to allow for a reasoned way of integrating multiple perspectives while designing educational games.

RUMBLEBLOCKS

The game we will be primarily discussing is called *RumbleBlocks*, which is an educational game designed to teach basic concepts of structural stability and balance to children in grades K-3 (ages 5-8 years old) [5]. The primary educational goals are for players to gain an understanding of three main principles of stability: objects with wider bases are more stable, objects that are symmetrical are more stable, and objects with lower centers of mass are more stable. The game follows a narrative of the player helping a group of stranded aliens on a number of foreign planets. In each level the player encounters an alien who is stranded on a cliff with their deactivated spaceship left off to the side of the world (see Figure 1). Players must build a tower out of blocks that is tall enough to reach the alien so that they can give the alien back his ship. In the process, they must also cover a series of energy dots with their tower so that the ship will receive power. Once the player has placed the ship on top of the tower, an earthquake is triggered when the ship powers up. If the earthquake topples the tower, or knocks the ship off the top, then the player must restart the level; if the tower remains standing, with the ship on top, then the player succeeds and moves on to the next level.

Previous analysis of *RumbleBlocks* [8,9] suggested that this domain possesses some issues with alignment between its mechanics and educational goals; however, this prior work could not provide enough detail to inform redesign. Previously, we showed that principle-relevant metrics, i.e. metrics from game log data which measure a student tower based on adherence to a particular principle, predicted success in a logistic regression for the wide base and symmetry principles, but not for the center of mass principle. This suggests that students adhering to the center of mass princi-

	Unprincipled	Principled
Successful	**Bad**	**Good**
Unsuccessful	**Good**	**Bad**

Figure 2. A matrix showing the possible alignment interpretations of student solutions based on how principled they are and success feedback that the game assigns to them.

ple would be receiving inconsistent feedback on their tower designs [9]. We examined clusters of student solutions based on extracted features from student game states to see how well they aligned with designer expectations and found a number of levels which deviated strongly from the designers' vision for a level [8]. Our current analysis looks to draw from our previous techniques with the motivation of digging deeper into the issue of misalignment and providing a fine grain view of player data capable of providing actionable design recommendations, whereas prior work stopped at diagnosing the existence of a problem. We make use of the prior datasets to help ground the approach in existing work.

ANALYSIS

At a high level, our approach involves capturing a picture of the space of solutions that students use to overcome in-game challenges. This solution space is generated by clustering the individual solutions created by actual students in the target population into a series of representative solutions. Once a collection of representative solutions is gathered, each one is evaluated using a principle-relevant metric (PRM), which measures how closely the representative solution embodies a certain target principle normalized across all other representative solutions to the same challenge. Finally, the PRM is compared to the positive or negative feedback designation that the game's mechanics assigned to the majority of individual solutions embodied by each of the representative solutions.

Using this approach, representative solutions can arrive at one of four designations, best thought of as the 2x2 matrix shown in Figure 2. Two quadrants in this matrix are desirable and, if solutions consistently land in either one of these quadrants, this indicates that the game is well aligned. Solutions that are highly principled would ideally be given a designation of successful, which would represent that the game is reinforcing target concepts to the student. Similarly, solutions that are unprincipled should be given a designation of failure, which would represent that the game is discouraging deviations from target concepts, allowing a student to learn from their mistakes. Solutions would ideally *not* fall into the other two quadrants, where principled solutions are discouraged or unprincipled solutions are reinforced. In these cases, the game is sending contradictory feedback to students, at best confusing them and at worst fostering misconceptions.

We analyze PRM alignment in terms of representative solutions because they a more concise representation of the solution space. Our goal is to help identify causes, and potential fixes for, cases of misalignment. Clusters help greatly in achieving this goal. They make it easier to investigate the causes of misalignment because solutions within a cluster should all be aligned or misaligned in the same way. Without clusters, one could employ other methods to know that a particular level is problematic but then one would have to resort to sifting through each individual solution one-by-one to figure out what the reason for the misalignment was. Additionally, we do not consider frequency information, or how many users used each representative solution, at this stage because this information is likely to vary by playtest population.

Data

The data we are using in this section comes from a formative evaluation of *RumbleBlocks* conducted in 2 local area schools using 174 students in the target demographic (5-8 year-olds). The evaluation took place in the context of a pre-post design over 4 days; it began with a pretest of target concepts on the first day, 2 sessions of roughly 45 minutes of gameplay each subsequent day, and ended on the final day with a counterbalanced posttest of the same target concepts. Throughout the study, the game was instrumented to log student actions at a high level of fidelity capable of being replayed through the game's engine. This replay approach allows us to perform a number of different analyses on the same dataset, allowing us to be more flexible and iterate on potential principle-relevant metrics [9].

Our novel analysis method assesses the degree to which success in playing the game aligns with educational objectives as the frequency with which solutions fall into the two desirable quadrants of Figure 2. This method starts by clustering student solutions. To generate student solution clusters with the *RumbleBlocks* data, we first generate a set of features using the conceptual feature extraction process, which we have reported on previously [8]. This process outputs a feature vector for each student solution that describes which structural patterns are and are not present within the solution. These patterns may correspond to individual blocks, pairs of blocks, other combinations of blocks, or even whole towers. We then use these feature vectors as input to standard clustering methods to yield a set of solution clusters for each level. We then view each cluster as a representative solution for that level.

For each representative solution we calculate the average value of each PRM on all the towers with that solution. The average PRM value is then interpreted as the canonical PRM for the representative solution. Finally, the PRM scores of all the representative solutions to the same level are normalized to make it easier to compare between solutions.

In *RumbleBlocks,* the PRMs correspond to calculable metrics from a student's tower; see Figure 3 for a visual representation. For levels targeting the "objects with wider bases are more stable" principle, the width of the tower's base is used as the PRM. For the "objects with lower centers of mass are more stable" principle, we calculate the tower's overall center of mass and take its height from the ground. For the "symmetrical objects are more stable" principle, we create a ray that extends from the center of the base of the tower through the center of mass and calculate the angle of this ray and its absolute difference from 90°. While this is not a perfect representation of geometric symmetry, in practice this measure adequately captures the concept as it exists in the *RumbleBlocks* dataset.

Figure 3. Examples of the 3 Principle-Relevant Metrics (PRMs) used in *RumbleBlocks*. The red line represents the width of a tower's base. The blue line represents the height of its center of mass, and the measure of the green angle is used for symmetry

Interpretation

To interpret the data, we are interested in finding two particular patterns within the representative solutions. In the first pattern, we are looking for instances where the game is providing incorrect feedback, either negative feedback to a principled solutions or positive feedback to an unprincipled solutions. To quantify this pattern, we compute a measure of misalignment for each level. This measure is calculated by taking the average error of the representative solutions, where the error for a solution is defined by its total distance (in terms of PRM score) from where it should be based on its correctness designation. For example, correct solutions with a positive PRM score would have an error of 0, whereas correct solutions with a negative PRM score would have an error equal to -1 times their PRM score. Similarly, incorrect solutions that have a negative PRM score would have an error of 0 and incorrect solutions that have a positive PRM score would have an error equal to their PRM score. We did not weight the solutions' error by their observed frequency because we are interested in finding places where the game provides misaligned feedback in general and not where it provided misaligned feedback to the play-testing population, which may differ somewhat from the release population.

In addition to misalignment, which exhibits incorrect feedback, we were also interested in identifying situations where we might be giving inconsistent feedback. To identify these levels, we compute a metric we call *discrimination*, which we define as the absolute difference between the average of the PRM scores for the correct and for the incorrect solutions. This measure is useful for identifying levels that have correct and incorrect solutions that receive similar

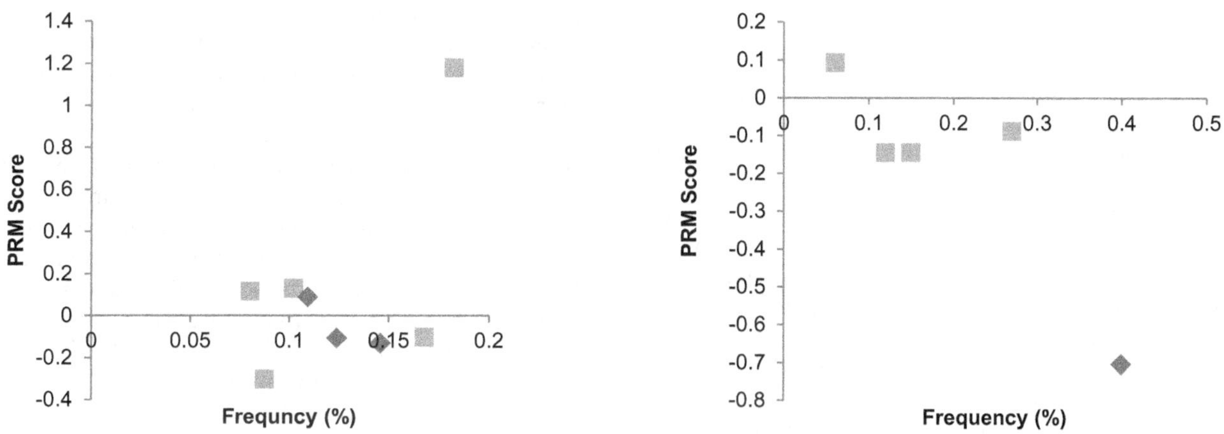

Figure 4. Two examples of the PRM score vs. Frequency charts. The x-axis shows the frequency with which students used each solution. The y-axis shows the PRM-score of each solution on the target PRM for that level. Green squares denote solutions that are >50% successful while red diamonds denote solutions which are ≤50% successful. The example on the left contains a prominent positive cluster while the example of the right contains a prominent negative cluster. Both of these examples show what would be considered good alignment to educational goals where highly principled solutions tend to succeed and highly unprincipled solutions tend not to succeed.

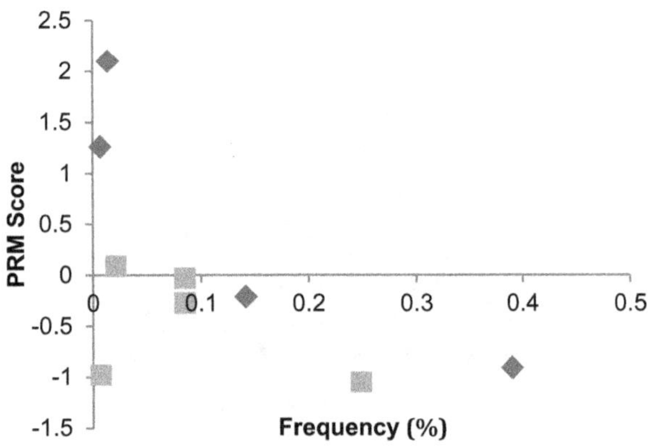

Figure 5. A plot of frequency of solution (as a percentage) vs. PRM score for all of the clusters on the Symmetry_07 level of RumbleBlocks.

Figure 6. Two example student solutions to the Symmetry_07 level. The solution on the left comes from a majority unsuccessful cluster while the solution on the right comes from a majority successful cluster.

PRM scores. This measure suggests places where some additional missing knowledge, in addition to the PRM, is determining success and failure.

Once levels of interest were identified, we plotted their data on charts like the ones show in Figure 4. In these charts each point represents a single representative solution, as determined by the clustering process. The y-coordinate of each point denotes that solution's normalized PRM score, while the coloring and shape of the point denotes the majority success designation of the representative solution. The x-coordinate shows what percentage of users in the testing population used a solution similar to the representative solution. We re-introduce usage frequency at this stage to help prioritize attention when grounding the data with corresponding screenshots. As per the 2x2 matrix in Figure 2, the ideal pattern to be observed is for successful points to appear high on the graph, and unsuccessful points to appear low on the graph.

For the purposes of this paper we will focus on two levels: one with high misalignment and another with low discrimination. For each of these levels, we visually inspected the PRM score vs. frequency plot. The first less desirable level is shown in Figure 5. In this example, there are two highly frequent solutions, the 2 points farther to the right, where one is mostly successful and the other is mostly unsuccessful, however they do not differ strongly in their PRM scores. When we examine screenshots of student solutions to this level we see the situation in Figure 6, where the tower on the left (an inverted T-shape) comes from the majority failure solution while the tower on the right (an arch shape) comes from the majority success solution. While it is clear from the examples that the left tower should fail (as it did frequently), it is important to remember that this level is designed to target the symmetry principle, which says a symmetrical structure should be more stable. Both solutions seen in these representative solutions are generally symmetrical, but one is considered a failure while the other is considered a success. This represents *RumbleBlocks* giving inconsistent feedback to players about the symmetry principle.

Another anomalous example can be seen in Figure 7, which shows a plot of the different solutions to the level CenterOfMass_10_PP. This level is used as part of an in game pre-post design. Because the level was used for pre- and posttest, it omits the energy ball mechanic and is based on a level designed to target the low center of mass principle. It is harder to attribute patterns in the chart to elements of level design because it lacks the energy ball mechanic and thus does not restrict players as much as normal game levels; however, an interesting pattern develops nonetheless. The distribution of how many students created each solution on this level is more evenly spread out, but among groups of solutions that are all relatively equal in PRM score, we see 2 solutions which are majority failure rather than success. Visually inspecting the solutions students created to this level, we see the pattern that arises in Figure 8, where an example from one of the nearby successful solutions is shown on the top and an example from each of the unsuccessful solutions is shown on the bottom. The salient feature to note among the unsuccessful solutions is the presence of the alien's spaceship on top of a single square block. This points to a nuance in the game's mechanics, where an additional constraint on game success is whether or not the spaceship falls off of the tower during the earthquake and not just that the tower continues to stand up. This opens the possibility, illustrated by the lower right quadrant of the matrix in Figure 2, that a student could build a perfectly reasonable tower that is judged as unsuccessful by the game because the spaceship falls off. This is an example of the more nuanced kind of alignment failure where a task requires an extra piece of unexpected knowledge to complete successfully.

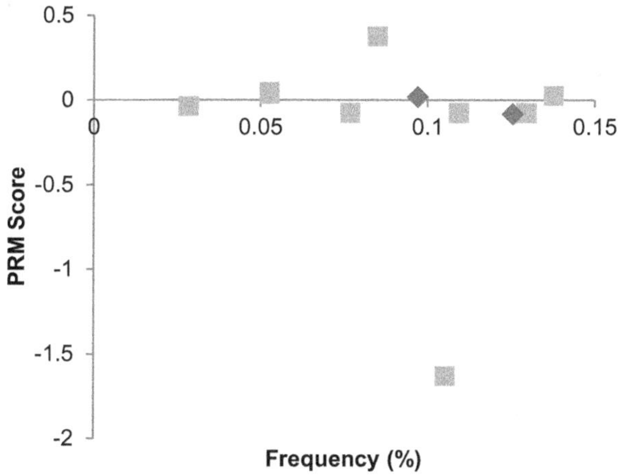

Figure 7. A plot of frequency of solution (as a percentage) vs. PRM score for all of the clusters on the CenterOfMass_10_PP level of RumbleBlocks.

The patterns we observed in our analysis of the Symmetry_7, and CenterOfMass_10_PP data were present in a number of other levels as well. As a pattern of salient features emerged, we wanted to see if there was further support in the structural data to support our conclusions. To do this we used the structural features generated through the conceptual feature extraction process and used a Chi^2 analysis to identify which structural features present in student solutions were more predictive of success. As the feature engineering process generated 6,010 potential features that could be present in a student solution, we had to apply Bonferroni correction to the analysis to control for the number of statistical tests. Fifteen substructures were found to be statistically significantly correlated with success after correction, however eleven of those substructures corresponded to the same grounded structure (referred to as "NT37") ultimately leaving five significant substructures, shown in Figure 9. Four of the structures, shown in the red region to the left of the figure, were negatively correlated with success while the remaining one, shown in the green region on the right, was positively correlated with success. At a high level, the same issue can be seen in Figure 9 as in Figures 6 and 8, where putting the spaceship on top of a single square block seems to lead to failure more commonly than putting it on top of a wider platform. This analysis would suggest that there is a more widespread issue with the mechanics of *RumbleBlocks* that goes beyond mere level design.

DESIGN IMPLICATIONS

As demonstrated by our analytical results, there is a clear misalignment between the feedback provided to students in *RumbleBlocks* and the principles that the game is trying to teach. This misalignment appears both in how discriminating the principles are in terms of success, as in the Symetry_7 example, and in potential troubles contributed by the secondary success criteria of the spaceship having to remain on top of the tower, shown in the CenterOfMass_11 example and the Chi^2 analysis. The results of our analysis can be filtered through the theories of the EDGE educational game design framework to reason about what the designers of *RumbleBlocks* might do to bring their game back into proper alignment.

Figure 8. Examples of student solutions on the CenterOfMass_10_PP level. The solution at the top comes from one of the majority successful clusters while the two at the bottom come from majority unsuccessful clusters.

Providing feedback that students can use to evaluate their conceptual understandings, is an important principle of learning that is advocated by many theoretical frameworks in the learning sciences [7,14,22]. Examining the alignment results, we see that there are cases where adherence to the target principle of a level does not translate into success for players. This would mean that if we want to have players learn the current principles of the game, we are not providing feedback that will actually help them to attend to their errors in thinking about those principles. If we look at the case of Symmetry_7 we see a pattern where successful and

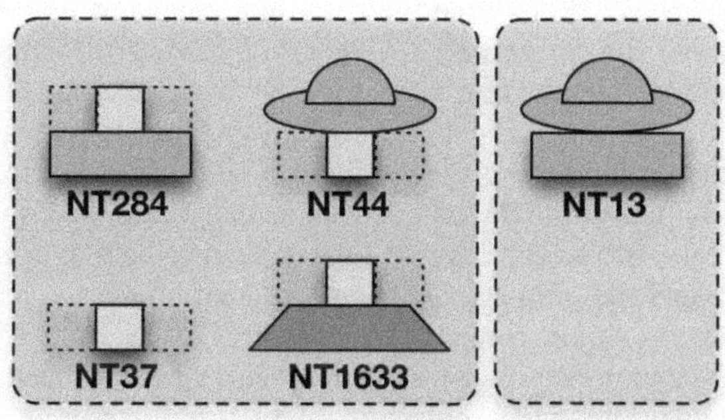

Figure 9. Rendered results of a Chi^2 analysis of structural features in *RumbleBlocks* which predict the success of a tower in the earthquake. Student solutions which contained the features in the red shaded region to the left were more likely to be unsuccessful in the earthquake while solutions which contained the feature in the green region to the right were more likely to be successful.

unsuccessful solutions are essentially the same in terms of PRM score. What is interesting about this particular example is that the unsuccessful solution is equivalent or better in terms of PRM score on both of the other two principles, wide base and low center of mass. This is because the principles used in *RumbleBlocks* are meant to be applied to single connected body structures, while the towers in the game are stacks of disconnected blocks. Using a design that involved connected structures was actually considered in the preliminary design phases of *RumbleBlocks* but initial prototype testing indicated that players found the disconnected structure to be more fun to play with. In terms of EDGE's Mechanics Dynamics and Aesthetics component, the designers also thought that having a disconnected block mechanic would allow for more interesting dynamics in the design. This situation highlights how difficult it can be to find a good balance between engagement and alignment and emphasizes the importance of analytics to help navigate this challenge.

One way that the designers of *RumbleBlocks* might address this issue is to consider new mechanics for the game that can better address the goals of the game. One such solution would be to introduce a mechanic that allows players to glue blocks together so that the blocks act more like the connected structures modeled by the principle-relevant metrics. As previously noted by the designers, this mechanical change would cause a resultant change in the dynamics experienced by the players because fully connected structures would react less to the in-game earthquake. A number of mechanical options could be considered to account for the drop in dynamics, such as adding in negative energy balls or more interesting terrain features such as ravines between the alien and their ship.

Another possibility for changing the mechanics could be to remove the spaceship entirely. This solution would address the alignment problems highlighted in the CenterOfMass_10_PP example as well as the Chi^2 analysis by removing the secondary success criteria of keeping the ship on the tower. Removing the spaceship mechanic could also preserve the interesting dynamics of having disconnected structures, which were valued by the designers, however, it adds other mechanical difficulties such as removing the mechanic for how players submit a solution – placing the ship on top of the tower – as well as damaging the narrative aesthetic of the game by no longer having the player trying to return the ship to the alien. Each of these mechanical changes can be filtered through the EDGE framework's MDA component and weighed against what the designers' wish to emphasize in redesign.

As an alternative to mechanical alterations to the game, the *RumbleBlocks* designers might choose to instead alter the educational goals to fit the experience they already have. While changing the goals of a game's design is generally uncommon, it may constitute a valid way of solving the problem. This solution would necessitate an examination of what kinds of knowledge players are employing as they interact with the game. To facilitate this exploration, we could develop a new set of principle-relevant metrics and see how success in the game aligns to these new metrics as opposed to the old ones. Keeping the EDGE framework's educational objective's component in mind, any alteration to the goals of the game would require that the designers create new external pre-posttests to allow for the measurement of how effective the game is at teaching the new goals.

While the EDGE framework helps to frame the directions the designers might take in iteration, it cannot easily inform which solution would be best. Our approach, along with *RumbleBlocks'* log replay system, could be used to consider the implications of each change. For example, if the designers wanted to explore adding in a glue mechanic between the blocks, the logs could be replayed with the change in place to examine how the various solutions would react differently in the earthquake. Alternatively, if the designers wanted to entertain changing the goals of the game then they could implement a new metric calculation within the replay system and see how this new metric performs as a principle-relevant metric for alignment. Rigorously evaluating which option is most promising would require the designers to run new playtests with players in their target demographic, but our proposed method of utilizing the replay system is a much less expensive way to focus on the most promising design.

DISCUSSION

We have demonstrated our approach to evaluating the alignment of an educational game against its stated educational goals. The technique relies on analytics of student gameplay data from which principle-relevant metrics can be calculated along with the structure of student solutions. Additionally, we have shown how these kinds of analysis can be employed while thinking across the components of the EDGE educational game design framework. It is our intention that this demonstration could serve to inspire the use of similar techniques to be employed in other educational game settings.

We believe that our process of evaluating the alignment of an open-ended educational game can be applied to other game contexts. For example one could imagine an educational game designed to teach the basics of planetary motion where the structural relations of student solutions would describe which bodies are orbiting which, rather than the simple rectangular adjacencies present in *RumbleBlocks*.

We also believe the process could be used for other educational games whose goals lie outside the domain of physics. Consider a hypothetical example of using McCoy's *Prom Week* [23], a social simulation game, to teach the nuances of the concept of social capital [29]. Students could be tasked with navigating a social simulation with the goal of asking their ideal date out to prom, but to do so they must properly curate their social capital in order to be able to ask their friends for assistance. The structural elements of student solutions in this example would be the structure of the social graph that students form as they play. A principle-relevant metric could be a quantification of their avatar's social capital, using any of the methods that exist in the social capital literature. It would be pedagogically important that accruing more social capital in the game actually leads to success in the game; otherwise students might learn to incorrectly conceptualize social capital.

At its core, our approach requires a way of grounding the educational objectives of a game in some kind of measurement. This measure could be a simple metric calculable from a game state, as in our *RumbleBlocks* example, or it could be a more complex composite measure. Secondly, our approach requires a way of capturing the space of solutions players employ on in-game challenges. For some games, such a space is straightforward to calculate but for more open-ended games, such as RumbleBlocks, it is helpful to be able to characterize solutions in terms of structural features. The particular systems we have used in our work are not strictly necessary for the general process, though they have simplified the process greatly.

While we believe our approach is sufficiently general to be applied to many games, it is important to note contexts where it might be less applicable. The notion of a principle-relevant metrics may not be appropriate to contexts where the content of a game is less easily quantified, for example in a serious game designed to change players' attitudes toward international conflicts [2]. Another place where the approach may be less useful is in games where the structural composition of a solution is less relevant to the educational goals of a game than the sequence of task that players perform. In these cases it may be more useful to generate features for student solutions based on the paths students take to arrive at the final solution rather than the solution itself. This would be similar to the work of Andersen *et al.* who use Playtracer to map players' paths through a game space [3].

In future work, we hope to explore additional ways to help educational game designers detect, diagnose, and resolve issues of alignment between their game designs and educational goals. In particular, we might investigate how to use the metrics in our current approach in a way that would not require as much visual inspection. If such an approach were developed, it could greatly reduce the load on designers looking to evaluate their games.

CONCLUSION

In this paper, we have demonstrated an approach to exploring how well an educational game's mechanics align to its stated target knowledge. Not only have we been able to measure whether or not an alignment issue exists, but we have also demonstrated how to employ an educational game design framework in thinking through how any alignment issues might be mitigated. It is our belief that the techniques we have shown here are generalizable to other contexts and would be a helpful aid in honing the design of other educational games. We hope others are able to find the techniques useful in their own situations.

ACKNOWLEDGMENTS

This work was supported in part by a Graduate Training Grant awarded to Carnegie Mellon University by the Department of Education #R305B090023 and by the DARPA ENGAGE research program under ONR Contract Number N00014-12-C-0284. All opinions express in this article are those of the authors and do not necessarily reflect the position of the sponsoring agency.

REFERENCES

1. Aleven, V., Myers, E., Easterday, M., and Ogan, A. Toward a Framework for the Analysis and Design of Educational Games. *Proc. DiGITEL 2010*, IEEE (2010), 69–76.
2. Alhabash, S. and Wise, K. PeaceMaker: Changing Students' Attitudes Toward Palestinians and Israelis Through Video Game Play. *International Journal of Communication 6*, (2012), 356–380.
3. Andersen, E., Liu, Y., Apter, E., Boucher-genesse, F., and Popovi, Z. Gameplay Analysis through State Projection. *Proc. FDG 2010*, ACM Press (2010).
4. Andersen, E., Liu, Y., Snider, R., Szeto, R., Cooper, S., and Popovi, Z. On the Harmfulness of Secondary Game Objectives. *Proc. FDG 2011*, ACM Press (2011).
5. Christel, M.G., Stevens, S.M., Maher, B.S., et al. RumbleBlocks: Teaching Science Concepts to Young Children through a Unity Game. *Proc. CGames 2012*, IEEE (2012), 162–166.
6. Clark, D.B., Tanner-Smith, E.E., and Killingsworth, S. *Digital Games for Learning: A Systematic Review and Meta-Analysis (Executive Summary)*. Menlo Park, CA, 2013.
7. Gee, J.P. *What video games have to teach us about learning and literacy*. Palgrave Macmillan, New York, 2003.
8. Harpstead, E., Maclellan, C.J., Koedinger, K.R., Aleven, V., Dow, S.P., and Myers, B.A. Investigating the Solution Space of an Open-Ended Educational Game Using Conceptual Feature Extraction. *Proc. EDM 2013*, (2013).
9. Harpstead, E., Myers, B.A., and Aleven, V. In Search of Learning: Facilitating Data Analysis in Educational Games. *Proc. CHI 2013*, ACM Press (2013), 79.
10. Hunicke, R., Leblanc, M., and Zubek, R. MDA: A Formal Approach to Game Design and Game Research.

Proc. of the AAAI Workshop on Challenges in Game AI, (2004), 1–5.

11. Isbister, K., Flanagan, M., and Hash, C. Designing Games for Learning : Insights from Conversations with Designers. *Proc. CHI 2010*, ACM Press (2010), 2041–2044.

12. Johnson, M.W., Eagle, M., and Barnes, T. InVis : An Interactive Visualization Tool for Exploring Interaction Networks. *Proc. EDM 2013*, (2013), 65.

13. Khaled, R. and Ingram, G. Tales from the Front Lines of a Large-Scale Serious Game Project. *Proc. CHI 2012*, ACM Press (2012), 69–78.

14. Koedinger, K.R., Corbett, A.T., and Perfetti, C. The Knowledge-Learning-Instruction Framework: Bridging the Science-Practice Chasm to Enhance Robust Student Learning. *Cognitive Science 36*, 5 (2012), 757–98.

15. Koedinger, K.R. and Nathan, M.J. The Real Story Behind Story Problems: Effects of Representations on Quantitative Reasoning. *The Journal of the Learning Sciences 13*, 2 (2004), 129–164.

16. Kohavi, R., Deng, A., Frasca, B., Longbotham, R., Walker, T., and Xu, Y. Trustworthy Online Controlled Experiments: Five Puzzling Outcomes Explained. *Proc. KDD 2012*, ACM Press (2012), 786–794.

17. Kohavi, R., Henne, R.M., and Sommerfield, D. Practical Guide to Controlled Experiments on the Web : Listen to Your Customers not to the HiPPO. *Proc. KDD 2007*, ACM Press (2007), 1–9.

18. Leighton, J.P. and Gokiert, R.J. The Cognitive Effects of Test Item Features: Informing Item Generation by Identifying Construct Irrelevant Variance. *Proc. NCME 2005*, (2005), 1–26.

19. Linehan, C., Kirman, B., Lawson, S., and Chan, G.G. Practical, Appropriate, Empirically-Validated Guidelines for Designing Educational Games. *Proc. CHI 2011*, ACM Press (2011), 1979–1988.

20. Lomas, D., Forlizzi, J.L., Koedinger, K.R., and Patel, K. Optimizing Challenge in an Educational Game Using Large-Scale Design Experiments. *Proc. CHI 2013*, (2013), 89–98.

21. Maciuszek, D. and Martens, A. Patterns for the design of educational games. In F. Edvarsen and H. Kulle, eds., *Educational Games Design Learning and Applications*. Nova publishers, 2010, 263–279.

22. Mayer, R.E. and Moreno, R. Nine Ways to Reduce Cognitive Load in Multimedia Learning. *Educational Psychologist 38*, 1 (2003), 43–52.

23. Mccoy, J., Treanor, M., Samuel, B., Reed, A.A., Wardrip-fruin, N., and Mateas, M. Prom Week. *Proc. FDG 2012*, ACM Press (2012), 235–237.

24. Miller, C.S., Lehman, J.F., and Koedinger, K.R. Goals and learning in microworlds. *Cognitive Science 23*, 3 (1999), 305–336.

25. Nacke, L.E., Drachen, A., and Göbel, S. Methods for Evaluating Gameplay Experience in a Serious Gaming Context. *Journal of Computer Science in Sport 9*, 2 (2010), 1–12.

26. Nathan, M.J. Knowledge and Situational Feedback in a Learning Environment for Algebra Story Problems. *Interactive Learning Environments 5*, 1 (1998), 134–159.

27. Nielsen, J. and Molich, R. Heuristic Evaluation of User Interfaces. *Proc. CHI 1990*, ACM Press (1990), 249–256.

28. Pashler, H., Bain, P.M., Bottge, B.A., et al. *Organizing Instruction and Study to Improve Student Learning (NCER 2007-2004)*. Washington, D.C., 2007.

29. Putnam, R.D. Bowling Alone: America's Declining Social Capital. *Journal of Democracy 6*, 1 (1995), 65–78.

30. Rau, M.A., Aleven, V., and Rohrbach, S. Why Interactive Learning Environments Can Have It All : Resolving Design Conflicts Between Competing Goals. *Proc. CHI 2013*, ACM Press (2013), 109–118.

31. Seif El-Nasr, M., Drachen, A., and Canossa, A., eds. *Game Analytics*. Springer London, London, 2013.

32. Wiggins, G. and McTighe, J. *Understanding by Design*. Pearson, 2005.

Brain Points: A Growth Mindset Incentive Structure Boosts Persistence in an Educational Game

Eleanor O'Rourke[1], **Kyla Haimovitz**[2], **Christy Ballweber**[1], **Carol S. Dweck**[2], **and Zoran Popović**[1]
[1]Center for Game Science, Department of Computer Science & Engineering, University of Washington
[2]Department of Psychology, Stanford University
{eorourke, christy, zoran}@cs.washington.edu, {kylah, dweck}@stanford.edu

ABSTRACT

There is great interest in leveraging video games to improve student engagement and motivation. However, educational games are not uniformly effective, and little is known about how in-game rewards affect children's learning-related behavior. In this work, we argue that educational games can be improved by fundamentally changing their incentive structures to promote the growth mindset, or the belief that intelligence is malleable. We present "brain points," a system that encourages the development of growth mindset behaviors by directly incentivizing effort, use of strategy, and incremental progress. Through a study of 15,000 children, we show that the "brain points" system encourages more low-performing students to persist in the educational game *Refraction* when compared to a control, and increases overall time played, strategy use, and perseverance after challenge. We believe that this growth mindset incentive structure has great potential in many educational environments.

Author Keywords

Educational games; growth mindset; incentive structures.

ACM Classification Keywords

H.5.0 Information Interfaces and Presentation: General

INTRODUCTION

Video games are famous for their ability to engage players and motivate them to perform complex, time-consuming tasks. Most children today are exposed to games on a daily basis; 92% of children ages 2 to 17 play video games, for an average of 20 to 33 minutes per day [16]. As a result, there is a growing interest in leveraging games to address the problem of student motivation in educational environments [11, 25, 23]. Game incentive structures, or the systems of rewards that are given to successful players, have elicited particular attention for their potential to motivate students [18]. However, games have produced mixed learning outcomes in the classroom [14, 21, 23], and the effects of in-game praise and rewards on motivation and learning are not well understood.

CHI 2014, April 26 –May 01 2014, Toronto, ON, Canada

http://dx.doi.org/10.1145/2556288.2557157

A growing body of research in psychology suggests that feedback such as praise can have varying, and sometimes negative, effects [24, 13]. Praising a student's inherent ability has been shown to promote the fixed mindset, or the belief that intelligence is unchangeable, while praising a student's strategies or effort promotes the growth mindset, or the belief that intelligence is malleable [24, 13]. Studies have shown that children with a fixed mindset view mistakes, challenge, and effort as negative indicators of their intelligence, while children with growth mindset view effort as positive and challenges as opportunities to learn [9, 15]. More importantly, holding a fixed mindset predicts static or decreasing academic performance over time, while holding a growth mindset predicts academic improvement [3, 12].

Many laboratory and classroom studies have shown that children's mindsets can be changed through careful intervention [3, 24, 17]. Directly teaching students that intelligence is malleable was shown to improve classroom motivation and grades compared to a control group [3]. Even minimal interventions, such as praising children for their strategy or effort (e.g., "you must have worked really hard!") instead of their ability (e.g., "you must be smart at this!") as they solve problems produces a growth mindset, as well as higher motivation and task persistence [24, 17]. This research suggests that the praise and rewards given to students in educational games could impact their behavior, and even have negative consequences if rewards inadvertently support the fixed mindset.

In this work, we show that making a fundamental change to a game's incentive structure can positively impact children's behavior. We present "brain points," a system that rewards students for their effort, use of strategy, and incremental progress. Unlike previous mindset interventions, this incentive structure provides children with real-time feedback as they work to develop growth mindset behaviors. Through a study of 15,000 children, we show that persistence and use of strategy is encouraged in the educational game *Refraction* through the introduction of this unorthodox incentive structure. We believe this method of promoting the growth mindset has great potential in many educational environments.

BACKGROUND

Psychologists have been studying motivation and academic achievement for decades, and many of their discoveries have important implications for the designers of educational technologies. Messages and rewards that support the growth mindset could be used to significantly improve the impact of such systems. In this section, we provide background on mindset research and discuss previous efforts to integrate growth mindset interventions into classrooms and educational tools. We also describe existing work on educational games, and suggest ways that the growth mindset could be used to improve their effectiveness.

Theories of Intelligence

Psychologist have shown that beliefs about the malleability of human attributes such as intelligence can have strong effects on motivation, reaction to challenge or failure, and academic achievement [3, 12, 15]. Individuals who hold a *fixed mindset* believe that they have a certain amount of intelligence, and that this is an unchangeable attribute. Studies have shown that people with a fixed mindset view challenging situations as "tests" of how much intelligence they have, and view effort and mistakes as indications of low ability [3, 15, 24]. On the other hand, individuals who hold a *growth mindset* believe that intelligence is malleable, and that people can increase their intelligence through hard work. They have been shown to value learning over performance, and view effort as a necessary part of the learning process [3, 15, 24]. These beliefs affect not only behavior but also academic achievement. In a longitudinal study of 373 seventh graders, Blackwell et al. showed that holding a growth mindset predicted improving grades over the two years of middle school, while holding a fixed mindset predicted static or decreasing grades [3].

A growing body of research shows that students' mindsets, and subsequently their behaviors and academic performance, can be changed through intervention [24, 3, 1, 12, 17]. One type of intervention involves changing the type of praise given to children when they are successful. In a now-famous 1998 study, Muller and Dweck showed that praise can have negative consequences when it supports the fixed mindset [24]. They gave fifth grade students a set of achievable problems and praised them for either their ability ("you must be smart at these problems") or their effort ("you must have worked hard at these problems"). Then they gave students very challenging problems on which they did poorly. Finally, they gave students another set of the original achievable problems. Students who received praise for their ability attributed their failure to lack of ability, and performed worse on the subsequent problem set, but students who received praise for their effort viewed the difficulty as a cue to try harder, and performed better on the subsequent problem set [24]. More recently, Gunderson et al. have confirmed the role of praise in mindsets, showing that the type of praise parents give to their young children at home predicts the child's mindset and desire for challenge five years later [13].

Another type of intervention involves teaching the growth mindset directly. Blackwell et al. taught a group of seventh grade students that intelligence is malleable during an eight-session workshop through readings and discussions about the neural connections that are formed in the brain when it works hard [3]. Before the intervention, students' math grades had been steadily decreasing (and this decline persisted for children in the control group), but after the intervention students grades improved significantly [3]. Aronson et al. also report the positive impact of a growth mindset intervention on the academic achievement of both African American and white college students [1]. The GPAs of both the African American and white students in the experimental condition were higher at the end of the academic quarter than those in the control condition [1].

The effects of these interventions on student motivation and academic achievement are impressive, and it would clearly be beneficial to integrate similar programs into educational technologies. Recently, efforts have been made to develop online materials that teach the growth mindset. Brainology, a for-purchase online program based on the Blackwell intervention, teaches students the scientific basis of the growth mindset through readings and interactive exercises [4]. In ongoing work, Paunesku and colleagues are studying the impact of integrating a praise-based intervention into the online educational website Khan Academy [19] with initial success [29]. However, we are not aware of any work that integrates the growth mindset into the incentive structures of educational games.

Games as an Educational Platform

Video games are increasingly recognized as a compelling platform for instruction that could significantly improve student motivation in the classroom [11, 25, 23]. While empirical evidence supporting learning outcomes of educational games is mixed [14, 21, 23], there have been clear successes that highlight the potential of games as instructional tools. In a comparative review of STEM game studies, Mayo found that some games produce a 7 to 40% positive increase in learning outcomes [23]. Games have been shown to increase time-on-task, an important indicator for academic success [21, 20], and also increase student motivation [27]. Researchers have noted that successful educational games are those designed around effective pedagogical practices, perhaps explaining some of the mixed learning outcomes [23, 25]. These results indicate the importance of grounding educational games in valid pedagogical theory.

Many researchers have explored how to most effectively integrate learning theories into games, and leverage game features to maximize student motivation, persistence, and learning [21, 7]. For example, Chase studied how the framing of tasks in a genetics game affects student persistence and learning. She found that students who are told their performance is dependent on both chance and skill persist more after failure than those who are told their performance is dependent on skill alone [7]. However, the effects of game features on student motivation are still not well understood.

To our knowledge, no existing research has explored how to improve in-game motivation and persistence through growth mindset incentives and feedback. We believe that educational games provide a set of properties that make them particularly conducive to introducing and incentivizing growth mindset concepts. Game narratives provide a forum for directly teaching about brain growth, weaving messages that support the growth mindset throughout the game world. Constant interactive feedback provides a medium for showing students that their effort translates into progress [10, 23]. But most importantly, game incentive structures provide a way to support and reward behaviors consistent with the growth mindset, such as persistence and use of strategy.

Experimental Hypotheses

The goal of this research was to study the impact of incentivizing productive effort and teaching the growth mindset in an educational game. To explore this question, we developed two versions of *Refraction*, a game designed to teach fraction concepts to elementary school students. The experimental version teaches and rewards growth mindset behavior by leveraging the game's narrative and incentive structure, while the control version provides a neutral view of intelligence. We expected children who played the experimental version to exhibit behaviors consistent with the growth mindset.

Hypothesis 1: *Players in the experimental condition will be more persistent and more strategic than players in the control.*

While we expected all players to be affected by the growth mindset intervention, we thought that players who struggle with *Refraction* would be most strongly influenced by our incentive structure that rewards effort. We expected them to be more strongly motivated to persist in the game.

Hypothesis 2: *Struggling players will be most strongly motivated by the experimental intervention.*

In addition to observing general behavior, we wanted to explicitly study how children in the two conditions reacted to challenge and failure. Following a similar model to that used in the 1998 Muller and Dweck study of the effects of praise on children [24], we designed an unusually challenging level to test children's persistence and performance. We expected children who played the experimental version of *Refraction* to react well to challenge, struggle, and failure.

Hypothesis 3: *Players in the experimental condition will react better to challenge than players in the control.*

To evaluate these hypotheses, we released both versions of *Refraction* to BrainPOP, a popular educational website for elementary school students that provides a game portal [5]. We analyzed data from over 15,000 players to determine the effects of incentivizing effort and teaching the growth mindset.

EXPERIMENT DESIGN

To explore the effects of teaching and supporting the growth mindset in educational games, we created two versions of *Refraction*, a game designed by our research group. One version teaches the growth mindset directly through the game's narrative, feedback, and incentive structures, while the other provides a neutral mindset and the incentive structure commonly found in educational games. In this section, we describe the two versions of *Refraction* in detail and discuss the rationale behind our designs.

Refraction

This educational puzzle game was designed by game researchers and learning science experts at the Center for Game Science to teach fraction concepts to elementary school students. The game was designed to support a conceptual understanding of fractions rooted in the concept of splitting [22]. To play, a child must interact with a grid that contains laser sources, target spaceships, and asteroids, as shown in Figure 1. The goal of the game is to satisfy target spaceships by splitting the laser into the correct fractional amounts and avoiding asteroids. The player uses pieces that either change the laser direction or split the laser into two or three equal parts to achieve this goal. To win, the player must correctly satisfy all the target spaceships at the same time. *Refraction* has been successful at attracting elementary school students, and has been played over 250,000 times on the educational website BrainPOP since its release in April 2012.

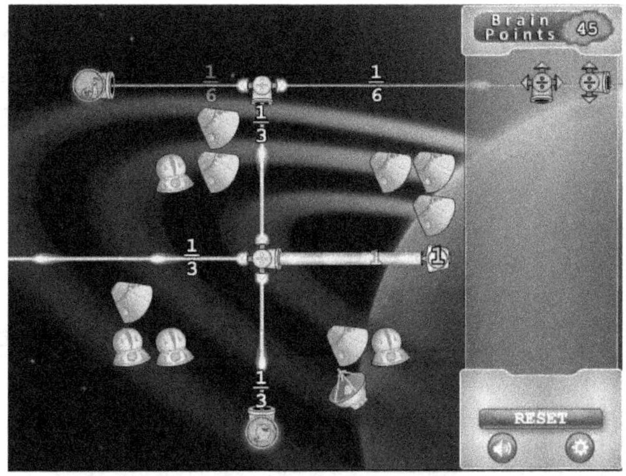

Figure 1. A level of Refraction. The pieces on the right are used to split lasers into fractional amounts and redirect them to satisfy the target spaceships. All ships must be satisfied at the same time to win.

Game Narrative

Both the experimental and control versions of *Refraction* are based on a central narrative. At the beginning of the game, players watch a 25 second introductory animation featuring Zuzu and Copper, characters who describe the game and its incentive structures. In the experimental version, we leverage this animation to teach players about the growth mindset directly, using language based on that used in the Brainology curriculum [4] and the Blackwell intervention [3]. In the control version, we present a neutral message about the importance of fractions. The text and art used in the animations are nearly identical, differing only in the messages they present to players. Screenshots are shown in Figure 2 and the full animation scripts are included in Table 1. We do not use audio in the animations because we cannot guarantee that players will have access to speakers or headphones. To accommodate different reading speeds, we added "Next" buttons that allow players to manually advance to the next part of the animation when they have finished reading.

Incentive Structures

Both versions of *Refraction* have point-based incentive structures designed to reward different types of behavior. For the experimental version, we designed a system of "brain points"

(a) (b) (c)

Figure 2. Figure (a) shows a screenshot of the introductory animation that teaches the growth mindset in the experimental version of Refraction. Figure (b) shows a corresponding screenshot in the control, which presents a neutral mindset about the importance of fractions. The animations use identical art and text wherever possible. Figure (c) shows the brain points interface in the experimental version. In this version players earn points for effort, use of strategy, and incremental progress as they work to solve levels, while in the control version players earn points each time they complete a level.

Experimental
Z: Hey Copper, guess what!
Z: Did you know that when you work hard and struggle, your brain gets stronger and SMARTER?
C: Whoa cool!
Z: In this game, when you work out your brain and try new ideas, you'll get BRAIN POINTS!
C: I want to get lots of brain points! Let's play, Zuzu!
Control
Z: Hey Copper, guess what!
Z: Did you know that you use fractions in all kinds of MATH?
C: Whoa cool!
Z: In this game, when you make the fractions on the spaceships you'll get FRACTION POINTS!
C: I want to get lots of fraction points! Let's play, Zuzu!

Table 1. The scripts for the introductory animations. The experimental animation teaches the growth mindset, while the control animation presents a neutral message about the importance of fractions. *Z* indicates Zuzu's line, and *C* indicates Copper's line.

that rewards children for their effort, use of strategy, and incremental progress. These types of behaviors support "learning" goals rather than "performance" goals, and rewarding similar behaviors with praise has been shown to promote the growth mindset [24, 13]. However, no existing growth mindset interventions have used point-based reward systems, so this is an entirely new method of teaching the growth mindset that is particularly well suited to the game context.

Children earn brain points while they are working to solve levels. We use a combination of four metrics that capture desirable strategic behaviors to determine when players should receive points. The *new hypothesis* metric captures each new idea the child tries. It triggers when the child makes two successive new moves with distinct pieces. The *board cleared* metric emphasizes stepping back to consider the puzzle from a fresh perspective. It triggers when there are at least two pieces on the laser, and the child returns all the pieces to the starting bin. The *math* metric captures incremental mathematical progress. It triggers when the child makes a target fraction for the first time. Finally, the *moves* metric captures effort. It triggers when the child makes ten distinct moves.

To earn brain points, the child must trigger two of these metrics. For example, a child might try a new hypothesis and then clear the board, earning five points. We require two metrics to be triggered because this makes the system more difficult to game, since the child cannot repeat his last sequence of moves to earn another point. Gaming the system is a problem in many educational domains [2], so we wanted to ensure that our point system rewarded desirable behaviors without being overly transparent. All metric data, such as the number of moves made so far, are cleared when the child earns a point so that subsequent points are earned from scratch.

Brain points are given to players in increments of five to make them more exciting. Each time the child triggers two metrics, she earns five points. When this happens, a small animated brain icon with a short message appears, as shown in Figure 2(c). The icon moves to the upper righthand corner of the screen, adding five to the total number of points shown in the brain points bar. The short message reflects the last metric the child triggered. The messages associated with the four metrics are "New Idea" for the *new hypothesis* metric, "Fresh Start" for the *board cleared* metric, "Math Effort" for the *math* metric, and "Working Hard" for the *moves* metric.

For the control version of *Refraction*, we designed a system of "fraction points" that reward children for completing levels. We chose to incentivize advancement through the level progression because this is a commonly used metric of success in video games, as Schell notes in his popular game design book [28]. Players earn five fraction points every time they win a level, displayed on the summary screen described in the next section. The total number of fraction points earned so far are shown in the upper righthand corner of the screen.

Summary Screens

Each time a child completes a level of *Refraction*, a summary screen is displayed. This screen is designed to reinforce the game narrative and provide an opportunity for children to reflect on their success or progress. Identical art is used in the experimental and control versions, but different messages are given to support either the growth mindset or a neutral mindset. The summary screen has three components: a progress indicator, a points message, and a praise message. Screenshots of summary screens are shown in Figure 3.

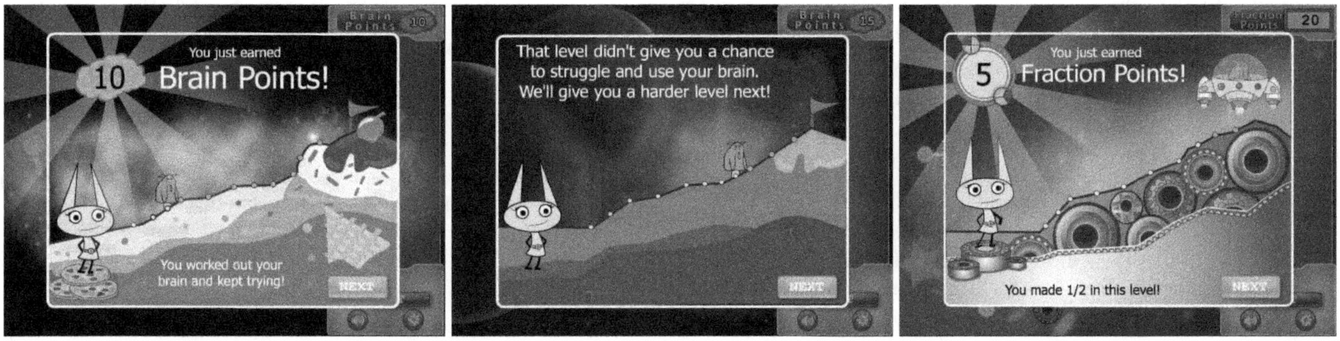

(a) (b) (c)

Figure 3. Screenshots of the summary screens. Figure (a) shows the summary screen that is displayed when the child earns brain points in the experimental condition, and Figure (b) shows the screen that is displayed when the player does not earn brain points. Figure (c) shows the control condition summary screen that is displayed every time the player wins a level. In all cases, the mountain represents progress through the current *Refraction* planet. Copper physically climbs the mountain in the experimental summary screens to symbolize the player's effort. In the control summary screen, Copper waits in his spaceship at the top of the mountain. The player advances to a new planet each time she earns 50 points.

Metric	Growth Mindset Praise Messages
New Hypothesis	You worked hard and tried new ideas!
Board Cleared	You worked hard and got a fresh start!
Math	You worked hard and used your math brain!
Moves	You worked out your brain and kept trying!

Table 2. The four growth mindset praise messages displayed at the bottom of the summary screen in the experimental version of *Refraction*. The praise message shown on a given screen is selected based on the brain points message the child saw most frequently during the level.

The *Refraction* world has seven different planets, each with unique level art. In both conditions, children advance to a new planet each time they collect 50 points, an exciting reward that highlights their progress through the game. Since this advancement is based on points, children in the experimental condition move forward based on their effort and strategy use, while children in the control condition move forward based on their performance. Each summary screen shows a mountain with ten dots that indicate the player's progress through the planet. The player moves up one dot for every five points earned, and completed dots are shown in yellow. When the player reaches the top of the mountain, a reward animation shows the orange character Copper flying to the next planet.

In the experimental version, an animation shows Copper climbing the mountain every time the child earns brain points, as in Figure 3(a). This physical climbing metaphor was designed to symbolize the hard work required to earn brain points and support the growth mindset. In the control version, Copper waits at the top of the mountain in his spaceship while newly acquired dots are highlighted in yellow, as in Figure 3(c). This presents a more neutral message, showing progress without symbolizing effort.

At the top of the summary screen, a message tells the player how many points were earned. Since players in the experimental condition earn points based on their behavior, this number changes dynamically. If a player does not earn any brain points on a given level, a message apologizing for not giving the player an opportunity to struggle is displayed, as shown in Figure 3(b). This message is based on Dweck's suggested growth mindset response to situations that do not challenge children or provide them with an opportunity to learn [9]. Players in the control condition always earn exactly five fraction points for each level completed.

At the bottom of the summary screen, a message praising the child's work in this level is shown. In the experimental condition, one of four messages is chosen, depending on which of the four brain point messages the player saw most frequently during the level. The possible messages, which are based on messages used in Muller and Dweck's praise-based intervention [24], are shown in Table 2. In the control condition, a message summarizing the fractions the child made in this level is shown. If the child won a level with spaceships that required 1/6 and 1/9 laser power respectively, the message would read "You made 1/6 and 1/9 on that level!"

Adaptive Level Progression

In order to effectively incentivize effort in the experimental version of *Refraction*, it was important to design a level progression that would provide every player with an opportunity to struggle, irrespective of their incoming skill level. To address this requirement, we created an adaptive level progression that was used in both versions of the game. Our design is based on the mastery learning model used in many knowledge tracing systems, in which students must display mastery of a concept before advancing to the subsequent concept [8]. The adaptive progression covers eleven mathematical concepts typically included in *Refraction*, which are listed in Table 3. We designed ten levels for each concept: one tutorial level that introduces the concept without providing additional pieces, and nine puzzles in which the player must correctly choose between splitter pieces to create the correctly valued fractions.

All children play the eleven concepts in the order listed in Table 3, but they move through the concepts at different speeds depending on their skill level. Every child plays the tutorial level for a given concept, and is then given levels from that concept until she either wins two levels under a performance threshold, or completes all nine levels for the concept. To win a level below the performance threshold, the player must complete the level in less than 1.5 times the minimum number of moves required to beat the level without making any mathematical mistakes. Mistakes are defined as moves that split the laser to make fractional values that are not needed to solve the level. For example, if a child is working on a level with a 1/9 target spaceship, she should never split the laser to make 1/2 or 1/4.

Every child will play between three and ten levels for each concept. The levels are given to all players in the same order, so every child plays the same first three levels for a concept, and some will continue on to play more levels. This means that many more children play the first three levels than play the ninth and tenth level.

Skipping Levels

For the growth mindset version of *Refraction*, we wanted players to think about their progress in terms of effort and strategy, symbolized by brain points, rather than in terms of the number of levels they have completed. As a result, we designed the summary screens and adaptive level progression in a way that minimizes the visibility of speed by making it difficult for children to compare the number of levels they have completed. One downside of this design is that it provides no way for players to back out of levels when they get stuck.

To address this issue and deter frustrated players from quitting the game, we added a "New Level" button that appears in each level after three minutes of play. Children are required to work on each level for at least three minutes, but then they are given an opportunity to move forward when they are stuck. To ensure that children notice the button, a tutorial message is displayed the first time it appears.

When a child clicks the "New Level" button, a summary screen is displayed. In the experimental version, if the child earns brain points before clicking the button, the standard summary screen shown in Figure 3(a) is displayed. If the child does not earn any brain points, the message "Work harder and use your brain on the next level to earn points!" is displayed in a screen similar to Figure 3(b). In the control version, children only earn points when they win levels, so the same summary screen with the message "Try again on a new level! To move up the mountain, save the spaceships!" is always shown. In all cases, the summary screen has a "Back" button that returns to the level and a "Next" button that advances to the next level in the current concept.

Challenge Levels

In addition to observing children's behavior as they interact with the standard game levels, we wanted to measure how they react to a particularly challenging level. In their 1998 study of praise, Muller and Dweck saw that failing to solve a very difficult problem affected children differently based on whether they received fixed or growth mindset praise [24]. We designed a similar test for *Refraction* players by giving them a "challenge level" 30 minutes after they started the game. This level had two 1/2 spaceships, and presented a tricky and unintuitive spatial problem. We used simple fractions because we could not guarantee that all players would have reached more complex concepts.

Order	Concept	Order	Concept
1	Halves	6	Halves and Fourths
2	Thirds	7	Thirds and Ninths
3	Fourths	8	Halves and Sixths
4	Ninths	9	Thirds and Sixths
5	Sixths	10	Fourths and Sixths
		11	Sixths and Ninths

Table 3. The fraction concepts covered in *Refracion*'s adaptive level progression. All children play the concepts in this order, but they advance through concepts at different speeds based on their performance.

Experimental	
Timing	*Message*
Tutorial	You won't earn points on this level, but it will let you challenge your brain and make it grow stronger!
Skip	You didn't master that challenge yet, but you can keep growing your brain by earning points on the next level!
Win	You beat the challenge! You really worked out your brain on that level.
Control	
Timing	*Message*
Tutorial	You won't earn points on this level, but it will let you show off your fraction skills!
Skip	You didn't beat that challenge, but you can use your fraction skills to earn points on the next level instead!
Win	You beat the challenge! You really used your fraction skills on that level.

Table 4. The three challenge level messages for each condition. The first message is shown during the challenge level tutorial, the second is shown when the level is skipped, and the third is shown when the level is won.

The challenge was framed as a special level separate from the standard game. We used an exciting animation to introduce the level, and designed a new background to accompany it. We wanted to measure whether any effects caused by the growth mindset intervention would transfer to levels where effort is not explicitly rewarded, so we did not give children points during the challenge level. We added a bright orange "New Level" button to the sidebar so that players could skip at any point. We also added a tutorial message highlighting the presence of the "New Level" button to make sure players knew it was available. The challenge level was identical in the two conditions except for the text displayed to children. There are three challenge-related messages: one shown at the beginning of the level, one shown when the child wins the level, and one shown when the child skips the level. These messages can be seen in Table 4.

METHOD

To gain an understanding of the effects of incentivizing productive effort and teaching the growth mindset in educational games, we studied how children play the experimental and control versions of *Refraction* on the popular educational website BrainPOP [5]. BrainPOP is best known for its curriculum resources, but it also provides an educational game portal designed for use in the classroom. The BrainPOP Educators community has over 210,000 members [6], and the website is used as a resource in around 20% of elementary schools in the United States (Traci Kampel, personal communication).

One benefit of using the BrainPOP game portal to study the impact of our growth mindset intervention is that it provides us with access to a large, diverse population of students, and allows us to quickly learn whether our intervention has promise in the classroom. However, one downside of this resource is that we know very little about the children who visit BrainPOP or the contexts in which they play. We cannot collect any demographic information, and while we know that the website is primarily used in schools, we cannot tell whether children are playing in the classroom, in a computer lab, or at an after-school program. We mitigate the effects of these uncontrolled variables by evenly distributing them between conditions through the use of randomization and large sample sizes. We are also unable to directly measuring learning through formal pre and post tests in this environment. Instead, we analyze how our intervention impacts observable in-game behaviors such as persistence, use of strategy, and reaction to challenge. These are key components of learning that capture how students react to our growth mindset system.

Our study has a single between-subjects factor *intervention* with two levels: experiment or control. To collect our data, we set up *Refraction* to randomly assign new players to either the experimental or control version of the game, and logged all interactions players made with the game or its interface. We only included new players who were not familiar with *Refraction* in our analysis, and only used data from a player's first session to control for issues with shared computers in schools. To track players, we stored their progress in the Flash cache, which allowed us to selectively include new players and exclude return sessions. One drawback of this method is that a player who clears the cache or changes computers will be treated as a new player by our system. While we cannot assess the seriousness of this risk, its effects will be evenly distributed across conditions. Furthermore, it is unlikely that children will clear the cache because this option is inconvenient to access and it deletes all saved game progress.

Another challenge of studying student behavior online is that average play times are typically small. Previous research conducted on BrainPOP shows that children play *Refraction* for about three minutes on average [26]. We expected our brain points system to influence student behavior even during this short period of play because previous studies have shown that very minimal interventions, such as praising children for their effort or strategies, can improve motivation and persistence [24, 17]. However, we filtered our data to ensure that all students included in our analysis had an opportunity to be influenced by our growth mindset intervention. The first growth mindset message presented to students is the introductory animation, so for both conditions we only included those who watched the entire introductory animation and made at least one move in the game. We also conducted our analysis with a stricter filtering criterion that only included students who completed the first four levels of the game. After four levels, 99% of players in the experimental condition have received brain points and seen the summary screen. Both analyses showed the same patterns of significance and led to the same conclusions, so we chose to present results for the looser filtering method that included more students in the analysis.

After filtering, our data set contained 15,491 players, with 7,807 players in the experimental condition and 7,684 in the control condition. These data were collected between September 3 and September 13, 2013. *Refraction* was featured on the front page of BrainPOP's game portal between September 3 and September 5, allowing us to attract large numbers of students. Since the data sets for the two conditions had different numbers of players, we randomly selected 7,500 players from each condition to include in our analysis.

DATA ANALYSIS AND RESULTS

We study the effects of our growth mindset intervention on children's behavior by analyzing a number of outcome measures, each of which is described in detail below. Before performing this analysis, we evaluated the Kolmogorov-Smirnov test to assess the normality of our data, and found that it was statistically significant for all of our outcome measures. We therefore use non-parametric statistical methods: a Wilcoxon rank sums test and an r measure of effect size for continuous variables, and a Chi-square statistic and a Cramer's V measure of effect size for nominal variables. We report effect sizes in addition to p-values to show the magnitude of the differences between our populations, since we are likely to find many significant differences due to our large sample sizes. For both tests, effect sizes with values less than 0.1 are considered *very small*, 0.1 are *small*, 0.3 are *moderate*, and 0.5 or greater are *large*.

The Growth Mindset Intervention Increases Persistence

We expected children who played the experimental version of *Refraction* to be more persistent than those who played the control version. To evaluate this hypothesis, we analyzed two outcome measures: the amount of time children spent playing the game, and the number of unique levels they played. Since BrainPOP offers many other games that teach fraction concepts, we expected children to quit *Refraction* when they became bored or frustrated. As a result, these measures capture how long children are willing to persist before choosing to leave the game.

We calculate active time by counting the number of seconds each child played *Refraction*, excluding menu navigation and idle periods with more than thirty seconds between actions. Our analysis showed that *intervention* has a significant effect on active time played, with children in the experimental condition playing a median of 118 seconds, compared to 89 for the control condition (Z=-8.61, p<0.0001, r=0.07). A graph of the active time for both conditions is shown in Figure 4.

We calculate the number of unique levels each child played by counting levels with at least one game action. Since *Refraction* has an adaptive level progression, each child plays a different set of levels based on their incoming skill. However, since children are randomly assigned to either the experimental or control condition, we expect skill to be evenly distributed across conditions. Our analysis showed that *intervention* has a significant effect on levels played (Z=-9.04, p<0.0001, r=0.07). Children in the experimental condition played more levels, a mean of 6.7 levels compared to 5.5 for those in the control. The median was 2 in both conditions.

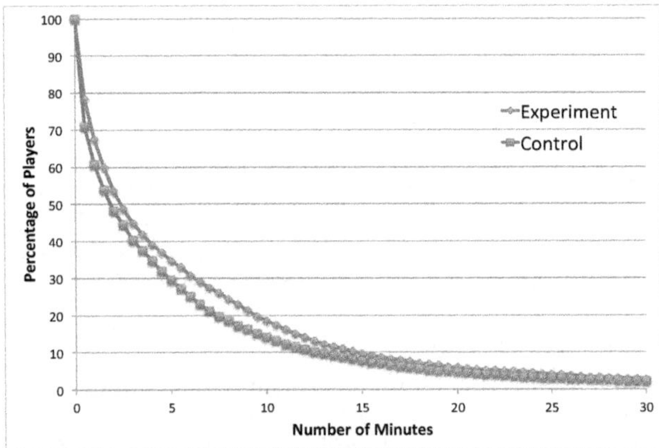

Figure 4. A graph showing the percentage of players in each condition who are still playing after a given number of active minutes. Children in the experimental brain points condition play significantly longer.

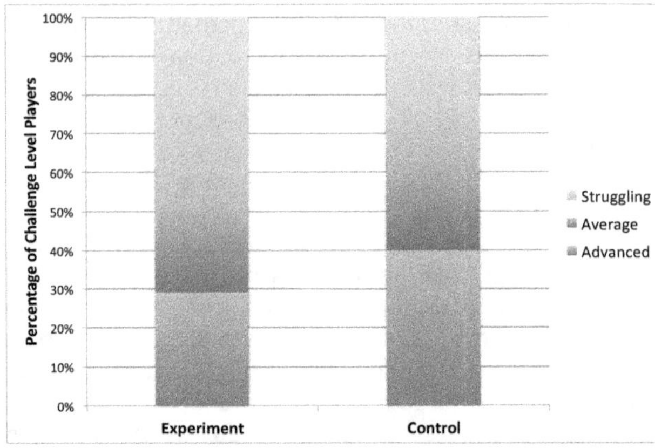

Figure 5. A graph showing the performance level distribution of players who persist for thirty minutes and reach the challenge level. The brain points version of *Refraction* is better at retaining struggling players.

These results suggest that children who play the growth mindset version of *Refraction* are more persistent than those who play the control version. They stay in the game significantly longer and play significantly more levels. However, both of these effects are very small. Given the BrainPOP environment, where the majority of children play for less than three minutes, this is not surprising. Therefore, the fact that we observe a 33% increase in median time played is encouraging, despite the small effect size.

The Intervention Promotes Growth Mindset Behavior

We expected children who played the experimental version of *Refraction* to display behaviors consistent with the growth mindset more frequently than those who played the control version. To evaluate this hypothesis, we analyzed an outcome measure that combines the four metrics used to award brain points to children in the experimental version. Recall from the Experiment Design section that we used a *new hypothesis* metric, an *empty board* metric, a *math* metric, and a *moves* metric to decide when to give brain points. In both versions of *Refraction*, we log an event every time one of the four metrics is triggered. We combine these four metrics to measure how frequently children exhibit the behaviors incentivized by the brain points system.

To combine the metrics, we summed the number of times each metric was triggered during play. Since children in the experimental condition play for significantly longer, they have more opportunities to trigger these metrics. To control for the amount of time played, we divided our combined metric by the number of minutes of active time played. This produced the average number of metric triggers per minute, our strategy outcome measure. Our analysis showed that *intervention* had a significant effect on this combined measure. Children in the experimental condition triggered an average of 2.49 metrics per minute, compared to 2.18 triggers per minute for the control (Z=-8.18, p<0.0001, r=0.07).

These results show that children who play the growth mindset version of *Refraction* learn to use the strategies incentivized by the brain points system. While the size of this effect is small, it is encouraging to see that such a short intervention can change the way children approach a problem, teaching them to exhibit growth mindset behaviors.

The Intervention Makes More Struggling Children Persist

We expected the experimental version of *Refraction* to encourage more struggling children to persist because effort was incentivized rather than speed or performance. To evaluate this hypothesis, we grouped players into three performance levels by measuring how quickly they mastered the first two concepts in the adaptive level progression. For each of the 483 players who mastered both concepts, we calculated the number of levels needed to complete the concepts. The minimum number of levels to master the concepts is six, and the maximum is twenty. To determine our grouping criteria, we ordered players by the number of levels they needed to master the concepts, and divided them into three equal groups. We consider children who complete the concepts in seven or fewer levels to be advanced, eight to ten levels to be average, and more than ten levels to be struggling.

To determine which types of players are encouraged to persist in each version of the game, we analyzed the performance level distribution of children who completed the first two concepts and reached the challenge puzzle that appears after thirty minutes of play. We found that *intervention* had a significant effect on performance level after thirty minutes (χ^2=8.00, p<0.05, V=0.13). As shown in Figure 5, 49% of children in the experimental version were labeled as struggling, 29% were advanced, and 22% were average, compared to 37% struggling, 40% advanced, and 23% average for the control. This suggests that our growth mindset intervention encourages more low performing students to persist for extended periods of time in *Refraction*.

The Intervention May Improve Reaction to Challenge

We expected children who played the experimental version of the game to react more favorably to an especially challenging level than children who played the control version. To evaluate this hypothesis, we analyzed children's behavior in the "Challenge Level" given to players thirty minutes into the game. Very few children play *Refraction* for long enough to reach the challenge level, so our analysis only includes 281 players from the experimental condition and 248 from the control condition.

First, we analyzed the time played and combined strategy outcome measures used previously. We found no significant effect of *intervention* on amount of active time played (Z=-0.81, *n.s*) or the number of strategy metrics fired per minute (Z=0.69, *n.s*). We also looked at whether children win the challenge level, skip by clicking the "New Level" button, or quit the game entirely. We did find a significant effect of *intervention* on win rate, most likely due to the uneven performance distribution at this point in the game. Children in the control condition won 18% of the time, compared to 11% for the experimental condition (χ^2=4.79, p<0.05, V=0.1).There were no significant differences in the skip rate (χ^2=2.0, *n.s.*) or the quit rate (χ^2=0.08, *n.s.*).

Finally, we studied how children were impacted by struggle by measuring how long children continued playing *Refraction* after the challenge level. We calculated the amount of active time children spent playing after this level, and while there was no significant effect, the results trend in the hypothesized direction of children in the experimental condition playing longer (Z=-1.71, p=0.088, r=0.07). They played for a median of 381 seconds after the challenge level, compared to 258 for children in the control condition, despite the fact that the remaining group of students in the experimental condition had a larger percentage of low performers.

We had hoped to see the increased persistence and use of strategy observed in the standard *Refraction* levels transfer to the challenge level, where effort was not explicitly rewarded through brain points. While it is possible that children in the experimental condition were less motivated to persist because they did not earn brain points on this level, it is also possible that we saw no effects due to the population of players included in this analysis. Children who play *Refraction* for more than thirty minutes on BrainPOP are unusual; they may be more persistent than average, and could already be inclined towards the growth mindset. Future research will need to explore this question in more depth in a environment where we can assess and control for children's incoming mindsets.

Despite the overall lack of difference in children's behavior during the challenge level, we measured a promising trend showing that children in the experimental condition may play longer after experiencing struggle and failure than children in the control condition. This trend suggests that even among the unusual group of children who play *Refraction* for over thirty minutes, our brain points intervention may affect how long they are willing to persist. This is especially encouraging because a larger percentage of the children who persisted until the challenge level in the experimental condition struggled with the game. However, this trend is not significant and will need to be confirmed through future research.

CONCLUSION

In this work, we show that making a fundamental change to an educational game's incentive structure can positively impact children's behavior. We present a new method of promoting the growth mindset through the "brain points" incentive structure. This system shows children how to practice and achieve growth mindset behaviors, in addition to teaching them the theory behind this mindset. The results from our preliminary study on BrainPOP are encouraging. Children were only exposed to our intervention for a short period of time, three minutes on average, and yet we were able to capture the effects it had on their behavior. Children in the experimental condition played longer and completed more levels than those in the control condition. They also learned to use the strategies incentivized by the brain points system, exhibiting strategic behavior more often than children in the control condition. Finally, an analysis of the children who played for thirty minutes showed that those in the experimental condition may persist longer after struggling with a challenging level than those in the control condition.

While the initial results are promising, this study has a number of limitations that we hope to address in future work. We know little about the children who play games on BrainPOP or the contexts in which they play, information which could help us better understand their behavior. Furthermore, children play for a very limited amount of time. While previous studies have shown that minimal interventions, such as praising students' hard work and strategies, can increase motivation and task persistence [24, 17], it would be valuable to understand how our system affects student behavior during longer play sessions. Finally, we could not directly measure how the intervention impacted student learning with formal pre- and post-tests in this work due to the nature of our online study. We plan to expand our understanding of the brain points intervention in future work by studying its effects in a fully controlled classroom environment.

Despite these limitations, our preliminary results suggest that growth mindset feedback has the potential to increase persistence and performance in educational games. We believe that the brain points incentive structure could be generalized and integrated into many game environments, and even adopted in other contexts to incentivize effort, strategic thinking, and persistence. Our brain points system was designed to reward the micro behaviors that are indicative of productive struggle in *Refraction*. This design could be applied to another application through the development of a context-specific metric for detecting effort and use of strategy. This metric could be used to provide real-time rewards that encourage growth mindset behavior in the new application. We hope that this method of promoting the growth mindset by directly rewarding desired behaviors can be adopted in many settings, and we plan to explore this possibility in future work.

ACKNOWLEDGMENTS

We thank creators of *Refraction* for making this work possible. In particular, we would like to recognize Barbara Krug and Marianne Lee who created the incredible art and animations for this study. We also thank Allisyn Levy of BrainPOP for promoting *Refraction*. This work was supported by the Office of Naval Research grant N00014-12-C-0158, the Bill and Melinda Gates Foundation grant OPP1031488, the Hewlett Foundation grant 2012-8161, Adobe, and Microsoft.

REFERENCES

1. Aronson, J., Fried, C. B., and Good, C. Reducing the Effects of Stereotype Threat on African American College Students by Shaping Theories of Intelligence. *Journal of Experimental Social Psychology 38* (2002), 113–125.
2. Baker, R., Walonoski, J., Heffernan, N., Roll, I., Corbett, A., and Koedinger, K. R. Why students engage in "gaming the system" behavior in interactive learning environments. *Journal of Interactive Learning Research 19*, 2 (2008), 185–224.
3. Blackwell, L. S., Trzesniewski, K. H., and Dweck, C. S. Implicit Theories of Intelligence Predict Achievement Across an Adolescent Transition: A Longitudinal Study and an Intervention. *Child Development 78*, 1 (2007), 246–263.
4. Brainology. http://www.mindsetworks.com/webnav/program.aspx.
5. BrainPOP. http://www.brainpop.com/.
6. BrainPOP Educators. http://www.brainpop.com/educators/home//.
7. Chase, C. The interplay of chance and skill: Exploiting a common game mechanic to enhance learning and persistence. In *Proceedings of the 2012 International Conference of the Learning Sciences* (2012).
8. Corbett, A. T., and Anderson, J. R. Knowledge tracing: Modeling the acquisition of procedural knowledge. *User Modeling and User-Adapted Interaction 4*, 4 (1995), 253–278.
9. Dweck, C. S. *Mindset: The new psychology of success*. New York: Random House, 2006.
10. Gee, J., and Shaffer, D. Looking where the light is bad: Video games and the future of assessment. (Epistemic Games Group Working Paper No. 2010-02), Madison: University of Wisconsin-Madison (2010).
11. Gee, J. P. *What Video Games Have to Teach Us About Learning and Literacy*. St. Martin's Press, 2008.
12. Good, C., Aronson, J., and Inzlicht, M. Improving adolescents standardized test performance: An intervention to reduce the effects of stereotype threat. *Journal of Applied Developmental Psychology 24* (2003), 645–662.
13. Gunderson, E. A., Gripshover, S. J., Romero, C., and Dweck, C. S. Parent Praise to 1- to 3-Year-Olds Predicts Children's Motivational Frameworks 5 Years Later. *Child Development 84*, 5 (2013), 1526–1541.
14. Harpstead, E., Myers, B. A., and Aleven, V. In search of learning: facilitating data analysis in educational games. In *Proceedings of the SIGCHI Conference on Human Factors in Computing Systems*, CHI '13, ACM (New York, NY, USA, 2013), 79–88.
15. Heyman, G. D., and Dweck, C. S. Children's Thinking about Traits: Implications for Judgments of the Self and Others. *Child Development 64*, 2 (1998), 391–403.
16. Kaiser Family Foundation. Key Facts: Children and Video Games, 2002. http://kaiserfamilyfoundation.files.wordpress.com/2013/04/5959.pdf.
17. Kamins, M. L., and Dweck, C. S. Person versus process praise and criticism: Implications for contingent self-worth and coping. *Developmental Psychology 35*, 3 (1999), 835–847.
18. Kapp, K. M. *The gamification of learning and instruction: game-based methods and strategies for training and education*. San Francisco, CA: Pfeiffer, 2012.
19. Khan Academy. http://www.khanacademy.org/.
20. Lee, J., Luchini, K., Michael, B., Norris, C., and Soloway, E. More than just fun and games: assessing the value of educational video games in the classroom. In *CHI '04 Extended Abstracts on Human Factors in Computing Systems*, CHI EA '04, ACM (New York, NY, USA, 2004), 1375–1378.
21. Linehan, C., Kirman, B., Lawson, S., and Chan, G. Practical, appropriate, empirically-validated guidelines for designing educational games. In *Proceedings of the SIGCHI Conference on Human Factors in Computing Systems*, CHI '11, ACM (New York, NY, USA, 2011), 1979–1988.
22. Martin, T., Smith, C. P., Andersen, E., Liu, Y.-E., and Popović, Z. Refraction time: Making split decisions in an online fraction game. In *American Educational Research Association Annual Meeting*, AERA (2012).
23. Mayo, M. J. Video Games: A Route to Large-Scale STEM Education? *Science 323* (2009), 79–82.
24. Mueller, C. M., and Dweck, C. S. Praise for Intelligence Can Undermine Children's Motivation and Performance. *Journal of Personality and Social Psychology 75*, 1 (1998), 33–52.
25. O'Neil, H. F., Wainess, R., and Baker, E. L. Classification of learning outcomes: evidence from the computer games literature. *The Curriculum Journal 16*, 4 (2005), 455–474.
26. O'Rourke, E., Butler, E., Liu, Y., Ballwebber, C., and Popović, Z. The effects of age on player behavior in educational games. In *Foundations of Digital Games*, FDG '13 (2013).
27. Ricci, K. E., Salas, E., and Cannon-Bowers, J. A. Do computer-based games facilitate knowledge acquisition and retention? *Military Psychology 8*, 4 (1996), 295–307.
28. Schell, J. *The Art of Game Design: A Book of Lenses*. Morgan Kaufmann Publishers, Burlington, MA, 2008, p.120.
29. Yeager, D. S., Paunesku, D., Walton, G. M., and Dweck, C. S. *How Can We Instill Productive Mindsets at Scale? A Review of the Evidence and an Initial R&D Agenda*. A White Paper prepared for the White House meeting on Excellence in Education: The Importance of Academic Mindsets, 2013.

Towards Automatic Experimentation of Educational Knowledge

Yun-En Liu[1], Travis Mandel[1],Emma Brunskill[2], and Zoran Popović[1]
[1]Center for Game Science, Computer Science & Engineering, University of Washington
[2]School of Computer Science, Carnegie Mellon University
{yunliu, tmandel, zoran}@cs.washington.edu, ebrun@cs.cmu.edu

ABSTRACT

We present a general automatic experimentation and hypothesis generation framework that utilizes a large set of users to explore the effects of different parts of an intervention parameter space on any objective function. We also incorporate importance sampling, allowing us to run these automatic experiments even if we cannot give out the exact intervention distributions that we want. To show the utility of this framework, we present an implementation in the domain of fractions and numberlines, using an online educational game as the source of players. Our system is able to automatically explore the parameter space and generate hypotheses about what types of numberlines lead to maximal short-term transfer; testing on a separate dataset shows the most promising hypotheses are valid. We briefly discuss our results in the context of the wider educational literature, showing that one of our results is not explained by current research on multiple fraction representations, thus proving our ability to generate potentially interesting hypotheses to test.

Author Keywords

Datamining; Games; Education

ACM Classification Keywords

H.5.0 Information interfaces and presentation: General

INTRODUCTION

Many disciplines have experienced an explosion of data in the past decade, transforming the way we do science [8]. Web-based software has led to a similar increase in data for the behavioral sciences. This is particularly exciting in these domains, as subjects are often costly, difficult to recruit, and may not be demographically diverse [15]. In the past, lack of subjects has often meant only sparse coverage of experimental spaces due. But now, for particular branches of the behavioral sciences in which humans can both remotely perform interesting tasks and are willing to do so, the increase in data means that we now have the potential to learn much more about how humans interact with software. But to take full advantage of these users, we first need effective tools to allow us to explore these new huge datasets.

To this end, we present an automatic experimentation and hypothesis generation framework designed for these big data scenarios. In the basic framework, the inputs are a target objective function on users, such as learning gains, and a set of factors that form a parameter space of possible experimental conditions, such as different learning interventions. We automatically bin users into experimental conditions, identifying the parameters with broadest impacts averaged across other factors. It then recurses on the best parameter setting as measured by the objective function, and finds the best setting of the remaining parameters, providing confidence intervals at each stage. This means both that we automate much of the experimental process, and also provide a much more thorough coverage of the hypothesis space. This frees the researcher to perform tasks that humans do best: deep data analysis and generation of hypothesis spaces for the system to explore.

Unfortunately, it is often the case that we do not possess full control over the user experience. For example, software companies may not want to expose many users to highly risky experimental conditions. Or, in a more extreme case, we may want to analyze already-collected data in a purely offline manner. To deal with these situations, our full framework uses importance sampling to simulate the desired user distributions given data drawn from a different distribution. This allows us to ask many different questions on already-collected data, allowing us to fully utilize previously collected data.

We demonstrate the power of our proposed framework in the educational domain, by implementing and running it offline on an data set with a sampling distribution different than the desired one. We show how our method can generate hypotheses about which parameters and their settings are best for encouraging near-transfer, and confirm these hypotheses with statistical tests on a completely different dataset. Some of our results match current educational theories, but some do not, suggesting further experiments to run either online or in a classroom. Of course, our framework has important limitations: for example, our greedy search may not explore effective parts of the hypothesis space in the presence of parameter interactions, or the data may be so noisy that we require prohibitive numbers of players to discover interesting information. Still, our ability to automatically find interesting parts of the hypotheses space suggests that this method may become a useful tool in behavioral research.

CHI 2014, April 26–May 1, 2014, Toronto, Ontario, Canada.
Copyright © 2014 ACM 978-1-4503-2473-1/14/04..$15.00.
http://dx.doi.org/10.1145/2556288.2557392

RELATED WORK

Online experimentation

Major companies such as Microsoft [19] and Amazon [20] have performed online experiments for years. For researchers, Mechanical Turk has proven to be quite helpful to many scientists looking for cheap, high-quality user data [18]. Games have also become an increasingly popular source for behavioral data, and have been used to study the effects of optional rewards [2] and tutorials [4]. More fine-grained methods, such as multi-armed bandits, have also been used in online settings to maximize click through rates of search results or article recommendations [25].

These web-based mass experimentation platforms have a few key benefits. Mechanical Turk has been shown to provide inexpensive, reliable results and has a demographic spread much wider than typical pools for social science research [10]. In the games domain, the observed behavior is "in the wild" [3], increasing external validity [33]. We build on this work by proposing a framework that automatically runs series of experiments depending on intermediate results, and use importance sampling to estimate the results when the sampling distribution does not match the desired one.

Scientific Discovery

Researchers in AI have been working for years to develop systems capable of generating scientific knowledge. This field, known as scientific discovery, has generated many such systems aimed at automating different scientific behaviors [21]. For example, Lee et al. used a feedback loop between the RL rule induction program and expert knowledge to identify potentially carcinogenic compounds [23]. Perhaps the most comprehensive example of such a system is Robot Scientist Adam, a fully automated robot capable of the full loop of hypothesis generation, experimental design, and data analysis in yeast genomics [17].

We focus on the automatic selection of experiments and introduce a new algorithm for choosing which ones to run. We differ in our source of data: automatically running experiments on humans introduces many problems not present in a laboratory setting. In some settings, such as education, there may be many experimental variables: instruction duration, number representation, ordering of concepts, problem type, hinting systems, etc.. In addition, we often want to both find general rules about how different factors affect student learning, but also the specific settings that optimize rate of learning and maximum transfer ability. We deal with both objectives with a greedy search strategy designed to find the "good" parts of the hypothesis space.

Educational Data Mining

Our example application runs experiments in the educational domain to identify factors contributing to variation in learning, a common theme in the educational data mining community. Intelligent tutoring systems, especially cognitive tutors [5], have been used for many experiments: for example, Rau et al. [29] test the usefulness of multiple fraction representations with self-explanation compared to single representations. Or in the educational games domain, Lomas et al. [26] used an educational game to run two large-scale experiments with many conditions on the effect of challenge on motivation and learning. We are not proposing a new tutor or game, but rather a method that gathers or uses existing data from some source (such as a tutor or game) to automatically run experiments with many factors. To the best of our knowledge, other EDM researchers have not proposed or used an automatic method for choosing and running experiments in a hypothesis space; nor have they used importance sampling to run multiple experiments on the same dataset with a different sampling distribution than desired.

BASIC FRAMEWORK

Here we present a simplified version of our framework, which requires full control over how players are sampled and is designed to run one experiment at a time. We will be investigating how varying the presentation of (fraction) number lines affects users' ability to answer future number lines. Fraction number line problems typically take the form of a line representing the reals, with at least two points marked for scale, and ask where new fractions should be placed or what fraction corresponds to some point. In the next section, we will extend this framework with importance sampling to allow us to run multiple analyses on the same dataset, and then present an implemented version of it that was able to automatically run parameter searches to find which types of number lines lead to maximal near-transfer to new number line questions, using data from an online educational game.

First, let's consider how a researcher might run an experiment.

1. The researcher hypothesizes about how one or more factors might impact a variable of interest, ex. different fraction representations or hinting systems might lead to different performance on future number lines.

2. If subjects are expensive, she cannot test more than a few of these factors simultaneously. Instead, she must decide which factors are most interesting: perhaps she compares a few different representations with no hinting systems.

3. She decides on an experimental procedure to test the role of this factor on the variable of interest, including whatever assessments are necessary. Here, this will likely involve the choice and refinement of existing number line tests, whether or not the players should participate online or come into the lab, and so on.

4. She runs the experiment, then collects and analyzes data.

5. Assuming the results become well-established and accepted, eventually another researcher may pick other factors to investigate, holding the already-studied ones constant. For example, perhaps symbolic representations are better in the initial experiment. Then the next experiment might test the effects of different hinting systems for symbolic fraction number lines.

From a research perspective, perhaps the most interesting part of this process is data analysis and hypothesis generation. The rest is needed to both gather data confirming or rejecting the hypothesis, and to ensure that there is sufficient statistical power even with a small number of subjects.

However, assume now that we have a constant stream of new users: say, several thousand per day. Furthermore, assume that they are interacting with a system under the experimenter's full control and are willing to participate in the experimental conditions and take any assessments necessary. Then, there is no difficulty in finding subjects, and the experimenter does not have to be present to run experiments. Furthermore, with so many users and control over the assignment of players to conditions, we can test many experimental conditions, not just a handful. Thus, the experimenter need not carefully select factor levels: she can simply specify the available factors and the system can explore them to identify the ones that seem most informative. Finally, statistical analysis becomes easier with clean experimental designs, though as we will show later we can continue to operate even if we do not have full control over which interventions are chosen.

Of course, the total number of experiments possible is combinatorial in the number of factors, so it is necessary to choose a search strategy. In this paper, we propose a greedy search: at each step, we choose a parameter and its setting that leads to the best performance when randomly selecting other parameters, then recurse on the remaining parameters. This leads to selecting parameters which are broadly effective at the top of the experiment tree (due to the randomization of other parameters), but which quickly narrows (due to the greedy setting of parameters with each step). This strategy is appropriate in a domain such as education where we both want to create generalizable knowledge about which dimensions of the parameter space are most effective, and also optimize some metric like learning gain. In other domains, such as psychology, the goal may simply be to find the factors that cause the largest differences between settings and so a different search strategy may be needed.

We formalize our framework in the following way. The experimenter specifies a *parameter space* P she is interested in exploring. The parameters that make up this space correspond to factors, in standard statistical parlance. Restricting ourselves to categorical variables for the time being, each parameter $p_i \in P$ has k_{p_i} settings $s_{p_i j}$, $j = 1 \dots k_{p_i}$, which correspond to factor levels. In addition, she specifies an *experimental set* E, $E \subset P$: these are parameters she wants the system to investigate. Letting our population of players be represented as X, she also provides an objective function $f : X \rightarrow R$ that produces a real value for each user.

Our algorithm can be thought of as a greedy depth-first search over the experimental set E, marginalizing over the parameters $P - E$. We describe it as follows.

- First, we test each setting of each parameter. To test a setting means to randomly assign some number of players N to an experimental condition with $p_i = s_{ij}$ and with all remaining variables $P - p_i$ set randomly.

- Each experimental condition C_q is specified exactly by a parameter $p_q \in E$ and its setting $s_{p_q j_q}$. Since there is one condition for each parameter setting, we have $q = 1 \dots \sum_{p \in E} k_p$. Let X_q be the set of players assigned to C_q. Let $F_q = \frac{1}{N} \sum_{x \in X_q} f(x)$.

- Once each condition has N players, we order the C_q from greatest to least by their associated objective values, F_q. We store the best node seen so far as B. We recurse on each condition in order, with parameter space $P - p_q$, experimental set $E - p_q$, objective function f, and setting $p_q = s_{p_q j_q}$.

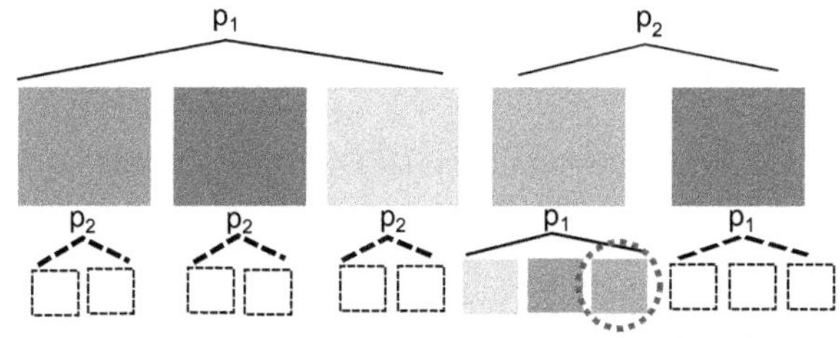

Figure 1. An illustration of the tree built by our algorithm with two parameters, p_1 and p_2. We first explore all individual parameter settings at the top of the tree, holding one parameter fixed to some value and randomizing over the other parameter. We order the nodes by function value and recurse, so that we hold p_2 to its best setting and vary p_1. In this work we stop once all nodes have been set for the first time, though with an exponential number of users we could explore all nodes.

Our algorithm is intuitively simple to understand. Its goal at each step is to order the parameter and associated parameter setting by how broadly positive of an impact they have, marginalizing over all remaining parameters in the parameter space. It then sets the best parameter to its best setting and repeats the process with all remaining parameters until it hits the bottom and has to backtrack to the next best parameter setting. Given enough players, the algorithm will eventually test all experimental conditions.

$P - E$ can be thought of as the generalization space of the results; none of these parameters are directly set, but they are always randomly selected at each stage. The generalization power of most standard studies is often both implicit and minimal, in the effort to control as many variables as possible. But in our framework it is made explicit, and as we will see later can reasonably be quite large, since we can muster so many players.

The algorithm can be stopped at any point, giving the experimenter a partial experimental tree and the current-best node, B. A common stopping choice might be to have it stop once it reaches the bottom for the first time, resulting in the greedy selection of good parameter settings. In this case, if $k_{p_i} \leq K$ and $|E| = M$, the number of experiments the system will run is $O(KM^2)$. Unfortunately, if there are particularly nasty interactions between parameters, nothing short of a full search of the experiment parameter space and its associated $O(K^M)$ runtime is guaranteed to find the globally optimal setting. An easy solution is for the experimenter to combine parameters likely to interact into a single parameter with many settings. Or, if we are assume that there are no more than J-way interactions between parameters, we could allow the algorithm to explore all combinations of parameters of size J at each level, resulting in approximately $O(K^{\binom{M}{J}}(\frac{M}{J})^2)$ experiments. N, the number of players assigned to each condition, must be chosen carefully to make good decisions in reasonable time.

FULL FRAMEWORK WITH IMPORTANCE SAMPLING

We are primarily interested in using games and online learning software. In these systems, we have the advantage that users are inexpensive, but the disadvantage that we may not have full control over our player sampling process. For example, game design constraints may make it difficult to give highly randomized interventions: a game with completely random levels may not be very fun to play. We also wish to be able to function in an offline setting in order to re-use existing datasets or if it is difficult to choose parameters for each new player in an online fashion.

We deal with both problems by extending our basic framework using importance sampling. Importance sampling is a commonly-used technique (ex. [14]) that allows us to estimate an expected function value from a desired distribution of the arguments, even though we can only sample from a different distribution of the arguments. This is accomplished by weighting our function evaluations. Specifically, let $f(x)$ be our objective function, $p(x)$ our desired distribution, and $q(x)$ our actual distribution. Then $E_p[f(x)] = E_p[f(x)\frac{q(x)}{q(x)}] = E_q[f(x)\frac{p(x)}{q(x)}]$. The last quantity is one we can estimate from data with $F_q = \frac{1}{N}\sum_{x \in X_q} f(x)\frac{p(x)}{q(x)}$, as long as we know both the sample and target distributions, and gives us an unbiased and consistent estimator. This technique allows us to run our full framework in offline situations with soft constraints on what interventions we can give to players, assuming that the dataset has non-zero probability for all possible settings of the experimental parameter set.

ASSESSMENT

We want to maximize player learning in our game. There are two challenges. The first is that players may quit at any time, so that an intervention may appear to be better just because it causes the least able players to quit. We deal with this by having short interventions and assessments, and assigning a score of 0 to players who quit before reaching the assessment. The second is that we need to be able to measure player knowledge. This is actually a major challenge: imagine the number of players we would lose by embedding a paper-and-pencil test in a free online game. In our implementation, we mitigate this problem by both embedding the test in the game itself, and only giving players a single question. For us, the resulting increase in noise of the objective function is offset by the large number of players we have. In other scenarios, longer tests may be a better choice.

While this is not a standard testing approach, we can do this because we are interested only in comparing expected assessment scores between different experimental conditions. At any particular stage, the population we are measuring, X_k consists of players who were directed into some particular condition C_k whose efficacy we wish to measure. The expected test score F_{C_k} for any player $x \in X_k$ for our randomized test is obtained by simply averaging over the test scores that we observe over all players, as long as players are sampled independently and identically distributed (from X). This approach bears some similarity to the one taken in domain sampling theory [11], one of the classical testing theories from psychometrics. We avoid many complications because we do not need to estimate single-user scores, only population-level ones, and our choice is justified because we are sampling directly from the population of interest.

To get a sense of how reliable our results are, we would like to establish confidence intervals for our assessment objective function. This is a non-trivial task, given that there is no a-priori knowledge of the objective function distribution, and we re-weight our samples with importance sampling. If we assume a stationary distribution of player scores, we can use a general resampling method known as bootstrapping [12], which repeatedly samples from our empirical data and calculates a test statistic on these resampled batches to estimate quantities relating to the original, unknown distribution. In our case, the test statistic is the mean, and we are interested in obtaining 95% confidence intervals of the mean. Since we have no guarantee of the symmetry of our sample mean around the true mean, we use the centered bootstrap percentile method [32]. Our framework does not depend on the method of calculating confidence intervals, however, so for certain classes of objective functions it may be considerably faster to calculate these intervals with closed-form solutions or more intelligent sampling methods.

EXAMPLE IMPLEMENTATION

Now that we have described our general automatic experimentation framework, we demonstrate its power with a full implementation in a specific setting, along with experimental results. Our platform is an educational game, with players gathered from a popular flash game website targeted at schoolchildren and teachers [9]. Taken together, our importance sampling method and our randomized assessments over populations will allow us to run the full system on a 2 x 2 x 4 x 4 experimental parameter space on a data set collected previously for a different use. This will allow us to discover what number line properties are most likely to lead to player near-transfer on a second, randomized test number line.

Treefrog Treasure

Treefrog Treasure is a platformer game that involves jumping through a jungle world and solving number line problems to reach an end goal. The player must navigate sticky, bouncy, and slippery surfaces and avoid hazardous lava to win successively more complex levels. Number line problems serve as barriers that the player must solve by hitting the correct target location, as shown in Figure 3. It has been played by over 5 million players worldwide.

Experimental Design

Our dataset was collected from June 3, 2013 to June 20, 2013. Players went through several tutorial levels before reaching the experiment levels. After cleaning our data, we had 34,197 players who made it past the tutorial.

We are trying to find the type of number line that leads to greatest player performance on a randomized test number

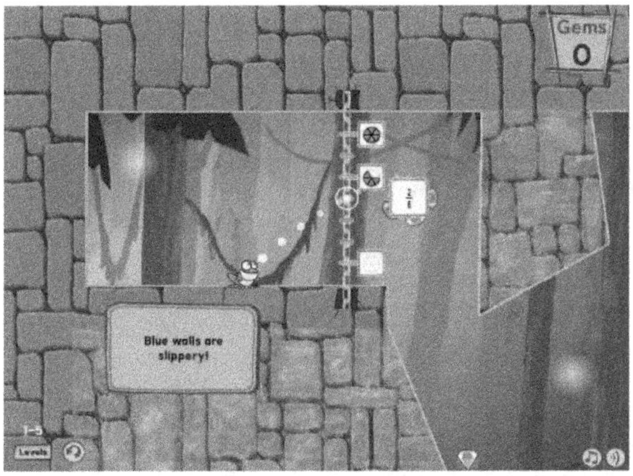

Figure 2. A screenshot of Treefrog Treasure, our source of users. Players navigate through a physics-based world, solving number line problems along the way. Notice that the number line has full tick marks, pie chart labels on the line, and a symbolic (ex. $\frac{a}{b}$) target representation. In our experiment, these are a few of the parameters we allow our system to automatically explore to determine which types of number lines lead to maximal near-transfer.

line. To do this, we consider each player as a sequence of many pairs of number lines, and treat each pair as an experimental unit. This gives us 361,738 pairs. This violates certain assumptions about the independence of variables in classical statistical tests, but greatly increases the amount of available data. We will strictly adhere to the correct assumptions when we validate our results on a new dataset, later, and we will see that our major results continue to hold.

We chose number lines in general as they are a popular pedagogical tool, and a fair amount of evidence exists suggesting that much whole and rational number knowledge is organized around a mental number line [6], [30]. Our experimental parameters alter the way number lines are presented, and can be seen in Table 1. We chose these parameters because they have all been the subject of previous research and are subject to varying amounts of controversy. Tick marks may allow students to find fractions directly through a double-counting method [22]. Hints are often considered necessary by educators [16], but can have negative effects when students "game" them [7]. Finally, there are many ways to represent fractions: pie charts and other area models, operators and linear models [27], magnitudes [30], standard symbolic notation, and so on. Showing multiple representations to students is widely thought to be useful, but may actually be worse than a single representation in some circumstances [29].

The parameter settings of the first number line in each pair constitutes the experimental condition. The full parameter set can be seen in Table 1. Our experimental set consists of Ticks, Animations, Backoff Hints, Target Representation, and Label Representation. We suspect that Target and Label representations are likely to interact, so we treat them as a single parameter, Representation, with four settings for Target and Label: Symbolic/Symbolic, Symbolic/Pie, Pie/Symbolic, Pie/Pie. This means that our results are meant to hold for dif-

Figure 3. The animation condition on the left shows the player how to divide up the number line. The backoff condition in the middle fills in labels and eventually tells the player where to hit. The ticks condition on the right either divide up the number line into segments when ticks are present, or leave it empty besides the 0 and 1 labels when ticks are absent.

ferent Fraction and Initial Labels values, which are always randomly chosen.

We show the results of our system on two objective functions.

1. *Correctness* 1.0 if the player answers the second number line correctly on the first try, 0.0 if they answer incorrectly or quit/restart before reaching it. This corresponds to fraction-placement ability.
2. *Persistence* 1.0 if the player eventually answers the second number line, 0.0 if they fail to answer it or quit/restart before reaching it. This corresponds to fraction-placement persistence.

Correcting sampling distributions

We want the number line parameter settings to be selected uniformly at random. Thus, if one experimental condition had a better objective function value than another, it would mean that some particular settings for the first number line (marginalized over the specific Fraction and Initial Label set) increased player performance across our randomized second number line.

Unfortunately, the dataset was collected for a different purpose, so the actual distribution is different than our distribution of interest. In this dataset, number lines are linked, two at a time. More specifically, the first two number lines always share the same value of Ticks, Animations, Backoff Hints, Target Representation, Label Representation, Initial Labels, and the Fraction denominator d. These are chosen uniformly at random. Then each number line in the pair has the Fraction numerator selected uniformly at random from 1 to $d-1$. Likewise, the second pair's parameters are selected (independently) using the same process, and so on.

This has several implications. The first is that certain fractions are over-represented relative to the desired uniform distribution over fractions. For example, $\frac{1}{2}$ is much more likely to be selected than $\frac{1}{9}$. The second is that half of our generated pairs will match on all parameters except the Fraction numerator due to the parameter pairing, and the other half will be independently and randomly generated from the process above.

As suggested above, we can use importance sampling to address these problems. This will up-weight the undersampled cross-pair links (second and third, fourth and fifth, etc.), and

Parameter	Settings	Interpretation
Fraction	Any $\frac{a}{b} \in (0,1), b \leq 9$	The target fraction the player must hit
Ticks	Present, Absent	For target $\frac{a}{b}$, we can display tick marks for each fraction $\frac{n}{b}$.
Animations	Present, Absent	If the player misses a target $\frac{a}{b}$, they might receive an lengthy pie chart animation showing how to divide up the number line into b parts.
Initial Labels	[0,1]	For target $\frac{a}{b}$, the proportion of labels of $\frac{n}{b}$ fractions shown at the start.
Backoff Hints	1, 2, 3, 4	The number of misses for target $\frac{a}{b}$ before the progressive hinting system fills in all labels for $\frac{n}{b}$ and displays the correct answer.
Target Representation	Symbolic, Pie	How the target fraction is displayed.
Label Representation	Symbolic, Pie	How fraction labels on the number line are displayed.

Table 1. The parameter space for our experiment.

down-weight the oversampled intra-pair links (first and second, third and fourth, etc.). For any experimental condition C_k, we have a set of parameters that are already set to some known value, and a set of parameters that should be uniformly random. This gives us the desired sampling distribution over the first number line. Since we also know that our desired objective function is some measure of performance on an independent, uniformly random second number line, this specifies the full desired distribution over pairs. But since we know the original distribution used to generate the data, we simply use importance sampling as above to reweight each objective function valuation in our dataset to calculate V_k, the expected player score under our desired distribution.

Results

Since we have at least one player in every experimental condition, it's possible to finish the depth-first search and generate the full experimental tree. However, even just the bottom of the tree contains 64 possible parameter setting combinations, making it difficult to show the full set of results. Instead, we show the parameters the algorithm greedily selected and its evaluation of the objective function for each of the different settings, stopping once it has set each parameter.

The results are shown in Figure 4. This is only a narrow, greedy slice of each experimental tree. At each stage, our algorithm finds the single parameter setting that maximizes the objective function, while averaging over all other parameters. It then sets this parameter to the best setting and repeats this process with the remaining parameters. Thus the Representation pie/pie setting is the broadest, best parameter setting among the entire experimental set in the *correctness* tree in Figure 4(a), the Backoff Hints 3 result is the broadest, best parameter setting only when the Representation is given to be pie/pie, and so on.

The confidence intervals given at each level of the tree grow wider as we go down. This is because data becomes sparser at each level, since we do not have control over the sampling distribution. In the basic online framework, the system would instead direct players to the condition in question, decreasing the amount of data near the top and increasing it near the bottom. Based on the amount of overlap present, we can guess that the results of the top and possibly second layer are reasonably trustworthy, but that we should be increasingly suspicious as we test more specific conditions.

An important question is whether the greedy method finds reasonable settings, in practice. We can of course construct examples such that for any deterministic strategy, the algorithm must perform an exponential search to find the best settings. This can be quite bad for large parameter spaces, though it is probably unlikely in practice. Since our original dataset contains samples from all over the experimental tree, we can exhaustively search all possible experimental conditions at each depth to see when the greedy search diverges. Our greedy selection of the *correctness* diverges from the global optimum on the third and fourth levels with average score 0.460 and 0.474, respectively. These values are well-within the greedy selection's confidence intervals as seen in Figure 4(a). Our greedy selection of in the *persistence* condition finds the globally best selection at each level of the tree. Thus we conclude that greedy selection is reliable in this particular domain, especially at the top of the tree where data are plentiful and only a few parameters are set.

Validation

Our results so far could be useful to a game designer, with appropriate validation on new players to avoid overfitting. However, we would like even more: we want our framework to suggest important parameters and likely-effective settings for further experimentation, or even to generate research results outright. Unfortunately, our methodology makes a number of assumptions that make standard statistical tests inapplicable, and runs so many experiments that it is virtually guaranteed to find spurious results. We can, however, use our results to generate hypotheses that are testable on a new dataset.

We use a second dataset, again sampled according to the same distribution as the original. This dataset consists of 9,675 players of Treefrog Treasure from June 20, 2013 to July 9, 2013. We did not use this dataset to help us develop our system, hence it is similar to the final test dataset common in supervised machine learning.

Recall that the first two number lines share most parameters, including all of our experimental parameters, so they can serve as our experimental condition. All other parameters are chosen independently of the experimental ones, so the conditions are comparable. The third number line is itself chosen randomly and independently from the first two, and can serve as our assessment.

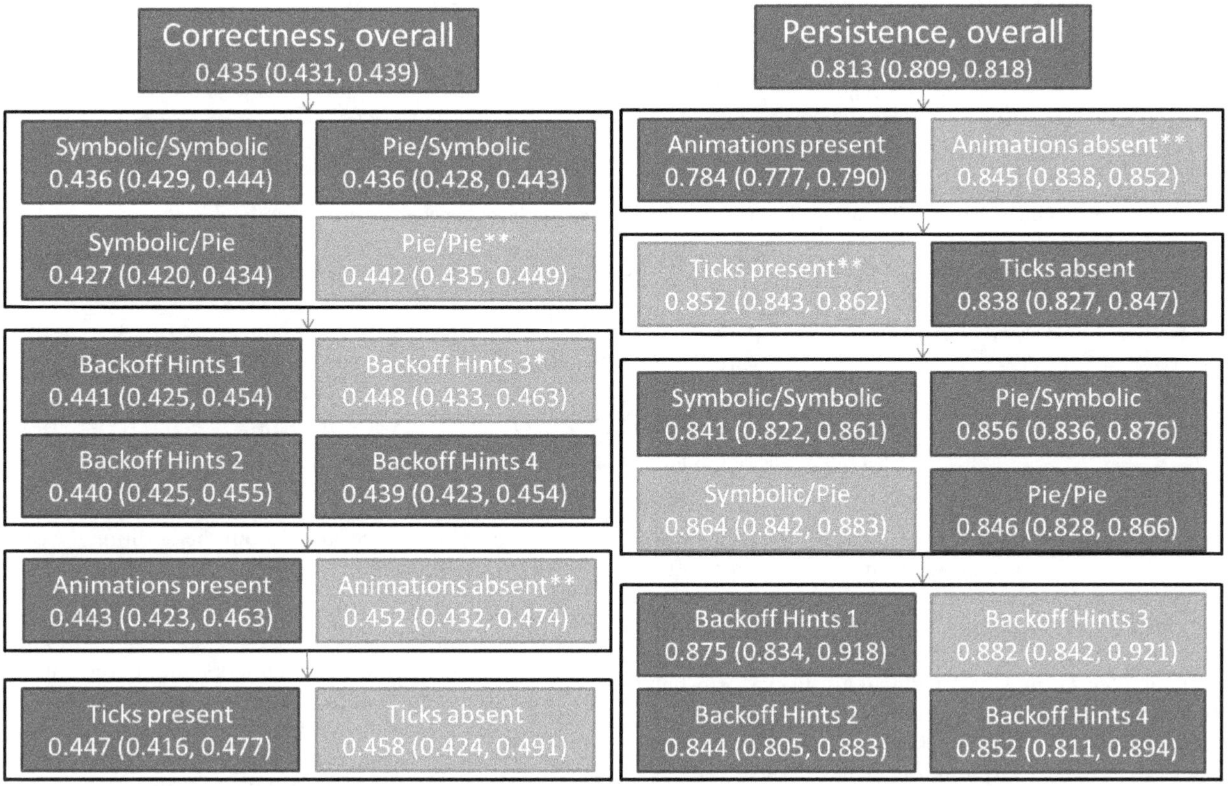

(a) Correctness (b) Persistence

Figure 4. A greedy slice of the experimental space explored, for two objective functions. Objective function evaluations are given with 95% confidence intervals, given by the centered bootstrap percentile method. Our algorithm conditions on more parameters as we go deeper down the tree, so that the results at the bottom have all experimental parameter values set according to their best observed settings. In addition, we will later statistically test the results on a separate dataset. * marks results that will be marginally significant, $p < 0.10$. ** marks results that will be significant, $p < 0.05$.

Thus, for any combination of parameter settings, we can ask whether players given number lines matching those criteria on the first two number lines performed better on the third than everyone else, a cross-sectional sampling scheme. We collect only one datapoint from each player, allowing us to meet the independence of samples criteria. Since both our objective functions are of the form "Pass" or "Fail", represented as 1.0 and 0.0 respectively, we use the χ^2 two sample test in each case. Other types of objective functions will in general have different appropriate tests, such as ANOVA or Mann-Whitney U.

Each experimental tree generates a large number of potential hypotheses; we will simply focus on the most basic ones, which is whether the chosen parameter settings lead to increasingly "good" outcomes as we go down the tree. Each comparison will be performance of players with the settings of the experimental parameters at that point, as compared to everyone else. The results are shown in Tables 2 and 3.

Remember that the wide confidence intervals at the deep ranges of the tree with many parameters set led us to suspect those results. Indeed, our statistical tests confirm this fact: we achieve significantly or marginally significantly better performance following our automatically-generated results at the top two layers, but mostly do not see significant effects on the bottom two. Thus our validation results are not surprising, and underscore the need for a validation set when running the system offline to avoid overfitting.

Finally, the effects may seem relatively weak, with a 2.4% increase from using the pie/pie representation on *correctness*. However, this is because we are measuring differences of interventions consisting of two numberlines and no explicit instruction. If a 10% difference in test scores after thirty minutes of instruction is good, then a 2% improvement after one minute may be reasonable. The extension of effective short interventions to effective long interventions is not trivial, and is left to future work.

DISCUSSION

Hypothesis Generation

Our primary purpose is to introduce an automatic experimentation framework. To demonstrate its utility, we have shown that we can use our implementation to discover interesting information and find potential educational hypotheses to further explore. We certainly do not claim that our findings are highly general, mature educational results. There are many caveats: the intervention is extremely short, the measured task is near-transfer onto a broadly randomized number line, the population is drawn from an online educational game, and so on.

Representation	Backoff Hints	Animations	Ticks	Mean	Other mean	Statistics
pie/pie	Any	Any	Any	0.431	0.407	$\chi^2(1, N = 9675) = 4.44, p = .0035$
pie/pie	3	Any	Any	0.447	0.410	$\chi^2(1, N = 9675) = 3.13, p = .077$
pie/pie	3	No	Any	0.471	0.411	$\chi^2(1, N = 9675) = 4.23, p = .040$
pie/pie	3	No	Yes	0.429	0.412	$\chi^2(1, N = 9675) = 0.15, p = .694$

Table 2. The results for correctness on the final validation set. The first line says that interventions with double pie charts are better than all others. The second line says that interventions with double pie charts and level 3 backoff hints are better than all others, and so on.

Animations	Ticks	Representation	Backoff Hints	Mean	Other mean	Statistics
No	Any	Any	Any	0.890	0.864	$\chi^2(1, N = 9675) = 14.18, p < .001$
No	Yes	Any	Any	0.896	0.870	$\chi^2(1, N = 9675) = 11.84, p < .001$
No	Yes	symbolic/pie	Any	0.892	0.876	$\chi^2(1, N = 9675) = 1.33, p = .249$
No	Yes	symbolic/pie	3	0.877	0.877	$\chi^2(1, N = 9675) < 0.001, p = 0.995$

Table 3. The results for persistence on the final validation set.

That being said, our results suggest broader hypotheses that could now be tested either in our framework, with lengthier interventions and more comprehensive assessments, or in a standard fashion in a school or lab setting. While the expert specified the parameter space, she did not need to decide particular parameter settings that were likely to perform better than others. This reduces our reliance on expert knowledge and makes it less likely that we will miss important results due to lack of extensive exploration.

As one example from our *correctness* results, we see that the pie/pie representation is significantly better than any other representation combination at improving player performance on a huge variety of number lines with both symbolic and pie chart representations for targets and labels. Educational experts that we spoke with found this to be quite interesting, since number lines almost always appear with symbolic notation. Not only is this a statistically significant result on an extremely rare representation combination that bears further research on its own, it also has potential implications for multiple representations research in general.

To explain further, the early math educational literature generally supports the notion of multiple representations in supporting learning [24], but only in certain circumstances. Many students have difficulty converting back and forth between different representations [31]. One of the reasons multiple representations may sometimes not be beneficial are that students simply opt to ignore presented number lines or informative diagrams when they are given with no added explanation [13]. In the fraction domain specifically, other researchers have found that multiple graphical representations may actually be harmful relative to single representations [1], unless accompanied by a self-explanation prompt.

Although our intervention number lines do offer hints, our number lines have no explanations nor prompts in the traditional sense. Yet using pie charts together with number lines lead to superior performance on the test line, compared to using number lines using the standard symbolic notation. Thus our system may have found an example where multiple representations are useful, without the additional explanation or support suggested by the literature.

We do not know why this is the case in our game, but one explanation might be that understanding symbolic notation may be more difficult than understanding pie charts, which at least are seen outside of the classroom. Then players who are not proficient with number lines may learn them faster or be more willing to play only when they can map them to a more familiar pie chart representation. The opposite possibility is that players have overfit in the classroom to number lines with symbolic notation. In this case, they would have difficulty answering the test number line questions that involve pie charts, and so the most profitable thing to practice would be the number line and pie chart combination. Though, we also note that pie/symbolic and symbolic/pie conditions are worse as well; perhaps the difficulty of mapping between three representations outweighs the potential benefits of seeing a pie chart target with a standard, symbolically-labeled number line.

Regardless of the explanation, our system was able to automatically find and run an interesting experiment that we would not have thought to try. The generated results were confirmed on a separate dataset, and differ in key ways with well-accepted literature, suggesting extensions to existing theories and further research to be done. This demonstrates the exploratory power of our method.

Finally, in this paper we have concentrated on parameters in an educational game; however, our method should be applicable to other domains, as well. For example, in the e-commerce domain, one could consider the parameter space of page layouts, checkout strategies, and item recommendation algorithm, with an objective function of clickthrough rate. Or a polling experiment on Mechanical Turk might ask which combinations of introduction, phrasing, question ordering result in the most consistent survey results. The key is to have a constant stream of users, and the ability to choose parameter settings for users and measure an outcome.

Limitations

Our work has important limitations. We wish to stress that the results are only strictly applicable to the user population they were generated from: in our case, players of our educational game. This can be mitigated in certain domains where demographics can be collected. When this is not possible, it may be best to treat the obtained results as hypotheses to test for future experiments on the desired population.

Furthermore, the algorithm is only as effective as the parameter space specified by the experimenter. It is entirely possible that the given parameters have negligible impacts on the objective function. In this case, the algorithm will greedily select parameter settings that appear very close to the global average, which may serve as a signal that a new parameter space should be devised. Researchers with a solid grasp of the underlying behavioral theories may be able to create more effective parameter spaces.

We also caution that problems arise in certain platforms, especially when users are not invested in the system. In the games domain, users can quit at any time; if a long intervention is desired, changes in the objective function may be caused by survivor bias induced by particular users leaving. As an example, an extremely difficult number line might appear to have a strong test score, but only because it caused all the players bad at answering number lines to quit. We control for this effect by having extremely short interventions so that the probability of quitting is low, and giving players who quit the lowest possible score. This protects us from spurious results caused by biased patterns of quitting, but also (intentionally) entangles learning and engagement. This issue is much less prominent in Mechanical Turk or software being used in schools by teachers, where the populations are more invested in finishing the intervention.

Also, this approach is focused only on exploring hypotheses related to the overall effects of system-controllable behaviors. Many factors such as age, gender, personality, performance, etc. are not directly controlled by the system, but are frequently studied in educational literature. For example, this system cannot identify different groups of people which need different interventions based on past performance. This type of useful adaptivity is challenging to achieve with limited data, and is left for future work.

FUTURE WORK

This is a new domain, only made possible in the past few years through the increasing use of the Internet. As such, there is a tremendous number of possible ways our framework could be extended or improved. We will list only a few of them.

Our implementation currently only handles standard, categorical factor experiments. This is not a fundamental limitation, but there is more work to be done to handle ordinal or numeric factors. Our system currently cannot deal with these variables because it does not know how to find the ideal parameter setting to use in a continuous range. One solution is to sample at random from numerical factors, then chop them into ranges that best separate the data as in regression trees. Another approach is to try using one of many well-known optimization techniques which attempt to find the best value, such as Covariance Matrix Adaptation.

As mentioned earlier, our search strategy in the space of experimental parameters is a staged, greedy selection designed for both maximizing the objective function value and finding which parameters are most important. This is appropriate in an educational domain. However, there are many other possible search strategies maximizing other goals. For example, a psychologist might care about variables causing the biggest difference in behavior, in which case a better strategy might be to choose parameters with greatest information gain, as often done in decision trees [28]. In this paper our results are taken from the offline case, where the search strategy is less important, but when players are committed to conditions online the search strategy is critical.

Future work includes investigating search strategies in the online case. If the researcher's interest is purely in mapping out the hypothesis space, one could imagine a search strategy that simply tries to find the most discriminative parameter at each level of the tree, using some well-known metric like information gain or Gini impurity. And departing from standard techniques, we could imagine a system that does a soft search over the parameter space to find the discriminative parts of the experimental tree. There are many online algorithms from the active learning and multi-arm bandit communities that attempt to do similar things, which can potentially be adapted to this framework.

CONCLUSION

Recent years have seen the emergence of large sources of user data. In this paper, we take advantage of these new data sources and propose a general, automated experimentation and hypothesis generation framework. This framework is specifically designed to automatically explore large hypothesis spaces in human behavioral research. Our importance sampling component allows the system to be used offline and when we have different distributions than the one of interest.

To show the usefulness of our framework, we implement it using an educational game. Using already-collected data, our system explores the hypothesis space for two alternative objective functions: maximizing player correctness and player persistence on a highly randomized test numberline. We find the most important parameters and their recommended settings and show that the greedy selection does a good job of finding the best settings at each level. We then confirm just a few of the most promising generated hypotheses on a already-collected, different data set. One of these hypotheses, generated from an unusual method of representing fractions on a number line, seems to be in opposition to recent work, which indicates that our system is indeed capable of automatically generating and testing interesting hypotheses that may not have been otherwise discovered.

ACKNOWLEDGEMENTS

This material is based upon work supported by the National Science Foundation Graduate Research Fellowship grant No. DGE-0718124, as well as the Office of Naval Research grant N00014-12-C-0158, the Bill and Melinda Gates Foundation grant OPP1031488, the Hewlett Foundation grant 2012-8161, Adobe, and Microsoft.

REFERENCES

1. Ainsworth, S. E., Bibby, P. A., and Wood, D. J. Analysing the costs and benefits of multi-representational learning environments. *Learning with multiple representations* (1998), 120–134.
2. Andersen, E., Liu, Y.-E., Snider, R., Szeto, R., Cooper, S., and Popović, Z. On the harmfulness of secondary game objectives. In *FDG* (2011).
3. Andersen, E., Liu, Y.-E., Snider, R., Szeto, R., and Popović, Z. Placing a value on aesthetics in online casual games. In *CHI* (2011).
4. Andersen, E., O'Rourke, E., Liu, Y.-E., Snider, R., Lowdermilk, J., Truong, D., Cooper, S., and Popović, Z. The impact of tutorials on games of varying complexity. In *CHI* (2012).
5. Anderson, J. R., Corbett, A. T., Koedinger, K. R., and Pelletier, R. Cognitive tutors: Lessons learned. *The Journal of the Learning Sciences 4*, 2 (1995), 167–207.
6. Ansari, D. Effects of development and enculturation on number representation in the brain. *Nature Reviews Neuroscience 9*, 4 (2008), 278–291.
7. Arbreton, A. Student goal orientation and help-seeking strategy use.
8. Berman, F., Fox, G., and Hey, A. J. *Grid computing: making the global infrastructure a reality*, vol. 2. Wiley. com, 2003.
9. BrainPOP. http://www.brainpop.com/.
10. Buhrmester, M., Kwang, T., and Gosling, S. D. Amazon's mechanical turk: A new source of inexpensive, yet high-quality, data? *Perspectives on Psychological Science 6*, 1 (2011), 3–5.
11. Churchill, Gilbert A., J. A paradigm for developing better measures of marketing constructs. *Journal of Marketing Research 16*, 1 (1979), pp. 64–73.
12. Efron, B., and Tibshirani, R. *An introduction to the bootstrap*, vol. 57. CRC press, 1993.
13. Gagatsis, A., and Elia, I. The effects of different modes of representations on mathematical problem solving. In *IGPME*, vol. 2 (2004), 447–454.
14. Hastings, W. K. Monte carlo sampling methods using markov chains and their applications. *Biometrika 57*, 1 (1970), 97–109.
15. Henrich, J., Heine, S. J., and Norenzayan, A. The weirdest people in the world. *Behavioral and Brain Sciences 33*, 2-3 (2010), 61–83.
16. Hume, G., Michael, J., Rovick, A., and Evens, M. Hinting as a tactic in one-on-one tutoring. *Journal of the Learning Sciences 5*, 1 (1996), 23–49.
17. King, R. D., Rowland, J., Oliver, S. G., Young, M., Aubrey, W., Byrne, E., Liakata, M., Markham, M., Pir, P., Soldatova, L. N., Sparkes, A., Whelan, K. E., and Clare, A. The automation of science. *Science 324*, 5923 (2009), 85–89.
18. Kittur, A., Chi, E. H., and Suh, B. Crowdsourcing user studies with mechanical turk. In *CHI* (2008).
19. Kohavi, R., Crook, T., Longbotham, R., Frasca, B., Henne, R., Ferres, J. L., and Melamed, T. Online experimentation at microsoft. In *Third Workshop on Data Mining Case Studies and Practice Prize* (2009).
20. Kohavi, R., Henne, R. M., and Sommerfield, D. Practical guide to controlled experiments on the web: listen to your customers not to the hippo. In *KDD* (2007).
21. Langley, P. *Scientific discovery: Computational explorations of the creative processes*. MIT press, 1987.
22. Larson, C. N. Locating proper fractions on number lines: Effect of length and equivalence. *School Science and Mathematics 80*, 5 (1980), 423–428.
23. Lee, Y., Buchanan, B., and Aronis, J. Knowledge-based learning in exploratory science: Learning rules to predict rodent carcinogenicity. *Machine Learning 30*, 2-3 (1998), 217–240.
24. Lesh, R., Post, T., and Behr, M. Representations and translations among representations in mathematics learning and problem solving. *Problems of representation in the teaching and learning of mathematics* (1987), 33–40.
25. Li, L., Chu, W., Langford, J., and Schapire, R. E. A contextual-bandit approach to personalized news article recommendation. In *Proceedings of the 19th International Conference on World Wide Web*, WWW '10, ACM (New York, NY, USA, 2010), 661–670.
26. Lomas, D., Patel, K., Forlizzi, J. L., and Koedinger, K. R. Optimizing challenge in an educational game using large-scale design experiments. In *CHI* (2013).
27. Moss, J., and Case, R. Developing children's understanding of the rational numbers: A new model and an experimental curriculum. *Journal for Research in Mathematics Education 30*, 2 (1999), pp. 122–147.
28. Quinlan, J. R. *C4. 5: programs for machine learning*, vol. 1. Morgan kaufmann, 1993.
29. Rau, M. A., Aleven, V., and Rummel, N. Intelligent tutoring systems with multiple representations and self-explanation prompts support learning of fractions. In *AIED* (2009).
30. Siegler, R. S., Thompson, C. A., and Schneider, M. An integrated theory of whole number and fractions development. *Cognitive Psychology 62*, 4.
31. Sierpinska, A. On understanding the notion of function. *The concept of function: Aspects of epistemology and pedagogy 25* (1992), 23–58.
32. Singh, K., and Xie, M. Bootstrap: A statistical method, 2008.
33. Stamper, J. C., Lomas, D., Ching, D., Ritter, S., Koedinger, K. R., and Steinhart, J. The rise of the super experiment. In *EDM* (2012), 196–200.

Spending Real Money: Purchasing Patterns of Virtual Goods in an Online Social Game

Donghee Yvette Wohn
Northwestern University
2240 Campus Drive, #2115
Evanston, IL 60208
yvettewohn@gmail.com

ABSTRACT
Researchers have found that "social" factors contribute to purchasing intentions of virtual goods in an online social game, but little is known about *actual* purchasing behavior. Study 1 examined the relationship between social factors and virtual goods purchasing patterns using large scale data obtained by server logs of an online social game. Exchange of virtual goods and number of friends increased the likelihood of spending real money compared to no spending. Among those who did spend real money, giving virtual goods to others was the strongest factor associated with the amount of spending. Study 2 examined purchasing patterns of players who spent real money: high real-money spenders were buying items for visual customization while low spenders were buying consumable items necessary to sustain playing the game.

Author Keywords
social game; virtual goods; big data; consumer behavior; social exchange; customization; e-commerce

ACM Classification Keywords
K.4.4. Electronic Commerce

General Terms
Human Factors; Design; Measurement.

INTRODUCTION
Purchasing virtual goods is increasingly becoming a common feature of virtual worlds and online games [3,9,16,24]. The global virtual goods market has been rapidly growing: one market report estimated that the global market value of virtual goods was $14.8 billion in 2012 and would increase at an annual growth rate of 12.5% to 2016 [6]. Moreover, sales of virtual goods—once seen only in massively multiplayer online games (MMOs) and social network sites based in Eastern Asia—are now becoming a common feature of social network sites in the United States and Europe, especially in social network game (SNG) applications [9,24].

Despite the prevalence of virtual good purchasing behavior in online games, there is little academic research that has examined *actual* virtual good purchasing behavior. Part of this is due to the fact that game companies do not share such information. Thus much of the research on virtual goods has been conducted from the player's (consumer's) perspective, and examining intention to purchase rather than actual behavior. Study 1 examines the relationship between behaviors captured by log data and players' actual spending behavior. This data-driven approach takes observable variables that are informed, but not exact proxies of psychological variables studied in prior research, providing a model that can be easily replicated in other game contexts. Study 2 examines spending patterns based on different types of virtual goods. By differentiating the spending behaviors of low and high real-money spenders, the results inform targeted design of virtual goods.

Understanding the factors that are associated with purchasing patterns of virtual goods is important to the HCI community because game companies are increasingly relying on sales of these goods as their main source of revenue. Traditionally, online games were subscription-based, requiring the player to pay a fixed amount every month or year to play the game. Now, newer games employ a free-to-play model, in which the game is free, but players can purchase virtual goods with real money to enhance their playing experience, whether that is to make their virtual character or space more visually pleasing, or to accelerate their progress.

Since most people play without purchasing anything, game designers must appeal to the pocket of the paying player without turning away the non-paying player in order to retain a large number of players. This poses a design challenge because the system must attract and retain two different types of players. This distinction is important because, as mentioned above, traditional online games with a single business model (subscription-based) were designed under the assumption of a uniform user.

Virtual Goods in Online Games
Most early online games—especially those popular in the Western hemisphere—did not require players to use real

CHI 2014, April 26 - May 01 2014, Toronto, ON, Canada

http://dx.doi.org/10.1145/2556288.2557074

money to buy virtual goods. For example, World of Warcraft had an internal economic system that required players to buy virtual goods with currency that could only be earned within the game. However, more game companies are now changing their revenue models to incorporate sales of virtual goods. In the context of online multiplayer games, which include MMOs and SNGs, one popular genre of virtual goods is that related to visual customization. These goods include clothing, hairstyles, and accessories for virtual characters (avatars), as well as furniture and home décor for virtual space. Another genre of virtual goods is related to game mechanisms, such as experience points. In many cases, these two genres are not mutually exclusive. For example, a piece of clothing may be aesthetically pleasing and be related to a game mechanism, such as enhancing certain skills.

Most often these virtual goods can be purchased from an in-game "store" that is run by the game company. Maple Story is a game that is a successful example of using virtual goods sales as a source of revenue: players can buy clothing for their avatars, digital pets, and items that are required to take care of the pet.

Not all virtual goods are purely eye candy. Farmville, for example, a SNG that lets players build a virtual farm, enables players to purchase virtual goods that will expedite their progress in the game. Kart Rider, an online social racing game, allows players to purchase virtual goods that will help themselves (such as a speed booster) or hinder others (such as a bomb).

Study Context: Puppy Red

This paper presents two studies that examine virtual goods purchasing behavior in the context of Puppy Red, a 3D social game service based in South Korea. Puppy Red is similar to social media services such as Webkins or Club Penguin and targets female players. Each player is provided with an empty island, which they can decorate with virtual goods.

Launched in 2003, the game has 5 million registered players and provides more than 15,000 different virtual items that range from avatar clothing and home decorations to pet accessories. Players create and dress up their own avatar and decorate their house. They can visit other players' houses, congregate in a public space, and engage in mini games or tasks within the game—such as picking apples—which will give them virtual currency in the form of beans.

Players can then use these beans to purchase clothes and animations for their avatar, furniture and decorations for their house, and food and accessories for their pets among others. The game operates on a free-to-play business model. There is no membership fee, but players have the option to purchase coins with real money. Coins are not necessary to play the game, but can be used to purchase special items. Some items can only be purchased with coins, while others can be purchased with both beans and coins.

ECONOMIC BEHAVIOR IN ONLINE GAMES

Much of the research on economic behavior in online games has been conducted in the context of MMOs such as World of Warcraft and Everquest. Players of MMOs can visually represent themselves through a virtual character, or avatar, and traverse in an immersive environment that resembles a physical space. The economy within the game emerges out of the activities of the aggregate behavior of individuals through complex mechanisms of individual and interactive behavior. Scholars found that activities that the behaviors players engage in within the game draw parallels to "real world" activities that economists call production, trade, consumption, and labor [17].

Although there have been studies on macro-economic trends in online games [3,4], there has been relatively little literature on micro-economic behavior, such as consumer behavior, that incorporates behavioral data. Studies on micro-economic behavior—in particular, purchasing behavior of players—have been limited by the difficulty in acquiring large enough samples. Only a small proportion of players actually spend real money to buy virtual goods in online games, which makes it extremely difficult for academics to identify the players who spend real money, even if there are tens of thousands of people who fall into this category. Industry statistics have shown that about 34 percent of people who played MMOs bought virtual goods and 23 percent bought goods in a social network game [23]. Even for Nexon, a company that is considered a successful case in terms of profiting from virtual goods sales—it operates at a 35 percent margin—only 90 percent of the people who play its games actually pay actual money [2].

The literature on virtual goods purchases mainly comes from two perspectives. The first is a player perspective, examining psychological motivations and decision processes that are involved in the purchase of virtual goods. In the context of MMOs, Nojima [20] looked at the relationship between players' motivations and revenue models, finding that certain motivations—such as immersion—are correlated with higher levels of spending. Lehdonvirta [17] identified several different motivations unique for explaining virtual goods purchases: advancement in status, competitive advantage, keeping up with other players, experiencing new content, customization, and self-expression. He found that players' attitudes towards virtual good purchases are correlated with their motivations. Researchers have also tested the technology acceptance model of how perceived usefulness and attitude leads to purchase intention of virtual goods through player surveys [5,18].

The second perspective taken by scholars studying virtual good purchases is a pragmatic one that focuses more on technical affordances or design factors that affect purchasing. For example, Oh and Ryu [21] looked at how game mechanics can be used to create and sustain demand for virtual goods. Hamari and Lehdonvirta [12] identified several mechanics that drive the desirability of virtual goods and then looked at how different types of game mechanics based on segmentation of players can generate repeated purchases or create settings for additional virtual goods.

These two perspectives are useful in understanding general purchasing behavior in an online environment, but this study will focus on the player perspective. In an online game that is inherently social in nature, interpersonal and group dynamics could strongly influence people's behaviors. The following section thus examines the social factors involved in purchasing behavior.

STUDY 1: SOCIAL FACTORS ASSOCIATED WITH SPENDING

Literature points to three social factors that have been empirically examined in the context of virtual goods purchases: social motivations, social presence, and social influence,

Social motivations have been found to be associated with spending. In the context of SNGs, researchers [24] found asked adult Facebook game players about whether or not they spent real money to buy virtual cash in the games. They found a significant positive correlation between social motivations (e.g., I play games on Facebook to... "find people like me," "to feel like I belong to a group") and spending. Motivation, however, is something that is difficult to examine with behavioral data, so we were unable to derive any testable hypotheses.

Social presence in a virtual environment has also been found to be positively correlated with purchasing intention [14]. Social presence is the feeling that an individual has that they are with other people in the virtual world [13], or the degree of salience of other people in an interaction [22]. In an experimental study, social presence and social interaction in Second Life were found to be positively related to purchase intention [14]. Social presence was also found to be positively correlated with purchasing intention of virtual goods in studies of Second Life [1] and Habbo Hotel [19].

The relationship between social influence and spending is mixed. Kim et al. [15] surveyed players of Cyworld and Habbo Hotel and, and found that players who had higher desire for online self-presentation were more likely to motivate their purchasing behavior. They explained that this self-presentation desire was driven by social norms [15]. However, although social influence has been hypothesized to predict spending in virtual worlds [10], empirical evidence has not been able to find a direct correlation between social influence and spending behavior in the context of Second life [11].

The above literature suggests that various social factors are correlated with spending. These constructs, however, are primarily psychological, requiring a self-report from the player. What has not been explored, however, is how social behaviors—such as exchange of virtual goods—and network factors—such as number of in-game friends—are associated with real-money spending. These factors do not require administration of a survey, and can be easily examined through log data by the designer. While not exact representations of the psychological constructs discussed above, these elements were selected with theories of social behavior in mind:

RQ1: *Are social factors (number of friends, giving and receiving virtual goods) associated with the likelihood of spending money in the game?*

The above research question examines how much social factors contribute to a player's *likelihood* to spend money in a game. However, do they explain the degree of spending? To our knowledge, consumer behavior literature has not examined this question, as studies have mainly looked at purchasing behavior as a dichotomous variable. If one were to look at spending as a continuous variable (i.e., how much money a player spends), would social factors still account for who spends more? We thus have an open research question that examines the relationship between social factors and the amount of real money spent by the player.

RQ2: *Are social factors (number of friends, giving and receiving virtual goods) associated with how much money a player spends in the game?*

One demographic factor to consider, especially in the context of this particular game, is age. Because the game caters to both under-age players and adults—and adults have more money to spend—these demographic groups should be examined separately.

RQ3: *Are there different spending patterns between adults and minors?*

Study 1 Methods

Tri-D provided access to three months of log data from Puppy Red. The company had been keeping track of all players' actions within the game for the entire seven years it had been in service, but did not provide all the data due to proprietary reasons. The log data comprised of demographic, behavioral and network variables that were recorded by the game server. Demographic data was based on the player's national ID information in their game account, which indicates birth date and gender. Behavioral data was captured when the individual performed a visible activity (i.e., clicking) that required a response from the main computer. This included the aggregate number of virtual items that were sent to other people by the player, aggregate number of virtual items received by the player, aggregate number of beans (virtual currency) collected by the player, and amount of real money (coins) spent in the game. The server also recorded when the player logged in and out, thus enabling us to calculate how frequently a player visits and how much time they spend on the site. The data also showed how many in-game connections, or "friends" the player has. Much like the concept of Facebook Friends, this was not an indicator of true friendship, but a signal that two players mutually agreed to officially connect with each other within the game.

Puppy Red players were mostly female (76.4%), aged nine to 85 (M=20.91, SD=14.927). However, age information was based on the account information, which may not reflect their actual age. The game required players to enter their government-issued ID number, which confirms their date of birth—this is a common form of authorization used in South Korea. Players who are 18 years old or younger must receive authorization from their parents through a mobile age-authentication system, a system commonly used in South Korea. Underage players who went through this authentication process would have their actual age reflected in their game profile. However, it is very probable that parents create the account and have their children use it.

Due to the nature of how age data was collected, it could be that some children used their parent's or grandparent's ID, but it would be unlikely for an adult to use a child's ID. Thus any effects of age seen in adult data should be interpreted with caution, but age in the data for children's behavior may be a more valid measure.

Membership length ranged from less than one year up to seven years. The lower quartile of players had been on the site for less than a year while the upper quartile consisted of players who had been on the site for four or more years.

Analysis was confined to players who accessed the site at least once during the past three months, as there were many who had been inactive during that timeframe. We defined these players as "active players" (N=264,934). Among this population, 69,269 players (26.1% of total active players) had spent real money at least once during the three-month period. We defined this sub-sample (N=69,269) of active players who had spent real money as "active spenders." Active spenders were mostly female (79.7%), aged nine to 53 (M=22.75, SD=14.77).

Study 1 Results

Modeling likelihood of spending real money

To identify the factors that contribute to spending, a Binominal Logistic Regression was conducted on the data of all active players. The dependent variable measured spending of real money, with "not spending any money" coded as 0 and "spending money" coded as 1. Independent variables included the two social interaction factors (giving and receiving virtual goods), and number of friends. Game-related variables included membership length, frequency of visits, time spent on the site, and number of harvested beans, as someone who is more invested in the game may be more inclined to spend more real money. Lastly, individual factors such as gender and age were included into the model.

Two models were created to see the added effect of social factors. The first model contained demographic and game-play variables (time spent, number of visits), while the second model added social variables (number of friends, virtual goods given and received). Both models were significant with a Hosmer & Lemeshow Goodness-of-Fit Test of the models' chi-square statistic (p<.001). Model 1 explained 78.5% of spending correctly (Nagelkerke R^2=.24) while Model 2 explained 83.7% of spending correctly (Nagelkerke R^2=.41). Adding the social variables made a significant change (p<.001) in the R^2. Variance Inflation factors (< 2.8) indicated that colinearity was not an issue.

As can be seen in Table 1, all coefficients are statistically significant, which is expected with such a large sample size,

	Model 1			Model 2		
Variables	Beta	Wald	Exp	Beta	Wald	Exp
Constant	-1.45**	16929.37	.23	-1.94**	16736.40	.14
Age	-.01**	2196.56	.99	-.01**	1660.26	1.10
Gender (Male)	-.04**	13.36	.96	-.09**	43.95	.55
No. of visits	.03**	2630.40	1.03	.02**	1066.02	1.02
Time spent in game	.00**	854.55	1.00	.00**	266.11	1.00
No. of beans	.00**	3004.64	1.00	.00**	655.93	1.00
Virtual goods given				.62**	7507.63	1.86
Virtual goods received				.04**	320.36	1.04
No. of friends				.02**	14137.55	1.02
Model Chi-square [df]	45,402.98 [5] (p<.001)			87,931.68[8] (p<.001)		
Block Chi-square [df]				40,869.38[3] (p<.001)		
% Correct Predictions	78.5			83.7		
Nagelkerke R square	.24			.41		

Dependent variable: spending/not spending, **p<.001

Table 1: Modeling likelihood of spending money among active players (N=264,934)

Variables	Model 1 Beta	Wald	Exp	Model 2 Beta	Wald	Exp
Constant	-1.45**	16929.37	.23	-2.56**	3480.44	.08
Age	.05**	287.37	1.01	.05**	272.81	1.05
Gender (Male)	-.08**	16.68	.92	.04*	4.35	1.02
No. of visits	.03**	1100.15	1.03	.02**	503.88	1.02
Time spent in game	.00**	537.62	1.00	.00**	186.53	1.00
No. of beans	.00**	1846.84	1.00	.00**	427.03	1.00
Virtual goods given				.57**	3493.38	1.76
Virtual goods received				.03**	102.12	1.03
No. of friends				.02**	8164.58	1.02
Model Chi-square [df]	22541.29 [5] ($p<.001$)			43501.05[8] ($p<.001$)		
Block Chi-square [df]				20959.75[3] ($p<.001$)		
% Correct Predictions	75.6			80.1		
Nagelkerke R square	.22			.39		

Dependent variable: spending/not spending, $*p<.05$, $**p<.001$

Table 2: Modeling likelihood of spending money among active players under age 19 (*N*=138,166)

thus interpretation of the coefficients should be focused more on the effect size, which can be seen through the odds ratio. Giving virtual goods (β=.62, odds ratio=1.86) to other players and receiving virtual goods (β=.04, odds ratio=1.04) from other players were positively related with likelihood to spend real money. Each additional friend increased the likelihood of spending real money by 1.02 (β=.02, odds ratio=1.02). Comparing spenders with non-spenders, a post-hoc T-test comparison of means indicated that spenders (M=46.09, SD=55.71) had more friends than non-spenders (M=7.34, SD=22.76), $t(264{,}932)=253.656$, $p<.001$.

In terms of demographic variables, younger players were more likely to spend real money and females were more likely to spend real money than males. However, variables related to game play had a minimum impact on the likelihood to spend. In particular, time spent playing the game and virtual currency earned within the game almost had no effect at all on the likelihood to spend.

As it could be that adults simply have more money to spend that children and teens, the same analysis was conducted only looking at the subset of the sample that was under the age of 19, which is the legal age in South Korea. The results in regards to the effect of social interaction variables were very similar (Table 2), showing a very strong positive relationship between giving virtual goods to others and the likelihood of spending real money. Age, however, had the opposite effect; among players who were under 19, older players were more likely to spend real money.

Explaining amount of money spent

As noted above, only 26% of the population had spent real money in the game. The range of money spent during the three-month period was 455 won (about \$.40) to 662,500 won (\$587.15) with the mean at 3,160 won (\$2.80). To identify the factors that contribute to how much more money is spent among those who spend money, a negative binomial regression was executed on just the population of active spenders, looking at the amount of real money spent as a dependent variable. Somewhat similar to an OLS regression, a negative binomial allows a continuous count variable to be the dependent variable, but is used when the dependent variable is over-dispersed (standard deviation is higher than the mean) and the distribution is skewed. In the case of this data, the skewness was 11; skewness under 2 is considered to be a normal distribution.

Independent variables were the same as the ones used for the first three hypotheses; these included social factors such as number of friends, giving and receiving virtual goods; as well as time spent on the site, number of visits, number of harvested beans, gender, and age.

The first model was for active spenders who were 19 years old and older (Table 3). The mean age for players in this group was 51 years. The regression model was significant (Likelihood ratio Chi-square= 2,620.77, df= 8, $p<.001$). Again, due to the large sample, results should be interpreted by looking at the effect size in addition to statistical significance. Social interaction factors were a positive indicator of spending, although they were extremely weak. Giving virtual goods to other players was positively associated with the amount of real money spent. Receiving virtual goods from other players and the number of friends had a very small effect close to zero.

Game variables had a weaker effect in explaining how much real money a player spends in the game. Spending more time in the game or playing more frequently had next to no relationship to amount spent. Also, having a large amount of virtual currency was not statistically related to spending more real money. Gender was insignificant and there was almost no effect of age.

	Beta	SE	Sig.
(Intercept)	9.38	.02	.000
Age	-.004	.00	.000
Gender (male)	.008	.00	.580
Time spent in game	1.99E-9	2.35E-10	.000
No. of visits	-.001	.00	.020
No. of beans	-1.77E-8	2.99E-8	.554
No. of Friends	.001	.00	.000
Virtual goods given	.056	.00	.000
Virtual goods received	.003	.00	.000

Table 3: Factors explaining amount of spending among active spenders 19 and older (*N*= 28,608)

The second model (Table 4) examined active spenders under 19 years of age, Likelihood ratio Chi-square= 2,015.45, df= 8, $p<.001$. Older players and females were more likely to spend more real money. Similar to the adult data, the amount of time spent in the game was weakly linked with using real money to buy virtual goods. Different from the adult data was a significant effect of gender: males were more likely to spend real money. Giving virtual goods was positively associated with amount of spending; receiving virtual goods was very weakly associated with amount of spending.

	Beta	SE	Sig.
(Intercept)	8.72	.03	.000
Age	.025	.00	.000
Gender (male)	.131	.02	.000
Time spent in game	1.18E-9	2.05E-10	.000
No. of visits	.001	.00	.036
No. of beans	9.60E-8	2.99E-8	.001
No. of Friends	.001	.00	.000
Virtual goods given	.053	.00	.000
Virtual goods received	.002	.00	.000

Table 4: Factors explaining amount of spending among active spenders under 19 (*N*= 40,661)

STUDY 2: PURCHASING PATTERNS: HIGH SPENDERS VS LOW SPENDERS

Study 1 looked at factors that contribute to likelihood of spending real money and factors that contribute to more spending of real money. However, the data did not provide any insights into what types of virtual goods were being purchased. The purpose of Study 2 was therefore to examine what kind of items players are purchasing and what currencies (real or virtual?) they are using to purchase those items because game had dual currencies: one that can be earned through play (beans), and another that can be purchased with real money (coins).

In the context of Puppy Red, it was difficult to compare the value of these two currencies because virtual currency requires time and effort inside of the game, while real money requires time and effort outside of the game. For certain currencies—such as gold in World of Warcraft or Linden dollars in Second Life—there are exchange systems where people can exchange real money for virtual currency. The famous "gold-farms" of China are a wonderful example of how people who want to save time purchase virtual currency from others [7]. However, not all items in the game can be bought with real money; in World of Warcraft, certain items can only be obtained by fulfilling a quest, and these items are not transferrable to other players. Similarly, in simulation games such as Farmville, there are items that can only be bought with real money, regardless of how much time one spends on the game. This raised additional questions about the relationship between players' behaviors in regards to the two different types of currency in an environment where the two currencies are not exchangeable:

RQ4: *What is the relationship between currency purchased with real money and currency earned through play?*

RQ5: *What are sales patterns of items by type of virtual good?*

RQ6: *What are the purchase patterns of high spenders vs. low spenders?*

Study 2 Method

Two separate data sets were obtained from Puppy Red: an item sales log and transactional data of players. The item sales log was an inventory list of all items and their sales during a one-month period, which included how many items were sold, what currency was used to purchase the item, and the price of the item. It did not contain any information on who the buyers were. The player transaction data was based on a random sample of 1,295 players who spent real money during the past three months as of the time of data collection. The game operator provided a log showing what items they bought and what type of currency (real or virtual) they used to purchase items.

First, categories of items were identified taking into consideration the existing taxonomy of items in the game's virtual shops and Lehdonvirta's [17] categorization of virtual goods. There were three main categories: avatar-oriented items, space-oriented items, and play-oriented items. Avatar-oriented items served the purpose of decorating or customizing the look of the avatar. An avatar is a virtual character that often represents the player and is created according to the player's preferences [8]. Items in this category included clothing items, beauty items—which can give variations on the avatar's hair and facial features—and accessories such as bags, jewelry, and gloves.

Space-oriented items were those that could be used for household decoration or landscaping. In the game, a humble house with bare furnishings and an empty island are provided to each player by default. Players can expand or renovate their space by purchasing items. Like avatar-oriented items, space-oriented items were all about visual customization. They include home décor such as wallpaper and furniture, and landscaping items such as ponds and bridges. Although some expensive items served utilitarian functions—for example, a ferris wheel could provide avatars a ride—but most items were merely decorative. Play-oriented items were perishable items that would assist raising pets or caring for crops. The consumable aspect made play-oriented items different from avatar or space-oriented items, because they diminish with use.

Study 2 Results

RQ4 inquired into the relationship between spending and the two types of virtual currencies. Results indicated that increased membership length generally increased the average amount of virtual currency that was being spent, suggesting that players become more efficacious in how to earn virtual currency. For real money, spending increased for players up to four years, then declined. This may be reflecting an exit pattern, or lack of new items that can be purchased with real money. However, given that the system generates new items every week, it is more likely to be the former explanation than the latter.

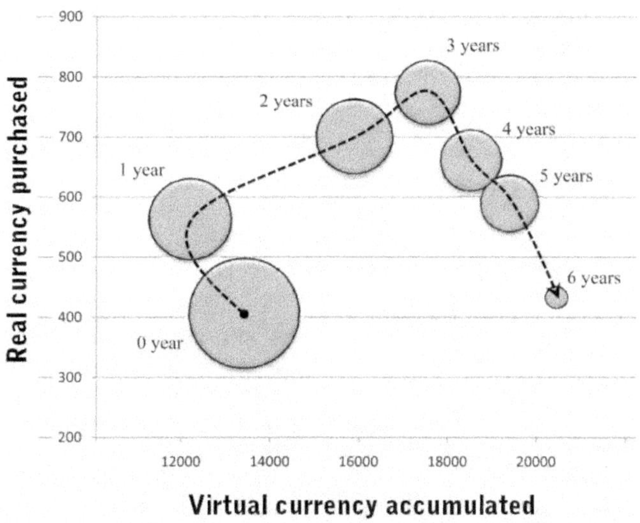

Figure 1: Relationship between amount of virtual currency accumulated (X-axis) and real currency purchased (Y-axis) based on membership duration

To see the relationship between the two different types of virtual currency, players were divided into seven groups in one-year intervals depending on how long they had been a member. As indicated in Figure 1, "0 year" indicates the player group whose membership period is less than 1 year and "6 years" are players who were on the site for more than six years but under seven years .The bubble size represents the number of players belonging to each group and the values of X- and Y-axis respectively indicate the groups' average amount of collected beans and coins bought with real money per month.

The "0 year" group has the largest player pool, but has the least amount of coins, indicating that newest players spend the least real money. The number of coins increases and peaks for players who were on the site for three or more years but less than four years, but subsequently declines.

To explore RQ4, item sales were aggregated within each category and the frequencies were converted to percentages (see Table 5). A price index for each category was calculated by dividing the average price of items affiliated to each category by the average price of total items. The price index for avatar items was 1.20, indicating that the price of avatar items are 1.20 times the average price of all items.

As mentioned above, Puppy Red uses two kinds of currency in parallel: coins (real money) and beans (virtual currency). There were noticeable differences regarding how people spent these different currencies. In terms of the quantity of items bought with real money, players spent most real money on avatar-oriented items (60.6%), followed by space-oriented items (26.8%) and play-oriented items (12.6%). However, the order was reverse with items bought using virtual currency (beans): players spent most beans on play-oriented (45.8%) items, followed by space-oriented (41.7%) and avatar-oriented (12.5%) items. This suggested that players are spending real money on items that enable visual customization, while items used for game mechanics were purchased with beans, which can be obtained through play. Play-oriented items required continuous replenishment, which may be why players were more inclined to purchase those items with beans.

Item category	Sales (Units)		Sales (Price)		Price index
	Beans	Coins	Beans	Coins	
Avatar	12.5	60.6	36.5	65.1	1.20
Space	41.7	26.8	41.3	28.0	0.78
Play	45.8	12.6	22.1	6.8	1.08
Total	100.0	100.0	100.0	100.0	

Table 5: Percentage of virtual goods spending patterns by category

This item-buying pattern is similar to that of the real world in the sense that people first satisfy basic needs to sustain living with hard-earned money and then allocate their extra resource into luxuries later. Players spent their beans to buy the play-oriented items in terms of necessities for sustaining services (such as feeding their pet), and then used real money to pursue the higher hierarchy of needs such as cosmetic products or cars.

Once virtual items are designed and released, the marginal cost for reproducing these items is close to zero for the characteristics of distribution of digital contents, therefore selling expensive items means higher profit to the service operator. The price index is a relative measure of how expensive the item is in comparison to other items. The price index of each item category in Table 5 shows that the price of play-oriented items (consumable items used to take care of pets or plants) is cheaper than avatar-related items. This indicated that despite the fact that "rearing" items were relatively less expensive to buy with coins compared to other items, players still chose to buy those items with beans.

To examine RQ5, players were divided into three groups based on their level of spending real money. These three groups were labeled "high spenders," "low spenders," and "non-spenders." Players who never spent real money were defined as non-spenders. Non-spenders did not spend real money to buy virtual items; they only used beans.

Spenders were players who had logged into the game at least once in the past three months and had spent real money at least once during that time. In this population, players had spent real money on virtual items ranging from $.05 to $210, with the mean amount at $9. High and low spenders in this player sample were defined by sorting the players by the amount they spent during the sampled period and then drawing a boundary that equates the aggregate sum of money spent between the high and low spenders; in other words, 89.7% (low spenders) cumulatively spent as much as the other 10.3% (high spenders).

Item-buying patterns between these two groups were examined by calculating the percentage of real money spent on each category of items then testing the significance of the difference between the two groups through means comparison T-tests. Low spenders spent 48.6% of their real money on play-oriented items mainly for taking care of their pets, followed by avatar (28.6%) and space (22.8%) items. In contrast, high spenders preferred to spend their money on items to customize their avatar (48.4%) and space (44.8%) rather than consumable play-oriented items (6.8%). The differences between these two groups were significant at the $p<.001$ level for all three item categories.

DESIGN IMPLICATIONS

In Study 1, log data of a 3D social game was used to examine factors that contribute to spending of real money. Using two regression models, results indicated that engaging in more social interaction, such as giving virtual goods, and having more in-game friends increased the likelihood of spending. However, social factors played a weaker role in terms of how much money players were spending.

Study 2 investigated what types of virtual items are sold and how the item-purchase patterns differ according to the extent of spending. High spenders mostly buy decorative avatar-oriented and space-oriented items using real money, while low spenders mostly buy consumable play-oriented items with hard-earned virtual currency.

The Effect of Social Factors

Time spent on site and earning virtual currency on the site had no effect on the likelihood to spend real money. This suggests that merely playing a lot on these sites doesn't encourage spending, but social playing does. In particular, giving virtual goods to other players was the strongest factor of all independent variables that contributed to whether or not the player spent real money. This suggests that game operators, when marketing their virtual goods to players, should focus on creating advertisements, promotional campaigns, or in-game quests that appeal to "gifting" behavior.

For example, Puppy Red sends out a weekly newsletter via email to its players informing them of the new items added to the virtual shop. Instead of presenting a static list of items, adding a persuasive message, such as "your friend may appreciate this new item" or framing certain items as a "perfect housewarming gift" may be a way to encourage players to purchase the item to give to their friend. Since giving virtual goods to others increases the likelihood that someone will spend real money, game designers may also want to provide reminders to players about their friends or even suggest reciprocity when the player receives a virtual item from another player.

Having more friends in the game also increased the likelihood of spending real money; this implies that game designers can devise in-game quests that encourage connecting with other people, or build more communication channels within the game to facilitate social interaction.

Social factors were strongly associated with whether or not an individual spent real money. However, they were not very strong in explaining *how much* money people spent. This suggests that different design strategies are required when trying to get people to spend more. Even with the weak associative value, social interaction factors can still contribute to significant increase in revenue when looking at large-scale populations. Of note, game-related factors, such as time spent and frequency of play, were not salient at all in explaining the extent of spending real money.

For both adults and minors, giving virtual goods to others in the game was the strongest positive factor associated with how much the player spends in the game. Time was a very weak factor. Time, which is often seen as a proxy of engagement, is strongly correlated to habit strength [25], so for game designers, efforts that are aimed at keeping players engaged in the game may not directly relate to their revenue. This may be particularly important for free-to-play games, because this indicates that players do not have to spend more time in the game to be spending money. Thus keeping the players engaged in the site in a short timeframe becomes just as important, if not more, than attracting players into the game. Constantly introducing new virtual goods that are related to aesthetics may be a way to retain high spenders.

People who had more friends were more likely to spend money than people who had less friends, but the added number of friends did not explain increased spending among spenders. These results suggest that the quality, not quantity, of social relationships within the site could affect why players spend more. Creating more features in the game that allow players to strengthen those strong ties could lead to more spending, while features in the game that allow players to build weak ties could encourage players who do not spend anything to spend at least something.

Age Differences in Spending

Among younger players, more virtual currency earned in the game was weakly but positively associated with real money spent in the game. This may seem counter intuitive, because if you had a lot of virtual currency, why would you want to use real money? However, the dual currency system of Puppy Red may work in their favor—as mentioned earlier, some virtual goods in Puppy Red can only be bought with real money. Thus one currency does not necessarily decimate the value of the other, and people who are more likely to purchase virtual items show the same pattern using both virtual and real currency. This suggests that having a dual currency system where the two currencies are not interchangeable can be advantageous to the game designer because it encourages the player to spend both time in the game and real money. However, this pattern was not present among older players. For players who were 19 years old or older, the amount of virtual currency they had in the game did not have any relation with the amount of real money they spent. This may be because the value of the time required to acquire virtual currency is greater for adults. Further exploration is needed to see why there are differences between adults and children, and if there are differences between adults who are playing for their own pleasure and adults who are playing because of a child.

High spenders vs. Low Spenders

The results of study 2 showed that players who spend a lot of real money purchase items that have decorative but no functional value, while players who spend a little money purchase items that are more consumable. This mirrors purchasing behavior of luxury items in the physical world and supports research on MMOs [3] that have found parallels between in-game economy and real-world economies.

From a marketing perspective, these results provide insights about how different marketing strategies should be used for these different sub groups. Currently, most gaming companies send out bulk newsletters, or have the same introductory screen when players log into the game. If the companies are able to identify what type of spender the player is, they will be able to deliver a more effective marketing strategy.

From a design perspective, it may be advantageous to keep the price range for consumable items narrow, since low spenders are the ones who are purchasing those items, and increase the price range for avatar and space-related items. Creating visually unique items, or limited-edition items may increase the appeal for high spenders.

Limitations

This study is based on log data of a social game service, which makes behavioral data more accurate than self-reported behaviors via surveys. However, this methodology has limitations in that it does not explain why the players are engaging in such behavior. Future studies should try to merge both player perception through surveys and pair it with behavioral data, which would provide more insight into why players engage in certain spending patterns or what elements of social interaction influence different types of spending.

The game service is based in South Korea where broadband penetration rate is high, youth have high Internet usage, and micro-payment services are widespread [21]. This may make our results difficult to generalize to all countries or cultures, especially as some studies have found that cultural differences in game play are associated with virtual goods spending [16]. However, these purchasing patterns at the very least may generalize to other collectivist cultures, and could be valuable to countries that are beginning to see rapid developments in micro-transaction revenue models involving virtual goods. These results may not generalize to all games, especially those games that are action-oriented or have more linear narrative-driven game play. However, findings may apply to the understanding behavior of players in games that have strong mechanisms for visual customization (e.g., avatar decoration, virtual space decoration) and caretaking (e.g., raising a pet, growing crops).

CONCLUSION

As selling virtual items become a major revenue source for social network and social game service operators, this study takes a big data analysis approach to factors that are associated with virtual goods purchasing patterns. This study tested variables that were informed by theory-based empirical studies, and while prior studies mainly examined behavioral intention, this study was able to examine actual behavior.

By examining actual behavior, this study found that social factors play different roles in terms of explaining an individual's likelihood of spending and the extent of their spending. Most consumer theories of purchasing do not make the distinction between these two concepts. This behavioral data suggests that the socio-psychological mechanisms involved in purchasing intention are different from those that are involved in how much money an individual spends, and informs development of future theories.

The results of this study also inform game design by identifying how different types of players based on their spending patterns. Study 1 suggests that game elements that enhance social presence, such as virtual goods exchange and having more in-game friends, are important in distinguishing real money spenders vs. non-spenders. When it comes to looking within spenders, however, Study 2 shows that there are major differences in purchasing patterns between high spenders and low spenders. Understanding player types from the perspective of how much they spend will allow for different strategies, especially in the design of different types of virtual goods and different types of marketing strategies of those goods.

ACKNOWLEDGMENTS

Thanks to staff at TriD and EK Na for providing access to log data.

REFERENCES

1. Animesh, A., Pinsonneault, A., Yang, S.-B., and Oh, W. An odyssey into virtual worlds: exploring the impacts of technological and spatial environments on intention to purchase virtual products. *MIS Quarterly 35*, 3 (2011), 789–810.
2. Campbell, C. Free-to-play's the future but not as we know it, says former Zynga and EA COO. *Polygon*, 2013. http://www.polygon.com/2013/9/11/4717122/free-to-plays-the-future-but-not-as-we-know-it.
3. Castronova, E., Williams, D., Shen, C., et al. As real as real? Macroeconomic behavior in a large-scale virtual world. *New Media & Society 11*, (2009), 685–707.
4. Castronova, E. *Synthetic worlds: The business and culture of online games*. University of Chicago Press, Chicago, IL, 2005.
5. Chung, D. Something for nothing: understanding purchasing behaviors in social virtual environments. *Cyberpsychology & behavior 8*, 6 (2005), 538–54.
6. Companies and Markets. *Global virtual goods market 2012-2016*. 2012.
7. Dibbell, J. The Life of the Chinese Gold Farmer. *The New York Times*, 2007.
8. Ducheneaut, N., Wen, M., Yee, N., and Wadley, G. Body and mind: A study of avatar personalization in three virtual worlds. In *Proc. CHI 2009*, (2009), 1151–60.
9. Greengard, S. Social games, virtual goods. *Commmunications of the ACM 54 (April)*, (2011), 19–21.
10. Guo, Y. and Barnes, S. Why people buy virtual items in virtual worlds with real money. *The Database for Advances in Information Systems 38*, (2007), 69–74.
11. Guo, Y. and Barnes, S. Purchase behavior in virtual worlds: An empirical investigation in Second Life. *Information & Management 48*, 7 (2011), 303–312.
12. Hamari, J. and Lehdonvirta, V. Game design as marketing: How game mechanics create demand for virtual goods. *International Journal of Business Science and Applied Management 5*, (2010), 14–29.
13. Heeter, C. Being there: The subjective experience of presence. *Presence 1*, (1992), 262–271.
14. Jin, S.-A.A. Modality effects in Second Life: The mediating role of social presence and the moderating role of product involvement. *CyberPsychology & Behavior 12*, (2009), 717–721.
15. Kim, H.-W., Chan, H.C., and Kankanhalli, A. What Motivates People to Purchase Digital Items on Virtual Community Websites? The Desire for Online Self-Presentation. *Information Systems Research 23*, 4 (2012), 1232–1245.
16. Lee, Y.-H. and Wohn, D.Y. Are there cultural differences in how we play? Examining cultural effects on playing social network games. *Computers in Human Behavior 28*, 4 (2012), 1307–1314.
17. Lehdonvirta, V. Virtual item sales as a revenue model: Identifying attributes that drive purchase decisions. *Electronic Commerce Research 9*, (2009), 97–113.
18. Mantymaki, M. and Salo, J. Teenagers in social virtual worlds: Continuous use and purchasing behavior in Habbo Hotel. *Computers in Human Behavior 27*, (2011), 2088–97.
19. Mäntymäki, M. and Salo, J. Teenagers in social virtual worlds: Continuous use and purchasing behavior in Habbo Hotel. *Computers in Human Behavior 27*, 6 (2011), 2088–2097.
20. Nojima, M. Pricing models and motivations for MMO play. In *Proc. DiGRA 2007*, (2007), 672–81.
21. Oh, G. and Ryu, T. Game design on item-selling based payment model in Korean online games. In *Proc. DiGRA 2007*, (2007), 651–657.
22. Short, J., Williams, E., and Christie, B. *The social psychology of telecommunications*. John Wiley & Sons, London, UK, 1976.
23. Takahashi, D. Free-to-play, virtual goods business models gain steam in games. *VentureBeat*, 2009.
24. Wohn, D.Y. and Lee, Y.-H. Players of Facebook Games and How They Play. *Entertainment Computing 4*, 3 (2013), 178–171.
25. Wohn, D.Y. The role of habit in social network game play. *Communication Research Reports 29*, 1 (2012), 74–79.

CADament: A Gamified Multiplayer Software Tutorial System

Wei Li, Tovi Grossman, and George Fitzmaurice
Autodesk Research, Toronto, Ontario, Canada
firstname.lastname@Autodesk.com

ABSTRACT
We present CADament, a gamified multiplayer tutorial system for learning AutoCAD. Compared with existing gamified software tutorial systems, CADament generates engaging learning experience through competitions. We investigate two variations of our game, where over-the-shoulder learning was simulated by providing viewports into other player's screens. We introduce an empirical lab study methodology where participants compete with one another, and we study knowledge transfer effects by tracking the migration of strategies between players during the study session. Our study shows that CADament has an advantage over pre-authored tutorials for improving learners' performance, increasing motivation, and stimulating knowledge transfer.

ACM Classification:
H5.2 [Information interfaces and presentation]: User Interfaces. - Graphical user interfaces.

Keywords:
Game; Multiplayer; Tutorial; Learning.

INTRODUCTION
Learning to use feature-rich software applications is a notoriously difficult task for new users. As such, there has been a long line of research on understanding and improving the learnability of software. As a result, numerous mechanisms for providing assistance have been proposed, such as online help, interactive tutorials, and video-based assistance.

Unfortunately, the process of learning to use such traditional mechanisms can be tedious, and research has shown users are resistant to relying on help systems [2]. To address this limitation, gamified approaches have been recently explored, in an effort to increase the engagement level of learning [13, 20, 23, 32]. Such approaches rely on design elements that are typical in games, such as feedback, guidance, time pressure, and rewards.

CHI 2014, April 26 - May 01 2014, Toronto, ON, Canada

http://dx.doi.org/10.1145/2556288.2556954

However, existing gamified approaches for software learning have not embraced the benefits of social and crowd-sourced learning solutions. In particular, there have been a number of studies that have shown the benefit of "over-the-shoulder" learning environments, where users can observe and acquire skills directly from their peers or user community [36]. Since many existing gamified approaches to software learning have been "single-player", they miss out on this potential benefit of social learning.

In this paper, we present CADament a new multiplayer online game system for learning to use AutoCAD, a feature rich software application for creating mechanical and architecture design. CADament is designed to be an online game that any number of players can join. All active players compete head-to-head, attempting to complete a series of short time-coordinated levels, faster than an opponent they have been matched up against. Two variations of this game are explored – one in which players see a split screen of their opponent's video while completing the levels, and one in which players review their opponents' video after each level has been completed.

By adding a multiplayer element, players have the opportunity for not only independent learning in an gamified environment, but also have the opportunity of acquiring new skills by observing the workflows and strategies of their opponents. Furthermore, the multi-player environment adds an additional competitive aspect to the gaming environment, potentially increasing a player's motivation to learn and improve.

After describing our system, we present an empirical evaluation of our system. In this study, we compare the two variations of our game, with a baseline help condition, where participants complete levels independently. We propose a user group study methodology where participants compete with one another, and we study knowledge transfer effects by tracking the migration of strategies between players during the study session. Our study shows that CADament has an advantage over pre-authored tutorials for improving learners' performance and stimulating knowledge transfer.

RELATED WORK
In this section, we review previous research in software learning, tutorial systems and gamified tutorials.

Software Learning

Since the early days of HCI research, software learnability has been an important research topic [12, 26]. Early results include Carrol et al.'s investigations of the learnability of word processing tools [2, 3, 24]. A full review of research on software learnability is beyond the scope of this article. We direct the reader to a recent survey on this topic [18].

Also particularly relevant to our work is the research of Twidale and colleagues on "over-the-shoulder" learning [36]. Such work states that although some people like to learn a system on their own, many prefer learning in a more social context. As such learning how to use a computer application is often a collaborative activity. Our multiplayer game system is designed upon this premise.

Software Tutorial Systems

Early work in software help indicated the importance of minimalist and task-centered help systems [2]. This is because of an active user's production bias [2, 3, 35], where a user does not want to take time away from the task to focus on learning about the system. Although static online help supports quick access, it can be difficult to communicate complex graphical operations through text.

Animated assistance strategies have been explored [5, 17, 25, 28, 29]. There has been some debate over the benefits of animated or video based assistance. Earlier work argued that such materials enforce a passive learning process, force users to work at the pace of the video, and may be detrimental to long term learning. However, recent work, such as ToolClips [17] and MixT [29], have shown clear benefits of using video based assistance for certain graphical operations. Pause-and-Play also provides a unique way to deliver video content, automatically pacing the video based on user progress [29]. Ambient Help [25] mimics an over-the-shoulder learning environment by looping videos of other user's workflows on a secondary ambient display. By automatically loading videos related to the user's current task, it was found that users discovered new concepts and workflows from the videos.

Alternatively, interactive tutorial systems can be integrated within the software application itself [1, 14, 20, 29, 31]. Stencils-based tutorials [20] overlay a stencil over a software application with a hole to click-through and guide a user to perform the correct steps. Fernquist et al. suggest that tutorial experiences should be as compelling as possible, so that users stay engaged [14]. The concept of flow [8] provides a general guideline for creating an engaging user's state of "optimal experience". Qualifying factors for achieving flow include: perceptions of clear goals, immediate feedback, and matched skills and challenges [4]. Lafreniere et al. [21] integrate video based demonstrations in interactive tutorials, where pre-recorded videos are generated by the user community.

Gamified Tutorials for Software Applications

Gamification is the use of design elements, which are characteristic for games, in non-game contexts [11]. Gamified systems have been used in many domains including educations [16, 30, 33]. The level of engagement that tutorials provide could potentially be increased by integrating gaming elements. To create engaging learning experiences, several games were designed for learning software, including the Microsoft Ribbon Hero [32], Adobe LevelUp [20], Jigsaw [13], and GamiCAD [23].

The above systems were primarily designed for single player user experiences, so their competition level is limited. Also, because the content of those games are pre-designed, the learning experience is not flexible and adaptive. When the player successfully covers the content, the educational experience has come to an end. Here, we proposed a general approach to apply multiplayer gamification in learning software applications. By providing a view into other player's strategies, users are continuously exposed to new content that they can adopt.

Because learning often happens in social environments, such as classrooms and schools, the multiplayer environments of modern games show promising applications in the educational domain [9, 15, 34]. However few games have been developed to support an over-the-shoulder learning experience. For example, multiplayer games for teaching math may not show exactly how other students do the addition tasks.

Recent research work has also investigated the educational benefits of 1-on-1 competitive games such as chess and StarCraft II [15]. However, in such games, one experienced player can only be directly challenged by another player in the same round. CADament leverages video streaming and broadcasting technology, and it allows one player to have many challengers.

Software Skill Contests

CAD drafting contests[1] are popular events among CAD software learners. Usually, competitors need to draw specified views of a given drawing problem, or model small objects within a designated time period, and submit their drawings or models using emails or a website. Informal CAD drafting contests often happen in CAD forums, where users challenge each other by posting and completing drawing and modeling tasks. Similarly, image editing contests, such as Layer Tennis[2], exist in the professional designer communities. The Photoshop contest is played through sequential alternating editing of an image using email or a web server. A common problem of those software contests is that the usage skills and techniques are difficult to be transferred to other learners, as players and spectators cannot observer their opponent's workflows.

[1] http://www.idea-online.org/competitions.html
2 http://layertennis.com/

In CADament, videos are recorded and live streamed from software users working on the exact same tasks, then videos are integrated in a competitive multiplayer gaming environment. We hope that the synchronized and context-based videos can improve the user's over-the-shoulder learning experience, while multi-player gaming creates a feeling of excitement and engagement.

MULTIPLAYER GAMIFICATION ELEMENTS

The emergence of the world-wide-web has made multi-player games extremely popular. In general, the game elements in single player games are also available in multiplayer games, such as an epic background story, rewards, time pressure, feedback and clear goals [23]. But multiplayer games have several unique elements.

Competition with Real players

Previous research into the experience of video games has shown the importance of the role of challenge in the engaging game experience [7, 19]. A game that allows for diverse people to play diverse ways is often more interesting and rewarding. Single player games challenge players through pre-designed levels and time pressure. Players are motivated by rewards and stimulus and play against pre-programmed challenges and/or AI-controlled opponents, which often lack the flexibility and ingenuity of regular human thinking.

Multiplayer games introduce different challenges in direct general competitions and head-to-head competitions. General competitions are based on the individual's score or relative standing [1]. Head-to-head competitions exist in many types of multiplayer games, such as racing, sports tournaments and MMORPG (massively multiplayer online role-playing game). In those games, people have different personal styles when playing against each other.

Sharing Game Play Experience

Sharing is a core element of multiplayer games, where players often share the same task space, common goals and challenges, unified feedback and performance metrics (such as leaderboards). Many multiplayer games setup real-time interactive communications among players to help them observe their opponents' actions and provide an immersive experience. This actually encourages learning by watching other players who exhibit different strategies.

For example, in Need for Speed World, a popular massively multiplayer racing game, drivers all share the same racing tracks and real time graphical effects during a race. Drivers not only see other cars' current positions and rankings in a map, they can also observe real time actions and techniques used by other players. In some other games, player's actions are shared after or between tasks. In Wordament, a successful word spelling game, players can only see other players' performance and answers during the breaks between tournaments. Some games have both forms of sharing. For instance, many racing games also provide recorded game replay for players to review their performance in the last racing event.

Pacing

The pace of video games is the rate at which players experience new challenges. It can be maintained at appropriate levels throughout the game [27], so that a game's design applies pressure but does not frustrate the player. Player fatigue can be also minimized by varying pacing during gameplay [10].

Multiplayer games often do not have a "pause key" as in a single player-game, since the progress of the game is synchronized among all players. For example, MMORPG games, such as World of Warcraft, never stop within a virtual persistent game world and continue to exist and evolve while a player is offline and away from the game. Other multiplayer games, such as Wordament, generate rapidly-short-iterating rounds. Slow periods follow intense ones and forced "time-outs". This type of lightweight design can offer opportunities to socialize, catch your breath and anticipate things to come. It often achieves a balance between competitive and enjoyable experiences while softening the impact of defeat. Rapidly-short-iterating rounds also assist the knowledge transfer by learning skills from many different players and help new users practice the same tasks multiple times.

DESIGN GOALS

In this section, we define four design goals, to guide the design of our multi-player software learning game.

Engaging

In terms of engagement, we aim to provide an environment that users will enjoy and be motivated to learn the software and improve their skill level. Competitive game play, including both head-to-head competition and general competition, helps learners strive to be better and creates a feeling of excitement and increases engagement level.

Knowledge Transfer

In general, we hope that the system can assist transferring knowledge among users. Over-the-shoulder learning [25, 36] is informal, spontaneous help – a given interaction that is often used by people to learn from their colleagues in their workplace. We create a similar environment to show other players' solutions within the context of the game.

Low Cost

Authoring tutorials for software applications is a time consuming process. We wish to create a system that can help experienced users easily share their knowledge and skills to novice users and lower the cost of authoring learning content. In multiplayer online games, every competitor is implicitly incentivized to be a content producer and create learning experience for other players.

Flexible

We hope the learning content and interactions are rooted in tasks that are relevant to the learner's needs and interests. We also want to balance between competitive and enjoyable experiences. The learning experience should match a learner's skill level to create an "optimal experience" or flow [8].

CADAMENT SYSTEM DESIGN

We design CADament, a competitive multiplayer online game for learning AutoCAD, which is a widely used software application for both 2D and 3D drafting and design. We choose AutoCAD for this project because 1) AutoCAD represents a large number of software applications with a direct manipulation interface; and 2) it is considered challenging to learn for novices [18]. A car racing theme was used.

Game Structure

CADament runs continuously in 30-seconds rounds, with a 30 second break between rounds. Players can join the game anytime and participant in the immediate next round with all online players. In each round, players solve a drafting task using AutoCAD. Each task, T_n, repeats in 3 consecutive rounds, with a break B in between each round, before being replaced by the a new task T_{n+1} (Figure 1). This rapidly-iterating round format should help the players learn skills from different challengers and allow new users to practice the same tasks multiple times.

T_n	B	T_n	B	T_n	B	T_{n+1}	B

Figure 1. Players have 30 seconds to complete the round's task (T_n) followed by a 30 second break (B).

Tasks

The tasks in the game were designed to help players to continuously increase their skills through progressive disclosure. For our prototype, we developed a set of tasks for the TRIM tool. An actual deployment could iterate through tasks for many different tools, or contain tasks requiring multiple tools. Tasks gradually increased in difficulty, and eventually looped back to the initial task.

Player Progress Feedback

CADament does not enforce a specific workflow, or a single approach that all players must follow. Instead, CADament compares each player's drawing with the pre-generated final result every time a command is executed, and reports the percentage of the task that has been completed. For example, if the task requires the user to trim 4 lines, then after trimming 3 lines a player's progress would be 75%.

Screen Sharing Game Modes

In our design we leverage a sharing mechanism to assist software learning and knowledge transfer. By sharing the screen of online players, we can create a mixed experience of head-to-head competition and over-the-shoulder learning. We explored two different game modes to allow players to see each other's screens, *Record & Replay (Replay)* and *Split Screen (Split).*

In *Record & Replay*, the players' screens are recorded during the competition. Players can watch their opponent's recorded video during the breaks between rounds. This allows users to focus on the skills used by their opponents.

In S*plit Screen*, players can see their opponent's screen in real-time while completing the tasks. The real-time sharing simulates a head-to-head competition experience, similar to many online multi-player games.

Both designs can simulate an over-the-shoulder learning experience. In the Replay mode, learning happens during the slower pace of the break period, and the player can focus entirely on completing the level during the round. In the Split mode, users have the opportunity to learn from their opponents strategies right away in the same round, instead of waiting for the next break.

User Interface During Rounds

During the rounds, each player competes against another online player to complete a drafting task using AutoCAD. At the beginning of each round, the initial drawing data will be automatically opened in AutoCAD.

In *Split* mode, every player produces a live broadcast of their AutoCAD screen area. A player sees their opponent's screen next to their own (Figure 2). Through the live streaming video, the player is able to observe her/his opponent's detailed actions. An overlay indicates the opponent's mouse behaviors and keystrokes (Figure 2).

In *Replay* mode, the opponent's live video stream is not displayed but is replaced by a blank image. Additionally, the players' application screen videos are saved and played during the 30 seconds break period.

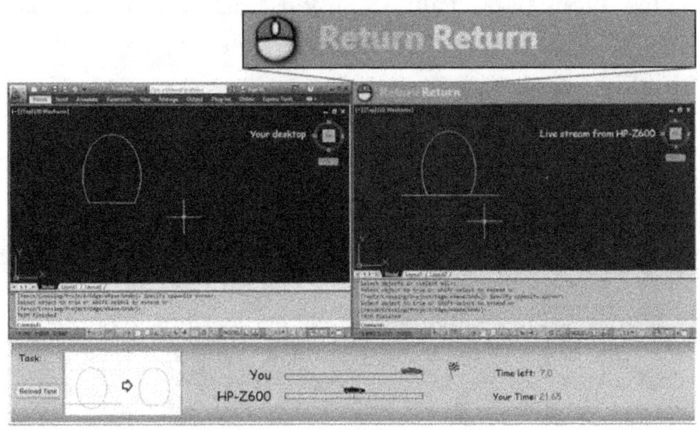

Figure 2. Competition mode. *Split* mode has players see their opponent (right side). For *Replay* mode, the region is replaced by a static image. Inset: Mouse/key-stroke visualization bar.

In both game modes, a task bar is also displayed below the main screen (Figure 3). A before-and-after image describes the goal of the current task. A timer starts counting down as soon as the round starts. The players' real time progress is visualized using two progress bars, and a waving checkered flag is displayed once a task is finished.

Figure 3. Task bar of CADament UI.

User Interface During Breaks

Figure 4 shows the view during the breaks between rounds. The performance data of a player and the player's opponent for the previous round are displayed on the left side of the screen. A ribbon is displayed for the winner of the head-to-head match-up. A leaderboard shows the rankings of all players currently competing, sorted first by the task completion percentage and then by speed (Figure 4). Additionally, in the *Replay* mode, a video player automatically plays the opponent's video after the round on the right (Figure 4A). Users can also replay the opponent's video during the 30 second break time by clicking the 'replay video' button.

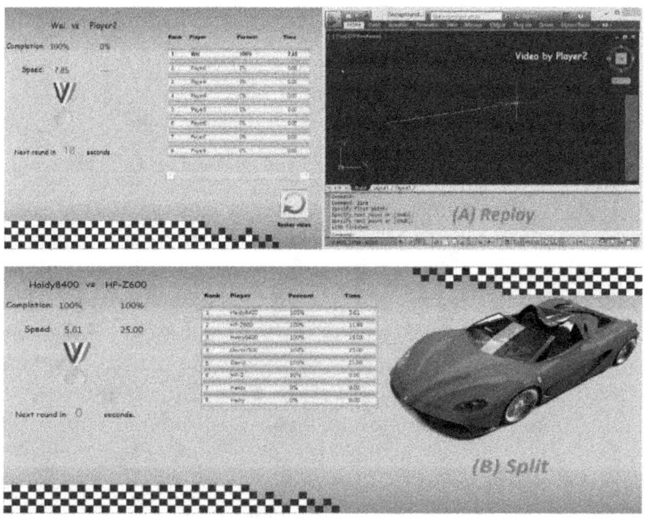

Figure 4 Screen of (A) *Replay* and (B) *Split* during breaks.

Matchmaking

At the beginning of each round, CADament matches each player with an opponent. The mapping from player to opponent is not one-to-one. That is, if player A is matched to player B, player B is not necessarily matched to Player A. This allows for more flexibility in the matchups. For example, all players (except the leader) could be matched against a player slightly better than themselves. Many-to-one matchups are also possible. For example, all players could be matched against the leader in a single round.

To create a balanced gameplay experience, CADament helps each player find the opponent 1) who can provide useful, diversified skill and knowledge to help the player complete the next task; and 2) whose skill level matches the player's level. In addition to the above requirements, there are two types of situations we try to avoid. First, if everyone plays against the top ranking player, a novice player may feel frustrated if she/he keeps being defeated by the best player. Second, if two novice players are always matched together, they might not learn anything from seeing each other's workflows.

Our matching algorithm is based on the rankings for the immediately preceding round:

1. The leader is matched to the second place player.
2. A player that successfully completed the last task will be matched with the player who was one rank above.
3. A player that did not complete the task will randomly play with one of the players who completed the task.
4. If no player completed the task, everyone will be matched with the player who has the highest task completion percentage.
5. When there are multiple candidate opponents, based on the above rules, the opponent is randomly selected from the candidates.

SYSTEM IMPLEMENTATION

We developed a system framework for our real-time multiplayer game using video sharing. In this framework, game progress controls, game data (tasks, player profiles), video streaming, and player matchmaking are managed using the cloud-based service, Microsoft Azure (Figure 5).

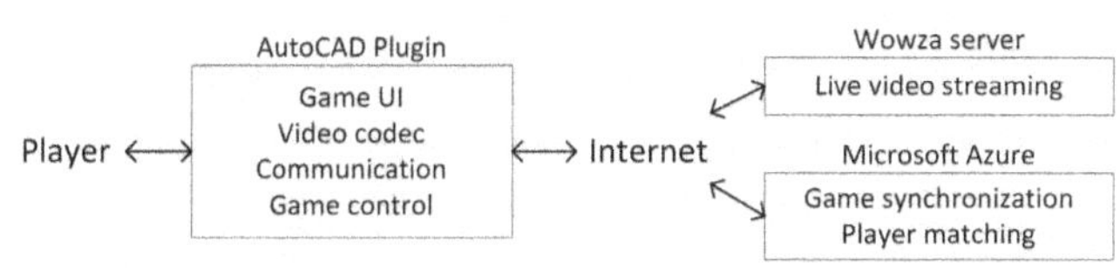

Figure 5. CADament system.

CADament updates a large amount of player's game data frequently in real time and synchronizes the game progress on every client. We used WebSockets (SignalR) in our client-server communication component, which enables high frequency updates from the server to support a real-time gaming experience. For sharing the players' screens and actions, screen captured videos need to be broadcasted over the internet. In the *Split* game mode, the action-viewing delay between one online player's action and the generated video being played at another player's game needs to be within an acceptable range. In order to achieve this goal, we deployed a live video streaming server (Wowza). Videos are encoded at each player's computer in real time, and then "fed" to the streaming (broadcasting) servers. Finally, they are distributed to multiple clients for viewing. We optimized the whole process so that the action-viewing delay is less than 2 seconds in our local lab intranet environment. In the *Replay* game mode, CADament records every player's screen stream to their local computer first, and then starts streaming based on demand when the round ends and an opponent needs to view the video.

USER STUDY

We performed an empirical user study to evaluate the CADament system. In particular, our goal of conducting this study is to answer three main questions: 1) Does our multiplayer software game improve learning, in comparison to single user learning experiences? 2) Which game mode is more effective, *Record & Replay* or *Split Screen*? 3)_What is the nature of knowledge transfer when players of different skill levels compete? To answer these questions, we performed a between-participants study with 3 conditions – one condition for each game mode, and a third baseline condition consisting of a single player tutorial environment.

Participants and Pre-Training

Twenty-four participants (13 female) between the ages of 19 and 30 were recruited via online postings in two universities. None of them had used AutoCAD. All participants played video games occasionally. Five of them play multiplayer online games regularly. One participant reported not playing any multiplayer video games at all.To conduct the study, we divide the 24 participants into 3 groups of 8, with each group being assigned to one of the conditions (Figure 6). For each group, we randomly choose 4 of them to serve as "trained" users, and spent 15 minutes to teach them how to use the TRIM tool. This allowed us to simulate an environment where both novices and experienced users were participating, introducing knowledge into the gaming environment.

The TRIM tool works by selecting a set of "cutting edges" and then selecting a set of lines to trim, at the point which they intersect a cutting edge. The order of steps which must be performed can be difficult for a new user to master, and there are many shortcuts which could be used to improve efficiency with the tool. As such, it serves as a good tool to use within a learning study [23].

To further understand the effects of knowledge transfer, we gave the trained participants two additional "tips" which we could reliably track the usage of throughout the study. The trained participants were split into two pairs. Pair A was taught Tip #1 and pair B was taught Tip #2. The two tips are typically exhibited by expert users, and can help users finish trimming tasks efficiently, but may not be immediately obvious to novices:

Tip #1 (Crossing), users can select multiple objects to trim by dragging the mouse over the drawing area.

Tip #2 (Select all), users can press the ENTER key and select all objects as cutting edges.

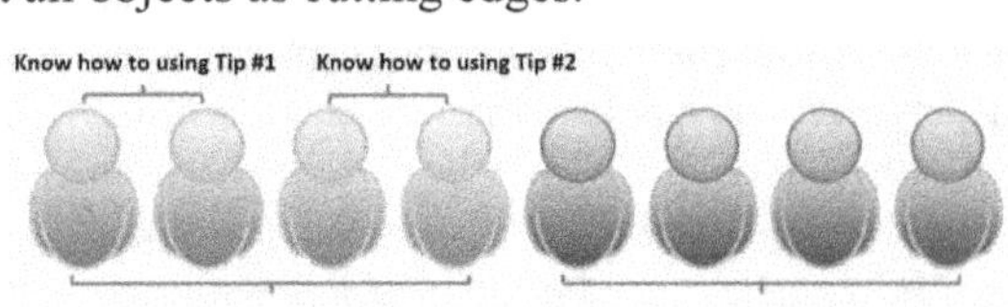

Figure 6. A user group has 4 untrained people and 4 trained people (two trained with tip #1, two trained with tip #2).

Conditions

The first two conditions were based on the two game modes of our system (*Replay* and *Split*). The group of 8 participants assigned to each of these conditions all completed the study together, in an 8-player session. Participants in this session could communicate, but could not verbally share any information related to learning how to complete the tasks.

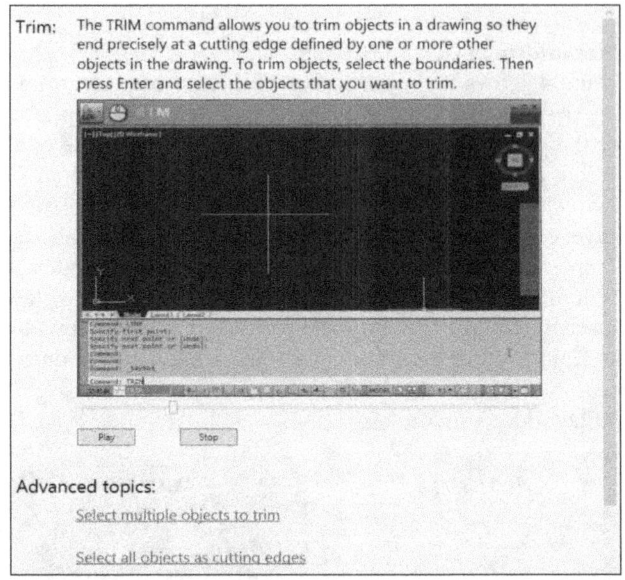

Figure 7. The tutorial webpage used in the *Tutorial* condition.

The third condition (Tutorial), which served as a baseline, was a non-gamified single-user environment. The 8 participants (4 of them were untrained) in this condition completed the study individually at separate times. The Tutorial condition was also performed using the CADament framework, but we removed all of the game elements (graphics, leaderboard, progress bars, racing theme and animations) from the system. Instead of playing with other people, participants in the 3rd condition worked alone on the drafting tasks, and were provided with a tutorial website (Figure 7). The website consisted of a main page that explained how to use the TRIM tool with text and a video. In addition, at the bottom of the page there were two links to pages that explained the two tips. These pages also included both text and a video. As such, the amount of information within the tutorial was equivalent to the information that the trained users were seeded with in the other two conditions. The webpage was available during the 30 second breaks. Similar to the Replay condition, participants could review material after the task, and between rounds. Apparatus

The study was conducted in a room with 8 PCs. A standard mouse and keyboard were connected to each PC. All PCs were connected to a local Gigabit Ethernet and the internet through a regular office connection. All displays had the exact same size (19 inches) and resolution (1600 by 1200). Separating panels were set up to prevent participants watching their neighbors' screens (Figure 8). While this environment is not a true representation of a distributed online environment, it provides a close approximation for the purpose of our research questions.

Figure 8. Study environment.

Procedure and Design

The study consisted of a series of 30-second rounds separated by 30-second breaks, as described in the design of the CADament system. A total of 12 training tasks were designed for the TRIM tool, and were presented in increasing order of difficulty. Each task was repeated for 3 rounds before moving to the next task.

To measure the users' learning progress, we also included a testing task. The same testing task was injected before the first task, and after the fourth, eighth and twelfth task. Each of these four instances was repeated for 3 rounds.

In addition, a warm-up task was included at the beginning of the study. The warm-up task used the LINE tool, and was used to familiarize participants with the study environment. The warm-up task was repeated 3 times.

In total, participants completed 48 training and testing rounds. Since the system ran on a timer, the study took 48 minutes. Participants answered a questionnaire and provided comments after all training rounds and test rounds were finished. The entire session took approximately 75 minutes, including the pre-training time.

Quantitative Results

Testing task times

Figure 9 shows the average completion times across all untrained users in each of the testing tasks. A time of 30s is assigned to rounds which were not completed. By the last task, untrained *Replay* users completed the testing tasks in 6.4 seconds on average, which is less than half of the time for the two other conditions. However, this effect did not reach a level of significance ($F_{2,9} = 3.80$, $p = 0.064$).

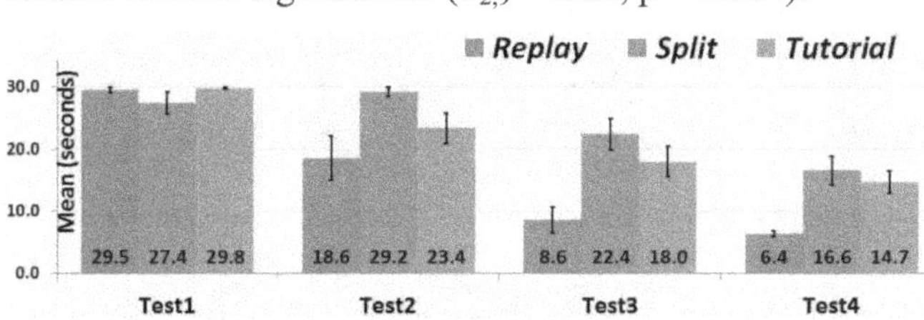

Figure 9. The average test completion times of untrained users in the three conditions.

Figure 10 compares the mean test completion time of all trained and untrained users for Test 4. It is interesting to see that in the *Replay* condition, the untrained users are faster than the trained users. In the other two conditions, the untrained users remained slower than the trained users. The post-hoc pairwise differences here, however, did not reach significance.

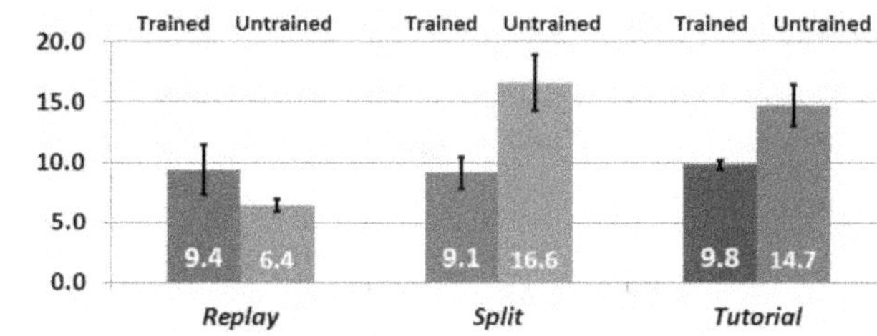

Figure 10. Compare trained and untrained group in Test 4.

Knowledge Transfer

To better explain the testing task results, we wanted to study how knowledge was being transferred from experienced users to novice users. In Figure 11 and Figure 12, we visualize each player's usage and exposure to a tip. Usage of a tip is shown as a solid red dot and exposure to the tip as an outlined dot (the player's opponent used the tip). Each row represents one of the six users who were not initially trained with the tip, and we show the trials in which either event occurs (usage or exposure) until the player has successfully completed three tasks using the tip, which indicates that a player has adopted that tip.

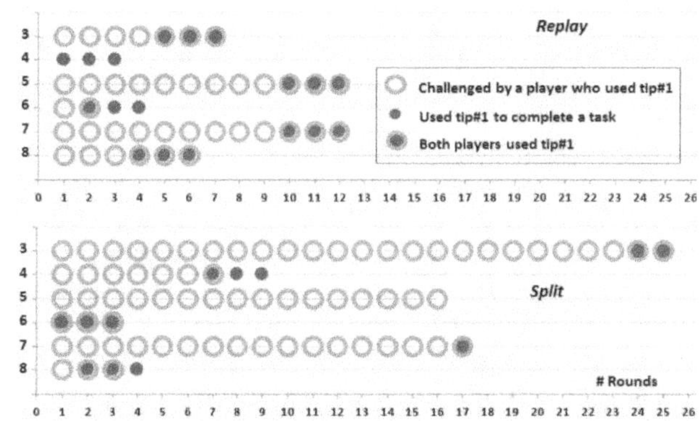

Figure 11. Tip #1 skill adoption progress for *Replay* and *Split*. The top two users were pre-trained, but not on Tip #1.

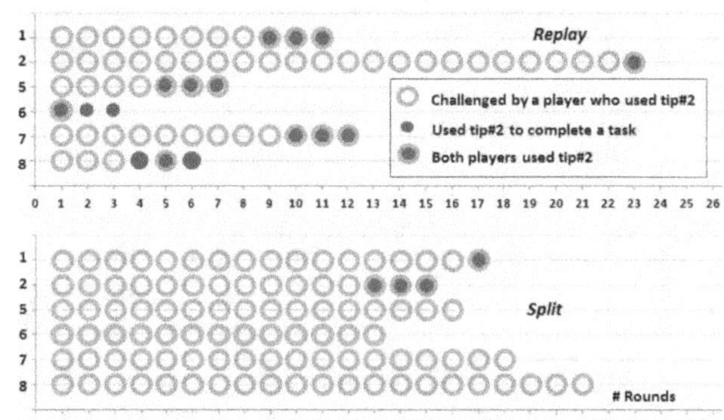

Figure 12. Tip #2 skill adoption progress for *Replay* and *Split*. The top two users were pre-trained, but not on Tip #2.

The top chart in Figure 11 shows that the 6 players in the *Replay* condition, who did not have any training on Tip #1 adopted this skill after an average of 5.7 exposures. Among those 6 participants, 2 participants learned the basic TRIM command during the pre-training (see Figure 6). The bottom chart shows that only 3 out of 6 players in the Split condition adopted Tip #1, after an average of 11.8 exposures. This difference is significant (t=2.05, P=0.043).

The results for Tip #2 are even more drastic. Figure 12 shows that 5 out of 6 players in the *Replay* condition adopted Tip #2, after an average of 9 exposures while in the *Split* condition, only 1 player adopted it, after an average of 16.6 exposures. This difference was also significant (t=-2.05, P=0.033).

Together, this indicates that the *Replay* condition provides for better knowledge transfer. Note that Tip #2 (Select All) seemed to be harder to distinguish from watching a video, which may explain the lower adoption rate.

Task Completion and Tip Usage

We next analyzed the untrained participants' skill progression over the training and testing tasks for the three conditions (*Replay*, *Split* and *Tutorial*). Specifically, we wanted to track and visualize if an untrained participant failed or succeeded to complete the task and if they used one or both tips (Figure 13).

The blue lines in Figure 13 indicate the outcome of a given trial for each untrained participant. Participants either failed, or succeeded using no tips, one tip or two tips, which is represented in the vertical axis. Each marker represents the exhibited behavior of the player's opponent for each round. For the Tutorial condition, a marker shows which webpage was displayed on the screen (main page, tip 1 or tip 2) for a trial. If the marker is filled-in, the user played the video associated with the tutorial content. It can be seen from Figure 13 that by the end of the study, all participants were able to complete the tasks successfully.

More importantly, Figure 13 again indicates that the *Replay* condition is more effective for learning, because every participant in this condition progressed from failing the tasks, to succeeding using both tips. In contrast, no untrained participant in the other two conditions ever completed a trial using both tips.

We can also compare the content that participants were exposed to throughout the study. In both of the multiplayer game conditions, the skill level of the opponents was adapted to each player's skill progress. For example, there are only a few markers under the blue lines in *Replay* and *Split* conditions. This implies that our match making algorithm tends to select more knowledgeable opponents for each player. However, in the self-learning tutorial condition (*Tutorial*), we can see that the tutorial content was very static. It shows that participants rarely accessed their tutorial content even as their skills progressed.

Qualitative Results

We measure perceptions of enjoyment, frustration, and usefulness through a survey given after all training rounds and test rounds were finished.

In the post-study questionnaire, participants were asked to rate 5 questions on a 1(strongly disagree) to 5 (strongly agree) Likert scale. We ran Wilcoxon Signed Ranks tests to compare their answers (Figure 14). The responses to question 1 and 3 were significantly different ($p<0.05$) between *Replay* and *Split*, and the responses to question 1, 3, and 5 were significantly different ($p<0.05$) between *Replay* and *Tutorial.*

The main result is that participants found the Replay system significantly more enjoyable and engaging than both the Split system and the Tutorial system. Although people did not indicate significant difference in terms of frustration level, it was clear that, in the Split condition, learners have difficulty to learn from their opponent's video while they were working on a cognitively demanding task at the same time.

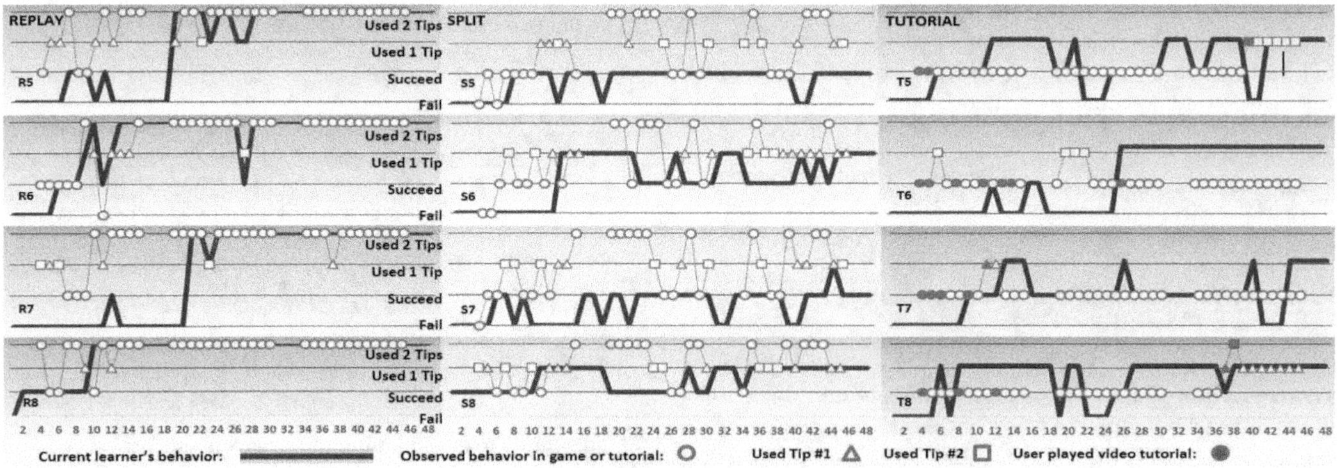

Figure 13. Skill level progression for Replay (left), Split (middle) and Tutorial (right) at 48 testing and training tasks.

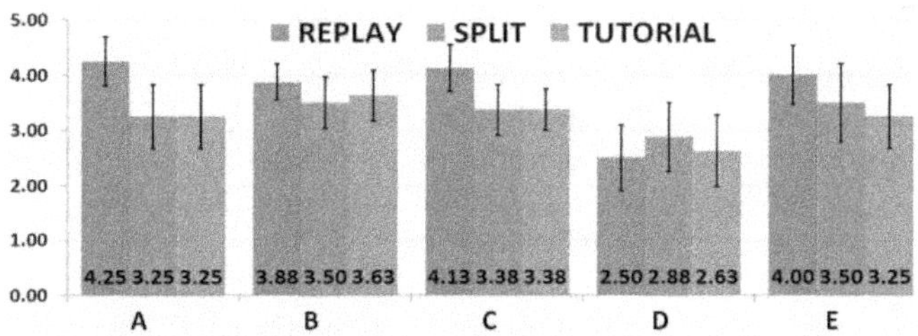

A. I enjoyed using this system.
B. This system is an effective learning tool.
C. The system provides an engaging experience.
D. Completing individual tasks was frustrating.
E. Seeing other people's video (tutorial) is helpful for learning how to use the TRIM tool.

Figure 14. Subjective results form the post study survey.

Comments and Observations

Participants' comments were also gathered inside the questionnaire. In general, many users commented that watching the video replay of how other people performed the same task was an effective way for learning software. One user said:

"...it is not easy to follow the prompt from the cmd (command). After a couple of game rounds, I figured it out by watching the others' replays."

CADament promoted competition. A participant commented:

"I wanted to win. This probably made me look for tricks to try to get ahead."

The design of repeating the same task multiple times did help novice users learn:

"Rationale for repeating tasks multiple times helped me feel more comfortable using the program. [I] was able to gradually improve [my] skill over time."

Participants in the *Split* condition suggested why they felt their performance was hindered:

"A window showing other player's actions is very useful but as the window [video] is real-time, it is hard to watch other player's action as you're doing your own task."

"During your task it is tough to work and see what other people were doing simultaneously."

But it is interesting to note some players developed their own strategy.

"I had watched half before trying the tricks out by myself with the remaining time."

"As there are 3 tries to each task, I watched in the 2nd trial and tried to imitated it during the 3rd if I didn't manage to get it in the first place"

Study participants were not allowed to talk about how to use the TRIM tool. However, they still were allowed to talk. During the study, we observed rich interactions among players. After the first few rounds, some players started to verbally challenge other players, especially when the leaderboard showed up. We summarized these behaviors into three main categories: 1) celebrations; 2) challenges to other players; and 3) comments on player ranking changes. Many online games offer a voice chatting room function. It would be reasonable to expect players to use similar verbal interactions during real online game play. Chatting could also be used as an extra channel for learning.

DISCUSSION AND CONCLUSION

Authoring software tutorials is a time consuming process. CADament presents a method for developing tutorials using multiplayer gamification. As an important advantage over pre-authored tutorials, each player generates a learning experience for the other player. On the other hand, when there is a shortage of experienced players, based on our video sharing design, pre-recorded video could also be used to simulate real players in the head-to-head competitions.

Software users also have difficulty to find tutorials based on their current skill level. It is encouraging that both multiplayer game designs of CADament generate adaptive learning content through match making and competing with other players (see Figure 13).

There are several reasons that performance did not improve as much in the baseline traditional tutorial condition. First, users may have been less motivated to work on improving their performance, since they were not in a competitive environment. Second, users may have seen a video for a tip, but not realized the implications of adopting that tip on their performance. In contrast, users in the two CADament conditions would see the tip by an actual user, and realize immediately that adopting the tip would be necessary to improve performance and stay competitive in the social learning environment.

In this paper we focused on three elements of multiplayer games: competition, sharing, and pacing. In the future, we would like to investigate other important elements in multiplayer online games, such as collaborative task solving and social communities. It would be interesting to further compare CADament to single player gamified tutorials and investigate the effect of skill retention. We also want to generalize the multiplayer gamification attributes to other software applications and higher level learning tasks.

We designed CADament, a multiplayer gamified tutorial system. Compared with existing gamified software tutorial systems, CADament generates engaging learning experiences through competitions. Active players compete head-to-head, attempting to complete a series of short time-coordinated levels. CADament is also a crowd sourcing platform for players to collaboratively produce learning content while they are competitively playing the game. We investigated two game designs, where over-the-shoulder learning was simulated at different pacing stages in the game. Our study shows that the multiplayer game has advantages over pre-authored tutorials for improving learners' performance. Specifically, our analysis and visualization shows that our multiplayer game prompted knowledge transfer.

AKNOWLEDGEMENT
Special thanks to my colleague, Justin Matejka and John Yee, for their continuous support throughout this project.

REFERENCES
1. Bergman, L., Castelli, V., Lau, T., and Oblinger, D. (2005). DocWizards: a system for authoring follow-me documentation wizards. *ACM UIST. 191-200.*
2. Carroll, J. M., and Rosson, M. B. (1987). *Paradox of the active user. Interfacing Thought Cognitive Aspects of Human-Computer Interaction.* MIT Press, 80-111.
3. Carroll, J. M. (1990). *The Nurnberg Funnel: Designing Minimalist Instruction for Practical Computer Skill.* MIT Press.
4. Chen, H., Wigand, R.T. and Nilan, M.S. (1999). Optimal experience of web activities. *Computers in human behavior.* 15(5), 585-608.
5. Chi, P., Ahn, S., Ren, A., Dontcheva, M., Li, W. and Hartmann, B. (2012). MixT: automatic generation of step-by-step mixed media tutorials. ACM UIST. 93-102.
6. Clark, R.E. (1983). Reconsidering research on learning from media. *Review of Educational Research, 53, 4,* 445-459.
7. Cox, A., Cairns, P., Shah, P. and Carroll, M. (2012). Not doing but thinking: the role of challenge in the gaming experience. *ACM CHI* 79-88.
8. Csikszentmihalyi, M. (1988). The flow experience and its significance for human psychology. *Optimal Experience: Psychological Studies of Flow in Consciousness.*15-35.
9. Delwiche, A. (2006). Massively multiplayer online games (MMOs) in the new media classroom. *Educational Technology & Society*, 9 (3), 160-172.
10. Desurvire, H., Caplan, M., and Toth, J.A. (2004). Using heuristics to evaluate the playability of games. In *ACM CHI.* 1509-1512.
11. Deterding, S., and Dixon, D. (2011). From Game Design Elements to Gamefulness: Defining "Gamification". *ACM MindTrek.* 9-15.
12. Dix, A., Finlay, J. E., Abowd, G. D. and Beale, R. (2003). Human Computer Interaction. Prentice-Hall.
13. Dong, T., Dontcheva, M.., Joseph, D., and Karahalios, K., Newman, M. W., Acherman, M. S., (2012). Discovery-based Games for Learning Software, *ACM CHI.* 2083-2086.
14. Fernquist, J., Grossman, T. and Fitzmaurice, G. (2011). Sketch-sketch revolution: an engaging tutorial system for guided sketching and application learning. *ACM UIST.* 373-382.
15. Foster, S., Esper, S. and Griswold, W. (2013). From competition to metacognition: designing diverse, sustainable educational games. In *ACM CHI.* 99-108.
16. Gee, J.P. (2003). *What Video Games Have to Teach Us About Learning and Literacy.* Palgrave Macmillan.
17. Grossman, T., Fitzmaurice, G. (2010). ToolClips: an investigation of contextual video assistance for functionality understanding. *ACM CHI.* 1515-1524.
18. Grossman, T., Fitzmaurice, G. and Attar, R. (2009). A survey of software learnability: metrics, methodologies and guidelines. ACM CHI. 649-658.
19. Juul, J. (2009) Fear of failing? The many meanings of difficulty in video games. The video Game Theory Reader 2. New York: Routledge, 237-252.
20. Kelleher, C. and Pausch, R. (2005). Stencils-based tutorials: design and evaluation. ACM CHI. 541-550.
21. Lafreniere, B., Grossman, T., and Fitzmaurice, G. (2013). Community enhanced tutorials: improving tutorials with multiple demonstrations. ACM CHI. 1779-1788.
22. Levelup, http://success.adobe.com/microsites/levelup
23. Li, W., Grossman, T., and Fitzmaurice, G. (2012). GamiCAD: a gamified tutorial system for first time autocad users. ACM *UIST*, 103-112.
24. Mack, R. L., Lewis, C. H., and CaREPLAYoll, J. M. (1983). Learning to use word processors: problems and prospects. *ACM Trans Inf Syst.* 1, 254-271.
25. Matejka, J., Grossman, T. and Fitzmaurice, G. (2011). Ambient help. *ACM CHI.* 2751-2760.
26. Nielsen, J. (1994). *Usability Engineering.* Morgan Kaufmann.
27. Pagulayan, R., Keeker, K., Wixon, D., Romero, R. and Fuller, T. (2003). User-centered design in games. The HCI Handbook: Fundamentals, Evolving Techniques and Emerging Applications. 883-905.
28. Palmiter, S. and Elkerton, J. (1991). An evaluation of animated demonstrations of learning computer-based tasks. *ACM CHI.* 257-263.
29. Pongnumkul, S., Dontcheva, M., Li, W., Wang, J., Bourdev, L., Avidan, S. and Cohen, M. F. Pause-and-play: automatically linking screencast video tutorials with applications. *ACM UIST.* 135-144.
30. Prensky, M. (2001). *Digital Game-Based Learning.* McGraw-Hill.
31. Ramesh, V., Hsu, C., Agrawala, M. and Hartmann, B. (2011) ShowMeHow: translating user interface instructions between applications. *ACM UIST.* 127-134.
32. RibbonHero, http://www.ribbonhero.com/
33. Rosas, R., Nussbaum, M., Cumsille, P., Marianov, V. etc. (2003) Beyond Nintendo: design and assessment of educational video games for first and second grade students. *Computers& Education,* 40 71–94.
34. Steinkuehler, C. (2007). Massively multiplayer online games & education: an outline of research. *CSCL*, 675-685.
35. Tuck, R. and Olsen, D. R. (1990). Help by Guided Tasks: Utilizing UIMS Knowledge. *ACM CHI.* 71-78.
36. Twidale, M. (2005). Over the Shoulder Learning: Supporting Brief Informal Learning. CSCW, 505-547.
37. Vorderer, P. and Bryant, J. (2006). *Playing Video Games: Motives, Responses, and Consequences (Routledge Communication Series)*, Routledge

Combining Crowdsourcing and Learning to Improve Engagement and Performance

Mira Dontcheva
Adobe Research
San Francisco, CA
mirad@adobe.com

Robert Morris
MIT Media Lab
Cambridge, MA
rmorris@media.mit.edu

Joel Brandt
Adobe Research
San Francisco, CA
joel.brandt@adobe.com

Elizabeth M. Gerber
Northwestern University
Evanston, IL
egerber@northwestern.edu

Figure 1. LevelUp for Photoshop is a crowdsourcing platform that combines learning and creative work. Workers learn photo editing skills, while improving real-world images. Interactive step-by-step tutorials teach workers new techniques and Challenge Rounds filled with images from different requester organizations test worker knowledge. The worker interface is shown on the left; several original and improved images are shown on the right.

ABSTRACT

Crowdsourcing complex creative tasks remains difficult, in part because these tasks require skilled workers. Most crowdsourcing platforms do not help workers acquire the skills necessary to accomplish complex creative tasks. In this paper, we describe a platform that combines learning and crowdsourcing to benefit both the workers and the requesters. Workers gain new skills through interactive step-by-step tutorials and test their knowledge by improving real-world images submitted by requesters. In a series of three deployments spanning two years, we varied the design of our platform to enhance the learning experience and improve the quality of the crowd work. We tested our approach in the context of *LevelUp for Photoshop*, which teaches people how to do basic photograph improvement tasks using Adobe Photoshop. We found that by using our system workers gained new skills and produced high-quality edits for requested images, even if they had little prior experience editing images.

Author Keywords

Crowdsourcing; training; games.

ACM Classification Keywords

H.5.2 User Interfaces: Graphical user interfaces

CHI 2014, April 26–May 1, 2014, Toronto, ON, Canada.
Copyright is held by the owner/author(s). Publication rights licensed to ACM.
ACM 978-1-4503-2473-1/14/04$15.00.
http://dx.doi.org/10.1145/2556288.2557217

INTRODUCTION

Many of today's crowdsourcing marketplaces are characterized by cheap labor and simple tasks that are easy for humans and hard for computers, such as tagging images, transcribing text, and ranking search results. For many reasons, platforms like Amazon's Mechanical Turk (MTurk) are ill-suited for complex creative tasks. While researchers have found some ways to remedy this problem [4, 12], crowdsourced creative work remains somewhat elusive, largely because most online workforces lack the expertise or motivation to produce high quality creative output. Some crowdsourcing marketplaces, such as oDesk[1] or 99designs,[2] offer the possibility of finding more advanced workers to accomplish specialized tasks, but specialized skills typically come at a higher cost.

One solution is to simply train the crowdworkers. Unfortunately, most crowdsourcing platforms are not designed to incorporate nuanced and sophisticated tutorials. As a result, it can be hard to help workers master the skills needed for complex creative work. There are a few exceptions to this status quo. Platforms like Samasource[3] and MobileWorks[4] do in-person training to teach crowdworkers computing skills, ranging from basic computer literacy to more advanced skills like web design. These skills are not only useful for the tasks these companies crowdsource, they are also highly valuable for the workers, most of whom come from the developing

[1] odesk.com
[2] 99designs.com
[3] samasource.com
[4] mobileworks.com

world. However, such training is costly, and more automated training tools are needed to help train workers while they engage in crowdsourced labor.

In our work, we help workers develop skills that are both useful for completing work in the crowdsourcing platform and potentially marketable in other contexts. Specifically, we introduce a platform that is both a training tool and a mechanism for producing crowdsourced results. We look specifically at photograph enhancement tasks as a representative form of creative work requiring complex skills. While it is becoming easier to capture high quality photos and apply premade filters, many enhancements are still beyond the reach of fully automated methods. To apply professional-level improvements, an individual must learn how to use many different tools. Moreover, they must gain skills in basic color theory and composition in order to correct white balance, adjust lighting, and crop images aesthetically.

Our training and crowd work platform, called *LevelUp for Photoshop*, is an interactive tutorial game for the popular photo editing software Adobe Photoshop. Through a series of interactive tutorials, LevelUp for Photoshop teaches people how to edit photographs one step at a time. Each interactive tutorial teaches a specific skill, such as how to crop to improve composition. As the workers complete the tutorials, they are encouraged to test their skills by improving real-world images. These images are submitted by requesters who want to crowdsource photo enhancements, such as the Wildlife Center for Silicon Valley, which needs high-quality photographs for the center website and brochures.

To understand the factors that influence learning outcomes and work quality, we carried out three deployments spanning two years with over ten thousand workers. We found that an interactive tutorial system is effective at teaching both novices and experts new skills. Moreover, with the right guidance, even novices were able to accomplish high-quality edits.

We offer three contributions to human-computer interaction research: First, we propose a crowdsourcing platform design that combines learning and labor to benefit both the workers and the requesters. Second, our studies extend existing research on motivating crowdworkers finding that real-world context drives workers to more closely follow directions. Finally, we offer guidelines for how platform designers can combine learning and crowdsourcing. Using these guidelines, we believe that a broad range of training environments could be transformed into crowdsourcing platforms.

RELATED WORK

In our work, we build on previous techniques used in crowdsourcing creative work [4, 8, 12, 13, 14, 16, 20] and suggest that a learning framework may further enhance creative crowd work. When the task to be crowdsourced is presented in the context of learning new skills, workers should be less likely to cheat or produce poor quality results; doing so not only harms the requester, it also subverts the learning objectives of the worker.

Learning is now increasingly happening online and opportunistically. To address this growing need for in-context help, some researchers have built interactive tutorial systems that lead users through tasks one step at a time [2, 17], while others have used game mechanics to incentivize users to keep learning [15, 7]. Games are not only useful for learning but also for crowdsourcing. There is an entire branch of the gaming community working on "serious games" or "games with a purpose." These are games that have another purpose beyond entertainment. For example, the ESP game was used to tag hundreds of thousands of images to improve image search [19], while FoldIt was used to discover new protein structures, which can be useful in creating better medication [6]. Like traditional crowdsourcing platforms, many games with a purpose ask users to do tasks that are easy for humans and difficult for computers. But beyond learning how to play the game and win, players do not learn skills that they are likely to use outside of the game. Consequently, while workers may enjoy the game experience, they are left with few marketable skills. For instance, FoldIt educates its players about the basics of amino acids and protein folding, but the target task does little to broaden skills that might be of use in biochemistry professions.

While there have been many different approaches to online learning and many different approaches to crowdsourcing complex tasks, to our knowledge, Duolingo[5] is the only project aside from ours that has combined the two and embedded crowdsourcing inside an environment for learning foreign languages. To date, most of Duolingo is devoted to traditional language instruction and the crowdsourcing task is presented as an optional translation feature, where users are offered a chance to test their language skills by helping translate documents from the Web. Since the project is yet to publish results, we don't know how well this approach works for both mastering a foreign language or for creating usable Web translations. In this paper we show evidence that a similar approach works well for learning how to edit images and for improving images supplied by real-world organizations.

SYSTEM OVERVIEW

In three deployments spanning two years, we explored how to combine crowdsourcing and learning. We built a novel platform, LevelUp for Photoshop, to support our exploration. It includes two parts (see Figure 2). First, users learn skills through interactive tutorials presented as "missions" and organized into levels. Second, at the end of each level, users test their skills in challenge rounds filled with images supplied by requester organizations.

Part I: Interactive tutorials

To make the learning experience seamless, we built LevelUp for Photoshop as a panel inside of Adobe Photoshop. All tutorials were created based on lessons from existing instructional books and were ordered by increasing difficulty level. Each tutorial contains a series of steps that guides players through common image improvements, such as removing red eye, straightening, or cutting out objects. To turn a static step-by-step tutorial into an interactive one, we associate each step with a user action, such as selecting a tool, creating a mask, or

[5]duolingo.com

LevelUp for Photoshop Platform

Part I: User learns skills with *interactive tutorials*

Level 1 - Mission 2: Brightness and Contrast

Step 1: Open a dull looking photo. Try our sample image to start.

User:

Step 2: Open the Image> Adjustments>Brightness/Contrast dialog. Click on the "Auto" button to automatically adjust the image. Play with the sliders to adjust brightness and contrast separately.

User:

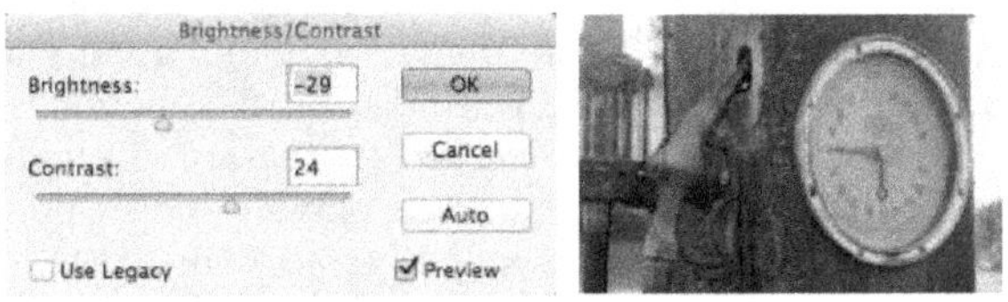

Mission Completed! You have earned 30 points!

Part II: User tests skills in *challenge rounds*

Level 1 - Challenge: Images from four requesters

User:

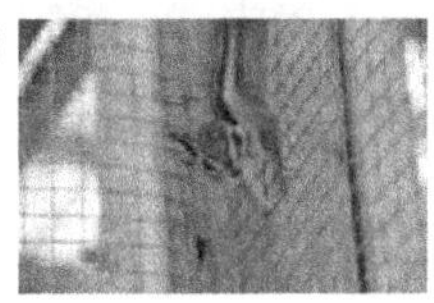

Step 1: This photo needs a lot of work. Start with the following improvements:
- Sharpen the image (25 pts)
- Adjust brightness (25 pts)

User:

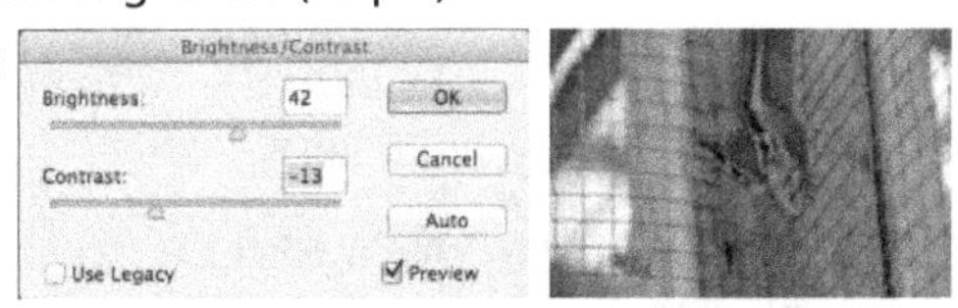

Step 2: Other ideas? Make additional improvements, and we will score the image for more points.

User:

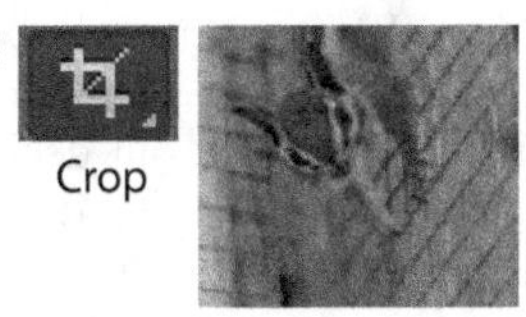

Step 3: Upload the image. Wildlife Center for Silicon Valley may use this image for their website, brochures, and newsletters.

Figure 2. LevelUp for Photoshop combines step-by-step learning with real world practice through interactive tutorials and challenge rounds

saving the image, and when the user performs the action, the tutorial continues to the next step. At any given time, only one step is visible and the user must complete it to see the rest of the tutorial. By displaying one step at a time and progressing only when the user completes the step, the system gives users immediate feedback on their progress. Our system does not offer subjective feedback on the quality of image improvements. That remains future work.

Each tutorial offers sample images, but users can also use their own images. The missions have to be completed in order, but can be repeated at any time. Each mission is associated with points, and the number of points increase with the difficulty of the mission. When they successfully complete missions, users can also earn badges, such as the "Dead-Eye Badge" for removing red eye with a single click per eye and the "Surgeon General Badge" for cutting out an object quickly. Badges such as the "Welcome Back" badge encourage players to come back a different day and continue editing images. The players can share their accomplishments through Facebook and Twitter and can compete against other players through a daily leaderboard available on the LevelUp for Photoshop website where users can also report problems and download the extension.

Part II: Challenge rounds

To support crowdsourcing we created a *challenge round* for each level, which offers images submitted by real-world organizations. We were inspired by the apprenticeship educational model, where students (e.g. aspiring chefs, hair stylists, or doctors) work on real problems as part of their training.

Unlike the interactive tutorials, the challenge round doesn't prescribe a set of steps for improving an image. Instead, it suggests improvements. For example, the challenge round for Level 1 (Challenge 1) suggests adjusting brightness and contrast and sharpening (see Figure 2). Additionally, each challenge round also lets the user improve the image in other ways and offers extra points for additional edits. Once the user edits an image, he is given the option of uploading the image for review by LevelUp for Photoshop staff for additional points and dissemination to requesters.

Requesters

In this paper we focus on the worker experience and thus did not implement a requester interface. However, we envision an interface similar to those of existing photo editing services (Tucia,[6] Photo Editing Company[7]). These interfaces require requesters to specify how their images should be improved. The improvements specified by the requesters can map to the suggestions given to workers in the challenge rounds. Requesters with little image editing knowledge may have difficulty specifying how an image should be improved. In such situations the challenge rounds can offer suggestions that are common across many images, such as adjusting lighting, cropping, and straightening.

Implementation

The LevelUp for Photoshop panel was implemented as an extension to Adobe Photoshop in ActionScript 3.0 using Adobe Extension Builder. To install LevelUp for Photoshop, users have to use the Adobe Extension Manager, which manages installation of extensions for all Adobe products. The panel includes twelve tutorials divided in three levels. To make the tutorials interactive, LevelUp continuously monitors Photoshop events (e.g., which tool was selected, which actions were performed). If a player successfully performs the requested behavior, the panel automatically proceeds to the next task. This gives players instant feedback on their performance.

To simplify deployment we bundled all images with the extension and thus had to limit the number of images available in the challenge rounds. Each challenge round offered the user a choice of editing up to 64 images provided by four different organizations. If extended to dynamically download images after the platform is installed, the challenge rounds can support any number of organizations and images. Uploaded images were stored on Amazon S3. To support a public leaderboard, we used the Nitro game engine.[8]

DEPLOYMENT 1: LEARNING NEW SKILLS.

In our first deployment, we focused on the interactive tutorials and wanted to understand how well they taught our workers new skills. Thus, we removed the challenge rounds and deployed a version of the panel that only included tutorials. While previous work has shown that interactive tutorials are effective [2, 15], we wanted to confirm that our design could quickly lead users to learn new skills. For this deployment, the panel included tutorials for: removing red eye, improving a smile by whitening teeth, removing wrinkles, objects, and other glitches, straightening a photo, masking, adjusting lighting, replacing colors, and improving composition.

We released LevelUp for Photoshop in September 2011 and collected data for one year. To evaluate this design, we used four sources of data. First, we instrumented the game panel and measured how many missions were completed by each player. Second, we surveyed players monthly to gather their feedback. In total, we collected 470 survey responses. Third, we carried out detailed interviews with six of our players (4 women, 2 men, ages 16-68, 2 novice, 4 advanced) to learn more about their game experience. Last, we analyzed data from the Adobe Product Improvement Program, which tracks how Adobe Photoshop users use the software over time. This final data source allowed us to compare user behavior before and after the game for 218 players (63 completed the game). This dataset included people who used Adobe Photoshop for at least 7 days before installing LevelUp for Photoshop and who had used the software for at least 7 days following installation of the game. Participation in the program is voluntary, which is why we were not able to analyze this data for all players.

Results

During the yearlong deployment, 5350 people downloaded and installed the game and completed at least one mission. Of the 5350 people, 62% completed Level 1, 49% completed Level 2, and 35% completed Level 3. Much of our survey and interview feedback was very positive. Of our 470 survey respondents, 86% reported enjoyed playing the game, 78% agreed that the game helped them learn something new, and 65% felt that they had learned the basics of photo editing. When asked why they stopped playing the game, 40% reported that they had finished the game. Only 4% reported that it was too easy or that they knew what it was trying to teach them, and 5% reported that they were just trying it out.

Was the interactive tutorial format effective?

In interviews users reported that the contextual interactive structure of the game was very useful. A lack of appropriate vocabulary can often be a stumbling block for people searching for tutorials, especially those who are just getting started with the software. Novices also reported that the step-by-step nature of the game design helped them focus on one tool at a time, rather than being overwhelmed by the entire interface. One user mentioned: "It got me to try things and gave enough instruction that I was able to rapidly make progress. Usually I get lost trying to find the item I am looking for."

Both novice and advanced users reported that they initially played the game to win points, but then revisited the game panel to refresh their memory and use the tutorials on their own images. This use of the panel was not intended but was an unexpected benefit.

Did players learn new tools and techniques?

In our surveys, players reported that some of their favorite aspects of the game included learning new tools and techniques, finding more efficient ways to perform tasks that were difficult, and the fact that it was fun to learn.

In interviews we heard similar things.

> P1: *"A lot of it is just accidental discovery. I blame myself, because I haven't been as diligent about reaching out and finding the resources. This is why I enjoyed this game. It was fun and the exercises were brief enough not to cause one to become frustrated. They introduced me to features and functions that I never knew existed."*

We also examined software use log data describing the behavior of 63 users before and after playing the entire game. We

[6] tucia.com

[7] photoeditingcompany.com

[8] bunchball.com

found that everyone tried new tools they had not used before installing LevelUp for Photoshop. After finishing the game, 83% of the users continued to use the new tools they were introduced to in the game.

Were players motivated by the points and badges?

In the forums, we received many questions about how to achieve certain badges, so while it's difficult to ascertain what percentage of players were motivated by the points and badges, it seems clear that many were incentivized by these game mechanics. During the yearlong deployment there were a number of prizes that were tied to points, which offered additional motivation, but despite the fact that the prizes were limited to the US and Canada, as many as 60% of the players were from other countries.

The design in our first deployment proved to be a useful way to teach new skills, but it needed modification before we could achieve our crowdsourcing objectives.

DEPLOYMENT 2: ADDING CHALLENGE ROUNDS

In our second deployment, our goal was to test whether skills taught in a tutorial could be applied to more open ended real-world tasks using a variety images. In this study, we tested our entire platform including both the interactive tutorials and the challenge rounds. However, we did not immediately open up the platform to real-world organizations. Instead, we presented the challenge rounds as another part of the game. We were curious to see whether on their own the challenge rounds were an engaging part of the platform.

Methodology

Deployment 2 started in September of 2012 and lasted four months. We analyzed data from three sources: (1) behavioral logs, which included the number of images edited and the types of edits that were performed, (2) qualitative assessments by workers from MTurk, who compared the original images to those uploaded by users of our platform, and (3) qualitative assessments by expert raters, which examined the quality of the edited images. Additionally, all players filled out a short survey specifying their experience level, gender, and locale.

For the qualitative assessments we created a subset of images to analyze by randomly sampling 552 users and selecting all of their images (2383 in total).

We collected task independent feedback from workers on MTurk using a paired comparison interface that showed two images (the original and an improvement) and asked them to select the image they believed would be more useful for a professional website. The placement of the original was randomized. Each job included twenty image pairs and paid $0.10. Two of the twenty pairs were used as golden standards. The golden standard pairs were created by expert raters. Each pair was evaluated by five different workers.

Inspired by previous work in creativity assessment [1, 9, 11], we also assessed the photo improvements systematically using expert raters who knew a lot more about the game environment and the suggested improvements. The expert raters gave each image two ratings, one for usefulness (1-3) and one for novelty (1-3).

The usefulness scale measured whether the edited image would be more valuable to the requester than the original image 3=*more useful than the original*, 2=*as useful as the original*, and 1=*less useful than original*. The novelty scale described the complexity of edits performed by the users. Users who used tools beyond those suggested by the challenge round, such as blurring part of the image or changing it from color to black and white, were given a *high novelty* rating (3). Users who stuck to the tools suggested by the challenge round but created novel effects were given a *medium novelty* rating (2). Finally, users who followed the directions and did exactly what they were asked performing only the suggested edits for each challenge round were given a *low novelty* rating (1). Figure 3 shows several images and the corresponding usefulness and novelty ratings.

As previous scholars have acknowledged [18], there are limits to creativity assessments as expert ratings are subjective. For this reason, we relied on established means for reaching inter-rater reliability [5]. First, the two raters rated 11% of the images. Since the inter-rater reliability between the two raters was high (Cohen's Kappa=0.96 $p<0.001$ for novelty and 0.92 $p<0.001$ for usefulness), we divided the remaining corpus between the two raters. Both raters were members of the research team.

All results reported as statistically significant used a Mann-Whitney U test with Bonferroni corrections to adjust for multiple comparisons and Type I error.

Results

3512 people (35%female) from 82 countries (35% from the US) participated and submitted 8068 images. Each image in our dataset was improved by at least 8 people. The majority of users (78%) reported that they were just starting to use Photoshop (novices). 11% said they had between 1 and 5 years of experience with the software (intermediates), and 4% said they had more than 5 years of experience (experts). 7% did not give an expertise level. Using the file names, we confirmed that 98% of the submitted images were improvements of the images embedded in the challenge rounds.

Worker performance: quantity

Consistent with our observations in Deployment 1, 74% of users completed Challenge 1, 57% of users completed Challenge 2, and 39% completed Challenge 3. Surprisingly, the number of images submitted in each round did not follow the same pattern. 48% of the images were submitted in Challenge 1, 26% were submitted in Challenge 2, and 26% were submitted in Challenge 3.

Of the 2613 users users who completed Level 1, 92% submitted at least one image. 31% submitted one image, 25% submitted two images, 20% submitted three images, and 24% submitted 4 or more images. Two people improved all 192 available images. Ten people improved over 100 images each. These ten motivated people submitted 21% of all of the submitted images, which is substantially lower than findings for MTurk, which show that the motivated individuals who do all the HITS for a task end up accomplishing almost half (46%) of all the work [10].

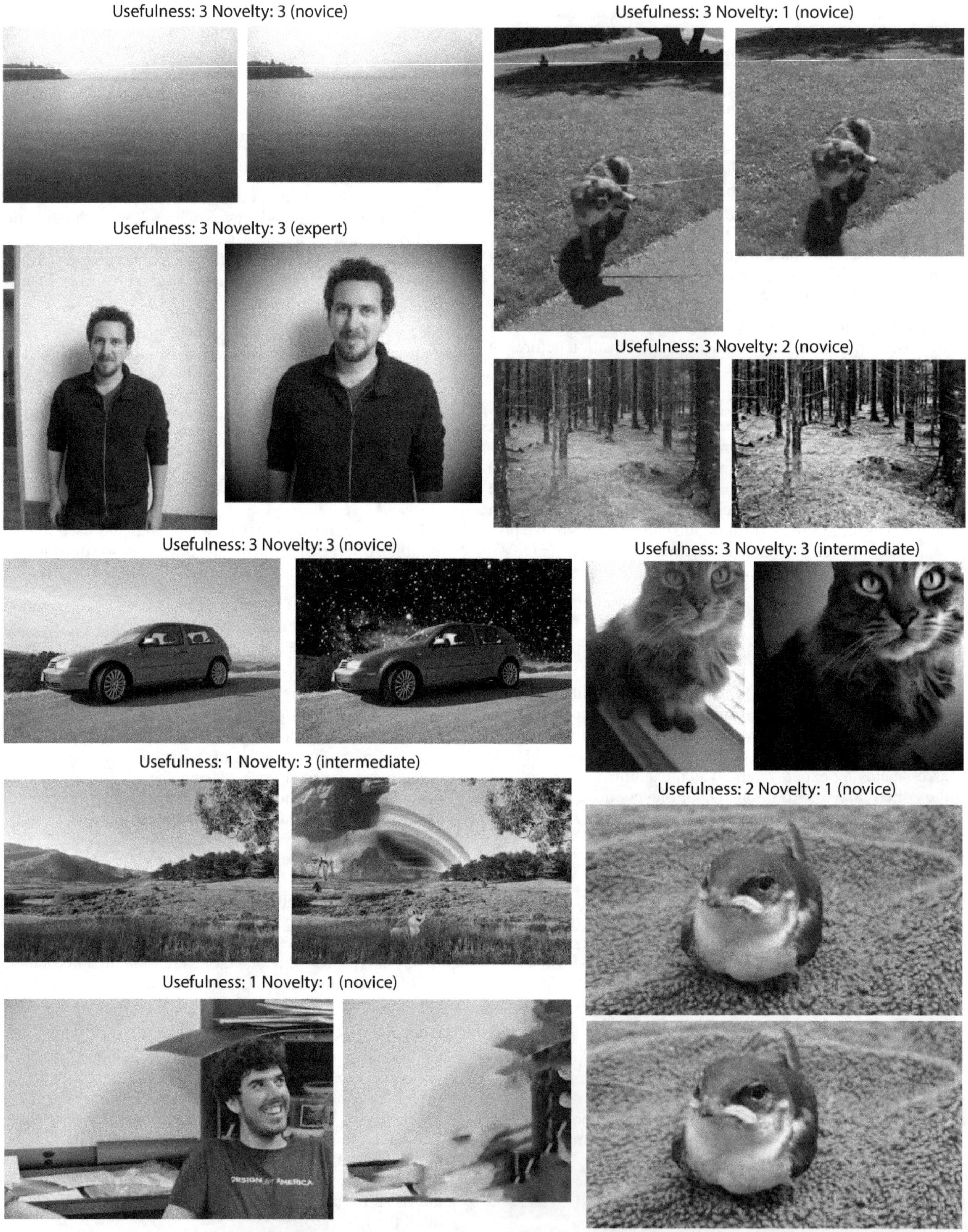

Figure 3. Here are some of the images submitted by our workers and their ratings for novelty and usefulness.

We analyzed the behavior of the 84 users who completed all challenge rounds and submitted at least ten images and found the following three patterns. 47% of users worked on roughly the same number of images in each challenge. 32% worked on a lot of images in the first challenge and almost none in the subsequent challenges. 16% worked on almost no images in the first two rounds but a lot in the final round. We believe that those who only worked on images in the first challenge were more interested in the interactive tutorials and seeing what the game had to offer. Those that only submitted images in the last challenge round may not have felt ready to tackle the challenge round until they had finished all of the tutorials. Finally, 39% had a strong preference among image categories, primarily working on images in one or two categories.

There was a strong preference for editing nature images over all other types of images. 30% of the edited images were outdoor nature scenes. 22% were animal images, 23% were people images and 24% were car images. We found no correlation between the expertise, gender, or age workers and the number or types of images improved.

Worker performance: quality

We used two methods to assess quality: (1) task-independent assessments from workers on MTurk (turkers) and (2) expert evaluation of novelty and usefulness.

Assessment by turkers

We collected 14760 total responses from 162 turkers. We excluded responses from workers who failed the golden standard comparisons more than 25%, which resulted in 6360 responses from 82 turkers for 2636 images. We found that for 25% of the submissions all turkers agreed that the submitted image was better than the original. For 37% for the submissions the majority of the turkers agreed that the submitted image was better than the original. The results were similar across player expertise. The turkers preferred improvements performed as part of Challenge 1 and Challenge 2. The majority of turkers agreed that 41% of submissions in Challenge 1 and 40% of the submissions of Challenge 2 were better than the originals, while in Challenge 3 only 25% were deemed better than the original by the majority of turkers. This may be due to the suggested edits. In Challenge 3, the suggestions were to convert the image to a square and remove glitches. A square composition is less common, and thus, the turkers may have preferred it less.

Assessment by expert raters

Of the 2383 images that were rated for usefulness and novelty, 69% were rated as more useful than the original, 15% were rated as less useful and 16% were rated to be about the same. The expert ratings are higher than those by the turkers, because the experts gave a high rating if a worker completed the task he was asked to do, even if the edit was not significantly better than the original. For example, if a worker cropped an image as a square in Challenge 3 and did not do anything too objectionable, such as crop across a face, the submission was given a rating of 3 for usefulness, even if the composition was not significantly improved by a square crop. 44% of users did not submit any images that were rated less useful than the originals. 20% of users did not submit even one image that was rated as useful. Previous work [4, 10] reported similar results with 10-30% error rate on Amazon Mechanical Turk for HITs without quality control measures. Figure 3 shows some of the more exceptional work submitted by the workers. Many users tried tools and techniques beyond those suggested by the challenge rounds. There were many who applied painterly effects to images, blurred the background or replaced some portion of the image. Some workers interpreted our instructions to do additional edits more liberally and attempted to do whimsical and funny edits. For example, some inserted cartoon characters, while others tried to communicate by adding text to the images.

The role of experience

When we compared users with different experience levels, we found that expert users received significantly more highly useful ratings (μ=2.833) as compared to novice (μ=2.54) and intermediate users(μ=2.43) ($p<0.0001$ for both). 86% of images edited by experts were rated as more useful than originals (69% for novices, and 62% for intermediate) and only 3% were rated as less useful (15% for novices and 19% for intermediates). This suggests that our rating rubric is consistent with real-world expectations. Similarly, experts received significantly more high novelty ratings (μ=1.55) as compared to novice (μ=1.21) and intermediate users (μ=1.27) ($p<0.0001$ for both). This is not surprising because experts should know how to use many more tools than novices and thus can improve images with a larger variety of techniques. 27% of the images edited by experts received a high novelty rating because they used tools beyond those suggested by the challenge rounds (9% for novices and 11% for intermediates).

Since our worker population is largely made up of novices (78%) and our training platform holds the most potential for those just getting started, we also analyzed the performance of novice users. Of the 552 users whose images we rated, 436 (79%) were novices. Of the novices, 339 (78%) submitted at least one image that was rated as useful. 184 (42%) only produced images that were rated as useful. These results are very encouraging, because they show that an interactive tutorial environment paired with less structured challenge rounds provides enough scaffolding to produce high quality work even from users who have little prior experience.

Surprisingly, in the set of images that were rated, we were not able to identify *cheaters*, i.e. people who were just trying to get points. We defined cheaters as people who got more than 50% of their images rated with 1,1 (i.e. less useful than the original and low novelty).

Challenge 1 vs Challenge 3

We found that significantly more images received "more useful" ratings in Challenge 3 than in Challenge 1 (76% in Challenge 3 vs 66% in Challenge 1 $p<0.0001$). We believe this is the case because only 40% of the users got to Challenge 3, and presumably these users were more motivated to learn and do a good job. In Challenge 1 many people might have been trying out the game and exploring its features, without trying to do a good job.

Wildlife Center for Silicon Valley (WCSV) provides high quality care and rehabilitation of injured, sick, and orphaned wildlife within the Silicon Valley Community. Through the dedication of approximately 120 volunteers, they care for over 4000 birds and mammals from over 150 species each year. "High quality images are critical for helping us obtain funding and recruit volunteers." - Janet Alexander, Director of Operations The images you edit will be sent to WCSV for their website, brochures, and newsletters.
Design for America (DFA) is a national training program for students interested in creating solutions to local challenges in their community in health, education, and the environment. With the help of more than 1200 students and professionals, they have touched the lives of 1000s of community members. "High quality images are critical for helping us recruit student and professional volunteers and raise money to support our programs." - Elizabeth Gerber, Founder The images you edit will be sent to DFA for their website, brochures, and newsletters.
Mira, LevelUp for Photoshop staff and player, wants to start a travel blog for family and friends. She just returned from Norway and has a large collection of images that she wants to put in her blog. "I try to capture the feeling of being there, but my photos often turn out dull. I know more people will read and enjoy my blog if I show nice images." - Mira The images you edit will be sent to Mira to help her start her blog.
Adobe Research is collecting a dataset of portrait photos for use in new research projects. "We want to build software that can fully interpret portraits of people and thereby enable creative manipulation of portraits that is both simple and fun. To do this, we need a large dataset of portrait photos in all their variety." -Jon Brandt, Principal Scientist The images you edit will be sent to Adobe Research for use in projects.

Table 1. The text describing the requester organizations.

We also found that images from Challenge 3 received significantly fewer high novelty ratings (10% vs 15% for challenge 1 $p<0.0001$). This is somewhat surprising, because workers could have used tools they learned in earlier levels to make additional edits beyond those suggested in Challenge 3. However, fatigue effects can affect creativity, so if users were more tired towards the end of the game, they may have been less willing to do additional creative edits.

While we observed a preference for editing nature images, we did not find the usefulness or novelty ratings for nature images to be significantly higher.

DEPLOYMENT 3: EXPLORING MOTIVATION STRATEGIES

In our third deployment, we added real-world context to the challenge rounds by embedding images from requesters. We curious whether certain types of organizations (e.g. non-profit vs for-profit) would receive better treatment and whether through the design of the game we could influence users to edit more images and do a better job. We collected images from four different organizations: a non-profit wildlife center, a non-profit student organization, a travel blogger, and a for-profit research organization that was collecting images for research projects. We placed these images in the challenge rounds and deployed two different versions of the game to test our two different designs.

Methodology

Deployment 3 started in March 2013 and lasted six months. In the *purpose* design, we included a lot of information about each organization, including a quote describing how the images will be used by the organization. In the *control* design we only listed the name of the organization. Table 1 shows all of the text we used in the purpose condition.

We randomly sampled 48 images from the images provided by each organization and placed them in the three challenge rounds. Unlike in Deployment 2, where each image category was pretty consistent, in this study the images were more varied, because the organizations provided the images they wanted to use in their marketing materials. So for example, the images from the wildlife center included images of wildlife as well as images of volunteers working in the wildlife center.

We analyzed data from five sources: (1) behavioral logs, which included the number of images edited and the types of edits that were performed, (2) qualitative assessments from workers on MTurk, (3) qualitative assessments from experts, (4) qualitative assessments from two requesters on how the edited images compare to the originals, and (5) surveys assessing the user experience.

To get feedback from the requesters, we used the same paired comparison interface that we showed to the workers on MTurk. We asked requesters to select the image they believed would be more useful to their organization. As with Deployment 2, we used the Mann-Whitney U test for all reported p values and applied Bonferroni corrections to address multiple comparisons.

Results

1290 people (648 purpose condition, 642 control condition, 27% female, 57% male) participated in Deployment 3 and worked on 2606 images. In the purpose condition we had 69% novices, 12% intermediates, 8% experts, and 11% who did not specify expertise. In the control condition we had 65% novices, 14% intermediates, 9% experts, and 12% who did not specify expertise.

We found no difference in the total number of images submitted between conditions. Similar to what we observed in Deployment 2, users preferred editing outdoor landscape images over other types of images. While we expected non-profit organizations to receive more attention from workers, we found little evidence to support this hypothesis. In the surveys users reported that they chose images not based on organization, but based on relevance to their lives. So, people edited outdoor landscape scenes more often, because many of their personal images were of outdoor scenes.

We found no significant difference between conditions in the qualitative turker assessment. Similarly, we found no significant difference between conditions or between organizations in the expert ratings for usefulness. But we did find a significant difference in the novelty ratings between the purpose and control conditions ($p<0.0001$). The control condition had a higher average novelty rating (control: $\mu=1.37$) than the purpose condition($\mu=1.22$). In the purpose condition 87% of images received a low novelty rating, while in the control condition 80% of images received a low novelty rating. We believe that people under the purpose condition were less willing to do more than the suggested edits because they wanted to do what was asked by the organization.

Requester feedback to the submitted images was positive. The Wildlife Center for Silicon Valley rated 76 submitted images. They rated 60% of the submitted images as better than the originals. Of the images that were submitted by novices (50 (66%)), they rated 92% as better than the originals.

Design for America rated 470 submitted images. They rated 20% of the submitted images as better than the originals. Of the images that were submitted by novices (271 (58%)), they rated 34% as better than the originals.

We collected 35 surveys and received qualitative feedback on the design of LevelUp for Photoshop and what could be improved. When asked what they liked most about the challenge rounds, workers listed new ways to learn ("I got to apply what I had just learned," "It's a nice ramp up from the previous lessons,""I like that I get to test the skills that I've learned.") and real-world impact ("It offers a sense of achievement beyond badges and points," "Having the opportunity to help real people/organizations out," "Working on real problems.") When asked what they liked least, workers reported that some of the images had poor resolution, the task felt repetitive, and that there was no feedback from the organizations. When asked whether they preferred the missions or the challenge rounds, almost all users (except for one) said that they preferred the missions or had no preference between the missions and the challenge round.

DISCUSSION

Our studies show that interactive learning can be combined with crowdsourcing to enhance both learning and worker performance. We found that an interactive tutorial system is effective at teaching both novices and experts new skills. Moreover, with the right guidance, even novices were able to accomplish high-quality edits. Furthermore, offering real-world context about a requesting organization motivates workers to more closely follow directions.

Design Implications for Creative Crowdwork

Designers of crowdwork platforms face many challenges in designing interactions that positively influence the requesters' and the workers' experiences. Our study highlights several design implications for crowdsourcing complex creative work. First, and perhaps most importantly, learning platforms can be an effective way to produce high quality creative work. If a particular creative skill is hard to find in traditional marketplaces, one solution is to offer workers a chance to learn this skill in exchange for producing work. This design approach can benefit both requesters and crowdworkers.

We also illustrate how simple it can be to adapt online learning tutorials to work with crowdsourcing systems. Many online learning platforms offer students a way to practice their skills, often through sample use cases that serve no purpose beyond pedagogy. In most photo editing tutorials, for example, students are given stock photos to improve. In our system we illustrate how stock photos can be replaced with third party images that are in genuine need of image enhancement. Similar substitutions could be made for other learning systems. We argue that this paradigm not only helps produce good crowdsourced work, but it also enhances the user experience and motivations of the workers.

Further, our challenge round design illustrates ways to capture labor from both novice and expert workers. For novices, it is important to provide specific, structured objectives. For experts, it is important to also make tasks somewhat open-ended, so they can utilize additional skills as appropriate. In our challenge rounds, experts were given the opportunity to make additional improvements to the image not specified by the requester. While there is a chance some workers might take this opportunity to overreach and perhaps make changes that are not appropriate, our experiments show that these behaviors are reduced when the needs of the requester are made explicit. Indeed, our findings also add further support to the notion that a sense of purpose can enhance motivation. When workers were given descriptions of the requester, they followed the instructions more closely and made more appropriate adjustments.

Future work

In future work we plan to extend the challenge round design to incorporate subjective feedback. Offering feedback is an integral part of learning and has been shown to be effective in crowdsourcing [20]. One possible design is to ask workers to rate images that others have submitted after they submit their own edits. Such an approach scales well, and potentially has both pedagogical benefits (reviewing others' work is an important part of instruction) and motivational effects (individuals are motivated by both opportunities to collaborate and to compete).

Limitations

Our worker pool was limited to those who voluntarily chose to use LevelUp for Photoshop, and we benefitted from tying our platform to a popular application. Not all tasks are amenable to being embedded into an existing application, and requesters may be limited to working with platforms such as MTurk. We believe that our approach could be applied on top of existing platforms, by integrating learning into tasks, but more research is necessary to further understand how payment would interact with learning motivations.

Many in the crowdsourcing community have focused on improving cost and throughput [3], but evaluating the cost and throughput of our platform was beyond the scope of this paper. Throughput for an in-app voluntary platform like LevelUp for Photoshop is heavily affected by marketing efforts and product release schedules. As a point of comparison, to improve all of the images edited in our experiments would have cost over $3200 on Tucia.

CONCLUSION

We present a novel platform that combines learning and crowdsourcing to benefit both workers and requesters. To understand the factors that influence learning outcomes and work quality, we carried out three studies over two years with over ten thousand workers. We found that:

- Workers enjoyed the interactive tutorial environment and learned new photo editing skills. All workers who completed all of the tutorials learned at least one new tool that they had not used prior to installing LevelUp for Photoshop, and 83% continued to use the new skills outside of the interactive tutorial game
- Even novice Adobe Photoshop users were able to complete basic photo editing tasks and improve images. 69% of images edited by novices were considered more useful than the originals as determined by expert raters blind to the experimental conditions. Additionally, the requesters who provided the images rated up to 92% of the images submitted by novices as more useful than the originals.
- Workers preferred work that helped them practice the skills they found most useful. For example, workers who wanted to improve their own landscape photos chose to work on crowdsourced tasks that involved outdoor scenes.
- Highlighting the purpose of the crowdsourced work changed the behavior of the workers. When the requester's origin was known and the purpose of the image enhancements was made salient, workers followed instructions more closely and made more appropriate adjustments.

ACKNOWLEDGMENTS

We thank all of the LevelUp for Photoshop players and Amazon Mechanical Turk workers. Also, we thank the Wildlife Center for Silicon Valley and Design for America for contributing images and working with us.

REFERENCES

1. Amabile, T. M. *Creativity and innovation in organizations*. Harvard Business School, 1996.
2. Bergman, L., Castelli, V., Lau, T., and Oblinger, D. Docwizards: a system for authoring follow-me documentation wizards. In *Proceedings of UIST* (2005), 191–200.
3. Bernstein, M. S., Brandt, J., Miller, R. C., and Karger, D. R. Crowds in two seconds: enabling realtime crowd-powered interfaces. In *Proceedings of UIST* (2011), 33–42.
4. Bernstein, M. S., Little, G., Miller, R. C., Hartmann, B., Ackerman, M. S., Karger, D. R., Crowell, D., and Panovich, K. Soylent: a word processor with a crowd inside. In *Proceedings of UIST* (2010), 313–322.
5. Cohen, J. A coefficient of agreement for nominal scales. *Educational and psychological measurement*, 1 (1960), 37–46.
6. Cooper, S., Khatib, F., Treuille, A., Barbero, J., Lee, J., Beenen, M., Leaver-Fay, A., Baker, D., Popovic, Z., and players, F. Predicting protein structures with a multiplayer online game. *Nature 446* (2010), 756–760.
7. Dong, T., Dontcheva, M., Joseph, D., Karahalios, K., Newman, M., and Ackerman, M. Discovery-based games for learning software. In *Proceedings of SIGCHI* (2012), 2083–2086.
8. Dow, S., Kulkarni, A., Klemmer, S., and Hartmann, B. Shepherding the crowd yields better work. In *Proceedings of CSCW* (2012), 1013–1022.
9. Guilford, J. P. *The nature of human intelligence*. McGraw-Hill, 1967.
10. Heer, J., and Bostock, M. Crowdsourcing graphical perception: Using mechanical turk to assess visualization design. In *Proceedings of SIGCHI* (2010), 203–212.
11. Kaufman, J. C., Plucker, J. A., and Baer, J. *Essentials of creativity assessment*, vol. 53. Wiley, 2008.
12. Kittur, A., Smus, B., Khamkar, S., and Kraut, R. E. Crowdforge: crowdsourcing complex work. In *Proceedings of UIST* (2011), 43–52.
13. Kulkarni, A., Can, M., and Hartmann, B. Collaboratively crowdsourcing workflows with turkomatic. In *Proceedings of the CSCW* (2012), 1003–1012.
14. Lewis, S., Dontcheva, M., and Gerber, E. Affective computational priming and creativity. In *Proceedings of SIGCHI* (2011), 735–744.
15. Li, W., Grossman, T., and Fitzmaurice, G. Gamicad: A gamified tutorial system for first time autocad users. In *Proceedings of UIST* (2012), 103–112.
16. Morris, R. R., Dontcheva, M., Finkelstein, A., and Gerber, E. Affect and creative performance on crowdsourcing platforms. In *Proceedings of ACII* (2013).
17. Pongnumkul, S., Dontcheva, M., Li, W., Wang, J., Bourdev, L., Avidan, S., and Cohen, M. F. Pause-and-play: automatically linking screencast video tutorials with applications. In *Proceedings of UIST* (2011), 135–144.
18. Puccio, G., and Murdock, Mary, E. *Creativity Assessment: Readings and Resources*. Creative Education Foundation Press, Buffalo, NY, USA, 1999.
19. von Ahn, L., and Dabbish, L. Labeling images with a computer game. In *Proceedings of the SIGCHI* (2004), 319–326.
20. Zhang, H., Dow, S., Kraut, R., and Kittur, A. Reviewing versus doing: Learning and performance in crowd assessment. In *Proceedings of CSCW* (2014).

A Game-Based Learning Approach to Road Safety: The Code of Everand

Ian Dunwell, Sara de Freitas, Panagiotis Petridis, Maurice Hendrix, Sylvester Arnab, Petros Lameras and Craig Stewart
Serious Games Institute
Coventry University, UK
idunwell@cad.coventry.ac.uk
+44 (0) 2476 158 201

ABSTRACT

Game and gamification elements are increasingly seeing use as part of interface designs for applications seeking to engage and retain users whilst transferring information. This paper presents an evaluation of a game-based approach seeking to improve the road safety behaviour amongst children aged 9-15 within the UK, made available outside of a classroom context as an online, browser-based, free-to-play game. The paper reports on data for 99,683 players over 315,882 discrete logins, supplemented by results from a nationally-representative survey of children at UK schools (n=1,108), an incentivized survey of the player-base (n=1,028), and qualitative data obtained through a series of one-to-one interviews aged 9-14 (n=28). Analysis demonstrates the reach of the game to its target demographic, with 88.13% of players within the UK. A 3.94 male/female ratio was observed amongst players surveyed, with an age distribution across the target range of 9-15. Noting mean and median playtimes of 93 and 31 minutes (n=99,683), it is suggested such an approach to user engagement and retention can surpass typical contact times obtained through other forms of web-based content. The size of the player-base attracted to the game and players' qualitative feedback demonstrates the potential for serious games deployed on a national scale.

Author Keywords

Game-based interfaces; road safety; gamification; attitudinal change; e-learning; serious games

ACM Classification Keywords

H.1.2 User/Machine Systems - Human Factors; K.8.0 Personal Computing: General - Games; K.4.1 Computers and Society: Public Policy Issue - Human safety

CHI 2014, April 26 - May 01 2014, Toronto, ON, Canada
Copyright 2014 ACM 978-1-4503-2473-1/14/04...$15.00.
http://dx.doi.org/10.1145/2556288.2557281

INTRODUCTION

The number of child pedestrians killed or seriously injured (KSI) on roads is a significant global issue. Statistics released by the World Health Organization place road traffic accidents as one of the leading causes of death worldwide, responsible for 1.26 million fatalities in 2000 [1], and the second leading cause of death amongst those aged 15-29. Hence, whilst this paper focuses on the specific case of the United Kingdom (UK), improving road safety is a significant global challenge [2]. As an emerging form of public e-health intervention, game based learning offers a potential avenue by which to reach demographics which are unresponsive to more formal methods of instruction, with the goal of fostering an attitudinal, and subsequently behavioural, change [3]. This may hold particularly true for the case of children aged 10-15, who present a unique road safety challenge in that their unsafe behaviour is predominantly linked to their failure to apply knowledge of safe practices [4], rather than lacking the knowledge itself.

In recent years it has become apparent that, while the game design community has developed mostly separately from the interaction design community, games can offer highly usable interaction experiences, especially when it comes to learning, motivation, user satisfaction and community formation. In a novel interaction design approach to addressing children's road-safety behaviours through game-based learning, Code of Everand was developed as a massively-multiplayer online (MMO) game for children, embedding abstract and social learning principles as a basis for instigating behavioural change.

In this paper, an analysis is presented of the game's reach to its target demographic, establishing some indicators of impact through self-reported surveys, qualitative interview, and statistics on game usage. The use of a game as not only a subject of research, but also a primary tool for data acquisition is an emerging concept [5], which allows for the analysis in this case of data arising from 99,683 players interacting with the game over a 5-month period. We couple these results to those from a national survey of 1,180 UK children, collected in an electronic format in a classroom-based context, and an online survey of 969 players, and qualitative interviews with a smaller group of participants, towards establishing key considerations for future interventions. The findings are of relevance not only in terms of the impact of the game on road safety, but also offer some insight into how players approach game-based interventions in general, and the specific case of web-based, open access, multiuser environments.

BACKGROUND

Accidents involving children represented 61% of all deaths and serious injuries on UK roads between 2000-2005 [6], emphasizing the need to promote safer behaviour and awareness amongst younger age groups. Further analyses have investigated the cause and likelihood of accidents within younger age groups: a study of 202 UK police reports and 826 coroner's records [7] analyzed fatal child accidents with the goal of identifying behaviours and groups best targeted by safety interventions. The results demonstrated higher fatality rates amongst males, suggesting that in particular the 11-15 age range represents a high-risk category, with the number killed or seriously injured (KSI) over a 1-year period (2001) four times greater than the 0-5 age range. Reaching this demographic with targeted safety interventions is a demanding task. Knowledge transfer alone has been shown to be inadequate [4]; often children are aware of the principles of safe crossing, but fail to enact them in practice. The causes of this are numerous, though key factors include peer-group pressure and perceived social norms [8], as well as overestimation of ability and underestimation of the likelihood and severity of injury [9]. Furthermore, since safety education programmes are frequently opt-in, they tend to be self-selecting and fail to reach the highest risk groups [10].

Entertainment media such as television have often been used to convey safety messages. However, as children's leisure time becomes increasingly fragmented across electronic gaming and social media [11], an emerging need exists for these technologies to be embraced by public health interventions to ensure important messages continue to reach at-risk groups. Furthermore, studies have demonstrated as many as 97% of UK children aged 11-15 play electronic games, and nine in ten UK children aged 5-15 live in a household with a games console [11]. The role, therefore, of HCI experts in understanding how to best utilize game-based media and translate psychological and pedagogical principles to effective digital interventions, is critical in retaining the capacity to reach and impact such audiences.

The project reported by this paper sought to capitalise on the popularity of electronic gaming amongst the target demographic to develop a targeted intervention conveying a road safety message in an intrinsically-motivating fashion. Existing evidence has already shown the efficacy of such games when seeking to induce attitudinal and behavioural change in a young age group, tackling for example topics such as treatment adherence amongst young cancer sufferers [3]. The mechanics, dynamics and aesthetics of a game-based intervention, when designed with pedagogical, psychological and participatory perspectives in the foreground can be effective in achieving the desired intervention outcomes. Similarly, the ability of the medium to reach demographics less responsive to more formal pedagogical approaches has been demonstrated alongside their potential to foster intrinsic motivation [12].

THE CODE OF EVERAND

The initial selection of a game-based medium was driven by the increasing distribution of childrens' time across emerging media, which in turn is reducing the audiences traditional messaging approaches such as television advertising can expect to reach. Whilst other examples of electronic games devised around the concept of road safety have been explored in various forms [13, 14], Code of Everand sought to be unique through its adoption of a massively multiplayer online (MMO) approach. Game-based learning was selected as an appropriate vehicle under the hypothesis that a game-based approach would demonstrate particular attraction to groups with higher risk levels, as identified in the previous section. This research highlighted males aged 11-15 as being at particularly high risk of death or serious injury in pedestrian accidents [6]. The game was developed to complement a wide portfolio of existing road safety interventions, which included approaches such as direct messaging and safety education in schools. As such, rather than seek to replicate these existing interventions, Code of Everand sought to explore a new means for encouraging children to socialize in a safe and positive environment during their leisure time, whilst reflecting upon and rehearsing their safety skills.

A key research question behind this design approach was whether a safety intervention could attract and retain a substantial UK audience when deployed as a free-to-play online serious game. In particular, as the game sought to reach at-risk groups who have limited engagement or exposure to other safety interventions, a concern was whether the "serious" nature of the game would limit its ability to compete for screen-time with leisure game equivalents. Gameplay remained at the forefront of the experience, in line with the view that engagement and entertainment should be foremost in such a context [15]. Towards this goal, storytelling and narrative aspects played a key role in the game's design, with players searching towards the long term goal of uncovering a mythical code, supported by a range of non-player characters with scripted dialogues. Players are provided with both a role to play and a context to play it in, ultimately leading to intervention and the desire to act. In essence this motivational approach is a the process of exposure, in which main protagonists are exposed to a sequence of events, motivating them to act and embark in a narrative journey. This was reinforced through the game's web presence, with short graphic novels and additional materials both adding to the world of Everand, and reinforcing positive safety messages.

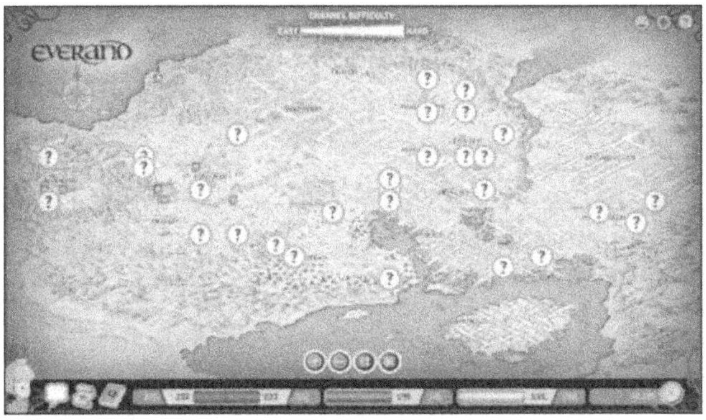

Figure 1. The world of Everand, intersected by ley-lines analogous to roads. Players are encouraged to exercise route-planning skills to navigate the land.

Figure 1 shows the world map of Everand, with its various locations and spirit channels. A range of social activities and elements existed within the game, encouraging and rewarding players for collaboration. Players assumed the role of powerful "Pathfinders", tasked with exploring the fantasy land of Everand and safely navigating "spirit channels" populated with a variety of monstrous creatures. As such, an abstract metaphor for road crossing was implemented, with basic road safety principles recreated in the virtual world: Pathfinders must carefully select their route, look both ways when crossing a spirit channel, and form peer-groups to enhance their safety and progression. Further images from the game are shown in Figures 2 and 3. Analogical transfer was embedded into the game through a this "crossing" mechanic, built around the spirit channels, with the player required to route-plan, using the map shown in Figure 1, to avoid crossing more dangerous spirit channels, and minimize the required number of crossings to reach their destination. On undertaking a crossing, they are confronted by creatures such as those shown in Figure 3, and must look right and left to defeat them in a turn-based game. Characters were able to accumulate experience points and "level up", in turn giving them more powerful abilities and the capability to attempt more challenging crossings; as illustrated in Figure 1, the colour of channels impacts the difficulty of the crossing, with green and yellow channels suited to lower-level players.

Additional elements common to story-driven and MMO games were implemented. On their arrival to the game, players were first presented with the opportunity to customise their character, being able to select a male or female avatar, and configure their appearance from a range of available options. Whilst the overarching narrative was conveyed through an introductory cutscene, a range of individual NPCs supported story development in-game, giving players a range of missions and quests which required they travel through the world of Everand. Hence, a typical player's experience was to create a character, arrive in the game's starting area, then communicate with NPCs and embark on a quest. On completing the quest, rewards could be used to upgrade their character with items such as armour, or "traps", "spells", and "tonics" to combat creatures during spirit channel crossings.

By socialising with other players, larger groups could be formed, with players collaborating to overcome creatures and cross safely. In addition to providing an environment which all players simultaneously co-habited, players also had pets ("critters"), which they were encouraged to take responsibility for. Figure 2 demonstrates a social mechanism whereby players were encouraged to compete and collaborate to pay tribute to their own type of critter, with the critter receiving the greatest daily tribute granting a bonus to all players with that critter type. Whilst ethical and safety considerations precluded the implementation of a method for open communication between players, players were able to communicate with one another using a collection of preset dialogue options and actions. This represented one the greatest design challenges, as without direct communication, limitations on socialisation may have impacted retention, as reflected by the results in this paper.

Figure 2. Game elements such as the 'critter court' shown here encourage players to collaborate and compete to gain advantages.

The game was made available from November 2009 to November 2011, accessible through a player embedded within a web page. As such, the interface was constructed to be operated using a mouse on a desktop PC. Prior to launch, it was promoted through online search and display advertising on child-oriented websites. Post launch, two week-long periods of advertising in the UK during children's prime viewing times was coupled with paid search to stimulate uptake. An additional question here, in light of the diminishing television audiences as noted in the previous section, was the relative value of television promotion when compared to online methods, and the results in this paper illustrate the comparative benefits of these methods.

Beyond reaching new audiences, a second rationale for the use of a game was its potential to communicate the safety message in a novel form, focusing on application and rehearsal of skills and knowledge, rather than their acquisition. This was an important goal, since other interventions have successfully transferred knowledge, and therefore a core road safety objective is not to communicate safe crossing principles to children, but rather to ensure they apply them in practice [4]. Hence, as a novel approach to road safety, multiple underlying pedagogic approaches were explored. It was hypothesized that models for attitudinal change may emerge from social learning [15], in the communities formed by the game, as well as analogical transfer [16] from the game's individual components. The game's design sought to support social aspects of learning through an in-game "buddy list", as well as through supplemental materials such as graphic novels available through the game's website.

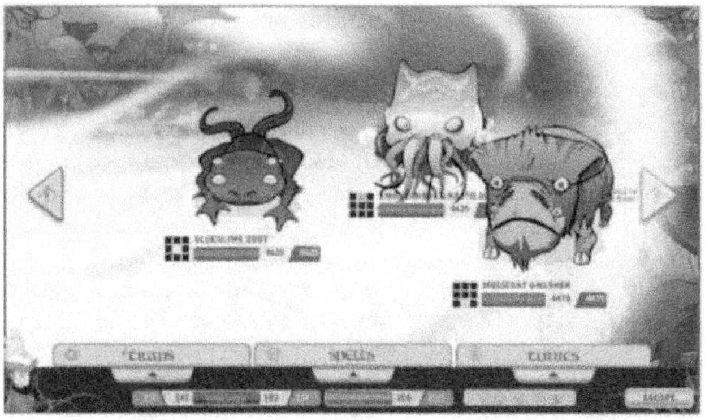

Figure 3. During a 'crossing', players must select the most appropriate traps and abilities to overcome creatures.

Understanding and validating analogical transfer is particularly salient to serious games, as the need to create a compelling game can often be at odds with the nature of the instructional material and learning outcomes the game seeks to convey [15]. Furthermore, in merging a real-world analogy to a fantasy game, a requirement is placed upon the player to identify the analogy as a first step in transferring skills learnt in-game to the real world. Whilst explicitly making the intent of the game clear to the player could accomplish this first step, and additional question was whether this could, in turn, reduce the appeal of the game, with children perceiving it as another safety intervention, rather than something with which they would willingly engage in their leisure time. In this case, the decision was made to avoid making the intent of the game explicit, with a view towards maximising the game's potential audience. The method in the following section hence sought to identify the proportion of players that had identified the analogy, and its value in impacting their attitudes and behaviours regarding road safety.

Impact also had the potential to occur in social interactions outside of the game, or through further reflection and learning stimulated by, but not necessarily transferred through, the game itself. Hence, the method described also sought to establish both the uptake of the game, to assess the viability of this and similar interventions as free-to-play MMO games, as well as providing an examination of the viability of the social and analogical learning mechanisms through a combination of survey, qualitative interviews, and analysis of the data arising from players' interactions with the game.

METHOD

Four data collection activities were used to gain insight into the efficacy, reach, and audience of Code of Everand: A nationally-representative survey (henceforth referred to as the "national survey"), a survey of the player-base, analysis of data from the game engine, and qualitative interviews with players. The process of analyzing the qualitative interviews was based on an inductive content analysis approach that led to the identification of different experiences when playing Code of Everand. Certain themes were derived from the qualitative analysis focused on transferability of play to real-worlds concepts, learning opportunities in game-based environments, conceptions of game-based content and scaffolding. An ethical review and approval for all components of the study was undertaken by Coventry University, UK.

The national survey was undertaken across 40 UK schools in December 2010. Surveys were completed in an electronic format by schoolchildren, with no incentive for participation in the survey. The total of 1,108 participants was representative of 28±5 participants per site. Participants were equally distributed in terms of gender (0.98 M/F n=1,108), with 43% of children aged 9-11 and 67% aged 12-14. Teachers provided informed consent *in loco parentis*, making clear to children they had the right to refuse to participate or opt-out at any stage, a message repeated in the survey itself. By comparison, the player survey was distributed via email invitation to parents of players, asking them to invite their child to participate, and completed online between February-March 2011. As a result the sample for this survey could be considered to be partly reflective of the user-base for the game (3.94 M/F, n=1,028), with an age distribution as shown in Table 1. Participation in this survey was incentivized with an in-game reward and prize draw.

Analysis of the databases held by the game engine relating to anonymized user behaviour was also undertaken. Informed parental consent was a principal consideration in this study, a consequence of this indirect method used for data capture. Children were required to provide as part of the sign-up process for the game to supply the email of a parent or guardian, who then authenticated their account for play after reviewing an agreement. No further information, which could be used for personal identification, was collected as part of the registration process, and these emails were held separate from the remainder of the data analyzed as personal data under the UK Data Protection Act. Parents of players consented to have this data used for research purposes as part of the sign-up process for the game. The data reported on by this paper represents a complete export of the game's database in May 2010, seven months after the game was made available via the Web. As the game engine does not facilitate text-chat or other methods for communication between players beyond pre-selected dialogue options, there was no risk personal data could be inadvertently collected through chat logs or similar mechanisms.

Age	Player Survey		National Survey	
	Male	Female	Male	Female
8 or less	82	17	17	18
9	81	13	71	69
10	103	23	114	117
11	122	26	108	114
12	85	17	128	140
13	65	18	89	81
14	39	12	21	21
15	22	12	0	0
16+	110	33	0	0
Unknown	67	22	0	0

Table 1. Age and gender distribution of player and national survey respondents

The final activity consisted of qualitative research with 31 participants: 28 children aged 10-12, selected on the basis of a single criteria: that they reported walking in the street without adults more than once a week, and 3 players who volunteered to participate in qualitative research following an advertisement on the game's website. These children were interviewed firstly on their pedestrian behaviour, then instructed to sign up to the game and keep a diary for 2-3 weeks. At the end of this period, the group was engaged a second time in a game-focused interview. This was supplemented by interviews with three existing players, who volunteered to participate following a request made by the game's welcome screen as well as on conclusion of the player survey. Each of these participants was also engaged twice, with a first interview focusing upon the game, and a second on their pedestrian behaviour. Interviews took place in the homes of children with a parent or guardian present. Prior to commencement, the aims and objectives of the research were discussed with the parent or guardian who consented to their child's involvement. Though the child was made aware they would be discussing the Code of Everand game, care was taken to avoid explicitly prompting or cueing responses linking the game to road safety to examine if children made this link automatically.

RESULTS

Results are separated into two sub-sections: the first reviews the overall uptake of the game, primarily in quantitative terms as a result of the two surveys and data from the game engine. The second reflects upon the perspectives of players towards the game as explored through qualitative interview and survey.

Uptake and Reach

Over the 7-month period between November 2009 and May 2010, the game attracted 99,608 unique account creations and 315,883 individual play sessions. From the national survey, 16% of participants had heard of Code of Everand, and of these 20% had gone on to play it (n=1,108), figures which, if replicated nationally, would generate a player-base roughly equivalent in size to that observed, assuming the age range recorded by the player survey (Table 1) was reflected in the user base. IP address geolocation showed this audience to be predominantly from the UK (88.1%), Republic of Ireland (3.5%), and US (2.5%), a consequence of the active promotion of the game though two 1-week periods of television advertising and paid search.

29% of players (n=954) reported hearing about the game through television advertising, 28% from an Internet site, and 21% from friends or school friends. This demonstrated that web-based promotion offered a significantly better return on investment than television advertising, each responsible for approximately half the player base (as word-of-mouth promotion would have occurred following a child becoming aware of the game through these mechanisms). This suggests that future interventions should consider carefully the use of television as a promotional medium, as well as recognising the importance of peer communication and supporting it to enhance the scale of the audience attracted to a game.

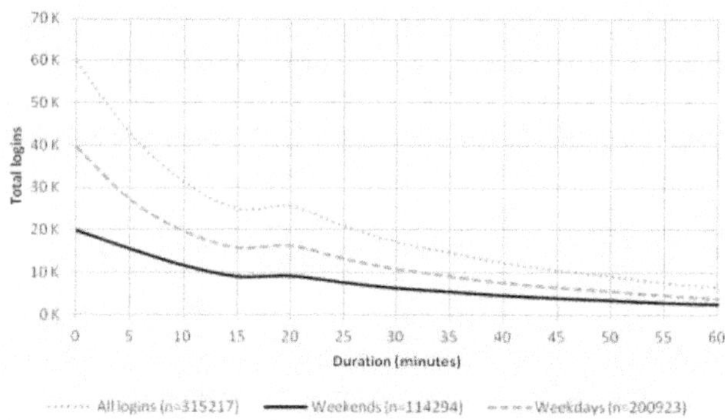

Figure 4. Duration of individual play sessions (n=315,217)

A clear in-game gender bias in avatar selection existed (4.56 M/F, n=99,608); this may have been due to the character creation process defaulting to a male avatar, with a link between time played and gender selection significant at $p<0.01$, with players with female avatars more likely to play for a longer period. However, a real-world gender bias is represented at a similar level in Table 1 (3.94 M/F, n=969). While this may have some implications of the comparability of the national survey and player survey it does also show that the game was very effective at addressing the target group of children most at risk, which shows a similar gender bias. 68.1% of players for whom data was available (n=969) had an avatar of the same gender as themselves. Notably females were more likely to play male characters than vice versa (70.2% of females played a character of the opposite gender, as opposed to 21.5% of males). The mean time spent playing Code of Everand (Figure 5) was 93 minutes (n=99,608), though the sample was characterized by outliers, with 28% of players experiencing the game for less than 15 minutes, and 14% for more than 2 hours. Hence the median of 31 minutes may be considered to be more representative of a "typical" playtime. With respect to the number of times players returned to the game, 52.4% of players logged in a single time, and for these players the mean playtime was 24 minutes. By comparison, 19.8% of players logged in twice, and 9.1% three times. As shown by Figure 4, 36.3% (n=315,883) of play sessions occurred on weekends.

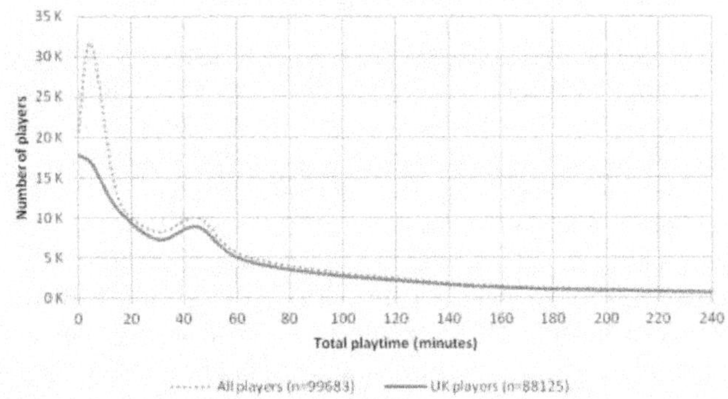

Figure 5. Total time spent playing by individual accounts (n=99,683)

As the player and national surveys asked identical questions on safety, comparison between individual questions was possible. However, the difference in samples and sampling methods (Table 1), as well as the differing contexts of the two surveys implies a need for caution when attempting to infer underlying causal factors. Figure 6 illustrates Likert responses for both national and player survey respondents for one of three groups of safety questions. Applying a non-parametric test (Mann-Whitney's U) in view of the distribution of the data yielded a range of significant results: Players were more likely to agree that they took the time to find a safe place before crossing ($Z=-5.912$, $p<0.001$), keep looking and listening as they crossed ($Z=-3.791$, $p<0.001$) and look both ways before crossing ($Z=-2.177$, $p=0.03$). Similarly, they reported higher levels of disagreement with negative, risky behaviour, being more likely to disagree that they crossed between parked cars where a safer place was nearby ($Z=-11.929$, $p<0.001$), cross regardless of whether traffic was coming ($Z=-11.516$, $p<0.001$), or run across the road without looking ($Z=-8.339$, $p<0.001$). Looking more specifically at concrete experiences, players were less likely to agree they had experienced incidences of thinking it was safe to cross, but realizing a car was travelling faster than they thought ($Z=-4.595$, $p<0.001$), and the same was true of forgetting to look as a consequence of using a mobile device ($Z=-11.163$, $p<0.001$). For questions on self-reported behaviour and experience, the overall weighted results were again in favour of more positive behaviour amongst players, with the only non-significant result at $p>0.05$ being on knowledge rather than behaviour.

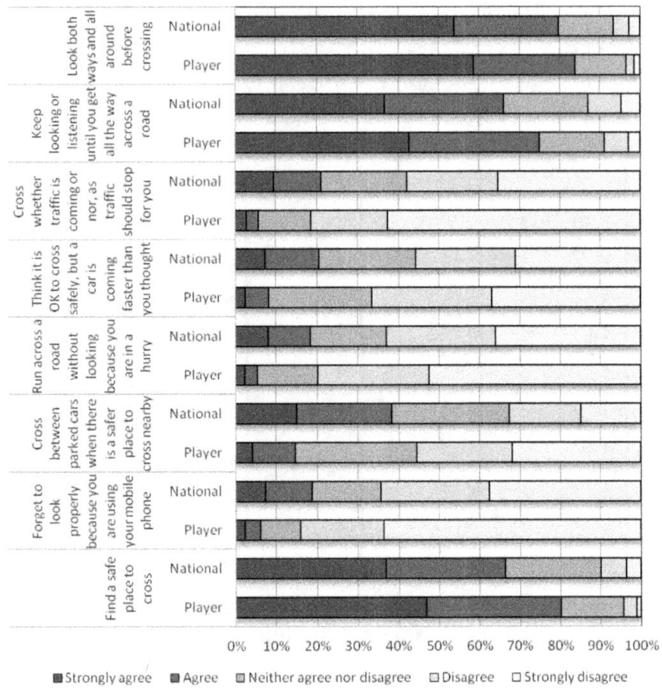

Figure 6. Comparison of Likert scale responses from the national sample (n=1,108) and players (n=814) to questions on frequency of dangerous and safe behaviour.

Whilst these multiple significances are an encouraging finding, possible underlying causes included a potential appeal of the game to an intrinsically safer audience, as well as the differing contexts of the surveys influencing their outcomes. To examine the former, the results for 337 players who had voluntarily supplied postcodes were compared against indices of multiple deprivation [17] to gain some insight into their socio-economic background. Indices of multiple deprivations are used within the UK to rank 32,482 (as of 2007) areas in order based on a range of social and economic metrics In Figure 7, these are arbitrarily grouped into 8 ranks, each containing 4,060 areas, with the data for players grouped by these ranks.

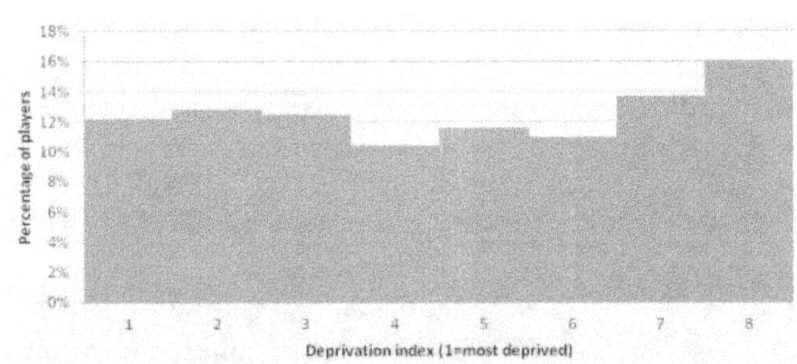

Figure 7. Histogram showing the distribution of players (n=337) by indices of multiple deprivation.

As can be observed, whilst the majority of players were indeed from the least deprived rank, the overall distribution proved broader than might have been expected and therefore it is reasonable to not consider players' social-economic status as a factor in or further analysis.

Players' Perspectives

Though the limited sample of 31 participants precludes a meaningful quantitative analysis of interview outcomes, one metric considered was the "top three" pieces of advice a child would give to a friend regarding road safety. Participants were asked this question in the initial and final interviews, and their responses compared to a list of best-practices to examine if their advice had changed and, if so, if it more closely matched desired road safety knowledge which Code of Everand sought to transfer. In initial interviews, four children across the sample identified these items: using zebra crossings, avoiding main roads, crossing in safer places, and avoiding busy junctions. In the follow-up interview after playing the game, this had increased to 13 children, suggesting play did have impact on their knowledge as well as their attitudes as reported in the previous section.

For learning to occur through analogy, a pre-requisite would be that players were capable of recognizing this analogy, and applying the tactics learnt in game to real-world problems. Key to this recognition were the spirit channels and crossing mechanics:

"I think the big ones [spirit channels] are like main roads cause the big blue ones stand out to me more like they are thicker main roads. But the long thin windy roads like this one here to me look like a village, like a little neighborhood or close, or cul de sac. It's a tiny road like just crossing the road." [Female, 12]

Similarly, other participants also recognized the analogy when confronted by the channels:

"The channels are like roads so you have to look left and right and then the monsters are like cars - sort of." [Male, 11]

Quantitative data (Figure 8) supported the assertion that many players had identified the analogy, with 46.8% of players (n=743) agreeing or strongly agreeing that 'I think about road safety' whilst playing. Also noteworthy was the level of disagreement with players to the statement that Code of Everand 'is boring because it is educational', with 61.2% disagreeing or strongly disagreeing, and only 12.8% of players agreeing or strongly agreeing. This suggests the perception of game-based learning amongst the majority of players who responded to the survey was positive, though the potential influence of self-selection bias should be considered. Irrespective, the overall uptake figures support the notion that there is little need to obscure a game's serious intent from players to ensure uptake. Participants who recognized the analogy frequently went on to reflect upon their own behaviour:

"I'm playing it and the next day I'm crossing this really busy road... this massive road... there's no crossing where I go on it. After a week of playing the game I thought: I'm not going to risk it. [...] I thought: cars are going four ways and you never really had time in the middle when the light switched. You can get injured. I just decided to be safe. The good thing is it influences you to be safe on the roads." [Male, 12]

"Normally, I have to admit, normally if there is a car coming I would wait for it to go past, but every now and again I would run across the road. Every kid does it. You can't say you don't do it, you can't say you will do it, but since playing this game I have taken more care of myself with crossing the roads, actually thought about... a minute ago I basically got run over [i.e. got defeated in Everand]. I have thought more carefully about the way I cross the road." [Female, 11]

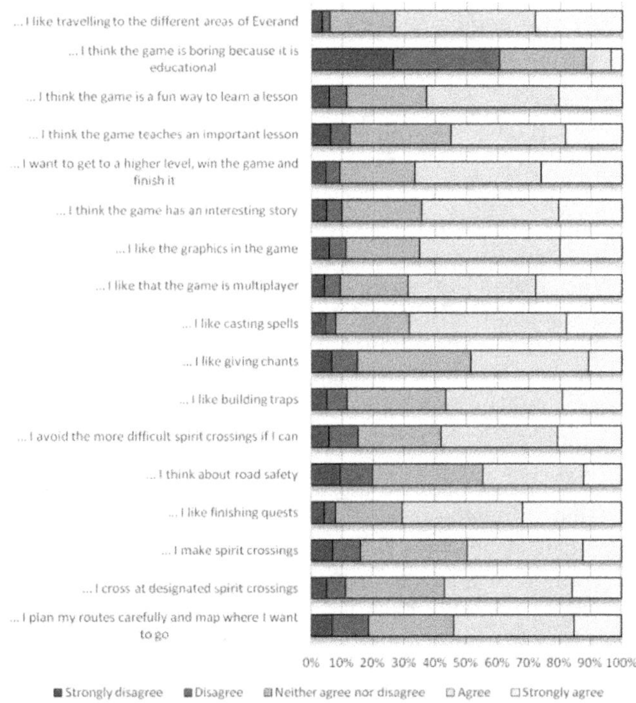

Figure 8. Likert scale responses from players (n=743) when asked about the various aspects of the game.

Attempting to create models for learning through analogy can be particularly challenging in a game-based environment, given the potential for players to seek to defeat a game as efficiently as possible, rather than take the route intended by designers. Consider, for example, the following child's perspective of their avatar - this player had learnt that, situationally, dying in game could be used to his advantage to save time on travel:

"He [my avatar] would be probably very very annoying. He'd be doing stupid things like killing himself. [...] I wouldn't do really stupid things, but if I was like him in this

game and I knew if I died I just could come back, I would just keep on trying things." [Male, 11]

Qualitative work demonstrated that usability within Code of Everand, though with some areas for improvement, was not a barrier to players' entry, a finding again reinforced by broadly positive responses to questions of the enjoyment of various game elements (Figure 8). A significant observation here related to the expectations of children with respect to how game-based content is conveyed. A tendency was observed to avoid reading text, and very few children in qualitative observation (n=31) referred to the substantive game manual, reflected in approaches which either built on trial-and-error or more-able partners:

"I just like to find out for myself because then I get used to the controls earlier" [Male, 11]

"It's better to play with someone [...]. Well it was a bit worrying at the start and [another male player, 10] told me what I had to do... he explained it first. That was ages and ages ago when we first got it." [Male, 10]

Entertainment games largely embrace spoken dialogue, and particularly with a young audience whose literacy skills may not yet be fully developed, text-heavy game content may easily be overlooked. If learning outcomes are similarly embedded, it is equally possible they may be overlooked. Code of Everand avoids this in-part though its implementation of analogical problem-solving though a predominantly visual approach, though to play and understand the game fully some appreciation of its depth is required whilst in turn implies reference to the manual. Some interviewees overlooked elements of gameplay such as using the correct trap types to match monsters, or the world map, as they were not sufficiently transparent.

Qualitative work also sought to understand the typical playtimes identified in the previous section. Analysis on the in-game "buddy" list, which allowed players to form friendship ties with other players, showed 14,100 players to have used the feature, generating a social network of 59,479 players from the total of 99,683. However, only 4.5% of social ties (2,685) were reciprocal. Observation of players (n=31) showed that in many cases the limited ability to communicate through pre-set dialogue options meant they approached a player, added them to their list, then went on their way: behaviour indicative of social interaction, but not in the a meaningful or deeper fashion that would be expected as a requirement for social learning.

DISCUSSION

Taken as a whole, the results show significant usage within the UK, supported by positive attitudes of players towards game based learning. In terms of ascertaining the receptiveness of a school-age audience to game-based road safety education, and engaging with a serious game in their leisure time, the results support the argument that children are willing to engage with serious games in a leisure context, and their realisation that the game has serious intent is not a barrier to entry (Figure 8). Evidence suggests that though the audience was predominantly male, females did make up around one in five players. Though playtimes and return visits preclude the ability to assert that social learning was occurring on a large scale over a long-term within the game, qualitative and survey data illustrate that in the shorter term, players were recognizing and reflecting upon the analogy to real world safety. It is again worth noting that as proven methods already existed for transferring the fundamental knowledge of safe crossing, Code of Everand focused upon encouraging children to apply this knowledge in practice, rather than reiterating the direct messaging aims of other methods of safety education. As such, whilst the ultimate impact of this recognition and reflection is hard to quantify, evidence suggests the game did achieve the objective of reaching a large UK audience for a significant contact time, and encouraged a proportion of this audience to reflect upon their existing safety knowledge in the context of the game.

A key benefit of the game based approach when compared to other interventions was its ability to attract a young audience for a period averaging 93 minutes, a notable achievement considering children were playing the game outside of a classroom context without extrinsic motivation. Similarly, that 16% of the nationally-representative sample had heard of the game (n=1,108), and that of these one in five had gone on to play it, demonstrates the appeal serious games can hold for this audience. Interest amongst the target audience was evident for game-based approaches to learning, with the majority of those surveyed disagreeing that the game's educational premise made it 'boring'. Evidence did emerge to support impact in the short-term on players of the game, and indeed there was no pre-requisite on minimum exposure time under the models of analogical transfer and scaffolded reflection built into the game. Qualitative interviews and larger scale statistics outlined in the previous section demonstrated recognition of the game's serious purpose and analogy, in many cases leading to reflection and self-reporting of attitudinal change by interviewees. Comparison of the player survey to the national survey also showed significantly safer behaviour amongst players, though a more rigorous control study approach would be required to demonstrate this conclusively, and would itself by limited due to the difficulty in obtaining concrete metrics of safer behaviour over the long term amongst participants within a practical sample size.

Though playtime durations were in excess of what might be expected from a visit to a static, informational website [22, 23], they were not indicative of the long-term retention often demonstrated by commercial massively-multiplayer online games. One factor behind this may have been the difficulty in realizing social aspects in the absence of the ability for players to directly communicate. Qualitative research supported this, as did analysis of the in game "buddy" list: when surveyed, 68% of players (n=618) purported to play the game alone, 9% with friends they met online, and 23% with parents, siblings, or friends from school. However, the in game 'buddy' list, which allowed players to record and track their friends, was used by only 14% (n=99,608) of players, and of the 59,479 social ties formed, only 2,685 were reciprocal. Within the smaller qualitative sample, the players who had made friends with other players tended to do so without any real sense of social connection. Either a player had approaches them, asked them to be friends, and they had said yes, or participants initiated the friendship; yet the entire encounter carried the same weight as acknowledging someone in the street: a clear example of social interaction, but not of meaningful social connection. Considering design methodologies for MMO worlds which emphasize the role of socializers in creating sustainable communities [19], this likely had a significant impact on user retention. More encouraging in this respect was the fact that 21% of players (n=969) signed up to Code of Everand after hearing about it from a friend or school friend, suggesting the game was discussed amongst children beyond the confines of its online environment.An open question in the national survey showed the most played game in the 9-15 age range was the PEGI-18 rated *Call of Duty* series (53% of boys and 12% of girls, n=1,108), demonstrating that this age group are widely engaging with adult gaming titles, compared to lower usage rates for child-oriented games such as *Club Penguin* (12% of boys and 13% of girls). Whilst Code of Everand was not intrinsically 'childish' in its design, this does demonstrate that appealing to such an audience in their leisure time requires interventions to compete with games aimed at a mature audience.

Taken in a wider context, this has implications for all interventions which seek to capitalize on social networking or other technology-facilitated social interactions, since interventions limited by policy preventing open communication amongst under-16s are likely to struggle when placed in competition with the adult-oriented sites and technologies which this audience reported to be widely using. Furthermore, when asked by open question what they felt were the greatest dangers affecting children their age, 16% of players (n=111) reported Internet-related threats; this was no doubt a consequence of the online nature of the survey, but nonetheless reflects a degree of wariness towards online social interactions amongst children who are frequently informed of the dangers they may pose. The specific chosen game-based interaction approach has a very clear appeal to the target audience of children aged 9-15, with a gender bias towards male players. An important part of this appeal is that the mechanics, dynamics and aesthetics of the game is deliberately not designed to be "childish", and focuses foremost on being fun and challenging. Even with this young age group some reflection can be expected and the scaffold pedagogical approach is suitable, provided that the analogy is not too difficult to spot.

CONCLUSION

A critique common to evaluations of digital games for learning is that evidence of high usage is not adequately supported by evidence of impact or reach to a target demographic. This is a particularly complex issue in the case of public health as digital games are typically deployed to enhance rather than replace other interventions, and therefore comparisons with existing methods of teaching or training can be of limited value. Similarly, in the specific context of road safety, differences between self-reported and actual behaviour makes survey or interview alone a limited tool for assessing behavioural changes. Hence, whilst the evaluation of Code of Everand presented in this paper cannot claim to conclusively demonstrate long-term change, the analysis of reach as well as impact presented a compelling case for the future consideration of game-based approaches to changing attitudes and behaviour in young audiences. Such approaches must capitalize on the findings of this study to anticipate exposure time at the early stages of design and develop and implement models for learning transfer accordingly.

If, as evidence suggests, the limited exposure times of players to the world of Everand were strongly influenced by difficulty in communicating and forming meaningful social ties, a need exists for careful review of reflection upon policy and its underlying ethical implications when creating social online environments for young audiences. If enabling direct communication is not viable, then as this study demonstrates, the resulting environment faces a challenge in engaging an audience widely interacting using social media and online games for which similar restrictions are not in place.

Despite these challenges, growing evidence, including that provided by this paper, suggests that the large-scale deployment of digital games for learning can attract and retain a sizable audience for a period likely to exceed that possible through more static web-based intervention [22, 23], or other media such as television advertising. By relying on players' ability to recognize and reflect on underlying road safety principles, Code of Everand followed widely accepted best practice approaches for serious games by putting gameplay elements before educational content [18]. It also demonstrates the need for careful and structured pedagogical design reflecting upon the typical playtimes of users; a factor which can be difficult to anticipate prior to launch due to the absence of similar large-scale studies. Certainly for the 9-15 audience, developers must be aware of the high level of competition for children's screen time as well as the games with which children currently engage, the majority of which may not necessarily be titles explicitly designed for a young audience. A model of analogical transfer requires considerable time investment of the part of the player, and it may be the case that alternative methods or mechanisms could prove more effective in delivering rapid outcomes. Developing these approaches and translating them to game design principles through careful reference to established pedagogies must by a key goal for future work.

ACKNOWLEDGMENTS

The authors would like to thank Simon Christmas (Simon Christmas Ltd), Rosemary Duff (Childwise) and Jenny Ehren (Childwise), who undertook the qualitative element of the research and have given permission for publication of their findings in this paper. They would also like to thank Simon Leggett (Childwise) for his support in analysing the data from the national survey. Code of Everand was developed by Area/Code, with the development of the game and its evaluation funded by the UK Department for Transport.

REFERENCES

1. C. Kapp, "WHO acts on road safety to reverse accident trends.," *Lancet* 362 (2003), 1125-1130.
2. T. B. Cole, "Global road safety crisis remedy sought: 1.2 million killed, 50 million injured annually," *Journal of the American Medical Association (JAMA)* 291 (2004), 2531-2532.
3. P. M. Kato, S. W. Cole, A. S. Bradlyn, and B. H. Pollock, "A Video Game Improves Behavioral Outcomes in Adolescents and Young Adults With Cancer: A Randomized Trial," *Pediatrics* 122 (2008), 305-317.
4. M. S. Zeedyk and L. Wallace, "Tackling children's road safety through edutainment: An evaluation of effectiveness.," *Health Education Research: Theory and Practice*, 18 (2003), 493-503.
5. E. H. C. Gámez, P. Cairns, J. Gow, J. Back, and E. Capstick, "Video games as research instruments," in *Proceedings of the 28th of the international conference extended abstracts on Human factors in computing systems*, Atlanta, Georgia, USA (2010), 4493-4496.
6. C. V. Platt, A. B. Clayton, S. M. Pringle, G. Butler, and M. A. Colgan, Road safety education for children transferring to secondary school. London, UK: Department for Transport (2003).
7. M. A. Elliott and C. J. Baughan, Adolescent road user behaviour: A survey of 11-16 year olds. Crowthorne, UK: Transport Research Laboratory Ltd. (2003).
8. D. J. Terry, M. A. Hogg, and K. M. White, "The theory of planned behaviour: self-identity, social identity and group norms," *British Journal of Social Psychology*, 38 (1999), 225-244.
9. V. J. Stretcher, J. A. Baumeister, J. Shope, C. Chang, M. H. Newport-Berra, A. Giroux, and E. Guay, "Intervention modalities to address relevant psychosocial predictors of driving behaviour among adolescents: Primary report, road safety research No. 70," London, UK: Department for Transport (2007).
10. K. Ampofo-Boateng and J. A. Thomson, "Children's perception of safety and danger on the road," *British Journal of Psychology*, 82 (1991), 487-505.
11. R. Pratchett, "Gamers in the UK: Digital play, digital lifestyles." London, UK: British Broadcasting Corporation (2005).
12. L. A. Annetta, M. R. Murray, S. G. Laird, S. C. Bohr, and J. C. Park, "Serious Games: Incorporating Video Games in the Classroom," *EDUCAUSE Quarterly*, 29 (2006).
13. P. Backlund, H. Engstrom, M. Johannesson, and M. Lebram, "Games for traffic education: An experimental study of a game-based driving simulator," *Simulation and Gaming*, 41 (2010), 145-169.
14. L. Renaud and S. Suissa, "Evaluation of the efficacy of simulation games in traffic safety education of kindergarten children," *American Journal of Public Health*, 79 (1989), 307-309.
15. M. Zyda, "From Visual Simulation to Virtual Reality to Games," *Computer*, 38 (2005), 25-32.
16. A. Bandura, Social Learning Theory. Englewood Cliffs, NJ: Prentice-Hall (1977).
17. K. J. Klauer, "Teaching for analogical transfer as a means of improving problem-solving, thinking and learning," *Instructional Science*, 18 (1989), 179-192.
18. M. G. Bradford, B. T. Robson, and R. Tye, "Constructing an urban deprivation index: a way of meeting the need for flexibility", *Environmental Planning A*, 27 (1995), 519-533.
19. R. Bartle, Designing Virtual Worlds. Berkeley, CA: New Riders (2003).
20. J. Dyck, D. Pinelle, B. Brown and C. Gutwin, "Learning from Games: HCI Design Innovations in Entertainment Software". in *Proceedings of Graphics Interface* (2003), 237-246.
21. A. H. Jørgensen, "Marrying HCI/Usability and computer games: a preliminary look", in *Proceedings of the third Nordic conference on Human-computer interaction*, ACM (2004), 393-396.
22. C. Liu, R. W. White, S. Dumais, "Understanding web browsing behaviors through Weibull analysis of dwell time", in *Proceedings of the 33rd International ACM SIGIR Conference on Research and Development in Information Retrieval*, SIGIR. ACM (2010) 379–386.
23. H. Weinreich, H. Obendorf, E. Herder, M. Mayer, M., "Not quite the average: An empirical study of Web use". *ACM Transactions on the Web*, 2 (2008), 5:1–5:31.

L.IVE: An Integrated Interactive Video-based Learning Environment

Toni-Jan Keith Monserrat[1] **Yawen Li**[2] **Shengdong Zhao**[1] **Xiang Cao**[3]
tjmonsi@gmail.com iamliyawen@gmail.com zhaosd@comp.nus.edu.sg xiangcao@acm.org
[1]NUS-HCI Lab, National University of Singapore, Singapore
[2]NUS Graduate School for Integrative Sciences and Engineering, National University of Singapore, Singapore
[3]Lenovo, Beijing, China

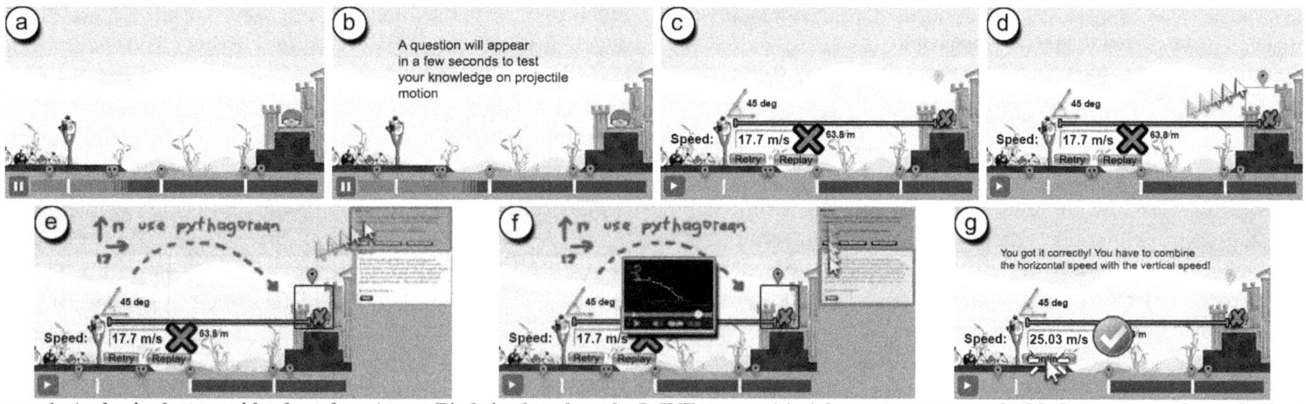

Figure 1: A physics lecture video based on Angry Birds is played on the L.IVE system (a). A lecturer uses an embedded text annotation to indicate a quiz is coming (b). The video is automatically paused with an in-place quiz that asks the speed required to hit the green target. Users' answers will be assessed and feedback given based on their individual responses (c). Users see a comment tag above the green target, and move the cursor over as the tag fades in (d). Clicking on the comment tag displays the comments on the side. Hovering over the comments reveals an associated annotation, which can be hand-drawn (e) or shown as a linked video (f). Correctly answering the quiz question advances the video (g).

ABSTRACT

In this paper, we introduce L.IVE: an online interactive video-based learning environment with an alternative design and architecture that integrates three major interface components: video, comment threads, and assessments. This is in contrast with the approach of existing interfaces which visually separate these components. Our study, which compares L.IVE with existing popular video-based learning environments, suggests advantages in this integrated approach as compared to the separated approach in learning.

Author Keywords

L.IVE; interactive video; video-based online learning

ACM Classification Keywords

H.5.1. Information interfaces and presentation: Multimedia Information Systems - Video

INTRODUCTION

Recently, video-based online learning environments have emerged as a hot topic in education. Some popular examples include Khan Academy, Udacity, edX, Coursera, and other websites that post their videos in YouTube educational channels. Together, they offer a great variety of courses and attract millions of users each month [2].

CHI 2014, April 26 - May 01 2014, Toronto, ON, Canada

ACM 978-1-4503-2473-1/14/04 $15.00.
http://dx.doi.org/10.1145/2556288.2557368

Although the content, design, and layout differ among these environments, they all have three interface elements to support key educational activities: videos to deliver the lecture content (learning), comment threads for sharing (discussion), and assessments to check learning progress (assessment) [5].

Despite their successes, current interface designs seem to have one drawback: the three components are presented separately, either by page layout or page separation (Fig. 2 *left*). This potentially creates additional burdens for learners to cognitively link different sources of information together, thereby impairing the effectiveness of their learning [1]. For example, a comment placed below the video may contain useful information for learners to understand the key lecture concepts; however, it can be easily overlooked, as most people tend to focus on the video. Furthermore, because the duration of each video typically spans at least a few minutes, it can be difficult for learners to identify which part of the video the comment is associated with.

Similarly, while it may seem natural to assess users' learning after watching a video segment, visually separating assessment questions from video content can make it harder for learners to recall the relevant information for answering questions. This may be less ideal as Constructivism suggests that it is beneficial to allow learners to explore and access relevant information "just-in-time," so they can better construct mental images for enhanced learning [4].

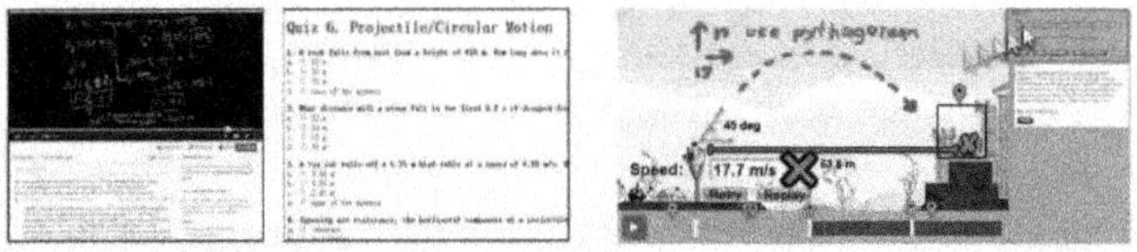

Figure 2: Current video-based learning environments visually separate the video, comments, and assessments (left). L.IVE tightly integrates the three components (right).

Therefore we propose an alternative design to visually integrate comment threads and assessment questions tightly with the video. We created the L.IVE (Integrated Interactive Video-based Environment for Learning) prototype to test the potential benefit of the proposed integrated approach as compared with the current separated approach. Our evaluation of 18 participants indicated that they learned more efficiently with the L.IVE integrated approach than with the baseline approach: participants showed 20% greater scores, measured as post-test performance compared with pre-test performance, when they experienced content with L.IVE. Our post-experimental questionnaire also indicated that most participants preferred the integrated approach as compared with the separated approach.

The concept of adding either comment thread or assessment to videos is not new. However, based on our analysis, users' benefit may be maximized when both comment thread and assessment are tightly integrated with the video. We developed L.IVE, the first system and design to integrate all three components and apply them in the context of online video-based learning. Further, we also contribute an architecture to facilitate the implementation of this integrated design on the web, where video-based learning systems are becoming increasingly popular. Finally, we conducted the first empirical evaluation to reveal the potential benefits of this integrated design for online video-based learning.

RELATED WORK

Numerous works have added various types of interactive elements in videos. Due to space constraints, we can only list a few representative ones. The Hvet Design [11] used links in videos to external information to improve user learning. NoteVideo reverse-engineered the video to convert visual glyphs of lecture notes into clickable links to make it easier for learners to access the different parts of video and has shown the new interface improves various learning tasks [9]. CWaCTool implemented in-place annotations and comments in video for sharing and discussing annotated information [10]. In-place annotation and in-context comment threads have also been tried in documents [12]. In addition, learning assessments have been included as part of games [3], and most recently be experimented in video [6].

While the previous work has provided inspirations, there has not been an attempt to integrate the three components of online video-based learning environment together. Furthermore, there hasn't been a formal evaluation to reveal the potential benefits/drawbacks of such integrated approach for learning and education, hence providing motivation for our work.

L.IVE SYSTEM

Our vision for the L.IVE system is for it to be an interactive video player that allows users to view lecture video, discuss with both the teaching staff and peers, and assess their learning within or in close proximity to the video itself. The goal is to tightly connect information presented from the different sources to provide an enriched, holistic learning experience.

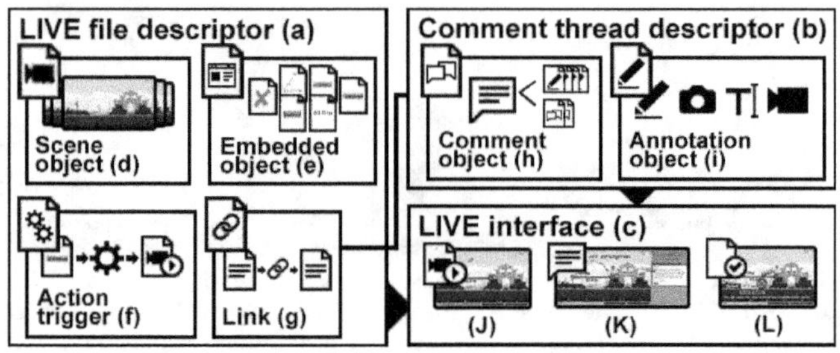

Figure 3. An overview of the l.ive system

Figure 1 illustrates an example of using the L.IVE system in a physics lecture on projectile motion. As in the example in the figure, educational information is often presented in three main formats: video, comment threads, and assessments. Though used somewhat differently, all three are equally important in working together to enhance the user's ability to learn efficiently. Existing systems separates these elements and may hamper with the user's ease of learning of abstract and complex information. Thus, there is a need for an interface design and underlying software architecture to support integrated organization and presentation of information that connects the three source components and allow users to easily interact with them.

System Implementation and Architecture

We constructed a data structure to organize the different interactive elements based on their spatial and temporal relationships to the video as well as their logical relevance to the lecture content. This hierarchy of information is described in two files called the *Interactive Video File Descriptor* (Fig. 3a) and the *Comment Thread Descriptor* (Fig. 3b). Both are JSON documents that are based on SIVA's interactive video XML document design but are modified to allow in-place objects in video rather than at pre-defined places (top, bottom, left, right) [8].

Interactive video file descriptor

The file descriptor defines four types of entities: a list of scene objects, a list of embedded objects, a separate list for action triggers, and a link to a comment thread descriptor (Fig. 3). *Scene Objects* (Fig. 3d) define the main videos (Fig. 1a) and their starting and ending times and can be linked to each other to provide a seamless flow to create one integrated timeline. *Embedded Objects* (Fig. 3e) define integrated interactive elements such as assessment forms, buttons for navigation, and additional in-place information (i.e., texts, sub-videos, and images, see Fig. 1b). They have a starting time of appearance and an ending time of appearance. The location of the element in the video space is defined by its x and y coordinates. *Action Triggers* (Fig. 3f) links to events, like showing or hiding interactive elements, are encapsulated in an action trigger's data definition. User interactions on elements will usually call these action triggers to issue a change in the interface. Link (Fig. 3g) is a vector that points to a separate comment thread descriptor for the L.IVE interface to load.

Comment thread file descriptor

All user annotations and comment threads are encapsulated in a separate file called a *Comment Thread Descriptor* (Fig. 3b). The separation of the comment thread descriptor and the interactive video file descriptor allows users to share the interactive video with their peers without copying the comment threads of the original interactive video. A comment thread descriptor contains a list of comment objects and annotation objects. Comment object is either a comment thread starter or a reply to a comment (Fig. 3h). A comment thread starter type has data connecting it to a scene object and holds x and y coordinate and a timestamp of the video. This visually integrates it to the video. A comment reply is connected to another comment data object, creating a comment thread. Annotation object is a user-created in-video annotation encapsulated in an annotation object (Fig. 3i) and is connected to comment data. Each annotation object can be any of these types depending on their encapsulated object data: free-hand drawing, text, image, or video. The annotation object's location is defined by its x and y data coordinates.

The system is implemented using three main web technologies: HTML5, Cascading Style Sheets (CSS), and Javascript (with JQuery 1.8 Library and JSON), which are responsible for the structure, style, rendering, and interactivity of all objects and action triggers in the L.IVE interface. The current mechanism of authoring a L.IVE video is through manually editing the markup language in a text editor. The WYSIWYG interface for authoring the L.IVE video is in current development.

USER STUDY

To evaluate our design, we performed an experiment to test the L.IVE interface and compare it with a current video-based online learning interface (baseline) (Fig. 2) to investigate any potential differences in their abilities to facilitate learning.

Participants: Eighteen participants (6 females), ranging in age from 20 to 29 years were recruited from within the university community to take part in the experiment. 15 of them have previous experience with existing online video-based learning environments.

Apparatus: The study was conducted using a desktop computer running on Windows 7 OS with the usual mouse-keyboard input. The L.IVE system's implementation was as previously described. The baseline system was implemented using HTML5, CSS, and JavaScript.

Task and stimuli: Two 10-minute biology videos from Khan Academy were selected as the lecture videos[1]. Each video has 10 comments and 3 assessment quizzes. All comments were selected from the existing comment threads on these videos from Khan Academy. We made some modifications to the comments by removing unrelated posts and answered some questions with text explanations and/or links to external information and videos. We also added x and y coordinates to fix appearance of linked videos on the L.IVE interface. The structure and appearance of comments for both conditions were the same. We also developed the assessment quizzes. Because assessments were not embedded in the baseline, they were implemented in the usual way: after every 2-3 minutes of a video segment, the users were taken to another page to complete the assessment. The timing of the assessment in the baseline is the same as in L.IVE.

Design and procedure: A within-participant design was used. Each participant watched both videos (v1, v2) using both interfaces (L.IVE, baseline). The order of the interfaces was counter-balanced while the order of the videos remained the same (e.g., participant 1 watched v1 using L.IVE, then watched v2 using baseline; participant 2 watched v1 using baseline, then watched v2 using L.IVE).

To measure the knowledge gain, for each video, a 10-question pre-test (before watching) and a 10-question post-test (after watching) were administered to each participant. The two sets of questions tests the same type of knowledge but were asked in slightly different ways (i.e. one question would be asked in identification form with a why question after, and the other question would be in essay form. The difference in the number of questions answered correctly in the pre- and post- tests was recorded. After they finished watching both videos using the two interfaces, participants shared their preferences and experience in an interview.

Before the experiment, participants were asked to spend about 2 minutes each to familiarize with the two interfaces. Each participant performed the entire experiment in one sitting, including breaks, in approximately 1 hour.

RESULTS

Two tailed t-Tests with 5% alpha-level revealed that there was a significant effect of interface type on difference of pre-test and post-tests scores. The percentage scores of participants using L.IVE interface (54.21%, pre-test score=.41, post-test score=8.3, gain=7.89) was significantly higher than when using the baseline interface (44.36%, pre-

[1] v1) http://bit.ly/14iSTFS
v2) http://bit.ly/15CQ3wB

test score=.37, post-test score=6.8, gain=6.43) ($t17 = 2.98$, $p < 0.01$). The L.IVE interface resulted in an additional 22% score as compared with the baseline interface. However, the overall learning time participants spent using the L.IVE interface (16 min 38 sec) were not significantly different from time spent using the baseline interface (15 min 44 sec) ($p = 0.62$). For embedded assessments, all participants eventually completed the assessments correctly after doing the experiment. Participants answered L.IVE and baselines assessments incorrectly, on average, 1.11 and 1.83 times, respectively. This indicates an average of 0.72 or 65% more unsuccessful attempts when using baseline.

In addition to the results above, the majority of participants preferred the design of the L.IVE system (13/18) over the baseline design (5/18). Participants expressed that the in-context annotations, comment threads and assessments were helpful in getting to know the bigger picture of the information. The ease of access to information in comments while watching video helped them understand and absorb more information. The in-context assessments also helped them to recall information.

DISCUSSION

The feedback of the participants also provided additional insights that can guide the design of future video-based learning environments. Although most participants preferred the L.IVE interface, a few participants still preferred the baseline interface as it allowed them to focus on the video first. This suggests that the L.IVE system may not be suitable for everyone; it is recommended that future video-learning environments provide an option for users to switch back to the traditional interface if they prefer.

In addition, while 10 comments are easy to manage, participants pointed out that an excessive number of comments may clutter the video interface and distract their attention. It is suggested that comments and annotations should be monitored and managed so that irrelevant ones can be filtered out and potential visual clutter can be minimized or avoided [7].

Lastly, participants suggested that it would be useful to allow personalized comments targeted to specific audiences instead of the entire viewing group. For example, a student may want to raise a question only for the teaching staff to look at; alternatively, one may want to start a discussion only with several of her close friends.

CONCLUSION

In this paper, we proposed an alternative design to visually integrate comment threads and assessment questions tightly within video. We implemented this alternative design in a prototyping L.IVE system and contributed a system architecture for organizing and presenting information from the three components on the web. Our evaluation of 18 participants indicated that they learned more efficiently with the L.IVE integrated approach than with baseline, showing 20% score gain with the former. Our post-experimental questionnaire and interviews revealed that most participants preferred the integrated approach as compared with the separated approach. Their input also highlighted potential challenges to watch for when deploying the system. In the future, we would like to evaluate L.IVE in a real online course setting and explore other values or experiences our integrated approach can bring to areas other than learning.

ACKNOWLEDGEMENT

This project is funded by the National Research Foundation (NRF) and managed through the multi-agency Interactive & Digital Media Programme Office (IDMPO) hosted by the Media Development Authority of Singapore (MDA) under Centre of Social Media Innovations for Communities (COSMIC).

REFERENCES

1. Ainsworth, S. and Van Labeke, N. Multiple Forms of Dynamic Representation. *Learning and Instruction 14*, 3 (2004), 241–255.
2. Faviero, B.B.F. Major players in online education market - The Tech. 2012. http://tech.mit.edu/V132/N34/education.html.
3. Harpstead, E., Myers, B.A., and Aleven, V. In-search of Learning: Facilitating Data Analysis in Educational Games. *In CHI '13*, (2013), 79.
4. Jonassen, D. Designing Constructivist Learning Environments. In *Instructional design theories and models: A new paradigm of instructional theory 2*. 1999, 215–239.
5. Kellogg, S. Online learning: How to make a MOOC. *Nature 499*, 7458 (2013), 369–371.
6. Macwilliam, T., Aquino, R.J., and Malan, D.J. Engaging Students Through Video: Integrating Assessment and Instrumentation. *Journal of Computing Sciences in Colleges 28*, 6 (2013), 169–178.
7. Mayer, R. Cognitive Theory of Multimedia Learning. In *The Cambridge handbook of multimedia learning*. 2005.
8. Meixner, B. and Kosch, H. Interactive Non-linear Video: Definition and XML Structure. *In DocEng '12*, (2012), 49.
9. Monserrat, T.-J.K.P., Zhao, S., McGee, K., and Pandey, A.V. NoteVideo: Facilitating Navigation of Blackboard-style Lecture Videos. *In CHI '13*, (2013), 1139.
10. Motti, V.G., Fagá, R., Catellan, R.G., Pimentel, M.D.G.C., and Teixeira, C. a. C. Collaborative synchronous video annotation via the watch-and-comment paradigm. *In EuroITV '09*, (2009), 67.
11. Tiellet, C.A.B., Pereira, A.G., Reategui, E.B., Lima, J.V., and Chambel, T. Design and evaluation of a hypervideo environment to support veterinary surgery learning. *In HT '10*, (2010), 213.
12. Zyto, S., Karger, D., Ackerman, M., and Mahajan, S. Successful classroom deployment of a social document annotation system. *In CHI '12*, (2012), 1883.

Persuasive Technology for Overcoming Food Cravings and Improving Snack Choices

Anne Hsu[1], Jing Yang[1], Yigit Yilmaz[1], Md Sanaul Haque[1], Cengiz Can[1], Ann Blandford[2]

Queen Mary, University of London
School of Electronic Engineering and Computer Science
Mile End Road, London, E14NS
{anne.hsu, j.yang, y.yilmaz, m.haque, c.can}@qmul.ac.uk

University College London
UCL Interaction Centre
Gower Street, London WC1E 7JG
a.blandford@ucl.ac.uk

ABSTRACT

A central challenge in weight management is the difficulty of overcoming desires for excessive and unhealthy food. Yet, studies show that when people are able to resist their desires for unhealthy choices, they experience pride and satisfaction. In order to alleviate the former and support the latter, we designed, implemented and tested a mobile application for improving snacking behavior. Our application delivers a food craving reduction intervention at the moment of need and allows users to track how often they successfully resisted cravings. Our craving reduction intervention is based on recent research that shows that food cravings can be reduced through imagery techniques. We conducted a week-long evaluation of our application, comparing the effectiveness of our application to a basic tracking application. We found that our imagery application significantly reduced both overall snacking and unhealthy snacking compared to a simple snack-tracking application.

Author Keywords

Persuasive technologies; behavior change; weight management; mobile; wellness; user-centered design

ACM Classification Keywords

H.5.m. Information interfaces and presentation (e.g., HCI): Miscellaneous. J.3. Life and medical sciences: Health.

General Terms

Human Factors.

INTRODUCTION

Persuasive technologies effect change through two primary (non-mutually exclusive) avenues: by targeting either external behaviors or internal attitudes. The overwhelming majority of existing persuasive technologies focus on external behaviors [1], e.g. a tracker for calorie consumption and exercise [1-5]. This is because external behaviors are more tangible, measurable, and thus easier targets for change. However, the distinction between influencing behavior vs. thought is often blurred: often influencing behavior also promotes new thoughts and awareness. For example exercise and calorie trackers increase user awareness of their activities and intake. Along these lines, there has been a recent increase in persuasive technologies designed for psychological influence by encouraging reflection and awareness about health related choices. These include a visual garden display to encourage emotional connection to one's levels of physical activity [6, 7], open-ended platforms for documenting and sharing health decisions, and a shared visual journal for diet and exercise [8].

It is important for persuasive systems to change attitudes as well as behavior because attitudes and psychological processes are the underpinnings of human choices and behavior [9-11]. Many technologies such as mobile applications are particularly well-positioned to deliver interventions that target psychological processes because they are pervasively by our side. These advantages of pervasive technologies have been summarized through a description of the many roles that such technologies play [12]: a device of 'kairos' that is always near at hand; the role of a concierge that offers guidance and information at the moment of need; a personal coach that can track personal goals and context; and a jester that can promote fun interactions (both personal and social). These properties of technological systems make them well suited for modifying psychology because they can evoke new thought processes and emotions in a timely fashion, customized to the persuasion context. For example, technologies can be synchronized with electronic diaries or sensing technologies [13] to know when contexts that prompt salient psychological states will occur. Finally, thoughts, feelings, and attitudes are highly personal, and technology-based systems have the potential for delivering personalized interventions that cater to this individual variation.

Designing for specific psychological constructs

In a movement towards more psychology-inspired design, recent persuasive health technologies have started applying

CHI 2014, April 26 - May 01 2014, Toronto, ON, Canada
Copyright @ 2014 ACM 978-1-4503-2473-1/14/04...$15.00.
http://dx.doi.org/10.1145/2556288.2557099

theories and strategies from psychology and health research [1, 3, 14-16]. While knowledge of context-general psychological principles is highly useful for persuasive design, it is also important to understand the specific psychological constructs that underlie the behaviors in a particular design context. Recent work has suggested that context-specific psychological constructs can be usefully investigated from the perspective of a decision theory framework [17]. Decision theory explains how behavioral choices are underpinned by psychological rewards and costs valuations [9]. Behaviors are chosen when they are associated with greater rewards and fewer costs. This notion of rewards and costs is fundamentally a hedonistic concept, relating to emotional experiences of pleasure and displeasure in the brain. An understanding of the rewards and costs associated with healthy and unhealthy behaviors can inform the design of persuasive health technologies: systems can then aim to increase the rewards and decrease the costs associated with healthy behaviors.

A recent study used such a decision theoretic approach to investigate the psychological constructs that discouraged and encouraged weight management behavior [17]. It was found that the need to restrict the pleasure of eating was one of the most widely experienced struggles involved in weight loss. On the other hand, another widely expressed view was that people felt good after resisting food temptations and making healthy choices. People felt pride, and satisfaction associated with being good to oneself and having self control. We wished to design an application that addressed both of these psychological weight loss constructs: to help people with their struggle against food temptations while simultaneously enhancing their ability to feel good about healthy choices. As a method of reducing the difficulty of unhealthy temptations, we look to recent research on the psychology of cravings, which describes both how cravings may be sustained in the mind and how they can be reduced. This is known as the Elaborated Intrusion (EI) Theory of Desire [18-21], which we describe briefly below.

Food Cravings: EI Theory of Desire

The Elaborated Intrusion (EI) Theory of Desire is a theory for how appetitive cravings (including food) are sustained through cognitive processes [18-25]. EI theory suggests that cravings involve a cycle of mental elaboration of an initial intrusive thought. Because these thoughts are initially pleasurable, the individual is motivated to elaborate the thought, and sustain the craving by retrieving cognitive associations and creating mental imagery of the target. These mental imagery elaborations recruit working memory functions and may include the senses of sight, taste, touch, and hearing. Because cravings are thus presumed to be sustained through specific cognitive processes, EI theory proposes that an alternative task that recruits similar mental resources could conversely disrupt the elaboration of desire-related intrusive thoughts and thus reduce cravings. Consistent with this idea, many studies have found that engaging in visual or olfactory imagery reduces the strength of food cravings, both for cravings induced in the lab [20-22] and naturally occurring 'in the wild' [25]. In contrast, auditory imagery tasks were not found to reduce cravings.

While the above results are very promising, they only measured self-reported decrease in craving levels and effects on consumption were not assessed. Our study will be the first to evaluate whether this method of craving reduction results in reduced consumption 'in the wild'. We designed and implemented a mobile application for improving snacking behavior. Our application is designed to alleviate the struggle for excessive consumption while enabling users to emphasize the times where they successfully made healthy choices by either choosing a healthy snack or resisting a snack entirely. Because previous research has shown that simple tracking is effective for improving eating habits [3], we assessed the effectiveness of our application for improving snacking by comparing its effects to that of a basic tracking application in a one week experimental study. Finally we discuss future directions for improving our application.

SYSTEM DESIGN: ICRAVE

We designed a technology we call *iCrave* to help people improve their snacking habits. iCrave is a simple mobile app that allows users to track their snack cravings and allows them to record whether they choose to have a healthy or unhealthy snack, or to forgo a snack. iCrave helps users in the moment of desire for unhealthy/excessive snacking by prompting a craving-reduction imagery task and allowing users to record their subsequent choices.

The usage of iCrave is as follows: When the user experiences a snack craving, they press the main 'iCrave' button. The application then shows a text prompt asking users to imagine a specific passive or active scene for 10 seconds, during which a 10 second countdown timer is shown. There were 20 different suggested visualizations based on those used in previous work, which appeared in block random order [21, 26]. This type of text-prompted imagery exercise has been shown in previous research to reduce craving intensity [18-24]. Because we wanted to check whether imagination intensity was correlated with effectiveness, and also to emphasize engagement with the visualization task, after the 10 second imagery task, we asked users to rate on a 5 point scale how vividly they imagined the scene, ranging from 'No image at all' to 'perfectly vivid, just like the real thing'. Then users were allowed to make one of three choices on the application, by either not eating at all and therefore 'saving' their craving, or choosing a healthy or unhealthy snack. If the user chooses to not eat at all, they are congratulated on 'saving' their craving and the system keeps track of a 20

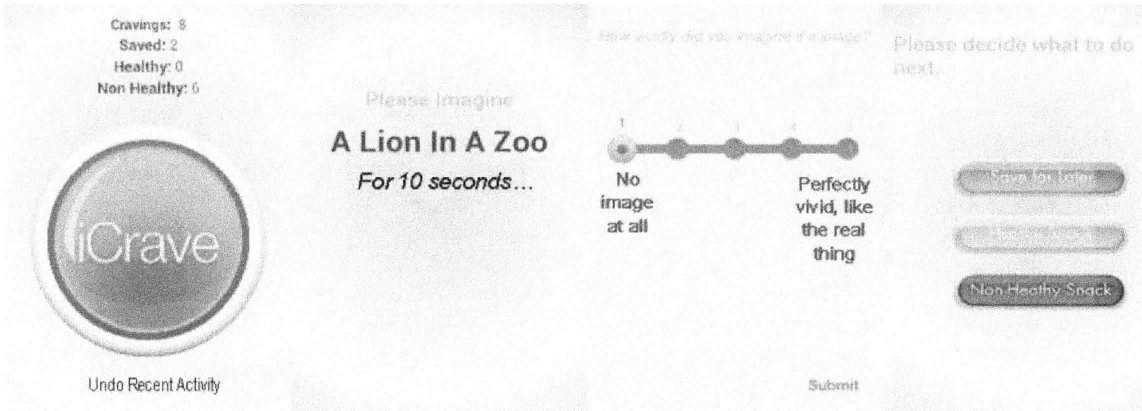

Figure 1. Screen shots of iCrave application

minute period, during which they are not allowed to choose to either eat or save a craving again. A 20 minute period was chosen because research has shown it takes at least 10 minutes for the brain to register fullness after consumption [27] and post-consumption experiences such as happiness and guilt peaked 5-30 minutes after eating [28]. If the user chooses to snack, there is no counter and they are allowed to snack again immediately. On the main screen a counter is shown that tracks total number of events of cravings, savings (no snacking), healthy and unhealthy snacks. We chose this simple level of tracking to minimize user burden while still offering a reasonable level of monitoring. Initial prototype evaluations verified that our design was simple and intuitive to use. An 'undo recent activity' button was provided to allow users to correct mistaken entries or report snacks they might have eaten while on the 20 minutes savings period. See Figure 1 for screen shots of our application. Below we summarize the main principles that inspired the design.

Enhancing rewards of healthy choices

Typically, when a person feels the temptation to consume excessive/unhealthy foods, there is little reward available for resisting the temptation. Previous work has found that people do feel good about resisting food temptations [17]. However, the moments of feeling good can be diminished as the moment becomes lost in memory. Current applications only track intake, and we do not know of any applications that specifically allow users to record moments where food is avoided. By recording moments of forgoing snacking despite experiencing cravings, we allow users to remember these moments of successful self control. Because we wanted to encourage the idea that forgoing immediate rewards should allow for greater rewards later, we called this event a 'saving' of the craving on the app.

Just in time intervention

One of the many heralded advantages of mobile applications is their ever-present nature, which allows them to deliver support at the moment of need. Along these lines, iCrave functions like an emergency aid response. When a snack craving hits, the user can use our application to obtain a 'just in time' delivery of our intervention. Thus our application operates at the key moment of necessity. While application-initiated interventions are also useful for weight loss, e.g., reminders and prompts, we feel it is also important to create applications where the onus is on the user to initiate to initiate engagement in order to promote user awareness. Thus our application was designed to enhance individuals' awareness of their snack cravings and promote a sense of agency in the user's efforts towards self control.

LITE PROTOTYPE EVALUATION

Before we implemented our full application, we tested general usability of our design on a 'lite' prototype. This 'lite' prototype allowed users to track craving savings and healthy vs. unhealthy snacks, but did not prompt the craving-reducing imagery task. The aim of our prototype pilot was to evaluate: whether the interface was intuitive to use; whether people would readily use the app during snack cravings; and whether it felt intuitive to use a 'save' button if the user chose to forgo snacking. As with our full application, if the user chose to 'save' their snack craving, they would not be able to use the application for 20 minutes. The prototype was deployed on a mobile-friendly web application so that it could be used on all mobile platforms. Our prototype did not store user data onto a database; individual user data (snack counts etc.) were stored in cookies in the individual's web browsers. We recruited 23 participants from the local community; all were healthy adults who had an interest in improving their snacking habits. They used our prototype app over a week-long period. Post-questionnaires verified that people were willing to use the app when they experienced a craving, and readily used the 'save' button when they felt they could forgo the snack. We also interviewed 13 participants and asked them about their experience using the app. Even when using just the lite prototype version, most felt the app helped them make healthier choices. *"It slowed down my rate of taking unhealthy foods and also motivated me." "After using this app I become cautious of taking junk food, started avoiding junk food." "I use the iCrave app to remind myself that I should control my appetite."* To evaluate usability, we asked how easy/hard they felt the app was to use. They all reported it was very usable. *'Very easy', 'simple', 'convenient', 'very user friendly, I like it very much'.* The main complaints were all centered on the fact that it wasn't deployed as an app and only as a mobile site. Given the positive qualitative results and positive survey results, we concluded that our prototype evaluation verified the basic usability of our design and warranted the implementation of our full application.

MAIN EVALUATION STUDY

Our full application extended the prototype version with the following additional features: When the iCrave button was pressed, the app prompts a 10s imagery task for craving reduction followed by a request for the user's vividness rating for the imagery task. We also implemented a simpler snack-tracker version for comparison purposes. We evaluated the effectiveness of our full iCrave application by comparing its effectiveness with the snack-tracker in a one-week between-subjects study. The snack tracker was almost identical to the full iCrave app, except that it did not prompt an imagery task or vividness rating, and did not provide the choice of a 'savings' button to record the forgoing of a snack. Thus, the snack tracker looked exactly like Figure 1 except that the two center screens were omitted, the 'save for later' button was not available in the right screen, and the 'saved' tally was not available on the home screen. Both the full iCrave and snack tracker apps were implemented on both iOS and Android platforms and recorded all user data on a secure database[1]. Participants were randomly assigned to one of two conditions. In the experimental condition, participants used our iCrave application during the week. In the control condition, participants used the snack tracker app. Participants in both conditions were asked to use the app when they experienced a snack craving and indicate whether they were going to consume a healthy or unhealthy snack before eating. Thus, any biases from reporting consumption beforehand would have applied to both groups.

Participants

48 participants were recruited from the local community through email lists at the university. Participants were recruited by asking for individuals who had an interest in improving their snacking habits. Participants were then randomly assigned to either condition (Experimental Condition: N=26, 10 females; Control Conditon: N=27, 8 females). There were 18 iOS users in each of the experimental and control conditions. The rest used the Android application. All participants were between 20-34 years of age except one who was 53. Participants were healthy adults over the age of 18. They were paid £7 each to participate in our study.

Procedure

Before the start of the experiment, participants were given a consent form along with a brief overview of the application and a short paragraph explaining standard portion sizes for common healthy and unhealthy snacks. Participants were provided a brief introduction to the app for their condition, explaining that it would allow them to track their consumption of healthy and unhealthy snacks. Participants in the experimental condition were also told that they could 'save' their cravings by resisting a snack altogether. All participants were then asked to fill out responses to a pre-study survey, which asked them to rate on a 7 point Likert scale, their motivation to snack more healthily, confidence in ability to snack healthily, likelihood of eating unhealthy snacks without thinking, strength of cravings for unhealthy snacks and snacks overall, ease of resisting unhealthy snacks, and the average number of unhealthy snacks and overall snacks they consumed a day. Participants were then instructed to use their app for the next week to try to improve snacking. At the end of the week, participants filled out a post-study survey asking them again to rate strength of cravings for unhealthy snacks and snacks overall, likelihood of eating unhealthy snacks without thinking, ease of resisting unhealthy snacks and the average amount of snacks they consumed per day the previous week. They were also asked to rate on a 7 point Likert scale how well they did in overcoming unhealthy snack habits during the week of the experiment compared to before.

Measurement

The main outcome variables of our experiment were the number of healthy, unhealthy, and overall snacks consumed in the two conditions. These values were stored in a database for each user (stored using an anonymous user id). As with our pilot study, we also compared post vs. pre experiment survey answers between the two conditions for questions that were asked both before and after the experiment. Finally we assessed whether vividness of imagery affects the snack choice. Post-experiment qualitative interviews were also conducted with seven participants who used the full iCrave app.

Quantitative Results

Pre-Study comparison of conditions

Based on our pre-study questionnaire, we verified that there were no significant differences between the participants in our two conditions: One-way ANOVA's showed there were no pre-experimental differences in BMI between our experimental (M=21.7; STD=2.9) and control (M=20.5;

[1] Both versions of the app were made available via the relevant app stores for the duration of the study. They should not be confused with https://sites.google.com/site/icraveapp/, which is a different app with a similar name.

STD=2.8) conditions p=.2. There also were no significant differences in age (p=.48), motivation to improve snacking (p=.53), confidence in ability to improve snacking (p=.60), tendency to engage in unhealthy snacking without thinking (p=.57), cravings for overall snacks (p=.43) and unhealthy snacks (p=.55), ability to resist unhealthy snacks (p=.40), and average daily consumption of snacks overall (p=.99), and unhealthy snacks (p=.79). Thus, we conclude that the characteristics of participants in our two conditions were well counter-balanced, enabling a valid comparison of the effects of our iCrave application vs. the snack-tracker.

Post-Study comparison: usage and snacking

We compared how consumption of healthy and unhealthy snacks, and overall app usage varied over time and between conditions. Overall usage is equivalent to the total snacks consumed on the tracker, and the total snacks plus savings for the full iCrave app. Mean overall usage over the whole week per participant was 7.2 times, STD=3.4 for the experimental condition and 8.3 times, STD=4.9 for the control condition. A repeated-measures ANOVA's with fixed effect of time (days into expt) of overall usage found no significant effect of condition, p=.39. A significant effect of time was found F(6,306)=2.71, p=.014, with marginal interaction of condition p=.09. Visual inspection of usage over time showed that while usage varied over days, overall decrease with time was small. This was confirmed using Ordinary Least Squares Pooled Errors (OLSPE) regression fit to usage data with parameters of condition and time, which revealed a small negative slope for the parameter of time: -.048, t(369)=2.8, p=.005. OLSPE fits to usage for individual conditions found slope for time=-.04, t(180)=2.9, p=.004 (experimental) and slope for time=-.05 t(187)=1.69, p=.09 (control). Thus, we conclude there was no significant difference between conditions in terms of the number of times the apps were used, and decrease in usage over time was small for both conditions.

Next we assessed how unhealthy snack consumption differed between participants in the two conditions, and whether this changed over time. We compared unhealthy snacking across conditions and time. A repeated measures ANOVA applied to unhealthy snack consumption found a significant effect of condition, F(1,306)=14.5, p=.0004, and no effects of time p=.43, and no significant interaction, p=.29. Thus, we conclude participants in our experimental condition consumed significantly fewer unhealthy snacks compared to the control condition (Experiment: M=1.65, STD=1.3 Control: M=3.5, STD=2.8) and this did not significantly differ over time (See Figure 2).

A similar analysis was applied to the consumption of healthy snacks consumed. While control condition participants consumed more healthy snacks, this difference was not significant, p=.27. There was a significant effect of time F(6,306)=2.37, p=.03, and no interaction, p=.5. As was the case for overall usage, visual inspection of trends over time showed that while consumption of healthy snacks varied over days, overall decrease with time was small. An OLSPE regression fit to data with parameters of condition and time revealed a small negative slope for the parameter of time: -.03, t(369)=2.0, p=.05. Thus, we conclude amounts of healthy snacks consumed did not differ signficantly between conditions. While there was variation in healthy snack consumption with time, the variation did not differ between conditions and the overall decrease over time was small.

We also analyzed overall consumption. We found that participants in the experimental condition consumed significantly fewer snacks overall compared to controls. Experiment: M=5.0, STD=2.8, Control: M=8.5, STD=5.0, (See Figure 2). Because we found no significant differences in consumptions of healthy snacks, this decrease in overall snack consumption was driven primarily by the fact that unhealthy snacks were reduced in the experimental condition while consumption of healthy snacks remained the same. A repeated measures ANOVA applied to overall snack consumption found significant effects of condition F(1,306)=9.2, p=.004, and time, F(6,306)=2.36, p=.03, with marginal interaction, p=.092. As before, OLSPE regression fit to the full data with parameters of condition and time found a small negative slope for time, -.045, t(369)=2.7, p=.007. Fits to individual conditions separately found slope for time=-.039, t(180)=2.8, p=.006 (experimental) and slope for time=-.05 t(187)=1.69, p=.09, (control).

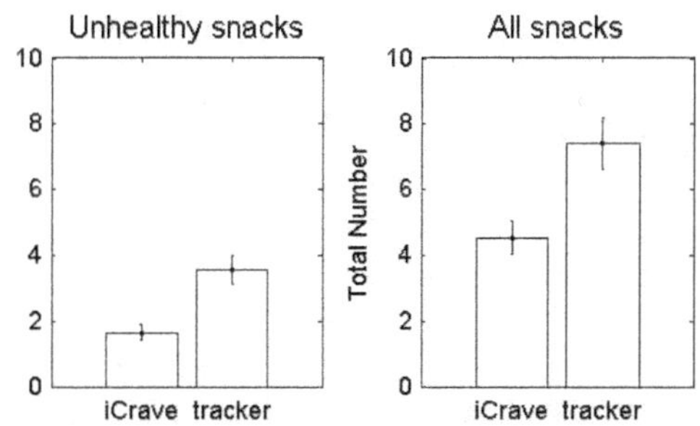

Figure 2. Means and standard errors of total snacks consumed over the week of the experiment. Users of the iCrave application consumed significantly fewer total overall snacks and total unhealthy snacks over a week, compared to users of a simple snack tracker.

Even though the iCrave app and snack tracker were very similar, it is possible that the fact that the hassle of the additional imagery task required by iCrave caused participants in the experimental condition to under-report their snack consumption. Thus, we also asked participants at the end of the study how many unhealthy snacks they consumed over the week. Results suggested participants in both conditions under-reported on the app. However, comparison of unhealthy snack consumption based on post-experiment reports, still supports the main findings that participants in the experimental condition consumed significantly fewer unhealthy snacks, F(1,51)=4.2, p=0.04.

Thus we conclude that our full iCrave app was more effective at reducing unhealthy snack consumption than a basic tracker.

We also checked that our application did not somehow increase the user's amount of snacking compared to the week before the experiment by drawing excessive attention to it. To do this we used t-tests to compare the average number of daily snacks reported in the post-experiment survey to the number reported in the pre-experiment survey[2]. Results analyzed over all participants in both conditions found that participants reported consuming fewer snacks during the week of the study compared to before, t(52)=2.3, p=.03. When these results were analyzed for each condition separately, we still found decreased snacking: the experimental condition results were near statistical significance, t(52)=1.9=.07, and the control condition results also showed reduced snacking but were not statistically significant. t(52)=1.3, p=.21. This analysis supports the premise that participants did reduce snacking during the week of the experiment and the iCrave app was more successful at reducing snack consumption through the reduction in unhealthy snacking.

	Mean rating	STD rating	p-value
iCrave	1.0	.85	0.02
tracker	.19	1.5	

Table 1: Perceived improvement in snacking. Answers were on a 7 point Likert scale of -3: 3 corresponding to Much Worse: Much Better

	Mean rating	STD rating	p-value
iCrave	0.4	1.1	0.009
tracker	-.5	1.4	

Table 2: Self-reported ease of resisting unhealthy snacks, where answers were on a 7 point Likert scale of -3: 3 corresponding to Extremely Hard: Extremely Easy.

[2]We also repeated analysis of all of our Likert response data assuming ordinal data using the Wilcoxon rank sum test for equal medians. All results and significance values remained virtually the same.

Post-Study comparison: survey answers

We conducted one-way ANOVAs comparing experimental vs. control participant's answers to the post-survey regarding how successful participants felt in overcoming unhealthy snacking habits, and how easy they found it to

	Mean rating	STD rating	p-value
iCrave	-.464	1.3	0.16
tracker	.11	1.5	

Table 3: Self-reported agreement to statement about likelihood eating unhealthy snacks without thinking where answers were on a 7 point Likert scale of -3: 3 corresponding to Completely Disagree: Completely Agree

	Mean rating	STD rating	p-value
iCrave	-.6	1.5	0.16
tracker	0.04	1.8	

Table 4: Self-reported agreement to statement about having strong cravings for unhealthy snacks where answers were on a 7 point Likert scale of -3: 3 corresponding to Completely Disagree: Completely Agree

resist unhealthy snacks during the week. Results showed participants in the experimental condition reported significantly greater perceived improvement in overcoming their unhealthy habit compared to controls (F(1,51)=5.4, p=.020), see Table 1, and found it easier to resist unhealthy snacks (F(1,51)=7.4, p=.009), see Table 2. While not reaching significance, but with trends in the right direction, experimental participants also reported being less likely to eat unhealthy snacks without thinking (F(1,51)=2.1, p=.16), see Table 3, and felt less strong cravings for unhealthy snacks (F(1,51)=2.1, p=.16), see Table 4, compared with control condition participants. Thus users of iCrave felt more successful about improving their snack habits and also felt more able to resist unhealthy snacks compared to users of the tracker.

Pre vs. Post-Study changes in survey answers

Another way of assessing the effects of the application is to compare the changes in answers to questions that were asked both pre and post experiment. Experimental participants showed significant changes in their answers to post-study survey questions compared to the same questions in the pre-study survey whereas control participants did not. Paired within-participant t-tests comparing pre vs. post answers for the same participants showed experimental participants after the week had significantly reduced cravings for snacks overall ($t(25)=5.27$, $p=3e-5$) and reduced cravings for unhealthy snacks ($t(25)=3.1$, $p=.005$), and found it much easier to resist unhealthy snacks ($t(25)=5.4$, $p=.1e-5$). Experimental participants also reported being less likely to consume unhealthy snacks without thinking in the post vs. pre survey, but this effect was not significant $p=.18$. In contrast, control participants only showed a significant decrease in their reports for cravings for snacks overall, $t(26)=2.2$, $p=.04$, and no other changes in post vs. pre study answers were significant.

Imagery vividness and snacking response
Previous work has shown that the vividness of imagery did not correlate with reductions in cravings [18]. To check whether this lack of correlation existed for craving reduction 'in the wild', we examined for experimental participants whether there were any differences in reported vividness of imagery corresponding to events where participants chose to either save, healthy snack, or unhealthy snack. A one-way ANOVA showed significant differences in vividness ratings across the different snack choices: Save: M=3.8, STD= 1.0; Healthy: M=3.8, STD=.92; Unhealthy: M=3.2, STD=.88 ($F(1,51)=10.8$, $p=3e-5$). Thus, we conclude that the vividness to which users were able to engage in the imagery task was related to the effectiveness of the app in improving snack choices.

Qualitative Results
Post-study interviews were conducted with seven randomly selected participants who participated in the experimental condition and used the full iCrave app for a week. Participants were asked about the external contexts as well as the inner thoughts and feelings that surrounded usage of iCrave. They were asked to describe moments where iCrave prompted them to either forgo a snack or choose a healthy snack, as well as moments where iCrave was not effective.

Moments of resisting snacking entirely
We asked participants to describe their experiences in instances where use of iCrave helped them resist snacking entirely. Responses supported the idea that cravings for snacks were indeed reduced. Participants reported the reduction in desire for food. *"There is a loss of appetite."*, *"it made me feel like I don't want to eat snacks." "The attraction of snacks is reduced."* Participants also described how the imagery task gave them the presence of mind to make better judgments and exert self control about snacking. E.g., *"Before I wanted a cookie...afterwards I felt it would be better that I did not eat a cookie." "Afterwards, I felt like I could control myself."*

Moments of choosing healthy over unhealthy snacks
We also asked participants what their experiences were when use of iCrave helped them choose a healthy snack. Responses suggested that in these instances, iCrave shifted initial unhealthy preferences towards healthier choices. E.g., *"Before, I wanted chocolate immediately. (Afterwards) I preferred the vegetable salad." "It made me prefer healthy food."* Similarly to the situations where iCrave heled participants avoid snacks entirely, participants described how iCrave gave them the presence of mind to choose a healthier option: *"I wanted chips, but afterwards, I felt it is better to eat something healthy." "After using the app, I wanted to order the healthy snack."* A few participants spoke of how iCrave caused them to reflect more generally on the importance of healthy choices: *"After using the app, I thought, ice cream is not good for body. I shouldn't just eat it, even when I'm not using the app." "With the app, I became more aware of the food (I chose)."*

Feeling good
All participants reported feeling good after the app helped them either avoid snacking or eat healthier snacks. E.g., *"I felt good avoiding the popcorn." "It was a good feeling to avoid the ice cream". "I felt happy to get healthy food". "I felt happy to change the choice of food so my life can be healthier."*

When iCrave did not work
We asked participants what their experiences were when iCrave did not help them avoid an unhealthy snack. These experiences appeared markedly different from the moments where iCrave did support healthier choices. Participants spoke of how the app didn't help them and they did not feel any shift in their cravings. E.g., *"I felt it could not help me this time." "Nothing changed, both before and after using the app I still wanted chicken." "It didn't work...the feeling was the same both before and after using the app."* These remarks suggest that iCrave worked by shifting preferences and mental states, and the situations in which iCrave was ineffective was when this shift did not occur.

DISCUSSION

Improving snacking in moments of temptation
Our results showed that engaging in imagery tasks, which have been shown to reduce self-reported craving levels in laboratory studies, can improve snacking behavior when performed at moments of food temptation. Qualitative interview results suggest that the craving-reduction imagery task influenced behavior in several ways. First, it may simply extinguish the desire for unhealthy foods. Second, it may shift preferences away from healthy foods and towards healthier foods. Third, it may reduce the initial desire enough to give users the presence of mind to make a more controlled choice informed by long term health rather than short term desires. Our user-log results showed that reported vividness of the imagery task correlated with moments where healthy snacks and no snacks were chosen,

supporting the idea that level of engagement in the imagery task was instrumental in influencing whether healthier choices were made.

Beyond momentary benefits

Our results hint at the possibility that the use of iCrave can provide wider benefits for snacking behavior beyond those moments of using the app. In post-experiment questionnaires, participants who used iCrave reported that they were more able to resist unhealthy snacks compared to those in the tracker condition. While this might have been purely due to the fact that they were using the full iCrave app, another possibility is that by practicing the imagery task, they learned a cognitive strategy for reducing desire, which they could implement even when they were not using the app. While results did not reach significance levels, users of iCrave also reported having overall fewer cravings for unhealthy snacks and being more aware of eating unhealthy snacks in comparison to users of the tracking app. Finally, in our qualitative interviews, some participants mentioned that iCrave prompted greater awareness of food choices even when they were not using the app. Longer term studies will be needed to verify the possible broader effects of using iCrave mentioned above that are suggested by our current work.

Open questions

Our study focused on the use of iCrave to improve snacking behavior. However, it would also be also interesting to know whether iCrave can improve the healthiness of consumption during meal as well as snacks. Though cravings are typically associated with snacks, they could also play a role in meal time consumption. The observations that iCrave appeared to shift preferences towards healthier foods and help induce a state of mind where one is able to make healthier choices, suggests that it may be useful for meals as well as snacks.

Another line of open enquiry is to understand in more detail the effectiveness of different individual components of iCrave. While our results found that imagery vividness correlated with healthy choices, it is unknown the extent to which a 10s delay without the imagery task might also be effective. Laboratory studies have shown that equivalent-length mind wandering tasks [22] and other cognitive tasks such as reciting the alphabet backwards [25] are not effective in reducing cravings. This suggests that a mere 10s delay without imagery would not be as effective in changing behavior. However, this remains to be empirically verified.

Another factor that may have contributed to the success of iCrave besides the imagery task and delay was the presence of the 'save' button. While our participants spoke of the imagery task shifting their choice preferences, it is possible that the mere possibility of being able to record moments of overcoming cravings also would be beneficial on its own, without a craving reduction task. Indeed, in user interviews for our lite prototype, which only contained a 'save' button, people reported enjoying recording their savings. However, the effectiveness of this savings button has yet to be systematically evaluated on its own.

Design implications

Our finding that a system which prompts an imagery task and records moments of overcoming temptation can improve snacking habits opens up questions about how the system might be designed to optimize effectiveness. One possibility is to allow users to engage in multiple repeats of the imagery task and/or to allow the user to select a new imagery task if the first imagery prompt is unappealing. Another option is to allow the user to choose whether they want to have an imagery task at all, thus allowing for more flexibility in usage. Additionally, a greater variety of craving reduction tasks can be incorporated to prevent adaptation. Previous laboratory studies have shown that other imagery tasks such as staring passively at dynamic black and white visual noise, olfactory imagery, and tactile-visual manipulation can also reduce cravings [18-21]. Other studies have shown that imagining indulging in ones favorite activities also can reduce cravings [25]. Thus future versions of iCrave can explore the usefulness of allowing users to create their own repository (e.g., text or photos) of craving reduction material.

Future versions of iCrave can incorporate additional features that enhance the rewards of forgoing snack cravings and reduce the strength of cravings. For example, the application can enhance the association of accumulated savings with future non-food rewards. One can imagine a personal treats store where the user could pre-specify the treats they would allow themselves if they overcame a certain number of cravings or went for a certain time period without unhealthy snacks. Another method for celebrating savings might be to include an option for social features where friends who are trying to snack less are connected together and updates can be posted when each successfully overcomes a craving, allowing others to give congratulations, feedback, or encouragement.

CONCLUSION

We implemented and tested iCrave, a mobile application designed to influence the specific psychological constructs that surround weight loss: the cost of resisting tempting foods and the rewards of feeling good about having self control. It is the first application to use the cravings reduction methods proposed by EI theory.

We evaluated the effectiveness of our application for improving snacking habits compared to that of a basic snack tracker in a one-week study. We found that while users of both iCrave and the tracker reported eating fewer snacks on average than they usually do, iCrave significantly reduced unhealthy snacking and overall snacking compared to the basic tracker. Users of our application also felt more successful in improving their snack habits, felt more able to resist unhealthy snacks compared to users of the simple tracker, reported significantly reduced cravings for snacks overall and reduced cravings for unhealthy snacks compared to before the week of using the application.

Our work demonstrates how a simple mobile app can help individuals overcome snack cravings and improve their snack habits. The design of our application was based on mitigating the discouraging psychological constructs of a desired behavior and enhancing the encouraging ones. iCrave represents one possible instantiation of the many design opportunities afforded through designing to alter the psychological constructs that underlie behavior. The success of our application demonstrates that this is a viable new approach for opening up the design space for persuasive technologies.

ACKNOWLEDGMENTS

We thank Vicky Cullen for helping us with practice interviews, and all participants for their contributions to the study. This research is partially supported by EPSRC Grant EP/G004560.

REFERENCES

1. Torning, K. and Kukkonen, H., Persuasive system design: state of the art and future directions. *Proceedings of the 4th International Conference on Persuasive Technology*, Springer, (2009), 30.

2. Brown, B., Chetty, G., and Harmon, E., A system for students to monitor diet and exercise. *Proceedings of CHI*(2012), 1807-1812.

3. Consolvo, S., McDonald, D., and Landay, J., Theory-Driven Design Strategies for Technologies that Support Behavior Change in Everyday Life. *Proceedings of CHI 2009*, ACM Press, (2009), 405-414.

4. Consolvo, S., Everitt, K, Smith, I I, and Landay, JA., Design requirements for technologies that encourage physical activity. *Proceedings of CHI 2006*, ACM Press, (2006), 457-466.

5. Lin, J, Mamykina, L, Lindtner, S, Delajoux, G, and Strub, H, Fish 'n' Steps: Encouraging physical activity with an interactive computer game. *UbiComp 2006: Ubiquitous Computing*, ACM Press, (2006), 261-278.

6. Consolvo, S., klasnja, P., McDonald, D., Avrahami, D. Froehlich J., LeGrand, L., Libby, R., Mosher, K., and Landay, J., Flowers or a robot army? encouraging awareness and activity with personal, mobile displays. *UbiComp 2008*, ACM Press, (2008), 54-63.

7. Baumer, E. P. S., Katz, S. J., Freeman, J. E., Adams, P., Gonzales, A. L., Pllak, J. P., Retelny, D., Niederdeppe, J., Olson, C. M., and Gay, G. K, Prescriptive Persuasion and Open-Ended Social Awareness: Expanding the Design Space of Mobile Health. *Proceedings of CHI 2012*, ACM Press, (2012), 476-484.

8. Brown, Brandon, Chetty, Marshini, Grimes, Andrea, and Harmon, Ellie, Reflecting on health: a system for students to monitor diet and exercise. *CHI'06 extended abstracts on Human factors in computing systems*, ACM Press, (2006), 1807-1812.

9. Fehr, E. and Rangel, A., Neuroeconomic Foundations of Economic Choice—Recent Advances. *Journal of Economic Perspectives*, 25, (2011), 3-30.

10. Oinas-Kukkonen, H and Harjumaa, M, Persuasive systems design: Key issues, process model, and system features. *Communications of the Association for Information Systems*, 24, (2009), 28.

11. Oinas-Kukkonen, H, A foundation for the study of behavior change support systems. *Personal and Ubiquitous Computing*, 17, (2013), 1123-1135.

12. Fogg, B. J., Eckles, D., Bogost, I., Consolvo, S., Holmen, E, Spasojevic, M, Ulm, J, Tanguay, S, Walker, S, and White, S, Mobile Persuasion: 20 Perspectives of the Future of Behavior Change, Fogg, B. J. and Eckles, D., Stanford Captology Media,Stanford, 2007.

13. Rachuri, K, Musolesi, M, Mascolo, C, Rentfrow, P, Longworth, C, and Aucinas, A, EmotionSense: A Mobile Phones based Adaptive Platform for Experimental Social Psychology Research. *Proceedings of the 12th ACM International Conference on Ubiquitous Computing*, ACM Press, (2010),

14. Maitland, J. and Chalmers, M., Designing for Peer Involvement in Weight Management. *Proceedings of CHI 2011*, ACM Press, (2011), 315-324.

15. Lee, M., Kiesler, S., and Forlizzi, J., Mining Behavioral Economics to Design Persuasive Technology for Healthy Choices. *Proceedings of CHI 2011*, ACM Press, (2011), 325-334.

16. Maitland, J., Towards Negotiation as a Framework for Health Promoting Technology. *ACM SIGHIT Record*, 1, (2011), 10-19.

17. Hsu, A. and Blandford, A., Designing for Psychological Change: Individuals' Reward and Cost Valuations in Weight Management. *Journal of Medical Internet Research*(2014),

18. May, J., Andrade, J., Batey, H., Berry, L. M., and Kavanagh, D. J., Less food for thought. Impact of attentional instructions on intrusive thoughts about snack foods. *Appetite*, 55, (2010), 279-287.

19. Andrade, J., Pears, S., May, J., and Kavanagh, D. J., Use of a clay modeling task to reduce chocolate craving. *Appetite*, 58, (2012), 955-963.

20. Kemps, Eva and Tiggemann, Marika, Modality-specific imagery reduces cravings for food: an application of the elaborated intrusion theory of desire to food craving. *Journal of Experimental Psychology: Applied*, 13, (2007), 95.

21. Harvey, Kirsty, Kemps, Eva, and Tiggemann, Marika, The nature of imagery processes underlying food cravings. *British Journal of Health Psychology*, 10, (2005), 49-56.

22. Hamilton, J, Fawson, S, May, J, Andrade, J, and Kavanagh, D J., Brief guided imagery and body scanning interventions reduce food cravings. *Appetite*, 71, (2013), 158-162.

23. May, J., Andrade, J., Panabokke, N., and Kavanagh, D., Images of desire: cognitive models of craving. *Memory*, 12, (2004), 447-461.

24. May, J., Andrade, J., and Kavanagh, D., Elaborated Intrusion Theory: A cognitive-emotional theory of food craving. *Current Obesity Reports*, 1, (2012), 114-121.

25. Knauper, B., Pillay, R., Lacaille, J., McCollam, A., and Kelso, E., Replacing craving imagery with alternative pleasant imagery reduces craving intensity. *Appetite*, 57, (2011), 173-178.

26. Baddeley, A D. and Andrade, J, Working memory and the vividness of imagery. *Journal of Experimental Psychology: General*, 129, (2000), 126.

27. Liu, Y., Gao, J. H., Liu, H. L., and Fox, P. T., The temporal response of the brain after eating revealed by functional MRI. *Nature*, 405, (29-6-2000), 1058-1062.

28. de, Lauzon B., Romon, M., Deschamps, V., Lafay, L., Borys, J. M., Karlsson, J., Ducimetiere, P., and Charles, M. A., The Three-Factor Eating Questionnaire-R18 is able to distinguish among different eating patterns in a general population. *J.Nutr.*, 134, (2004), 2372-2380.

The Effects of Embodied Persuasive Games on Player Attitudes Toward People Using Wheelchairs

Kathrin M. Gerling, Regan L. Mandryk, Max Birk, Matthew Miller, Rita Orji
Department of Computer Science
University of Saskatchewan
110 Science Place, Saskatoon, SK, S7N 5C9
firstname.lastname@usask.ca

ABSTRACT
People using wheelchairs face barriers in their daily lives, many of which are created by people who surround them. Promoting positive attitudes towards persons with disabilities is an integral step in removing these barriers and improving their quality of life. In this context, persuasive games offer an opportunity of encouraging attitude change. We created a wheelchair-controlled persuasive game to study how embodied interaction can be applied to influence player attitudes over time. Our results show that the game intervention successfully raised awareness for challenges that people using wheelchairs face, and that embodied interaction is a more effective approach than traditional input in terms of retaining attitude change over time. Based on these findings, we provide design strategies for embodied interaction in persuasive games, and outline how our findings can be leveraged to help designers create effective persuasive experiences beyond games.

Author Keywords
Embodied Interaction; Persuasive Games; Attitude Change; Disability.

ACM Classification Keywords
K.8.0 [Personal Computing]: General - Games.

INTRODUCTION
People using wheelchairs face barriers in their lives, many of which are created by the people around them: research has shown that the general population holds negative attitudes toward people with disabilities, and that perceptions of disability influence how people with disabilities are treated [18]. This is a problem because able-bodied individuals often function as gatekeepers in settings that directly influence the quality of life, for instance, in education, employment, and leisure [24].

Disability awareness – empathy and a positive attitude regarding people with disabilities [39] – is an important step towards fostering positive attitudes and behaviour towards people with disabilities [18]. Various efforts have been made to help promote positive attitudes, such as the use of materials that help able-bodied individuals to better understand capabilities of people using wheelchairs (e.g., online videos [9]), or materials that let able-bodied people experience challenges that individuals with disabilities face (e.g., simulation exercises [15]). However, these approaches assume that able-bodied individuals have a volitional drive to understand people with disabilities; there is little logic in interventions for attitude change that require proactive participation because those who most need to change their attitude are also the least likely to participate. Game-based interventions can provide this missing motivation for participation, and persuasive games – games that are designed with the primary purpose of changing a user's behavior or attitude – have been applied successfully in domains such as sustainability, international conflict resolution, and health (see persuasivegames.com). Therefore, persuasive games for attitude change toward people using wheelchairs are a promising intervention.

Although there are a number of persuasive strategies that can be employed to change attitudes or behaviours [12, 27] within a game, one of the most successful approaches in persuasive games is the use of simulation [29]. Game-based simulations allow the player to experience different perspectives, try out solutions to a problem, and observe the outcome of their choices on a time scale not possible in the real world. Traditionally, persuasive games focus the simulation in the game world, while interaction with the game is handled through conventional input devices. However, the concept of *embodied interaction* [10] in human-computer interaction suggests that interaction with the game could be made physical – incorporating the user's own body and movements. Embodied interaction has been effective in interventions in other domains, such as learning [21] and health [36]. In the context of mobility disabilities, motion-based game control offers an interesting design opportunity: embodied interaction can be applied to allow players to physically experience challenges that persons using wheelchairs face, potentially strengthening the persuasive experience and resulting in improvements not only to awareness, but also to attitude. However, research in the field of disability simulation suggests that simulating

CHI 2014, April 26 - May 01 2014, Toronto, ON, Canada
Copyright 2014 ACM 978-1-4503-2473-1/14/04...$15.00.
http://dx.doi.org/10.1145/2556288.2556962

disability in able-bodied people may not be very effective and can lead more to frustration than understanding [13].

In this paper, we ask the question of whether persuasive games can be used to change *attitudes* towards people using wheelchairs. Furthermore, we ask whether the use of *embodied simulation* (i.e., simulation controlled through embodied interaction) strengthens the persuasiveness of the game intervention. To answer these questions, we developed a persuasive game that simulates common challenges in the use of wheelchairs. To study the impact of embodied simulation in games, we created two versions – one that is controlled directly with a wheelchair, and one that uses a traditional gamepad. We present results of a study with 40 participants exploring the effects of embodied interaction in our persuasive game. We assess participant attitudes one week prior to our intervention, immediately following gameplay, and after one week to explore attitudes over time, and we combine this information with player experience measures to further understand the effects of embodying interaction. Our results show that the game intervention successfully raised awareness for challenges that people using wheelchairs face, and that embodied interaction is a more effective approach in terms of sustaining attitude change over time.

RELATED WORK

We provide an overview of persuasive games. We show how embodied interaction can foster persuasion, and how embodied simulation relates to disability simulation.

Game-Based Persuasion and Attitude Change

Persuasive Technology aims to bring about desirable change by shaping and reinforcing behavior or attitude about an issue, action, or object [1, 12]. Various terms have been used to describe games designed for purposes other than entertainment, such as serious games (used to describe games that are designed to entertain, educate, and train players [37]) and persuasive games (used to describe video games that mount procedural rhetoric effectively [6]). Regardless of the terminology, these games focus on persuading players using various design strategies [9]. For the purpose of this paper, we define persuasive games as games that are designed with the primary purpose of changing a user's behavior or attitude using persuasive strategies [12]. Persuasive games provide advantages over non-game interventions, including the motivation of participation [35], and the ability to trigger attitude change using indirect approaches by engaging users in play (e.g., by allowing for peripheral messages based on in-game conflicts rather than on an obvious rhetorical approach). Persuasive games have affected behaviour or attitude in a variety of domains, including smoking cessation [17], energy consumption [2], and healthy eating [3].

Persuasive Simulation Games

A number of persuasive strategies have been developed that can be applied to persuasive game design. For instance, Fogg [12] developed seven persuasive tools, and Oinas-Kukkonen [27] built on Fogg's strategies to develop 28 persuasive system design principles, such as *Customization* or *Self-Monitoring*. Out of the strategies, *Simulation* is one of the prominent examples that can easily be transferred into games. It provides the means for a user to observe the cause-and-effect linkage of their behavior by encouraging users to observe and experience the world (or some aspect of it) in a simulated environment. It allows players to live and feel the world from another person's perspective, and has been found to be an effective one-size-fits-all approach that is capable of motivating positive change in the majority of the players without demotivating others [28].

An example of a persuasive simulation game is *Darfur is Dying* [34], a web-based game that allows players to experience the difficulty of living among modern genocide and the hardship faced by Darfurian refugees with the aim of promoting attitude and behaviour change. Similarly, *Sweatshop* [8] is an online simulation game that allows players to experience the cause-and-effect of stakeholder actions in the textile industry to encourage actions that impact workers positively. These games are examples of how simulation games can be employed for attitude change by exposing the players to the experience of real-world scenarios during play. Hence, persuasive games employing simulation can also be considered for motivating positive attitude change towards persons with disabilities.

Disability Simulation

Disability simulation is an approach towards helping able-bodied persons experience life from the perspective of a person with a disability [15]; it relies on the embodiment of the disability to evoke empathy and a better understanding of disabilities. It is frequently applied in the context of mobility disabilities, e.g., disabilities that require the use of wheelchairs, where able-bodied persons are invited to exclusively use a wheelchair for a certain amount of time to experience challenges associated with wheelchair use [13].

While some studies claim that wheelchair simulations help improve attitudes towards persons with disabilities [15], others report that they do not provide an accurate experience (e.g., because blindfolding a sighted person will result in an entirely different experience than that of a person with a visual impairment), are overly challenging (e.g., because the able-bodied person is unfamiliar with the assistive device), and may ultimately lead to frustration [13]. A 2007 meta-analysis of disability simulation [11] reports only small positive effects of disability simulation, and underlines the importance of adequate challenges allowing able-bodied persons to cope with the situations that they experience in order to create effective simulations.

Game-Based Disability Simulation

Virtual environments have been applied to simulate the effects of different disabilities; Lewis et al. [19] build on a popular game engine to demonstrate the effects of visual impairments, and in the context of simulating mobility disabilities, Pivik et al. [27] present a video game that invites able-bodied children to navigate a virtual environment that simulates the use of the wheelchair. The game is played using a mouse; results of a user study show higher awareness of barriers related to mobility disabilities, but no improvement of attitudes towards persons with disabilities. In this context, one problem related to game-based disability simulation could be the fact that they lack the physical dimension of disability simulations in the real world, and do not allow players to experience the effects of a mobility disability in a way that encourages them to be more empathetic towards people with disabilities.

Disability Simulation and Embodied Interaction

In our work, we leverage the effects of embodied interaction. Dourish [10] defines embodied interaction as a participatory process with a strong physical dimension; when individuals interact, meaning is given to that interaction through the embodiment of their interaction (e.g., the physicality of their bodies), and by the fact that it takes place in the context of the world. In Human-Computer Interaction, embodied interaction has been approached from the context of tangible interaction where real-world objects are integrated into interaction [16], and in motion-based interaction where users apply their body as input device [20]. In game development, video games with motion-based control schemes have been created to augment physical experiences (e.g., sports [25]) or engage broader audiences in play. Research results show that the physical aspect of embodied interaction – particularly perceived effort – can be exploited to shape the user experience [21]. Furthermore, results show that the inclusion of motor actions leads to an increase in the effectiveness of interventions in health persuasion [36], suggesting that embodied interaction can be applied to increase the effects of persuasive games.

By combining a simulation game with wheelchair input, players could experience the physical aspect of a mobility disability in a virtual environment, thereby maintaining the benefits of the embodied experience. However, using a virtual environment allows for a carefully crafted player experience with challenging, yet achievable game tasks that convey the core challenges of using a wheelchair while controlling the level of frustration among players. This approach could create a basis for further reflection upon the situation of persons using wheelchairs.

BIRTHDAY PARTY: AN EMBODIED PERSUASIVE GAME

We explore embodied interaction in persuasive games using wheelchair game input. We designed *Birthday Party*, a wheelchair-controlled persuasive game in which players have to complete a series of wheelchair-related challenges.

Background

Based on previous work investigating common barriers faced by persons using wheelchairs [23] and considerations for the design of disability simulations [13], we created *Birthday Party*, a persuasive game in which players control an avatar – a person using a wheelchair –to navigate a city and arrive at a friend's birthday party on time. On the way, the player has to stop at different locations to pick up items for the party, but the player is running late, so completing all tasks quickly is important. The game is comprised of an overworld, i.e., a map that shows the stops the player needs to make, in a top-down perspective. One mini-game is integrated in the overworld and played from a top-down perspective; the other games are played from a side-scrolling perspective and triggered at specific locations.

Mini Game Challenges

The game features four mini-games that the player needs to complete to arrive at the party.

Crossing the street. This mini game is integrated into the overworld, and is triggered repeatedly throughout the game. Whenever the player arrives at an intersection, the game zooms in: cars are moving by quickly, and the player has to safely navigate the wheelchair to the other side of the street. If a car comes up to the player while she is crossing the street, the car stops, a honking sound is played, and the player receives a time penalty for blocking traffic.

Grocery store. When entering the grocery store, players are shown a list of items that they are supposed to pick up (cake, whipping cream, candles). Players need to navigate the store to find all items. Challenge is created in two ways: first, players have to avoid puddles of water on the ground by moving the wheelchair out of the way; if they fail to do so, they slow down. Second, players have to use their arm to reach up to shelves and collect the items; sometimes, they will be out of their reach, and they will have to try and find the item in another location.

Bookstore. In the bookstore, players have to pick up additional items (birthday card, wrapping paper) to bring to the birthday party, and find the check-out. Challenge is created by having to navigate different levels of the store without being able to use escalators. Players have to watch out for elevators instead; additionally, they need to use their arm to grab items from the shelves similar to the grocery store. Finally, players must steer around piles of books on the floor, otherwise the obstacles will slow them down.

Park. In the last mini game, the player arrives at a park to collect three flowers (tulip, chrysanthemum, rose) to bring to the birthday party. Challenge is created by the introduction of stairs that the player must avoid. Because the player must avoid stairs, flowers that are too close to the steps cannot be obtained, and must be found elsewhere.

After completing all mini games, the game returns to the top-down view of the overworld and the player has to navigate the street until she arrives at her friend's house. There, feedback on overall player performance is provided, and the game ends.

Figure 1. Overview of the mini game challenges included in *Birthday Party*: Crossing the street (upper left), grocery shopping (upper right), browsing through a bookstore (lower left), and visiting a park (lower right). Each of the games features challenges specific to the use of wheelchairs, e.g., completing time critical tasks, avoiding obstacles, or finding accessible pathways.

Game Input
To study the effects of embodied simulation in persuasive games, there are two types of game input.

Wheelchair-based (embodied) input. In this condition of the game, wheelchair-based input is implemented in two ways, depending on the current view. (1) Top-down view: Players navigate the world by moving the wheelchair forward (moving up on the map), backward (moving down on the map), turning it to the left (moving left), and turning it to the right (moving right). (2) Side-scrolling view: If the player moves the wheelchair forward, the avatar moves from left to right, gradually speeding up. If the wheelchair is moved back, the avatar slows down. Turning the wheelchair to the left or right will result in the avatar 'switching lanes' in the game; this way, it is possible to avoid obstacles. In order to lift the arm of the avatar, the player has to raise her arm.

Traditional game input. In this condition, the player uses an Xbox 360 gamepad as input to the game. The control scheme is implemented in a way that closely matches the wheelchair (embodied) input. In the top-down view, the game is controlled by using the D-Pad: pushing up (moving up on the map), pushing down (moving down on the map), pushing to the left (moving left) and pushing right (moving right). In the side-scrolling view, the player uses the D-Pad similarly to the way wheelchair input is used; pushing up and down to speed up or slow down, and pushing left and right to 'switch lanes'. To raise the arm of the avatar, the right thumbstick is pushed up.

Implementation
The game was implemented in C# using Microsoft XNA Game Studio 4.0 and the Microsoft Kinect SDK alongside the KINECT^{Wheels} toolkit [14] for wheelchair input.

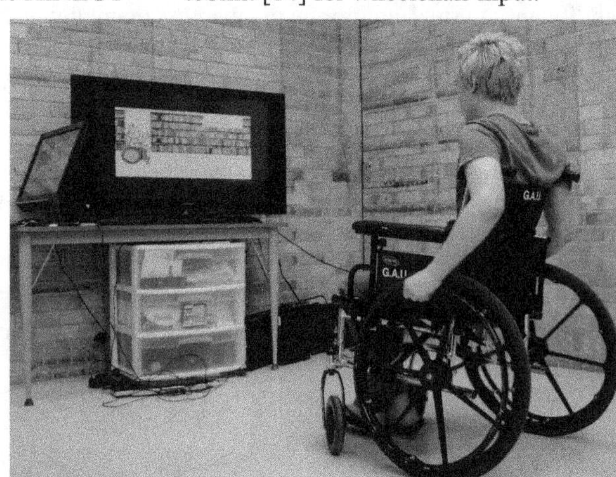

Figure 2. Wheelchair-based game input.

EXPERIMENT DESCRIPTION

We conducted a mixed-methods experiment to study how embodied simulation affects player attitudes.

Study Design

The presented study is a 2 (input) by 3 (time) factor design with input as a between-subject factor (embodied simulation or simulation), and time as a within-subject factor (1 week prior to intervention, immediately post, one week post). Participants first provided informed consent, and then completed an online survey that assessed attitudes toward disability and included demographic questions. One week later, participants played Birthday Party in one of the two input conditions. After completing the game, participants completed a post-play questionnaire that assessed attitudes toward disability and player experience. Between one and two weeks later, participants completed the follow-up questionnaire assessing attitudes toward disability. On study completion, participants received $20.

Participants and Setting

The game was played in a university laboratory on a 42 inch Panasonic TV screen. Participants used an Xbox 360 controller in the gamepad condition and a standard manual wheelchair with the foot pedals removed (for safety when entering and leaving the chair; see (Figure 2) in the wheelchair condition. Forty participants (21 female, mean age=28.43, SD=6.26) took part in the experiment.

Measures

Performance Logging

The game software logged all in-game actions and calculated a variety of performance measures; we discuss the following aggregate measures: *overall time*, the total time (in seconds) required to complete all tasks in the game. Furthermore, we include *errors*, the total number of errors (e.g., wrong selection, hitting obstacle) made in a session.

Player Experience	
PRE	m *(SD)*
Positive Affect	2.89 (0.85)
Negative Affect	1.38 (0.52)
POST	
Positive Affect	2.75 (0.82)
Negative Affect	1.64 (0.59)
Competence	2.69 (0.88)
Autonomy	2.85 (0.88)
Relatedness	2.91 (0.89)
Immersion	3.07 (0.77)
Intuitive Controls	2.84 (0.89)
Enjoyment	3.35 (0.71)
Effort	3.69 (0.55)

Attitudes to Disability	
PRE	m *(SD)*
Inclusion	2.82 (0.66)
Discrimination	2.94 (0.74)
Gains	3.69 (0.54)
Prospects	2.06 (0.68)
POST	
Inclusion	2.78 (0.76)
Discrimination	3.19 (0.83)
Gains	3.72 (0.62)
Prospects	1.84 (0.7)
Follow-Up	
Inclusion	2.74 (0.71)
Discrimination	3.18 (0.74)
Gains	3.68 (0.53)
Prospects	2.18 (0.84)

Table 1. Descriptive Statistics.

Player Experience Measures

We collected a variety of player experience measures immediately following play using standardized scales commonly used in the assessment of player experience. Descriptive statistics are displayed in Table 1.

Enjoyment and Effort. We assessed intrinsic motivation using the *interest-enjoyment* and *effort-importance* subscales of the Intrinsic Motivation Inventory [35]. Participants rated their agreement on a 5-point Likert-scale, (1=strongly disagree, 5=strongly agree). **Pleasure.** To determine overall pleasure, we assessed emotional valence using the Positive Affect Negative Affect Schedule (PANAS) [38], in which participants are asked to state their level of agreement with 20 emotion adjectives on a scale (1=very slightly or not at all, 5=extremely), resulting in a score for *positive affect* and *negative affect*. **Need Satisfaction.** To deconstruct experience, we used the Player Experience of Need Satisfaction Scale (PENS) [35], which assesses *competence*, *autonomy*, *relatedness*, *immersion*, and *intuitive control*. Players agree with statements using a 5-pt Likert-scale (1=strongly disagree, 5=strongly agree).

Attitude Measures

Table 1 shows descriptive statistics for attitude measures.

Attitudes to Disability Scale. We assessed attitudes towards disability using the Attitudes to Disability Scale (ADS) [30], which was developed by the World Health Organization Quality of Life project to assess attitudes toward people with physical or intellectual disabilities. The scale has been tested with over 3700 participants and shows good reliability (α >.70). Participants rated their agreement on a 5-point Likert scale (1=strongly disagree, 5=strongly agree), resulting in the following constructs: *Inclusion*. Higher ratings indicate lower inclusion of people with a disability. *Discrimination*. Higher ratings indicate higher awareness of discrimination between people with and without a disability. *Gains*. Higher ratings indicate a positive attitude towards people with a disability, by focusing on the gains of disabilities. *Prospects*. Higher ratings indicate a negative attitude towards people with disability, by focusing on their prospects.

Research Questions

We gathered this variety of measures to enable us to answer a series of research questions using planned comparisons.

1. Did the players invest more effort with different input types (embodied simulation, simulation)?
2. Did the different input types result in different in-game performance?
3. Did the different input types yield different play experiences?

We included these questions to study how embodied simulation influences interaction with persuasive games. We expected that differences in player experience may promote differences in player attitude change:

4. Did the game produce changes in attitudes toward disability, particularly persons using wheelchairs?
5. Did embodying simulation affect the efficacy of attitude change persuasion?
6. Did attitude changes last after the intervention?
7. Did embodying simulation make a difference on the lasting impact of attitude changes?

We were particularly interested in whether changes in player attitudes are sustained over time, and whether effects are stronger when applying embodied interaction.

Data Analysis

Inter-group comparisons (simulation, embodied simulation) for play experience, affect, and performance were made using independent-samples t-tests. As attitudes were measured three times over the experiment, we conducted RM-ANOVA on the scales that measured attitude. Planned pairwise comparisons were made with α=.05. Distributions of all data were inspected and met assumptions of normality. We report η^2 for all F-tests, whereas Cohen's d shows effect size for all other significant effects. Following guidelines for qualitative research by Marshall and Rossman [22], we iteratively developed a coding scheme for qualitative data grounded in the data focused on perceptions of wheelchairs and people with mobility disabilities. We identified the following four prominent topics: (1) wheelchair-themed video games as an opportunity to experience challenges that persons using wheelchairs face, (2) effects of wheelchair input on perceived competence within the game, (3) the reflection upon one's own abilities, and (4) usability issues related to wheelchair- and controller-based game input.

RESULTS

We organize our results by the research questions. First, we report quantitative results from the planned comparisons; we then provide explanations from the qualitative analyses.

Experience Resulting From The Input Types

Our first research questions relate to the experience depending on whether the simulation was embodied (wheelchair input) or traditional (gamepad input).

1. Did players invest more effort with different input types?
Yes. An independent samples t-test showed that players who used embodied simulation reported greater levels of effort (t_{38}=2.119, p=.041, d=.67) than those using gamepad.

2. Did the different input types yield different performance?
Yes. Independent samples t-tests show a significant increase in time (t_{38}=6.103, p≈.000, d=1.93) and errors (t_{38}=5.271, p≈.000, d=1.67) when using the wheelchair over the gamepad (Figure 3). Participant comments highlight an awareness of these differences: "*using the wheelchair felt disabling*" (P36, embodied simulation), and it "*did not let me perform to my expectations in the game that I had for myself*" (P43, embodied simulation).

3. Did different input types yield different play experience?
Independent-samples t-tests showed that there were no differences in the enjoyment of the game (t_{38}=0.712, p=.481), or in any of the measures of player satisfaction of needs (Competence: t_{38}=1.125, p=.268; Autonomy: t_{38}=0.687, p=.496; Relatedness: t_{38}=0.180, p=.858; Immersion: t_{38}=0.055, p=.957). In addition, there was no difference in the ratings of intuitive control (t_{38}=0.002, p=.999) or change in positive (t_{38}=1.814, p=.078) or negative (t_{38}=0.278, p=.782) affect. However, qualitative results suggest that participants playing the wheelchair simulation strongly focused on the effects of the input device, whereas participants using traditional game input reflected upon in-game challenges: "*The wheelchair made me feel restricted and less competent than a traditional input device and me sitting or standing*" (P53, embodied simulation) - "*[it is] interesting to note the different challenges one has when in a wheelchair - such as finding the elevator, or not being close enough to the shelf to reach an item*" (P19, traditional simulation). Also, participant quotes show that the wheelchair was perceived to be a challenging device and had an impact on how participants perceived their in-game abilities: it was "*difficult, challenging, enlightening. Using the wheelchair actually felt disabling in the game.*" (P36, embodied simulation).

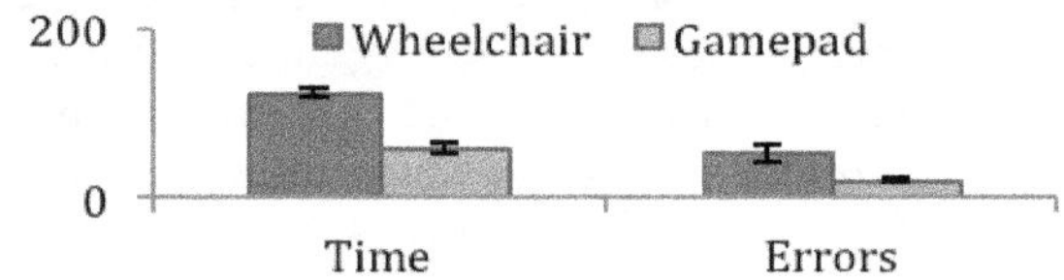

Figure 3. Time (ms) and errors for both input types.

Summary of Experience Results
The wheelchair input inspired more effort and resulted in significantly worse performance in the game; however, this did not transfer to different ratings of perceived competence. As such, players were likely attributing the difficulty of control (and resulting performance) to the input device, and not their own ability. Interestingly, the ratings for intuitive control were not different, suggesting that neither input device was more intuitive than the other. Because the embodied simulation inspired more investment of effort, took longer, and resulted in more in-game errors, we next investigated whether embodied input promoted attitude change differently than traditional input.

Efficacy Of The Persuasive Game Intervention

The next group of questions relate to the efficacy of the intervention for promoting attitude change.

4. Did the game yield changes in attitudes toward disability?
Yes. Attitudes as measured by the ADS immediately after play were significantly improved from the same attitudes measured one week prior to play for discrimination ($F_{1,38}$=7.1, p=.011, η^2=.16) and prospects ($F_{1,38}$=7.2, p=.011, η^2=.16), but not for inclusion ($F_{1,38}$=0.1, p=.712) or gains ($F_{1,38}$=0.2, p=.700). Qualitative results showed that the game prompted players to reflect upon their own situation and

compare their lives to persons using wheelchairs. For example, the game made them "*realize how difficult it is to use a wheelchair*" (P13, embodied simulation) and "*think of how real life is when one is in a wheelchair*" (P11, traditional simulation).

5. Did embodying simulation affect the efficacy of attitude change persuasion?

Yes. Planned pairwise comparisons of the interaction between time and input type show that post-play attitude changes in prospects were significant for wheelchair users (p=.031, d=.40), but not gamepad users (p=.126), whereas the changes in discrimination were significant for gamepad users (p=.027, d=.48), not but wheelchair users (p=.150), see Figure 4. Comments suggest that players using the wheelchair focused on real-world challenges, e.g., that the game "*made me grateful that I am not confined to a wheelchair*" (P4, embodied simulation) and that it "*made me realize how difficult it would be for disabled [people] to live*" (P50, embodied simulation). Players of the traditional simulation reflected upon in-game challenges, stating that the game gave them "*the perspective of that person and makes me realize how easy I have it and how grateful and thankful I should be for my ability to do things without extra challenges*" (P49, traditional simulation) and made them "*understand some of the struggles people in wheelchairs face*" (P48, traditional simulation).

6. Did attitude changes last after the intervention?

Comparisons of follow-up attitudes to pre-play attitudes showed that the changes in discrimination were still present after a week ($F_{1,38}$=5.6, p=.024, η^2=.13); however, the changes in prospects were not ($F_{1,38}$=1.5, p=.222).

7. Did embodying simulation make a difference on the lasting impact of attitude change (i.e., discrimination)?

Yes. Planned pairwise comparisons of the interaction between time and input type show that users of the embodied simulation sustained changes in discrimination (p=.028, d=.41), whereas users of the regular simulation did not (p=.299) – the attitudes of gamepad users had returned to pre-play levels, whereas attitudes of wheelchair users sustained the change (see Figure 4).

Summary of Attitude Changes

The premise and gameplay was successful at eliciting attitude changes. The traditional simulation was more effective in fostering immediate attitude changes regarding the discrimination faced by people with disabilities; however, the embodied simulation was better at cultivating longer-term changes in attitudes regarding discrimination. In addition, the embodied simulation was more effective than the traditional simulation at changing short-term attitudes regarding the prospects of people with disabilities. Although these attitude changes did not remain significant when measured one week later, Figure 4 shows that the trend for longer-term attitude change is similar to the effects for discrimination – the embodied simulation seems to better promote sustained attitude change.

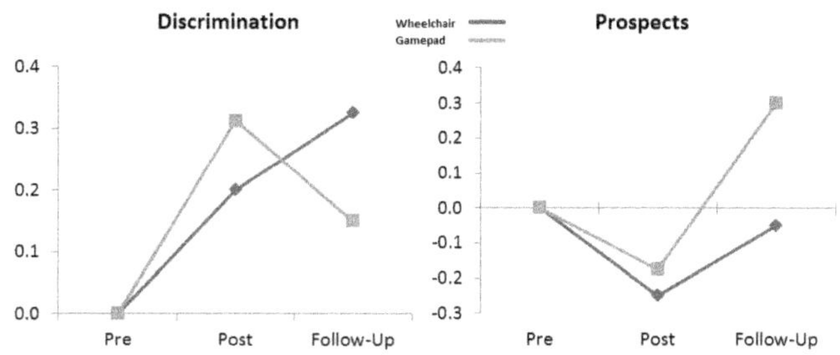

Figure 4. Mean attitude change for prospects and discrimination over time by input type. Data are normalized by player to show change from the baseline value (pre-play). Improvements in attitude are reflected in higher values for discrimination and lower values prospects.

DISCUSSION

This paper investigates the role of embodied interaction in persuasive games designed to promote positive attitudes towards persons using wheelchairs. In this section, we discuss our findings in terms of psychological aspects of persuasion and traditional disability simulation.

Persuasive Games for Attitude Change toward Disability

Our work shows that persuasive games are an effective tool to foster positive attitudes toward people using wheelchairs. Our findings support the idea that game-based disability simulation can be applied to make individuals more aware of problems that people with disabilities experience, and that games help by allowing players to experience these challenges in the playful context of a game. In this section, we provide insights into how *Birthday Party* affected attitudes, outline how embodied interaction contributed to the persuasive effect, and discuss how game-based embodied disability simulation can combine the advantages of disability simulation with those of persuasive games.

The Role of Embodied Interaction

Our results agree with findings from psychology that suggest that embodied interaction can contribute to attitude change [7, 36]. Although our study shows no difference in player experience between the traditional and embodied simulations – suggesting that both game versions were perceived in a similar fashion from the perspective of games user research – the two versions had differing effects on player attitude change. Our results show that embodied simulations have advantages over traditional simulations in terms of the impact of the intervention and in sustainability over time. These findings fall in line with prior research on attitude change through embodied interaction and allow for interpretation by established theories.

Theories that Explain Attitude Changes

Positive effects of embodied interaction have been shown on depth of processing, recognition, and acceptance of information [26]. Psychological theories explain that embodied interaction may have higher persuasive power, because: (1) it conveys information through a peripheral channel, avoiding the precise processing of arguments, which can be immediately rejected. Therefore, the message is more likely to be accepted (Elaboration Likelihood Model) [31]; (2) it adds full-body motion to process information not only through eyes, ears, or tactile feedback, but through a proprioceptive experience that allows for deep processing and longer recognition (Perceptual Symbol Systems) [4]; and (3) observing oneself performing the embodied interaction, followed by the reflection of which attitudes prompted the demonstration of a behaviour, could motivate a shift in attitude (Self Perception Theory) [5].

In the context of our game, we show that compared to traditional game input – which emphasizes the challenge internal in the game – embodied interaction may also draw attention to the challenges external to the game. While the persuasive game itself allowed us to convey the message that people using wheelchairs experience different challenges in their everyday life, embodied interaction allowed participants to have a first-hand experience using a wheelchair, forcing players to put themselves in the same situation as a person using a wheelchair. Doing so poses the question of how a player could reject a person using a wheelchair if she could be in the same situation. To solve this conflict, participants seem to temporarily reduce their prospects towards people with disabilities, and increase awareness of discrimination. The proprioceptive experience of the embodied interaction leads to deeper processing of the differences, but not the prospects, between people with disabilities and able-bodied individuals, and stabilizes the change of attitude over time. This would explain why the embodied simulation led to improved attitude in terms of discrimination, and not prospects.

Game-Based Embodied Disability Simulation

In contrast to traditional disability simulation that takes place in real-world settings [15], game-based disability simulation offers the opportunity of creating a protected environment in which players can experience challenges associated with specific disabilities, e.g., the use of wheelchairs. While previous approaches toward disability simulation have applied traditional game input and therefore omitted the physical dimension, our work shows that embodied interaction can in fact be a means of re-introducing the physicality of traditional disability simulation while maintaining the advantages of video games, i.e., the opportunity to balance difficulty to create achievable challenges that do not discourage players.

Designing Effective Embodied Persuasive Games

Our work shows that the interface affects how player attitudes are influenced by persuasive games, and that designers need to consider these effects when creating embodied persuasive games. In the following section, we outline challenges and opportunities that can be leveraged to support the creation of effective persuasive games.

Designing Physical Player Input in Embodied Persuasion

Embodied interaction naturally includes a physical dimension. In game development, this aspect has previously been approached from the perspective of exergame design, i.e., games that aim to provide physically stimulating experiences, and draw from intense physical player effort to create a challenging player experience [25]. In embodied persuasion, additional considerations are necessary to design adequate physical player input.

Understand the difficult role of physical player effort in the persuasive context. Motion-based games such as exergames have previously integrated physical effort to challenge players and improve player experience. In the context of embodied persuasive game design, this principle has potential beyond player experience. Our findings support suggestions by previous work stating that physical effort may contribute to persuasion [21]: our results show that that the *physical effort of embodied simulation may promote lasting attitude change*. Therefore, designers wishing to invoke attitude changes in players can build upon embodied interaction to facilitate persuasion. In this context, it is important to carefully balance the role of physical effort. For instance, a game that aims to promote positive attitudes towards persons using wheelchairs needs to allow players to see that despite the impact of a disability, individuals can still be physically competent and overcome physically challenging situations.

Effects of Embodied Game Interaction on Persuasion

Our results show that it is important to consider the impact of embodied interaction when designing persuasive games.

Be aware that the usability of embodied game input has an impact on persuasion beyond player experience. Our results reveal interesting differences in the way players attribute difficulties related to the input device. Participants who used a gamepad generally seemed to make a distinction between challenges related to the input device, and in-game challenges. In contrast, *when using embodied input, participant comments show that participants associated usability issues caused by the input device with the persuasive context*, i.e., players who found it hard to control the game with a wheelchair concluded that navigating a wheelchair is a difficult task. The perception of difficulties related to interaction with motion-based input is interesting when considering findings that suggest that the position of our body influences how we feel about a matter (e.g., negative affect increases if body is in an uncomfortable position) [7], an effect that may play a role in embodied persuasive games.

Understand that embodied interaction may divert player attention from in-game content. Our results show that participants using embodied game input focused on the input device. In addition to increasing game difficulty, embodied interaction may also divert player attention from in-game content, potentially reducing the persuasive power of game mechanics and narrative. When employing embodied input, designers have to account for this aspect by creating *intuitive embodied game input that allows for easy entry into play*. Furthermore, understanding that the embodiment has been shown to increase player focus on the input device is an important step towards adjusting the pacing of the game by *balancing in-game challenge, story elements, and stretches of physically demanding interaction* in a way that allows players to attend to each element.

LIMITATIONS AND FUTURE WORK

A general challenge in the evaluation of persuasive games that address socially sensitive attitudes is the measurement of attitudes and the risk that participants may provide socially desirable answers. We applied the Attitudes to Disability Scale (ADS) [30], which is an explicit measure, meaning that participants are required to consciously reflect upon their opinions. The inclusion of implicit measures of attitudes, as demonstrated by [1], can provide additional insights into subconscious attitudes. Additionally, there are four other aspects of our study design that need to be considered when generalizing the results. First, our study only addresses one type of mobility disability (wheelchair use), and future work needs to explore whether our approach can promote positive attitudes toward persons with other disabilities. Second, players using the wheelchair took longer to complete the game and thus experienced a longer exposure to our intervention; this may have affected the persuasive process. Third, although we did measure the development of participant attitudes over time, our post measurement took place one week after the intervention. To further study the effects of embodied interaction in persuasive games, conducting a longer-term study with post measurements that take place after a longer period of time might provide insight into how attitudes develop over time; increasing the frequency of the intervention may also affect attitude change. Finally, embodied interaction as explored in this paper is only suitable for persuasive technologies that include a strong physical dimension easily captured by a system, e.g., intuitive game controls that can be combined with other game mechanics in persuasive game design. For persuasive games that cannot build on physical attributes, exploring alternative approaches towards embodied persuasion might be valuable, e.g., leveraging the fact that certain postures and facial expressions have been demonstrated to facilitate persuasion [7].

CONCLUSION

Persuasive games can be an effective means of changing player attitudes or behaviours. Our work demonstrates that embodied interaction can be successfully applied to support the process of persuasion. It is a step toward capitalizing on the positive relationship between embodiments and persuasive processes studied in psychology, and applying it to video game design, thus further contributing to theoretically-grounded approaches toward persuasive game design. Applying embodied interaction in a persuasive game for promoting positive attitudes towards people using wheelchairs opens up new perspectives for disability simulation. By combining the strengths of video games with aspects of traditional disability simulation, game-based disability simulation can be a powerful tool to allow able-bodied individuals to better understand challenges that people with disabilities face. This research demonstrates that embodied persuasive games can be applied to foster positive attitudes towards persons using wheelchairs, potentially reducing barriers between able-bodied people and people with disabilities. Thereby, embodied persuasive games can help promote inclusion and make an important contribution to the ultimate goal of improving the quality of life of people with mobility impairments.

ACKNOWLEDGMENTS

We thank all participants for their contribution during evaluation. We thank our CHI reviewers for their helpful comments and NSERC and the GRAND NCE for funding.

REFERENCES

1. Alhabash, S. and Wise, K. PeaceMaker: Changing Students' Attitudes Toward Palestinians and Israelis Through Video Game Play. *International Journal of Communication* 6, (2012), 356-380.
2. Bang, M., Torstensson, C. and Katzeff, C. The PowerHouse: A Persuasive Computer Game Designed to Raise Awareness of Domestic Energy Consumption. *Persuasive Technology*. (2006), 123–132.
3. Baranowski, T., Baranowski, J., Cullen, K. W., Marsh, T., Islam, N., Zakeri, I., Honess-Morreale, L., & demoor, C. (2003). Squire's Quest!: dietary outcome evaluation of a multimedia game. *American journal of preventive medicine*, *24*(1), 52-61.
4. Barsalou, L. W. Perceptual Symbol Systems. *Behavioral and Brain Sciences* 22, 4 (1999), 577-660.
5. Bem, D. J. Self-perception: An alternative interpretation of cognitive dissonance phenomena. *Psychological Review* 74, 3 (1967), 183.
6. Bogost, I. Persuasive Games on Mobile Devices. Fogg, B.J. Eckles, D.(eds): *Mobile Persuasion*, (2007).
7. Briñol, P. and Petty, R.E. Embodied Persuasion. In: Semin, G.R. & Smith, E.R. (Eds.): *Embodied grounding*. Cambridge University Press, Cambridge (2008).
8. Brown, A. Q&A: Littleloud talks guilt and gaming with Sweatshop. 2011. http://www.wired.co.uk/news/archive/2011-07/22/sweatshop-q-and-a/viewgallery/269289.
9. Columna, L., Yang, S., Arndt, K., and Lieberman, L. Using Online Videos for Disability Awareness. *Journal of*

Physical Education, Recreation & Dance 80, 8 (2009), 19-24.

10. Dourish, P. *Where the Action is. The Foundations of Embodied Interaction*. MIT Press (2004).
11. Flower, A., Burns, M.K., Bottsford-Miller, N.A. Meta-Analysis of Disability Simulation Research. *Remedial and Special Education 28*, 2 (2007), 72-79.
12. Fogg, B.J. *Persuasive Technology: Using Computers to Change What We Think and Do*. Morgan Kaufmann, 2003.
13. French, S. Simulation Exercises in Disability Awareness Training: a critique. *Disability, Handicap & Society 7*, 3 (1992), 257-266.
14. Gerling, K.M., Kalyn, M.R., and Mandryk, R.L. KINECT^{Wheels}: Wheelchair-Accessible Motion-Based Game Interaction. In: *EA of CHI 2013*, ACM (2013).
15. Grayson, E. and Marini, I. Simulated disability exercises and their impact on attitudes toward persons with disabilities. *International Journal of Rehabilitation Research 19*, (1996), 123-131.
16. Ishii, H. and Ullmer, B. Tangible Bits: Towards Seamless Interfaces between People, Bits and Atoms. In: *Proc. of CHI 1997*, ACM (1997), 234-241.
17. Khaled, R., Barr, P., Noble, J., Fischer, R. and Biddle, R. 2007. Fine tuning the persuasion in persuasive games. *Persuasive Technology*. (2007), 36–47.
18. Krahé, B. and Altwasser, C. Changing Negative Attitudes Towards Persons with Physical Disabilities: An Experimental Intervention. *Journal of Community & Applied Social Psychology* 16, (2006), 56-69.
19. Lewis, J., Brown, D., Cranton, W., and Mason, R. Simulating visual impairments using the Unreal Engine 3 game engine. In: *Proc. of SeGAH 2011*, IEEE (2011).
20. Loke, L. and Robertson, T. Moving and Making Strange: An Embodied Approach To Movement-Based Interaction Design. *ACM TOCHI 20*, 1 (2013).
21. Lyons, L., Slattery, B., Jimenez, P., Lopez, B., and Moher, T. Don't Forget about the Sweat: Effortful Embodied Interaction in Support of Learning. In: *Proc. of TEI 2012*, ACM (2012), 77-84.
22. Marshall, C. and Rossman, G.B. 2011. *Designing Qualitative Research*. Sage Publishers: Thousand Oaks, CA, USA.
23. Meyers, A.R., Anderson, J.J., Miller, D.R., Shipp, K., and Hoenig, H. Barriers, facilitators, and access for wheelchair users: substantive and methodologic lessons from a pilot study of environmental effects. *Social Science & Medicine 55*, (2002), 1435-1446.
24. Miller, S.R. Attitudes toward Individuals with Disabilities: Does Empathy Explain the Difference in Scores between Men and Women? *Annals of Behavioral Science and Medical Education* 16, 1 (2010), 3-6.
25. Mueller, F., Edge, D., Vetere, F., Gibbs, M.R., Agamanolis, S., Bongers, B., and Sheridan, J.G. 2011. Designing Sports: A Framework for Exertion Games. In: *Proc. of CHI 2011*, ACM (2011), 2651-2660.
26. Niedenthal, P. M., Barsalou, L. W., Winkielman, P., Krauth-Gruber, S., and Ric, F. Embodiment in attitudes, social perception, and emotion. *Personality and Social Psychology Review* 9, 3 (2005), 184-211.
27. Oinas-Kukkonen, H. and Harjumaa, M. A systematic framework for designing and evaluating persuasive systems. *Persuasive Technology*, (2008), 164–176.
28. Orji, R., Mandryk, R.L., Vassileva, J., and Gerling, K.M. Tailoring persuasive health games to gamer type. In: *Proc. of CHI 2013*, ACM (2013), 2467–2476.
29. Orji, R., Vassileva, J., and Mandryk R. L. Modeling the Efficacy of Persuasive Strategies for Different Gamer Types in Serious Games for Health. User Modeling and User-Adapted Interaction: Special Issue on Personalization and Behaviour Change (in press).
30. Power, M., & Green, A. The WHOQOL-DIS Group The Attitudes to Disability Scale (ADS): development and psychometric properties. *Journal of Intellectual Disability Research 54*, 9 (2010), 860-874.
31. Petty, R. E. and Cacioppo, J. T. The elaboration likelihood model of persuasion. *Communication and Persuasion*, Springer (1986), 1-24.
32. Pivik, J., McComas, J., Macfarlane, I., and Laflamme, M. Using Virtual Reality to Teach Disability Awareness. *J. Educational Computing Research 26*, 2 (2002), 203-218.
33. Przybylski, A.K., Weinstein, N., Murayama, K., Lynch, M.F., & Ryan, R.M., The ideal-self at play: The appeal of video games that let you be all you can be. *Psychological Science*, 2011, 23 (1), 69-76.
34. Ruiz, S., York, A., Stein, M., Keating, N., Santiago, K. Darfur is Dying. 2009. http://www.darfurisdying.com/.
35. Ryan, R. M., Rigby, C. S., & Przybylski, A. K., Motivational pull of video games: A self-determination theory approach. *Motivation and Emotion* 30, (2006).
36. Sherman, D.K., Gangi, C., and White, M.L. Embodied cognition and health persuasion: Facilitating intention-behavior consistency via motor manipulations. *Journal of Experimental Social Psychology 46*, (2010), 461-464.
37. Stokes, B. Videogames have changed: time to consider 'Serious Games'? *The Development Education Journal*, (2005), 6–13.
38. Watson, D., & Clark, L. A. The PANAS-X: Manual for the positive and negative affect schedule-Expanded Form. Iowa City: University of Iowa (1994).
39. Wilson, S. and Lieberman, L. Disability awareness in physical education. *Strategies 13,* 6 (2000), 29-33.

Spent: Changing Students' Affective Learning Toward Homelessness Through Persuasive Video Game Play

Dana Ruggiero
Bath Spa University
Newton St. Loe, Bath BA29BN
d.ruggiero@bathspa.ac.uk

ABSTRACT
To investigate whether a persuasive game may serve as a way to increase affective learning about homelessness, this study examined the effects of procedural rhetoric and ethos in a video game designed to put the player in the shoes of an almost-homeless person. Data were collected from 5139 students across four states. Examination revealed that playing the game or doing the reading significantly increased the affective learning score after treatment with the game group scoring 1.57 points higher and the reading group scoring .66 points higher out of a score of 6. Findings indicate that students who played *Spent* sustained significantly higher scores after three weeks. Overall, findings suggest that when students play a video game that is designed using persuasive mechanics an affective change can be measured empirically.

Author Keywords
Affective learning; persuasive mechanics; video games.

ACM Classification Keywords
I.2.6. [**Learning**]; Concept learning and Knowledge acquisition

INTRODUCTION
Approximately 3.5 million people, 1.35 million of them children, are likely to experience homelessness in a given year in the United States [31]. On any given night 656,000 to 744,313 people experience homelessness [31]. Due to the recent foreclosure crisis, homelessness has been on the rise, and families living on the edge of homelessness face more and more tough choices every day. In 2003 children under the age of 18 accounted for 39% of the homeless population, and the number of homeless families with children has increased significantly over the past decade [31]. People who suffer from homelessness are citizens, immigrants, white, Asian, Hispanic, black, working full time, unemployed, veterans, addicts, and teenagers with all levels of education – these are similar demographics to people that play video games. There are over 183 million active gamers in the United States, over half of the population log onto virtual worlds to plan virtual battle, save virtual lives, and wage virtual war against inequalities like famine and poverty in make- believe lands. The immense immersive power of video games may be able to solve real world problems that affect millions of people on a daily basis, like homelessness, but to support that claim there is a need to examine the effect that playing a specific type of video game has on the affective learning of its players.

CHI 2014, April 26–May 1, 2014, Toronto, Ontario, Canada.
Copyright ©ACM 978-1-4503-2473-1/14/04...$15.00.
http://dx.doi.org/10.1145/2556288.2557390

Research in learning video games has focused very much on content or procedural knowledge [4, 5, 18]. However, new subsets of learning games, called persuasive games, have become more prevalent over the last ten years. Persuasive games are aimed at changing the attitude or behavior of the game players towards a particular topic (e.g., homelessness). The content in a persuasive game is what drives the persuasion necessitating a strong framework in the processes that drive affective change. This paper examines the change in affective learning experienced by students in grades 7-12 (ages 12 to 18) after playing the persuasive game *Spent.*

VIDEO GAMES AND AFFECTIVE LEARNING
Affective learning in games focuses on variables such as self-efficacy, feedback, social skill development, and transfer of learning. For the purposes of this study, a review of studies that relate to affective domain processes of motivation and engagement in learning follows. An early gaming study [37] by Paperny & Starn evaluated the effectiveness of action games dealing with health issues and learner characteristics (n=718) in a high school with students ages 13-18. The findings suggest that games produced significant knowledge gain and positive affective change towards the game as opposed to traditional instruction. The researchers found that students with low SES enjoyed and learned from games more than other students, demonstrating that games can be more motivating and engaging depending on student background. This early study led the way for more recent research into how games for learning contribute to affective change in different populations.

Another component of affective learning, and one that also relates to cognitive learning as well is the part that motivation plays in learning through games. Motivation as an affective process has been explored through game studies in various contexts. Okolo [34, 35] had confounding findings where drill and practice games were used with special education middle school students, to teach basic skills. The first study on keyboarding skills found that the process of game play had a detrimental affect on continuing motivation, while the second study on math skills found that game play had a facilitating affect on continuing motivation. These findings suggest that the subject area that the game falls under is a factor in whether or not motivation is facilitated. Conversely, Kashibuchi & Sakamoto [21] found that gaming with reversal role-playing using (n=279) 2nd and 3rd year high school students in Japan, facilitated conceptual knowledge most, and there were no effects of experimental situations on motivation.

Research on games designed around social issues is comparatively scarce in the field of learning sciences. Two key studies on affective learning focus on AIDS and homelessness respectively. Cahill [9] used descriptive quantitative methodology in a large-scale study (n=3829) with 5th-8th graders involving AIDS education. Using a simulation game the findings suggest that learning experience was enhanced and motivation toward subject were developed. Second, a dissertation by Lavender [24] explores how the perception of homelessness can be affected through game play. Lavender created a game called *Homeless: It's No Game* and had adults play the game and than complete a survey to measure if perception of homelessness had changed. This quantitative study had three participant groups; playing the game, reading about homelessness, or control with a pre-post survey administered immediately and two weeks later; no significant effect was found.

PERSUASIVE GAMES

Persuasive games have been studied in various contexts with differing definitions over the past forty years. Predating the invention of the computer, humans have used play and games for teaching necessary skills and socialization for millennia [19, 28]. Games explicitly created to change attitudes and behavior date back to 1790, when British publishers of the *New Game of Human Life* advised parents to play the board game with their children and "request their attention to a few moral and judicious observations explanatory of each character as they proceed & contrast the happiness of a virtuous and well spent life with the fatal consequences arriving from vicious & immoral pursuits" [26].

In 1843 a board game released in the US called *Mansion of Happiness* gave instructions that instructed players to make good and moral decisions to gain the seat of happiness. Moreover, Milton Bradley created the *Checkered Game of Life,* in 1860 with the intention "to forcibly impress upon the minds of youth the great moral principles of virtue and vice." While a commercial success that helped launch Bradley's board game business, there is no evidence that it had any moral affect on the minds of children [26].

The 1960s and 1970s witnessed a surge of multiplayer simulations. Given credibility by the Rand Foundation, which developed a number of persuasive games for use in the Cold and Vietnam wars, most of these were intended for education, training, and exploring alternative courses of action [1] with some persuasive purposes. For example, sociologists at Johns Hopkins developed *The Life Career Game, The Family Game, The Representative Democracy Game, The Community Response Game* and *The Consumer Game* with game aims at the player learning the necessity to defer gratification through persuasion techniques [26].

Persuasive games today are an established part of video game landscapes. They have attracted the attention of the media [2, 32] academics [7, 9, 42], and funding agencies such as the MacArthur Foundation. How persuasive games persuade is a combination of several mechanisms grounded in game studies and communication theory.

HOW PERSUASIVE GAMES PERSUADE

How can video games "modify or change values, wants, and beliefs of others"? Attempts at analyzing persuasion date back to ancient Greece; according to Aristotle persuasion is achieved through rhetoric, and three parts that include ethos, pathos, and logos [12]. Ethos uses claims about the persuader's moral character and his or her trustworthiness, an important aspect of the persuasion process if it is to be effective [14]. Pathos is an emotional appeal to secure the goodwill of the listener while logos is the reasoned argument that appeals to the listener's rational mind. Aristotle's categorization has been elaborated over time but is still useful for analysis of persuasion [7]. An important addition to the definition of persuasion is Burke, who in 1969 defined it as the use of words by human agents to form attitudes or induce actions in other human agents [33]. While the term 'words' is limiting, Burke does also include non-verbal means of communication.

However, decades of research on advertising and marketing have confirmed that persuasion is a complex phenomenon dependent on many interrelated factors that make the cross-effects of these factors difficult to separate [33]. Factors such as the interest of receivers of the message, their level of education, their knowledge of the issue, their cultural background, their feelings about the originator of the message, the medium used for the persuasive message, and competing factors all influence the success or failure of an attempt at persuasion [33].

Persuasive games use several mechanisms of persuasion that have been posited by game researchers, including: immersion, flow, engagement, procedural rhetoric, and ethos.

Immersion

Immersion is the experience of being transported to an elaborately simulated place that takes over all attention and becomes enveloping [30]. Technology has increased the power of immersion through video games, "it seems that games as persuasive technology hold much promise for changing people's attitudes: games are by nature interactive, and people tend to retain more impressions" [23]. Related to immersion is the concept of agency, which Murray [30] describes as the satisfying power to take meaningful action and see the results of our decisions and choices. Agency helps immersion build when our actions in the video game are appropriate to the game narrative, strengthening the belief in the consistency of the game world.

Flow

Flow has been a theory posited by some game theorists [3] that games are compelling because players are in a highly energized state of concentration and focus [13]. Flow is achieved when the level of the challenge and the level of the player's skill in in dynamic tension, creating a highly focused state of mind. Amory [3] posits that the player can assimilate tacit knowledge through the process that is then assimilated and constructed after emerging from the state of flow.

Engagement

Engagement is closely related to flow where the player finds the game so engrossing that they assimilate facts and values without realizing they are doing so [39]. Research [36, 42] supports the claims made above that games increase engagement through flow, immersion, and agency. Accordingly when players are more engaged with the game, they are more likely to see the situation from the perspective presented in the game. Yee and Bailenson [46] placed college age students in a virtual environment where they used avatars that resembled elderly people. The researchers tested the attitudes of the subjects towards the elderly and found that the computer simulation increased empathy toward people with similar traits to that of the avatar and decreased players' stereotypes of the elderly. Another study on engagement by Goldsworthy, Barab, & Goldsworthy [18] found that adolescents with ADHD who played a simulation game performed significantly better than the control group on measures of engagement. Both of these studies demonstrate that games with a persuasive message can affect engagement through manipulation of the immersion elements within the game context. Engagement in *Spent,* the game chosen for this experiment is triangulated among three modalities. The player is the character and makes decisions as they would in real life, he or she has the ability to ask for help using social media, and every action is measured on a sliding monetary scale.

Procedural Rhetoric and Ethos

Both procedural rhetoric and ethos are Aristotelian theories of persuasion updated by Bogost [7] and Evans [14]. While Bogost defines procedural rhetoric as "the practice of using processes persuasively" [7], Evans argues that rhetoric is not enough and includes ethos or "persuasion by empathy, fact, and integrity" [14]. The *McDonald's Videogame* and the *Redistricting Game* are used to demonstrate where procedural rhetoric and ethos are exhibited through gameplay. The *McDonald's Videogame* is an anti-advertising game, where games are a satire of specific companies and their business practices [43].

By demonstrating that every action in the game has consequences, which are built into the game structure by the designers, the rhetoric and ethos of these procedures not only allow the player to learn through game play but also are a more effective and longer-lasting way of assimilating information [7]. While Evans [14] argues that rhetoric alone is not enough, his use of the *Redistricting Game* to demonstrate the power of procedural ethos is important to this study because it examines not only the message being sent but the messenger and the final outcome for integrity, empathy, and fact.

MEASURING IMPACT OF PERSUASIVE GAMES

Having established how games can persuade is there a way to determine how effective they are? How many students who play *Food Force,* a game that puts them in the shoes of a World Health Organization food worker and that has been downloaded 4 million times [11], retain an interest in the politics of food distribution after game play concludes? *America's Army,* a game developed by the U.S. Army, has had players dedicate more than 160 million hours of game time [11] but how many of those players actually enlist in the Army? Games that are intended to lead to actions are easier to evaluate because you can measure the effect. For example, the effectiveness of a game that is aimed at persuading people to visit a website can be calculated by the number of players who clicked through from the game to the website.

When measuring a game without such concrete goals, such as the intention to influence the players' change in affective learning by experiencing what it's like to be almost homeless, this influence is more difficult to measure. In order to measure a change in affective learning by playing a persuasive game, this research propose to first establish whether or not there is a significant change when playing a game designed to be extremely persuasive through the use of both mechanics and topic. Thus, the following research question was proposed:

R1: To what extent does affective learning differ immediately ***and three weeks*** *after playing the persuasive game Spent for the game treatment group, controlling for gender and hours playing video games, as measured by the Affective Learning Inventory (ALS) compared to the control and comparison groups?*

METHODS

This study used a quasi-experimental design with control and two treatment groups to compare the effects of playing a persuasive game on affective learning towards homelessness. The population of this study consisted of adolescents in grades 7 through 12 (ages 12 to 18) in formal education settings in the Midwestern U.S. The sample consisted of adolescents in grades 7 through 12 in public, private, and religious schools in four states of the Midwestern U.S. Using a purposive sampling [20] an email was sent to all principals of schools in Indiana, Michigan, Illinois, and Ohio asking them to forward a letter of introduction to their teachers. Given the nature of the study it was nearly impossible to get a probabilistic representational sample and a total of 346 classrooms agreed to participate. Ninety-four classrooms agreed to participate but did not start the project or completed only the demographic information; thirty-one classrooms did not complete the three-week posttest; twenty classrooms had fifty percent or more unlabeled student data; and one classroom had only three students. In total, 200 classrooms (n= 5139 students) completed the study. Twenty-four classrooms were from religious schools, eleven were from private schools, and 165 were from public schools. As this study does not introduce novel teaching methods it was approved through the Institutional Review Board (IRB) as exempt research and every teacher who agreed to participate had their entire class enrolled in the study.

Pretest-posttest control group design [10] occurred in two steps. The first step was where matching was employed on individual classrooms to ensure that there was equal representation in the pretest and no pretest groups. Second, randomization occurred for the experimental condition. For example, using a Solomon design, classes were assigned to game, reading, or control with a pretest and two posttests: one, immediately after treatment and a second at three weeks after the treatment. The pretest was used to ensure that the control and treatment groups were equivalent. Additionally classrooms were matched using the following variables: state, setting, and grade. This was done to minimize variance in the scores due to contextual effects and to create equal numbers for each of the treatment and control groups. This was done to ensure that across states, setting, and grade there were an equal number of classrooms participating in each of the groups. To do this a model was developed that looked at the total number of classes participating in each grade. After that the model split those classes in each grade by state and the type of school setting. Finally classes were randomly assigned to one of the three groups (control, reading, or game).

Group	Pretest	Treatment	Post-Immediate	Post-3 weeks
T1 (Game)	O1	X	O2	O3
T1 (Game)		X	O4	O5
Control	O6		O7	O8
Control			O9	O10
T2 (Reading)	O11	X	O12	O13
T2 (Reading)		X	O14	O15

Key: T= Treatment, O= Observation, C= Control

Table 1. Solomon Design of Experimental Groups

Affective Learning Scale (ALS)

The dependent variable was defined as the average score on the Affective Learning Scale (ALS) [41]. ALS has participants indicate their level of agreement with statements pertaining to the experience of that particular day in class.

Reliability and validity

Scott and Wheeless reported a .96 Cronbach's alpha reliability for ALS, demonstrating a very high internal consistency that is explained by the semantic structure of the survey questions. Preliminary analysis of the ALS scores for this study found a similar high Cronbach's alpha reliability (.944). Statements in this scale are highly circular asking similar questions with slight differences (the beginning of every sentence is the same and only one word changes), overlapping so using an average score is most reasonable. The Affective Learning Scale measures current emotions and positive internalized attitudes toward content, a temporary condition of intention to complete a task, and a positive belief in accomplishing a task. The measure above was chosen after reviewing studies that have been completed over the course of the last twenty years that profiled affective learning in educational settings [22, 28, 38]. Similar reliability (Cronbach's alpha=.941) has also been demonstrated in the Kearney study [22] using the ALS. The reason for using this instrument was two fold: (1) this measure is reliable and has been tested multiple times using the same age group as the research study; and, (2) this measure looks specifically at affective learning as identified by Bloom as "an increasing internalization of positive attitudes toward content or subject matter" [22].

Independent Variables

The independent variables of this study were group membership (i.e., game, reading, and control group assignments) controlling for gender, hours playing video games at home, and pretest scores on the ALS. Students were asked to provide demographic information such as gender, age, number of hours playing video games, and volunteer experience with the homeless.

Control, Game, and Reading Group Assignments

Using matching protocols [10] classes were matched first by variables (e.g., grade, state, setting) and then randomly assigned to either the game, reading, or control group to ensure equivalency across the participant. This was done to ensure that an equal number of students were assigned to each of the control, reading, and game groups from each of the grades, states, and school settings. The matching failed over the course of the data collection due to classrooms dropping out of the study and students not completing the measures. This led to an unbalanced design with different amounts of classrooms in each group.

The game

Spent is a text based game developed by the McKinney advertising studio in cooperation with the Durham Homeless Coalition. The player starts off with a scenario that they are a single parent, have no job, and just lost their home. The gameplay starts when the player is challenged to see if they could survive on $1000 for the next month. After securing a job the player is faced with a series of choices including finding housing, paying for car insurance, joining the union, and buying food. Every decision has an effect on the player's money barometer and the challenge is to make the choices you would normally make in your own life but on the limited financial means that the player currently has available.

The reading

Written in the first person this account is of the first night of homelessness and the experiences that lead to and follow from living on the edge of financial ruin. Published by the Huffington Post the author leads the reader through carrying all of their belongings, finding a safe place to sleep, getting a job interview, buying food, and applying for benefits. The reading level of this article is grade 5.

PROCEDURE

In the fall of 2011 9816 emails were sent to every school in Indiana, Ohio, Illinois, and Michigan asking principals to forward an email invitation to participate in the study. A total of 200 classrooms (n=5139 students) completed the study by June 2012.The researcher contacted each teacher that expressed interest in participating in the study via email in March 2012. Upon receiving the approval of the Institutional Review Board (IRB) the researcher began recruiting individual classrooms for the experiment to be conducted in the spring 2012. The researcher sent a hyperlink to each teacher to an online video that discussed the research procedures. Each teacher also filled out a Qualtrics™ survey with his/her preferred research dates, and pertinent demographic data about their students. Once the teachers watched the video and were instructed in the research procedures, they were assigned to game, reading or control groups. The researcher was not present to administer the study and teachers were given a detailed instruction sheet on how to proceed. Off-site research allowed access to larger research subject pools relevant to the research questions and allowed participation research at a site from which research would otherwise not be conducted. Critical elements such as fostering communication, encouraging subject participation, and optimizing data collection and management were handled through email, Qualtrics™, and online video.

A week prior to the research date, teacher participants received a reminder email with a basic survey that asked them to provide classroom data such as volunteer activities related to homelessness, how often they used computer games in their classroom, and subject area specialization, including whether or not they have talked about homelessness and any community service projects that the school is involved in relating to homelessness. This was used in the data conditioning process to determine if any outliers were the result of these individual classroom variables. The survey was in Qualtrics™ with multiple-choice and open-ended questions. This information was used to gain a clearer understanding of how the variables related to the school and classroom settings. Related to the research questions and the research by Lenhart et al. [25] the number of hours spent playing video games could have an effect on ALS scores. There is no prior research that examines hours playing video games at home and hours playing video games at school in relation to affective learning, thus the researches hypothesize that these variables may have an impact and account for them in data analysis.

For game and reading groups, on the assigned research day the teacher escorted their class to the computer lab and started the study. Teachers read a brief introduction telling the students how to log on to Qualtrics™ and take the pretest, the length of time to play the game or read the story, and how to access the posttest. Each teacher received a short script to be followed for the treatment section and the follow up. Students logged onto individual computers and accessed the Internet. Each student received a slip of paper that had the URL listed for the game (www.playspent.org) or reading and the tinyURL (www.tinyurl.com) for the Qualtrics™ survey. First students took the pretest on Qualtrics™. They then played *Spent* or read a first-person narrative about being homeless for approximately 30 minutes. Then they accessed the Qualtrics™ survey site again to complete the posttest measure. The pretest and posttest measure asked for the students' name, gender, school, state, and grade to ensure proper identification of the student on all three tests. To ensure confidentiality surveys were matched and de- identified by a third party not associated with the research study prior to any data analysis. This occurred for all research groups.

For control groups, on the assigned research day the teacher escorted their class to the computer lab and started the pretest. Students logged onto individual computers and accessed the Internet. Each student received a slip of paper that had the tinyURL for the Qualtrics™ survey. Students accessed the Qualtrics™ survey site to complete the pretest measure. Three weeks later the class returned to the computer lab on the assigned research day. Students logged onto individual computers and accessed the Internet. Each student received a slip of paper that had the tinyURL for the Qualtrics™ survey. Students accessed the Qualtrics™ survey site to complete the measure. The measure was made up of one scale. Participants in the game, reading and control groups took the

ALS. The treatment groups took the ALS immediately before and after playing the game or reading and the control group took the scale without playing the game. Each group completed the scale three weeks later to test for long-term sleeper effect.

DATA ANALYSIS

Hierarchical Linear Modeling (HLM) was chosen for the data analysis of the current study because the data were reported by students nested in classrooms, with the classroom receiving the assignment of control, game, or reading group. HLM is a multi-level multiple regression technique that is useful in analyzing nested data [8]. In order to proceed with HLM analysis, the number of levels in the data needed to be specified and models needed to be constructed. The current study data were best described in two levels: student level (level 1), and classroom and teacher level (level 2).

$$ALS\ Immediate\ Post\ Test$$
$$= \beta_{0j} + \beta_1(Gender) + \beta_2(Hours\ Playing\ Games\ at\ Home)$$
$$+ \beta_3(Hours\ Playing\ Games\ at\ School) + \beta_4(ALS\ Pretest) + r$$
$$\beta_0 = \gamma_{00} + \gamma_{01}(Game) + \gamma_{02}(Reading) + U_{0j}$$
$$\beta_{1j} = \gamma_{10} + U_{1j}$$
$$\beta_{2j} = \gamma_{20} + U_{2j}$$
$$\beta_{3j} = \gamma_{30} + U_{3j}$$
$$\beta_{4j} = \gamma_{40} + U_{4j}$$

Figure 1. Immediate Post-test Model

$$ALS\ Three\ Week\ Post\ Test$$
$$= \beta_{0j} + \beta_1(Gender) + \beta_2(Hours\ Playing\ Games\ at\ Home)$$
$$+ \beta_3(Hours\ Playing\ Games\ at\ School)$$
$$+ \beta_4(ALS\ Immediate\ Post\ Test) + r$$
$$\beta_{0j} = \gamma_{00} + \gamma_{01}(Game) + \gamma_{02}(Reading) + U_{0j}$$
$$\beta_{1j} = \gamma_{10} + U_{1j}$$
$$\beta_{2j} = \gamma_{20} + U_{2j}$$
$$\beta_{3j} = \gamma_{30} + U_{3j}$$
$$\beta_{4j} = \gamma_{40} + U_{4j}$$

Figure 2. Three-Week Post-test Model

Level 1 was represented by student background such as; hours playing games at home and at school, pretest score, and gender which are unique across students. Teacher and classroom background variables such as treatment grouping and grade level represented level 2.

RESULTS

Students in both the reading and game group increased their affective learning score immediately after treatment and both factors were statistically significant in their difference from the control group. While students in the reading group had .667 (p<. 0001) points higher than the control group, the game group had a 1.57 (p<. 0001) increase over the control group. This could be interpreted to mean that the game had a greater impact on affective learning and that it is the persuasive game mechanics of *Spent,* rather than the subject that relates to this finding.

The change from ALS pretest to ALS immediate posttest for the control group can be explained by carry over effect as these tests were taken back to back. The game group gained an approximate 2.4 points, which is a significant change. Additionally, the reading group gained an approximate 1.5 points immediately after treatment. The changes in scores may be explained by the fact that students had to travel to a computer lab and take part in a special assignment rather than the normal day-to-day classwork.

Source DV: Immediate Posttest ALS	Coefficient	Standard Error	Approx. d.f.	P-value
CONTROL	3.833	.059	197	p<0.01
GAME	1.578	.170	197	p<0.01
READING	.667	.180	197	p<0.01
GENDER	-.057	.048	2330	.244
GAMES HOME	.011	.005	2330	.042
ALS PRETEST	.545	.019	2330	p<0.01

Figure 3. Immediate Posttest results

In summary the model as a whole is significant in predicting the immediate posttest score on ALS. Individual level 1 variable gender, is not a significant predictor of the immediate posttest score on ALS, but hours playing games at home and ALS pretest are significant predictors of ALS immediate posttest score. This may imply that the more hours students play games at home, the more they enjoyed and found interesting, the game *Spent*.

Overall, the reading and game groups showed a significant difference from the control group score. This may imply that immediately after treatment students felt that the activity was different and engaging compared to daily classroom activities. One thing that is not explained by the data is the lower pretest score for the control group. One possible explanation is the lower number of control group classrooms (n=24). An additional possible explanation is that teachers informed their students of the control group assignment and this affected the control group score.

Three weeks after the treatment the game group showed a significant difference, .736 points (p<. 001) from the control group while the reading group did not, .102 points (p=.553). The practical significance of these findings is weak. One possible explanation for this finding is that after three weeks with no additional exposure to the game or reading the students were not as engaged or interested in the material. However, the game group is statistically higher than the control group on the ALS three-week posttest.

All three groups decreased in their affective learning scores but only the game group showed a significant change from the posttest to the three week posttest as measured by paired sample t-tests. This could be interpreted to mean that playing the game increases affective learning temporarily but the effect is not sustained over the long term. The reading group had a significant point difference from pre test to posttest but did not differ significantly from posttest to three-week posttest, as measured by paired sample t- tests.

Source DV: Three Week Posttest ALS	Coefficient	Standard Error	Approx. d.f.	P-value
CONTROL	3.026	.046	197	p<0.01
GAME	.736	.164	197	p<0.01
READING	.102	.173	197	.553
GENDER	.001	.051	3451	.987
GAMES HOME	.003	.003	3451	.241
GAMES SCH	-.006	.006	3451	.299
ALS IMMEDIATE POSTTEST	.010	.018	3451	.584

Figure 4. Three-week Posttest results

This could be interpreted to mean that reading about homelessness immediately increases affective learning and decreases but not in a significantly different way than the control group.

In summary none of the groups sustain their ALS score from immediate posttest to three-week posttest. However, the game group does score significantly higher on the three-week posttest than the control group. Both the reading group and the control group decrease to pretest level after three weeks and there is no significant difference between these groups.

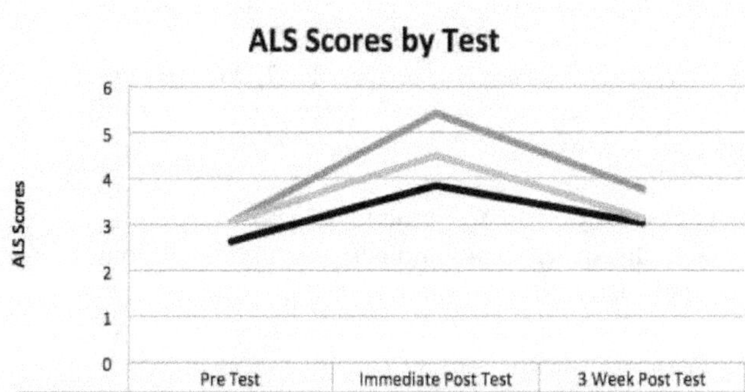

	Pre Test	Immediate Post Test	3 Week Post Test
Control	2.62243	3.833264	3.026905
Game	3.0524	5.411577	3.763186
Reading	3.0491	4.500636	3.129898

Figure 5. Affective Learning Scores from pretest, to immediate post test to three-week posttest.

DISCUSSION

First and foremost this study is significant because it is currently one of very few studies that empirically measured the persuasive effectiveness of a game aimed at a social issue and found statistically significant results. There are multiple anecdotal reports and case studies available on social issue games, but this is one of the first that took a large-scale quantitative approach to measuring affective learning using a publicly available social issue game. Additionally, the study used an empirical methodology that is verifiable with measures routed in valid and reliable statistical approaches. Simply stated, this study found statistically significant results within the protocols of the study, using parametric tests and reached conclusions that are supported by current literature.

Playing *Spent* or completing the reading significantly increased the affective learning score immediately after treatment with the game group scoring 1.57 points higher and the reading group scoring .66 points higher out of a score of 6. This finding showed that there is a significant impact on affective learning whether the students read or play the game. That in itself doesn't relate significance, but what does matter is that the game group scored both significantly higher than the control group and almost a full point higher than the reading group in the immediate posttest. The data did support the prior research [24, 27] that playing the game would lead to a higher level of affective learning. Although subjects who were a part of the game group scored significantly higher than the reading group, the game group was not significantly different than the reading group. Both activities positively affected the affective learning score significantly over the control group. However, it is interesting to note that students in the game group increased two times over the reading group. One possible explanation for this finding is that the game elements and interactivity increased affective learning. Prior research supports this [2, 4, 23] and the students in the game group were experiencing the same content as the students reading in addition to the persuasive game.

Another potential explanation for the significant statistical and practical increase in scores on the ALS for the game group is that the pretest score was based off of subjects not having any prior experience with the game. Therefore the pretest scores were homogenously low across all groups and the game group was significantly different than the control group at the immediate posttest due to the game elements. The combined explanation of the prior research supporting an increase in affective learning and no prior activity resulting in low pretest scores indicates the differential impact of game play on affective learning over reading or control group scores.

This finding is both interesting and expected. It was expected that the students who played the game to be more engaged and affected than those who did nothing. What was unexpected was that students who read would not be statistically different than the students who play the game. However, it has been seen before in games research [45] where there is no statistical difference between groups when measuring abstract concepts like affective learning.

All three groups affective learning score decreased from the immediate posttest, but the game group was significantly different from the control group in a positive direction. This means that after three weeks the students that played the game were still more engaged and motivated in the topic of homelessness than the students who had not played the game. While affective learning scores peaked at the immediate posttest and then went down during the three- week interval, the game group was still more positive than the other groups. However, while the reading group and control group decreased to pretest level the game group was significantly higher statistically than the control group after three weeks. One explanation for this finding may be that the mechanics of the game that initially increased the ALS score were sustainable after three weeks leading to a higher, albeit less peaked, affective learning score than the control or reading groups.

One possible interpretation of this finding is that the game *Spent,* with its persuasive mechanics, has a higher residual effect on affective learning when students think about homelessness. This more positive affective learning could possibly link to a more positive attitude towards the homeless. Prior research [5, 6, 18] supports this finding. Practical significance of this finding links to the statistical significance. Students that are more engaged and motivated by the game immediately after playing are able to sustain that engagement and motivation in the topic of homelessness over the course of three weeks. Games can manufacture psychological changes as shown here and supported by the work of the above studies as well as Foster & Mishra [16] and Mishra & Foster [29].

In the big picture this study was both statistically and practically significant in the field of measuring persuasive games. This is a first step in a barren area of research and for that reason alone this study will open up new paths to future research. All of the major findings were statistically significant with a solid methodology and research framework that created a replicable study that can be used with any persuasive game that fits the criteria discussed in the introduction. Moreover, this study is the first step on lining up more research on this process. Moving forward is the key to the utility of this study and lessons learned during the process will help further this field of research.

This study examined the effects of playing a persuasive game on affective learning. Data were collected from 5139 middle and high school students across 200 schools in four states. The treatment conditions were randomly assigned to each classroom after matching and included a control group (only took the tests), a game group, and a reading group each within a Solomon design (no pretest for half the participants). There were statistically significant positive changes to the game group after three weeks, a first step in closing the gap that exists in persuasive game research.

CONCLUSION

Games about poverty and homelessness are creating opportunities for new conversations about social issue awareness in the global community [40]. Games such as *Spent*, designed to demonstrate that homelessness is a matter of circumstances and not character, take an interactive approach to raising awareness about major issues in our society. Homelessness is not declining in the United States [31] and awareness through education, whether formal or informal, without explicit instruction needs to rely on other mechanisms. Persuasive mechanics in conjunction with game elements can provide motivation for players to actively engage in social issues through gameplay. As demonstrated in this study, active engagement can lead to a change in affective learning and could, in the future, lead to a change in behavior. We do not yet have the empirical evidence to suggest that *Spent* and social issues games can provide impetus for action, but we are getting closer as a games community. In a world where poverty and homelessness are becoming more prevalent and inaccurate stereotypes about the poor still abound, it's important that we find ways to measure the impact of social issue games.

ACKNOWLEDGMENTS

I would like to thank all the teachers and students that participated in this study.

REFERENCES

1. Abt, C. (1970). Serious Games. New York: The Viking Press.
2. Alkan, S., & Cagiltay, K. (2007). Studying computer game learning experience through eye tracking. *British Journal of Educational Technology, 38(3),* 538-542.
3. Amory, A. (2006). Game object model version II: a theoretical framework for educational game development. *Educational Technology Research and Development,* 54, 1-27.
4. Barab, S., Sadler, T., Heiselt, C., Hickey, D., & Zuiker, S. (2007). Relating narrative, inquiry, and inscriptions: Supporting consequential play. *Journal of Science Education & Technology, 16(1),* 59-82.
5. Barker, J., Brinkman, L., & Deardorff, M. (1995). Computer intervention for adolescent children of divorce. *Journal of Divorce & Remarriage, 23(3),* 197-213.
6. Bartholomew, L.K., Gold, R.S., Parcel, G.S., Czyzewski, D.I., Sockrider, M.M., Fernandez, M. et al. (2000). Watch, discover, think, and act: Evaluation of computer-assisted instruction to improve asthma self-management in inner-city children. *Patient Education and Counseling, 39(2-3),* 269-280.
7. Bogost, I. (2007). *Persuasive Games: The Expressive Power of Video Games.* Cambridge, MA: The MIT Press.
8. Bryk, A.S., & Raudenbush, S.W. (1992). Hierarchical Linear Models in Social and Behavioral Research: Applications and Data Analysis Methods (First Edition). Newbury Park, CA: Sage Publications.
9. Cahill, J.M. (1994). Health works: Interactive AIDS education videogames. *Computers in Human Services,*

11(1), 159-176.
10. Campbell, D. T., Stanley, J. C., & Gage, N. L. (1963). *Experimental and quasi-experimental designs for research.* Boston: Houghton Mifflin.
11. Clarren, R. (2006). Virtually dead in Iraq. Salon, September 16, 2006. Retrieved October 12, 2011 from www.salon.com/ent/feature/2006/09/16/americasarmy/
12. Cooper, L. (1932). *The Rhetoric of Aristotle.* EnglewoodCliffs, NJ: Prentice-Hall.
13. Csikszentmihalyi, M. (1990). *Flow:The psychology of optimal experience.* New York: Harper & Row.
14. Evans, M. A. (2011). Procedural Ethos: Confirming the Persuasive in Serious Games. *International Journal of Gaming and Computer-Mediated Simulations (IJGCMS), 3*(4), 70-80. doi:10.4018/jgcms.2011100105
15. Frasca, G. (2001). *Videogames of the Oppressed: Videogames as a means for critical thinking and debate.* Georgia Institute of Technology, Atlanta, GA.
16. 44.Foster, A. N., & Mishra, P. (2009). Games, claims, genres & learning. In R. E. Ferdig (Ed.), *Handbook of Research on Effective Electronic Gaming in Education*: Information Science Reference.
17. Gee, J.P. (2007). *Good video games + good learning: Collected essays on video games, learning and literacy.* New York: Peter Lang
18. Goldsworthy, R.C., Barab, S.A., & Goldsworthy, E.L. (2000). The STAR project: Enhancing adolescents' social understanding through video- based, multimedia scenarios. *Journal of Special Education Technology,15(2)*, 13-26.
19. Huizinga, J. (1955). Nature and significance of paly as a cultural phenomenon. In K. Salen, & E. Zimmerman (Eds), *The game design reader: A rules of play anthology* (p. 96-120). Cambridge: MIT Press
20. Johnson, B., & Christensen, L. B. (2012). *Educational research: Quantitative, qualitative, and mixed approaches.* Thousand Oaks, Calif: SAGE Publications.
21. Kashibuchi, M., & Sakamoto, A. (2001). The educational effectiveness of a simulation/game in gender education. *Simulation & Gaming, 32(3)*, 331-343.
22. Kearney, P. & McCrosky, J. (1980). Relationships among teacher communication style, trait and state communication apprehension, and teacher effectiveness. In D. Nimmo (Ed.), *Communication Yearbook 4* (pp.533-551). New Brunswick, NJ: Transaction Books.
23. Khaled, R. (2007). *Culturally-Relevant Persuasive Technology.* Victoria University of Wellington, Wellington, NZ.
24. Lavender, T. (2011) "Video Games as Change Agents -- The Case of Homeless: It's No Game," *The McMaster Journal of Communication*: Vol. 7: Iss. 1, Article 2.
25. Lenhart, A., Kahne, J., Middaugh, E., Macgill, A. R., Evans, C., & Vitak, J. (2008). Teens, video games, and civics. Pew Internet & American Life Project, September, 16.
26. Lepore, J. (2007). The Meaning of Life. *New Yorker,* 83(13), 38-43
27. Lieberman, D. A. (2001). Management of chronic pediatric diseases with interactive health games: Theory and research findings. The Journal of Ambulatory Care Management, 24(1), 26–38.
28. McCrosky, J. (1992). *An introduction to communication in the classroom.* Edina, MN: Burgess International Group, Inc.
29. Mishra, P., & Foster, A. (2007). The claims of games: A comprehensive review and directions for future research. In C. Crawford, D. A. Willis, R. Carlsen, I. Gibson, K. McFerrin, J. Price & R. Weber (Eds.), *SITE'18* (Vol. 2007, pp. 2227-2232). Association for the Advancement of Computing in Education (AACE).
30. Murray, J. (1997). *Hamlet on the Holodeck: The Future of Narrative in Cyberspace.* Cambridge, MA: MIT Press.
31. National Law Center on Homelessness and Poverty, "Annual Report", Washington D.C., March 5, 2011
32. Ochalla, B. (2007). *Who Says Video Games Have to be Fun? The Rise of Serious Games.* Retrieved November 3, 2011 from www.gamasutra.com/view/feature/
33. O'Keefe, D. J. (2002). *Persuasion: Theory and Research.* Thousand Oaks, California: Sage Publications, Inc.
34. Okolo, C.M., & Others, A. (1990). Learning dis- abled students' acquisition of keyboarding skills and continuing motivation under drill-and-practice and game conditions. Learning Disabilities *Research, 5(2)*, 100-109.
35. Okolo, C.M. (1992). The effect of computer-assisted instruction format and initial attitude on the arithmetic facts proficiency and continuing motivation of students with learning disabilities. *Exceptionality: A Research Journal, 3(4)*, 195-211.
36. Padgett, L.S., Strickland, D., & Coles, C.D. (2006).Case study: Using a virtual reality computer game to teach fire safety skills to children diagnosed with fetal alcohol syndrome. *Journal of Pediatric Psychology,31(1)*, 65-70.
37. Paperny, D.M., & Starn, J.R. (1989). Adolescent pregnancy prevention by health education computer games: Computer-assisted instruction of knowledge and attitudes. *Pediatrics, 83(5)*, 742.
38. Plax, T., Kearney, P., McCrosky, J., & Richmond, V. (1986). Power in the classroom: VI. Verbal control strategies, nonverbal immediacy and affective learning. *Communication Education, 35*, 43-55.
39. Quinn, C., (2005). *Engaging Learning: Designing e-Learning Simulation Games.* Hoboken, NJ: Pfeiffer Essential Resources.
40. Ruggiero, D. (2013) Persuasive Games as Social Action Agents: Challenges and Implications in Learning and Society. *International Journal of Gaming and Computer-Mediated Simulations (IJGCMS), 5*(4).
41. Scott, M. & Wheeless, L. (1975). Communication apprehension, student attitudes, and levels of satisfaction. *Western Journal of Speech Communication, 41.* 188-198.
42. Thomas, R., & Cahill, J. (1997). Using an interactive computer game to increase skill and self-efficacy regarding safer gender. Health *Education & Behavior,24(1)*, 71-86.

43. Tiwari, N., "Cow slaughtering with Ronald McDonald", July 5, 2006, Retrieved from CNET News on February5, 2012.
44. Tuzun, H. (2007). Blending video games with learning: Issues and challenges with classroom implementations in the Turkish context. *British Journal of Educational Technology, 38(3),* 465-477.
45. Van Eck, R. (2006). The effect of contextual pedagogical advisement and competition on middle- school students' attitude toward mathematics and mathematics instruction using a computer-based simulation game. *Journal of Computers in Mathematics & Science Teaching, 25(2),* 165-195.
46. Yee, N. & Bailenson, J. N. (2006). *Walk A Mile in Digital Shoes: The Impact of Embodied Perspective- Taking on The Reduction of Negative Stereotyping in Immersive Virtual Environments.* PRESENCE 2006.

Incentives to Participate in Online Research: An Experimental Examination of "Surprise" Incentives

Andrew T. Fiore
Facebook, Inc.
& UC Berkeley
atfiore@fb.com

Coye Cheshire
School of Information
UC Berkeley
coye@ischool.berkeley.edu

Lindsay Shaw Taylor
Dept. of Psychology
UC Berkeley
shawtaylor.lindsay@gmail.com

G.A. Mendelsohn
Dept. of Psychology
UC Berkeley
jermend@berkeley.edu

ABSTRACT
The recruitment of participants for online survey research presents many challenges. In this work, we present four experiments examining how two different kinds of "surprise" financial incentives affect the rate of participation in a longitudinal study when participants are initially solicited with either an appeal to intrinsic motivation to participate in research or one that also offers extrinsic financial incentives. We find that unexpected financial incentives ("existence surprises") presented to people who click a recruitment advertisement focused on intrinsic incentives lead to a lower recruitment rate than do the same incentives offered to those who clicked an advertisement that led them to expect it. However, when potential participants expect a financial incentive, surprising them with a higher amount ("amount surprises") yields a higher recruitment rate. We interpret these results in the context of crowding theory. Neither type of surprise affected ongoing participation, measured as the number of questions and questionnaires completed over the course of the study.

Author Keywords
Incentives; Motivation; Online research recruitment.

ACM Classification Keywords
H.5.m. Information interfaces and presentation (e.g., HCI): Miscellaneous.

INTRODUCTION
Surveys are an important and increasingly pervasive part of the arsenal of tools employed by HCI researchers, as well as information, computer, and social scientists more broadly (cf. [23]). Even as large-scale behavioral data analysis provides powerful insights into *what* people are doing with computational systems, surveys provide complementary information about *why* and *how* people behave as they do.

Best practices for recruiting participants for postal mail, telephone, and face-to-face surveys have much in common with those for online surveys (cf. [12]). Yet recruiting participants in online environments also presents new challenges, such as how to format and deliver surveys and reminders and what kind of bias to expect in terms of who responds [14]. At the same time, web-based surveys offer enormous advantages to researchers who might otherwise lack the financial resources to conduct large-scale population studies [36].

For such researchers, it is important to understand how different kinds of incentives and the manner in which they are presented might promote or depress interest, recruitment, and ongoing participation among participants who may have varying motivations for taking part in a study. Crowding theory [11, 15, 24, 30] offers a framework not previously applied in the context of large-scale research recruitment for understanding how extrinsic financial incentives may "crowd out," or displace, intrinsic motivation, whereas the same incentives may "crowd in," or amplify, existing extrinsic motivation.

In this paper, we present four experiments to examine the impact of two levels of extrinsic financial incentive ($15 and $60, paid in three installments) combined with four different recruitment ads, varying in their appeals to intrinsic or extrinsic motivations to participate in research, on the participation rate in a longitudinal survey study. In particular, we focus on two kinds of incentive surprises: the "existence surprise," when a financial incentive is revealed to participants who were not expecting one, and the "amount surprise," when a financial incentive is expected but the amount is higher than participants were led to anticipate.

We find that "existence surprises" have little benefit with respect to successful recruitment into a study and, at the lower incentive level, in fact incur some penalty as compared to offering the same amount advertised in advance, consistent with a "crowding out" effect. By contrast, "amount surprises" yield higher recruitment rates as compared to the same financial incentive presented up front, consistent with extrinsic motivation being "crowded in."

SURVEY RECRUITMENT AND INCENTIVES
Techniques for recruiting survey participants have a long history of adapting to new media, from the use of postal mail to the telephone and now the Internet. Throughout this

CHI 2014, April 26 - May 01 2014, Toronto, ON, Canada
Copyright 2014 ACM 978-1-4503-2473-1/14/04...$15.00.
http://dx.doi.org/10.1145/2556288.2557418

progression, researchers have strived to maximize response rates in order to reach representative samples efficiently. Yet as Tourangeau [33] discusses, response rates have declined in recent years due to a number of factors: greater difficulty in reaching potential participants, due to societal changes such as the increase in people living alone and technological changes like caller ID; more people declining to participate once contacted; and more people proving unable to participate, perhaps due to language barriers arising from demographic shifts.

Potential participants may have a variety of reasons for choosing to participate in a survey or to decline — no survey or incentive will be universally compelling. Different respondents may value the relevance of the survey's topic to them, the effort involved in participating, the worth of incentives offered, and the merits of the organization conducting the survey differently in making their participation decisions [19]. In the present study, we hold constant the topic, effort, and the sponsoring organization and focus on how extrinsic incentives shape these decisions when paired with advertisements invoking intrinsic and extrinsic motivations in the context of an online survey.

Incentives for Participation

Survey researchers often provide material or financial incentives as well as the promise of contributing to the advancement of scientific knowledge in exchange for respondents' time and willingness to answer questions. However, differences in how and when individuals are compensated for survey participation can sometimes dramatically affect how the incentives influence recruitment and retention. In mail surveys, pre-paid financial incentives, such as a dollar bill in the envelope with the survey, significantly increase participation, but payment upon completion typically does not [9, 31]. Church found that pre-paid incentives generated an average increase in response rate of 19% [9]. Some researchers focusing specifically on online surveys have found both pre-paid and post-paid incentives to be largely ineffective [4], though others suggest that post-paid incentives have more potential in online contexts than they do offline [13]. Indeed, post-paid £10 electronic gift cards offered in a follow-up online survey invitation produced response rates 9% higher as compared to participants offered no incentive, although no such effect was found with smaller £5 incentives [22]. Mixing online and postal-mail messages with pre-paid cash incentives showed promise for recruiting online respondents, although overall recruitment rates may still lag behind those resulting from mail messages alone [28, 29].

Lottery draws, in which an extrinsic incentive is awarded to a randomly selected subset of participants after completion of the survey, seem to be more effective in boosting participation in online surveys [16, 4, 35, 20]. A meta-analysis of studies using predominantly lottery-style material incentives conducted by Göritz [18] found that, on average, the incentives led to a 2.8% increase in initial response rate and a 4.2% increase in retention rate over conditions without incentives, though as Fan and Yan [14] and Messer and Dillman [28] point out, this is a modest effect. Lottery draws can be more cost-effective than paying every participant, as even very small payments of US$10 or less quickly become prohibitively expensive with the large sample sizes that survey researchers often seek [10].

Material incentives can take many forms: goods, services, cash, check, or other financial implements such as gift certificates or pre-paid debit cards. The latter are not necessarily equivalent to their nominal cash value — indeed, Birnholtz and colleagues [2] found that US$5 gift certificates, whether delivered by postal mail or email, induced significantly lower participation rates than did US$5 in cash. For online research, however, cash is impractical; incentives that can be delivered electronically are faster and easier for both researchers and participants [14].

Intrinsic and Extrinsic Motivation

Although material incentives have the potential to increase participation under the right circumstances, one concern for researchers is that they might at the same time undermine individual motivations to participate in scientific research if they are seen as a controlling or even coercive enticement to elicit responses or behaviors for researchers. Moreover, respondents who seek material compensation may differ in important ways from those who participate out of their desire to add to scientific knowledge or support the aims of the organization conducting the survey. The concern regarding the impetus to participate in research can be considered in terms of a tradeoff between extrinsic and intrinsic motivations for taking part in a study. Extrinsic motivations are those that can be satisfied through indirect compensation, usually financial in nature [30]. On the other hand, intrinsic motivations are a more direct form of compensation, "undertaken for one's immediate need satisfaction" [30] (p. 539). Intrinsic motivations include doing tasks for their own sake, for a sense of accomplishment, or for obligations associated with one's personal identity [26]. We define intrinsic and extrinsic incentives as those that appeal, respectively, to intrinsic and extrinsic motivations.

It is important to note that some researchers use these terms somewhat differently; for example, Tuten and colleagues [34] take intrinsic cues to be those central to the recruitment message and extrinsic cues to be peripheral to it, including not only material prizes but also pleasing sounds and colors in the recruitment advertisement. Despite this conceptual difference, Tuten and colleagues operationalized intrinsic and extrinsic approaches to recruitment similarly to the present study, with advertisements for the "opportunity to contribute to an important study" vs. the "opportunity to win valuable prizes" [34] (p. 18).

Crowding theory

Motivation is neither strictly individual nor strictly situational; instead, it depends on the interplay of individual value disposition (cf. Bilsky and Schwartz [5]) with situational factors such as the type of incentives offered and whether they match the individual's expectations. Extrinsic incentives can increase participation for some individuals, yet research shows that extrinsic rewards can lead to *lower* participation when they "crowd out" — that is, dampen or displace — one's own intrinsic motivation [11, 24, 30]. For example, a small payment for a task one was willing to do anyway may seem at best unnecessary and at worst insulting; relatedly, a token financial incentive may seem to assign a low value to a task with inherent non-financial worth. However, the opposite can also occur ("crowding in") if the extrinsic incentive increases the perceived marginal financial benefit of performing the task [15]. In addition, non-financial (e.g., social) incentives can enhance intrinsic motivation, such as reputation from one's peers or recognition of unique contributions, leading to increased participation without crowding out existing motivation [7, 8, 25, 32].

AN EXPERIMENTAL EXAMINATION OF "SURPRISE" FINANCIAL INCENTIVES

We present a series of four experiments to examine the effects of incentives on survey participation as part of an extensive web-based longitudinal survey project. Our primary research goal is to investigate the effect of "surprise" financial incentives — that is, those not initially advertised or different from what was advertised — on the following outcomes of interest among participants initially solicited by different advertisements designed to appeal to intrinsic and extrinsic motivations:

(1) Rate of **interest** in learning more about the study
(2) Rate of successful **recruitment** into the study
(3) Amount of **ongoing participation** in the study
(4) **Cost effectiveness** in generating responses

We operationalize *interest* as the click rate on the recruitment ads, computed by measuring the fraction of targeted users who clicked a recruitment ad. We calculate the *successful recruitment rate* as the fraction of ad-clickers who completed informed consent and an intake questionnaire, which was presented immediately afterwards. We measure *ongoing participation* in two ways: the number of questionnaires completed and the total number of questions answered over the course of the study. Finally, we assess the *cost effectiveness* of different incentives with respect to the outcomes above by computing the number of recruited participants per $1000 spent, the per-participant average incentive value paid per completed question, and the across-participants cost per 100 questions answered.

Based on the logic of crowding theory described above, we expect to find evidence of crowding out in the form of decreased participation when individuals are recruited *solely* through a request to be part of social research (intrinsic incentive) but later discover that they will be paid for their effort after they have already shown interest in participating. Second, when individuals are recruited with a promise of extrinsic financial compensation from the beginning, we expect higher levels of subsequently revealed extrinsic financial compensation to "crowd in" — that is, amplify — existing motivation to participate.

This work consists of theoretically informed field experiments, but we do not make separate theoretical hypotheses for all of the various conditions in our experiments. Instead, our intention is to explore the results of our experiments in light of our baseline predictions. The purpose of this research is primarily to examine the relationship between intrinsic and extrinsic motivations to participate in research and to help researchers make informed decisions about incentives and recruitment in web-based surveys and other forms of research requiring the solicitation of participants. Additionally, this study adds to the growing collection of empirical research on intrinsic and extrinsic incentives and how they interact in observed social behavior.

Method Overview

Through a partnership with a large American online dating site, we recruited participants for a longitudinal study of online relationship formation through "pop-over" advertisements that appeared on users' screens when they visited the dating site during several one-week periods in 2009 and 2010. We conducted four experiments, described below, in different waves of recruitment for this online dating study, using two combinations of advertisement and incentive in each experiment.

Each person was assigned to only one condition across all four experiments reported below; that is, there was no overlap in samples among the experiments. Potential participants were shown at most one ad during the recruitment period for their wave. Only those who visited the site during that period had the opportunity to see an ad. A button on each ad labeled "Tell me more" took users to the informed consent page, while a button labeled "No, thanks" closed the advertisement.

Users who clicked "Tell me more" were presented with an informed consent page, which explained that the study would last several weeks and would involve several questionnaires during the study period about attitudes, dispositions, and behaviors related to online relationship formation. Those who agreed to participate were taken immediately to the first questionnaire. Periodic follow-up emails were sent to notify participants when new questionnaires were available, which a state machine determined based on participants' previous responses, and to remind them of pending questionnaires. All participants were sent at least three questionnaires, and those who continued responding were sent as many as 17; the same state machine rules for questionnaire assignment were used

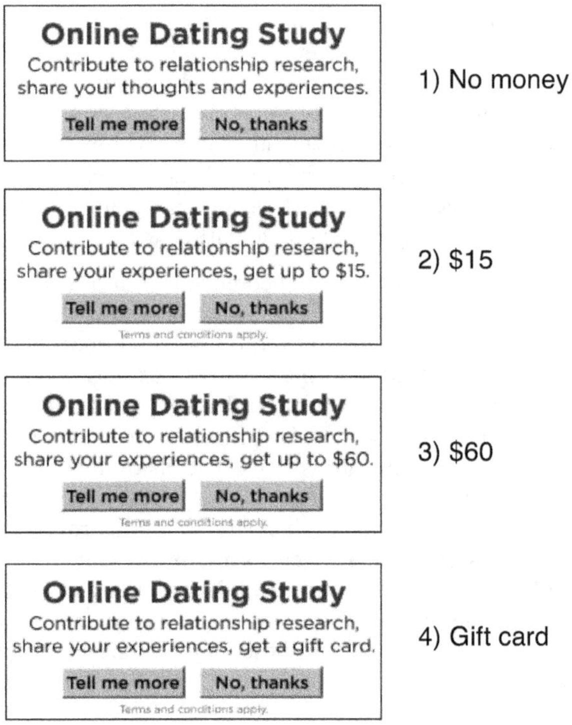

Figure 1. Recruitment advertisements

in all conditions of the experiments reported here. Participants were free to withdraw via our web site at any time, at which point we would stop sending them emails.

Recruitment Ads

Across the four experiments, we used four different recruitment ads to invite users of the dating site to participate in the study. Some participants saw an ad that made no mention of money (even though some would learn later that they would receive gift cards), while others saw ads promising a gift card or ads that mentioned US$15 or US$60 amounts specifically. The "no money" advertisement asked potential participants to "Contribute to relationship research, share your thoughts and experiences." Thus, we consider the no-money message to be an appeal to intrinsic motivations only. The three other advertisements also asked potential participants to "Contribute to relationship research, share your experiences" but explicitly offer a gift card or a quantity of money ("get a gift card," "get up to $60"). We consider these three messages to appeal to both intrinsic and extrinsic motivations. The four different recruitment ads are displayed in Figure 1.

Financial Incentives

Financial incentives were offered to participants in the form of Amazon.com gift codes. These gift codes were delivered via email and could be entered into Amazon.com to use their value immediately. We chose incentive values of $15 and $60 to represent typical and unusually high levels of compensation for an online study. Furthermore, we designed a payment schedule to strike a balance between immediate reward and longer-term incentive for continued participation in a longitudinal sequence of questionnaires. Payments were scheduled so that participants would receive part of their payment shortly after completing the first questionnaire and the rest after they responded to requests for follow-up questionnaires during a six-week period. All participants who met these milestones received the promised payment amounts. Participants in a $60 incentive condition received $30 upon completing the first questionnaire and two additional $15 payments at three weeks and six weeks from their start date if they continued participating by answering at least one questionnaire in each three-week period. Those in a $15 incentive condition were paid $5 at first followed by two $5 payments at three weeks and six weeks.

Experimental Conditions

The conditions in the following experiments resulted from various combinations of the four recruitment advertisements with either the $15 or $60 financial incentives, as described in detail for each of the experiments below. We employed only combinations in which the payment was *at least as much as promised in the ad*. That is, some participants learned after clicking on the ad that they would be getting a financial incentive when none had been mentioned in the ad or that they would get a larger incentive than promised by the ad, but they were never offered less than what the ad stated. Although these conditions involve a form of deception, the ultimate offer was always more favorable than the initial promise in terms of financial incentives, not less.

The combinations that offered a greater incentive than what the ad promised are what we consider the "incentive surprise" conditions. Conditions with "no money" recruitment ads that later revealed a financial incentive ($15 or $60) after the potential participant clicked on the ad are examples of an "existence surprise" (Experiments 1 and 2). An ad mentioning $15 paired with a subsequently revealed $60 incentive is slightly different: it offered a higher actual payment than the *specific amount* shown on the advertisement, an "amount surprise" (Experiment 3). In this case, the *fact* of a financial incentive is not a surprise, but the *amount* is. Moreover, for this condition, we can easily identify the exact difference between the payment users expected when choosing to learn more about the study and what they expected when agreeing to participate ($60 – $15 = $45). A different kind of "amount surprise" is presented in Experiment 4, where an ad promising a financial incentive of unspecified value is paired with two different levels of incentive — here, the surprise is contingent on what people expect the amount to be for a typical study.

Sampling and Assignment

The design of the online dating study required that we recruit waves of participants in geographic clusters within the United States. These geographic clusters varied in size, so the total sample size varies among the experiments presented here. For each experiment, all users of the dating site within

	Condition 1A	Condition 1B	
Incentive offered in ad	None	$15	
Actual incentive	$15	$15	
Targeted *N*	38,536	38,395	
Click rate	1.45%	1.69%	**
Clicked *N*	558	648	
Recruitment rate (among clicked)	33.9%	41.2%	*
Recruitment rate (among targeted)	0.49%	0.70%	
Recruited *N*	189	267	
Questionnaires completed (*M* and *SD* per recruited)	4.57 [3.08]	4.43 [2.88]	*n.s.*
Questions completed (*M* and *SD* per recruited)	128.2 [85.7]	133.0 [87.6]	*n.s.*
Incentive cost per question completed per participant (*M* and *SD* per recruited)	$0.10 [$0.04]	$0.10 [$0.04]	*n.s.*
Estimated incentive cost per 1,000 participants	$12,820	$13,300	

* $p < .05$ ** $p < .01$ *** $p < .001$ *n.s.* not significant

Table 1. Results from Experiment 1

	Condition 2A	Condition 2B	
Incentive offered in ad	None	$60	
Actual incentive	$60	$60	
Targeted *N*	12,069	11,936	
Click rate	0.89%	1.83%	***
Clicked *N*	108	218	
Recruitment rate (among clicked)	50.9%	48.2%	*n.s.*
Recruitment rate (among targeted)	0.46%	0.88%	
Recruited *N*	55	105	
Questionnaires completed (*M* and *SD* per recruited)	5.33 [3.41]	5.29 [2.94]	*n.s.*
Questions completed (*M* and *SD* per recruited)	150.7 [95.7]	157.2 [95.4]	*n.s.*
Incentive value per question completed per participant (*M* and *SD* per recruited)	$0.42 [$0.17]	$0.41 [$0.18]	*n.s.*
Estimated incentive cost per 1,000 participants	$63,294	$64,452	

* $p < .05$ ** $p < .01$ *** $p < .001$ *n.s.* not significant

Table 2. Results from Experiment 2

the designated geographic clusters were randomly assigned to one of two conditions. In Experiments 1, 2, and 3, approximately equal numbers of users were randomized into each condition ($P = .50$). For Experiment 4, we employed a weighted randomization process to assign more users to condition A ($P \approx .95$) than to condition B ($P \approx .05$), proportional to the availability of incentive funds.

Experiment 1: Comparing two ads with the same $15 incentive

Method

All users of the online dating site in a major metropolitan area, approximately 77,000 people (33% female, 61% male, 6% gender unknown; median age 41), were randomly assigned to be recruited with one of two advertisements: (1A) the ad that did not mention money (Figure 1.1), or (1B) the ad offering "up to $15" (Figure 1.2). After clicking the ad, those in both conditions were offered the $15 incentive.

Results

Condition 1B, with the $15 ad, yielded higher click and recruitment rates than did condition 1A, with the no-money ad (Table 1). Users targeted with the $15 ad clicked it 16.6% more often than those targeted with the no-money ad, 1.69% vs. 1.45%, $\chi^2\ (1) = 7.0, p < .01$. After clicking the $15 ad, users in condition 1B were successfully recruited 21.5% more often than those who clicked the no-money ad (1A), 41.2% vs. 33.9%, $\chi^2\ (1) = 6.5, p < .05$.

The average number of questionnaires and questions completed per participant (Table 1) did not differ significantly by condition. The cost of incentives paid per question completed, averaged on a per-participant basis, was the same in both conditions, $0.10.

Discussion

It is not surprising that an ad that offered a financial incentive (1B), appealing to both extrinsic and intrinsic motivations, would generate more interest than one that did not offer a financial incentive and appealed only to intrinsic motivation (1A). However, among those who clicked each ad to find an identical offer of a $15 incentive, a significantly higher proportion of those who knew about the incentive from the start also went on to join the study. It is possible that the people who clicked the no-money ad were relatively more intrinsically and less extrinsically motivated — whether dispositionally or momentarily — than those who clicked the $15 ad, leading to a lower recruitment rate when presented with the same financial incentive.

Experiment 2: Comparing two ads with the same $60 incentive

Method

A random sample of dating site users from 10 U.S. states and 5 additional metropolitan areas, approximately 24,000 people (32% female, 59% male, 9% gender unspecified; median age 41), were randomly assigned to be recruited with one of two advertisements: (2A) the ad that did not mention money (Figure 1.1), or (2B) the ad offering "up to $60" (Figure 1.3). After clicking the ad, those in both conditions were offered the $60 incentive.

Results

Condition 2B, with an ad that promised up to $60, resulted in a click rate twice as high (+106%) as in the no-money ad condition, 1.83% vs. 0.89%, χ^2 (1) = 38.2, $p < .001$ (Table 2). But the percentage of ad-clickers who were successfully recruited did not differ significantly between conditions.

Questionnaires and questions completed per recruited participant did not differ significantly by condition. The cost of incentives paid per question completed was the same in both conditions, just over $0.40.

Discussion

The design of Experiment 2 mirrors that of Experiment 1 but with a $60 payment and ad instead of a $15 one. While the click rate for the $60 ad vs. the no-money ad is unsurprisingly dramatically higher, the recruitment rate among people who click is the same in the two conditions. We might expect the same pattern of results as in Experiment 1 — that people who clicked the no-money ad would not be as motivated by the financial incentive as those who clicked the $60 ad — but in this case it seems that the substantial value of the incentive was sufficient to override this tendency.

Experiment 3: Comparing two financial incentive ads with the same $60 incentive

Method

A random sample of dating site users from a major metropolitan area, approximately 15,700 people (31% female, 57% male, 12% gender unspecified; median age 41), were randomly assigned to be recruited with one of two advertisements: (3A) the ad offering "up to $15" (Figure 1.2), or (3B) the ad offering "up to $60" (Figure 1.3). After clicking the ad, those in both conditions were offered the $60 incentive.

Results

The $15 and the $60 ad did not differ by click rate (Table 3). But among those who clicked an ad, those in condition 3A with the $15 ad were successfully recruited 31.3% more often than those than in condition 3B with the $60 ad, 57.0% vs. 43.4%, χ^2 (1) = 4.7, $p < .05$.

As in previous experiments, the average number of questionnaires and questions completed per successfully recruited participant did not differ significantly by condition. The cost of incentives paid per question completed was also the same in both conditions, approximately $0.40.

	Condition 3A	Condition 3B	
Incentive offered in ad	$15	$60	
Actual incentive	$60	$60	
Targeted *N*	7,920	7,757	
Click rate	1.70%	1.84%	*n.s.*
Clicked *N*	135	143	
Recruitment rate (among clicked)	57.0%	43.4%	*
Recruitment rate (among targeted)	0.97%	0.80%	
Recruited *N*	77	62	
Questionnaires completed (*M* and *SD* among recruited)	6.12 [2.78]	5.47 [2.76]	*n.s.*
Questions completed (*M* and *SD* among recruited)	157.2 [95.4]	150.7 [95.7]	*n.s.*
Incentive value per question completed per participant (*M* and *SD* among recruited)	$0.39 [$0.17]	$0.41 [$0.16]	*n.s.*
Estimated incentive cost per 1,000 participants	$61,308	$61,787	

* $p < .05$ ** $p < .01$ *** $p < .001$ *n.s.* not significant

Table 3. Results from Experiment 3

Discussion

The two ads in this experiment did not vary in terms of intrinsic vs. extrinsic incentives — both mentioned a financial incentive, in contrast to Experiments 1 and 2, where one of the ads in each study appealed only to intrinsic motivation. Instead, the ads in Experiment 3 varied in terms of the value of the financial incentive offered. The ads did not differ in terms of click rate, but those in the $15 ad condition who were presumably pleasantly surprised to find after clicking that the true incentive was $60 were successfully recruited into the study at a significantly higher rate than those who found that they would receive the $60 incentive they already expected.

Experiment 4: Comparing $15 and $60 incentives with the same ad

Method

A random sample of dating site users from 10 U.S. states and 5 additional metropolitan areas, approximately 229,500 people (34% female, 61% male, 5% gender unspecified; median age 41), were recruited with the advertisement offering a "gift card" (Figure 1.4). They were randomly

	Condition 4A	Condition 4B	
Incentive offered in ad	Gift card	Gift card	
Actual incentive	$15	$60	
Targeted *N*	217,589	11,912	
Click rate	1.48%	1.39%	*n.s.*
Clicked *N*	3,220	165	
Recruitment rate (among clicked)	35.2%	55.8%	***
Recruitment rate (among targeted)	0.52%	0.77%	
Recruited *N*	1,134	92	
Questionnaires completed (*M* and *SD* among recruited)	4.59 [2.98]	4.89 [3.11]	*n.s.*
Questions completed (*M* and *SD* among recruited)	131.6 [82.3]	135.7 [84.6]	*n.s.*
Incentive value per question completed per participant (*M* and *SD* among recruited)	$0.10 [$0.04]	$0.45 [$0.17]	***
Estimated incentive cost per 1,000 participants	$13,160	$61,065	

* $p < .05$ ** $p < .01$ *** $p < .001$ *n.s.* not significant

Table 4. Results from Experiment 4

assigned to be offered one of two incentives after clicking the ad: (4A) the $15 incentive, or (4B) the $60 incentive.

Results

The ads in conditions 4A and 4B did not differ by click rate, as expected because the same ad was used in both conditions. The click rate across conditions was 1.47% (Table 4). However, among those who clicked the ad, the rate of successful recruitment was 58.5% higher when the subsequent incentive offered was $60 (4B) as compared to $15 (4A), 55.8% vs. 35.2%, χ^2 (1) = 27.8, $p < .001$.

The average number of questionnaires and questions completed per recruited participant did not differ significantly by condition. But he cost of incentives paid per question completed was substantially greater in condition 4B, $0.45 vs. $0.10, t (91.9) = –19.6, $p < .001$.

Discussion

This experiment differs from the previous three in that it compares two different incentive levels with the same ad, one that promises a financial incentive of unspecified value. In this case, the amount of the incentive constitutes a type of surprise, especially for the condition offering $60, which is likely higher than most people would expect for a web-based survey study. Because the same ad is used in both conditions, the click rate does not differ between them. But those who were subsequently offered the $60 incentive were recruited at a 58% higher rate than those who were offered $15, allowing a direct estimate of the increase in effectiveness due to the larger incentive among people motivated to click the an ad that mentions an extrinsic incentive.

DISCUSSION

These four experiments demonstrate significant and in some cases substantial effects on survey recruitment rates due to different combinations of advertisements and financial incentives. Interestingly, these differences did not extend to measures of ongoing participation; once recruited, participants did not differ significantly in how actively they participated in any of the experiments, even though full payment of the incentives required that participants continue to complete questionnaires. Instead, any differences in the number of responses gathered by condition were due entirely to upstream differences in click and recruitment rates.

Incentives, Motivation, and Surprise

Existence Surprises

Our analysis compares survey participation with different types of incentive surprises. The existence surprise conditions in Experiments 1 and 2 were compared with conditions where the incentive offered matched what was mentioned in the ad, while the participants in the surprise conditions were shown ads that did not mention an extrinsic incentive at all. With the $15 incentive (Experiment 1), the recruitment rate was lower for people in the surprise condition, suggesting that people who clicked the no-money ad, which played on the desire to contribute to research, were less motivated by the financial incentive than those who clicked an ad that explicitly mentioned the incentive.

The recruitment rate with the no-money ad was 33.9%. By way of comparison, a separate non-experimental recruitment wave outside of the four experiments reported here, using the no-money ad followed by no subsequent offer of a financial incentive, produced a significantly higher recruitment rate of 42.1% out of 627 people who clicked the ad, χ^2 (1) = 8.1, $p < .01$. That is, people who clicked the same ad and were subsequently offered $15 were recruited at a lower rate than those who were offered no financial incentive at all[1]. One interpretation of this result, consistent with crowding theory, is that people intrinsically motivated by the no-money ad were actually demotivated — had their intrinsic motivation crowded out — by the offer of a relatively small financial incentive. Crowding out occurs when intrinsic motivation is undermined in a way that leads to a loss of self-determination or individual control. Financial payments that are contingent on performance negatively affect the desire

[1] Because the separate wave was not part of the main experimental design and involved a different sample, we provide this comparison only as a point of interest and not a primary result.

to complete a given task. In addition, by attaching a monetary value to the task, a financial incentive invites a comparison with the perceived economic value of the task. Thus, a task that might first seem interesting on its own may seem like a bad deal when it is attached to a precise monetary figure. In our experiment, the existence surprise of $15 may be enough to undermine existing intrinsic motivation, but not large enough to provide an overriding extrinsic motivation to join the study.

By contrast, no such difference was evident in Experiment 2, where clickers of the no-money ad were surprised with a $60 incentive. In this case, they joined the study at the same rate as those who clicked the ad that offered $60 from the start. While lower recruitment rates, consistent with crowding out, were evident with the $15 existence surprise, it appears that the substantially greater value of the $60 incentive overrode this effect. This does not necessarily mean that intrinsic motivation was *not* crowded out in the $60 surprise condition. As prior research on crowding effects shows (aptly titled "Pay enough or don't pay at all"), *small* compensations may lead to lower effort when compared to an equivalent situation with no compensation at all [17]. However, when higher payments are offered for the same task, individuals exert higher effort because the financial incentive is viewed as attractive compensation for the required task, perhaps sufficient to fully compensate for the intrinsic motivation that was crowded out. In our study, $60 appears to pass the threshold for attractive compensation.

Amount Surprises

In Experiment 3, we compared outcomes for potential respondents who clicked the $15 ad were subsequently surprised with a $60 incentive with outcomes for those who clicked the $60 ad and were then offered the expected $60. Even though the amount ultimately offered was the same, those in the amount surprise condition were 31% more likely to join the study. One interpretation of this result is that the same $60 incentive performed better with the $15 ad because it was better *relative to participants' expectations* than it was with the $60 ad, where it merely met expectations. Because the click rates and subsequent participation levels for the two ads were not significantly different, this was essentially a more efficient way to spend the higher amount in terms of participants recruited and thus responses gathered. Moreover, since all participants clicked an ad that appealed to extrinsic as well as intrinsic motivations from the start, the increased participation when presented with a higher-than-expected incentive is consistent with the notion of crowding in — that is, the existing motivation is amplified by an unexpected incentive consistent with that motivation.

The results of Experiment 4, where $15 and $60 incentives were paired with an ad that offered a gift card of unspecified value, are harder to interpret in terms of an amount surprise. One might argue that this scenario is better termed a "delayed reveal" in both conditions, but we believe that $15 is more typical of the amount typically offered for participating in an online survey, if a financial incentive is offered at all. By this logic, the $60 condition would constitute an amount surprise, and indeed we see a similar pattern of results to Experiment 3, with a significantly higher recruitment rate for the $60 condition as compared to the $15 condition.

Cost Effectiveness

An additional contribution of this work is to quantify the relative cost of obtaining responses under different incentive conditions. Across our four experiments, in the $15 incentive conditions, the estimated incentive cost per 1,000 participants based on participant-level averages was approximately $13,000, while in the $60 incentive conditions, it was more than four times as much.

The larger financial incentive improved participation rates substantially, but rates remained low in absolute terms, with no more than 0.97% of the targeted sample successfully recruited in any condition. Moreover, ongoing participation was unchanged even with the $60 incentive. Thus, the coverage of the sampling frame was poor and no more data was obtained per participant even with the high incentive level, making it hard to argue for the use of such expensive incentives in the present context of recruitment via a web advertisement for the sake of promoting recruitment and ongoing participation. Of course, the desire to compensate participants for their efforts is in many cases a compelling reason to offer incentives anyway.

Limitations

We have presented four experiments of different advertisement and incentive combinations in recruiting for a longitudinal survey study of online dating behavior. Because the present set of experiments was embedded in the observational dating study, some decisions made in service of the larger study may complicate the interpretation of the experimental results. In this section, we discuss potential limitations to our claims that may result for the present work.

Purely Extrinsic vs. Mixed Incentives

In Experiments 1 and 2, the ads we designed do not allow us to directly compare appeals to intrinsic motivation with purely extrinsic motivation. Rather, they represent intrinsic-only and *intrinsic-plus-extrinsic* pitches. The no-money ad (#1) was designed to appeal to intrinsic motivation to contribute to scientific research and improve online dating. The other ads, #2 and #3, use an appeal that combines an abbreviated version of this pitch with the mention of a gift card or dollar amount. We believe this combination is the most ecologically valid way to present extrinsic incentives, since a strictly extrinsic pitch with no additional context ("Participate and get $15") is both uncommon in recruitment for academic studies and also more likely to be seen as a scam when presented in a web advertisement. Thus, we did not believe this to be a viable approach to recruitment for the dating study. Future work that uses a different recruitment medium may be able to examine the performance of extrinsic-only pitches as well.

Payment Parallelism and Response Volume

We found no difference in ongoing participation in any of our experiments, but one limitation applies specifically to those analyses in Experiment 4, when the actual incentive amount differed: the payment schedules for the $15 and $60 conditions were not perfectly parallel. In the $15 condition, participants received $5 after completing the first questionnaire and two additional $5 payments at three weeks and six weeks if they continued completing questionnaires. In the $60 condition, on the other hand, participants received $30 after the first questionnaire and two additional payments of $15 each on the same schedule. Aside from the different total amounts, which constituted the experimental manipulation, the conditions differed in that $15 participants received a third of the total in each payment, while $60 participants received half in the first payment and a quarter in each subsequent payment. The primary confound that could result from this difference is that participants in the $60 condition may be relatively less motivated to continue participating after the first questionnaire because they had already received a greater proportion of their payment, as compared to the $15 condition or a hypothetical alternative $60 condition with three equal $20 payments. Thus, we cannot rule out the possibility that if we had used a balanced $20-$20-$20 payment schedule for the $60 condition, we might have found a significant difference in ongoing participation as compared to the $15 condition.

CONCLUSION

We have presented four experiments examining two types of financial incentive surprises in the recruitment of participants for an online survey study. "Existence surprises" performed poorly relative to comparison conditions where the existence of an incentive and its exact amount were not a surprise. We believe this finding may be due to a "crowding out" effect in which intrinsic motivation to participate is dampened, or the intrinsic worth of participation devalued, by the later presentation of an extrinsic incentive. A $15 surprise incentive yielded recruitment rates that were significantly lower than those produced with an equivalent but expected incentive (Experiment 1), and in fact were also lower than those for a separate sample that was offered no financial incentive at all. Even the $60 surprise incentive, an unusually large amount for an online study, only achieved parity in terms of participation rate with the same incentive when it was expected (Experiment 2).

"Amount surprises," where the fact of an incentive was known from the start but the amount was higher than expected, performed better than comparison conditions where the amount ultimately offered was exactly as initially advertised (Experiment 3) or was a typical amount for an online study (Experiment 4). Surprising people recruited via an ad that appeals to extrinsic financial motivation with a higher-than-expected incentive yielded substantially better recruitment rates. However, this advantage did not extend to measures of the volume of subsequent participation on a per-participant basis.

For researchers who wish to recruit participants online, a few recommendations follow from the present work. First, surprising people who are already intrinsically motivated to participate in a study with a financial incentive may be counterproductive. If financial incentives are offered, they work more efficiently when they are part of the recruitment pitch from the start. Second, when people are aware that a financial incentive is offered, a surprisingly high amount can motivate more of them to participate. The same $60 incentive produced a higher recruitment rate when it was a surprise than when it was disclosed in advance.

Finally, it is important to note that an intrinsic pitch and an extrinsic pitch may attract qualitatively different respondents, whose predisposition to respond may also vary with the context in which the recruitment takes place, in this case an online dating site. Future work should examine how self-selection bias may result from intrinsic vs. extrinsic approaches in additional online contexts.

ACKNOWLEDGMENTS

This work was supported in part by NSF HSD-IIS 0624356. We would also like to thank our anonymous reviewers for their valuable feedback and suggestions.

REFERENCES

1. Andrews, D., Nonnecke, B., and Preece, J. (2003). Electronic Survey Methodology: A Case Study in Reaching Hard-to-Involve Internet Users. *International Journal of Human-Computer Interaction* 16 (2), pp. 185–210.
2. Birnholtz, J.P., Horn, D.B., Finholt, T.A., and Bae, S.J. (2004). The Effects of Cash, Electronic, and Paper Gift Certificates as Respondent Incentives for a Web-Based Survey of Technologically Sophisticated Respondents. *Social Science Computer Review* 22 (3), pp. 355–362.
3. Bosnjak, M., and Tuten, T.L. (2001). Classifying Response Behaviors in Web-based Surveys. *Journal of Computer-Mediated Communication* 6 (3).
4. Bosnjak, M., and Tuten, T.L. (2003). Prepaid and promised incentives in Web surveys: An experiment. *Social Science Computer Review* 21 (2), pp. 208–17.
5. Bilsky, W., and Schwartz, S.H. (1994). Values and personality. *European Journal of Psychology* 8, pp. 163–181.
6. Camemer, C.F., and Hogarth, R.M. (1999). The Effects of Financial Incentives in Experiments: A Review and Capital-Labor-Production Framework. *Journal of Risk and Uncertainty* 19 (1–3), pp. 7–42.
7. Cheshire, C. (2007). Selective Incentives and Generalized Information Exchange. *Social Psychology Quarterly* 70 (1), pp. 82–100.
8. Cheshire, C., and Antin, J. (2008). The Social Psychological Effects of Feedback on the Production of Internet Information Pools. *Journal of Computer-Mediated Communication* 13 (3).

9. Church, A.H. (1993). Estimating the effect of incentives on mail survey response rates: A meta-analysis. *Public Opinion Quarterly* 57 (1), pp. 62–79.

10. Cobanoglu, C., and Cobanoglu, N. (2003). The effect of incentives in Web surveys: Application and ethical considerations. *International Journal of Market Research* 45 (4), pp. 475-488.

11. Deci, E.L. (1971). Effects of Externally Mediated Rewards on Intrinsic Motivation. *Journal of Personality and Social Psychology* 18, pp. 105–115.

12. Dillman, D.A., Smyth, J.D., and Christian, L.M. (2008). *Internet, Mail, and Mixed-Mode Surveys: The Tailored Design Method.* New Jersey: John Wiley & Sons.

13. Evans, J.R., Mathur, A. (2005). The value of online surveys. *Internet Research* 15 (2), pp. 195–219.

14. Fan, W., and Yan, Z. (2010). Factors affecting response rates of the web survey: A systematic review. *Computers in Human Behavior* 26, pp. 132–139.

15. Frey, B.S., and Jegen, R. (2001). Motivation Crowding Theory: A Survey of Empirical Evidence. *Journal of Economic Surveys* 15 (5), pp. 589–611.

16. Frick, A., Bächtiger, M.-T., and Reips, U.-D. (2001). Financial incentives, personal information and drop-out in online studies. In U.D.-Reips & M. Bächtiger (Eds.), *Dimensions of Internet Science*, pp. 209–219. Lengerich: Pabst.

17. Gneezy, Uri, and Rustichini, A. (2000). Pay Enough or Don't Pay At All. *Quarterly Journal of Economics* 115 (3), pp. 791–810.

18. Göritz, A.S. (2006). Incentives in Web Studies: Methodological Issues and a Review. *International Journal of Internet Science* 1 (1), pp. 58–70.

19. Groves, R.M., Singer, E., and Corning, A. (2000). Leverage-Saliency Theory of Survey Participation: Description and an Illustration. *Public Opinion Quarterly* 64 (3), pp. 299–308

20. Heerwegh, D. (2006). An investigation of the effect of lotteries on Web survey response rates. *Field Methods* 18 (2), pp. 205–220.

21. Holm, S. (1979). A simple sequentially rejective multiple test procedure. *Scandinavian Journal of Statistics* 6 (2), pp. 65–70.

22. Khadjesari, Z., Murray, E., Kalaitzaki, E., White, I.R., McCambridge, J., Thompson, S.G., Wallace, P., Godfrey, C. (2011). Impact and Costs of Incentives to Reduce Attrition in Online Trials: Two Randomized Controlled Trials. *Journal of Medical Internet Research* 13 (1), article e26.

23. Lazar, J., Feng, J.H., and Hochheiser, H. (2010). *Research Methods in Human-Computer Interaction.* Hoboken, NJ: John Wiley & Sons.

24. Lepper, M.R., and Greene, D. (1978). *The Hidden Costs of Reward: New Perspectives on the Psychology of Human Motivation.* Hillsdale, NY: Erlsbaum Publishers.

25. Ling, K., Beenen, G., Wang, X., Chang, K., Frankowski, D., Resnick, P., and Kraut, R.E. (2005). Using social psychology to motivate contributions to online communities. *Journal of Computer Mediated Communication* 10.

26. March, J.M. (1999). *The Pursuit of Organizational Intelligence.* Malden, MA and Oxford, UK: Blackwell.

27. McCrae, R.R., and Costa Jr., P.T. (1987). Validation of the five-factor model of personality across instruments and observers. *Journal of Personality and Social Psychology* 52 (1), pp. 81–90.

28. Messer, B.L., and Dillman, D.A. (2011). Surveying the general public over the Internet using address-based sampling and mail contact procedures. *Public Opinion Quarterly* 75 (3), pp. 429–457.

29. Millar, M.M., and Dillman, D.A. (2011). Improving response to web and mixed-mode surveys. *Public Opinion Quarterly* 75 (2), pp. 249–269.

30. Osterloh, M., and Frey, B.S. (2000). Motivation, Knowledge Transfer, and Organizational Forms. *Organization Science* 11, pp. 538–550.

31. Porter, S.R. (2004). Raising Response Rates: What Works? *New Directions for Institutional Research* 121, pp. 5–21.

32. Raban, D. (2009). Self-presentation and the value of information in Q&A websites. *Journal of the American Society for Information Science and Technology* 60 (12), pp. 2465–2473.

33. Tourangeau, R. (2004). Survey Research and Societal Change. *Annual Review of Psychology* 55, pp. 775–801.

34. Tuten, T.L., Bosnjak, M., Bandilla, W. (1999). Banner-advertised Web surveys. *Marketing Research* 11 (4), pp. 16–21.

35. Tuten T.L., Galesic M., and Bosnjak M (2004). Effects of immediate versus delayed notification of prize draw results on response behavior in Web surveys: An experiment. *Social Science Computer Review* 22 (3), pp. 377–384.

36. Wright, K.B. (2005). Researching Internet-based populations: Advantages and disadvantages of online survey research, online questionnaire authoring software packages, and web survey services. *Journal of Computer-Mediated Communication* 10 (3).

37. Yamagishi, T., and Cook, K.S. (1993). Generalized Exchange and Social Dilemmas. Social Psychology Quarterly 56 (4), pp. 235–248.

Combining Body Pose, Gaze, and Gesture to Determine Intention to Interact in Vision-Based Interfaces

Julia Schwarz[1], **Charles Marais**[2], **Tommer Leyvand**[2], **Scott E. Hudson**[1], **Jennifer Mankoff**[1]
Carnegie Mellon University[1], Microsoft[2]
{julia.schwarz,scott.hudson,jmankoff}@cs.cmu.edu, {cmarais,tommerl}@microsoft.com

ABSTRACT
Vision-based interfaces, such as those made popular by the Microsoft Kinect, suffer from the Midas Touch problem: every user motion can be interpreted as an interaction. In response, we developed an algorithm that combines facial features, body pose and motion to approximate a user's *intention to interact* with the system. We show how this can be used to determine when to pay attention to a user's actions and when to ignore them. To demonstrate the value of our approach, we present results from a 30-person lab study conducted to compare four engagement algorithms in single and multi-user scenarios. We found that combining intention to interact with a "raise an open hand in front of you" gesture yielded the best results. The latter approach offers a 12% improvement in accuracy and a 20% reduction in time to engage over a baseline "wave to engage" gesture currently used on the Xbox 360.

Author Keywords: Free-space interaction; vision-based input; user engagement; input segmentation; learned models

ACM Classification Keywords: H.5.2 [Information interfaces and presentation]: User Interfaces - Graphical user interfaces.

INTRODUCTION
Recent commercialization of skeletal tracking using depth-sensing cameras holds the promise of bringing free-space, gestural interaction into our everyday lives. One common property that these free-space interfaces share is that they all leverage computer vision to interpret a user's actions (i.e., vision-based interfaces, or 'VIs'). One challenge these VIs present is the Midas Touch Problem: VIs are "always on" and therefore everything a user does may be interpreted as an interaction [12].

This paper addresses the question of *user engagement:* determining when a system should pay attention to a user's actions, and when to ignore them. We describe a machine learning-based algorithm which combines facial features, body pose and body motion to approximate a user's intention to interact, and show how this can be used to make VIs more robust.

CHI 2014, April 26–May 1, 2014, Toronto, Ontario, Canada.

http://dx.doi.org/10.1145/2556288.2556989

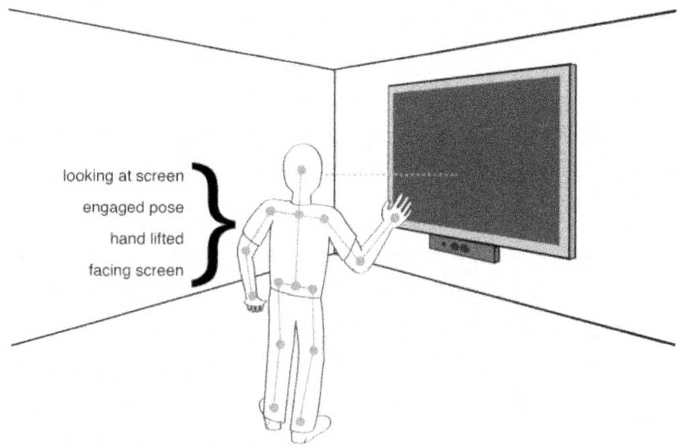

Figure 1. Our system combines results from a collection of individual classifiers to determine a user's intention to interact with a vision-based interface.

To better understand the role of gaze, body pose, and gesture in determining intention to interact, we ran a formative study to identify a set of non-verbal signals people use to communicate intention to interact with vision-based systems, and then trained a set of binary classifiers to recognize these signals. We then used regression analysis to combine these results into an overall intention to interact score, estimating the likelihood of a user's intention to interact (Figure 1).

To illustrate the immediate and practical benefits of using our approach, we built a full-body vision-based interface, and ran a 30-person lab study comparing four different user engagement algorithms in single and multi-user scenarios. We compared an approach that used only our intention to interact score, and two hybrid approaches that combined the intention to interact score with an explicit gesture. Additionally, we include the "wave to engage" algorithm currently used on the Xbox 360 as a benchmark.

Our study results demonstrated that our intention-to-interact metric was useful in determining engagement. Further, by combining this intention-to-interact metric with an easy-to-execute gesture yields even better results, offering a 12% improvement in accuracy and a 20% reduction in time to engage over the baseline "wave to engage" gesture used on the Xbox 360.

Our contributions are twofold. First, we highlight the value of incorporating information about a user's body pose and motion when determining intention to interact. Second, we show that using an intention-to-interact metric facilitates more accurate and faster engagement detection without requiring users to execute complicated gestures (a common practice today).

RELATED WORK

There has been a wide body of work exploring detection of user engagement, as well as the related question of user attentiveness. These efforts have spanned areas such as desktop interfaces, educational systems, games, driver analysis, human-robot interaction, and human-computer interaction.

For example, Mota estimates a young learner's interest level by analyzing posture data obtained from a pressure-sensitive chair. Mota combined neural networks (posture detection) and Hidden Markov Models to detect engagement at an overall accuracy of 77% [16]. Smith et al. are able to use a single commodity camera to track features such as blinks, gaze direction and mouth movement which can be used to estimate driver's attention level [23]. In the domain of computer interfaces, Asteriadis [1] shows how to perform face detection and tracking to estimate user attentiveness at a computer using only a web camera. Asteriadis is able to correctly detect attentiveness for 88% of a set of 22,000 annotated test frames. Nakano et al. explore conversational attentiveness using gaze transition 3-gram patterns to determine a user's interest in a conversation. They use these insights to develop a multimodal conversational agent which asks probing questions when users are about to lose interest [17]. Our work extends these findings in two ways. First, we address the related question of *determining user engagement*, that is, whether to pay attention to a user's actions, or to ignore them. Second, we demonstrate the value of examining not just the eyes and head but the entire body when determining engagement.

User engagement is important in the domain of human-robot interaction, since a robot must decide whether to pay attention to or ignore a user's actions. Michalowski et al. use a spatial model combined with gaze tracking to determine user engagement with a robot receptionist [14]. Interestingly, the authors observe that in the process of coding the video, they were able to guess a user's engagement by looking at their body motions, suggesting that body motion is a valuable cue to consider. Rich et al. expand on Michalowski's work to include linguistic information such as conversational adjacency pairs and backchannels in their model [20].

In contrast to human robot-interaction, the question of user engagement in single-user desktop interfaces is so trivial that it is almost overlooked. When multiple users are present in a desktop interface, the problem is more complex. One solution is to let each user have control of a finite region [9,24]. When space is limited, several users can share a region [18].

In VIs, a user's body is always tracked. This 'always on' property brings many challenges [12] as users have no natural clutching mechanism [10]. As a result, a person who wants to sip a drink in their living room, for example, may unintentionally trigger music through an inadvertent gesture. This problem is compounded when multiple users are present. When in groups, VIs must know who to pay attention to and who to ignore.

Current VIs use a variety of rules to determine when to begin and end an interaction. For example, the Kinect Dashboard interface on Xbox 360 begins an interaction when it sees a hand wave [15], and ends an interaction when the user leaves the visible area. Several games (see e.g., [8,19]) ask the user to raise one or both hands to begin interacting, and end an interaction either at the end of a game or when the user leaves the scene. StrikeAPose [26] leverages blob tracking to provide a clever "teapot" gesture to detect engagement. Unfortunately, relying solely on explicit gestures is often inaccurate, time-consuming, and not particularly intuitive.

Predictive models have also been applied to detecting engagement. This research largely relies on facial features and gaze tracking to measure interest level. One of the most sophisticated examples is the work of Bohus and Horvitz on predicting intention to interact [4] in open-world dialogue systems [5]. They describe an in-situ model looking at face position and orientation, as well as trajectory. This could be used to predict intention to interact with a kiosk three seconds before an actual interaction with a minimum false positive rate of 5%.

This paper builds off of Bohus et al.'s contribution in two primary ways. First, Bohus' system is primarily intended for spoken dialogue with a machine, whereas our model is intended for non-verbal interactions. The fact that the interactions are all gesture-based, and not voice- or gaze-based, makes the engagement detection problem even more difficult, as there is no input modality change to serve as an additional cue or backup indicator. Second, our intention to interact model incorporates body pose and motion, something Bohus specifically mentions as a potential area of future work.

The use of body pose and motion in determining user's interest level has received additional attention thanks to the advent of inexpensive body tracking systems like Kinect [13]. Bianchi-Berthouse [3] provide an overview of the role of body movement in gameplay, and propose investigating changes in body motion to understand how a user is playing a game. Further, in [2], Bianchi-Berthouse discuss the relationship between body movement and interest level in a game, and show how this relationship can be leveraged to

	# train frames	# test frames	test accuracy	model weight
Engaged stance	189,778	54,359	93.8%	0.67*
Hand lifted above waist	53,182	10,037	98.4%	0.15*
Looking at screen	N/A	N/A	N/A	0.12*
Waving	56,634	16,933	92.5%	0.11*
Hand raised above head	57,344	10,168	92.3%	0.08*
Body facing screen	54,796	7,296	87.4%	-0.05*

Table 1. Test set accuracy of binary classifiers used in our algorithm (train and test data obtained from separate users), as well as weights assigned to each classifier in our final computation. Accuracy refers to per-frame accuracy (# of correct video frames / total # of frames) of detecting a gesture. For example, 98.4% in the hand lifted above waist row indicates that this classifier correctly detected the hand lifted above for 98.4% of gestures. Because "looking at sensor" used built-in face detection algorithm, accuracy numbers are unavailable. Weights marked * are statistically significant (effectively contributed to estimation), $p < 0.05$.

use body motion to enhance gaming experience. In [21], Sanghvi et al. use body lean angle, slouch factor, quantity of motion (computed by looking at pixel-based silhouette motion), and body contraction to determine a student's interest level in playing a game with a robot game companion. Lastly, Kapoor [11] combines facial features, body posture and system state information to determine interest level in a game.

Our work builds on top of the aforementioned research by illustrating how gaze, body pose, and motion can be used in concert in determining a user's intention to interact with vision-based interfaces. Further, we demonstrate the value of combining our intention-to-interact metric with explicit gestures in determining user engagement. This approach offers a new way of thinking about user input: taking account *intention to interact* at the system level. This suggests that future input systems may benefit from directly incorporating uncertainty [22] into the dispatch process.

CHARACTERIZING INTENTION TO INTERACT

To better understand the role of body pose, motion and facial features in determining intention to interact, we ran a formative study exploring how people naturally engage with others, and how they might engage with a vision-based interface. We recruited 16 participants (mean age 25, 2 female, all Caucasian), none of which has experience with VIs.

Participants stood approximately 2.5m away from a VI setup consisting of a depth-sensing camera and 30-inch 1080p display. First, we asked participants to demonstrate how they would get the attention of another person pictured on the display. Second, participants demonstrated how they would "wake up" the system from a sleeping state using gesture, and then pretend to select buttons on a screen (using gesture). Participants repeated each task five times when sitting and standing, and task order was counterbalanced.

We recorded video, depth and skeleton data for each participant in our formative study. One of the authors watched these videos to find common factors that would indicate intention to interact. The following signals were found to be relevant (Table 1): 1) user is looking at the screen, 2) user's hands are lifted above the waist, 3) user is waving one or both hands, 4) user raises a hand above their head, 5) user's body is facing the screen, and 6) user's posture is attentive (arms are not crossed, hands are far away from the head, at least one hand has non-zero velocity).

One feature (one or more hands lifted above waist) was largely due to the type of interaction we were asking users to complete, which was pretending to select buttons in an interface. Not all interfaces have this requirement, indicating that any model that focuses on this feature may be over-specific. This feature, however, can be easily removed in the intention-to-interact model to expand the generalizability of our result to different VIs. The importance of features specific to the interaction at hand should not be understated: in practice interaction-specific features are quite important to generate robust models.

COMPUTING AN INTENTION TO INTERACT METRIC

Based on observations from our formative study, we developed six binary classifiers to detect the body poses and gestures described above.

Our first classifier – *user is looking at camera* – was computed using commodity face detection on the video feed provided from our camera [25]. The remaining five classifiers (*hand is above the waist*, *hand is lifted above head*, *attentive posture*, *body facing sensor*, and *waving*) were trained using hand-labeled frames from a subset of clips gathered during our formative study, as well as clips subsequently gathered by the authors.

We labeled and trained each classifier using Visual Gesture Builder, a tool shipped with Microsoft's Xbox SDK. Visual Gesture Builder uses features such as relative joint angles and joint motion to learn gesture and body pose classifiers using the ADABoost [7] algorithm. Each classifier was trained using ADABoost with 1000 weak classifiers; we also mirrored joint data to account for a lower rate of left-handed users. Body poses were labeled irrespective of whether the user was actually engaged, and we ignored joints below the waist to make classifiers agnostic to whether users were standing or sitting. Table 1 shows statistics regarding accuracy of our binary classifiers. Statistics are presented based on a set of test clips obtained from a subset of users in our formative study (train and test data obtained from different users).

Our intention-to-interact score is a value between zero and one (inclusive), representing an estimation of the likelihood of a user's intention to interact. The intention-to-interact score is computed using a weighted combination of the six classifiers above; the output of each binary classifier is treated as a zero or one. We used clips recorded from a pilot of our experiment (see below) to get ground truth measurement of engagement for running a regression.

For each clip we recorded the user's ground truth engagement as well as output from our classifiers every 30 msec. In total we collected 16,893 frames over 13 clips. We then ran a linear regression over our features to determine weights that best predicted engagement. Feature weights for the intention-to-interact model are in Table 1. All features significantly contributed to the result estimation ($p < 0.05$), and coefficient of determination (R^2) was 0.66.

We were surprised to see a low weight on hand raised above head and a negative weight on body facing sensor. We posit that this is because the hand raised above head gesture occurred infrequently and that users were almost always facing the sensor regardless of whether they were interacting or not. Interestingly, body pose – not gaze – had the highest weight. This suggests that in the context of VIs (where users may be looking at an interface but have no intention to interact) body pose is more telling than gaze.

In our user study, we used a threshold to determine when a user transitions from *disengaged* to *engaged*, and vice versa. A final component in development of our engagement algorithm was in determining an appropriate threshold: when a user engages and when she disengages.

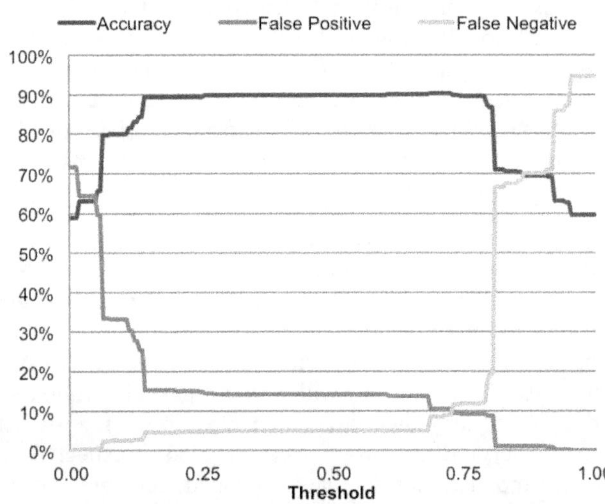

Figure 2. Users transitioned from not engaged to engaged when their intention to interact scores reached a threshold. This figure illustrates the tradeoff between accuracy, false positives, and false negatives at different threshold levels.

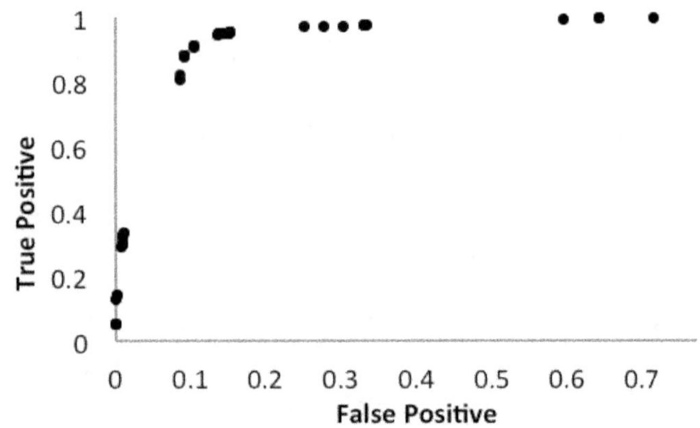

Figure 3. ROC curve for intention to interact model. A' (area under ROC curve) = 0.88.

Figures 2 and 3 illustrate the accuracy tradeoffs of using different thresholds to determine engagement. We used the same 16,893-frame dataset used in computing classifier weights for this analysis. Figure 2 displays curves illustrating tradeoff between false positives, false negatives, and accuracy at different threshold levels, and Figure 3 shows an ROC curve comparing accuracy tradeoff of different thresholds. Based on this analysis, we determined that a threshold between 0.685 and 0.705 offered the highest overall per-frame accuracy in determining intention to interact of 90%, however as will be seen in future sections, this threshold should be adjusted according to the cost of false positive and false negative classifications.

EVALUATION

To demonstrate the value of our intention-to-interact approach, we ran a 30-person lab study comparing three different engagement algorithms, both in single and multi-user scenarios. As a baseline, we used a direct port of the "wave to engage" gesture on the Xbox 360, and compared this engagement method to three of our own methods: a protocol that used only our intention-to-interact score, and two hybrid protocols that combined the intention-to-interact score with a gesture. Our experiment focused on testing the following hypotheses:

***H1:** Making use of the intention-to-interact metric leads to higher accuracy when determining user engagement.*

We picked this hypothesis because it tested the overall percentage of time that the system correctly interpreted a user's intention to interact (or not) with a system.

***H2:** Making use of the intention-to-interact metric reduces the number of accidental engagements when compared to using only a gesture.*

This hypothesis is useful to test because while overall accuracy is important, a key aspect of any VI (and the core problem behind Midas touch) is reducing accidental engagement.

***H3:** Making use of the intention-to-interact metric leads to faster engagement with the system compared to explicit gesture.*

An important consideration regarding the usability of vision-based systems is the ease and speed with which users can begin to use an interface. Therefore, we chose this hypothesis to ensure that the intention-to-interact metric, while accurate, would better enable users to engage with VIs in a timely manner.

***H4:** Making use of the intention- to-interact metric leads to faster engagement handoff between users.*

Whether in the living room, kitchen or operating room, VIs often must determine whom amongst a set of possible users to pay attention to. Furthermore, being able to hand off system control between users is also important. We chose this hypothesis to ensure that our intention-to-interact model offered improvements in multi user as well as single user scenarios.

System Description

We built a simple gesture-controlled interface for our study using a pre-release version of the Xbox One Kinect. Software was implemented in C++ and ran on Windows. We used an Xbox One Kinect camera to capture depth images and track skeletons; our system ran at 30 frames per second.

The interface was a simple 'bop the mole' game, where users need to engage and move a hand-controlled cursor over as many targets as possible, then disengage and do some secondary task. Our VI was designed to work for single and multi-user scenarios. Users could also see a small "Picture-in-Picture" (PiP) view of the scene, and get feedback about when they were engaged in the PiP. Users controlled a body-relative screen cursor, one cursor per hand.

Our system recorded depth and skeleton data, as well as results from individual binary classifiers, intention-to-interact scores, and ground truth engagement as determined by the game state. In addition to implementing the classifiers and regression described in the model, we also implemented a direct port of the wave recognizer currently shipped on the Xbox 360 to provide a baseline comparison.

We developed a player engagement protocol to compare algorithms. Our protocol assumes at most one engaged player at any given moment. Engaged users became disengaged when they satisfied a disengagement criteria. If no user was engaged, the player with the highest engagement score (above some threshold) became engaged.

Procedure

We ran two studies to compare our engagement algorithms in different scenarios. The first study was aimed at determining engagement speed and accuracy for a single player. The second study explored a multi-user scenario, specifically, the time to hand off control to another player.

We recruited 30 participants for our single person study (3 female, mean age 32). We used all participants from the single person study in addition to 9 more males and 1 female (mean age 35) for our multi-user study. All participants were professionals in the IT industry and had moderate to high experience with using the Kinect. Participants knew nothing about the internal workings of our algorithm and did not participate in gathering of training data. However, the skewed distribution of participants (mostly male, IT professionals) is a limitation of the study. In particular, our participants may have had prior experience with triggering the "wave to engage" gesture, making it more challenging to demonstrate the benefit of the intention to interact score over the baseline.

The experimental setup was identical for both studies. Participants stood or sat in a living-room sized alcove 2.5m away from a 65" (165.1cm) display, raised 1.5m from the floor. Our Xbox One Kinect camera was located directly underneath the display. Figure 1 illustrates our experimental setup. The experimenter sat in the alcove with participants, giving instructions and moving participants through conditions of the experiment.

Figure 4 provides an overview of the study procedure. In both experiments, participants were asked to repeatedly engage with the system and select a series of buttons, then disengage from the system. To ensure participants tried to engage quickly our game kept a score of the number of buttons selected. In both studies, each participant session was broken into two blocks, one standing block and one sitting block. All conditions were tested in each block. In both studies block and condition order was counterbalanced. For each condition the experimenter explained the engagement method to participants and participants were given one minute to practice.

The experimenter described the wave condition and wave combined with score condition as "wave your hand to engage", the hand lifted combined with score condition as "raise your hand and make sure it is open". During piloting, users appeared to be at a loss for what to do in the score

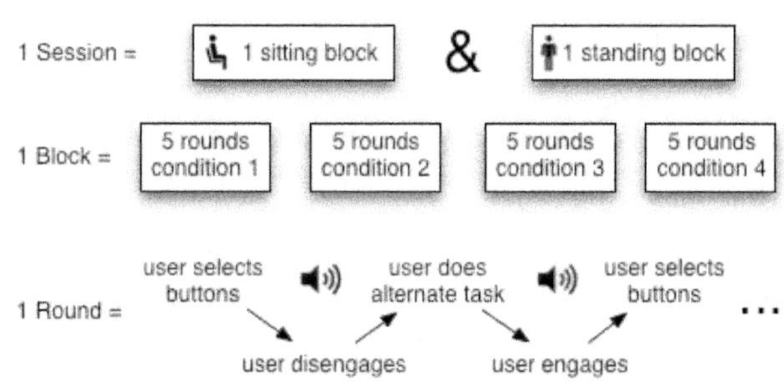

Figure 4. Overview of study design for single user scenario. Each user participated in a single session. Condition and block order were counterbalanced. The multi-person scenario used pairs of participants who were asked to take turns selecting buttons with no alternate task.

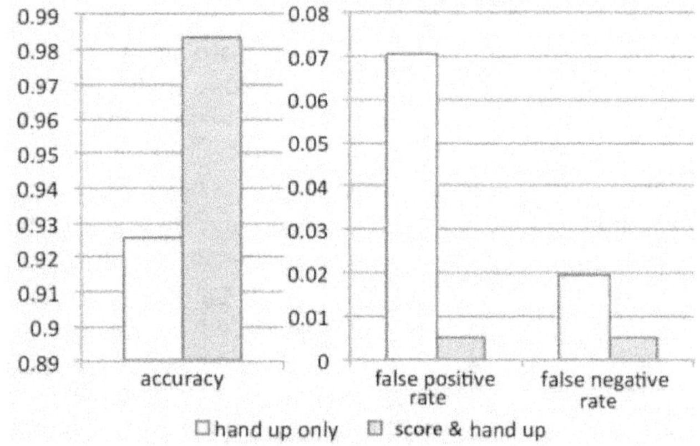

Figure 5. Accuracy and false positive rates comparing a hand raised and hand raised & score algorithm from 3-person pilot study. Error bars omitted due to insufficient data.

only condition unless they were given a specific action to perform, so we told them to "either raise your hand", or "wave".

At the end of each session participants filled out a brief questionnaire asking them which engagement method they preferred. Condition order was counterbalanced to control for order effects.

Study 1: Single Active Player

In our first study, we aimed to compare engagement speed and accuracy across conditions. Within each block, users alternated between selecting buttons on a screen and doing some other task. The latter was randomly selected from a set of tasks designed to mimic what a user may want to do during regular usage. A set of seven alternate tasks were picked from an initial expert brainstorming session, and then these seven tasks were narrowed down to five tasks based on feedback from pilot runs of our study. The tasks were: "Talk on your phone", "Look to the side", "Cross your arms", "Walk over to and move an object from one location to another" and "Browse email on your mobile device."

For each block, users selected buttons for five seconds, and then performed the randomly selected task for five seconds. Users were given audio and visual cues to switch tasks. Each round was repeated five times.

Study 2: Multiple Users

The aim of our second study was to compare time to hand off control to another user between conditions. The high level procedure of the study is described above. Users participated in pairs, giving us a total of 20 pairs. For each pair, each user had a designated color, indicated in the PiP display. In each block users had to engage and select as many of their colored buttons as possible. Button color would alternate every five seconds (indicated by a chime). Users were penalized in the game if they stayed engaged while another person's buttons were visible, thus motivating users to disengage as quickly as possible after selection. This was repeated 20 times per block.

Conditions

For both studies, we compared three engagement algorithms to the baseline wave to engage gesture, resulting in four experimental conditions.

C1: Wave Gesture (control) Our control condition aimed to very closely mimic the "wave to engage" interaction currently shipped on Xbox 360. For this we implemented a direct code port of the wave recognizer on Xbox 360. The engage criterion for this condition was recognition of the Xbox 360 wave gesture, and disengagement occurred 250ms after both of the user's hands were below the waist.

C2: Score only This condition used only our intention-to-interact score to determine engagement and disengagement. The engagement criterion for this condition was based off of a smoothed intention-to-interact score. We smoothed the intention-to-interact score in our implementation using (for simplicity) an exponential smoothing filter [6] with a smoothing factor of 0.8, applied every frame. Our smoothing factor was determined from observations during pilot runs of the study.

Users became engaged when their intention-to-interact score rose above 0.69. This threshold was found to provide a relatively low false positive rate of 10% while maintaining an overall accuracy (on our training dataset) of 95% (see Figure 2). Users became disengaged when their intention-to-interact score dropped below 0.1, which offered a nice tradeoff between false positives, true negatives and false negatives.

C3: Score Combined with Wave Gesture Another way to reduce false positive engagement is to add an additional gesture requirement. The score combined with wave condition used the same threshold of 0.69, this time with an unsmoothed score, and also required that the user complete the Xbox 360 wave gesture. Users disengaged when their unsmoothed intention-to-interact score dropped below 0.1.

C4: Score Combined With Hand Raised and Open We were also curious to see if an easy-to-execute, but error-prone gesture ("hand raised and open") could be combined with the intention to interact score to create a fast yet accurate engagement protocol. In this condition we required the unsmoothed intention-to-interact score to again be above 0.69 and that at least one of the user's hands was above the waist and open.

We used a hand state classification algorithm similar to what is shipped in the Kinect for Windows SDK v1.7 for hand state detection. Disengagement was the same as in C3.

To verify our intuition that the hand raised and open gesture would generate too many false positives to be practical, we ran a three-person pilot of the full study described below on six runs of three different people (total of 1,785 frames), hand labeled these frames according to whether the user was engaged with the system, and compared accuracy and false positive rates (see Figure 5).

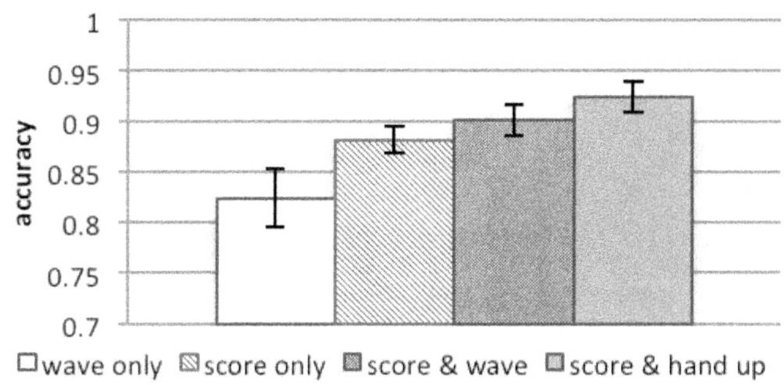

Figure 6. Mean of per-frame accuracy across users, single person study. Bars represent 95% CI.

Using just hand up and open had an accuracy and false positive rate of 93% and 7% respectively, while the combined model had an accuracy and false positive rate of 98% and 0.5%. Results from this preliminary study indicate that this simple gesture, while easy and fast, was not accurate enough for detection of user engagement, and that an additional metric such as our intention-to-interact score would be necessary to better determine user engagement.

Data

During our study, we recorded depth and skeleton data for all runs, and recorded binary classifier results, as well as an engagement score every 300ms. We were able to automatically determine ground truth because the study interface controlled programmatically the user's engagement state (Figure 4). During the study the experimenter made sure that users were on task and switched tasks in a timely manner.

In total, we recorded 1305 clips, representing 191,905 frames of data, 1,200 engagements, 1,200 disengagements, and 3,200 engagement handoffs across the single and multiple person study. Two users from our single person study had corrupt data or failed to complete the study in an attentive manner and were removed from analysis. To ensure that all data samples were independent, we performed all analysis on a per-user basis. The statistics presented below are based on 28 per-user samples in our single person study, and 20 per-pair samples in our multiple person study.

As ground truth we recorded the each user's expected engagement, based on the task that they were currently doing. In the single person study, the ground truth was based on whether users were supposed to be performing button selection or the distractor task (see Figure 4). In the multiple person study, the ground truth was based on which user was asked to select the buttons. To account for user reaction time (the time between when the chime sounds and the user actually starts switching tasks), we ignored all data one second after a chime in all conditions. In the analyses presented below, all data were normally distributed, or log transformed to become normally distributed.

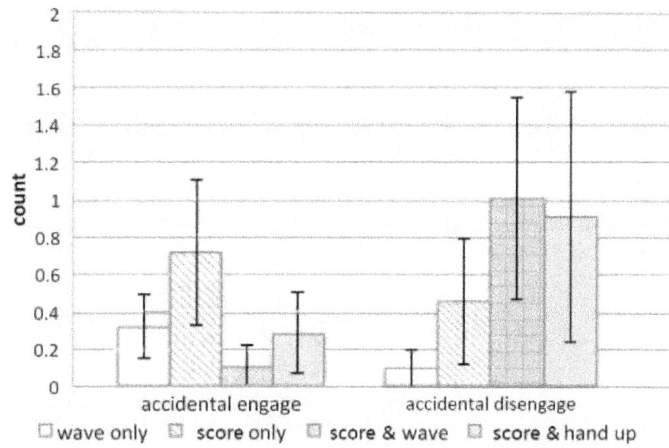

Figure 7. Mean number of accidental engagements and disengagements per user in single person study. Bars represent 95% CI.

Results and Discussion

Our hypotheses were largely confirmed, with the exception of H2, which was partially confirmed. Below we describe these results with respect to each specific hypothesis.

H1: *Making use of the intention-to-interact metric leads to higher accuracy when determining user engagement.*

Our results indicate that using an intention-to-interact score leads to higher accuracy over the baseline wave to engage condition. All analyses for this hypothesis were performed on data from the single person study. To determine impact of condition on overall accuracy, we used several measures.

First, for each user we measured per-frame accuracy (# frames correct / total number frames) after ignoring all frames within one second of a chime. This number was chosen to ensure that the cutoff was considerably less than the fastest possible engagement method. However, this metric unfairly biases situations where users are accidentally engaged for a long time (i.e. they fail to disengage). Therefore, we also counted the number of accidental engagements and accidental disengagements per user for each condition (out of a total of 40 engagements and 40 disengagements per user). Accuracy was computed on a per-user basis. Figure 6 shows results comparing overall accuracy, while Figure 7 show results comparing number of accidental engagements and accidental disengagements in our system.

Using our engagement score combined with a hand up and open gesture yielded the highest per-frame accuracy, at 92.4%, while wave only was at 82.3%. We log transformed our per-frame accuracy to normalize the distribution. A repeated measures ANOVA on the log-transformed data comparing per-frame accuracy indicated a difference across conditions ($F(3, 81)=21.68$, $p < 0.01$), and a post-hoc test applying Bonferonni correction indicated that the three methods leveraging the intention-to-interact score had higher mean accuracy than wave only ($p < 0.01$ in all cases).

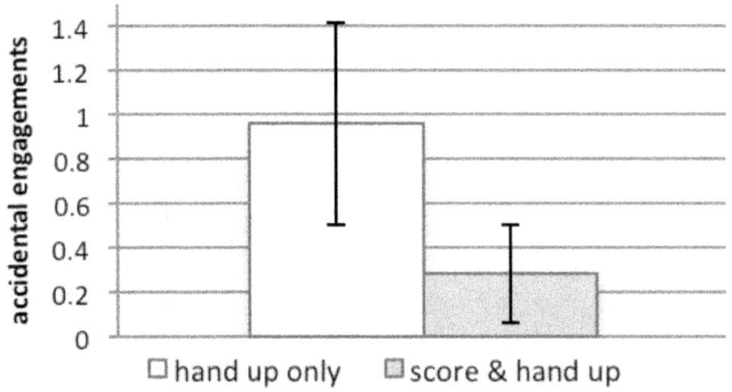

Figure 8. Post-hoc comparison of accidental engagements with and without an intention to interact score (single person study) when using a hand up and open gesture.

There are two possible explanations for this difference. First, the wave gesture takes a considerable time to engage. Also, the disengage condition for our wave only method caused a failure to *disengage* in some cases. This failure to disengage was a surprising result, which caused accuracy to drop significantly for the wave gesture. To reduce the impact on prolonged failures to disengage, we also counted the number of accidental engagements per user in our single person session. Figure 7 compares number of per-user accidental engagements and disengagements. A detailed analysis of accidental engagement will be presented in the next section.

One interesting observation is that our intention-to-interact score led to more accidental disengagements than using an explicit gesture. This is not surprising as our intention-to-interact metric measures *intention to interact*, and not *intention to disengage*. In future work we suggest developing a separate *intention to disengage* metric to reduce accidental disengagement.

H2: *Combining intention-to-interact with an explicit gesture reduces the number of accidental engagements when compared to using only an explicit gesture.*

Our study did not show that the combining of a wave gesture with our intention-to-interact score helped reduce accidental engagement (Figure 7, left). One likely reason for this is that the wave gesture was already specifically tuned to reduce false engagement, at the cost of other factors such as engagement speed (see *H1*). Additionally, the number of accidental engagements per user was already very low in all conditions, at less than 0.8 false engagements out of 40.

While the intention-to-interact score did not perform significantly better than the wave gesture, a post-hoc analysis showed that the engagement metric does reduce false engagement when using the raise hand up gesture.

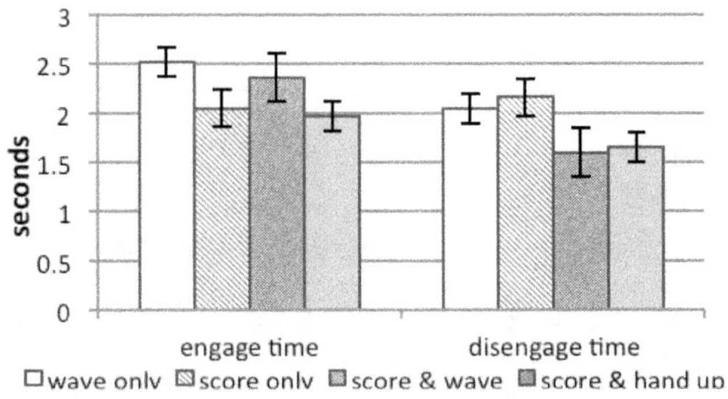

Figure 9. Mean time to engage, disengage in single person study, across users. Bars represent 95% CI.

For our post-hoc analysis, we simulated a "hand up and open" engagement gesture by replaying depth and skeleton data collected from our study, and this time used hand up and open as the engagement criteria, hands dropped as disengagement criteria. We recorded binary classifier results, ground truth, and computed engagement. One recording from our study was thrown out due to corrupt data, yielding a total of 27 data points per condition.

Figure 8 shows results of our post-hoc comparison. A *t*-test indicated that the intention-to-interact score did lead to significantly fewer accidental engagements between the hand up only condition and the intention-to-interact score combined with hand up condition ($t(26)=2.62$, $p < 0.05$). Specifically, accidental engagement dropped from 0.96 accidental engagements in the open hand up only condition to 0.29, a 70% reduction in accidental engagements.

H3: *Making use of the intention-to-interact metric leads to faster engagement with the system compared to explicit gesture.*

Analysis of data from our single person study indicates that using an intention-to-interact score leads to faster engagement time than the baseline wave to engage gesture. Specifically, average time to engage with wave was about 2.5 seconds while average time to engage in the score-only condition and the score combined with hand up condition was about 2 seconds, yielding a 20% reduction in engagement time (Figure 9).

A repeated-measures ANOVA across all conditions indicated a statistically significant difference between average engagement times ($F(3, 81) = 9.66$, $p < 0.01$). Post-hoc tests applying Bonferroni correction indicated a statistically significant difference in time to engage between using the wave gesture and our score only at $p < 0.05$, as well as a difference between wave only and hand up & score ($p < 0.05$). The fastest engagement method was obtained using intention-to-interact combined with a hand up and open.

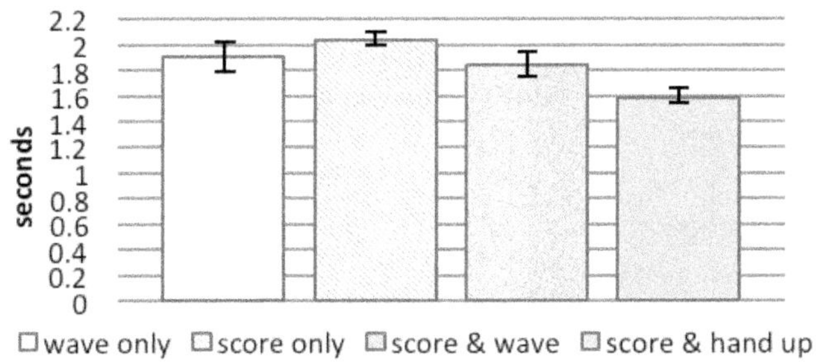

Figure 10. Mean time to hand off control in multi-person study, across users. Error bars represent 95% CI.

H4: Using an intention-to-interact score leads to faster engagement handoff between players.

For this analysis, we only used data from our multi-person study. Surprisingly, handoff time was slowest in the intention-to-interact score only condition (Figure 10). We posit that this was because time to disengage was quite high in the intention-to-interact score only condition (due to smoothing of the intention-to-interact score). Since our scenario required that the currently engaged user first disengage before another user can take control, a high disengagement time would increase handoff time as well. The high disengagement time in our intention-to-interact only condition was a result of aggressive smoothing of the intention-to-interact score.

Nevertheless, this study once again illustrated the benefits of combining the intention-to-interact score with a hand up and open gesture. Specifically, we found that handoff time in the intention-to-interact score combined with hand up condition was significantly lower than handoff time in the wave only condition. Time to switch dropped from 2.04 seconds (wave) to 1.59 seconds, a 22% reduction. A repeated measures ANOVA confirmed a significant difference across conditions ($F(3, 57) = 28.40$, $p < 0.01$), and post-hoc tests using Bonferroni correction confirmed a difference between wave only and hand up combined with score at $p < 0.05$. Note that the degrees of freedom in this analysis are different from previous analyses because we are analyzing results from the multiple person study, which had 4 conditions, and 20 pairs of users completing each condition.

Subjective Gesture Preference

Questionnaire data collected during both studies showed a strong preference for the hand up and open gesture compared to the wave gesture (Figure 11). Interestingly, people strongly preferred the hand up combined with intention-to-interact score condition to the score only condition. One explanation for this could be that in the score only condition users did not know exactly what they should do and thus could not be sure that their actions would lead to an engagement. This further speaks to the need of always combining an intention-to-interact score with some gesture so that users can always know what action will trigger engagement.

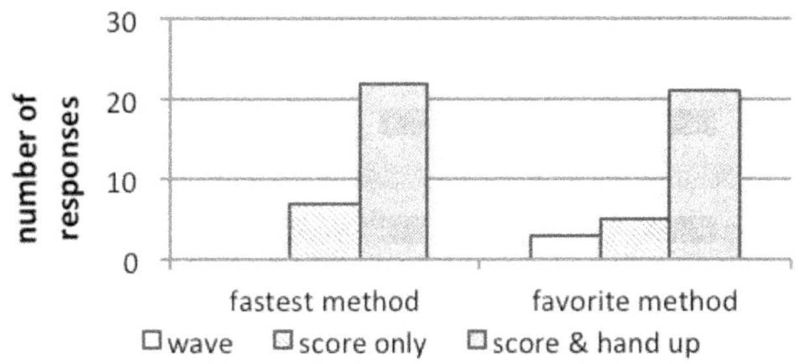

Figure 11. Gesture preference from questionnaire (single person study).

Limitations

Our studies and subsequent analysis demonstrate the benefit of using an intention-to-interact metric for determining intention to interact with vision-based systems. Nevertheless, there are a few limitations we should note.

Foremost, we smoothed our model score considerably to reduce false engagements and disengagements, which caused an unusually high disengagement time. However, even with aggressive smoothing we were able to show benefit over our baseline. Secondly, our baseline engagement, to which we compared, may not be the fastest or most accurate method available across all of the research literature. We chose it primarily because it was an example of a commercially available, in-the-wild engagement detection algorithm that was highly tuned and tested.

CONCLUSIONS AND FUTURE WORK

In this paper, we argue for the inclusion of an intention-to-interact metric when determining user engagement in vision-based input systems. We used a collection of binary classifiers that looked at a user's body pose, motion, and gaze to approximate the likelihood that a user intends to interact with an interface.

Results from two 30-person lab studies indicate that while an intention-to-interact metric by itself is useful, the full power of our intention-to-interact score becomes evident when combined with an easy-to-execute but error-prone activation gesture. Our intention-to-interact metric allows vision-based input systems to accurately detect user engagement without requiring overly complex gestures.

This work opens up several avenues of future work. First, our model for intention to interact focuses largely on detecting engagement with the system. However, the model could be further improved if we included intention to disengage. Second, we have demonstrated the value of using body pose and gesture in determining intention to interact, and believe that these findings are relevant to other types of vision based scenarios, such Human-Robot Interaction and dialogue management systems. Finally, the model offers a new way of thinking about and segmenting user input: generating an *intention-to-interact score* and dispatching user input according to this score, suggesting that future input systems may benefit from directly incorporating uncertainty [22] into the dispatch process.

ACKNOWLEDGMENTS

The authors thank Chris Harrison for his assistance, as well as the members of the Xbox NUI Team for their feedback and support. The authors would also like to thank Tyler Murphy for his assistance with Figure 1. This work was funded by a Microsoft Graduate Research Fellowship and NSF Grant IIS1217929. Icons from Figure 4 were by Jessica Lock and Mellonie Manohar from The Noun Project.

REFERENCES

1. Asteriadis, S., Karpouzis, K., and Kollias, S. Feature extraction and selection for inferring user engagement in an hci environment. *Human-Computer Interaction*, Springer-Verlag (2009), 22–29.

2. Bianchi-Berthouze, N. What Can Body Movement Tell Us About Players' Engagement? *Measuring Behavior '12*, ACM Press (2012), 94–97.

3. Bianchi-Berthouze, N. Understanding the role of body movement in player engagement. *Human Computer Interaction 28*, 2 (2013), 42–75.

4. Bohus, D. and Horvitz, E. Learning to Predict Engagement with a Spoken Dialog System in Open-World Settings. *SIGDIAL '09*, ACM Press (2009), 244–252.

5. Bohus, D. and Horvitz, E. Dialog in the open world: platform and applications. *ICMI-MLMI '09*, ACM Press (2009), 31–38.

6. Brown, R.G. *Exponential Smoothing for Predicting Demand.* Little, 1956.

7. Freund, Y. and Schapire, R.E. A Decision-Theoretic Generalization of On-Line Learning and an Application to Boosting. *Journal of Computer and System Sciences 55*, 1 (1997), 119–139.

8. Harmonix. Dance Central. 2012. http://www.dancecentral.com.

9. Hartmann, B., Morris, M.R., Benko, H., and Wilson, A.D. Pictionaire: supporting collaborative design work by integrating physical and digital artifacts. *CSCW '10*, ACM Press (2010), 421–424.

10. Hinckley, K., Pausch, R., Goble, J.C., and Kassell, N.F. A survey of design issues in spatial input. *UIST '94*, ACM Press (1994), 213–222.

11. Kapoor, A., Picard, R.W., and Ivanov, Y. Probabilistic combination of multiple modalities to detect interest. *ICPR '04.*, IEEE Computer Society Press (2004), 969–972.

12. Kjeldsen, R. and Hartman, J. Design issues for vision-based computer interaction systems. *PUI '01*, ACM Press (2001), 1–8.

13. Kleinsmith, A. and Bianchi-Berthouze, N. Affective Body Expression Perception and Recognition: A Survey. *IEEE Transactions on Affective Computing 9*, Preprint (2012).

14. Michalowski, M.P., Sabanovic, S., and Simmons, R. A spatial model of engagement for a social robot. *Advanced Motion Control '06*, IEEE Computer Society Press (2006), 762–767.

15. Microsoft. Xbox 360 + Kinect. http://www.xbox.com/kinect.

16. Mota, S. and Picard, R. Automated posture analysis for detecting learner's interest level. *In CVPR Workshop on HCI*, (2003).

17. Nakano, Y. and Ishii, R. Estimating user's engagement from eye-gaze behaviors in human-agent conversations. *IUI '10*, ACM Press (2010), 139–148.

18. Pawar, U.S., Pal, J., Gupta, R., and Toyama, K. Multiple mice for retention tasks in disadvantaged schools. *CHI '07*, ACM Press (2007), 1581–1590.

19. Rare. Kinect Sports. 2010. http://www.rareusa.com/games/kinect-sports.

20. Rich, C., Ponsler, B., Holroyd, A., and Sidner, C.L. Recognizing engagement in human-robot interaction. *HRI '10*, IEEE Computer Society Press (2010), 375–382.

21. Sanghvi, J., Castellano, G., Leite, I., Pereira, A., McOwan, P.W., and Paiva, A. Automatic analysis of affective postures and body motion to detect engagement with a game companion. *HRI '11*, ACM Press (2011), 305–312.

22. Schwarz, J., Hudson, S.E., Mankoff, J., and Wilson, A.D. A Framework for Robust and Flexible Handling of Inputs with Uncertainty. *Proceedings of the 24th annual ACM symposium on User interface software and technology UIST '11*, ACM Press (2010), 47–56.

23. Smith, P., Shah, M., and da Vitoria Lobo, N. Determining Driver Visual Attention With One Camera. *IEEE Trans. on Intelligent Transportation Systems 4*, 4 (2003), 205–218.

24. Stødle, D., Hagen, T., Bjorndalen, J., and Anshus, O. Gesture-based, touch-free multi-user gaming on wall-sized, high-resolution tiled displays. *Journal of Virtual Reality and Broadcasting 5*, 10 (2008), 1860–2037.

25. Viola, P. and Jones, M.J. Robust Real-Time Face Detection. *International Journal of Computer Vision 57*, 2 (2004), 137–154.

26. Walter, R., Bailly, G., and Laboratories, T.I. StrikeAPose : Revealing Mid-Air Gestures on Public Displays. (2013), 841–850.

Wave to Me: User Identification Using Body Lengths and Natural Gestures

Eiji Hayashi[1]
ehayashi@cs.cmu.edu

Manuel Maas[2]
manuel.maas@gmx.de

Jason I. Hong[1]
jasonh@cs.cmu.edu

[1]Human-Computer Interaction Institute
Carnegie Mellon University
5000 Forbes Ave. Pittsburgh PA 15213, USA

[2]Institute of Cryptography and Security
Karlsruhe Institute of Technology
Kaiserstraße 12, 76131 Karlsruhe, Germany

ABSTRACT
We introduce a body-based identification system that leverages individual differences in body segment lengths and hand waving gesture patterns. The system identifies users based on a two-second hand waving gesture captured by a Microsoft Kinect. To evaluate our system, we collected 8640 gesture measurements from 75 participants through two lab studies and a field study. In the first lab study, we evaluated the feasibility of our concept and basic properties of features to narrow down the design space. In the second lab study, our system achieved a 1% equal error rate in user identification among seven registered users after two weeks following initial registration. We also found that our system was robust even when lower body segments could not be measured because of occlusions. In the field study, our system achieved 0.5 to 1.6% equal error rates, demonstrating that the system also works well in ecologically valid situations. Lastly, throughout the studies, our participants were positive about the system.

Author Keywords
User Identification; Gesture; Natural User Interface;

ACM Classification Keywords
H.5.2 User Interfaces: Interaction styles.

INTRODUCTION
Many future visions of interactive computing have us moving away from keyboard and mouse interactions, opting instead for natural user interfaces that bridge the physical and virtual worlds. These natural user interfaces might include input modalities such as speech, handwriting, or gestures. Here, we focus just on physical gestures.

While there has been a great deal of exploration into what the user experience might be like for gesture-based interfaces in smart environments, there has been little work on how one might manage user identification. In GUI-based systems, a user specifies his identity by choosing it from a list of users or typing a user ID; the system then typically asks for a password to verify the claimed identity.

CHI 2014, April 26–May 1, 2014, Toronto, Ontario, Canada.
Copyright ©ACM 978-1-4503-2473-1/14/04...$15.00.
http://dx.doi.org/10.1145/2556288.2557043

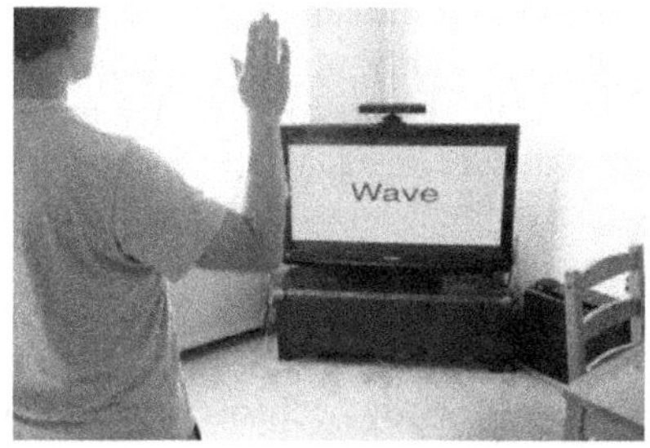

Figure 1. The proposed system can identify users based on 2 seconds of hand waving gesture measured by a Microsoft Kinect.

However, this approach assumes the existence of displays and keyboards (either physical or virtual), which may not hold or make sense, especially if gesture-based interfaces become popular. For example, many electric appliances, such as air conditioners, room lights, thermostats, and stereos, have limited input and output capabilities, but could potentially benefit from gesture-based controls as well as personalization based on user identification. A simple example would be turning on an air conditioner with a gesture and setting a personalized temperature based on user identification. Other examples might include being able to access game consoles, parental controls, personalization for electric appliances like DVRs, or showing some personalized information on wall displays (such as today's schedule or feeds from SNSs). Furthermore, many of these applications will be deployed in places with reasonably good physical security, such as homes, meaning that user identification can be designed in favor of usability over security.

In this paper, we investigate a novel body-based identification scheme that uses a two-second hand wave gesture captured by a Microsoft Kinect to identify users (Figure 1). We evaluated our system through three user studies. In our first study, we evaluated the feasibility of using body segment lengths as well as four natural gestures for user identification. Our analysis showed that body segment lengths and gesture patterns were not reliable enough when used separately; however, when we combine body lengths with a natural gesture, the system achieved reasonable performance. Furthermore, we found that a hand-waving gesture yielded the best performance among the four gestures. In our second user study, we further evaluated hand-waving gesture through a two-week lab study. The study showed that user identification was stable over this timeframe and performed well when trained with data from two sessions. In our third study, we tested our system in participants' living rooms. Our system still had good performance here, where environmental conditions were not controlled and some partial body occlusions occurred. Finally, throughout the three studies, our participants reported that they were positive about body-based identification system.

In summary, we make the following three research contributions. First, we measured, in the context of user identification, the reliability of body segment lengths and gesture data extractable from Microsoft Kinect's standard APIs. Second, we developed a body-based identification system that works on the basis of body segment lengths and hand-waving gesture patterns, and evaluated it through three user studies consisting of 75 participants in total. Third, we measured the robustness of our body-based identification to partial-body occlusions, the reliability over a two week period, robustness against environmental changes, and participants' responses to the system.

RELATED WORK

Many pieces of past work have leveraged gestures captured by sensors for user identification and authentication. User identification and authentication are similar but distinct concepts. User identification is a process where a system identifies a user among a set of pre-registered users and verifies the identity, whereas user authentication is a process where a system verifies whether a user is actually the pre-registered user that he claims to be [12]. In other words, a system performing user identification does not know a user ID, whereas one performing user authentication does.

Several lines of past work have used gestures with devices for authentication. For example, Chong et al. used discrete gestures consisting of a series of orientations as a password for mobile phones [1]. Jiayang et al. used a tri-axis accelerometer that yielded 2% false rejections and 12% false acceptances for authentication [9]. Patel et al. developed a system that authenticates users to public terminals through gestures captured by a mobile device [18]. Mayrhofer and Gellersen used a shaking gesture for device-device authentication [16].

There have also been authentication systems using Microsoft Kinect. For example, KinWrite authenticates users based on handwriting in mid-air [23]. With BroAuth, a user touched her own and her virtual partners' bodies in a sequence to authenticate [15]. For all of the systems above (mobile and Kinect), users need to first register and memorize a secret gesture. Although this approach has advantages on small devices where typing text is hard, the memorability of these gestures is not clear, especially if there are multiple gestures that need to be memorized. In contrast, our system uses a hand-waving gesture for all users; thus, it does not require any memorization.

Kam et al. proposed a hand-gesture-based authentication system for surveillance cameras that requires the same gestures for all users. The system authenticated people based on a series of eight pre-determined gestures [10]. In a more HCI related domain, biometric-rich gestures [17] required users to perform the same multi-finger gesture on touch displays (e.g., touch a display with five fingers and then close the fingers). Their system achieved an equal error rate (EER) ranging from 6.6% to 18.9%, depending on the gestures. Our work differs from these works in that it combines body segment lengths and gestures to improve performance, and uses a two-second hand wave gesture rather than series of gestures or multi-finger gestures.

Biometrics are another class of research using sensor data for user authentication / identification. Biometrics can be classified into two categories [8]. The first category leverages users' *physiological* properties, such as fingerprints (e.g., [1,14]), face, or voice. For example, Heusch et al. developed face authentication with a 2.4% EER under controlled background and light conditions. However the EER became 13.49% under uncontrolled background and light conditions [6]. Wan et al. demonstrated a 4.03% EER using voice [24]. Schmidt et al. developed HandsDown, which identified users based on hand contour [21]. Our paper explores a new design space for user identification in the context of gesture-based interfaces.

Human body sizes, primarily studied in the context of ergonomics design [4,20], can be another physiological property used for biometrics. In 2010, Microsoft released the Microsoft Kinect, which uses a depth camera to identify individuals as well as gestures. Although the details of the Kinect user identification algorithm have not been disclosed, Leyvand et al. as well as Gantenbein reported that the identification was based on a person's height, face, and clothing [2,11]. The user identification is done without explicit user inputs because it is primarily designed for user identification during gaming. As a result, its accuracy is relatively low. Our work investigates ways of improving user identification using a Kinect.

The second category is *behavioral* biometrics, which authenticates / identifies users based on behavioral characteristics, such as key typing pattern [19] and gait patterns [5]. For example, Mäntyjärvi et al. achieved 7% to 19% EER for gait pattern authentication [11]. These approaches are related to our system in a sense that users are identified based on individual differences extracted from common behaviors. However, as far as we know, natural gestures, such as hand-waving gesture, have not been studied in the context of behavioral biometrics.

Finally, there are systems that combined multiple biometrics [7]. Snelick et al. demonstrated that combining fingerprint and face recognition could achieve a 0.64% EER [22]. These pieces of past work focused on achieving high accuracy to improve security. In contrast, our work

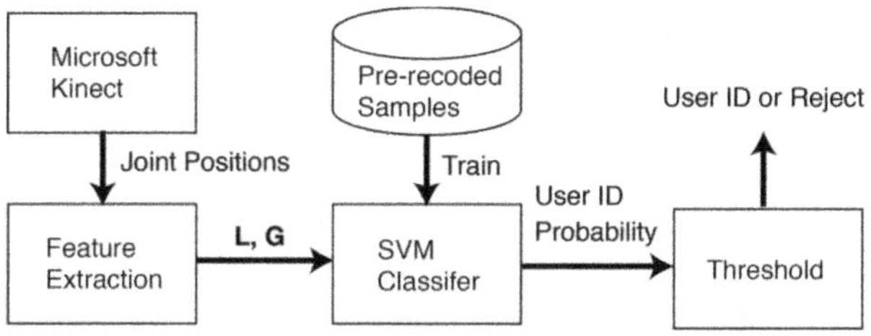

Figure 2. Overall algorithm of body-based identification. A body length feature vector (L) and a gesture feature vector (G) are extracted from joint positions. The vectors are concatenated and used for user identification with a SVM classifier trained with pre-recorded samples.

focuses on achieving high usability with reasonably good security by combining multiple factors.

BODY-BASED USER IDENTIFICATION

Our body-based user identification makes use of both physiological and behavioral properties of users, namely body segment lengths and gestures. We decided to use both of these properties because our preliminary analysis indicated that neither of them was reliable enough for user identification by itself. Our prototype consists of a computer, a display for showing the user instructions, and a Microsoft Kinect.

At a high level, our system works as follows (Figure 2). First, the system is trained by recording users performing a pre-specified gesture (e.g., hand waving). The recordings contain trajectories of three-dimensional positions of users' joints. In the training phase, our system extracts a body length feature vector and a gesture feature vector from the recordings. These two vectors are concatenated and used to train a SVM model that identifies the users. The system trains pair-wise SVM classifiers using a polynomial kernel (exponent=1) with logistic models for all possible pairs of users, and combine these classifiers to build a multi-class classifier that predicts user IDs with probabilities. We also tried Decision Tree, k-Nearest Neighbor, and Naïve Bayes as classifiers. Based on evaluations using a subset of our data, we chose SVM as well as its kernel and parameters.

Once the model is built, the system identifies the users and verifies their identities when they repeat the gesture once. The system extracts the two feature vectors, feeds them into the classifier, and predicts a user ID with a probability. When the probability is higher than a pre-defined threshold, the system accepts the user as the predicted user. Otherwise, the system rejects the user as a stranger. The system needs this threshold because, without the threshold, any person can be identified as one of the registered users. All registered users perform the same gesture, so the system discriminates users based on systematic differences in body segment lengths and gesture patterns. In the following, we describe the process more in detail.

Measurements of Gestures

Our system measures gestures with a Microsoft Kinect using APIs provided in Microsoft Kinect SDK 1.5. When a

Features	Description	# of features
Positions	10, 30, 50, 70, and 90 percentiles of wrist positions for each axis	15
Angles (hand - wrist-elbow)	Max, min and mean of the 3D angles consisting of hand-wrist-elbow	3
Angles (wrist-elbow-shoulder)	Max, min and mean of the 3D angles consisting of wrist-elbow-shoulder	3
Speeds	Mean absolute speed of hand, wrist and elbow calculated in 3D	3
Accelerations	Mean absolute acceleration of hand calculated in 3D	1
# of gesture sequences	Mean cross freq. of wrist positions. 0 for static gestures	1

Table 1. 26 features consisting of a gesture feature vector.

user stands in front of the Kinect and raises her dominant hand to shoulder level, the system initiates a measuring process. The system then asks the user to perform a hand-waving gesture (or other gestures in the user study #1). While a user is performing the gesture, our system records the trajectories of 21 joints [3] every 20 milliseconds. In total, the system obtains 100 three-dimensional position measurements of the 21 joints over two seconds. In our studies, data was processed off-line using Matlab and Weka. Processing one measurement took less than 0.5 seconds on a Macbook Pro with 2.6GHz Intel Core i7.

Gestures

Our body-based identification requires all registered users to perform the same gesture. In user study #1, we tested four gestures (hand waving, come-over, one-hand raised, and phone-to-ear) in two postures (standing and sitting), to investigate which gesture yields the best results. Based on the results from the study, we used hand-waving gestures in user studies #2 and #3.

We chose the four gestures to be tested in the study #1 as follows. First, we wanted gestures that people were familiar with performing, so that people could easily repeat the same pattern. Second, we wanted gestures that could be performed by one arm, because gestures performed by other parts of the body (e.g., nodding) could be too simple to discriminate between many users. We also avoided gestures requiring synchronizing movements from multiple body parts as we felt these would be too complicated for most users to reproduce precisely. Furthermore, we hypothesized that there would be a trade-off in reproducibility and discriminatory power. For example, complex gestures that require a lot of arm movements should have very distinct performance profiles across users; however, precisely reproducing these gestures could be difficult for users. In contrast, simple gestures that involve little movement should be easy for users to reproduce but might be performed similarly by other users, as well.

Considering these, we chose two *kinetic* gestures that involved continuous arm movements (hand waving and come-over), and two *static* gestures that involved little movement (one-hand raised and phone-to-ear gestures) to be investigated in the user study #1.

Feature Vectors

For each measurement, the system extracts a *sample* consisting of a body segment length vector and a gesture vector. Our system calculates the Euclidian distances between 17 pairs of adjacent joints. The distances are averaged over the 100 captured frames to mitigate sensor noise. Gesture features are extracted from the trajectory of joints of the user's dominant arm, relative to the user's head. From this trajectory, our system extracts 26 features that comprise a gesture feature vector (see Table 1). Except for the position features, all features were calculated in three-dimensional coordinates. We initially extracted more features, then, chose these features based on evaluation with a subset of our data. While these features worked reasonably well to demonstrate feasibility of our concept, we do not claim these are the best features.

Evaluation Metrics

In our body-based identification, there are two types of errors: false acceptances and false rejections. False acceptances denote the cases where a registered user is identified as a different user. False rejections denote cases where a registered user is rejected. The False Acceptance Rate (FAR) and False Rejection Rate (FRR) were calculated as shown in the Eq. (1) and (2).

$$FAR = \frac{Number\ of\ False\ Acceptances}{Number\ of\ Identifications} \tag{1}$$

$$FRR = \frac{Number\ of\ False\ Rejections}{Number\ of\ Identifications} \tag{2}$$

We used Equal Error Rates (EER) to evaluate performance of the body-based identification rather than the classification accuracy because false acceptances are more serious errors than false rejections, and simple classification accuracies do not make a distinction between the two types of errors. EER is the error rate where FAR and FRR become equal when changing the threshold for rejections. Therefore, smaller EERs indicate better performance.

In this paper, to calculate EER, we simulated having seven registered users to avoid the effects of having a variable number of participants. Our three studies consisted of 36, 25, and 12 participants. If we used all participants as registered users when calculating EERs, we cannot easily compare our results across studies, especially since user identification becomes more difficult when the number of users in a dataset increases. Additionally, for our expected use cases (e.g., home situations), we felt it would not be common to have more than seven registered users. Thus, in the following analyses, we randomly chose 10,000 combinations of seven participants from a dataset, and calculated EER over all combinations.

USER STUDY #1: FEASIBILITY EVALUATION

The overall goal of this lab study was to investigate basic properties of body segment lengths and gesture patterns captured by Microsoft Kinect. Additionally, we chose the most promising gesture among the four gestures based on the result. The chosen gesture was further investigated in the following studies.

Participants

We recruited 36 participants from an existing university recruiting website meant for the general public. Out of the 36 participants, 14 were male and 22 were female. Participants were 32.6 years old on average, ranging from 19 to 64. Twenty-three participants were university students, two were university staff employees and the other eleven were employed. Participants were 168cm tall, on average (SD=10.2), and weighed 78.0kg (SD=22.0). We paid $40 for completing the study.

Data Collection

The lab study consisted of two sessions. All sessions were conducted in the same windowless room, to avoid sunlight interference with the Kinect measurements. Both sessions took about 40 minutes to complete. In the first session, we explained that our system recorded participants' gestures using a Microsoft Kinect and identified them using their gestures as well as their body segment lengths. We then asked participants to perform the four gestures both standing and sitting, 10 times each. Participants stood three meters away from the Kinect. While standing, participants were asked to move half a meter to the left and back between measurements to mitigate habituation. While sitting, we asked participants to stand up and sit back down between measurements for the same reason. Half of the participants started the measuring session standing and the other half started sitting. We counterbalanced the order of the gestures using a Latin square. Three days later, in the second session, we repeated the procedure except explanation of our system. At the end of study, we asked participants to fill out a survey.

We collected 80 (10 samples times eight gesture-posture pairs) for each participant. In total, we collected 5760 samples from the 36 participants. Each sample consisted of a body segment length and a gesture feature vector. All data was processed off-line after the study. Thus, participants were not given feedback about the classification results.

Evaluating Feature Vectors Separately

Before combining the body segment length and gesture feature vectors, we started by analyzing them separately to understand their properties.

Performance Within Session and Posture

As baselines for the following analyses, we first investigated the consistency of the body segment length and gesture feature vectors in the same session and posture through 10-fold cross validation.

Figure 3 shows that identification through body segment lengths alone had EERs around 0.6% in the standing conditions and 1.5% in the sitting conditions. This indicates that the body segment lengths measurements were consistent in the same postures in one session. Additionally, the come-over gesture had low EERs relative to other

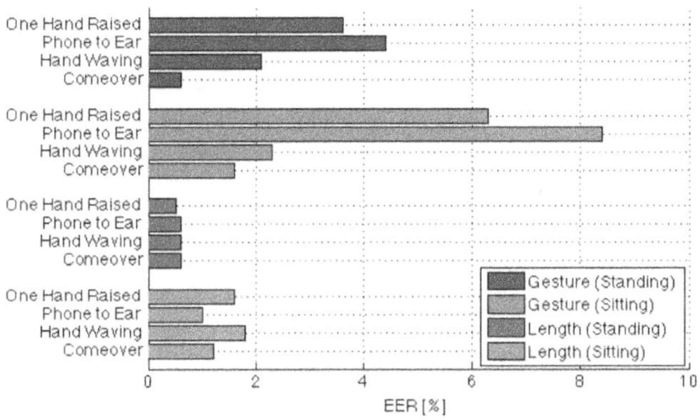

Figure 3. Equal Error Rates (EER) for user identification using one feature vector. Classifiers were evaluated with samples in the same posture as in the first session using 10-fold cross validation. Smaller EERs denote better performance.

gestures. In other words, the hand motions of the come-over gesture varied more between participants relative to other gestures, and thus have greater discriminatory power.

Performance Across Session and Posture

To evaluate robustness of the body segment lengths and gesture feature vector, we tested our system against samples measured in different sessions or postures. The results were similar for all gestures, and so for brevity, we only show the results for the hand waving gesture (Figure 4). We trained samples in the standing condition in the first session. Then, we calculated EERs using the samples of the standing condition in the second session and of the sitting condition in the first session as test sets. We include EERs calculated in Figure 3 as baselines.

Across sessions, the EERs were much higher. Thus, the feature vectors are not very repeatable across sessions. The EERs calculated for body segment length feature vectors and gesture feature vectors increased 20 fold and 5 fold respectively compared to the baselines. This finding indicates that, to further improve the performance, we need to train the classifier on samples acquired from multiple sessions to account for systematic sensor and performance imprecision across sessions.

Furthermore, across postures, the EERs calculated using just the body segment lengths feature vector increased over 80 fold. The EERs calculated from the gesture feature vector for hand waving also increased by a factor of 5. These results suggested that body segment length feature vectors were sensitive to postures and that we needed to train a separate SVM classifier for each posture.

The source of the inconsistencies in the measurement of body segment length remains unclear. We held the environment in which we took measurements constant, so environmental causes were unlikely. Rather, we suspect the inconsistencies across sessions may be caused by clothing changes across sessions. This hypothesis could explain why the samples within sessions are consistent but the samples

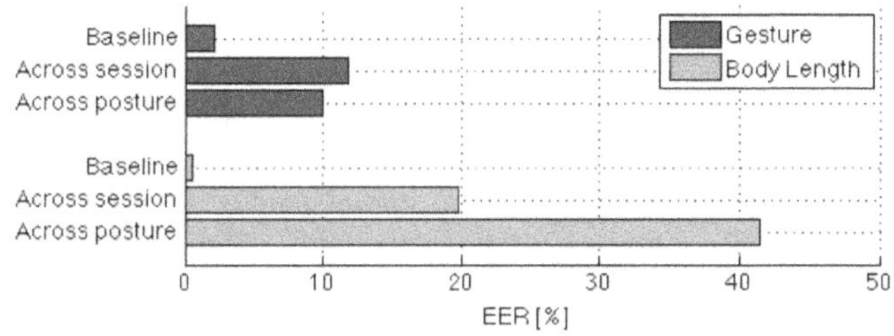

Figure 4. EERs with hand waving across sessions or postures. When classifiers were tested with samples in different sessions or postures, the EERs became higher. Note that the x-axis scale is different from that in Figure 3.

across sessions are inconsistent. However, further study is necessary to confirm the hypothesis.

Evaluation of Body-Based identification

We found that, when used separately, neither the body segment length nor the gesture feature vector was consistent enough to identify users reliably. Next, we evaluated identification performance using both feature vectors.

The previous analysis indicated that we needed to train our classifier with samples collected in difference sessions to achieve better performance. However, in this study, we have only two sessions. Therefore, we decided to train our classifiers only using samples from the first session to separate training and test sets clearly. We evaluate training with multiple sessions in the next study.

Dataset

For all samples, we concatenated body-lengths feature vectors and gesture feature vectors. For each gesture-posture pair, we trained SVM classifiers using samples collected in the first session, and evaluated with samples collected in the second session.

User Identification

Figure 5 shows EERs for each posture-gesture pair. For instance, when the hand waving gesture feature vector was combined with the body segment lengths feature vector, our system obtained 4.3% and 6.2% EERs in the standing and sitting conditions respectively. For other gesture-posture pairs, the EERs range from 2.6% to 7.6%. Thus, across sessions, our system performed much better by combining both body segment lengths and gestures when compared to either one separately as shown in Figure 4. This shows

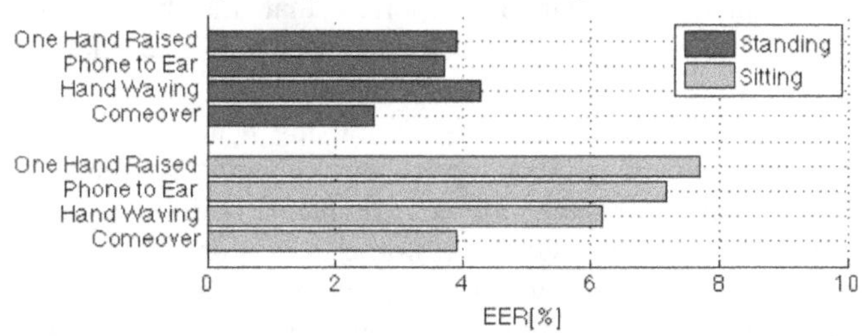

Figure 5. EERs for gesture-posture pairs. The system was trained with samples collected in the first session and tested with samples collected in the second session.

Gesture	Naturalness	Ease of Use	Security
One Hand Raised	4.0	5.0	3.0
Phone to Ear	2.0	4.0	3.0
Hand Waving	4.0	5.0	3.0
Come-over	2.0	4.0	3.0

Table 2. The numbers represent the median of the five-point Likert scale ratings by the participants. Higher numbers denotes positive ratings.

feasibility and effectiveness of the user identification based on both body segment lengths and gesture patterns.

Survey Results

At the end of the second session, we asked participants to complete a post-test survey. We asked participants to rate our body-based identification in terms of naturalness, ease of use, and security on a five-point Likert scale. For instance, with regard to naturalness, we asked how strongly participants agreed or disagreed a statement "using body lengths and hand waving to log into systems is natural" where 5 stands for strongly agree and 1 stands for strongly disagree. We used "logging in" as an example because it was easy to understand for users and it was one of the typical use cases of user identification. For the remainder of this section, we denote the median of the ratings in parentheses. See Table 2 for a summary of results.

The participants rated both the one-hand raised gesture and hand waving as natural (4.0) and very easy to use (5.0). For example, P11 commented, "I feel that the waving gesture is most appropriate for a login process because it has a connotation of welcoming and saying 'hello', which seems to feel right for a login screen." Indeed, the one-hand raised and hand waving gestures are common greetings that initiate human-human interactions. Thus, it makes sense that participants reported that these gestures were a natural form of identification—the common initiation of many human-computer interactions.

Participants rated body-based identification as neutral in terms of security (3.0). One explanation could be that participants were not familiar with the security properties of behavioral biometrics. P15 had concerns in using gestures for identification. She commented, "For the purpose of logging into a system, I would feel more secure if I could select a gesture, or motion, that I feel is somewhat unique to me, [...] and therefore less likely to be copyable."

In summary, participants reported that the body-based identification system was natural and easy to use, thought its level of security was unclear. We agree that impersonation is possible by mimicking a user's gestures especially when an attacker has body lengths similar to a target user. However, for environments with reasonable physical security, such as homes, or for non-critical applications, usability may be favored over security. Furthermore, applications requiring more security could still make use of our work, but it should be complemented by additional techniques.

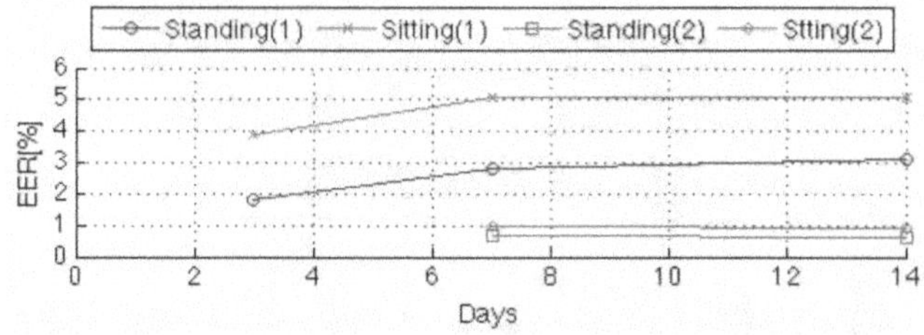

Figure 6. EER for each condition along with the number of days from the first session. The numbers in parentheses denote the numbers of sessions used to train the system. Training the system with samples from two sessions significantly improved performance.

USER STUDY #2: TWO WEEKS EVALUATION

For our second user study, we chose to investigate performance when trained with samples collected in two sessions, as well as longer-term robustness of users' gesture patterns. In this study, we only tested the hand-waving gesture because it was the most promising—it had low EERs and was well liked by users. Gestures were measured in the same manner as the first study (in two postures and 10 samples for each posture in each session). We conducted the measurements in four sessions: on the first day, three days later, one week later, and two weeks later.

We recruited 27 participants using an existing university recruiting website meant for the general public. Out of the 27 participants, 20 participants were male and 7 were female. Their ages ranged from 19 to 62 years old with a mean of 29.7. Sixteen participants were university students, four were university staff employees and seven were otherwise employed. Their average height was 173cm (SD=9.8) and their average weight was 75.1kg (SD=21.1). None of them participated the previous study. We paid $50 for completion of the study.

Performance over a Two-Week Period

Figure 6 shows how the EERs changed over time. In Figure 6, Standing (1) shows the EERs in the standing condition when samples obtained in the first session were used as a training set. According to the figure, the EERs were constant around 3% one week later and two weeks later. Similarly, in the sitting condition (i.e., Sitting (1)), the EERs were around 5.1%. The results were consistent with the results from our first study, indicating that the performance of body-based identification was stable for two weeks.

Training Classifiers with Samples from Two Sessions

The results in our first study indicated that training a SVM classifier with samples collected in different sessions would improve the performance. Standing (2) and Sitting (2) in Figure 6 show EERs obtained when the samples in the first and second session were used as a training set, and the samples in the third and fourth sessions as test sets. As we expected, the performance was improved significantly. In the standing and sitting conditions, the EERs were 0.7% and 0.9%. Furthermore, the EERs were constant in the two-weeks period. These results suggest that samples from two different dates should be enough to represent variations of

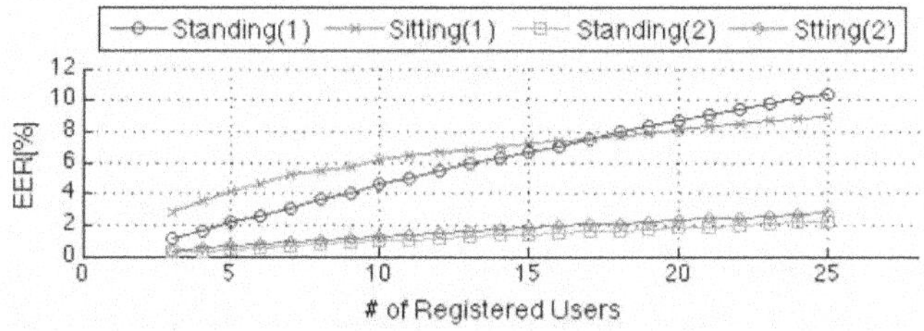

Figure 7. EER for each condition along with the number of registered users. The numbers in parentheses denote the numbers of sessions used for training. When the number of registered users increased, EERs increased almost proportionally

features, and that training SVM classifiers with samples from two dates addresses the variation in body segment length measurements and gestures effectively.

Effect of Numbers of Registered Users

As stated earlier, in this paper, we calculate EERs based on the assumption that the system has seven registered users. However, in practice, the system may have different numbers of registered users. Thus, we investigated how the number of registered users affected EERs. For each N (N=3, 4, …, 25), we randomly chose 10,000 combinations of N participants, and calculated the EERs among the combinations. The classifiers were trained using either the samples from the first session or the samples from both the first and the second sessions as training sets. We used the samples obtained in the fourth session as a test set.

Figure 7 shows the EERs for different numbers of registered users for each condition. Generally, the EERs increase proportionally to the number of registered users. When the system was trained with samples from the first session, the EERs were 10.4% and 9.0% for 25 registered users in the standing and the sitting conditions respectively. Likewise, when trained with samples from the first and the second session, the EERs were 2.3% and 2.8% respectively (N=25). These results are very encouraging. Considering that our system requires only performing a waving gesture for two seconds to identify a user among 25 registered users, the EERs less than 3% were surprisingly low.

Robustness to Partial-Body Occlusions

In our studies, participants stood or sat three meters away from the Kinect to allow our system to capture the participant's entire body. However, in practice, capturing entire bodies may be difficult—for example, if a user is too close to the Kinect or if there are objects in the room obstructing part of the camera's view.

To estimate the impact of partial-body occlusions on performance, we ran simulations with body segment length feature vectors that only included segment lengths above the spine—using joints from shoulders to hands and heads.

Figure 8 shows the EERs with simulated occlusions along with EERs without occlusions. Classifiers were trained either using samples from the first session (Standing (1) and Sitting (1)) or using samples from the first and second sessions (Standing (2) and Sitting (2)) as training sets. For both cases, samples from the fourth session were used as a test set. Figure 6 shows that the estimated effects of the partial-body occlusions are limited. On average, the EERs increase by just by 0.96% (σ=0.40%). In other words, our body-based identification system worked reliably even if lower body segments were occluded.

USER STUDY #3: FIELD STUDY

In our two lab studies, we demonstrated that the body-based identification performed well in identifying users. However, the lab studies were conducted in a well-controlled procedure (e.g., using a window-less room and controlling a distance between participants and a Kinect). To evaluate the body-based identification system in more ecologically valid situations, we conducted a field study.

We recruited five households (12 participants) by posting flyers in a local neighborhood. Out of the 12 participants, five were male and seven were female. Their age ranged from 18 to 42 years old with a mean of 33 years old. Seven participants were employed, two were students and three were unemployed. Their average height was 159.5cm (SD=11.4) and their average weight was 56.9kg (SD=6.9). None of them participated the previous studies.

This study consisted of three sessions at their homes. The three sessions took place on different days in a week depending on participants' availabilities. The gaps between sessions were not controlled because the results of the study #2 indicated that days from registration had limited impact on the performance. However, successive sessions had at least one-day gap between them to have some distractions between sessions.

For each session, we collected data in their living rooms. We put a Microsoft Kinect on their TVs and asked participants to perform waving gestures in front of the TVs as if they were interacting with the TVs. All living rooms had windows to outside, and room lights were kept as the participants configured prior to our visits. This gave us a variety of infrared and visible light conditions.

We collected 10 hand-waving gestures in two postures, just as in our second study. In the standing posture, participants were asked to stand in positions where they felt confortable,

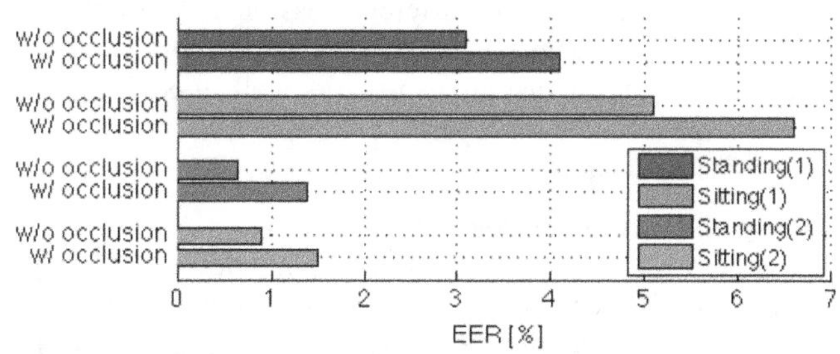

Figure 8. We simulated occlusions by using body part locations only above spines. On average, the EERs became only 0.74% higher.

assuming that they would be interacting with the TVs using gestures. All participants stood two to three meters away from TVs facing to them. In the sitting posture, we asked participants to sit as they usually did in their living room. Eight participants sat on couches, two sat on chairs, and two sat on cushions placed on the floor. After the third session, the participants were asked to fill a post-survey followed by brief interviews based on their responses to the survey. The first and the second session took about 15 minutes, and the third session took about 45 minutes to complete. We paid $40 for completion of the study.

As we anticipated, we observed partial-body occlusions in the subset of samples. The occlusion occurred in the samples from six participants in the sitting posture. For those samples, tables placed between TVs and participants occluded participants' legs. We used classifiers trained with body segment lengths above the spine, as we did in the simulation of partial-body occlusion, to perform user identification with these samples.

In the less controlled study design described above, we collected samples with natural variations in participants' postures, orientations and distances between a Kinect in addition to light condition changes and some occlusions.

User Identification

We trained classifiers for each posture either using samples from the first session, or from the first and the second sessions. Each classifier was tested with samples collected in the third session (Figure 9). When the first session was used as a training set, the EERs of the standing and sitting posture were 3.4% and 5.3% respectively. The EER values were close to the result in the second study (3.8% and 5.1%). When we trained the SVM classifiers with the first and second sessions, the EERs were 0.5% and 1.6% for the standing and the sitting posture respectively, which were also comparable to results (0.9% and 1.0%) in the study #2.

During the study, we noticed that the participants' sitting posture varied more than we observed in our lab studies. We suspect that the participants in this study were more relaxed than ones in the lab study because this study was conducted in their living rooms. However, the EERs remained almost same as ones from the lab studies. This finding offers additional support that we can compensate the variations in the features by training the system with samples obtained in two different sessions. Additionally, the results obtained in this field study show that the body-based identification system also works well in ecologically valid situations with partial body occlusions and environmental changes.

Survey and Interview Results

In the survey, we asked questions about how well body-based identification could be used in practice. First, we asked how many people they would want to register to this system, and who those people would be. They answered that, on average, they wanted to register 5.2 users (SD=1.1).

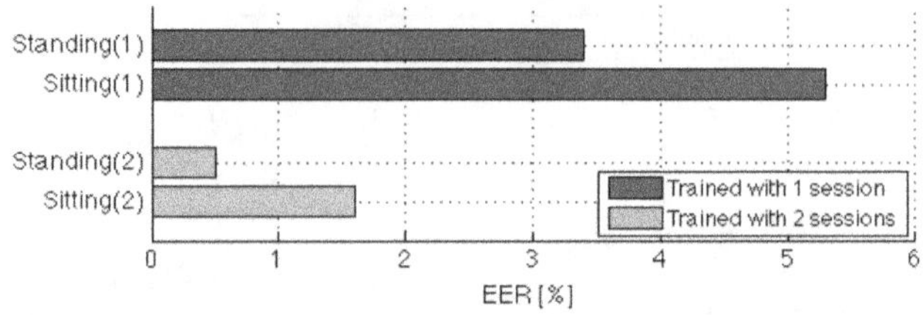

Figure 9. EERs obtained in a field study. Overall, the EERs remained similar to the results in the study #2 showing robustness of the system to environmental changes.

Most of the users were people they were living with (e.g., family members and roommates). Four participants mentioned that they wanted to register one or two friends who visited their home frequently. These responses validate our assumption of having roughly seven registered users, as assumption we made in calculating EERs.

We then asked participants to rate the statement "I will use body-based identification system if it is available on home electric appliances such as TVs" using a five-point Likert scale (1=strongly disagree and 5=strongly agree). Participants responded they agreed with the sentence with a median of 4.0. Although we have to be careful of possible novelty effect, these ratings are encouraging.

We further asked participants for what purposes they wanted to use the body-based identification. Five participants mentioned parental controls. P1 said, "I want control what my child can do with electric appliances such as TVs. They quickly learn how to use remotes. So, it's difficult to stop them using a TV. But, if the TV checks [users'] heights, it will be easy." Two participants mentioned personalization as a potential use case. P5 commented, "If a TV automatically turns on and shows a TV program that I regularly watch when I wave to it, that would be great. I don't need to search a remote." P7 noted, "If I have a wall display, and I can check personalized information such as today's schedule, subjects of received emails, local weather by waving to it in a busy morning, that would be useful." Although these responses were speculative, they indicate that participants saw value for body-based identification in practical situations.

We also asked participants to rate the statement, "It is acceptable that the body-based identification system requires two sessions of data (20 waving gestures for one posture) to register a user" using a 5-point Likert scale. Participants generally agreed with the sentence with a median of 4. Two participants chose strongly agree, eight chose agree, and two chose disagree. P2 commented, "Registration happens only once. So, I don't care. Once I'm registered, it's pretty quick." On the other hand, P9 said, "Doing 10 waving [gestures] would be OK. But, it's troublesome if I need to do more than that." These responses are encouraging because the current un-optimized training process was acceptable for the majority of participants. However, further investigation would be necessary to shorten the process.

LIMITATIONS

While our results are encouraging, there are a few caveats to our findings that represent fruitful opportunities for future work. In our user studies, we did not provide feedback about user identification results to avoid biasing users. However, for real deployments, the system should provide feedback, which would affect how users perform gestures. Some users may consciously reproduce their individual gesture patterns; moreover, some may game the system by registering distinct waving patterns to be easily identified. Investigation of these user behaviors could be interesting follow-up research.

Furthermore, in the second study, two weeks may not be long enough to evaluate the long-term robustness of the system. In the third study, we collected data at participants' living rooms; however, it was not a field deployment (e.g., we still have sessions). As a result, participants' responses to our survey were speculative. A longitudinal deployment of a body-based identification will provide further insight into these issues.

Finally, we do not claim that the features we use and the models we employ are optimal. Our system performed reasonably well using a simple model and feature set, but it would be possible to further optimize performance using other interesting features and models.

DISCUSSION

While our body-based identification was reasonably accurate, there is still a room for improvement. One opportunity is to improve the precision of the body segment length measurements. We found that, within the same session, body segment lengths were reliable, but were unreliable across sessions. We suspected that this would be primarily because participants' clothing changed between sessions. Because we did not control participants' clothing, we think our results reflect variations caused by different clothing. Moreover, in the second study, there were two participants wearing baggy clothing; however, it did not affect our system's performance. While these indicate that real-time joint extraction in the Kinect SDK is reasonably robust, more computationally expensive processing could yields better results in user identification.

Additionally, we found that the performance of body-based identification depends on consistency in postures. However, in practice, it would be ideal for body-based identification to be reliable regardless of the posture variations. Our results offer some hints in this vein. Specifically, we found that removing some body segment lengths from the body segment length feature vector did not significantly affect performance. Consequently, we could omit body segment lengths that have imprecise readings in different postures to stabilize performance across postures.

Similarly, users' orientations to a Kinect could affect performance. A Kinect extracts the three-dimensional position of users' joints. Thus, theoretically, body-based identification should be robust to changes in relative orientations between a user and a Kinect. Moreover, in the use cases where a Kinect is placed near the device that users interact with (e.g., in our third study), users naturally face to the Kinect. Thus, the orientations would be less of an issue. In contrast, in the use cases where we put a Kinect in a room and users interact with devices placed at many different positions in the room, users are unlikely to face to the Kinect. As a result, users' bodies could occlude their gestures and/or body lengths measurements could become less robust. Further investigation would be necessary for these use cases.

Furthermore, the registration process could be improved. In our analyses, we trained the system using 20 samples collected on two different days for each standing and sitting postures. Although, in our field study, majority of participants reported that it was acceptable, requiring data from two sessions could pose challenges in practice.

It is also possible to improve the user identification algorithm. One possible approach is to build models that represent how the feature values measured for the same user could vary. We did build such models and found that they did not perform well (not reported in this paper due to space constraints). However, we still believe that there are opportunities in this direction. Another approach would be to build a layered classifier combining other factors amenable to natural user interfaces, such as face recognition, to improve the overall performance of user identification. An upper layer classifier can use predictions from lower layer classifiers, such as body-based identification, face recognition and voice recognition to perform combined user identification. As we demonstrated, using multiple factors has great potential in improving overall performance in user identification.

One interesting implication for gesture-based interfaces would be the usefulness of recognizing both gestures and users' identities. Currently, gesture-based interface systems recognize what gesture users are performing. Then, the systems execute the same commands regardless of users performing the gestures (e.g., when a TV recognizes a user performing hand waving, the TV turns on). However, if a system can recognize both gestures *and* users' identifies, the system can personalize execution of the commands (e.g., turning on a TV *and* showing program that a specific user prefers). The first lab study suggested that users also could be identified when performing other gestures. This could be an interesting direction for future research.

CONCLUSION

We proposed body-based user identification: a new form of user identification based on the body segment lengths and a hand-waving gesture. We evaluate the system through two lab studies and one field study consisting of 8,640 samples from 75 users in total. Our first lab study explored the basic feasibility of the system, in terms of properties of body segment length and four different gestures. Based on the results, we chose a hand waving gesture as the most promising gesture to be used in subsequent studies.

Our second lab study showed the robustness of our system over a two-week period, as well as robustness to partial body occlusions. Our study also showed that training the system using samples collected on two different days effectively addresses the variations in the body segment length measurements and hand-waving measurements. The EERs improved from 3.0% to 0.7% when trained with samples collected on two different days compared to when trained with samples collected on a day.

Finally, our field study demonstrated that our proposed system worked well in ecologically valid situations, in terms of different environments and partial occlusions. Our system achieved an equal error rate ranging from 0.5 to 1.6% when trained with samples from two sessions.

Given our encouraging results, we believe that this paper makes a first step toward the vision of more natural and usable user identification seamlessly integrated with gesture-based interfaces.

REFERENCES

1. BioLab University of Bologna. Finger Print Verification Competition. Retrieved Sep. 13, 2013. https://biolab.csr.unibo.it/fvcongoing/UI/Form/IJCB2011.aspx
2. Douglas Gantenbein. Helping Kinect Recognize Faces. Retrieved Sep. 13, 2013. http://research.microsoft.com/en-us/news/features/kinectfacereco-103111.aspx
3. Microsoft. Kinect for Windows SDK. Retrieved Sep. 13, 2013. http://msdn.microsoft.com/enus/library/hh855347
4. Corlett N.E., and Clark S.T. 1995. The Ergonomics of Wrokspaces and Machines: A Design Manual. CRC Press. 1995.
5. Gafurov, D. A Survey of Biometric Gait Recognition: Approaches, Security and Challenges, *NIK-2007 Conference*. 2007.
6. Guillaume,H., and Sébastien M. A novel statistical generative model dedicated to face recognition. Image and Vision Computing. vol. 28, Issue 1, 2010, 101-110.
7. Jain, A., Nandakumar, K., and Ross, A. Score normalization in multimodal biometric systems, Pattern Recognition, vol. 38, Issue 12, 2005, 2270-2285.
8. Jain, A., Bolle, M.R., and Pankanti, S. Biometrics: Personal Identification in Networked Society. Springer. 2005.
9. Jiayang, L., Lin, Z., Jehan, W., and Venu V. User evaluation of lightweight user authentication with a single tri-axis accelerometer. In *Proc. of MobileHCI*. 2009.
10. Kam L., Konrad, J., Ishwar, P., Towards Gesture-Based User Authentication, *Advanced Video and Signal-Based Surveillance,* 2012, 282-287.
11. Leyvand, T., Meekhof, C., Wei, Y., Sun, J. and Guo, B. Kinect identity: Technology and experience. IEEE Computer Society. Computer Magaznine, April, 2011, 94–96.
12. Cranor L. F. and Garfinkel S. Security and Usability Designing Secure System That People Can Use. O'Reilly Media. 2005.
13. Mäntyjärvi, J., Lindholm, M., Vildjiounaite, E., Makela, S.M., and Ailisto, H. Identifying users of portable devices from gait pattern with accelerometers. In *Proc. of ICASSP*. vol. 2, 2005, 973-976.
14. Maltoni, D., Maio, D., Jain, K.A., and Prabhakar, S. 2005. Handbook of Fingerprint Recognition. Springer.
15. Maurer, M. E., Waxenberger, R., and Hausen, D. BroAuth: evaluating different levels of visual feedback for 3D gesture-based authentication. In *Proc. of the International Working Conference on Advanced Visual Interfaces*. 2012, 737-740.
16. Mayrhofer, R. and Gellersen, H. Shake well before use: two implementations for implicit context authentication. *IEEE Transactions on Mobile Computing*, vol.8, no.6, 2009, 792-806.
17. Napa, S.B., Kowsar, A., Katherine, I., and Nasir, M. Biometric-rich gestures: a novel approach to authentication on multi-touch devices. In *Proc. of SIGCHI*. 2012, 977-986.
18. Patel, S.N., Pierce, J.S., and Abowd, G.D. A gesture-based authentication scheme for untrusted public terminals. In *Proc. of UIST* , 2004, 157–160.
19. Peacock, A., Ke, X., and Wilkerson, M. Typing patterns: A key to user identification. IEEE Security and Privacy, vol. 2, Issue 5, 2004, 40-47.
20. Pheasant, S., and Haslegrave, M.C. Bodyspace: Authropometry, Ergonomics and the Design of Work. CRC Press. 2005.
21. Schmidt, D., Chong, M.K., and Gellersen, H. HandsDown: hand-contour-based user identification for interactive surfaces. In *Proc. of NordiCHI*, 2010, 432–441.
22. Snelick, R., Uludag, U., Mink, A., Indovina, M., and Jain, A. Large-scale evaluation of multimodal biometric authentication using state-of-the-art systems. *IEEE Transactions on Pattern Analysis and Machine Intelligence,* vol.27, no.3, 2005, 450-455.
23. Tian, J., Qu, C., Xu, W., and Wang, S. KinWrite: Handwriting-Based Authentication Using Kinect. In *Proc. of* Annual Network & Distributed System Security Symposium, 2013.
24. Wan, V., and Renals, S. Speaker verification using sequence discriminant support vector machines. *IEEE Transactions on Speech and Audio Processing.* vol.13, no.2, 2005, 203- 210

Haptic Turk: a Motion Platform Based on People

Lung-Pan Cheng, Patrick Lühne, Pedro Lopes, Christoph Sterz, and Patrick Baudisch
Hasso Plattner Institute, Potsdam, Germany
{firstname.lastname}@hpi.uni-potsdam.de

ABSTRACT

Motion platforms are used to increase the realism of virtual interaction. Unfortunately, their size and weight is proportional to the size of what they actuate. We present *haptic turk,* a different approach to motion platforms that is light and mobile. The key idea is to replace motors and mechanical components with humans. All haptic turk setups consist of a *player* who is supported by one or more *human-actuators*. The player enjoys an interactive experience, such as a flight simulation. The motion in the player's experience is generated by the actuators who manually lift, tilt, and push the player's limbs or torso. To get the timing and force right, timed motion instructions in a format familiar from rhythm games are displayed on actuators' mobile devices, which they attach to the player's body. We demonstrate a range of installations based on mobile phones, projectors, and head-mounted displays. In our user study, participants rated not only the experience as player as enjoyable (6.1/7), but also the experience as an actuator (4.4/7). The approach of leveraging humans allows us to deploy our approach anytime anywhere, as we demonstrate by deploying at an art festival in the Nevada desert.

Author Keywords

Haptics; force-feedback; motion platform; immersion.

ACM Classification Keywords

H5.2 [Information interfaces and presentation]: User Interfaces. - Graphical user interfaces.

INTRODUCTION

For a long time, the key to immersion in interactive experience and games was sought in photorealistic graphics [8]. More recently, game makers made games more immersive by requiring players to physically enact the game such as with Wii (http://wii.com) and Kinect [26]. With graphics and user interaction now part of many games, many researchers argue that *haptics and motion* are the next step towards increasing immersion and realism, i.e., applying the forces triggered by the game onto the player's body during the experience.

While some game events can be realistically rendered using one or more vibrotactile actuators (e.g., driving over gravel in a racing game [14]), a much larger number of gaming events result in *directional* forces, such as centrifugal forces pulling at a steering wheel or a car bumping into the railing. Such events have been simulated using motion platforms [27]. Motion platforms are able to move one or more users around and have been used to add realism to flight simulators [22] and theme park rides.

Unfortunately, the size and weight of motion platforms tends to be proportional to what they actuate. As a result, motion platforms not only tend to be prohibitively expensive, but also large and heavy and thus stationary, limiting their use to arcades and lab environments.

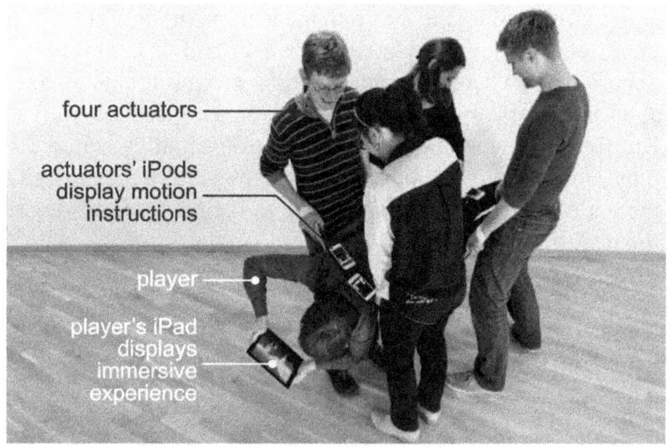

Figure 1: Haptic turk allows producing motion experiences anywhere anytime. Here, the suspended player is enjoying an immersive hang gliding game. The four *actuators* create just the right physical motion to fill in the player's experience.

In this paper, we present *haptic turk,* a software platform that allows experiencing motion anywhere there is people. Its key idea is to substitute the motors and mechanical components of traditional motion platforms with humans.

HAPTIC TURK

Haptic turk is a motion platform based on people. The name is inspired by the 18th century chess automaton "The Turk" [20] that was powered by a human chess master.

The specific configuration shown in Figure 1 involves one *player* located in the center. The player is enjoying an immersive experience, here a first-person simulation of flying a hang-glider, running on a hand-held device (iPad). In the shown setup, the player can steer the hang-glider by tilting the iPad.

The main difference to regular video games is that the player's experience comes with *motion*—this motion is administered by *human-actuators* who *manually* lift, tilt, and push the player around. Here there are four of them.

To get the timing and force right, all actuators receive timed motion instructions in a format familiar from rhythm games (see Figure 3 for a preview). In the set-up shown in Figure 1, actuators receive these motion instructions on

CHI 2014, April 26–May 1, 2014, Toronto, Ontario, Canada.
Copyright ©ACM 978-1-4503-2473-1/14/04...$15.00.
http://dx.doi.org/10.1145/2556288.2557101

their mobile devices (here iPods and iPhones) that they have attached to the player's body.

During the experience, actuators execute the motion instructions displayed on their respective device by moving the part of the player's body assigned to them. At the moment shown in Figure 1, for example, the two actuators left of the player lift up their side of the player, causing the player to be rotated ("rolled") towards the camera.

Haptic turk generates these motion instructions so as to feed into the player's experience. As actuators perform their motion instructions, they therefore contribute to the *player's* experience, making it richer and more immersive.

A haptic turk experience *may* incentivize actuators to perform their best by measuring and scoring how well they match their motion instructions in terms of timing, position, and force—using the inertial measurement unit (IMU) in their mobile device. However, we obtain a better player experience by scoring actuators as a group, as this encourages actuators to synchronize during cooperative moves. But finally, several participants in our user study stated that they simply enjoyed supporting the player, suggesting that the act of providing an experience to the player provides all the necessary incentive.

WALKTHROUGH

We now illustrate the haptic turk platform at the example of the specific configuration from Figure 1 (four actuators with mobile devices) and a hang glider experience we call *team flight*. The actual experience takes three minutes and contains 14 motion event groups (25 individual actuator movements overall). We present selected scenes that allow us to illustrate the design elements.

Figure 2: The *team flight* hang glider experience has started: The actuator display is blank, actuators are relaxed.

As illustrated by Figure 2, the experience starts out in calm weather and the player's hang glider is in a neutral, horizontal position. Accordingly, the *actuator displays* are blank. This instructs all actuators to stand upright, relaxed, shoulders dropped—a position that actuators can sustain with minimum effort. We design our experiences to bring actuators back to this position frequently to avoid fatigue. Note that the actuator displays show the timelines of *all* actuators so as the help actuators see "the big picture" and to synchronize their actions.

Up/down-bars: The player is approaching a big fan located on the right and the hang glider is about to get caught by the fan's draft. Haptic turk reflects this by rendering *up/down* motion instructions. The bars enter the actuator display from below and travel up the screen as the hang glider is approaching the fan (Figure 3a). This leverages the visual language of, for example, *dance dance revolution* (www.konami.com/ddr). As the bars reach the actuators' *bullseyes* at the top of the screen, the respective actuators execute the instructions. Motion instructions take about seven seconds to reach the bullseye. This is essential as it allows actuators to get ready so as to perform their motion *on time,* i.e., in sync with the player's experience.

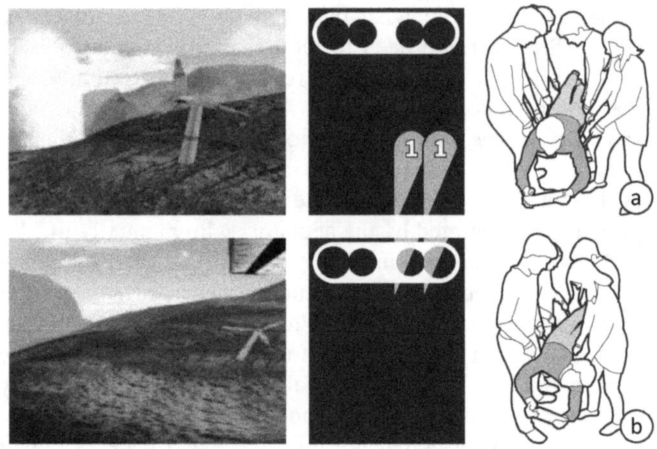

Figure 3: (a) The player is about to get caught by the draft of a fan "lift to +1" motion instructions appear, and (b) are executed as they reach the actuator's bullseyes.

The shown up/down bars in the two right columns reach the bullseye exactly at the moment the player enters the draft of the fan. The up/down bars are labeled "1"; the two actuators right of the player therefore lift their side of the player to position "1", which is waist height. This causes the player to be rotated or "rolled" to the left, as the player's hang glider is pushed sideways by the fan.

The two up/down bars have round heads, which demands actuators to move up *abruptly*, right at the moment the round head fills the round bullseye. Actuators continue to hold the player at +1 height, then return *smoothly* to the relaxed position, as demanded by the bars' diagonal tails.

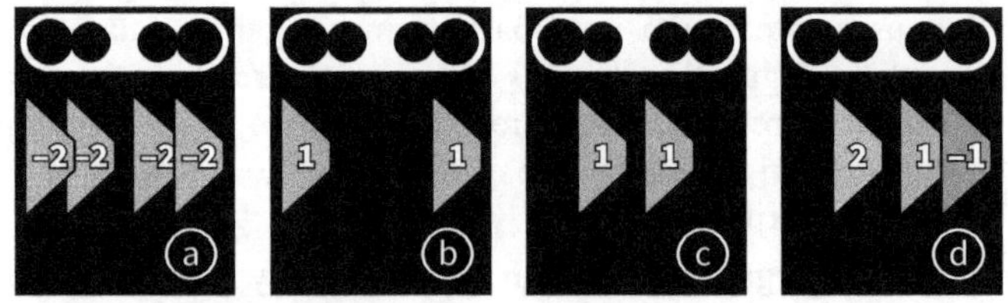

Figure 4: Up/down bar representations for (a) drop, (b) face down tilt, (c) face up tilt, and (d) up-left tilt-roll.

Up/down bars are haptic turk's most versatile design element and they are used to render the vast majority of motion events. As shown in Figure 4, up/down bars come with values from -2 to +2, with +2 'chest level', +1 'waist level', *blank* 'relaxed', -1 'knee level', and -2 'foot level'. Redundant color-coding makes the display more glanceable (sun orange means up; grass green means down). The main idea behind up/down bars is that they show actuators exactly what to do, yet, with experience, allow them to see the big picture.

Large movements & anticipation: Figure 5 shows how haptic turk performs a large motion event. Here the player enters a tornado, which causes the player's hang glider to shoot up into the air. Haptic turk renders this by instructing all four actuators to abruptly lift the player to '+2' the chest level. To make the player's experience even more intense, haptic turk instructs actuators to first lower the player slightly in anticipation *and then* to perform the vertical '+2' move.

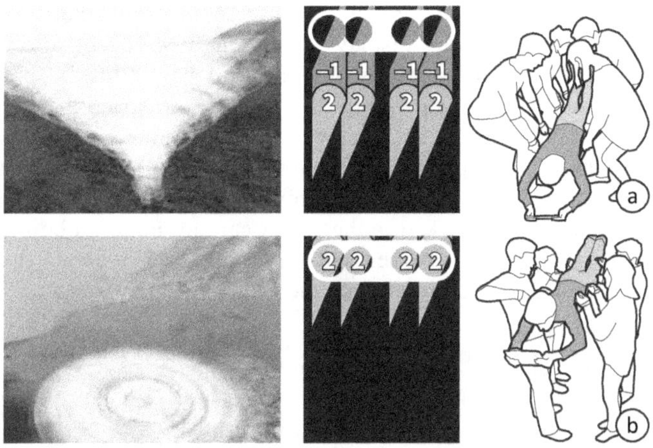

Figure 5: Right before the player enters the tornado, haptic turk lets players anticipate the move by lowering the player.

Collisions: In Figure 6, the player's hang glider collides with an object, here a blimp approaching from the left. Haptic turk renders the event as a pair of "bump" instructions on the left. As the bump events reach the bullseyes, the left two actuators bump the player using their thighs.

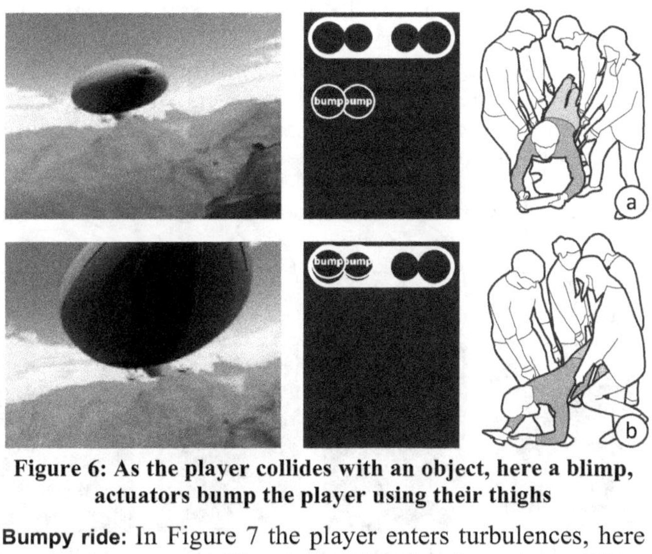

Figure 6: As the player collides with an object, here a blimp, actuators bump the player using their thighs

Bumpy ride: In Figure 7 the player enters turbulences, here created by a group of fans pointed at the player from different directions. Haptic turk responds by creating 'shake' instructions for all actuators, which each actuator executes as an unsynchronized vertical shake.

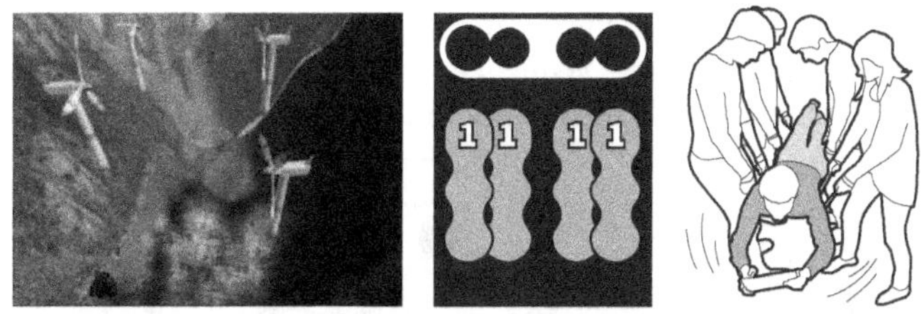

Figure 7: The fans cause an unsynchronized vertical shake

Horizontal motion: In Figure 8, the player is entering the field of a *very* powerful fan that propels the glider quickly out over the desert. Haptic turk emphasizes the onset of this movement with a horizontal move event, which actuators execute by taking a step into the specified direction. After all, the shown implementation of haptic turk is *mobile*, allowing actuators to walk around during the experience.

Figure 8: This fan produces a strong wind that shoots the player off horizontally, rendered as *horizontal* motion

Special effects: The concept of haptic turk is broader than just motion. Figure 9 shows two effects that we have explored, i.e., water and heat. They are administered by an additional "special effects" actuator.

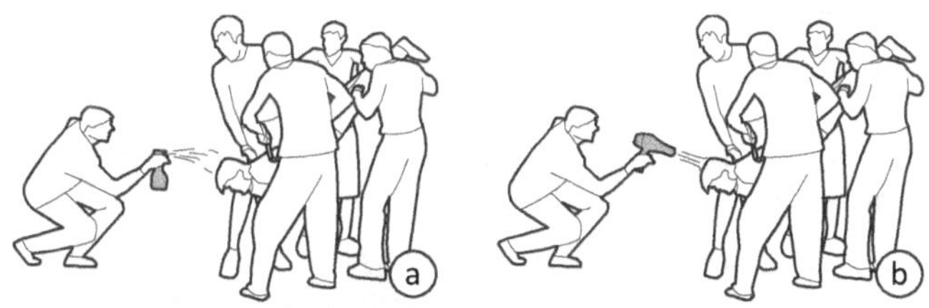

Figure 9: This *special effects actuator* (a) sprays water at the player as the player enters a waterfall and (b) uses a hair dryer to emulate a hot breeze, as the player crosses over into the desert terrain in Figure 8.

Landing: Finally, the player has reached the destination: a temple in the middle of the desert. As the player approaches the ground, haptic turk generates landing instructions, as shown in Figure 10.

Figure 10: To land the player, the front actuators whip up the player to +2, while the back two set down the player's feet.

These were all simple scenes, taken from an experience designed to be calm and serene, as one would expect a hang-glider experience to be. Figure 11 shows a more action packed game sequence we created—note how the actuator display now handles multiple actions at once.

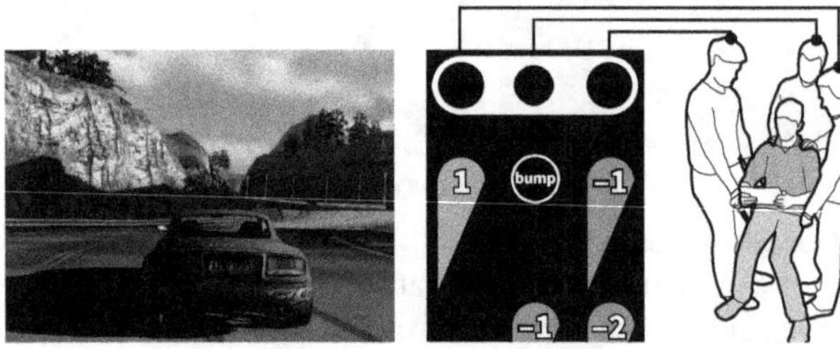

Figure 11: More action-packed games, such as our car racing game contains faster sequences of motion instruction. (This experience is administered by 3 actuators, thus 3 timelines)

GETTING THE TIMING RIGHT: PREEMPTIVE WARNING

The main technical challenge behind haptic turk is to get the timing right, i.e., to make sure that actuators provide force exactly at the moment required by the player's experience. This is a challenge because actuators' are inherently subject to human response time and thus delay. The mean response time for humans to react to a simple visual stimulus is 220ms [17], to which we add network delay and human movement. This duration is substantially longer than the 50ms humans tolerate in delayed haptic feedback [15].

For pose changes, we found this delay to not cause too much of an issue as long as we simulate a vehicle that moves *smoothly*. Hang gliders, for example, change their position only gradually in response to their pilots shifting their weight around. Here, haptic turk simply displays a preview of the expected goal pose as soon as the player starts to steer; this gives actuators ample time.

The true challenge comes from instantaneous events, such as the forces resulting from a user colliding with an object. Haptic turk addresses this challenge with two approaches.

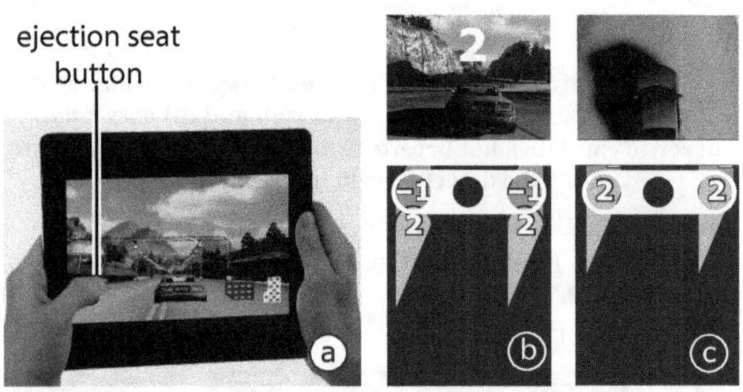

Figure 12: Delaying a game event using a countdown: (a) In response to the player pressing the 'eject' button, (b) haptic turk renders up/down bar. (c) When the countdown runs down, the actuators eject the player—well prepared.

#1: Countdown events. Haptic turk cannot speed actuators up, but it can slow reality down—by adding a countdown. We use this approach for all player actions where precision matters, either because they result in a high force or because that are performed by multiple actuators in synchrony. The ejection seat button in the racecar of our racing game, for example, uses a three-second countdown before it fires. The countdown not only adds drama to the game, but, more importantly allows haptic turk to give actuators advance warning. This is essential, as it allows actuators to throw the player up in the air in synchrony.

Only certain game events can plausibly be fitted with a countdown. For other events, such as those resulting from physical collisions, haptic turk creates timely responses through "anticipation".

#2: Anticipate collisions. Rather than waiting for the collision to happen, haptic turk continuously checks for the *possibility* of an upcoming collision. Whenever, a collision is likely, haptic turk displays a *possible bump* event, allowing actuators to get ready. We call this haptic turk's "presponse" mechanism. Haptic turk probes the space the user is likely to reach in the next seconds using *probe lines* (Figure 13, inspired by imaginary reality games [2]). In team flight, for example, we send probe lines forward, as this is the only direction the glider can go. Each probe line is as long as the player can travel in the 7 seconds that actuator displays project into the future.

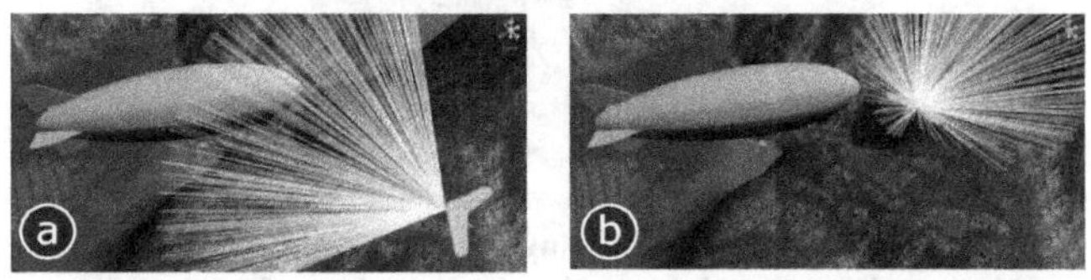

Figure 13: (a) Haptic turk's debug view: the hang glider on the bottom right continuously sends out probe lines (~1000 on a MacBook Pro). Here some of them detect a blimp (shown in red). (b) As the player turns right to avoid the blimp, no more probe lines are reaching the blimp.

At every frame, haptic turk counts how many probe lines predict a collision. If a collision seems likely (>30%) haptic turk injects a motion event into the actuator displays (Figure 14a). It renders the motion instruction's opacity so as to reflect the probability of the event, so 70% opacity represents a 70% probability. Haptic turk then continuously updates the actuator display.

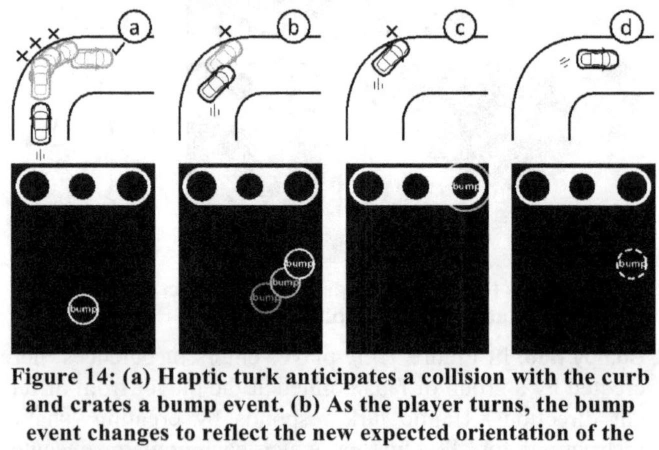

Figure 14: (a) Haptic turk anticipates a collision with the curb and crates a bump event. (b) As the player turns, the bump event changes to reflect the new expected orientation of the bump. (c) If the car stays the course, the collision takes place. Otherwise, (d) the bump event dissolves.

As the player navigates, the expected collision time tend to change. The motion instructions may thus speed up if the player steers into the obstacle or they may slow down if the player turns to hit the obstacle more tangentially. At the same time, the expected collision probability and thus the opacity of the motion instructions will vary. If the probability ever drops below a threshold (<15%), haptic turk removes the bump instruction—a "false alarm".

To enable probe lines, all the in-game objects have their own "colliders" and corresponding motion instruction. The tornado in the hang gliding game, for example, has a cylindrical collider. Probing it triggers the -1/+2 up/down bars shown earlier.

ONE PLATFORM, MANY CONFIGURATIONS

The haptic turk software is a general-purpose platform for creating motion experiences based on people. In the examples shown above, we used one particular hardware set-up based on mobile devices, one for each actuator. This installation was designed with ubiquitous use in mind in that it only requires devices that users are likely to carry with themselves at all times. In the following, we show other hardware configurations we have explored.

Display/sensing configurations

Figure 15a shows another mobile set-up. It reduces hardware requirements further by running on two iPads—one for the player and a single shared iPad for the actuators.

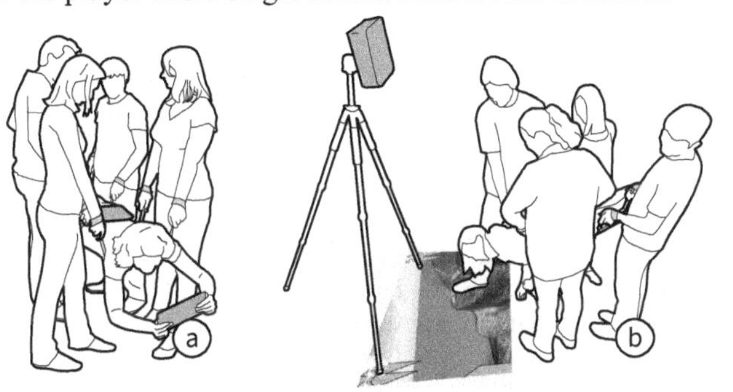

Figure 15: (a) Haptic Turk running on two iPads (b) The walk-up installation, designed for museums etc., is designed to minimize per-user start-up time. This version integrates player and actuator display into a single projection.

Figure 15b shows one of our *walk-up* installations designed for use at tradeshows, museum exhibits, and art shows. Walk-up installations do not require participants to bring anything and we designed them to minimize per-player set-up time. The shown version integrates player display and actuator display and projects onto the floor. This version allows players to control the game using a simulated delta, which we implemented by attaching an iPod to a bar.

We also combined our walk-up installation with a head-mounted display (*Oculus Rift,* http://oculusvr.com) as shown in Figure 16. It allows users to look around in the virtual environment. As the head mounted display is closing out reality, it delivers a higher level of immersion than any of the other installations. We deployed this version at Burning Man 2013 (see section "Deployment", Figure 25).

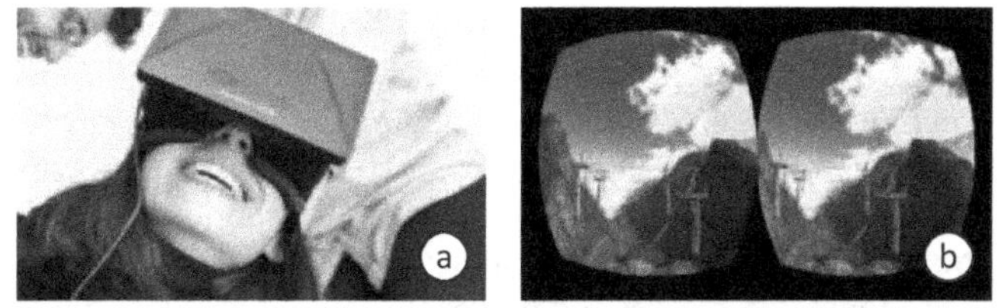

Figure 16: This installation uses a head-mounted display for the player experience (and projection as actuator display).

Finally, we may record haptic turk experiences and share them as "haptic turk movies". People downloading the movie may then render the experience on any installation they have access to. While this could be done by using any video format that allows for timed annotations (e.g., mpeg 7), we feel that the most effective format is to overlay the actuator instructions directly onto the video stream (as in Figure 15b). This allows us to share on *any* medium that transports video, including web pages, file sharing services, and YouTube.

Mechanical configurations

All designs shown so far use four actuators to keep the player suspended. We initially had actuators hold the player directly (Figure 20), but then added the *slingshots* shown in Figure 17 to reduce actuator fatigue, increase player safety, and to soften potential proxemics issues. The shown design we made from the seat cushions of foldable chairs (*Folding stool Stockholm II* by *Lectus*), curtain bars, and linen ribbon. Slingshots can be rolled up to carry.

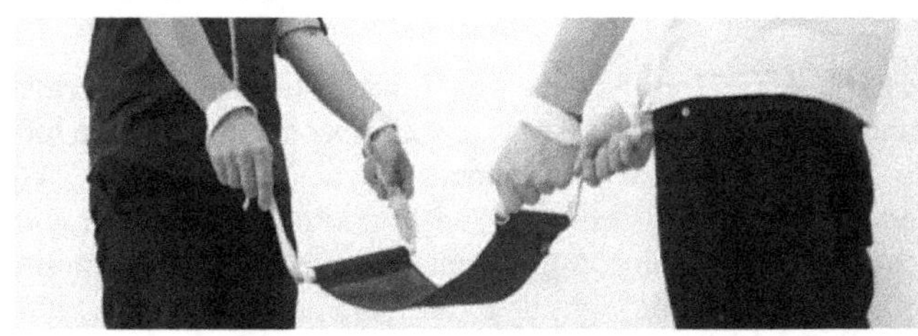

Figure 17: We made these custom *slingshots* to reduce actuator fatigues, increase player safety, and soften proxemics.

Figure 18 shows some of the alternative mechanical configurations we have explored. The shown designs (a, b, c) allow three experiences that require an upright player pose, such as car racing, (b, c, d) provide additional physical support to the player, thereby reducing actuator fatigue. They allow playing with fewer actuators and/or people with a wider range of physical abilities.

Figure 18: Haptic Turk configurations: (a) racing game based on two actuators, (b) chair and (c) swing allow for single-actuator use, and (d) in swimming pool.

Actuator interfaces

The actuator interface presented earlier in the "walkthrough" section was the result of a series of iterations. Figure 19 shows two earlier designs for context. Our initial "level and arrows" design (Figure 19a) caused split attention, but most of all it caused ergonomic issues: Since this display style only indicated the desired player tilt, but no absolute height, actuators tended to spend most of their time in non-neutral postures, resulting in substantial fatigue.

We consequently switched to a model that instructed actuators using a notion of absolute height (Figure 19b). The 2x2 layout also showed the actuator instructions of up to four actuators, allowing actuators to better synchronize.

Figure 19: Earlier versions of the actuator interface: (a) Initial version based on the metaphor of a two-dimensional level. Only for bumping events did we use the time-line metaphor. (b) This second helped us get actuators into the neutral position, thus improved actuator ergonomics. (c) The current actuator interface. The thick bullseye highlights the actuator's timeline.

The interface, however, was limited in that it provided actuators with too little preview of upcoming events, which is a truly essential requirement for actuator displays. We addressed this by lining up the four timelines at the top of the display and unifying all instructions to fit the timeline format—which brought us to the version shown throughout this paper (Figure 19c). It performed very well throughout studies and deployment.

CONTRIBUTION & BENEFITS

The main contribution of this paper is a new mechanism for creating a motion platform—based on humans. We present user interfaces and a system of motion instructions, three display and four mechanical configurations, interactive experiences, and two approaches to address lag.

The main benefit of our approach is *ubiquitous availability*. (1) *Instantaneous:* Since the underlying units—people—are incredibly flexible, users may obtain new experiences simply by downloading them from a network "into the actuators". This means that the actuators that formed a hang glider a second ago may now serve as a car or battle robot. This way, haptic turk reduces the sharing of motion experiences to the sharing of data files. (2) *Available:* Haptic turk runs on equipment that is orders of magnitude cheaper and more space-efficient than the technical equipment it emulates. In particular, the mobile versions of haptic turk could potentially reach millions of users by leveraging the existing install base of mobile devices. (3) *Everywhere:* We have deployed haptic turk not only in the lab and the student cafeteria but also at a desert festival, i.e., a hostile environment that would make it hard to deploy an actual motion platform. A single person was able to bring the equipment on the plane.

LIMITATIONS

Limitations of our approach include that it requires multiple people, is tiring, and that human actuators cannot rival a computerized motion platform in terms of responsiveness and reliability. In particular, a real time unpredictable event is difficult to handle in our current system. For example, if players controlling a racing game swerve and hit a wall, this hit is difficult to predict. This makes the event difficult to haptically render by our system, as it does not leave enough time to properly prepare actuators for their action. Haptic turk runs in to similar issues if *multiple* events become possible at a given moment.

In addition, there are all the risks that come with motion equipment in the first place, such as motion sickness and the risk of injury. The approach may also raise proxemics considerations, the extent of which should be expected to vary across cultures. We address some of these issues with the design of slingshots that reduce actuator fatigue, increase player safety, and soften proxemics issues, but these are certainly only a partial solution.

In exchange to the proxemics issues, haptic turk delivers not only force feedback, but also a human-to-human experience that lets people interact in a new way. While we initially expected that competing to win the rhythm game would be the main incentive for actuators, the physical activity itself and, in particular, the social nature of the setup turned out to be the main driving force that made people participate in studies and experimental deployment.

RELATED WORK

The work presented in this paper is related to interaction concepts, such as Wizard of Oz as well as motion platforms.

Wizard of Oz and Crowdsourcing

Haptic Turk shares some characteristics with Wizard of Oz systems, such as the aforementioned Turk [18]. Researchers use the wizard of oz method to speed up prototyping [6] and to give users new experiences [7].

Haptic Turk is different from crowdsourcing, such as Amazon's Mechanical Turk (www.mturk.com/mturk), which focus on *recruiting* workers. However, haptic turk could use crowdsourcing platform such as TaskRabbit (www.taskrabbit.com), CommunitySourcing [13] and Friendsourcing [3] to help recruit actuators.

Motion Platforms, Exoskeletons & Mobile Haptics

A wide variety of force feedback devices have been used to enhance the realism of virtual reality interactions including virtual object manipulation and motion simulation [18].

Motion simulators simulate motion by shaking, lifting or tilting players or groups of player sitting or standing on them. They are intensively used in driving and flight simulation for both training and entertainment purposes [22].

Most of them are based on a Stewart platform [27], which has six degrees of freedom driven by six hydraulic cylinders as actuators.

HapSeat [5] achieves motion simulation with lower cost and a more compact form factor by actuating the user's head and hands. The fact that users perceive motion mainly using their visual, auditory, vestibular, and kinesthetic systems [4,10] allows this project to limit actuation to arm- and headrests.

Researchers also showed that vibrotactile feedback may generate the illusion of self-motion [25]. Tactile Brush [14] uses this haptic illusion and renders vibrotactile strokes on the user's back using a grid of actuators in the chair.

Exoskeletons are wearable machines not only for amplifying users' motion but also providing force feedback. There are different kinds of exoskeletons, such as [11,19] that use different actuators (pneumatic, hydraulic and strings) to help users perform six or more degrees of freedom tasks either in the real or the virtual world. They can provide large forces, but are also heavy and large because of their actuators and mechanical parts. *FlexTorque* [29] offers an exoskeleton in a portable form factor; it provides force feedback to the arm of a user playing shooting games.

Mobile Haptics Lopes et al. [21] proposed a mobile force feedback device, which relies on electrical muscle stimulation to actuate the user's opposing muscles to counter the current input motion. GyroTab [1] produces torque in a mobile form factor based on a gyroscopic effect. Yano et al. [30] proposed a handheld haptic device that uses a laser range finder to control a linear servomotor that touches users fingertips so that users can touch the object remotely. Han et al. [9] proposed a handheld haptic device that integrates a linear servomotor and a solenoid–magnet pair located under a membrane to simulate huge and subtle kinesthetic feedback when the finger touches the membrane. Another mobile haptic device is POKE [23], which uses an air pump and silicon membranes on the front side to poke the caller's face remotely.

IMPLEMENTATION

We implemented the haptic turk platform and the experiences (hang glider and racing) in C# and JavaScript on the Unity3D engine (http://unity3d.com). We then deploy to notebook computers (we used Mac OSX, but can also deploy to Windows and Linux) and mobile devices (we used iOS, but can also deploy to Android). By switching to the professional version of Unity3D, we obtained the ability to deploy to the oculus rift.

The actuators' mobile devices sample their accelerometers and gyros 60 times a second and assess actuators' performance by comparing these readers with the received motion instructions in terms on tilt, roll, and acceleration.

Haptic turk connects devices using WiFi. Informal testing showed a mean latency of 32ms, which is faster than the earlier discussed 50ms delays that humans tolerate in a haptic response. Haptic turk achieves this with off-the-shelf components, so we found no need for more sophisticated network synchronizations methods such as Delay Measurement Time Synchronization [24].

To run an experience, one person starts the haptic turk app as "host", which makes this person the "player" for the first round (Figure 20a). (b) All other users join the session as actuators. (c) Haptic turk indicates each actuator where to stand with respect to the player. The actuators Velcro-strap their devices to the indicated part of the player's body.

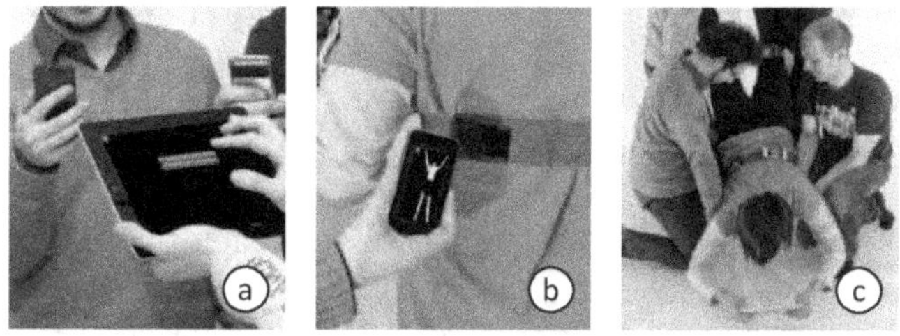

Figure 20: Setting up a haptic turk session via WiFi: (a) player starts a session, (b) joining actuator are assigned a position on the player's body, (c) play.

LAB STUDY

To validate our approach, we conducted a user study. Our main objective was to verify that the haptic experience does indeed produce an enjoyable experience—for players and for actuators.

Experience

In teams of six (player, four motion actuators, one special effects actuator) participants played the *team flight* hang glider experience, parts of which we presented in the walkthrough section.

Interface

We ran the team flight experience on the walk-up virtual reality setup of haptic turk already shown in Figure 16, i.e., players experienced the world through a head mounted display (an Oculus Rift). Actuators saw their instruction on the computer screen in front of the player.

To assure that all participants enjoyed the same experience, we set the hang glider experience to autopilot. This limited player's interaction abilities to looking around using the oculus rift, but assured that all participants encountered the same events. It also allowed us to always complete the experience in a fixed amount of time (3min), thereby creating a controlled experience also for the actuators.

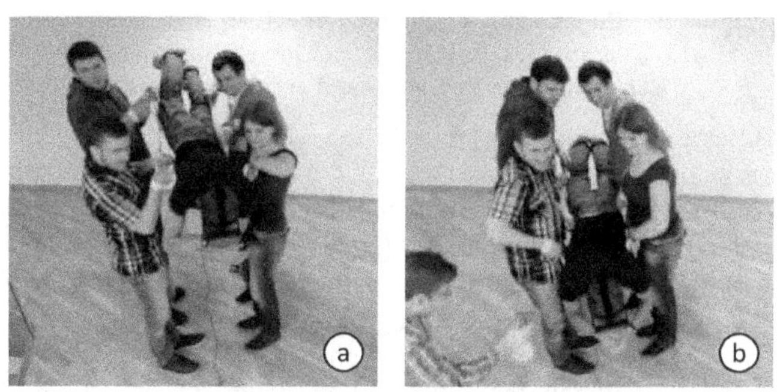

Figure 21: One team of participants playing *team flight*

Similarly, there was no actuator/actuator team scoring, so that the only reward for actuators was the opportunity to affect the player, plus the experience itself.

Procedure

We brought in participants in groups of 2, 3, or 4 and filled in experimenters so as to reach the 5 people required to play (plus we provided one experimenter for the water special effects). We then played one round of the team flight experience for each participant, so that each participant had the opportunity to be player exactly once.

With each new group, we provided two minutes of training during which we explained the handling of the slingshots, the actuator display and how high to lift the player for the four types of up/down bars, which track each actuator was expected to follow, and how to wear the oculus rift.

Participants played once as a player and 1-3 times as a actuator, according to their group size. Within these constraints, player/actuator order was counterbalanced. After all participants of a group were done playing and turking, all participants filled in questionnaires about their experience. We then released the group of participants and brought in the next group. Running a group of 2-4 participants took 10 to 15 minutes.

Participants

We recruited 14 participants (4 females) from our university. Their age ranged from 20 to 28 years (mean 23.6), BMI from 19-25 (mean 22.3). We recruited participants in groups of 2-4, i.e., participants were familiar with some of their actuators/co-actuators, but never all of them.

Results

Figure 22 summarizes our results.

As players, participants rated their experience on average as 6.1 (SD=0.7) on a 7-point Likert scale (1=unpleasant, 7=enjoyable)—so clearly as enjoyable.

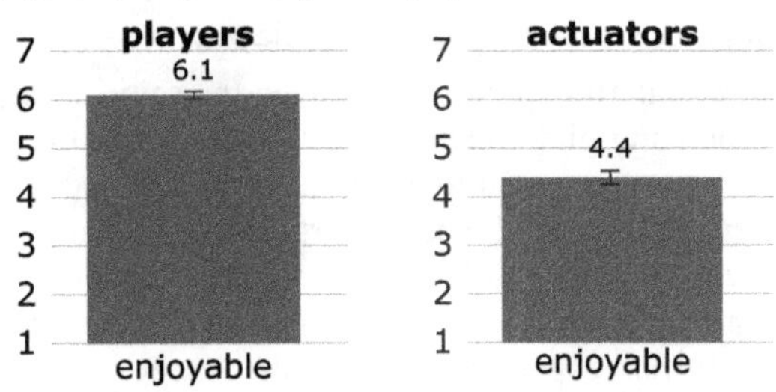

Figure 22: Players rated gameplay as 6.1, so clearly enjoyable. Also as actuators, participants enjoyed the experience. Error bars are +/-1 standard error of the mean.

Overall, players preferred the large motion events. Five players stated that they liked the intense motion resulting from lifting, shaking and bumping. Another player stated that he particularly enjoyed whole-body movements, such as being lifted or being swung forward—more so than being tilted and rolled. Along the same lines, three participants stated that they did not enjoy the extensive landing period in which they were tilted down. One participant described tilting as uncomfortable.

Accordingly, when asked about the most impressive moment of their player experience, 11 participants picked the intense -1/+2 boost caused by the tornado. One player expressed that "the changes in altitude were amazing and immersive". Another player explained that he enjoyed the moment when he bumped into the blimp.

Players rated that the actuators "were pushing me at the wrong/right time" as 5.4 (SD=0.8), i.e., they were satisfied with the actuators' timing.

As actuators, participants rated the experience as actuator as less enjoyable than as players, yet still on the "enjoyable" side (M=4.4, SD=1.2).

Very obviously, the actuators' experience was strongly driven by their perception of players' experience. Actuators felt that their performance contributed to player's experience (M=5.4, SD=1.3) (the "contribution" bar in Figure 22). Our observations match this. Five actuators said that they enjoyed seeing their players scream and giggle. One actuator said "it's fun to play this with your friends and see their reactions as they fly." And one simply stated "it's fun to watch." One participant would have enjoyed an even better view of what the player is experiencing. While we thought of the special effects role as being less exciting, one actuator said he would have also liked to take on that role.

The most likely reason for the lower score on enjoyment was fatigue. Seven actuators mentioned fatigue. One actuator mentioned that fatigue kicks in after two rounds of turking. Another actuator said "The person we moved was too heavy for me and I was smaller than the other players so my arms end at a lower height." Two actuators mentioned that lifting the player to level +2 repeatedly had caused fatigue.

To learn more about proxemics, we asked participants who they would play team flight with. They indicated that they would play with friends (14/14) and family (10/14), but only 1/14 felt it was appropriate to play with the public. Given that this study had forced participants to play with a group of mostly strangers, this suggests that subjective satisfaction may improve further if experienced in a closer circle of friends and family. One participant explicitly said that she would enjoy playing haptic turk with her kids.

The human-human nature of haptic turk polarized participants. While 7/14 participants responded that they would have preferred an experience administered by a mechanical motion platform, 5/14 stated that they preferred being actuated by humans (Figure 23).

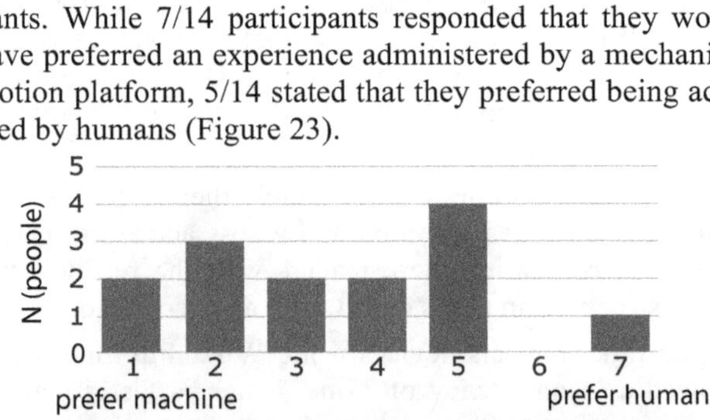

Figure 23: Some participants preferred haptic turk, other would have preferred a mechanical motion platform.

This suggests that these participants found an enjoyable quality in the human element. This is interesting, especially given that the actuators were assigned to them for the purpose of the experiment and not the friends or family that participants would have liked to play with.

In summary, our simple study provides some initial validation for the haptic turk concept. Most importantly, participants very much enjoyed the player experience. The actuator experience, while still enjoyable, could be improved by longer breaks and by giving the choice of who to play with.

EXPERIMENTAL DEPLOYMENT

Encouraged by the results of the study, we decided to try an experimental deployment of haptic turk and the *team flight* experience at an art festival in the Nevada desert (burning man, http://burningman.com). Our goal was to learn more about the social dynamics of haptic turk—outside the lab.

We again opted for the walk-up VR haptic-turk set-up previously shown in Figure 16. As shown in Figure 24, we adapted the set-up to the hostile desert environment by placing the projector in a box equipped with air filters, etc. The entire installation (minus the generator, which we acquired on site) was transported, set up, and run by *one* of the authors, emphasizing haptic turk's potential to deliver motion experiences anytime anywhere.

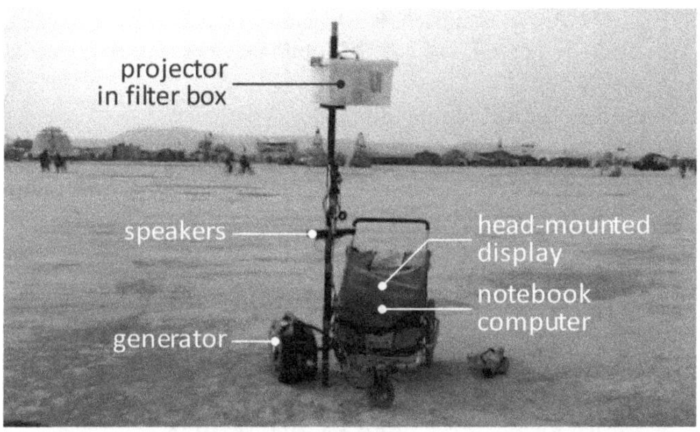

Figure 24: Our walk-up installation with head mounted display at the Burning Man art festival in the Nevada desert. A plastic box with fans protected the projector from desert dust.

We ran the installation only at night. While players wore the oculus rift, the projector projected a copy of the rift display with overlaid actuator display onto the desert ground, which served as actuator display (Figure 25). As before, we ran the team flight experience in autopilot and without additional incentives for actuators.

On three nights, we ran about 100 attendees. Player weights ranged from an estimated 100 pounds to a self-declared 200 pounds. While the venue did not afford running questionnaires, we observed attendees and videotaped four of the runs for further analysis.

Players recruited actuators

Unlike a lab study, our set-up had to begin by attracting its own audience. Every run unfolded as follows. An attendee or a small group of 2-3 attendees would walk by and inspect the installation. There was no particular attract mode, but the projection showed the game running.

Whenever an attendee was interested in playing, they would convince their friends to turk for them. Groups, however, were small—never large enough to play. We then encouraged attendees to recruit strangers as additional actuators. This typically took them a minute or two ("can you help us play a video game?") and was simplified by the friendly atmosphere of the event.

While most attendees recruited to be able to play, several attendees "gifted" the experience to a friend—oftentimes their boy/girlfriend—i.e., they recruited actuators, but then stepped back and let their friend take on the role as player while they actuated.

Given the constant competition for visual attention at the festival, it was essential for us to get started as quickly as possible. To get started in about a minute, we assigned actuator positions, helped actuators into the slingshots, and taught them about how high to raise lower at the individual up/down bars. We then filled in one actuator position ourselves, which allowed us to start right away and instead coach the other actuators as the experience was unfolding.

Figure 25: A player wearing the oculus rift. Our installation projected the actuator interface (overlaid onto the game world) onto the desert ground. This player weighed 200 pounds.

Observations

As during the study, the large motion events were favorites for players and actuators and led to audible expressions of joy. Upon "landing", several players were visible taken by the immersion of the experience and typically required a few seconds to find their way back to reality.

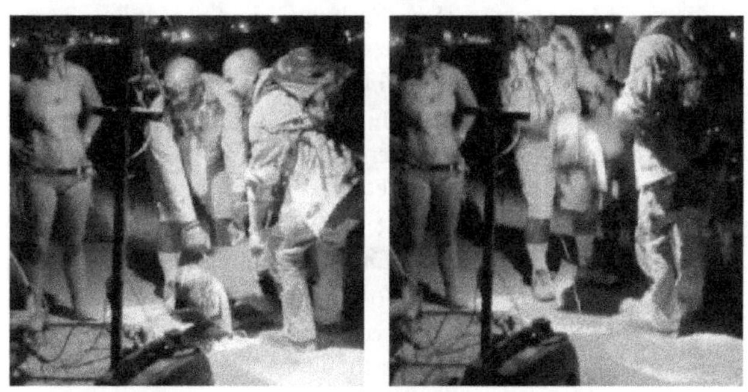

Figure 26: A player entering a tornado.

Among actuators, the most popular scenes were again the large motion events, but also the rocky ride sequence in which actuators had the opportunity to shake up the player a bit. One player reported motion sickness.

None of the actuators mentioned fatigue this time. The reason could be that, unlike our study, most attendees actuated only once, very few of them twice. This suggests that the fatigue threshold for this particular 4-person setup is around 3-5 min for this particular young athletic audience.

CONCLUSION

We have presented haptic turk, an approach to having motion experience everywhere. With haptic turk, we tackle this challenge orders of magnitude cheaper, more space efficient, and faster-to-deploy than the technical equipment it is inspired by. By leveraging the existing install base of mobile devices, haptic turk has the potential to reach hundreds of millions of users. As a side effect, haptic turk produces an interesting new social experience.

As future work, we plan on using haptic turk to apply force feedback to players' hands and to use haptic turk for virtual reality, rehabilitation, and for rapid prototyping haptic machinery. We also plan on exploring how to give actuators a more active role, e.g., by allowing them to slip into the role of game world characters and to *control* game events.

ACKNOWLEDGEMENTS

We thank Caro Fetzer for her help modeling the team flight 3D world.

REFERENCES

1. Badshah, A., Gupta, S., Morris, D., Patel, S., and Tan, D. GyroTab: a handheld device that provides reactive torque feedback. *Proc. CHI '12,* 3153–3156.
2. Baudisch, P., Pohl, H., Reinicke, S., Wittmers, E., Luehne, P., Knaust, M., Koehler, S., Schmidt, P. and Holz, C. Imaginary Reality Gaming: Ball Games Without a Ball. *Proc. UIST '13.*
3. Bernstein, M.S., Tan, D., Smith, G., Czerwinski, M., and Horvitz, E. Personalization via Friendsourcing. *TOCHI 08, 17,* 2, 6:1–6:28.
4. Berthoz, A. *The Brain's Sense of Movement (Perspectives in Cognitive Neuroscience).* Harvard University Press, 2000.
5. Danieau, F., Fleureau, J., Guillotel, P., Mollet, N., Lécuyer, A., and Christie, M. HapSeat : Producing Motion Sensation with Multiple Force-feedback Devices Embedded in a Seat. *Proc. VRST '12,* 69–76.
6. Davis, R.C., Saponas, T.S., Shilman, M., and Landay, J.A. SketchWizard: Wizard of Oz Prototyping of Pen-based User Interfaces. *Proc. UIST '07*, 119–128.
7. Dow, S.P., Mehta, M., MacIntyre, B., and Mateas, M. Eliza Meets the Wizard-of-oz: Blending Machine and Human Control of Embodied Characters. *Proc. CHI '10*, 547–556.
8. Gaggioli, A. and Breining, R. Perception and cognition in immersive Virtual Reality. *Emerging Communication: Studies on New Technologies and Practices in,* 71–86.
9. Han, B., Kim, S., Lim, S., Pyo, D., and Kwon, D. Physical mobile interaction with kinesthetic feedback. *Proc. HAPTICS '12*, 571–575.
10. Harris, L.R., Jenkin, H., Zikovitz, D., et al. Simulating self motion I: cues for the perception of motion. *Virtual Reality 2,* 6 (2002), 75–85.
11. Hayashi, T., Kawamoto, H., and Sankai, Y. Control method of robot suit HAL working as operator's muscle using biological and dynamical information. *Proc. IROS '05,* 3063–3068.
12. Heer, J. and Bostock, M. Crowdsourcing graphical perception: using mechanical turk to assess visualization design. *Proc. CHI '10,* 203–212.
13. Heimerl, K., Gawalt, B., Chen, K., Parikh, T., and Hartmann, B. CommunitySourcing: engaging local crowds to perform expert work via physical kiosks. *Proc. CHI '12,* 1539–1548.
14. Israr, A. and Poupyrev, I. Tactile Brush : Drawing on Skin with a Tactile Grid Display. *Proc. CHI '11,* 2019–2028.
15. Jay, C., Glencross, M., and Hubbold, R. Modeling the effects of delayed haptic and visual feedback in a collaborative virtual environment. *TOCHI 14,* 2 (2007).
16. Kittur, A., Chi, E.H., and Suh, B. Crowdsourcing user studies with Mechanical Turk. *Proc. CHI '08,* 453–456.
17. Kosinski, R.J. A literature review on reaction time. http://biae.clemson.edu/bpc/bp/lab/110/reaction.htm, 2012.
18. Laycock, S.D. and Day, A.M. Recent Developments and Applications of Haptic Devices. Computer Graphics Forum 22, 2 (2003), 117–132.
19. Lee, S., Park, S., Kim, M., and Lee, C.-W. Design of a force reflecting master arm and master hand using pneumatic actuators. *Proc. ICRA '98,* 2574–2579.
20. Levitt, G.M., *The Turk, Chess Automation*. McFarland & Company, Incorporated Publishers, 2000.
21. Lopes, P. and Baudisch, P. Muscle-Propelled Force Feedback: Bringing Force Feedback to Mobile Devices. *Proc. CHI '13,* 2577-2580.
22. NASA Vertical Motion Simulator. http://www.nasa.gov/centers/ames/research/technology-onepagers/vms.html. .
23. Park, Y., Beak, K., and Nam, T. The roles of touch during phone conversations: long-distance couples' use of POKE in their homes, *Proc.* CHI '13, 1679–1688.
24. Ping, S. *Delay Measurement Time Synchronization for Wireless Sensor Networks.* Berkeley, CA., 2003.
25. Riecke, B.E., Schulte-Pelkum, J., Caniard, F., and Bulthoff, H.H. Towards Lean and Elegant Self-Motion Simulation in Virtual Reality. *Proc. IEEE VR '05,* 131–138.
26. Shotton, J., Fitzgibbon, A., Cook, M., Sharp, T., Finocchio, M., Moore, R., Kipman, A. and Blake, A. Real-time human pose recognition in parts from a single depth image. In Proc. CVPR '11, 1297-1304.
27. Stewart, D. A Platform with Six Degrees of Freedom. *Proc. Institution of Mechanical Engineers 180,* 1 (1965), 371–386.
28. Telban, J., Cardullo, M., Telban, R.J., Wu, W., and Cardullo, F.M. Motion Cueing Algorithm Development: Initial Investigation and Redesign of the Algorithms. 2000.
29. Tsetserukou, D., Sato, K., and Tachi, S. ExoInterfaces: novel exosceleton haptic interfaces for virtual reality, augmented sport and rehabilitation. *Proc. AH '10,* 1:1–1:6.
30. Yano, H., Miyamoto, Y., and Iwata, H. Haptic Interface for Perceiving Remote Object Using a Laser Range Finder. *Proc. WHC '09*, 196–201.

Audience Experience in Social Videogaming: Effects of Turn Expectation and Game Physicality

John Downs[1], Frank Vetere[1], Steve Howard[1], Steve Loughnan[2], Wally Smith[1]
[1] Department of Computing and Information Systems, The University of Melbourne, Australia
[2] School of Psychological Sciences, The University of Melbourne, Australia
jdowns@student.unimelb.edu.au, {f.vetere, sloughnan, wsmith}@unimelb.edu.au

ABSTRACT

Videogames are often played socially with both co-players and audiences. Audience members' experiences are not well understood, nor are the factors of videogaming sessions that influence their experience. We conducted a study to examine the effects of game physicality and turn anticipation on audience members' experiences in social videogaming sessions. Pairs of participants played games under three conditions of physicality (controller-based, Wii, and Kinect) and their expectation of turn-taking was manipulated. Their enjoyment, game engagement, social engagement and sense of participation were measured. We found that the introduction of turn-taking into the session had positive effects for audience members – both *anticipated* and *residual play effects* – and that Kinect gameplay resulted in a more enjoyable experience for audience members. We argue that audience members' experience changes as they become more active within a session, and suggest there are design opportunities between purely active 'players' and passive 'audience members'.

Author Keywords

Audience experience; social gaming; physical videogames; turn-taking.

ACM Classification Keywords

H.5.m. Information interfaces and presentation (e.g., HCI): Miscellaneous.

INTRODUCTION

HCI has recently turned its attention to videogaming and the ways in which games can be designed to support or promote different types of sociality (e.g. [23]). However, there has been little consideration given to the differences in roles within a gaming situation. Videogames are frequently played in the presence of people who act as audience members – those who are not actively playing, but who are nevertheless engaged in the game and are an integral part of the social situation. The experience of videogame audience members is poorly understood, which inhibits our ability to design games to enhance their experience. In this work we seek to understand how audience members enjoy and engage with games.

CHI 2014, April 26 - May 01 2014, Toronto, ON, Canada

ACM 978-1-4503-2473-1/14/04...$15.00.
http://dx.doi.org/10.1145/2556288.2556965

There may be many reasons why an individual might be in the role of audience member rather than playing the game. Pre-existing social roles might direct participants in one direction or another – for example, a parent might suggest their child play a game while they stand aside in a supporting role. There may be constraints on the number of active players – fewer controllers than participants, or a game that only supports a limited number of players. Or, individuals may simply prefer to watch from the sidelines.

Advances in gaming technologies and shifting consumer demands have led to increasingly physical and mimetic games, and these games lend themselves to use by a variety of people who do not fit the stereotypical gamer profile [8]. As such, one factor that might influence the experience of audience members is the level of physicality of the game being played. Work within HCI has suggested that physical interfaces are inherently more engaging and present unique social characteristics (e.g. [2,23]). It seems reasonable to expect that these increasingly physical forms of gameplay also lend themselves to a more performative situation: a player jumping, ducking, and punching certainly seems more engaging and enjoyable to watch than one who is pressing buttons on a controller, and the division between those standing up to play and those sitting back watching becomes more striking. While HCI has examined how players are influenced by game physicality (e.g. [22]), to our knowledge there have been no experimental studies to date looking at how the physical control of games and the visibility of these controls might influence the experience of those watching.

Another factor that might influence the audience's experience is the anticipation of their own play. That is, there may be a difference between a person who spends the entire gaming session watching and a person who watches knowing that they will soon take a turn to play themselves. In many social gaming scenarios turn-taking is a core part of the situation, but the effect of turn-taking is not well understood. More generally, the social situation in which a game is played will be influenced by a number of factors;

prior work (e.g. [24]) has examined how sociality affects players' experiences, but has largely neglected audiences.

From a theoretical perspective, an account of audience experience will contribute to our understanding of social gaming and social computing more generally [17,23]. Audience members occupy an interesting and underexplored space between 'user' (player) and 'non-user' [18]. From a practical perspective, game designers and marketers should consider audiences when planning and designing games, and it is important that they understand the social and physical influences on audience members' experiences in order to broaden the appeal of their games.

In this paper, we outline an initial account of audience experience in physical videogaming sessions. We begin by reviewing the HCI literature, experimental and qualitative, looking at the physicality of game controllers and the sociality of gameplay. We then describe a study that was conducted to investigate the effects of physical gameplay and turn-taking on the audience members' experience.

RELATED WORK

Social Gameplay

The experience of gaming with another person is generally regarded as having different, usually more positive, characteristics than playing alone. Voida & Greenberg [23] described console gaming as having intensely social characteristics, seen as a place for players with varied levels of skill and different levels of status to come together, and to be given equal time and opportunity to take a turn or participate.

The effect of the presence of co-actors (almost always a co-player) has also been studied experimentally. For example, Weibel et al. [24] examined the effect of playing a videogame with a human compared with playing against a computer on the players' subjective experience of spatial presence (being 'in the game'), flow, and enjoyment. By manipulating the players' expectations of an opponent (in fact, all players played against a computer) they found that the experience of playing against a perceived human was more enjoyable and also resulted in higher levels of presence and flow.

Similarly, Ravaja et al. [16] examined the experience of social gameplay by varying the opponent type (computer, stranger, or friend) and measuring various experiential constructs. They found that playing against a human rather than a computer led to higher levels of engagement, arousal, and spatial presence, and that these effects were generally amplified further when playing against a friend over a stranger.

Physical Gameplay

In recent years researchers and the gaming industry have turned their attention to videogames that require physical activity of varying degrees. Videogames now exist on a continuum from using traditional controllers with simple buttons and knobs, to using physical controllers with varying degrees of natural mapping, to employing whole-body interaction using the Kinect and other similar systems.

The gestures required to engage in physical videogame play are, by their nature, more performative and publicly visible than the types of interactions commonly associated with traditional videogame play. Through physical movements a player's game manipulations are made available to other co-actors and become a resource for sociality [2,7]. As such, the increasing role of physicality in videogames should be considered a core part of the sociality of games and gaming technologies.

Players' relationships with these physical games have been explored in a number of ways, including understanding their usefulness as promoting a form of exercise [14], as well as ascertaining how the changing forms of game control are leading to different types of player experiences. Bianchi-Berthouze [2] conducted a series of experiments to examine the effect of controller type on engagement. The more physical controllers emphasized higher levels of movement. She found that movement was positively correlated with game engagement. Similarly, Skalski et al. [20] examined the effect of the naturalness of the control mapping on game enjoyment, concluding that a more natural controller results in higher levels of player enjoyment.

A review of the above experimental studies, and others, was provided by Vanden Abeele et al. [22]. They noted that although the literature generally indicates that natural controllers present advantages over traditional game control systems, the marked differences observed in these studies' results – both in nature and extent – may reflect methodological differences, making cross-study comparisons fraught. Additionally, each of these studies focuses exclusively on the experience of players; none of them speak to how game physicality might influence the behavior and experiences of those who are watching.

Effect of Physicality on Sociality

As certain genres of games become increasingly physical [8], there is also a need to understand the social effects of these systems and their place within gaming contexts.

Whitson et al. [25] argued that as console games become more physically oriented, they are becoming more grounded in the physical spaces they inhabit, and as such encourage a more dynamic exchange between the 'game world' and the 'real world'. This, in turn, provides co-players and audience members an increased opportunity to be part of the gaming situation through their observation of and communication with the player and each other, and therefore to become engaged in the game.

There is little published experimental work examining the intersection of physical and social gaming [22]. One such study was an experimental comparison of physical and traditional controllers conducted within pairs of co-players

[2]. The researchers measured a number of characteristics of the social setting and found that some did differ with higher levels of physicality. Specifically, the players' reported engagement was higher with a physical controller, and video analysis showed they were more vocal and more willing to use non-game gestural movements when using the physical controller. However, the small and homogenous sample (10 pairs of participants, all female) make it difficult to draw strong conclusions from this study [22].

Vanden Abeele et al. [22] performed a similar study evaluating two types of controller (traditional and physical), and measured a variety of experiential factors. In general their results were consistent with expectations – physical controllers were perceived as increasing the players' sense of spatial presence, but at the cost of lower perceived control. Enjoyment was not directly measured in this study. Their results also indicated a gender difference, which they suggest may be due to males' tendency to be more competitive and to adjust their gameplay strategies accordingly. However, it should be noted that in both of these studies [2,22], no aspect of the social situation was manipulated. Additionally, the social relationship between group members was not controlled. As such these studies would be better characterized as studies of videogame controller physicality within a fixed social setting, rather than examining the sociality of physically controlled games.

If we consider the broader HCI literature outside of experimental work, there is some consideration given to the sociality of physical gameplay. Harper & Mentis [7] described "the mocking gaze", a sense of playful derision of the active player of a Kinect game, who must perform oddly exaggerated physical gestures in order to be recognized by the sensor technology. They argued that this leads to a sense of social fun, and that the gestures provide a resource for play and for gentle mocking of family members within the safe space of a videogame.

Similarly, Downs et al. [6] described the ways in which the physical nature of Kinect gameplay enables different types of social play. This includes the types of mocking and derision described by Harper & Mentis [7], as well as the emulation of players' movements, the provision of sports-like commentary, the peculiarities of the sensor's technical abilities and the resulting effects on players' avatars, and the use of the Kinect games' video replay features to capture and re-experience moments.

Audiences and Audience Experience

Games are complex social systems that afford a variety of social roles to emerge. If we consider collocated console games, these roles can be seen to be on a continuum, with the most active roles involving full co-play, and the most passive being co-present others who pay no attention to the game. Between these two extremes lie a variety of types of 'audience' – those who are not actively playing the game but are, to some degree, engaged in the game experience [6,7].

De Kort et al. [10] highlighted the importance of spectatorship in videogame play, but noted that an understanding of "social processes and interpersonal dynamics (is) underrepresented" in the HCI game literature. They presented several phenomena from the field of social psychology that may be relevant to understanding the experience of social videogaming for all of the individuals involved, regardless of their social role.

One such phenomenon is evaluation apprehension, or more broadly, social facilitation effects (see [1] for a review). These effects suggest that the performance of a player will be affected by the presence of a co-player or a spectator, and depending on factors such as the player's experience with the game, the influence may be facilitatory or inhibitory on their performance. Social facilitation effects have been empirically assessed with games [9]. However, social facilitation effects focus on the player's instrumental game performance, not their overall experience (such as fun or engagement).

Returning to the HCI literature, when Harper & Mentis [7] described the idea of passively watching a co-present player play a Kinect game, they suggested that this is a form of "selfishness" since they will be gaining enjoyment from mocking the player without allowing themselves to be subjected to the same ridicule.

In each of these examples, the research has primarily focused on the experience of the player, not that of the audience member. There is relatively little literature specifically examining the role of audience members or spectators of technological systems, within the field of videogaming or more broadly.

One notable exception was Reeves [17], who constructed a framework for understanding the role of spectators of public interfaces and their role transitions as they become more or less involved in the system. This work is most relevant to public interactions, but aspects are germane to the consideration of audiences of videogaming. The framework includes the concepts of 'manipulations' and 'effects' – the interactions necessary to interact with a system and the resulting output. Public systems tend to require and promote more obvious manipulations and present larger, more visible effects.

As videogames begin to require more physical exertion and larger, more obvious gestures [19], and as there continues to be a trend toward larger television screens, we can see that games are becoming more publicly oriented. Consider, for example, the difference between playing a Kinect game and a game on a Nintendo DS or Apple iPad – the console game's control system and screen both lead to a more social experience [23]. If nothing else, Reeves' framework [17] suggests that if games continue to follow this trajectory of increasing physicality, audiences around console games will only become a more prevalent phenomenon.

Some researchers have presented case studies of spectatorship within specific games, usually qualitative in nature. In an interview-based study of the audio channel by spectators of Super Street Fighter IV, Su & Shih [21] highlighted the importance that the gaming technology plays in enabling spectatorship experiences. Cheung & Huang [3] presented an account of the spectatorship experience of Korean games of StarCraft II and argued that the information asymmetry between players and spectators (i.e. only the players know their underlying strategy and likely next actions) leads to the spectators' entertainment, both through anticipation and also through the added pleasure of providing analysis, commentary, and predictions. Although it might seem that information asymmetry would be reduced in a collocated, physical gaming scenario, Downs et al. [6] noted that audience members observing Kinect gaming often engaged in commentary and speculation from the sidelines. Similarly, O'Hara et al. [15] observed that while spectators in a public screen-based game were often reluctant to participate directly, they were engaged by some of the social aspects of the game such as the competitiveness between the two cities in which the game was run.

Although some of this literature hints at the audience experience of gaming, there is little examination of these experiences explicitly, and few attempts to ascertain the types of social, technological, and game-related factors that might influence audience experience. Other areas, such as theatre and performance art (e.g. [11]), explore the nature of audiences generally, but the implications of this work for audience of interactive games in a home environment are unclear. In the following sections we present a study that examines the sociality of physical console gaming and looks specifically at the experience of audience members.

STUDYING AUDIENCE EXPERIENCE IN PHYSICAL VIDEOGAMING

Based on these areas of previous work, and in the absence of directly related studies of audiences in videogaming situations, we set out to investigate two conjectures: that audience members' experiences are affected by both their own participation in the session and the characteristics of the game itself.

The level of participation in a gaming session has not been manipulated in the literature we reviewed. In all cases, social gaming studies have been conducted using co-players or players' perceptions of mediated co-player presence. Based on the principle of social facilitation [1] it would be expected that the player's performance (and, perhaps, experience) would be affected by a co-present non-player; it is less clear what the non-player's experience may be.

It is also difficult to make specific hypotheses about the nature of the effects of game physicality based on prior experimental work. As observed by Vanden Abeele et al. [22], experimental studies of gaming controller effects tend to have inconsistent and sometimes wildly divergent results. They suggest that this is due to a wide variation in the games and controllers used across studies, in their experimental procedures and measures, and in their participant sampling. Another potentially confounding factor is that in many cases these studies compare games using controllers for which they were not designed.

Our study begins to address the issues of audience experience in social videogaming sessions. We aimed to isolate the effects of different levels of physicality on the audience's experiences. We operationalize *physicality* as the amount of visible physical activity performed by the player. In addition we explore how the shifting roles of an audience member throughout a session might influence their experience; specifically, we examine how the introduction of turn-taking (i.e. the anticipation of having a future turn) might change the audience's experience.

METHOD

Participants

74 pairs of friends (148 participants) were recruited for this study. Seven pairs were removed due to violations of experimental protocol, leaving a total of 67 pairs (134 participants). Participants were not reimbursed but were provided with snacks and beverages throughout their session. Participant demographics are detailed below.

At the beginning of each session participants were randomly assigned to one of two roles:

- Participant P_A, who was led to believe they would be the player for all four game rounds; or
- Participant P_B, who was led to believe they would be the audience member for all four game rounds and would not actually play the games themselves.

Experimental Design

A 3 × 4 mixed model design was employed. Game physicality was manipulated as a between-groups factor with three levels (low, medium, and high physicality) and turn expectation was manipulated across four rounds as a within-subjects factor. Each group participated in all game rounds, each with one game lasting ten minutes. In total each experimental session lasted approximately one hour.

The experiments were conducted in a laboratory. Two rooms were used – one for the 'low physicality' condition and the other for the 'medium' and 'high physicality' conditions. The laboratory rooms included one-way windows; behaviors and conversations were not recorded, however the experimenter did casually observe participants to ensure that the technology worked correctly.

Participant groups were randomly assigned to one of the three physicality conditions. In the 'low physicality' condition, players would use a traditional gamepad-style controller that had no requirement for any motion except button-pressing and turning knobs. In the 'medium physicality' condition players would need to perform simple gestural movements, isolated to one limb, using a gestural control system. In the 'high physicality' condition, players would perform large or whole-body movements, generally involving multiple limbs, using a whole-body control system.

The participants' expectation of turn-taking was manipulated through the use of four game rounds. At the beginning of round 1, P_A was told that they would play all four rounds, and P_B was told they would always be the audience member. However, between rounds 1 and 2 the participants were informed that the experimenter had changed their mind and that in round 3, P_B would play the game and P_A would watch. Round 2 proceeded as round 1 had (P_A playing, P_B watching), and in round 3 the participants swapped roles (P_A watched and P_B played). In round 4 they returned to the original configuration (P_A playing, P_B watching). This manipulation is summarized in Table 1.

	Round			
	1	2	3	4
P_A	Play	Play	Watch *Already played*	Play
P_B	Watch *No play expectation*	Watch *Expect play*	Play	Watch *Already played*

Table 1. Rounds and turn-taking manipulations.

Due to this manipulation, P_B's expectation about the turn-taking nature of the session was altered during the session: in the first round P_B watched and expected not to have a turn; in the second round they watched again but expected to have a turn later; in the third round P_B did in fact have a turn; and in the fourth round they watched having now had a turn.

Participants were fully debriefed on the deception at the conclusion of the session. No participants indicated they guessed the deception during the session; at the beginning of each session all P_As expected to play throughout the entire session and all P_Bs expected to watch.

Games

Games were selected that were similar enough to compare (within the physicality condition), but that required different types of physical movements (to mitigate rehearsal effects and fatigue between game rounds). After a review of game titles for all three platforms we determined there were no suitable games that were designed for all three platforms, and so decided to use similar but slightly different game titles for each condition. We evaluated a number of games and selected those that fit within a common theme (sports-themed mini-games), and attempted to choose games that had comparable levels of fun and quality while using different physical motions within each physicality condition.

We considered using a custom game, or using non-standard controllers with existing games, but this would have resulted in a less naturalistic experiment. Although the use of different games may present a potential confound to the study design we believe that our approach presents the best tradeoff between full experimental control and ecological validity.

For the 'low physicality' condition a Sony PlayStation 3 gaming system was used with a standard wireless controller, and the games were diving, track running, archery, and swimming, all from the game title 'London 2012: The Official Videogame of the Olympic Games'. For the 'medium physicality' condition a Nintendo Wii gaming system was used with a single Wii Remote with built-in MotionPlus, and games were table tennis, bowling, wakeboarding, and golf, all drawn from the game title 'Wii Sports Resort'. For the 'high physicality' condition an Xbox 360 with Kinect sensor were used, and games were boxing (from the title 'Kinect Sports') and skiing, golf and tennis (from 'Kinect Sports: Season 2').

Groups played all four games within whichever physicality condition they were assigned to, but the order of games was counterbalanced between participant groups.

Measurement of Dependent Variables

All participants completed a short demographic questionnaire at the beginning of the session. In addition, at the end of each game round participants completed a 30-item questionnaire. In the case of round 1, this was completed before the participants were informed of the upcoming player switch in in round 3. Each item was on a 7-point Likert-style scale (from 'strongly disagree' to 'strongly agree', with 4 representing neutral). Both the player and audience member completed these questionnaires, although the wording for some items was reversed depending on the participant's role. The order of items was randomized for each questionnaire version.

The questionnaire included items measuring the following constructs: *enjoyment* (the level of fun the participant had), *mood* (the participant's emotional state), *game engagement* (how immersed in the game the participant felt), *social engagement* (how immersed in the social situation the participant felt), and *subjective participation* (the extent to which the participant felt an active part of the gaming session). Multiple items were used to measure each construct. Post-study analysis found that Cronbach's alpha was above 0.7 for each subscale, so the arithmetic mean of the items in each subscale was calculated and acted as the dependent variable for subsequent analyses. Dependent variables generally did not correlate highly with one another. One exception was enjoyment and mood (R=.77); as a result of its high correlation and similar item list, mood has been excluded from the reported analyses. Further details about the questionnaire are published separately [5].

In addition, manipulation check items were included to assess the participants' subjective performance (i.e. how well they felt they played) and physicality (i.e. how physically active they felt the player was).

RESULTS

Except where stated, statistical tests reported are mixed-model analyses of variance (ANOVAs) with post-hoc *t* tests. Eight missing post-round questionnaire responses were imputed using the Expectation-Maximization function in SPSS 21.0. Effect sizes are reported as partial η^2 and are interpreted as small ($\leq .01$), moderate (.06) or large ($\geq .14$) [4]. Because P_A and P_B are non-independent samples (due to being drawn from the same pairs), data for each participant type were analyzed separately. In the analyses below we principally discuss the results from P_B, since they were predominantly the audience member.

Participant Demographics

Participants' mean age was 23.69 years (standard deviation 6.68 years). Although condition assignments were random, participants in the Wii condition were slightly older (mean=26.00 years, standard deviation=8.13 years). 68% of participants were male. Most participants were regular gamers: only 20% reported they played games 'rarely' or 'never'. 51% of participants reported they sometimes played games socially (with others present in the room), and 41% reported they sometimes played games with the other participant they had come to the experiment with. 93% of participants had prior experience using the Wii, and 44% had prior experience with the Kinect.

Effect of Game Physicality on Subjective Physicality

Separate one-way ANOVAs were performed for P_A and P_B, and each showed a significant effect of physicality (for P_A, $F_{2,265}$=95.08, p<.001, SE=.16, η_p^2=.42; for P_B, $F_{2,265}$=107.48, p<.001, SE=.14-.15, η_p^2=.45). Both participant types reported significantly higher subjective physicality in the Wii condition (M_A=5.23, M_B=5.48) compared to the Controller condition (M_A=2.83, M_B=3.22), and in the Kinect condition (M_A=5.75, M_B=6.06) compared to the Wii condition, although the difference was not as large. Although analyses were separated, both are shown in Figure 1. P_A consistently rated physicality as very similar to, but slightly lower than P_B, but the significance of this effect could not be assessed using inferential statistics.

Effect of Game Physicality on Subjective Performance

Separate one-way ANOVAs were performed for P_A and P_B and showed a significant main effect of physicality on subjective performance (for P_A, $F_{2,265}$=14.73, p<.001, SE=.16, η_p^2=.10; for P_B, $F_{2,265}$=7.34, p=.001, SE=.14-.15, η_p^2=.05). Both participant types rated subjective performance as significantly lower in the Wii condition (M_A=4.69, M_B=5.09) than the Controller condition (for P_A, M_A=5.75, p<.001; for P_B, M_B=5.59, p=.01) and the Kinect condition (for P_A, M_A=5.75, p<.001; for P_B, M_B=5.85,

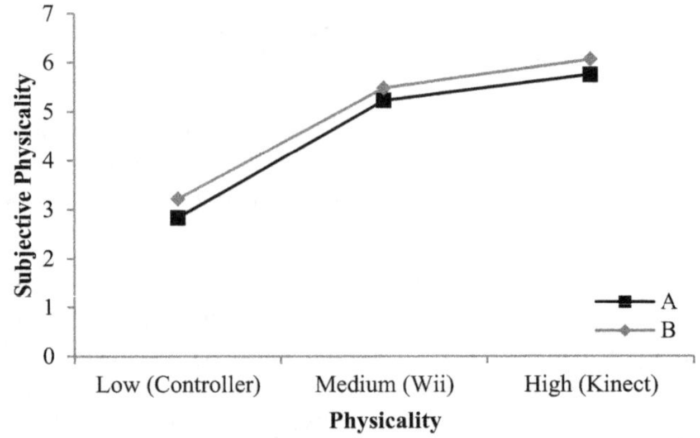

Figure 1. Subjective physicality as a function of physicality condition, by participant type.

p<.001). The differences between the Kinect and Controller conditions were not significant.

Repeated measures ANOVAs showed no significant main effects of round number on subjective performance for either participant.

Effects of Physicality Condition

We now focus our attention on the experience of participant P_B. A significant main effect of physicality condition was found for enjoyment ($F_{2,64}$=3.94, p=.02, SE=.16, η_p^2=.11). Post-hoc tests showed the Kinect condition (M_B=5.67) was rated significantly more enjoyable than the Wii condition (M_B=5.05, p=.01). There were no significant differences between the Kinect and Controller (M_B=5.25) conditions, or between the Wii and Controller conditions.

Although other constructs (game engagement, social engagement, or subjective participation) generally showed a similar pattern of results (Figure 2), no significant main effects were observed. In addition, breaking down each physicality condition by mini-game showed no significant differences in these constructs.

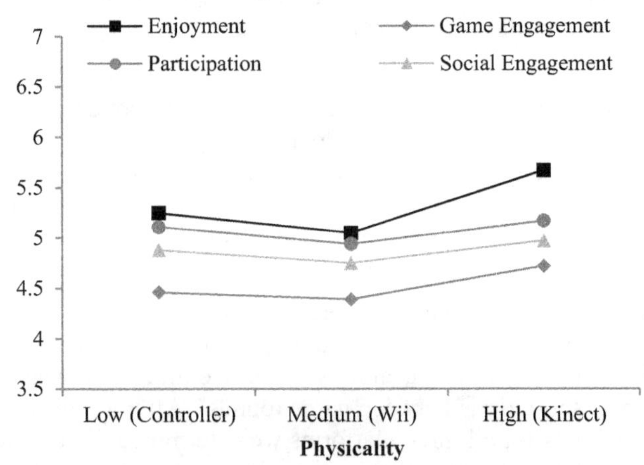

Figure 2. Enjoyment, subjective participation, game engagement and social engagement as a function of physicality condition, for participant P_B.

Effects of Round Number

For participant P_B, a significant main effect of round number was found for enjoyment ($F_{3,192}$=20.35, p<.001, SE=.10-.13, η_p^2=.24), game engagement ($F_{3,192}$=40.55, p<.001, SE=.12-.15, η_p^2=.39), subjective participation ($F_{3,192}$=71.69, p<.001, SE=.07-.18, η_p^2=.53) and social engagement ($F_{3,192}$=6.41, p<.001, SE=.11-.14, η_p^2=.09) (Figure 3).

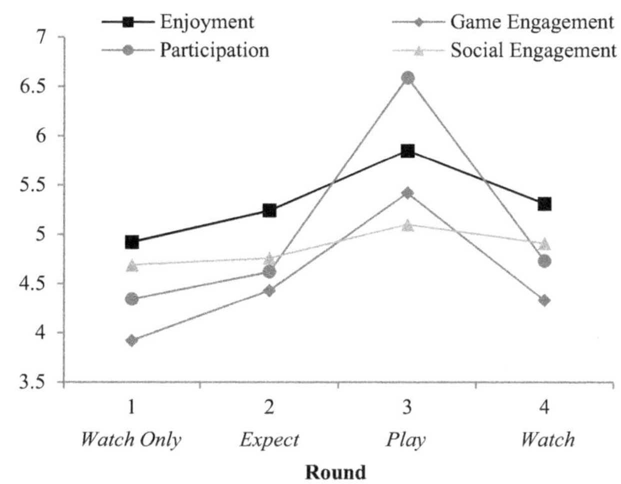

Figure 3. Enjoyment, subjective participation, game engagement and social engagement as a function of round for participant P_B.

Enjoyment post-hoc tests showed that round 1 (M_B=4.92) was rated as significantly less enjoyable than rounds 2 (M_B=5.24, p=.01), 3 (M_B=5.85, p<.001) and 4 (M_B=5.31, p=.001). Significant differences were also seen between rounds 2 and 3 (p<.001), and rounds 3 and 4 (p<.001), but not between rounds 2 and 4 (p=.49).

Game engagement post-hoc tests showed that participants rated engagement significantly lower in round 1 (M_B=3.92) than in rounds 2 (M_B=4.43, p<.001), 3 (M_B=5.42, p<.001), and 4 (M_B=4.33, p=.004). Significant differences were also seen between rounds 2 and 3 (p<.001), and rounds 3 and 4 (p<.001), but not between rounds 2 and 4 (p=.45).

Subjective participation post-hoc tests showed that players rated their subjective participation significantly lower in round 1 (M_B=4.34) than in rounds 3 (M_B=6.59, p<.001) and 4 (M_B=4.73, p=.02). Although subjective participation was rated higher in round 2 (M_B=4.62) than round 1, this difference was not significant (p=.09). Significant differences were also seen between rounds 2 and 3 (p<.001) and rounds 3 and 4 (p<.001), but not between rounds 2 and 4 (p=.36).

Social engagement post-hoc tests showed that social engagement was significantly lower in round 1 (M_B=4.69) than in round 3 (M_B=5.10, p<.001), and in round 2 (M_B=4.76) than round 3 (p=.001). No significant differences were observed between rounds 1 and 2 (p=.34) or between round 4 (M_B=4.91) and any other rounds.

Interactions of Round Number and Physicality

No interaction effects were significant. We have not discussed them here, with one exception. For enjoyment (Figure 4), in the Wii and Kinect conditions the same general pattern was observed as in Figure 3. For Wii, a significant difference was seen between rounds 1 (M=4.61) and 2 (M=4.99, p=.03), rounds 1 and 3 (M=5.74, p<.001), rounds 2 and 3 (p=.01), and rounds 3 and 4 (M=4.88, p=.002). In the Kinect condition, significant differences were seen between rounds 1 (M=5.30) and 2 (M=5.64, p=.049), rounds 1 and 3 (M=6.12, p<.001), and rounds 1 and 4 (M=5.62, p=.046), and rounds 2 and 3 (p=.002), and rounds 3 and 4 (p=.01). However, the controller condition showed significant differences between rounds 1 (M=4.83) and 3 (M=5.67, p=.01), and rounds 1 and 4 (M=5.42, p=.02), but not between rounds 1 and 2 (M=5.08, p=.40) or rounds 3 and 4 (p=.30). Although the overall interaction effect was not significant, we provide these details to add context to our later discussion.

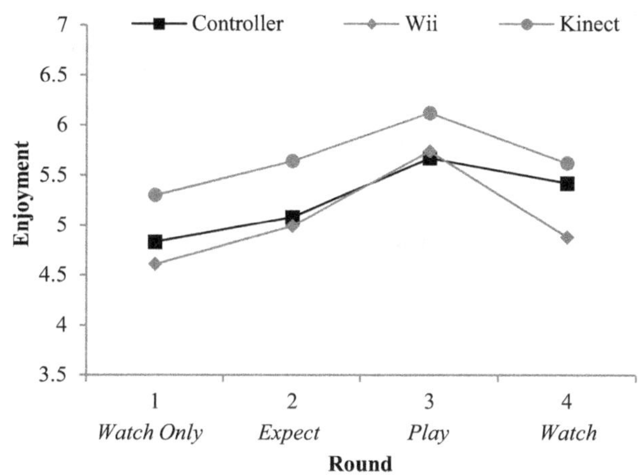

Figure 4. Interactions of round number and physicality condition, for participant P_B enjoyment.

DISCUSSION

From these results we can identity four distinct effects. First, when participants played the game themselves they reported higher levels of enjoyment, game engagement, subjective participation, and social engagement than when watching. While this may seem obvious, it is an important validation of the underlying assumption that playing and watching games are different experiences. Second, there is an *anticipated play effect*: when participants were told they would have a turn themselves their experience changed. Third, these changes in experience persisted beyond their own turn, lasting even when they knew they would not have another turn – we term this the *residual play effect*. Fourth, there is an effect of game physicality on audience enjoyment. In the following sections we discuss these effects in more detail.

Anticipation and Turn-Taking

We observed a clear effect of round order. Audience members found the session more enjoyable after being told they would be having a turn themselves (i.e. between rounds 1 and 2), and this effect persisted through all subsequent rounds. Their engagement in the game followed a similar pattern. This suggests that at the point where audience members found out that they would be more actively involved in the session they became more engaged in the game itself, and their enjoyment also increased. It is interesting to consider how these two factors (enjoyment and game engagement) might be related. For example, at the point when an audience member is told they will have a turn, they might become conscious of future evaluation by the other participant, and therefore pay more attention to (i.e. become more engaged in) the game. This increased engagement may act as a mediator of their enjoyment.

Somewhat surprisingly, social engagement was only affected when the participant actually had a turn. In contrast to game engagement, the social engagement construct measures the participant's sense of being part of a team, and of being attentive to and attended to by the other person. One's own direct participation in the game would not immediately seem to affect these directly. A possible explanation is that the active player is dividing their attention between the game and the social situation. While they feel that they are giving a high level of attention to the audience member, they are in fact generally more absorbed in the game and have fewer attentional resources available for socialization than they might assume, but subjectively sense that they are attentive to the social situation. In contrast, the audience member has more resources available to evenly split their attention and is more cognizant of their split attention. Future work could attempt to validate the existence of such an 'audience attentiveness bias', and how it might change in the presence of evaluative and non-evaluative audience members (similar to the implications made by social facilitation theory [1]).

Passive and Active Audiences

Overall, there is a characteristic pattern for several of the effects we observed: in round 1 they are lowest; in round 2 they increase; in round 3 they peak; and in round 4 they return to round 2 levels. We assume that the differences between rounds 1 and 2 are due principally to the revelation that the audience member will, in fact, have a turn. Of course there may be other factors at play: the player may generally become more used to the control system of the game after the first round, or might adapt their play style on the basis of knowing there is now a potential competitor. However, we did not set up the situation to be competitive, we found no evidence of a novelty effect (when a player might be unfamiliar with the game controls), and we did not observe a significant change in either participant's performance by round. As such we argue that the turn-taking manipulation is the most likely candidate for any changes in audience experience after round 1.

The characteristic pattern described above seems to indicate that once an audience member becomes aware that they will have a turn, their involvement in the session shifts from being strictly a passive audience member into an 'active audience member' (the *anticipated play effect*). This provides additional support to prior work that suggests that there may not be a strict dichotomy between 'player' and 'audience', but that an individual can sit along a continuum between these extremes [6]. Interestingly, we found that their experience changes for the entire duration of the session – even once they have had a turn and sit back down to watch again (the *residual play effect*).

The interaction of physicality and round on enjoyment may provide some clues to this phenomenon. When using a traditional controller the audience member has little reference for what it is like to be the player of the game; using Reeves' terminology [17], the manipulations that the player performs are secretive and not publicly available. As such, when the experimenter reveals that the audience member will have a turn, they have no physical frame of reference for what this experience might be like, and their enjoyment does not shift until they actually have a turn themselves. At this point they more fully appreciate and understand the game. In contrast, in the Wii and Kinect conditions the player's actions are public and obvious from the start of the session, and so the audience member is able to appreciate what their own involvement will entail from the point at which they find out they will take a turn. However, the interaction effects we speak of here were not significant, and so these explanations require further study and the factors require further correlation with other variables.

Game Physicality

There was a significant effect of physicality condition on audience enjoyment: Kinect games were rated as the most enjoyable for audience members. Interestingly, Wii games scored lower than controller-based games even though they included elements of physicality. There are several possible reasons why this might be the case.

Some prior work (e.g. [12]) has found evidence of Wii games being less preferable than traditional controller-based games on the basis that they provide less fine-grained control to players. While it could certainly be argued that Kinect games also provide only gross control mechanisms, without the tangible presence of a controller (such as a Wii Remote) there is less potential for direct comparison between Kinect- and controller-based games. The experience of playing a Kinect game feels qualitatively different to either a Wii-based or controller-based game. In Wii games, if players expect a high degree of control and do not get it their performance may be impaired, and as their performance degrades this could in turn negatively influence audience experience.

Indeed, we found that participants' subjective game performance ratings were slightly but significantly lower for Wii games than for Kinect or controller games. This could suggest that the Wii games were, on average, more difficult than the games in the other conditions. It is certainly plausible that a player struggling with a game or its controls will be less interesting to watch than a player who plays expertly.

Another potential explanation is that the games used in this study are less visually interesting to watch, or that participants are simply fatigued with Wii gaming or its aesthetic. Over 90% of our participants had used a Wii before. This made it difficult to compare the experiences of audience members who had prior Wii experience with those who did not; however, we conducted such a comparison for the Kinect condition (41% of the participants in the Kinect group had used a Kinect before, and we compared those who had with those who had not). No significant differences were observed, suggesting that platform novelty may not be a key determinant of experience.

A more interesting possibility is that Wii gaming exists in a zone between controllers and full-body gaming: a well-designed controller game might be interesting to watch with one's full attention on the screen, and a Kinect game might be interesting to watch splitting one's time between the screen and observing the (often exaggerated) full-body gameplay. Wii games still promote this dual attention between the screen and player, but the gestures that players perform are less interesting to watch. Further work would be needed to disentangle the factors of the game design, platform novelty and physicality.

Design Implications

Although this work is intended principally to inform an understanding of audience experience, the findings do suggest that there may be design implications that future work could extend and validate. The suggestion that the mere foreknowledge of having a turn changes an audience member's experience leads to the implication that notions of a strict dichotomy or barrier between a player and an audience member are problematic and limiting.

Most commercial games, including the ones used in this study, are designed to be played by one or two players at a time. However, there is an opportunity to expand the design space of games to include additional gradations of 'audienceship'. For example, it may be possible to allow different degrees of participation by audience members. Morrison et al. [13] presented suggestions to enable crowds of sports spectators to interact with each other and the wider stadium environment, although these were specific to large-scale events. When considering more private, physical gaming technologies like the Kinect, one can imagine using the sensor's capabilities to detect the presence of audience members and allow them to participate in various ways, if they so choose. Similarly, 'second screen' interactions (such as those enabled by the Wii U GamePad and SmartGlass for Xbox) might provide opportunities for audience members to participate in games beyond standing up and playing directly.

These results may also have implications for the design of turn-taking mechanisms in games. In many games turn-taking is achieved by manually swapping players at a suitable point in the gameplay (e.g. at the end of a level or mini-game, or when a character loses a life). Our results suggest that by declaring a turn-taking session ahead of time the experience of audience members will differ.

CONCLUSIONS

In this paper we have argued that audiences are frequently a part of social gaming situations, but that their experiences are not well understood. The main aim of this paper has been to describe an experimental study of social videogaming audiences within the context of physical gaming. We found that the experience of audience members changes when they are informed that the gaming session involves turn-taking rather than mere observation. At this point audience members seem to shift from a passive to an active state, even before and after they have their own turns, and this active state results in higher levels of enjoyment and engagement with the game. We introduced the terms *anticipatory* and *residual play effects* to describe these changes in experience based on the introduction of turn-taking. However, contrary to expectations, increasing levels of physicality did not necessarily lead to a more positive audience experience. While Kinect gameplay was rated as more enjoyable for audience members than other types of gameplay, Wii gaming was rated as the least enjoyable. Several potential reasons for this finding were suggested, including issues with game control, novelty, difficulty, or having intrinsically uninteresting gestures.

Of course, this study only considered the influence of two factors on audience experience. There are other factors that are likely to be equally interesting and important, and we hope that future work will attempt to isolate how other situational (e.g. room configuration), social (e.g. watching friends vs. strangers) and game design factors (e.g. competitive vs. collaborative games) shape audience experience. We also only considered the experience of a single audience member at a time; undoubtedly, larger audiences will have very different social processes and dynamics that will influence the experience.

We also temper the results of our physicality manipulation on the basis that different games were used in each of the conditions. Although we went to great lengths to mitigate any confounding factors, the differences between the games used in each condition may have affected the physicality manipulation results in unexpected ways.

Additionally, the sizes of the differences observed are often in the order of one scale point. Nevertheless, we are encouraged by the statistical effect sizes that were observed (most of the significant effects are moderate to high strength), and also note that the majority of participants tended to score highly in general, potentially resulting in a compressed scale – few participants would rate a social gaming session as a negative experience, whatever factors may be manipulated.

Finally, as noted above, this study considered 'audience member' and 'player' as a strictly dichotomous separation. Our findings suggest that audiences are in fact much more complicated and nuanced, and we hope further work and future game designs will begin to color in this gap.

ACKNOWLEDGMENTS

We acknowledge the contributions of The University of Melbourne Statistical Consulting Centre, the Interaction Design Lab's Usability Expert Review Panel, and the Institute for a Broadband-Enabled Society.

REFERENCES

1. Aiello, J.R. and Douthitt, E.A. Social facilitation from Triplett to electronic performance monitoring. *Group Dynamics: Theory, Research, and Practice 5*, 3 (2001), 163–180.
2. Bianchi-Berthouze, N. Understanding the role of body movement in player engagement. *Human Computer Interaction 28*, 1 (2013), 1–36.
3. Cheung, G. and Huang, J. Starcraft from the stands: Understanding the game spectator. *Proc. CHI 2011*, ACM Press (2011), 763–772.
4. Cohen, J. *Statistical Power Analysis for the Behavioral Sciences*. Psychology Press, 1988.
5. Downs, J., Vetere, F., Howard, S., and Loughnan, S. Measuring audience experience in social videogaming. *Proc. OzCHI 2013*, ACM Press (2013).
6. Downs, J., Vetere, F., and Howard, S. Paraplay: Exploring playfulness around physical console gaming. *Proc. INTERACT 2013*, Springer (2013), 682–699.
7. Harper, R. and Mentis, H. The mocking gaze: The social organization of Kinect use. *Proc. CSCW 2013*, ACM Press (2013), 167–180.
8. Juul, J. *A Casual Revolution: Reinventing Video Games and Their Players*. MIT Press, Cambridge, MA, 2009.
9. Kimble, C.E. and Rezabek, J.S. Playing games before an audience: Social facilitation or choking. *Social Behavior and Personality 20*, 2 (1992), 115–120.
10. De Kort, Y.A.W., IJsselsteijn, A., and Gajadhar, B.J. People, places, and play: A research framework for digital game experience in a socio-spatial context. *Social Psychology 6*, 2 (2007), 823–830.
11. Latulipe, C., Carroll, E.A., and Lottridge, D. Love, hate, arousal and engagement: Exploring audience responses to performing arts. *Proc. CHI 2011*, ACM Press (2011), 1845–1854.
12. Limperos, A.M., Schmierbach, M.G., Kegerise, A.D., and Dardis, F.E. Gaming across different consoles: Exploring the influence of control scheme on game-player enjoyment. *Cyberpsychology, Behavior, and Social Networking 14*, 6 (2011), 345–350.
13. Morrison, A., Bell, M., and Chalmers, M. Visualisation of spectator activity at stadium events. *Proc. IV 2009*, IEEE Computer Society (2009), 219–226.
14. Mueller, F., Gibbs, M.R., and Vetere, F. Design influence on social play in distributed exertion games. *Proc. CHI 2009*, ACM Press (2009), 1539–1548.
15. O'Hara, K., Glancy, M., and Robertshaw, S. Understanding collective play in an urban screen game. *Proc. CSCW 2008*, ACM Press (2008), 67–76.
16. Ravaja, N., Saari, T., Turpeinen, M., Laarni, J., Salminen, M., and Kivikangas, M. Spatial presence and emotions during video game playing: Does it matter with whom you play? *Presence: Teleoperators and Virtual Environments 15*, 4 (2006), 381–392.
17. Reeves, S. *Designing Interfaces in Public Settings: Understanding the Role of the Spectator in Human-Computer Interaction*. Springer, London, 2011.
18. Satchell, C. and Dourish, P. Beyond the user: Use and non-use in HCI. *Proc. OzCHI 2009*, ACM Press (2009), 9–16.
19. Simon, B. Wii are out of control: Bodies, game screens and the production of gestural excess. *Loading... 3*, 4 (2009).
20. Skalski, P., Tamborini, R., Shelton, A., Buncher, M., and Lindmark, P. Mapping the road to fun: Natural video game controllers, presence, and game enjoyment. *New Media & Society 13*, 2 (2010), 224–242.
21. Su, N.M. and Shih, P.C. Virtual spectating: Hearing beyond the video arcade. *Proc. British HCI 2011*, ACM Press (2011).
22. Vanden Abeele, V., De Schutter, B., Gajadhar, B., Johnson, D., and Geurts, L. More naturalness, less control: The effect of natural mapping on the co-located player experience. *Proc. FDG 2013*, ACM Press (2013).
23. Voida, A. and Greenberg, S. Wii all play: The console game as a computational meeting place. *Proc. CHI 2009*, ACM Press (2009), 1559–1568.
24. Weibel, D., Wissmath, B., Habegger, S., Steiner, Y., and Groner, R. Playing online games against computer- vs. human-controlled opponents: Effects on presence, flow, and enjoyment. *Computers in Human Behavior 24*, 5 (2008), 2274–2291.
25. Whitson, J., Eaket, C., Greenspan, B., Tran, M.Q., and King, N. Neo-immersion: Awareness and engagement in gameplay. *Proc. Future Play 2008*, ACM Press (2008), 220–223.

Exploiting Thermal Reflection for Interactive Systems

Alireza Sahami Shirazi, Yomna Abdelrahman, Niels Henze, Stefan Schneegass, Mohammadreza Khalilbeigi†, Albrecht Schmidt

VIS, University of Stuttgart
Stuttgart, Germany
{firstname.lastname}@vis.uni-stuttgart.de

†Technische Universität Darmstadt
Darmstadt, Germany
khalilbeigi@tk.informatik.tu-darmstadt.de

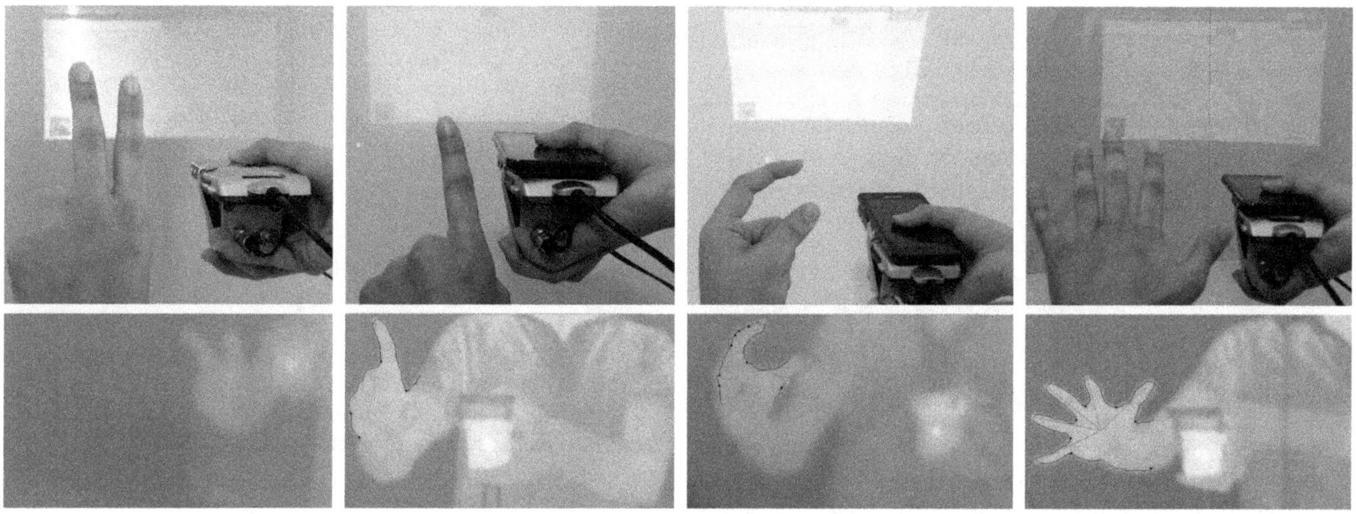

(a) Aluminum (b) Glass (c) MDF (d) Tile

Figure 1: We explored the thermal reflectivity of different surfaces for interaction with projected surfaces. The thermal reflectivity allows to sense users that perform in-air gestures inside and outside the thermal camera's direct field-of-view. Four of the eight surfaces we analyzed and which can be found in normal office environments are presented above.

ABSTRACT

Thermal cameras have recently drawn the attention of HCI researchers as a new sensory system enabling novel interactive systems. They are robust to illumination changes and make it easy to separate human bodies from the image background. Far-infrared radiation, however, has another characteristic that distinguishes thermal cameras from their RGB or depth counterparts, namely *thermal reflection*. Common surfaces reflect thermal radiation differently than visual light and can be perfect thermal mirrors. In this paper, we show that through thermal reflection, thermal cameras can sense the space beyond their direct field-of-view. A thermal camera can sense areas besides and even behind its field-of-view through thermal reflection. We investigate how thermal reflection can increase the interaction space of projected surfaces using camera-projection systems. We moreover discuss the reflection characteristics of common surfaces in our vicinity in both the visual and thermal radiation bands. Using a proof-of-concept prototype, we demonstrate the increased interaction space for hand-held camera-projection system. Furthermore, we depict a number of promising application examples that can benefit from the thermal reflection characteristics of surfaces.

CHI'14, April 26 – May 01 2014, Toronto, ON, Canada

ACM 978-1-4503-2473-1/14/04?$15.00.
http://dx.doi.org/10.1145/2556288.2557208

ACM Classification Keywords

H.5.2 [Information interfaces and presentation]: User Interfaces. - Graphical user interfaces.

Author Keywords

heat; thermal imaging; reflection; camera-projector system; roughness

INTRODUCTION

Thermal cameras operate in the far-infrared (F-IR) band and provide a heat map of a scene without an additional illumination source. As thermal cameras are light invariant and robust to illumination and color changes, they have been used for various applications, such as surveillance systems [48] and medical applications [47]. In the field of human-computer interaction, thermal imaging has been recently used to determine users' body pose, emotions [30], and for face recognition [22]. Due to their unique properties, thermal cameras have shown remarkable opportunities for interactive systems [14, 15, 23]. In these systems, a thermal camera is not only used to detect the users' position and body parts but also to trace heat trails left behind by body parts touching a surface.

Another unique property of thermal cameras results from objects' varying reflectivity in different electromagnetic wavebands. Brass, for example, diffuses visible radiation whereas it is practically a mirror in the far infrared spectrum. As shown in Figure 2, a surface that seems non-reflective for a human observer and an RGB camera, is a mirror for thermal radiation. Previous work considered such thermal reflection from surfaces as noise [23] and developed approaches to filter them out [37]. In contrast, we propose to exploit *thermal reflection* as a unique characteristic of thermal radiation and use it for interactive systems. If a thermal camera faces towards a surface that reflects thermal radiation in a specular manner the surface gains properties of a thermal mirror for the camera. In addition to its direct field-of-view, a thermal camera can thereby sense the space besides and even behind the camera through the thermal mirror (see Figure 2). For user-surface interaction, this extends the interaction space beyond the space between the camera and a surface. It enables sensing a human body and hand gestures in areas that are not directly visible from the camera's position. While recent prior work has used time-of-flight imaging to also detect objects that are not in the camera's direct field-of-view [36], thermal imaging can provide a more detailed picture, is more robust and requires little computational power.

In this paper, we investigate how thermal reflectivity, which has been considered as noise in previous work [23, 37], can be exploited for creating novel interactive systems. We overview the laws of physics to explore which surfaces diffuse visual light but provide specular thermal reflectivity. Such surfaces can be used with normal visual displays such as video projectors but at the same time enable a thermal camera not only to observe its direct field-of-view but also the space besides end behind the camera. We build a handheld camera-projection prototype that uses thermal imaging. The system supports on-surface interaction and mid-air gestures in the camera's direct field-of-view. In addition, it can also trace body movements outside the camera's direct field-of-view. Using the prototype, we assess the thermal reflectivity of common surfaces which can be found in many offices and living rooms. We envision further promising use cases that can benefit from this phenomenon.

This paper makes the following contributions:

- Investigation of thermal reflection and how it can be used to build novel interactive systems extending the interaction space beyond the field of view of the camera.
- Implementation of a thermal camera-projection prototype as the proof-of-concept allowing users standing in front of a surface to perform hand gestures outside the thermal camera's direct field of view.
- Analysis and assessment of the reflection characteristics of different surfaces that can be found in our vicinity.
- Discussion of four promising application examples that can benefit from thermal reflection.

The paper is structured as follows: after reviewing the related work, we discuss the physical properties of thermal and visual radiation. We then present an interactive prototype that exploits thermal reflection to extend the interaction space beyond the camera's direct field of view. Afterward, we use the prototype to assess the reflection characteristics of common materials in the visual and the thermal spectrum. Finally, we discuss a number of potential areas of application.

RELATED WORK

Enabling natural gestural and touch-based interaction techniques is one of the main goals of human-computer interaction research. In the following, we discuss prior work in three different areas aimed to provide natural interaction using (1) thermal imaging, and techniques used for recognizing human gestures to interact with (2) stationary as well as (3) mobile projected screens.

Thermal Imaging

Thermal cameras have been used for various purposes, including health-related applications, user recognition, and to build interactive systems. Wong et al. used thermal imaging and proposed algorithms to detect persons' head positions and parameter ratios such as the height and the width of objects [48]. Such algorithm were not only used for anti-theft surveillance systems, but also applied in nursing homes for monitoring Alzheimer patients and preventing them from leaving the nursing home without being attended to. The same approach is used for faint detection [47]. Pham et al. proposed a system for posture analysis in a dense crowd of people to detect irregular behavior using thermal imaging [29].

Face recognition remains one of the most challenging tasks in computer vision. By utilizing the light independent properties of thermal imaging, a vast enhancement in the performance of face recognition can be achieved [22]. Thermal imaging has not only been used to recognize faces but also to classify facial expressions [19] and it has also been shown that by measuring the temperature of a user's face it is possible to determine the cognitive load and the emotional state [30].

Thermal imaging has recently also been used as a sensor for enabling the interaction with arbitrary surfaces [14, 15, 23]. This is achieved by integrating thermal imaging and existing computer vision techniques to improve user surface interaction by utilizing advantages of thermal imaging to overcome common RGB and depth cameras' drawbacks. Daisuke and Koskue, for example, used short-lived heat traces that result from the heat transfer from one object to another as means for interaction and created an interactive

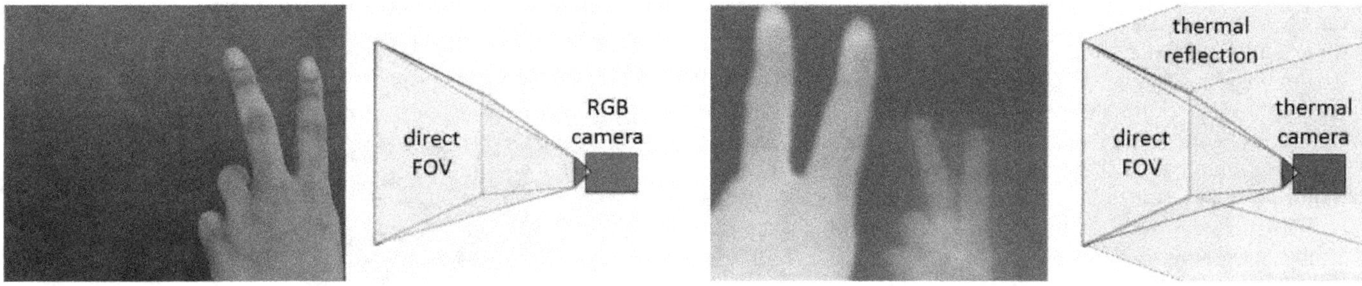

Figure 2: A standard RGB camera observes objects in the direct field of view as shown on the left. Through thermal reflection, a thermal camera facing a surface such as brass shown on the images also observes objects besides and behind the camera.

tabletop surface [14]. Larson et al. used heat traces caused by fingers touching a surface and detected pressure for interaction on surfaces [23]. They reported that the thermal reflectivity of surfaces induces noise for their system.

Interaction with Projected Surfaces

Touch and mid-air gestures are common techniques to interact with projections. These are typically detected using either RGB, infrared (IR), or depth cameras. There exists a large body of work focusing on detecting and tracking hands and fingers to enable multi-touch and mid-air gestures using RGB cameras [7, 21, 18, 25]. Such systems typically use skin color detectors [18] or template matching [21] to segment the hand and then calculate contour and convexity defects [25] to identify fingers.

Infrared imaging is a popular technique to enable multi-touch and mid-air gesture when interacting with projection screens [13, 12, 17, 40, 41]. In such systems, the space behind the screen is typically illuminated with an infrared source and all except the infrared light is blocked from the camera using an infrared-pass filter. This technique has been widely used for tabletop interaction by combining a rear-mounted IR camera and a projection unit. Using the depth map provided by depth cameras is another approach for detecting touch and hand gestures on projected screens [27, 42, 43, 44]. These systems generally utilize either a 2D view above the surface [43, 27] or a selective 2D projection of 3D sensed data [44] for processing users input on or above the surface using common 2D computer vision techniques.

Ubiquitous Mobile Interaction

Our research is also related to previous work on interaction with mobile projectors. According to the work by Rukzio et al. [32], interaction with mobile projected displays can be divided into four categories. A common approach is to separate input and output and use the touchscreen of a mobile phone [10] or a touch sensor for input [3]. Researchers have also investigated input for mobile projection by moving and gesturing with the projector itself [3, 5, 39] or by aiming with the projector at objects in the environment [33]. Although these solutions allow users to focus on the projection and perform intuitive gestures, tracking the projector's movements requires additional hardware equipment to be installed in the room or mounted on the projector unit.

Directly touching the projection screen with the fingers [46, 11] or using a stylus [4] is another approach to interact with mobile projections. However, such a setup requires users to be very close to the projection leading to a small projection area and large shadows on the projection. Another solution is to use mid-air finger pointing and hand gestures to interact with the projection [26, 8]. The SixthSense system [26], for example, offers a set of mid-air hand gestures to support interaction with the projection. The system uses a color-based approach to track fingers. ShadowPuppets [8] provides shadow gestures as input to a handheld projector system by casting hand shadows for co-located collaborative scenarios. Winkler et al. [45] have argued that it is more preferable to perform gestures besides or even behind the projector. This is not possible with current handheld projectors-camera systems as both face the same direction and the projection and sensing spaces overlap. Thus, users occlude the projection while performing mid-air gestures in front of the camera. A thermal camera, however, can detect direct interactions on a surface and mid-air gestures as well as users interaction out of the camera's direct field-of-view for instance behind the camera.

THERMAL REFLECTIVITY

Thermal radiation, as a result of energy transitions of molecules, atoms, and electrons of a substance, is continuously emitted by all matter whose temperature is above absolute zero. The spectrum and intensity of blackbody radiation depends on the object's temperature as expressed by the Planck's and Stefan-Boltzmann laws. The radiation emitted by objects at room temperature falls into the infrared region of the spectrum, which extends from 0.76 to 100 micron. The human body's net radiation is, for example, around 142 watt (W), with a skin temperature of 33°centigrade (C), at an ambient temperature of 22°C, and a peak wavelength of 9.5 micrometer (μm).

When radiation strikes a surface it is partially absorbed, partially reflected, and the remaining part, if any, is transmitted. Based on the first law of thermodynamics the sum of absorbed, reflected, and transmitted radiation is equal to the incident radiation. For fully opaque surfaces the transmissivity is zero, thus, the sum of absorptivity and reflectivity is one. The absorptivity is independent of a surface's temperature. However, it depends on the temperature of the source at which the incident radiation is generated. The reflectivity of a surface depends not only on the direction of the incident radiation but also on the direction of the reflection. Surfaces are assumed to reflect in two manners: specular and diffuse. In specular (mirror-like) reflection, the angle of reflection equals the angle of the radiation beam. For diffuse reflection the radiation is reflected equally in all directions regardless of the incident radiation's direction. The reflectance of a surface depends on its roughness and the wavelength of radiation strikes [2]. If the wavelength is smaller than the surface roughness, light is scattered diffusely. For wavelengths much larger than the roughness dimensions, the radiation is specularly reflected as from a mirror [37]. Beckmann & Spizzichino reports that reflectance is specular if the roughness (R_a) is smaller than one eighth ($^1/_8$) of the wavelength and otherwise diffuse [1]. The smaller the roughness, the higher the reflectivity: reflection from smooth and polished surfaces is mirror-like, whereas it is diffuse from rough surfaces [37]. Surfaces with roughness smaller than approximately 1.18 micrometer (μm) reflect a human's radiation (with a peak wavelength of 9.5 μm) in specular manner.

A thermal camera produces thermograms of a surface based on the incident radiation from the surface. This radiation includes the energy the surface emits (based on its temperature) as well the reflection of objects' radiation from the surrounding. If the reflectivity of all objects is diffuse the camera only views the objects in its direct field of view. However, if a surface reflects radiation in a specular manner, it acts as a mirror for the thermal camera. Thus, the camera is additionally able to view objects which are out of its direct field of view but visible through the surface's reflection. With such surfaces it is possible to extend the camera's field of view and the space of interaction, respectively.

Objects reflect thermal radiation and visual light differently. Surfaces made of different metals or with a smooth paint can act as a mirror in the thermal spectrum and can still be used for visual projection. Other materials such as transparent glass and plastic are transparent for visual light but still a mirror for thermal radiation. In the following, we show how the reflection of thermal radiation can be exploited to build interactive systems that can sense body gesture in front, besides and even behind a thermal camera. We show that a wide range of materials exist that diffuse visual light and can thus be used for projecting visual content but still reflect thermal radiation. As the human body radiation is in the F-IR range, we are interested in surfaces that have high specular reflectivity for F-IR radiation but diffuse reflectivity in the visual spectrum.

PROTOTYPE

In the following, we describe the design of our prototype that is used as proof-of-concept to explore the concept of thermal reflectivity and investigate opportunities for interactive systems. The prototype runs a sample application that highlights the usage mid-air gestures and on surface interaction using a single portable thermal camera. It further allows to have an ad-hoc mobile setup and transforms any surface into an interactive canvas.

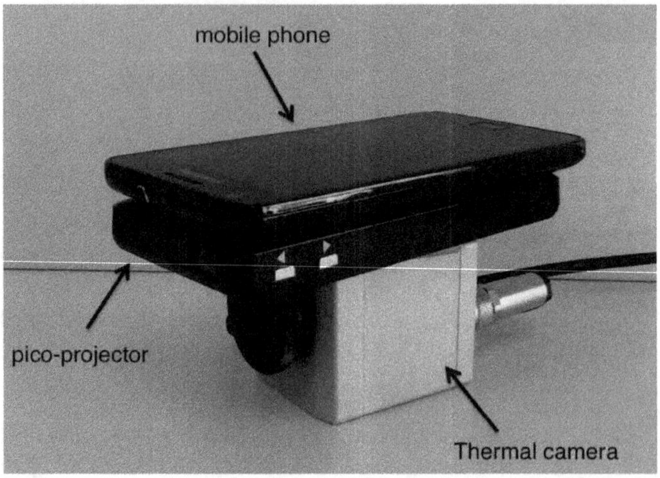

Figure 3: The prototype consisting of a thermal camera, a pico-projector, and a smartphone that has been used for the experiment.

Hardware Unit

As shown in Figure 3, our prototype consists of a smartphone augmented with a pico-projector (MicroVision) and a thermal camera (Optris PI160) . The thermal camera is a contactless sensor that measures the temperature of objects in its field of view. The optical resolution is 160 x 120 pixels and it has a frame rate of 120Hz. The camera is able to measure temperatures between -20°C and 900°C. It operates with a thermal sensitivity of 0.08 Kelvin represented by the noise equivalent temperature difference (NETD) [1]. The wavelengths captured by the camera are in the spectral range between 7.5μm and 13μm. The lens we use in the following provides a is 23° x 17° field of view. The thermal camera is faced in the same direction as the pico-projector.

The camera uses USB as power source as well as to transfer data. It provides raw data in one of three formats: pre-processed energy values, temperature values, or YUV-color values. A dynamic link library (DLL) allows to access the camera through inter-process communication. In our implementation we dynamically link the DLL into our application. We utilize the 16-bit color values from which we can compute the corresponding temperature based on the specification of the thermal camera.

Algorithm

We implemented a Google Maps application which allows users to pan and zoom the map information either by directly touching the projection surface or performing mid-air hand gestures. In order to recognize touch input and hand gestures we the used OpenCV library[2] for image processing and feature extraction. For each retrieved frame from the thermal camera pre-processing is required before extracting the features. The pre-processing includes the following steps: noise filtering, background subtraction, and thresholding.

[1]NETD refers to the electronic noise that is interpreted as a temperature difference of an object

[2]OpenCV: `http://opencv.org/` (last access 15.01.2014)

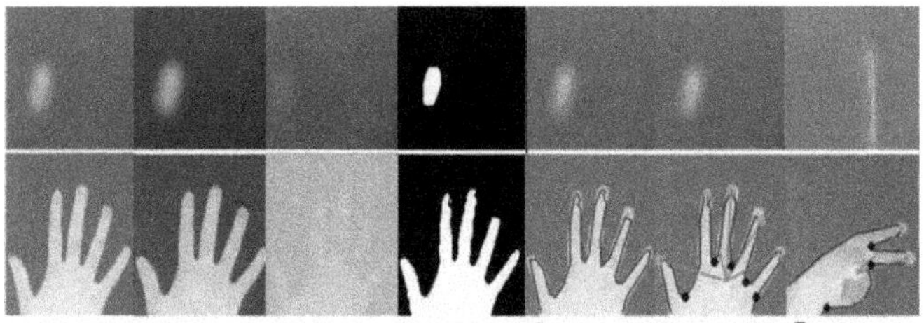

Figure 4: Feature extraction in different steps of the algorithm. The top row shows the features extracted from the heat trace on a surface, the bottom row presents features retrieved from an in-air gesture.

Noise filtering: As the first step we apply a filter to reduce the noise in the image provided by the camera. Similar to [23], we use a 5 x 5 pixels median filter. Then, we convert the image to gray scale and reapply the median filter for better noise reduction.

Background subtraction: To remove the background, a model is computed using an accumulated weighted model for each pixel. It is chosen to allow a dynamic adaptation of the background. The dynamic update is dependent on the learning rate parameter (α) that controls how fast the background model is updated which is essential to detect heat traces. The α value lies between zero and one and can be adjusted to either maintain heat traces until they start decaying or disappear completely. The higher α, the more sensitive the background model becomes to changes in the image sequence. We systematically tested the algorithm with different α values and α = 0.1 showed the best result. Old heat trace lasts in the foreground for detection yet are merged to the background fast enough to enable interaction on the same spot.

Thresholding: We use Otsu's thresholding method [28] for identifying parts of the image that are relevant to detect body parts and heat traces. The thresholding algorithm separates parts of a human's body such as hands and fingers as well as heat traces from the rest of the foreground. This method assumes the existence of two classes of pixels and aims to set the threshold to have minimal class overlap. Since the interactive parts stand out in the image, it separates the image into two classes (interactive part and the remaining foreground). An additional morphological closing operation is applied to enhance the boundaries of the segmented foreground and shrink the background.

Heat trace detection: The heat transmitted from the user's hand to the surface leaves a trace that could be detected by searching for contours in the image and examining the area, shape, and temperature of the contour. The gesture mapping is implemented by matching the shape of the contour detected. In our system we consider two types of interaction on surfaces, that is, touch-points or swiping in any arbitrary direction. By fitting the contour to a circle/eclipse or a line using Hough Transform [9] the interaction type is determined. By tracking the center of the detected line-shape

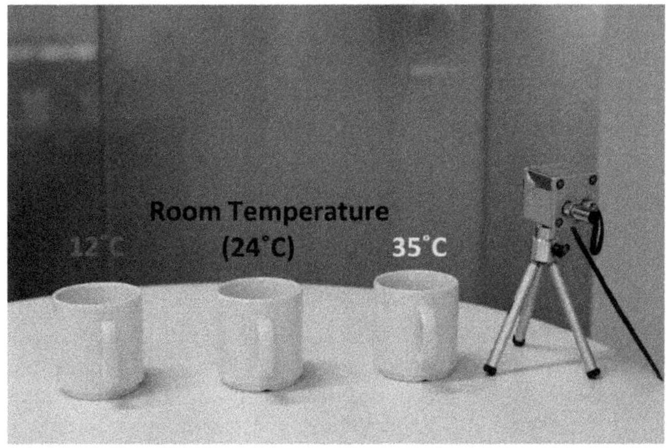

(a) Three coffee cups with different temperatures.

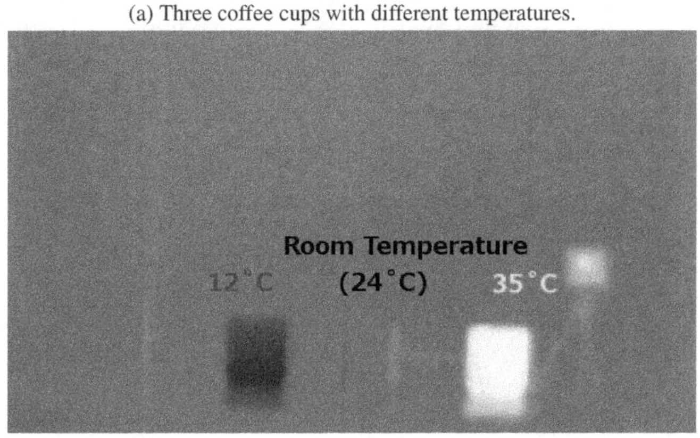

(b) Thermal image of the coffee cups with different temperatures.

Figure 5: When an object has a temperatures that is very similar to the temperature of the background, there is no clear difference between the object and the background in the thermal image. Whereas, as higher the temperature difference is the easier the object segmentation becomes.

contour the direction of swipe gestures is recognized. The center of the contour is computed by getting the spatial moment of the extracted contour. By detecting this trace, we can differentiate between directly touching a surface and the hovering above it. Figure 4 shows step by step processing for detecting the touch-point interaction on the surface as well as mid-air gestures.

No calibration is required for detecting heat traces if the amount of pressure that is applied to a surface by the user is not important. Otherwise, the pressure can be detected through a calibration process and determining the number of frames the heat trace lasts (β). With two levels of pressure (high pressure and low pressure) the number of frames in which the trace persists is identified and stored. During the interaction the number of frames are compared to stored β values to deduce the pressure level of the interaction. This calibration is processed after noise filtering and before background subtraction due to the fact that we adjust the background subtraction learning rate (α) in such as way that we do not view old heat traces. This results in latency for detecting the pressure level. The latency depends on the camera frame rate as well as the decay rate of the heat trace on the surface.

Hand and finger detection: Hand and finger detection is considered as one of the most challenging tasks using ordinary RGB cameras. Such a task is achieved either by using skin color filter [6, 31], relying on a color map of the human skin, or by instrumenting the hands using colored gloves [16, 38] to extract and track the hand. Since the hands have a different temperature than the room temperature, they can be robustly segmented from the image in any lighting conditions using thermal imaging. Our algorithm computes the convex hull and convexity defects of the hand contour. To determine the hand center, we moreover calculate the average depth points of the defects. The finger tips are then identified as points which have local maximum distance to the computed hand center. This approach allows detecting the hand and fingers at any orientation with all possible cases (fist, open hand, 1-5 fingers). Figure 4 presents the procedure of extracting a hand and its finger tips.

Hand gesture detection: Approaches to detecting hand gestures include model-based and view-based approaches. Model-based approaches utilize a 3D hand model for tracking, which makes it a complex and challenging, yet not very robust [34] task. However, view-based approaches uses the hand and finger information extracted and matches these features to patterns for hand gesture recognition. We have utilized this approach by tracking fingertips and computing their relative distance. We have implemented for instance, the pinch and pan gestures for zooming in and out by tracking the relative distance between the finger tips over the image sequence captured. The approach can be used in real-time without any latency or delay.

Robust detection of hands and fingers through the processing pipeline explained above depends on the sharpness and contrast of the thermal images. In order to retrieve a sharp image the roughness of the surface should be as low as possible (e.g., smooth and polished surfaces). Surfaces with high roughness disturb the sharpness of the image rendered from the reflected heat waves, making the detection process very challenging. The contrast of objects in the thermal images also depends on the object's temperature and the thermal imaging sensitivity. If the object's temperature is similar to the surface (e.g., both have room temperature), the object may neither be visible through the reflection nor in the direct field of view (cf., Figure 5).

Changes in the temperature of surfaces or fingertips after a long interaction session decreases the robustness of the system. Such a limitation does not apply to mid-air gestures.

As described above, there is a latency for detecting the pressure level. This latency relays on the surface material and is directly proportional to the decay of the trace. In order to differentiate between hovering over a surface and mid-air gestures we defined a set of feature constraints. We use, for example, the heat traces for interaction on the surface and at least two fingertips the in-air.

Surface	β (High Pressure)	β (Low Pressure)	R_a Roughness
Tile	200 (1.7 sec)	60 (0.5 sec)	0.04
Glass	220 (1.8 sec)	100 (0.8 sec)	0.004
Acrylic (transparent)	170 (1.4 sec)	40 (0.3 sec)	0.005
Acrylic (white)	160 (1.3 sec)	44 (0.4 sec)	0.06
Acrylic (mate)	250 (2.1 sec)	48 (0.4 sec)	3.49
MDF	120 (1.0 sec)	50 (0.4 sec)	0.11
Polished Wood	260 (2.2 sec)	70 (0.6 sec)	1.48
Polished Wood (glossy painted)	400 (3.3 sec)	120 (1.0 sec)	0.11
Aluminum Plate	0 (0.0 sec)	0 (0.0 sec)	0.33

Table 1: The surfaces used for the experiment. The β represents the number of frames and the respective time in seconds the heat trace lasts.

EXPERIMENT

We conducted an experiment to explore the thermal radiation characteristics of various surfaces found in a normal office or home environment. We focused on surfaces that reflect thermal radiation and can serve as a projection surface. Such surfaces can be turned into interactive surfaces with a large interaction space even outside the camera's direct field of view.

Based on our pre-observation of several office and home environments, we choose frequently used surface materials for our experiment. We considered nine surfaces for the experiment (cf., Table 1). We tested shiny tiles, transparent glass, transparent acrylic, white acrylic, medium-density fiberboards (MDF), polished wood, and aluminum plates. We used the prototype and experimentally tested each surface. The α value was set to 0.1 during the whole experiment.

Observations

In general, shiny surfaces showed enough reflectivity to be used with our prototype. We examined the properties of the thermal reflectivity and whether it is sufficient to detect mid-air gestures outside of the camera's direct field of view for each of the nine surfaces. For all surfaces except the polished wood and the aluminum plate, the reflectivity is high and the camera provides images with enough sharpness and contrast to detect mid-air gestures. Figure 1 shows the images provided by the thermal camera next to a visual photo of the recorded scene for four of the nine surfaces that we tested in the experiment. While glass has the highest reflectivity, the aluminum plate is more diffuse and provides blurry reflection. The polished wood is completely diffuse and provides unclear image through reflection. Therefore, we decided to paint the normal wood board and repeat the experiment. We used a glossy white color for painting the board. The color added a layer to the wood that reflects thermal wavelengths. However, the reflectivity is not as good as the MDF, for instance.

Surface Roughness

As described above, the reflectivity of a surface depends on its roughness. We measured the roughness of the surfaces used in the experiment according to ISO 4287. The

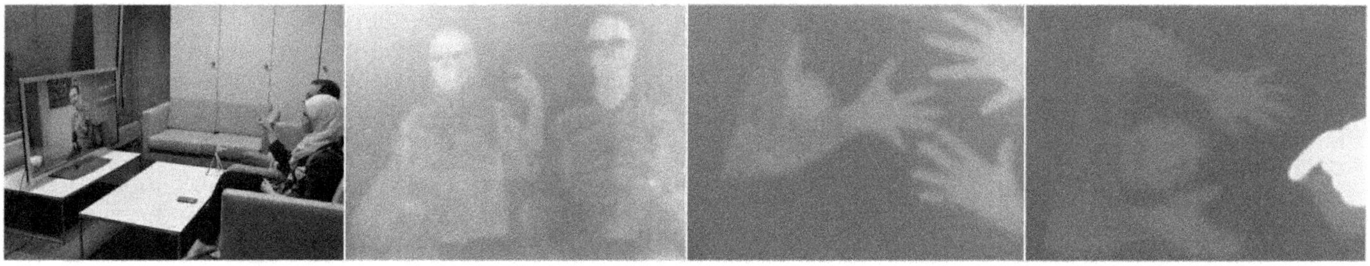

Figure 6: A thermal camera facing a TV can monitor users sitting behind the camera through thermal reflection (left images). Facing a living room table from the top an ad-hoc tabletop setup can be created. The right images show two persons interacting while the thermal camera solely observed through thermal reflection and by observing one user through reflection and other one in the direct field of view.

topography of the surfaces were measured with a spinning micro lens confocal microscope [35, 24] (50x magnification, 0.8 numerical aperture, optical resolution below 50 nm). The roughness Ra was calculated with the NIST reference software [3] according to ISO 4287 from a representative slice along the measured surface. Table 1 shows the roughness of the surfaces. The glass has the smallest roughness, whereas the polished wood has the highest one. The smaller the roughness value, the more mirror-like is the surface. Painting the wood decreases its roughness by more than 90%.

Heat trace decay

The speed of heat trace decay depends on the surface's material. Therefore we measured the number of frames the heat trace last on each of the nine surfaces (β) after a finger is lifted from the surface. We measured the β values for touch with high and low pressure. Table 1 shows the values for all surfaces. While the heat trace stays very long on glass, it decays very fast on acrylic. For the aluminum plate no heat trace is left behind, hence, the β value is zero.

LIMITATIONS

It should be mentioned that the described approach has its own limitations. The object's temperature plays an important role for object detection. When objects have a similar temperature as the background there is no clear difference between objects and background in the thermal image (see Figure 5). This makes it very hard to detect such objects. Whereas, a higher temperature difference between object and background makes objects segmentation much easier. The sensitivity of the thermal camera in measuring of temperature should be also taken into account.

The spatial configuration is another important factor. The camera has a limited viewing angle. Therefore, the interaction space through thermal reflectivity is also limited. A movement of the camera and, in general, a change in its spatial configuration with the surface results in rendering a new interaction volume based on thermal reflectivity.

Furthermore, the approach cannot be used with every surface. Surfaces should be smooth and polished to have a mirror-like reflectivity in the thermal frequency range. It is particularly critical when it is used in combination with projection. Best surfaces for thermal imaging, such as glass, cannot be used for projection and vice versa. The best combinations are surfaces that are diffuse for projection and reflective for thermal imaging.

POTENTIAL USE CASES

We envision that thermal reflection can be used for a variety of applications. In the following we describe four potential applications in which thermal reflectivity can enlarge the interaction space and consequently opens up novel possibilities for interaction in front of surfaces that reflect thermal radiation.

Interactive (Mobile) Projection

Given the recent technological advances in manufacturing pico-projectors, we already witnessed mobile phones equipped with an embedded pico-projector. The projector extends the space for visualizing information beyond the mobile phone's display. Using current commercial systems, users interact with such systems through the phone's display. Equipping the pico-projector with a camera allows users to interact in front of the camera using mid-air gestures. Using RGB cameras in such a setup forces the user to perform the gestures in front of the camera which results in occlusion. Winkler et al. [45] already indicated that enabling users to perform gestures behind the phone might result in higher performance.

We envision that future mobile phones can be equipped with a combination of a thermal camera and a pico-projector. If the projector projects on a surface that is a mirror for the thermal camera, the camera can also observe gestures performed besides or even behind the camera and the phone. Hence, the user can perform gestures without occluding the projection. This advantage of an increased interaction radius can not only be used for mobile projectors but also for stationary projectors. Equipping a stationary projector with a thermal camera and using a surface that reflects thermal radiation as projection screen enables to create a setup with large interactive space. The advantage is that projector and camera can be co-located which leads to a very simple setup. Users can interact directly on the surface in the camera's direct field of view as well as while being behind or besides

[3]National Institute of Standards and Technology: `http://physics.nist.gov/VSC/jsp/` (last access 15.01.2014)

the projector. However, finding a proper surface is essential to use this setup.

Interactive TVs

With the increasing success of inexpensive commercial sensing technologies such as depth cameras (e.g., Microsoft Kinect[4]), they have been used widely for sensing natural gestures at home. The typical setup consists of an RGB camera or a depth camera that is situated above or below the TV. Thereby the camera is looking at the living rooms. It can observe gestures performed in their direct field of view.

We envision that thermal cameras to be integrated into TV's remote controllers (RC) or another mobile device and leverage thermal reflectivity once the device aims at the TV (see Figure 6). This can be used in an ad-hoc scenario while holding the RC in the hand and doing bimanual interactions. For example, using the RC for activating the Electronic Program Guide (EPG) and using hand gestures for navigating through the EPG. Further, the RC can be on the living room table looking towards the TV so users can perform mid-air gestures while sitting on the sofa behind the camera. This setup may provide a larger interaction space compared to setups with depth or RGB cameras. However, it requires a specific spatial arrangement of the camera and the TV.

Interactive tabletops

A typical vision-based setup to create an interactive tabletop is orienting a projector and a camera at a table that can serve as a projection screen. Camera and projector are either located above or below the surface. Each setup has its own shortcomings [41]. In a top-projection setup the user's body parts can occlude the projected image. In a rear-projection setup it becomes challenging to capture objects that are on top of the surface or hover above. Another proposed approach is to place projector and camera at the side of the interactive surface [41]. In this setup, a difficult overhead installation of the projector is avoided. Further, the camera and projector are oblique and the occlusion problem is minimized.

Using a thermal camera as the sensing camera together with a reflective surface can enable setups that further reduce occlusion or increase the interaction radius (see Figure 6). When the thermal camera is oblique and the surface reflects thermal radiation, its field of view is extended. Interaction can mainly take place outside of the projection space to avoid occlusion. To have a surface that reflects human body thermal radiation, its roughness should be smaller than $1.18\mu m$. Typical tables provide this reflectivity and further surfaces can be easily created by, for example, painting a smooth wood surface glossy.

Wearable Computing

The miniaturization of computing devices has led to new types of devices that users can wear and use in various contexts (e.g., Google Glass). Interaction with such wearable devices is of great importance. Various sensors such as infrared cameras [20] have been proposed to facilitate full-body interaction. However, these sensors might be sensitive to illuminations. Further, with such camera, the user must hold the hands in the camera's direct field of view to be observable by the camera.

Considering Google Glass, for example, its RGB camera provides the opportunity to be used for observing mid-air gesture. Substituting the RGB camera with a thermal camera in front of a reflective surface, the interaction space is enlarged. Users can perform interaction behind/beside themselves out of their sight while their gestures are still visible for the camera. Furthermore, such a camera works in any light condition which is very useful for wearable devices. However, not all surfaces can be used for interaction.

CONCLUSION

RGB and depth cameras are widely used to build interactive systems by research and industry. Users can interact with such systems while they are in the camera's direct field of view. In such systems, occlusion may occur if the interaction space overlaps with the projection volume. As such cameras are sensitive to illumination or color changes, thermal cameras have been proposed as a robust alternative. A unique property of thermal cameras results from objects' varying reflection characteristics in different electromagnetic wavebands. A surface that diffuses visual light can still reflect thermal radiation. In previous work, thermal reflection has only been considered as noise. In this paper we exploit thermal reflection to build novel interactive systems.

Surfaces that either diffuse visual light or are transparent for visual light can be used as projection screen but still reflect thermal radiation. Using such common surfaces we can extend the area observable by a thermal camera beyond its direct field of view. Using such a setup we built a camera-projector system that can monitor users in front of the camera but also besides and even behind the camera. After reviewing the laws of physics we present an interactive prototype system used to explore the characteristics of different materials. We show that a wide range of surfaces is suitable for projection and can also provide an enlarged interaction space through thermal reflection. Through four application examples that could benefit from thermal reflection we demonstrate that the concept is widely applicable.

Current thermal cameras, the algorithms that have been developed for thermal imaging, and the resulting systems are all optimized to reduce thermal reflection. We assume that by developing cameras, algorithms, and systems that are optimized to exploit thermal reflection we can further extend the range of surfaces that can be used for interaction through reflection. We further believe that using thermal cameras beyond the niche applications where they are currently used can bring down their cost dramatically.

A comprehensive assessment of further gestures and their recognition rate is an interesting direction which can be subject of future work. In particular, to develop algorithms that are optimized to exploit thermal reflection. Various use

[4]Microsoft Kinect - **http://www.microsoft.com/en-us/kinectforwindows/**(last access 15.01.2014)

cases can be implemented that benefit from using thermal reflectivity for interaction.

ACKNOWLEDGMENTS
We are very grateful to Prof. Dr. James Fogarty (University of Washington) for his valuable feedback on this paper. We also thank Mr. Ahmad Faridian and Mr. Wolfram Lyda (ITO, University of Stuttgart) for helping us with the measurement of surfaces roughness. This work is funded by the German Research Foundation within the SimTech Cluster of Excellence (EXC 310/1).

REFERENCES
1. Beckmann, P., and Spizzichino, A. *The scattering of electromagnetic waves from rough surfaces*. Artech House Radar Library, 1987.
2. Bennett, H., and Porteus, J. Relation between surface roughness and specular reflectance at normal incidence. *Journal of the Optical Society of America 51* (1961).
3. Blasko, G., Feiner, S., and Coriand, F. Exploring interaction with a simulated wrist-worn projection display. In *Proceedings of the International Symposium on Wearable Computers* (2005), 2–9.
4. Cao, X., and Balakrishnan, R. Interacting with dynamically defined information spaces using a handheld projector and a pen. In *Proceedings of the Symposium on User interface software and technology* (2006), 225–234.
5. Cao, X., Forlines, C., and Balakrishnan, R. Multi-user interaction using handheld projectors. In *Proceedings of the Symposium on User interface software and technology* (2007), 43–52.
6. Ciaramello, F. M., and Hemami, S. S. Real-time face and hand detection for videoconferencing on a mobile device. In *Proceedings of the Workshop on Video Processing and Quality Metrics for Consumer Electronics* (2009).
7. Cohen, C. J., Beach, G., and Foulk, G. A basic hand gesture control system for pc applications. In *Proceedings of the Workshop on Applied Imagery Pattern Recognition* (2001), 74–79.
8. Cowan, L. G., and Li, K. A. Shadowpuppets: supporting collocated interaction with mobile projector phones using hand shadows. In *Proceedings of the Conference on Human Factors in Computing Systems* (2011).
9. Duda, R. O., and Hart, P. E. Use of the hough transformation to detect lines and curves in pictures. *Communications of the ACM 15*, 1 (1972), 11–15.
10. Greaves, A., and Rukzio, E. Evaluation of picture browsing using a projector phone. In *Proceedings of the Conference on Human computer interaction with mobile devices and services* (2008), 351–354.
11. Harrison, C., Benko, H., and Wilson, A. D. Omnitouch: wearable multitouch interaction everywhere. In *Proceedings of the Symposium on User interface software and technology* (2011), 441–450.
12. Henze, N., Löcken, A., Boll, S., Hesselmann, T., and Pielot, M. Free-hand gestures for music playback: deriving gestures with a user-centred process. In *Proceedings of the Conference on Mobile and Ubiquitous Multimedia* (2010), 16:1–16:10.
13. Hilliges, O., Izadi, S., Wilson, A. D., Hodges, S., Garcia-Mendoza, A., and Butz, A. Interactions in the air: adding further depth to interactive tabletops. In *Proceedings of the Symposium on User interface software and technology* (2009), 139–148.
14. Iwai, D., and Sato, K. Heat sensation in image creation with thermal vision. In *Proceedings of the Conference on Advances in computer entertainment technology* (2005), 213–216.
15. Iwai, D., and Sato, K. Limpid desk: see-through access to disorderly desktop in projection-based mixed reality. In *Proceedings of the Symposium on Virtual reality software and technology* (2006), 112–115.
16. Iwai, Y., Watanabe, K., Yagi, Y., and Yachida, M. Gesture recognition by using colored gloves. In *Proceedings of the Conference on Systems, Man, and Cybernetics* (1996), 76–81.
17. Izadi, S., Hodges, S., Taylor, S., Rosenfeld, D., Villar, N., Butler, A., and Westhues, J. Going beyond the display: a surface technology with an electronically switchable diffuser. In *Proceedings of the Symposium on User interface software and technology* (2008), 269–278.
18. Kane, S. K., Avrahami, D., Wobbrock, J. O., Harrison, B., Rea, A. D., Philipose, M., and LaMarca, A. Bonfire: a nomadic system for hybrid laptop-tabletop interaction. In *Proceedings of the 22nd annual ACM symposium on User interface software and technology* (2009), 129–138.
19. Khan, M. M., Ingleby, M., and Ward, R. D. Automated facial expression classification and affect interpretation using infrared measurement of facial skin temperature variations. *ACM Transactions on Autonomous Adaptive Systems 1*, 1 (2006), 91–113.
20. Kim, D., Hilliges, O., Izadi, S., Butler, A. D., Chen, J., Oikonomidis, I., and Olivier, P. Digits: freehand 3d interactions anywhere using a wrist-worn gloveless sensor. In *Proceedings of the Symposium on User interface software and technology* (2012), 167–176.
21. Koike, H., Sato, Y., and Kobayashi, Y. Integrating paper and digital information on enhanceddesk: a method for realtime finger tracking on an augmented desk system. *ACM Transactions on Computer-Human Interaction 8*, 4 (2001), 307–322.
22. Kong, S. G., Heo, J., Boughorbel, F., Zheng, Y., Abidi, B. R., Koschan, A., Yi, M., and Abidi, M. A. Multiscale fusion of visible and thermal ir images for illumination-invariant face recognition. *International Journal of Computer Vision 71*, 2 (2007), 215–233.

23. Larson, E., Cohn, G., Gupta, S., Ren, X., Harrison, B., Fox, D., and Patel, S. Heatwave: thermal imaging for surface user interaction. In *Proceedings of the Conference on Human Factors in Computing Systems* (2011), 2565–2574.

24. Lyda, W., Zimmermann, J., Burla, A., Regin, J., Osten, W., Sawodny, O., and Westkämper, E. Sensor and actuator conditioning for multiscale measurement systems on example of confocal microscopy. In *SPIE Europe Optical Metrology*, vol. 7389 (2009).

25. Manresa, C., Varona, J., Mas, R., and Perales, F. Hand tracking and gesture recognition for human-computer interaction. *Electronic letters on computer vision and image analysis 5*, 3 (2005), 96–104.

26. Mistry, P., Maes, P., and Chang, L. Wuw - wear ur world: a wearable gestural interface. In *Proceedings of the Conference on Human Factors in Computing Systems (extended abstracts)* (2009), 4111–4116.

27. Murugappan, S., Vinayak, Elmqvist, N., and Ramani, K. Extended multitouch: recovering touch posture and differentiating users using a depth camera. In *Proceedings of the Symposium on User interface software and technology* (2012), 487–496.

28. Otsu, N. A threshold selection method from gray-level histograms. *Automatica 11*, 285-296 (1975), 23–27.

29. Pham, Q.-C., Gond, L., Begard, J., Allezard, N., and Sayd, P. Real-time posture analysis in a crowd using thermal imaging. In *Proceedings of the Conference on Computer Vision and Pattern Recognition* (2007), 1–8.

30. Puri, C., Olson, L., Pavlidis, I., Levine, J., and Starren, J. Stresscam: non-contact measurement of users' emotional states through thermal imaging. In *Proceedings of the Conference on Human Factors in Computing Systems (extended abstracts)* (2005), 1725–1728.

31. Raheja, J. L., Das, K., and Chaudhary, A. Fingertip detection: A fast method with natural hand. *arXiv preprint arXiv:1212.0134* (2012).

32. Rukzio, E., Holleis, P., and Gellersen, H. Personal projectors for pervasive computing. *IEEE Pervasive Computing 11*, 2 (2012), 30–37.

33. Schmidt, D., Molyneaux, D., and Cao, X. Picontrol: using a handheld projector for direct control of physical devices through visible light. In *Proceedings of the Symposium on User interface software and technology* (2012), 379–388.

34. Stenger, B., Thayananthan, A., Torr, P. H., and Cipolla, R. Model-based hand tracking using a hierarchical bayesian filter. *Transactions on Pattern Analysis and Machine Intelligence 28*, 9 (2006), 1372–1384.

35. Tiziani, H., Haist, T., and Reuter, S. Optical inspection and characterization of microoptics using confocal microscopy. *Optics and lasers in engineering 36*, 5 (2001), 403–415.

36. Velten, A., Willwacher, T., Gupta, O., Veeraraghavan, A., Bawendi, M. G., and Raskar, R. Recovering three-dimensional shape around a corner using ultrafast time-of-flight imaging. *Nature Communications 3* (2012).

37. Vollmer, M., Henke, S., Karstädt, D., Möllmann, K., and Pinno, F. Identification and suppression of thermal reflections in infrared thermal imaging. In *Proceedings of Inframation*, vol. 5 (2004), 287–298.

38. Wang, R. Y., and Popović, J. Real-time hand-tracking with a color glove. In *ACM Transactions on Graphics*, vol. 28 (2009), 63:1–63:8.

39. Willis, K. D., Poupyrev, I., and Shiratori, T. Motionbeam: a metaphor for character interaction with handheld projectors. In *Proceedings of the Conference on Human Factors in Computing Systems* (2011), 1031–1040.

40. Wilson, A. D. Touchlight: an imaging touch screen and display for gesture-based interaction. In *Proceedings of the Conference on Multimodal interfaces* (2004), 69–76.

41. Wilson, A. D. Playanywhere: a compact interactive tabletop projection-vision system. In *Proceedings of the Symposium on User interface software and technology* (2005), 83–92.

42. Wilson, A. D. Depth sensing video cameras for 3d tangible tabletop interaction. In *Proceedings of Workshop on Horizontal Interactive Human-Computer Systems* (2007).

43. Wilson, A. D. Using a depth camera as a touch sensor. In *Proceedings of the Conference on Interactive Tabletops and Surfaces* (2010), 69–72.

44. Wilson, A. D., and Benko, H. Combining multiple depth cameras and projectors for interactions on, above and between surfaces. In *Proceedings of the Symposium on User interface software and technology* (2010), 273–282.

45. Winkler, C., Pfeuffer, K., and Rukzio, E. Investigating mid-air pointing interaction for projector phones. In *Proceedings of the Conference on Interactive tabletops and surfaces* (2012), 85–94.

46. Winkler, C., Reinartz, C., Nowacka, D., and Rukzio, E. Interactive phone call: synchronous remote collaboration and projected interactive surfaces. In *Proceedings of the Conference on Interactive Tabletops and Surfaces* (2011), 61–70.

47. Wong, W. K., Lim, H. L., Loo, C. K., and Lim, W. S. Home alone faint detection surveillance system using thermal camera. In *Proceedings of the Conference on Computer Research and Development* (2010), 747–751.

48. Wong, W. K., Tan, P. N., Loo, C. K., and Lim, W. S. An effective surveillance system using thermal camera. In *Proceedings of the Conference on Signal Acquisition and Processing* (2009), 13–17.

MisTable: Reach-through Personal Screens for Tabletops

Diego Martinez Plasencia, Edward Joyce, Sriram Subramanian
Department of Computer Science,
University of Bristol, UK
{diego.martinez-plasencia, ej0502, sriram.subramanian}@bristol.ac.uk

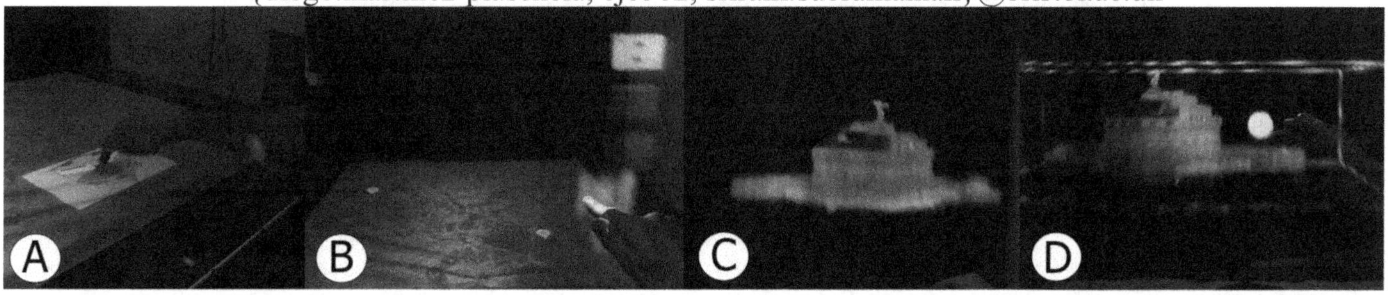

Figure 1. (A) MisTable combines a personal fog screen per user, a common tabletop and Kinect. This extends tabletops with additional interactive spaces: (B) personal 2D contents and storage on the personal screens and (C) 3D contents above the tabletop. (D) Augmenting real objects such as hands or tangibles is also possible.

ABSTRACT
We present MisTable, a tabletop system that combines a conventional horizontal interactive surface with personal screens between the user and the tabletop surface. These personal screens, built using fog, are both see-through and reach-through. Being see-through provides direct line of sight of the personal screen and the elements behind it on the tabletop. Being reach-through allows the user to switch from interacting with the personal screen to reaching through it to interact with the tabletop or the space above it. The personal screen allows a range of customisations and novel interactions such as presenting 2D personal contents on the screen, 3D contents above the tabletop or augmenting and relighting tangible objects differently for each user. Besides, having a personal screen for each user allows us to customize the view of each of them according to their identity or preferences. Finally, the personal screens preserve all well-established tabletop interaction techniques like touch and tangible interactions. We explore the challenges in building such a reach-through system through a proof-of-concept implementation and discuss the possibilities afforded by the system.

Author Keywords
See-through displays; tabletops systems; reach-through displays; fog screens.

ACM Classification Keywords
H.5.m. Information interfaces and presentation (e.g., HCI):

CHI 2014, April 26 - May 01, 2014, Toronto, ON, Canada.
Copyright 2014 ACM 978-1-4503-2473-1/14/04 $15.00.
http://dx.doi.org/10.1145/2556288.2557325

INTRODUCTION
In most tabletop systems the tabletop's surface becomes a shared space for information sharing and collocated collaboration while the space around it becomes a space for social interaction and discussion. The always visible shared surface of a tabletop encourages collaboration, but it also limits the opportunities for customizing the views for each user around the table.

Recognizing this limitation, researchers have proposed systems that combine tabletops with tablets and other personal devices which can offer a level of customization and view management through the screen of this personal device. Although elegant, such solutions require access to user's personal devices and can be cumbersome to initiate collaborations. In this paper we take a different approach. We provide a personal space between the user and the tabletop in the form of a see-through display which also allows the user to physically reach through it to interact with the table.

MisTable is a novel tabletop system that explores this concept of a reach-though personal display. These personal displays are presented between each user and the tabletop surface providing a display surface to show relevant content to the user (Figure 1b) while at the same time allowing users unhindered visibility and access to contents on the tabletop surface (Figure 1a). This feature of MisTable to create a see-through and reach-through display surface between the user and the tabletop surface opens a range of novel interaction possibilities.

Besides being able to use the personal screen as an auxiliary display surface to store content (Figure 1b), MisTable can now use the space above the tabletop surface to present 3D content that is personalized to a user (Figure 1c). More interestingly, being a reach-through display means users can poke their hands right through the personal screen and interact with the 3D content (Figure 1d).

The resulting system extends the capabilities of a common tabletop, aligning three interactive spaces, each of them with different dimensionalities and collaborative implications: the tabletop becomes a space for shared 2D interaction; personal screens hold personal 2D tasks and the volume above the tabletop supports 3D contents/interaction. All three spaces are within the users' reach, allowing them to easily migrate contents among spaces (e.g. drop a content on the tabletop to share it or in the volume above to reveal its 3D representation). Also, all three spaces stay in the users' line of sight, allowing them to keep peripheral awareness of other users and tasks.

We implement the personal screens on MisTable using a laminar curtain of fog [16]. Unexplored challenges exist when using fog as a personal screen. At short distances fog displays suffer from uneven brightness across the display. To enable reaching through the fog, one should consider the direction of fog flow and the projector throw direction to minimize turbulences and shadows while maximizing the screen brightness. Through a proof-of-concept prototype we measure the brightness profile of our fog display using a colorimeter and create a brightness compensation algorithm to create a uniform brightness profile. We finally explore the features enabled by MisTable through example implementations of relevant interaction opportunities.

This paper makes the following contributions; a) A novel system that combines a conventional tabletop with a personal screen that is both reach-through and see-through. b) An implementation of the personal screen using a laminar curtain of fog with technical details on brightness profiles and colour gamut at different angles c) An exposition of interaction possibilities enabled by MisTable through our proof-of-concept system.

All pictures in the paper and the accompanying video figure are taken in standard indoor lighting conditions, the room lights were not dimmed during filming or edited in any way after shooting. The images were taken using a canon EOS550 camera with 1/60 shutter speed and 3.5 aperture and ISO 400.

The rest of the paper is structured as follows. We start with the related work followed by a description of the concept of MisTable. We then provide detailed information on the design and implementation of the personal screen before presenting a collection of interaction possibilities enabled by MisTable. The paper then finishes with a short discussion and conclusion.

RELATED WORK

View enhanced tabletops allow personalized information to be presented to each user, which is one of the possibilities enabled by our personal screens. Several tabletop systems have been proposed that provide personalised information either using personal overlays or enabling transitions with personal devices. *Lenses* [29] provide local changes to views in selected regions of the tabletop allowing a user to inspect new information locally. However, these changes are visible to all users of the tabletop and can potentially occlude shared content causing interference to other users.

Systems like WeSpace [10], LUMAR [23] or E-conic [22] include multiple displays to alleviate interference. However, since it is not possible to see-through these displays they are often pushed to the periphery of the interaction space, like in WeSpace [10]. This usually leads to a loss in the awareness of other user's actions. To overcome this loss of awareness most systems use different forms of cursor and hand embodiments [22].

Lumisight [19], Ulteriorscape [14] and TaPS [20] overlay tabletop surfaces with diffusion control materials to create regions within the surface which are only visible from specific viewing angles. Thus each user around the tabletop can see a different personal view based on their seating position. However, the projection surface is still shared and users can accidentally occlude other's personal contents when interacting with the shared surface. MisTable detaches the personal space from the tabletop surface, while maintaining direct line of sight of the tabletop.

MisTable can present and allows interaction with 3D content on and above the tabletop surface. Most tabletop 3D systems [7], like the ImmersaDesk [6] or the responsive workbench [1] use shutter glasses to present stereoscopic contents for up to two users. Other systems like TADS [8] or PiVOT [15] support more users using auto-stereoscopic technologies. In all these systems, the display surface always lies behind the user's hands, which can cause problems due to incorrect depth occlusions. Users' hands occlude contents even if their hand penetrates the virtual content, which does not fit the way occlusions happen in the real world.

Placing a see-through display between the user and the tabletop can solve this issue. Other authors use see-through HMDs, either to augment a tabletop [2] or even a whole ecosystem of displays and spaces [3]. However, this forces users to be instrumented and partially occludes users' faces, hiding facial expressions and affecting social interaction.

SpaceTop [18] uses a see-through display over a regular desk and a depth camera. This transforms the space behind the display into a continuous 2D/3D interaction space that keeps some resemblances with our approach. Toucheo [9] uses a half-silver mirror similar to a virtual workbench [25] several centimetres above a tabletop. Such a see-through display between the user and the tabletop can be beneficial. They detach the location of personal contents from the tabletop avoiding accidental occlusions from other users' hands. Depth occlusions like the fingers reaching into virtual objects can also be reproduced (to our knowledge, none of them does). But their see-through element does not allow users to reach through the display. This limits direct interaction with the tabletop forcing users to move their hands around or below the display to interact with the surface behind.

Solutions exist that allow users to reach the space behind the image plane. Some approaches place a common display behind a lens at a distance that allows the formed image to appear to float in front of the lens. Virtual Panel [4] uses this feature to provide privacy lenses above a tabletop. iBall [12] and CrystalBall [5] add a transparent ball to create the illusion of a spherical display. Even though the image surface appears to float in front of the lens, it is actually displayed on the lens surface, so any object placed between the image surface and the lens will destroy the illusion. As a result, it is not possible to place a tabletop which is visible through the floating image (e.g. in VirtualPanel the tabletop is not visible through the privacy lenses). These approaches are unsuitable for our requirements.

A thin curtain of fog particles [16] can be used to create a translucent diffusion surface. Rakkalolainen et al. [27] explore their potential to display different images on each side of the screen and to see through them in a 2D face to face game and a 3D modeller. They also propose using them to create an extended desktop, in an office environment, visible from both sides.

We take this exploration further, illustrating how fog screens can be used in combination with tabletops to align three different interaction spaces (the all shared 2D tabletop, the personal 2D screen and 3D contents above the tabletop). The reach-though feature (not explored in [27] either) becomes a key element. First, it preserves tabletop interaction. Secondly, it allows users to easily move contents among interactive spaces and content's representation can be tailored according to space they occupy (e.g. a picture of a building could reveal a 3D representation when dropped in the 3D volume). Other possibilities, such as relighting tangibles or users hands/arms had never been explored either.

MISTABLE: SEE- AND REACH- THROUGH SYSTEM

MisTable is a tabletop system that combines a conventional tabletop system with personal fog screens between the user and the tabletop surface. Unlike solid see-though screens, MisTable allows the user to interact with the tabletop in a conventional way. Unlike reach-though screens using lenses, the space behind the display in MisTable can contain other objects (e.g. the tabletop or the users' hands). MisTable's personal screens are both see-though and reach-through allowing users to interact with the tabletop in a conventional way (see Figure 1a), but at the same time extending it in several unique ways.

The personal screens provide a personal auxiliary interactive surface that can be used to undertake individual tasks or store personal contents [28], as show in Figure 1b. The same screen can also be used to create an additional interaction volume above the tabletop surface. By tracking the user we can present 3D contents with motion parallax and perspective correction depth cues. When the user reaches in to interact with the 3D content we can provide correct occlusions such as the user's hand penetrating the 3D content. Stereo techniques are available as explained in [26]. Furthermore, the personal screen can be used to re-light objects on the tabletop surface. For example, tangible objects or user's hands can be augmented with additional digital information.

The personal screen provides direct line of sight and access to the different interaction spaces (screen itself, tabletop and volume above it). Users can stay aware of each others' actions and effortlessly switch between interacting with the personal screen to the tabletop surface or the interaction volume. This allows users to easily break in or out of shared tasks to better support mixed focus collaboration [29].

Users can also move contents freely between these interaction spaces. Moving contents between the tabletop and the personal screen allow users to share it with others or to get exclusive ownership over it. Content representation can also be adapted to the presentation space where they are moved. A content dropped in the volume above the tabletop can enable 3D manipulation techniques. A content moved to a personal screen can change its appearance or display controls according to the identity/preferences of the user.

FOG SCREENS FOR TABLETOPS

Commercial fog-based displays such as FogScreen® or IO2's HelioDisplay have demonstrated their ability to create thrilling experiences at TV shows, exhibitions, fashion events and concerts. Presenters can enter the stage through a fog curtain displaying impressive special effects.

Rakkalolainen et al. [26] reported artefacts affecting these systems (projector to observer distance over 5 meters). However, projection on these displays in the short range (like in our tabletop context) raises several challenges. First of all, fog and mist produce a non linear scattering of the light [26]. Contents projected on a fog screen become more dim as the angle between the incident light and the observer increases (e.g. to the sides of the screen). While this effect is not so important in a theatre or TV stage (the long distance makes all rays to the observer almost parallel), it has a great impact when the observer is close to the screen. Besides, reaching with an arm through the screen affects the flow of fog, producing turbulences that affect projection and, if the projector is not carefully located, arms can cast shadows on the display.

We start with an analysis of these issues and propose a feasible design to use fog displays in conjunction with tabletops. Our implementation of the fog screen is adapted from the design proposed by Kakashara [16]. Specific details about the implementation of our screen and fog distribution system are provided later in the paper.

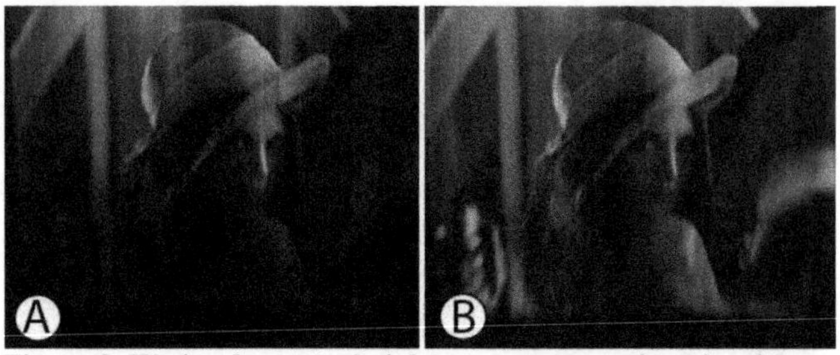

Figure 2. We implement a brightness compensation algorithm. (a) Normal and (b) corrected images.

Brightness correction

Brightness across the screen varies greatly when the observer is close to it. The spot on the screen between the user and the projector is blinding bright and the colours wash off as the image spans to the sides. This attenuation is a function of the angle between the incoming light hitting a point of the screen and the observer. We studied the brightness profile of our screen using a colorimeter and implemented a brightness compensation algorithm to attenuate brightness differences across the screen. The results of applying this algorithm are visible in Figure 2.

In order to characterise the behaviour of our screen, we projected different colours (i.e. white, red, green and blue) into a small target region of the screen and measured the colour profile using a Konica Minolta CS100a colorimeter (Figure 3a). We took three sets of ten measures of the colour profile (white, red, green and blue) at nine different angles, for a total of 1080 samples. Measures below five degrees were impractical as luminance was above the upper limit of 49,900 cd/m^2 supported by our colorimeter. The experiment was performed in a dark room without any other light sources or windows.

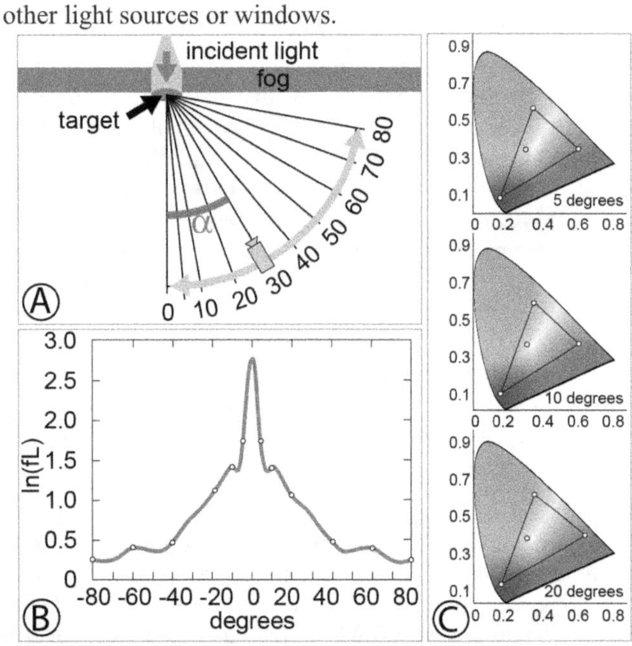

Figure 3. (a) Measurements taken and (b) brightness profile obtained. (c) Colour gamuts show no changes in chromacity.

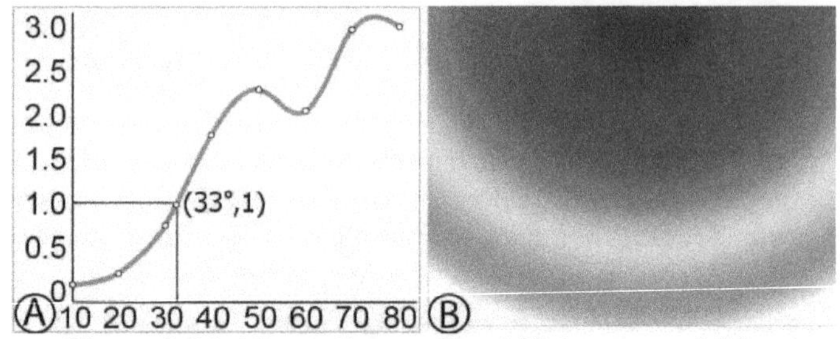

Figure 4. (a) Attenuation profile at 33 degrees and (b) resulting mask used.

Figure 3.c present colour gamuts at different angles, representing the chromacity of the colours that can be generated. We found no differences in chromacity related to the angle. Although one might expect differences due to changes in refractive index with wavelength, we believe that the number of particles across our fog screen is high enough to counterbalance for these differences.

Figure 3.b shows the brightness profile obtained in a logarithmic scale (as perceived by the human eye), with intermediate points approximated using cubic splines. Brightness is remarkably higher at small angles and it decreases almost linearly above 15 degrees. Brightness becomes impractical below 75degrees.

We use the information of our brightness profile to produce an attenuation correction mask that creates a uniform brightness profile across the screen. Figure 4.a shows the attenuation distribution used to correct the image in Figure 2 for a reference brightness at 33 degrees (centre of the screen).

Figure 4.b shows the attenuation mask computed according to the attenuation function and the relative position of the observer and the projector. The blue region corresponds to parts of the image where the brightness needs to be reduced. The purple region corresponds to those parts that need to be over saturated. Note the secondary purple ripple corresponding to the local maximum present at 60 degrees in our brightness profile. Our approach is a best effort approach, given the capabilities of our projector. There are situations in which it is not possible to achieve the desired colour. These are visible as white regions in Figure 4.a.

Turbulence and direction of the fog

A fog based system is made of particles of water. If the particles of water are too large then they can condense in the hands of the user making the user's hand wet when interacting with the fog curtain. Using a particle size of around 0.4 microns makes fog float around user's arms, avoiding condensation. The curtain of fog particles must be enclosed between two laminar flows of air to avoid turbulence and maximize image quality [16].

This laminar flow gets disrupted as the user reaches the hand through the screen. While not so important for general purpose fog screens, when used in our context, user's locus of interaction will be many times behind the screen (on the

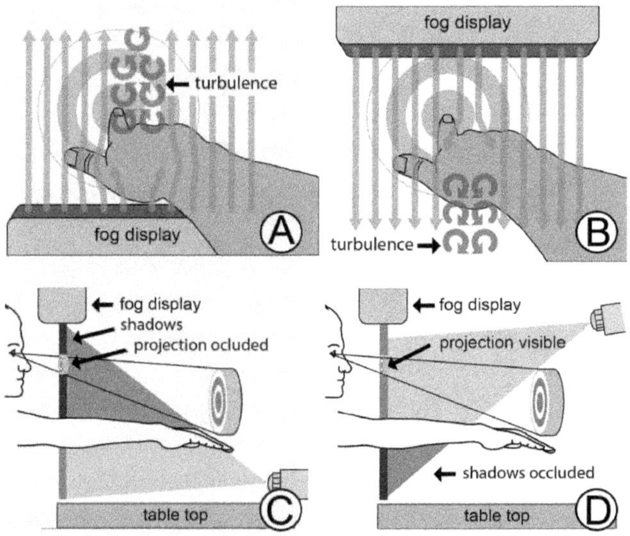

Figure 5. (a) Fog rising from below causes turbulences in the observer's locus of attention. (b) Fog falling from above causes turbulences below the arms. (c) Projecting from below causes shadows on the screen. (d) Shadows hidden below the user's hands with top projection.

tabletop or on an object floating above it). In this case, these turbulences can have a significant impact (Figure 5a).

To ease this problem, in our system the fog is dropped from above. In this case (Figure 5b), when a user extends their arm through the screen, it is the space below the arm that becomes turbulent. This space is most often occluded by the user's own arm. Furthermore, with the user's focus of attention on the target from above the arm rather than below a turbulent region below the extended arm causes minimal impact on the task. On the other hand, fog rising from below (like in Displair or HelioDisplay) would cause visible turbulent regions in the region of the user's focus of attention.

Location of the projector

The location of the projector illuminating the fog screen is another important factor to consider when it is used in a tabletop context. Commercial medium size displays, like HelioDisplay (30 inches) place a projector behind the screen projecting upwards towards the users. Although placing the projector below has the inconvenience that when the user looks directly into the projector the bright spot becomes visible, the regions around it get the benefit of the higher luminance values around the bright spot.

However, when a user reaches the arm to interact with 3D objects above the tabletop, shadows will be cast in the space behind the hand and the projector. In a bottom-up projection (as with HelioDisplay), these shadows would occlude big parts of the screen and particularly, the target that the user is reaching (see Figure 5c). For these reasons, MisTable, places the projector above the opposite side of the table, avoiding direct line of sight of the projector. Thus, shadows are projected in the space below the arms which, in general is occluded by the arm itself (Figure 5d).

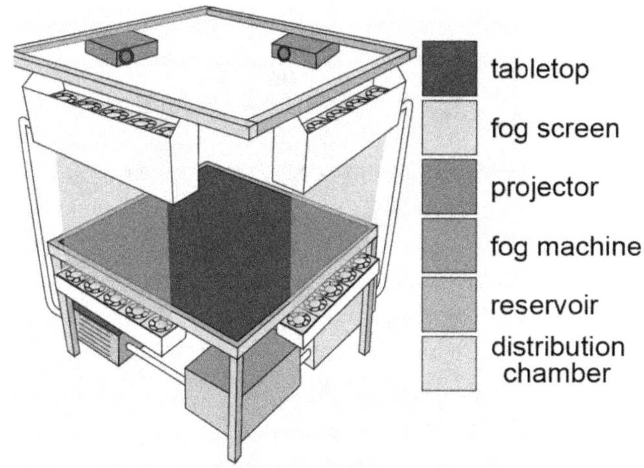

Figure 6. Main elements in MisTable include: a tabletop system, personal fog screens and projectors; and a fog distribution system.

The projector is located so that the observer can visualize the top part of the screen with an angle to the projector rays of 10 degrees. This avoids the brightest parts of the image that blind the user and eliminates shadows due to users' hands. The resulting screen is visible to an observer at 30 cm from the fog screen with a projector to observer angle between 10 to 65 degrees. This range is chosen from our brightness distribution profile to maximize image brightness and avoid glaring. Footprint and scalability issues were also considered. Placing the projectors at bigger distances would allow a more reduced and brighter range of the brightness profile to be used, but it would also increase the footprint of the system and make it more difficult to scale for four users.

IMPLEMENTATION OF MISTABLE

The basic elements of MisTable are shown in Figure 6 and include: a conventional tabletop of size 86x86 cm, a fog distribution system, personal fog screens, a tracking system and a software component.

Fog distribution system

The fog distribution system in MisTable contains a fog machine, a reservoir and a fog distribution chamber. We use a glycerine based continuous fog machine. Preliminary versions used piezoelectric foggers and water, but we found it difficult to achieve a stable fog generation and fog tended to condense in the pipes. Fog thickness was also lower than that produced by glycerine based machines.

Two chambers are used to hold and distribute the fog. The first one (reservoir) stores a volume of 70 litres of fog and is important to allow a steady supply of fog. When the fog machine is on, pressurized fog could travel all the way to the personal screens. The reservoir helps prevent fog bursts. Then, the second (distribution) chamber creates a negatively pressurized chamber that drags the fog and delivers it through the pipes to the personal screens. One fan per screen, controlled using pulse width modulation

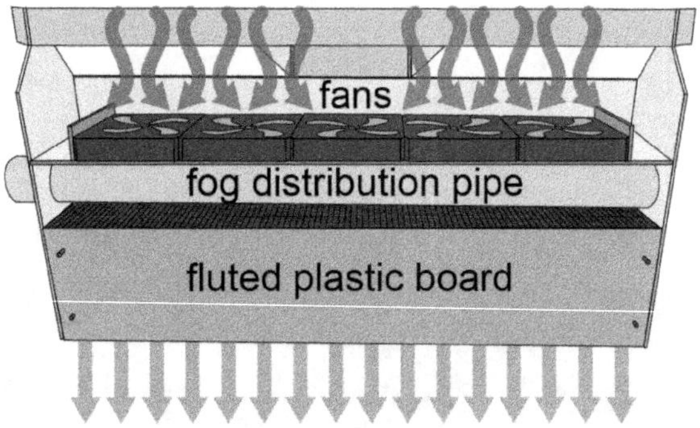

Figure 7. Detail of the personal screens showing the distribution pipe, the fans and the fluted board that create the laminar flow.

created this negative pressure and assures an equal amount of fog reaches each screen.

Personal fog screens

We built two personal fog screens of 60x47 cm at two adjacent sides of the tabletop, designed as shown in Figure 7. The screens have a fog distribution pipe, with a slit of 15 mm at the bottom. We used 12 cm fans to blow air around the pipe into a stack of fluted plastic below it. Adjusting the speed of the fans, we create a laminar flow of air to drag the fog. The speed must be slow enough for the flow to remain laminar, but fast enough to cover the total height of our screen. Extractors below the screen capture the fog and stabilize the image at its bottom part.

Users sensing

Personal 2D contents presented on the fog screen are correctly visible independent of the user's location. Presenting 3D contents, however, requires tracking the users' heads to support motion parallax and perspective correction depth cues. Our prototype uses Kinect to track the users head position and to track hand gestures on and above the tabletop surface. Its limited field of view (~57° horizontal FOV) meant we used two Kinects, one to cover the space above the tabletop and another to track the head of the users around MisTable.

A four degrees of freedom head tracking (position and rotation around the vertical axis) was implemented using the Kinect SDK and OpenCV. Background subtraction and depth based thresholding was used to segment user's heads. Contours detected were approximated by ellipses and their major axis was used to identify the rotations of the users' heads (i.e. to better approximate the position of the eyes).

dSensingNI [17] was used to detect fingers, hands and tangibles above the tabletop. The information about the fingers and hands is used to build an approximate 3D model of the users' arms. These models are used to account for incorrect depth occlusions as explained later in the paper. The initial position of the hand when it appears into the volume above the tabletop is used to identify to which user the hand (and the connected fingers) belongs to. This is important to allow each user to interact with personal

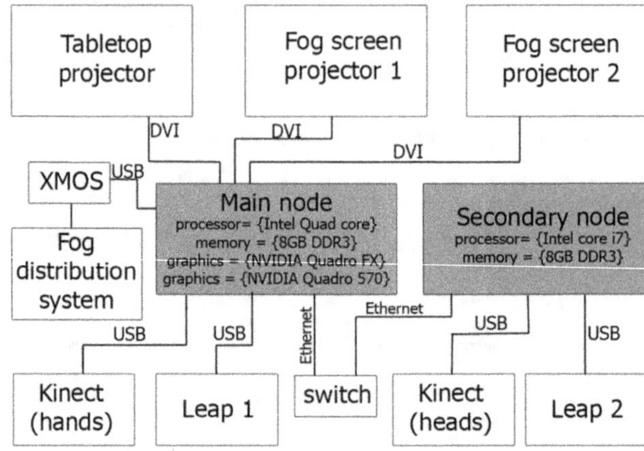

Figure 8. Component diagram of Mistable.

contents that might only be present for him/her. dSensingNI could not detect precise interactions on the personal screens. A leap motion device was added at the top of each fog screen for this task.

This selection of devices granted us accurate user registration without user instrumentation, but we expect that future sensing technologies, with a bigger FOV, range and accuracy, will allow more simple arrangements to be used.

Software Component and System Architecture

The system, detailed in Figure 8, is built around a workstation using two graphics cards, in order to connect all three graphical outputs (tabletop and personal screens) to the same computer. We built a software framework in C++, using the OGRE3D rendering engine. The brightness compensation algorithm was implemented as an NVIDIA CG shader. This shader requires computations that are expensive and could potentially interfere the real time requirements of the system. To avoid this, we compute our brightness attenuation mask using a low resolution texture (128x86 pixels), which is then applied to the full resolution of our image (1024x768). This results in a sub sampling of the brightness profile and linear interpolation is used for intermediate pixels. An XMOS XC-1A board was used to control the fog distribution chamber and fans in the fog screens. The Kinect used to track users' hands and fingers and the Leap for the first user were also connected to this computer. A secondary node was introduced to leverage the computing requirements of the application. The second Kinect and its head tracking algorithm were executed in this secondary node. The Leap used to detect finger interactions from the second user was also connected to this computer. Both nodes were connected through a switch and a local ethernet connection, using the OSC/UDP to deliver finger and head tracking messages.

EXPLORING INTERACTION OPPORTUNITIES

MisTable extends the capabilities of a conventional tabletop in many novel and unique ways, aligning interactive spaces for personal 2D and 3D tasks in the line of sight and within arm's reach of the users. Through our proof-of-concept

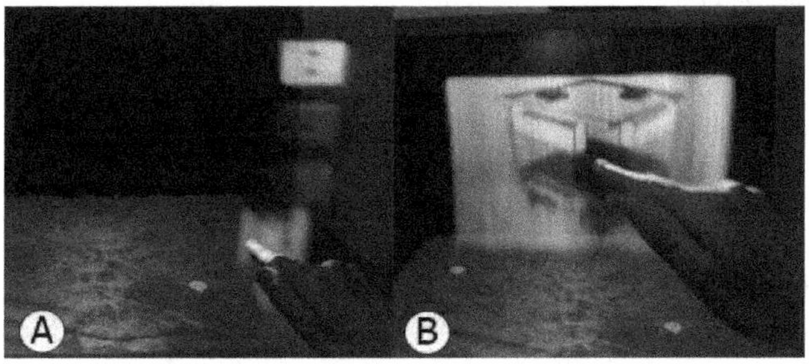

Figure 9. (a and b) The personal screen can be used as a space to undertake individual tasks. At the same time, users stay aware of the tabletop and can join at any time.

implementation we explored many of these new features and we describe them below.

Personal screens for mixed focus collaboration

Figure 9 illustrates the capabilities of our personal screens as an auxiliary interaction territory [28] and storage space [21]. Each screen contains a side menu to store user's personal contents. Users can select from contents from the side menu using a simple crossing gesture (Figure 9a) and interact with them using standard finger interaction gestures (Figure 9b). As long as the user's hand is approximately within the plane of the fog, all user's finger movements are interpreted to mean interaction with the personal screen. So pausing the finger on an image selects it and moving the finger moves the content. However, if the user makes a quick inward gesture from the personal screen towards the tabletop, the selected content is pushed towards the tabletop surface where it becomes available to all other users.

As soon as the system detects this pushing gesture, the content on the personal screen changes its perspective to give the appearance of it falling onto the tabletop. This gives the user clear visual confirmation of the system's action and the final position of the content on the tabletop. Similarly, the user can direct this pushing action towards another personal screen and the content gets dropped as an icon in the other user's screen. A simple confirmation mechanism can be implemented to check that the receiver wants to accept this content. However in our current implementation the content merely appeared at the centre of the second user's personal screen.

Users can also pick contents from the tabletop and bring them to their screen. When the user makes a quick and deliberate lifting gesture with their finger above the tabletop surface, the content controlled by the finger starts moving up towards the user's personal screen. The personal screen presents the content in such a way that it appears to be moving out of the table and onto the personal screen.

Our current implementation only supports simple finger tracking and recognition, so the content is always moved to the personal screen in the direction of the finger lift gesture. However, with finger identification (like [11]) the system can detect whether the personal screen belongs to the user or not

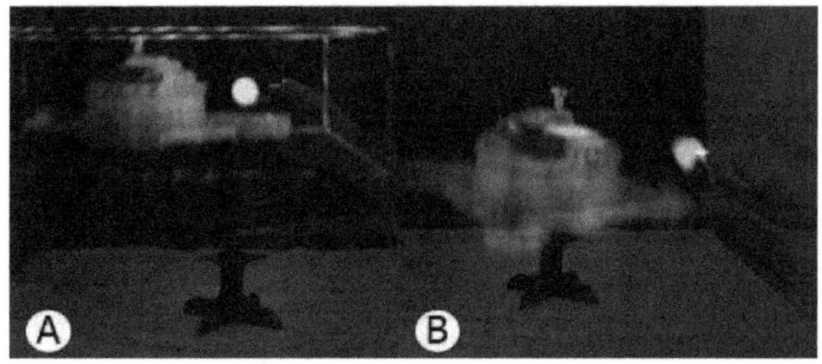

Figure 10. MisTable supports different types of 3D interaction: (a) Direct 3D interaction, (b) multitouch finger interaction.

and request permission of the personal screen owner before dropping content onto the personal screen.

Direct, indirect and tangible 3D interaction

MisTable uses a conventional multi-touch table, but the volume above it can display 3D contents and other interactive augmentations. To interact with them, MisTable can borrow well-established interaction techniques from the 3D user interface community. However, it can also reuse techniques from traditional tabletop systems, providing a rich and flexible range of techniques.

For example, Figure 10a. shows a user manipulating a 3D object directly with his hands, in an implementation of a virtual hand technique. Users can also rotate the object around constrained (i.e. vertical and horizontal) axes by sliding their fingers up-and-down or left-and-right (Figure 10.b). Finally, tangible objects can be used to rotate the object using bimanual interactions. Users can easily switch between these interaction techniques to adapt to the interactions style that best suits the application context.

Brightness control to adjust visibility

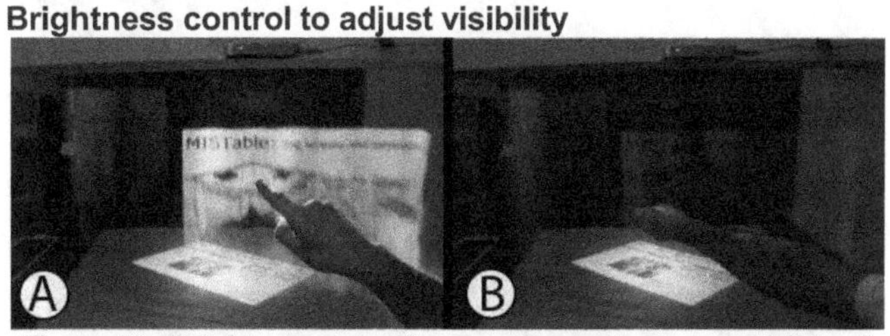

Figure 11. Brightness control can make content more visible of more see-through. (a) Contents can adapt to the user locus of interaction, becoming more visible when interacted, or (b) transparent when the user reaches through the screen.

The brightness of the fog display can be used to increase or decrease the visibility of the contents projected onto it. Increasing the brightness enhances the visibility of the contents on the fog display, while lowering brightness increases the visibility of the elements behind it (e.g. hands, tabletop, tangibles, etc.).

Figure11 illustrates how brightness control is used in our system to adapt to the locus of interaction of the user. Initially, when the user's hands are not detected by the system, MisTable uses a medium brightness that allows both contents on the personal screen and contents on the tabletop to be visible. When the user reaches the personal screen to interact with it (as seen Figure 11a), the brightness of those contents (the picture) are increased to enhance visibility. Other contents not in focus are dimmed, allowing the user to see through them better. If the user puts their arm through the screen contents can be made more transparent providing better visibility through it (Figure 11b). Our system makes brightness control a property of each object on the personal screen. Depending on the context of interaction this parameter can be manipulated to either bring it to the user's attention or to fade it away leaving the user to focus on the tabletop, other objects or the users around the tabletop.

Within a collaborative context, brightness control could also be used to raise awareness of ownership and provide personal overlays over the 3D contents displayed. 3D objects above the tabletop could be equally visible to all users when they are located above the central part of the table, as they can be considered a shared content. When a user grasps an object and moves it closer to their end of the table, its visibility to this user can be enhanced while other users' visibility can be reduced. This could represent the user's intention to get exclusive control of the object and accompany granting ownership of the object to the user, allowing him/her to access extra functionality. These are simple examples of the potential of this technique. Its major difference when compared to any tabletop where object brightness can be dynamically controlled is that brightness also affects the see-through component of the content.

Depth perception of 3D contents

MisTable can provide a range of 3D depth perception cues. Perspective correction and motion parallax allow objects to be correctly presented according to the position of the user, and a variety of stereo techniques are supported [26].

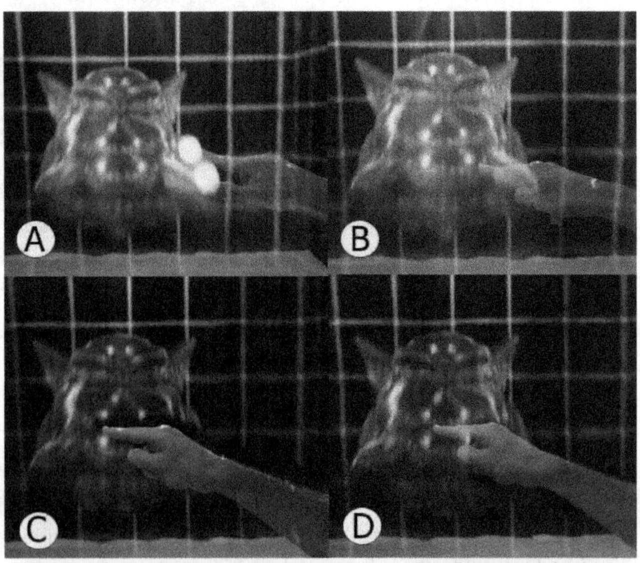

Figure 12. Techniques used to enhance depth perception: (a) 3D cursors on the fingertips. (b) These get occluded when inside the object. (c) An approximate, black 3D model of the hand allows the user to see his hand though the fog. (d) Parts of the hand inside the object do get occluded.

MisTable also deals with false occlusions to facilitate depth perception when users' hands reach into objects. We implemented two techniques, illustrated in Figure 12. In Figure 12a, user's fingertips are overlaid with bright white spots, as proposed in [27]. Spots represent 3D cursors to provide the user with a clear indication of the point of interaction. When the cursor penetrates an object, it disappears inside the it, providing the user with feedback that they are actually inside the object (Figure 12b). Even though the 3D cursors become invisible, the virtual object is still incorrectly presented over the user hand, even if that part of the hand is actually outside the object. Background lines are also incorrectly overlaid on the hand.

Figure 12c shows a second approach where we use brightness control and the 3D hand representation to create a more realistic presentation. Using the approximate 3D hand model obtained through the tracking system, we present the hand in black (no lighting applied), so the parts of the display where the hand model is visible are highly see-though. This allows users to see their real hands when outside of an object (Figure 12c). When the finger penetrates an object, the part of the darkened hand model gets occluded inside and the 3D object overlaps the parts of the user's hands inside the object (Figure 12d). This creates correct occlusions, where parts of the objects can overlap a user's hands and can provide the users with an additional and valuable depth perception cue.

Augmenting real objects

The ability of MisTable to augment real object enables some of the benefits of spatial augmented reality systems like Illuminating Clay[24], SandScape [13]and URP [30]. In those approaches projection happens on the same surface of the objects, so the effects are visible to all user, and can reveal registration problems to some users. In MisTable, projection happens on each users' fog screen, so the effect is only correct from their position. This allows us to create different effects on the same object for each user or to minimize hindrance to other users.

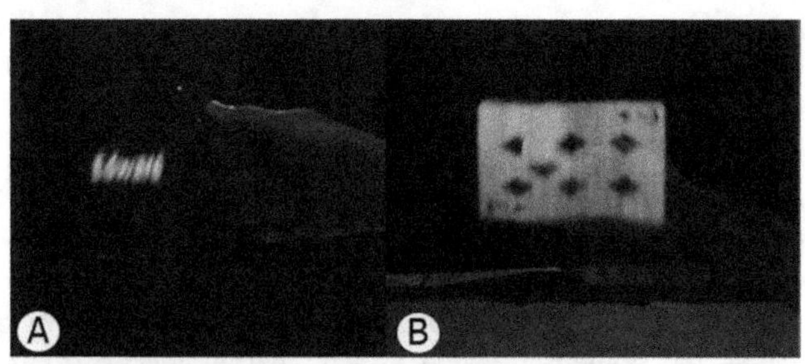

Figure 13. MisTable can relight different real objects. (a) a cup with its owner's name on it (b) content overlaid on a user's hand.

Augmentation can be applied to both tangible objects and to parts of the users' bodies. Figure 13a shows a cup of tea augmented with its owner's name, while Figure13b shows content projected on the hand of a user. These two examples illustrate the ability of MisTable to augment and personalise the appearance of real objects.

This could be used to provide embodiments and increase awareness of collaborative tabletop tasks. When other users are interacting with content on the tabletop, both their hands and the content get overlaid with a common (yellow) colour in the observer's screen. This informs a user about another users' locus of interaction providing additional task awareness to the observer. Because these overlays are personalised to each user different forms of embodiments and awareness cues can be overlaid to each user to allow better contextualising of the cues. Other elements, like tangibles or the whole users' silhouette could also be augmented this way.

We can also augment a user's appearance to create better effects in a gaming scenario. For example, the dungeon master in dungeons and dragons can have different avatars overlaid on the other players to create a more compelling gaming scenario.

DISCUSSION

This paper has focused on exploring the interaction opportunities raised by using fog based personal screens around a tabletop system. Our implementation of MisTable allowed us to explore these possibilities, focusing mostly on image quality and user interaction.

Other aspects related to the usage of MisTable should also be considered when designing interactive experiences for MisTable. Touchless and 3D interaction (when users interact with their fog screens or above the tabletop) forces users to keep their arms stretched, which is known to cause fatigue. Performance might also be affected due to the lack of tactile feedback.

Secondly, these touchless contents will float in the space between the users. A high density of objects could clutter visibility of other users, affecting social interaction. The fact that other users cannot effectively judge what another user is seeing through his/her screen (i.e. contents can be tailored/different for each user, and they are only correct from their point of view), could also introduce disruptions in the collaborative workflows. This could lead to situations in which one user could think another user is looking at him/her, while he/she is actually looking at a personalized content. Peripheral awareness of other user's actions and our inherent ability to tell when somebody is actually looking into our eyes should help avoiding these issues.

There are also elements that need to be considered when building and deploying a MisTable system. MisTable can be used in normal indoor lighting conditions and all images in this paper and the accompanying video was shot in the presence of ambient light. However, the location where it is deployed can impact the quality of the system. MisTable relies on a laminar curtain of fog to create the personal display surfaces. Open spaces, or any space with air currents can distort these laminar flows making the system unusable.

One needs to take great care in building the fog distribution and extractor system. Fog leaks or even fog pushed away from the extractors when users interact with the system can have an impact on the continuous use of the system for extended periods of time. When used continuously, these leakages could fill the room with fog and affect image quality. The projector image would get scattered before reaching the fog screens leaving a visible light path from the projector to the personal screen. It could also interfere with the tracking devices used, given fog's ability to scatter or even reflect the IR light on which many tracking technologies rely. Our experience has shown that in extreme cases a fog leak can trigger a smoke alarm. This is something to be aware of during the initial stages of system development where leaks are more likely to occur.

Our implementation required a complex arrangement of devices. This choice allowed us to accomplish the kind of user registration required to explore the range of interaction possibilities of MisTable. However, user's head tracking is not necessary if only 2D content is going to be presented on the fog screen. This scenario still enables important interaction possibilities (e.g. personal territories detached from the shared surface, storage space for user's personal contents, line of sight visibility of the tabletop for mixed focus collaboration). The hardware arrangement in this situation would be minimal.

CONCLUSIONS

MisTable is a tabletop system that combines a conventional horizontal interactive surface with personal screens between the user and the tabletop surface. We used a projected fog based display to create the personal screens that are both see-through and reach-through. We examine various design issues and through a prototype demonstrate that such systems can be built. We further explore various interaction possibilities enabled by MisTable. For example, MisTable allows the creation of a new interaction volume above the tabletop surface where interactive content (both 2D and 3D) can be presented. MisTable is able to accomplish this while preserving the social interactions enabled by tabletops. We believe these features illustrate the potential of MiSTable as a novel tabletop system to support new forms of interaction and collaboration.

ACKNOWLEDGEMENTS

We thank Matt Sutton for taking the images and the video. This work is supported by European Research Council (Starting Grant Agreement 278576) under the Seventh Framework Programme.

REFERENCES

1. Agrawala, M., A.C. Beers, I. McDowall, B. Frohlich, M. Bolas, and P. Hanrahan, *The two-user Responsive Workbench: support for collaboration through individual views of a shared space*, in *ACM SIGGRAPH*. 1997, ACM Press. p. 327-332.

2. Benko, H., E.W. Ishak, and S. Feiner, *Cross-dimensional gestural interaction techniques for hybrid immersive environments*, in *IEEE VR*. 2005. p. 209-216.
3. Butz, A., T. Hollerer, S. Feiner, B. MacIntyre, and C. Beshers, *Enveloping users and computers in a collaborative 3D augmented reality*, in *ACM IWAR*. 1999. p. 35-44.
4. Chan, L.-W., H. Ting-Ting, L. Jin-Yao, H. Yi-Ping, and H. Jane, *On top of tabletop: A virtual touch panel display*, in *IEEE TABLETOP*. 2008. p. 169-176.
5. Chan, L., Y.-F. Chuang, M.-C. Yu, Y.-L. Chao, M.-S. Lee, Y.-P. Hung, and J. Hsu, *Gesture-based interaction for a magic crystal ball*, in *ACM VRST*. 2007, ACM Press: Newport Beach, California. p. 157-164.
6. Czernuszenko, M., D. Pape, D. Sandin, T. DeFanti, G.L. Dawe, and M.D. Brown, *The ImmersaDesk and Infinity Wall projection-based virtual reality displays*. SIGGRAPH Computer Graphics, 1997. **31**(2): p. 46-49.
7. Grossman, T. and D. Wigdor, *Going Deeper: a Taxonomy of 3D on the Tabletop*, in *IEEE TABLETOP*. 2007. p. 137-144.
8. Gu, Y., A. State, and H. Fuchs, *A practical multi-viewer tabletop autostereoscopic display*, in *IEEE ISMAR*. 2010. p. 147-156.
9. Hachet, M., B. Bossavit, A. Cohe, and J.B. de la Rivi, *Toucheo: multitouch and stereo combined in a seamless workspace*, in *ACM UIST*. 2011, ACM Press: Santa Barbara, California, USA. p. 587-592.
10. Hao, J., D. Wigdor, C. Forlines, and S. Chia, *System design for the WeSpace: Linking personal devices to a table-centered multi-user, multi-surface environment*, in *IEEE TABLETOP*. 2008. p. 97-104.
11. Holz, C. and P. Baudisch, *Fiberio: a touchscreen that senses fingerprints*, in *ACM UIST*. 2013, ACM Press: St. Andrews, Scotland, United Kingdom. p. 41-50.
12. Ikeda, H., H. Naemura, T. Harashima, and J. Ishikawa, *i-ball: Interactive information display like a crystal ball.* , in *SIGGRAPH*. 2001. p. 122.
13. Ishii, H., C. Ratti, B. Piper, Y. Wang, A. Biderman, and E. Ben-Joseph, *Bringing Clay and Sand into Digital Design — Continuous Tangible user Interfaces*. BT Technology Journal, 2004. **22**(4): p. 287-299.
14. Kakehi, Y. and T. Naemura, *UlteriorScape: Interactive optical superimposition on a view-dependent tabletop display*, in *IEEE TABLETOP*. 2008. p. 189-192.
15. Karnik, A., D. Martinez, W. Mayol-Cuevas, and S. Subramanian, *PiVOT: personalized view-overlays for tabletops*, in *ACM UIST*. 2012, ACM Press: Cambridge, Massachusetts, USA. p. 271-280.
16. Kataoka, A. and Y. Kasahara, *Method and apparatus for a fog screen and image-forming method using the same*. 1993, US patent 07985755: US.
17. Klompmaker, F., K. Nebe, and A. Fast, *dSensingNI: a framework for advanced tangible interaction using a depth camera*, in *ACM TEI*. 2012, ACM Press: Kingston, Ontario, Canada. p. 217-224.
18. Lee, J., A. Olwal, H. Ishii, and C. Boulanger, *SpaceTop: integrating 2D and spatial 3D interactions in a see-through desktop environment*, in *ACM CHI*. 2013, ACM Press: Paris, France. p. 189-192.
19. Matsushita, M., M. Iida, T. Ohguro, Y. Shirai, Y. Kakehi, and T. Naemura, *Lumisight table: a face-to-face collaboration support system that optimizes direction of projected information to each stakeholder*, in *ACM CSCW*. 2004, ACM Press: Chicago, Illinois, USA. p. 274-283.
20. Mollers, M. and J. Borchers, *TaPS widgets: interacting with tangible private spaces*, in *ACM ITS*. 2011, ACM Press: Kobe, Japan. p. 75-78.
21. Muller-Tomfelde, C., *Tabletops - Horizontal Interactive Displays*. 2010: Springer Publishing Company, Incorporated. 484.
22. Nacenta, M.A., S. Sakurai, T. Yamaguchi, Y. Miki, Y. Itoh, Y. Kitamura, S. Subramanian, and C. Gutwin, *E-conic: a perspective-aware interface for multi-display environments*, in *ACM UIST*. 2007, ACM Press: Newport, Rhode Island, USA. p. 279-288.
23. Olwal, A. and A. Henrysson, *LUMAR: A Hybrid Spatial Display System for 2D and 3D Handheld Augmented Reality*, in *Artificial Reality and Telexistence*. 2007, IEEE Computer Society. p. 63-70.
24. Piper, B., C. Ratti, and H. Ishii, *Illuminating clay: a 3-D tangible interface for landscape analysis*, in *ACM CHI*. 2002, ACM Press: Minneapolis, Minnesota, USA. p. 355-362.
25. Poston, T. and L. Serra, *The virtual workbench: dextrous VR*, in *VRST*. 1994, World Scientific Publishing Co., Inc.: Singapore, Singapore. p. 111-121.
26. Rakkolainen, I., *Measurements and Experiments of the Immaterial Virtual Reality Display*, in *3DTV Conference: The True Vision - Capture, Transmission and Display of 3D Video*. 2008. p. 37-40.
27. Rakkolainen, I., T. Hollerer, S. Diverdi, and A. Olwal, *Mid-air display experiments to create novel user interfaces*. Multimedia Tools Appl., 2009. **44**(3): p. 389-405.
28. Scott, S.D., M. Sheelagh, T. Carpendale, and K.M. Inkpen, *Territoriality in collaborative tabletop workspaces*, in *ACM CSCW*. 2004, ACM Press: Chicago, Illinois, USA. p. 294-303.
29. Tang, A., M. Tory, B. Po, P. Neumann, and S. Carpendale, *Collaborative coupling over tabletop displays*, in *ACM CHI*. 2006, ACM Press: Montreal, Quebec, Canada. p. 1181-1190.
30. Underkoffler, J. and H. Ishii, *Urp: a luminous-tangible workbench for urban planning and design*, in *ACM CHI*. 1999, ACM Press: Pittsburgh, Pennsylvania, USA. p. 386-393.

What is a Device Bend Gesture Really Good for?

Teemu Ahmaniemi
Nokia Research Center
Espoo, Finland
teemu.ahmaniemi(at)nokia.com

Johan Kildal
Nokia Research Center
Espoo, Finland
johan.kildal(at)nokia.com

Merja Haveri
Cresense Ltd.
Helsinki, Finland
merja.haveri(at)cresense.com

ABSTRACT

Device deformation allows new types of gestures to be used in interaction. We identify that the gesture/use-case pairings proposed by interaction designers are often driven by factors relating improved tangibility, spatial directionality and strong metaphorical bonds. With this starting point, we argue that some of the designs may not make use of the full potential of deformation gestures as continuous, bipolar input techniques. In two user studies, we revisited the basics of deformation input by taking a new systematic look at the question of matching gestures with use cases. We observed comparable levels of UX when using bend input in different continuous bipolar interactions, irrespective of the choice of tangibility, directionality and metaphor. We concluded that device bend gestures use their full potential when used to control continuous bipolar parameters, and when quick reactions are needed. From our studies, we also identify relative strengths of absolute and relative mappings, and report a Fitts' law study for device bending input.

Author Keywords

Device deformation, bend input, Organic UI, absolute mapping, relative mapping, Fitts' law

ACM Classification Keywords

H.5.2 [Information interfaces and presentation]: User Interfaces - Input devices and strategies, Haptic I/O.

INTRODUCTION

Deformable user interfaces (DUIs) have gained considerable interest in recent years. The development of flexible display technology has made it possible to conceive devices that can be bent, twisted or otherwise deformed while the display still produces high resolution images in non-planar configurations. Concept devices such as Gummi [26], Nokia Kinetic Device [15] and PaperPhone [17] provide attractive scenarios based on deformable devices equipped with a flexible display and deformation sensors.

CHI 2014, April 26 - May 01 2014, Toronto, ON, Canada
Copyright 2014 ACM 978-1-4503-2473-1/14/04...$15.00.
http://dx.doi.org/10.1145/2556288.2557306

Device deformation caused by the interaction can be measured, and different sets of deformation input gestures can be used to manipulate the user interface of a device.

The catalogue of input deformation gestures proposed in the literature is already substantial. Similarly, many use cases for device deformation input have been proposed, both as part of flexible device concepts and as the basis for interaction tasks in research studies. Generally, the use cases proposed in the literature were selected to highlight the strengths and benefits of device deformation input in interactions, as we illustrate below. This profusion of plausible gesture/use-case pairing examples shows how versatile deformation input gestures can be for the design of new interactions. What we have not found are systematic validations of such choices in user studies. As a consequence, we feared that this versatility might be compensating for the shortcomings of some sub-optimal pairings of gestures with use cases. In other words, some selected use cases might under-utilize the real potential of deformation gestures. This would be the case if, for instance, a particular deformation gesture did not offer the best possible UX but still could "do the job".

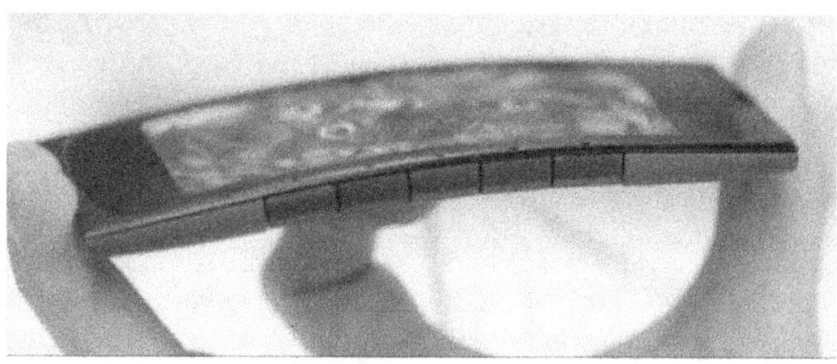

Figure 1. Prototype device with bendable display and deformable back cover made out of aluminum stripes

In this paper, we re-visit the basics of flexible interaction in order to contribute towards addressing this question. By reviewing the literature, we first identify successful criteria that have been followed for the pairing of input deformation gestures with use cases. Following, we report two user studies. The first one, referred to as pilot study, was conducted using a non-functional flexible handheld device, exploring the affordances of a two-handed flexible form factor in the context of typical mobile computing interaction use cases. It also collected *a priory* preferences when compared with touch (both interactions were imagined at this stage). The second one is a full experimental study that we conducted using a new functional, high-fidelity deformable device that included a high-resolution flexible display (see Fig. 1). When building this prototype, we took particular care in achieving a highly-polished finish and mature aesthetics. With this, we wanted to convey the perception of product-like quality, so as to avoid the bias that raw prototypes can often imprint on the UX. In this second study, we focused on just one of the basic building blocks of deformation gestures: device bending. We investigated the adequacy of bend input for four abstracted typical use cases, from the subjective perspective of our participants.

As part of the second experiment, and in the spirit of revisiting the basics, we also conducted a Fitts' Law study using this new bendable device. To our knowledge, no previous such study has been reported, and we considered it an indispensable piece in order to understand device bend input in relation to other input techniques. We avoided conducting a direct performance comparison with a conventional touch interface in this second study, as this was not our goal in this paper. Early examples of such controlled performance comparison studies between deformation and touch can be found in [3] and [14].

RELATED WORK

Form factors and deformation gestures

The most significant contributions to the literature on flexible interactions have mainly been made during the last decade. Early work considered (at least at a conceptual level) amorphous form factors that could be molded, somewhat freely, with the awareness of a computer [19, 28] However, since the formal introduction of Organic User Interfaces (OUIs) to HCI [32], and coinciding with the advent of flexible visual display technology, *paper-like* thin form factors have motivated much of the work in this area. Gummi is an early example of a thin and flexible computer concept [26] followed by concepts such as paper-like GUI windows [9], and thin devices with form factors inspired by smartphones [17], tablets [31], as well as rollable [12] and foldable [11] computers. Thin and flexible non-computational paper-based form factors are very familiar to everyone: traditional books, stacks of paper sheets, notepads, etc. This prior familiarity motivated a series of observation studies from which catalogues of deformation gestures for hypothetical thin and flexible computers were obtained, such as in [9, 18, 33]. From all the implementations and concepts that we find in this part of the literature, *bend gestures* (i.e., curving over the flat surface of a flat device) stand our as an omnipresent building block in interaction designs.

Besides highly-flexible paper-thin devices, a different breed of more volumetric form factors has also been proposed in the last years, often inspired by existing smartphone or tablet form factors. An example of this is the already-mentioned Nokia Kinetic Device [15, 21], in which flexible interactions were mainly supported for two families of gestures: device *bending* and *twisting*. Examples of other similar form factors are found in e.g., [7, 8, 20], where bending and twisting gestures are also predominant, together with squeezing the interface.

Research conducted with all these form factors and input deformation gestures has led authors to propose many use cases and applications. Some patterns emerged here as well. Understandably, when interacting with paper-like form factors, the model of the traditional book had a strong influence. The main interaction with that traditional technology is leafing or turning pages. Several versions of device-bending gestures have been proposed to turn pages one by one in either direction [26, 30, 35] or to browse fast through the many pages of an e-book [34]. Other popular use cases for bend gestures in the literature are: zooming or scaling the information on the screen [3, 5, 8, 13-15, 18, 26], selecting an item or triggering an action in a gaming environment [15, 36], switching the order of stacked layers of information [6], and visualizing non-planar intersections in a 3D space [29].

Successful gesture/use-case pairings

Most of the pairings of deformation gestures and use cases in the literature appear reasonably convincing to the reader. The nature of the rationale behind the success of such pairings varies from case to case. In our review of the literature, we have identified various themes along which successful pairs of deformation gesture and use case have been achieved. The first one is *Tangibility*. This concept is closely linked to Tangible User Interfaces (TUIs), and by extension it is also present in DUIs. It refers to the ability of the user to obtain information or feedback from the system by touching it and feeling its physicality and configuration, as the interaction progresses. Tangibility is often presented as a feature that is missing in touchscreen interactions [10]. Thus, providing tangibility to an interface by making it flexible is a beneficial contribution in many cases. For example, in [34] bend gestures were used to turn the pages of an e-book, evoking the "good feeling" that the tangibility of a real book provides. Similarly, in a study investigating the combination of deformation gestures and touch to manipulate images, the participants reported that bending and twisting the device conveyed a sense of "physically working" with the images [14].

Another theme for the successful pairing of deformation gestures and use cases that we have identified in the literature is *Directionality*. This is understood as the coherent relationship between the actual movement of a deforming device in space and the direction in which the information on the display moves, either in reality or metaphorically. Some examples include scrolling information up and down by twisting a device [15], turning pages of a book to the left and to the right by bending the left, right or both sides of the device [17, 34], zooming or scaling information by bending the whole device (making it concave or convex [15]), and rotating information by twisting the device [14]. There is often high consensus about the appropriateness of the gesture/use-case pairs regarding directionality, except for some ambiguity in the polarity of the mapping for gestures with weaker directional cues, such as twist, as noted in e.g. [17].

One additional important theme that we have identified is pairing deformation gestures and use cases according to *Metaphors* that form mental models for the interaction [17]. This theme is not necessarily orthogonal with tangibility and directionality. In fact, most of the examples given for the other two themes could also be classified as metaphors. However, in some cases the metaphor aspect described in the literature is so powerful that it fully justifies the action/use-case pairing. A clear example is crumpling the device to delete a document [18].

The potential of device bend gestures

Indeed, the versatility of input with deformation gestures has been demonstrated under many use cases, use scenarios, areas of application and with different form factors. However, versatility does not guarantee the optimal use of its potential. In simple interactions (e.g., 0-dimensional binary selections), equally simple input actions are already used as the norm (e.g., a binary button). Introducing a deformation gesture for a binary action (e.g., bending the device a certain threshold amount) expands the set of options available for the interaction designer. However, using deformation to perform binary selections can be wasteful in complex interactions, since deformation can easily handle other more complex input tasks.

Each deformation gesture is a continuous (often bipolar) high-resolution input technique that can take many intermediate positions between two extremes, given its high shape resolution [25]. Thus, we can say that a deformation gesture uses its full potential when controlling a continuous parameter dexterously (with high-precision requirements), while also providing enhanced tangibility, directionality and metaphor-strengthening in the context of a particular use case. With this understanding as our starting point, we conducted two user studies to find out which use cases naïve users believe continuous bend input gestures suit best, and how they related to tangibility, directionality and metaphor themes, as discussed earlier.

Target Acquisition and Fitts' law

In this exercise of revisiting the basics of input deformation, we noticed that there are no Fitts' Law studies conducted with deformable interfaces reported in the literature. As a common method for assessing the efficiency of an interaction technique, we decided that it was important to address this gap. Fitts' law [4] predicts the movement time (MT) to a target of width W within a distance D from the starting position:

$$MT = a + b\log(\frac{D}{W} + 1) \qquad \text{(eq. 1)}$$

In the equation, a and b are system-specific constants, and the logarithmic term is often called the Index of Difficulty (ID). This model has been mostly applied to pointing tasks, such as selecting targets with a desktop mouse [2] or interacting in augmented environments [1, 24]. Closest to our area of interest, the suitability of Fitts' Law for force-based interfaces was investigated in [22, 23, 27]. Raghu *et al.* [22] found a very good fit (R^2=0.993) with Fitts' model in their experiment with finger-based force input and visual feedback. In their study, the applied force was directly mapped to cursor position which had to be moved to a target region. Ramos *et al.* [23] used a force-sensitive stylus to explore pressure-sensitive UI widgets. In position control task using dwell time selection (as in this study) they also found a relatively good fit (R^2=0.84) with Fitts' model. Scott *et al.* [27] had a device that could sense bending and twisting forces in a rigid body that did not deform. In that study, the correlation with Fitts' model was not so good, and the authors argued that, when limb movements are negligible, Fitts' model is not valid. This argument provides an interesting viewpoint for our study, particularly because the experiment settings are very similar. However, unlike in the references mentioned, the devices introduced in this study are clearly deformable, even when the movements of the users' hands during the deformation are rather small. We believe that, in addition to the magnitude of limb movements, the mapping of the applied force to the actual interface actions plays an even more significant role in interaction predictability.

PILOT STUDY

The aim of the pilot study was to explore the affordances of a two-handed flexible form factor in the context of typical mobile interaction use cases. We conducted the study with an appearance model made of plastic and silicone, which could be bent and twisted. In the central (flexible) section of the model there was a color-printed image mimicking the screen of the device (see Fig. 2). Similar studies have been conducted before, but using non-functional [18] and functional [17] hardware that were paper thin.

Figure 2. The appearance model used in the pilot study

Test setup/procedure

Eight participants (4 female, 4 male, 31-49 years old), all employees of Nokia, took part in the study. The first phase of the study was a think-aloud exploration of the prototype and its affordances. We asked participants to take the model in their hands and describe freely what it could be used for in a user interface, in the broadest sense. The only piece of information given was that it could be deformed with the hands.

In the second phase, participants saw screenshots of a set of typical interactions, printed on a handout. We asked them to imagine carrying out each interaction both by deforming the interface and by using a multitouch display. We selected multitouch for comparison because it is the currently-dominant input technique with mobile devices. In order to quantify their answers, participants rated their preference on a scale ranging from -2 to 2, where negative and positive ratings stood for better suitability of touch and deformation interactions respectively. The interaction use case examples shown, were: *horizontal scrolling*, *vertical scrolling*, *zooming in/out*, *3D map navigation*, and *browsing web content (up/down/left/ right/select)*.

Results

During the free exploration phase, participants spontaneously proposed sets of use cases that could suit the deformable form factor they were inspecting. We analyzed the transcripts of the think-aloud sessions and grouped the proposed use cases by families. As a result, we identified the following six families of application areas: *distorting images*, *volume control*, *playing games*, *web browsing*, *zooming or scaling*, *menu navigations and selections*.

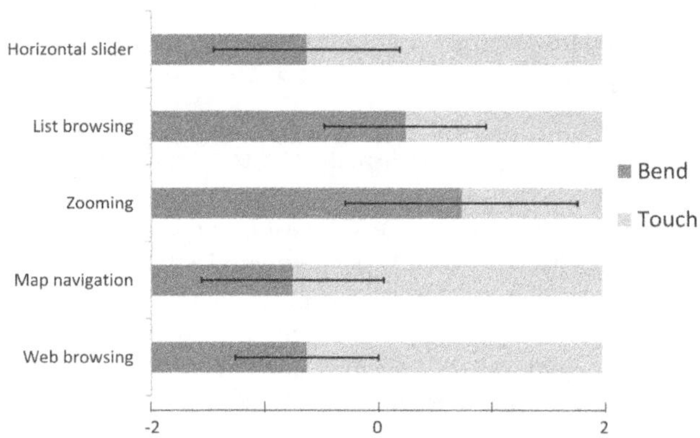

Figure 3. Preference rating of touch and deformation as input method in selected interactions.

Figure 3 shows a summary of the preference ratings that we collected in the second phase of the pilot study (deformation *vs.* touch interactions, both nonfunctional). *Zooming* was the use case rated as most appropriate for device-deformation interactions (better than multitouch), in line with previous similar studies [17]. The second most appropriate use case for deformation gestures was thought to be *List Browsing* (i.e., a 1D navigation scenario). In this case, deformation and touch received similar ratings of appropriateness. The rest of the interactions were thought to be better suited for touch input.

Discussion and conclusions

The results of the pilot study hint towards *zooming* being the most intuitive and clearest interaction for device deformation gestures. Further, according to Figure 3, it was generally preferred over the well-established multitouch pinch gesture.

The fact that in the other proposed use cases touch received similar or more favorable preference ratings did not come as a big surprise. All participants were proficient users of touch interaction on a daily basis, and our study did not provide the opportunity to try out the behavior of the systems with a functional prototype. This is a limitation that was addressed in the next study that we describe, with a bendable functional prototype.

EXPERIMENTAL STUDY ON BENDING INTERACTION

We conducted a full controlled experimental user study using a hi-fi functional prototype. Our aim with this second study was to provide participants with the opportunity to actually try out interactions with a high-quality deformable device, in a variety of use scenarios. By doing this, we expected to collect subjective data from the users that shed light onto the question about which use cases were more appropriate to be executed with device deformation gestures.

To design this study, we reduced the scope of input deformation gestures to *device bending* only. As discussed in the introduction, device bending, in its various forms, is arguably the most common device deformation gesture proposed in the literature. In our pilot study, the use case with best acceptance (i.e., zooming) was executed with a basic two-handed whole-device deformation gesture. For the sake of convention, we will hereinafter use the following terminology for this gesture:

- **Bend in**: the user bends the device so that the middle part of the device gets closer to the user forming a convex arc.
- **Bend out**: the user bends the device so that the middle part of the device gets further from the user forming a concave arc.

We further focused on investigating the appropriateness of use cases that, *a priory*, could be expected to make the most from the potential of device-bending gestures. As advanced in our introductory discussion, this very simply meant that we did not consider use cases in which device bending was used to trigger binary actions. Although perfectly eligible for such use cases, a device-bend gesture has the characteristic of being able to control a one-dimensional continuous parameter in two directions dynamically, ideally with a neutral position between two polarity directions. From this premise, we collected examples of classic interactions that fulfill these requirements, such as parameters that are typically controlled using a slider in a GUI. Based on observation and on examples already proposed in the literature, we narrowed down our selection to four use case areas that loosely related to tasks involving: (i) zooming or scaling visual information, (ii) controlling the position of an object, (iii) editing the properties of an image, and (iv) controlling the speed of movement of an object.

One additional criterion to select these four use case areas was that they related in different ways to the three themes for pairing gestures and use cases identified earlier: tangibility, directionality and metaphor. For example, we judged that zooming by bending was strong in that it had a strong directional component in the z axis, matching very well the direction in which the device deformed. In contrast, adjusting a graphical property of an image (such as its contrast or brightness), was lacking any clear vectorial component in space. To give another example, adjusting the speed of movement of an object could have, through an appropriate metaphor (e.g., pushing an accelerator pedal), both a directional and a tangible component that might be less strong in some of the other cases.

In each experimental session, the first task was always (i) (matching the size of two circles), while the other cases (ii, iii, iv) were presented in quasi-counterbalanced order. With the size-matching task, we made two different implementations. One implementation (called *absolute* in this paper), was an absolute mapping between the angle of bend and the size of the circle (minimum size when fully bent in, and maximum size when fully bent out). The other implementation (called *relative*), mapped the angle of bend deformation to the speed of change of the size of the circle (maximum shrinking/growing speeds when fully bent in/out respectively, with no change in size when the device remained flat with no deformation). We implemented the other three interactions in their *absolute* version only. By making two implementations for the size-matching interaction, we wanted to perform a comparison of these two options that was both quantitative and qualitative, and get a sense of the effect of this design parameter. In addition, we were curious to see how each type of implementation of the same deformation gesture behaved when confronted with Fitts' laws' model.

Prototype device

Deformability introduces challenges to the construction of the device. If the device is deformable, not only the display, but also the supporting parts and electronic components need to tolerate deformations. This has been one of the major reasons why devices with bendable displays are not yet commercially available. To make the device durable, some limitations in the deformation have to be set, which also limits the degrees of freedom in the interaction. The device introduced in this paper solves some of the durability issues while still allowing for enough deformation to convey a clear sense of flexible hardware to the hands that manipulate it without affecting performance in demanding dexterous actions, and preventing the physical fatigue that extended interactions with larger deformations can cause [16].

The prototype device used in the current study (see Figure 4) consisted of a 4.47 inch OLED display with HD resolution (1280x720 pixels). The display was attached to the top of the device on a plastic board. The back cover of the device was made out of aluminum strips, allowing deformation. The strips were attached to each other using a mechanism that limited bending beyond a certain angle. The maximum bending angle in each direction was 15°.

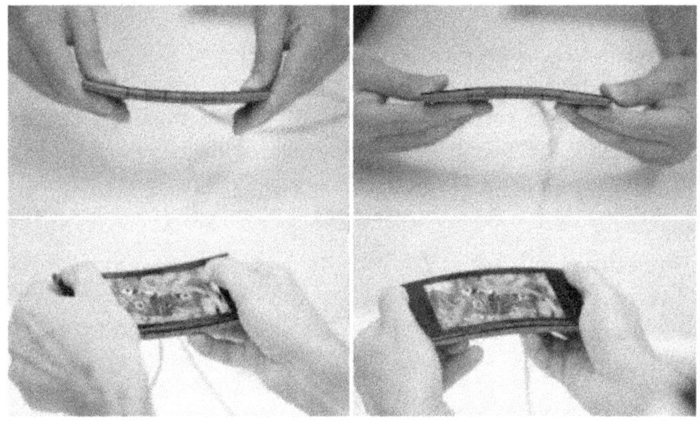

Figure 4. Prototype device allowing bending out (left) and bending in (right) gestures.

The deformation of the device was measured with strain gauges attached to the plastic board under the display. The sensor data acquisition and the display control took place in an external driver hardware to which the device was tethered. The sensors were sampled with 10bit resolution (1024 levels) at 100 Hz, and the refresh frequency of the display was 60 Hz. The experiment software was running on a Windows PC and written in C# language.

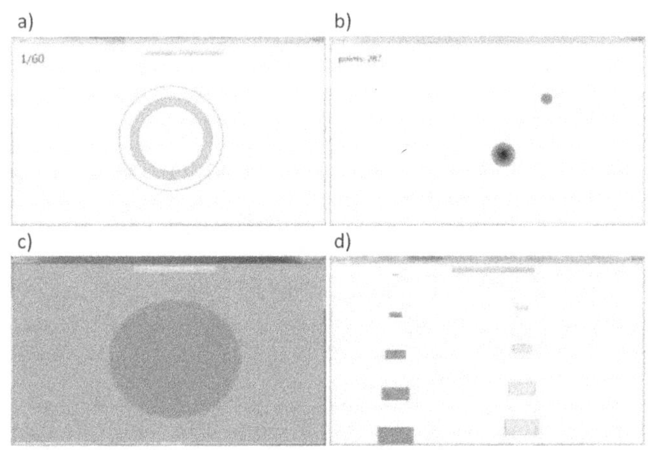

Figure 5. Interaction examples and tasks in the experiment. a) Size matching, where the task was to fit the red circle inside the boundaries of the blue circle. b) Height control, where the task was to hit the red ball by altering the height of the moving green ball. c) Color depth control, where the task was to match the inner circle color with the background color. d) Speed control, where the task was to match the speeds of the columns of moving blocks close to each other.

Test setup

Sixteen participants (8 females, 8 males, 30-47 years old) with various backgrounds took part in the experiment. The whole experiment took approximately 45 minutes to complete, and a movie ticket was paid as compensation. The experiment was arranged in a quiet room equipped with the prototype hardware, an experimenter laptop, a video camera, and a table with two chairs. The experimenter sat next to the participants while conducting the test. The size matching experiment was conducted first, followed shortly by the concept evaluation experiment.

Size matching experiment (Fitts' law)

In the size-matching interaction, participants saw two circles on the screen: a thick blue and a thin red circles. When the participant bent the device, the size of the red circle changed. The participant was asked to fit the red circle inside the boundaries of the blue circle (Figure 5a).

Procedure

There were two sessions in the size-matching experiment, one in each condition (absolute/relative). The order of the conditions was alternated for each participant. In each session, there were 60 trials consisting of different target sizes (blue circle thickness) and distances (target size difference from previous trial). The orders of target sizes and distances were randomized and organized so that consecutive trials were always to different scaling directions (i.e. smaller-bigger-smaller-bigger…). Dwell time was used for target selection: the user had to stay inside the target area (inside the blue circle boundaries) for 0.5 seconds to complete the trial, after which the next trial immediately started, with a new target. A simple progress bar indicating dwell time was visible on the screen above the circles (see Figure 5a). After each session, a task load index questionnaire (Raw NASA-TLX) was filled out, assessing the subjective workload generated in each condition.

Results

We analyzed the sensor data for each trial in the size-matching experiment: target acquisition time as a function of distance to the target and target width. In terms of the mapping condition, absolute mapping led to significantly shorter task completion time. With absolute mapping, the average task completion time was 2.13 second, whereas the relative mapping yielded 2.93 seconds in average ($t(15)=12.1$, $p<0.01$). See Figure 6.

The data from each condition were aligned for Fitts' model (eq. 1). For each ID value, an average value was calculated from all the trials of all participants. A linear regression was calculated to estimate the goodness of fit (R^2) to the model (see Figure 7). The fit was better in the relative mapping condition (R^2=0.626) than in the absolute mapping condition (R^2=0.206). The corresponding Pearson correlations between task time and ID were 0.79 and 0.45, respectively.

We also estimated the applied torques in both conditions. We did this by logging sensor readings during each trial and mapping them to the approximate range of torques of the device. In the absolute mapping condition, the estimated average torque was significantly higher than in the relative mapping condition (0.15 Nm *vs.* 0.11 Nm, $t(15)=20$, $p<0.01$).

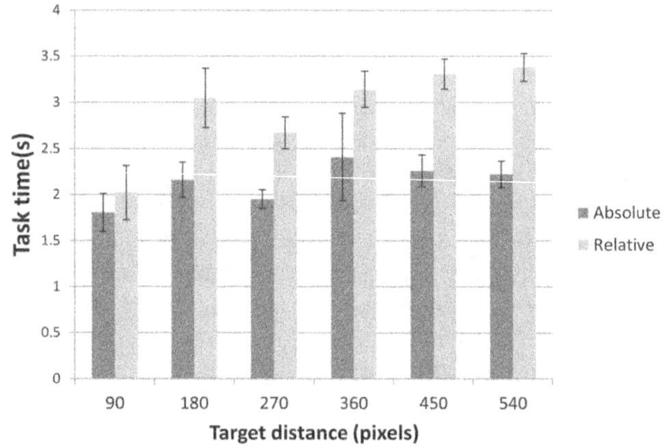

Figure 6. Task-completion times by distance-to-target in both mapping conditions (size-matching task). Average completion time was significantly shorter with absolute mapping.

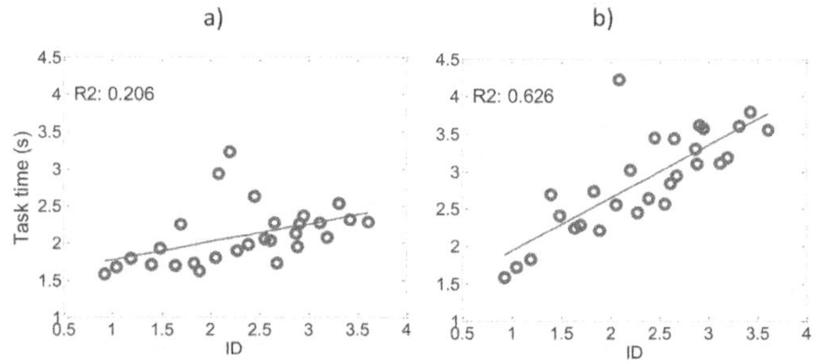

Figure 7. Fitting the task time of absolute (a) and relative (b) mapping conditions to Fitts' model (size-matching task).

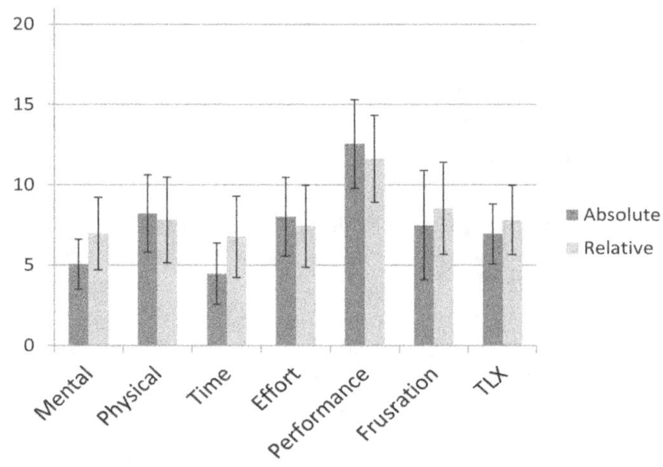

Figure 8. Raw NASA TLX ratings of absolute and relative mapping conditions (size-matching task).

Ergonomic aspects of the interaction in both conditions were assessed with a task load index questionnaire. In our assessment of the subjective workload in each condition (using a 21-point Raw NASA-TLX questionnaire), we did not find any significant differences in the Task Load Index measured for each condition ($TLX_{absolute}$=6.94, $TLX_{relative}$=7.81; t(15)=1.38, p=0.19). Similarly, none of the sub-categories in the questionnaire showed any significant differences between the conditions (Figure 8).

Concept evaluation experiment

In the concept evaluation part, bend interaction was applied to: 1) height control in a simple game, where the user could control the vertical position of a moving ball, 2) color depth control, where the user could change the color of the circle to match the background color, and 3) speed control of moving blocks on the screen, to match the speed to another column of moving blocks on the screen. Participants' task was to evaluate the easiness of the interaction, the enjoyment during the session, and the suitability of bend gesture to that particular interaction concept.

Procedure

In the concept evaluation part, the three interaction concepts were presented one by one, in semi-counterbalanced order. The participants used each interaction concept freely for approximately 5 minutes.

In the position control concept, two balls were presented on the screen: a moving green ball and a static red ball (Figure 5b). The green ball moved from left to right, and the participant could control the vertical position by bending the device. The task was to hit the red ball with the green ball. A successful hit granted points, suggesting a game-like experience. After the green ball had crossed the screen, a new green ball emerged from the left side of the display, and a new red ball was presented in a new vertical position.

In the color-depth control concept, participants were asked to bend the device to change the depth of the color of a big circle on the screen (Figure 5c). When the color was within a 15% range (8-bit RGB value) from the background color for 1s, a next background color was introduced and the next trial started. Like in the size-matching task, a progress bar on top of the display indicated the time spent on the target color range.

In the speed control concept, two columns of blocks were presented on the screen (Figure 5d). The left column, consisting of dark blue blocks drawn in perspective, appeared to be moving either towards or away from the participant, with constant speed. Participants were able to control the speed of the right column, consisting of light blue blocks, by bending the device. Bending *in* moved the blocks towards the user and bending *out* made the blocks move away from the user. By keeping the device unbent, the blocks remained stationary. The task was to match the speed of the right column to that of the left column. When the speeds of both columns were within a 15% range from each other for 1s, the next speed level was presented on the left column, and a new trial started.

Results

In the concept evaluation part of the experiment, participants evaluated each interaction concept (the pairing of bend input with each one of the tasks) with respect to easiness, enjoyment and suitability, using 9-point likert scales. These attributes were also evaluated in the size-matching part of the experiment, after both mapping condition sessions. The ratings of each attribute in all concepts are presented in Figure 9. The only significant difference that we observed was on the easiness ratings (F(4, 60)=2.9, p=0.024), suggesting that the speed control task was perceived as the most difficult one.

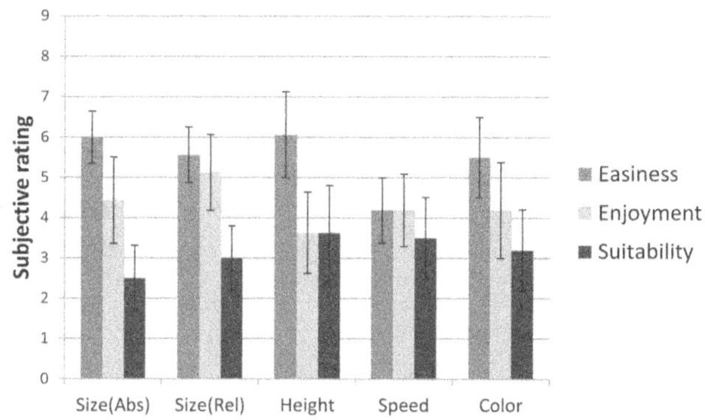

Figure 9. Subjective ratings of the interaction concepts in the concept evaluation.

Participant Interview

Participants were interviewed regarding each session, with the aim to clarify the benefits, challenges and required further development of the interaction scenarios. Also, for each interaction, participants were asked to comment on the comparison between using device bending and how they imagined it would have been to use touch.

Results

We used Affinity Diagramming to analyze the data from the discussions conducted after each experiment, and we identified the following main themes:

- Physicality of bending
- Differences between absolute and relative mapping
- Bend versus touch in size matching
- Directionality of bend
- Further development ideas and other applications

Related to the physical demand of the interactions, 10 out of 16 participants mentioned that bending can be physically heavy, particularly if the interaction session is long in duration. Another concern, raised by 4 participants, was that bending cannot be done with one hand only. On the other hand, 6 participants mentioned that bending is a very natural way to interact with the device.

Table 1. Proposed applications for bend, *n* indicates the number of participants putting forward the proposal

Interaction	Examples	*n*
Zooming	Zooming or scaling of maps, images, text, camera, games	12
Image editing	Editing photos (brightness, contrast, colors), editing camera settings	9
Reading	Reading news, articles, email, books by bending to navigate between pages	7
Map information	Finding hidden information on maps, restaurants, museums, shops etc.	4
Navigation	Navigation between applications, web browser tabs or menus.	6
Browsing large amounts of information	Browsing mailbox contents, folders, images, photos, music	9
Quick reactions	Mute, on/off, calendar alarms, alarm clock, calls, switching the device on/off, switching applications on/off	5
Games	Angry birds slingshot, bomb dropping, speed controlling (running, driving and flying), following a track (cars, pacman), treasure hunt, baking, tetris	16

A general comment concerning differences between absolute and relative mappings was that absolute is too sensitive (9 participants) and relative is too slow (12 participants), even "sticky" and "hindered by inertia". The sensitivity of the absolute mapping was also considered less accurate and requiring more effort to complete the task.

In the size-matching task, when comparing bending (as experienced in the test) and multitouch pinching (as known through previous experience), 8 participants preferred bending while 4 participants preferred pinch gestures. The rest of the participants did not have an opinion. When asked why bending was better, the main reasons given were:

- Fingers do not cover the screen while zooming (4)
- It feels more natural (4)
- Pinch requires more precision, which is difficult while moving (2)
- No need for releasing the grip of one hand while interacting (1)

Some participants had concerns about how the bending angle was mapped to directions of the interaction (i.e., the polarity of the mapping). None of the participants were confused in the size-matching or speed-matching tasks, Seven participants reported problems in the color-shifting task (i.e. which way was dark/bright appeared unclear) and 4 participants in the position control task (i.e. ambiguity about which way corresponded with displacing up/down).

Most of the improvement ideas dealt with *fine tuning the mappings* and *adding system feedback*. As the above comments about the mappings suggest, participants wished to see a compromise between the sensitive absolute mapping and the slower relative mapping. On the other hand, this fast-slow dimension was seen as an opportunity for different types of interaction. While browsing large amounts of data or reaching far away targets, rapid response and sensitivity would be preferred. But when higher accuracy and interaction with small details is needed, slower and smooth response was thought to work better.

The need for system feedback was raised by many participants. The most frequent request (9) was for additional visual feedback in order to improve the interaction. Tactile (7) and auditory feedback (4) were also proposed. The additional feedback was thought to be useful for indicating successful task completion, such as reaching the target or the end of dwell time.

When asked about the potential applications of similar bend interactions, participants identified many areas showing potential. We grouped them thematically and we present them summarized in Table 1.

DISCUSSION

Our comparison of absolute and relative mappings of device-bending to interface-action showed different strengths for each one of them. In the target acquisition (size-matching) task, we found that the absolute mapping led to significantly shorter average time to complete task, compared with the relative mapping. In contrast, the correlation with Fitts' law was much higher in the relative mapping condition. However, the correlation was still much lower than what has been found in similar studies dealing with force input [22, 23] (0.63 vs. 0.84-0.99). This could be caused by the unfamiliarity with device deformation input, which is rather different from pressing a rigid surface with a finger or stylus. Also, the actual average applied torque (a good proxy for the total muscle effort required) was clearly lower with the relative than with the absolute mapping. These findings suggest that relative mapping was more appropriate for extended use of the interaction. Although raw NASA-TLX failed to capture these differences from a subjective perspective, other subjective data from the study (comments from the interviews) also suggested that absolute mapping required more effort, and that relative was less efficient. We believe that, to some extent, the lower efficiency obtained with the relative mapping was due to our particular implementation. From these findings we interpret that an optimal mapping of bending angle to change rate of the circle size can provide a more ergonomic and more natural solution than absolute mapping.

When bending was compared to pinching in the size-matching task, half of the participants preferred bending. This is a particularly interesting finding, and it proves that bending could work equally well or even better than touch in some contexts of use. Looked at it from the perspective of the driver themes identified at the beginning, bending to zoom or scale information could be more successful than pinch in multitouch because it combines enhanced tangibility, better spatial directionality and at least as strong a metaphor. Additional strengths of bend over pinch captured in our study include that the display is not occluded by fingers, and that both hands can remain gripping the device throughout the interaction (in line with e.g. [14], [3]) This result is further supporting that *bend to zoom* can be a particularly successful pairings of a device deformation gesture with a use case.

In the quantitative concept evaluation part, we only find a significant difference in the *easiness* metric, where speed control appeared to be the most difficult use case for device bending. We suspect that a factor influencing this was the visual complexity of the graphic representation: two moving columns of blocks and a progress bar indicating the trial success. In contrast, speed control was one of the two tasks in which polarity of the mapping was not reported to be confusing, possibly because of better coherence between directionality and action in the mental model created by the users [17]. With the four generic tasks for the control of continuous parameters that we devised, participants found enough inspiration to produce many concrete use case examples. All the ones that inspired our tasks were spelled out: zooming, image editing, gaming and navigation. However, it was very interesting to find participants proposing also some of the *classic* discrete interactions that have been repeatedly proposed to be used with deformation gestures. *Reading,* with its iconic page-turning binary action, occupied a category of its own. As we already acknowledged, it is evident that the strong tangible, directional and metaphorical links of a discrete bend gesture with the action of turning a page are enough justification to sacrifice the capacity for continuous control in such a use context. In addition, we also received requests for discrete deformation gestures to be used in *quick reactions* which are presumably also forceful. In these cases, the perceived sturdiness of a deformable device plus the ability to deform it in a casual way may have motivated these use cases.

CONCLUSIONS

In this paper we have taken a step back and reconsidered some of the basic premises for the use of deformation gestures in interaction. In particular, we were intrigued by the reasons behind the most common pairings of specific deformation gestures with specific use cases in the literature. We identified that *enhancing tangibility*, bringing *spatial directional coherence* and, forming a strong *metaphoric bond* between action and use case were the most common drivers in gesture/use-case selections in the literature. In addition, and focusing on device bending specifically, we thought it necessary to investigate two other foundational aspects about this relatively new input technique: the effect of different mapping strategies and their compliance with Fitts' model.

Our main goal in this study was to understand what use cases intrinsically suit input deformation gestures best. We investigated this question in a pilot user study (using a non-functional prototype) and in a full experimental user study. Our findings are indicative of the high versatility of dynamic device bending to control any kind of continuous bipolar interaction accurately. Additionally, we provide data to suggest that our analysis of the main drivers for action/use-case pairing selections (tangibility, directionality, metaphors) has value beyond bipolar continuous control use cases, *a priori* more optimal. Examples are some iconic discrete actions, such as page turning in reading applications, and quick reactions.

Regarding the type of mapping, we identified strengths for both absolute mapping (superior performance) and for relative mapping (superior usability, particularly in lengthy interactions). In addition, relative mapping showed a better match with Fitts' model. We conclude that bending may suit equally well non-directional manipulations (such as color depth control) and clearly-directional manipulations (such as speed or height control). Similarly, the metaphorical character of the interaction did not influence the subjective ratings. Thus, we may argue that any continuous parameter requiring high resolution input could be controlled with dynamic bend, as long as the implementation is completed carefully.

REFERENCES

1. Ahmaniemi, T.T. and Lantz, V.T. Augmented reality target finding based on tactile cues. In *Proc. ICMI'09*, ACM (2009) 335-342.
2. Akamatsu, M. and MacKenzie, I.S., *Movement characteristics using a mouse with tactile and force feedback.* International Journal of Human-Computer Studies, 1996. **45**: p. 483-493.
3. Burstyn, J., Banerjee, A., and Vertegaal, R. FlexView: an evaluation of depth navigation on deformable mobile devices. In *Proc. TEI'13*, ACM (2013) 193-200.
4. Fitts, P.M., *The information capacity of the human motor system in controlling the amplitude of movement.* Journal of Experimental Psychology, 1954. **47**(6): p. 381-391.
5. Gallant, D.T., Seniuk, A.G., and Vertegaal, R. Towards more paper-like input: flexible input devices for foldable interaction styles. In *Proc. UIST'08*, ACM (2008) 283-286.
6. Girouard, A., Tarun, A., and Vertegaal, R. DisplayStacks: interaction techniques for stacks of flexible thin-film displays. In *Proc. CHI'12*, ACM (2012) 2431-2440.

7. Goyal, N. COMET: Collaboration in Mobile Environments by Twisting. In *Proc. ECSCW'09* (2009)
8. Herkenrath, G., Karrer, T., and Borchers, J. Twend: twisting and bending as new interaction gesture in mobile devices. In *Proc. Extended Abstracts on CHI'08*, ACM (2008) 3819-3824.
9. Holman, D., Vertegaal, R., Altosaar, M., Troje, N., and Johns, D. Paper windows: interaction techniques for digital paper. In *Proc. CHI'05*, ACM (2005) 591-599.
10. Ishii, H. Tangible bits: beyond pixels. In *Proc. TEI'08*, ACM (2008) xv-xxv.
11. Khalilbeigi, M., Lissermann, R., Kleine, W., and Steimle, J. FoldMe: interacting with double-sided foldable displays. In *Proc. TEI'12*, ACM (2012) 33-40.
12. Khalilbeigi, M., Lissermann, R., Muhlhauser, M., and Steimle, J. Xpaaand: interaction techniques for rollable displays. In *Proc. CHI'11*, ACM (2011) 2729-2732.
13. Kildal, J. Interacting with Deformable User Interfaces: Effect of Material Stiffness and Type of Deformation Gesture. In *Proc. HAID'12*, Springer Berlin Heidelberg (2012) 71-80.
14. Kildal, J., Lucero, A., and Boberg, M. Twisting touch: combining deformation and touch as input within the same interaction cycle on handheld devices. In *Proc. MobileHCI'13*, ACM (2013) 237-246.
15. Kildal, J., Paasovaara, S., and Aaltonen, V. Kinetic device: designing interactions with a deformable mobile interface. In *Proc. Extended Abstracts on CHI'12* ACM (2012) 1871-1876.
16. Kildal, J. and Wilson, G. Feeling it: the roles of stiffness, deformation range and feedback in the control of deformable ui. In *Proc. ICMI'12*, ACM (2012) 393-400.
17. Lahey, B., Girouard, A., Burleson, W., and Vertegaal, R. PaperPhone: understanding the use of bend gestures in mobile devices with flexible electronic paper displays. In *Proc. CHI'11*, ACM (2011) 1303-1312.
18. Lee, S.-S., Kim, S., Jin, B., Choi, E., Kim, B., Jia, X., Kim, D., and Lee, K.-p. How users manipulate deformable displays as input devices. In *Proc. CHI'10*, ACM (2010) 1647-1656.
19. Murakami, T. and Nakajima, N., *DO-IT: deformable object as input tool for 3-D geometric operation.* Computer-Aided Design, 2000. **32**(1): p. 5-16.
20. Murata. *Murata's Flexible Remote*. Available from: http://techcrunch.com/2011/09/23/muratas-flexible-remote-lets-you-control-your-tv-with-bending-and-twisting-motions/.
21. Nokia. *NRC developed Nokia Kinetic prototype demoed at Nokia World 2011.* 2011 [cited 2013 12.9.2013]; Available from: http://research.nokia.com/news/12110.
22. Raghu Prasad, M.S., Purswani, S., and Manivannan, M. Modeling of Human Hand Force Based Tasks Using Fitts's Law. In *Proc. ICoRD'13*, Springer India (2013) 377-386.
23. Ramos, G., Boulos, M., and Balakrishnan, R. Pressure widgets. In *Proc. SIGCHI conference on Human factors in computing systems* (2004) 487-494.
24. Rohs, M., Oulasvirta, A., and Suomalainen, T. Interaction with magic lenses: real-world validation of a Fitts' Law model. In *Proc. CHI'11*, ACM (2011) 2725-2728.
25. Roudaut, A., Karnik, A., Lochtefeld, M., and Subramanian, S. Morphees: toward high "shape resolution" in self-actuated flexible mobile devices. In *Proc. CHI'13*, ACM (2013) 593-602.
26. Schwesig, C., Poupyrev, I., and Mori, E. Gummi: a bendable computer. In *Proc. CHI'04*, ACM (2004) 263-270.
27. Scott, J., Brown, L., and Molloy, M., *Mobile Device Interaction with Force Sensing*. Pervasive Computing, ed. H. Tokuda, et al. Vol. 5538. 2009: Springer Berlin Heidelberg. 133-150.
28. Sheng, J., Balakrishnan, R., and Singh, K. An interface for virtual 3D sculpting via physical proxy. In *Proc. GRAPHITE'06*, ACM (2006) 213-220.
29. Steimle, J., Jordt, A., and Maes, P. Flexpad: highly flexible bending interactions for projected handheld displays. In *Proc. CHI'13*, ACM (2013) 237-246.
30. Tajika, T., Yonezawa, T., and Mitsunaga, N. Intuitive page-turning interface of e-books on flexible e-paper based on user studies. In *Proc. MM'08*, ACM (2008) 793-796.
31. Tarun, A.P., Wang, P., Girouard, A., Strohmeier, P., Reilly, D., and Vertegaal, R. PaperTab: an electronic paper computer with multiple large flexible electrophoretic displays. In *Proc. Extended Abstracts on CHI'13*, ACM (2013) 3131-3134.
32. Vertegaal, R. and Poupyrev, I., *Organic User Interfaces.* Commun. ACM, 2008. **51**(6): p. 26-30.
33. Warren, K., Lo, J., Vadgama, V., and Girouard, A. Bending the rules: bend gesture classification for flexible displays. In *Proc. CHI'13*, ACM (2013) 607-610.
34. Watanabe, J.-I., Mochizuki, A., and Horry, Y. Bookisheet: bendable device for browsing content using the metaphor of leafing through the pages. In *Proc. Ubicomp'08*, ACM (2008) 360-369.
35. Wightman, D., Ginn, T., and Vertegaal, R. Bendflip: examining input techniques for electronic book readers with flexible form factors. In *Proc. INTERACT'11*, Springer-Verlag (2011) 117-133.
36. Ye, Z. and Khalid, H. Cobra: flexible displays for mobilegaming scenarios. In *Proc. Extended Abstracts on CHI'10*, ACM (2010) 4363-4368.

SurfacePhone: A Mobile Projection Device for Single- and Multiuser Everywhere Tabletop Interaction

Christian Winkler[1], Markus Löchtefeld[2], David Dobbelstein[1], Antonio Krüger[2], Enrico Rukzio[1]

[1]Ulm University
Ulm, Germany
{firstname.name}@uni-ulm.de

[2]DFKI
Saarbrücken, Germany
{firstname.name}@dfki.de

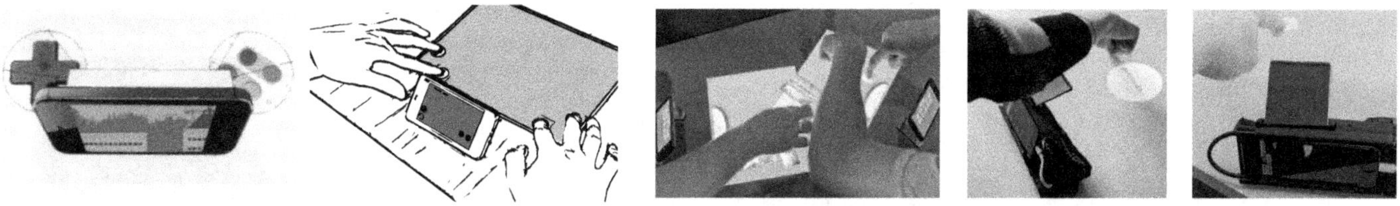

(a) (b) (c) (d) (e)

Figure 1: The evolution of the SurfacePhone design. Starting with design sketches (a, b) over concept prototypes for multi-user interaction (c) to a fully implemented phone case for iPhone5 that supports gesture tracking (d) and touch recognition (e) using the phone's camera and accelerometer.

ABSTRACT

To maintain a mobile form factor, the screen real estate of a mobile device canIn this paper we present SurfacePhone; a novel configuration of a projector phone which aligns the projector to project onto a physical surface to allow tabletop-like interaction in a mobile setup. The projection is created behind the upright standing phone and is touch and gesture-enabled. Multiple projections can be merged to create shared spaces for multi-user collaboration. We investigate this new setup, starting with the concept that we evaluated with a concept prototype. Furthermore we present our technical prototype, a mobile phone case with integrated projector that allows for the aforementioned interaction. We discuss its technical requirements and evaluate the accuracy of interaction in a second user study. We conclude with lessons learned and design guidelines.

Author Keywords

Projector Phone; Interactive Surfaces; Mobile Multi Display Environment

ACM Classification Keywords

H.5.3 Information Interfaces and Presentation: Computer-supported cooperative work

INTRODUCTION

Mobile computing devices have caught up with their desktop counterparts in terms of computing power and even display resolution. But in terms of display real estate they are limited to maintain a small mobile form factor. The more power and content is made available on our mobile companions the higher become users' needs to perform more complex tasks. This creates demand for bigger displays which inevitably leads to increased form factors. To overcome this problem, an increasing number of devices focuses on multi-display solutions. Besides devices based on multiple physical displays such as [8], projector phones set out to enable the exploration of large-scale content and support collaboration in a mobile setting.

In such mobile multi-display environments (MMDEs) the information is displayed across different screens, that are often spatially seperated and not in the same field of view. While a MMDE consisting of multiple physical displays easily allows for the extension of the screen real estate, it is still limited by the maximum size of the device. A MMDE consisting of a combination of physical and projected displays, however, allows an increase in screen estate to a much higher degree while still keeping the small form-factor, and can be used for collaboration and sharing. However the display setup of current projector phones such as the Samsung Galaxy Beam is often characterized by two displays being visually separated. This setup precludes many of the prevalent sharing and collaboration techniques that are well known and investigated for example in today's tabletop systems. In contrast, our setup allows to recreate such tabletop-like interactions in mobile scenarios with a private and a public display. In this paper we present SurfacePhone, a novel configuration of a MMDE that consists of a physical and a projected display. It is able to project a second display right behind itself, while it is standing on a surface (compare Figure 1d).

The investigated setup allows for collaboration and sharing as well as advanced single-user interactions. The projected display is touch- and gesture-enabled and additionally orientation aware. This allows connecting multiple projected displays into one combined display (see Figure 1c). In this paper we present the design process of the SurfacePhone. Starting with the considerations for such a system and the envi-

CHI 2014, April 26–May 1, 2014, Toronto, Ontario, Canada.

http://dx.doi.org/10.1145/2556288.2557075

sioned usage concepts, we then present two prototypes that have been evaluated in user studies. The initial concept prototype allowed us to easily evaluate the concepts and ideas. The technical mobile phone case prototype (hard- and software open sourced) was developed to show and evaluate the technical feasibility of the SurfacePhone concept. We conclude with design guidelines based on our study results.

RELATED WORK

There has been an ever increasing interest in mobile projection interfaces in the last five years [5, 6, 15, 21]. Initial investigation of the advantage that a mobile phone with integrated projector can deliver has been done by Hang et al. [5]. Harrison et al. demonstrated the capabilities of a body-worn system [6]. All these systems demonstrate that pico projectors integrated into a mobile device allow for an increased display size and that the explored applications and interaction benefit from it significantly. Therefore the SurfacePhone integrates a mobile projector instead of a secondary physical display. This allows to maintain a small form factor while generating a significantly bigger secondary display.

MMDE devices have been not only explored in research [10, 8, 3, 21, 14], there are also commercially available devices such as the Nintendo DS or the Kyocera Echo. With Codex [8], Hinckley et al. created a dual-display device that allows for re-orientation of two physical hinged displays. Besides, they also explored different application scenarios for different configurations as well as novel interaction techniques. Nevertheless the display arrangement of the here presented SurfacePhone has not been mentioned nor explored in the related work.

Kane et al. explored with Bonfire a laptop equipped with a pico-projector that allows to create a secondary display right next to the notebook [10]. Even though the SurfacePhone also makes use of a similar configuration, one of its main aspects is to explore collaboration on a potentially mutual interactive surface with multiple devices. As a consequence, we present new sharing techniques between displays and devices and dynamic merging of their projections which lead to new public/private scenarios. Furthermore, the SurfacePhone improves on touch accuracy and portability and for the first time, evaluates touch and gesture recognition which could not have been carried out before.

The ad-hoc combination of multiple mobile devices is another possibility [9, 11]. For instance, the work of Lyons et al. [13] would allow to create such a setting. While there is evidence that different spatial arrangement of displays can have an impact in a mobile setting [2], it has been ignored in most MMDE investigations [3, 8]. A large body of literature also investigated partially mobile configurations with one fixed display and one mobile [4, 16, 17]. Those configurations mainly have been employed to create a personal display which interacts with a shared public display [4, 18]. In those settings the orientation of the displays to each other can be fluently changed since they are not coupled. The SurfacePhone takes a very similar approach, it combines a public and personal display that keep their spatial alignments.

The most related work to SurfacePhone is PlayAnywhere [19]. Just like PlayAnywhere the SurfacePhone can create an ad-hoc display on, e.g., a table and just like PlayAnywhere it allows for touch interaction. The main difference between those two systems is that beside SurfacePhone being a truly mobile device, it also provides an additional personal display to manage private content.

SURFACEPHONE CONCEPT

The design of the SurfacePhone concept encompasses the position of the projected surface in relation to the phone, the position and orientation of one SurfacePhone to other SurfacePhones in the environment, and the modalities to interact with screen and projected display in either scenarios. Further, we distinguish between *single device/single user* (SDSU), *single device/multi user* (SDMU), and *multi device/multi user* (MDMU) scenario groups.

Position and size of projection

Hinckley et al. [8] showed that a range of very private to very public and collaborative application scenarios can be supported, depending on the spatial relation of dual-screen postures. The projection in front of the mobile device would resemble the laptop posture or the display configuration, it is a very private setup. This is because the projection is mainly visible to the user facing the device. In such a configuration the projection could show a soft keyboard. A projection to either sides of the phone would imitate the setup of Bonfire [10], where the projected surface is still within easy reach of the user, but more public than in the laptop scenario.

These two configurations have been explored intensively but a projection behind an upright standing phone has been neglected so far. This setup – the SurfacePhone – consists of a public projected display and a private display (as can be seen in Figure 2a) and presents a more collaboration oriented setup. To some extent, it resembles the Battleship setup of Codex [8], albeit the difference that the primary user is able to see both the phone display and the projected display. In this setup, there is a clear separation between the private phone and the public projection that is visible and within reach to people in the near vicinity. This comes at the expense of a slightly more difficult interaction with the projection as the user has to circumvent the phone to touch the projection.

Additionally, this MMDE setup is in line with the findings of Cauchard et al. [2]. When the user is sitting in front of the upright standing phone, the phone's display as well as the projection are in the same field of view. This allows the SurfacePhone to split the information between these two displays without risking visual separation effects.

Details of our technical prototype can be found in section *Implementation*. But to give an idea of the size and position of the projection early-on: through experimentation we found an optimal (undistorted) projection behind the phone to be around 17cm $\times$ 14cm in size, 14cm behind the phone and 4cm to the left of the center of the device. The projection, thus, is three times as big as the 4" screen of the iPhone 5.

Configurations

The SurfacePhone can be used alone, or by multiple users using one or multiple SurfacePhones.

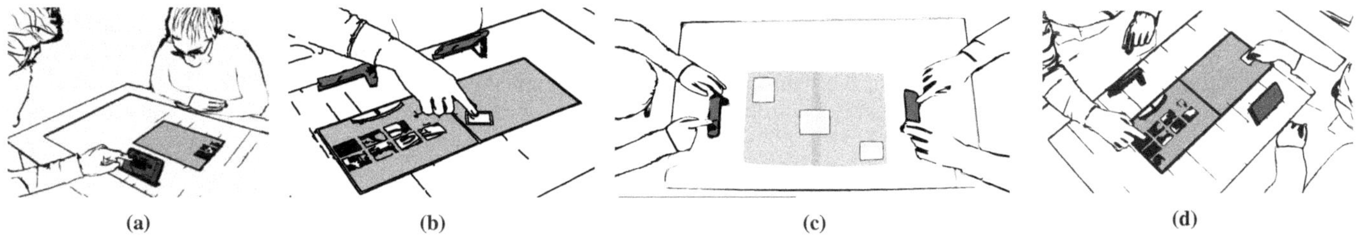

Figure 2: SDMU: (a) One user is presenting pictures to another user. MDMU: (b) Sitting next to each other on the same side with the projections merged at the short side. (c) Two users sitting face to face with the projections merged at the long side. (d) Two users sitting face to face with the projection merged at the short side.

Single-device, single user (SDSU)

This configuration can be used, for instance, to overcome the fat-finger problem on mobile devices by outsourcing e.g. controls of a game (compare Figure 1b) to the projection or showing the main view of the game on the projection. Apart from that, the projected display could be used as general secondary display, for instance, showing a task manager or notifications of applications currently running on the device. Finally, phone screens are very useful for augmenting the reality of the user, but cannot serve publicly visible augmentation. The projection on the other hand could be used to augment a real playboard with projected tokens. For example it could project chess tokens on a real board to play against the computer or a human opponent.

Single-device, multi-user interaction (SDMU)

Leveraging the inherent differences in publicity of the displays, the SurfacePhone can be used for several sharing tasks in small groups (compare Figure 2a). For instance, the projection of the phone can be used to present pictures or slides to a small group of people. The screen of the SurfacePhone can be used to browse the content and decide which content should be shown on the projection. Advantages of using SurfacePhone in this scenario include that users do not have to give out their phone to other people; that the content can be presented to all people simultaneously; and that only specific pictures or slides for presentation can be selected to address time or privacy constraints. Finally, the projection can also be touch- or gesture enabled, giving the viewers the possibility to interact with the pictures or slides. Similarly, the setup is also suitable for games such as blackjack: The person playing the bank controls the game from the screen. Other players sit in front of the projection and use touch interaction.

Multi-device, multi user interaction (MDMU)

Finally, when more than one user brings their SurfacePhone to the table, projections can be merged at different sides forming larger shared surfaces. These can be used for collaboration, e.g. data sharing, as well as competitive scenarios such as gaming. Depending on the scenario and the familiarity of the participants, different setups support different degrees of collaboration.

Sitting next to each other on the SAME SIDE (Figure 2b) is the most intimate setup as both the projections as well as the phone screens are visible to both users. This setup, for example, could be useful to collaboratively search for holiday trips. Users can first explore offers on their personal devices, then share it to the surface. Being able to also see other users' phone screens may significantly improve communication in collaborative planning.

On the opposite, sitting FACE TO FACE (Figure 2c) merging the long side of the projections is the most distant setup. It suits users unfamiliar with each other, as well as competing opponents in a game for instance. In both cases, users have private interaction on their mobile display, using it to selectively share content on the projected surface. Also, the own projected display is likely not within easy reach of other parties making it more personal for each user.

Sitting face to face, but at the same time NEXT TO each other (Figure 2d) combines properties of both aforementioned setups. In this setup, users keep their private view on their mobile screens, but expose their projected surface to be easily reachable by the other party. Therefore, the setup particularly emphasizes familiar use cases of interactive surfaces, encouraging participants to manipulate all objects on the surface. Two users may also sit round the corner of the table which is in general equivalent to the previous case, but allows more easily to come round and take a look on the other user's private display when both users desire so.

Finally, groups > 2 merge projections at ARBITRARY SIDES in their center. Obviously, no general rule for the visibility of phone screens or reachability of projections can be determined. However, like people do when playing games involving hand cards, users can arrange to ensure the required visibility and privacy.

Interaction Techniques

In the following we will discuss required interaction techniques for the SurfacePhone that suit aforementioned application and usage scenarios. Here we draw from users' experience and familiarity with smartphones and tabletop systems. The technical feasibility of the here described techniques will be addressed in the implementation section of the technical prototype.

With today's prevalence of multi-touch interaction users would expect to be able to interact with the projected content using *direct touch*. This includes long touches and double-touches, to allow for a richer input set through different touch modalities. Furthermore, gestures like directional swipes are common on tabletops and should be supported as well. As the phone camera is watching the scene from above, mid-air gestures above the projection could also be considered.

Another interesting space of interaction lies *around* the projection. As the phone camera is seeing an up to ten times larger space around the projection, invisible buttons around the projection are possible. Similarly, gestures that cross the edges of the projection could be supported, for example, to move content to another user's projection that is currently not merged.

As the SurfacePhone is a mobile device, movement of the device can be measured using the built-in motion sensors and the optical flow of the camera's video stream. The projection could, for example, be changed from showing display-fixed content that moves with the device to showing a dynamic peephole into world-fixed content. Any table could thus become the personal virtual desktop that is explorable by moving the SurfacePhone like a flashlight over the table.

A regularly occurring task when using the SurfacePhone is to transfer content from the screen to the projection and vice-versa. Following on [1] we can distinguish between three main categories of transfer-techniques that can be supported: *direct*, *binned*, and *mediated* transfer.

- *Direct transfer* is used to transfer an item from a specific position on the phone to a specific position on the projection or vice-versa. For this category we propose to use *Human Link*. The body of the user is conceptually used as a medium to transfer the content between the two displays (cf. [20]). The user touches the content that they want to transfer on the phone and then, simultaneously or in quick succession, touches the point in the projection where they want to place it or vice versa (Figure 3a).
- *Binned transfer* uses a bin element on one or either displays that is used to place content items in the bin that then can be transferred using a form of *direct transfer*. For instance, to place a whole word in the scrabble game, users can position the letters on the bench (the bin) on their phone screen in correct order and then transfer them altogether by swiping over the target positions on the projection (Figure 3b). Similarly, users could select pictures on their phone to a bin and then fan them out on the projection with a finger swipe.
- *Mediated transfer* uses a proxy or gate element through which content is transfered. To transfer a object simply drag&drop it on the *proxy* (Figure 3c).

CONCEPT PROTOTYPE

To explore and evaluate the SurfacePhone concept, we built a prototype to validate that the proposed display configuration is actually desirable and usable. Through the placement of a standard mobile phone on a multi-touch surface it is easily possible to simulate the projection behind the phone. This allows us to test users' experiences providing a more robust, responsive, and clearer multitouch surface than would have been possible through developing a technical prototype (which we present later on) in the same time.

Implementation

The hardware setup consists of a Samsung PixelSense table running Microsoft's Windows 7 and Surface SDK; further two HTC HD 7 running Windows Phone 7.5 which offer a stand to arrange the phone on a table more easily. Markers placed below the phones allow them to be tracked by the table. Our software framework creates a 23cm $\times$ 18.5cm sized virtual projection 9cm behind and 3cm to the left of the phone. This size exceeds the projection size that is supported by our technical prototype by 33%. As phone manufacturers surely are able to build devices that support projections of these dimensions by using short-throw lenses or curved mirrors, we assume the projection size fits a realistic usage scenario. The devices communicate over Wi-Fi. As soon as phones are moved such that projections intersect, a merged projection is created. This merged projection can either be a graphically highlighted union of the individual projections, or something different like a shared playboard within the concave hull of the projections' corners.

Applications

Single-user game "escape" (SDSU)

The "escape" game represents the SDSU category by supporting external controls on the projection in a single-user game. The task of the game is to escape monsters by moving the character horizontally and vertically on a play field without other obstacles. When playing the game on the mobile phone, the on-screen controls and finger of the user cover parts of the play field on the phone. By "outsourcing" the controls to the projection behind the phone, thus providing free sight on the whole play field, we assume users will perform better in the projected mode (Figure 4a).

Multi-user presentation (SDMU)

In this application the SurfacePhone is used to present pictures or slides to a small group of people in two different ways: Either the user publishes thumbnails to the projection by dragging the thumbnail on the *proxy* at the top of the phone screen. The audience can then use standard multi-touch techniques for rotating and enlarging the pictures to their will (Figure 3c). The other possibility is that users browse their content on the projection and present items fullscreen on the

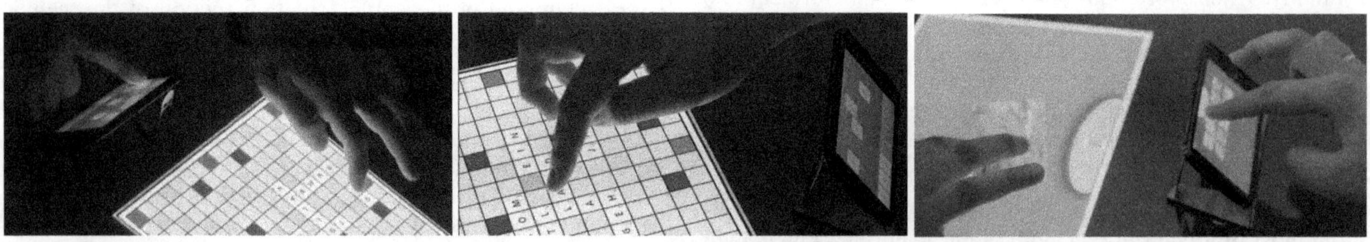

(a) Direct transfer: A user places a scrabble piece at a precise position on the board through simultaneous touch. **(b) Binned transfer: Elements from the bin element (here the bench) on the phone are placed on the projection using *touch-swipe*.** **(c) Mediated transfer: The presenter drags another picture on the proxy element at the top of the phone.**

Figure 3: Three techniques for content transfer between displays.

(a) Single-user "Escape" game: The game controls are "outsourced" to address the fat-finger problem with on-screen controls.

(b) Multi-user sharing from projection: the presenter selects images to be displayed on the phone screen.

(c) Multi-device: Both users have pieces for a collaborative puzzle they are supposed to solve on the merged projection.

Figure 4: Three of the five apps used in the concept study (see Figure 3 for the remaining two apps).

phone by double tapping them (Figure 4b). Different to the first way, the user gives up their privacy for the benefit of having a larger space themselves that can be quicker explored.

Multi-device picture sharing (MDMU)
The exemplary picture sharing – which would similarly work with other content types – is very similar to the SDMU presentation application. Users publish their thumbnails to the surface by using the *proxy* or *Human Link* techniques as in the presentation application. As soon as more than one device and user merge their projections by intersecting them, the merged space can be used to share all sorts of personal data. Thumbnails then belong to the joint surface, allowing all participants to explore pictures through multitouch operations and transfer them to their phone using one of the aforementioned techniques. When one of the participating users withdraws from the merged state the merged view is split and the separate projections retain prior items and positions on their side. If items have not been moved to the phone, these items are moved back to the projection of the owner. This feature shall give users a simple means of privacy control as they can withdraw with items that they only want to present but not give away.

Multi-device scrabble game (MDMU)
The scrabble application (Figures 3a and 3b) particularly emphasizes the private display on the mobile phones. It shows a standard scrabble playboard on the merged projections. The phone screens show the letters available to the users and a virtual bench on the bottom where words can be arranged with the letters using drag&drop. On their turn, users either use the *Human Link* technique to place any letter, no matter if on the bench or not, by touching the letter and the target position on the playboard. Alternatively, they first put the letters to place in correct order on the bench and then swipe over the empty fields on the board to place these letters. Depending on whose turn currently is, the board changes its orientation to face the corresponding user. Letters can be taken back to a precise position on the phone using *Human Link* or to a random position by double tapping them.

User Study

With the first user study we assess the quality of the overall SurfacePhone concept and its several components using the presented concept prototype. Using the four aforementioned applications we assess input techniques (e.g. *Human Link* and *proxy*), output (e.g. size and visibility of displays) and possibly occurring problems such as undesired occlusions of the projection and physical demands of the MMDE.

We follow a qualitative approach using think aloud, structured interviews, and video analysis as no similar system is available for comparison. We had 16 participants who took part in pairs to create a more realistic collaborative environment. Their average age was 26 years, (ranging from 23 to 31 years) and six of them were female. All participants except one owned a mobile touchscreen phone and three of the participants had prior experience with multi-touch tables.

Procedure
First we explained the concept of the SurfacePhone by showing them a concept design (similar to Figure 5a) of the technical prototype and to convince them that similar devices can be built we demonstrated a Samsung Galaxy Beam projector phone. Finally, the experimenter briefly explained the prototype, how it works, and the different configurations (SDSU, SDMU, MDMU) which also represented the different phases of the study.

After that, both participants tried all four applications (one each for SDSU and SDMU, two for MDMU) for approximately eight minutes each. Before each application participants were given time to test the concepts relevant in that phase, for instance, merging of projections and different transfer techniques, until they had no further questions. In single-device applications they took turns in acting as user or audience/spectator. In multi-device applications both users operated their own device simultaneously. To ensure a constant learning curve, the order of applications was always the same, going from single-device and single-user to multi-device and multi-user applications, thereby constantly gaining in complexity. Before each multi-user application, users were allowed to choose device positions (see MDMU before) that fit the task according to their opinion.

For the study the participants had to use all aforementioned applications. For the picture presentation applications (SDMU) both participants acted as presenter and observer in turns. For the picture presentation in MDMU mode we added two tasks. One task was to share pictures that contained Waldo with your partner and the other was to solve a 3×3 puzzle collaboratively on the merged projection space.

While participants were continuously motivated to share their experiences aloud, after each configuration (SDSU, SDMU, MDMU) they filled out a questionnaire regarding the configuration and contained tasks. The questionnaire asked for experience with the applications as well as physical demand, fatigue, visibility of content, feelings regarding privacy, etc.

After the study we let participants fill out the Post-Study System Usability Questionnaire (PSSUQ [12]). The study was video captured and later qualitatively analyzed. The textual answers were later analyzed using axial coding.

Results

In terms of preferred interaction technique, to transfer information between the two screens, most participants favored *touch-swipe*. Comparing *touch-swipe* and *Human Link* in the scrabble game, 15 of the 16 participants preferred *touch-swipe*. When comparing *touch-swipe*, *Human Link* and *proxy*, nine participants preferred *touch-swipe* and five would rather use the *proxy* technique. This is also reflected in the physical demand. Ten participants stated that *Human Link* has the highest physical demand and four found *proxy* to have the highest demand. The same was reflected in their rating of success, 12 participants said they were most successful with the *touch-swipe* and two thought they would be better with either *Human Link* or *proxy*. In their comments the poor performance of *Human Link* became pretty obvious. A majority (9 out of 16) stated that when using the *Human Link* they had the problem that when they touched the phone's screen and tried to touch the projection the phone would slide away. This was especially seen as an advantage of *touch-swipe*.

We asked the participants whether they developed a strategy to solve the puzzle and image tasks. All participants agreed that they followed a certain strategy. From the video analysis and the comments two strategies were particular promising. Three couples would actually change their original sitting position so that they would sit next to each other, allowing both participants to view each others phone displays, helping them to identify the correct pictures before putting them on the surface. Three other couples divided the work between in each other so that one participant would move the pictures from the phone to the projection and the other would arrange the puzzle parts in the projection.

To evaluate a possible adoption of such a device we asked the participants whether they would recommend such a device to their friends and if so what would be the necessary circumstances. All but one participant answered that they would recommend it. Most of the participants found fulfillment of hardware constrains such as reasonable size and battery life to be mandatory. Privacy was desired by all participants as a needed feature and most of them thought that presenting pictures by selecting them on the phone screen and have the projection show them is more reasonable than the other way round. Ten participants stated that they like that they don't need to pass their device around when presenting to groups.

The preferred combination of devices and users was MDMU. Participants found the possibilities that arise from having a mobile device that ad-hoc can create a complex mobile multi-display environment very attracting. Besides games such as Battle Ships, Poker and Black Jack the collaborative editing of documents, e.g. layouts of newspapers, was seen as possible application scenarios. Two participants mentioned the case of ad-hoc meetings for example to collaboratively investigate construction plans on a construction site.

The results of the PSSUQ are underlining these results. In the overall usability rating the SurfacePhone scored 84.8% as a mean of system usefulness (87.3%) and interface quality (81.9%). Overall, the results of the PSSUQ indicate that the SurfacePhone is a useful new device to extend screen space in single- and multi-user applications.

TECHNICAL PROTOTYPE

The positive results of the first study motivated us to build a technical SurfacePhone prototype that can support aforementioned interactions. Our aim with this prototype is twofold: Firstly, we want to investigate the technical requirements and challenges for such a device and find solutions for them. Secondly, we want to conduct another user study that delivers quantitative measures how well touches and gestures can be performed by users and detected by the system. Additionally we want to provide everything needed to create a SurfacePhone prototype to the community. From this we hope to spark further discussions.

Hardware Design

As no similar device configuration has been presented so far, we started from scratch. We chose the iPhone platform, since it was the only mobile platform that allowed two different outputs on screen and projection at that time. After we tested several different projection engines (e.g. TI DLP 2 or Microvision PicoP) attached to the backside of the device, it became obvious that without a fitting short-throw lens that is not available, the size of the projection would become too small. We solved the problem by attaching a mirror to the top of the phone and the projector to its bottom. This way the distance from projector to surface is more than doubled and sufficient to create a projection much larger than the phone screen.

Our prototype consists of an iPhone 5 plus projector case as depicted in Figure 5a. Both projector and mirror are 4cm to the right of the iPhone camera which is the minimum distance required for projector and mirror not to appear in the wide-angle view of the phone camera. In the camera image that is sampled at 640×480 the projection appears between $P_{TopLeft}\{183, 238\}$, $P_{BottomRight}\{590, 316\}$, thus takes up 407px in X and 78px in Y direction. Obviously, specifically the resolution in Y direction is quite small and the projection is not centred in the image. Nonetheless, this is the best compromise we found between maximizing the size of the projection and still completely seeing the projection in the camera.

Implementation

Following our previous design considerations, the prototype should support direct touch on the projection, different touch modalities, gestures, and tracking of other nearby SurfacePhones.

The software of the SurfacePhone is implemented in Objective-C and C++ on iOS with the help of OpenCV and openFrameworks modules. First we calibrate intrinsic and extrinsic camera parameters using printed chessboard and projected chessboard patterns respectively. Having the parameters we can map the projected area from object space to an interpolated orthogonal view of the projected region (see Figure 6a) and use this for tracking. In a final SurfacePhone device this would only have to be performed once.

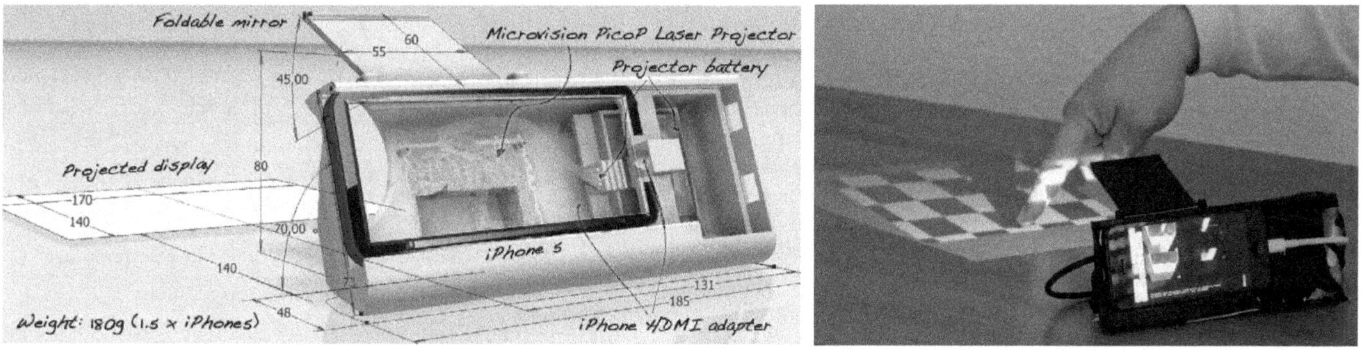

(a) The technical prototype design (dimensions in mm). (b) The implemented prototype.

Figure 5: Design and instantiation of the SurfacePhone prototype that tracks finger touches using in-built camera and accelerometer. The red border (for illustration) in (b) is the relic of perspective counter distortion. The phone shows raw camera image (top-left), background-image (bottom-left) and finger tracking with green dot at recognized fingertip (top-right).

For the tracking to work robustly at arbitrary locations we must make sure that different lighting conditions are handled. We can let the iPhone automatically adjust exposure and focus of the camera to the center of the image to adapt to different conditions. However, we need the user's finger for a correct estimation. Therefore, in step 3, we ask the user to present their finger for 2 seconds to the center of the camera while we lock correct exposure and focus for future interaction.

Finger Position

In step 4, we capture a still frame for subsequent background subtraction. As the background of interaction can be arbitrary we use background subtraction to separate moving fingers from the background. This step is automatically performed whenever the device comes to rest on a plain surface. Since we constantly measure the accelerometer at 100Hz we can quickly recognize whenever the user starts and stops moving the device.

Our following tracking process runs at 22 FPS. To eliminate shadows as best as possible we first convert the camera image to the HSV space and then work on the saturation channel. The literature recommends working on the hue channel to eliminate shadows, but we found that desk colors are often very similar to skin colors which is why we use the saturation channel that works more reliably in our scenario. After background subtraction we find blobs using openCV's contour finding algorithm. Because of the steep camera angle in our setup, blob area sizes can range from a few pixels to sizes that fill half of the image. This makes the classification of correct blobs more difficult. Further, we cannot rely on standard CV techniques like convexity defects for finding fingertips as often there is only one finger plus parts of the thumb in our image which do not provide the defects information. Instead, the algorithm we developed first computes the convex hull of the contour and its normalized approximation. Then, for each point on this new contour that has a tangential slope of less than 15° with its surrounding points, it calculates a probability that this point is the fingertip by minimizing equation:

$$P(Fingertip) = \frac{(SCD * W_{SCD} - DCP * W_{DCP} + SA)}{AREA} \quad (1)$$

- where SCD is the second closest distance of the point to the corners of the bounding box. A finger should create a very rectangular bounding box where the fingertip lies almost at the center of the smaller side of the rectangle yielding small distances to the two closest corner points;
- where DCP is the summed distances between the point and corner points of the bounding box that lie on or outside of the edge of the camera frame. A correct fingertip of a pointing finger will always have maximum distance to the hand center. As we do not see the hand the corner point is only an average guess;
- where SA is the estimated area of the fingertip above the current point. This is calculated as the sum of distances between up to 15 surrounding points on the contour to both sides. Correct fingertips should yield smaller results than arbitrary shapes with peak endpoints;
- where $AREA$ is the size of the blob;
- and where W_{SCD} and W_{DCP} are weights found by experiment set to 10 and 5.

Finally we have to decide which blob represents the primary finger, which one is a possible second finger and which ones are not of interest. Our blob sorting and filtering algorithm favors blobs with fingers, high finger probabilities, less circular shape (to filter out hand areas) and lower Y position (to filter out shadows appearing below fingers).

Finger Touch and Touch Modalities

To support different *touch modalities* we cannot rely on the 2D camera image as small changes in depth are indistinguishable from small changes in height for touch recognition. Kane et al. in their Bonfire system used a combination of posi-

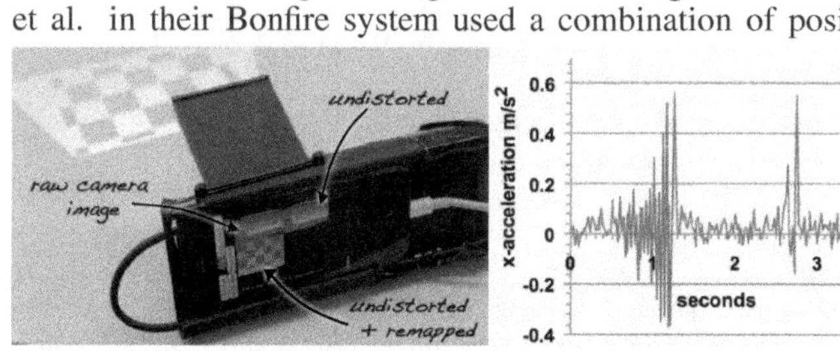

(a) Calibration proof mode: The projector projects a chessboard, the screen shows different proof views. **(b) First a strong, then a light touch, logged on the SurfacePhone.**

Figure 6: Implementation details

tion tracking using the camera and touch recognition using an accelerometer that measures the touch vibration on the table [10]. This approach seems the most promising as the hardware is readily available in most (projector) phones – in contrast to e.g. [6, 19]. However, their camera angle was almost orthogonal which simplified finger tracking. Further, they used the accelerometer of a laptop that shares a much larger space with the surface than our prototype and therefore allowed to work with simple thresholds. Correctly classifying touches with the SurfacePhone is thus bigger challenge.

Furthermore, when relying on surface vibrations for touch detection we cannot distinguish between touch down and up events to, for example, classify a touch as "long touch". Similarly, double taps cannot be recognized as successive events since the second vibration could overlay the first one. We can, however, recognize the intensity of the touch quite well since light and strong touches create distinct vibration patterns (see Figure 6b). These two modalities, light and strong, can, for instance, be used to start dragging of an item using a strong touch.

For the touch detection we measure the current acceleration in X direction every 10ms. Then we compute the touch vibration as the difference between the averaged sum of the absolute amplitudes of the recent 150ms (15 values) and the previously calibrated sensor noise. Based on thresholds we then decide whether the measured vibration corresponds to a strong, a light, or no touch at all. The default strong threshold is twice the default light threshold. As not all surfaces transport vibrations equally, we also implemented a detection procedure that vibrates the SurfacePhone with a constant pulse and measures the resulting phone vibration. Based on our tests with different tables, lightweight tables will be good mediums resulting in low phone vibrations (down to $0.1m/s^2$) and good touch recognition whereas strong tables will not pass on the vibration very well, resulting in phone vibrations up to $0.5m/s^2$. Through this procedure we can adjust the default thresholds to increase touch accuracy on different tables.

Gesture Recognition
Since in our setup we only see small parts of the user's hand, gesture support of hand postures does not make much sense. However, we can well recognize gestures that are based on a trajectory of movement such as directional gestures (left, right, top, down swipes) or more complex gestures like a circle. Finger trajectories that do not end in touches are simply analyzed for long directional movements or otherwise handed to the 1$ gesture recognizer by Wobbrock et al. [22].

Detection of other SurfacePhones
Although not fully integrated into our prototype yet, we evaluated the use of Qualcomm's Vuforia on the SurfacePhone using *projected* frame- and image markers. Our interest was to see how the steep camera angle and the much lower resolution of the projected image compared to printed markers affects the recognition algorithm. Fortunately, the recognition worked better than expected. Frame markers of a size of $1/8$ of the projection size are perfectly recognized as soon as they are completely visible in the scene. Image targets are recognized even up to a $1/50$ of the projection (see video figure).

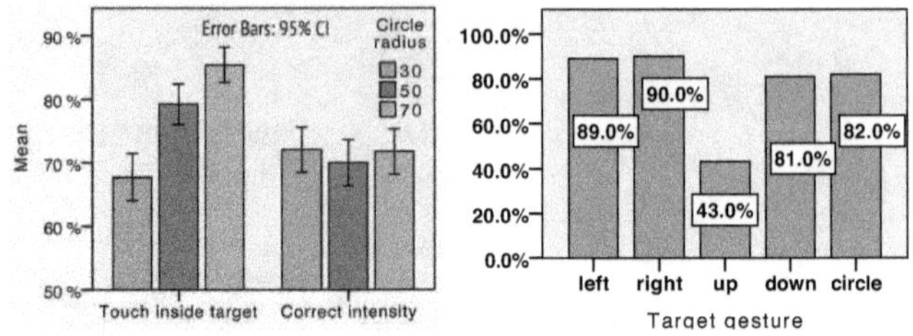

(a) Touch performance. (b) Gesture performance.

Figure 7: Results of the second study.

Technical evaluation
For the technical evaluation we recruited 15 untrained right-handed participants (5 female) of an average age of 27 years (ranging from 22 to 65 years).

Evaluation procedure
In the first part of the study, we asses multi-modal finger touch. The projection shows circles the user has to touch. There are three different sets of circle radius (30, 50, 70px respectively 1.75, 2.9, 4.0cm physical diameter) that each are arranged in a grid of 3×4 circles (cf. Figure 8) that span the projection area. Additionally, each target exists once for light and once for strong touch, marked with a big L or S (see Figure 1e). Thus, in total there are $3 \times 12 \times 2 = 72$ different targets split across three circle groups. After a test round, each participant performs 2 successive study rounds (resulting in 2160 touches overall). The order of circle size sets is counterbalanced and the display order of targets randomized. Participants can take as much time as they need to perform the touch.

In the second part of the study participants performed the gesture (circle, swipe left, right, top, down) that was written on the projection. Again, users performed one test and two study rounds of 4×5 gestures in random order (resulting in 500 recorded gestures overall).

Results and Discussion
Overall, 93% of user touches were recognized (7% have been performed too light to be recognized), 71% of these were hit with the right intensity and 77% of targets at the right position (see Figure 7a). Furthermore, we measured that clearly misclassified fingertips ($\delta > 300px$ off the target center) have been responsible for about 12% of false position recognition.

Factorial repeated-measures ANOVA on the touch data reported significant main effects of *circle radius*, *target position in Y direction*, but not *target intensity* at the $p < .05$ level (Greenhouse-Geisser corrected) on positional accuracy. Post-hoc analysis using Bonferroni corrected pairwise comparison of means revealed significant differences ($p < .05$) between small and middle and small and large sized circles as well as target heights 140px/340px and 240px/340px. Thus, the larger targets have been and the farer they have been away from the device, the better they have been hit in terms of position. Touch intensity recognition is statistically independent of both target position and circle radius.

Left and right gestures yielded recognition rates around 90%, down and circle gestures around 80%. Only the up gesture performed significantly worse than all others with only 43% (Figure 7b). The reason for this is that the tracker confused

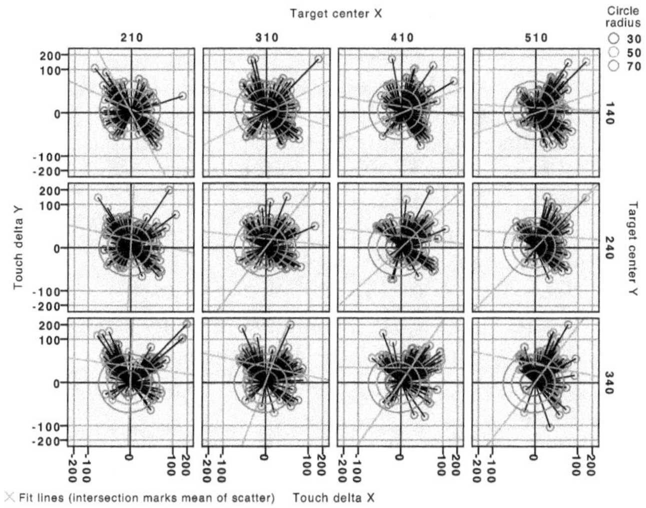

Figure 8: Participants touches visualized by target position and target radius. The orange fit line indicates general under-/overshooting.

44% of up gestures with the circle gesture. This may be due to the fact that after performing the correct up gesture participants moved their hand down and to the right to their default position, which the recognizer that evaluates the gesture after the hand has left the frame may have misinterpreted.

We also wanted to know if users would show a similar over- and undershooting behavior as they do on touchscreens (cf. [7]). Figure 8 depicts all performed touches except for the far outliers ($\delta > 300px$). From the touch distribution and their mean marked by the crossing of the fit lines we can conclude that the target position indeed has an effect on over-/undershooting in both X and Y direction. Targets to the lower-right are more overshot than targets to the upper left. However, overshooting is only compensated for farer targets without transforming into obvious undershooting as on touchscreens [7]. We assume the reason for this is that due to the steep viewing angle of the user on the projection the fat-finger problem only exists close to the device and decreases with increasing distance from the device. Also, perspective misjudgment may counter-balance overshooting. The issue of overshooting may thus also explain the significant effect of Y direction on touch accuracy mentioned before.

Regarding personal experiences, all participants thought that the device is already usable in many scenarios but maybe not for tasks like text entry (3 participants). Similarly, 10 participants stated that the difference between light and strong touches was difficult to learn, maintain (especially after performing the same intensity multiple times before switching), or to perform. For three female users the threshold for strong touch was set too high, for two male users rather too low. Overall, light touches have been slightly but significantly better ($p < .05$) recognized than strong touches (75% vs. 68%).

Overall, the results of the exploration and study of the second prototype reveal that a working SurfacePhone with the features (touch, drag&drop through multi-modal touch, gestures, and merging of projections) used in the first study can be built with today's mobile phone hardware. These findings underpin the overall concept but also show that the restriction to standard mobile phone hardware leaves room for the improvement of the system's accuracy. In the following we present suggestions towards that matter.

LESSONS LEARNED AND GUIDELINES

Through our explorations and studies we learned the following lessons and concluded guidelines for the SurfacePhone and its interface design:

1. In our study all participants cherished having the private display. Therefore, applications designed for the SurfacePhone should always consider its proper usage in innately not very private mobile scenarios.
2. Where possible, interaction techniques should be used that do not require simultaneous interaction on both displays. Besides the visual separation, though small, the user has no hand available to keep the phone in place.
3. The *proxy* was seen as an advantage in the SDMU case where the screens are divided between the users and nobody wanted to intervene on the display of the other. In multi-device scenarios with merged and thus larger displays, transfer techniques that support precise placement (like *touch swipe* and *human link*) should be favored.
4. Interface elements placed to the top left side of the projected display will not be affected by the fat-finger problem. Specific to our implementation, interactive elements should also have a radius of at least 50pixel to ensure a good accuracy.
5. Users should receive feedback about their touch intensity (e.g., a color meter around their touch) to support their mental touch model. Further, touch thresholds should be personally adaptable to account for anatomic differences.
6. Multi-modal touch decreases the accuracy of touch recognition as sometimes users touch too light while they try to keep the intensity below the threshold for strong touches. Thus multi-modal touch should be disabled whenever the interface gets by with single touch plus gestures to increase the accuracy to at least 93%.
7. The proposed automatic calibration of touch thresholds only makes sense up to the physical limits of surface vibrations. For thicker surfaces this especially means that light and strong touch thresholds move closer together, possibly resulting in more falsely recognized strong touches. Thus, strong surface materials (e.g. stone) should be avoided.
8. The system should account for overshooting with an offset function to increase accuracy of finger position tracking.

CONCLUSION AND FUTURE WORK

In this paper we presented the SurfacePhone, a novel configuration of a physical display and a projector that are aligned to allow ad-hoc Tabletop interaction in a mobile setup. We explored its design space and identified new single- and multi-user application scenarios with tailored interaction techniques. Our evaluation using our concept prototype indicates that the device is suited for a variety of everyday scenarios. We also learned which setups and transfer techniques users preferred in different scenarios. Later we demonstrated how the SurfacePhone can be built with only today's commodity phone hardware and the help of a specialized case and state-of-the art techniques for finger tracking and multi-modal touch recognition. Results of a quantitative user study on touch and gesture tracking accuracy revealed that the present prototype would already be applicable to many single- and multi-user scenarios and how it could be further improved, for instance, by counterfeiting typical overshooting behavior and personal adaptation of touch intensity. Overall, we can conclude that the SurfacePhone makes for a new and interesting device for ad-hoc collaboration.

In this work we concentrated on re-creating Tabletop scenarios with personal mobile data. However, there is a large potential of mobile scenarios that include movement of devices on or off the table as interactions. For instance, could the phone projection be used as peephole on a large desktop in joint learning scenarios, or games could involve tasks of which some can better be performed while holding the phone in hand and others better while placing the phone on the table. We leave this for future work, likewise further improvements to our technical prototype.

The SurfacePhone software, STL print files of the hardware, and assembly instructions are available for download http://uulm.de?SurfacePhone.

ACKNOWLEDGMENTS

This work has partly been conducted in the context of the DFG Emmy Noether research group *Mobile Interaction with Pervasive User Interfaces*.

REFERENCES

1. Bachl, S., Tomitsch, M., Kappel, K., and Grechenig, T. The effects of personal displays and transfer techniques on collaboration strategies in multi-touch based multi-display environments. In *Proc. of*, INTERACT'11, Springer (2011), 373–390.
2. Cauchard, J. R., Löchtefeld, M., Irani, P., Schoening, J., Krüger, A., Fraser, M., and Subramanian, S. Visual separation in mobile multi-display environments. In *Proc. of*, UIST '11, ACM (New York, NY, USA, 2011), 451–460.
3. Chen, N., Guimbretiere, F., Dixon, M., Lewis, C., and Agrawala, M. Navigation techniques for dual-display e-book readers. In *Proc. of*, CHI '08, ACM (New York, NY, USA, 2008), 1779–1788.
4. Greenberg, S., Boyle, M., and Laberge, J. PDAs and shared public displays: Making personal information public, and public information personal. *Personal Technologies 3*, 1-2 (Mar. 1999), 54–64.
5. Hang, A., Rukzio, E., and Greaves, A. Projector phone: a study of using mobile phones with integrated projector for interaction with maps. In *Proc. of*, MobileHCI '08, ACM (New York, NY, USA, 2008), 207–216.
6. Harrison, C., Benko, H., and Wilson, A. D. OmniTouch: wearable multitouch interaction everywhere. In *Proc. of*, UIST '11, ACM (New York, NY, USA, 2011), 441–450.
7. Henze, N., Rukzio, E., and Boll, S. 100,000,000 taps: analysis and improvement of touch performance in the large. In *Proc. of*, MobileHCI '11, ACM (New York, NY, USA, 2011), 133–142.
8. Hinckley, K., Dixon, M., Sarin, R., Guimbretiere, F., and Balakrishnan, R. Codex: a dual screen tablet computer. In *Proc. of*, CHI '09, ACM (New York, NY, USA, 2009), 1933–1942.
9. Hinckley, K., Ramos, G., Guimbretiere, F., Baudisch, P., and Smith, M. Stitching: pen gestures that span multiple displays. In *Proc. of*, AVI '04, ACM (New York, NY, USA, 2004), 23–31.
10. Kane, S. K., Avrahami, D., Wobbrock, J. O., Harrison, B., Rea, A. D., Philipose, M., and LaMarca, A. Bonfire: a nomadic system for hybrid laptop-tabletop interaction. In *Proc. of*, UIST '09, ACM (New York, NY, USA, 2009), 129–138.
11. Kauko, J., and Häkkilä, J. Shared-screen social gaming with portable devices. In *Proc. of*, MobileHCI '10, ACM (New York, NY, USA, 2010), 317–326.
12. Lewis, James R. IBM computer usability satisfaction questionnaires: Psychometric evaluation and instructions for use. Technical 54.786, Human Factors Group.
13. Lyons, K., Pering, T., Rosario, B., Sud, S., and Want, R. Multi-display composition: Supporting display sharing for collocated mobile devices. In *Proc. of*, vol. 5726 of *INTERACT '09*. Springer, Berlin, Germany, 2009, 758–771.
14. Matsumoto, T., Horiguchi, D., Nakashima, S., and Okude, N. Z-agon: mobile multi-display browser cube. In *Extended Abstracts of*, CHI '06, ACM (New York, NY, USA, 2006), 351–356.
15. Molyneaux, D., Izadi, S., Kim, D., Hilliges, O., Hodges, S., Cao, X., Butler, A., and Gellersen, H. Interactive environment-aware handheld projectors for pervasive computing spaces. In *Pervasive Computing*, vol. 7319. Springer, Berlin, Heidelberg, 2012, 197–215.
16. Schmidt, D., Seifert, J., Rukzio, E., and Gellersen, H. A cross-device interaction style for mobiles and surfaces. In *Proc. of*, DIS '12, ACM (New York, NY, USA, 2012), 318–327.
17. Seifert, J., Simeone, A., Schmidt, D., Holleis, P., Reinartz, C., Wagner, M., Gellersen, H., and Rukzio, E. MobiSurf: improving co-located collaboration through integrating mobile devices and interactive surfaces. In *Proc. of*, ITS '12, ACM (New York, NY, USA, 2012), 51–60.
18. Shirazi, A. S., Döring, T., Parvahan, P., Ahrens, B., and Schmidt, A. Poker surface: combining a multi-touch table and mobile phones in interactive card games. In *Proc. of*, MobileHCI '09, ACM (New York, NY, USA, 2009), 73:1–73:2.
19. Wilson, A. D. PlayAnywhere: a compact interactive tabletop projection-vision system. In *Proc. of*, UIST'05, ACM (New York, NY, USA, 2005), 83–92.
20. Wilson, A. D., and Benko, H. Combining multiple depth cameras and projectors for interactions on, above and between surfaces. In *Proc. of*, UIST '10, ACM (New York, NY, USA, 2010), 273–282.
21. Winkler, C., Seifert, J., Reinartz, C., Krahmer, P., and Rukzio, E. Penbook: Bringing pen+paper interaction to a tablet device to facilitate paper-based workflows in the hospital domain. In *Proc. of*, ITS '13, ACM (New York, NY, USA, 2013), 283–286.
22. Wobbrock, J. O., Wilson, A. D., and Li, Y. Gestures without libraries, toolkits or training: a $1 recognizer for user interface prototypes. In *Proc. of*, UIST '07, ACM (New York, NY, USA, 2007), 159–168.

Is Once Enough? On the Extent and Content of Replications in Human-Computer Interaction

Kasper Hornbæk[1], Søren S. Sander[1], Javier Bargas-Avila[2], Jakob Grue Simonsen[1]
[1]Computer Science, University of Copenhagen, Njalsgade 128, DK-2300 Copenhagen, Denmark
[2]Google/YouTube, User Experience Research CH-8002 Zürich, Switzerland
kash@diku.dk, s.s.sander@mail.dk, javier.bargas@me.com, simonsen@diku.dk

ABSTRACT
A replication is an attempt to confirm an earlier study's findings. It is often claimed that research in Human-Computer Interaction (HCI) contains too few replications. To investigate this claim we examined four publication outlets (891 papers) and found 3% attempting replication of an earlier result. The replications typically confirmed earlier findings, but treated replication as a confirm/not-confirm decision, rarely analyzing effect sizes or comparing in depth to the replicated paper. When asked, most authors agreed that their studies were replications, but rarely planned them as such. Many non-replication studies could have corroborated earlier work if they had analyzed data differently or used minimal effort to collect extra data. We discuss what these results mean to HCI, including how reporting of studies could be improved and how conferences/journals may change author instructions to get more replications.

Author Keywords
Replications.

ACM Classification Keywords
H.5.m. Information interfaces and presentation (e.g., HCI): Miscellaneous.

INTRODUCTION
A replication attempts to confirm an earlier study's findings, sometimes in conditions almost identical to the original study, sometimes in conditions that differ with respect to manipulations, setting, or measures. Replications thereby help establish whether a finding can be repeated – increasing confidence in its validity – and describe the conditions under which it holds or fails. They also help weed out studies whose results cannot be validated by independent research teams or under slightly different conditions. Therefore, replications help generalize findings and ensure intersubjectivity [24], and are a key to making science cumulative. A recent special section in the journal *Science* called replications the "scientific gold standard" [21]; Bazerman [2] wrote that "in replication the private chimera becomes the communal fact".

CHI 2014, April 26 - May 01 2014, Toronto, ON, Canada

http://dx.doi.org/10.1145/2556288.2557004

In Human-Computer Interaction (HCI), the discussion of the extent and value of replications recurs. For example, a series of events at the ACM CHI conference ([51], www.replichi.org) has promoted replications. Another example is a much debated paper on usability evaluation [11] that discussed the lack of replication in HCI. It argued that reviewers do not value replications and that replications are often not published, despite their potential value in nuancing earlier results. Zhai et al. [53] reported a replication of a study of target expansion by changing how the original study presented target expansion and how errors in performance were analyzed. They motivated the need for this replication by writing "although rarely done in the field of human computer interaction, important research results should be replicated for soundness and sustained development of a research topic" (p. 179).

In fields outside HCI, studies have shown that the literature contains few replications [e.g., 8,26,46] though some argue that a substantial number of replications exist [e.g., 23,39]. The success of meta analyses in some fields, most prominently medicine, presupposes studies that replicate each other [19]. In some fields it has been shown that replications often fail to find support for the claim they were supposed to replicate [2,48], though also this finding varies across fields [cf. 23]. In several highly publicized cases, initial claims of spectacular results have not been reproduced in spite of determined efforts by several independent research teams. Examples include cold fusion [18] and the ability of certain microbes to sustain growth by substituting arsenic for phosphorous [43].

To our knowledge no study has systematically investigated replications in HCI. Thus we do not know (a) the extent of replications in HCI or (b) the content of those replications. The present paper reports a study of replications identified through systematically examining conference proceedings and journals. We code the extent and content of replications, analyze the replications found, and discuss the relation between them and the studies being replicated. We believe that our work will (i) strengthen discussions of replications in HCI by providing data on the extent and content of replications, and (ii) assist in developing HCI-specific guidelines for replications that will facilitate more and better replications.

RELATED WORK

Replications have been much discussed in the literature on scientific methodology [e.g., 24,45]. Usually, replications are taken to mean the confirmation of the results of one study in a second, independent study [45]. Despite the importance of original, first discoveries in science, many have argued that there is too much emphasis on such discoveries [e.g., 20], and consequently less on replications.

The question of what constitutes a replication is hard to answer. In a strict sense, a study cannot be replicated because the investigator, setting, time of study, and instrumentation will differ [45]. In a less strict sense, most scholars rely on some classification of replications. Makel et al. [31] distinguished "direct" replications (attempting to follow the same experimental recipe) and "conceptual" replications ("original methods purposefully altered to test the rigor of the underlying hypothesis", p. 538). In a similar manner, Rosenthal [45] distinguished "fairly precise" and "fairly imprecise" replications. Kelly et al. [26] distinguished four types of replication: (i) Literal replications, where both the measures and the manipulations of an earlier experiment are reused (i.e., both the independent and dependent measures); (ii) operational replications, where the manipulations were replicated but other dependent measures were collected; (iii) instrumental replications, the opposite of operational replications, that is, they replicate measures but change the manipulations; and (iv) constructive replications that involve "an attempt to achieve equivalent results using an entirely original methods recipe" [26, p. 339], hence attempting to ensure external validity by varying both manipulations and measures.

Other papers offer complementary types of replication. Hendrick [15] also distinguished four types of replications: A (a) "strict replication" aims at repeating the study as exactly as possible, focusing on the procedure and context; it matches the literal replication discussed above; (b) a "partial replication" repeats some factors of a study, but introduces deliberate changes to others (covering Kelly's operational and instrumental replications); (c) a "conceptual replication" uses a completely different procedure (as Kelly's constructive replications); and (d) a "systematic replication" combines a strict replication with variations in the conceptual variables. Hendrick [15] argued that a systematic replication can both certify existing findings and potentially extend the scope of their applicability. Tsang and Kwan [48] differentiated six types of replications, defined by the type of population (same data set, same population, or different population) and type of measurement and analysis (same as the original study or different). The main difference to Kelly et al.'s categorization is that Tsang and Kwan consider reanalysis of the original data as a replication, and therefore list "Checking of analysis" and "Reanalysis of data with different methods" as types of replication.

Many studies investigate the extent to which replications are published: The number of replications they find differs widely. Some studies find few or no replications. For example, Sterling [46] found no replications in a sample of 362 articles from psychology journals. In marketing, one paper showed that replication rates were 1.2% [8], whereas a paper covering psychology papers since 1900 found 1.07% replications [31]. Other studies find many replications. Neuliep and Crandall [39] found more than 20% replications in *Journal of Personality and Social Psychology*, and more than 50% of the papers comprised several studies, attempting within a single paper to replicate findings. Some studies have suggested that replications often fail to replicate the original results [48]. These differences in findings may in part reflect differences among fields, in part differences in the definition of replication.

Jones et al. [23] studied replications in the field of human factors. They found 50% to 75% replications by selecting eight papers published in one year of the journal *Human Factors* and looking at citations to those papers in a sixteen-year window. Jones et al. sampled across papers retrieving different number of citations, and found that more highly cited papers were more likely to be replicated. Most of the replications (87% - 94%) were conceptual (in the sense of [15]) and many (19% - 37%) were conducted by the authors of the paper being replicated.

Replications have been much discussed in HCI [e.g., 11,40,51]. Newman [40] argued that much research in HCI present radical solutions, that is, new paradigms to solve problems in interaction. By definition, radical solutions change the problem to be addressed substantially. In contrast, engineering research often enhance existing solutions or methods. Radical solutions do not emphasize existing solutions/methods and do not do incremental refinement; hence, in our reading of Newman, they do not lead to a focus on replicating existing findings. Greenberg and Buxton [11] argued that there is a lack of replications at the ACM CHI conference, claiming reviewer reluctance towards replication studies as one reason. The RepliCHI series of events [51] initiated a discussion of replications in HCI. Among other things, participants in the RepliCHI events have proposed that the CHI conference should create a venue for presenting replications (which happened in 2013). In addition to these general discussions of replications, many influential papers in HCI have included some type of replication [e.g., 7,53].

However, to our knowledge no study has assessed the extent of replications published in the field of HCI or tried to analyze a sample of replications so as to understand their findings relative to the original studies or how replications might be improved.

METHOD

The aims of this study are to (a) discover the extent of replication in HCI research, and (b) characterize the replications done, in particular their type, their results, and the differences to the studies being replicated.

Browsing for Replications

One approach to identifying replications is to search for papers that might contain replications. Unfortunately, no generally accepted terminology for replications exists (authors use "follow up study", "reproduce results", etc.), making the selection of appropriate query terms difficult. Neuliep and Crandall [39] pointed out that most replications are not labeled as such; Makel et al. [31] found that only 68% of 500 psychology papers containing the term replication were actually replications. Moreover, it is difficult to use searching to estimate the frequency of replications. At the time of writing, a search on Google Scholar on "human computer interaction" and "replication" returns more than 21,000 entries.

Another approach is to identify a set of papers and investigate how frequently they have been replicated. Jones et al. [23] took that approach in studying how many papers from the 1991 volume of the journal *Human Factors* had been replicated, by whom, and how frequently. This approach has the disadvantages that the sample of papers is crucial to the findings, that replication rates are obtained only for older papers (not current ones), and that the sample size that can be treated is usually small.

A third approach is to browse a set of publication outlets; this was done by for instance Neuliep and Crandall [39]. The drawback of that approach is that replications in HCI most likely are infrequent; studies in other fields typically find low rates. A large number of studies must therefore be examined to characterize replication studies. Nevertheless, we chose to browse publication outlets for replications; this is the preferred method in studies of replications in other fields (e.g., [39]).

We examine four key outlets for research in HCI (see Table 1). We browsed all full papers from the years 2008 to 2010 of a key conference on human-computer interaction and three highly-ranked journals. We had no reasons to expect replications being more frequent in conference proceedings than in journals, so we examined both types of outlet.

Publication outlet	*Papers*	*Eligible*	*%*
ACM Conference on Human Factors in Computing Systems (CHI)	590	265	62
ACM Transactions on Computer-Human Interaction (TOCHI)	63	28	6
Human-Computer Interaction (HCI)	32	22	5
International Journal of Human-Computer Studies (IJHCS)	206	114	27
Total	891	429	100

Table 1. Publications browsed for replications (2008-2010).

Criteria for Eligibility

Before considering whether a paper contains a replication, we checked each paper on certain criteria for eligibility. In particular, a paper must:

- *be empirical.* We do not include literature reviews or papers that theoretically justify or predict particular findings.
- *include quantitative data.* While qualitative studies may build on and relate to earlier findings, such studies typically rely on other notions of overlap among studies than replication [32]. Thus, we restrict our sample to papers that include quantitative data.
- *report an experiment.* This criterion was added for three reasons. First, we wanted to compare the size of effect found in a replication to that of the original study. The notion of effect, and its quantification in effect size, presupposes a comparison of two or more treatments. Second, research may be thought of as descriptive, relational, or experimental [44]. Replications are most likely to be found in experimental research because descriptive and relational research is often exploratory, aiming to describe new phenomena or contexts of use. Third, almost all earlier studies of replications either explicitly or implicitly focus on experiments (e.g., [26]). We wanted to compare our results to these studies.
- *study human interaction with user interfaces.* Although interested in HCI in a broad sense, we did not include papers that simulate computational models or that compare algorithms without data on users' interaction.

As shown in Table 1 about half of the papers published in the outlets were eligible under these criteria.

What Counts as a Replication?

To code the eligible papers, we fixed a set of operational criteria for determining if a given paper is a replication. In the present paper, a replication is considered an *attempt to confirm, expand, or generalize an earlier study's findings.* Hence, a replication investigates the reported findings, resulting in either consolidation or potential invalidation or reduction in scope of the original study's findings. Note that this description of replications does not entail a particular philosophy of science or position on falsification as a scientific ideal.

We operationalize this general formulation as follows.

- A replication must name and reference the original study it replicates; if it did not, it would be very hard to determine if a paper replicated another study. It must also discuss its findings against that earlier study.
- A replication must collect data that relate to the original study; it must express some kind of intent to confirm/expand/generalize that study. We looked for hints about this in the abstract, introduction, method, and discussion sections. The rationale is that if an original study is not mentioned in these sections, it has

not influenced the design or the analysis, and the original study is unlikely to be replicated. In some cases we also analyzed the related work section, for instance when the hypotheses or rationales for a study were developed in that section.

- A replication must concern an original study outside of the paper under consideration; attempts to confirm, expand, or generalize results from earlier parts of a paper are not treated as true replications.
- A replication need not use the word replication or any synonym thereof to be coded as a replication.
- A replication must seek to confirm, expand, or generalize an existing study; using earlier results does not qualify as replication. For instance, a paper may use a questionnaire, validated in an earlier study, to measure a particular construct without being considered replication. Likewise, using a previously established model does not in itself count as a replication (e.g., many studies use Fitts's law to model performance with an input device, but do not attempt to confirm, expand, or generalize that law).
- A replication must seek to confirm, expand, or generalize an existing study; discussing results in relation to earlier work does not make for a replication. For instance, Morris et al. [36] studied SearchBar, a tool for storing, browsing, and querying web search history. In the discussion they noted, "One particularly surprising result was the extensive use of browser tabs among our participants […]. This is in contrast with results reported by Weinreich et al […]" (pp. 1214-1215). We do not consider this paper a replication because the contrast to Weinreich et al. is of minor importance and because the goal of the study was not to compare to the findings by Weinreich et al.

If a paper contains a replication, we distinguish several types based on the literature reviewed earlier (e.g., [26,39]); the types are mutually exclusive:

- *Strict replications* use the same independent and dependent variables as the original study, and attempt to reproduce that study as closely as possible.
- *Partial replications* use deliberate modifications of earlier research, with the aim of testing them in different settings, with different demographic groups of participants, or other operationalizations of variables.
- *Conceptual replications* or *constructive replications* investigate earlier findings, but using different measures, manipulations and settings.

In addition to these types, we include a *number comparison*. This replication type was not seen in the literature, but only in studies that were eligible but did not replicate a finding about differences in means (typically, the difference between means from two experimental conditions) but instead looked at the absolute value for some dependent variable.

We also coded a type of work that is sometimes called replication, but in a much looser sense than the above. A paper with *related experiments* contains several studies that attempt to re-find or challenge each other's findings (i.e., a intra-study replication). For instance, Hoggan et al. [16] investigated adding feedback to touchscreens, reporting two experiments that differed only in the quality of the tactile actuator used to generate the feedback. We do not consider such studies to be replications because they lack the independent scrutiny of earlier research findings that replications offer.

Checking Coding

The above codes were developed over a number of iterations and then applied to papers by the four authors and two research assistants. To test the successfulness of the coding, one rater (the first author) coded a subset of 20% of the papers coded by each of the other raters. Inter-rater agreement using Cohen's kappa indicated substantial to perfect agreement [28]: For eligibility, $\kappa = .9$ (range .7-.99), for replication, $\kappa = .8$ (range .75-.87), and for other codes it was $\kappa = .9$ (range .85-.97).

In addition to the above checks, we also contacted authors from each of the papers that were classified as replications (N = 28). The aim was to let authors input their views. We report outcomes of this coding check in the results section.

Example of Coding

Coding papers was difficult. To give a sense of the complexity involved, we describe some considerations in the coding of a single paper.

Escape [52] is an interactive technique that aims to help users select targets on the touch screens of mobile devices, in particular when targets are small or occluded. It does so by associating a target (say, a pin on a map) with a direction. The user then makes a gesture in the direction associated with a target to select it. The paper describes two experiments; the first compares Escape to an earlier technique called Shift [50]. The first part of the experimental results compare the performance of Shift and Escape; with no other information, this would be an example of building on earlier work (by reusing Shift) but not of replicating a finding. Had the paper for instance repeated the same conditions as in the earlier study of Shift (which included that technique and two baseline conditions) it could have rechecked the earlier findings (for instance, that Shift is faster than unaided touch for small targets). The last part of the results in Yatani et al.'s paper, however, compares directly to Shift by noting [52, p. 290]:

> Although Escape's task time outperformed our reimplementation of Shift in this study, Escape's performance is only marginally better than the original published results […] for targets 12 pixels or less, and is somewhat worse for targets 18 pixels or greater.

Yatani et al. then report a second experiment that compares their implementation of Shift to the original implementation of Shift (see [52], Figure 9 on p. 291). In the terms of the coding scheme presented above, this is a *number comparison*. The second experiment compares some variations on Escape and is not an independent replication (although the paper does contain *multiple studies*). It does not qualify as *related experiments* because the experiment focused on studying new independent variables rather than attempting to re-find the results of the first experiment.

RESULTS

First we discuss how many replications our sample contains and then we turn to the content of those replications.

Frequency of Replication

Among the eligible papers we found 28 papers that contained replications in some form (see Table 2). This is 6.5% of the eligible papers and 3.1% of the full sample. The list of 28 replications can be obtained from the authors; in the present paper we discuss some of them [1,3,5,6,10, 12,13,14,25,29,30,33,38,41,42,47,49,52]. Heer and Bostock [14], for instance, used crowdsourcing to replicate classic results in graphical perception; Pietriga and Appert [42] introduced new types of lenses for magnifying data and compared their performance to earlier work.

Across outlets, the percentage of eligible papers and replications vary. TOCHI and CHI have the lowest number of eligible papers (44% and 45%, respectably), while IJHCS has 57% and HCI has 69%. One outlet contained no replications (TOCHI), while others had more (HCI 5%, IJHCS 6%, CHI 8%) relative to the number of eligible papers. We see no pattern across outlet type to generate eligible papers or papers with replications.

Half of the papers classified as replications explicitly mentioned doing replications, for instance by noting that they "broadly replicate the work of Fitzmaurice and Buxton" [49, p. 2232] or "attempted to replicate results reported by Litman et al." [6, p. 313]. This is more frequent than reported in other fields, where replications are rarely identified as such [39]. Whereas 11 papers did not mention any stem of the word replication, three papers used replication in another sense from that intended here and one paper argued that it did not do a replication [38], even though we classified it as such.

Type	*N*	*%*
Replication	28	7
Strict	3	1
Partial	8	2
Conceptual	17	4
Multiple studies	150	35
Related experiments	67	16
Number comparison	6	1
Eligible papers	429	100

Table 2. Three types of eligible papers. A paper can be simultaneously in the categories Replication, Multiple Studies, and Number Comparison. The subtypes Strict, Partial, and Conceptual are mutually exclusive and exhaustive.

Types of Replication

Table 2 shows the types of replications that were coded; the types attempt to capture the relation between the replication and the initial study. Few *strict replications* were coded (3 of the eligible studies). The paper by Heer and Bostock [14] is one example, as they attempted to do at least two studies that mimicked the setup and measures of earlier studies of graphical perception, changing only the setting in which the study was done (crowdsourced rather than in a lab). Most replications change aspects of the study they replicate, either a little (8, partial replications in Table 2) or much (17, conceptual replications). Nacenta et al. [38] was classified as a *partial replication*. They reused earlier work but adapted implementations, the experimental setup, and the performance measures collected. An example of a *conceptual replication* is the paper by Chen and colleagues [5]. They integrated previous work on two-handed command selection and empirically investigated some benefits of using two hands and of merging commands. Although they compare directly to earlier work (e.g., p. 738), the implementations of interaction techniques and the experimental setup were different.

Papers Reporting Multiple Studies

Among the papers in the sample, 17% contained *multiple studies* (35% of the eligible papers). This number varies among outlets; in particular journals contain more multiple-studies publications (HCI: 44%; TOCHI: 21%; IJHCS: 20%) than conferences (CHI: 14%). Paper length is one explanation of this difference.

Among the papers that contain *multiple studies*, 67 (16% of the eligible papers) were coded as *related experiments*. For instance, Moscovich and Hughes [37] conducted several experiments on multi-touch input. They justified their second experiment by noting: "in the light of Experiment One, we expect that one hand would be better able to coordinate control of an object's position, orientation, and size." (p. 1279). In our analysis, this paper and other papers classified as *related experiments* are conceptually different from replications: while they add credibility and variation to the evidence presented, they are not providing the independent scrutiny possible in replications by independent researchers.

Content of Replications

The content of replications helps answer five questions that we think are of importance to understand how replications are done. We discuss those questions in turn.

Are earlier findings confirmed?

A key purpose in conducting replications is to either confirm earlier findings or show that they do not hold. Among the replications reported, half re-find the effect identified in earlier papers; in one case [6] a study fails to find an effect that an original study had also failed to find.

The remaining half of the replications show mixed results ($N = 7$, 25%), fail to replicate findings ($N = 3$), or could not be coded by all coders ($N = 4$). Showing mixed results and failing to replicate are interesting because they help qualify and scope earlier results. In [38], for instance, the authors noted – after having reported results of a study on how to mitigate difficulties in moving a mouse pointer between screens next to each other – that "the previous findings may seem to contradict the results of the initial evaluation of Mouse Ether" (p. 784). Casiez and Vogel [3] compared to an earlier study and noted that (p. 1714):

> This confirms the results found by Zhai [...] while extending it to a wider range of stiffness values. However, Zhai found a 47% difference between the isotonic and isometric rate control devices, which may be explained by the 6 DOF docking task or the different device form factors he used.

How do authors compare to earlier findings?

We were also interested in how authors compared to the original study. Many replication studies (N = 22) used general terms to compare to the original studies. They might write that results are "consistent with" the study being replicated [e.g., 4,13,29], that they "match earlier work" [14], or that they "are similar to those presented by [...]" [10]. Some studies argue that they "replicate" earlier findings, without qualifying how or to what extent [e.g., 30]. The use of these general terms means that the comparison to earlier findings is mostly binary, either confirming or failing to confirm.

Before analyzing the sample, we were curious if HCI researchers would use the large literature on going beyond binary outcomes (confirm/non-confirm) toward quantifying effects [44]. Although six papers used effect sizes to report results, only two papers used effect sizes to compare to earlier work. Hartmann and colleagues [13] noted in discussing their results that "the difference in effect sizes between framing without and with exposure to the website is consistent with findings of related previous studies" (p. 862). Another study used a variant of effect sizes (sigma scores) to discuss their results against other work [6].

The frequent binary comparisons used in most replications leave the reader wondering about the data behind the comparisons. Findlater and McGrenere [9] studied adaptive menus and held a hypothesis about the difference between two menus types, called High and Low: "The difference between High and Low would replicate previous findings [...]" (p. 1251). They succeed in supporting that hypothesis, but it is not clear how the strengths of the findings compares to the two original studies they replicate. Heer and Bostock [14] replicated earlier work on graphical perception and wrote that they obtained results consistent with earlier work (p. 208). This was supported by a graphical comparison and statistics: "we found a significant effect of plot density (F(3,2415) = 3.49, p = 0.015) but not of background density (F(4,2415) = 0.44, p = 0.779), consistent with Stone and Bartram's findings". However, the effect found by Heer and Bostock is much lower (d = 0.13) than that of original study by Stone and Bartram (d = 1.58 or d = 0.79)[1]. These effect sizes are hard to estimate, but if the difference is as large as the d-values suggest, then the consistency among findings is an apt description at the level of binary significance testing, but not when looking at the actual effects. Both of the studies we have discussed above are exemplary in many respects, but their replication component seems unnecessarily binary.

A few papers compare to earlier work in a non-binary way without using effect size. The techniques for doing so include plotting results against those from original studies [3,10,14] or formulating models of performance [10]. The latter helps comparing across studies, for instance by reducing pointing performance to throughput. Comparisons were sometimes enriched with simple percentages. Chapuis et al. [4] wrote that "Performance results for Point and Bubble cursors are consistent with those in [...]", but added "our participants perform faster overall: 10.6% faster for Bubble cursor and 9.6% faster for Point cursor." (p. 1398).

Whose work is replicated?

Most studies replicate the work of other researchers (N = 22). The remainder either replicates their own work (N = 2) or do both (N = 6, e.g., [1]). Note that these cases refer to work reported outside of the replication paper. Although most replications succeed in reproducing earlier studies to the extent that they may be replicated, it is sometimes hard. Some researchers create independent implementations of earlier user interfaces [e.g., 38,52]; in some cases this necessitates extra evaluations to ensure that the new implementation works as in the original study [52].

What counts as a finding?

We had expected that replications attempted to investigate findings from earlier papers and – because we looked for replications in experiments – that those findings would be differences between experimental conditions (e.g., differences in means). This did not always happen.

Six studies do *number comparisons* [e.g., 12,41,50]. Thus, instead of comparing to earlier findings (e.g., differences in means) they compare the numbers from a particular condition directly to numbers in an original study. For instance, Grimes et al. [12] compared the accuracies obtained with a new EEG classification methodology to those from an earlier studies by writing "we were able to replicate classification accuracies reported in previous work (e.g. our accuracies of 92.3% accuracy at 30 seconds is comparable to Gevins' 2-way accuracy of ~95% using 27.5 second windows [...])" (p. 841). The key point in *number comparisons* is that the comparison is not made to results of the experimental manipulation (in [12] that would have been task difficulty) but to raw values (in [12] accuracy). Another example is [33] that obtains a correctness rate in

---

[1] We estimated $d = 2*\mathrm{sqrt}(df_n*F/df_d)$ from F-values in the Heer and Bostock paper (those in the quote) and from the Stone and Bartram paper (p. 3, hypotheses 3).

gesture guessing of 46% and compares it to earlier work. *Number comparisons* do not use the experimental component of the paper (which is a necessary to be classified as replication), but instead just checks or relates to a value from the original study. We have not seen this in studies of replications in other fields.

Some studies reuse conditions. To simplify, assume that a replication study builds on an original study that has two conditions, *oldUI* and *controlUI*: presumably, findings that compare these conditions could be interesting to replicate. The replication study may include both of these, and compare them to a new interface, *newUI*. This is done in several cases [e.g., 25,35,41]. In such replications, one could easily check any of the *oldUI* vs. *controlUI* findings, but many studies refrain from doing so. For instance, Karlson and Bederson [25] studied thumb input, building on two earlier interfaces ThumbSpace and Shift. In comparing those interfaces they included a control condition (DirectTocuh), which had been used in the original studies. Karlson and Bederson (study 1) did not in check the earlier findings. With the above discussion of effect size in mind, they could have compared the effect sizes of, for instance, the DirectTouch versus ThumbSpace comparison to the ones in the original study. We consider Karlson and Bederson's study excellent, but from the perspective of replication they could have added even further to our body of knowledge by considering findings relational and by comparing effects, rather than values. In all fairness to Karlson and Bederson, doing such comparisons is hard because earlier papers may not report their data clearly, making the extraction of key statistics hard.

What do authors' of replications think?

As part of this study we contacted authors of studies that had been coded as replications (N = 28). Although we promised not to quote their responses or name individual studies, the patterns in their responses are interesting.

Twenty-three authors responded to our request, representing 82% of the coded replications. Out of those answers, 19 (83%) confirmed our coding, though 13 (57%) reported that while their work contained replication, their study was not planned as a replication. They emphasized that their main goal was not to replicate an original study, but to research new/additional topics and extend the original work substantially.

Four authors (17%) disagreed with our coding. Three authors pointed out that this coding depends heavily on our definition of "replication". They noted differences to the original studies, such as different experimental setup, variables, and research goals. All of the four replications under dispute were coded as partial or conceptual replications, due to the major differences to the original studies. One author in particular disagreed with our coding and mentioned that even if prior work was replicated, the study's main goal was not to replicate anything. Thus, the disagreement with our coding stems from more rigorous definitions of what a replication is than the one we adopted.

The data are in line with other findings reported here. Most replications in HCI are not conducted to replicate earlier findings; typically they seem a byproduct of the necessity to compare new data to prior work.

DISCUSSION

This review of a selection of HCI papers has shown a 3% replication rate. The analysis of replications shows that they mainly confirm earlier findings and that comparisons to earlier studies are often simple. The notion of replication proved difficult, as evidenced by the work taken to code replications and by the authors' comments on papers that we consider replications. Next we discuss these findings and their implications for HCI.

What can we Learn from Replication Studies?

There are two main lessons to be drawn from the 28 replications found in the sample. First, the replications are valuable in that some show that independent research teams can repeat earlier work [49]. In some cases they qualify earlier work [30], suggest that we might not be sure of an earlier finding [38], show that a finding outside of HCI also apply to our field [13], or do an empirical test that explains earlier, seemingly contradictory findings [5]. These examples show that in as far as HCI is an empirical science, replications improve cross-study validity of findings. Although it has been argued that replications are hard because some phenomena in HCI are volatile [27], replications also help see how changing user expectations and technologies affect what we thought we knew.

The second benefit of replications is that they often are specific about what is kept constant and what is changed in empirical work: they motivate *why* a replication is needed. Thereby, critical reasoning about validity issues in earlier work is brought to the fore.

Why so few Replications?

Lack of replications in other fields has shown to be detrimental to proper scientific practice and development of the fields [2,19,48]. Why, then, do HCI researchers not replicate more frequently? Many explanations suggested in other fields probably also hold for HCI, including lack of prestige in replicating, lack of success of replication initiatives, and difficulty in getting replications published. Our analysis has revealed five further points. First, some papers in our sample attempt to improve interaction techniques presented in earlier work. They miss an opportunity, at least in our view, to check if the earlier findings about a technique hold and instead go on to "beat" earlier work with a better technique. This was also evident in the comments from authors, where many explained that they were not trying to replicate, but just to propose new interaction techniques; their focus is on new interaction techniques, not on consolidating earlier work. Thus, building upon earlier studies is widespread, whereas discussing against and replicating them are not.

Second, some papers downplay replication. In [47], Takayama and Nass reported a study that we read as downplaying its replication contribution. They wrote "While this study is similar to Moon's (1998) experiment of computer source proximity in the interviewing context, this paper is the first test of the effects of source proximity in the driving content and the first to investigate effects of source proximity upon physical performance in a safety-critical situation" (p. 176). They might as easily have written "This study replicates the finding of Moon (1998) on computer source proximity in interviewing within a driving context. This provides a first test of the effects of source proximity upon physical performance in a safety-critical situation". Whether that formulation is compatible with the authors' goals is not the point, nor is the specific example the key issue. Mainly, we argue that HCI outlets might be changed in the future, so that authors can more easily write the latter variant and get their work published.

Third, HCI is a multi-disciplinary field, drawing for instance on natural science, social science, and engineering. These fields bring different conceptions of empirical enquiry and of replication to HCI; we already discussed this for qualitative studies. Because of this mix of fields, HCI researchers need both to contribute technology, demonstrate utility to users, and show implications of design. In that mix, replications may end up as a low priority.

Fourth, the distinction between a formative study (e.g., a user study of a new interface) and summative study (e.g., an experiment comparing several variants of interface) might explain the replication rate. Whereas formative studies are useful in driving technological refinements, only summative studies can qualify as a replication. Whereas formative studies change with new technologies and new use contexts, summative studies often use theories and models that abstract from the substantive to the conceptual domain (in the terms of [34]). The low replication rates may be a symptom of priority to empirical studies that evaluate technology, rather than to empirical studies that summarize and challenge conceptual insights.

Fifth, while we emphasize "few" replications, a more positive view may be that HCI is doing well compared to older and more mature fields. We have opted for the rather negative view because of the lack of systematic attempts to replicate work, because of the promise of replications to help emphasize conceptual insights, and because of their utility as a vehicle to clarify, share, and improve experimental work.

Implications and Recommendations

Our papers have some implications for HCI researchers and for editors/chairs in HCI. Note that we are *not* arguing that all studies, or even a majority of studies, should replicate earlier work. We also *do not* want to imply that experiments are a better research method than other methods (see a general discussion in [34] and a HCI-specific discussion in [17]). Rather, our intent is to give a number of recommendations to be taken into serious consideration when designing and reporting experiments for HCI.

How to improve reporting of experiments?

Based on our reading of papers, we think that reports of experiments in HCI, both replications and non-replications, may be improved in several ways:

- Distinguish reuse from replication. Sometimes it is easy to add data analysis to corroborate earlier results.
- Distinguish effect sizes from numbers. What we have called *number comparisons* is to be distinguished from comparing to earlier results (e.g., using effect sizes).
- Include baselines from earlier studies. Instead of just "beating" the best technique from an earlier study, consider including earlier baselines to allow replications of effects.
- Share material from experiments. Some authors had to re-implement interactive techniques and struggled to get the details right. We can help others do that more easily. Also, sharing data allows reanalysis, what some consider a replication [48].
- Describe similarities and differences to earlier work. What is varied and what is kept constant?
- Signal if something is a replication (for instance in the abstract, as in [29]).
- Some papers contain many results, making it hard to identify key comparisons. Compare to the key findings of the work being replicated, not just select findings.
- Discuss against earlier work. All replications discussed against earlier work; in a sample of 102 eligible, non-replication papers from CHI 2010, only 18% had references in the sections following their discussion.
- Authors who write papers containing *multiple studies* (35% of the eligible papers in our sample) may apply the thinking about replications propose here to their intra-paper comparisons, for instance by using effect sizes or by considering the type of replication done.

How to change HCI outlets?

We suggest that editors/chairs rethink their instructions to authors and reviewers. Other fields have seen proposals on how to improve replication rates, such as open science collaboration, journals dedicated to replications, and repositories for replications. For HCI, the guides for submissions for the four outlets we studied could be revised. The instructions for journals, for instance, suggests that "The paper **must be original in some way**: either in its insights, its results, or its approach" (HCI), "... **publishes only original** and significant research papers" (TOCHI), and "...**publishes original research** over the whole spectrum" (IJHCS). The emphases are ours. CHI 2014 authors are told that "it is not just helpful but essential that the submission's **contribution be original**, going beyond any work already reported in other journals or conference proceedings". They can select a contribution type called "Validation and refutation" which mentions replications, though it is not prominent to authors (or reviewers) and seems to contradict the emphasized instructions.

These instructions focus on novelty and originality of research, which works against the publication of replications. The gap between the urge for novelty and adopting replication as a scientific gold standard [21] must be addressed. As discussed earlier, outlets could change their focus from novelty to significance of contributions or, alternatively, just research quality. Incidentally, this approach has been taken by some venues already (e.g., PLOS one). In addition, a dedicated section should mention how the outlet handles submissions with replications. No guideline among the four mentions the word "replication". Increasing the number of prestigious venues that explicitly accept replication studies will lead to more of such contributions in the long run.

The recent discussions in RepliCHI also warrant some comments based on our data. Our key concern is that the definition of replication is less straightforward than some discussions at RepliCHI suggests. The definition of replication was difficult to us as well as the authors we contacted. We applaud the suggestion by John [22] of marking replications at submission time and the CHI 2014 initiative that makes replication as a contribution type (though we prefer them to continue to be part of main track of the conference).

Limitations

This study has a number of limitations that we would like to flag and discuss how to mitigate in future work. First, coding replications is complex. Thus we share with many studies [e.g., 31] the limitation that "if research articles are not framed as replications, then they were not categorized as such" (p. 541). The exclusion of qualitative studies from the sample and of *related experiments* may also be seen as a limitation. Second, we chose to use browsing of publication outlets as a strategy for identifying replications. Third, much more could be done on the dialogue with authors on why they chose to replicate (e.g., on when they do not replicate or on the barriers to replication). Fourth, the coding of replications presupposes much knowledge about the replications' research area. For most papers we lack that, perhaps over-emphasizing what authors have written.

CONCLUSION

We have studied replications in HCI through browsing papers from journals and publications. Three percent replications were identified and analyzed. We have suggested several implications of the analysis for HCI outlets that could increase replication rates.

ACKNOWLEDGMENTS

We are grateful to Malene Jacobsen and Mathias Andersen for help in coding. We also thank the many authors that answered our questions about their work carefully and patiently. Sebastian Boring and Antti Oulasvirta commented on the draft, which helped us immensely.

REFERENCES

1. Appert, C., Chapuis, O., and Pietriga, E. High-precision magnification lenses. In *Proc. CHI* (2010), 273–282.
2. Begley, C.G. and Ellis, L.M. Drug development: Raise standards for preclinical cancer research. *Nature 483*, 7391 (2012), 531–533.
3. Casiez, G. and Vogel, D. The effect of spring stiffness and control gain with an elastic rate control pointing device. In *Proc. CHI*, (2008), 1709–1718.
4. Chapuis, O., Labrune, J.-B., and Pietriga, E. DynaSpot: speed-dependent area cursor. In *Proc. CHI* (2009), 1391–1400.
5. Chen, N.Y., Guimbretière, F., and Löckenhoff, C.E. Relative role of merging and two-handed operation on command selection speed. *International Journal of Human-Computer Studies 66*, 10 (2008), 729–740.
6. D'Mello, S.K., Graesser, A., and King, B. Toward Spoken Human–Computer Tutorial Dialogues. *Human–Computer Interaction 25*, 4 (2010), 289–323.
7. Egan, D.E., Remde, J.R., Gomez, L.M., Landauer, T.K., Eberhardt, J., and Lochbaum, C.C. Formative design evaluation of superbook. *ACM Transactions on Information Systems (TOIS) 7*, 1 (1989), 30–57.
8. Evanschitzky, H., Baumgarth, C., Hubbard, R., and Armstrong, J.S. Replication research's disturbing trend. *Journal of Business Research 60*, 4 (2007), 411–415.
9. Findlater, L. and McGrenere, J. Impact of screen size on performance, awareness, and user satisfaction with adaptive graphical user interfaces. In *Proc. CHI* (2008), 1247–1256.
10. Forlines, C. and Balakrishnan, R. Evaluating tactile feedback and direct vs. indirect stylus input in pointing and crossing selection tasks. In *Proc. CHI,* (2008), 1563–1572.
11. Greenberg, S. and Buxton, B. Usability evaluation considered harmful (some of the time). In *Proc. CHI* (2008), 111–120.
12. Grimes, D., Tan, D.S., Hudson, S.E., Shenoy, P., and Rao, R.P. Feasibility and pragmatics of classifying working memory load with an electroencephalograph. In *Proc. CHI,* (2008), 835–844.
13. Hartmann, J., De Angeli, A., and Sutcliffe, A. Framing the user experience: information biases on website quality judgement. In *Proc. CHI* (2008), 855–864.
14. Heer, J. and Bostock, M. Crowdsourcing graphical perception: using mechanical turk to assess visualization design. In *Proc. CHI* (2010), 203–212.
15. Hendrick, C. Replications, strict replications, and conceptual replications: Are they important? *Journal of Social Behavior & Personality*, (1990).
16. Hoggan, E., Brewster, S.A., and Johnston, J. Investigating the effectiveness of tactile feedback for mobile touchscreens. In *Proc. CHI* (2008), 1573–1582.

17. Hornbæk, K. Some Whys and Hows of Experiments in Human–Computer Interaction. *Foundations and Trends in Human–Computer Interaction 5*, 4 (2013), 299–373.
18. Huizenga, J.R. *Cold fusion: The scientific fiasco of the century* (1992).
19. Hunter, J.E. and Schmidt, F.L. *Methods of meta-analysis*. Sage, 2004.
20. Ioannidis, J.P. Why most published research findings are false. *PLoS medicine 2*, 8 (2005), e124.
21. Jasny, B.R., Chin, G., Chong, L., and Vignieri, S. Again, and again, and again…. *Science 334*, 6060 (2011), 1225–1225.
22. John, B. Avoiding "It's JUST a Replication", *RepliCHI 2013 Workshop*.
23. Jones, K.S., Derby, P.L., and Schmidlin, E.A. An investigation of the prevalence of replication research in human factors. *Human Factors, 52*, 5 (2010), 586–595.
24. Kaplan, A. *The Conduct of Inquiry: methodology for behavioral science*. Chandler, San Francisco, CA, 1964.
25. Karlson, A.K. and Bederson, B.B. One-handed touchscreen input for legacy applications. In *Proc. CHI* (2008), 1399–1408.
26. Kelly, C.W., Chase, L.J., and Tucker, R.K. Replication in experimental communication research: An analysis. *Human Communication Research 5*, 4 (1979), 338–342.
27. Lallemand, C., Koenig, V., and Gronier, G. Replicating an International Survey on User Experience: Challenges, Successes and Limitations. *RepliCHI 2013 Workshop*.
28. Landis, J.R. and Koch, G.G. The measurement of observer agreement for categorical data. *Biometrics*, (1977), 159–174.
29. Lee, E.-J. Flattery may get computers somewhere, sometimes: The moderating role of output modality, computer gender, and user gender. *International Journal of Human-Computer Studies 66*, 11 (2008), 789–800.
30. Lee, E.-J. I like you, but I won't listen to you: Effects of rationality on affective and behavioral responses to computers that flatter. *International Journal of Human-Computer Studies 67*, 8 (2009), 628–638.
31. Makel, M.C., Plucker, J.A., and Hegarty, B. Replications in Psychology Research How Often Do They Really Occur? *Perspectives on Psychological Science 7*, 6 (2012), 537–542.
32. Marshall, C. and Rossman, G. B.. *Designing qualitative research,* Sage (1999).
33. Martin, B. and Isokoski, P. EdgeWrite with integrated corner sequence help. In *Proc. CHI* (2008), 583–592.
34. McGrath, J.E. Methodology matters: Doing research in the behavioral and social sciences, in *Human-computer interaction* (1995), Morgan Kaufmann, 152-169.
35. Moffatt, K. and McGrenere, J. Steadied-bubbles: combining techniques to address pen-based pointing errors for younger and older adults. In *Proc. CHI* (2010), 1125–1134.
36. Morris, D., Ringel Morris, M., and Venolia, G. SearchBar: a search-centric web history for task resumption and information re-finding. In *Proc. CHI* (2008), 1207–1216.
37. Moscovich, T. and Hughes, J.F. Indirect mappings of multi-touch input using one and two hands. In *Proc. CHI* (2008), 1275–1284.
38. Nacenta, M.A., Mandryk, R.L., and Gutwin, C. Targeting across displayless space. In *Proc. CHI* (2008), 777–786.
39. Neuliep, J.W. and Crandall, R. Everyone was wrong: There are lots of replications out there. *Journal of Social Behavior & Personality*, (1993).
40. Newman, W. A preliminary analysis of the products of HCI research, using pro forma abstracts. In *Proc. CHI* (1994), 278–284.
41. Olwal, A., Feiner, S., and Heyman, S. Rubbing and tapping for precise and rapid selection on touch-screen displays. In *Proc. CHI* (2008), 295–304.
42. Pietriga, E. and Appert, C. Sigma lenses: focus-context transitions combining space, time and translucence. In *Proc. CHI* (2008), 1343–1352.
43. Reaves, M.L., Sinha, S., Rabinowitz, J.D., Kruglyak, L., and Redfield, R.J. Absence of detectable arsenate in DNA from arsenate-grown GFAJ-1 cells. *Science 337*, 6093 (2012), 470–473.
44. Rosenthal, R. and Rosnow, R. *Essentials of behavioural research.* McGraw-Hill (1991).
45. Rosenthal, R. Replication in behavioral research. *Journal of Social Behavior & Personality*, 5, 1990, 1-30.
46. Sterling, T.D. Publication decisions and their possible effects on inferences drawn from tests of significance—or vice versa. *Journal of the American statistical association 54*, 285 (1959), 30–34.
47. Takayama, L. and Nass, C. Driver safety and information from afar: An experimental driving simulator study of wireless vs. in-car information services. *International Journal of Human-Computer Studies 66*, 3 (2008), 173–184.
48. Tsang, E.W. and Kwan, K.-M. Replication and theory development in organizational science. *Academy of Management Review 24*, 4 (1999), 759–780.
49. Tuddenham, P., Kirk, D., and Izadi, S. Graspables revisited. In *Proc. CHI* (2010), 2223–2232.
50. Vogel, D. and Baudisch, P. Shift: a technique for operating pen-based interfaces using touch. In *Proc. CHI* (2007), 657–666.
51. Wilson, M.L., Mackay, W., Chi, E., Bernstein, M., Russell, D., and Thimbleby, H. RepliCHI-CHI should be replicating and validating results more. In *Extended Abstracts of CHI* (2011), 463–466.
52. Yatani, K., Partridge, K., Bern, M., and Newman, M.W. Escape: a target selection technique using visually-cued gestures. In *Proc. CHI* (2008), 285–294.
53. Zhai, S., Conversy, S., Beaudouin-Lafon, M., and Guiard, Y. Human on-line response to target expansion. In *Proc. CHI* (2003), 177–184.

Binding the Material and the Discursive with a Relational Approach of Affordances

Huatong Sun
University of Washington
Tacoma
Tacoma, WA
huatongs@gmail.com

William F. Hart-Davidson
WIDE Research Center
Michigan State University
East Lansing, MI
hartdav2@msu.edu

ABSTRACT
As Norman's vision of affordances developed twenty-six years ago is unable to address complex challenges faced by today's designers, we outline a view of affordances as discursive relations in HCI design. This argument is framed in the discussion of a larger trend of work beyond the HCI field, the scholarship on relational affordances from the fields of communication and organization studies. Through comparison and interrogation, we maintain a relational approach of affordances that bind the material and the discursive will help us to address design issues such as discursive power, cultural values, performed identities, mediated agency, and articulated voices in this increasingly globalized world and design culturally sensitive technology for transformation and emancipation. With a few cases, this paper deciphers the hidden power relationship of interaction design and suggests ways of we should design for social affordances.

Author Keywords
HCI; affordance; culture; ideology; identity; discursive; materiality; HCI4D; critical design; cross-cultural design.

ACM Classification Keywords
H.5.2. Information interfaces and presentation: User Interfaces—Theory and methods

INTRODUCTION
Since the term "affordances" was introduced to the HCI community as "perceived and actual properties of the thing" by Norman [44, p.9] twenty-six years ago, the concept of affordances has been one of the most influential concepts in the field. Following this tradition, abundant HCI work uses affordances, program functions, and product features interchangeably. Indeed affordance also receives high interest and much attention beyond the field, and researchers from multiple disciplines are attracted by its "constraining and enabling" feature that arises from the materiality of a technology [28, 30, 34, 36, 49, 62]. For example, communication scholars and sociologists welcome a middle position between technological determinism and social constructivism this feature brings as they endeavor to decipher the complex interactions between communication technology and the society. Organization theorists are fascinated by its utility and potential to explore the mutual constitution of technology and organizations through the technology appropriation process of information systems. In those literatures, the concept of affordances is treated in a relational manner, different from Norman's approach. Most interpret an affordance as one or more emergent properties rather than as intrinsic features of a technology. In this view, affordances arise from the interactions between the actor and his/her surrounding contexts—it is an "interaction quality" [56, p.74].

In this paper we look at the values and benefits a relational approach to affordances bring to the HCI community and discuss how these fresh insights inform design practices at a time when HCI designs must deal with a broader range of cultural, social, aesthetic, and ethical dimensions due, in part, to globalization. We argue that Norman's vision of affordances developed 26 years ago is unable to adequately address the complex challenges faced by today's HCI designers. Leaving aside rapid technological advancement, today's HCI landscape is dramatically different, influenced by heightening user participation in an increasingly globalized world. Issues such as identity, agency, power, structure, politics, and social justice compete for designer's attention alongside traditional metrics (e.g., effectiveness and efficiency) in our design process, as shown in research areas such as postcolonial computing [31, 32, 39, 47], feminist HCI [6, 7], and critical design [5, 8], along with new development in areas such as cross-cultural design [48, 56], ICT4D and HCI 4D [27, 57], and value sensitive design [11, 21, 41]. All these changes ask us to look beyond the view of affordances as intrinsic properties of technology and to adopt a more robust view of affordances that would

CHI 2014, April 26 - May 01 2014, Toronto, ON, Canada

ACM 978-1-4503-2473-1/14/04©$15.00.

connect the material with the discursive for technology design.

Extending the work of Sun [53, 54, 55, 56]—one of the authors—on culture-sensitive design, we outline a view of affordances as discursive relations in HCI design to approach contested issues such as identity, agency, voice, and social justice in design situations where culture and political economy are foregrounded and where the feelings, attitudes, and emotions of individual users may be shadowed in structures of power, ideology, history, dominance, and epistemology. This argument is framed in the discussion of a larger trend of work beyond the HCI field, the scholarship on relational affordances from the fields of communication and organization studies. Through comparison and interrogation, we propose that a relational approach of affordances that bind the material and the discursive will help us to address design issues such as discursive power, cultural values, performed identities, mediated agency, and articulated voices in this increasingly globalized world and design culturally sensitive technology for transformation and emancipation. With a few cases, this paper deciphers the hidden power relationship of interaction design and suggests ways of how we should design for emergent affordances. It is also a response to the recent call for critical design methodology [5, 8].

Our goal here is to offer an initial articulation to start a cross-disciplinary conversation on culturally, socially, and ethically informed HCI design issues with the point of departure being the concept of affordances. Following the Vygotskian sociocultural approach, we see affordances as action possibilities in much the same way that Kaptelinin and Nardi [33] delineated in their mediated action perspective. In our case, we bring in key concepts from communication studies (i.e., a constitutive model of communication) and from organizational studies (i.e., materiality) to sketch a structured framework of affordances that begins to explore social abilities and constraints on both the macro level and micro level, particularly in cross-cultural design contexts. The exploration is intended to enrich the heated discussion on materiality in HCI [e.g., 30, 49, 62] by attending to the aspects of situatedness and structuration of affordances, issues important to culturally sensitive design, along with a view of materiality informed by organizational studies and sociology. This is an especially important step to draw our attention to critical, discursive design issues amidst an era of globalization. We hope this paper will sparkle more engaging conversation and inspire more work along these lines.

Ideology of the interface and the hidden power relationship of affordances

Technology has politics and is never value free [20, 43, 64]. As a matter of fact, the interface of a computing technology is the manifestation of its implicit politics and ideology. For example, Tayoma states that "(t)he fundamental GUI interface (files, pages, buttons) poses unique challenges in HCI4D" [57]. The Macintosh's desktop interface that is built on the discursive practices and cultural values of a white male office worker might not make sense to users outside of Western culture [50].

In our experiences of working with under-represented users, we witnessed those moments of frustration and discomfort users had with well-intentioned designs. A native American user was disappointed and even upset to see that the artifacts of an online museum were chronicled with a colonist view of history rather than their own. A blind user felt isolated by a feature particularly requested by a nonprofit organization serving people with disabilities: "Text-only websites put me in the back of the bus"—comparing the experience of getting another web version with the experience of Rosa Parks, an African-American civil rights activist who refused to sit in the back of the bus during the time of segregation. A cultural stakeholder in an online archival collection published by a University library expressed concern that access to the artifacts, sacred objects to members of the community from which they originate, would be limited by an information architecture designed for Western scholars rather than community members. Those moments lead us to a riveting question: How might design features that aim to improve efficiency and effectiveness end up hurting a user's feelings and morale, distancing him from his own community, isolating her from other users, and/or labeling him as "other"? In a search for answers to these questions, we came to realize that the current HCI language and terminology does not help to interpret these issues. We believe a view of affordances as dialogic, discursive relations can begin to help us to examine these types of design issues more closely and find ways to create alternatives to design process and workflow as well as novel solutions.

A RELATIONAL APPROACH OF AFFORDANCE

A relational approach of affordances is not entirely new. Sun [53] describes how affordances were defined in a relational way in Gibson's original definition: an affordance is "equally a fact of the environment and a fact of behavior. It is both physical and psychical, yet neither. An affordance points both ways, to the environment, and to the observer" [23, p. 129]. Affordances describe a three-way relationship between the environment, the organism, and an activity [4, 17]. Considering that Gibson's goal for advancing the concept of affordances was to counter the dualism of meaning vs. action in modern psychology, it makes sense that affordances are mapped as relationships "within a frame of being and acting" [17, p.118]. Clearly, in the beginning, affordances were considered as emerging from the context of material encounters between actors and objects.

Insights from the communication field: A constitutive model of communication

Gibson's relational treatment of affordances is attractive to communication scholars and sociologists as it brings a fresh angle to study the role of technology in our lives, one of the fundamental research questions in communication studies. Hutchby [28] plays a key role in making Gibson's work accessible to the fields of communication studies, sociology, cultural studies, and organization studies [9]. He defines affordances as "functional and relational aspects which frame, while not determining, the possibilities for agentic action in relation to an object. In this way, technologies can be understood as artefacts which may be both shaped by and shaping of the practice humans use in interaction with, around, and through them" (p. 444). His view of affordances is "grounded in a conception of the *constraining*, as well as *enabling*, materiality of the technology as worldly object" (ibid, emphasis added); here, materiality is not necessarily related to something physical.

Hutchby's introduction is as influential to social scientists as Norman's work has been for the HCI design community. In the communication field, the notion of affordances "offers a reconciliation between the two opposing poles" (ibid) for people who are tired of the debate between technological determinism and social constructivism. Here the "constraints and unique possibilities" affordances offer can help us "avoid the arbitrariness of the radical constructivist position" and "evade the equally unilateral epistemology associated with technological determinism" [29, p. 33]. The opportunities brought by the affordances also works with an increasingly popular model of communication at that time, a constitutive model of communication that believes communication creates meanings rather than simply transmits. For example, a designer who expects users to use a technology as designed follows a transmission model of communication unconsciously. In contrast, a designer who embraces a constitutive model of communication would expect users to creatively modify the technology and include those opportunities in the design for the generation of new meanings. As a result, affordances become popular among communication scholars who explore the complex relationship between technologies and society (e.g., [3, 25, 42, 63]).

Two patterns surface from this discussion: First, as communication scholars are most interested in the grand issues of agency "in the causal flow between technology and society" [3, p. 24], attention to specific technologies' affordances shifts to the plural form of communication technologies (rather than a particular technology) for a larger group of users generally. This also occasions a shift toward the broader sociocultural context. In contrast, HCI studies of technology affordances often occur on the micro level—the immediate context [42]. Second, a relational affordances view looks beyond program functions to inspect the *social* capabilities that certain communication technologies enable. Here the shift is toward an interest in social interactions surrounding (and giving rise to) affordances. Of course, these two patterns are consistent with the search for developing a synthetic perspective on the materiality of technology and its social uses. As a result, technology use narratives and case studies tend to illustrate various ways of connecting affordances with sociocultural issues such as agency, identity, and values on a macrosocial level with a constitutive model of communication [25, 63].

Maybe because of the tendency to inspect the grand issues of technology and society, the term "affordances" also tends to be invoked rather loosely by this group of scholars. Other than Hutchby [28, 29], affordances are often simplified and represented as "possibilities and constraints." In her data-grounded primer about digital media, Baym characterizes the affordances of digital media as "packages of potentials and constraints, for communication" [3, p. 17]. While this touches the essence, it remains rather vague for people unfamiliar with the concept, even after seeing her further explanation, "the social capabilities technological qualities enable" [3, p. 44]. Similarly, in an article that explores networked individualism [63], the key term "social affordance" that also appears in the title line is curtly summarized as "possibilities," lacking a sophisticated treatment we would see from some other work about social affordances we review below.

While the relational approach of affordances used in the communication field has its own weaknesses as described above, the application of a relational approach of affordances does bring something illuminating to HCI design. Particularly its discursive angle and strong orientation to social interactions of a technology and its favor for agency (both human agency and technological agency) [42] is something we search for in a more socially, aesthetically, and ethically-oriented HCI design. Within this context, it might be easier to understand why Norman's vision of affordances is critiqued as a narrow one. When technology is treated as a neutral and value-free vehicle to implement social change, its affordances may also be abstracted from its surrounding sociocultural contexts and placed in "a kind of no-man's land"[1].

It should be noted that framing affordances in the context of a "causal flow between technology and society" is especially likely to downplay the values of relational affordances. According to Slack and Wise [51], a causal approach is reductive, failing to account for "the contingent play of a wider variety of factors," or "a set of dynamic, changing, and interrelated connections or relations" (p.116).

Insights from the organization studies field: Materiality towards situatedness and structuring

While communication scholars and sociologists integrate technological agency and human agency through a relational approach of affordances to focus on social interactions on a macroscopic level, researchers from organization sciences and information systems pursue a similar approach to examine organizations on both a macroscopic and microscopic level, developing a sophisticated relationship between materiality and social interaction [19, 34, 35, 36, 38, 59]. Due to their object of inquiry (work practices and the systems that support them), their inspections of technological affordances are more closely aligned to HCI research in terms of scope and unit(s) of analysis.

Organizational theorists share a similar interest with communication scholars in studying the co-constitution processes of technology and sociocultural contexts. They approach organizational contexts as "structures" [24] but understand that the dual influence of technology and action are both in play [16, 45]. Affordances are advocated as "a promising approach to overcome the subject-object and agency-structure dichotomies that have stifled much of the research at the intersection of technology and organizations" in earlier frameworks such as structuration [24], practices, or emergent views [19, p. 237].

This goal is achieved though a sophisticated conceptualization of materiality. Influenced by "the material turn" in social science and built on Hutchby's early work [28] in which he characterizes materiality as "constraining and enabling," a group of information systems researchers regard materiality as the "capabilities that afford or constrain action," which is what makes digital artifacts *material* [34]. To build the argument, Leonardi illustrates that the connotation of materiality for digital artifacts includes any of the three dimensions: the physical matter, the practical instantiations of abstract ideas, and/or something that has significance for a current task. It is the last two dimensions that make digital artifacts (e.g., software) material even though they may lack physical substance. Therefore, "materiality is not a causal force of social outcomes but a fundamental human condition tied to the material anchorage of human agents and what is often perceived as the inexorable reality that everything that happens cannot but happen in a 'here and now' (the leitmotif of situatedness)" [36, p. 9]. Clearly, materiality cannot be reduced as technical features and conditions, but it is deeply embedded in an activity: "materiality is not a property of artifacts, but a product of the relationships between artifacts and the people who produce and consume them." Therefore materiality orients towards both situatedness and structuring forces.

Being relational from its nature, this treatment of materiality bends towards "the material conditions and material consequences" related to sociocultural considerations of design practices [62, p. 57]. It aligns with one aspect of "the material turn" that is being unfolded in the HCI field. In addition to this aspect, the material turn in the HCI also includes the attention to the material nature of computation and that to the material interactions driven by ubiquitous computing and tangible interactions [49].

In this context, affordances are regarded as "constituted in relationships between people and the materiality of the things with which they come in contact" [59, p.146]. Out of the constitutive relationship, materiality stays stable, "independent of people, but affordances do not" [34]. On the one hand, materiality as a constraint provokes similar technology use (and thus affordances) across organizations: an email client is used for email communication between users. On the other hand, materiality as a generative resource enables diverse and unique uses (and thus affordances) for individual users across different contexts: an email client functions as a personal calendar system. A rough metaphor would see the materiality of technology as a picture frame, and a variety of affordances cultivated by that technology as those pictures that could be fit in the frame. Clearly an affordance approach based on materiality introduces more room to handle structuring forces and cultural influences in organizations.

However, this approach still has a few rough spots, which surface when taking social interactions into account as organization researchers reflect [19]. First, we need a hierarchy model of affordances that could address multiple levels of IT design issues. What vocabulary could be used to pinpoint broad social interactions and more immediate use actions neatly? Second, for a relational affordance approach that aims to connect and reconcile a Cartesian perspective (e.g., the subject-object, structure-agency, and determinism vs. voluntarism) to be used in "a truly relational manner," it needs to encompass a variety of social influences in the structural context. One big problem in these types of organization studies is that individual users may disappear in the crowd. Most of the time users are reduced into faceless, one–dimensional human being, collapsed into a social role such as "patients" or "customers." Their feelings, values, identities, and even pains may go unnoticed in organizations. Indeed the concept of materiality itself tends to focus more on the situatedness rather than structuring forces, and so it is not common to see or hear the struggles of individual users experience within structures of discursive power.

AFFORDANCES AS DIALOGIC, DISCURSIVE RELATION FOR CULTURALLY SENSITIVE DESIGN

A relational approach to affordances is not a novelty in the HCI field, either. Informed by activity theory, a group of scholars [1, 4] advances a relational view of affordances. [4] asserts that "[a]ffordances are not properties of objects in isolation, but of objects related to subjects in (possible) activities" (p. 59). Following this line of inquiry, researchers explore how affordances arise from actions and serve as properties of interactions between people and technologies [33, 53, 54, 55, 56, 61].

This group of researchers cites two problems with the view expressed in Norman's early work: First, affordances are regarded as technology properties that derive from an artifact, and it is "a one-dimension relationship only centering on an artifact" [56, p. 73]. Second, this view tends to discount sociocultural influences during interactions as a consequence of the qualities of a network being placed only on one tool (or actor). Yet we should apply a historical perspective to understand the limitation of Norman's view. When Norman claims affordances as "the perceived and actual properties of the thing, primarily those fundamental properties that determine just how the thing could possibly be used" [44, p. 9], he strips away rich contextual influences by reducing complex relations to intrinsic properties of interactive technologies. However, he emphasizes the role of designers in the design process by treating affordances as designed features, and points out that one of the designer's goals is to make design cues clearer. Therefore this vision has advanced the field by linking affordances to interface design directly when the focus of the field was previously more on usability rather than on user experience.

The landscape has changed dramatically after two and half decades. HCI design approaches are more and more culturally, socially, aesthetically, and ethically informed. As a result, a reductive vision of affordances as intrinsic design features will not help us to address many crucial design issues in this increasingly globalized world where social media and social computing play a more important role. Particularly in contexts such as cross-cultural design and HCI4D when culturally-sensitive designs are involved, and when values, identities, power, and voices need to be addressed, we must have a relational approach to affordances that follows a constitutive model of communication for meaning creation (as applied by communication scholars) and that originates from the materiality towards both the situatedness and structuring to bind the subject-object and agency-structure dichotomies.

To address culturally sensitive design issues, Sun [56] defines affordances thus: "Affordances describe the action possibilities posed by an artifact in use and associate the artifact with practices. They emerge as the material and the discursive are fused together during technology use." Here affordances are characterized as relations that come from the fusion of the material and the discursive, not the material and the social—a dualism we commonly see in the literature of science and technology studies. Since the material is further elaborated in the previous section, we turn here to look at the discursive more closely. While discourse is social itself, it further emphasizes a tendency towards a) design concerns for discursive power, cultural values, performed identities, mediated agency, and articulated voices, and b) design situations which constitute "a layer of embedded cultural power relationships (or culturally negotiated positions of power and subordination) atop already pervasive power structures in society, organizations, and designer-user relationships" [39, p. 75]. As a *critical* design approach, an emphasis on the discursive resonates with heuristics for the proposal of critical design [5]. In addition, the discursive dimension is connected with the communicative nature of a technology. Its innovation suggests an active process of meaning construction according to the constitutive model of communication, which values the constructive subjectiveness of individual users arising from the intersection of the material and the discursive.

Affordances are a key component of the Culturally Localized User Experience (CLUE) approach [56], a design philosophy and methodology to create culturally sensitive design for local users. This framework places concrete use activities on center stage, a component that is often missing in current cross-cultural design literature and practice. In the CLUE framework, Sun regards local culture as the dynamic nexus of contextual interactions that manifests numerous articulations of practices and meanings to replace a taxonomic view of culture. The framework advocates a holistic, integrated vision that takes user experience as both situated action and constructed meaning. It proposes a dialogical, cyclical design process to integrate action and meaning in cross-cultural design in order to make a technology usable and meaningful to local users.

As a significant extension of the CLUE, the view of affordances as discursive relations suggests the three traits:

Affordance as dialogic relation

Relations surfacing from affordances are dialogic. As Sun describes, "dialogicality is a key feature here as affordance comes from the milieu of the artifact, user, and activity" [56, p. 74]. This dialogic character comes from the intellectual tradition of Bakhtin's work [2], rhetorical genre theory [40, 52], and a constitutive model of communication. As a dialogic relation, technological affordance unfolds and develops as a result of the interplay of habituated uses and sociocultural influences. For example, LINE, the mobile messaging application developed in Japan, began an interesting feature for mobile chat apps to show the status of a message and informs users whether a message is read or not. This creates pressures for users on the receiving end, but it seems to work well with Japanese users who value the courtesy of responding messages in a timely fashion.

Binding the material and the discursive

Regarding affordances as discursive relations binds materiality and discursive power, integrating action and meaning, and articulating "the contingent interplay of a wider variety of factors" to create sensible designs in local cultural contexts.

This view represents a three-way dialogic relationship between a technology, a user, and a user's concrete activity, situated in a specific context. Sun [56] claims affordances arise from a dual mediation process—mediation of action and mediation of meaning— as part of a "mediation property" (p. 225). This suggests that the process of binding the material and the discursive is to connect the situatedness and the constructiveness of technology use, and therefore to integrate action and meaning for creating designs that are at once sensitive to local discursive culture and conscious of power relationships of that structure, aiming for transformation and emancipation. In this regard, technical features cannot be neutral since affordances are inherently value-laden, particularly in the context of globalization where there exists much power and struggle. A goodwill design does not necessarily help or (emotionally) support the targeted users, as shown in the case of text-only web versions for blind users.

Instrumental affordance and social affordance

A structured model of affordance helps to address design issues at different levels of scope. Based on an activity theory model [4], a three-level affordance structure consists of operational affordance, instrumental affordance, and social affordance. Different levels of affordance interact and evolve through the process of technology enactment in the milieu of technology, user, and activity. Social affordances arise out of instrumental affordances through user's interactions in local contexts, and thus the same instrumental affordance might lead to different social affordances and support different social uses when affordances are realized in different contexts. Furthermore, different local cultures will nurture different social affordances. Here, "social" refers to social interactions on various levels including the individual, the community, and the society level and cultural level as related to the discursive aspect of human action. Issues of agency, identity, dominance, ideology, and power often are associated with social affordances but occasioned and encountered in concrete terms in instrumental affordances.

AFFORDANCES UNFOLDING IN A MURKY GROUND OF TIPPING POWER RELATIONSHIP

Technology affordances unfold in this praxis of use and develop as a result of the interplay of habituated uses and sociocultural influences, usually shadowed in certain power relationship. Originating from materiality, technology affordances do not come from the void. The traits of "enabling and constraining" imply certain positions, gestures, and power relationships that comes from the network, or as [36] describes: "a fundamental human condition tied to the material anchorage of human agents" and " the inexorable reality that everything that happens cannot but happen in a 'here and now'." And this is why we say technology has politics, and interfaces manifest hidden ideologies of which designers and users might not be fully aware.

Many goodwill designs seem to nurture good instrumental affordances, but they can miss the complexities of social affordances. In a service-learning project to develop a CMS-based website for a local nonprofit organization that serves people with disabilities, the client required students to develop a text-only web version to complement the current one as their website has been critiqued by vision-impaired users due to accessibility problems. However, our user research found that the text-only version often suffers from poor content maintenance and out-of-date information. As we interviewed vision-impaired users, one blind user announced firmly that he did not want to access a text-only website because he felt he was placed in the back of the bus. Instead he asked student designers why not aim for an accessible website and thus a more inclusive design for everyone from the beginning. In this case, a goodwill design that intends to make blind user's browsing experience easier ended up strengthening the digital divide that already existed and further marginalized the user group it was created to serve. This reminds us to be careful to attend to multiple levels of affordance.

Affordances also may come with unequal relations of power, and user agency in the network is a process of power distribution: some groups of users are privileged while some might be ignored, marginalized, or even oppressed. Lewis [37] points out the decline of the newspaper business and subsequent job losses of journalists and editors is a result of the tension between the ideology of the journalism profession and the ideology of arising digital platforms for news-making, and of the collide of "a one-way publishing mindset" and "a multi-way network." For the entire 20th century, the cultural logic of the journalism profession is journalists' control for information, i.e., "journalists, acting in their normative roles, ought to wield gatekeeping control over news content on behalf of society" (p. 845). In contrast, the emerging digital media platform promotes a logic of openness and participation that affords ordinary users opportunities to take part in news-making and distribution. However, those opportunities for parajournalists (or citizen journalists) take information control away from news professionals and may displace many of them out of the workforce, which makes professionals wonder how much control they would need to give up to encourage civic participation even though they embrace the ideal. This case clearly shows affordances are not designed features. Particularly, social affordances are not the same for every user, and sometimes one man's meat is another man's poison.

Facebook Japan case: Ideology, power, and capitalism

A view of affordances as discursive relations could inform design practices on both the micro level and macro level for wise intervention strategies. In this age of globalization when power is transferred from "the colonial state" to "more remote international corporations whose sole responsibility is to their shareholders" [14], the relationship between discursive power and local values are made even more intricate through technological affordances. The recent development of the Facebook Japan website tells a compelling story of how cross-cultural design practices are complicated by power and political economy.

As the U.S.-based Facebook has rapidly risen to be the world's largest social networking website with a billion users [12], many local SNS websites were kicked out of the game [15]. However, Facebook had a difficult battle to win the hearts of Japanese Internet users due to its distinctive feature that require users to use real names for profiles. This feature, which made Facebook a huge success in American culture where it originated, conflicts with Japanese Internet culture, where users like to use pseudonyms to interact with each other either for bonding with old friends or for bridging new connections with a different conceptualization of privacy. Over 75% of Japanese social media users chose to use pseudonyms around the time of 2009 [46], a feature supported by the top Japanese SNS website Mixi at that time. Consequently Facebook's penetration rate had been stagnant at 3% for a long time until fall 2011, long after a Japanese version was released in 2008 and after a Facebook office was opened in Tokyo in September 2010.

Facing such strong resistance from local users, the global IT giant Facebook determined to conquer this strategically important online market—Japan has been on the top three list of the largest markets globally for advertising, including mobile advertising [18]. Facebook pushed forward with bold localization initiatives while sticking to their real-name policy. As a result, the technological affordances of Facebook Japan site began to unfold and develop, incorporating habituated uses and sociocultural influences. It finally claimed victory over the local service Mixi in September 2012 after morphing into a professional networking site for Japanese users, similar to LinkedIn, as local users are more comfortable using their real names for professional networking. Facebook Japan peaked at 17.12 million users by the end of 2012, but that number has since dropped to 13.78 million by June 2013, a decline of 19.5% drop in less than half a year [58].

This case shows the tension between power and discourse behind cross-cultural design is never settled, and colonial relationships still persist [31]. They do not just affect users in developing countries but everywhere, including an affluent country with a well-developed, unique and independent Internet culture as Japan. An unfortunate design message that was promoted in the Facebook Japan case—that only one social networking modality can be honored in the global village—is perhaps more alarming and disturbing than similar cases occurring in other developing countries. The impression is one of digital colonialism: that a local social network service is doomed before this juggernaut no matter how hard local users fight. This message, inadvertent though it may be, also conflicts with the design goal of "pluralism" we would like to advocate in the third wave of HCI research [6, 10, 26].

The tipping of power relations can indeed be driven by the greed of capitalism and, at the same time, sheltered by the political economy of social media [22]. Facebook provides a free platform for its users to share their social network experiences with friends, and it makes profits through targeted advertising with the commodification of their data. van Dijck [60] expounds that the real-name policy is a tool for a platform owner like Facebook to access, control, and utilize user's data for business revenues in the era of big data. The business goal is packaged in an ideology that advocates a uniform and authentic online identity for integrity, because multiple identities or an inauthentic identity fails to meet advertiser's "truthful" requirements and would hurt "the clarity and coherence" of the data. In fact, the redesign of the Facebook Timeline feature is one that clearly aligns with business goals to improve the process of data gathering and data analysis. As a result, "(t)he linear, narrative structure dominating the visible user interface not only cajoles more information out of the user but also channels data input into a more uniform format" (p. 206).

A view of affordances as discursive relations could inform design practices on both the micro level and macro level for intervention. On the micro level, Facebook improves instrumental affordance with design features such as the Timeline to make user task of updating one's status easier. Therefore, they enhance the social affordance of presenting and staging one's identity online, but purposefully ignore the affordance of networking in anonymity. Why? From the macro level, while it is technically feasible to nurture for social affordances that resonate with local preference for certain mode of privacy, Facebook chose not to due to the discursive reality (the ideology of promoting an American social networking mode in postcolonial conditions) combined with the material reality (truthful data required by the quest for profit). As a result, we see a troubled design that excels in effectiveness and efficiency across the globe but fails to articulate the voices of certain local users.

Indeed, seeing the discursive power on the macro level will help designers come up with wise intervention strategies overall. In this case, an exploration solely on the micro level would lead to a naïve recommendation that a better design could be devised at the time when Facebook Japan would respect local cultural values fully, outlined in the early work by one of us [56, p. 251]. However, the findings from the macro level indicate that that might hardly happen considering the commercialistic nature of a transnational corporation. Therefore a set of design strategies and tactics that only address the micro level will not be successful here.

A critical understanding of how the material and the discursive are tied together in this case does not suggest that we have to submit to the pervasive ideology and power structure. Instead, as HCI designers, we are interested in how to bring this understanding to our design process in order to empower our users. Considering the enabling and constraining characteristics of materiality, as users are "cajoled" to present their truthful user data most of the time, they also learn how to better present and stage themselves for self-promotion. Platform owners like Facebook may need to respond to user's needs as users can choose not to stay as long as there is more than one SNS from which to choose. For example, users could choose to maintain multiple online identities across platforms. In our personal transnational experiences, we found it more efficient to maintain different identities by utilizing different SNS technologies.

CONCLUSION

One of the design challenges we face is how to best address issues such as discursive power, cultural values, performed identities, mediated agency, and articulated voices in this increasingly globalized world in order to design culturally sensitive technology for transformation and emancipation. While we have seen the increasing appreciation for the value and role of culture in HCI design, many times culture is treated in a taxonomic manner. And the influence of power relationships has only been emphasized recently through the proposal of postcolonial computing [31, 32, 39, 47]. This might explain why much of HCI4D work stays on the instrumental level, lacking a critical and reflexive perspective. The ambition of designing for the bottom of the economic pyramid cannot be truly achieved if we ignore power struggles in those contexts and only seek technologically sound solutions. Similarly, the same empathy is needed when we design for minority user groups locally. The instrumental affordance a designer plans for may not cultivate the social affordances that would empower users and transform lives for the better.

We present our preliminary explorations on affordances as discursive relations in this paper. Building on Sun's view of affordances as "a dialogic relation" to inform design across cultures [56], we further develop it into a view of discursive relations to particularly address critical design issues concerning identity, power, and discourse at this stage of the globalization process when power is transferred from old colonial states to transnational corporations [14]. The discursive view of affordances is primarily informed by a constitutive model of communication and a sophisticated treatment of materiality. The former brings insights to HCI design practices to examine the complex interactions between interactive technologies and the broader society surrounding issues such as agency, identities, and voices. The latter, as a reflection and an uptake of the material turn that is happening in the HCI field [e.g., 30, 49, 62] and beyond. Therefore we outline the three traits of affordances and conduct an exploration on a few cases. While most of the intellectual roots presented here are credited to the fields of communication, sociology, and organizational studies, we see they can also be traced to software studies and critical computing, and critical studies of media technologies prior to computing technology.

We hope this article will raise awareness of the struggles of identity, agency, power, ideology, and dominance in the design process through the lens of relational affordances among the HCI community. When we design a technological product, we are not just making users' lives easier with a more efficient or effective product, nor are we merely making them happier so that they would resonate with the lifestyle the product promotes. We must also be conscious of design consequence that the introduction of the particular product will influence. We may tip the balance of a power relationship and change the status quo as well.

As a result, we will not conclude this paper with detailed design implications, but instead we will end by pointing to a positive example of systems design that takes positive social change as its primary goal.

The Mukurtu project (mukurtu.org) is a community development initiative, started in Australia for the Warumungu Aboriginal community. It has produced a web-based content-management system and a set of ethical processes for tailoring guidelines for archiving and sharing information via the CMS. The aim of the project is to provide indigenous community groups with digital resources for cultural heritage preservation as well as providing the means to do this work in accordance with community values. The project leaders recognized, from the outset, that archival work is value-laden and that information systems often have built-in assumptions about access and representation that can threaten the core goals of cultural heritage preservation work. Where communities' ability to represent themselves—via descriptions and images of artifacts, places, and people—become threatened, so do core human values of individual and collective sovereignty.

Arguably the most innovative features of the Mukurtu CMS lie in an administrative layer (sitting on top of the popular Drupal CMS) that grants users the ability to establish customized cultural protocols for what can be seen, shared, and edited [13]. These protocols form the baseline logic for each archive/cultural heritage project developed in the tool. The result is a new workflow for the process of creating a web-based repository of digital objects that begins with setting access preferences rather than by propagating a default set of roles, permissions, and views. As the project leader Kimberly Christen reflects, those features challenge the idea that "information wants to be free," a deeply Western value that tends to grant access and write access privileges to the powerful in ways that can seriously endanger the rights of indigenous groups to represent themselves [13].

How can we not only change the world, but change the world *for the better*?

REFERENCES

1. Albrechtsen, H., Andersen, H. H. K., Bødker, S., & Pejtersen, A. M. (2001). *Affordances in Activity Theory and Cognitive Systems Engineering*: Riso National Laboratory, Roskilde.
2. Bakhtin, M., M. (1981). *The Dialogic Imagination Four Essays*. Austin: University of Texas Press.
3. Baym, N. (2010). Personal connections in the digital age. UK, Polity.
4. Baerentsen, K., & Trettvik, J. (2002). An Activity Theory Approach to Affordance. In *Proc. NordiCHI* '02, ACM, 51-60.
5. Bardzell, J., and Bardzell, S. (2013). What is "critical" about critical design? In *Proc. CHI* '13, ACM, 3297-3306.
6. Bardzell, S. (2010). Feminist HCI: Taking stock and outlining an agenda for design. In *Proc. CHI* '10, ACM, 1301-1310.
7. Bardzell, S. & Bardzell, J. (2011). Towards a feminist HCI methodology: social science, feminism, and HCI. In *Proc. CHI* '11, ACM, 675-684.
8. Bardzell, S., Bardzell, J., Forlizzi, J., Zimmerman, J., & Antanitis, J. (2012). Critical design and critical theory: the challenge of designing for provocation. In *Proc. DIS* '12, ACM, 288-297.
9. Bloomfield, B, Latham, Y, & Vurdubakis, (2010). Bodies, Technologies and Action Possibilities: When is an Affordance? Sociology 44(3). 415-433.
10. Bødker, S. (2006). When second wave HCI meets third wave challenges. Proc. of NordiCHI'06, ACM Press.
11. Borning, A. and Muller, M. (2012). Next Steps for Value Sensitive Design. In *Proc. CHI* '12, ACM, 1125-1134.
12. Chilana, P., Holsberry, C., Oliveira, F., Ko, A. (2012).Designing for a billion users: A case study of Facebook. In *Proc. CHI* '12, ACM, 419-431.
13. Christen, K. (2012). Does Information Really Want to be Free? Indigenous Knowledge Systems and the Question of Openness. International Journal of Communication, 6, 2870-2893.
14. Choudry, A., Majavu, M., & Wood, L. (May 2013). Struggles, strategies and analysis of anticolonial and postcolonial social movements. Interface, 5(1),1-10.
15. Cosenza, V. (December 2013). World map of social networks. http://vincos.it/world-map-of-social-networks/
16. DeSanctis, G., and Poole, M. S. (1994). "Capturing the Complexityin Advanced Technology Use: Adaptive Structuration Theory," Organization Science (5:2), pp. 121-147.
17. Dourish, P. (2001). *Where the action is*. Cambridge, MA: MIT Press.
18. eMarketer. (August 3, 2012). US to Top Japan as World's Biggest Mobile Ad Market. http://www.emarketer.com/newsroom/index.php/top-japan-worlds-biggest-mobile-ad-market/
19. Faraj, S. & Azad, B. The materiality of technology: An affordance perspective. In Leonardi, P., Nardi, B. & Kallinikos, J. (eds), Materiality and Organizing: Social Interaction in a Technological World (pp, 237-258). New York: Oxford University Press.
20. Friedman, B. (Ed.). (1997). *Human values and the design of computer technology*. New York: Cambridge UP.
21. Friedman, B., and Nathan, L.P. (2010). Multi-lifespan information system design: A research initiative for the HCI community. In *Proc. CHI* '10, ACM, 2243-2246.
22. Fuchs, C. (2012). The political economy of privacy on Facebook. Television & New Media 13 (2): 139-159.
23. Gibson, J. J. (1979). *The Ecological Approach to Visual Perception*. Boston: Houghton Mifflin.
24. Giddens, A. (1984). *The Constitution of Society*. Berkeley, CA: University of California Press.
25. Graves, L. (2007). The affordances of blogging: A case study in culture and technological effects. *Journal of Communication Inquiry 31,* 4, 331–346.
26. Harrison, S. Tatar, D. and Sengers, P. (2007). The three paradigms of HCI. Ext. Abstracts CHI 2007, ACM.
27. Ho, M., Smyth, T., Kam, M., & Dearden, A. (2009). "Human–computer interaction for development: The past, present, and future," Information Technologies & International Development, 5(4), URL: http://itidjournal.org/itid/article/view/420/188.
28. Hutchby, I. (2001a). "Technologies, Texts and Affordances," Sociology (35:2), pp. 441-456.
29. Hutchby, I. (2001b). *Conversation and technology: From the telephone to the Internet*. Cambridge, UK: Polity Press.
30. Jung H, & Stolterman E. (2012). Digital form and materiality: propositions for a new approach to interaction design research. In *Proc. NordiCHI* '12, ACM, 645- 654.
31. Irani, L. Dourish, P. (2009) Postcolonial interculturality. In Proc. IWIC 2009, ACM Press, 249-252.
32. Irani, L., Vertesi, J. Dourish, P., Philip, K., Grinter, R. (2010). Postcolonial Computing: A Lens on Design and Development. In *Proc. CHI '10*, ACM, 1311-1320.
33. Kaptelinin, V., and Nardi, B. (2012).Affordances in HCI: Toward a mediated perspective. In *Proc. of CHI'12*, ACM, 967-976.
34. Leonardi, P. M. (2010). Digital materiality? How artifacts without matter, matter. First Monday, 15(6). Retrieved from http://firstmonday.org

35. Leonardi, P. M. (2011). When flexible routines meet flexible technologies: Affordance, constraint, and the imbrication of human and material agencies. MIS Quarterly, 35, 147–167.

36. Leonardi, P., Nardi, B. & Kallinikos, J. (2013). Materiality and Organizing: Social Interaction in a Technological World. New York: Oxford UP.

37. Lewis, S. (2012). The tension between professional control and open participation. Information, Communication & Society; 15(6) 836-866.

38. Markus, ML, & Silver, MS. (2008). A Foundation for the Study of IT Effects: A New Look at DeSanctis and Poole's Concepts of Structural Features and Spirit. *Journal of the Association for Information Systems, 9*(10/11), 609-632.

39. Merritt, S. & Stolterman, E. (2012). Cultural hybridity and participatory design. PDC' 2012, 73-76.

40. Miller, C. R. (1984). Genre as Social Action. *Quarterly Journal of Speech, 70*(2), 151-167.

41. Nathan, L. P., & Friedman, B. (2010). Interacting with policy in a political world: Reflections from the Voices of the Rwanda Tribunal project. interactions, 17(5), 56-59.

42. Neff, G., Jordan, T., & McVeigh-Schultz, J. (2012). Affordances, Technical Agency, and the Politics of Technologies of Cultural Production. Journal of Broadcasting & Electronic Media 56(2), pp. 299–313,

43. Nissenbaum, H. (2005). Values in Technical Design. In *Encyclopedia of Science, Technology and Ethics*. New York: Macmillan.

44. Norman, D. A. (1988). *The Design of Everyday Things*. New York: Basic Books.

45. Orlikowski, W. J. (1992). The Duality of Technology: Rethinking the Concept of Technology in Organizations. *Organization Science, 3*(3), 398-427.

46. Orita, A., & Hada, H. (2009). Is that really you?: an approach to assure identity without revealing real-name online. In *Proc. of the 5th ACM workshop on Digital identity management,* ACM, 17-20.

47. Philip, K., Irani, L., Dourish, P. (2012). Postcolonial Computing: A Tactical Survey. Science, Technology, & Human Values, 7(3), 3-29.

48. Rau, P., Plocher, T., & Choong, Y. (2012). Cross-cultural design for IT products and services. Boca Raton, FL: CRC Press.

49. Robles, E., and Wiberg, M. (2010). Texturing the "Material Turn" in interaction design. In *Proc TEI'10,* ACM, 137-144.

50. Selfe, C. L., & Richard J. Selfe, J. (1994). The Politics of the Interface: Power and Its Exercise in Electronic Contact Zones. *College Composition and Communication, 45*(4), 480-504.

51. Slack, J. D., & Wise, J. M. (2005). Culture + Technology: A primer. New York: Peter Lang.

52. Spinuzzi, C. (2003). *Tracing Genres through Organizations: A Sociocultural Approach to Information Design*. Cambridge, MA: MIT Press.

53. Sun, H. (2004). *Expanding the scope of localization: A cultural usability perspective on mobile text messaging use in American and Chinese contexts.* Doctoral dissertation, Rensselaer Polytechnic Institute, Troy, NY. http://www.localisation.ie/resources/Awards/Theses/sun_diss.pdf.

54. Sun, H. (2006). The triumph of users: Achieving cultural usability goals with user localization. *Technical Communication Quarterly, 15*(4), 457-481.

55. Sun, H. (2009) Designing for a dialogic view of interpretation in cross-cultural IT design. In *Proc. HCI International 2009,* 4, Springer-Verlag, 108-116.

56. Sun, H. (2012). Cross-cultural technology design: Creating culture-sensitive technology for local users. New York: Oxford UP.

57. Tayoma, K. (2010). Human-Computer Interaction and Global Development. Foundations and Trends in Human-Computer Interaction, 4(1), 1-79.

58. Torres, I. (June 6, 2013). Japanese netizens seen moving away from Facebook. Available at http://japandailypress.com/japanese-netizens-seen-moving-away-from-facebook-0630137/

59. Treem, J.W. & Leonardi, P.M. (2012). Social Media Use in Organizations: Exploring the Affordances of Visibility, Editability, Persistence, and Association. Communication Yearbook, 36, 143-189.

60. van Dijck, J. (2013). 'You have one identity': performing the self on Facebook and LinkedIn. Media, culture, & society, 35(2), 199-215.

61. Vyas, D., Chisalita, C., & van de Veer, G. (2006). Affordance in interaction. In *Proc. of the 13th Eurpoean conference on Cognitive ergonomics,* ACM, 92-99.

62. Wiberg, M., Ishii, H., Dourish, P., Vallgårda, A., Kerridge, T., Sundström, P, Rosner, D., and Rolston, M. (2013). Materiality Matters. *Interactions 20*, 2, 54-57.

63. Wellman, B., Hasse, A., Boase, J., Chen, W., Hampton, K., Diaz, I., & Miyata, K. (2003). The Social Affordances of the Internet for Networked Individualism. Journal of Computer-Mediated Communication, 8, 3, 0-0.

64. Winner, L. (1980). Do Artifacts Have Politics? *Daedalus, 109*(1), 121-136.

The Turn to Practice in HCI: Towards a Research Agenda

Kari Kuutti
University of Oulu
Department of Information Processing Science
P.O Box 3000, 90014 Oulu
Finland
kari.kuutti@oulu.fi

Liam J. Bannon
TrentoRISE/ Aarhus University/ University of Limerick
liam.bannon@ul.ie

ABSTRACT

This paper argues that a new paradigm for HCI research, which we label the 'practice' perspective, has been emerging in recent years. This stands in contrast to the prevailing mainstream HCI paradigm, which we term the 'interaction' perspective. The 'practice turn', as it has been dubbed in the social sciences, provides a conceptual frame to organize a variety of issues emerging in more recent HCI research. While this approach has been present in certain strands of HCI research for some time, it has not been articulated fully to date. In this paper, we provide a short account of the main tenets of this perspective, and then show how it can illuminate some of the recent debates within HCI. Our argument is one which does not seek to replace extant HCI theories, but rather to provide an alternative, complementary theoretical lens which may illuminate the present confusion among both researchers and practitioners as to the direction of HCI. The paper articulates a set of issues which can help direct HCI research programs, as well as highlighting the potential contribution of the HCI field to this practice approach itself, in terms of a more nuanced understanding of emerging practices.

Author Keywords

Research; interaction; practice; theory; methodology

ACM Classification Keywords

H.5.2 [Information Interfaces and Presentation]: User Interfaces — Theory and methods;

General Terms

Design, Human factors, Theory.

INTRODUCTION

While HCI has always been an arena where different disciplines mix, and where a variety of theoretical approaches and research methods have been used, it would appear that more recently this eclecticism has become even more pronounced. Indeed, in a recent review of theory in HCI, Rogers states: "...there is no longer a coherent set of aims or goals, or accepted classification of contributing disciplines. It seems anything goes and anyone can join in" [32, p. xii]. We have always had debates in the community about the definition of the HCI field, and where exactly are its borders. Indeed, some have raised the question as to whether the term itself should be retired, as it seems so problematic and limiting in terms of the issues being addressed in HCI research today [1]. This might indicate that the HCI field is in crisis, but in this paper we rather argue that at least some of the apparent confusion in the field can be understood as tensions between competing, dare we say it, 'paradigms' of enquiry in HCI [18]. We are aware of the over-use or misuse of this term in much recent academic debate, but hope to show, in this paper, that the term may indeed be warranted. Our argument is not that one paradigm is necessarily superior to the other, but rather that each paradigm orients to a particular kind of research program, and admits different objects and activities into its mode of enquiry. We label these two distinct paradigms in HCI as the Interaction paradigm and the Practice paradigm.

Briefly, HCI studies within the Interaction paradigm have tended to focus on momentary and ahistorical HCI situations, that are not crucially connected to a particular time and space; the focus is on the snapshot of the interaction at the moment, usually focused on an individual, centered on the human-machine dyadic relationship itself. Methods have traditionally come from the psychological sciences, involving controlled short-term, lab-oriented studies with individuals engaged in pre-determined experimental tasks. The Practice paradigm, on the other hand, examines historical processes and performances, longer-term actions which persist over time, and which must be studied along the full length of their temporal trajectory; they are situated in time and space, and are dependent on many features of the surrounding material and cultural environment, which cannot be simply seen as a surrounding "context", but must be interwoven within the practice. This necessarily involves coordination with others (implicitly or explicitly). Research methods have often been qualitative, *in situ*, observational studies, extended over time, studying an overall activity, involving people,

CHI 2014, April 26 - May 01 2014, Toronto, ON, Canada
Copyright 2014 ACM 978-1-4503-2473-1/14/04...$15.00.
http://dx.doi.org/10.1145/2556288.2557111

artifacts, organizational routines and daily practices. The methods of enquiry adopted by the 2 paradigms thus differ, with one being more experimental, the other more developmental and phenomenological in orientation.

We posit that the Interaction paradigm has held sway for many years, indeed defining mainstream HCI. Our argument is that the current turbulence in the field is brought about by an increasing realization that this paradigm, while effective in handling certain problems and issues, is, like any perspective, blind to other issues. Further, these areas of blindness have become more pertinent in recent years as a result of changes in the nature of technology, and in the ways that technological infrastructures are being developed and appropriated into a variety of societal forms. Whilst the notion of interaction between human and machine has not gone away, the need to consider how the technology fits into our everyday practices has grown. As a result, there has been a relative loosening of the mainstream experimentalist hold on what counts as quality HCI research, allowing into the community a variety of alternative perspectives with their own conceptual frames, epistemologies, and methods. Our purpose is not to attempt a history of these changes in the field, but to argue that certain of these competing frames have some elements in common, and it is these elements we wish to explore in this paper, under the banner of the Practice paradigm. Note that this does not mean that the Interaction paradigm is somehow wrong, or must disappear. Rather, we state why there is a need to explicate a novel paradigm to handle the raft of new challenges posed by this emerging situation. We hope to provide a conceptual frame within which these emerging issues can be debated and explored. We believe that the practice and interaction perspectives are complementary in certain respects, framing the field in particular ways.

'Practice' as a potential research focus has been identified in the social sciences for some time, and there has been a decades-long process, 'a turn to practice', where practice has slowly gained a legitimate position as a fundamental unit of analysis [34, 26, 27]. We believe that themes are emerging in HCI that echo those seen as central in the practice discussion in the social sciences – without to date acknowledging this existing discussion. Our interpretation is that a new research focus is emerging within the HCI field, a focus that can be tentatively labeled as "computer-supported practice". The difference between the discussions in HCI and those in the social sciences is that while the practice turn in the social sciences has been an openly partisan, programmatic and reflective movement to create a new research focus, in HCI it has been and remains tacit, spontaneous, and unsystematic, without any articulated program or indeed a clear recognition of this practice orientation. The mere fact of naming this perspective and articulating some of its features in this paper may in itself be helpful for the HCI field. Given that practice-oriented research in the social sciences has reached a more mature stage, there is also the likelihood that investigating this social science field may help our understanding of current HCI.

As we will see, one can discern a practice orientation in certain studies within HCI at least since the 1980s, so it is not a complete novelty to the community. Thus far it has, however, been more of an undercurrent, existing on the fringes, rather than being mainstream. In the last few years this 'fringe' has become more mainstream, and has been challenging aspects of the Interaction paradigm. The Interaction paradigm is hardly going to disappear (for the good reason that it is still brimming with unresolved problems), so what we expect is that the two perspectives need to be understood as different ways of 'carving Nature at its joints", to use Plato's famous phrase.

For example, while discussion about the "context" of interaction has long been a part of the Interaction paradigm, the interaction between human and computer is always at the center, in a privileged position, while everything else is considered as a "context" to this primary interaction, that impacts on, but can be treated independently from the basic interaction. The Practice paradigm requires us to "decenter" this privileged position of interaction, as noted in [30], and to consider this human- machine interaction as only one factor among several that are interesting and important. The Interaction paradigm usually takes the situation it studies as static: except for the change brought by the novel technology itself, the general situational context is considered as given, and often immutable. The Practice paradigm, on the other hand, views the current situation as the momentary result of a historical evolution, which is constantly under the influence of a variety of forces; over a period of time it may, and probably will, change, and it is important to anticipate the potential for such evolution. The paradigms differ also with respect to the scope of the changes intended. For the Interaction paradigm, the scope of the intervention is viewed as changing human actions by means of novel technology. For the Practice paradigm, a whole practice is the unit of intervention; not only technology, but everything related and interwoven in the performance is under scrutiny and potentially changeable, depending on the goals of the intervention. Thus the changing technology is but one of the options.

Some implications of this shift away from a focus on interaction between person and artifact, and towards a more encompassing view of human activity and practices in a setting, can be found in recent work e.g. [16]. This broadening of the scope of intervention has implications for the 2 paradigms in terms of their stance towards the values and politics of their actors. The Interaction paradigm eschews any need for politics in its analysis, or for cultural specificity, focusing on the modalities of interaction in the here and now, isolated from other activities and from most features of the setting. The Practice paradigm necessarily includes aspects of values and thus the cultural and political, in the origins and development of the practice.

The structure of the paper is as follows: we first give a general outline of the practice approach, list the major schools of thought within it and identify the main issues identified within practice research. Then the paper analyzes two IT sub-disciplines – IS and CSCW – where practice theories have surfaced more explicitly than in HCI to date. The result is that this focus on practice differs across these areas: while the practice approach has gained some acceptance in mainstream IS and HCI, it has been much more prominent (even though not labeled explicitly) in CSCW – especially European CSCW, as well as in the participatory design (PD) sub-community of IS. We then proceed to show how this practice approach might help organize and frame certain HCI concerns. Practice as a research focus is quite different to interaction, and requires different approaches for its study, and different measures for evaluation. Practice research in the social sciences can serve as an example and reference point for how this might be done. A simple replication will not be sufficient however, as much of the social science practice research has tended to focus on organizational settings, and not to focus on the ways artifacts can also change practices. Because of their experience with these matters, we might expect CSCW and PD researchers to lead this practice turn. We note that the weaknesses of social science practice research to date allow for the possibility that HCI research might eventually contribute back to the general practice discussion, especially concerning the role of *artifacts* and the *emergence of new practices*.

THE 'PRACTICE TURN' IN THE SOCIAL SCIENCES

One of the most significant developments in the social sciences in recent years has been a re-orientation in how the object of research is conceived, often referred to as the 'turn to practice' [34, 26]. Reckwitz [31] provides one conceptual frame for orienting to different kinds of social science practice theories. He distinguishes between 'traditional' and 'cultural' theories. Traditional explanations are based on either individual needs (*homo economicus*) or on social norms (*homo sociologicus*). The critiques of the rational choice model underlying *homo economicus* are legion [24, 25]. Likewise, *homo sociologicus* has also come underfire, especially from the ethnomethodologists. For Reckwitz, cultural theories challenge the traditional two extremes as being too narrow and limiting, and maintain that human actions take place in a cultural context that allows humans to interpret the world and thus make their actions meaningful. All practice theories are cultural in this respect, but according to Reckwitz there is a second division between cultural theories, based on what is the base of the social, and thus not all cultural theories are practice-oriented.

Practice theories do not locate the origin of the social in the mind, discourse, or interaction, but in 'practices' - routines consisting of a number of interconnected and inseparable elements: physical and mental activities of human bodies, the material environment, artifacts and their use, contexts, human capabilities, affinities and motivation. Practices are wholes, whose existence is dependent on the temporal interconnection of all these elements, and cannot be reduced to, or explained by, any one single element. Practices are relatively stable performances, ways how things get done, continuously produced and reproduced. Practices are also the substrate for the shared understanding and perception of the world, for common language games and the formation of shared identities. For social scientists, practices are the minimal units of analysis where essential and interesting social issues all come together in a natural and authentic way and become accessible for study. From a practice perspective the world is a network of performances that are durable, because the ways of doing things are coded in minds, bodies, artifacts, objects and texts, and connected together so that the result of performing one activity serves as a resource for another.

The practice perspective creates a radical shift in perspective, as noted by an organizational researcher:

> "...A focus on practice challenges us to bridge different levels of analysis, and to do so in different ways. The orthodox language of social science, including organizational studies, carves up phenomena into three levels: from the very micro (what people say and do); to the meso (routines); to the macro (institutions). (...) 'practice studies' as a field forces us to reground our study of organizational activities in terms of phenomena that are actually done, as they become evident in the here-and-now. And this in turn requires us, arguably, to reconceptualize the idea of levels." [26, p. 1309].

There are a number of approaches to how practices are conceptualized and studied, commonly called practice theories – a family of different approaches connected together by a network of historical and conceptual similarities. The overview here follows Nicolini's recent account [27]. Note that the use of the term 'theory' by Nicolini and others in describing the variety of practice approaches can lead to some confusion, as these perspectives are not what many would term theories *per se*, but we use the term here for convenience, following Nicolini's usage.

What is meant by the concept of practice is a debated topic since the time of Aristotle, and tracing its provenance is a worthwhile endeavor. According to Nicolini the historical and philosophical roots of practice theories can be directly traced to the groundwork done by Marx, Heidegger and Wittgenstein, who each in their critiques of contemporary philosophy gave practices a pivotal role in the development of their own systems. Marx legitimized 'practice' both as an object of study and as an analytical category, and also connected it with both sociality and historicity. Heidegger's project was to renew philosophy by focusing on ontology and being, and he took embodied practical interaction with the environment, 'being-in-the-world', as the starting point. Wittgenstein studied meaning in language and found that shared practices are both the origins of, and are made possible by, language, and they serve as the measure for the correctness and usefulness of a language used. Both Heidegger and Wittgenstein, independent of the different origins of the projects, ended up seeing practices as the central foundation for their critical projects. The influences of Marx, Heidegger and Wittgenstein have in various ways and combinations led to a number of different lines of thought on notions of practice in the social sciences.

In an insightful forthcoming paper entitled "The Concept of Practice" [35], Kjeld Schmidt shows how the term moved centre-stage at the time of the Enlightenment, through an examination of the work of the French Academy of Sciences from the late 17th to the late 18th century, which undertook an exceptionally comprehensive and detailed study of the work practices and techniques of hundreds of trades. This was conducted because they had an understanding of the importance of the practical reasoning conducted by these people in their daily work, and wished to have it documented in great detail in order to explicate it. However, this body of knowledge, as Schmidt points out, was then forgotten with the rise of the Industrial Revolution in the late 18th century, as the focus switched to the machine. Indeed, Schmidt states: "..two centuries after the onslaught of the Industrial Revolution actual work practice remained managerially and academically uninteresting." [35, p. 6]

Nicolini has identified six main schools of practice theories: the 'praxeology' of Giddens and Bourdieu, practice as tradition and community, practice as activity, practice as accomplishment, practice as 'the house of social' – direct followers of Heidegger and Wittgenstein, and practice as discourse. Very briefly, a word or two on each of these:-

Praxeology: The 'praxeology' of both Giddens and Bourdieu holds that social life is a series of contingent and continuously evolving practices, and that institutions, power, and social norms can be understood through structures and connections between practices.

Practice as tradition and community: The work of Jean Lave and Etienne Wenger would be an example. Their theory of legitimate peripheral participation sees learning both related to, and a specific form of, a particular practice, - a social process whereby a novice obtains a legitimate role that grows along with their skills and capabilities, and which is characterized by participation, commitment, belonging and identity.

Practice as activity: The cultural historical "activity theory" approach, which emerged from the Soviet Union through the early work of Vygotsky and developed more fully by A. Leont'ev, is the practice approach that has most pushed the earlier ideas of Marx on practice. In this approach, the notion of human activities fuelled by motives is the fundamental unit of analysis. Nicolini sees this as one of the most radical approaches to practice, emphasizing many issues not discussed by other theories, and one having an interventionist program of changing practices 'from the inside'. Activity Theory has also developed one of the more detailed conceptual apparatuses for articulating practice.

Practice as accomplishment: Although it is not fully correct to call ethnomethodology a theory because of its opposition to the very notion of 'theory', Nicolini characterizes it as an approach that sees practice as an accomplishment. For ethnomethodology practices are locally produced by using a selection of certain 'ethno-methods' of interaction that make practices, and thus all social activity, possible. These ethno-methods are the central object of ethnomethodological studies.

Practice as the 'house of the social': Nicolini uses Theodore Schatzki as an example of those researchers developing further Heidegger's and Wittgenstein's thoughts. For Schatzki the meaningfulness of human actions has a central role. This is historically formed and different from abstract rationality. Practices form the natural horizons for meaningfulness.

Practice as discourse: Nicolini classifies both the conversation analysis tradition and Foucault's work as practice theories focusing on discourse. Conversation analysis tries to understand the social organization of linguistic conduct, and its origins are in ethnomethodology. Foucault's approach is different; he is interested in material and discursive practices that regulate social life.

Although these approaches differ in many ways, there are also a number of common features; Nicolini lists them as follows:-

1. A *process and performative view on social life*: structures and institutions are realized through practices; practices are local and timely and they have histories.

2. The *critical role of materiality* of human bodies and artifacts; there are no practices without them.

3. A *different role of agency and actor* than in traditional theories: 'homo practicus' is both the bearer of practices in his or her mind and body, and the one who produces the practices in action.

4. Seeing *knowledge as a capability to act* in practices in meaningful and productive way.

5. The *centrality of interests and* motivation in all human action and a corresponding focus on power, conflicts and politics.

Nicolini's account of practice theories is important, not in proposing any form of meta-theory, but because it shows that despite the diversity of practice theory perspectives (which he uses the bulk of his book to elaborate), they all –

perhaps surprisingly – share a number of ontological and epistemological commitments about practices as objects of study. Given that some of the practice theories listed among Nicolini's schools (Heideggerian phenomenology, ethnomethodology, Activity Theory) serve as the major foundations of current HCI research, this may lead one to question the commonly held perception that HCI theory is in a somewhat chaotic state, e.g. [32]. So, instead of fragmentation there is actually an underlying common ground. The underlying commonalities noted do not make the theories directly commensurable, but they surely open up the possibility for some dialogue, and for exploring the use of different theoretical frames in complementary ways, as Nicolini explicitly notes.

Seeing social life as consisting of practices that have to be studied as wholes is a radical ontological commitment, leading to a complication and restructuring of the whole research process. As characterized by Miettinen et al:

> "In sum, 'practice' has not only a theoretical agenda but a methods one, as well. Studying a living practice 'here and now' and relating it to the history of practice and to larger institutional contexts is an extraordinary challenge." [26, p. 1314].

The practice approach has opened up a potential for better explanations of phenomena than heretofore, and a possibility to alleviate many of the dichotomies that have been plaguing social sciences, such as *social vs. material*, *mind vs. body*, and *knowledge vs. action*.

Because practices are contingent, mediated and cannot be understood without reference to the particular place, time and concrete historical context where they occur, they can only be studied 'close-up'. This is in a sharp contrast with many social science approaches that take isolated features of human behavior and study them at a distance, through modeling and generalization.

Further, if one is interested in real-life practices, they must be studied where they occur, in their natural setting, as bringing them into the laboratory is impossible. There may be practices to be studied in the laboratory as well, but they are not the same ones as in everyday life. In studying practice, many other widely used data collection methods also have their problems:

> "... for studying practices, one needs to employ an internally coherent approach where ontological assumptions (the basic assumption about how the world is) and methodological choices (how to study things so that a particular ontology materializes) work together. For example, studying practices through surveys or interviews alone is unacceptable. These methods are, in fact, as unsuitable for studying work practices as they are unfaithful to the processual ontology that underpins the ethnography of the practice approach." [27, pp. 217-218].

After this very brief description of social science practice theories, let us turn to how such approaches have informed HCI and related fields.

THE INFLUENCE OF PRACTICE THEORIES IN IS, PD & CSCW

While explicit concern with practice theories is a relatively novel phenomenon in HCI, that is not to say that many of the issues have not surfaced in HCI and allied fields over the years. We briefly examine what has happened within the related fields of information systems (IS) – incorporating the field of Participatory Design (PD), and computer-supported cooperative work (CSCW), with respect to practice and practice theories, before turning to practice concerns in the HCI field itself.

Information systems

IS has a long connection with practice-oriented theorizing, and the first attempts to use Giddens' structuration theory in IS appeared in the early 1990s [23, 28]. This can be related to the shifting focus in the closely related organizational studies (OS) field, which according to Nicolini [27] in the 1990s moved from studying organizations as things towards studying them as discourses and processes, which generated a fertile ground for practice theories. Over the years practice-oriented research has penetrated most of the subfields in OS and become a well-established genre of research. Because of the significant overlap between IS and OS research communities and publication channels, research drawing from practice theories has also become rather popular within IS. The interest in materiality, embodiment and artifacts has, however, remained rather weak in IS research, as noted in a well-cited framework paper [29]. Indeed, we would critique much recent IS research for its over-elaborate articulation of theoretical frames and consequent neglect of the details of practical work activities and settings.

One of the sub-areas of IS has been, however, radically different in this respect. It is the Scandinavian Participatory Design (PD) tradition, which emerged at the end of the 1970s as an opposition movement against both the then dominant systems-theoretical, and alternative socio-technical, traditions in IS design [5]. Scandinavian PD was (and still is) very much practice-oriented: the starting point is the recognition of worker knowledge and skills enmeshed in their everyday work practices. Scandinavian PD has also emphasized agency, emancipation and empowerment. It has also brought forward a distinct new set of methods for studying practices. Small wonder that one of the most substantive theoretical accounts in Scandinavian PD – Pelle Ehn's 1988 book [11] – draws heavily from the three foundations of practice theories: Marx, Heidegger and Wittgenstein. Although PD has lost some of its emancipatory and empowering flavor since the pioneering days of the 1970's, being viewed by some as a mere technique for improving the quality of IT products, the PD community has maintained a core concern with workplace practices.

CSCW research

The practice approach has been embraced within the field of computer supported cooperative work (CSCW), and especially within the distinct European CSCW community (ECSCW). While the interests of the US CSCW community were more diverse (including social psychology-oriented 'groupwork'), the research agenda in Europe was strongly influenced in the early 90s' by sociologists from Lancaster, whose work practice studies had begun to intersect with work done by the systems engineering development group there [e.g., 3]. It so happened that the sociological approach adopted by the majority of the social scientists was ethnomethodological in character. Thus ethnomethodology had a strong role in defining the CSCW research agenda in Europe, and correspondingly it became practice-oriented and has remained so, while the US CSCW community has always been more heterogeneous in this respect.

Other sociologists have also been involved, e.g. the studies on cooperative work conducted by Schmidt and colleagues [36]. What Schmidt so elegantly argues is that practice is not mere 'doing', or simple execution of pre-defined rules, but crucially involves reasoning in the 'doing'. The work that people perform is not simply the following of pre-ordained rules, but necessarily involves the local interpretation of these rules in the light of the evolving situation. Thus, work is not the execution of pre-ordained rules, but neither is it completely *ad hoc*. There is a notion, shared among other workers, of what it means to perform the work competently. This is the 'practice' which is common to the workers. Or, as Schmidt puts it, " *the concept of 'practice' focuses on normatively governed contingent action* " [35, p. 9]. This conceptual approach has provided a solid basis on which to develop a research program for CSCW, where practice has been a central concern [36].

There has also been a long-standing interest among ECSCW researchers in the application of Soviet-inspired Activity Theory, another approach with a strong practice base [20]. Within the CSCW community the practice approach to IT design has had the possibility to grow and mature, and by the end of the 1990s, it had started to influence the mainstream HCI research field. A unique feature of European CSCW is the serious interest in, and theorizing about artifacts, in the form of both studies on coordination mechanisms [37] and mediation [8]. Not all aspects of the practice approach in CSCW are equally developed, however: interest in both agency and power has been rather muted. Thus CSCW and PD complement each other in this respect.

STEPS TOWARDS A PRACTICE ORIENTATION IN HCI

The practice orientation in HCI has a more complicated history. In the early days of HCI, the dominant paradigm in cognitive psychology, the human information-processing (HIP) approach, was the conceptual framework used. The focus was on the relationship between the human and the computer, via the interface, with the goal of engineering a better fit between the physical and mental state of the 'user' and the interface of the machine. While much useful work was done, and indeed, continues to be done within this framework, by the end of the 80's this 'first wave' of traditional theoretical frames began to be questioned as to their relevance to the design of user interfaces [2]. A scan of the book chapters in [9] provides an indication of the feeling of unease within the community as to its ongoing purpose and relevance. Laboratory studies as a method of acquiring knowledge about how interfaces were used, or for the design of new systems, were shown to have limited applicability [38, 21].

There began an opening out to new ideas and theoretical frames – activity theory, action theory, linguistic theories, the language–action perspective, phenomenology, etc. It was also at this time that HCI began to open up to PD ideas, albeit often in a 'watered-down" form. None of these approaches became mainstream during the 90's in HCI, although they all had adherents. For others, the lessons to be learned from the perceived failure of the HIP research program for HCI was to eschew "theory" altogether, and concentrate on more mundane practical matters of usability, seeking to develop measures and methods that would help in designing more usable systems – developing guidelines for "user-centred" design (UCD). The resulting research was practical and utility-oriented: designing interfaces that enable us to do something at all; designing interfaces that enable us to do something 'better' than previously; and devising methods that enable us to design and manage designing.

While some of the UCD approaches engaged with users in the design process, influenced by PD approaches, others did not. Most of the UCD approaches stayed away from 'theory'. The focus on practical observations, at times in actual work situations, did mean that UCD practitioners observed human work practices, but this rarely became a central feature of the work. Research was still centred on the Interaction, not the Practice, paradigm. The opening up of HCI to the field of design helped to move some aspects of the HCI research program out of the formal lab experimentation tradition into a more open, "design thinking" arena, allowing for design explorations into such topics as ambiguity and playfulness in design [13]. However, this design turn in HCI, worth further investigation in its own right, did relatively little to contribute to the understanding of ongoing work practices – other than those involving the designer's own creative activities, such as sketching, for example.

HCI as a field had become very eclectic, consisting of a mix of theoretical positions, personal reflections, and simple observational studies, combined with technology explorations. From the outside, this led to the view that the field was conceptually weak, or perhaps chaotic. But the seeds of the practice turn were present from quite an early stage. Certain practice-oriented elements appear from the outset of the '2nd wave' of HCI research in the 1980s [7]. Lucy Suchman's book *Plans and Situated Actions* in 1987 and the studies of the Work, Practice and Technology (WPT) group she led at Xerox PARC, and some practice theories like Activity Theory came along during the 1980s and 1990s [6, 19], but the focus in mainstream HCI remained at the level of interaction and usability of systems. During the 1990s interest in what surrounds interaction (i.e. the 'context' of the interaction) grew stronger, also affecting more practical UCD approaches - e.g., the Contextual Design method pays some level of attention to aspects of work practices [4]. The broadening of the areas of IT application outside the workplace, and the widespread use of mobile technology launched what has been termed the '3rd wave' of HCI at the turn of the millennium [7], bringing in even more practice elements, in particular the interest in embodiment and personal experience. In recent years we have entered another phase, where the scope of HCI applications has expanded rapidly and questions of agency, engagement, materiality and even social responsibility have become fashionable. It is interesting to note, however, that despite the parallel between the new 'paradigms', 'waves' or 'turns' in HCI and the 'practice turn' discussion in the social sciences, the connection between the two fields has hardly been recognized at all.

In this short paper we cannot provide a detailed review of this emergence of interest in practice, but we can point to a number of topics that have begun to be explored by HCI researchers, all of which we believe link to this turn to practice. Briefly, we note:-

Understanding the "context" of interaction: One of the central issues in HCI has been the notion of 'context' in interaction. For some time it has been supposed that context influences what happens in interaction and how it is experienced, resulting in attempts to define richer and richer contexts. But 'practice' can be interpreted as the ultimate context: *practices are where interactions take place in real life*. But there is also a gestalt shift involved: while formerly interaction is the foreground and context the background, with practices, interaction is no longer at the center, but is one aspect among many, serving its specific part in the performance. It can be studied and understood only through this whole performance, not separately.

An interest in "appropriation"[33, 39]: The recent interest in how people take ownership of artifacts and shape them to their own purposes and practices clearly relates to this practice turn, as it examines the ways in which designed "things" become assimilated into an ongoing set of routines.

The push towards research 'in the wild': With respect to research methods, the suggested program for in-the-wild studies carries a clear mark of a practice orientation:

> The shift towards conducting in-the-wild studies has largely come about from a growing interest in how pervasive technologies can be designed to enhance and become part of the everydayness of life. In-the-wild studies show how people come to understand and appropriate technologies in their own terms and for their own situated purposes. [32, p 73]

Interest in solving complex real-world problems: In recent years a cluster of research topics has emerged in HCI which is historically grounded, shaped around complex real world problem spaces, and conceived as a response to these problem. Kaptelinin and Nardi analyse this emergence in their book [17], and as examples they give topics such as sustainable HCI, interactive and collaborative technologies for development (ICTD), crisis informatics, comparative informatics, and collapse computing. These are often explicitly studied from a practice point of view, as in the TOCHI September 2013 special issue.

Materiality: Practice approaches see materiality of the world as one of the central resources for the realization of practices. Therefore the recent interest in both material aspects of interaction, and digital artifacts as a form of materiality is a very interesting parallel, e.g. [41, 14].

Embodiment: In recent years, HCI has finally engaged in a substantial way with the role of the body in human activities and performances. Much of this work has taken its inspiration from the phenomenological approach of Merleau-Ponty. The book by Dourish [10] helped turn many researchers in HCI towards aspects of this topic.

Performance: One of the central insights of the practice approach is their processual and performative nature. Again, there has been increasing interest in various forms of process and performance in HCI and design, e.g. [22, 40].

Digital ecologies: The extension of analysis from individual artifacts towards a family of artifacts is a step in broadening our viewpoint on the world about us e.g. [12, 15]. However, it needs to be extended to include the practices that surround these artifacts, the ways that humans appropriate and shape these artifacts, as the focus needs to be not on artifacts *per se* but on *artifacts-in-use*. The change and evolution of digital ecologies only becomes meaningful when linked to corresponding practices, as artifacts and practices co-evolve. Every practice has a particular set of artifacts that make it possible.

The explicit mention of practices in research: The September 2013 issue of TOCHI was devoted to "practice-lens" approaches to sustainable HCI. The Editorial for the issue discusses the decentering of the human-computer interaction element, the dynamics of practices and practices as the unit of intervention. [30].

While this list of emerging HCI topics may at first appear to be rather disparate and have little in common, we believe that, at a deeper level, there can be uncovered themes which resonate with a practice-based approach, as distinct from the earlier mainstream Interaction approach. A practice lens approach should help us to perceive these underlying relationships.

TOWARDS A PRACTICE-BASED RESEARCH AGENDA IN HCI

We have shown that an increasing number of practice-oriented research programs have emerged in HCI in recent years. We believe that it is time to seek a common conceptual foundation for these programs, through reflecting on some of their common origins and concerns. The practice frame we have articulated here allows us, through the notion of practice, to align a number of currently disparate research threads into a relatively coherent research program. The movement towards practice research has thus far however been rather unsystematic, partial, and tacit. We suggest that much can be gained by making it more systematic, comprehensive, and reflexively conscious. A characteristic of recent HCI research has been to take one isolated aspect of practice – be it embodiment or empowerment, for instance – and make it the focus. But studying isolated aspects of practices will not lead to the benefits that a holistic practice approach is capable of offering.

The different nature of the units of analysis leads to different research settings and methodological selections. There are various approaches to practice research, but in HCI there is a common unifying goal to understand practices that are changing, where the change is often due to the introduction of information technology. This gives a better common ground to seek common foundations and construct values and norms with respect to validity and quality of research. In any case, the recognition of commonalities can give a boost to the internal discussions and the search for more coherence within the field.

One central issue is the question concerning *emergent practices*. The goal of the proposed research program is to develop our capability to transform practices through technology. Practices cannot be fully preplanned; it is only possible to provide a set of arrangements and resources, put in the hands of participating humans, who then try to use whatever is available to accomplish their goals. The end result is eventually a transformed new practice that may be close to the initial vision or not. During the transformation new practices emerge, a process whereby the change happens. The ultimate goal of the research program is to understand the dynamics of this transformation and emergence: why and how it happens, and what are the ways to facilitate and support it. This is taking place in real situations and places, between real stakeholders, under real conditions of politics and power.

An essential ingredient in understanding these dynamics is to understand the role of computer artifacts in the emergence and transformation of practices; what are artifacts for practices, and what are our possibilities in influencing what happens through changing the artifacts? In this respect we have not progressed very far, but there are a number of promising openings – for instance with respect to materiality and the complexity of artifacts, and to mediation of practices by artifacts. The notion of practice gives us a possibility to connect and align these separate efforts.

Approaches privileging individualistic "user needs" or macro-level "organizational systems" are no longer sufficient, as we grapple with the complexities of digital ecologies and usage practices. The individual user cannot be the unit of analysis -- user needs are not a homogenous mass, but consist of sets of needs, differentiated and separated from each other depending on the practice. Practices are a shared resource among a community of people. Neither is the "organizational system" a monolithic structure; it is composed of a number of smaller systems, each serving the needs of a particular practice. And wherever these systems have connecting points and commonalities, it is important to maintain the relative independence of each of them. Practices and artifacts co-evolve, different practices are in different phases of maturity, they evolve at a different pace. If the connections and links between systems are made fixed and permanent, it may paralyze the evolution of those practices that are changing faster than others. How do we handle such issues in systems design, and what technical infrastructures are required?

There is the potential to open up a theoretical discussion between approaches as to what it means to do practice-oriented HCI research and further expand that into a general practice-oriented research program, giving order and direction to the whole HCI field. The participatory design and European CSCW communities, due to their experience and dedication to practice research issues, may serve an important role as catalysts for this development.

CONCLUDING REMARKS

The paper has posited that we are witnessing the emergence of a major new paradigm within the HCI field, concerned with the concept of computer-supported practices. The earlier interaction paradigm still has value for answering certain HCI questions, but from a practical point of view, in terms of our understanding of how ICT supported practices emerge and develop, the practice paradigm encompassing bodies, artifacts, performances, and routines provides a more encompassing frame, giving us a variety of conceptual resources to understand important issues of appropriation and assimilation of technology into everyday life. Developing a set of methodological tools and guidelines as to how they should be utilized is the next step.

This Practice program being advocated is clearly not without risks, although this has not been a major focus in this paper. Recently, researchers at Siegen, who have been influential in developing one version of a practice-based approach to HCI-related research, articulated some of these difficulties:

"Practice-orientation is a labor-intense, risky, and long-term research approach. To be able to conduct in depth field studies in real world settings and to roll out innovative IT artifacts, one needs to build trustful cooperation with practitioners and their management. A considerable part of the research efforts are dedicated to satisfy the practitioners' problems which are not always academically interesting. In addition, the technical artifacts, which we build and roll out, need to be technologically well performing, stable, and usable. Hence, an open challenge is to develop design approaches to observe appropriation phenomena in a timely and cost efficient way, not deformed by technical issues in a disturbing sense. Finally, practice-orientation is a risky research framework. Design case studies can break for a variety of different reason of which many are not under the control of the researcher". [42, p. 510].

We are aware that recent efforts in articulating this Practice paradigm, including ours, have only scratched the surface. More work is needed both analytically and empirically to elucidate this perspective, and to develop its research agenda. We look forward to being a part of this emerging research program.

ACKNOWLEDGMENTS

The authors thank Abi Sellen & Dave Randall for their advice, and all of our reviewers for their comments. Emil Aaltonen foundation has supported the research by KK for this paper. LB has been supported by TrentoRise, Trento; PIT Centre, Aarhus University; & Lero, University of Limerick.

REFERENCES

1. Bannon, L. J. Reimagining HCI: Toward a More Human-centered Perspective. *interactions* 18 (4) (July): 50–57. (2011).
2. Bannon, L., & S. Bødker, S. Beyond the interface: Encountering artifacts. In J. Carroll (Ed.), *Designing Interaction: Psychology at the Human Computer Interface* (pp. 227–253). New York: Cambridge University Press (1991).
3. Bentley, R., J. A. Hughes, D. Randall, T. Rodden, P. Sawyer, D. Shapiro, & Sommerville, I. "Ethnographically-Informed Systems Design for Air Traffic Control." In *Proc. of ACM CSCW'92, pp.* 123–129. (1992)
4. Beyer, H. and Holtzblatt, K. *Contextual design: Defining customer-centered systems*. Morgan Kaufmann, San Francisco. (1997)
5. Bjerknes, G., Ehn, P. & Kyng, M. ed. *Computers and Democracy - a Scandinavian Challenge*. Gower Publishing Ltd., Avebury, (1987).
6. Bødker, S. A human activity approach to user interfaces. *Human Computer Interaction* 4: 171–195. (1989)
7. Bødker, S. "When Second Wave HCI Meets Third Wave Challenges." In *Proc. of the 4th NordiCHI Conference*, 1–8. (2006).
8. Bødker, S. & Andersen, P. B. "Complex Mediation." *Human-Computer Interaction* 20 (4): 353–402. (2005).
9. Carroll, J. M. (Ed.). *Designing interaction: Psychology at the human-computer interface (Vol. 4)*. Cambridge Univ. Press, New York (1991).
10. Dourish, P. *Where the action is: the foundations of embodied interaction*. The MIT Press, Cambridge, Mass. (2004).
11. Ehn, P. *Work-Oriented Design of Computer Artifacts*. Arbetslivscentrum, Stockholm. (1988).
12. Forlizzi, J. The product ecology: Understanding social product use and supporting design culture. *International Journal of Design, 2*(1), 11-20. (2007).
13. Gaver, B., Dunne, T., & Pacenti, E. Design: cultural probes. *interactions*, *6*(1), 21-29. (1999).
14. Gross, S., Bardzell, J., & Bardzell, S. Structures, forms, and stuff: the materiality and medium of interaction. *Personal and Ubiquitous Computing*, 1-13. (2013).
15. Jung, H., Stolterman, E., Ryan, W., Thompson, T., & Siegel, M. Toward a framework for ecologies of artifacts: how are digital artifacts interconnected within a personal life?. In *Proc. of the 5th NordiCHI Conference* (pp. 201-210). ACM. (2008).
16. Kaptelinin, V. & Bannon, L. J. Interaction Design Beyond the Product: Creating Technology-Enhanced Activity Spaces. *Human--Computer Interaction*, vol 27, no. 3, pp. 277-309, (2012)
17. Kaptelinin, V., & Nardi, B. Activity theory in HCI: Fundamentals and Reflections. Synthesis Lectures Human-Centered Informatics, 5(1), 1-105. (2012).
18. Kuhn, T.S. *The Structure of Scientific Revolutions*. Chicago: University of Chicago Press, (1962).
19. Kuutti, K., Activity Theory as a potential framework for human-computer interaction research, in B. Nardi (Ed.) *Context and Consciousness: Activity Theory and Human Computer Interaction*, MIT Press: Cambridge. p. 17-44. (1996).

20. Kuutti, K. "The Concept of Activity as a Basic Unit of Analysis for CSCW Research." In *Proc. of the 2nd ECSCW Conference*, pp. 249-264. (1991).
21. Landauer, T.K. "Let's Get Real: A Position Paper on the Role of Cognitive Psychology in the Design of Humanly Useful and Usable Systems." In J. M. Carroll (Ed.) *Designing Interaction*, 60–73. Cambridge University Press, New York. (1991).
22. Light, A., & Wright, P. The panopticon and the performance arena: HCI reaches within. In *Human-Computer Interaction–INTERACT 2009* (pp. 201-204). Springer Berlin Heidelberg. (2009).
23. Lyytinen, K.J., and O.K. Ngwenyama. "What Does Computer Support for Cooperative Work Mean? A Structurational Analysis of Computer Supported Cooperative Work." *Accounting, Management and Information Technologie* 2 (1): 19–37. (1992).
24. Macy, M.W. & Flache, A. Beyond Rationality in Models of Choice. *Ann. Rev. Sociol.*, vol 21, pp. 73-91. (1995).
25. March, J. G. How Decisions Happen in Organizations. *Human-Computer Interaction*, Vol. 6, pp. 95-117. (1991)
26. Miettinen, R., Samra-Fredericks, D. & Yanow, D. "Re-Turn to Practice: An Introductory Essay." *Organization Studies* 30 (12): 1309–1327. 2009.
27. Nicolini, D. *Practice Theory, Work, & Organization. An Introduction.* Oxford University Press, Oxford, UK. (2013).
28. Orlikowski, W.J. "The Duality of Technology: Rethinking the Concept of Technology in Organizations." *Organization Science* 3 (3): 398–427. (1992).
29. Orlikowski, W.J., and S.V. Scott. "Sociomateriality: Challenging the Separation of Technology, Work and Organization." *Annals of the Academy of Management* 2 (1): 433–474. (2008).
30. Pierce, J., Strengers, Y., Sengers, P., and Bødker, S. Introduction to the special issue on practice-oriented approaches to sustainable HCI. *ACM Trans. Computer-Human Interaction* 20, 4, Article 20 (September 2013), 8 pages. (2013).
31. Reckwitz, A. "Toward a Theory of Social Practices: A Development in Culturalist Theorizing." *European Journal of Social Theory* 5 (2): 243–263. (2002).
32. Rogers, Y. *HCI Theory*. Morgan & Claypool Publishers, San Rafael, Ca. (2012).
33. Salovaara, A., Höök, K., Cheverst, K., Twidale, M., Chalmers, M., & Sas, C. Appropriation and creative use: linking user studies and design. In *Proc. of CHI 2011 Extended Abstracts* (pp. 37-40). ACM. (2011).
34. Schatzki, T. R., Knorr-Cetina, K. & Savigny, E. Von. *The Practice Turn in Contemporary Theory*. Routledge, London. (2001).
35. Schmidt, K. The concept of 'practice': What's the point? To be published in the *Proc. of 11th International Conference on the Design of Cooperative Systems (COOP 2014)*. (forthcoming 2014)
36. Schmidt, K. *Cooperative Work and Coordinative Practices. Contributions to the Conceptual Foundations of Computer-Supported Cooperative Work (CSCW).* Springer, London. (2011)
37. Schmidt, K. & Simone, C. "Coordination Mechanisms: Towards a Conceptual Foundation of CSCW Systems Design." *Computer Supported Cooperative Work* 5 (2/3): 155–200. (1996).
38. Thomas, J. C., & Kellogg, W. A. Minimizing ecological gaps in interface design. *Software, IEEE*, *6* (1), 78-86. (1989).
39. Stevens, G., Pipek, V., & Wulf, V. Appropriation infrastructure: mediating appropriation and production work. *Journal of Organizational and End User Computing (JOEUC)*, *22*(2), 58-81. (2010).
40. Vines, B. W., Wanderley, M. M., Krumhansl, C. L., Nuzzo, R. L., & Levitin, D. J. Performance gestures of musicians: What structural and emotional information do they convey?. In *Gesture-based communication in human-computer interaction* (pp. 468-478). Springer Berlin Heidelberg. (2004).
41. Wiberg, M., Ishii, H., Dourish, P., Vallgårda, A., Kerridge, T., Sundström, P., & Rolston, M. Materiality matters – experience materials. *interactions*, *20*(2), 54-57. (2013).
42. Wulf, V., M. Rohde, V. Pipek, and G. Stevens. "Engaging with Practices: Design Case Studies as a Research Framework in CSCW." In *Proceedigns of CSCW 2011,* ACM, pp. 505-512. (2011).

CHI 1994-2013: Mapping Two Decades of Intellectual Progress through Co-word Analysis

Yong Liu[1], Jorge Goncalves[1], Denzil Ferreira[1], Bei Xiao[2], Simo Hosio[1], Vassilis Kostakos[1]
[1]Department of Computer Science and Engineering, University of Oulu, Finland
[2]Abo Akademi University, Finland
[1]firstname.lastname@ee.oulu.fi, [2]xiaobei89@gmail.com

ABSTRACT
This study employs hierarchical cluster analysis, strategic diagrams and network analysis to map and visualize the intellectual landscape of the CHI conference on Human Computer Interaction through the use of co-word analysis. The study quantifies and describes the thematic evolution of the field based on a total of 3152 CHI articles and their associated 16035 keywords published between 1994 and 2013. The analysis is conducted for two time periods (1994-2003, 2004-2013) and a comparison between them highlights the underlying trends in our community. More significantly, this study identifies the evolution of major themes in the discipline, and highlights individual topics as popular, core, or backbone research topics within HCI.

Author Keywords
Co-word analysis; bibliometric study; conceptual evolution; HCI; cohesion; coherence

ACM Classification Keywords
K.2. History Of Computing: Theory.

INTRODUCTION
The CHI conference has a long and rich history. In the last 20 years alone its 3152 publications have shaped and defined the field of human-computer interaction, making CHI a flagship HCI venue characterized by its strong multidisciplinarity. In this paper, we are interested in mapping how the landscape of the HCI field has evolved, as reflected in the record of CHI publications.

Harrison et al. [16] characterized the field of HCI into three intertwined and non-exclusive paradigms: human-factors; classical cognitivism/information processing based; and phenomenologically-situated. This simplified categorization makes it challenging to understand the field's evolution as a whole. As the authors note, it is difficult to assess "marginal" contributions that are hard to precisely place. HCI is indisputably a multidisciplinary field requiring a more in-depth analysis to reveal the intricacies of its evolution.

To contribute towards understanding the big picture of HCI evolution, we analyzed CHI's publications keywords since 1994, and for our convenience, we divided them into two 10-year periods: 1994-2003 and 2004-2013. Between 1994-2003, CHI was predominantly focused on fixed (or non-mobile) HCI. Since 2004, however, the field has grown at a high pace, due to the introduction of extended abstracts and electronic proceedings. The popularity of mobile phones, ambient media and social technologies has shifted HCI research towards mobile and social interaction, while new issues involving humans, such as crowdsourcing and privacy have taken the spotlight. We attempt to study and analyze HCI research foci transitions and reflect on their drivers and present status.

CHI 2014, April 26–May 1, 2014, Toronto, Ontario, Canada.

ACM 978-1-4503-2473-1/14/04...$15.00.
http://dx.doi.org/10.1145/2556288.2556969

Our analysis relies on techniques from hierarchical cluster and graph theory, through the use of co-word analysis artifacts such as strategic diagrams and graphs. Co-word analysis is part of the co-occurrence analysis methods. It is a widely-applied bibliometric approach to describe the interactions among concepts, ideas, and problems and to explore the concept network within a scientific area [7,8]. A recently published paper of a *co-citation* analysis of the CHI proceedings [2] focused on authorship aspects of the proceedings and citation metrics for papers. Here we focus on the concepts that reflect our community and their evolution over time.

Co-word analysis rests on the assumption that a paper's keywords constitute an adequate description of its content as well as the links the paper established between problems: two keywords co-occurring within the same paper are an indication of a link between the topics to which they refer to [9]. The presence of many co-occurrences around the same word or pair of words points to a locus of strategic alliance within articles that may embody a research theme [9,30].

More importantly, by measuring the association strength of terms produced in a specific scientific discipline, co-word analysis allows researchers to identify key patterns and trends within the area [13,18,20]. It is assumed that a specific keyword with adequate frequency refers to a particular research topic while a cluster or pattern of keywords refers to a specific research direction or research theme. A change of research theme (*i.e.*, declining or emerging research interest) as well as the change of research topics within a research theme implies a paradigm change.

RELATED WORK
The main concepts we use in our analysis are *keywords*, *networks*, and *clusters*. *Keywords* appear on research papers, and two keywords appearing on the same paper are linked to form a *network* (or graph) of keywords. Analysis of this network helps us identify *clusters* (a set of closely-related keywords).

Our co-word analysis reduces a large space of descriptors (*i.e.*, keywords) into a network graph (*i.e.*, multiple related smaller spaces). Easier to comprehend but still retaining crucial information, this approach visualizes the interrelated concepts [11] and intellectual structure of a discipline into a map of the conceptual space of this field, and a time-series of such maps produces a trace of the changes in this conceptual space [13]. Co-word analysis has been widely utilized in mapping the conceptual networks of a diversity of disciplines, like business intelligence [29], consumer behavior [22], software engineering [11], patent analyses [10], biology [1,9], education [25], and library and information science [13,20,30]. As such, it makes sense to apply this technique to enrich our understanding of CHI.

Given a network of keywords, we can use network analysis and strategic diagrams to characterize the field. Keywords and clusters have different properties, depending on how they are linked with each other. For instance, bridges between two nodes (*i.e.*, linked nodes) in a network perform a valuable function in allowing communication and facilitating the flow between otherwise isolated regions of the network, also known as *structural holes* [24]. The greater the number of bridges associated with a research topic or theme, the more it serves to connect otherwise isolated research topics or themes. Keywords with a great number of structural holes serve as the *backbone* of the whole network. If these are removed from the network, the whole network will collapse into a number of separated and unconnected research sub-fields, therefore losing its scientific cohesion and identity.

When computing a network's *core-periphery* structure, it becomes possible to determine which nodes are part of a densely connected core (*i.e.*, with a higher number of bridges) and which are part of a sparsely connected periphery [5,26]. Core nodes are typically well connected to peripheral nodes. Peripheral nodes are sparingly connected to a core or to each other. In a keyword network it is expected that, as the body of knowledge grows, peripheral nodes become core nodes, thus allowing for the emergence of new peripheral nodes. Research topics with a high core value delimit the main body of HCI knowledge, and represent important knowledge-growing points of the main body of the field.

In our work we rely on two graph theory concepts to map the field of HCI: *density* and *centrality*, defined as follows:

- *Density*, or internal cohesion, measures the *strength of the links that tie together the cluster of keywords* making up the research theme. This can be understood as a measure of the theme's development [17,22]. Density offers a good representation of the cluster's capacity to maintain itself and to develop over the course of the time in the field [7,17]. The *higher* the density, the more *coherent* the cluster is and the more likely it is to contain inseparable expressions;

- *Centrality* measures the *degree of interaction of a theme with other parts* of the network [24]. In other words, it measures the strength of external ties of a research theme to other research themes, and can be referred to as a measure of the importance of a theme in the development of the entire research field [22]. The greater the number and the strength of a theme's connections with other themes, the more central this theme will be to the whole network [3].

By combining both concepts we then created *a strategic diagram*. Strategic diagrams are two-dimensional plots that have been widely used in prior co-word analysis studies [7,11,20,22]. The *x-axis* shows the *strength of interaction between a specific research theme with others* (*i.e.*, centrality). The *y-axis* reflects the density of the research theme, or the *internal cohesion of a specific research theme* (see **Figure 1**).

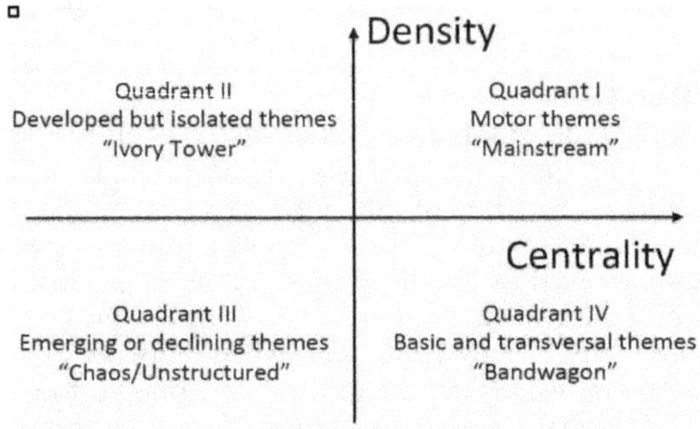

Figure 1. Strategic diagram's degree of density and centrality.

The location of a given research theme within this strategic diagram characterizes the theme in the context of the whole discipline:

Quadrant I (**Figure 1**, top-right): both internally coherent and central to the research network in question. Known as the motor-themes of the discipline given that they present strong centrality and high density;

Quadrant II (**Figure 1**, top-left): coherent but low centrality themes. These themes are internally well structured and indicate that a constituted social group is active in them. However, they have rather unimportant external ties resulting in specialized work that is rather peripheral to the work being carried out in the global research network;

Quadrant III (**Figure 1**, bottom-left): weakly developed with marginal interest in the global research network. These themes have low density and low centrality, mainly representing either emerging or disappearing themes;

Quadrant IV (**Figure 1**, bottom-right): weakly structured themes. These are strongly linked to specific research interests throughout the network but are only weakly linked together. In other words, prior works in these themes is under-developed yet transversal, with potential to be of considerable significance to the entire research network.

DATA

The ACM digital library provided us data on the papers published at the CHI conference between 1994 and 2013. According to Bradford's law [6], a fundamental theory in bibliometric analysis, a small core of publications will account for a sizeable portion of the significant literature in terms of citations received (*i.e.*, as high as 90%), while attempts to gather 100 percent of it will add articles to the core at an exponential rate [14]. Considering the relevance of the CHI conference to the field of HCI, an analysis on the CHI articles should enable us to attain a fair overview of the field's development: a total of 3152 CHI articles (full papers and notes) were published between 1994 and 2013, containing 16035 keywords (mean of 5.09 per article) (see **Figure 2**). For a small number of papers we had to manually extract the keywords from the electronic version of the manuscript (PDF) using a script.

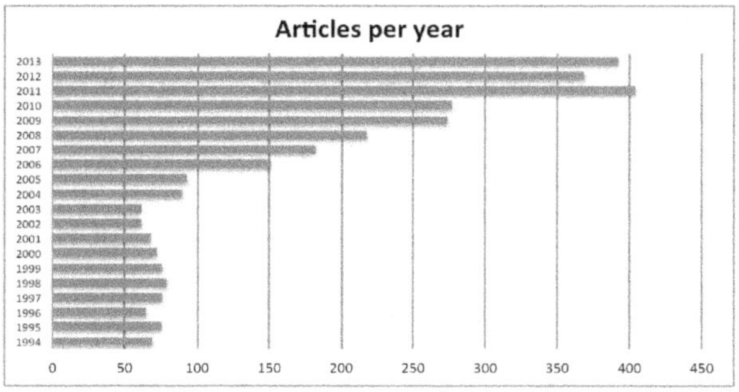

Figure 2. Number of publications per year at CHI.

The sample was split in two datasets of ten years each, to investigate the paradigm change in HCI over the past 20 years. The number of the papers published in 1994-2003 (N=702) is smaller than the number of the papers published in 2004-2013 (N=2450), suggesting that the research in HCI has grown considerably in the last ten years. We manually standardized the keywords through synonyms mergence (*e.g.*, "mobile devices" and "handheld devices" were merged; "ubicomp" and "ubiquitous computing" and so on) and *filtered broad* items (*e.g.*, "HCI" and "human computer interaction") [18,20,27,30]. The *synonyms mergence* considered the top 2029 keywords that appear at least twice in a dataset with regard to the merging of singular and plural forms of nouns, gerunds, nouns, abbreviations and acronyms.

The frequency of keywords follows a power-law distribution (see **Figure 3**) with an alpha of 3.46 (R^2=0.51), indicative that the research structure of HCI in the past 20 years is a *scale-free network*, a network where a small number of popular nodes (*i.e.,* keywords) act as hubs connecting other concepts. These hubs shape the overall network, which in this case reflects the intellectual structure of HCI represented by and through keywords. This scale-free characteristic suggests that a small number of popular keywords can capture major research directions and major influences in the field [20,30]. Therefore, in our analysis we retained only those keywords which appeared more than six times during 1994-2003, or more than 14 times during 2004-2013. Thus, 94 keywords were selected for the period of 1994-2003 (total frequency=1154), covering 556 (79.2%) of the 702 papers published during this period. Similarly, for the period of 2004-2013, 95 keywords were selected (total frequency=2692), covering 1602 of the 2450 papers published, *i.e.*, 65.3% of the publications. With fewer but popular keywords we could then reliably characterize the entire network of keywords.

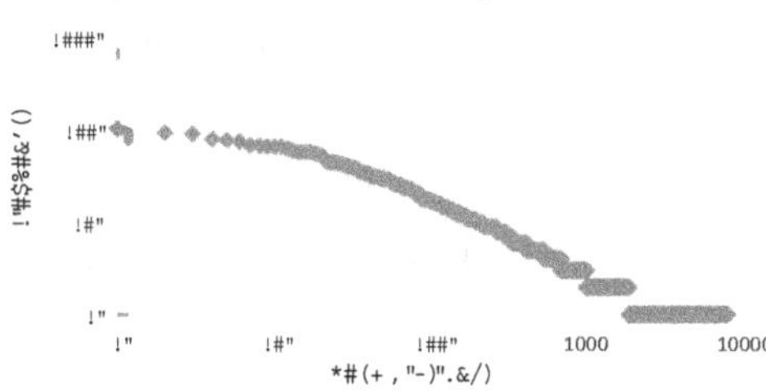

Figure 3. Power-law distribution of keyword frequency (in logarithmic scale). Power-law distributions resemble a straight line when on logarithmic scale.

RESULTS

Identifying the major research themes

First, we conducted hierarchical clustering using Ward's method with Squared Euclidean Distance as the distance measurement [28]. We adopted a supervised clustering method to reach as many clusters as possible while maintaining content validity and cluster fitness [18,20,30]. The 94 keywords for the 1994-2003 samples led to 14 clusters (labeled as A1-A14, in **Table 1**). Each cluster represents a research theme or subfield [20,30]. Similarly, the 95 keywords of 2004-2013 samples led to 14 clusters (labeled as B1-B14, in **Table 2**). The top-3 most frequent keywords are shown in bold, and are used to label each cluster [18,20,30]. In **Tables 1** and **2** we show for each theme:

- *Keywords*: the set of keywords that constitute this theme;
- *Size*: the number of keywords in the theme;
- *Frequency*: how often, on average, a keyword in this theme appears in our dataset;
- *Co-word frequency*: how often, on average, two keywords in this theme appear on the same paper;
- *Cohesion coefficient*: measures the extent to which when a keyword of this theme appears on a paper then another keyword of this theme also appears on a paper. Indicates the *similarity* or *dissimilarity* of keywords in a theme. Themes with *higher cohesion coefficient* are *more developed* or *bridging* research themes [20];
- *Centrality*: the degree of interaction of a theme with other parts of the network [24]. We calculate a localized version of this metric using the standard value 2 for the K-step reach. Thus, our centrality metric evaluates how the keyword connects all other keywords that can be reached through 2 connections;
- *Density*: measures the internal cohesion, or the strength, of the links that tie together the cluster of keywords making up the research theme [7,17]. To minimize the possible bias caused by the different sample sizes of the two periods, when calculating the overall network density, we rely on a binary version of the keyword co-occurrence matrix. This matrix only uses values 1 ("connected") or 0 ("not connected") to characterize every pair of keywords.

We constructed two strategic diagrams to visualize the cohesion and maturity of the research themes in HCI, using the centrality and density of each cluster as proposed by [7,11,18,20,22]. We plotted a strategic diagram for each period of analysis: 1994-2003 and 2004-2013 (**Figure 4a** and **Figure 4b**, respectively), based on Tables 1 and 2. The plots' origins are set to the average centrality and density across all the clusters for the designated sample, *i.e.*, (0.571, 2.305) for 1994-2003 and (0.635, 3.127) for 2004-2013. Comparing the intellectual structure of other fields (as shown in **Figure 5**), HCI lacks motor themes, and has lots of under-developed, but transversal research themes (see **Figure 4**).

We also calculated the overall network density for each network, to analyze whether the whole research field became more cohesive or not. The overall density of the HCI intellectual map has increased from 0.148 in 1994-

2003 to 0.206 in 2004-2013, meaning that the research field has become more cohesive over time.

Keyword network maps

For each of the two periods in our datasets we constructed a granular network of keywords using the following procedure. Each keyword is represented as a node in a graph, and we link together keywords that appear together on a paper. In **Figure 6 and 7** we show the result of this process for each of the two periods of analysis. We note that in these figures the size of a node is proportional to the frequency of the keyword, and the thickness of links is proportional to the co-occurrence correlation for that pair of keywords. Nodes of the same color belong to the same cluster, as presented next. To reduce visual clutter we only show a subset of the complete networks, omitting weaker ties and isolated nodes. A downside of this simplification is that, for example, "privacy" in Figure 6 appears to be disconnected from its own cluster. This is simply because weaker links are not included. Popular, core and backbone topics of HCI research

We next focused our analysis on individual keywords rather than underlying themes. A core-periphery analysis was conducted to determine the core research topics in the field from the perspective of the whole network structure. Twenty keywords (concentration=0.824) and 28 keywords (concentration=0.841) were identified to be the core research topics of the whole network in 1994-2003 and 2004-2013 respectively. Keywords or research topics were categorized as follows:

- *Popularity*: how frequently a research keyword is used;
- *Core*: [0-1] how connected is a research keyword with other topics;
- *Structural holes*: how connected is a research keyword with other otherwise distinct topics, thus supporting the topic structure (*i.e.*, the *backbone* of the field).

A higher core value indicates a topic that is well connected to other topics. A higher structural holes count suggests a keyword that brings together otherwise isolated topics. Topics with high scores on both of these metrics can be considered as the driving force for advancements in the field: without these topics, the field of HCI would be fragmented. We show these results in **Tables 3** and **4**.

ID	Keywords	Size	F	CW-F	Cohesion	Centr.	Density
A1	**computer supported cooperative work, interaction design, computer-mediated communication**, awareness, media spaces, audio, social interfaces	7	18.42	34.14	0.767	0.981	2.048
A2	**world wide web, empirical study, email**, Internet	4	15.25	27	0.662	0.532	2.500
A3	**ubiquitous computing, augmented reality, tangible user interface**, ethnography, mobile computing, PDA, learning, GOMS, education, mobile/handheld devices, groupware	11	13.90	21.90	0.437	0.888	0.909
A4	**visualization, user interface design, cognitive modeling**, evaluation, navigation, direct manipulation, agents, user modeling, animation, graphical user interfaces, design rationale, two-handed interaction, metaphor, prototypes, trust, haptic, mobile phone, pen computing, design, two-handed input, intelligent systems, speech recognition, intelligent interfaces	23	10.34	13.78	0.353	1.160	0.174
A5	**input devices, virtual reality, information visualization**, interaction techniques, 3D user interfaces, motor control, virtual environments, human performance	8	16.62	30.12	0.734	0.655	2.179
A6	**user interface, user studies, usability**, methodology, Empirical Evaluation	5	15	24.2	0.468	0.570	1.600
A7	**Fitts' law, information retrieval, hypertext**, browsing	4	18	33.25	0.624	0.465	4.000
A8	**children, educational applications, participatory design**, design techniques	4	13.25	25	0.795	0.287	3.833
A9	**multimedia, Interface design, collaboration**, video, mouse, gestures, field study, e-commerce, hypermedia, privacy, social computing	11	8.81	16.09	0.876	1.069	0.473
A10	**user-centered design, usability testing, usability engineering**, design process, videoconferencing	5	9.6	15.4	0.715	0.368	1.400
A11	**eye tracking, eye movements, multimodal interfaces**, gaze	4	8	14.25	0.855	0.376	2.000
A12	**annotation, digital libraries, documents**, dynamic query	4	7.5	10.5	0.617	0.276	1.167
A13	**programming by demonstration, end-user programming**	2	8.5	12	0.609	0.195	4.000
A14	**information foraging, information scent**	2	8	16.5	1.001	0.184	6.000

Table 1. Major research themes in HCI during 1994-2003 (size, frequency (F), co-word frequency (CW-F), cohesion, centrality (Centr.), density)

ID	Keywords	Size	F	CW-F	Cohesion	Centr.	Density
B1	***mobile phone***, **sustainability**, ***ethnography***, online communities, HCI4D/ICTD, health, persuasive technology, motivation, *user-centered design*, behavior change, community	11	30.09	30.27	0.358	0.899	1.036
B2	***ubiquitous computing, privacy***, **mobile**, *augmented reality*, wearable computing, *field study*, *mobile computing*, context-aware, *navigation*, *haptic*, large displays, human-robot interaction, music, computer vision, GPS, feedback, mobile interaction	17	26.94	28.58	0.416	1.064	0.654
B3	***visualization, collaboration, user interface***, wikis, *social computing*, tagging, *annotation*, personal information management	8	30.62	35.5	0.516	0.866	1.393
B4	***mobile/handheld devices, gestures, Fitts' Law***, touch screens, text entry, pointing, touch	7	36	43.71	0.470	0.631	3.619
B5	***computer-mediated communication, computer supported cooperative work, eye tracking***, communication, *empirical study*, *trust*, *videoconferencing*	7	30.71	36	0.496	0.722	2.048
B6	***user studies, interaction techniques***, **web search**, *input devices*, personalization	5	26.4	28.2	0.442	0.642	1.500
B7	***design***, **games**, ***usability***, user experience, older adults, accessibility, memory	7	30.14	32.14	0.368	0.790	1.476
B8	***children, tangible user interface***, **multi-touch**, *education*, tabletop, *learning*	6	34	44.16	0.551	0.748	3.333
B9	***evaluation, information visualization, interaction design***, *participatory design*, assistive technology, *Methodology*, design methods, creativity, *prototypes*, Security, *end-user programming*	11	25.63	27	0.419	0.842	0.855
B10	**social networks, SNS, social media**, twitter, Facebook	5	25.6	34	0.705	0.453	3.700
B11	**crowdsourcing, human computation**	2	23	25.5	0.533	0.268	7.000
B12	***awareness, video***, **families**, coordination	4	19	23.5	0.690	0.449	2.167
B13	**multitasking, attention, interruption**	3	25.33	31	0.656	0.293	9.000
B14	**emotion, affect**	2	18	24.5	0.792	0.236	6.000

Table 2. Major research themes in HCI during 2004-2013 (size, frequency (F), co-word frequency (CW-F), cohesion, centrality (Centr.), density)

#	Popular Topic (Frequency)	Core Topic (Coreness value)	Backbone Topic (Structural holes)
1	**CSCW** (50)	**CSCW** (0.375)	**CWCW** (42)
2	**world wide web** (35)	two-handed interaction (0.355)	**world wide web** (31)
3	**ubicomp** (28)	**ubicomp** (0.226)	**interaction design** (31)
4	**visualization** (27)	**world wide web** (0.222)	**user interface** (30)
5	input devices (27)	**CMC** (0.191)	**visualization** (29)
6	**user interface** (26)	**information retrieval** (0.186)	input devices (27)
7	**virtual reality** (26)	**infoviz** (0.171)	**interaction techniques** (27)
8	Fitts' law (24)	awareness (0.161)	**CMC** (26)
9	**infoviz** (23)	tangible user interface (0.160)	**ubicomp** (25)
10	**augmented reality** (22)	**virtual reality** (0.160)	**information retrieval** (24)
11	**interaction design** (22)	**user interface** (0.159)	**multimedia** (24)
12	**interaction techniques** (21)	**augmented reality** (0.149)	**infoviz** (23)
13	**information retrieval** (20)	**children** (0.148)	**children** (23)
14	tangible user interface (20)	user studies (0.146)	**virtual reality** (22)
15	**CMC**(20)	**multimedia** (0.145)	Fitts' law (22)
16	**children** (20)	**interaction techniques** (0.142)	Interface design (22)
17	**multimedia** (20)	**visualization** (0.142)	mobile computing (20)
18	user studies (18)	**interaction design** (0.137)	empirical study (20)
19	user interface design (18)	hypertext (0.133)	**augmented reality** (19)
20	cognitive modeling (18)	ethnography (0.113)	agents (19)

Table 3. Summary of popular, core and backbone topics of HCI in 1994-2003. In bold are keywords that appear in every column.

#	Popular Topic (Frequency)	Core Topic (Coreness value)	Backbone Topic (Structural holes)
1	**mobile phone** (67)	**handheld devices** (0.229)	**ubicomp** (44)
2	**ubicomp** (65)	**gestures** (0.229)	**collaboration** (43)
3	**visualization** (62)	**collaboration** (0.226)	evaluation (43)
4	**handheld devices** (60)	**mobile phone** (0.224)	**mobile phone** (41)
5	**CMC** (59)	**CMC** (0.211)	**children** (39)
6	**gestures** (59)	**ubicomp** (0.210)	**visualization** (38)
7	**user studies** (58)	**CSCW** (0.208)	**design** (38)
8	**collaboration** (57)	touch (0.207)	**gestures** (34)
9	**privacy** (54)	**children** (0.203)	**user studies** (34)
10	**CSCW** (52)	evaluation (0.195)	**CSCW** (34)
11	**design** (49)	**privacy** (0.161)	**CMC** (33)
12	**children** (48)	**user studies** (0.158)	**mobile** (32)
13	sustainability (45)	**design** (0.153)	**handheld devices** (31)
14	ethnography (45)	education (0.152)	**games** (29)
15	evaluation (43)	learning (0.149)	ethnography (28)
16	**infoviz** (43)	**games** (0.146)	**augmented reality** (28)
17	**mobile** (42)	**visualization** (0.146)	social computing (28)
18	**TUI** (38)	**TUI** (0.142)	**privacy** (27)
19	**games** (38)	touch screens (0.134)	**social networks** (26)
20	Fitts' Law (37)	**mobile** (0.134)	mobile computing (25)
21	online communities (36)	tabletop (0.123)	sustainability (24)
22	HCI4D/ICTD (35)	**augmented reality** (0.117)	**infoviz** (24)
23	interaction design (35)	communication (0.116)	education (24)
24	**augmented reality** (34)	**infoviz** (0.115)	learning (24)
25	participatory design (33)	**social networks** (0.113)	communication (24)
26	**social networks** (33)	awareness (0.112)	**TUI** (23)
27	usability (33)	SNS (0.109)	awareness (23)
28	crowdsourcing (32)	wikis (0.106)	participatory design (22)

Table 4. Summary of popular, core and backbone topics of HCI in 2004-2013. In bold are keywords that appear in every column.

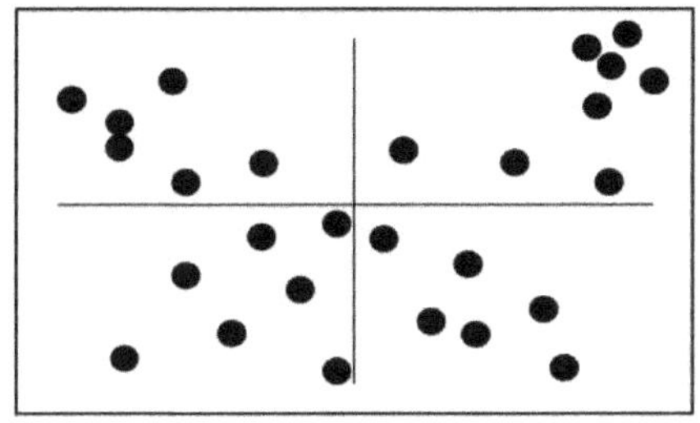

Psychology [21]

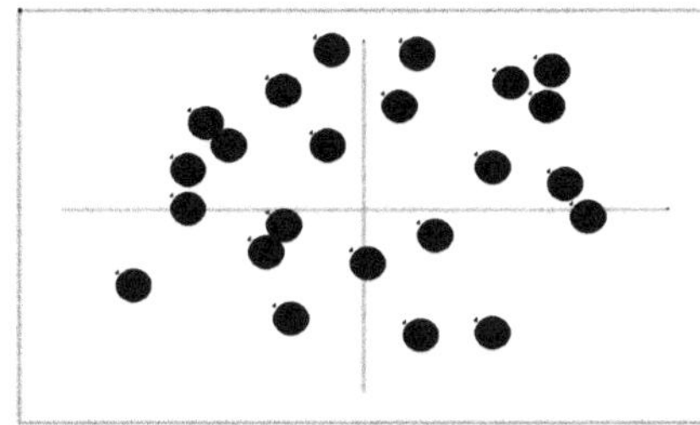

Consumer Behavior [22]

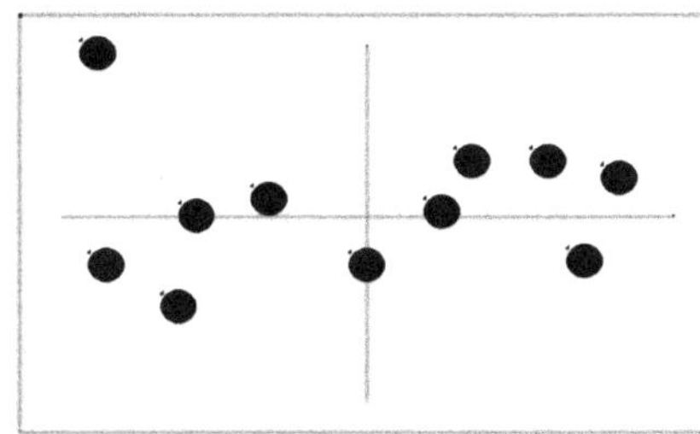

Software Engineering [11]

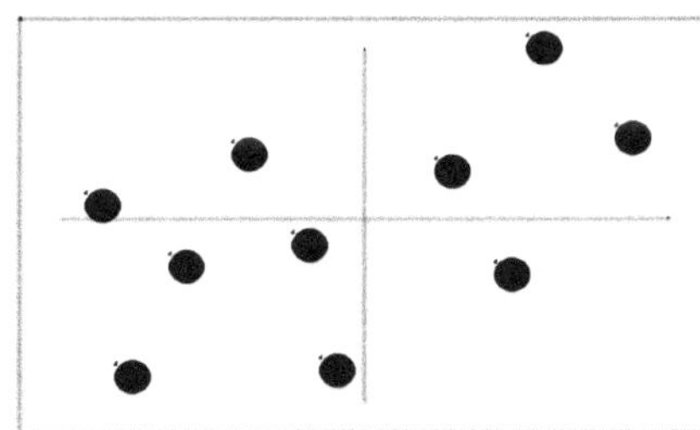

Stem Cell Research [1]

Figure 5. Indicative strategic diagrams from other scientific disciplines.

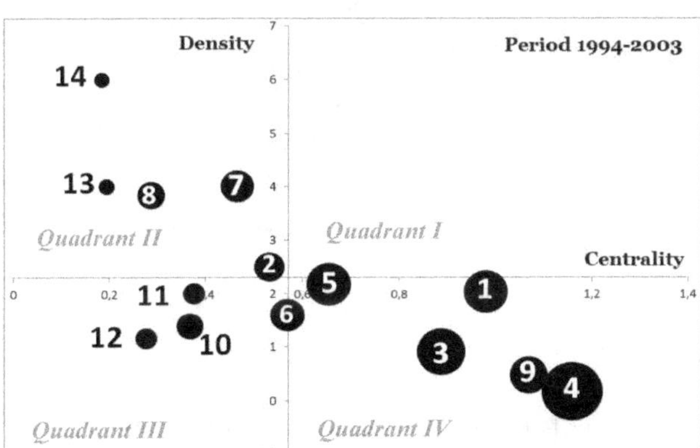

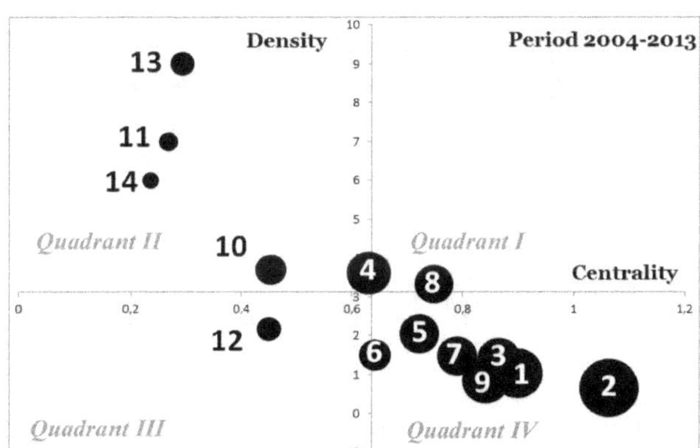

Figure 4. Strategic diagram for CHI for the period 1994-2003 (left), and 2004-2013 (right).

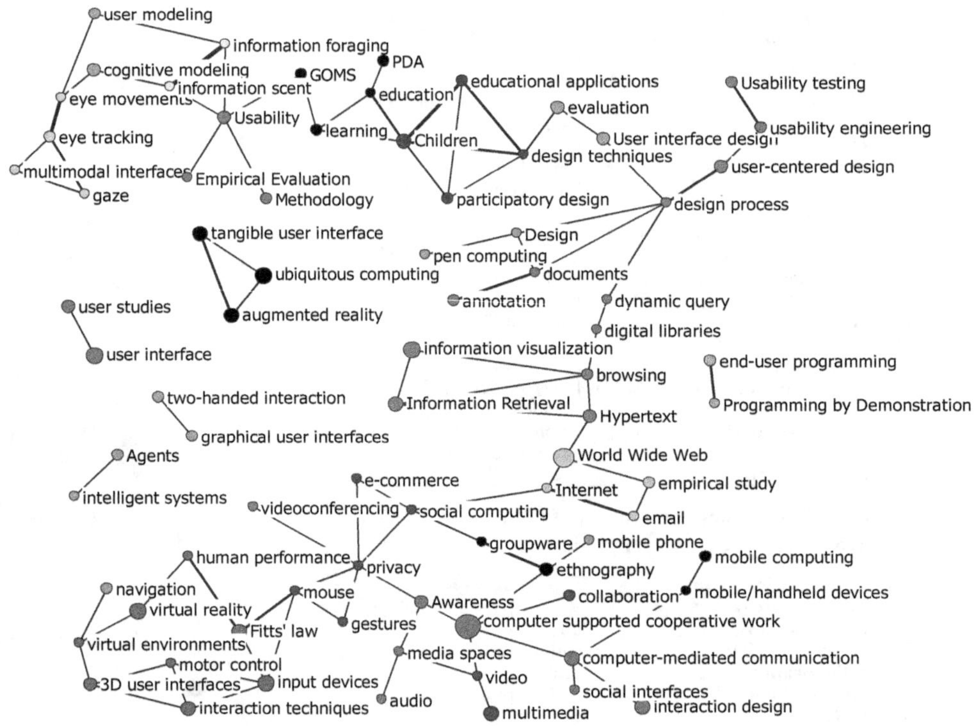

Figure 6. Keywords networking map 1994-2003 (the line represents the link between two keywords with correlation coefficient ≥ 0.14). An interactive version of this graph is available at http://goo.gl/BAjyMt.

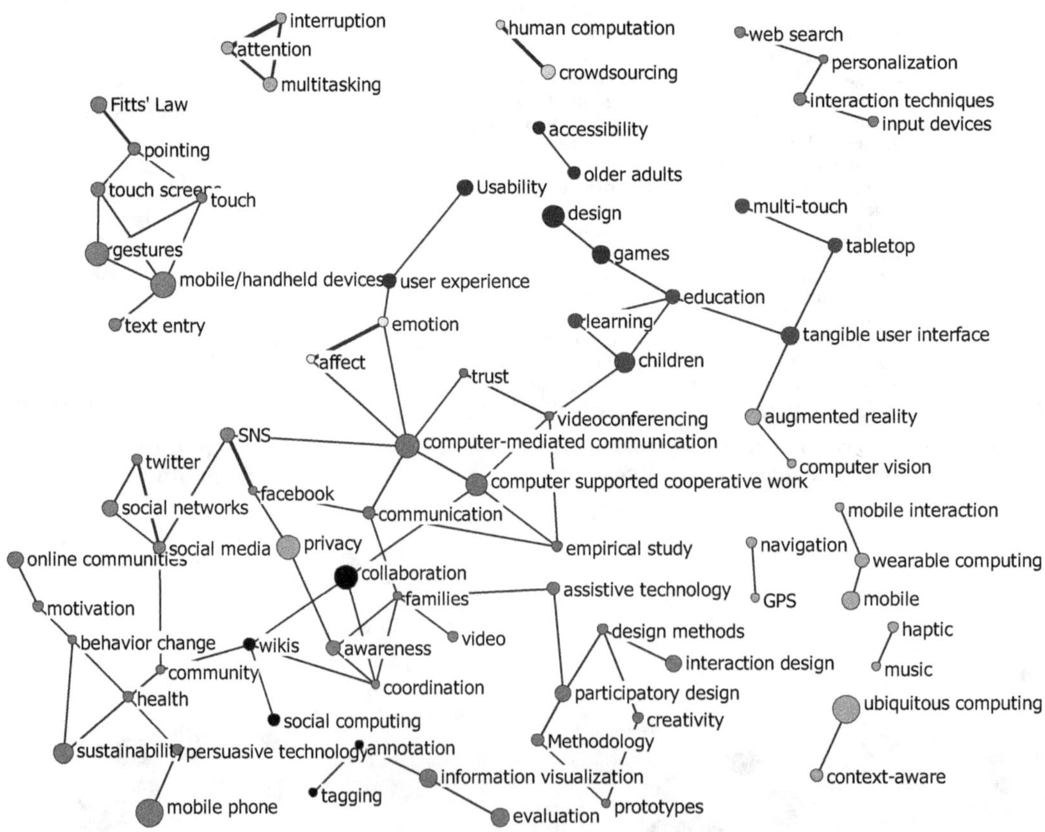

Figure 7. Keywords networking map 2004-2013 (the line represents the link between two keywords with correlation coefficient ≥ 0.09). An interactive version of this graph is available at http://goo.gl/v8j1Nh.

DISCUSSION

Underlying trends within HCI

While previous work [16] has outlined major paradigms within the field of HCI, our work provides a novel perspective towards seeing the big picture within our discipline. Our analysis has identified a number of research themes that are based on the co-presence of keywords on published papers – as opposed to a tacit interpretation of the field and its methods. Thus, our findings reflect the research that was *actually* conducted and published, not how a researcher would subjectively or intuitively map the field. Orthogonal to this analysis we add the dimension of time, and focus on analyzing our field in two distinct periods. This gives us the benefit of hindsight when interpreting our findings for the first period (1994-2003), since we are able to validate our claims for that period on the subsequent period of analysis.

1994-2003

In **Figure 4a**, quadrant II, we observe clusters A2 (www), A7 (hypertext), A8 (children), A13 (end-user programming) and A14 (information foraging) have a high density but low centrality. This indicates that these research topics are fairly isolated from other research topics but internally well connected. In particular, research in clusters A13 and A14 is less popular, and in hindsight we observe that in period 2004-2013 these clusters have disappeared.

In quadrant III, clusters A6, A10, A11 and A12 exhibit low centrality and density. These are indicative of research topics that are either emerging or fading, with a higher likelihood of change. In hindsight we can identify that one of these clusters was actually fading (A12: digital libraries), while the other three emerging (A6: methodology, A10: user-centered design, A11: eye tracking).

In quadrant IV, clusters A1 (CSCW), A3 (ubicomp), A4 (visualization), A5 (UI design) and A9 (multimedia) have high centrality but low density, sign of an important yet immature research topic in the field. Their importance is evidenced by the frequency in which the keywords appear, often leading to more concrete research subfields. In hindsight, new conferences were spun-off from these clusters: Ubicomp in 2001 and Pervasive in 2003 (from A3), and IUI in 1997 (from A5).

Surprisingly, we found no research topics in quadrant I, *i.e.*, with a high centrality and density. Closest to quadrant I we found cluster A5 (input devices, virtual reality, information visualization), with a high centrality, reflective of an important area for CHI as a conference and HCI as a field in the early days of computer-human interaction.

2004-2013

In **Figure 4b**, in quadrant I we find B8 (children, tangible user interfaces, and multi-touch), the maturing theme relating to children and learning through the use of tangible and tabletop technologies. Our analysis suggests that these themes are likely to become motor themes in the future.

In contrast, located in quadrant II are clusters B4, B10, B11, B13 and B14, clusters with high density but low centrality, well-focused and developed research topics, yet fairly isolated from other research topics. Some of these themes focus on relatively recent technology and trends (*e.g.*, B11: crowdsourcing, B10: social networks, B14: emotion & affect) that have not had time to establish strong ties to other research themes. Yet some of these themes represent more traditional work that has remained relatively isolated (B4: text entry & Fitt's law, B13: multitasking).

In quadrant III we expect clusters that are emerging or fading. Here we find theme B12 (awareness, video), which is most likely a fading theme judging by its relatively small frequency.

Finally, themes in quadrant IV are likely to be core and transversal for HCI. Here we find multiple clusters (B1, B2, B3, B5, B6, B7, and B9) of high frequency. Given that these large clusters have low density, they are evidence of field expansion during this time period. We note that in the period 1994-2003 new conferences emerged from themes in this quadrant that went on to become mainstream, and so we may expect the same from these themes here.

Trending topics

Next, our analysis focused on specific topics or keywords. A limitation of our previous analysis was that some of the research themes contained multiple and diverse keywords, making it hard to precisely characterize each theme. Here we overcome this challenge by conducting a core-periphery analysis of individual keywords to more precisely map their role and evolution over time.

1994-2003

For the period 1994-2003, 14 of the 20 keywords appear as popular, core and backbone topics *simultaneously* (**Table 3**, in **bold**). This indicates a consistency between research interests, knowledge acquired, as well as effort to maintain the field. In contrast, the research topics of "*tangible user interface*" and "*user studies*" are popular and core topics, but have a relatively low number of structural holes. This indicates that whilst these research topics have the potential to prosper the field, they are not the '*backbone'* during the period.

As yet another example, research topics of "*input devices*" and "*Fitts' law*" are popular and backbone topics, but are not core topics, indicating that research on these topics has not yet effectively extended the knowledge landscape of the field. Interestingly, research topics of "*mobile computing*," "*empirical study*" and "*agents*" were not popular or core research topics, but they played an important role in bridging different research efforts to establish an internally cohesive research field of HCI (*i.e.*, higher structural holes count).

Lastly, despite the research on "*two-handed interaction*," "*awareness*," "*hypertext*" and "*ethnography*" effectively extending the HCI knowledge scope (*i.e.*, high core and structural holes count), a limited attention was given to these research topics (*i.e.*, low popularity).

2004-2013

Compared to the period of 1994-2003, we identified a higher number of keywords (N=28) as core research topics for the period of 2004-2013, indicating growth of the knowledge field of HCI (**Table 4**). Of the top 28 keywords, 18 keywords were simultaneously popular, core and backbone topics (**Table 4**, in **bold**). "*Sustainability*" and "*ethnography*" are both popular and backbone research topics, however not core topics. "*Education*," "*learning*," "*communication*" and "*awareness*" are both core and backbone research topics, but not hot topics. These results suggest that an increased attention towards these topics is required in order to develop and maintain the development of the field.

Many keywords are found to exist only in one group: "*Fitts' law*", "online *communities*," "*HCI4D/ICTD*," "*interaction design*," "*usability*," "*crowdsourcing*," "touch," "*touch screens*," "*tabletop*," "*SNS*," "*wikis*," "*social computing*" and "*mobile computing*." These keywords indicate a *paradigm change* in the field, as they disappear or emerge. In addition, despite their popularity, if the keywords are neither in the core or backbone topics, they are potentially a mismatch of research efforts.

In summary, comparing the popularity of the keywords between the two periods, *only* 42 of 94 keywords (44.7%) between 1994-2003 are found again as top keywords between 2004-2013 (italic font in table 2). In other words, most top research topics of the first ten years were *replaced* by new research topics in recent years. The whole field witnessed a *paradigm change* during this period.

Fluxionary Research

The field of HCI grew considerably in the last 10 years, from an average of approximately 70 (1994-2003) to 245 publications per year (2004-2013). We observed an overall increase in research clusters' centrality (from 0.571 in 1994-2003 to 0.635 in 2004-2013), and density (from 2.305 in 1994-2003 to 3.127 in 2004-2013) (Figure 4a and Figure 4b, respectively). This means that HCI is becoming increasingly cohesive. However, the field is lacking a major driving theme that could potentially accelerate this process, but instead consists of multiple themes competing for recognition despite cooperating with each other.

While the underlying dynamics of themes point to gradual maturity, the field has witnessed a recent explosion in the number of specific topics or keywords. Overall keyword centralization has decreased from 31.04% in 1994-2003 to 26.79% in 2004-2013, indicating that the leading research keywords are constantly becoming less central in the network. This is inevitable given that more new research connections have been established between different research topics in the later ten years.

For example, our analysis reveals that "social networks" and "crowdsourcing" are completely new research themes established during 2004-2013, located in quadrant II, clusters (B10, B11) (**Figure 4b**). However, this should not come as a surprise if the reader takes into account the emergence of several social networking web sites during this period (*e.g.*, Facebook and Twitter opened to the general public in 2006, Google+ in 2011). Similarly, crowdsourcing presents itself as an emerging research theme in 2004-2013 even though the first publication with this keyword only appeared at CHI in 2009. However, due to its rapid growth it has in merely 4 years positioned itself as an important emerging research paradigm despite its low centrality and therefore weak connection to other research paradigms. During the same time period, in clusters B13 and B14, "multi-tasking" and "emotion" are hand-in-hand with the highest density. This indicates a cluster that contains "inseparable" expressions that are usually co-present, much unlike the previous cluster in which, more often than not, only one of those keywords appear.

In parallel to the emergence of research themes, there are others that *decline* or *merge*. For instance, "End-user programming," and "information foraging," from clusters A13 and A14, have faded from the landscape of HCI research as major independent research subfields.

A theme can also merge with others for several reasons, such as the introduction of novel technology leading to appropriation, or because a new advance is beneficial to both fields. For example, in the early days of CHI, "annotation" from A12 took form in physical documents. With the availability of collaborative tools, such as "wikis", and social "tagging" (from cluster B3), annotation is now in the context of digital formats. Another example is the merging of "computer supported cooperative work" from cluster A1 with "eye tracking" from cluster A11 resulting to cluster B5 in 2004-2013, as eye-tracking methodologies began to be used in collaborative settings, such as [23].

Research themes merging can lead also to new research topics: "ubiquitous computing," "augmented reality," and "ethnography" (from A3) and "visualization," "user interface design," and "cognitive modeling" (from A4) triggered the creation of three novel subfields: "mobile phone," "sustainability" and "ethnography" (B1); "ubiquitous computing," "privacy" and "mobile" (B2); and "visualization," "collaboration" and "user interface" (B3). Research on the older topics is now intertwined with these new topics, contributing to the appearance of several research directions like sustainability [4], large-scale ethnography [12] and ubiquitous public displays [15,19].

Where is the accumulated knowledge?

As it stands, the only tradition in HCI is that of having no tradition in terms of research topics. HCI has a long enough history for knowledge to accumulate, but to what extent has this happened? Do prior studies help us when it comes to new technologies? Judging from our findings the answer is no, when a new technology comes along it seems that researchers start from scratch leading to relatively isolated research themes. There seems to be no single well-defined way to study a new technology in the context of HCI. As a result, different approaches or perspectives are adopted when studying a new technology, leading to a relative fragmentation within HCI.

Reflecting on our own experience, we believe that the accumulated knowledge in HCI is almost exclusively grounded on very specific technological contexts. For instance when it comes to improving the design of a mouse, previous studies on ergonomics are helpful. But when the mouse is replaced by a touch-screen or voice input, previous findings on mouse performance tend to be inapplicable. This is not an HCI phenomenon: the transition from gramophone to music tapes to CDs to iPods had a similar effect on multiple disciplines. Due to the rapid pace of technology designed for humans, however, knowledge in HCI tends to be highly contextual instead of universal like in the field of biology or physics. So we argue that by nature HCI research is like nomads chasing water and grasslands, making it challenging for the community to accumulate knowledge.

Of course, the Human in HCI does not change as rapidly as technology, even though practices and habits do. Hence one potentially solid ground for HCI to develop accumulated knowledge is on the human aspects of HCI, and this was acknowledged in the session "celebrating the psychology of human-computer interaction" in CHI 2008 [2]. However, our analysis shows that this is far from likely to happen in the community, with no discernable research theme emerging on this topic.

Note that a motor theme should be derived from well-established knowledge (high density), and have implications to new HCI topics (high centrality). Therefore, the existence of accumulated knowledge that is applicable to the context of new technologies is an important condition for the formation of motor-themes. Based on the above discussion, we believe that the 'nomads' nature of HCI research largely contributes to the lack of motor theme in the field.

Should CHI break up into multiple conferences?

The diversity of the CHI conference, and more broadly of the HCI field, has often prompted discussion. The diversity of the papers submitted to the CHI conference often backfires when authors feel that their work is not evaluated by 'true' experts, or indeed by someone of an appropriate background. Furthermore, researchers complain that some kind of work is "more valued", specifically raising the issue of one-off novelty experiments being preferred over laborious system development. On the other hand, researchers feel that the diversity of the field is one of its key strengths. Thus, the issues of rigor, diversity, and reviewing process become intertwined in discussion. We attempt to relate our findings to this discussion and shed some light on the underlying processes of our discipline and how we should approach rigor and diversity.

First, our results show that HCI *is* a diverse field. However, the field is diverse not in the sense that it consists of multiple disconnected research themes, like a pot-pouri, but in the sense that there are a lot of links within and between diverse themes, rather like a cobweb. In fact, only a handful of clusters fall in Quadrant II (isolated themes) in Figure 4, with most large clusters falling in Quadrant IV (transversal themes) indicating an expansion of the field.

Our results also show that over time, the themes *have* become more cohesive, while at the same time there is a much larger number of topics or keywords in the discipline. To a large extent, this is stimulated and driven by factors external to the community, for instance through the introduction of new technological products and services (*e.g.*, iPhone, Facebook) that have a direct impact on humans' life. As technology advances, and the rate of innovation remains high, we can expect this trend to remain: more new topics will constantly be of relevance to the HCI community.

The key insight we obtain from our results is that any breakup of the CHI conference today, or the HCI field, is likely to be pointless in a few years. The community simply lacks the motor themes along which a potentially meaningful break up could be achieved (Quadrant 1 in Figure 4). Our community is slowly maturing in terms of themes, but is not transversally mature and the recent expansion of topics is likely to delay this process.

A further insight from our analysis attests to the value of diversity in our community. We identify many instances where topics merge or interact with each other in unpredictable ways, sometimes establishing new themes, sometimes declining. This strong interaction is indicative of the adaptability of our community, constantly evaluating alternative approaches and attempting to conquer new ground. A break up of the community would only hinder this process, making it much harder to cope with the introduction of new topics. This diversity and constant state of flux is crucial in assimilating and dealing with new topics.

The polycentric nature of the knowledge map of HCI, as opposed to a unicentric one, reveals a key property of our community. Our analysis of the keywords making up the various clusters suggests that when a new technology is introduced, our community tackles it and approaches it from a number of perspectives. For instance, the introduction of tabletop technology prompted usability and Fitts' law studies, studies on security and privacy, studies on education and learning. Similarly the introduction of smartphones and social media has been tackled from multiple perspectives. This pluralism is a characteristic of our community, for better or worse.

In summary, our analysis suggests that the HCI community:

- is having to deal with an increasing number topics that are externally driven (*e.g.*, new products, services, advances in other sciences);
- is responding to this challenge by maintaining a diverse yet intertwined research profile which remains in flux;
- is gradually maturing in terms of its themes, but it is simply not transversally mature enough to undergo a meaningful breakup.

LIMITATIONS

We considered only a single source of publications, the CHI conference, which despite being the flagship conference of the discipline has a strong geographical bias with most papers coming from the US, UK and Canada [2]. The fact that no journals were included in our analysis means that work on topics more likely submitted directly to journals is likely to be underrepresented in our sample.

Furthermore, the CHI conference has an acceptance rate of about 24%, so most papers that were submitted to CHI were eventually published somewhere else – and therefore not included in our sample. Finally, a crucial issue is the extent to which keywords accurately reflect the contents of a paper. It is not clear whether all authors follow the same approach for assigning keywords to their papers, and this is likely to lead to some inconsistencies. Also, it is possible that some change of keyword frequency may come from a change in practices of how authors assign keywords. However most of the keywords refer to specific technologies, rather than generic concepts that can be used interchangeably due to authors' habit. So we feel that it is very unlikely that the change of major keywords during the two periods comes from authors' habits.

CONCLUSION

In summary, our findings suggest that the field of HCI has undergone dramatic change in the past 20 years. We can see a clear paradigm change from the top keywords list, more than half of which in 1994-2003 have disappeared from the top list of 2004-2013. No research theme seems to be immune from the influence of evolution. Rapid technology change, including the prevalence of mobile devices and technologies and the availability of new service like SNS and crowdsourcing appear as a sort of driving force.

From the perspective of the whole network, the study reported an enhanced cohesion of the field. The overall network density increased while the whole network became more internally connected. This implies progress towards the formation of a concrete research field of HCI as a whole. However, the results also indicate unmatched research efforts on hot, core and backbone topics in recent years, suggesting an ongoing and rapid paradigm shift.

REFERENCES

1. An, X.Y. and Wu, Q.Q. Co-word analysis of the trends in stem cells field based on subject heading weighting. *Scientometrics 88*, 1 (2011), 133–144.
2. Bartneck, C. and Hu, J. Scientometric analysis of the chi proceedings. *Proc. CHI 2009*, ACM Press (2009), 699–708.
3. Bauin, S., Michelet, B., Schweighoffer, M.G., and Vermeulin, P. Using bibliometrics in strategic analysis: "understanding chemical reactions" at the CNRS. *Scientometrics 22*, 1 (1991), 113–137.
4. Blevis, E. Sustainable interaction design: invention & disposal, renewal & reuse. *Proc. CHI 2007*, ACM Press (2007), 503–512.
5. Borgatti, S.P. and Everett, M.G. Models of corer/periphery structures. *Social Networks 21*, (1999), 375–395.
6. Bradford, S.C. Sources of information on specific subjects. *J. Information Science 10*, 4 (1985), 173–180.
7. Callon, M., Courtial, J.., and Laville, F. Co-word analysis as a tool for describing the network of interactions between basic and technological research: The case of polymer chemsitry. *Scientometrics 22*, 1 (1991), 155–205.
8. Callon, M., Courtial, J.P., Turner, W.A., and Bauin, S. From translations to problematic networks: An introduction to co-word analysis. *Social Science Information 22*, 2 (1983), 191–235.
9. Cambrosio, A., Limoges, C., Courtial, J.P., and Laville, F. Historical scientometrics? Mapping over 70 years of biological safety research with co-word analysis. *Scientometrics 27*, 2 (1993), 119–143.
10. Chang, P.-L., Wu, C.-C., and Leu, H.-J. Using patent analyses to monitor the technological trends in an emerging field of technology: a case of carbon nanotube field emission display. *Scientometrics 82*, 1 (2010), 5–19.
11. Coulter, N., Monarch, I., and Konda, S. Software engineering as seen through its research literature: A study in co-word analysis. *J. of the American Society for Information Science 49*, 13 (1998), 1206–1223.
12. Dalsgaard, P. and Eriksson, E. Large-scale participation: a case study of a participatory approach to developing a new public library. *Proc. CHI 2013*, ACM Press (2013), 399–408.
13. Ding, Y., Chowdhury, G.G., and Foo, S. Bibliometric cartography of information retrieval research by using co-word analysis. *Information Processing & Management 37*, 6 (2001), 817–842.
14. Garfield, E. The mystery of the transposed journal lists—wherein Bradford's Law of Scattering is generalized according to Garfield's Law of Concentration. *Current Contents 17*, (1971), 5–6.
15. Goncalves, J., Ferreira, D., Hosio, S., Liu, Y., Rogstadius, J. Kukka, H. and Kostakos, V. Crowdsourcing on the spot: altruistic use of public displays, feasibility, performance, and behaviours. *Proc. UbiComp 2013*, ACM Press (2013), 753–762.
16. Harrison, S., Tatar, D., and Sengers, P. The three paradigms of HCI. *Proc. CHI 2007*, ACM Press (2007), 1–21.
17. He, Q. Knowledge Discovery through Co-Word Analysis. *Library trends 48*, 1 (1999), 133–159.
18. Hu, C.-P., Hu, J.-M., Deng, S.-L., and Liu, Y. A co-word analysis of library and information science in China. *Scientometrics*, (2013).
19. Kukka, H., Oja, H., Kostakos, V., Gonçalves, J., and Ojala, T. What makes you click: exploring visual signals to entice interaction on public displays. *Proc. CHI 2013*, ACM Press (2013), 1699–1708.
20. Liu, G.-Y., Hu, J.-M., and Wang, H.-L. A co-word analysis of digital library field in China. *Scientometrics 91*, 1 (2011), 203–217.
21. Marc, M., Courtial, J.-P., Senkovska, E.D., Petard, J.-P., and Py, Y. The dynamics of research in the psychology of work from 1973 to 1987: From the study of companies to the study of professions. *Scientometrics 21*, 1 (1991), 69–86.
22. Muñoz-Leiva, F., Viedma-del-Jesús, M.I., Sánchez-Fernández, J., and López-Herrera, A.G. An application of co-word analysis and bibliometric maps for detecting the most highlighting themes in the consumer behaviour research from a longitudinal perspective. *Quality & Quantity 46*, 4 (2011), 1077–1095.
23. Nguyen, D. and Canny, J. MultiView: spatially faithful group video conferencing. *Proc. CHI 2005*, ACM Press (2005), 799–808.
24. Nielsen, A. and Thomsen, C. Sustainable development: the role of network communication. *Sustainable development: the role of network communication 18*, 1 (2011), 1–10.
25. Ritzhaupt, A., Stewart, M., Smith, P., and Barron, A. An investigation of distance education in North American research literature using co-word analysis. *Int. Review of Research in Open and Distance Learning 11*, 1 (2010), 37–60.
26. Rombach, M.P., Porter, M., Fowler, J., and Mucha, P. Core-Periphery Structure in Networks. (2013), 1–27.
27. Wang, Z.-Y., Li, G., Li, C.-Y., and Li, A. Research on the semantic-based co-word analysis. *Scientometrics 90*, 3 (2011), 855–875.
28. Ward, J.H. Hierarchical Grouping to Optimize an Objective Function. *J. of the American Statistical Association 58*, 301 (1963), 236–244.
29. Vaughan, L., Yang, R., and Tang, J. Web co-word analysis for business intelligence in the Chinese environment. *Aslib Proceedings 64*, 6 (2012), 653–667.
30. Zong, Q.-J., Shen, H.-Z., Yuan, Q.-J., Hu, X.-W., Hou, Z.-P., and Deng, S.-G. Doctoral dissertations of Library and Information Science in China: A co-word analysis. *Scientometrics 94*, 2 (2013), 781–799.

"Narco" Emotions: Affect and Desensitization in Social Media during the Mexican Drug War

Munmun De Choudhury[1] **Andrés Monroy-Hernández**[1] **Gloria Mark**[2]

[1] Microsoft Research
One Microsoft Way
Redmond, WA 98052 USA
{munmund, andresmh}@microsoft.com

[2] Department of Informatics
University of California, Irvine
Irvine, CA 92697 USA
gmark@uci.edu

ABSTRACT

Social media platforms have emerged as prominent information sharing ecosystems in the context of a variety of recent crises, ranging from mass emergencies, to wars and political conflicts. We study affective responses in social media and how they might indicate desensitization to violence experienced in communities embroiled in an armed conflict. Specifically, we examine three established affect measures: negative affect, activation, and dominance as observed on Twitter in relation to a number of statistics on protracted violence in four major cities afflicted by the Mexican Drug War. During a two year period (Aug 2010-Dec 2012), while violence was on the rise in these regions, our findings show a decline in negative emotional expression as well as a rise in emotional arousal and dominance in Twitter posts: aspects known to be psychological markers of desensitization. We discuss the implications of our work for behavioral health, facilitating rehabilitation efforts in communities enmeshed in an acute and persistent urban warfare, and the impact on civic engagement.

Author Keywords

affect; desensitization; social media; crisis informatics.

ACM Classification Keywords

H.5.3. Group and Organization Interfaces; Asynchronous interaction; Web-based interaction.

INTRODUCTION

People living in regions facing warfare or political conflict are often exposed to protracted violence that have negative mental and physical side-effects. For instance, research has shown that prolonged exposure to violence, through media reports, direct observation, word-of-mouth or victimization can bear detrimental impacts on people's affective, and behavioral processes [1]. It can also lead to emotional habituation or numbing, known as "desensitization." Affective desensitization has implications for mental health as it can lead to cognitive performance decline, attentional impairment [20], and is a stressor of the onset of PTSD (post-traumatic stress disorder), an anxiety disorder associated with harmful physiological outcomes [30].

CHI 2014, April 26 - May 01 2014, Toronto, ON, Canada

ACM 978-1-4503-2473-1/14/04...$15.00.
http://dx.doi.org/10.1145/2556288.2557197

The Mexican Drug War is an example of the type of armed conflict that has exposed people to persistent acts of violence. Since the war started in, many Mexican cities have seen a rapid increase of shootings and homicides that, on occasions, affect innocent civilians. Furthermore, the conflict has triggered an increase of criminal activities such as extortions, and kidnappings affecting the general population [24]. This generalized violence in some Mexican cities, coupled with constrained information reporting on news media, have contributed to the emergence of citizen alert networks using platforms like Twitter and Facebook to inform and collectively grieve, critique, and express frustration about the violence in the streets [25].

Previous research in crisis informatics has demonstrated the role of social media as a lens to understand how society copes with crises and how communities leverage these tools for civic engagement and social support [21,39,27,34,35]. In this paper, we use social media to examine the evolution of affective reactions to persistent violence, and to study whether affective desensitization may be manifested on social media, focusing on the Mexican Drug War. As a first step to this investigation, we focus particularly on Twitter, because of its prominent adoption in the Mexican population—35% of Mexicans are online, of which 82% use social media, and 58% of social media users use Twitter [38].

Given the politically complex and highly contested nature of conflict, we first utilize a multi-prong approach to gauge the context of violence in four major cities in Mexico during Aug 2010 and Dec 2012 (Monterrey, Reynosa, Saltillo, Veracruz). The data sources include: government statistics on homicides, web search interest in violence-related phrases, and social media data from Twitter and a highly popular anonymously curated "narco" blog. Thereafter, we define psychological measures to operationalize affective responses and possible desensitization in Twitter postings of individuals impacted by the conflict: *Negative Affect, activation or arousal, and dominance*.

Our findings show that, while violence was consistent, or in some cases on the rise in the cities we study, Twitter posts discussing the cities indicate a numbing of emotional responses and aggressive expression over time—both of which are known attributes of affective desensitization [6]. Specifically, negative affect shows decline over time, while activation and dominance measures show an increase.

As our data is observational, a causal relationship cannot be inferred; however the results *do* suggest a significant link between exposure to violence due to the ongoing urban warfare in Mexico, and anxiety and post-traumatic stress symptomatology gleaned from social media. Our analyses also contribute to the literature on crisis informatics in general and violence in Mexico in particular, and extend beyond looking at determinants of violence and violence intensity, into studying its consequences manifested on social media. We also discuss the possible implications of our research for civic media.

RELATED WORK

There has been an increased interest in HCI research in understanding how citizens use social technologies to respond to crises: from natural ones: earthquakes and floods, to manmade ones: wars and terrorist attacks [9,26]. As social media becomes a prominent communication channel, the motivation to study the use of these platforms during crises, comes in part, from a desire to understand how society copes with those events. Our work builds on this prior literature in crisis informatics by investigating how social media can be used to gauge the well-being of a society experiencing prolonged violence. There is limited research in this area e.g., [21] that investigate citizens' affective responses to crisis, even specifically to the Mexican Drug War [26], albeit focused on a US border town. However, to our knowledge, the crisis informatics literature, despite studying a wide range of crises (e.g., [9,26]), has not examined emotional expression of citizens experiencing urban warfare. Our study will investigate emotional responses manifested in social media during a crisis and has implications for public health officials, as social media could potentially be used as a barometer of negative psychological impact on citizens.

However, although not related to crisis informatics, recent research on social media use has demonstrated that it can reveal a variety of behavioral and affective trends. Kramer [19] utilized posts made on Facebook to determine a measure of societal happiness; whereas Golder and Macy [14] found that positive and negative affect expressed on Twitter can replicate known diurnal and seasonal behavioral patterns across cultures. Affect and behavior mined from Facebook and Twitter posts has also been known to be reflective of behavioral [13] and public health concerns [28].

Another thread of research relevant to our work comes from psychology, where the impact of trauma and crisis in the society on the affective responses of people has been widely investigated [22,40]. A critical consequence of a crisis experience is affective desensitization, a well-studied topic in behavioral health domains. Researchers have studied how individuals chronically exposed to violence might experience a decrease in affective and even physical reactions [7]. This phenomenon, affective desensitization, is characterized by the numbing of (negative) emotional reactions to events that typically would elicit a strong response, as well as by an increase in aggressive behavior [6,18]. Additionally, research has shown that even brief exposure to violence both in the physical world [11] and through the media (from television, to video games, and the Internet), can result in affective desensitization [6,7].

The rich body of studies on affect due to trauma, and associated desensitization has all been done in laboratory settings, or with surveys, with homogeneous samples. To our knowledge, they have never been investigated with social media. Social media provides an opportunity to study whether desensitization to violence can be detected on a macro scale by studying the affective responses of people as a consequence of trauma. Due to its archival record, reactions to societal violence can be tracked longitudinally.

Weaving together these observations from prior work, along with the known unique context of social media use in Mexico as a mechanism of expression during the ongoing armed conflict [25] provides us an opportunity to study the affective responses of people enmeshed in the chronic violence, and the possible manifestation of desensitization on Twitter.

BACKGROUND AND RESEARCH QUESTIONS

Drug War in Mexico: An Overview

The Mexican Drug War is an ongoing armed conflict among rival drug cartels fighting each other for regional control and against the Mexican government forces and civilian vigilante groups. It was reported in 2011 that this Drug War had taken 60,000 lives [4] and has displaced between 230,000 and 1.6 million people. However unconfirmed reports set the homicide statistics over 100,000 victims that include cartel members (~90% [16]), law enforcement personnel, officials, journalists, and innocent civilians. Beyond mere body counts, these numbers over time are taking a hidden psychological toll on citizens as well: forced disappearances of people, for instance, take a huge emotional toll on the families and the community [23]. Furthermore, small business owners are extorted and threatened with death by petty criminals taking advantage of the climate of fear [8].

Given the acuteness of the circumstances, and as a consequence of weakened and censored traditional media along with the failure of the local governments in appropriate public communication [25], blogs and social media accounts [15] have emerged that attempt to report gory details, warnings, and alerts about the ongoing violence in various cities as they unfold—increasing the average civilian's exposure to the crisis.

The hijacking of the control over violence has also led to a continuing deterioration of the Mexican social fabric, and has been known to lead to detrimental impact on behavioral health, apparent in symptoms of post-traumatic stress and anxiety. In fact, as early as 2010, local health officials had reported a significant increase in the number of people seeking mental health help with post-traumatic stress disorder (PTSD) induced by drug-related violence [26]. Similarly, the international news media have reported how Mexicans are "numb to carnage" [2] and even kids are "exposed to such violence that they're desensitized" [17]. These observations motivate our work to study the affective responses of people manifested in social media in the light of the ongoing armed conflict, and also investigate whether affective desensitization may be present.

Research Questions

In the context of the ongoing urban warfare in Mexico and the context described above, we aim to investigate the following core question: *can social media signal how people's affective reactions to violence change as they get exposed to persistent violence?* In the following paragraphs we will flesh out our research questions.

First, in order to characterize affective reactions via people's social media postings, we rely on the following measures:

1. *Negative Affect (NA).* A broad emotional dimension, that indicates the level of displeasure of an emotion; e.g., *sad* has a higher measure of NA than *bored.*
2. *Activation.* An established dimension of affect that measures the intensity of an emotion, or arousal [12]. As an example, while *frustrated* and *infuriated* are both negative emotions, *infuriated* is higher in activation.
3. *Dominance.* Another well-studied dimension of affect, that represents the "controlling power" of an emotion [12]. For instance, while both *fear* and *anger* are negative emotions, *anger* is a dominant emotion, while *fear* is a submissive emotion.

We now discuss the relationship of these affective measures to desensitization. Studies have indicated desensitization to be associated with the attenuation or elimination of cognitive, emotional, and, ultimately, behavioral responses to a stimulus [31]. Hence operationally, desensitization manifests itself with numbing (or lowering) of negative emotions, i.e., failure to respond appropriately to the anticipated negative consequences of a violent situation. This motivates our first RQ:

> **RQ 1:** *How does the expression of NA in social media change over time, subject to prolonged violence? In particular, what kind of changes in NA would characterize affective desensitization on social media?*

Observing violence may additionally create or accentuate feelings associated with aggressive thoughts [31]. People may thus habituate emotionally to the display of aggression, although their general fear of crime and violence may become enhanced. These aggressive thoughts can often manifest in the form of increased emotional arousal, and the expression of more dominating feelings [11]. We address these notions in our second and third RQs:

> **RQ 2:** *How does the expression of activation in social media change over time, subject to prolonged violence exposure? In particular, what kind of changes in activation would characterize affective desensitization on social media?*

> **RQ 3:** *How does the expression of dominance in social media change over time, subject to prolonged violence exposure? In particular, what kind of changes in dominance would characterize affective desensitization on social media?*

Finally, literature in crisis informatics [21,27,34,35], and research on the drug war-related violence in Mexico [25] has demonstrated that given such extraordinary circumstances, people are likely to use social media (e.g., Twitter) to express frustration, grievances, or simply to share instantaneous information to alert fellow citizens about violent clashes, or to seek and provide social support. Such community practices are often driven by social norms (e.g., helping each other, seeking and providing support) or as an objective way of ensuring safety in one's surroundings amid ongoing warfare. Cognizant of these observations, it is likely that the level of people's social media activity during such situations would not change with any desensitization. We present our final RQ:

> **RQ 4:** *How does the level of social media use change over time, subject to prolonged violence exposure? In particular, what kind of changes in social media activity would characterize affective desensitization on the platform?*

DATA AND METHODS

Our data collection proceeded in two parts: Twitter data that we used to infer affective responses referring to four Mexican cities, and statistics on ongoing drug war violence.

Twitter post (Spanish)	Translated in English
lamenta edil de san pedro plagio y homicidio de empresario <url> #monterrey	*mayor of san pedro regrets kidnapping and murder of businessman <url>#monterrey*
voy viendo lo de los ahorcados en #saltillo estoy en shock! en que momento?? gente cuidense mucho y tomen precauciones!!!	*I just saw that people were hanged in #saltillo I am in shock! when was that? be careful and take precautions!*
que bueno que hayan detenido a este hombre que destazaba hombre para hacerlos pasar por carne y venderla #reynosa <url>	*It is good that they have arrested this man was butchering people to make them pass by meat and sell it #reynosa <url>*

Table 1. Example city-specific postings on Twitter.

Social Media Data

We utilized Twitter's Firehose stream, made available to us via a contract with Twitter. We collected all of the Spanish postings with hashtagged mentions (e.g., #cityname) of one of the four Mexican cities of interest: Monterrey, Reynosa, Saltillo, and Veracruz, between Aug 2010 and Dec 2012 *(retweets were disregarded)*. Example posts are given in Table 1. We did experiment with focusing on only geocoded Twitter posts to accurately collect postings from the residents of the four cities. However, the proportion of geocoded posts was extremely low (under 1%), and hence less likely to be representative of the affective state of the social media users in the cities in our investigation. City hashtags would likely capture the general affective state in a city, as they were explicitly marked to refer to the city, and therefore more appropriate to use to characterize affective responses than drug war specific hashtags, like #mtyfollow, used in [25]. Statistics of the posts per city are given in Table 2.

	Monterrey	Reynosa	Saltillo	Veracruz
tweets	672,310	501,313	608,936	1,336,478
users	91,044	19,068	28,267	81,589
tweets/user	7	26	22	16
tweets/day	778.14	580.22	704.79	1546.85

Table 2. Statistics of Twitter data on the four cities.

Violence Data

Data on homicides by the Government of Mexico

A concrete proxy of violence in a location, although often a conservative estimate, is the official number of homicides that are reported over a period of time at that location. We referred to the data gathered from the National Institute of Statistics and Geography (*www.diegovalle.net/projects.html #url=%23datasets*) to obtain monthly aggregates of the number of homicides in each of the four cities we focus on, affected by the drug wars from Aug 2010 to Dec 2011 (Monterrey, Reynosa, Saltillo, Veracruz). Since this source did not have statistics from 2012, we referred to the website of the "Executive Secretariat of the National Public Security System" (*www.secretariadoejecutivo snsp.gob.mx*) to obtain comparable monthly aggregates of homicides for 2012.

Google Search Trends on Drug War Violence in Mexico

We conjecture that an objective measure of the degree of violence in a location could also be the tendency of individuals to look for information and news on violent events at the same location. Hence we referred to Google Trends (*www.google.com/trends*) to obtain "search interest" measures in monthly averages over a variety of violence related phrases that we handcrafted specific to the drug war context in Mexico (we chose "Spanish" as the default language). Specifically, we used an iterative approach by starting with 10 terms from the "death" category of the prominent psycholinguistic lexicon: Spanish Linguistic Inquiry and Word Count or LIWC (*www.liwc.net*), and then expanded this term set using co-searched terms suggested by Google and one of the researcher's familiarity with the drug war context in Mexico. These phrases included (all searches also included the word "mexico" for additional specificity): *asesinato, cadaver, calcinado, falleció, fosa*, homicidio*, incinerar*, luto, matanza, matar, morir, muere.*

Postings on Blog del Narco (BDN)

A crucial aspect of the drug war context in Mexico was that much of Mexico's mainstream media, especially television stations and local newspapers, had shied away from covering killings and naming the cartels involved. This is because Mexico has become one of the world's most dangerous countries for journalists [10]. Between 2005 and 2010 ~ 66 reporters were killed, with 12 more disappearing, according to the National Human Rights Commission (NHRC).

Given the constraints of statistics reported in traditional media, we therefore resorted to unofficial (citizen) reporting of drug war violence; of these, the Blog del Narco (BDN) (*www.blogdelnarco.com*) edited by an anonymous curator is the most notable, has gained much popularity over the years, and has also been a subject of controversy. This blog publishes graphic details of spiraling violence in different Mexican cities [3]. As of September 2013, the number of followers of the blog on its Twitter account (@InfoNarco) was ~135K. Also, according to a book by the blogger herself, in 2012, the blog "recorded an average of 25 million monthly hits and was ranked among the 100 most-visited websites in Mexico by Alexa, and in the 4,000 for the world" [3].

Using a web crawler we collected all of the postings on BDN in our period of interest: Aug 2010 to Dec 2012. We collected the text of all of the post titles, the post itself and the timestamp of its posting. We calculated the number of postings in monthly aggregates to obtain a time series of the volume of the blog's postings. The total number of posts was 6,880 with an average of 7.9 postings per day during our period of study. Additionally, we obtained monthly snapshots of #followers of BDN's Twitter account over the same period of analysis. Twitter's Firehose stream was again used for the purpose. We conjecture that the audience size of the blog on social media (as indicated by the number of Twitter followers) gives a notion of its visibility and popularity in the greater violence-affected community.

Usage of Narco Language

The persistent drug war related violence in Mexico saw the emergence of a terminology that was attributed specifically to drug cartel informants, and to describing the drug war victims. While it initially emerged in colloquial speech and news media, it slowly and steadily made its way into social media like Twitter as well. For example: "*encobijado*", "*encajuelado*", "*encintado*", are names given to those killed in drug-related violence based on how their body was found. *Encintado* refers to a body found suffocated in packing tape; *encobijado* is wrapped in a blanket, and *encajuelado* is stuffed in a car trunk.

narcotunel*	levantado*	capo*	ejecuci*
narcotúnel*	narcomanta*	sicari*	ejecuta*
encobijad*	narcomensaje*	decapit*	balea*
encajuelad*	narcocorrido*	degolla*	plagi*
levanton	narcoejecucion*	destaza*	balacera*
levantón	narcoejecución*	ahorca*	

Table 3. List of narco words.

Our motivation was to leverage the volume of usage of this colloquial "narco language" on Twitter into gauging, as another complementary signal, the expression and reporting of drug war-related violent events in our four cities of interest and during the time period of this study. We first created an ensemble of "narco words" by combining information reported in local and national press in Mexico, and lists of words published by the Royal Spanish Academy (official arbitrator of the Spanish language) [37]. A list of these words is given in Table 3.

In order to obtain the volume of usage of these words on Twitter, we utilized the ensemble of posts we collected over the four cities, and followed a regular expression matching exercise on the content of the post to determine if it mentioned a particular 'narco' word. Like other data sources, we constructed monthly aggregates thereafter by computing the mean proportion of posts in each month that contained one or more narco words. We obtained approximately 14.5K narco word-containing posts in the case of Monterrey, 17.9K in the case of Reynosa, 16.6K for Saltillo, while 20.8K for Veracruz. Example Twitter posts mentioning popular narco words are given in Table 4.

In the following sections, we utilize these data sources to first establish the persistent nature of violence in our regions of interest, and then examine the four RQs we set up in the early part of the paper.

Twitter post (Spanish)	Translated in English
jornada violenta ayer en #monterrey deja saldo de 5 ejecutados <url> @milenio	*violent day yesterday in #monterrey leaves 5 executions <url> @milenio*
@trackcoahuila delincuentes se dan a la fuga tras breve balacera con militares en v. carranza y figueroa en #saltillo // esta confirmado???	*@trackcoahuila criminals on the run after a brief shootout with soldiers in v. Carranza and Figueroa on # saltillo // is this confirmed???*
ejecutan a mujer, pkm ya con estas van 80 ejecutadas, malditos narcos #verfollow #veracruz #pozarica	*woman executed, wtf there's been 80 women execute, damn narcos # verfollow #veracruz #pozarica*

Table 4. Sample posts showing use of narco words.

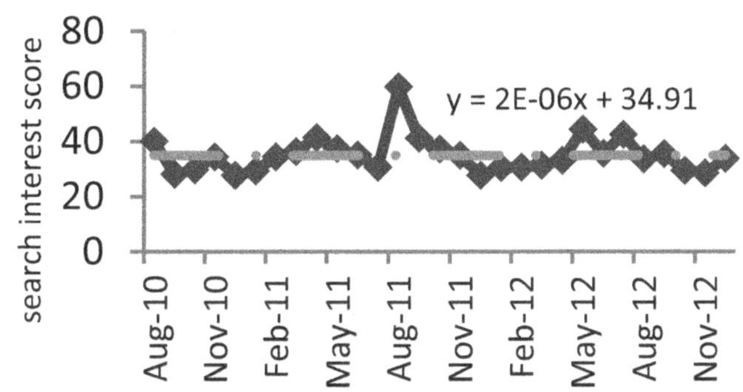

Figure 1. Distributions of search interest scores on violent terms specific to Mexico.

PERSISTENCE OF DRUG WAR VIOLENCE IN MEXICO

We first begin by discussing how our sources of data convey the persistence of drug war related violence in Mexico, beyond what is indicated by government reported homicide statistics. The purpose of this analysis is to establish factual evidence that demonstrates the ongoing nature of drug war violence in Mexico in general, and the four cities in particular during our period of analysis.

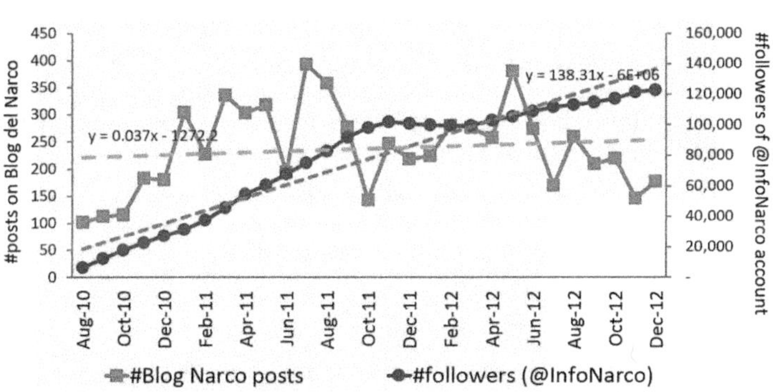

Figure 2. Number of posts on BDN, and number of followers on its Twitter account over time.

Violence-related Search Interest, BDN Statistics

The web search data from Google Trends (Figure 1) show that search interest specific to the violence keywords has a stable trend throughout—notice the linear trend fit. Also, we notice that the number of postings on BDN and its number of Twitter followers (Figure 2) show a slight increase (the positive slope of the linear trend fit). Specifically, for search interest score the mean values are 34.09 in 2010-11 and 35.61 in 2012 (little change; $p=.2$ based on independent sample t-test). The same for the number of posts on BDN is an average of 227.88 in 2010-11 and 240.57 in 2012 which indicates a slight increase ($p<.05$ based on independent sample t-test). In the case of the Twitter follower count of the blog as well, we observe the mean #followers in 2012 (=109,698) to be greater than that in 2010-11 (=54,948) (significant change $p<10^{-5}$, per independent sample t-test). Together, these observations imply the presence of persistent drug war related violence during our period of study.

How well do these aggregate countrywide statistics match up to the city-specific government reported homicide counts? Compared to the city-specific numbers, we find that the distributions of search interest scores show positive correlations with number of homicides: for Monterrey $r^2=.33$ ($p<10^{-8}$); Reynosa $r^2=.28$ ($p<10^{-15}$); Saltillo $r^2=.31$ ($p<10^{-15}$); and Veracruz $r^2=.42$ ($p<10^{-4}$). In the case of number of postings on BDN, correlations with #homicides are positive as well: for Monterrey $r^2=.57$ ($p<10^{-10}$); for Reynosa $r^2=.34$ ($p<10^{-14}$); for Saltillo $r^2=.41$ ($p<10^{-15}$); and for Veracruz $r^2=.27$ ($p<10^{-14}$). In the same light, positive correlations between the number of homicides in each city and number of BDN's Twitter followers are noted: Monterrey $r^2=.17$ ($p<10^{-11}$); Reynosa $r^2=.13$ ($p<10^{-11}$); Saltillo $r^2=.48$ ($p<10^{-11}$); and Veracruz $r^2=.25$ ($p<10^{-11}$).

In essence, the positive values of the correlation coefficients suggest that search interest scores, number of postings on BDN and its number of Twitter followers additionally support the government data on homicides reflecting the ongoing urban warfare in the cities of interest.

Narco Language Use

Next, we shift gears to exploring levels of violence in the four cities of interest (Monterrey, Reynosa, Saltillo, and Veracruz). Here we present the volume of Twitter posts corresponding to each city that contain a narco word, between Aug 2010 and Dec 2012 (Figure 3).

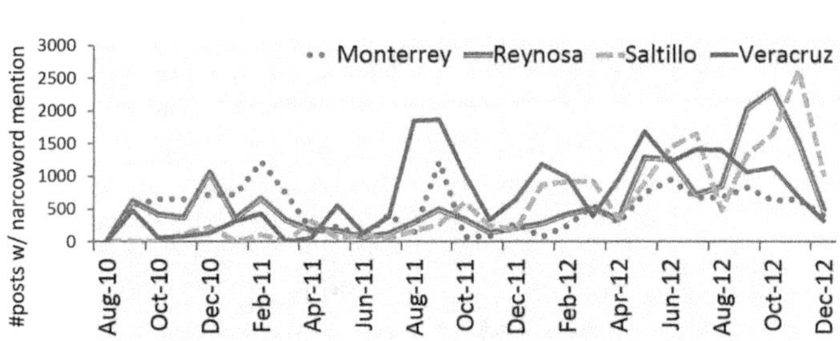

Figure 3. Volumes of Twitter posts containing narco words.

Each of the four distributions shows an increasing trend, implying that usage of narco-specific language gradually evolved on Twitter in the light of the ongoing urban warfare situation. For instance, the per month mean volumes of narco word-containing posts in 2010-11 are: 464.5 (14%) for Monterrey, 341.4 (22%) for Reynosa, 141.7 (15%) for Saltillo, and 488.9 (28%) for Veracruz. On the other hand, the same numbers in 2012 are higher: 554.2 (18%) for Monterrey, 1005.3 (29%) for Reynosa, 1180.2 (32%) for Saltillo, 1039.5 (30%) for Veracruz. Across the entire period, Pearson correlation coefficient comparing narco word use with number of homicide yields positive values: r^2=.41 ($p<10^{-5}$) for Monterrey, r^2=.29 ($p<10^{-5}$) for Reynosa, r^2=.33 ($p<10^{-4}$) for Saltillo, and r^2=.46 ($p<10^{-6}$) for Veracruz. Thus over time, while the number of homicides in the cities were consistent or on the rise, use of narco language increased, providing us additional evidence of ongoing violence.

RESULTS

Having established evidence for persistent violence over the two year period, we now address our research questions.

RQ 1-3: NA, activation and dominance

Measuring NA, activation, dominance. We first discuss our method of computing NA, activation, and dominance values in Twitter posts. First, to compute *NA*, we utilize LIWC (Spanish version), which identifies over 64 behavioral and psychological dimensions (e.g., "insight", "certainty", "perception") in text. LIWC's emotion categories are large in size, broad in semantics, and have been validated for affect computation on Twitter [12,14].

We focus on the words and word stems available in the *negative affect* categories in LIWC: "negative emotion", "sadness", "anger", "anxiety" and "inhibition". We compiled a *negative affect* lexicon for Spanish text. Based on regular expression matching of the words in the lexicon with the content of a Twitter post, we determined a measure of *NA* as the ratio of the number of negative words in the post to the number of words in the post.

	decrease in NA in 2012 over 2010-11	*t*-stat (w.r.t. #homicides)	*p*-value
Monterrey	41.11%	2.2481	1.12e-11
Reynosa	20.76%	1.1925	7.96e-11
Saltillo	12.52%	1.9845	1.66e-11
Veracruz	35.87%	1.6393	0.000197

Table 5. Change in NA in 2012 compared to 2010-11. We also show the results of statistical significance comparing *NA* over time and number of homicides for the corresponding cities over time, using a paired *t*-test (df=29).

For the other two measures, activation and dominance, we utilized the ANEW lexicon [5] that provides a set of normative emotional ratings for a large number of words in the English language (~2000). For our purpose, we constructed a Spanish resource for the same with the help of translations from two Spanish proficient individuals. To compute activation and dominance, we followed a regular expression match exercise, as with NA measurement. Thereafter, using the corresponding activation (and dominance) values of each such word from ANEW, we

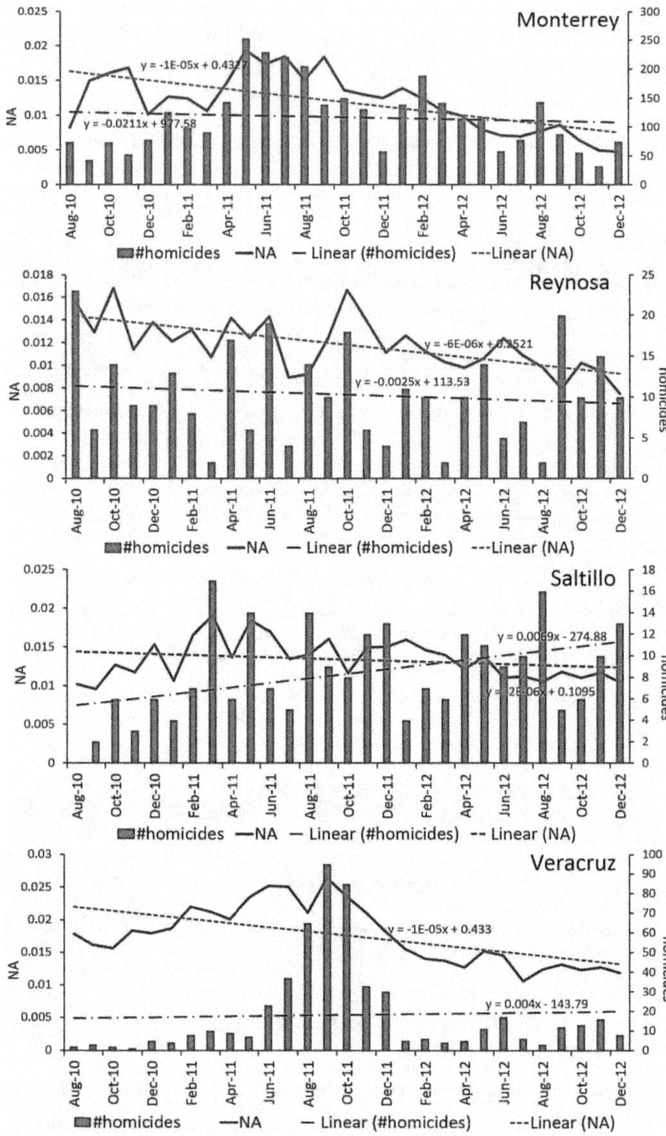

Figure 4. NA and government reported homicide statistics over time for the four cities.

determined a mean measure of activation (and dominance) per post, and thereafter computed monthly averages.

Findings. Figure 4 shows the trends of *NA* expressed on Twitter over time for each of the four cities: Monterrey, Reynosa, Saltillo, and Veracruz. It also shows the corresponding government reported statistics of homicides, and the respective linear trends for both. From the slope of the trendlines it is clear that, like before, homicides over time show either an increasing trend or a consistently stable trend, and NA for each of the cities shows decreasing trends. Results of a paired *t*-test comparing the trends of the number of homicides (monthly units) with that of *NA* yields statistical significance (see Table 5).

Delving a little deeper, notice that actually towards the beginning of the time period of analysis, i.e., early on in 2010 or early 2011, the peaks in number of homicides are actually correlated with those in NA. However over time, especially in 2012, that ceases to be the case. In Table 5, we observe that in 2012, the mean NA per month was between 12-41% *less* than the mean *NA* per month (i.e., between Aug 2010 and Dec 2011) for all of the four cities. In fact, the Pearson correlation coefficient between the NA distribution and the homicide distribution shows that for each city, in 2010-11 they were highly correlated (Monterrey r^2=.81, Reynosa r^2=.61, Saltillo r^2=.76, Veracruz r^2=.63). Whereas in 2012 they followed either an inverse relationship or are uncorrelated: Monterrey r^2=.53, Reynosa r^2=-.37, Saltillo r^2=-.58, Veracruz r^2=.07. (We also compare these correlations per city in 2010-11 and in 2012 for significance using Fisher's *r*-to-*z* test. See Table 6).

	Monterrey	Reynosa	Saltillo	Veracruz
	NA			
2010-11	0.81	0.61	0.76	0.63
2012	0.53	0.37	0.58	0.07
z-score	1.26$^+$	0.75	0.78	1.57*
	activation			
2010-11	0.84	0.41	0.52	0.83
2012	0.06	0.07	0.19	0.09
z-score	2.72**	0.86$^+$	0.9$^+$	2.57**
	dominance			
2010-11	0.82	0.41	0.49	0.84
2012	0.41	0.13	0.08	0.16
z-score	1.69*	0.71	1.07$^+$	2.48**

Table 6. Fisher's *r*-to-*z* tests, that compare the correlations of measures (NA, activation, dominance) in 2010-11 with 2012. Here $^+$ *p* < .2; * *p* < .05; ** *p*< .01.

From the literature, we know that affective desensitization is not an instantaneous phenomenon: rather it happens as a consequence of the convergence of prolonged exposure to real-world and media violence [18]. Along those lines, it appears that the decreasing trend or lowered correlation with number of homicides may be associated with the Twitter users' exposure to the ongoing drug war situation which results in numbing of their negative reactions predominant in the early phases: this could indicate evidence of affective desensitization. *Hence, in the context of RQ 1, lowered NA over time manifested on Twitter may be indicative of affective desensitization.*

Next, in Figure 5 we show activation manifested in the Twitter posts of the four cities over time, along with number of homicides, and their respective linear trend fits. Over time, from the trends of activation, we observe a general increase (ref. the slopes of the linear trend fits for the cities), implying that Twitter users mentioning the four cities in their postings, were increasingly using higher intensity emotions. To elaborate further, we observe that in 2012, the mean activation per month was between 9.9-71% *greater* than the mean activation per month (i.e., between Aug 2010 and Dec 2011) for all of the four cities (Monterrey= 9.9%; Reynosa= 36.7%; Saltillo= 70.8%; Veracruz= 20.5%).

This is also supported by the fact that the Pearson correlation coefficient comparing the activation distribution and homicide distribution gives considerably *lower* (even uncorrelated) values in 2012 than in 2010-11 (ref. Table 6 for details): (2010-11) Monterrey r^2=.84, Reynosa r^2=.41,

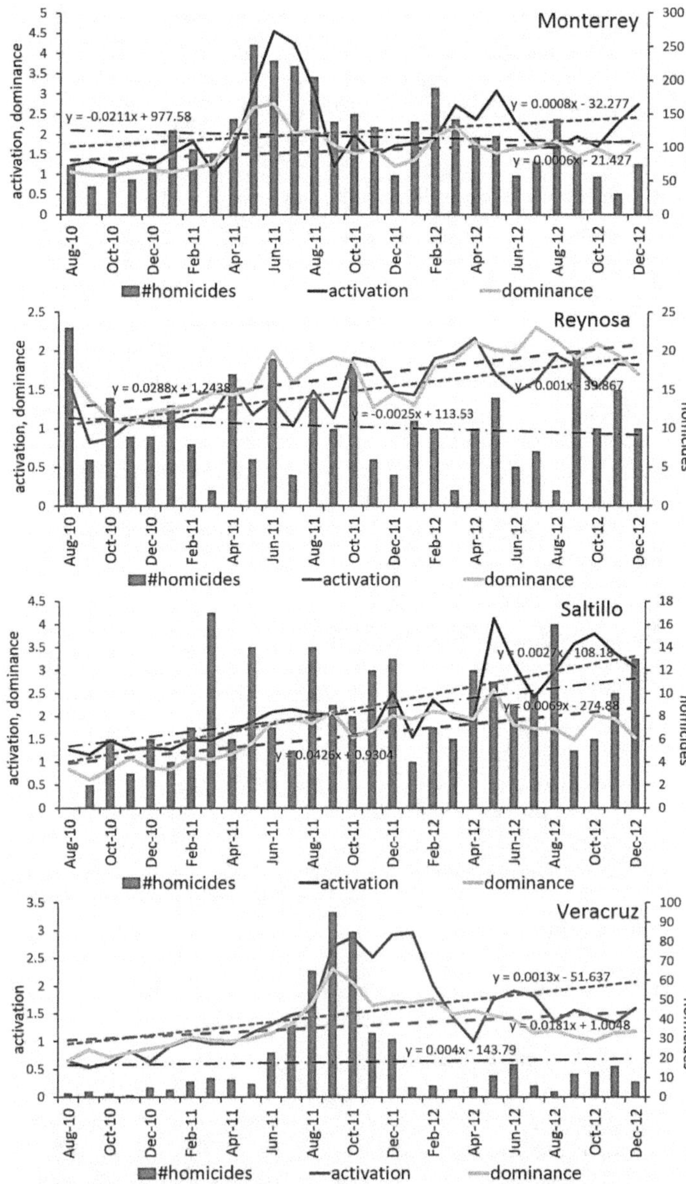

Figure 5. Activation and dominance over time for the four cities. Govt. reported homicide statistics are also shown.

Saltillo r^2=.52, Veracruz r^2=.83; (2012) Monterrey r^2=-.06, Reynosa r^2=-.07, Saltillo r^2=.19, Veracruz r^2=-.09. In other words, activation is more reflective of homicide rate early on in our analysis; however it ceases to do so in the later period, indicating possible aggressive tone in Twitter posts [33].

Finally, in Figure 5 we also show the levels of *dominance* in Twitter posts of the four cities over time, along with fit linear trends. Like before, *dominance* shows a rise with persistent violence (ref. the slope of the linear fit), indicating that users are increasingly using dominating and aggressive emotions. We observe that in 2012, the mean *dominance* per month was between 8.6-41.7% *greater* than the mean *dominance* per month (i.e., between Aug 2010 and Dec 2011) for all of the four cities (Monterrey= 8.6%; Reynosa= 29.3%; Saltillo= 41.7%; Veracruz= 9.2%).

Like in the case of the *activation* measure, a Pearson correlation coefficient comparing the *dominance* distribution and homicide distribution gives *lower* (and even uncorrelated) values in 2012 than in 2010-11 (ref. Table 6 for details): (2010-11) Monterrey r^2=.82, Reynosa r^2=.41, Saltillo r^2=.49, Veracruz r^2=.84; (2012) Monterrey r^2=.41, Reynosa r^2=-.13, Saltillo r^2=-.08, Veracruz r^2=-.16.

To summarize here, rising trends of *activation* and *dominance* over time show signs of aggression in Twitter postings related to the four Mexican cities—a key aspect that characterizes *affective desensitization* [18]. With the persistent number of homicides in the four cities over the time period between 2010 and 2012, it is consistent with the idea that prolonged exposure to violence is associated with desensitization in terms of users' affect expression, with a habituated tendency to display aggression in their day to day postings on social media. *Per RQs 2 and 3 these observations show that affective desensitization on social media may manifest itself via raised levels of activation and the dominance of emotional postings.*

RQ 4: Levels of social media use

Finally, we present the distributions of the levels of Twitter activity (number of postings) in each of the four cities, for the time period of our analysis. The mean number of posts in monthly aggregates are shown (Figure 6). Like with Figures 1-3, we also show the # homicides per month, and fit linear trend lines for both distributions. The volume of postings for Monterrey and Reynosa show fairly stable trends (ref. slopes of the respective trend fits), whereas Saltillo and Veracruz show an increasing trend. Note that these trends are either considerably highly correlated with the number of homicides—e.g., Monterrey (r^2=.46; $p<10^{-10}$), Reynosa (r^2=.51; $p<10^{-20}$), Saltillo (r^2=.43; $p<10^{-9}$), or show marginal positive correlation—e.g., Veracruz (r^2=.002; $p<10^{-7}$).

Combining these observations, we conclude that unlike the three affective measures, exposure to violence does not correlate with lowered levels of Twitter activity in the four cities. In fact, as one would expect, given an ongoing urban warfare situation, users resorted to using social media tools over the entire period of our analysis consistently, probably conforming to community practices of providing social support and spreading safety information and alerts to concerned citizens [25]. *Per RQ 4, we therefore observe that social media activity do not show a pattern of a decreasing trend in the context of prolonged exposure to violence.*

DISCUSSION

Our findings have demonstrated how chronic exposure to violence as a consequence of urban warfare in Mexico is associated with lowered affective responses in Twitter posts of citizens experiencing the violence, leading to possible signs of desensitization in their social media postings. These observations extend the literature on crisis informatics. The Drug War in Mexico is a political conflict that has witnessed weakening of government and traditional media in their ability to keep communities informed of the violence. Twitter has acted as a unique platform allowing affected people to express their emotion, be it their frustration, or grievances and anger about their circumstances anonymously or pseudonymously, amid feelings or perception of threat or terror. This has helped create a counter-narrative to the mainstream media coverage—an aspect that can eventually inform historical accounts about the time period. Our findings can also help researchers build theories about socio-psychological responses to crisis, as well as help compare citizens' thoughts and feelings with their habitual states prior to the upheaval. Additionally, understanding how long certain negative emotional states linger may give an alternate sense of the severity and longevity of a crisis.

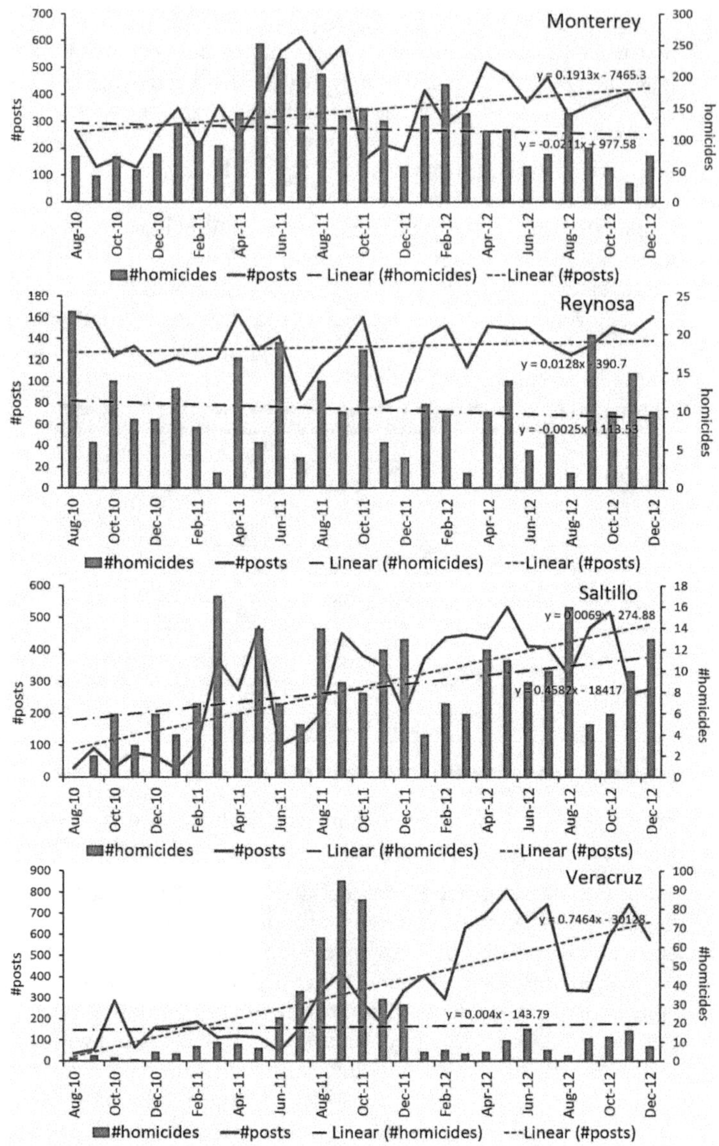

Figure 6. #posts and homicide stats over time for the four cities.

Practical and Design Implications

This research bears implications for public health. Timely attention to communities exposed to violence, experiencing psychological challenges or likely desensitization holds promise in improving rehabilitation efforts in a protracted war context. This is currently a challenge with government or agency administered surveys, because of the large temporal gaps in which they are administered and due to their observations being mostly retrospective. The surveys thus lack the contextualization that is needed to associate the manifested affective concerns to actual circumstances people face. Complementing these surveys with near real-time information about people's affective reactions from social media seems to be an effective way of informing national or international healthcare policies, programs, interventions, and prevention strategies, as well as decisions about the allocation of humanitarian aid.

Our findings also bear implications for the role of civic media during times of prolonged crises. Prior work has indicated that social media has enabled Mexicans to create citizen alert networks, where traditional new media has weakened [25]. While we do not for sure know what people's intrinsic motivations for participation in this case are, we can speculate that strong emotions motivated them to take some risks and use to social media to reach collective action. However, as people experience affective desensitization, it is possible that these collective efforts weaken. More generally, if people rally around common causes when they are passionate about them, then losing that passion could threaten collective action, and perhaps a desensitized society might be less likely to be civically engaged.

As researchers and designers, we therefore need to build information channels that particularly cater to such unique circumstances, and help people gain awareness of the possibility of experiencing *affective desensitization*. Empowering people with tools and platforms that can provide them with psychological and emotional support in the context of widespread affective numbing constitutes a design direction worthy of future exploration.

Limitations and Future Directions

Our findings, however need to be interpreted with caution:

Causality. First and most importantly, we acknowledge that our study is purely *correlational*. In the absence of ground-truth knowledge about affective desensitization in the society or in social media, we cannot draw causal conclusions regarding whether prolonged violence exposure actually leads to desensitization in people embroiled in the armed conflict. An important future extension would be to collect quantitative evidence of desensitization in the cities affected by the ongoing violence, and examine if our findings, as derived from social media, are predictive of that.

Alternative explanations. Certainly, there could be alternative explanations behind our observations. It is possible that with the protracted nature of the warfare ultimately individuals adapt to the environment—a process that may appear as desensitization. Perhaps the society slowly makes its way to normalcy and people try to recover the behaviors they experienced before the violence escalated [21]. However, even if this is the case, we feel that a process of returning to normalcy would involve some degree of desensitization to be able to go about normal day-to-day life. In this light, an analysis of the topics of the social media postings in the cities under consideration, and supplementing with qualitative interviews with affected people may provide insight. It is also possible that people have started to self-censor their Twitter posts out of fear of retaliation—an aspect that may manifest as desensitization.

In fact, desensitization may also be because of exhaustion or long-term stress over time—e.g., simply being wary of the ongoing crisis, instead of being overtly distressed, grieving, or angry. Future research may reveal whether there were corresponding changes in people's daily activities and behavior as well, or whether the affective changes on Twitter were primarily in people's perspectives and thoughts.

Context. Finally, Twitter users who share information about a city could be affected by the war directly, through friends and family, indirectly as a bystander, or not affected but simply cognizant about the violent situation. Such distinction might bear a relationship to the degree to which a person shows affective desensitization; however, we do not distinguish between those roles. Investigating these nuances of impact of violence on a person's geosocial context forms interesting directions for future research.

Social Network, Cultural Effects. There are also a number of empirically motivated questions around network effects of affective expression and desensitization. Are there network contagion attributes to these phenomena? If so, what kind of attributes of the individual (e.g., personality, gender, age, socio-economic status) that make some more vulnerable to the desensitization process than others? Finally, our work is a case study on one (but notable) ongoing armed conflict in a unique cultural context: in the future it would be interesting to study how our findings generalize to other violence-laden crises in the world, and perhaps other online social platforms.

CONCLUSION

Through a large-scale quantitative study around the Mexican Drug War, we have demonstrated the nature of affective changes in social media posts by people exposed to this protracted violence. First, we used official homicide statistics as well as unofficial data (search interest, "narco" language use on Twitter, activity on and visibility of a prominent "narco" blog) to establish factual evidence of ongoing violence in four major Mexican cities in 2010-12. Thereafter, we quantified the affective responses of people in their Twitter posts through the measures *negative affect*, *activation*, *dominance*. While violence was on the rise in our regions of interest, our findings showed a decline in negative affect as well as a rise in emotional arousal and dominance in Twitter posts: aspects that are known to be psychological correlates of desensitization. We discussed how our findings may augment mental health related rehabilitation efforts in crisis afflicted communities, and how civic media might need to adapt to address this psychological challenge.

ACKNOWLEDGMENT

This material is partly supported by NSF grant #1218705.

REFERENCES

1. Anderson, C. A., & Bushman, B. J. (2002). The effects of media violence on society. *Science*, *295*(5564).

2. Archibold, R., and Cave, D. (2012). Numb to Carnage, Mexicans Find Diversions, and Life Goes On. NYT.
3. Blog del Narco (2013) *Dying for the Truth: Undercover Inside the Mexican Drug War by the Fugitive Reporters of Blog del Narco.* Feral House.
4. Booth, W. (2012). Mexico's crime wave has left about 25,000 missing. Washington Post.
5. Bradley, M.M., & Lang, P.J. (1999). Affective norms for English words (ANEW). Gainesville, FL. *The NIMH Center for the Study of Emotion and Attention.*
6. Bushman, B. J., & Huesmann, L. R. (2001). Effects of televised violence on aggression. *Handbook of children and the media*, 223-254.
7. Carnagey, N., Anderson, C. and Bushman, B. (2007). The effect of video game violence on physiological desensitization of real-life violence. *J Experimental Social Psychology,* 43(3), 489-96.
8. Cawley, M. (2013). La Extorsión Llega a Cifras Récord en México. *http://es.insightcrime.org/noticias-del-dia/la-extorsion-llega-a-cifras-record-en-mexico*
9. Cheong, M. & Lee, V. (2010). A microblogging-based approach to terrorism informatics: Exploration and chronicling civilian sentiment and response to terrorism events via Twitter. *Info Sys Frontiers 13*, 1, 45–59.
10. Committee to Protect Journalists. (2011). *For journalists, coverage of political unrest proves deadly.*
11. Davidson, R. J., Putnam, K. M., & Larson, C. L. (2000). Dysfunction in the neural circuitry of emotion regulation--a possible prelude to violence. *Science.*
12. De Choudhury, M., Counts, S., & Gamon, M. (2012). Not all moods are created equal! Exploring human emotional states in social media. In *Proc. ICWSM.*
13. De Choudhury, M., Counts, S., Horvitz, E., and Hoff, A. (2014). Characterizing and Predicting Postpartum Depression from Facebook Data. In *Proc. CSCW 2014.*
14. Golder, S.A. and Macy, M.W. (2011). Diurnal and Seasonal Mood Vary with Work, Sleep, and Daylength Across Diverse Cultures. *Science 333*, 1878–1881.
15. Gómez Leyva, C. El exitoso Blog del Narco. 2010. *http://impreso.milenio.com/node/8855061*
16. Hernández, E. M., and Castro, R. M. (2012). El Presidente de las 83 mil ejecuciones. *http://www.zetatijuana.com/ZETA/reportajez/el-presidente-de-las-83-mil-ejecuciones/*
17. Hopewell, J. (2013). In Mexico, violent art imitates life. Variety.com.
18. Huesmann, L. R., & Taylor, L. D. (2006). The role of media violence in violent behavior. *Annu. Rev. Public Health*, *27*, 393-415.
19. Kramer, A. D. I. (2010). An unobtrusive behavioral model of "gross national happiness". In *Proc. CHI.*
20. Kendall, P. C., and Hammen, C. (1995). *Abnormal psychology.* Boston: Houghton Mifflin.
21. Mark, G., Bagdouri, M., Palen, L., Martin, J., Al-Ani, B., and Anderson, K. Blogs as a Collective War Diary. In *Proc. CSCW 2012.*
22. Mehl, M. R., & Pennebaker, J. W. (2003). The Social Dynamics of a Cultural Upheaval Social Interactions Surrounding September 11, 2001. *Psychological Science*, *14*(6), 579-585.
23. Michaelsen, M. (2012). Mental Health and Labour Supply–Evidence from Mexico's Ongoing Violent Conflicts. *Ruhr Economic Paper*, (378).
24. Miroff, N. (2012). Mexico's drug war is at a stalemate as Calderon's presidency ends. Washington Post.
25. Monroy-Hernández, A., Kiciman, E., De Choudhury, M., & Counts, S. (2013). The new war correspondents: The rise of civic media curation in urban warfare. In *Proc. CSCW 2013*. 1443-1452.
26. O'Connor, K. A. (2013). Narco-Trauma: The Phenomenology of Post-Traumatic Stress among Binational Students at the Border.
27. Palen, L. and Vieweg, S. The emergence of online widescale interaction in unexpected events: assistance, alliance & retreat. *In Proc. CSCW* 2008. 117–126.
28. Paul, M., J.; and Dredze, M. (2011). You are What You Tweet: Analyzing Twitter for Public Health. In *Proc. ICWSM '11.*
29. Rodriguez, O. (2010). Narco-blogger beats Mexico drug war news blackout. Huffington Post.
30. Rosenberg, M., O'Carroll, P., and Powell, K. (1992).Violence is a public health problem. *Journal of the American Medical Association*, 267, 3071–3072.
31. Rule, B. G., & Ferguson, T. J. (1986). The effects of media violence on attitudes, emotions, and cognitions. *Journal of Social Issues*, *42*(3), 29-50.
32. Shirk, D. A. (2010). Drug violence in Mexico: data and analysis from 2001–2009. *Trends in Organized Crime*, *13*(2-3), 167-174.
33. Sparks, G., & Sparks, C. (2002). Effects of media violence. *Media effects: Advances of theory & research.*
34. Starbird, K. and Palen, L. (2012). (How) Will the Revolution be Retweeted?: Information Propagation in the 2011 Egyptian Uprising. *Proc. of CSCW'12.*
35. Starbird, K., Palen, L., Hughes, A.L., & Vieweg, S. Chatter on the red: what hazards threat reveals about the social life of microblogged information. *In Proc. CSCW* 2010. 241–250.
36. Stevenson, M. Mexico Battles New 'Drug Language' To Describe Horrifying Violence. Huffington Post, 2011.
37. Tejeda, A. G. (2010). La Real Academia reconoce el lenguaje del crimen organizado: *http://www.jornada .unam.mx/2010/10/28/cultura/a03n1cul*
38. Urbán, A., and Acre, H. (2013). Crece en México número de usuarious de internet: *http://www.eluniversal.com.mx/finanzas/102437.html*
39. Vieweg, S., Hughes, A., Starbird, K., and Palen, L. (2010). Microblogging During Two Natural Hazards Events: What Twitter May Contribute to Situational Awareness. In *Proc. CHI 2010*, 1079-1088.
40. Zarowsky, C. (2000). Trauma stories: Violence, emotion and politics in Somali Ethiopia. *Transcultural Psychiatry*, *37*(3), 383-402.

A Pool of Dreams: Facebook, Politics and the Emergence of a Social Movement

Clara Crivellaro, Rob Comber, John Bowers, Peter Wright, Patrick Olivier
Culture Lab
School of Computing Science
Newcastle University, UK
{c.crivellaro/rob.comber/john.bowers/p.c.wright/patrick.olivier}@ncl.ac.uk

ABSTRACT

In this paper we present insights from an empirical analysis of data from an emergent social movement primarily located on a Facebook page to contribute understanding of the conduct of everyday politics in social media and through this open up research agendas for HCI. The analysis focuses on how interactions and contributions facilitated the emergence of a collective with political will. We lay out an exploration of the intrinsic relationship between cultural memories, cultural expression and everyday politics and show how diverging voices co-constructed dynamic collectives capable of political action. We look at how interactions through the Facebook page challenge traditional ways for conceiving politics and the political. We outline possible research agendas in the field of everyday politics, which are sensitive to the everyday acts of resistance enclosed in the ordinary.

Author Keywords

Social media; discourse; activism; collectives; politics

ACM Classification Keywords

H.5.m. Information interfaces and presentation (e.g., HCI): Miscellaneous.

INTRODUCTION

There has been increasing interest in the role of social media and the design of systems to serve a socio-political function [5], and in the facilitation of the mobilization and organization of social movement for socio-political action and social change [26]. Social movements have been defined as "collective challenges, based on common purposes and social solidarities, in sustained interaction with elites, opponents, and authorities" [34]. Research in this field has focused on the mobilization of social actors [39, 40], the role of storytelling in social movements [6], and the development of systems to support civic engagement for reflection and action [19]. Other research strands have examined the role of technology as an active political agent [9] and the necessity for bottom up approaches to the design of system in support of grassroots practices [23]. However, the HCI community is just beginning to understand the way social media enable members of the public and communities to construct collectives of social movements to affect change in the politics of everyday life.

In this paper, we explore the role of social media in facilitating the emergence of social movements and the potential for an understanding of the political as complex, contingent and contextual, embedded in the concerns of everyday life. We situate this work within a discourse analysis of the Facebook (FB) page of a local activist group concerned with the redevelopment of a derelict outdoor swimming pool. The social movement evolves from the re-imagining of the pool, as a multiplicity of perspectives fosters a political potential to affect change. This political potential is exposed on the FB page as a representation of posters' opinions and wishes assembled on the page.

We contribute the findings of an empirical investigation, which shows how the appropriation of FB technology is intertwined with the creation of a social movement and its mobilization in socio-political action. The paper makes this contribution through an exploration of the 'work' of socio-political discourse in social media and an empirical analysis of the evolution of collectives through everyday rhetoric. We provide a theoretical framework for the analysis, looking at the way power is performed through everyday rhetoric, as the study of "who is trying to do what to whom with emphasis on how and why they are doing it" ([15] p.5). Through these contributions we challenge traditional understanding of politics and the political, and how we can conceive of HCI interest in technology and everyday politics.

BACKGROUND AND RELATED WORK

The role of social computing in socio-political action has been an area of interest in a variety of disciplines, where the communication [3], medium [36], and design of technology [18, 10] are understood to play a significant role. In this regard, HCI research has focused on developing 'socio-technical' systems to support social movements achieving their goals [5], to support community action [1], urban

CHI 2014, April 26 - May 01 2014, Toronto, ON, Canada
Copyright 2014 ACM 978-1-4503-2473-1/14/04...$15.00.
http://dx.doi.org/10.1145/2556288.2557100

activists practices [18], collective expression [7] and creative and critical engagements with technology in order to support vibrant political communities [8]. Such work ranges from the design of systems for recruitment of individuals to political causes [18, 26], to the requirements of systems to support socio-political action, such as citizen science [1] and health promotion [29]. In this final instance, Parker et al. [29] argue for a thorough understanding of the context in which technologies operate to facilitate and enable collectives to affect social change. Equally, [24] underline the necessity to understand existing cultural practices in uses of social media in order to foster radical approaches to the design and co-design of systems to support meaningful civic engagement. To this end researchers have looked at the potential of design to open up spaces in which to contest, question and challenge matters of concern [4, 8]. Importantly, such work explores how technology and participatory design processes create agonistic spaces where discussions can engender innovative solutions amongst divergent 'voices' [4, 8].

In this way, social media have been largely regarded as one space offering opportunities for alternative discursive modes, broadening participation in political discourses, and activism. As social media and interactive systems have come to be enmeshed in everyday life, they are contributing to the change of the very notion of the public sphere [28], the modalities and spaces where we come together to discuss what matters to us. For instance, [14] argue for the democratic potential of social media to increase political participation where the quality of deliberation can benefit from affordances such as identifiability and information access. However, scholars have questioned to what extent these online practices are stimulating meaningful political participation and 'deepening' democracy in any significant way [37].

Attention has also been drawn to the uncertain interpersonal dynamics of such discursive spaces, and the need for facilitation in forming and co-constructing thoughtful political opinions and arguments [14, 36, 25]. For instance, Mascaro et al. show, through empirical data analysis from a Facebook activist group, how administrators have considerable control in setting agendas, and debates, but that equally the most contentious debates emerged through posters' engagement with the group [25]. Their findings highlighted a structural evolution on the media page where engagement and the role of administration changed over time. Through analysis of data from Twitter, Segerberg and Bennet [2, 33] find similar gatekeeping mechanisms in online practices, encouraging certain organizing actions and preventing others. Equally, Uldam and Askanius, examining the affordances of Youtube's architecture as a platform for political debate in the context of media activism, highlighted a complex interplay between political expression and censorship [36].

There has been considerable skepticism in regard to online activists' practices, seen as ephemeral and limited in relation to the change they wish to achieve, with studies questioning the value of online and social media practices, also referred to as 'Slacktivism' [31, 22, 27]. Yet, other scholars have highlighted the potential of these practices, in providing an organizational aid for protests [32], raising awareness in relation to marginalized citizen's concerns and rights [35], and also as providing a new space to enter in dialogue with the State. In this regard, [30] analyzed how local activists appropriated a social media site, generating alternative modalities of dialogue with the government, thus questioning the efficacy of existing 'official' channels of communication between citizens and the State.

At the core of these studies lies the idea that technology cannot 'do' social change for people, but it can facilitate those processes. Research should therefore endeavor to build an understanding of why and how people become advocates for social change, the mechanisms that bring people together and how collectives are formed [29]. With this paper, we focus on a case study of small-scale socio-political action, where we are interested in understanding the mechanisms at play in the emergence of a social movement among citizens engaged in discussions on a FB page in order to affect the changes they wish for in their everyday life. We seek to shed light on the complexities of social movement formation for everyday socio-political action for change and further understand the relationship between cultural expression and socio-political action.

FRAMEWORK AND METHODOLOGY

We utilized a discourse analysis approach that focuses on understanding what people *'do'* with their talk and the resources they use in the construction of the self, other and alternative realities [38]. Discourse analysis (DA) is helpful for this study as it looks at how people's versions of the world are gathered to perform social action and how these personal versions of the world can counter real and potential alternatives. DA recognizes the power inherent in an utterance to produce and construct objects and subjectivities that delineate modalities of what can be seen, said and acted upon [11]. In this sense what is said is inextricably linked to what is done and can be done. A Foucauldian approach to discourses analysis [11] emphasizes the way that through discourse, power is exercised throughout society. That is the manner in which through talk we produce knowledges and meanings in whose terms 'things' are done. This approach to knowledge production and its constitutive practices, however, points towards disciplinary practices that entrap and preclude possibilities for social actors to produce alternatives to the existing power structures [12]. Sometimes Foucault makes for a fatalistic impression as if we are locked into modes of saying and therefore doing, which replicate existing power structures in society, which we are incapable of changing.

Hauser [16] offers an alternative approach to understanding discourse, which recognizes social actors' fundamental capacity to challenge the status quo and expose opportunities for alternatives to emerge. Hauser locates the possibilities for social action in and through everyday talk: "*through discourse, social actors produce society*" ([15] p.112), whereby everyday talk (what he calls "vernacular rhetoric") has both a reflective and a constitutive function in society. It is through everyday talk that social actors express their values, where what is to be considered meaningful is attained through discursive practices and processes of negotiation within and between social groups. Hauser emphasizes the roles of memory and narrative in society for their potential to generate common understanding among people, and motivate common action. In recent years, the study of rhetoric has expanded to include visual representations, everyday talk, graffiti, music and bodily displays [16], and we argue can extend to the study of technology and social media in the course of political action. We therefore propose a broader understanding of politics, across everyday life, and as the process of negotiation that social actors undertake in deciding how they should live together and what should be considered meaningful [21].

Hauser's model of vernacular rhetoric identifies political resistance in seemingly mundane acts performed by ordinary people in their daily lives [16]. This model highlights how the *'rubbing up'* of multiple, diverging opinions (*'polyvocality')* has the potential to engender alternatives to dominant power structures. Social movements' everyday talk, in Hauser's terms, *performs power*, often in unnoticed ways, through mundane acts that construct social movements through expressions of *solidarity*. By expressing our own opinion or position, we can oppose, support, or negate the position of others. In so doing, everyday talk collectivizes through '*markers of positionality*' (e.g. use of particular language, or other modes of identification) generating explorations of alternative meanings. It also creates *'negative bonding'* with the opposition to ascertain and define the movements' visions and aims, and performs, what Hauser calls, '*acts of gentle violence'* to comply with the values underpinning the movement [16]. In this respect, Hauser suggests social movements' talk is at once inclusive and exclusive, defining participants whose discourse displays membership and bonds of ambition. '*Acts of gentle violence'* might thus be slight or subtle omissions, intentionally labeling someone or something as 'our' or 'their', 'us' or 'them'.

By exploring interactions in everyday talk as elements of change we can question the complexities of power relations in society and of personal and collective agency [16]. This theoretical perspective informs our analysis, highlighting the necessity to develop analytic sensitivities that uncover resistance in seemingly mundane acts. By shifting our focus to "*discourses that originate under the surface of an official discourse [...] a model of vernacular rhetoric may detect spontaneous moments of an alternative consciousness of reality as they form and emerge*" ([16], p.45).

In this paper, we explore the use of FB as a platform that enables people to co-construct 'alternative' possibilities through everyday talk, facilitating the formation of social collectives with a political potential to affect change. We argue therefore that FB can be seen as technology by which power is performed, exposed and concealed through the multiple layers which comprise digital objects: the semantic layer, such as the content of a post, the network layer, which connects digital objects to other informational networks and a third layer establishing positions among users and digital objects [20].

CASE STUDY

Tynemouth is a small seaside town situated in the North East of England. The town has 17,075 inhabitants and hosts a number of visitors and surfers each week. "Tynemouth Outdoor Swimming Pool" is a derelict site located on Tynemouth seafront. The open-air swimming pool, designed to be filled with seawater by the incoming tide, first opened to the public in 1925. The swimming pool was an important attraction for local families and tourists when lidos and open-air swimming pools became symbols of civic pride and progress. Following the arrival of overseas holiday packages, indoor leisure centers and the monitoring and regulation of health and safety, the pool fell in disuse and became derelict in the 1980s. In 1996 the local council converted the site into a natural 'rock pool' intended to host the natural flora and fauna by filling it with concrete, sand and rocks. However, the design of the natural rock pool never functioned as originally conceived, and the site went through further dereliction causing disappointment in the local community. In recent years several proposals to convert the site back to its original use, had been put forward by private investors to the local council unsuccessfully.

The 'Friends of Tynemouth Outdoor Pool' (FoTOP) FB page was set up in 2010 by a group of four local residents with the aim of probing public interest regarding the possibility of reconverting the site to its original use. The page, set up for "*those who are interested in the past, present and future of Tynemouth Outdoor Pool*", remained fairly inactive (having only 9 followers) for a period of two years. The page gained sudden and significant interest following the publication of the council's planning proposal[1] on August 6th 2012 to convert the site into a multipurpose facility comprising of a beach volley court and an open-air theatre. Under UK planning law, once a planning application is submitted, the general public has a relatively short period (3-8 weeks) to express 'material' objections on the council website. The FoTOP FB page swiftly extended into a public forum, (growing from 9 to

[1] http://goo.gl/BOZ5ea

4463 followers within the first 48 hours, then to 8000 within the first month), where memories, opinions, discussions relating to the site and the possibility to reinstate the swimming pool unfolded. Public engagement on the social media page crystallized into an active campaign. The administrators of the page started a counter-consultation in order to collect 'official' data to present to the local council. This was publicized on the FB page on August 16th, and on the streets. The campaigners convened a flash-mob protest on the pool site on August 19th, which around 200 people attended. They also organized mainstream media coverage where the FB page campaign was further publicized. Residents also submitted online formal objections to the council proposal on the council website and wrote directly to the local mayor. The campaign was successful to the extent that the council withdrew its proposal on August 24th. Thereafter a number of offline meetings and *'critical friends events'* took place, where volunteers and professionals convened to probe prospects of restoring the pool as a community project. FoTOP initiated cooperation with the council in order to bring the project to fruition. The group produced their own planning proposal[2] to redevelop the pool, benefiting from voluntary and free professional help attained through the FoTOP page. The proposal was submitted on January 14th 2013 and the group is currently fundraising to make the swimming pool project a reality.

Our analysis covers the interactions taking place on the social media page. We focus primarily on the emergence of the social movement and campaign as it is played out on the FB page alone from the day the council proposal was published on the FoTOP page. Although FB interactions are just one part of the campaign, we look at how the movement was formed prominently through those interactions and the way social media become the site where socio-political, cultural and economic contexts are articulated and developed [10]. That is, the FB page is a site for the production of the social movement reflecting and enabling the offline actions of the movement through shared articulation of values, aims and achievements.

ANALYSIS

The data set was retrieved through the FB graph API and comprises of 620 parent-posts and 3987 comments (a total of 4607 digital objects) that were posted on the page between August 2012 and January 2013. We conducted qualitative analysis of the data set with a discourse analysis approach [38]. The empirical data were coded and three analytic clusters were inductively generated: 'memories and nostalgia for the future', 'nurturing a political potential', and 'activating the political'. In each area, we look at how the functionalities and architecture of FB were appropriated to make it a tool for political discussion and action. We report pseudonymised quotes from the data set to illustrate discursive processes in temporal order (confirmatory responses are omitted from this paper for lack of space). Through this we chart the process in which FoTOP formed as a social movement capable of political action.

[2]http://goo.gl/gPQgos

Memories and Nostalgia for the Future

The FB page functions as a repository of life moments - memories inviting others to remember, imagine and project their visions into the future. Old black and white photographs and old film footage of the swimming pool prompt stories and memories of the site when it was in use. As stories and memories accumulate, further stories and memories are posted in response to one another. These acts of remembrance sketch out moments of childhood, growing up, learning to swim, and social events that took place on the site: swimming galas, picnics with family members and neighbors. Here is a typical example.

"All of our neighbours used to meet in there we loved it ,even when i look at it now it stirs millions of childhood fun filled memories, we always sat in the same spot, and as soon as mam dozed off to sleep i used to get my three sisters and climb over onto the beach, it was all such a big adventure .best years of my life,xxxxx" (Julie , 08.14.12)

It is notable here how the poster creates a vivid reminiscence of the past, connecting the pool to their habits as a family, to their cheeky unruliness as children, and to its status as a meeting point for their neighborhood. This is underlined by quantifiers: *all* of the neighbors met at the pool, *millions* of memories are stirred. The glimpses of the past given by such vignettes enable other posters to respond with and intertwine their reminiscences. The posts take on semi-ritualistic properties, whereby posters deposit their memories one after the other. Consider the following pair:

"I remember going there with mam and dad and my 2 brothers I learnt to swim there." (Tom, 08.15.12)

"I learnt to swim in this pool as a little girl..." (Suzy, 08.15.12)

As a pair, the posts link up and intertextually reinforce each other, linking the end of the first with the beginning of the second to create a cultural ideal of children learning to swim with their families. In the terms of Ingold [17], the reminiscences invite the reader to fill the gaps, respond to and establish affinity with others. They operate as temporal windows across time and space: "tracing a path that others can follow, they offer guidance without specification" [17]. Indeed, it is their very under-specification, which allows people to associate their experience with other's stories and which gives the vignettes relevance across space and time. The stories and memories enable an imagining, which the readers and posters can project onto their own families and onto future generations.

"I have only known this pool in its current state yet got to see my dads photos and hear stories of it as a pool, I'd love to see this outdoor pool restored to its original use, so my kids get a chance to experience this pool – people don't need a sea side theatre – it wouldn't get used." (Fiona, 08.20.12)

This post indicates how the stories of the pool can elicit support from those who did not actually experience it in its heyday and how these stories give the basis for endeavoring action and resistance. However, posts questioned such acts of remembrance as unhelpful *"cosy nostalgia"*.

"Guys, we're talking about years ago now... Its never going to be like that again, its one of those things where they look at it as a statue, will never be taken down... Nor will it be changed, I would love for it, but the likelihood of it happening?" (John, 08.15.12)

The post here makes an appeal to a kind of "realism" to counter the imaginings based in reliving the past, by suggesting that returning to the past might be akin to creating something lifeless and fixed. However the discourse is carefully articulated so that the poster is presented as a fellow reader, as one of the "guys" who "would love for" things to be changed. Here those who deposit memories and remember are discerned from those who observe these enactments, and offer a discursive reflection about it. This acceptance is in turn challenged.

"Stick with it John *Yep... its not gonna be the same, but the council just want to concrete it over and turn it into a raised artificial beach. The cheapest solution to their problem. [...] if we dont give it a go... we'll kick ourselves" (Ben, admin, 08.16.12)*

As the FB page gathers more public attention, FB's multimodal functionalities begin to be seen as a way to build support. Photographs and links to related successful projects add to people's responses and reflections. The next extract entails the possibility that enhancing people's nostalgia will promote the campaign.

"[...] Also can photos be added to the group as I'm sure many people in the local area will have photos of the pool being used all those years ago. just might help to get more likes and help people feel nostalgic about it all?![...]" (Harriet, 08.19.12)

In this case posting photographs on the FB page is a means to *perform* nostalgia and persuade others to 'like' the page and support the cause. As photographs and narratives prompt envisioning and re-imagining of the pool, they come to intertwine with other arguments: links to official documents regarding heritage legislations; documents of council consultations that led to the current planning proposal; and successful open-air swimming pools. This 'meshwork' of rhetorical resources is used to inspire, validate and synthetize the "dream" in real-life contexts.

Nurturing a 'political potential'

Discussions in relation to the possibility of reinstating the pool unfolds, as well as explicit political discourses related to demands for activities for families and children, healthy lifestyles, effective economic regeneration of the area, and discourses expressing a general dissatisfaction with the current and previous council's management of the town. Various people bring their own socio-political issues to the page, recognizing the possibility of seeing their wishes and desires brought to fruition.

" [...] Try to not make it too expensive to get in please as it will put a lot of people off.... And the public who would of appreciated the most would be put off coming [...]" (Charlotte, 08.17.12)

"i am now of an age when it would be so good to have that pool [...] as with two active grandsons i could watch them every min and feel safe [..] while in the healthy sea air.[...]" (Sue, 08.15.12)

"Another thought...in the aftermath of the Olympics, the government supposedly want to encourage more sport, and it would be a great time to introduce a pool [...]. Also, by encouraging exercise in a fun way, people can lose weight and get healthy, so reducing costs to the NHS." (Thom, 08.16.12)

"I've been having a think about some of the issues that would make it difficult to turn it into a pool. I'm just stating them so we are all aware. [...] these are things that I don't know the solutions to [...]. But if you want to launch a credible opposition to the current plans you need to be clued up. Good luck as ever and see you on Sunday!" (Truman, 08.17.12)

Posters are discursively engaging with social, economic and political mechanisms at play in the construction of society. These initiate processes of discursive negotiation on how they should go about opposing the council proposal and restoring the pool. It is notable how the use of different pronouns, 'we', 'you', and 'they' indicate different modalities of participation and degrees of (devolution or retention) of responsibility in respect to the matter. While there is notable enthusiasm for the redevelopment of the pool, and posters connect this possibility to other political concerns, the discourse of the page is not unanimous.

"Am I the only person who thinks it is absolutely ridiculous to even consider restoring the pool!? let's start being sensible about this, rather than giving into childhood nostalgia!"(Nick, 08.15.12)

"It would definitely be better put to use as something else OTHER than a swimming pool. I have named a couple of ideas earlier. What else do you lot think it could be turned into?? [...] DEFFO NOT A FREEZING, OPEN AIR SWIMMING POOL, NO THANK YOU." (Rachel, 08.16.12)

The poster above links into arguments previously made. In this way she presents herself as a positive thinker, not to be rejected for contradicting the idea of redeveloping the pool. Indeed this prompted discussions on the feasibility and costs of developing a heated pool. However several posters were keen to formulate a sense of the majority view and recognised the impossibility of reaching unanimity.

"There are no public outdoor pools in the north east - plenty of skateboard parks and restaurants though - looking at the comments far more people for it than against it so the majority say its a great idea - the price of diplomacy is that not everyone can agree - but facts are facts. :-) BRING BACK THE POOL." (Gemma, 08.17.12)

FB's functionality whereby people can scroll down and read other's people posts, is used to show where opinions may incline. The display of different comments on the page is used to validate the formation of a collective whose aims are beyond simply dissenting the council proposal.

"surely the people who make the decisions about the whole issue should read all these comments, at the end of the day it is us the normal everyday family who would use this facility, an artificial beach is crazy. [...] Let us bring back a sense of community through fresh air and family enjoyment. Lets get behind this campaign" (Bob, 08.16.12)

The statement above, challenging and critiquing the authority, *"the people who make the decisions"*, is directed to the FoTOP page readers and posters to initiate a collective that politically validates people' wishes and opinions as they unfold. The continued collective discourse exposes social actors' realization of the efficacy of FB as a channel by which a variety of modalities of expressions close to their everyday socio-cultural lives can be voiced.

We have seen some very positive changes in our world by using social media [...] Let's not be misled by statements from our Council of what the majority what [want] *- it has been made clear today that the restoration of our open air pool is what we really want (Tina 16.08.12)*

"I am glad this page is here, finally the public gets a say" (Joe, 16.08.12)

The FoTOP page is presented as addressing the lack of dialogue with the local council and a subsequent lack of understanding of people's daily realities and wishes. With this emerging political consciousness, the FB page begins to represent, for these posters, a potentially impactful form of expression. The FB page offers a platform where discursive processes take place, but also where a community of support is formed, one that can make the pool a reality.

"Consider forgetting about the council having the funding or the resource (or vision...) to develop this as a serious project on their own [...] call and visit the outdoor pools who have established a sustainable model, figure out how much money you need, raise it from multiple interested parties, craic on and run it as a social enterprise. Consider it not least cos you're onto a winner." (Simon, 16.08.12)

"Now why didn't we think of that! Lets stop this farce of an application first and look at developing our own funding strategy, using the MASSIVE skill base that has surfaced on here over the last 48 hours!" (Ben, admin, 17.08.12)

The focus here shifts from the council to the political potentials of the emerging movement itself, which now comprises a constituency offering a range of voluntary and professional help to facilitate the pool redevelopment.

Activating the political

The rubbing together [16] of these discourses delineates a polyvocal collective, fostering a process of political consciousness by which posters become more aware of what they want and come to perceive the FoTOP page as a political space. In this regard, the FB functionality of 'likes' and comments are considered means to call the council proposal into question.

"according to the current application lodged with planning for the artificial beach, 5 public consultations have revealed that no-one actually wants the pool back!!! The more people we get on here... ie "likes" and especially positive comments will go along way to disproving this." (Ben, admin, 08.16.12)

Following the significant number of memories, opinions and discussions shared on the FoTOP page, the administrator proposes to collect opinions in a way that can to be used 'officially', as evidence to the local council.

"This FB page is a testament to how passionate you all are about the pool, and how you would like to see it used [...] However we need to turn all of this energy into something a little more useful, [...] I am going to set up a an online form which we'll use to collate responses and opinions in a way that can be used 'officially' and in a way that will have a little more credibility than a FB page..." (Ben, admin, 08.17.12)

The statement above marks an important moment in three ways. First, the administrator openly recognizes contributions on the FoTOP page. Second, by positioning his action (i.e. setting up an online form), as a means for collective action (i.e. "we'll use to collate responses and opinions") the admin starts an "official" campaign. Third, it heightens the credibility of the administration and the campaign through recognition of existing political power structures and "official" channels. The statement also illustrates how the administrator does not see FB as an "official" political tool. The campaign proceeds through a multidirectional approach to action. A flash-mob protest takes place on site on August 19th, providing mainstream media coverage. FB posters contribute to the group's "official" counter consultation, write to the local council and formally object the proposal. The campaign successfully forces the council to withdraw its proposal.

"so proud to be part of something so special [...] we don't need to resort to back handed tactics or violent protests to get what we want, sometimes just a bit of well mannered but firm objection (backed by 7000) can get the job done! Well done and keep up the good work, I hope we will find a solution that suits everyone!" (Lesley, 08.25.12)

The poster expresses here the close feeling developed in relation to the campaign and the formation of a collective striving towards the same aims. Being heard and obtaining their wishes (victory) are displayed as a rare achievement. The poster presents the quantified support of likes as one of the elements contributing to their 'victory'. However, the validity, lack of identifiable information and geographical provenance of 'likes' are questioned and so is the consensus relating to the redevelopment of the pool.

"Sorry to put a downer on your jubilation, but the number of people who like your fb page do not necessarily agree that the pool should be reinstated. Also, your group represents a minority of residents and therefore is a minority voice." (Sarah, 08.24.12)

"So what if everyone who likes this page is not a local [...]. Change can be brought about by and I think we have proved there is sufficient support to at least attempt this challenge for future generations." (Angela, 08.25.12)

The ability to bring together a large number of people into a common cause simply through 'liking' a page creates a previously unknown constituency. The mundane act, 'like', creates a strength and support that can be used politically by the group to endeavour the redevelopment of the pool. In this regard FB functionality of 'Insights' provides the administrators with detailed data analysis of the numbers of people, gender, age, location, language spoken, and sources of like (recommended, mobile, on page). This information is used to suggest that through 'friends of friends' the group is a much larger political 'constituency' than its actual membership. The knowledge of quantification of the admin allows him to paint a picture of the state of the campaign that without FB wouldn't be able to attain.

"our Facebook page data tells us that we actually have a grand total of 1,047,591 friends between us [...] Imagine what we could achieve with that many supporters [...] The fact that so many people are actively participating, talking, debating (and even just reading) demonstrates how much we all care about this [...]. But what's even more exciting is that you're all part of what could potentially be one of the North East's biggest and most exciting coastal regeneration projects in a long, long time. This is how history is made, folks [...]" (Ben, admin, 08.27.12)

The quantification of likes and FB Insight enables the admin to prompt excitement for the campaign and establishing a sense of support with FB others, whereby the page acts as bonding mechanism among people. For the page admin, contributors and 'likers' of the FoTOP page are now equally considered part of the campaign. However, opposing political purposes are continually expressed, diverging opinions intersect on the page exposing a multiple, polyvocal collective, in the Hauserian sense [16].

"Regeneration...I'm so confused as to why residents say no to the councils proposals... I live in Whitley Bay and it upsets me to see the area so run down, the shops empty. May be residents need to start shopping locally and supporting local business we all need to put extra effort into helping rebuild the towns, but it starts with us not the council." (Pauline, 08.30.12)

Here the poster disconnects with the campaigners' motivations for dissent. She places herself 'out' of the emergent movement, but 'in' the collective of residents who share the same town, initiating a reflective process in relation to a broader proactive attitude beyond the cause.

"the residents want something worthwhile to draw in visitors. The council just wanted to stick a cheap, meaningless plaster on an eye sore..." (Roy, 08.30.12)

"[...] This group does not exist simply to upset the council. [...] All I would do is ask you to read some of the posts/comments on this page and keep an open mind." (Gavin, 08.31.12)

The movement is here presented as a committed collective with a proactive and positive attitude and the posts on the page are used to engender public understanding on the matter. Indeed once rhetorical connections are made between intertwined personal recollections and opinions, criticism relating to the return of the pool, is countered. These connections enable a strong sense of a collectivity to emerge, a sense of 'we' and what is 'ours', even to the point that negative thinking should be discouraged.

"as a child I was one of hundreds of children who every summer enjoyed that pool [...] and without romantic dreams and the enthusiasm of these people a fantastic piece of our heritage will just be another eyesore on our beautiful coastline and remember it is not just the people of Tynemouth that remember and loved this pool so quite frankly if you cannot be positive about this perhaps it would be better to keep your opinion about this to a minimum" (Rob, 09.01.12)

As the campaigners endeavor into making the outdoor pool a reality, they also come to realize the 'dream' is a big challenge, one that requires self-belief and positive thinking and a degree of like-mindedness. The control of the administrator over the content of the timeline, and the comments that are allowed, is also significant.

"Hi P. constructive and/or critical feedback is always welcome. So, if you've got some in depth research, or inside/industry knowledge, or some solid financials/projections to back any of this up, or even if you know anyone who has, it would be great if you could share it/them with us. [...] you also now appear to be insulting and patronizing over 8,000 people while you're doing it. [...] Everyone else, you may want to read this: http://en.wikipedia.org/wiki/Troll_(Internet) I'll be quite happy to delete any comments that are solely designed to provoke, rather than offer constructive debate." (Ben, admin, 09.03.12)

Unconstructive provocations on the page are singled out. The administrator takes on an editorial control to ensure that both positive contributions and constructive debates are taking place providing 'acceptable parameters' of participation. For the next poster these are essential requirements for the group in order to face the task ahead.

"[...] I must say I feel very passionate in the quest to re-open what was once an extremely popular community facility. In the main the comments on this page have been extremely constructive and professional. At the end of the day we really do need to work in partnership with our local council, who [...] have very much listened to the 'community' and abandoned their original redevelopment plans. Now we have arrived at this point let's keep the momentum and work alongside our council to bring this dream back to a reality. [...] I am a professional businessperson who would be more than willing to offer some of my time to this worthy project" (Dale, 30.08.12)

The poster's reflection initiates the prospect and necessity to cooperate with the local council in order to realize the pool as a project. It is notable the use of pronoun "we" and "I" denoting the interplay between personal feelings and agency and collective agency in the attainment of common good. In the next post the potential realization of the pool project through cooperation with the council produces enthusiasm also in relation to other future prospects.

"my family are very excited about this proposal getting the full backing off NCC, hopefully we can all work together and try to rebuild Tynemouth [...]" (Claire, 01.17.13)

The poster here presents the possibility of rebuilding the town itself as a collective matter that can be achieved through dialogue and cooperation between residents and the local council.

DISCUSSION

The visibility of posters' memories and discussions facilitated the process of ascertaining what was meaningful among them. The interactions on the FB page became a prominent means by which a collective capable of affecting material change formed. The findings challenge the way we conceive of politics, exposing the possibilities for an understanding of the political as a matter of everyday life and embedded in ordinary people's mundane acts. In the following section, we discuss how HCI might conceive of: the ways we design to support social actors in discourse; how digital objects and functionalities can be appropriated into everyday political acts; and how everyday ways of doing and saying, including the use of digital systems, constitutes the political.

Collectivizing discourses

Hauser suggests that cultural memory relates to questions of power in two ways: how people draw resources from the past to shape their present and future; and how people resist attempts by others to distort and appropriate their memories and experiences [15]. The seemingly mundane acts of sharing memories and old photographs on the FB page may be considered as *implicit acts of political resistance* and *solidarity* as those memories were antithetical to the council's proposal. They synthesized the 'dream' and invited others to associate and join in acts of imagination, resistance and solidarity. Nostalgia, often understood as inert dwelling in the past, here is about the awakening of a set of values, inscribed in personal meanings, which collectively 'make' the outdoor pool. It is the exposure of individual and 'private' values that, allowing the discovery and recognition of commonalities, engenders the formation of collectives [30]. Studies in HCI and related fields have illustrated the benefits of shared subjective experiences and opinions for citizen activism and social movements [3, 2, 6, 30]. For instance [6] highlighted how crowd-sourced storytelling helped people with similar life experiences collectively define an issue and act upon it in a sensitive context. This study shows such processes extended to cultural expressions and memory in everyday talk.

Yet, as FB pages are open to anyone to contribute to, the polyvocality of diverging opinions around the issue was manifest. These engendered discursive and reflective processes towards the definition of the movement aims and a political consciousness with a broader sense of activism. Prior research has underlined the necessity for political spaces fostering discussion through the exposure of a multiplicity of perspectives in the quest of common solutions [8, 4]. However, we account for a tension between multiple perspectives and the attainment of material change. As the movement's aims are defined (the redevelopment of the pool), posters discourage negative contributions and the page admin suggests censoring what he considers unconstructive provocations. While issues of censorship of opinions limiting productive discourse were highlighted in other studies of political discourse in social media such as [25, 36], Hauser provides a nuanced reading for these behaviors. In his terms, these *'acts of gentle violence to conform'* exemplify the way, once relations are established in social movements through affiliation, a demand for commitment and allegiance to the aims of the movement is required [16]. Thus we recognize that *what collectivizes also excludes* in the struggle to affect material change. Future work might consider the ways in which the 'administration' of social media can go unseen, and design in relation to this by exposing the 'gentle violence' of political participation. Likewise, we might use digital systems to expose the ways citizens are excluded in traditional political systems.

Appropriation of Facebook functionalities

HCI research has explored social media systems as political actors offering broadcasting mechanisms to foster activism in health contexts [29] and as tool for citizen participation and protest organization in countries of political conflict [39, 40]. For instance, [39] indicated how people in Tunisia appropriated FB to turn a network of friends into a platform for political activism. In the current study the FB page is not just used to raise awareness on the issue and organize offline protests, but also as a forum for discussion, where public opinion develops. The FB page structure, facilitating the visibility of discourses, is used to generate further discussions, engender understanding, and indicate where people's values may lie. The page is appropriated as representation of the political will of the people assembled on it, as a living document of their wishes and opinions [21]. It is used as a display of resistance and support, and as an argument upon which the campaign and plans to produce a counter proposal to reinstate the pool, develop.

Qualitative (memories, opinions, visuals, links) and quantitative data (likes and quantification) work together to form the movement's discourses. In this respect the mundane act of pressing 'like', establishes a network of support and affiliations entailing consequences [10]. 'Likes' and corresponding quantification are appropriated as a means to distribute information, raise belief in the campaign and, as perceived by posters, apply pressure to authorities. While some posters and the page admin interpret 'likes' (and quantification) as valid expressions of support, others dispute such interpretation. It is the hidden articulations behind the 'likes' [20], their ambiguous and polysemic meaning, which allows their use as rhetorical means. Crucially important is not only data collection, but also its interpretation, i.e. the 'story' that is constructed with it. The work of 'likes' in this sense, is intertwined with the 'work' of memories and opinions displayed on the FB page.

Research into citizen science, [1, 26] highlights how data collection was seen as a way to promote activism, influence and apply pressure, but equally how it depended on interpretation. This study can lead to important questions in relation to data collection and its use. Future work might explore the affordances of online digital objects (i.e. beyond the like button) to make articulations more transparent and dynamic facilitating the visibility of discursive processes and assisting collective interpretation.

Everyday talk and politics

FB multimodal communication opens avenues for different modalities of cultural expression and participation, embracing some of the diversity of everyday talk. FB provides a space where people can formulate their cultural voice [13]. Cultural expressions of individuals who in their everyday life perform a multiplicity of roles (citizen, parent, tourist, shop keeper, etc.) comprise personal values and memories as well as economic and political discourses. The findings illustrate a complex notion of the 'civic', one in which personal stories, opinions and wishes blur with communitarian duties to achieve public good [24]. The study presents a challenge to the dichotomy between private and public, the social and the political. What is personally meaningful and what civic might be are contextual, contingent and dynamic affairs that are produced through discursive processes in any given social group [15].

In our findings, FB interactions and data play a crucial role in the formation of the movement, but are also perceived by the admin as not 'officially' valid, at least not alone. This exemplifies, in Hauser's model, the way social movements can be aware of forms of governance and regulation and have an intrinsic need to react to those in power [16]. However, Hauser suggests, unofficial and official discourses should not be conceived in opposition, but in dialogical relationship with one another, illustrating the diversity of ways social actors strive to achieve change. In this way we can begin to conceive of the political as existing across everyday life, rather than existing solely in official spaces allocated to it. Building on [10], the findings suggest an understanding of politics as the result of social actors' complex reflexive and discursive processes to negotiate and ascertain what is common and meaningful in order to affect the changes they wish in their everyday life. Thus political consciousness starts with the visibility and the recognition of everyday acts of resistance performed by ordinary people [16].

As technology becomes the site where socio-cultural, economic and political contexts evolve [10], we argue for the necessity for HCI to develop methods and sensitivities to recognize and increase our understanding of the impact of technology on social actors' everyday rhetorical forms. Our findings show how the FB page rendered different ways of 'seeing' the world (memories, opinions and 'likes') into 'objects' that could be seen, talked about and acted upon, which led to dynamic processes of negotiation among people. By interpreting 'likes' as merely mundane acts, and online activism in terms of individual moral cleansing [22], we are in danger of failing to understand the ability of social actors to display political resistance and the diversity of ways in which they participate in affecting change.

CONCLUSION

The FB page provided the visibility for cultural expressions (personal memories, stories, etc.) and opinions relating to the issue of the pool that sparked discussion and debate among posters. In the context of the planning proposal, these were ways of saying and doing, which allowed individuals, and the collective, to begin to shape the outdoor pool as a possible reality. The appropriation of FB's functionalities and exposure of the social actors' discursive processes had a central role in facilitating the construction of a common vision and the definition of the movement. Hauser's theoretical model of everyday talk [15, 16] can help us recognize agency and political resistance in everyday talk and the mechanisms at play in social movement formation in everyday politics. This opens up avenues for nuanced ways in which we can conceive of politics and activism in HCI. We call for future work to look more closely at the mechanisms at play in the politics of participation and power relations in social movements and design for and expose the nuances of complex discursive processes to action for change.

ACKNOWLEDGMENTS

This research was funded by the AHRC Creative Exchange Knowledge Exchange Hub and the EPSRC Digital Economy Theme Social Inclusion through the Digital Economy Research Hub (EP/G066019/1).

REFERENCES

1. Aoki, P.M., Honicky, R.J., Mainwaring, A., et al. A vehicle for research: using street sweepers to explore the landscape of environmental community action. In *Proc CHI 2009*, ACM (2009), 375-384.
2. Bennett, W.L. and Segerberg, A. Digital media and the personalization of collective action. *Information, Communication & Society 14*, 6 (2011), 770–799.
3. Bennett, W.L. and Segerberg, A. The Logic of Connective Action. *Information, Communication & Society 15*, 5 (2012), 739–768.
4. Björgvinsson, E., Ehn, P., and Hillgren, P.A. Participatory design and "democratizing innovation". In *Proc. PDC 2010*, ACM (2010), 41-50.
5. Dearden, A. and Light, A. Designing for e-Social Action An Application Taxonomy. In *Proc Design Reaserch Society Conference 2008*, Sheffield Hallam University (2008)
6. Dimond, J.P., Dye, M., Larose, D., and Bruckman, A.S. Hollaback !: The Role of Collective Storytelling Online in a Social Movement Organization, In *Proc. CSCW 2013,* ACM (2013), 477–489.

7. Disalvo, C., Maki, J., and Martin, N. MapMover : A Case Study of Design-Oriented Research into Collective Expression and Constructed Publics. In *Proc. CHI 2007,* ACM (2007), 1249–1252.
8. Disalvo, C., Nourbakhsh, I., Holstius, D., Akin, A., and Louw, M. The neighborhood networks project: a case study of critical engagement and creative expression through participatory design, In *Proc. PDC 2008*, ACM (2008), 41-50.
9. DiSalvo, C. *Adversarial Design (Design Thinking, Design Theory)*. The MIT Press, 2012.
10. Dourish, P. HCI and environmental sustainability: the politics of design and the design of politics, In *Proc. DIS 2010*, ACM(2010), 1-10.
11. Foucault, M. *The Archeology of knowledge*. Tavistock, 1972.
12. Foucault, M. *Power/Knowledge : Selected interviews and selected writings 1972-1977*. C.Gordon Edition, New York: Harvester WheatSheaf, 1980.
13. Fraser, N. Rethinking the public sphere: a contribution to the critique of actually existing democracy. *Social Text* 25-26, (1990), 56–80
14. Halpern, D. and Gibbs, J. Social media as a catalyst for online deliberation? Exploring the affordances of Facebook and YouTube for political expression. *Computers in Human Behavior* 29, 3, (2013), 1159–1168
15. Hauser, G.A. *Vernacular voices: the rhetoric of publics and public spheres*. University of South Carolina Press, 1999.
16. Hauser, G., A., McClellan, D., E. Vernacular Rhetoric and Social Movements: Performances of Resistance in the Rhetoric of the Everyday. In Stevens, Mckenzie, S. and Malesh,P., *Active voices : composing a rhetoric for social movements*, SUNY Press, 2010.
17. Ingold, T. *Lines : A Brief History*, Routledge, 2007.
18. Kuznetsov, S., Paulos, E., and Gross, M. WallBots: interactive wall-crawling robots in the hands of public artists and political activists. In *Proc DIS 2010*, ACM (2010), 208–217.
19. Kuznetsov, S. and Paulos, E. HCI , Politics and the city : engaging with urban grassroots movements for reflection and action. *Ext. Abtracts CHI 2011*, ACM (2011), 2409-2412.
20. Langlois, G. and Elmer, G. The research politics of social media platforms. *Culture Machine 14*, (2013), 1–17
21. Latour, B., Weibel,P. *Making Things Public: Athmosphere of Democracy*, MIT Press, 2005.
22. Lee, Y.-H. and Hsieh, G. Does slacktivism hurt activism?: the effects of moral balancing and consistency in online activism. In *Proc. CHI 2013*, ACM (2013), 811-820.
23. Light, A. The Unit of Analysis in Understanding the Politics of Participatory Practice, In *Proc PDC 2010*, ACM (2010), 183-186.
24. Mainsah, H. and Morrison, A. Social media, design and civic engagement by youth: a cultural view. In *Proc. PDC 2012*, ACM (2012), 1-9.
25. Mascaro, C.M. and Goggins, S.P. Brewing up citizen engagement: the coffee party on facebook. In *Proc. C&T 2011*, ACM (2011), 11-20.
26. Massung, E., Coyle, D., Cater, K.F., et al. Using crowdsourcing to support pro-environmental community activism. In *Proc. CHI 2013,* ACM (2013), 371–380
27. McCafferty, D. Activism vs. slacktivism. *Communications ACM* 54, 12 (2011), 17-19.
28. Monroy-Hernández, A., Farnham, S., Kiciman,E., et al. Smart societies: from citizens as sensors to collective action, *Interactions 20, 4* (2013), 16–19.
29. Parker, A., Kantroo, V., Lee, H.R., et al. Health promotion as activism: building community capacity to effect social change. In *Proc CHI 2012*, ACM, (2012), 99–108.
30. Pietrucci, P. Poetic publics: agency and rhetorics of “netroots” activism in post-earthquake L ' Aquila, *The Journal of Community Informatics* 6, 3 (2013), 1–13.
31. Rotman, D., Vieweg, S., Yardi, S., et al. From slacktivism to activism: participatory culture in the age of social media. In *Proc CHI 2011,* ACM (2011), 819–822.
32. Saeed, S., Rohde, M., and Wulf, V. Analyzing political activists' organization practices: findings from a long term case study of the european social forum. *CSCW 20*, 4-5 (2011), 265–304.
33. Segerberg, A. and Bennett, W.L. Social Media and the Organization of Collective Action: Using Twitter to Explore the Ecologies of Two Climate Change Protests. *The Communication Review 14*, 3 (2011), 197–215.
34. Tarrow, S. *Power in Movement*, Cambridge University Press, 1994.
35. Tayebi, A. Planning activism: using social media to claim marginalized citizens' right to the city. *Cities 32*, (2013), 88–93
36. Uldam, J. and Askanius, T. Online civic cultures: debating climate change activism on youtube. *International Journal of Communication 7*, (2013), 1185–1204.
37. Varnelis, K. *Networked Publics*. The MIT Press, 2008
38. Wodak, R., Krzyzanowski, M. *Qualitative Discourse Analysis in the Social Sciences*, Palgrave Macmillan Press, 2008.
39. Wulf, V., Aal, K., Ktesh, I.A., et al. Fighting against the wall: social media use by political activists in a palestinian village, In *Proc CHI 2013,* ACM (2013), 1979–1988
40. Wulf, V., Misaki, K., Atam, M., et al. 'On the ground' in Sidi Bouzid: investigating social media use during the tunisian revolution, In *Proc CSCW 2013*, ACM (2013), 1409–141.

Shared Values/Conflicting Logics: Working Around E-Government Systems

Amy Voida[1], Lynn Dombrowski[2], Gillian R. Hayes[2] & Melissa Mazmanian[2]

[1]School of Informatics and Computing
Indiana University, IUPUI
amyvoida@iupui.edu

[2]Department of Informatics
University of California, Irvine
{ldombrow, hayesg, mmazmani}@uci.edu

ABSTRACT

In this paper, we describe results from fieldwork conducted at a social services site where the workers evaluate citizens' applications for food and medical assistance submitted via an e-government system. These results suggest value tensions that result—not from different stakeholders with different values—but from differences among how stakeholders enact the same shared value in practice. In the remainder of this paper, we unpack the distinct and conflicting interpretations or logics of three shared values—efficiency, access, and education. In particular, we analyze what happens when social services workers have ideas about what it means to expand access, increase efficiency, and educate the public that conflict with the logics embedded in the e-government system. By distinguishing between overarching values and specific logics, we provide an analytic framework for exploring value tensions as values are enacted in practice.

Author Keywords

E-government; Social Services; Values

ACM Classification Keywords

H.5.3. [Information Interfaces and Presentation]: Group and Organization Interfaces—Computer-supported cooperative work

INTRODUCTION

All technology has politics [32]. E-government systems—technology used to engage citizens and support public sector operations and services [4]—are even more explicitly political. They reflect values from the very political context in which they are borne: the values of the lobbyists and advocates who frame narratives and influence opinions about these technologies; the values of the elected officials who vote on whether or not these technologies should receive funding; the values of the many bureaucrats who determine in what contexts the technologies will be used, for what kinds of end-users the technologies will be designed, against what criteria they should be evaluated, and what organizations will design and mange these technologies; and the values of the workers and citizens who engage with these technologies and enact values through use and non-use.

CHI 2014, April 26 - May 01 2014, Toronto, ON, Canada

ACM 978-1-4503-2473-1/14/04...$15.00.
http://dx.doi.org/10.1145/2556288.2556971

It should come as no surprise, then, that these many values can be in conflict—surfacing, for example, in debates over whether e-government systems should be designed to support managerial values of efficiency and cost-effectiveness or to foster democratic values, such as equality or engagement (e.g., [4, 6, 13]). Human–computer interaction researchers have been strong advocates for engaging with a breadth of stakeholders and negotiating value conflicts in situations such as these (e.g., [19]). To the extent that values of import can be identified in advance of or in parallel to design—whether through the use of value-sensitive frameworks and heuristics (e.g., [8]) or fieldwork (e.g., [1, 17])—these methods often enable value tensions to be anticipated and negotiated in ways that have shown promise in enabling more empathic technology design. However, research has yet to explore the possibility that even when core values align, tensions may still exist about how to achieve desired ends, or what these values mean in practice.

In this research, we unpack data from fieldwork conducted at a social services site where the workers evaluate citizens' applications for food and medical assistance submitted via an e-government system. Given the political nature of this field site, we were surprised at the extent to which core values are, in fact, aligned. Social services workers expressed very similar goals and values to those reflected in the e-government system. Yet values tensions still exist—a result of different interpretations or logics about these shared values and about how they are best achieved in practice. In the remainder of this paper, we unpack the distinct and conflicting interpretations or logics of three shared values—*efficiency*, *access*, and *education*. In particular, we analyze the impact on work practices and client relationships when social services workers have ideas about what it means to expand access, increase efficiency and educate the public that conflict with the logics embedded in the e-government system.

By distinguishing between overarching values and specific logics, we provide an analytic framework for exploring values tensions as values are enacted in practice. We argue that research engaged with values and design will need to consider not only the potentially differing values across stakeholders but also the various assumptions about, implications of, and orientations towards how to put values into practice to fully engage with and address values tensions.

THE VALUES OF E-GOVERNMENT

A growing subset of the e-government research literature engages explicitly with the values embodied in and fostered by e-government systems (e.g., [4, 6, 13]). At the coarsest level of granularity, discourses about e-government systems often reflect the highly value-laden nature of the political context in which they have arisen [31]. Conservative discourses, for example, tend to emphasize values of cost savings and efficiency while liberal discourses tend to reflect values of equality—fostering universal access or closing the digital divide. Additional discourses, which often reflect conflicting values as well, include discussions about democratic participation, education, organizational reform, dependency, consumerism, and information security, among others (e.g., [14, 30, 33]). Three values, in particular, are foregrounded prominently in the e-government literature and are most salient to our own research—access, efficiency, and education.

The value of *access* is most commonly invoked in reference to the design and evaluation of new service channels—new media that are used to enable access to governmental services (e.g., [23, 24]). Access is a multi-faceted construct that encompasses the physical availability of information and communication technologies [25] as well as the 'how to' skills that are necessary to make those technologies useful [2, 21]. Access is also understood to require social support, whether through public awareness of the availability and relevance of these technologies [10] or through the help of local intermediaries assisting with access [7]. Generally, issues of access have been central to researchers interested in reducing the digital divide (e.g., [2, 21]).

The value of *efficiency* is most commonly invoked as a rallying cry to encourage public administration to become more streamlined and cost-effective (e.g., [13]). Heeks, for example, argues that information systems make governments more efficient by cutting processing costs and enabling strategic connections across and within governmental agencies [12]. Efficiency is advocated most strongly by proponents of New Public Management, a style of public administration that applies private sector values to the management of public sector services (e.g., [13]). While such an emphasis may be prudent, there are significant concerns that private sector values alone may be too limited a basis for the future of e-government [4, 6]. Researchers arguing for a "public value" perspective, in contrast, argue that governmental information systems should support values and policy goals that come from the public [6]. This perspective reflects a more situated understanding of values, derived within a given sociotechnical context [18].

Within the literature on e-government systems, the value of *education* is typically foregrounded in discussions about the extent to which these systems provide citizens with information about governmental operations and services [22]. The value of education can also be seen in efforts to support citizen reflection on political issues, efforts aimed toward fostering democratic dialogue [14] and civic participation [26].

Beyond the discussion of individual values, the field of e-government has also engaged in broader debates over which values, whose values, and whether or not a conversation about 'values' is helpful in moving the domain forward. West, for example, argues that the politicization of e-government is problematic as it stands to limit funding [31]. He contends that if these systems are foregrounded as being solely technical and apolitical, the future of e-government is less apt to stall out in political quagmire. However pragmatic this perspective may be, it conflicts with a legacy of research in science and technology studies and human–computer interaction asserting that all technology is political; all technology embodies some values and not others (e.g., [1, 8, 32]).

There are numerous vigorous dialogues and debates related to values within both the e-government and human–computer interaction literature. Nevertheless, there are some resonances between some of the research in each domain. Researchers from both domains, for example, have asserted the need for a more situated understanding of values [3, 6, 17]. And researchers from both domains have also come to question whose values predominate (e.g., [1, 6, 16, 27]).

In both the e-government and the human–computer interaction literature, much of the emphasis has been on identifying the values in play. When researchers in either domain unpack values tensions, they refer to conflicts between different values held by different stakeholders. We extend these bodies of research to describe values tensions that arise even when the values in play *have* been successfully identified and even when those values are *not* conflicting or contested. We provide empirical evidence to demonstrate that not only do we need to understand values as situated in and contingent upon a particular sociotechnical context, but in addition, any given value has to be understood as capable of being enacted in multiple, conflicting ways within that context.

METHOD

We carried out qualitative fieldwork at the social services office responsible for processing all of the applications that are submitted via an online e-government system by residents of one California county. We interviewed 12 participants within the first year of the new system's deployment and analyzed the data iteratively and inductively.

Research Context

The Mail-In Center

We undertook this research at the social services office responsible for processing all applications that are submitted by residents of one California county via the e-government system, Benefits CalWIN. This county is 1 of 58 counties in California and services a population of ~3 million residents. Like many across the state, this county suffers from an underutilization of social services; citizens are not receiving the help for which they are legally entitled. The rollout of a public-facing online application system is seen by stakeholders—including government employees and community-based advocates—as a key investment in increasing participation.

In the county in which we carried out this research, applications submitted online are processed at the "Mail-In Center." This name reflects a long-standing distinction between two types of offices where applications are processed: (1) the open-to-the-public social services offices, staffed by people trained to serve clients who travel to the office and apply in a face-to-face meeting and (2) the Mail-In Center, staffed by people trained to serve clients who apply remotely (historically, through the mail via paper-based forms). In addition to processing 17 different paper-based applications, workers at the Mail-In Center now also process applications submitted via two online systems—Benefits CalWIN, the public-facing web portal, and One-e-App, a system designed for certified ombudsmen at community-based organizations to submit applications on clients' behalf. In this research, we have focused on the use of Benefits CalWIN. One-e-App has very different affordances and involves additional stakeholders and additional politics that are beyond the scope of this paper.

Benefits CalWIN

Benefits CalWIN is the public-facing online portal for individuals and families to apply for government-subsidized social services, including nutrition, health, and financial assistance (CalFresh, Medi-Cal, and CalWorks). Application data submitted via Benefits CalWIN is imported directly into the social services' internal database, through which the eligibility determination process for each social service is managed.

A confluence of three events is key to understanding the context of work and use of Benefits CalWIN at the time of this study:

- *Rollout of Benefits CalWIN.* Benefits CalWIN was launched in January 2011 and had been in use for 4 months prior to our first interview and for 12 months prior to the remainder of our interviews (see the timeline for data collection below).
- *Departmental Hiring Freeze.* Because of the tenuous economic situation in the state prior to and during this study, the Mail-In Center had been operating under a hiring freeze for several years. Managing the increased workload of the remaining employees was a key concern, as was ensuring that clients were receiving assistance within a mandated timeframe.
- *Increase in the Number of Applications.* The recession works as a double-edged sword for social services. At the same time that the Mail-In Center was prevented from hiring additional staff, the demand for social services spiked. This increase in the number of applications occurred during the same timeframe in which Benefits CalWIN was rolled out. During this timeframe, one administrator cited a 50% increase in the number of applications received; another administrator verified that there was a 40% increase in the county beneficiaries pool.

Participants & Data Collection

Data collection at this field site began in May 2011 when one researcher interviewed a social services administrator who oversees more than 1400 staff members distributed among 7 different offices. This interview lasted 90 minutes and provided a high-level orientation to the social services organization and their deployment of the e-government system, Benefits CalWIN. This interview also enabled us to build rapport and gain entre at the Mail-In Center.

Eight months after that initial interview, in January 2012, an administrator at the Mail-In Center organized a three-day visit for one researcher. During that visit, the researcher interviewed 11 additional social services workers for one hour each. Because of concerns about employee workload, interviews were limited in duration so as not to interfere with the functioning of the center. Due to regulations about the privacy of client data, the researcher was not able to tour employee workspaces or observe their use of any of the systems they use to carry out their work. All interviews were conducted in the center's conference room.

The 11 additional interviewees represented five different positions in the organizational hierarchy, from the on-site manager who directs the center, to supervisors in multiple middle management positions, and eligibility technicians who process the social services applications and determine eligibility. We also interviewed an administrator responsible for implementing social services policy mandates within the county. With the permission of informants, interviews were audio recorded and transcribed.

To protect anonymity, we refer to participants as either being eligibility technicians (a class of six individuals with eligibility technician as their job title) or administrators (an aggregate class of six individuals including directors, managers, and supervisors). We also refer to all participants with female pseudonyms to protect the anonymity of the small number of male informants in this study (one eligibility technician and one administrator).

Data Analysis

Because of the fixed and intensive period of interviews, all data analysis occurred after data collection. We conducted our data analysis iteratively and inductively using open coding, memoing and affinity diagramming techniques (e.g., [5]). In our first round of data analysis, we primarily tried to disentangle the various practices associated with different job descriptions and phases of the application (intake) process. In our second round of data analysis, we began to draw out themes related to the goals of the participants' work and the frustrations they experienced processing applications submitted through the online system. Subsequent rounds of data analysis and re-engagement with the research literature helped us to shift our framing from goals to values and to tease apart the different and sometimes conflicting logics for enacting these values present within the sociotechnical system.

SHARED VALUES/CONFLICTING LOGICS

In our interviews with social services workers and through our exploration of the Benefits CalWIN system, we found that the same values discussed in the e-government literature—*access*, *efficiency*, and *education*—were key values in our research context, as well. These values manifest through the ways in which social services workers describe their jobs, in general, and their interactions with clients, in particular. These values are even corroborated by language on the front page of the Benefits CalWIN website, which promises access ("apply"), efficiency ("fast and easy"), and education ("learn about" and "get more information") [Fig. 1].

Given that the social services workers and the e-government system appear to share the same set of core values, we were initially surprised by the amount of frustration voiced by the informants in this research. A sizable amount of research in values and design, after all, emphasizes the identification of shared values as being key to successful technology adoption (e.g., [19]). However, in examining the frustrations that came up repeatedly in interviews, we discovered significant tensions between how the social services workers understand each of these values and how the system reflects these same values.

In this paper, we discuss the ways in which the values of *access*, *efficiency* and *education* are enacted in the sociotechnical system through two distinct logics—the logics of the system and the logics of the social services workers. By "logics of the system" we refer to how the infrastructure and interface of the system direct lines of action and engagement, suggesting how values are instantiated in the technology[1]. By "logics of the social services workers" we refer to how people in various positions within the organization think about values and how they describe putting those values into practice[2]. By articulating these distinct and often conflicting logics we are able to locate many of the social service workers' frustrations at the place where these logics fail to align.

Figure 1. The client portal to Benefits CalWIN

Expanding Access

Both the social services workers and Benefits CalWIN evidence a value for expanding access, although how access is operationalized differs. The online system supports clients' 'getting in the door,' providing twenty-four hour web access for individuals to submit an initial application. Yet, the social services workers understand access more broadly; they describe an understanding of access that doesn't stop once the initial application has been submitted. Social services workers want to support applicants through the entire intake process and are frustrated by the ways in which the online system hampers their efforts.

Benefits CalWIN provides an additional "access point" to apply for social services. Social services workers recognize that an online portal reduces many of the barriers for individuals and families to submit applications.

> *Benefits CalWIN is another resource to allow our population to utilize a variety of access points. In the traditional method you must walk in ... [which] is not effective for all populations and demographics.... Truly successful access means a variety of port methods based on an individual comfort zone.* (Gloria, Administrator)

> *It gives people more opportunities of how to apply, because I think a lot of people can be really hurting and hungry and*

---

[1] These values may have been intentional or unintentional consequences of the design process.

[2] We present our results under categorical labels that reflect the perspective of our informants—they perceive their values and goals to be their own and to be distinct from that of the system. However, we want to be clear that we believe all values are enacted within complex sociotechnical systems. To be more precise, albeit linguistically unwieldy, "logics of the social services workers" are their logics as influenced by their use of the system and through their interactions with clients who also use the system. The "logics of the system" are the logics (a) that the social service workers attribute to the system through their experiences working with clients who have used the system and (b) that we have been able to verify through an analysis of the features of the public-facing online portal.

so forth and just not want to come into the office. (Alicia, Eligibility Technician)

On the website, applicants are advised that they can "complete an application" online and that the "process may take 10 to 20 minutes." CalFresh applicants are also advised that they "have the right to submit an application with just your name, address and signature." The logic of the system, then, suggests that access is operationalized as 'getting in the door'—submitting an initial application.

In contrast, the workers at the Mail-In Center view access as both 'getting in the door' *and* as navigating the remainder of the application (intake) process. From this perspective, the system's logic of access is problematically incomplete.

'Getting in the Door'

Social services workers have experienced numerous ways that Benefits CalWIN expands access through a reduction in the travel and opportunity costs associated with getting to the social services office.

> *We have had applications come in at 2am, 3am, 5am.... People that are nurses that come home at 2am and are wide-awake. They are not making enough money, so they apply at 2 in the morning. We know because it shows the date and time when they submit the application.* (Sara, Administrator)

> *Many of our clients, the reason they do it online is because they don't want to deal with our offices, and I don't blame them.... because our offices are pretty hairy. Sometimes even 'out the door' hairy.* (Alicia, Eligibility Technician)

Benefits CalWIN is also viewed as supporting the value of access by reducing the stigma that might be associated with being seen applying for social services in person.

> *This is not traditionally someone who would have accessed our services. This is where a little bit of hesitancy of walking into social services offices... and that stigma that they feel that it adds to it.... So we are seeing that population take advantage of the technology to get their family's needs met but still maintain the perceived anonymity they desire.* (Gloria, Administrator)

Benefits CalWIN enables individuals to apply for multiple social services at once, and many of the Mail-In Center's eligibility technicians have been trained to process applications for multiple social services. In contrast, when individuals apply for social services via most other methods, they must submit a separate application for each social service, even if all of the applications are submitted as part of one face-to-face visit. Each application requires redundant information, partially overlapping documentation, and, sometimes, different eligibility technicians to process the application.

> *That's one of the benefits of this, by doing it electronically, it also adds the potential of them getting screened and evaluated for CalFresh, where in the past, if they were only doing MediCal, and that's it, they are out the door, you are done. So that means the client, after they get out, if they get out, they have to come back in and submit another application to apply. So now, they are doing it simultaneously.* (Ruby, Administrator)

> *I'd like to see a universal approach to the families' needs.... I think Benefits CalWIN is definitely an example of that. It's a one-stop screening tool that allows a family to sort of pre-assess whether they may be eligible, and they can apply for everything that they are potentially eligible for at one time. It's a one-stop tool. I think the more we remove the individual barriers that each individual program may have, the easier it is for access.* (Gloria, Administrator)

The social services workers acknowledge certain up-front advantages offered by Benefits CalWIN—the system's logic of access expands clients' ability to 'get in the door' and submit an initial application. However, this same logic also undermines social services' attempts to assist clients in navigating the entire application and intake process.

Navigating the Intake Process

When clients apply for social services via Benefits CalWIN, they are required to submit basic information online, including their name and address. However, this initial application is merely the beginning of a multi-phase "intake" process. After the applications have been assigned to eligibility technicians at the Mail-In Center, those eligibility technicians call the applicants for a phone interview that serves several important functions. First, it allows the eligibility technician to clarify any ambiguous information that was submitted online and to acquire any additional information that might be needed. The interview also allows the eligibility technicians to advise applicants of any additional documentation they will need to provide, to educate applicants about their rights and responsibilities, and to set expectations for continuing interactions with social services. After the interview, the applicant and eligibility technician typically coordinate the exchange of any additional documentation that may be needed and are in contact to address any remaining questions that the applicant might have.

Benefits CalWIN allows people to submit applications with minimal information—a small subset of the information that will be needed eventually. Although social services workers understand the multi-phase nature of the intake process, they have found that clients who apply online have different expectations of the process and frequently think they are "done" once they have clicked the submit button.

> *I think they just go online, and they just think that they don't have to do anything else. Because maybe they don't know.... This is my thinking: they just go online and don't even give you the right phone number sometimes.... And they are just thinking: "Okay, I am done. I am just going to have to wait for my benefits."* (Ana, Eligibility Technician)

> *They think it is easier: "Oh, I will just do the application and that will be it." But it's more than... just doing an application online.* (Selena, Eligibility Technician)

Once eligibility technicians have received applicants' initial information, they must ensure that there is appropriate justification for making an eligibility decision. None of the informants in this research reported ever having received a Benefits CalWIN application containing all of the information and documentation required for them to actually verify eligibility.

> *When you go public access... the majority [of applications] do not come in complete.* (Gloria, Administrator)

> *One that is completely filled out? We never have any of those. We can have all the questions answered, but... we never have any where all the documents are there.* (Alicia, Eligibility Technician)

> *The system allows them to skip questions and even skip important questions.... It's really not beneficial to not trouble them because in the end, we are going to have to trouble them anyway because we have certain regulations and information that we need. So if they skip those questions, all it does is make our interview longer and the letters we write to them longer, the checklist that we write to them longer."* (Alicia, Eligibility Technician)

So while in most cases, the online application does not require applicants to enter all of the necessary information, in some instances, the system does not even request it.

> *The application is not comprehensive. It doesn't have everything we need. It doesn't ask for vehicles. It doesn't ask for the absent parent. We have a lot of single parents, and it does not ask for that information... but it is still stuff that the workers need to enter, so they are doing all this manually.* (Raquel, Administrator)

Here, the logic of the system embodies the value of access by reducing the initial informational overhead for applicants, but in doing so, leads applicants to have an incomplete understanding of and incorrect expectations about the end-to-end application process. Ambiguity about what information is actually needed to complete the intake process creates tensions between eligibility technicians and applicants. For example, one eligibility technician reported talking to an applicant who became somewhat confrontational after being asked to provide additional information.

> *You try to help them.... "No problem, I just need this from you." "Why do you need that?" "Because we need to, you know, we have your income here, and you have to provide.... That's how it is."* (Ana, Eligibility Technician)

Social services workers find themselves frustrated by the system's logic that does not make explicit what information is and is not required to complete the eligibility determination process fully or require applicants to enter all of the requisite information. In turn, the social services workers report being hampered in their efforts to support applicants through all phases of the intake process.

Increasing Efficiency

Both the social services workers and Benefits CalWIN demonstrate a priority of increasing efficiency. However, like access, the ways in which efficiency is understood by the workers and operationalized by the system differ. If efficiency is about processing information as quickly and easily as possible to approve benefits for eligible applicants, it requires getting information both *quickly* and *accurately*. However, Benefits CalWIN appears to privilege speed over accuracy, reflecting an assumption that information is objective and that data entry can unproblematically be outsourced to clients. Social services workers, left to clear up all the mistakes and confusion, value accuracy, as well, and saw the need for more dialogic interaction to help get the information "right."

Transferring Objective Information

Benefits CalWIN fosters efficiency through the transfer of so-called 'objective information' from the applicant to the social services worker. Applications submitted via Benefits CalWIN appear in the Mail-In Center's virtual queue, and any information that clients enter or documents that they upload are accessible to social services' staff.

> *Once the client has punched in their information, we have a way of transposing all the information in the system, so it's less work for us... we don't have to punch in the last name or social security, the system will automatically do it for us. I think that for us, it cuts time for us to process.* (Jada, Eligibility Technician)

> *You have more information, meaning they are filling out more information from the get go, you have where they were working, where they have checking accounts, banking accounts, whatever it is that their situation is. If they fill it out, I know it.* (Paula, Administrator)

Yet, these workers report that, overall, applications submitted via Benefits CalWIN take *longer* to complete than do their in-person counterparts. For social services workers, then, efficiency does not merely relate to the speed of data entry. Efficiency refers to the ease and expediency with which all of the information and documentation can be obtained and verified. And for the social services workers, any initial benefits from offloading data entry to the client are thwarted by the drawn-out and frustrating process of trying to remotely obtain and verify all this information.

> *I am going to say it doubles the difficulty of our job. At least doubles it. And not only that, but it takes longer. Because it takes longer for us to get it to them and it takes longer for them to get things back to us. So it really complicates the whole process.* (Alicia, Eligibility Technician)

> *It's just more work because... they are online so they don't have to come in and they think it is just going to be faster for them to be approved there.... But we still have to do the interview; we still have to send the letters and get the verifications. So, it's a little bit more work for us.* (Selena, Eligibility Technician)

A Dialogic Process to Get it "Right"

Participants recounted numerous ways that Benefits CalWIN undermines the efficiency of the intake process, from failing to error-check data to stopping short of supporting the kind of synchronous and asynchronous communication that makes up a significant part of the intake process. Eligibility technicians rely on the dialogic interview process to verify much of the information that is entered via Benefits CalWIN.

> *And a lot of people... they fill it in and don't do it right. That's why we do the interviews. We call them and verify everything.* (Selena, Eligibility Technician)

> *Yesterday, a client didn't put on her social [security number, a unique identifier in the United States] on there, but her birth date was on there. The birth date and the last name matched a different record with a social. So, do we use that or not? I wasn't able to contact the client so we are going to try and appreg it [register the application] without [the social security number]... and just try to let it get going that way.... Those questions are not answered as quickly as... if the client was standing there.* (Paula, Administrator)

> *Back in the day, I remember getting up to 10 applications a day, but it was so much easier, because I had the client in front of me where if I didn't understand a question or an answer I could easily clarify [with the client]. Where these workers don't have that advantage.* (Raquel, Administrator)

In addition to having to verify information that may or may not have been entered correctly, eligibility technicians also have to verify information submitted for questions that are frequently misinterpreted by clients. For example:

> *If the client goes online and he sees the question "How much do you make?" they go by the net [instead of gross], right?... They don't know. You can't assume that they are doing it right, so you have to talk to them.* (Ana, Eligibility Technician)

However, one of the biggest impediments to the efficiency of the intake process is the extreme difficulty that eligibility technicians report in contacting clients for the follow-up interview. To protect the privacy of client data, follow-up communication must happen via phone, postal mail, or in person. Eligibility technicians attempt to contact applicants first via phone, but the synchronous nature and unpredictable contexts of phone communication make connecting challenging, particularly with the ubiquitousness of mobile devices.

> *Now with everyone having cell phones, I hear some workers tell me that, gosh, they call their clients while they are driving, or they are picking up their kids, and they don't want to ask, "Well, do you have time for an interview?".... Our best time to contact the client is not necessarily their [best] time even though [the contact information they entered in the system] says "Call me between this time and this time." And even when you do they are in the middle of something.... You know life happens, it happens to all of us. I think that can be challenging too, for our workers, and they are like: "We have deadlines. When am I going to get this done?" But they feel bad for the client, too.* (Raquel, Administrator)

> *Those kinds of things are always challenging because we don't have the luxury of the client just sitting there in the office for an hour waiting for us to ask them for information. They are out, at school, at work... so you have limited time to try to call them or talk to them, and then is it a place where I can talk to you?* (Paula, Administrator)

If the eligibility technicians are unable to connect with applicants via phone, they are forced to resort to postal mail, which draws out the intake process and undermines the initial efficiencies of an online system.

> *Sometimes it is kind of frustrating, because if you can't get ahold of the client, you have to do everything by paper, pretty much. Because if I can't talk to them, I can't process the application. We can't do that. We have to talk to someone. So, you have to send the appointment letter. Sometimes they don't respond to the appointment letter. So, you have to send the second one... And if they do not respond after 30 days, you deny the case. If you do get ahold of the client, pretty much sometimes or most of the time, you have to make the appointment to come in for face-to-face. So in my opinion... it's double work.* (Ana, Eligibility Technician)

In addition, certain documentation must be handled on paper, by fax, or in person, even if the applicant initially applies online. In some cases, an application that is initiated expediently online can stall awaiting follow-up paperwork.

> *They are not willing to give you the information or mail it in or fax it in.... You call them, say, "We need this and this to evaluate. I can't evaluate if I don't have your income, and it's based on income so I need something." So they say they will send it to me and I never get anything. If the 30th day comes and we haven't received anything, we have to deny the case.* (Selena, Eligibility Technician)

> *It is all fantastical online. They don't have to go to the office, fine. But* still *we are mandated to give them information that is in hard paper: example the voter registration form, forms that say, "I agree with the rules of using the electronic card." The signature at the end of the form saying, "I agree with what I have reported," which is this income, people in the home, et cetera.... So we have still this exchange of paperwork although some can be scanned, but there are things that we have to send to them that they have to sign and send to us. There is nothing that we can do yet electronically.* (Sonia, Administrator).

The logic of the system, then, appears to instantiate a view of efficiency that is limited to enabling clients to enter their application information online. But this view conflicts with the logic of the social services workers, who understand efficiency to require not just the entry of information but the provision of information that is "right" and verifiable so that they and/or the system can compute an eligibility determination. Their experiences suggest that gathering the right information requires more dialogic interaction than the system supports.

Promoting Education

Both the social services workers and the system, Benefits CalWIN, promote education. Yet, again, they operationalize this value in different ways. While the logic of the system suggests an understanding of education that is limited to the provision of information, the logic of the workers focuses on ensuring that applicants understand that information and are, in the end, empowered as applicants and potentially clients moving forward.

Making Information Available

The logic of the system suggests that education is enabled through the display of information. As clients step through the application workflow online, they can read information including rules about what services may be applied for if the applicant creates an account or not, a list of documents that "you might want to gather… to help you complete the application," notices about what services and under what conditions they will need to appear in person at the social services office, as well as a four-page, PDF file "cover sheet" that includes numerous programmatic definitions and rules governing eligibility for various programs. One eligibility technician was quite skeptical, however, about whether applicants actually read any of the information that is posted, an apprehension that research in the privacy domain suggests may be well grounded [20]:

> *You know, when you go online you don't read everything. You just try and go fast through the application….* (Ana, Eligibility Technician)

Fostering Understanding and Empowerment

In addition to skepticism about whether or not clients read the information posted by Benefits CalWin, numerous social services workers also articulated a logic of education that extends beyond the provision of information. For these workers, education entails engaging in a dynamic exchange to ensure that clients understand the information, understand how it applies to them, and can project forward in time to imagine the implications of a variety of scenarios in which they might find themselves in the future. These workers understand education as leading to empowerment, a necessary component for individuals to become self-advocates in a complicated governmental bureaucracy.

For the social services workers at the Mail-In Center, the process of educating and empowering clients begins in a critical interview during the intake process. One administrator describes eligibility technicians as being "expert interviewers." When conducting interviews in person, eligibility technicians are confident of their ability to assess whether or not applicants truly understand the information they are discussing. They report reading applicants' body language and providing additional clarification as needed. They also visually step applicants through the sometimes-intimidating quarterly status report.

With Benefits CalWIN applicants, however, this educational process happens over the phone, and eligibility technicians are concerned about their ability to perceive confusion and dynamically troubleshoot when applicants claim that they understand, even though they do not.

> *We go over everything just as we would if they were in person. But like I said, it is difficult because they are over the phone, so they are not looking at your face or at your eyes and they can just say, "Yeah, I understand. I can go to jail and that there are penalties or I can be sanctioned. Yeah, sure."* (Selena, Eligibility Technician)

The prospect of educating clients about the quarterly status report also presents new challenges.

> *When we first started about a year ago, for me it was very, very difficult to explain something to our clients, something that I felt I needed to show them. I felt like they visually had to see it versus trying to explain it over the phone. Sometimes I think there is still that difficulty, 'cause they have to provide a quarterly status report. I try to be as thorough as possible, but it is so much easier when a client is in front of you and [you] just say, "This is when you applied. You are going to get a report that looks like this [she holds a piece of paper in front of herself and points to it] and this is when we are going to need it." And I can even circle when we are going to need it.... But I think that was... the hardest thing for me to do. Where it was just me-showing-you versus me-trying-to-explain-to-you. And you know, sometimes I think... it might be a little more difficult for the clients... because I can't show them a QR7 [the quarterly status form] and they don't know what it looks like. So I don't know if they are understanding: "What is this crazy lady explaining to me?" you know?* (Lucia, Eligibility Technician)

The social services workers in intake also understand that the education they provide is valued throughout the organization; educating clients early in the process helps prevent confusion and extra work for many parties down the road.

> *The workers in continuing, case maintenance, [and] call handling do get upset if we don't explain [the longer-term process] to them [our clients]: "Why didn't you guys explain?" They will tell their supervisors, "Can you guys at the next supervisors meeting let people in intake just to remind their workers...". So this worker goes back to her supervisor upset, "I had to go out there to stop what I was doing just for this address change where it could have been taken care of over the phone. In the next supervisors meeting, can you remind intake to explain?"* (Sara, Administrator)

If clients aren't adequately educated and empowered to take ownership of their cases, they run the risk of missing deadlines or deliverables and losing their program eligibility and therefore their benefits.

> *The risk we take is that if we haven't had that encounter in which we could explain exactly what it is and we could not be sufficiently there to help with that then we risk that we have situations where we approve them now, but three months later we lose them.* (Sonia, Administrator).

In the long run, a lack of client education and empowerment can cause additional work for everyone if those clients resubmit an application and end up back in the queue at the Mail-In Center.

MISMATCHES AMONG LOGICS

Our analysis of data gathered from interviews with social services workers and corroborated against our exploration of the features of Benefits CalWIN demonstrate the following: *Even when core values are shared across entities in a sociotechnical system, mismatches in the way values are understood and put into practice can create significant tensions* [Table 1]. During the rollout of Benefits CalWIN in this particular county, these mismatches: caused

Table 1. Overview of conflicting logics and the issues that arise from their mismatch

Value	Logic of the System	Logic of the Workers	Issues that Arise from the Mismatches between Logics
Access	Enabled by lowering the barriers to entry and instantiated in the system by providing a 'low cost' avenue for applying for social services.	Enabled by *both* getting people in the door and helping them navigate the entire intake process.	The logic of the system can impede access to the service by complicating or hindering the acquisition of required information and by creating misleading expectations about how the process will play out. Social services workers, therefore, have to take on extra work to contact applicants, explain the process, procure additional information, and sooth frustrated applicants.
Efficiency	Created through the transfer of objective information from the applicant. This logic assumes that necessary information can be easily identified and entered into the system by the applicant without intervention.	Created when people are guided though the process of providing information. Information is not always objective and can be difficult to find and format without support.	The logic of the system creates extensive additional work for the eligibility technician, who has to go back and forth with client to get information "right" in order for the system to assess whether or not the applicant is eligible for social services.
Education	Supported by ensuring that information is available online without consideration for whether people will read and understand the posted information given the format or context in which it is presented.	An ongoing process that holds empowerment as an end goal. Education emerges slowly through dialogue, interaction, and explanation in modalities that are usable and understandable to the applicant.	The logic of the system does not educate clients in an authentic and reliable way that leads to empowerment and self-advocacy. This leads to confusion and frustration for both parties and potential issues in maintaining the service for the client.

misunderstandings between clients and eligibility technicians; created communication delays between clients and eligibility technicians; caused additional administrative overhead; impeded access to the service for clients; and raised questions about the potential for clients enrolled via the online system to become self-advocates. Tensions that have arisen from mismatches among logics are substantial and have the long-term potential to undermine system use.

LOGICS & THE INTERPRETABILITY OF VALUES

By making an analytic distinction between values and logics, we have foregrounded the multiple interpretability of values. So, beyond asking questions about *what* values should or do drive design and *whose* values should or do predominate, we also have to ask questions about *how* those values are operationalized and embodied. Values are enacted through the use of technology much in the same way that meaning is constructed through use [9]. So just as multiple interpretations arise of the meaning of a single technology [28; 29], multiple interpretations of a single value arise, as well. This insight also builds on prior work suggesting how narratives of technology use in popular culture can portray alternative visions of the 'same' core value [11] by revealing how such tensions emerge in organizational functioning.

The human–computer interaction research exploring value tensions has focused thus far on easing conflicts between multiple, different values that come into conflict in design, often the result of multiple stakeholders wanting to emphasize different values. Building on this work, our research suggests that designers need to engage with a more nuanced and thornier question: how to identify and resolve value tensions that arise when values are shared—tensions that arise from multiple conflicting interpretations of how to best achieve and promote a shared value.

By making this analytic distinction between values and logics, we also affirm the importance of understanding values in practice—exploring how different stakeholders in a sociotechnical system understand and enact a given value in the context of their work. Making this distinction requires a new unit of analysis. It may also require a longitudinal perspective; just as the meaning of information evolves over time [15], the meaning of values may evolve, as well.

Design, then, needs to be understood not only in participatory, reflective, and empathic ways—involving a breadth of stakeholders and acknowledging a plurality of values—but also in an ongoing and iterative way. Design needs to accommodate the evolution of entire sociotechnical systems that occur when technology is deployed, when work practices change, and when the way in which shared values are enacted may change, as well.

In conclusion, our research demonstrates that there are multiple logics—ways of enacting a single value—within a sociotechnical system. Our research reaffirms just how messy and difficult to contend with values are in design contexts, even when the stakeholders share beliefs about the core values that are important.

REFERENCES

1. Alsheikh, T., Rode, J.A., & Lindley, S.E. (2011). (Whose) value-sensitive design? A study of long-distance relationships in an Arabic cultural context. In *Proc. CSCW*. New York, NY: ACM Press, pp. 75–84.
2. Bélanger, F. & Carter, L. (2006). The effects of the digital divide on e-government: An empirical evaluation. In *Proc. HICSS*. Los Alamitos, CA: IEEE Computer Society, pp. 81–88.
3. Borning, A. & Muller, M. (2012). Next steps for value sensitive design. In *Proc. CHI*. New York, NY: ACM

Press, pp. 1125–1134.

4. Chadwick, A., & May, C. (2003). Interaction between states and citizens in the age of the internet: "E-government" in the United States, Britain and the European Union. *Governance 16* (2), 271–300.
5. Corbin, J. & Strauss, A. (2007). *Basics of qualitative research: Techniques and procedures for developing grounded theory.* Thousand Oaks, CA: Sage Publications.
6. Cordella, A., & Bonina, C. (2012). A public value perspective for ICT enabled public sector reforms: A theoretical reflection. *Government Information Quarterly 29* (4), 512–520.
7. Dombrowski, L., Voida, A., Hayes, G.R. & Mazmanian, M. (2012). The social labor of service mediation: A study of the work practices of food assistance outreach. In *Proc. CHI.* New York, NY: ACM Press, pp. 1977–1986.
8. Friedman, B., Kahn, P.H. & Borning, A. (2006). Value sensitive design and information systems. In P. Zhang & D. Galletta (Eds.), *Human-computer interaction in management information systems: Foundations* (pp. 348–372). Armonk, New York: M.E. Sharpe.
9. Gadamer, H.G. (2005). *Truth and method.* (2nd ed.). (J. Weinsheimer & D.G. Marshall, Trans.). London, UK: Continuum Publishing Group.
10. *Hearing to review federal nutrition programs: Hearing before the Subcommittee on Department Operations, Oversight, Nutrition, and Forestry, of the Committee on Agriculture, 111th Cong., 41* (2010) (testimony of Nancy Swanson).
11. Harmon, E. & Mazmanian, M. (2013). Stories of the smartphone in everyday discourse: Conflict, tension & instability. In *Proc. CHI.* New York, NY: ACM Press, pp. 1051–1060.
12. Heeks, R. (2008). Benchmarking e-government: Improving the national and international measurement, evaluation and comparison of e-government. In Z. Irani & P. Love (Eds.), *Evaluation of information systems* (pp. 257–296). Burlington, MA: Butterworth-Heinemann.
13. Hood, C. (1991). A public management for all seasons. *Public Administration, 69* (1), 3–9.
14. Jaeger, P.T. (2005). Deliberative democracy and the conceptual foundations of electronic government. *Government Information Quarterly, 22* (4), 702–719.
15. Kidd, A. (1994). The marks are on the knowledge worker. In *Proc. CHI.* New York, NY: ACM Press, pp. 186–191.
16. Knobel, C.P. & G.C. Bowker. (2011). Values in design. *Communications of the ACM 54* (7), 26–28.
17. Le Dantec, C.A., Poole, E.S. & Wyche, S.P. (2009). Values as lived experience: Evolving value sensitive design in support of value discovery. In *Proc. CHI.* New York, NY: ACM Press, pp. 1141–1150.
18. Meynhardt, T. (2009). Public value inside: What is public value creation? *International Journal of Public Administration 32* (3–4), 192–219.
19. Miller, J.K., Friedman, B., & Jancke, G. (2007). Value tensions in design: The value sensitive design, development, and appropriation of a corporation's groupware system. In *Proc. GROUP.* New York, NY: ACM Press, pp. 281–290.
20. Milne, G.R. & Culnan, M.J. (2004). Strategies for reducing online privacy risks: Why consumers read (or don't read) online privacy notices. *Journal of Interactive Marketing 18* (3), 15–29.
21. Mossenburg, K., Tolbert, C., & Stansbury, M. (2003). *Virtual inequality: Beyond the digital divide.* Washington, D.C: George Washington University Press.
22. Norris, D. F. & Reddick, C.G. (2013). Local e-government in the United States: Transformation or incremental change? *Public Administration Review 73* (1), 165–175.
23. Pieterson, W. & vanDijk, J. (2007). Channel choice determinants: An exploration of the factors that determine the choice of a service channel in citizen initiated contacts. In *Proc. dg.o.* Digital Government Society of North America, pp. 173–182.
24. Reddick, C.G. & Turner, M. (2012). Channel choice and public service delivery in Canada: Comparing e-government to traditional service delivery. *Government Information Quarterly 29* (1) 1–11.
25. Riggins, F.J. & Dewan, S. (2005). The digital divide: Current and future research directions. *Journal of the Association for Information Systems 6* (12), 298–337.
26. Sæbø, Ø., Rose, J., & Flak, S. (2008). The shape of e-participation: Characterizing an emerging research area. *Government Information Quarterly 25* (3), 400–428.
27. Sengers, P., Boehner, K., David, S. & Kaye, J. 'J.' (2005). Reflective design. In *Proc. Critical Computing.* New York, NY: ACM Press, pp. 49–58.
28. Sengers, P. & Gaver, B. (2006). Staying open to interpretation: Engaging multiple meanings in design and evaluation. In *Proc. DIS.* New York: ACM Press, 99–108.
29. Voida, A. (2008). Exploring a technological hermeneutic: Understanding the interpretation of computer-mediated messaging systems. (Doctoral dissertation, Georgia Institute of Technology, 2008).
30. Wastell, D.G. (2002). Organizational discourse as a social defense: Taming the tiger of electronic government. In E.H. Wynn, E.A. Whitley, M.D. Myers & J.I. DeGross (Eds.). *Global and organizational discourse about information technology* (pp. 179–195). Norwell, MA: Kluwer Academic Publishers.
31. West, D.M. (2005). *Digital government: Technology and public sector performance.* Princeton, NJ: Princeton University Press.
32. Winner, L. (1980). Do artifacts have politics? *Daedalus 109* (1), 121–136.
33. Yildiz, M. & Saylam, A. (2013). E-government discourses: An inductive analysis. *Government Information Quarterly 30* (2), 141–153.

Rethinking Plan A for Sustainable HCI

Bran Knowles, Lynne Blair, Paul Coulton, Mark Lochrie
Lancaster University, Lancaster, UK
b.h.knowles@lancaster.ac.uk, lb@comp.lancs.ac.uk, p.coulton@lancaster.ac.uk, mark@barterproject.org

ABSTRACT

This paper challenges the sustainable HCI community to move away from a focus on *demand* and instead address climate change as a *supply* problem. We identify a new route to impact, namely addressing the psychological barriers that interfere with political mobilization toward limiting the use of fossil fuels. Five barriers are explored as a means of refocusing research objectives for the community.

Author Keywords

Sustainability, climate change, supply, psychological barriers, activism

ACM Classification Keywords

H.5.m. Information Interfaces and Presentation (e.g. HCI): Miscellaneous

INTRODUCTION

Having recently undertaken an extensive survey analysis of sustainability research in computing [18], which details the many and varied research activities in the area, this paper is inspired by a concern that sustainable HCI seems to be focusing too much effort on a series of minimal-impact solutions for an increasingly serious and imminent sustainability problem, namely climate change. While we intend to underscore the scale and urgency of the challenge by citing important new climate change research [1, 16, 21], we are by no means the first in the sustainable HCI community to point out the insufficiency of the historical and ongoing emphasis on incremental reductions in energy consumption as a response to this challenge. As one example, Mankoff [19] notes that even if we pursue this strategy alongside efforts such as smart grid and other IT solutions, 'the maximum impact [computing] can have is .6 percent of global energy emissions, assuming that we had a systemic impact on all energy wasted post-grid (not just home heating and cooling in a few households in one or two developed countries).' Since the average annual growth in emissions for the past 160 years is approximately 1.8% [16], and from 2000 to 2010 appears to be closer to 2.3% growth [1], this means our maximum potential impact is *not even enough to offset this rate of growth*, let alone enable overall *reductions*.

CHI 2014, April 26–May 01 2014, Toronto, ON, Canada.

http://dx.doi.org/10.1145/2556288.2557311

For those who recognize the scale of this challenge and the limitations of the tools sustainable HCI has identified for addressing it, the natural question is 'What if sustainability doesn't work out?' [25]. Here we see the emergence of Collapse Informatics [26], which pragmatically proposes a Plan B: 'If, as increasingly seems likely, humanity is unable to prevent dramatic global change, then adaptation to these transformations will be of growing relevance' [25]. This strategy is in clear contrast to the mainstream line of research (Plan A) that focuses on preventing climate change through incremental reductions in energy consumption.

Plan B is most certainly not a substitute for Plan A; neither do Plan A and Plan B constitute a sufficient response to the climate change problem. Plan A needs to respond to the growing concern that mainstream preventative strategies are minimal-impact and insufficient. It is surely time to re-imagine a more effective preventative agenda for sustainable HCI.

An ostensibly intuitive adjustment to Plan A would be to aim to enable consumers to make significantly greater carbon savings, for example to explore how to break through the current ceiling of 5–15% energy reductions demonstrated by persuasion and eco-feedback [7].[1] However, the core of the problem is that, if we adopt two degrees Celsius above pre-Industrial levels as the 'safe' limit for climate change (cf. [13]), in practical terms this means that our proven fossil fuel reserves are approximately 4–5 times the amount we are able to safely burn before passing this limit [1, 20]. This suggests that we cannot succeed by addressing climate change as a *demand* problem alone.

To the extent that the issue of *supply* is explored at all within HCI, it is typically within the context of 'peak oil' as a potential catalyst for collapse [25]. In contrast, the real problem is we simply have too much available to burn. Any serious commitment to climate change, therefore, must involve a strategy for getting fossil fuel companies to leave as much as 80% of their assets *in the ground*. By understanding the current barriers to doing so, we can begin to develop HCI solutions that affect these barriers. We propose a shift toward aiming to affect these barriers to political mobilization as a means of shortcutting to more systemic change, as called for by numerous voices in HCI (e.g. [10, 24, 29]).

ROUTES TO IMPACT FOR SUSTAINABLE HCI

If there is any hope that fossil fuel companies will be convinced to leave 80% of their assets in the ground as needed to

[1] Note that 80% carbon reduction targets, as in the UK's Climate Change Act, refer to national footprints, of which only part is accounted for by domestic energy use.

avert climate 'disaster' [21], it lies in the masses mobilizing in a way that influences policy reform. Important work is being done to understand how we might overcome the psychological barriers that are currently preventing us from taking action on climate change (e.g. [5, 6, 28]), and we propose below an initial five-point strategy for addressing the issues raised by this research. There is currently some research being done by HCI in these areas — and space permitting we will attempt to acknowledge precedents — but our intention is a) to reiterate the importance of increasing such efforts as core to the sustainable HCI agenda, as well as b) to unify them within a strategy for shifting emphasis toward supply. We offer these up in their current form to garner community feedback that can be incorporated into a more comprehensive publication exploring the potential contributions from HCI in these areas.

Addressing Values: Toward Caring

Periods of prosperity, and the economic security this brings, tend to breed bigger-than-self concern for issues such as equality, civil rights, and protecting the environment [22]. In contrast, authoritarian and self-enhancement values — which have been shown to lead to reduced concern for issues such as climate change and sustainability [5] — tend to be strengthened by the feelings of economic insecurity currently being exacerbated by global recession.

Sustainable HCI often attempts to resolve this problem by leveraging concern about the economy into pro-environmental behavior, by designing feedback mechanisms that translate environmentally beneficial behavior change into cost savings (as discussed in [17]). Sustainable HCI could have a greater impact by specifically seeking to develop interactions and interventions that activate *self-transcendent* values that have been shown to increase concern about sustainability [5]. This has the potential to foster the emotional capacity to care about climate change, counteracting the pervasive reinforcement, particularly by advertising, of *self-enhancement* values associated with erosion of such concern. To be clear, this goes beyond [24] who notes that current interventions tend not to motivate additional or more significant behavior change. Although designing in such a way as to reinforce self-transcendent values may contribute to greater conservation behaviors [6], more importantly, it is essential for motivating the kinds of actions that can make a more significant difference.

Addressing Material Insecurity: Toward Caring Enough

As raised elsewhere (e.g [3, 8]), sustainable HCI tends to design for people who have the luxury to care about sustainability. In the context of fostering lasting concern that can motivate political action (while also seeking a sustainability solution that advances social justice around the world), it is important to note that transitional nations that are ramping up their industrialisation, such as China, India and Brazil, see the objective of raising standards of living as far more pressing and *real* than the projected problems of climate change. This is best expressed by the statement from a Chinese spokesman that, 'You cannot tell people who are struggling to earn enough to eat that they need to reduce their emissions' [22]. In other words, a perceived inability to meet basic needs (i.e. material insecurity) is a major impediment to taking action for climate change. Material insecurity is not just a problem for developing nations, however. It appears to be on the rise in recent years in comparatively wealthy nations, causing people to increasingly rate economic concerns as their top priority [22].

The strategy described previously to address values may go some way toward elevating climate change as a priority, but this would be further helped by developing interventions that are designed specifically to increase feelings of material security. Here, the goals of sustainable HCI and HCI for Development (HCI4D) might overlap. But increasing material security could also be achieved, for example, by developing tools to help communities maximize and retain their wealth, as being explored through projects such as BARTER (barterproject.org). At the same time, however, as this has the potential to reinforce self-enhancement values (e.g. personal wealth), we suggest that successful approaches would emphasize values associated with community feeling and improved collective wellbeing, as represented by the spirit of Transition Towns [15].

Addressing Survival Anxiety: Toward Desire for Change

By promoting consumer reductions as its primary avenue to impact, sustainable HCI has reinforced a framing of the climate change solution as 'sacrifice'. This 'sacrifice' frame collides with notions of 'progress' as a continual march toward human improvement, which has become integral to our notions of what it means to be successful humans. 'Sacrifice' may therefore trigger what psychoanalysts call 'survival anxiety' [28], i.e. not just anxiety about our physical survival, but also about the survival of our notion of ourselves as special and capable of remaking the world according to our wishes. When this human identity is threatened, we are more likely to think irrationally and engage in destructive behaviors.

Nordhaus & Shellenberger [22] argue that this is the root cause of the 'failure' of environmentalism to date, namely that environmentalism promotes a 'politics of limits, which seeks to constrain human ambition, aspiration, and power rather than unleash and direct them' [22, p. 17]. As others have suggested (e.g. [12]) — albeit in different terms — in order to overcome the disruptive influence of survival anxiety, sustainable HCI needs to replace rhetoric about sacrifice (and, indeed, 'collapse') with a vision of sustainability as the fulfilment of human potential. While partially a marketing challenge for sustainability generally, positive contributions in this area would include the design of aspirational futures, e.g. through exploration of design fictions [2, 27]. Additionally, it would be useful to conduct more fundamental research into ways of (re)framing necessary changes in ways that are psychologically palatable.

Addressing Disavowal: Toward Empowerment

An especially common form of denial of the reality of climate change is *disavowal*, which works to deflect anxiety by systematically distorting the truth. Disavowal tends to entrench thinking that climate change is 'none of my fault' while simultaneously increasing feeling that 'it is all my fault' [28], neither of which is helpful for promoting positive action. As noted by [10], sustainable HCI tends to locate the onus of responsibility for sustainability on the shoulders of individual consumers. We suggest this may feed this de-motivating spiral of disavowal.

Instead, sustainable HCI can work to disrupt this disavowal by providing greater clarity about the power relationships in play that contribute to the climate change problem. For example, visualizations or artistic or creative interventions may be utilized to powerfully showcase the data and facts that face us, illustrating complex inter-relationships between different agents, and capturing externalities presently hidden from public view. The ways in which the fossil fuel industry has systematically distorted the truth about climate change and influenced legislation (see [9] for examples) is one area where HCI and persuasive techniques may be employed to help people gain a sense of proportion about their own role in climate change as a necessary first step for identifying targets (e.g. the fossil fuel industry, politicians) for positive actions one can take, and spurring individuals and/or communities to take these actions. End User Development (EUD) is another important emerging field that aims to facilitate end-user empowerment [23] and could be utilized by citizens to further 'spread the word' of climate change realities.

Addressing Helplessness: Toward Activism

The previous routes to impact focus on creating the conditions for people to be psychologically able to care about climate change and to want to do something about it. These are necessary but insufficient for generating the kind of political force needed for instigating meaningful policy change. Especially when people are fired up about the need to do something, struggling to identify steps that can be taken toward affecting change can provoke fatalism (e.g. 'We're all doomed, so what's the point?'). A similar exasperation can result from feelings that current methods of participation are insufficiently influential, e.g. being able to add one's name to an online petition.

Beyond designing for democratic participation in policy making [14], a necessary contribution from sustainable HCI, therefore, would be to innovate technologically-mediated or technologically-enhanced forms of *activism* (cf. [29]). As part of this effort, research that explores the history of successful political movements with a view toward revealing specific qualities that any design for activism should aim to support would help ensure that the resulting activism has a maximally positive impact for the cause. A further exciting opportunity is in more fully understanding the potential for the use of crowd-sourcing to better enable the sharing of 'problems and associated solutions, together with their underlying rationale' [23] (cf. climatecolab.org), particularly how to do so in ways that can produce genuinely powerful ideas and the emergence of a broadly shared 'vision'.

DISCUSSION

Like everyone else, sustainable HCI researchers experience a psychological struggle with certain aspects of climate change. The initial years of sustainable HCI may be a manifestation of a particular kind of anxiety that is prone to 'omnipotent thinking' and employs a range of 'quick fixes' to the problem of climate change (and sustainability more broadly) (cf. [28, p. 33]). The inconvenient side effects of pursuing a route to sustainability based on these (consumption based) quick fixes is that 1) it 'deflect[s] pressure for government to adopt ambitious and potentially unpopular policies and regulations' [6], and 2) it reinforces the narrative that 'all will be well', a message that people are all too ready to believe. The recent interest in Collapse Informatics, however, seems to reflect the encroachment of helplessness, that there may be nothing sustainable HCI can do to help avert climate change. To the extent that this is grounded in the hope that the beginnings of collapse might serve as a psychological impetus for undertaking societal overhaul, Collapse Informatics may be seen as optimistic; but this hope does not align with the evidence [4, 22] that crisis tends to fuel the very emotional management strategies we have discussed which currently serve to prevent us from making headway on climate change. Hence our insistence on strengthening preventative efforts.

Ultimately, we are offering the same suggestion for sustainable HCI researchers that they might offer the general pubic: to overcome helplessness, sustainable HCI researchers need new opportunities to engage in activism. Depending on the style of researcher, this may include confrontational forms such as 'adversarial design' [9] or 'quieter' forms of 'design activism' (cf. [11]). But assuming that sustainable HCI undertakes a strategy for affecting the supply side of climate change, the community cannot avoid being political. Becoming comfortable with being contentious is part of the work sustainable HCI researchers need to do to construct their identity as activists. Further discussions such the CHI'13 panel on activism are needed to explore the implications of this changing job description. In particular, strategies are needed for resolving the apparent tension that many of the research activities suggested here (and by other voices in the community) that can make a significant difference for sustainability are not easily justified in terms of their 'business case'; and indeed, attempting to make sustainable HCI a commercially viable proposition may be a significant contributor to the explosion of persuasive technology. In other words, while certainly no easy task, sustainable HCI researchers will likely have to affect significant change in mindset amongst funding bodies and mainstream publication venues as the core form of activism, in part by making it clear why the current, more easily funded Plan A is just not sufficient.

CONCLUSION

The 'HCI route' is certainly not the only route to addressing the five areas outlined in this short work. However, given the large volume of work currently targeting sustainability issues in HCI, our aim is to stimulate discussion on the balance and value of this HCI research and open up possible avenues for higher impact research. We passionately believe that HCI can and should aspire to loftier goals and have greater impact in this arena.

We propose that any engineering solutions to climate change proposed by sustainable HCI *can only succeed if they are cou-*

pled with political action toward affecting the supply of fossil fuels, and that one route to promoting this political action is to address the barriers currently preventing this action. We hope that the challenge we have outlined is more inspiring than the current Plan A. We recognize that this may be on the edge of what is considered within the HCI remit, but we anticipate creative responses in these areas that may significantly re-shape the boundaries of sustainable HCI.

ACKNOWLEDGMENTS

This work is partially funded by 1) the Digital Economy programme (RCUK Grant EP/G037582/1), which supports the HighWire Centre for Doctoral Training (highwire.lancs.ac.uk), and 2) EPSRC grants EP/K012584/1 and EP/I033017/1, in collaboration with Michael Hallam of the Ethical Small Traders Association.

REFERENCES

1. Berners-Lee, M., and Clark, D. *The Burning Question*. Profile Books Ltd., 2013.
2. Bleecker, J. Design fiction: A short essay on design, science, fact and fiction. *Near Future Laboratory 29* (2009).
3. Brynjarsdóttir, H., Håkansson, M., Pierce, J., Baumer, E., DiSalvo, C., and Sengers, P. Sustainably unpersuaded: how persuasion narrows our vision of sustainability. In *Proc. CHI '12*, ACM (2012), 947–956.
4. Crompton, T., and Kasser, T. *Meeting environmental challenges: The role of human identity*. WWF-UK Godalming, UK, 2009.
5. Crompton, T., and Kasser, T. Human identity: a missing link in environmental campaigning. *Environment 52*, 4 (2010), 23–33.
6. Crompton, T., and Thøgersen, J. *Simple and Painless: The limitations of spillover in environmental campaigning*. WWF-UK, February 2009.
7. Darby, S. The effectiveness of feedback on energy consumption. *A Review for DEFRA for the LIterature on Metering, Billing and Direct Displays* (2006).
8. Dillahunt, T., Mankoff, J., Paulos, E., and Fussell, S. It's not all about "green": Energy use in low-income communities. In *Proc. UbiComp '09*, ACM (2009), 255–264.
9. DiSalvo, C. *Adversarial Design*. The MIT Press, 2012.
10. Dourish, P. HCI and environmental sustainability: the politics of design and the design of politics. In *Proc. DIS '10*, ACM (2010), 1–10.
11. Fuad-Luke, A. *Design activism: beautiful strangeness for a sustainable world*. Earthscan, 2009.
12. Håkansson, M., and Sengers, P. Beyond being green: simple living families and ICT. In *Proc. CHI '13*, ACM (2013), 2725–2734.
13. Hansen, J., Sato, M., Kharecha, P., Beerling, D., Masson-Delmotte, V., Pagani, M., Raymo, M., Royer, D. L., and Zachos, J. C. Target Atmospheric CO2: Where Should Humanity Aim? NASA. *Goddard Institute for Space Studies, Columbia University Earth Institute* (2008).
14. Hirsch, T., and Anderson, K. Cross currents: Water scarcity and sustainable CHI. In *Proc. CHI EA '10*, ACM (2010), 2843–2852.
15. Hopkins, R. *The Transition Handbook*. Green Books, Totnes, UK, 2008.
16. Jarvis, A., Leedal, D., and Hewitt, C. Climate-society feedbacks and the avoidance of dangerous climate change. *Nature Climate Change 2*, 9 (2012), 668–671.
17. Knowles, B. Re-imagining persuasion: designing for self-transcendence. In *Proc. CHI EA '13*, ACM (2013), 2713–2718.
18. Knowles, B., Blair, L., Hazas, M., and Walker, S. Exploring sustainability research in computing: where we are and where we go next. In *Proc. UbiComp '13*, ACM (2013), 305–314.
19. Mankoff, J. HCI and sustainability: a tale of two motivations. *interactions 19*, 3 (May 2012), 16–19.
20. McKibben, B. Global warming's terrifying new math. *Rolling Stone* (2012).
21. McKibben, B. Do the math [video]. Available at `http://documentaryheaven.com/do-math-movie/`, 2013.
22. Nordhaus, T., and Shellenberger, M. *Break Through: Why We Can't Leave Saving the Planet to Environmentalists*. Mariner Books, Boston, 2009.
23. Paternò, F. End user development: Survey of an emerging field for empowering people. *ISRN Software Engineering* (2013).
24. Strengers, Y. A. Designing eco-feedback systems for everyday life. In *Proc. CHI '11*, ACM (2011), 2135–2144.
25. Tomlinson, B., Patterson, D. J., Pan, Y., Blevis, E., Nardi, B., Silberman, S., Norton, J., and LaViola, Jr., J. J. What if sustainability doesn't work out? *interactions 19*, 6 (Nov. 2012b), 50–55.
26. Tomlinson, B., Silberman, M. S., Patterson, D., Pan, Y., and Blevis, E. Collapse informatics: augmenting the sustainability & ICT4D discourse in HCI. In *Proc. CHI'12*, ACM (2012a), 655–664.
27. Wakkary, R., Desjardins, A., Hauser, S., and Maestri, L. A sustainable design fiction: Green practices. *TOCHI 20*, 4 (Sept. 2013), 23:1–23:34.
28. Weintrobe, S. *Engaging with climate change: Psychoanalytic and interdisciplinary perspectives*. Routledge, 2013.
29. Woodruff, A., Hasbrouck, J., and Augustin, S. A bright green perspective on sustainable choices. In *Proc. CHI '08*, ACM (2008), 313–322.

HaptiMoto: Turn-by-Turn Haptic Route Guidance Interface for Motorcyclists

Manoj Prasad[1], **Paul Taele**[1], **Daniel Goldberg**[2], **Tracy Hammond**[1]
Sketch Recognition Lab, Dept. of Computer Science & Engineering[1] and Department of Geography[2]
Texas A&M University
{manoj.prasad,ptaele,daniel.goldberg,hammond}@tamu.edu

ABSTRACT
A national study by the Australian Transport Safety Bureau revealed that motorcyclist deaths were nearly thirty times more prevalent than that of drivers of other vehicles. These fatalities represent approximately 5% of all highway deaths each year, yet motorcycles account for only 2% of all registered vehicles in the United States. Motorcyclists are highly exposed on the road, so maintaining situational awareness at all times is crucial. Route guidance systems enable users to efficiently navigate between locations using dynamic visual maps and audio directions, and have been well tested with motorists, but remain unsafe for use by motorcyclists. Audio/visual routing systems decrease motorcyclists' situational awareness and vehicle control, and thus elevate chances of an accident. To enable motorcyclists to take advantage of route guidance while maintaining situational awareness, we created HaptiMoto, a wearable haptic route guidance system. HaptiMoto uses tactile signals to encode the distance and direction of approaching turns, thus avoiding interference with audio/visual awareness. Our evaluations demonstrate that HaptiMoto is both intuitive and a safer alternative for motorcyclists compared to existing solutions.

Author Keywords
Tactile interface; vibro-tactile; advanced traveler information system; route guidance.

ACM Classification Keywords
H.5.2.g. Information Interfaces and Representation (HCI): Haptic I/O.

INTRODUCTION
Navigational support tools are valuable resources for motorists and motorcyclists alike, and paper maps have been the norm for many years until the introduction of modern technological solutions such as commercial GPS systems, virtual displays, and turn-by-turn audio and visual navigation devices. With Advanced Traveler Information Systems (ATIS), vehicle drivers have access to information for planning routes, viewing traffic conditions, looking up restaurants, and so on [10]. The most common utility of ATIS is in-vehicle route guidance and navigation system (IRANS) [7], which serves dual purposes of route planning and guidance. The route planning feature is used to plan a driving route between two known locations, while the route guidance feature is used to provide turn-by-turn guidance to drivers in motion. A combined dynamic visual and audio interface is most common for providing in-transit route guidance information to drivers. One notable example is Google Maps, a popular route guidance application for drivers, which uses a visual interface for providing the driver's current location on a map, the upcoming turn, and the distance to that turn. Google Maps also uses an audio interface to alert drivers of the approaching turning direction and distance.

However, these audio/visual interfaces are not suitable for motorcyclists, since they require their visual and auditory channels to maintain awareness of the environment around them. Such interfaces could obstruct the motorcyclist's view, decrease their acoustic awareness, and magnify their inattention while traveling, which in turn raises the probability of being involved in an accident [7, 9]. Audio interfaces have also been proven in military field tests to throw off team commanders' sense of direction from other audio inputs; commanders donning wearable audio devices (e.g., earbuds) only realize gunfire being directed at them after observing other team members with unimpeded listening ducking for cover. The human ear is very good at focusing in on certain sounds while blocking out others. While not a concern for motorists whom are accustomed to blocking out outdoor noises while driving, this can be detrimental to motorcyclists in those cases where outdoor sounds are crucial to their situational awareness.

In addition, a national study by the Australian Transport Safety Bureau revealed that motorcyclist deaths were nearly thirty times more prevalent than that of drivers of other vehicles [1]. Motorcyclist fatalities represent approximately 5% of all highway deaths each year, yet motorcycles account for only 2% of all registered vehicles in the United States [2]. The U.S. Center for Disease Control and Prevention report on motorcycle accidents further reveals that over 34,000 motorcyclists were killed and an estimated 1,222,000 persons were treated in the emergency room in the United States for nonfatal motorcycle-related injuries from 2001 to 2008 [5].

CHI 2014, April 26–May 1, 2014, Toronto, Ontario, Canada.

ACM 978-1-4503-2473-1/14/04..$15.00.
http://dx.doi.org/10.1145/2556288.2557404

Alternatively, current smartphone navigation systems encourage touch interaction; a simple swipe might be needed to clear an incoming text message or phone call, or even awaken the screen to view the map for approaching turns. On the other hand, any touch interaction is hazardous for motorcyclists, whom must keep one hand on the brake and the other on the gas at all times. Requiring touch interaction for motorcyclist navigation would be akin to a car interface requiring drivers to use their right foot while driving and, furthermore, requiring that the driver take off their shoe before interacting with that interface, since common motorcycle gloves will not work with a smartphone. Thus, there is a need to create an interface for a hands-free in-transit route guidance system that also does not reduce motorcyclists' situational awareness.

Haptic interfaces supply information through touch feedback, and can be used in situations where the visual and audio medium is overloaded with information. According to multiple resource theory [64], visual, audio, and tactile channels can be used by individuals to acquire information without drastic increases in brain processing resources for most situations. With motorcyclists, visual and audio channels are already overtaxed due to the noise from the motorcycle itself, elevating the danger of causing an accident. The use of a tactile modality for providing directional cues is further supported by van Erp's framework for choosing an information modality [62] and by experiments conducted by Cao, *et al.* [11].

Our hypothesis is that a tactile modality is effective for communicating turn-by-turn information to motorcyclists. Therefore, we propose HaptiMoto, a haptic interface system for in-transit route guidance that provides turn-by-turn information to motorcyclists during travel. The scope of our contributions do not include route planning, which are obtained through Google Maps on a smartphone kept in the motorcyclist's pocket, but focus instead on the valuable activity of communicating directions while motorcycling. The contributions of our work include:

1. Enumerating the differences in haptic interface design requirements between pedestrian and motorcyclist route guidance.
2. Locating optimal placement of tactors on a haptic vest for motorcycle route guidance.
3. Designing a set of tactile signals to encode direction and distance for approaching turns.
4. Identifying travel scenarios capable of evaluating a route guidance system for motorcyclists.
5. Demonstrating the effectiveness of a tactile medium to communicate turn-by-turn directions to motorcyclists, including the ability of users to perceive and understand tactile signals, react appropriately to directional cues, and perform appropriate turns with HaptiMoto.

RELATED WORK

While there is extensive research in tactile navigation interfaces for pedestrian and car navigation [7, 10], research in analogous tactile route guidance interfaces for motorcyclists is limited. Thus, our work is significantly influenced by existing work in interfaces for other forms of navigation, as well as by psychophysical experiments on tactile sensitivity, multiple task management, and change blindness to haptic cues [21, 59, 64].

Human Factors Research in Tactile Interfaces

Research on orienting users with tactile interfaces includes conveying driving directions [14, 26, 59, 63], bicycle navigation [44, 56], and pedestrian navigation [13, 43]. Van Erp examined the navigation of pilots, motorists, and soldiers, and devised a theoretical framework to decide the appropriateness of a communication modality based on the primary and secondary task [62]. For a motorist, driving is a task secondary to navigation, while the reverse is true for motorcyclists. Van Erp [62] suggests the use of a tactile modality in such circumstances, including dual-task environments (e.g., navigation and driving). There is less workload for cueing tasks when haptic cues are used in combination with audio or visual cues, rather than with audio or visual cues alone [16, 63]. Additionally, research comparing tactile and auditory modalities to convey driving directions in cars shows tactile input works better than auditory [11], further motivating the use of haptics for motorcycle navigation.

Poppinga, *et al.* [44] designed Tacticycle, an interface using a combination of the visual and tactile medium to navigate bicyclists. Tacticycle uses "drift to destination" to guide bicyclists by providing the destination's direction relative to their orientation like a compass, but was not designed to either efficiently navigate between two locations or alert them of approaching turns. Tacticycle's typical use cases were also limited to short routes and slow navigation. Steltenpohl and Bouwer [56] designed a vibrotactile belt called Vibrobelt to provide turn-by-turn navigation signals for bicyclists, where signals are provided at 50 m and 10 m before upcoming turns. We contend that bicyclists are instead similar to pedestrians; bicyclists' have ample time to respond to navigational cues due to much slower travel speeds and can more easily pull over to the side of the road to confirm navigational aspects. Vehicle speed also determines when a bicyclist needs to be warned of upcoming turns; low speeds and small variations in bicyclist speeds allow designers to signal riders at predefined distances before a turn (e.g., Vibrobelt), while motorcyclists can travel anywhere between 10-75 mph. Motorcyclists cannot afford to be distracted by navigational cues due to a higher average and wider range of speeds, especially since they share the travel speed hazards of motorists and the exposed vulnerabilities of bicyclists and pedestrians. The vibrotactors' positions in Tacticycle's handlebars and Vibrobelt's belt are also not appropriate stimulus locations for motorcyclists, since these will increase change blindness [23].

Tactile direction cueing for motorists has been shown to be effective and tested in several configurations, including on a three-by-three array of tactors on a chair [59], an eight-by-eight array of tactors on seats [14, 63], and left and right haptic sensations on a steering wheel [16]. An *on-thigh* vibro-tactile belt containing eight tactors around the thigh successfully alerts pilots of plane orientation, with two tactors specifying the line representing the direction of gravity [51, 52]. Researchers have found haptic driving modalities safer than electro-tactile or force-feedback systems while driving cars [12]. When compared to a visual navigation display, the tactile navigation display did not increase motorists' mental workload. We believe motorists have smaller workloads than motorcyclists, and our motivation focuses on building a usable vibro-tactile guidance system that does not increase motorcyclists' workload.

Tactile Interfaces for Pedestrian Navigation

Pedestrian navigation systems are designed to accommodate various pedestrian types, such as tourists in unfamiliar environments [43, 58], soldiers in sensitive environments [13, 17, 18], and vision-impaired individuals in bustling environments [27, 39], whom use tactile alerts, smartphone vibration alerts, or wearable devices such as vibrotactile belts and vests. The literature provides ideas about affordances and analogies that could be used for designing vibro-tactile signals to provide directions. The *magic wand* interaction metaphor points the device at a distant object to learn more about its presence, and accesses its corresponding information [20]. Users must often scan their surrounding by either turning their bodies or physically waving the mobile device with their arms stretched out forward, or turning their bodies around with the mobile device in their possession [35, 36]. This has been used for different purposes, such as improved guidance for the visually-impaired [34], flexible routes for wandering tourists [48], and streamlined meetups for social groups [65]. Although the *magic wand* metaphor has proven to be effective and intuivite [35, 48, 65], it requires user motion that is not feasible for motorcyclists whom must keep their body and hands in a fixed location. The *sixth sense* metaphor is often used with wearable devices such as multiple vibrating tactors, enabling users to derive the location or navigation of their target destinations in relation to their current location and orientation [13, 31, 41, 42, 43, 46, 50, 58]. *Sixth sense* interfaces benefit users through more passive interaction (i.e., no additional user motion), but has a steeper learning curve for understanding the directional meaning of the feedback.

Sixth Sense haptic systems include tactile belts and vests. In general, haptic belts [19, 40, 54] outperform early haptic vests that generated straight-lined patterns [28, 49], as tactile belts allow for 360 degrees of location feedback. Recent vest improvements support relative point vibrations on the back of the user (e.g., left, forward, right) during navigation [13, 17, 18], allowing for more sophisticated navigation. We have experimented with both belts and vests in our work with motorcycles, and discovered that the hips and waist receive a significant amount of vibrational noise from the motorcycle. This made a tactile belt impractical for our use, and we instead chose a tactile vest that affords the "tap on the shoulder" analogy [45].

Psychophysical Research

Auditory directional signals perform better than visual directional signals for motorcyclists, as they reduce visual overload [15, 32, 57] while still presenting high priority and intermittent information [10]. For motorcyclists, the use of the auditory channel comes with certain limitations and increased risk as it reduces acoustic awareness. Motorcyclists need to have acoustic awareness in order to respond to unexpected events [9]. Moreover, external noises such as engine or wind turbulence noise could make directional signals inaudible. At 70 mph, the wind turbulence is approximately 100 dB and is a major source of noise at high speeds [9]. The Psychological Refractory Period (PRP) states that when two tasks require simultaneous response, users decide on performing one task and queue the response for the secondary task. The delay in performing the queuing task is called the PRP period, which reduces the attention in detecting critical events caused by the PRP effect [25]. The PRP effect further motivated us to not overload motorcyclists' visual or auditory channels.

The effectiveness of the tactile medium depends on the perception of the tactile stimulus, which is dependent on the stimulus strength, count, location, environmental change blindness, and user sensitivity [22]. Users can distinguish up to twelve different angles of directional information, with errors in judgment within 10° to 17° [61]. The HaptiMoto vest provides tactile signals on the rear shoulders and lower-center back, as shown to be effective by prior experiments [45].

Change blindness is induced when multiple stimuli are presented simultaneously on similar medium, which can reduce communication effectiveness. Driving involves both visual and auditory input mediums of the user, so change blindness is higher when the user is provided audio/visual directional cues. Change blindness is higher for tactile stimulus when it is applied to moving parts of the body or close proximity to other tactile stimulus [23, 53]. For example, motorcyclists use their arms to steer, while their arms and legs are close to the vibrational noise of the motorcycle. Thus, it is ineffective to provide tactile direction stimulus to either the arms or the legs of motorcyclists. The tactors in the HaptiMoto vest are located on the upper part of the body, and also away from moving parts of the body or those close to motorcycle vibration (e.g., hips, waist). Errors caused from change blindness can be further reduced by repeating the tactile signals [22].

Navigation research supports the use of turn-by-turn route guidance for navigating users; turn-by-turn signals can be associated to view-action pairs, where a driver gets a directional signal for a turn and performs the corresponding turning action [60, 15]. According to Dingus [15], directional information is sufficient for route guidance and any other information is potentially disruptive. Information about a turn signal should contain three important parts to it: which direction to turn, at what specified distance, and onto which specific road.

The timing of the tactile signals and the amount of time between them are as important as the directional information, where timing should take into account the user's reaction time, decision-making time, and maneuvering time. The reaction time for drivers is between 0.75 seconds and 1.50 seconds, with 2.50 seconds being the preferred reaction time for roadway navigation design [33, 37]. Navigation timing can also depend on a fixed distance approach [55] or a lead distance approach [10]. In one fixed distance approach [55], the first message was given 365 meters before a turn on parkways, 213 meters on a four-lane road, and 122 meters on a two-lane road, while the second message was given 61 meters before the turn. The lead distance approach also depends on the speed of the vehicle [10]. It is defined as the distance before a user needs to be warned of an approaching turn for them to make the turn comfortably, and suggests an equation for the minimum, ideal, and maximum lead distance required for a user to make any turn. The lead distance and timing of the directional signal can be calculated from the vehicle's speed.

Given a driving task for a certain distance and a travel route, several standard measures exist to determine the effectiveness and attentional demands of the task at hand, including the NASA TLX Subjective Workload Test [24, 38, 55]; reaction time required to respond to directional cues [55]; Subjective Workload Assessment Test (SWAT) [32, 47]; number of correct, incorrect, missed, and near-miss turns [32]; mean velocity, absolute deviation in velocity, and variance in acceleration, where higher variation means navigational cues take more attention disrupting the speed of the vehicle [32]; and total driving time to complete a route [38]. In our evaluation, we measure the motorcyclist's completion time and also their number of correct, incorrect, and missed turns.

DESIGN AND IMPLEMENTATION

Our system consists of a tactile vest with adjustable straps to fit different users and an accompanying mobile Android app. The vest is equipped with a LilyPad Arduino [3], a BlueSMiRF Bluetooth module [4], and also three LilyPad Vibe Boards (i.e., vibrational tactors) [6] located at the lower back and rear left and right shoulders (Figure 1(a)). The mobile app provides GPS location updates, the user's alignment, and a processing unit for calculating directional cues. The directional cues are communicated to the Arduino via Bluetooth, where the Arduino serves as the microcontroller for the navigation system by activating the vibrational tactors indicating the directional cues. We selected these components specifically for their lightweight characteristics and seamless integration into the vest's fabric with conductive threads (Figure 1(c)), since integrating the vibe boards with clothing improves how users perceive tactile stimulus [29].

The design choice for presenting directional cues involves sending tactile signals to the user's rear shoulders (Figure 1(b)), since users found the locations both intuitive and effective in communicating navigational information without prior directional training for the domain of walking [45]. That is, users naturally turned in the same direction as the received signal without prior instruction, which they described as akin to "a tap on the shoulder". We were further motivated by this design choice for motorcycling compared to other locations, since it was less prone to interference from vehicle vibration and air turbulence [23, 53]. Moreover, the co-location of haptic cues and target direction (i.e., left and right tactors mapping to the left and right direction, respectively) reduces the number of turning errors committed by the user [26]. We also selected the length of our tactile signals' pulse lengths as 300 ms for navigational cues, since users perceived pulses on their rear shoulder less than 500 ms in duration as analogous to being pulled or tapped toward that side (e.g., pulling the left shoulder back to turn left) and greater than 700 ms in duration as analogous to being pushed toward the other side (e.g., pushing the left shoulder forward to turn right) [45]. The number of these pulses encodes the relative distance to an upcoming turn, and the duration between pulses and the number of these pulses are dimensions that serve to encode the sense of urgency or nearness to that turn [62, 63].

From our evaluations, we discovered several key differences between pedestrian and motorcycle navigation. First, people require less awareness of their surroundings while walking compared to motorcycling due to its slower speed. That is, the perception and timing of directional signals presented is crucial for motorcyclists. Second, the lead distance to convey direction for motorcycling is larger than for walking due to motorcycle's higher travel speeds. Third, pedestrians can change orientation at any direction with walking, while motorcyclists are restricted by the road's orientation during travel. Therefore, we do not rely on the motorcyclists' orientation to calculate the directional cue for the next turn.

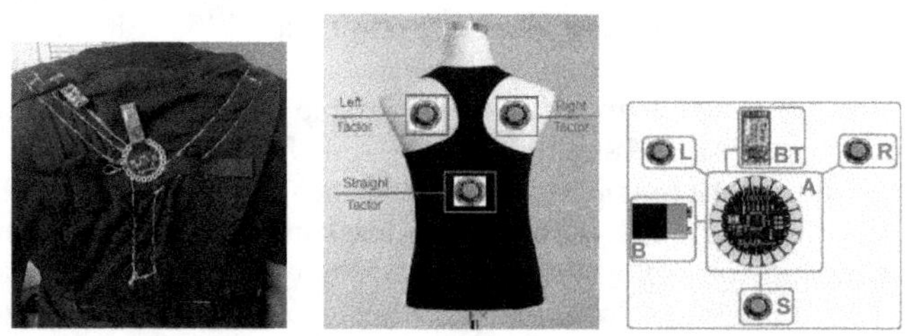

(a) The vest. (b) The tactors. (c) The schematic.

Figure 1: The HaptiMoto vest with Lilypad Arduino (A), battery (B), BlueSMiRF (BT), and Vibe Boards (L,R,S).

The timings of the directional cues were specifically adapted for motorcycle route guidance as four primary directional signals: left, right, straight, and U-turn. The tactile signal dictionary is shown in Figure 2. Directional haptic cues are provided either every three seconds or fifteen meters traveled except for U-turns, which are provided continuously.

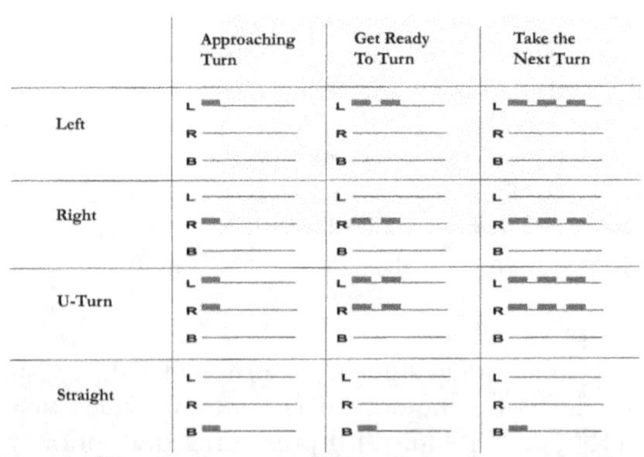

Figure 2: The dictionary of HaptiMoto's tactile signals.

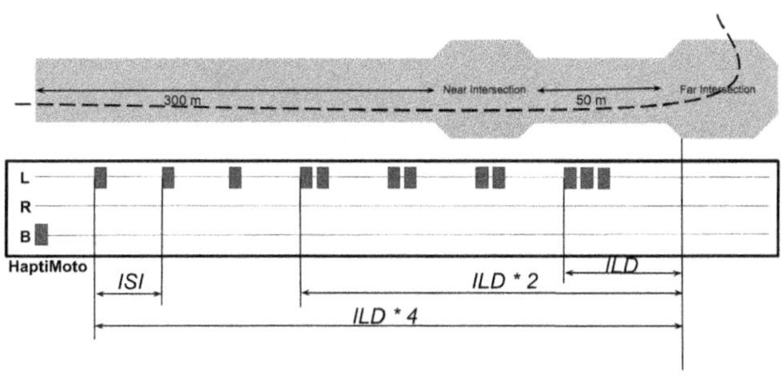

Figure 3: An example of the tactile signals presented to users before an approaching left turn, where *ILD* is *Ideal Lead Distance (x)* and *ISI* is *Interstimulus Interval* (i.e., either 3 seconds or the time taken to travel 15 meters).

We encode the direction of the approaching turn by the location of the vibro-tactile stimulus, and the distance to the approaching turn by the number of pulses. Tactile signals for turns are provided at $4x$, $2x$ and x distance intervals before the turn, where x is the ideal lead distance proposed by design guidelines from the United States' Department of Transportation [10]. Users receive a straight signal when they are beyond $4x$ distance from the location of the approaching turn, a single shoulder pulse every three seconds between $4x$ and $2x$ distance, two shoulder pulses every three seconds between $2x$ and x distance, and three shoulder pulses every three seconds within x distance:

1. *Minimum lead distance* = (speed * 1.637) + 14.799
2. *Ideal lead distance (x)* = (speed * 1.1973) + 21.307
3. *Maximum lead distance* = (speed * 2.22) + 37.144

Figure 3 illustrates the timings of the tactile signals during motorcycle travel. Single pulses for tactile signals activate for 300 ms, while multiple pulses activate for 150 ms.

EVALUATION

The central aim of our evaluation is on the feasibility of haptic motorcycle navigation, which we evaluated in two parts: the usability of HaptiMoto's tactile signals with no training and users' motorcycling abilities with HaptiMoto guidance for three scenarios. As such, we evaluated our design using a study population on four distinct circuits, with the purpose of testing the following hypotheses:

1. The users perceive and understand the tactile directional cues (*h1*).
2. The users react appropriately to tactile directional cues (*h2*).
3. The users understand a tactile directional cue well enough before approaching a turn and comfortably makes that turn (*h3*).

Before motorcycling, we introduced users to HaptiMoto by having them wear the vest and ensuring the tactors fit snuggly against their shoulders and center of their back. We then required users to wear a safety helmet, gloves, shoes, and jacket. Each tactile signal was presented to them to ensure that users perceived it, but they were provided no explanation on the meaning of any signal given to them. All of our users are also experienced motorcyclists.

Evaluation I

In order to evaluate the users' ability to perceive and understand (i.e., *h1*) and react to (i.e., *h2*) haptic cues for direction, users motorcycled into an open parking lot while wearing the vest and reacted to the vest's tactile commands as they interpreted them. Starting at a pre-specified starting point, we asked users to accelerate to a speed of between 20 to 30 mph before reaching a second point in the circuit marked by red traffic cones. We anticipated users responding to the provided directional instruction, which was a single pulse chosen randomly that specified one of four possible directions of either straight, left, right, or back, as soon as they reached the specified speed. Each direction was tested four times in a random sequence for a total of twelve directions. The experimenter noted the number of correct and incorrect turns made during each task, and we used the overall turn accuracy as the metric to evaluate hypotheses *h1* and *h2*.

Evaluation II

The second evaluation tested the ability of users to perceive haptic cues, react to them, and make turns comfortably (*h1, h2, and h3*) through four different circuits, all presented randomly to the user, and included double turns, single turns, straightaways, turns after 50 meters, and turns after 150 meters. The circuits were chosen to reflect common driving scenarios faced by motorcyclists while in motion. The distance of 150 meters between intersections was chosen from road and highway guidelines [8, 37]. According to road geometric design guidelines, the minimum distance between intersections should be 150 meters for roads with 20 mph speed limit. 50 meters is the recommended minimum distance between intersections for roads with 10-20 mph speed limits [8, 37]. The number of turns made in the correct direction, made at the correct intersection, nearly missed, and missed were recorded.

Figure 4(a) shows Circuit I with two intersections separated by 150 meters, where users would travel 150 meters before reaching the first intersection. The user would then have to decide on which direction to turn and the intersection on which they have to turn into, where the order and turn sequence was given at random. Figure 4(b) shows Circuit II with two intersections separated by 50 meters. The first two circuits helped us evaluate the users' ability to follow the navigation signals and perform turns correctly while traveling on a straightaway. Figure 3 shows an example scenario of tactile signals instructing users to turn.

Circuits III and IV reflect scenarios where turns are made in quick succession from one street to the next (Figures 4(c) and 4(d)). Users motorcycled on a 150 meter-long straight path to the first intersection in the circuits, where they sometimes attained significant speeds, and were instructed to turn either left or right by the tactile signal, before driving an additional 50 meters straight for another left or right turn. This scenario tested the users' ability to make turns in quick succession with HaptiMoto guidance.

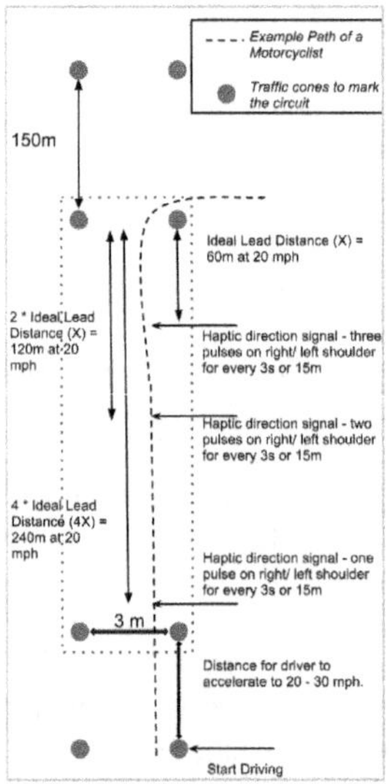

(a) Intersection separated by 150 m (Circuit I).

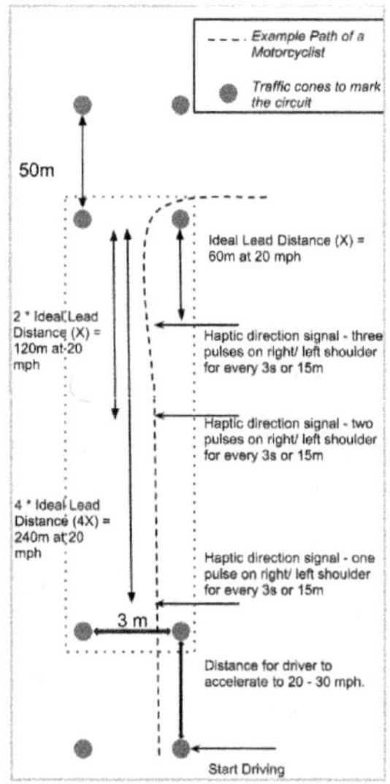

(b) Intersection separated by 50 m (Circuit II).

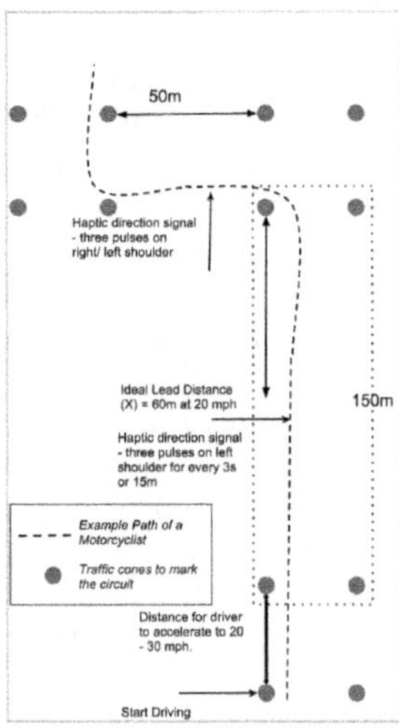

(c) Circuit with two turns in quick succession (Circuit III).

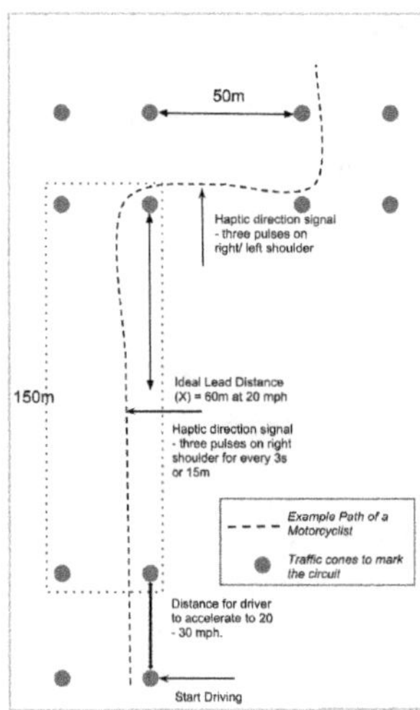

(d) Circuit with two turns in quick succession (Circuit IV).

Figure 4: The circuits used in our user study.

We then asked users to motorcycle on the four circuits shown in Figure 4 at random with the HaptiMoto vest's directional cues. Users motorcycled on a parking lot with both real and distractor turn cones, and we asked them to accelerate to between 20 and 30 mph, where the ideal lead distance x is 60 meters at 20 mph and 110 meters at 30 mph. For this evaluation, users received one-, two-, and three-pulse notifications as elaborated in the description of HaptiMoto's implementation.

RESULTS

We recruited 16 participants in our user study, all male and between the ages of 25 and 30 years, inclusive. Each participant in the first part of the study performed a total of 48 turns for four directions (i.e., left, right, straight, back), where everyone performed the intended turn with 100% accuracy.

Figure 5 shows the results from Circuits I and II. For Circuit I, each participant performed tasks for each turn and intersection twice in random order. Together, the participants performed 52 correct left turns, 52 correct right turns, and 12 missed left and right turns from out of 128 turns performed. Six of the missed turns were due to being improperly fitted with the vest and thus not being able to detect the vest's tactile signals, at which point the vest was fitted on them again. Figure 5(a) shows the results from the data points where users could perceive the tactile signals, in which all users successfully chose the correct direction to turn. Seven users from the starting point of the circuit chose the nearer intersection to turn when HaptiMoto instead guided them to the farther intersection, while one user missed the nearer intersection and made the turn at the farther intersection.

For Circuit II, participants performed each turning task once, for a total of 16 data points on each turn and intersection. Participants had to perform 32 turns each for left and right directions, and they all chose the correct direction to turn for each turning task. Figure 5(b) shows the number of correct turns and intersections made. Of a total of $32N \times N4 = 128$ turns, there were nine instances when a participant chose to turn at the nearer intersection when HaptiMoto instead guided the user to the farther intersection, and one instance where a participant turned at the farther intersection instead of the nearer one.

Figure 6 shows the performance of users for Circuits III and IV. Seven of those data points dropped stem from users' inability to perceive tactile signals, due to an improper vest fit. Each of the sixteen users had to perform 128 turns in total, choosing the correct direction in 100 instances while not being able to perceive the tactile signal in 28 instances. From a total of 50 instances in which a user makes a left turn at the first intersection, two instances involved the user missing the second turn at the appropriate intersection. In those two instances, users made the turn 25 m after the intended intersection. Figure 6(a) illustrates the number of correct and incorrect turns from users for Circuit III. Of the 50 total instances in which a user makes a right turn at the first intersection, seven of those instances involved the user missing the second turn at the appropriate intersection. In those seven instances, users made the turn 25 m after the intended intersection. Figure 6(b) illustrates the number of correct turns and the seven wrong instances for Circuit IV.

On a scale of 7, with 1 being the lowest usability rating and 7 being the highest, the mean rating for HaptiMoto's usability is 5.33 and its standard deviation is 1.11. The mean and standard deviation of the user ratings on the tactile signals for left, right, straight, and back are 6.12 ± 1.14, 6.2 ± 0.94, 6.2 ± 0.94, and 5.8 ± 1.68, respectively.

DISCUSSION

We can see from Evaluation I that users were able to perceive and understand the haptic cues (*h1*) and their intent (*h2*). While some users reported interpreting tactile signals for U-turns as straight or vice versa, this confusion did not seem to affect the accuracy for performing turns. In Evaluation I, users did not perceive the tactile signal for 40 of the instances,

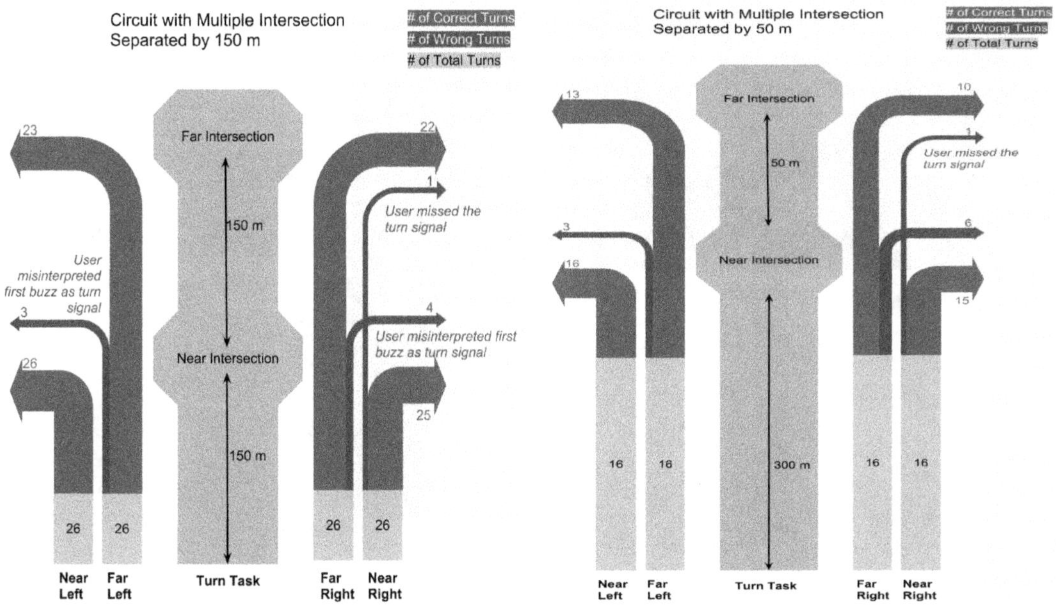

(a) Circuit with intersection separated by 150 m.

(b) Circuit with intersection separated by 50 m.

Figure 5: Results from Evaluation II, with an illustration of the number of turning tasks performed and number of correct turns made in (a) Circuit I and (b) Circuit II from two intersections.

which we attribute to the looseness of the HaptiMoto vest. However, the results show that users did not have problems perceiving or understanding the haptic cues when the HaptiMoto vest was properly fitted.

Evaluation II shows that users could employ the haptic cues for choosing appropriate turns (*h3*), and also shows the errors while choosing a turn. The users chose correct turns with 91% accuracy in Circuit I, 84.4% in Circuit II, and 92.3% in Circuits III and IV. Seven of the eight errors were caused by users choosing to turn at the nearer intersection when they were instead guided to the farther intersection. These errors were due to users misinterpreting the tactile signals. The users reported that they made the turn after receiving two pulses for turning rather than three pulses, for which they were given no prior initial instruction. The three pulses were explained after the first mistake, and the users performed the turning task accurately in following turns. While there was some minor adapting to the system, we pleasantly discovered that users needed almost no instruction for the direction or distance feedback provided by the system, which emphasized the system's intuitiveness.

In the cases of Circuits I and II, one user missed making a turn for each circuit at a nearer intersection due to speeding too fast, and instead turned at the farther intersection. This user reported that he had reacted to the tactile signal too late to safely make the turn, so he continued on to the next intersection and turned there. This demonstrated that the tactile signals were strong enough to at least cause motorcyclists to be aware of correct turns that may be missed due to situations such as aggressive motorcycling. Although we did not consider this scenario when designing HaptiMoto, we would like to keep the tactile signal's intensity at levels where motorcyclists may still be made safely aware of turns.

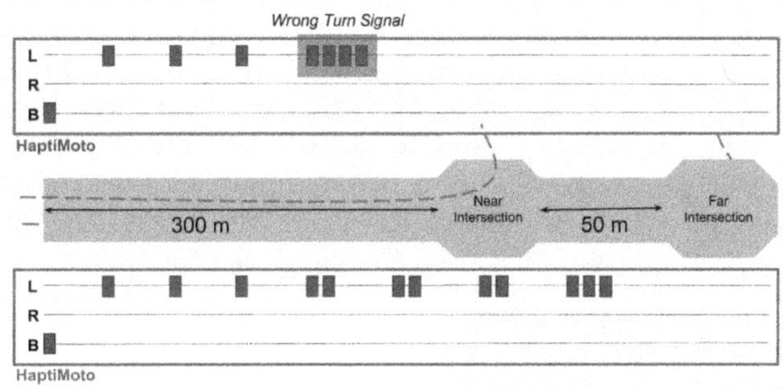

Figure 7: An example scenario where two sequentially GPS updates causes error in HaptiMoto navigation.

Additionally, there were nine instances from Circuit II in which users turned at the nearer intersection as HaptiMoto attempted to navigate them to the farther intersection. These errors occurred from a latency bug with the mobile app's built-in GPS feature, since HaptiMoto relies on the frequency and accuracy of the Android platform's GPS updates. These update can create instances where two GPS update events were received sequentially. While Android enables developers to set a minimum distance traveled or time elapsed between two location update events, there were some instances when these conditions were not met. As a result, this bug can cause two tactile signals to be grouped together as one. For instance, when a motorcyclist is 150 m away from the intended turn while traveling at 20 mph, HaptiMoto would send out a haptic signal to, say, the motorcyclist's left

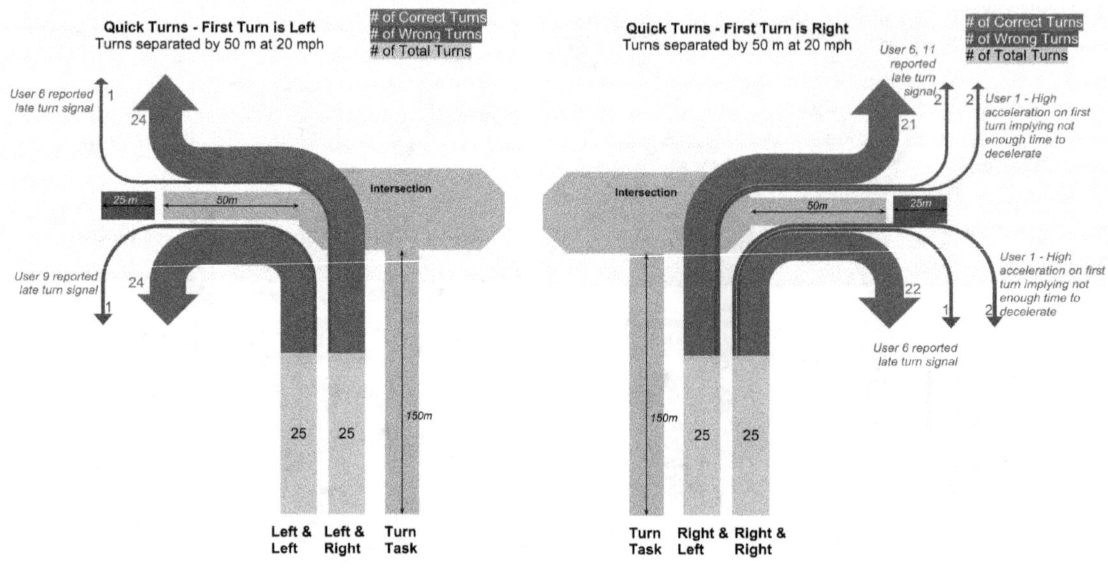

(a) (b)

Figure 6: Results from Evaluation II, with an illustration of the number of turning tasks performed and number of correct turns made in (a) Circuit III and (b) Circuit IV from two turns in quick succession.

shoulder (Figure 7). The next tactile signal would then not be sent to the user until they have traveled an additional fifteen meters or three seconds. For the problematic case however, there were instances when such conditions were not met in-between GPS updates. The location updates were instead sent sequentially, resulting in two turn signals being sent simultaneously. We show this in Figure 7 on the right side of the route. The number of pulses in a signal determines the turn to be taken by the user, but when two turn signals are sent simultaneously, the users receive two separate two-pulse signals perceived as a single four-pulse signal. Since we observed users perceiving any signal which has more than three pulses as turning, they would therefore incorrectly make a turn immediately. We later addressed this bug by adding an additional time-elapsed check during the location update event.

We also observed that when users performed two turns in quick succession with HaptiMoto, there were nine instances from four users where they missed making the second turn (Figure 7). These users reported two different reasons for unsuccessfully making the second turn. Firstly, if they accelerate too quickly after making the first turn, it was difficult for them to decelerate in time to successfully make the second turn. Secondly, they reported instances when HaptiMoto's tactile signal for turning was received too late to safely make the turn. Our system is limited by the pace of Android's GPS updates, and therefore has some limitations in providing prompt tactile signals for turning. Since all four users were comfortably able to make a turn 25 m later after the second turn (i.e., 75 m later after the first turn), we can safely assume that HaptiMoto is able to support navigation of quick turns in succession when turns are separated by more than 75 meters. The errors indicate that motorcyclists require a minimum duration of time to make a turn [33, 37]. Otherwise, when the directional cues are presented within the ideal lead distance from the turn, they are more probable to miss making the turn [10].

Our results support haptic vests' viability as a motorcycle navigation interface, which employs the co-location of haptic cues and target direction [26, 49] and the encoding of warning lead distance with pulse count [10, 22]. Overall, we observed twelve user errors in the study due to weak contact between the user's body and tactors, as similarly noted in [28, 29, 61]. Turning direction accuracy also shows the discreteness and clearness of the haptic cues, with minimal interference from vehicle vibration noise [53]. Participants had suggested using a continuous vibrotactile signal instead of a three-pulse signal just prior to turning. However, our rationale for not implementing a continuous signal in this case is that it would distract the motorcyclist's attention away from the road and could also be perceived as annoying [30].

FUTURE WORK

One result from our user study revealed a flaw in the timing of HaptiMoto's tactile signals, which depended on Android's GPS update frequency that could affect users' navigation performance. We will work on a solution that will accommodate changes in GPS update frequencies. Another future work involves developing additional usability studies for HaptiMoto at higher speeds (e.g., 30-75 mph) above our current studies' range of 20-25 mph. We observed users' perception of the tactile signals decreased at faster speeds, and would like to expand HaptiMoto for alleviating issues from motorcyclists' increased workload in detecting navigational signals while traveling at faster speeds. Another future work we are working on is comparing HaptiGo with audio feedback, which has thus far shown haptic pulses to outperform audio feedback. Lastly, we would like to test HaptiMoto for navigation through complex junctions.

CONCLUSION

The primary purpose of this paper was to develop a wearable tactile navigational interface and demonstrate its effectiveness. Specifically, we tested three hypotheses: 1) haptic cues can be understood by motorcyclists, 2) motorcyclists can understand the haptic cues' intent, and 3) haptic cues can be used to perform routine motorcycle tasks. We designed an adjustable vest with vibrotactile sensors embedded on the the rear shoulders and center back, identified and implemented the minimum required information for route guidance (i.e., next turn direction, distance to approaching turn, and street to turn onto), and designed HaptiMoto's tactile signals to accommodate the information for route guidance. Lastly, we evaluated the system on three scenarios to test our three hypotheses. Our results show that HaptiMoto is an intuitive system that supports our hypotheses.

ACKNOWLEDGMENTS

We greatly thank Stephanie Valentine for her help in stitching circuits on the HaptiMoto vest, and the Texas Transportation Institute for their help in identifying no-traffic circuits in College Station, Texas for our user studies.

REFERENCES

1. Report on transportation accidents in australia. `http://tinyurl.com/rgxcd`, 2005.
2. National highway traffic safety administration, traffic safety facts, 2007.
3. Arduino website. `http://www.arduino.cc/`, 2012.
4. Bluesmirf product page. `http://tinyurl.com/oghbno5`, 2012.
5. Center for disease control and prevention (cdc), motorcycle crash-related data, 2012.
6. Lilypad product page. `http://tinyurl.com/k4oql7z`, 2012.
7. Barfield, W., and Dingus, T. A. *Human factors in intelligent transportation systems*. Psychology Press, 1998.
8. Book, G. A policy on geometric design of highways and streets, 2011.
9. Brown, C. H., and Gordon, M. S. Motorcycle helmet noise and active noise reduction. *Open Acoustics Journal* (2011).
10. Campbell, J. L., Carney, C., and Kantowitz, B. H. Human factors design guidelines for advanced traveler information systems (atis) and commercial vehicle operations (cvo). Tech. rep., 1998.
11. Cao, Y., Van Der Sluis, F., Theune, M., Nijholt, A., et al. Evaluating informative auditory and tactile cues for in-vehicle information systems. Automotive UI (2010).
12. Chang, W., Hwang, W., and Ji, Y. G. Haptic seat interfaces for driver information and warning systems. *International Journal of HCI* (2011).
13. Cummings, D., Lucchese, G., Prasad, M., Aikens, C., Ho, J., and Hammond, T. Haptic and ar interface for paratrooper coordination. CHINZ (2012).
14. de Vries, S. C., van Erp, J. B., and Kiefer, R. J. Direction coding using a tactile chair. *Applied ergonomics* (2009).
15. Dingus, T. A., and Hulse, M. C. Some human factors design issues and recommendations for automobile navigation information systems. *Transportation Research Part C: Emerging Technologies* (1993).
16. Ege, E. S., Cetin, F., and Basdogan, C. Vibrotactile feedback in steering wheel reduces navigation errors during gps-guided car driving. WHC (2011).
17. Elliott, L., van Erp, J., Redden, E., and Duistermaat, M. Field-based validation of a tactile navigation device. *Haptics* (2010).
18. Elliott, L. R., Schmeisser, E. T., and Redden, E. S. Development of tactile and haptic systems for u.s. infantry navigation and communication. HI (2011).
19. Erp, J. B. F. V., Veen, H. A. H. C. V., Jansen, C., and Dobbins, T. Waypoint navigation with a vibrotactile waist belt. *ACM Trans. Appl. Percept. 2*, 2 (Apr. 2005), 106–117.
20. Fröhlich, P., Oulasvirta, A., Baldauf, M., and Nurminen, A. On the move, wirelessly connected to the world. *Commun. ACM* (2011).
21. Gallace, A., Tan, H. Z., and Spence, C. The failure to detect tactile change: A tactile analogue of visual change blindness. *Psychonomic Bulletin & Review* (2006).
22. Gallace, A., Tan, H. Z., Spence, C., et al. Numerosity judgments for tactile stimuli distributed over the body surface. *Perception* (2006).
23. Gallace, A., Zeeden, S., Röder, B., and Spence, C. Lost in the move? secondary task performance impairs tactile change detection on the body. *Consciousness and cognition* (2010).
24. Hart, S. G., and Staveland, L. E. Development of nasa-tlx (task load index): Results of empirical and theoretical research. *Human mental workload* (1988).
25. Hibberd, D. L., Jamson, S. L., and Carsten, O. M. J. Managing in-vehicle distractions: evidence from the psychological refractory period paradigm (2010).
26. Ho, C., Tan, H. Z., and Spence, C. The differential effect of vibrotactile and auditory cues on visual spatial attention. *Ergonomics* (2006).
27. Johnson, L., and Higgins, C. A navigation aid for the blind using tactile-visual sensory substitution. EMBS (2006), 6289–6292.
28. Jones, L. A., Nakamura, M., and Lockyer, B. Development of a tactile vest. HAPTICS (2004).
29. Jones, L. A., and Sarter, N. B. Tactile displays: Guidance for their design and application. *HFES* (2008).
30. Kaaresoja, T., and Linjama, J. Perception of short tactile pulses generated by a vibration motor in a mobile phone. WHC (2005).

31. Lin, M.-W., Cheng, Y.-M., Yu, W., and Sandnes, F. E. Investigation into the feasibility of using tactons to provide navigation cues in pedestrian situations. OZCHI (2008), 299–302.
32. Liu, Y.-C. Comparative study of the effects of auditory, visual and multimodality displays on drivers' performance in advanced traveller information systems. *Ergonomics* (2001).
33. Lunenfeld, H. Human factor considerations of motorist navigation and information systems. VNISC (1989).
34. Magnusson, C., Molina, M., Rassmus-Gröhn, K., and Szymczak, D. Pointing for non-visual orientation and navigation. NordiCHI (2010).
35. Magnusson, C., Rassmus-Gröhn, K., and Szymczak, D. The influence of angle size in navigation applications using pointing gestures. HAID (2010), 107–116.
36. Magnusson, C., Rassmus-Gröhn, K., and Szymczak, D. Scanning angles for directional pointing. MobileHCI (2010), 399–400.
37. Marek, M. A. Roadway design manual. Tech. rep., 1998.
38. Parkes, A. M., Ashby, M. C., and Fairclough, S. H. The effects of different in-vehicle route information displays on driver behaviour. VNIS (1991).
39. Pielot, M., and Boll, S. Tactile wayfinder: Comparison of tactile waypoint navigation with commercial pedestrian navigation systems. LNCS.
40. Pielot, M., Henze, N., and Boll, S. Supporting map-based wayfinding with tactile cues. MobileHCI (2009).
41. Pielot, M., Poppinga, B., Heuten, W., and Boll, S. 6th senses for everyone!: the value of multimodal feedback in handheld navigation aids. ICMI (2011).
42. Pielot, M., Poppinga, B., Heuten, W., and Boll, S. A tactile compass for eyes-free pedestrian navigation. INTERACT (2011).
43. Pielot, M., Poppinga, B., Heuten, W., and Boll, S. Pocketnavigator: studying tactile navigation systems in-situ. CHI (2012).
44. Poppinga, B., Pielot, M., and Boll, S. Tacticycle: a tactile display for supporting tourists on a bicycle trip. In *MobileHCI* (2009).
45. Prasad, M. A., Taele, P., Olubeko, A., and Hammond, T. A. Haptigo: A navigational 'tap on the shoulder'. HAPTICS (2014).
46. Raisamo, R., Nukarinen, T., Pystynen, J., Mäkinen, E., and Kildal, J. Orientation inquiry: a new haptic interaction technique for non-visual pedestrian navigation. EuroHaptics (2012).
47. Reid, G. B., and Nygren, T. E. The subjective workload assessment technique: A scaling procedure for measuring mental workload. *Human mental workload* (1988).
48. Robinson, S., Jones, M., Eslambolchilar, P., Murray-Smith, R., and Lindborg, M. "i did it my way": moving away from the tyranny of turn-by-turn pedestrian navigation. MobileHCI (2010).
49. Ross, D. A., and Blasch, B. B. Wearable interfaces for orientation and wayfinding. Assets (2000).
50. Rümelin, S., Rukzio, E., and Hardy, R. Naviradar: a novel tactile information display for pedestrian navigation. UIST (2011).
51. Salzer, Y., and Oron-Gilad, T. A comparison of" on-thigh" vibrotactile, combined visual-vibrotactile, and visual-only alerting systems for the cockpit under visually demanding conditions.
52. Salzer, Y., Oron-Gilad, T., and Ronen, A. Vibrotactor-belt on the thigh–directions in the vertical plane. Haptics.
53. Shivakumara, B., and Sridhar, V. Study of vibration and its effect on health of the motorcycle rider. *Online Journal of Health and Allied Sciences* (2010).
54. Srikulwong, M., and O'Neill, E. A comparison of two wearable tactile interfaces with a complementary display in two orientations. HAID (2010).
55. Srinivasan, R., and Jovanis, P. P. Effect of selected in-vehicle route guidance systems on driver reaction times. *HFES* (1997).
56. Steltenpohl, H., and Bouwer, A. Vibrobelt: tactile navigation support for cyclists. IUI (2013).
57. Streeter, L. A., Vitello, D., and Wonsiewicz, S. A. How to tell people where to go: comparing navigational aids. *International Journal of Man-Machine Studies* (1985).
58. Szymczak, D., Rassmus-Gröhn, K., Magnusson, C., and Hedvall, P.-O. A real-world study of an audio-tactile tourist guide. MobileHCI (2012).
59. Tan, H. Z., Gray, R., Young, J. J., and Traylor, R. A haptic back display for attentional and directional cueing. *Haptics-e* (2003).
60. Thorndyke, P. W., and Hayes-Roth, B. Differences in spatial knowledge acquired from maps and navigation. *Cognitive psychology* (1982).
61. van Erp, J. B. Absolute localization of vibrotactile stimuli on the torso. *Percept. Psychophys.* (2008).
62. van Erp, J. B., Kooi, F. L., Bronkhorst, A. W., van Leeuwen, D. L., van Esch, M. P., and van Wijngaarden, S. J. Multimodal interfaces: a framework based on modality appropriateness. vol. 50 of *HFES* (2006), 1542–1546.
63. van Erp, J. B., and Van Veen, H. A. Vibrotactile in-vehicle navigation system. *Transportation Research Part F: Traffic Psychology and Behaviour* (2004).
64. Wickens, C. Multiple resources and performance prediction. *Theoretical Issues in Ergonomics Science* (2002).
65. Williamson, J., Robinson, S., Stewart, C., Murray-Smith, R., Jones, M., and Brewster, S. Social gravity: a virtual elastic tether for casual, privacy-preserving pedestrian rendezvous. CHI (2010).

Experimental Evaluation of User Interfaces for Visual Indoor Navigation

Andreas Möller [1], Matthias Kranz [2], Stefan Diewald [1], Luis Roalter [1], Robert Huitl [1], Tobias Stockinger [2], Marion Koelle [2], Patrick Lindemann [2]
[1] Technische Universität München, Arcisstraße 21, 80333 Munich, Germany
[2] Universität Passau, Innstraße 43, 94032 Passau, Germany
andreas.moeller@tum.de, matthias.kranz@uni-passau.de, {stefan.diewald, roalter, huitl}@tum.de, {tobias.stockinger, marion.koelle, patrick.lindemann}@uni-passau.de

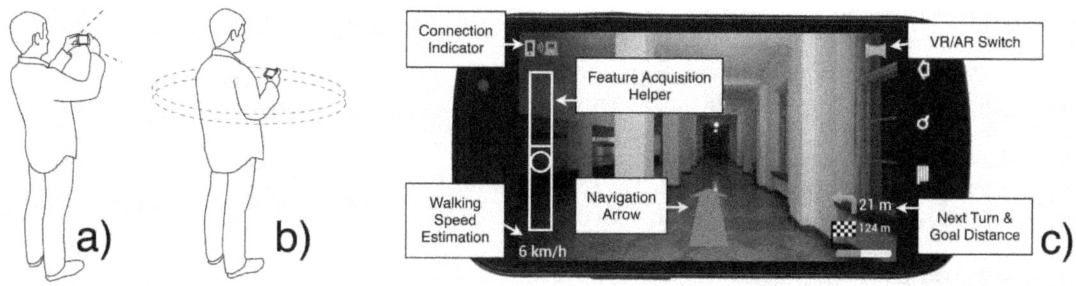

Figure 1. We present and evaluate a novel user interface for indoor navigation, incorporating two modes. In augmented reality (AR) mode, navigation instructions are shown as an overlay over the live camera image and the phone is held as depicted in Picture a). In virtual reality (VR) mode, a correctly oriented 360° panorama image is shown when holding the phone as in Picture b). The interface particularly addresses the *vision-based* localization method by including special UI elements that support the acquisition of "good" query images. Screenshot c) shows a prototype incorporating the presented VR user interface.

ABSTRACT
Mobile location recognition by capturing images of the environment (visual localization) is a promising technique for indoor navigation in arbitrary surroundings. However, it has barely been investigated so far how the user interface (UI) can cope with the challenges of the vision-based localization technique, such as varying quality of the query images. We implemented a novel UI for visual localization, consisting of Virtual Reality (VR) and Augmented Reality (AR) views that actively communicate and ensure localization accuracy. If necessary, the system encourages the user to point the smartphone at distinctive regions to improve localization quality. We evaluated the UI in an experimental navigation task with a prototype, informed by initial evaluation results using design mockups. We found that VR can contribute to efficient and effective indoor navigation even at unreliable location and orientation accuracy. We discuss identified challenges and share lessons learned as recommendations for future work.

Author Keywords
Virtual Reality; Augmented Reality; Indoor Navigation; Visual Localization; Mobile Interaction.

CHI 2014, April 26 - May 01 2014, Toronto, ON, Canada

ACM 978-1-4503-2473-1/14/04...$15.00.
http://dx.doi.org/10.1145/2556288.2557003

ACM Classification Keywords
H.5.m. Information Interfaces and Presentation (e.g. HCI): Miscellaneous

General Terms
Human Factors; Design; Measurement.

INTRODUCTION AND MOTIVATION
Imagine you are at the airport, at a mall or in a museum and your smartphone gives you directions to your departure gate, that hot new fashion store, or the famous Dalí painting you want to visit. While mobile navigation is omnipresent outdoors, it is not inside buildings. Reliable *indoor* navigation is still a "hot topic". While researchers are still looking for the optimal localization method, appropriate novel user interfaces for these scenarios have to be investigated.

An analysis of existing indoor localization techniques (which we discuss in the Background section), shows *visual localization* to have multiple advantages to concurrent methods for indoor usage. Using computer vision, this technique captures and matches images of the environment with previously recorded reference images of known locations. However, we found that existing user interfaces (UIs) for pedestrian navigation are not appropriate for that (relatively new) technique, since they do not particularly address the characteristics of *visual* localization. As the device uses the camera to orientate and position itself, visual localization works similar to human orientation and wayfinding (e.g., based on landmarks and salient objects). The technical implications of this localization method should be reflected in the user interface to the advantage of both the UI and the underlying localization mechanism. In that way, the UI can benefit from the strengths of visual localization, and the (perceived and actual) localization quality can be improved through UI elements and the user interactions with them.

In this paper, we implemented a novel UI concept for an indoor navigation system which is specially fitted to visual localization, and we provide a first evaluation of this UI, based on experimental simulation, compared against the conventional augmented reality (AR) technique. Moreover, our work represents an example for interweaving the UI and the underlying localization technique of an indoor navigation system to the advance of both, arguing that localization and UI should be treated jointly for being most effective.

The structure of this paper is as follows: We begin with presenting related work, where we focus on existing user interfaces for navigation systems and on the particularities of visual localization. Subsequently, we describe the implemented interface concept and UI elements. We introduce the conducted study and discuss our experimental findings in a comprehensive way. We finally share lessons learned in order to inform the design of future visual indoor navigation systems.

BACKGROUND AND RELATED WORK

Discussion of Visual Localization and Other Techniques

First, we discriminate visual localization against other techniques to localize a device inside buildings, and outline the advantages of visual localization. By visual localization, we understand the usage of computer vision to correlate query and reference images by characteristic properties (so-called feature matching). We explicitly do not comprise marker-based approaches (e.g. [17]) by this term.

Feature matching has the advantage that image can be captured with the device's camera at any location, which then serve as query images. No augmentation of the infrastructure with fiducial markers (i.e., points of reference) is necessary any more. Other infrastructure-based approaches, e.g. WLAN fingerprinting [9], require dense coverage of access points. This coverage is in many buildings not available, and it costs money and effort to establish.

Furthermore, a common camera-equipped smartphone is sufficient for visual localization. By contrast, approaches based on signal metrics, such as angle (AOA) or time of arrival (TOA), require special hardware, such as directional antennas or ultra-accurate timers [10]. Signal-*strength*-based measurements are feasible with common hardware, but the location often can only be determined within a radius of 1 m or more [9], even in laboratory tests. In the real world, where the typical density of access points is mostly lower, expected localization accuracies are likely to be inferior to those in controlled experiments. Fiducial markers provide exact localization only at locations where such markers are placed. Apart from these "key locations", the position needs to be estimated with relative positioning techniques, such as dead reckoning.

With a database of sufficiently densely recorded reference images, visual localization can be performed at almost any location and on centimeter level [19]. Based on the position of feature points, even the pose (i.e., the viewing angle) can be detected, which is usually not the case with other approaches. However, the image database must be built up once (by mapping the environment) and updated regularly when buildings and objects therein significantly change.

There are several concrete implementations of camera-based location recognition systems [4, 17, 19]. Hile and Borriello correlated a floor plan or a previously captured reference image to estimate the device's pose and to calculate an information overlay [4]. However, the system only works for static images. Mulloni et al. [17] relocalized a phone by recognizing visual markers and displayed the new location on a map. Schroth et al. [19] presented localization approaches through feature-based image matching, but without focusing on a specific user interface.

UIs for Pedestrian Navigation Systems

After having motivated the visual localization technique, we provide an overview of pedestrian navigation user interfaces. Kray et al. [7] use sketches, maps or pre-rendered 3D views according to the quality of the location estimate or device capabilities. Butz et al. [3] propose a simple directional arrow when localization accuracy is high, and suggest to use a 2D map and more additional cues in case of decreasing accuracy.

Besides rendered graphics, augmented reality (AR) is considered an intuitive way to visualize a location and has been used in manifold ways [1]. In AR, virtual elements are superimposed over a live camera view, so that users do not need to translate between the virtual representation and the real world [18]. Liu et al. [11] presented a smartphone-based indoor navigation system with superimposed directional arrows and textual navigation instructions. They found that adapting the interface to the users' preferences is particularly important. AR can also convey information beyond navigation instructions. Narzt et al. visualized elements in a car navigation system that are invisible in the real world, such as highway exits that are hidden behind a truck [18]. Similar ideas could be adapted for pedestrian navigation. Miyashita et al. [12] used AR for a museum guidance system. Augmentations enhanced exhibits with additional information. Visitors were guided along a predefined route through the museum when they searched with their phone for the next AR object. An AR system which employed floor-projected arrows as way directions was evaluated better in terms of usability than a map-based system [20].

Researchers also recognized the value of landmarks for orientation (particularly for outdoor pedestrian navigation). Hile et al. [5] created route descriptions that include geo-tagged images as additional cues besides textual instructions. A similar approach is presented by Beeharee and Steed [2]. Miyazaki et al. [13] use panoramic images to provide additional information on surrounding buildings in an AR-like manner, but the location must have been determined before with GPS or manually on a map. Mulloni et al. suggested different perspectives for displaying panoramas [16]. They found that by top-down and bird's eye views of a panorama, users were quicker to locate objects in the environment than using a frontal view.

UI Challenges with Visual Localization

When going beyond key-point localization, as used in many prior systems [4, 17], towards continuous guidance, as known from outdoor navigation, new challenges emerge. In that case, the visual system must capture query images on a regular basis. The challenge is here that quality and distinctiveness of the query images impact the location estimate. Ideal query images are crisp and show characteristic areas with lots of visual information. However, the camera-visible scene can happen to be blurred due to motion of the device, or can be not sufficiently unique (e.g., plain corridors often look very similar). The pose of the device plays a role as well – the typical orientation when holding a phone (about 45° downwards) entails that rather the floor is visible to the camera, but not corridors and rooms and the objects therein (which would be good candidates for reference images).

USER INTERFACE CONCEPT

Our implementation is based on the UI concept we have presented in earlier work [14]. It includes a panorama-based view as a complement to Augmented Reality and proposes different visualizations for motivating users to record "good" query images. The concept is dedicated to visual localization and conceived as "live interface" during the entire navigation process, i.e., it is used not only for (re-)localization at a certain point on the route, but allows continuous guidance. Additionally, it is prepared for the use of context-based services by interacting with objects in the environment.

Augmented and Virtual Reality

The interface consists of two modes for continuous guidance: *Augmented Reality* (AR) and *Virtual Reality* (VR). *Augmented Reality* enhances the video seen by the smartphone's camera by superimposing navigation information, such as a directional arrow. Since users need to hold the phone upright for visual localization (so that the camera can see the environment), this seems a reasonable interface for a visual localization system. Users hold the phone as illustrated in Fig. 1a) and "look through" the phone in order to see the augmentation directly on their way. However, this pose might be inconvenient for long-term or frequent use (e.g. in unknown environments).

The alternative mode is *Virtual Reality*, which can be employed also when the phone is carried in a lower position. It displays pre-recorded images of the environment (downloaded from a server) that are arranged to a 360° panorama on the mobile device. Navigation arrows are directly rendered into the panorama, so that their orientation is fixed in relation to the virtual 360° view. This is expected to have several advantages. First, the device can be held in a more natural and comfortable way, as illustrated in Fig. 1b), since no alignment of the overlays with live video is required. Second, we expect that the "hard-embedded" navigation arrows provide a more reliable navigation, as they also show the correct way in the panorama if the orientation estimate is not perfectly accurate. Furthermore, in case no reliable localization estimate is possible, the frequency in which panoramas are updated can be lowered. Hence, we expect VR to be more robust than the more conventional AR view.

Specially Designed UI Elements For Visual Localization

Dedicated UI elements for the visual localization method shall help to improve localization accuracy. We assume that a visual localization system can determine its location better when the device is held upright, as if taking a photo. In that pose, the camera points at regions in eye height, such as exhibits, posters or signs, which are potentially more discriminative motives for feature matching than if the camera were pointed downwards. Consequently, if localization certainty has reached a lower bound (this value could e.g. be determined by the localization system or by user preferences), an indicator prompts the user to actively point at regions containing more visual features. The user is thereby asked to bring the phone from a pose as in Fig. 1a) to one as in Fig. 1b). Four indicator types fulfilling that purpose are proposed:

- *Text Hint*: A notification to raise up the phone appears until the pose is such that sufficient features are visible.
- *Blur*: The live video view turns blurry; the closer the device is moved to a feature-rich position, the sharper the image becomes. This metaphor is inspired by an autofocus camera, motivating the user to find the "best" shot.
- *Color Scale*: A colored scale, ranging from red to green, indicates the quality of the current scene for relocalization. The user should steer the indicator into the green area.
- *Spirit Level*: The user must align the bubble of a spirit level in the middle of the scale to find the ideal inclination, so that the camera points at a feature-rich region.

Involving the user to help the system improve its position accuracy has already been used in other contexts for self-localization. For example, Kray et al. [8] asked users whether they can see certain landmarks from their point of view in order to perform semantic reasoning about their position.

Another way to draw the users' attention to feature-rich objects is to explicitly highlight them in the viewport. Object highlighting is motivated by an additional benefit for the user: context-based services. Like this, stores in a mall, individual shop windows, or even doors and doorplates can become points of interaction. However, a convenient side effect is that typical "interaction areas" like posters or signs often have a very characteristic appearance and therefore also serve well as reference images for localization (we though have to note that they are also subject to frequent change, see Discussion section). If they attract the user's attention and are focused with the smartphone's camera, they implicitly help improve the system's certainty of the location estimate.

ANALYSIS OF CONCEPT EVALUATION

A non-functional mock-up of the proposed UI concept has been evaluated in an online survey in prior work [14]. We summarize and analyze the results of this evaluation as a starting point for our investigation of the concept's effectiveness in practice. Extending on this prior work, we developed a working system which was evaluated in a laboratory study.

Research Questions and Results Summary

Perceived Accuracy and User Preference for AR/VR

In order to have subjects estimate how they perceive accuracy in the AR and VR modes, videos of a pre-recorded sample navigation task were played back alongside with the simulated output of the system. The video demonstrations contained the simulated field of vision (i.e., the "reality") in the upper part, and the simulated visualization on the smartphone in the lower part. In four videos for each mode, different types of errors (position, orientation, both error types together) were induced to the system's location estimate, so that the simulated output changed accordingly. Subjects rated the perceived accuracy and quality of the guidance instructions they saw in the videos. In the individual ratings of each video, AR was preferred in case of reliable localization, but VR was perceived as more accurate when errors were introduced. The panoramas in VR helped subjects to orientate themselves even if the location estimate of the system was incorrect. However, when asked which method subjects would generally prefer, 58% chose AR. This inconsistency motivated us to gain a deeper understanding of users' preferences.

Understandability and Level of Distraction

Subjects rated four visualizations (text hint, color scale, blur, spirit level) with respect to how likely it would make them raise the phone. The most effective visualizations were the text instructions and spirit level metaphor, followed by color scale and blur. Furthermore, subjects compared two object highlighting visualizations: *Frame* showed a rectangle around the object of interest, while *Soft Border* showed a semi-transparent overlay, smoothly fading out at the borders. We hypothesized that *Soft Border* better hides the inherent inaccuracy and jitter effects of object tracking due to the lack of a sharp border, adding to a more stable, calm visualization. As a consequence, distraction from the navigation task would be reduced with *Soft Border* compared to *Frame*. In fact, subjects rated the *Soft Border* visualization equally attention-raising as *Frame*, but at the same time less distracting.

Discussion and Motivation for Experimental Evaluation

We draw the following conclusions and lessons learned from this initial evaluation, which motivate us to a further iteration of the presented concept, and to an experimental evaluation.

1. A questionnaire-based survey with mockup videos might not reveal the true strengths and weaknesses of AR and VR modes. Users did not actually navigate in a building and thus could not evaluate certain aspects in situ (e.g., the experience on a small screen, or the additional effort to carry the phone). Moreover, using the interfaces while walking (secondary task) might have produced different results than evaluating them in a video (primary task).
2. Subjects perceived the VR mode to be more reliable in case of inaccurate localization. However, they widely preferred AR in a direct ranking, which seems contradictory. We hypothesize that in situ, preference for AR would be lower, since the phone must be carried in an uncomfortable pose for AR to work. Such physical usage factors cannot be determined in an online study. AR probably appeared in the mockup as the more elegant solution, compared to a "flip book" impression of VR.
3. No combined evaluation of AR and VR has been performed to see which mode subjects actually use more frequently in a navigation task.
4. The additional UI elements (indicators to raise the phone up) were only evaluated in terms of understandability, but not in terms of effectivity. Results do not tell if these elements really lead to more detected features and thus to improved localization. It was only examined which of the *Frame* and *Soft Border* visualization is believed to be less distracting (based on mockup videos), but not what was their actual effect based on actual object tracking.

PROTOTYPE

In order to evaluate the previously presented UI in an experiment, we built a prototype in Android 2.3[1] following the tool requirements in [15]. We implemented the described VR and AR modes as shown in Fig. 1c). Users can either manually switch between VR and AR with a button on the top right of the screen, or the system can switch modes automatically based on the gravity sensor readings. In an upright pose as in Fig. 1a), the system switches to AR; in a pose as in Fig. 1b), the VR visualization is selected. Based on empirical trials, we set the threshold angles to an inclination of 35° for switching to AR, and to an inclination of 30° for switching back to VR.

Simulation of Self-Localization and Navigation

We implemented the navigation mechanism with a Wizard-of-Oz (WOz) approach [6]. This allow us to modify the accuracy of position and orientation estimates throughout the different study conditions. Further, WOz enables comparable conditions for all participants. A live localization system would not guarantee reproducible behavior in all trials.

We built a WOz app (see Fig. 4) to control the navigation instructions that subjects see on a predefined path in a reproducible way. With this app, the experimenter sends location information to the subject's device at the desired position of the route, and can deliberately trigger localization and orientation errors. The subject's device uses this information to render the VR or AR visualization accordingly (see Fig. 1c).

The navigation interface on the subject's device is implemented with OpenGL ES 2.0. For VR, it displays 360° panorama images of key locations and draws the navigation arrow on top. For AR, the directional arrow is anchored to virtual "key point" locations similar to VR, except that it is overlaid on live video from the rear camera. The panorama photos of the route used in the experiment and the associated walking arrow directions for each key point have been prepared and stored in the WOz app. For both AR and VR, the compass was used to auto-rotate the visualization, accounting for device orientation. In VR, users could also drag and hold panoramas to rotate them manually; lifting up the finger re-enabled auto-rotation.

Elements Specific To Visual Localization

Out of the four suggested indicators to motivate users to raise the phone up (*Text, Blur, Color, Spirit Level*), we chose a combination of the spirit level metaphor and a text hint, as these two were evaluated best in prior work [14]. The indicator can

[1]As of July 2013, still >33% of devices run Android 2.3 or lower (http://developer.android.com/about/dashboards/index.html, last visited: September 2013)

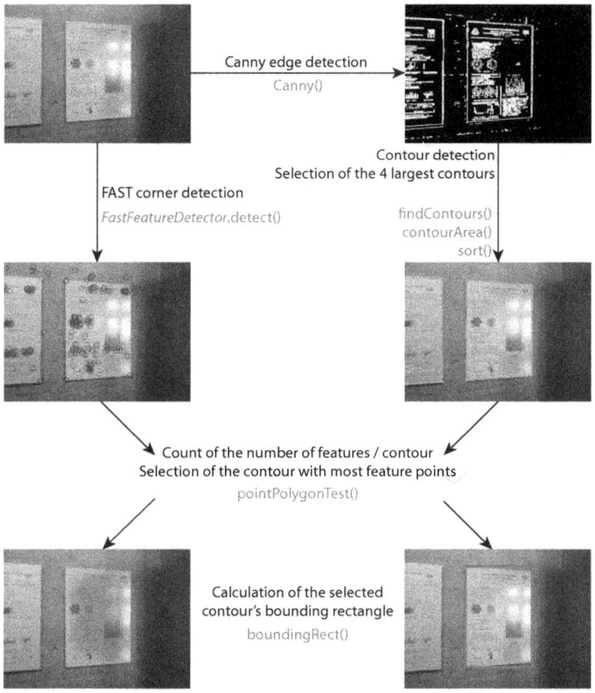

Figure 2. General proceeding for detecting and highlighting objects with two different visualizations: a soft border overlay, supposed to be less distracting (left), and a rectangular frame (right). Best viewed in color.

either pop up automatically when the number of visible features falls below a definable threshold, or it can be triggered through the WOz app. For the automatic trigger, we used a FAST feature detector from the OpenCV framework for Android to detect the number of features in the camera's live image. The anticipated position of the device (90° angle) is determined by the phone's gravity sensor.

We also implemented an object highlighting function which we trimmed to detect posters on uniform backgrounds using the image processing pipeline depicted in Fig. 2. For each frame, a contour detection is applied after edges have been enhanced by a Canny edge detector. The contour containing the most FAST features is regarded as the most interesting object in the scene, and is highlighted. We created two visualizations: for the *Frame* highlight, a red rectangle is drawn; for *Soft Border*, a semi-transparent texture with gradient borders is drawn at the position of the chosen contour.

EXPERIMENTAL EVALUATION

We evaluated the described user interface concept regarding its ability to deal with the previously exposed challenges. By these experiments, we aim at verifying the results of the initial mockup's evaluation. We conducted three experiments, covering the following aspects of the navigation interface: (1) efficiency, perception and convenience of AR and VR under different accuracy conditions, (2) effectivity of UI elements specific to vision-based localization, and (3) convenience and distraction of object highlighting.

In all experiments, subjects used a Samsung Galaxy S II (4.3-inch screen, 8 megapixel camera); the WOz app ran on a

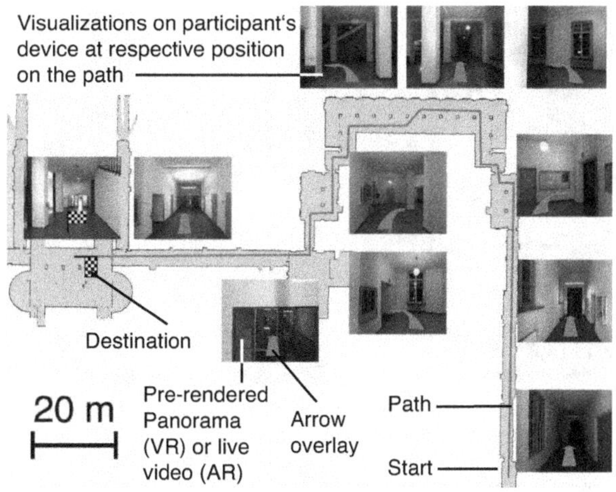

Figure 3. The indoor path used for the navigation task in the study (220 meters), alongside with some sample images and route instructions as they were displayed on the subjects' phone. Best viewed in color.

Samsung Nexus S (4-inch screen). Both devices had a screen resolution of 480×800 pixels.

Participants and Design

12 people (11 males, 1 female) between 23 and 27 years (average age: 24, standard deviation = 1.3) participated in the study. Most subjects were students; none were involved in our research project. No compensation was paid. The experimental design of all three experiments was within-subjects.

Experiment 1: Navigation using VR and AR

Hypotheses

We hypothesize that users reach their navigation destination faster with VR than with AR, i.e., that VR is more efficient **(H1)**. Further, similar to the online study, we suppose that VR will be perceived to be more accurate in case of errors **(H2)**. Although subjects preferred AR over VR in the online evaluation [14] (despite the higher perceived accuracy of VR), we hypothesize that VR would be generally favored in a hands-on study **(H3)**.

Task and Measurements

Subjects performed a navigation task in a university building on a path of 220 meters length (see Fig. 3), using both the AR and the VR mode. The accuracy of the system's location estimate was varied in four conditions (*No Error*, *Position Error*, *Orientation Error*, *Combined Error*), for both AR and VR. Consequently, each user traversed the path eight times. We decided to use the same path in all conditions for better comparability, but counterbalanced the order of conditions with a 4×4 Latin square to weigh out learning effects over all conditions. Subjects were asked to rely only on the given instructions, so that they could not be sure whether the path would not vary.

Navigation instructions were fed into the subject's phone by the experimenter (Wizard of Oz). The experimenter walked approx. one meter behind the subject and sent the appropriate panoramas in VR mode (and directional arrows in AR mode) to the subject's phone using the WOz interface (see Fig. 4,

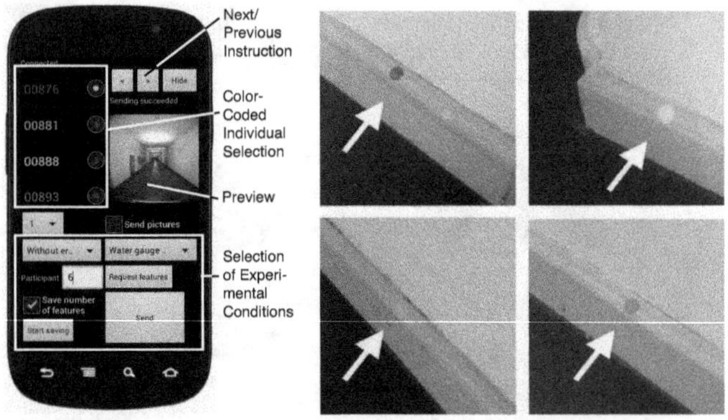

Figure 4. The WOz app for controlling visualizations on the subject's device and simulating localization errors (left). Markers in the corridors (right) helped the experimenter to trigger visualizations at identical locations for similar experimental conditions. Best viewed in color.

left). Colored labels in the app and on the skirting board (see Fig. 4, right) helped the experimenter to choose the correct image at the same locations.

In error conditions, the experimenter replaced correct images and instructions twice by short sequences of misplaced (*Position Error*) and misoriented panoramas (*Orientation Error*). Those errors were introduced at the same locations for all participants. Start and end time of each run (from receiving the first panorama until reaching the destination) were measured by the device. Users were asked to "think aloud" while using the system and answered a questionnaire after each run.

Results of Experiment 1

Efficiency

Subjects were in average 25 seconds faster to reach their destination with VR (averagely 2:39 minutes for the 220 m path) than with AR (averagely 3:04 minutes), which is a significant difference according to a paired sample t-test ($p = 0.002$, $\alpha < 0.05$), and confirms **H1**. With VR, no significant time differences between conditions were found. With AR, differences between conditions were partly significant. Subjects were slower in the *Orientation* and *Combined Error* condition than in the *No Error* or *Position Error* condition (see top right table in Fig. 5). This signifies that AR works worse in case of (particularly orientation) errors.

Accuracy Perception

Subject rated the perceived accuracy in the conditions *Without Error*, *Position Error*, *Orientation Error* and *Combined Error*. Subjects were presented the following statements: *"The system seemed to know well where I am"* (relating to the position estimate), *"The system seemed to know well in which direction I am looking"* (relating to the orientation estimate), *"The navigation instructions were always correct"* (relating to the perceived correctness of individual instructions), and *"Overall, I found the guidance accurate"* (relating to the general guidance accuracy).

Agreements to each statement were indicated on a symmetric 7-step Likert scale where -3 corresponds to "strongly disagree" and +3 to "strongly agree". Fig. 5 summarizes the responses in box plots. As the response format approximates an interval-level measurement, the mean values are indicated in the diagram in addition to medians. However, in the following we only use medians (M) and non-parametric tests to report the results. α denotes the level of significance; W denotes the test statistic in Wilcoxon signed-rank tests.

Both in VR and AR mode, subjects clearly identified position and orientation accuracy differences between the *No Error* and the respective error condition. The Wilcoxon signed-rank test showed p-values below the significance level of $\alpha < 0.05$ for differences in position accuracy (AR mode: $W = 15$, $p = 0.037$, $\alpha < 0.05$; VR mode: $W = 28$, $p = 0.021$, $\alpha < 0.05$) and slightly higher p-values for orientation accuracy (AR mode: $W = 19.5$, $p = 0.073$, $\alpha > 0.05$; VR mode: $W = 55$, $p = 0.005$, $\alpha < 0.05$). This indicates that subjects were able to generally identify the induced position and orientation errors.

However, only with AR, p-values below 0.05 were observed for differences in perceived correctness between error and no error conditions ($p = 0.015$ for position and $p = 0.034$ for orientation). The perceived correctness of instructions was rated significantly higher for VR than for AR. With *Position Error*, rating medians were 3 for VR and 1 for AR ($W = 6$, $p = 0.030$, $\alpha < 0.05$). With *Both Errors*, medians were 2.5 for VR and 1.5 for AR ($W = 3.5$, $p = 0.023$, $\alpha < 0.05$). Only with *Orientation Error*, medians were slightly above significance (VR: $M = 2$; AR: $M = 1$; $W = 4.5$, $p = 0.065$, $\alpha > 0.05$). Those results indicate that VR is generally considered to be more accurate than AR (which supports **H2**).

Convenience and User Preference

Asked for the preferred system, 50% decided for VR, 33% for AR, and 17% were undecided (supporting **H3**). This strong tendency is presumably not only grounded in the quality of navigation instructions, which were perceived to be better in VR, but also in the convenience when using the system. Subjects found carrying the phone more convenient in VR ($M = 2$) than in AR ($M = 0$), which is a significant difference ($W = 0$, $p = 0.009$, $\alpha < 0.05$) The required upright position for carrying the phone in AR was physically constraining. One participant said that it could work *"well for 200 meters, but not more"*. Most subjects found it embarrassing to pass by other people in that pose, because others might fear being recorded. This problem was not given in VR, because the camera in that case pointed towards the floor.

Experiment 2: Effect of Vision-Specific UI Elements with Combined Interface

Hypothesis

We hypothesize that the spirit level indicator actually makes subjects point at areas with more visual features and thereby increases localization accuracy. More precisely, we expect that the visibility of the indicator increases the average number of visual features in the captured images **(H4)**.

Task and Measurements

Subjects performed a navigation task on the path shown in Fig. 3, but in opposite direction as in Experiment 1, so that the path was not already too familiar. Three times during the walk, a relocalization procedure, as it would be required from

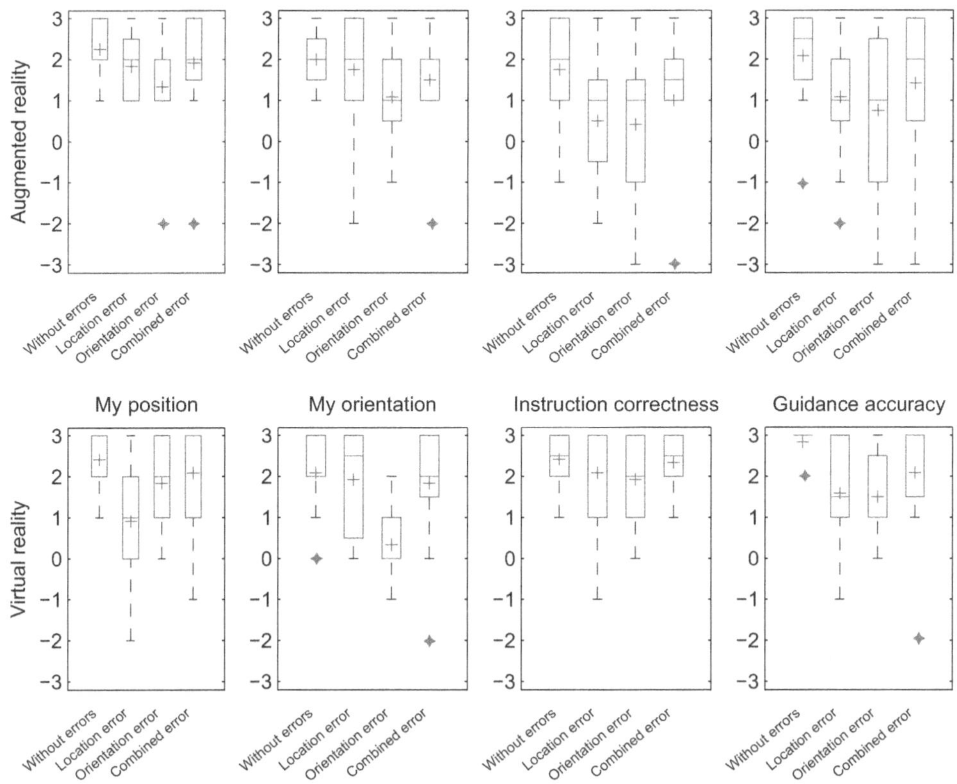

Mode	Condition	Time m:ss	Avg./ Mode
AR	No Errors	2:52	3:04
	Position	2:53	
	Orientation	3:23	
	Combined	3:07	
VR	No Errors	2:36	2:39
	Position	2:41	
	Orientation	2:44	
	Combined	2:36	

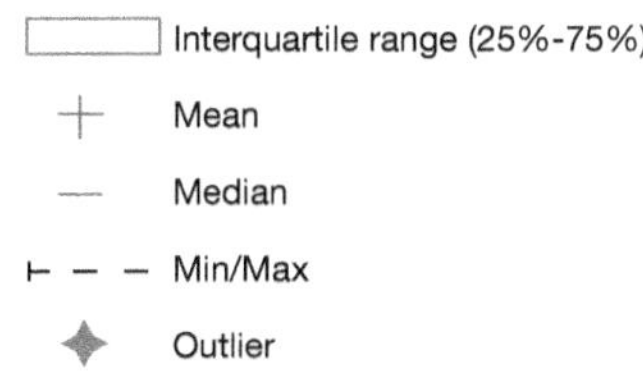

My position: The system seemed to know well where I am.
My orientation: The system seemed to know well in which direction I am looking.
Instruction correctness: The navigation instructions were always correct.
Guidance accuracy: Overall, I found the guidance accurate.

Figure 5. ***Left:*** **Perceived guidance accuracies in experimental conditions of AR and VR interfaces. The box plots visualize the level of agreement to the statements on the bottom right. (on 7-step Likert scales ranging from -3 to +3).** ***Top right:*** **Task completion time using VR and AR. In AR, Subjects on average took 25 seconds longer, and differences between conditions were higher. Best viewed in color.**

time to time in a self-contained system, was simulated. The experimenter triggered a spirit level visualization (cf. Fig. 1c) to appear on the subjects' device. The indicator told subjects to collect enough features for relocalization. As soon as subjects raised the phone until the bubble was centered on the scale, the indicator disappeared and a location update (i.e., the correct arrow/panorama) was displayed. To increase the degree of realism, the interface automatically switched between the AR and VR visualization based on the phone's inclination, as described in the *Prototype* section. Subjects were not given any instructions how they should carry the phone.

We logged the inclination of the phone (whether it was carried down or upright), whether the feature indicator was currently shown or not, as well as the number of detected FAST features (all in one-second intervals). After the experiment, users answered a questionnaire.

Results of Experiment 2

Reliable localization requires 100 to 150 features in the image (empirical values). While the indicator was visible, the average number of detected features per frame rose from 42 to 101. Given that the amount of frames in which more than 150 features were detected was 20.7% with active indicator, and 8.1% with inactive indicator, the indicator significantly increased the probability for successful re-localization, which confirms **H4**. While those ratios may in overall appear low, it has to be kept in mind that in practice, a certain amount

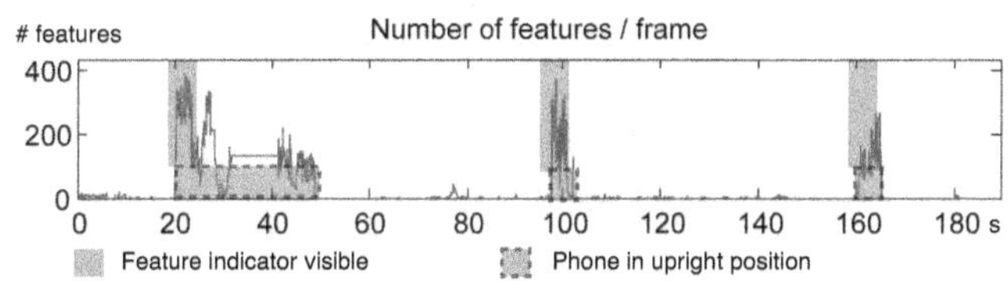

Figure 6. When the feature indicator is visible (light blue), users move the phone up (green) and more visual features are detected per frame. This diagram exemplarily shows one subject's data. Best viewed in color.

of frames will always be subject to motion blur, and 20% of frames with sufficient features still yields on average 5 frames per second (at 25 frames per second), which is sufficient for continuous visual localization. Fig. 6 illustrates, based on an exemplary excerpt of the experiment's data, how the number of features per frame was correlated with the phone inclination and the state of the indicator.

The experiment also showed that subjects preferred the lower carrying position for VR mode, compared to the upright pose for AR mode. They only raised the phone when told so by the visualization, but soon returned to the more comfortable carrying position. None of the subject deliberately chose to carry the phone upright which would have activated AR mode.

Subjects responded that they found the pose-dependent switch between AR and VR convenient (median of agreement M = 2.5). They also understood the meaning of the indica-

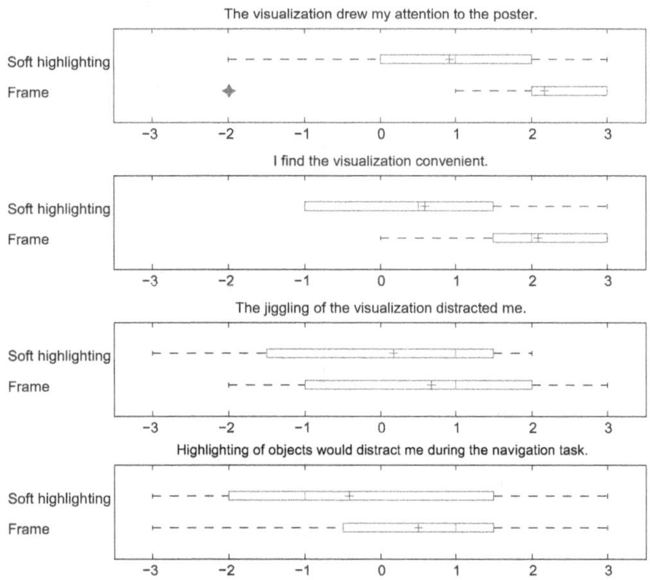

Figure 7. User feedback on *Frame* and *Soft Highlight* object visualization. Answers were given on a 7-step Likert scale, ranging from -3 (strongly disagree) to +3 (strongly agree). For symbol legend see Fig. 5.

tor: they agreed with M = 3 to the statement *"What I should do when the indicator appeared was clear to me"*, and with M = 3 to the statement *"I have been motivated by the indicator to raise the phone up"*.

Experiment 3: Object Highlighting Methods

Hypothesis

We hypothesize that highlighting objects might have a distracting effect, but that a soft border can reduce the effect size, compared to a simple rectangular highlighting **(H5)**.

Task and Measurements

We evaluated the two ways of highlighting objects, *Frame* and *Soft Highlight*, as described earlier and illustrated in Fig. 2. Our algorithm is currently optimized to detect square, feature-rich objects out of a uniform background. This applies to, e.g., a poster on a wall, which we chose as scenario for evaluating the object highlighting mechanism. It was tested beforehand that the posters could be robustly recognized. Subjects pointed at the posters using both highlighting visualizations. Feedback was afterwards collected by a questionnaire.

Results of Experiment 3

The results are summarized in Fig. 7. On a Likert scale from -3 to +3, subjects indicated that *Frame* drew more attention to the poster (M = 3) than *Soft Highlight* (M = 1). Given that the visualization signals a possibility to interact with the object, they found *Frame* more convenient (M = 2) than *Soft Highlight* (M = 0.5). The semi-transparency of *Soft Highlight* complicated readability of text on the poster. Regarding distraction, the visible contours of the *Frame* visualization were perceived as more unstable. During a navigation task, subjects would be more distracted by *Frame* (M = 1) than by *Soft Highlight* (M = −1). Although this is a tendency towards **H5**, this difference was not significant. However, we found significant differences between *Frame* and *Soft Border* for attention and convenience ratings (Student's t-test, $p < 0.05$).

GENERAL DISCUSSION AND LESSONS LEARNED

We now discuss the findings of Experiments 1–3, also in comparative view to the initial mock-up study [14], and formulate lessons learned. We also report on issues that have not been addressed explicitly in our presentation of results, but which have become evident in the course of our study or were explicitly mentioned by participants when "thinking aloud".

VR as Main Visualization

VR mode turned out to be advantageous in several ways. In Experiment 1, it brought subjects significantly faster to the destination, independently of the accuracy condition. Further, the perceived correctness of instructions was higher in VR than in AR, which made the system more reliable even when panoramas were incorrect with relation to position and orientation. Navigating using VR was also more convenient from a practical point of view, since this visualization did not require subjects to hold up the phone all the time (which was perceived to be physically uncomfortable). Experiment 2 confirmed this, where subjects almost "automatically" chose VR when they had the choice how to carry the phone. An additional argument in favor of VR manifested through the "think aloud" technique, where multiple subjects reported that they felt like unwantedly recording or "stalking" other passers-by when walking around with active camera in AR mode.

In the direct vote, subjects clearly preferred VR over AR, in contrast to the initial mock-up study, where subjects liked the AR visualization better. This contradiction could be explained due to the fact that the AR UI might have appeared more appealing in the simulation, and that subjects could not really compare both in practice. Moreover, the physical constraints of AR – the required pose of the phone – seem to be a "knock-out criterion". Hence, we see the hands-on results as more plausible and more in line with the results for efficiency and convenience, which were likewise in favor of VR.

We thus recommend, as a guideline, the VR mode as primary interface for a visual navigation system. Particularly when localization accuracy is not perfect, it allows still reliable and fast guidance, compared to AR.

AR and Feature Indicator to Improve Localization

The AR view, by contrast, can play out its strengths in two cases. First, it can help to improve feature collection using the feature indicator. In the study, the spirit level visualization contributed to a rise of visual features in query images, thus increasing the probability of reliable re-localization. Hence, a visual navigation system could switch to AR mode when the location estimate is too inaccurate even for the robust VR mode, and ask and motivate users to relocalize themselves by pointing at a feature-rich scene.

Second, AR can integrate object highlighting which likewise may contribute to feature-rich query images. It also provides an anchor for interaction with those objects (a detailed analysis of location-based services via an AR interface, however, is beyond the scope of this paper). We have investigated two highlighting visualizations and found that *Frame*-based highlighting of interesting objects contributed to high attention of users, but at the same time distracted them stronger during navigation. The *Soft Highlight* visualization reduced visual jiggling, but aroused less visual attention and resulted in worse readability of text on posters and signs. As another guideline, a way to combine the advantages of both visualizations could be to use *Soft Highlight* for peripheral objects during a navigation task in order not to distract subjects too much, and to employ the *Frame* visualization once a user focuses an object with the phone.

Automatic AR/VR Switching

Since both VR and AR are useful components of a vision-based navigation interface, future work will have to investigate how both can be combined even better. We need to examine which events could serve as triggers to select them automatically, in addition to the quality of the location estimate (see Fig. 8) and the phone's inclination.

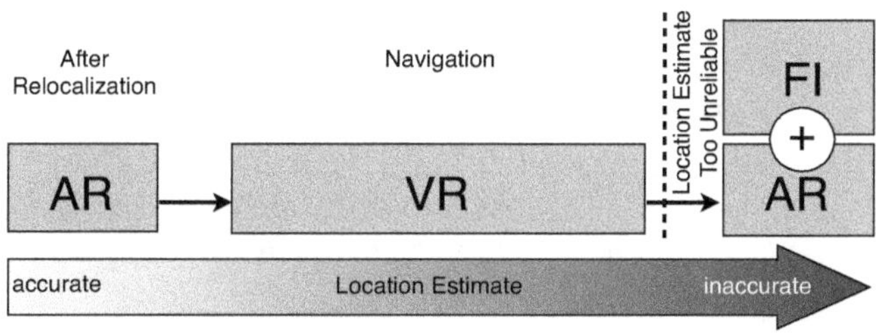

Figure 8. VR is used as main interface during navigation. AR is either used directly after re-localization (to highlight objects of interaction), or when the location estimate becomes too unreliable and a re-localization has to be enforced using an additional feature indicator (FI) element.

Discrepancies between Real and Virtual World

The photorealism of panorama images and the visible landmarks (e.g. posters, exhibits, fire extinguishers) contribute to a simpler identification of a location. However, the real environment often does not look exactly like the recorded panorama images. While color-invariant feature descriptors can minimize the matching problem for the localization algorithm, differences in lighting conditions and exposure changes between subsequent panoramas have been negatively noticed by subjects. However, it did not hinder them in finding their route. To some extent, image post-processing (e.g., exposure correction) could solve this issue.

An advanced solution could choose appropriately from multiple reference sets (e.g. recorded at day and at night) by the time of day. Mapping of (especially crowded) buildings, however, will often have to take place at night when they are closed for the public, and therefore exhibit significantly different lighting conditions than at day. In order to ease mapping of landmarks between panoramas and the real world, characteristic objects could be highlighted in the interface with a similar approach to what we presented in this paper.

Another challenge are permanent changes to the real environment. Posters or advertisements might be replaced from time to time (i.e., within several weeks). As an example, Fig. 9 shows two advertisements in the reference dataset which were not present any more at time of the user study two months later. This is problematic in two ways: Such distinctive objects expose characteristic features and are thus important for visual localization. As a consequence, image matching could fail after a change in the real world. Second, also humans use landmarks for orientation. When they see, e.g., a poster in the VR panorama image, they might search for this poster in the real environment to orientate themselves, which could be irritating if it is not present any more.

Figure 9. Advertisements that were present in the reference dataset (left) but have been removed at the time of the study (right) were irritating for users, as such salient points often serve as landmarks for orientation.

A possible solution for that problem could be crowd-based updates. Query images users take with their smartphone cameras can be included as new textures and continuously update the reference dataset. However, more profound changes in buildings (such as construction works) that entail detours require not only texture updates, but also adaptions of the underlying 3D model and a different navigation path, which might eventually require re-mapping (parts of) the building.

Frequency of Panorama Updates

Subjects reported that the frequent updates of the panorama images in VR mode (every few meters or less, independent of the walking speed) were partly irritating, especially when not permanently looking at the screen. Since each panorama was slightly different in perspective and lighting, they had to "re-check" their position in reference to the panorama each time they looked back at the display. Some stated to have used mostly the distance indicator (showing the distance to the next turn), and to have looked at the panorama only for double-checking when approaching the turn location.

This leads to the idea of varying the frequency in which panoramas are updated during a path. Instead of showing always the closest view to the current location estimate, a reduced set of panoramas could be used along the route, illustrating particularly the turns and difficult parts. This could reduce the cognitive effort required for visually matching panoramas with the real world, at similar quality of guidance.

LIMITATIONS

Although the evaluation presented in this paper provides valuable insights, it also has limitations. First, this work evaluated interfaces with simulated localization data. This was necessary to test the ability of AR and VR interfaces to cope with varying levels of accuracy. Simulations can however not fully model a self-contained system. For example, although the usage of the spirit level indicator resulted in more visible features, this study cannot tell whether this increase actually would lead to more reliable localization. It is subject to future work to evaluate our UI concept, which we have shown to be sound and useful, with an underlying live-working visual navigation system. Further, it was not part of this work to evaluate the accuracy of visual localization.

However, we have shown that VR mode provides reliable guidance even with low (simulated) accuracy, making the UI adequate to work on top of a variety of visual localization systems, including such with lesser accuracy. As we have tested responses to various error types and levels of accuracy, we believe that the results will be transferable to a broad range of real-world cases.

CONCLUSION AND FUTURE WORK

We have presented a user interface adapted to some unique challenges of visual indoor navigation, and evaluated a working prototype in a hands-on study. Our concept combines virtual and augmented reality elements, and proved in quantitative and qualitative experiments to provide reliable navigation instructions even with inaccurate localization. It actively contributes to feature acquisition which improves positioning certainty. We identified challenges of visual localization and outlined ways for solving them. We believe that vision-based approaches are a promising technique for indoor navigation. Future work will have to evaluate approaches addressing the mentioned challenges in real-world studies, with a larger user base, and with a live localization system.

REFERENCES

1. Azuma, R. A survey of augmented reality. *Presence-Teleoperators and Virtual Environments 6*, 4 (1997), 355–385.
2. Beeharee, A. K., and Steed, A. A natural wayfinding exploiting photos in pedestrian navigation systems. In *Proc. of the 8th Conf. on Human-Computer Interaction with Mobile Devices and Services (MobileHCI)*, ACM (2006), 81–88.
3. Butz, A., Baus, J., Krüger, A., and Lohse, M. A hybrid indoor navigation system. In *Proc. of the 6th Intl. Conf. on Intelligent User Interfaces (IUI)*, ACM (2001), 25–32.
4. Hile, H., and Borriello, G. Positioning and orientation in indoor environments using camera phones. *Computer Graphics and Applications, IEEE 28*, 4 (2008), 32–39.
5. Hile, H., Vedantham, R., Cuellar, G., Liu, A., Gelfand, N., Grzeszczuk, R., and Borriello, G. Landmark-based pedestrian navigation from collections of geotagged photos. In *Proc. of the 7th Intl. Conference on Mobile and Ubiquitous Multimedia (MUM)*, ACM (2008), 145–152.
6. Kelley, J. F. An empirical methodology for writing user-friendly natural language computer applications. In *Proc. of the SIGCHI Conf. on Human Factors in Computing Systems (CHI)*, ACM (1983), 193–196.
7. Kray, C., Elting, C., Laakso, K., and Coors, V. Presenting route instructions on mobile devices. In *Proc. of the 8th Intl. Conf. on Intelligent User Interfaces (IUI)*, ACM (2003), 117–124.
8. Kray, C., and Kortuem, G. Interactive positioning based on object visibility. In *Mobile Human-Computer Interaction (MobileHCI)*, S. Brewster and M. Dunlop, Eds., vol. 3160 of *Lecture Notes in Computer Science*. Springer Berlin Heidelberg, 2004, 276–287.
9. Li, B., Salter, J., Dempster, A., and Rizos, C. Indoor positioning techniques based on wireless LAN. In *1st IEEE Intl. Conf. on Wireless Broadband and Ultra Wideband Communications* (2006), 13–16.
10. Lim, H., Kung, L., Hou, J., and Luo, H. Zero-configuration, robust indoor localization: Theory and experimentation. Tech. rep., Univ. of Illinois, 2005.
11. Liu, A., Hile, H., Kautz, H., Borriello, G., Brown, P., Harniss, M., and Johnson, K. Indoor wayfinding: Developing a functional interface for individuals with cognitive impairments. *Disability & Rehabilitation: Assistive Technology 3*, 1-2 (2008), 69–81.
12. Miyashita, T., Meier, P., Tachikawa, T., Orlic, S., Eble, T., Scholz, V., Gapel, A., Gerl, O., Arnaudov, S., and Lieberknecht, S. An augmented reality museum guide. In *Proc. of the 7th IEEE/ACM Intl. Symposium on Mixed and Augmented Reality*, IEEE (2008), 103–106.
13. Miyazaki, Y., and Kamiya, T. Pedestrian navigation system for mobile phones using panoramic landscape images. In *Intl. Symposium on Applications and the Internet (SAINT)*, IEEE (2006).
14. Möller, A., Kranz, M., Huitl, R., Diewald, S., and Roalter, L. A mobile indoor navigation system interface adapted to vision-based localization. In *Proc. of the 11th Intl. Conf. on Mobile and Ubiquitous Multimedia (MUM)*, ACM (2012), 4:1–4:10.
15. Möller, A., Kray, C., Roalter, L., Diewald, S., and Kranz, M. Tool support for prototyping interfaces for vision-based indoor navigation. In *Workshop on Mobile Vision and HCI (MobiVis) on MobileHCI 2012* (2012).
16. Mulloni, A., Seichter, H., Dünser, A., Baudisch, P., and Schmalstieg, D. 360 ° panoramic overviews for location-based services. In *Proc. of the SIGCHI Conf. on Human Factors in Computing Systems (CHI)*, ACM (2012), 2565–2568.
17. Mulloni, A., Wagner, D., Barakonyi, I., and Schmalstieg, D. Indoor positioning and navigation with camera phones. *Pervasive Computing, IEEE 8*, 2 (2009), 22–31.
18. Narzt, W., Pomberger, G., Ferscha, A., Kolb, D., Müller, R., Wieghardt, J., Hörtner, H., and Lindinger, C. Augmented reality navigation systems. *Universal Access in the Information Society 4*, 3 (2006), 177–187.
19. Schroth, G., Huitl, R., Chen, D., Abu-Alqumsan, M., Al-Nuaimi, A., and Steinbach, E. Mobile visual location recognition. *IEEE Signal Processing Magazine 28*, 4 (2011), 77–89.
20. Walther-Franks, B., and Malaka, R. Evaluation of an augmented photograph-based pedestrian navigation system. In *Smart Graphics*, Springer (2008), 94–105.

Digitally Driven: How Location Based Services Impact on the Work Practices of London Bus Drivers

Gary Pritchard[1], John Vines[1], Pam Briggs[2], Lisa Thomas[2] and Patrick Olivier[1]

[1]Culture Lab,
School of Computing Science,
Newcastle University, UK
{firstname.lastname}@ncl.ac.uk

[2]PaCT Lab,
Department of Psychology,
Northumbria University, UK
{firstname.lastname}@northumbria.ac.uk

ABSTRACT

This paper examines how an occupational group has adapted to the demands of working with a Location Based Service (LBS). Instead of following a rigid timetable, London's bus drivers are now required to maintain an equal distance between the bus in front and the one behind. Our qualitative study employs ethnographic fieldwork and in-depth semi-structured interviews to elicit drivers' perspectives of the new system and show how it has modified their driving and general work conditions. We explore how passengers influence the movement of the bus and how the technology frames bus drivers' relationships to their managers and commuters. This work contributes to our understanding of the impact of LBS in the workplace and shows how technological imperatives can be established that cause unanticipated consequences and gradually undermine human relationships.

Author Keywords

Public Transport; Location Based Services; LBS; Location Based Devices; LBD; Auto ethnography; Ethnography.

ACM Classification Keywords

H.5.m. Information interfaces and presentation (e.g., HCI): Miscellaneous.

INTRODUCTION

Digital technologies have become an integral part of modern travel. Increasingly, transport companies are seeking to support passengers by providing location based services (LBS) that can alert them to when the next train or bus is arriving and maintain schedules between vehicles to deliver a more regular service. In this paper we focus on the ways the implementation of an LBS - the iBus and its associated headway timing system - has changed the work practices of London bus drivers. These technologies help drivers co-ordinate with one another, make services more efficient and ensure an even distance is kept between buses on the same route. While most of these technologies have been introduced to enhance the reliability, frequency and passenger experience, they also impose significant changes to traditional bus driving work practices. Ge et al. [16] suggest that LBS and driver monitoring have the capacity to improve staff behaviour - reducing fraud and improving efficient driving in taxis, for example - but we must also be aware that 'panopticon' workplace monitoring practices can adversely affect staff morale [39]. The idea of a panopticon has been inherently linked to LBS monitoring systems. The premise is one of complete surveillance without knowledge of when and where one is being explicitly watched. In the modern workplace, new forms of "electronic panopticon" [2, p.2] are implemented in the hope that, with constant yet covert surveillance, employees will become more compliant.

The work context in this study is bus transport - an area where HCI research has been eclectic. Prior work has studied systems to support traffic regulation at junctions [4], technologies to assist conductors [1], studies of media sharing among commuters [23], in-bus information systems for the visually impaired [35], and systems to encourage fuel-efficient driving habits [25]. In the specific context of London buses, prior work has studied the introduction of new automated fare collection systems [21] and the lived experiences of passengers [19]. However, no work has examined the impact LBS can have on these important transportation systems, nor the implications for drivers and their long-established work practices.

In our study we adopted an ethnographic approach, using qualitative fieldwork. Our contribution to the field is threefold. First, we advance HCI's understanding of the ways LBS can change driving behaviour, relationships in the workplace and experiences of public transportation. Second and more generally, we add to our understanding of the role of such systems in surveillance and control, illustrating the ways LBS can change workplace power dynamics. Finally, we suggest ways to improve the implementation of LBS in this workplace.

CHI 2014, April 26 - May 01 2014, Toronto, ON, Canada

ACM 978-1-4503-2473-1/14/04...$15.00.
http://dx.doi.org/10.1145/2556288.2557156

RELATED WORK

Outside of the workplace, the use of LBS to share information with family and friends has become popular, particularly amongst young people [32]. Research has illustrated the benefits of using LBS to support communication among family members and friends [e.g. 2, 3, 7, 34]. There have also been studies reporting the privacy concerns around location data sharing [6, 8]. Unsurprisingly, people are more willing to share location data with friends and family than with colleagues [7].

LBS studies conducted within the workplace are relatively scarce. Those studies that exist tend to be office-based and focus on the protection of lone workers [26] or on raising awareness between co-workers—such as the use of 'active badges' for worker monitoring in a research institution [17], and public broadcasts of the relative location of colleagues [27] (e.g. at work, at-home). Such interventions were well received, but crucially they were opt-in systems designed to support worker collaboration. Mandatory use of LBS monitoring in the workplace is often resisted as it can result in changes to time-management, workload and morale [21]. In a study exploring the implementation of GPS-monitoring for parole officers to supplement parolee supervision in the US, Shklovski et al. found that the technology radically transformed their relationships [28]. Previously held organisational values of reintegration and progression deteriorated, giving way to a new standard of surveillance and recidivism. Parole officers maintained that although the technology offered new ways to keep track of parolees, more human interaction was preferred.

When more stringent systems are introduced for top-down performance monitoring [22, 29, 36] workers often report concerns about privacy and invasiveness [38, 39]. Even when privacy principles can be established and upheld, resistance to LBS monitoring is strong [39]. This can be mediated however by perceived risk to the worker and by trust in the employer [24]. Lone workers or vulnerable individuals can accept that their job carries significant risk and that some type of monitoring is desirable. A study of 387 employees in the US, UK and India, found that employees overwhelmingly resisted workplace monitoring [36]. However, those who perceived themselves as vulnerable, who had higher levels of self-efficacy and greater levels of trust in their employer 'were more amenable to monitoring' [p.229].

Trust and employer disclosure are two of the key components of the predictive models of LBS acceptance [20, 32]. In the workplace, intentions to use LBS have been identified as a function of three factors: (i) the perceived usefulness of the technology; (ii) trust in the LBS provider and (iii) willingness to disclose information to the employer. In considering this current study, we would predict that the relationship between employer and employee be important. What is distinctive in this work however is the way in which the usefulness of LBS within the London transport system can be contested by a number of different parties—not simply employer and employee, but the passengers themselves. As we will see, the proposed passenger benefits of LBS are not to be taken for granted.

LONDON'S BUS NETWORK

London has one of the world's largest bus networks; facilitating over 1.8 billion passenger journeys a year on 7,500 buses servicing over 700 different routes [31]. This form of public transport is an integral part of London life and it is estimated that 90 percent of Londoners live less than 400 meters from one of the Capital's 19,500 bus stops.

London Buses, a subsidy of *Transport for London* (TfL) are in charge of contracting out different routes to the 17 companies operating bus routes in London. London Buses also control the age and specifications of vehicles and allocate routes through a tendering system where operators bid to run them for a 5 year period. Operators have to work within guidelines set by TfL and are in charge of driver recruitment and vehicle procurement. TfL are the local government body responsible for setting bus routes and service levels. They also monitor service quality, manage bus stations and stops, set fares, assist drivers in the case of diversions and traffic accidents and provide passenger information. This body also incorporates a bus command and control hub called *CentreComm*.

Timetables, bus bunching and the headway system

Before 2009 London's buses ran to a timetable. Copies were displayed at bus stops and on TfL's website, listing the times a bus was scheduled to arrive at named locations. Although timetables are designed to schedule buses evenly, anyone familiar with the old adage, *"You wait ages for a bus and then two come along at once"*, will recognize that buses regularly bunch together, creating an unreliable service and long waiting times. Bunching occurs because even if a bus is slightly late it will pick up extra passengers who would have taken the next bus. These additional commuters delay the bus even further and cause the bus behind to run ahead of schedule as it has fewer people to pick up. Eventually, this bus will catch the one in front.

In 2009 the 'headway' system was adopted as a corrective measure to avoid bus bunching. Instead of publishing a specific time, the headway approach uses LBS to measure the distance between buses. Instead of a published timetable, notices now state the estimated time between services (e.g. 'services run every 5-7 minutes'). The iBus terminal, fitted on all London buses, contains a GPS-based system that provides drivers with an LCD display informing them how far the bus in front and behind are (Figure 1). The driver is expected to keep an equal distance between the two within a two-minute time frame. All buses are monitored externally by controllers at CentreComm who watch 2 to 3 routes at a time, to an accuracy of 10 metres [9]. The controllers can request the driver to moderate their driving via on-screen prompts or verbally through a radio.

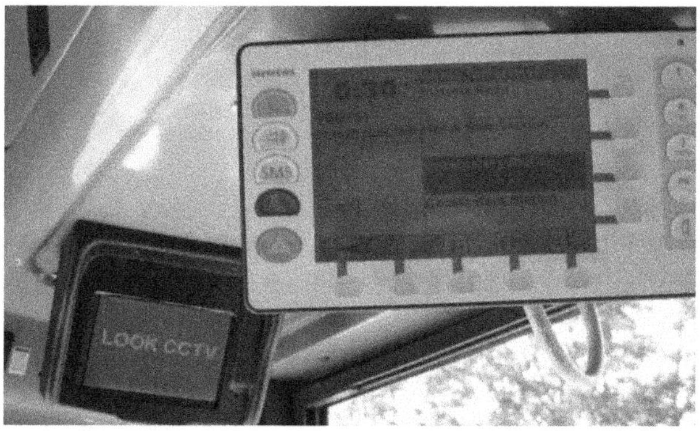

Figure 1. The iBus terminal

METHOD

Inadvertently, data collection began five years ago when the lead author was given special dispensation to join a bus-drivers' football team. This involved training sessions, competitive games and frequent social gatherings where he gained an interest and appreciation for how technology impacted the working lives of this occupational group. This was a popular topic of conversation among drivers who frequently mused about how their jobs had changed over the years. This background and awareness provided the motivations and cornerstone of this research.

When the formal research commenced, our cordiality with this group greatly eased access. Ethnographic fieldwork consisted of riding on different buses with our participants, both when they were driving and when they were not. While riding a bus with participants, they were asked to provide a commentary on the driver's performance and speculate on the specific motivations for each passenger encounter or subtle driving technique. While riding a bus with a participant driving, the researcher kept a detailed log of the journey, and sat on the seat nearest the driver. Officially, passengers are supposed to stand behind a yellow-painted line and are forbidden to talk or distract the driver. Despite this, our participants would regularly beckon the researcher to stand by the cab. Drivers were enthusiastic about relaying the intricacies of their work and these observations fed into semi-structured interviews with 10 bus drivers and one ex-bus driver who now has a position working closely with controllers. All participants, with the exception of Lesley, were male and this reflects the gender makeup of the profession. Details of drivers, their age and length of service is provided in Table 1. All names have been changed and ages and length of services given in bands to protect participant confidentiality

A total of 8 routes were observed two or three times each. Half of these journeys were with a participant driving and half with a participant riding along with the researcher. The journey time for a typical route was an hour. The lead researcher is also a native Londoner and was able to draw on his experiences of being a bus passenger in the city.

Name	Age	Service	Name	Age	Service
Peter	40-45	26-30 years[1]	Frank	40-45	10-15 years
Tony	60-65	10-15 years	Mark	50-55	24 years
Jim	46-50	10-15 years	Keith	40-45	10-15 years
Mike	60-65	10-15 years	Lee	30-35	0-5 years
Ron	65-70	6-10 years	Lesley	40-45	0-5 years

Table 1: Research participants

The lead author's close social connections with most participants granted us 'insider status' and motivated them to be incredibly helpful during fieldwork. This afforded the opportunity to contact drivers after the interview phase to ask them to clarify points and pose follow-up questions. After fieldwork we also received a number of text messages from interviewees relaying details that they thought were important but neglected to mention during fieldwork. These informal relationships also helped us to triangulate our data by double-checking assertions made by other drivers.

The lead author's personal history with this occupational group made our research bear the hallmarks of auto ethnography, a method that to date has only been employed selectively in HCI [11]. It is characterized as an 'autobiographical genre of writing and research that connects the personal to the cultural' [12, p.739]. A benefit of this approach is giving an insider's view of the research subject. Due to this familiarity, it is unhelpful to characterize data analysis as a segregated process in our research. Analysis began in the field when we decided what issues appeared to be relevant and what questions were important to ask drivers. After fieldwork, all interviews were anonymised and transcribed. Following Glaser and Strauss [17] this data along with our fieldwork diary was coded at the sentence to paragraph level to develop themes [17]. This data was then reassembled using selective quoting to illustrate these themes.

FINDINGS

Three themes were identified from our analysis of the data: *driving modification*, *surveillance and control*, and *passenger and driver interaction*.

Driving modification

This section highlights the how LBS has caused bus drivers to modify their driving behaviour through the requirement to respond to the iBus prompts, by continually altering and managing their pace, and by enforcing new professional standards on their work practices.

Responding to the headway system

Three of our participants were very positive about the iBus and headway system. Tony, who started driving buses in

[1] Peter began working as a conductor at 15.

the early 80s, likes to treat the demands of keeping an equal headway as a type of game, enjoying the challenge that the system demands:

> *"I prefer it like it is because you've only got to glance up at a bus stop and you can see straightaway how early or late* [you are]. *If you've got to slow down, you stay at a bus stop a little bit longer so you know the traffic lights will be red by the time you get there. Whereas if you're running late, you'll hopefully get the green light."* (Tony)

Tony's positive attitude towards the headway system stood him apart from most drivers who were contemptuous of it. Mike reflected nostalgically about the bus timetable that he used to work to and articulated a sense of disorientation and uncertainty in his work since the introduction of the new system: *"you don't know where you are now. When you had the old timetable system you knew where you're supposed to be and that."* Jim was more candid and forthright in his opinion: *"Basically,* [it] *is the biggest load of shit going, because it don't work. It don't work, it's the worst thing they've ever brought out."*

Overall, drivers felt the LBS created an additional burden to their work and made it more stressful. Frank felt that the new system took away his agency and resented that he couldn't use his situational knowledge to drive the bus optimally. This implies that the new system deskills the driver and marginalizes them from the various driving decisions they used to be able to make:

> *"They can tell us to slow down. That can be infuriating because you're doing your job, you're going at the rate of what the traffic conditions and the passenger conditions are allowing you."* (Frank)

Frank believed that the essence of bus driving had been lost. To maintain a headway drivers often had to slow down in what they felt were inappropriate places. During fieldwork, we observed some of these frustrations first hand when Jim had to pull over to the side of the road for 5 minutes. During this time, he called the researcher over and said these type of interruptions were one of the worst things about his job. Others complained that this heavily-mediated driving style caused them grief from passengers:

"The other day when I was told to lose a bit of time on the bus in front, there was this woman on the bus, who, because I was driving slowly, was getting really upset about it: *"Why are you driving so slowly?" I said, "I've got to lose a bit of time. I'm too close to the bus in front." She was getting really, really worked up about it."* (Ron)

Passenger anger was all too evident during fieldwork, often aimed at what they saw as unnecessary delays to their journey. Frustration was especially fierce on mornings as people travelled to work or had transport connections to make. The need to drive to the demands of headway created additional work, as drivers needed to expel emotional labour in interactions with passengers frustrated with the irregular movement of the bus.

Speeding up and slowing down

As a safety issue, drivers were not supposed to be told to drive faster in order to make up time. However, some drivers confessed to doing this. Jim explained how sometimes: *"You've just got to floor it in between stops"*. A number of the drivers described feeling pressurized to drive faster even though safety and driving law made them reluctant to do so. This created greater pressure for drivers: *"There's a lot of pressure for you to accelerate to bring that needle back, if you know what I mean."* (Peter). Some drivers resented this and refused to be coaxed into driving fast. There was still a range of driving strategies they could employ without actually driving faster:

> *"If you start slowing down and looking left and right at a junction, you keep going on, you are driving effectively on road conditions. If the lights have changed red when you are approaching them, if you back off, ideally they will go around and you can get through that second set of lights. No point racing up to them."* (Frank)

During fieldwork drivers' interactions with the researcher would vary greatly depending on whether he had to make up time or not. On some journeys, it was not possible to speak to the driver until the end of the route. On being asked how they make up lost time, a couple of drivers even admitted to driving past passengers: *"Drive straight past them* [...] *Especially if somebody said to me the day before, "Oi, you fucking arsehole, I've been waiting half an hour"* (Frank). Others admitted to only being motivated to move fast if they were near the end of a shift or their lunch break:

> *"You don't want to be late. If you're late, sometimes, you just have to swallow it. "Right, there's nothing I can do about it," and you're late. Other than that, you will put your foot down and will be quite upset when there are people at bus stops putting their hand up or ringing the bloody bell."* (Jim)

Slowing down a bus or 'losing time' is a different activity altogether. Unlike making up time, this is something that controllers can, and often do, ask drivers to do via the iBus terminal. This can cause distress as a lot of drivers feel they are at the mercy of traffic conditions and other drivers:

> *"There is nothing worse than when you're trying to lose time. You can guarantee that the lights will all be green and every driver will be absolutely so charming. They'll flash to let you out and you're thinking, "No, please go. I'm trying to lose two minutes."* (Ron)

On two occasions, drivers called the researcher to the front of the bus to vent his anger towards the faceless controllers who were asking them to slow down. The most straightforward method of slowing down a bus is to park it at a bus stop. While this tactic is the one recommended by TfL, bus drivers do not enjoy employing it as they get complaints from customers. They also have difficulty in communicating why they are stopped and the demands of the headway system as opposed to a more traditional timetable. Instead, most drivers employ a variety of strategies to discretely slow down the journey:

"If you do it discretely you don't have to ask, and it is only poodle along, break, put your handbrake on, turn round, open the doors, lower the bus. There are ways. Everything takes seconds, but everything works into that minute. It doesn't take long to lose that minute." (Keith).

When needing to lose time, we witnessed that drivers regularly gave more attention to passengers and spent a greater amount of time on routine activities like opening and closing the bus doors and pulling away more gently. Other participants described how they had to change their attitude and behaviour towards other drivers on the road:

"As a bus driver, you do feel you have to be an assertive driver because nobody will let you out. When you're running early, you do the opposite and traffic tries to let you out". (Frank)

Frank explained how he adapts his driving personality depends on the demands of the headway system. The drivers have to continually move between rather selfish and altruistic approaches to driving.

Enforcement of professional standards

Driving behaviour was also adjusted as the tracking systems on their buses had prevented the drivers transgressing some workplace rules. As Ron articulates, controllers have the ability to ascertain the location of all buses in real-time. This annoyed him greatly because in the past he parked at bus stops to do some shopping or carry out other errands:

"The disadvantage is there is absolutely no chance you can slope off anywhere because they know exactly where you are. They know the times that you arrive at every bus-stop. Every single thing is recorded." (Ron)

Jim vented his dislike of being closely monitored at work and explains how it has prevented him from taking unsanctioned breaks:

"The iBus is a pain in the arse, they know exactly where you are. I used to go off route in the old days round my mate's house [...] for an hour and a half, and then pick my time up on the way back up the next time. No one knew anything. Now they know exactly where you are."

Another driver relayed a story of a colleague actually taking his bus out of service in order to transport a horse from one field to another:

"I do know of someone actually transporting a horse. It was a driver, he actually took his horse to move it to another field [...] all on the hush-hush." (Keith)

Others spoke about how they used to compete with each other to see how many times they could drive around a round-a-bout with passengers on board. One driver spoke proudly of managing to do it twelve times with a vehicle full of passengers. Although some travellers complained, he asserted he was a new driver and wasn't sure what exit to take. Two drivers also admitted that prior to iBus they were able to cover-up minor accidents they had. Even a minor traffic accident now means drivers have to fill in paperwork, something many begrudged.

Surveillance and control

Here we explore driver's perceptions of LBS as a source of surveillance, how controllers use the information provided by LBS to control drivers and also the ability of drivers to resist the controlling qualities of this technology.

The feeling of being monitored

The introduction of LBS has initiated a new form of surveillance on London's buses. Half of the drivers made Orwellian references when articulating concerns about how LBS impacted upon their privacy: *"When it first came, it was like this Big Brother thing. Personally people didn't like it."* (Frank). Most drivers, especially those who had worked on the buses for some time, spoke about having to psychologically adjust to these new forms of monitoring. However, greater experience and exposure to LBS lessened their concerns and most eventually adopted a philosophical stance: *"At the end of the day, if you have done nothing wrong you have got nothing to worry about. You know? That is what it boils down to."* (Keith).

Others however saw a clear benefit in LBS when used in conjunction with CCTV. CentreComm allowed the police and other emergency services to locate buses near incidents and get access to the CCTV cameras both inside of the bus and surrounding areas. Drivers argued that their provision had helped combat terrorism and crime:

"Like, when that drummer Lee Rigby[2] was killed . We had a group go up to the CentreComm, [...] where they can monitor everything, a lot of the guys that dispatched the first set of ambulances, police cars, were able to watch it in real-time from the CCTV cameras around." (Lesley)

In a similar vein, Ron recounted an occasion where the monitoring system was central to solving a murder. One driver, Keith, proudly declared during an interview that CCTV allowed them to be *"the eyes and ears of London"*. Here we can hear echoes of Workman who found workers were less likely to object to monitoring if they felt themselves especially vulnerable [36]. The difference here is the drivers perceive the city and not themselves to be in need of extra caution and invigilation.

Continual controller intervention

Controllers are required to intervene when they feel a driver is not maintaining headway. This caused a level of

[2] Lee Rigby was an off duty British Army soldier who was attacked and killed on the streets of London on 22 May 2013.

animosity directed toward them from drivers: *"They're against you. The controllers are against the drivers."* (Jim). In the first instance, controllers would prompt the drivers to modify their driving through a text message delivered to the iBus terminal. This created an unwelcome distraction from driving and introduced a further level of emotional labour:

> *"You have got the controllers texting in to the iBus. The driver is supposed to be concentrating on his driving, not looking at a screen in the corner to read these text messages."* (Lesley)

There were also numerous instances of the technology not working properly. Keith describes being told to slow down before he had even begun his journey:

> *"They text me at the stand, "Keep an eye on your headway. Hold back for two minutes." I did, I hadn't left. I waited two minutes, and then came another text, "Driver, please mind your headway." I radioed and said, "I haven't even left yet."*

During one journey, while waiting to drive a route the bus was delayed as another bus had parked in the wrong place at the garage. The controllers didn't have this information and Keith became visually agitated as he tried to explain the situation over the radio to them after the journey had started. Among drivers, it was understood that the system contained glitches and would occasionally give controllers false information regarding the location of buses. This created further stress and extra work for drivers who had to communicate with controllers over the radio. This new workload was further added to as controllers would send a radio message to drivers if they had not responded to a text prompt. This caused an additional unwanted distraction as it worked to slow drivers down even further:

> *"Controllers expect you to answer them straightaway. Now, if you were doing it to the letter of the law, you would have to pull over, put the handbrake on and put it in neutral to answer them."* (Frank)

As Frank explains, responding to a radio message is not just a simple task of talking. In the UK it is against the law to use handheld telephones and radios while driving, and it is against company policy to talk on the radio while driving in public. Therefore even the simplest of responses involves pulling over and potentially losing time:

> *"CentreComm get terribly upset if you don't pull over and stop the bus. Ideally, they'd like you to switch everything off. They say, "We can't hear you," which is a load of bollocks."* (Ron)

Lesley found the coercion by controllers so stressful that she left the job after six weeks:

> *"Training was alright, and then when you are actually out there driving, you have got the controllers moaning at you, your iBus is beeping, and you have got the controller moaning at you through that. You have got passengers on top, and you just think, no."*

Finally, if a driver continues to not respond to the headway system, they are called into the office for a formal discipline hearing. Although nearly all of the drivers we spoke to did their best to maintain headway, two resisted, primarily as slowing down delayed their breaks or leaving times. Here Jim recounts a time when maintaining headway would have meant stopping the bus and finishing work late. He refused and this led to a disciplinary hearing:

> *"I've been in* [a disciplinary] *once. I said to them I ain't doing it, because they want me to finish later as well, even with my last trip. I said, "You can't make me do overtime, it's against the law, and I will not do overtime unless I want to do overtime". They're not going to tell me.* [...] *They can have me in every week for all I care; I don't care. They're not making me do overtime."* (Jim)

Passenger and driver interaction

Our final theme explores how bus travel is quite distinct from other forms of public transportation in the greater degree of interaction between passengers and drivers and also in the frequency of stops. This has implications on the ability of drivers to maintain headway, and headway impacts upon the relationships drivers have with their passengers.

During fieldwork it became apparent that the headway system had strained the passenger-driver relationship. The high levels of driver-passenger interaction in bus transportation made bus driving less predictable, especially in terms of the length of time it took passengers to enter and leave the vehicle. The need to get them on and off the bus quickly in order not to fall behind caused drivers to categorize passengers into distinct groups. Experience endowed them with the perception that certain 'types' of passengers were likely to be slow and make maintaining headway more difficult. In particular, older people and parents with young children were seen to take a disproportionate amount of time getting safely on and off the bus. A popular in-joke among drivers involved referring disparagingly to older passengers as 'wombles', the large fictional rodents in a popular British children's stop-animation TV show. The drivers perceived a similarity between the way wombles were unencumbered in their movement and the way the free public travel offered to all Londoners over 60. During fieldwork, Rodney, a driver in his 30s, spoke frankly about his views of this age group:

> *"It's not like they have anything to do other than ride the bus* [...] *They DO slow down the bus, they get on slow and get off slow. You can't move until they are sitting down. This can lose 1 minute a bus stop and soon enough, you are running late."*

Talking to older passengers during ethnography, it became apparent that they not only relied on the bus service as a mode of transportation but also valued interactions with drivers. It was a common complaint that this affability has been lost. Parents with young children, particularly those accompanied by a pushchair, were a further source of driver frustration. The following offers an extreme view, highlighting how this group is stigmatized and resented due to the time it takes them to board and disembark:

> "[They're] *lazy bastards. Give the kids fresh air. They go one stop on the fucking bus when the kids could have five minutes in the fresh air, instead of having a smelly armpit hanging over its head. It proper annoys you."* (Jim)

On numerous occasions the researcher witnessed the driver roll his eyes at the sight of a shopper laden with heavy bags or an unsteady older person because he knew they would slow him down. As well as their perceptions towards different categories of passengers, it also became apparent that the technology also directly impacted upon work practices. When a driver is at a stop and sees someone running to get on the bus, they make a judgment whether to wait for them or drive on. Some drivers admitted that the headway system had made them less considerate. They would assess variables such as how much effort a passenger was exerting to get to the stop, whether the passenger might cause further delays (i.e. being older or a parent with young children) and how much longer they would have to wait for the next bus. Tony admitted that if the bus behind him is getting too close, he will forgo his usual considerate nature.

> *"It depends on how fast they were running and how far behind they are. If I was running late and I knew that there's a bus just a minute behind."*

During a ride-a-long when one of our participants was driving a bus, the driver received numerous prompts to say they were not maintaining headway and the bus behind was catching up. At the next stop a prospective passenger flagged down the bus and asked if it was going to Harrow-on-the-Hill. The driver peered at the passenger's large 2-seater pushchair, smiled and said, *"Yes love, but the long way round. You're better off getting the next bus which will be a more direct route for you darling."* After our participant's shift the researcher commented that he was impressed that he found time to give the passenger travel guidance. He laughed and confessed: *"Ha ha, I was bullshiting. Both buses take the same route, I was just trying to make up time"*.

Occasionally, the iBus system would ask the driver to slow down, especially if it is too close to a bus ahead. This aspect of the system also greatly affected the relationship a bus driver has with their passengers. Some of our participants admitted to becoming irritable if customers asked them questions about why they were running slow.

> *"I have said, "Hold on, I'll tell you at the next bus stop" or something like that. But the trouble with a lot of passengers is they don't realise that we've got a schedule to keep."* (Tony)

While the requirement to interact with passengers when they board could be time consuming in some cases, innovations in recent years has reduced the time-burden this places on drivers. Recent years has seen the introduction of the Oyster Card, a prepaid card intended to reduce cash transactions and eliminate the need for drivers to check travel passes. Frank asserted that this development has made his job easier:

> *"When you have people get on with, 'Travel cards', you have to scrutinise the date more than anything else...Then, different areas have different zones. With the card, you go on the noise...One bleep: yes; two bleeps: no."*

Frank articulates the benefits in reallocating the function of dispensing and scrutinizing travel cards from drivers to computers. Most drivers were in agreement with Frank, talking about the difficulty and time-intensive activity of inspecting travel passes, especially as many passengers held the pass too far away for the driver to read accurately or obscured important details with their fingers (this was routinely done by passengers who attempt to travel with invalid passes). Oyster took over this wearisome task and the driver just had to take notice of audio signals.

Other drivers took the contrary view however, feeling that the Oyster system had created additional work for them. Jim and Mike explained how they received more *"aggro"* since the introduction of the card. Often passengers would get on the bus and have no money left on their cards: *"Then they turn round and say, "I've just put £5 on it". "Well, where's your receipt then?"* (Jim). Mike noted that a lot of passengers who do not have money on their card would typically only have large banknotes on them and no small change to pay for a ticket. During fieldwork, it was noted that drivers would have two or three of these 'problem passengers' per route (although this varied depending on the area of London). Other drivers we spoke to confirmed this perception, arguing that, rather than enhancing the efficiency of the bus service, the Oyster card has mystified the payment process and introduced additional barriers that contribute to delays. These were delays that became increasingly difficult to manage in relation to the headway system with its frequent prompts and interruptions from controllers.

As a final point, our participants complained that the Oyster card altered the nature of their work and eliminated the passenger-interaction some valued. One of our participants, Keith, reminisces about this:

> *"It takes a lot of the one-on-one away from you. A lot of people don't even acknowledge the driver, because they just get on and go, "Beep" and walk past, as if you weren't in the cab. Whereas you used to have to deal* [with them]. *"* (Keith)

DISCUSSION

Our findings highlight the various ways the introduction of LBS on London's buses has affected long-established work practices and relationships. While LBS and the headway system was introduced to improve the efficiency of this public service, they have also been applied as a way of managing drivers and introducing new surveillance mechanisms from controllers and TfL. Through careful, value-sensitive ethnographic work, we have shown how LBS technologies can come to fail both employees and consumers - driving priorities based on digital performance data that have reduced driver autonomy, damaged the driver-passenger relationship and led to the most vulnerable of the passengers becoming stigmatized.

The issue of reduced driver autonomy directly addresses employee wellbeing. A large research literature has demonstrated that employees can only cope with increases in job demand when they are also given greater autonomy to make decisions. The Demand-Control model [33] shows that work related stress is the interaction between two key constructs: job demands and decision latitude. In the current study, decision latitude would reflect both the level of skill and creativity the bus drivers can bring to the job and also the autonomy they have to make decisions. Effectively, then, our bus drivers have entered a vicious circle in which the demands placed upon them by various new monitoring technologies cannot be ameliorated by increased decision-latitude—ironically because those same technologies have removed driver autonomy. They no longer feel free to drive at appropriate speeds or to respond to customer demands in an appropriate manner. Effectively, any kind of playfulness or creativity in their work has now been eliminated.

Deskilling and reskilling: the driver's changing role

The ways in which technology can come to fundamentally change job roles is well rehearsed in the function allocation literature that was particularly prevalent in the 1990s. At this time the rapid introduction of new technologies into workplaces necessitated a consideration of the distribution of work between humans and machines [12]. Early work was essentially Taylorist in its approach - the machine would fit into a carefully articulated workflow process in order to improve productivity. Such an approach eschewed a nuanced understanding of the broader context for workplace activity [37]. Subsequently a number of studies brought a critical perspective to function allocation, arguing that the changes associated with a new technology are inevitably mediated by the communities it serves [5] and that at the outset, a full understanding of the *richer context* of work is essential [37].

Such perspectives are still valuable now as we consider the work role changes described in the current study. Specifically, we see here how a complex set of technologies has fundamentally changed driver function; from removing the interpersonal interaction with the customer at the boarding point (*Oyster*), to removing timetabling decisions and, ultimately, compromising the drivers ability to make safe decisions in relation to speed and to address passenger care and comfort (headway). There is no doubt that the introduction of monitoring technology has helped curb mischievous driver behaviour and it is likely that it has improved scheduling from the passenger perspective (although that is not something we explicitly addressed in this study). However the technology has also 'bitten back' [30] in the sense that it has created some unfortunate unintended consequences, which include increased workload and reduced autonomy leading to unsafe driving and in some cases, passenger discrimination.

The passenger perspective

In the few documented passenger studies in relation to LBS, the use of mobile devices to deliver and communicate real-time transit information was shown to have positive influences on passenger satisfaction, reducing perceived wait time, sense of security and public transport usage (14]. Certainly, in the web-based survey conducted by Ferris et al., a new set of passenger applications provided by the Seattle OneBusAway system was well received and passengers were able to plan their travel much more effectively and reduce wait-time. Crucially, their study addressed only the communication of bus location to passengers and remained silent on the issue of whether the same information was used to drive bus-driver behaviour [14]. Yet here is the crux of the issue in our own study. The sharing of information either between drivers or between passengers would not seem to be the divisive issue. Instead, the direct surveillance of drivers by controllers has changed the way that drivers respond to passengers.

In a rather different approach to passenger satisfaction, Foth et al. [15] noted that passengers place a high value on the subjective personal experience of riding the bus. Consequently they intend to explore interventions designed to make the whole journey more enjoyable, noting that: 'Instead of focusing on efficiency and speed of each of these steps, we will focus on making the experience more enjoyable and meaningful' [15, p3]. It is particularly interesting to us that this is the only other study we have found to take an ethnographic approach. This work is useful in that the authors are at pains to distinguish between the passenger experience of *waiting* for the bus as opposed to the experience of *boarding* the bus—when, as we've seen, LBS surveillance systems may generate unfortunate unintended consequences, particularly for those passengers with mobility difficulties or more complex needs and who are slower to board the bus.

Implications for design

Our findings raise a number of design implications around how future systems should grant the driver greater autonomy and awareness, supporting them in applying their situated knowledge of routes in a flexible fashion, while at the same time, enhancing the passenger experience.

First, the introduction of iBus system transferred the responsibility of managing the buses' pace from the driver to the controller. One side effect of this is frequent miscommunication between drivers and controllers, often resulting in drivers pulling over and having to explicitly respond to controller requests. One clear area for design innovation therefore is in *new feedback mechanisms to support awareness between drivers and the remote controllers*. A simple resolution to this problem might be in providing the driver a set of predetermined 'responses' through a button-based interface on their dashboard. This would allow them to "acknowledge" the controllers request, or communicate if there is a reason why that request might be difficult to adhere to (i.e. "traffic" or "passengers"). Driver-controller communication might also be improved by providing additional contextual information related to a specific bus without requiring explicit action from the driver. For example, controllers could have greater awareness of passenger numbers by having access to real-time Oyster card data and how long the vehicle is stationary while dropping-off and loading passengers. Taking this idea further, we could also imagine that the iBus system could be better integrated with other existing location based services that provide information on street traffic (e.g. Google Maps Traffic feature). Providing this additional information on passengers and the influence of traffic might mitigate some of the problems of misunderstandings between drivers and controllers, and provide evidence for drivers who feel controllers requests are unreasonable.

Second, there are also opportunities to extend the iBus system to *improve communication and relationships between the drivers and passengers*. Many drivers described difficulties in explaining the headway system to passengers, especially in circumstances where it was necessary to drive slowly or wait at bus stops. While the passengers likely enjoyed the new service and absence of bus-bunching, it was difficult for them to understand how the service was run in practice. We might consider then how displays within the bus and at bus stops might be used to display spatial representations of the distances between buses on the same route.

Finally, there needs to be an *increase in the involvement of drivers in the design of role-transforming technologies*. A surface level analysis of the current role of the driver is that it has become increasingly complex since the implementation of the iBus terminal and the headway system. However, the drivers' role has always been technically complex and required expertise in navigation, time-keeping, relating with passengers and more. Much of the negativity surrounding iBus related to the ways this new technology is at odds with established practices of drivers to manage their bus independent of controllers. Poor training exacerbated this negativity and by drivers not having a complete comprehension of how the system worked. Many of our sample were unfamiliar with using digital technology and an argument can be made that iBus introduced an implied ageism into this workplace. Much like the original aims of co-operative design in Scandinavia, the drivers might have been provided the opportunity to learn about this new technology prior to its introduction and feel confident to challenge some of the decisions influencing its design.

LIMITATIONS AND FUTURE RESEARCH

Our study was conducted in the United Kingdom, a place with specific cultural conventions when using public transport. Indeed, there are significant differences between transport provision and passenger behaviour in London and almost any other part of the UK. Therefore, some of the insights from our findings are of course limited to our site and future work would benefit from exploring the role of LBS and monitoring technologies on similar work practices in other sites. Our focus on a small group, in order to receive rich and vivid accounts of the experience of technology in their workplace, limited our sample size. Furthermore, while the closeness to the ethnographer supported the elicitation of candid reports, analytical distance was more difficult to achieve.

CONCLUSION

We have provided an initial exploration of the way LBS has been integrated into the working lives of London bus drivers and altered their relationships with customers and colleagues. We have illustrated the complex, and at times, cynical coping strategies of drivers and the varying ways they changed their behaviour to meet the demands of this new system. Our methodological strategy meant that we sacrificed berth, in terms of number of participants, for depth of understanding of the perspectives of drivers. As a result our study affords a valuable insight into how LBS can change the nature of work and how employees integrate and cope with the expectations it places upon them.

ACKNOWLEDGMENTS

This work was supported by TSB ALIP 3/4 project SALT (2377-25137) and RCUK Digital Economy Program grant no. EP/G066019/1 SiDE.

REFERENCES

1. Ashok, A., Beck, C. and Quagliara, N. Ri-Ri: assisting bus conductors in madras (Chennai). In *Proc. CHI EA 2007*, ACM Press (2007), 2031-2036.
2. Bain, P., and Taylor, P. Entrapped by the 'electronic panopticon'? Worker resistance in the call centre. *New Technology, Work and Employment 15, 1* (2000), 2-18.
3. Brush, A., Krumm, J. and Scott, J. Exploring end user preferences for location obfuscation, location-based services, and the value of location. In *Proc. UbiComp 2010,* ACM Press (2010), 95-104.
4. Bhouri, N., Balbo, F., Pinson, S. and Tlig, M. Collaborative agents for modelling traffic regulation systems. In *Proc. WI-IAT 2011*, IEEE (2011), 7-13.
5. Bijker, W.E. *Of Bicycles, Bakelites and Bulbs: Towards a Theory of Socio-Technical Change*. MIT Press, Cambridge, 1997.
6. Boesen, J., Rode, J. A., and Mancini, C. The domestic panopticon: location tracking in families. Proc *UbiComp 2010,* ACM Press (2010), 65-74.

7. Consolvo, S., Smith, I. E., Mattews, T., LaMarca, A., Tabert, J. and Powlwdge, P. Location disclosure to social relations: why, when, & what people want to share. In *Proc. CHI 2005*, ACM Press (2005), 81-90.
8. Dahl, Y. and Holbø, K. Value bias of sensor-based assistive technology: case study of GPS tracking system used in dementia care. In *Proc. DIS 2012*, ACM Press (2012), 572-581.
9. Dodson, S. The next stop should be Helsinki. *The Guardian*, 28th February 2008.
10. Dziekan, K. and Kottenhoff, K. Dynamic at-stop real-time information displays for public transport: effects on customers. *Transportation Research Part A: Policy and Practice 41, 6* (2007) 489-501.
11. Efimova, L. Weblog as personal thinking space. In *Proc HT 2009*, ACM Press (2009), 289-298.
12. Ellis, C. and Bochner, A. B. Auto-ethnography, personal narrative, reflexivity: researcher as subject. In N. K. Denzin and Y. S. Lincoln (Eds.) *Handbook of Qualitative Research*, 733-768. Sage, London, 2000.
13. Fallon, E., Bannon, L. and McCarthy, J. (Eds.) *ALLFN 1997, Revisiting the Allocation of Functions Issue: New Perspectives*. IEA Press (1997), 73 –88.
14. Ferris, B., Watkins, K. E. and Borning, A. Onebusaway: behavioural and satisfaction changes resulting from providing real-time arrival information for public transit. In *Proc. of Transportation Research Board 90th Annual Meeting* (2010).
15. Foth, M., Schroeter, R. and Ti, J. Opportunities of public transport experience enhancements with mobile services and urban screens. *IJACI 5, 1* (2013), 1-18.
16. Ge, Y., Liu, C., Xiong, H. and Chen, J. A taxi business intelligence system. In *Proc. SIGKDD 2011*, ACM Press (2011), 735-738.
17. Glaser, B. and Strauss, A. *The Discovery of Grounded Theory: Strategies for Qualitative Research*. Transactions, Chicago, 1967.
18. Harper, R. H. R. *Why Do People Wear Active Badges?* Rank Xerox Research Centre, 1993.
19. Inglesant, P. and Sasse, M. Usability is the best policy: public policy and the lived experience of transport systems in London. In *Proc. BCS-HCI 2007*, BCS Press (2007), 35-44.
20. Junglas, I., and Spitzmüller, C. A research model for studying privacy concerns pertaining to location-based services. In *Proc. HICSS 2005*, IEEE Press, 180-189.
21. Lathia, N. and Capra, L. How smart is your smartcard?: Measuring travel behaviours, perceptions, and incentives. In *Proc. UbiComp 2011*, ACM Press (2011), 291-300.
22. Lee, S. and Kleiner, B. H. Electronic surveillance in the workplace. *Management Research News 26 (2/3/4)* (2003), 72-81.
23. McNamara, L., Mascolo, C. and Capra, L. Media sharing based on colocation prediction in urban transport. In *Proc. MobiCom 2008*, ACM Press (2008), 58-69.
24. Olson, J. S., Grudin, J. and Horvitz, E. A Study of Preferences for Sharing and Privacy. In *Proc. CHI 2005*, ACM (2005), 1985-1988.
25. Pace, T., Ramalingam, S. and Roedl, D. Celerometer and idling reminder: persuasive technology for school bus eco-driving. In *Proc. CHI EA 2007*, ACM Press (2007), 2085-2090.
26. Peng, J. A Survey of Location Based Service for Galileo System. In: proc. *Computer Science and Computational Technology 2008*, IEEE (2008), 737-741.
27. Sellen, A., Eardley, R., Izadi, S. and Harper, R. The whereabouts clock: early testing of a situated awareness device. In *Proc. CHI EA 2006*, ACM Press (2006), 1303-1312.
28. Shklovski, I., Vertesi, J., Troshynski, E. and Dourish, P. The commodification of location: dynamics of power in location-based systems. In *Proc. UbiComp 2009*, ACM Press (2009), 11–20.
29. Spitzmüiller, C. and Stanton, J. M. Examining employee compliance with organizational surveillance and monitoring. *Journal of Occupational and Organizational Psychology 79* (2010), 245-272.
30. Tenner, E. *Why Things Bite Back: Technology and the Revenge of Unintended Consequences*. Vintage, 1996.
31. Tfl (2013) 'Modes of Transport'. *Transport for London*. http://www.tfl.gov.uk/corporate/modesoftransport
32. Thomas, L., Little, L., Briggs, P., McInnes, L., Jones, E. and Nicholson, J. Location tracking: views from the older adult population. *Age and Ageing*, (2013), 1–6.
33. Van der Doef, M and Maes, S. The job demand-control (-support) model and psychological well-being: a review of 20 years of empirical research. *Work & Stress 13* (1999), 87-114.
34. Vasalou, A., Oostveen, A. and Joinson, A. N. A case study of non-adoption: the value of location tracking in the family. In *Proc. CSCW 2012*, ACM Press (2012), 779-788.
35. Venard, O., Baudoin, G. and Uzan, G. Experiment and evaluation of the RAMPE interactive system for the mobility of blind people in public transport. In *Proc. Assets20'08*, ACM Press (2008), 271-272.
36. Workman, M. A field study of corporate employee monitoring: attitudes, absenteeism, and the moderating influences of procedural justice perceptions. *Information and Organization 19* (2009), 218-232.
37. Wright, P., Dearden, A. and Fields, B. Function allocation: a perspective from studies of work practice. *Int. J of Human Computer Studies 52*, 2 (2000), 335-355.
38. Zhou, T. The impact of privacy concern on user adoption of location-based service. *International Management & Data Systems 111*, 2 (2011), 212-226.
39. Zweig, D. and Webster, J. Where is the line between benign and invasive? An examination of psychological barriers to the acceptance of awareness monitoring systems. *Journal of Organizational Behaviour 23* (2002), 605-633.

Smart Flashlight: Map Navigation Using a Bike-mounted Projector

Alexandru Dancu
t2i lab, Chalmers
alexandru.dancu@gmail.com

Zlatko Franjcic
Qualisys AB and Chalmers
zlatko.franjcic@chalmers.se

Morten Fjeld
t2i lab, Chalmers
fjeld@chalmers.se

ABSTRACT
While mobile phones affect our behavior and tend to separate us from our physical environment, our environment could instead become a responsive part of the information domain. For navigation using a map while cycling in an urban environment, we studied two alternative solutions: smartphone display and projection on the road. This paper firstly demonstrates by proof-of-concept a GPS-based map navigation using a bike-mounted projector. Secondly, it implements a prototype using both a projector and a smartphone mounted on a bike, comparing them for use in a navigation system for nighttime cycling. Thirdly, it examines how visuo-spatial factors influence navigation. Our findings will be useful for designing navigation systems for bikes and even for cars, helping cyclists and drivers be more attentive to their environment while navigating, providing useful information while moving.

Author Keywords
Bike; GPS; Navigation; Smartphone; Pico-projector; Visuo-spatial; Field of View

ACM Classification Keywords
H.5.m. Information Interfaces and Presentation (e.g. HCI): Miscellaneous

INTRODUCTION
Most mobile device interfaces today use a "stop-to-interact" paradigm [4]. This enables design for general-purpose interaction but makes several assumptions about the mode of operation, such as using both hands and holding the display still. This poses a challenge when designing interfaces for interaction in motion. This paper examines the design and use of projectors and smartphones mounted on bicycles.

A common smartphone application is digital map-based navigation of urban settings. This task requires switching focus between the device and the terrain. Handheld devices thus impose limitations on our behavior and separate us from the physical environment, which could be part of the information domain if we could project onto it when and where needed, allowing the user to move without requiring stopping to look at a handheld screen.

CHI 2014, April 26–May 1, 2014, Toronto, Ontario, Canada.
Copyright © 2014 ACM ISBN/14/04. $15.00.
http://dx.doi.org/10.1145/2556288.2557289

Figure 1. Driving a bike equipped with the Smart Flashlight.

Here, we study nighttime map navigation using GPS, as we compare a mounted smartphone's display versus a projection onto the road. We note that projectors are getting more powerful and accessible, potentially allowing for daytime use. The key contributions of this paper are:

(a) Demonstrating by proof-of-concept that navigation of an urban setting using a projected map is possible;

(b) Designing an experiment focused on subjective feedback that compares navigation while cycling between a map projected on the road with one displayed on a mounted smartphone;

(c) Discussing visuo-spatial factors that influence interface design for interaction in motion

RELATED WORK
Designing for interaction in motion is necessary since mobile devices are worn and used at almost all times. Instead of having the user stop to interact with the mobile device, the system design could be adapted to support perception of digital information while maintaining spatial awareness during motion. Some examples of activities that could make use of interaction in motion are walking, running, cycling, swimming, or driving a car [4]. A similar system to the one demonstrated here used a bike-mounted projector as an augmented headlight to display speedometer data[1]. Findings from exploratory bike trips using handlebar-mounted smartphones reported that map navigation is possible while cycling

[1] `http://youtu.be/Nfkl-XMASrk`

[6]. It was reported that by not offering turn-by-turn navigation, the bike rider could be more aware of the environment, but most cyclists had to stop to read the map anyway, "since they found it too small" [6]. In a stationary indoor study involving memorizing locations on a map, smartphone displays were compared with handheld projectors. For that task and context, spatial memory improved 41% when using projectors [3]. Our focus is not to compare display sizes. Rather, we compare the use of smartphones and projectors for navigation outdoors while in motion. Previous work by Rowland et al. on designing interactive experiences for cyclists employed mobile phones mounted on the bicycle's handlebars or worn on the cyclist's lower arm [7]. They found that for map navigation, adapting digital media to the cycling activity was essential. They used audio instructions to support a "heads-up approach", however the user still had to stop to interact. We note that safety remains a challenge, as interaction with a device in traffic will generally be less safe than passive, stationary use [8].

Automotive ergonomics state humans are comfortable with eye movements of 15 degrees above or below the line of sight, and can easily tilt their heads 30 degrees upward or downward [5]. These field of view parameters are relevant when designing systems presenting visual digital information while moving. Research on car driver attention and behavior revealed how map system configuration (audio, visual, or audio-visual) inside a car influences eye glance frequency [2].

Informed by work in the area of interaction in motion, the design of interactive experiences for cyclists, and findings from the study of car drivers' visual capacity, we verify if map navigation is possible using a bike-mounted projector and compare it with a smartphone display for the use of GPS-based navigation during nighttime cycling. We then discuss factors influencing interaction in motion.

EXPERIMENT

We conducted an experiment comparing two conditions, each using GPS navigation while cycling: mobile phone display versus projection on the pavement in front of the bike. GPS map navigation is considered a skilled activity where users should support their navigation with the system and not follow instructions blindly [1]. Design choices are drawn from recent GPS navigation guidelines suggesting active drivers are "interpreting, ignoring, re-using instructions while also combining them with related information from the environment and their own route knowledge" [1]. Experiment leaders indicated start and finish for the four routes. Subjects cycled for over 20 minutes and had 20 minutes to complete a questionnaire. Recruits were required to be able to ride a bike. Novelty effect was addressed by choosing university students as subjects, having more routes, and providing subjects time to get them acquainted with the technology. These findings, together with the goal of designing for interaction in motion, led us to not have audio or turn-by-turn instructions in our study. Instead, subjects were instructed to identify their need to turn solely from visual information, given as a route and their location on it. We wanted subjects to be more aware of their surroundings in order to use their visuo-spatial capabilities, allowing a heads-up approach instead of following instructions blindly.

Figure 2. Images selected from experimental video recordings: projector (left) and mobile display (right).

Apparatus and Interfaces

The map and navigation application OsmAnd [2] was running on the 4.7" display of an LG Optimus 4X 4D (Android 4.0) smartphone with a screen resolution of 720x1280 pixels. The pico-projector was a Brookstone HDMI Pocket Projector with a resolution of 854x480 pixels, connected to the smartphone via an MHL adapter. The projected display had the shape of a trapezoid, with an area of $0.72m^2$, shown one meter in front of the bike. To mount this equipment on the bike, a commercial mobile phone holder was used, while for the projector we designed our own holder and had it 3D printed. Cycling routes were created using the Viking application[3]. Runkeeper, an application for tracking sport activities, collected information on the route travelled (distance, time, and speed). Subjects were asked to wear a helmet with an attached GoPro video camera to record the journey.

Task and Data

Each subject received a bike equipped with a mobile phone and a small projector mounted to the handlebars, and the helmet. They were instructed to follow routes on a map displayed on the mobile phone screen or the light projected on the pavement (Figure 2). In the projector case, we covered the phone display. Using the map and current GPS location, depicted by a blue arrow, the subject followed a route displayed in pink. Based on this visual information, the subject had to identify when and where to make turns. The subject stayed at the center of the map, which rotated so that "up" on the map always represented the direction of movement. After completing the routes, each subject was asked to complete a questionnaire. The study was completed at night in the city center of a medium-sized city. Total length of routes with recorded data exceeded 90 km. For quantitative analysis we collected the travelled route, distance, time, and speed. We counted the head tilt frequency by analyzing the videos filmed with a head-mounted camera. Subjects then completed a questionnaire comparing usability of the two devices and their subjective assessment of the perceived task workload using a modified NASA Task Load Index. We chose to focus on subjective

[2] `http://osmand.net/`

[3] `http://sourceforge.net/projects/viking/`

feedback because this work was an initial test to check if map navigation is feasible while cycling.

Pilot Study

A within-groups pilot study was performed to ensure the general usefulness and feasibility of the prototype. The aim was both to confirm that the projected light was appropriate for navigation, and to design the final experiment. Six persons (four females and two males) aged between 24 and 50 years (M=34.5, SD=8.89) tested our prototype. We chose several routes throughout the city, with distances varying between one to three kilometers. Initially, each subject was given two arbitrary routes from the set of all available routes. Thereafter, they completed a questionnaire and we subsequently conducted an interview, taking into account their questionnaire answers. We used the collected data for an informal assessment of our prototype to incrementally adjust the system and the experiment. We concluded that because subjects might not be familiar with navigation while cycling, letting them first ride with the projector-based system would introduce two new aspects at once, and thus would be more difficult than beginning with the mobile phone. This observation contributed to the decision in the final design to have four shorter routes (less than a kilometer) instead of two longer routes. This way, the subjects would have more time to learn, to get familiar with the prototype, and also take more time to form an opinion and make a better assessment.

Experiment Results

The final experiment was a 2 x 4 (device: mobile phone, projector; trial: 1-4) within-subjects design using four different routes with a balanced distribution of the number of trials across route-device combinations, and a strict alternation of mobile (M) and projector (P) across the different routes (M-P-M-P or P-M-P-M). The number of subjects was 16, out of which were 7 females and 9 males of ages between 21 and 33 (M=25.8, SD=2.98). subjects completed four routes and a questionnaire whose results are presented below. Each questionnaire section is reflected in the following sections.

Mobile or Projector

The aim of this section was to compare preference and usability of the two displays. The subject could choose between the mobile and projector as answers to questions about which was easier to use, safer, helpful, fun, kept road and traffic more visible, and which kept attention on the route (Figure 3). For 69% of subjects, the projector-based system was easier to use, and 75% found it safer to use. Regarding support for navigation, 69% of subjects stated the projector helped them more than the mobile phone. Similarly, route attentiveness was perceived as being higher with the projector-based system for 63% of subjects. In 69% of all cases subjects reported, road and traffic visibility was reported as higher with the projector-based system.

Task Workload

The goal of this section was to assess the perceived task workload. The subject rated the mental, physical, and temporal demand, as well as frustration level and their perceived map checking frequency, on a seven-point Likert scale where one

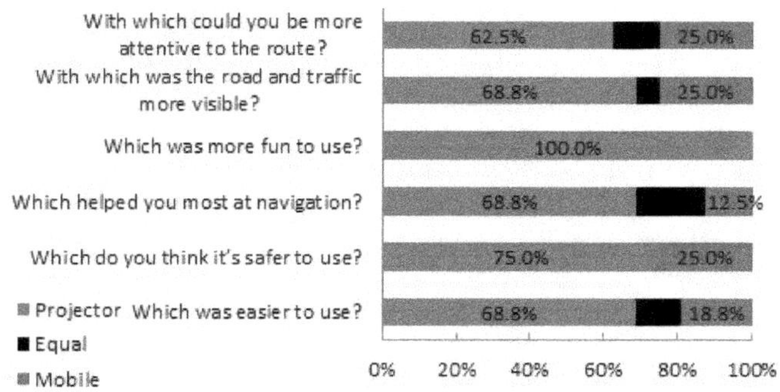

Figure 3. Users' system preferences among the six criteria for projector (blue) and mobile display (red): attention, road visibility, traffic visibility, navigational aid, safety, and ease of use.

meant "Very Low" or "Very Little" and seven meant "Very High" or "Very Much". Additional comments in clear text were encouraged to justify or clarify the ratings and are presented in the next subsection. The reported task loads and relative map check frequency were compared across devices. Paired t-tests for each of the questions revealed a significant effect of device type on mental load ($t = -3.27$, $df = 15$, $p < 0.01$). On the other hand, the type of device had no significant effect on neither the other task load aspects nor the map checking frequency.

User Feedback

Most of the subjects appreciated the large projector display for navigation because it increased the map's clarity, making street names visible. One subject mentioned that it aided in planning the route—the projector freed them to observe and be aware of their surroundings. The projected map was natural to look at, helping them to see the way ahead, letting them feel secure about when to turn. In contrast, some reported missing turns with the phone display, as it was easy to forget about the small device. The safety concerns of looking down into a small mobile screen caused some stress, whereas looking at the projection was much less distracting, allowing peripheral vision to remain on the road. But this was not universal: some subjects preferred the mobile instead, as they could keep the map in memory and focus fully on traffic, with one writing how the greater effort to glance at the mobile encouraged better memory.

Projector Visibility

The goal of this section was to assess if the map was visible enough for navigation and to find out what conditions affected its visibility. All subjects (100%) considered the projected map was visible enough for navigation. The main factors affecting visibility were light sources (from street lights or cars) and ground irregularities (leaves, cobblestones, or other patterns) also causing vibrations.

DISCUSSION

While display size and position are important factors for interaction in motion, the former was not the focus of our research. Similar to the research of Kaufmann and Ahlström [3], our study focused on comparing map navigation using a smartphone versus a portable projector. However, in our study, we evaluated two alternative display types for map navigation during cycling and factors other than display size affecting this task. One such visuo-spatial factor was eye-to-digital information distance (EI), which can be understood as the radius of a circle whose center is the cyclist's face and ends at the phone view or the projected view (Figure 5). In our study, the map was either visible at an arm's length from the eyes of the cyclist or on the ground in front of the them. Besides EI, another factor is normal-view-to-digital information distance (NVI). There is thus a distance between the normal view and the information displayed by the mobile and by the projection. For the cyclist, the normal view is ahead, towards the road. The normal view is characterized by the field of view (FOV) and the line of sight directed ahead (A) (Figure 5). If digital information is presented outside of the FOV, the cyclist's head is required to move towards that information. In our study, the information was the map, requiring a head tilt to enable seeing the projection view (B) or the phone view (C) (Figure 5).

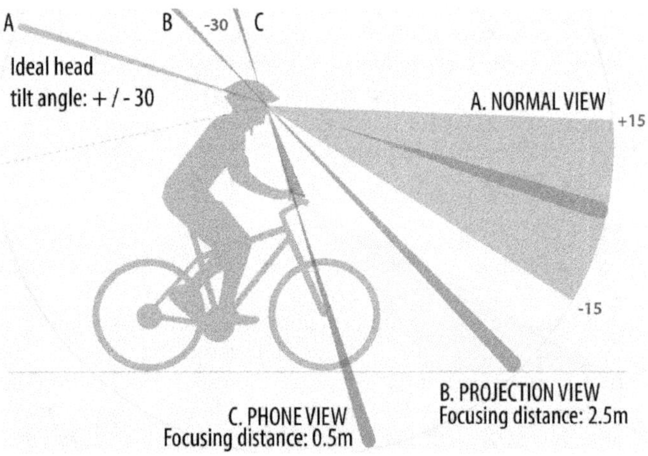

Figure 4. Line of sight and field of view in: A) normal view, B) projection view, and C) phone view.

The mobile's EI is less than the projector's, so the eye focuses faster on the projection. This is because the projection is closer to the normal view and in the FOV, as suggested by one subject. The NVI for the mobile is larger than it is for the projector, resulting in a larger angle during the head tilt. This difference in information placement, together with display size, could be the reason why the mental demand is perceived higher for the mobile phone than for the projector display. For the projected map, we noticed that head tilts had shorter duration and smaller angles, probably because the projected map is closer to the field of view. The experiment provided statistically non-significant data on head tilt frequency differences between devices. However, the data for both devices was remarkably close to the eye glance frequency found by researchers studying car driver attention and behavior for different GPS configurations [2].

CONCLUSION AND FUTURE WORK

This paper presented a mobile system, Smart Flashlight, designed to evaluate bicycle map navigation using a mobile phone versus using a projector. The mobile phone display could be used for navigation during the day, while the projector could serve as both flashlight and map during the night. This interaction method for navigation could be applied to other settings, such as hiking, swimming, or driving. To reliably measure and test objective factors such as completion time and head tilt frequency, we suggest i) controlling subject's cycling proficiency, ii) controlling subject's map navigation skills, and iii) controlling the GPS performance.

ACKNOWLEDGEMENTS

Special thanks to Weiquan Lu, Barrie James Sutcliffe, Pawel Wozniak, and Asim Evren Yantac. This work was supported by the EU FP7 People Programme (Marie Curie Actions) under REA Grant Agreement 290227 and 289404.

REFERENCES

1. Brown, B., and Laurier, E. The normal natural troubles of driving with gps. In *Proceedings of the 2012 ACM annual conference on Human Factors in Computing Systems*, ACM (2012), 1621–1630.
2. Jensen, B. S., Skov, M. B., and Thiruravichandran, N. Studying driver attention and behaviour for three configurations of gps navigation in real traffic driving. In *Proceedings of the SIGCHI Conference on Human Factors in Computing Systems*, CHI '10, ACM (New York, NY, USA, 2010), 1271–1280.
3. Kaufmann, B., and Ahlström, D. Studying spatial memory and map navigation performance on projector phones with peephole interaction. In *Proceedings of the SIGCHI Conference on Human Factors in Computing Systems*, CHI '13, ACM (New York, NY, USA, 2013), 3173–3176.
4. Marshall, J., and Tennent, P. Mobile interaction does not exist. In *CHI '13 Extended Abstracts on Human Factors in Computing Systems*, CHI EA '13, ACM (New York, NY, USA, 2013), 2069–2078.
5. Peacock, B., and Karwowski, W. *Automotive ergonomics*. Taylor & Francis London; Washington, 1993.
6. Pielot, M., Poppinga, B., Heuten, W., and Boll, S. Tacticycle: Supporting exploratory bicycle trips. In *Proceedings of the 14th international conference on Human-computer interaction with mobile devices and services*, ACM (2012), 369–378.
7. Rowland, D., Flintham, M., Oppermann, L., Marshall, J., Chamberlain, A., Koleva, B., Benford, S., and Perez, C. Ubikequitous computing: designing interactive experiences for cyclists. In *Proceedings of the 11th International Conference on Human-Computer Interaction with Mobile Devices and Services*, ACM (2009), 21.
8. Strayer, D. L., Drews, F. A., and Crouch, D. J. A comparison of the cell phone driver and the drunk driver. *Human factors: The journal of the human factors and ergonomics society 48*, 2 (2006), 381–391.

Partially Intelligent Automobiles and Driving Experience at the Moment of System Transition

Key Jung Lee[1], Yeon Kyoung Joo[1], Clifford Nass
Stanford University, Stanford, CA, USA
keyjlee@stanford.edu, jusibel@stanford.edu, nass@stanford.edu

ABSTRACT

The current study (*N* = 49) took a user-centered approach to explore how level of automation (pedal automated, wheel automated or fully automated driving) and the interface modality (switching automation on or off via touch or voice control) in automated vehicles influence drivers' perceived experience and performance. The results found that full or wheel automation in vehicles was perceived significantly more intelligent than pedal automation. Furthermore, drivers in the pedal automation condition reported greater nervousness when using the touch interface than the voice interface. This tendency was not found among drivers in the full and wheel automation conditions. Drivers who used the voice interface to control automated driving had fewer driving mistakes than those who operated the touch interface. Our findings have important psychological and practical implications for designing a user interface for automated vehicles.

Author Keywords

Automated car; partial automation; in-car interfaces; safe driving; situational awareness

ACM Classification Keywords

H.5.2. Information interfaces and presentation (e.g., HCI): User interfaces

INTRODUCTION

Driverless car KITT in a famous American TV series is no longer science fiction. Although there has been incredible progress in control technology for automated vehicles [1], little attention has given to human factors regarding how drivers would respond to and interact with the automated vehicles [7]. Much of the early work on automation was conducted in the context of aviation systems [5, 9]. Researchers in road vehicle automation have adopted the assumptions of aviation automation and explored the effects on drivers' situational awareness, stress, and negative affect [2, 9, 10]. More recent work tested the different level of automated systems (e.g., steering wheel automation, gas/brake automation) on driving performance and mental workload [12]. Evidence indicates that automation decreases mental workload and enhances the psychological well-being of the driver [1, 9].

CHI 2014, April 26-May 1, 2014, Toronto, Ontario, Canada.
Copyright 2014 ACM 978-1-4503-2473-1/14/04...$15.00.
http://dx.doi.org/10.1145/2556288.2557370

However, little is known about what drivers experience at the moment of transition between computer control and driver control in automated vehicles. Drivers' subjective experience during a transition can exert a significant influence on their perception of the technology and on their driving performance. Thus, the present work attempts to understand human factors in a partially or fully automated vehicle at the moment of system transition. Our ultimate goal is to conduct a series of empirical studies to provide a set of psychological principles that will guide the design of a vehicle interface that gives effective, real-time support for drivers of a partially intelligent vehicle (PIV).

Automated Driving System Transition

Automation in vehicles such as adaptive cruise control (ACC) and a Stop & Go system is already playing an important role in the current automobiles [1, 10]. However, there are certainly concerns about the technology [11]. One of the concerns is that drivers may experience difficulty reclaiming control [6]. For instance, a driver may feel vulnerable after receiving back control from the automation system. The driver's negative experience during the moment of system transition can significantly influence his affect, cognition and performance. To our knowledge, no empirical study has given attention to this topic.

We think that the modality that the driver uses to switch automation modes will have a significant influence on the transition experience. Studies have found that control modality in vehicles can affect safety, performance, and driver experience [3]. Both voice interface and touch interface have advantages and disadvantages, dependent upon certain conditions (see [3]). Since the pedal automation still requires a driver's hand control whereas wheel and full automation does not, level of automation may influence a driver's perceived usability of touch/voice interface. In sum, the current study examines how relationship between different level of automation (manual,

[1] Both authors contributed equally to this paper.

pedal, wheel, and full automation) and types of modality (voice and touch) to control such automation influences driver attitudes, negative affect and behavior.

METHOD

Participants & Experimental Design

49 undergraduate students (21 male) with a valid driver's license participated in the study. Their ages ranged from 18 to 27 ($M = 20.73$, $SD = 1.71$). The present study had a total of seven conditions, six experimental and one baseline control conditions. Level of automation constituted the first between-subject variable, with three levels: pedal, wheel, and full. Interface modality constituted the second between-subject variable, with two levels: mode switch by touch vs. mode switch by voice command. The participants were randomly assigned to only one of the seven conditions. Participants in the control condition were neither given any features of automation.

Driving Simulator, Course & Procedure

The driving simulator (Realtime Technolgies, Inc.) comprised a front vehicle cab with force-feedback steering wheel, accelerator and brake pedals, and OE automotive seats. The visual display 'windscreen' was projected on a six-foot rear projection screen. The pre-programmed driving course was about 4.5 miles long. During the experiment, participants, except those in the control condition, activated and deactivated the automation features for four times in total. All participants drove manually to start the simulation. When participants reached the first stop sign, a text message displayed on the screen, "please enable automation." The computer then either partially or fully controlled the driving of the vehicle for a minute. After one minute, a second message was presented, "please disable automation." The second automated driving segment, one minute in duration, was prompted in an open road. The third, three-minute automated driving segment occurred on a straight, rural road. The fourth automated driving segment was prompted in the business area for a minute. No specific event followed after the final transition. After completing the simulation, all participants completed an online questionnaire regarding their experience driving in the simulator. The whole study lasted approximately 50 min.

Independent Variables

Level of Automation

Level of automation had three levels: pedal (only gas/brake pedals were automated), wheel (only steering wheel was automated), and full (both wheel and pedals were automated). The automation mode was displayed on an iPad attached to the center console.

Type of Modality Interface

A simple modal switch was used when invoking automation. Half of participants switched their automation modes by using a touchscreen interface, and the other half of participants used a voice interface. In the touchscreen interface condition, participants activated automation by touching the "Automation is ON" button on the iPad. To reclaim control, they pressed the "Automation is OFF" button. In the voice interface condition, participants used their voice to give the command "Auto Drive" to activate the system and "Manual Drive" to reclaim control. The software OpenEars was used to identify the two voice commands.

Dependent measures

Self-reported measure: perceived intelligence of the car

Participants were asked to indicate how accurately certain adjectives described the car that they just drove (1= describes very poorly, 10 = describes very well). A principle component analysis (PCA) revealed that five items – *intelligent, advanced, high-tech, smart,* and *sophisticated* – were highly correlated and descriptive of the perceived intelligence of the car. The index was calculated by averaging the unweighted values of all five items ($\alpha = .95$, $M = 6.07$, $SD = 2.14$).

Self-reported measure: nervousness during the automation to manual driving system transition

To measure the degree of nervousness that the participants experienced during the system transition, participants reported how much they agree/disagree with statements such as "I felt insecure" and "I felt unsafe" (1 = strongly disagree, 10 = strongly agree). A PCA revealed that six statements – *worried, uncomfortable, not relaxed, unsafe, insecure,* and *nervous* – were descriptive of nervousness. The index was calculated by averaging the unweighted scores of all six items ($\alpha = .92$, $M = 4.86$, $SD = 1.86$).

Self-reported measure: situational awareness (SA)

A total of seven statements from Endsley's SART [4] were adopted and modified by the authors to measure SA. Participants rated how accurately statements such as "I had a good amount of information about the situation" described their state of mind at the moment of certain events happened during the simulation (1 = not at all accurate, 10 = very accurate). A PCA revealed that four of the items – *The situation was familiar, I had enough mental capacity to understand the situation, I knew how to handle the driving situation,* and *I was able to find a way to avoid getting accident* – were descriptive of drivers' SA. Averaging the unweighted values of all four statements constituted the SA score ($\alpha = .88$, $M = 6.53$, $SD = 2.19$).

Behavior measure: road edge excursion

Driving performance measures, including the number of road edge excursions, centerline crossing, and speeding incidences was automatically collected by the simulator. In the present study, only the total number of road edge excursions within 150 meters after the system transition

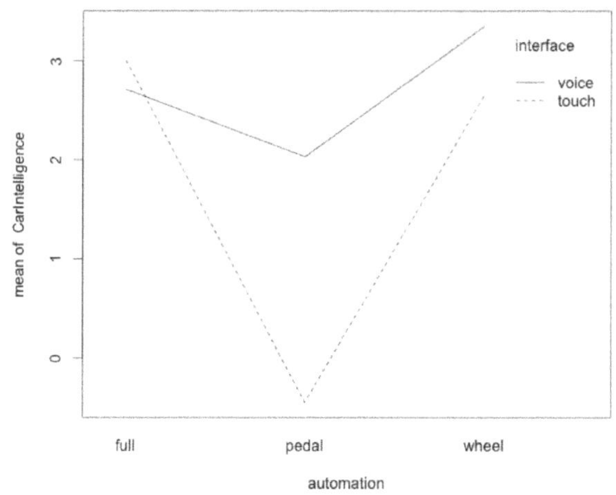

Figure 1. Mean of Car Intelligence.

from automated to manual driving was analyzed (M = .30, SD = .85, min = 0, max = 4.14). Other variables did not provide meaningful differences due to the design of the study, and thus, excluded from the analysis.

RESULTS

Car Intelligence. We adjusted *car intelligence* by subtracting the control group's (baseline) rating of *car intelligence (M* = 4.06*)* from each participant's *car intelligence* score, and conducted a 2 x 3 analysis of variance (ANOVA) with automation and interface modality as independent variables. There was a significant main effect for automation type, $F(2, 36) = 3.44, p < .05, \eta^2 = .16$ (see Figure 1). A least significant difference (LSD) post-hoc analysis revealed that participants in the full (M = 3.03, SD = 1.63) and wheel (M = 2.75, SD = 1.84) automation conditions rated the car's intelligence significantly higher than those in the pedal automation condition (M = 1.29, SD = 2.04), p = .02. Between the two partial automation conditions, the wheel condition (M = 2.75, SD = 1.84) led to a greater perception of car intelligence than the pedal condition (M = 1.30, SD = 2.24), p = .05.

Nervousness. The nervousness data were entered into the same 2 x 3 ANOVA above. There was a significant main

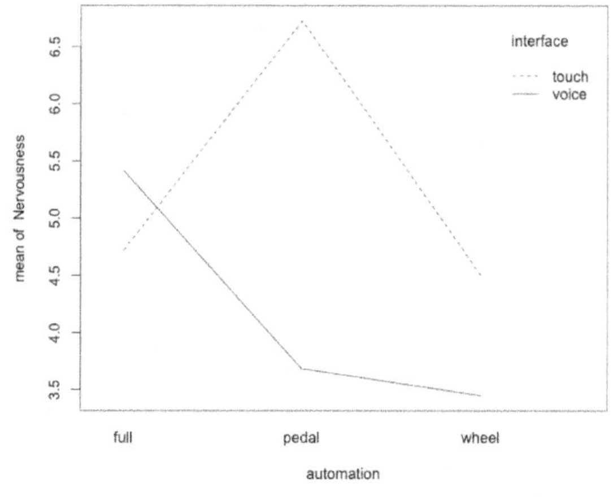

Figure 2. Mean of Nervousness.

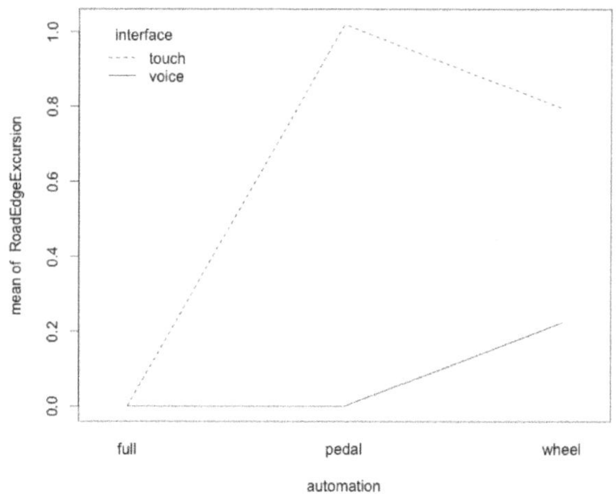

Figure 3. Mean of Road Edge Excursion.

effect of control modality, $F(1, 32) = 5.83, p = .02, \eta^2 = .14$ and an interaction effect between interface modality and level of automation, $F(2, 32) = 5.79, p = .007, \eta^2 = .27$ (see Figure 2). Regardless of automation type, the use of the touch interface (M = 5.47, SD = 1.81) led to a greater sense of nervousness than the voice interface (M = 4.25, SD = 1.74). Decomposing the interaction using simple effect t-tests revealed that with pedal automation, the touch interface (M_{pedal} = 5.14, SD_{pedal} = 1.76) led to a greater feeling of nervousness than the voice interface (M_{pedal} = 5.14, SD_{pedal}= 1.76), $t = 3.26, p = .01, \eta^2 = .25$. However, such difference between the two interfaces was found neither in the full nor wheel automation conditions.

Road Edge Excursion. Baseline-adjusted road edge excursions within 150 meters of the automated driving to driver control transition were entered into a general linear model using a Poisson distribution with interface modality and automation as independent variables. The mean of road edge excursion for the control group was zero. There was a significant main effect of switch modality, b = -2.09, p = .01 (see Figure 3). When participants were using the voice interface, they exited the road edge less frequently (M = .07, SD = .2) than participants who used the touch interface (M = .64, SD = 1.23).

Situational Awareness (SA). The SA data were evaluated by a 2 x 3 ANOVA with automation and interface modality as the independent variables. No main effects on SA (*ps* > .41) were found but there was a marginally significant interaction, $F(2, 36) = 2.80, p = .07, d = .65$. Due to lack of power, decompositions of interaction revealed non-significant differences of modality on three levels of automation.

Additional Analysis. We explored how much time drivers took to reach stable performance after the transition from automated to manual driving. A repeated-measures ANOVA employing participant and time as independent variables and road edge excursion as a dependent variable was conducted. A main effect on time was not significant, $F(10,480) = 1.09, p = .37$. However, our descriptive data suggested that the transition from automated to manual driving impaired driving performance for a short period of time. Starting at 15 meters after the transition, road edge excursions increased (M_{max} = .06), but after 30 meters, it appeared to stabilize (M = .04).

DISCUSSION AND CONCLUSION

This study examined how the type of vehicle automation controls and the modality of switching between automated control and driver control of the vehicle would influence drivers' experience and driving performance. The results showed that a vehicle with full or wheel automation was perceived more intelligent than that of pedal automation. This finding implies that a vehicle with automated pedals would not appear to be as great a technological advance, since adaptive cruise control similar to such automation already exists in current vehicles, and has existed for some time.

In addition, drivers in the pedal automation condition stated a greater degree of nervousness when operating the touch interface than the voice interface. Full and pedal automation conditions did not show a significant difference. This finding indicates that a system that requires drivers to use their hands to operate both the steering wheel and control automation with hand controls can lead to increased nervousness among drivers.

Lastly, the behavioral data showed that drivers had fewer road edge excursions when they used the voice interface. This suggests that drivers are less likely to suffer accidents when their visual attention is not distracted by operating the car interface. The results confirm the findings of previous studies [8] that information for drivers should be presented across various sensory modalities to avoid cognitive overload. As evidenced by previous studies [3], perceived negative affect and driving behavior found in the present study indicate that a speech recognition in-car interface seemed to require less cognitive and physical work load than a touch-based interface, particularly when the computer controlled steering.

The current study has theoretical and practical implications for designing a user interface for automated vehicles. Previous studies have reported that different levels of automation exert differential impact on users' driving experience [7]. Our results showed that drivers' experience of automation technology could be different depending on the modality of car interface they operate while driving [7]. When drivers need to conduct any secondary task that requires coordinated hand movement or visual attention, a touch interface can cause greater distraction than a voice interface. One of the key findings is that not all levels of automation were perceived as equally advanced by drivers, and, thus, the type of automated systems may differently influence drivers. Moreover, a subtle interface feature touch vs. voice command can bring a significant difference in usability and performance of drivers at the moment of system transition in automated vehicles.

ACKNOWLEDGMENTS

This work is published posthumously for Clifford I. Nass, who passed away on November 2, 2013. The other authors dedicate this article to him. This research was sponsored by Toyota's Collaborative Safety Research Center.

REFERENCES

1. Brookhuis, K. A., van Driel, C. J., Hof, T., van Arem, B., & Hoedemaeker, M. Driving with a congestion assistant: mental workload and acceptance. *Applied Ergonomics*, *40*,6 (2009), 1019-1025.
2. Cottrell, N.D., and Barton, B.K. The role of automation in reducing stress and negative affect while driving. *Theoretical Issues in Ergonomics Science 14,* 1 (2013), 53-68.
3. Graham, R., & Carter, C. Comparison of speech input and manual control of in-car devices while on the move. *Personal Technologies*, *4,* 2-3 (2000), 155-164.
4. Endsley, M. Toward a theory of situation awareness in dynamic systems. *Human Factors, 37,* 1 (1995), 32-64.
5. Jensen, R. S. The boundaries of aviation psychology, human factors, aeronautical decision making, situation awareness, and crew resource management. *The International Journal of Aviation Psychology*, *7,* 4 (1997), 259-267.
6. Parasuraman, R. Designing automation for human use: Empirical studies and quantitative models. *Ergonomics, 43,* 7(2000). 931-951.
7. Schmidt, A., Dey, A. K., Kun, A. L., and Spiessl, W. Automotive user interfaces: human computer interaction in the car. In *CHI'10 Extended Abstracts on Human Factors in Computing Systems* (2010), 3177-3180.
8. Sklar, A.E., and Sarter, N.B. Good vibrations: Tactile feedback in support of attention allocation and human-automation coordination in event-driven domains. *Human Factors: The Journal of the Human Factors and Ergonomics Society*, *41*, 4 (1999), 543-552.
9. Stanton, N.A., and Marsden, P. From fly-by-wire to drive-by-wire: Safety implications of automation in vehicles. *Safety Science*, *24,* 1 (1996), 35-49.
10. Stanton, N. A., Young, M. S., Walker, G. H., Turner, H., and Randle, S. Automating the driver's control tasks. *International Journal of Cognitive Ergonomics*, *5,* 3 (2001), 221-236.
11. Wickens, C.D. *Engineering Psychology and Human Performance*. Columbus, OH: Merrill, 1992.
12. Young, M.S., and Stanton, N.A. What's skill got to do with it? : Vehicle automation and driver mental workload. *Ergonomics*, *50*, 8 (2007), 1324-1339.

mobile phone users, and (c) additional parameters for the request, such as how long the request is active, the minimum number of responses needed per location within the specified area, and what constitutes a location for that request (see Figure 1a).

After a user installs the Slide to GeoPoll application on her Android phone, it replaces the normal keyguard mechanism setup on the phone. Each time the user turns off the phone, the application queries a task managing service on the GeoPoll website for a list of possible requests that the user can potentially help to produce a response for; this list is determined based on the user's location and whether or not the request has been previously responded to by the user at that or nearby locations. The application selects a random request from the list of possible requests and presents that request as an optional task on the mobile phone's unlock screen. When the user next turns on the phone, she can perform the task before performing a slide to unlock gesture to use the phone; alternatively, she can ignore the task if she is too busy to, does not want to, or is not in a position to be able to answer the question, and simply unlock the screen (see Figure 1b). That task will continue to remain as a possible request of the user until she has ignored it more than three times.

The Slide to GeoPoll application will submit user responses to the GeoPoll website. Because the user's location when she unlocks the phone may differ from when she last turned off the phone prior to that unlock, the server must check to confirm that the location at which the response was made satisfies the criteria and parameters of the data collection request. If it does not, it is simply discarded. However, if it matches the criteria and parameters of the request, then that information is stored to a database. Because the intent of the service is to produce a collection of public datasets, all requests can be browsed—and the respective datasets can be viewed and downloaded—from the GeoPoll website (see Figure 1c).

Slide to QuantifySelf Application

Our second application is Slide to QuantifySelf. This application allows users to enhance existing practices in personal health data collection, in order to better track and refine their personal habits. Questions include *"have you eaten lunch yet"* and *"are you happy right now?"* This information is, at present, collected solely for the information of the user, but could ultimately be provided to a healthcare professional monitoring the health of the user. This application builds on a growing trend of personal health and fitness datametrics, which has given rise to wearable sensors (*e.g.,* Fitbit [13], Jawbone Up [23]), personal tracking applications (*e.g.,* MoodPanda [32], Momento [31]), and social media applications (*e.g.,* Fitocracy [14]).

Li *et al.* [27] argued that personal informatics and self-reflection can help a person to improve his or her own quality of life. In a few instances, a simple sensor can be

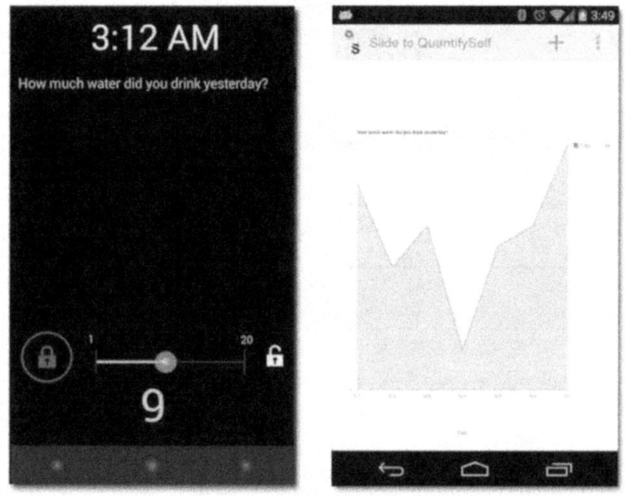

Figure 4. Slide to QuantifySelf application.

used to collect this information over time (*e.g.,* an accelerometer to measure how many steps a person has walked and a scale to measure how much a person weighs). However, there is an abundance of other information which cannot be collected automatically (*e.g.,* how a person feels emotionally) that the user would need help to collect. Often times, the burden of remembering and being prepared to manually capture this information is high [37] and thus it is a challenge to have a useful and detailed enough set of data needed for review and self-reflection.

Slide to QuantifySelf allows the user to track information about herself each time she unlocks her phone (see Figure 5). The application allows the user to specify the set of information to ask herself about throughout the day and the conditions for which to collect any specific piece of information (*i.e.,* when and how often to ask the user particular questions). The application stores this information as time-series data for the user. When the user wants to review her life patterns, the application graphs the information on timelines to support self-reflection.

Slide to Cure

Amazon's Mechanical Turk [3] has popularized the concept of using an online crowd as workers who can complete tasks which require human intelligence (or HITs) at a relatively low cost to companies and developers who need the work completed. The low pay for completing tasks reduces the likelihood that the available online set of workers is a sufficiently broad workforce capable of attacking any problem. Furthermore, the time it takes for tasks to get completed largely depends on the set of workers who are online who can perform the specific work at any given time and how much compensation is provided for completing the work. Although researchers have previously shown that a plausible approach to using the Mechanical Turk for completing human intelligent tasks in a timely manner is to keep the crowd actively engaged on fake tasks until a real one arises. The scalability of this approach as a long term

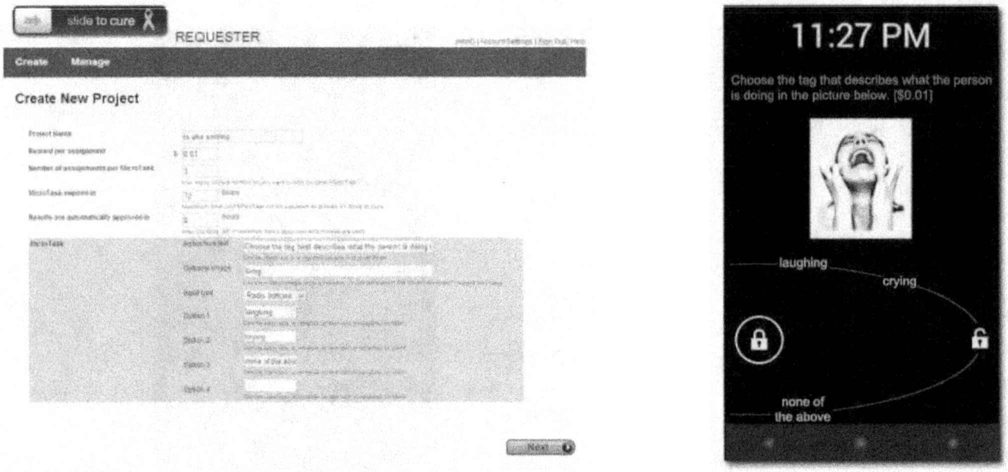

Figure 5. Slide to Cure application.

solution, however, has not been evaluated for tasks which require immediate responses but may not arise all the time (such as to help provide answers for visually impaired users [5]). Is having to pay a crowd to complete fake tasks until a real task is needed by a visually impaired user a cost that can be afforded?—the amount might seem low to the general population but not to users with visual impairments.

We have developed a website called Slide to Cure to allow people who need work done to create and deploy microtasks that can be performed by mobile phone users when they unlock their devices (see Figure 5). Similar to the application described above, after a user installs the Slide to Cure application on his Android phone, it replaces the normal keyguard mechanism setup on the phone (see Figure 5). Each time the user turns off the phone, the application connects to the Slide to Cure database and receives a random microtask which still requires work. When the user turns on his phone, the microtask is displayed as an optional task on the unlock screen, which the user can complete if he is able to and interested in doing so. Tasks which the user ignores more than three times are automatically removed from the list of possible ones to show again to that user in the future.

Our system allows for work to be completed differently from the Mechanical Turk in that work could, in theory, be pushed to an available mobile workforce of more than 1.3 billion people. The significantly larger workforce means that work can get accomplished quickly. We believe that benevolent motivations such as contributing their pay to donate to a non-profit/charity will keep the crowd motivated to complete microtasks. Although that aspect of the demonstration app is not developed, we can require requesters to register a PayPal or Amazon Payments account with their profile when they use the Slide to Cure website. As with the Mechanical Turk, microtasks are not available to the crowd until the funds needed to pay for the work have been transferred to the Slide to Cure website.

When each microtask is approved, the payment is added to the larger collection of money donated monthly to a charity. Although we suspect that the worldwide market for HITs is not yet large enough to support this many users, it is nonetheless worth considering that, were we to harness only 1% of daily unlocks (from our study, on average 52.8 per user, per day), the work capacity worldwide would be 686.4 million unlocks. Paid at $0.01 per HIT, this would represent $6,864,000 generated, per day, for charity.

CONCLUSION AND FUTURE WORK

As the project continues, we will seek out additional uses for the sorts of microtasks we have described. We will also seek to implement our platform on a wider array of devices. We will also explore other sorts of activities at the unlock screen. For example: if users were presented with two unlock widgets, one that is the 'normal' unlock, and one which would cause $0.01 to be donated to charity, which would they choose, when, and why? Along with this, we will seek to understand the relative mental difficulties of the various tasks and the effects of modulating difficulty on the cell phone usage and answer accuracy.

We will also seek to integrate microtasks into a wider array of circumstances and devices. Tablet unlocking, computer, indeed, all portable electronics, offer the potential for microtasks at login time. Further, other moments, such as idle, interruptible moments of use, might provide an opportunity for the completion of additional microtasks.

In this paper, we have described the concept of Slide to X, replacing the unlock screen of mobile phones with a screen that allows users to perform optional microtasks. We also describe our deployment study, in which 10 participants performed thousands of such microtasks over the course of two weeks. We demonstrated that users unlock their phones with high regularity, and at the vast majority of locations visited, indicating that unlock screens could potentially serve as a replacement for prompted alerts in all manner of ubiquitous computing applications. We also described our applications, which hold the potential to unlock the potential of smart phone unlocking to better support data collection, personal metrics, and HIT task completion.

REFERENCES

1. von Ahn, L., Maurer, B., McMillen, C., Abraham, D., Blum M. (2008) reCAPTCHA: Human-Based Character Recognition via Web Security Measures. Science, 321(5895), 1465–1468.s
2. Alt, F., Shirazi, A.S., Schmidt, A., Kramer, U., and Nawaz Z. Location-based crowdsourcing: extending crowdsourcing to the real world. NordiCHI 2010: 13-22
3. Amazon Mechanical Turk. https://www.mturk.com/mturk/welcome
4. Bauer, J.S., Consolvo, S., Greenstein, B., Schooler, J.W., Wu, E., Watson, N.F., and Kientz, J.A. ShutEye: encouraging awareness of healthy sleep recommendations with a mobile, peripheral display. CHI 2012: 1401-1410
5. Burton, M.A., Brady, E.L. Brewer, R., Neylan, C., Bigham, J.P, and Hurst, A. Crowdsourcing subjective fashion advice using VizWiz: challenges and opportunities. ASSETS 2012: 135-142
6. Chaudhri, I., Ording, B., Anzures, F. A., Van Os, M., Lemay, S. O., Forstall, S., & Christie, G. (2011). Unlocking a Device by Performing Gestures on an Unlock Image. U.S. Patent No. 8,046,721 B2. Washington, DC: U.S. Patent and Trademark Office.
7. Chen, W. C., Cheng, Y. M., Sandnes, F. E., & Lee, C. L. (2011). Finding suitable candidates: the design of a mobile volunteering matching system. In Human-Computer Interaction. Towards Mobile and Intelligent Interaction Environments (pp. 21-29). Springer Berlin Heidelberg.
8. Consolvo, S., Klasnja, P.V., McDonald, D.W., Avrahami, D., Froehlich, J., LeGrand, L., Libby, R., Mosher, K., and Landay, J.A. Flowers or a robot army?: encouraging awareness & activity with personal, mobile displays. UbiComp 2008: 54-63
9. Dearman, D., and Truong, K.N. Evaluating the implicit acquisition of second language vocabulary using a live wallpaper. CHI 2012: 1391-1400
10. Dey, A.K, Wac, K., Ferreira, D., Tassini, K., Hong, J.H., and Ramos, J. Getting closer: an empirical investigation of the proximity of user to their smart phones. Ubicomp 2011: 163-172.
11. Eagle, N. txteagle: Mobile Crowdsourcing. HCI (14) 2009: 447-456
12. Falaki, H., Mahajan, R., Kandula, S., Lymberopoulos, D., Govindan, R., and Estrin, D. (2010) Diversity in Smartphone Usage. Proc. MobiSys '10, ACM, 179-194.
13. Fitbit. http://fitbit.com
14. Fitocracy. https://www.fitocracy.com/
15. Froehlich, J., Chen, M.Y., Consolvo, S., Harrison, B.L., and Landay, J.A. MyExperience: a system for in situ tracing and capturing of user feedback on mobile phones. MobiSys 2007: 57-70
16. Frost, M., Doryab, A., Faurholt-Jepsen, M., Kessing, L.V., and Bardram, J.E. Supporting disease insight through data analysis: refinements of the monarca self-assessment system. UbiComp 2013: 133-142
17. Gartner. Gartner Forecast: Mobile Phones, Worldwide, 2011-2017, 2Q13 Update.
18. Gupta, A., Thies, W., Cutrell, E., and Balakrishnan, R. mClerk: enabling mobile crowdsourcing in developing regions. CHI 2012: 1843-1852
19. Guy, R.T., and Truong, K.N. CrossingGuard: exploring information content in navigation aids for visually impaired pedestrians. CHI 2012: 405-414
20. Ha, J. H., Chin, B., Park, D. H., Ryu, S. H., and Yu, J. (2008) Characteristics of excessive cellular phone use in Korean adolescents. CyberPsychology & Behavior, 11(6), 783-784.
21. Hara, K., Le, V., Froehlich, J. Combining crowdsourcing and google street view to identify street-level accessibility problems. CHI 2013: 631-640
22. Hicks, J., Ramanathan, N., Kim, D.H., Monibi, M., Selsky, J., Hansen, M.H., and Estrin, D. AndWellness: an open mobile system for activity and experience sampling. Wireless Health 2010: 34-43
23. Jawbone Up. https://jawbone.com/up
24. Khang, H., Woo, H. J., & Kim, J. K. (2012). Self as an antecedent of mobile phone addiction. International Journal of Mobile Communications, 10(1), 65–84.
25. Klasnja, P., Harrison, B.L., LeGrand, L., LaMarca, A., Froehlich, J., Hudson, S.E. Using wearable sensors and real time inference to understand human recall of routine activities. Ubicomp 2008: 154-163
26. Lockout Mobile Security (2012). Mobile mindset study. https://www.mylookout.com/downloads/lookout-mobile-mindset-2012.pdf.
27. Li, I., Dey, A.K., and Forlizzi, J. Understanding my data, myself: supporting self-reflection with ubicomp technologies. Ubicomp 2011: 405-414
28. Lowry, C. S., & Fienen, M. N. (2013). CrowdHydrology: Crowdsourcing Hydrologic Data and Engaging Citizen Scientists. Ground Water, 51(1), 151-156.
29. Lyons, K., Skeels, C., Starner, T., Snoeck, C.M., Wong, B.A., Ashbrook, D.: Augmenting conversations using dual-purpose speech. UIST 2004: 237-246
30. Meacham, J. W. (2013). Alternative unlocking patterns. U.S. Patent No. 8,504,842 B1. Washington, DC: U.S. Patent and Trademark Office.
31. Momento. http://www.momentoapp.com/
32. MoodPanda. http://moodpanda.com/
33. National Science Foundation. Award Abstract. http://www.nsf.gov/awardsearch/showAward?AWD_ID=1331439
34. Oulasvirta, A., Rattenbury, T., Ma, L., and Raita, E. (2012) Habits make smartphone use more pervasive. Personal and Ubiquitous Computing, 16(1), 105-114.
35. Patel, S.N., Kientz, J.A., Hayes, G.R, Bhat, S., and Abowd, G.D. Farther Than You May Think: An Empirical Investigation of the Proximity of Users to Their Mobile Phones. Ubicomp 2006: 123-140
36. SeeClickFix. http://seeclickfix.com/apps
37. Truong, K. N., & Hayes, G. R. (2009). Ubiquitous computing for capture and access. Foundations and trends in human-computer interaction, 2(2), 95-171.
38. Twitch. http://twitch.stanford.edu/
39. Verkasalo. H. (2009) Contextual patterns in mobile service usage. Personal Ubiquitous Computing, 13(5), 331-342.
40. UTest. http://www.utest.com/
41. Waze. http://www.waze.com/

Slide to X: Unlocking the Potential of Smartphone Unlocking

Khai N. Truong, Thariq Shihipar, Daniel Wigdor
Department of Computer Science
University of Toronto
khai@cs.toronto.edu, thariq.shihipar@alum.utoronto.ca, daniel@dgp.toronto.edu

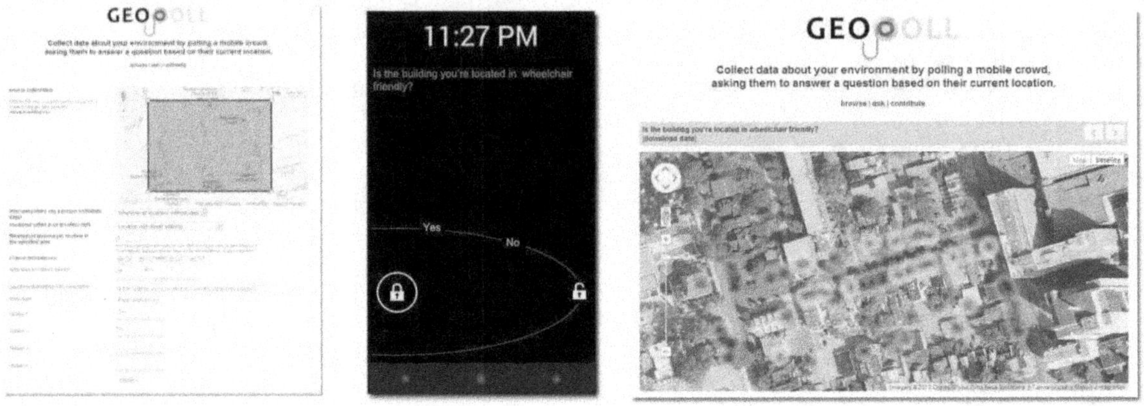

(a) (b) (c)

Figure 1. A Slide to X application—Slide to GeoPoll. (a) Interface for creating a Slide to Geopoll task (b) Slide to GeoPoll screen unlock interface, and (c) the GeoPoll webpage for viewing and downloading the content collected by mobile phone users

ABSTRACT

Unlock gestures are performed by billions of users across the world multiple times a day. Beyond preventing accidental input on mobile devices, they currently serve little to no other purpose. In this paper, we explore how replacing the regular unlock screen with one that asks the user to perform a simple, optional task, can benefit a wealth of application domains, including data collection, personal-health metrics collection, and human intelligence tasks. We evaluate this concept, which we refer to as Slide to X. Further, we show that people are willing to perform microtasks presented through this interface and continue to do so throughout the day while they visit different locations as part of their daily routines. We then discuss how to implement this concept and demonstrate three applications.

Author Keywords

Dual-purpose interaction; microtasks; phone unlock.

ACM Classification Keywords

H5.2 [Information interfaces and presentation]: User Interfaces – Input devices and strategies

CHI 2014, April 26 - May 01 2014, Toronto, ON, Canada

ACM 978-1-4503-2473-1/14/04…$15.00.
http://dx.doi.org/10.1145/2556288.2557195

INTRODUCTION

According to Gartner, by the end 2013, there will be 1.3 billion smartphones in active use worldwide [17]. Largely to reduce accidental input, most touchscreen-based phones and tablets require that a gesture be performed in order to unlock the device (*e.g.,* [6, 30]). Previous work has found that, on average, adult users unlock their phone between 10-200 times per day. This suggests that, worldwide, at least 13 billion unlock gestures are performed on a daily basis. Given a measured 3cm per unlock gesture performed in an average time of 1.72 seconds (found in our study), we estimate that humanity is spending 6.2 million man-hours sliding fingers approximately 390,000 km (roughly the distance to the moon) – every day – all for the sake of reassuring our phones that we are, in fact, acting intentionally.

To be sure, preventing accidental inputs is important. However, we see this as a tremendous opportunity to harvest that time and physical activity to other aims. We believe that these unlocking gestures, instead of simply acting as wasted movements, could be redirected to far greater effect. In this paper, we examine replacing the regular unlock screen with a dual-purpose one asking the user to perform a simple, optional task while unlocking. We demonstrate this concept, which we refer to as Slide to X, can enhance geo-location data, assist in biometric data collection, and provide sustenance for those in need – while preserving the use of a gesture to reduce accidental input. Each of these applications share a common workflow: the user or a third party defines a set of questions which can be easily and quickly answered with a single gesture. Those questions are presented to the user in place of the traditional 'unlock' UI for their phone. The user can then to choose to answer the question, or bypass it by performing a traditional unlock. The answers which are provided are then shared back to the party specifying the question, along with any necessary contextual information (such as, geo-location).

While Slide to X applications holds promise, it is clear serious questions must be answered about their viability, as each relies on particular usage patterns of the phone, as well as users' willingness to answer Slide to X questions. We sought to understand these issues through a deployment study, in which participants were presented with abstract tasks in place of their unlock screen over a two-week period. In this paper, we thus make three contributions:

1. *The use of micro-tasks as a replacement for traditional phone unlocking.*
2. *A study of regular unlocking patterns and of users' willingness to perform micro-tasks in that context.*
3. *A set of three example applications which demonstrate the Slide to X concept.*

We begin by reviewing related work, before describing our study and our applications in more detail.

RELATED WORK

In this section, we review previous studies and findings which lay the foundation for our research and the Slide to X concept. We first present previous research which has examined smartphone usage patterns; we discuss how their findings suggest that users will interact with the phone's unlock screen an ample number of times per day, and thus the unlock screen can potentially be augmented and harnessed to complete a large amount of work. We then discuss research projects which have explored using mobile phone users to complete human-intelligent tasks and collect data. Finally, we describe prior research of dual-purpose interactions, focusing specifically on applications for mobile devices.

Smartphone Usage Patterns

Researchers have conducted studies to examine how often people use their phones on a daily basis [12] and the reasons why [20, 24]. Falaki *et al.* [12] have shown that users interact with their phones on average 10-200 times a day. A recent study by Lookout Mobile Security [25] found that 58% of adult smartphone users do not go an hour without checking their phone. Khang *et al.* [24] have identified compulsive anxiety as a factor in mobile phone addiction, while Ha *et al.* [20] have shown that Korean adolescents who report excessive cellular phone use expressed more depressive symptoms, higher interpersonal anxiety, and lower self-esteem than people who use their phones at a lower frequency. Oulasvirta *et al.* [34] showed that 18-35% of the time, users interact with their phone only briefly out of their habit of checking dynamic content. Finally, Verkasalo [39] showed that, on average, over 50% of the time spent on mobile devices is at home, over 25% is on the move, and the remainder is at work.

Although past research suggests that people use their phones a large number of times per day at different locations, because the user can customize how soon the phone's lock screen becomes active after it sleeps, the actual frequency of presentation of the unlock screen is not known. Thus, one of the questions that we attempt to answer in our study is how often users see the unlock screen, and actually proceed to unlock the phone.

Mobile CrowdSourcing & In-Situ Data Collection

Patel *et al.* [35] and Dey *et al.* [10] have shown that on average the mobile phone is on the user's body or within-arm's reach more than 75% of the time. Thus, not surprisingly, mobile phones have been used for *in situ* data collection purposes, such as experience sampling [15,25] and life-logging [22, 31]. Klasnja *et al.* [25] studied how mobile phones can be used for in-situ experience sampling via regular (hourly, daily, *etc.*) cellphone surveys. A key issue they identify with such a method is identifying opportune times to pose surveys and avoid disruption.

There are also many potential applications that could be developed if the billions of mobile phone users across the world can be leveraged as a potential source of workers for performing data collection and human-intelligence tasks. Examples of such commercial and research applications include crowdsourcing work that needs to be completed for companies and developers [1,11,18] (including testing of mobile apps in the wild [40]), to providing up-to-date traffic information [1], and participating in citizen science [28] and community activism [36].

Many of the crowdsourcing applications described above envision that users will complete requested tasks for free or small payments. However, it is unclear whether small payments or none at all could attract mobile phone users in all parts of the world and keep them motivated to continue to complete work (*e.g.,* beyond the initial month in which people may use applications because of their novelty factor). For example, Alt *et al.* [1] developed and evaluated whether a mobile application could be used for location-based crowdsourcing. In their study, nine participants completed only 30 total tasks over the course of 2 weeks. This demonstrates that people are willing to work; however, further research must explore how to motivate continued participation. Later in this paper, we propose a different way to motivate participation in mobile crowdsourcing.

Dual-Purpose Interactions with Mobile Devices

The concept of performing a single interaction with a mobile device to complete two actions has been explored previously in a number of contexts. Lyons *et al.* [29] have shown that speech which is "socially appropriate in the context of human-to-human conversations" can also be used to provide instructions to a mobile computer, such as to navigate and interact with the user's calendar. The UbiFit Garden [8], ShutEye [4] and MONARCA 2.0 [16] systems demonstrate that the background screens on mobile devices can be used to convey health information; as the user uses her phone, she would also see information which would support self-reflection about specific aspects of her health. Dearman and Truong showed that a Vocabulary Wallpaper [9] could display place-specific phrases and translations to help the user develop vocabulary in a second language through implicit learning which occurs while she uses the phone for other explicit reasons. Because the interface for ShutEye [4] and MONARCA 2.0 [16], and Vocabulary WallPaper [9] were all implemented as live wallpapers for the Android OS, they were displayed on the lock screen as well as on the home screen. Thus, even when the user turns on the phone to glance at the time or unlocks the screen to use the phone, she may gain information from those actions.

When interacting with the Slide to X interface on the lock screen, the user can both unlock the screen while also producing input to complete an additional task. This concept has been proposed in a number of similar applications: Lock Screen Query [33] and Twitch [38]. Applications of supported by these interfaces overlap with one another, not surprisingly, because many of them have been previously explored by the research community (*e.g.*, crowdsourcing and collection of geo-tagged information about the environment). Thus, what is introduced in Swipe to X, Lock Screen Query [33] and Twitch [38] is the augmentation of the lock screen as a way to get users to perform tasks while they unlock their phones. This concept itself is a next step that extends prior work; *i.e.*, now the lock screen is not only altered to display useful information (as done in previous work such as Vocabulary Wallpaper [9] and ShutEye [4]) but also designed to receive input to complete a task while also unlocking the screen. Our contribution, as shown in this paper, is to answer research questions which will help to inform the design of applications which use such a dual-purpose unlock screen interface to collect data. For example, it is important to know how long on average the phone stays asleep before it is unlocked so that tasks can be selected and assigned to users without the assignment expiring before the user has a chance to complete the task.

STUDY

The success or failure of a Slide to X application hinges on two factors. First and foremost, the user must be willing to answer simple questions when unlocking their phones. Second, some applications require broad or particular context coverage (either temporal or spatial) from unlocking actions throughout a user's day, and thus would require that users unlock regularly, or at particular locations. To shed light on these two issues, we conduct a study to answer four questions, the first two of which relate to context coverage:

1. *How often, throughout the day, do users unlock their phones?* (*i.e.*, what is our temporal coverage?)
2. *What is the distribution of phone unlocks across the places the user visits during the day?* (*i.e.*, what is our geolocation coverage?)

These issues of coverage are of critical importance to many applications. In our Slide to QuantifySelf application, for example, collecting information at the appropriate time is essential (*e.g.*, determining users' coffee consumption by asking "have you had a coffee in the last hour?"). In our Slide to Geopoll application, location coverage is also critical (*e.g.*, mapping wheel chair accessibility by asking people about their current building). In general, it is our goal to understand if Slide to X microtasks could replace the use of location or time-based alerts for many applications.

In addition to our questions about coverage, we also sought to understand users' willingness to perform microtasks as a part of the unlocking action. In particular, we wished to begin to find answers to these questions:

3. *How often are users willing to perform Slide to X unlocking?*
4. *How intensive a question are users willing to answer when unlocking?*

We conducted a study in which experimental software was installed on participants' own phones to track their usage. Our software replaced their phone's unlock screen, allowing us to modulate the presentation of information at unlock time. In addition to answering the above research questions, we took the opportunity to collect additional information about our participants' phone unlocking habits.

Participants

We recruited 10 paid ($20) participants between the ages of 19-23 (3 female) from the local community using online advertising. Participants were selected for our two-week study based on their phone's compatibility with our apparatus (any version of Android 2.3 or later was allowed, with a preference for newer phones given the battery usage needs of our tracking software).

Apparatus

Software

We developed and installed experimental software on each participant's handset. The software was written in Java with a minimum Android API level of 10. Android was targeted as the distribution platform, because it exposes APIs for overriding the phone's unlock screen. The software was forked off on an open-source project called LinguaLock under the Apache 2.0 License. The software stored data locally on the phone's SD card in a CSV file format; thus, no internet connectivity or backend server was required,

The apparatus was instrumented to perform three fundamental tasks: collect position data, collect usage data, and present the participant with various types of unlock screens:

1. Position data: Every 10 minutes, the user's geospatial position was recorded using the Android location APIs (whether the phone's screen was on or off). The APIs ensure that the most accurate means available is employed. Tracking participants allowed us to assess the 'spatial coverage' of their unlocking gestures.

2. *Usage data:* Further, every time the phone's screen was turned on, the event was recorded, as was the time and location of each unlocking activity.
3. *Slide to X functionality:* When a participant unlocked her phone, she was presented with one of several possible unlock screens: (a) a traditional, Android unlock screen, (b) a simple mathematical question, meant to abstract cognitive load and provide a question with ground-truth to test participant effort, (c) an introspective questions about health (*e.g., "how happy have you felt in the past hour"*), meant to understand if users are able to meaningfully sample their experiences during the time it takes to unlock their phone; or questions about recent activities (*e.g., "in the last hour, have you had any coffee"*), meant to test if users are willing to quickly perform recall when unlocking their phone.

The answers provided to each question were recorded, as was the time spent between screen power-on and the eventual completion of the unlock action.

To ensure sufficient data collection, participants were not given the choice to override the Slide to X functionality. While we advocate for a design in which a traditional unlock gesture is always available, we believe this compromise in external validity allowed us to enhance our collection of both quantitative data and post-task feedback.

Procedure

We instructed the 10 participants to use their phones as per usual but with our experimental apparatus running on their phones for two weeks. We asked participants to return to the lab for a follow-up interview and post task questionnaire at the end of the two weeks. Due to scheduling difficulties, time in the field varied from 14 to 20 days. All data are included in our analysis.

Because all input to our apparatus is participant-initiated, the lower bound on the number of data points per participant was not controlled. The software was configured so that Slide to X questions were presented only occasionally. The rate of presentation was set as follows: at the beginning of each day, a pseudo-random value p was computed with a uniform distribution in the range of (0.25, 0.75). Each time the phone was activated, the apparatus would either display a question (probability of p), or a traditional unlock screen (probability of 1-p). This distribution was chosen based on early testing, which found that asking a question on every unlock was too onerous. The range was set to allow us to collect feedback about the reasonableness of a given frequency. Questions were posed using a random without-replacement method.

RESULTS

Over the course of the study, the ten participants unlocked their phones a total of 16,398 times. Of these, a question was posed 8,118 times, and a simple unlock screen displayed a total of 8,280 times.

The average number of daily unlocks was highly variable across participants: the minimum mean was 4.82 (std dev=8.75) per day (participant P8), the maximum mean was 105.24 (std dev=35.11) by P1. P8 was an outlier in this respect – the next lowest was 20.07 (std dev=18.97) by P3. The average number of Slide to X questions answered per day, per participant, was 49.83 (std dev=28.95).

All but 1 participant reported in the post-task questionnaire that they checked their phone immediately after waking up and immediately prior to going to sleep each night. We therefore used unlocking activity as a proxy for the beginning and end of each user's day when computing various descriptive statistics.

Participants were asked in the post task questionnaire if they would be willing to continue the study for another period of the same length for the same compensation ($20) – all but one volunteered. This suggests that the compensation was sufficient for the task. Given the average of 772 questions per participant, this resulted in a rate of pay of $0.026 per question.

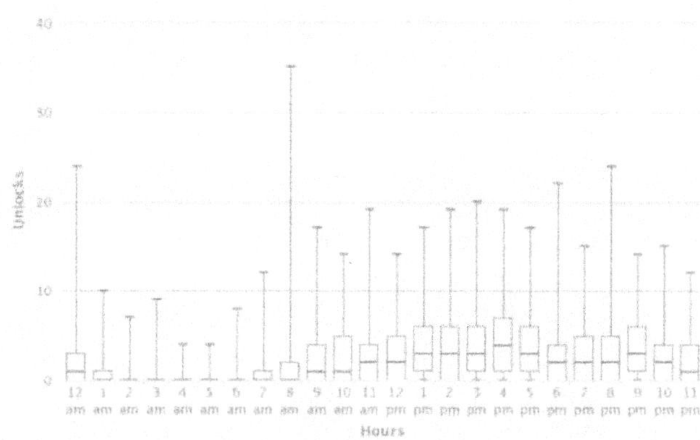

Figure 2. Hourly distribution of unlocking actions.

Unlocking Distribution & Frequency

As mentioned above, 9 out of 10 participants indicated that they checked their phone immediately upon waking up and immediately before going to sleep each night. Phone usage typically tapered off during meal times (12pm-1pm and 6pm-8pm), and peaked in early afternoon (3pm-5pm) and late evening (8pm-10pm). On average, participants unlocked their phones 4.3 times per waking hour. Unlocks happen on average 25.8 minutes apart (std dev=150.7).

Participants were asked in the post task questionnaire whether the frequency of Slide to X questions was *too low*, *too high*, or *just right*. 8 of 10 participants reported the current frequency of questions was reasonable, while 2 reported that they were too frequent. None of the participants noted a difference in frequency on days with a lower p value than on days with higher values. Seven of the 10 participants noted that, while the overall frequency of being asked a question was reasonable, greater variety in the questions and less redundancy (*i.e.,* seeing the same question less frequently) was desired.

Participants were asked in the post-task questionnaire to list situations where the Slide to X behavior was problematic. All reported that activities requiring frequent unlocking were sometimes frustrating (*e.g.,* carrying on a conversation via SMS). They also indicated the occasional need to find information quickly (*e.g.,* time of arrival of the next bus). For this reason, we advocate for a design in which a traditional unlock gesture is always available—allowing the user to bypass a task when she is unable or unwilling to complete it.

Location Distribution

Using our persistently recorded GPS data, we analyzed the coverage of 'locations visited' in unlocking actions. To eliminate noise from the GPS readings and to cluster movements that might happen within buildings, we defined a *visit* location as one where 3 or more consecutive recorded locations were within a 500m radius. These thresholds were set *post hoc*, after interviewing participants and presenting them with their location data.

We found that participants visited an average of 2.58 locations per day (std dev = 1.02). Although this seems low, it is consistent with what is commonly reported in the literature as the number of places a person visits on a daily basis. We note it is because the location data is collected once every 10 minutes, and a visit is denoted only if 3 consecutive readings fall within an area of 500 m radius. This means that the participant has been inside of an area for at least 30 minutes. We also found that, participants unlocked their phone at least once during 90% of their visits to any given location (std dev=0.18).

Overall, 45% of the unlocking actions took place in the visited locations, and 55% happened while the participants were on the move. That 55% of unlocking actions which took place on the move is important because they happened in locations that are not the places where the user stays for very long and suggests that unlocking has broad spatial coverage.

In the post-task questionnaire, participants were asked to describe the situations in which they did not choose to unlock their phones, and whether the Slide to X functionality impacted those decisions. 4 of 10 participants indicated that they were always less likely to unlock their phone in certain social contexts, such as small gatherings or meetings. 3 of 10 participants indicated that, because of the increased unlocking time, Slide to X further decreased the probability that they would unlock their phone in those contexts. We leave it to the reader to decide whether this is a positive or negative impact of our framework.

Ground Truth

We did not allow users the option of skipping questions, so we aimed to understand if and when users would intentionally answer a question incorrectly (or without looking at the answers) in order to unlock their phone. 9 out of 10 participants reported occasionally 'skipping' questions in this manner and of those, 7 said they primarily answered questions incorrectly due to time constraints and not based on the type of questions answered.

Thus to study our ground truth we included a class of questions with definite answers that all participants were able to answer correctly, specifically simple math questions (*e.g.,* 'What is 4×8?'). We found that 81% (std dev = 0.19) of the math questions were answered correctly with 4 participants answering the questions correctly at least 95% of the time.

Unlocking Performance

To determine the difficulty added through a Slide to X interface, we recorded the time required between screen activation and successful unlock of the phone, differentiated by whether a regular unlock screen or Slide to X question was displayed.

The mean time across all participants for a 'regular' unlock was 2.15 seconds (std dev=0.75). In contrast, across all Slide to X question types, the mean time was 3.22 seconds (std dev=1.67), with math questions requiring 3.27 seconds (std dev=1.5), health related questions requiring 3.31 seconds (std dev=1.83), and recall questions requiring 3.14 seconds (std dev=1.58). Questions which participants felt were difficult were those which left them unsure of their response or those which needed extra time to perform a deep recall in order to answer.

"I didn't know how to rate how busy or alert I was, either I was doing work or I wasn't." –P8

"The questions that took the longest were the ones that I needed to look back on and remember like 'how many conversations have you had in the past hour'. Things like 'Have you had water in the past hour' were easy." –P9

DISCUSSION

We now discuss how the results validate the viability of Slide to X as a method that can facilitate in the completion of wealth of tasks which require human intelligence and effort. First, we discuss the context coverage of unlocking actions. Then we discuss participants' willingness to perform Swipe to X gestures.

Coverage

In our study, participant unlocked their phones between 4.82-105.25 times a day on average (20.07-105.25 times if we remove a participant who unlocked his phone much fewer than the next least participant). While participants were surprised by how often they used their phones, this matches with previous the findings from research by Falaki *et al.* [12]. Participants found that the plots of their phone usage over time correlated very well with their daily patterns. As a result, their unlocking pattern is a possible proxy for their daily routines. Our results showed that almost all participants unlocked their phones immediately after they wake up and before they go to sleep. Participants checked their phones regularly throughout the day while they are awake, and this tapers off during their meal times and peaks twice—once in the afternoon and once at night. We also learned that participants check their phones at least once at 90% of the locations they visit. On average, participants visit 2.58 places a day, and 45% of their unlocks happen in those places where they stayed for 30 minutes or longer, while the remaining 55% happens on the move.

In all, our findings show that the unlocking action has broad temporal and spatial coverage. It happens at a high frequency, on average 4.33 times per waking hour. Unlocks happen on average 25.8 minutes apart (std dev=150.7). 77.6% the unlocks that happened during our study happened within 15 minutes or sooner of the previous unlock. These findings demonstrate that unlocks happen very frequently and validate that augmenting the unlock screen is a potentially effective way to get tasks completed by users promptly, and if it requires broad context coverage (*e.g.,* experience sampling or in-place data collection).

Willingness

We found that overall participants thought the frequency at which they were presented with questions was reasonable. Answering the questions required an additional 1.64 seconds to their unlocking action. On the whole, however, participants did not find the interface to be disruptive to daily use. On a Likert scale from 1-5, with 1 being not disruptive at all and 5 being highly disruptive, participants rated their experience answering questions as a part of the unlocking action an average of 2.4 (std dev=1.17). However, the interface did impact 3 of our participants in that the increased unlocking time influenced their decision to unlock their phone or not in different contexts.

In all, the findings suggest that participants were willing to answer questions, but that questions could be disruptive. It is important for a design to include a mechanism which would allow the users to simply unlock the phone as they normally would without requiring them to answer the question. Additionally, the interface must conform with the phone's operating system settings users have applied for when a screen lock should occur. In this manner, users can turn on or off their phone and perform quick tasks (such as texting) without being slowed down by the augmented unlock screen. Finally, it is important to consider (1) how to determine the questions that are of interest to the user or ones that they want to ignore and (2) to adjust the tasks that they are asked to perform based on this information.

Motivation

Motivation for answering questions can come from either internal (self-interest) or external (monetary) sources.

In regards to self-interest, participants found that the novelty and personal relevance of the questions made them appealing to answer. For example, P8 remarked that she had no interest in tracking her exercise and would find such questions annoying, but questions about food and calorie consumptions would be more interesting to her.

Other question types may require compensation as motivation. We used math questions as an example of a question type with no intrinsic internal motivation. We found that participants were generally truthful in their responses, with 81% (std dev 0.19) correct answer rate. Furthermore, at least 4 participants answered the questions almost every time (95% correct or greater).

When asked if they would continue with the study at the same compensation rate of $20 for two weeks, all but one of the participants volunteered. This suggests that users were willing to complete tasks at a very small rate of pay ($0.026 per question). It is important to note, however, that users in this study were incentivized at a flat rate, not on a per question basis, so future research should examine how a per-question payout may impact motivations.

SLIDE TO X INTERFACE AND APPLICATIONS

In this section, we present Slide to X, our interface designed to provide users with an optional task that they can perform while unlocking their phones. Then we will discuss three potential applications of the Slide to X interface. Motivated by some of the real world problems recently explored by the HCI community: crowd-sourced generation of map data about the accessibility of the physical environment [19, 21], quantified self [27], and computing for social good [7], we demonstrate how to leverage mobile phone users' ability and desire to complete a short optional task as a potential way to:

- **Slide to GeoPoll** – produce context data for a specified geographical area;
- **Slide to QuantifySelf -** help users more easily collect information about themselves; and
- **Slide to Cure – offer users** work to receive payment that is donated to a charity.

Slide to X Interface

Slide to X is a software library which forked off an open-source project called LinguaLock under the Apache 2.0 License. The software was written in Java with a minimum Android API level of 10. Again, we targeted Android as the distribution platform, because it exposed APIs for overriding the phone's unlock screen. The interface performs three steps automatically when it is installed on a phone: first, it creates a unique user ID based on the device's default user profile; second, it subscribes for screen on and off actions from the operating system; and third, it subscribes for periodic location updates. When the screen is turned off, the software generates a packet composed of the user ID, the most recent location information, and a future time value (which takes into consideration how much time must pass after the screen has been turned off before the unlock screen can be shown again to the user). This packet is dispatched to a task managing service, which then responds with a microtask that will be presented to the user when the screen is next turned back on.

The time value is used by the task managing service to filter for tasks which will not expire before the unlock screen may next appear. The software obtains this task at screen turn-off time instead of turn-on in order to ensure that the screen is shown immediately to the user (instead of needing to wait for it to communicate with the task managing service which searches its database for a task that can be assigned to the user and then transferred that back to the interface).

The augmented lock screen itself has three parts:

1. a clock, which allows users who only want to check the time to be able to do so easily;
2. a question, which may include a picture; and
3. the slide to unlock widget, which includes the possible answers.

The slide to unlock widget can either display radio options (or multiple choice answers), a Likert scale, or a rating slider. To select a particular answer, the user simply touches the lock icon on the left side of the widget, drags it to the answer she wants to select and releases. An unlock icon is always present on the right side of the widget. This allows for the user to always be able to unlock the screen quickly using the same motion without needing to consider the question or the answers.

Once the user has completed a sliding action, the answer is reported back to the task managing service so that it can release the task assignment (if no answer was provided) or record the answer and close the assignment (if an answer was provided).

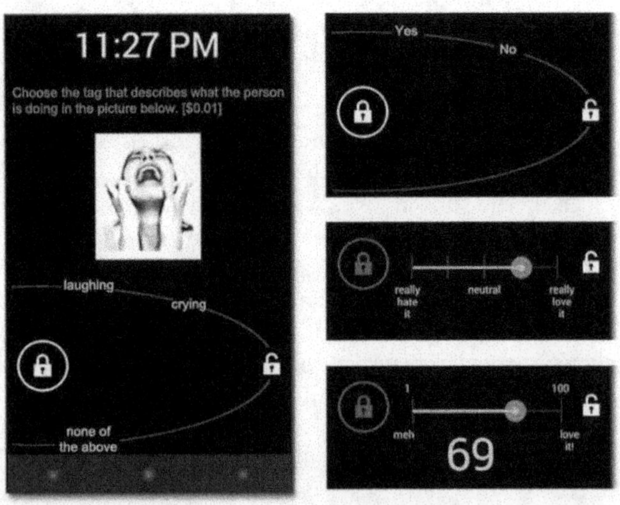

Figure 3. The Slide to X interface. Left shows the three parts to the unlock screen: a clock, the question with an optional image, and a slide to unlock widget. Right shows three possible variations of the slide to unlock widget: multiple choice answers, a Likert scale, and a rating bar.

The task managing service can either be online or on the same device. An online version of the task managing service is developed in PhP and can be accessed through web requests. It consists of a library for inserting, editing, deleting tasks, assigning and removing tasks, and to store and retrieve completed work/responses submitted by the user. Because it is a PhP library, an application developer simply installs it on a Website and directs the Android application they develop to that URL. The interface for creating questions online can be customized without needing to write additional PhP code. Alternatively, if the application being developed is for personal use, an Android version of the task managing service is also available to be imported and used by the application. More information about how the task managing service works will be described in the applications described below.

Slide to GeoPoll Application

We now discuss the first application of the Slide to X interface—using it to collect information about the environment.

Much information about the world still does not exist in an easy to access database. For example, information about how accessible streets and intersections are to the visually or motor impaired are not readily available and need to be collected. Prior researchers have asked online crowds to label previously captured StreetView images as a way to produce this information. However, these images may not always be up-to-date and occlusions can prevent online crowds from providing accurate judgments about the accessibility of streets and intersections for others. Motivated by these challenges, we developed Slide to GeoPoll, a system which leverages a mobile crowd to provide in-place data about the physical environment. Because the mobile phone user is asked to provide information about the place she is currently located at, this enables map information to be collected more accurately and furthermore for information beyond what can be extracted from Google StreetView to also be gathered.

For example, an extension of work by Hara *et al.* [21] is to determine whether different buildings in an environment are wheelchair friendly or not (that is, can a person in a wheelchair not only enter the building, but also navigate throughout the space and access different stories in that building). This information would be difficult for an online worker to judge simply from Google StreetView images and is best provided by someone who has visited and is located in the building. Additionally, if one wanted to map how noisy people think different parts of the city are, this information is both subjective and non-visual.

We have developed a website to allow anyone to request mobile phone users to help collect specific information within a specified geographic area when they unlock their phones. The requester simply specifies (a) the geographic area in which she wants context information to be collected (b) the question and possible responses to be asked of

Twitch Crowdsourcing: Crowd Contributions in Short Bursts of Time

Rajan Vaish[1], Keith Wyngarden[2], Jingshu Chen[2], Brandon Cheung[2], Michael S. Bernstein[2]

[1] UC Santa Cruz
Santa Cruz, CA
rvaish@cs.ucsc.edu

[2] Stanford University HCI Group
Stanford, CA
{kwyngard, jingshuc, msb}@cs.stanford.edu

ABSTRACT

To lower the threshold to participation in crowdsourcing, we present *twitch crowdsourcing*: crowdsourcing via quick contributions that can be completed in one or two seconds. We introduce Twitch, a mobile phone application that asks users to make a micro-contribution each time they unlock their phone. Twitch takes advantage of the common habit of turning to the mobile phone in spare moments. Twitch crowdsourcing activities span goals such as authoring a census of local human activity, rating stock photos, and extracting structured data from Wikipedia pages. We report a field deployment of Twitch where 82 users made 11,240 crowdsourcing contributions as they used their phone in the course of everyday life. The median Twitch activity took just 1.6 seconds, incurring no statistically distinguishable costs to unlock speed or cognitive load compared to a standard slide-to-unlock interface.

Author Keywords

Crowdsourcing, microtasking, mobile crowdsourcing

ACM Classification Keywords

H.5.2 [Information interfaces and presentation]: User Interfaces. – Graphical User Interfaces.

INTRODUCTION

Mobilizing participation is a central challenge for every crowdsourcing campaign. Campaigns that cannot motivate enough participants will fail [25]. Unfortunately, many interested contributors simply cannot find enough time: lack of time is the top reason that subject experts do not contribute to Wikipedia [29]. Those who do participate in crowdsourcing campaigns often drop out when life becomes busy [21]. Even seemingly small time requirements can dissuade users: psychologists define *channel factors* as the small but critical barriers to action that have a disproportionate effect on whether people complete a goal [27]. Despite this constraint, many crowdsourcing campaigns assume that participants will work for minutes or hours at once, leading to a granularity problem [3] where task size is poorly matched to contributors' opportunities. We speculate that a great number of crowdsourcing campaigns will struggle to succeed as long as potential contributors are deterred by the time commitment.

CHI 2014, April 26 - May 01 2014, Toronto, ON, Canada

ACM 978-1-4503-2473-1/14/04...$15.00.
http://dx.doi.org/10.1145/2556288.2556996

To engage a wider set of crowdsourcing contributors, we introduce *twitch crowdsourcing*: interfaces that encourage contributions of a few seconds at a time. Taking advantage of the common habit of turning to mobile phones in spare moments [24], we replace the mobile phone unlock screen with a brief crowdsourcing task, allowing each user to make small, compounded volunteer contributions over time. In contrast, existing mobile crowdsourcing platforms (e.g., [12,16,22]) tend to assume long, focused runs of work. Our design challenge is thus to create crowdsourcing tasks that operate in very short time periods and at low cognitive load.

To demonstrate the opportunities of twitch crowdsourcing, we present *Twitch*, a crowdsourcing platform for Android devices that augments the unlock screen with 1–3 second volunteer crowdsourcing tasks (Figure 1). Rather than a typical slide-to-unlock mechanism, the user unlocks their phone by completing a brief crowdsourcing task. Twitch is publicly deployed and has collected over eleven thousand volunteer contributions to date. The system sits aside any existing security passcodes on the phone.

Twitch crowdsourcing allows designers to tap into local and topical expertise from mobile users. Twitch supports three unlock applications:

1) *Census* envisions a realtime people-centered world census: where people are, what they are doing, and how they are doing it. For example, how busy is the corner café at 2pm on Fridays? Census answers these questions by asking users to share information about their surroundings as they navigate the physical world, for example the size of the crowd or current activities (Figure 1).

2) *Photo Ranking* captures users' opinion between two photographs. In formative work with product designers, we found that they require stock photos for mockups, but stock photo sites have sparse ratings. Likewise, computer vision needs more data to identify high-quality images from the web. Photo Ranking (Figure 1) asks users to swipe to choose the better of two stock photos on a theme, or contribute their own through their cell phone camera.

Figure 1: Twitch crowdsourcing asks for one to two seconds of users' time each time they unlock their phone. From left to right: Census (crowd size), Census (attire), Photo Ranking, and Structuring the Web.

3) *Structuring the Web* helps transform the written web into a format that computers can understand. Users specify an area of expertise — HCI, the Doctor Who television series, or anything else of interest on Wikipedia — and help verify web extractions relevant to that topic. Each unlock involves confirming or rejecting a short extraction. In doing so, users could power a fact-oriented search engine that would directly answer queries like "heuristic evaluation creator".

After making a selection, Twitch users can see whether their peers agreed with their selection. In addition, they can see how their contribution is contributing to the larger whole, for example aggregate responses on a map (Figure 2) or in a fact database (Figure 5).

We deployed Twitch publicly on the web and attracted 82 users to install Twitch on their primary phones. Over three weeks, the average user unlocked their phone using Twitch 19 times per day. Users contributed over 11,000 items to our crowdsourced database, covering several cities with local census information. The median Census task unlock took 1.6 seconds, compared to 1.4 seconds for a standard slide-to-unlock gesture. Secondary task studies demonstrated that Twitch unlocks added minimal cognitive load to the user.

Our work indicates that it may be possible to engage a broad set of new participants in crowdsourcing campaigns as they go about their day or have a few spare moments. In the following sections, we introduce twitch crowdsourcing in more detail and report on our public deployment and field experiments.

RELATED WORK

Crowdsourcing has demonstrated the potential to support goals ranging from search engine support [6], classifier training [28], and even real-time interaction [5,19]. However, these systems often are limited in the amount of topical and local expertise they can assume. To address this limitation, txtEagle [12], mCrowd [30], and mClerk [16] have sought to engage new sets of users through mobile crowdsourcing. However, these mobile crowdsourcing applications assume longer stretches of participation from crowd workers; twitch crowdsourcing aims to capture more incidental, ad-hoc opportunities. Bentley et al. characterize micro-moments by short (~10 second) time periods when attention can be taken away from a current task [1,4]. Twitch crowdsourcing demonstrates that these micro-moments are ideal platforms for interaction. Applications such as adaptive flashcards [13] operate on similar insights, but Twitch is unique in its design as an unlock screen.

Twitch: Census

Previous efforts have spread sensor-oriented crowdsourcing tasks through mobile phones [30]. Crowd-sensing applications likewise draw on humans-in-the-loop to trigger sensing actions or review results [26]. Scaling up sensor networks, MetroSense provides a people-centric paradigm for urban sensing [8]. Census also complements sensor technologies to track transportation habits [15] and mobile phone-based remote sensing platforms [11].

Twitch: Photo Ranking

User-generated photo voting platforms often succeed through a motivating goal, such as Kitten War [32]. However, while stock photography portals such as iStockPhoto [33] exist, none provide a vast collection of free to download images. In parallel, computer vision has demonstrated the importance of crowdsourcing large datasets [28]. Rankr [20] aims to rank images, ideas and priorities via a mobile phone application; however, it requires dedicated users and is not integrated into users' general flow. Photo Ranking is also inspired by the Matchin game, which demonstrates that twitch crowdsourcing can complement game strategies [17].

Twitch: Structuring the Web

Campaigns such as FreeBase [34] and dbPedia [35] have demonstrated the opportunities available when crowds help structure the information available on the web. Automatic

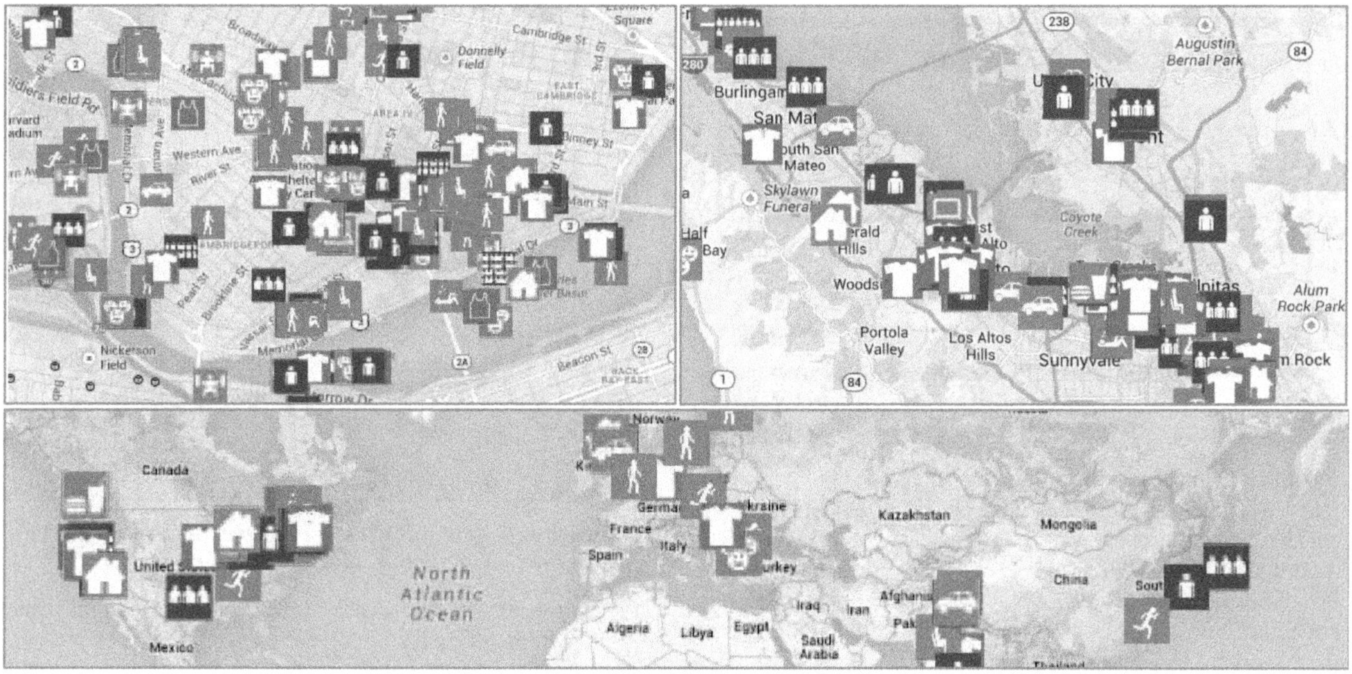

Figure 2: Subsamples from the worldwide Census activity generated by Twitch. Upper left: Cambridge, Massachusetts. Upper right: Bay Area, California. Bottom: worldwide.

information extraction techniques such as ReVerb [14] can be augmented by crowd verification [18]. Twitch generalizes these interactive techniques and allows users to contribute to essentially any topic of interest.

TWITCH CROWDSOURCING

We address difficulties in mobilizing crowd participation by tapping into brief moments of users' time. While waiting for an elevator, a meeting, a walk signal, or cafeteria service, it can be difficult to resist glancing at the phone [24]. Rather than making this temptation harder or less desirable, we take advantage of these short bursts to encourage people to make small contributions towards solving impactful problems. We call this approach *twitch crowdsourcing*: engaging with participants in a convenient fashion in short bursts.

While there any many possible short bursts of time in users' daily lives, we focus on one that users already expect to be a small task: the mobile phone unlock screen. A slide-to-unlock gesture is useful for preventing accidental activation of the phone, but there is no reason why the unlock needs to be a slide gesture. We replace the unlock screen with a small crowdsourced task that takes roughly the same amount of time to complete. In doing so, the user contributes to crowdsourcing goals they want to support without taking extra time out of their day.

Twitch crowdsourcing interactions are very brief, so it is important that users can complete the tasks extremely quickly. Likewise, crowdsourcing is not the user's primary task, so these tasks must be lightweight and not distracting. We frame the design of our twitch crowdsourcing applications around the following principles:

- Availability: summon the task with a single button press
- Quick completion: contribute within a couple of seconds
- Low cognitive load: do not distract users from their primary task
- Value: volunteer toward a worthwhile goal
- Personal impact: maximize the uniqueness of the user's contributions [2]
- Longevity: keep tasks interesting after many repetitions
- Feedback: situate the user's effort as directly contributing to the larger crowdsourcing goal
- Privacy: do not circumvent standard phone security

To maximize value and personal impact, we focus not on paid crowdsourcing (e.g., Amazon Mechanical Turk) but on activities to which the user might want to volunteer their time. Because twitch crowdsourcing happens while users are mobile, tasks that take advantage of the user's local, physical context are particularly attractive. In addition, by lowering the threshold to contribution, we hypothesize that even busy topical experts might be able to contribute. Thus, we also explore opportunities to capture expertise, much like Wikipedia.

TWITCH

Twitch is an Android application that appears when the user presses the phone's power/lock button (Figures 1 and 3). When the user completes the twitch crowdsourcing task, the phone unlocks normally. Each task involves a choice between two to six options through a single motion such as a tap or swipe.

To motivate continued participation, Twitch provides both instant and aggregated feedback to the user. An instant

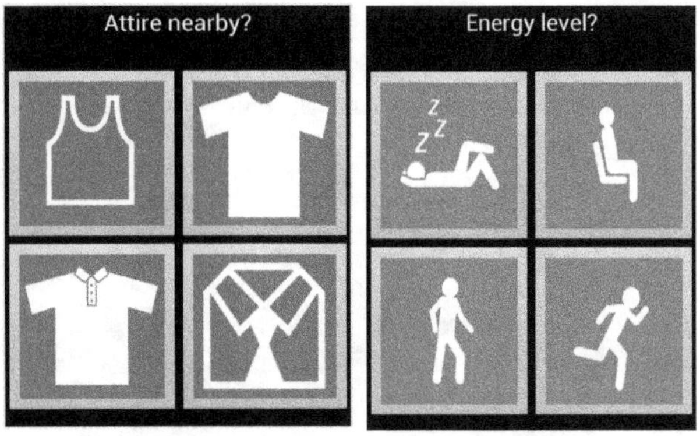

Figure 3: Census tasks, activity and energy level.

feedback display shows how many other users agreed via a fadeout as the lock screen disappears (Figure 4) or how the user's contributions apply to the whole (Figure 5). Aggregated data is also available via a web application, allowing the user to explore all data that the system has collected. For example, Figure 2 shows a human generated map from the Census application.

To address security concerns, users are allowed to either disable or keep their existing Android passcode while using Twitch. If users do not wish to answer a question, they may skip Twitch by selecting 'Exit' via the options menu. This design decision has been made to encourage the user to give Twitch an answer, which is usually faster than exiting. Future designs could make it easier to skip a task, for example through a swipe-up.

Below, we introduce the three main crowdsourcing applications that Twitch supports. The first, Census, attempts to capture local knowledge. The following two, Image Voting and Structuring the Web, draw on creative and topical expertise. These three applications are bundled into one Android package, and each can be accessed interchangeably through Twitch's settings menu.

Census

Despite progress in producing effective understanding of static elements of our physical world — routes, businesses and points of interest — we lack an understanding of human activity. How busy is the corner cafe at 2pm on Fridays? What time of day do businesspeople clear out of the downtown district and get replaced by socializers? Which neighborhoods keep high-energy activities going until 11pm, and which ones become sleepy by 6pm? Users could take advantage of this information to plan their commutes, their social lives and their work.

Existing crowdsourced techniques such as Foursquare are too sparse to answer these kinds of questions: the answers require at-the-moment, distributed human knowledge. We envision that twitch crowdsourcing can help create a human-centered equivalent of Google Street View, where a user could browse typical crowd activity in an area. To do so, we ask users to answer one of several questions about

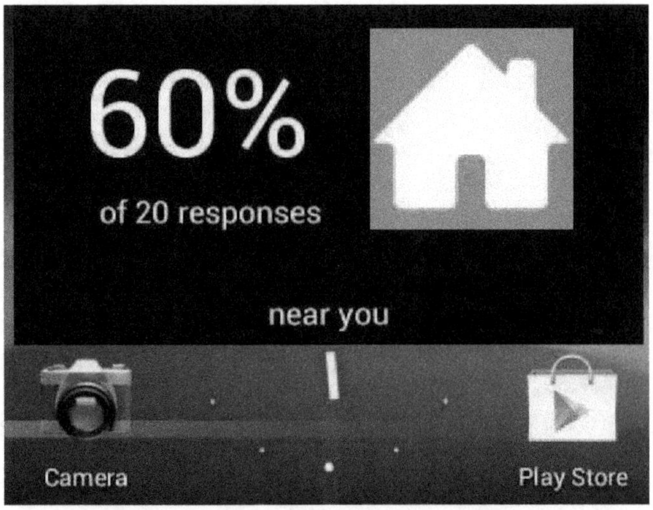

Figure 4: Instant feedback shows people agreeing with the user in her location.

the world around them each time they unlock their phone. Users can then browse the map they are helping create.

Census is the default crowdsourcing task in Twitch. It collects structured information about what people experience around them. Each Census unlock screen consists of four to six tiles (Figures 1 and 3), each task centered around questions such as:

- How many people are around you?
- What kinds of attire are nearby people wearing?
- What are you currently doing?
- How much energy do you have right now?

While not exhaustive, these questions cover several types of information that a local census might seek to provide. Two of the four questions ask users about the people around them, while the other two ask about users themselves; both of which they are uniquely equipped to answer. Each answer is represented graphically; for example, in case of activities, users have icons for working, at home, eating, travelling, socializing, or exercising.

To motivate continued engagement, Census provides two modes of feedback. *Instant feedback* (Figure 4) is a brief Android popup message that appears immediately after the user makes a selection. It reports the percentage of responses in the current time bin and location that agreed with the user, then fades out within two seconds. It is transparent to user input, so the user can begin interacting with the phone even while it is visible. *Aggregated report* allows Twitch users to see the cumulative effect of all users' behavior. The data is bucketed and visualized on a map (Figure 2) on the Twitch homepage. Users can filter the data based on activity type or time of day.

Photo Ranking

Beyond harnessing local observations via Census, we wanted to demonstrate that twitch crowdsourcing could support traditional crowdsourcing tasks such as image

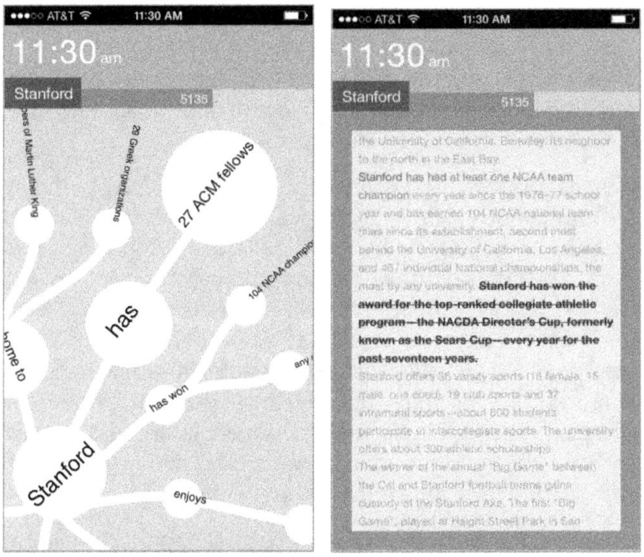

Figure 5: Verifying a web extraction animates a new branch onto the knowledge graph (left). Rejecting the extraction shows how far the user is in the article (right).

ranking (e.g., Matchin [17]). Needfinding interviews and prototyping sessions with ten product design students at Stanford University indicated that product designers not only need photographs for their design mockups, but they also enjoy looking at the photographs. Twitch harnesses this interest to help rank photos and encourage contribution of new photos.

Photo Ranking crowdsources a ranking of stock photos for themes from a Creative Commons-licensed image library. The Twitch task displays two images related to a theme (e.g., Nature Panorama) per unlock and asks the user to slide to select the one they prefer (Figure 1). Pairwise ranking is considered faster and more accurate than rating [17]. The application regularly updates with new photos.

Users can optionally contribute new photos to the database by taking a photo instead of rating one. Contributed photos must be relevant to the day's photo theme, such as Nature Panorama, Soccer, or Beautiful Trash. Contributing a photo takes longer than the average Twitch task, but provides an opportunity for motivated individuals to enter the competition and get their photos rated.

Like with Census, users receive instant feedback through a popup message to display how many other users agreed with their selection. We envision a web interface where all uploaded images can be browsed, downloaded and ranked. This data can also connect to computer vision research by providing high-quality images of object categories and scenes to create better classifiers.

Structuring the Web

Search engines no longer only return documents — they now aim to return direct answers [6,9]. However, despite massive undertakings such as the Google Knowledge Graph [36], Bing Satori [37] and Freebase [7], much of the knowledge on the web remains unstructured and unavailable for interactive applications. For example, searching for 'Weird Al Yankovic born' in a search engine such as Google returns a direct result '1959' drawn from the knowledge base; however, searching for the equally relevant 'Weird Al Yankovic first song', 'Weird Al Yankovic band members', or 'Weird Al Yankovic bestselling album' returns a long string of documents but no direct answer, even though the answers are readily available on the performer's Wikipedia page.

To enable direct answers, we need *structured* data that is computer-readable. While crowdsourced undertakings such as Freebase and dbPedia have captured much structured data, they tend to only acquire high-level information and do not have enough contributors to achieve significant depth on any single entity. Likewise, while information extraction systems such as ReVerb [14] automatically draw such information from the text of the Wikipedia page, their error rates are currently too high to trust. Crowdsourcing can help such systems identify errors to improve future accuracy [18]. Therefore, we apply twitch crowdsourcing to produce both structured data for interactive applications and training data for information extraction systems.

Contributors to online efforts are drawn to goals that allow them to exhibit their unique expertise [2]. Thus, we allow users to help create structured data for topics of interest. The user can specify any topic on Wikipedia that they are interested in or want to learn about, for example HCI, the Godfather films, or their local city. To do so within a one-to-two second time limit, we draw on mixed-initiative information extraction systems (e.g., [18]) and ask users to help vet automatic extractions.

When a user unlocks his or her phone, Structuring the Web displays a high-confidence extraction generated using ReVerb, and its source statement from the selected Wikipedia page (Figure 1). The user indicates with one swipe whether the extraction is correct with respect to the statement. ReVerb produces an extraction in Subject-Relationship-Object format: for example, if the source statement is "Stanford University was founded in 1885 by Leland Stanford as a memorial to their son", ReVerb returns {Stanford University}, {was founded in}, {1885} and Twitch displays this structure. To minimize cognitive load and time requirements, the application filters only include short source sentences and uses color coding to match extractions with the source text.

In Structuring the Web, the instant feedback upon accepting an extraction shows the user their progress growing a knowledge tree of verified facts (Figure 5). Rejecting an extraction instead scrolls the user down the article as far as their most recent extraction source, demonstrating the user's progress in processing the article. In the future, we envision that search engines can utilize this data to answer a wider range of factual queries.

FIELD DEPLOYMENT AND EVALUATION

This paper hypothesizes that short bursts of crowdsourcing can be embedded in users' everyday activities. We focus our evaluation on the two main components of this claim. First, *is it possible to crowdsource meaningful tasks in short bursts of time?* Can Twitch attract sufficient volunteer usage to achieve its goals via short interaction bursts? Second, *it is possible to embed these tasks in users' everyday activities?* Are the tasks sufficiently quick and easy that users can complete them without excessive burden?

To answer these questions, we pursued two evaluation strategies. First, we publically deployed Twitch and attracted 82 volunteer users over one month. We used this data to investigate naturalistic usage, collect crowdsourced data, and gather qualitative feedback. Second, we performed two field experiments on Twitch users to compare Twitch's time cost to a standard slide-to-unlock gesture, and a study of cognitive load using a working memory instrument called the 2- and 3-back test [23].

Android Deployment

To examine Twitch's ability to attract naturalistic crowdsourced data, we began with a public deployment. In doing so, we focused on unlock statistics, timing data, location demographics, and duration of usage.

Method

We released Twitch on Google Play, a public marketplace for Android applications. We then used social networks and email lists to spread word of the application to individuals who would be willing to try the research prototype. This process resulted in 82 volunteer users installing the application and completing at least one Twitch task. While Twitch contained all of the applications, its focus and default setting was Census.

The application saved a timestamp each time a user pressed the power/unlock button and launched a Twitch unlock, and another timestamp each time the user completed a Twitch task. To address privacy concerns, we tied all data to a randomly generated phone identifier. Finally, to complement our quantitative metrics, we emailed all users of Twitch roughly three weeks after they began using the application with an invitation to complete a brief survey about their experiences.

Results

During the study period, 82 participants completed 11,240 Twitch tasks to unlock their phones. The task completion rate was 37.4%; other times, users pressed the power button but did not complete the task, most likely just checking the time or notifications without unlocking the phone.

Active Twitch users kept using the application for a significant length of time. As expected for free smartphone applications on a public marketplace, many window shoppers dropped off early: about half (46.4%) of those who downloaded Twitch within the study period uninstalled it within a day. However, among the remaining users who kept the application for at least one day, the average duration of use was 31.9 days (median 30.9 days), One month of usage indicates a significant time and effort investment from these volunteers.

Census, the default Twitch application, received by far the most attention, with 9,717 responses from around the world (Figure 2), including the United States, Europe, India and Asia. The cities with the greatest number of responses were Cambridge, MA; Stanford, CA; and Pittsburgh, PA. Large numbers of responses also came from India and Japan. The resulting data is quite densely populated (Figure 2). The data indicates insights such as when cafes shift from work activities to social life, how many people are in a building early in the morning and late at night, and where people who work in downtown tend to go to exercise.

Roughly one fifth of users switched to try the Structuring the Web application, resulting in 334 responses. Across a range of topics such as "Google", "Android", "Earth", and "United States", Twitch users evaluated 181 unique statements from Wikipedia run through ReVerb. Users marked 41.4% of total extractions as correct.

At the end of the field study, we sent an online survey to 57 users who optionally provided their emails when installing the application. Sixteen participants filled out the survey in three days, with thirteen participants from the United States and three participants from Panama, Canada, and India. Participants generally enjoyed using Census (median Likert score 5 of 7), and found it only slightly distracting (median = 3.5). Participants who self-selected to switch to Image Ranking enjoyed it as well (median = 6).

Twitch discourages skipping tasks — it involves a two-tap exit via a context menu — making it possible that some users would deliberately answer incorrectly just to quickly unlock their phone. However, most participants reported making their selections honestly and accurately (median = 6). Roughly half of participants (56%) never felt the need for a skip button or gesture.

In order to motivate our users to continue using Twitch, and to encourage longevity, we have complemented all the applications with immediate feedback that tells users the percentage of others agreeing. Users moderately enjoyed the popup feedback (median = 5.5). In addition, we provided a web interface where users are able to view their data on a crowdsourced activity map; participants reported that the site had some effect on motivating them to contribute further (median = 5).

Open ended responses reinforced that the application was *"very lightweight [...] I'm sure I answered over 100 questions effortlessly."* One area of improvement: when users were not moving, Census tasks in particular became repetitive and thus annoying. Some participants wished the immediate feedback to be richer or less precisely tuned to their location so that it reports more data. A few

Field deployment Twitch unlock times (N=11,014)

Activity	Median	Mean
Slide-to-unlock	1421 ms	1956 ms
Census: people	1583 ms	2077 ms
Census: activity	1910 ms	2077 ms
Census: energy	1688 ms	2177 ms
Census: dress	1499 ms	2033 ms
Photo ranking	1579 ms	2438 ms
Structuring the web	2900 ms	3510 ms

Table 1. Answer times for Twitch usage in the wild.

participants were conscious of their location identification. Those users who used Image Ranking enjoyed the experience, but as the application switching was not particularly discoverable (a design decision to make the public application simpler), many weren't aware of its existence. One of the users shared her experience: "*The beautiful pictures brought happiness to the moment*".

Most participants felt that concerns about privacy were addressed (median = 5); however, some users uninstalled the application due to privacy concerns with location tracking. Redundant tasks and privacy concerns were the core reasons reported for uninstalling the application.

Participants' biggest requests for improving Twitch involved adding variety to the tasks or making tasks appear less frequently. Others wanted more intelligent automatic task selection: we believe this may be possible using the onboard phone sensors.

Field Experiments: Speed and Cognitive Load

For twitch crowdsourcing to succeed, tasks must be quick and low in cognitive load. If a task is too slow, users will opt out or give quick, unthoughtful responses. Likewise, if a task requires too much mental effort, users will have to disengage from whatever they are doing just to unlock their phones, which is undesirable. In a pair of field experiments tied to our deployment, we investigate the impact that Twitch has on the speed of unlocking users' phones and on cognitive load.

Method: Speed Experiment

To compare unlock times to a standard unlock interface; we included a simple slide-to-unlock screen in Twitch when the application was publicly deployed. Slide-to-unlock is similar to the default Android screen lock (called Slider). Thus, slide-to-unlock acts as a speed baseline to compare with rest of the Twitch applications. Once a week, Twitch displayed the slide-to-unlock screen instead of the selected Twitch task, along with a message stating that this temporary unlock interface was part of our field experiment. We compare user speed on the slide-to-unlock test against the rest of Twitch applications, examining whether Twitch tasks are noticeably slower or faster than a standard Android unlock. Speed is calculated in milliseconds from the moment Twitch is visible until the user completes the task.

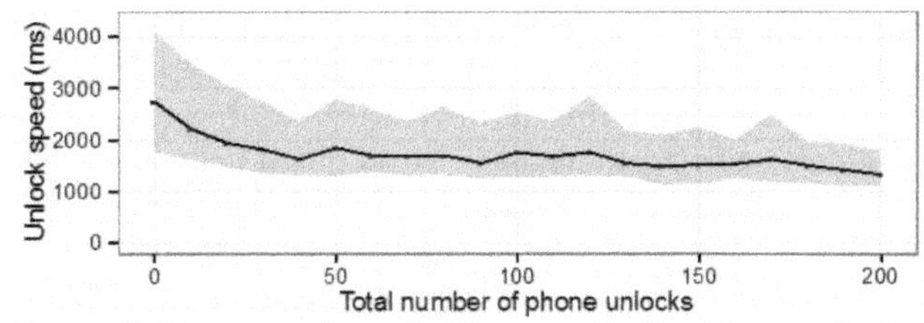

Figure 6. Response times decline over the first forty unlocks. The line indicates the median; band is the interquartile range.

Results

In naturalistic usage via a dataset of 11,014 unlocks (Table 1), slide-to-unlock took users a median of 1.39 seconds to unlock their phone (average 1.89). Median Census unlocks took between 1.49–1.89 seconds (average 2.01–2.49 seconds). Photo Ranking took 1.58 seconds (average 2.44). The median Structuring the Web unlock took 2.09 seconds (average 2.98 seconds), as it requires more reading.

We next tested whether the Twitch unlocks were in fact slower than a standard slide-to-unlock interface. As is common with reaction time data, Twitch duration data are not normally distributed; even after transformation, the data were heteroskedastic and thus not amenable to parametric statistics. Thus, we use the Friedman test on medians, a nonparametric equivalent of the ANOVA with blocked designs. We compared median unlock times between Twitch tasks for users who completed at least 100 unlocks and tried all Census activities, excluding Structuring the Web and Photo Ranking because fewer users had tried it (N=22 users). The Friedman test revealed a significant effect of Twitch activity on unlock time ($\chi^2(4)=24.4$, $p<.001$). Post-hoc paired Wilcoxon signed rank tests using Bonferroni correction between conditions revealed that the "current activity" Census task was significantly slower than all other Census tasks and slide-to-unlock (all $p<.05$), but there were no other significant differences between conditions.

Thus, while Twitch tasks may be slightly slower than a standard slide-to-unlock gesture (100–300ms), the difference is so slight in comparison to the variance that the two are not currently statistically distinguishable. There is clearly variability across Twitch tasks: Census's current activity task is 300–400ms slower than the others, possibly because it is the only categorical (non-scalar) response amongst the Twitch tasks, which impacts visual search.

Users quickly acclimated to Twitch, with median response time dropping from 2.7 seconds in the first ten unlocks to 1.6 seconds by the fortieth unlock (Figure 6). Given that users are unlocking their phones many times each day, they approach optimal performance quickly.

Method: Cognitive Load Experiment

To understand whether twitch might distract or annoy users, we turn to measures of cognitive load. In particular, we adopt a working memory task known as the 2-back and 3-back test [10,23]. The 2-back test displays a stream of

English letters, one at a time, and the participant must indicate for each letter whether it is the same as the letter that was displayed two letters ago. For example, if the previous letter stream were E, U, S, I, and the current letter were Y, the correct answer would be 'Different'; if the current letter were S, the answer would be 'Same'. Following previous work [10], we sample so that that the correct answer is 'Same' with probability 1/7. The 3-back test is identical to the 2-back test except the distance is three letters instead of two, making the task more difficult. To further load working memory, we likewise inject a Twitch Census activity or a Photo Ranking activity with probability 1/7 between letters. Twitch activities add to cognitive load but do not impact the correct answer — they do not count as a letter.

We performed a within-subjects field experiment to test how much each Twitch activity would negatively impact performance on the memory task. For each round of the study, the participant performed a series of 2- or 3-back tasks with random Twitch activity injections until they had completed all of the Twitch activities. One study factor was Twitch activity: we randomized the order of Twitch unlock screens that got injected into the task stream, including a slide-to-unlock control, for each round of the study. The second factor was memory task: participants rotated through rounds of 2-back or 3-back tasks until all Twitch activities had been tested in each condition. We randomized whether 2-back or 3-back tasks appeared first for each participant. The study continued for six rounds, three in each memory task condition. The study typically took fifteen minutes.

We recruited participants from the set of active Twitch users, so they would already be familiar with the applications. In exchange, participants received a raffle ticket for an Android tablet. Drawing on prior work [24,31], we instructed participants to go on a walk outdoors following a predefined path at one of two major universities or (alternatively) following any safe route in their neighborhood. In forcing participants to walk, we made sure that users would need to look around to answer Census questions.

We measured reaction time and task accuracy on the memory task. In particular, we grouped each reaction time and accuracy measurement with the Twitch activity that occurred just before the task. Thus, we measured how much of an impact each unlock screen had on the next 2- or 3-back instance, compared to baselines of no unlock (3-back instance preceded by a 3-back instance) and slide-to-unlock.

Our hypothesis was that Twitch would incur a cost to working memory accuracy and reaction time compared to a slide-to-unlock or no unlock gesture. However, we hypothesized that this cost for most Twitch tasks would be similar to the cost of a simple slide-to-unlock.

3-back task performance (N=5405 tasks)

Previous Screen	Median	Mean	Accuracy
Back task	1194 ms	1802 ms	90%
Slide-to-unlock	1724 ms	2228 ms	87%
Photo ranking	1506 ms	2009 ms	86%
Census: people	1737 ms	2332 ms	87%
Census: activity	1679 ms	2000 ms	93%
Census: energy	1881 ms	2238 ms	93%
Census: dress	2229 ms	2445 ms	95%

Table 2. Median and mean delay times for answering 3-back tasks in the cognitive load study. 2-back results are similar.

Results

Fourteen Twitch users completed the study. The population was worldwide, centered in areas with the most Twitch users. Participants completed 5,405 back tasks.

As with many reaction time measurements, timing data was non-normal after dropping outliers. Unlike the previous study, it was possible to retain homogeneity of variance and approach normality by applying a transformation. Such transformations are common when analyzing reaction time data. We use a generalized power transformation called a Box-Cox transformation, which algorithmically searches for the power λ that best fits a normal distribution. For our data, λ=-.25, a reciprocal fourth root transformation of the data. We transform timing data for our statistical analysis, but report raw milliseconds to aid interpretability.

The median task took 1.2 seconds to answer for both the 2-back and 3-back conditions when no Twitch activities were interposed (mean 1.68 for 2-back and 1.80 for 3-back, Table 2). Slide-to-unlock caused the task to take a median 1.7 seconds (mean 2.2). All Twitch tasks except Census clothing had similar delays, 1.7–1.8 seconds (mean 2.0–2.3). We performed a two-way ANOVA controlling for participant, using transformed delay as dependent variable, and memory task and Twitch activity as independent variables. The ANOVA found a significant main effect of Twitch activity ($F(6, 5378)=25.8$, $p<.001$). Post-hoc Tukey comparisons found no significant differences in delay between any Twitch activities and the slide-to-unlock control (all $p>.55$). All activities, including the slide-to-unlock control, were significantly slower than the previous task being another back task (all $p<.001$).

We compared accuracy across conditions using a logistic regression, again controlling for participant. Memory task was significant ($\beta=-0.45$, $z=-4.3$, $p<.001$), indicating that 3-back tasks produced less accurate performance than 2-back tasks. However, none of the Twitch activities or the control slide-to-unlock activity had a significant impact on accuracy.

Thus, contrary to our hypothesis, Twitch activities had no measurable impact on accuracy or delay for the working memory task compared to a standard slide-to-unlock gesture. While unexpected, this is good news for Twitch:

Twitch activities may not meaningfully distract the user from their daily activities while using their phone.

DISCUSSION

Twitch crowdsourcing can extend beyond the three applications outlined in this paper: opportunities include citizen science, accessibility, education, and scientific discovery. Users might participate in micro-tutoring sessions by marking an English-language sentence as correct or incorrect to help language learners from the developing world and K-12 education. They might answer short survey questions (e.g., txtEagle and Jana [12]), help power accessible interfaces for other users, collate local news, or direct lost people in their neighborhood. Of course, while we have focused on volunteer crowdsourcing, it may be possible to add a microtask marketplace to Twitch so that users can make money as they go about their day.

Longevity and retention are challenges for every crowdsourcing campaign. In our deployment, the median Twitch user was active for one month. (One month out of a forty-day field deployment period is longer than we expected for users of research software.) Moving forward, we believe that the key to long-term usage is finding design opportunities that match users' intrinsic motivation. Similar to gamification, twitch crowdsourcing cannot make an uninteresting application more attractive, but it can empower an already viable design. Our results indicated that users would be more likely to continue using the application if they see their progress and value toward the larger goal. In response, we have been developing far richer feedback for the Structuring the Web application (Figure 5).

In our vision of twitch crowdsourcing, tasks are fast and impose little cognitive load. However, many worthwhile crowdsourcing goals may not easily fit this definition. Structuring the Web is nearing this limit, taking roughly three seconds per unlock. We believe that it may be possible to break longer task into smaller ones that can be completed serially across multiple screens. This might enable a user to execute a long task through multiple unlocks, with each fragment taking less than 2 seconds.

Reciprocally, some users have slightly longer stretches of time to contribute, for example while waiting for a meeting to start. Twitch crowdsourcing could apply in these situations as well, for example by allowing users to launch a standalone application or ask the unlock screen to keep cycling through new tasks without disappearing. To maintain users' desired level of security, Twitch allows users to add its unlock screen after an Android native unlock. The effect is extremely similar to the passcode unlock on the Apple iPhone: users must both swipe to unlock and enter a passcode. Moving forward, we believe that it would be possible to create Twitch tasks that could function as security locks as well. One possible approach would be to integrate a user-determined security swipe pattern into the motion needed to complete a Twitch task. For example, users could tap to indicate their answer, and then swipe a gesture password from that starting position to verify their identity.

Our deployment underscored that a stream of fresh tasks is required to keep Twitch interesting. This is possible with applications like Structuring the Web, but Census suffered from boredom in repeat usage. The system could be extended to assign microtasks more intelligently. For example, location-based tasks should be distributed among nearby users and topic-based text extractions and other tasks should be distributed among experts and enthusiasts in each field. Private groups could split up and share their own tasks among friends and coworkers. Likewise, the system could learn to regularly swap stale tasks for fresh ones.

CONCLUSION

This paper presents *twitch crowdsourcing*, an approach to crowdsourcing based on quick microtasks that encourage short bursts of contribution. Our Twitch application augments the lock screen on mobile phones to harness users' spare moments for short tasks. Unlocking a mobile device via a Twitch microtask takes tenths of a second longer than a standard unlock — so little that the two were not statistically distinguishable in our field experiment. Our study, designed to determine the mental workload imposed by Twitch, revealed that our twitch crowdsourcing tasks likewise do not impose a more significant cognitive load than a simple swipe-to-unlock motion. In a public deployment, Twitch collected over eleven thousand data points to help build a census of local activity, rank stock photos, and structure the web.

Reducing concerns about effort, time, and motivation are key steps to greater volunteerism in crowdsourcing. We suggest that small contributions made in short bursts during spare seconds can be aggregated to accomplish significant, customized tasks without placing an undue burden on volunteers. We envision that this approach could bring experts into the crowdsourcing fold, overcoming their historical tendency to stay out because of large time commitments. If we succeed in involving a broader set of participants and topic experts, they could unlock many new opportunities for research and practice in crowdsourcing.

ACKNOWLEDGEMENTS

The authors thank the Stanford HCI Group and MIT UID Group for testing in-progress prototypes. This work was supported by Google Research and HTC.

REFERENCES

1. Anttila, A., Experience, U., Corporation, N., Jung, Y., Specialist, D., and Tower, A. Discovering Design Drivers for Mobile Media Solutions. *Proc. CHI EA '06*, (2006).
2. Beenen, G., Ling, K., Wang, X., et al. Using social psychology to motivate contributions to online communities. *Proc. CSCW '04*, (2004).

3. Benkler, Y. *The Wealth of Networks: How Social Production Transforms Markets and Freedom.* Yale University Press, 2007.
4. Bentley, F., Tullio, J., Metcalf, C., Harry, D., and Massey, N. A time to glance: Studying the use of mobile ambient information. *Proc. Pervasive '07 Workshop: Ambient Information Systems*, (2007).
5. Bernstein, M.S., Brandt, J., Miller, R.C., and Karger, D.R. Crowds in two seconds: enabling realtime crowd-powered interfaces. *Proc. UIST'11*, (2011).
6. Bernstein, M.S., Teevan, J., Dumais, S., et al. Direct Answers for Search Queries in the Long Tail. *Proc. CHI'12*, (2012).
7. Bollacker, K., Evans, C., Paritosh, P., Sturge, T., and Taylor, J. Freebase : A Collaboratively Created Graph Database For Structuring Human Knowledge. *Proc. SIGMOD '08*, (2008).
8. Campbell, A.T., Eisenman, S.B., Lane, N.D., Miluzzo, E., and Peterson, R.A. People-centric urban sensing. *Proc. WICON '06*, (2006).
9. Chilton, L.B. and Teevan, J. Addressing People's Information Needs Directly in a Web Search Result Page. *Proc. WWW 2011*, (2011).
10. Cohen, J., Forman, S., Braver, T., Casey, B.., Servan-Schreiber, D., and Noll, D.C. Activation of the Prefrontal Cortex in a Nonspatial Working Memory Task With Functional MRI. *Human Brain Mapping I*, (1994), 293–304.
11. Das, T. PRISM : Platform for Remote Sensing using Smartphones. *Proc. MobiSys '10*, (2010).
12. Eagle, N. txteagle : Mobile Crowdsourcing. *Proc. IDGD '09*, (2009).
13. Edge, D., Whitney, M., and Charlotte, C. MemReflex : Adaptive Flashcards for Mobile Microlearning. *Proc. MobileHCI '12*, (2012).
14. Fader, A., Soderland, S., and Etzioni, O. Identifying relations for open information extraction. *Proc. EMNLP '11*, (2011).
15. Froehlich, J., Dillahunt, T., Klasnja, P., et al. UbiGreen : Investigating a Mobile Tool for Tracking and Supporting Green Transportation Habits. *Proc. CHI'09*, (2009).
16. Gupta, A., Thies, W., Cutrell, E., and Balakrishnan, R. mClerk: Enabling Mobile Crowdsourcing in Developing Regions. *Proc. CHI'12*, (2012).
17. Hacker, S. and Ahn, L. Von. Matchin: Eliciting User Preferences with an Online Game. *Proc. CHI'09*, (2009).
18. Hoffmann, R., Amershi, S., Patel, K., Wu, F., Fogarty, J., and Weld, D.S. Amplifying community content creation with mixed initiative information extraction. *Proc. CHI '09*, (2009).
19. Lasecki, W., Miller, C., and Bigham, J.P. Warping time for more effective real-time crowdsourcing. *Proc. CHI'13*, (2013).
20. Luon, Y., Aperjis, C., and Huberman, B.A. Rankr: A Mobile System for Crowdsourcing Opinions. *Springer Berlin Heidelberg*, (2012).
21. Luther, K. and Bruckman, A. Leadership in online creative collaboration. *Proc. CSCW '08*, (2008).
22. Narula, P., Gutheim, P., Rolnitzky, D., Kulkarni, A., and Hartmann, B. MobileWorks: A Mobile Crowdsourcing Platform for Workers at the Bottom of the Pyramid. *Proc. HCOMP '11.*
23. Ophir, E., Nass, C., and Wagner, A.D. Cognitive control in media multitaskers. *PNAS 106*, 37 (2009).
24. Oulasvirta, A., Tamminen, S., Roto, V., and Kuorelahti, J. Interaction in 4-Second Bursts : The Fragmented Nature of Attentional Resources in Mobile HCI. *Proc. CHI '05*, (2005).
25. Poteete, A.R., Janssen, M., and Ostrom, E. *Working together: collective action, the commons, and multiple methods in practice.* Princeton University Press, 2010.
26. Ra, M., Liu, B., Porta, T. La, and Govindan, R. Medusa : A Programming Framework for Crowd-Sensing Applications Categories and Subject Descriptors. *Proc. MobSys'12*, (2012).
27. Ross, L. and Nisbett, R.E. *The person and the situation: Perspectives of social psychology.* Mcgraw-Hill, 1991.
28. Su, H., Deng, J., and Fei-fei, L. Crowdsourcing Annotations for Visual Object Detection. *Proc. HCOMP'12*, (2012).
29. Taraborelli, D., Mietchen, D., Alevizou, P., and Gill, A. Expert participation on Wikipedia: barriers and opportunities. *Wikimania 2011*, (2011).
30. Yan, T., Marzilli, M., Holmes, R., Ganesan, D., and Corner, M. mCrowd - A Platform for Mobile Crowdsourcing. *Proc. SenSys '09*, (2009).
31. Yu, C.-H. Mobile continuous reading. *Ext. Abs. CHI '12*, (2012).
32. Kitten War. http://www.kittenwar.com/.
33. iStockPhoto. http//www.istockphoto.com.
34. Freebase. http://www.freebase.com/.
35. dbPedia. http://dbpedia.org/.
36. Google Knowledge Graph. http://goo.gl/6cCKVP.
37. Microsoft Bing Satori. http://binged.it/10nFdH0.

Crowdsourcing the Future: Predictions Made with a Social Network

Clifton Forlines[1] Sarah Miller[1]
[1]Draper Laboratory
Cambridge, MA
cforlines@gmail.com, smiller@draper.com

Leslie Guelcher[2] Robert Bruzzi[2]
[2]Mercyhurst University
Erie, PA
{lguelc84, rbruzzi}@mercyhurst.edu

ABSTRACT

Researchers have long known that aggregate estimations built from the collected opinions of a large group of people often outperform the estimations of individual experts. This phenomenon is generally described as the "Wisdom of Crowds." This approach has shown promise with respect to the task of accurately forecasting future events. Previous research has demonstrated the value of utilizing meta-forecasts (forecasts about what others in the group will predict) when aggregating group predictions. In this paper, we describe an extension to meta-forecasting and demonstrate the value of modeling the familiarity among a population's members (its social network) and applying this model to forecast aggregation. A pair of studies demonstrates the value of taking this model into account, and the described technique produces aggregate forecasts for future events that are significantly better than the standard Wisdom of Crowds approach as well as previous meta-forecasting techniques.

Author Keywords

Social Network; aggregation; forecasting; crowd-sourcing; meta-forecast; Bayesian Truth Serum.

ACM Classification Keywords

H.5.3 [Group and Organization Interfaces]: Computer-supported cooperative work, Theory and models.

INTRODUCTION

Through forecasting future events, we are able to make better decisions about actions we can take in the present. As individuals, we routinely make forecasts about the future and use them to guide our actions; activities such as deciding to bring an umbrella to work or to take the stairs rather than the elevator are all made with our future-selves in mind. The happiness and well-being of our future-selves is largely a result of our ability to forecast our future environment accurately in the present.

CHI 2014, April 26 - May 01 2014, Toronto, ON, Canada

ACM978-1-4503-2473-1/14/04$15.00.
http://dx.doi.org/10.1145/2556288.2556967

Outside of our personal lives, decision makers in many fields rely on the predictions made by individual experts. Researchers have long understood that aggregate estimations built from the individual opinions of a large group of people often outperform the estimations of individual experts [8,23]. The research field of Collective Intelligence contains a growing volume of work centered on this premise. The use of the Unweighted Linear Opinion Pool (ULinOP, a fancy term for group mean) has proven to be a robust method of aggregating judgments that often outperforms more complex techniques [9]. For example, in the domain of weather forecasting, "ensemble averaging" (another domain-specific term for arithmetic mean) is currently the gold standard and is rarely if ever beaten by alternative aggregation schemes [5]. However, recent research has shown that combining forecasts through averaging can sometimes lead to poor prediction performance in the field of political judgment [24], often because the performance of the individuals themselves is low. Because knowledge and forecasting ability resides in a small subset of the population, group forecasts are often incorrect when majority voting is applied [14,21].

Indeed, group forecasting is significantly more complicated than individual forecasting as characteristics of the group come into play. Groups benefit from the diversity of the knowledge of their members; but groups are hindered by inefficient communication among group members, social cognitive biases such as groupthink, and difficulties in combining the individual forecasts into accurate group forecasts. This paper focuses on the last of these problems – the accurate aggregation of individual predictions into group forecasts. Specifically, we focus on a new method that better identifies which members of the group are in a position to provide high-quality forecasts so that their contribution can be given more weight when creating an aggregate prediction.

In this paper, we present this new method for weighting and combining forecasts and present the results of an experiment in which an objective measure of prediction performance quantifies the benefits of this approach. This new approach extends previous aggregation techniques by recognizing that the familiarity among the members of the group is highly heterogeneous and by incorporating a model of the group's social network into the aggregation process.

MOTIVATION

The Intelligence Community (IC) is tasked with collecting information from a wide variety of sources and combining this information to produce accurate forecasts about world events (for example questions, see Table 1). Clearly, the impact of forecasts made in the IC can have large consequences; as such, even small improvements to the accuracy of forecasts made by groups can have large real-world impacts. More often than not, these forecasts are not made by an individual, but rather are the output of a team.

The authors of this paper participated in the Aggregative Contingent Estimation (ACE) Program sponsored by IARPA. The goal of the ACE program was "to dramatically enhance the accuracy, precision, and timeliness of forecasts for a broad range of event types, through the development of advanced techniques that elicit, weight, and combine the judgments of many intelligence analysts" [**Error! Reference source not found.**]. Beyond forecasting world events, the techniques presented in this paper have applications in the areas of medicine, educational testing, politics, and economics.

PRIOR WORK ON AGGREGATE JUDGMENTS

Research into methods for combining individual judgments into accurate group judgments has been the subject of a great deal of research over the past 100 years. As such, a detailed account of this literature is beyond this paper.[1] The field is still an active research area, and the introduction of ubiquitous networking has opened the door to the exploration of systems that query and combine judgments from a large numbers of diverse individuals in real-time. This section attempts to outline some of the efforts that most closely relate to the work presented in this paper.

Weighted and Unweighted Opinion Pools

The term Wisdom of Crowds refers to the general process of "taking into account the collective opinion of a group of individuals rather than a single expert [when] answer[ing] a question" [23]. It is most often used to describe the phenomenon that the mean answer of a group is often more accurate than any one individual's answer.[2] As discussed in the introduction, simple averaging or majority voting is a surprisingly robust method for aggregating individual judgments into accurate group judgments. Researchers have found that alternatives to simple averaging work well in specific domains [4,11,27], but the ULinOP, or arithmetic mean, works well in a large number of cases [9]. Indeed, many crowd-sourcing techniques assume that the average answer is correct, and focus instead on either gathering that average quickly or even estimating the group average from a subsample of the population [7].

With respect to combining forecasts of future events, there is ample evidence that forecast accuracy can be significantly improved through combining multiple individual forecasts, and that simple techniques (such as the ULinOP) often outperform more complex methods [3]. This said, theoretical arguments have been made that no linear combination of forecasts provides an optimal combination [20], suggesting that further work is required in the field.

Prediction Markets and Collaboration

A popular alternative to linear averaging for aggregation is the use of a prediction market. Prediction markets (as their name implies) are markets that can be used to aggregate information from market participants about the likelihood of future events (e.g., [26]). Generally, these markets are highly accurate and compare favorably with the ULinOP.

Recent work has focused on leveraging the combined benefits of ULinOP and Prediction Markets [10].These hybrid approaches, which average the prediction of several methods (so called "poll of polls"), have shown promise, and have performed well in recent U.S. election forecasting.

Prediction Markets rely on a large number of participants and are inherently "zero sum" in their reward structure. As such, they do not foster collaboration among individual forecasters who are seen as competing, although there is inherent information sharing in the market due to buy/sell pricing. Recent work on the role of collaborative approaches to combining expert predictions have shown very good results [25]. In this work, small teams working collaboratively to come up with consensus forecasts were able to outperform linear averaging techniques for a large percentage of forecasting questions examined.

Another related area of collaboration that has received a good deal of attention in recent years is collaborative, or social, search [2,6,13]. Researchers have identified that searchers often query their social network for answers [6], and have demonstrated that there is value in leveraging people's beliefs about the knowledge of other individuals when reading responses to crowd-sourced answers [13].

Forecaster Knowledge and Quality Assurance

Much work has been completed on methods to improve aggregate forecasts through applying quality assurance methods to the answers given by individuals. Because of the popularity of on-line crowd-sourcing tools like Amazon Mechanical Turk, many groups used to provide aggregate answers include a number of individuals who provide unreliable answers in order to quickly receive their compensation. Research into automatically identifying these poor and malicious performers [18] and into filtering out low-quality answers through making multiple comparisons among judgments [21] can help improve aggregate answers in many cases.

One particular method of filtering out poor answers/ forecasters is through the use of a "gold question" [15,17].

[1] For a good overview of techniques see [3,10].

[2] Galton's original demonstration of this effect [8] used the group median rather than the mean.

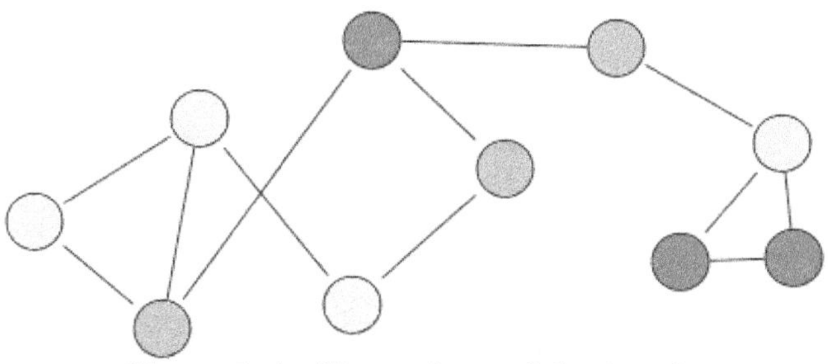

Figure 1. An illustrative social network.

A gold question has a known answer and is a question that the experimenter has determined has a high level of diagnostic value. Those forecasters who can answer the gold question correctly have a high probability of answering the question of interest correctly. While the value of such questions has been demonstrated, it is difficult to generate gold questions quickly and reliably for many topics of interest [16].

Prelec [19] introduced the intriguing notion that a meta-prediction could act as a sort of common gold question with a high level of diagnostic value for factual and forecasting questions. A meta-prediction is an individual's expectations concerning other people's forecasts, and can be elicited at the same time as an individual's personal forecast.

Prelec's Bayesian Truth Serum (BTS) [19] is the fundamental aggregation method that we base our aggregation approach on. In a simple variation of the technique, each individual forecaster provides not only their own forecast about a question, but also their meta-forecast about the average answer from the group as a whole. Forecasters who can predict what others will say are generally better forecasters themselves. The BTS algorithm produces a BTS score, which is itself an indicator of expertise. Through using BTS scores to weight individual forecasts in the aggregation process, one can assign greater importance to the "experts" identified by BTS and thus outperform the traditional ULinOP Wisdom of Crowds technique. For reference, we have found improvements in aggregate forecasting performance in the range of 5-10% when using the BTS technique.

The research described in this paper stems from the observation that the current BTS approach to eliciting and using the meta-forecast from an individual assumes that the individual's knowledge of the group is uniform. Intuitively, one knows that this knowledge is *not* uniform, and in fact can be highly disparate. For example, an individual has varying degrees of knowledge about different subpopulations and even individuals in a larger group. Furthermore, this knowledge is often directional (for example, the authors of this paper know a lot more about the views and beliefs of the President of the United States than vice versa) and is dependent on topic areas (for example, the equipment manager of a sport team probably know a lot more about players' equipment preferences than their political leanings).

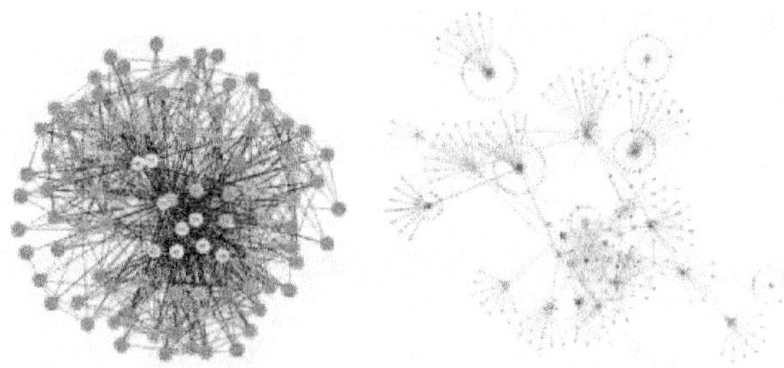

Figure 2. Two social network topologies that should greatly influence the value of meta-forecasts.

The motivation behind this investigation is to start to understand if an appreciation for this heterogeneity can be useful when generating aggregate forecasts. Toward this end, we investigate the usefulness of meta-forecasts made about familiar and unfamiliar group members, and describe an elicitation and aggregation technique that produces superior aggregate forecasts for a diverse set of forecasting questions.

ILLUSTRATIVE EXAMPLE

The baseline idea is to amend the BTS technique so that BTS scores are influenced by our understanding of the population's social network. The BTS approach to aggregation works by suppressing the answers from certain (highly predictable) people when it comes to averaging the groups' overall answer. Each individual is asked to model the distribution of answers given by the group, and as discussed previously, one's knowledge of the group is decidedly nonuniform.

One's view of the group as a whole is greatly influenced by the social network of that group, such as the one depicted in Figure 1. In this example, Alice (shown in red) is more closely familiar with the opinions and knowledge of her immediate neighbors (green) in this network than with those people further away from her (yellow, and then purple). In this example, Alice's opinion of the group is greener than the group actually is; thus, her meta-forecasts should be influenced more by the green members than those farther removed from Alice in the graph.

One can hypothesize that groups with a highly connected social network will result in inferior traditional BTS aggregations because each individual "knows" quite a lot about the knowledge of the group as a whole, which is what they're being asked to estimate. With this knowledge of the opinions of others shared among the group, the BTS technique would do little to identify the experts in the population.

Consider the two network topologies shown in Figure 2. The network on the left represents a highly connected network, such as you might find residing in a

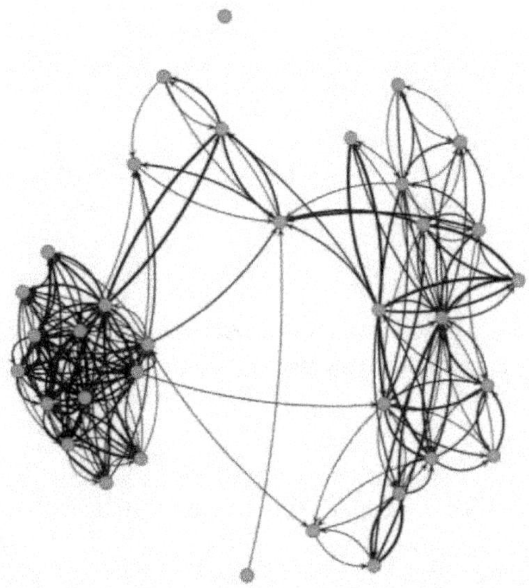

Figure 3. The social network of the pilot study investigation.

single location and working closely with one another. The network on the right would represent an organization with several remote locations that each includes a highly connected team connected to the overall organization by a small number of individuals. As we hypothesize that the value of the meta-forecast depends greatly on the familiarity among group members, understanding the social ties among the group may prove to be an important task when creating aggregate forecasts.

MEASURING FORECAST PERFORMANCE

In the two studies discussed in this paper, individual and group performance on forecast problems was measured using the Brier score [1]. The Brier score quantifies the accuracy of a probability forecast by computing the average squared deviation between predicted probabilities for a set of events and the (eventual) outcomes (detailed in Eq. 1).

$$BrierScore = \frac{1}{n}\sum_{t=1}^{n}\sum_{i=1}^{r}(f_{ti} - o_{ti})^2$$

where:

- f_{ti} is the forecast probability
- o_{ti} is the binary indicator of the event outcome
- r is the number of possible outcomes
- t is the number of forecast instances

Equation 1. Measuring forecast accuracy [1].

The range of Brier scores is [0,2] where 0 indicates a 100% accurate prediction and 2 an inaccurate prediction. Applying the Brier scoring rule requires knowledge of the actual resolution for the forecasting problem. Consequently, Brier scoring can only be performed after the forecasting problem has closed and truth is known.

PILOT INVESTIGATIONS

To begin investigating the usefulness of a knowledge network model for BTS-based forecasting, we designed a simple pilot experiment using students from [removed for blind review]. In this pilot study, 34 students answered 15 factual questions and 15 forecasting questions covering 4 topic areas: the Arab Spring, European Economics, North Korea, and Professional Sports.

In addition to providing a prediction (for forecasting questions) or a confidence (for factual questions), each student gave a BTS meta-prediction for the distribution of the groups' answers as well as predictions about the answers and confidences of other individual students. These other students included both students that they had previously indicated that they knew well as well as students that they did not know.

Modeling the Social Network of Student Forecasters

Before asking the factual and forecasting questions, we began by eliciting information from the 34 students that would help us build a simple knowledge network model. In this questionnaire, students were asked to rate their overall familiarity with each of the other students in the study on a 0-5 scale, with 0 indicating that they did not know the other student and 5 indicating that they knew the other student very well. With these connections in hand, we were able to build a social network model of this pilot study population. Figure 3 illustrates the model of the overall familiarity among students in the pilot study population.

Figure 3 clearly shows an important feature of our pilot population, namely that it is heterogeneous in terms of interconnectivity. After observing the two large cliques in

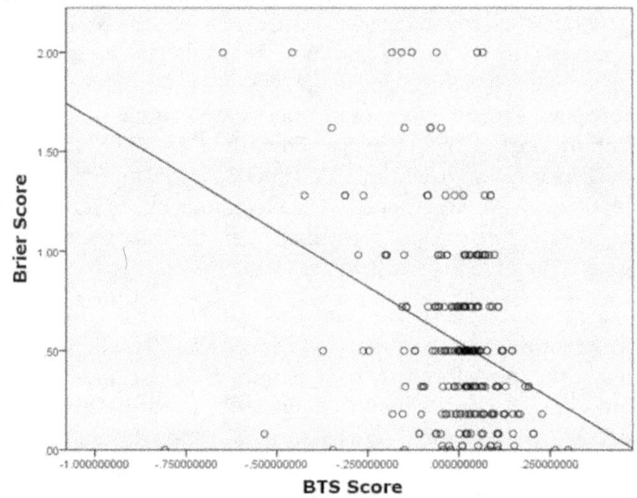

Pearson Correlation	-.326
Sig. (2-tailed)	<.001
N	309

Figure 4. BTS score is a good predictor of forecast performance. Lower Brier scores are better; higher BTS scores indicate expertise.

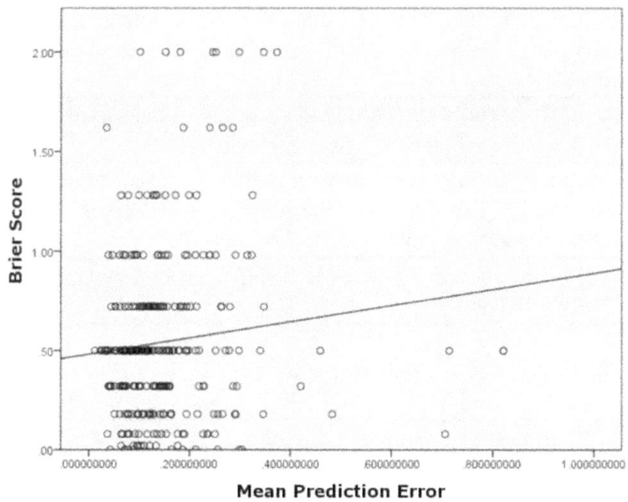

Pearson Correlation	.106
Sig. (2-tailed)	.062
N	309

Figure 5. Participants ability to predict other individuals' answers (X axis) and their own Brier score (Y axis).

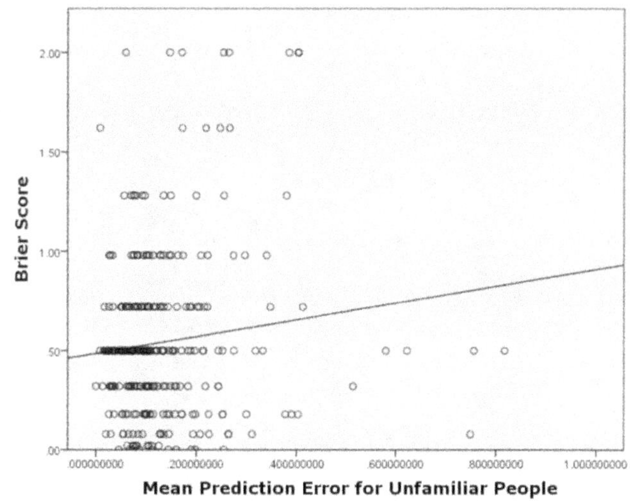

Pearson Correlation	.117
Sig. (2-tailed)	.040
N	309

Figure 6. Ability to correctly predict the answers of other unfamiliar individuals (X axes) vs. one's own Brier score (Y axes). Lower error when predicting others' forecasts is correlated with better Brier scores for one's own predictions. Not shown, the nonsignificant correlation between ability to predict answers of other familiar individuals and Brier score.

this population, we discussed this finding with our graduate research assistant, who informed us that these cliques represented first and second-year students, respectively. The students who bridged these two groups are either taking courses ahead or behind the typical schedule, or acting as teaching assistants and student leaders.

Pilot Study Analysis and Results

First, we looked at the performance of BTS meta-predictions about the whole group. BTS scores were calculated as described in [19]. As expected, an individual's BTS score (which is immediately available when a forecast is made) was a good predictor of their performance as measured by the Brier score (which can only be calculated after truth is known). Figure 4 shows the relationship between BTS score and Brier score for this population.

Overall, we were happy to see that the BTS aggregation technique performed well with a population that had such a heterogeneous familiarity with one another. In addition to the group meta-predictions used to generate Figure 4, we asked participants to give meta-predictions about other individual students. These students included students that they knew well as well as those whom they did not know.

Overall, an individual's ability to predict other individuals' answers did not significantly correlate with Brier score. Figure 5 shows the relationship between participants' ability to predict other individuals' answers (X axis) and their own Brier score (Y axis). In this chart, the X axis shows the mean absolute error between an individual's prediction of others' forecasts and those people's actual forecasts. Lower (leftmost) positions on the X axes equate to better prediction of others' answers. While better predictions of others' answers did correspond to better (lower) Brier scores, this relationship was not significant.

While a participant's overall ability to predict others' answers was not predictive of their own ability to accurately answer questions and give forecasts (Figure 5), a different picture emerged when we looked separately at predictions of familiar and unfamiliar individuals. In general, one's ability to predict other individuals' answers, *whom one does not know*, correlates significantly with Brier score, while one's ability to predict other individuals' answers *whom one does know* did not. Figure 6 shows the significant relationship between participants' ability to correctly predict other unfamiliar individuals and their own Brier score.

Figure 6 suggests that the ability to correctly predict the answers of other unfamiliar individuals (X axes) is related to one's own Brier score (Y axes). Being able to predict others' answers indicates that you have a relatively high level of accuracy, but only for individuals whom you do not know well. This somewhat surprising relationship between familiarity and ability to predict others' answers and the accuracy of one's own forecasts indicates that there is value in modeling the social network of a group of forecasters. While interesting, the cause of this relationship is unclear. Perhaps the ability to predict the forecasts of a familiar group member demonstrates familiarity with that individual

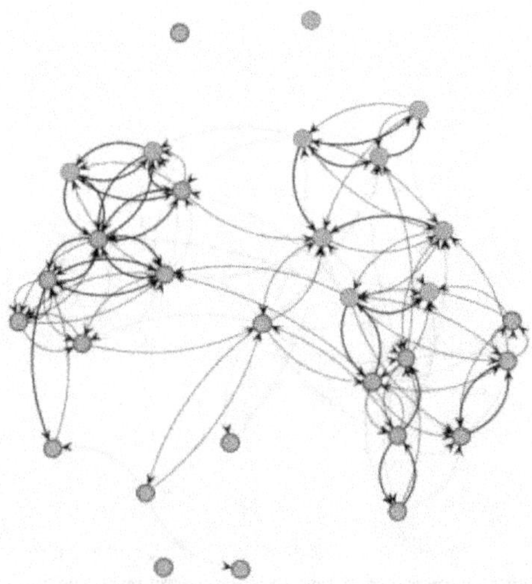

Figure 7. The social network of our study population. (Note that the weakest ties have not been drawn for clarity, which has the effect of isolating some nodes in this figure.)

and their opinions rather than knowledge about the forecast question itself. Perhaps other issues are at play. As this pilot experiment was not designed to answer this question definitively, one should be wary of putting too much confidence into the difference in correlation between familiar and unfamiliar individuals. What is clear is that additional research is needed to further explore this space.

MAIN EXPERIMENT

Given the evidence gathered in the pilot study indicating that there was value in looking at the social ties between individuals when considering their meta-predictions, we set out to design a follow-up study to investigate this relationship more closely. 30 students were recruited and asked to answer 10 forecasting questions, as well as provide meta-predictions and recommendations about fellow students.

To model our population, we began by asking each participant to rate their overall familiarity with every other student in the study on a 0-5 scale. This activity was repeated, with the variation that each student was asked to rate their familiarity with every other student's knowledge and opinions of four topic areas – Iran, North Korea, Europe, and Israel. The overall social network for this study population is shown in Figure 7. This study included 10 forecasting questions shown in Table 1. In addition to forecasting these 10 questions, participants gave BTS meta-predictions for the population as a whole, as well as predictions about other individuals in the study.

Additionally, knowing that peers are often good judges about their peers [2,6,13], we asked each student to pick the three students from the population that they felt would give the best answers to each of the 10 questions.

Will Israel officially announce that it recognizes the Armenian genocide before 1 April 2013? **(Mean Brier 0.24)**
Will the Republic of Macedonia be a NATO member before 1 April 2013? **(Mean Brier 0.19)**
Will any country officially announce its intention to withdraw from the Eurozone before 1 April 2013? **(Mean Brier 0.19)**
Will Iran sign an IAEA Structured Approach document before 1 April 2013? **(Mean Brier 0.16)**
Will Moody's issue a new downgrade of the long-term debt rating of the Government of Germany between 30 July 2012 and 31 March 2013? **(Mean Brier 0.36)**
Will Standard and Poor's downgrade the United Kingdom's foreign long-term credit rating at any point between 18 June 2012 and 1 April 2013? **(Mean Brier 0.49)**
Will the United Nations Security Council pass a new resolution directly concerning Iran between 17 December 2012 and 31 March 2013? **(Mean Brier 0.22)**
Will the sentence of any of the seven Italian experts convicted of manslaughter for failing to "adequately warn" about the L'Aquila earthquake be reduced, nullified, or suspended before 1 April 2013? **(Mean Brier 0.45)**
Before 1 April 2013, will substantial evidence emerge that Iran has enriched any uranium above 27% purity? **(Mean Brier 0.46)**
Will the United Kingdom's Liberal Democrats and Conservatives remain in a coalition through 1 April 2013? **(Mean Brier 0.23)**

Table 1. Forecasting questions from the main experiment and the mean Brier scores for study participants.

One-on-One Meta Predictions

Given the evidence from the pilot study, we designed a simple scoring mechanism that took advantage of all of the information gathered from the One-on-One predictions. This score would be used to weight individual forecasts when creating group aggregate forecasts. This score was calculated by looking at all possible pairs of forecasters in the group and transferring points among them in a zero-sum manner. Consider the following example, illustrated in Figure 8. The Red and Green participants make individual

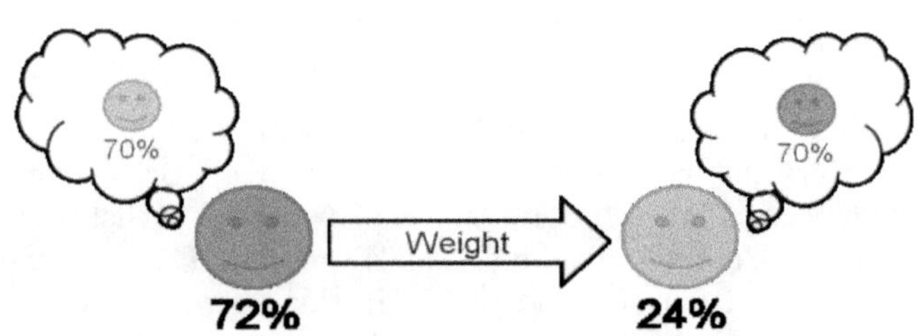

Figure 8. Weight transfer from One-on-One meta-predictions.

predictions about a question of 72% and 24%, respectively. They both predict that the other's answer was 70%. In this case, the Green participant did a much better job of predicting the Red participant than vice versa; as such, points are transferred from the Red participant to the Green participant. After all possible pairs of forecasters are examined in this manner, their individual forecasts are weighted by their final score. This has the combined effect of heavily weighting individuals who are good at predicting others while being difficult to predict themselves – both qualities of the BTS approach. Furthermore, this One-on-One method takes advantage of the nonuniform knowledge among participants as it samples all possible pairs rather than the group as a whole.

Equation 2 details the means by which the point-transfer is calculated. There are many such functions that should suffice, but this specific function was chosen as it is symmetric around zero (errors is either direction result in the same score transfer).

$$weightTransfer = \left| \ln \frac{metaPrediction}{actualPrediction} \right|$$

Equation 2. The transfer of points between pairs of participants is calculated using the ratio of meta-prediction to actual prediction.

Our study included two variations of the One-on-One approach in which the score transfer was scaled by the social ties between the pair. In one variation, familiarity increased the transfer of points, and in another variation, unfamiliarity did.

One limitation of the One-on-One approach is that to fully sample the pairs in a group, N*(N-1) meta-forecasts are needed. While any one individual only needs to make N-1 of these, this can still be burdensome for large groups. As such, we divided our population of 30 students into three groups of 10 (shown in Figure 9). These groups were built to include both strong and weak connections, and the use of multiple groups allowed for repeated measurements in our study, resulting in better statistical power.

Aggregation Methods and Design

Given our model of the social network and One-on-One aggregation design, we compared the following six aggregation techniques.

ULinOP. The mean forecast for the members of each group. This aggregate forecast is the traditional Wisdom of Crowds approach.

All-Stars. Because every participant picked the top students in the study to answer each question, we simply weighted each participant's answer by the inverse of their average rank when creating the aggregate forecast.

BTS Weighted. After calculating a BTS score using each participant's meta-prediction for the group as a whole, we weighted individual forecasts by the normalized BTS score to produce an aggregate forecast for the group.

One-on-One. This method used the One-on-One meta-predictions to calculate a weight for each forecaster using the method described in a previous section of this paper.

One-on-One Ties Make Stronger. In this variation, strong social ties (e.g., familiarity) increased the transfer of points between pairs of participants. This approach had the effect of giving participants who were good at meta-forecasting the answers of people they knew well more weight. As familiarity (F) was measured on a 0-5 scale, the point transfers were scaled by (F+1) in this variation.

One-on-One Ties Make Weaker. In this variation, strong social ties (e.g., familiarity) decreased the transfer of points between pairs of participants. This approach had the effect of giving participants who were good at meta-forecasting the answers of people they did not know well more weight. As familiarity (F) was measured on a 0-5 scale, the point transfers were scaled by 1/(F+1) in this variation.

Overall, our study design was:

10 binary forecasting questions x
3 groups x
6 aggregation methods =
180 measurements

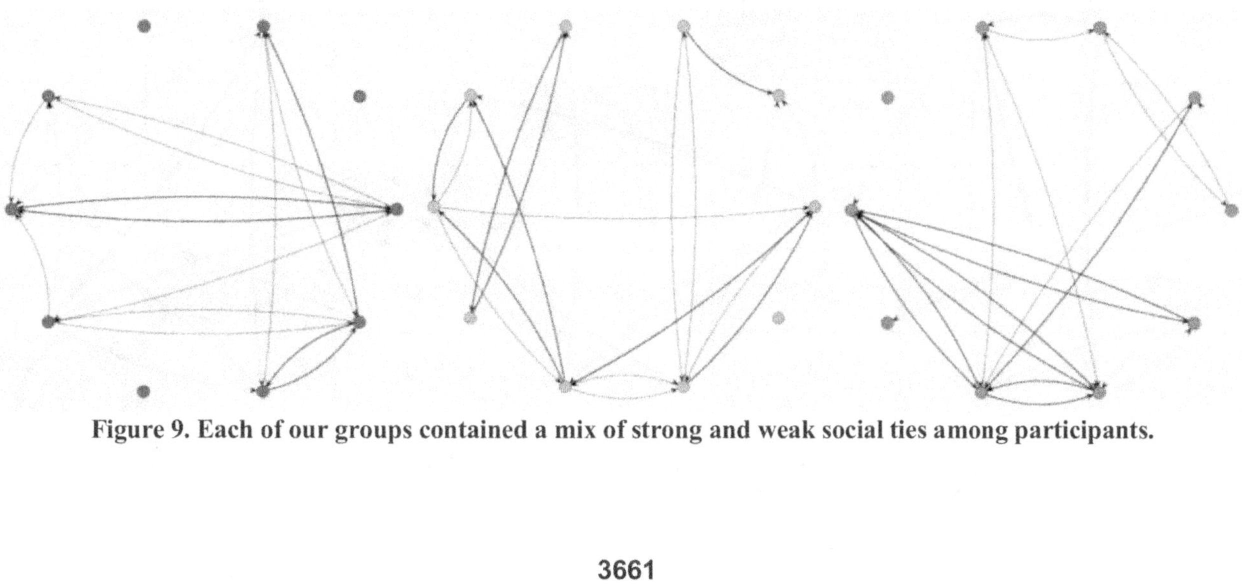

Figure 9. Each of our groups contained a mix of strong and weak social ties among participants.

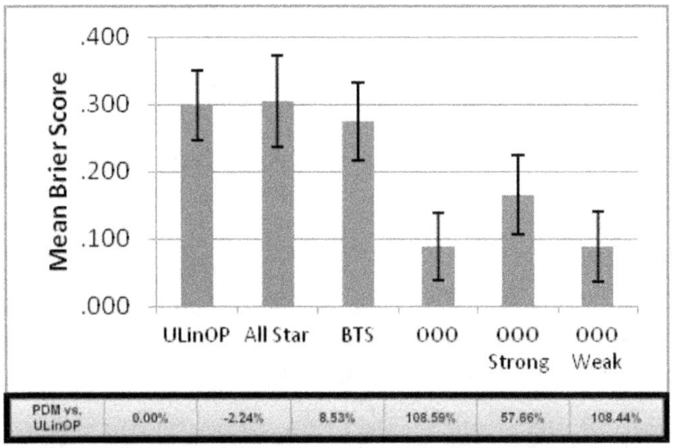

Figure 10. Mean Brier scores for each of the six aggregation methods. (Below) The PDM between each aggregation method and the ULinOP.

Results

Overall, we saw significant differences among the 6 aggregation methods for the 10 forecasting questions included in this study. A Repeated-Measures Analysis of Variance (ANOVA) using Brier Score as the dependent variable, Aggregation Method as a 6-level within-group contrast, and using Group ID as a 3-level between subjects factor showed a significant main effect for Aggregation Technique on Brier Score ($F_{5,130}$ = 4.871, $p<0.001$, $\eta^2=0.158$). The mean Brier score (mean of each group for each forecast question) for each of the six aggregation techniques is shown in Figure 10. The Percent Difference in Means (PDM) between each aggregation technique and the ULinOP was -2.24%, 8.53%, 108.59%, 57.66%, and 108.44% for the All-Star, BTS, One-on-One, One-on-One Ties Make Stronger, and One-on-One Ties Make Weaker techniques, respectively.

Table 2 shows pairs of techniques that were significantly different from one another according to a post-hoc, pair-wise analysis of the results. After adjusting these multiple pair-wise comparisons using Bonferroni, our results suggest significant differences between the three One-on-One techniques and the ULinOP, All Star, and BTS techniques.

DISCUSSION

Overall, these results suggest that the One-on-One approaches do a significantly better job at identifying individual forecasters who should be weighed more heavily when creating aggregate forecasts.

Interestingly, the All-Star method performed poorly, indicating that these participants were not good at picking fellow students who would provide good forecasts. While the BTS approach did not produce a significantly improved forecast over the ULinOP in this study, we expect that this is due to low statistical power as we are seeing an absolute difference of around 9% PDM, which is in line with other BTS results. All variations of the OOO weighting approach work well. As found in the pilot study, one's ability to predict people you know well is not as good an indicator of expertise as one's ability to predict people you don't know.

The studies described in this paper were part of a two-year effort into forecast aggregation. As part of this larger effort, we did investigate models that looked toward an individual's previous performance. While this type of "leaderboard" weighing did help, it was not as valuable as one would hope. In the current study, it's not the case that a single amazing individual contributed to the good scores of the OOO techniques. It was the case that for any single question, there was often an individual whose weight was noticeably higher than the other individuals, but this person changed from question to question. An individual who could accurately answer such a diverse collection of questions would be a rarity indeed; however, the OOO technique seems to help identify the specific individual who is best able to answer a specific question.

	ULinOP	All Star	BTS	One-on-One	One-on-One Strong	One-on-One Weak
ULinOP	-	p=1.0	p=1.0	**p<0.001**	**p<0.001**	**p<0.001**
All Star	p=1.0	-	p=1.0	**p<0.001**	**p<0.001**	**p<0.001**
BTS	p=1.0	p=1.0	-	**p<0.001**	**p<0.05**	**p<0.001**
One-on-One	**p<0.001**	**p<0.001**	**p<0.001**	-	**p<0.005**	p=1.0
One-on-One Strong	**p<0.001**	**p<0.001**	**p<0.05**	**p<0.005**	-	**p<0.01**
One-on-One Weak	**p<0.001**	**p<0.001**	**p<0.001**	p=1.0	**p<0.01**	-

Table 2. Post-hoc, pair-wise comparisons between aggregation techniques. Significantly different pairs are shown in bold. Adjusted for multiple comparisons using Bonferroni.

As with any experiment, there are considerations that the reader should make when interpreting the results and their applicability to real-world scenarios. The following paragraphs attempt to outline some of the threats to the external validity of this study and our results.

The major limitation of applying this technique to many real-world scenarios centers on the difficulty and expense of sampling the social ties among the members of a group. Our studies used a relatively stable and reasonably-sized population of students. Through questionnaires, we were able to model the social network of these populations once and apply this model to our analysis. In other areas, it may not be possible or practical to gather the necessary relationship data to apply the One-on-One technique. Many populations are too large to measure in their entirety (e.g., movie reviewers on Netflix) or are too unstable to build a static model of the network (e.g., product reviewers on Amazon.com). Other populations, such as relatively static organizational teams, are more amenable to modeling. While not explored in the current research, existing social networks (such as Facebook and LinkedIn) may be good environments to explore these techniques. The reader should consider their population of interest and the potential difficulties in building their social network model when thinking about the application of this paper's technique to their aggregation problem.

This work was primarily motivated by the needs of the Intelligence Community and aims to help improve their ability to make accurate group forecasts about future events. While we have discussed the application of these techniques to other important fields (medicine, education, economics, etc.), it is hard to argue that in any field, group forecasts would not improve by aggregating the individual forecasts of experts. While it is widely understood that experts themselves can often fail when making predictions [24], better input into an aggregation engine should produce better output. Our study participants consisted of students enrolled in intelligence programs. While these students are impressive and quite knowledgeable, as students they should not yet be considered experts in their field. As such, future work should include studying the aggregation of expert forecasters so that the results of the study better match the intended use cases.

In this set of experiments, we investigated a small number of binary forecasting questions concerning world events in four topic areas. While binary questions have the benefits of being relatively easy to score and are relatively easy to determine the outcome of, these considerations should not limit the types of forecasting questions that new aggregation techniques are subjected to. Many real-world forecasting questions have multiple possible outcomes, or are better phrased as point predictions rather than discrete outcomes (e.g., the future price of oil). Future work should include extending the One-on-One techniques to these other question types, and should include extending the forecast topic areas to other important domains, such as medicine, politics, education, and economics. Similarly, forecasting is only one of a number of worthwhile judgments to explore in this line of research. Medical diagnostics, pathology, and forensics are all types of judgments that might benefit from the techniques described in this paper, although they were not studied per se. Future work should include investigations into other types of collective judgments, the aggregation of which is made easy by our increasingly networked culture.

Looking ahead, many of the open questions in the field of forecast aggregation center on the accurate elicitation of individual forecasts and (in our case) the elicitation of the meta-forecast and a population's social network. The CHI community is in an excellent position to contribute to both of these challenges, and we are pursuing collaborative efforts to extend the art in these areas.

CONCLUSION

Overall, we were encouraged to see the value in One-on-One meta-predictions and the value of incorporating familiarity (e.g., social ties) into meta-prediction methods. Looking ahead, we are interested in further improving our ability to apply these techniques to larger groups (with significant N*(N-1) problems) and would like to investigate subsampling pairs from the population. Similarly, our approach used a simple score transfer function, and the space of such functions should be looked into. Finally, we recognized that this study used three small groups with a mixture of levels of connectivity. It would be good to investigate the value of social network influenced meta-predictions in populations with strong and weak social ties.

The results show that there are significant benefits to employing a One-on-One meta-prediction weighting scheme when aggregating individual forecasts into group forecasts. The base One-on-One technique produced a 108.59 PDM score when compared with ULinOP aggregation. It is our hope that the strong results presented in this initial study, mediated by the reservations discussed in this paper, motivate others to join us as we continue to investigate improvements to aggregate judgments.

ACKNOWLEDGMENTS

This work was supported by the Intelligence Advanced Research Projects Activity (IARPA) via the Department of Interior National Business Center contract number D11PC20058. The U.S. Government is authorized to reproduce and distribute reprints for Government purposes not withstanding any copyright annotation thereon. Disclaimer: The views and conclusions expressed herein are those of the authors and should not be interpreted as necessarily representing the official policies or endorsements, either expressed or implied, of IARPA, DoI/NBC, or the U.S. Government.

REFERENCES

1. Brier, G.W., "Verification of Forecasts Expressed in Terms of Probability," *Monthly Weather Review*, 78, 1950, pp. 1-3.
2. Chi, E.H., "Information Seeking Can Be Social," *IEEE Computer*, Vol. 42, No. 3, IEEE Press, pp. 42-46.
3. Clemen, R.R., "Combining Forecasts: A Review and Annotated Bibliography," *International Journal of Forecasting*, 5, 1989, pp. 559-583.
4. Dawid, A., DeGroot, M., Mortera, J., Cooke, R., French, S., Genest, C., Schervish, M., Lindley, D., McConway, K., and Winkler, R., "Coherent Combination of Experts' Opinions," *TEST*, Vol. 4, Issue 2, 1995, pp. 263-313.
5. Du, J., "Hybrid Ensemble Prediction System: a New Ensembling Approach," preprints, Symposium on the 50th Anniversary of Operational Numerical Weather Prediction, University of Maryland, College Park, Maryland, June 14-17, 2004 (5 pp.).
6. Ehrlich, K., Shami, N.S. "Searching for Expertise," *Proceedings of the ACM Conference on Human Factors in Computing Systems*, (CHI 2008), ACM Press, 2008.
7. Ertekin, S., Hirsh, H., and Rudin, C., "Learning to Predict the Wisdom of Crowds," Presented at Collective Intelligence Conference (arXiv: 1204.3611), 2012.
8. Galton, F., "Vox Populi," *Nature*, Vol. 75, 1907, pp. 450-451.
9. Genre, Kenny, Meyler, and Timmermann, "Combining Expert Forecasts: Can Anything Beat the Simple Average?" *International Journal of Forecasting*, Vol. 29, Issue 1, 2013, pp. 108–121.
10. Graefe, A., Armstrong, J.S., Jones, R., and Cuzan, A., "Combining Forecasts: An Application to Election Forecasts," APSA Annual Meeting, 2011.
11. Hegselmann, R. and Krause, U., "Opinion Dynamics Driven by Various Ways of Averaging," *Computational Economics*, 25, 2005, pp. 381-405.
12. IARPA Aggregative Contingent Estimation (ACE). http://www.iarpa.gov/Programs/ia/ACE/ace.html
13. Jeong, J.W., Morris, M.R., Teevan, J., and Liebling, D., "A Crowd-Powered Socially Embedded Search Engine," *Proceedings of the Seventh International AAAI Conference on Weblogs and Social Media (ICWSM 2013)*, Boston, MA, July 2013.
14. Law, E. and von Ahn, L., "Input-Agreement: a New Mechanism for Collecting Data Using Human Computation Games," *Proceedings of the SIGCHI Conference on Human Factors in Computing Systems (CHI '09)*, ACM, New York, 2009, pp. 1197-1206.
15. Le, J., Edmonds, A., Hester, V., Biewald, L., "Ensuring Quality in Crowd-Sourced Search Relevance Evaluation: The effects of Training Question Distribution," *Proceedings of the SIGIR 2010 Workshop on Crowdsourcing for Search Evaluation (CSE 2010)*, 2010.
16. Miller, S., Forlines, C., Regan, J., "Exploring the Relationship Between Topic Area Knowledge and Forecasting Performance," *Proceedings of the Human Factors and Ergonomics Society Annual Meeting*, Vol. 56, No. 1, 2012, pp. 318-322.
17. Oleson, D., Sorokin, A., Laughlin, G., Hester, V., Le, J., Biewald, L., "Programmatic Gold: Targeted and Scalable Quality Assurance in Crowd Sourcing," *Proceedings of the ACM SIGKDD Workshop on Human Computation (HCOMP '11)*, ACM, New York, NY, USA, 2011.
18. Ipeirotis, P.G., Provost, F., and Wang, J., "Quality Management on Amazon Mechanical Turk," *Proceedings of the ACM SIGKDD Workshop on Human Computation (HCOMP '10)*, ACM, New York, NY, USA, 2010, pp. 64-67.
19. Prelec, D., "A Bayesian Truth Serum for Subjective Data, *Science,* 306, 2004, pp. 462-466.
20. Ranjan, R. and Gneiting, T., Combining Probability Forecasts," *Journal of the Royal Statistical Society: Series B (Statistical Methodology)*, 72, pp. 71–91.
21. Sun, Y. and Dance, C., "When Majority Voting Fails: Comparing Quality Assurance Methods for Noisy Human Computation Environment," Presented at Collective Intelligence Conference, 2012.
22. Sun, Y., Roy, S., Little, G., "Beyond Independent Agreement: A Tournament Selection Approach for Quality Assurance of Human Computation Tasks," *Proc. of: Human Computation,* San Francisco, California, USA, 2011.
23. Surowiecki, J., *The Wisdom of Crowds*, New York: Doubleday, 2004.
24. Tetlock, P., *Expert Political Judgment*, Princeton University Press, Princeton, NJ, 2006.
25. Ungar, L., Mellers, B., Satopää, V., Tetlock, P., and Baron, J., "The Good Judgment Project: A Large Scale Test of Different Methods of Combining Expert Predictions," *AAAI Fall Symposium Series,* 2012.
26. Wolfers, J. and Zitzewitz, E., "Prediction Markets, *Journal of Economic Perspectives, American Economic Association*, V 18, No. 2, '04, pp. 107-126.
27. Yaniv, I., "Weighting and Trimming: Heuristics for Aggregating Judgments under Uncertainty," *Organizational Behavior and Human Decision Processes*, 69, 1997, pp. 237-249.

Cognitively Inspired Task Design to Improve User Performance on Crowdsourcing Platforms

Harini Alagarai Sampath
IIIT, Hyderabad
India
harini@research.iiit.ac.in

Rajeev Rajeshuni
IIIT, Hyderabad
India
rajeshuni.rajeev@research.iiit.ac.in

Bipin Indurkhya
IIIT, Hyderabad
India
bipin@iiit.ac.in

ABSTRACT
Recent research in human computation has focused on improving the quality of work done by crowd workers on crowdsourcing platforms. Multiple approaches have been adopted like filtering crowd workers through qualification tasks, and aggregating responses from multiple crowd workers to obtain consensus. We investigate here how improving the presentation of the task itself by using cognitively inspired features affects the performance of crowd workers. We illustrate this with a case-study for the task of extracting text from scanned images. We generated six task-presentation designs by modifying two parameters — *visual saliency of the target fields* and *working memory requirements* — and conducted experiments on Amazon Mechanical Turk (AMT) and with an eye-tracker in the lab setting. Our results identify which task-design parameters (e.g. highlighting target fields) result in improved performance, and which ones do not (e.g. reducing the number of distractors). In conclusion, we claim that the use of cognitively inspired features for task design is a powerful technique for maximizing the performance of crowd workers.

Author Keywords
Crowdsourcing; Cognitive Psychology; Task Design; Visual Saliency; Working Memory; Mechanical Turk; Eye Tracking

ACM Classification Keywords
H.5.2. Information Interfaces and Presentation (e.g. HCI): Miscellaneous

INTRODUCTION
Crowdsourcing is an emergent paradigm for leveraging human intelligence to solve computationally difficult tasks. Microtask markets like Amazon's Mechanical Turk (AMT) provide a platform for requesters to recruit human users (*crowd workers*) to perform tasks like handwriting recognition, image and speech annotation, and translation, which are difficult to fully automate on the computer. These microtasks on crowdsourcing platforms range from simple web searches to creative design and ideation.

CHI'14, April 26–May 1, 2014, Toronto, Canada.

ACM 978-1-4503-2473-1/14/04...$15.00.
http://dx.doi.org/10.1145/2556288.2557155

Unlike typical organizations, the nature of communication between the requester and the worker in a crowdsourcing platform is mostly asynchronous. Requesters post a *Human Intelligence Task (HIT)* online using a task template, which is taken up (at some later time) by one or more workers to solve. There is no direct interaction (physical or virtual) between the requester and the worker. This lack of direct supervision makes it difficult to extract high-quality work from a heterogeneous set of crowd workers.

Current approaches in literature to ensure quality in crowdsourcing platforms can be grouped into three major categories [19].

- Filtering workers: Special qualification tasks are provided to choose the right set of workers, or responses from crowd workers are accepted or rejected based on their performance on gold data [4].
- Aggregating responses: Same task is posted to multiple crowd workers and their responses are aggregated [14] through majority voting, ranking or clustering.
- Modifying task design: The task design is modified to reduce the cognitive load on workers, or to make it inefficient for workers to provide meaningless responses.

The research described here falls under the third category. Our ultimate goal is to develop a system that learns what parameters of the task design are optimal to maximize the performance of any crowd worker, given some information about his or her background. As a first step towards this goal, we present here an experimental study of how different task designs affect the performance of a crowd worker. Our approach incorporates insights from the cognitive psychology research.

RELATED RESEARCH
In the existing research, the role of multiple HIT parameters on the performance of crowd workers has been investigated. Mason *et al.* explore the role of financial incentive [21], and conclude that paying more for each task generates more quantity but does not necessarily guarantee quality. Huang *et al.* [13] use learning models to predict the optimal task parameters (pay per HIT, number of labels to extract per image, number of images per HIT) for image labeling task. Little *et al.* [20] propose an iterative model of task design, in which the output of one crowd worker is sent as input to the second crowd worker.

In another study, where crowd workers had to rate [15] quality of Wikipedia articles, Kittur *et al.* used task designs —

one in which users had to provide ratings on a Likert scale and another in which they had to answer a set of questions before rating the article. They found that the responses obtained from the second design were more reliable because, in this design, completing the task in good faith requires as much effort as providing a meaningless response.

INSIGHTS FROM COGNITIVE PSYCHOLOGY

The above-mentioned approaches do not consider how the features of the task presentation itself, like its visual presentation and semantics, affect the performance of crowd workers. However, researchers in cognitive psychology have long been aware that these factors can have a major influence on the efficacy and quality of the solution offered, even for simple tasks. A classical example is the *Mutilated checkerboard puzzle*, where one is asked if an 8x8 grid with two of the diagonally opposite corners removed (so a total of 62 squares remain) can be covered by 31 2x1 tiles (Fig. 1 left).

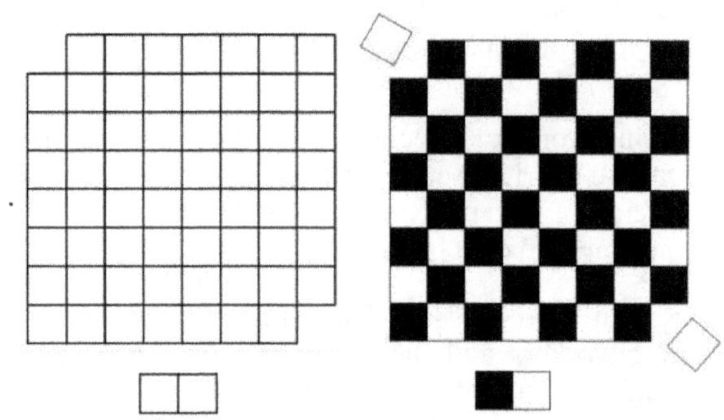

Figure 1: Mutilated checkerboard puzzle: (left) original version, (right) with overlaid grid pattern

Typically, participants take a long time and make many attempts to solve the problem before giving up in frustration [9, 17]. However, if the problem is presented in a slightly different way, with a checkerboard pattern of alternate black and white squares overlaid on the grid (Fig. 1, right), after a bit of trial and error, the participants quickly conclude that the problem cannot be solved. This is because one 2x1 tile always covers exactly one black and one white square irrespective of where it is placed. But the 62-square grid is missing two tiles of the same color.

Only few researchers have investigated the role of cognitive factors in crowdsourcing. Heer *et al.* [12] conducted a series of graphical perception experiments on Mechanical Turk, and found that the results from the web-based experiments replicated the already known results from cognitive psychology about graphical perception. Morris *et al.* [23] explored the role of affective priming in a task where workers had to come up with unusual uses for given objects. In this study, crowd workers were primed with both images and music of positive, negative and neutral affect. They found that the performance of crowd workers improved when they were primed with positive-affect music. The nature of priming used by the authors is effective in influencing the crowd worker's judgment in a creative task, but there are other cognitive phenomenon that can also be used to improve the performance of crowd workers in more realistic task settings.

We explore here various task presentations that are inspired by existing research in cognitive psychology. We use a typical form-digitization task, and generate multiple task-presentation designs (referred to as *templates* from now on). There have been other instances where improving the performance in form-digitization task has been examined. In Shreddr [5], the authors propose shredding a form into individual fields for digitization. While this is one possible task design, we explore here how several task designs can be generated by varying multiple cognitive parameters. In the rest of the paper, we describe the cognitive theories that motivated the design of each of the templates, and our experiments to measure how they effect the performance of crowd workers.

FORM-DIGITIZATION TASK

The objective in this task is to extract three fields (*patient name, patient identification number, patient illness*) from a handwritten insurance form as shown in Fig. 2. The structure of the form is such that each of these fields has one distractor field with potential for confusion: Member Name, Group ID, and Treatment Sought respectively. We refer to this form as $T_{baseline}$ in the rest of this paper.

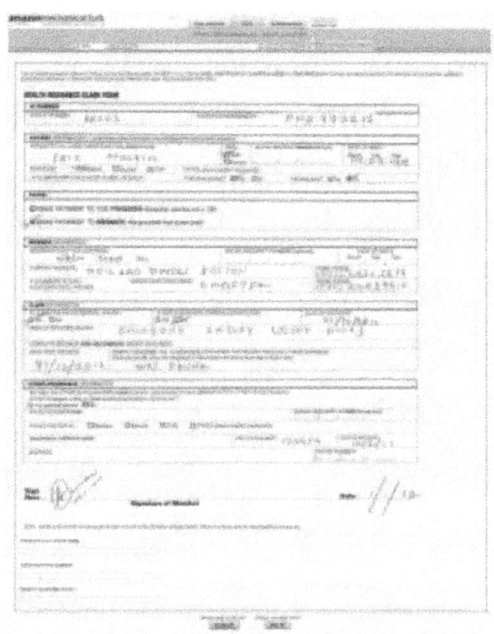

Figure 2: $T_{baseline}$: Sample insurance form

To complete the form-digitization task, the user needs to read the task description, identify the target field in the form, remember its contents and type those contents in a target text box. By generating multiple cognitively inspired templates, we attempt to reduce the possibility of errors in each of these steps. Next, we describe theories that motivated the design of our templates, and experiments to determine their efficacy.

VISUAL SEARCH

Visual search is one of the important paradigms in attention research. One of its key findings [28] is that searching for a target which differs from distractors in one feature (disjunctive search) is faster than searching for a target which shares features with distractors (conjunctive search). This is illustrated in Fig. 3. It is also known that the response time to find a target item increases roughly linearly with the number of items in the search space [30].

Figure 3: Searching for a blue circle is faster in the panel on the left as compared to panel on the right. The left panel illustrates disjunctive search where the target stands out from distractors. The right panel illustrates conjunctive search where the target shares features with the distractors.

In the form-digitization example, identifying the target field can be modeled as a conjunctive search problem, as the target field shares features with the distractor fields. To avoid the crowd worker from digitizing a distractor field, and to reduce the effort needed to identify the target field, this conjunctive search problem needs to be transposed to a disjunctive search problem. This can be achieved in two ways: by making the target field visually salient so that it *pops out* from the rest of the form, or by reducing the number of distractor fields so that the search space is smaller, thereby making it easier to identify the target field.

The role of highlighting in increasing search performance has been explored in other instances in literature. Fisher *et al.* [8] found that highlighting by color improved the performance of participants in a digit-search task, and highlighting works best only when it is predictive of the target-distractor status of the items displayed. Wickens *et al.* [29] found that discriminating multiple information domains with different intensities improves performance in a map search task. In our experiment, we were interested in understanding the role of increasing visual saliency in an environment where the crowd worker is trying to optimize his or her time by performing as many tasks as possible in a given time. In this case, we hypothesized that increasing visual saliency of the target would not only reduce search time but also reduce the cognitive load associated with searching, and hence improve the accuracy of results.

We generated two templates to transpose the form-digitization task into a disjunctive search. In the first template ($T_{highlight}$), we highlighted what we wanted the workers to digitize as shown in Fig. 4. In the second template ($T_{searcheff}$), we systematically varied the number of distractors in the search space as shown in Fig. 5. We hypothesized that this will not only speed up the worker's response time, but also increase accuracy by focusing the worker's attention to only the fields that needed extracting.

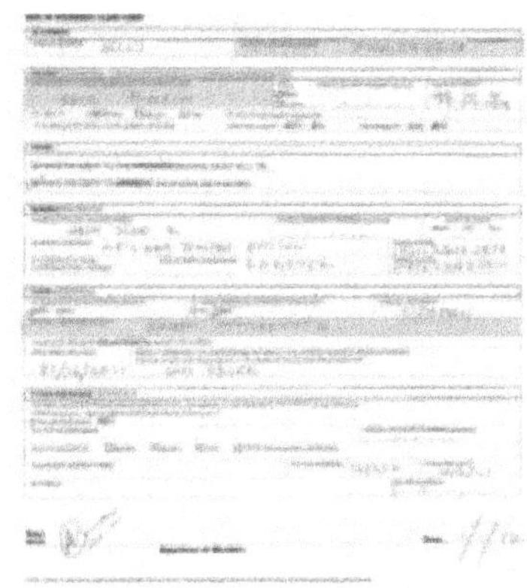

Figure 4: $T_{highlight}$: Visual saliency is manipulated by highlighting the target fields

Experiment I - Role of Visual Saliency

Design

Data was collected from AMT for each of the three templates - $T_{baseline}$, $T_{highlight}$ and $T_{searcheff}$ over four consecutive days. Each day was divided into four 6-hour time slots (starting times are as follows : S1 - 00:00, S2 - 06:00, S3 - 12:00, S4 - 18:00). This was done to ensure sufficient geographical coverage of crowd workers across time zones. A batch of Human Intelligence Tasks (HITs) was posted to AMT in each time slot. Each batch contained 100 images of a particular template type. Each HIT had two assignments. This resulted in 800 responses for each template (4 (Number of days) x 100 (Number of HITs/day) x 2 (Number of assignments/HIT)). The distribution of templates across the slots was counterbalanced. Each HIT was offered a payment of 2 cents.

Procedure

The batches were scheduled to be posted automatically. Crowd workers were asked to extract three fields: a) Name of the patient, b) Identification number, and c) Name of the illness for which the patient received the treatment.

All the responses received were compared against the ground truth data for the forms (manually generated) and the payments were released. The following factors were *not* considered while comparing for accuracy: a) changes in case ('Name' vs. 'name'), b) presence of extra spaces ('R. Name' vs. 'R.Name'), and c) minor punctuation changes ('this is illness.' vs. 'this is illness'). For the analysis reported here, we used the aggregate of length-normalized Levenshtein distance between the response and the ground truth for the three fields as the operational definition of accuracy. This measure takes a value in the range [0 1]. A value closer to 1 indicates higher accuracy.

Analysis

In our design, there were no restrictions on the number of HITs that could be completed by a crowd worker. Our data indicates that the distribution of tasks among the workers was

IDENTIFICATION NUMBER: RC603391

(a) No distractors

BRIEFLY DESCRIBE THE CONDITION(S) FOR WHICH THE PATIENT RECEIVED THESE SERVICES: (You can usually copy the diagnosis or description of service from the provider bill.) OsteoArthritis

GROUP (EMPLOYER) NAME: TECHMAHINDRA

IDENTIFICATION NUMBER: CV 321011

(b) One target and two distractors

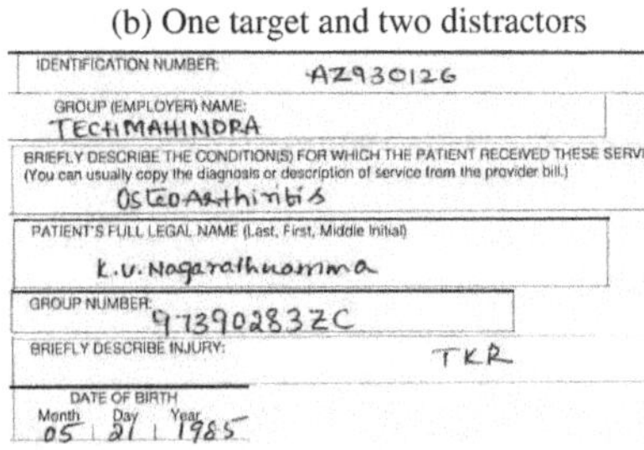

IDENTIFICATION NUMBER: AZ930126

GROUP (EMPLOYER) NAME: TECHMAHINDRA

BRIEFLY DESCRIBE THE CONDITION(S) FOR WHICH THE PATIENT RECEIVED THESE SERVICES: (You can usually copy the diagnosis or description of service from the provider bill.) OsteoArthritis

PATIENT'S FULL LEGAL NAME (Last, First, Middle Initial): K.V. Nagarathnamma

GROUP NUMBER: 9139028 3ZC

BRIEFLY DESCRIBE INJURY: TKR

DATE OF BIRTH Month Day Year 05 21 1985

(c) One target and six distractors

Figure 5: $T_{searcheff}$: The number of distractors are varied.

not uniform as shown in Fig. 6: 56% of the workers accepted less than 5 HITs. Conversely, 80% of the tasks were finished by just 25% of the crowd workers.

In light of this skewed distribution, we used a linear mixed-effects analysis [3] to understand the relationship between accuracy and the templates. The template was considered to be the fixed effect and crowd workers as the random effect. WorkerIDs obtained from AMT were used to identify the individual crowd workers in the analysis. P-values reported here were obtained by the likelihood ratio tests of the full model with the fixed effect against the model without the effect. Similar analysis has been reported in [11].

Figure 6: Task distribution among Crowd Workers.

Results

Our results indicate that $T_{highlight}$ had the highest accuracy of the three templates. This was significantly higher than the accuracy obtained from $T_{baseline}$ (p <0.05). There was no significant difference between $T_{searcheff}$ and $T_{baseline}$. The accuracies obtained are presented in Table. 1

Within the template $T_{searcheff}$, we examined if search efficiency of a form can predict the accuracy. We defined search efficiency of a template as $X_{searcheff} = \frac{\eta_T}{\eta_N}$, where η_T is the number of fields to extract and η_N is the total number of fields in the form. We constructed a linear model of accuracy as a function of $X_{searcheff}$. However, this model was not significant (p = 0.186), indicating that the search efficiency did not predict the accuracy.

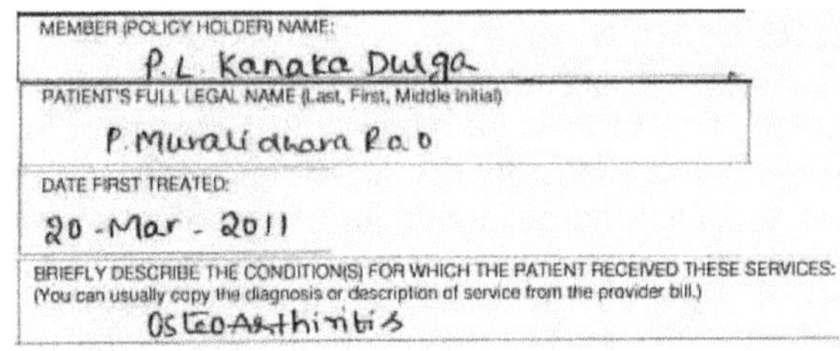

MEMBER (POLICY HOLDER) NAME: P.L. Kanaka Durga

PATIENT'S FULL LEGAL NAME (Last, First, Middle Initial): P. Muralidhara Rao

DATE FIRST TREATED: 20-Mar-2011

BRIEFLY DESCRIBE THE CONDITION(S) FOR WHICH THE PATIENT RECEIVED THESE SERVICES: (You can usually copy the diagnosis or description of service from the provider bill.) OsteoArthritis

(a) The target field (*patient name*) has a high semantic similarity with the distractor (*member name*).

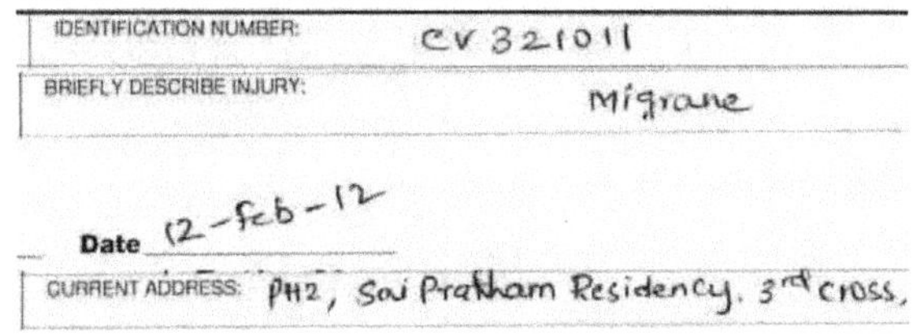

IDENTIFICATION NUMBER: CV 321011

BRIEFLY DESCRIBE INJURY: Migrane

Date 12-feb-12

CURRENT ADDRESS: PH2, Sai Pratham Residency, 3rd cross,

(b) The target field(*patient identification number*) is not similar to the distractors

Figure 7: T_{tdsim}: The semantic similarity between the target and the distractors is varied.

To investigate further, we annotated the data for the nature of errors. We found that most of the errors in template $T_{searcheff}$ were caused by the users transcribing a wrong field — e.g., *group number* instead of *patient identification number* in Fig. 5b. While highlighting the target fields makes them both visually and semantically salient, reducing the number of distractors makes the target fields visually salient, but a confusion with semantically similar fields is possible. This led us to investigate the role of semantic similarity between the target and distractors as a separate template.

Experiment II - Role of semantic similarity

Visual search literature shows that the search efficiency decreases as the visual similarity between the target and the distractor increases, and increases as the similarity among the distractors increases. This means that the most efficient search will happen when the user searches for a conspicuous target among homogeneous distractors. The same argument can be extended to the semantic dimension: It is easier for the user to find a target field of interest when the semantic similarity between the question and target fields is higher.

We used Latent Semantic Analysis (LSA) [18] to compute these similarity values. LSA provides a cosine value that reflects the semantic distance between any two pieces of text. A cosine value of +1 denotes identical texts, and values near 0 denote unrelated texts. In a form with one target and M distractor fields, d_i is defined as the semantic distance (cosine value from LSA) between the label of the target and i^{th} distractor field.

$d_i = LSA(Target, Distractor_i), 1 \leq i \leq M$

The Target-Distractor Similarity and Distractor-Distractor Similarity metrics for the given template are then given by

$X_{TDSim} = \max[\sum_{i=1}^{M} d_i]; X_{DDSim} = \frac{1}{\binom{M}{2}}[\sum_{i,j=1}^{M} d_i.d_j]$

A large value for X_{TDSim} indicates that the target is semantically very similar to the distractor. Similarly, a large value for X_{DDSim} indicates that the distractors are semantically homogeneous. We hypothesized that in a template with a small value for X_{TDSim} and a large value for X_{DDSim}, the target field would be salient and hence easier for the user to spot.

Procedure

We generated multiple templates (T_{tdsim}), each with one target field and three distractor fields as shown in Fig. 7. The templates were generated such that their X_{TDSim} and X_{DDSim} values spanned the possible range of [0,1]. These templates were then posted to AMT. The design was similar to Experiment I. Templates were posted over four consecutive days, counterbalanced across four time-slots. In all, 800 responses were obtained.

Results

We constructed a linear mixed model with X_{TDSim} and X_{DDSim} as the fixed effects and workers as the random effect. We found that the model was significant ($p < 0.05$). This suggests that the target-distractor similarity and the distractor-distractor similarity predict the accuracy obtained from a template. Though the accuracy obtained with T_{tdsim} was less than with $T_{highlight}$, this difference was not significant ($p > 0.1$). The accuracies obtained are shown in Table 1

Discussion

We generated three templates ($T_{highlight}$, $T_{searcheff}$, T_{tdsim}) to make the target field salient in both visual and semantic sense. We found that highlighting the target fields yielded the best accuracy. Reducing the number of distractors in an attempt to improve the search efficiency of the template did not yield any significant result. Though the search efficiency of the template did not predict the accuracy obtained, the semantic distance between the target and the distractor fields was a predictor of the crowd worker's performance. Highlighting the target fields achieves saliency in both visual and semantic dimensions.

Template	Mean	SD
$T_{baseline}$	0.873	0.134
$T_{highlight}$	0.979	0.077
$T_{searcheff}$	0. 919	0.24
T_{tdsim}	0.966	0.20

Table 1: Accuracy for visual search templates

While the data from AMT indicates $T_{highlight}$ and T_{tdsim} perform better than $T_{searcheff}$ and $T_{baseline}$, it is not possible to ascertain from the AMT data if this is because the crowd workers found it easier to locate the target fields in $T_{highlight}$ and T_{tdsim}. Hence we conducted an eye tracking study in laboratory conditions to investigate this further.

Experiment III - Visual Saliency - Eye tracking study

The goal of this eye tracking study was to verify if the crowd workers spend more time looking at the target fields in template $T_{highlight}$ compared to $T_{baseline}$, and if locating the target field is indeed faster in T_{tdsim} compared to $T_{searcheff}$.

Stimuli

All the tasks were posted on the AMT's requester sandbox, a simulated environment provided by AMT. We used the sandbox because HITs on the sandbox look exactly like on the actual platform and ensures that only participants in the experiment would be able to see the HITs.

Participants

Thirteen participants took part in the study, who were all undergraduate computer science students.

Design

A within-group design was used where each participant viewed forms from the three templates: $T_{baseline}$, $T_{highlight}$ and $T_{searcheff}$. The presentation order of the templates was randomized.

Procedure

Each participant was told that they would have to solve a task using AMT and an introduction to AMT-specific terms and activities (e.g. accepting a HIT, submitting a HIT etc.) was provided. Apart from this, no instructions were given to the participants. In particular, the exact nature of the task was not disclosed to them. The participants used a computer in a separate room and there was no interaction with the experimenter. This was done to simulate the AMT conditions, as an actual crowd worker does not interact directly with the requesters. The participant were told that they would be provided equivalent of 2 cents for every HIT they complete and were asked to complete as many HITs as possible. Each participant was allowed to finish 20 HITs after which the experimenter interrupted and told them that they have finished the task. The presentation order of each of the templates was controlled and randomized. The eye movements of the participants were recorded using a Tobii X120 eye tracker.

Results

We defined *areas of interest (AOI)* around the target fields in $T_{highlight}$ and $T_{baseline}$. The total fixation duration (in seconds) in the target fields was calculated as the sum of duration of all the fixations in the AOI. We also computed the total time spent by the participants to complete each HIT. The HIT-completion time was measured as the time (in seconds) between accepting and submitting the HIT.

No significant difference was found in HIT-completion time between $T_{highlight}$ and $T_{baseline}$ ($p > 0.1$). However, the total fixation duration on the target fields in $T_{highlight}$ was significantly higher than $T_{baseline}$ (df = 12, t = 2.72, p = 0.02) indicating that the participants spent more time looking at the target fields in $T_{highlight}$ compared to $T_{baseline}$. This is also reflected in the heat-maps generated from the eye-tracking data

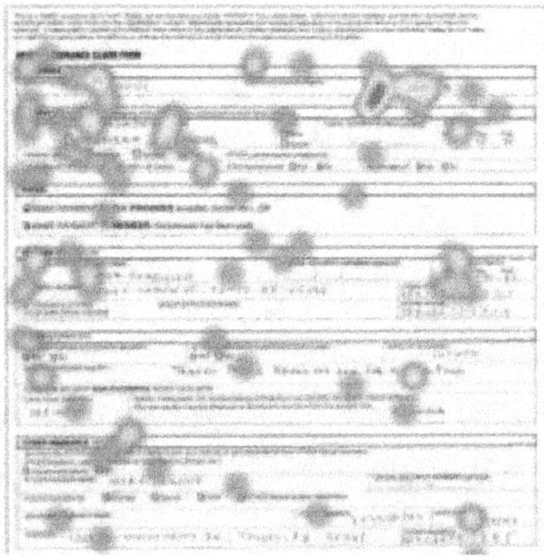

Figure 8: Heat map for $T_{baseline}$. Participants' attention is drawn to the target as well as to the distractor fields.

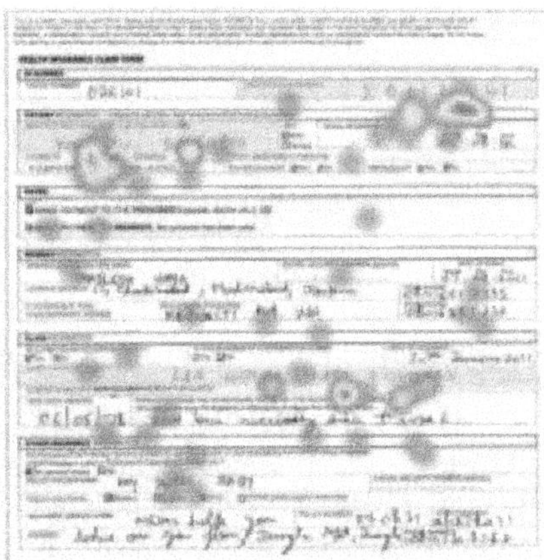

Figure 9: Heat map for $T_{highlight}$. Participants' attention is more concentrated on the highlighted target fields.

for these templates (Fig. 8 and Fig. 9). It can be seen that while the participants have fixated on the distractor fields in template $T_{baseline}$, the fixations are mostly concentrated on the highlighted fields in template $T_{highlight}$, thereby explaining the higher accuracy in template $T_{highlight}$.

We measured the time to first fixation as the time (in seconds) from when the template was shown to until the start of the first fixation within an area of interest. We found that the time to first fixation in T_{tdsim} (Mean (SD) : 18 (11)) was significantly (t = 6.14, df = 10 p = 0.004) faster than $T_{searcheff}$ (Mean (SD) : 31(10)). This validates the hypothesis that the target fields are easier to find in T_{tdsim} compared to $T_{searcheff}$.

WORKING MEMORY

Working memory is a limited capacity system that temporarily maintains information and acts as an interface between human perception, long-term memory and action [1]. Working memory is in many instances considered as a measure of cognitive load associated with a task. In the digitization task, users need to hold the information from the image in their working memory before they type it in the response boxes. Given that the requester has no knowledge of the existing cognitive load of the crowd worker, it is imperative that the working memory requirements are kept to a minimum to avoid performance degradation.

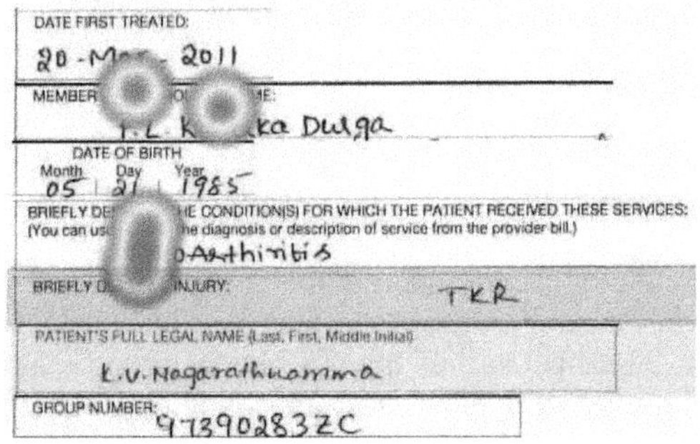

Figure 10: Sample heat map for $T_{searcheff}$. The target fields are highlighted for easier visualisation. Participants viewed the images without highlighting. One can see that the participant's attention is drawn to the semantically similar distractors.

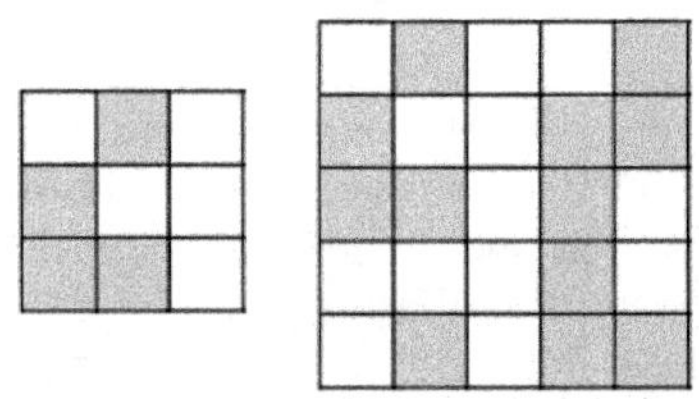

Figure 11: Spatial-Span Task for two matrix sizes. Participants are asked to reproduce the shading pattern. Performance in this task degrades as the size of the matrix increases.

Various studies have explored the limits of the working memory. For example in the digit-span task, the participants are asked to remember a sequence of numbers and repeat them back immediately. It has been found that as the length of the sequence increases, the performance breaks down. Similarly, in the spatial-span task (Fig. 11), the participants are provided with matrices in which half the cells are shaded, and are asked to remember and reproduce the pattern. Here again, accuracy decreases as the size of the matrix increases. Though the limits of working memory varies depending on the task, context and individual, it is generally agreed that it is possible to hold less than ten items in working memory without performance degradation [22].

It has been shown that training users to associate different items into chunks that could be remembered as a whole improves working memory [24]. In a related experiment using a block-copying paradigm, Ballard *et al.* [2] found that subjects remember either the color or the position of the tiles in the block, and make repeated saccades to the source figure to confirm if they have copied the tile correctly. It is argued that the human brain plans its action so as to reduce the working memory requirements, and acquires new information as they are needed just-in-time using eye movements [6].

This suggests two ways to reduce working memory constraints on the user: a) by priming them to remember information as chunks, or b) by ensuring that the users can acquire new information just-in-time by making saccades. Based on this, we generated two variants of the task template.

In the first variant (T_{chunk}), we asked the users to extract shorter segments of data from the form for the *patient identification number* field. The *patient id* is an eight-digit randomly-generated alphanumeric string. We asked the users to extract the first two alphabets and the next six digits from the *patient id* into separate response boxes (Fig. 12). We hypothesized that this would prime the users to chunk them, and thereby improve performance.

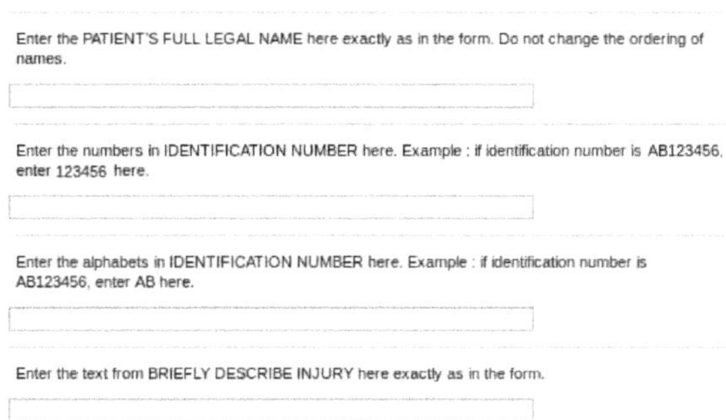

Figure 12: In T_{chunk}, crowd workers were asked to extract information in parts

In the next variant (T_{closer}), we placed the response boxes near the fields to be extracted as shown in Fig. 13. We hypothesized that this would again reduce the need for the workers to commit all the content to their working memory. Instead, they need only parse short chunks of information at a time, and use the direct visual feedback to validate their response.

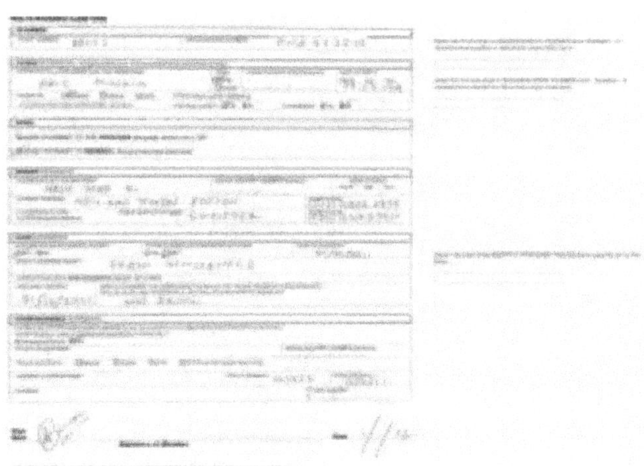

Figure 13: In T_{closer}, working memory was manipulated by altering the location of the response boxes

Recent research on applying rational analysis to interactive behavior [10] shows that, when the cost of accessing information is lower, users tend to adopt a *perceptual-motor* strategy over a *memory-intensive* strategy. We hypothesized that when the response boxes are proximal to the target field, participants would choose a *perceptual-motor* strategy where they would make multiple eye-movements between the response box and the target field to acquire information, but choose a more *memory-intensive* strategy when the response boxes are placed further.

Experiment IV - Role of Working Memory

Procedure

The procedure was similar to Experiment I. Three templates $T_{baseline}$, T_{chunk} and T_{closer} were used. For each template, 100 images were posted over four days across four templates. Each HIT had two assignments. As before, 800 responses were collected for each template and there were no restrictions on the number of HITs a crowd worker could accept.

Results

The analysis used linear mixed models as in Experiment I. There were no significant differences in the accuracy obtained for *patient id* between $T_{baseline}$ and T_{chunk}. However, T_{closer} performed significantly better than both $T_{baseline}$ ($p < 0.05$) and T_{chunk} ($p < 0.05$). The accuracies obtained are tabulated in Table 2. To confirm if the crowd workers indeed used visual feedback in T_{closer}, we conducted an eye-tracking study.

Template	Mean	SD
$T_{baseline}$	0.873	0.134
T_{closer}	0.973	0.115
T_{chunk}	0.884	0.17

Table 2: Accuracy for working-memory templates

Experiment V - Working-Memory eye-tracking study

The goal of this experiment was to validate the hypothesis that in template T_{closer}, the crowd workers acquire new information as needed just-in-time using eye movements. This would mean that the number of saccades between the response boxes and the form would be higher in T_{closer} compared to $T_{baseline}$.

Stimuli

The experiment was conducted using two templates from the previous study: $T_{baseline}$ and T_{closer}. All the tasks were posted on the AMT's requester sandbox, a simulated environment provided by AMT. We used this because HITs on the sandbox look exactly like on the actual platform and ensures that only the participants in the experiment would be able to see the HITs.

Participants

Twenty-five participants (12 female and 13 male) took part in the study. All of them were undergraduate computer science students (Age: Mean = 20.1 SD = 1.6).

Design

A within-group design was used where each participant viewed forms belonging to the two templates, $T_{baseline}$, and T_{closer}. The presentation of the templates was randomized.

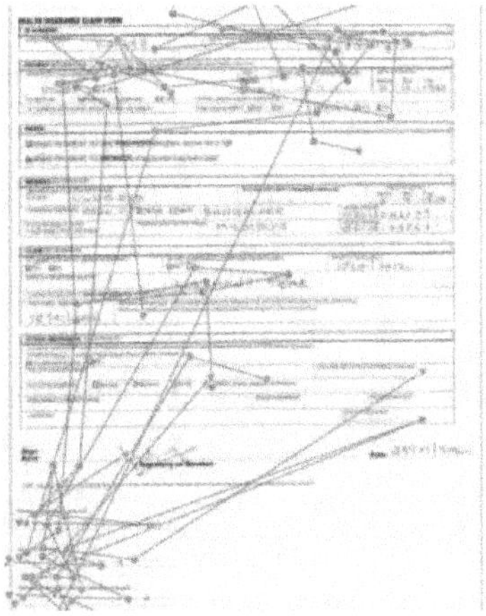

Figure 14: Sample saccade map for template $T_{baseline}$. The number of saccades between the target fields and response boxes are lesser compared to T_{closer} (shown in Fig. 15) indicating that workers favor a memory-intensive strategy.

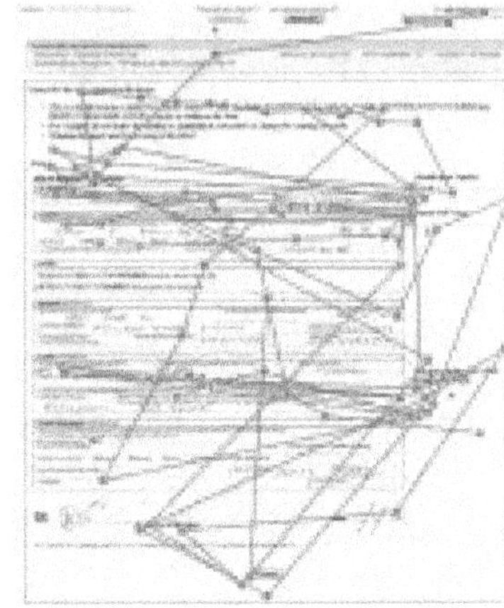

Figure 15: Sample saccade map for template T_{closer}. The number of saccades between the target fields and response boxes are more compared to $T_{baseline}$ (shown in Fig. 14) indicating that workers favor a perceptual-motor strategy.

Procedure

The procedure was similar to the earlier eye-tracking study. Participants were given an overview of AMT-specific terms. The exact nature of the task was not disclosed, and there was no interaction with the experimenter. Participant were told that they would be provided equivalent of 2 cents for every HIT they complete, and were asked to complete as many HITs as possible. The experimenter allowed each participant to finish 20 HITs. The presentation order of the templates were controlled and randomized. The eye movements were recorded using a Tobii X120 eye tracker.

Results

The accuracy obtained in T_{closer} (Mean (SD) = 0.8(0.1) was significantly (t = 2.01, p = 0.09) higher than $T_{baseline}$ (Mean (SD) = 0.71(0.2). The saccades for templates $T_{baseline}$ and T_{closer} are shown in Fig. 14 and Fig. 15 respectively. The number of saccades was measured by defining an area of interest around the response boxes and the target fields. We found that the total number of saccades between the response boxes and the target fields in T_{closer} (Mean(SD) = 11.64(3.88)) was significantly higher (t = 4.6, p = 0.001) than $T_{baseline}$ (Mean(SD) = 6.55(2.50)). We hypothesize that, similar to the earlier work of Ballard *et al.* [2, 6], this indicates that T_{closer} allows participants to commit less information to the working memory and obtain information just-in-time, thereby explaining the superior performance with template T_{closer}.

Discussion

The results from the AMT show that T_{closer} produces better performance for the *patient id* field than $T_{baseline}$ or T_{chunk}. Results from the eye-tracking study show that in T_{closer}, participants make more saccades between the target fields and the response boxes. This allows them to obtain information just-in-time and reduces the need to commit information to the working memory.

In crowdsourcing platforms, participants would like to finish as many tasks as possible in a given amount of time. In T_{chunk}, dividing the *patient id* resulted in the need for an extra response. We hypothesize that this results in the crowd workers perceiving this task-design as the one with a lower economic utility [27], thereby leading to a poorer performance. We plan to investigate this in our future research.

VISUAL SALIENCY VS. WORKING MEMORY

To understand the interaction between visual saliency and working memory, we created a template $T_{combination}$ as shown in Fig. 16. This template combines the best of the visual search ($T_{highlight}$) and working memory (T_{closer}) templates. The target fields were highlighted and the response boxes were moved closer to the target fields. Similar to earlier cases, the templates were posted to AMT and responses were collected.

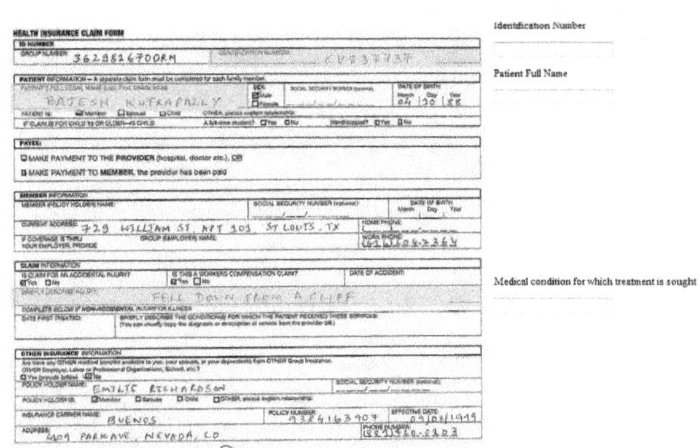

Figure 16: In $T_{combination}$, target fields were highlighted and response boxes were moved closer

Results and Discussion

Comparing $T_{combination}$, $T_{highlight}$ and T_{closer} using linear mixed models, considering the task design as the fixed effect and the crowd workers as the random effect, we did not find any significant differences in the performance between any of these templates ($p > 0.1$). The accuracies obtained are presented in Table 3.

Template	Mean	SD
$T_{baseline}$	0.873	0.134
$T_{highlight}$	0.979	0.077
T_{closer}	0.973	0.115
$T_{combined}$	0.982	0.15

Table 3: Accuracy for best-performing templates

One possible explanation for this result is as follows: since in T_{closer} the text boxes were placed closer to the target fields, it also served to increase the visual saliency of the target fields. To investigate this, we compared the total fixation duration on the target fields between $T_{baseline}$ and T_{closer} from the eye-tracking study. We found that the fixation time on the target was significantly higher ($t = 2.22$, $p = 0.02$) in T_{closer} (Mean(SD) = 22.5(14.2)) than $T_{baseline}$ (Mean(SD) = 15.2(10.9)). This confirms that T_{closer} also serves to increase the visual saliency. This is illustrated in Fig. 17.

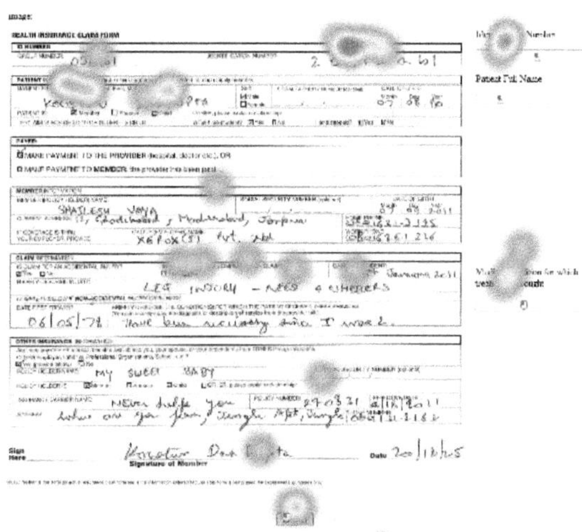

Figure 17: This sample heat map shows that T_{closer} also results in an increased visual saliency of the target fields.

DISCUSSION

In this paper, we demonstrated that different task presentations affect crowd performance significantly. Our experiments show that highlighting the target fields, which reduces the search time, and moving the response boxes closer to the target fields, which reduces the working-memory load, result in higher accuracy compared to the baseline condition. Templates that increased the perceived workload of crowd workers (e.g. chunking) resulted in a poorer performance.

One limitation of the data obtained from AMT is that we can consider only its accuracy aspect. The timing (latency) aspect of this data is not reliable, for we do not know how crowd workers spend their time between accepting a HIT and submitting it. We found large variances in the latency data from AMT, which we could not account for. We plan to address this in our future research. It would also be interesting to explore the effect of the expertise the crowd workers may acquire while doing the tasks. For instance, Deshpande [7] has shown that the interface and navigation design influences users' adaptation to the task, and affects their learning performance in e-learning environments. It would be interesting to study the role of task-design to facilitate adaptation in crowdsourcing context as well.

Current approaches to improve quality control in crowdsourcing put the onus of quality entirely on the worker. Our study shows that the requester can improve the quality by providing better task designs. Moreover, one can take a scientific approach to optimizing the task design by applying principles of perception and cognition.

The prospect of applying cognitive principles to crowdsourcing is exciting. There is a growing body of work in crowdsourcing which shows that many laboratory tasks like decision-making [25], graphical perception [12] and evaluating user-interfaces [16] could be reliably replicated in crowdsourcing platforms. However, we believe care should be exercised in importing principles from cognitive psychology. Most of these principles are based on controlled experiments conducted with abstract stimuli, and they typically explore bottom-up processes. In crowdsourcing environments, on the other hand, the crowd worker's perception is strictly task-oriented. Even in our study, some templates (e.g. chunking) based on well-established cognitive principles did not lead to an improved performance.

CONCLUSION AND FUTURE WORK

We focused here on the form-digitization task to demonstrate the efficacy of cognitive principles to task design, but a similar approach can be applied to other domains like speech processing [26], where there is also a need to reduce the cognitive load of crowd workers. We believe that exploring cognitively inspired task designs to improve the performance of crowd workers is a promising line of enquiry for both cognitive psychology (to understand how its principles apply to real problems) and human computation (to generate better task interfaces).

Our ultimate goal is to build domain-specific recommendation systems that could predict performance given a task-design, and suggest effective templates to the requesters. To this end, we plan to identify features that could predict the performance of crowd workers in a given domain. Using these features and the data collected from crowd workers (similar to those described in this paper), we plan to implement a learning system to predict the performance for a new task design. We envision that such a system would empower the requesters with a concise methodology for selecting a task template that maximizes the return of investment, by saving time and improving quality.

ACKNOWLEDGEMENTS

The initial stage of this research was supported in part by a grant from the Xerox Corporation under their Open Innovation program.

REFERENCES

1. Baddeley, A. Working memory: Looking back and looking forward. *Nature Reviews Neuroscience 4*, 10 (2003), 829–839.
2. Ballard, D. H., Hayhoe, M. M., Pook, P. K., and Rao, R. P. Deictic codes for the embodiment of cognition. *Behavioral and Brain Sciences 20*, 04 (1997), 723–742.
3. Bates, D., Maechler, M., and Bolker, B. lme4: Linear mixed-effects models using s4 classes.
4. Biewald, L., and Van Pelt, C. Distributing a task to multiple workers over a network for completion while providing quality control, 2011. WO Patent 2,011,159,434.
5. Chen, K., Kannan, A., Yano, Y., Hellerstein, J. M., and Parikh, T. S. Shreddr: pipelined paper digitization for low-resource organizations. In *Proceedings of the 2nd ACM Symposium on Computing for Development*, ACM (2012), 3.
6. Clark, A. *Supersizing the Mind: Embodiment, Action, and Cognitive Extension: Embodiment, Action, and Cognitive Extension*. Oxford University Press, USA, 2008.
7. Deshpande, Y. *Adaptivity and Interface Design: A Human-Computer Interaction Study in E-Learning Applications*. PhD thesis, Indian Institute of Technology, Guwahati, January 2014.
8. Fisher, D. L., and Tan, K. C. Visual displays: The highlighting paradox. *Human Factors: The Journal of the Human Factors and Ergonomics Society 31*, 1 (1989), 17–30.
9. Gamow, G., and Stern, M. *Puzzle-math*. Macmillan, 1958.
10. Gray, W. D., Sims, C. R., Fu, W.-T., and Schoelles, M. J. The soft constraints hypothesis: a rational analysis approach to resource allocation for interactive behavior. *Psychological review 113*, 3 (2006), 461.
11. Green, S., Heer, J., and Manning, C. D. The efficacy of human post-editing for language translation. In *Proceedings of the SIGCHI Conference on Human Factors in Computing Systems*, ACM (2013), 439–448.
12. Heer, J., and Bostock, M. Crowdsourcing graphical perception: using mechanical turk to assess visualization design. In *Proceedings of the SIGCHI Conference on Human Factors in Computing Systems*, ACM (2010), 203–212.
13. Huang, E., Zhang, H., Parkes, D. C., Gajos, K. Z., and Chen, Y. Toward automatic task design: A progress report. In *Proceedings of the ACM SIGKDD workshop on human computation*, ACM (2010), 77–85.
14. Ipeirotis, P. G., Provost, F., and Wang, J. Quality management on amazon mechanical turk. In *Proceedings of the ACM SIGKDD workshop on human computation*, ACM (2010), 64–67.
15. Kittur, A., Chi, E. H., and Suh, B. Crowdsourcing user studies with mechanical turk. In *Proceedings of the SIGCHI conference on human factors in computing systems*, ACM (2008), 453–456.
16. Komarov, S., Reinecke, K., and Gajos, K. Z. Crowdsourcing performance evaluations of user interfaces. In *Proceedings of the SIGCHI Conference on Human Factors in Computing Systems*, ACM (2013), 207–216.
17. Korf, R. E. Toward a model of representation changes. *Artificial intelligence 14*, 1 (1980), 41–78.
18. Landauer, T. K. Latent semantic analysis. *Encyclopedia of Cognitive Science* (2006).
19. Law, E., and Ahn, L. v. Human computation. *Synthesis Lectures on Artificial Intelligence and Machine Learning 5*, 3 (2011), 1–121.
20. Little, G., Chilton, L. B., Goldman, M., and Miller, R. C. Exploring iterative and parallel human computation processes. In *Proceedings of the ACM SIGKDD workshop on human computation*, ACM (2010), 68–76.
21. Mason, W., and Watts, D. J. Financial incentives and the performance of crowds. *ACM SigKDD Explorations Newsletter 11*, 2 (2010), 100–108.
22. Miller, G. The magical number seven, plus or minus two: Some limits on our capacity for processing information. *The psychological review 63* (1956), 81–97.
23. Morris, R., Dontcheva, M., and Gerber, E. Priming for better performance in microtask crowdsourcing environments. *Internet Computing, IEEE 16*, 5 (2012), 13–19.
24. Olesen, P. J., Westerberg, H., and Klingberg, T. Increased prefrontal and parietal activity after training of working memory. *Nature neuroscience 7*, 1 (2003), 75–79.
25. Paolacci, G., Chandler, J., and Ipeirotis, P. Running experiments on amazon mechanical turk. *Judgment and Decision Making 5*, 5 (2010), 411–419.
26. Parent, G., and Eskenazi, M. Speaking to the crowd: Looking at past achievements in using crowdsourcing for speech and predicting future challenges. In *INTERSPEECH* (2011), 3037–3040.
27. Toomim, M. Economic utility of interaction in crowdsourcing. In *Workshop on Crowdsourcing and Human Computation at CHI* (2011).
28. Treisman, A. Perceptual grouping and attention in visual search for features and for objects. *Journal of Experimental Psychology: Human Perception and Performance 8*, 2 (1982), 194–214.
29. Wickens, C. D., Ambinder, M. S., Alexander, A. L., and Martens, M. The role of highlighting in visual search through maps. In *Proceedings of the Human Factors and Ergonomics Society Annual Meeting*, vol. 48 (2004), 1895–1899.
30. Wolfe, J. M. Guided search 2.0 a revised model of visual search. *Psychonomic bulletin and review 1*, 2 (1994), 202–238.

Searching for Myself: Motivations and Strategies for Self-Search

Catherine C. Marshall
Microsoft Research
1065 La Avenida, Mountain View, CA, 94093, US
cathymar@microsoft.com

Siân Lindley
Microsoft Research
21 Station Road, Cambridge, CB1 2FB, UK
sianl@microsoft.com

ABSTRACT
We present findings from a qualitative study of self-search, also known as ego or vanity search. In the context of a broader study about personal online content, participants were asked to search for themselves using their own computers and the browsers and queries they would normally adopt. Our analysis highlights five motivations for self-search: as a form of identity management; to discover reactions to and reuse of user-generated media; to re-find personal content; as a form of entertainment; and to reveal lost or forgotten content. Strategies vary according to motivation, and may differ markedly from typical information-seeking, with users looking deep into the results and using image search to identify content about themselves. We argue that two dimensions underpin ways of improving self-search: controllability and expectedness, and discuss what these dimensions imply for design.

Author Keywords
Self-search; ego search; vanity search; autosurveillance; identity; aggregation; doppelganger; archive.

ACM Classification Keywords
H.5.m. Information interfaces and presentation (e.g., HCI): Miscellaneous.

INTRODUCTION
As social networking sites evolve and personal content is increasingly hosted online, search engines are a central way users seek online content about themselves. In 2004, a Harris poll revealed that 40% of adults in the US had performed an ego or vanity search; in 2009, a Pew Internet poll found that the majority of adults (57%) had searched for their own name [16]; and in 2008, to support their work on query log privacy, Jones and her colleagues used Yahoo's query logs to establish that as many as 30% of users conducted a vanity search over the 70-day period of their study [13]. *Thus, people do conduct vanity searches, and some may conduct them regularly.*

CHI 2014, April 26 - May 01 2014, Toronto, ON, Canada
Copyright 2014 ACM 978-1-4503-2473-1/14/04...$15.00.
http://dx.doi.org/10.1145/2556288.2557356

When people search for themselves this way, they may encounter content they have generated themselves, but they may also find public records, stories from local newspapers, items from commercial data repositories, and unfamiliar material about themselves. This diverse material is brought together as a search engine results page (SERP), which may act as a form of dynamic profile or self-presentation [17]. If favorable, the SERP can serve as a résumé; anecdotal reports point to the success of having a business card that exhorts the recipient to 'google me', rather than providing a static URL [25]. Indeed, at one time Google issued business cards to support the phenomenon [22]. However, the SERP may also present links to a variety of confounding sites: those about doppelgangers, pages assembled by aggregators and data miners, and social media content the search's subject hoped would remain hidden.

In this paper, we report findings from a qualitative study that begins to investigate this type of search, which we will refer to as *self-search*, focusing specifically on participants' interaction with the SERP. Our research aims to understand the motivations and strategies behind self-search, as well as the obstacles searchers face and surprises they encounter. Building on these results, we consider what our analysis implies for the design of search engine interaction.

Thus far, self-search has been the province of personal branding books, a sideline of the digital identity literature, and an implicit aspect of named entity information retrieval. In this paper, we shift self-search and the SERP from the periphery to the research focus. We begin with a brief discussion of related work before turning to a description of the overarching study, focusing on the part of data collection and analysis that is relevant to self-search. After we present the self-search results, we explore their implications: how can self-search be rendered more effective? How can we better support people's ultimate aims in seeking this type of personal information?

RELATED WORK
Research on self-search lies at the intersection of digital identity management, information-seeking, personal information management (PIM), and privacy; we will draw

on all four areas to inform the interpretation of our results. Self-search (also known as vanity search, ego search, and autosurveillance [7]) has also captured the popular imagination; thus we will touch on recent privacy and identity management books aimed at non-researchers.

Where self-search has been examined, it is often in the context of improving search results or protecting privacy. In the case of the former, researchers have sought to predict whether a query is a name [2] or have explored self-search in the context of rare queries [26]. In the latter case, researchers have pointed to the risks of revealing identity through self-search, highlighting the implications for privacy and data surveillance [13,23]. Other researchers have examined self-search in the context of narcissism (albeit healthy narcissism), situating it in the development of digital identity [20]. Their aim was twofold: to develop a method for distinguishing between self-searches (as part of a broader phenomenon of people searches) and other types of search engine-based information seeking, and to characterize the phenomenon's relative prevalence in overall search engine use. A technique of the sort these researchers describe is likely to be important in providing computational support for self-search.

Self-search sometimes falls under the operational rubric of PIM: people may search for themselves as an implicit part of managing their outward-facing personal information [14]. The key distinction is that we are focusing on how people encounter themselves and their footprints in the process of self-search rather than in common PIM tools. By looking in some detail at how people negotiate self-search, we hope to provide a new perspective on managing the visible traces of one's own online identity. Such ideas resonate with Marchionini's notion of proflection [17], the construction of a digital presence in online resources via explicit action and monitoring implicit online activities.

While research on self-search is fairly sparse, it features prominently in non-scholarly guides to digital identity management, where it is highlighted as a key activity in 'personal branding' [1,7] and 'protecting your internet identity' [4]. People are increasingly worried about "*how much sensitive information about ourselves we voluntarily consign to others in exchange for social interaction, a discount, or simply to access a product or service*" [4, p. viii]. Self-search is a diagnostic tool that can be used to debug a digital identity, to answer the question of what's out there, possibly out of most people's control [10]. These guides distinguish self-search from traditional information seeking in two important ways: First they emphasize that self-search is aimed at uncovering one's digital footprint, the impression made as results are combined and taken as a whole (as opposed to information seeking, which is aimed at a per-document notion of relevance). Secondly, they highlight the distinction that the results presentation (the SERP) is directed at an imagined audience, rather than at the original searcher. Taken together, these two emphases make this aspect of self-search unique.

RESEARCH AIMS

The findings reported in this paper are from a study that aimed to understand how people conceptualize online content about themselves, be this through collections that they have curated (e.g. on sites such as Flickr and Pinterest), traces they have left (e.g. on social network sites), or content created by others that is about them. We were interested in people's awareness of the breadth of this online content, how they kept track of it, and whether they made any efforts to back it up or archive it. A key part of this research relates to self-search. Findings from this study that relate to archiving and managing online content are covered in [15]; in this paper, unpublished findings that focus on self-search are presented. We aim to understand how people search for themselves, what they expect to find, where surprises lie (both pleasant and unpleasant), and what they would like to do with the results. We then consider what our analysis implies for the design of search engines.

METHOD

We interviewed 14 people, 8 in the UK and 6 in the US. To reach participants with a spectrum of external web footprints, we recruited two types of people: those whom we expected to have a significant online presence, including creative output (e.g. amateur musicians), and those with normal social networking habits (e.g. regular Facebook users). Two digital natives (young adults) were among our recruits, since we are aware they might have distinctive online practices and relationships with their 'virtual possessions' [21]. Participants were given a £40/$65 gift voucher in appreciation of their time. Table 1 (included from [15]) summarizes participants' characteristics. The same pseudonyms are used in both papers.

Participant	Age	Gender	Based	Details
Harry	35	M	UK	Amateur musician, consultant
Charlie	36	M	UK	Amateur musician, academic
Jacob	27	M	UK	Amateur musician, sound designer
Oliver	48	M	UK	Amateur photographer, academic
Ava	38	F	UK	Blogger/tweeter, e-learning professional
Thomas	32	M	UK	Blogger/tweeter, lobbyist
Jane	32	F	UK	Stay-at-home mum
Sophie	18	F	UK	Student embarking on a gap year
Ann	50	F	US	Tech writer, amateur musician
Kim	50	F	US	Novelist, blogger and stay-at-home mom
Lynn	37	F	US	Admin, videographer
Todd	33	M	US	Journalist, fact-checker
Mary	31	F	US	Non-profit administrator
Vincent	20	M	US	Student, math nerd

Table 1. Participants' pseudonyms and backgrounds.

The interviews were semi-structured and open-ended, and lasted between 90 minutes and 3 hours. They consisted of three segments: an online tour, a self-search exercise, and reactions to a set of design sketches for an integrated personal archive. The self-search exercise was motivated by our desire to turn up content the participant had forgotten, or was unaware of. However this portion of the interview often became multi-faceted, as the participants encountered unexpected content, and considered how they appeared to others through the lens of the SERP. Self-search data also appeared in other interview segments, primarily during online tours, e.g. when participants forgot where they had stored something, and needed to search for it explicitly.

To initiate a discussion of self-search, we asked participants if they had ever searched for themselves on the Web; all had done so for a variety of reasons. We then asked them to search for content about or by themselves as they normally would; they were able to choose the search engine, the starting point (e.g. the whole Web or a social media site like Facebook), and use input terms that seemed appropriate to them. The searches were conducted on participants' own computers, so normal personalization may have occurred. We urged them to discuss the value and appropriateness of individual results, usually through multiple results pages.

The interviews were audio-recorded and transcribed for analysis. We also collected screen snaps and photos to document portions of the interviews. To re-analyze the data, we extracted portions of the transcripts concerned with self-search, and used thematic analysis to code them and identify common themes and underlying patterns.

FINDINGS

Although the interview provoked the self-searches that we observed, our discussions with participants highlighted various circumstances in which the activity would normally occur. These ranged from self-search as a relatively common online housekeeping task, to a focused effort in preparation for an event like a job search. Self-search also fell under the rubric of more traditional information seeking tasks, like re-finding familiar content, such as a blog post the participant wrote, or discovering new material, such as commenters' reactions to that blog post.

We do not wish to make any strong claims about the regularity or frequency of self-search on the basis of our qualitative findings. Indeed, it is quite possible that participants may have forgotten specific instances of self-search, especially if it was embedded in a broader task (such as re-finding). Furthermore, since self-search is apt to carry with it a stigma of narcissism, some participants were quick to assert that for them, it was done infrequently. However, none of our participants claimed they had never tried a self-search, most seemed fairly familiar with the results, including content that was not about themselves (such as content related to doppelgangers), and some admitted to conducting regular self-searches. So while Ann said she'd last searched for herself "*years ago*", Mary said she did it "*every couple of years... to make sure there's nothing out there that I don't know about*", and Lynn who was an avid Facebook user, said "*I hate having stuff about me online*". She performed self-searches regularly.

This brief overview points to a number of different motivations for conducting self-searches. In the following, we consider in more detail what these motivations are. We also relate these to self-search strategies, since how people look for themselves online and interact with the resulting SERP is contingent on why they are doing it. Finally, we consider how searchers' motivations shape what they expect to find, and what types of results they consequently perceive as surprising. We sum up these findings in a framework that juxtaposes familiarity of the material with how and whether it can be controlled.

Self-Search Motivations

What provokes people to search for themselves? In the following, we tease apart five motivations that emerged in our analysis. We focus on the first (identity management) in particular, as this practice is associated with strategies that are distinct from other information-seeking practices; in this case the SERP may function as a form of dynamic profile. Other motivations we discuss more briefly include the need to re-find familiar content or discover new content; these are familiar tropes in the information retrieval literature (e.g. [6, 12]). We also consider self-search in the name of entertainment, and as a way of curating archival material.

Self-search in pursuit of identity management

As past research has pointed out, managing one's online presence and multiple personas is a significant and consuming endeavor [9]. Self-search may act as quality control on proflection; participants use self-search to check how well they are curating their online identities, and whether intervention is necessary. Are various personas adequately represented? Are they reasonably distinct? If a unified presentation of self is desired, is this integrated online presence available via the SERP? Finally, if circumstances have changed, is one's SERP up-to-date?

While some proflective self-searches are performed with online identity itself as the focus, others are performed prophylactically: participants place themselves in the role of a specific searcher—a prospective employer or an ex-boyfriend or girlfriend—to speculate on what that person will find. This way a person can potentially avoid exposing content they don't want the prospective searcher to see, or they can identify unwanted porosity between distinct and purposefully separate portions of an online identity.

Two aspects of proflective self-search emerged in our data: (1) managing the appearance of the SERP as a whole; and (2) identifying specific pieces of content that the participant wanted to weed out. While these aspects are inter-related, they were associated with different strategies and suggest different implications. We deal with each separately, first discussing motivations, then covering associated strategies.

Managing the appearance of the SERP as a whole. As they searched for themselves, participants reacted to the SERP as an artifact in its own right. Specifically, they seemed concerned with the relative rankings of different sites, content repetition and its effect, and doppelgangers. While these elements may be difficult to control, participants had adopted strategies to influence their SERP, especially with an eye to particular audiences.

The aspect of self-search that changed most frequently, and was often the source of some mild surprise, was the order in which the SERP presented results and the auto-complete terms the search engine suggested. Todd, a journalist, noted that although nothing was missing that he expected to see on his semi-annual self-search *("it's always been the same stuff")*, there was nevertheless "*more stuff that I would rather see higher up, like that story from China was a story that I enjoyed doing. ... It's a good example of something in my portfolio that I wish was higher.*" He went on to contrast the article he had written with other genres of material he was encountering on his SERP: "*So then when I see this weird Quora user page so prominent, or that MyLife thing, it just seems like something is not working quite correctly there. Because it's not relevant to me. And if you clicked on it, and were curious about me, I don't know how relevant it would be to somebody who wanted to find out something about me.*" Similarly, Charlie (an amateur musician) noted that his band's name did not appear as an auto-complete, saying "*that's sad.*" Like SERP position, the presence or absence of auto-complete terms was a part of participants' search engine-based identity.

A second, related, feature of the SERPs was the presence of doppelgangers. While search engine features such as Google Profiles have been introduced to support people in distinguishing themselves from their doppelgangers in search engine results [8], our analysis revealed that users have a more complex relationship with their doppelgangers than simply wishing to be separate from them. Most participants were aware of who their doppelgangers were and some were playfully competitive with them. So in addition to showing an interest in the ranking of their own content, they also pitted themselves against bartenders, homeopaths, writers and musicians who shared their names. Indeed, some participants adopted strategies to underpin this competitive element of self-search; Oliver had never searched for his full name, only entering his rather distinctive surname, which allowed him to "*compete with a curry*", as well as with his brother, to add interest to his self-search results. Doppelgangers are also essential in obscuring one's own activities. We discuss this later, as a strategy of sorts for maintaining anonymity. By contrast, doppelgangers can also stand in as a proxy for one's own presence. Jane, who did not appear on the SERP for her own name, noted "*sometimes it's quite nice to see that there's successful Jane Taylors out there doing well, I think, ah that must be a good name, a successful name.*"

Finally, participants noted that novel content can be lost or devalued through repetition (in spite of search engines' use of sophisticated duplicate detection algorithms). Ann, who like several of our other participants, had an academic persona and an artistic one, commented on the degree to which the same content recurs: "*You publish a few things, and it's just one giant echo chamber... you have to try really hard to not have a million things on the Web. Because you put one thing, and it gets copied.*"

Strategies for managing online identity. Clearly, it is difficult to control the ranking of search results, and even more so to influence the presence of doppelgangers in a SERP. However, participants did adopt various strategies in an effort to influence the SERP as a whole. These included adopting online identities that could be distinguished from prominent doppelgangers, using pseudonyms to create distinct online identities, and even embracing sites that were likely to appear high in the rankings. We consider these in turn.

Some participants specifically tailored online content that they were in control of with search in mind. Often this meant specifically curating online identities. For example, Kim had adapted her online identity to distinguish herself from a well-known actress by adding her middle name. Searching for her full name would then pull up her "*writing persona*", which meant her Amazon author's page would be included prominently in the results. Where participants wished to separate out different elements of their online activities, multiple identities were often adopted. Charlie pointed out the absence of any of his musical efforts in an initial search for his name: "*I don't have any music associated with my name. I have a different name for that, my artist's name or whatever*", and Ann used several different pseudonyms to control which sites would appear on the SERP, using "*BitBucket for the nerd persona*" and SoundCloud for her musician persona. Online identities were often managed with a specific audience in mind (e.g. prospective employers). Thus, Charlie described self-search as "*having a little look in the mirror in terms of what a potential employer's going to see, so I want to be aware of, ok if they search my name they're going to see this this this and this.*" For him, separating out his musical persona was key to managing his professional identity.

Interestingly, for some participants anonymity trumped any desire for a SERP-based online identity. Lynn said: "*I am thankful for [a woman whose name is spelled similarly], who is a jewelry designer, so when you search my name, she [comes up]. There's like three pages of [links to her pages]. I'm going, 'thank god this woman exists.'*" Her concern with anonymity was in large part motivated by the dissonance between a previous identity in the entertainment industry and her current professional identity in the corporate world: "*I make sure I don't have an online presence. Especially when some things that I work on can be misconstrued as offensive. I worked on a film called [provocative name redacted]. So if I'm job hunting and people look me up, I don't want them to say, 'oh this woman's worked in porn. Let's hire her.'*" She later clarified, "*When you're gay, you don't know. Because I always look at it from a perspective of, who's going to search for me? People who want to hire me, or work with me, or something. So I try and keep it clear. ... Because I can't control it, and I'm reliant on somebody else's belief system.*"

Some participants saw embracing social media as a way of having some control over the way a SERP appears. Because certain social media sites were apt to appear high in the rankings, using them to curate a presence meant that a self-search would produce content that was under their control, and would represent them in a satisfactory way. Ava commented, "*If you use social media in the right way then if someone searches for you, you can make sure that the results that they find are about you and not about someone else, and therefore you are in control of it*". By making public the profiles she was happy for her professional peers to see (such as Twitter), while hiding others (such as Facebook) from search results, she felt in control of the image she was presenting via the SERP related to her name.

Similarly, Thomas invested heavily in his own website, preferring to put content there as a way of participating in debates about local issues, rather than on other forums or blogs. This was partially about retaining control of the content, and partially about building up his own "*asset*" rather than adding value to someone else's. "*I'll write it on my site and link to it and that's mainly about having control over it and getting the search results, so if I've written something interesting then people may as well come and read it on my site.*" His view of the SERP was "*if I didn't have my own website then it wouldn't look like that would it? So there is definitely a reason for having a website of your own [... and] another reason for having a Twitter feed.*"

As a final strategy in managing a SERP-as-profile, some participants sought to avoid personalized results, since they felt they would be misled about what others would see. Although several participants were aware of personalization and disliked it, they were uncertain how to turn it off. Todd said, "*I don't know whether it's set right now. I think it might be the default...*" and Kim said, "*But Google's strange, because it will pull up things you've already pulled before. ... I don't know what normal people would see.*"

Weeding out unwanted personal content. Presenting a coherent identity—either as a unified person or as an activity-centered persona—via a SERP is difficult. Participants relied on certain sites being visible only to certain audiences as a way of preserving their privacy in an online (and very public) space. Making sure there were no rogue elements within a SERP entailed weeding out unwanted content, and this meant a robust approach to search. Unlike traditional information-seeking where the SERP is abandoned if the desired content isn't found on the first few pages, participants went deep into the search results and often repeated searches using different modifiers, as a way of doing a form of what Charlie termed "*auditing*". Important types of unwanted content included social network sites that unexpectedly showed up in search results, pages that aggregators constructed about participants from multiple sources, and references to past careers and deeds that participants would prefer to forget, particularly in the form of photos.

Even those participants who used social network sites carefully and with a view to enhancing their SERP were sometimes surprised by what search engines presented to them. Ava, who noted that controlling social media means a degree of control over the SERP itself, was surprised to find Pinterest near the top of her SERP. She described it as "*completely different from anything else that I do online ... I don't even know if I would really like to engage either my friends or my professional contacts, because it is just really housewifey.*" She left the website open as a reminder to herself to change the privacy settings once the interview was finished. Other boundaries between distinct online identities also revealed themselves to be too porous for comfort. Ann found her "real" and "hacker" personas mixed "*because I 'liked' the hacker dojo*" on Facebook, and Ava discovered an aggregation site that seemed to draw content from pages that she had 'liked' on Facebook (which was itself hidden from the SERP). This left her wondering if she should 'unlike' the pages within Facebook, so as to prevent this apparent information leak. Aggregation sites, which compile and mix results from different sources (including among others, telephone book listings, property records, court records, blogs, and social media profiles and status postings) were notable in the way they surprised and often disturbed the participants. They were perceived as interfering with the construction of multiple coherent identities, since they drew together content that was normally kept distinct [3], and as compromising privacy, since they dip into public data that was normally obscure or difficult to obtain, and so violate participants' expectations of privacy through obscurity [11,27].

Participants frequently remarked on how many aggregators they had seen, the mysterious sources of their information, and whether they would be apt to use one of them. A few participants had ignored the aggregator sites in the past, and so the interview was their first real encounter with their content. For Kim, it was PeekYou: "*Oh, and it's me, isn't it? What is it? I guess I could click on it. I've never seen it.*" Todd, who was fairly tolerant of the aggregators' information practices, explained his ambivalence: "*You'll see these kind of weird companies that seem to suck up information.... Actually I'm curious. 'Create a free account to see all 2 results.' Or sign in with one of my social network links. Facebook. Twitter. I have no desire to do that. ... location [redacted]. That's where I went to college. So I haven't lived there in almost 10 years. They just pulled some stuff from my website it looks like. Or maybe not from my website. ... So this doesn't make me want to give them my information and sign up as a useful resource ... People must.*"

Paradoxically, participants felt that the sites' inaccuracies and out-of-date information were also a problem. For example, Charlie referred to "*ancient*" information in Zoominfo and Ann noted, "*What am I doing in France? All my domains are still around.*" The sites routinely misidentified their subjects, mixing hard-won identities with those of doppelgangers. After Lynn clicked on a SERP link to 123movies.info, she was disturbed to see not only her picture and text from her IMDB page, but also a photo of two people she did not recognize; a 2007 newspaper page; a 1965 yearbook page; and a photo of a tour group. Unfamiliar content had been mixed with important identity surrogates: "*This must've been pulled from IMDB. I don't know. I have no idea where they would've gotten this photo. MySpace or Facebook before I made it secure. ... I have no idea who these people are. ... And the class of 1965—I'm definitely not in the class of 1965.*"

Finally, and most importantly, the aggregators seem to violate emerging social norms, which acknowledge that you should have control over certain elements of your online identity, and reciprocity principles (people are given information that they would not willingly supply to others). Participants were explicitly aware of these violations. With a sense of outrage, Lynn reported: "*So this one [search result] even has my dad's house from 10, 15 years ago, and my school. See? I just hate these sites. They just make me mad. They're just mining, mining, mining. Like, oh, there are my parents. Y'know. What's your father's middle name, that's a security question on bank accounts. It's so irritating.*" Even during the interview, she began writing email to say, *'stop posting crap about me.'*

Strategies for finding unwanted content. Our findings illustrate some of the difficulties of controlling unwanted content. Participants were not always sure about the sources of leaks, or how to discover more without revealing more. They did, however, show a range of strategies that differ from typical information seeking in pursuing this content. These included diving deep (multiple pages) into the SERP, performing image searches, and trying to check up on content that may or may not have expired.

Information seeking research has long established that Internet searchers usually do not go beyond the first page or two of results [12]. By contrast, self-search appears to be one instance in which multiple SERP pages are viewed; this exception may well be a manifestation of the fact that self-search is usually performed surmising the eyes of others. Although our self-search exercise was artificial, participants seemed to be familiar with results that occurred quite far down in the rankings (if participants seemed engaged by self-search results, we allowed them to keep going through them until they stopped of their own accord).

In addition to going deep into the results, some participants also adapted their searches to focus on media types of particular concern, usually photos. Four participants called out image search as an important component of their self-search strategies. Mary perceived Google image search as an easy technique to reveal things that had gone awry and to quickly turn up content that was difficult to find with normal Web search. She told us, "*I love image search. Because this is easy. I don't have to dig. I can do an image search, and nope! That's not me. It's very efficient. I can see if I've been linked in any blogs or anything like that. Now I feel safe.*" Kim also performed image searches on herself, although as a blogger, she found this technique far less efficient than Mary did: "*The other thing that I do once in a while that kind of disturbs me more if I do a search for myself and then do images. That one, sometimes there's some strange stuff. I mean, it's fascinating that it knows [that it's me]. So it pulls up a lot of stuff that I put on my blog. So obviously Abraham Lincoln is not me.*"

Another aspect of auditing one's online presence may involve tailoring searches. This was especially the case for participants with common names and a minimal Internet presence, and for some, finding any content about themselves proved tricky. Jane said, "*I just don't come up [in the SERP] .. and then if I do [enters a tailored search term] .. if you put 'Jane Taylor University of [name redacted]' I came up on the Contact Us page for my department, which isn't really surprising*". Another of Jane's strategies was to enter the search term 'Jane Taylor Facebook', as she expected that if any further content would come up, it would be linked to the social networking site. Other participants searched within sites like Facebook and Flickr, or commented on other portals. Sophie noted, "*I wouldn't expect it to come up if I just typed in my name, but at school cos I was involved in drama a lot I wouldn't be surprised if something came up about plays and things like that, cos in school we have our own Facebook called [name redacted] .. but that was all private*".

In summary, when self-search plays a role in identity management, the SERP is often interpreted holistically as a form of profile. Because users do not have direct control over the SERP's appearance, strategies to influence it are usually indirect, through engaging with social media sites or investing in one's own website. The presence of doppelgangers can be interpreted in a variety of ways, from playful competitors to useful cover, and were in general received much more positively than other peripheral search results, such as aggregation sites, which seemed to pollute one's online identity, often by conflating online identities or by revealing irrelevant (but personal) details.

Self-search for discovery

A second motivation for self-search was to discover new content, often in connection with user-generated media. This content may be in the form of comments on or reviews of creative efforts; the search may also be performed to find reuse or even plagiarism. Discovery searches might be performed fairly frequently if the participant has reason to believe that there might be interesting new content.

Reactions to creative efforts. Participants involved in creative efforts were on the lookout for reviews and listings of their output (although they might be wary of running into negative reviews). Kim reported digging deeply into the SERP via self-search (in addition to searching by her book's title) to find new reviews when her novel was first released: "*Especially when my book first came out [I searched for myself], to see what reviews were coming up on it. And what people are saying and stuff. It's been a year-and-a-half now so sales are much slower. And so there's not much action. Or change. And so I don't tend to do it as much.*" Similarly, Charlie said he kept an eye out for people discussing his band's music and performances "*...sometimes I've searched for like [band name redacted], or if I've played a gig recently maybe search on Twitter, see if there's anything…*" In fact, even those participants who were concerned with the stigma of self-search allowed themselves discovery searches. For example, Harry said: "*… the only time I've ever searched for myself online was when I searched for [band name redacted] online, so that was good to look for reviews and gig listings and stuff … it would be the only way I'd know that a particular website would be advertising our gig, so that was quite good …*"

Reuse of self-generated content. For participants who posted content they had created online, self-search had the additional motive of discovering and tracking reuse. If reuse verged on plagiarism, or was done without the desired permission, participants were sometimes angered, and motivated to track down the offender. Oliver recounted the reuse of his photos (a common practice—see [18]) with and without permission: "*Some of them- the photographs, mostly people have asked, but I've occasionally- for example, when Northern Rock [a UK bank] crashed, I took a picture of the queue, and that was ripped off and used without commission in blogs.*" He had also noted an instance of reuse for a set of PowerPoint slides, a practice which he usually attempted to thwart by disseminating PDF files: "*…I went to give a presentation. I can't remember if they asked or if they [just posted the slides]. Especially in PowerPoint format. I'm not so keen on that. ...If I go and give a talk, normally I would give them a PDF version ... But stuff just leaks, and sometimes that gets, you know, reused without the credit and so on.*"

Strategies for discovery. Because discovery is a standard information-seeking activity, it is perhaps better supported than examining the SERP as a profile. Two strategies stand out in this regard, alerts and image search. Although alerts may be associated with self-search (the Pew survey notes that this is an uncommon practice for maintaining one's digital footprint [16]), among our participants, alerts were generally employed in a discovery function. Image searches on the other hand served several different functions.

Alert tools in our study included Google Alerts, although some participants were content to use alerts for specific services, such as Twitter or Facebook, where they felt they were most likely to be discussed or tagged. Jane described her feelings towards a (now retired) Facebook feature, in which a selection of recent photos appeared at the top of the profile page: "*especially now the new Facebook's got like horrid pictures of you in your profile page, I feel like I need to keep going online and checking that there's not really awful pictures there showing in that top band…*". Other participants focused on references to their websites from other sites. Thomas described, "*… I will go and have a look and see how [my website] has been linked in [from other sites] and sometimes I will comment on sort of how it has been described.*"

In addition to the role we discussed earlier in weeding out undesirable content from the SERP, image search also helped participants track reuse. Of course, participants who were amateur photographers were anxious to check the use of their photos, but image search also proved to be an easy way of understanding how ideas proliferated and were adapted by others. For example, Oliver was interested to watch how some of his diagrams propagated within his own academic community: "*If you search on my thing, which is [topic redacted], say, and go to Google Images. ... That's mine. And then this is an adaptation of mine, so it's kind of interesting to see how it propagates – how people take one and then adapt it.*"

In summary, self-search is a means for discovering content about oneself, undertaken especially when the searcher expects to find reviews of or responses to content they have published online, or when they wish to understand how their content propagates through the web.

Self-search for re-finding

A third motivation for self-search is to return to content one has published or shared online, either as an intentional effort (e.g. a scholarly paper, a photo, or music) or as a smaller digital trace that refers to something else (e.g. a blog comment or product review). Charlie said, "*sometimes I'm searching my name so I can get to a paper, because maybe I don't have a copy.*" On the other end of the spectrum, Kim described searching for her own comments to recover facts she had found; these comments would be difficult to retrieve by other means. The searches also had the advantage of returning her writing in context: "*And I've noticed that if I post a lot on [a local blog], I actually want to go back and retrieve comments [that I've written]. Like I'll do research, and I'll say, dah-dah-dah. And later I'll think, what did I dig up in that research? I will actually go into Google and search for my name on [the local blog] and whatever the topic was and I'll find my previous post.*"

Re-finding familiar content is described in greater detail as an information-seeking activity in [6].

Self-search for entertainment

A fourth motivation we wish to highlight briefly is self-search for entertainment. This was described by a minority of participants, but we include it to emphasize that not all self-search is connected with serious endeavors. Indeed even earnest self-search might be concealed to some measure under the auspices of curiosity, and may feature aspects of playfulness as participants compete with their doppelgangers for SERP position and rediscover forgotten content. But further to these, some self-searches were undertaken explicitly for fun. Sophie commented on a practice that she and her friends had adopted: "*if you're just with a group of friends or something, or on the iPad, just lazing around, then quite often people just Google everyone in the room and see what comes up.*" Image search was a key part of this activity, possibly since images are easier to browse and are more entertaining to view as a group.

The archival value of self-search

A final aspect of self-search worth mentioning is the discovery of forgotten content. Participants did not necessarily describe searching with this goal in mind, so it is difficult to characterize as a motivation. However, it was notable that some participants found content that was truly unexpected. While in some cases this content was somewhat trivial ("*So I have two SoundCloud accounts because one I made when I forgot that I had the other one. [laughs]*" – Ann), others were more meaningful. For example, Charlie came across reviews of a track he had remixed a year ago but subsequently forgotten, and Lynn found a haiku she had written for a contest (and won), again less than a year before: "*This is the haiku contest I won this past Christmas! This I don't mind. I wrote a haiku about fruitcake, and I got an honorable mention.*"

DISCUSSION AND IMPLICATIONS

When we look across the range of motivations for self-search, focusing in particular on the SERP as a dynamic profile of the participant, we can pull out two dimensions that are salient to our goal of improving self-search: *controllability* and *expectedness*. By controllability, we mean the ability to intervene in and change what is out there, either directly or by changing one's online behavior; by expectedness, we are referring to whether the participant has seen the material before, and whether they know how it got there (its source and provenance). While we might tease out other dimensions, we are choosing to focus on these two because they bear on both technology and policy.

Controllable and expected content may arise through social media, or through Web publishing. For example, people may post public Instagram photos on their own accounts; they may create Facebook profiles that come up high on the SERP; or they may publish public comments on blog posts. The self-searcher expects to see these items, and can take them down or mark them private at will.

Next are controllable, but unexpected, items: for example, candid photos may be taken by a friend, put on Facebook, and tagged. Once the self-searcher is aware of this content, it can be untagged or similarly rendered less visible via the SERP. On the other hand, if the unexpected material is flattering, the self-searcher might find it desirable to push it further up in the SERP. However, in this category, we also find social media material the self-searcher expected to be private through obscurity, but which somehow has become visible (Facebook 'likes' are notorious in this regard).

Uncontrollable expected content stems from recent data practices. For example, some public records (arrests, phone listings, address databases) have become accessible online, and have found their way onto SERPs. In the US, services such as BlockShopper publish public real estate records such as home sales history and neighborhood information; Zoopla offers an equivalent service in the UK. Even content that self-searchers had a hand in creating may not fall under their direct control (e.g. media published on a collaborator's SoundCloud account), simply due to circumstances. This type of material may figure prominently if it is not outranked by other kinds of content.

Uncontrollable and unexpected content can be the result of old data being posted online. Forgotten content such as Usenet posts and articles in newspaper archives falls under this rubric, as do aggregator results (which may or may not be controllable through social means), current reviews, and other types of published material.

Framing an Audience-Directed SERP

As our framework shows, being in control of online content about oneself is a multifaceted problem that appears not to be completely solvable; even participants who had relatively sophisticated online and self-search practices were occasionally surprised by apparent information leaks. However, the controllability dimension does suggest some implications for design, which draw in particular on the idea of the SERP viewed holistically, as a kind of profile page. In particular, the idea of *building* a SERP that presents a desirable (or at least acceptable) face, in addition to attempting to *weed out* isolated pieces of content that in fact the user has little control over, is key to our recommendations here. We are aware of different types of sophisticated services which assist users in manipulating their SERPs (e.g. reputation.com) or in creating a coherent online identity (e.g. claimID.com), but we use our results to explore a few lightweight approaches.

First of all, we highlight the potential for control over the order of social media content. It seems mutually beneficial for search engine providers and end-users to have relevant social media content appear highest on a person's SERP. Thus, giving users some control over the order of search results that relate specifically to themselves (e.g. specifying the order in which Twitter and LinkedIn appear) is one possibility. The SERP may also be tailored for a specific audience. If the person conducting a search is connected to the target through a shorter path on Twitter or LinkedIn, perhaps these sites could be prioritized; thus a friend would see different results than a prospective employer. Stretching this idea further, users might be permitted to perform a kind of "reverse personalization," tailoring the results of a search for themselves to meet the needs of different imagined searchers, such as family members vs. colleagues. Of course, this relies on the search engine's ability to accurately categorize searchers, but relationships that have been specified through social networks may allow users to dictate preferences here. For example, Facebook friends could also be presented with Pinterest or Instagram feeds in a SERP, whereas these could be hidden from people who are only connected via LinkedIn. Finally, the existence of relationships through social network sites may also act as a pointer to who is being searched for when doppelgangers are present, enabling friends to find selected content, while also supporting the general anonymity through obscurity that some users also valued.

Secondly, we highlight awareness of content that one is nominally in control of but that has the potential to 'leak'. Stutzman and Kramer-Duffield have explored the sources of Facebook users' expectations about these boundaries [24]. For example, when participants sign up for social network sites, they rarely expect their content to be visible to aggregator services, even though they have unwittingly exposed it. This becomes even more problematic because these sites frequently mix online identities that have been curated as separate. Allowing users to work backwards and identify privacy settings that underpin such leaks would help them understand the actual effects of their choices and would help them refine specific settings (e.g. by using real data exposure to say, "I think everybody should be able to see this, but not this"). Such episodes could be used as a provocation for sending messages to social network contacts who have posted undesirable content, or to reveal the sources of public data that aggregators draw upon. Thus, users would be aided in adjusting privacy options where control is permitted, and reaching a better understanding of the leaks' source where it is not. Of course, some aggregation services are unlikely to reveal their sources. However, presenting details in the SERP that allow inferences to be drawn could be useful; for example, specifying when a site obtained a photo could imply which social network site is responsible for the leak.

For content that is completely beyond one's control, being able to put some kind of "watch" on it would at least remove the need to continually dig deep into the search results to see if it persists or has been altered. In instances where content is deeply undesirable or compromises security, bids for removal that do not require the provision of further details seem essential. Finally, some of these public data sources of what is perceived to be private data become a matter of policy, not technology.

The Process of Self-Search

The above discussion brings to the fore how the results of self-search can be used. However, the process of self-search is also worth considering in design. While search is typically cast as something that produces results, rather than something with an experiential aspect, this is clearly not the case here (and indeed, recent research points to the potential for richer design around search in general [5]).

Our results suggest four ways to support the process of self-search: (1) assist in query formulation (to help people distinguish themselves from their doppelgangers and to find unexpected content); (2) show changes in the SERP over time (e.g. webpages' relative rankings); (3) present results organized around specific content; and (4) reveal the effects of personalization. In the first case, some participants' self-search strategies (e.g. 'Jane Taylor Facebook') simply turn up familiar content, but novel results can be important, as demonstrated by participants' enthusiasm when they found unexpected content they had created themselves. Secondly, changes in the SERP over time might help users identify the source of information leaks, draw comparisons with their doppelgangers, discover the progress (both desired and not) of various pages in the rankings, and know how long unwanted content has been present for. Our third suggestion capitalizes on users' interest in how specific pieces of content, such as mp3 files or photos, have been reused, commented upon, or have otherwise attracted attention. Finally, the effects of personalization are important to self-search, yet most users don't know how to control them. Not only do they want to turn personalization off, but they also want to ask questions like, "what would people professionally connected to me see?" Such features are similar to those used by businesses in managing their online presence, but our results suggest that everyday users may also find such content of interest.

The presence of doppelgangers represents an interesting instance whereby results that are largely irrelevant to a search may enrich the experience. There was an element of competition here that could be played upon, for example by showing how search rankings change over time. But we also saw genuine interest in who these people were and how well they were doing in their own lives. The fact that some of our participants appreciated the anonymity provided by their doppelgangers means that simply excluding them from a SERP would be a mistake. Interestingly, this may be an instance whereby if search results could be wholly accurate, for example by using separate 'entities' for doppelgangers, the shift may not be appreciated. This suggests that, on the one hand, users may value a SERP that contains doppelgangers and makes their relative rankings clear; on the other, being alerted to the presence of new content, and drawing together content that is about the user as some form of dashboard, which shows where it is hosted, if it has been reused or tagged, and even if it has disappeared, may be valuable.

CONCLUSION

Self-search is a practice that is usefully distinguished from other types of information seeking. Our results show that the activity typically stems from a handful of distinct motivations, and raises new concerns. We look in particular at the SERP as a form of dynamic profile, one that might make productive use of elements like doppelgangers, and might highlight unwanted porosity between personas and stand as a straw man that exposes privacy vulnerabilities. In so doing, we examine ways in which the SERP can be made more useful for the self-searcher, as well as to the self-searcher's imagined audience.

ACKNOWLEDGMENTS

We are grateful to our patient participants and to Richard Banks, Abigail Sellen and Tim Regan, who were part of the research team that designed the study described here.

REFERENCES

1. Beal, A. and Strauss, J. *Radically Transparent: Monitoring and Managing Reputations Online*. Wiley, Indianapolis, 2008.
2. Bich, V., Gerasoulis, A. and Glover, E. Systems and methods for predicting if a query is a name. US Patent, 11 October 2007. http://www.google.com/patents/US20070239735. Accessed 7 January 2014.
3. boyd, d. and Crawford, K. *Six provocations for big data*. Oxford Internet Institute, 21 September, 2011.
4. Claypoole, T. and Payton, T. *Protecting Your Internet Identity*. Rowman & Littlefield, Lanham, 2012.
5. Dörk, M., Carpendale, S. and Williamson, C. The information flaneur: A fresh look at information seeking. *Proc. CHI 2011*, ACM (2011), 1215-1224.
6. Dumais, S., Cutrell, E., Cadiz, J.J., Jancke, G., Sarin, R. and Robbins, D. Stuff I've Seen: A system for personal information retrieval and re-use. In *Proc. SIGIR 2003*, ACM (2003), 72-79.
7. Gehl, R. Ladders, samurai, and blue collars: Personal branding in Web 2.0. *First Monday 16*, 9 (2011).
8. Google Profiles. http://www.google.com/+/learnmore/profile. Accessed 7 January 2014.
9. Gross, B. Names of our lives. In *Proc. CSE 2009*, IEEE (2009), 747–752.
10. Henry, A. How to clean up your online presence and make a great first impression. *Lifehacker*, 28 November 2012. http://lifehacker.com/5963864. Accessed 7 January 2014.
11. Herzog, W. and Stutzman, F. The case for online obscurity, *California Law Review 101*, (2013), 1-35.
12. Jansen, B., Spink, A. and Saracevic, T. Real life, real users, and real needs: A study and analysis of user queries on the Web. *IP&M 36*, 2 (2000), 207-227.
13. Jones, R., Kuman, R., Pang, B. and Tomkins, A. Vanity fair: Privacy in querylog bundles. In *Proc. CIKM 2008*, ACM (2008), 853-862.
14. Jones, W. and Teevan, J., eds. *Personal Information Management*. UW Press, Washington, 2007.
15. Lindley, S., Marshall, C.C., Banks, R., Sellen, A. and Regan, T. Rethinking the web as a personal archive. In *Proc. WWW 2013*, (2013), 749-760.
16. Madden, M. and Smith, A. *Reputation Management and Social Media*. Pew Internet & American Life Project, 26 May 2010.
17. Marchionini, G. *Information Concepts: from Books to Cyberspace Identities*. Morgan & Claypool, 2011.
18. Marshall, C.C. and Shipman, F. The ownership and reuse of visual media. In *Proc. JCDL 2011*, ACM (2011), 157-166.
19. Mayfield, A. *Me and My Web Shadow: How to Manage Your Reputation Online*. A&C Black Publishers, 2010.
20. Nicolai, T., Kirchhoff, L., Bruns, A., Wilson, J. and Saunders, B. The self-Googling phenomenon: Investigating the performance of personalized information resources. *First Monday 14*, 12 (2009).
21. Odom, W., Zimmerman, J. and Forlizzi, J. 2011. Teenagers and their virtual possessions: design opportunities and issues. In *Proc. CHI 2011*, ACM (2011), 1491-1500.
22. Pash, A. Order free Google business cards for a limited time. Lifehacker. 1 May 2009. http://lifehacker.com/5236055/order-free-google-profile-business-cards-for-a-limited-time. Accessed 7 January 2014.
23. Soghoian, C. The problem of anonymous vanity searches. *ISJLP 3*, 2 (2007), 297-316.
24. Stutzman F. and Kramer-Duffield, J. Friends only: Examining a privacy-enhancing behavior in Facebook. In *Proc. CHI 2010*, ACM (2010), 1553-1562.
25. Trapani, G. Forget the business card. Just Google me. *HBR Blog Network*, 10 August 2009. http://blogs.hbr.org/trapani/2009/08/forget-the-business-cardjust-g.html. Accessed 7 January 2014.
26. Yao, T., Zhang, M., Liu, Y., Ma, S. and Ru, L. Empirical Study on Rare Query Characteristics. In *Proc. WI-IAT 2011*, Vol. 1. IEEE (2011), 7-14.
27. Zimmer, M. Privacy on planet Google: Using the theory of contextual integrity to clarify the privacy threats of Google's quest for the perfect search engine. *J. Bus. & Tech. Law 109*, 3 (2008), 109.

Finder Highlights: Field Evaluation and Design of an Augmented File Browser

Stephen Fitchett
Dept. of Computer Science
University of Canterbury
Christchurch, New Zealand
saf75@cosc.canterbury.ac.nz

Andy Cockburn
Dept. of Computer Science
University of Canterbury
Christchurch, New Zealand
andy@cosc.canterbury.ac.nz

Carl Gutwin
Dept. of Computer Science
University of Saskatchewan
Saskatoon, Canada
gutwin@cs.usask.ca

ABSTRACT

Navigating to files through a hierarchy is often a slow, laborious, and repetitive task. Recent lab studies showed that file browser interface augmentations, such as Icon Highlights and Search Directed Navigation [15], have the potential to reduce file retrieval times. However, for this potential to be realised in actual systems, further study is necessary to address two important issues. First, there are important design and implementation challenges in advancing the research prototypes previously evaluated into complete interactive systems that can be used for real work. Second, it is unknown how real users would employ these systems while engaged in actual work; would the potential performance improvements suggested by the earlier lab studies be realised? We therefore describe the design, implementation, and longitudinal field study evaluation of Finder Highlights, a file browser plugin for the OS X 'Finder' that adds support for Icon Highlights and Search Directed Navigation. Study results confirm that the augmentations are effective in reducing real-world file retrieval times, with retrieval times 13% faster when using Finder Highlights compared to the standard tool (10.6 s versus 12.2 s), while also emphasising important differences between lab and field studies. In summary, the paper strongly suggests that large-scale deployment of interface augmentations to file browsers, particularly Icon Highlights, will have a marked effect in improving users' real-world file retrieval.

Author Keywords

File navigation; prediction; file retrieval; revisitation

ACM Classification Keywords

H.5.2 User Interfaces: Theory and methods

INTRODUCTION

Every day, millions of computer users retrieve files from their file systems. Although there are many interface techniques for retrieving files, such as search tools and recent file lists, studies have shown that the predominant method of access is to navigate through a hierarchy using a file browser [3].

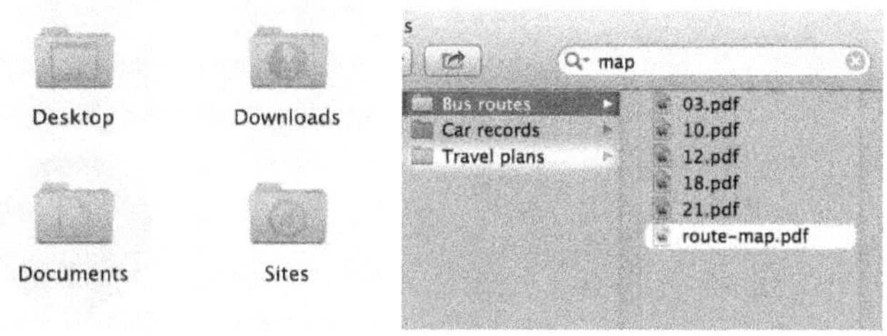

(a) Icon Highlights (b) Search Directed Navigation

Figure 1: Icon Highlights and Search Directed Navigation, as implemented in Finder Highlights. Highlighted items are those most likely to be accessed next (IH, as yellow circles) or those that match the search query (SDN, as white cutouts).

Importantly, this frequent activity of navigating to a file is known to be slow, typically taking 12-17 seconds per retrieval [6]. There is therefore a pressing need and opportunity for interfaces that improve navigation-based file retrieval.

Previous work introduced two such interface techniques, called Icon Highlights (IH) and Search Directed Navigation (SDN) [15]. IH visually emphasises files and folders in the browser that are predicted to be more likely to be chosen, based on their access history. SDN also highlights items, but does so based on their match to a filename query explicitly typed by the user. Both techniques are designed to augment the normal behaviour of a file browser interface, with the highlighting intended to reduce visual search time for salient targets at each level of the hierarchy. For example, with SDN, if the user types "Spain", the folder "Countries" would be highlighted, as would the target "Spain" once "Countries" was opened. As summarised later in the paper, an important part of the design objective for IH and SDN is to maintain and augment the key benefits of navigation-based retrieval, which allows users to take a series of reliable steps towards their target by moving through the hierarchy.

A lab study of Icon Highlights and Search Directed Navigation demonstrated their strong potential [15]. Participants performed navigation-based file retrievals much more quickly when using IH and SDN than when using a standard, non-augmented file browser. Subjective preferences also strongly favoured IH and SDN.

These findings are important in suggesting the potential for improving a core interaction that is used many times a day by most computer users. However, the results only demonstrate a *potential* – they improved performance when used in a lab setting that applied several experimental constraints.

Factors that limit the external validity of the findings, or that raise risks to generalisability, include both technical aspects of system behaviour and methodological constraints.

On the technical side, the evaluated browser augmentations were intentionally rudimentary, and they limited interaction to only the key interface features under study. They therefore excluded many of the interface components that would normally be present in a file browser, such as the following:

1. *Tools* – the evaluated systems eliminated navigation tools normally available in real file browsers, such as shortcuts, search features, buttons to go 'back' or 'up', etc.
2. *Views* – the evaluated systems permitted only a single-window icon view, whereas real file browsers allow extensive view configuration, including file trees, list details, thumbnails, and so on.
3. *Integration of IH and SDN* – a real-world file browser might be expected to support both IH and SDN, but the evaluated systems separated their support.
4. *Naïve back-end algorithms* – the evaluated systems made unrealistic simplifying assumptions to enable prediction of upcoming file selections.

On the methodological side, as with any lab study, aspects of the empirical methodology constrained external validity:

1. *Artificial and Static File Hierarchy* – the study used an artificial file hierarchy of static content, which differed from the user's real file system in terms of size, structure, content, and importantly, familiarity.
2. *Revisitation Patterns* – participants were required to repeatedly revisit files within a short experiment, creating unrealistically dense revisitations.
3. *Task Stimuli* – rather than retrieving files when needed for actual work, participants retrieved them in response to a filename cue, when other cues may be more realistic [7].

Our intention is not to criticise the previous study. We believe it used an appropriate method for determining the potential of IH and SDN. However, these technological challenges and methodological issues need to be addressed before the potential of these systems can be realised in actual interactive systems. We therefore describe the design, implementation and longitudinal evaluation of a real-world file browser supporting Icon Highlights and Search Directed Navigation. Called 'Finder Highlights', the system is a plugin to Finder, the standard OS X file browser. Finder Highlights was evaluated in a four-week longitudinal study of real use. Results confirm that the techniques can improve file retrieval times and are subjectively preferred over standard techniques. Analysis of file retrieval performance shows that retrieval times when using Finder Highlights (mean 10.6 s) were 13% faster than retrievals accomplished without it (mean 12.2s). However, many participants did not use SDN, associating it with rarely-used search interfaces. This distinction between favourable lab study results for SDN (where all participants employed its features and benefited from them) and the field study results (where many participants ignored it) validates our motivation for the study. The finding also corroborates several prior studies showing that lab studies often produce more positive results than field studies [9, 11, 18, 26].

The primary contribution of this paper is positive field study results for Finder Highlights, particularly those that demonstrate the effectiveness of IH in supporting real work. Secondary contributions include important methodological observations on the difference between prior lab results and results in the field, as well as design and algorithmic extensions to IH and SDN for use in a real-world file browser.

BACKGROUND

There is extensive prior literature on file retrieval. This includes studies of how users organise and retrieve both physical (e.g., [21]) and computer files (e.g., [25, 2], the performance impact of hierarchical structure (e.g., [10, 5]), and analysis of the use of enhanced interfaces, such as search, for file retrieval (e.g., [2, 3, 7, 8]). Although there has been extensive research on personal information management and file retrieval, including substantial improvements in the area of search systems, recent studies show that file navigation – the process of traversing through a file hierarchy in order to obtain a file – remains the dominant method for retrieving files [2, 3, 8]. Bergman [3] offers four explanations for this preference: 1) it is consistent and reliable; 2) it is cognitively lightweight, in that users can rely on recognition to identify folders and files, rather than having to recall a file name; 3) the retrieval processes of pointing and clicking may become partially automated with experience; and 4) the use of a hierarchical structure may reflect real-world relationships, assisting sense-making. Other retrieval methods, such as search, while valuable when needed, are often used as methods of 'last resort' when navigation-based retrieval fails [3, 25], in part due to their higher cognitive load [4].

The following subsections briefly review three key area of related work: the use of predictive highlighting in user interfaces; the interface augmentations for file navigation that motivated this work; and an algorithm for predicting upcoming user actions in user interfaces.

Predictive Highlighting

Considerable previous research has explored predictive highlighting, for example to highlight commands [16, 23], menu items [13], document locations [1] and files [24, 15]. Its use has also been suggested to support email revisitation [12].

The success of highlighting interfaces has been mixed. While they have often been beneficial (e.g., [1, 15, 24]), other studies have shown them to provide little benefit (e.g., [13, 16]). Possible reasons for these differing levels of success include conflicts between highlight appearance and other use of colour [13], how effectively users can predict highlights [29], how much additional information highlights provide [23] (for example, benefits may be lower for spatially consistent interfaces), and the level of prediction accuracy [13].

Icon Highlights, HoverMenus, Search Directed Navigation

Fitchett et al. [15] described three interface augmentations for file browsers, called Icon Highlights, Hover Menus, and Search Directed Navigation. These augmentations addressed three particular performance constraints of the file retrieval task: *visual search constraint*, the need to visually search for an item among those displayed in each folder view; *levels constraint*, the need to take an explicit user action at every level of the hierarchy; and *practice constraint*, the limitation on performance improvement across successive retrievals.

Icon Highlights (Figure 1a) is designed to ease the visual search constraint by highlighting items that are predicted to be more likely for upcoming access. Highlight prominence is based on the score from a predictive algorithm (called AccessRank, described below), normalised based on the maximum score of items in the same folder and by the size of the folder's access history. Items that are predicted to be more likely are consequently highlighted more prominently than others. The number of highlighted items in a folder is limited to promote visual saliency.

Hover Menus (not shown) are designed to ease the levels constraint by allowing users to bypass intervening hierarchical levels and jump directly to predicted items. A pop-up menu on every folder icon provides this shortcut access.

Search Directed Navigation (Figure 1b) is designed to ease the practice constraint by bringing some of the benefits of file navigation to the results of search queries. When the user types a query with SDN, the system highlights items that match the query or contain descendants that match the query. The design intention is to help users learn the navigation-based methods for future retrievals of the same file. SDN used two highlight levels: a prominent highlight for previously visited matched items and their ancestors, and a dim highlight for previously unvisited matches.

Each of these augmentations was separately evaluated in a single lab study, with a non-augmented file browser used as a baseline comparator. Experimental tasks involved navigating through an artificially-generated file hierarchy to repeatedly select one of ten different target files. To reduce extraneous experimental factors, the file hierarchy was constructed so that all folders at a given level contained the same number of items, and all folder content was displayed without scrolling.

Experimental results showed that all three interfaces improved file retrieval times in comparison to the standard file browser. Subjective preferences and workload measures also favoured the augmented interfaces. Icon Highlights was particularly efficient when retrieving previously visited files in an unstable view (as occurs, for example, when icon views are reflowed to match a changing window configuration). SDN was the most preferred method overall, and was ranked as being the least frustrating and requiring the least effort. Hover Menus, while preferred to the standard browser, was rated as the most mentally demanding of the three augmentations.

AccessRank

The AccessRank algorithm [14] predicts upcoming user actions based on past actions. Specifically designed for deployment within user interfaces, AccessRank emphasises both accuracy and stability of results over time. The need for stability stems from the expertise benefits that users gain when interface elements remain in predictable spatial locations [10].

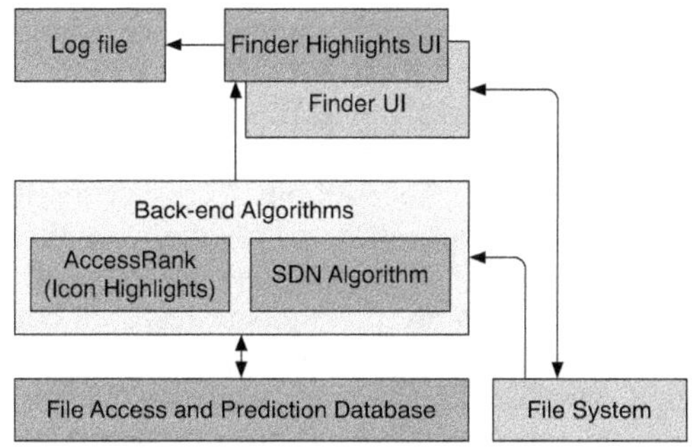

Figure 2: High-level architecture of Finder Highlights. Grey cells represent system components, blue cells represent parts of Finder Highlights, and arrows indicate information flow.

AccessRank calculates a score for each item by multiplying together several weighted values, with the weighting determined by a parameter. These values include a *Markov weight*, based on Markov chains [22] (a statistical model of events over time), as well as a *Combined Recency and Frequency* (CRF) weight [19], which efficiently considers every past access of an item with a bias towards more recent accesses.

AccessRank results are normally ranked by score, however, to facilitate prediction stability, two items can only swap places in subsequent rankings if the score of the lower-ranked item exceeds that of the higher ranked item by a required amount.

BASELINE FINDER USAGE DATA

Before developing Finder Highlights, we conducted a four-week field study that logged details of Finder usage. This study was originally used to characterise file retrieval activities. In this paper we further use these logs to calibrate AccessRank parameters for Icon Highlights and to provide a baseline description of Finder usage, used for between subjects comparison of Finder usage with that of Finder Highlights. The original logs were gathered by a tool installed on the computers of 25 participants (11 female, 14 from computer science departments) running Mac OS X 10.6 or 10.7, aged between 20 and 64 (mean 31.9, s.d. 11.0). Logs recorded details of all file retrievals, including navigation and search.

FINDER HIGHLIGHTS

In order to investigate the real-world feasibility of IH and SDN (the most promising augmentations in [15]), we developed Finder Highlights, a fully functional plugin for the Finder, the standard OS X file browser. A high-level architecture of Finder Highlights is shown in Figure 2. It consists of a user interface layer (Finder Highlights UI) that extends the OS X Finder. Finder Highlights UI requires file access predictions, which are provided by two different algorithmic components. The first of these serves Icon Highlights predictions, and uses modifications and extensions to AccessRank that were required to enable AccessRank to support mutable, hierarchical data (e.g., to support score changes when a file is moved between folders). The second component is new, and serves predictive augmentations within SDN. Both the Finder and the predictive algorithms draw on data from the file system. The algorithms store data about retrievals and predictions in a database, and the Finder Highlights UI writes data describing all user interactions to a log file.

We describe the design and implementation of Finder Highlights in three sections. First, we describe the interface design challenges and solutions in integrating IH, SDN, and existing functionality in a real browser. Second, we detail the algorithmic extensions to AccessRank necessary to allow strong file retrieval predictions. Third, we describe the algorithm developed to support SDN. To reiterate, these interface and algorithm extensions are prerequisite research contributions that enable Finder Highlights to support real file retrievals. Although described in the context of the OS X Finder, the algorithms are designed to be platform independent.

Interface Design

Design challenges of integrating IH and SDN

IH and SDN were originally implemented and evaluated separately, but real-world use might require both to be integrated within a single browsing interface. Achieving this integration raises substantial design challenges, as both IH and SDN use highlighting to guide users to items within each folder view, although the basis for their highlighting is very different (AccessRank predictions for IH, and query matches for SDN).

Concurrently displaying IH and SDN highlights would, in theory, provide users with access to the most complete set of information. However, we believed that this combined visualization would be hard to learn, visually cluttered, and potentially distracting. We therefore chose to show only one form of highlighting at a time.

IH highlights are shown without any explicit user request or action. They are displayed as yellow 'spotlights' over items, with the spotlight adapting to the size and shape of items in the folder view (e.g. Figure 1a, Figure 4). The blur level and brightness of each highlight varies based on the confidence of the associated prediction. Strongly predicted items, such as the *Documents* folder in Figure 1a, have bright highlights with a crisp border, while weakly predicted items are dimmer and more blurred.

SDN highlights are shown in place of Icon Highlights whenever the user explicitly types a query into the SDN search field (as shown in Figure 1b). Like IH highlights, SDN highlights match the shape and size of highlighted items. However, to help users discriminate between IH and SDN highlights, they use clearly discriminable display methods. When SDN is active (by typing into the SDN search field), a semitransparent grey overlay is displayed over the view, with white 'cutouts' to indicate the highlighted items (Figure 1b). SDN uses two levels of visual prominence: previously visited search term matches have crisp borders; unvisited ones, blurred.

Design challenges in supporting multiple views

Finder Highlights supports all of the Finder's view types, some of which are shown in Figure 3. We iteratively refined highlighting methods across view types, trying to balance visual saliency with aesthetics and clutter, resulting in some subtle variations between views. For example, Finder Highlights uses circular spotlights for icon view when the labels are beneath the items (Figure 3a), but a rectangular spotlight when the labels are to the right of the item (Figure 3b).

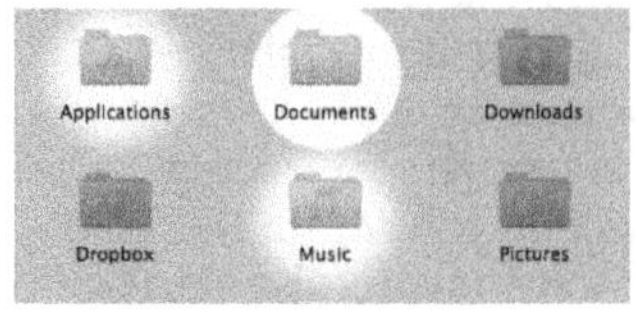

(a) Icon view (labels beneath icons)

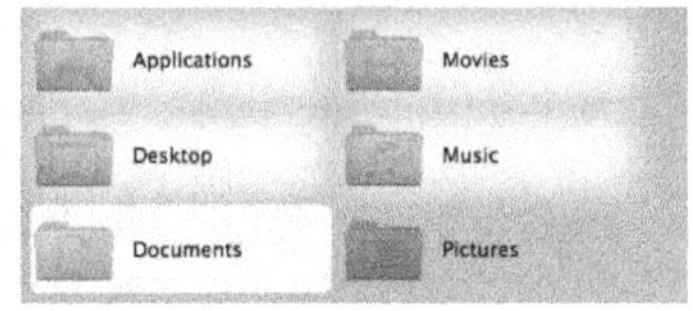

(b) Icon view (labels on right of icons)

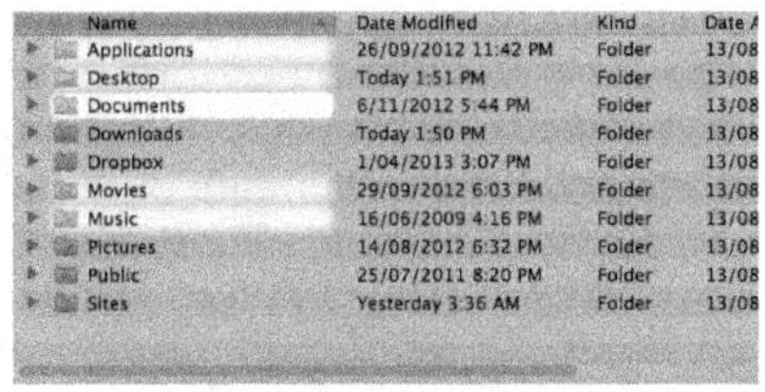

(c) List view (Details view on Windows)

Figure 3: SDN highlights shown in different views.

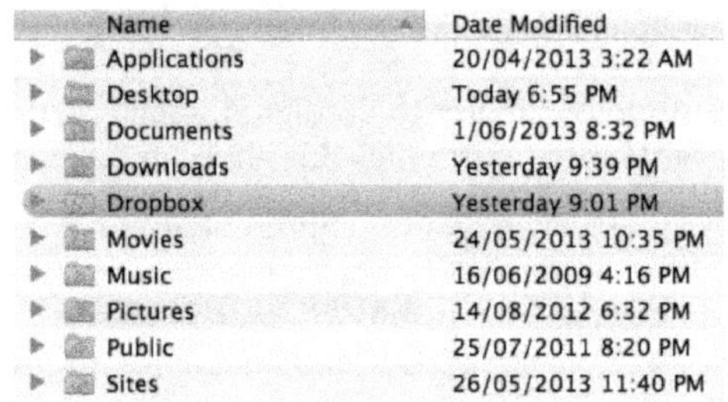

Figure 4: Icon Highlights in list view.

For column view (Figure 1b), list view (Figure 3c), and Cover Flow views, a shorter, wider rounded rectangle highlight appears around the item's icon and filename. The maximum blur level of a highlight is linearly scaled for highlights less than 48 pixels high, as pilot testing revealed that short highlight rectangles are not sufficiently salient when using the same blur levels as larger regions.

Design challenges of competing with other visual features

File browsers such as the Finder offer a range of features that potentially conflict with highlighting, such as colour labels (e.g., item 'Dropbox' in Figure 4) and the use of colour in icons. SDN's highlighting method mitigates these concerns by uniformly applying a grey 'transparency' over all items except those highlighted. The use of yellow highlights in IH, in contrast, can conflict with other colour cues. IH applies two methods to mitigate the problem. First, in icon view, where there is a large amount of whitespace, IH spotlights are drawn *behind* icons, allowing their assigned colour to be unaffected by the IH spotlight. In other views, where there is inadequate whitespace to provide a sufficiently salient spotlight behind the item, the design solution is a compromise: highlights are drawn *on top* of the underlying view, combining colours as in a subtractive colour model (i.e., with colour values approaching black). This ensures that the highlight is visible without affecting text readability or the visibility of other content.

To reduce visual clutter and promote visual saliency of highlighted items, a maximum of seven IH highlights are shown in each folder. When the content of multiple folders are visible at once (e.g., multiple columns in column view), the highlight limit is applied to each folder individually.

Design challenges of integrating SDN and search

SDN and Finder's search feature are designed for differing use cases; for example, SDN supports folder- and file-name queries only, whereas search supports more advanced queries. However, both techniques are activated by typing a query into a search field. Providing multiple search fields in the file browser would clutter the browser interface and would be likely to confuse users, so Finder Highlights integrates SDN within Finder's existing search field (Figure 1b).

To achieve this, Finder Highlights adds a menu, activated by clicking on the search icon on the left of the field, allowing users to switch between search and SDN. The current mode is indicated by placeholder text in the field. New windows default to SDN mode unless created in response to a search related event (for example, via the system's Spotlight search feature). The Find command and its menu shortcut focus the active window's search field in its current search mode, while holding down the option key while using the command instead activates the other search mode. A progress indicator in the search field indicates an incomplete search. When opening a folder while SDN is active, Finder Highlights automatically scrolls to show the first highlighted item.

Extending AccessRank for Icon Highlights

IH uses a modified and extended version of AccessRank [14] to determine item highlights. The original AccessRank algorithm assumed a homogeneous dataset of independent items where every access carries the same weight. This section describes enhancements to AccessRank that better support predictions of hierarchical data, as well as describing the calibration of AccessRank parameters for use with file retrieval.

Configuring AccessRank parameters for Icon Highlights

AccessRank has two parameters which affect the accuracy and stability of its results: λ is the weighting between Markov and CRF algorithms (see earlier), and δ is the required threshold for items to swap ranks. These parameters are intended to be manipulated based on the characteristics of each application, requiring calibration.

Simulations on the baseline Finder usage data (described above), conducted using a similar method to the original AccessRank evaluation [14], confirmed the suitability of AccessRank for predicting file retrievals. We selected $(\lambda, \delta) = (1.65, 1)$ for subsequent use in IH, a configuration that provided the best-performing combination of accuracy and stability. Here, δ refers to a relative threshold for two items to swap places (i.e., for $\delta = 1$ an item's score must exceed that of a higher ranked item by at least 100% in order to swap places), which performed slightly better than an absolute threshold as used in the original version of AccessRank.

We also significantly lowered the weighting of retrievals made outside the Finder, so that items retrieved in this way were not given as prominent highlights as those retrieved within the Finder. Simulations showed that this modification substantially improved prediction accuracy, as files consistently retrieved without the Finder (e.g., using 'Open Recent' menus) are rarely also retrieved within the Finder.

Location-specific adaptations

The original version of AccessRank treated the entire dataset as a single homogeneous dataset, meaning that predictions and data describing actions did not need to account for any consideration of the 'location' or context in which they were made. Icon Highlights, in contrast, is designed to provide feedback to the user regarding predictions within a particular location (the current folder). Five modifications were made to the way that AccessRank scores are used by Icon Highlights to account for its use in file navigation, as follows.

First, scores for items within each folder are normalised relative to the maximum score of other items in the same folder. This ensures that at least one previously retrieved item will always be highlighted prominently by IH.

Second, AccessRank's stability delta is only applied when displaying physical folder locations. It is thus not applied to dynamic locations (e.g., search results), which vary with context and where highlight stability has little logical value.

Third, the highlight score for an alias or shortcut is that of the item it references, and opening the alias records a retrieval for the referenced item. The aim is to assist subsequent retrievals of that file regardless of the path taken to it.

Fourth, to remove the effect of navigation errors corrupting prediction accuracy, both file accesses and ancestor folder accesses are recorded only when the file is opened. For the purposes of AccessRank's Markov model, the previous item is always the previously accessed file, rather than any ancestor folders, with transitions recorded from this previous file to all path components of the subsequent file retrieval.

Fifth, OS X's *Quick Look* feature allows an item to be quickly previewed without opening a separate application. Once a preview window is shown, users can switch between items using the keyboard. To attempt to distinguish between use of Quick Look as a substitute for opening a file, and for skimming through a list a files, Finder Highlights records a retrieval only when a preview is visible for at least five seconds.

Updating scores after changes to the hierarchy structure

Finder Highlights stores its data based on file paths. When an item is moved or renamed, it carries its score and history data to its new path, and references contained in the Markov model are updated. When an item is deleted, its data is removed.

We consider three types of items when moving or deleting items. *Files* are leaf nodes in the hierarchy, *containers* are the direct parents of files, and *intermediaries* are the parents of containers or other intermediaries. If a file is moved or deleted, its container may still be an area of active work. If an intermediary is moved or deleted, this may be more indicative of a more fundamental change in the hierarchy structure. A given folder may act as both a container and an intermediary in different contexts.

Accordingly, containers and intermediaries are treated differently when updating CRF weights. If the child of an intermediary is removed, its CRF weight is subtracted from the intermediary's weight recursively up the hierarchy. However, if the child of a container is removed, the container's CRF score is *not* affected. A moved item's CRF weight is added to its new ancestors, regardless of whether it is a file or folder.

Recording simultaneous retrievals
The Finder allows users to select and open multiple files simultaneously as part of a single retrieval event, for example to view a series of photos. To prevent this resulting in excessive score increases for ancestor folders, Finder Highlights records only a single access for each file or ancestor folder observed in a simultaneous retrieval.

Algorithm for Search Directed Navigation
Icon Highlights guides users to predicted items within the current folder. Its backend algorithm does not need to inspect descendent files and folders until their parent folder is opened. Search Directed Navigation, in contrast, provides visual feedback that guides users to descendent files and folders that match a search term query at any lower level of the hierarchy. Search terms are case-insensitive, and the search is initiated and refined for every successively typed character.

The SDN algorithm is designed to provide rapid and accurate feedback to the user. It does so by using an *index of visited items* and *search prioritisation*, described below.

Index of visited items – immediate highlights for previous items
The index of visited items records all files, folders, and their ancestors that have been opened, regardless of the method by which they were opened. The index is stored on disk as a sorted list of file and folder paths. The SDN algorithm also stores in memory a sorted list of all potential lookup keys, which are the successive substrings of each file or folder name (for example, the filename "finderHigh-CHI.14" would generate substrings "finder", "High", "finderHigh", "CHI", etc). A match occurs when a query matches the start of any lookup key; in this way, all results for a query can be found using binary search in $O(\log(n) + m)$ time, where n is the number of key-path pairs, and m is the number of matches for the query. The index is updated in response to file management events, such as moving, renaming, or deleting items or their ancestors. When a search term is entered, the index is searched and results are returned in a tree form that mirrors the file hierarchy. Consequently, for previously visited items SDN can give essentially immediate feedback.

Search prioritisation
Following initial feedback generated through the index, the SDN algorithm performs an exhaustive breadth-first search of the subtrees displayed in the current folder. This is necessary to generate results for previously unvisited parts of the file hierarchy. Matches are dynamically added to the results.

Although the search is exhaustive, it is prioritised to maximise the speed with which highlights are identified. Once a folder is highlighted its priority is reduced (because finding more matches will not generate further changes to the current folder), so folders that have no current highlights are searched first. Further, user folders (such as *Documents* and *Downloads*) are prioritised above system folders.

Location and query changes are common while SDN is active, as users traverse their hierarchy or refine their query. The SDN algorithm ensures that any additional searching is minimised when these changes occur, retaining or refining existing results where possible.

The SDN algorithm can optionally use OS X's Spotlight index to improve search performance. It issues a concurrent search term to Spotlight, restricted to descendent items of the current folder which have names starting with the SDN query.

FIELD EVALUATION OF FINDER HIGHLIGHTS
The primary objective of this research is to learn how techniques similar to IH and SDN are used in the real world. Finder Highlights addresses the interface and algorithm design issues described above, allowing for such an evaluation.

Finder Highlights was deployed in a four-week-long field study, logging details about Finder usage, IH predictions and SDN searches. To protect privacy while maintaining an ability to identify revisitations, logs recorded hash codes of file paths, rather than the original paths. Logs were stored locally on participants' computers until the end of the study.

Procedure
Twenty OS X 10.8 users (4 female) participated in the study, aged between 23 and 66 (mean 32.0, s.d. 9.8), with 19 submitting data at the end of the study. Self-reported daily computer use ranged from 1 to 14 hours per day (mean 7.2 hours). Participants were recruited from a range of sources: four were tertiary students (three in computer science), eight were university staff or faculty (seven in computer science), and eight worked outside academia.

Communication with participants occurred online. They were instructed to download the Finder Highlights software and to watch a three minute video that briefly explained the techniques. The video directed participants to use their computers as normal during the study, and to use the techniques as little, or as much, as they liked. After four weeks, participants were sent instructions to uninstall the software, submit their logs, and complete a post-study survey.

Log File Data Analysis
Ultimately, the techniques included in Finder Highlights are intended to reduce file retrieval times. However there are complexities in determining these times from interaction logs. In particular, certain assumptions must be made to establish an objective time at which the retrieval began (in contrast, lab experiments can begin timing at the point an artificial stimuli is shown). In our analyses, retrieval time measurements were determined to begin at the later of (1) the time a browser window was opened; (2) the time of the first navigation event after either another retrieval, use of another browser window, or a file management task (e.g. moving an item); and (3) a navigation event that was more than 30 seconds after the previous one. Time measurements ended when a file was opened. Retrievals of items on the desktop were excluded, since Finder Highlights had no effect on the desktop interface.

To further characterise retrievals, we also analysed *step times* – the time between opening successive folders while navigating to a file. Steps were excluded from the analysis if they included: an upwards step through the hierarchy; use of history

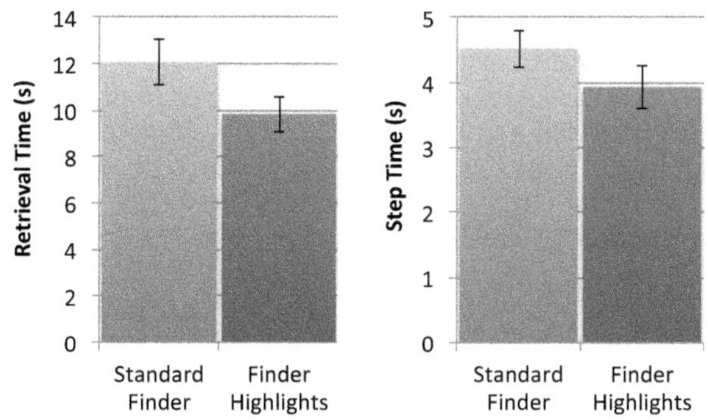

Figure 5: Non-search retrieval and step times with and without Finder Highlights, showing the effect of Icon Highlights. Error bars ± 1 st. err.

buttons, sidebar links, search, or another window; a change in the view configuration; file management activities (e.g., moving a file); or if the step took longer than 30 seconds.

Baseline between-subjects comparisons were performed between logs from the standard Finder (described previously) and from Finder Highlights. The two sets of logs were analysed with exactly the same assumptions using exactly the same analysis tools; in particular, the assumptions for measuring retrieval and step times were identical. All times were log-transformed for statistical analyses (both ANOVA and unpaired t-tests) to reduce the skew of the data.

Retrieval Times and Step Times

We conducted between-subjects analyses of retrieval and step times using Finder and Finder Highlights logs. The Finder logs contained data about 1689 retrievals, while the Finder Highlights logs contained 2521.

The mean retrieval time with Finder Highlights was 10.6 s (s.d. 3.4), 13% faster than the Finder mean of 12.2 s (s.d. 4.7): $T_{42} = 2.7, p < .01$. The mean for the Finder retrieval times is supported by a recent result from Bergman et al. [6], which reported a similar mean Mac OS X file retrieval time of 12.6 s.

More exact comparison of retrievals is possible by separating the Finder Highlights logs between those retrievals conducted using Icon Highlights, and those using Search Directed Navigation, as described below.

Icon Highlights

To examine the independent contribution of Icon Highlights, we excluded retrievals that involved search-based interfaces. Results were similar to the overall results above, which is best explained by the low proportion of retrievals using search or SDN (see below). Mean retrieval times with IH were 9.8 s (s.d. 3.3), compared to 12.1 s (s.d. 4.8) without it – $T_{42} = 3.1, p < .005$. To eliminate the possibility that this difference in retrieval times is explained by differences between the participants' file structures (rather than by the retrieval interfaces themselves), we compared the mean depth of retrieved files between the studies, with no significant difference. Further, a comparison of step times confirms that participants selected targets within the folder view more quickly when IH was available (mean 3.9 s, s.d. 1.4) than when using the standard Finder (mean 4.5 s, s.d. 1.5) – $T_{43} = 2.0, p < .05$. Importantly, as IH is intended to reduce visual search time by highlighting likely targets, this reduction provides strong evidence that this design intention is fulfilled. Both step and retrieval times for IH are summarised in Figure 5.

Search Directed Navigation

In the earlier lab study, SDN was highly efficient and extremely well received by participants [15]. Results from the field study, however, are very different; not because SDN was inefficient or disliked, but rather because many participants never used it. It was actively used by only 4 of the 19 participants, who used it in between 1% and 44% of navigational steps (mean 14%); these participants averaged 9.8 retrievals and 89 steps using SDN. This contrast between extremely positive lab study results and substantially neutral findings due to disuse in the field amplifies the motivation for our research, in migrating analysis from the lab to the real world.

The lack of data on active use of SDN complicates its rigorous analysis. Further, as SDN introduces new functionality – guiding users to files through the hierarchy in response to a search term – there are difficulties in determining an appropriate baseline for comparison. Limited insights can be gained by comparing steps times following SDN activation for the four participants who used it (mean 2.9 s, s.d. 1.3) to other steps made by the same participants (3.8 s, s.d 1.7), however statistical tests are inappropriate due to the above reasons.

Step Times with Correct and Incorrect Highlighting

Highlighting functionality is likely to assist users when their intended target is highlighted, but may distract when other items are highlighted and the target is not. To investigate this issue, we categorised all IH steps in one of three ways to produce an analysis factor *step type*: *positive highlights*, where the selected item was highlighted; *negative highlights*, where other items were highlighted and the selected item was not; and *no highlights*, where no items were highlighted. We also categorised steps in the baseline Finder logs in the same way, by first determining which items *would* have been highlighted, had IH been available.

An ANOVA with between-subjects factor *study* and within-subjects factor *step type* showed a significant effect of *step type* – $F_{2,82} = 9.4, p < 0.001$. With Finder Highlights, step times were fastest with *positive highlights* (3.4 s), followed by *no highlights* (3.9 s) and *negative highlights* (5.1 s). In the baseline data, step times were 4.2 s for *positive highlights* and *no highlights*, and 5.3 s for *negative highlights*. This result provides further evidence that IH, when providing correct predictions, was successful in helping users quickly identify and select targets. Additionally, negative highlights did not result in any noticeable change in performance.

The slow times for *negative highlights* can be partially explained by the variability in folder sizes: in the Finder Highlights study, folders with *negative highlights* contained many more items (mean 73.9, s.d. 111.3) than either *positive highlights* (mean 21.8, s.d. 16.5) or *no highlights* (mean 24.2, s.d. 22.5). This is likely because large folders have a smaller percentage of highlighted items, and are therefore more likely to produce *negative highlights*.

Statement (paraphrased)	Strongly Disagree (1)	Disagree (2)	Neutral (3)	Agree (4)	Strongly Agree (5)	Mean
Icon Highlights						
IH was useful	0	2	3	9	5	3.9
IH reduced cognitive load	0	3	7	5	4	3.5
Would like IH as permanent feature	0	4	3	8	4	3.6
Predictions seemed accurate	0	2	1	14	2	3.8
Could predict if target would be highlighted	0	1	4	8	5	3.9
Highlighting technique clear and intuitive	0	0	2	11	6	4.2
Search Directed Navigation						
SDN was useful	3	2	9	2	3	3.0
SDN affected file retrieval behaviour	2	2	10	2	3	3.1
Would like SDN as permanent feature	2	2	9	2	4	3.2
Results seemed accurate	0	0	4	2	4	4.0
SDN made it harder to use search	4	6	1	3	0	2.2
Confused between SDN and search	5	5	1	3	0	2.1
Highlighting technique clear and intuitive	0	0	2	4	6	4.3

Table 1: Participant agreement with statements about IH and SDN

Further analysis of steps showed that 46.5% had *positive highlights*, 29.3% had *negative highlights*, and 24.2% had *no highlights*. In contrast to the 46.5% of selected items that were highlighted, an average of 22.5% of items were highlighted in each folder, suggesting that the AccessRank prediction algorithm provided good predictions of upcoming file selections. The average rank of a revisited item in its folder was 3.4 (18.2% of all steps opened a top-ranked item), while an average of 3.0 items were highlighted at each step.

Questionnaire Responses

After four weeks of use, participants completed a post-study questionnaire that gathered both quantitative subjective responses (using five-point Likert scales from 'strongly disagree' (1) to 'strongly agree' (5)) and participant comments. The quantitative responses are summarised in Table 1, which shows abbreviated forms of the Likert-scale questions asked.

Likert scale responses reflect the log results above. Participants responded more favourably to the question 'IH is useful' (14 responses above neutral, 2 below) than for the equivalent question with SDN (5 above neutral, 5 below). Participants also felt the IH predictions were accurate (16 above neutral, 1 below) and predictable (13 above neutral, 1 below), and that its highlighting technique was clear and intuitive (17 above neutral, none below). The positive response for the predictability of highlighting is important, as prior research has shown that users can more quickly identify targets using pre-attentive search if they know in advance that they will be highlighted in a particular way [29].

Icon Highlights

The survey also asked participants to rate the effect of IH on retrieval times and error rates. Participants generally stated that it improved retrieval times (7 felt it made them faster, 1 slower), especially when retrieving previously visited files (15 faster, none slower). IH also had a positive impact on perceived error rates (7 reported fewer errors, none more).

The participants' general comments on IH referred to it being most useful when navigating through many successive directories, when lots of items in a folder had similar names, and when revisiting specific items – particularly in large folders. However, a number of comments suggested possible refinements: (1) that too many items were highlighted towards the end of the study (one participant), which could be rectified by reducing the per-folder highlight limit; (2) that there was not enough difference between prominent and dim highlights (one participant), which could be rectified by calibrating the highlighting formula; (3) that the highlight colour was not visually appealing or should be customisable (six participants); (4) a lack of keyboard navigation, which would be useful to move between highlighted items (one participant); and (5) confusing interaction between highlights and existing colour labels (one participant), which suggests the need for refining the colour blending methods used in Finder Highlights.

The participants' comments also suggested a perception that the techniques might be most effective for users with disorganised file structures. *P8: "There is more and more mess on my hard drive, so it is useful to highlight files that I actually use."*. Indeed, IH may be of more benefit to 'pilers' than 'filers' (terms used to describe file organisation behaviour [21, 28]); those with disorganised hierarchies may be more reliant on visual search, perhaps due to larger folder sizes or less inherent knowledge of file locations.

While IH was designed to help retrieve files, one participant said that its benefits were primarily in reducing *organisation* time. This participant had previously made extensive use of OS X's manual colour labelling feature, meaning that IH provided no additional benefit at retrieval-time. However, he commented that it was a very useful automatic replacement for manual labelling. Another unexpected use, referred to in comments from four participants, was that sometimes the *absence* of highlights was particularly useful. For example, in ordered lists of movie files, the highlighted items would indicate which had already been watched, and the first unhighlighted item following them would correspond to the video they wanted to watch next. In another example, a participant sometimes knew a target item would not be highlighted, and could ignore highlights to speed up visual search.

Search Directed Navigation

As expected, considering its relatively infrequent and light use, the dominant response for questions concerning use of SDN was neutral. However, as supported by the logs, a minority of the participants found it useful, with three expressing strong agreement regarding its usefulness.

Those who used it appreciated the context it provided, using it both as a search substitute and in place of some navigation tasks. P5: *"Just loved it! Unlike the normal search, my current path stays the same, and I don't have a list of items coming from nowhere... I was comfortably guided through what I wanted. Sometimes [with normal search] several files match the query and the results are all [shown together]. Here I can easily focus on the one file I was looking for. No ambiguities."*

P4 commented that SDN resulted in lower error rates than search, and facilitated learning of item locations, in line with its design goals: *"Sometimes I will use [Spotlight search], but if a file doesn't appear that I am looking for, I am no closer to finding it. With Search Directed Navigation... I was able to use a starting top level folder as a starting point. This allowed me to usually find my file much more quickly, and with more success, but I also got the benefit of being reminded of where I stored the file and other files that I passed on the way."*

P6 also mentioned this property, commenting *"I really liked the way it seemed to teach the directory structure to me; traditional find would hide the structure from me"*, and referring to IH as a way to retrieve files faster, but SDN as a way to remember his structure.

However, most participants rarely or never used SDN. Common reasons for this were that participants already knew where their files were (12 participants), do not use search much (8), forgot or did not think to use it (4), prefer traditional search interfaces (2), do not navigate to files much (2) or that it was too slow to find results (2). One participant commented that he would have used SDN frequently had it supported navigation to highlighted items using the keyboard. Two participants did not realise that SDN only searched filenames, and were confused by this, with another suggesting that a content searching option would be useful. A common theme in the explanation for the lack of use of SDN was a reluctance to resort to search, which confirms results of previous studies suggesting that search is often used as a method of last resort [2, 3, 7, 8].

Despite the low uptake, the strong positive reactions from those who used it suggest that SDN can be a valuable tool once people are familiar with it.

Discussion

To briefly summarise, conducting a real world evaluation of IH and SDN required addressing several user interface design challenges in extending and integrating the previously reported research prototypes into a viable file browser. It also required several extensions to existing algorithms. Results of a four-week field study in which real users employed Finder Highlights for their everyday file retrieval activities showed that IH reduced file retrieval times and was enthusiastically received by users. SDN was ignored by most users, but appreciated by those who used it.

Methodology – Lab versus Field

The results of the lab study and field study are very different. In the lab, SDN caused marked performance improvement and strongly positive subjective assessments, but in the field, it was rarely used. This finding underlines and reiterates methodological concerns previously identified in several HCI studies [9, 11, 26]. The need for cross validation across multiple methods is well known (e.g., [18]), but it remains relatively uncommon in HCI. There are several disincentives for advancing beyond lab studies – the *potential* of innovative interface concepts can be established quickly and with strong rigour in controlled experimental studies; advancing beyond lab studies requires arduous and refined system engineering; and longitudinal evaluation is difficult to conduct, not least because of the difficulty of finding participants who will make a long term commitment to experimental software. Although these disincentives are substantial, the results in this paper exemplify both the limits of lab studies and the value of field studies. We hope to stimulate more evaluations of novel interactive systems that go beyond the lab.

Overcoming Barriers to Adoption

It seems likely that SDN can improve user performance in file retrieval tasks, as suggested by the lab study and the enthusiasm of those who used it. However, until users have their first experience of its benefits, they have little reason to try to exploit it, as doing so requires an overhead in learning and adapting to its new functionality. The barriers to adopting new and ultimately more efficient interface methods were examined by Scarr et al. [27]. There are abundant opportunities for further research on methods that help users identify and capitalise on unused interface methods that will ultimately assist them in becoming more efficient with computing tools, with 'Skillometers' providing one recent example [20].

Prediction Versus Interaction

IH and SDN use sophisticated algorithms to predict the user's upcoming actions. The algorithms' predictions are currently deployed to improve the user's *manual* methods for file retrieval – they help users identify targets and learn the navigational actions required to facilitate improvement over time. However, there is an interface design tension between the accuracy of the predictive algorithm and the interface methods used to present those predictions. For example, if AccessRank or any other algorithm had near perfect prediction, then it would be near pointless to require the user to manually retrieve the file; instead, the system could autonomously open the file on the user's behalf. There are interesting research opportunities in analysing the theoretical and design challenges of different interface methods for working with algorithmic predictions, with some of the issues discussed in [17].

CONCLUSION

Finder Highlights is a robust and real software system that augments the OS X file browser, the Finder, with techniques designed to improve navigation-based file retrieval. It was designed and implemented in order to test Icon Highlights and Search Directed Navigation, two techniques that earlier lab studies showed to have strong potential for improving file retrieval. We presented the interface and algorithmic design challenges associated with advancing from the lab to the field. The algorithmic advances, in particular, represent research contributions that can be reused by future researchers working on interfaces that predict upcoming user actions.

A four week field study of Finder Highlights showed marked differences between the lab and field results. While the field study results show that the potential of Icon Highlights identified in the prior study is realised in the field, the lab study results for Search Directed Navigation did not fully translate to the field. The findings have clear implications for the design of future file browser interfaces, which should incorporate features similar to those of Finder Highlights, and for HCI experimental methodology. We hope to see more novel interactive techniques tested in the field as well as the lab.

ACKNOWLEDGEMENTS

This work was partially funded by Royal Society of New Zealand Marsden Grant 10-UOC-020. Thanks to the anonymous participants for their time and efforts.

REFERENCES

1. Alexander, J., Cockburn, A., Fitchett, S., Gutwin, C., and Greenberg, S. Revisiting read wear: analysis, design, and evaluation of a footprints scrollbar. In *Proc. CHI '09* (2009), 1665–1674.
2. Barreau, D., and Nardi, B. A. Finding and reminding: file organization from the desktop. *SIGCHI Bull. 27*, 3 (1995), 39–43.
3. Bergman, O., Beyth-Marom, R., Nachmias, R., Gradovitch, N., and Whittaker, S. Improved search engines and navigation preference in personal information management. *ACM TOIS 26*, 4 (2008), 1–24.
4. Bergman, O., Tene-Rubinstein, M., and Shalom, J. The use of attention resources in navigation versus search. *Personal and Ubiquitous Computing 17*, 3 (2013), 583–590.
5. Bergman, O., Whittaker, S., Sanderson, M., Nachmias, R., and Ramamoorthy, A. The effect of folder structure on personal file navigation. *JASIST 61*, 12 (2011), 2300–2310.
6. Bergman, O., Whittaker, S., Sanderson, M., Nachmias, R., and Ramamoorthy, A. How do we find personal files?: the effect of os, presentation & depth on file navigation. In *Proc. CHI '12* (2012), 2977–2980.
7. Blanc-Brude, T., and Scapin, D. L. What do people recall about their documents?: implications for desktop search tools. In *Proc. IUI '07* (2007), 102–111.
8. Boardman, R., and Sasse, M. A. "stuff goes into the computer and doesn't come out": a cross-tool study of personal information management. In *Proc. CHI '04* (2004), 583–590.
9. Chiasson, S., Biddle, R., and van Oorschot, P. C. A second look at the usability of click-based graphical passwords. In *Proc. SOUPS '07* (2007), 1–12.
10. Cockburn, A., and Gutwin, C. A predictive model of human performance with scrolling and hierarchical lists. *HCIJ* (2009), 273–314.
11. Duh, H. B.-L., Tan, G. C. B., and Chen, V. H.-h. Usability evaluation for mobile device: a comparison of laboratory and field tests. In *Proc. MobileHCI '06* (2006), 181–186.
12. Elsweiler, D., Harvey, M., and Hacker, M. Understanding re-finding behavior in naturalistic email interaction logs. In *Proc. SIGIR '11*, ACM (2011), 35–44.
13. Findlater, L., Moffatt, K., McGrenere, J., and Dawson, J. Ephemeral adaptation: the use of gradual onset to improve menu selection performance. In *CHI '09* (2009), 1655–1664.
14. Fitchett, S., and Cockburn, A. Accessrank: predicting what users will do next. In *Proc. CHI '12* (2012), 2239–2242.
15. Fitchett, S., Cockburn, A., and Gutwin, C. Improving navigation-based file retrieval. In *Proc. CHI '13* (2013), 2329–2338.
16. Gajos, K. Z., Czerwinski, M., Tan, D. S., and Weld, D. S. Exploring the design space for adaptive graphical user interfaces. In *Proc. AVI '06* (2006), 201–208.
17. Gajos, K. Z., Everitt, K., Tan, D. S., Czerwinski, M., and Weld, D. S. Predictability and accuracy in adaptive user interfaces. In *Proc. CHI '08* (2008), 1271–1274.
18. Hertzum, M. User testing in industry: A case study of laboratory, workshop, and field tests. In *Proceedings of the 5th ERCIM Workshop* (1999), 59–72.
19. Lee, D., Choi, J., Kim, J.-H., Noh, S. H., Min, S. L., Cho, Y., and Kim, C. S. On the existence of a spectrum of policies that subsumes the least recently used (lru) and least frequently used (lfu) policies. *SIGMETRICS Perform. Eval. Rev. 27*, 1 (1999), 134–143.
20. Malacria, S., Scarr, J., Cockburn, A., Gutwin, C., and Grossman, T. Skillometers: reflective widgets that motivate and help users to improve performance. In *Proc. UIST '13* (2013), 321–330.
21. Malone, T. W. How do people organize their desks?: Implications for the design of office information systems. *ACM Trans. Inf. Syst. 1*, 1 (1983), 99–112.
22. Markov, A. The theory of algorithms. *American Mathematical Society Translations* (1960).
23. Matejka, J., Li, W., Grossman, T., and Fitzmaurice, G. Communitycommands: command recommendations for software applications. In *Proc. UIST '09*, ACM (2009), 193–202.
24. Moon, J. M., and Fu, W.-T. Effects of spatial locations and luminance on finding and re-finding information in a desktop environment. In *Proc. CHI '09*, ACM (2009), 3365–3370.
25. Nardi, B., Anderson, K., and Erickson, T. Filing and finding computer files. *Proc. East-West HCI* (1995), 162–179.
26. Nielsen, C. M., Overgaard, M., Pedersen, M. B., Stage, J., and Stenild, S. It's worth the hassle!: the added value of evaluating the usability of mobile systems in the field. In *NordiCHI '06* (2006), 272–280.
27. Scarr, J., Cockburn, A., Gutwin, C., and Quinn, P. Dips and ceilings: understanding and supporting transitions to expertise in user interfaces. In *Proc. CHI '11* (2011), 2741–2750.
28. Teevan, J., Alvarado, C., Ackerman, M. S., and Karger, D. R. The perfect search engine is not enough: a study of orienteering behavior in directed search. In *Proc. CHI '04*, ACM (2004), 415–422.
29. Treisman, A. Perceptual grouping and attention in visual search for features and for objects. *J Exp Psychol [Hum Percept] 8*, 2 (1982), 194.

PIM and Personality: What do our Personal File Systems Say About Us?

Charlotte Massey, Sean TenBrook, Chaconne Tatum, Steve Whittaker
University of California at Santa Cruz,
High St, Santa Cruz, 95064.
{cmassey, stenbroo, ctatumdi, swhittak}@ucsc.edu

ABSTRACT
Individual differences are prevalent in personal information management (PIM). There is large variation between individuals in how they structure and retrieve information from personal archives. These differences make it hard to develop general PIM tools. However we know little about the *origins* of these differences. We present two studies evaluating whether differences arise from *personality traits,* by exploring whether different personalities structure personal archives differently. The first exploratory study asks participants to identify PIM cues that signal personality traits. While the aim was to identify cues, these cues also proved surprisingly accurate indicators of personality. In a second study, to evaluate these cues, we directly measure relations between structure and traits. We demonstrate that Conscientiousness predicts file organization, particularly PC users' desktops. Neurotic people may also keep more desktop files. One implication is that systems might be customized for different personalities. We also advance personality theory, showing that personal digital artifacts signal personality.

Author Keywords
Personal Information Management; file systems; individual differences; personality.

ACM Classification Keywords
H.5.m. Information interfaces and presentation (e.g., HCI): Miscellaneous.

INTRODUCTION
Personal Information Management (PIM) is a fact of life; all of us spend time every day organizing personal information, both to facilitate its later retrieval and to manage our tasks. One repeated observation in PIM is *individual differences* in how people structure and retrieve personal information. However less attention has been paid to the *reasons* for these differences. This is an important question because differences in organizational structure have direct consequences for retrieval [5], task management [36], and for stress [8]. And despite improvements in desktop search, search has not replaced the need to actively organize personal files. Navigation through one's personally organized file system is still people's preferred way to find their information, underscoring the importance of understanding different organizational strategies [4].

CHI 2014, April 26-May 01 2014, Toronto, ON, Canada
Copyright is held by the owner/author(s). Publication rights licensed to ACM.
ACM 978-1-4503-2473-1/14/04...$15.00.
http://dx.doi.org/10.1145/2556288.2557023

There are clearly many potential causes of individual differences in PIM. One classic individual difference is between *filers* and *pilers*. Prior work speculates that these differences partially arise from different work responsibilities [3, 36] or individual cognitive processing style [19]. However, so far no PIM research has directly explored whether differences arise from *personality traits*. In personality theory, traits are defined as habitual patterns of behavior, thought, and emotion [26]. The consensus in personality theory is there are 5 main personality traits of Openness, Conscientiousness, Extraversion, Agreeableness, and Neuroticism [15, 21]. Such traits may directly influence how people organize information. We can therefore ask whether Neurotics organize personal information differently, and whether there are effects of other personality factors such as Conscientiousness or Openness.

A new approach to this question is suggested by recent work on personality examining relationships between people's personal *physical* environments and their personality. This approach explores whether personal environments, e.g. bedrooms or offices, directly signal their owners' personality traits. [16, 17] shows that strangers inspecting an unoccupied college dorm room can reliably determine how Open and Conscientious the owner is, based on *cues* such as travel souvenirs or a wide variety of books and music. Inspectors are moderate at judging other traits, apart from Agreeableness. However there are sometimes discrepancies between what room inspectors *think* are accurate trait cues, and what *actually* are reliable cues. So for example, while inspectors *thought* that towels strewn on bedroom floors indicated the owner's Disagreeableness, *in reality* formality of décor is a better cue.

Although [17] shows reliable relations between personal physical environments and certain personality traits, less research has explored the *digital* domain. We know that public aspects of information spaces, such as Facebook profiles or personal web pages are deliberately designed to convey identity [1, 11, 18, 29, 35]. However does personality also affect how we organize less public aspects of our personal digital collections that others aren't intended to see? Do our personalities affect how we organize personal files?

We examine whether *organization of personal archives* reflect personality. We ask, for example, whether Conscientiousness people have smaller overall archives, and do they more actively use folders and the desktop? Do Open individuals have large amounts of pictures and music and so forth? We focus on personal archives including documents, music and folders. We exclude email organization as this largely involves processing information sent by others, rather than generating, finding and organizing personally relevant information [37]. We address the following questions:

- *Is there a relationship between people's personality and their organization of personal digital archives?*
- *How does personality affect organizational strategies?*
- *Can strangers identify structural cues that signal personality based on how a person organizes their personal archives?*

We use two different methods. Our first exploratory study presents people ('analysts') with structural information about how a stranger's personal digital archive is organized. We ask these analysts to first identify what structural aspects of the archive provide *cues* to the archive owner's personality, e.g. an organized Desktop reveals Conscientiousness. We then ask analysts to *predict* the owner's personality traits using these cues. In the second study, we test the validity of the structural cues identified in the first study. Participants complete a standard personality survey. We analyze the structure of their personal digital archive, using a program that generates structural information including number of files, files/folder, use of the desktop etc. We then assess whether and how owners' personality predicts objective structural properties of their personal archives.

Overall we demonstrate relations between PIM and personality. The first study generated a set of cues about which aspects of PIM structure signal personality, surprisingly showing that people may be able to use such structural information to reliably predict overall personality traits. The second study found that Conscientiousness and Neuroticism predict objective characteristics of people's personal archives, in particular desktop usage.

RELATED WORK

PIM and Individual Differences

PIM is an active research area, with new theoretical frameworks [23, 37] building on pioneering empirical studies examining how people organize their information [5, 25]. More recent work demonstrates that organizational structure predicts how successful people are at refinding personal information [5]. The importance of PIM for daily work means that many new software systems have been developed to improve organization and retrieval of personal information. These include sophisticated search tools [10] and faceted classification [7]. However these new organizational tools have not replaced the hierarchical file system: users still prefer to organize and retrieve information by navigating their personal file hierarchy [4, 34].

Malone [25] documented individual differences in how people organize paper archives that he called *filing* and *piling. Filers* organize collections into fine-grained subclassifications of semantically related items, whereas *pilers* make shallower collections involving large classes of heterogeneous objects related by temporal rather than semantic association. Email research has found similar strategies. Some people create complex folder structures to organize incoming messages (filers), while others leave many messages in the inbox relying on inbox scanning for retrieval (pilers) [36]. Although these simple strategy classifications have subsequently been refined [12, 19], there is consensus that there are distinct individual differences in organizational strategies. Work exploring the relations between organizational strategy and retrieval has shown that shallower broader organizations promote more effective and successful retrieval [5]. However there has been little systematic examination of the causes of these individual differences, which we explore here.

Personality Traits and Their Relation to Physical Environments

'Big-Five' personality theory has reliably identified 5 main *traits* [15,16,21,26]: *Openness to Experience:* how curious/imaginative vs. cautious/habitual a person is, expressed by a preference for novelty and independence; *Conscientiousness*: organized vs. careless, expressed by self-discipline and goal seeking; *Extraversion:* outgoing vs. solitary, expressed by tendencies to seek out and enjoy others' company; *Agreeableness*: friendly vs. cold, expressed by co-cooperativeness and trust of others; *Neuroticism:* nervous vs. confident, expressed by how much one experiences negative emotions and is able to control these. Together these traits are known by the acronym OCEAN [21]. Standard reliable personality surveys have been developed where survey responses correlate with observable behaviors or trained analysts' evaluations for most traits [15, 26].

Classic personality theory involves inferring traits from *observable behaviors* such as language use, non-verbal communication, interview style, and appearance [15,26]. More recent personality research has broadened to examining *personal artifacts and physical spaces*, in part because traits such as Openness have proved more difficult to detect from observable behaviors.

Gosling [16,17] has systematically examined relations between personality and personal *physical* environments. In each study, the owners ('targets') of that environment complete a standard personality survey. Next observers ('analysts') who do not know the owner inspect the target's environment, examining it for trait cues: for example how tidy it is, whether it contains photos of friends and family, diverse books and music, or inspirational posters. On the basis of their inspection, analysts fill out a personality survey assessing the target's personality. The key question is *whether analysts' personality assessments match the targets' self-evaluations*. For both dorms and offices analysts can identify Openness and Conscientiousness accurately. They are inaccurate at judging Agreeableness and moderately good at the remaining traits.

Gosling explains these relations between personality and physical environment in terms of three separate mediating mechanisms [16,17]. *Identity Claims* are when people *intentionally* structure personal environments to signal aspects of their personality to *others*. *Emotion Regulation* is *self-directed* organization occurring when people actively design personal environments to influence their mood. And *Behavioral Residue* is when people *unconsciously* leave informative traces in their environment following past actions. Behavioral Residue is a side-effect of everyday actions and is not *intentionally* created to affect self or others, in contrast to Identity Claims and Emotion Regulation.

Personal file systems are not generally intended for public viewing, or to be seen by others, so we anticipate that in our study, organization will be most affected by Behavioral Residue, somewhat affected by Emotion Regulation and relatively unaffected by Identity Claims.

Gosling's work also suggests possible *cues* for personality in the digital realm: Openness might be cued by a tendency to acquire more digital information, in particular varied types of files, e.g. music and pictures. Conscientiousness might be signaled by more systematic file organization. It is less obvious what might be reliable digital cues to Neuroticism, Agreeableness and Extraversion, and so our first study set out to explore this.

Intentional Identity Claims: Profiles and Personality

Although there is little prior work on digital archives and personality, much recent work has addressed how people use other digital media, such as profiles to *intentionally* signal personal characteristics to others. People's Facebook and online dating profiles are actively crafted to signal personal characteristics [6, 11] and this has been explained using Goffman's account of self-presentation [14]. More indirect aspects of one's online profile such as number of friends, density of friendship networks or language used online also predict personality [1, 6, 18, 29]. Personality can also be detected from the contents of personal web pages [35]. Another approach has explored how personality relates to online preferences (e.g. Facebook 'likes') or the content people access. Personality can be inferred from browsing logs [9, 13, 20, 24]. Kosinski et al [24] analyzed a massive collection of Facebook 'likes', finding that 'likes' predict various demographic, behavior and personality characteristics, most reliably Openness.

Digital Collections

Some previous work has examined collections of *digital possessions* and shown that personality traits can be predicted from the content of music collections [31]. Other work explores how digital collections (particularly music and photos) relate to Identity and Emotion Regulation [27]. Finally, work on physical mementos examines how these are organized around the home to support different functions. Public mementos are placed in social locations and chosen to promote conversation or signal shared family values, whereas private ones are meant to engender deeper emotions and facilitate self-regulation [28]. However none of these studies of possessions has tried to relate the *structure* of digital collections to the owner's personality.

STUDY 1: IDENTIFYING PERSONALITY CUES FROM STRUCTURE

This was an exploratory study to determine whether people ('analysts') could identify structural cues about a stranger's (target's) personality by examining their archive. Following Gosling [17], we expected analysts to be able to identify structural personality cues. We also wanted to see whether they could use these to accurately infer personality traits.

There were three steps to the procedure:

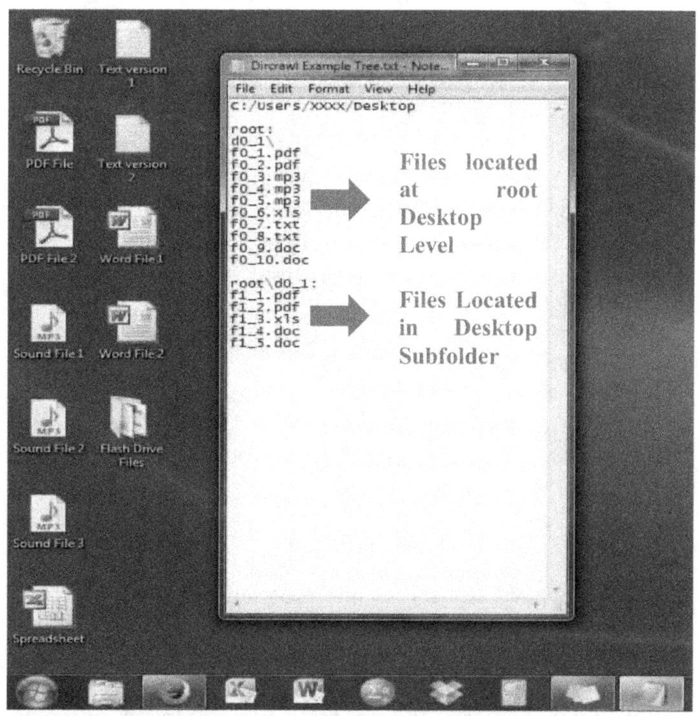

Figure 1: Automatic structural analysis for the Desktop. Open window shows dircrawl automatic anonymized analysis of structure for desktop revealing: one folder and 10 objects that are unfiled on the desktop and one desktop subfolder containing 5 objects.

- Analysts identified which structural attributes of the target's personal archive they thought served as *cues* to different personality traits,
- We determined targets' actual personality traits using a standard survey,
- Analysts judged the target's personality traits based on structural cues. We compared these with target's survey self-assessments allowing us to determine *judgment accuracy*.

Method

Profiling Targets and Generating Structural Information from Target Archives

Profiling Personality: We first recruited targets and profiled their personality. We then programmatically analyzed their archives to generate cues for analysts. We administered the 44 item Big Five Inventory (BFI) [15, 21] to an initial 8 target volunteers, and from them we selected a subset of 4 targets who were distinct in terms of their Big 5 personality traits. This was to ensure variability across different traits in our targets, allowing us to assess multiple personality traits. Our procedure asked analysts to compare two target's traits and we wanted those traits to be distinct.

Generating Structural Information: For the selected 4 targets (who were all PC users), we extracted structural information about their digital archives by running a program ('dircrawl') that analyzes their file organization. The program also automatically anonymizes all file and folder names, while retaining file type information (e.g. docx, ppt, pdf). Retaining file types should allow an analyst to tell that a target has a large collection of movies or documents, but not the names or content of those files. Sample outputs for a target's desktop are shown in Fig. 1, along with the specific desktop that generated those outputs. The first line of the output in each cluster of files (beginning with "root:") shows the folder's location within the folder hierarchy followed by the anonymized names of the files in that folder. In this case the program was started at the desktop level, so the first cluster (under root:) is the desktop folder itself, which contains one folder (d0_1) and 10 files labeled (f0_1.pdf to f0_10.doc). Note that while each *name* is anonymized, file *type* (pdf, mp3, txt, doc etc.) is preserved. The next cluster (root\d0_1:) lists the contents of the subfolder the user created on the desktop (d0_1), which contains 5 objects f1_1.pdf to f1_5.doc.

We explained several sample program outputs to analysts, showing them how different file structures were represented in the program and walked them through a key, listing various file types. We did not provide summary outputs, e.g. total number of files, or mean files per folder, as we did not want to prejudice analysts about what might be significant structural cues.

To generate target data for the study, we used dircrawl to collect data from 4 separate folder locations for each target: Documents, Desktop, Pictures, and Videos folders. We also interviewed each target to rule out the possibility that they kept personal data in other idiosyncratic places. Information about music was not collected in this study because the majority of music files are automatically organized within applications such as iTunes, undermining the potentially predictive nature of personality and file/folder organization behaviors.

Analysts were only shown personal files. We excluded system files as these are not actively organized by the targets themselves [32]. Based on the different applications that our targets used, personal files were defined by inclusion as: Microsoft office files (e.g. doc, docx, xls, pptx, etc), Mac productivity files (e.g. pages, keynote, etc), picture files (e.g. jpg, png, tiff, etc.), music files (e.g. mp3, m4a, wav, etc.), video files (e.g. mov, wmv, avi, etc.), and zip, txt, mid, csv, rtf, wpd, msg, pdf, and mp4 files. We did not observe any targets using Open Office files (.odt, etc). Folders that contained only system files were also removed so as to avoid the appearance of spurious empty folders.

Personality Trait Analysis

Participants: Twelve analysts were asked to examine the structural information obtained by the dircrawl program and to use it to determine the target's personality type, giving their assessment of their Big 5 traits [21]. Analysts were mostly aged 18-21, drawn from a first year psychology class recruited via online sign-ups. They completed the study for course credit.

Training on Structural Attributes: We first explained the program outputs to the analysts, showing them various illustrative examples of non-anonymized personal archives alongside their structural output. We showed how the outputs provided information about file and folder structure as well as file types. Once analysts confirmed that they understood how outputs related to the original archives, we explained that their task was to use similar anonymized outputs to determine the target's personality traits.

Training on Personality Traits: We briefly explained the Big Five personality traits providing capsule summaries of each and ensured that analysts understood each trait's definition. Analysts were allowed to consult these personality trait definitions throughout the study and encouraged to ask clarifying questions at any point if they were unsure about either personality definitions or dircrawl program outputs.

Procedure and Motivation: Each analyst judged the personality of two targets. To provide motivation we told analysts to adopt the role of a Crime Scene Investigator recruited to provide expert character analysis derived from structural analysis of the digital archives. Analysts looked at the structural information on a computer. There were 4 separate dircrawls for each target (starting at Documents, Desktop, Pictures, and Videos folders), meaning that analysts looked at 8 different text files, presented two at a time side-by-side (Desktops for the two targets, then Documents, etc.).

Identifying Trait Cues: To determine what analysts perceived to be important *cues* to personality, we elicited qualitative descriptions about the exact structural information were using to infer each personality trait. We also asked participants to compare and contrast the two targets for a given trait and explain how they used each target's structural information to formulate an assessment for that trait. These responses were audio recorded, and transcribed. Participants were allocated an hour for the task, although the average time taken was only 27 minutes.

Trait Judgments: Analysts also recorded their personality judgments on a set of 5 scales (one for each personality trait) where the ends of each scale represented the relevant trait anchors, e.g. Introvert-Extravert. Participants manually marked a point on a continuous scale for each target trait (e.g. if the analyst judged the target as an extreme Introvert they would give a score of exactly '1' and extreme Extravert a score of exactly '5' for that trait). We measured exact scale position for each trait, accurate to one sixteenth of an inch.

Results

Cues to Different Traits

We collected user comments about which aspects of structure signaled *cues* for each trait. Analysts noted multiple structural attributes as cues for a given trait and the same attribute was proposed for multiple different traits. The following content analysis was based on the 12 interviews. Consistent with Gosling [17] they provided more examples and were more confident about Openness and Conscientiousness than other personality traits.

Analysts readily provided cues for the *Openness* trait, and had clear views about how structure related to Openness. 11 analysts provided Openness cues, although one was uncertain about the reliability of the cue they provided. *Archive size*, particularly *overall number of pictures* and *videos* were all thought to signal Openness. Targets with more total files were thought to be more Open (6 analysts). Targets with many picture and video files were thought to be especially Open (8 analysts):

A7: I rate that person a 5 (highest score) in Openness, just because they had ***a lot of images and had a lot of files.***

Another important cue to Openness was general *lack of organization*; 4 analysts judged the target to be Open when their information was piled on the desktop or at shallow levels of the file hierarchy.

A10: But Y is more Open, he has way more pictures, ***even though they're not organized.***

Analysts were also able to identify clear cues signaling *Conscientiousness,* consistently focusing on *organization*. Altogether, 9 analysts provided cues to Conscientiousness. All were confident about the cues they provided. Four described *general levels of organization*:

A6 Their folders were ***pretty organized****, so they were both pretty Conscientious.*

Three identified *greater use of folders*. The following analyst identifies a lack of Conscientiousness indicated by empty folders and unfiled items:

A12: For Conscientiousness, ***Y, had lots of empty folders and then there were tons of unsorted things.***

Unfiled desktop information indicated lower Conscientiousness:

A11: X was more organized. And Y wasn't like a mess, but ***they had a lot of stuff on their desktop***

Another analyst focused on *within* folder organization analyzing whether folders contained *consistent file types*.

A1: X seemed pretty good at sorting things, so I guess that's Conscientiousness because a lot of their ***folders had very similar file types.***

Analysts found it harder to identify cues to *Extraversion*. Nine provided cues, although two were unsure of what they proposed and one analyst failed to provide any cues, saying that identifying cues was too hard. As with Openness, 5 analysts felt Extraverts were more likely to have *more files* overall and, specifically, *more pictures*:

A8: ***Y has a lot of pictures and he has more documents****.*

Three analysts thought that Introverts were more likely to be *highly organized*, and Extraverts more haphazard:

A12: I put by a 1 (extreme Introvert) based on the file structure ***- it seems like they are less chaotic and less spontaneous and more organized.***

Analysts also found *Agreeableness* cues much harder to determine. Only 6 provided cues, with 3 of these being unsure, and 2 others saying it was hard to specify cues. There was a partial focus on *number of files* and *organization*, but often there was a lack of confidence in this judgment:

A2: For Agreeableness, X seems like ***they don't have many files*** *so, like, they don't want to be in the limelight I guess.*

In the same way, analysts found it hard to provide cues for *Neuroticism*. Only 6 provided cues, one of whom was uncertain about the cues provided. Three analysts were unable to provide any cues. Cues focused on *number of files* (4 analysts), and *level of organization* taken to indicate a desire to control and avoid anxiety.

A12: X, maybe it could be like ***they're super organized because they have a lot of anxiety, which causes them to be orderly****.*

Analysts Trait Judgments Are Accurate

Comparison between Analyst and Target Evaluations: While the focus of this study was to generate cues we also explored the *accuracy* of analysts' judgments based on these cues. For all 12 analysts, we correlated *analyst's evaluations* of each trait with the ground truth of the *target's own self-evaluation* of that trait. Despite having just 24 observations (2 for each of 12 analysts), correlations were significant for Openness r(22)=0.412, p=0.045. None of the other individual trait correlations were significant. However when we combined *all traits* in a single correlation, judgments were accurate. After removing missing data points, for all 5 traits combined, there was a significant correlation: (r(112)=0.224,p=0.016).

Overall the results are encouraging, suggesting analysts can both identify structural cues and use these to accurately infer personality traits particularly Openness. Although Conscientiousness judgments were inaccurate participants were nevertheless able to generate plausible cues for this trait. Analysts were unconfident about cues for other traits, and their judgments less accurate.

OBJECTIVE RELATIONS BETWEEN PERSONALITY AND PERSONAL ARCHIVE STRUCTURE

The first study suggested analysts could identify cues and infer some personality traits from structural information about a stranger's archive. Our second study explored this relationship more directly by assessing whether specific *self-reported personality traits* predicted *objective structural characteristics* of a person's personal archive.

Analysts in our first study oriented to the following cues: (a) total number of files, (b) extent to which people imposed organization on these files by foldering them, (c) use of privileged locations such as the Desktop, and (d) number of media files such as music or photos. Results suggested that these were reliable cues to Openness, so we evaluated these in study 2. We explored Conscientiousness as our analysts' comments and prior work [17] suggest this trait might be inferable from archival properties. In addition we explored a potential cue for Neuroticism based on a trend observed in previous pilots of this study.

Method

Participants and Personality Assessment: We collected personality profiles from 62 participants (23 PC users and 39 Mac users). We obtained self-reported personality traits using the same Big Five Personality survey as in the first study. Again participants were recruited from a first year psychology class and their ages were 18-21. All participants had owned their laptop for at least one year.

Analyzing Personal Archives: We used the same dircrawl program as the first study, run on four major file locations (Documents, Desktop, Pictures, and Music). In contrast to the first study, we analyzed Music rather than Videos as both the literature and the participants in our first study suggested Music was important, and few of our participants kept large numbers of videos. To obtain informed consent from our participants, we first demonstrated our dircrawl analysis program showing how it generates anonymized structural data. Participants were encouraged to ask questions and allowed to withdraw if they did not want to participate. None withdrew.

Participants were asked about other locations where they actively organized personal files. One participant mentioned Downloads, but we excluded this because they did not actively organize information within it. Another mentioned Dropbox, but we this was excluded because as a shared resource it may have been organized by others. Files in My Music and My Photos folders are an ambiguous case; they are personal files, but are often automatically organized by the system, such as iTunes or iPhoto. Files from these locations were included in measures of total number of files, but excluded from analyses of active organization due to the higher likelihood that they had been automatically organized for the user.

Properties of Archives: We examined the following structural variables derived from dircrawl:

Total files: All personal files located in all four default folder locations combined (Desktop, Documents, Music, and Pictures). This gave an overall measure of the *size* of the person's archive.

Total files in actively organized locations: All files in the Documents and Desktop folders. We are interested in active organization so this variable excluded files from the Pictures and Music folders as these were more likely to be automatically organized (e.g. iTunes, iPhoto, etc).

Files/folder: Average number of files per folder in actively organized locations (Documents and Desktop). This gave us a measure of a person's propensity to impose organization on actively managed information.

The Desktop's salience makes it a privileged location for personal archives. It is actively used for task management and reminding about outstanding tasks [25, 37]. We therefore included two specific measures of Desktop usage.

Total desktop files: Number of files located in the entire Desktop folder.

Percentage of Desktop files in organized folders: Percentage of total desktop files that are located in subfolders rather than scattered unorganized at the root level of the Desktop space. This provides a measure of the extent to which the desktop is organized versus cluttered.

Gosling's work [17] also suggests the importance of media such as music and books in revealing personality traits, so we also measured:

Total music files: Total number of music files across all folder locations.

Total picture files: Total number of picture files across all folder locations.

All of these archival metrics were highly skewed, so, to run analyses to determine their relationships with personality traits, they were each log transformed.

Archive Property	Mean	Median	Std. Dev.
Total Files	15320.1	9330	24174.2
Total Files in Actively Organized Locations	5395.9	864	21925.5
Files/Folder in Actively Organized Locations	18.9	13.2	16.4
Total Desktop Files	4745.2	272	21827.9
Percentage Desktop Files Organized in Folders	75.1	98.3	40.5
Total Picture Files	11287.3	5239	19214.6
Total Music Files	2929.45	1551	3994.5

Table 1: Descriptive statistics prior to log transformation

Our predictions are derived from our first study and Gosling's findings about personality in physical environments [17]. Based on Study 1 and Gosling's findings we expected Openness and Conscientiousness to predict PIM practices. We were also interested in looking into a potential relationship between Neuroticism and the desktop based on a trend seen in prior pilots of this study. We repeatedly observed that Neurotic participants kept more items on the Desktop possibly to reduce anxiety about forgetting ongoing tasks involving those items. Predictions and results are presented separately for each trait.

Results

Descriptive statistics prior to log transformation of each variable are presented in Table 1.

Conscientiousness Predicts Organization

Conscientious people have clean, organized, neat, and uncluttered physical spaces [17]. Our initial study also suggested Conscientiousness cues such as having "more things organized," as well as "[having] less stuff." Lack of conscientiousness was signaled by "a lot of files on their desktop." We therefore predicted Conscientious individuals would have:

- ***Fewer files overall,*** **because they don't keep superfluous information.**
- ***Fewer files per folder*** **because they should be more actively organizing.**
- ***Fewer files*** **on the** ***Desktop,*** **to keep their workspace clear.**
- ***Higher percentage of desktop files organized into folders*** **to actively manage ongoing tasks.**

We used regressions to test whether total number of files in actively organized locations, number of files per folder, number of desktop files, and percentage of foldered desktop files are significantly related to Conscientiousness. Variables were also centered to control for multi-collinearity. We conducted one regression rather than multiple correlations to avoid the risk of generating spurious significant results following multiple statistical tests.

As OS affects organization [5], we conducted separate analyses for PC and Mac users. We tested 2 models for each. Model 1 tested Total Files and Files per Folder as predictors. In addition we tested the interaction, Total Files X Files per Folder, to determine whether tendency to organize is mediated by total number of files. Model 2 adds desktop variables: Total Desktop files and Percentage of foldered Desktop files.

For PC users (see Table 2) Model 1 is not significant (R^2=.108,F=0.689,p=.571), but if we include Desktop variables the regression is highly significant (R^2=.709,F=7.297,p=.001), and all variables have significant effects. Model 2 indicates Conscientious PC users keep fewer files overall, confirming our first hypothesis. However, files per folder is *positively* related to conscientiousness, which contradicts what we expected. One explanation is that Conscientious individuals are less likely to create 'failed folders' [36] that are empty or contain one or two files only. Again contradicting our hypothesis, Conscientious people keep *more* files on the Desktop, possibly to better manage their tasks. However as expected they are active in foldering these. Fig 3 shows the

	Model 1 General Organization			Model 2 Desktop Organization		
	Coef.	SE	P	Coef.	SE	P
Intercept	3.611	.152	.000	2.280	.262	.000
Total Files (Documents & Desktop)	.012	.083	.884	-.362	.087	.001
Files/Folder	.243	.200	.240	.443	.128	.004
Total Files X Files/Folder	.110	.096	.270	-.148	.060	.026
Desktop Files				.145	.053	.015
Desktop Files in Self-Created Folders				.212	.062	.004
	R^2	F		R^2	F	P
	.108	.689	.571	.709	7.297	.001

Table 2: Nested lagged regression of the general organization metrics and the desktop organization metrics related to Conscientiousness for PC users.

interaction between total files and active organization indicating that the relationship is moderated by the total number of files, with files/folder only being predictive of Conscientiousness when people have low numbers of files. This may be explained by the fact that it is more cognitively demanding to systematically folder when one has large numbers of files, making it hard even for Conscientious participants to keep data organized.

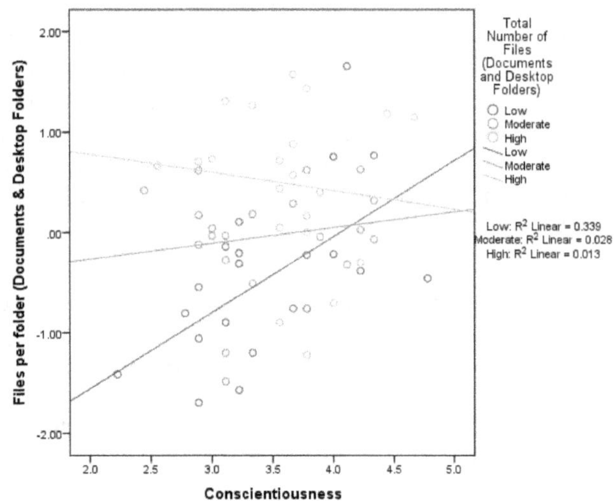

Figure 3: Relations between Total Number of files and Files per folder and Conscientiousness: Conscientiousness predicts active foldering only when people have fewer files

For Mac users the regression analysis was only significant for Model 1 (R^2=.222,F=3.327,p=.031). The interaction was the only significant predictor, indicating a similar mediating relationship between total number of files and files per folder as was found for PC users. However, including the desktop terms did not improve the regression. This suggests that Mac users have a very different relationship with the desktop space. Whereas for PC users it is a space that seems to be related to Conscientiousness, for Mac users this is not the case.

Openness

Cues for identifying Openness in physical spaces include distinctive, stylish, and unconventional spaces and varied CDs and magazines [17]. Participants from our initial study also reported that they relied on the total number of files for determining Openness, although this is not what Gosling found. From this we hypothesize that:

- **Open participants should have more *total files, more music and more picture files* because of a desire to expose themselves to a broad range of stimuli**
- **Open individuals should have more varied *types* of files**

Regression analyses were run, again separating Mac and PC users, to test whether total number of files overall, total number of picture files, and total number of music files are significantly related to Openness. We again include an interaction term to allow for the fact that increased number of music and picture files may mean different things based on the total number of files overall. Variables were again centered to control for multi-collinearity.

Contrary to our predictions, neither model was significant, For PC users: (R^2=.350,F=1.829,p=.161) and for MAC users (R^2=.120,F=.896,p=.495) confirming Gosling's findings that Openness is not predicted by total files, amount of music, and amount of pictures. Gosling's findings would argue instead that it is the *variety* of music and pictures that indicate Openness. However filetype variety was unrelated to Openness (R^2=.031,F=.568,p=.572) for MACs and (R^2=.165,F=1.876,p=.181) for PCs.

Neuroticism

Neuroticism is not well predicted in physical spaces [17]. Participants from our initial study also reported difficulties identifying cues to Neuroticism. However, other pilot studies we have conducted consistently suggest a relationship between neuroticism and use of the desktop space. This may be because anxious people keep more of their files on the desktop to avoid forgetting active to-dos. Based on this our prediction for neuroticism is:

- **Neurotic participants should have more desktop files because of concerns about forgetting important tasks.**

We conducted a simple regression combining all users to see if total number of desktop files was a significantly related to Neuroticism. The regression was not significant (R^2=.043,F=2.706,p=.105) but it does appear to be trending in the predicted direction. However one characteristic of the desktop is that its 'messiness' may fluctuate with workload. Given that our sample was made up of a student population we took into account students' work cycle where the beginning of an academic term marks a reset. We expected desktop effects to be most pronounced for students tested late in the quarter as work piles up. When we ensured that we sampled participants tested at least halfway through the academic term (N = 45) this same regression becomes significant (R^2=.144,F=7.418,p=.009) indicating that high number of files on the desktop relates to Neuroticism. Future iterations of this work will be necessary to confirm the validity of this relationship.

DISCUSSION AND CONCLUSIONS

Our finding that people's personality affects how they organize is important for PIM theory. It demonstrates that PIM behaviors are not entirely *functional*. Rather than someone's file system being rationally organized to maximize retrieval, our results suggest that organization is partially driven by aspects of the users' personality. However it could still be true that a match between personality and organization may optimize retrieval and future work could test this.

This study presents a new approach to understanding individual differences in PIM practices. There are various technical implications to these findings. Personality factors may help address pernicious problems in the *design* of PIM tools, allowing us to target tools to different user traits. A well-documented barrier to the widespread adoption of PIM tools is that users employ very different strategies for the same organizational tasks [23,36]. We have shown that personality is one source of these differences, although other factors such as job type [3] may also be important. Our results allow us to predict organizational style once we have profiled personality. Tools might therefore provide personality based defaults based on different user personality traits. Thus, it may be that for PCs, Conscientious users may want tools that provide greater support for task management and the Desktop. Neurotics may also want to organize ready access to their Desktops. While personalization has been proposed previously, as far as we are aware, this is the first research to make *specific recommendations* about how it might be implemented to respect personality differences. There is also growing concern about how personal information management practices can cause knowledge workers stress and anxiety [8]. Devising PIM practices that suit one's personality might also reduce such stress.

We also contribute to new theoretical approaches to the study of personality that examine *possessions* rather than *observable behaviors* as signals of personality. While prior personality work has explored mechanisms of Identity Claims and Emotion Regulation [1, 16, 17, 29], we believe our study is the first to look at digital *Behavioral Residue*. File systems are usually private, and we extend other work demonstrating relationships between traits and *public* aspects of digital behavior such as active construction of profiles, or active digital behaviors such as browsing, language use or Facebook 'likes' [1, 6, 18, 29]. Conscientiousness was related to smaller archives and more Desktop files with these being organized into folders, presumably to support reminding and task management.

We also found interesting differences between PC and MAC users; for PC users, systematic active use of the desktop related to Conscientiousness, while this was not true for MAC participants. Another intriguing aspect of our findings concerned the interaction between traits and the total amount of information stored. While Conscientious people stored less information overall, the effects of Conscientiousness are most marked for participants who stored lower amounts of information. These people seemed less likely to create spurious unused folders. We also found that as workload increased, Neurotics reacted by keeping more files on the desktop. This could be to decrease anxiety over forgetting pending work tasks and to-dos.

There are limitations to our study. Our analytic program Dircrawl does not provide *spatial* organizational information which some users thought could be related to personalitytraits. Future work should explore this. There is also evidence that people are increasingly storing materials in the *cloud* [32], which we didn't examine here. We also focused on actively organized archives, but it might also be interesting to include temporary locations such as Downloads or Trash, although there are clearly issues about when to record representative usage, as many participants periodically clear these out. In addition our participant pool was homogeneous and more diverse populations should be explored.

Another issue concerns intriguing inconsistencies between our two studies. Why were analysts able to accurately detect Openness in study 1, but we could not find relationships in study 2? It seems that our analysts had access to information that was not captured by the summary statistics tested in study 2. Prior work suggests *variety* of music and magazines are strong Openness cues, and it may be that our hypotheses need to be refined. We carried out a simple analysis of variety of file *types,* but it may be that other properties such as age, length of file name, creator and so forth might offer more reliable indicators of variety and hence Openness.

The opposite was true for Conscientiousness. We were able to detect relations between objective organization and Conscientiousness. Intriguingly, study 1 shows analysts clearly oriented to the correct structural properties although their final judgments were inaccurate. This may be because certain relations are unexpected. Our regression model showed counterintuitive relations, e.g. Conscientious people have *more* desktop files and *more* files per folder. Our findings on Neuroticism make intuitive sense although they are not predicted by theory, and need to be explored further.

An interesting future direction concerns the organization of *shared* tools such as Dropbox or GoogleDrive. Prior work suggests that collaborators experience difficulties in co-organizing such folders [30, 32, 33]. However theoretically we could examine whether shared tool organization reveals traces of *all* participants' personalities or whether more *dominant* team members' personality is most clearly stamped on the shared archive.

Future work should continue to explore these novel relations between personality and personal digital archives. That work could extend personality theory exploring relations between possessions and personality. Enhanced understanding will also address outstanding issues surrounding personalization and customization that has been a substantial barrier to the adoption of general PIM tools.

REFERENCES

1. Bachrach, Y., Kohli, P., Graepel, T., Stillwell, D.J, Kosinski, M. Personality and patterns of Facebook usage. *Proc WebSci*, ACM Press (2012) 36–44.
2. Barreau, D., & Nardi, B. A. Finding and reminding: file organization from the desktop. *ACM SigChi Bulletin*, *27*(3) (1995) 39-43.

3. Bellotti, V., Ducheneaut, N., Howard, M., Smith, I., & Grinter, R. E. Quality versus quantity: E-mail-centric task management and its relation with overload. *HCI*, *20*(1) (2005), 89-138.

4. Bergman, O., Beyth-Marom, R., Nachmias, R., Gradovitch, N., & Whittaker, S. Improved search engines and navigation preference in PIM. *ACM (TOIS)*, *26*(4) (2008), 20-58.

5. Bergman, O., Whittaker, S., Sanderson, M., Nachmias, R., & Ramamoorthy, A. The effect of folder structure on personal file navigation. *Journal of the ASIST*, *61*(12) (2010) 2426-2441.

6. Boyd, D. Friendster and publicly articulated social networking. *Proc. CHI* (2004), 1279–1282.

7. Cutrell, E., Robbins, D., Dumais, S., & Sarin, R. Fast, flexible filtering with phlat. *Proc CHI,* ACM Press. (2006) 261-270.

8. Dabbish, L. A., & Kraut, R. E. Email overload at work: an analysis of factors associated with email strain. *Proc. CSCW,* ACM Press(2006) 431-440.

9. De Bock K, Van Den Poel D (2010) Predicting website audience demographics for Web advertising targeting using multi-website clickstream data. *FI 98(1)* (2010) 49–70.

10. Dumais, S., Cutrell, E., Cadiz, J. J., Jancke, G., Sarin, R., & Robbins, D. C. Stuff I've seen: a system for personal information retrieval and re-use. *Proc. SIGIR,* ACM Press. (2003) 72-79.

11. Ellison, N., Heino, R., & Gibbs, J. Managing impressions online: Self-presentation processes in the online dating environment. *JCMC 11*, 2 (2006), Article 2.

12. Fisher, D., Brush, A. J., Gleave, E., & Smith, M. A. (2006, November). Revisiting Whittaker & Sidner's email overload ten years later. *Proc. CSCW*, ACM Press (2006) 309-312.

13. Goel S, Hofman JM, Sirer MI (2012) Who does what on the Web: Studying Web browsing behavior at scale. *Proc ICWSM* ACM Press (2012) 130–137.

14. Goffman, E. *The presentation of self in everyday life.* Anchor: New York, 1959.

15. Goldberg, L. R. The development of markers for the Big-Five factor structure. *Psychological assessment*, *4*(1) (1992) 26-39.

16. Gosling, S. *Snoop: What your stuff says about you.* Basic Books. (2009)

17. Gosling, S. D., Ko, S. J., Mannarelli, T., & Morris, M. E. A room with a cue: personality judgments based on offices and bedrooms. *Journal of personality and social psychology*, *82*(3) (2002) 379-394.

18. Gosling, S. D., Gaddis, S., & Vazire, S. Personality Impressions Based on Facebook Profiles. *Proc. ICWSM* ACM Press (2007) 123-130.

19. Gwizdka, J. Email task management styles: the cleaners and the keepers. *Proc. CHI,* ACM Press. (2004) 1235-1238.

20. Hu J, Zeng H-J, Li H, Niu C, Chen Z. Demographic prediction based on user's browsing behavior. *IWWWC,* (2007) 151–160.

21. John, O. P., Donahue, E. M., & Kentle, R. 'The Big Five: Factor Taxonomy. *In Handbook of Personality: Theory and Research* (1990) 66-100.

22. Joinson, A.N. Looking at, looking up or keeping up with people?: Motives and use of Facebook. *Proc. CHI* ACM Press (2008) 1027–1036.

23. Jones, W. *Keeping Found Things Found.* Morgan Kaufmann. (2010).

24. Kosinski M, Kohli P, Stillwell DJ, Bachrach Y, Graepel T. Personality and website choice. *ACM WebSci* (2012) 251–254.

25. Malone, T. W. How do people organize their desks?: Implications for the design of office information systems. *ACM TOIS*, *1*(1) (1983) 99-112.

26. McCrae, R. R., & Costa, P. T. Validation of the five-factor model of personality across instruments and observers. *Journal of personality and social psychology*, *52*(1) (1987) 81.

27. Odom, W., Pierce, J., Stolterman, E., & Blevis, E. Understanding why we preserve some things and discard others in the context of interaction design. *Proc .CHI*, ACM Press. (2009) 1053-1062).

28. Petrelli, D., Whittaker, S., & Brockmeier, J. AutoTopography: what can physical mementos tell us about digital memories? *Proc CHI*, ACM Press (2008) 53-62.

29. Quercia D, Lambiotte R, Kosinski M, Stillwell D, Crowcroft J (2012) The Personality of popular Facebook users. *Proc CSCW,* ACM Press (2012) 955–964.

30. Rader, E. Yours, mine and (not) ours: social influences on group information repositories. *Proc CHI,* ACM Press (2009) 2095-2098.

31. Rentfrow, P. J., & Gosling, S. D. The do re mi's of everyday life: the structure and personality correlates of music preferences. *Journal of personality and social psychology*, *84*(6), (2003) 1236-1258.

32. Tang, J., Drews, C., Smith, M., Wu, F., Sue, A., & Lau, T. Exploring Patterns of Social Commonality Among File Directories at Work. *Proc CHI,* ACM Press (2007) 951-960.

33. Tang, J., Brubaker, J., & Marshall, C. What Do You See In The Cloud? Understanding the Cloud-Based User Experience through Practices. *HCI – INTERACT* (2013) 563-572.

34. Teevan, J., Alvarado, C., Ackerman, M. S., & Karger, D. R. The perfect search engine is not enough: a study of orienteering behavior in directed search. *Proc CHI,* ACM Press (2004) 415-422.

35. Vazire, S., & Gosling, S. D. e-Perceptions: personality impressions based on personal websites. *Journal of personality and social psychology*, *87*(1), (2004) 123-132.

36. Whittaker, S., & Sidner, C. Email overload: exploring personal information management of email. *Proc. CHI,* ACM Press (1996) 276-283.

37. Whittaker, S. Personal information management: from information consumption to curation. *ARIST*, *45*(1) (2011) 1-62.

Show Me the Invisible: Visualizing Hidden Content

Thomas Geymayer
Graz University of Technology
geymayer@icg.tugraz.at

Markus Steinberger
Graz University of Technology
steinberger@icg.tugraz.at

Alexander Lex
Harvard University
alex@seas.harvard.edu

Marc Streit
Johannes Kepler
University Linz
marc.streit@jku.at

Dieter Schmalstieg
Graz University of Technology
schmalstieg@icg.tugraz.at

ABSTRACT

Content on computer screens is often inaccessible to users because it is hidden, e.g., occluded by other windows, outside the viewport, or overlooked. In search tasks, the efficient retrieval of sought content is important. Current software, however, only provides limited support to visualize hidden occurrences and rarely supports search synchronization crossing application boundaries. To remedy this situation, we introduce two novel visualization methods to guide users to hidden content. Our first method generates awareness for occluded or out-of-viewport content using see-through visualization. For content that is either outside the screen's viewport or for data sources not opened at all, our second method shows off-screen indicators and an on-demand smart preview. To reduce the chances of overlooking content, we use visual links, i.e., visible edges, to connect the visible content or the visible representations of the hidden content. We show the validity of our methods in a user study, which demonstrates that our technique enables a faster localization of hidden content compared to traditional search functionality and thereby assists users in information retrieval tasks.

Author Keywords

Hidden Content; Off-Screen Content; Occluded Content; Visual Linking.

ACM Classification Keywords

H.5.2. Information Interfaces and Presentation: Graphical User Interfaces

INTRODUCTION

When analyzing multiple data sources and documents simultaneously, not all information can be kept in plain sight. There are several causes for information being hidden from a user. First, many documents contain more content than can sensibly be displayed at a time, making it necessary to show only a small fraction of the information contained. We refer to the visible section of a document as its viewport, which, in order to read the whole document, must be changed through scrolling and zooming. Second, it is common that many (partially) occluding application windows are open, potentially covering relevant information. A third cause of content being hidden are minimized windows. To manage limited screen-space, users regularly minimize windows, which may contain important information. Finally, relevant information may be contained in unopened or not accessed documents.

Common strategies to identify relevant information include *searching* and *brushing*. Users can *search* for specific keywords and explore the context of individual occurrences. While zooming and scrolling can be used to manually search through content, most applications also provide a built-in search function that highlights occurrences of a search term. Often, users can advance the viewport of the application to the next matching term. *Brushing* is similar to searching, but instead of an explicit query, the query is implicitly given by selecting an existing item. Further occurrences of the selected item may be highlighted and/or linked. Brushing is common in visualization tools and text-editors.

By going through all open application windows and searching or brushing in each application in turn, users are able to eventually access all relevant information. As search functions are also available for searching through online documents and files stored on disk, all types of initially hidden content could possibly be explored. For certain tasks this kind of workflow is sensible. It is, for example, sufficient for looking up words in a dictionary, where each term has one entry.

There are, however, other tasks where seeing a global structure between individual pieces of information is highly relevant. Consider a user investigating the causes of a crisis in a company. The investigator needs to tie together information from multiple sources. These may involve dozens of reports with hundreds of pages each, multiple spreadsheets documenting money flow, web exposes of other companies involved, travel routes of employees, etc.

If the investigator finds an interesting fact, she will typically want to cross-reference other occurrences of the fact. For many documents this is inefficient using the sequential search approach. In this paper, we introduce techniques that instead let users see an overview of all occurrences, no matter in which document they are contained or if they are visible or hidden, and jump directly to the most interesting occurrence(s).

CHI'14, April 26–May 1, 2014, Toronto, ON, Canada.
ACM 978-1-4503-2473-1/14/04$15.00.
http://dx.doi.org/10.1145/2556288.2557032

Directly accessing all content, both visible and hidden, poses a number of challenges. To address these challenges, we elicited six requirements that a technique for visualizing hidden content needs to address. This list evolved out of an initial set of requirements which we based on our experience with designing visualization interfaces for application domains such as systems biology and our own needs when working on search tasks. We then created multiple prototypes, which we informally evaluated with users, leading us to the following final set of requirements:

R I: Mental map. Users should be aided in building a mental map of the explored documents. Ideally, this overview should make use of the investigator's spatial memory by pointing out occurrences at their actual position on the desktop (if occluded), or at least preserve relative arrangement of occurrences (if currently not on the desktop). For such a mapping, it is necessary to communicate the information's *location* or at least the *direction* in which information can be found.

R II: Indicate occurrences & relevance. Sources or sections mentioning a search term multiple times tend to be more relevant compared to documents or parts that only contain a few mentions of a term. Thus, users may want to prioritize densely populated documents or sections in their search. To support this requirement, visual cues should indicate the amount of information available at a specific location or in a certain direction.

R III: Fast previews. To enable users to quickly judge whether looking at a specific region in a document in detail could be interesting, getting fast previews of hidden content should be possible.

R IV: Fast navigation. Fast navigation between all available chunks of information is essential for an efficient exploration. Once a user has chosen to closely investigate a piece of hidden information, it should be possible to quickly navigate there with minimal interaction.

R V: Heterogeneous sources. The integration of information from different sources is essential to capture all types of hidden content. The technique should connect information from open application windows, minimized windows, and documents which are only present as a file on a disk or available on the Internet. All sources should be handled in a unified manner to allow for all types of hidden content.

R VI: Changing content. The technique must be able to accommodate arbitrary changes to the content presented on the desktop. In particular, the arrangement of windows on the desktop can change at any time: Windows can be moved, resized, minimized, or closed. Moreover, the content and viewport of windows may change at any time, possibly removing existing information, adding new information, or changing location and visibility of information.

In addition to content being hidden, visible content can also be overlooked [4]. While traditional highlighting techniques such as color work reasonably well on a uniform background, a cluttered environment, e.g., due to many windows, or other factors such as large display sizes can increase the chances of relevant content being overlooked [14]. A remedy for overlooking content are visual links [21], explicit edges connecting individual pieces of information.

Our contribution are two novel visualization techniques for hidden content and their combination with visual links into one sophisticated information exploration system that integrates multiple applications and data sources. First, we present **smart links**, a see-through visualization to extend visual links to occluded content. Second, for out-of-screen content, we present a combination of visual links and **smart previews**, aiding the user in quickly estimating the amount of relevant information and allowing accelerated navigation to the information. Additionally, we show how minimized windows and information from files on disk can be integrated into the visualization. Using these two techniques, we provide guidance to all aforementioned types of hidden content. We conducted an exploratory user study evaluating the performance of our hidden content visualization methods relative to standard search functionality. The results of this study indicate that visualization of hidden content is superior to traditional methods in both quantitative and qualitative measures.

RELATED WORK

As mentioned previously, the two main reasons for available content not being considered is that it is *hidden*, i.e., not visible to the user, or that it is *overlooked* even though it is technically visible [4]. We first discuss techniques to show and access hidden content, followed by techniques that help avoid overlooking content.

Hidden Content

For hidden content, we distinguish between techniques that reveal occluded or out-of-viewport content that could be shown within the given display space and techniques that visualize off-screen content.

A common strategy to reveal **occluded content** are see-through interfaces that cull away the foreground to reveal the background. A prominent example are magic lenses [5], which in their general form can not only remove foreground but also alter the representation in arbitrary ways. Magic lenses are typically invoked manually and locally (only the elements within a 'lens' are changed), a characteristic that is not suitable for search tasks. While completely transparent windows [11] and user interface elements [12] have been evaluated in the past, in practice they are rarely used when reading and interacting with content in window managers. An approach that uses transparency for 'unimportant' window regions is described by Ishak and Feiner [18], while Baudisch and Gutwin introduce 'multiblending' [1], as a smarter alternative to alpha blending that considers multiple image features and makes the blending results more readable. A more sophisticated approach is taken by Waldner et al. [29], who superimpose 'clip-outs' of occluded content on top of occluding components. They use a measure of salience to reveal salient occluded content in regions where the occluding elements are not salient. Steinberger et al. [20] additionally scale unimportant content to reveal occluded content. None of these approaches use a semantic measure of relevance, i.e., consider what is currently relevant to a user. Search tasks, however, inherently require revealing specific semantic elements.

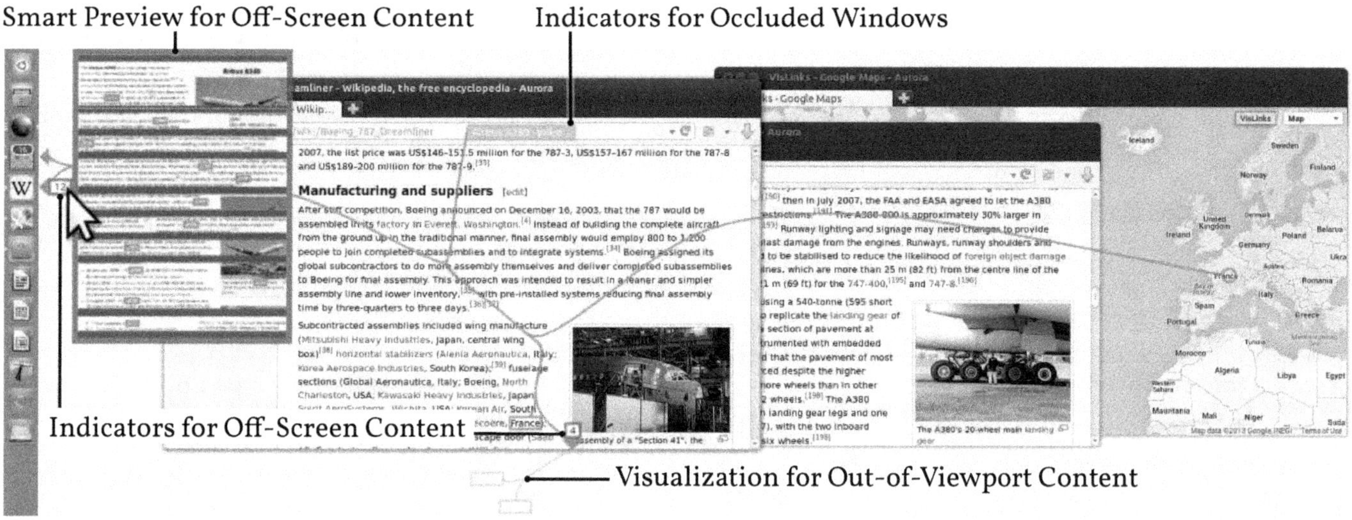

Figure 1: Visualization of occluded, out-of-viewport, and off-screen content. Multiple browser windows and files stored on the computer contain occurrences of the search term “France”. Most occurrences are either outside one of the browser's viewports, which is indicated by arrows and links to the out-of-viewport locations, or are occluded by another window, which is indicated by semi-transparent red window labels. The arrows pointing to applications in the taskbar indicate off-screen content in a minimized window (Wikipedia) containing 12 occurrences of the search term and 16 files found by the desktop search engine. Hovering over an arrow, reveals a smart preview showing the regions of the documents containing occurrences.

A common strategy to visualize **off-screen** content are marks rendered within the visible area that point to off-screen content. Baudisch and Rosenholz introduce *halos* [2], circles with the center at the (off-screen) point of interest and a radius chosen so that a segment of the circle intersects with the display. Similar in spirit are *wedges* [10], a technique that uses triangle instead of circles. Users can infer the location of the point from the size and position of the circle or triangle segment. A problem of halos and, to a lesser extend of wedges, is scalability and clutter if many targets should be indicated. To remedy this, Waldner et al. [27] introduce arrows that aggregate multiple proximate points of interest and indicate how many items are aggregated with the size of the arrow. Highly abstracted document previews are another technique to visualize off-screen content. Eick and Ball use such abstract representations for visualizing software [9]. Hearst combines them with a visualization of the search term density in specific regions of text [13]. This technique has been extended by Dieberger and Russel [8] to consider multiple search terms and enable fast navigation and preview. The occurrences of search terms can also be superimposed on the scroll bar [6], a technique that is nowadays, for example, employed in web browsers and in software development tools. However, all of these tools and techniques use very abstract representations. We believe that using a representation that preserves the appearance of the document under inspection will provide additional benefit to users. In our work we combine both, marks to indicate the presence of off-screen context and on-demand smart previews to minimize clutter and enable efficient discovery of and navigation to off-screen content.

Overlooked Content

Search combined with highlighting is a common method to minimize overlooking of content. The highlighting typically employs adding a colored frame, but other methods such as magnifying search terms [25] or interesting parts while shrinking [16, 17] or even completely removing other content is possible [3]. Such methods are also used for generally ‘interesting’ content [16]. Stoffel et al. use a similar approach for thumbnail previews, where they distort important terms, while preserving the layout of the document [22].

A different approach is to employ connectedness [19], i.e., visual links [7], as a method to highlight occurrences of a search term, which are beneficial especially in a cluttered environment such as in an information visualization system [7, 23, 24, 26, 27] or on large screens where not all content is in a user's field of view [14, 28]. Hoffman et al. [14] have evaluated various techniques to help users locate windows on large displays and found that links (trails) outperform conventional highlighting (frames); similar results have been found for conventional displays [21]. We believe that visual links are the most powerful method to point to content distributed over the screen, especially in a highly heterogeneous environment spanning multiple windows and various types of documents, and consequently have chosen to combine them with methods to visualize hidden content in this paper.

VISUALIZING HIDDEN CONTENT

For visualizing hidden content we take two steps: indicating that relevant content is hidden in the first place, and revealing the hidden content on demand. We introduce novel techniques to visualize **occluded content**, i.e., content that is occluded by other windows, **out-of-viewport content**, i.e., content that is outside of the application window but within the limits of the display, and **off-screen content**, i.e., content that is outside of the available display space or that is in closed, minimized,

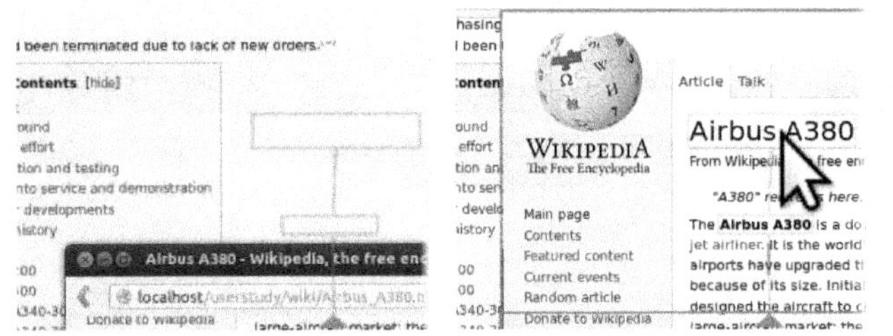

(a) (b)

Figure 2: (a) Smart links pointing to out-of-viewport occurrences of a search term. (b) Hovering over a smart link reveals a semi-transparent overlay showing the actual content.

or not accessed documents. All of these techniques are integrated with visual links to create a strong visual connection between all related pieces of information—hidden as well as visible—resulting in an information exploration interface that makes hidden content easily accessible and reduces the risk of overlooking content (see Figure 1).

Visualizing Out-of-Viewport Content

Relevant content is often hidden due to the limited viewport size. Large portions of content can be situated in virtual space outside of a window's viewport. We distinguish two cases of out-of-viewport content: (1) The target region is outside the current viewport, but would be visible on the screen if the application's viewport was extended, and (2) the target region is outside the screen. We consider the latter case as off-screen content, which is treated in a later section.

For the former case we use *smart links*: semi-transparent outlines—one for each target region—that indicate the location of invisible target regions (Figure 2(a)) and are connected to other visible or hidden occurrences with visual links. Smart links clearly indicate the occurrence and relevance of hidden content (R II) and support a user's mental map (R I). If the user hovers over a target region outside the application's viewport, as shown in Figure 2(b), all of the application's content that fits on the desktop is rendered in order to provide context to the otherwise 'disembodied' target region, thus providing fast previews of the hidden content (R III). When the user selects such a target region, the application's viewport is automatically centered around the region, allowing the user to immediately continue working with the application at the chosen position, thus facilitating fast navigation (R IV).

Visualizing Occluded Content

To direct the user's attention to windows containing occluded content, we use markers, connected to visual links, as shown in Figure 3(a) that contain the title of the windows where relevant content was found. We chose this approach over showing direct links to occluded content (as we do for out-of-viewport regions), since user-feedback indicated that direct links produce too much clutter. When hovering over such a marker, we overlay the hidden window semi-transparently and highlight and connect the relevant content (R III), as shown in Figure 3(b). To avoid interference with the background window, the overlay can optionally be shown completely opaque.

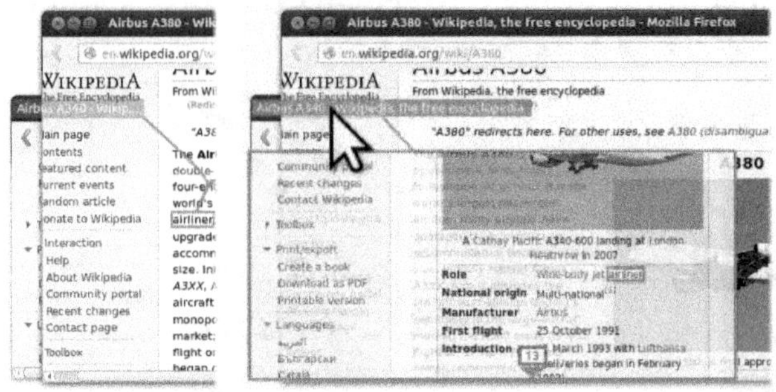

(a) (b)

Figure 3: (a) A marker showing a part of the window title indicates occluded content. (b) Hovering over the marker reveals a transparent preview of the occluded window, including highlights for the occluded content.

To ensure fast navigation to the occluded region (R IV), a click with the mouse on the overlay moves the respective window to the top of the window stack, thus permanently revealing the occluded information.

Visualizing Off-Screen Content

If a target region is located either outside the screen, within a minimized windows, or in unopened files, it is not possible to draw a link to a specific target region. Instead, we visualize off-screen content by drawing an arrow pointing into the direction of the target, or at the icons representing the minimized windows and unopened files. To avoid clutter in cases where multiple target regions are off-screen, we only draw a single arrow for each icon or window edge. For the latter case we adjust the arrow to point towards the center of gravity of all outside regions. Additionally, we draw a text label next to the arrow to show the number of hidden target regions in the given direction (see Figure 1). These encodings indicate occurrences and relevance (R II).

To get an overview of the whole document (R I) and to enable fast navigation (R IV), we provide a *smart preview* of the complete document, which appears when hovering over the arrow. For search tasks, it is reasonable to assume that users are only interested in those parts of the document that contain relevant information. We use this consideration to present the user with a more compact preview where regions containing no relevant information are clipped, freeing up space for increasing the size of interesting areas (see Figure 4). In this way, all hidden regions of the document are presented at once. To decide which areas should be removed, we first calculate bounding boxes of all highlighted regions, then loop through all bounding boxes and mark regions with a certain margin above and below as important and finally hide all unmarked and therefore unimportant regions (see Figure 4(c)).

These smart previews can be zoomed and panned to explore all target regions in detail (R III). To facilitate orientation (R I), the current viewport of the application is highlighted using a rectangle in the preview. Once a target region has been identified by the user, clicking on the target region hides

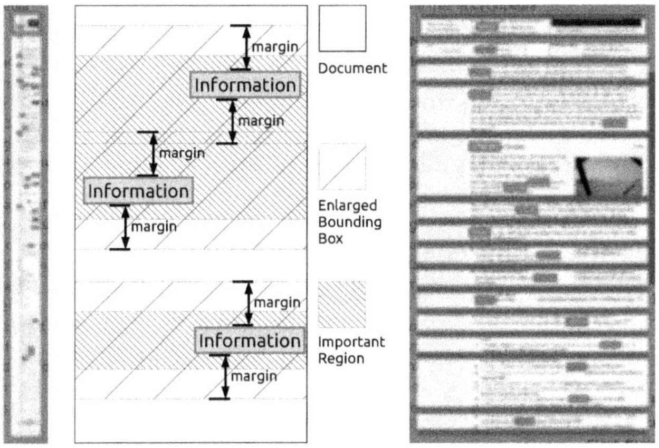

(a) (b) (c)

Figure 4: Smart preview. (a) A preview of a complete web page with the relevant regions highlighted. The necessary scaling makes it hard to recognize information. (b) All regions containing relevant information are detected and embedded within a bounding box, that makes sure some context is retained. Overlapping bounding boxes are merged. (c) By clipping the unimportant regions much more detail for the relevant parts is revealed.

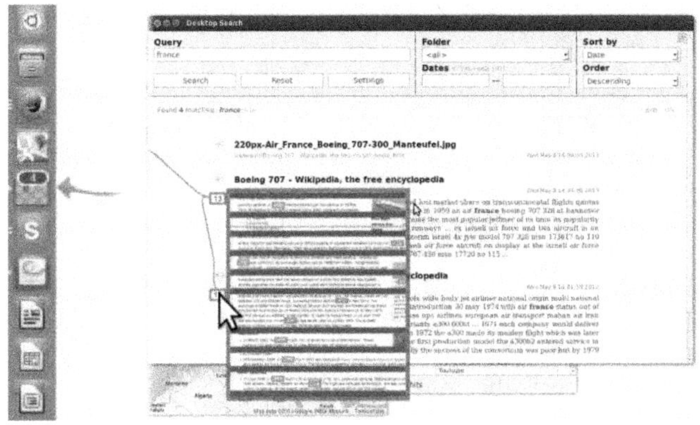

(a) (b)

Figure 5: Links to unopened documents. (a) The icon of a desktop search engine is marked with an arrow. The number shown inside the icon indicates the number of documents containing the current search term. (b) Within the desktop search engine, occurrences are highlighted and smart previews are provided.

the preview and scrolls the document to the location of the requested information (R IV).

When using the smart preview for **minimized windows**, we draw an arrow next to the application's icon in the task bar to indicate that it contains target regions. Upon hovering over the arrow, the smart preview is revealed (see Figure 1). When the user selects a target region, the minimized window is restored and the viewport is centered on the selected target.

Information may also only be available in **unopened documents**. To integrate unopened documents, we query a desktop search engine to find occurrences of search terms. Similar to our approach for minimized applications, we draw an arrow next to the desktop search engine's icon in the task bar and show the number of documents found within the icon, as shown in Figure 5(a). When opening the search engine, we highlight the search term in the search engine's previews and provide smart previews to reveal the details, as shown in Figure 5(b).

IMPLEMENTATION

To fully integrate heterogeneous data sources (R V), we implemented a central service written in C++, which runs in the background as a standalone application and accepts connects from other applications taking part in the visualization. These other applications are integrated using a minimally invasive approach through the use of a plug-in API or minor modifications of the application source code, if no API is provided [27]. The data exchange between the server and the clients is handled using WebSockets. To add the described user interface components on top of the existing screen content, we create a transparent Qt window which we render using OpenGL.

After the server has received a user-triggered search string, it forwards the request to every connected client application, enabling each application to add its regions. Upon receiving a request, each client searches its content for instances of the requested identifier and reports back the bounding boxes of all found occurrences. For simple selection types, like individual words, bounding boxes already provide an accurate approximation of the relevant region. To highlight and link more complex shapes, such as objects in a map or graph, a client is free to use arbitrary polygons for representing its regions.

Visual links are drawn between all highlighted regions. The naive approach that connects all highlighted regions to a common center results in a cluttered visualization. To remedy this, we bundle links using force-directed edge bundling [15], an algorithm based on an iteratively refined system of control points, attracting each other. The system is initialized by calculating the center of gravity of all occurrences. Then, the highlight region closest to the center of gravity is determined, and all other regions are connected to it. Moving the center of gravity avoids an artificial branching point. Next, all links are subdivided into segments of approximately equal length and finally, force-directed edge bundling is applied. Due to potentially large differences in the length of individual links, the forces affecting a single link can change rapidly, leading to sharp corners in the link routes. To address this issue, we apply a geometric smoothing on the points forming the link routes after executing the bundling algorithm.

All rendering output is directed to an off-screen buffer first. This buffer is twice the size of the screen and copied into the fullscreen window. Using hardware accelerated texture filtering, the visualization is automatically smoothed while being downscaled. The use of alpha-transparency allows blending with the desktop content. Screen pixels that are not covered by the visualization are masked, to allow mouse events passing through. In this way, the user can interact with all content that is not covered by our visualization.

For rendering see-through visualizations and smart previews, the client application is required to send an image of its content to the server. We use a hierarchical tile map, where each level consists of a single or multiple tiles, which add up to a full preview image of the client application's content at a specific zoom level. Using different resolution images for the individual zoom levels, we create tiles in a resolution that is sufficient for a single level of zoom. As the user zooms into the preview or moves the viewport, missing tiles are asynchronously requested from the corresponding client application.

While working in a desktop environment, the arrangement of opened windows can change at any time (R VI). As this possibly affects the position and occlusion of regions, we need to react to such changes. Current operating systems usually do not allow receiving notifications for changes in windows of other applications. As a workaround, we use a window monitoring component, which periodically requests a list of all opened windows, including their geometry and stacking order, and compares this information with the previous state. If any changes are detected, the server triggers the recreation of the visualization for all active identifiers.

As a proof of concept, we have integrated several widely used applications into our system. A browser add-on allows searching for words or phrases matching a given search identifier. The bounding boxes of all found occurrences, both within and out of the current viewport, are sent back to the server for further processing. As a non-textual example, we have used the Google Maps JavaScript API[1] to create a mash-up which supports the search for geographic locations by name and the retrieval of corresponding screen coordinates on the map. Retrieving the name of a location on a map and querying by this name is also supported. For connecting minimized windows and the desktop search engine, the location of the associated icons needs to be known. Therefore, we query the list of windows in the task bar and calculate the exact location of each icon using the known icon sizes. To retrieve the data for the smart preview for unopened files, they are opened in the background in their respective applications while visual feedback is suppressed.

For a basic integration with our system (to show the number and location of elements) applications need to implement a simple WebSockets protocol, which all modern browsers support. For a full integration, applications need to provide imagery of hidden areas for the preview, which is typically supported in either the GUI library or the graphics API.

Our implementation is open source and can be downloaded at `http://hidden-content.caleydo.org`. Due to the use of cross-platform libraries, our implementation runs on Linux, Microsoft Windows, and Apple OS X. Our technique can be used interactively on all operating systems and is usually able to update all visualizations within half a second. Getting imagery for showing a smart preview of a hidden document requires roughly the same time it takes to open an additional tab in a browser. Due to the delay of an application notifying our system of viewport changes like scrolling and window resize operation a short delay until the graphics elements update is unavoidable. During our study no user raised any concerns regarding the performance of our implementation.

[1] `https://developers.google.com/maps/documentation/javascript/tutorial`

EXPLORATORY USER STUDY

We conducted an exploratory user study to evaluate our hidden content visualization technique for three desktop scenarios of varying difficulty. The scenarios involved up to twelve web browser windows. To gather meaningful feedback, a major part of the study focused on an informal post test interview about the used hidden content visualization techniques. We recruited 18 participants from a local university (aged 20 to 37, 3 females) with a background in computer graphics and visualization. 10 participants indicated that they have experience with visual data analysis.

Techniques

As baseline condition we used the **standard searching and highlighting** technique of the web browser (Firefox), synchronized across all browser windows, to isolate the effect of our visualization. Participants could mark (brush) words in the web browser and press a keyboard shortcut (*CTRL+F*) to search the document for the marked word. The found terms use the default colored box to highlight all occurrences. Pressing the *Enter* button repeatedly advanced to the next occurrence of the word within the same application. As an alternative method, participants could also type the search term into a text field. To search for the same term in a different application window, participants only had to switch the window and continue with the inspection of the highlighted occurrences. A new search term replaced the previous one. Switching windows was possible through standard operating system features.

We tested the baseline condition against our fully functional, real-time **hidden content visualization** implementation, as described before. The ability to interact with all types of links was provided, which either brought covered windows to the front or scrolled the regions outside the viewport into sight. The procedure to trigger a search was identical to the one used in the baseline condition.

Tasks and Apparatus

Participants were asked to perform three information analysis tasks, with thirteen desktop windows opened concurrently. The desktop was presented to the participants on a 22" monitor with 1920 × 1080 pixels. Participants were seated approximately at the same distance from the monitor. No restrictions where enforced during the test, i.e., users were allowed to move or to rearrange windows. All tasks dealt with properties of aircrafts and airports. To generate two setups with equivalent complexity, we have altered two original data sets taken from Wikipedia to include the exact same number of hidden and visible regions for different properties.

The default window setup is shown in Figure 6. We placed a master browser window on the left side of the screen which

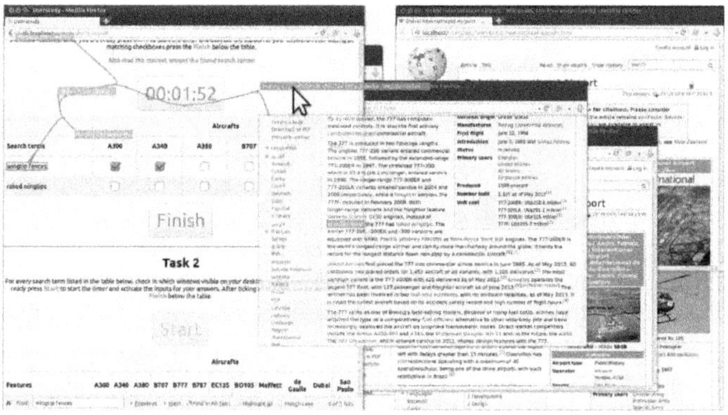

Figure 6: Window setup for the user study. Twelve browser windows are randomly arranged. Another window on the left, is used by the participants to start new trials and indicate their answers.

was used to start a new trial and indicate answers. Twelve additional windows were randomly distributed across the whole screen, each approximately one third the size of the screen. The synchronized highlighting and guidance functionality was provided among all thirteen windows. Due to the large number of windows, participants were confronted with numerous overlapping windows and covered regions. Also, the shown documents were about six to ten times larger than the viewports they were displayed in.

We consciously avoided tabbed browsing, i.e., nested window management, in the study, since it would have made the design more complex and we were primarily interested in testing the performance of our techniques with larger numbers of (partially) overlapping windows.

We designed the following tasks with increasing complexity:

Task 1 was designed as a simple information retrieval task testing the effectiveness of finding information. Participants had to find a single keyword in a subset of the open windows. They were additionally asked to take information from the context area of the search results into account. Participants should tell whether each of the six aircrafts described within the documents is controlled using a yoke or a side-stick. For two aircrafts the information was unavailable and no answer was required.

Task 2 was designed as a more complex search task testing the efficiency of locating documents containing relevant information. Participants were asked to tell the experimenter which of two given keywords were contained within every of the twelve browser windows. The windows contained none, one, or both keywords.

Task 3 was designed as a research task testing the effectiveness of finding information. It required long content interaction, using three search terms, scanning through entire paragraphs, and reasoning. Participants were asked to find all aircrafts equipped with a certain number of engines. The number of engines was indicated by a specific phrase. Participants had to read the context surrounding the phrase, as some documents contained the given phrase even though the aircraft had a different number of engines. Out of the six documents describing an aircraft, three contained the requested number of engines. For the remaining aircrafts, participants where asked which of them have two more features installed, resulting first in two and finally one matching aircraft.

Design and Procedure

The study was conducted as a within-subjects experiment over the described two conditions and the three tasks for each condition. For each task, we measured task completion time and correctness. To start a trial, participants clicked on a button located in the master window on screen. The same window included check boxes for answering the questions and completing the trial. We automatically measured the time between the initiation and competition of a trial. Prior to each task, participants were given a warm-up period, which allowed them to become familiar with the technique and the content of the application windows. After each condition, participants were required to assess their subjective satisfaction with the technique on a questionnaire containing six questions. After the hidden content visualization condition, we presented them with an additional questionnaire, comparing the individual approaches we employ for the different kinds of hidden content. Upon completion of the experiment, the participants were asked to take part in an unstructured interview.

Participants completed all three tasks twice, once with each technique. To avoid learning effects due to knowledge of the data, all tasks where available with two different sets of keywords or features. To reduce the influence of learning effects due to the repetition of tasks, the order of the conditions and the assignment of the task sets was counterbalanced.

Hypothesis

The goal of the user study was to compare the effectiveness and efficiency of our hidden content visualization techniques and traditional search for finding hidden content. We formulated the following three hypotheses for this experiment:

[H1] Using the hidden content visualization leads to a faster retrieval of hidden data. Our techniques visualize all hidden regions that are placed within the boundaries of the screen and offers a preview for regions which are outside the screen. By interacting with these links, every hidden region can be accessed with one or two clicks. Thus, we expect our hidden content visualization to be faster than a sequential search through all hidden regions.

[H2] With the hidden content visualization fewer errors are made. Because we visualize every occurrence of a search term, we expect users to miss fewer occurrences than by stepping through all windows and occurrences within windows sequentially.

[H3] Visualizing hidden content has a positive impact on understanding the spatial distribution of the data. Our hidden content visualization either shows the exact location of hidden regions or points towards the direction where they can be found. Thus, we hypothesize that it is easier for users to orient themselves within the data, if our visualization technique is

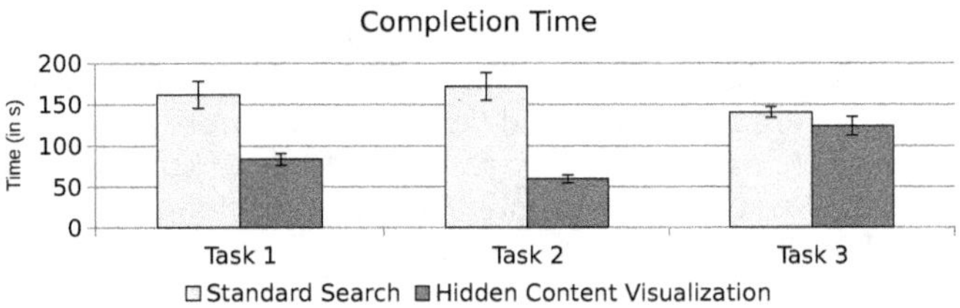

Figure 7: Mean completion time with standard error. Our hidden content visualization performs significantly better for tasks with a lot of unrelated content (Task 2) or only simple information retrieval (Task 1). For the research task (Task 3) the differences are not significant.

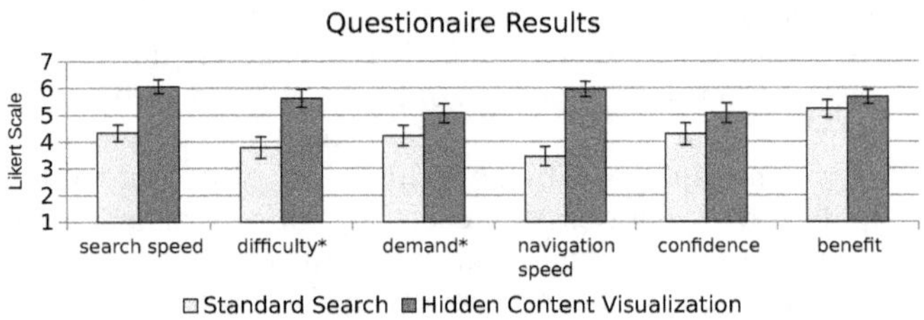

Figure 8: Mean questionnaire results given on a seven point Likert-scale. Higher results are better in all cases (* elements have been inverted).

used. As a consequence, we also expect it to be easier for users to locate data they have not yet explored.

Results

We measured the time participants needed to complete each task, the correctness of the reported numbers, and subjective assessments, which were given on a seven-point Likert scale. As no category tested entirely positive for being normal distributed, all measures were evaluated using non-parametric tests. Wilcoxon signed rank tests ($\alpha = .05$) were used for completion time, error rate, and the subjective task evaluation. The results comparing the individual approaches used by our hidden content visualization were analyzed using Kruskal-Wallis tests ($\alpha = .05$). Timing results are illustrated in Figure 7, and questionnaire results are provided in Figure 8 and 9.

Our analysis revealed a difference in completion time between the techniques for Task 1 ($W = 141$, $p < .005$) and Task 2 ($W = 171$, $p < .001$). We found no significant difference in completion time between the techniques for Task 3 ($W = 80$, $p = .085$).

The average number of errors was very low for all tasks and techniques (traditional search: 0.05; hidden content visualization: 0.04). There was no measurable difference to be found for error.

We found a significant difference for the questionnaire items *subjective search speed* ('I could find the hidden content quickly.') ($W = 129$, $p < .005$), *subjective difficulty* ('It was very hard to find all hidden elements.') ($W = 106$, $p = .022$), and *subjective navigation speed* ('I could navigate to hidden content very quickly.') ($W = 135$, $p = .003$). The differences in *subjective demand* ('The task was very mentally demanding.') ($W = 70$, $p = .07$), *subjective confidence* ('I am sure I did not miss any highlighted elements.') ($W = 49$, $p = .08$) and *subjective benefit* ('The technique would be beneficial for my every day computer work.') ($W = 38$, $p = .29$) were not statistically significant.

Observations and Feedback

All participants quickly developed successful strategies using our hidden content visualization. Once a new search process is initiated, the viewport of each application is moved to contain the first occurrence of the search term. This allowed the fastest participants accessing the required information directly in the see-through visualization or smart preview without moving the viewport to the highlighted regions. This strategy could even be completed with the lowest zoom-level. Most participants, however, zoomed in one level, which eased the reading of the preview.

For regions outside the viewport, participants developed different strategies. If both regions outside the viewport and outside the screen appeared at the same time, participants most often used the smart preview only, because it also includes regions outside the viewport. About half of the participants clicked on the regions to scroll them into sight; the other half hovered over the region and read the information directly from the superimposed see-through preview. Many participants stated that they did not recognize regions outside the viewport very often and they would prefer the system treating these regions like regions outside the screen. Some participants thought that this visualization is only useful with a maximum of two or three windows.

If multiple windows containing scrolled-away content had large overlapping areas, some participants had problems to recognize which window each visualization belongs to. In the interview, they mentioned it would be useful to use different colors for different windows or have the covered window marker also for partially covered windows.

In the hidden content visualization condition, no participant used the window manager to switch between open windows. Most of them mentioned that the hidden content visualizations enables them to locate target windows and regions faster than before. Two participants stated that they would like to have the indicators for found information inside the task-bar or window list, as they think a one-dimensional search within a linear list is faster than a two-dimensional search for highlights on the whole screen.

With a small amount of interesting content, participants sometimes were slower at marking a search term, initiating a new visualization process, opening the smart preview and zoom/scroll to the location than simply scrolling there. Some participants also mentioned that they think the hidden content visualization is not useful for simple search tasks involving little content, but gets increasingly useful with complex tasks involving multiple windows.

Participants said that they would especially like to see the visualization feature to support tabs within applications and connect spreadsheet applications as well as code editors and documentations. Additionally, integrating a call hierarchy or

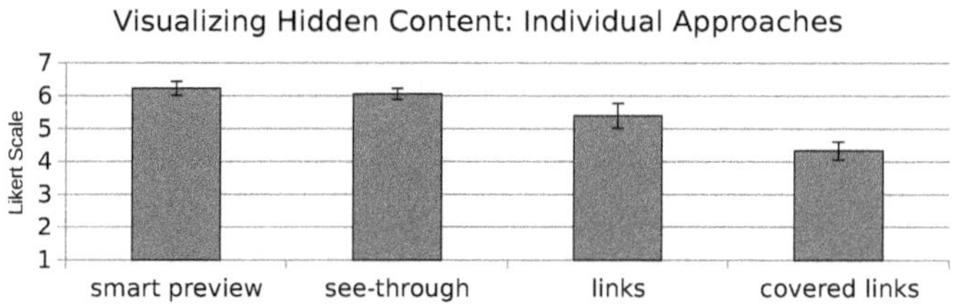

Figure 9: Mean questionnaire results for the different approaches combined our hidden content visualization given on a seven point Likert-scale. No significant difference was found in the data.

references to a variable inside a software development environment was considered as a useful extension. Also enhancing the smart preview by showing only headings of the previewed document and expand or navigate to the sections content on demand would increase the acceptance as an everyday tool.

One participant tried to use scrolling within a see-through preview and stated in the interview the scrolling would be a useful extension to the preview.

Discussion

Based on the significantly lower task time achieved with our hidden content visualization for Task 1 and 2 and the higher subjective search and navigation speed, we conclude that *H1* is supported, and our hidden content visualization leads to a faster retrieval of hidden content. The results also indicate that the usefulness of our technique increases with the number of windows containing no relevant content. For Task 2 only half of the windows contained relevant content, which caused participants using standard search to check twice as many windows as required. Task 3 required far less navigation to different windows and, additionally, involved a reduced number of windows during each step. The largest part of the task required retrieving and combining information from the content. We believe that the major time-consuming activity for Task 3 was understanding and interpreting content instead of navigation and that this resulted in no significantly faster results for our hidden content visualization. Due to the low error rate, we can neither accept nor reject *H2*. Based on the participant feedback that our visualization helps not to miss elements, it might be possible to confirm this hypothesis in a more extensive study. Because all participants stated that our visualization helped them to get a better location awareness inside documents, we conclude that *H3* is also supported.

The overall positive user feedback, in particular for the smart preview and the see-through visualization of the smart links (see Figure 9), indicates that visualizing hidden content is a useful tool especially for complex information retrieval tasks possibly with a high amount of unrelated content.

CONCLUSIONS AND FUTURE WORK

In this paper we presented techniques for visualizing search terms in areas of documents that are covered by other windows, outside the window's current viewport, outside the screen, contained in a minimized window, or in unopened files. We introduced smart previews that allow efficient exploration of content outside visible areas by providing a content-sensitive, space conserving, compressed preview of the whole document's virtual area, whereas smart links paired with a transparent overlay and click-to-show functionality allows for a fast navigation to covered content.

Future work will aim to reduce the visual clutter that may arise when a large number of regions are selected. We envision a combination of more sophisticated bundling algorithms, context-preserving routing [21], and smart fading of the links over time to further improve the situation.

Moreover, to improve temporal consistency and reduce lag, we plan to extend our system to track changes of relevant objects over time and incorporate temporal coherence into the layout planning. This would also allow us to avoid radical layout changes resulting from small changes (such as scrolling by a single line) in the underlying scene.

Finally, we want to pick up comments from study participants and plan to integrate our hidden content visualization techniques with an integrated development environment such as Eclipse, where search tasks and visiting all references and modifications of specific variables are crucial tasks in developing and debugging software.

ACKNOWLEDGMENTS

The authors wish to thank Manuela Waldner for her important suggestions. This research was funded by the Austrian Science Fund (FWF): P22902 and J 3437-N15, the government of Styria (A3-22.M-5/2012-21), the Austrian Research Promotion Agency (840232), and the Air Force Research Laboratory and DARPA grant FA8750-12-C-0300.

REFERENCES

1. Baudisch, P., and Gutwin, C. Multiblending: displaying overlapping windows simultaneously without the drawbacks of alpha blending. In *Proceedings of the SIGCHI Conference on Human Factors in Computing Systems (CHI '04)*, ACM (2004), 367–374.

2. Baudisch, P., and Rosenholtz, R. Halo: a technique for visualizing off-screen objects. In *Proceedings of the SIGCHI Conference on Human Factors in Computing Systems (CHI '03)*, ACM (2003), 481–488.

3. Baudisch, P., Xie, X., Wang, C., and Ma, W.-Y. Collapse-to-zoom: Viewing web pages on small screen devices by interactively removing irrelevant content. In *Proceedings of the ACM Symposium on User Interface Software and Technology (UIST '04)*, ACM (2004), 91–94.

4. Bezerianos, A., Dragicevic, P., and Balakrishnan, R. Mnemonic rendering: an image-based approach for exposing hidden changes in dynamic displays. In *Proceedings of the ACM Symposium on User Interface Software and Technology (UIST '06)*, ACM (2006), 159–168.

5. Bier, E. A., Stone, M. C., Pier, K., Buxton, W., and DeRose, T. D. Toolglass and magic lenses: the see-through interface. In *Proceedings of the Conference*

on Computer Graphics and Interactive Techniques (SIGGRAPH '93), ACM (1993), 73–80.

6. Byrd, D. A scrollbar-based visualization for document navigation. In *Proceedings of the ACM Conference on Digital Libraries (DL '99)*, ACM (1999), 122–129.
7. Collins, C., and Carpendale, S. VisLink: revealing relationships amongst visualizations. *IEEE Transactions on Visualization and Computer Graphics (InfoVis '07) 13*, 6 (2007), 1192–1199.
8. Dieberger, A., and Russell, D. Exploratory navigation in large multimedia documents using context lenses. In *Proceedings of the Hawaii International Conference on System Sciences (HICSS '02)* (2002), 911–917.
9. Eick, S., Steffen, J., and Sumner, E.E., J. Seesoft-a tool for visualizing line oriented software statistics. *IEEE Transactions on Software Engineering 18*, 11 (1992), 957 –968.
10. Gustafson, S., Baudisch, P., Gutwin, C., and Irani, P. Wedge: Clutter-free visualization of off-screen locations. In *Proceedings of the SIGCHI Conference on Human Factors in Computing Systems (CHI '08)*, ACM (2008), 787–796.
11. Harrison, B. L., Ishii, H., Vicente, K. J., and Buxton, W. A. S. Transparent layered user interfaces: An evaluation of a display design to enhance focused and divided attention. In *Proceedings of the SIGCHI Conference on Human Factors in Computing Systems (CHI '95)*, ACM (1995), 317–324.
12. Harrison, B. L., Kurtenbach, G., and Vicente, K. J. An experimental evaluation of transparent user interface tools and information content. In *Proceedings of the ACM Symposium on User Interface and Software Technology (UIST '95)*, ACM (1995), 81–90.
13. Hearst, M. A. TileBars: visualization of term distribution information in full text information access. In *Proceedings of the SIGCHI Conference on Human Factors in Computing Systems (CHI '95)*, ACM (1995), 59–66.
14. Hoffmann, R., Baudisch, P., and Weld, D. S. Evaluating visual cues for window switching on large screens. In *Proceedings of the SIGCHI Conference on Human Factors in Computing Systems (CHI '08)* (2008), 929–938.
15. Holten, D., and van Wijk, J. Force-directed edge bundling for graph visualization. *Computer Graphics Forum (EuroVis '09) 28*, 3 (2009), 983–990.
16. Hornbaek, K., and Frøkjær, E. Reading of electronic documents: The usability of linear, fisheye, and Overview+Detail interfaces. In *Proceedings of the SIGCHI Conference on Human Factors in Computing Systems (CHI '01)*, ACM (2001), 293–300.
17. Hornbæk, K., and Frøkjær, E. Reading patterns and usability in visualizations of electronic documents. *ACM Transactions on Computer-Human Interaction 10*, 2 (2003), 119–149.
18. Ishak, E. W., and Feiner, S. K. Interacting with hidden content using content-aware free-space transparency. In *Proceedings of the ACM Symposium on User Interface Software and Technology (UIST '04)*, ACM (2004), 189.
19. Palmer, S., and Rock, I. Rethinking perceptual organization: the role of uniform connectedness. *Psychonomic Bulletin and Review 1*, 1 (1994), 29–55.
20. Steinberger, M., Waldner, M., and Schmalstieg, D. Interactive self-organizing windows. *Computer Graphics Forum 31*, 2pt3 (May 2012), 621–630.
21. Steinberger, M., Waldner, M., Streit, M., Lex, A., and Schmalstieg, D. Context-preserving visual links. *IEEE Transactions on Visualization and Computer Graphics (InfoVis '11) 17*, 12 (2011), 2249–2258.
22. Stoffel, A., Strobelt, H., Deussen, O., and Keim, D. A. Document thumbnails with variable text scaling. *Computer Graphics Forum 31*, 3pt3 (2012), 1165–1173.
23. Streit, M., Kalkusch, M., Kashofer, K., and Schmalstieg, D. Navigation and exploration of interconnected pathways. *Computer Graphics Forum (EuroVis '08) 27*, 3 (2008), 951–958.
24. Streit, M., Lex, A., Kalkusch, M., Zatloukal, K., and Schmalstieg, D. Caleydo: Connecting pathways and gene expression. *Bioinformatics 25*, 20 (2009), 2760–2761.
25. Suh, B., Woodruff, A., Rosenholtz, R., and Glass, A. Popout prism: Adding perceptual principles to Overview+Detail document interfaces. In *Proceedings of the SIGCHI Conference on Human Factors in Computing Systems (CHI '02)*, ACM (2002), 251–258.
26. Viau, C., and McGuffin, M. J. ConnectedCharts: explicit visualization of relationships between data graphics. *Computer Graphics Forum 31*, 3pt4 (2012), 1285–1294.
27. Waldner, M., Puff, W., Lex, A., Streit, M., and Schmalstieg, D. Visual links across applications. In *Proceedings of the Conference on Graphics Interface (GI '10)*, Canadian Human-Computer Communications Society (2010), 129–136.
28. Waldner, M., and Schmalstieg, D. Collaborative information linking: Bridging knowledge gaps between users by linking across applications. In *Proceeding of the IEEE Symposium on Pacific Visualization (PacificVis '11)*, IEEE (2011), 115–122.
29. Waldner, M., Steinberger, M., Grasset, R., and Schmalstieg, D. Importance-driven compositing window managment. In *Proceedings of the SIGCHI Conference on Human Factors in Computing Systems (CHI '11)*, ACM (2011), 956–968.

"Maybe It Was a Joke" - Emotion Detection in Text-Only Communication by Non-Native English Speakers

Ari Hautasaari[1], Naomi Yamashita[1], Ge Gao[1,2]

[1]NTT Communication Science Labs
2-4 Hikaridai, Seika-cho,
Soraku-gun, Kyoto, Japan
ari.hautasaari@lab.ntt.co.jp
naomiy@acm.org

[2]Department of Communication
Cornell University
Ithaca NY 14850 USA
gg365@cornell.edu

ABSTRACT

Previous studies have shown that people can effectively detect emotions in text-only messages written in their native languages. But is this the same for non-native speakers? In this paper, we conduct an experiment where native English speakers (NS) and Japanese non-native English speakers (NNS) rate the emotional valence in text-only messages written by native English-speaking authors. They also annotate all emotional cues (words, symbols and emoticons) that affected their rating. Accuracy of NS and NNS ratings and annotations are calculated by comparing their average correlations with author ratings and annotations used as a gold standard. Our results conclude that NNS are significantly less accurate at detecting the emotional valence of messages, especially when the messages include highly negative words. Although NNS are as accurate as NS at detecting emotional cues, they are not able to make use of symbols (exclamation marks) and emoticons to detect the emotional valence of text-only messages.

Author Keywords

Computer-mediated communication; text-only communication; non-native speaker; emotion;

ACM Classification Keywords

H.5.2 [Information Interfaces and Presentation]: Group and Organization Interfaces - Web-based interaction.

INTRODUCTION

Accurately detecting and understanding emotional states is central to all human communication. In text-only communication, however, detecting the intended emotional tone can be difficult due to the lack of non-verbal cues in text-only mediums [9, 25, 27]. Misunderstandings sometimes occur even between native speakers who try to exchange emotional cues via text-only messages [12]. This problem may be more salient in communication between native speakers (NS) and non-native speakers (NNS).

CHI 2014, April 26 - May 01 2014, Toronto, ON, Canada
Copyright 2014 ACM 978-1-4503-2473-1/14/04...$15.00.
http://dx.doi.org/10.1145/2556288.2557215

Unfortunately, this is likely an issue that multilingual group members often face when contacting each other since their communication patterns are closely connected to their geographical distribution [17]. For example, when a native Japanese speaker who lives in Japan wants to contact his native English-speaking colleagues in the U.S., they will have to rely largely on text-based mediums (such as SMS or email) to overcome the time difference between their locations [14].

In addition to the limitations imposed by communication mediums used among multilingual group members, NNS may have particular difficulty in understanding the connection between the syntactic structure of a text-only message and the emotional nuances expressed by words [22] due to limited exposure to their second language. Indeed, both anecdotal and empirical evidence show that NNS generally have limited exposure to English beyond a classroom [2, 11]. Thus, it may be hard for NNS to discern the emotion expressed in a message when the wording of an English sentence does not include any direct expressions of the author's emotional state (e.g., "I am happy" vs. "I finally arrived"). To reduce such misunderstandings between NS and NNS in text-only communication, it is important to consider ways to support accurate emotion detection [12].

In this paper, we aim to uncover how native English speakers and Japanese non-native English speakers differ in detecting the emotional valence of text-only messages. Our main research questions are: Can non-native English speakers accurately detect the emotional valence of text-only messages written by native English speakers? What types of messages are problematic for non-native English speakers when detecting the emotional valence? Do native and non-native English speakers rely on the same cues to detect the emotional valence? If not, what types of cues do they rely on? Answering these questions will provide a foundation for designing text-only communication systems that support accurate emotion detection among native and non-native speakers.

In the remainder of this paper, we will discuss the related work on emotion detection in text-only communication, describe our experimental design and report our findings. Lastly, we will discuss our results in relation to previous work and draw design implications for the development of supporting tools for text-only communication between NS and NNS.

RELATED WORK

Emotion Detection in Text-Only CMC

Difficulties in emotion detection from text-only messages have been addressed by previous computer-mediated communication (CMC) theories. The Social Presence theory implies a radical claim that emotional tone is hard to detect from text-only messages. It states that problems in emotion detection are induced by the lack of non-verbal cues and intonation in text-only CMC environments. The limited range of available cues inhibits the use of full range of emotional and interpersonal information [24]. The Social Information Processing (SIP) theory, however, presents a more moderate claim. It suggests that emotional information is available in any CMC environment, including text-only communication, but it takes longer for interlocutors to detect this information [25].

Recent HCI/CSCW literature has largely supported the view of SIP. For example, Hancock et al. (2007, 2008) concluded that native English speakers are able to successfully detect positive and negative emotions in a text-only chat. Gill et al. (2008) also reported some similar findings where native English speakers were accurate in detecting more complex emotions such as joy and anger expressed in blog texts [7, 8].

Words as Emotional Cues in Text-Only CMC

It is worth noting that emotion detection is not only decided by receiver's ability to figure out what information is useful, but also by how a message is originally written by the author. In the context of text-only communication, previous research suggests that authors tend to adjust their emotional expressions to the medium to help receivers detect the intended emotions [27].

Previous works indicate a variety of cues that authors may use to exchange emotional information with receivers, including words, symbols and emoticons [1, 10, 26]. As for the use of words, authors who portray positive emotions use more words overall compared to actors portraying negative emotions [10]. Authors acting or experiencing negative emotions use fewer words [9], more affective words, words conveying negative feelings and negations [10]. Angry authors use more affective language and negative words as opposed to joyful authors who use more positive words [7].

The words used by the author have a strong impact on how NS detect the author's emotional tone. For instance, NS who follow a chat conversation rely mostly on negations and negative words to detect between author's positive and negative emotions [10].

Symbols and Emoticons as Emotional Cues in Text-Only CMC

Besides words, emotions in text-only CMC can be expressed through symbols, such as exclamation marks (!), and emoticons. Emoticons are representations of facial expressions constructed of symbols (e.g., :)), numbers and letters (e.g., 8D). Emoticons punctuate text-only messages by indicating pauses of emotional expression that would occur in spoken dialogue (e.g., laughter) [21].

Previous work has shown that native speakers rely on exclamation points, such as exclamation marks, to detect between their chat partner's positive and negative emotional states [10]. Also, the presence of emoticons strengthens the intensity of the verbal message [3], especially in the case of negative emotions [26]. In general, positive emoticons are associated with positive socio-emotional communication and negative emoticons are associated with negative socio-emotional communication [3].

These studies have shown that native speakers are able to draw accurate perceptions of an author's emotional state even when the available cues are limited. With all previous evidence showing how native speakers use different cues to detect emotions in text-only messages, we wonder whether and how the exchange of cues would work between NNS receiver and NS author. More specifically, whether non-native speakers use different types of cues than native speakers to detect emotions in text-only messages?

Emotion Detection by Non-Native Speakers

In this study, we focus on emotion detection by non-native English speakers (NNS) in complete text-only messages. Previous studies by both Russell (1983) and Romney et al. (1997) reported implications that NNS may have trouble detecting English emotion terms accurately [22, 23]. More precisely, NNS tend to recognize some, but not all nuances associated with English language emotion words even when they are fluent in the second language [22].

Besides individual emotion words, NNS may also not be familiar on how emotional tone is exchanged in symbols and emoticons in text-only messages. For example, Nishimura (2006) highlighted differences on how symbols, punctuation and spelling are used to emphasize text-only communication in English and Japanese. Further, emoticon styles, usage and variety differ widely across cultures and languages. Consequently, the context and sentiment associated with a given emoticon is dependent on the language backgrounds of the author and the receiver [18].

These studies altogether imply the possibility that NS and NNS may differ on how they detect emotions in text-only messages. Yet, little is known on what cues NNS rely on to detect emotions, what kind of messages are particularly problematic for NNS, and what causes the discrepancies between how NS and NNS perceive the same emotions. Answering these questions would inform the design of future systems for assisting NNS to accurately detect emotions in text-only CMC.

CURRENT STUDY

In the current study, we analyze how Japanese non-native English speakers detect the emotional valence of text-only messages written by native English-speaking authors.

Research Questions

In this paper, we use quantitative and qualitative data analysis to examine the following hypotheses and research questions.

Accuracy of emotional valence detection in text-only messages written by NS authors.

As mentioned in previous sections, native English speakers are able to successfully detect emotions in text-only CMC. For non-native speakers, however, emotion detection can be difficult due to their lack of fluency in the second language. Thus, we hypothesize that:

H1: Generally, NS will detect the emotional valence of a message more accurately than NNS.

In addition, we ask whether NS and NNS accuracy of detecting the emotional valence is affected by the presence or absence of highly positive or negative words in the message.

RQ1: Does the lexical sentiment of a message affect the accuracy of detecting the emotional valence for NS and NNS?

Cues for detecting emotional valence of text-only messages.

Previous works show that the emotional tone of a text-only message can be detected based on certain cues, including words, symbols and emoticons [1, 15, 26]. However, NNS may detect the emotional tone expressed in individual English words differently from NS [22, 23]. Furthermore, the use of symbols [16] and emoticons [18] in text-only communication differs between languages. Based on these, we wonder whether NNS rely on same cues as NS to detect the emotional valence of text-only messages written by native English speakers.

RQ2: Do NS and NNS make use of different types of cues (e.g., words, symbols, and emoticons) when detecting the emotional valence of text-only messages? If so, what type?

METHOD

Overview

To test our hypotheses and answer our research questions, we tested whether the language fluency (NS vs. NNS) and lexical sentiment of a message (positive vs. negative vs. objective) influenced the participants emotional valence rating and cue annotation accuracy. During the experiment, NS and Japanese NNS participants rated the emotional valence in a set of text-only messages written by native English-speaking authors. After that, we asked all participants to indicate the cues (words, symbols and emoticons) in each message that they used to resolve the emotional valence of the message.

Authors of all messages were also required to rate the emotional valence of their own messages and annotate the cues they used to generate their emotional valence rating. By doing this, we got a gold standard (i.e., author rating) for comparing the accuracy of emotional valence detection and cue annotation between NS and NNS.

Participants

There were 20 native English speakers (NS) and 20 non-native English speakers (NNS) that participated in this study. All NS participants had received their primary education (from the age of 6 to 18, elementary school to high school) in English speaking countries. All NS participants reported English as their only native language.

The NNS participants in this study were all Japanese native speakers. They all had spent less than two years in English speaking countries. They speak English as their second language, but not fluently. We required a minimum score of 750 in the TOEIC[1] English proficiency test for all NNS participants.

Materials for Participants

Categorization of Messages Based on Lexical Sentiment

We extracted a total number of 98 messages from Facebook with the authors' consent, which formed the initial message pool for our experiment materials. All messages were public status updates written by native English-speaking authors. None of the messages included photos, videos, hyperlinks, or any other additional content besides text.

In order to get an equal distribution of messages with different lexical sentiment (positive, negative and objective), we categorized all messages using a software called SentiWordNet[2]. We used SentiWordNet to identify and count the proportion of emotional words in each message (Table 1). SentiWordNet includes a human rated synset classification of words with three numerical scores in the positive, negative and objective scales [6]. We input all words in each message to SentiWordNet and identified the sentiment score of each individual word.

The lexical sentiment of each message was calculated as the ratio of highly positive words to highly negative words (rated over 0.5 in a 0-1.0 scale)[3]. In total, 33.67% of messages were categorized as positive, 32.65% were categorized as negative and 33.67% were categorized as

[1] Test of English for International Communication

[2] http://sentiwordnet.isti.cnr.it/

[3] SentiWordNet allows user feedback on the values assigned to each individual word. In this paper, we used the values as of April 15th, 2013.

	Rater	Sampling message with cue annotations	Rating scale and results	Emotional valence according to the rating
Lexical sentiment	SentiWordNet	Holy moly that flight was freakin' scary :O The WIND was nuts :O They almost diverted us to another Tokyo airport. Hats off to the pilots :) OMG :O	#Positive words = 0 #Negative words = 1	Negative
Author rated valence & cue annotation	NS author of the message	Holy moly that flight was freakin' scary :O The WIND was nuts :O They almost diverted us to another Tokyo airport. Hats off to the pilots :) OMG :O	4 on a 7-point scale	Neutral
Participant rated valence & cue annotation	NS participants	Holy moly that flight was freakin' scary :O The WIND was nuts :O They almost diverted us to another Tokyo airport. Hats off to the pilots :) OMG :O	5 on a 7-point scale	Slightly positive
	NNS participants	Holy moly that flight was freakin' scary :O The WIND was nuts :O They almost diverted us to another Tokyo airport. Hats off to the pilots :) OMG :O	2 on a 7-point scale	Negative

Table 1. Example of a message with lexical sentiment calculated by SentiWordNet, gold standard rating and cue annotation by NS author, and participants' ratings and cue annotations by NS and NNS (overlap between author's and participants' annotation is indicated in green, and additional annotations are indicated in yellow).

objective (i.e., messages that had neither positive or negative lexical sentiment). Table 1 includes an example of a message with a negative lexical sentiment (negative words indicated in red).

All messages were fully anonymized, excluding all person names, profile photos, and other personal information. We combined these messages in to one dataset and randomized their order.

Author Rating and Cue Annotation

To compare the accuracy of participants' emotional valence detection and cue annotation on each message, we use the authors' emotional valence ratings and cue annotations as the gold standard. We asked all authors to rate each of their own messages for the emotional valence in a 7-point Likert scale (1 = very negative, 4 = neutral, 7 = very positive). Secondly, we asked them to annotate the words, symbols and emoticons in each message that reflected their rating. The author annotations were used to calculate the cue selection accuracy of NS and NNS. Table 1 includes an example of author rating and cue annotation.

Procedures

In the experiment, we asked both NS and NNS participants to read a set of messages (N=98). In the first step, they rated the emotional valence of each message. After that, they annotated all cues in the messages (i.e., words, symbols and emoticons) that they were using to determine their emotional valence rating in the first step (Table 1). The task instructions for NNS participants were given in Japanese.

NNS participants were allowed to use English to Japanese bilingual dictionaries during the experiment, so that their emotional valence rating and cue annotation would not be heavily influenced by their individual English language abilities (grammar, vocabulary, etc.).

Measures

Participants' emotional valence detection in the message: Both NS and NNS participants rated their evaluation of the emotional valence of each given message on a 7-point Likert scale (1 = very negative, 4 = neutral, 7 = very positive). The rating score reflects the participants' emotional valence detection in the message. The consistency of emotion ratings given by NS (Krippendorff's α = .68) and NNS (Krippendorff's α = .64) formed a reliable scale.

Participants' cue annotation in the message: Both NS and NNS participants annotated three types of cues from the messages (words, symbols and emoticons), that influenced their emotional valence rating on the given message.

RESULTS

We conducted Mann-Whitney U tests to explore if NS and NNS detect the emotional valence in each type of messages differently. Non-parametric test was used because the data was not normally distributed.

Emotional Valence Rating Accuracy

Our *H1* and *RQ1* discussed the differences in NS and NNS ability to detect the emotional valence of NS authors' messages. To verify our *H1*, we firstly calculated participants' emotional valence rating accuracy. Participants' rating accuracy is calculated as a correlation (Spearman's correlation coefficient) with the author ratings. We then compared the average correlation of NS and NNS.

Accuracy of Emotional Valence Detection between NS and NNS

To explore our *H1*, we conducted a Mann-Whitney U test on the effect of language proficiency (NS vs. NNS) to emotional valence rating accuracy (N=98). The result fully supported our *H1*. A Mann-Whitney U test showed a significantly higher correlation between NS and author ratings compared to the correlation between NNS and author ratings (r_{NS}=0.51, r_{NNS}=0.41; Z=4.26, p<.05). This indicated that NS participants could detect the emotional valence of NS authors' messages more accurately than NNS participants.

Accuracy of Emotional Valence Detection in Messages with Different Lexical Sentiment

In our *RQ1* we asked whether the lexical sentiment of a message would affect the accuracy of emotion detection for NS and NNS. To answer this research question, we conducted a Mann-Whitney U test on the effect of lexical sentiment of a message (positive vs. negative vs. objective) on the emotional valence rating accuracy for both NS and NNS.

The results indicated that the NS and NNS participants' accuracy of detecting the emotional valence followed a similar pattern (Figure 1). More specifically, both NS and NNS were most accurate at rating the emotional valence of messages with positive lexical sentiment, and least accurate at rating messages with negative lexical sentiment. This effect was significant with both NS (r_{POS}=0.57, r_{NEG}=0.45; Z=2.23, $p<.05)^{\dagger}$ and NNS (r_{POS}=0.46, r_{NEG}=0.35; Z=2.53, $p<.05)^{\circ}$. Similarly, the rating accuracy for messages with positive lexical sentiment was higher than rating accuracy for messages with objective lexical sentiment for both NS and NNS, but this result was significant only for NS (r_{POS}=0.57, $r_{OBJECTIVE}$=0.47; Z=3.45, $p<.05)^{\ddagger}$.

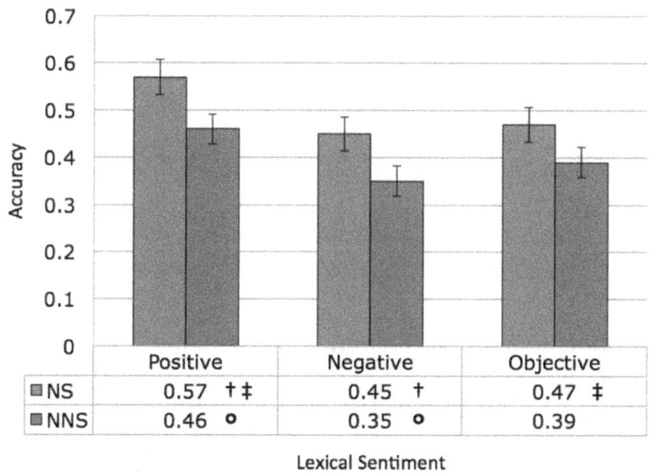

Figure 1. NS and NNS emotional valence rating accuracy for messages with positive (N=33), negative (N=32) or objective (N=33) lexical sentiment.

These results answered our *H1* and *RQ1*. They indicated that the participants' language background and the lexical sentiment of a message had an effect on the participants' accuracy of detecting the emotional valence of the text-only messages.

Cues for Assessing Emotional Valence

Our *RQ2* discussed the differences in NS and NNS ability to annotate proper emotional cues in NS authors' messages. To answer this research question, we firstly calculated the participants' cue annotation accuracy. NS and NNS cue annotation accuracy is indicated by Spearman's correlation coefficient with author cue annotations (match or no match). Empty author annotations (i.e., no cues selected by author) are handled as either 1 (no cues selected also by participant) or 0 (cues selected by participant).

Accuracy of Emotional Cue Annotation between NS and NNS

In our *RQ2* we asked whether NS and NNS participants would use different types of cues (e.g., words, symbols and emoticons) to generate their emotional valence rating. To answer this research question, we first used the authors' annotations as a gold standard to compare whether there are differences in the accuracy of cue annotation between NS and NNS.

The results given by Mann-Whitney U test did not show any significant difference in the cue annotation accuracy between NS and NNS (r_{NS}=0.62, r_{NNS}=0.66; Z=-1.28, p=*n.s.*). However, after splitting all messages based on their lexical sentiment (Figure 2), our data showed that the cue annotation accuracy was significantly higher in messages with positive lexical sentiment compared to negative lexical sentiment for both NS (r_{POS}=0.69, r_{NEG}=0.47; Z=2.88, $p<.05)^{\dagger}$ and NNS (r_{POS}=0.74, r_{NEG}=0.60; Z=3.15, $p<.05)^{\circ}$. Similarly, the cue annotation accuracy was significantly higher in messages with positive lexical sentiment compared to objective lexical sentiment for both NS (r_{POS}=0.69, $r_{OBJECTIVE}$=0.54; Z=2.53, $p<.05)^{\ddagger}$ and NNS (r_{POS}=0.74, $r_{OBJECTIVE}$=0.61; Z=2.23, $p<.05)^{**}$.

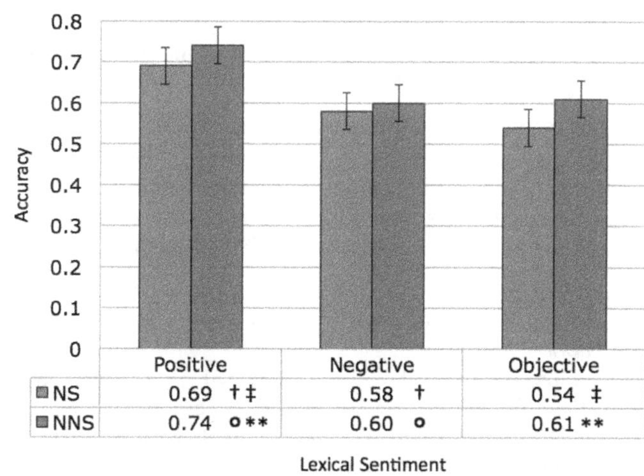

Figure 2. NS and NNS cue annotation accuracy in messages with positive (N=33), negative (N=32) or objective (N=33) lexical sentiment.

These results answered the first part of our *RQ2*. They indicated that participants' accuracy on annotating proper emotional cues varied with the lexical sentiment of a message.

NS and NNS Annotation of Words, Symbols and Emoticons as Emotional Cues

As shown in Table 1, the participants also annotated words, symbols and emoticons that were not included in the author annotations. To explore the second part of our *RQ2* and answer what different types of cues NS and NNS make use of, we examined the discrepancies in word, symbol and emoticon annotations between NS and NNS in all messages (N=98).

First, we calculated the ratio of additional words selected by NS and NNS. Secondly, we calculated the ratio of symbols and emoticons selected by NS and NNS from all messages (N=98). For symbols, we focused on exclamation marks since previous work has indicated that they are used as one NS author strategy to express emotions in text-only messages [10].

We did not find any significant difference in the ratio of words selected as emotional cues between NS (M=0.31, SD=0.17) and NNS (M=0.30, SD=0.16) from all messages (N=98). Furthermore, we tested the word annotation accuracy based on the gold standard author annotations separately, and found no significant difference between NS and NNS (r_{NS}=0.62, r_{NNS}=0.65; Z=-0.97, p=*n.s.*). However, our results indicated that NS chose exclamation marks and emoticons significantly more frequently than NNS (Table 2).

	Exclamation Marks	Emoticons
NS	0.57	0.32
NNS	0.29	0.07
	χ^2 = 14.87, p<.05	χ^2 = 18.35, p<.05

Table 2: Ratio of exclamation marks and emoticons selected by NS and NNS.

These results partially answered the second part of our *RQ2*. They indicated that NS annotated significantly more symbols (exclamation marks) and emoticons as emotional cues from messages than NNS. Variance on word selection turned out to be the same between NS and NNS.

Emotional Valence Rating Accuracy between NS and NNS in Messages Including Symbols and Emoticons as Emotional Cues

A Mann-Whitney U test indicated that NS were significantly more accurate in their emotional valence rating for messages that included exclamation marks or emoticons than NNS (r_{NS}=0.78, r_{NNS}=0.69; Z=3.39, p<.05). Furthermore, a Mann-Whitney U test showed that NS were significantly more accurate than NNS at rating the emotional valence of messages where the lexical sentiment was positive (r_{NS}=0.67, r_{NNS}=0.57; Z=2.02, p<.05) or negative (r_{NS}=0.70, r_{NNS}=0.49; Z=3.48, p<.05) and the messages included exclamation marks or emoticons

The emotional valence rating accuracy of NS did not vary with the lexical sentiment when messages included exclamation marks and emoticons. However, NNS were significantly less accurate at detecting the emotional valence when a message included exclamation marks or emoticons and its lexical sentiment was either positive (r_{POS}=0.57, $r_{OBJECTIVE}$=0.69; Z=-2.34, p<.05) or negative (r_{NEG}=0.49, $r_{OBJECTIVE}$=0.69; Z=-3.23, p<.05).

These results answered the second part of our *RQ2*. Altogether, our results indicated that NS and NNS use similar words to detect the emotional valence of text-only messages. However, NS make use of symbols (exclamation marks) and emoticons significantly more than NNS. Furthermore, our results showed that the lexical sentiment of a message (positive and negative vs. objective) had an effect on NNS rating accuracy, but not on NS rating accuracy when the messages included exclamation marks and emoticons.

DISCUSSION

In summary, we found the following results on NNS detection of emotional valence in text-only messages written by native English-speaking authors:

- NNS were significantly less accurate than NS at detecting the emotional valence of English messages written by native English speakers.
- NNS were least accurate at detecting the emotional valence of messages where the lexical sentiment was negative.
- NNS were as accurate as NS at detecting the proper emotional cues in messages.
- NNS were significantly less accurate than NS at detecting the emotional valence of messages that included symbols (exclamation marks) and emoticons.

While the differences may seem relatively small, the effect size (Cliff's delta ranging from δ=0.32 to δ=0.67) indicates the robustness of our results. In the next sections, we discuss our findings in relation to previous work in more detail.

Explanation of the Findings

Why are NNS less accurate than NS at detecting the emotional valence of text-only messages?

We hypothesized that NS are more accurate at rating the emotional valence of text-only messages than NNS (*H1*), and our results fully supported this. In our related work section, we discussed some previous works that gave an indication on why this might be the case: NNS may have trouble detecting the nuances in single emotion words even when they are advanced second language learners [22].

What makes our results unique is that while previous work has focused on the semantic similarity of individual emotion words in multiple languages, we analyzed emotional valence detection in full text-only messages. Furthermore, we calculated the accuracy of NS and NNS emotional valence detection based on author ratings for each message. Our results indicated that even when more contextual information is available (i.e., complete messages), NNS have trouble detecting the emotional valence accurately.

Previous research suggests that emotional responses to emotional expressions may differ between first and second languages depending on the first language background [4]. Thus, first language background may explain some difficulties that the Japanese NNS in this study faced when rating the emotional valence of text-only messages.

How did the lexical sentiment of a message affect NNS emotional valence rating?
In our *RQ1*, we asked whether the lexical sentiment of a message has an effect on the emotional valence rating accuracy of NS and NNS. Our results indicated that both NS and NNS were most accurate at detecting the emotional valence of messages that included highly positive words. This result is also related to the cue selection accuracy (*RQ2*), where both NS and NNS were most accurate at detecting emotional cues in messages with positive lexical sentiment.

Previous works suggested that NS make use of negative words and negations to detect between author's positive and negative emotional states [10]. NNS had particular problems with detecting the emotional valence of messages that included highly negative words as opposed to highly positive words. Furthermore, as depicted in Figure 2, NNS were least accurate at detecting the emotional cues in messages with negative lexical sentiment.

One likely explanation for this discrepancy is that while NNS can successfully detect the important emotion words, they may not be familiar with the nuances of negative English words when used as part of sarcastic and cynical messages. Indeed, some NNS participants routinely wrote "*maybe it was a joke*" as an additional explanation for their emotional valence rating in negative messages if they were not confident that they understood the emotional nuance correctly.

How come NNS were less accurate in their emotional valence ratings but this did not hold true for emotional cues?
Our second research question (*RQ2*) asked whether NS and NNS rely on same cues when detecting the emotional valence of a text-only message. Despite the fact that NNS were significantly less accurate at detecting the emotional valence in each message (Figure 1), our results showed that NS and NNS were as accurate at detecting proper emotional cues from the messages (Figure 2).

Permitting the use of bilingual dictionaries for NNS might have helped the NNS participants rate each message more accurately. Interestingly, however, the use of bilingual Japanese to English dictionaries did not solve the problem for NNS to accurately detect the emotional valence of the text-only messages. One possible explanation is that dictionaries may have helped the NNS detect the proper emotion words, but did not help in perceiving them properly. In case the NNS would have had a longer tenure in an English speaking country, their emotional valence rating accuracy would likely be closer to that of NS.

Why NNS did not rely on symbols and emoticons when detecting the emotional valence of text-only messages?
As suggested in previous work, native English speakers often rely on symbols (exclamation marks) and emoticons to detect emotions in text-only messages [1, 9, 15, 26]. However, our results concluded that NNS make use of exclamation marks and emoticons significantly less than NS when detecting the emotional valence of messages (Table 2).

Previous research has highlighted the differences in the use of symbols [16] and emoticons [18] between different languages. The pragmatic use of emoticons may also differ in the native language of the NNS. For example, Japanese emoticons may not convey emotions same as Western emoticons [26], but may serve a different, more complex purpose in socio-emotional communication [13, 28].

One possible explanation for our results is that the Japanese NNS may not be familiar with the Western emoticons (e.g., :O or :P) and their relation to the verbal content of a message. Another possible reason for the Japanese NNS not to rely on the available emoticons is the lower expressiveness of Western emoticons compared to Japanese emoticons (e.g., _|￣|○ meaning: disappointment) [28]. In short, NNS may be unable to detect the connection between the verbal emotional content and the symbols and emoticons depending on how they are used in the NNS native language.

Design Implications
In this paper, we concluded that NNS were significantly less accurate at detecting the emotional valence of text-only messages compared to NS. However, our results also implied that NNS did not have trouble detecting the relevant words used as emotional cues in each message.

Secondly, we highlighted a discrepancy between NS and NNS annotation of symbols (exclamation marks) and emoticons as emotional cues in the messages. In short, NNS did not make use of the available emoticons when detecting the emotional valence of a text-only message written by NS authors.

Based on these results, we propose two design implications for a system to bridge the gap between NNS receiver's and NS author's understanding of the emotional tone conveyed in a text-only message.

1) *System for classifying the lexical sentiment in emotion words based on non-native speaker's ratings.*

Existing software for automatic analysis of emotions conveyed in words and sentences are tuned based on native English-speakers' evaluations (e.g., SentiWordNet [6], LIWC [19]). For example, the system used in this paper, SentiWordNet, includes a numerical score for positive-negative polarity of subjective terms based on human ratings [6]. Based on results in this paper, the existing systems may not adequately predict NNS understanding of the emotional nuances in individual words and messages.

A system that would gather human annotations of emotion words specifically by non-native speakers would be one solution to alleviate the problem highlighted in this paper. For example, synset classification of emotion terms rated by NNS could be compared to a classification rated by NS (e.g., SentiWordNet). In case of discrepancies in the ratings, the system could let the NS author know about the possible misunderstanding the word choice may cause for NNS receivers.

A less transparent approach would be to automatically replace the emotion words with disparate ratings in NS and NNS synsets to the closest matching synonym only for NNS receivers. While this approach would be less transparent for the NS authors, it would impose a lower burden on them, as well as on other NS who receive the same message (e.g., one-to-many messages).

2) *System for translating emotional cues in symbols and emoticons for non-native speakers.*

Previous research has implied that symbols (exclamation marks) and emoticons help NS to determine between positive and negative emotions [10] and the strength of the emotion [3, 26]. However, our results indicated that not all available cues are useful for NNS (i.e., exclamation marks and emoticons).

Due to the variety of emoticons in different languages, NNS may have difficulties connecting the verbal emotional content in their second language to the symbols and emoticons. Thus, simply replacing the emoticons with the closest equivalent in the NNS native language may not be helpful. However, since the NNS in our study relied mostly on words to detect the emotional valence of a message, a solution that would translate the emotional tone of the emoticon verbally to NNS receivers would likely be helpful. For example, the basic human emotions (anger, disgust, fear, sadness, surprise, anticipation, trust, joy/happiness [5, 20]) could be used to automatically translate the emotional tone of symbols and emoticons to NNS receivers.

Informing the NS author about low expressivity of symbols and emoticons as emotional cues for the NNS may help prevent misunderstandings between NS and NNS. A transparent approach would be a system that would assist NS authors to translate their emotional expressions in symbols and emoticons. This would not lower the amount of cues available for NS receivers, but rather give NNS more verbal cues to detect the emotions conveyed in text-only message.

Future Directions

For future studies, we are interested in expanding this study to authors and participants with different language backgrounds. For example, NNS whose native language is closer to the grammatical and conceptual structure of English, or have had a longer tenure in an English speaking country might perceive emotions in English text-only messages differently. Thus, adjusting the native language of the authors and/or the language background of the participants may yield different results. We are also interested in expanding this study to include multiple emotional dimensions (e.g., joy, anger, sadness, etc.). Further, we are interested in how our results may apply to various conversational contexts, such as when the author and receiver are familiar with each other.

CONCLUSIONS

Accurately detecting emotions in text-only CMC is difficult even for native speakers. Authors need to employ alternative strategies for expressing their emotional states as opposed to when using rich communication channels [9, 15, 25]. Yet, little is known on how non-native speaking receivers detect the emotions in text-only messages written by native speaking authors based on these cues.

By looking at how accurately Japanese non-native English speakers were able to detect the emotional valence in text-only messages, we have been able to identify key problems in multilingual distance communication. When detecting the emotional valence of messages, non-native English speakers are not able to reach the accuracy of native English speakers. Furthermore, non-native English speakers have particular problems detecting the emotional valence when text-only messages include highly negative words as opposed to highly positive words.

Despite their problems in detecting the emotional valence of a message, Japanese non-native English speakers are able to accurately detect the proper emotional cues, particularly words, from text-only messages. However, while native speakers rely on symbols (exclamation marks) and emoticons to detect the emotional valence, non-native speakers are unable to make use of these cues. In other words, even when native English-speaking authors include emotional cues in their messages that both native and non-native speakers are able to accurately detect, non-native speakers detect the emotion expressed with these cues differently.

This study highlights challenges for socio-emotional communication in text-only mediums between native English-speaking authors and non-native English-speaking receivers. Especially when the majority of communication is done over text-only mediums (such as email or instant messaging), misunderstandings in emotion detection between native and non-native speakers can have detrimental effects in interpersonal and work relationships. We hope that this work illustrates the discrepancies between how non-native speakers detect emotions in text-only communication, and how native English speakers express them as message authors.

ACKNOWLEDGMENTS
We would like to thank all Facebook message authors who agreed to let us use their public status updates as part of our dataset. We would also like to extend our gratitude to the anonymous reviewers for their insightful comments and suggestions for improving this paper.

REFERENCES
1. Aman, S. and Szpakowicz, S. Identifying expressions of emotion in text. In *Proc. TSD 2007* (*LNCS 4629*), Springer (2007), 196-205.
2. Benson, M.J. Attitudes and motivation towards English: A survey of Japanese freshmen. *RELC Journal 22, 1* (1991), 34-48.
3. Derks, D., Bos, A.E.R. and von Grumbkow, J. Emoticons and online message interpretation. *Social Science Computer Review, 26, 3* (2008), 379-388.
4. Dewaele, J-M. The emotional weight of *I love you* in multilinguals' languages. *Journal of Pragmatics 40, 10* (2008), 1753-1780.
5. Ekman, P. An argument for basic emotions. *Cognition and Emotion 6* (1992), 169–200.
6. Esuli, A. and Sebastiani, F. SentiWordNet: A publicly available lexical resource for opinion mining. In *Proc. LREC 2006*, 2006, 417-422.
7. Gill, A.J., French, R.M., Gergle, D. and Oberlander, J. The language of emotion in short blog texts. In *Proc. CSCW 2008*, ACM (2008), 299-302.
8. Gill, A.J., Gergle, D., French, R.M. and Oberlander, J. Emotion rating from short blog texts. In *Proc. CHI 2008*, ACM (2008), 1121-1124.
9. Hancock, J.T., Gee, K., Ciaccio, K. and Lin, J.M-H. I'm sad you're sad: emotional contagion in CMC. In *Proc. CSCW 2008*, ACM (2008), 295-298.
10. Hancock, J.T., Landrigan, C. and Silver, C. Expressing emotion in text-only communication. In *Proc. CHI 2007*, ACM (2007), 929-923.
11. Hyland, F. Learning autonomously: Contextualising out-of-class English language learning. *Language Awareness 13, 3* (2004), 180-202.
12. Kato, Y., Kato, S. and Akahori, K. Effects of emotional cues transmitted in e-mail communication on the emotions experienced by senders and receivers. *Computers in Human Behavior, 23, 4* (2007), 1894-1905.
13. Miyake, K. How young Japanese express their emotions visually in mobile phone messages: A sociolinguistic analysis. *Japanese Studies 27, 1* (2007), 53-72.
14. Mok, D., Carrasco, J.A. and Wellman, B. Does Distance Still Matter in the Age of the Internet?. *Urban Studies 46, 13* (2009), 2747-2783.
15. Murphy, K. L. and Collins, M. P. Development of communication conventions in instructional electronic chats. *Journal of Distance Education 12, 1–2* (1997), 177-200.
16. Nishimura, Y. Linguistic innovations and interactional features of casual online communication in Japanese. *Journal of Computer-Mediated Communication 9, 1* (2006) http://onlinelibrary.wiley.com/doi/10.1111 /j.1083 - 6101.2003.tb00356.x/full (accessed: 15.9.2013).
17. Olson, G.M. and Olson, J.S. Distance matters. *Human-Computer Interaction 15, 2* (2000), 139-178.
18. Park. J., Barash, V., Fink, C. and Cha. M. Emoticon style: Interpreting differences in emoticons across cultures. In *Proc. ICWSM 2013*, AAAI Press (2013), 466–475.
19. Pennebaker, J. W., Francis, M. E. and Booth, R. J. Linguistic inquiry and word count. Mahwah, NJ: Erlbaum Publishers (2001).
20. Plutchik, R. *The Psychology and Biology of Emotion.* New York: HarperCollins (1994).
21. Provine, R.R., Spencer, R.J. and Mandell, D.L. Emotional expression online: Emoticons punctuate website text messages. *Journal of Language and Social Psychology 26, 3* (2007), 299-307.
22. Romney, A.K., Moore, C.C. and Rusch, C.D. Cultural universals: Measuring the semantic structure of emotion terms in English and Japanese. In *Proc. National Academy of Sciences 94, 10* (1997), 5489-5494.
23. Russell, J.A. Pancultural aspects of the human conceptual organization of emotions. *Journal of Personality and Social Psychology 45, 6* (1983), 1281-1288.
24. Short, J., Williams, E. and Christie, B. *The Social Psychology of Telecommunications*. New York: Wiley (1976).
25. Walther, J. Interpersonal effects in computer-mediated interaction: A relational perspective. *Communication Research 19* (1992), 52-90.
26. Walther, J. and D'Addario, K.P. The impacts of emoticons on message interpretation in computer–mediated communication. *Social Science Computer Review 19* (2001), 324-347.
27. Walther, J.B., Loh, T. and Granka, L. Let me count the ways: The interchange of verbal and nonverbal cues in computer-mediated and face-to-face affinity. *Journal of Language and Social Psychology 24, 1* (2005), 36-65.
28. Yuasa, M., Saito, K. and Mukawa, N. Emoticons convey emotions without cognition of faces: An fMRI study. In *Proc. CHI 2006*, ACM (2006), 1565-1570.

TransPhoner: Automated Mnemonic Keyword Generation

Manolis Savva, Angel X. Chang, Christopher D. Manning and **Pat Hanrahan**
Computer Science Department, Stanford University
{msavva, angelx, manning, hanrahan}@cs.stanford.edu

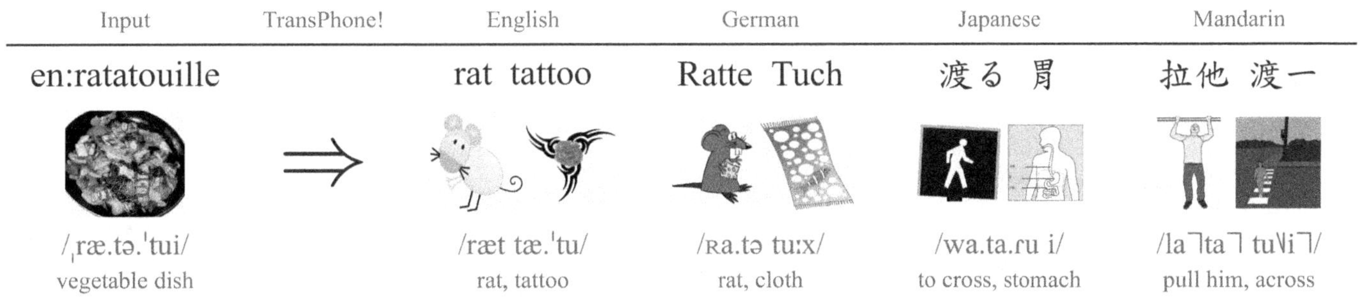

Figure 1. TransPhoner: a system that given terms in one language generates phonetically similar, highly imageable keywords. These keywords can aid learning of foreign language vocabulary and can serve as memorable pronunciation guides (click keywords for audio).

ABSTRACT

We present *TransPhoner*: a system that generates keywords for a variety of scenarios including vocabulary learning, phonetic transliteration, and creative word plays. We select effective keywords by considering phonetic, orthographic and semantic word similarity, and word concept imageability. We show that keywords provided by TransPhoner improve learner performance in an online vocabulary learning study, with the improvement being more pronounced for harder words. Participants rated TransPhoner keywords as more helpful than a random keyword baseline, and almost as helpful as manually selected keywords. Comments also indicated higher engagement in the learning task, and more desire to continue learning. We demonstrate additional applications to tasks such as pure phonetic transliteration, generation of mnemonics for complex vocabulary, and topic-based transformation of song lyrics.

Author Keywords

Mnemonic keywords

ACM Classification Keywords

H.5.m Information Interfaces and Presentation (e.g. HCI): Miscellaneous

General Terms

Languages; Human Factors; Design.

CHI 2014, April 26–May 1, 2014, Toronto, Ontario, Canada.

http://dx.doi.org/10.1145/2556288.2556985

INTRODUCTION

"The limits of my language means the limits of my world."
— Ludwig Wittgenstein

Learning vocabulary is a hard and laborious task, whether memorizing foreign language words or mastering complex terminology. Mnemonic keywords are a learning tool that can be applied to vocabulary learning and other tasks. For example, the keywords and images in Figure 1 can facilitate learning and recall of the English word ratatouille. We present *TransPhoner*: a cross-lingual system that given words in one language, suggests phonetically and semantically relevant keywords in the same or another language.

Prior work has shown that keyword association can improve memorization and pronunciation of foreign vocabulary [2, 13]. However, to the best of our knowledge, there are no existing methods for generating such keywords automatically. To use mnemonic methods, teachers and learners expend considerable effort in manually generating mnemonic material.

Our main contribution is a keyword generation system, with design principles grounded in results from cognitive psychology. To empirically evaluate the effectiveness of TransPhoner keywords we used them for the concrete application of foreign language vocabulary learning. In a human participant study, we found that TransPhoner keywords improve short-term learning performance significantly, with the effect being stronger for harder words. Study participants rated TransPhoner keywords higher on a helpfulness scale compared to a baseline random keyword condition. Finally, we present additional applications of TransPhoner to illustrate the variety of scenarios where keyword generation can be beneficial.

RELATED WORK

Our research is enabled by prior work in psycholinguistics and natural language processing, and related to computational systems for assisting language learning.

Natural Language Processing

Recent NLP research has automatically re-spelled English words to create spellings that clarify pronunciation [18]. The focus was on using phonetically unambiguous English syllables to correct for phonetic inconsistencies in English orthography (spelling). In contrast, we jointly consider phonetic similarity, imageability and semantics to find effective mnemonic keywords in any target language.

Mapping the script of a word from one language to a conventional form in another while preserving pronunciation is the goal of machine transliteration systems—most commonly used for proper nouns (names of people, places and organizations). A recent survey is provided by Karimi et al. [21]. Transliteration approaches differ from our task in that they aim to retrieve typical, commonly accepted transliterations from one language to another. They do not aim to output strings of semantically meaningful words in the target language, nor are they concerned with memorability or learning of a source language term.

Mnemonic Keyword Strategy

Psychologists have long known that mnemonics are a powerful learning strategy [30]. In the specific scenario of vocabulary learning, mnemonic keywords are words presented in addition to the foreign word and its translation. Mnemonic keywords have been extensively studied and are an established learning strategy amongst educators [9, 34]. Fig 2 provides an example. The keyword "cook" is associated with the German for kitchen: "Küche". Typically context is provided in the form of a sentence or image linking keyword with foreign word: "Imagine your kitchen and a *cook* in it".

Keywords are selected to be phonetically similar to the foreign word and highly *imageable*. Imageability is defined as the ease with which a word gives rise to a sensory mental image [31]. High imageability keywords make it easier to visualize interactions between the keyword, foreign word form and underlying concept.

The pioneering work of Atkinson et al [2] showed the effectiveness of keywords for improving vocabulary learning and was followed by studies confirming recognition and recall improvements in a variety of conditions [13, 15, 32]. However, as far as we are aware, our work is the first exploring computational methods for generating mnemonic keywords.

Computer-Assisted Language Learning

The application of technology to language learning has a long history of prior work [1, 22]. We focus on the automated generation of keywords that can help to link a word form—either visual or auditory—with a mental image, an important prerequisite before learning can occur.

Some CALL systems have addressed pronunciation training by using speech recognition to evaluate learners and assist them in correcting mistakes [11]. Other systems have used virtual simulations of real-life contexts to facilitate learning [20]. We demonstrate that our mnemonic keyword generation system can assist vocabulary learning and can thus be integrated with other CALL methods in comprehensive language learning systems.

LINGUISTICS TERMINOLOGY

Although TransPhoner keywords can be used for a variety of tasks, for clarity of exposition we focus on foreign language learning and use conventional terminology from linguistics. A *foreign* language is one in which a learner is not completely fluent. *Native languages* are the languages in which a learner has attained fluency, usually at an early age. Each language has at least one associated writing system, which we call a *script*, and a spoken language which obeys a set of phonological rules.

We represent pronunciations using the International Phonetic Alphabet (IPA) notation [19]. The IPA organizes and categorizes a comprehensive inventory of vowels and consonants exhibited in human speech and can be used as a language-agnostic transcription of *phones*: the basic sound units of speech. Each language uses a different subset of phones conceptualized as language-specific *phonemes*: the basic units of the phonology of that language that can distinguish meaning.

Phonemes are combined to form pronunciations of words. A phoneme can be viewed as a set of phones considered equivalent under the phonetics of a particular language. For example, the English phoneme /k/ occurs in words such as "kit" (IPA: [$\mathrm{k^h}$ɪt]) and "skill" (IPA: [skɪl]) but the physical sound (i.e. phone) is different. "Kit" is pronounced with the phone [$\mathrm{k^h}$] (aspirated k) whereas "skill" is pronounced with [k] (unaspirated k). In English these are so called *allophones* but in other languages such as Thai, they represent different phonemes and can be used for semantic distinctions.

Analogously, a *grapheme* is the smallest semantically distinguishing unit in a written language. Examples of graphemes include alphabetic letters in alphabets (e.g. a, ω), ideograms such as Chinese characters (e.g. 木, 字), and syllabic characters such as the Japanese kana (e.g. あ, ヒ).

DESIGN PRINCIPLES

We look at prior research on effective mnemonic keywords to lay out a set of design principles for a keyword generation system. At a high level, the mnemonic keywords should be memorable and have high reminding power for both the foreign word and the native translation. This requirement implies the following desirable properties for the generated keywords:

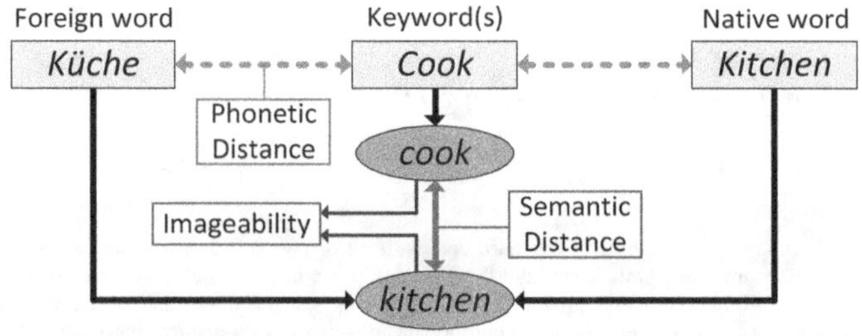

Figure 2. Illustration of the mnemonic keyword learning strategy. Effective keywords are phonetically similar to the foreign word, correspond to highly imageable concepts, and are semantically close to the concept. Concepts in dark blue circles, word forms in light blue boxes.

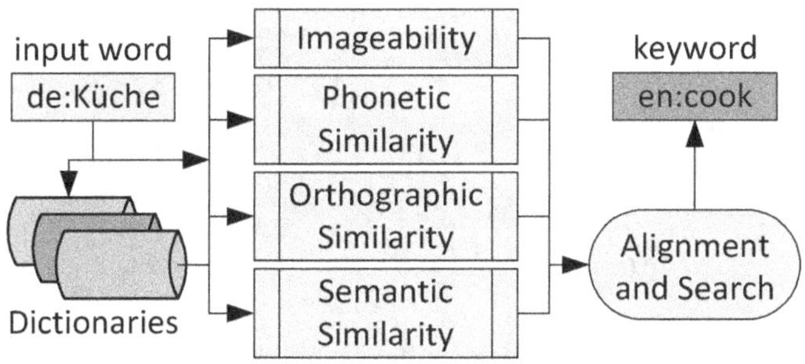

Figure 3. The TransPhoner system architecture: input words in a given foreign language are looked up and evaluated against words in a target native language using several similarity and quality measures. An alignment and search algorithm optimizes suggested keyword choice to give highly imageable, phonetically and semantically proximal keywords to be used as mnemonics for the input word.

Language	Dictionary	IPA Pronunciations	# Words
English	Scrabble list[2]	`www.dictionary.com`	63,261
French	FreeDict[3]	FreeDict	7,452
German	FreeDict	Rule-based[4]	80,235
Japanese	EDICT[5]	Rule-based	213,829
Mandarin	CEDICT[6]	CJKlib[7]	104,528

Table 1. Dictionary data used by our system. Dictionaries provide word lists and definitions. IPA pronunciations are retrieved from pronunciation dictionaries, or by using rule-based systems for languages with regular grapheme-to-phoneme mappings.

- *Phonetically similar*: aid recognition and generation of pronunciation
- *Highly imageable*: improve memorability and learnability
- *Semantically related*: help associate word form to concept

Our goal is to demonstrate that we can computationally generate keywords that are effective for learning vocabulary and guiding pronunciation. There are several dimensions along which a system such as this can be adjusted to generate better results for particular tasks. However, the focus of our paper is to present results utilizing simple, sensible defaults.

The architecture of our system is illustrated in Fig 3. Information for input words is retrieved by searching available dictionaries. Measures of word imageability, phonetic similarity, orthographic similarity and semantic similarity are then used to evaluate candidate keywords from the appropriate target language dictionary. The results are combined in a joint objective function and a search algorithm is used to optimize for the best candidate keyword.

LANGUAGE RESOURCES

Before applying a computational method to our problem, we need data sources for the orthography, definitions and pronunciations of words in all desired source and target languages. We retrieve this data from dictionaries (see Table 1). We use the IPA as a common representation for pronunciations to facilitate cross-language comparison. The IPA transcriptions were annotated with syllable separators (syllabification) using a rule-based system for English[1] and French, or induced directly during the rule-based transcription to IPA for German, Japanese and Mandarin.

[1] `github.com/codyrobbins/syllabify`

We also need to reason about word semantics, and to connect word concepts between languages. For the former, we use WordNet [29], a lexical ontology with senses (meanings) for English words. Many words have multiple senses—an example is "bank" which can refer to a financial institution or to a river bank. For the latter, we use the Universal WordNet (UWN) [10], which connects other languages to the English WordNet. UWN also provides a weighted score for the degree to which a given word reflects each candidate sense. From the senses of each word, we retrieve definitions for computing imageability scores and semantic similarity between words.

SIMILARITY MEASURES

Orthographic similarity is useful for languages with similar scripts, since associating the written word forms in two languages can be effective for learning. However, phonetic similarity is more important in general as it helps in remembering the pronunciation of a word, and in avoiding pitfalls due to differences of script-to-phonetic mappings between languages. For example, "ch" is pronounced /ç/ in German, similar to the initial consonant in "hut", rather than English "chat".

An imageability measure is critical for selecting memorable keywords that are easy to associate with the word concept being learned. Finally, semantic similarity to the target word concept is useful for facilitating the forming of associations between foreign words and their native language translations.

Orthographic Similarity

A simple way to measure similarity of written form is using orthographic distance. For words in the same script we use a simple edit distance (Levenshtein distance) between their graphemes (letters). The Levenshtein distance [26] counts the number of operations (insertions, deletions and substitutions) that are required to transform one string into the other.

Phonetic Similarity

To compute phonetic similarities between pronunciations of words in different languages we consider each word as a sequence of phones from that word's IPA transcription. Again, we use a Levenshtein distance, now with a weight matrix defining the cost of substituting one phone for another, to compute the phonetic distance between two words. We search for an alignment (mapping of phones in one word to those of another) such that the Levenshtein distance is minimized.

Many phonetic similarity methods exist—a survey is provided by Kondrak [24]. We use the phonetic similarity defined by the ALINE phonetic alignment system which has been shown to align cognates between languages [23]. This scheme categorizes vowels and consonants in separate feature spaces where each phone is represented as a vector of values. Each feature dimension has an associated weight used in computing the overall distance between phones.

[2] `code.google.com/p/scrabblehelper/`
[3] `www.freedict.org/en/`
[4] `korpling.german.hu-berlin.de/~amir/Text2IPA_German.pl`
[5] `www.csse.monash.edu.au/~jwb/edict.html`
[6] `cc-cedict.org/wiki/`
[7] `code.google.com/p/cjklib/`

We simplify the ALINE algorithm by omitting phone expansions (i.e. no special costs for matching two phones to one, or one phone to two). We handle matching of syllable breaks by adding a constant match score $C_{sep} = 20$, and a mismatch cost $C_{skip} = -10$, as defined by ALINE. The phone feature set used by ALINE is not complete—a few phones are considered equivalent (e.g. /i/, /ɪ/), so we add an extra weight for preferring exact phone matches[8].

Word Imageability

Unlike the other similarity components, methods for computing word imageability are largely unstudied. We describe a simple approach which aims to take into account word familiarity and easiness of acquisition as proxies for word imageability. Though not our focus here, an investigation and evaluation of approaches for computing imageability is an interesting avenue for future work.

A large corpus of imageability ratings for words is not available. However, studies in cognitive psychology have shown that word imageability is highly correlated with age of acquisition (AoA), an estimate of the average age at which children acquire a word [5, 16, 28, 33]. We therefore use a corpus of AoA ratings for more than 50,000 English words by Kuperman et al. [25], as well as other word features such as familiarity and part of speech to compute imageability ratings. We then propagate imageability values to other languages using the inter-language mappings from UWN.

We begin by estimating the imageability of English words in the Kuperman corpus of AoA values using a linear regression method. Additional word features for this regression come from the MRC Psycholinguistic Database [37] which contains linguistic and psycho-linguistic attributes of English words. Importantly, it contains imageability values for 4579 words derived from several previous corpora [7, 8, 16]. We normalize this imageability to be between 0 and 1, and then train a linear regression model using AoA, familiarity, and part of speech feature values from the Kuperman corpus.

We then compute the imageability of foreign words and English words not covered by the Kuperman corpus from words with known imageability using a two-step averaging scheme:

$$I_W(w) = \sum_{(a_i,s_i)\in S(w)} \frac{a_i I_S(s_i)}{\sum_j a_j} \quad ; \quad I_S(s) = \sum_{(b_i,w_i)\in W(s)} \frac{b_i I_W(w_i)}{\sum_j b_j}$$

where $I_W(w)$ and $I_S(s)$ are the imageability values of a word w and sense s respectively, and $a_i; b_i$ are the word-sense association weights from UWN. Words not covered by UWN are given an imageability value of 0, under the assumption that rare words will be unfamiliar to most people, and consequently are unlikely to be highly imageable. Figure 4 plots a histogram of the resulting imageability values.

Semantic Similarity

We use a simple bag-of-words [27] (BoW) model over WordNet sense definitions to approximate relatedness of word concepts. We represent each sense as a vector of counts of words

[8]ALINE output values are divided by 100 to make them comparable with similarities from other components.

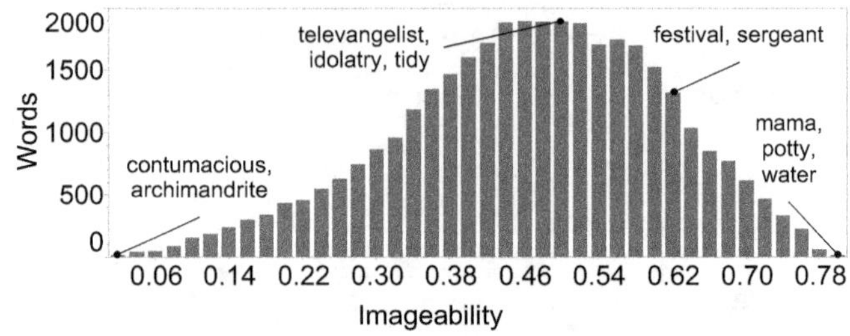

Figure 4. Histogram of imageability for 35,000 English words. Example words annotated. Imageability ranges between 0 and 1 on the horizontal.

occurring in the sense definition. We filter the BoW vector to include only nouns, verbs, adjectives and adverbs. Part of speech tagging is done using the Stanford POS tagger [35]. The BoW vector for a word is then represented as a weighted sum of the BoW vectors for each sense of that word. The similarity between two words is computed using the cosine distance between the BoW representations: $sim(w_1, w_2) = v_{w_1} \cdot v_{w_2} / \|v_{w_1}\| \|v_{w_2}\|$ where $v_w = \sum_{(a_i,s_i)\in S(w)} a_i v_{s_i}$ and v_{s_i} is the BoW vector representation of sense s_i.

We chose to use a simple approach for approximating semantic similarity—many alternatives exist from extensive work in Natural Language Processing [36]. Similarity measures over the WordNet hierarchy, or more advanced methods such as Latent Semantic Analysis or word embeddings trained with neural networks are easy to incorporate.

FINDING CANDIDATE KEYWORDS

We combine the similarity measures in an objective function and search for good keywords given particular input words.

Combined Objective Function

Since we do not constrain our system to single words on either input or output side, we consider sequences of words for our objective function. Given a sequence of words in a foreign language W_f as input, we find the sequence of words W^* from all candidate target native language word sequences W_n such that it maximizes a weighted combination of phonetic similarity σ_p, imageability I, semantic similarity σ_s, and orthographic similarity σ_o.

$$W^* = \operatorname*{argmax}_{W_n = w_1,\dots w_n} \alpha_p \sigma_p(W_n, W_f) + \alpha_o \sigma_o(W_n, W_f) + \alpha_s \sigma_s(W_n, W_f) + \alpha_i I(W_n) \text{ where}$$

$$\begin{aligned} \sigma_p(W_n, W_f) &= -\texttt{LevDist}(\texttt{phones}(W_n), \texttt{phones}(W_f)) \\ \sigma_o(W_n, W_f) &= -\texttt{LevDist}(\texttt{chars}(W_n), \texttt{chars}(W_f)) \\ \sigma_s(W_n, W_f) &= \texttt{sim}(\texttt{BoW}(W_n), \texttt{BoW}(W_f)) \end{aligned}$$

$$\texttt{BoW}(W) = \sum_{i=1}^{n} \texttt{BoW}(w_i); \quad I(W) = \sum_{i=1}^{n} I(w_i)$$

The components of the objective function each assign a quality score to a candidate keyword. The relative importance of these components and the independent efficacy of each at aiding language learning is an interesting research question

Input	English	German	French	Japanese	Mandarin
en:watermelon /ˈwɔ.təɹ.ˌmɛ.lən/ watermelon	water million /ˈwɔ.təɹ ˈmɪ.lyən/ water, million	Rotte mahlen /ʀɔ.tə maː.lən/ herd, grind	voiture main lune /vwa.ˈtyʁ mɛ lyn/ car, hand, moon	夜手メゾン /jo te me.zoɴ/ night, hand, house	苜塍密林 /mu˥˩ təŋ˥ mi˥˩.lin˧˥/ clover, flying dragon, jungle
de:Gesundheit /gə.zʊnt.haɪt/ health	gazette height /gə.ˈzɛt haɪt/ gazette, height	Gesamtheit /gə.zamt.haɪt/ entirety	goût zone chatte /gu zon ʃat/ relish, area, cat	偽善者手 /gi.zeɴ.ʃa te/ hypocrite, hand	革新海 /kɤ˧˥.ɕin˥ xai˨˩˦/ innovation, sea
ja: お早う /o.ha.joː/ Good morning	Ohio /oʊ.ˈhaɪoʊ/ Ohio (state)	Ohrhörer /oːɐ.høː.ʀɐ/ earphones	eau ration houx /o ʁa.ˈdjo u/ water, ration, holly	オヒョウ /o.hjoː/ halibut (fish)	五花肉 /u˨˩˦.xua˥.ʐou˥˩/ pork belly (food)

Table 2. Representative TransPhoner keyword results between several pairs of languages. Input word on the left, with source language indicated by the prefix. When targeting the same language, the input words are removed from the output candidate list. See supplemental materials for more results.

which is beyond the scope of this paper. For the examples presented here, we found $\alpha_p = \alpha_s = \alpha_i = 1$ and $\alpha_o = 0.5$ to provide good results.

Search Algorithm

To efficiently search over candidate matches, we use dynamic programming with either a phone-based trie or a character-based trie [14]. Tries are useful because we search over word sequences. For single word outputs, iterating over all words in a dictionary would suffice.

We take all words in the target language and create a phone-based trie. Potential phone matches are taken from the position in the trie. The cost of the match is the phonetic distance between the phones. This allows for re-using the computed Levenshtein distance between words with common prefixes. Whenever a word is matched, we loop back to the root of the trie, adding a syllable break between words. We also add the cost for selecting the matched word, incorporating non-phonetic similarity costs.

At each stage, we use a beam of N-best choices to ensure that we do not prune choices which may not be the closest phonetic match but have high scoring imageability or semantic similarity to the foreign word. This also allows us to generate N-best keyword lists from which a user can choose.

EXAMPLE OUTPUT KEYWORDS

Table 2 gives some example results of top keyword sequences suggested by TransPhoner when given the input words in the leftmost column. Output keywords are given in all five languages for which we have dictionary data. Keyword output is achieved at near-interactive rates, usually on the order of a second per source-target language pair, largely determined by the size of the target language dictionary.

EVALUATION EXPERIMENT

To evaluate the quality of keywords generated by TransPhoner we compared against manually selected keywords in the concrete application context of foreign language vocabulary learning. Prior work by Ellis et al. [13] has shown that manually chosen keywords can facilitate vocabulary learning. Our experimental goal was to show that we can generate equally effective keywords in this scenario with a direct evaluation metric: recall of learned words.

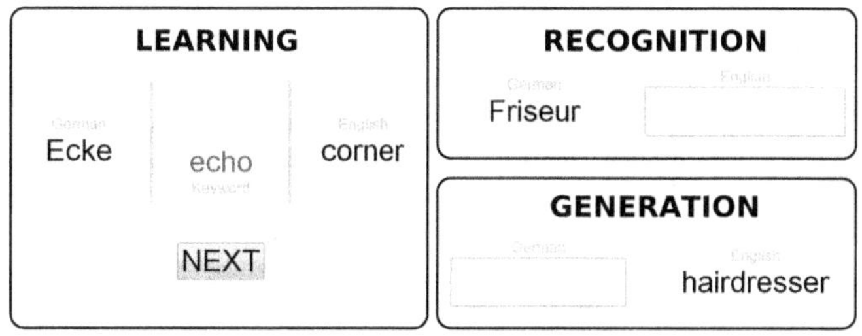

Figure 5. Screenshots of our vocabulary learning study interface.

Vocabulary Learning Study

We hypothesized that presenting TransPhoner keywords to people while they learn vocabulary improves learning performance by increasing new word retention. Ideally, this improvement would match or exceed the one imparted by manually chosen mnemonic keywords. To test this hypothesis, we carried out a vocabulary learning study. We used the evaluation set of 36 German words and manually chosen keywords by Ellis et al. as a comparison baseline. In addition, we randomly sampled from the 25000 most frequent English words to create a *random* keyword control condition. We thus have four conditions for keywords: *none*, *random*, *manual* and *TransPhoner*. As an example, for the German word "Friseur" (hairdresser), the *random* keyword was "opal", the manually chosen keyword by Ellis et al. was "freezer", and the automatically generated TransPhoner keyword was "frizzy".

Participants

We recruited participants from the Amazon Mechanical Turk workplace. Participants were required to not have any exposure to German and to be fluent in English. In total, we recruited 100 participants (60 male) with an average age of 32.3 years ($SD = 9.9$). Participants were compensated with \$1.70 for the study and told a \$0.10 bonus is available for average scores higher than 70%. To account for workers who did not earnestly attempt the task, we filtered any participants with average scores lower than 25%. This leaves 19 participants each for *none* and *manual* conditions, and 18 each for *random* and *TransPhoner* conditions.

Procedure

Fig 5 shows our web-based study interface. We designed the interface to match the experimental procedure of Ellis. Participants were randomly assigned to one of the four conditions.

They first took a short demographic survey and read instructions introducing the task. In keyword conditions, participants were instructed to do their best to *"imagine a visual scene connecting the given keyword with the English meaning, and the sound of the German word"*.

The study proceeded in three phases: learning, recognition and generation. First, participants were shown a block of 12 word pairs and asked to memorize the association. Keywords were shown in the center (except in the *none* condition). Words were pronounced twice, two and seven seconds after being shown. When the participant was ready, they proceeded by clicking a next button. The screen was blanked for one second, and the next word was shown. Order of presentation was randomized between participants.

Next, participants had to input the English meaning of the same 12 German words (re-randomized order) in a recognition phase. The word was again pronounced twice at the same intervals. Participants had a total of 10 seconds for input, after which the screen was blanked for one second and the next word was shown. Finally, participants were asked to give the German word for each English translation in the generation phase, spelling the German words as best as they could.

After one stage of learning–recognition–generation, the procedure was repeated with two more blocks of 12 words for a total of 36 words. Participants were instructed that the first stage was for training while the other two would be scored.

Design

The experiment was a mixed between- and within-subjects factorial design with the keyword condition {*none*, *random*, *manual*, *TransPhoner*}, participant {1...74}, word {1...36} and task {*recognition*, *recall*} as factors. All participants provided a recognition and generation response for each of 36 words for a total of 5328 responses.

The dependent measure was the recall score computed by comparing participant responses with the correct translation. We allowed for imperfect spellings by using the Levenshtein distance between participant response and the correct word, dividing by maximum possible distance and subtracting from 1 to create a normalized score between 0 and 1. Scores above 0.5—corresponding to at least half of the characters matching—were given partial credit equal to the score, while lower values were considered incorrect. Common synonyms such as "pants" and "trousers" were also considered correct. At the conclusion of the task, we also asked participants in the keyword conditions to judge the keywords for helpfulness in learning foreign vocabulary on a 5-point Likert scale, as well as to provide optional comments on the task.

Study Results

Vocabulary learning scores

Table 3 summarizes the average participant scores and keyword helpfulness ratings across conditions. The *none* condition had the lowest scores, followed by *manual*, *random* and finally the *TransPhoner* condition with a combined score of 76.1%. Interestingly, the difference between *random* and

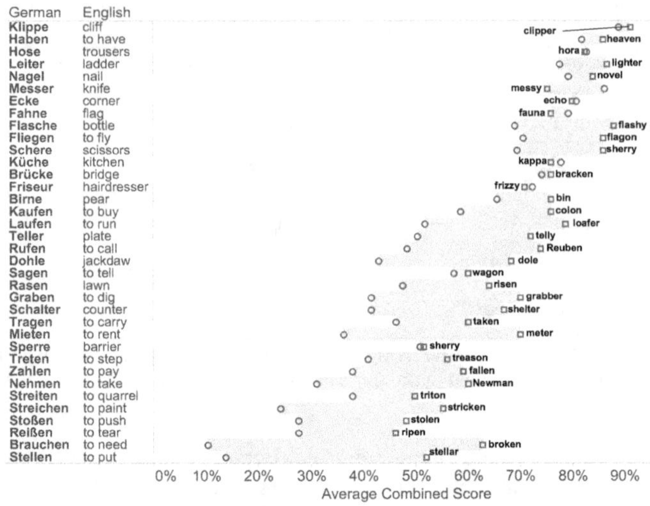

Figure 6. Comparison of average participant scores in conditions *none* (blue circles) and *TransPhoner* (red squares with keyword) for all words. Words ordered by decreasing mean score (easiest to hardest).

manual conditions is small, an observation we discuss later, in light of participant comments.

Fig 6 plots participant score improvement per word between the *none* and *TransPhoner* conditions. TransPhoner keywords significantly improve learning, with the effect being more pronounced for harder words. In general, verbs are harder to learn, a result agreeing with prior work [13].

Keyword helpfulness ratings

The mean keyword helpfulness ratings (see Table 3) were lowest for *random*, followed by *TransPhoner* and *manual*. All pairwise keyword rating differences were significant under Wilcoxon rank-sum tests with Bonferroni-Holm correction ($p < 0.001$ for all, except *manual–Transphoner* $p < 0.05$). Random keywords were generally disliked—an observation reflected in comments by study participants. The better performing *manual* and *TransPhoner* conditions had polarized ratings (almost purely 1 or 5 ratings). This polarization is not unexpected since some participants can have low affinity for keyword-based vocabulary learning, an observation also reflected in participant comments.

Keyword similarity scores

Table 3 also reports the normalized similarity scores between keyword and target word for all 36 German words used in the study. Unsurprisingly, randomly selected keywords had the lowest score along all dimensions. TransPhoner keywords had the highest overall (0.87) and phonetic (0.84) similarities, while manual keywords had higher semantic (0.25) similarity and imageability (0.65). Overall similarity and phonetic similarity were found to have a statistically significant positive correlation with combined learner scores (Pearson's $r(3526) = 0.06, p < 0.01$ and $r(3526) = 0.8, p < 0.001$ respectively). We did not find a significant correlation between either semantic similarity or imageability and the learner scores.

Further investigation of the effect of different forms of similarity between keyword and target word on learner perfor-

Condition	Rec %	Gen %	Comb %	Helpfulness	Overall Sim.	Phonetic Sim.	Semantic Sim.	Imageability
None	60.6	60.7	60.7	—	—	—	—	—
Random	68.1	66.9	67.5	2.09	0.40	0.38	0.11	0.32
Manual	69.3	64.4	66.8	**3.78**	0.78	0.72	**0.25**	**0.65**
TransPhoner	**76.4**	**75.9**	**76.1**	3.46	**0.87**	**0.84**	0.15	0.51

Table 3. Left side: average participant recognition, generation and combined vocabulary learning scores, and keyword ratings. Right side: average normalized target word to keyword similarity and imageability scores.

mance is an interesting avenue for future work. We noted that with English as a target language, the phonetic similarity dimension tends to strongly constrain word choice. In contrast, in target languages with higher phonetic-to-semantic multiplicity, such as Mandarin and Japanese, jointly optimizing phonetic similarity along with semantic similarity and imageability becomes easier.

Statistical analysis

We standardized all continuous numeric data by subtracting the mean and dividing by the standard deviation. Standard ANOVA does not account for per-word and per-participant variation leading to increased risk of type II errors. We therefore used mixed effects models which support both fixed effects and random effects (such as stimulus word and participant), and which are commonly used in psycholinguistics [3]. A good introduction for the HCI community is provided by recent work in machine translation post-editing [17]. Following this work, we also report significance results using likelihood-ratio (LR) tests—a measure equal to twice the difference between the log-likelihood of the model and the null hypothesis.

We fit a mixed effects model with keyword condition and logarithm of time spent learning the word as fixed effects, and both word and participant as random effects[9]. There was a significant main effect of the keyword condition on average participant score $\chi^2(3, N = 5184) = 7.87, p < 0.05$. We performed follow-up pairwise Welch's t-tests with Bonferroni-Holm correction between all keyword conditions. The mean score differences were all significant at $p < 0.001$, except *manual–TransPhoner* at $p < 0.01$, and *random–manual* (not significant $p = 0.07$). All keyword conditions performed better than no keywords, including *random* likely due to participants being primed to use a mnemonic strategy.

The absence of a significant difference between manual and random keywords seems surprising. However, we note that we used the *manual* condition keywords in a different way than Ellis et al., since the original work prompted participants with complete sentences containing the keywords (which were emphasized). Furthermore, the *random* condition likely resulted in participants reverting to a strategy of coming up with their own keyword. This hypothesis is supported by comments from *random* condition participants who complained about the quality of the keywords and stated that they came up with their own keywords. Prior work has shown that even when not asked to use keywords, participants come up with their own and use them effectively, which makes it difficult to control the participant learning strategy [13].

[9]Other independent variables such as age and gender had no significant effect, and interactions between keyword condition and learning time were not found. We used the `lme4` R package and optimized fit with maximum log-likelihood [3].

Participant comments

Though comments at the conclusion of the study were optional, more than half of our participants provided them. Comments from *manual* and *TransPhoner* condition participants were overwhelmingly positive indicating that they thoroughly enjoyed the task, and would like to continue taking similar experiments. Some examples include: *"Very interesting way for learning a new language"*, *"keywords really helped"*, *"I have always wanted to learn German but this HIT has really opened up that it might be really hard but it could be done by me"*. One of the negative comments mentioned the potential interference effect of keywords with target word meaning: *"I remembered them far better than I remembered the meaning of the word for some reason"*.

Despite improving performance over no keywords, the *random* keyword condition garnered largely negative comments: *"I didn't think the keyword helped in most cases – better off trying to make the sound fit with the english word"*, *"I actually felt like the keywords threw me off a bit"*, *"I do better when I make my own connections."* and *"The keywords made it harder for me. I like to make up my own keywords. For someone who didn't do that already, it might help"*. The latter comments indicate that some participants in the *random* condition compensated by creating their own keywords. A similar comment even occurred in the *none* condition: *"This was very difficult even using word association"*, reflecting that participants may use keywords even when not prompted to do so.

Summary

Our results are consistent with prior studies in keyword-based vocabulary learning. Short-term recognition and generation are improved by TransPhoner keywords, with the effect being larger for recognition. Though detailed evaluation of keyword-based learning is beyond our scope, and covered by much prior work, these results indicate that automatically generated keywords can significantly facilitate vocabulary learning, with performance matching or exceeding manual keywords. We note that our experiment only tested short-term effects. However, a retention study over a period of 10 years has shown that the positive effect of keywords carries over into long-term retention [4].

OTHER APPLICATIONS

So far, we focused on generating mnemonic keywords for foreign vocabulary learning. However, the TransPhoner system can be used in various other scenarios as well. Examples include: retrieval of images for generated keywords, transliteration within one language for clarifying pronunciation or

SAT Word	Meaning	Keywords
camaraderie	mutual trust and friendship	camera diary
subservient	obey others unquestioningly	sub servant
querulous	complaining in a whining manner	Queen rule loss
nonchalant	feeling or appearing casually calm	noon shall law neat
vicissitude	change of circumstances or fortune	visit side dude

Table 4. SAT vocabulary and example mnemonic phrases from top 10 results generated by TransPhoner.

creating mnemonics for complex words, and pure phonetic transliteration of tourist guide book phrases.

Keyword Images

Providing images for the generated keywords may facilitate the formation of a mental image. Though we do not empirically evaluate this hypothesis, we can easily retrieve relevant images for keywords from the web. TransPhoner currently uses the Google Image API to demonstrate this functionality (examples shown in Fig 1).

Complex Word Mnemonics

By matching rare complex words against shorter, more frequent keywords in the same language, we can create mnemonic keyword phrases for learning the complicated words. This is similar in spirit to the re-spelling work of Hauer et al. [18], using complete words instead of syllables, and optimizing for memorability as well as phonetic similarity. Table 4 gives examples for words taken from a list of vocabulary covered by the Scholastic Aptitude Test (SAT) exam, commonly taken by high school students in the United States.

Pure Phonetic Transliteration

When learning foreign word pronunciations, transliterations formed with the phonetically closest keywords in the target language can be effective as pronunciation guides. In fact, such keyword transliterations are designed manually and marketed as pronunciation learning guide books [12]. Table 5 shows some example phrases found in this series of books, the transliterations provided by the authors, and corresponding transliterations generated by TransPhoner. In general, TransPhoner transliterations are at least as close to the input language pronunciation as the manually designed phrases. Most importantly, TransPhoner generates these transliteration suggestions in seconds, whereas the effort in authoring them from scratch is considerable.

Topic-based Homophonic Transformation

TransPhoner can be used to automatically suggest topic-based homophonic transformations of word sequences. An application of this is in creating novel, phonetically similar interpretations of song lyrics–usually for comedic effect–known as *soramimi* or *mondegreen*. An example is in Table 6. We use all WordNet hyponyms under a given topic as candidate replacement words and for each phrase we compute phonetic similarity between original words and all candidates, offering the top 5 closest matches as suggestions.

LIMITATIONS AND FUTURE WORK

In our implementation we relied on dictionary data sources for phonetic information. A more robust approach could handle out-of-dictionary words by estimating pronunciation through grapheme to phoneme conversion systems [6]. Such systems would also help us deal with word pronunciations which are context-sensitive. For example, the Japanese "人" for person can be pronounced as /hi.to/, /d͡ʑiɴ/ or /niɴ/ depending on the context of the character. We have also not investigated how to transfer the prosody and pitch contours of utterances from one language to another. These attributes are particularly important for tonal languages such as Mandarin.

Input	"Slanguage" Books	TransPhoner
fr:Merci beaucoup /mɛʁ.ˈsi bo.ˈku/ Thank you very much	Mare-see-bow-coo /mɛər si boʊ ˈkɔː/ $\sigma_p = 0.82, \sigma = 0.92$	Meg-see-boo-coup /mɛg si bu ku/ $\sigma_p = 0.83, \sigma = 0.90$
ja: 楽しむ /ta.no.ʃi.mu/ To enjoy	Ton-know-she-Moo /tʌn noʊ ʃi mu/ $\sigma_p = 0.80, \sigma = 0.89$	Ta-gnaw-she-moo /tɑ nɔ ʃi mu/ $\sigma_p = 0.90, \sigma = 0.93$
zh: 薄烤饼 /po˧˥.kau˨˩˦.piŋ˨˩˦/ Pancake	Bow-cow-bing /boʊ kaʊ bɪŋ/ $\sigma_p = 0.51, \sigma = 0.65$	Paw-cow-ping /pɔ kaʊ pɪŋ/ $\sigma_p = 0.80, \sigma = 0.87$

Table 5. Some phrases with transliterations provided by "Slanguage" guide books [12], and corresponding transliterations by TransPhoner. Normalized phonetic (σ_p) and overall (σ) similarity values between input and output given for comparison.

Original	Food Topic	Gambling Topic
Sweet dreams are made of this	Sweet creams are made of this	Sweet deals are made of this
Who am I to disagree	Who am I to daiquiri	Who am I to lottery
I travel the world and the seven seas	I travel the world and the saffron seas	I raffle the world and the seven seas
Everybody's looking for something	Everybody's looking for dumpling	Everybody's looking for gambling

Table 6. Example of phonetic transformation constrained by topic: lyrics from the song "Sweet Dreams" by Eurythmics are transformed to be semantically closer to the topics of "food" and "gambling".

Another avenue for future work is generation of longer phrases and incorporation of language models to form grammatically valid sentences. An interesting empirical question is whether keyword sequences which are also valid sentences are better for learning. Richer stimuli such as context sentences connecting keyword and foreign word, related images, and animations could be integrated with such a system to further facilitate learning.

Finally, methods for tuning the generation of keywords for different tasks and types of users would be valuable to explore. For instance, we may tune keywords for younger learners by restricting them to more basic and imageable words, through an age of acquisition threshold.

DISCUSSION

Benefit of mnemonic keywords

We empirically saw that TransPhoner keywords improve short-term vocabulary learning, a result in agreement with existing research. Why are keywords helpful for learning? One hypothesis advocated by prior work is that keywords make learning more fun and engaging. For instance, the initial phases of foreign language learning require absorbing thousands of new words and can be discouraging, especially when approached mainly through rote repetition. Likewise, memorization of complex terminology for academic topics is intimidating to many students.

Though rote memorization is effective for learning, it is unfortunately also monotonous and discouraging, especially given the unfamiliar phonetics and orthography of a new language. Keywords and visual imagery can make the process more enjoyable, especially for younger learners. As such, keywords are a tool to surmount the initial learning hump and accelerate learning by facilitating associations at a point when the learner lacks knowledge necessary to form them independently. Keywords provide a learning scaffold that can engage learners and can also inspire them to come up with their own mnemonics.

The comments from our study indicate that participants enjoyed learning when keywords were carefully selected, and want to continue learning with keywords. Several participants explicitly requested to be informed when more similar learning tasks are available. In contrast, participants disliked random keywords and indicated their unhappiness with the task. Since the difference between these two conditions was the choice of keywords, we see that well chosen keywords can strongly engage and motivate learners, and that badly chosen keywords can have the opposite effect.

Implications for practical learning

Much research has shown that keywords are effective learning aids. However, application to actual learners and classrooms has been restricted. Teaching materials with keywords are scarce—the LinkWords system being a notable exception.[10] Creating such material requires considerable time and effort. Furthermore, each student responds differently to particular keywords, so success is largely contingent on tailoring them to the student's learning affinities. Therefore, a system for suggesting candidate mnemonic keywords can be invaluable for making keyword learning practically feasible and broadly accessible. Used in conjunction with other learning strategies, such a system can have tremendous positive impact.

CONCLUSION

We have presented TransPhoner, a cross-lingual system for generating mnemonic keywords. We evaluated TransPhoner keywords with a web-based vocabulary learning study and found that they lead to improved recall, with the effect being more prominent for harder words. Investigating the efficacy of TransPhoner keywords for specific learner demographics, and measuring the degree to which recall improvements lead to longer term retention are both interesting avenues for further research.

We also demonstrated how TransPhoner keywords are useful in a variety of other scenarios: as mnemonics for aiding learning complex vocabulary, as pronunciation guides for tourists and traveling professionals, and as suggestions for inspiring creative word plays.

The potential impact of mnemonic keyword systems is broad. In modern societies, knowledge of multiple languages is critical, so any improvement in learning languages can have significant long-range effects. Furthermore, the keyword mnemonic can easily be applied to other kinds of information such as country capitals or elements of the periodic table.

We hope our results will inspire further work on methods for mnemonic-based teaching and learning. Beyond increasing learner performance, integration of keyword-based techniques in learning tools may benefit teachers by allowing for easier design of effective teaching materials. Finally, psycholinguistics researchers studying mnemonic keyword learning strategies stand to benefit from a system that can generate keywords with different phonetic and semantic properties.

We have barely scratched the surface of the multi-faceted domain of mnemonic keywords. There is great potential for follow-up work on incorporating keywords in HCI systems to aid creative writing tasks, to provide on-the-spot pronunciation guides for tourists, and to assist people in learning a variety of material.

[10] `www.linkwordlanguages.com`

ACKNOWLEDGMENTS

We thank Gabor Angeli, Katherine Breeden, Matt Fisher and Daniel Ritchie for their help. The first author was supported by a Stanford Graduate Fellowship. The images in Figure 1 were released to the public domain by www.openclipart.com users: nicubunu, massimo, chrisdesign, palomaironique, chudq and stevelambert. The ratatouille image is by Flickr user Marcus Guimarães.

REFERENCES

1. Arnold, N., and Ducate, L. *Present and future promises of CALL: From theory and research to new directions in language teaching*. Computer Assisted Language Instruction Consortium, 2011.
2. Atkinson, R. C., and Raugh, M. R. An application of the mnemonic keyword method to the acquisition of a Russian vocabulary. *Journal of Experimental Psychology: Human Learning and Memory 1*, 2 (1975), 126.
3. Baayen, R., Davidson, D., and Bates, D. Mixed-effects modeling with crossed random effects for subjects and items. *Journal of Memory and Language* (2008).
4. Beaton, A., Gruneberg, M., and Ellis, N. Retention of foreign vocabulary learned using the keyword method: A ten-year follow-up. *Second Language Research 11*, 2 (1995), 112–120.
5. Bird, H., Franklin, S., and Howard, D. Age of acquisition and imageability ratings for a large set of words, including verbs and function words. *Behavior Research Methods, Instruments, & Computers 33*, 1 (2001), 73–79.
6. Chen, S. F. Conditional and joint models for grapheme-to-phoneme conversion. In *INTERSPEECH* (2003).
7. Clark, J. M., and Paivio, A. Extensions of the Paivio, Yuille, and Madigan (1968) norms. *Behavior Research Methods, Instruments, & Computers 36*, 3 (2004), 371–383.

8. Cortese, M. J., and Fugett, A. Imageability ratings for 3,000 monosyllabic words. *Behavior Research Methods, Instruments, & Computers 36*, 3 (2004), 384–387.
9. de Groot, A. M., and Van Hell, J. G. The learning of foreign language vocabulary. *Handbook of bilingualism* (2005), 9.
10. De Melo, G., and Weikum, G. Towards a universal WordNet by learning from combined evidence. In *Proceedings of the 18th ACM conference on Information and knowledge management*, ACM (2009), 513–522.
11. Ehsani, F., and Knodt, E. Speech technology in computer-aided language learning: Strengths and limitations of a new call paradigm. *Language Learning & Technology 2*, 1 (1998), 45–60.
12. Ellis, M. *French Slanguage*. Gibbs Smith, 2012.
13. Ellis, N. C., and Beaton, A. Psycholinguistic determinants of foreign language vocabulary learning. *Language learning 43*, 4 (1993), 559–617.
14. Fredkin, E. Trie memory. *Communications of the ACM 3*, 9 (1960), 490–499.
15. Fritz, C. O., Morris, P. E., Acton, M., Voelkel, A. R., and Etkind, R. Comparing and combining retrieval practice and the keyword mnemonic for foreign vocabulary learning. *Applied Cognitive Psychology 21*, 4 (2007), 499–526.
16. Gilhooly, K. J., and Logie, R. H. Age-of-acquisition, imagery, concreteness, familiarity, and ambiguity measures for 1,944 words. *Behavior Research Methods & Instrumentation 12*, 4 (1980), 395–427.
17. Green, S., Heer, J., and Manning, C. D. The efficacy of human post-editing for language translation. In *Proceedings of the SIGCHI Conference on Human Factors in Computing Systems*, ACM (2013), 439–448.
18. Hauer, B., and Kondrak, G. Automatic generation of English respellings. In *Proceedings of NAACL-HLT* (2013), 634–643.
19. International Phonetic Association. *Handbook of the International Phonetic Association: A guide to the use of the International Phonetic Alphabet*. Cambridge University Press, 1999.
20. Johnson, W. L., Marsella, S., and Vilhjalmsson, H. The DARWARS tactical language training system. In *Proceedings of I/ITSEC* (2004).
21. Karimi, S., Scholer, F., and Turpin, A. Machine transliteration survey. *ACM Computing Surveys (CSUR) 43*, 3 (2011), 17.
22. Kern, R. Perspectives on technology in learning and teaching languages. *TESOL Quarterly 40*, 1 (2006), 183–210.
23. Kondrak, G. A new algorithm for the alignment of phonetic sequences. In *Proceedings of the 1st North American chapter of the Association for Computational Linguistics conference*, Association for Computational Linguistics (2000), 288–295.
24. Kondrak, G. Phonetic alignment and similarity. *Computers and the Humanities 37*, 3 (2003), 273–291.
25. Kuperman, V., Stadthagen-Gonzalez, H., and Brysbaert, M. Age-of-acquisition ratings for 30,000 english words. *Behavior Research Methods 44*, 4 (2012), 978–990.
26. Levenshtein, V. I. Binary codes capable of correcting deletions, insertions and reversals. In *Soviet physics doklady*, vol. 10 (1966), 707.
27. Manning, C. D., Raghavan, P., and Schütze, H. *Introduction to information retrieval*, vol. 1. Cambridge University Press Cambridge, 2008.
28. McDonough, C., Song, L., Hirsh-Pasek, K., Golinkoff, R. M., and Lannon, R. An image is worth a thousand words: Why nouns tend to dominate verbs in early word learning. *Developmental science 14*, 2 (2011), 181–189.
29. Miller, G. A. WordNet: a lexical database for English. *Communications of the ACM 38*, 11 (1995), 39–41.
30. Paivio, A. Mental imagery in associative learning and memory. *Psychological review 76*, 3 (1969), 241.
31. Paivio, A., Yuille, J. C., and Madigan, S. A. Concreteness, imagery, and meaningfulness values for 925 nouns. *Journal of experimental psychology 76*, 1p2 (1968), 1.
32. Sagarra, N., and Alba, M. The key is in the keyword: L2 vocabulary learning methods with beginning learners of Spanish. *The Modern Language Journal 90*, 2 (2006), 228–243.
33. Stadthagen-Gonzalez, H., and Davis, C. J. The Bristol norms for age of acquisition, imageability, and familiarity. *Behavior Research Methods 38*, 4 (2006), 598–605.
34. Takač, V. P. *Vocabulary learning strategies and foreign language acquisition*, vol. 27. Multilingual matters, 2008.
35. Toutanova, K., Klein, D., Manning, C., and Singer, Y. Feature-rich part-of-speech tagging with a cyclic dependency network. *NAACL* (2003).
36. Turney, P. D., Pantel, P., et al. From frequency to meaning: Vector space models of semantics. *Journal of artificial intelligence research 37*, 1 (2010), 141–188.
37. Wilson, M. MRC psycholinguistic database: Machine-usable dictionary, version 2.00. *Behavior Research Methods, Instruments, & Computers 20*, 1 (1988), 6–10.

AudioCanvas: Internet-Free Interactive Audio Photos

Simon Robinson, Jennifer Pearson, Matt Jones
Future Interaction Technology Lab, Swansea University, SA2 8PP, UK
{ s.n.w.robinson, j.pearson, matt.jones } @swansea.ac.uk

ABSTRACT
In this paper we present a novel interaction technique that helps to make textual information more accessible to those with low or no textual literacy skills. AudioCanvas allows cameraphone users to interact directly with their own photos of printed media to receive audio feedback or narration. The use of a remote telephone-based service also allows our design to be used over a standard phone line, removing the need for data connections, which can be problematic in developing regions. We show the value of the technique via user evaluations in both a rural Indian village and a South African township.

Author Keywords
QR codes; camera phones; audio; developing regions.

ACM Classification Keywords
H.5.2 User Interfaces: Input devices and strategies; Interaction styles; H.5.1 Multimedia Information Systems: Audio I/O.

INTRODUCTION
In many developing, rural regions, low textual literacy rates prevent large proportions of the population from accessing information from flyers, posters, maps or other text-based media. In addition to this, while mobile phones are relatively widespread, internet or data connections, and hence online information access, are not widely the norm. There are several reasons for this, varying from region to region. In some places, the pricing structures and business models are not attractive to users. Users may also appreciate "internet-free" methods due to the lack of a reliable data signal, or their greater comfort and familiarity with making conventional telephone calls. As a result of both low textual literacy, which prevents people from reading printed media, and poor internet connectivity, which prohibits online translation or information enquiry, accessing information in many underdeveloped regions can prove exceedingly difficult.

To address these issues, several voice-based telephone services have been proposed (such as [5]). These audio-only tools are intended to provide spoken information in local languages, accessible via low-end devices. However, the use of purely audio makes it difficult to, for example, get an overview of

CHI '14, April 26 – May 1 2014, Toronto, ON, Canada.

ACM 978-1-4503-2473-1/14/04...$15.00.
http://dx.doi.org/10.1145/2556288.2556993

1. Take a photo of the item using the phone's camera 2. Use the photo as a canvas to select areas of interest 3. Listen to information about the selected region

Figure 1. Interacting with the AudioCanvas system. From left to right: (1) the user takes a photo of an item, which then (2) becomes a canvas to interact with audio content related to the object. (3) audio content is provided over the telephone system; no data connection is required.

a voice space, navigate through disparate content regions, or quickly locate a certain item. Printed media, on the other hand, is entirely visual, providing simple overviews and navigation, but has clear issues with regards to textual literacy.

We saw an opportunity to connect these two spaces in a novel way, taking advantage of the fact that while access to internet-connected devices is minimal, in many areas people own at least a low-end cameraphone or featurephone, and smartphones are increasingly price accessible. This popularity of camera-capable phones, coupled with local-language voice services, offers potential for creating interactive audio photos.

AudioCanvas is a fusion of Interactive Voice Response (IVR) services and physical objects, as illustrated in Fig. 1. Our design allows users to take a photograph of printed media and use the picture as a canvas for interaction with related audio. The system automatically dials a remote telephone-based voice service, and allows users to touch areas of interest on their own photo—titles, captions, adverts or images, for example—to hear audio narration for their selection. Our novel design uses precisely-placed QR codes as reference points, allowing it to transmit the user's touch coordinates via DTMF tones over a standard phone line, and ensuring that the service can be used without an internet connection in the contexts we describe.

BACKGROUND
Previous work has augmented physical artefacts with digital media. DigitalDesk [12], for example, used precisely positioned projectors and cameras to retain paper's affordances but allow documents to be manipulated digitally. More recently, Mistry et al. [7]'s pico projector system allowed objects to be queried for information by framing them with coloured finger tags. Other designs, such as Audio d-touch [2] used custom markers to create user-friendly tangible interfaces. Unlike AudioCanvas, these examples focus on *direct* interactions with objects; e.g., manipulating physical items to control digital interactions. Our approach differs, letting people use their

own photos of items to act as canvases to interact with audio. Other augmentation designs, such as Listen Reader [1], OCR methods, or commercial options,[1] have required either a *client-side* metadata database or realtime internet access for their functionality. A major advantage of our design, then, is that the client is completely independent of the media used. This independence—particularly relevant in the regions where we created AudioCanvas—means that updates or internet access are not required to support additional items in the future.

Previous work has used digital codes for partially automating paper-based tasks. Parikh et al. [8] focused on QR codes in rural developing contexts, allowing form fields to be scanned one-by-one to enter data. Klemmer et al. [4] used barcodes in page margins to recall audiovisual interview transcripts. However, these approaches required preloaded content, unlike our artefact-independent method. Snap 'n' Grab [10] provided South African taxi users with access to media via photos, having similar internet-free goals to our design. The prototype uses barcodes around a printed icon, which are photographed and sent via Bluetooth to a server phone (also in the taxi), which then returns relevant media. Our approach does not require a local server, as all communication is via a normal telephone connection to a remote voice service.

Interactive photos

Our design turns photographs into interactive touch canvases for communicating with telephone-based services. Frohlich [3]'s related technique allowed interaction with paper photos to request audio. The design supported only one track per image, however, and also required a separate projector. Suzuki et al. [11] demonstrated the use of photos of physical objects as interaction tools, but required a marker on *each* object (cf. [8]). More similar to our design is Seifert et al. [9]'s technique which turns hand-drawn sketches into interactive prototypes. However, our approach focuses on audio interaction, rather than a conversion of photos into digital facsimiles.

Many mobile augmented reality applications are able to add overlays or web links to physical artefacts. Daqri,[2] for example, uses QR codes for tracking; others, such as Blippar[3] or Shortcut,[4] have used image recognition. However, these approaches require a data connection and a large download for every scan. Furthermore, they focus entirely on augmenting a photo or camera preview with visual content. Our system uses QR codes to encode a coordinate grid and phone number on a photographed object, instead. The aim is to add audio to the experience—without requiring an internet connection—rather than just providing a different way to enter a website address.

AUDIOCANVAS

AudioCanvas affords rich experiences with physical objects, allowing any marked-up item to become a touch panel to interact with remote audio resources (see Fig. 1). Our approach uses two precisely placed QR codes on printed media to support detection of the position of the user's selections on their photo of an item. To interact with the system, the user positions their phone to take a photo. When both codes are detected, a photo is taken automatically, and the phone dials the voice

[1]leappad.com; [2]daqri.com; [3]blippar.com; [4]kooaba-shortcut.com

Figure 2. Using AudioCanvas. Left: (1) translating instructions; (2) finding out about a movie from its poster; (3) listening to a newspaper. Right: the interaction afforded – touching the photo to hear the audio.

service in the background. Selecting any region on the photo (with fingers on touchscreens or the joypad on a feature phone) passes the coordinates to the voice service, which plays back the appropriate audio immediately, removing the need for IVR navigation. A video of the technique accompanies this paper.

Figure 2 shows the audio browsing interaction afforded, and our prototype in use in several scenarios. The system was designed specifically for use where internet access is sparse or unaffordable, and where low textual literacy levels prevent people from reading printed media. The interaction afforded clearly resonates with Medhi et al.'s design guidelines for interfaces for non-literate and semi-literate users (see [6]), allowing audio-based captioning on demand without any connection beyond a standard phone line.

AudioCanvas is not meant to be a competitor to automatic translation systems. This is partially because such services can require extensive online interaction. More importantly, though, the aim here is to provide a technique through which the content provider or community members can produce appropriate interpretations or comments to supplement the media item in both textual and visual elements. For example, touching on form fields might explain in useful terms the reason this data is required and what it might be used for, in the same way a proximate might guide in person.

Implementation

AudioCanvas has two components: a local client (which we focus on in this paper), and a remote voice service. The client is a mobile phone application that is used to take a photo of an object, allow panning, zooming and selection, and help the user interact with the remote service. The voice service is a standard IVR system, where DTMF (i.e., phone keypad) tones over a standard phone line control the interaction.

Our novel client design uses two separate QR codes on printed media to detect the position of the interactive area within a photo taken by the user. The codes are positioned at opposite corners of the item – one at the bottom left and another at the top right. The bottom left code contains the telephone number of the interactive voice service, and an identifier for the item

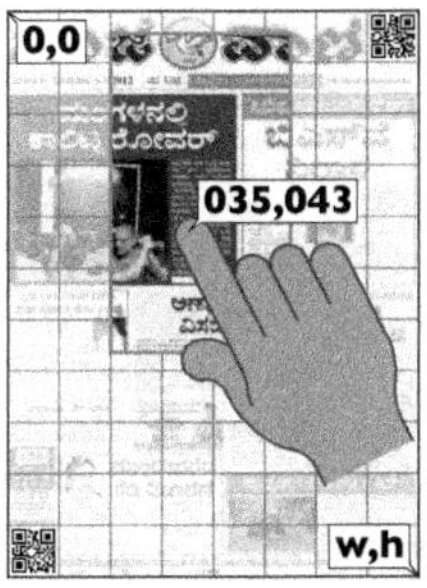

Figure 3. The AudioCanvas coordinate system. Touch point coordinates on the user's photo of an object are calculated based on the distance between and relative sizes of the two QR codes detected on the item. The resolution of the coordinate grid is high enough to allow zooming in to the image and very precise selections, if necessary. Touching a point causes a six-digit DTMF-encoded request for the relevant audio to be sent to the voice site. The audio is played over the phone line in response. The grid is not visible during usage (see Fig. 2).

(e.g., the issue and page number of a newspaper). The top right code is used for coordinate calibration and image alignment (we automatically straighten and skew correct the image).

Figure 3 shows the layout of marked-up objects, and illustrates how touch coordinates are interpreted. Based on the sizes and positions of the two QR codes, the exact position of a touch on the photo can be converted to a location on the physical object without the client application requiring any knowledge about the object itself. This design allows almost any object to be used for interaction, with the system able to calculate exact coordinates within the media automatically. When a user touches the picture they have taken, the coordinate of the current touch point is sent as DTMF tones to the remote telephone service indicated by the lower left QR code. The voice service then plays the relevant audio in response.

Our initial prototype was created using an Android phone, allowing direct touch interactions with photos. It caters directly to the increasing number of users in developing regions who have or will own smartphones. The use of QR codes, rather than more complex image recognition, means that lower-end feature phones are capable of providing AudioCanvas interaction. A feature phone compatible J2ME version of the design is in development. While this type of handset does not offer the same affordances as a smartphone (i.e., directly touching photos), the image is easily navigable via the phone's joypad. We have also developed a mobile tool to allow easy creation of new items by, for example, NGOs or companies who wish to mark-up their printed material or products with AudioCanvas content. This tool works in a similar way to the client, and allows product designers or authors to highlight parts of the photo to create an audio area. Audio annotations can then be created on the fly, or added from a local file and sent to the voice server via the phone line.

EVALUATION

We conducted two user evaluations in separate locations to trial the AudioCanvas technique, aiming to test over a range of literacies (both textual and technological). Our main aim in trials was to observe usage of the system and gather qualitative feedback from users. Experienced local researchers (who were not associated with the system) were employed in both cases to manage studies and translate information from participants.

The first study took place in a village near Devrayandurga, Karnataka, India, with Kannada-speaking participants who were textually illiterate and largely unfamiliar with mobile devices. Twenty-two participants (11M; 11F, aged 22–65) were recruited for individual 30 min trials in this location.

The second study took place in Langa, a township in Cape Town, South Africa, with isiXhosa-speaking participants who had low-to-moderate literacy in isiXhosa, but none in English. Thirty-six participants (6M; 30F, aged 18–45) were recruited for six 60 min group trials (4–8 participants per session). Participants requested focus group evaluations in Langa as this setup was more comfortable – many came to the session with friends or other family members, and were reluctant to participate individually. We provided four AudioCanvas-enabled phones during these sessions, feeling that group-based participation was the best compromise to allow us the opportunity to evaluate the system with this potential user base.

Media

The media items used in the Indian study were a phone bill and a map of Bangalore. Text was in both English and Kannada (participants could read neither) and audio was given in Kannada. Media used in the South African study included a newspaper, product packaging and several local flyers. These items were written in English, with audio provided in isiXhosa.

The items used in both evaluations were of various physical sizes, from A3 to A6, aiming to encourage participants to experiment with all aspects of the system, including framing the item for the automatic photograph, panning and zooming around the image, and finding and listening to audio areas. It is important to note that none of the objects contained indications as to where audio was available. That is, with the exception of the two QR codes, the original media was unchanged, and participants had to discover audio areas independently.

Procedure

Studies began with a demonstration of the system (individually in India; groups in South Africa). Participants were not familiar with smartphones, so part of this demonstration involved a basic introduction to touchscreens. Following this, participants were asked to use AudioCanvas to take photos of the media items and interact with the audio content, exploring for as long as they wished. No specific tasks were given; we aimed to allow exploration rather than forced usage. At the end of the study, participants rated usefulness (1–10; 10 high – a familiar feedback scale in both cases) and ease of use (five attributes – see Table 1; India only, due the group-based setup in South Africa). The study concluded with a semi-structured interview.

Results

All participants enjoyed using the system, and many expressed a desire to be able to have the app pre-installed on the next generation of their phones. Feedback given by participants indicated a strong appreciation of the design, and shows its potential usefulness in regions where textual and technological literacy levels are low. The average usefulness scores given were 8.1 (s.d. 1.90) in India and 8.4 (s.d. 2.07) in South Africa.

These results are strengthened further by user comments during the tasks. For example, participants in the Indian evaluation commented: *"it will be very useful for illiterate people, especially in our village," "it may be useful to me in learning English better," "it is easy to use once you get used to it,"* and *"I can access a lot of information which I otherwise*

Ease of use, in terms of:	Rating (s.d.)
Focusing the camera and taking the initial photo	4.9 (2.0)
Panning and zooming around the photo	6.2 (1.3)
Selecting specific points of interest within the photo	6.3 (1.2)
Getting information back from each section	6.3 (1.2)
Finding the audio areas in a photo	5.1 (2.0)

Table 1. Indian study participants' ratings (1–7 Likert-like scale; 7 high).

could not have accessed." Participants in the South African group studies felt similarly: *"I can see this as something that could really help me and empower people," "for me it's very easy and there's nothing I don't like about it," "it works like music, now I can listen to articles"* and *"it's perfect and easy."*

Over both studies, all except one participant said they regularly found themselves in a situation where they needed information they could not read. When in this situation, participants confirmed that they either asked someone else (e.g., a friend or other proximate) to read text for them, or were not able to read it at all. In post-study interviews, all participants suggested that AudioCanvas would be useful for people unable to read. Other scenarios were also given – for example, after using AudioCanvas, one noted its usefulness for helping with sensitive information, such as when filling in a private form without the need to resort to others; and several participants pointed out opportunities for helping with language learning.

Participants in the Indian trials also gave ratings for ease of use (see Table 1). The average for three of the five scores was high, in excess of 6 out of 7. However, due to a lack of familiarity with cameraphones, some participants did find it difficult to frame and take the initial photograph, causing lower scores for this attribute, and comments such as: *"getting the barcodes in view is challenging"* and *"[it was] difficult for me because I couldn't fit in the barcodes."* Many participants tried framing the image in a skewed or slanted manner, only just managing to accommodate the QR codes. The majority of these initial difficulties with the camera were overcome during the study with additional time spent using the application.

The ease of locating audio areas in a photo was also ranked lower on average. This result was somewhat to be expected, as there were no explicit visual indications of where audio could be found on any of the items. Participants found audio areas more difficult to locate on the map due to the lack of obvious places for feedback. The phone bill, with its structured layout, and more familiar context, was more engaging, and participants eagerly explored photos for audio. Given that there were no extra visual indications of audio areas, the rating given is very encouraging. Similar behaviours were also observed in South Africa, with participants keenly exploring local flyers, but less able to find audio on more image-heavy items.

DISCUSSION AND CONCLUSIONS

In this paper we have presented AudioCanvas – a novel photo interaction method that pairs audio with printed media. The design allows users with low textual literacy levels to interact directly with self-taken photos of physical items by touching regions on-screen. A remote voice service provides audio content, accessed via a standard phone line to ensure it can be used without a potentially costly network data connection.

Our evaluations with both Indian and South African participants who have low technology familiarity, and mixed levels of generally low literacy, show promising results for the ease of use and popularity of our design. The majority of participants enthusiastically embraced the AudioCanvas design, and saw value in the concept despite some initial difficulties in using the technology. Comments made with regards to the usefulness and novelty of the interface were also extremely encouraging. This evidence suggests that AudioCanvas can provide users who are unable to read text—either due to literacy or language issues—an alternative means of access to printed media via mobile phones. We believe, as illustrated by our experiments, that the technique could be particularly beneficial to those in impoverished areas where low-literacy is common, and where data connections are not yet available or attractive.

ACKNOWLEDGMENTS

This work was funded by EPSRC grant EP/J000604/2. We thank Ram Bhat and Minah Radebe for managing studies.

REFERENCES

1. Back, M., Cohen, J., Gold, R., Harrison, S. and Minneman, S. Listen reader: an electronically augmented paper-based book. In *Proc. CHI '01*, ACM (2001), 23–29.
2. Costanza, E., Giaccone, M., Kueng, O., Shelley, S. and Huang, J. Ubicomp to the masses: a large-scale study of two tangible interfaces. In *Proc. UbiComp '10*, ACM (2010), 173–182.
3. Frohlich, D. Audiophotography. Springer (2004).
4. Klemmer, S., Graham, J., Wolff, G. and Landay, J. Books with voices: paper transcripts as a physical interface to oral histories. In *Proc. CHI '03*, ACM (2003), 89–96.
5. Kumar, A., Rajput, N., Chakraborty, D., Agarwal, S. and Nanavati, A. WWTW: the world wide telecom web. In *NSDR workshop, SIGCOMM '07*, ACM (2007).
6. Medhi, I., Gautama, N. and Toyama, K. A comparison of mobile money-transfer UIs for non-literate and semi-literate users. In *Proc. CHI '09*, ACM (2009), 1741–1750.
7. Mistry, P., Maes, P. and Chang, L. WUW – wear ur world: a wearable gestural interface. In *Proc. CHI '09: Extended Abstracts*, ACM (2009), 4111–4116.
8. Parikh, T., Javid, P., K, S., Ghosh, K. and Toyama, K. Mobile phones and paper documents: evaluating a new approach for capturing microfinance data in rural India. In *Proc. CHI '06*, ACM (2006), 551–560.
9. Seifert, J., Pfleging, B., Hermes, M., Rukzio, E. and Schmidt, A. Mobidev: a tool for creating apps on mobile phones. In *Proc. MobileHCI '11*, ACM (2011), 109–112.
10. Smith, G. and Marsden, G. Providing media download services in African taxis. In *Proc. SAICSIT '11*, ACM (2011), 215–223.
11. Suzuki, G., Aoki, S., Iwamoto, T., Maruyama, D., Koda, T., Kohtake, N., Takashio, K. and Tokuda, H. u-Photo: interacting with pervasive services using digital still images. In *LNCS*, vol. 3468. Springer (2005), 190–207.
12. Wellner, P. Interacting with paper on the digitaldesk. *Communications of the ACM* 36.7 (1993), 87–96.

The Impact of Visual Contextualization on UI Localization

Luis A. Leiva and Vicent Alabau
PRHLT Research Center, Universitat Politècnica de València
{luileito,valabau}@dsic.upv.es

ABSTRACT
Translating the text in an interface is a challenging task. Besides the jargon and technical terms, many of the strings are often very short, such as those shown in buttons and pull-down menus. Then, as a result of the lack of *visual* context in the traditional localization process, an important ambiguity problem arises. We study three approaches to solve this problem: using plain gettext (baseline condition), using gettext plus being able to operate the UI, and translating the UI in-place. We found that translators are substantially faster with plain gettext but commit a significantly higher number of errors in comparison to the other approaches. Unexpectedly, the mixed condition was slower and more error-prone than in-place translation. The latter was found to be comparable to plain gettext in terms of time, although some strings passed unnoticed as the UI was operated. Based on our results, we arrive at a set of recommendations to augment localization tools to improve translator's productivity.

Author Keywords
Localization; L10n; Internationalization; i18n; Translation

ACM Classification Keywords
H.5.2 User Interfaces: Prototyping, Interaction styles; D.2.2 Design Tools and Techniques: User interfaces

INTRODUCTION
Designing products and services that are intended to support more than one language is a challenging task. Translation is just one of the activities of software localization, yet the most important overall [1, 2]. So much so that when a product is translated into a new culture it becomes a *new* product [7].

On the UI, some texts may be confusing or offensive for a particular cultural target. Even more, UIs often introduce additional subtleties such as jargon, specialized words, and technical terms. This can be an obstacle for speakers of lesser known tongues because of a non-familiar vocabulary [4], and may prevent the access to cultural resources that are otherwise available in other languages.

What is more important, many of the strings that have to be translated are often very short, such as those shown in buttons and pull-down menus. Therefore, an important ambiguity problem arises as a result of the lack of visual context in the traditional localization process. A string may appear in more than one situation on the UI with completely different translations, e.g., the same word may behave as a verb when placed in a button, but also as a noun if attached to a label. Misinterpretation of these differences could result in major issues for the users of the application [5, 9].

It has been shown that context brings systematic variation in cognitive functioning and performance [6]. Hence, coupling translations with the UI from which all messages were drawn should help translators to better disambiguate, and today there is software to achieve this effect. However, we are not aware of any empirical evaluation of this capability among the research literature. As such, the impact of visually contextualized localization approaches still remains largely unexplored. We therefore contribute to HCI with a rigurous and comprehensive study on the influence of the visual context on translation quality and translator's productivity.

BACKGROUND AND RELATED WORK
UI localization is the process of translating and adapting (source) texts in UI buttons, menus, or headings, in order to support different (target) languages or "locales". To achieve this goal, these source texts must be decoupled first from the source code of the UI, basically by wrapping each string with a translation-capable function. A very popular tool to do so is GNU gettext, although other utilities such as Qt Linguist follow similar principles. Then, strings are exported to a file so that translators can use either a regular text editor or specialized applications; just to name a few: Pootle, Crowdin, Verbatim, and Launchpad. However, the main problem with these applications is that translators often do not have access to the UI from where the source texts were extracted.

Some general-purpose translation tools such as TRADOS or Google Translator Toolkit support visually contextualized translation, although they are oriented to translate *content* like text documents or static web pages. This means that most UI elements cannot be localized, e.g., buttons, placeholders, drop-down lists, etc. For that reason, a number of more sophisticated approaches to support UI localization have risen recently. For instance, dedicated localization tools for the desktop include Passolo, Catalyst, or RCWintrans; which seldom support more than one programming language but allow to perform contextualized translations. A more interesting approach is ScreenMatch [3], a platform-independent system to assist software translators by showing UI screenshots alongside each translatable string.

In addition, it is worth mentioning that what all these tools display as UI is not the actual UI end users will operate, just a static visualization, and may therefore be outdated over

CHI 2014, April 26–May 1, 2014, Toronto, Ontario, Canada.

ACM 978-1-4503-2473-1/14/04..$15.00.
http://dx.doi.org/10.1145/2556288.2556982

time. Consequently, we believe that translators should be able to access the actual UI being translated. In this regard, applications like SmartLing or Drupal translations, featuring a gettext-like interface alongside the current web-based UI, may help to overcome such limitation. However, this capability has not yet been formally assessed.

EVALUATION

Intuitively, being able to access the actual UI should provide translators with better disambiguation capabilities and thus improve the quality of the produced translations. This should come at the expense of an increase in the time spent localizing, since localizable elements must be located on the UI and sometimes operated. Also, some elements may not be obvious (or even possible) to locate. Such is the case of error messages or dynamic content that disappear after a short amount of time. However, if translations are properly contextualized the final outcome would result in fewer errors to amend, resulting hopefully in higher productivity. Therefore, we formulated the following hypotheses:

H1. Visual context improves localization quality.
H2. When the UI is available, translations are finished later.
H3. In-place localization leaves strings untranslated.
H4. Visual context improves translator's productivity.

To test these hypotheses, we studied three UI localization possibilities, ranging from no visual context at all to a pure visually contextualized translation approach (see Design section). We developed a small airline website (Figure 1), by drawing inspiration from actual airline websites. The source language was English, and we decided to localize the website into Spanish. We noticed that some lexical ambiguities were evident. For instance, 'delayed' is a neutral word in English but can be both masculine and feminine in Spanish, depending on the context of the string. However, in the absence of context, it is usually translated using its masculine form.

Participants

Thirty participants aged 24–37 ($M = 30.3$, $SD = 4.1$) were recruited via email advertising. All were native Spanish speakers with an advanced English level according to CEFR[1] and had had previous experience as translators. Participants performed the assigned tasks at a dedicated laboratory room, and were rewarded with a gift voucher at the end of the evaluation.

Design

Participants were assigned to exactly one condition (between-subjects design). People were randomly split into 3 groups of 10 users each: one group would use a gettext-based application (GT condition), other group would use gettext plus being able to operate the UI when desired (GTVIS condition), and the other group would use in-place translation (VIS condition). An alpha level of .05 was used for all statistical tests. There were no departures from normality (verified by the Shapiro-Wilk test, n.s.) or homoscedasticity (verified by Levene's test, n.s.). Hence, we used the one-way ANOVA test to compare the differences between the 3 conditions, followed by post-hoc pairwise comparisons where applicable.

[1] `http://www.coe.int/lang-CEFR`

Apparatus

The website was coded in PHP and was manually internationalized using PHP's `gettext()` function. This way, all translatable messages could be automatically extracted using the `xgettext` command. Overall, the website comprised 92 strings of 1.99 words each on average ($SD = 1.87$).

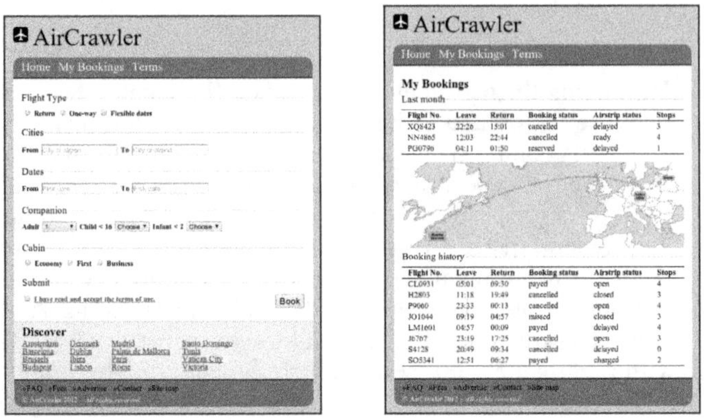

Figure 1: Screenshots of the website used in the study. The website comprised 5 sections in total.

For the baseline approach, GT, we used the traditional way of localizing interfaces at present, which is based on the GNU gettext model; i.e., the text is decoupled from the UI and is delivered as a PO file to the translator, who then uses a dedicated localization tool. Typically, such localization tools feature two sections: one that displays the resource strings (the texts in the PO file) and other that allows the translator to enter the target strings (the translated text); see Figure 2.

For the mixed approach, GTVIS, each string was augmented with a link to the page where such string appeared. Links opened in a dedicated browser tab so that, if desired, the translator could browse each page and see the context of the task.

For the in-place translation approach, VIS, we instrumented the calls to the PHP `gettext` function to mark the localizable elements. Then, using JavaScript, these elements would be edited on the very same UI. By CTRL+clicking on an element, a pop-up dialog asked the user to enter the translation, which was then stored in a plain text log file.

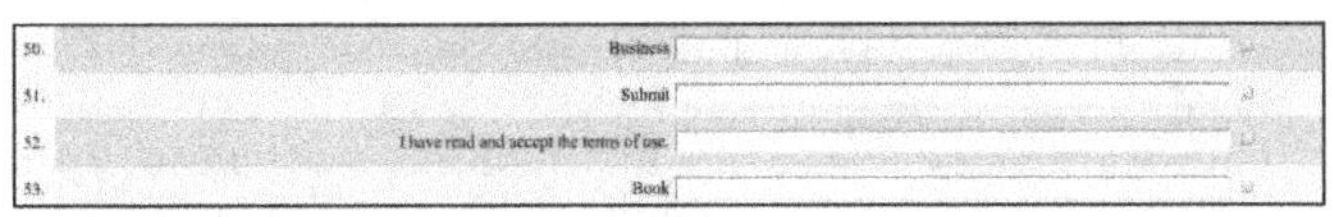

Figure 2: A typical localization interface. This is in turn the tool we used for GT and GTVIS conditions.

It was ensured that the airline website would be as similar as possible to that of an actual airline company, i.e., there were city names, dates, or loan words such as 'premium' or 'business'. As such, some messages were not required to be translated. For these cases, it was assumed that a VIS user would not submit a translation. Then, to align the capabilities of the other groups to that of this group, the gettext editor featured a checkbox near each target input field. This way, by clicking on a checkbox, GT and GTVIS users would indicate that the source string should not be translated (Figure 2).

Procedure

Each participant was briefly introduced to the localization approach assigned to them for about 5 minutes, including a motivating discussion on the importance of software localization. No restrictions were set regarding time to complete the task, using auxiliary tools such as online dictionaries, and so on. All participants were given the following statement: *"You have been hired to localize the website of an airline company. You are expected to deliver a translation as professional as possible."* By giving this high-level articulation, we expected that our hypotheses would be clearly assessed: being able to navigate the pages of the site while localizing them would provide GTVIS and VIS users with enough context to disambiguate properly. Therefore, these users should produce better translations than GT users, who were not shown the site. VIS users were expected to perform slower than the other participants, since the UI had to be operated at any time in order to translate the strings. However, it was expected that their translations would be of the highest quality, since the visual context would be always available.

For **H1**, quality was measured with the Human-targeted Translation Edit Rate (HTER): the number of word post-edits required to change a submitted translation into a valid reference [8]. For **H2**, we measured the time to complete the task (in minutes); whereas for **H3**, we counted the number of strings edited. Finally, for **H4**, we evaluated translator's productivity as follows. In the translation industry, productivity is measured in words per day. This assumption is reasonable if the provided translations are of high quality, and thus an additional round for reviewing them is not required. However, in UI localization some translations might be irresolvable without a proper context, regardless of how professional the translator is. As a result, more than one reviewing round may be needed. Hence, we define *raw* productivity as the number of *correct* words per day. We should emphasize that, since all wrongly translated strings would require to be re-submitted in a real-world localization workflow, *actual* productivity would be much affected by the turnaround time, which typically spans from 2 to 7 business days [5].

RESULTS

While inspecting the data, we found a GT user that took an unusual amount of time to complete the task. This participant took exactly 46 minutes to complete the task, while the rest of GT users spent 13 minutes on average, and therefore was removed from the analysis. He was asked about this unusual delay, and stated that *"translations can change completely according to the context of the sentence on the website. In addition, I found an important problem while determining the gender of some words, since in English adjectives are neutral but in Spanish they can be masculine, feminine, or both. [...] I had to browse other airline websites to give a more accurate picture of how to translate these sentences properly."*

Overall, GT users translated 81.11 strings (*SD* = 1.76) in 12.73 minutes (*SD* = 5.03), with an HTER of 34.60% (*SD* = 6.06). The remaining strings were accepted by clicking on the checkboxes, revealing that all strings were reviewed by all GT users. As shown in Figure 3a, it becomes clear that gettext-based approaches allow to entirely localize the website, since all strings are shown to the translator. Meanwhile, GTVIS users localized 79.88 strings (*SD* = 3.95) in 33.44 minutes (*SD* = 12.99). On average, they consulted the website 56.55 times (*SD* = 42.64), which accounted for 20% of the total task time. (Time spent on the translatable website was measured by looking at the focus/blur events on that website.) Then, the remaining time was spent either on the gettext editor or at auxiliary websites such as dictionary or thesaurus sites. This time HTER was more competent, 19.14% (*SD* = 8.22). On the other hand, VIS users localized 71.6 strings (*SD* = 4.92) in 19.84 minutes (*SD* = 8.26), with a very competent HTER of 10.79% (*SD* = 3.64).

We observed that problematic sentences are often those with few words, as there is an important ambiguity problem. In general, shorter sentences (up to 2 words) are more error-prone. In this regard, we found a moderate correlation: the longer the sentence, the more likely it will be successfully translated with GT $[r(292) = -0.34, p < .001]$ or GTVIS $[r(300) = -0.29, p < .001]$. With VIS, the correlation is smaller $[r(269) = -0.21, p < .001]$ because ambiguities can be properly solved with contextual information. In the next section we provide some examples of sentences that can be easily translated with and without visual context.

ANOVA revealed that differences between groups were statistically significant for all measures, i.e., HTER $[F_{2,25} = 35.84, p < .001, \eta_p^2 = 2.87]$, time $[F_{2,25} = 11.52, p < .001, \eta_p^2 = 0.92]$, number of localized strings $[F_{2,25} = 17.52, p < .001, \eta_p^2 = 1.40]$, and raw productivity $[F_{2,25} = 8.77, p < .001, \eta_p^2 = 0.70]$. Effect sizes suggested a high practical significance. Post-hoc pairwise comparisons using the t-test with Bonferroni correction revealed that GT translations were of significantly worse quality than GTVIS, and VIS produced the highest quality results. Unexpectedly, no time differences between VIS and GT were found. GTVIS users were significantly slower than the other approaches, and VIS localized significantly less strings than GT and GTVIS. As expected, no differences between GTVIS and GT were found in this regard, since both groups saw all localizable strings. Productivity results are discussed next.

DISCUSSION

It can be observed that GT allowed users to complete the task sooner than the other approaches (Figure 3b). This was unsurprising, as gettext aims for a completely sequential workflow while the other approaches required to interact with the UI. However, we must remark that less time does not necessarily mean higher productivity. Actually, if translation errors are found then more iterations between translators and developers are likely to happen, which would lead to higher turnaround times for companies [5]. For instance, assuming that all translation errors would be fixed after a second pass over the GT data, participants would have needed on average 10 additional minutes, which is comparable to the time GTVIS users spent browsing the UI. This is nevertheless an upper bound, since not being able to access the UI would probably result in more than one review cycle for GT users.

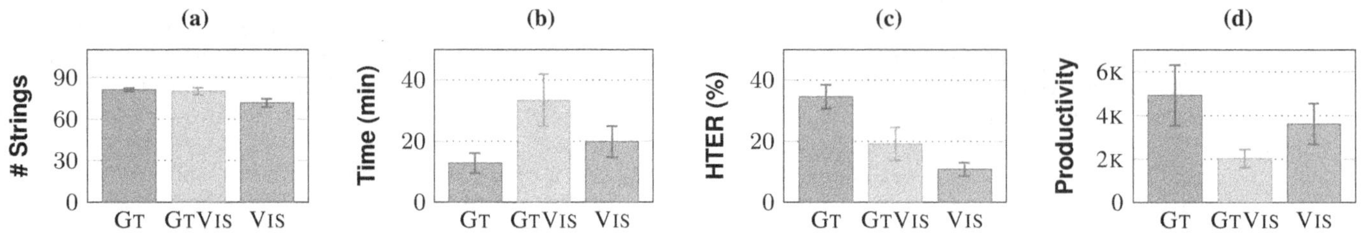

Figure 3: Evaluation results. Error bars denote 95% CIs. Productivity (3d) is estimated as the number of correctly translated words per day.

On the contrary, a visually contextualized localization tool facilitates the disambiguation of messages that depend on the UI context for a proper interpretation, leading to higher-quality translations (Figure 3c). As a result, the number of iteration cycles and refinements over the localization process would be dramatically shortened. This is interesting for software localizers, as well as for companies that decide to go global, since time is often a scarce resource and translation errors can be exceedingly costly. Unexpectedly, GTVIS quality was significantly worse than VIS. While the visual context is always available to VIS users, in GTVIS it is the translator's decision to check the context by inspecting the UI, which was often skipped to save time (29% of the strings in our data).

A deep analysis of the productivity reveals that VIS is statistically comparable to GT, and so both can produce the same number of correct words per day (Figure 3d). The reason is that HTER is much higher in GT but in VIS some strings were not localized. A particular example were error messages, which tend to have more words on average (e.g. 'Please fill in the required form fields'), and thus their actual meaning is easier to notice in the absence of visual context. In general, messages composed by one or two strings should be translated with visual context, as their meaning depend on the UI element; e.g. buttons ('Book'), labels ('One way', 'Display unit'), or date fields ('From', 'To'). More practical examples can be found in Muntés-Mulero *et al.* [5, p.3].

On the other hand, GTVIS is significantly less productive than the other approaches. In fact, we observed that VIS leads to significantly faster translation time if compared with GTVIS. As hinted by 3 participants, *"[gettext] strings are not sorted by page, so I had to switch often from page to page, which may slow down the overall task time."* Indeed, if we discount the time GTVIS users spent searching for the strings on the UI, then there would be no differences between GTVIS and VIS, as indicated by the Bonferroni-corrected pairwise t-test.

In consequence, we argue that pure visually contextualized localization tools should be complemented with a gettext-like interface to reach *all* resource strings. On the other hand, while screenshots are a very useful approach to allow translators to get an overview of the visual context of the task, we recommend gettext-like interfaces to be complemented with pointers to the actual UI elements to safely save lookup time. This could be implemented by e.g. dynamically generating screenshots were each resource string is highlighted whenever the translator is localizing it on the gettext editor. Currently, the UI context is provided via textual descriptions, or not at all [3]. Therefore, we hope researchers and practitioners will consider this work when developing new software localization tools.

CONCLUSION

This paper puts forward the fact that the impact of visual contextualization on UI localization can be considerable, leading to significant effects on translation quality and translator's productivity. In short, when the visual context is available to the translator, better translations are produced. Additionally, raw productivity is comparable to the traditional workflow if translations are edited in-place. Furthermore, if the translator needs to locate the UI elements without an additional aid, productivity may decrease significantly. We thus recommend current localization tools be augmented with pointers to the actual UI elements, clearly highlighting them, if possible.

ACKNOWLEDGMENTS

This work is supported by the 7th Framework Program of the European Commision (FP7/2007-13) under grant agreements 287576 (CASMACAT) and 600707 (tranScriptorium).

REFERENCES

1. Dunne, K. J., Ed. *Perspectives on Localization*. John Benjamins Publishing Company, 2006.
2. Keniston, K. Software localization: Notes on technology and culture. Working Paper #26, MIT press, 1997.
3. Kovacs, G. ScreenMatch: providing context to software translators by displaying screenshots. In *Proc. CHI EA* (2012).
4. Leiva, L. A., and Alabau, V. An automatically generated interlanguage tailored to speakers of minority but culturally influenced languages. In *Proc. CHI* (2012).
5. Muntés-Mulero, V., Adell, P. P., España-Bonet, C., and Màrquez, L. Context-aware machine translation for software localization. In *Proc. EAMT* (2012).
6. Nardi, B. A., Ed. *Context and consciousness: Activity Theory and Human Computer Interaction*. MIT Press, 1996.
7. Russo, P., and Boor, S. How fluent is your interface? designing for international users. In *Proc. CHI* (1993).
8. Snover, M., Dorr, B., Schwartz, R., Micciulla, L., and Makhoul, J. A study of translation edit rate with targeted human annotation. In *Proc. AMTA* (2006).
9. Sun, H. Building a culturally-competent corporate web site: an exploratory study of cultural markers in multilingual web design. In *Proc. SIGDOC* (2001).

Improving Machine Translation by Showing Two Outputs

Bin Xu[1] Ge Gao[2] Susan R. Fussell[1,2] Dan Cosley[1]

[1]Department of information Science
Cornell University
Ithaca NY 14850 USA

[2]Department of Communication
Cornell University
Ithaca NY 14850 USA

{bx55, gg365, sfussell, drc44}@cornell.edu

ABSTRACT
We propose to improve real-time communication between people who do not share a common language by foregrounding potential problems in machine translation. We developed a prototype chat tool that displays two parallel translations of each chat turn, with the thought that comparing the translations might both highlight problems and provide resources for resolving them. We conducted a user study to investigate how people use and like such an interface compared to a standard one-translation interface. On balance, users preferred two translations to one, using them to both notice differences and infer meaning from uncertain translations, with no increase in workload. This suggests that this interface may help improve cross-lingual communication in practical applications and lays the groundwork for a larger design space around systems that highlight possible errors to support communication.

Author Keywords
Machine translation; multiple translations

ACM Classification Keywords
H.5.3. Information interfaces and presentation (e.g., HCI): Group and Organization Interfaces.

INTRODUCTION AND BACKGROUND
Machine translation (MT) systems have been used to support cross-lingual communication for decades, with the goal that one day, high-quality machine translation services will support transparent conversation between people who share no language in common. However, translation is not there yet, especially in unrestricted domains such as the kind of informal communication that is a cornerstone of building trust [1]. MT services still frequently make errors and lack both the specific and the cultural context of the conversation, causing asymmetries and inconsistencies [8] and reducing their utility for cross-lingual communications.

Still, MT systems may help bridge language barriers when human translators are unavailable or expensive, and there are many real-world cases, from tourism to teamwork, where there is little or no linguistic common ground. Thus, much work has gone into improving the algorithms behind these systems. However, errors persist, and interfaces that simply present translated text hide the fact that there are alternative word translations, alignments, and so on.

Showing these alternatives may have value. Studies on back-translation systems show that retranslating a speaker's translated messages back to the speaker's language improves awareness of how messages are processed by MT, thus improving communication quality [7]. Crowdsourcing systems like Monotrans [5] and DuoLingo use human judgment to find and correct flaws in MT by iterating through translations. Google's Translate interface allows users to view alternate translations for individual words and phrases and also shows alignments between elements of the original and the translated text.

THE IDEA: SHOWING MULTIPLE TRANSLATIONS
These ideas suggest that rather than hiding their flaws, MT systems might foreground them in ways that make the problems easier to see, exposing seams in the technology [5] and providing resources to better use the translations. In this paper, inspired by ensemble learning approaches and by the saying "two heads are better than one", we explore the idea of showing multiple parallel translations generated by different engines. Our hope is that this will allow CMC (computer mediated communication) systems that use MT services can implicitly provide information about confidence and alternatives that people can interpret based on redundancies and differences between the translations.

We first explored this idea by translating both English and Chinese conversational turns to the other language using the Google, Bing, and Youdao engines and showing them to both Chinese and English-speaking members of the research lab. In general, we found that when the translations are redundant, either in part or completely, those parts of the translation tended to be both syntactically and semantically correct. Thus, we expect that reading

CHI 2014, April 26 - May 01 2014, Toronto, ON, Canada

ACM 978-1-4503-2473-1/14/04 $15.00.
http://dx.doi.org/10.1145/2556288.2557171

redundant text will increase people's confidence that they understand their partner's intent.

When the translations are not redundant, the situation is more complicated. We expect people will often be able to infer their partner's intent by using redundant aspects to align the translations and their knowledge of the conversational context to choose elements from both translations that make the most sense.

At other times, especially as translation quality declines, they won't be able to make sense of the two translations at all. In this case, we expect there to be some benefit because the fact that something amiss with the translations is clearer than if there is only one translation, and people will realize this and initiate clarifications more quickly when they are needed—but there will be cost in processing the extra text.

Finally, there will be times when one translation is high quality and one is low quality, and in these cases showing two translations is pure cost with no benefit.

We expect that the relative frequency of these different cases will depend on the particular translation engines, language pairs, topics of conversation, and phrasing and word choices, and this will affect the usefulness of the system. On balance, we expect that with two translations rather than with one, people will be more confident in both the partner's intent and the progress of the conversation, and that this will be worth the effort of reading an additional translation. This, in turn, should lead to less clarification work, quicker clarification when it is needed, and smoother conversations overall.

Experimental prototype

We developed a prototype to present our idea in the context of real-time conversation supported by MT. Our scenario was to support chatting between partners who do not both have enough fluency in a common language to have an effective conversation in it. The system has two main parts, the messenger window and the MT backend. We chose to present only two translations because in pilots people reported three translations caused much more workload than two, and chose Google and Bing because they are competitive in quality while using distinct algorithms [9].

When one person sends a message, it first goes to our own server, which forwards the request to Google and Bing. Once the translations are received it sends them to the partner, whose client displays them, always in the same order so that people would get used to the characteristics of each engine. In pilot testing there was no additional noticeable delay introduced by generating two translations instead of one.

USER STUDY

We conducted a within subject user study to investigate how people use and react to showing two translations. Each participant used both the two-translation interface described above and a one-translation interface that was identical except that it presented only one translation. For the one-translation version we used Google, because it is slightly better than other engines in Chinese-English translation [9].

Tasks and data collection

We designed a chatting task to represent a typical informal conversation scenario that might occur when meeting new people either casually or in new work teams. Because it is hard to find Chinese students who can't speak at least some English at a U.S. university, in this study we focused on only the English speakers and used two Chinese confederates from Mainland China to be their partners. They were trained to conduct conversations in a natural, consistent way without steering the conversation.

Participants were instructed to discuss at least three things about themselves and learn at least three things about their partners; we suggested six possible topics but allowed them to use others as well. Each participant spoke to each confederate in two separate sessions; in one they used the single translation interface and in the other they used the two-translation version. We counterbalanced the order of confederates and interfaces.

During the task participants followed a think-aloud protocol. We explained that the goal of our study was to evaluate the system and that we would record their voice and their chatting on the computer simultaneously, and asked them to say aloud everything that went though their mind. Confederates wore headphones so as not to hear participants' voices. We asked partners to chat for 15 minutes in each session; the average time for the single- and two-translation cases was 16.5 minutes (SD=3.1) and 15 minutes (SD=5.2) respectively. After each session, there was a survey asking about their experience during the task, including workload (based on the NASA TLX scale [4]).

After completing both sessions, participants filled out a short post-survey asking their preference between the two interfaces and strategies they used when making sense of the two translations, along with a short (3-5 minute) interview about how they felt about two interfaces, preferences between them, strategies for using them, and suggestions for improvement.

We used an online research recruitment website to recruit 8 participants (5 female, 3 male; ages 18-23 with a median of 20), who were all U.S. citizens at a large northeastern U.S. university. They were native English speakers unable to speak Mandarin Chinese and in the pre-survey rated themselves as frequent users of IM chatting tools, but not of MT tools. Quotes are labeled by participant number.

RESULTS

Figure 1(a) shows the two-translation chat window. Figure 1 also illustrates several ways translation pairs varied for participants: being similar like the first pair in (a), being partly different like `"blue Berry"` vs. `"blueberry"` in

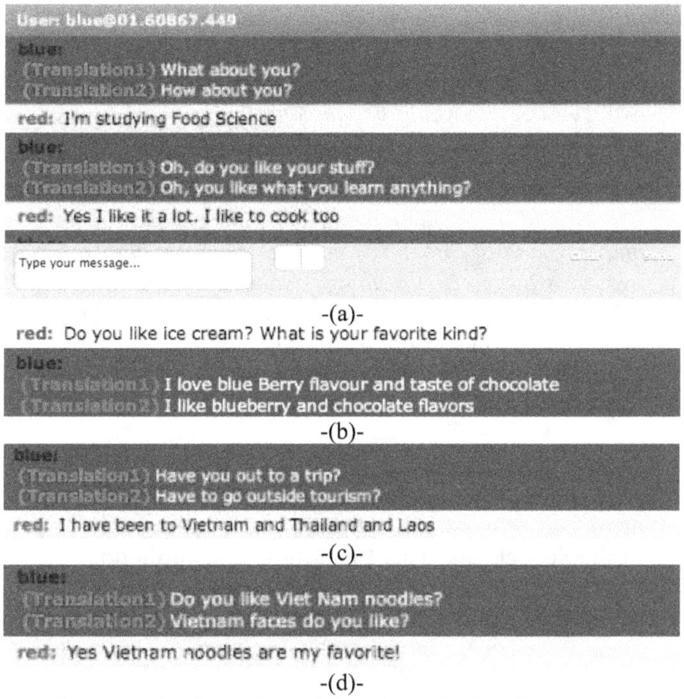

Figure 1. (a) Snapshot of the chat window in the two-translation case, with three additional samples (b, c and d).

(b), being different and one has information being absent in the other one, like "learn anything" in (a)'s second pair, being different but semantically related like "trip" and "tourism" in (c), and finally being different and one is higher quality like the pair in (d). We computed the Levenshtein string edit distance between translations, where small distances usually correspond to similar translations and larger distances tend to be more distinct. The average difference was 36% of the length of the translation, which means that engines often generated quite different translations even on these short, informal texts.

People overall preferred two translations

Interviews showed that 7 of the 8 participants preferred the two-translation interface: *"I definitely like the double translation better than the single translation. In cases where the message is a little bit confusing or vague, the fact that you have a second option to look at is pretty nice."* (P5) and *"I prefer the double ...if one translator didn't get it maybe the other one could have provided more clarity."* (P4) This is corroborated by participants' ratings of the usefulness of having a second translation when one was confusing as 6.1 (SD=0.99) on a 7-point Likert scale (1 is least helpful), demonstrating fairly strong liking for it. All participants reported using both translations at least some of the time on the survey.

Differences invite questions, and sometimes choices

We expected that by examining both translations people would become more aware of both specific problems with particular translations and of the potential for errors. This tended to happen when the translations were different: participants in the think-aloud process would often read the two translations, but only when they were different. Often they then just composed a reply, but some differences led to further reflection. For example, when P1 saw Figure 1(b), she said, *"It is kind of interesting the 'blueberry' in translation 1 was separated and 'Berry' was capitalized, where the translation 2 just had 'blueberry'. And the chocolate was 'taste of chocolate' and 'chocolate flavors'."*

This often took the form of thinking about the quality or accuracy of the two translations. For example, when P5 saw "You now what subject?" and "What is your current discipline?" he said, *"The second translation is definitely more accurate, probably is towards what the other person wants to say ...you know 'what subject' really does not make any sense, whatsoever, so 'what is your current discipline' is definitely a valid question."*

This idea of comparing the translations, and looking for differences, was a persistent theme in how people thought about the interface: *"...while sometimes they were fairly similar ...sometimes they were different enough that I could look at the two and compare them."* (P7)

Differences also help people infer meaning

The snippet from P5 above shows that when one translation is clearly better, people tended to rely on it. However, people sometimes also use parts of both translations, with the differences helping people guess about their partner's intent: *"...sometimes the organization of words was different and sometimes that would help me sort of come to a meaning, understanding of what they're trying to communicate."* (P6) For example, when P1 saw the second pair in Figure 1(a), she said, *"...wording stuff is different. And one says 'do you like your stuff'...and the other is 'oh you like what you learn anything'. I mean, between the two it was easy to figure out what is being asked (about study)."*

This was seen as useful even when the differences were small: *"I think the two translations was a lot easier to use, even though sometimes they didn't vary by much, but sometimes that little variation helped a lot."* (P1)

Even when both translations were flawed, people could often still use them if the flaws were complementary: *"...sometimes they'd both be kind of incorrect but in different ways so I think it's good to have them both kind of work together so you can get what it is they're trying to say."* (P8) In these cases, people might not try to infer the exact, best translation, but to have a good enough idea of the partner's intent to continue the conversation. Often there was enough commonality or redundancy to make this guess. For example, when P1 saw the pair in Figure 1(c), she said *"I got a question, 'have you out to a trip', and the second is 'have to go outside tourism'. Obviously it is about trip, about touring"* to help her infer topics. However, one participant found having two flawed translations to be more confusing than one: *"I think with two, if they were both confusing then it was hard for me to judge which one was more correct, but if it were just one I could try to figure out, I think, what they meant."* (P3)

Similar translations are not so helpful

We had thought that participants would also benefit from redundancy in translations that would give them confidence that the redundant parts were correct. However, we did not see much evidence of this. Instead, when the translations were the same it was not helpful: *"...it was definitely better when they were different, when they would return different results, to use them both. ...if they were the same then that would make me feel more confident, but most of the time the results when they were the same, even when they were still fairly correct they still both had like the same errors."* (P7).

Two translations were not harder than one

We measured users' response time to partners and found no significant difference between the one- and two-translation conditions on average (14.7 vs. 15.2 seconds respectively). Likewise, on the self-reported NASA TLX workload questions, there was no significant difference between the conditions, and participants reported no workload concerns during post-experiment interviews.

DISCUSSION AND CONCLUSION

The lack of difference in workload, participants' preference for two translations over one, and their feedback that differences between translations helped them infer partner's meanings all suggest that showing two translations has promise, at least in this population, setting, and task. Our guess is that the workload was perceived as no higher because extra effort spent on reading two translations was made up for by the gains in understanding they provided.

More study will be needed to identify the tasks, language pairs, and other characteristics of conversational contexts that make showing two translations more and less valuable. More generally, as second language fluency improves, the value of two translations (and MT in general) eventually will fall below just conversing in a common language. Still, there may be times or topics where a person would rather express themselves in their native language and use MT tools to supplement their own proficiency.

In those cases strategies such as this that help people get the most out of MT will still matter. Multiple translations of words (as Google Translate provides) or whole turns, back-translations, keyword highlighting [3] and other visual clues [2] all may help people detect and recover from problems by foregrounding flaws in ways that also provide resources for recovery. In the case of showing two translations, the implementation is not complex and the value is good, suggesting that this is a practical idea for real systems.

We also see this as an interesting case of the general idea of foregrounding system flaws. As technology improves, these strategies may not matter for MT: *"...it would be really nice if the computer could figure out eventually and only give you one message because it'll be easier to talk to the person because it'll be faster: you wouldn't have to read two messages, it would be one, and then you could message quicker and it'll be more fluid."* (P5)

But for now, *"it's still really nice to have two messages, like I speak with other people in different like in Russian and stuff and like often it's not very accurate and so having two translations helps things, so that's definitely cool."* (P5) More generally, we hope this case encourages other designers of tools where the technology plays an active, but imperfect, role in shaping communication [5] to think about ways the interface can help users make the most of it.

ACKNOWLEDGMENTS

This research was funded by NSF grant #1318899. We also thank Xi Yang, Cen Guo, Bridget Rudgers, Ivy Huang, Leslie Setlock, and Tina Yuan for their contributions.

REFERENCES

1. Chevrier, S. Cross-cultural management in multinational project groups. *J. World Business*, *38*, (2003), 141–149.
2. Finch, A., Song, W., Tanaka-Ishii, K., & Sumita, E. Picotrans. Using pictures as input for machine translation on mobile devices. In *Proc. IJCAI 2011*. AAAI Press (2011), 2614–2619.
3. Gao, G., Wang, H.-C., Cosley, D., & Fussell, S. R. Same translation but different experience: the effects of highlighting on machine-translated conversations. In *Proc. CHI 2013,* ACM Press (2013), 449–458.
4. Hart, S. G., & Staveland, L. E. Development of NASA-TLX (Task Load Index): Results of empirical and theoretical research. *Human mental workload*, 1, (1988), 139–183.
5. Hu, C., Bederson, B. B., Resnik, P., & Kronrod, Y. Monotrans2: A new human computation system to support monolingual translation. In *Proc. CHI 2011*, ACM Press (2011), 1133–1136.
6. Sengers, P., & Gaver, B. Staying open to interpretation: engaging multiple meanings in design and evaluation. In *Proc. DIS* 2006, ACM Press (2006), 99–108.
7. Shigenobu, T. Evaluation and usability of back translation for intercultural communication. *Usability and Internationalization. Global and Local User Interfaces*. Springer (2007), 259–265.
8. Yamashita, N., & Ishida, T. Effects of machine translation on collaborative work. In *Proc. CSCW 2006,* ACM Press (2006), 515–524.
9. Zhang, R. P., Pan, Y., & Yang, Y. (2012). A comparative case study of Google and Bing translation. In *Proc. ICERI 2012*, 3669–3673.

Diversity for Design: A Framework for Involving Neurodiverse Children in the Technology Design Process

Laura Benton[1], Asimina Vasalou[1], Rilla Khaled[2], Hilary Johnson[3] and Daniel Gooch[1]

[1]Institute of Education
London, UK
{l.benton, a.vasalou, d.gooch}@ioe.ac.uk

[2]Dept. of Digital Games
University of Malta
rilla.khaled@um.edu.mt

[3]Dept. of Computer Science
University of Bath, UK
h.johnson@bath.ac.uk

ABSTRACT

The neurodiversity movement seeks to positively reframe certain neurological conditions, such as autism spectrum disorders (ASD) and dyslexia, by concentrating on their strengths. In recent years, neurodiverse children have increasingly been involved in the technology design process, but the design approaches adopted have focused mostly on overcoming difficulties of working with these children, leaving their strengths untapped. We present a new participatory design (PD) framework, Diversity for Design (D4D), which provides guidance for technology designers working with neurodiverse children in establishing PD methods that capitalize on children's strengths and also support potential difficulties. We present two case studies of use of the D4D framework, involving children with ASD and dyslexia, showing how it informed the development and refinement of PD methods tailored to these populations. In addition, we show how to apply the D4D framework to other neurodiverse populations.

Author Keywords

Participatory design; children; neurodiversity; autism; dyslexia.

ACM Classification Keywords

H.5.2. User Interfaces: User-centered design.

INTRODUCTION

The term 'neurodiversity' refers to a subset of neurological conditions, which typically result in a child being labeled as having special educational needs (SEN). These conditions include (among others) attention deficit hyperactivity disorder (ADHD), autism spectrum disorders (ASD), dyslexia, anxiety disorders and intellectual disabilities [4]. Neurodiversity seeks to reframe how these conditions are viewed by arguing that they constitute alternative cognitive processing styles occurring across a wide spectrum. This perspective offers a new way of thinking about the involvement of these children in design by recognizing that these conditions have associated *strengths* alongside the *deficits* that often define them. Indeed, as Armstrong [4] points out, the view of these different cognitive styles as disabilities is dependent on the social and cultural context of the individual; for instance in a pre-literate society dyslexia would not be seen as a disability at all.

The benefits technology can bring to children with SEN are now widely acknowledged within the child-computer interaction research community. More researchers are now seeking to involve them within the technology design process through approaches such as participatory design (PD), where users are actively involved throughout the design process [12,14]. However, there is a tendency for this work to focus predominantly on how to overcome the *difficulties* of working with these children e.g. [1,14,23].

The importance of revisiting how disability is viewed in HCI has recently been discussed. Armagno [3] has argued in favor of applying a social model of disability, which shifts the focus from the functional limitations of individuals to problems resulting from limits of environments, barriers and cultures. He highlights the need for methodologies that adopt this alternative model such that the solutions developed by designers, responsible for creating and developing interactive digital products, are not also subject to the same limitations [3]. In employing the neurodiversity perspective, Dalton [9] has called for the specific development of "neurodiverse design protocols and methods – for example, for participatory design".

While the moral proposition of neurodiversity raises questions for designers, the development of design methods that balance children's strengths or weaknesses requires time and careful consideration. Technology projects often have tight schedules, and designers are rarely experts in the subject matters they pursue. In following Armagno and Dalton's suggestions, if design methods are informed by incorrect assumptions and preconceptions of the neurodiverse community, resulting technologies may serve to further marginalize these groups.

In this paper, we provide designers with a framework that guides them in adapting PD to account for neurodiversity. The framework facilitates the development of PD methods, which direct designers' attention to children's strengths, while supporting their difficulties. We demonstrate how the framework can be used in practice through two cases studies, the first involving children with ASD and the second involving children with dyslexia. These examples illustrate

CHI 2014, April 26 - May 01, 2014, Toronto, ON, Canada.

ACM 978-1-4503-2473-1/14/04...$15.00.
http://dx.doi.org/10.1145/2556288.2557244

the flexibility of the framework in accommodating designers' resources and preferences, and demonstrate how the resulting methods evolve on the basis of theory and practice. Our framework serves as a unifying resource that can guide the development and documentation of new PD methods for neurodiverse children. In guiding designers to record and justify their methodological decisions, our framework can contribute towards capturing designers' tacit knowledge, facilitating a deeper understanding of designerly practices. Finally, we propose that the implications of our framework can go well beyond the neurodiverse population to empower individuals from the wider population by reinforcing their strengths.

BENEFITS OF NEURODIVERSITY TO PD

There are a significant number of children labeled as "gifted and talented" who have also been diagnosed with a neurological condition such as ADHD, ASD, or dyslexia [24]. Armstrong [4] has identified characteristic strengths associated with different neurodiverse conditions. These strengths are presented in Table 1 alongside some of the difficulties that typically define the conditions, although we note that these characteristic strengths/difficulties are not necessarily observed in *all* individuals diagnosed with these conditions. Furthermore many associated characteristics can be viewed as either a strength or as a difficulty depending on the situation or the lens through which it is viewed.

Alper et al. [2] highlight that gifted children with diverse needs are "at risk of growing frustrated or bored with existing interactive technologies because their needs…are not well understood or identified". This emphasizes the importance of involving them directly in the technology design process rather than using proxies, such as parents, carers or teachers, to make design decisions on their behalf.

Creativity is a strength commonly associated with all of these conditions. Creativity is a much-debated concept and while there are many definitions of the term, most refer to the generation of ideas that are both novel and appropriate [29]. Creativity is viewed as a key skill within PD, with Warr and O'Neill [29] proposing "the more creative we are in design, the greater the probability of designing useful and usable software applications and software". The creative strengths of neurodiverse individuals along with other talents such as, for example, the spontaneity and risk-taking of individuals with ADHD, or the strong visual-spatial skills and innovative thinking of individuals with dyslexia, could result in extremely valuable, and potentially unique, contributions to the design of new technology.

While adapting PD to support the involvement of children has been relatively common for over a decade [15], recently some researchers have begun recognizing the strengths of neurodiverse children. After involving children with high-functioning autism (HFA) in the design of a technology-enhanced learning environment, Frauenberger et al. [12] stated that they "have a tendency to become very good at what they like, whatever skill that might be" and emphasized the importance of their input within the end product. Gibson et al. [13] also highlighted the positives of working with 'difficult' children in mainstream classes, which can frequently include those with ADHD, stating that "the benefits far outweigh the problems". These benefits included strengthening the enjoyment of the group, quickly understanding the need for a "different and fun" product, and being more innovative and less inhibited in their ideas.

Despite this movement, within the HCI community there remains a tendency to focus on the barriers that need to be overcome to enable the participation of neurodiverse children

Associated Characteristics (✓ = a strength and **x** = a difficulty)	**ADHD**	**ASD**	**Dyslexia**	**Anxiety disorders**	**Intellectual disabilities**
Spontaneous and high energy/Restless	✓ x				
Divergent or innovative thinkers	✓		✓		
Creative (in specific areas)	✓	✓	✓	✓	✓
Risk-takers/Impulsive	✓ x				
Attention to details or high precision	✓			✓	
High focus (related to interests)/Distractible	✓ x	✓ x	✓ x		
Strong systemizers/Obsessive routines		✓ x			
Prodigious memory/Poor memory		✓	x		
Visual-spatial skills		✓	✓ x		x
Exceptional talents in very specific areas		✓			✓
Ability to see "big picture"			✓		
Social skills		x			✓
Reading, writing and/or spelling abilities			x		
Cognitive abilities					x
Communication skills		x	x		✓
Intense phobias				x	

Table 1. Characteristic strengths and difficulties associated with neurodiverse conditions [4]

e.g. [1,11,23]. Guha et al. [14], for example, have developed a model for involving children with special needs more generally within the technology design process. The authors propose three layers to their model including (1) level of children's involvement; (2) nature/severity of disability; (3) availability/intensity of support. This model has combined best practice from special education teaching with technology development [19], but as Fohlin [10] points out, the second layer of this model can be viewed as "an obstacle that needs to be overcome" in the third layer. Exemplifying researchers' focus on the limiting factors of neurodiversity, Dalton [8] conducted a meta-review of papers in the ACM digital library (1999-2013) referencing dyslexia or autism and found "no paper made any positive mention of any aspect of either of these conditions".

In reflecting on the challenges of PD more generally, Sanders et al. [27] observe that it can be "difficult for many people to believe they are creative and behave accordingly". PD methods must thus support a design environment in which individuals feel comfortable and confident generating and sharing creative ideas alongside designers. Crafting design environments that provide the best possible opportunities for children to realize their potential and make meaningful design contributions becomes even more critical in the context of neurodiversity. Armstrong [4] discusses the importance of *niche construction* in the education of neurodiverse children. This concerns adapting the environment to match the particular needs of an individual, to maximize strengths and minimize weaknesses. In this spirit, Kärnä et al. [19] propose a framework for involving children with special needs in technology design and development, called Children in the Centre (CiC). CiC has five levels, with the central component focusing on the children's interests, strengths and needs, which can facilitate the emergence of the children's potential and hidden skills. CiC therefore acknowledges children's limitations, whilst not restricting participation to being exclusively limitation-centric. Though Kärnä et al. describe rich examples of applying CiC to a technology design project, they do not present a practical framework that can guide future work. In summary, recognizing the importance of neurodiversity in HCI highlights a need for a flexible framework that can guide technology designers in the development of PD methods that support the specific capabilities of children from different neurodiverse populations. One way to achieve this is through the application of niche construction. The following section introduces the TEACCH program, which is based on this philosophy, and forms the foundation of our PD approach.

D4D: A FRAMEWORK FOR NEURODIVERSITY IN PD

TEACCH (Treatment and Education of Autistic and related Communication handicapped CHildren) is an evidence-based program that has been used internationally in the education of individuals with autism for over 30 years. Mesibov et al. [22] explain that the aim of TEACCH is not "being normal", but rather for individuals with autism to function as comfortably and effectively as possible within society. The primary link between TEACCH and the neurodiverse movement is the focus on the fundamental strengths of the condition. Although Mesibov et al. [22] do acknowledge "all programs should work on both strengths and deficits to some extent", they emphasize that the priorities of TEACCH are on strengths. The TEACCH program incorporates a *Structured Teaching* intervention approach. Structured Teaching is "an array of teaching or treatment principles and strategies" based on the understanding of and respect for the 'Culture of Autism', that can be applied to each person's particular situation [24,32]. These principles include the following:

(1) ***Understanding Culture***: TEACCH recognizes and responds to autism as a culture i.e. the "characteristic and predictable patterns of thinking and behavior" observed in the condition [22]. Examples of these characteristics include strengths related to, and preferences for, *visual processing* and following *routines* [28].

(2) ***Tailoring to the Individual***: TEACCH is premised on the philosophy that its application should be flexible and individualized, enabling its' concepts and methods to be relevant for a wide range of "developmental levels and behavioral profiles" [22]. Whereas the first principle targets typical ASD characteristics, here the focus is on characteristics specific to the individual, including "skills levels, talents, special interests, personality, feelings, quirks and potential" [22]. An example would be to theme a particular activity for a child with an interest in World War I with prominent WWI figures or battles.

(3) ***Structuring the Environment:*** TEACCH incorporates "situational modifications" to help mitigate potential difficulties by matching the environment to an individual's "abilities and ways of understanding and learning" [22]. One example of this is to set a predictable sequence of activities to make the environment more comprehensible and prevent anxieties related to uncertainty or surprises.

(4) ***Providing Supports***: TEACCH provides supports to make the specific activities more understandable to the individual [28]. Examples of supports include providing visual representations or physical demonstrations of task instructions to reinforce verbal explanations.

In abstracting the key TEACCH principles, it becomes apparent that the program's philosophy can be generalized to a wider neurodiverse population. Moreover, as Mesibov et al. [22] highlight, characteristics of ASD can also exist in conditions such as ADHD and OCD, as well as in typically developing children, for instance the attention to detail in ASD and OCD. This suggests that structuring the environment or incorporating supports that capitalize on typical ASD strengths could benefit children with other neurodiverse conditions associated with similar strengths (or difficulties). In using TEACCH to inform a framework for PD methods that broadly support the participation of neurodiverse populations, we must therefore consider how these four key principles can apply to PD.

A typical PD session centers on a design activity and collaboration between participants. The potential for collaboration and creativity is influenced by how the design activity has been crafted. Therefore, the construction of the design environment, and how strengths are promoted and weaknesses are accommodated (*structuring the environment* and *providing supports*) should be informed by the typical characteristics of the neurodiverse culture as well as by each participating child's own talents and strengths (*understanding culture* and *tailoring to the individual)*. Fig. 1 presents our proposed PD framework for neurodiversity, which we call *Diversity for Design (D4D)*.

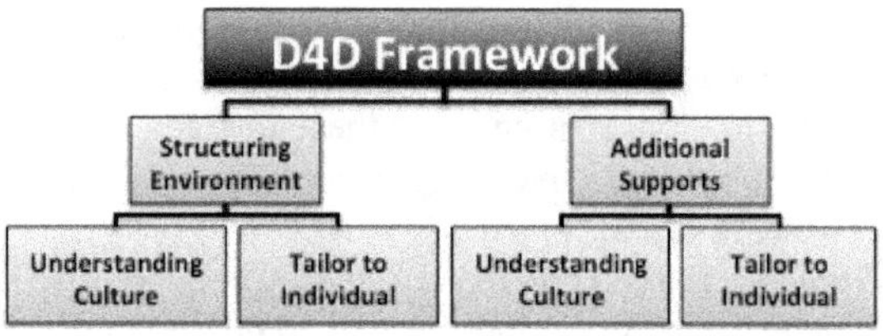

Figure 1: Diversity for Design (D4D) framework

We intentionally employ the term *framework*, as opposed to method or tool, as the term reflects the necessary flexibility D4D provides designers in developing methods appropriate to their specific context and constraints, whereas *method* implies more rigidity and precise replication. In considering designers' agency and need for flexibility in conducting design research, the D4D framework *guides them* in tailoring their PD methods to enable the participation of neurodiverse populations. To demonstrate how our D4D framework for neurodiversity can be employed in practice, we present two case studies, one using PD to inform math software for children with ASD, and the second employing PD during the development of software to assist children with dyslexia with their reading difficulties.

CASE STUDY 1: DEVELOPING PD METHODS FOR CHILDREN WITH ASD

The first case study describes a project that aimed to involve children with HFA and Asperger's Syndrome (AS) in the development of an intelligent tutoring system for helping children with ASD at Key Stage 3 (aged 11-14) to learn math. The lead designer in the project had two years to work with children on designing certain aspects of the system. This timeframe enabled taking an iterative stepwise approach to the process of developing a PD method for children with ASD. Here we describe those steps.

Theoretically-informed PD

Our first step involved reviewing existing literature in order to identify the typical strengths (e.g. visual-spatial skills) and preferences (e.g. preference for structure and routines), as well as potential difficulties (e.g. distractibility) of children with ASD, particularly those relevant in a PD context. The TEACCH characteristics of the Culture of Autism [22] played an important role here, as did other key literature within the field of autism, e.g. [5,16].

We then undertook a critical review of existing PD methods and techniques for children, e.g. [14,15,20], to provide inspiration for features that could be incorporated into a PD method for children with ASD. We selected PD features that we believed would either capitalize on the strengths or support the difficulties associated with ASD, both in terms of structuring the design environment or providing appropriate supports within the design activities. Next, we determined which of the features could be applied to benefit the wider ASD population, and which could be tailored to the individual child participants. The PD method established through this process is as follows (PD features responsive to ASD characteristics are presented in small caps, with the number of the corresponding feature from the D4D framework summarized in Fig. 2 in brackets):

In preparing the sessions, it was important to identify children's HOBBIES AND INTERESTS (8) through e.g. surveys or discussions with their guardian, with the aim to integrate them into PD – either within the overall design task, specific activities, or as a form of reward for participating. Children with ASD often have exceptional knowledge or skills in areas related to their special interests [22] and therefore integrating these into the design process allows them to contribute their knowledge/skills. Moreover, it was essential to choose design task CONTENT APPROPRIATE FOR THE CHILDREN'S ABILITY LEVEL (9) to mitigate any concerns about failure. Also due to preferences for routine and potential auditory sensitivities, each session was to take place in a QUIET/FAMILIAR ENVIRONMENT (1), e.g. in a separate classroom at the children's school.

In providing structure to the sessions, we would use a VISUAL SCHEDULE (5) for displaying each of the activities, using both text and images, and also a set of rules agreed on by all participants to guide appropriate behavior during sessions. This would be visible throughout the session with a child TICKING OFF EACH ACTIVITY (6) on completion. To capitalize on the children's visual strengths the session would begin with A VISUAL RECAP (2) of what happened in the previous session (if appropriate), incorporating images of activities undertaken during the past session, a summary of the main achievements and how they linked to the current session. Next, the current sessions would be VISUALLY INTRODUCED (2), involving references back to activities displayed on the schedule and explanations of what each would entail. Where possible all ACTIVITIES WOULD INTEGRATE VISUAL COMPONENTS (14). Each session would finish with a SUMMARY OF THE SESSION AND AN INTRODUCTION TO WHAT WOULD HAPPEN NEXT WEEK (2), to highlight what the children had achieved and to prevent anxieties about unknown, upcoming activities. To reflect the systemizing approach of children with ASD each session would FOLLOW A SIMILAR STRUCTURE (3), i.e. same start/end, and design activities would be CONSISTENTLY STRUCTURED (15) wherever possible. Lastly, the sessions would ideally be SCHEDULED AT THE SAME TIME AND PLACE (4) each week to provide some familiarity for the children.

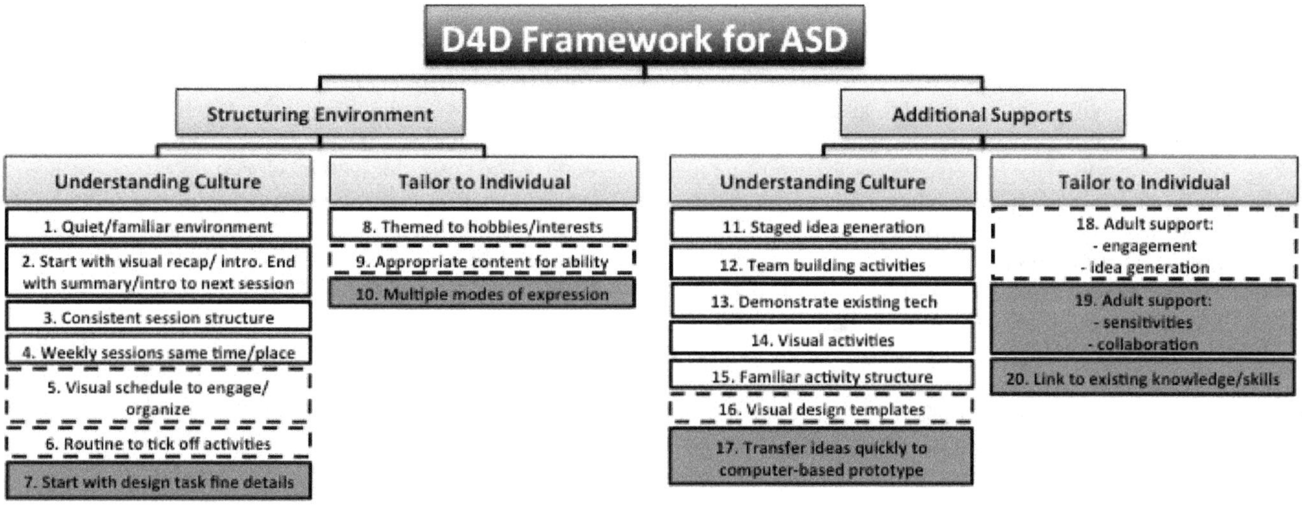

Figure 2: D4D framework applied to the development of PD features for the ASD population

In performing design work within sessions, during initial sessions we would incorporate fun, structured ACTIVITIES FOCUSED ON BUILDING TEAM RAPPORT AND SKILLS (12), e.g. Lego building challenges, to help the children feel comfortable and confident about working in a collaborative design environment. In introducing the main design task, SIMILAR EXISTING TECHNOLOGY WOULD BE DEMONSTRATED (13) and critiqued, to build on the children's reality-based creativity style. The IDEA GENERATION PROCESS WOULD BE SPLIT INTO EXPLICIT STAGES (11) and incorporate VISUAL DESIGN TEMPLATES (16), to guide the process of generating and documenting individual ideas, and combining these with other design team members. If a child appeared to be struggling to make progress an ADULT WOULD INTERVENE AND PROVIDE ADDITIONAL SUPPORT (18) to enable the child to successfully complete the activity.

Fig. 2 summarizes how the various features were informed by our D4D framework. White boxes (with solid or dashed lines) indicate PD features that were informed by theory. Next, we describe how our method was trialed with children with ASD, and additionally how we refined it by reflecting on our design practice.

Practice-informed PD: one-to-one workshops

Our second step involved applying our theoretically-inspired PD method in one-off design workshops with individual children with HFA/AS (see [6] for full details). The aim of these workshops was to explore the children's strengths and difficulties during participation within typical design activities. Given our inexperience with the user group at the time, we intentionally used one-to-one design sessions to create a safe design context that was easier for us to control. Ten children with HFA/AS aged 11-14 from three specialist ASD schools participated in the workshops.

Our original literature review highlighted the talent, knowledge and focus children with ASD can have within areas related to their special interests. Therefore, we tailored the design task to match a common interest of children with ASD (and children in general): computer games [21]. To draw links with the intelligent tutoring system we sought to inform, the children were asked to design a *math-based* computer game for their peers. Each session involved four activities: 1) introduction to the workshop, 2) discussion of the child's previous experience of math and computer games, and demonstration of existing math games, 3) generation and documentation of design ideas, 4) physically drawing an interface design of best idea using provided art materials. These activities drew from features of our D4D framework for ASD presented earlier. The findings from these workshops are discussed below with the resulting implications in bold.

Our workshops revealed the need to **evolve existing features** due to difficulties that children faced. We found that VISUAL DESIGN TEMPLATES (16), in particular, needed to provide more guidance to children in the initial idea generation phase. At the beginning of sessions, when children were provided with a blank design template on which to document their ideas, many struggled to generate any. However, once we changed our protocol to incorporate example ideas and partially completed interface designs, children were able to expand on the ideas given, and in some cases generate their own idea(s) where previously they had been unable to do so.

We also discovered **emergent uses,** as features we had included were sometimes used in unexpected ways. The VISUAL SCHEDULE (5) worked well to prepare the children for which activities would be encountered during the workshop. To our surprise, it also proved useful as a tool for re-engaging any children who became distracted during the session, enabling them to see where they were and resume from where they had left off more easily.

Our workshops highlighted the **flexibility** required for certain features, such as the provision of ADULT SUPPORT (18). An adult facilitator was present to re-engage some of the children if they became distracted. This facilitator was additionally able to support children who initially struggled with idea generation by providing them with inspiration and verbal encouragement. At the same time, we observed the importance of applying tacit knowledge about each child in providing support. For example, interventions that supported some children would stifle others, who remained engaged throughout and enthusiastically shared their own ideas without verbal prompts. Moreover, our sessions demonstrated the importance of tailoring content to the individual child participant's ability level. During the demonstration of existing math games, although the difficulty of the demonstrated levels was intentionally kept low, it still proved too difficult for some. An inability to understand the game had a strong negative impact on engagement. For example, instead of documenting his ideas, one boy wrote 'I hate the basketball', referring to the game he had been unable to understand. We thus modified this protocol to ensure that children's abilities be established in advance where possible, and to rely on video demonstrations rather than direct interaction with software, to avoid uncertainties about appropriate content level.

Finally, certain features such as the ROUTINE OF TICKING OFF ACTIVITIES (6) gained more **prominence** than originally intended. Many of the children appeared to enjoy this routine and some explicitly asked to tick off the last activity at the end of the session. This suggested to us that this responsibility could be further leveraged, thus in subsequent sessions this role was explicitly 'assigned' to a child.

From our workshops, we observed that while most of our proposed PD features enabled children to participate, others required modification. This prompted a first iteration of our PD method (see Fig. 2): while 10 of our original features remained the same (solid white boxes), five others were revised based on our insights (dashed boxes).

Practice-informed PD: collaborative workshops

In a third and final step, we applied the iterated PD method in a new design context involving two design teams of children with ASD, see [7]. The collaborative nature of this step created new demands, thus we anticipated adapting or adding new features. The method was used over six design workshops, with each design team involving three children with HFA aged 12-13, two researchers (one undertaking an interaction designer role), and one teaching staff member from the children's school. Our objective in the workshops was to explore children's preferences for types of feedback and rewards, to inform the design of the math tutoring system. As in the first series of workshops, we chose a design task related to computer games.

Our design workshops demonstrated a need to **evolve existing features**. Varying levels of ADULT SUPPORT were present throughout, and our facilitators focused on supporting engagement and idea generation. At the same time, however, we discovered individual difficulties that needed to be accommodated to enable the children to share their many ideas most effectively. For instance, one child was sensitive to touching paper, and thus required the facilitator to write/draw his ideas on the paper-based templates. Others struggled to work in teams, did not listen to each other's ideas, and were hyper-critical. Adult intervention was required to reposition the workshop as a collaborative activity. These emergent needs led us to redefine the role of ADULT SUPPORT (19) to additionally include responding to specific sensitivities and collaboration patterns to facilitate equity in participation.

Our experiences also highlighted the need to **introduce new features**. In one of the design teams, children initially found it challenging to generate design ideas. As a response, the teaching assistant directed them to generate ideas for a very specific aspect of the feedback system. This enabled children to begin generating focused ideas, which were later expanded and integrated in a wider variety of feedback mechanisms. Focusing early design sessions on the FINER DETAILS OF THE DESIGN TASK (7) and then extending the design context in later sessions is therefore one way to match the detail-focused processing style of children with ASD. A second feature concerned children's expressive preferences in sharing their ideas. We observed quickly that some children with artistic talents preferred to draw their ideas and appeared to lack confidence in sharing their ideas verbally, while others seemed restricted by their drawing ability, but were able to eloquently describe their ideas verbally. Children's individual expressive strengths evolved over the course of the sessions and evidenced the need to support MULTIPLE MODES OF EXPRESSION (10) by providing opportunities to share ideas verbally or visually.

After the fourth and fifth design sessions, one of the researchers converted the paper-based design ideas into videos of a digital prototype of the math game. The children asked to watch each video several times, which helped them generate ideas about how to improve the feedback and reward design. Children with ASD typically think about things in a concrete way, therefore CONVERTING PAPER-BASED DESIGN IDEAS VERY QUICKLY INTO CONCRETE COMPUTER-BASED REPRESENTATIONS (17) of the design product fit with their reality-based style of creativity.

During the sessions it became clear that some of the children had extensive knowledge of computer games. For example, one boy suggested useful game design resources to the researchers, and was able to analyze the many games he had played to reflect on what made them successful. This knowledge came to guide the team's idea generation, highlighting the importance of being able LINK THE DESIGN ACTIVITIES TO EXISTING KNOWLEDGE/SKILLS (20) of individual participants by identifying relevant skills in advance and explicitly encouraging a child to contribute to a design activity that links to their specific strengths.

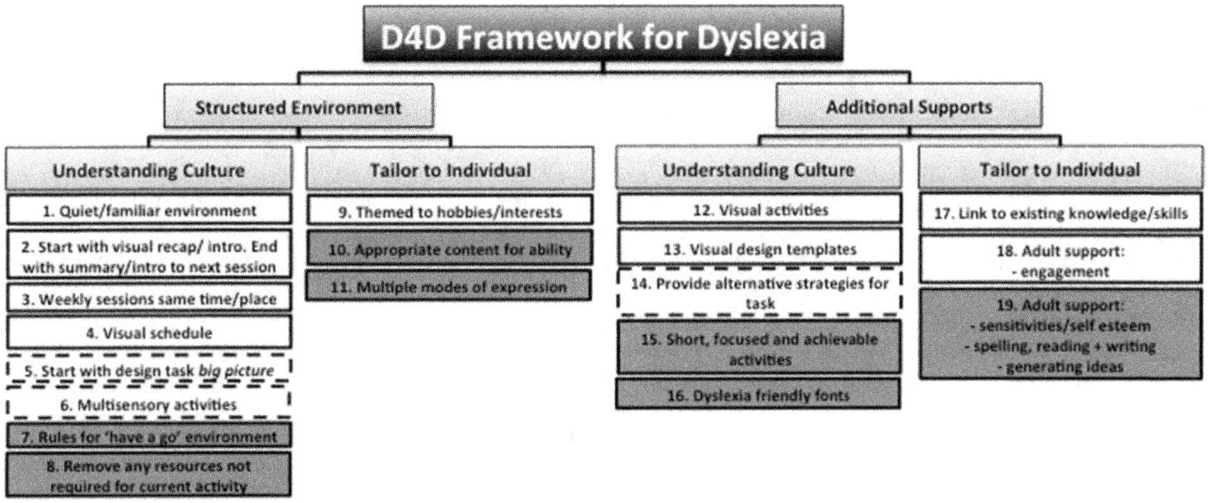

Figure 3: D4D framework applied to the development of PD features for a dyslexic population

Our collaborative workshops showed that while most of our PD features worked well in the new context, we needed to **evolve one feature**, and introduce four additional features (see grey boxes in Fig. 2).

CASE STUDY 2: DEVELOPING PD METHODS FOR CHILDREN WITH DYSLEXIA

Our second case study concerns an ongoing EU-funded project aimed at developing a learning tool to help dyslexic children between the ages of 9-11 improve their reading and writing skills. Given that our design research stage has been limited to one year, we had less time to develop a PD method, thus this case presents a considerable contrast to the previous one. As stated earlier, characteristics of ASD can also exist in other conditions, including dyslexia [26]. Thus, we built on the foundations laid during our previous case study. We describe the stepwise process of method development we used in the following sections, with the number of the corresponding feature in the D4D framework summarized within Fig. 3 in brackets.

Theoretically-informed PD

Our first step involved identifying typical strengths, preferences, and potential difficulties of children with dyslexia from the literature. We relied, in particular, on a recent review of dyslexia [26], which enabled us to identify shared characteristics between ASD and dyslexia. As presented in Table 1, two overlapping characteristic strengths are a high focus on activities related to interests, and strong visual-spatial skills. These similarities suggested that PD features previously developed in the context of ASD to support these strengths would be transferable to this context. These features were:

- Building on existing talents by theming design workshop to HOBBIES/INTERESTS (9) and capitalizing on CHILDREN'S EXISTING KNOWLEDGE OR SKILLS (17) during idea generation
- Taking advantage of visual strengths by Including A VISUAL RECAP (2) of the previous session followed by a VISUAL SCHEDULE (4) of design activities; integrating VISUAL COMPONENTS (12) within design activities where possible; and using VISUAL DESIGN TEMPLATES (13) for documenting ideas

Our review also revealed overlapping difficulties between ASD and dyslexia, such as anxieties related to failure, the unfamiliar, or the unknown. The PD features originally developed to overcome these difficulties were:

- Incorporating APPROPRIATE CONTENT FOR THE CHILD'S ABILITY LEVEL (10) to help mitigate failure
- Conducting session in QUIET/FAMILIAR ENVIRONMENT (1) and scheduling sessions at the SAME TIME/PLACE EACH WEEK (3) to limit unknown factors
- Providing an INTRODUCTION TO THE CURRENT SESSION and WHAT WILL HAPPEN THE NEXT WEEK (2) to ensure the child knows what to expect

Next, we reviewed existing applications of PD to establish how to capitalize strengths and support difficulties specific to children with dyslexia, focusing both on the broad level and at the level of the specific individual. In shaping our PD method to be specific to dyslexic children, we introduce the 'BIG PICTURE' OF THE DESIGN TASK (5) first, focusing on specific design components during later sessions as a way to capitalize on dyslexic children's global processing style. We employ a MULTISENSORY APPROACH (6) in design activities, incorporating visual elements to maximize typical visual strengths, and kinesthetic elements e.g. Lego-based tasks, to enable children to participate in ways more natural for them. Furthermore, ALTERNATIVE STRATEGIES FOR COMPLETING THE DESIGN TASK (14) would be provided to promote independence and encourage metacognitive thinking, e.g. providing different sources of idea inspirations, as dyslexic children tend to overgeneralize negative experiences.

Practice-informed PD: observations and interviews

Our second step involved balancing our theoretically-informed PD method with best practice notions from teachers. We conducted observations and interviews in two UK primary schools and two specialist dyslexia-teaching centers to capture strategies used by teachers to support neurodiversity, which would be useful to employ during PD. The lead researcher observed and took detailed notes documenting the teaching strategies employed by the teachers during one-to-one, small group and entire class literacy lessons. The same researcher then interviewed five of these teachers, including one mainstream primary school teacher, two SEN teachers, and two specialist dyslexia teachers. The interviews focused on teaching strategies witnessed during observations, including how teachers engaged children, built on their strengths to increase their confidence, selected appropriate content, supported particular difficulties, incorporated children's interests, and integrated technology into their teaching.

This step suggested a need for inclusion of two **additional features**. The specialist teachers sought to create a non-threatening environment where children felt confident enough to 'have a go'. This led to us ADAPTING THE RULES (displayed on the visual schedule) (7) to emphasize 'having a go' at an activity and to clarify that there were no 'wrong answers'. We also learned that specialist teachers employed a quick succession of short literacy tasks to keep children engaged, and constructed sessions with key achievable targets that children would not 'fail'. Thus, design activities incorporated into the PD method would be SHORT, FOCUSED AND ACHIEVABLE (15), with all tasks having precise objectives, being explained as simply as possible, and lasting no more than 10 minutes. Finally, in witnessing children's reading difficulties in practice, we proposed to **evolve the feature** ADULT SUPPORT (19) to include help with spelling, writing and reading, and for text to be avoided wherever possible.

Practice-informed PD: collaborative workshops

In a third and final step, we applied our revised PD method in three design workshops involving a single design team, comprised of four children with reading/writing difficulties, one researcher undertaking an interaction designer role, and one teaching staff member from the children's school who knew the children well. All children were aged 9-10 and were undergoing dyslexia assessment. The workshops were targeted at informing the design of a game forming part of a larger learning tool, for children aged 9-11. In particular, the goal was to generate design ideas for the game's navigation and reward systems.

Our work with children revealed further difficulties that **introduced new PD features**. Children frequently became distracted from current activities by resources for previous activities, such as the pens for ticking off activities on the visual schedule. This sensitized us to remove RESOURCES NOT APPLICABLE TO THE CURRENT ACTIVITY FROM VIEW (8) to maintain the children's focus on the activities. Difficulties the children encountered also required us to **evolve existing features**. For example, the VISUAL SCHEDULE (4) that detailed the structure of the workshop included the words 'The End', but unknowingly, we had used an elaborate font that was difficult for children to discern. While in this instance, reading the text itself was not essential, difficult-to-read text can lower children's confidence, potentially affecting their willingness to contribute to design activities. This highlighted the importance of overriding any aesthetic choices and using a DYSLEXIA FRIENDLY FONT (16) at all times. The workshops also **evolved existing features**, such as having MULTIPLE MODES OF EXPRESSION (11), with the children not only expressing their ideas visually via drawing and verbally during group discussions, but also sometimes with acting, using materials as props, e.g. using a board rubber to show how they interact with their mobile phone.

Fig. 3 summarizes how each of these steps was informed by our D4D framework. White boxes indicate theoretically-inspired features, with features appropriated from the ASD method presented in solid lines. Grey boxes represent features that were proposed by teaching practices and the design workshop sessions.

ADAPTING THE D4D FRAMEWORK

In illustrating the practical application of the D4D framework, we break down our process into a series of steps a designer might employ for another neurodiverse population. We use children with ADHD as an example.

Understand the Culture of ADHD: Examine the ADHD literature to identify the typical characteristics of the culture of ADHD, including strengths, preferences and difficulties. Reflect on how these might manifest within a PD context. Consider supplementing theoretical views with design research, such as observations or interviews with both the children and the adults that work with them, or trial design activities and workshops.

Understand the Individual Children: Consider how the method will be tailored to the individual children participating in the session. Identify in advance the children's ability levels in relation to the design task content, their existing knowledge/skills as well as hobbies/interests and how these could be linked in with the design activities. Decide on whether to involve an adult already familiar with the children, such as a teacher, for providing relevant information and additional support.

Structure the Environment and Provide Supports: Determine the implications of these insights within the context of the designer's tacit knowledge on the environment structure and types of supports required, focusing especially on capitalizing strengths and supporting known difficulties. For example, a detail-focused or global processing style requires consideration of the initial presentation of the design task, while a particular preferred information presentation style impacts on what and how information in the visual schedule should be presented.

DISCUSSION

Many designers do not have experience of working with neurodiverse populations. Over continuous exposure to a neurodiverse population, designers can develop the expertise necessary to engage such individuals in design activities, but the time constraints of most technology projects do not allow for this. Furthermore, within PD, participants can play multiple roles, at various levels of involvement [17]. For meaningful participation, neurodiverse children require support to emphasize their strengths, and provisions to mitigate their difficulties. This enables a deeper level of involvement where designers 'learn with' the participants during the design process rather than simply 'learning about' [17]. We found that children were most suited to contributing ideas and evaluating different design options. However, as some children also had extensive technical knowledge/skills, they additionally had the potential to contribute towards assessing technical feasibility and developing design prototypes. The present paper proposed a new framework, D4D, to guide designers in supporting the meaningful participation of neurodiverse children. Our contribution is not in developing a novel PD method, as many of the features we identified in our neurodiverse PD methods are not novel. Rather it is the adaptation of the TEACCH education principles as a design framework that scaffolds designers in the creation of new PD methods for children with a range of neurodiverse conditions, guiding them to identify the specific combination of PD features most appropriate for their target population. The implications of our work are three-fold.

First, in many research projects involving neurodiverse children, methods are generated "on the fly" for use within specific project bounds. Often, only minimal details are provided about these methods, their rates of success, and reasons underlying success or failure. This makes it difficult for the research community to learn from each other's experiences. In hoping that HCI researchers will employ the D4D framework, and document the resulting methods, we aspire to *create a common point of reference and a practical resource that is enriched over time to benefit those working with neurodiverse children*. Indeed, given the overlap of characteristics between some of these conditions, PD methods developed for one condition can become reusable and transferable to another.

Second, researchers may hesitate to rigorously document their methods because of the complexity of methodological choices both at the inception and application stage. Additionally, parties involved in design activities draw on tacit knowledge and prior experiences. Reflecting on our case studies, the lead designer drew on experiences of conducting design workshops, observations of how teachers intervened in challenging situations, and conversations with individual children or their parents regarding the children's interests or difficulties. These influences led to new PD features guided by, and subsequently captured within, the D4D framework. The framework can thus serve to *capture and model designers' strategies and tacit knowledge longitudinally providing us with more insight into the often-elusive nature of design practice.*

Third, a practical contribution of our work is to demonstrate a *process through which the D4D framework can guide the development of features for incorporation in PD*, informed by theory and practice. Importantly, this process is flexible to the practices of different designers and their constraints. Case Study 1 presented an in-depth approach, where sufficient time was available to undertake iterative testing of the different feature sets with the target population. Case Study 2 presented a lightweight approach that partly reused the method from the first case study, and replaced the more time-consuming and resource intensive design workshops with ethnographic work. Whereas Case Study 1 is strongly informed by design practices including children, Case Study 2 takes a more teacher-centric approach.

An important feature of our process is the acknowledgement that methods are not only proposed but also practiced. Although theory was initially used to develop each PD method, the D4D framework facilitated the incorporation of insights gained from our application of these methods. Neurodiverse conditions, which entail a range of specific talents and difficulties, create an additional demand to reflect and capture the practice of design methods in a more *iterative* process. The D4D framework of neurodiversity therefore guides initial method construction, but also scaffolds reflection and further development. As systematically evaluating the outcomes of this framework is beyond the scope of this work, it would be valuable if designers using D4D evaluated and reported on the outcomes of their methods with different populations; potentially considering the quantity, quality and/or novelty of ideas generated using their method.

A final contribution of our work is the documentation and development of two PD methods for ASD and dyslexia. We note, however, that given the limited scope of our paper, the frameworks presented here should be viewed as illustrative rather than fully comprehensive, and may not cover a complete set of PD features for all children with ASD or dyslexia, let alone the wider neurodiverse population.

We conclude with some optimism about the far-reaching implications of neurodiversity for HCI. Kapp et al. [18] have argued that "many neurological conditions have variable traits, fluid boundaries among one another, a continuous nature within the general population, and strengths beyond or as part of significant challenges". While we have highlighted the many commonalities between different neurodiverse conditions, it is important to acknowledge that these conditions exist on a spectrum. Indeed, there is often no clear line demarcating a formal diagnosis of a neurodiverse condition. Consequently, many children remain undiagnosed, and characteristics typically associated with neurodiverse conditions can also be found throughout the child population. We argue that taking a strength-focused individualized approach to involvement in PD is a philosophy that can benefit the wider child population. It allows us to focus on each child's capability set, rather than consider where children are in accordance with a baseline. Guided by our framework, PD can be adapted to help maximize any child's potential for making meaningful contributions to the design process. This draws parallels with the work of Van Rijn [25] who highlights the challenges of designers working with 'extreme' user groups they share little in common with, and how insights from designing with one particular group can actually contribute to an understanding of how to design for any user group. We therefore hope HCI researchers begin to consider how a neurodiverse approach might apply more generally within the child population, as well as to teams of children with mixed cognitive styles.

ACKNOWLEDGMENTS

This research was partly funded by the EU FP7 ICT project iLearnRW (project number: 318803). We would like to thank all the fantastic teachers and pupils who participated in our studies and also our reviewers for their thoughtful critiques and comments that helped to strengthen this paper.

REFERENCES

1. Al-Wabil, A., Meldah, E., Al-Suwaidan, A., and AlZahrani, A. Designing Educational Games for Children with Specific Learning Difficulties: Insights from Involving Children and Practioners. *ICCGI '10*, IEEE (2010), 195–198.
2. Alper, M., Hourcade, J.P., and Gilutz, S. Adding reinforced corners: designing interactive technologies for children with disabilities. *Interactions 19*, 6 (2012), 72–75.
3. Armagno, G. The Role of HCI in the Construction of Disability. *Proc. of HCI Ethics '12*, BIS Ltd. (2012).
4. Armstrong, T. *Neurodiversity*. Da Capo, 2010.
5. Baron-Cohen, S. Autism: The Empathizing-Systemizing (E-S) Theory. *Ann NY Acad Sci 1156*, 1 (2009), 68–80.
6. Benton, L., Ashwin, E., Johnson, H., Grawemeyer, B., and Brosnan, M. IDEAS: An interface design experience for the autistic spectrum. *Proc. CHI '11*, ACM (2011), 1759–1764.
7. Benton, L., Johnson, H., Ashwin, E., Brosnan, M., and Grawemeyer, B. Developing IDEAS: Supporting children with autism within a participatory design team. *Proc. CHI '12*, ACM Press (2012), 2599–2608.
8. Dalton, N.S. Neurodiversity & HCI. *Proc. CHI'13*, ACM (2013), 2295–2304.
9. Dalton, N.S. Neurodiversity HCI. *Interactions 20*, 2 (2013), 72-75.
10. Fohlin, R. Designing for Special Education Schools Involving Children with Intellectual Disabilities in the Design Process. *SIDeR '13*, (2013).
11. Foss, E., Guha, M.L., Papadatos, P., Clegg, T., Yip, J., and Walsh, G. Cooperative Inquiry Extended: Creating Technology with Middle School Students with Learning Differences. *Journal of Special Education Technology 28*, 3 (2013), 33-46.
12. Frauenberger, C., Good, J., and Keay-Bright, W. Designing technology for children with special needs: bridging perspectives through participatory design. *CoDesign 7*, 1 (2011), 1–28.
13. Gibson, L., Gregor, P., and Milne, S. Case study: Designing with difficult children. *Proc. IDC '02*, (2002), 42–52.
14. Guha, M.L., Druin, A., and Fails, J. Designing with and for children with special needs: An inclusionary model. *Proc. IDC '08,* ACM (2008), 61–64.
15. Guha, M.L., Druin, A., and Fails, J.A. Cooperative Inquiry revisited: Reflections of the past and guidelines for the future of intergenerational co-design. *Journal of Child-Computer Interaction 1*, 1 (2013), 14–23.
16. Happe, F. and Vital, P. What aspects of autism predispose to talent? *Phil Trans R Soc B: Biological Sciences 364*, 1522 (2009), 1369–1375.
17. Harder, M.K., Burford, G., and Hoover, E. What is Participation□? Design Leads the Way to a Cross-Disciplinary Framework. *Design Issues 29*, 4 (2013), 41–57.
18. Kapp, S.K., Gillespie-Lynch, K., Sherman, L.E., and Hutman, T. Deficit, Difference, or Both? *Autism and neurodiversity 49*, 1 (2013), 59–71.
19. Kärnä, Eija, Nuutinen, Jussi, Pihlainen-Bednarik, Kaisa, Virpi, V. Designing Technologies with Children with Special Needs□: Children in the Centre (CiC) Framework. *Proc. IDC '10*, ACM (2010), 218–221.
20. Large, A., Nesset, V., Beheshti, J., and Bowler, L. "Bonded design": A novel approach to intergenerational information technology design. *Library & Information Science Research 28*, 1 (2006), 64–82.
21. Mazurek, M.O., Shattuck, P.T., Wagner, M., and Cooper, B.P. Prevalence and Correlates of Screen-Based Media Use Among Youths with Autism Spectrum Disorders. *J Autism Dev Dis 42*, 8 (2011), 1757–1767.
22. Mesibov, G.B., Shea, V., and Schopler, E. *The TEACCH approach to autism spectrum disorders*. Springer, New York, 2007.
23. Millen, L., Cobb, S., and Patel, H. A Method for Involving Children with Autism in Design. *Proc. IDC '11*, ACM (2011), 185–188.
24. Montgomery, D. *Gifted and Talented Children with Special Educational Needs: Double Exceptionality*. Routledge, 2013.
25. Van Rijn, H. Meaningful encounters: Explorative studies about designers learning from children with autism. Dcotoral Thesis (2012).
26. Rose, J. *Identifying and Teaching Children and Young People with Dyslexia and Literacy Difficulties*. 2009.
27. Sanders, E.B.-N. and Stappers, P.J. Co-creation and the new landscapes of design. *CoDesign 4*, 1 (2008), 5–18.
28. TEACCH. TEACCH Approach. 2013. http://teacch.com/about-us/what-is-teacch.
29. Warr, A. and O'Neill, E. Understanding design as a social creative process. *Proc. Creativity & Cognition '05*, ACM (2005), 118–127.

Canine-Centered Interface Design: Supporting the Work of Diabetes Alert Dogs

Charlotte Robinson[1], Clara Mancini[1], Janet van der Linden[1], Claire Guest[2], Rob Harris[2]

[1]Open University
Milton Keynes MK7 6AA, UK
{charlotte.robinson, clara.mancini, janet.vanderlinden} @open.ac.uk

[2]Medical Detection Dogs
Great Horwood MK17 0NP, UK
{claire.guest, rob.harris} @medicaldetectiondogs.org.uk

ABSTRACT
Many people with Diabetes live with the continuous threat of hypoglycemic attacks and the danger of going into coma. Diabetes Alert Dogs are trained to detect the onset of an attack before the condition of the human handler they are paired with deteriorates, giving them time to take action. We investigated requirements for designing an alarm system allowing dogs to remotely call for help when their human falls unconscious before being able to react to an alert. Through a multispecies ethnographic approach we focus on the requirements for a physical canine user interface, involving dogs, their handlers and specialist dog trainers in the design process. We discuss tensions between the requirements for canine and the human users, argue the need for increased sensitivity towards the needs of individual dogs that goes beyond breed specific physical characteristics, and reflect on how we can move from designing *for* dogs to designing *with* dogs.

Author Keywords
Diabetes Alert Dog; human-animal interaction; animal-computer interaction; user-centered design; multispecies ethnography

ACM Classification Keywords
H.5.m. Information interfaces and presentation

INTRODUCTION
It is estimated that, worldwide, 371 million people currently suffer from diabetes, a serious disorder in sugar metabolism [25]. Insulin treatment to manage diabetes can cause sudden drops in blood glucose levels, which are known as hypoglycaemic attacks. Since these attacks can be fatal [31], they are greatly feared by diabetes patients. To try and prevent them, wearable hypoglycaemia alarm machines have been researched and developed which use skin conductance or glucose sensors [2, 6]. However, these machines have a certain margin of error and are often not a practical stand-alone solution to manage day to day hypoglycaemic attacks [10].

As a result, Diabetes Alert Dogs (DAD) have increased in popularity over the last two decades. DADs are paired with human diabetes patients and are trained to warn their owners of oncoming hypoglycaemic attacks, giving them time to call for help or take steps to prevent the attack [23]. Diabetic alert dogs use their olfactory capabilities to detect changes in blood sugar in real-time [5, 33] and act as an early-warning system for their assisted humans with shorter reaction times and higher precision than existing alarm machines, thus significantly contributing to their owners' quality of life and safety [23]. However, some hypoglycaemic attacks can be so sudden that the owner falls into a coma before being able to react to their dog's alert. If no other humans are around, the dog is then unable to help further, left alone with the unconscious person. But what if technology existed that empowered the dog to take action even in a situation such as this?

Recently there has been an increase in the availability of technological artefacts for companion animals (e.g. programmable pet-food feeders [20], remotely-played interactive pet toys [8,18] location pet tracking devices [29,17,12,28,], and "doggie doorbells" [19]). However, many of these technologies are for leisure or for pet-owner convenience. Indeed, so far there has been very little attention to researching and developing technology that can support the work of animals such as DADs in tasks of critical importance. Therefore we are interested in investigating how computing technology can be designed to assist animal workers in tasks they are already performing. More specifically, our work aims to investigate the development of a system that enables a dog to remotely call for help on their owner's behalf, precisely for those situations in which the owner is unable to act upon their dog's alert.

HCI recognises the importance of user-centred design in order to best support humans in their tasks and daily life. Consistent with this, the growing area of Animal-Computer Interaction (ACI) aims to develop a user-centred approach to

CHI 2014, April 26 - May 01, 2014, Toronto, ON, Canada.
Copyright 2014 ACM 978-1-4503-2473-1/14/04…$15.00.
http://dx.doi.org/10.1145/2556288.2557396

the design of technology intended for animals, in order to best support both their welfare and work [13,15]. To this effect, ACI aims to develop frameworks that can account for species-specific characteristics both at the level of usability and user experience, involving animals in the design process as participants and design contributors. However, pursuing user-centred design for non-human users presents unique challenges due - on the one hand - to sensory, ergonomic, cognitive, and cultural differences between canines and humans, and - on the other hand - to the difficulty of relying on verbal communication, so often relied upon by interaction designers. Recently researchers have begun to explore the possibility of adapting HCI research methodologies which combine verbal communication with observational techniques [14,33]. However, this work is yet to be concretely applied in the context of specific interaction design projects for and with animals. Thus here we explore how existing HCI verbal and nonverbal methodologies such as multispecies ethnography and iterative dynamic prototyping, combined with ethologically informed behavioural observation, can be concretely applied to develop specific user-centred interface designs for assisting the work of DADs.

The contribution of this paper is therefore twofold: 1) we acknowledge DADs as a specific user group and explore ways of eliciting their unique requirements and integrating their input in the design process, in order to prototype and evaluate a range of interfaces for a canine alert system; 2) we identify a number of design and methodological implications for the development of user-centred canine interfaces, thus contributing to the development of ACI as a research area.

SCENARIO

Dan has Type 1 diabetes and lives in fear of hypoglycaemia. Like approximately 25% of diabetic patients [3], he has developed 'unawareness' over the years and cannot tell when he is going hypo. Dan's dog, Buddy, is trained to alert hypoglycaemia in Dan by nudging him persistently until Dan acknowledges him and goes to test his blood sugar levels. Many times, Buddy's alerts have prevented Dan from undergoing a full-on hypoglycaemic attack, allowing him to restore his blood sugar with food or drink before it becomes dangerously low. Dan feels lucky to have an alert dog by his side; knowing his dog will alert him has dramatically improved his quality of life.

Scenario A

One day, Dan's partner is out and he is home alone. Buddy smells Dan's blood sugar dropping and gives him an alert by persistently nudging Dan. However, Dan's levels have dropped so quickly that he has already become unaware of his surroundings. Buddy can tell that Dan is going hypo and continues nudging and pawing at him. Buddy even brings Dan his blood testing kit, as he is trained to do when his persistent nudging does not work. However, it is too late: Dan has slipped into a coma. Buddy paces back and forth, distressed that Dan is unresponsive. He knows his owner is in trouble but there is no one else in the house he can alert; he is now powerless at his owner's side.

Scenario B

When Dan, at home alone with Buddy, starts having a hypoglycaemic attack, Buddy knows how to use his special alert system to remotely contact Dan's partner and./or other friends or family, as soon as Dan has become unconscious. Unless Dan is conscious and intentionally stops the alert by typing in an override code, the system is preconfigured to send an SMS to relevant people, who are prompted them to call him and to call emergency services if he doesn't answer. If none of them responds within a set time, the system calls emergency services directly with GPS coordinates of Dan's house. Buddy paces worriedly for a few minutes, but then help arrives. Dan's chances of avoiding brain or heart damage, or even death, have just skyrocketed and Buddy has been spared hours of stress.

What would the part of the system that Buddy uses look like? How would Buddy engage with it? How would his sensorial, ergonomic, cognitive and cultural characteristics, together with the characteristics of the tasks and his working environment, inform the interface design for such a canine alarm? And, critically, how would the researchers developing such a system figure out what kind of interface Buddy might want to do his job? In order to address these questions, we conducted ethnographic research at the UK's leading DAD training center. Working alongside dogs and their trainers, we explores ways of uncovering requirements of such an alarm by involving the dogs themselves in the design process. We took part in training practices to learn how trainers communicate with the dogs; interviewed human-dog partnerships to understand their needs; and engaged in rapid prototyping sessions with the dogs to identify their preferences.

RELATED WORK

Alarm systems

Care home alarm systems and pervasive care monitors [16,27] have been developed to enable vulnerable (e.g. older or less-abled) people to remotely call for help. These systems have been found to provide peace of mind and improve quality of life for those who actively choose to use such systems [1]. Many types of alarm are available, examples including tethered hanging pull-cord alarms, wearable alarms triggered by either intentionally pressing a button, or magnetic quick-release alarms that clip on to clothing and are triggered upon a fall or sudden movement. Although there are anecdotes of dogs being trained to hit an emergency button on a phone, existing alarm systems are not designed for canine use and pose major usability challenges for users with the ergonomic and cognitive characteristics of a dog. This lack of canine usability means that dogs are unable to become proficient in their use and thus cannot be expected to use such systems reliably, particularly at critical times.

Technologies for Working Dogs

However, the development of technology to enhance canine performance in specific tasks is not unprecedented. For example, military researchers have created wearable haptic systems to remotely communicate with and control dogs employed in explosive-sniffing operations. Researchers at Auburn University also developed a similar canine interface allowing a handler to remotely communicate with and maneuver their dog through vibration and sound feedback [4] through impervious terrain during search and rescue operations. Both of these systems place the dog in a reactive position, as though they were part of the operational apparatus, rather than allowing them to proactively use the technology to carry out a task or communicate with their human partner.

In contrast, the Georgia Tech FIDO (Facilitating Interactions for Dogs with Occupations) project aims to support communication between dogs and their handlers. The authors have developed a wearable device which allows dogs to remotely signal to their handlers via a tangible interface attached to a vest worn by the dog [9]. Here the dog takes an active role in deciding whether to engage with the technology. However, in this work the exploration of the design problem space from the perspective of canine usability or user experience is limited to a brief discussion of canine physiological characteristics; moreover it is unclear what role canine users might have had in the design process. With such canine technologies being developed, there is a need to pointedly consider the design process to ensure that the dog's requirements as a user are met. This is important to ensure that the technology appropriately supports canine workers while safeguarding their welfare. Although momentum in designing for dogs is growing, appropriate design protocols still need to be developed.

Animal-Computer Interaction

Animal-Computer Interaction is about researching and designing user-centered technology for and with animals [13,15]. In this regards, there is a growing interest among researchers to develop methodological approaches and protocols to enable nonhuman users, such as working dogs, to participate in the process as design contributors. In relation to canine workers, Helton [7] highlighted how studying their working behavior could help develop technologies to assist them in their tasks. Indeed, Resner's early proposal of a canine-centered design framework [22] carefully considered canine physiological and behavioral characteristics, as well as communication and interaction patterns between humans and dogs. More recently, Wingrave *et al.* [35]'s Canine Amusement and Training game for dogs and their owners, was also directly informed by canine behavioral patterns, partly thanks to the collaboration of an expert dog trainer with the development team. While the needs of the canine users and their humans are clearly taken into account, this research does not question how the dogs themselves might be allowed to take part in the development process.

Recent work in multispecies ethnography [32,14] investigated how the use of wearable canine tracking technology influences the interactional dynamics between dogs and humans. In particular Mancini *et al.* [14] explored the mechanisms by which both parties might make sense of the technology and by which the technology might change them and their relationship. To try and understand what the perspective of the dogs on the technology might be, the authors' methodological framework combines canine behavioral observations informed by ethological expertise and ethnographic accounts from dog owners or handlers who have familiarity with individual dogs. Here we are interested in exploring how such an approach could be applied within the context of specific interaction design projects.

Westerlaken and Gualemi [33] proposed the use of biosensors embedded in the animal's surroundings to measure their vital signs and make ethnographic observations more objective. Although such measures might complement behavioral observations, their interpretation is non-trivial, particularly in relation to an animal's experiences [26]. Measuring biometric parameters more directly indicative of experiential states (e.g. EEG, EMG) still requires the use of wearable equipment sufficiently obtrusive to interfere with measuring. On the other hand, the use of non-obtrusive ambient sensors to measure other parameters requires infrastructures which may be difficult to set-up in field settings, where ethnographic research typically takes place. Therefore, at least for now, ethologically informed observation of the animal's spontaneous behavior and responses to technological artifacts within specific interactional contexts remains the most viable way of enabling animals to participate in the design process.

For example, Lee *et al.* [11] employ preference testing techniques developed within animal welfare science to evaluate their haptic wearable human-poultry interface for remote tactile interaction from the animal's perspective. The authors allow their animal participants to choose between different options and measure the strength of their preference based on the animals' behavior. With this in mind, our research takes a multispecies ethnographic approach which combines ethnographic accounts from expert dog trainers or assisted owners with direct behavioral observation within specific interactional contexts.

FIELD STUDIES

We conducted our research at a leading DAD training facility, with the active co-operation of the trainers, clients (who have already been or are waiting to be paired with a dog) and dogs who frequent the facility. Our research aimed at identifying requirements for designing the canine interface of a remote alert system. Consistent with our methodological approach, our fieldwork was organized in three subsequent phases aimed at progressively uncovering requirements for a technology that would enable DADs to remotely summon help for their assisted humans. A key aim of our fieldwork was to identify ways of enabling the dogs themselves to participate in the requirement elicitation process as design contributors. The fieldwork phases were as follows:

1. To begin with our aim was gaining an in-depth understanding of the problem space, and existing practices both in terms of ongoing pre-placement training and in terms of relationship between dog and their assisted human. To achieve this, we spent two full working weeks at the training facility collecting qualitative data about the working environment, daily activities of dogs and humans, and working challenges faced by both. For this phase of the research we gathered field notes, audio and video recordings; and to develop an awareness of the challenges involved we actively took part in training activities by assisting the trainers with various tasks. We relied on these trainers as intermediaries between us and the dogs, and as interpreters of the canine behavior and body language we observed during our time there. Although we did reference canine behavior resources for our own background knowledge, in general we viewed our role in the design space as interaction designers and depended on trainers, handlers, owners, and puppy socializers as the source of knowledge specifically relevant to that particular context. This initial work enabled us to hypothesize design opportunities for potential technological interventions.

2. Next our aim was investigating how the opportunities previously identified could be turned into concrete designs to meet the specific needs of individual dog-human pairs. In particular, in this phase we worked closely with two pairs who were visiting the research facility for a week for training purposes. We spent the week learning more about the health, daily habits and activities, and shared history of the human and canine partners, and directly observing their interactional dynamics both ordinarily and specifically during alerting episodes. We conducted semi-structured interviews with the two clients, and observed both clients and dogs, gathering data in the form of field notes, as well as audio and video. In this phase we did not actively take part in training activities in order not to interfere with the delicate interactional dynamics between the members of established partnerships. The outcome of this phase was the identification of possible features (e.g. shapes, sizes, materials, weight, location, interaction mechanisms) for a canine alarm system.

3. Findings from the previous phase informed the design of a range of prototype canine interfaces for an alert system, which were presented to two dogs (one from the human-canine pair we had worked with and one in early training) in order to explore their requirements. We were seeking to understand the dogs' responses to different components of the interfaces, particularly the mechanism through which the dog would trigger the alarm. We spent several hours, distributed over a period of two weeks, training the dogs to engage with our prototypes, video recording these interactions. Later, we reviewed the video footage together with the trainers to discuss the canine body language. These observations gave us insight into what design features would be appropriate for individual canine users from an ergonomic and cognitive perspective. Through their direct engagement with the prototypes, the dogs gave us an indication of what they might *want* from such an interface.

FINDINGS

Here we show how our findings contributed to our understanding of the design space, the needs of both members of these human-canine partnerships, and how the dogs' participation might inform the design of a canine interface of a remote alarm system.

Understanding the design space

During our initial fieldwork, we studied the daily routine training and social interactions of dogs, trainers, and other personnel at the facility. We specifically aimed to uncover particular challenges the dogs and their assisted humans might face, and whether there might be potential for a technological intervention that could assist the dogs in their work. We wanted to find out what goes in to training these dogs in the first place, and how they alert their humans when they detect dangerously low or high blood glucose levels.

We observed that all dogs at the facility, like many scent detection dogs, undergo "clicker" training. A clicker is an instrument that makes a distinct clicking sound every time a trainer presses it. It is used to reinforce a desired behavior and is one way in which trainers communicate with the dogs during training sessions. At this facility, clicker training follows the popular Pryor framework [21]. Initially, dogs are taught to associate clicking with a reward (usually treats). As their training progresses, the dogs learn to interpret the sound of the click to mean "*Yes! Keep doing that!*" or "*yes! Do that again!*", which thus guides their behavior. In this way, we observed 'conversations' between dogs and their handlers, where the dog was trying to guess the behavior that would result in a click and the trainer would have to be careful to click the exact moment the dog performed the desired action. DAD trainers use this method to teach a dog to distinguish the smell of low blood sugar in a sweat or breath sample (at first in generic biological samples, later in samples from the specific human with whom they have been paired).

If clicker training is done in small enough intervals of behavioral change on the dog's part (e.g. first just glancing at an object, then holding the glance for a few seconds), it can be used to teach behavior that would be very unlikely for the animal to do spontaneously (e.g. staring intently at an object for several seconds, which is how some dogs learn to alert). The following extract from a training session with a young scent detection dog in training, a male black Labrador "D1", illustrates the back-and-forth dynamic nature of clicker training in this context. Here, D1 is at his very early stages of doing click work on scent discrimination and is working with two trainers (T1 and T2) who are co-operating to interpret his performance:

> The dog approaches the first of two lined-up small plastic pots, each of which contains a biological sample with the scent he is learning to recognize. He sniffs the pot and gets a click for this. Out of the dog's sight, the pots are then

switched but he approaches the first pot again (which now contains a sample with an irrelevant scent). T1 mentions that D1 is signaling based on a prediction of the trainers' behavior (i.e. that they will always place the relevant sample in the first pot), as opposed to actually signaling because he is smelling the target sample.

In response to this, T1 replaces the pot with a target, and this time, even though D1 noses the target several times, T1 refrains from clicking until D1 has 'held' his attention (nose to the pot) a bit longer than before. Then D1 gets clicked for just examining the pot, with T1 commenting:

T1: "There was a big blow out, then, on the inhalation and exhalation".

T2: "Yes, I saw".

To extinguish the undesirable 'guessing' behavior, D1 is then presented again with an irrelevant sample and T1 tells him that he is a 'good boy' for paying attention to the sample a fraction of a second less. Then the pots are switched again so that the first pot now contains again the target sample. D1 sniffs the pot but T1 waits until he sniffs it again, this time longer, before clicking.

T1: "I'm looking for a difference of behavior [the extension of him staying with the sample versus looking at the (doggie treat) pouch]".

T2: "Yes that makes sense. You want him to show slightly more attention to the scent sample itself before he looks at you expecting his treat- got it."

The next time D1 is presented with a blank he gives it a quick sniff and immediately looks towards T1's pouch, and he is told 'yes' and gets a treat. This happens two times in a row. Next he is presented with target and gives it a distinct sniff, holding his attention half a second longer than the he had for the blank, and immediately gets a click. T1: *"I'm looking for a difference of behavior* [the extension of him staying with the sample versus looking at the (doggie treat) pouch]*".*

T2: *"Yes that makes sense. You want him to show slightly more attention to the scent sample itself before he looks at you expecting his treat- got it."*

The next time D3 is presented with a blank he gives it a quick sniff and immediately looks towards T1's pouch, and he is told 'yes' and gets a treat. This happens two times in a row. Next he is presented with target and gives it a distinct sniff, holding his attention half a second longer than the he had for the blank, and immediately gets a click.

During training sessions like the one above, we noticed that the trainers maintained a continuous dialogue between themselves, checking how the other was interpreting the situation, or getting the other's feedback. Similar to the "talk aloud" technique used in HCI studies, this dynamic verbal collaboration is standard practice for these particular trainers and provided us with a real-time verbal guide to canine body language and allowed us to pick up on some of the subtleties of the training process that we might otherwise have missed. This, in turn, allowed us to identify and later discuss certain requirements with a better understanding (for example, the need to reinforce behavior on discrete actions).

Once the dog has learned to distinguish a particular smell, trainers are able to get the dog to alert when the smell becomes present. We noticed that different dogs alert in different ways. Some alerts are passive, such as a dog sitting by its owner and staring at them in an intent manner. Others are aggressive, where the dog physically jumps on, pulls the clothing of, or nudges the owner until they have their attention. We learnt that dogs are often taught an escalation process, so many dogs will begin with a passive alert and get progressively more aggressive until they perceive that their human has acknowledged their alert. Once they have acknowledged the alert verbally, the human then checks their blood glucose to determine if the dog is alerting correctly. If the blood test confirms that the alert is correct, the dog gets praise and a reward (e.g. a treat, attention, play time).

One recurrent theme we identified was the problem of reliability in recognizing the dogs' alerts. Occasionally, a dog's owner could not distinguish between when the dog was alerting and when the dog was merely spontaneously performing a similar behavior. To address this issue, the practice of teaching the dog to retrieve a particular object, called a bringsel, is becoming popular (see Figure 1). A bringsel is a distinct tube or "U" shaped object that usually hangs from a dog's collar and that the dog uses only in specific circumstances. The concept originated from search and rescue dogs, who were trained to only take the bringsel in their mouth when they had found a missing or injured person. Holding the bringsel in their mouth would therefore unambiguously signal that the dog had found something, thus the handler would be sure of what the dog meant.

Figure 1. DAD in training dog holding a bringsel in the typical gesture made to communicate to his handler.

Due to the difficulties posed by the training process based on long-term conditioning and associations, we realized that an alarm system should be integrated within existing practices, for example, by embedding new functionalities within objects, such as bringsels, which are already in use.

Understanding the partnership's needs

To understand the needs of the users of our prospective alarm system, we worked closely with two clients of the training organization who were visiting the research facility to participate in training sessions with their respective dogs and who had expressed interest in integrating a remote call emergency alarm system into their lives. The first pair was an established partnership, whereas the second pair was a newly formed partnership doing their initial training exercises as a team. Additionally, we interviewed trainers and staff about their overall client demographics, and discussed examples of challenges that many of their clients face related to hypoglycemia alerts. Here we report our findings in relation to one of the pairs we worked with.

The pair included an adult female, C1 with Type 1 Diabetes with a long established partnership with her dog, D1, a male Labrador. C1 had impaired awareness, thus could not always notice signs of impending hypoglycemia. Thus her dog's warnings were especially important to her as they could make the difference between her falling into coma or not. Furthermore, C1 lived in a flat alone with her alert dog, so if she did slip into a coma, no one would be there to call for help, which made prevention critically important. At the beginning of her visit to the facility, C1 reported that she was not sure whether her dog was always alerting accurately. In response to her concern, the training team at the facility observed the dog's behavior throughout the week finding that the dog was alerting consistently correctly, however it was the client who did not always notice her own hypoglycemic episodes since she was already experiencing impaired awareness as a result of her dropping blood glucose levels. Indeed the dog appeared to be highly attuned to the client, frequently looking in her direction or walking over to her and visibly sniffing the air with his nose. Even when the dog was outside playing with other dogs, he would run back every few minutes unprompted, sniff the air around the client, then return to playing. On several occasions the dog was observed getting up close to her face to sniff. Trainers mentioned that while most dogs check on their human periodically, this dog was especially vigilant about checking on his human, and that their strong partnership and bond was clear.

In discussions with the client, we learned that when she did miss her dog's alert and slipped into hypoglycemic coma, the moment she woke up the dog was always right by her side or face, staring at her worriedly. At times the client also would wake up with bruises on her arm that appear to be from the dog nudging and pawing her, presumably trying to wake her up. Medical response teams have also reported that when they found the client unconscious, they also found the dog lying by her side. From this information, the trainers thought that D1 makes an extended effort to wake his owner up and then does not leave her side until she either wakes up on her own or someone arrives to help. In the subsequent phase of our study we realized how D1's attachment to his owner and his unwillingness to leave her side during a hypoglycemic episode would have a drastic influence on the design of the alarm system.

On her part, C1 was used to spending time alone both in and outside her home, for example driving or going on long walks. She therefore felt that the system should be wearable, and specifically requested that such a device would be lightweight and as small as possible. However, such a human requirement was at odds with canine ergonomics, for which a larger and heavier interface would be more appropriate. While for a human a small and lightweight wearable (and perhaps not too eye-catching in order not to attract unwanted attention) interface might be ideal, a dog would have a hard time engaging with such a device: dogs do not have the dexterity of humans and, for example, it is notoriously difficult to train dogs who assist people with disabilities to operate small, fiddly devices such as light switches. Therefore we realized that the design of the canine interface would have to somehow accommodate apparently diverging requirements.

Additionally, as mentioned above, many dogs tend to have a preference for manipulating objects and exploring their surroundings with their mouth, thus a canine interface is likely to need to be 'mouthable' or perhaps, more specifically, 'bitable'. This made us realize that the part of the device intended for the dog to interact with should not contain any electronic components, as these might not withstand the pressure of a dog's bite.

Understanding the dogs' responses

Since our goal was to see how they responded to various design ideas, in designing initial prototypes, we took into account the fact that we would need to test a variety of prototype features with the dogs. To facilitate this, we designed the prototypes modularly, in order for each functional component to be interchangeable with equivalent alternatives. By creating prototypes made of interchangeable components, on a base that could easily be attached to a support (e.g. a wall, someone's belt loop), we aimed to achieve flexibility in the testing process to make the most of our training sessions and limited time with the canine participants. We developed a system with the following three components (shown in Figure 2):

Base: Physically representing a space that could hold eventual electrical components; a 'dummy' of lightweight wood was used. All prototypes had wooden bases with rounded corners for safety and to minimize catching.

Trigger: The electric switch mechanism that will serve to trigger the emergency alarm software. We looked at three different types: a co-called kill switch that triggers upon separation of the two components; a magnetic (reed) switch that triggers upon separation of two components; and a pull-cord switch, that triggers when enough pressure is applied to release the switch.

Bringsel: The 'tuggy' part for the dog to actually take in its mouth and pull on, to trigger the alarm call. This is the one part of the system that the dog directly manipulates to interact with the system.

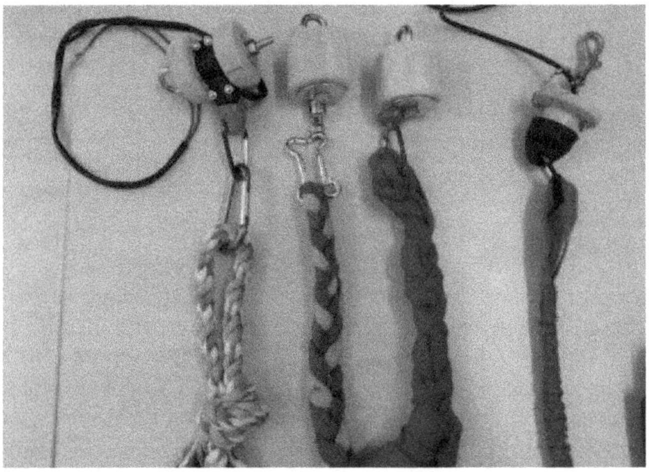

Figure 2. Physical prototypes used during testing, consisting of wooden base, trigger mechanism, and bringsel, or 'tuggy 'part for the dog to interact with.

During testing, much of our focus was on the ergonomic experiences associated with a range of trigger mechanisms. For example, the strength required for the pulling action, the tactile sensation when pulling, the sound produced by the triggering mechanism, the smell of the materials and other physical stimuli. Specific trigger mechanisms we used include:

• A pull-cord switch (much like those used for pulling a cord to turn on and off a light). This switch made a distinct 'clicky' sound and offered resistance to traction.

• Quick-release "kill" switch, such as those used on motorboats, which attach to the boat operator so that if the operator falls overboard the engine immediately stops. This switch provides little resistance, is lightweight, makes no sound and appears to simply pop off.

• Quick-release magnet, such as those used in care homes for quick-pull alarms. This switch offers more resistance and is considerably harder to pull off.

Testing

Two dogs, D1 and D2, engaged with testing the prototypes. D1 was a certified dog from the partnership referenced above, whereas D2 was another working dog at the facility trained to alert for different scent detection. D1 learned the verbal command to 'pull tuggy' within one training session. He engaged with a hanging pull-cord tuggy that was modeled after the ones already installed in his owner's care home. Initially, the dog was instructed to go 'pull tuggy'; upon which he would take the bringsel part of the prototype in his mouth and pull, producing a click and causing the tuggy to detach. Once he learned this command, the command was paired with a specific behavior on the part of the client (i.e. the client C1 mocking a collapse). D1 quickly associated this behavior with having to go over to the tuggy and pull on it, then bringing it back to C1, who was still laying on the ground. We noted that the trainers expressed interest in taking advantage of the built-in click of one of the prototypes, and of the detaching aspect of all of the prototypes, as a distinct event which could be reinforced in training. In this respect, the system needs to offer the dog two forms of feedback: one is to do with reinforcing the trained behavior and one is to do with informing the dog that he has successfully engaged with the device. The former is a training requirement whereas the latter is an interaction design requirement. In interaction design, it is essential that the system provides feedback to let the user know it has completed an action. We have considered using a clicking noise for this purpose given that it is a sound that the dogs are already familiar with from training reinforcement; however, other noises or feedback mechanisms could be explored instead to avoid possible confusion for the dog. For example, from our initial testing it appears that detachment of the mechanism might be promising. In one instance, when D1 was presented with a detaching prototype with no click, the detaching mechanism failed to work and he could not get it to detach. Rather than give up, the dog continued to pull until he broke the base of the prototype; it appeared that he was waiting for some feedback (either a click or a detachment or both), and continued pulling until this happened (see Figure 3).

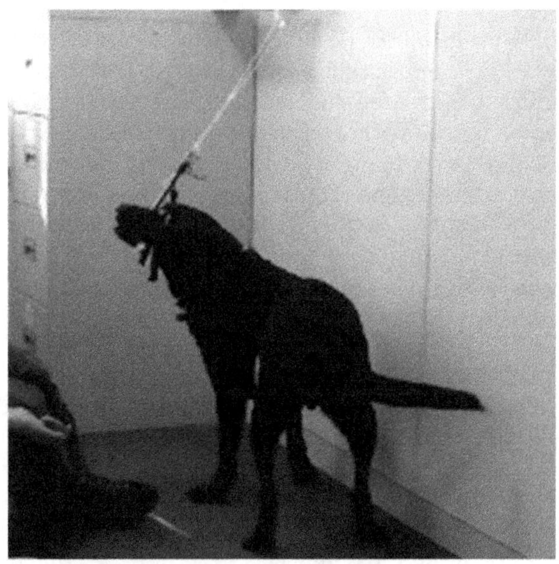

Figure 3. Still image from video showing D1 pulling on the 'tuggy' to trigger the interface mechanism. Here the wooden base is attached to the wall.

Initially, C1 and D1 were in close proximity (approximately 3 feet) from the alarm prototype. However, in real-life circumstances, a client might be anywhere in their home when they experience an attack. To explore this, in subsequent sessions, C1 'collapsed' farther and farther from the prototype, until she was behind a corner. At this point, D1 would no longer engage with the prototype. His walking slowed and he gave hesitant body language, staying by the 'collapsed' client rather than walking away from her. In subsequent sessions where the client was again in eyesight of the prototype, D1 again engaged with it. We concluded that a requirement for this particular dog, is that the device must not be out of the line of sight of his owner when she collapses. We concluded that the dog wanted to be able to keep an eye on his owner as he was used to watching her, while waiting for help or for her to wake up, and leaving her out of his sight even for a moment to engage with the prototype was not something he was willing to do. This further reinforced our observation, in the previous section, that the device needed to have some level of portability, even if the client was only to use it within their home.

In evaluating our prototype with magnetic detachment trigger, we noticed that magnets were useful for their level of customizability with regards to the amount of pressure necessary to cause detachment (e.g. for stronger or more forceful dogs, stronger magnets could be used). However, we observed that the prototypes that use magnets to detach had the side effect of being attracted to nearby metal objects, such as filing cabinets. For example, in an instance where D2 was walking by a filing cabinet carrying in his mouth a bringsel with a magnet mechanism in his mouth, the bringsel was pulled towards the cabinet, much to the confusion of D2. Further consideration and testing will be needed to address these types of issues (e.g. the use of electromagnets could be explored).

Overall, we identified positive and negative aspects for each type of trigger mechanism. Moving forward, design solutions might need to combine different solutions for different functions. For example, it may be necessary to simultaneously employ a separate detachment mechanism to give unambiguous feedback to the dog (as with the magnet solution) with a reliable trigger mechanism to activate the alarm (as with the pull-cord solution), allowing for greater flexibility when designing and when integrating a design into homes with existing alarms (e.g. pull-cord).

DISCUSSION

Our study has shown how a methodology involving dogs, their handlers and their trainers in a multi-species ethnographic approach results in an in-depth understanding of the problem space we are designing for: supporting the work of DADs. In particular, our study has uncovered a number of specific requirements to form part of the design of a canine centered interface for an alarm system for DADs. By working on a specific project this work raises important questions about what it means to be designing for and with canine users.

Designing for Multi-Species Partnerships

Our findings highlight that designing for assistance dogs means designing for a human-canine intimate partnership as a unit. Although this is a symbiotic partnership, each member within it has their individual user requirements between which there may be tensions (e.g. the human's requirement to wear something small and unobtrusive vs the dog's requirement to interact with something 'grabbable' and 'mouthable'). Therefore designing for such multispecies partnerships is a mediation process similar to that which would be undertaken in any interaction design project aiming at developing human technology with stakeholders who have diverging requirements.

These human-canine partnerships share practices to support unambiguous communication between the two (e.g. the use of the bringsel) and we have seen how it is important not to alter such practices in order not to confuse the dog thus compromising their alerting performance, particularly in critical situations. Therefore any technological intervention aiming at supporting the alerting work of the dog needs to be embedded in existing practices and the tools utilized within them (e.g. by developing something similar to a technologically enhanced bringsel). This is indeed consistent with findings from research about the adoption of human alert systems.

Designing for Canine Users

When designing for canine users we need to be aware of their specific needs and capabilities as users. Dogs from different breeds may have different physical (e.g. size) and behavioral (e.g. tendency to bite, tug or nudge; levels of concentration) characteristics for which different artefacts may be more or less suitable. Indeed, when describing the development of a technologically enhanced wearable jacket to aid communication between humans and dogs, Jackson *et al.* [9] emphasize the need to adjust the positioning of sensors on the body of the canine users, to different canine body types.

However, beyond physical and behavioral characteristics immediately associated with breeds and types of dog, our research has highlighted the need to be sensitive to the individual characteristics of the canine user, as shaped by their personality, training and history (e.g. anxieties, likes, dislikes). We have seen that the needs of a dog who has been with his human handler for several years, and who has experienced many problematic hypo attacks, may require a design that is specifically attuned to his anxiety. We argue that designers need to be prepared to listen out for these specific, more subtle requirements, and engage with the dogs as individuals with their particular personalities and stories, in order for a better informed design to emerge.

From designing for to designing with

As we have seen, user-centered design means going beyond just accounting for the physiological or even cognitive characteristics of specific user groups to try and understand the subtleties that make up the individuality of real users and their lives. Participatory Design [24] moves from the assumption that this cannot be achieved without the active participation of the users, that is without bringing users into the *conversation of the design process* But what language should designers use to have a design conversation with dogs?

We have found that rough, interchangeable, thus easily modified prototypes could act as catalysts of such a conversation by enabling us and the dogs to engage in a rapid exchange of stimuli and responses. Indeed, van der Linden *et al.* [30] found that the use of physical prototyping can help both designers and users explore novel interactions which would otherwise be difficult to grasp even when designing with humans. Here it is important to emphasize the possibility of quickly and easily changing the physical prototypes in response to the dog's reactions, in order to maintain the *flow of the conversation*. For example, we have seen how D1 did not appear to fully engage with the prototype until we identified the point at which the detachment mechanism of the prototype offered him enough resistance. We therefore propose the use of *rapid physical prototyping* to enable nonhuman users such as dogs to actively participate in the conversation of the design process. But how can designers interpret the dogs' responses in order to gradually achieve the design that the dogs might want?

Stamp Dawkins [25] proposes the use of behavioral observation as a way of assessing what an animal wants. She argues that understanding what an animal wants is not about interpreting their subjective experience but rather acknowledging what they require based on specific evolutionary adaptations. Perhaps the same might be said of adaptations the animal has developed through training or life experiences which result in the animal demonstrating individual propensities or which a design needs to account for. These adaptations and propensities might express themselves through: readiness in engaging with an artifact or in grasping its functionalities (e.g. being mouthy and pulling hanging objects); repeating interactional patterns in an attempt to complete an action (e.g. pulling repeatedly a cord until a cord breaks); positioning within a space (e.g. sitting next to the collapsed human and refusing to leave their side). We propose that future work in ACI focuses on exploring, articulating and validating such patterns.

CONCLUSION

Using a multi-species ethnographic approach we conducted a field study over three phases working with assistance dogs, their handlers and trainers towards a canine-centered interface design for a Diabetes Alert system. The field study uncovered a number of requirements for such a system, some specifically relevant to the human handler, and others of particular relevance to the canine user. Indeed our investigation showed that we are effectively designing for the human-canine partnership as a unit, which - though intimately symbiotic - may place conflicting individual demands on the design. We also argued that, while it is important that the design process takes on board the specific canine user needs and capabilities, it is now time for researchers to look beyond characteristics directly related to the breed and type of dog. Instead researchers should be prepared to delve into the intricacies of an individual dog's life, their unique personal history, their foibles, and particular likes and dislikes, in order to move towards better informed designs. Whilst this research has focused on the specific example of canine users assisting human users with Diabetes, we anticipate that the methodological approach, and possibly some of the requirements, will be relevant to other assistive partnerships between human and canine users. Through the process of *rapid physical prototyping* sessions, combined with behavioral observation, our research approach critically questions and reflects upon the way in which dogs can participate in iterative interaction design processes. Our research thereby seeks to address the core questions of what it means to design with animals as a part of ACI's wider research agenda to widening participation with non-human users.

ACKNOWLEDGMENTS

The authors are grateful to Daniel Mills for his support and also to the staff and clients (both human and canine) of Medical Detection Dogs, Milton Keynes, UK.

REFERENCES

1. Alwan, M., Dalal, S., Mack, D., Kell, S., Turner, B., Leachtenauer, J., & Felder, R. (2006). Impact of monitoring technology in assisted living: outcome pilot. Information Technology in Biomedicine, *IEEE Transactions* on, 10(1), 192-198.
2. Bergenstal, R. M *et al.* (2010). Effectiveness of sensor-augmented insulin-pump therapy in type 1 diabetes. *New England Journal of Medicine*, 363(4), 311-320.
3. Bilous, R., Donnelly, R. (2010) *Handbook of Diabetes*. 4th Edition. John Wiley & Sons Ltd., Chichester, 96–97.
4. Britt, W. R., Miller, J., Waggoner, P., Bevly, D. M., & Hamilton Jr, J. A. (2011). An embedded system for real-time navigation and remote command of a trained canine. *Personal and Ubiquitous Computing*, 15(1), 61-74.
5. Chen, M., Daly, M., Williams, N., Williams, S., Williams, C., & Williams, G. (2000). Non-invasive detection of hypoglycaemia using a novel, fully biocompatible and patient friendly alarm system. BMJ: *British Medical Journal*, 321(7276), 1565.
6. Corstjens, A. M., Ligtenberg, J. J., van der Horst, I. C., Spanjersberg, R., Lind, J. S., Tulleken, J. E., Meertens, J., & Zijlstra, J. G. (2006). Accuracy and feasibility of point-of-care and continuous blood glucose analysis in critically ill ICU patients. *Critical Care*, 10(5), R135.
7. Helton, W. S. (2009). Overview of Scent Detection Work. *Canine Ergonomics: The Science of Working Dogs*, 83.
8. iPetCompanion; ipetcompanion.com/
9. Jackson, M. M., Zeagler, C., Valentin, G., Martin, A., Martin, V., Delawalla, A., Blount, W., Eiring, S., Hollis, R., & Starner, T. (2013). FIDO-facilitating interactions for dogs with occupations: wearable dog-activated interfaces. *In Proceedings of the 17th annual*

international symposium on International symposium on wearable computers (pp. 81-88). ACM.

10. Joseph, J. I., Hipszer, B., Mraovic, B., Chervoneva, I., Joseph, M., & Grunwald, Z. (2009). Challenges in Glycemic Control in Perioperative and Critically Ill Patients: Clinical Need for Continuous Glucose Monitoring in the Hospital. *Journal of diabetes science and technology*, 3(6), 1309.
11. Lee, P., Cheok, D., James, S., Debra, L., Jie, W., Chuang, W., & Farbiz, F. (2006). A mobile pet wearable computer and mixed reality system for human–poultry interaction through the internet. *Personal and Ubiquitous Computing*, 10(5), 301-317.
12. Loc8tor Pet: loc8tor.com/uk/pets/
13. Mancini, C. (2011). Animal-computer interaction: a manifesto. *Interactions*, 18(4), 69-73.
14. Mancini, C., van der Linden, J., Bryan, J., & Stuart, A. (2012). Exploring interspecies sensemaking: dog tracking semiotics and multispecies ethnography. Proceedings ACM UbiComp, 143-152.
15. Mancini, C. (2013). Animal-computer interaction (ACI): changing perspective on HCI, participation and sustainability. In ACM CHI'13 EA, 2227-2236.
16. Miskelly, F. G. (2001). Assistive technology in elderly care. *Age and ageing*, 30(6), 455-458.
17. PawTrax: pawtrax.co.uk/
18. PetCube: petcube.net
19. Pet Doorbell Mat: petdoorbellmat.net
20. PintoFeed Intelligent PetFeeder: pintofeed.com/
21. Pryor, K. (2002). *Clicker training for dogs*. Ringpress.
22. Resner, B.I. (2001). Rover@Home: Computer Mediated Remote Interaction for Dogs. Media Arts and Sciences MS, Cambridge, Massachusetts Institute of Technology.
23. Rooney, N. J., Morant, S., & Guest, C. (2013). Investigation into the Value of Trained Glycaemia Alert Dogs to Clients with Type I Diabetes. *PloS One*, 8(8), e69921.
24. Schuler, D., & Namioka, A. (Eds.). (1993). *Participatory design: Principles and practices*. Routledge.
25. Shaw, J. E., Sicree, R. A., & Zimmet, P. Z. (2010). Global estimates of the prevalence of diabetes for 2010 and 2030. *Diabetes research and clinical practice*, 87(1), 4-14.
26. Stamp Dawkins, M. (2012). *Why Animals Matter: Animal Consciousness, Animal Welfare and Human Well-Being*. Oxford University Press, Oxford-NY.
27. Stanford, V. (2002). Using pervasive computing to deliver elder care. *Pervasive Computing*, IEEE, 1(1), 10-13.
28. Track My Cat: trackmycat.com/
29. Tractive: tractive.com/
30. van der Linden, J., Rogers, Y., Waights, V and Taylor, C. (2012). A blended design approach for pervasive healthcare: bringing together users, experts and technology. *Health Informatics Journal*, 18(3), 212–218.
31. van Belle, T. L., Coppieters, K. T., & Von Herrath, M. G. (2011). Type 1 diabetes: etiology, immunology, and therapeutic strategies. *Physiological reviews*, 91(1), 79-118.
32. Weilenmann, A., & Juhlin, O. (2011, May). Understanding people and animals: the use of a positioning system in ordinary human-canine interaction. *Proc. ACM CHI'11,* 2631-2640
33. Westerlaken, M., & Gualeni, S. (2013). Digitally complemented zoomorphism: a theoretical foundation for human-animal interaction design. *Proc. ACM DPPI'13*, 193-200.
34. Wells D, Lawson SW, Siriwardena N (2008) Canine responses to hypoglycaemia in patients with Type 1 diabetes. *Altern Complem Med14*: 1235–1241.
35. Wingrave, C.A., Rose, J., Langston, T., LaViola Jr, J.J. (2010). Early Explorations of CAT: Canine Amusement and Training. *In CHI 2010: Monsters Attack! Proc. CHI'10*, ACM Press, 2661-2664.

Co-constructing Child Personas for Health-Promoting Services with Vulnerable Children

Pontus Wärnestål[1, 3], Petra Svedberg[2, 3], Jens Nygren[2, 3]

[1]Halmstad University
School of Information Science
P.O. 823, Halmstad, Sweden
+46 35 16 76 96
pontus.warnestal@hh.se

[2]Halmstad University
School of Social and Health Sciences
P.O. 823, Halmstad, Sweden
+46 35 16 78 63
{petra.svedberg, jens.nygren}@hh.se

[3]The CHIPS Study Group
Halmstad University
P.O. 823, Halmstad, Sweden
chips@hh.se

ABSTRACT
The availability of health-promoting resources for young children diagnosed with cancer who are transitioning from intensive care to everyday life is limited. In the context of designing digital peer support services for children who are considered vulnerable due to clinical and age-related aspects, there are several challenges that put critical requirements on a user-centered design process. This paper reports on a new method for co-constructing child-personas that are tailored for developing health-promoting services where empirical data is restricted due to practical and ethical reasons. In particular, we are proposing to focus children design workshop sessions on salutogenesis, and complement this with a pathogenic perspective by interviewing healthcare professionals and parents. We also introduce the use of proxy personas, and redemption scenarios in the form of comicboards, both collaboratively constructed by children and designers through storytelling. By applying four progressive steps of data collection and analysis we arrive at authentic child-personas that can be used to design and develop health-promoting services for children in vulnerable life stages.

Author Keywords
Digital peer support, personas, participatory design, interaction design, user experience, social interaction, vulnerable children, methodology.

ACM Classification Keywords
H.1.2 [User/Machine Systems]: Human factors.

H.5.2 [User Interfaces]: User-Centered Design.

K.4.2 [Social Issues]: Assistive technologies for persons with disabilities.

1. INTRODUCTION
Children who are diagnosed with cancer undergo intensive and long treatments that expose them and their families to physical, mental and social challenges [12]. Thanks to advances in treatment protocols most children survive the disease and have the potential to live a long life with a quality of life comparable to their peers. Transitioning from a period of intensive treatment to everyday life results in difficulties that are unique for each individual and for which they need professional support [34]. The availability of such support is limited and resources are often offered in a hospital setting and intermittently [39]. However, this transition can be facilitated by social support mediated by peers on whom the child can rely and who share similar experiences [35]. The availability of peer support services that are not restricted by the clinical, geographical, age-related and logistic limitations of face-to-face interaction associated with this user group are, however, limited [36].

In our work, we aim at developing *digital peer support services* (DPS) directed towards children surviving from cancer in order to facilitate health-promoting social connectedness to other children with similar experiences. Development of novel resources has to involve the children themselves in the design process to allow for inclusion of their perspectives on challenges of survival and on how to integrate such services into their everyday life [9, 37]. Involving children in a user-centered design process enables designers to meet the children's worldview, their cognitive and emotional developmental stage, age and gender [32], as well as their requirements on usability and experiential quality [36]. User-involvement in a design process can be achieved through a variety of user-centered design (UCD) techniques and methods, such as cooperative and participatory design [33, 4], contextual design [3], and design based on personas [7, 30, 29, 8, 16].

In the context of designing health-promoting and social digital services for children who have survived cancer, there are several challenges that put critical requirements on a user-centered design process. First, although it is acknowledged that children have the right to be heard in matter that affects their lives, health, and care, they are often viewed as *vulnerable* subjects due to their dependence on adults. In regard to participation, it is essential to protect children from harms associated with involvement. It is of particular importance to carefully handle consent to

CHI 2014, April 26 - May 01 2014, Toronto, ON, Canada
Copyright is held by the owner/author(s). Publication rights licensed to ACM.
ACM 978-1-4503-2473-1/14/04 $15.00.
http://dx.doi.org/10.1145/2556288.2557115

participation, confidentiality, as well as research context and activities [14]. Further development and adaptation of methodology is needed to ensure that children's perspectives and rights are preserved. Second, children who have experiences from a severe disease are seen as even more vulnerable in relation to participation and therefore several gatekeepers restrict their participation. Such restrictions consist of ethical boards, healthcare professionals, parents [5], and ultimately, the children's own willingness to participate in processes designed by researchers or designers [14]. Third, the specific characteristics of this user group (e.g. age-span, medical history, geographic spread, and clinical restrictions) make it difficult to recruit, meet, and engage the children on a regular basis for long-term participatory design work. *Persona-driven* design that takes these considerations into account could be a powerful tool for user involvement in the design context outlined above.

Faced with these challenges, our research question becomes: *How can we develop high-quality, authentic personas for digital peer support service design for children who have survived cancer?* This paper describes and discusses a method for co-construction of personas with children in sensitive design contexts.

2. CHILD-CENTRIC DESIGN OF HEALTH SERVICES

A UCD approach can be viewed from several perspectives, such as practice, philosophy, framework, theory, or process. The common ground for all perspectives is heavy involvement of end-users in all phases of a design process in order to gain empathy for – and understand – the end-users' motivations, behaviors, and experience goals [38]. In our case, we discuss the UCD approach mainly from a process and practice perspective.

2.1 Ethical Considerations

Generally, children should be involved in research related to their health [37]. However, it can be difficult to recruit children for research that remind them about the difficulties they have experienced in relation to disease or treatment. Recruitment depends on both the children's own willingness to participate and the views and beliefs of gatekeepers' (i.e. parents, nurse, doctor, or the children themselves) about the children's ability to participate in the research [5]. Thus, children's own views and opinions in persona driven design can be limited by various gatekeepers that prohibit access to specific children due to ethical or clinical restrictions. In order to address this challenge, we developed an approach based on differences between a *salutogenic* orientation and a *pathogenic* orientation towards health [2]. A salutogenic orientation focuses on factors that maintain and promote health and wellbeing, whereas a pathogenic orientation focuses on factors that are related to disease and treatment. We predicted that gatekeepers would limit access to children with experience from cancer treatment in the development of a DPS. To accommodate this, we used a salutogenic orientation to incorporate aspects that are inherent to the users and their motivations, behaviors, and goals related to everyday life at home, with friends and family, and in school. We used a pathogenic orientation to incorporate stakeholders' views on the challenges and limitations related to disease and treatment that a DPS has to deal with. This study was approved by the regional ethical board (dnr 2011/307).

2.2 Methodological Considerations

The specific methodological implications for a child-centric design process in this context is that a UCD process needs to be customized to fit the design space for (a) children users, (b) the domain of health-promoting, social services, and (c) sensitive contexts. These three qualities are not explicitly addressed by generic persona-driven methods developed for adult, professional users in a productivity- or efficiency-oriented domain. The traditional principles rather regard goals such as minimizing work [8] and to increase productivity and reduce costs. For children's interaction with technology in terms of digital toys, games, and other more experience-oriented products, such as social media platforms, principles beyond productivity and effectiveness have to be acknowledged [1, 27].

The natural extension of a UCD approach for children is the emerging field of Child-Computer Interaction (CCI). CCI was early predominantly approached by adapting standard, industrial practices to child contexts, e.g. usability testing with children [19]. As the field matured, co-creative aspects have been voiced as an important part of CCI, such as Druin's work on cooperative inquiry [10, 18], and the initiatives stemming from the Scandinavian participatory design approach [32, 22]. Recently, children's participation in a UCD process have been extended to include the roles *users*, *testers*, *evaluators*, *informants*, *design partners*, and *experience design innovators* [15]. Such advances address the needs of developmental abilities of children when involving them in the design process. However, it is difficult to directly implement standard interview and participatory design techniques for young children because of difficulties with abstraction and verbalizing conceptual problem solving [1]. To address this, the persona approach has been developed and customized for specific user groups, such as child-personas [1, 27].

Along these lines, our design approach takes a user-centered, co-creative perspective, where the use of child-personas plays an important role. The design context for children who have survived cancer is of a sensitive nature, where ethical considerations need to be addressed regarding what topics can be handled during interviews and workshops in order to ensure a healthy environment for all participants [25]. This puts additional requirements on the design methodology, since the restrictions inherent in this sensitive design context limit the ways user data can be collected compared to traditional approaches.

Initiate | Design | Build | Test | Maintain

Phases	Discovery	Modeling	Ideation	Refinement	Evolution
Activities	Literature review/Audit Stakeholder interviews User interviews Co-creative workshops	Personas Scenarios Requirements	Sketching	Prototyping	Usability Testing Implementation Support Quality Assurance
Participants and Roles	Children as *informants* Children as *designers* Stakeholders as *informants*	Children as *informants* Children as *designers*	Children as *designers* Children as *innovators*	Children as *evaluators*	Children as *testers* Stakeholders as *informants*

Figure 1. Design process overview, showing phases, activities, and roles as part of larger service development process. The figure is simplified, as there are iterative overlaps between the different phases.

3. METHOD: THE DESIGN PROCESS

Figure 1 gives an overview of our design process, as part of a larger service development process, and shows the user-involvement in each phase.

The purpose of the *Discovery* phase is to assess and characterize the user group from various perspectives and establishing what their needs and behavior patterns are. Armed with data from literature, stakeholder interviews with healthcare professionals and parents, user interviews and observations, we move on to the *Modeling* phase where the collected data is interpreted and explained through models such as personas, and scenarios describing personas' end goal resolutions.

In the following, we focus on the key activities when bridging the Discovery phase with the Modeling phase in this particular context: persona co-construction for the design of health-promotion activities with, and for, children in sensitive contexts.

3.1 Focus Group Interviews

Fifteen children, 8-12 years of age, were recruited for the initial focus group interviews. Applying the strategy of approaching the children from a salutogenic orientation, we encountered no difficulties in the recruitment of children and the various gatekeepers gave access to both children and their parents for interviews and design sessions.

The children and their parents were informed both orally and in writing about the purpose, structure, and confidentiality of the study before they gave their informed consent. They were also informed that the participation was voluntary and that they could withdraw from the study at any time.

The recruited children had a cancer diagnosis and were under maintenance treatment, or in remission, at a pediatric oncology department in Sweden. The interviews explored the children's own experiences of friendship in the context of everyday life following cancer treatment to capture salutogenic perspectives on friendship. Interviews focused on children's motivations, frustrations, and behaviors in everyday life settings (e.g. home, school, and health care) by elaborating on why friends want to hang out and how friends can help or support each other, when they hang out and what they do when they are together. Focus groups were designed to meet the needs of children involved, which meant adaptation of group size (three children), composition (gender and age matched) and location (child-friendly environment selected by the families) [20, 6]. The focus groups had a semi-structured approach, with (a) an introductory icebreaking phase, (b) an interview phase, and (c) a closure phase were the conversation was rounded up and participants had the opportunity to speak up on participation. A mixture of creative techniques – including brainstorming, draw and tell, listing and open questioning – assisted the children in talking and expressing themselves [11].

The focus group content was analyzed through qualitative content analysis with an inductive approach in order to describe the phenomenon friendship in a conceptual form [24, 13, 11]. This model was central for the salutogenic focus in the continued development of stakeholder interviews and subsequent workshop sessions.

3.2 Stakeholder Interviews

An important pre-cursor to successful design is to consider stakeholder input. Stakeholders typically include business-oriented roles and subject-matter experts [16]. In our domain of (Scandinavian) healthcare, stakeholders are various healthcare professionals, parents and various roles from local childhood cancer associations.

In UCD processes, stakeholder interviews are often performed prior to user involvement. In this particular case, we knew in advance that the pathogenic perspective would be off-limits when interacting with the children, so it was important to let the children's views on the salutogenic perspectives influence the themes discussed with the stakeholders. Based on children's salutogenic descriptions of friendship and health, the stakeholder interviews could shed light on *pathogenic* aspects relevant to the development of a DPS in terms of observed experiences of disease, treatment, and difficulties in the transition to everyday life.

Stakeholders were recruited with a high-level organizational perspective. A few additional roles were identified organically, until an idea of the multiple stakeholders that exist in relation to a DPS emerged. In total, nine health care professionals were interviewed: one medical specialist/doctor, one clinic leader (doctor), one oncology nurse, two consultancy nurses, two play/occupational therapists, and one sibling supporter (nurse). We also interviewed one representative from a local childhood cancer patient association and four parents of children treated for childhood cancer. Interviews were semi-structured and scheduled one-to-one to get unfiltered perspectives on discrepancies and consistencies in opinions. Stakeholders were interviewed about the health care organization's long-term strategies, objectives, predictions, and perceived challenges and possible positive and negative effects of introducing a DPS, when and how it should be deployed in the existing health care process, and insights about the children in the DPS target group [39]. The analysis aimed at grouping associated descriptions into an affinity diagram to discover relationships among ideas and interviewee input [23]. Emerging themes were clustered based on likeness to form categories that were used to start building the experience framework for a DPS design. Categories were graphically organized and described to identify where the stakeholders interact with the end-users and when and where the end-users would most likely benefit from and use the DPS.

The stakeholder analysis provided the basis for placing the conceptual model of friendship in the context of opportunities and constraints that are associated with childhood cancer survival. It also gave valuable pointers on "wicked problems" surrounding this domain [39], such as the inherent conflict of privacy and integrity even though a DPS encourages sharing of experiences online, or the balance between encouraging outdoor physical activity for increased wellbeing potentially opposing the introduction of more "screen time" by introducing a new digital service to the children. These problem frames were useful in setting up the tasks and scenarios in the design workshops, as well as being incorporated in the resulting persona descriptions.

3.3 Design Workshops

The third step in the data collection process was to involve the children again. This time in a generative, creative set of themed design workshops, loosely corresponding to the UCD steps of persona and scenario development.

A series of three design workshops were held for two groups of children. The first group consisted of three boys aged 11-12, and the second group consisted of two girls aged 11-13. For each workshop, 3-4 adult researchers and professional designers participated (including one workshop facilitator), so that even design pairs of one child and one adult could be formed.

Each workshop session lasted three hours, including breaks. Workshop 2 and 3 started with a summary of the previous workshop, allowing children to re-visit the character descriptions from Workshop 1 and scenarios created in the Workshop 2, as well as critique and adjust the material if necessary. All sessions had different themes, and built on each other in a progressive manner. The underlying theme for all workshops was that of comics. Having a familiar, recurring theme such as comics makes the design process more understandable for the participants [25].

3.3.1 Workshop 1: Character Construction

The first session was focused on creating characters. The participants worked in pairs of one adult and one child. One researcher took the role as session facilitator with the responsibility to lead the activities and keep track of time, etc. This activity had two main purposes: First, for the participants to get to know each other, and to build trust in the pairs by creating a fictive character together. Second, to set up characters that would form the base for story creation in the subsequent workshop.

Adults and children both contributed to create one character per pair. At the end of the session the various teams' characters were presented to the whole group. Throughout the creation process, the researchers listened in on the children's reasoning about the characters' attributes, and asked follow-up questions about decisions made in the character design process.

The facilitator led the character construction process by asking questions that the children-adult teams would discuss and incorporate into their character. The battery of questions started with concrete, tangible pieces of information (such as "where does your character live?", "what family members live in his/her house?", "what is his/her name?" , and "does Jacob have any pets?"). With basic demographics in place the facilitator moved on to more value-oriented questions concerning the character's likes, dislikes, hobbies, and interests (e.g. "what does Jacob like to do after school?"). At this stage, other fictive characters in the created character's social sphere naturally began to emerge, such as best friends, siblings, sports coaches, etc. These characters were used in subsequent questions about behavior patterns and frustrations related to friendship and peer support (e.g. "what does Jacob and his best friend Stefan do when they want to have fun?", and "what does Jacob tell Stefan when he is sad?"). The latter set of the facilitator's questions was informed by the themes of friendship discovered in the focus group interview analysis (see Section 3.1), combined with themes derived from the stakeholder interview analysis (see Section 3.2). This allowed the teams to approach sensitive issues as part of the character construction. This also gave the children more control of the sensitive issues, since they could safely project them on the fictive characters, or completely ignore them if they so desired. The character sketches and supplementary data were compiled after the workshops into "proxy personas". Figure 2 shows an example of a proxy persona, presented in the form of a comicboard.

Figure 2: Part of the comicboard presentation of the proxy persona "Jacob".

3.3.2 Workshop 2: Comic Boarding

The second session was focused on creating stories around the characters from Workshop 1. After presenting the characters created in Workshop 1 to the teams, the teams were allowed to make adjustments to the characters. When the teams were happy with the characters, the story-creation process started. The stories were created as comics, roughly following [26]. The teams paired up in the same way as in the previous workshop of one adult and one child. The workshop lasted approximately three hours. In preparation for this workshop, a set of story introductions and endings featuring the created characters had been prepared (Figure 3).

The story introduction to each storyline was set a priori, and based on theories of friendship and peer support [35, 11]. The introduction was framed as a sensitive and socially

Figure 3: Sample start and end panels for redemption scenarios used in Workshop 2.

problematic situation for the character, which called for redemption. Each story had a selection of end panels that were also designed a priori. The end panels consisted of possible positive outcomes from the problem introduced, framed as a positive social interaction with e.g. a friend, peer, or family member. The task was to create redemption scenarios connecting the given starts and ends in order to get the children's perspective on how such experiences are shaped. The storylines featured several of the characters created in previous workshops. That is, the characters could all play a role in each scenario, allowing the teams to explore themes of friendship, social support, as well as covering relations to e.g. parents, teachers, and siblings. Throughout the story-creation process researchers learned about how the children reasoned regarding social interaction and peer support. In terms of design process, this step is analogous to context scenario creation [16], featuring the (proxy) personas in the form of comicboard characters.

3.3.3 Workshop 3: Design Session

The third workshop was focused on ideation, and was facilitated by a designer. The now familiar teams of one child and one adult designer and/or researcher worked on sketching solutions that would connect to the comicboard redemption scenarios from the previous workshop. However, the design solutions were allowed to stray in terms of both design and content, since the main focus was to get yet another opportunity to capture the interests and motivations from the children. Some ideas were in themselves promising design directions, whereas some ideas were naive, or highly unrealistic for implementation. However, all ideas and data were captured and discussed by all participants at the end of the session, were equally important for the Modeling phase (see Figure 1) regardless of whether they were potential design directions by themselves, or merely ideas that could be incorporated in not yet explored DPS design directions.

The first part of the workshop the teams worked with pen

Figure 4: A ten-year old girl prototyping her tablet-based Question-and-Answer video chat app.

and paper to connect ideas to the comicboard stories. In the second part the teams started building simple interactive

Steps:	1. Focus groups	2. Stakeholder interviews	3. Design workshops	4. Modeling
Types of data	• Interview transcripts • Video footage	• Interview transcripts	• Characters (proxy personas) • Redemption scenarios (comics) • Video footage	• Affinity diagrams
Findings	Conceptual descriptions of friendship.	Roles and effects of a DPS from a pathogenic perspective. "Wicked" design challenges. Onboarding and positioning of service in relation to existing healthcare processes.	Scenario insights on behaviors, attitudes, motivations regarding friendship, relations, peer support, and redemption strategies.	Categories and behavioral dimensions for boys and girls in the user group.
Progression of persona construction	Discovering central salutogenic concepts (i.e. friendship, peer support) that need stakeholder input.	Defining the context (i.e. vulnerability, friendship with peers, and surrounding environments such as hospital, home, school. Friendship cancer/disease aspects.	Building character and story: Narrative constructs based on the concept and context captured in scenarios.	Complete primary personas (Anton and Julia)

Table 1. Summary of the empirical data from the Discovery phase (steps 1-3) and the persona construction progression in the Modeling phase (step 4).

artifacts using prototyping software such as POP[1], assisted by the facilitator and present interaction designers. Figure 4 shows one of the girls prototyping an interactive question-and-answer video chat app where friends can ask the peer community for tips on any subject.

4. ANALYSIS AND INSIGHTS

For the purpose of clarity, we view the Modeling phase as a qualitative analysis of the collected data, which results in one or more models of the problem. In particular, the target models for our purposes are (a) personas, and (b) context and key-path scenarios [16] that will guide the creative work on design solutions. The use of comics naturally encouraged character creation and storytelling, which effectively facilitated the transfer of characters and stories into personas and scenarios in the post-workshop modeling steps.

To summarize, the empirical basis that feeds into the Modeling phase (see Figure 1) consists of:

- A conceptual model of friendship and peer support based on salutogenesis (from the focus group interviews).
- Pathogenic perspectives from stakeholder interviews (healthcare professionals and parents).
- Proxy personas co-created by children and designers in the workshops.
- Stories about friendship, sensitive contexts, and redemption scenarios co-created by children and designers, featuring the proxy personas.
- Initial sketches of solutions that fit the redemption comicboard stories, co-created by children and designers.
- Dialogue between children and researchers and designers captured from the three workshops.

In order to model this rich data, a qualitative analysis on the material was made. Three researchers wrote down terms that occurred in the proxy persona descriptions, and combed the comicboards for details about behaviors, motivations, goal fulfillment, technology use, social platform interaction, and channels (analog and digital). The "wicked problems" and other pathogenic input from stakeholders were then added, along with additional concepts derived from quotes from the child-researcher dialogues during the workshops. All terms were put on post-it notes and assembled on a big wall, where they were grouped based on similarity in an iterative and collaborative fashion. Each move or grouping was done with an articulated intention behind it (e.g. "*I'm moving category X to theme Y because of Z*"). This allowed clusters to emerge and form categories in an affinity diagram. In total, 40 categories were formed, and structured into eight themes. For example, the theme *Creativity* consisted of categories such as *Building*, *Drawing*, and *Taking Photos*.

[1] POP prototyping tool: http://popapp.in

Julia Hansson, 11 years old

Quote

I always got my phone with me – I have my whole life in it!

Backgrund

Julia lives with her mother and father in Eldsberga, just outside the city of Halmstad, Sweden. She does not have any siblings, but her family has got two cats.

She spends her spare time with friends and likes to go shopping. She also enjoys photographing, and sharing her photos on Instagram.

Juila thinks school is rather boring, but she knows that it is important to get good grades. The subject she likes the least is History.

Touchpoints

School

Consultancy Nurse

Childhood Cancer Foundation

Appstore/Instagram/YouTube

Family

Characteristics and feelings

High sense of duty.
Wants to excel in school.
Wants to be independent.
Creative and imaginative.
Emotionally mature.
Dares to ask for advice.

Social

Friends and family are important.
Does her homework with friends.
Keeps constant contact through her phone (SnapChat, FaceTime and Instagram).
Can sometimes feel left outside.
Wants to belong.

Behavior

Constantly checking Instagram.
Likes to document and collect things (photos, videos, accessories).
Rarely plays games on the phone.

Environments

Home.
School.
Shopping center.
At friends' houses.
In the car.
Hospital during check-ups.

Clinical

Treated for: **Leukaemia**
Diagnosed: 5 years ago (at age 6)
Discharged: 2 years ago (at age 9)
Check-ups: Annually
Everyday Effects: Scars, memories of pain and social isolation.

Frustrations

Does not like to wash dishes.
Does not want to miss school.
Feeling stressed about school.
Gets reminded of the disease by her scars.

Anton Lundberg, 10 years old

Quote

I want to be able to do the fun things: to play with my friends and build worlds in Minecraft!

Backgrund

Anton lives with his mother, father, and younger sister Alice (8 years old) in a townhouse in Halmstad, Sweden. Anton's older brother Joakim (18 years old) has moved to Lund to study.

Anton plays floor ball once a week. He enjoys playing video games in his spare time, and Skypes with his friends who play on the same server.

Anton enjoys school, but he doesn't like Math and homework. He loves going snowboarding in the mountains on the winter holiday with his family.

Touchpoints

After-school center

School

Consultancy Nurse

Childhood Cancer Foundation

Steam/Appstore/YouTube

Family

Toy store

Toy catalogue (print and online)

Characteristics and feelings

Curious.
Wants to be independent.
Creative and imaginative.
Emotionally mature.
Wants to do fun, exciting, and friendly things.
Likes surprises.

Social

Family is important.
Plays with friends at school.
Misses his brother Joakim.
Likes to set up surprises for the family.
Both plays and teases his sister Alice.

Behavior

Likes to draw.
Likes to build things (huts, lego, Minecraft, ...)
Plays online video games frequently.

Environments

Home.
After-school center
School.
The soccer field, the backyard, the forest.
The Floorball Center.
Backseat of the car.
Hospital for check-up.

Clinical

Treated for: **Leukaemia**
Discharged: 5 years ago (at the age of 5)
Check-ups: Annually
Everyday Effects: Physically healthy. No memories of disease, but suffer from mild concentration difficulties due to treatment.

Frustrations

Sometimes socially insecure (missed out on peer activities due to hospitalization).
Waiting is boring.
Wants to play, but is often tired.

Figure 5: Persona overview of Anton and Julia showing e.g. background, touchpoints, environments, behaviors, medical history, and social aspects of their lives. The shaded panels indicate categories primarily emanating from pathogenic perspectives.

Some categories contain sub-categories, which can have multiple connections. The category *Building* is for example split into *Digital Construction* (with atomic data points such as *Minecraft*[2] and *Toca Boca Builders*[3]) and *Analog Construction* (e.g. *Playing with Lego* or *Building a Treehouse*). *Minecraft* also belongs to the category *Computer Games*, in the *Consume* theme, whereas *Building a Treehouse* also belongs to the theme *Physical Outdoor Activities*.

This rich, multi-level affinity diagram forms the basis for morphing the proxy personas into authentic, high-quality personas.

It was noticed early on that certain categories were intimately tied to gender. For example, in the intersection of the themes *Technology*, *Creativity*, and *Social Interaction* girls were oriented towards taking photos and sharing them on Instagram, whereas the boys built Minecraft worlds together online while Skyping. Based on the persona-creation process advocated by [8] and [16] this led us to create two primary personas: one boy (Anton) and one girl (Julia). Figure 5 shows the one-sheet overview of Anton and Julia, a ten-year old boy and an eleven-year old girl who were treated for Leukemia.

From a methodological point of view, the progression of the persona's richness is based on four steps, summarized in Table 1. Anton's and Julia's persona descriptions (see Figure 5) contain interpreted data from focus group interviews, stakeholder insights derived from the interview analysis, as well as a distillation of the proxy persona attributes and social redemption scenarios discovered in the three design workshops. The personas manifest the synthesis of the pathogenic and salutogenic perspectives. The pathogenic orientation is most evident under the "Clinical" and "Frustration" headings of the persona descriptions. The other four headings are mainly derived from the salutogenic orientation. However, content in these headings are verified and complemented by pathogenic perspectives. For example, the characteristic "emotionally mature" was verified by both parents and healthcare professionals. The characteristic "Wants to play" (described by children, and part of Anton's persona) was complemented with "but is often tired" in the "Frustrations" heading from parent interviews. The result of such syntheses emphasizes the necessity of both the salutogenic and pathogenic perspectives when developing personas for a DPS in this domain.

5. DISCUSSION

In qualitative studies the reliability and validity is not linked to truth and evidence, rather to trustworthiness, which deals with readers' ability to track and verify a rigorous and relevant research process [21]. The trustworthiness is discussed through the following qualitative lenses, based on social and design research criteria: objectivity, dependability, credibility, relevance and transferability [17, 40, 1].

5.1 Objectivity

Objectivity is addressed by asking if this technique allows researchers and designers to create authentic personas that truly represent the children in question. The persona-driven design method is to support designers to overcome subjective notions of their end-users and avoid solutions based on introspection. The method presented here consists of multiple data sources to cover as many aspects as possible of the design context. Furthermore, several researchers interpreted the data both individually and collaboratively. As an extension to the work of [1], this method is designed to let the end-users (i.e. children) take initiative when it comes to creating the proxy personas' behaviors, motivations, and experience goals, as well as crafting the scenarios in the comicboards. The subjective step involved in this process is the qualitative interpretation of interview data. However, as this is carried out in a rigorous fashion, by several researchers, the subjectivity is reduced.

5.2 Dependability

Dependability deals with the repeatability of this process, so that future researchers or designers are enabled to repeat the work – even though we do not expect the results to be identical [40]. Since the children's participation was entirely focused on the salutogenic aspects of the research question, and because the stakeholder involvement was focused on pathogenic conditions and limitations, it is probably possible to apply the same approach to a different target group with other forms of vulnerability or that operates in a different context. However, generalizing this method to *any* child-persona creation process for *any* sensitive context is beyond the claims of this paper. In order to provide comparisons, this approach needs to be implemented in other design projects.

5.3 Credibility (Internal Validity)

Throughout the co-construction process feedback from the children played a crucial role in shaping of personas. Proxy personas and comics that were developed based on outcomes from each workshop were returned for verification by the children at the start of next workshop to validate the interpretations made by the design team between workshops. Furthermore, to obtain feedback on the results obtained from interviews and workshops we arranged a final session for children and parents that had participated in the various stages of the process. In this session, the entire process was outlined and results and conclusions were presented visually, and orally explained by researchers and designers. The session enabled communication of participant's reflections on summarized results and interpretations that had been made by researchers and designers throughout the process. This

[2] http://minecraft.net

[3] http://tocaboca.com/game/toca-builders/

feedback together with subsequent amendments helped to strengthen credibility of the final result from the perspective of the participants involved in the research process.

5.4 Relevance

As our stakeholder interviews have verified, there is a clear relevance of a DPS in this domain. To be relevant, the service should provide a strategic (long-term) and salutogenic perspective on the children's interaction and experience. On a more tactical level, the relevance from the end-users' point of view is captured in the needs of the personas. Here, relevance deals with e.g. what channels and platforms the DPS should reside on in order to be relevant (i.e. successfully deployed and used). This is addressed throughout the contact with the children, where researchers carefully noted what apps, services, and technological platforms and channels were popular among the children (as exemplified in the persona overview in Figure 5). A third perspective on relevance is that this method addresses a need for a customized child-centered design methodology that accommodates persona data collection in sensitive contexts surrounding healthcare services for children. The generative power captured in personas and accompanying scenarios has the potential to overcome some of the creational aspects that strict participatory design with children sometimes lacks [1].

5.5 Transferability

Transferability is concerned with the extent to which the results can be generalized or applied to other contexts or settings. A persona deliverable for any project is specific. It lies at the essence of the method that the personas themselves can be re-used only to a point [16]. This method does not extend that per se. Anton and Julia are specifically crafted for DPS design for children with a specific medical history. The re-usability of this approach lies instead in the structure (questions, workshop setup, etc.), and – to a certain extent – the data collected throughout this process.

6. CONCLUSIONS

The motivation behind the research reported on herein stems from methodological constraints put forward by the specifics of vulnerable children in health-related, sensitive contexts. As design thinking and UCD practice find their way into processes that aim to cater for patient experience in healthcare [31] there is a growing need to customize methods and techniques originally devised for more traditional applications and domains.

In particular, we have provided insights and resolutions to difficulties that can arise in a user-centered persona-driven design process where empirical data from end-users are restricted due to clinical and ethical reasons. In particular, by combining the salutogenic (from the children) and pathogenic (from adult stakeholders) perspectives we could learn about aspects related to both health and disease that are important for the design of authentic, child-centered personas. By employing proxy personas and co-constructing social redemption scenarios in the form of comics in collaboration with children, designers and children could investigate complex themes of friendship and wellbeing, peer support and relationships, and the role of social technology in everyday life together. By a four-step methodological progression, these insights were sculpted into authentic personas that can continue to support and drive the design process forward into ideation, prototyping, production, and testing stages.

An often-overlooked part of the nature of design is that the design process itself is a designed object. By providing reflections on the details of how a design process is planned, and unfolds, this work contributes to the accumulation of knowledge on how to shape the design process itself based on domain-specific requirements.

Even though our objective is to design digital services and IT artifacts, the methodological mindset that underlies this work is applicable even in processes where a digital artifact or service is not necessarily the outcome. Thus, this paper responds to the call of [28] – that human-centered design should increasingly be implemented within healthcare.

ACKNOWLEDGMENTS

We thank Susanne Lindberg and Eva-Lena Einberg for their contribution to planning, implementation, and analysis of interviews and workshops. We also thank our children and adult research participants and gratefully acknowledge the grants from the Swedish Research Council, the Swedish Research Council Formas, the Swedish Childhood Cancer Society, the Knowledge Foundation, and the Swedish Governmental Agency for Innovation Systems (Vinnova).

REFERENCES

1. Antle, A. 2008. Child-Based Personas: Need, Ability and Experience. *Cognition, Technology and Work* 10(2), 155-166.
2. Antonovsky, A. 1979. *Health, Stress and Coping*. San Francisco: Jossey-Bass.
3. Beyer, H., Holtzblatt, K.. 1997. *Contextual Design: Defining Customer-Centered Systems*. San Francisco: Morgan Kaufmann.
4. Bødker, S. 1996. Creating conditions for participation: Conflicts and resources in systems design, *Human Computer Interaction*, 11(3), 215-236
5. Coyne, I. 2010. Accessing children as research participants: examining the role of gatekeepers. *Child: care, health and development*, 36(4), 452-454.
6. Coyne, I., Hayes, E., Gallagher, P. 2009. Research with hospitalized children. Ethical, methodological and organizational challenges. *Childhood*, 16(3), 413-429.
7. Cooper, A. 1999. *The Inmates are Running the Asylum*. Macmillan Publishing.
8. Cooper, A., Reimann, R., Cronin, D. 2007. *About Face 3: The Essentials of Interaction Design*. Wiley.
9. Druin A. 2002. The role of children in the design of new technology. *Journal of Behavior and Information Technology*, 21(1), 1-25.

10. Druin, A. 1999. Cooperative Inquiry: developing new technologies for children with children. In *Proceedings of the SIGCHI Conference on Human Factors in Computer Systems*, CHI'99, ACM, New York, NY, USA, 592-599.
11. Einberg, E., Svedberg, P., Enskär, K., CHIPS study group, Nygren, J. M. 2013. Friendship relations from the perspective of children with experience of cancer treatment. *Manuscript in preparation*.
12. Eiser, C. 2007. Beyond survival: quality of life and follow-up after childhood cancer. *Journal of Pediatric Psychology* 32(9), 1140–1150.
13. Elo, S, Kyngäs, H. 2008. The qualitative content analysis process. *Journal of Advanced Nursing*, 62(1), 107–115,
14. Fargas-Malet, M., McSherry D., Larkin, E. & Robinson, C. 2010. Research with children: methodological issues and innovative techniques. *Journal of Early Childhood Research*, 8(2), 175–192.
15. Garzotto, F. 2008. Broadening children's involvement as design partners. In *Proceedings of the 7th conference on Interaction Design and Children*. ACM, New York, NY, USA, 186-193.
16. Goodwin, K. 2009. *Designing for the Digital Age: How to Create Human-Centered Products and Services*. Wiley.
17. Guba, E.G., Lincoln, Y.S. 1989. *Fourth Generation Evaluation*. California: Sage Publications.
18. Guha, M. L., Druin, A., Fails, J. A. 2013. Cooperative Inquiry revisited: Reflections of the past and guidelines for the future of intergenreational co-design. *International Journal of Child-Computer Interaction*, 2013, 1(1), 14-23.
19. Hanna, E., Ridsen, K., Czerwinski, M., Alexander, K. J. The role of usability research in designing children's computer products. In: A. Druin (Ed.), *The Design of Children's Technology*. Morgan Kaufman, San Francisco, 1999, 4-26.
20. Heary, C. M., Hennessy, E. 2002. The use of focus group interviews in pediatric health care research. *Journal of Pediatric Psychology*, 27(1), 47-57.
21. Hevner, A., March, S., Park, J., and Ram, S. 2004. Design Science in Information Systems Research. *MIS Quarterly* 28(1), 75-105.
22. Iversen, O. S., Dindler, C. 2013. A Utopian Agenda in Child-Computer Interaction. *International Journal of Child-Computer Interaction,* 1(1), 14-23.
23. Kolko, J. 2011. *Exposing the Magic of Design*. Oxford University Press.
24. Krippendorf, K. 2004. *Content Analysis: An Introduction to Its Methodology*. 2nd ed. Sage publication Inc.
25. Lindberg, S. 2013. Participatory Design Workshops with Children with Cancer: Lessons Learned. In *Proceedings of Interaction Design and Children* (IDC'13), 332-335. June 24-27, 2013, New York (NY), USA.
26. Moraveji, N., Li, J., Ding, J., O'Kelley, P., Woolf, S. 2007. Comicboarding: Using comics as proxies for participatory design with children. In *Proceedings of CHI '07*, ACM, 1371-1374. San José, USA.
27. Moser, C., Fuchsberger, V., Tscheligi, M. 2011. Using Probes to Create Child Personas for Games. In *Proceedings of ACE'2011*. Lisbon, Portugal.
28. Mullaney, T., Pettersson, H., Nyholm, T., Stolterman, E. 2012. Thinking Beyond the Cure: A Case for Human-Centered Design in Cancer Care. *International Journal of Design*, 6(3), 27-39.
29. Pruitt, J., Adlin, T. 2006. *The Persona Lifecycle*. San Francisco: Morgan Kaufmann.
30. Pruitt, J., Grudin, J. 2003. Personas: Practice and Theory. In *Proceedings of the 2003 Conference on Designing for User Experience*, ACM Press, New York.
31. Robert, G. 2007. *Bringing User Experience to Healthcare Improvement: The Concepts, Methods and Practices of Experience-based Design*. Radcliffe.
32. Ruland CM, Starren, J., Vatne, TM. 2008. Participatory design with children in the development of a support system for patient-centered care in pediatric oncology. *Journal of Biomed Inform*. 41(4), 624-35.
33. Schuler, D., Namioka, A. (1993). *Participatory Design: Principles and Practices*. L. Erlbaum Assoc. Inc., Hillsdale, NJ, USA.
34. Sprangers MA, Schwartz CE. 1999. Integrating response shift into health-related quality of life research: a theoretical model. *Soc Sci Med*. 48(11), 1507-1515.
35. Solomon P. 2004. Peer support/peer provided services underlying processes, benefits, and critical ingredients. *Psychiatric Rehabilitation Journal* 27(4), 392-401.
36. Stinson, J. N., White, M., Breakey, V., Chong, A.L, Mak, I, Low, K.K., Low, A.K. 2011. Perspectives on quality and content of information on the internet for adolescents with cancer. *Pediatric Blood and Cancer*. 15, 57(1):97-104
37. Söderbäck, M., Coyne, I., Harder, M. 2011. The importance of including both a child perspective and the child's perspective within health care settings to provide truly child-centred care. *Journal of Child Health Care*. 15(2):99-106.
38. Wright, P., McCarthy, J. Empathy and Experience in HCI. In *Proceedings of CHI 2008*. April 5-8, 2008, Florence, Italy, 637-645.
39. Wärnestål, P., Nygren, J. 2013. Building an Experience Framework for a Digital Peer Support Service for Children Surviving from Cancer. In *Proceedings of Interaction Design and Children* (IDC'13), 269-272. New York (NY), USA, June 24-27, 2013.
40. Zimmerman, J., Forlizzi, J., Evenson, S. 2007. Research through design as a method for interaction design research in HCI. In *Proceedings of the SGCHI Conf. on Human Factors in Computing Systems*, 493-502. ACM, New York.

Balancing Design Tensions: Iterative Display Design to Support *Ad Hoc* and Multidisciplinary Medical Teamwork

Diana S. Kusunoki[1], Aleksandra Sarcevic[1], Nadir Weibel[2], Ivan Marsic[3], Zhan Zhang[1], Genevieve Tuveson[4] and Randall S. Burd[4]

Drexel University[1]
Philadelphia, PA 19104
{dsk38, aleksarc, zz87}
@drexel.edu

UC San Diego[2]
La Jolla, CA 92093
weibel@ucsd.edu

Rutgers University[3]
Piscataway, NJ 08854
marsic@rutgers.edu

Children's Nat'l Med Ctr[4]
Washington, DC 20010
{gtuveson, rburd}
@childrensnational.org

ABSTRACT
In this paper, we describe how we developed an information display prototype for trauma resuscitation teams based on design ideas and feedback from clinicians. Our approach is grounded in participatory design, emphasizing the importance of gaining long-term commitment from clinicians in system development. Through a series of participatory design workshops, heuristic evaluation, and simulated resuscitation sessions, we identified the main information features to include on our display. Our results focus on how we balanced the design tensions that emerged when addressing the *ad hoc*, hierarchical, and multidisciplinary nature of trauma teamwork. We discuss the implications of balancing role-based differences for each information feature, as well as two major design tensions: process-based vs. state-based designs and role-based vs. team-based displays.

Author Keywords
Participatory design; information displays; design tensions; teamwork; healthcare; trauma resuscitation.

ACM Classification Keywords
H.5.0. Information interfaces and presentation (e.g., HCI): General

INTRODUCTION
This paper presents the select findings from an ongoing iterative design process, the goal of which is to develop ideas for technological innovation and to support *ad hoc*, multidisciplinary medical teamwork during trauma resuscitation. Awareness, cooperation, and information sharing are crucial for teamwork in the resuscitation setting; trauma teams work under extreme time pressure while stabilizing critically injured patients and addressing life-threatening injuries. Although we see opportunities for technological innovation, we recognize that designing for emergency scenarios is challenging for several reasons. First, trauma teams are *ad hoc*, hierarchical, and involve medical professionals from multiple disciplines, leading to a diversity of information needs. Second, the resuscitation environment—the trauma bay—is complex and filled with medical equipment, imposing physical design constraints. Finally, resuscitations are safety-critical events in which teams deal with incomplete information and unpredictable problems, adding even more design constraints.

CHI 2014, April 26 - May 01 2014, Toronto, ON, Canada
Copyright 2014 ACM 978-1-4503-2473-1/14/04…$15.00.
http://dx.doi.org/10.1145/2556288.2557301.

To address these challenges and, at the same time, create a design process that would support both researchers and practitioners in achieving common understanding across disciplines, we rooted our approach in participatory design (PD) [12,18]. In particular, we combined observations from our previous fieldwork with an iterative design process, rapid prototyping, and PD techniques to develop solutions that will meet the needs of these dynamic and multidisciplinary teams. Throughout the process, we created and evaluated a dozen prototypes using empirically accessible events and practitioner participation that ranged from design workshops, interviews, heuristic evaluation of paper prototypes, and simulated resuscitation events with entire teams using a high-fidelity prototype.

As an outcome of this process, we gained an understanding of role-based differences in information needs, and conceptualized several design tensions, two of which played a critical role in guiding our design decisions:

(1) The biggest design tension was between using *process-based*, checklist-driven designs that present information organized by the order of activity, and using *state-based*, snapshot-like designs that present information about patient and teamwork status. A state-based design was preferred because it allowed team members to observe treatment outcomes and trends in patient information.

(2) Another design tension was between creating individual, *role-based* displays that suit the needs of each role, and creating a *team-based* display that meets the needs of all roles as a team. A team-based design was preferred, but it required methods for reducing biases due to the multidisciplinary and hierarchical nature of trauma teams.

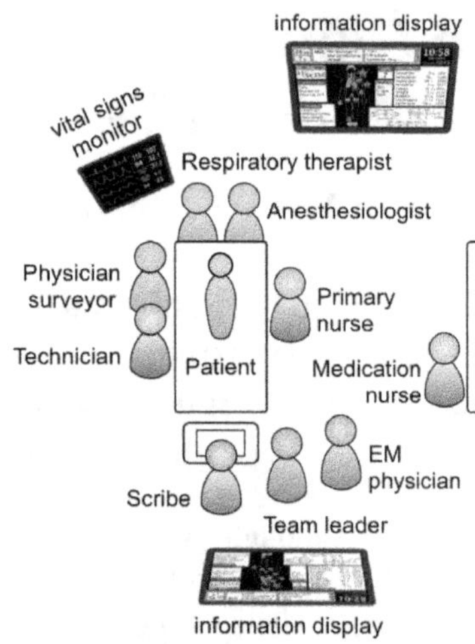

Figure 1. Team organization and layout of the trauma bay.

In addition to serving as mechanisms for analyzing the evolution of a design, these design tensions show the kinds of considerations HCI researchers must make when developing information technologies for *ad hoc*, hierarchical, and multidisciplinary teams.

BACKGROUND, RELATED WORK & CONTRIBUTIONS

Emergency Resuscitations: Overview

The process of trauma resuscitation is one of the most challenging in healthcare, requiring a team to focus on common tasks for a short time period (20-30 minutes, on average), while adapting to complex and changing circumstances driven by patient status. Unlike other clinical settings, patient management during resuscitation relies on emerging rather than existing information, demanding fast and effective cooperation among many disciplines [2]. Resuscitation teams are heterogeneous, consisting of clinicians with different roles, specializations, experience levels, ranks, and work responsibilities. Each role is strategically positioned (Figure 1): *respiratory therapist* and *anesthesiologist* at the head of the bed managing airway; *physician surveyor* at the side evaluating the patient; *bedside nurses* on both sides administering treatments; *scribe* at the foot of the bed documenting the event; and *leader* and *emergency medicine (EM) physician* in the back overseeing team activities. Trauma teams follow the Advanced Trauma Life Support (ATLS) protocol for patient evaluation that focuses on the major physiological systems: **A**irway, **B**reathing, blood **C**irculation, and **D**isability or neurological status ("ABCD") [1]. While the protocol serves as a mechanism by which teams articulate their work, task coordination is still dynamic and changes with patient needs. Despite the extensive amounts of information teams must process, few information technologies are available to support their work. Information is shared verbally, with a high cognitive load of integrating data due to the lack of external memory aids [20]. Scribes record the information produced by the team on flowsheets and team leaders at our research site use a checklist to manage protocol tasks. These artifacts, however, are paper-based and rarely used for real-time decision making. Vital signs monitors are currently the only electronic displays in trauma bays at most hospitals.

Related Approaches to Designing Information Displays

An important challenge to implementing computerized support in emergency medicine is the need to efficiently synthesize and present information. One way to address this challenge is through shared information displays.

Information displays have been developed in medical and emergency response settings using a variety of approaches. The Ecological Interface Design (EID) approach [5], for example, highlights the importance of studying work domains at different levels of abstraction and hierarchy, and deriving display requirements based on this top-down work domain analysis (WDA). In contrast, Holzman [11] and Parush et al. [19] derived requirements for their information displays using bottom-up approaches, such as observations, interviews, and analysis of team communications. Our approach was also bottom-up, but relied on participatory design (PD) to understand the domain and elicit the information needs of individuals and teams. Other researchers have used PD techniques as well. For instance, Bardram et al. designed their AwareMedia system for an operating ward based on field studies and a series of design workshops with a group of clinicians [3]. Kyng et al. used participatory design to develop interactive systems for emergency response [14], while Kristensen et al. used design workshops in highly realistic settings ("future labs") to develop ideas for supporting emergency medical services during major incidents [13]. Where we differ, however, is in using PD as a vehicle to not only understand the domain and develop ideas, but also to manage design tensions that emerged from the design process. We see design tensions and associated challenges acknowledged in the HCI and CSCW literature [e.g., 6,7,9], but discussions on how to address and balance these tensions are lacking.

Our work makes the following contributions to HCI:

- Discussion of PD as a vehicle to manage design tensions that emerge from designing shared displays based on feedback from users with different information needs.
- Contextualized examples of why certain design directions work or do not work.
- Descriptions of role-based differences for targeted information presentation.
- Prioritized list of information types for display.

OUR APPROACH: FROM FIELD STUDIES TO AN ITERATIVE DESIGN PROCESS

The display design and evaluation process was preceded by several years of fieldwork, providing the basis for building shared knowledge with all participants. Our interdisciplinary team is composed of ten researchers and practitioners at four institutions, and involves HCI

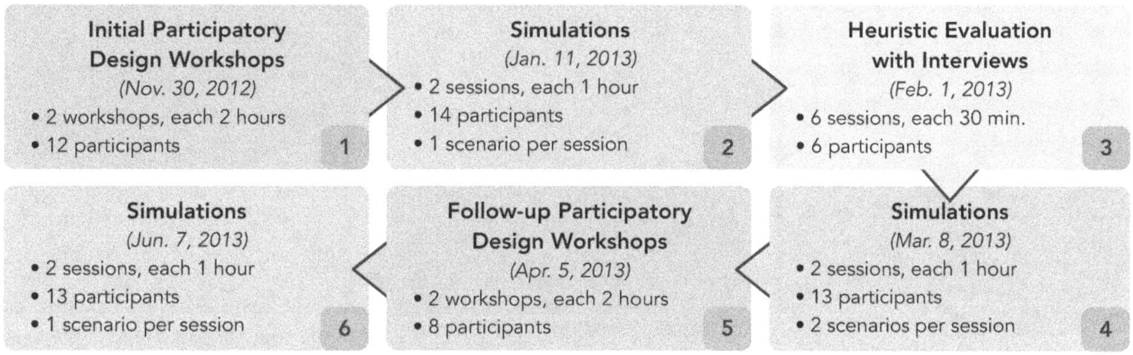

Figure 2. Display design and evaluation process: Phases and timeline of data collection sessions.

researchers and ethnographers, computer scientists, engineers, and clinical experts. Over the years, we have used different methods to engage with the domain: observations of live and simulated resuscitations, interviews with trauma team members, and micro-analyses of live video recordings [e.g., 20]. As an important part of the participatory design process, these field studies revealed the problems of coordination and information overload, access, and retention. It was through this fieldwork that a display solution emerged to synthesize the information about patient status and team activities. Our collaborators at the research site—a Level I trauma center at a pediatric teaching hospital in the U.S. Mid-Atlantic region—supported this idea, and installed two large wall monitors in the trauma bay. The results we report in this paper are from the first phase of the iterative design process, which focused on the design and development of the display prototype.

Display Design and Evaluation Process

Over the course of eight months (November 2012 – June 2013), we conducted six design and evaluation phases, with each phase including two or more data collection sessions for a total of 16 sessions: four participatory design workshops, six simulation sessions with entire resuscitation teams, and six heuristic evaluation sessions (Figure 2).

Participatory Design Workshops

We started with two participatory design workshops to create preliminary designs (Phase 1, Figure 2), and followed up with another set of workshops focused on display functionality (Phase 5, Figure 2). The main purpose of these workshops was to understand clinicians' perceptions of what information was critical to their work and how they needed this information displayed. We used the PD technique called PICTIVE [17] to provide an environment where users with diverse perspectives have equal opportunity to engage in the design process. Participants were asked to (a) discuss the most recent resuscitation in which they participated, (b) create display sketches based on their individual needs, (c) engage in a group design activity to create a shared display, (d) rank the priority of the information features based on their role, and (e) discuss any concerns with using the display. After several design iterations and evaluation sessions, we conducted two follow-up design workshops (Phase 5, Figure 2). The format was similar to the initial workshops, but focused on eliciting input on display functionality. We also used these workshops to validate prior findings.

Simulated Resuscitations in a Realistic Setting

We performed three sets of simulations (Phases 2, 4, and 6 in Figure 2) to both gather design requirements and evaluate display prototypes. Simulation sessions were conducted in an actual trauma bay with the equipment normally available to teams. In each of the hour-long sessions, we oriented teams to the display functionality. Following this brief overview, teams performed two to four resuscitations using a high-fidelity mannequin based on clinical scenarios ranging from moderate to demanding that were developed by medical experts. Participants were then asked to indicate up to five features they found useful (liked) and up to five features they did not find useful (disliked) on a paper copy of the display using stickers color-coded based on role. If an information feature did not receive a "like" or "dislike," we considered it neutral. Each session concluded with a discussion about team communication, information features and display design.

Prototypes were displayed using two 42" wall-mounted monitors showing the same information (Figure 1). Data capture varied between simulation sessions; the goal was to experiment with different data capture mechanisms for the entire system development. We first inputted information onto the display using a digital pen and paper flowsheet used by scribes. During the second set of simulations, the prototypes drew data via digital pens from both the flowsheet and the leader's paper checklist. A confederate scribe acted as the 'Wizard of Oz' in our third simulation session, inputting information using a computer interface.

Heuristic Evaluation with Interviews

The purpose of heuristic evaluation sessions (Phase 3, Figure 2) was to get feedback individually from each participant and their ideas for improving the display design. We asked participants to rate the display based on a set of criteria adapted from previous work on heuristic evaluation for ambient and peripheral displays [15,16]. Participants were instructed to explain their reasoning behind each

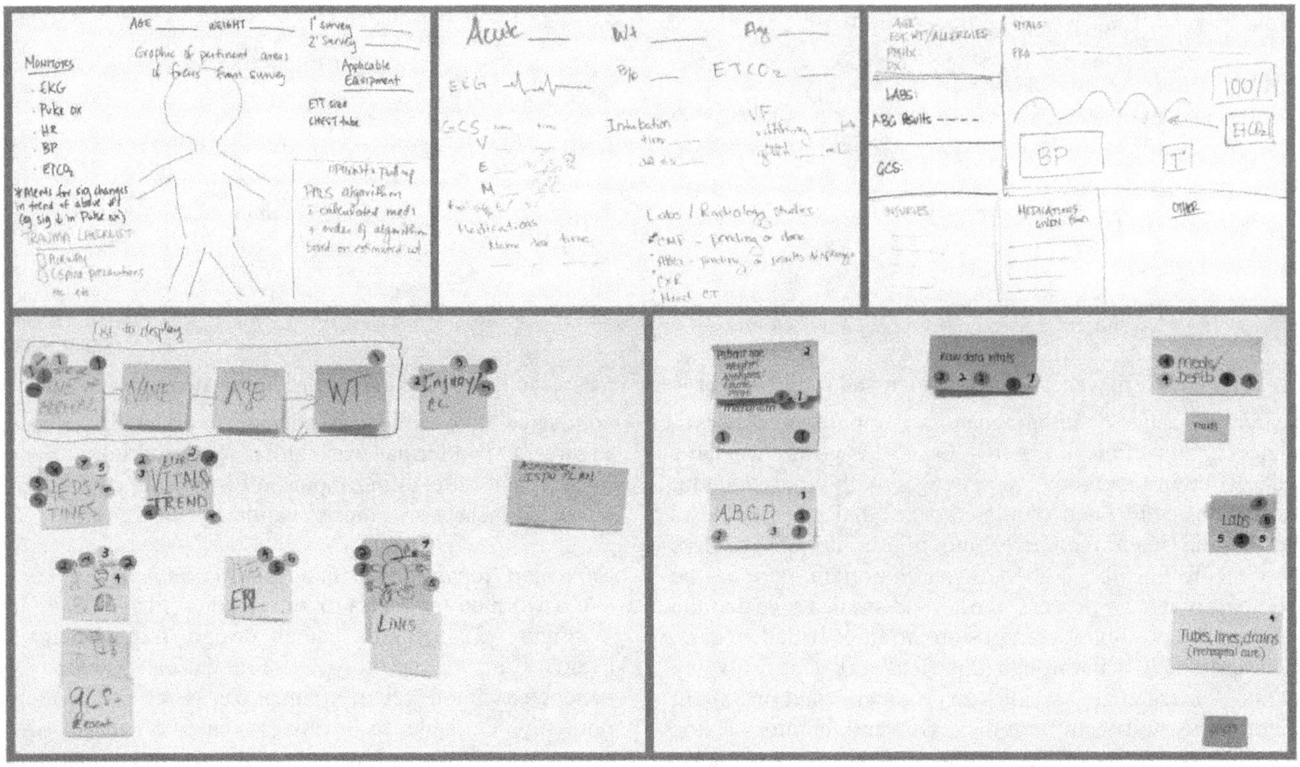

Figure 3. Participants' individual designs (three samples of sketches out of 12, top row) and group designs (bottom row).

rating and write notes on the paper prototype to show what they meant. Each session concluded with questions about concerns they had about using this display, and what they believed was the purpose of the display.

In summary, the types of participant feedback differed with each design and evaluation activity. We received feedback based on participants' own design ideas and perceptions of information needs through participatory design workshops. We also received feedback through heuristic evaluations using paper prototypes. Finally, we elicited feedback based on using the actual display prototype in the context of work through simulation sessions. This mix of feedback types ensured a holistic approach to design while minimizing methodological biases tied to each of the approaches.

Participants

Of the 39 unique participants involved in the design and evaluation process, 21 attended two or more sessions (Table 1). Repeated participation was allowed between but not within phases (Figure 2). Our participants were clinicians who regularly perform trauma resuscitations, with experience levels ranging from a few months to more than 30 years. We recruited participants to represent all core team roles for data collection activities to replicate the composition of actual teams. Participation was voluntary and participants were compensated for their time.

Roles	Partic. (N=39)	Avg. Exper. (yrs.)
Anesthesiologist	5	5
Bedside nurse	9	9
EM physician	4	5
Physician surveyor	6	4.5
Respiratory therapist	5	4
Scribe	4	14
Surgical team leader	6	3

Table 1. Participant demographics.

Data Analysis

Analyses were conducted to identify trends on all artifacts, design feedback, and other data collected throughout the process (i.e., design sketches, annotated paper displays, rankings, likes and dislikes, photographs, and audio and video recordings of discussions). Individual designs from workshops were transcribed into a matrix to analyze the information features each role included in their designs. The features were then grouped by type and sorted by number of times they were included in designs. Group designs were transcribed in a similar manner by grouping information features by type and recording the top five ranks that each role assigned to features. Likes and dislikes assigned to information features during simulations were also calculated to analyze the feedback trends over time. Information features were again grouped by type into main categories (e.g., header, ABCD, treatments, and orders); the percentages of people who liked and disliked each feature were then calculated as (the first term in the equation is because only one vote per category was allowed):

$$\frac{\text{\# of votes}}{\text{\# of items in category}} \times \frac{1}{\text{\# of people who voted}} \times 100$$

Discussions were transcribed and analyzed to supplement the findings from design artifacts, feedback, and prototypes.

Information features & team roles that included them in their individual designs	Simulation 1, v2 ✓	Simulation 1, v2 ✗	Simulation 2, v4 ✓	Simulation 2, v4 ✗	Simulation 3, v5 ✓	Simulation 3, v5 ✗
Header	**34.3%**	**12.9%**	**38.6%**	**1.4%**	**44%**	**0%**
Patient demographics	All team roles					
Pre-hospital information	Anesthesiologist, bedside nurse, physician surveyor, scribe, respiratory, leader					
Vital signs	**N/A**	**N/A**	**N/A**	**N/A**	**N/A**	**N/A**
Numeric values	Respiratory, anesthesiologist					
Live waveforms	Scribe, respiratory, anesthesiologist					
Trends	Scribe					
Patient evaluation findings (ABCD)	**21.4%**	**42.9%**	**21.4%**	**19.6%**	**25%**	**17.5%**
Checklist of steps	Physician surveyor, EM physician					
Findings and procedures under ABCD	Leader 1, leader 2, scribe, respiratory, EM physician					
Findings and procedures by type	Anesthesiologist 1, anesthesiologist 2, respiratory, bedside nurse, scribe					
Body with representations of findings	Physician surveyor, EM physician					
Treatments (medications and fluids)	**54.8%**	**2.4%**	**N/A**	**N/A**	**70%**	**0%**
Medications and fluids separated	Bedside nurse, scribe, respiratory					
Medications and fluids combined	Anesthesiologist, respiratory, leader					
Laboratory and radiology orders/results	**14.3%**	**14.3%**	**14.3%**	**30%**	**30%**	**30%**
Radiology tests ordered	Bedside nurse					
Labs and radiology tests ordered	Leader					
Labs ordered and results	Anesthesiologist, scribe, EM physician					
Lab results	Respiratory					
Lab results and radiology tests ordered	Scribe, respiratory					

Table 2: Role preferences for different information features and participants' attitudes toward major components of the display expressed through the percentage of likes (✓) and dislikes (✗) during 3 sets of simulations (N/A = not included in display).

FINDINGS: ROLE-BASED DIFFERENCES & TENSIONS

The hierarchical nature of trauma teams and the multiplicity of responsibilities, disciplines, and training levels naturally led to a diversity of information needs. As we found through fieldwork, patient data that was meaningful to one team member may go unnoticed by other team members. While each role has particular information needs, we also observed several roles with overlapping needs that allow them to coordinate tasks. This mix of information needs became evident as we were designing and evaluating display prototypes, revealing both role and design tensions. Due to space limitations, we show only six designs (out of 13 iterations), four of which were tested with users.

Role Tensions Around Information Features

Eight categories of information emerged from participants' group designs during the initial workshops (Figure 3). The categories included (ranked by perceived importance): (1) header with patient information; (2) vital sign values, waveforms, and trends; (3) findings from ABCD steps; (4) medication names, dosages, and administration times; (5) procedures, access types and their locations; (6) laboratory and radiology orders and results; (7) fluid types and amounts; and (8) disposition plan. Role-based differences in information needs emerged through analyzing the information features in individual designs, rankings in group designs, and likes and dislikes on prototypes tested in simulations (see Table 2 and Figure 5 for summary).

Header: Patient Demographics and Pre-Hospital Information

All individual designs included a portion at the top with patient information such as age, weight, mechanism of injury, name, pre-hospital interventions, medical history, timer, arrival time, and allergies (Figure 3). For group designs, header included all information from individual designs except pre-hospital interventions, name, and timer. Although suggested initially, patient name, gender, allergies, and medical history were found least useful and did not propagate to the initial prototypes. All but two participants ranked the header as most important during the workshops. Similarly, throughout simulation testing, the header was the most popular feature of the display, stabilizing with an increasing percentage of likes (Figure 5).

The most debated portion of the header, however, was pre-hospital interventions. During the first set of simulations (v2, Figure 4), EM physicians, physician surveyors, scribes, and leaders disliked pre-hospital information because it was not as useful as the other header features. The design tested in the second set of simulations omitted pre-hospital information (v4, Figure 4), and the header received only one dislike from a respiratory therapist. Pre-hospital information, however, emerged as important again during the second set of design workshops. After including pre-hospital information again with a more efficient layout (v5, Figure 4), users liked this version the best (Figure 5).

Vital Signs

Individual designs suggested three ways of monitoring the patient's vital signs: *numeric values*, *live waveforms*, and *trends* during resuscitations (Table 2). Only leaders and a physician surveyor did not include vital signs in their designs, noting they were keeping in mind that a separate monitor for vitals was present. The vital signs feature was ranked as second most important in both group designs, and

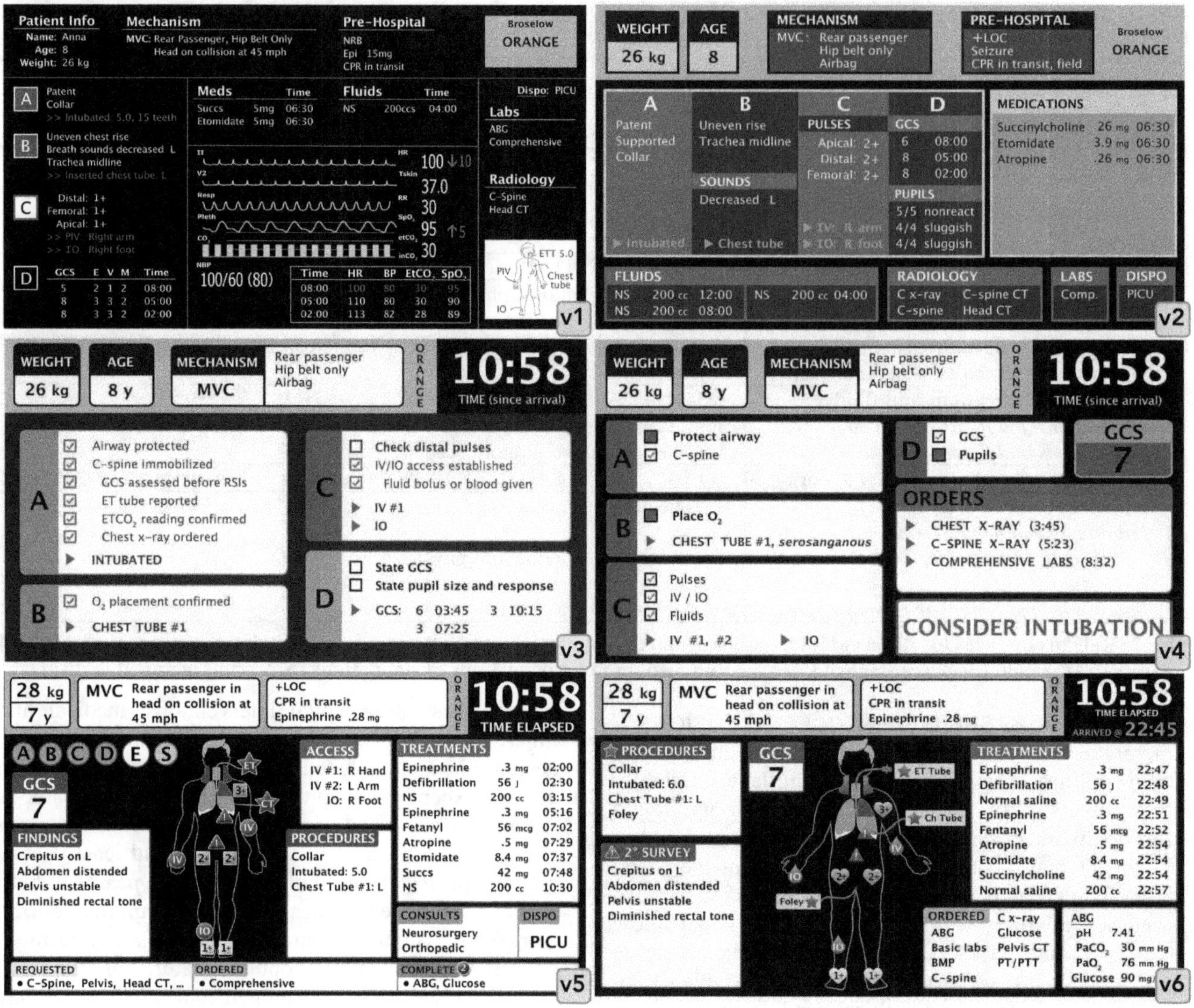

Figure 4. Evolution of display designs, moving from a process-based (v1-v4) to a state-based design (v5, v6).

most roles liked it. Scribes needed both waveforms and trends to record this data and alert the team about vital signs changes. Respiratory therapists and anesthesiologists highlighted the importance of numeric vital signs for real-time feedback on the effectiveness of their treatments.

Vital signs are currently omitted from our display prototype until we can determine how to efficiently incorporate them into the design and stream data to the display. Vital signs are critical to patient care so we made sure to have a vital signs monitor when testing our display during simulations. Throughout the project, we have been working with the biomedical engineering department to develop a technical solution so teams can view both vital signs and our information display. Several options were discussed, including: (1) splitting the screen with vital signs and resuscitation information; (2) feeding vital sign data into a section within the information display; (3) displaying resuscitation information on the front screen for leadership roles and vital signs on the back screen for the anesthesiologist and respiratory therapist; and (4) adding a second set of screens for augmenting vital signs.

Patient Evaluation Findings from ABCD Protocol Steps

Information about ABCD ranked third overall. Individually, all participants from both initial workshops incorporated elements of ABCD in their designs using four methods (Table 2). The *first* method was a basic checklist of the steps; once the team completes a step, it turns green or is checked off. The *second* method was a list of abnormal findings and procedures under each ABCD step. The *third* method was extracting the elements of ABCD (e.g., a neurological exam score [Glasgow Coma Score], abnormal findings, and procedures) and then separating them into different display sections. The *fourth* method was an image of the body with visual representations of abnormal findings and procedures. This feature was part of a physician surveyor and an EM physician's designs in conjunction with a basic checklist. A respiratory therapist's design also followed the fourth method, but in conjunction

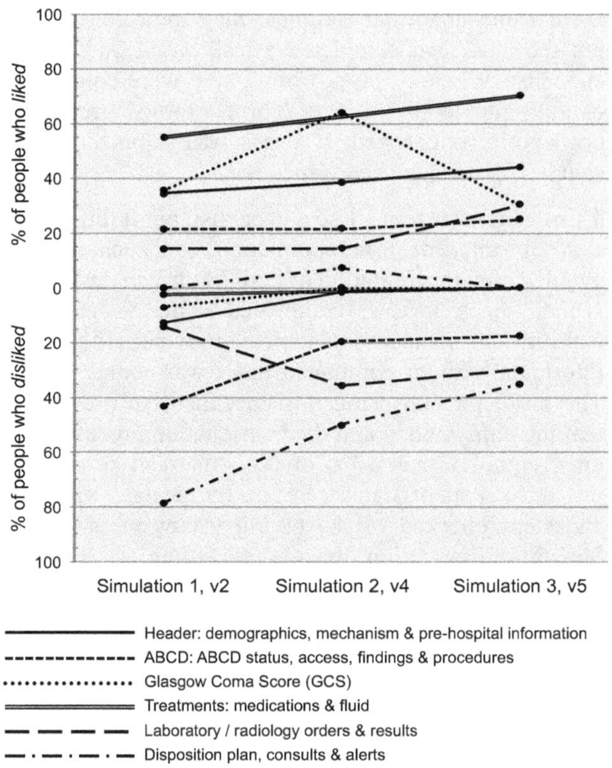

Figure 5. Evolution of participants' attitudes toward different components of the display evaluated in 3 sets of simulations.

with the more detailed second method of abnormal findings and procedures under each step. Both groups used the second method in their group designs; the first group also added an image of the body.

We grouped these four methods into two types of information: (1) *process-based* (first and second method of presenting information organized by the order of activity) and (2) *state-based* (third and fourth method of presenting information about patient and teamwork status). After experimenting with these different methods, we found that the state-based combination of the third and fourth method (Figure 4, v5) was the most effective, as indicated by an increasing percentage of likes and decreasing percentage of dislikes (Table 2 and Figure 5).

Where we saw the most discussion surrounding ABCD from both participants and research team members was during the major shift from a list of abnormal findings and procedures under each step (second method, v2, Figure 4), to using the checklist-driven method in versions 3 and 4 (Figure 4). Emergency medicine physicians generally did not find the information about ABCD useful because it relates to the responsibilities of another role (surgical team leader). A bedside physician noted after a simulation that the checklist-driven information was not helpful because the primary survey assessment (ABCD steps) is his main focus with all of this information already in his mind, so having it on the display is distracting. A leader had similar feelings about the checklist-driven method, noting in heuristic evaluations that the display just mirrored the information from the paper checklist in his hand. Participants' notes on paper prototypes from heuristic evaluations suggested that we could simplify each step and remove the less critical checklist items (v3, Figure 4). Scribe nurses in heuristic evaluations and simulations suggested providing numeric values and descriptive findings to make the checklist format more useful.

Treatments: Medications and Fluids

All participants, with the exception of a physician surveyor and two EM physicians, included treatments such as medications, fluids, and defibrillation in their individual designs. Medications and fluids were also included in both group designs. Participants responded positively to having treatments on the prototype even though medications ranked as fourth and fluids ranked as seventh most important. Despite these positive reactions, we had to remove fluids and medications in design versions 3 and 4 due to technical difficulties until we could capture and display this information accurately in version 5 (Figure 4).

Where participants differed, however, was in the ways they suggested treatments should be formatted (Table 2). Some roles did not find it necessary to have fluids on the display because it is possible to look at the physical bag to see how much fluid has been given. Some participants only needed the ordered amount of fluids or dosage of medications, while others preferred the amount that has actually been received by the patient or the time medications were administered (e.g., scribe nurses). After reviewing this issue with participants in the second set of workshops, we decided to combine medications and fluids into one running list called 'treatments' (v5, Figure 4). Participants in the last set of simulations responded positively to having this single, detailed list (Figure 5).

Laboratory and Radiology Orders and Results

Participants needed a way to manage their orders and results for laboratory ("labs") and radiology studies, ranking this information as sixth. Information about lab orders only made it to one group's design. There were, however, different perceptions about the ways in which this information should be configured on the display (Table 2). The design evolved from separate lists of radiology and lab orders, to a combined list with timestamps when ordered, to a scrolling list divided by status of requested, ordered, and completed labs, to a final small list of orders with a separate section with lab results (Figure 4).

DISCUSSION: DESIGN TENSIONS

We next present the implications of two major design tensions we encountered throughout the process: process-based vs. status-based designs and role-based vs. team-based displays. As we describe each of these tensions, we discuss the findings that guided our decisions, as well as the approaches we used to resolve these tensions.

Process-Based vs. State-Based Designs

The biggest tension we encountered was between using process-based and state-based designs. The design evolution of the ABCD section demonstrates this tension well, as it moved from a process-based to a state-based design. *Process-based designs* followed a checklist-driven style and presented information organized by the order in which ABCD steps were performed. In design versions 1 to 4 (Figure 4), information was presented under each step, and the ABCD layout was used to represent the progression of the resuscitation process. *State-based designs* (v5 and v6 in Figure 4) presented a snapshot of the system's state, organizing information by the type of information produced by team activities (i.e., findings, procedures, pulse levels, and intravenous access) and their location on the patient's body. Both designs presented either *patient status* (findings and values of the patient's physiological condition) or *team status* (whether the team has performed a task).

While other researchers discussed design tensions in terms of assumptions about feasibility [9], we learned about trade-offs through trial and error. In doing so, we found an effective combination of design approaches that suited the nature of teamwork in the resuscitation context and provided concrete, contextualized examples of why certain design directions did or did not work. Versions 1 and 2 had a process-based design with patient status information. Versions 3 and 4 also had a process-based design, but presented team status information. Finally, version 5 and 6 had a state-based design with patient status information. We next describe the nature of each combination and responses we received during evaluations.

Process-Based Design and Patient Status Information

The ABCD feature of the first two designs (v1, v2 in Figure 4) was process-based, showing patient status information. We tried this configuration first because it was the most prominent in individual and group designs. Each section of ABCD had a list of both normal and abnormal findings in the order reported by the team. At the bottom of each section, we included a list of completed procedures, which participants liked the most in the first set of simulations. With this layout, however, participants felt the display was cluttered and unfamiliar because it was difficult to find information. Several participants noted that the display was not dynamic in that the information did not seem like it would update when the status of the patient changes or when the team reassesses the patient. More was needed to make the display useful than just duplicating the information that teams gather while performing each step.

Process-Based Design and Team Status Information

We thought the display might be more useful if we presented information at the teamwork level with a layer of the leader's interpretation about the team's progress. The next two designs (v3, v4 in Figure 4) were, therefore, organized by evaluation steps, but instead of showing normal and abnormal findings, they indicated whether or not the team had completed a task based on the leader's checklist. When all tasks from a step were completed, the overall step letter (A, B, C, or D) turned green and the checkbox was checked. If a task was skipped, the overall step letter and checkbox turned red.

This design was much like a checklist, but it did not require a strict order of task completion. As such, the design avoided a major limitation of activity-driven designs, which is their focus on tasks anticipated at the design stage and inability to manage unanticipated events [5]. Even so, information about completed tasks was found ineffective. The problem with using this checklist-like presentation is that the human body and the resuscitation process are much more complex than a list of tasks that can be checked off just once. Patient status can rapidly change, with findings and steps checked off becoming irrelevant or inaccurate. Showing information linearly according to process also requires time to analyze trends. Users wanted task status represented through the information that the task produced. Furthermore, checklists are meant to catch errors in tasks that teams do routinely, which the leader at our site already does. After using this display in simulations, participants echoed that they needed abnormal findings, laboratory and radiology results, completed procedures, and treatments.

State-Based Design and Patient Status Information

Once we gained a better understanding of how to present the most important information features, we experimented with a large image of the patient's body in the last set of designs (v5 and v6 in Figure 4). Although we included an image of the body in the first version, it was not feasible at that time because we just started to narrow down the information to display and the image was then too small to be useful. With the latest designs, normal and abnormal findings were included in the ABCD feature again, but in visual form, using images and icons to indicate the current status of the patient's airway, breath sounds, pulses, intravenous access locations, and procedures. We extracted the most liked features from ABCD in previous designs—Glasgow Coma Score, procedures, and intravenous access—then separated them into their own sections on the display. Abnormal findings from the secondary survey were also added in a separate section marked 'findings' with icons on the body showing these findings. Some participants liked the idea of using an image of the body to superimpose information graphically, while others preferred the textual lists, thus we kept both.

Summary

As we experimented with different display configurations, we realized that both patient and teamwork information could be more accessible if we abandoned the checklist-like, process-based method. Our most recent design (v6, Figure 4) has patient information within state-based elements that in turn indicates team status without having to organize information using a process-based structure. Unlike EID-driven medical displays, which focus on patient data [5], our display also incorporates information about teamwork (i.e., status of phases, tasks, activities). User feedback throughout the process showed that listing information according to ABCD steps was ineffective. To make the ABCD feature valuable—after all, the entire resuscitation process centers around findings from ABCD steps—information had to be grouped to allow quick access to and analysis of treatment outcomes and trends in patient information. Instead of presenting information based on relevance to a system component (in our case, **A**irway, **B**reathing, **C**irculation) or the team's progress using checklist data, we believe that information organized into chunks showing a snapshot of the process is more effective because information can be compared within a category. Our final design is independent of the current workflow practices, making the display more flexible and amenable to modifications with future workflow and protocol changes. Finally, using a PD approach allowed us to design a display tailored specifically to the resuscitation setting, but also develop a template with key information features adaptable to other hospital contexts [6,7].

Role-Based vs. Team-Based Displays

The second major tension we observed was between creating *role-based displays* that individually suit the needs of each role and creating a *team-based display* that meets the main information needs of all roles as a team. The tradeoffs of displaying individual versus group activities are also about the required amount of user attention [9]. Much of discussion with participants and within research team focused on this tension. Several considerations became apparent while developing and testing the display.

On one hand, designing different displays for each role has its advantages—it helps avoid the influence of the team's hierarchy and heterogeneity on the design to best meet each role's information needs. Mounting displays tailored for each role (at least eight displays in our case), however, is not as cost- or space-effective as two or three common displays mirroring the same information. Multiple displays in a small space may also introduce confusion about where to look and each display would need to be strategically placed. If a role arrives late (which happens often), other roles may have difficulty managing information on multiple displays while covering the duties of the missing role.

On the other hand, designing a team-based display that summarizes the key information also has its advantages—all team members share the same information to "get on the same page," and it is easier to know where to access information. The notion of "getting on the same page" was a recurring theme throughout the design process when participants described the main purpose of the display. This finding resonates with previous work that argued for common displays in group settings to support establishing common ground and conventions [7,8,21]. In addition, team-based displays have been proposed in other safety-critical settings characterized by multidisciplinary teams, precisely because they allowed for efficient common grounding [e.g., 3,4,10]. There are still disadvantages in that it is difficult to reconcile different needs, especially because team hierarchy and vocal participants could influence the information selected to display. Despite these challenges, we chose this second approach because it emphasizes efficiency and consistency.

Reconciling Information Needs

Although it is difficult to reconcile various information needs and address role hierarchy when developing a shared display, we used several strategies to minimize the effects of these factors. First, we had each participant create their ideal display to suit their role, discuss the various information features, reach consensus, and then create a design as a group (Figure 3). This strategy allowed us to understand the detailed role-based information needs that may be lost through group design activities. Second, we encouraged participants to include as many information features as possible when creating their group designs, because they would be able to individually rank the top five information features they needed the most. Information ranking provided participants with equal opportunity to voice their opinion, despite any differences in power and outspokenness; it also acknowledged these differences in the process of identifying individual priorities and those shared across roles. This approach helped us determine the overall rank order of group needs by analyzing the ranks assigned by participants. We used a similar strategy in simulation sessions. Instead of ranking their top information items, participants rated information features on the display using "like" and "dislike" stickers. Rating and follow-up discussions provided feedback about their experiences using our display designs, which allowed us to further examine how roles were affected. Top-down methods such as work domain analysis (WDA) [5] can also be used to understand role differences and shared information needs, but the level of granularity to describe those needs is much coarser than that of our approaches.

To quantify the potential effect of our approaches, we analyzed individual designs and compared them to the consensus-based group designs. We checked if some roles compromised more than others, in that fewer information items suggested in their individual designs propagated to the group design. Similarly, we analyzed rankings from simulations to see if any roles compromised in the group design and whether they were the least satisfied with the display design. Results from these analyses showed that we included most of the information features proposed in individual and group designs, with each role compromising on only three features or less. Although our display did not include vital signs, we made sure to have a separate vital signs monitor during simulations. Until we included labs and radiology results in our final design, anesthesiologists, scribes, and respiratory therapists compromised the most without this feature. While scribes had three unaddressed features, they included the most features in their designs (total of 32 between two scribes), which made it difficult to meet all of their needs. Even so, we incorporated most features except name, pupils size, and Glasgow Coma Score details (score for eye opening, verbal response, and motor response). No particular role appeared dissatisfied more than others with the final design we tested (v5, Figure 4).

CONCLUSION

Through participatory design workshops, heuristic evaluation, and simulated resuscitations, we identified and prioritized the information features that trauma resuscitation teams require to coordinate their work. Taking an iterative participatory design approach was critical to balancing role tensions, as well as two major design tensions that emerged during the design process. We first described in detail the role-based tensions surrounding each information feature and how our designs evolved to meet the needs of different roles. We then discussed two major design tensions that emerged—*process-based* vs. *state-based* designs and *role-based* vs. *team-based* displays—and how we reached balance through different approaches. Our work has implications for HCI researchers interested in (1) using participatory design to develop shared information displays for hierarchical and multidisciplinary teams, and (2) designing information displays to support *ad hoc*, time-critical teamwork. The next phase of our research will focus on implementing and refining the display prototype for use during real trauma resuscitations.

ACKNOWLEDGMENTS

This work is supported by the National Library of Medicine of the National Institutes of Health under Award Number R21LM011320-01A1 and partially by the National Science Foundation Award No. 1253285. We thank the medical staff at the research site for participating in this study.

REFERENCES

1. American College of Surgeons. *Advanced Trauma Life Support® (ATLS®)*, 8th Edition, Chicago, IL, 2008.
2. Barach, P. and Weinger, M.B. Trauma team performance. In *Trauma: Emergency resuscitation, perioperative anesthesia, surgical management*, Informa Healthcare USA, Inc., New York, NY, 2007.
3. Bardram, J.E., Hansen, T.R., and Soegaard, M. AwareMedia: A shared interactive display supporting social, temporal and spatial awareness in surgery. *Proc. CSCW 2006*, ACM Press (2006), 109-118.
4. Bowers, J.M. and Martin, D. Informing collaborative information visualization through an ethnography of ambulance control. *Proc. ECSCW 1999*, 309-330.
5. Burns, C.M. and Hajdukiewicz, J.R. *Ecological Interface Design*. CRC Press, 2004.
6. Fitzpatrick, G. and Ellingsen, G. A review of 25 years of CSCW research in healthcare. *Computer Supported Cooperative Work 22*, 4-6 (2013), 609-665.
7. Gross, T. Supporting effortless coordination. *Computer Supported Cooperative Work 22*, 4-6 (2013), 425-474.
8. Grudin, J. Partitioning digital worlds: focal and peripheral awareness in multiple monitor use. *Proc. CHI 2001*, ACM Press (2001), 458-465.
9. Gutwin, C. and Greenberg, S. Design for individuals, design for groups: tradeoffs between power and workspace awareness. *Proc. CSCW 1998*, ACM Press (1998), 207-216.
10. Heath, C.C. and Luff, P. Collaborative activity and technological design: Task coordination in London underground control rooms. *Proc. ECSCW 1991*, 65-80.
11. Holzman, T.G. Computer-human interface solutions for emergency medical care. *interactions 6*, 3 (1999), 13-24.
12. Kensing, F. and Blomberg, J. Participatory design: Issues and concerns. *Computer Supported Cooperative Work 7*, 3-4 (1998), 167–185.
13. Kristensen, M., Kyng, M., and Palen, L. Participatory design in emergency medical service: designing for future practice. *Proc. CHI 2006*, ACM Press (2006), 161-170.
14. Kyng, M., Nielsen, E.T., and Kristensen, M. Challenges in designing interactive systems for emergency response. *Proc. DIS 2006*, ACM Press (2006), 301-310.
15. Mankoff, J., Dey, A.K., Hsieh, G., Kientz, J., Lederer, S., and Ames, M. Heuristic evaluation of ambient displays. *Proc. CHI 2003*, ACM Press (2003), 169-176.
16. Matthews, T., Rattenbury, T., and Carter, S. Defining, designing, and evaluating peripheral displays: An analysis using activity theory. *Human-Computer Interaction 22*, (2007), 221-261.
17. Muller, M.J. PICTIVE: Democratizing the dynamics of the design session. In *Participatory Design: Principles and Practices*. Erlbaum Associates Inc., Hillsdale, NJ, 1993, 211–239.
18. Muller, M.J. Participatory design: the third space in HCI. In *Human-Computer Interaction: Development Process*. CRC Press, Boca Raton, FL, 2003, 165–185.
19. Parush, A., Kramer, C., Foster-Hunt, T., Momtahan, K., Hunter, A., and Sohmer, B. Communication and team situation awareness in the OR. *Journal of Biomedical Informatics 44*, (2011), 477-485.
20. Sarcevic, A., Marsic, I., and Burd, R. S. Teamwork errors in trauma resuscitation. *ToCHI 19*, 2 (2012), article 13.
21. Wallace, J.R., Scott, S.D., Lai, E. and Jajalla, D. Investigating the role of a large, shared display in multi-display environments. *Computer Supported Cooperative Work 20*, 6 (2011), 529-561.

Error Related Negativity in Observing Interactive Tasks

Chi Thanh Vi, Izdihar Jamil, David Coyle, Sriram Subramanian
Department of Computer Science, University of Bristol, UK.
{Chi.Vi; David.Coyle; Sriram.Subramanian}@bristol.ac.uk

ABSTRACT
Error Related Negativity is triggered when a user either makes a mistake or the application behaves differently from their expectation. It can also appear while observing another user making a mistake. This paper investigates ERN in collaborative settings where observing another user (the executer) perform a task is typical and then explores its applicability to HCI. We first show that ERN can be detected on signals captured by commodity EEG headsets like an Emotiv headset when observing another person perform a typical multiple-choice reaction time task. We then investigate the anticipation effects by detecting ERN in the time interval when an executer is reaching towards an answer. We show that we can detect this signal with both a clinical EEG device and with an Emotiv headset. Our results show that online single trial detection is possible using both headsets during tasks that are typical of collaborative interactive applications. However there is a trade-off between the detection speed and the quality/prices of the headsets. Based on the results, we discuss and present several HCI scenarios for use of ERN in observing tasks and collaborative settings.

Author Keywords
EEG; BCI; Error Related Negativity; ERN, Tabletop

ACM Classification Keywords
H.5.2 [Information interfaces and presentation]: User Interfaces - Graphical user interfaces;

INTRODUCTION
Off-the-shelf Electroencephalogram (EEG) headsets are becoming widely available at affordable prices and improving signal quality enabling a growing number of interactive applications for competitive gaming [13] or task classification [16]. Typically, EEG studies focus on Event Related Potential (ERP) which is the time- and phase-locked brain response following an event. A popular example is P300, a positive signal that is elicited about 300ms after the process of decision making. It has been widely used to recognize an intended selection of a speller [15] or an object on a multi-touch surface [27].

CHI 2014, April 26–May 1, 2014, Toronto, Ontario, Canada.

http://dx.doi.org/10.1145/2556288.2557015

Error Related Negativity (ERN) is another form of ERP that can be triggered in the brain when a user is aware of the obvious error(s) or confused about the last decision made in a time-critical task or the application behaves differently from their expectation [4, 8]. For example, ERN would be produced when pressing the LEFT key while intending to press the RIGHT key in a time critical multiple choice task. Previous studies have shown that ERN signals usually appear and peak within 150ms of the committed action [9]. Often ERN is detected offline using an averaging of EEG signals around the event onset from multiple trials (e.g. [4, 18]). However, recent studies demonstrate that ERN can be detected online and on a single-trial with expensive, clinical headsets (e.g. [5, 8]) and commodity headset (e.g. [23]). This opens ERN's use in interactive applications where the system can provide assistance once it can detect that the user is aware of their accidental action (i.e. in gaming or spatial navigation).

To date most examples of ERN have focused on detecting the signal by recording signals from the executer of the task. Recent endeavors [6, 19, 22] suggest that ERN signals even appear while observing another user making errors. These studies confirm the existence of negative potential within 250ms after the event onset and analysis of the signals' origin confirm that they are ERNs. This is useful in scenarios where the executer is not aware of their error but that error is spotted by an observer or supervisor. In current studies, the observer did not have much opportunity to anticipate the executer's actions and often relied on the answer displayed. In HCI scenarios, the executer's actions may become visible to the observer even before the action is committed. For example, in collaborative tabletops, an observer has awareness of an executer's actions through their reaching gesture [21].

We investigate the effect of anticipation in an observing task where the outcome of an action is revealed before that action is committed which has not been investigated with ERN in an observing task before. This can have many applications in pair-programming, collaborative tabletops and emergency response applications. We first investigate these anticipation effects with an expensive clinical EEG system to demonstrate that the signal is present and can be detected. Following this we investigate if an Emotiv headset has the similar detection capability.

We start by repeating an experiment from van Schie et al. [22] with an Emotiv headset to demonstrate that Observer ERN can be detected in a single trial and online basis, with the accuracy up to 64%, using a commodity headset.

After that, we investigated the anticipation effect in observing tasks when one person observes another person committing errors. Our results show that there are ERN-like patterns detected in the observer's EEG about 368ms after the initial movements happened and 55ms before the errors are committed. Following this result, we then show that the Emotiv headset can capture these patterns in the same experiment settings. Finally, we discuss the implications of our results on interactive applications.

The contributions of this paper are: (a) we demonstrate that off-the-shelf EEG devices like an Emotiv EEG headset can capture ERN in an observing task from channels in the frontal-central part of the brain; (b) we investigate the anticipation effects in collaborative settings demonstrated by the ERN detected in an observer's EEG signals before the action is committed; (c) through a final experiment we show that these anticipation effects can still be demonstrated using off-the-shelf EEG devices such as the Emotiv EEG headset.

RELATED WORK

EEG and Passive Brain Computer Interface

In the field of physiological computing, EEG is widely chosen because of its high temporal resolution, ease of use and the reasonably low cost. EEG-based BCI system for healthy users has been gaining interest because of its reliability and usability; opening them for creating new types of applications [29]. Because of this, passive BCI (beside active BCI and reactive BCI) was proposed as one type of new BCI systems [28, 29]. It can be defined as a BCI system that processes neural activity arising from users' involuntary control. An example of this is ERN, an error-potential used to correct a user's erroneous action.

Error Related Negativity (ERN)

ERN is a form of an ERP triggered in the brain when a person makes a mistake or the application behaves differently from their expectation [4]. This pattern is produced in a person's brain when they are aware of the obvious error(s) that they have made; either through system feedback or individual realization [8]. ERN peaks within 150ms after the action onset and has amplitude varied in accordance with the awareness of the mistake. Interestingly, ERN also appears when the user is confused about their last decision [4]. This pattern has been discovered by researchers using both expensive devices [4, 8] and commodity devices (such as Emotiv) [23]. ERN is useful in interactive applications when it is detected immediately following the triggered moment. To this end, researchers have looked at detecting this pattern in real-time, and on a single trial basis with accuracy up to 80% [3, 8, 20]. Vi and Subramanian [23] showed that this detection can be done using a low-cost and off-the-shelf headset like Emotiv with around 65% accuracy. This makes ERN more accessible to game developers and other consumer application designers.

Error Related Negativity (ERN) in Observing Task

Recent endeavors [1, 6, 19, 22] suggest that ERN signals even appear while observing another user making errors. For example, Miltner et al. [19] reported the generation of an ERN potential when participants observed errors committed in a choice reaction time (RT) task. Moreover, van Schie et al. [22] reported an ERN pattern elicited in an observer when observing another person performing a modified Eriksen flanker task [7]. Other researches have confirmed these results by showing observed ERN following observations of other's errors [1, 19]. These results suggested that similar neural processes trigger the detection of a person's own error as well as the detection of others. Interestingly, de Bruijn et al. [6] aimed to disentangle the dependency of ERN on error or reward. Their results show that the performance monitoring as reflected by the ERN is error-specific and not directly dependent on reward. As a result, our study focuses on the error awareness of the observers.

To date, all studies of ERN in observation tasks only look at situations where the outcome of the action becomes visible around the moment where the action is committed (e.g. in [22]). Furthermore, these studies focus on detecting the ERN pattern using averaging methods for the purpose of confirming the pattern's existence. We are not aware of studies that investigate the context where the observer can anticipate the executer's actions through their gestures towards the target.

In these contexts, anticipation effects can cause the observer to trigger an ERN before the moment when the executer finishes the action. Successfully detecting this pattern can be useful in many HCI applications such as collaborative tabletops, pair-programming and emergency response scenarios.

EXPERIMENT 1: ERIKSEN FLANKER TASK ON PC

The purpose of this experiment is twofold: first to validate, based on the study in [22] and [6] that we can detect the ERN signal on an observer using off the shelf brain sensing technology; second to verify that the ERN pattern can be detected using the classifier presented in [23] using an off the shelf headset.

Task and Procedure

Each participant performed the experiment paired with an actor. We used an actor in all of our experiments to trigger the ERN signal on the participant. Only the participants wore an Emotiv EEG headset which has the ability to capture EEG signals of 14 channels in the 10-20 international system. Participants were told about the experimental goals to explain why they had to wear the EEG headset and not the actor. Participants were not aware of the actor's role and were led to believe that the actor is another participant. As the window of recognizing the ERN signal is very small, the role of the actor is to perform certain actions that will maximize the ERN detection from the observer during the task period.

The experimental procedure is similar to the task carried out in [4] and [7]. To mimic the experimental conditions for a typical Flanker task experiment and reduce noise in data collection (such as in [4]), both the actor and observer were seated side by side in front of a screen in a dimly lit room. Participants were told to sit comfortably and minimize body, facial, and eye movement as well as to blink as infrequently as possible during the task.

Figure 1. Observation of Flanker Task with the executer (left) and the observer (right)

Trial: Each trial began with a black screen for 3s, followed by a fixation dot in the center of the screen for 200ms. After that, the screen remains clear for 200ms before one of four stimuli was displayed for 300ms. There were two types of arrows, each type had two stimuli: congruent stimuli (<<<<< and >>>>>) and incongruent stimuli (<<><< and >><>>). All four stimuli were used in our trials in random order. At a viewing distance of about 100cm, the visual angle of the arrow stimuli was 0.4° vertically and 0.6° horizontally, and between them was 0.3° space. The executer was asked to press the direction key as soon as they saw the stimulus to indicate the direction of the middle arrow. The input device used for this key press was a remote control (Genius Media Pointer). The pressed key (< or >) was displayed for 1s afterward. Note that the executer can be either the participant or the actor depending on the trial condition, as explained below.

The observer was then asked to rate the correctness of their last action by choosing one of three options: *1. Sure correct*, *2. Do Not Know*, and *3. Sure Incorrect*. This was input through a mini keypad.

Practice trials: Participants were asked to perform a version of the Flanker task where they had to press one of two keys to specify the direction of a central arrow that was bounded by flanker arrows. This was done to make the participant familiar with the task that will be performed by the actor giving them an idea of what to expect as quick as possible when the stimuli appears.

Each participant performed a practice block of 40 trials where they had to press the direction key and rate the correctness of their action in each trial. During this time, the actor sat beside the participant and played a dormant role. In these trials, the directional arrows, which appeared on the screen after participants pressed a button, were exactly like the pressed button. We did not collect EEG signals or any data during practice block.

Experimental Trial: After finishing the practice block, the participant and the actor switched places. The actor now had to press the directional keys and the participant (the observer) rated the actor's last performance. However, the actor hid her hands under a box to prevent the observer from seeing which button was physically pressed (see Figure 1). The observer was instructed to focus on the screen to judge the correctness of the actor's answers. As in [1, 19] participants were instructed to silently count the number of incorrect selection. However, the result displayed on the screen was independent of the button press: 40% of the time the computer displayed a wrong answer (the 'pressed button' is opposite of the middle arrow of the stimulus). This allowed us precise control of the experiment settings.

The actor performed 4 blocks of 50 trials each with 3 minutes break after each block. We collected 200 trials from each participants of the experiment. We recruited 6 university students, aged between 21 and 29 years old to give us a total of 1200 trials for this experiment.

Data Collection and Analysis

The EEG signals were captured from the Emotiv headset. Although Emotiv is an off-the-shelf headset, its ability of capturing EEG signals were validated by previous studies such as in [23, 24]. EEG signals were divided into 2s length epochs; 1s before and 1s after the key press moment. With the sampling frequency at 128Hz the length of each epoch is 256 samples. The first 200ms (about 25 samples) of each epoch were used to remove DC offset following which all epochs were filtered in 3-8Hz to remove components that are not in the ERN frequency bands of that particular epoch. Our chosen band ([3 – 8Hz]) was narrower compared to [22] ([1-10Hz]) but still keeps valuable information about ERN that is at least in part in the θ-freq band (4-7Hz) [17].

We then employed the classifying method described in [3] and validated in [20, 23] to analyze the data. It can be summarized as follow. For each channel, we used the holdout method where half of the trials (100 trials) were used for training via a logistic regression technique and other half were used for testing. We performed a t-test on the classifier output for each channel per user to check if there was a significant difference between two types of output (correct and incorrect epochs). Here, there were two categories to classify: correct or incorrect. Epochs were divided as correct and incorrect trials based on the participants ratings. "*Do not know*" rated epochs were removed from the analysis (~5% of 1200 trials in total).

The classifier performed the classification on a single trial basis. The result then was compared with the ground truth of each trial. This holdout method has advantages of large training and testing datasets, and fast processing time. It also mimicked an online working version where a coefficient matrix is extracted for each user through performing a training block (the first consecutive half number of trials), this is used for detecting ERN pattern online (the second consecutive half). To minimize the bias of this method, no samples of the first half was used in the second half. Also in the training set, the number of correct trial was randomly picked so that it equals the number of the incorrect trials. This classification model was trained blindly (with no estimation of the expected accuracy) and test it on an unseen, fixed test set. As this approach was not repeated for a set of parameters, it should not cause any over-fitting effect.

Result

Using the above method, our results reveal significant differences in classification rates (for correct and incorrect epochs) for FC5, F7, and F3 channels. The classification rate for the rest of the channels was not significantly better than chance.

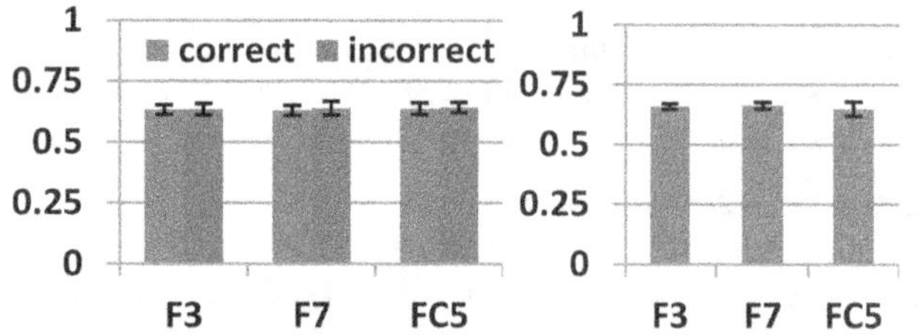

Figure 2. Mean classifier accuracy (left) and AUC (right) for different channels with error bars.

Figure 2 shows the average accuracy of three sensing channels. These three channels correspond to the frontal lobe which is in line with the literature about the origin of ERN (the Anterior Cingulate Cortex - ACC) [26]. Figure 3 illustrates the average EEG signals at F3 and F7 over all epochs belonging to two cases: correct and incorrect. Here, the averaged EEG signals for correct and incorrect over all trials and all participants are displayed in blue and red, respectively. For the incorrect trials (the red curve), we can see an ERN-like pattern (a negative peak followed by a positive peak) at around 250ms after the actor's committed action (the black vertical line). Note that as a convention, ERPs are usually plotted upside down.

We did a Receiver Operating Characteristic (ROC) Analysis to investigate the efficiency of the classifier by evaluating its discriminating power. ROC analysis uses two distinct inputs: hit rate (or true positive rate) and false alarm rate (or false positive rate) as two separate performance measures. Figure 4 shows ROC curves for F3 and F7 channels. The further the curve is from the diagonal line, the more effective the classifier. The area under the curve (AUC) gives an indication of the performance of the classifier. An AUC of 1 indicates a perfect classifier and 0.5 indicates a random chance of classification. Our classifier achieves an averaged value of 0.66 over these three channels (F3, F7, and FC5). Their AUC are shown in Figure 2 (right).

Discussion

This study demonstrates that Emotiv EEG headset is capable of capturing EEG signals with sufficient quality for a classifier to be able to detect ERN pattern with an accuracy of about 65%. The characteristic of detected ERN patterns is similar to previous studies using more expensive devices [22]. Our results further demonstrate that the classifier described in [3] and validated in [20, 23] can be used to detect ERN in observer tasks. This means an interactive application can have a similar classifier detecting both observer and executer ERNs with minimal modification to the software.

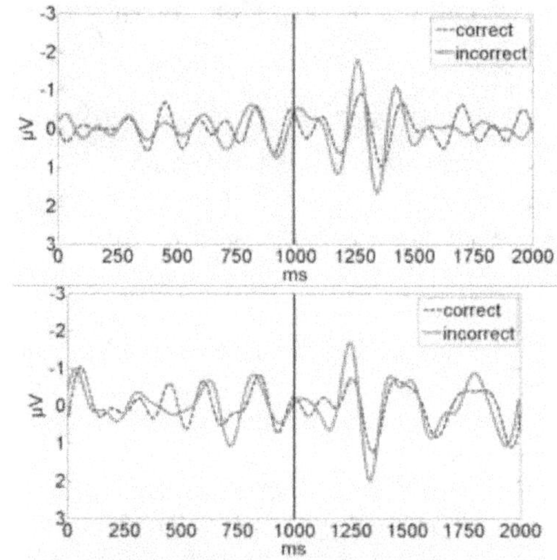

Figure 3. Average EEG signals at channel F3 (top) and F7 (bottom).

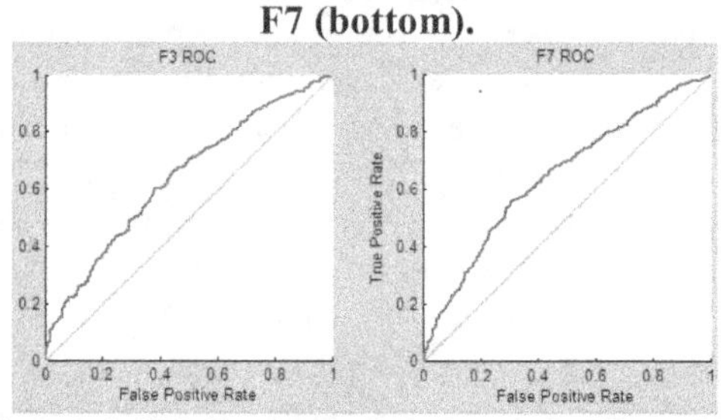

Figure 4. ROC curves for channels F3 and F7

One example of interactive tasks that can benefit from our results is in pair programming where two programmers work together as partner, on the same machine, to complete a programming work with their roles switched frequently [25]. One programmer is the driver, who performs all "on computer" tasks. The other is the observer or navigator who reviews each line of code and points out the errors as it is being written. Usually this error correction process requires the observer to interrupt the programming process, point out the location of the errors in his opinion either using his hand or using the mouse/keyboard that the driver is controlling.

However, our experiment results suggest that monitoring the appearance of ERN in the observer's EEG can speed up this error correction process. Each action of the driver is considered a trial of a multiple choice RT task. If the

ERN is detected in the observer's brain, it can be used to pinpoint the whereabouts of the error (e.g. highlighting the code section) which is 250ms after the action's committed moment. The system can also provide suitable suggestions based on the context of the location where the error was triggered. This can happen either with or without the error awareness of the executer.

In addition, we believe the detection accuracy can be enhanced by improving the visibility and awareness of the performer's actions through better visualization. This will elicit higher amplitude of ERN which can improve the classification rate. More detailed implications of this study to HCI are discussed at the end of this paper.

OBERSEVER ERN IN A TABLETOP TASK

In the first study the participant did not have any opportunity to see the actions of the actor and often relied on the answer displayed. In collaborative HCI scenarios like around a tabletop, a participant can usually anticipate the executer's actions through their gestures which reveal the outcome of an action before that action is committed.

The awareness caused by anticipation gives the observer more time to form an opinion on the action. This could potentially reduce the time-critical aspect of the ERN leading to a low signal quality. Alternatively, the observer may reach an opinion of the executer's action as soon as they see the initial cues. In this case, we may detect a good quality ERN in the observer well before the executer has even completed the action.

We are not aware of any experimental investigation of the effect of anticipation in an observing task where the outcome of an action is revealed before that action is committed. Therefore we extended the duration between start and committed moments of the actor's action to investigate this effect. We also aimed to determine the moment when the observer elicits an ERN. Successfully detecting this opens a rich design space of interest to HCI such as collaborative tabletops and pair-programming.

Experiment Setup

Each experimental session involved two users – an executer and an observer seated around a rear-projected FTIR interactive table of height 76cm. The executer was an actor trained to do this study while the observer was our experiment participant. The executer and observer sat opposite to each other so that they were aware of each other's movements and actions (similar to the setup in [22]). The projection area of the table was 72cm x 48cm (resolution 1024x768 pixels) and touch detection was done through a Point-Grey Dragonfly 2 camera.

All participants performed the task with the same actor (the person at the top in Figure 5). However, participants were led to believe that the actor is just another participant like themselves. In order to study the effect of anticipation, we had two experimental conditions – a *close layout* and *far layout*.

In the *close layout* the actor's buttons (size 100x100 pixels each) were placed right under their hands and next to each other. The participant would struggle to see the actors hand movement limiting their ability to anticipate the outcome before the actor commits to the action. Any ERN elicited in the participant (observer) in this condition would be because of the committed action of the actor.

In the *far layout* the two confirmation buttons were placed close to the left and right edges of the table (200 pixel gaps to left and right edges with 524 pixels distance between them; 80 pixels gap from two buttons' centers to the edge of the actor's table side). The actor was asked to keep his hands touching two touch sensors placed on his side of the table (see the table's top edge in Figure 5, right). In order to select a response the actor had to lift one hand from the rest position and move towards the button. This action took approximately 400ms giving the participant sufficient time to anticipate the actor's actions. The actor's other hand was left in the rest position touching the sensor during this action.

Task and Procedure

Each participant wore the EEG cap of the BE-MRI System from EbNeuro. In this experiment, 19 electrodes were used (Fp1, Fp2, F7, F3, Fz, F4, F8, T3, C3, Cz, C4, T4, T5, P3, Pz, P4, T6, O1, O2). This system has higher sampling frequency, larger coverage, and has access to Cz channel compare to Emotiv EEG headset. Participants observed and gave feedback about the correctness of the actor's performance in an Eriksen flanker task.

Each trial began with a black screen for 3s, followed by a fixation dot in the center of the screen for 200ms. After that, the screen remains clear for 200ms before one of four stimuli was displayed at the center of the table for 300ms. All four stimuli were used in a random order.

In both *close* and *far layouts* (Figure 5 left and right), the actor then touched one of two buttons to indicate the direction of the middle arrow. In *close layout* there is no noticeable hand movement whereas in the *far layout* the actor has to reach the button to make a selection.

After the answer button was selected, it was highlighted in red for 1s before turning back to the initial color. This is to re-enforce to the observer the actor's selection. The participant was then asked to rate the correctness of their last action by choosing one of three options: 1. Sure correct, 2. Do Not Know, and 3. Sure Incorrect. During the experiment, the observers were asked to minimize their body and facial movements as well as blink as infrequent as possible. They were also instructed to guess the outcome of each answer as quick as possible although they could input that answer at their own pace. As in [1, 19] participants were instructed to silently count the number of incorrect selection. Since it was not possible to control the ratio of correct and incorrect trials to the extent done in Experiment 1, the actor was asked to keep the incorrect selection rate to between 25 and 30%. The actor received practice to minimize difference in action between correct and incorrect gestures.

Each participant performed 2 blocks of 80 trials each per layout. The order of presentation of the blocks was controlled using a Latin square to reduce order effects. Participants received 3mins break between blocks and the whole experiment took about 90mins per participants including about 40mins of setup time.

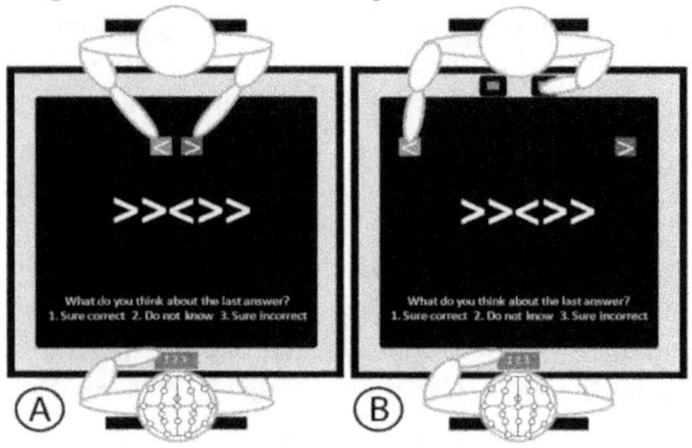

Figure 5. Tabletop Flanker task a) close, b) far layout.

Ten participants (7 males) between the age of 19 and 31 volunteered for the study. All were from the local university and did not participate in the earlier experiment. All participants had normal or correct-to-normal vision, and none of them were color blind. Also no participant had undergone brain surgery or had any known neurological disorders. Participants wore EEG cap during the experiment. Participants received a financial compensation for their participation in the study.

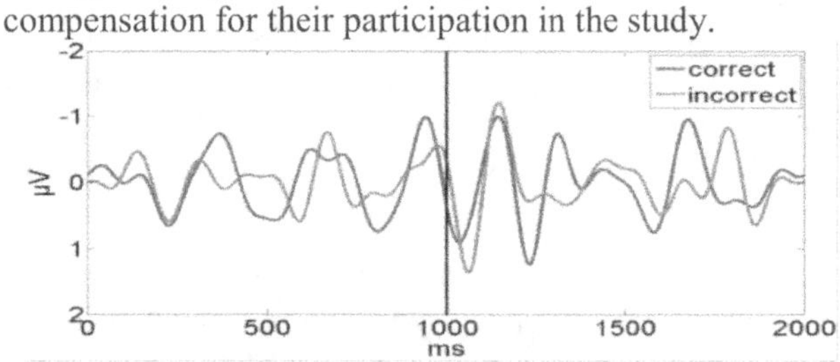

Figure 6. Averaged signals of the 'close' layout at Cz

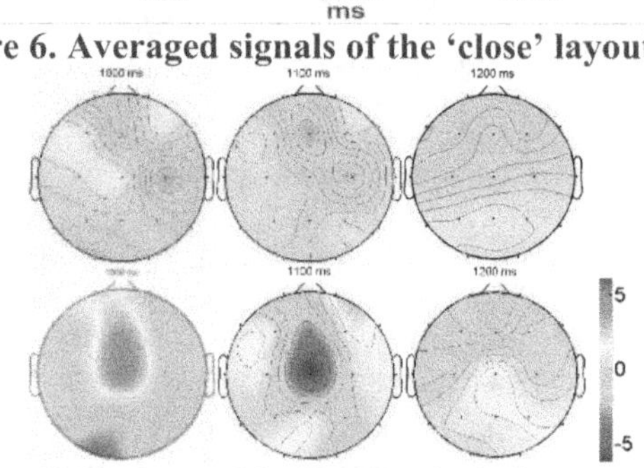

Figure 7. Topographic distribution of correct trials (top) and incorrect trials (bottom) in the 'close' layout at the intervals: key press (left), 100ms after (middle), and 200ms after (right).

Data Collection and Analysis

EEG signals were collected using the BE-MRI System from EbNeuro. The sampling frequency was set at 4 KHz and electrode impedance was below 5 KΩ. EEG signals were then down sampled to 1 KHz before being divided into 2s epochs around the touching moment, which is also the moment that the results were displayed or the touched button was highlighted in red. It is also assumed to be the moment when participants became aware that the actor had or had not made a mistake. Epochs were averaged, filtered, and divided into groups as in prior experiment.

Result

We collected 3200 trials, 1600 each for close and far layout. The number of incorrect trials was 27% in the close layout and 30% in the far layout. 7 trials in the close layout and 30 in the far layout were rated as "*Do Not Know*" by the participant.

Close Layout Analysis: Figure 6 shows the averaged signals in Cz channel in the close layout. It can be seen that there is a difference, however small, between incorrect trials (red curve) and correct trials (blue curve). Latency of the highest peak after the touch button was pressed was 140ms. However, the topographic distribution (Figure 7) shows a clear difference between correct and incorrect trials around the time of the peak. It can be seen that there is a high density of negative EEG at the central and frontal area around the latency of the highest peak after the key press onset (Figure 7, middle).

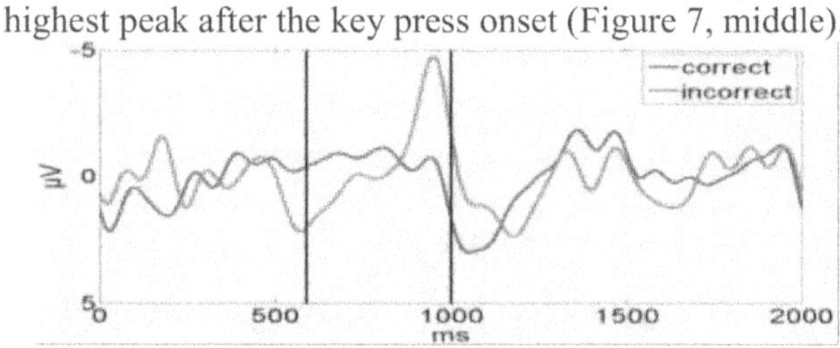

Figure 8. Averaged signals of the 'far' layout at Cz

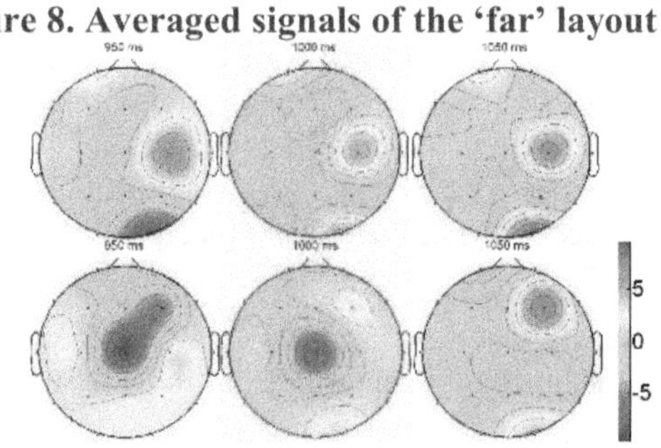

Figure 9. Topographic distribution of correct trials (top) and incorrect trials (bottom) in the 'far' layout at the intervals: 50ms before key press (left), key press (middle), and 50ms after key press (right).

Far Layout Analysis: In the far layout, the differences can be seen clearer with the averaged EEG signals in Figure 8. The left vertical line depicts the averaged moment that the actor lifted up his hand and started to reach to the answer button. The right vertical line depicts the moment that the actor pressed the answer button. It took the actor averagely 428ms (correct trials) and 423ms (incorrect trials) to touch the answer. There was no significant difference found between these two durations ($p > 0.05$).

The signals peak at 55ms before the answer buttons were touched. The topographic distribution (Figure 9) shows a clear difference (in the density of negative EEG at the frontal and central area) between correct and incorrect trials at the time of the peak (~ 50ms before button touch, left figures) and at the time of the touch (middle figures).

Using the same classifying method described in the previous experiment, we found that several channels in the frontal-central area of the brain yield successful classification. More details are in depicted in Figure 10. The highest classification rates are from channel Cz for both *close layout* (correct/incorrect = 70.43%/68.71%) and *far layout* (correct/incorrect = 73.02%/72.40%).

We also calculated the AUC for the above channels. Their values are plotted in Figure 11. Overall, the classifier achieved averaged AUC values of 0.6733 for the *close layout* and 0.6602 for the *far layout*.

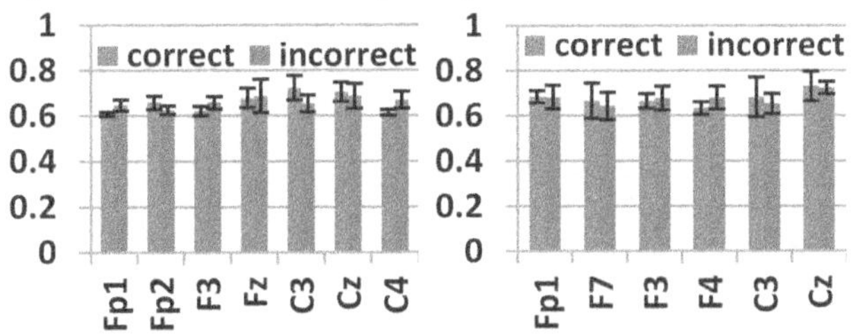

Figure 10. Classification rates of *close layout* (left) and *far layout* (right) with error bars

Discussion

The result of this experiment demonstrates that ERN can be detected in an observer in both hand layouts. It also shows that there is an anticipation effect where the ERN pattern in the observer's mind appears about 55ms before the touching action is committed.

The experiment mimicked a classic Flanker task to keep our experimental settings in line with other research in this area. Interactive applications can trigger ERN using a similar paradigm. It may be possible to detect the ERN pattern earlier by making the actor's movement clearer to the observers that can trigger the awareness sooner.

It is worth noting that the classifier used is a light-weight module which can provide an output in less than 1ms for a 1kHz sample once the β coefficient matrix is known for that participant (tested in Matlab ®R2013a 64 bit, Intel® Core™ i3 CPU 3.10GHz, 8GB RAM). This means any interactive application could act on an executer's action based on the ERN of an observer. For example, in collaborative tabletops a user could be asked for a stronger confirmation if the system detects an ERN in the observer. This could also benefit peer-learning activities where the observer and executer can constantly switch roles to learn from each other.

A drawback of this study is that the EEG cap is an expensive clinical system that is cumbersome to wear, tethered and does not lend itself to applications that require the observer to move freely within the experimental environment. This further limits the possibility of both the observer and the executer wearing the cap in a realistic environment. The following experiment aims to address this drawback.

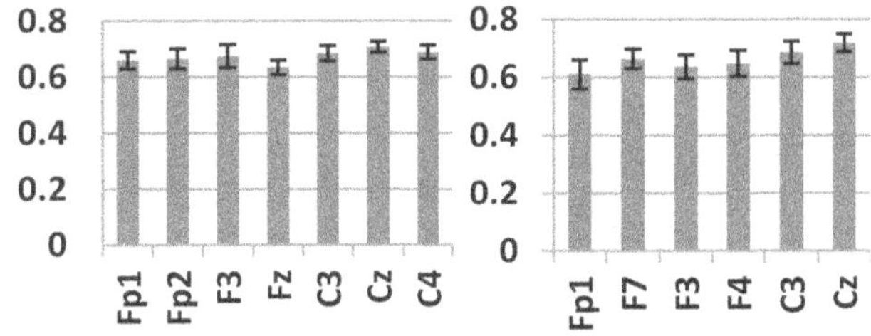

Figure 11. AUC for *close* (left) and *far layouts* (right) with error bars

TABLETOP OBSERVER ERN WITH EMOTIV

The purpose of this experiment is to see if the Emotiv EEG headset can be used to detect the same pattern as in experiment 2. This would then open up the use of observer ERN to a wide range of interactive applications by detecting and predicting errors in observers' mind.

Task and Procedure

The experimental setup, task and procedure were identical to the previous experiment. We recruited 11 participants (8 males), aged between 20 and 31 years old. None of them took part in previous studies. The experiment took about 60mins per participant. This shorter experiment time, compared to the previous experiment, was due to the shorter setup time needed for Emotiv headset.

As with experiment 2, we collected 320 trials per participants yielding a total of 3520 trials from all participants of the experiment for both *close* and *far layouts* with 1760 trials each. The number of incorrect trials was 26% in the *close layout* and 28% in the *far layout*. 19 trials in the *close layout* and 34 in the *far layout* were rated as "Do Not Know" by the participant.

Data Collection and Analysis

Signals were collected at a sampling frequency of 128 Hz using the Emotiv EEG Neuroheadset. They were then divided into 2s epochs around the touching moments, which is also the moment that the results were displayed. The analysis was the same as in previous experiment.

Result

Close layout: Figure 12 shows average signals at channel AF3 in the *close layout* over all participants and all trials. It can be seen that there is a difference between incorrect trials (red curve) and correct trials (blue curve) at the latency of 188ms after the moments where the button answers were pressed. This pattern has a negative peak appeared within the time period of 250ms after the event onset, similar to previous studies such as in [6, 22].

Far layout: Figure 13 shows the averaged EEG signals for the *far layout* over all participants and all trials. There is also an ERN-like pattern which peaks at about 3ms after the answer button was touched. This indicates that if this is the ERN pattern, the observer must have the judgment about the actor's action's correctness about 250ms before which also is an indication that the observers have made the decisions before the answer buttons were touched.

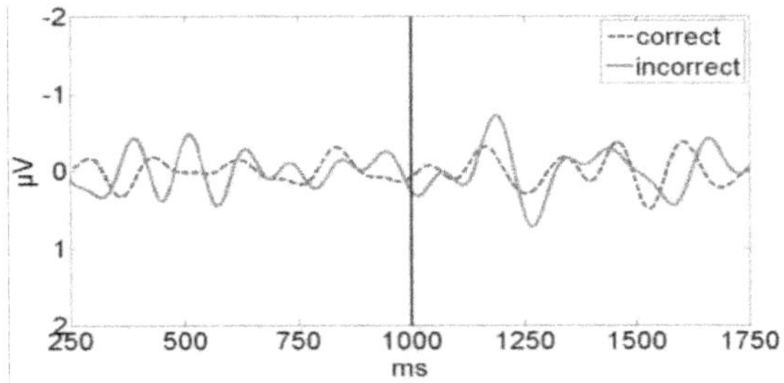

Figure 12. Averaged signals of the close layout at AF3. The vertical line is the button touched moments

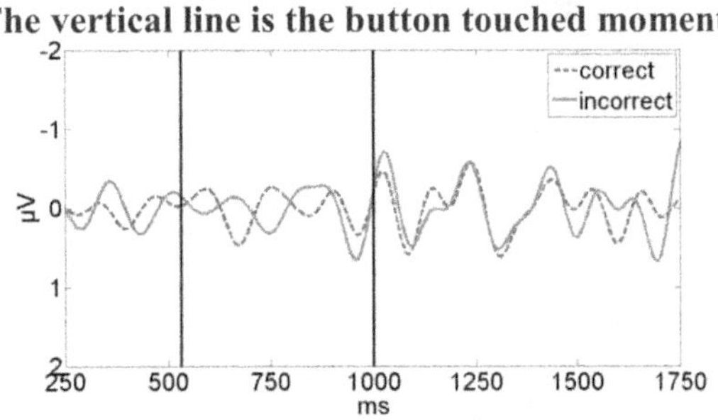

Figure 13. Average signals of the far layout at F3. The left vertical line is the averaged hand lift-off moments, the right vertical line is the button touched moments.

Between Figure 6 & Figure 12 and Figure 8 & Figure 13, we observer similar ERN-like patterns (negative peaks 140ms after touch moments in Figure 6; 188ms after touch moments in Figure 12; 50ms before touch moment in Figure 8; 3ms after touch moment in Figure 13).

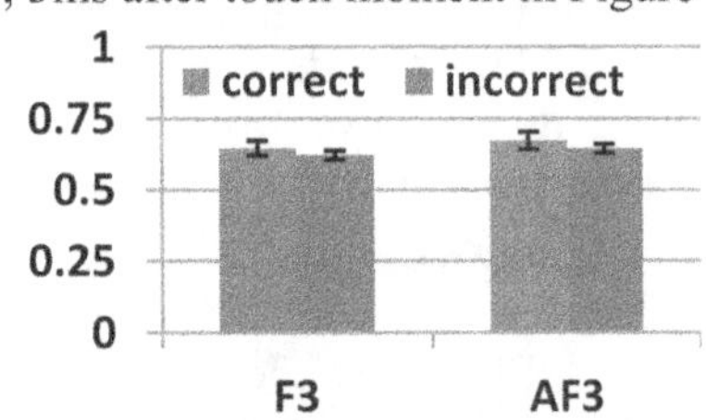

Figure 14. Classification rates with error bars

Using the same classifying method described in the first experiment on the collected signals from Emotiv device, we found that in close layout, channel AF3 yields the classifying results with 67.32% of correct trials were classified as correct and 64.57% of incorrect trials were classified as incorrect. Additionally, in far layout, channel F3 yields the successful classification with classification rates for correct and incorrect trials are 65.03% and 62.30% respectively (see Figure 14).

Additionally, we calculated the area under the curve (AUC) values for channels AF3 and F3 to justify how well the classifier performs on these two channels. Our obtained results show that AUC for channels AF3 and F3 were 0.6483 and 0.6486 respectively.

Discussion

The results from this experiment show that it is possible that ERN can be observed in collaborative tasks from the observers' EEG. Although the channels that show the detection are limited to AF3 (*close layout)* and F3 (*far layout*), it is an indication that an off-the-shelf EEG headset such as Emotiv is capable of detecting this pattern. As a result, other commodity headsets which have access to these channels can also harness the advantage of detecting ERN pattern in observing tasks.

There is a shift in latency of the ERN peaks between experiments 2 and 3. The latency differences of about 40ms (*close layout*) and 60ms (*far layout*) are due to the devices used in each experiment; EbNeuro BE-MRI system (~USD 10k) and Emotiv headset (~USD 300). We can postulate many reasons for the difference:

- The buffer used in each device is different. While Emotiv headset waits for the buffer to be filled before pushing signals toward the receiving Bluetooth dongle, EbNeuro pushes the signals continuously for each collected data sample. As the process of continuously pushing signals requires much more expensive Digital Signal Processing (DSP) module, this reflects the price difference between the two devices. Furthermore using Bluetooth to transfer might add to the latency.
- While EbNeuro pushes signals continuously at the original sampling frequency (4KHz), Emotiv samples EEG signals internally at 2KHz then down samples it to 128Hz. This can introduce latency.

From the experiment's results, it can be seen that there is a trade-off between how early the ERN pattern in observing tasks can be observed vs. the prices and quality of EEG headsets. Although the differences are small (from about 40ms to 60ms), they should be considered carefully to fit with the goals of each interactive task.

DISCUSSION

In addition to the benefit of correcting one's own errors, ERN has the potential to enrich interactive applications in the collaborative working setting. The results from our studies can provide guidance on how best to begin harnessing ERN for such interactive experiences. From our results, HCI designers can employ ERN in interactive tasks to pinpoint the executer's error's whereabouts, which can be from 50ms before to 250ms following the triggered action, depend on the interaction technique.

The usefulness of executer' and observer' ERNs in interactive tasks depends on the usage context and the designer's creativity in making use of it. Here we suggest some applications to highlight design possibilities.

Collaborative tabletop settings

Groupware applications use embodiments to help people stay aware of the presence, location and movement of users in collaborative tasks [11]. They can either be real embodiments which make use of the actual physical body of the user or virtual embodiments which are digital representations of users (e.g. Telepointers [10]).

In these settings, real and virtual embodiments both provide obvious information of awareness to other group users. Therefore, an observer can judge quickly about the correctness of the action being performed. However, this information is not accessible unless the observers provide feedback to the performer or the system. This is a time consuming process and can interrupt the performance.

Our results show that an integrated ERN detection module can be used to monitor an ERN's appearance in the observers. As the classification time is about 1ms with the coefficient matrix known, the detected ERN can be used to trace back the time period where the observer thinks the performing user made a mistake or is confused about their action. Although these time periods range from 50ms before to 250ms following the committed action, careful task design can help to shorten this range to specific time points. This is due to different interaction techniques providing different awareness to the observers leading to different ERN triggered moments. Therefore, HCI designers should design their applications to maximize the in order to trigger clearer ERNs.

As a simple example, an action of a performer leading to an observer ERN can result in an ignorable pop-up menu that can help revert or discuss based on the source of ERN in the observer. Rather than merely automate the action's reversion, ERN can serve as an information point for discussion and clarification between the collaborators. The pop-up menu can then provide contextually relevant information including an "undo" item.

The goal is to maximize group awareness of individual's actions without disrupting the work-flow of the task. Further contextual studies can explore this trade-off.

War-rooms / Emergency response

In emergency scenarios, it is crucial to give instructions and make decisions. ERN can be integrated into the Emergency Management Information System [14] so that each decision that has been made can be crossed checked by the observers/ supervisors in the same team. If the executer is made aware that other teammates thinks a mistake is about to be made by the performing action, it can be avoided before it is made. Moreover, if the mistake is already committed, the system can sense if an ERN appears in an observer's brain to speed up the correction.

Gaming scenarios

Usually in shooting games and MMORPGs gamers team up to act against other teams. Here, every decision needs to be precise and made in a timely manner. ERN could be integrated to provide a new tool to team members to observe and react to each other's actions. Detected ERNs from teammates can be combined and displayed as feedback to every continuous action say in the form of an overlay window. This can give gamers an idea of where and when they committed a mistake, which could add to the game tactics a new dimension. This ERN communicating channel, beside verbal and chatting ones, can be used to improve the teamwork and strategic analysis skills during the game hence make it more challenging between teams. However, the mechanism to trigger error-events has to follow an oddball paradigm in the context of a reaction time task.

Limitations of the classification method

Our classifier is based on a linear regression method described in [3] and validated in [20, 23] for single trial ERN detection. Applying this method provides classifying rates of up to 73% accuracy. [23] evaluated the usefulness of different ERN detection accuracies and showed that when integrating an ERN detection module in an interactive application a classifier with 65% accuracy is as good as a classifier with 80% accuracy. Moreover, if a system has very high accuracy (less error rate), it may promote hasty commitment to selections [12] and thereby increase the cost of recovery from an error.

In addition, our classifier requires input EEG signals ±1s around the time-locked event which means that it can detect the ERN pattern 1s after the action. However it can be used to pinpoint the ERN's triggered moment which can be up to 50ms before the action. Despite the delay, this form of ERN detection can still be useful in many applications like in the earlier outlined case of Pair programming. A 1s delay will not affect the benefit of ERN in such activities especially when we can highlight the code-section that is in question. Additionally, other classifier methods can improve accuracy and reduce the window size of input signals leading to earlier detection of the ERN after it is triggered. For instance, a BCI competition on customized classifier increased classification rates of P300 up to 96.5% and motor imaginary up to 94.2% [2].

Moreover, the selection of channels is based on a set of t-tests on the output of the training set. Then, the test set was used to remove under-the-chance classification rate channels as a beta-correction method. A more robust method (e.g. bootstrapping) can be used here to reduce the chance of selecting randomly significant channels.

CONCLUSION

The experiments described in this paper offer some valuable guidelines for HCI designers. We show that ERN patterns can be detected in an observing task using an off-the-shelf EEG headset on a single trial basis. Moreover, we show the anticipation effects in collaborating work where ERN can be detected before a committed action in the observer's mind. We then extended our finding to a commodity headset to show that it can also detect the anticipation effect through the existence of ERN. In our discussions, we suggested novel ways in which HCI applications can benefit from ERN in collaborative and observing environments.

ACKNOWLEDGEMENTS

We thank Dr. Jade Thai (CRICBristol, University of Bristol) and Dr. Rafal Bogacz (University of Oxford) for their help in providing access to the EbNeuro equipment.

REFERENCES

1. Bates, A. T., Patel, T. P. and Liddle, P. F. External Behavior Monitoring Mirrors Internal Behavior Monitoring. J. of Psychophysiology281-288. 2005.
2. Blankertz, B., Muller, K., Krusienski, D. J., Schalk, G., Wolpaw, J. R., Schlogl, A., Pfurtscheller, G., Millan, J. R., Schroder, M. and Birbaumer, N. The BCI competition III: validating alternative approaches to actual BCI problems. IEEE Trans. Neural Syst. Rehabil. Eng. 2006.
3. Christoforos, A., Dimitris, T., Niall, A. and David, H. Temporally adaptive estimation of logistic classifiers on data streams. ADAC, 3, 3 243-261. 2009.
4. Coles., M. K. S. a. M. G. H. Performance Monitoring in a Confusing World: Error-Related Brain Activity, Judgments of Response Accuracy, and Types of Errors. Proc. of JEPHPP, 26, 1 141-151. 2000.
5. Dal Seno, B., Matteucci, M. and Mainardi, L. Online detection of P300 and error potentials in a BCI speller. Computational Intelligence and Neuroscience. 2010.
6. De Bruijn, E. R. A. and von Rhein, D. T. Is your error my concern? An event-related potential study on own and observed error detection in cooperation and competition. Frontiers in Neuroscience, 6. 2012.
7. Eriksen, C. and Schultz, D. Information processing in visual search: A continuous flow conception and experimental results. Attention, Perceptionn & Psychophysics, 25, 4 249-263. 1979.
8. Ferrez, P. W. and Millán, J. D. R. You are wrong!: automatic detection of interaction errors from brain waves. Proc. of IJCAI. 2005.
9. Ganushchak, L. Y. and Schiller, N. O. Brain errormonitoring activity is affected by semantic relatedness: An event-related brain potentials study. J. Cognitive Neuroscience, 20, 5 927-940. 2008.
10. Greenberg, S., Gutwin, C. and Roseman, M. Semantic Telepointers for Groupware. OZCHI. 1996.
11. Gutwin, C. and Greenberg, S. A Descriptive Framework of Workspace Awareness for Real-Time Groupware. CSCW, 11, 3 411-446. 2002.
12. Gutwin, C. and Cockburn, A. Improving list revisitation with ListMaps. AVI. ACM. 2006.
13. Hjelm, S. I. and Browall, C. Brainball - using brain activity for cool competition. NordiCHI. 2000.
14. Kristensen, M., Kyng, M. and Palen, L. Participatory design in emergency medical service: designing for future practice. CHI. ACM. 2006.
15. Krusienski, D. J., Sellers, E. W., McFarland, D. J., Vaughan, T. M. and Wolpaw, J. R. Toward enhanced P300 speller performance. Neuroscience Methods2008
16. Lee, J. C. and Tan, D. S. Using a low-cost electroencephalograph for task classification in HCI research. UIST. 2006.
17. Luu, P., Tucker, D. M. and Makeig, S. Frontal midline theta and the error-related negativity: neurophysiological mechanisms of action regulation. J. Clin Neurophysiol, 115, 8 1821-1835. 2004.
18. Miltner, W. H. R., Braun, C. H. and Coles, M. G. H. Event-related brain potentials following incorrect feedback in a time-estimation task: Evidence for a neural system for error detection. Cognitive Neuroscience. 1997.
19. Miltner, W. H. R., Brauer, J., Hecht, H., Trippe, R. and Coles, M. Parallel brain activity for self-generated and observed errors. 2004.
20. Parra, L., Alvino, C., Tang, A., Pearlmutter, B., Yeung, N., Osman, A. and Sajda, P. Linear Spatial Integration for Single-Trial Detection in Encephalography. NeuroImage, 17, 1 223-230. 2002.
21. Pinelle, D., Nacenta, M., Gutwin, C. and Stach, T. The effects of co-present embodiments on awareness and collaboration in tabletop groupware. GI. 2008.
22. van Schie, H. T., Mars, R. B., Coles, M. G. H. and Bekkering, H. Modulation of activity in medial frontal and motor cortices during error observation. Nature Neuroscience, 7, 5 549-554. 2004.
23. Vi, C. and Subramanian, S. Detecting error-related negativity for interaction design. CHI. ACM. 2012.
24. Vi, C., Takashima, K., Yokoyama, H., Liu, G., Itoh, Y., Subramanian, S. and Kitamura, Y. D-FLIP: Dynamic and Flexible Interactive PhotoShow. Springer. 2013.
25. Williams, L. and Kessler, R. Pair Programming Illuminated. Addison-Wesley Longman. 2002.
26. Yeung, N. and Cohen, J. D. The Impact of Cognitive Deficits on Conflict Monitoring: Predictable Dissociations Between the Error-Related Negativity and N2. Psychological Science, 17164-171. 2006.
27. Yuksel, B. F., Donnerer, M., Tompkin, J. and Steed, A. A novel brain-computer interface using a multi-touch surface. CHI. 2010.
28. Zander, T., Kothe, C., Jatzev, S. and Gaertner, M. Enhancing Human-Computer Interaction with Input from Active and Passive Brain-Computer Interfaces. 2010.
29. Zander, T. O. and Kothe, C. Towards passive brain–computer interfaces: applying brain–computer interface technology to human–machine systems in general. Journal of Neural Engineering, 8, 2. 2011.

Dynamic Difficulty Using Brain Metrics of Workload

Daniel Afergan[1], Evan M. Peck[1], Erin T. Solovey[2], Andrew Jenkins[1], Samuel W. Hincks[1], Eli T. Brown[1], Remco Chang[1], Robert J.K. Jacob[1]

[1]Tufts University
Medford, MA USA

[2]Drexel University
Philadelphia, PA USA

{afergan,epeck02,ajenki01,shincks,ebrown,remco,jacob}@cs.tufts.edu, erin@cs.drexel.edu

ABSTRACT
Dynamic difficulty adjustments can be used in human-computer systems in order to improve user engagement and performance. In this paper, we use functional near-infrared spectroscopy (fNIRS) to obtain passive brain sensing data and detect extended periods of boredom or overload. From these physiological signals, we can adapt a simulation in order to optimize workload in real-time, which allows the system to better fit the task to the user from moment to moment. To demonstrate this idea, we ran a laboratory study in which participants performed path planning for multiple unmanned aerial vehicles (UAVs) in a simulation. Based on their state, we varied the difficulty of the task by adding or removing UAVs and found that we were able to decrease errors by 35% over a baseline condition. Our results show that we can use fNIRS brain sensing to detect task difficulty in real-time and construct an interface that improves user performance through dynamic difficulty adjustment.

Author Keywords
BCI; passive brain-computer interface; dynamic difficulty; fNIRS; near-infrared spectroscopy; workload; UAV

ACM Classification Keywords
H.5.m. Information Interfaces and Presentation (e.g. HCI): Miscellaneous

INTRODUCTION
Task difficulty can induce a wide variety of cognitive and emotional states that can impact performance [16]. A problem that exceeds an individual's skill set can be overwhelming and cause anxiety, while a problem that does not utilize a person's skills may result in boredom and apathy. When users are in states of anxiety or boredom, they do not focus on their task, learn less, are less productive, and more prone to errors [30]. Minimizing anxiety and boredom during a task can keep people in a state of *flow*, helping a user maintain focus on the current task and perform well.

CHI 2014, April 26 - May 01 2014, Toronto, ON, Canada

http://dx.doi.org/10.1145/2556288.2557230

To keep people in an optimal state, *dynamic difficulty adjustment (DDA)* systems automatically modify the difficulty of the task in real-time. By monitoring user state and adapting the system when it detects detrimental states, a dynamic difficulty system improves performance and helps users maximize their amount of productive work. However, DDA systems face two primary challenges. First, DDA systems must infer a correct model of the user's skill level and willingness to engage in a task. This can be particularly difficult when performance metrics are hard to define or are not indicative of skill, or as skill improves. Second, DDA systems must subtly change difficulty level while not obtrusively interfering with the task in order to not interrupt presence and degrade performance [24, 41].

While there has been considerable research on DDA systems, there are few examples of DDA systems outside of gaming environments, where behavioral metrics are often a good indicator of performance and difficulty. Finding these indicators in the real world is challenging, but the benefits of systems with dynamic difficulty are widespread. For example, in computer-assisted learning environments, the system could calibrate the pace of learning or materials to the understanding of each individual. These principles can also be applied towards task allocation in order to use physiological signals to calibrate the amount of work given to a user or balance task load across team members.

In this paper, we demonstrate a set of adaptation techniques and triggers to address some of the traditional problems with using physiological input to DDA systems in the real world. As an example of a task allocation environment, we construct a system that aids operators in path planning for unmanned aerial vehicles (UAVs) and use input from *functional near-infrared spectroscopy (fNIRS)* brain sensing to model the operator's state. By using the confidence in its output, we construct an adaptive system that is more robust to the noise of physiological input. Finally, by being careful with our manipulation of visual elements, we prevent disrupting the user's mental model of the system. The UAV operator scenario is an ideal testbed to control task allocation because the path planning system is composed of discrete elements, each of which carries a level of independent workload.

In particular, we show that we can use fNIRS to model a user's working memory load in real time and use this signal as an indicator of difficulty in multitasking scenarios. We propose that fNIRS has specific advantages in being applied to DDA systems. It is a lightweight and non-intrusive sensor, and can be affixed to the forehead while allowing users to still function normally. Additionally, it has been found to be resistant to movement artifacts in comparison to other sensors [35]. Because of this, it is ideal for a passive input, where users still perform a task normally but the system knows and adjusts to their overall cognitive state.

By applying fNIRS to a DDA system that supports UAV route planning, we find that we are able to improve task performance. We suggest that this is because we aid users in avoiding harmful cognitive states, thereby maintaining a state of *flow*. In this paper, we make the following claims:

- **We show that we can build a brain-computer interface that uses task allocation as means for dynamically matching the task to the user.** We apply functional near-infrared spectroscopy to detect signals in the prefrontal cortex that correlate with working memory load, using this signal as a proxy for the user's engagement with a task. We demonstrate that this system decreases operator error by 35% over a baseline condition, holding speed and other factors constant.

- **We suggest adaptive strategies that circumvent traditional problems with biocybernetic systems and make adaptation feasible for DDA systems in the real world, such as UAV path planning.** To minimize the impact of misclassifications, we only trigger the adaptive mechanism when the system has a high confidence in its modeling. To prevent disrupting the user's mental model of the system, we only modify those visual elements that the user has no reason to monitor.

Application: UAV Path Planning

For our testbed scenario, we use an unmanned aerial vehicle (UAV) software simulator. UAV operation lends itself well to task allocation because difficulty adjustments because operators go through periods of boredom and high workload, both of which lead to operator attention inefficiencies, delays, and degradations in performance measures [14]. Unmanned aircraft are an increasingly common solution used by the military for surveillance, intelligence, and combat. They are also frequently used for humanitarian assistance and disaster relief to assess damage and conduct search and rescue missions, as well as for transporting cargo and passengers.

Workload for a UAV operator is inherently dynamic. As autonomy capabilities improve, there is increasing interest in giving individual operators responsibility for multiple autonomous vehicles. Because of varying demands for each UAV, sometimes a lower number of UAVs will cause more work and we cannot measure operator workload based solely on number of vehicles [12]. A successful dynamic difficulty system would better optimize distribution of workload and the utilization of human resources to maximize performance. In addition, control systems could be alerted when more or fewer UAV operators are needed. However, such a system requires the user's state be captured in real-time, as performance metrics alone might not accurately reflect the mental demands of a UAV operator's current scenario. Although this study is based on a UAV simulation, we posit that it is generalizable to most systems with variable levels of workload that can be modified by task allocation.

BACKGROUND AND RELATED WORK

Flow and Dynamic Difficulty

As defined by psychologist and philosopher Mihaly Csikszentmihalyi, *flow* is the state of complete immersion in a task induced by achieving an ideal balance between the skills of the user and the challenge of the user's task [10]. When this balance is met, a user will typically experience a clear sense of goals, focused concentration, loss of self-consciousness, altered sense of time, increased sense of control, increased motivation, and a merging of action and awareness [10]. As depicted in Figure 1, keeping users in the flow state provides a positive emotional experience and avoids boredom, frustration, anxiety, or apathy [15, 26].

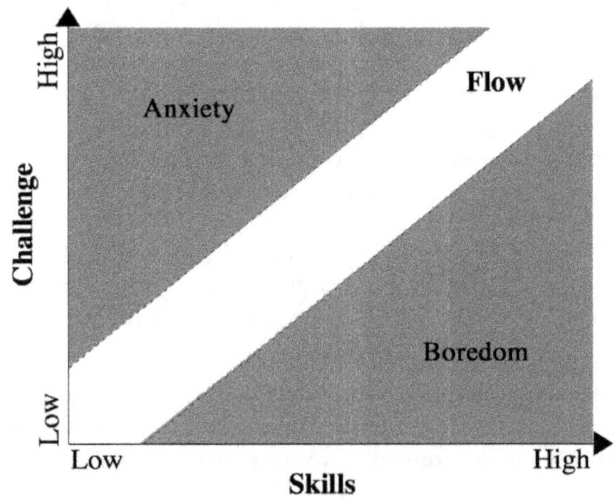

Figure 1. A two-dimensional model of flow

To capitalize on these benefits, designers have attempted to automatically maintain a user's flow state through the use of *dynamic difficulty adjustment (DDA)*, or adapting the challenge of a task automatically based on a model of the user's current skills. Research has shown that game players, for example, experience faster performance gains and feel more in control when the difficulty increases based on their skill [24, 39]. Scenarios that adjust difficulty according to performance keep the player more immersed than those that simply adjust difficulty over the course of gameplay [32]. Outside of the gaming industry, DDA systems can be used to accommodate the transition of users from novice to expert [6] — a central application of adaptive interfaces.

Dynamic Difficulty Psychophysiological Metrics

Psychophysiological signals can be used to determine player boredom and anxiety [8], and many researchers have looked at how these affect performance and flow [15, 32, 33]. Chanel et al. found that playing at different levels of difficulty will give rise to different emotional states and those emotional states (and the underlying conditions) can be assessed using physiological measures [8]. These signals can also be used passively to modify a scenario by determining a user's affective, or emotional, state [15]. Participants' skills improve more and the participants find the simulations more enjoyable when the level of challenge is altered due to affective or mental state rather than their performance [33]. In addition, research has found that boredom and frustration/anxiety are distinguishable from each other and from flow, and that they can be classified with high levels of accuracy [8, 33].

The sympathetic and parasympathetic nervous sytem are susceptible to effects of cognitive state. Unobtrusive sensors such as electrocardiograph (EKG) electrodes or Galvanic Skin Response (GSR) can be used to find changes in a participant's physiological state. Heart rate variability and interbeat interval (IBI) measured from EKG can correspond to arousal levels. In addition, IBI standard deviation and GSR mean have been found to rise and peak as subjects' challenge states change from boredom to flow, but then fall again once the challenge becomes too difficult and subjects reach a state of anxiety, indicating that these physiological signals fall once the user becomes disengaged [16]. These signals are a good complement to fNIRS. However, they measure affective state and how the user feels about the challenge and are not necessarily descriptive of how the user's skills interact with the difficulty of the task.

Brain-sensing can be used to focus on a user's mental state. Clinical studies using electroencephalogram (EEG) have found significant results that can be used for dynamic adaptations, such as that left frontal lobe activity is correlated with positive emotions and motivation and that frontal theta rhythms are maximized when the challenge was also at its peak [15]. EEG can also find attentional engagement and affective workload in first-person shooters [1]. The key step in creating an affective loop is to identify appropriate classifiers that correlate biosignals and the actual affective state of the users. Fairclough et al. also found significant differences in EEG signals as task load in an n-back task changed and that systolic blood pressure (SBP) increases with task demand, peaks when task demand reaches the maximum challenge, and then decreases once the task is too challenging [15].

While the literature on using EEG as input to adaptive systems is quickly growing, it has historically been extremely sensitive to movement artifacts without careful filtering methods. We investigate the use of fNIRS as a less-explored device in comparison to EEG and complementary in many of its characteristics. In the next section we provide a more detailed description of fNIRS and its benefits for use in DDA systems.

fNIRS and Prefrontal Cortex

fNIRS uses near-infrared light to detect levels of oxygenated (HbO) and deoxygenated hemoglobin (HbR) on the surface of the prefrontal cortex. Light at this wavelength penetrates biological tissue and bone but is absorbed by hemoglobin in the bloodstream, and has similar vascular sensitivity to fMRI [21]. Since neural activity is accompanied by increased oxygen demands in order to metabolize glucose, much like fMRI, fNIRS can detect activation at localized areas of the brain. For a more in depth validation of fNIRS signals in comparison to fMRI, we refer to Strangman et al [38]. fNIRS detects slow trends of hemodynamic changes, and is thus more appropriate for detecting overall state rather than event-related responses.

Recently, fNIRS has increasingly been leveraged to research users because it is considered to be safe, comfortable, relatively robust to movement artifacts, and can be designed for portability. In addition, it is resilient to head movement, facial movement, ambient noise, heartbeat, and muscle movement [17, 35]. This is critical for complex environments where the user must be able to function freely and normally.

Predictive models have been used to differentiate the fNIRS signal between levels of workload [4, 20, 28, 34], verbal and spatial working memory [19], and game difficulty levels [17]. Furthermore, it has been used to determine periods of cognitive multitasking [36, 37], levels of expertise [7], preference [25, 29], and emotion [40].

fNIRS is a viable technology to monitor the brain activity of UAV pilots in ecologically valid environments. Previous work has shown that mean oxygenation levels increase as the number of vehicles in a simulation increases, but then drop once the operator is tasked with too many elements [2, 7, 22].

Passive Brain-Computer Interfaces

Traditional active and reactive BCIs use physiological signals as input to directly control an application, such as moving a cursor/object, selecting an option, or other intentional actions. In contrast, passive BCIs are based on "reactive states of the user's cognition automatically induced while interacting in the surrounding system" [44]. Passive inputs assess user state and use that to help control interaction without direct or intentional effort from the user. These systems supplement direct input with implicit input, typically derived from physiological sensors attached to the user, in order to trigger commands based on user state. Jacob et al. anticipated the notion of the passive physiological monitoring in 1993 [23], and recent advancements in physiological sensors has allowed them to become feasible. Physiologically-sensed signals represent user state and can provide additional, implicit input to systems. Driven by more efficient monitors and the computational power and algorithms to process large quantities of data in real-time, modern technology can more affordably integrate passive systems and has spawned research into passive biocybernetic adaptation [15].

Adaptations triggered by passive input face two primary challenges: to accurately model the user's cognitive and emotional state and to sensibly adjust the system based on this model. The model must be very cautious since users are often in a different mental state during offline calibration and online feedback [42].

BCI helps solve the first challenge of passive systems by providing user models that tap more directly the source of user state. Cutrell and Tan suggest that the implicit commands inferred from a user's changing brain activity may be the most promising, universal application of BCI [13]. Explicit brain-issued commands suffer disproportionally from errors and have a limited range of input, whereas implicit commands offer purely additional information without the user's deliberate attention, and the user does not see misclassifactions, nor have to spend additional cognitive resources recovering from these errors.

There are currently few examples of passive, real-time BCI systems that objectively improve user performance in a system. Prinzel et al. built an EEG-based adaptive automation system that alternated between manual and automated modes for a joystic tracking task and auditory pitch counting task [31]. Wilson and Russell designed a similar system based on an EEG engagement index for single-operator single-UAV systems and found success with slowing the UAV down or presenting alert in order to maintain engagement levels [43]. Solovey et al.'s *Brainput* system was able to adapt a scenario where an interactive human-robot system changed its state of autonomy based on whether it detected a particular state of multitasking [37] and Peck et al. demonstrated a passive, implicit adaptive movie recommendation system [28].

FNIRS AS INPUT TO DYNAMIC DIFFICULTY

In this paper, we explore whether we can improve performance by using fNIRS brain sensing as input to a dynamic difficulty system. To investigate this topic, we run a user study on an an task allocation system. As our testbed, we use a simulation designed for UAV path planning [18]. In this simulation, UAV operators are tasked with directing multiple UAVs at once, similar to an air traffic control task. Since this task can either be overwhelming or overly simple, we use fNIRS input to intelligently add or remove UAVs in order to provide an ideal challenge to the user. Mirroring the two primary challenges of DDA systems, we pose the following research questions:

- Can we use fNIRS to identify periods of low and high difficulty as operators perform a navigation task with multiple UAVs?
- Can we use real-time fNIRS data as input to a dynamic difficulty system and improve operator performance?

In the following sections, we describe the UAV simulation task, the details of our Brain-Based Dynamic Difficulty Engine, and the experimental design of our study.

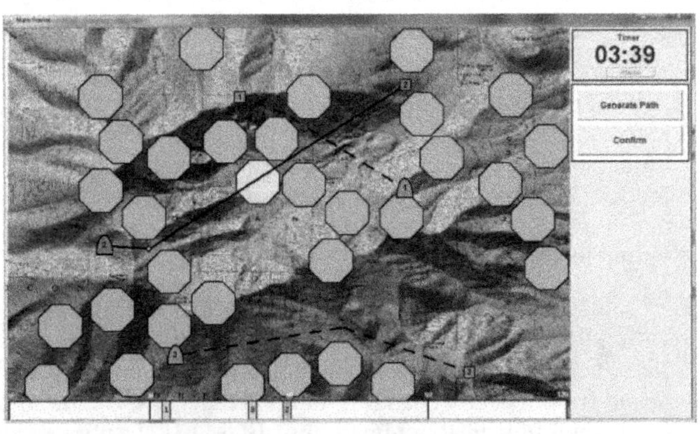

Figure 2. View of UAV operator simulation. Participants guided UAVs to targets while avoiding dynamic obstacles.

UAV SIMULATION TASK

We used a single-operator multiple-UAV system designed by a human automation research laboratory [18]. In the UAV navigation task, participants (or operators) were shown an overhead view of a map with UAVs (displayed in Figure 2) and instructed to guide the UAVs to a sequence of targets as quickly as possible while avoiding obstacles. Participants controlled between three and seven UAVs. Operators were instructed that obstacles, shown as teal octagons, were no-fly zones, and that while UAVs could fly through them, there would be a large penalty for doing so. If entered, obstacles should be exited as soon as possible. Leaving UAVs idle for a long period of time would also result in a penalty, so participants were motivated to balance performing the task quickly and without collisions.

The participants were instructed that they were part of a team of UAV operators and that vehicles would be passed off from their control to other operators, and other operators' vehicles would be passed to them. Thus, participants were prepared for vehicles to appear and disappear during the task. Intermittently, UAVs would be added or removed to modify the operator's current challenge level. To prevent disruption of the user's mental model of the scenario, UAVs were only removed if there were no obstacles in its path, meaning that the UAV should not demand any of the user's attentional resources and thus the user would not be distracted by the change. A pilot study showed that participants found this less disruptive than removing vehicles that needed path modifications, since a UAV could disappear during interaction. Overall, scenarios were hard-coded in order to guarantee consistency in obstacle density and path distance.

Interface Details

The vehicles were shown in pink and were numbered, with each UAV having a corresponding numbered target. When operators clicked on a UAV, that UAV and its target would become red and the user could click anywhere on the map to create a waypoint (indicated by a yellow diamond). When the user pressed "Generate Path," a path was created that included the starting position of the UAV, all of the waypoints, and the target. Once the participant pressed "Confirm," the vehicle would begin to follow the path.

The obstacles intermittently moved, so users could add more waypoints, move existing waypoints, or delete waypoints in the UAV's path. The currently selected path was shown as a solid black line, while other UAVs' paths were shown as dashed lines. When a vehicle's path crossed into an obstacle, the obstacle would turn bright yellow until the obstacle was cleared. Every time the vehicle reached a target, a new target would appear. Along the bottom of the map was a timeline so that operators could see when the UAVs would reach their targets, and a timer was on the top right.

BRAIN-BASED DYNAMIC DIFFICULTY ENGINE

In order to identify user states that correlate with periods of low or high difficulty, we depend on a number of analytical components that we call the *Brain-Based Dynamic Difficulty Engine*. In this section, we describe the process of calibrating our system to recognize periods of low and high difficulty as the user interacts with an interface. We also describe our adaptation mechanism that attempts to increase or decrease the difficulty of the user's task.

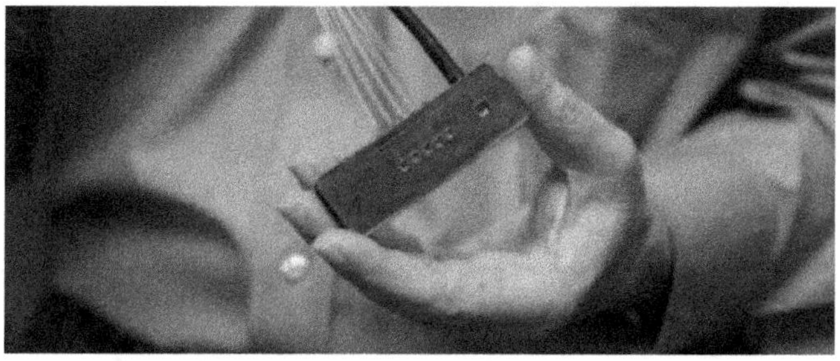

Figure 3. An fNIRS sensor that contains five light sources (only four were used) and one detector.

Equipment
We used a multichannel frequency domain Imagent fNIRS device from ISS Inc. (Champaign, IL) for data acquisition. The system used two probes (shown in Figure 3), one on each side of a subject's forehead, to measure changes in oxygenated and deoxygenated hemoglobin in the prefrontal cortex. Each probe had four sources, each emitting infrared light at two near-infrared wavelengths (830 nm and 690 nm), and one detector. The source-detector distances ranged from 1.5 to 3.5 cm and the system sampled at 11.79 Hz.

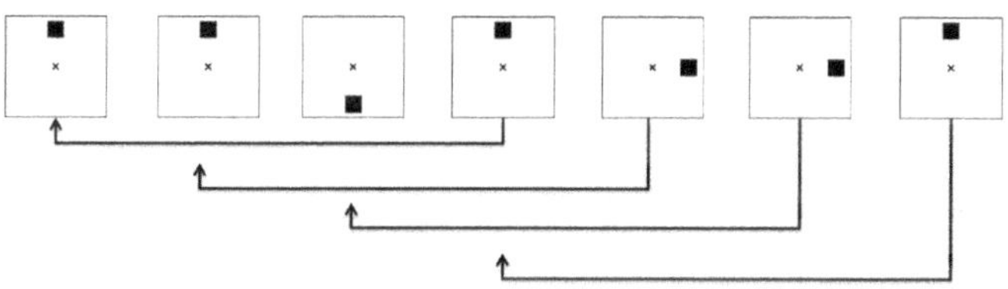

Figure 4. 3-back task. Participants were instructed to respond if the current square appeared at the same location as the one presented three trials back in the sequence.

Calibration Task
In order to identify fNIRS signals that determine periods of high and low periods of difficulty, participants first completed a series of visuospatial n-back trials. The n-back test is widely used and has been established and proven to incite increasing levels of short-term working memory as n increases [5, 27] as well as yield distinguishable fNIRS signals [11, 29]. Participants were shown a screen with a square and an X in the middle, with flashing black boxes (see Figure 4), and were asked to indicate if the currently presented stimulus was the same as the stimulus presented n trials previously. In order to induce levels of low and high difficulty, participants performed 1-back and 3-back trials. Because each participant only has to recall the last stimulus during a 1-back but has to remember the last three stimuli during a 3-back, the 3-back incites significantly higher cognitive load. Each trial consisted of 10 stimuli, each being displayed for 500 ms with an interstimulus interval of 2000 ms. Each trial totalled 25 seconds and was followed by a 15 second break. Participants completed 30 trials and were allowed to take a longer break after every 10 trials.

Filtering the fNIRS Signal
During the n-back task, raw fNIRS data was collected by Boxy (fNIRS acquisition software from ISS, Inc.) and sent to a specialized analysis system which was built in-lab using MATLAB. There, the system calculated the time series of change in light intensity compared to an initial baseline period of 30 seconds for each of our 16 information channels (2 probes x 4 light sources x 2 wavelengths). The signals were filtered for heart rate, respiration, and movement artifacts using a third-degree polynomial filter and low-pass elliptical filter. Further details of these algorithms can be found in [29, 37].

Modeling Difficulty
Previous work that used fNIRS to detect workload in UAV operator tasks took advantage of changes in the oxygenated hemoglobin signal. By calculating the mean and linear regression slope of operators' oxygenated hemoglobin levels in the prefrontal cortex, they were able to see signal differences that correlated with the number of UAVs and task difficulty [3, 7] Thus, for each n-back trial, we constructed an example of 32 features (16 information channels x 2 descriptive features) in order to build our model of user difficulty. We then fed each of these examples into LIBSVM, an integrated software for support vector classification [9], where we used a linear kernel to prevent overfitting the data [11]. In addition, we did a parameter search for the C and γ, the cost and gamma parameters for the machine learning model, in order to find the best model for each individual user. This technique uses the training data to build a support vector machine in order to classify new input and give a probability estimate. Finally, after building the model, we used 10-fold cross-validation to ensure that the model was accurate. For system implementation, see Figure 5. We used an individualized model for each user (Figure 6 is for illustration purposes), and this model was able to predict difficulty level while each user was performing the UAV task.

Classifying New fNIRS Data in Real-Time
After the model was created, we were able to predict user state in real-time by using a sliding window of the same size as our n-back trial length (25 seconds) on new, incoming fNIRS data. For each window of data, we used the same filtering techniques as the training series data and extracted the same mean and slope features.

Predictions and confidence values were sent to the UAV simulation software in real-time, which kept track of recent classifications and calculated its own prediction of user state by averaging the previous 8 seconds that were received from the model. Whenever the confidence average was above 80% for either low or high difficulty levels, a UAV would be added or removed, respectively. We base our confidence average off of results obtained from pilot studies. The adaptation was used to raise or lower the overall difficulty and challenge of the simulation when appropriate. This ensured that we would only make an adaptation if the system was confident in the

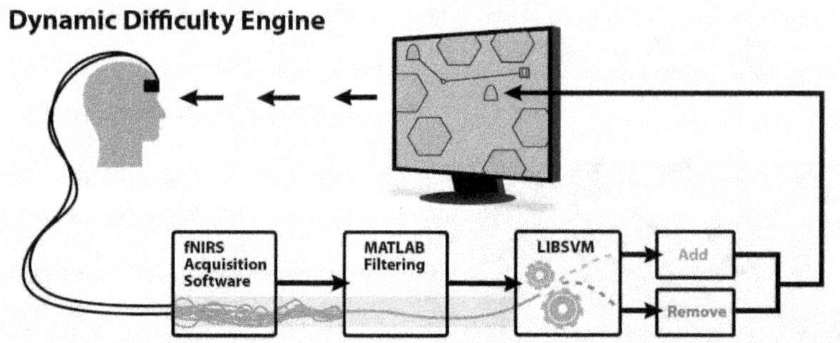

Figure 5. Diagram of our closed-loop dynamic difficulty adaptation engine. Raw signals acquired the fNIRS device are filtered, then used to classify user workload. When we are confident that the user is in a suboptimal state, we appropriately add or remove UAVs in order to provide the right amount of work.

user's state. In the following sections, we compare the success of this adaptation with a non-adaptive condition.

EXPERIMENTAL DESIGN

Training and Calibration

Participants first went through a self-guided slideshow explaining UAV simulation. They then practiced the simulation, spending five minutes controlling three UAVs and five minutes controlling seven UAVs. Our initial pilot tests showed that three UAVs was the minimum to incite workload, and that seven UAVs was the maximum that a single operator could handle without frustration. After this section, they were then described the calibration task – n-back task – and practiced a 1-back and 3-back task. Once the calibration task began, participants performed 30 n-back trials, 15 each of 1-back and 3-back trials, with a 15 second break between trials in order to allow their brain to return to resting state. The data from these trials was used to train our classifier. Although each participant had an individual model, the overall trends are shown in Figure 6.

UAV Scenario - Adaptive vs. Non-Adaptive

We compared our fNIRS-based adaptations to a control condition where UAVs were randomly added and removed. Thus, the independent variable in this experiment is the extent to which the system adapts to the user's state: *adaptive* and *non-adaptive*.

- In the *adaptive condition*, UAVs were added and removed according to brain signals correlating with low workload and high workload. We posit that extended periods of low and high workload cause boredom and anxiety, and lead to periods of disengagement and decreased performance. Thus, when the system was confident that the user was in a state of low or high workload, one UAV would be added or removed, respectively. After a UAV was added or removed, there was a 20 second period where no more vehicles were added or removed. This was done to prevent the user from having to rapidly switch contexts.

- In the *non-adaptive condition*, the simulation did not keep track of user state and intermittently added and removed UAVs (a random interval between 20 and 40 seconds). This timing was determined based on a series of pilots to correspond as closely as possible to the average number of additions/removals we observed in the adaptive condition.

All participants ran one ten-minute trial of each condition. The order of conditions was counter-balanced across subjects and participants wore the fNIRS device during both trials so they did not notice a difference between the two conditions.

Dependent Measures

In order to evaluate the success of the system, we analyzed the following dependent measures:

- *Successes:* the number of UAVs that reached the target without entering a no-fly zone
- *Failures:* the number of UAVs that entered at least one no-fly zone on the way to the target.
- *Obstacles entered:* the total number of no-fly zones that planes entered during operation. This metric differs from failures because a UAV can enter multiple no-fly zones in a single flight.
- *Distance in obstacles:* the total distance (in pixels) that UAVs travelled in no-fly zones during operation. This measure helps us understand how quickly users were able to recover from these mistakes.
- *Average neglected UAVs:* a neglected UAV is idle waiting for a route or having a no-fly zone in its route and needing redirection. This metric refers to the avg number of neglected UAVs at any given moment during operation.

RESULTS

The study included twelve participants (five male) between the ages of 18 and 26. All participants were right-handed, had no history of brain injury and had normal or corrected-to-normal vision. Informed consent was obtained for all participants. This experiment was approved by our institutional review board.

Improved Performance: Fewer Failures, Collisions

Across conditions, participants controlled roughly the same number of UAVs over time, averaging 4.41 UAVs in the adaptive fNIRS condition and 4.69 UAVs in the non-adaptive

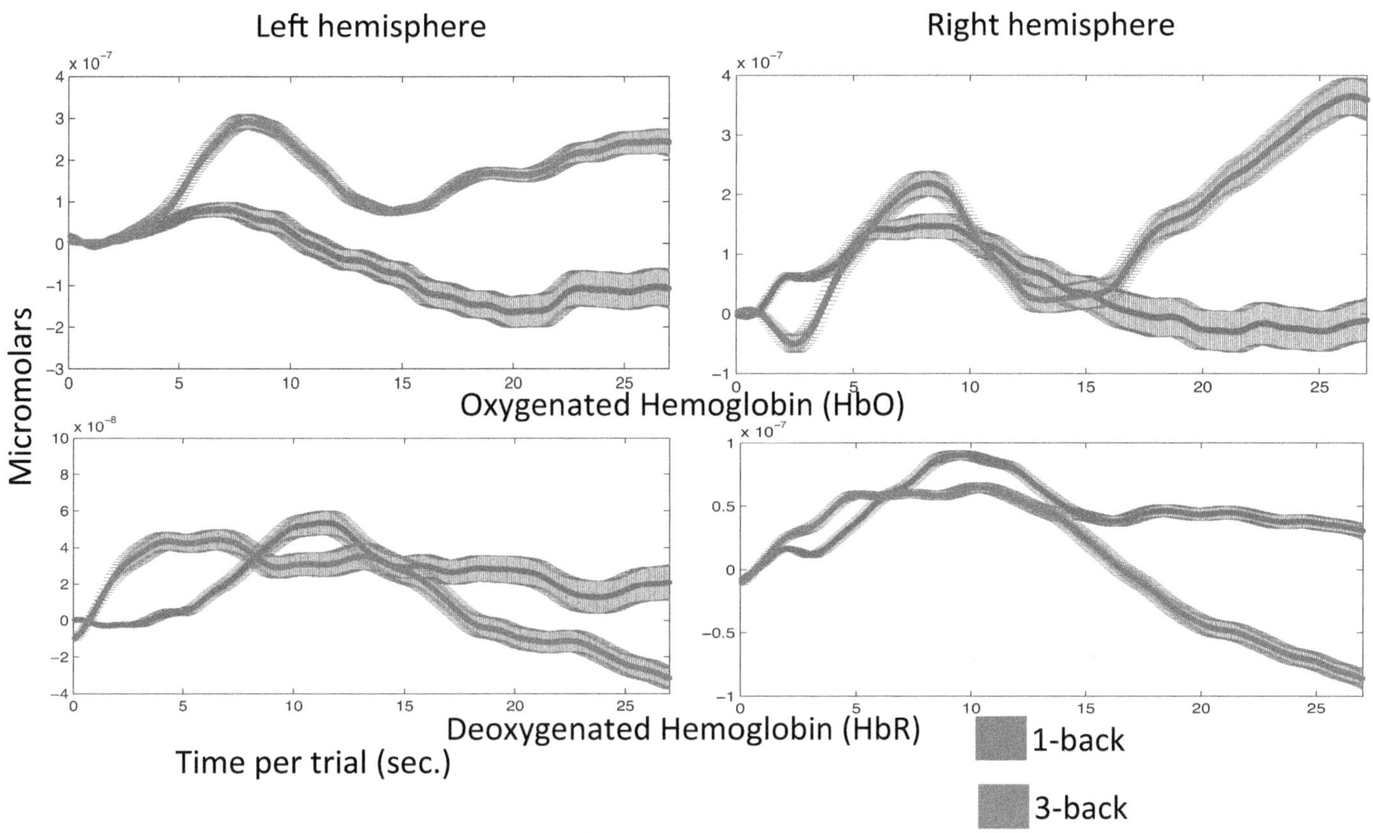

Figure 6. Although we model each participant individually, the fNIRS signal exhibited general trends as participants completed 1-back and 3-back trials. Plotting the mean change in HbO and HbR across all training trials and all participants (15 trials * 12 participants) shows that the 1-back task is correlated with a drop in HbO and increased levels of HbR, while the 3-back task induces an increase in HbO and decrease in HbR. The standard error of the mean is shown with the width of the plots.

condition (no significance in number of UAVs). Participants completed the same number of successful trials across conditions, so there was no significant difference in completion rates. However, their failure rate was significantly higher in the non-adaptive condition. With a paired t-test, we found that participants had significantly fewer failures in adaptive condition ($M = 3.25, SD = 2.14$) than the non-adaptive condition ($M = 5, SD = 1.95$) ($t(11) = 3.17, p < 0.01, Cohen's\ d = 0.92$). In addition, although there was no significant difference in the number of obstacles that appeared in the UAVs' paths across conditions (since the obstacles randomly moved over time), participants entered an average of 4.75 ($SD = 2.77$) no-fly zones in the adaptive condition and 7.42 ($SD = 2.81$) no-fly zones in the non-adaptive condition ($t(11) = 4.14, p < 0.01, Cohen's\ d = 1.2$).

While we did not see a change in number of successful trials, this is to be somewhat expected, since the operators' ability to complete their main objective was not affected by condition. However, the significant decrease in failures as well as variables associated with failures shows that users prevent degrades in performance. One likely explanation is that participants are paying more attention to the simulation and stay more engaged in the task.

Increased Awareness: Quicker Error Correction

We also measured the number of pixels that the UAVs traveled while in no-fly zones, an indicator of how aware the operators were that the UAVs were in obstacles. With a paired t-test, we found that participants traveled significantly less distance in obstacles in the adaptive condition ($M = 101.38, SD = 91.43$) than the control condition ($M = 206.39, SD = 179.1$) ($t(11) = 2.84, p < 0.05, Cohen's\ d = 0.82$). This means that they were more attentive to the appearance of obstacles in the adaptive condition and did a better job of avoiding the obstacles once the obstacles appeared. Participant also neglected UAVs less, having fewer average UAVs that needed attention. Participants had an average of 1.14 ($SD = 0.13$) neglected UAVs in the adaptive condition, with 1.37 ($SD = 0.29$) neglected UAVs in the non-adaptive condition ($t(11) = 2.78, p < 0.05, Cohen's\ d = 0.80$).

DISCUSSION

We presented a working dynamic difficulty system that used brain activity to determine when to perform task mitigations. In the background section of this paper, we described two primary challenges for DDA systems. First, DDA systems must accurately model the interaction between user skills and the challenge of their task. Second, DDA systems must modify the challenge to keep users in a state of flow *without* being disruptive. Mirroring these challenges, we posed research

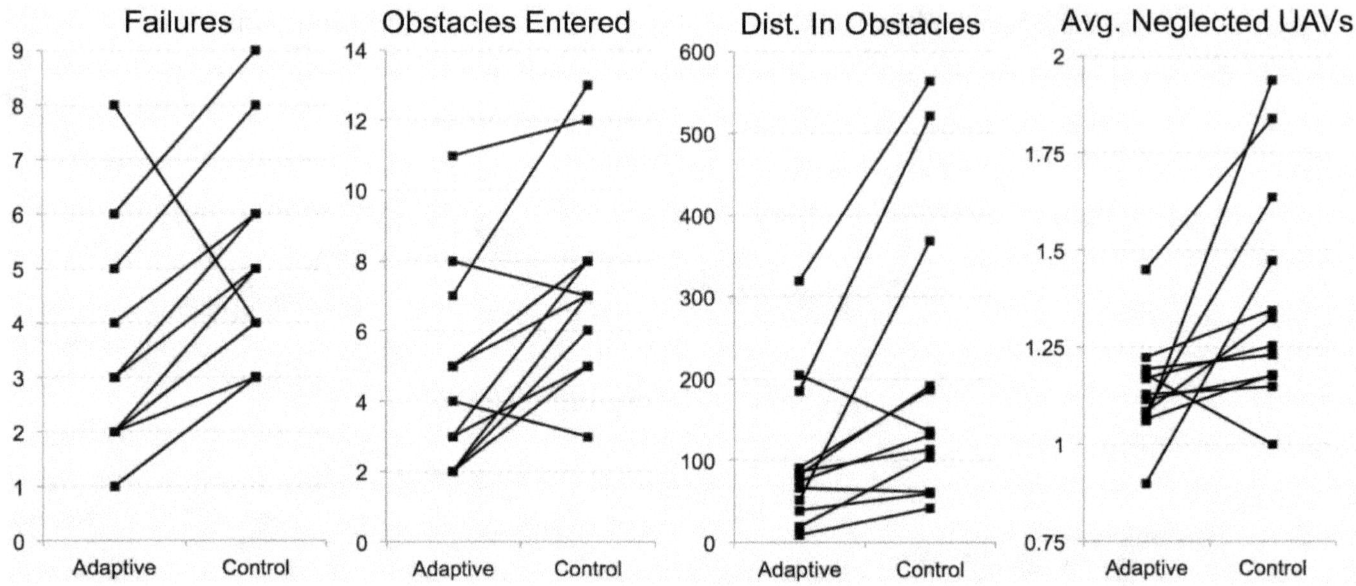

Figure 7. We use a slopegraph to plot the effects of condition on UAV operator performance for each participant. The following four measures showed significantly ($p < 0.05$) better performance in the adaptive condition interface (upward sloping lines), and at least ten of the 12 subjects performed better in the adaptive condition in each of these measures.

questions asking whether using fNIRS as input could address these challenges in a UAV operator task. In this section, we explore the implications of our study as it relates to these questions, beginning with the second of these challenges.

Using fNIRS to Minimize Disruption

It is worth reemphasizing the benefits of using fNIRS for ecologically valid evaluations of user state. Its resistance to movement artifacts in comparison to other many other sensing technologies means that users are able to engage with their task under fewer constraints. Earlier, we mentioned that an important goal of DDA systems was to minimize disruption within the context of adaptation. However, this disruption can also apply to the constraints required by measurement tools. Allowing the user to interact naturally will be important to consider if DDA systems are to be driven by physiological input in the future. While our system still requires users to be tethered by wires and fibers, there is a growing body of research that suggests that fNIRS will become even more lightweight and unobtrusive in the future [2, 41].

Mapping Working Memory to Difficulty

Our results indicate that we were able to model the working memory load of the user in the UAV scenario using fNIRS. Participants who interacted with the adaptive system saw performance boosts in the form of fewer failures and fewer collisions in comparison to a non-adaptive condition. Incorrectly modeling user state would have negatively impacted performance by pushing users into a potentially harmful state such as boredom or overload. Therefore, we were able to model user state sufficiently enough in a real-time environment to improve performance. Although misclassifications are inevitable, one of the challenges of applying adaptations is deciding when to take action. Our system shows that using a timeseries of confidence classifications can aid the user by only adapting when we are fairly certain of user state.

However, one criticism for using working memory as a proxy for difficulty is that high working memory load may in fact be an indicator of engagement with a task. While we caution against mindlessly mapping working memory to difficulty, the UAV experiment exemplifies a larger classification of tasks where measuring high working memory load can indicate harmful user states. In multitasking scenarios, increasing the amount of mental effort required to accomplish a primary task necessarily decreases the available resources for secondary tasks.

We also believe that the user's increased awareness in the adaptive condition, as demonstrated by distance travelled inside obstacles and neglected UAVs, suggests that our adaptive mechanism successfully preserved the user's mental model of the scenario while modulating their challenge level.

Our system has measurable benefits, with no direct input from the user. This is advantageous because the user may not detect when he or she is disengaging, and will not have time or the extra cognitive capacity to indicate when the workload is overwhelming; continuously inputting information explicitly would be annoying and distracting.

This system is independent of the simulation software package and thus can be applied to any operator scenario. The predictions are sent as text strings (consisting of the prediction and the confidence rates) over TCP/IP, and a we have developed a generic Java class that reads in these predictions and gives moving averages of the predictions. Stripling et al. emphasize the need for a "robust user-friendly closed-loop training environment" that can produce automated methods for adaptive manipulations in complex simulations [39], and this system seeks to do that based on brain signals.

CONCLUSION

Dynamic difficulty adjustment is a valuable tool to keep people in an ideal state to learn better and perform better, while also enjoying the experience. As physiological sensors become more prevalent and the signal processing techniques continue to improve, passive systems will become easier to implement, more accurate, and more commonplace.

In this paper, we presented our system, the Brain-Based Dynamic Difficulty Engine, which uses fNIRS brain signals to dynamically adjust the difficulty level of a given task. Our system is real-time and passive, which is ideal for real world conditions such as UAV operations where the operators need to perform tasks and cannot tell the system when difficulty level is inappropriate. We demonstrated that our system can significantly decrease the operator's failure rate by 35% compared to randomly adding and removing over time, holding other factors constant. In addition, the operators exhibited higher level of awareness in dealing with UAVs that had immediate concerns. These results suggest that our system is beneficial to operators, and that fNIRS and other brain sensing techniques for DDA can be used for regulating user state and producing improved performance.

ACKNOWLEDGMENTS

We thank Beste Yuksel, Jordan Crouser, Francine Lalooses, Tomoki Shibata, Shiwan Zuo, Alvitta Ottley, Lane Harrison, David Young, Sergio Fantini, and Angelo Sassaroli from Tufts University, as well as Jamie Macbeth, Missy Cummings, and Alina Griner from MIT HAL. We also thank the NSF for support of this research (NSF Grants Nos. IIS-1065154 and IIS-1218170). Any opinions, findings, conclusions, or recommendations expressed in this paper are those of the authors and do not necessarily reflect the views of the National Science Foundation.

REFERENCES

1. Allison, B., and Polich, J. Workload assessment of computer gaming using a single-stimulus event-related potential paradigm. *Biological Psychology 77* (2008), 277–283.
2. Ayaz, H., Shewokis, P. A., Bunce, S., Izzetoglu, K., Willems, B., and Onaral, B. Optical brain monitoring for operator training and mental workload assessment. *NeuroImage 59*, 1 (2012), 36–47.
3. Ayaz, H., Shewokis, P. A., Bunce, S., and Onaral, B. An optical brain computer interface for environmental control. In *IEEE EMBC 2011* (2011), 6327–6330.
4. Ayaz, H., Willems, B., Bunce, S., Shewokis, P. A., Izzetoglu, M., Hah, S., Deshmukh, A., and Onaral, B. Cognitive workload assessment of air traffic controllers using optical brain imaging sensors. *Advances in Understanding Human Performance: Neuroergonomics, Human Factors Design, and Special Populations* (2010), 21–31.
5. Baddeley, A. Working memory: looking back and looking forward. *Nature Reviews Neuroscience 4*, 10 (2003), 829–39.
6. Bederson, B. Interfaces for Staying in the Flow. *Ubiquity* (2004).
7. Bunce, S. C., Izzetoglu, K., Ayaz, H., Shewokis, P., Izzetoglu, M., Pourrezaei, K., and Onaral, B. Implementation of fNIRS for monitoring levels of expertise and mental workload. In *Foundations of Augmented Cognition. Directing the Future of Adaptive Systems*. Springer Berlin Heidelberg, 2011, 13–22.
8. Chanel, G., Rebetez, C., Betrancourt, M., and Pun, T. Boredom, engagement and anxiety as indicators for adaptation to difficulty in games. In *Proc. Entertainment and Media in the Ubiquitous Era*, ACM Press (2008), 13–17.
9. Chang, C., and Lin, C. LIBSVM: a library for support vector machines. *Transactions on Intelligent Systems and Technology* (2011), 1–39.
10. Csikszentmihalyi, M. *Flow: The Psychology of Optimal Experience*. HarperCollins, 1991.
11. Cui, X., Bray, S., and Reiss, A. L. Speeded near infrared spectroscopy (NIRS) response detection. *PLOS ONE 5*, 11 (2010).
12. Cummings, M., and How, J. The Impact of HumanAutomation Collaboration in Decentralized Multiple Unmanned Vehicle Control. *Proc. IEEE 100*, 3 (2012), 660–671.
13. Cutrell, E., and Tan, D. BCI for passive input in HCI. In *Proc. CHI 2008*, ACM Press (2008).
14. Donmez, B., Nehme, C., and Cummings, M. L. Modeling Workload Impact in Multiple Unmanned Vehicle Supervisory Control. *IEEE Transactions on Systems, Man, and Cybernetics - Part A: Systems and Humans 40*, 6 (2010), 1180–1190.
15. Fairclough, S., Gilleade, K., Ewing, K. C., and Roberts, J. Capturing user engagement via psychophysiology: measures and mechanisms for biocybernetic adaptation. *International Journal of Autonomous and Adaptive Communications Systems 6*, 1 (2013), 63–79.
16. Giakoumis, D., Vogiannou, A., Kosunen, I., Moustakas, K., Tzovaras, D., and Hassapis, G. Identifying Psychophysiological Correlates of Boredom and Negative Mood Induced During HCI. *Bio-inspired Human-Machine Interfaces and Healthcare Applications* (2010), 3–12.
17. Girouard, A., Solovey, E. T., and Hirshfield, L. M. Distinguishing Difficulty Levels with Non-invasive Brain Activity Measurements. *INTERACT 2009* (2009), 440–452.
18. Griner, A. Human-RRT Collaboration in UAV Mission Path Planning. *Master's Thesis, Massachusetts Institute of Technology* (2012).
19. Hirshfield, L., Gulotta, R., and Hirshfield, S. This is your brain on interfaces: enhancing usability testing with functional near-infrared spectroscopy. In *Proc. CHI 2011*, ACM Press (2011).

20. Hirshfield, L. M., Solovey, E. T., Girouard, A., Kebinger, J., Jacob, R. J. K., Sassaroli, A., and Fantini, S. Brain Measurement for Usability Testing and Adaptive Interfaces: An Example of Uncovering Syntactic Workload with Functional Near Infrared Spectroscopy. In *Proc. CHI 2009*, ACM Press (2009).
21. Huppert, T., and Hoge, R. A temporal comparison of BOLD, ASL, and NIRS hemodynamic responses to motor stimuli in adult humans. *NeuroImage 29*, 2 (2006), 368–382.
22. Izzetoglu, K., Ayaz, H., and Menda, J. Applications of Functional Near Infrared Imaging: Case Study on UAV Ground Controller. In *Foundations of Augmented Cognition*. Springer Berlin Heidelberg, 2011, 608–617.
23. Jacob, R. J. K., Leggett, J. J., Myers, B. A., and Pausch, R. Interaction Styles and Input/Output Devices. *Behaviour and Information Technology 12*, 2 (1993), 69–79.
24. Jegers, K. Pervasive game flow: understanding player enjoyment in pervasive gaming. *Computers in Entertainment (CIE) 5*, 1 (2007).
25. Luu, S., and Chau, T. Decoding subjective preference from single-trial near-infrared spectroscopy signals. *Journal of Neural Engineering 6* (2008).
26. Nacke, L., and Lindley, C. Flow and immersion in first-person shooters: measuring the player's gameplay experience. In *Proceedings of the 2008 Conference on Future Play: Research, Play, Share*, ACM Press (2008), 81–88.
27. Owen, A. M., McMillan, K. M., Laird, A. R., and Bullmore, E. N-back working memory paradigm: a meta-analysis of normative functional neuroimaging studies. *Human Brain Mapping 25*, 1 (2005), 46–59.
28. Peck, E., Yuksel, B., Ottley, A., Jacob, R. J. K., and Chang, R. Using fNIRS Brain Sensing to Evaluate Information Visualization Interfaces. In *Proc. CHI 2013*, ACM Press (2013).
29. Peck, E. M., Afergan, D., and Jacob, R. J. K. Investigation of fNIRS brain sensing as input to information filtering systems. *Augmented Human 2013* (2013).
30. Pekrun, R., Goetz, T., Daniels, L. M., Stupnisky, R. H., and Perry, R. P. Boredom in achievement settings: Exploring controlvalue antecedents and performance outcomes of a neglected emotion. *Journal of Educational Psychology 102*, 3 (2010), 531–549.
31. Prinzel, L. J., Freeman, F. G., Scerbo, M. W., Mikulka, P. J., and Pope, A. T. Effects of a Psychophysiological System for Adaptive Automation on Performance, Workload, and the Event-Related Potential P300 Component. *Human Factors: The Journal of the Human Factors and Ergonomics Society 45*, 4 (2003), 601–613.
32. Qin, H., Rau, P., and Salvendy, G. Effects of different scenarios of game difficulty on player immersion. *Interacting with Computers 22*, 3 (2010), 230–239.
33. Rani, P. Maintaining optimal challenge in computer games through real-time physiological feedback mechanical engineering. *Pulse* (2005).
34. Sassaroli, A., Zheng, F., Hirshfield, L. M., Girouard, A., Solovey, E. T., Jacob, R. J. K., and Fantini, S. Discrimination of Mental Workload Levels in Human Subjects with Functional Near-Infrared Spectroscopy. *Journal of Innovative Optical Health Sciences 1*, 2 (2008), 227–237.
35. Solovey, E. T., Girouard, A., Chauncey, K., Hirshfield, L. M., Sassaroli, A., Zheng, F., Fantini, S., and Jacob, R. J. K. Using fNIRS Brain Sensing in Realistic HCI Settings: Experiments and Guidelines. In *Proc. UIST 2009*, ACM Press (2009), 157–166.
36. Solovey, E. T., Girouard, A., Jacob, R. J., Lalooses, F., Chauncey, K., Weaver, D., Parasi, M., Scheutz, M., Sassaroli, A., Fantini, S., and Schermerhorn, P. Sensing cognitive multitasking for a brain-based adaptive user interface. In *Proc. CHI 2011*, ACM Press (2011).
37. Solovey, E. T., Schermerhorn, P., Scheutz, M., Sassaroli, A., Fantini, S., and Jacob, R. Brainput: Enhancing Interactive Systems with Streaming fNIRS Brain Input. In *Proc. CHI 2012*, ACM Press (2012).
38. Strangman, G., Culver, J. P., Thompson, J. H., and Boas, D. A. A Quantitative Comparison of Simultaneous BOLD fMRI and NIRS Recordings during Functional Brain Activation. *NeuroImage 17*, 2 (2002), 719–731.
39. Stripling, R., Coyne, J., Cole, A., Afergan, D., Barnes, R. L., Rossi, K. A., Reeves, L. M., and Schmorrow, D. D. Automated SAF adaptation tool (ASAT). In *Foundations of Augmented Cognition*. Springer Berlin Heidelberg, 2007, 346–353.
40. Tai, K., and Chau, T. Single-trial classification of NIRS signals during emotional induction tasks: towards a corporeal machine interface. *Journal of Neuroengineering and Rehabilitation 6* (2009), 39.
41. Tan, D., and Nijholt, A. Brain-Computer Interfaces and Human-Computer Interaction. In *Brain-Computer Interfaces*. Springer London, 2010, 3–19.
42. Vidaurre, C., Kawanabe, M., von Bünau, P., Blankertz, B., and Müller, K. R. Toward unsupervised adaptation of LDA for brain-computer interfaces. *IEEE Transactions on Biomedical Engineering 58*, 3 (2011), 587–97.
43. Wilson, G. F., and Russell, C. A. Performance Enhancement in an Uninhabited Air Vehicle Task Using Psychophysiologically Determined Adaptive Aiding. *Human Factors: The Journal of the Human Factors and Ergonomics Society 49*, 6 (2007), 1005–1018.
44. Zander, T. O., Kothe, C., Welke, S., and Rötting, M. Utilizing secondary input from passive brain-computer interfaces for enhancing human-machine interaction. In *Foundations of Augmented Cognition, Neuroergonomics and Operational Neuroscience*, Springer Berlin Heidelberg (2009), 759–771.

Measuring the Effect of Think Aloud Protocols on Workload using fNIRS

Matthew Pike*, **Horia A. Maior***†, **Martin Porcheron**†, **Sarah Sharples**‡ **and Max L. Wilson***

*Mixed Reality Lab
University of Nottingham
Nottingham, UK

†Horizon Doctoral Training Centre
University of Nottingham
Nottingham, UK

‡Human Factors Research Group
University of Nottingham
Nottingham, UK

{psxmp8, psxhama, psxmp9, sarah.sharples, max.wilson}@nottingham.ac.uk

ABSTRACT

The Think Aloud Protocol (TAP) is a verbalisation technique widely employed in HCI user studies to give insight into user experience, yet little work has explored the impact that TAPs have on participants during user studies. This paper utilises a brain sensing technique, fNIRS, to observe the effect that TAPs have on participants. Functional Near-Infrared Spectroscopy (fNIRS) is a brain sensing technology that offers the potential to provide continuous, detailed insight into brain activity, enabling an objective view of cognitive processes during complex tasks. Participants were asked to perform a mathematical task under 4 conditions: nonsense verbalisations, passive concurrent think aloud protocol, invasive concurrent think aloud protocol, and a baseline of silence. Subjective ratings and performance measures were collected during the study. Our results provide a novel view into the effect that different forms of verbalisation have on workload during tasks. Further, the results provide a means for estimating the effect of spoken artefacts when measuring workload, which is another step towards our goal of proactively involving fNIRS analysis in ecologically valid user studies.

ACM Classification Keywords

H.5.2 [Information interfaces and presentation]: User Interfaces. - Evaluation/methodology.

Author Keywords

functional near-infrared spectroscopy; fNIRS; BCI; human cognition; Think Aloud Protocol; HCI

INTRODUCTION

The Think-Aloud Protocol (TAP) is a widely used research method [23], utilised in a variety of research fields including Human Computer Interaction. Since TAP will use resources from verbal working memory, it is fair to assume that the inclusion of spoken protocols will potentially affect cognitive processes due to use of available resources. Consequently, TAPs may affect performance in tasks, and also measures of workload during studies.

CHI 2014, April 26–May 1, 2014, Toronto, Ontario, Canada.

ACM 978-1-4503-2473-1/14/04..$15.00.
http://dx.doi.org/10.1145/2556288.2556974

To analyse the potential impact that a TAP may have on an individual, we use a direct measure through the brain monitoring technology Functional Near-InfraRed Spectroscopy (fNIRS). fNIRS has received recent focus in HCI research for its amenability for more ecologically valid study conditions [17, 33]. While some brain sensing techniques like functional Magnetic Resonance Imaging (fMRI) require minimal or no movement from users, fNIRS can be used while seated naturally at a computer [33]. Further, because fNIRS measures blood oxygenation and deoxygenation rather than electrical signals like Electroencephalography (EEG), fNIRS permits more natural movements associated with using a computer without being subject to significant artefacts in the data. Although the suggestion is that fNIRS can be used more easily within natural, ecologically valid user study conditions, current research is still limited to performing controlled simple Working Memory tasks (e.g. [33, 30]).

In the context of HCI, TAP is typically used as an evaluation method to elicit insights into participants thoughts and strategies during usability and user studies. TAP, however, has also been used in other settings, such as cognitive psychology and social sciences [7], to understand phenomena such as user mental models, expertise, and problem solving. As well as being a core part of user studies, verbalisations are also closely related with Working Memory, as both the interpretation of words in the task and the integration of thoughts involve the phonological loop [38]. Consequently, to integrate fNIRS measurement within a typical user study that might involve a TAP, we have to be aware of how one will affect the other. There are various forms of TAP, including retrospective, which occurs after a task has been completed, and concurrent, which occurs during a task. Of concurrent forms of TAPs, there is both invasive, which involves directly questioning participants, and passive, which simply encourages participants to maintain verbalisations about their thoughts and actions. Because fNIRS measurements are taken during tasks, this paper focuses on concurrent TAPs.

In the following sections, we first review related work on TAPs, Working Memory and mental workload, fNIRS sensing and other technologies. The paper continues by describing a user study examining the impact of a) nonsense verbalisations, b) passive concurrent think aloud, and c) invasive concurrent think aloud, compared to a baseline of silent non-verbal working memory. We then present the results of the study, discuss the findings in terms of what we can learn about the impact of TAP on mental workload in general, and recommendations for using fNIRS measurements in an HCI user study.

RELATED WORK

This section presents three key areas of related work: 1) TAP and their effect on Cognition, 2) Working Memory (WM) models and the Prefrontal Cortex (PFC), and 3) Brain sensing techniques in HCI including fNIRS.

Think-Aloud Protocols

Ericsson and Simon's seminal work on verbal reporting of participants thought process is the most cited amongst Think Aloud Protocols [29]. Prior to this work, little consideration was made to the type of verbalisation produced by participants under study conditions [16]. In their original discussion of TAP, Ericsson and Simon [11] distinguish between 3 distinct levels at which verbalisations occur. Levels 1 and 2 are described as being valid representations of a participant's mental state, since they are verbalising information stored in short term memory and are representative of the participant's current state. Level 3 requires access to long term memory and influences what would otherwise be their typical state. Ericsson and Simon's version (Levels 1 and 2) of the protocol is strictly non-intrusive, and researchers implementing the protocol are restricted to simply using the verbal prompt -"Keep talking"- to avoid influencing the participant, and ensuring that the reported data relates solely to the task. To distinguish between other forms, we refer to this type of TAP as Passive (PTAP) for the remainder of this paper.

In practice, however, it has been shown that many researchers incorrectly implement or misreport the TAP they are using [23]. Many practitioners of TAP prefer to question participants at level 3 to obtain coherent, actionable utterances relating to the system under evaluation, rather than inferring results from level 1 and 2 utterances. Researchers have attempted to formalise this level of questioning [9, 16]. We characterise these approaches under the umbrella term Invasive TAP (ITAP). With ITAP, researchers are free to probe the user's mental model, but Ericsson and Simon would disregard the findings at these levels stating that they have been influenced. Under ITAP, a practitioner is able to prompt the participant with more probing questions - "Why did you do X?".

Working Memory

In an attempt to characterise and model the cognitive processes involved when a participant is partaking in a TAP, we draw on research into Working Memory (WM)[5], a specific system in the brain which "provides temporary storage and manipulation of information" [2]. WM [5, 3, 4] processes information in two forms: verbal and spatial, and has four main components (Figure 1): a visuo-spatial sketch pad holding information in an analogue spatial form (e.g. colours, shapes, maps, etc.), a phonological loop holding verbal information in an acoustical form (e.g. numbers, words, etc.), an episodic buffer dedicated to linking verbal and spatial information in chronological order and finally, a central executive acting as supervisory system and controlling the information from and to its "slave systems".

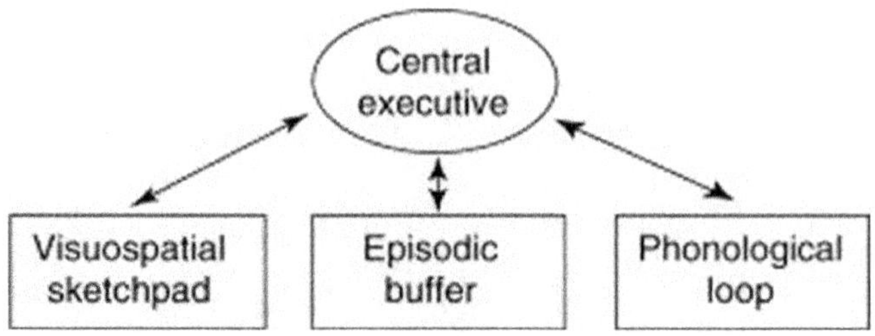

Figure 1. Baddeley's Working Memory Model

Additionally, Baddeley describes the concept of Long-term memory (LTM), which represents a different storage location to working memory. LTM is unlimited in space and is responsible for storing information that is no longer in working memory.

We can relate a number of concepts described by Ericsson and Simon to the working memory model described by Baddeley. For example, Ericsson and Simon note that verbalisations at level 1 and 2 occur within short term memory. We can further characterise this with Ericsson and Simon stating that TAP will utilise the Phonological loop as it is verbal in nature. Tasks under which the TAP is performed may also interact with other components of the working memory model. Tasks involving imagery or mental rotation, for example, will utilise the visuo-spatial sketchpad since they are spatial, whereas verbalising occurs in the phonological loop. For such tasks under TAP conditions the two concepts of the model will be activated, with the central executive mediating information flow between the two. The episodic buffer may also have a role under ITAP conditions, since the protocol will require access to memories that are not in the immediate short term memory. We would not expect the Episodic buffer to be utilised in the PTAP condition.

In addition to the WM model, we can also consider the Information Processing Model [39] and Multiple Resource Model [38] proposed by Wickens. Wickens describes that necessary resources are limited and aims to illustrate how elements of the human information processing system such as attention, perception, memory, decision making and response selection interconnect. We are interested in observing how and when these elements interconnect under TAPs. Wickens describes three different 'stages' (see STAGES dimension in Figure 2) at which information is transformed: a perception stage, a processing or cognition stage, and a response stage. The first stage involves perceiving information that is gathered by our senses and provide meaning and interpretation of what is being sensed. The second stage represents the step where we manipulate and "think about" the perceived information. This part of the information processing system takes place in WM and consists of a wide variety of mental activities. We can observe that TAP will likely affect each of these elements since the protocol introduces additional sensory inputs, which require potential comprehension and will sometimes require a response (specifically under ITAP).

Wickens also proposes the Multiple Resource Model [38], illustrated in Figure 2. The elements of this model overlap with the needs and considerations of evaluating complex tasks which could be analysed and affected by the inclusion of a TAP. He describes the aspects of cognition and the multiple resource theory in four dimensions: STAGES, MODALITIES, CODES and the VISUAL PROCESSING (see Figure 2).

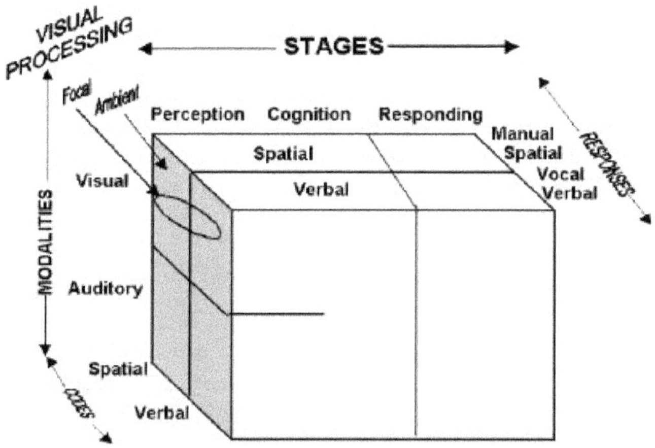

Figure 2. The 4-D multiple resource model, by Wickens

One of the key roles of the Multiple Resource Model is to demonstrate the hypothesised independence of modalities and use this to design tasks. We know for example that the inclusion of TAP will introduce additional Auditory resource requirements, since the participant will hear their own verbalisations. This in turn will require additional Perception from the participant and will draw on their Verbal coding resources and Vocal Verbal responses.

The Prefrontal Cortex (PFC) is the anterior part of the frontal lobes of the brain and is considered central to the function of WM, dealing with executive and attention processes [19]. Miller and Cohen defines the representations in the PFC as "attentional templates, retrieval cues, rules, or goals" [27], and many researchers agree that PFC function is one of Baddley's executive control [1]. Conversely, Rushworth reports that not all PFC subregions are essential for working memory [32]. The PFC is the region of the brain that we targeted during this study since there is significant evidence to support its role in WM [6, 8]. In addition to the PFC, Brocas area is located within the frontal lobe and is linked with speech production [12].

Brain Sensing Techniques

There are several brain sensing technologies available for research, including (but not limited to) fMRI, EEG, and fNIRS, which are summarised in Table 1. Each of these technologies have different strengths and weaknesses, as discussed by Tan and Nijholt [34, Chapter 1].

Functional Magnetic Resonance Imaging (fMRI) is a functional neuroimaging technique that associates detected changes in blood flow (hemodynamic response) to brain activity. fMRI is typically used for applications requiring high spatial resolution, but requires people to lay very still, and precludes the use of a computer. Participants are unable to interact directly with a system, but can respond to visual stimuli through the use of mirrors. Li et. al [22] for example, used real time fMRI to control the animation speed of a virtual human runner.

Electroencephalography (EEG) typically uses between 16 and 64 sensors on the scalp to detect varying electrical charge within the brain. With the introduction of commercially available bluetooth EEG sensors, like the Emotiv[1], EEG has become an affordable option for brain sensing [10]. For evaluation, however, EEG data is susceptible to motion artefacts, and so producing averages for periods of interaction provides limited insight. Pike et al [31] proposed, that EEG data was most valuable when combined visually with recorded TAP data, as statements of confusion, or pauses in verbalising ones actions, coincided with and were qualified by EEG data.

fNIRS uses blood oxygenation, rather than electrical levels, for determining the activation of areas in the brain, where more blood flow indicates higher activity. Recent research has shown that because blood-flow in the brain is less affected by body movement, fNIRS may be a more appropriate brain sensing technology for evaluation [17, 30, 21]. Because it takes several seconds for blood to flow to the brain [37], fNIRs has been largely discounted for real-time interaction with systems.

EXPERIMENT DESIGN

The aim of this study was to investigate how verbalisation and TAPs affect cognition and the thought process during user study tasks. We produced three research questions:

- How can we identify the impact of TAPs on human cognition and mental workload using fNIRS?
- What are the most suitable measures to sense such an impact?
- How can we sense the reduction of available resources due to integrating a TAP concurrently with a task?

To answer these research questions, a theoretical understanding of TAPs, human cognition, mental workload and the interconnection between these concepts is required. Wickens' Multiple Resource Model [38] can describe the relationship between the available resources and task demands. When performing a task, a person perceives both their own verbalisation and/or external stimuli as an Auditory modality. During 'think aloud' we also process information (make decisions, store memories, retrieve memories, etc.), and output them as a response (e.g. as a Vocal Verbal encoding). Therefore, TAPs might have an impact on all three stages (perception, cognition and response) of the Multiple Resource Model. According to the model, a TAP is a verbal/linguistic activity, therefore the codes of its cognition stage is Verbal. Consequently, we chose a task (described further below) that was easy to verbalise and involves continuous use of the phonological loop, such that different verbalisation conditions would interact with the task.

[1] http://www.emotiv.com/

Technique	Physical Property	Sensitivity to Motion	Portability	Spatial Resolution	Temporal Resolution	Cost
fMRI	Magnetic	Very High	None	High	Low	Expensive
EEG	Electrical	High	Portable	Low	High	Reasonable
fNIRS	Optical	Low	Portable	High	Low	Moderate

Table 1. Summary of Brain Sensing technologies

Primarily, we wanted to compare the different concurrent TAPs against a baseline of not verbalising. In order to check whether simply using your voice creates an artefact in the fNIRS data, as opposed to thinking and talking, we also included a second baseline of repeatedly verbalising the word 'blah'. Type of verbalisation, as primary independent variable, created four conditions:

1. Task Only (Baseline - B1)
2. Task + "Blah blah blah" (Baseline - B2)
3. Task + Passive Concurrent TAP (PTAP)
4. Task + Invasive Concurrent TAP (ITAP)

We designed a repeated measures, within-participants study to compare these conditions, where participants solved eight mathematical problems. Conditions and tasks were counterbalanced using a Latin-square design.

Hypotheses

We had a number of hypothesis that we sought to investigate whilst conducting this study relative to performance, cognition, and participants' grouping based on mathematical performance (High and Low performing groups):

HP - There will be a significant difference in performance between verbal conditions.

HC - There will be a significant difference in cognition between verbal conditions.

HP and HC were drawn from Wickens 4D Multiple Resources Model [38]. Both TAP and mathematical tasks should primarily use verbal working memory in the modality, encoding, and processings dimensions. Consequently, the demands imposed by various verbal conditions may affect the total workload element, and workload may then affect performance.

HC.S - There will be a significant difference in cognition between verbal conditions for high performing participants.

HC.W - There will be a significant difference in cognition between verbal conditions for low performing participants.

Depending on how well participants performed during the four conditions, we distinguished between high performing participants (top half) and low performing participants (bottom half) [26]. These groups were formed to investigate whether TAPs have a different impact on cognition relative to the participants grouping.

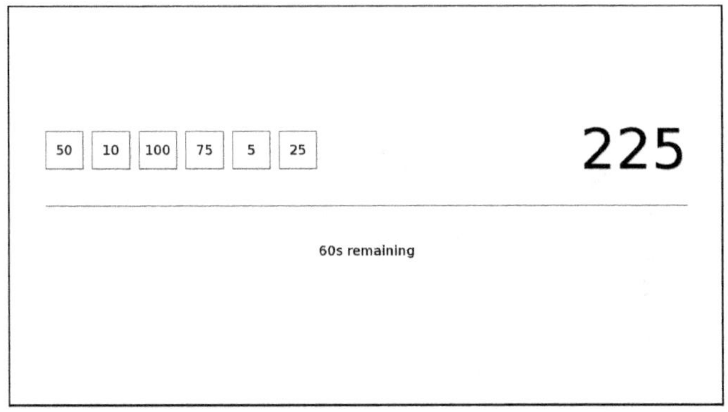

Figure 3. A screenshot of the task

Task

In order to determine how TAPs affect the different stages of the Multiple Resources Model, the task had to be chosen carefully such that verbalisation could potentially interrupt the process. The first criterion, therefore, was that the task should primarily use the phonological loop, and thus be a verbally oriented task. Second, the task had to involve continuous use of the phonological loop, and so a simple and discrete memory task was not sufficient. Third, the task had to be verbalisable for the TAPs, which also meant that a memory task was not sufficient. Fourth, the task also had to have various levels of difficulty to enable control over the primary task mental demands; according to the resource vs demands model [25] harder tasks would increase demand and thus reducing participant's resources for engaging in the TAP. Finally, performance on the task had to be measurable in order to determine the effect of verbalisations. Based upon these five criteria, we decided on using a mathematics task. Participants were provided with a set of six numbers and had to get as close as possible to a target final number. This problem is a variation on what is commonly known as the countdown problem[2]. Each number may be used only once (although there is no requirement to use every number), and participants have 60s to reach as close to the target number as possible, using four operators: addition, subtraction, multiplication and division.

36 versions of the task were created to be used across the four conditions, at various levels of difficulty. To classify their difficulty, one researcher and two independent judges rated the difficulty of each problem. Difficulty was judged in four categories: easy, quite easy, quite hard, and hard. Inter-rater agreeability was confirmed with a Cohen's Kappa test, where

[2]based on the mathematical challenge presented to contestants of the popular UK TV quiz show "Countdown"

the researcher achieved scores of 0.6419 (substantial agreement [20]) with the first independent judge, and 0.8571 (almost perfect agreement) with the second. This agreement was used to ensure that problem difficulty was balanced between conditions.

Participants

Twenty participants (14 male, 6 female) with an average age of 28.55 years were recruited to take part in the study. Participants were recruited from the University of Nottingham, and included a mix of staff members and students from a range of disciplines. All participants had normal or corrected vision and reported no history of head trauma or brain damage. The study was approved by the school's ethics committee. Participants provided informed consent, and were compensated with £15 in gift vouchers.

Procedure

Participants were first introduced to the task that they would be completing during the study. They were given two practice runs of the task (under baseline conditions) to familiarise themselves and reduce the impact of learning in their first condition. Once comfortable with the requirements of the task, participants were fitted with the fNIRS brain imaging device, which was placed upon their forehead targeting the PFC. At this point participants entered the recorded section of the study. During this stage, participant input was captured, verbalisations were recorded via microphone, and brain data was captured on a separate, calibrated machine.

Participants partook in four conditions which were counterbalanced using a latin square rotation. Each condition began with a tutorial and practice session. The tutorial session was used to train the participant on how to verbalise according to the specific TAP being used in the particular condition. The practice session would then serve as an opportunity to trial the technique prior to beginning the test itself and thus reducing the interference on the first task in each condition. Each condition included eight of the tasks described above.

For each of the eight tasks in each condition, participants were given sixty seconds to attempt the problem. All calculations were performed mentally; pen and paper was not provided. After the sixty seconds had elapsed (or if the participant decided to proceed prior to this), participants were prompted to enter the number they had achieved during the calculation period. To avoid participants simply entering the target number, they were prompted to recall their solution. The solutions provided by participants were recorded by the researcher on paper and later digitalised.

After each condition, participants completed a standard NASA TLX form to subjectively rate their mental workload during the task. Each condition concluded with a thirty second rest period where the participants were asked to remain still, relax and empty their mind of thoughts.

The study was conducted in an office-like environment. This was an important consideration as many brain based studies are conducted under strictly controlled lab settings. The office environment provides a more naturalistic and ecologically valid setting.

Measurements and Equipment

We collected various types of data during the study. The data can be categorised into two groups: Performance during the study (P), and Cognition (C).

Task Accuracy - P

We measured task performance according to distance from the target answer for each of the 36 problems across the four conditions. Because the target varied, we used measured distance from the target as a percentage, which was subtracted from 100%. 100% represented the correct answer, 95% as being 5% from the target, and so on. As the results tended towards the target, task accuracy was analysed. To provide incentive to submit actual rather than ideal answers, we also measured whether participants could recall the solution to their answer.

Task Time - P

Task time was measured for each of the 36 problems performed across the four conditions. We note that participants were not encouraged to solve the problem in the shortest possible time, rather, they were asked to get as close possible to the target.

NASA-TLX questionnaire - C

We used the NASA-TLX questionnaire, a subjective workload assessment tool [15], based on the weighted average ratings of six subscales including, in order: Mental Demand, Physical Demand, Temporal Demand, Performance, Effort and Frustration. Each participant was asked to self rate their mental workload using the NASA-TLX once after each condition. We additionally investigated each of subscales independently.

fNIRS data - C

fNIRS data was recorded using an fNIRS300 device and the associated COBI Studio recording software provided by Biopac Systems inc. The headband shaped device is a sixteen-channel transducer for continuous Near Infrared Spectroscopy (NIRS). The headband consists of four infrared (IR) emitters operating on a range between 700 to 900 nm, and ten IR detectors. The device is placed on the PFC targeting the Brodmann area 10 (BA10). Oxygenated hemoglobin (HbO) and deoxygenated-hemoglobin (Hb) are both strong absorbers of light, whereas skin, tissue and bone are mostly transparent to NIR light, this property is typically referred to as the *optical window* [18]. The tissue is radiated by the light sources and the detectors receive the light after the interaction with the tissue. See Figure 4 [13] for an illustration of how the headband is positioned, and to visualise the path that the light follows during operation.

Preprocessing was performed to transform raw data from the device into oxygenation values using the Modified Beer-Lambert law (MBLL) [36]. We also applied filtering algorithms to remove high-frequency noise, physiological artefacts such as heartbeats and motion derived artefacts. To perform this preprocessing step we used the Matlab Toolbox,

NIRS-SPM [40]. We performed de-trending using a discrete cosine transform with a high frequency cut off of 128 seconds. The baseline was removed, and low pass filtering was performed with a Gaussian filter with a width of 1 second. We also considered the delay induced by the hemodynamic response [36] by omitting the first 10s of the trial when processing the data [30].

The Biopac fNIRS device used in this study provides 16 channels of brain data readings. A channel is defined by the relationship between a source and detector pair as shown in Figure 4. From the MBLL we receive Hb, HbO and TotalHb (Hb + HbO) values for each channel. Measures were synthesised by combining specific channels averages to form a single measurement. Channels 3,4,5,6 were used to represent the left side and channels 11,12,13,14 formed the right side in these measurements. An overall measurement was produced by averaging the data from all 16 channels(see Figure 4).

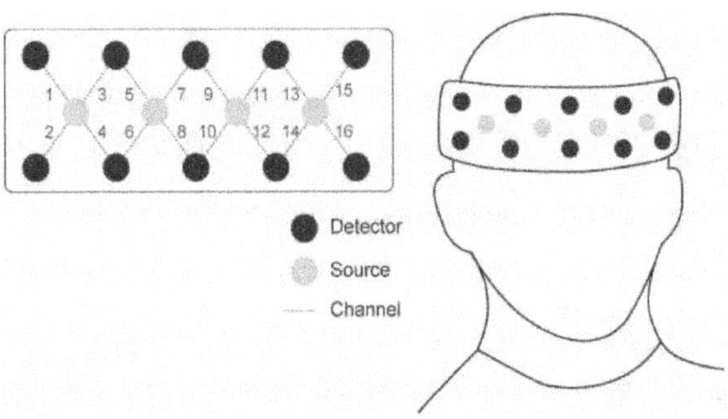

Figure 4. Sensor layout for the Biopac fNIRS used

Experiment Software

When designing the study we placed a strong emphasis on automating the running of the study and collection of the associated data. With the exception of the brain data, all other measures were collected from a single program. We developed this program using PEBL: The Psychology Experiment Building Language [28]. The language provides a convenient set of features including accurate experiment timing and predefined psychology/study procedures such as demographic questionnaires. Of particular relevance to this study was the pre-defined, computerised version of NASA-TLX.

RESULTS

We began by checking for ordering effect. A one way repeated measure ANOVA showed that participants performed significantly slower in the first condition they experienced, while average time to complete the subsequent conditions was even ($F(19, 3) = 2.816, p < 0.05$). An LSD post-hoc ANOVA test also showed that average scores also improved between the first condition they experienced and the last ($F(19, 3) = 2.271, p < 0.05$).

Performance

Against hypothesis HP, our analysis showed no significant difference in task accuracy between conditions. We found no significant difference in performance between any of the four conditions, however, under the TAP conditions, participant performance slightly improved. There was also no difference in the number of tasks correctly calculated in each condition. We hypothesised that, ITAP under time pressure would cause performance to drop, but instead these results support the findings of McDonald et al. [24] who found that neither form of TAP affected performance.

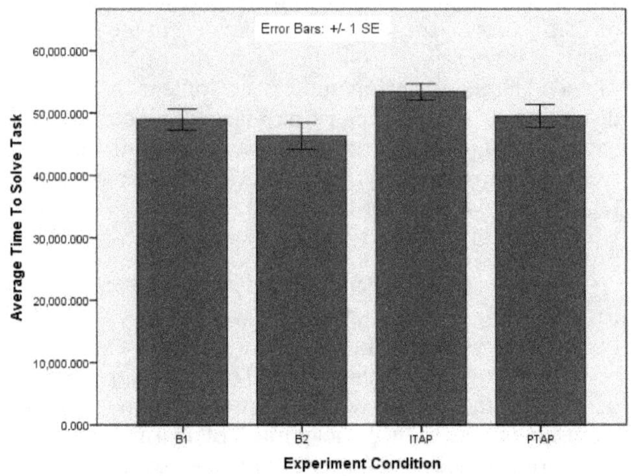

Figure 5. Mean time to solve a set of tasks

A significant difference was found in terms of time to complete tasks (Figure 5). As perhaps expected, participants took significantly longer to solve tasks in the ITAP condition ($F(17, 3) = 9.895, p < 0.01$) relative to the other three conditions (B1: $p < 0.005$, B2: $p < 0.001$, PTAP: $p < 0.05$). PTAP was not significantly different to B1 or B2. This time difference was likely created by the additional time required to explain decisions being made. Participants were not asked to solve the tasks in the shortest amount of time, but were encouraged to get as close to the target answer as possible. As such this metric is a measure of the participants natural behaviour under a given condition.

Mental Workload: Subjective measure

In support of hypothesis HC, we found significant differences between conditions in the NASA-TLX scales: Mental Effort, Mental Demands, and Physical Demands. Against our own intuitions, each of these measures demonstrated higher demands for B2 compared to the other conditions (see Figure 6). A Wilcoxon signed-rank test showed that B2 created significantly more mental effort than B1 ($Z = -2.058, p < 0.05$), and it required more mental demands ($Z = -2.292, p < 0.05$). The difference between B2 and PTAP was only $p = 0.075$ and there was no significant difference between ITAP and the other conditions. Participants also rated B2 as being physically more demanding than the other conditions (B1: $p < 0.05$, PTAP $p = 0.067$, and ITAP $p < 0.05$). This is to say that participants found the additional utterance of a nonsense word whilst solving the maths problems induced a greater physical demand than other conditions (see Figure 6). Correlations between performance scales from unweighted NASA-TLX and performance data were found. This includes

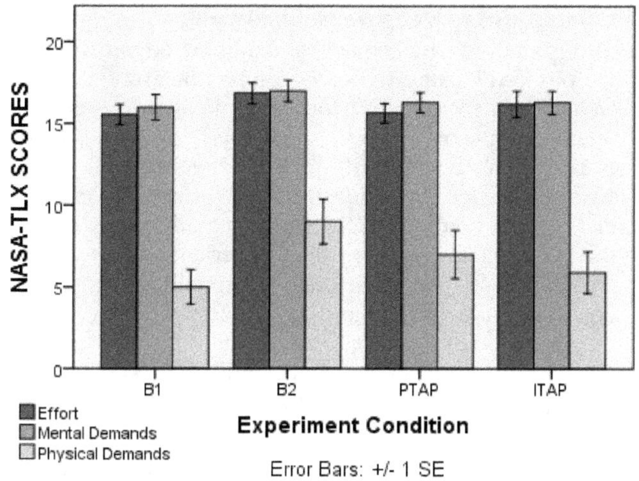

Figure 6. Means for three sub-scales of NASA-TLX

a negative Pearson correlation between NASA-TLX Performance scale and distance from target $r = -252, n = 80, p = 0.024$, indicating that participants were rating their performance as worse, when in fact it was better. Two positive Pearson correlations between NASA-TLX Mental Demands and Temporal Demands when compared with time to solve a problem were also found: $r = 0.340, n = 80, p = 0.002$, and $r = 0.408, n = 80, p = 0.001$ respectively.

Mental Workload: fNIRS

Further supporting HC, our analysis found a significant difference in brain region activation in both right and left inferior PFC during the experiment conditions.

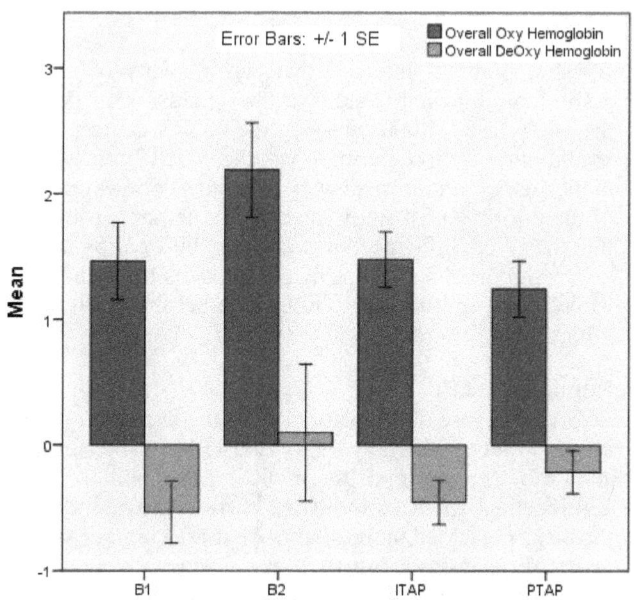

Figure 7. Overall HbO and Hb levels for each condition

As shown in Figure 7, OverallHbO were significantly higher during B2 compared to all other conditions (PTAP: $p < 0.05$, ITAP: $p = 0.064$). We also noted an effect on the rest time at the end of each conditions: values at rest after B2 were significantly higher than values at rest after B1 ($p = 0.05$).

Peck et al [30] found a negative correlation between fNIRS levels of Hb and the subjective ratings from NASA-TLX Mental Demands scale. Tasks that created more mental effort were accompanied by lower levels of Hb. We were unable to confirm these finding across all participants, however we found a positive correlation between performance data (distance from target) and fNIRS overall Hb, $r = 0.228, n = 80, p = 0.04$. This possibly complements Peck's correlation assuming that when mental demands are high to the point of overload, performance decreases and therefore Hb follows. This assumption ties well with the Limited Resource Model presented by Megaw [25].

There was also a strong positive Pearson correlation ($r = 0.474, n = 80, p < 0.001$) between the fNIRS readings Hb left and Hb right.

Mathematics Skill

Peck et al [30] found differences in participants depending on their ability to analyse both pie and bar charts. Similarly, we believed that mathematical propensity would affect an individuals performance under differing TAPs, with the assumption that high performers would better cope with TAPs, while lower performers would be impaired as a result of reduced resources (from TAP).

High Performers

The high performing group rated ITAP as being more mentally demanding (Wilcoxon signed-rank test with $Z = -1.89, p = 0.059$) and requiring more mental effort (Wilcoxon signed-rank test with $Z = -1.98, p = 0.048$) when compared against PTAP. A Spearman negative correlation for the strong mathematicians between the NASA-TLX Mental Demands scale and the fNIRS Hb levels on the right side of the PFC ($r = -0.348, n = 40, p = 0.028$) confirms Peck's [30] findings. High performers also demonstrated a positive Spearman correlation between distance from target and fNIRS Hb on the left side of the PFC ($r = 0.344, n = 40, p = 0.03$). Weighted NASA TLX score also positively correlated with time taken to solve a problem ($r = 0.399, n = 40, p = 0.01$).

Low Performers

For the low performing group we observed an agreement between weighted NASA-TLX score and fNIRS overall Hb. There was the same significant difference from a Wilcoxon Sign Rank test in both NASA-TLX and fNIRS ($Z = -1.78, p = 0.074$) between PTAP and ITAP. Participants workload measured with both NASA-TLX and fNIRS is marginally higher in PTAP than ITAP. This result is opposite to what was observed with the high performing group.

DISCUSSION

fNIRS, Language and Mental Workload

Activations in the left side of the prefrontal cortex are known to occur during semantic, relative to nonsemantic, tasks that relate or involve "the generation of words to semantic cues or the classification of words or pictures into semantic categories" [14]. Due to the physical placement of our fNIRS device on participants foreheads, we can discount the interaction between Broca's area and our results as it does not fall within the reach of our device. Because fNIRS was sensitive to the B2 condition, we developed two premises (interpretations) of the results:

1. fNIRS is particularly picking up the part of the brain that is activated during B2 and therefore the signal received by fNIRS is higher, or

2. fNIRS is picking up an indicator related to mental workload and that B2 induces more workload. The reason behind this is the non-compatibility and non-complementarity of B2 with the mathematical reasoning task, rather than the compatibility of verbalisation protocols from PTAP and ITAP with the mathematical reasoning task.

One way to distinguish between these two is to look at the participants performance data and subjective ratings (the NASA-TLX scores) together with fNIRS. If the first premise is true, you would not expect a difference in mental workload (in the subjective scores) between the verbalisation conditions. Additionally, you would not expect any relationship between performance or NASA-TLX data with fNIRS readings. We found significant difference between verbalisation conditions in NASA-TLX scores and we also found correlations between fNIRS data with both performance and NASA-TLX. If fNIRS would pick up information related to language generation, you would expect significant difference in fNIRS data between verbalisation conditions and the silent condition (which we did not find, see Figure 7). With this in mind, we propose that fNIRS is not an indicator of how many words you are saying, but is sensitive to mental workload and human cognition (therefore provides support for the second premise).

Using the fNIRS alone we were unable to identify the significant differences we were expecting. However we found the fNIRS data to be complementary to existing measures such as performance and NASA-TLX. Considering the number of marginally significant results($p < 0.075$), we believe that increasing the number of participants would increase power, reduce type II error, and positively impact our findings.

High and Low Performers

If generalisable, our findings suggest that for high performers PTAP is the more suitable protocol and that ITAP is better suited to low performers. One possible explanation for this is that high performers have an existing procedural structure in which they operate, so interrupting this procedure (as is experienced under ITAP) potentially interferes with their natural behaviour. For low performers, however, such structure is not present and verbalising via PTAP is potentially troublesome, as they are being forced to verbalise a process that is absent or unnatural for them. The introduction of carefully chosen prompts, however, may encourage non-experts to describe how they are struggling and provide useful insight into how researchers may help these types of users in the future.

Using fNIRS to Measure Mental Workload

In this study we looked at evaluating the cognitive impact of various TAPs using fNIRS as a novel measurement. fNIRS was chosen for its non invasive application, portability and relative resilience to motion artefacts. We found the device to be suitable ecologically for HCI style user study settings, with the device providing minimal distraction and interference. After completing the study, we informally questioned the participants regarding their experience with wearing the fNIRS device. No participant described feeling particularly uncomfortable during the study, some did however state that they began to experience some discomfort towards the end of the study. We advise that studies utilising fNIRS should aim to keep sessions below 1 hour in a single sitting.

We believe that fNIRS is well suited to HCI evaluation and usability testing. We believe that the inclusion of this novel new measurement complements existing evaluation measures such as NASA-TLX. fNIRS benefits from having the properties of being both an objective and continuous measure allowing for accurate, time correlated recording during evaluation and testing studies, especially when compared to the subjective one time snapshot rating achieved via NASA-TLX. We must also note the potential negatives associated with this type of technology. fNIRS is an emerging technology and as such does not have the associated supporting research proving its correctness. Studies have correlated the measurements to those observed with fMRI [35], specifically the BOLD signal. Additionally, in the current state of technology, fNIRS can only be used to detect a level of workload (high or low), leaving a distinct lack of mapping between the readings recorded with fNIRS and the actual cognitive or emotional states. For example, detecting frustration under a evaluation study would be a useful measure, but is not currently obtainable from fNIRS.

Another point of interest, that can possibly be considered a shortcoming of this study is the exclusion of performing the study task without wearing the fNIRS device. Doing so would allow us to determine whether fNIRS affected performance or behaviour in anyway. We did ask however, as a part of the informal post study interview, whether participants felt that they were influenced in some way by wearing the device; no one reported such an effect. This does leave the potential for a follow up study to examine whether there was indeed an effect.

Running a TAP

One of our research questions was to investigate two think aloud protocols (namely PTAP and ITAP). The study results should be seen as a positive indicator that both TAPs do not significantly affect or influence participants ability to solve the tasks presented in the study. We used a high demand tasks and participants performance was not negatively affected in any way. Contrarily, we observed a slight improvement in participants' performance under TAP conditions, confirming with McDonald [24] that using the TAPs during the task did not have a negative influence on participants' performance.

Reflecting on Wicken's Multiple Resource Model, using multiple resources that are complementary and compatible with the task in hand might have a positive impact on performance in the case of non multitask resource overload. Between the four conditions, participants performed the worse in Condition B2 where they had to repeatedly say 'Blah' during task solving. This was due to a higher workload generated by the condition, sensed with both fNIRS and NASA TLX subjective scale.

The TAPs conditions differed when compared between the expertise level of participants. The high performing group rated ITAP as being more mentally demanding requiring more mental effort when compared against PTAP. This result was also confirmed with the fNIRS data. Conversely for the low performing group, PTAP was the one that was more mentally demanding.

CONCLUSIONS

The aims of this research were a) to investigate how *verbalisations* might affect the use of fNIRS in increasingly ecologically valid user studies, and b) to provide insights into how different forms of verbalisations affect mental workload and performance in user studies. In order to achieve our aims, we compared nonsense verbalisations with different forms of concurrent TAP: passive and invasive. One of our primary findings was that non-complementary verbalisations, as opposed to complex verbalisations, created higher levels of mental workload. In particular, nonsense verbalisations created higher mental workload, across measures, than Invasive TAP where participants discussed their mathematical problem solving options. Consequently, we can conclude that the use of TAPs in user studies is fine as long as the discussion uses words relating to solving the task. We saw a slight increase in mental workload for Invasive TAP compared to Passive TAP, indicating that some Invasive TAP verbalisations may not have been directly conducive to solving the task. None of the nonsense verbalisations supported the task.

The findings about non-complementary language were hidden within the subjective, reflective, self-assessments included in NASA TLX; ratings had high variance, and results were only evident in some of the sub-scales. Further, we saw no difference in task performance between conditions. The objective measure obtained from the fNIRS however, provides a clear indication of the participants' mental workload whilst completing the study tasks. Because there were no differences between the silent baseline and TAP conditions, we can conclude a) that fNIRS measurements were not largely affected by verbalisation itself, and b) that fNIRS can be used to determine mental workload objectively during tasks if verbalisations remain task-related.

Overall, we provide three main contributions: 1) we provide novel insights into the underlying cause of increased mental workload created by TAPs *during* tasks; 2) we provide a novel example of using fNIRS to measure cognition during a more complex task than prior work; and 3) we provide an example to show that fNIRS is suitable for use with tasks that involve verbalisation. Our results make a positive step towards proactively using fNIRS as an evaluation tool within realistic HCI user studies.

ACKNOWLEDGMENTS

This work was partially supported by the EPSRC ORCHID project (EP/I011587/1) and the Horizon Doctoral Training Centre at the University of Nottingham (EP/G037574/1).

REFERENCES

1. Aron, A. R., Robbins, T. W., and Poldrack, R. A. Inhibition and the right inferior frontal cortex. *Trends in cognitive sciences 8*, 4 (2004), 170–177.
2. Baddeley, A. Working memory. *Science 255*, 5044 (1992), 556–559.
3. Baddeley, A. The episodic buffer: a new component of working memory? *Trends in cognitive sciences 4*, 11 (2000), 417–423.
4. Baddeley, A. D. Is working memory still working? *European psychologist 7*, 2 (2002), 85–97.
5. Baddeley, A. D., and Hitch, G. Working memory. *The psychology of learning and motivation 8* (1974), 47–89.
6. Braver, T. S., Cohen, J. D., Nystrom, L. E., Jonides, J., Smith, E. E., and Noll, D. C. A parametric study of prefrontal cortex involvement in human working memory. *Neuroimage 5*, 1 (1997), 49–62.
7. Charters, E. The use of think-aloud methods in qualitative research an introduction to think-aloud methods. *Brock Education* (2013).
8. D'Esposito, M., Detre, J. A., Alsop, D. C., Shin, R. K., Atlas, S., and Grossman, M. The neural basis of the central executive system of working memory. *Nature 378*, 6554 (1995), 279–281.
9. Dumas, J. S. *A practical guide to usability testing*. Intellect Books, 1999.
10. Duvinage, M., Castermans, T., Dutoit, T., Petieau, M., Hoellinger, T., Saedeleer, C., Seetharaman, K., and Cheron, G. A P300-based quantitative comparison between the Emotiv Epoc headset and a medical EEG device. In *IASTED* (2012).
11. Ericsson, K. A., and Simon, H. A. *Protocol analysis*. MIT press, 1985.
12. Fadiga, L., Craighero, L., and DAusilio, A. Broca's area in language, action, and music. *Annals of the New York Academy of Sciences 1169*, 1 (2009), 448–458.
13. fNIR Devices LLC. *fNIR Imager & COBI Studio Manual*. Biopac, 2013.
14. Gabrieli, J. D., Poldrack, R. A., and Desmond, J. E. The role of left prefrontal cortex in language and memory. *Proceedings of the national Academy of Sciences 95*, 3 (1998), 906–913.
15. Hart, S. G., and Staveland, L. E. Development of nasa-tlx (task load index): Results of empirical and theoretical research. *Human mental workload* (1988).

16. Hertzum, M., Hansen, K. D., and Andersen, H. H. Scrutinising usability evaluation: does thinking aloud affect behaviour and mental workload? *Behaviour & Information Technology 28*, 2 (2009), 165–181.

17. Hirshfield, L. M., Solovey, E. T., Girouard, A., Kebinger, J., Jacob, R. J., Sassaroli, A., and Fantini, S. Brain measurement for usability testing and adaptive interfaces: an example of uncovering syntactic workload with functional near infrared spectroscopy. In *Proc. CHI*, ACM (2009), 2185–2194.

18. Izzetoglu, M., Bunce, S. C., Izzetoglu, K., Onaral, B., and Pourrezaei, K. Functional brain imaging using near-infrared technology. *IEEE Engineering in Medicine and Biology Magazine 26*, 4 (2007), 38.

19. Kane, M. J., and Engle, R. W. The role of prefrontal cortex in working-memory capacity, executive attention, and general fluid intelligence: An individual-differences perspective. *Psychonomic bulletin & review 9*, 4 (2002), 637–671.

20. Landis, J. R., and Koch, G. G. The measurement of observer agreement for categorical data. *Biometrics* (1977), 159–174.

21. Leanne, M., and Robert, J. Using brain measurement to evaluate reality based interactions. *Challenges in the Evaluation of Usability and User Experience in Reality Based Interaction 5* (2009), 19–20.

22. Li, X., Xu, L., Yao, L., and Zhao, X. A novel HCI system based on real-time fmri using motor imagery interaction. In *Foundations of Augmented Cognition*. Springer, 2013, 703–708.

23. McDonald, S., Edwards, H. M., and Zhao, T. Exploring think-alouds in usability testing: an international survey. *Professional Communication, IEEE Transactions on 55*, 1 (2012), 2–19.

24. McDonald, S., and Petrie, H. The effect of global instructions on think-aloud testing. In *CHI*, ACM (2013), 2941–2944.

25. Megaw, T. The definition and measurement of mental workload. *Evaluation of human work, Eds. Esmond N. Corlett, and John R. Wilson* (2005), 525–551.

26. Miles, J., and Shevlin, M. *Applying regression and correlation: A guide for students and researchers*. Sage, 2001.

27. Miller, E. K., and Cohen, J. D. An integrative theory of prefrontal cortex function. *Annual review of neuroscience 24*, 1 (2001), 167–202.

28. Mueller, S. Pebl: The psychology experiment building language (version 0.10).[computer experiment programming language]. *Retrieved Nov* (2012).

29. Olmsted-Hawala, E. L., Murphy, E. D., Hawala, S., and Ashenfelter, K. T. Think-aloud protocols: a comparison of three think-aloud protocols for use in testing data-dissemination web sites for usability. In *CHI*, ACM (2010), 2381–2390.

30. Peck, E. M., Yuksel, B. F., Ottley, A., Jacob, R. J., and Chang, R. Using fNIRS Brain Sensing to Evaluate Information Visualization Interfaces. In *CHI*, ACM (2013).

31. Pike, M., Wilson, M. L., Divoli, A., and Medelyan, A. CUES: Cognitive Usability Evaluation System. In *EuroHCIR2012* (2012), 51–54.

32. Rushworth, M. F., Nixon, P. D., Eacott, M. J., and Passingham, R. E. Ventral prefrontal cortex is not essential for working memory. *The Journal of Neuroscience 17*, 12 (1997), 4829–4838.

33. Solovey, E. T., Girouard, A., Chauncey, K., Hirshfield, L. M., Sassaroli, A., Zheng, F., Fantini, S., and Jacob, R. J. Using fNIRS brain sensing in realistic HCI settings: experiments and guidelines. In *Proc. UIST2009*, ACM (2009), 157–166.

34. Tan, D. S., and Nijholt, A. *Brain-Computer Interfaces: applying our minds to human-computer interaction*. Springer, 2010.

35. Toronov, V., Webb, A., Choi, J. H., Wolf, M., Michalos, A., Gratton, E., and Hueber, D. Investigation of human brain hemodynamics by simultaneous near-infrared spectroscopy and functional magnetic resonance imaging. *Medical physics 28* (2001), 521.

36. Villringer, A., and Chance, B. Non-invasive optical spectroscopy and imaging of human brain function. *Trends in neurosciences 20*, 10 (1997), 435–442.

37. Villringer, A., Planck, J., Hock, C., Schleinkofer, L., and Dirnagl, U. Near infrared spectroscopy (NIRS): a new tool to study hemodynamic changes during activation of brain function in human adults. *Neuroscience letters 154*, 1 (1993), 101–104.

38. Wickens, C. D. Multiple resources and mental workload. *The Journal of the Human Factors and Ergonomics Society 50*, 3 (2008), 449–455.

39. Wickens, C. D., Gordon, S. E., and Liu, Y. *An introduction to human factors engineering*. Pearson Prentice Hall Upper Saddle River, 2004.

40. Ye, J. C., Tak, S., Jang, K. E., Jung, J., and Jang, J. NIRS-SPM: statistical parametric mapping for near-infrared spectroscopy. *Neuroimage 44*, 2 (2009), 428–447.

An EEG-based Approach for Evaluating Audio Notifications under Ambient Sounds

Yi-Chieh Lee[1], Wen-Chieh Lin[1], Jung-Tai King[2], Li-Wei Ko[2,3], Yu-Ting Huang[1], Fu-Yin Cherng[1]
[1]Dept. of Computer Science, [2]Brain Research Center, [3]Dept. of Biological Science and Technology
National Chiao Tung University, Taiwan
be341341@gmail.com, wclin@cs.nctu.edu.tw, {jtchin2, lwko.brc, tinahuang79, fufu22710}@gmail.com

ABSTRACT
Audio notifications are an important means of prompting users of electronic products. Although useful in most environments, audio notifications are ineffective in certain situations, especially against particular auditory backgrounds or when the user is distracted. Several studies have used behavioral performance to evaluate audio notifications, but these studies failed to achieve consistent results due to factors including user subjectivity and environmental differences; thus, a new method and more objective indicators are necessary. In this study, we propose an approach based on electroencephalography (EEG) to evaluate audio notifications by measuring users' auditory perceptual responses (mismatch negativity) and attention shifting (P3a). We demonstrate our approach by applying it to the usability testing of audio notifications in realistic scenarios, such as users performing a major task amid ambient noises. Our results open a new perspective for evaluating the design of the audio notifications.

Author Keywords
audio notifications; usability testing; human cognition; electroencephalography (EEG); mismatch negativity

ACM Classification Keywords
H.1.2 User/Machine Systems: J.3Life and Medical Sciences

General Terms
Human Factors; Design; Measurement.

INTRODUCTION
Auditory icons, earcons, and warning sounds have been widely used in computers, consumer electronics, and traffic-control devices. Audio notifications also play critical roles in assistive technologies for the visually impaired; they are a powerful tool for human computer interfaces and can be used to assist users to work more effectively [3]. Generally speaking, the design goals of audio notifications are that they should be short and clear, and allow users to recognize and understand their meanings easily [3, 29]. However, a notification's effectiveness at attracting users' attention is also important. An inappropriate audio design may distract users' concentration, even to the point of danger. Hence, a good audio notification design should take into account not only users' preferences but also the notification's perceptual effects upon users' cognitive states.

CHI 2014, April 26–May 1, 2014, Toronto, Ontario, Canada.

http://dx.doi.org/10.1145/2556288.2557076

Existing approaches for evaluating the preference and effectiveness of audio notifications often rely on questionnaires, or measures of users' performance, such as response time and hit rate [26]. While these approaches provide means of evaluating various audio notifications, they are limited with regard to analysis of users' cognitive states, such as alertness level and attention shifting. Previous studies [14, 24] have shown that humans' behavioral performance is a rather indirect indicator of their cognitive state and may not be consistent with it at all. Hence, failure to assess cognitive state in usability testing might lead to an incorrect evaluation [24]. Despite the wide applications of audio notifications, there has been little research aimed at developing objective measurement of perceptual or cognitive activities for audio-notification evaluation. Moreover, as an audio notification often plays a supporting role in our interaction with machines, its influence to the major task on auditory perception and cognitive state should not be ignored.

Recently, brain-sensing technologies have been used to evaluate users' cognitive state directly [7, 28] and research attempts have been made to integrate them into usability testing in the HCI field [12, 24]. Nevertheless, previous work of using EEG or other brain-sensing technologies [12, 24, 31] focused on investigating users' workload or visual tasks, and these techniques have rarely been used to measure auditory tasks. As auditory stimulation is attention-grabbing [3] and humans can hardly avoid hearing it, it is thus very important to assess the perceptual effects of sound and users' cognitive state when we evaluate audio notifications for HCI design.

In this paper, we propose to apply EEG technology to evaluate human auditory perception and attention allocation in usability testing. We exploit two types of neural responses, called mismatch negativity (MMN) and P3a, which can be detected in our brains when we hear novel sounds. Depending on the characteristics of a sound and a user's cognitive state, different degrees of the MMN and P3a responses would be induced. While various studies in cognitive science have investigated MMN and P3a, most still use simplified sounds, such as pure tones and beeps, in their experiments. Although some research used repetitive tones and natural sounds [20], there is still a significant gap between MMN/P3a studies and HCI applications.

Therefore, we conducted two experiments to determine whether MMN and P3a could be new indicators to enhance the usability testing of audio notifications. If so, this would allow audio designers to use our approach to objectively assess the impact of their audio design upon users, and to improve their design accordingly. In addition, we suggest some possible future applications of MMN and P3a research to HCI.

This paper makes three primary research contributions:

(1) *Extending prior studies and verifying that MMN and P3a can be induced by complex audio stimuli.* This extension is critical for applying MMN and P3a to HCI research as MMN and P3a experiments have rarely been conducted on stimuli in daily life such as audio notifications and ambient noises.

(2) *Suggesting a new method for objectively evaluating audio notifications.* Existing paradigms for verifying the effectiveness of audio notifications mostly require subjects to pay attention to the stimuli. However, Sussman et al. [30] have shown that if subjects expect audio notifications to occur, the impact on their sound perception is the same but the influence on their attention state is clearly different. Therefore, we introduce an objective approach for audio evaluation that can be conducted without users' attention, i.e., a passive and unobtrusive way to evaluate audio notifications.

(3) *Demonstrating that MMN and P3a could enhance the audio usability testing in scenarios where the evaluated task is supporting.* Users operate across a wide variety of environments in their daily lives, and this certainly influences the perceptual effects of audio notifications. Moreover, users undertake tasks that require different amounts of mental workload, and this too would tend to affect the evaluation results. We introduce an appropriate approach for considering these complex factors in usability testing of audio notifications.

RELATED WORK AND BACKGROUND

Audio Notifications

Auditory icons and earcons are audio notifications commonly used in consumer products and by mobile services. Gaver [13] first introduced auditory icons, which map a specific event to a sound heard in everyday life such that users can easily remember the icon without learning. In contrast to auditory icons, earcons [2] are nonverbal messages represented by abstract musical tones that users have to learn and memorize.

Brewster [3] suggests that auditory interfaces should avoid annoying sounds because they may disturb other people in the same environment. Furthermore, one should avoid basing the meaning of an audio notification on its intensity, since a loud sound may grab too much of a users' attention and could even cause a delay in their handling the problem. Hence, it is necessary to carefully evaluate the perception and effectiveness of audio designs.

Graham [11] compared the effectiveness of auditory icons and earcons as vehicle collision warnings. He found that auditory icons had shorter reaction time but higher risk of false-positive responses. Edworthy [5] also suggested that the real-world sounds are more suitable for monitoring tasks, while earcons are more appropriate for the warning systems as they can effectively attract the user's attention. Lemmens et al. [17] studied whether audio notifications help subjects react faster in a picture categorization task. Their results showed that both auditory icons and earcons reduce subjects' response time, as compared to the quiet condition.

Conventionally, response time, hit rate, and questionnaires have been used to evaluate the effectiveness and impact of auditory icons and earcons. However, these prior audio-evaluation approaches have some limitations. Fagerlönn et al. [8] indicated that non-expert users do not necessarily feel comfortable about giving suggestions or feedback on a detailed level. Other studies [24, 28] also pointed out that performance measurement could not take into account users' changing cognitive state, such as mental workload during an interactive process. In fact, previous studies [1, 18] had suggested that audio-notification designers should consider the context of use, especially when the users are under complex and high mental-workload conditions. Nevertheless, measuring human perception is difficult because users' experiences and perceptions vary from time to time [18]. To help designers objectively measure the perceptual effectiveness of their audio designs, we need a method to complement prior evaluation approaches.

Brain-Sensing for Evaluation

Several studies [28, 31] have applied brain-computer interface (BCI) to HCI. Zander and Kothe [33] proposed *passive* BCI, which records human cognitive state without the purpose of voluntary control. Using *passive* BCI can enrich HCI and help monitor actual user states during interaction. To understand the perceptual influence and the degree of attention shifting associated with particular audio notifications, we need a more efficient evaluation method. One possible solution is to make use of physiological indicators, such as functional near-infrared spectroscopy (fNIRS) or event-related potentials (ERPs) via EEG device. fNIRS is a non-invasive imaging method involving the quantification of chromosphere concentration resolved from the measurement of near-infrared light attenuation, or temporal or phasic changes. Although fNIRS is an adequate tool for monitoring cognitive states, it is not suitable for quick perceptual tasks [24]. In contrast, as ERPs are brain responses directly related to specific sensory, motor, or cognitive events, they provide higher temporal resolution in analyzing the various stages of neural processing associated with related behaviors [20]. Therefore, in this study, we utilize ERPs to analzye the effectiveness of various audio notifications.

Mismatch Negativity

An ERP component well known to be related to sound processing is the MMN, which is a change-specific negative potential over fronto-central sites. The latency of MMN is about

100-250 ms, and it is elicited by a subject's preattentive discrimination between a recurring standard sound and a deviant sound [20]. For example, when subjects are seeing a movie and hearing an oddball sequence of sounds, in which a rare deviant sound is interspersed among a series of frequent standard sounds, the repetitive standard sound forms a memory trace and MMN will be evoked if a new (deviant) sound does not match this auditory memory. This means that humans' auditory system can use preattention to distinguish the differences between two sounds, including intensities, pitches, locations, and durations [23, 16]. Moreover, MMN reflects not only the physical characteristics of deviant sounds (e.g., intensity, frequency, duration), but also more abstract representations of complex auditory rules, such as melody, speech, and rhythm [20].

The amplitude and latency of MMN depend on the differences between the deviant and standard sounds, with larger differences inducing larger amplitudes and shorter latencies [20]. MMN amplitude may also positively correlate with hit rate [22], where the correlation between MMN response and behavioral performance is investigated across various frequencies of the same sound. These studies suggest that MMN is a good indicator for audio perception and an objective measurement for the discriminability of a sound.

P3a

A fronto-central positive component, P3a, often occurs around 200 ms to 300 ms after the stimulus onset, i.e., somewhat later than MMN, and is related to the orienting responses towards deviant stimuli [6]. When deviant stimuli attract more of a subject's attention, the amplitude of P3a becomes larger. Although increasing the difference between the deviant and standard stimuli often enlarges the MMN and P3a amplitudes at the same time [20], this tendency holds under proper conditions [22]. Previous research has indicated that P3a would also be modulated according to different cognitive states such as workload and attention [25, 30]. Based on these studies, MMN is more likely related to involuntary attention switching, while P3a is more likely to reflect the level of active attention orienting.

Oddball Paradigm

A common task used in MMN and P3a studies is the oddball paradigm, in which a series of auditory or visual stimuli with different occurrence probabilities are used to assess neural reactions to unpredictable events [20]. An auditory oddball paradigm usually includes a frequent tone as standard stimuli and a less frequent tone as deviant or novel stimuli. When infrequent stimuli are inserted in the series of standard stimuli, MMN and P3a – which as we have seen are associated with novelty detection and attention-switching towards deviant events – will be evoked [6], and the occurrence probability of frequent and infrequent stimuli will influence the level of MMN and P3a. Typically, the cumulative duration ratio of deviant stimuli is controlled at 10%-30% of the cumulative duration of standard stimuli [20]. However, some studies still found stable MMN when 50% of deviant stimuli were used [27].

RESEARCH GOALS

Our goal is to explore the possibility of applying EEG to the evaluation of the effectiveness of audio notifications under more realistic conditions that are suitable for HCI applications. In the first experiment, we used ambient noises and audio notifications as stimuli to gain an understanding of how these auditory stimuli affect users' perception. Though prior studies have found that MMN can be evoked under complex standard stimuli such as repetitive tones or natural sounds [20], these cannot represent real conditions. Thus, a novelty of our experiment design was that we used ambient noises instead of repetitive sounds as the standard stimuli, and audio notifications as the deviant stimuli. This brought our experimental conditions closer to real-world scenarios, thus potentially extending the applications of MMN and P3a for audio evaluation.

In the second experiment, we explored the benefits of MMN and P3a for analyzing subjects' perception of sounds and their attention shifting while evaluating audio notifications in a more complex and realistic situation, where subjects simultaneously performed multiple tasks with auditory and visual modalities. We manipulated each subject's cognitive state by controlling the difficulty of the game (the card game Pairs in this case), to test if human perception of sound and attention shifting could be affected by users' mental workload, and if these influences resulted in the deflection of MMN and P3a.

METHODS

We modified the oddball paradigm to evaluate the effectiveness of six audio notifications in two sets of ambient noises.

Deviant Stimuli: Audio Notifications

Six audio notifications were used as deviant stimuli: Dev1 (Do, 500 ms), Dev2 (Do, 500 ms), Dev3 (Tri-tone, 500 ms), Dev4 (Ding, 500 ms), Dev5 (Horn, 700 ms) and Dev6 (Bell, 700 ms). All deviants were presented via loudspeakers. The intensity of each deviant was set at 72 dB SPL, except that of Dev2 which was set at 78 dB SPL. Dev1 and Dev2 were the same digitally generated piano chords, but with different intensities, to allow us to assess the effect of intensity on audio notification. Dev3-Dev6 were four of the default audio notifications used on Apple iPhones to notifying their users about incoming messages.

Standard Stimuli: Ambient Noises

Two sets of ambient noises recorded at real-life venues were used as the standard stimuli: the first was recorded in a club, and included conversations of males and females, some music, and background noise; the other was recorded on a city street and included traffic sounds and other street noise. The intensities of the two ambient noises were controlled to between 70 to 75 dB SPL, which was a comfortable level for the subjects in our test scenarios. The experimental setting and information regarding auditory stimuli are presented in Figure 1.

Procedure

We set a period of 700 sec as a testing block (Figure 1). The total time of all deviants appearing in each block was controll-

	Standard Stimuli	Deviant Stimuli
Experiment 1	Club Ambient	Dev1 – Dev6
	City Street Ambient	Dev1 – Dev6
Experiment 2	Club Ambient	Dev1, Dev2
	City Street Ambient	Dev1, Dev2

Figure 1. List of experimental procedures and auditory stimuli. All deviant stimuli are randomly scattered in a testing block. The occurrence probability of each deviant is equal.

ed so as to not exceed 30%, i.e., 210 sec. The interval between each deviant stimulus was at least 3.4 sec. To avoid subjects generating expectations of the audio notifications, and to collect enough trials, the interval between any two consecutive deviant stimuli was randomly varied in the range of 3.4 to 6.8 sec. In each block, all six deviant stimuli were randomly scattered with equal probability of occurrence and played as an overlay to the ambient noise while the chosen set of standard stimuli (i.e., either city street noise or club noise) was played continuously. Figure 1 shows our paradigm design. We took the EEG data recorded between each pair of consecutive deviants as the standard trials and those recorded while each audio notification appeared as the deviant trials. We obtained approximately 120 deviant trials in each testing block. At the beginning of each block, standard stimuli (ambient noise) would be played for 10 sec, data from which was not recorded.

EEG Recording and Data Analysis

We used a non-invasive EEG cap as measurement equipment. The EEG was recorded using a NeuroScan system with 32 Ag-AgCl electrodes and a bandpass filter of 0.01-100 Hz. Although 32-channel EEG data were recorded, we only used single-channel (Fz) ERP information for analysis as previous studies had shown that MMN has its maximal amplitude at Fz which is usually treated as the representative location of the MMN source [20, 22]. Additionally, for practical considerations of usability testing, it would be advantageous if fewer EEG channels (implying a cheaper, portable EEG device) are proved to be sufficient for a quick evaluation. We adopted an open-source Matlab toolbox, EEGLAB, to process EEG data, which was digitized with a 1000 Hz sampling rate and bandpass filtered at 1-50 Hz off-line. The epochs used for averaging were 600 ms long, starting 100 ms before and ending 500 ms after the stimulus onset. The pre-stimulus period (100 ms) was set as a baseline. All epochs with voltage variations exceeding $100\mu V$ were automatically rejected; the rejection rate varied from 5%-10%. Then, all epochs of the same standard (or deviant) stimuli were averaged. For MMN and P3a analysis, the response to the standard stimuli was subtracted from the response to each deviant stimuli. The peak amplitudes and latency of MMN and P3a were measured separately from the most negative peak occurring at 100-220 ms and the most positive deflection within 220-320 ms at the location of electrode Fz (Figure 2). Mauchly's test and Greenhouse-Geisser corrections were applied to verify if the data violated the assumption of sphericity. Repeated-measures (RM) ANOVAs were conducted, and the Tukey's method for multiple comparisons was applied in post-hoc tests.

EXPERIMENT 1: AUDIO EVALUATION BY MMN AND P3A

The goal of this experiment was to extend prior MMN and P3a studies to the evaluation of audio notifications in the HCI field, by bringing the experiment design closer to real-life scenarios. Figure 1 indicates the procedure and auditory stimuli involved this experiment.

Participants and Device

Thirty healthy, right-handed subjects (12 females; 20-25 years old) with normal or corrected-to-normal vision participated in this experiment. None of the subjects had any history of brain disease, drug use, or hearing problems. None had any musical expertise. After completing the entire experiment (about 2 hours), subjects were rewarded with 16 USD for their time. We used an LCD monitor (22 inches, 1920×1080 pixels) to show videos and visual tasks. Audio stimuli were presented via loudspeakers (Altec Lansing 2.0 ch, VS2620), which were placed at a distance of 60 cm in front of the subjects, at 30° to their left- and right-hand sides. A decibelmeter was used to adjust the intensity of audio stimuli before all experiments.

Task

There were two sessions intended to test the relationship between the MMN, P3a and behavioral performance in experiment 1. All subjects attended both sessions.

Session 1. We only recorded the subjects' behavioral data for the audio notifications. The subjects were seated in a comfortable chair and instructed to visually stare on a white cross sign in the center of the screen before the experiment began. Once the experiment started, they watched a subtitled silent video pre-chosen by themselves, and continuously heard an ambient noise. They needed to respond via the keyboard as fast as possible once they heard any of the six audio notifications.

Session 2. The subjects watched the same silent video along with the same ambient noise as in Session 1, but they were asked to ignore all auditory stimuli while their EEG data were recorded during the entire session.

Each session comprised four testing blocks: two using club ambient noise and two using city street ambient noise as standard stimuli. Between any two consecutive blocks, subjects had three minutes to rest. The order of the four blocks for each subject were randomly arranged. During each session with a given subject, at least 40 trials were collected for each audio notification in a session.

Results of Experiment 1

Session 1: Behavioral Performance

Behavioral responses were defined as 'hit trials' if subjects pressed the keyboard within 2 sec after a deviant stimulus had played. We computed the average reaction time and hit rate for each audio notification. Only the reaction time of the hit

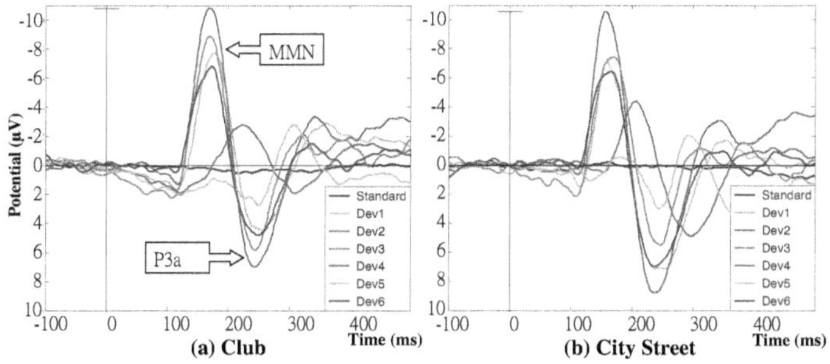

Figure 2. MMN (100-220 ms) and P3a (200-320 ms) curves in the context of two ambient noises: (a) Club; (b) City Street.

trials were used to compute the averaged reaction time. We performed a two-way RM-ANOVA (2 ambient noises × 6 deviant stimuli) to analyze the relationship between each audio notification. Mauchly's test indicated that the sphericity was not violated.

Figure 3(a)(b) shows the average reaction time (RT) associated with each audio notification within each type of ambient noise. The results did not reveal significant effects of the type of ambient noises (F=.056, p=.812). We found Dev5 had statistically significant differences with the other deviants under both types of ambient noises (p<.05). Additionally, Dev4 differed significantly from Dev2 (p=.02) and Dev3 (p=.01) in the context of city-street ambient noise. There were no statistically significant differences between any two of Dev1, Dev2, Dev3 and Dev6 in either ambient-noises context.

Figure 3(c)(d) shows the average hit rate of each audio notification within each type of ambient noise. There was a main effect of deviants on hit rate (F=4.32, p<.002). It can clearly be seen that Dev4 and Dev5 had lower hit rate than the other deviants, especially in the context of club ambient noise. There was a statistically significant difference between Dev4/Dev5 and the other four deviants (p<.05). The average hit rates of Dev1, Dev2, Dev3 and Dev6 in the club background were higher than their hit rates in the city-street background, while Dev4 and Dev5 had lower hit rates in the club background. This implies that subjects' behavioral performance on audio notifications might be influenced by ambient noises.

Session 2: MMN and P3a

An RM-ANOVA was used to determine if audio stimuli induced different MMN and P3a potentials. Mauchly's test indicated that the assumption of sphericity was not violated. We used 95% as the confidence level to determine the statistically significant difference.

Club Ambient Noise. Figure 2(a) shows the grand-peak ERP curves elicited by each deviant stimulus and the standard stimulus (club ambient noise) on the Fz channel. Each curve was obtained by averaging the ERPs of all subjects' trials. There was a main effect of different audio notifications on MMN amplitude (F=288.8, p<.0001). Except for Dev5, all deviants elicited a significantly larger negative deflection than the standard stimuli in the 100-220 ms interval after the stimuli onset. This showed typical MMN responses. As our results closely replicated those of previous studies [32], it seems appropriate to use MMN amplitude and latency to explore the discriminability of audio notifications in the context of different ambient noises.

The MMN amplitude of each deviant is shown in Figure 4(a), which reveals a ranking of the different deviants' amplitudes: Dev2 > Dev3 > Dev1 > Dev6 > Dev4 > Dev5 (p<.01 in all post-hoc comparisons). We observed that Dev3 and Dev4 had the same intensity and duration, but their MMN amplitudes had a statistically significant difference (p<.001). A similar result was also found with regard to Dev5 and Dev6 (p<.001). These results revealed that two deviants' MMN could be very different despite their intensities and durations being the same. According to previous studies, following the occurrence of MMN, a positive ERP component P3a would be elicited over the frontal-central area (Fz channel) [25]. Our results also clearly replicated this P3a response around 220-320 ms, as indicated in Figure 2(a). Figure 4(c) plots the P3a amplitude of the six deviants. There was also a main effect of different deviants on P3a amplitude (F=36.12, p<.001). One can clearly distinguish their differences. Dev1, Dev2, Dev3 and Dev6 showed more positive deflection than Dev4 and Dev5. No statistically significant difference was found between Dev4 and Dev5 (p=.39), on the one hand, and on the other, Dev1 and Dev6 (p=.87).

City-Street Ambient Noise. The ERP curves of all deviants in the context of city-street ambient noise also exhibited typical MMN responses (F=127.46, p<.0001), with the exception of Dev5 (Figure 2(b)). Figure 4(b) shows the ranking of the deviants based on their MMN amplitudes: Dev2 > Dev3 ≥ Dev1 ≥ Dev6 > Dev4 > Dev5, where p<.05 in all post-hoc comparisons except Dev1/Dev3 (p=.14), and Dev1/Dev6 (p=.52). Additionally, there was a main effect of different deviants on P3a amplitude (F=93.6, p<.001). Dev2 had the largest positive potential, while Dev1 (p=.005) and Dev6 (p=.008) had greater positive potential than Dev3.

Discussion

MMN and P3a Reflect Multiple Properties of a Sound. By manipulating only the intensity of two of the deviant stimuli – Dev1 and Dev 2 being the same sound, but at 72 dB and 78 dB, respectively – we found statistically significant differences between both their MMN and P3a amplitudes. When an audio notification was louder, the subjects were more likely to notice it and paid more attention to it. This finding replicated previous research [23, 20] that the physical characteristics of different sounds can be reflected by the ERP components, MMN and P3a.

Although physical characteristics of sounds, such as intensity and frequency, can greatly affect brain response, they are not the only factors influencing MMN. For example, Dev3 and Dev4 had almost the same intensity and duration, but their MMN amplitudes differed greatly. This supports the idea that MMN is not only influenced by the intensity and duration of a sound [20]. The same phenomenon was also observed in the case of different notifications that had the same decibel level or duration, e.g., Dev5 and Dev6.

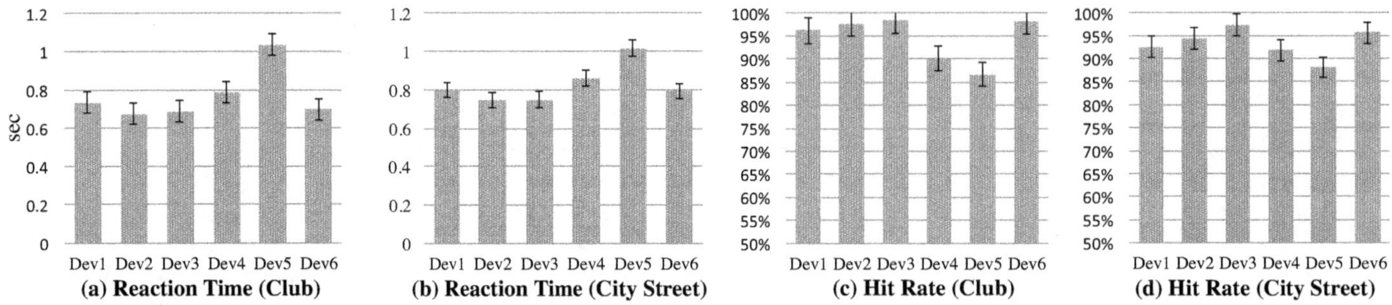

Figure 3. (a) and (b) are average reaction times associated with each audio notification, computed from the hit trials of all subjects, while (c) and (d) are the average hit rates of each audio notification.

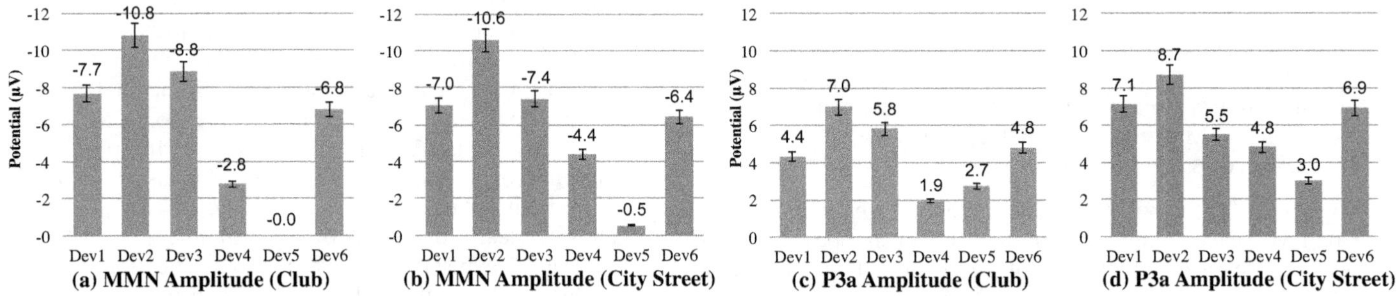

Figure 4. (a) and (b) are MMN amplitudes in the context of the two different sets of ambient noise, while (c) and (d) are P3a amplitudes in the two different sets of ambient noise.

Some audio notifications had an effect on the latency of MMN and P3a. Both Dev4 and Dev5 had longer latency when compared with the other four deviants, regardless of the type of ambient noises (Figure 2). This long latency suggest that the deviant required more time to be detected and perceived. This could be because of other properties of the sound, such as melody or timbre, and more experiments will be needed to make a determination. We also found a ranking order among the MMN amplitudes of the different audio notifications (Figure 4(a)(b)). This shows that audio notifications could be discriminated by brain response. However, the ranking order of the deviants by MMN amplitude was not exactly the same as their ranking by P3a. This indicated that MMN and P3a may not be mutually dependent. For instance, Dev1 and Dev3 had similar MMN potentials in the city-street background, but Dev1 had larger P3a potential than Dev3. This is not surprising, as MMN and P3a actually reflect auditory perception and involuntary attention shifting, respectively [20]. In other words, MMN shows how well a subject detects a sound while P3a shows how much the subject's attention is shifted towards it. Thus, it can be supposed from the above example of Dev1 and Dev3 that these two deviants were detected by brains at a similar level, but they led to different degree of attention resource allocation.

Behaviorial Performance v.s. MMN and P3a. In general, the behavioral data (Figure 3) can provide a simple evaluation of audio notifications, but they cannot discriminate clearly between all audio notifications well. On the other hand, MMN and P3a clearly revealed the ranking order of different audio notifications. This suggests that they can provide additional information for evaluating audio notifications. In particular, MMN and P3a can reflect the impact of audio notifications on subjects' perception and attention shifting. Given that this deeper analysis of auditory perception and attention is possible, a better evaluation approach to the evaluation of audio notifications is likewise possible.

In fact, MMN and P3a can help to analyze behavioral performance. For example, Dev5 had a longer reaction time and a lower hit rate than the other deviant stimuli in Figure 3. The reason for this cannot be learned from behavioral performance alone, but MMN and P3a may provide some clues. Indeed, Dev5 induced the lowest MMN potential in both ambient-noise backgrounds. This implies that it is difficult for users to discriminate Dev5 from ambient noises. A similar observation can also be made with regard to Dev4. These findings are in agreement with those of previous studies [22], with a relatively more simple experimental setting (i.e., modulating frequency of the same audio stimuli). They suggested that MMN amplitude might positively correlate with the hit rate and negatively correlate with the RT.

Effect of Ambient Noises. Our six audio notifications also exhibited different ERP responses with the two types of background sounds. We found that P3a amplitudes of four audio notifications (i.e., except Dev3 and Dev5) exhibited significant differences between the two ambient noises, while the MMN amplitudes of Dev3, Dev4, and Dev5 also were significantly different depending on ambient noises. This implies that the subjects' perception of a deviant sound and attention shifting to the deviant sound, were both influenced by the type of background sounds. Furthermore, though audio notifications can be discriminated amid different ambient noises, their discriminability might be influenced by the discrepancy between them and those ambient noises. In fact, previous studies have shown that ambient noises would influence not only the performance of human [1, 18] but also creative cognition [19]. Our findings indicated that EEG method is a useful tool for verifying audio perception in the context of different types of ambient noises.

P3a Might Be a Major Factor for Hit Rate. Dev1, Dev2 and Dev6 in the context of city-street noise had lower hit rates than in the context of club noise. In particular, Dev1 and Dev2 showed a noticeable decrease. This may be because the Do chord was harder to discriminate from city-street ambient noise. To better understand the cause, we can analyze Dev1's and Dev2's MMN and P3a. From Figure 4(c)(d), one can clearly see that both the Dev1's and Dev2's P3a amplitudes had a large increase in the city-street context (as compared with the club context). This finding might lead us to presume that P3a was a major factor for hit rate decreasing amid city-street ambient sounds, and imply that an appropriate degree of attentional allocation was important [25], i.e., that *too much* attention shifting may actually cause a lower hit rate. Moreover, both Dev1's and Dev2's MMN amplitudes, as shown in Figure 4(a)(b), were almost the same across the two ambient noises. This further confirms that P3a was a major factor for hit-rate change [25]. A similar finding can also be observed and inferred from Dev3: the P3a amplitudes of Dev3 had no statistically significant difference between the two types of ambient noises, and neither did its hit rates. It should be noted that Dev3 had a larger MMN amplitude amid club ambient noise than amid city-street ambient noise, but this did not affect Dev3's hit rate.

In summary, subjects' behavioral results provide us with a basic understanding of the efficiency of different audio notifications [14, 24], but may not reveal the causes for the differences between them, or their relationship with attention shifting. On the other hand, the MMN and P3a results in the present study may provide information about the brain activity that may help us better analyze the auditory perception of, and attention shifting associated with audio notifications. Therefore, behavioral results should be supplemented with more objective physiological responses, to gain a fuller understanding of the different effects of audio notifications in the context of various ambient noises.

EXPERIMENT 2: AUDIO EVALUATION WITH VISUAL TASK

Experiment 1 demonstrated that MMN and P3a can be used to evaluate audio notifications under more realistic experimental conditions than those have been attempted in the past. Another important factor that interferes with audio perception is the user's cognitive state. In particular, devices generally emit audio notifications to notify a person who is occupied by some tasks. It is therefore important to consider the level of attention shifting and task complexity when evaluating audio notifications. The effectiveness of supplementary notifications will be influenced in part by users' current need to concentrate on something else. Hence, in Experiment 2, we modified the previous auditory oddball paradigm and manipulated subjects' mental workload to explore if and how their auditory perception and involuntary attention shifting would be influenced by their cognitive state. It is hoped that our EEG-based approach can be applied to the usability testing of audio notifications in complex and realistic scenarios, in which subjects' mental workloads include some visual tasks.

Twenty-two subjects (ten females), all of whom had previously participated in Experiment 1, consented to take part in Experiment 2. The settings of Experiment 2 were identical to those of Experiment 1 except that we used the Pairs game to control subjects' workload and attention. To maintain the focus of the study and avoid exhausting the subjects, we used only two deviant stimuli (Dev1 and Dev2) while adopting the same two types of ambient noises as standard stimuli. With this design, we concentrated on investigating how a user's audio perception is affected by their mental workload and the intensity of audio notifications (Figure 1).

Task

We modified the auditory oddball paradigm of Experiment 1 as follows. Instead of watching a video, subjects were required to play a Pairs game. Pairs is a card game in which all the cards are laid face down at the start. The player turns over two cards at a time. If two cards drawn at the same time match, they stay face up; otherwise, they are placed face down. The game can be learned quickly, despite the different levels of mental workload that are required for different levels of difficulty [4]. In this experiment, we varied the difficulty level of the game to control the subjects' mental workload, following Warnock et al. [4] suggestion that playing a Pairs game with 6×4 cards and a 60-second time limit is a useful way to quickly build subjects' mental workload.

Hence, we designed the game with two difficulty levels: one using 6×4 cards and the other using 2×2 cards. All subjects could easily complete the 2×2 version, which was designed to keep subjects engaged in the game but without too much workload. Each subject was trained for 10 minutes before the experiment. EEG recording started 15 sec after a game began. In the task of 2×2 Pairs game task, the subjects had to complete consecutive games continuously. If a subject could not complete a game within 10 sec, a new game would start. This avoided the subjects expending too much mental workload. In the task of 6×4 Pairs game task, subjects had to play at least five games continuously in a testing block and were required to complete each game to the best of their ability. The success rate and completion time were recorded. If the subjects found all the matched pairs in a game or the 60-second time limit expired, the game would immediately restart. We set the length of a testing block as 350 sec, because this experiment only used two deviant stimuli. Subjects took at least five minutes' rest between each testing block. Experiment 2 had four testing blocks for each ambient noise. For each subject, we collected approximately 40 trials for each deviant in each difficulty level.

Results of Experiment 2

Figures 5(a)(b) and 5(c)(d) show the results obtained from a three-way RM-ANOVA analysis (2 ambient noises, 2 deviants, and 2 workloads). Mauchly's test indicated that the sphericity was not violated. With regard to MMN response (Figure 5(a)(b)), whether the subjects' workload was high or low, there were statistically significant differences between Dev1 and Dev2 in both ambient-noise contexts ($p<.05$). With regard to P3a response (Figure 5(c)(d)), there was a significant difference in the workload factor ($F=27.03$, $p<.001$): larger P3a amplitude was observed in the context of the higher workload level (6×4 Pairs). Except for Dev2 in the context of city-street ambient noise, the P3a amplitudes of Dev1 and Dev2 had statistically significant differences between high workload and low workload. Furthermore, comparing the results of MMN and P3a as shown in Figures 5(a)(b) and 5(c)(d), we also observed that all P3a amplitudes were higher amid the city-street ambient noise, whereas no similar trend was apparent in the MMN-potential results.

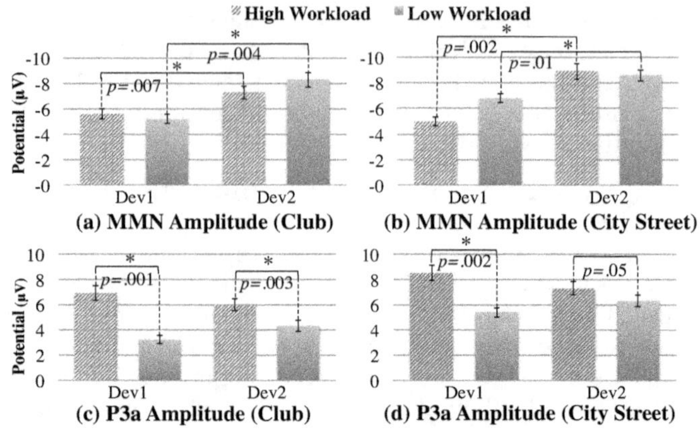

Figure 5. (a) and (b) are MMN amplitudes in the two different ambient noises. (c) and (d) are P3a amplitudes in the two different ambient noises. An asterisk indicates a statistically significant difference ($p<.05$).

Discussion

In this experiment, we modulated subjects' mental workload to investigate its influence on the human perception of, and attention to, audio notifications. Except for Dev2 in the city-street background, we found that the P3a amplitudes of both deviants differed significantly across high and low mental workloads, while MMN amplitudes exhibited no similar phenomenon. This implies that regardless of a user's mental workload, their auditory perception ability is almost the same. This finding is in agreement with those of a prior study [30].

On the other hand, our finding with regard to P3a suggests that subjects allocate more attentional resource to an audio notification when they have higher mental workloads. This finding is inconsistent with earlier research [30]. There are two possible explanations. First, because we used the Pairs game to control subjects' mental workload and focus, audio notifications may have operated more like distractors than notifiers in pervious studies. If a user is concentrating on an assignment, their attention may be involuntary shifted more by obvious audio notifications, and in an extreme case, they might even be frightened by an audio notification if they are too concentrated on a task. Second, the standard stimuli used in this experiment and previous studies [30] are very different; we used ambient noises while previous studies used pure tones. As the context of realistic ambient noise may also influence a subject's cognitive state [19], this should be considered when evaluating the effectiveness of audio notifications.

Taken as a whole, therefore, our findings in experiment 2 suggest us to believe that audio notifications should be designed more carefully, especially when the end-users' mental workload levels are expected to be high. Our results may also suggest that using a louder audio notifications in a higher workload situations might not be useful. From Figure 5(c)(d), we can observe that when the audio intensity is small (Dev1), mental workload has a stronger influence on attention shifting, as its P3a varies more. Conversely, if audio intensity is large (Dev2), workload has a weaker influence upon attention shifting. Although the audio notifications applied in this experiment were irrelevant to the Pairs game, it may be useful in future research to design the task-relevant experiments, e.g., incorporating audio alerts in online gaming scenarios or audio notifications in social media.

EEG-BASED APPROACH TO AUDIO EVALUATION

Comparison to Previous Studies

As the past studies [24, 28] have mentioned, it is difficult to measure and quantify a person's cognitive state during interaction. Although some questionnaires, e.g., NASA-TLX, can be used to investigate a subjects's cognitive state, these surveys are performed off-line after the subject completes a task. As the subject has to recall his/her experience of the experiment, questionnaires may be easily influenced by external factors [24]. Previous studies [30] have shown that users' expectations regarding tones would cause different attention states. Hence, experimental results are probably biased where only reaction time and hit rate have been used to evaluate the effectiveness of notification tones. Our approach allows us to conduct audio evaluation passively, i.e., the subject does not need to pay full attention to the audio notifications to be evaluated. This is consistent with the real-world role of audio notifications, and allows the evaluation procedures to be dovetailed into the real application scenarios.

Our experiments also revealed the impact of sound intensities upon MMN and P3a amplitudes. A prior study [11] pointed out that some notifications alter users to alert quickly, but can also result in higher error rates, especially in environments characterised by high mental demand. This is probably because these audio notifications attract too much attention and lead the users to be distracted from their primary task. We also observed from our experiments that ambient noises can influence MMN and P3a. Therefore, how to keep a balance between auditory perception and attention allocation is an important issue.

Potential Applications of MMN and P3a in HCI

The phenomena of MMN and P3a have been extensively studied within the field of cognitive science. Many studies have applied MMN to clinical practices [16]; however, MMN and P3a have rarely been applied to HCI. We have extended prior work to demonstrate that MMN and P3a can have applications in HCI. Drawing on previous studies on MMN and P3a in cognitive science, we found a number of potential future applications for HCI, and make the following suggestions.

User Experience. Past studies of MMN and P3a have validated many basic physical properties of sound – such as frequency, intensity, and timbre – that are easy to convey and that form memory meanings [22, 23]. Recently, several researchers have begun to test the effects of complex sound stimulation, such as speech sound and composed music (melody, harmony and rhythm). Moreover, subjects' experience of auditory perception has also been investigated, e.g., familiarity with the sounds, learning and/or memory effects [9], and the emotional effect of content [10]. MMN and P3a could help us analyze the impact on audio perception and attention shifting of audio notifications being learned, as well as understand how sound influences users emotionally. MMN and P3a can also measure the changes in users' experience of audio tones.

Adaptive Interface. According to Wetzel et al. [21], who investigated involuntary and voluntary attention shifting on subjects of different ages by P3a. They found that the same auditory stimuli would induce different P3a and cause stronger or weaker distraction in different age groups. Prior work also confirms that trained experts (e.g., musicians) would have the discrepancy with general users on MMN and P3a for the same auditory stimulation. Alcohol and drugs would also influence the users' perception [20]. MMN and P3a have also been studied in single-subject level in recent years. Therefore, MMN and P3a may inspire more diverse ways for the design and evaluation of audio notifications. These findings also suggest that designers should pay more attention to the impact of audio notifications for different user groups.

Context of Use. Depending on the purpose of the notification, designers must also take into account the end-users' likely environments and mental states. Past study [15] on the effect of ambient sounds was mainly conducted such that subjects were focused and prepared to evaluate deviant sounds. However, people process many familiar environmental sounds effortlessly. As such, a change in environments could cause a variety of effects, such as attention being distracted; while ambient sounds that may encourage productivity have also recently been studied [19]. The evaluation of audio notifications when the user is performing a major task is also very important. Whether audio stimuli are relevant or irrelevant to the major task may cause different auditory perception and attention shifting.

The studies [9, 10, 15, 19, 20, 21, 22, 23, 16] mentioned above showed that audio-notification design needs more serious perceptual consideration and EEG-based approaches may be good candidates for its evaluation. Nevertheless, discrepancies inevitably exist between the experimental conditions in cognitive science studies and the real-life situations, so findings may need to be verified or modified if they are to be of use to practical HCI applications.

LIMITATION

There are currently a wide variety of audio notifications, and they are used extensively in technical devices. Despite the diversity of audio notifications, we only chose a small set of them in our experiments, since the goal of this paper is to introduce a new approach for audio evaluation. Recent studies have also extended MMN and P3a to the analysis of emotion, sound learning, memory consolidation, and even the semantic meaning of a sound [20], e.g., whether voices belong to family members or strangers. In our future work, we would like to evaluate more sounds and explore related topics and potential applications.

CONCLUSION

In this study, we have proposed an objective method for evaluating audio notifications. In the first experiment, we verified that MMN and P3a can be used to measure audio notifications in more realistic scenarios. In the second experiment, we demonstrated that this EEG-based approach can be used when the subjects perform major complex tasks, by directly evaluating the changes in users' auditory perception at different levels of workload in the course of an interactive process. Based on the findings of these two experiments, measurement of MMN and P3a can be successfully applied to the usability testing of audio notifications. Moreover, our approach provides a new means by which HCI researchers can investigate the impact of sounds upon individuals' auditory perception and mental states. We believe that this EEG-based approach can open new perspectives for evaluating the human experience of sound.

ACKNOWLEDGMENTS

We thank the anonymous reviewers for their insightful comments. This work was supported in part by the National Science Council (101-2628-E-009-021-MY3 and 102-2221-E-009-082-MY3) and the UST-UCSD International Center of Excellence in Advanced Bioengineering sponsored by the Taiwan National Science Council I-RiCE Program under grant number: NSC-102-2911-I-009-101.

REFERENCES

1. Barrass, S., and Frauenberger, C. A communal map of design in auditory display. In *Proc. ICAD* (2009).
2. Blattner, M. M., Sumikawa, D. A., and Greenberg, R. M. Earcons and icons: their structure and common design principles. *Hum.-Comput. Interact. 4*, 1 (1989), 11–44.
3. Brewster, S. A. Non-speech auditory output. *Human Computer Interaction Handbook, Lawrence Erlbaum Associates* (2002), 220–239.
4. David, W., Marilyn, M.-L., and Stephen, B. The role of modality in notification performance. *INTERACT* (2011), 572–588.
5. Edworthy, J. Does sound help us to work better with machines? A commentary on rauterberg's paper 'about the importance of auditory alarms during the operation of a plant simulator. *Interacting With Computers 10* (1998), 401–409.
6. Escera, C., Alho, K., Schröger, E., and Winkler, I. Involuntary attention and distractibility as evaluated with event-related brain potentials. *Audiology and Neurotology 5* (2000), 151–166.

7. Ewing, K., and Fairclough, S. The impact of working memory load on psychophysiological measures of mental effort and motivational disposition. *Human Factors: A system view of human, technology and organisation* (2010), 1–11.
8. Fagerlönn, J., and Liljedahl, M. Awesome sound design tool: a web based utility that invites end users into the audio design process. In *Proc. ICAD* (2009).
9. Gottselig, J. M., Brandeis, D., Hofer-Tinguely, G., Borbély, A. A., and Achermann, P. Human central auditory plasticity associated with tone sequence learning. *Learning & Memory 11*, 2 (2004), 162–171.
10. Goydke, K. N., Altenmüller, E., Möller, J., and Münte, T. F. Changes in emotional tone and instrumental timbre are reflected by the mismatch negativity. *Cognitive Brain Research 21*, 3 (2004), 351–359.
11. Graham, R. Use of auditory icons as emergency warnings: evaluation within a vehicle collision avoidance application. *Ergonomics 42*, 9 (1999), 1233–1248.
12. Grimes, D., Tan, D. S., Hudson, S. E., Shenoy, P., and Rao, R. P. N. Feasibility and pragmatics of classifying working memory load with an electroencephalograph. *CHI* (2008), 835–844.
13. Helander, M. G., Landauer, T. K., and Prabhu, P. V. Auditory interfaces: Handbook of human computer interface. *Elsevier Science* (1997).
14. Hollands, J. G., and Wickens, C. D. *Engineering psychology and human performance.* Prentice Hall New Jersey, 1999.
15. Kirmse, U., Jacobsen, T., and Schröger, E. Familiarity affects environmental sound processing outside the focus of attention: An event-related potential study. *Clinical neurophysiology 120* (2009), 887–896.
16. Kujala, T., Tervaniemi, M., and Schröger, E. The mismatch negativity in cognitive and clinical neuroscience: Theoretical and methodological considerations. *Biological Psychology 4* (2007), 1–19.
17. Lemmens, P. M. C., Bussemakers, M. P., and Haan, A. D. Effects of auditory icons and earcons on visual categorization: the bigger picture. *In Proc. ICAD* (2001), 117–125.
18. McGregor, I., Larsson, P., and Turner, P. Evaluating a vehicle auditory display: comparing a designer's expectations with listeners' experiences. In *proc. ECCE* (2011), 89–92.
19. Mehta, R., Zhu, R. J., and Cheema, A. Is noise always bad? Exploring the effects of ambient noise on creative cognition. *JCR 39*, 4 (2012), 784–799.
20. Näätänen, R., Paavilainen, P., Rinne, T., and Alho, K. The mismatch negativity (MMN) in basic research of central auditory processing: A review. *Clinical Neurophysiology 118*, 12 (2007), 2544 – 2590.
21. Nicole, W., Andreas, W., Stefan, B., and Erich, S. The development of involuntary and voluntary attention from childhood to adulthood: A combined behavioral and event-related potential study. *Clinical Neurophysiology 117* (2006), 2191–2203.
22. Novitski, N., Tervaniemi, M., Huotilainen, M., and Näätänen, R. Frequency discrimination at different frequency levels as indexed by electrophysiological and behavioral measures. *Cognitive Brain Research 20*, 1 (2004), 26–36.
23. Pakarinen, S., Takegata, R., Rinne, T., Huotilainen, M., and Näätänen, R. Measurement of extensive auditory discrimination profiles using the mismatch negativity (MMN) of the auditory event-related potential (ERP). *Clinical Neurophysiology 118* (2007), 177–185.
24. Peck, E. M., Yuksel, B. F., Ottley, A., Jacob, R. J. K., and Chang, R. Using fNIRS brain sensing to evaluate information visualization interfaces. In *CHI* (2013), 473–482.
25. Polich, J. Updating P300: an integrative theory of P3a and P3b. *Clinical neurophysiology 118*, 10 (2007), 2128–2148.
26. Rafa, A., and Catherine, G. Usability of non-speech sounds in user interfaces. *In Proc. ICAD* (2008).
27. Satu, P., Minna, H., and Risto, N. The mismatch negativity (MMN) with no standard stimulus. *Clinical Neurophysiology 121* (2010), 1043–1050.
28. Solovey, E., Schermerhorn, P., Scheutz, M., Sassaroli, A., Fantini, S., and Jacob, R. Brainput: enhancing interactive systems with streaming fNIRS brain input. In *CHI* (2012), 2193–2202.
29. Stavros, G., Simon, J., Tim, J., and Eamonn, O. Auditory icon and earcon mobile service notifications: intuitiveness, learnability, memorability and preference. *CHI* (2009), 1513–1522.
30. Sussman, E., Winkler, I., and Schröger, E. Top-down control over involuntary attention switching in the auditory modality. *Psychonomic Bulletin and Review 10*, 3 (2003), 630–637.
31. Vi, C. T., and Subramanian, S. Detecting error-related negativity for interaction design. *CHI* (2012), 493–502.
32. Winkler, I., Teder, Sälejärvi, W., Horváth, J., Näätänen, R., and Sussman, E. Human auditory cortex tracks task-irrelevant sound sources. *Neuroreport 14*, 16 (2003), 2053–2056.
33. Zander, T. O., and Kothe, C. Towards passive brain–computer interfaces: applying brain–computer interface technology to human-machine systems in general. *J. Neural Eng. 8*, 2 (2011), 025005.

faBrickation: Fast 3D Printing of Functional Objects by Integrating Construction Kit Building Blocks

Stefanie Mueller, Tobias Mohr, Kerstin Guenther, Johannes Frohnhofen, Patrick Baudisch
Hasso Plattner Institute, Potsdam, Germany
{firstname.lastname}@hpi.uni-potsdam.de

ABSTRACT

We present a new approach to rapid prototyping of functional objects, such as the body of a head-mounted display. The key idea is to save 3D printing time by automatically substituting sub-volumes with standard building blocks—in our case Lego bricks. When making the body for a head-mounted display, for example, getting the optical path right is paramount. Users thus mark the lens mounts as "high-resolution" to indicate that these should later be 3D printed. faBrickator then 3D prints these parts. It also generates instructions that show users how to create everything else from Lego bricks. If users iterate on the design later, faBrickator offers even greater benefit as it allows re-printing only the elements that changed. We validated our system at the example of three 3D models of functional objects. On average, our system fabricates objects 2.44 times faster than traditional 3D printing while requiring only 14 minutes of manual assembly.

Author Keywords: rapid prototyping; 3D printing; design iteration; building blocks; physical prototyping.

ACM Classification Keywords: H.5.2 [Information interfaces and presentation]: User Interfaces.

General Terms: Design; Human Factors.

INTRODUCTION

The recent development in rapid prototyping tools, such as laser cutters, milling machines, and 3D printers [8], allows users to prototype one-off objects and to iterate over designs. These tools offer sufficient shape complexity and resolution to allow prototyping functional objects, such as the body of a head-mounted display with its bosses and mounts for holding the lenses, the head-strap, etc.

While 3D printers can create objects with the necessary level of detail, they are also very slow. Since printing time is largely proportional to the volume of the printed object, fabricating the body of the head-mounted display shown in Figure 1d takes hours on current 3D printers (14:30h on our Dimension SST 1200es). Even printing with multiple heads [6] achieves only a constant speed-up.

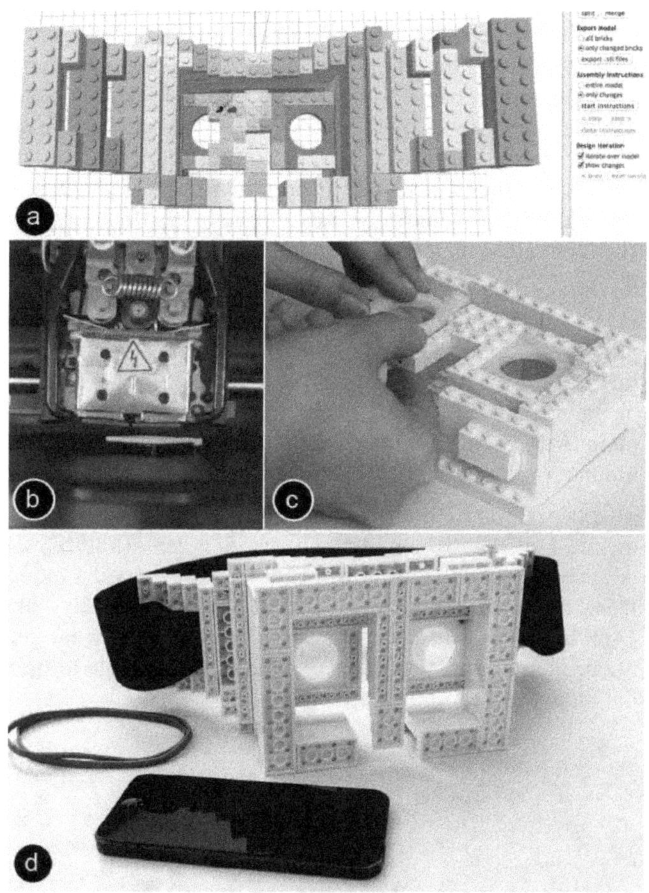

Figure 1: Let's fabricate this head-mounted display body quickly: (a) The exact shape of the lens mounts matters; the user thus marks them as "high-resolution" in faBrickator and (b) prints them. (c) faBrickator shows the user how to create everything else from Lego bricks and how to insert the 3D printed part. (d) Done in 67 minutes instead of the 14:30h for 3D printing.

Yet speed is mission critical: while printing can be done over night, this still limits designs to a single iteration per day. Thus a typical iteration process easily adds up to a week—even though the actual design work may not have taken longer than a day. As a result, in today's common design workflow, the 3D printer forms the bottleneck.

Experienced designers tend to address the problem by mixing fabrication techniques and weaving in prefabricated objects into the fabrication process. However, this requires a good amount of ingenuity and experience.

CHI 2014, April 26–May 1, 2014, Toronto, Ontario, Canada.

http://dx.doi.org/10.1145/2556288.2557005

We propose addressing the problem by limiting 3D printing to where it is necessary—we use a much more rapid technique, the assembling of Lego bricks, everywhere else.

FABRICKATION: FAST 3D PRINTING WITH BRICKS

Figure 1 illustrates the rapid prototyping workflow we enable with our system faBrickator. faBrickator is a system that substitutes parts of 3D models with Lego bricks. Users specify, which areas they want to have executed in full detail, i.e., by the 3D printer. faBrickator then substitutes everything else with Lego bricks. Based on building instructions generated by faBrickator, users assemble the Lego part while the 3D printer is printing. Since it reduces the volume that needs to be 3D printed, faBrickator speeds up the fabrication process. While faBrickator already speeds up the fabrication of the initial prototype, it saves even more time when subsequently iterating over segments since users only have to reprint the parts that actually changed rather than reprinting the entire model.

Walkthrough: printing a head-mounted display body

In the following example session, the user rapidly prototypes the body of a head-mounted display using faBrickator. In order to get the optical properties of the display right, the exact shape and position of the lens mounts is crucial; the user thus decides to 3D print the lens mounts while fabricating the rest of the design in Lego.

The user starts by modeling the body of the head-mounted display in a 3D editor, here *Blender* (Figure 2). Alternatively, many users will choose to download a model from the web. The shown model would normally take 14:30h to 3D print. By using faBrickator to limit what gets 3D printed to the lens mounts, the user will be able to print the model in 67 minutes instead.

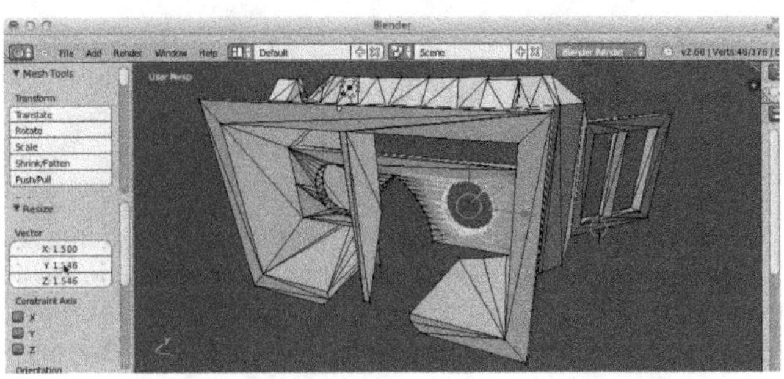

Figure 2: Walkthrough: The user has created a model of a head-mounted display body in *Blender*.

#1 Loading and legofication: The user is currently editing the model in Blender (Figure 2). As the user exits the *edit* mode, the 3D model is automatically loaded into faBrickator, initiated by the *Blender* plug-in we provide. In faBrickator (Figure 3), the user hits the *legofy*-button, which causes faBrickator to display a naïve legofication of the model, i.e., one that consists only of Lego's smallest building blocks—the 1x1 plates (Figure 3b). The user now hits the *layout*-button (Figure 3c). faBrickator responds by grouping the 1x1 plates into larger plates and bricks, so as to minimize the overall number of bricks. faBrickator also

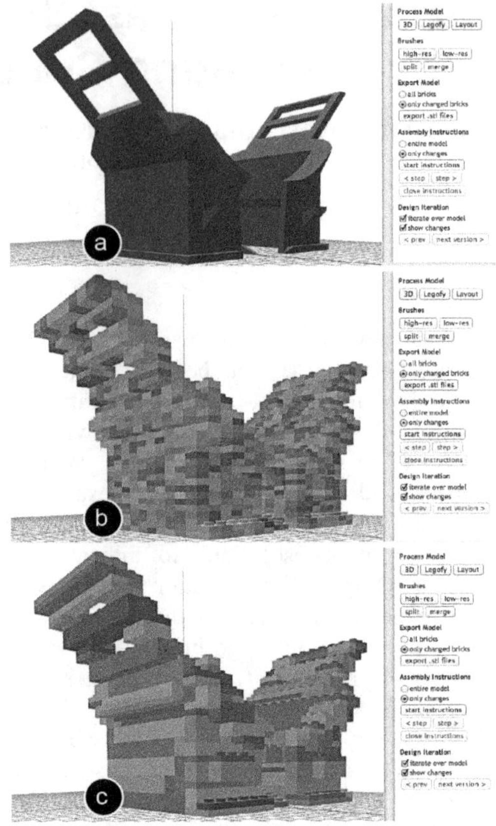

Figure 3: (a) The model is loaded into faBrickator, (b) legofied into 1x1 Lego plates, and (c) layouted.

assures a stable design in this step by iterating over the brick layout until all components are connected.

#2 Marking the high-res areas of the model: Figure 4 demonstrates how the user defines the regions that need to be 3D printed. (a) The user brushes the region around the lens mounts with the *high-res* brush. (b) This tells faBrickator to execute this area in full detail. The system responds by changing the preview accordingly. By default, faBrickator merges the marked area to a single 3D-printed block. The user repeats the process for the other lens opening.

Figure 4: Using the *high-res* brush the user defines the region that will be 3D printed in full detail.

#3 Printing and assembling: To print, the user *exports* the model. This creates a 3D printable .stl file for each of the two lens mounts. The user then sends the files to the printer using the 3D printer software (in our case *CatalystEX*).

As soon as the 3D model has been sent to the printer, the user starts assembling the Lego part of the model. As shown in Figure 5, faBrickator provides animated assembly instructions that show how to assemble bottom-up, layer-by-layer. This helps to minimize the time needed for assembly.

67 minutes after the design was sent to the printer, the 3D printer is done fabricating the two lens mounts. Each brick bears a unique ID embossed into one of its sides (Figure 5b). This helps the user to quickly place them into the partially assembled Lego model.

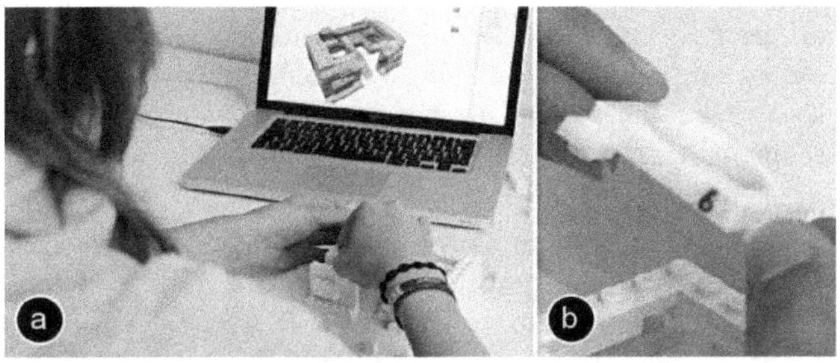

Figure 5: (a) Assembly instructions highlight the next brick in blue. (b) Each 3D printed part has a unique ID.

Figure 6 shows the assembled body of the head-mounted display with the accurately fitted lenses, which took 25 minutes to assemble. The overall fabrication time was thus still bound by the 3D printer, so that the 67 min is the final time for the entire fabrication. In this case, a speed-up of a factor of 12.99.

The main benefit of our approach is that it can change the fabrication process from overnight printing to something that can be carried out multiple times a day. This allows users to perform several design iterations in a day that would otherwise have stretched out over the course of a week.

Figure 6: The final faBrickated model.

Switching from low-res to high-res parts later on

faBrickator allows users to change their mind later on in that it allows replacing additional Lego bricks with 3D printed parts. Figure 7 illustrates this, continuing our walkthrough: the optics of the head-mounted display work great, but after wearing the device for a while, the user notices that it does not sit comfortably on nose and fore-

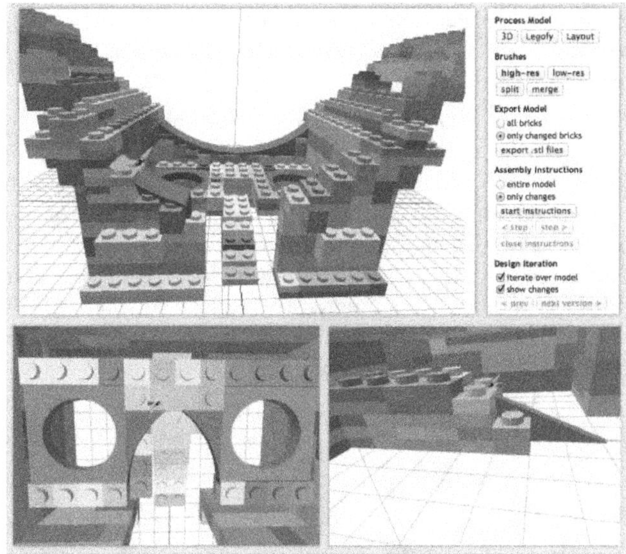

Figure 7: Making the forehead and nosepiece high-res for more comfort.

head. The user goes back into faBrickator to create more ergonomic forehead and nose pieces.

As shown in Figure 7, the user marks the forehead and nose regions as *high-res,* then exports and 3D prints them. Figure 8 shows how the user removes the corresponding Lego bricks from the faBrickated head-mounted display body and replaces them with the printed parts. This iteration took 3:55 hours including assembly.

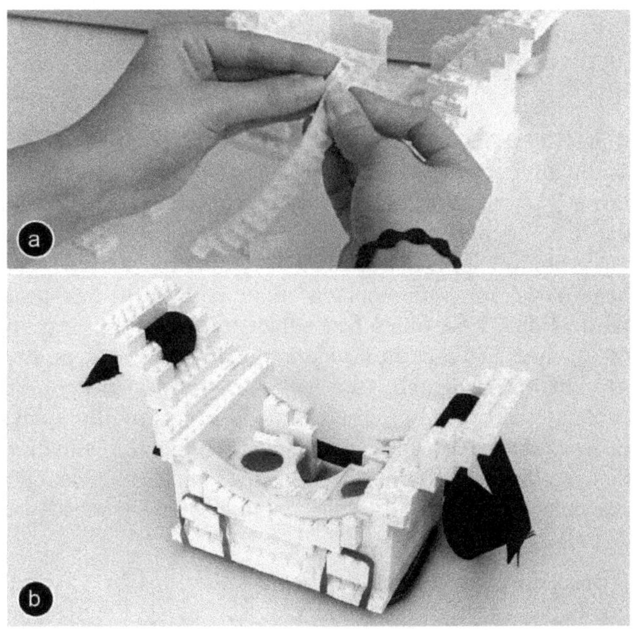

Figure 8: (a) Replacing bricks with the 3D printed parts for the head. (b) The assembled model.

FASTER ITERATION THROUGH LOCALIZED CHANGES

The second key benefit of faBrickator is that helps users iterate more quickly. Rather than reprinting the entire object, faBrickator allows users to make *local* changes to an already printed object. As this allows for faster design iteration, it allows users to iterate more and thus ultimately leads to better designs [1].

Back in the 3D editor *Blender,* the user extends the nosepiece so as to perfectly fit the user's nose. After the user exits the edit mode in *Blender,* faBrickator aligns the current version of the 3D model with the previously printed one to minimize the number of bricks that need to be re-fabricated. Figure 9a shows how faBrickator highlights all bricks that changed compared to the last version. (b) The user now rebuilds the nose piece and (c) after printing exchanges it with the one that didn't fit perfectly.

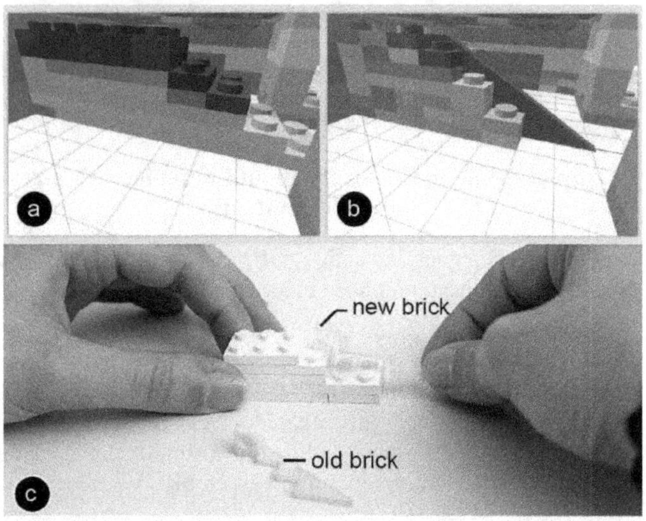

Figure 9: (a,b) faBrickator highlights what changed between two model versions. (c) The user then reprints only the part that changed.

CONTRIBUTION, BENEFITS, AND LIMITATIONS

The main contribution of this paper is a novel approach to fast 3D fabrication and a system called faBrickator that implements this approach. The main idea is to complement 3D printing with construction kit building blocks. The main benefit of our approach is that it allows for faster fabrication—2.44 times faster than traditional 3D printing on average (see section *Validation*). This allows users, such as industrial designers, to achieve several design iterations in a day that would otherwise extend across multiple days. faBrickator's approach is especially beneficial in situations that underlay external constraints such as changing customer needs and thus require many subsequent iterations.

faBrickator implements additional speed-ups by (1) printing in low-detail where possible, i.e., using Lego bricks, (2) allowing for fast iteration by limiting reprinting to those regions that have actually changed, (3) minimizing the effort for manual assembly by using different sized Lego bricks. As a side effect, it also allows repairing objects that are partially broken. Unlike approaches that are entirely based on Legos, our approach allows creating precise parts for regions that require additional accuracy.

On the flipside, faBrickator trades in detail for speed. While suitable for iteration, the partially legofied objects do require a full 3D printing process eventually, i.e., before being deployed. There is also a modest amount of manual effort required, since users need to assemble the Lego part of the object manually.

Finally, as discussed in the introduction, faBrickator applies to *functional* objects, i.e., objects that have shape constraints only in specific areas, which is commonly the case for objects that fulfill a functional purpose. Most of the speed-up faBrickator achieves results from the fact that a given functional purpose can be implemented in many different forms, allowing faBrickator to choose the one that can be fabricated fastest. This approach, however, does not lead to benefits when designing objects where the entire shape matters, such as artistic or decorative shapes.

IMPLEMENTATION

faBrickator is built in *CoffeeScript* using the *constructive solid geometry* library for its geometry operations. We also provide a *Blender* Plugin written in *Python* for easier file exchange between *Blender* and *faBrickator*.

#1 File Exchange between Blender and faBrickator

Our *Blender* plugin automatically exports the 3D model as an .stl file into a predefined folder as soon as the user exits the *edit* mode. faBrickator automatically detects if a new .stl file appears in the folder and imports it accordingly. The *Blender* plugin runs in a separate thread to prevent interference with *Blender's* editing functionality.

#2 Legofying: converting the 3D model into Legos

Figure 10 shows how faBrickator converts the 3D model into Lego's smallest building blocks—the 1x1 Lego plates. faBrickator first determines the bounding box of the model and extends it to the full multitude of a 1x1 Lego plate (8x8x3.2mm). Afterwards, faBrickator fills the bounding box with Lego plates in those positions that are either inside the model or share a portion of the volume with it. The remaining locations are left empty.

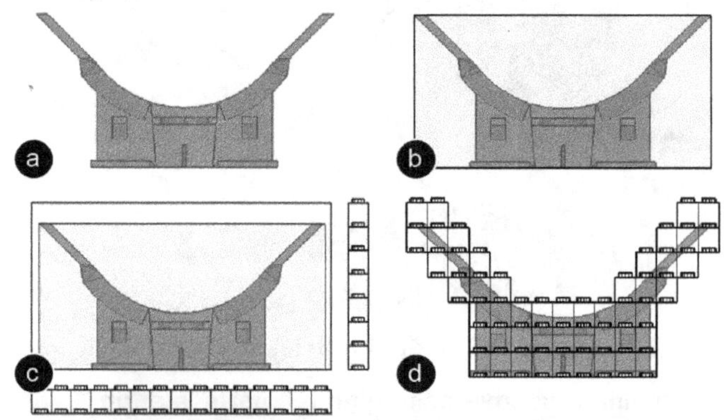

Figure 10: Legofying: (a) model, (b) bounding box, (c) extended bounding box, (d) legofied model.

#3 Layouting Lego Bricks

faBrickator's layout algorithm optimizes for two things: it minimizes the number of bricks used for assembly while maximizing stability. For layouting, we use the layout algorithm proposed by Testuz et al. [22]. The algorithm works as following: (1) it merges the 1x1 plates into larger Lego bricks, (2) it creates a connectivity graph representing the brick layout, (3) it identifies weak points in the graph (unstable connections), and (4) tries to relayout the bricks at these positions in a different way to erase the weak points.

#4 Converting Lego bricks into 3D printable bricks

When users select a Lego brick with the *high-res* brush, it is converted into a 3D printable brick. In order to generate the 3D printable brick, we use a Boolean *intersection* of the Lego brick with the original 3D model geometry (see Figure 11).

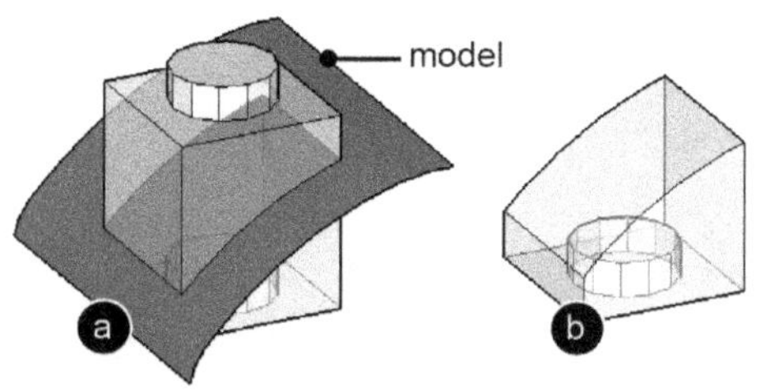

Figure 11: The 3D printable brick is a result of a Boolean intersection of the model and the Lego brick.

#5 Merging and splitting Lego bricks

When users select several bricks using the *merge* brush, they are merged into a single compound 3D printable brick. In our initial approach, we used the Boolean *union* operation to merge the bricks, which turned out to be very expensive. The reason is that the side faces of the two Lego bricks that should be merged are always co-planar, which is the most expensive case for a *union* operation.

Instead faBrickator uses a *tagging* approach for merging. As can be seen in Figure 12a, faBrickator tags each side of a Lego brick according to its orientation in space (e.g., side-y, side+y). In order to merge two bricks, we simply identify the matching neighbor sides by their tag and remove the sides since they would be inside the compound brick (Figure 12b). If later on users apply the *split* brush, we just enable the sides again.

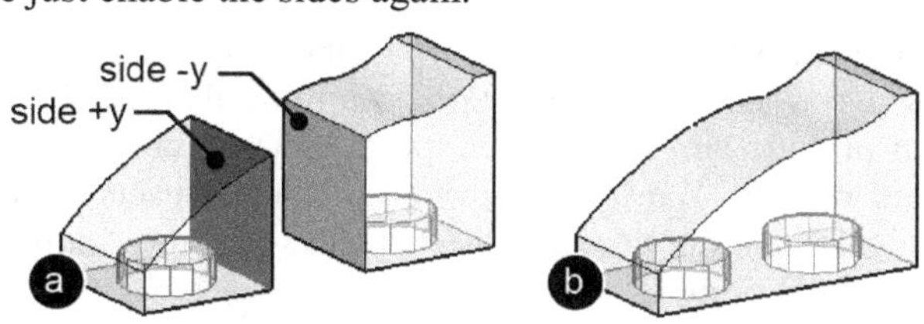

Figure 12: Merging: (a) The sides of each brick are tagged according to their orientation. (b) We use this to identify, which sides need to be removed for merging.

#6 Detecting the completeness of knobs and tubes

In order to ensure a stable brick layout, faBrickator needs to detect working knobs on a 3D printable brick. Only complete knobs can be used to make a connection with another brick. A knob is only complete if all of the knob's faces were inside the model before the intersection with the model (see Figure 13). If a part of the knob lays outside the model, it is cut off during the intersection and the knob is no longer functional.

A regular Boolean *intersect* determines inside and outside faces in the process of calculating the intersection. However, as the result the *intersect* operation only returns a geometrical volume from which it is difficult to tell if the knob is complete or not. faBrickator therefore has its own *intersect* operation that stores the meta-information about inside and outside faces in *tags*. Before the intersection, all the faces of a knob are tagged with the *knob-tag* (Figure 13a). During the *intersect,* faBrickator tags, which faces are *inside/outside* of the model (Figure 13b). Afterwards, we check if there is any face that was with the *knob-tag* that also has the *outside-tag.* If there is none the knob is complete. We use the same mechanism for the tubes on the bottom side of the bricks.

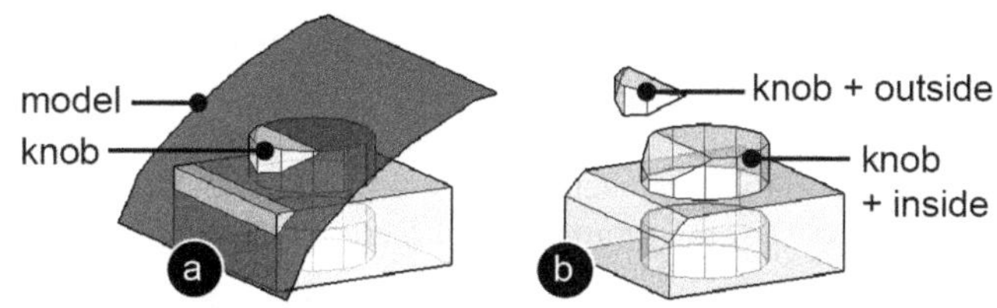

Figure 13: Detecting the completeness of knobs: (a) During intersection, we (b) tag if a part of the knob lies outside the model.

#7 Calculating changes between design iterations

When users iterate over a model, faBrickator displays which part of the model changed. For this, we first align the new 3D model with the old 3D model because faBrickator allows users to rotate the 3D model in *Blender* and to move it around freely. In order to align the two models, faBrickator calculates a transformation matrix based on the distance of specific model features to a reference point—we use the point of origin. The triangles of a model are not suited as model features because even small changes of the model result in a completely different tessellation during the export from a 3D modeling program (e.g., *Blender*).

In order to create a representation of the model that is comparable, we merge the triangles into larger sides based on their orientation. First we merge neighbor triangles that have the same normal into larger convex polygons. In a second step, we merge all convex polygons with the same normal into a side. We use these sides for comparison (i.e. their outline) and after finding a match, calculate the transformation matrix and align the models.

Now that the models are aligned, we legofy the new model. Afterwards, we determine which parts changed by calculating the differences based on the 1x1 Lego plates. If a plate was added or removed, the part changed. For bricks that were marked as *high-res* 3D printed bricks in the old model, we use a volume comparison to determine changes. For bricks that did not change, we copy the brick layout of the old model to minimize the number of bricks that need to be reassembled.

#8 Eliminating Non-Manifold Geometry

When downloading models from the online platform *Thingiverse*, we experienced that many 3D models have invalid geometry, i.e. are not manifold/watertight. Therefore, we identified and cleaned the faulty geometry in the program *meshlab* before we further processed it with faBrickator.

VALIDATION

Beside the head-mounted display body, we *faBrickated* two additional example objects we downloaded from *Thingiverse*. faBrickator fabricates the three objects 3.11 times, 2.75 times, and 1.45 times faster (avg. 2.44 times) than traditional 3D printing while requiring only 14 minutes of manual assembly on average. How much faBrickator speeds up the prototyping process depends on how much volume can be substituted with bricks.

Figure 14 shows the first model: a soap bar dispenser that dispenses small flakes of soap when the sled is moved back and forth. It consists of two pieces: (1) the body that holds the soap and that the user moves with his dominant hand in the sled, and (2) the mount for the razor blades and the sled.

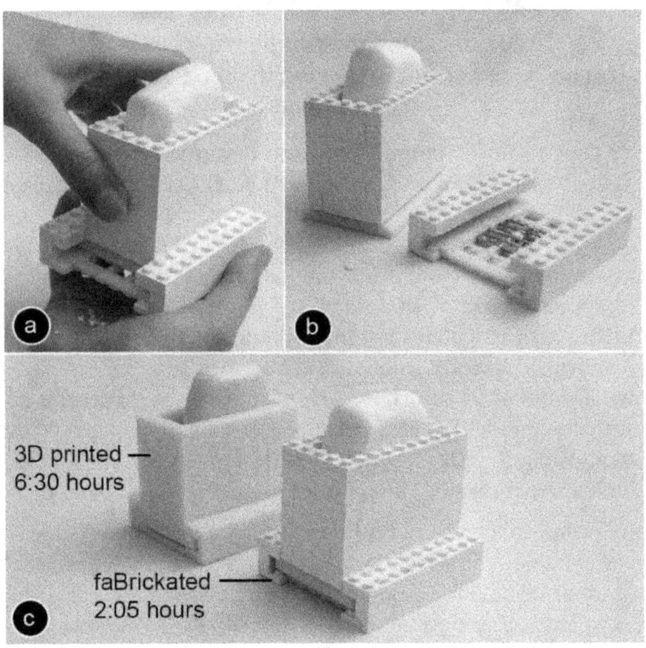

Figure 14: (a,b) This soap dispenser only takes (c) 2:05h and 5 minutes assembly compared to the 6:30h of traditional printing.

Producing this object with traditional 3D printing takes 6:30h compared to only 2:05h printing and 5 minutes assembly when using faBrickator (casing: 0:51h printing and 3 minutes assembly, razor blade: 1:14h printing and 2 minutes assembly). This is an improvement of a factor 3.11 for 3D printing time.

Figure 15 shows the second model: a "penny ballista" that allows ejecting a penny with a rubber band. The ballista consists of a mount for the penny and the ballista body with a sled.

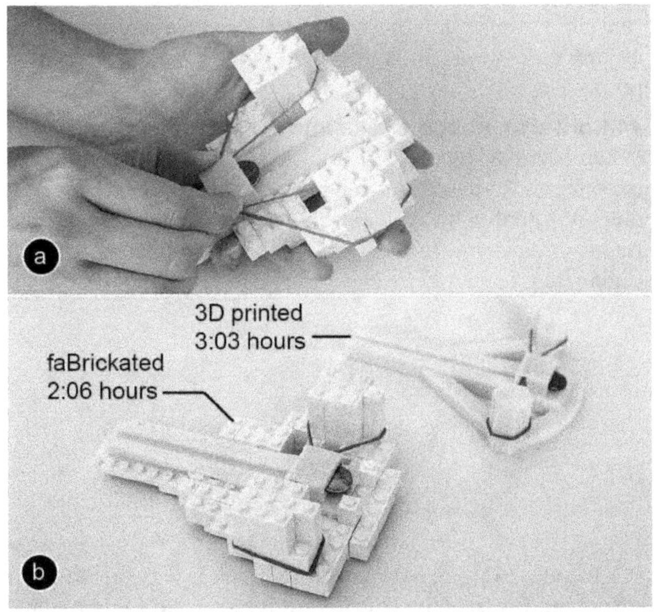

Figure 15: (a) A faBrickated penny ballista takes (b) only 2:06h for printing and 11 minutes for assembly compared to 3:03h when 3D printing entirely.

Using 3D printing, this model takes 3:03h compared to 2:06h printing and 11 minutes assembly when using faBrickator (penny mount: 0:59h printing, ballista body: 1:07h printing and 11 minutes for assembly). This is an improvement of a factor 1.45 for 3D printing time.

The third model is the already presented head-mounted display body with the lens mounts and the head and nose parts. When using faBrickator, it took 5:17 hours for 3D printing and only 25 minutes for assembly (lens mounts: 0:33h and 0:34h, forehead piece top: 1:26h, forehead pieces bottom: 0:41h and 0:44h, nose bridge: 0:25h, nose: 0:54h). This is an improvement of a factor 2.75 for 3D printing time, which for the completely 3D printed model is 14:30h.

While these examples give first insights into potential time-savings when using faBrickator, we think that faBrickator will provide an even greater speed-up when creating very large objects. We hope this will encourage users to start designing and fabricating objects that exceed the volume of current 3D printers.

RELATED WORK

The work presented in this paper builds on personal fabrication, fast fabrication of three-dimensional objects, and brick-based assembly.

Personal Fabrication

Personal fabrication devices such as 3D printers, milling machines, and laser cutters allow users to rapidly fabricate one-off physical objects [8]. The traditional workflow in personal fabrication requires users to first create a digital model in a CAD program. A range of projects in HCI lower the entry barrier to 3D modeling by restricting the space of possible objects to chairs (*SketchChair* [19]), plush animals (*Plushi* [10]), furniture (*FurnitureFactory* [13]), lamps (*SpatialSketch* [26]), and dresses (*Dress-up* [24]). Recently, researchers proposed interfaces that do not only allow the design of passive objects, but also the design of interactive prototypes. *Midas* [17] enables users to prototype capacitive touch layouts with a vinyl cutter. *Printed Optics* [25] and *Papillon* [1] create optical sensors and display elements. Finally, *Sauron* [18] allows creating interactive controllers via optical marker tracking.

Interactive Fabrication

Interactive fabrication systems [27] do not require the user to model the entire object before fabrication, but offer an alternation between user and system control. Since users need to wait for the machine after each input, fast fabrication is a key element of interactive fabrication systems to keep users in the flow [3]. *ModelCraft* [20] allows users to annotate on a paper model and then implements the changes by reprinting the model. *CopyCAD* [4] enables users to copy geometry from existing objects using a milling machine. *constructable* [11] re-introduces speed and precision using a fast laser cutter and a system of constraints. Other systems combined traditional fabrication with interactive fabrication: *Position-correcting router* [16] automatically corrects the user's routing path according to a loaded 3D model. *FreeD* [30] is a milling machine that can stop its spindle to prevent users from making mistakes.

Fast Fabrication of Three-Dimensional Objects

While 3D printers can create the most complex shapes, they are also very slow. Different approaches try to reduce printing time by either massively parallelizing the printing process using multiple heads [6] or by assembling objects layer-wise from prefabricated voxels of equal size [7]. However, as printing resolution increases, fabrication gets slower since more voxels or layers need to be fabricated. Laser cutters on the other side are fast, but can only cut 2D pieces. *LaserOrigami* [12] showed how to use a laser cutter to create 3D objects by cutting and folding an acrylic sheet in a single integrated process.

Complementing Objects with 3D Printed Parts

Several projects used 3D printed parts to repair or to complement existing physical objects. In *Hybrid reAssemblage* [29] the authors repair broken vases by first scanning their geometry and then replacing the part with a 3D printed structure. This process is also common in medicine for replacing parts of broken bones [20]. Petchkowvsky [14] finally enhanced existing physical objects with additional 3D printed features that perfectly blend into the shape and texture of the existing object. faBrickator, in contrast, combines existing bricks with custom 3D printed parts to speed up the rapid prototyping process while assuring accuracy in the areas that need more detail.

Making Objects From Bricks

The hardest problem in building any 3D object from bricks is the automatic generation of a constructable brick layout. Researchers proposed different algorithms, such as using a cost function for simulated annealing [5], evolutionary algorithms [15], beam search [28], and cellular automata [23]. Besides aiming at minimizing the overall number of bricks, an additional focus is on stability, i.e. to prevent bricks from falling off [22]. faBrickator extends these layout algorithms for its 3D printed bricks, which have irregular shapes and therefore additional constraints that need to be taken into account.

CONCLUSION

In this paper, we presented a new approach to rapid fabrication and our system—faBrickator—that implements this approach. The key idea is to substitute sub-volumes of 3D models with standard building blocks. We demonstrated how the modular approach of faBrickator is especially useful when iterating over a design since only the parts that changed are reprinted – not the entire model.

As future work, we plan to extend faBrickator so as to work with a wider range of building blocks and objects in order to further decrease printing time. We also plan to improve the assembly instructions according to the Lego specification. Finally, we aim at automating the assembly process by building on existing tools that are able to assemble standard Lego bricks [9].

ACKNOWLEDGEMENT

We thank the 3D printing lab of the Berlin Institute of Technology for sharing their 3D printing resources, Alexandra Ion for helping with the 3D prints, and Serafima Gurevich for feedback.

REFERENCES

1. Brockmeyer, E., Poupyrev, I., Hudson, S. PAPILLON: Designing Curved Display Surfaces With Printed Optics. *Proc. UIST'13*, 457-462.
2. Buxton, B. *Sketching User Experiences: Getting the Design Right and the Right Design*. Morgan Kaufmann, '07.
3. Csikszentmihalyi, M. *Flow: The Psychology of Optimal Experience*. Harper Perennial Modern Classics, '08.
4. Follmer, S., Carr, D., Lovell, E., Hiroshi, I. CopyCAD: remixing physical objects with copy and paste from the real world. *Adjunct Proc. UIST '10,* 381-382.
5. Gower, R., Heydtmann, A., Petersen, H. LEGO: Automated Model Construction. *European Study Group with Industry. Study Report '98,* 81–94.
6. Hansen, C. J., Saksena, R., Kolesky, D. B., Vericella, J. J., Kranz, S. J., Muldowney, G. P., Christensen, K. T., Lewis, J. A. High-Throughput Printing via Microvascular Multinozzle Arrays. *Advanced Materials '13, Vol. 25, Issue 1.*
7. Hiller, J., Lipson, H. Methods of Parallel Voxel Manipulation for 3D Digital Printing. *Proc. SFF Symposium '07,* 200-211.

8. Gershenfeld, N. *Fab: The Coming Revolution on Your Desktop--From Personal Computers to Personal Fabrication.* Basic Books, '07.
9. Lego Assembler, 2010. http://mikeshouts.com/Lego-made-3D-printer-that-builds-Lego-out-of-Lego/
10. Mori, Y., Igarashi, T. Plushie: an interactive design system for plush toys. *SIGGRAPH '07, No. 45.*
11. Mueller, S., Lopes, P., Baudisch, P. Interactive Construction: Interactive Fabrication of Functional Mechanical Devices. *Proc. UIST '12,* 599-606.
12. Mueller, S., Kruck, B., Baudisch, P. LaserOrigami: Laser-Cutting 3D Objects. *Proc. CHI'13*, 2585-2592.
13. Oh, Y., Johnson, G., Gross, M., Do, E.Y. The Designosaur and the Furniture Factory. *Proc. DCC'06*, 123-140.
14. Petchkovsky, G. Mixing Digital Sculpture with Real Objects. '12.
15. Petrovic, P. Solving the LEGO brick layout problem using evolutionary algorithms. *Tech. rep., Norwegian University of Science and Technology '01.*
16. Rivers, A., Moyer, I.E., Durand, F. Position-correcting tools for 2D digital fabrication. *Proc. SIGGRAPH'12 (TOG), Vol. 31, Issue 4, No. 88.*
17. Savage, V., Zhang, X., Hartmann, B. Midas: Fabricating Custom Capacitive Touch Sensors to Prototype Interactive Objects. *Proc. UIST '12,* 579-588.
18. Savage, V., Chang, C., Hartmann, B. Sauron: Embedded Single-Camera Sensing of Printed Physical User Interfaces. *Proc. UIST'13*, 447-456.
19. Saul, G., Lau, M., Mitani, J., Igarashi, T. SketchChair: an all-in-one chair design system for end users. *Proc. TEI '11*, 73-80.
20. Science News, skull implant, 2013. https://www.sciencenews.org/article/plastic-implant-replaces-three-quarters-mans-skull
21. Song, H., Guimbretière, F., Lipson, H., Hu, C. ModelCraft: Capturing Freehand Annotations and Edits on Physical 3D Models. *Proc. UIST '06*, 13-22.
22. Testuz, R., Schwartzburg, Y., Pauly, M. Automatic Generation of Constructable Brick Sculptures. *Proc. Eurographics '13,* 81-84.
23. Van Zijl, L., Smal, E. Cellular automata with cell clustering. *Proc. Automata '08,* 425-441.
24. Wibowo, A., Sakamoto, D., Mitani, J., Igarashi, T. DressUp: a 3D interface for clothing design with a physical mannequin. *Proc. TEI '12*, 99-102.
25. Willis, K.D.D., Brockmeyer, E., Hudson, S.E., Poupyrev, I. Printed Optics: 3D Printing of Embedded Optical Elements for Interactive Devices. *Proc. UIST '12,* 589-598.
26. Willis, K.D.D., Lin, J., Mitani, J., Igarashi, T. Spatial sketch: bridging between movement & fabrication. *Proc. TEI '10*, 5-12.
27. Willis, K.D.D., Xu, C., Wu, J.K., Levin, G., Gross, M.D. Interactive fabrication: new interfaces for digital fabrication. *Proc. TEI '11*, 69-72.
28. Winkler, D.: Automated brick layout. BrickFest, 2005.
29. Zoran, A., Buechley, L. Hybrid reAssemblage: An Exploration of Craft, Digital Fabrication and Artifact Uniqueness. *Leonardo Journal '13, Vol. 46, Issue 1.*
30. Zoran, A., Paradiso, J.A. FreeD: a freehand digital sculpting tool. *Proc. CHI'13,* 2613-2616.

Understanding Physical Activity through 3D Printed Material Artifacts

Rohit Ashok Khot
Exertion Games Lab
RMIT University, Australia
rohit@exertiongameslab.org

Larissa Hjorth
RMIT University
Melbourne, Australia
larissa.hjorth@rmit.edu.au

Florian 'Floyd' Mueller
Exertion Games Lab
RMIT University, Australia
floyd@exertiongameslab.org

ABSTRACT
In this paper, we advocate a novel approach of representing physical activity in the form of material artifacts. By designing such material representations, we aim to understand what these artifacts might offer in terms of reflecting upon physical activity. For example, what types of affect do material artifacts, representing ones' physical activity create for the user? In order to advance this understanding, we designed a system called SweatAtoms that transforms the physical activity data based on heart rate into 3D printed material artifacts. We conducted an "in the wild study" by deploying our system in six households where participants were experiencing five different material representations of their physical activity for a period of two weeks each. We found that the material artifacts made participants more conscious about their involvement in physical activity and illustrated different levels of engagement with the artifacts. Along with reporting the gained insights from the deployments, we offer reflections on designing material representations for physical activity. We hope that our work will inspire designers to consider new possibilities afforded by digital fabrication to support user's experience with physical activity by utilizing interactive technologies at our disposal.

Author Keywords
Physical exercise; personal informatics; quantifiable self; 3D printing; digital fabrication; entertainment

ACM Classification Keywords
H.5.m. Information interfaces and presentation (e.g., HCI): Miscellaneous.

INTRODUCTION
Studies have pointed out that a lack of awareness about physical activity may lead to a sedentary lifestyle [3,36]. In response, there has been a growing interest in building technologies that sense and collect personally relevant information such as bodily responses to physical activity and provide users with opportunities for self-monitoring and reflection [25]. For example, devices like heart rate monitors inform users about their exercise intensity by measuring the heart rate during a physical activity session while pedometers count the number of steps taken in a day. Studies suggest that regular use of these devices can increase the user's motivation towards physical activity [3,25,36]. However, the majority of the existing approaches mainly target the virtual medium (such as screen-based output) to provide a portrayal of physical activity [3,4,8,9,17,19]. On one hand, the virtual medium is beneficial for data visualization because of its interactive capabilities (such as allowing for zooming into data) and support for dynamic updates on the data. On the other hand, the virtual medium has some limitations as to what can be experienced with it, as argued by Vande Moere [39] and Victor [41]. For example, the virtual medium requires a flat display surface that is less perceivable in daylight and demands visual attention [40]. The "picture under the glass" effect [41] caused by a 2D display surface also makes the virtual medium mainly suitable for 2D representations of data since onscreen 3D visualization can suffer from problems such as occlusion, distortion and navigational issues [35]. Additionally, Ullmer and Ishii [37] worry that the virtual mode of information entirely focuses on the visual form and neglects other senses. Ishii [18] reminds us that "*our visual and auditory sense organs are steeped in the sea of digital information, but other bodies remain imprisoned in the physical world*". As being physically active happens in this physical world, we see an opportunity to explore complimentary design strategies beyond virtual visualizations to support physical activity.

Recently, with the rapid advancements in digital fabrication technology, devices like 3D printers are becoming more accessible for public use. Gershenfeld [11] envisions that 3D printers will soon be found in every home and people will regularly use them to create, share and copy material artifacts. As a result, design and HCI researchers are now increasingly considering the role of digital fabrication in HCI [28]. This has motivated us to advocate an innovative approach of representing physical activity data in the form of material artifacts. By material artifacts we mean physical objects that are constructed using a digital fabrication process [30]. By incorporating the digital fabrication

CHI 2014, April 26 - May 01 2014, Toronto, ON, Canada

ACM 978-1-4503-2473-1/14/04...$15.00.
http://dx.doi.org/10.1145/2556288.2557144

process of 3D printing for constructing material artifacts based on physical activity, our research also aims to explore a "physical–digital–physical" mode of interaction, where physical energy is first invested in generating digital data such as heart rate, which is then converted back to a material form, re-entering the physical world. Vande Moere [39] argues that a material representation carries a meaning beyond the data itself as it "*can be touched, explored, carried and even possessed*" [39], thus potentially encouraging people to reflect on their behavior yielding more engaging and educational experiences. Additionally, a recent study by Jansen et al. [20] compared virtual and material visualizations of physical data and found that visualizations of data in material form can be easier to understand for the user because of the material's 3D features. In sum, material representation can offer many opportunities. However, it remains unclear how to design such material representations to support physical activity.

In order to contribute to an understanding of material representations of physical activity, we conducted an "in the wild" [33] study on our prototypal system "SweatAtoms" [21,22]. SweatAtoms transforms physical activity data based on heart rate into five different 3D printed material artifacts. We deployed SweatAtoms in 6 households to present findings from the system in use. Although invoking behavioral change was of general interest to us, we focused primarily on eliciting richer reflections on physical activity and understanding the affect material artifacts, representing one's physical activity, can have on users. Through the deployments, this research contributes the following: 1) Insights gained from the design and deployment of the SweatAtoms systems in households that illustrate various affects of material representations on individual's physical activity experiences. 2) An initial understanding of the interrelationship between material representations and physical activity.

RELATED WORK

Li et al. [25] argued that visualization plays an important role in motivating users towards physical activity because it helps users to reflect upon their performance and to gain insights into their physical activity levels. However, Vande Moere [39] points out that physical activity data such as heart rate is often very abstract in nature, and "*has no natural counterpart that can be graphically reproduced.*" Therefore, it becomes the designer's responsibility to create meaningful mappings of physical activity data for the user. We next discuss how designers have previously approached this issue.

Visualization using numbers and graphs

Most of the commercial applications built around sensing technologies such as heart rate monitors use numbers and graphs to show data from recent and past physical activities of users on screens[1]. Numbers and graphs take little screen space and can be easy to interpret, however there can be usability and interpretation issues when it comes to large data sets [16].

Visualization using virtual metaphors

Lin et al. [26] and Consolvo et al. [4] built systems in which physical activity is represented using virtual metaphors such as a virtual fish and garden flowers respectively. The designers believe that virtual metaphors can be more engaging, motivating and easy to glance at when compared to graphs and numbers. Moreover, the authors believe that such virtual metaphors can develop empathy in users motivating them to exercise more. However, living metaphors can sometimes discourage participants from doing the desired activity: for example, in the fish-based metaphor, people did not want to look at the fish when they were inactive because they knew their sedentary activity would make the fish sad [26].

Visualization using interactive art displays

Fan et al. [8] utilized a variety of abstract virtual visualization patterns to display the number of steps users have taken in a day. Their study revealed that people found abstract visualizations engaging. Some artists have also explored the use of physical activity data for artistic and musical performances [7]. George Khut [23] explored an interactive abstract visualization of heartbeat data while the Interactive Institute [17] created a Brainball game controlled by player's brain waves.

Visualization using physical metaphors

Similar to virtual metaphors, people have also looked at physical metaphors to make people aware of their sedentary lifestyle and prompt them to be physically active. For example, Breakaway is a sculpture-based metaphor system by Jafarinaimi et al. [19], where the sculpture starts to yawn if the user remains seated for a long time.

Visualization using playful systems

Prior work has also attempted to facilitate play experiences around the sensed bodily responses of physical activity. For example, Run Zombie Run [34] is a mobile app that prompts users to jog using a game-based narrative while Berkovsky et al. [2] have looked at virtual game rewards in exchange of physical activity, which suggests that rewards can be an important design consideration when building systems to support physical activity.

Rethinking visualization of physical activity

The above mentioned relevant literature suggests an emphasis on using a virtual medium to represent physical activity whereas non-virtual (material) representations have not been explored much, possibly because of the scarcity of

[1] E.g.: http://runkeeper.com, http://fitbit.com

resources that could support material visualizations. However, with the recent advancements in 3D printing technology, we see an opportunity to explore material representations of physical activity as an alternate design strategy. We believe the way energy is spent (subtracted) during physical activity is reversely analogous to the way a 3D printer works where a 3D model is constructed by adding up materials layer by layer on the print bed. This has motivated us to build a system called SweatAtoms that utilizes 3D printing to represent physical activity.

SWEATATOMS

SweatAtoms is a 3D modeling and printing system that transforms physical activity data into 3D printed material form (Figure 1). We utilize the constructive solid geometry technique [5] and preprogrammed patterns to generate 3D designs. These models are then printed, using a 3D printer, forming an aesthetic and informative expression of physical activity data in material form. Next, we discuss our design process to determine the material representations for our study.

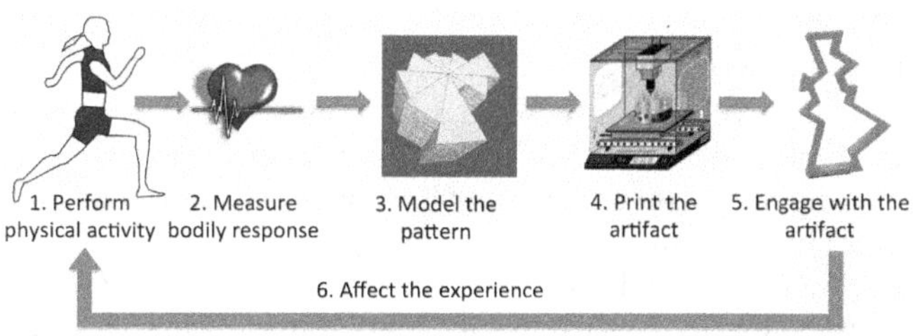

Figure 1: The SweatAtoms system in action: 1) User performs a physical activity 2) Her heart rate is measured 3) A 3D model is created based on the heart rate pattern 4) User prints the 3D model 5) User engages with the printed artifact 6) Engagement with the artifact affects her current (and possibly future) physical activity experience.

Design process: Mapping heart rate to 3D design

Our design process involved investigation into the design space surrounding material representation, digital fabrication (3D printing) and physical activity. To help us explore each of these design spaces, we held regular meetings with available experts in each of the above-mentioned areas. For example, we had lengthy discussions with two junior level interaction designers (1 male and 1 female) and three senior contemporary artists (1 male and 2 female) on possible representation choices. We also talked to an expert (1 male), working on 3D printing from last two years, to identify current limitations and possibilities of state-of-the-art 3D printers. Finally, we also spoke to three designers of exertion games (3 male, 1 senior and 2 junior) as well as two physical activity trainers (2 male) to identify the aspects of physical activity that should be highlighted in a material form. Below we summarize the key aspects of each design space that we identified after the discussions.

Aspects of physical activity

We chose heart rate data as a first exploration to represent physical activity as the physical activity trainers suggested to us that heart rate data is commonly used to analyze physical activity performance and progress towards a set health goal [1]. We discussed with them the finer details of heart rate data such as six heart rate zones (resting, recovery, aerobic, anaerobic, speed and alarming) [1], and got an insight on how these zones can be utilized to convey varied information related to physical activity: for example, the resting heart rate is a good indicator of a user's physical inactivity (sedentary lifestyle). Exertion game designers also recommended us to look at the frequent changes in the heart rate data to uncover interesting patterns and insights on physical activity routine.

Aspects of material representations

We decided on the following design strategies suggested by Consolvo et al. [4] for creating material representations that could facilitate richer reflections on physical activity:

- **Abstract and reflective:** The material representation should not only reflect certain aspects of physical activity but should also be aesthetically pleasing.
- **Public:** Users should be able to wear the artifact or keep them on display in their home. However, care should be taken to conceal any personal information that a user might not want to share in the public space.
- **Unique:** Each artifact should appear unique and differentiable from the rest of the artifacts.
- **Positive:** The material artifact should be a positive reinforcement for doing physical activity.

Aspects of digital fabrication

After having a discussion with the digital fabrication practitioner, we gained an understanding of the limitations and capabilities of the current 3D printers. For example, we realized that the current printers are not capable of printing complex shapes, which limited our possible representation choices. Additionally, we also considered the printing time (which increases with the complexity and density of a selected shape) as well as the sustainability of the material (environmentally friendly). As a result, we chose to print small shapes using a biodegradable material called Polylactic acid (PLA) and selected the Cube 3D printer [6] for fabrication because of its polished look and its interface which we found easy to use.

Taking the above discussed aspects into account and after many design iterations and fabrication trials, we decided on five material representations of physical activity. The technical details and descriptions of the representations are provided in Table 1 and Figure 2 respectively. Below we briefly describe each of the representations.

Representation 1: Graph

"Graph" is an "abstract and reflective" representation where each recorded heartbeat per minute is mapped to a point in XY space. The plotted points are then extruded to achieve a suitable thickness for 3D printing. The idea behind this representation was to mimic a virtual graph and to offer detailed information on heart rate in a material form.

Representation 2: Flower

"Flower" is an "abstract and unique" representation where unlike the "graph" representation; we only capture significant changes (±20 beats per minute) to the heart rate and then represent them in a floral pattern. The length of the petal increases with the heart rate while the width of the petal captures the duration of that heart rate intensity. We intend it to serve as a wearable jewelry item that captures the variations in heart rate through a floral pattern and signifies how heartbeats have evolved over a day.

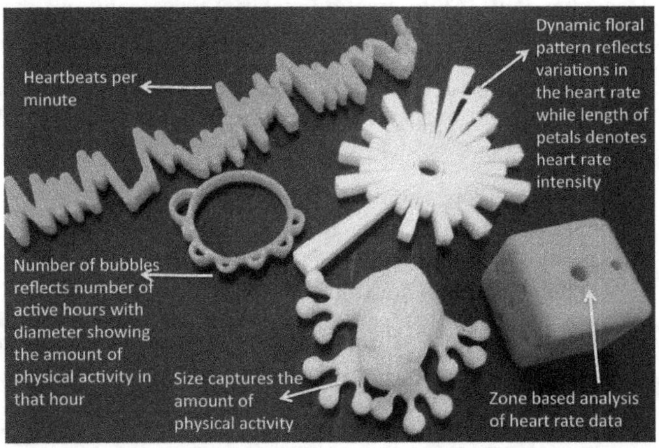

Figure 2: Five material representations of physical activity, each depicting a different aspect of physical activity.

Representation 3: Frog

"Frog" is an "abstract and positive" representation, which serves as a playful reward for doing physical activity. The size of the frog is scaled based on the amount of physical activity done in a day.

Representation 4: Die

"Die" is an "abstract and reflective" representation where six faces of the die depict the amount of time spent in each of the six zones of heartbeat data. We intend the die model to serve as a playful object that can also be stacked together to support comparison between physical activities on different days.

Representation 5: Ring

"Ring" is a "reflective and public" representation where the circles around the ring denote the number of active hours in a day. We define an active hour as an hour where the heart rate is above the resting zone. The diameter of the circle increases with increase in the heart rate and the ring is designed to be a wearable item.

Table 1: Summary of the selected five designs

Representation	Max. dimensions (l × w × h) (mm)	Avg. print time (mins)
Graph	120 × 80 × 4	20
Flower	40 × 40 × 4	25
Frog	20 × 20 × 20	30
Die	16 ×16 × 16	35
Ring	20 × 20 × 4	10

SWEATATOMS IN ACTION: IN THE WILD STUDY

We conducted an "in the wild" study [38] to understand the impact of material artifacts on the behavior and experience of an individual engaged in everyday physical activity. Given the exploratory nature of our design work, we focused on gathering a rich set of opinions rather than a majority of opinion. As such, our work leans on the idea of cultural probing [9] and "in the wild" [33] studies that aim to encourage reflective thinking about a system.

Recruitment

We deployed the system in 6 households across a large metropolitan city for a period of 2 weeks. We recruited participants using the snowball method. We had one participant from every home except for the one where a couple (Frank and Kate as changed names) was interested to participate together in our study, which we welcomed. There were 4 male and 3 female participants with their age varying from 26 to 52 years (average 34). The sample size of 7 participants is in-line with the previous studies on cultural probing [9,10,13,15]. We asked the participants about their level of physical activity in a week (low 1-2 days, medium 3-4 days, high more than 4 days) and also about their most common physical activities (see table 2).

Table 2: Demographic details of the participants.

Name (changed) & Age (years)	Occupation	Level of physical activity	Common physical activities
Alicia (52)	Manager	Medium	Jogging, cycling
Alan (30)	Engineer	High	Gym training
Kelly (43)	Architect	Medium	Tennis, cycling
Frank (29)	Student	Medium	Karate, cycling
Kate (27)	Student	High	Yoga, cycling
Chad (32)	Consultant	Low	Gym training
Dave (26)	Teacher	Low	Cycling, walking

Setup

We supplied each participant with a heart rate monitor (Polar H7) [32], an iPod Touch (5th generation) with the installed Polar Beat application and a Cube 3D printer with 2-3 PLA plastic filament tubes as printing material. The heart rate monitor was paired up with the iPod using the Bluetooth low energy protocol. Following the cultural probing practice, we also provided diaries and asked participants to reflect upon their experience on our system.

Procedure

We installed the SweatAtoms system and 3D printer in every household. Then, we introduced the participants to the system, study procedure and how to understand each artifact. As our intention was to make the printer a part of the home, we placed the printer according to the participants' wishes (which we noted). We also went through the process of printing one object to make participants familiar with the printing process. We then interviewed participants about their daily routines in terms of physical activity. For quick reference, we provided every participant with an A3 poster detailing the study steps to be followed.

Tasks in the morning

We asked the participants to wear the heart rate monitor and start the Polar beat application on the provided iPod while starting their day (usually around 7-8 am). Participants were then asked to continue any usual routine including any physical exercise throughout the study's duration.

Tasks in the evening

We asked the participants to stop the Polar Beat application and to take off the heart rate monitor in the evening (usually around 5-7 pm). Once the heart rate monitoring was stopped, the recorded data was sent automatically to our SweatAtoms application. The SweatAtoms application then generated five material representations in the Stereo-Lithography (STL) format from the received heart rate data. We then converted the generated STL files into the required print file formats (.cube) and emailed them to the participants. (due to the taxing nature of the study, we did the conversions for the participants). To print the material representations, participants were required to copy these files on a USB stick and print them one by one by attaching the USB stick to the 3D printer. This process could have been simplified by wirelessly accessing the 3D printer; however, it would have required modifying the participants' personal Wi-Fi settings, which we chose not to interfere with. The printing time varied for every object based on the participants' level of physical activity (and thus the object size) every day, but typically it took around 90-120 minutes for printing all five objects.

Data source

To gain insights into the underlying motives and experiences of the participants, we asked the participants to maintain a daily diary. We visited each household two times (first and last day) and spent around 4-5 hours with each participant. Based on the participants' needs (such as difficulty in running the 3D printer), we visited some of them more frequently. Additionally, we were in contact with everyone through emails and phone calls. In the conversations, we focused on how they used the SweatAtoms system and gathered their thoughts and experiences with it. We also took notes and recorded audio, which was then coded and analyzed for common themes.

FINDINGS

Deployment of material artifacts representing physical activity not only led us to identify new insights and opportunities but also raised some questions. We describe below our key findings from the deployment of the system.

Intervention

Participants welcomed the system and the study setup in their home with excitement.

Accommodating the 3D printer

Participants usually placed the 3D printer in their living room space close to a window to nullify potential print smell, as seen in Figure 3.

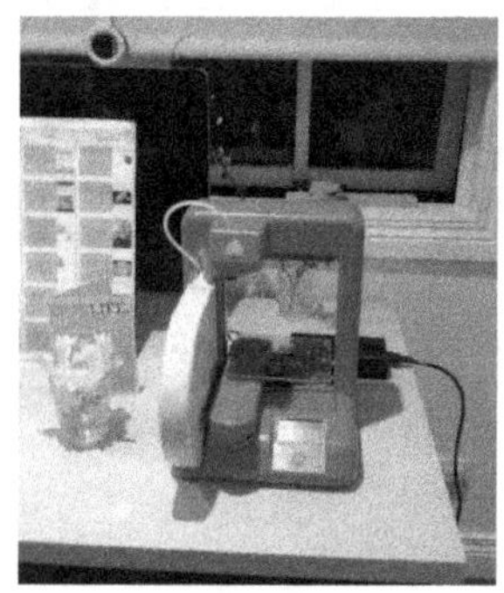

Figure 3: Participants tried to make the printer fit into their home ambience.

Alan, being a technologically oriented person, kept the printer along with his other tech gadgets in a separate room. Kate was particularly happy with the size of the printer as it fitted into an empty window space. Frank and Kelly said that they would not have liked a bigger printer than this. Interestingly, Kelly felt the printer being a part of her household. For example, as the printer was kept near to an open window, she tried to conceal its appearance from the outside with cardboard to prevent someone stealing it. The printer worked smoothly for the entire study duration in all households except one. At Alan's house, we had to recalibrate the print offset and replace the print filament. There were no complaints about the printer smell; however, Frank and Kate commented that the printing noise is affecting their concentration when studying. As a result, they moved their study activity to a different room while the printing was taking place.

Accommodating the artifacts

Frank bought one box to keep all his objects together while Kelly utilized the envelopes of promotional campaigns to keep objects sorted according to each day. We found it noteworthy that a participant went out of his way and bought a box, as we had not previously seen such commitment in some of our prior work with participants.

Lessons learned

The size of the 3D printer is the key to finding an appropriate place in a household. Designers should also consider printer noise, as it could be an issue.

Engagement with the process

All the participants were enthusiastic about seeing their heart rate reflected in material artifacts despite the lengthy process of printing all five objects every day (Figure 4).

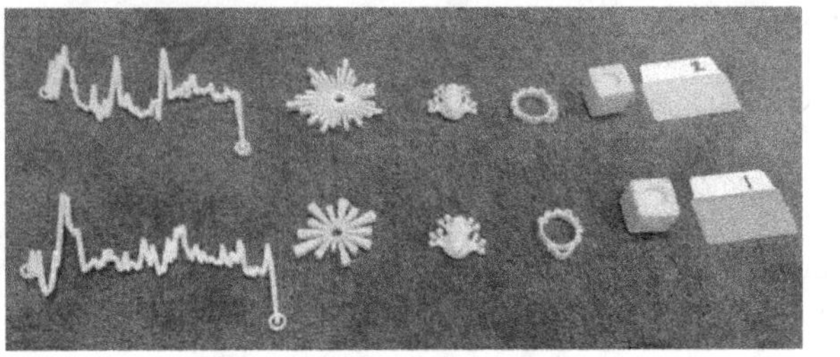

Figure 4: Participants were enthusiastic to see how their reflected heart rate evolved in different material forms as the study progressed. Participants arranged their objects according to day and used sticky notes for assigning days.

Engaging with the heart rate monitoring

Participants felt that heart rate was an appropriate measure of representing their physical activity. Five participants were curious to see how their physical activity was reflected in the artifacts at the end of day, while the remaining two participants tried to confirm whether the artifacts correctly portrayed their physical activity. Two participants had previous experiences of wearing a heart rate monitor but they never wore it continuously for 8 hours. Four participants felt a little uncomfortable in wearing the heart rate monitor continuously for 8 hours every day and they wished to have a strapless heart rate monitor instead. Three participants did not like the idea of continuous monitoring and suggested us to track heart rate only during an exercise.

Engaging with the 3D printing process

Most participants printed artifacts every night before going to bed, two participants skipped printing on a couple of days and then did bulk printing on the weekend to cover the backlog. All participants were excited initially to see the printing process, however, their interest in watching the print process faded over time. Frank mentioned, "*in the beginning, it was exciting to see objects printing small, big, like a recap of my physical activity... later it became time consuming.*" He further added that he would prefer to have objects delivered to him in a mailbox rather than doing the printing at home daily. Kelly and Chad also pitched a same idea. Alan on the other hand got excited about 3D printing and tried to learn more about the printer's capabilities and current trends in 3D printing. All participants enjoyed the opportunity of changing colors of the plastic filament and wished to have more colors in order to print everyday artifacts in different colors. Participants were also satisfied with the size of the artifacts. However, Kelly wanted to print a bigger "Flower" so that she can rest her wine glasses on them.

Four participants, however, did not like the idea of printing objects every day; rather, they wanted to make printing more flexible. For example, Chad added: "*I should be able to choose when and what data I can print*", while Frank and Kate inquired: "*Can we print an object representing heart rate from both of us?*"

Lessons learned

Designers should allow participants to customize their experience by letting them choose when and what information needs to be printed. Additionally, there might be an opportunity for designers to combine physical activity data from multiple people and represent them in one object. Similarly, designers should look into utilizing strapless heart rate monitors for a study.

Engaging with the artifacts

The "Frog" was the favorite artifact, as all participants got affectionate with it immediately. Participants particularly adored the idea that the frog gets bigger if they exercise more. Kelly felt *"it is like burning your body fats and putting them on the frog"*. The majority of the participants kept frogs stacked on top of their computer screens and near their working desks (Figure 5). Frank and Kate competed against each other by doing more exercise in order to get a bigger frog. Kate read from her diary (while holding the printed frogs from her and her husband's data): "*see, how little I am doing in comparison to my husband ☹*". Alan, being a very active person, liked the "Graph" artifact as it clearly displays his performance during various physical activities. He particularly enjoyed the frequent high and low peaks in the artifacts showing how dynamic his day was. Chad stacked the graphs from all days next to each other, which was helpful for him to monitor his progress. Interestingly, Frank and Kate had different views about the "Graph": Kate mentioned "*the graph is not very exciting as we can see the same on a virtual screen. It would be like printing something that we have already seen. I don't like that.*" Four participants found the "Flower" artifact aesthetically pleasing and mentioned various ways of using them in their everyday life: Alicia felt that she could wear them as earrings; Dave, on the other hand, was interested in a flower garden and stacked all flower artifacts next to each other on a desk. The "Ring" artifact was less appreciated as participants felt it does not convey much meaning to them.

Moreover, participants also questioned its utility. Dave replied, "*One has only 10 fingers, then how many rings can he wear?*" Three participants found the "Die" informative as it made them realize about their sedentary lifestyle. Kate was particularly unaware about the time she spends sitting each day and was glad that we included the "Die" artifact in the study communicating this information to her.

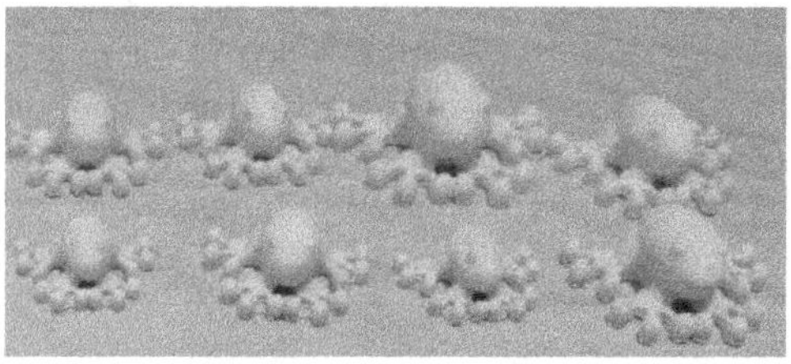

Figure 5: Participants liked the frog and the way it scales with their physical activity. It also became the object for public display and reflective conversations.

Cherishing artifacts

Participants had several ideas of using the printed artifacts in the future. Dave, for example, created a clock using all his printed artifacts as shown in Figure 6. He plans to hang it on the wall of his study room. Kate who liked the "Flower" model described: *"I would fill a glass bowl with water and then put candles on the printed flower and let it float on the water surface, it would make a great decoration for my house."* Chad had a great physical workout session on one day of the study. Looking at the printed artifacts of that day, he happily said: "*I am going to cherish today's graph...see how dynamic it is...I would put it on my shelf to remind me that I did well.*" It was heartening to see that participants took interest in correlating and arranging the objects together.

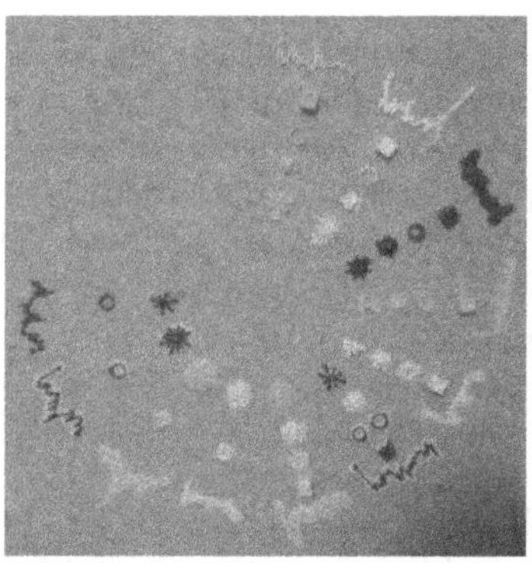

Figure 6: Dave created a wall clock using his printed objects to remind him about how his heart rate evolved over time.

Most participants were happy with the selected design choices for representing their physical activity, however, Kelly, Alicia and Dave were also willing to design their own objects.

Four participants raised issues of sustainability and pondered over the utility of objects in their life. For example, Kelly asked what would she do with so many of such artifacts, if she keeps on printing them each day. Frank and Chad had a common suggestion of making them all interlock with each other to create a bigger sculpture. Kelly put forward the idea of Lego bricks to construct a skyscraper of physical activity over time while Dave suggested printing of the objects only on selective or special days rather than everyday. Three participants wished for a provision to recycle the artifacts.

Conversations around artifacts

Many participants showed their printed artifacts to neighbors and visitors to their home. These artifacts generated a sense of curiosity and conversations among the visitors who did not know what the design actually meant. Participants were enthusiastic to explain the meaning to them. Kate on weekends does voluntary work for young girls at a school. At an annual science and technology event, which happened during the first week of the study, she enthusiastically spoke about the system to the girls. She plans to give some artifacts to the girls "*as a token of her heart*". Chad similarly gave a few of his artifacts to his mom and sister who came to visit him one day during the study. Alicia is planning to incorporate the system in her IT services office. She says: *"I would like to use an approach like this for a reward and recognition program that we are starting. We were thinking about giving out big stars but that is lame in comparison with letting them print out 3d trinkets and the more they need to be rewarded the bigger they are - plus the more they can print."*

Lessons learned

Although people's interest in the printing process faded over time, their interest in the artifacts appeared to be more persistent over time. Designers can learn from the "Frog" design and should map a similar reward structure into their design. For example, the participants welcomed scaling the size of an artifact as a reward to the invested efforts in physical activity. Participants took interest in decorating their homes with the artifacts, and these artifacts also became a topic of conversion. The "Frog" also prompted healthy competition among participants for getting bigger frog. These narratives suggest that personalized artifacts if designed carefully, have an ability to extend engagement with physical activity. For example, although participants appreciated the aesthetics of artifacts, their utility as well as sustainability was equally important to participants.

Relating to physical activity

Most participants became more conscious about their physical activity routines and started to take their heart rate data more seriously with time. Alan said: "*I used to see my heart rate data on my mobile, but this is different, now I can not only touch and feel my data, but I can also show it to the world, I care more about my heart rate now.*" Alicia confirmed, "*My trainer was so happy to see my progress, thanks for letting me participate.*" This supports findings from previous research where participants gained awareness about themselves from a visualization method [21]. Besides physical activity, participants also tried to understand their daily routines from the printed material artifacts. Frank said: "*It was great to know about the self and my activities throughout the day from the printed artifact (graph): when I went to university, when I came back (by looking at large peaks in the graph), when I sat idle (by looking at lower peaks)*". However, Frank and Alicia initially had difficulties in interpreting the "Flower". Alicia thought Flower is like clock that shows her physical activity of the entire day around the clock. Referring to a large petal in Flower, she said, "*see I was most active around 2 pm, when I had to rush twice to office for work.*" After discovering that Flower is not clocklike timely representation of physical activity, she felt slightly disappointed and suggested to make such alternations to Flower design. Kelly and Chad expressed the need of designing artifacts that are easier to interpret similar to the "Graph" and "Frog" artifacts.

Although we did not target an immediate behavioral change with the artifacts among the participants, there was anecdotal evidence of increased physical activity amongst them. For example, Alicia confirmed her increased physical activity to us in an email (Figure 7). She added, *"but the main thing is I am out on my bike and am aware of my heart. In the past, if I exercised on Saturday I would have said that I deserve to rest on Sunday :)"* Dave resumed his weight training after a long time to see its reflection on the artifacts. He mentioned: "*It's been ages since I did that [...] but now this study prompted me to start weight training again*". We find these examples illustrative of people's rekindled interest in physical activity. Kelly emphasized that "*it's the Frog, that makes me jog more*", while Frank and Kate said that they did more physical activity to get a bigger frog at the end of the day.

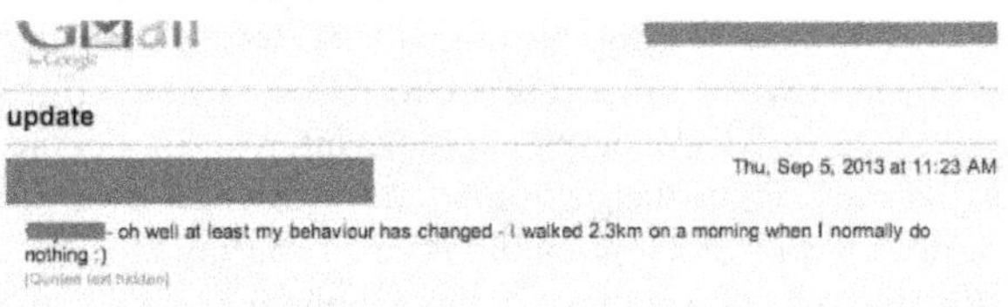
update

Thu, Sep 5, 2013 at 11:23 AM

- oh well at least my behaviour has changed - I walked 2.3km on a morning when I normally do nothing :)

Figure 7: Engagement with the artifacts encouraged a participant to go for a walk.

Significance of personalized material artifacts

During the follow-up interviews, we asked the participants what difference a material artifact made over the virtual counterpart. Most participants answered affirmatively that the physical form and the support for sensory capabilities like touch and feel makes the material artifacts more special than the virtual ones. Kate added that "*[on a mobile phone] you look at your heart rate and then forget about it, here [addressing the material artifact] you cannot, it is more persistent*".

During the follow-up interviews, participants also mentioned that they care more about these artifacts because they contain their personal data and are printed by them at home. Referring to the "Flower" and "Graph" artifacts, Kate mentioned, "*this is me and my data, you cannot get this in the market.*"

Lessons learnt

3D printing was new for all the participants, although all of them had heard about it. We worked with the vision that in 10 years time, most people will have a 3D printer in their home just like a 2D printer today, and therefore, we intend to explore the future interactions associated with today's technology. Although further studies are needed to eliminate any doubts about novelty effects, our interview data suggests that participants' interest in the printing process faded over time; however, participants' interest in the artifacts appeared to have persisted over time. Participants mentioned that the objects matter to them because they reflect their personal data and activities, making them unique, as they cannot be "bought at a shop", as mentioned by Kate. Furthermore, the statement made by three participants that they would rather get the objects delivered to them in the mail rather than printing them at home (to avoid the printing noise), further suggests that the participants were able to differentiate between the appeal of 3D printing and personalized 3D artifacts. Therefore, we argue that giving a physical form to the ephemeral experience of physical activity can facilitate a deeper engagement with the data. Secondly, personalized material rewards also prompted physical activity amongst people who otherwise was spending time sedentary.

DISCUSSION

We discuss below the experiences that the material representations of physical activity elicited for our participants.

Material artifacts as an autotopography

Miller [29] argued that individuals like to express themselves with material artifacts that embody their lives, personalities, emotions and achievements. Our participants expressed themselves by placing the "Frogs" on their computer monitors and decorating their home with "Flowers". Such an arrangement of material artifacts as physical signs to spatially represent the identity of an individual is called "*autotopography*" [14]. This autotopographical collection of material artifacts put on display not only becomes the public representation of the self and craftsmanship [12] but also serves as a memory landscape to the owner triggering reminiscence [38]. As such, our study supports the theory of autotopography. Interestingly, the autotopography was driven mainly by the aesthetic rather than the embodied information in the artifacts. For example, the "Frog" was readily displayed in the home ambience despite containing very little and abstract information about an individual's activity; in contrast, other more informative models like "Graph" and "Die" did not become a part of people's home ambience except for Chad, he placed his "Graph" on the living room wall for public display to cherish his best workout day. Designers therefore should consider building artifacts that are easy to interpret, although the embodied information can be as little as "*I did more physical activity*".

Material artifacts as personalized rewards

According to the Goal Setting Theory [27], incentives are important to sustain a user's interest in an activity. Participants liked getting artifacts at the end of the day as a reward and a testimony to their invested physical efforts. It seemed that material rewards could contribute to an increase in physical activity for some participants. Participants enjoyed how the "Frog" scaled based on their physical activity and they did more physical activity to get a bigger "Frog". Participants appreciated this scaling, even though a bigger "Frog" required more printing time. We believe that the perceived value of the artifact among the participants also increased with the time they waited for it to get printed. Therefore, in future works, it could be interesting to examine the relationship between printing time and size of the reward.

Previous research on archiving and souvenirs suggests that material artifacts can be cherished more than virtual objects because of their higher visibility in the surroundings and low replication possibilities [13,24]. Our findings support this argument, as participants liked the fact that these artifacts are unique and cannot be purchased elsewhere. Additionally, they also liked that these artifacts embodied their personal heart rate data. As a result, we see further opportunities for using material artifacts as personalized rewards to physical activity that can readily be displayed and consider it an interesting design space for designers to explore in the future.

Material artifacts for reflection and reminiscence

Participants mentioned that the material artifacts prompted reflection and reminiscence on past physical activities. Sometimes participants encountered difficulties in understanding the meaning conveyed by these artifacts (the "Flower" in particular). These issues however encouraged conversations and fuelled recall about past activities. We believe that ambiguity in meaning encourages participants to expand their interpretation of physical activity data and thus could facilitate a richer reflection about the self and past activities [15].

Material artifacts have a tendency to disappear into the background, which Miller calls as the "humility of things" [29]. For example, unlike a virtual representation that calls for instant user attention, a material artifact can sit quietly in the surroundings and may not seek attention. We believe this property can be harnessed as an alternative design strategy to provide passive tracking of physical activity and to encourage delayed feedback on data. For example, material artifacts can be built that passively monitor user's physical activity and which are seen only when the user is looking for them. We see an opportunity for designers by engaging with these notions to provide users with additional opportunities for reflection on their physical activity.

CONCLUSION

The contribution of this work is the first conceptual understanding of the relationship between material representations and physical activity. With the deployment of our system SweatAtoms through an "in the wild" study, we explored how participants' relationship to physical activity can be affected through design. We hope that our work inspires different ways of reflecting upon embodiment and material representations, especially, in the context of physical activity and sensing technology. We also encourage design researchers to consider and incorporate digital fabrication in their HCI design practice: in particular, designers should consider not only trying to print things that already exist in the material world, but rather consider that there is an opportunity to print things from data that exists only in the digital world, such as heart rate. We also foresee an opportunity of having personal 3D printers at home, as these printers can produce unique material artifacts that are never as good as coming from large fabrication houses, but are more personal representations of one's life. In the future, we envision people crafting their world with moments from their lives, using data that was previously only seen in digital form but now re-entering their physical world in an embodied material form.

REFERENCES

1. Benson, R., and Connolly, D. *Heart rate training*, Human Kinetics, 2011.
2. Berkovsky, S., Coombe, M., Freyne, J., Bhandari, D., and Baghaei, N. Physical activity motivating games: virtual rewards for real activity. In *Proc. CHI'10*, ACM (2010), 243-252.
3. Bravata, M.S., Smith-Spangler, C., Sundaram, V., Gienger, A.L., Lin, N., Lewis, R., Stave, C.D., Olkin, I. and Sirard, J. Using Pedometers to Increase Physical Activity and Improve Health: A Systematic Review. *JAMA*, 298(19), 2007, 2296-2304.
4. Consolvo, S., McDonald, D.W. and Landay, J. Theory-driven design strategies for technologies that support behavior change in everyday life. In *Proc. CHI'09*, ACM (2009), 405-414.
5. Constructive solid geometry http://evanw.github.io/csg.js/, 2013.
6. Cube 3D printer. http:// cubify.com/cube/index.aspx.
7. Donnarumma, M. http://marcodonnarumma.com.
8. Fan, C., Forlizzi, J. and Dey, A. A Spark Of Activity: Exploring Information Art As Visualization For Physical Activity. In *Proc. Ubicomp '10*, ACM (2010), 81-84.

9. Gaver, W.W., Dunne, A., and Pacenti, E. Cultural Probes. *Interactions*, 1999, 21-29.
10. Gaver, W. W., Bowers, J., Boehner, K., Boucher, A., Cameron, D., Hauenstein, M., Jarvis, N., and Pennington, S. Indoor weather stations: investigating a ludic approach to environmental HCI through batch prototyping. In *Proc. CHI '13*, ACM (2013), 3451-3460.
11. Gershenfeld, N. *Fab: The Coming Revolution on Your Desktop–from Personal Computers to Personal Fabrication*. Basic Books, 2007.
12. Goffman, E. *The Presentation of Self in Everyday Life*, Penguin Books, 1959.
13. Golsteijn, C., Hoven, E. van den, Frohlich, D. and Sellen, A. Towards a More Cherishable Digital Object. In *Proc. DIS'12*, ACM (2012), 655-664.
14. Gonzalez, J. A. Autotopographies. In *Prosthetic Territories. Politics and Hypertechnologies*, Westview Press, 1995, 133–150.
15. Hallnäs, L. and Redström, J. Slow Technology; Designing for Reflection. *Journal of Personal and Ubiquitous Computing*, Springer-Verlag, 2001, 201-212.
16. Herman, I., Melancon, G., and Marshall, S. M. Graph visualization and navigation in information visualization: A survey. *IEEE Trans. Visual. Comput. Graph*. 6, 10, 2000, 1–21.
17. Hjelm, S.I., Browall, C., Brainball-using brain activity for cool competition. In *Proc. NordiCHI'00*, (2000).
18. Ishii, H. Tangible bits: beyond pixels. In *Proc. TEI'08*, ACM (2008), xv-xxv.
19. Jafarinaimi, N., Forlizzi, J., Hurst, A. and Zimmerman, J. Breakaway: an ambient display designed to change human behavior, In *Proc. CHI EA'05*, ACM (2005), 1945-1948.
20. Jansen, Y., Dragicevic, P. and Fekete, J.D. Evaluating the Efficiency of Physical Visualizations. In *Proc. CHI '13*, ACM (2013), 2593-2602.
21. Khot, R. Sweat-atoms: crafting physical objects with everyday exercise. In *Proc. CHI EA '13*, ACM (2013), 2701-2706.
22. Khot, R., and Mueller, F. Sweat-atoms: turning physical exercise into physical objects. In *Proc. CHI EA '13*, ACM (2013), 3075-3078.
23. Khut, P.G. *Development and Evaluation of Participant-centred Biofeedback Artworks*, unpublished thesis manuscript, University of Western Sydney, 2006.
24. Kirk, D.S. and Sellen, A. On human remains: Values and practice in the home archiving of cherished objects. *ACM TOCHI* 17, 3, 2001,1-43.
25. Li, I., Dey, A. and Forlizzi, J. Understanding my data, myself: supporting self-reflection with ubicomp technologies. In *Proc. UbiComp '11*, ACM (2011), 405-414.
26. Lin, J. L., Mamykina, L., Lindtner, S., Delajoux, G. and Strub, H.B. Fish'n'Steps: Encouraging physical activity with an interactive computer game. In *Proc. Ubicomp'06*, Springer (2006), 261-278.
27. Locke, E., and Latham, G. *A theory of goal setting and task performance*, Prentice Hall, 1990.
28. Mellis, D., Follmer, S., Hartmann, B., Buechley, L. and Gross, M.D. FAB at CHI: digital fabrication tools, design, and community. In *Proc. CHI EA '13*. ACM (2013), 3307-3310.
29. Miller, D. *The comfort of things*. Polity, 2008.
30. Mota, C. The rise of personal fabrication. In *Proc. C&C '11*, ACM (2011), 279-288.
31. Munson, S.A., and Consolvo, S. Exploring Goal-setting, Rewards, Self-monitoring, and Sharing to Motivate Physical Activity, In *Proc. Pervasive Health 2012*, 25-32.
32. Polar heart rate monitors, http://www.polar.com/en/products.
33. Rogers, Y. Interaction Design Gone Wild: Striving for Wild Theory. *Interactions* 18, 4, 2011, 58-62.
34. Run Zombie Run, https://www.zombiesrungame.com/.
35. Shneiderman, B. Why not make interfaces better than 3d reality? *IEEE Comput. Graph. Appl.* 23, 6, 2003.
36. Tudor-Locke, C., Bassett, B.R., and Swartz, A.M. A preliminary study of one year of pedometer self-monitoring. *Annals of Behavioral Medicine*, 28, 2004, 158-162.
37. Ullmer, B., and Ishii, H. Emerging frameworks for tangible user interfaces. *IBM systems journal 39*, 3.4 (2000), 915-931.
38. Van den Hoven, E. 2004, Graspable Cues for Everyday Recollecting. PhD thesis, Technische Universiteit Eindhoven, The Netherlands.
39. Vande Moere, A. Beyond the tyranny of the pixel: Exploring the physicality of information visualization. In *Proc. IV'08*, IEEE (2008), 469-474.
40. Vande Moere, A. and Patel, S. Analyzing the design approaches of physical data sculptures in a design education context. In *Proc. VINCI'09,* 2009, 1-23.
41. Victor, B. A brief rant on the future of interaction design, http://worrydream.com/ABriefRantOnTheFutureOfInteractionDesign/, 2013.

Supporting the Design and Fabrication of Physical Visualizations

Saiganesh Swaminathan[1] Conglei Shi[2] Yvonne Jansen[1]
Pierre Dragicevic[1] Lora Oehlberg[1] Jean-Daniel Fekete[1]
[1]Inria
firstname.lastname@inria.fr
[2]HKUST
clshi@cse.ust.hk

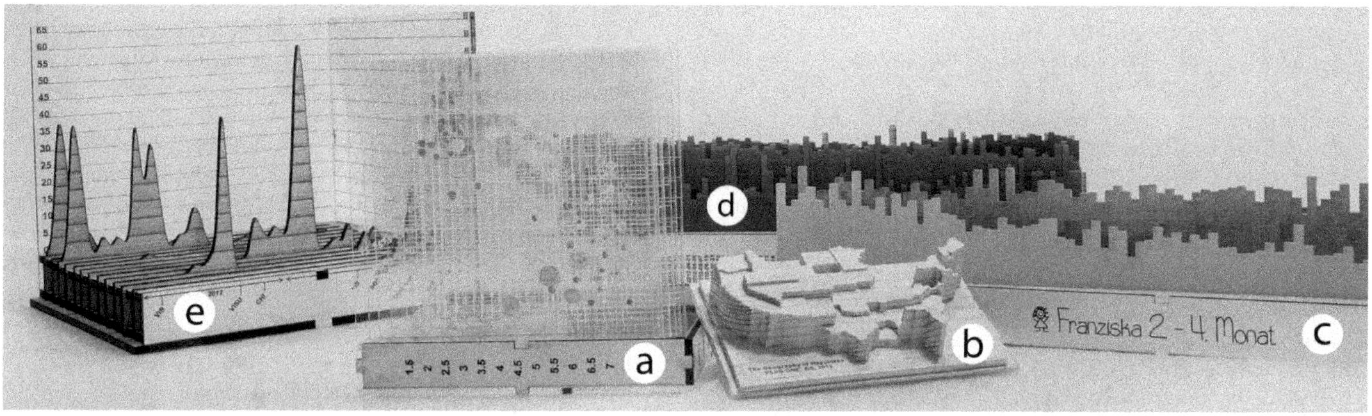

Figure 1. Physical visualizations created with our fabrication tool, MakerVis: a) a layered scatterplot modeled after Rosling ; b) a prism map showing relative happiness in US states computed from Twitter sentiments; c), d), e) layered bar charts and line charts crafted by end users.

ABSTRACT

Physical visualizations come in increasingly diverse forms, and are used in domains including art and entertainment, business analytics, and scientific research. However, creating physical visualizations requires laborious craftsmanship and demands expertise in both data visualization and digital fabrication. We present three case studies that illustrate limitations of current visualization fabrication workflows. We then present MakerVis, a prototype tool that integrates the entire process of creating physical visualizations, from data filtering to physical fabrication. Design sessions with three end users demonstrate how tools such as MakerVis can dramatically lower the barriers to producing physical visualizations. Observations and interviews from these sessions highlighted future research areas, including customization support, using material properties to represent data variables, and allowing the reuse of physical data objects in new visualizations.

Author Keywords

Physical visualization; digital fabrication; infovis.

http://dx.doi.org/10.1145/2556288.2557310

ACM Classification Keywords

H.5.2 Information Interfaces and Presentation: User interfaces; D.2.2 Design Tools and Techniques: User interfaces

INTRODUCTION

Visualization systems beyond traditional desktop settings offer radically new ways of interacting with data, an emergent area of research [17, 12]. In particular, *physical visualizations* — visualizations that map data to physical matter instead of pixels — are an information medium that promises to be more compelling [9], more expressive [19], and in some cases more effective than on-screen setups [13]. A wide range of physical visualizations have already been crafted by artists, analysts and scientists, for various purposes ranging from infotainment to goal-oriented tasks [5].

However, creating physical visualizations remains a major bottleneck. While digital fabrication technologies are increasingly accessible [30], most software tools that drive fabrication machines focus on static object models, ignoring data-driven content. Conversely, a wealth of software tools exist for creating on-screen visualizations [28, 32], but do not support the creation of physical objects. In addition to the fundamental differences between physical objects and graphical content (e.g, physical objects are three-dimensional rather than flat, and are subject to physical forces such as gravity and friction), fabrication machines have unique constraints that differ from those of computer displays and 2D printers.

There is no integrated tool for building physical visualizations; it is a laborious and time-intensive process. It requires complex workflows, a heterogeneous set of tools, and expertise in both data visualization and fabrication. The lack of cross-domain tools ultimately limits a designer's abilities to create physical visualizations of larger-scale data, to reuse an existing physical design with new datasets, or to rapidly iterate through possible design variations. This paper addresses these problems through the following contributions:

- We present case studies and discuss users' current design and fabrication process for physical visualizations, and current tools' support during this process;
- We introduce *MakerVis*, a physical visualization design tool prototype that imports users' raw data tables and produces digital fabrication-ready design files (see Figure 1 for examples);
- We present an observational study of three end users who used MakerVis to create a physical visualization of personal data;
- Based on our observations, we identify key design requirements and research challenges for physical visualization design tools.

By developing tools for creating physical visualizations, our work bridges the gap between information visualization and digital fabrication. Not only does it offer visualization experts renewed access to physical media, but it also dramatically expands the application range of digital fabrication technologies. Our work also aims to facilitate the replication of research on effective physical visualization designs [7].

BACKGROUND & RELATED WORK

We draw on research literature from information and digital fabrication to inform our work. In the following section we address the importance of physical visualization, and briefly discuss related work from information visualization and digital fabrication that impact the creation of physical visualizations. We explain the problems that each area tries to address and review current tools that attempt to address them. We explain why the design and fabrication of physical visualizations creates unique problems that neither community is currently able to properly address.

Physical Visualizations

Roughly defined, a physical visualization maps data to physical form instead of pixels or ink [13]. People have externalized information in physical form since before the invention of writing, e.g., in the form of clay tokens [25]. Although flat surfaces – i.e., clay tablets, then paper and ink, and later computer screens – became a more convenient media for data visualization, physical visualizations are becoming more popular. One revealing trend is the explosion of data sculptures, i.e., aesthetic physical visualizations created by designers and artists to support informal reflection about data [19]. An increasing variety of data sculptures are being created, exhibited and shared, from small data jewelry (Figure 4) to large-scale museum installations (Figure 3).

In addition to artistic applications, physical visualizations are increasingly considered for their potential to support analytical tasks. In the mid-20th century, companies and research scientists already used physical visualizations for practical purposes [5]. More recently, Hans Rosling used physical visualizations to explain population growth and income inequalities, and General Motors started using 3D LEGO visualizations to track car failures [5]. Consistent with numerous psychology studies suggesting that physical object manipulation can enhance cognition [1], recent studies suggest that in some cases physical visualizations can be more effective than on-screen visualizations for communicating and analyzing data [9, 13]. Additionally, a variety of data exploration tasks can be carried out by simply rearranging modular physical visualizations [2, 12, 29].

Physical visualizations have the potential to dramatically enrich and complement paper and computer displays. They bridge the gap between artistic and pragmatic visualization [15], and between casual and traditional infovis [21]. Physical visualizations can not only be useful to analysts by faithfully conveying complex, three-dimensional data, but also by inheriting all of the practical and social advantages of everyday objects: they can be "touched, explored, carried, or even possessed" [19]. Moreover, they are constantly "on" and are therefore convenient as ambient displays [12].

Information Visualization: Problems and Tools

The goal of information visualization (or simply *visualization*) is to help humans make sense of data using vision and perception. It translates data into a visual form, mapping data attributes to visual attributes (e.g., shape or color). These primitive shapes are then combined into visual representations such as bar charts, line charts, scatterplots, or choropleth maps. To be optimally effective and support "external cognition" [3], this process is informed by experience and knowledge of the capabilities of the human visual system.

Historically, all data visualizations were hand-crafted. Two-dimensional visualizations were created with a pencil and a ruler on paper, while physical visualizations were made using hand tools [2, 13, 5]. The process of hand-crafting both types of visualizations is laborious and requires considerable expertise. In the last 30 years, researchers have developed many computer tools to simplify the creation of visualizations for screen and printed media (e.g., [28, 14, 10]).

Modern charting systems such as Tableau [28] now support many types of visual representations and offer GUIs to interactively tune visual parameters and polish the produced output. Popular statistical and numerical-computing tools offer charts that can be extensively customized through scripting, requiring programming skills. Support for full customization and creative exploration is still an active research topic [31]. Nonetheless, the process of generating effective visualizations on screen and paper is now accessible to a large audience with little training, and produces high-quality output. However, for physical visualizations, this is not yet the case.

This is partly due to a lack of an appropriate conceptual model. Modern tools rely on the visualization reference model introduced by Card et al. [3]. The model identifies a visualization "pipeline" with four main stages: *raw data* is transformed into *processed data*, which in turn is mapped into an *abstract visual form*, then refined into a full visual specification, the *visual presentation*. Most of the research on the architecture of visualization toolkits and tools has focused on identifying how to split this conceptual pipeline into software components offering the appropriate level of functionality. This model has been only recently adapted to account for physical visualizations [12], where an additional stage, the *physical presentation*, captures the presentation medium.

Existing toolkits and systems are intended for flat physical presentations, providing essentially 2D visualizations (sometimes using projections from 3D models). The primitives managed by existing systems take for granted the unified raster display abstraction, which allows any image to be specified and rendered on any screen (CRT, LED) or 2D printing technology (laser, ink-jet) transparently. However, the raster model is not appropriate to produce general physical visualizations. There is no unified description of a 3D physical model that can be turned into an efficient set of instructions for a fabrication machine.

Additionally, visualization systems typically automate all pipeline transformations, supporting interaction by allowing users to alter the pipeline at different levels and have the screen dynamically updated [12]. However, in the case of physical visualizations, pipeline transformations may be semi-automated or entirely manual (e.g., physical assembly), and most interactions are deferred to the physical object (e.g, reordering data by rearranging parts) [12]. Specification of interactions for physical visualizations is still at an early stage: existing physical visualizations use ad-hoc or opportunistic interactions, far from any general operational model of physical interaction.

In summary, existing visualization systems cannot be easily adapted to support physical visualizations; neither their conceptual model nor their graphical model is appropriate for physical construction.

Digital Fabrication: Problems and Tools

In digital fabrication, digital *design files* are passed to computer-controlled manufacturing machines to create physical objects. Although many different machines exist, there are two main approaches to digital fabrication. Subtractive techniques (e.g., laser cutting, CNC milling) cut away or remove material. Additive techniques (e.g., 3D printing) build up material layer-by-layer. In addition, fabrication techniques can be either 2D or 3D: laser cutters operate on flat sheets of material, while CNC mills and 3D printers produce 3D solid objects. Materials and manufacturing techniques are tightly coupled. The choice of manufacturing technique may limit the types of materials available for use, and vice versa.

The primary challenge when fabricating objects is to ensure that they physically embody specific physical properties. Most properties must be negotiated by the designer on a case-by-case basis. However, necessary properties often include:

Manufacturability. A digitally-specified object can exist virtually while being impossible to physically manufacture. While several thousand objects models are freely available on the Internet, these models may or may not be at the right scale, or be tailored for a particular fabrication technique. Some software tools attempt to address this issue. For example, *Chopper* [18] partitions 3D digital models into parts that fit within the working volume constraints of a 3D printer. Research tools such as crdbrd [11] and commercial tools such as Autodesk *123DMake*[1] cut 3D models into 2D slices.

Assembly & Fit. Multi-part objects must be easily assembled – and sometimes disassembled – into a well-fitting object. Designers must choose from a wide range of attachment techniques [8], define design specifications (e.g., joint location, feature dimensions, clearance between parts) and iterate to identify the right design for assembly. To computationally facilitate design for assembly, Lau et al. [16] devised a tool that takes IKEA-style 3D models and applies formal grammars to identify the parts and connectors needed to build it.

Balance & Stability. Once fabricated and assembled, objects usually need a stable resting state. Professional CAD software (e.g., AutoDesk Inventor[2]) facilitate design iteration through physics simulation, while the tool *Make It Stand* specifically helps design physically stable 3D virtual objects by carving or deforming them [22].

Strength. Fabricated objects need to support their own weight and withstand human forces from normal use. Again, professional CAD software provides simulation and visualization tools for design iteration. Similarly, the *Sculpteo*[3] Web App for 3D printing offers a heatmap stress visualization on the 3D object preview, which is updated as the user changes the object's dimensions.

While professional CAD tools have extensive design and fabrication support, they require considerable training. Meanwhile, tools for general audiences focus on the fabrication of existing designs. Helping non-experts both design and fabricate is an active research topic. *SketchChair* [23] lets users sketch 2D profiles of chairs that are then extruded and transformed into design files for laser cutters or CNC mills. *Midas* [24] lets users design customized touch-sensors, producing both fabrication-ready design files and assembly instructions. Direct manipulation tools for digital fabrication enable users to concurrently design and fabricate [20].

One promising approach for lowering the barrier to design and fabrication is *parametric design*, i.e., letting users build specific classes of objects by specifying their parameters [26]. For example, *BoxMaker*[4] lets users specify the dimensions of a box and automatically generates 2D stencils with finger joints. Although it only creates boxes, infinite variations are possible. Similarly, our goal is to facilitate the design and fabrication of a particular class of objects –physical visualizations– without the necessity for domain-specific expertise in digital fabrication. As a result, MakerVis treats physical visualizations as parametric objects whose final shape is driven by both raw data and user preferences.

[1] `http://www.123dapp.com/make`

[2] `http://www.autodesk.com/inventor`

[3] `http://www.sculpteo.com`

[4] `http://boxmaker.rahulbotics.com/`

CASE STUDIES

To illustrate the difficulty of crafting physical visualizations, we discuss current practices through four real-world case studies taken from a curated list of data sculptures and physical visualizations [5]. All four designs were documented online and involved varying degrees of manual, automated and computational work.

Manual Fabrication

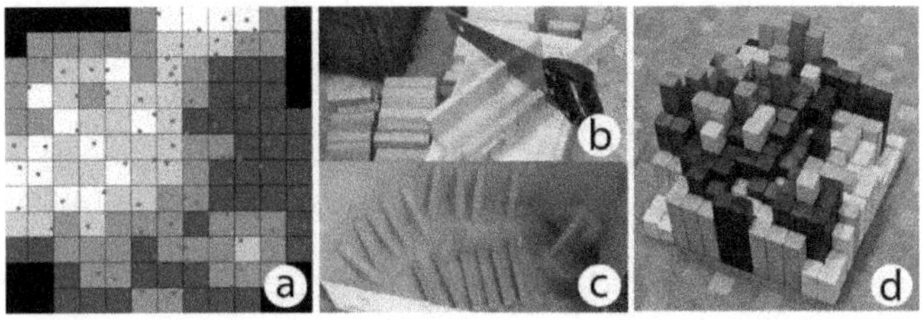

Figure 2. Building a 3D heatmap. Image courtesy of Doug McCune.

Doug McCune constructed a 3D heatmap (Figure 2), showing the performance of elementary schools in San Francisco. With the help of a computer, McCune divided the entire city area into 12×12 squares and computed a weighted score for school performance per square (see Figure 2a). Score values were then converted in heights. McCune then cut 144 pieces of wood according to these heights using a hand saw, which he now does not recommend (Figure 2b). After spray-painting each bar according to its height (Figure 2c), he glued the bars to a base for the final design (Figure 2d).

Apart from the initial steps of data collection and transformation, this visualization was created entirely by hand. This fabrication approach is not only very labor intensive, but also less accurate than digital fabrication.

Semi-Automatic Fabrication, Standard Software

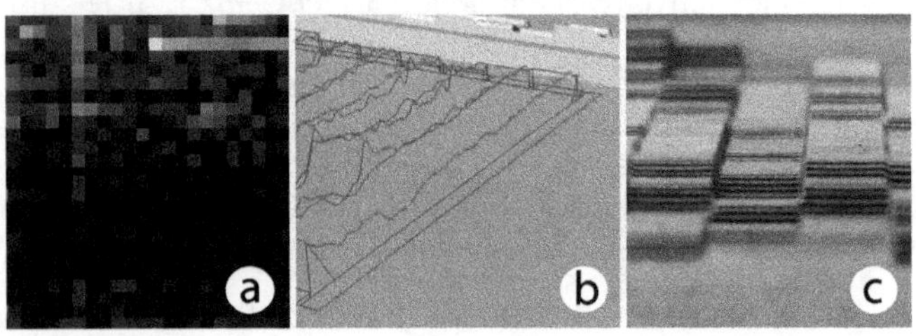

Figure 3. Building a data sculpture. Image courtesy of Moritz Stefaner.

The emoto data sculpture (Figure 3c) shows the emotional response to the London 2012 Olympic games based on Twitter traffic [27]. The visualization began as a heatmap visualization in Tableau (Figure 3a), and then was transformed into 3D shapes using Grasshopper (Figure 3b), a graphical algorithm editor for Rhino 3D. The model was fabricated using a CNC milling machine (Figure 3c).

Emoto is digitally created from start to finish, therefore ensuring a data-accurate physical visualization. However, it involved a sequence of different software tools to transform the original data set into fabrication-ready design files. This hinders iterative design; every early-stage change (e.g., filtering data) requires a manual re-execution of the entire process.

Semi-Automatic Fabrication, Custom Software

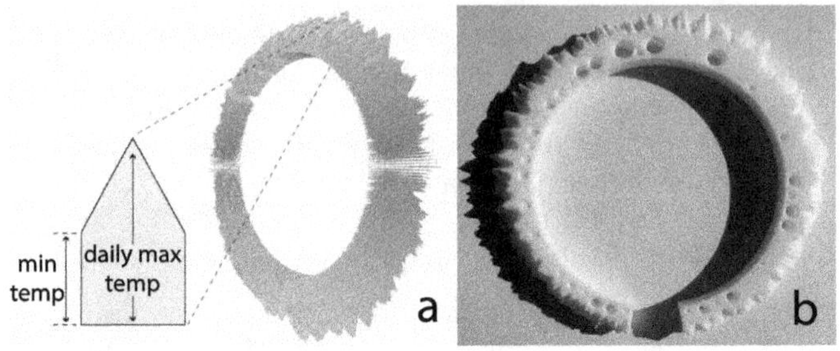

Figure 4. Building a data bracelet. Image courtesy of Mitchell Whitelaw.

Mitchell Whitelaw created a bracelet showing one year of temperature and rain fall data from Canberra (Figure 4b). He first used the Processing programming environment[5] to generate a 2D shape for each day (Figure 4a). His program arranged these shapes radially and connected them to form a continuous 3D object. He then used MeshLab[6] to remove redundant vertices and normalize all faces of his model to make it ready for 3D printing. Whitelaw finally used the 3D modeling software Blender[7] in order to subtract cylinders representing rainfall data (also generated by a Processing program) and to finalize the three-dimensional model (see Figure 4a). The model was exported and sent to the on-line 3D printing service Shapeways[8] (see Figure 4b).

This example shows how creating non-conventional visualizations may require writing custom software. On-screen visualizations also may require writing custom software, although several programming toolkits are available.

With this approach, designers with programming skills are able to precisely control and define the design. However, the 3D models created by Processing are still not immediately suitable for fabrication; converting to fabrication-ready files require additional steps. These steps must be explicitly repeated if the design needs changes or adjustments.

(Nearly) Fully-Automated Fabrication

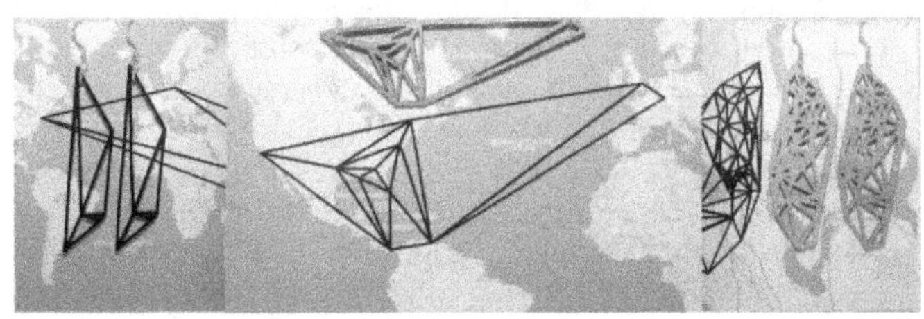

Figure 5. Pendants created with meshu.io. Image courtesy of Meshu.

Meshu.io[9] is a Web service where users create jewelry from their travel data, without any prior knowledge of fabrication. Users either grant the service access to their existing social media data, or manually enter cities. A 2D mesh is built that

[5] `http://processing.org/`
[6] `http://meshlab.sourceforge.net`
[7] `http://www.blender.org`
[8] `http://www.shapeways.com`
[9] `http://meshu.io/`

spans the visited cities as represented on a map. Users then select the material and fabrication technique (3D printing or laser cutting). The object is remotely fabricated and mailed to the user, together with a map that decodes the visualization.

Unlike previous case studies, this approach requires no expertise on visualization or fabrication. Users only need to upload data and fine-tune parameters. On the other hand, they have very little control over the final design. The visualization is very specific, and the service only allows the user to re-orient the object and select the fabrication material. Also, while most of the process is automated (from the user's perspective), it takes several weeks to receive the object.

Summary

These case studies illustrate the need for tools that integrate the entire design workflow of physical visualizations, from data processing to final object fabrication. This integration is important not only for making data-accurate visualizations, but also for supporting fast iteration cycles.

MAKERVIS

In this section we discuss and motivate the features – workflow, visualizations and fabrication technologies– currently supported by MakerVis. We then review its user interface, and discuss its implementation.

Features Supported

MakerVis is an initial proof of concept prototype that offers a deeper understanding of users' needs and technical challenges in building design tools for physical visualizations.

Although MakerVis acknowledges all stages in the workflow, we chose to not focus on the earliest and latest stages of the workflow which address more general information visualization and digital fabrication problems. MakerVis only has a basic support for data transformation (i.e., filtering out data points); more elaborate data processing operations are delegated to specialized tools such as Tableau [28]. Concerning the later stages, the support for final customization (e.g., adding a personalized title to a visualization) is limited and primarily delegated to specialized vector graphics and 3D authoring tools. The use of standard formats (i.e., CSV as input and SVG or STL as output) greatly facilitates this process.

As the number of possible physical visualizations is overwhelming (see [5]), we chose to focus on pragmatic visualizations (such as Figures 2 and 3) instead of more artistic data sculptures (such as in Figures 4 and 5). A large family of such visualizations consist of layered (also called 2.5D [6]) visualizations, or stacked 2D visualizations. These are well-suited for displaying complex temporal datasets. MakerVis supports layered bar charts, layered line charts, layered scatterplots and prism maps.

All of the layered physical visualization designs are modular and rearrangeable: layers can be taken out from the base to be reordered or laid out separately. This makes these visualizations more interactive and allows users to perform a range of infovis tasks by direct physical manipulation [2, 29, 12].

Figure 1a shows a laser-cut physical layered scatterplot displaying fertility and life expectancy of the largest countries in the world across the last 60 years, as famously commented by Hans Rosling[10]. Figure 1b shows a CNC-milled prism map displaying the happiness levels of US states in 2011, extracted from Twitter sentiments[11]. The other physical visualizations from Figure 1 have been crafted by end users and will be discussed in MakerVis Design Session section.

MakerVis has extensive support for laser cutters and basic support for 3D printing and CNC milling (through an STL export function). Laser cutting is one of the most popular fabrication techniques in fab labs, in part due to its speed and efficiency, and its ability to cut a wide range of materials. As a 2D fabrication technique, it can be challenging to create 3D visualizations, but it is well-suited to layered visualizations.

Workflow and User Interface

MakerVis's user interface is shown Figure 6. The workflow involves six steps: 1) loading the data, 2) selecting a type of visualization, 3) mapping the data dimensions to visual variables, 4) setting the visualization's geometry, 5) setting the fabrication machine and parameters, 6) downloading the design file. Breaking down the workflow in different steps helps novices learn the software. However, users are not restricted to these steps and can return to a previous step at any point.

After loading a data file in the CSV format (*step 1*), the user can choose an initial visualization type (*step 2*). The *step 3* involves dragging data dimensions to visualization dimensions in a similar way to Tableau [28]. Bar charts and line charts have three dimensions: *Slices*, *X axis* and *Y axis*, while scatterplots offer *Radius* and *Color* as extra dimensions. In Figure 6, the user loaded data on electricity consumption of 10 countries across 10 years, and chose a layered bar chart where each slice is a country, and each country is an extruded 2D bar chart showing electricity consumption over time.

After all visualization dimensions are mapped, MakerVis immediately shows a 3D preview of the physical visualization, together with the stencils for the laser cutter (the stencils follow the design described by [13]). The 3D preview shows the properties of the selected material, including its thickness, color, and texture. In order to give a better idea of the actual size of the physical visualization, the 3D visualization sits on a 30×30 cm base that users can physically recreate, and the laser stencils are shown in 1:1 scale.

The 3D and laser stencil previews are both interactive. On the laser stencil preview, each tab contains a separate sheet to be laser-cut. The user can reposition individual pieces – which can help save material – and change the material selected for each piece. As the material changes, pieces are moved to a tab that corresponds to a sheet of the new material. All available materials are stored in human-readable files.

Step 4 consists of tuning the visualization's geometry. Geometry parameters include the size and spacing of elements (e.g., bars for layered bar charts) and font sizes. These parameters

[10] `http://tinyurl.com/rosling`

[11] `http://tinyurl.com/geohappiness`

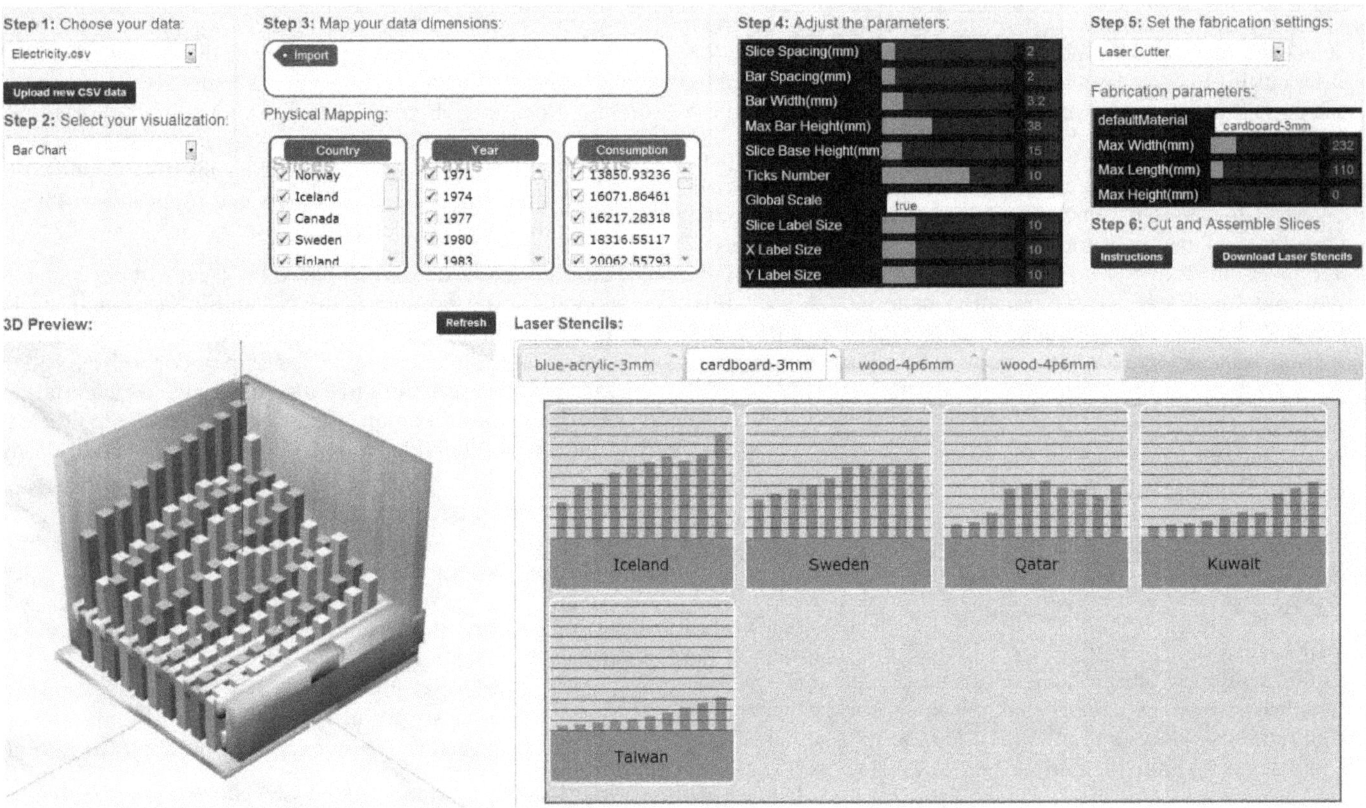

Figure 6. Screenshot of the MakerVis prototype. The control panel is on the top, from Step 1 (left) to Step 6 (right). The previews are shown below.

help adjust design features, aesthetic features and assembly or manufacturing features. Changes in any of these parameters are directly reflected on the two previews.

The user can change fabrication techniques or adjust parameters, such as default material and sheet size for laser cutters (*Step 5*). Once the user is satisfied with the design, she can finally download the design file (e.g., laser stencil, 3D model) and its assembly instructions (*Step 6*). Currently, assembly instructions are general guidelines for assembling laser-cut designs and customizing objects (e.g., using spray paint to change material color). Alternatively, the design file can be customized with separate software (e.g., CorelDraw for laser stencils, SketchUp for 3D models) before fabrication.

Implementation and Extensibility

MakerVis is a web application built on top of NodeJS, D3, JQuery and ThreeJS frameworks. It uses Java as a backend to process SVG boolean operations requests that are currently not supported by Web browsers. Supported input file formats are CSV and topoJSON, used for creating prism maps. Export formats are SVG for laser stencils and STL for 3D printers and CNC mills, both standard file types for fabrication.

Adding New Material

Laser cutter materials are specified in human-readable JSON files. Currently supported parameters are *name*, *thickness*, *color* and *texture*. Texture points to a bitmap file that is rendered in both the 3D preview and the laser stencil preview. Users can therefore easily add new materials; in principle, MakerVis could interface with a local supply chain or a remote fabrication service that sends these JSON files.

Adding New Visualizations

MakerVis can be extended to support new layered visualizations. An abstract layered visualization class holds methods for i) generating the individual 2D visualization layers, ii) adding physical assembly features for laser cutters (e.g., joints), iii) specifying the way layers need to be geometrically assembled, iv) generating the parameter panels, v) generating a 3D model and vi) generating laser stencils.

Most of these methods do not need to be overriden. The default laser stencil generation method uses a layout manager that employs a simple bin packing algorithm to lay out visualization parts on each laser sheet. Parts are distributed across sheets based on their material. The default method for generating 3D models extrudes the parts, assembles them and merges them. The parts are assembled as specified by the assembly logic (step iii), above), which is an array of 3D translations and rotations that are applied to individual parts.

The 2D visualization that appears on each layer needs to be implemented, but D3 can assist in this process. The physical visualization's geometrical parameters also need to be implemented. The parameters are listed separately by way of a JSON file. Once these two steps are completed, users can immediately test their design with MakerVis.

Support for Fabrication Process and Limitations

Our goal is to explore the problem space for tools that support the creation of physical visualizations, and not to implement a exhaustive, fully-fledged tool. We therefore discuss the extent to which MakerVis currently supports fabrication, and suggest directions for future extensions.

As discussed in Background & Related Work, supporting fabrication involves helping users ensure that their design meets specific physical properties. In a parametric design tool such as MakerVis, three strategies can be considered:

S1. Provide *user feedback* through simulation and visualization, a strategy typically used by professional CAD tools,
S2. Ensure that the property is met *by design*, i.e., is satisfied for all possible parameter values,
S3. *Constrain* the ranges of possible parameter values so that the desired property is always met.

We recommend against **S3** because users should not be restricted in their explorations; the importance of a property is ultimately the designer's judgement. For example, balance may not be critical for a hand-held object or a data jewelry. MakerVis employs a mix of **S1** and **S2**. More specifically:

Manufacturability. All visualizations are compatible with 2D and 3D fabrication machines (**S2**). For laser cutting, MakerVis distributes parts across sheets (**S2**) and the preview reveals parts that are larger than sheets (**S1**). Although size constraints are not yet supported for 3D machines, their working areas could also be shown in the preview (**S1**).

Assembly Fit. MakerVis supports assembly fit by design (**S2**). All visualizations except the prism map include a sliding mechanism that lets users take layers apart and rearrange them. For parts that need to be glued, MakerVis uses finger joints whose size and location are automatically computed from the visualization's geometry and material thickness. These assembly features can be easily added to new visualization types. In the future, we envision a tool that supports a range of attachment designs (e.g., press-fits) [8] and lets users further explore the design space of physical interactions with visualizations [2, 12, 29].

Balance & Stability. Our current visualizations are stable by design (**S2**), as their weight is distributed on a flat, solid base. However, visualizations could be added in the future that may not be inherently balanced. In this case, users may benefit from seeing a physics simulation on the 3D preview (**S1**). Visualizations could also be post-processed to ensure balance (**S2**) as proposed by [22], although only carving – not deformation – can be used, since in our case geometry encodes data. Similarly, visualizations with floating parts such as 3D scatterplots could be post-processed into physically plausible objects by automatically adding support material (**S2**).

Strength. Although MakerVis generally produces robust visualizations, users are allowed to make arbitrarily thin features. The 3D preview (**S1**) can help users detect such issues, but solidity can be difficult to predict as it also depends on material. Future tools could assist users by showing a visualization on the 3D preview (**S1**), similar to that provided by Sculpteo.

MAKERVIS DESIGN SESSIONS

We organized design sessions to observe how users would use MakerVis in practice and to collect user feedback. We sent an announcement on two of our lab's mailing lists. To be eligible participants needed to have personal data that they wanted to visualize. Four people replied; we invited three of them to each participate in an afternoon-long design studio. No compensation was offered to participants beyond the final physical visualization, which they could keep.

User Profiles

Our users were one professor and two PhD students from our team who were not involved in this project. While they have both experience and interest in data and infovis, they had little or no training in fabrication. We summarize their demographic profiles and users' self-rated expertises on a 5-point Likert scale in the table below.

User	Dataset	Age	Sex	Infovis Expertise	Fabrication Expertise
1	Baby	35	F	4	2
2	Training	29	M	4	1
3	Projects	29	M	4	1

Procedure

The participant's task was to create a physical visualization, from loading the data to assembling the final object. To ensure the task was feasible given time constraints, we asked users to send us their data files in advance in order to clean and process the data into a suitable CSV file for MakerVis. As our prototype does not support elaborate data transformations, we also pre-computed aggregated datasets for each user. All three users sent time-series data that was compatible with our three layered-visualization designs.

Sessions were held in a research fab lab. We only offered laser cutter fabrication due to the long build times of 3D printers and CNC milling machines (1 hour for the laser cutter vs. about 10-20 hours for 3D printing or CNC milling). The material provided were 2-5 mm sheets of cardboard, plywood, clear acrylic, and four colors of opaque acrylic. The sheets of material were stored in a cabinet, while spray paint in 10 colors was visible on the workbench.

At the beginning of each session, we gave the user a short introduction to the concept of layered 3D visualization. We then asked the user to create a physical visualization using MakerVis. We provided no initial instruction for the tool, as the GUI already includes explicit steps. We provided help only when necessary. We encouraged users to talk aloud and offer verbal comments. After the session, we conducted semi-structured interviews. Interviews were recorded and design sessions were partially videotaped.

Timing

The times spent on each phase were similar across all three users. An entire design session lasted three to four hours. Users spent about one hour exploring MakerVis and converging on a design. They then spent about one hour customizing and decorating the laser stencils in an external vector editing

Figure 7. Photos from the design sessions: a) a user working on a layered bar chart design, b) a user extracting a visualization's structural parts from a laser cutter, c) a user assembling a physical bar chart.

application — suggested by the researcher as soon as the user asked for a decoration feature not provided by MakerVis. The laser cutting took 45 to 90 minutes depending on the material used. The finishing and assembly phase took 15 to 30 minutes depending on whether or not the user wanted to physically customize their visualizations (e.g., apply colors).

First User – Baby Data

The first user supplied us with data that she had collected on her baby daughter's activity during the first months of her life. This time-series data included sleeping hours, breastfeeding hours, and diaper changes across 3 months.

Initially, the user experimented with different visualizations and data mappings. She then focused on a layered bar chart and spent 20 minutes adjusting its geometry. However, she looked at other aggregated datasets in parallel by opening another instance of the tool. While tuning the geometry, she asked for calipers to measure her finger size, so that that slices of the final physical visualization could be easily removed.

The user asked to see materials, despite the textures displayed on the 3D preview. She was not satisfied with the range of colors provided in opaque acrylic (4 colors), so she decided to use clear acrylic and spray paint instead (10 colors).

While graphically editing the laser stencils generated by MakerVis, the user relabeled the time axis by week instead of by date, as the age of young babies is often described in weeks. She also replaced the default font with a more casual font that she downloaded from the Web, and added a title (see final design on Figure 1c – time labels are on the back face).

From the interview, the user seemed to enjoy the experience of making a physical visualization, even though she felt the process was a bit long. When asked if she got any new insights about the data, she reported being surprised about sleeping time not decreasing over time, but then remembered this was accurate. She also pointed at a peak in diaper changes and commented it was "crazy" but a "cool reminder".

When the user was asked how she could improve her physical visualization, she commented that data-specific additions were important, such as week units for babies. When asked whether the final visualization looked like what she had imagined while using MakerVis, she said she "expected it to be a bit smaller", but was "finally happy with the size". Finally, when asked what she would do with the object she replied:

> "I will put it up in the living room and show to people. You can imagine the scenario: you are all sitting in the living room, you have visitors and take pieces out of it and everyone can look at a part of the visualization."

Second User – Training Data

The second user supplied us with his father's self-looged cycling activity data over the course of 8 months, with multiple performance measures per trip such as average heart rate, distance traveled, and average speed.

The user explored all three visualizations in parallel (bar charts, line charts and scatterplots) by opening several instances of MakerVis. He finally chose bar charts then went on to tune the geometry. At this point the user asked to see the actual material. The final result is shown in Figure 1d.

When asked if the final object matched his expectations, the user reported that "the size was too big, but actually I didn't have any idea how it would look". When asked about possible data insights, the user replied he was not too familiar with the data, and built this physical visualization as a gift to his father. When asked if he would use this type of tool again, the user said that he would do so only in a fab lab context because it is important to be able to play with the object physically.

Third User – Project Activities

This user supplied us with time-series data on commits in a versioning repository containing several research projects he was involved in over the first two years of his PhD thesis.

While exploring designs, the user wanted to aggregate his data by week instead of the monthly aggregation that we had prepared. One researcher produced the requested data but when the data was ready, the user had already converged to a design. Since MakerVis cannot save designs, we took a screenshot of the geometry parameters then replicated these settings on the new dataset.

After the design was finalized, the user was disappointed to realize that there was not enough plywood to build his visualization. He then manually rearranged the laser stencils on the preview to fit the available material. Using the vector graphics editor, he also added conference deadlines on the time axis. After the parts were cut, he re-emphasized laser-engraved axis labels and lines by tracing with a pen. The final result is shown in Figure 1e.

When asked about his overall experience of building the visualization the user reported that "it was easy, but for the tweaking you needed an external editor", and that axis customization was important. When asked about missing features, he commented that the 1:1 scale on the laser stencil preview was useful, but a zoom feature would have reduced the need for scrolling. The user also reported under-estimating the size of the final visualization. When asked if he would use a fully-functional version of MakerVis in the future, he replied:

> "I am wondering for which kind of data I will use the tool. For standard data, no; but for personal data, yes. Or to give or show to people, especially if you can customize it, tweak everything, personalize it, really personalize the final visualization. It's for someone, so you want specific stuff."

DISCUSSION

Our user observations suggest that MakerVis helps create physical visualizations and has low entry requirements as a fabrication tool. Our interviews confirm that none of the users would have been willing to spend the necessary time for creating one without the tool. They were all satisfied with the results they obtained and could imagine creating more physical visualizations of personal data in the future. One of our users left stating "I feel like I accomplished something."

The three design sessions also identified shortcomings that were not salient earlier. We identified four major topics that demand further research:

Personalization. One of our users' main interests was personalization. Users want detailed control over all decorative aspects of the visualization they create, as they are already investing effort and resources into the creation of an object. Producing a finely-tuned design is more important than for on-screen visualizations, where users can always save the current state and improve it later on.

MakerVis only provides limited control over scale and axis design. All users therefore chose to use an external graphical editor. We identify two possible problems with this approach:

1. Any modifications done after exporting cannot be brought back into the tool. For example, should the user realize that she made a mistake when filtering her data, she would would have to redo her modifications in the external tool.
2. Such interventions can easily break the design. Separate pieces need to fit together and be correctly aligned, e.g., for scales to make sense.

Future versions of MakerVis should allow users to hand-tune their designs within the tool, especially text-based decorations as used for scales, labels, and titles. MakerVis should also help users ensure that these modifications do not change the data displayed or violate a desired physical property (manufacturability, assembly fit, balance & stability, strength). However, a design tool should also allow to export designs for further customization with external tools. Users would do this, as always when hacking a system, on their own risk since such actions "void the warranty" that all the pieces will fit and the displayed data is correct.

Material. When crafting their physical visualizations, our users were confronted with both the constraints and expressive potential of physical material. MakerVis already allows users to assign different parts to different materials; we noticed that users sometimes used material color to encode categorical data. This suggests that future versions of MakerVis should explicitly support material properties as "visual" variables, such as texture, elasticity, transparence or shininess.

Preview. MakerVis renders approximate textures for available materials. With a wider variety of materials, more realistic rendering is needed. Despite the digital preview, all our users asked to see and to hold actual materials before finishing their design. Optical and haptic properties require elaborate equipment to emulate. Overall, it seems difficult if not impossible to give a preview of the real object. Our users also consistently underestimated the size of the final physical visualization. Therefore, effectively conveying physical scale, perhaps using anchoring [4], seems important.

Reuse. Some of our users were disappointed by MakerVis' inability to save and load designs. Such tools should let users share designs and reuse an existing design with new datasets. However, supporting reuse with very different datasets (either in terms of size or type) may be hard. Data can also change after a physical visualization has been created, making the object obsolete. Ideally, the tool should let users create physical visualizations that can be later updated with new data.

CONCLUSION

Despite the democratization of fabrication technologies, software tools are still needed to help users design and fabricate complex objects. In particular, building physical visualizations is still a laborious process, that requires expertise in both information visualization and digital fabrication.

We explored the possibilities behind a tool that integrates the entire physical visualization design workflow, from data filtering to physical fabrication. Using our prototype, users proficient in data visualization but not fabrication could easily create their own physical visualization. Their main request was for more opportunities for customization to highlight events with personal significance. In the future, a study involving users proficient in digital fabrication but not data visualization will yield a better understanding of user needs.

MakerVis will be released as an open source project to support ongoing research on physical visualizations, by facilitating the implementation of more visualization types and different fabrication and assembly techniques.

ACKNOWLEDGEMENTS

We thank our participants and reviewers for their helpful and useful comments. This work was partially supported by SENG Overseas Research Awards, HKUST.

REFERENCES

1. Anderson, M. Embodied cognition: A field guide. *Artificial Intelligence 149*, 1 (2003), 91–130.
2. Bertin, J. Graphique et mathématique : généralisation du traitement graphique de l'information. *Annales. Économies, Sociétés, Civilisations.*, 1 (1969), 70–101.
3. Card, S. K., Mackinlay, J. D., and Shneiderman, B. *Readings in Information Visualization: Using Vision to Think*. Morgan Kaufmann, Jan. 1999.
4. Chevalier, F., Vuillemot, R., and Gali, G. Using concrete scales: A practical framework for effective visual depiction of complex measures. *Visualization and Computer Graphics, IEEE Transactions on 19*, 12 (2013), 2426–2435.
5. Dragicevic, P., and Jansen, Y. List of physical visualizations. tinyurl.com/physvis, 2013. [Online; accessed 04-Sep-2013].
6. Dwyer, T. *Two-and-a-half-dimensional Visualisation of Relational Networks*. PhD thesis, School of Information Technologies, Faculty of Science, University of Sydney, 2005.
7. Gaines, B. R. Modeling and forecasting the information sciences. *Information Sciences 57* (1991), 3–22.
8. Genc, S., Messler Jr, R. W., and Gabriele, G. A. A systematic approach to integral snap-fit attachment design. *Research in Engineering Design 10*, 2 (1998), 84–93.
9. Gwilt, I., Yoxall, A., and Sano, K. Enhancing the understanding of statistical data through the creation of physical objects. In *Proc. ICDC2012* (2012), 117–126.
10. Heer, J., Card, S. K., and Landay, J. Prefuse: A toolkit for interactive information visualization. In *ACM Human Factors in Computing Systems (CHI)* (2005), 421–430.
11. Hildebrand, K., Bickel, B., and Alexa, M. crdbrd: Shape fabrication by sliding planar slices. *Comp. Graph. Forum 31*, 2pt3 (May 2012), 583–592.
12. Jansen, Y., and Dragicevic, P. An interaction model for visualizations beyond the desktop. *IEEE TVCG* (Nov. 2013). To appear.
13. Jansen, Y., Dragicevic, P., and Fekete, J.-D. Evaluating the efficiency of physical visualizations. In *Proc. of CHI 2013*, ACM (2013), 2593–2602.
14. Jean-Daniel Fekete. The InfoVis Toolkit. In *Proc. InfoVis 2004*, IEEE Press (October 2004), 167–174.
15. Kosara, R. Visualization criticism-the missing link between information visualization and art. In *Proc. of Information Visualization, IV'07*, IEEE (2007), 631–636.
16. Lau, M., Ohgawara, A., Mitani, J., and Igarashi, T. Converting 3d furniture models to fabricatable parts and connectors. In *Proc. of ACM SIGGRAPH 2011*, SIGGRAPH '11, ACM (2011), 85:1–85:6.
17. Lee, B., Isenberg, P., Riche, N., Carpendale, S., et al. Beyond mouse and keyboard: Expanding design considerations for information visualization interactions. *IEEE TVCG 18*, 12 (2012).
18. Luo, L., Baran, I., Rusinkiewicz, S., and Matusik, W. Chopper: partitioning models into 3d-printable parts. *ACM Trans. Graph. 31*, 6 (Nov. 2012), 129:1–129:9.
19. Moere, A. Beyond the tyranny of the pixel: Exploring the physicality of information visualization. In *Proc. IV'08*, IEEE (2008), 469–474.
20. Mueller, S., Lopes, P., and Baudisch, P. Interactive construction: interactive fabrication of functional mechanical devices. In *Proc. of UIST 2012*, ACM (2012), 599–606.
21. Pousman, Z., Stasko, J., and Mateas, M. Casual information visualization: Depictions of data in everyday life. *IEEE TVCG 13*, 6 (2007).
22. Prévost, R., Whiting, E., Lefebvre, S., and Sorkine-Hornung, O. Make it stand: balancing shapes for 3d fabrication. *ACM Transactions on Graphics (TOG) 32*, 4 (2013), 81.
23. Saul, G., Lau, M., Mitani, J., and Igarashi, T. Sketchchair: an all-in-one chair design system for end users. In *Proc. TEI 2011*, ACM (2011), 73–80.
24. Savage, V., Zhang, X., and Hartmann, B. Midas: fabricating custom capacitive touch sensors to prototype interactive objects. In *Proc. of UIST 2012*, ACM (2012), 579–588.
25. Schmandt-Besserat, D. *How writing came about*. University of Texas Press, 1996.
26. Shah, J. J. *Parametric and feature-based CAD/CAM: concepts, techniques, and applications*. Wiley. com, 1995.
27. Stefaner, M., Hemment, D., and Studio NAND. Emoto. tinyurl.com/emotovis, 2012. [accessed 2013-03-30].
28. Stolte, C., and Hanrahan, P. Polaris: A system for query, analysis and visualization of multi-dimensional relational databases. *IEEE TVCG 8* (2002), 52–65.
29. Stusak, S., Tabard, A., and Butz, A. Can physical visualizations support analytical tasks? Vis '2013 (poster) (Nov. 2013). In press.
30. Tanenbaum, J. G., Williams, A. M., Desjardins, A., and Tanenbaum, K. Democratizing technology: pleasure, utility and expressiveness in DIY and maker practice. In *Proc. CHI 2013*, ACM (2013), 2603–2612.
31. Victor, B. Drawing dynamic visualizations. vimeo.com/66085662, 2013. [Online; accessed 18-Sep-2013].
32. Viegas, F. B., Wattenberg, M., van Ham, F., Kriss, J., and McKeon, M. Manyeyes: a site for visualization at internet scale. *IEEE TVCG 13*, 6 (Nov. 2007), 1121–1128.

MixFab: A Mixed-Reality Environment for Personal Fabrication

Christian Weichel[1] Manfred Lau[1] David Kim[2] Nicolas Villar[2] Hans Gellersen[1]

[1]Lancaster University
Lancaster, United Kingdom
{c.weichel, m.lau, h.gellersen}@lancaster.ac.uk

[2]Microsoft Research
Cambridge, United Kingdom
{b-davidk, nvillar}@microsoft.com

ABSTRACT

Personal fabrication machines, such as 3D printers and laser cutters, are becoming increasingly ubiquitous. However, designing objects for fabrication still requires 3D modeling skills, thereby rendering such technologies inaccessible to a wide user-group. In this paper, we introduce *MixFab*, a mixed-reality environment for personal fabrication that lowers the barrier for users to engage in personal fabrication. Users design objects in an immersive augmented reality environment, interact with virtual objects in a direct gestural manner and can introduce existing physical objects effortlessly into their designs. We describe the design and implementation of *MixFab*, a user-defined gesture study that informed this design, show artifacts designed with the system and describe a user study evaluating the system's prototype.

Author Keywords

personal fabrication; direct manipulation; 3D printing; mixed-reality; 3D modeling

ACM Classification Keywords

H.5.2. Information Interfaces and Presentation: User Interfaces - Interaction styles

General Terms

Design; Human Factors

INTRODUCTION

Personal fabrication of 3D objects has been spurred by rapid advances in printing tools and techniques. The quality, speed, capability and ease of use of 3D printers is rapidly increasing while cost is going down, enabling wider audiences as "makers" of physical objects. The outcome of the process is distinguished by the immediate presence it has in the real world - physical, tangible, and usable in a real world sense. The front-end of the process is in stark contrast; the tools that help users design things they would like to make still reside on flat computer screens.

In this paper, we introduce a new system, MixFab, to support design for personal fabrication with a mixed reality approach.

CHI 2014, April 26 – May 1, 2014, Toronto, Ontario, Canada.

http://dx.doi.org/10.1145/2556288.2557090

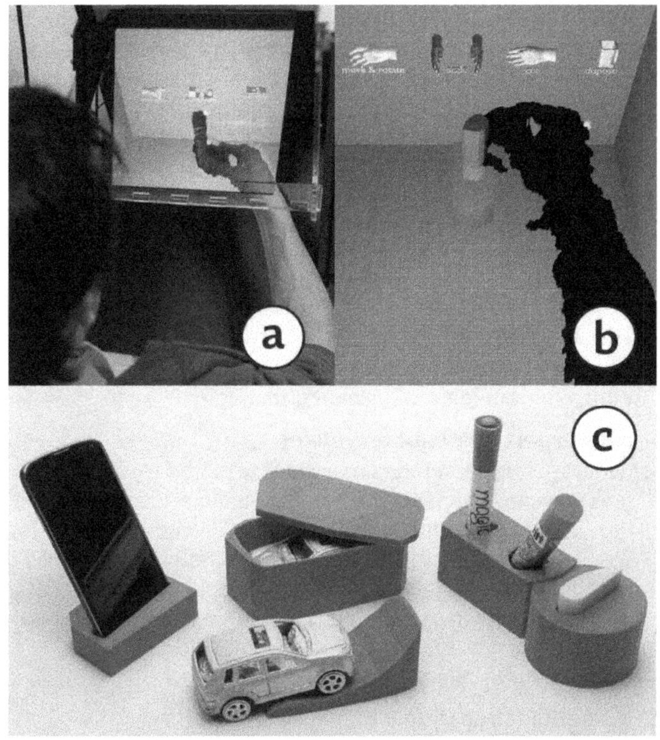

Figure 1. MixFab: mixed-reality environment for personal fabrication. (a) a user positioning a physical object in the MixFab prototype system, (b) screenshot of a user manipulating a virtual object, (c) 3D printed objects created with the system.

The system is aimed to lower the barrier for casual design of 3D content, and to enable a design experience where the digital model of an artifact-to-be-made is created in a physical work space that affords direct manipulation and interaction with artifacts that are real. To this end, the system integrates three core concepts: (1) use of immersive augmented reality to provide a 3D visualization of the artifact under construction projected in the real world; (2) support for users to shape artifacts directly with their hands, replacing the need for advanced modeling skills with intuitive gestures; (3) enabling use of real artifacts in the design process such that new artifacts can be shaped to fit existing ones.

MixFab's mixed-reality environment is by virtue of a Holodesk-like structure [11] where the user sees virtual content merged with the real world. Users can introduce physical artifacts as size-reference or to capture their shape – Figure 1a shows a user placing a glue-stick inside a virtual object to create the glue-stick's virtual replica in place. In Figure 1b the just created glue-stick replica (green object) is manipulated as if it was still a physical entity; by virtue of gesture recognition, users can directly manipulate virtual and physical objects alike. Hands and other physical artifacts properly occlude other objects and face-tracking provides a parallax-corrected image, creating important depth-cues.

We make four contributions in this paper. First we propose and implement an immersive mixed-reality environment by combining an augmented reality setup, gesture recognition and 3D scanning capabilities. Our second contribution is a set of user-defined gestures for 3D modeling obtained through a study in which we observe how users would perform basic tasks unconstrained by any system or augmentation. We then present MixFab's design environment, which is based on these gestures. It is centered around direct and natural interaction with virtual artifacts, effortless integration of physical objects into the design process and a self-explanatory interface. Fourth, we perform a user study evaluating the design decisions of MixFab and providing evidence that especially the effortless integration of existing objects is of value.

RELATED WORK

MixFab is related to personal fabrication, mixed-reality modeling environments and gestural interaction.

Non-expert fabrication systems

Several semi-commercial products seek to enable non-engineers to design objects for personal fabrication machines, typically by providing a feature-reduced version of traditional CAD systems [1, 2]. Others reduce the complexity of the modeling task by specializing on a specific purpose. For example, SketchChair [23] lets users draw chairs and produces the patterns required to fabricate them, while Plushie [18] follows a similar idea for stuffed toys.

Personal fabrication with existing objects

Using existing objects in the design process has been explored in a variety of ways. Follmer et al. focus on mixing objects to create new ones. KidCAD [10] lets children combine the 2.5D shape of their toys, while CopyCAD [9] enables the reuse of 2D shapes in a CNC milling setting.

Constructable [19] extends the 2D contour reuse by copying textures to workpieces. A camera takes a photo of the texture and transfers it on the part using a laser-cutter. Enclosed [27] uses electronic components as handles and size references during enclosure design. It automatically adds cutouts to the enclosure patterns so that the components can be mounted.

MixFab lets users remix existing objects, use them to construct new shapes and as a physical size reference, combining the features above in one system.

Mixed-reality modeling environments

Anderson et al. use tangible proxies to create and shape virtual objects [3]. Tangible building blocks that can sense their spatial configuration are used to create the models; a 3D scanner for scanning clay figures is also proposed. The clay based modeling is extended by Sheng et al. [25] who use clay for direct, fine-grained manipulation. Arisandi et al. introduce tangible tools such as a hammer or a knife, for modeling in an augmented reality (AR) environment [4]. MirageTable is a general-purpose mixed-reality environment targeting collaborative scenarios, that supports physics based interaction with existing physical objects [5].

Designing fabricable objects in an AR setting has been explored. Modeling-in-Context uses a single photo as reference for size, perspective and ratio [16]. Situated Modeling takes this a step further by stamping primitives into an augmented 3D space, designing artifacts in their designated place [15].

MixFab provides a mixed-reality environment, in which users can interact naturally without the need to wear props [4, 15] or being constrained by physicality [25].

Gesture-based systems

Shape creation has been transported into virtual space in a variety of ways. Some let users deform models using both hands [20, 17]; others use the motion of the hand [24] or its curvature [12] to define the shape.

Gestures for 3D manipulation and navigation can be distinguished between symbolic and natural gestures. FingARtips [7] introduces finger-based augmented reality interaction with haptic feedback. The Perceptive Workbench uses pointing in combination with 3D objects [26]. Kim et al. propose a set of symbolic gestures for 3D modeling [14] by studying the interaction with real world objects. Data Miming follows a natural gesture approach, in that they do not prescribe a set of gestures but record users unconstrained hand movement [12].

Whereas related work often has author-defined gestures, we inform our gesture-set by a user defined gesture study [29].

Hand pose recognition

Hand pose recovery often relies on user augmentation. Surface Drawing utilizes gloves [24], others use reflective markers [14]. Oka et al. [21] require only a camera in the environment and no user augmentation. For an overview of hand pose recognition techniques, see [22]. We implemented an appearance based approach using a single depth-camera, requiring no user-worn equipment or prior calibration.

MIXFAB

At MixFab's core is an immersive mixed-reality system creating a high permeability between the virtual and physical world. It enables new and exciting interactions that were not possible with each component taken by itself.

We implemented MixFab's physical configuration by building upon the Holodesk frame [11], although other hardware implementations may also be used. The setup superimposes virtual content with the real world by using a beam-splitter and a display mounted at a 45 degree angle. It provides an interaction volume roughly the size of modern 3D printers. A depth camera placed at the top of the frame provides data for interaction within the system. We further add a motorized turntable, to the bottom of the frame, for 3D scanning.

Our processing pipeline is designed to specifically support seamless interaction between virtual and physical objects, blurring the border between the two. The main components of this pipeline are:

Gesture Recognition which is solely based on the depth-data provided by the Kinect serves as input modality for the interaction with virtual objects. It does not require any user-augmentation or prior calibration.

3D Shape Acquisition is supported at a trade-off between time and precision. One can capture the rough shape of an object in real-time or acquire a more precise scan in about a minute. Physical objects can be captured anywhere in the frame, allowing their placement relative to virtual objects.

Sketch Recognition enables users to describe objects they want to create without having to be very precise.

Mesh data manipulation serves as back-end for object creation, acquisition and manipulation. We support complex operations (e.g. constrained Delaunay triangulation or plane segmentation) required for object acquisition, and *constructive-solid geometry* operations for shape manipulation which produce 3D printable models.

USER STUDY: USER-DEFINED 3D MODELING GESTURES

In previous work, hand gestures are typically defined by the respective authors, rather than users [14, 20]. We are interested in what gestures users would intuitively perform to create and manipulate objects, also to inform our subsequent system design. To this end we conduct a user-defined gesture study with a methodology similar to Wobbrock et al. [29].

Tasks and Procedure

Each participant was subsequently given a set of tasks (order determined using a balanced latin square). For each task, they were shown one or two images of the desired outcome and asked to perform a gesture to create that desired outcome. Participants were instructed to imagine the objects depicted on the images as being displayed in front of them.

After each gesture, users were asked to rate the gestures suitability and how easy it was to perform, both on a rating scale from 1 (very unsuitable / very hard) to 5 (very suitable / very easy) . Once all ten tasks were completed, all users completed a survey querying their age and gender. We further asked for prior CAD experience and how much that experience influenced the proposed gestures (Rating scale, 1 no experience / no influence to 5 a lot of experience / strong influence). Users were seated at a table with a camera placed a meter above the surface, resulting in an interaction area of about 60 × 50 cm.

Upon completion of the study, the recorded video material was transcribed and coded to extract the suggested gestures. Quantitative data collected through the questionnaires, as well as user agreement [29] is used to judge the quality and confidence of users in the proposed gestures.

We invited twelve participants from various departments at our university. Half of the participants were female with age ranging from 19 to 42 (M=30.83 years, SD=7.47). Eight users reported no experience with CAD (overall M=2.08, SD=1.31) and thus little influence of prior experience (M=2, SD=1.53).

Results and Observations

All participants were able to propose a gesture for every task, sometimes more than one in which case they were asked to report the one they preferred. In the following we report gestures that were proposed by at least two or more participants.

	Task / Gesture	c	s	e / A
Create Primitives	**create box**			0.42
	draw outline	7	3.86	4.57
	hand boundaries	3	4.00	5.00
	create cylinder			0.37
	hand boundaries	6	4.33	4.83
	draw outline	4	4.00	4.00
Rotating and Translating	**move box**			0.33
	1h grab & move	4	5.00	5.00
	2h grab & move	4	4.50	5.00
	1h push	4	5.00	5.00
	rotate box			0.40
	1h grab & rotate	7	4.57	4.86
	2h grab & rotate	2	5.00	3.50
	2h rotation	2	4.50	5.00
Scale	**scale 1 axis**			0.71
	compression	10	4.80	5.00
	scale 3 axis			0.26
	compression	5	3.80	4.80
	corner pinch & resize	3	3.67	4.00
Plane Cut	**plane cut**			0.35
	karate	5	4.00	4.20
	knife	4	2.25	4.25
	points	3	4.33	4.33
Scan	**object scan**			0.17
	dwell time	4	3.50	4.50
Add Material	**add material**			0.31
	stuff	4	4.00	4.50
	gap trace	4	3.50	4.50
	filling tool	2	2.50	3.00
Remove	**remove object**			0.22
	wipe	4	5.00	5.00
	move out	3	4.33	5.00
	smash	2	4.50	4.50

Table 1. List of tasks and corresponding gestures (described by more than one user) during the study. c is the count of how many users suggested the gesture, s is the reported suitability and e is the reported easiness. A the agreement among the users as defined by Wobbrock. Gestures recommended for each task group are written in italic.

Creating primitives

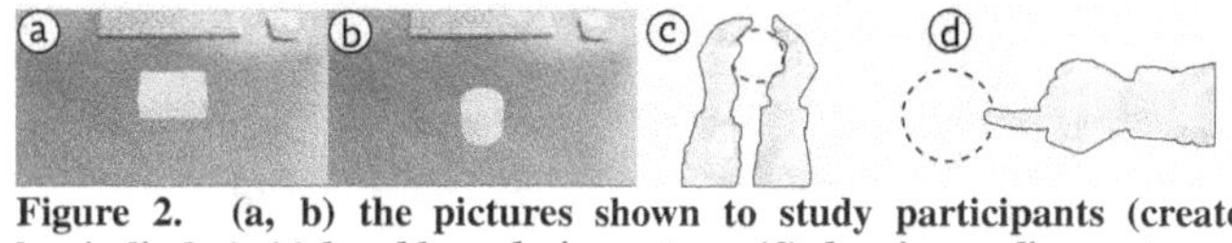

Figure 2. (a, b) the pictures shown to study participants (create box/cylinder), (c) *hand boundaries* gesture, (d) *drawing outline* gesture

While creating primitives has no equivalent in the physical world, describing 3D shapes is a common task. When creating boxes, three users choose a method similar to *Data Miming* [12] and define the shape by describing it using their hands (hand boundaries gesture). In case of the cylinder, a majority preferred to describe the shape using the curvature of their hands. Drawing the outline of the shape with the index finger and extruding it into 3D space was proposed by a majority when creating boxes, and by a third of the participants suggested it for cylinders.

Rotating and translating

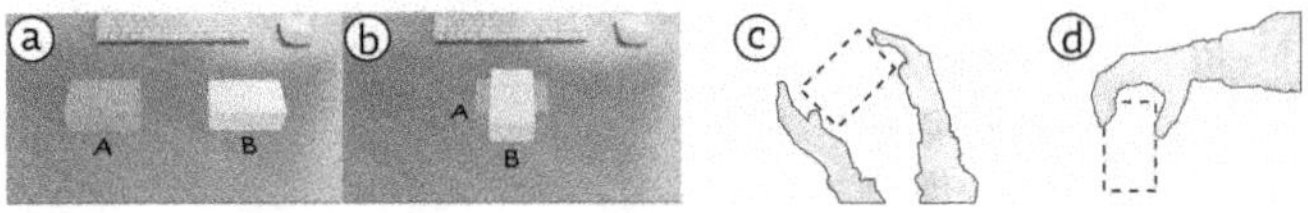

Figure 3. (a, b) the pictures shown to study participants (Rotate/move box from A to B), (c) *two-handed grab and rotate* gesture, (d) *one-handed grab* gesture

Rotating and moving objects are everyday tasks performed using two variants of the same gestures: one-handed vs. two-handed. The pictures shown to the participants contained a keyboard and a mouse next to the virtual object, as a size reference. It seems that the size of virtual object was interpreted differently by each participant, leading to the use of one hand if the object is perceived to be small or both hands if the object is perceived to be large.

Scaling

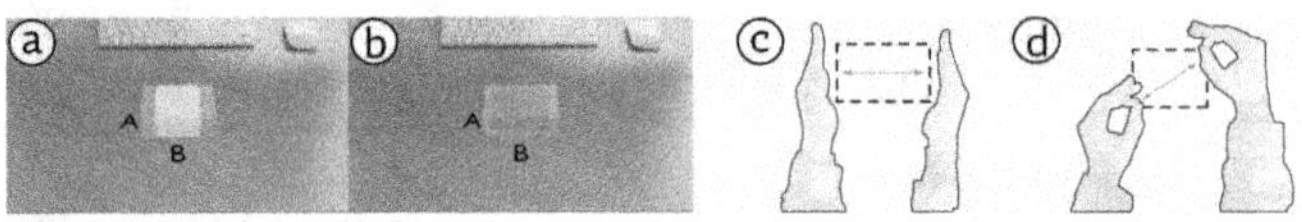

Figure 4. (a, b) the pictures shown to study participants (scale 1DOF/3DOF from A to B), (c) *compression* gesture, (d) *corner pinch & resize* gesture

Ten out of twelve users suggested the same gesture: compression. Both hands are placed around the object and changing their distance, changes the objects size.

Plane cut

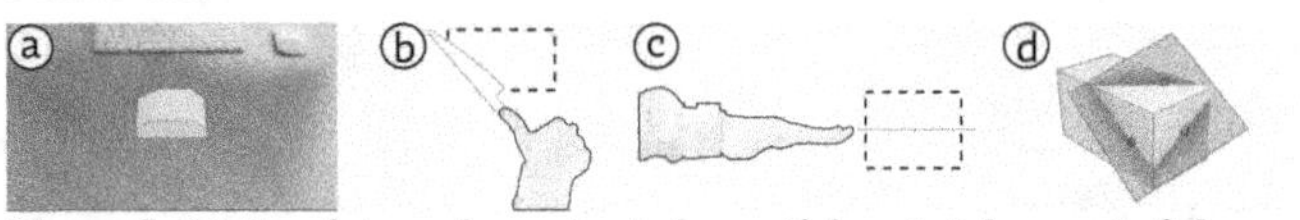

Figure 5. (a) the picture shown to study participants (plane cut of shapes from box), (b) *knife* gesture, (c) *Karate* gesture, (d) three *points* defining a plane

Cutting a slice of an object is a daily task (e.g. cutting a slice of bread or cheese). Users without CAD experience proposed gestures resembling such actions. Four users moved their flat hand or thumb where they wanted to cut, miming a knife. Five users indicated how they wanted to cut by performing a "Shuto" (Knife Hand) motion from Karate. Those experienced in CAD, suggested that one might select three points on the object to define a plane used for cutting.

Adding material

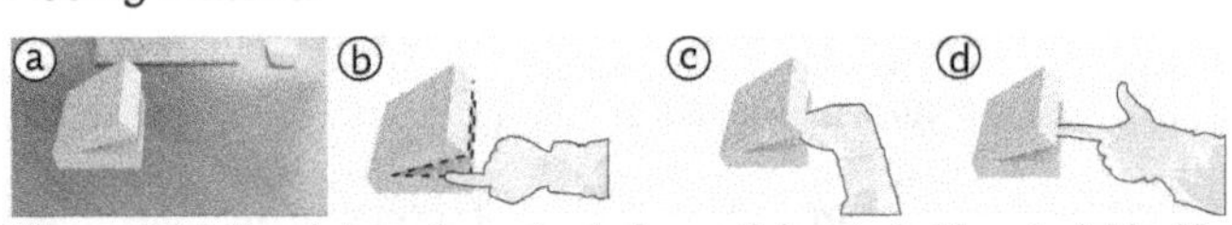

Figure 6. (a) the picture shown to study participants (add material inside gap), (b) *gap trace* gesture, (c) *stuff(ing)* gesture, (d) *filling tool* gesture

Most users suggested a "stuffing motion" as if they were to take a handful of material and put it onto the object. Others traced the gap they wanted closed with the index finger and confirmed again using a stuffing gesture or by pressing a button. We believe that the "gap-trace" gesture is an artifact of the picture that demonstrated the task: the gap to close was of regular and linear nature. Suggestions would most likely be different when manipulating more organic shapes.

Scanning objects

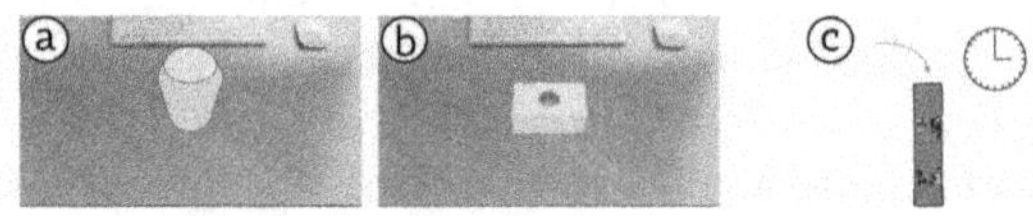

Figure 7. (a, b) the picture shown to study participants (positive scan of existing cup, negative imprint of cup in box), (c) the *dwell time* action

Transforming physical objects to virtual ones proved to be the most challenging task; to some extent because it is difficult to convey the need of the operation without a system being present. Participants proposed a variety of actions (agreement score: 0.17), but only one was mentioned multiple times: dwell time. Users place the object in the desired position, move their hands away and wait for a certain amount of time.

Removing objects

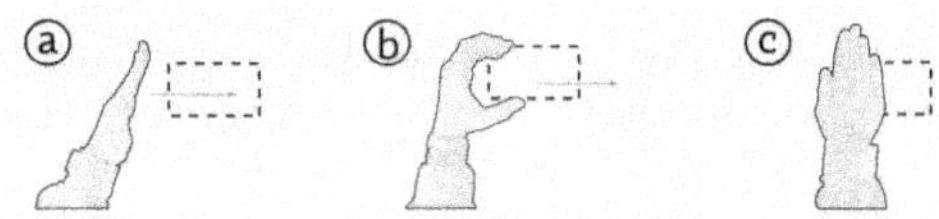

Figure 8. (a) *wipe* gesture, (b) *move out* gesture, (c) *smash* gesture

Removing objects is a daily task. We often throw things away, place them elsewhere or deform them prior to disposal. The gestures suggested for removing objects tend to resemble such actions. *Wipe* and *move out* – the two most prominent gestures – have the same intent: move the object out of the workspace. Wiping objects (moving a hand fast from one side to the other, hitting the object) was suggested more than *move out* and rated easier/more suitable.

Discussion

We observe a similar pattern as Wobbrock *et al.* in that user agreement is inversely proportional to the task complexity [29]. More complex tasks (such as object scan) have low user agreement scores, whereas more simple ones (such as rotation or translation) yield higher agreement amongst users. Despite low agreement rates, suitability and easiness remain at high levels, suggesting confidence in the proposed gestures.

To choose an appropriate gestures for each task group, we use the count of how often a gesture was suggested as main metric. In cases where the suggestion count is not distinctive, we decide based on suitability and easiness rating. The gestures recommended for each task are marked in italic in table 1.

For most task groups suggestion count, easiness and suitability are sufficient criteria, except for the creation of primitives. When looking at box and cylinder creation separately, we'd be required to choose different gestures for each of them which is undesirable as it would be likely to cause confusion with users. Adding the suggestion counts within the task group however, yields a slight preference for the *draw outline* gesture (11 suggestions vs. 9 for *hand boundaries*).

USER INTERFACE

MixFab's user interface is centered around the gestural creation, modification and assembly of objects. The user mainly interacts with "gestural icons" and the virtual objects being created and assembled (Figure 9).

Gestural icons depict a certain hand pose, showing the user what gesture to perform to trigger a certain action or change a certain property. All hand icons translate to gestural input (e.g. draw outline), and all non-hand icons translate to automation (e.g. scan object). To perform an action, the user first selects the appropriate icon and then either performs the gesture (e.g. scales the object) or waits for the system to complete its task. The icons are context-sensitive, hence inform the user about the possible operations of the system.

Virtual objects displayed in MixFab can have three different states. Inert objects that and cannot be modified without selecting a gestural icon, is colored in a slightly transparent gray (inert state). Once an object becomes modifiable using a gesture, it turns yellow (inactive state). Objects that are currently being modified, are colored green (active state). This color-coding provides feedback about the current system state, especially the grasping of objects. It allows users to determine whether the system recognizes them as engaged in a gesture and what influence their movement will have on the scene.

Creating objects

There are four ways users can create objects: drawing an outline, having the system capture the outline of a physical artifact, 3D scan an existing object or load an existing 3D model.

Draw outline

Users can draw the outline of primitive shapes on the floor of MixFab, using only their index finger. The system then recognizes the sketch as either a circle or rectangle and extrudes it to 3D space. The height of the object is set by the height of the hand above the systems ground. Once the height is as desired, the other hand taps the floor to fix the height.

Capture outline

Capturing the 2D outline and extruding it to 3D space is a simple but fast method to capture an object's shape. Users can place existing objects anywhere in the frame and after a fixed dwell time, the system captures the outline and automatically extrudes it to the existing object's height. Users can manipulate the object's height, by indicating the height with one hand and confirming it with the other.

3D scan

The MixFab frame has a turntable built in which serves to rotate objects so that objects of more complex shapes can be scanned. To scan an object, the user selects the "scan object" icon, and places the physical object together with the scanning rig on the turntable (Figure 11). The system then waits until all hands are out of the frame before it starts rotating the object to capture it from all sides. Once scanning is complete, the virtual object appears where the existing one was placed.

Load model

CAD drawn models can incorporate functional aspects or higher-resolution details than what the built-in 3D scanner is able to capture. When the user selects the "load model" icon, a grid of scaled-down models is provided from which the user can select the desired model (by selecting icons). The new object is then placed in the center of the frame.

Manipulating objects

Once an object has been created, it can be manipulated in three ways: translation & rotation, scaling and cutting off parts of the object.

Translation & Rotation

Translation and rotation is performed using a one-handed grabbing gesture, much like one would grab a cup. If the object is grabbed so that the hand intersects the object, it attaches to the user's hand so that the object can be moved freely within the interaction volume. Grabbing any point away from the object lets users change the object's orientation. A lever is formed between the base of the object and the hand-tip, which is then used to rotate the object. Translation and rotation both snap to common values (e.g. the floor for translation and 0/90 degrees for rotation).

Scaling

Objects can be uniformly scaled using a two-handed compression gesture. Users place their hands on either side and the scaling factor is a function of their distance. We implemented relative, yet direct scaling using a fixed control-display gain. When users first assume the compression posture, their hand distance is identified as 100% scale. Changing the distance between both hands then scales the object.

Cutting

Cutting objects removes material, rather than splitting objects. To perform a cut, the user indicates the desired position of the cut using their flat hand ("Shuto"/Karate gesture) along the X-axis. Tapping on the ground with the other hand confirms the cut. If the user indicates the cutting position with the right hand, the right side of the cutting plane is discarded; indicating with the left hand removes the left side.

Assembling objects

Object assembly combines two objects, either by adding them together or by subtracting one from the other. Fusing two objects can be used to add material or refine the shape of an object. Subtracting one object from the other is commonly used to create holes or cavities to hold other objects.

There is no specific gesture for assembly. Object assembly is simply a matter of selecting the way the two objects are to be combined. Union or difference of meshes are symbolized with a plus or a minus sign respectively (Figure 9).

WALKTHROUGH: CONSTRUCTING A DESK ORGANIZER

We illustrate the systems use by constructing a desk organizer (Figure 9h) that will hold a pen and a glue-stick.

We start with creating the base shape by drawing a circular outline (Figure 9a). The system recognizes the drawing as a circle, beautifies it and offers the outline for extrusion. We set the height using one hand; the height snaps to 5mm increments and is displayed just above the object. To confirm the height, we tap with the other hand (Figure 9b).

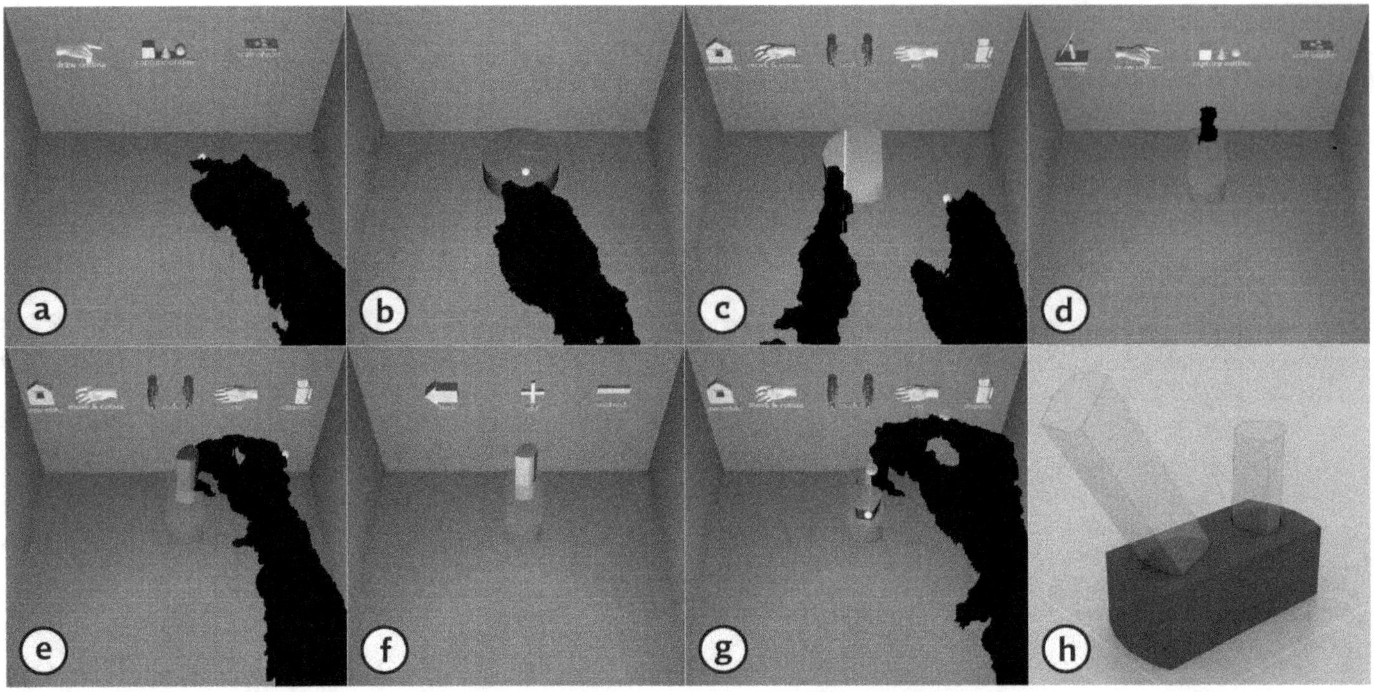

Figure 9. MixFab's user interface: (a) a user drawing an object's outline, (b) setting the height of the cylinder, (c) plane cuts of the cylinder, (d) capturing the shape of a physical object (glue-stick) positioned in the virtual one, (e) moving an object (glue-stick) upwards by grabbing it with one hands, (f) object assembly (difference of glue-stick with existing virtual shape), (g) rotating an object (pen), (h) the desktop organizer (blue)

To create the semi-rectangular shape of the organizer, we cut off both sides. First we cut off the right side of the object by indicating the cut position with the right hand and confirming with the left. To cut the left side, we repeat the procedure, this time holding the left hand where we want to cut and confirming with the right one (Figure 9c).

Next, we create the first hole which will hold the glue-stick. We position the real glue-stick where we want the hole to be within the virtual object. Once in position, we select "capture outline" and move our hands out of the frame (Figure 9d). The system then captures the outline of the glue-stick and extrudes its height. Confirming that initial height with the left hand, turns it into a virtual glue-stick replica.

As the glue-stick was standing on the ground of the frame, the virtual glue-stick replica is on the ground as well. If we were to assemble the object as it is, we would create a hole through the whole shape. To have some material at the bottom of the hole, we grab the virtual glue-stick, move it a few millimeters up and release it to fix it in that position (Figure 9e).

Eventually we assemble the virtual glue-stick and the previously created base to create the hole for the stick. After selecting assembly, we are asked to choose the method of assembly (Figure 9f). Choosing subtract removes material where the glue-stick was, leaving a hole of correct size and position.

Lastly we repeat the steps above for the pen, placing it in its desired position, capturing its outline, extruding it and moving it up a few millimeters. To make the pen easier to access, we tilt it forward by grabbing at a point in space, forming a lever with which the object is re-oriented (Figure 9g). Once in correct position and orientation, we assemble the virtual pen replica resulting in the final desktop organizer (Figure 9h).

SYSTEM IMPLEMENTATION

We built a prototype to implement the MixFab system by using *Holodesk's* hardware frame [11]. Holodesk provides an immersive environment with an interaction volume roughly the size of modern 3D printers. Our hardware differs in that we use a Kinect for Windows rather than a Kinect360 and mirror setup, and have a turntable built into the frame for 3D scanning. Most importantly, on the software side, we employ a different processing pipeline and provide a gesture-based interface rather than a physics-based one.

System Hardware

The hardware consists of a display mounted at a 45 degree angle, being reflected through a 50/50 half-mirror into the interaction space. A Microsoft Kinect depth sensor mounted at the top of the frame is used for capturing the interaction with the system, while a second camera placed between the display and half-mirror is used to implement perspective correction through face tracking. A motorized turntable for 3D scanning is built into the floor of the frame (Figure 10).

Calibration

Two cameras need to be calibrated once (not per user): the facetracker and the Kinect. The facetracking camera is calibrated to a plane perpendicular to the half-mirror (Figure 10f). As the dimensions of the frame are known, the exact position and orientation of the facetracking camera (and thus faces tracked) can be mapped to real-world coordinates. The

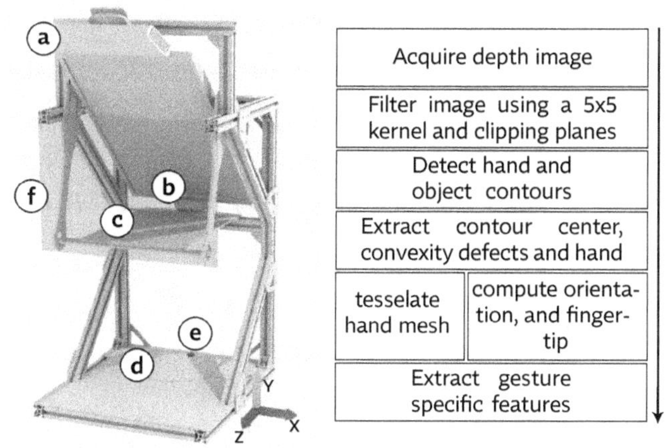

Figure 10. [left] The MixFab hardware (a) Microsoft Kinect depth sensor, (b) webcam used for face tracking, (c) 50T/50R half-mirror, (d) motorized turntable, (e) common world origin (virtual), (f) face-tracker calibration plane (virtual). [right] MixFab 's general processing pipeline

Kinect is calibrated using its RGB camera by placing a laser-cut calibration pattern at a fixed location on the bottom of the frame. Using an approximation of the depth-to-RGB transformation, we can map depth data to the real world coordinate system with respect to a common origin (Figure 10e).

General Processing and Gesture Recognition

MixFab follows an appearance based approach to hand posture and gesture recognition that requires no prior calibration or user augmentation. Depth data from the Kinect is processed to extract a set of features which is later used by specialized gesture recognizers. We rely solely on the depth image, as the half-mirror occludes the hands in the color image.

The general processing pipeline is as follows: first we acquire a depth frame from the Kinect, filter it using a 5x5 kernel, remove points using previously defined clipping planes and tessellate the remaining points to provide an occlusion mesh; all of which is implemented in OpenCL. Then we find all connected components touching the image border, with an area greater than A_{hand}. For each such contour, we compute its center, orientation via the Hu moments and finger-tip which is the convexity defect farthest along the principal axis.

Touching the floor

To implement touch input on the floor of the frame, we threshold the Y component of the finger-tip [28]. As the floor surface is flat and we map the Kinect depth-data to real-world coordinates with an origin in the floor plane, we set $d_{surface} = d_{max} = 0$ and $d_{min} = 20$mm.

Sketch recognition

Sketches drawn on the floor are represented as 2D polygons $p_1, \ldots, p_N$ which we simplify using the Douglas-Peucker algorithm [8] and an edge-angle based filter (all adjacent edges with an enclosing angle less than α_{join} are joined). We consider the sketch to be a rectangle if it's average segment length $\frac{1}{N}\sum_{i=1}^{N-1}|p_i - p_{i+1}|$ is less than L_{rect}. A circle has it's center at the center of the polygon and its radius is the average distance of each point to that center. Rectangles are the bounding rectangle of the polygon.

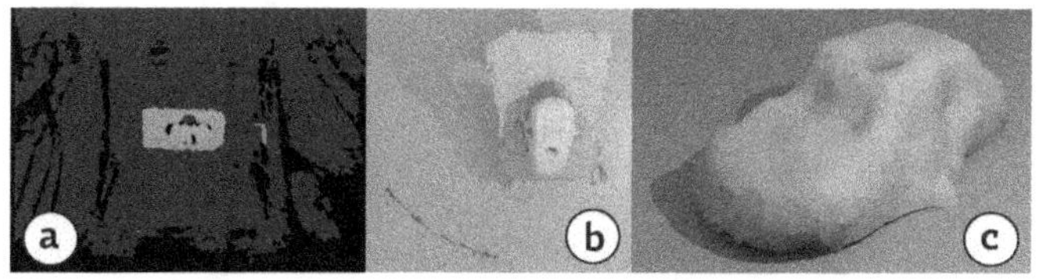

Figure 11. The object scanning process. ***(a)*** **The Kinect depth data (white) is filtered using clipping planes (purple), leaving some noise (red),** ***(b)*** **the scanned object (white) contains that noise (red). Removing noise and scanning table (green) and closing remaining holes results in the scanned object** ***(c)*** **.**

Open hands: plane cut and scaling

Open hands (Figure 5c) pointing along the Z-axis, result in a local minimum of the contour arc length. We exploit those observations and threshold the arc-length L of the hand contour going back d_{hand}mm. An "open hand" posture is recognized when the arc-length is less than L_{max}.

Grabbing

A not-grabbing hand forms several convexity defects [6]. If a defect with an angle greater than α_{min} and depth greater than d_{open} is found, the hand is considered to be in an open state. If no such defect is found, the hand is considered to be in a grabbing state. While maintaining a grabbing pose, the finger-tip detection heuristic does not work reliably. Part of the grabbing pose is to bend the hand compared to the arm, causing the finger-tip to move away too far from the orientation axis previously computed. The real tip of the hand and origin of the hand contour form another convexity defect, which is approximately stable when the correct posture is maintained. Kalmann filtering yields a usable hand-tip estimation.

Wiping

When performing the wiping gesture, users move their flat hand from one side of the frame to other in a speedy fashion. To detect that gesture, we continuously sample the contour centers X component with a fixed window size w (corresponding to the time in which the gesture has to be performed). If all points in that window are equidistant, their distances monotonously inc-/decreasing and the start/end points are at least d_{width} apart, a wipe gesture was performed.

Contour capturing

MixFab's processing pipeline distinguishes between hand and object contours, if they are not connected (see previous section). All contours are subject to perspective distortion, which we correct using the previously acquired calibration. To capture the outline of an object, we build the convex hull of all object contours in the frame. Thus, objects can be grouped and produce a smooth shape from the noisy Kinect data, but we also slightly reduce precision. We further find the hightest point within the hull, making that the initial extrusion height.

Object scanning

3D scanning in MixFab uses Kinect Fusion and a custom built turntable/scanning rig. Kinect Fusion estimates the camera to world coordinates using the *iterative closest point* (ICP) algorithm. ICP implicitly requires geometric features to converge, resulting in a poor scanning performance on "uninteresting" scenes. Normally Kinect Fusion is used on a room scale, with enough clutter so that the ICP based camera tracking works well. In MixFab however, we scan single objects only, resulting in severe alignment errors without our scanning rig.

After filtering the depth image using clipping planes, there is still a some degree of noise left (Figure 11a). Due to the sparse nature of the images produced by the clipping, noise has a drastic impact on the camera tracking and thus scanning performance. To alleviate those issues, we designed a scanning table with an extreme width to height ratio, that aids Kinect Fusion in producing its camera alignment.

Once an object has been scanned, the resulting mesh data has to be cleaned. The noise integrated during scanning has to be removed, the scanning table has to be removed, holes have to be closed and the mesh has to be made watertight.

The scanning process begins with integrating plane-clipped point clouds into the *truncated signed distance function* (TSDF) representation maintained by Kinect Fusion. Once the object has been captured from all sides, the TSDF is transformed to a tri-mesh. All unconnected components with less than c_{noise} faces are removed. The scanning table surface is found by computing the largest connected component using a threshold of the discrete RMS curvature as connectivity condition. We then fit a plane to the scanning table vertices and rotate the mesh, so that the scanning table is in the XZ plane. All vertices and faces closer than d_{cut} to the scanning table plane are removed. We remove unconnected components with less that $\frac{1}{2}c_{noise}$ faces, as well as non-manifold vertices/faces and fill gaps less than c_{hole} units in arc length.

The resulting mesh is likely to contain holes – at least one from cutting away the scanning table. We smooth the mesh (thus hole boundaries) using Laplacian smoothing. For each remaining hole, we fit a plane to the boundary vertices, project those vertices to that plane and compute a Constrained Delaunay triangulation (CDT), hence closing the hole. In a last step, we remove non-manifold vertices/edges created by the CDT and fill the resulting gaps (Figure 11c).

The mesh processing pipeline is implemented using the *Visualization and Computer Graphics Library*, *sgCore* and *qHull*. It takes 30 seconds to complete one revolution of the turntable and less than 10 seconds to perform the mesh processing.

USER STUDY: SYSTEM EVALUATION

In this study, we evaluated the interaction cycle, design decisions and prototype implementation of MixFab. We were interested in how well non-engineering users could use the system. During the study, we collected primarily qualitative feedback to gain insight to the experience of using the system.

Tasks and Procedure

Participants were first asked to sign a consent form and given an introduction to the system. We started by introducing the idea of designing objects for 3D printing by showing example objects created with MixFab (Figure 1c). They were then shown the "desktop organizer" walk-through (Figure 9) and given five minutes to familiarize themselves with the system.

Building things

To guide users during their exploration of the system, we asked them to replicate the desktop organizer example. The

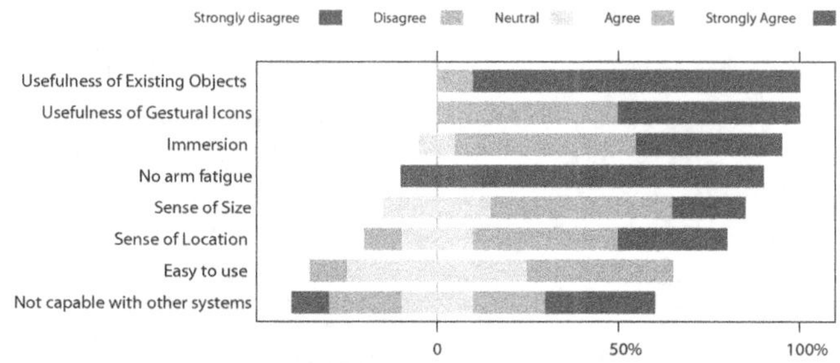

Figure 12. Agreement distribution of the post-task questionnaire. The further bars extend to the right (relative to zero), the more users agree.

glue-stick and pen were provided and we guided users when necessary. Once the example was completed, we asked users to design a phone dock and provided our phone dock example (Figure 1c). Participants could use their own phone or an LG Nexus4 we provided. Users were encouraged to design the object on their own, but were assisted when necessary.

Semi-structured interview

Upon completion of all design tasks, we presented users with a set of statements and asked them to rate how much they agreed with each of them, on a 5-point Likert scale. We then went into a semi-structured interview asking about their experience, trying to gain insight into the usability of the system.

Participants

We invited 10 participants (5 female) from various departments on our campus. Participants were between 19 to 31 years old (M=24.3 years, SD=4.52), and all were right-handed. All except one participant had no experience with CAD systems or an engineering background (Rating scale, 1 a lot of experience to 5 no experience, M=4.56, SD=1.01).

Results and Discussion

Creation, Preparation, Assembly

MixFab's construction mechanism was quickly understood by all users. Knowing when to create a new object, modifying it and assembling two objects seemed to pose no problem for the participants. User 2 reported that *"when I was told to create the phone-dock I had a strategy in my head, thus knowing when to use a physical object."* The method of assembling objects to create new ones, was particularly well received – some users said that they *"[...] very much liked this way of putting things together, to compose objects"* (U6).

Using existing objects

Using existing objects during the design process was deemed useful by all users (100% agreement, Figure 12). Not having to measure objects and being able to place them in their desired position was highlighted by users *"I very much liked [...] the thing that you can bring real physical objects in there."* (U6). Being able to use an existing object as starting point or base for designing new ones was mentioned as one of the benefits of the system: *"I like the idea of being able to put my phone in there and design something around it."* (U8). The effortless integration of existing objects was even considered fun: *"[...] it's fun because you know there is no sort of effort required to replicate existing objects."* (U1)

Natural object manipulation

For interaction to be natural users to feel immersed and have a sense of object size and location. 90% of the participants agreed that they were immersed into the system. A majority of users (70%) agreed that they had a sense of size and location of objects as well as their hands (U10: *"I liked that the objects were as big as they are in reality."*). Users had no issues with selecting the gestural icons, further indicating that they had a sense of where things were in the frame. Manipulating objects was reported to be easy (U3: *"it felt easy to create and manipulate 3D objects compared to other systems which I image would take quite a bit of competency"*) and interacting with the system felt natural (U8: *"I liked how natural [...] the way I interacted with it [felt]"*).

Usability

Several usability aspects are subsumed under "ease of use": navigating within the system, ergonomic aspects and implementation specific artifacts. Finding their way around the system posed no greater challenge to users (U2: *"it [the system] is easy to comprehend; it's self-explanatory."*); partly because of the gestural icons. While interacting with the system, users at times asked what to do next but shortly afterwards selected the appropriate icon and continued on their own; all users reported that the gestural icons were useful (Figure 12).

Mid-air gestural interaction runs the risk of inducing arm-fatigue when used for an extended period of time. During our study, 9 of 10 users reported no arm fatigue. When using MixFab , many of the gestures are performed on the floor of the system and are often interleaved with short pauses of rest. As users sit close to the system, they do not have to extend their arms very far, further reducing the risk of arm fatigue.

The accuracy of the gesture recognition had the biggest impact on usability. Some users found it hard to execute precise movements (U5: *"sometimes I wished that it was more accurate"*, U6: *"the system is very sensitive, it was hard to really make accurate movements."*) or had trouble with disengaging from a gesture. Most of the issues revolved around moving objects (U8: *"when you were moving and let go it was jumping a bit"*). Others however, found the precision to be sufficient. When asked if precision was a problem, user 7 answered: *"no, that was easy"*. Overall, users agreed that the system was easy to use (Figure 12).

Using other systems

Our study participants had no experience with CAD and modeling tools. When asked if they would be able to design the items they designed during the study with other systems, 40% answered that they would be capable of doing so, despite no prior experience. Some users expected our system to be the way items are commonly designed: *"I have never used any of the CAD tools, but I think it's kind of like this one"* (U7).

DISCUSSION AND FUTURE WORK

The results of our study provide evidence that MixFab can be used by non-expert users to design meaningful objects for fabrication. Integrating existing objects was found particularly useful by all participants. Interaction with the system is natural, by virtue of the gestures proposed during the user-defined gesture study and the mixed reality setup. Users have a sense of size and location of the object they're designing.

In MixFab existing objects first have to be digitized before they can be used which is beneficial in that it allows us to e.g. scale and alter the object. Using the physical object as tangible proxy however, would likely increase immersion. We could introduce recursion by designing an object, fabricating it and introducing its physical manifestation back into the design process, making it semi-interactive fabrication.

Capturing existing objects comes at a detail vs cost trade-off. Our prototype can capture a crude form of objects in real-time, a more detailed one can be had at a small time cost. This trade-off is likely to shift towards an increased level of detail at decreasing costs. Other material properties, such as color and texture will likely be capturable in the near future. With recent advances in appearance fabrication and 3D printing such features could also be physically reproduced.

The mixed-reality environment of MixFab helps users to get a sense of size of the objects they're designing, bringing both closer together. In the MixFabs prototype implementation objects look artificial however. Immersion could likely be increased by providing a more realistic object representation taking environmental lighting, proper material appearance and texture into account. Stereoscopy, in combination with the head-tracking, would further improve realism.

Not having to wear special equipment increases immersion thus naturalness of the interaction; not having to go through a calibration procedure prior to using the system increases the users readiness to engage with the system. Being free of user-augmentation and calibration comes at a cost, however: precision and accuracy. To some extend this is caused by the coarse spatial resolution of consumer depth cameras – something that is likely to change in the near future. A model-based hand tracking approach or specialized sensors hand-tracking sensors [13] are bound improve precision.

Gestural modelling is less precise than traditional CAD environments. First, the RGBd sensor limits attainable precision, compared to i.e., a mouse; something that will get better as such sensors improve. Second, gestures themselves can limit precision. It is hard, for example, to accurately place an object in mid-air without haptic feedback. MixFab currently implements snapping to the ground when moving objects, or snapping to 45 degree increments when rotating. Extending this approach to tool-specific constraints (as in Interactive construction [19]) will improve gestural modeling precision, and enable users to design symmetrical, reflected and parallel features - something that is not yet possible in MixFab.

CONCLUSION

In this paper we have presented MixFab – a mixed-reality environment for personal fabrication. We described the system rationale, user-defined gesture study that informed its gestures and its implementation. The system was evaluated in a user study showing that users were successfully able to use the system – even considered it fun. We have presented a set of objects designed with the system, demonstrating its expressive enough to create meaningful and useful objects. We found the effortless integration of existing objects and mixed-reality environment creates an engaging and immersive environment to create content for personal fabrication.

ACKNOWLEDGMENTS

We would like to thank John Hardy for the helpful implementation tips and support. This work was supported by the EU Marie Curie Network iCareNet under grant number 264738.

REFERENCES

1. Autodesk 123D Design. `http://www.123dapp.com/design`.
2. TinkerCAD: Mind to design in minutes. `https://tinkercad.com/`.
3. Anderson, D., Frankel, J. L., Marks, J., Agarwala, A., Beardsley, P., Hodgins, J., Leigh, D., Ryall, K., Sullivan, E., and Yedidia, J. S. Tangible interaction + graphical interpretation: a new approach to 3d modeling. In *Proc. SIGGRAPH* (2000), 393–402.
4. Arisandi, R., Takami, Y., Otsuki, M., Kimura, A., Shibata, F., and Tamura, H. Enjoying virtual handcrafting with tooldevice. In *Adjunct Proc. UIST* (2012), 17–18.
5. Benko, H., Jota, R., and Wilson, A. Miragetable: Freehand interaction on a projected augmented reality tabletop. In *Proc. CHI* (2012), 199–208.
6. Bradski, G., and Kaehler, A. *Learning OpenCV: Computer Vision with the OpenCV Library*. O'Reilly Media, Incorporated, 2008.
7. Buchmann, V., Violich, S., Billinghurst, M., and Cockburn, A. Fingartips: Gesture based direct manipulation in augmented reality. In *Proc. GRAPHITE* (2004), 212–221.
8. Douglas, D. H., and Peucker, T. K. Algorithms for the reduction of the number of points required to represent a digitized line or its caricature. *Cartographica: The International Journal for Geographic Information and Geovisualization 10* (1973), 112–122.
9. Follmer, S., Carr, D., Lovell, E., and Ishii, H. Copycad: remixing physical objects with copy and paste from the real world. In *Adjunct Proc., UIST* (2010), 381–382.
10. Follmer, S., and Ishii, H. Kidcad: digitally remixing toys through tangible tools. In *Proc. CHI* (2012), 2401–2410.
11. Hilliges, O., Kim, D., Izadi, S., Weiss, M., and Wilson, A. Holodesk: direct 3d interactions with a situated see-through display. In *Proc. CHI* (2012), 2421–2430.
12. Holz, C., and Wilson, A. Data miming: inferring spatial object descriptions from human gesture. In *Proc. CHI* (2011), 811–820.
13. Kim, D., Hilliges, O., Izadi, S., Butler, A. D., Chen, J., Oikonomidis, I., and Olivier, P. Digits: freehand 3d interactions anywhere using a wrist-worn gloveless sensor. In *Proc. UIST* (2012), 167–176.
14. Kim, H., Albuquerque, G., Havemann, S., and Fellner, D. W. Tangible 3d: hand gesture interaction for immersive 3d modeling. In *Proc. EGVE* (2005), 191–199.
15. Lau, M., Hirose, M., Ohgawara, A., Mitani, J., and Igarashi, T. Situated modeling: a shape-stamping interface with tangible primitives. In *Proc. TEI* (2012), 275–282.
16. Lau, M., Saul, G., Mitani, J., and Igarashi, T. Modeling-in-context: user design of complementary objects with a single photo. In *Proc. SBIM* (2010), 17–24.
17. Llamas, I., Kim, B., Gargus, J., Rossignac, J., and Shaw, C. D. Twister: a space-warp operator for the two-handed editing of 3d shapes. In *ACM SIGGRAPH* (2003), 663–668.
18. Mori, Y., and Igarashi, T. Plushie: an interactive design system for plush toys. In *ACM SIGGRAPH* (2007).
19. Mueller, S., Lopes, P., and Baudisch, P. Interactive construction: interactive fabrication of functional mechanical devices. In *Proc. UIST* (2012), 599–606.
20. Nishino, H., Utsumiya, K., and Korida, K. 3d object modeling using spatial and pictographic gestures. In *Proc. VRST* (1998), 51–58.
21. Oka, K., Sato, Y., and Koike, H. Real-time fingertip tracking and gesture recognition. *Computer Graphics and Applications, IEEE 22*, 6 (2002), 64–71.
22. Pavlovic, V. I., Sharma, R., and Huang, T. S. Visual interpretation of hand gestures for human-computer interaction: A review. *IEEE Trans. Pattern Anal. Mach. Intell. 19*, 7 (July 1997), 677–695.
23. Saul, G., Lau, M., Mitani, J., and Igarashi, T. Sketchchair: an all-in-one chair design system for end users. In *Proc. TEI* (2011), 73–80.
24. Schkolne, S., Pruett, M., and Schröder, P. Surface drawing: creating organic 3d shapes with the hand and tangible tools. In *Proc. CHI* (2001), 261–268.
25. Sheng, J., Balakrishnan, R., and Singh, K. An interface for virtual 3d sculpting via physical proxy. In *Proc. GRAPHITE* (2006), 213–220.
26. Starner, T., Leibe, B., Minnen, D., Westyn, T., Hurst, A., and Weeks, J. The perceptive workbench: Computer-vision-based gesture tracking, object tracking, and 3d reconstruction for augmented desks. *Machine Vision and Applications 14*, 1 (2003), 59–71.
27. Weichel, C., Lau, M., and Gellersen, H. Enclosed: A component-centric interface for designing prototype enclosures. In *Proc. TEI* (2013), 215–218.
28. Wilson, A. D. Using a depth camera as a touch sensor. In *Proc. ITS* (2010), 69–72.
29. Wobbrock, J. O., Morris, M. R., and Wilson, A. D. User-defined gestures for surface computing. In *Proc. CHI* (2009), 1083–1092.

Model of Visual Search and Selection Time in Linear Menus

Gilles Bailly[1] Antti Oulasvirta[1] Duncan P. Brumby[2] Andrew Howes[3]
[1]Max Planck Institute for Informatics and Saarland University
[2]UCL Interaction Centre, University College London
[3]School of Computer Science, University of Birmingham

ABSTRACT

This paper presents a novel mathematical model for visual search and selection time in linear menus. Assuming two visual search strategies, serial and directed, and a pointing sub-task, it captures the change of performance with five factors: 1) menu length, 2) menu organization, 3) target position, 4) absence/presence of target, and 5) practice. The novel aspect is that the model is expressed as probability density distribution of gaze, which allows for deriving total selection time. We present novel data that replicates and extends the Nielsen menu selection paradigm and uses eye-tracking and mouse tracking to confirm model predictions. The same parametrization yielded a high fit to both menu selection time and gaze distributions. The model has the potential to improve menu designs by helping designers identify more effective solutions without conducting empirical studies.

Author Keywords

Linear menus; User Performance; Mathematical predictive models; Visual search; Eye-tracking.

ACM Classification Keywords

H.5.2. Information Interfaces and Presentation (e.g. HCI): Miscellaneous

INTRODUCTION

Menus are used on numerous applications and systems for presenting, organizing, and selecting commands. However, designers reportedly struggle with menu design [5]. While many research papers focus on novel interaction techniques (e.g. [38]), and others on human factors (e.g. [6, 9, 32, 33, 36]), surprisingly few develop predictive models of users' performance with menus [7, 8, 10, 12, 14, 16, 21, 28]. Predictive models are an efficient way of encapsulating scientific knowledge. They synthesize phenomena that are typically fragmented across several studies, and they capture subtle interactions among multiple factors in an empirically verifiable form. They can help designers to design more efficient menus by informing choices without expensive empirical studies. Once matured enough, models can be incorporated into interactive design tools [5, 16, 25].

CHI'14, April 26–May 1, 2014, Toronto, Canada.

http://dx.doi.org/10.1145/2556288.2557093

Models of menu performance can be divided into two categories: cognitive simulations and mathematical models. Simulation models such as ACT-R models [3, 8] and EPIC models [19, 21, 27] explain the progression of search by reference to underlying cognitive processes, such as perception, attention, and memory. Mathematical models such as the SDP model [12, 14] are nonlinear regression equations that predict selection time as a function of external factors such as menu length, target position and practice. These models expose fewer details about the process but may be less complex and more straightforward to apply.

Our goal is to advance the scope and validity of mathematical models of *linear menus*, a widely used menu type in desktop applications and consumer electronics. We assume that tasks, including both searching and pointing, are performed using one of a number of strategies. In practice, the strategy space for perceptual/motor tasks, even very simple ones, is known to be large [23, 39] but here we explore a few key points in the space. We focus on two searching strategies: 1) Directed search makes use of knowledge, including knowledge of locations acquired through practice, alphabetic and semantic knowledge, to programme saccadic eye movements that jump to the vicinity of the target location or directly to its location. 2) Serial search starts with the first menu item and moves from one item to the next until the target is located or the menu is exhausted. In practice a user would combine elements of these strategies depending on the reliability of available of knowledge. For example, directed search might be combined with serial search in proportion to the reliability of location memories and the available relevance scores. In some situations location knowledge will be highly reliable and in others it will be the relevance scores that are more reliable. Finally, 3) we also explore two pointing strategies: *Find-and-point* and *Track-and-point*.

In our current model these strategies are expressed as probability distributions of gaze. A distinct advantage of this model formulation is that it allows deriving both distributions for gaze points on the menu as well as selection time from the same parametrization. These predictions can be checked against eye tracking data.

To parametrize and evaluate the model, we collected an extensive dataset. Although the constituent processes of menu selection have been heavily studied in psychology, the menu selection task has been hard to study for the purposes of modeling. Multiple factors must be controlled, the apparatus like eye-trackers are complex, and the studies must be long enough to gauge practice effects. Our model is informed by a study that replicates and extends the Nielsen [36] menu selection task in order to cover more factors. The experimental design controls 1) menu length, 2) menu organization, 3) target position, 4) absence/presence of target, and 5) practice. These factors were chosen to extend the coverage of modeling to a larger number of empirically reliable findings reported in the literature. Particularly important is the effect of menu organization, which we cover with three frequent layouts: alphabetical, semantic, and unordered. Moreover, we reveal a *last item effect*: items that are positioned toward the end of the menu are faster to select. The data confirms some existing findings and yields new observations of subtle interactions among the factors that our model tries to capture.

GOALS AND RELATED WORK

In our view, an ideal predictive model covers phenomena which are replicated, shown to bear large effect sizes, concern features that designers can affect, and are widespread in real designs. We visited empirical findings on linear menu search and gathered a list of six phenomena which serves as the goal for our modeling efforts. We review them and discuss what is left out of our model due to this scoping. We also briefly review how existing models address these phenomena.

Menu Performance Phenomena

1. Menu length: Users are faster at searching menus with fewer items [2, 9, 36]. More precisely, search time to the same target position increases as the number of items in the menu increase. This effect can be explained by the fact that, on average, it will require more time to localize a random target in a longer menu [1, 14, 21, 38].

2. Menu organization: The organization of items in the menu affects selection time. In particular, semantic and alphabetic organizations of items are faster than unordered layouts [10, 18, 32, 33]. This is explained by learning in visual search: experienced users learn to skip items in the menu. The relationship between alphabetic and semantic organization is more nuanced. For targets with unknown labels, semantic organization is faster than alphabetic organization [32]. However, for target with known labels the evidence is mixed: One study found no difference [32], but two others suggest that alphabetic is faster [10, 33].

3. Target position: Users are faster at selecting targets that are closer to the top of the menu [9, 14]. This effect is large and only partially explained by pointing time. Visual search strategies can explain the effect [37]: Users can follow a *serial search* strategy, reading items one by one from the top of the list until reaching the target [9, 21, 29]. Users can use a mix of serial and random search (with or without replacement) [20, 21]. In both cases, search time is a linear function of target position. Moreover, the second item can sometimes be faster to select [8, 9]. Finally, we will reveal below that items that are positioned toward the end of the menu are faster to select (Fig. 2). We call this phenomenon *last item effect*).

4. Absent target: Scanning a menu that does not contain the target takes longer than scanning one with it. This can be explained by exhaustive visual search: Novice users have to scan all items to ensure the target is absent.

5. Practice: Performance improves with more experience with the same menu [14, 26, 40]. One explanation is that when the layout is stable, users remember the location of items and can directly glance at them [40]. Moreover, three studies [10, 32, 33] show that the effect of organization disappears with practice [8].

6. Mouse control: Users mainly exhibit two strategies to coordinate its movement with the eyes: 1) a single move once the target item has been located by visual search and 2) the tracking strategy where the cursor trails the eye gaze [9]. The latter one decreases time and the contribution of pointing, because the cursor is already closer to the target. The mouse cursor can also be used to tag an item while the eyes are free to move elsewhere and access additional knowledge [15].

Our decision to focus on these effects leaves out some other phenomena for future work. One such effect is naming: Item labels that are clearly associated with the target goal are quicker to localize [6, 33]. Another one is distractors: Searching for a number among letter distractors is faster than searching for a letter [2]. The density of items impacts also visual search [17, 35]. Related to this is the saliency effect: Items that are salient in terms of color or size can be easier to localize. We believe that our scope is justified on the basis that all six effects have been replicated and bear large effects.

Overview of Previous Models

The main difference between mathematical and simulation models is that the latter have a richer description of visual search strategies and assume it to dominate total selection time. Our goal is to incorporate their findings to a mathematical model.

Mathematical models: The models pre-dating the SDP model assume a linear relationship between item position and search time [28]. The *SDP* model (Search-Decision-Pointing) [12, 14] is a regression model using four variables and seven parameters to predict total selection time. Contrary to the simulation models, it has only a random model of search and it places more emphasis on decision and pointing time. The four predictors are: *Number of items*, *item frequency*, *spatial consistency* and *item position*.

SDP covers some of the phenomena mentioned above: 1) the **S**earch component predicts that the time to localize an item increases linearly with the number of items in the menu. However, the position effect is only explained by pointing time, not by localization time. 2) The **D**ecision component predicts that the time to decide among items depends on the "entropy" of their relative frequencies in previous selections. It is given by the Hick-Hyman law. 3) The **P**ointing component is based on Fitts' law [30] and predicts that items closer to the top are faster to select. Furthermore, mouse movement starts *after* search. 4) Finally, an *expertise* scalar modulates the components by the number of repetitions with an item. With practice, performance shifts from being dominated by search (linear) to decision (logarithmic). 6) The model includes a scalar "predictability" variable (1: unchanging, 0: constantly changing order) that predicts a detrimental effect of spatial consistency. With these assumptions, the

SDP model has been extended to scrolling lists and hierarchies [12], square and circular layouts [1] and interaction with constrained devices [13].

Simulation models mainly refer to visual search as the explanatory factor for the above effects. *EPIC* (Executive Process Interactive Control) [27] consists of a production-rule cognitive processor and perceptual motor peripherals. Their execution is limited by temporal and capacity limitations posed by the cognitive infrastructure [19, 21, 22]. Four strategies are distinguished for menus [21]: serial search (one menu item processed at a time), parallel search (many items processed at the same time), random search, and systematic search. The last two are combination of the others. Data suggested that parallel search with both random and systematic search matched well observed data.

ACT-R/PM [8] extends ACT-R [3], which is also a production rule architecture. It differs from EPIC in the details of the visual search process [35]. ACT-R/PM posits a systematic, top-to-bottom search with eye fixations on menu items that share features with the target item [3]. In constrast, EPIC posits a 50/50 blend of random and systematic search with eye fixations determined by the number of menu items visible in the fovea. However, a study found that neither EPIC nor ACT-R is a good characterization users' behavior [9]. The assumptions concerning mouse movements also differ. EPIC predicts, similar to SDP, that there is a single aimed mouse movement from the initial position to the target item once the target has been located. Timing of this movement should be governed by Fitts' law [30]. ACT-R, on the other hand, predicts that the mouse should "trail" the eyes such that once the target is located, there is an approximately constant and short distance to the target. This predicts multiple mouse movements that are correlated with the number of eye movements.

MODEL OVERVIEW

The model has four input variables: target position (1-16), menu length (8-16), menu organization (unordered, alphabetical, semantic), and number of previous encounters with the item (1-12). The model is in a mathematical form that allows deriving both total menu selection time and gaze distribution. The assumption is that the total time to select an item consists of time spent in two consecutive subtasks–search and pointing–and both are affected by learning (Figure 1):

- **Search** uses the recruitment of eye gaze and memory recall to identify the position of the target in the menu by scanning it. We follow previous simulation models [20, 21] and assume two search strategies:
  - **Serial search** consists of top-to-bottom reading of items that, with practice, allows more skipping. This is modeled as a uniform distribution from the beginning of the menu to the target.
  - **Directed search** consists of a direct attempt at moving the eyes on top of the target. At first such attempts are random, as the user tries to guess the location, but with more exposure they become more accurate. We model directed search as a normalized Gaussian distribution centered on the target.

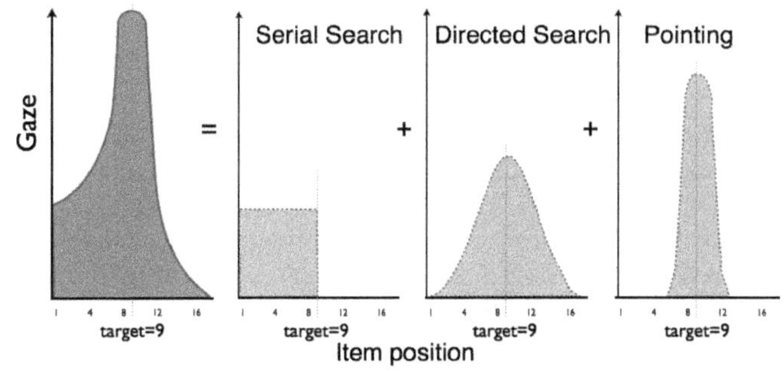

Figure 1. We predict total selection time as a gaze distribution that is the sum of three components: Serial search, Directed search and Pointing.

- **Pointing**: After localizing the target, the target is selected by pointing. Pointing time is modeled with Fitts' law, like in previous models. However, like [8], we assume two starting locations of the cursor: 1) the first at the top of the menu, 2) the other from a constant distance in the vicinity of the target (trailing).
- **Learning**: Our learning model is a power law of practice model [34] which is parametrized for each search component. The negative exponential form of the law implies that largest gains are achieved in the first repetitions, and the gains diminish rapidly after that.

Total Selection Time

Total selection time T is the sum of time spent in serial search T_s, directed search T_d, and pointing T_p:

$$T(\theta) = T_s(\theta) + T_d(\theta) + T_p(\theta) \quad (1)$$

where $\theta = (l, t, P)$ is a vector containing the four input variables: length of the menu l, position of the target t, and a vector giving the number of previous encounters with the items in the menu P (practice).

An original aspect is to explain *where* (e.g., on which item) the eyes spend time. The total time for selecting target t is the sum of the gaze time required for each item i of the menu. The relationship between total time and the gaze distribution for each component is:

$$T(\theta) = \frac{1}{R}\sum_{i=0}^{i=l} G_s(i,\theta) + G_d(i,\theta) + G_p(i,\theta) \quad (2)$$

where G_s, G_d, G_p estimate the numbers of gaze points (serial, directed, and pointing) captured using an eye-tracker with a sampling rate of R. In our studies, $R = 50Hz$.

Serial search

Serial search refers to the top-to-bottom inspection of items. Items after the target are not visited. With practice, users not only skip more items but also spend less time on each visited item. For this reason, the number of gaze points on each item in a menu is not constant but decreases as a function of repetitions. The number of gaze points for i when looking for target t is:

$$G_s(i,\theta) = \begin{cases} a_s \times \exp(-b_s \times p_i) + c_s & \text{if } i \le t \\ 0 & \text{otherwise} \end{cases} \quad (3)$$

where a_s, b_s, c_s are the parameters of the learning model, while p_i is the number of previous encounters with item i.

Directed search

In directed search the user tries to glance directly at the target. Attempts are initially more random, but the spread of gaze distribution decreases with more repetitions. As experienced users have memory about the general location of the target, they can glance at the neighborhood of the target and, eventually, directly move the eyes to it [11]. As in serial search, we assume that experienced users also skip more items and spend less time reading them than novices.

We thus model this distribution of gaze with a normal distribution centered on the target item t. Probability for item i in the menu is given by its probability density function $\psi_{t,\sigma_d^2}(i)$ modulated by the power law of learning:

$$G_d(i, \theta) = \psi_{t,\sigma_d^2}(i) \times (a_d \times \exp(-b_d \times p_i) + c_d) \quad (4)$$

where σ_d is the standard deviation reflecting the spread of the search area. a_d, b_d and b_d are the empirical parameters of the learning model. Note that the sum in Eq. 2 ranges from the first item to the end of the menu ($i \in [1, l]$), but not longer, because we assume that users only search inside the menu.

The spread σ_d reflects the accuracy of memory-directed search and depends on the number of previous encounters p_t with the target. The amplitude of the distribution reflects the amount of time spent in the search area and is affected by the power law of practice. We assume that the spread σ_d is also affected by menu length: Longer menus have more uncertainty and users are more likely to visit more items:

$$\sigma_d(i) = l \times a_\sigma \exp(-b_\sigma \times p_i) + c_\sigma \quad (5)$$

where a_σ, b_σ and c_σ are the parameters of the learning model. Note that two learning components affect the gaze distribution: The first affects the tendency to engage in directed search (amplitude), the second the accuracy of perceptual memory (spread).

Pointing

Pointing is the time the eyes spend on the target to make the selection after it has been localized. The pointing time is predicted by Fitts' law [30]:

$$T_p = a + b \times log_2(1 + ID) \ with \ ID = \frac{D}{W} \quad (6)$$

where ID is the index of difficulty. In our model, D_t is the distance from the cursor position to the target position when starting the pointing task. Evidence [9] suggests that the cursor sometimes trails the eye gaze and can be in the vicinity of the target when this one is localized. However, the distribution of these two strategies (starting from the top vs. starting in the vicinity) is not known. The average distance D_t is thus defined with a weighing parameter α:

$$D_t = \alpha \times d_t + (1 - \alpha) \times d_0 \quad (7)$$

where α reflects the relative usage of the two strategies; $d_t = t * W$ is the distance from the top of the menu to the target and d_0 the distance from the cursor to the gaze when using the trail strategy. We assume that $d_0 = 0$.

$$T_p = a + b \times \log_2(1 + \alpha \times t) \quad (8)$$

We can thus estimate G_p. However, to account for the fact that users can see 2-5 items in the neighborhood of the gaze point, we revisit the equation 8. We add a normal distribution $\psi_{t,1.1}(i)$ that covers the dispersion of gaze in the items around the target:

$$G_p(i, \theta) = a_p + b_p \times \log(1 + \alpha \times t) \times \psi_{t,1.1}(i) \quad (9)$$

where $\psi_{t,1.1}$ is a normal distribution centered around the target t with a standard deviation equal to 1.1. This reflects that 95% of the gazes are in the users' (extended) fovea.

Absent items

We also provide a simple model for deciding that an item is not in the menu. We assume that search time here only depends on menu length. If users do not know the menu content ($p = 0$), they inspect *all* items. They then become quicker at detecting missing items. The model is:

$$T_a(\theta) = a_a \times exp(-b_a \times P_a) + c_m \quad (10)$$

where a_a, b_a, c_a are three components of the learning model. We expect here having a large b_a reflects that users quickly acquire knowledge about absent targets.

DATA COLLECTION

The experimental design is based on and extends Nielsen [36]. In the experiment, a label is shown and the participant must click the corresponding item as quickly as possible. Distinctive properties of the method include:

- eye fixation and mouse movement data are collected to understand visual search and pointing behavior (cf. [9])
- item selections are repeated multiple times to understand practice effects
- three different organizations of the items are included (unordered, alphabetical, semantic).

Participants, Apparatus and Setup

Twenty one participants (13 females), ages 18 to 26 years (mean=21.1, σ=3.54), were recruited by email list advertisements, and paid 45 euros for participation. All participants had normal or corrected-to-normal vision, were familiar with WIMP interfaces, and used menus regularly.

The experiment was conducted on a windows PC and a 20 LCD display at 1280x960 resolution. A traditional optical mouse was used. All Participants used the same sensitivity and acceleration of the mouse.

We used an 1750 Tobii eye-tracker. The sampling data rate is 50Hz (raw eye movement data points every 20 ms); the latency was 20ms and the spatial resolution is 0.25 degrees (0.19cm on the screen) while the height of an item is 0.75 cm. The distance of the users' eyes from the screen was 65cm. It means that participants can simultaneously focus on 3 items if we consider a fovea of 2 degrees.

Experimental Design

The experiment used within-subjects design with four independent variables: *Menu length*, *Menu organization*, *Practice*, and *Target location* as the main factors. Menus contain 8, 12 or 16 items that are common menu lengths in current applications [31]. We tested three menu organizations: Unordered, Alphabetical and Semantic organization. In the semantic organization, logical groups contained 4 items for all menu lengths. 4 items were chosen because it is the average number of items per logical groups according to [4]. Logical groups were separated by an horizontal line (separator) like traditional linear menus. To investigate the impact of practice, participants carried out 12 blocks per menu. Each item is selected the same number of times. Additionally, we added a missing item in each block. The order of menu length as well as menu organization was counter-balanced between participants. Participants searched one menu organization per session. Menu length was counter-balanced between menu organization. For each layout, participants performed at least 4 blocks. Finally, the order of items was randomized within block. In summary, we have: 22 participants x 3 Menu configurations x 3 Menu Length x 12 blocks (depending on menu length) x (8-12-16 items) = 39,564 selections.

Task and materials

The task consists of selecting the target as fast as possible. Each trial starts with a single button on the screen. As soon as the cursor enters in the button, the stimulus (label of the target item) appears just above the button (to avoid possible occlusion). The selection task started as soon as participants pressed the button. The label then disappears and the menu appears. The task finishes when participants activate the *correct* target and then the menu disappears. In the case of missing items, it finishes when participants press the space bar.

We identified several kinds of stimuli in the literature on menus: the explicit target name, a synonym, the definition of the target or an icon [6, 33]. In this experiment, we used the explicit target name to avoid confound effect.

The same set of items was used for each menu organization. The set of items was changed for each menu length. The set of words that we used is a subset of the list that can be found in [18] with minor modifications: no items in the menu have more than 3 letters length difference. This modification was used to reduce potential saliency effects.

To assess the validity of semantic groupings, seven participants were asked to rate the semantic relatedness (0 to 100) of 120 pairs. Item-pair order was scrambled and the respondents did not know if they originated from a semantic menu or not. We found that items that are in the same semantic group had average relatedness of 44.4 (σ = 26.0) whereas other items had 16.0 (σ=10.0). A two-sample unequal variance t-test found this difference to be statistically significant, $t(47) = -6.828, p < 0.0001$.

Procedure

After introduction to the task, the eye tracker was calibrated. During the experiment, participants took a break every 50 selections. We forced the minimum duration of the break to 1 minute to avoid fatigue. Breaks between conditions were used to re-calibrate the eye-tracker. The experiment was split into 3 sessions of 90 minutes each. The time between two sessions was from 0 to 7 days depending of the schedule of the participants. Participants were instructed to select items as fast as possible. They were not instructed about the layout and the length of the menu they will use. Finally, before the experiment, participants performed a calibration task consisting of selecting a target in a menu with a single item.

RESULTS

To preprocess the data, we removed trials in which selection times were greater than 3 SDs from the mean and trials in which the participant did not correctly select the target on the first attempt. Using these criteria, 3.83% (1,515 out of 39,564) of trials were excluded. In all subsequent analysis, one block has 3 repetitions.

Inferential statistics

To gain an overview of the data we carried out a series independent Organization × Practice × Target position ANOVAs on the selection time data. Table 1 provides a summary of the results of this analysis. To simplify our discussion, we focus on the effects that the experiment was designed to replicate and extend: (1) practice effect, (2) target position effect, (3) absent target effect, (4) menu length effect, and (5) menu organization effect. These effects are shown in Figure 2.

Practice effect. Table 1 shows that there was a consistent effect of Block, reflecting that users became faster at locating the target with repeated practice at searching the same menu. Table 1 also shows that there were significant interactions between Block and the other factors.

Target position effect. There was a robust effect of Target position on search time (see Table 1). To understand this effect, Figure 2 plots selection time as a function of target position for different menu lengths for the first (2-a) and last block (2-b) of trials. It can be seen that during the first block, selection time tends to increase with target position. By the last block of trials, this target position effect has decreased (i.e., the curve has flattened).

Absent target effect. Recall that on some trials the menu did not contain the target (an absent target trial). On these trials the participant had to press the space bar to indicate that it was absent. Response times are shown in the Figure 2a -b (at 0 on the x-axis). It can be seen that participants were initially very slow at making these absent target decisions during the first block of trials (particularly for 12- and 16-item menus). By the last block of trials, participants were very quick at indicating when there was an absent target.

Length	Organization (O)	Practice (P)	Target (T)	OxP	OxT	PxT	OxPxT
8	**	***	***	n.s.	***	*	**
12	***	***	***	***	***	***	n.s.
16	***	***	***	***	***	***	*

Table 1. Summary of main effects and interactions for search time data. Note: * p < .05, ** p < .01, *** p < .001

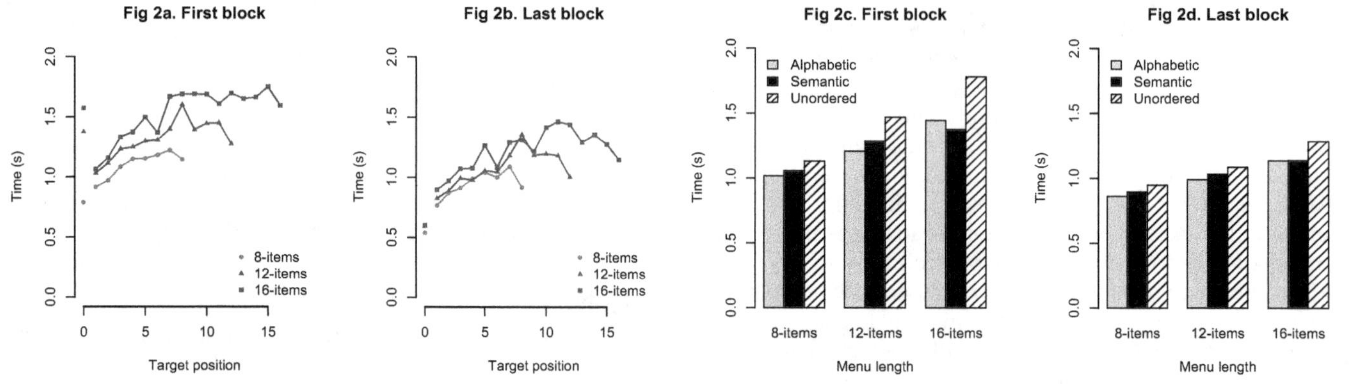

Figure 2. The effects of target position (left panels) and organization, and practice interaction (right panels) on selection time.

Menu length effect. The data replicate Nilsen's menu length effect: selection times were longer for targets in a given position when the menu contained more items. To test this effect, we performed a Length × Organization × Practice × Target-position ANOVA on a subset of the data: trials in which the target was in position 1 to 8. As expected, there was a significant main effect of menu length, $F_{2,40} = 70.44, p < .001$. However, there was also a significant Length × Block interaction, $F_{6,120} = 8.84, p < .001$. With practice, the effect decreases from the first to the last block (Figure 2a b).

Menu organization effect. Figure 2c d shows the menu organization effect. Participants were faster at selecting targets when the menu had either an alphabetic or semantic organization compared to when it had an unordered organization. Reflecting this observation, statistical analysis shows that there was a consistent main effect of menu organization across (see Table 1). There was also significant organization × block interactions for the longer 12-item and 16-item menus. As can be seen in Figure 2, these interactions reflect that with practice the menu organization effect diminished.

In contrast with the Nilsen experiment, we observed a *last item effect*: Items that are positioned toward the end of the menu are faster to select. It is the opposite of what would be expected by the Fitts' law. We return to this effect later in the paper and show that our model explains this effect as well as the previous effects and their interaction with practice.

Observations of Pointing Strategies

We here report observations for pointing. We return to gaze distributions in the Modeling section.

The model of pointing in Eq. 9 assumes that there are two strategies of mouse control and the proportion of these is regulated by the parameter α. Figure 3 shows two examples of cursor controls for the same target position: on the left trailing behavior, on the right the single move behavior. To better understand cursor control and to derive α, we looked at the position of the cursor upon localizing the target. To identify this moment, we used a simple heuristic: we assumed localization to take place at the beginning of the last fixation to the target item (Figure 3). This estimate is conservative, because it does not take into account the time needed to identify

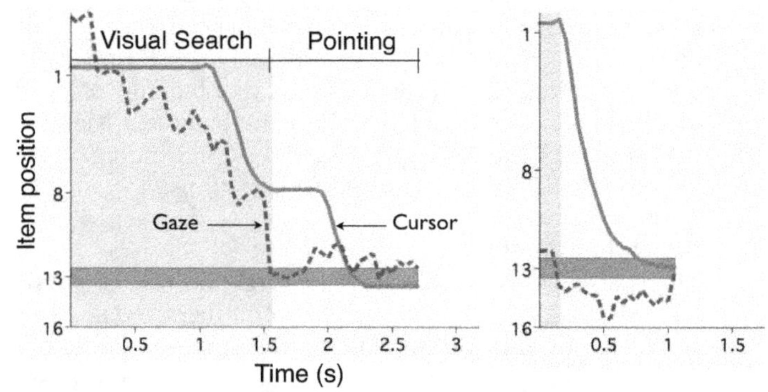

Figure 3. Two cursor control strategies for selecting the target 13 (dark grey). Left: The cursor (solid) trails the eyes gaze (dash). Right: A single mouse move when the target has been localized.

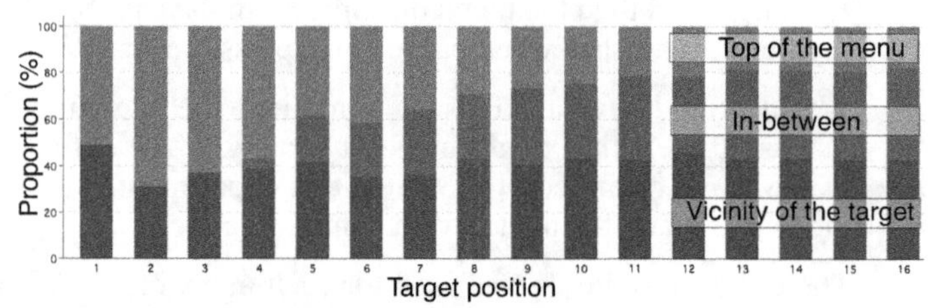

Figure 4. Proportion of three cursor movement strategies: trailing (on the target +/- 0.5 items), single move (top of the menu; +/- 0.5 items), and intermediate (between).

the target. Figure 4 shows the relative proportion of mouse strategy according to the target position. Data confirm our assumption that pointing and search are not always sequential.

MODELING

In this section, we estimate parameters and report model fit. Unlike previous models of menu selection, our approach allows assessment at three levels of granularity: *Selection time for menu*, *Selection time for targets*, and *Gaze distribution*. We used trials containing no missing gaze data (85% of the trials). This is important because we derive selection time from the gaze distribution (integration). Two participants were removed due to incompatibility with the eyes tracker (less than 65% of valid trials). It results in 19690 trials aggregated between participants.

Parameter Estimation

The model consists of 4 independent variables. For each menu organization, we have 12 parameters, 5 of which are shared by all menu organizations. Five parameters were estimated by analysis of user performance in selected conditions. The rest were solved using ordinary least squares (OLS), but insisting on theoretically sound value ranges. Note that we assume that both visual search strategies depend on menu organization: Unordered (U), Alphabetic (A), Semantic (S) [10, 18, 32, 33]. The parameters of Eq. 3, 4, 5 are thus fitted separately for each menu type.

Serial seach: Parameters a_s and b_s were obtained by OLS. For the three menu types, this yielded a_s =[U: 2.04; A: 1.48; S: 1.05] and b_s =[U: 0.15; A: 0.07; S: 0.09]. Second, we assume c_s is the same for every menu. This reflects the observation that an expert user can directly glance at the target *regardless* of the menu organization. We estimated c_s based on our Fitts' law calibration task to be $c_s = 0.2$. Notice that all parameters (a_s, b_s, c_s) are positive, describing that users abandon serial search with practice. We also note that they spend more time in serial search with the unordered menu ($a = 2.1$) that with the two other organizations [1.48, 1.05].

Directed search: The two parameters a_d =[U: 4.83; A: 4.28; S: 4.36], b_d =[U: 0.03; A: 0.03; S: 0.03] of the power law of practice, as well as the three describing the spread of directed search, σ_a =[U: 0.14; A: 0.14; S: 0.27], σ_b =[U: 4e-9; A: 1e-9; S: 5e-9] and σ_c =[U: 1.2; A: 1.5; S: 1.24], were obtained using OLS. That all parameters are positive reflects that not only users spend less time on each item but they also reduce the search area. Additionally, b_d, σ_b and σ_b are very similar whatever the menu organization indicating that the organization only impacts the initial amplitude and the initial size of search area. Finally, $c_d = c_s = 0.2$.

Pointing: We used data from the Fitts' law calibration task to estimate the parameters of Eq. 9 as $a_p = 10.3$ and $b_p = 4.8$. We consulted Figure 4 to set $\alpha = 0.4$. These parameters are organization-independent.

Absent target: We used OLS on the data of absent items and set the parameters to: $a_m = 3.75$, $b_m = 1.14$, and $c_m = 23.8$. We assume these parameters to be independent of menu organization, because every item is read.

Pre-search gaze

Figure 5 shows deployment of gaze on the stimulus before searching the menu. This occurs because users in the study processed the stimulus even a couple of milliseconds after having opened the menu. To cover this in the model, we added a component *Pre-search*: a normal distribution centered around the stimulus location (above the menu). It reflects the dispersion of gaze around the stimulus. We assume this component to be constant:

$$G_{pre}(i) = a_{pre} \times \psi_{S,\sigma_{pre}}(i) \tag{11}$$

where $a_{pre} = 6$, $\sigma_{pre} = 1.0$ were defined using OLS. The two parameters are, respectively, the amplitude of the normal distribution and the standard deviation (spread). $S = -0.5$ is the position of the stimulus.

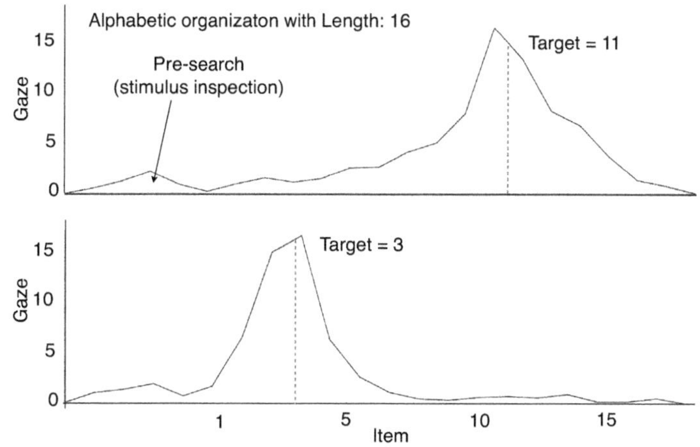

Figure 5. Gaze distribution for the target 3 and 11 aggregated across users. The plot shows that gaze occurs also in the vicinity of the stimulus (above the menu).

Model Fit

We report fit for three levels of analysis: *Selection time for Menu*, *Selection time for Target* and *Gaze Distribution*. The parameter values reported above were utilized for all three levels. Models fit are based on the whole data set. We also report at the end of this section a 2-fold cross-validation to avoid possible overfitting. All predictions for the whole design of the experiment are given in Supplementary Materials.

Selection time averaged for menu: Empirical data matched the predictions well for organization, length, and practice, as shown in Figure 6. Model fit was $R^2 = 0.95$ ($pred = 0.93 \times emp - 0.01$) for Unordered, $R^2 = 0.89$ for Alphabetic ($pred = 1.09 \times emp - 0.09$) and $R^2 = 0.78$ for Semantic ($pred = 1.84 \times emp - 0.74$).

Selection time per target: Model fit was $R^2 = 0.76$ for Alphabetic ($pred = 0.76 \times emp + 0.24$), 0.71 for Unordered ($pred = 0.87 \times emp + 0.25$) and $R^2 = 0.61$ for Semantic ($pred = 0.43 \times emp + 0.54$). While the absolute value is inferior to the menu-level prediction, many more observations must be predicted [1]. Figure 7 shows a sample of observed vs. predicted values for the different conditions. The model predicts the known effects of target position, menu length, and practice. It also predicts that selection time does not linearly increase with target position. More surprisingly, it predicts the decrease in selection time for the last item (last item effect). These two last effects can be explained by the Eq. 4, which models gaze distribution by a normal distribution centered around the target. When the target is the last in the menu, the predicted gaze distribution is effectively "cut" for items after the menu, lowering the total amount of gaze for that target item. This reflects the observation that users hardly look at the area below the menu. We also observe a limitation of our model for the semantic organization. Selection time increases quickly as a function of target position, especially for the first block. This can be explained by the serial search

[1] We reanalyzed Cockburn et al.'s data [14] for selection time per target. Their fit is at $R^2 = 0.42$ for this task. The analysis was based on data available at **www.cosc.canterbury.ac.nz/~andy/publs/chi07/**.

component. We assumed that users inspect all items from the top of the menu to the target. We hypothesis that users can skip more items with the semantic menus by using logical groups and separators.

Gaze Distribution. This prediction task has 13,800 points to predict (gaze for each item according to target, length, organization and practice). However, empirical data match the model surprisingly well, yielding a fit of $R^2 = 0.90$ for both Unordered ($pred = 0.90 \times emp + 0.05$) and Alphabetic ($pred = 0.85 \times emp + 0.40$) and $R^2 = 0.76$ for Semantic ($pred = 0.81 \times emp + 0.92$). One sample is shown Figure 8. We provide more examples in Supplementary Materials.

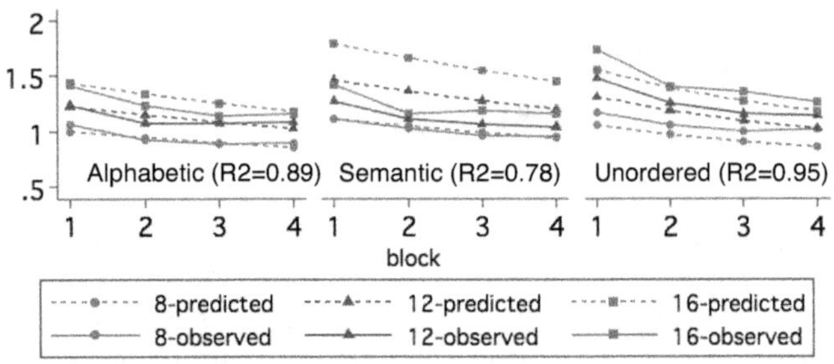

Figure 6. Observed vs. predicted menu selection times by menu organization, menu length an practice.

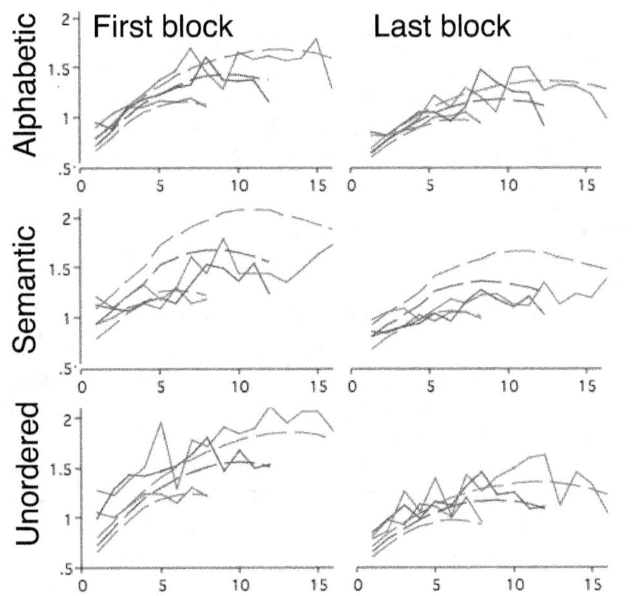

Figure 7. Observed (solid) vs. predicted (dash) menu selection time per target, organization length for the first and last block

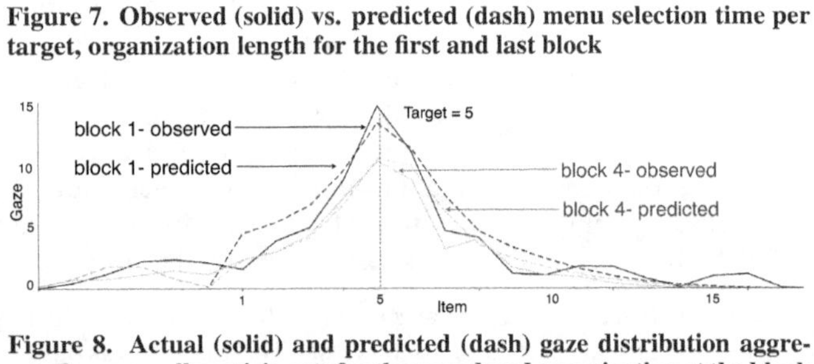

Figure 8. Actual (solid) and predicted (dash) gaze distribution aggregated accross all participants for the unordered organization at the block 1 (black) and block 4 (grey).

Cross-validation

We performed a 2-fold cross-validation analysis to test the generalizability of our model. We calibrated the model parameters on half of the participants and tested it on the others. The R-squared is still high at the menu level (A: 0.91; S: 0.86; U: 0.87), target level (A: 0.64; S: 0.52; U: 0.56) and item level (A:0.85; S: 0.81; U:79).

DISCUSSION

The present paper advances the understanding of menu performance by providing a mathematical model that better accounts for pointing behavior and visual search. It achieves this by combining assumptions about search and pointing strategies that have been identified by previous literature but never modeled in a single model.

We proposed a novel formalization to capture these behaviors. Instead of modeling sequences of elementary operations, like in cognitive simulations, or a linear sum of time spent in sub-tasks, we model the distribution of gaze. The benefit is that the area under the curve is an estimate of the total selection time. Thus, the same model can be used for predicting both dependent variables. The data support the assertion that modeling visual search distributions is a promising approach to mathematical modeling of linear menu performance. The predicted distributions not only yield a good fit but they provide insight into the process of search.

We conclude with a critical appraisal of the model in the light of six criteria for predictive models by Jacobs and Grainger [24]:

1. **Plausibility**: Are the assumptions of the model psychologically plausible?
2. **Explanation**: Is the theoretical explanation reasonable and consistent with what is known?
3. **Interpretability**: Do the model and its parameters make sense?
4. **Descriptive adequacy**: Does the model provide a good description of the observed data?
5. **Complexity**: Does the model capture the phenomenon in the simplest manner?
6. **Generalizability**: Does the model predict the characteristics of data that will be observed in the future?

Plausibility. We modeled pointing time with Fitts' law as previously, but with the additional assumption that the distance to target depends on the selected pointing strategy. One strategy starts from the top, the other trails the eyes. The two strategies were included in previous work but never in a single model [9]. Visual search was also modeled by assuming two strategies: serial and directeded search. The direct search component makes the assumption that search is random in the beginning of experience, but becomes gradually more accurate. It thus subsumes a model of random search assumed in previous works (e.g [14]). Unlike the SDP model [14], our model does not assume a separate component for decision. More work is needed to understand the role of decision processes in menu selection.

Explanation. The model increases our ability to cover important design factors by a single model. The model covers the effects of menu organization, absent item, and target position, as well as the previously modeled factors of menu length and experience. The model also describes the"last item effect" that was not reported in the literature and is counter-intuitive.

Interpretability. Our modeling assumptions come from previous work. Moreover, the model increases the interpretability of mathematical models in this area by linking selection time to gaze. The model makes predictions of gaze distribution that are verifiable with eye-tracking data.

Descriptive adequacy. The model not only provides a high fit at the menu level but also at the target and gaze level. This multi-level approach decreases the risk of over-fitting and better describes the collected data. It is the main difference with previous models.

Complexity. Our model is more complex if measured by the number of free parameters, but the ratio of parameters against explained observation points favors our model. A single parametrization was used to describe 13800 gaze points, 432 target-level selections, and 36 menu-level selections.

Generalizability. To test the generalizability of our model, we provided a cross-validation result that were mostly favorable to our model. However, novel experiments should be carried out to test generalizability to completely different contexts, for example including other menu organizations, layouts, etc.

We see two opportunities to develop the model further. First, more work is needed to cover other common features of linear menu designs (e.g., icons) as well as more complex menu *systems* that include hotkeys, toolbars, and hierarchical menus. This means that semantic relatedness among items must be modeled to predict their effect on navigation and exploration behavior [16]. Second, although we are now better able to model search strategies, our model only predicts averaged behavior. This unfortunately can make the approach "fragile" to the sample of users. Were the distribution of strategies to change in the sample, the averaged prediction may not hold.

Future work also needs to consider a more thorough exploration of the strategy space implied by the statistical distribution of menu relevance and the cognitive constraints. For example, Smith et al. [39] reported a multi-dimensional analysis of the space of possible typing strategies and showed that the assumption that people adopt rational strategies can be used to predict performance. We are currently building a similar analysis of menu search that is aimed at revealing the details of how directed and serial search strategies are combined depending on (1) the availability and precision of relevance and location knowledge and (2) the ecological distribution of relevance and organizational factors in real-world menus.

ACKNOWLEDGMENT

We thank M. Scholtes, M. Staudte and A. Bulling. This research was funded by the Max Planck Centre for Visual Computing and Communication and the Cluster of Excellence for Multimodal Computing and Interaction at Saarland University.

Experimental data and model derivation calculations at www.gillesbailly.fr/menumodel.

REFERENCES

1. Ahlström, D., Cockburn, A., Gutwin, C., and Irani, P. Why it's quick to be square: modelling new and existing hierarchical menu designs. In *CHI '10*, ACM (2010), 1371–1380.
2. Anderson, J., and C., L. *The Atomic Components of Thought*. L. Erlbaum Associates Inc., 1998.
3. Anderson, J. R., Matessa, M., and Lebiere, C. Act-r: a theory of higher level cognition and its relation to visual attention. *Hum.-Comput. Interact. 12*, 4 (Dec. 1997), 439–462.
4. Bailly, G., Lecolinet, E., and Nigay, L. Flower menus: a new type of marking menu with large menu breadth, within groups and efficient expert mode memorization. In *AVI '08*, ACM (2008), 15–22.
5. Bailly, G., Oulasvirta, A., Timo, K., and Hoppe, S. Menuoptimizer: Interactive optimization of menu systems. In *UIST'13, ACM. To appear* (2013).
6. Brumby, D. P., and Howes, A. Good enough but I'll just check: web-page search as attentional refocusing. In *Proceedings of the Sixth International Conference on Cognitive Modeling* (2004), 46–51.
7. Brumby, D. P., and Howes, A. Strategies for guiding interactive search: An empirical investigation into the consequences of label relevance for assessment and selection. *HumanComputer Interaction 23*, 1 (2008), 1–46.
8. Byrne, M. Act-r/pm and menu selection: Applying a cognitive architecture to hci. IJHCS 55 (2001), 41–84.
9. Byrne, M. D., Anderson, J. R., Douglass, S., and Matessa, M. Eye tracking the visual search of click-down menus. In *CHI '99*, ACM (1999), 402–409.
10. Card, S. K. User perceptual mechanisms in the search of computer command menus. In *CHI '82*, ACM (New York, NY, USA, 1982), 190–196.
11. Card, S. K., P., T., and Newell, A. *The Psychology of Human-Computer Interaction*. L. Erlbaum Associates Inc., 1983.
12. Cockburn, A., and Gutwin, C. A predictive model of human performance with scrolling and hierarchical lists. *HumanComputer Interaction 24*, 3 (2009), 273–314.
13. Cockburn, A., and Gutwin, C. A model of novice and expert navigation performance in constrained-input interfaces. *ACM Trans. Comput.-Hum. Interact. 17*, 3 (July 2010), 13:1–13:38.

14. Cockburn, A., Gutwin, C., and Greenberg, S. A predictive model of menu performance. In *CHI '07*, ACM (2007), 627–636.
15. Cox, A. L., and Silva, M. M. The role of mouse movements in interactive search. In *Annual Meeting of the Cognitive Science Society*, Lawrence Erlbaum (2006), 1156–1161.
16. Fu, W.-T., and Pirolli, P. Snif-act: a cognitive model of user navigation on the world wide web. *Hum.-Comput. Interact. 22*, 4 (Nov. 2007), 355–412.
17. Halverson, T., and Hornof, A. J. Local density guides visual search: Sparse groups are first and faster. In *Proceedings of the Human Factors and Ergonomics Society 48th Annual Meeting* (2004).
18. Halverson, T., and Hornof, A. J. The effects of semantic grouping on visual search. In *CHI EA '08*, ACM (N, 2008), 3471–3476.
19. Halverson, T., and Hornof, A. J. A computational model of active vision for visual search in humancomputer interaction. *HumanComputer Interaction 26*, 4 (2011), 285–314.
20. Hornof, A. J. Cognitive strategies for the visual search of hierarchical computer displays. *Hum.-Comput. Interact. 19*, 3 (Sept. 2004), 183–223.
21. Hornof, A. J., and Kieras, D. E. Cognitive modeling reveals menu search in both random and systematic. In *CHI '97*, ACM (N, 1997), 107–114.
22. Hornof, A. J., and Kieras, D. E. Cognitive modeling demonstrates how people use anticipated location knowledge of menu items. In *CHI '99*, ACM (1999), 410–417.
23. Howes, A., Lewis, R. L., and Vera, A. Rational adaptation under task and processing constraints: implications for testing theories of cognition and action. *Psychological Review 116*, 4 (2009), 717–751.
24. Jacobs, A. M., and Grainger, J. Models of visual word recognition: Sampling the state of the art. *Journal of Experimental Psychology: Human perception and performance 20*, 6 (1994), 1311.
25. John, B. E., Prevas, K., Salvucci, D. D., and Koedinger, K. Predictive human performance modeling made easy. In *CHI '04*, CHI '04, ACM (N, 2004), 455–462.
26. Kaptelinin, V. Item recognition in menu selection: the effect of practice. In *INTERACT '93 and CHI '93*, CHI '93, ACM (1993), 183–184.
27. Kieras, D. E., and Meyer, D. E. An overview of the epic architecture for cognition and performance with application to human-computer interaction. *Hum.-Comput. Interact. 12*, 4 (Dec. 1997), 391–438.
28. Lane, D. M., Napier, H. A., Batsell, R. R., and Naman, J. L. Predicting the skilled use of hierarchical menus with the keystroke-level model. *Hum.-Comput. Interact. 8*, 2 (June 1993), 185–192.
29. Lee, E., and McGregor, J. Minimizing user search time in menu retrieval systems. *Human Factors 27*, 2 (1985), 157–162.
30. MacKenzie, I. S. Fitts' law as a research and design tool in human-computer interaction. *Hum.-Comput. Interact. 7*, 1 (Mar. 1992), 91–139.
31. Malacria, S., Bailly, G., Harrison, J., Cockburn, A., and Gutwin, C. Promoting hotkey use through rehearsal with exposehk. In *CHI '13*, ACM (2013), 573–582.
32. McDonald, J. E., Stone, J. D., and Liebelt, L. S. Searching for items in menus: The effects of organization and type of target. *Proceedings of the Human Factors and Ergonomics Society Annual Meeting 27*, 834 (Oct. 1983), 834–837.
33. Mehlenbacher, B., Duffy, T. M., and Palmer, J. Finding information on a menu: linking menu organization to the user's goals. *Hum.-Comput. Interact. 4*, 3 (Sept. 1989), 231–251.
34. Newell, A., and Rosenbloom, P. S. The soar papers (vol. 1). MIT Press, Cambridge, MA, USA, 1993, ch. Mechanisms of skill acquisition and the law of practice, 81–135.
35. Nilsen, E., and Evans, J. Exploring the divide between two unified theories of cognition: modeling visual attention in menu selection. In *CHI EA '99*, ACM (1999), 288–289.
36. Nilsen, E. L. *Perceptual-motor control in human-computer interaction*. PhD thesis, Ann Arbor, MI, USA, 1991. UMI Order No. GAX91-35659.
37. Norman, K. L. *The Psychology of Menu Selection: Designing Cognitive Control at the Human/Computer Interface*. Greenwood Publishing Group Inc., Westport, CT, USA, 1991.
38. Sears, A., and Shneiderman, B. Split menus: effectively using selection frequency to organize menus. *ACM Trans. Comput.-Hum. Interact. 1*, 1 (Mar. 1994), 27–51.
39. Smith, M. R., Lewis, R. L., Howes, A., Chu, A., and Green, C. More than 8,192 Ways to Skin a Cat : Modeling Behavior in Multidimensional Strategy Spaces. In *Proceedings of the 30th Annual Conference of the Cognitive Science Society*, B. C. Love, K. McRae, and V. M. Sloutsky, Eds., Cognitive Science Society (Austin, Tx, 2008), 1441–1446.
40. Somberg, B. L. A comparison of rule-based and positionally constant arrangements of computer menu items. In *CHI '87*, ACM (1987), 255–260.

Towards Accurate and Practical Predictive Models of Active-Vision-Based Visual Search

David E. Kieras
Electrical Engineering & Computer Science
University of Michigan
Ann Arbor, MI 48109 USA
kieras@umich.edu

Anthony J. Hornof
Computer and Information Science
University of Oregon
Eugene, OR 97403 USA
hornof@cs.uoregon.edu

ABSTRACT
Being able to predict the performance of interface designs using models of human cognition and performance is a long-standing goal of HCI research. This paper presents recent advances in cognitive modeling which permit increasingly realistic and accurate predictions for visual human-computer interaction tasks such as icon search by incorporating an "active vision" approach which emphasizes eye movements to visual features based on the availability of features in relationship to the point of gaze. A high fidelity model of a classic visual search task demonstrates the value of incorporating visual acuity functions into models of visual performance. The features captured by the high-fidelity model are then used to formulate a model simple enough for practical use, which is then implemented in an easy-to-use GLEAN modeling tool. Easy-to-use predictive models for complex visual search tasks are thus feasible and should be further developed.

Author Keywords
Cognitive architecture; GOMS; human performance modeling; visual acuity; visual search.

ACM Classification Keywords
H.5.2. [Information Interfaces and Presentation]: User Interfaces - evaluation/methodology, screen design, theory and methods; H.1.2 [Models and Principles]: User/Machine Systems – Human factors; Human information processing.

INTRODUCTION
Visual search pervades everyday computer usage, such as the simple task of finding an icon on a smartphone. Icons that are always in the same location on the home screen and used often will be found quickly, but icons that are used occasionally or that change their position often as new applications are added will require visual search. Designing systems that support faster visual search will improve usability.

Figure 1 shows four pairs of icons from the Apple iPhone. Each pair shows two icons used for the same application, an older version (on the top or left of each pair) and a recent redesign (on the bottom or right of each pair). Each redesign does a better job of emphasizing the primary visual features of color, shape, and size (rather than detailed visual information) and is thus easier to distinguish than the older version in the near periphery. This can be seen by trying to describe each icon while holding your gaze fixed on the crosshairs. Vision psychology has long understood that, for objects that are away from the point-of-gaze, the primary visual features such as color, shape and size can be more easily perceived than the detailed features, and that primary features are thus very effective for guiding the eyes in visual search [30]. But not all visual designs utilize these human abilities.

Figure 1. A set of icons from the iPhone interface.

Graphic designers discuss visual designs such as the icons in Figure 1 using terms such as "clutter" versus "simplicity" [22] perhaps without realizing that in part what they are discussing is which visual features can be perceived at a shorter *eccentricity* (angular distance from the point of gaze), which will in turn lead to more efficient eye movements. Interface design can benefit when designers, including anyone designing a web page, understand fundamental human performance abilities, but this is often not practical. For as long as human-computer interaction has been studied, researchers have been working to address this problem by developing theoretical models and design tools that simulate people using computer interfaces to do tasks, so that these simulations can stand in as real users early in the design cycle to help guide a designer to a usable interface that will fit well with

CHI 2014, April 26 - May 01 2014, Toronto, ON, Canada
Copyright © 2014 ACM 978-1-4503-2473-1/14/04...$15.00.
http://dx.doi.org/10.1145/2556288.2557324

fundamental human perceptual, cognitive, memory, and motor abilities [4, 27].

Some cognitive modeling research focuses on developing the cognitive architectures (the software frameworks for building the models) and identifying appropriate parameters and settings for general classes of models, such as [7, 9, 20, 27, 28]. Other work aims more at making the modeling easier to use for everyday designers, such as GLEAN [21], Distract-R [25], and perhaps most notably the CogTool project [2, 12, 14, 27]. The work presented here contributes to both fronts, first introducing and validating an innovation that permits a cognitive architecture to more accurately simulate human vision, and then showing this innovation implemented and used within an easy-to-use modeling environment.

The modeling work presented here, partially reported previously in [16], goes beyond previous cognitive modeling of icon search (such as [7]) by incorporating a more advanced simulation of visual perception and ocular motor processing, and stands in contrast with mathematical modeling of human performance (such as [5]) in which empirically-derived relationships such as Fitts' Law are used to explain features of performance data without reference to the underlying cognitive architecture mechanisms in the human user; rather, architecture-based approaches seek to develop and apply a reusable unified theory in human-computer interaction [4, 20].

This paper presents cognitive models of a visual search task akin to icon search. First, the search task is described. Second, a high fidelity model is built using the EPIC cognitive architecture [20] to explore perceptual parameter and other settings necessary for the task. Third, the key components of the model are extracted and carried over to a lower-fidelity modeling environment, GLEAN [21], which lends itself to use by practitioners. The paper provides a specific approach for predicting visual search performance in HCI tasks that could be integrated into easy-to-use predictive analysis tools, complements and advances other approaches for predicting visual performance in HCI visual search tasks, and demonstrates the value of building these models using a cognitive architecture that distinguishes the human invariants from the task-specific knowledge.

THE TASK

This modeling work applies contemporary modeling techniques to explain a data set from the literature, in this case a very early eye movement study of visual search published by Williams in 1966 [29, 30], who ventured into experimental territory commonly avoided even today. The task involved visual search of a very large number of objects varying in size, color, and shape, each with a unique two-digit label. The 100 objects consisted of all combinations of 4 sizes, 5 colors, and 5 shapes.

Figure 2 shows a re-creation of a small portion of a search field used in the experiment. The entire display is 39° × 39° of visual angle. Search objects ranged from 0.8° to 2.8° in size and were randomly distributed across the field. Participants were precued with the numerical label of the target. The key to the experimental design is this: On most trials, participant were also precued with some combination of the color, size, and shape features of the target. For example, in Figure 2, if the target is the large triangle at the center, the precue could be just "59" (the number-only precue) or "blue 59" (the color-only condition) or "very large triangle 59" (the size and shape condition). All combinations of size, color, and shape precues were tested in addition to the number-only precue. The specifications appeared first in the center of the display; when a button was pressed, the search objects were added to the display. The participant pressed another button when he or she had located the specified object.

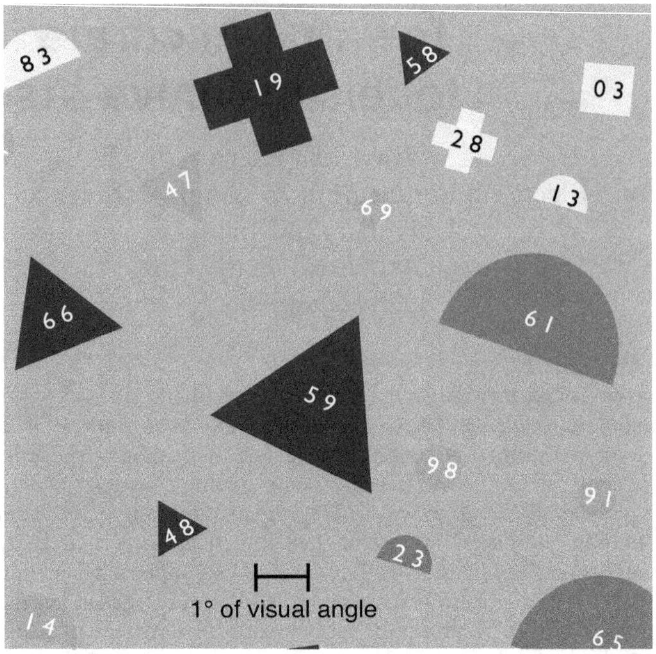

Figure 2. A reproduction of a portion of the display used in the Williams (1966) visual search experiment. The user's task was to search for an icon given a number and some combination of color, shape, and size. For example, for the trial shown here, the precue might be "small green 23".

Eye movements were recorded with a corneal-reflection film camera system and scored by hand. The total number of fixations were counted, and classified by whether they fell on objects whose size, color, and shape matched the specifications. The hypothesis is that if a specification is an effective precue for visual guidance, more fixations should be on objects matching the precue than expected by chance. Williams approximated reaction time (RT) measures by counting the number of fixations and dividing by 3.25, the observed average number of fixations per second.

The Observed Data

Figure 3 shows the average number of fixations that participants needed to find the target for each of the eight precue conditions. The most pronounced effect is that the target can be found with the least number of fixations any time that color is specified in the precue. Specifying size helps less to reduce the number of fixations. Specifying shape helps only a little.

Figure 4 shows the proportion of fixations that landed on objects that had a feature specified in the precue, for each of the eight precue types. This shows the most interesting phenomenon captured by the Williams experiment, that during visual search participants tended to look at objects with whatever features were included in the precue. They especially did this for color. When no features were specified in the number-only condition, there was a chance likelihood that fixations landed on the correct color, size, or shape (which was respectively 20%, 25%, and 20%). When color was specified, roughly 60% of the fixations were on objects with the target color. Specifying the size also helped participants to increase their fixations on objects of the target size. Specifying the shape did not help much. Fewer fixations were needed because the fixations that were made were more likely to land on the target.

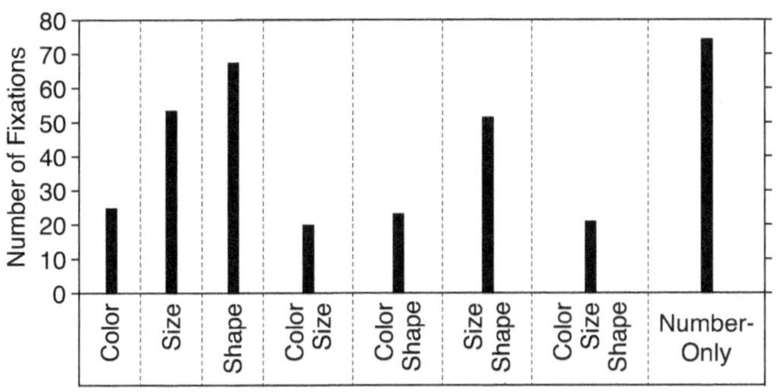

Figure 3. The average number of fixations observed for each precue type from the Williams experiment [29, 30].

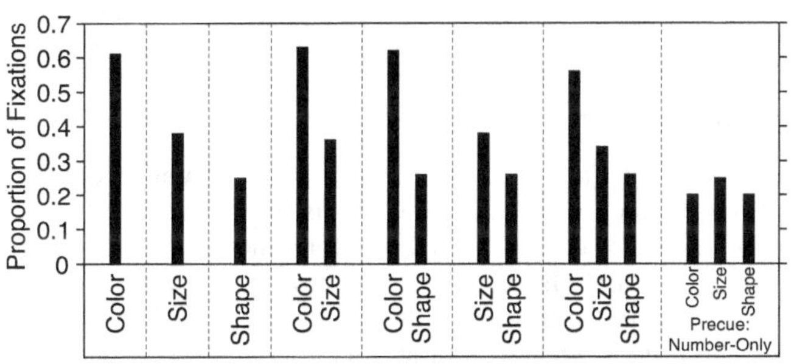

Figure 4. The proportion of fixations landing on objects with the features specified in the precue, for the eight precue types.

It is clear from the results that color is the strongest cue for visual guidance, resulting in the highest proportion of fixations on matching objects (about 0.6) and the fewest fixations (about 20). Size comes next, and shape is a distant third. There is a tendency for each precue to have a smaller effect if a stronger precue is also present. If only the label is provided (the number-only precue), the fixations on objects that match the target properties is at chance level, and the number of fixations is large (about 72).

The data reveal a high number of repeat fixations. If every object that was examined received exactly one fixation, on average half of all candidate objects would be examined. For example, in the number-only condition, on average fifty objects would be fixated. This implies some form of inefficiency or unreliability in the search process, wherein objects are looked at repeatedly and at a very high rate. For example, the 72 fixations in the Number-only condition implies a repeat rate of about 30%. Williams reports a small number (3%) of immediate repeat fixations, but does not report repeat fixations over longer time periods.

In contrast, recent observation (such as Peterson et al. [24]) and modeling [15] of repeat fixations suggests that repeat fixations are relatively rare, around 5%, implying a good memory for previous fixations, and almost all are performed immediately, being due to recognition (encoding) failures rather than failures of the memory for previous fixations. However, these results were obtained in search tasks involving many fewer objects and that took much less time than Williams' task. Perhaps the much higher repeat rate in these results is due to time decay of the fixation memory. In fact, in Peterson's task, repeat fixations at long lags become more frequent if the trial has gone on for an usually long time [Peterson, personal communication]. This issue will be important in modeling the Williams data.

Williams did not report confidence intervals nor apply conventional statistical analyses for what is basically a descriptive study. However, the reported details imply that there are many thousands of fixations underlying the reported proportions, so their binomial confidence intervals would be almost invisibly small on these graphs. Thus we can take the data as being very reliable statistically.

THE MODELING APPROACH

Active Vision

The modeling approach used here closely follows the notion of *active vision* which is argued eloquently by Findlay and Gilchrist [6] and which characterizes visual behavior in terms of the eye movements that are made to reorient the high-resolution vision at the center of the gaze to different items of interest. Active vision is markedly different from traditional approaches to visual attention which have ignored both the role of eye movements and extra-foveal information (information within roughly 2° to 10° of the point of gaze) and which have relied primarily on RT rather than eye movements as the primary dependent measure.

A key process in any visual search task is choosing the next object for inspection. A variety of studies (see [6] for a review) have shown that this choice is strongly influenced by the color, shape, size, orientation, and other visual properties of nearby objects. This phenomenon is called *visual guidance*. In the active vision framework, these properties are available in extra-foveal or peripheral vision to some extent, meaning that visual attention, which in the context of normal visual activity is almost synonymous with where the eye is fixated, is a process of selecting for detailed examination one of a large number of objects currently perceived to be in the visual scene, and doing this selection on the basis of the visual properties available in extra-foveal vision.

Though the importance of color in visual search is well-documented [26], in the active vision framework, color is not specially privileged in some way, but rather, various direct measurements simply show that the color of an object is visible over a wide range of eccentricity and object sizes (e.g. [8]), and so can often serve as an effective cue about where to look next. The relative ineffectiveness of shape is likewise not due to a fundamental problem with shape, but rather that in many cases recognizing the shape requires resolving detailed features that can only be seen close to the fovea. As an extreme of shape recognition, the text label involves very fine features requiring foveation unless the text is very large [1].

The EPIC Cognitive Architecture

The Williams results can be modeled using the EPIC (Executive Process-Interactive Control) architecture for human cognition and performance [19, 20]. EPIC provides a general framework for simulating a human interacting with an environment to accomplish a task, and directly supports an active vision approach to visual search as demonstrated in [9].

The EPIC architecture consists of software modules for the simulated task environment or device that interacts with a simulated human, which consists of perceptual and motor processor peripherals surrounding a cognitive processor. The device and all of the processors run in parallel with each other. To model human performance in a task, the cognitive processor is programmed with production rules that implement a strategy for performing the task. When the simulation is run, the architecture generates the specific sequence of perceptual, cognitive, and motor events required to perform the task, within the constraints determined by the architecture and the task environment.

Figure 5 shows the visual system of EPIC. The *eye processor* explicitly represents differential retinal availability in terms of *acuity functions* that specify whether each visual property (feature) of each object is currently

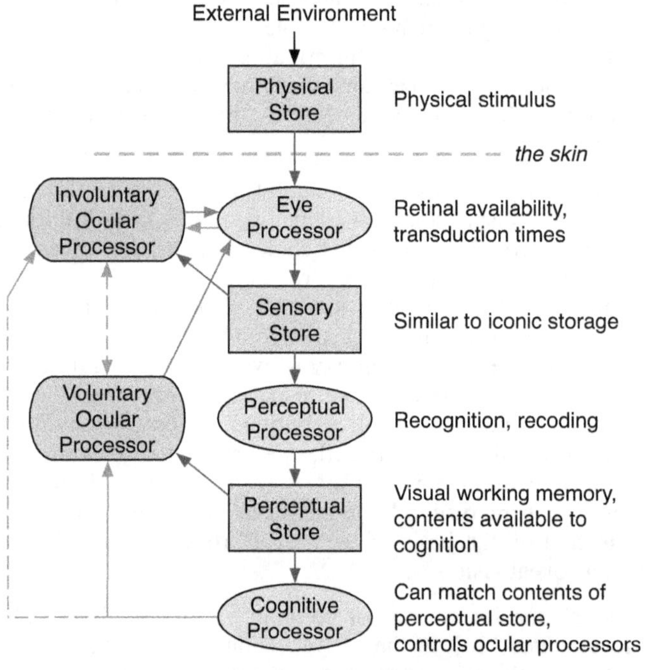

Figure 5. EPIC's visual system.

visible as a function of the size of the object and its eccentricity. The currently available visual properties for each object are represented in the *sensory store*; the *perceptual processor* then encodes the properties of each object, possibly in relation to other objects, and passes the encoded representation on to the *perceptual store* where they are available to the cognitive processor to match the conditions of production rules. The perceptual store thus contains the current representation of the visual world that cognition can make decisions about, including decisions about where to move the eyes next by commanding the *voluntary ocular motor processor*. The perceptual store retains the representations for all objects currently visible, with more information and detail available for objects that have been fixated.

There are two senses of *size* in this model: the physical size of the object in degrees of visual angle and its encoded size which corresponds to the precue specification from *small* to *very large*. The acuity functions use the physical size of the object to determine whether visual features (including the encoded size) is perceptually available given the object's eccentricity, and the strategy uses the encoded size to focus the search when that feature is available.

Persistence of the visual perceptual store

When the eyes move away from an object, the properties of the object persist in the sensory store for a short time (e.g. 200 ms) after which the perceptual processor notes that the property in the perceptual store no longer has sensory support. After a relatively long time, the property is removed from perceptual store. However, if the the object disappears completely, the object and its properties will be removed from the perceptual store fairly quickly.

The concept is that as the eyes move around the visual scene, a complete and continuous representation of the objects in the scene is built and maintained in the perceptual store, allowing the cognitive processor to make decisions based on far more than the properties of the currently fixated object. The notion that this information persists for a considerable time as long as the scene is present is supported by studies summarized by Henderson & Castelhano [10] in which subjects are tested for their memory of a previously fixated object and retention times of at least several seconds long are observed.

Figure 6 illustrates how visual information flows through EPIC's physical, sensory, and perceptual stores by showing the contents of these memories at a single point in time. The left panel shows the physical store—an encoding of all objects and features in the world. The gray concentric circles at the bottom left show the current location of EPIC's eyes, currently on the yellow cross *88*. The small gray circle has a 1° radius corresponding to the fovea; the larger gray circle is a calibration ring of 5° radius. This view of the physical store permits a person running a model to monitor its progress; high fidelity with the original visual display is not needed. The middle panel shows the sensory store—the objects and features that are currently visible to the eyes. Feature availability is determined by the acuity

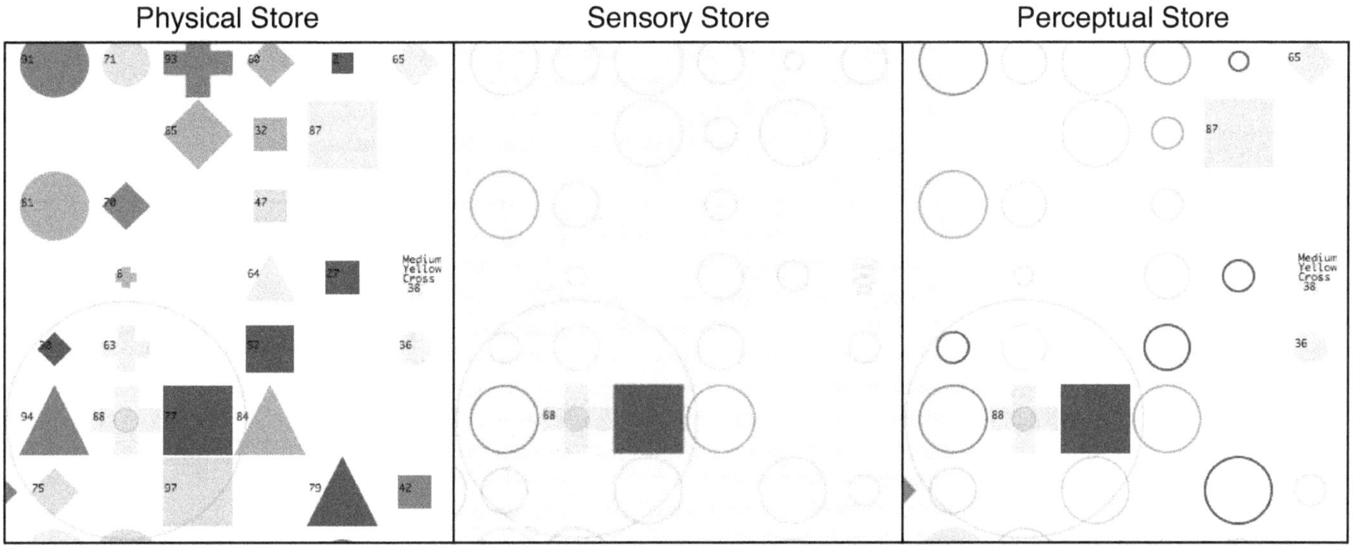

Figure 6. A snapshot of EPIC's physical, sensory, and perceptual stores. The eyes are currently fixating the yellow cross *88*.

function. The right panel shows the perceptual store—the visual information that has persisted from the last few gaze fixations on the other objects whose numbers are visible.

THE EPIC MODEL

Constructing an EPIC model for the Williams task required a choice of (1) visual acuity parameters, (2) a parameter for the decay time of visual properties in the perceptual store that are no longer sensorily supported, and (3) a set of production rules that implement the visual search strategy. The strategy and the values for the parameters were varied in a manually conducted iterative search to maximize the goodness of fit to the data. Each of these model inputs will be described briefly.

Acuity functions

Visual acuity functions were specified for the size, color, shape, and text properties to model how visual properties can be recognized in peripheral vision depending on the eccentricity, size, and property involved. The functions are derived from the literature on visual perception (such as [1, 8]) which show how, in the periphery, the features of larger objects are more recognizable than the features of smaller objects. An object's color is more visible in the periphery than the object's shape, which in turn would be more visible than the object's text label whose small size would require a fixation to be recognized. Text acuity is thus specified as being available within 1° of the current eye position, corresponding to the conventional definition of foveal vision. For other features, a quadratic psychophysical acuity function determines the availability of object properties based on the eccentricity and the size of the object, with some random noise added. Thus, the size, color, and shape functions are quadratic threshold functions for object size s that depend on eccentricity e and a random noise component X, specified as follows:

$$threshold = ae^2 + be + c$$
$$P(available) = P(s + X > threshold)$$
$$X \sim N(s, vs)$$

Since comprehensive parametric data on extra-foveal acuity for different visual properties is lacking in the empirical literature, the parameters for these functions were determined with an iterative search in which the acuity function parameters and retention time were adjusted to maximize the goodness of fit with the observed data. Because the differences in availability are strongest at larger eccentricities and because these differences are primarily determined by the quadratic coefficient of the acuity function, the other parameters of the acuity functions were kept constant to simplify the parameter search.

Figure 7 shows the availability functions for color, size and shape that were used in the model. The functions were set with parameter values of v=0.7, b=0.1, c=0.1 for all three features, and the parameter of a was set to 0.035 for color, 0.2 for size, and 0.3 for shape. The functions converge to 0.9 at 0° to provide for an optional 10% encoding error, analogous to the encoding errors used in previous models [9, 15, 18], though this was not used in this model. Instead, an additional step function was imposed at 1° such that, like

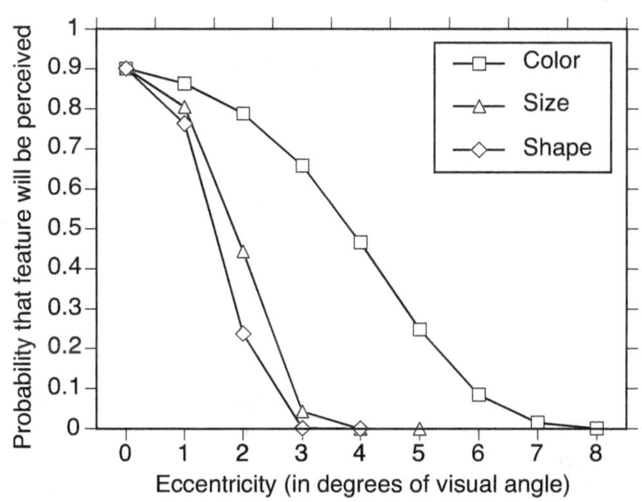

Figure 7. The acuity functions used in the EPIC model.

the text property, color, size, and shape were also fully available in the fovea.

The availability for every property of every object is recomputed whenever the eye is moved. The sensory store in Figure 6 shows what is currently available around the fixation point after several fixations. Objects whose location, but no other properties, are known are represented as light gray open circles. Objects which are close enough to the current fixation point to have their color available, but not their shape, are represented as colored open circles.

Perceptual store persistence time

Once a property of an object is visible, that property is attached to the object representation in the visual perceptual store where it can serve to match conditions of production rules. The visual perceptual store is persistent in that as long as an object is within the visual field, its properties, once acquired, will persist for up to several seconds even after the eyes move [10], and can thus serve as a memory for previous fixations [15]. The perceptual store in Figure 6 shows EPIC's perceptual store several seconds into the visual search. The duration parameter was estimated iteratively, starting with the 4 s lower bound determined in [15]. The reported results here used a value of 9 s.

Task strategy

The visual search strategy in the model is an application of a basic strategy, shown in Figure 8, that has been used in several EPIC visual search models (such as [11]). There are two threads of execution: (1) Nomination rules in the first thread propose objects to fixate based on available visual properties, and also nominate a random choice. Choice rules then pick a single candidate from the nominated objects according to a priority scheme, and launch an eye movement to the chosen candidate. The nomination thread then either starts over, or terminates if the other thread had found the target. (2) Comparison rules in the second thread wait for all relevant properties of the fixated candidate to be fully visible and either respond if it is a target, or discard the candidate if not. Given the typical 100 ms transduction and encoding times for visual properties and the 50 ms production rule cycle time, the overlapped processing provided by the two threads enables the time between successive eye movement initiations to be short, about 250 to 300 ms, which is commonly observed in high-speed visual search tasks.

For the Williams model, the strategy nominates candidate objects that have the precued properties, such as the precued color or shape. The fixation memory effect is implemented by only nominating objects whose text property is unknown—not currently present in the visual perceptual store—either because the object was never fixated or because it was fixated a long time ago and the representation has decayed The priority scheme for choosing a fixation target was originally implemented as picking the object with the most matching properties, which required a large number of rules for each combination. However, the acuity functions dictate that if color is available, shape and size are not very relevant. So a more parsimonious single-property priority scheme that mirrors the relative acuities is used in this version of the model: An object with a matching color is chosen over one with a matching size over one with a matching shape. This scheme is an optimization to favor the most-available information over the-less available information.

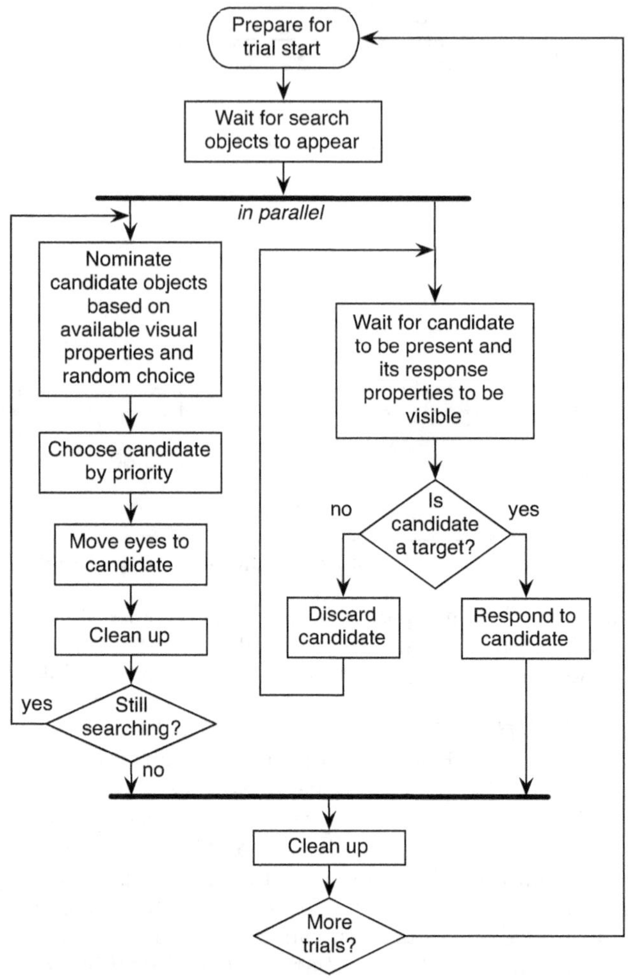

Figure 8. Flowchart for the search task strategy.

EPIC MODEL RESULTS

The model was run for 500 trials in each experimental condition, which was determined to produce stable predicted values, and the predicted eye movement and response time data were compared to the observed data.

Figure 9 shows the predicted and observed proportion of fixations that landed on objects that had a feature specified in the precue, corresponding to Figure 4. Clearly the fit is very good using the acuity function and perceptual store persistence parameters listed above; R^2 = .99; average absolute error (AAE) = 3%.

Figure 10 shows the predicted and observed number of fixations. Again there is a very good fit (R^2 = 0.98, AAE = 12%). The observed and predicted RTs in Figure 11 fit well (R^2 = 0.98 and AAE = 9%), although there is a general tendency for the model RTs to run slightly longer than Williams' results. Given the unusual methodology used to

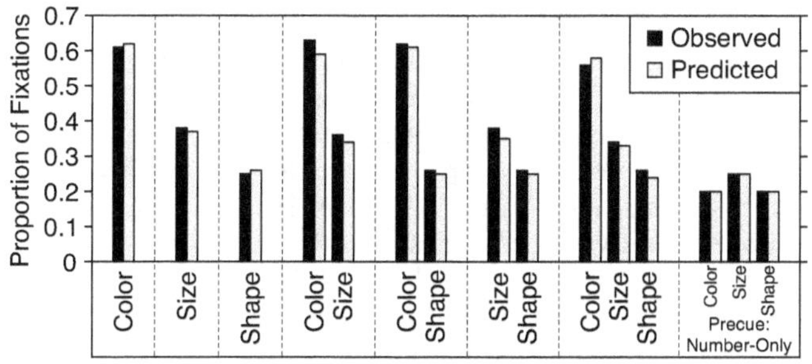

Figure 9. Observed and predicted proportion of fixations landing on objects with the features specified in the precue, for the eight precue types.

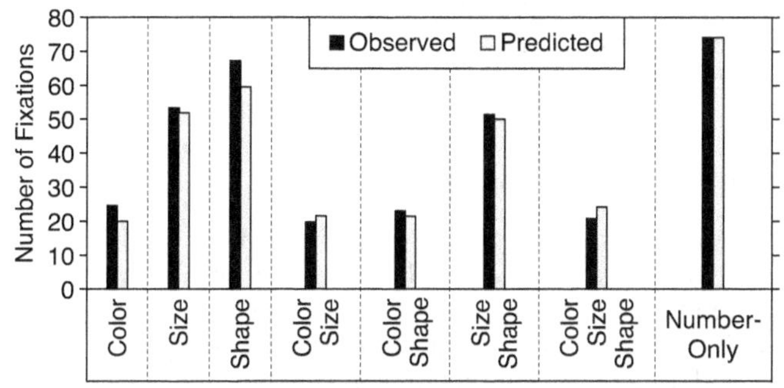

Figure 10. Observed and predicted number of fixations for each precue type.

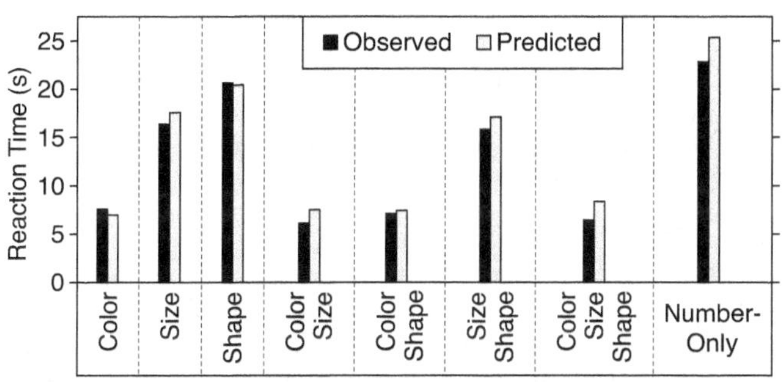

Figure 11. Observed and predicted RTs for each precue type.

measure the RTs, it is not clear that attempting to improve the fit would be worthwhile.

In an analysis of the model output, the proportion of repeat fixations was found to increase substantially as the perceptual store duration was decreased, and the number of fixations increased. The persistence parameter was adjusted to produce the overall good fit on the number of fixations shown in Figure 10, and the proportion of repeat fixations on search objects was then determined with the final parameter value. The range was 11% repeats in the best condition to 33% in the Number-only condition. This proportion was highly linear with the predicted number of fixations, with an intercept = –.03, slope = 0.01, and R^2 = 0.95. Thus the loss of fixation memory over time accounts for the excess number of fixations in the data.

Generality of the strategy and obtained parameter values

The three inputs to the model were the acuity functions, the perceptual store persistence time, and the task strategy. Each of these contribute to the fit of the model: The task strategy makes use of the most visible properties of the objects to guide the search efficiently and uses the persistent information in the visual store to avoid repeat visits to objects, but the effectiveness of this depends on how long the information persists. This task strategy should generalize to visual search tasks in which the visual field lacks an overall structure to guide the search, and the target has to be located based on its visual features. The strategy, acuity function parameters, and persistence time parameter should apply to similar tasks such as with radar displays using military-standard icons (such as in [23]).

But other displays would likely require different acuity parameters and a variation on the task strategy. For example, some of the complex icons used in desktop and mobile devices, such as the older icons in Figure 1, lack a dominant color. Many icons also lack a distinguishing size or shape. If no distinguishing features are visible in the periphery, then a strategy that uses such features would be less useful, and performance might be more like the number-only condition in this study.

High-Fidelity Model Success

The success of this EPIC model to account for the Williams data means that a very demanding search task can be described with an architecture and model based on active vision principles—different visual properties are differentially effective in visual search primarily because they have different visual acuity characteristics. In addition, the capacious but limited memory for previous fixations will fail more often if the search task goes on for a long time, resulting in inefficient repeat fixations on objects. All these factors can be explained with the EPIC model, using architectural features, parameter values, and strategies similar to those used to model other search tasks.

THE CHALLENGE FOR PRACTICAL MODELING

Applying models of human performance in the evaluation of interface designs has been a important goal for HCI theory since Card, Moran, and Newell's seminal work [4, 17]. However, there is a difficult tradeoff between the high-fidelity models like EPIC that are central to the research effort of modeling human performance, and practical low-fidelity easy-to-use models necessary for HCI application. GOMS modeling is the most common example of such a practical approach, and has a track record of model successes that are both scientifically valuable and practically useful [13, 14]. The key important characteristic of these practical model techniques is *ease of model construction* which requires first, a simple modeling language (as in GOMS) that is far easier than production rules, and second, that the details of psychological processes must be thoroughly encapsulated in the modeling system [17]. So can visual search times be predicted to a useful degree with a very simple model?

Guidelines for Low-Fidelity Prediction of Visual Search

The empirical literature on visual search, together with the modeling results of this task and others in the EPIC framework, identifies several characteristics of visual search that can serve as guidelines for a simple and practical method for predicting visual search. These guidelines are as follows:

1. In general, sample objects without replacement so that they are seldom revisited. The empirical results, explained by the model mechanisms of encoding failures and memory for previously fixated objects, is that in small search tasks completed in a few seconds, the revisit rate is about 5%. The model results for this task, which could take a much longer time, produced a higher revisit rate, about 11-33%, mostly due to memory failures.

2. *Treat the color feature as widely available if the objects are reasonably large and the color is prominent,* such as for objects 1° or larger with a single color.

3. Treat other object properties such as encoded size and shape as narrowly available except for very large objects. Generally, the object must be fixated for these properties to be visible.

4. In general, text must be fixated to be recognized.

5. Fixate adjacent items only if their available visible properties have not ruled them out as candidates. While a common observation is that the closest relevant object tends to be fixated next, this could simply be due to the shape of acuity functions resulting in closer objects being more likely to have their visual guidance properties available.

5. Set each fixation time to a constant in the range of 250 to 300 ms.

An Approximate Algorithm for Predicting Visual Search

These guidelines for predicting visual search can be combined into a simple algorithmic model of visual search such as the following:

1. Start with a list of all the to-be-searched objects in the visual field each marked as unknown color and unvisited.
2. Set n, the number of fixations, to zero.
3. Repeat the following:
   If a color is specified:
      For each object, use the availability function to determine whether its color is available. If it is, add the color to that object in the list.
      If the specified color is available for one or more unvisited objects in the list, choose one of those objects at random.
      If the specified color is not available for an unvisited object, choose an object with unknown color at random.
   If a color is not specified, choose an unvisited object at random.
   Make the chosen object the current object, make its location the current eye location, mark it as visited, and increment n. If it is not the target object, repeat with the new eye location. If it is, the search is done.
4. Estimate the proportion of repeat fixations with the formula (n * .01 - .03), floored at 0. Add this proportion to n, and multiply by 300 ms/fixation to yield the approximate search time.

The GLEAN Model

A GOMS model of the Williams task was implemented using the GLEAN cognitive modeling system [21]. GLEAN is a simulation environment similar to EPIC, but with a much simpler cognitive architecture directly inspired by the Card, Moran, and Newell [4] Model Human Processor, and whose cognitive processor is directly programmed in terms of procedural GOMS models using GOMSL, a formalized version of the earlier NGOMSL notation. GOMSL includes a visual search operator `Look_for` which takes a list of property value pairs (e.g. `Color is Red`) and examines the content of the visual processor's store of visual objects, locates the first object that has the specified property-value pairs, and stores the name of the object in working memory under a supplied tag. This tag can then be used to identify the object for later operators, such as pointing a mouse to the object. In the GOMS tradition, the time required for the `Look_for` operator is a single *Mental* operator with a time constant of 1.2 or 1.35 s [14].

When expressed in GOMSL, the complete model for the Williams task is very simple, as shown in Figure 12. This version uses all four properties to identify the target object; if fewer properties are specified, the `Look_for` operator would use only the specified properties. For brevity, the Acquire Probe method is not shown; it simply examines each field of the probe and stores the size, color, shape, and label under the corresponding tags. The brevity and simplicity of this model compared to the intricacy of the EPIC or other full-fledged cognitive architecture models is striking. This simplicity is the principal argument for trying to develop computational architectures such as GLEAN that are based on GOMS [17].

Two GLEAN models were run. The two models were identical to each other from the perspective of the analyst (the person) using GLEAN—both used the exact same GOMSL code shown in Figure 12. The first model used the current GLEAN system in which every `Look_for` operator is assigned a constant time of 1.2 s. The second model used

```
Define_model: "Williams 67 task"
Starting_goal is Perform Search_task.

Method_for_goal: Perform Search_task
Step 1. Accomplish_goal: Perform Trial.
Step 2. Goto 1.

Method_for_goal: Perform Trial
Step 1. Accomplish_goal: Acquire Probe.
Step 2. Keystroke X.
Step 3. Wait_for_visual_object_whose
   Event_type is New
   and_store_under <new_object>.
Step 4. Look_for_object_whose
   Color is <color>, Encoded_size is <size>,
   Shape is <shape>, Text is <label>
   and_store_under <found_object>.
Step 5. Keystroke X.
Step 6. Return_with_goal_accomplished.
```

Figure 12. The GOMSL model for the Williams task when all precue properties are specified.

an augmented version of the GLEAN system in which the time required for a `Look_for` operator was determined using an implementation of the "approximate algorithm" described above, and in which the same acuity function described for the EPIC model was used to determine the availability of each object's color feature.

GLEAN Model Results

The first model, using the current GLEAN system with a constant `Look_for` operator time, was run for a single iteration. (All subsequent runs would have been identical.) The model produced a short constant RT of 1.92 s regardless of the precue specifications. This RT was primarily determined by the Mental operator time regardless of the cue specifications, the number of objects, or their visual characteristics. The model is seriously inaccurate, with an R^2 of 0.0 and an overall AAE = 80%.

The second model, using the GLEAN system augmented with the enhanced `Look_for` operator and the color-only acuity function, was run for 500 trials on each condition. Figure 13 shows the model's RT predictions. The predictions are much less accurate than the EPIC model and consist of only two values—a short one for color-guided search and a long one for a random search. Because the size and shape acuity functions were not used, the model is not accurate in these conditions. Despite this oversimplification, the R^2 over this data is a respectable 0.91; the AAE for the color-guided and Number-only search is reasonably good at 11%, and overall is 26%. Despite the serious over-prediction for the non-color precues, the predictions are much more accurate than when predicting search time using the Mental operator.

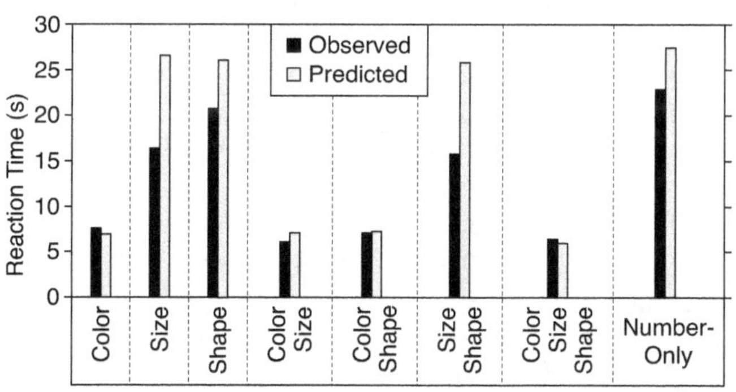

Figure 13. Observed and predicted RTs for the augmented GLEAN GOMS model.

Low-Fidelity Model Success

Even in this preliminary highly simplified form, the augmented version of the `Look_for` operator would produce much more accurate results than the original GOMS Mental operator version. Further accuracy could be obtained by working with additional data sets, and by including the object size and shape in the algorithm using representative acuity functions. The best approach to further this line of development of practical models for visual search would be to develop additional EPIC models for visual search tasks of realistic stimuli, harmonize them with the model for the Williams task, and update the algorithm and its parameters accordingly. To avoid misleading appearances of accuracy, the GLEAN implementation would need to gracefully and visibly default to the standard Mental operator predictions when outside the bounds supported by the EPIC models.

CONCLUSION

This work presents extensions to existing cognitive modeling frameworks that permit models to more accurately characterize the processes of "active vision" in HCI tasks such as by incorporating into the modeling frameworks visual acuity functions which account for the gradual decrease in feature availability for objects as they appear at greater eccentricities from the point of gaze. These extensions will make it possible for contemporary modeling approaches to predict the benefits of simplified icons, such as in Figure 1, that can be distinguished based on peripherally-visible features rather than just fine details. These extensions can (and we believe should) be incorporated into both high fidelity modeling frameworks such as ACT-R [7] and easy-to-use modeling tools such as CogTool [27] and Distract-R [25].

This work shows that practical modeling of visually intensive tasks can be made more accurate without requiring additional effort from the analyst. It also demonstrates the benefits of decoupling the human invariants such as visual acuity functions from the encoding of the procedural skill needed to do a task—the augmented GLEAN provided a substantially better fit using the exact same encoding of procedural knowledge.

There is great value in the cognitive-architecture approach of modeling the human, task, and device each as separate entities. This will contribute to modeling frameworks that can predict performance across a wide range of existing and not-yet-imagined HCI tasks. This may be difficult to accomplish with models that characterize overall HCI performance simply as combinations of smaller-scale empirical relationships as in [5], which does not provide as clear a decomposition into the components responsible for the task performance. For example, the mediocre fit to some of the conditions shown in Figure 13 is easy to explain—the architecture simply does not make use of the possible extra-foveal availability of size or shape cues. Adding these would be straightforward and would improve the fit.

Cognitive modeling is well within reach of most interface designers as demonstrated by both unpublished and published [2, 3, 12, 13] successes and as supported by efforts to make such models not only easy-to-generate [14, 21, 25] but also increasingly flexible and veridical, such as with the work presented here which takes us further along the road towards accurate and practical predictive models of active-vision-based visual search.

ACKNOWLEDGMENT

This work was supported by the Office of Naval Research under grants N00014-10-1-0152 and N00014-13-1-0358 to the first author.

REFERENCES

1. Anstis, S. M. (1974). A chart demonstrating variations in acuity with retinal position. *Vision Research*, *14*(7), 589-592.
2. Bellamy, R., John, B., & Kogan, S. (2011). Deploying CogTool: Integrating quantitative usability assessment into real-world software development. In *Proceedings of the 2011 International Conference on Software Engineering*, 691-700.
3. Callander, M., & Zorman, L. (2007). Usability on patrol. In *CHI '07 Extended Abstracts,* 1709-1714.
4. Card, S. K., Moran, T. P., & Newell, A. (1983). *The Psychology of Human-Computer Interaction*. Hillsdale, NJ: Lawrence Erlbaum Associates.
5. Cockburn, A., & Gutwin, C. (2009). A predictive model of human performance with scrolling and hierarchical lists. *Human-Computer Interaction*, *24*(3), 273-314.
6. Findlay, J. M., & Gilchrist, I. D. (2003). *Active Vision: The Psychology of Looking and Seeing*. Oxford University Press.
7. Fleetwood, M. D., & Byrne, M. D. (2006). Modeling the visual search of displays: A revised ACT-R/PM model of icon search based on eye tracking data. *Human-Computer Interaction, 21*(2), 153-197.
8. Gordon, J., & Abramov, I. (1977). Color vision in the peripheral retina. II. Hue and saturation. *J. Opt. Soc. Am.*, *67*(2), 202-207.
9. Halverson, T., & Hornof, A. J. (2011). A computational model of "active vision" for visual search in human-computer interaction. *Human-Computer Interaction*, *26*(4), 285–314.
10. Henderson, J. M., & Castelhano, M. S. (2005). Eye movements and visual memory for scenes. In G. Underwood (Ed.), *Cognitive Processes in Eye Guidance*. (pp. 213-35). Oxford University Press.
11. Hornof, A. J., & Kieras, D. E. (1997). Cognitive modeling reveals menu search is both random and systematic. In *Proceedings of CHI '97*, 107-114.
12. John, B., Starr, S., & Utesch, B. (2012). Experiences with collaborative, distributed predictive human performance modeling. In *CHI '12 Ext. Abs.*, 437-452.
13. John, B. E., & Kieras, D. E. (1996). Using GOMS for user interface design and evaluation: Which technique? *ACM Transactions on Computer-Human Interaction*, *3*(4), 287-319.
14. John, B. E., Prevas, K., Salvucci, D. D., & Koedinger, K. (2004). Predictive human performance modeling made easy. In *Proceedings of CHI 2004*, 455-462.
15. Kieras, D. (2009). The persistent visual store as the locus of fixation memory in visual search tasks. In R. Cooper & D. Peebles (Eds.), *Proceedings of the Ninth International Conference on Cognitive Modeling*, UK.
16. Kieras, D. (2010). Modeling visual search of displays of many objects: The role of differential acuity and fixation memory. In D. D. Salvucci & G. Gunzelmann (Eds.) *Proceedings of the 10th International Conference on Cognitive Modeling,* August 6-8, 2010, Philadelphia.
17. Kieras, D. E. (2007). Model-based evaluation. In J. A. Jacko & A. Sears (Eds.), *The Human-Computer Interaction Handbook* (2nd ed.). (pp. 1191-208). Mahwah, NJ: Lawrence Erlbaum Associates.
18. Kieras, D. E., & Marshall, S. P. (2006). Visual availability and fixation memory in modeling visual search using the EPIC architecture. In *Proceedings of the Annual Meeting of the Cognitive Science Society,* 423-428.
19. Kieras, D. E. (2004). *The EPIC Architecture: Principles of Operation*. Retrieved from http://www.eecs.umich.edu/~kieras/docs/EPIC/EPICPrinOp.pdf
20. Kieras, D. E., & Meyer, D. E. (1997). An overview of the EPIC architecture for cognition and performance with application to human-computer interaction. *Human-Computer Interaction*, *12*(4), 391-438.
21. Kieras, D. E., Wood, S. D., Abotel, K., & Hornof, A. (1995). GLEAN: A computer-based tool for rapid GOMS model usability evaluation of user interface designs. In *Proceedings of UIST '95*, ACM, 91-100.
22. Maeda, J. (2013, June 12). The future of design is more than making Apple iOS flat. *Wired Magazine*. Retrieved from http://www.wired.com/opinion/2013/06/the-future-of-design-is-more-than-making-apple-ios-flat/
23. Osga, G., Van Orden K., Campbell, N., Kellmeyer, D., and Lulue D. (2002). *Design and Evaluation of Warfighter Task Support Methods in a Multi-Modal Watchstation*. Space & Naval Warfare Center, San Diego, Technical Report 1874.
24. Peterson, M. S., Kramer, A. F., Wang, R. F., Irwin, D. E., & McCarley, J. S. (2001). Visual search has memory. *Psychological Science*, *12*(4), 287-292.
25. Salvucci, D. D., Zuber, M., Beregovaia, E., & Markley, D. (2005). Distract-R: Rapid prototyping and evaluation of in-vehicle interfaces. In *Proc. of CHI '05*, 581-589.
26. Sanders, M. S., & McCormick, E. J. (1987). *Human Factors in Engineering and Design* (6th ed.). New York, New York: McGraw-Hill.
27. Teo, John, & Blackmon. (2012). CogTool-Explorer: A model of goal-directed user exploration that considers information layout. In *Proc. of CHI '12*, 2479-2488.
28. Vera, A. H., John, B. E., Remington, R., Matessa, M., & Freed, M. A. (2005). Automating human-performance modeling at the millisecond level. *Human-Computer Interaction*, *20*, 225–265.
29. Williams, L. G. (1966). *A Study Of Visual Search Using Eye Movement Recordings*. Technical Report, Honeywell Inc., St. Paul Minnesota, Feb. 28, 1966. NTIS AD0629624.
30. Williams, L. G. (1967). The effects of target specification on objects fixated during visual search. *Acta Psychologica*, *27*, 355-360.

Understanding Multitasking Through Parallelized Strategy Exploration and Individualized Cognitive Modeling

Yunfeng Zhang and Anthony J. Hornof
Computer and Information Science
University of Oregon
Eugene, OR 97403 USA
{zywind, hornof}@cs.uoregon.edu

ABSTRACT
Human multitasking often involves complex task interactions and subtle tradeoffs which might be best understood through detailed computational cognitive modeling, yet traditional cognitive modeling approaches may not explore a sufficient range of task strategies to reveal the true complexity of multitasking behavior. This study proposes a systematic approach for exploring a large number of strategies using a computer-cluster-based parallelized modeling system. The paper demonstrates the efficacy of the approach for investigating and revealing the effects of different microstrategies on human performance, both within and across individuals, for a time-pressured multimodal dual task. The modeling results suggest that multitasking performance is not simply a matter of interleaving cognitive and sensorimotor processing but is instead heavily influenced by the selection of subtask microstrategies.

Author Keywords
Cognitive modeling; high performance computing; model comparison; multimodal; multitasking; task strategies.

ACM Classification Keywords
H.1.2 [User/Machine Systems]: Human information processing; I.6.4 [Model Validation and Analysis]; I.2.0 [General]: Cognitive simulation.

INTRODUCTION
A contemporary lack of understanding of the human ability to multitask—to pursue two goals in parallel, with each goal requiring and competing for the same human information processing components such as the high resolution vision at the point of gaze—puts humans in peril in human-computer interaction contexts [13]. As manufacturers race towards profit and consumers towards perceived social and lifestyle benefits, this lack of understanding of fundamental multitasking abilities paves the road for new interface designs that cause great harm [15]. As with seatbelt use, sweeping reform will not likely take place until it is mandated by law [19] but the first hurdle we face on the road to improving contemporary driving safety (as well as regaining a human social presence in the physical world of everyday life) is to determine the contemporary equivalent of "crash testing" human-computer interfaces to better understand how people are likely and able to interleave computer use with other primary life-critical tasks.

Since the dawn of HCI, cognitive modeling has been making progress in providing theory and methods needed to predict the usability of routine behavior on standalone devices for well-defined user tasks with clear goal and task structures [3]. Paper-based cognitive modeling [3] has evolved into computational cognitive modeling [11] which permits increased complexity and predictive power in the models. Eye tracking has emerged as a powerful technique for revealing in greater detail how people are truly interacting with devices [6] and can also reveal nuanced interactions between parallelized task hierarchies [8].

Recent theoretical advances, especially the work of Howes, Lewis, and Vera [9] on cognitively-bounded rational analysis, have opened the door for even more rigorous theoretical exploration and determination of the cognitive strategies that people use when multitasking. In addition to exploring strategies, there is also the challenge of appropriately exploring and adjusting a model's perceptual, motor, and memory parameters to capture an individual's "personal equation" [17], though much contemporary cognitive modeling and predictive engineering still presumes a single hypothesized average user.

This paper presents recent advances in all of these areas of cognitive modeling by presenting a rigorous exploration of cognitive strategies and individualized parameters for a highly-interactive multimodal dual task. This project pushes the boundaries of computational cognitive modeling by employing a high-performance computing cluster to explore a large strategy and parameter space. All told, this paper reveals the nuanced strategies with which humans accomplish complex optimized multitasking performance.

THE MULTIMODAL DUAL TASK
The multimodal dual task experiment was originally designed by Ballas, Heitmeyer, and Perez at the Naval Research Laboratory [1], and has already proven useful for exploring multitasking performance through cognitive modeling [7, 12]. The work presented here models the data collected from our replication of the experiment [8], in which eye movement data were collected to inform detailed analysis and modeling.

CHI 2014, April 26 - May 01 2014, Toronto, ON, Canada
Copyright 2014 ACM 978-1-4503-2473-1/14/04...$15.00.
http://dx.doi.org/10.1145/2556288.2557351

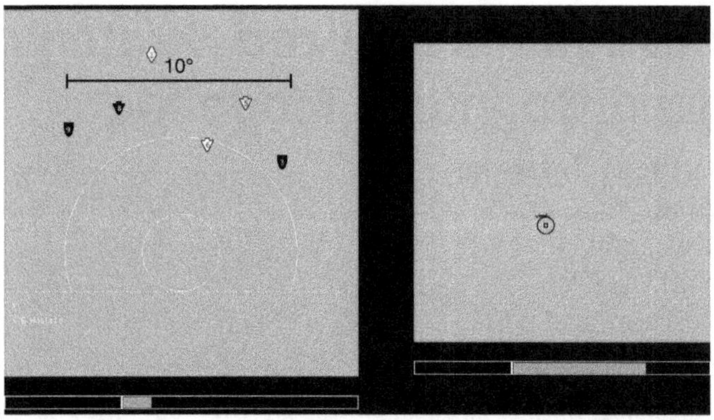

Figure 1. A screenshot of the multimodal dual-task display.

Figure 1 shows a screenshot of the display used in the dual task experiment. On the left is the classification task, and on the right is the tracking task. The classification task requires the participant to monitor icons or "blips" that move down the classification window and to key-in, with the left hand, the blip number and its "hostility" classification as soon as the blip changes color from black to red, green, or yellow. Red indicates hostile, green indicates neutral, and yellow indicates unknown such that the participant needs to further study the blip's shape, speed, and direction to determine its hostility based on a set of memorized rules. The tracking task requires the participant to keep the cursor (the circle) on a randomly moving target using the joystick with the right hand. When the cursor is within 20 pixels of the target, the cursor is green and the participant earns money. When the cursor is more than 40 pixels away from the target, the cursor is red and the participant loses money. Participants earned financial bonuses in both tasks based on carefully designed payoff schemes that reward fast and accurate performance.

To study the effects of perceptual information on multitasking performance, two factors were manipulated, each with two conditions: (a) *peripheral visible* or *peripheral not visible* and (b) *sound on* or *sound off*. In the peripheral-not-visible conditions, the contents of the window that the participant was not currently looking at were hidden using a gaze-contingent display. This simulates a task environment in which two windows are separated by enough distance such that the contents of the peripheral window cannot be monitored with peripheral vision. In the sound-on conditions, spatialized auditory cues were played to indicate a blip's appearance and color change in the classification window.

Twelve participants completed the experiment on three consecutive days. Performance improved slightly from day to day, but with no clear indication of shifts in strategy. The data presented here are from the third day, and from the ten participants who achieved good overall performance. More details of this experiment are discussed in [8].

Figure 2 shows the overall dual task performance by plotting the average classification time against the root-mean-square (RMS) tracking error, for each of the four conditions, with a different plot symbol for each of the two

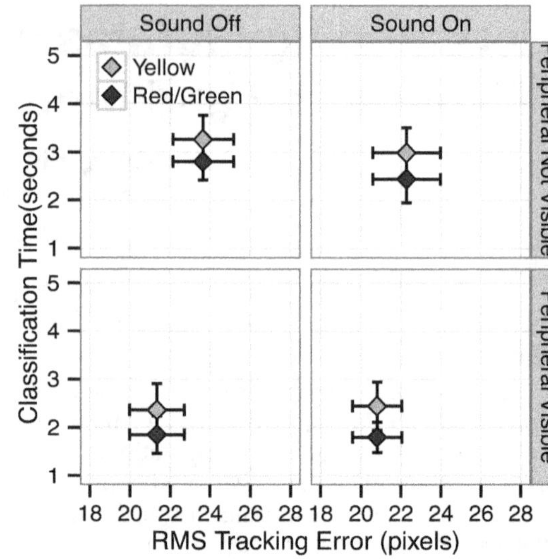

Figure 2. The classification time and tracking error across the four conditions, for yellow and red-and-green blips, and the 95% confidence intervals (CI) of the participant means.

kinds of blips. The general trend is that more perceptual information resulted in better performance in both the classification and the tracking task. For example, note in Figure 2 that the performance shown in the bottom right panel, in which both auditory and visual peripheral cues were present, is better than in the top-left panel, in which there were no peripheral cues. However, the effect of sound is only significant when the peripheral window is not visible, as is suggested in that the performance shown in the top right panel is better than in the top left panel, but the performance shown across the two bottom panels is roughly the same.

Figure 3 summarizes the most important eye movement data from the experiment. These data measure the time spent to complete each of the four steps involved in classifying a blip: (a) Initiate the eye movement from the tracking window to the classification window (the radar); (b) once on the classification window, find the target and move the eyes to it; (c) keep the eyes on the blip until its visual features are identified and then move the eyes back to tracking; and (d) after the eyes are back on tracking, key-in the classification. The main differences in the eye movement data across the four conditions are: (a) The eyes-to-radar time and the eyes-to-target time are shorter in the peripheral visible conditions; and (b) the eyes-to-radar time is shorter when sound is on in the peripheral-not-visible conditions. These differences could no doubt contribute to the effects observed in Figure 2, which we set out to investigate through cognitive modeling.

THE COMPUTATIONAL COGNITIVE MODEL

The models presented in this paper are built using the EPIC (Executive Process-Interactive Control) cognitive architecture [11]. EPIC provides a general software framework for simulating humans interacting with a task environment. It models a human as an information processing system with a cognitive processor and various perceptual and motor processors. The cognitive processor

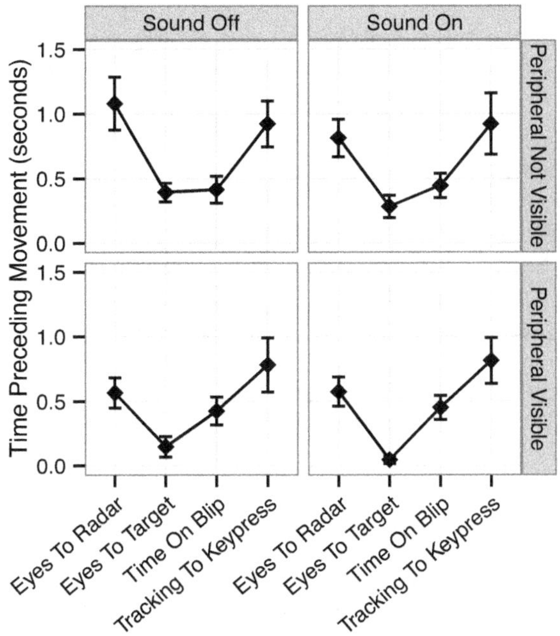

Figure 3. The time preceding the eye and hand movements needed to classify a blip. (The radar is the classification window.)

decides what actions to take based on perceptual information and preprogrammed task strategies which are written by an analyst as a set of IF-THEN statements called production rules. EPIC is particularly well-suited for exploring multitasking strategies; it only enforces sequential processing for motor activities, such as to constrain the hands to execute only one movement at a time. Perceptual information flows into the visual and auditory processors in parallel, though visual acuity degrades as objects move farther away from the center of the gaze. The cognitive processor can execute multiple production rules in a single 50 ms cycle. This view on multitasking—that serial processing bottlenecks only exist in the motor processing stage—is supported by previous psychological studies (e.g., [18]).

Figure 4 illustrates the basic structure of the multitasking strategy that we identified for the multimodal dual task (in [7]). The strategy consists mainly of two independent sets of production rules, represented abstractly by the top and the bottom state transition diagrams in the figure. One set of production rules summarized in the figure passes control of the ocular motor (eye movement) processor back and forth between the two tasks, while another set of rules passes control of the manual motor (hand movement) processor back and forth. This independent interleaving of ocular and manual motor processing was found (in [7]) to explain performance better than a hierarchical task decomposition, and is thus used across all strategies and all conditions.

The transition of the ocular motor processing from tracking to classification does not mean that the eyes are instructed at that point in time to move to the classification window. The decision of when to actually move the eyes is handled

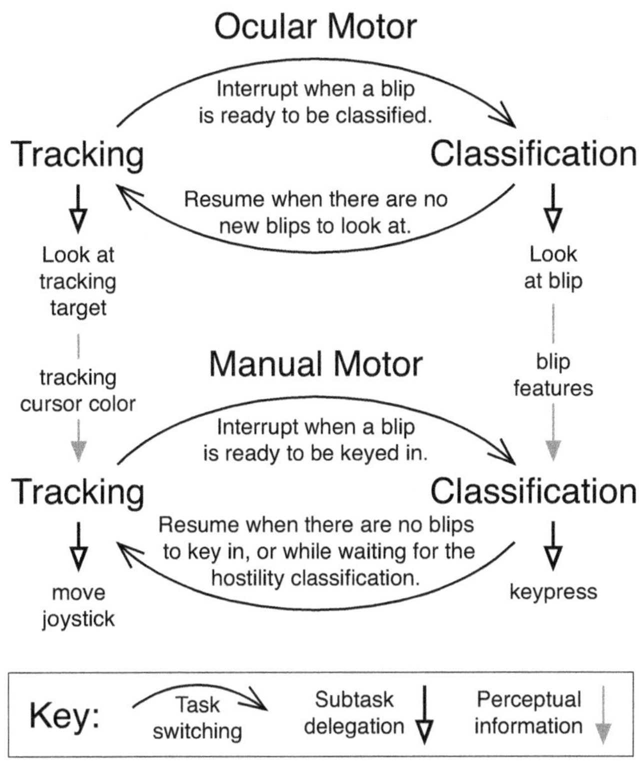

Figure 4. State transition diagrams showing the independent interleaving of the ocular motor (eye movement) and manual motor (hand movement) processing in the dual task model.

by decisions within the strategies which will be discussed later. Across all strategies, however, the decision of when to transition the ocular motor processing to classification is handled differently in different experimental conditions. The transition occurs in the peripheral-visible conditions when a blip color-change is detected, in the sound-on conditions when an auditory cue is detected, and in the sound-off and peripheral-not-visible condition when a self-paced periodic glance is initiated.

Some aspects of this basic strategy can be modified to represent variations in participant behaviors, such as to prioritize one task over the other, and this paper explores these variant strategies. In a previous study [7], we demonstrated that one variant strategy could fit the average participant performance. The present study goes beyond the previous study and introduces a modeling technique which provides a new principled approach to addressing some general theoretical modeling issues such as how to (a) systematically find strategies that explain the data, (b) minimize the model's degrees of freedom, and (c) explore a large strategy-and-parameter space in a reasonable amount of time.

STRATEGY AND PARAMETER SPACE EXPLORATION

A Systematic Approach for Exploring Strategies

For many tasks, a reasonable high-level structure for the task, such as that shown in Figure 4, can be identified through straightforward task analysis. But for many such tasks, the lower-level subtasks might be accomplished with numerous different substrategies, or *microstrategies* [5].

This view, that people exert cognitive control to select alternative task strategies, stands in contrast with modeling work (e.g., [16]) that assumes fixed strategies. As demonstrated by Gray and Boehm-Davis [5], people use different microstrategies even for tasks as simple as mouse-clicking under different task settings. Thus, it is necessary to explore many microstrategies to determine which strategies best explain human multitasking performance.

Conventional cognitive modeling studies (such as [16]) often present only one model that fits the human data. This is problematic because to show that a certain task strategy is necessary to explain the human data, one also needs to show that other strategies *cannot* fit the data [14]. With little or no information given about what other strategies were explored and why some strategies were ruled out, the modeling results and the conclusions based on them cannot be properly evaluated.

In the last decade, cognitive modeling researchers have started to explore strategies more systematically. Some studies (e.g., [2, 9, 10]) have explored strategies that can be numerically parameterized, such as in deciding how many keys to press before switching tasks, by sampling these parameters at regular intervals and executing all of the resulting strategies. Though this method is effective, many strategies that people actually employ include alternatives that cannot be parameterized numerically, such as in deciding whether to move the mouse before or after finding a target. To explore the effects of these sorts of alternative task strategies, Kieras and Meyer [12] proposed a bracketing heuristic in which a fastest-possible model and a slowest-reasonable model are used to "bracket" a reasonable range of task performance. However, the fastest and the slowest models may be hard to determine because the effects of all possible substrategies can be hard to predict without actually trying them all.

This paper proposes a systematic approach for exploring strategies, and applies it to the multimodal dual task model. The main idea of this approach is to organize plausible strategies into a well-defined multi-dimensional space with each dimension representing one aspect of the task that can be accomplished with alternative microstrategies. These dimensions can include alternatives that cannot be parameterized numerically. The strategy space can be thought of as a multidimensional grid, with each point in the grid representing a specific combination of microstrategies, with each microstrategy from a different dimension. By exploring all the strategies defined by the strategy space, we can see the complete range of the model's predicted task performance.

Table 1 shows the strategy space defined for the multimodal dual task. The strategy space consists of five dimensions, each of which contains two to three alternative microstrategies, and each of which relates to the task switching and subtask delegation shown in Figure 4. Dimension 1 controls how the model delegates the tracking subtask. Dimensions 2, 3, and 4 control when the model moves the eyes from the tracking window to the classification window, and where exactly it puts the eyes in the classification window. Dimension 5 controls how the model will sometimes switch manual motor from classification to tracking in the middle of a classification.

Dimension 1. How judiciously to track the target.
- **Joystick-Nonstop (JNS).** Track whenever possible.
- **Joystick-To-Green (JTG).** Track whenever necessary to keep the tracking cursor green.

Dimension 2. When to move the eyes to the classification window after seeing a blip change color.
- **Immediate-Eyes-To-Blip (IEB).** Move immediately.
- **Track-Then-Eyes-To-Blip (TEB).** Continue tracking until the tracking cursor is green and then move.

Dimension 3. When to move the eyes to the classification window after hearing an auditory cue.
- **Immediate-Eyes-To-Sound (IES).** Move immediately.
- **Track-Then-Eyes-To-Sound (TES).** Track until the auditory cue is classified and then move the eyes.

Dimension 4. In the peripheral-not-visible conditions, where exactly to put the eyes in the classification window when switching to the classification task.
- **Look-Window-Center (LWC).** Go to the center.
- **Look-Sound-Location (LSL).** Go to the exact location of the spatialized sound.
- **Look-Prior-Blip-Location (LBL).** Go to a blip location recalled from a previous visit.

Dimension 5. What to do with the hands after acquiring the visual features of a yellow blip but while waiting for the hostility classification to be retrieved from memory.
- **Keypad-Then-Joystick (KTJ).** Wait for the retrieval, key in the response, and then resume tracking.
- **Joystick-Until-Classification (JUC).** Track while waiting.
- **Interruptible-Tracking-Preparation (ITP).** Track while waiting but permit an immediate interruption upon retrieval.

Table 1. The strategy space explored in the dual task model. The space includes five strategic dimensions with each dimension having two or three alternative microstrategies.

These dimensions relate to some important general issues in multitasking. For example, Dimension 2 explores the effect of prioritizing one task over another. Dimensions 3 and 4 explore to what degree can people utilize information in auditory cues to assist with a secondary task. Dimension 5 examines what extent of overlapping is possible between the cognitive processes of one task (classifying a blip) and the manual motor processes of another (manual tracking). All of these issues are critical for understanding human performance in a wide range of multitasking contexts such as coordinating with specialists while piloting a drone, operating a navigation system while driving a car, or using a smartphone while walking down the street. By exploring this strategy space, we may learn something about the strategies that people use for general classes of time-critical, multimodal multitasking.

A Principled Approach for Setting Model Parameters

Aside from strategy exploration, another hurdle in conducting principled cognitive modeling is finding parameter settings that accurately characterize task-specific cognitive, perceptual, and motor capabilities. Default settings have been established for many parameters based on past psychological research, but for some tasks, parameters have not been established. To set these unknown parameters, a common practice is to sample many different settings until the model fits the data, but this approach increases the model's degrees of freedom and weakens its predictive power.

A more principled way to set the model parameters, advocated by Howes et al. [9], is to calibrate them using data sets that are not used to evaluate the model's goodness of fit. This will reduce the variability of the model when fitting the evaluation data, and hence increase the model's predictive power. We adopted this approach and calibrated the following parameters for our dual task model:

- *Text recoding time.* This parameter determines how long it takes to recognize the blip ID. It was calibrated using the fixation time on red and green blips.
- *Speed and direction recoding time.* This parameter determines how long it takes to acquire the yellow blips' visual features for hostility classification. It was calibrated using the fixation time on yellow blips.
- *Tracking coefficients.* These parameters determine the tracking movement time for any tracking distance. They were calibrated by fitting a Fitts' law equation to the long tracking movements extracted from the tracking error data (see [20] for a full discussion of this).
- *Glance interval.* This parameter determines how often the model should check for new blips in the sound-off and peripheral-not-visible condition. It was calibrated using the eye movement data from that condition.

None of these parameters were fitted directly to the evaluation data, which are the classification time and the RMS tracking error. This greatly reduces the model's degrees of freedom. However, not all parameters could be calibrated. Our model still has one free parameter—the hostility recoding time for yellow blips. Based on some preliminary exploration, we determined that the hostility recoding time could range from roughly 100 ms to 1200 ms, and so we sampled the parameter at 100 ms intervals to find the best-fitting setting for each participant. The parameter settings were explored in conjunction with strategy exploration using our parallelized cognitive modeling system, which we introduce next.

A Parallelized System for Cognitive Modeling

Fully exploring strategic dimensions and parameter settings requires a large number of models. In our case, there are 72 different strategies (the combinatorial product of the five strategy dimensions) and 12 settings for the hostility recoding time parameter, resulting in 864 models. Running one dual task model takes about 1 minute on a single core 1.8 GHz machine, and so running 864 models would require about 14 hours. If we were to model individual participant performance, this number would be multiplied by the number of participants. This long execution time makes it impractical to explore a large strategy and parameter space using a traditional modeling system on a contemporary desktop or laptop computer.

To solve this computational problem, we built a parallelized cognitive modeling (PCM) system that utilizes a computer cluster to speed up this large scale exploration. The specific cluster used here is part of the University of Oregon's Applied Computational Instrument for Scientific Synthesis. Though previous research [4] used a computer cluster to explore model parameters, our system pushes the boundary further by using a cluster to also explore task strategies.

Figure 5 shows the components of the PCM system and illustrates how it generates and parallelizes multiple models at once. The system takes three files as inputs: the basic model, the parameter space, and the strategy space. The basic model defines the basic structure of the strategy, such as the one shown in Figure 4, using production rules; it also includes slots that will be filled in later with specific parameter and strategy settings to generate complete models. The parameter space defines the ranges and sampling intervals for the model's free parameters. The strategy space includes instructions about how to modify

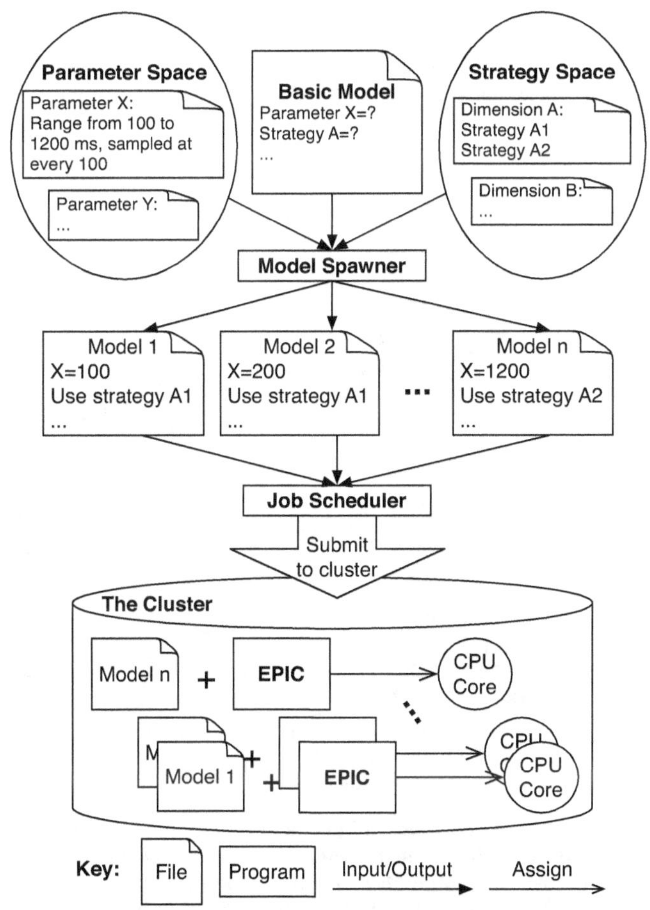

Figure 5. The components of the Parallelized Cognitive Modeling (PCM) system.

the basic model to implement each microstrategy. The instructions include which production rules to modify, and what conditions and actions to add and delete. The three files are fed into the *model spawner*, which parses the parameter definitions and the strategy modification instructions. The spawner then modifies the basic model to generate versions of the model that together span across all possible strategy and parameter settings. The generated models are then arranged by the *job scheduler* which assigns each model to run on a CPU core in the cluster. By using the PCM system, the original 14-hour running time on a desktop machine is reduced to less than 20 minutes. This enables us to conduct truly large scale modeling and to collect much more comprehensive results than has been feasible in previous cognitive modeling studies.

RESULTS

Modeling The Average Human Performance

This section presents the results of using the parallelized cognitive modeling (PCM) system to explore the strategy and parameter space defined earlier for the multimodal dual task. Figure 6 compares the predictions of all 864 models with the aggregated human data. As in Figure 2, each panel plots the average classification time against the RMS tracking error for one of the four conditions. The diamonds show the human data. The data clouds show the model predictions, with one data point per model. The results for yellow blips and for red-and-green blips are shown separately. The more the clouds fall within the human data brackets, the better the models explain the observed data.

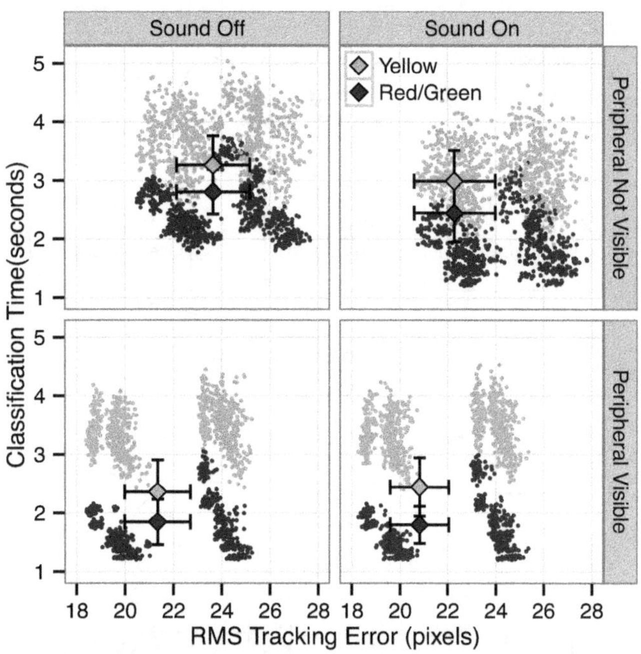

Figure 6. The observed and predicted classification time and RMS tracking error for each of the four experimental conditions. The diamonds show the participant means and the 95% CIs. The clouds show the predictions from the 864 different models, with the light gray plot symbols for yellow blips and the dark gray symbols for red and green blips.

Though the clouds in Figure 6 span large areas, the clouds still show trends that are similar to those observed in the human data. These trends include: (a) The clouds in the bottom panels are generally lower and more to the left than those in the top panels indicating that, in the peripheral-visible condition, the models predict better performance for both classification and tracking; (b) the clouds in the top-left panel are higher and more to the right than those in the top-right panel indicating that, in the peripheral-not-visible conditions, the model predicts better performance for both tasks when auditory cues are present; and (c) the clouds in the bottom two panels look virtually the same suggesting that, when the peripheral window is visible, the model predicts that auditory cues have no effect. All of these effects are consistent with the human data, suggesting that the model's basic strategy captures the main effects of the experimental conditions.

Though the models predict the effects of auditory and visual cues, they do not fit the human data in all conditions. Particularly in the peripheral-visible conditions, the human data fall between the two parts of the clouds as opposed to on the clouds. Figure 7 shows that the left and right parts of the clouds shown in each frame in Figure 6 result from the two Dimension 1 microstrategies. The left part of the cloud is produced by the Joystick-Nonstop (JNS) microstrategy, and the right part is produced by the Joystick-To-Green (JTG) microstrategy. The JNS microstrategy clearly produces a smaller tracking error than the JTG microstrategy. In all conditions, the human data are closer to the predictions of JNS than to those of JTG, which suggests that the participants tried hard to optimize tracking

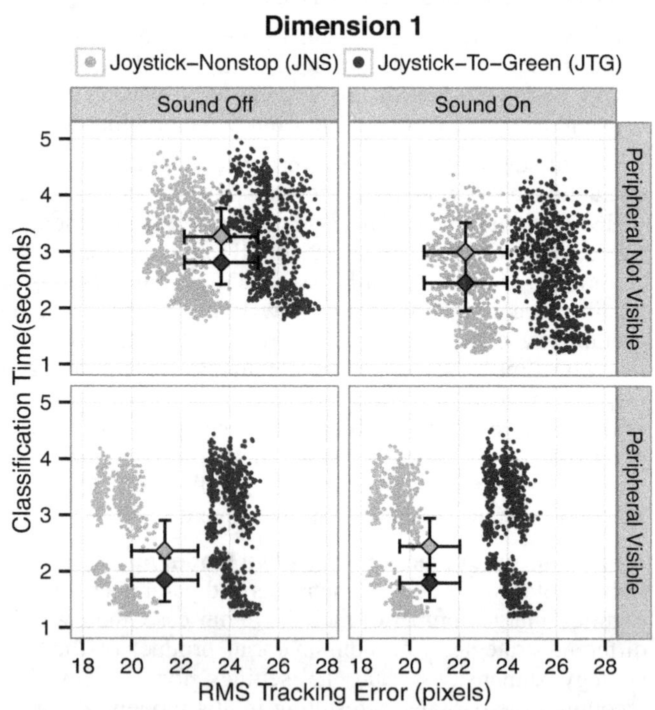

Figure 7. The effect of the microstrategies of Dimension 1. The data are the same as in Figure 6, but the clouds are shaded differently to distinguish the two microstrategies.

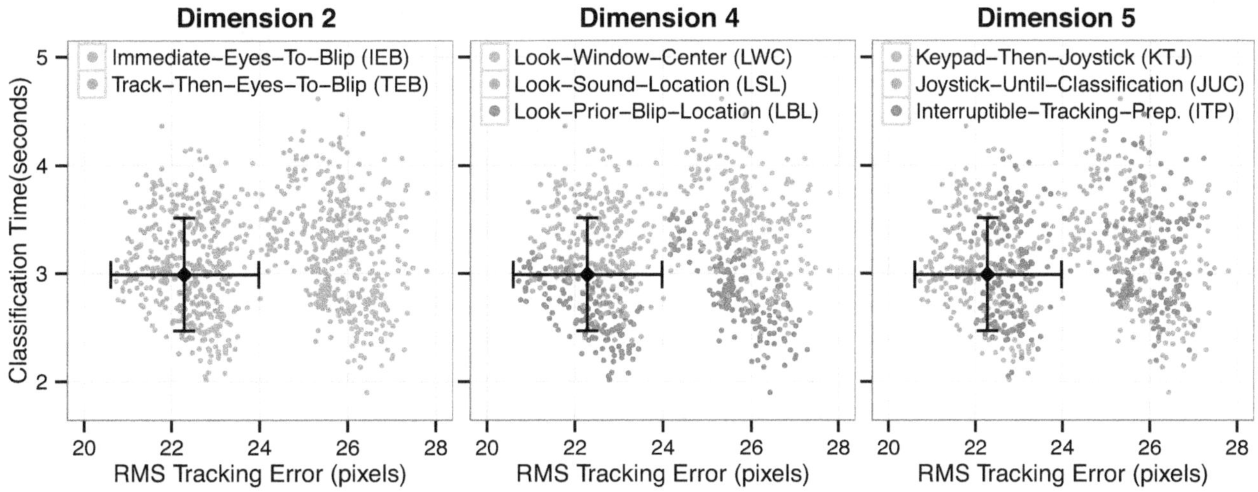

Figure 8. The effects of different microstrategies from Dimensions 2, 4, and 5 shown in different colors. Each panel shows the human data and model predictions for the sound-on and peripheral-not-visible condition.

performance. The difference in the cloud densities between the top two panels and the bottom two panels suggests an interaction between peripheral visibility and some other aspect of the model.

Figure 8 continues the examination of the effects of microstrategies for Dimensions 2, 4, and 5 to find out which strategies explain the data better. The results for Dimension 3 are not shown because the microstrategies in that dimension did not generate a range of different predictions. Each panel in Figure 8 shows only the results from the sound-on and peripheral-not-visible condition, and for yellow blips. The effects of microstrategies in other experimental conditions are similar.

The first panel in Figure 8 shows the effect of Dimension 2. There is a small difference between the Immediate-Eyes-To-Blip (IEB) microstrategy, which immediately moves the eyes to the classification window, and the Track-Then-Eyes-To-Blip (TEB) microstrategy. The prediction cloud of TEB is generally higher and more to the left than that of IEB, which illustrates that, between the two microstrategies, TEB prioritizes tracking whereas IEB prioritizes classification. However, judging from this graph alone, it is unclear which strategy leads to a better overall payoff. Answering this question requires a more comprehensive analysis, presented later.

The second panel in Figure 8 shows the effect of the Dimension 4 microstrategies, which control where to look in the classification window. Because the Look-Window-Center microstrategy usually requires additional visual search to find the blip, it is not surprising that it predicts the longest classification time (the yellow cloud). It is, however, surprising that the Look-Sound-Location (LSL) microstrategy (the blue cloud) takes longer to classify the blip than the Look-Prior-Blip-Location (LBL) microstrategy (the green cloud), which performs the best in both tasks. Further examination of the model shows that LSL is slower because extracting the location information from sound requires roughly 200 ms under the EPIC cognitive architecture, and this delay exceeds the average time to put the eyes on the target by selecting a prior blip location from memory.

The third panel in Figure 8 shows the effect of the Dimension 5 microstrategies, which decide what to do with the hands after a blip has been fixated but before the hostility classification has been retrieved such that the blip's classification could be keyed-in. The Joystick-Until-Classification (JUC) and Interruptible-Tracking-Preparation (ITP) microstrategies use this time to perform the tracking task, whereas the Keypad-Then-Joystick microstrategy stays idle until the classification is retrieved. Intuitively, Strategies JUC and ITP should outperform ITP in both the classification and tracking tasks because they perform the two tasks simultaneously. However, the graph shows that although Strategies JUC and ITP predict better tracking performance, they also predict slightly longer classification time. Further examination of the model shows that prioritizing manual tracking sometimes postpones the classification response. This low-level interaction between the two tasks may be overlooked by theory-based qualitative reasoning but is easily captured by quantitative computational modeling.

In all three panels of Figure 8, the human data (the brackets) have a large variance across the predictions of all of the microstrategies. This again suggests that all participants did not use the same microstrategies. Individualized models are needed to explore how different participants likely selected different microstrategies and how this likely led to individual performance variations.

Modeling The Individual Performance

Figure 9 illustrates how the average-performance model fails to capture individual participant performance variations. The graph superimposes the observed data from each of the ten participants on the model predictions. To simplify the presentation, only the results for yellow blips are shown. As can be seen in the top panels, the observations for individual participants fall mostly on the

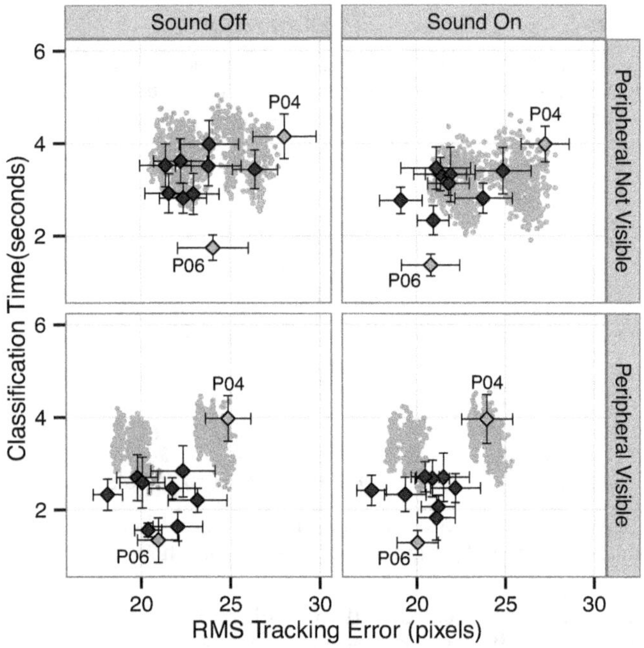

Figure 9. The individual data for each of the ten participants (the diamond-shaped plot symbols) compared to the predictions of the model built for the aggregated human data (the gray clouds). P04 and P06's data are indicated.

clouds, and in the bottom panels mostly between and below the clouds. That the clouds do not envelop the human data across all conditions shows that the model as it stands cannot fully account for individual participant performance.

Individualized models are needed to explain individual performance. Participants have different cognitive, perceptual, and motor capabilities and to generate accurate predictions for each participant these differences need to be reflected in the model's parameter settings for each participant. Such individualized parameter settings can be obtained by calibrating the parameters using individual data rather than aggregated data. Then, the strategy and parameter space can be explored in the same manner as was done for the average-performance model, but this time to find the best-fitting model for each individual participant.

Figure 10 shows the results of this individualized modeling for the top performer P06 and the bottom performer P04. (Again, only the results for yellow blips are shown.) Note how the prediction clouds for each condition shift across the two participants. When compared to Figure 9, it can be seen that the individualized-parameter models explain the individual data better than the model that was parameterized based on the aggregated human data. The plots for P06 in Figure 10 show that the clouds now approach P06's data more closely than the clouds in Figure 9. The top two panels for P04 in Figure 10 show the prediction clouds readily encompassing P04's data whereas, in the top two panels in Figure 9, P04 fell at the edge of the clouds. It is only through individualized modeling that we are able to account for the divergent behaviors in the top and bottom performers.

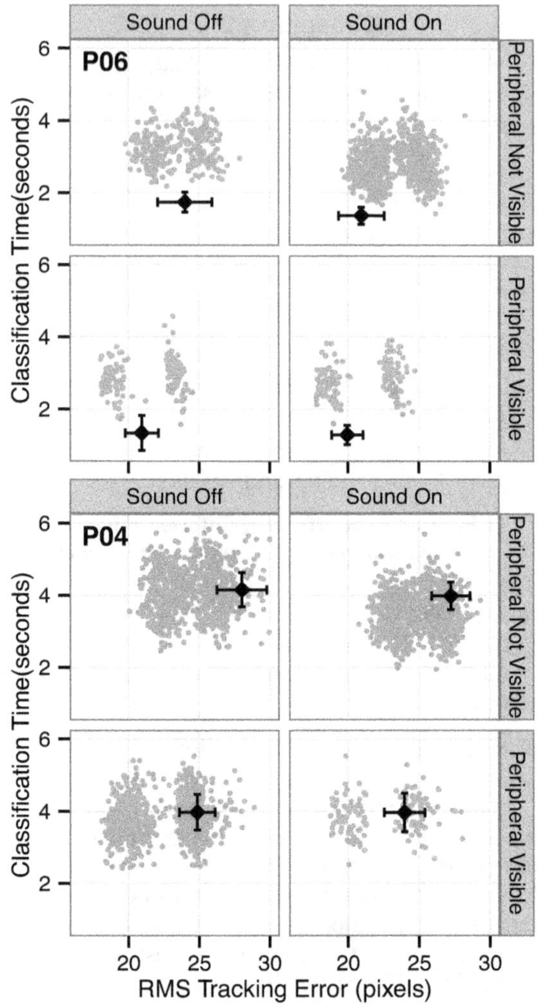

Figure 10. The observed data and predictions of the individualized models for P06 and P04.

The Best-Fitting Individualized Models

One benefit to building individualized models is that it helps to reveal the strategies that lead to good task performance, which has implications for training and personnel selection. This section thus compares the strategies of the top and bottom performers to identify the optimal microstrategies for this task.

Table 2 shows the best strategy and parameter settings produced by the PCM system to account for the performance of each of the ten participants, and to account for the average performance. The individualized models are sorted from best to worst participant performance as determined by the bonus that each participant earned. The best fitting strategy and parameter settings were determined by finding the model with the lowest average absolute error (AAE) in its prediction of each participant's classification response time (RT) and tracking error (TE). Table 2 illustrates which microstrategy selections appear to have contributed to good overall performance, and to some participants performing better than others.

	Participant	Strategy Dimension Dim1	Dim2	Dim3	Dim4	Dim5	Hostility Recoding Time (ms)	RT and TE (AAE)	Participant Bonus
Top Performers	P06	JNS	IEB	IES	LBL	ITP	200	14%	$17.86
	P20	JNS	IEB	IES	LSL	JUC	300	6%	$17.85
	P07	JNS	IEB	IES	LBL	ITP	200	13%	$17.63
	P17	JNS	TEB	TES	LBL	KTJ	100	7%	$17.16
	P10	JNS	IEB	IES	LSL	JUC	500	8%	$16.61
Bottom Performers	P11	JNS	TEB	TES	LWC	ITP	100	15%	$16.45
	P09	JNS	TEB	TES	LSL	JUC	200	9%	$14.75
	P12	JNS	TEB	TES	LWC	ITP	200	7%	$14.75
	P16	JTG	IEB	IES	LWC	JUC	500	8%	$14.13
	P04	JTG	TEB	TES	LWC	JUC	900	5%	$11.94
	AP Model	JNS	TEB	TES	LWC	ITP	100	8%	

Table 2. The best fitting strategies and hostility recoding times for the individualized participant models and for the average-performance (AP) model.

For Dimensions 1 and 5, nearly all participants selected the same high-payoff microstrategies. For Dimension 1, nearly all used the Joystick-Nonstop (JNS) microstrategy and, for Dimension 5, the Joystick-Until-Classification (JUC) and Interruptible-Tracking-Preparation (ITP) microstrategies. As discussed earlier and as illustrated in Figures 7 and 8, these microstrategies lead to better tracking performance and roughly the same level of classification performance compared to the other microstrategies in Dimensions 1 and 5. That nearly all participants appeared to employ these high-payoff microstrategy selections suggests that, for some strategic dimensions, given appropriate motivation and feedback, all participants are able to optimize rather than just satisfice in their performance, as in [9].

However, for Dimensions 2, 3, and 4, it seems that some participants were more successful than others at finding high-payoff microstrategies. As can be seen in Table 2, the top five performers tended to use, for Dimension 2, the Immediate-Eyes-To-Blip (IEB) microstrategy; for Dimension 3, Immediate-Eyes-To-Sound (IES); and for Dimension 4, Look-Prior-Blip-Location (LBL) and Look-Sound-Location (LSL). Whereas the bottom five performers tended to use, for Dimension 2, Track-Then-Eyes-To-Blip (TEB); for Dimension 3, Track-Then-Eyes-To-Sound (TES); and for Dimension 4, Look-Window-Center (LWC). It appears as if at least some of the observed differences in multitasking performance can be explained in terms of microstrategy selection.

The top performers somehow found the high-payoff microstrategies. For Dimensions 2 and 3, IEB and IES are better than TEB and TES because the first two prioritize classification over tracking whenever there is a blip to classify, which is a good decision given how little the tracking target typically drifts in the time that is required to key-in a classification, and how quickly classification-delay penalties accrue; that the IES microstrategy appears to have been used by top performers suggests that it is not worth spending the time required to decode the auditory cue to assist with classification—it is better to just look at the blip as soon as possible. For Dimension 4, LSL and LBL perform better than LWC because LSL uses sound and LBL uses memory to find the active blip, both evidently more quickly than the LWC approach of essentially saying "I'll figure it out when I get there." It appears as if the bottom performers failed to adopt these more efficient microstrategies, perhaps because they took more work, or perhaps because the benefit of adopting them was not clear.

Comparing the strategies of the average-performance model (the bottom row in Table 2) with those of the individualized models shows that the conventional approach of modeling the average human performance may not lead to the most accurate model. As can be seen in Table 2, the microstrategies of the average-performance model are more similar to those of the bottom performers than those of the top performers, and the average-performance model's estimated hostility recoding time (100 ms) is shorter than most of the participants' estimated times. If we were to base our conclusions on the results of the average-performance model, we might conclude that the participants did not find the optimal microstrategies (such as LBL and LSL in Dimension 4) and that participants seemed to be very fast at classifying hostility. The individualized models, however, suggest that the participants were not very fast at hostility classification (the average encoding time is 320 ms) but were able to compensate for it with faster strategies. Fitting a model to average human data will sometimes lead to incorrect conclusions. Individualized modeling may be necessary to understand human multitasking performance.

DISCUSSION

This paper demonstrates that multitasking performance might be best understood with highly parallelized microstrategy exploration in the context of individualized computational cognitive modeling. By running and analyzing 8,640 models on a cluster-based parallelized cognitive modeling system, we showed that the difference between the top and bottom performers did not appear to result from their intrinsic perceptual, cognitive, and motor capabilities but rather from their skill at orchestrating a complex symphony of microstrategy selection, coordination, and execution. The effect of microstrategy selection on overall task performance suggests that multitasking is not accomplished by simply interleaving subtasks but rather with a controlled process that involves many micro-decisions which together determine overall task performance.

The cognitive modeling work presented here has powerful implications for the design of user interfaces intended for use in multitasking scenarios which, in the age of mobile computing, includes pretty much all computer interfaces. First, our modeling results suggest that effective multitasking might only occur when manual motor processing can be managed independently of ocular motor processing across two tasks or devices. Given the high demand of both ocular and manual motor processing when using touchscreen interfaces, it is questionable whether contemporary smartphones lend themselves to effective multitasking. Second, that microstrategies can so dramatically impact multitasking performance suggests that interface designers, if they wish to design a highly effective user interface, should thoughtfully consider how their designs will support a range of efficient microstrategies. Parallelized strategy exploration and individualized cognitive modeling may be key to understanding and ultimately accommodating human performance in time-pressured multitasking settings.

ACKNOWLEDGMENTS
This project was funded in part by NSF grant IIS-1017593 and, for the computer cluster, NSF grant OCI-0960354. The opinions expressed are strictly those of the authors.

REFERENCES
1. Ballas, J., Heitmeyer, C., and Perez-Quinones, M. (1992). Evaluating two aspects of direct manipulation in advanced cockpits. In *Proceedings of CHI*, 127–134.
2. Brumby, D. P., Salvucci, D. D., and Howes, A. (2009). Focus on driving: How cognitive constraints shape the adaptation of strategy when dialing while driving. In *Proceedings of CHI*, 1629–1638.
3. Card, S. K., Moran, T. P., and Newell, A. (1983). *The psychology of human-computer interaction*. Hillsdale, NJ: Lawrence Erlbaum Associates.
4. Gluck, K. A., Stanley, C. T., Moore, L. R., Reitter, D., and Halbrügge, M. (2010). Exploration for understanding in cognitive modeling. *Journal of Artificial General Intelligence, 2*(2), 88–107.
5. Gray, W. D. and Boehm-Davis, D. A. (2000). Milliseconds matter: An introduction to microstrategies and to their use in describing and predicting interactive behavior. *J. Exp. Psychol.: Applied, 6*(4), 322–335.
6. Halverson, T. and Hornof, A. J. (2011). A computational model of "active vision" for visual search in human-computer interaction. *Human-Computer Interaction, 26*, 285–314.
7. Hornof, A. J. and Zhang, Y. (2010). Task-constrained interleaving of perceptual and motor processes in a time-critical dual task as revealed through eye tracking. In *Proceedings of the 10th International Conference on Cognitive Modeling, 97–102*.
8. Hornof, Zhang, and Halverson (2010). Knowing where and when to look in a time-critical multimodal dual task. In *Proceedings of CHI*, 2103–2112.
9. Howes, A., Lewis, R. L., and Vera, A. (2009). Rational adaptation under task and processing constraints: Implications for testing theories of cognition and action. *Psychological Review, 116*(4), 717–751.
10. Janssen, C., Brumby, D., Dowell, J., Chater, N., and Howes, A. (2011). Identifying optimum performance trade-offs using a cognitively bounded rational analysis model of discretionary task interleaving. *Topics in Cognitive Science, 3*(1), 123–139.
11. Kieras, D. E. and Meyer, D. E. (1997). An overview of the EPIC architecture for cognition and performance with application to human-computer interaction. *Human-Computer Interaction, 12*(4), 391–438.
12. Kieras, D. E. and Meyer, D. E. (2000). The role of cognitive task analysis in the application of predictive models of human performance. In J. M. Schraagen, S. F. Chipman, V. L. Shalin, & V. Shalin (Eds.), *Cognitive task analysis* (pp. 237–260). Mahwah, NJ: Erlbsum.
13. Olson, R. L., Hanowski, R. J., Hickman, J. S., and Bocanegra, J. (2009). *Driver distraction in commercial vehicle operations*. Technical report #FMCSA-RRR-09-045. U.S. Department of Transportation.
14. Roberts, S. and Pashler, H. (2000). How persuasive is a good fit? A comment on theory testing. *Psychological Review, 107*(2), 358–367.
15. Richtel, M. (2009, December 6). Promoting the car phone, despite risks. *New York Times*. Retrieved from http://www.nytimes.com.
16. Salvucci, D. and Taatgen, N. (2008). Threaded cognition: An integrated theory of concurrent multitasking. *Psychological Review, 115*(1), 101–130.
17. Sanford, E. C. (1888). Personal equation. *The American Journal of Psychology, 2*(1), pp. 3–38.
18. Wickens, C. D. (2002). Multiple resources and performance prediction. *Theoretical Issues in Ergonomics Science, 3*(2), 159–177.
19. Williams, A. F. and Lund A. K. (1986). Seat belt use laws and occupant crash protection in the United States. *Am. J. Public Health, 76*(12), 1438–1442.
20. Zhang, Y. and Hornof, A. (2012). A discrete movement model for cursor tracking derived from moment-to-moment tracking data and the modeling of a dual-task experiment. In *Proceedings of the 56th Human Factors and Ergonomics Society Annual Meeting, 1000–1024*.

How Does Knowing What You Are Looking For Change Visual Search Behavior?

Duncan P. Brumby, Anna L. Cox, Jacqueline Chung, Byron Fernandes
UCL Interaction Centre
University College London
London WC1E 6BT UK
Brumby@cs.ucl.ac.uk

ABSTRACT
When searching a display, users sometimes know what the target is but sometimes do not. It has generally been assumed that for this latter case people must engage in a deeper semantic evaluation of items during the search process. This idea is central to Information Foraging theory. But do people actually spend longer assessing items when engaged in a semantically demanding search task? We investigate this by having participants locate target items in 16-item menus. Participants were either told exactly what to look for (known-item search) or they were told the category that the target belonged to (semantic search). Participants were faster and more accurate at known-item searches. Eye-movement data show that this was because participants were more likely to skip over items when performing known-item searches. Contrary to expectation, we found limited empirical evidence to support the idea that deeper semantic evaluations of items lead to longer gaze durations (this occurred only when items were arranged very close together). This finding is important because it reveals how people adopt different eye gaze strategies depending on the kind of search activity they are engaged in.

Author Keywords
Visual search; menus; information foraging; eye-tracking.

ACM Classification Keywords
H.5.2 User Interfaces: evaluation/methodology, screen design, theory and methods; H.1.2 User/Machine Systems: human factors, human information processing.

INTRODUCTION
Computer users spend a great deal of time looking at and searching displays, whether that be launching an application from a menu on a smartphone or finding the cheapest flight to Toronto on a webpage. It is perhaps not surprising then that since the inception of HCI there has been a sustained interest in studying visual search [3,4,6,7,9-11,13,15].

CHI 2014, April 26–May 1, 2014, Toronto, Ontario, Canada.

http://dx.doi.org/10.1145/2556288.2557064

Across the literature, a basic distinction can be made in the kind of search tasks that users have been asked to perform. In one tradition, the user is given a precise description of the target item that must found. We refer to this as *known-item* search, and a number of studies have investigated this in detail [3,6,7,15]. An everyday example of this kind of search might be launching the Angry Birds application on a smartphone. This is a relatively simple search task because the user knows precisely what it is they are looking for. It has therefore been assumed that items need only be assessed in terms of their surface features [5,10,17,19]

In contrast to known-item search, there are many instances in which the user has a clear goal in mind but only a vague idea of how the target will be specified. We refer to this as *semantic* search. Studies have investigated this kind of search, with a particular focus given to how people look for information on the Internet [2,4,8]. Information foraging theory [9,16] has been highly influential for understanding this activity because it describes how people go about assessing the semantic relatedness of items to their search goal – that is, the *information scent.* Given that it takes time to retrieve information from memory, it has long been speculated that assessments of items should be longer during semantic search than during known-item search [17,19].

In this paper, we investigate differences in how people perform known-item and semantic searches. These tasks have been extensively studied in the literature, but separately – there have been surprisingly few attempts to compare how people perform these different kinds of search tasks. What few studies there have been have found that known-item searches are faster and more accurate than semantic searches [12,13]. However, these early studies did not make use of eye-tracking techniques to investigate underlying changes in search strategy. If semantically assessing an item incurs an added time cost we might expect this to be reflected in eye movement data: Fixations to items should be longer during semantic searches than during known-item searches. We provide the first direct test of this hypothesis.

A further aspect of search behavior that concerns us here is the observation that people often do not sequentially look at every item in turn when scanning through a menu – occasionally items are skipped. This item skipping behavior has been documented in known-item searches [5,10] as well as semantic searches [4]. It is generally assumed that the reason people skip over items while searching is that they accumulate enough visual information to rule-out an item while it is in peripheral vision. We test a novel prediction of this account: People should be more likely to skip items when performing known-item searches than semantic searches. This is because items can be assessed on the basis of visual features during known-item searches. Hence, items can be assessed quickly and on the basis of partial information available from peripheral vision. In contrast, assessing the semantic meaning of an item requires it to be read carefully. Hence, items must be directly fixated. We investigate this skipping hypothesis by varying the physical distance between menu items, as this will determine how much visual information is available from each eye movement: more items can be assessed within a single fixation when items are placed closer together [10].

METHOD

Participants

Thirty-three participants (six male) were recruited through the UCL Psychology Subject Pool to take part in the study. Participants were between 19 and 21 years of age. All were native English speakers, with normal or corrected-to-normal vision, and experienced computer users.

Materials

A target item had to be found in a menu containing 16 items. Each item in the menu was a single word, which was sampled from a dataset (adapted from [18]) of 560 unique words (with character length $M = 6.2$, $SD = 2.0$, range: 2 – 12). The words in this dataset were organized into natural categories. There were 14 top-level categories (e.g., animal, building, entertainment), with each of these separated into four mid-level categories (e.g., bird, farm animal, tropical fish, and wild animal are all members of the animal category). Finally, for each mid-level category there were 10 instances (e.g., bluebird, canary, starling, eagle, hawk are all members of the bird sub-category). Using this dataset it was possible to generate menus in which every item in the menu came from a different mid-level category.

Menu items were arranged in a single vertical list, one item per line. The vertical separation between items was varied between conditions (see design). The first item in the menu was positioned 80 pixels from the top of the screen. All text was presented in an Arial font, size 10. Stimuli were presented on a 17-inch TFT monitor set at a resolution of 1280 by 1024 pixels. Eye movements were recorded using a Tobii 1750 eye tracker. The sampling rate of the eye tracker was 50 Hz, with gaze point accuracy of less than 0.5 degrees of visual angle. The experimental software ran on a Dell Optiplex machine with 1 GB of RAM running Microsoft Windows XP. An optical mouse was used, set at the 'medium' speed via the system control panel.

Design

A 2 x 3 (search type x layout) within-subjects design was used. We varied the target description that was given to participants between different search type conditions. For known-item searches, participants were given the target word (e.g., find the word canary). For semantic searches, participants were given a mid-level category description of the target (e.g., find a type of bird). For the manipulation of menu layout the vertical separation between items was systematically varied from a small gap (17 pixels, 0.40° visual angle), to a medium gap (35.5 pixels, 0.85° visual angle), to a large gap (55 pixels, 1.3° visual angle).

Procedure

Participants were informed that they would be required to search menus to locate a target item and that they would be given either the precise label for the item that had to be found in the menu or they would be given a category label for the item. This target description was given at the start of each search trial. After reading it, participants started the trial by clicking on a button on the screen. This made the target description disappear, and the menu was displayed beneath it. Participants were told that there was only a single target item in each menu and that they had to locate it as quickly as possible. Participants selected an item by clicking on it with the mouse. If an incorrect selection was made, participants were instructed to make another selection from the same menu after being shown the target information again. The trial ended when the participant had successfully selected the target. Before proceeding to the next trial, participants were given feedback on the time taken to locate the target. The purpose of this feedback was to reinforce the instruction to locate the target quickly.

Each participant completed 84 menu search trials, divided into six blocks of 14 trials each (grouped by each of the search type x gap size experimental conditions). Each block had an initial set of four practice trials, followed by 10 critical trials. Each trial consisted of a unique (and automatically generated) menu. The order in which each condition was experienced was partially counter-balanced between participants: Half of the participants did all of the known-item searches before the semantic searches, or vice versa. Within each search type, the order in which each display layout was experienced was randomized across participants (but held consistent across conditions). Participants were given the opportunity for a short break after completing each block of 14 trials. The eye tracker was calibrated before the start of each block to ensure accurate gaze tracking. Participants were seated approximately 60-70 cm from the monitor throughout the experiment. The entire experiment took approximately 30 minutes to complete.

Figure 1. Search time as function of target position.

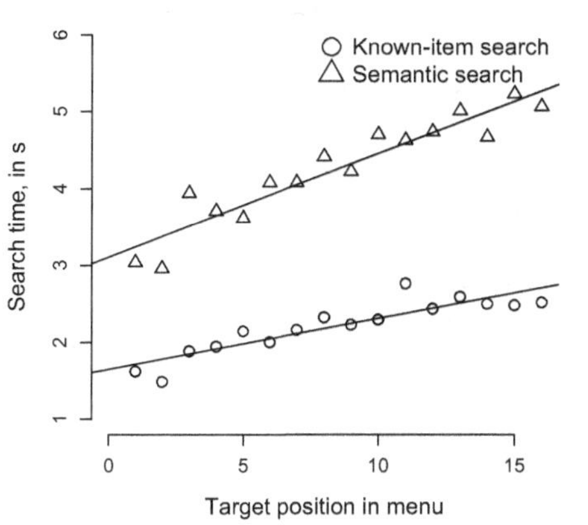

Figure 2. Duration of item visits by condition.

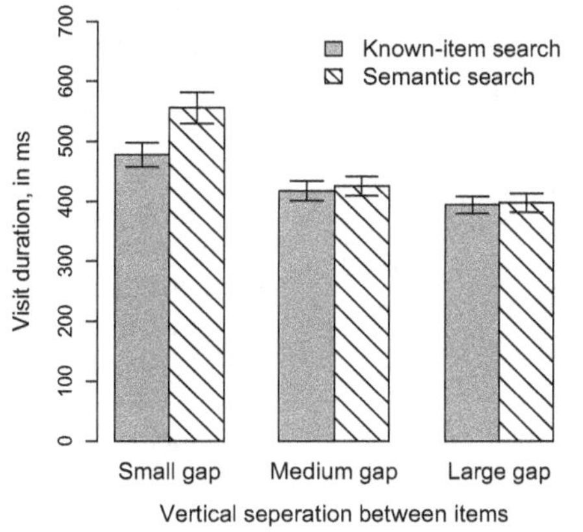

Figure 3. Distance between item visits by condition.

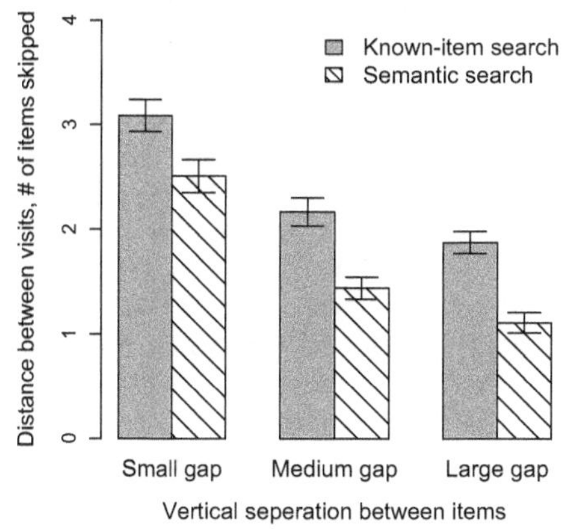

RESULTS

A 2 x 3 (search type x layout) repeated measures ANOVA was used, with a .05 significance level for judging the significance of effects. We excluded trials from the analysis in which the participant did not correctly select the target item on the first attempt. Accuracy was generally very high, but participants did make more errors when performing semantic searches (M = 18%, SD = 12%) than known-item searches (M = 1%, SD = 4%), $F(1, 32) = 139.20$, $p < .001$. There was no significant main effect of layout nor was there a significant interaction.

In terms of search time, participants were faster at locating targets when performing known-item searches (M = 2.21, SD = 0.45) than semantic searches (M = 3.68, SD = 0.77), $F(1, 32) = 269.80$, $p < .001$. Search times also became slower as the size of the vertical gap between items increased from a small gap (M = 2.76, SD = 0.93), to a medium gap (M = 2.88, SD = 0.87), to a large gap (M = 3.20, SD = 1.05), $F(2, 64) = 20.18$, $p < .001$. There was no significant interaction. In addition to this basic analysis, we also consider how search time varies as a function of the position of the target within the menu. Figure 1 shows that there is a simple linear relationship between search time and target position for both known-item searches, $y = .14x + 3.11$, $R^2 = 0.80$, and for semantic searches, $y = .07x + 1.65$, $R^2 = 0.89$. The larger slope and intercept for the semantic search model suggest a slower and more deliberate assessment strategy during this kind of search.

We next consider eye movement data to understand how participants were assessing items during search. For each search trial, we define a *visit sequence*. To do this, we map each fixation to the nearest item in the menu (up to a maximum distance threshold), before collapsing multiple contiguous fixations to the same item together. The resulting visit sequence describes the order in which items in the menu were assessed as well as the duration of each of these assessments. From this we can calculate for each trial the mean duration of visits as well as the mean distance between consecutive visits.

Figure 2 shows the mean duration of item visits across conditions. It can be seen that there is a significant search-type by layout interaction, $F(2, 64) = 6.14$, $p < .01$. Follow-up tests of this interaction show that item visits were longer for semantic searches than known-item searches, but only when there was a small gap between each item, $F(1, 32) = 11.91$, $p < .005$. When there was a larger gap between items (medium or large), there was no effect of search type on the duration of item visits, F's < 1. It can also be seen that the duration of item visits increased when items were closer together; that is, there was a main effect of gap size on visit durations, $F(2, 64) = 49.51$, $p < .001$.

Figure 3 shows the distance between consecutive item visits. This provides an indication of the mean number of items that were skipped over from one visit to the next during a search trial. For example, imagine a sequence in which items 1, 3, 6, 7 are visited. The number of items skipped between each visit is then 1, 2, 0, giving a mean of 1 item being skipped between visits for this sequence. Figure 3 shows that participants tended to skip over more items between visits when performing known-item searches than when performing semantic searches, $F(1, 32) = 23.52$, $p < .001$. Participants also skipped over more items when they were closer together, $F(2, 64) = 30.83$, $p < .001$. The interaction was not significant.

Finally, we consider how often participants selected the target item straight after visiting it for the first time – we refer to this as self-terminating search [11]. This measure gives an index of how often the target was missed on the first pass. There were more self-terminating search trials for known-item searches (M = 86%, SD = 20%) than for semantic searches (M = 61%, SD = 21%), $F(1, 32) = 89.94$, $p < .001$. This suggests that when performing known-item searches participants rarely missed the target when it is within their gaze. There was no effect of gap size nor was there a significant interaction.

DISCUSSION

The results of this study show how eye gaze strategy is influenced by the kind of search activity a user is performing. We found that during known-item searches participants were more likely to skip over items when searching a menu and were more likely to select the target immediately after locating it. In contrast, during semantic searches participants were more likely to assess items in turn. This finding could potentially inform the development of real-time gaze tracking systems that try to infer a user's search intentions based on their eye movements [20].

We found limited empirical evidence to support the intuitive idea that assessing the semantics of a label during search – inferring an item's *information scent* –is reflected in longer item gazes. Our results show that item gazes were longer for semantic searches but only when items were arranged close together. These longer gazes probably occurred because the close proximity of items allowed participants to assess multiple items with a single fixation. Consistent with this we also found that participants were more likely to skip over items when searching tightly packed menus. In contrast, when items were placed farther apart, assessments had to occur individually, and we found no evidence to suggest that semantic assessments incur an added time cost per assessment in this situation. We should however remain mindful that it is difficult to rule out the possibility that participants might have been accessing the semantic meaning of an item from memory *after* the focus of gaze had moved on to the next item in the menu [1].

One way to explore these explanations in more detail is to model these data. There is a long tradition of modeling menu selection tasks and various accounts of the underlying cognitive and perpetual-motor processes have been put forward [3,6,7,9-11]. We might speculate that Hornof's model [10] should be able to account for the item skipping behavior observed here. However, this model currently lacks a mechanistic account of the memory retrieval process required for semantic search. This could be reconciled by incorporating elements from Fu and Pirolli's model [9], which provides a detailed account of this process. Of particular interest to us though is recent work by Myers et al. [14] who use Reinforcement Learning techniques to explain the emergence of various eye movement strategies in a visual search task. Future work is necessary to ascertain whether these models can capture the data reported here.

ACKNOWLEDGEMENTS

We thank Gilles Bailly, Antti Oulasvirta, and Andrew Howes for encouraging us to publish this work, as well as our reviewers for their constructive feedback.

REFERENCES

1. Anderson, J.R., Bothell, D., & Douglass, S. Eye movements do not reflect retrieval: Limits of the eye-mind hypothesis. *Psychological Science, 15*, (2004), 225-231.
2. Aula, A., Khan, R.M., & Guan, Z. How does search behavior change as search becomes more difficult? *Proc. CHI '10*, ACM (2010), 35-44.
3. Bailly, G., Oulasvirta, A., Brumby, D.P., & Howes, A. Model of visual search and selection time in linear menus. *Proc. CHI '14*, ACM (2014).
4. Brumby, D.P. & Howes, A. Strategies for guiding interactive search: An empirical investigation into the consequences of label relevance for assessment and selection. *Human-Computer Interaction,23,*(2008),1-46.
5. Byrne, M.D. ACT-R/PM and menu selection: Applying a cognitive architecture to HCI. *International Journal of Human-Computer Studies, 55,* (2001), 41-84.
6. Card, S.K., Visual search of computer command menus. In H. Bouma and D. Bouwhuis (Eds.) *Attention and Performance X*, LEA, 1984, 97-108.
7. Cockburn, A., Gutwin, C., & Greenberg, S. A predictive model of menu performance. *Proc. CHI '07*, ACM (2007), 627-636.
8. Cutrell, E. & Guan, Z. What are you looking for? An eye-tracking study of information usage in web search. *Proc. CHI '07*, ACM (2007), 407-416.
9. Fu, W.-T. & Pirolli, P. SNIF-ACT: A cognitive model of user navigation on the world wide web. *Human-Computer Interaction, 22,* (2007), 355-412.
10. Hornof, A.J. Cognitive strategies for the visual search of hierarchical computer displays. *Human-Computer Interaction, 19,* (2004), 183-223.
11. Lee, E. & MacGregor, J. Minimizing user search time in menu retrieval systems. *Human Factors, 27*, (1985), 157-162.
12. McDonald, J.E., Stone, J.D., & Liebelt, L.S. Searching for items in menus: The effects of organization and type of target. *Proc. Human Factors and Ergonomics Society Annual Meeting,* HFES (1983), 834-837.
13. Mehlenbacher, B., Duffy, T.M., & Palmer, J. Finding information on a menu: Linking menu organization to the user's goals. *Human-Computer Interaction, 4,* (1989), 231-251.
14. Myers, C.W., Lewis, R.L., & Howes, A. Bounded optimal state estimation and control in visual search: Explaining distractor ratio effects. *Proc. CogSci 2013*, Cognitive Science Society (2013), 1049-1054.
15. Nilsen, E.L. *Perceptual-motor control in human-computer interaction.* Report 37, The Cognitive Sci. & Machine Intelligence Lab. Univ. of Michigan (1991).
16. Pirolli, P., *Information Foraging Theory: Adaptive Interaction with Information.* Oxford University Press, 2009.
17. Rieman, J., Young, R.M., & Howes, A. A dual-space model of iteratively deepening exploratory learning. *International Journal of Human-Computer Studies, 44,* (1996), 743–775.
18. Yoon, C., Feinberg, F., Hu, P., et al. Category norms as a function of culture and age: Comparisons of item responses to 105 categories by American and Chinese adults. *Psychology and Aging, 19,* (2004), 379-393.
19. Young, R.M., Rational analysis of exploratory choice. In M. Oaksford and N. Chater (Eds.), *Rational Models of Cognition.* Oxford University Press, 1998, 469-500.
20. The all-telling eye, *The Economist*, 22 Oct 2011. http://www.economist.com/node/21533362.

Automated Nonlinear Regression Modeling for HCI

Antti Oulasvirta
Max Planck Institute for Informatics and Saarland University

ABSTRACT
Predictive models in HCI, such as models of user performance, are often expressed as multivariate nonlinear regressions. This approach has been preferred, because it is compact and allows scrutiny. However, existing modeling tools in HCI, along with the common statistical packages, are limited to predefined nonlinear models or support linear models only. To assist researchers in the task of identifying novel nonlinear models, we propose a stochastic local search method that constructs equations iteratively. Instead of predefining a model equation, the researcher defines constraints that guide the search process. Comparison of outputs to published baselines in HCI shows improvements in model fit in seven out of 11 cases. We present a few ways in which the method can help HCI researchers explore modeling problems. We conclude that the approach is particularly suitable for complex datasets that have many predictor variables.

Author Keywords
Predictive modeling in human–computer interaction; Multivariate nonlinear regression models; Model selection.

ACM Classification Keywords
H.5.m. Information Interfaces and Presentation (e.g. HCI): Miscellaneous

INTRODUCTION
Predictive models are used in human–computer interaction (HCI) in theory construction, user-interface (UI) design, adaptive UIs, and UI optimization. This paper addresses *multivariate nonlinear regression equations*, a popular approach to modeling (the literature provides useful introduction [9]). As a concrete example, consider Fitts' law. Although at times presented as a linear model, it is a nonlinear one: Given movement amplitude (A) and target width (W) (predictor variables), Fitts' law predicts movement time T (response variable) as $T = a + bID = a + b\log_2(2A/W)$. Fitts' law is linear only *after* the nonlinear transformation that yields ID. However, nonlinear models are not limited to pointing tasks; in fact, they are used in many modeling papers in the HCI field.

HCI researchers have preferred regression because it supports many research goals. Firstly, regression is a "white box" approach: equations allow scrutiny against pragmatic and theoretical assumptions. Also, predictions can be computed rapidly, which makes regression models useful in online applications such as adaptive interfaces and interface optimization. Thirdly, it is flexible: a pragmatic researcher can improve model fit by introducing more free parameters and predictor variables, though at the expense of parsimony and generalizability.

This Note addresses the issue that identifying nonlinear models can be a grueling enterprise since the number of (theoretically) possible models grows exponentially with the number of predictor variables. While present-day tools support parameter estimation and analytics of predefined equations, they do not adequately support the process of identifying equations with desirable qualities. We work from the observation that a nonlinear regression model can be produced by a sequence of operations starting with a *linear* model. Fitts' law, for example, can be obtained when one starts with a linear model with A and D as predictor variables, applying first division and then $\log_2$.

We present an algorithmic approach for exploring model spaces like this. The method is aimed at finding the best function that maps experimental variables (predictors) to a response variable while respecting researcher-defined constraints to the function. It is a stochastic local search method that permits control of the model's content and the search process. In its design, we have paid attention to the specific nature of 1) prediction tasks and 2) goals in modeling in HCI.

The method allows the researcher to set constraints that aid in striking a balance among parsimony, consistency with assumptions, and model fitness. Instead of working with one equation at a time, the researcher can work with *sets* of models found via changes in constraints that guide the search algorithm. The requirement of complete pre-knowledge is relaxed. Such capability can be useful for four purposes:

1. Identifying a "lower bound" for optimal model fit
2. Seeing whether a problem is "modelable" in the first place
3. Exploring alternative models that conform to the desired constraints
4. "Brute force" modeling – acquiring a model for applications wherein theoretical plausibility is unimportant

For evaluation, we compare generated models to those reported in the HCI literature. The datasets range from pointing tasks to menu selection and multitouch rotations. The method did find improvements in more than half of the cases and showed comparable performance in the others. The results were particularly promising for complex datasets with more predictors and observations.

CHI'14, April 26–May 1, 2014, Toronto, Canada.

http://dx.doi.org/10.1145/2556288.2556999

BACKGROUND AND APPROACH

The available tools do not adequately support the task of automatically identifying multivariate nonlinear models. Firstly, the tools previously developed within HCI [14, 16, 17] support model fitting, diagnostics, and visualizations but have been limited to predefined pointing models (e.g., in the work of Fitts, Welford, and Mackenzie). Secondly, although the general statistical packages[1] allow a researcher to enter arbitrary nonlinear models, they support only parameter estimation, not the identification of models. Thirdly, while some tools do support *automatic* exploration of nonlinear models, they do not support a larger number of predictors (e.g., xuru.org supports one). Finally, a recent interactive tool [10] supports the construction of models with visualizations, but the process is manual and time-consuming.

We build on optimization solutions [12] to the "symbolic regression" problem [6]. We propose a variant of stochastic local search methods motivated by four observations of HCI. First, HCI modeling often favors particular operations on terms. Next, the number of predictors is relatively small and typically limited by that of independent variables in the experiment wherein the data are collected. This number typically lies in the range 1–6. These two observations imply that *variable selection* [9] is not a significant challenge but the control of terms in the equation is. In contrast, automated tools in, for example, chemistry [15] target problems with hundreds of predictors and need different controls. Thirdly, our examination of some of the existing models (see Table 1) suggested that a *linear* model with all predictors as separate terms can serve as an initialization for search. Fourth, HCI models are typically based on averaged point data. Thus, model fitting is significantly faster than with unaveraged data. These observations imply that even local search may yield good results.

METHOD

Our model assumes repeated observations of a response variable Y in independent conditions $x_1, ..., x_k \subset X$. Value Y_i in condition x_i follows the model

$$Y_i = \sum_{j=1}^{m} \beta_j f_j(x_i) + \epsilon_j, \qquad (1)$$

where coefficients β are free parameters. The task of the algorithm is to find the functions $f_j(x)$ that maximize model fitness (e.g., R^2). It achieves this by performing a sequence of operations on terms in each iteration. The operations are the familiar algebraic (addition, exponentiation, etc.) and transcendental (exponential, logarithmic, and trigonometric) operations. Unary operations (e.g,. log) involve a single term and binary ones (e.g., multiplication) two. At present, we cover 16 operations, but this range is extendable.

Our method is *stochastic local search*, a random search method [12]. Stochastic local search includes a probabilistic decision criterion that allows it to get past local maxima. Stochastic hill climbing is a baseline method for biologically inspired methods such as genetic algorithms [5].

[1] E.g., SPSS, Stata, R, SAS, Matlab, Maple, and Statistica.

Moreover, we hybridize this method with a hill climbing method (greedy search). Hill climbing methods examine neighbor candidates locally and select the best neighbor. The probability with which it will perform greedy local search (steepest ascent) versus stochastic search can be controlled by the user on the basis of time constraints.

In our implementation, search starts with a *linear* model with every predictor separately as a term. In every iteration, we take the model with the highest fitness value, generate a set of neighbors, and evaluate them. The strategy here on depends on the outcome: if an improvement was found, *all* single-operation neighbors are examined, for finding the best improvement (steepest-ascent hill climbing); if no improvements were found, the neighborhood is searched more deeply via generation of multi-operation variants. The best candidate is always selected. However, we use the Metropolis criterion [12] to stochastically accept a candidate that is poorer than the best known, if it is not too much worse and if many rounds have passed without improvements. A tabu list keeps track of already visited models and prevents re-accessing them.

User controls

Our prime goal has been to provide sufficient control over the process and outcomes. The user can change:

1. The maximum number of free parameters
2. The types of operations permitted
3. The maximum number of operations allowed per term
4. The maximum number of neighbors generated in each iteration
5. A seed equation for search with a list of terms that are not to be changed
6. Stochasticity factor: with a zero value, search is deterministic and favors steepest ascent to find a local maximum quickly; with a higher value, search is slower and stochastic, but it has an improved chance of finding the optimum
7. Fitness function: R^2, AIC (Akaike Information Criterion), AIC_c (AIC corrected for sample size), and BIC (Bayesian Information Criterion) [1, 9]

Implementation

The algorithm is implemented in Python and uses OLS (ordinary least squares) for fitting. The program is operated from the command line by a user specifying an input file and parameters. By default, variables are treated as scalars, but dummy coding can be applied for categorical variables. It prints intermediate results to display and file and can be stopped during search. The program outputs the best equation found with coefficients and reports a few statistics of model fit and residuals, along with some simple diagnostics (e.g., p-values for coefficients).

Limitations

The tool does not eliminate the researcher's responsibility for model quality but insists on new tasks [1]. One such task is encoding domain knowledge. For instance, Eq. (1) does not allow free parameters *within* a term (e.g,. ax^b), but this can be avoided via searching in stages and encoding them

				Baseline			This paper	
#	Dataset	Predictors*	n	k	Model provided in paper	R^2 **	Best model found***	R^2
1	Stylus tapping (1 oz)[8]	A,W	16	2	$a + b\log_2(2A/W)$	.966	$a + b\log_2(A/W)$	.966
2	Reanalyzed data [8]	A,W_e			$a + b\log_2(A/W_e + 1)$	.987	$a + b(\log_2(\log_2 A) - W_e)$	.981
3	Mouse pointing [8]	A,W	16	2	$a + b\log_2(A/W + 1)$	.984	$a + b\log_2(A/W)$	.973
4		A,W_e			$a + b\log_2(A/W_e + 1)$	.980	$a + b\log_{10}(A/W_e)$	.978
5	Trackball dragging [8]	A,W	16	2	$a + b\log_2(A/W + 1)$	.965	$a + b\log_2(A - (W^3)^4)$	.981
6		A,W_e			$a + b\log_2(A/W_e + 1)$	.817	$a + b(A/(1 - e^{\log_{10} W_e}))$	.941
7	Magic lens pointing [13]	A,W, S	16	3	$a + b\log_2(D/S + 1) + c\log_2(S/2/A)$	.88	$a + b(1 - 1/A) + cW^9$	.947
8	Tactile guidance [7]	N,I,D	16	3	Eq. 8-9, nonlinear	.91, .95	Nonlinear ($k = 3$)	.980
9	Pointing, angular [3] Exp. 2	W, H, α, A	310	4	Eq. 33, ID_{pr}, nonlinear	.953	Nonlinear ($k = 4$)	.962
10	Two thumb tapping[11]	ID,$T_{elapsed}$	20	6	Eq. 5-6, quadratic	.79	$a + b(T^2_{elapsed}/ID)$	.929
11	Menu selection[2]	B,I,D,W,Fr	10	6	Eq. 1-7, nonlinear	.99,.52	Nonlinear ($k = 6$)	.990

Table 1. Benchmarking automatic modeling against previously published models of response time in HCI. Notes: n = Number of observations (data rows); k = Number of free parameters; * All variable names from the original papers, except I is interface type (dummy coded); ** = As reported in the paper; * = Some equations omitted due to space restrictions**

to fixed terms. A second is deciding on a meaningful fitness score – we currently use R^2, but this can be changed to cross-validation metrics. A third is model diagnostics. For instance, the use of OLS assumes collinearity and homogenous error variance [9]. The latter is probably an unrealistic assumption in many HCI datasets. Analytics are needed to examine the consequences. Fourthly, the equations are not always elegant and require manual "beautification." Fifthly, since the outputs are multivariate models with case-specific semantics, we cannot offer tools for plotting or diagnostics.

EVALUATION

We evaluate the method with a benchmark against published models. We then consider two exploration exercises and finally a more complex modeling case. Our intent is not to propose that the outcomes should replace published models but to test whether the method *could have* aided in the exploration of model spaces.

Benchmarking with published datasets

The datasets shown in Table 1 cover traditional pointing tasks with 2–3 predictors (datasets 1–6), more complex pointing models (7 and 9), and more complex compound tasks that involve visual attention and cognition (8, 10, and 11). To match the prediction task to those in the corresponding papers, we use the same input data, including the predictor variables. Moreover, we cap the number of free parameters (k in Table 1) at the one reported in the paper and use the same fitness metric (unadjusted R^2). Second-order predictors – i.e., variables derived from independent variables, such as ID [8] – are not included in the input data. Search parameters (i.e., stochasticity factor and number of operations allowed per iteration) were set by hand for each case after experience obtained in a few trials. A MacBook Pro 2.8 GHz with 8 GB of RAM was used for all results reported here. Every dataset was given a minimum of 1 hour 30 minutes of runtime, but the winner was often found much sooner.

Table 1 shows the results: the models identified by the method improved on model fitness in seven of the 11 cases. Model fit was the same in one case. Interestingly, the method "found Fitts' law" for Fitts' original data from 1954 (Dataset 1). In three cases the outcomes were inferior. Two conclusions are drawn:

1. Pointing datasets 1–6 provide the least room to improve, since the R^2s are high to begin with.
2. The method is more successful when there are more predictors. The improvements obtained for datasets 7–11 range from small (8, 9, and 11) to medium (7) to large (10).

Constraining of model exploration

To emulate theory-oriented modeling, we took Dataset 11 and limited the transformations $(1/x, log_2(x), *, /, +, -)$ to match the equations in the original paper. Many models were found, the best having three parameters and $R^2 = 0.90$.

Modeling of multiple datasets with a single model

We also considered modeling multiple datasets with a single model. Here, as in some pointing papers, the model terms are kept the same but free parameters fitted per dataset. We tested this feature in an exercise covering three datasets (1, 3, and 5) that use D and W to predict T. The best model we found had $R^2 = 0.97$.

The case of multitouch rotation gestures

To evaluate performance when there are substantially more observations and predictors, we obtained the dataset of a recent study of multitouch rotations [4]. In the study, five factors were controlled: angle (3 levels), direction (2), x-position on the surface (4), y-position on the surface (3), and diameter (4), yielding an experimental design with 288 cells. The response variable is movement time T. We estimate the search space to be on the order of 10^{12}. The original paper did not present a model, and Fitts' law [8] yields a low fit ($R^2 = 0.28$).

Our input data contain averaged movement time from trials without contact loss. On the basis of the conclusion of the paper [4], we divided the prediction task into three subtasks: 1) all data, 2) clockwise rotations only, 3) and counterclockwise rotations only. Because no reference model existed, we allowed more time (96 hours) to search. The same setup was used as previously.

For the case with all data, a model was found with seven parameters and a fit of $R^2 = 0.672$. For the counterclockwise case, the best model had 11 parameters and a fit of $R^2 = 0.730$. The method was more successful in the clockwise-only case. The best model too had 11 parameters and $R^2 = 0.835$. However, the method also found a model with seven free parameters and $R^2 = 0.827$. Also, a simpler model, with four parameters and $R^2 = 0.805$, was found:

$$a + bx_1 + \frac{c \cos x_2^3}{e^{\cos \frac{1}{x_0^2} - log_{10}(x_1 \times x_3)}} + d \tan x_3 \tag{2}$$

Here, variables $x_0, ..., x_3$ refer to x-position, y-position, angle, and diameter, respectively. Further analysis is not possible, for reasons of space, but the results show that performance is satisfactory also for harder problems.

SUMMARY AND CONCLUSION

This paper has presented a proof-of-concept for automated nonlinear regression modeling in HCI. It builds on the observation that many HCI problems involve a small number of predictors, averaged point data, and preference for simple models. The implementation offers multiple controls to constrain and guide search. It runs on a regular computer and produces the first results in a matter of seconds.

It is perhaps unsurprising that better models can be found with a search algorithm, because we have defined these tasks such that they involve relatively small search spaces – at least for a computer. However, the results confirm that the approach is sensible. For tasks involving one or two predictors, the results are comparable to those in the literature when model fitness is considered. For tasks involving two or more predictor variables, it found models that improve on the reference papers'. For instance, the original model of Dataset 10 had six free parameters, but the method found a superior model with only two free parameters.

We hope that automated modeling can aid in both pragmatic and theoretical efforts. The ability to obtain a model automatically can accelerate research in pragmatic pursuits like adaptive UIs and UI optimization. On the other hand, for theoretically oriented researchers who previously regarded modeling as an arcane enterprise, it might lower the barrier of entry. However, we want to warn against "fishing" in theory-construction. Although the method helps with the process of identifying models, it is the modeler's responsibility to explain the terms and parameters.

Two challenges stand out for future work. First, performance should be improved, perhaps by using a tree representation for equations [6] and genetic algorithms instead of local search. Second, to better assist the identification of theoretically plausible models, we need visualizations and more interactive ways to construct models.

ACKNOWLEDGEMENTS

This research was funded by the Max Planck Centre for Visual Computing and Communication and the Cluster of Excellence on Multimodal Computing and Interaction at Saarland University. We thank Miikka Miettinen, Gilles Bailly, Michael Rohs, Andy Cockburn, Stephanie Wuhrer, Timo Kötzing, and Miguel Nacenta. Code and data are shared on the project homepage.

REFERENCES

1. Bunke, O., Droge, B., and Polzehl, J. Model selection, transformations and variance estimation in nonlinear regression. *Statistics: A Journal of Theoretical and Applied Statistics 33*, 3 (1999), 197–240.
2. Cockburn, A., Gutwin, C., and Greenberg, S. A predictive model of menu performance. In *Proc. CHI'07*, ACM Press (2007), 627–636.
3. Grossman, T., and Balakrishnan, R. A probabilistic approach to modeling two-dimensional pointing. *ACM TOCHI 12*, 3 (2005), 435–459.
4. Hoggan, E., et al. Multi-touch rotation gestures: performance and ergonomics. In *Proc. CHI'13*, ACM (2013), 3047–3050.
5. Juels, A., and Wattenberg, M. *Stochastic hillclimbing as a baseline method for evaluating genetic algorithms.* 1994.
6. Koza, J. R. *Genetic Programming: vol. 1, On the programming of computers by means of natural selection*, vol. 1. MIT press, 1992.
7. Lehtinen, V., et al. Dynamic tactile guidance for visual search tasks. In *Proc. UIST'12*, ACM Press (2012), 445–452.
8. Mackenzie, I. S. *Fitts' law as a performance model in human-computer interaction. Doctoral dissertation.* University of Toronto: Toronto, Ontario, Canada, 1991.
9. Motulsky, H. J., and Ransnas, L. A. Fitting curves to data using nonlinear regression: a practical and nonmathematical review. *The FASEB journal 1*, 5 (1987), 365–374.
10. Muhlbacher, T., and Piringer, H. A partition-based framework for building and validating regression models. *Visualization and Computer Graphics, IEEE Transactions on 19*, 12 (2013), 1962–1971.
11. Oulasvirta, A., et al. Improving two-thumb text entry on touchscreen devices. In *Proc. CHI'13*, ACM Press (2013), 2765–2774.
12. Rao, S. S., and Rao, S. *Engineering optimization: theory and practice.* John Wiley & Sons, 2009.
13. Rohs, M., and Oulasvirta, A. Target acquisition with camera phones when used as magic lenses. In *Proc. CHI'08*, ACM Press (2008), 1409–1418.
14. Schedlbauer, M. J. An extensible platform for the interactive exploration of fitts' law and related movement time models. In *Ext Abs. CHI'07*, ACM Press (2007), 2633–2638.
15. Searson, D. P., Leahy, D. E., and Willis, M. J. Gptips: an open source genetic programming toolbox for multigene symbolic regression. In *Proc. IMECS'10*, vol. 1 (2010).
16. Soukoreff, R. W., and MacKenzie, I. S. Generalized fitts' law model builder. In *Ext Abs. CHI'95*, ACM (1995), 113–114.
17. Wobbrock, J. O., Shinohara, K., and Jansen, A. The effects of task dimensionality, endpoint deviation, throughput calculation, and experiment design on pointing measures and models. In *Proc. CHI'11*, ACM Press (2011), 1639–1648.

Understanding Digital and Material Social Communications for Older Adults

Alexis Hope[1,2], **Ted Schwaba**[2], **Anne Marie Piper**[2]
[1]MIT Media Lab, [2]Northwestern University
ahope@media.mit.edu, TedmondSchwaba2014@u.northwestern.edu, ampiper@northwestern.edu

ABSTRACT

Online technologies are promising for helping older adults maintain social connectedness, particularly with younger people, yet many older adults resist or participate minimally in the mainstream technologies used by younger members of their social network. We present results from an interview study involving 22 older adults (age 71-92) to understand communication preferences and values related to social media. Seniors articulate many concerns with online social media, including the time required for legitimate participation, the loss of deeper communication, content irrelevance, and privacy. Additionally, older adults engage in social practices that could be supported by online social technologies, but they rarely use such tools. The theme of material social communications emerges from our data, and we examine this in context of online social media. We conclude with design considerations for the development of social media for older adults, and as part of this we describe the notion of bridging technologies as a framework for intergenerational communication design.

Author Keywords

Older adults, social media, social network sites, materiality.

ACM Classification Keywords

H.5.m. Information Interfaces and Presentation (e.g. HCI): Miscellaneous

INTRODUCTION

People age 65 and older are one of the fastest growing groups of Internet users in the United States [44], and this demographic is beginning to use social media more and more [15, 30]. However, Internet and social media use drops off significantly for people age 75 and older [44]. Only 34% of people in the *G.I. Generation* (born in 1936 or earlier) [43] use the Internet and 21% have home broadband [44]. For members of the G.I. Generation who are online, fewer than 20% use social network sites, play games online, rate things online, read blogs, listen to podcasts, or use instant messenger [43].

CHI 2014, April 26 - May 01 2014, Toronto, ON, Canada

http://dx.doi.org/10.1145/2556288.2557133

While younger seniors are embracing online social technologies [2], their parents, many of whom are still living, are neglected in this trend. Because the strength of social support networks in late life is related, both positively and negatively, to health [29], it is important to support the needs and social goals of members of the G.I. Generation. Unfortunately, people in late older adulthood who stand to benefit most from online social interaction are precisely the individuals who are least likely to adopt such technology.

This paper examines the current generational divide in online social media and social network site (SNS) adoption, focusing on the needs and preferences of people in late life. The reasons for this divide are complex, and issues of technology access and skill are important. However, there are many older adults with sufficient technology access and ability who do not use online social media. Why do older adults resist using mainstream social media sites or only participate minimally, particularly when many younger members of their social network are active on such sites? Which communication channels and social media forms are most meaningful to people in late life?

The contribution of this paper is a qualitative analysis of older adults' perceptions and usage of social media. We present results from an interview study with 22 older adults age 71 to 92 years old, 17 of whom are members of the G.I. Generation. Study participants are well-educated, active in their communities, have access to computers and the Internet, and express an interest in improving communication with their social network. Even among this exceptional population, only eight of the 22 participants use social media. While social media plays an important role in how young people form and maintain social capital [16], we find that it is far less important to older adults. Instead, as prior work indicates [12, 28], phone calls, e-mails, and letters serve older adults' needs. Seniors articulate many concerns with online social media, including the time required for participation, expectations of reciprocity, content irrelevance, and privacy. These are recurring themes that have been presented throughout the literature on older adults, but here we put them in context of social media, providing new insights into how and why seniors use and abstain from online social technologies. For example, older adults report helping people in their social network by researching, disseminating, and archiving information, but they rarely use social media sites that could assist with these activities. A central theme in our data involves the importance of material communications, and we describe the ways in which social communications for older adults span digital and physical spaces. We conclude with design considerations for the development of future social communication technologies that stand to engage members of the G.I. Generation, and as part of this we discuss the notion of bridging technologies as a framework for intergenerational communication design.

RELATED WORK

It is well documented that people in old age interact with others far less than in youth [19, 21]. Socioemotional selectivity theory asserts that the social and emotional goals of older adults differ from younger populations [6]. Older adults value self-achievement and the development of self-concept less than younger populations, but they place higher value on regulation of emotion. Older adults are motivated to stay connected with people in their social network with whom they already have a strong connection [6], and a perception that the end of life is near shifts one's social and emotional goals towards strengthening existing emotionally fulfilling relationships rather than pursing novel social partners. In contrast, mainstream SNSs may help people form and maintain "weak ties" [14], or loose connections between individuals [20]. Compared to younger adults, older adults are less concerned with the goal of information seeking, in which novel social partners are often the best sources and are especially valuable in fulfilling this goal. Contact with family, particularly siblings, takes on new importance in old age and a disruption of those bonds may be related to depression [9]. Older adults are generally more satisfied with interpersonal relationships and their lives overall [13].

Intergenerational family communication is often asymmetrical, where older adults put more effort into communication than their children and grandchildren [27, 28, 33]. Even if communication is reciprocal, grandparents may do more work to structure the interaction [11]. Lindley et al. [26, 28] discuss the notion of "heavyweight" and "lightweight" communications, with older adults seeking heavyweight communications that are personalized, human, and require a commitment of time. They state that older adults "want to feel that real contact has been made with someone, that a level of intimacy has been reached, and that they have put something of themselves into the act, or indeed the art, of communication," [28]. Our findings suggest that materiality is important in the heavyweight communications older adults seek.

Related work shows that face-to-face contact is the most frequently used means of communication between grandparents and grandchildren followed by landline telephone, mobile phones, and then occasional letters or cards [35], yet there is much to learn about intergenerational communication practices in context of social media. Those with mobile phones were more likely to use SMS and e-mail to stay in contact as well. Grandparents also do not use traditional forms of contact (e.g., face-to-face communication, telephone calls) in a compensatory way [8]. That is, grandparents who meet with their grandchildren more often face-to-face also call them more frequently. Older adults may prefer communication in a written form as it gives them more time to construct and think about what they want to write [22]. Similarly, older generations may value material artifacts that represent social connectedness over analogous digital objects. Older adults are part of the "Kodak Culture" [7], or the generation of people who grew up with and value printed photos, and this plays a role in the importance of material social communications.

Studying online interactions and aging has been an important research topic for several years. Greater use of the Internet as a communication tool has been associated with lower levels of late life social loneliness [37] and enhanced quality of life and well-being [41]. Online activity also allows seniors to regain control over their personal and social life, which may have become compromised due to age-related changes, by connecting with others and seeking information online [32]. Analysis of a newsgroup for older people had higher numbers of replies to messages and therefore showed a higher degree of responsiveness and reciprocity compared to a newsgroup with younger users [42], leading to positive social experiences. Even with potentially positive outcomes, motivating and encouraging seniors to engage in online social interaction is challenging. Selwyn [36] reports that older adults tend to perceive the Internet as a functional tool and may be ambivalent about its use for social interaction. Older adults also have privacy concerns and are afraid of identity theft [17].

SNSs designed specifically for older adults (e.g., Eldr, SeniorFriendFinder) are typically aimed at helping seniors establish intragenerational social contacts. However, the younger generations with whom older adults want to connect use different tools (e.g., Facebook) [1]. The seniors who use SNSs such as Facebook tend to be younger [2], use it to stay connected with family, and joined because of the influence or help of a family member or friend [38]. While older adults may have fewer friends on an SNS than younger users, their friend groups have a wider distribution of ages [34], indicating that they are using such services for intergenerational communication. Prior work indicates that the perceived usefulness of SNSs, trust in SNSs, and frequency of Internet use are indicators of an older adult's willingness to join an SNS [5].

BUILDING ON AND EXTENDING PRIOR WORK

The present study replicates previous research on technology and social media use among seniors but also offers new, nuanced findings to further expand our collective knowledge of the social communication practices of older adults. Several large-scale quantitative studies on social media use (e.g., [2, 44]) provide a foundation for understanding the behaviors of older adults who are active online, but these studies do not provide a deeper analysis of reasons for non-use or minimal use. Moreover, these larger studies tend to group seniors (people over age 65) together into a single demographic instead of understanding individual cohorts, such as the G.I. Generation, which the present paper examines.

Our study confirms and extends findings from several recent studies. For instance, older adults who do not use SNSs most commonly cite lack of interest rather than lack of knowledge or skill [38], and our research unpacks reasons for this disinterest that are not articulated in prior work. We also confirm older adults' concerns about privacy [17], perceptions of social media as a forum to seek attention and publicity [17,

25] and dislike of the public nature of SNSs [25]. Building on this, we provide details of older adults' attitudes regarding how and which content should be shared via online social media (i.e., conditions under which one should share medical, political, or religious information).

This paper also replicates and extends findings by Lindley et al. [28], who five years ago examined the communication practices of older adults (age 55-81) through a focus group study, and work by Dickinson and Hill [12], who also studied older adults' (age 70-90) communication practices involving technology through focus groups and interviews. These studies examine seniors' practices of "keeping in touch" more broadly, whereas this paper focuses specifically on the role of social media in how older adults maintain communications. Importantly, these qualitative studies should be considered together to reach saturation and enable formulation of theory [18]. Our research provides converging evidence and support for earlier themes such as the role of "heavyweight" communications [26, 28], but we also extend this by analyzing the importance of paper-based and hand-written communications in light of the growing presence of digital social media.

Our analysis provides new insights into what is social media for older adults and how digital social media does not directly support older adults' communication preferences. We found that some social relationships are based in letter writing and seniors intentionally avoid using electronic media because of this history. Other seniors regularly share (through postal mail) printed newspaper articles and crossword puzzle clippings with their social contacts. These physical artifacts are important social media for this generation, and we learned of instances where seniors have performed this ritual of paper social media exchange for over 60 years. Others perform the social work of filling communication gaps by printing off e-mails to share with their peers who do not use computers. Still others create original articles and publications in which they distribute to their social contacts in printed form. Themes such as the importance of personalized correspondence and letter writing have been noted in prior work [12, 26, 28], but our contribution is to examine these practices through the lens of social media, enabling an exploration of the intertwined nature of media form and meaning [31] and an analysis of how digital social communications marginalize the values of older demographics.

METHOD

We conducted semi-structured in-home interviews with 22 older adults (age 71-92; mean age=80.9, stdev=5.8; 15 females) to understand attitudes towards social media as well as how they communicate with members of their social network given the presence of online technologies. We recruited older adult participants by sending a paper letter in the mail to members of a university database of people interested in research opportunities. The recruitment letter focused on attracting participants with an interest in improving communication with family and friends. Our initial plan was to recruit older adults who are social media users, but early conversations with participants indicated resistance to social media that in and of itself merited further exploration. For that reason, we did not screen participants for technology ownership or use but rather recruited participants based on an interest in improving communication with one's social network.

While we targeted people in the G.I. Generation (age 77 and older), we allowed participants to include other family members age 70 or older in the interview. Thirteen participants were interviewed with a family member (usually a spouse) and nine participants were interviewed on their own. Participants who were interviewed on their own typically described their own life history and social networks, whereas participants interviewed in dyads described shared histories and friendships. Interviews lasted approximately one hour. Except for one participant, all interviews were conducted in participants' homes, allowing us to better understand the contexts in which they lived. As part of the interview, some participants showed us artifacts (e.g. handwritten letters) to aid discussion or demonstrate their broader interests and personalities.

The older adult population we recruited is exceptional in that they are well-educated (several people have a graduate degree) and either own or have communal access to a computer and the Internet. All older adults we interviewed are retired, but they are active in their communities and selective in the activities they pursue. Study participants are involved with what we call "serious hobbies," including conducting research for oneself or others, starting and managing a medical foundation, journalism, discovering a family's genealogy, participation in the League of Women Voters, and political activism.

All interviews were audio recorded and transcribed. Interview transcripts and photographs of supporting materials collected during interviews were analyzed using a thematic approach [18]. Through inductive analysis we iteratively identified themes in the data. We treat informant language with care and unpack the meaning behind the ways in which participants describe their needs, values, and preferences for technology and non-technology based communication.

FINDINGS

We describe participants' access to and use of computers as well as the ways in which older adults communicate with people in their social network, including a few examples of social media. All participants articulated concerns with mainstream social media, which we explore in detail. Interestingly, older adults manage and provide valuable resources to members of their social networks in ways that could be supported by online technologies, yet they rarely use such systems. While many older adults use e-mail, material social communications are of central importance to the older adults we study.

Technology Access and Ability

Using the computer is a dedicated activity for older adults, and some participants describe computer use as a hobby. All participants except two have at least one household computer, and all but five participants use a computer daily. As with the broader population of older adults, our participants are diverse in technical ability and amount of experience with computers. OH (age 83, male) explained, *"I use the computer all the time but I don't operate it. I look over her shoulder. I don't press the keys or operate the mouse."* JK (89+[1], M) and JD (83, F) described no interest in using a computer, even though they are available for use at nearby libraries for free. MD (75, F) was the only participant who said that she would like to use the family computer but lacked the skill to do so. On the other extreme, RO (87, M) has owned and used multiple computers since the early 1980s, LL (81, F) described first using a computer in 1987, and KW (81, F) writes her own programs in Visual Basic for bookkeeping.

Participants describe having one person as the primary owner and operator of the household computer. For households with multiple computers, each family member claimed ownership over a particular computer. A single e-mail account that is shared between a couple is common, but one person is typically responsible for this e-mail account, resulting in interesting sharing practices that we describe below.

Communications Landscape

To understand opportunities for improving social communications of older adults, we first examine the ways in which seniors currently communicate. This section echos prior work [12, 28, 33, 39], so we briefly summarize our results in order to characterize our interview participants.

While eight of 22 older adults report using social media, they prefer to communicate through telephone calls, emails and written letters. Participants described tailoring both the message content and channel to the recipient's availability and preferences while considering the perceived affordances of each mode of communication [28]. In agreement with earlier work [12, 28, 33], our data also show a preference for telephone calls because of their dynamic nature that better approximates a "real conversation." E-mail, the "bedrock of communication" for older adults [44], was used by 17 of our 22 participants. Many participants valued email for utilitarian purposes, using it to schedule events but noting its structured, less conversational nature. Participants contrasted e-mail with the material practice of letter writing, which affords a personal touch [28]. Our findings suggest that letter writing is an art, a hobby, and a social practice for the generation of adults in our study. Letter writing allows older adults to communicate with strong ties and reconnect with ties that have become weak while affording varying degrees of formality depending on the content, tone, and even the choice of paper used. The older adults in our study mostly eschewed text messaging and video chat. Three participants used text messaging to communicate with younger generations:

> *"The only way I can communicate with [my grandson] is by texting. If I call him, he won't pick up and I'll leave a message. But, right away– like two seconds later, if I text him, he'll answer the text within seconds. He just won't pick up the phone." (KB 71, F)*

Two participants (a husband-wife pair, age 82 & 83) described using video chat for communication, as a scheduled event to "see the new babies" in the family.

[1]University IRB prevents disclosure of individual ages for people over age 89. Participants over 89 are reported more generally as age 89+.

Usage of Online Social Media

We expected social media to play a more central role in this group of older adults' communication practices, yet fewer than half of participants (8 of 22) report using social media. Study participants use Facebook (n=7), Twitter (n=1), LinkedIn (n=1), Words With Friends (n=1), JewishGen (n=1), and a news station blog (n=1). Five participants use Facebook daily, and one participant reported using Twitter daily. Only three participants said they post messages to Facebook.

> *"We engage in some repartee with people on Facebook... I will do a lot of kibitzing or teasing, or agreeing or disagreeing, the random remarks of three words a piece... but I don't spend a lot of time doing that..." (TW 83, M)*

Two other participants mentioned "lurking" on Facebook, or watching what people are doing without posting content.

> *"I follow them [her children] on Facebook because they always put pictures of the babies... I always check Facebook to see who's posted what during the day, and I don't necessarily respond to it. In fact my daughter accuses me of stalking because she says, 'You don't write anything, you just check,' and I say, 'Yes, that's right, I just check.' ((laughter))" (MW 82, F)*

A few participants used social media sites beyond Facebook and described the benefits of these sites. RO (87, M) said, *"LinkedIn is entirely different from Facebook. It's really professionally oriented."* Regarding her nightly routine, MW (82, F) explained, *"Every night before I go to bed, I try to get caught up with my Words With Friends games, but I've got, I think 18 of them going now so it that takes a little while..."* LL (81, F) has connected with family members online via JewishGen. One participant (KB 71, F) enjoys Twitter *"'cause it's quick. It's 120 characters, and you can follow people and see what different people are doing, like celebrities or music artists."*

The majority of participants asserted that not using social media was a choice rather than something they would like to use but cannot because of reasons such as technology access or skill [38]. Indeed, many participants explicitly said they could learn to use Facebook, for example, if they wanted.

> *"I don't mind learning things... I just don't feel the need to learn Twitter and Facebook. I like computers and the more they can do with them the better. I'm not against learning new things, but I just don't want to get out there in the public with every Tom, Dick, and Harry." (SK 89+, F)*

Concerns with Online Social Media

All participants, even social media users, expressed concerns with mainstream social media. Participants mentioned a range of issues, including limited time, lack of privacy, and irrelevance of information. Interestingly, when we first brought up the term social media, many participants responded with the phrase, "I'm not interested."

Social media is for younger people

While we probed for use of social media sites that are designed for seniors, participants regularly referenced mainstream websites where the majority of users are younger. Naturally, older adults commented on this aspect, stating that one reason for not using websites such as Facebook and Twitter is that they are for younger people and not people their age. DH (76, F) stated, *"I'm the age group that doesn't use it... I really do think partly as function of age, you know, we didn't grow up with it."* More broadly, participants are aware of intergenerational differences in communication. LL (81, F) explained, *"[My children and grandchildren] use forms of communication that I don't use. They don't write letters."* One participant offered a contrary opinion and believes that older adults are missing out by not using social media. This participant described how she uses social media, specifically Twitter, to connect with younger family members:

> *"I think it's a bonding thing. I think it's wonderful... So many grandmas and grandpas of [granddaughter's] friends, they don't even know what Twitter is... They're missing out on experiencing what their grandkids [use], which is, social media." (KB 71, F)*

Social media requires a time commitment and reciprocity

Although all of our participants are retired, they are discriminating in how they choose to spend their time. E-mail and other forms of communication occupy seniors' time, and the perceived time required for social media participation may be a deterrent. JO (85, F) commented, *"[Facebook is] not even something I think about that much... I have so much e-mail to do, and I go down the e-mail and you see Facebook and you just go [delete]."* Seniors anticipate that SNS participation requires a great time investment because it may open up new social relationships, most likely with weak ties, that require maintenance. JO continued, *"There are some [Facebook messages] that say... 'Do you know these people?' Well, I don't even open it because if I did know those people, I don't want to know them any better now."* RO (87, M) elaborated, *"[Facebook is] trying to entice you to make more friends and we have enough friends."* Another participant, LH (80, F), explained, *"I haven't wanted to get involved [with Facebook] 'cause it takes...a couple hours a day. I don't wanna spend that much time on a computer."* KB (71, F) said, *"Facebook is too much work to really get into it... 'Cause if I let 150 cousins follow me, then I'd always have to be commenting on things, and, it's just too much work."* Similar expectations of reciprocity in communication have been reported related to time pressures of responding to e-mail [28].

The content is unimportant and trivial

Many participants described the content on social media sites as unimportant and trivial. DH (76, F) said, *"I also don't like the trivial nature of it... It's too much information on stuff that's not important. I'm not interested in that."* Several examples seniors gave about the content they perceive as trivial involved postings about where or what one is eating.

Information about weak ties or social contacts who are seen infrequently may also be perceived as unimportant. For example, JO (85, F) explained, *"I'll look at a Facebook [post] and it'll say, [Sue], who I know, has put on a new picture."* She continued, *"Well, [Sue] lives out in San Diego and I don't see her from one year to the next. I don't care if she puts a new picture. That doesn't grab me so I don't open it."*

The perception of unimportant content is coupled with a view of the immediacy of information resulting in postings that are not well thought out. LL (81, F) explained, *"It's meaningless....nothing to write home about, just kind of instantaneous 'this popped into my mind.' "* KW (81, F) commented, *"These [Twitter and Facebook] strike me as totally useless. Why not just use the telephone?... For one thing you don't...stop and think ahead of time what you're going to be doing."* Participants contrasted the "trivial" nature of online interactions with the depth and thoughtfulness of letters.

> *"I look upon my letters as compositions... When I do a letter I work maybe three or four hours. It's not a work of art but it's something like that. It's a well-written piece. I can go back and look at stuff I've written and it's self-satisfying... Condensing a message to 140 characters, which I know you have to do on one of them, it ruins the language." (LL 81, F)*

Analyzing letter writing practices helps reveal what seniors consider to be important and non-trivial communications. Several seniors describe the time commitment and gratification associated with letter writing, which we discuss in detail below, and this stands in stark contrast to the lightweight digital interactions provided by social media. Writing letters and e-mails enables not only immediate reflection on communication [28] but also provides self-satisfaction to older adults who revisit correspondence at a later date.

Privacy on social media is limited and unclear

In agreement with prior work [17], many participants mentioned privacy concerns and the potential negative results of putting personal information online. OH (83, M) stated, *"They know what your buying habits are, what your interests are, and who your friends are and that's enough for me not to get in to those programs."* Older adults mentioned privacy issues regarding their own information but also the information that younger family members put online. They raised concerns that photos of their grandchildren "not in very flattering situations" might influence future employment.

Understanding which information is public and which is private is a challenge for older adults. TW (83, M) said, *"Facebook has changed its rules about five times...and it's never possible to judge whether or not something is going to be private on Facebook."* KW (81, F) said she goes as far as not having an Internet connection to protect files on her computer. She explained, *"I don't want people getting into my database, and I don't believe all this garbage about how you can protect files. I don't think there is any sure protection."* Providing seniors with a private network may address this concern [40].

Related to privacy, several older adults mentioned that social media is not a place to discuss religious or political views. However, many of our participants discuss political and religious views outside of social media, at in-person discussion groups, for example. KB (71, F) commented, *"I don't like to put it out there... On social media, I would never talk about religion, politics..."* This attitude is in contrast with the way younger populations use social media to voice one's beliefs.

Lack of credibility and negative influence

Older adults expressed concerns about the credibility of information on social media and the influence it has. One participant, AD (79, M), stated, *"We don't use it [Facebook]... The reason is because there's filth in it... We don't get involved with all that junk."* Other participants described content on social media as "inaccurate", "gossip", and "rumors". Older adults in our study want news from venerated sources, most often from a printed newspaper. RO (87, M) said, *"The current events that I'm interested in I want from the New York Times or the Washington Post... I like to make sure it's reliable when I read it and pass it along."*

While social media is a powerful platform for sharing official news stories, older adults in our study did not perceive this as a benefit. Interestingly, the fact that people can comment on news stories shared via social media was perceived as slanting the article and negatively influencing others' thoughts. When we described the ability to share news via social media, RO, a former journalist, explained, *"But then as it gets passed around and people comment, it gets totally distorted and unreliable."* Several participants identified social media as a persuasive tool, and believed that those using it may have sinister intentions. These participants were concerned with information sources, credibility, and whether they can trust it. SK (89+, F) said, *"I think they're [people on social media] trying to change people's minds, or at least infiltrate them... I think a lot of them are trying to win others to their thought... I wouldn't ever put anything like that on Facebook or Twitter..."* Here again we see that due to concerns about manipulation and inaccuracy, social media is not considered an appropriate place to discuss political or religious views.

Social media engenders constant communication

Older adults do not want constant communication and may withdraw from locations that promote connectivity or purposefully avoid technology for this reason [3]. A few participants echoed this sentiment, mentioning that they disliked social media because of the constant stimulation and communication it provides. Older adults may use SNSs minimally or sporadically to maintain limited connectivity [23], or as in our data, resist SNSs altogether as a way of avoiding constant contact with others. While mobile phones have been cited by older adults as the culprit for "always on" behavior [28], older adults in our study suggested social media more broadly was the source of constant communication behaviors. LL (81, F) said, *"It's a need to be in touch with people all the time. It's constantly having to be connected to another person. It's like the umbilical cord."* There is a time and place for communication for older adults [28], and they purposefully structure their lives and home environments to support this goal [3].

> *"I consider television an inappropriate device for the home. I also consider the Internet inappropriate for the home... The purpose of the home is, you come home at the end of the day to rest, relax, and cut off contact with the outside world. So I consider these things not helping me to cut off contact." (KW 81, F)*

The act of not communicating is an important way in which older adults may indicate their wellbeing to family. JK (89+, M) rarely calls his sons and waits for them to contact him. He said, *"I usually don't call them for two reasons. First of all, how can I select what's a convenient time for them? And second is, if I call them, they might feel that I'm being neglected or that I need help...and that's not the case."* Here we see that by not calling his sons, JK communicates his wellbeing and independence.

Figure 1. Letter sent to inquire as to whether a friend was still alive.

Managing and Contributing to One's Social Network

Older adults manage and contribute to their social networks in many ways, yet the majority of seniors do so without modern online technologies. Part of growing older is dealing with more frequent deaths of people within one's social network [19, 21, 6, 26], and several participants mentioned this challenge. KW (81, F) said, *"My friends keep dying. ((laughs)) Very annoying."* JK (89+, M) explained that he no longer writes as many letters because so many of them have been returned to him as undeliverable. He showed us a letter he sent to one of his friends, in which he playfully inquired whether or not his friend was alive (see Figure 1). This letter was returned by his (living) friend, along with a response letter. For JK (89+, M), letter writing was often an attempt to find out whether or not the recipient had passed away. He explained, *"I'm sorry to say that the last two letters I wrote to my old boss, who I stayed in touch with, it looks like he's dead... There again, I've lost communication."* While reconnecting with "people from long ago" is a goal, older adults are cautious about this. LL (81, F) described sending paper photos to clarify and verify a relationship with a relative found from a genealogy website.

Seniors may help fill gaps in communication. We learned of many instances where they print and share e-mail correspondence, particularly for a spouse who does not use the computer or e-mail. AD (79, M) explained, *"If they [daughters] say something interesting [via e-mail] about people we know, I'll print it out and give it to her [wife] and some other people at church who don't have computers. I usually distribute about six or seven..."* This social communication support is typically intragenerational as seniors are filling communication gaps for people their age who do not use a computer.

Several older adults described doing research for other people in their social network, typically for younger family members. LL (81, F) said, *"I'm a very good resource person. I enjoy that. It makes me feel good."* The act of doing research for another person contributes to the older adult's identity and self-worth [26]. Interestingly, older adults described printing and mailing content to the recipient. Some did this

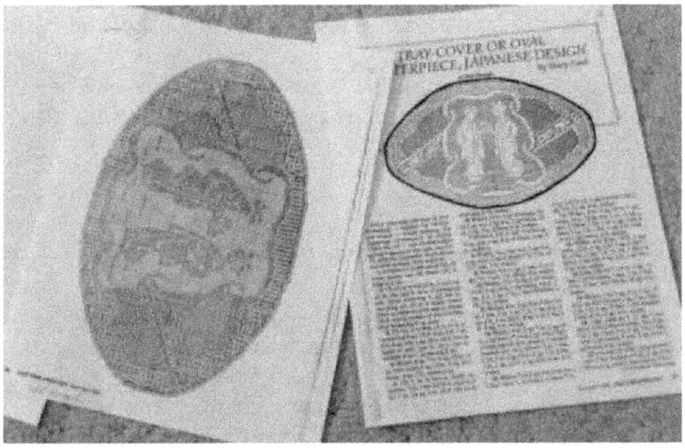

Figure 2. Crochet newsletter created by one participant.

even when the recipient was a younger relative who uses e-mail. A related activity involves generating and distributing new content to social contacts. RO (87, M), a former journalist, showed us an article about a political issue that he wrote and distributed to fellow retirement community residents. KW (81, F), a former librarian, worked for multiple years on one of several crochet newsletters where she interweaves history with a how-to guide (see Fig. 2). She calls it a "zine" and distributes it in paper form.

Overall older adults are more interested in one-on-one communication [28], but we learned of instances when they performed mass communication to their social network, often to an extended family group concerning a family member's illness. This provides an opportunity for online social technology support. LK (74, F) described using e-mail to avoid "getting a million phone calls" when updating family on her mother's illness. The asynchronous nature of e-mail allowed LK to manage communications, particularly during an emotional time where telephone calls do not disguise such feelings [12]. TW's (83, M) son was in an accident and his other son set up *"a communication circuit that was really rather privatized. It was a utilization of the Facebook routine as best we could make it... It became a news posting, day-by-day, for the family."* Several participants noted the importance of keeping this information private when shared online. In general, seniors seem willing to use social media or SNSs to communicate such issues if they can ensure privacy.

Older adults also contribute to their social networks by assembling and preserving genealogical archives (e.g., [33]). This work typically occurs within an extended family group and includes gathering, storing, and distributing photos [39]; yet seniors did not describe using online services to support this work. Uniquely, TW (83, M) distributed his collection of 40,000 digital family photos to his children via portable hard drives. More commonly, older adults maintained physical albums for children and grandchildren to view as entertainment [39].

Importance of Paper-Based Social Communications

A recurring theme involves material social communications. Paper-based artifacts play a particularly important role in the correspondence practices of older adults in our study. Participants described the "art" or "poetry" of writing letters. Older adults perceive letter writing to be more personal than electronic communication [12, 28], and our participants described handwritten letters as "more thoughtful" as the time spent writing a letter conveys care towards the recipient. Several other themes around paper-based social communications emerged from our data and provide a more nuanced understanding of letter writing and exchanging paper artifacts.

Participants described having a different mindset when they compose a handwritten letter versus an e-mail, and multiple people compared letter writing to poetry. LK (74, F) said, *"I know I have a totally different thought process when I'm sending an e-mail versus writing a letter... I guess it's [like] writing a poem..."* While the formality and cultural conventions of writing letters is viewed negatively by some seniors [12], our study participants as a whole valued writing letters. However, participants noted that composing a letter on a computer has advantages. Older adults appreciate being able to revise their letters using a word processing program and several mentioned using the computer because they have illegible handwriting in old age. Several older adults described printing out typed letters and sending them in the mail. LL (81, F) said, *"I would print it out and mail it Pony Express because I find it a lot more satisfying."* Others, like LR (89+, F) for example, print and archive e-mails that are important to her.

Multiple participants used the word "correspondence" to describe communications that are long-term, composed, well thought out, and often, but not always, hand-written. Even if not hand-written, correspondence is most often sent through the mail and only occasionally through e-mail. TW (83, M) uses e-mail if a quick or short response can be made. In contrast, he says, *"I am very laborious about putting a letter together...unless it looks right and sounds right, and is really well constructed, I don't want to send it out..."*

The social practice of writing letters is important to some participants despite its apparent anachronism. MW (82, F) said she *"grew up in a tradition where...Sunday afternoon you sat there and you wrote your letters, you wrote your correspondence for the week, and that's how you got caught up with everybody."* JD (83, F) described being mocked for writing letters when it is "out of style." What was interesting is that some of the most tech savvy study participants, who are also social media users, were the strongest advocates of letter writing. We learned of social relationships that are based in the media form of hand-written letters. This was most common between older adults and their intragenerational contacts. JD has been corresponding with a pen pal for twenty years, and hand-written letters are of central importance to their relationship. LL mentioned a 12 year letter-writing relationship. LK described a similar pen pal and her preference for physical letters over e-mail. She said *"Our whole history's writing letters back and forth. We've avoided purposely e-mailing unless it's something really important that we had to tell each other."* She continued, *"Usually nothing is that critical."*

We learned of many examples in which the medium itself influences how the message is perceived [31]. The selection of paper on which a letter is written, for example, is important. MW (82, F) explained, *"I still have friends in my generation who like to sit down and read the letter, and furthermore they like it on carefully selected paper..."* Participants mentioned using embossed stationery, notecards, or home-made cards depending on the occasion. The act of correspondence may also include sharing material artifacts that demonstrate an understanding of the recipient's interests [28] as a way of showing care and thoughtfulness. In turn, they felt cared for when someone else sent them material communication artifacts. KW (81, F), for example, has clipped newspaper crossword puzzles for a friend since they roomed together in college, and she has continued this tradition over the years, sending her friend a weekly batch of puzzles. Occasionally her friend reciprocates with newspaper clippings of interest from the local paper. LK (74, F) said she uses *"commemorative stamps... I try to choose stamps that are relevant to that particular person."* LL (81, F) explained, *"I'm always clipping things, clipping articles. I will save them until I write to the person."*

DISCUSSION

This paper presents an analysis of older adults' communication values and preferences related to social media. While extensive prior work reports older adults' attitudes and behaviors around keeping in touch as well as social media usage, our unique contribution is an in-depth qualitative analysis of late life social communication practices through the lens of social media. By analyzing older adults' practices of keeping in touch in context of mainstream social media, we examine how existing online sites and services could better support seniors' social communication needs and goals. Our analysis provides a foundation for designing more inclusive social communication technologies for the current oldest generation, the G.I. Generation, but also provides a long-term view of designing communication systems for seniors given the rapidly changing landscape of digital social media.

Design Considerations

Designing for older adults is a challenge, as the population is heterogeneous and perpetually changing. Older adults have idiosyncratic needs related to computer accessibility and technical skill, but there is also great variation among each generation of older adults. Age is only one dimension used to understand this population. As described earlier, our participants are active in their communities, well-educated, and have access to a computer and the Internet. We study this elite population of older adults to understand their concerns with social media, given that they have the means and resources to use such sites if desired. Based on our analysis, we highlight key issues to consider when designing social media primarily for members of the G.I. Generation, approximately 18 million older adults in the United States, the vast majority of whom currently do not use social media.

Social media for older adults should foster strong tie relationships. Older adults may avoid using social media if they perceive joining a site as an obligation to maintain communications, particularly with weak ties. Promoting weak tie relationships may actually deter use. Indeed, several participants intentionally limited the number of weak ties that they had (e.g., by restricting the number of friends on Facebook or by removing people from a newsletter distribution list) in order to focus on strong ties in their network.

Existing social media is considered lightweight by many older adults, and this stands in contrast to their desire to engage in thoughtful communication that often requires an investment of time and attention to composition [26, 28]. For example, many of our participants who use social media also engage in letter writing, a practice which they describe as time-consuming. Lightweight communication through social media (e.g., Words With Friends, terse humorous replies on Facebook) has a place, but it is a supplement to, rather than a replacement for, deep and thoughtful communication.

Older adults often want to connect with younger family members, who are active on mainstream social media sites. Many of our participants recognize that younger family members are active users of sites such as Facebook. New sites or systems that are created should integrate with existing mainstream platforms in seamless ways to encourage participation by younger family members.

Older adults find value in doing research for members of their social network and may play an important role in the social question and answer behavior of younger people. Currently this interaction is likely to occur offline or through e-mail. Seniors described the work of sending paper newspaper articles and e-mails pertaining to grandchildren's research projects.

Older adults are more interested in one-on-one communication than mass communication to a broader audience [28], *but certain situations are exceptions to this.* For example, the ability to share family medical updates via a private social media forum is valuable to older adults. Seniors emphasized that the most important qualities of this are privacy of information and knowing with whom information is shared.

Older adults want news from venerated sources and do not feel that political and religious views should be shared on social media. Reading the news from a printed newspaper is common and was stated as a preference by the vast majority of participants. The ability to add comments to new stories on social media is viewed negatively as it may "distort" the news story.

For older adults, material social communications afford expression of thoughtfulness and concern, and the medium and meaning of social media are intertwined. An opportunity to integrate paper-based or hand-written artifacts into an online experience may resonate well with this generation. Similarly, the ability to give digital social media artifacts a physical dimension (i.e., by printing) may be received positively.

Towards Inclusive Social Media Design for Older Adults

A short-term view of inclusive social media design considers the needs of specific cohorts of older adults, as we describe above. A long-term view, however, considers a rapidly changing communications landscape, where the technologies of today will be replaced by new interaction paradigms of tomorrow, which will again displace the oldest generation. This trend is visible in younger generations of older adults. Consider the Baby Boomers[2] who are active on sites such as Facebook, but who are less likely to use sites and services that are popular with Millennials[3] (see [43] for a full analysis).

A long-term research program aimed at supporting late life communication involves designing *bridging technologies* that meet the needs of different generations, who each prefer different interaction styles and user interfaces. Systems such as Wayve [26] and Tlatoque [10] act as intergenerational bridges for communication. Studying this broader class of bridging communication technologies is important, and designers must deeply understand age-related needs pertaining to accessibility as well as cultural practices and preferences of different generational cohorts, as we describe in this paper. For example, a bridging system that is tailored to the G.I. Generation may incorporate paper interfaces, penmanship, or other media that enable depth of thought, reflection, and personalization desired by these seniors.

The overarching theme of this and related work is that seniors want to connect with their strong ties and they put considerable effort into crafting well thought out, meaningful communications. Analyzing the communication practices of seniors in context of digital social media highlights that the oldest generation's social communication needs and values are marginalized: older adults lament that the forms of expression afforded by material social communications are lost with online social media. For older adults, social media "ruins the language" and such lightweight interactions pale in comparison to the letter-based compositions on which they work. Although some seniors exploit digital social media, indeed we learned of instances of communicating with grandchildren over Facebook and Words With Friends, we argue that technology should better support older adults' communication needs and preferences, enabling depth of thought, careful and reflective composition, and personalization. These are qualities that are valued by older adults [28] but not often supported by existing digital social media.

Examining late life communication practices through the lens of social media also reveals a need to reconsider how we evaluate meaningful use of online social media by seniors. Current theories of how people use online social media, form identities, and maintain relationships in online spaces focus on younger populations. The signifiers of online social status for a young adult, such as content of one's profile or number of friends on a SNS [24, 4], are likely to manifest in far different ways with older adults. Older adult social status is better understood by examining the strength or closeness of relationships rather than quantity, the quality and credibility of information shared on one's profile, and the presence of both digital and paper-based media that represent social relationships (e.g., printed photo albums, hand-written letters). A more holistic view of *what is social media* for seniors is required.

[2]U.S. population born between 1946-1964

[3]U.S. population born between 1977-1992

CONCLUSION

This paper explores older adults' attitudes and uses of online social media. We studied older adults who are interested in improving communication with their family and friends, yet these seniors rarely use social media to connect with members of their social networks. As a whole, older adults value deeper, well thought out, carefully crafted social communications that are achieved through telephone calls, e-mails, and written letters. Issues of privacy, information credibility, and content relevance are key reasons for not using social media. Participation on social media sites requires a time commitment and there are expectations of reciprocity. Encouraging seniors to connect with weak ties may deter use. While older adults perform many social functions that could be supported by online technologies, few seniors use such systems. We hope that understanding seniors' concerns with social media and the ways in which they manage and interact with their social networks will inform the design of more inclusive online technologies as well as additional research into technologies that serve as a bridge for intergenerational communication.

ACKNOWLEDGEMENTS

We thank Chelsea Kim for her help with data collection and transcription. We thank our study participants for their time.

REFERENCES

1. Arjan, R., Pfeil, U., and Zaphiris, P. Age differences in online social networking. In *Proceedings of ACM CHI* (2008), 2739–2744.
2. Bell, C., Fausset, C., Farmer, S., Nguyen, J., Harley, L., and Fain, W. B. Examining social media use among older adults. In *Proc of Hypertext and Social Media* (2013), 158–163.
3. Birnholtz, J., and Jones-Rounds, M. Independence and interaction: understanding seniors' privacy and awareness needs for aging in place. In *Proc of CHI*, ACM (New York, NY, USA, 2010), 143–152.
4. boyd, d. Why youth (heart) social network sites: The role of networked publics in teenage social life. In *Youth, identity, and digital media*, D. Buckingham, Ed., MIT Press, Cambridge (2008).
5. Braun, M. T. Obstacles to social networking website use among older adults. *Comput. Hum. Behav. 29*, 3 (2013), 673–680.
6. Carstensen, L. Socioemotional selectivity theory and the regulation of emotion in the second half of life. *Motivation and Emotion 27*, 2 (2003), 103–123.
7. Chalfen, R. *Snapshot versions of life*. Bowling Green State University Popular Press, OH, 1987.
8. Cherlin, A., and Furstenberg, F. *The New American Grandparent: A Place in the Family, a Life Apart*. Basic Books, New York, 1986.
9. Cicirelli, V. G. Feelings of attachment to siblings and well-being in later life. *Psychology and Aging 4*, 2 (1989), 211–216.

10. Cornejo, R., Tentori, M., and Favela, J. Ambient awareness to strengthen the family social network of older adults. *Comput. Supported Coop. Work 22*, 2-3 (2013), 309–344.
11. Davis, H., Vetere, F., Francis, P., Gibbs, M., and Howard, S. 'I wish we could get together': exploring intergenerational play across a distance via a 'Magic Box'. *Intergen. Relat. 6*, 2 (2008), 191–210.
12. Dickinson, A., and Hill, R. Keeping in touch: Talking to older people about computers and communication. *Educ Gerontology* (2007), 613–630.
13. Diener, E., and Suh, M. Subjective wellbeing and age: An international analysis. In *Annual review of gerontology and geriatrics*, K. Schaie and M. Lawton, Eds., Springer, New York (1997), 304–324.
14. Donath, J., and boyd, d. Public displays of connection. *BT Technology Journal 22*, 4 (2004), 71–82.
15. Duggan, M., and Smith, A. Social media update 2013. *Pew Internet and American Life Project* (2013).
16. Ellison, N., Steinfeld, C., and Lampe, C. Spatially bounded online social networks and social capital: the role of facebook. In *ICA* (2006).
17. Gibson, L., Moncur, W., Forbes, P., Arnott, J., Martin, C., and Bhachu, A. Designing social networking sites for older adults. In *Proc of BCS Interaction Specialist Group* (2010), 186–194.
18. Glaser, B., and Strauss, A. *The Discovery of Grounded Theory: Strategies for Qualitative Research.* Aldine Publishing Company, Chicago, 1967.
19. Gordon, C., and Gaitz, C. Leisure and lives. *Handbook of Aging and the Social Sciences 1* (1976), 310–341.
20. Granovetter, M. The strength of weak ties: A network theory revisited. In *Social structure and network analysis*, P. Marsden and N. Lin, Eds., Sage (1982).
21. Harvey, A., and Singleton, J. Canadian activity patterns across the life span: A time budget perspective. *Canadian Journal on Aging 8* (1989), 268–285.
22. Kanayama, T. Ethnographic research on the experience of japanese elderly people online. *New Media and Society 5* (2003).
23. Karimi, A., and Neustaedter, C. My grandma uses facebook: Communication practices of older adults in an age of social media. *Technical Report 2011-1116-04* (2011).
24. Lampe, C., Ellison, N., and Steinfield, C. A familiar face(book): profile elements as signals in an online social network. In *Proc of CHI* (2007), 435–444.
25. Lehtinen, V., Nasanen, J., and Sarvas, R. "A Little Silly and Empty-Headed" – Older Adults' Understandings of Social Networking Sites. In *Proc. HCI* (2009), 45–54.
26. Lindley, S. E. Shades of lightweight: supporting cross-generational communication through home messaging. *Univers. Access Inf. Soc. 11*, 1 (2012), 31–43.
27. Lindley, S. E., Harper, R., and Sellen, A. Designing for elders: exploring the complexity of relationships in later life. In *Proc of BCS-HCI* (2008), 77–86.
28. Lindley, S. E., Harper, R., and Sellen, A. Desiring to be in touch in a changing communications landscape: attitudes of older adults. In *Proc of CHI*, ACM (New York, NY, USA, 2009), 1693–1702.
29. Lubben, J., and Gironda, M. Centrality of social ties to the health and well-being of older adults. *Social work and health care in an aging society* (2003), 319–350.
30. Madden, M. Older adults and social media. *Pew Internet and American Life Project* (2010).
31. McLuhan, M. *Understanding Media: The Extensions of Man.* McGraw Hill, New York, 1964.
32. McMellon, C., and Schiffman, L. Cybersenior empowerment: How some older individuals are taking control of their lives. *Jour of Applied Geront 21* (2002).
33. Moffatt, K., David, J., and Baecker, R. M. Connecting grandparents and grandchildren. In *Connecting Families: The Impact of New Communication Technologies on Domestic Life*, C. Neustaedter, S. Harrison, and A. Sellen, Eds., Springer (London, 2012), 173–193.
34. Pfeil, U., Arjan, R., and Zaphiris, P. Age differences in online social networking a study of user profiles and the social capital divide among teenagers and older users in myspace. *Comp in Human Behav 25* (2009), 643–654.
35. Quadrello, T., Hurme, H., Menzinger, J., Smith, P. K., Veisson, M., Vidal, S., and Westerback, S. Grandparents use of new communication technologies in a european perspective. *Eur J Ageing* (2005).
36. Selwyn, N. The information aged: A qualitative study of older adults use of information and communications technology. *Jour of Aging Studies 18* (2004), 369–384.
37. Sum, S., Mathews, R., Hughes, I., and Campbell, A. Internet use and loneliness in older adults. *Cyberpsychol Behav 11* (2008).
38. Sundar, S. S., Oeldorf-Hirsch, A., Nussbaum, J., and Behr, R. Retirees on facebook: can online social networking enhance their health and wellness? In *Proc of CHI* (2011), 2287–2292.
39. Tee, K., Brush, A. J., and Inkpen, K. Exploring communication and sharing between extended families. *Int. J. Hum.-Comput. Stud. 67*, 2 (2009), 128–138.
40. Waycott, J., Vetere, F., Pedell, S., Kulik, L., Ozanne, E., Gruner, A., and Downs, J. Older adults as digital content producers. In *Proc of CHI*, ACM (New York, NY, USA, 2013), 39–48.
41. Xie, B. Older chinese, the internet, and well-being. *Jour of Long Term Home Health Care 8* (2007).
42. Zaphiris, P., and Sarwar, R. Trends, similarities and differences in the usage of teen and senior public online newsgroups. *TOCHI 13* (2006).
43. Zickuhr, K. Generations 2010. *Pew Internet and American Life Project* (2010).
44. Zickuhr, K., and Madden, M. Older adults and internet use. *Pew Internet and American Life Project* (2012).

Never Too Old: Engaging Retired People Inventing the Future with MaKey MaKey

Yvonne Rogers[1], Jeni Paay[2], Margot Brereton[3], Kate Vaisutis[3], Gary Marsden[4], Frank Vetere[5]
[1]UCLIC, University College London, UK, y.rogers@ucl.ac.uk
[2]Research Centre for Socio-Interactive Design, Aalborg University, Denmark, jeni@cs.aau.dk
[3]Queensland University of Technology, Australia {m.brereton, k.vaisutis}@qut.edu.au
[4]Computer Science Dept., University of Cape Town, South Africa
[5]Interaction Design Lab, The University of Melbourne, Australia, f.vetere@unimelb.edu.au

ABSTRACT
Within HCI, aging is often viewed in terms of designing assistive technologies to improve the lives of older people, such as those who are suffering from frailty or memory loss. Our research adopts a very different approach, reframing the relationship in terms of wisdom, creativity and invention. We ran a series of workshops where groups of retirees, aged between early 60s and late 80s, used the MaKey MaKey inventor's toolkit. We asked them to think about inventing the future and suggest ideas for new technologies. Our findings showed that they not only rose to the challenge but also mastered the technology, collaborated intensely together while using it and freely and at length discussed their own, their family's and others' relationship with technology. We discuss the value of empowering people in this way and consider what else could be invented to enable more people to be involved in the design and use of creative technologies.

Author Keywords
Aging, creativity, MaKey MaKey, toolkits, invention, future technology, retired people

ACM Classification Keywords
H.5.2 [Information Systems]: Information Interfaces and Presentation - *user interfaces*; K.4.2 [Computers and Society]: Social Issues.

INTRODUCTION
There is a stereotyped view that when people retire they go off on cruises, play golf and then don their slippers. While a few do, most have less money to live on, and prefer to do other things, such as spend more time with their grandchildren, take up new hobbies, participate in local activities, potter, make, tinker and/or keep fit. As part of this transition into retirement, many continue and even increase their use of technology. Being on the Internet, and keeping in touch via email and Skype have become part of their daily life – just as it has for everyone else. There is a concern, however, that after retiring, people's knowledge and use of technologies – especially new ones – will decline (as they are no longer exposed to them at work or get training). As a result, they may miss out on new opportunities that could widen their horizons, and help them manage and enjoy their lives further in unknown ways.

CHI 2014, April 26 - May 01 2014, Toronto, ON, Canada
Copyright 2014 ACM 978-1-4503-2473-1/14/04…$15.00.
http://dx.doi.org/10.1145/2556288.2557184

How might this gap be bridged, especially with the continued development of more affordable, accessible and exciting technologies? To date, HCI researchers have largely been concerned with the downside of aging; focusing on assistive technologies that can help compensate for people's frailties and the assumed needs that arise when getting older, such as more social engagement, help with exercising and increased memory aids [e.g., 13, 29]. While this approach has helped establish a global agenda for enabling older people to live independently for longer, it overlooks another side of growing older, where people do not consider themselves in need of such technological care and who otherwise feel they still have a lot they can give back to society and their communities. Moreover, contrary to popular belief many people remain active well into their retirement – and sometimes more so – than when they were at work, socially, physically and mentally [cf. 26].

Our research is concerned with breaking down the 'old' stereotypes and reframing the relationship between aging and technology in ways that is more in tune with how people live after work. The focus of this paper is how retired people can contribute to future technological design and user experience – rather than being, themselves, the subject of technological assisted living. In particular, we are interested in how older people can explore, suggest and invent new ways of using technology for themselves and others. Instead of considering what researchers might provide for them – in terms of age related needs – we ask them to think about what possibilities new technologies suggest. Our motivation is driven by a desire to tap into their wisdom and know-how, built up over a lifetime.

So, how might retirees (ranging from those who have just given up work to those who have been retired for many years) be inventive in this way? Central to our approach is providing toolkits and resources to encourage creative thinking – something that is often overlooked when growing older (cf. [13]). We are interested in discovering what happens when retirees are allowed to imagine and be inspired by new technologies, through extending their existing skills and abilities, while learning new ones that do not make them feel stupid or uncomfortable.

In the last few years, a number of DIY toolkits have become commercially available and affordable, that offer new opportunities for people to be inventive and creative, comprising electronics and software that are also relatively easy to get started and experiment with e.g., Arduino, Senseboard, Lego Mindstorms. So far, most have been aimed at children or adult learners to enable them to begin to program through rapid creation of small electronic gadgets and digital tools [11, 23]. MaKey MaKey has even broader ambitions: being promoted as a creative toolkit that anyone can use. It claims to be *"a simple Invention Kit for Beginners and Experts."* We wanted to see how retired people took up this challenge and what they thought of turning *"everyday objects into touchpads"* [15]. Would they see new possibilities and think of how it could be used in innovative and unexpected ways for themselves and others?

To answer our research question we ran a series of creative workshops where small groups of retired friends, aged between early 60s and late 80s assembled and played with the MaKey MaKey toolkit. Our findings showed all groups, not only rising to the challenge of being inventive, but also mastering the technology, playing intensely together and afterwards generating a diversity of ideas while discussing freely and at length their own, their family and other's relationship with technology. An unexpected finding was the pivotal role of actively collaborating to play music together in a highly coordinated way and how this triggered subsequent discussions and idea generation. We discuss the findings of our study in terms of how our study has demystified 'old' stereotypes while opening up a new debate about the relationship between wisdom, creativity and technology. We end by discussing what other kinds of technology toolkits could be developed that could be used by all ages to encourage creative doing, playful thinking and collaborative imagining.

BACKGROUND

Technology, in its various forms, plays an integral and sometimes greater role in retiree's lives than when they were at work [30]. Many people who have retired during the last 20 years or so have been using IT at home and work for a long time: using word processing, email, Skype, Facebook and the Internet to do a diversity of things (such as pay their bills, buy goods, search on topics, and so on). They have tried and used various devices (PCs, laptops, tablets, smartphones). Many are more determined than ever to lead a full life and this often means embracing what technology has to offer them in their lives.

While some still shy away from technology, fearing they might not be very good at it, those who did not have contact with technology during their lives before retirement may now find they have the time to explore and experiment with it [e.g. 26]. Using a tablet to watch movies or TV online, or find a recipe, etc., is proving to be a much less daunting way of getting started with technology compared with 10 years ago, when struggling to learn how to connect to the internet or use a spreadsheet package on a PC. This new interest in technology is coupled with a motivation that comes from being physically distant from family and friends, and not being as mobile. It provides a new found way of keeping in touch with family, friends, and interest groups and clubs. Furthermore, it offers them opportunities to widen what they did before, e.g. researching genealogy and family trees, and try out new things online, such as playing games, blogging and joining online dating sites. However, at the same time, the frustrations of using technology can become magnified for those who are new to it. Many don't want to bother others, nor do they want to appear to be stupid in front of others, not knowing or remembering what to do.

It goes without saying, that as we grow older, we become aware of our aging bodies and minds, especially when our joints start to creak and need replacing, we need to wear more than one pair of glasses, and we begin to forget our friend's names and what we went upstairs for. Much has been written about developing technologies that can help older people live more independently, especially for those with identified illnesses, such as Alzheimer's and other forms of dementia while doing their everyday tasks [13]. Commercial services are now available that use sophisticated sensor-based systems to monitor, detect and notify deviations from someone's everyday routines, such as if they have fallen. Other systems have been developed that encourage older people to connect with each other through creating digital content and sharing photos [29].

What people say, regardless of age, depends on how they are asked and how the new technology is explained to them. Instead of simply asking older people what they think, some researchers have tried to engage them more by using a form of a form of participatory design to develop future technologies. However, designing can prove challenging. For example, in an early study [17], a group of 5 older people found it difficult to design functions when asked to develop software for a mobile phone that the designers thought would be helpful to them. Instead, the participants found it easier to critique the software. Similarly, in a more recent study, elderly people with memory loss found participating in the design process sometimes arduous and somewhat abstract, especially when hypothesizing about technologies that do not already exist [14].

This raises the question of how to engage older people in participatory design when designing specific solutions for technologies with which they might not be familiar. On the one hand, it has been suggested that because they are not fixated on a particular kind of technology they may generate more novel ideas [8]. However, by the same token, they may fixate on what is familiar to them and not see how this could be extended or augmented by new technologies. This argument, however, applies to everyone regardless of age; the extent to which someone becomes fixated on what they know versus the ability to break away and generate new ideas based on what might be possible, exemplifying the tensions that arise between working with participants to gather information versus working with them to leverage their creative abilities. The Living Labs concept takes a more hands-on approach with the objective of enabling older people to be more directly involved, for example, the ambient kitchen [19] and the interactive doll's house [12]. The rationale is that this way of envisioning the future through interacting with a physical model or life-sized mock-up can help explain better and demonstrate more concretely a proposed system. Others introduce them to 'sandpits' where they explore current and emerging technologies in a playful and creative way helping them see potential implications for their lives [12]. Another approach is to sensitize designers more to particular needs. Pairing design students with older people can open their eyes to seeing the world of aging differently [7]. Newell et al. [18] worked with actors, script writers and directors to create dramatic performances which when showed to design students increased their awareness of the different characteristics, needs and wants of other people.

But underlying many of these approaches is an assumption that the purpose of the project is to design for older people who need help in some capacity. This view means the technology design is very much constrained by a deficit/ compensatory model, instead of a more pro-active approach of focusing on engagement with a view to empowerment. Here, technology is designed and created by older people themselves, for more life-affirming activities, such as reminiscing, generating digital content and socializing [10]. A recent study that has adopted a more engaging stance demonstrated that when adults in their eighties and nineties were shown how to create and share personally meaningful digital content, it helped them build connections with their peers [29]. It seems the act of engaging with the technology to create something, rather than using it for monitoring or consumption, was key. Instead of us designing for old people's frailty and asking *"what technology do you need?"* we should consider inviting older people themselves to design and use technology to conjure up applications and experiences we have not thought of, and ask, *"what can you do or make with this technology?"* [24].

Part of the answer may lie in the kind of tools provided as to what they engender and encourage. Props, videos, and low-tech materials have all been used to elicit responses, prompt idea generation and discussion. Cultural probes [9] for example, have successfully been used to provoke participants to record playful and creative ideas, thoughts and desires in a range of contexts used to inspire design. Wallace et al. [28] suggest the use of more crafted objects and prototypes, designed around a particular theme, to encourage reflection and *"gentle ways to access complex notions and experience"*. Another approach has been to encourage older people to critique the organizers' 'silly' ideas and concepts [27]. The objective here is to get the participants to see new possibilities, challenging their existing assumptions and conventional views.

An alternative approach is to empower people through providing new technologies and/or teaching them a new skill, such as basic electronics or programming and inviting them to use this to envision and create, themselves [6]. Interactive tabletop apps [20] and mixed reality tools [1] were developed to encourage creative, equitable and imaginative participation. These early technologies were often complex, requiring a technician and/or expert facilitator to program and control them during a workshop, limiting participants in how they could explore and develop their own ideas when using them. The newer generation of creative materials (e.g. conductive ink), craft technologies and DIY construction tools (3D printers, laser cutters) have lowered the entry level, providing opportunities for a wider range of people to use them to design the future. New toolkits, with little or no programming are appearing, using "friendlier than usual" or visual programming languages e.g. Lego Logo [22]. Moreover, this emerging homemade technology movement offers new possibilities for anyone to be an inventor; designing, building and rethinking the world of objects in physical/digital environments in fun and creative ways. Inspired by these new forms of technology toolkits and their low entry barriers, we wanted to see if they could inspire creativity in mature participants; whether it allowed them to be creative about technology designs or if the current generation of technologies, like previous ones, were too intimidating to use.

AIMS

The aims of our study are: firstly, to investigate how retirees learn, construct and play with the MaKey MaKey inventor's toolkit and, secondly, to see what this hands-on experience suggests to them about future technology uses and experiences. The objective was to see whether playing with everyday materials and electronics led to creativity and invention, and if so, what forms it took.

METHODOLOGY

Our approach can be viewed as a form of participatory design insofar as it aims to bring power to the voice of those often excluded from design while tapping into the wisdom and 'domain' knowledge of retired people through including them as full participants in design conversations and activities [cf. 1, 16]. We ran 6 workshops, lasting between 2-3 hours, with groups of 2-3 friends who were between their early 60s and late 80s. Much has been written about how to run workshops and the role of facilitation, different activities and resources, including how best to engage older people [14]. We designed our workshops to be playful and collaborative to inspire creativity and inventiveness. They were structured around a series of activities to provide sufficient training and then free time to play and discuss new ideas. For the first part, our role was central, giving instruction, facilitation and encouragement. For the second part, it was in the background, enabling the participants to take over and control the flow of conversation.

The groups were instructed to learn, assemble, create and play with the MaKey MaKey toolkit, followed by having an in-depth discussion over tea and cake. The sessions were held in one person's kitchen, to provide a familiar and rich sensory environment for thinking about everyday objects and activities and how they might be augmented and combined to do things in new ways.

The MaKey MaKey toolkit

MaKey MaKey was developed by MIT researchers Jay Silver and Eric Rosenbaum together with SparkFun Electronics. The toolkit comprises a printed circuit board with an Arduino microcontroller, alligator clips and a USB cable. It uses the HID protocol to communicate with a computer to send key presses, mouse clicks, and mouse movements. There are six inputs (the 4 arrow keys, the space bar and a mouse click) positioned on the front of the board that alligator clips are clipped onto in order to connect with a computer via the USB cable (see Figure 1). The other ends of the clips can be attached to any non-insulating object, such as a vegetable or piece of fruit. Thus, instead of using the computer keyboard buttons to interact with the computer, external objects such as bananas are used. The computer thinks MaKey MaKey is just like a keyboard or mouse. An example is to play a digital piano app using bananas as keys rather than keys on the computer keyboard. When they are touched they make a connection to the board, and MaKey MaKey sends the computer a keyboard message.

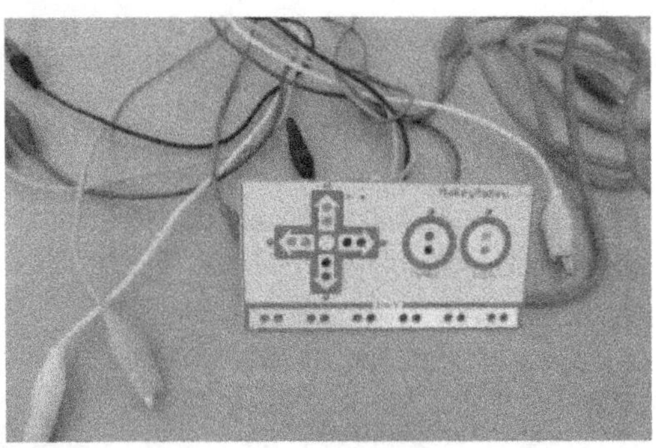

Figure 1. MaKey MaKey components: board, alligator clips with plastic sheaths and USB cable to connect to computer

The groups were shown how to play music together using the kit. Three musical apps were provided – a piano, a guitar and a set of drums/percussion (see Figure 2). A bowl of fruit and vegetables were provided to select from for the input.

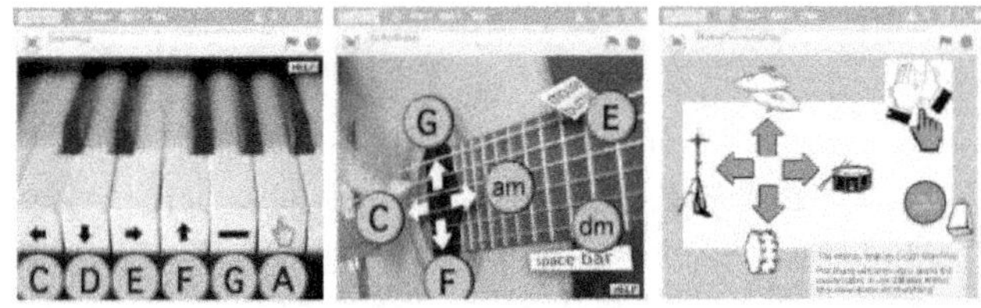

Figure 2. Screen shots of the piano keyboard, guitar chords and drum/percussion apps provided

Each instrument allowed only six sounds; the piano comprised the notes of C, D, E, F G and A; the guitar had the chords of Am, C, Dm, E, F and G, and the drums had cymbals, snare drum, bass drum, hi-hat and cowbell. This constraint meant that the mappings could be quickly learnt, set up easily and the mappings remembered when played with.

Participants

Six groups of three friends in three Australian cities were recruited. When asked, most preferred to say they were in their early or late 60s, 70s or 80s. We chose to respect their way of saying how old they were (see Table 1). They were from a diversity of backgrounds; some had done quite different jobs, including being a social worker then a church minister, a teacher then a Member of Parliament and a geologist then a palm reader.

Group no.	Partici-pant*	Age bracket	Former work
1	Sally	Late 60s	Teacher/MP
	Joan	Late 60s	University admin
	Jean	Late 60s	Social worker/Minister
2	Carol	Early 80s	Census interviewer
	Jill	Late 80s	Home duties
3	Felix	Late 70s	Refrigeration Mech.
	Raymond	Late 80s	House Painter
4	Charles	Late 70s	Cook on a ship/Navy
	Liz	Early 70s	Knitting Pattern tester
	Barry	Early 70s	Football coach
5	Sarah	Mid 60s	Building business
	Rhonda	Mid 60s	Admin/Home duties
	Cecily	Mid 60s	Business Owners
6	Grant	Mid 70s	Geologist/Palm Reader
	Richard	Late 60s	Journalist/Lecturer
	Trevor	Mid 70s	Engineer

Table 1: The six groups who took part in the workshops (*not real names)

Procedure

The workshops were run so as to enable sufficient time for groups to learn, construct, play, discuss, generate ideas and reflect on the session. After introducing the project, a short video was shown of someone playing a piano using bananas instead of piano keys. The idea was to show the participants what was possible. The MaKey MaKey toolkit was demonstrated next. The participants were asked to help by selecting pieces of fruit or vegetables and connecting them to the alligator clips and the board (see Figure 3). They were then asked to connect the USB cable and play with the different instruments using the fruit/vegetable inputs. They then set up their own kits and played with the different musical instruments. Next, we asked them to come up with a tune they would like to play together as an ensemble.

Figure 3. Attaching the MaKey MaKey alligator clips to pieces of fruit and vegetables, the circuit board and the laptop

We prepared a card with the words and notes of 'Twinkle Twinkle Little Star' so they could follow it together – a familiar tune. The next stage involved exploring what else they thought they could make with the kit and asking them if they were inspired to share and teach it to others. Finally, there was an open discussion over tea that was led by the participants discussing and sharing experiences. We ended with a free-reeling conversation as it can encourage a range of topics to be covered and creative ideas to be generated. Each workshop lasted about 2 hours.

FINDINGS

When asking participants about themselves and what they had done in their lives, they told us how they had lived through incredible changes. One mentioned how they had used slate and ink/nibbed pens and another regaling how they had watched the first man walk on the moon. They exclaimed how they were not frightened of technology but not everyone uses it to the same level. Some used it much more since they had retired, including playing games, like online Scrabble every night, and using Facebook to keep up with the activities of family and friends. Others had begun using it less, and viewed Skype and email as old hat. Some were very open while others were more reticent. The same with their actual age; some people prefer to say roughly how old they are while others are only too proud to announce their age.

In the first workshop, we ran into some technical difficulties. One of the Bluetooth speakers would not work properly and one of the drum apps got stuck in a loop on one of the laptops. So we decided ad hoc to just use two of the set-ups. This proved to be fortuitous as it meant that two of the participants had to make a circuit, which meant one holding the earth alligator clip and the other holding onto them. As shown in Figure 4, it made for greater closeness, awareness and much fun amongst them. In subsequent workshops, some of the groups played just one instrument together using one laptop while others shared one laptop between two. The groups of two had a laptop each, but still reached over to share the same one when playing.

Figure 4. Group 6 holding and touching each other and each tapping a fruit/vegetable input to play music together

All sessions were videoed and viewed by all investigators. An investigator who was at the session then transcribed the conversations and the interactions that took place. Transcriptions were reviewed by all researchers, who independently categorized and themed them in terms of activity and conversation, using an iterative and open form of thematic analysis [2]. The themes derived from the different researchers were categorized under the headings of (i) experiences of engaging with the toolkit, (ii) idea generation and (iii) reflections on technological change.

(i) Experiences of engaging with the toolkit

Confidence To begin, the participants were a bit apprehensive when interacting with the MaKey MaKey toolkit. They were not sure how serious they should be but some were quick to point out afterwards how much fun other participants were having while playing with the fruit, *"she was enjoying herself, wasn't she"*, while encouraging each other, *"aren't we having fun!"* The groups soon lost their inhibitions and grew in confidence as they watched and learned to put the components together. For example, one participant said *"I'm a dinosaur but I couldn't wait to get my hands on it."*

Enjoyment The participants all enjoyed experimenting with the toolkit and fruit/vegetables. For example, while selecting which vegetable to 'plug in' to the configuration, one participant in Group 1 suggested, *"Maybe a potato?"* As her friend grabbed one, she jibed, *"the other one"*, making them all laugh. Later on in the same session, to celebrate the successful playing of a tune, one of them popped a tomato into her mouth and said, *"I think I am going to eat the bass drum"*.

Intimacy To play a sound, the participants had to create a circuit, which meant holding onto the earth alligator clip and touching a piece of fruit. If they weren't holding the earth alligator clip they had to touch the person that was. They figured out this need to touch or hold onto each other early on and how to make a circuit through doing so. They also experimented with different fruit and vegetables as to which were the best as inputs. Some were found to be good conductors (e.g. tomato, carrot) and others less so (e.g. apple, potato). In the process of trying out the different ones, they talked about why this might be the case and then more generally about conductivity.

The women held on to each other and tapped the fruit, while sometimes the men held the fruit and tapped on each other's arms or hands until they grew more comfortable, eventually holding onto each other even after they had finished playing. They were very considerate of each other, but some groups also teased each other. For example, there was much hilarity in Group 4 when they discovered that they weren't holding onto the right earth lead. Through observing their laughter and from their comments afterwards it was clear that they enjoyed playing together immensely in this intimate way.

Coordination Working together as a group was quickly understood as central to mastering the fruit/vegetable instruments. As observers, we were surprised by the sheer determination that some of the oldest participants displayed when connecting the difficult and fiddly alligator clips to the circuit board. Often they asked each other for help, *"something is not right? Help, [Ray]. Help!"* or offered to help each other – but all were keen to manage it without our intervention. In general, working together to successfully master a tune came naturally to the groups as they connected the MaKey MaKey kits, found the correct notes for the tune, demonstrated to each other how to earth, and organized who would play which notes, *"I'll do C, D. You be E, F. Glen, you're G, A. Sorted."* They saw it very much as a joint effort, even when they were playing on different instruments. For example, while one of the participants in Group 2 tried to pick out an old tune from memory on her fruit piano, the other started banging on her drum fruit, saying, *"There you are, I'll give you a bit of encouragement"*.

Creativity All groups explored the option of one person holding the earth wire while others contacted them physically, either by holding hands, holding their wrist, or simply just poking them with a finger. Once they understood the idea of needing to complete a circuit, they thought creatively about how to make this happen, including removing the plastic sheath from the alligator clip, licking their finger before touching the fruit, and touching the MaKey MaKey circuit board directly when the earth wire was out of reach. In choosing fruit, one participant in Group 1 had a theory that characteristics of the fruit influenced the conductivity, saying, *"Let's go the lemon, it's more acidic, I can put my theory to the test"*.

Each group found a different way of matching up the fruit to the notes in order to figure out how to play a tune as they experimented with fruit music making. Inventiveness happened as they learned how to 'do the fruit'. Two women in Group 5 watched patiently while their less musical friend persevered with trying to remember which fruit was which note in the tune. One appeared to be desperate to have a turn herself but was keen not to interrupt her friend. The three men in Group 6 quickly arranged who was playing which instrument and methodically laid the fruit in order of the notes of the scale. Several of the other groups also adopted this strategy (e.g. see Figure 5). These groups talked about the idea of matching the name of the fruit with the piano note that it would play, for example, the apple should be the note A and the cucumber the note C. Group 4 made up a rhyme on the fly: *"Kiwi E"*. They interacted and shared notes/fruit and worked closely together to play the tune. A more pragmatic approach, used by Group 3, was to line the fruit up in order of the tune they were trying to play, so that they just had to play the fruit from left to right.

Figure 5. The fruit and vegetables all lined up to match the notes of the piano keyboard

When assigning fruit and vegetable to the drums, some participants made associations between the type of fruit and the characteristics of the instrument it operated. For example, one participant commented, *"Oh yes, an apple for the big bass drum"*. For others, the fruit actually "became" the instrument itself. While moving the fruit aside to make room for the tea, one person commented, *"I'll shift the keyboard for you"*, referring to the line up of connected fruit, not the computer keyboard. In fact, the assignment of fruit to instrument was so strong that some people were hesitant to experiment with set ups other than the piano, claiming, *"I don't know, I'm not a guitarist"*, or *"I wouldn't know how to play a guitar"*, and then joking, *"except on CD, I'm alright with them!"*

Mastery All groups played at least one round of Twinkle Twinkle Little Star and some embarked on playing other tunes, too. Once they had successfully mastered a tune, each group spontaneously cheered or clapped, laughed and smiled. *"Hooray! It's only taken us half an hour!"* Group 1 exclaimed when the challenge was finally met. Sometimes, they even suggested that they add a level of complexity to the activity, by coordinating two set ups, *"Hey, duets, piano and guitar"*. Group 2 was happy to celebrate half way though the set up task, when they managed to pick out a tune from only 3 pieces of connected fruit, exclaiming, *"You see, the music's coming out already!"* at which point they laughed joyfully.

(ii) Idea generation

All the groups relished the challenge of learning to assemble and then play with the fruit/vegetable instruments. They viewed this as a great achievement – having never done anything like it before. After finishing playing and having demonstrated mastery, all but one group readily engaged in conversation, reflecting upon technology in their lives and proposing design ideas. The groups came up with lots of ideas about what else they could do with the toolkit. Moreover, they discovered that making and playing together, however childlike it appeared at first, was a catalyst for imagining, free thinking and exploring. Ideas are fragile. People can be cautious to volunteer them and they are easy to squash, but in a positive environment like this they flourish. The shared experience seemed to create a positive and relaxed atmosphere, in which they freely bounced ideas around.

Sharing Several ideas emanated from the participants' experiences and specific interactions when playing the fruit/vegetable instruments. In particular, the music-making activity had them thinking about the people with whom they would like to share directly the experience that they had just had themselves, namely, their children and grandchildren. They often spontaneously made comments, such as, *"that would be fun for children, wouldn't it?"* and it would be useful, *"certainly for entertaining the grandchildren, when the whole family is over for tea"*. This was common across all groups and one of the first things to be mentioned. They assumed that other grandparents would love to show it to their adult children and grandchildren to see what they thought of it. Moreover, rather than just showing them it they were keen to use MaKey MaKey to engage them in a family activity. They saw it as, *"good for interacting with the grandchildren, yes, not on my own. Once they got the idea they'd get going very quickly. They're very savvy"*. They were tickled at the thought of being able to interact with their grandchildren on their level and perhaps even to impress them with some technology they had mastered but which their grand children hadn't heard of yet.

Experimenting In talking about technology use, one participant in Group 3 suggested the MaKey MaKey toolkit could be used by kids *"experimenting with different articles to see if they worked or not, and learn which items will conduct signals and which don't"*. The kit would make it possible to design activities involving children that offered *"so much more than just sitting, there, watching TV"*.

Another theme in one group was to think about the older generation, i.e., their parents generation, in their 80s or 90s, who were sometimes in nursing homes, and/ or living with dementia. Rather than just sitting, or passively watching TV, they suggested that activities such as those with MaKey MaKey would keep their minds active, engage them in a playing together and having fun. They also talked about the ability to make interaction devices much bigger and more graspable than computer keys for older people with limited dexterity, as one participant said *"I think getting older that the little dials are a real problem. Like the mobile phone really drives me insane...I can't do it...the idea of making it bigger is a great idea"*.

The sequencing of notes in order to play a tune led them to ideas about how the toolkit could be extended to help with other kinds of sequencing that is integral to other activities, such as learning to read, to spell, to count, and even learn colors. Drawing on their reflections about today's children Group 1 talked about the sequencing difficulties that children with dyslexia have in learning to read and how the physical touching and interactive feedback of sound and visuals could help them with the sequencing of letters and phonetic sounds required to spell words correctly and to learn to read. *"It could make them want to read more to you. Instead of them getting frustrated because they are having difficulty. Make it more interesting rather than words and numbers on a page. Because they are doing it themselves. Getting the desire"*.

Humor The most concrete and detailed ideas arose from a synergy of humor, practical needs and the physicality of the experience with the kit, itself. For example, they were tickled by the idea of photographing the neighbor's cat if it tried to eat their cat's food. Group 2, when talking about extending the uses of the fruit, had the idea that if children would not eat their fruit, then having the system react in some way (e.g., change in volume of musical note) to a bite being taken out of a piece of connected fruit, might encourage them to eat it. This same group turned around the idea of kids needing to monitor aging parents, to imagine a set up using the MaKey MaKey, where parents monitor their children to make sure they are doing their homework when they are supposed to be.

Surrounding context A number of objects in the environment served as inspiration for suggesting new ideas. While some were obvious and specific suggestions, like using with Play-Doh or Lego, others made more abstract suggestions, for example, *"anything that's got a moisture content, or metal – it's a bit hard to put a probe in a metal object"*. Seeing a trampoline in the garden, Group 5 commented on what a good activity that was for children and how bouncing on the trampoline might serve as an input for MaKey MaKey, with different parts of the bouncy mat acting as different inputs. Other ideas for some kind of technological intervention included the chickens in the garden that could be tagged somehow, the fridge in the kitchen that could be instrumented to see who was eating what, the banana that could serve as a phone and lights that could be dimmed. Other practical ideas included measurements, fractions, cooking – even devising a system that would encourage children to clean up after cooking.

(iii) Reflections on technological change

Rather than thinking about how they might use MaKey MaKey to design for themselves, the groups first began to think about today's children and what was wrong with their use of technology (e.g. constantly using Facebook, playing video games and not communicating much face to face) and how activities with MaKey MaKey might help them interact with others more. Groups 1, 4, 5 and 6 noted how children needed to be able to express themselves better in conversation, to use their imaginations more, to develop coordination and memory and that many needed help in learning to read, write, and count. As one participant said, *"I think we intervene too often"* and *"we are stymieing our kid's creativity"*. They thought that the MaKey MaKey kit *"might get them to use their imaginations more"*, adding that if they were a child, they would think of things to do with it. Instead of consuming digital content, they suggested wittily, that children could eat the fruit and move on. Another one said, *"I think it would stimulate anyone of any age. Not just old people. Young people sometimes just need something to play with without being organized – let them be and see what they could come up with themselves."*

While discussing other possibilities for uses of the MaKey MaKey toolkit, many of the participants spontaneously talked about the problems they have with current technologies, in the hope that something like MaKey MaKey might help solve some of them. Group 1 shared both work-based and home-based technology issues, talking about the simplicity of physical operations of household appliances like washing machines, which stop when you open them and wanting this kind of physical manipulation for use with technologies, for example, lifting the lid of a photocopier to stop and start it. Their experiences with using technology was revealing, *"because in something new, things are supposed to be intuitive, a lot of things aren't intuitive"*. They talked about the complexity of interfaces with everyday objects like gym equipment, modern ovens, set-top boxes, DVD players, remote controls for home entertainment systems, swipe card travel systems, online booking systems, mobile phones, and iPads, lamenting that *"if we only use six of the buttons on a remote, then why are all those other buttons there?"* In talking about the interface problems for these devices (most of which were not age-related but simply bad design and classic usability), they complained *"the instruction books are so boring, and go on for hundreds of pages, so why can't they tell you something simple...it must be there"*. They also talked about how they shared digital information and their use of Dropbox and shared calendars. One participant mentioned a desire for a coordinated car booking system with her husband, but wanted the input to be intuitive, *"it should be quite simple... something like... typing in "I need the car.""*

Lost through advances Throughout the conversations, the participants commented on technological change and how things were different for children these days. They noted how children were likely to spend more time chatting online rather than developing skills in conversation, talking face to face. They suggested children needed to learn in more interactive ways rather than persevering with less engaging ways, like they used to. While children nowadays had a huge variety of toys available to them, for example, *"dolls of every nationality"*, the downside of so much choice was that perhaps they didn't get to exercise their imaginations enough. One also exclaimed that the shift from analogue to digital technology meant that children had far less experience of tinkering with analogue technology and so were less likely to understand the science or mechanics of it, instead memorizing sequences of commands.

The participants also lamented on what has been lost as a result of technological advances in their lifetime, such as letter writing, paper diaries, and history. But they also recognized the great power of technology, and in many of their ideas and designs were seeking to reconcile new technology with old ways of doing things by suggesting that kits like MaKey MaKey could get children to use their imaginations more, spend more time together creating things rather than being online, and to transform activities such as exercise and reading to be more fun through making them more interactive.

DISCUSSION

Our study has shown how all the retirees very much enjoyed using the MaKey MaKey toolkit. An unexpected finding was how much they were prepared to collaborate their efforts in a combination of playful, very serious and humorous ways to master the shared task of playing different notes of a tune together. Moreover, following their accomplishment they were far less inhibited and the conversation flowed in terms of other possibilities and design ideas for a diversity of uses. As well as generating ideas, it provided them with a platform from which to reflect about the future of technology, especially for children. In particular, they were able to use their experiences to project about how such technology might be designed to change children's use of technology to be more creative, imaginative and mindful. Although there may have been a perception that they were not inventors, the design conversations that took place were as rich as one might expect from any age group and their strategies of drawing on local context, devices and needs were also typical design strategies as found by [3].

The participants expressed that they felt the kit was targeted more for others and not themselves; that they were more users than designers of technology, accepting technological change but not creating it. They were all willing to have a go with the kit and enjoyed doing so in the company of friends, but they saw it more as an opportunity for an activity, perhaps one to share with the grandchildren, than a pathway to invention. In discussions they saw more immediate application than far-reaching applications, and they drew upon their immediate surroundings and recent physical experiences and felt needs within society for inspiration, in particular the needs of other generations, their grandchildren and parents.

Irrespective of their own perceptions, everyone was willing to play with the kit, enjoyed it when they did and came up with interesting design ideas. This leads us then to consider the qualities of kits and activities that can enable everyone to take part. As Perner-Wilson et al. [21] point out, *"re-creating a design is a good place to start"*. The activity of creating and playing a tune with musical fruit, as seen in MaKey MaKey videos, proved to be a good way to engage the participants and make them feel comfortable and confident to engage in exploratory conversations. Perner-Wilson et al. [21] also point out that functional transparency or legibility of designs is important, so that it is clear how things work and how to reproduce them. The retirees in our study were able to see how to use the MaKey MaKey through a simple demonstration and through doing themselves. The kit was easy to use apart from the fiddliness of the alligator clips, and it was legible – the participants could figure out how to use it with minimal instruction.

MaKey MaKey is largely a toolkit for thinking about new forms of input to map onto existing forms of digital apps, such as music making, photo taking and so on. What would it take to create equivalent forms of new output (physical or digital) that could enable people to be even more creative and fire up their imagination? What qualities of new kits might support greater invention? While the next step-up electronic toolkits have a wider range of building blocks, actuators and sensors, they require a level of programming in order to be configured to create interesting devices with complex behaviors. More complex kits invariably suffer from limitations in the kinds of components and configuration and connection possibilities, or from the barriers to entry created by the need to learn how to use and program them. A challenge for HCI, therefore, is how to fold more computational power into a toolkit so that it provides more inventing power that does not require them to learn program as a separate skill.

Buechley and Perner-Wilson [6] have suggested the kit-of-no-parts approach to building electronics from a diverse palette of craft materials, is more personal, understandable and accessible than the construction of technology from a kit of predetermined components. Their Lilypad Arduino kit [5] enables electronics to be easily embedded into fabrics and craft materials to give them new behaviors and capabilities, allowing people to "make it personal" and exercise their creativity. Perner-Wilson et al. [21] found that craft workshops were most effective because they used existing skills from a diverse group so that each person's skill was a valuable resource for others. One participant might be an expert at sewing whereas another is good with electronics. In their workshops, participants indicated that they all felt a measure of confidence in some kind of skill.

Retired people have a diverse range of skills gained through life's experience. As we age, rather than becoming a homogeneous category to be designed for, we grow more diverse rather than less, by virtue of our different life experiences in different bodies (see also [4]). Toolkits, such as MaKey MaKey, can enable retired people to combine kit skills with their existing skills, expanding their design repertoires and their capability to design. The challenge for toolkit inventors is to find ways to tap into the huge diversity of skillsets of retired people.

CONCLUSIONS

People learn by doing and creating and so enabling people to do through accessible and empowering kits is a key means to engaging retired people in designing their own futures. It is important then that future kits not only support contained "activities" but rather that they come to mind to be adopted and adapted in support of meeting everyday needs. As Suchman [25] argues, a large part of design occurs in use, as people adapt systems in artful integration practices in order to meet their everyday needs. Supporting artful integration in everyday use by augmenting existing technologies should be an objective for effective kits. Kits could make it easier to generate expressive creative output as well as input. There is scope to create many more kits that allow exploration of new forms of sensors, buttons, actuators, wireless communications and new ways to program. But, perhaps most importantly, as evidenced by our study, is that future toolkits need to have the social affordance of being easy and fun enough to play with, use and demonstrate so that they, or knowledge about them will be passed around and shared, enthusing, enabling and empowering others to do, learn and create. Finally, while we look different on the outside as we age, we are the same on the inside. As our participants showed in the workshops so much stays the same; the toolkits allowed them to have fun, rib each other, and not worry about what others think of them. Such wisdom and playfulness should be nurtured and valued when inventing the future of technology.

ACKNOWLEDGEMENTS

The research was partially funded by an EPSRC dream fellowship awarded to Yvonne Rogers and an Australian ARC Discovery project, number 11010199.

NOTE

Gary Marsden died suddenly and unexpectedly while we were revising the paper.

REFERENCES

1. Bratteteig, T. and Wagner I. Spaces for participatory creativity. *CoDesign 8*, 2-3, (2012), 105-126.
2. Braun, V. and Clarke, V. Using thematic analysis in psychology. *Qualitative Research in Psychology* 3, 2 (2006), 77–101.
3. Brereton, M. and McGarry. B. An observational study of how objects support engineering design thinking and communication: implications for the design of tangible media. In *Proc. CHI 2000*, ACM Press (2000), 217-224.
4. Brereton, M. Habituated objects: everyday tangibles that foster the independent living of an elderly woman. *interactions 20*, 4 (2013), 20-24.
5. Buechley, L., Eisenberg, M., Catchen, J. and Crockett, A. The LilyPad Arduino: using computational textiles to investigate engagement, aesthetics, and diversity in computer science education. In *Proc. CHI 2008,* ACM Press (2008), 423-432.
6. Buechley, L. and Perner-Wilson, H. Crafting technology: reimagining the processes, materials, and cultures of electronics. *ACM TOCHI, 19*, 3 (2012), Article 21.
7. Coleman, R. and Myerson, J. Improving life quality by countering design exclusion. *Gerontechnology, 1*, 2 (2001), 88-102.
8. Davidson, J.L. and Jensen, C. Participatory Design with Older Adults: An Analysis of Creativity in the Design of Mobile Healthcare Applications. In *Proc. Creativity and Cognition* (2013), 114.
9. Gaver, W., Dunne, T. and Pacenti, E. Cultural probes. *interactions, 6*, 1 (1999), 21-29.
10. Greenhalgh T., Procter R., Rouncefield M., Dewsbury G. and Wherton, J. ATHENE: assistive technologies for healthy living in elders. In *Proc. of 2nd Digital Economy All Hands Meeting,* (2011).
11. Hodges, S., Scott, J., Sentance, S., Miller, C., Villar, N., Schwiderski-Grosche, S., Hammil, K. and Johnston, S. .NETGadgeteer: A New Platform for K-12 Computer Science Education. In *Proc. SIGCSE '13,* ACM Press (2013), 391-396.
12. Lim, C.S.C., Frohlich, D. M. and Ahmed, A. The challenge of designing for diversity in older users. *Gerontechnology 11,* 2 (2012), 297.
13. Lindsay, S., Brittain, K., Jackson, D., Ladha, C., Ladha, K. and Olivier, P. Empathy, Participatory Design and People with Dementia. In *Proc. CHI 2012,* ACM Press (2012), 521-530.
14. Lindsay, S., Jackson, D., Schofield, G. and Olivier, P. Engaging older people using participatory design. In *Proc. CHI 2012*, ACM Press (2012), 1199-1208.
15. MaKey MaKey toolkit. http://www.makeymakey.com/
16. Malmborg, L., Binder, T. and Brandt, E. Elderly's everyday practices as a design approach. *Workshop at NordiCHI* (2012), Copenhagen, Denmark.
17. Massimi, M., Baecker, R. and Wu, M. Using Participatory Activities with Seniors to Critique, Build, and Evaluate Mobile Phones. In *Proc. ASSETS 2007* (2007), 155-162.
18. Newell, A.F., Morgan, M.E., Gibson, L. and Forbes, P. Experiences with professional theatre for awareness raising. *Interacting with Computers 23* (2011), 594–603.
19. Olivier, P., Xu, G., Monk, A. and Hoey, J. Ambient kitchen: designing situated services using a high fidelity prototyping environment. In *Proc. PETRA 2009,* ACM Press (2009), Article 47.
20. Pantidi, N., Rogers, Y. and Robinson, H. Is the Writing on the Wall for Tabletops? In *Proc. Interact 2009*, Springer (2009), 125-137.
21. Perner-Wilson, H., Buechley, L. and Satomi, M. Handcrafting textile interfaces from a kit-of-no-parts. In *Proc. TEI 2011*, ACM Press (2011).
22. Resnick, M. Behavior construction kits. *Comm of ACM 36*, 7 (1993), 64-71.
23. Richards, M., Petre, M. and Bandara, A. Starting with Ubicomp: using the SenseBoard to introduce computing. In *Proc. SIGCSE 2012,* ACM Press (2012), 583-588.
24. Rogers, Y. and Marsden, G. Does he take sugar?: moving beyond the rhetoric of compassion. *interactions 20,* 4 (2013), 48-57.
25. Suchman, L. A. Practice-based design of information systems: Notes from the hyper-developed world. *The information society* 18, 2 (2002), 139-144.
26. Taylor, P. Growing Old in America: Expectations vs. Reality. *Pew Research Social & Demographic Trends Report.* (2009).
27. Vines, J., Blythe, M., Lindsay, S., Dunphy, P., Monk, A. and Olivier, P. Questionable Concepts: Critique as a resource for designing with eighty somethings. In *Proc. CHI 2012*, ACM Press (2012), 1169-1178.
28. Wallace, J., McCarthy, J., Wright, P.C. and Olivier, P. Making design probes work. In *Proc. CHI 2013,* ACM Press (2013), 3441-3450.
29. Waycott, J., Vetere, F., Pedell, S., Kulik, L., Ozanne, E., Gruner, A. and Downs, J. Older Adults as Digital Content Producers. In *Proc. CHI 2013,* ACM Press (2013), 39-48.
30. Zickuhr, K and Madden, M. Older adults and internet use. *Pew Report.* pewinternet.org/Reports/2012/Older-adults-and-internet-use.aspx (2012).

What's on Your Mind?: Investigating Recommendations for Inclusive Social Networking and Older Adults

Chris Norval[1], John Arnott[1]
[1]School of Computing
University of Dundee
Dundee, Scotland, UK, DD1 4HN
{chrisnorval, jarnott}@computing.dundee.ac.uk

Vicki L. Hanson[2,1]
[2]GCCIS
Rochester Institute of Technology
Rochester, New York, USA
vlh@acm.org

ABSTRACT
Social networking sites (SNSs) are becoming increasingly popular as a method for social interaction. While research has reported benefits associated with components of SNS usage, a digital divide has emerged between younger and older users. SNSs can be useful for communicating with family members and helping one feel digitally included; however, there are a wide range of reasons why many older adults choose not to use this kind of technology. We present a series of user studies investigating the barriers and challenges that SNSs can present to older users. These user studies led to the derivation of user recommendations to mitigate these barriers. The recommendations were then evaluated within a comparative evaluation which involved 25 older adults completing tasks on two interface versions of a simulation SNS. We present the recommendations and the methods of their creation and evaluation. Implications for developers of SNSs are discussed.

Author Keywords
Social networking sites; older adults; recommendations; inclusive design; comparative evaluation

ACM Classification Keywords
H.5.3. [User Interfaces]: User-centered design; Prototyping; Screen design (e.g., text, graphics, color)

General Terms
Human Factors

INTRODUCTION
Social Networking Sites (SNSs) have grown in popularity in recent years. Facebook, for example, currently has over 1.1 billion monthly active users[1]. Both in the UK and US it was reported that between 64% and 72% of online adults use SNSs [3, 18].

[1]https://newsroom.fb.com/Key-Facts

CHI'14, April 26–May 1, 2014, Toronto, Canada.
ACM 978-1-4503-2473-1/14/04.
http://dx.doi.org/10.1145/2556288.2556992

Researchers from different fields have investigated reasons and implications for this rise in popularity. Such research has suggested that intensity of Facebook usage is positively associated with life satisfaction and social trust [21], and the use of some Facebook components are associated with increased social capital [5, 21] and reduced loneliness [5].

Additionally, researchers have found that SNSs can be a beneficial online platform for older adults as a communication platform with family members [1, 8, 9, 14, 17, 20]. Using social media, where, for example, children or grandchildren live far away, is suggested to help older adults who feel disassociated with family events [8].

Despite these positive associations and benefits of use, younger adults are considerably more likely than older adults to be using them. Ofcom found that 92% of 16-24 year old respondents have set up an SNS profile, compared with 25% of respondents over 65 [18]. Similarly, Pew Research Center's report observes that 89% of the respondents aged 18-29 use SNSs, compared with 43% of over 65s [3].

A lack of interest and purpose have been suggested as leading reasons for the low uptake amongst the older population [7, 9, 13, 16, 20]. This signifies a digital divide and a problem for older adults if SNSs are used more widely for communication and diffusion of information. We believe that by considering the needs and opinions of older adults, a more acceptable and useful platform for online communication can be provided.

This research aims to explore measures to make SNSs more inclusive by creating user-centred recommendations for developers of such sites. These recommendations attempt to avoid common barriers which can prevent older adults from choosing to use SNSs. These suggested improvements aim to support older adults who would potentially be interested in using a SNS, but don't for a variety of reasons, rather than those that find SNSs uninteresting or without purpose. While the recommendations do not contain a solution to every problem, we believe that they are a positive step in identifying potential solutions to key barriers.

Additionally, despite sharing similar concerns, such as privacy, many younger adults continue to use SNSs in order to enjoy social inclusion [10]. While many of the concerns may not be unique to older adults, we support that developing for 'extra ordinary' users helps improve the service for people of all ages [19].

This paper describes the process of creating and validating the recommendations, outlines an exploratory comparative evaluation to explore their impact and provides context into modifications that aided participants in completing tasks through observational notes and empirical results. We lastly open a discussion around design considerations, and how developers can improve SNSs for a wider range of people.

RELATED WORK

Exploring the Lack of Participation

From the literature, several barriers and reasons for not using SNSs are raised from participant discussions. For many of the studies, older adults could not see the purpose, or benefit, of using SNSs [7,9,13,16,20]. Participants were content with their existing methods of communication, such as telephone, SMS and email [13]. Lehtinen et al. argue that showing clear benefits and purposes of using a SNS is vital if we are to introduce older adults to this technology.

Lehtinen et al. observed that current SNSs *"do not seem to fit the everyday communication of older adults well"* [13]. This was supported by arguments that older adults find intentional self-presentation as not socially acceptable, and online communication as "cold". SNSs were perceived as "places for dating or celebrities, not for themselves". This was additionally observed by Gibson et al., with older adults commenting on negative feelings of being "on display" [9].

Preconceptions can be a barrier, such as if one was to encounter negative media stories involving SNSs [9, 24]. This can lead to older adults being put off from joining such a site. Mikkola and Halonen found that while Facebook was used very little by participants, they all knew what it was, viewing the site as "useless time consuming" [16]. At times, negative media coverage has led to misconceptions and concerns about the behaviour of SNSs [9,24].

Privacy has been shown to be a major barrier in the literature, being described as a "major concern" and "very important" [7, 9–11, 13, 14, 16, 17, 20, 23, 24]. A degree of distrust was observed by Mikkola and Halonen, reporting that some older adults were afraid of joining Facebook [16]. The group discussions held by Xie et al. had a strong emphasis on privacy, being described as the "primary concern" and "key perceptual barrier to adoption" [24].

While SNSs designed specifically for older adults do exist, they have generally not had a large uptake [6]. This may in part be due to a lack of family members on these sites, a lack of critical mass, people not knowing that they exist or little being done to address the actual barriers faced by older adults.

A number of other barriers exist, such as a fear of committing social blunders, a lack of confidence, a lack of skill, concerns over security and abusive other users [7, 13, 20, 24]. Much of the literature overlaps, with several emerging themes. These themes, such as a lack of purpose, incompatibilities, preconceptions of SNSs and privacy, are all suggested as important reasons as to why participation with older adults on SNSs is so low. We hold that exploring and understanding these themes is the first step to providing an improved online environment and opportunity for older adults to explore SNSs.

Older Adults, SNSs, Requirements and Usability

A variety of evaluations and usability studies have been undertaken with a variety of different types of systems. Chou et al. conducted 'think-aloud' interviews with 5 adults over 55 years old in Taiwan while they used Facebook [7]. Inconveniences were categorised before being turned into user requirements, which were then combined with general web guidelines [12] generated from existing research. Chou et al. go on to argue that Facebook can be improved for older adults through the use of these requirements [7].

Karahasanović et al. report a list of needs and requirements at both an individual and group level for elderly people and sites with user generated content (such as SNSs) [11]. Requirements such as ease of use, a need for control and a concern about the skills required to stay up to date were all found to be important to participants.

Gibson et al. discuss how participants used Ning[2], an open source social platform, to create their own closed-off social network [9]. This custom SNS had the underlying purpose of providing information on upcoming events and classes. Gibson et al. suggest that a clear purpose and a community focus, rather than on any individual, may be one of the key reasons for the site's uptake. The SNS was additionally not publicly available to anyone outside the group, with users expressing greater feelings of security. A secure and focused SNS may be seen as more acceptable for this age group, conditional on careful behaviour and design considerations.

Many of the suggestions from the literature focus on technical requirements which do little to address issues relating to how the site behaves. Little attention has also been given to investigating the impact of these requirements in a controlled evaluation. There is a need for research which addresses both of these aspects. By evaluating our recommendations using a comparative evaluation, we can begin to understand how much of an impact these changes can make, and promote them to developers and researchers.

CREATION OF RECOMMENDATIONS

Focus Groups

To generate the recommendations, two focus groups were held with separate groups of Internet users over 60 years old. Participants were recruited from the SiDE user pool [22], a collection of over 800 volunteers, mostly over 65, who have been recruited through local organisations, groups or clubs for accessibility research. Both focus groups were audio recorded and transcribed so that qualitative analysis could take place. Participants were given a £10 gift voucher.

The first focus group involved 8 people (4 male, 4 female; aged 61-80, M = 67.9, SD = 5.8), two of whom were SNS users, two were previously SNS users and four were non-users. A mixture of backgrounds was sought to explore a range of opinions from different experiences. The

[2] http://www.ning.com/

non-users had mostly high-level concerns (such as privacy, security) whereas the users had specific examples of barriers that they had experienced and overcame (e.g. difficulties accessing privacy settings, frequent unsolicited emails). These examples were generally more specific and informed. The experiences of those who had previously overcome barriers in their early stages of use were recognised as valuable for identifying potential problems for new users.

This led to SNS users being specifically recruited for the second focus group. 7 people were recruited (5 female, 2 male; aged 63-78, M = 68.7, SD = 5.2). Due to a misunderstanding during the selection process, one participant was not a SNS user. Many of the participants who used SNSs did so for communication with family and friends, describing it as beneficial for themselves.

Participants of both focus groups were asked to discuss positive and negative opinions of SNSs alongside improvements that could be made. Conversations were steered through a number of topics by the lead researcher, such as how the participants used SNSs, why they started using them, why they chose not to use them and how those sites could be made more suitable.

Qualitative Analysis

To analyse the focus group transcripts, thematic analysis [2] was used to categorise and find themes relating to both positive and negative aspects of SNS usage from quotes in the transcripts. For example, one participant commented that *"You've got to keep the information really simple and with simple terminology"*. Quotes were then coded with one or more themes, such as "Terminology".

A further stage of thematic analysis was conducted with two key qualitative papers in the literature [9, 13], chosen due to their relevance in the field. This aimed to investigate theoretical saturation and congruity. Text from the literature, e.g. 'they were anxious to retain their privacy' [9], was coded in the same way as text from the transcripts. Findings in the literature were coded as new themes, unless a new theme overlapped with one from the transcripts, whereupon the existing theme was used.

Including these two papers in the later stages of thematic analysis enabled us to verify the consistency of our themes with other research. A high amount of overlap appeared between our themes and those from the two papers. This suggests that many of our themes generalise to beyond the small sample sizes of the focus groups. Themes such as a lack of purpose, privacy concerns and negative media stories were present in both the literature and the transcripts.

Some themes were unique to the focus groups, such as frequent and unsolicited emails to the user, difficulties experienced when trying to deactivate an account, constantly changing interfaces, confusion over financial cost and feelings of invasion regarding friend suggestions. Other themes were unique to the literature, such as a fear of social blunders and a desire for partial anonymity, mass distribution of messages and off-the-record (temporary) messages.

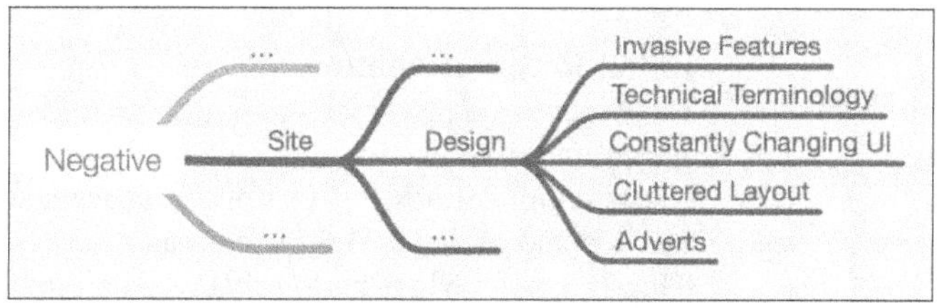

Figure 1. A subset of the themes. The sub-themes are all relating to people raising concerns over the design of specific sites.

While thematic analysis usually encourages refinement toward a small collection of abstract themes, maintaining the granularity and specificity of our themes was necessary to preserve the wide range of issues. Our solution was to categorise similar themes into sub-themes throughout the coding process, refining the analysis while maintaining granularity. This generated a large mind map structure, with abstract themes near the center and more specific themes near the outside. Figure 1 shows a subset of the themes.

Identifying the Recommendations

Traversing from higher to the lower levels of the mind map provided context into each granular theme (e.g. 'Negative' > 'Don't like SNSs' > 'Worried' > 'Privacy' > 'Lack of Transparency'). Recommendations for developers were then derived from this process by a researcher. From the above example, a recommendation was identified to 'Clarify and simplify privacy and account settings', as this would likely help users who were worried about the lack of transparency regarding privacy settings. Additional context was gained by consulting the quotes which were coded under the sub-theme in question. This aimed to avoid misinterpretations during the process of deriving the recommendations.

The sub-themes on the right of Figure 1 are all categorised as issues with the design of specific SNSs. Some recommendations that were derived from this subset include *using a simple layout* and *avoiding technical terminology*, *adverts* and *frequent changes to the interface*. 'Invasive Features' is an example of where quotes were utilised. Participants described friend suggestions and unsolicited emails as invasive. This led to a recommendation to avoid such invasive functionality.

Themes were treated equally when identifying the recommendations, regardless of originating from the transcripts or the literature. Each recommendation involved suggesting a way to either eliminate a concern or support a positive feature. In cases of themes relating to a positive feature, the recommendation suggested supporting that feature. In cases of themes relating to a concern, the recommendation attempted to identify the root cause of the problem and suggest a method to bypass this concern. If a possible solution could be identified by the researcher then it was included as a recommendation. Some themes, however, could not be addressed by a recommendation, e.g. 'Negative' > 'Not Interested' > 'I am happy without it'. In this case, 'I am happy without it' is at the lowest level of granularity. Neither the parent themes or coded quotes identify a way to 'solve' this reason for not using a SNS.

		Initial Recommendations	CUI	MUI
Design & Behaviour	1.1	Have increased privacy by default.	X	√
	1.2	Avoid invasive functionality and emails (e.g. friend suggestions).	⋈	⋈
	1.3	Clarify implications of functions to prevent social blunders.	†	√
	1.4	Reduce and moderate fake accounts.	⋈	⋈
	1.5	Clearly label navigation to privacy, email and account settings.	X	√
	1.6	Avoid targeting specific age groups (e.g. over 65).	√	√
	1.7	Avoid pressurising techniques, reminders or features to encourage contributions.	X	√
	1.8	Avoid games, apps and irrelevant functionality.	X	√
	1.9	Avoid similar designs to sites where people hold negative assumptions. *	X	Sub
User Control	2.1	Provide control to delete content.	†	√
	2.2	Provide control to delete account if desired.	†	√
	2.3	Clarify and simplify privacy and settings.	†	√
	2.4	Allow control over what emails (if any) the user wishes to receive.	†	√
	2.5	Allow partial anonymity if desired.	X	X
	2.6	Allow simple removal of contacts.	√	√
	2.7	Allow categorization of contacts.	X	X
	2.8	Give users control of which contacts see what content.	X	X
	2.9	Allow for mass distribution of messages. *	⋈	⋈
	2.10	Allow for session, or 'off-the-record' private messages. *	X	X
	2.11	Provide moderation/report functionality. *	†	√
	2.12	Focus on a specific purpose (e.g. club or group). *	X	X
Generalisable Beyond SNSs	3.1	Use a simple, but bold, layout on the site.	Sub	Sub
	3.2	Reduce or avoid advertisements.	X	√
	3.3	Clarify if the site has a financial cost or is free.	√	√
	3.4	Reassure users that suitable security measures are in place (e.g. SSL/https).	⋈	⋈
	3.5	Provide support to explain/help/guide users through tasks.	⋈	⋈
	3.6	Avoid unnecessary complexity when changing settings or completing tasks.	Sub	Sub
	3.7	Avoid drastic and frequent changes to the site.	⋈	⋈
	3.8	Avoid technical terminology.	√	√
	3.9	Avoid using 'small print' checkboxes for additional services/information sharing.	√	√
	3.10	Reduce or avoid emails to the user by default.	X	√
	3.11	Follow accessibility guidelines.	⋈	⋈

√ = Recommendation met X = Recommendation not met Sub = Subjective (debatable)
† = Recommendation somewhat met (e.g. difficult to find, unclear) ⋈ = Difficult to implement/represent for study

Table 1. The list of initial recommendations prior to the evaluation. Additionally shows which recommendations were met in each UI version. CUI = Control UI, MUI = Modified UI. Those marked with an * are discussed further in the Results section, which should be consulted before use.

The process resulted in the generation of 32 initial recommendations, shown in Table 1, to mitigate concerns or support positive features identified in the focus groups and literature. At this stage, the recommendations consist of potential solutions interpreted by the researcher from the analysis. The next step of the research is to evaluate the individual recommendations for participant agreement (validity), as well as the overall impact of the initial set of recommendations to investigate reliability.

EVALUATION

To explore the impact of the recommendations, we developed a system and recruited non-SNS users to partake in a comparative evaluation. Non-SNS users were chosen to explore the impact of the recommendations for people who had never used a SNS before, simulating new users. Additionally, SNS users would likely skew results toward the control interface in an evaluation due to familiarity.

This approach led to a few challenges. It is difficult to develop a control site which does not follow any of the recommendations as this would require a conscious effort on the part of the developer to discard good design practice (SNSs commonly adhere to some, but not all, of the recommendations presented in this paper). Our solution to this was to investigate the impact that the recommendations may have on an existing SNS. This raises further challenges due to our requirement of non-SNS users as participants. Ethical considerations (the lack of consent from contacts or friends, requiring participants to sign up to a service) and the difficulty of conducting a controlled study on such a diverse site also surfaced in early stages of planning the study.

The solution resulted in a combination of these options. An offline likeness to Facebook was developed, providing the main functionality (e.g. creating content, 'unfriending' contacts and changing settings) and controls of the system.

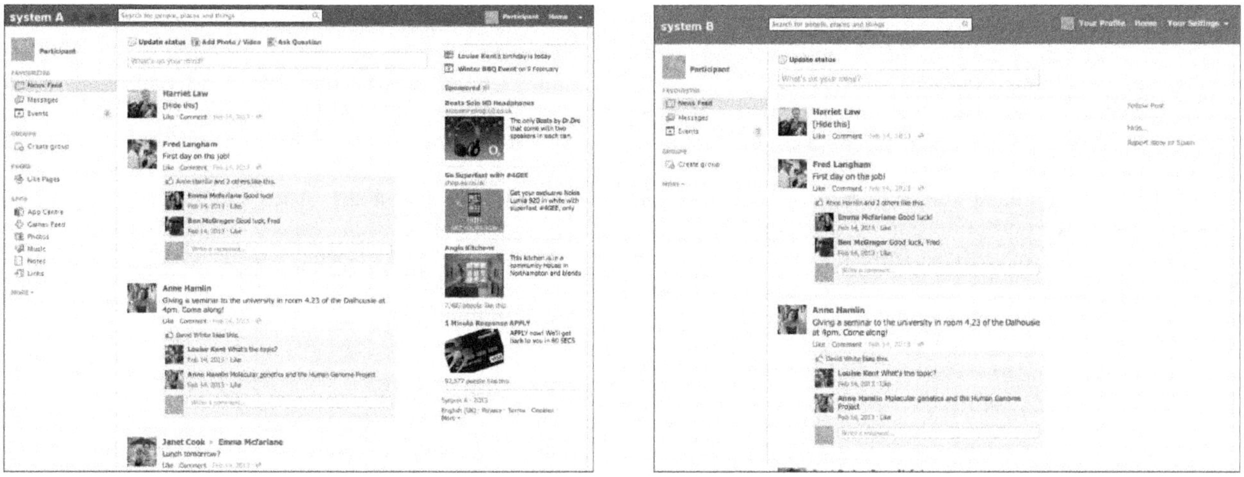

Figure 2. Homepages of the Control UI (left) and Modified UI (right).

A similar approach has previously been used to comparatively identify improvements to Facebook privacy controls [15]. Creating our own prototype allows alternative interfaces, and attempts to simulate the experiences faced by new users of the site while avoiding the above ethical issues. This method, however, comes with reduced real-world applicability, as participants communicate on the prototype with pre-generated users representing real-life contacts.

Prototype System

The system used for the study has two user interface (UI) versions, the 'Control UI', which was strongly influenced by Facebook (as of December, 2012), and the 'Modified UI', which adapts the Control UI to follow recommendations as indicated in Table 2. These two interfaces are presented to the participants as 'System A' and 'System B' respectively.

The implementation of the Modified UI relied on identifying alterations to the UI that aligned with the recommendations. Since many of the recommendations are subjective in nature, subjectivity was needed in order to implement these into the prototype. While some followed a logical progression, e.g. recommendation 3.2 led to the removal of adverts, some were the interpretation of the researcher. An example may be how the navigation buttons to settings were labelled, or the simplification of the interface. The goal of this study was to explore how one might utilise the recommendations and the subsequent impact that these changes would have.

Not all recommendations are listed in Table 2. There are three reasons for this. Firstly, 5 recommendations (1.6, 2.6, 3.3, 3.8 and 3.9) were included in both UI versions (and therefore not listed as changes) due to being met by Facebook (and subsequently the Control UI). For example, non-technical terminology is used on both the Control UI and the Modified UI. Facebook also does not specifically target age groups in the same way that, for example, some SNSs do for adults over 65.

Secondly, 7 recommendations (1.2, 1.4, 2.9, 3.4, 3.5, 3.7 and 3.11) were outlined in Table 1 as difficult to represent in the study. As an example, the true implications of simulating frequent changes to the UI were not practical in an hour-long session. Another recommendation suggested the use of a support section of the site. This was avoided to prevent tasks from being overly easy to complete, potentially detracting from other findings of the study.

Thirdly, since the system is a simplified representation, some of the more sophisticated features of Facebook were not

Change	Rec.(s)
Removal of advertisements and reminder bar	1.7, 3.2
'Pages' and 'Apps' moved to under 'More' on left navigation bar	1.8, 3.1
Changed the colour of the header	1.9
Header size increased	1.5, 3.1
Font of content slightly increased in size	3.1
Drop-down box for settings pages labelled with 'Your Settings'	1.5
Add text to clarify who will be able to see a new status update	1.3
Location and tagging removed when creating a status update	1.8
Default frequency of email notifications set to least frequent option	3.10
Default privacy setting set to 'Friends'	1.1
Buttons to change privacy settings moved to the top of the privacy settings page	2.3, 3.6
'Quick Settings' tab added to settings page which contains suggested settings	2.2, 2.3, 2.4, 3.6
Removal of 'Subscribers', 'Apps', 'Mobile', 'Payments', 'Advertisements' and 'Gifts' tabs from the settings page	1.8, 2.3, 3.1
Hovering the cursor over content makes the report and delete/hide box appear directly	2.1, 3.6, 2.11

Table 2. Table showing the changes made to the Modified UI and the relevant recommendation(s). Codes can be looked up in Table 1.

implemented. Functionality such as the 'Chat' feature, uploading photographs and the 'list' controls were often simulated (i.e. an inactive link) or omitted. In such cases, neither UI version had the functionality to meet this criterion. Additionally, since some of the recommendations would drastically modify the focus or functionality of the prototype, such as by changing the purpose of the site and integrating anonymity and temporary private messages, the decision was taken to omit these from the prototype. This related to the aim of the study, an example of how developers can utilise the recommendations that are relevant to the design and purpose of their SNS. Hence, the prototype utilised the recommendations which maintained the main functionality and purpose of the Control UI.

Due to these reasons, the evaluation of the prototype is, in essence, a case study into the impact of the recommendations on a theoretical site. This site shares many of the same functionality and design aspects as Facebook, as is the case with many other SNSs. The study should therefore not be viewed as an evaluation of Facebook itself.

METHOD

30 participants, who were all non-SNS users but Internet users with no severe cognitive impairments, were recruited from the SiDE user pool [22] to partake in the study. None were participants of either focus group. Of the 30 participants, one did not attend, three did not wish to complete the comparative evaluation part of the study and one wasn't able to due to having a visual impairment. While having no visual impairment was a prerequisite for this study, this was not discovered for this participant during the recruitment process. Subsequently, they could not complete the comparative evaluation part of the study. The four participants who did not, or could not, complete the comparative evaluation wished to complete the questionnaire to evaluate the recommendations. This resulted in 25 (aged 64-86, $M = 71.2$, $SD = 5.07$) participants for the comparative evaluation and 29 (aged 64-89, $M = 72.3$, $SD = 6.30$) for the questionnaire. Participants were given a £10 gift voucher.

The study was conducted in a private testing lab with two separate computers. Each computer had its own monitor, mouse and keyboard which were positioned perpendicular to each other. The participant could not see both screens at the same time, while the researcher could view both screens without moving and potentially distracting the participant.

For each participant, the computer running each version of the UI remained the same for the duration of the session. Participants could therefore associate each UI with a physical computer to make it easier to differentiate between 'System A' and 'System B' when later answering questions relating to that UI version. Each computer had an identical, but separate, prototype database which was reinitialised and repopulated using a 'Seed' file for every participant. This ensured that there were 16 (simulated) users and pre-generated content on each system, which remained consistent for every participant, regardless of deletions or modifications of content during prior sessions.

For the comparative evaluation, participants were asked to attempt 11 tasks on both UI versions, described in Table 4. These represented tasks that were identified in the earlier focus groups as important for the participants to be able to do. Participants attempted each task on one of the two UI versions before moving on to the second UI. The order of which UI version the task started with alternated for each participant and each task to counterbalance the study and mitigate practice effects. For the second part of the study, a questionnaire was completed measuring agreement with each individual recommendation.

Data Collection

After each task was attempted on both systems, participants answered a Likert question on paper asking which system (UI version) they preferred completing the task on. This 5 point Likert question ranged from "System A greatly" (Control UI) to "System B greatly" (Modified UI) with a neutral point of "No Opinion". This resulted in eleven of these answers for each participant (one for each task) for the study. After all tasks were attempted, participants completed two System Usability Scale (SUS) questionnaires [4], which each provided a 0-100 score relating to the usability of the corresponding UI version. In addition to this, we noted whether a participant successfully completed each task, allowing completion rates to be investigated. Observational notes were taken when problems were encountered.

The second part of the study consisted of a series of Likert questions aimed at measuring agreement (validity) with 31 of the 32 recommendations. One recommendation (3.11) which promotes the use of accessibility guidelines was not included in the questionnaire due to a strong existing body of support for accessible design, as seen in the WAI-AGE guidelines[3]. Recommendations with a median response that demonstrates agreement are considered verified and accepted. Those with a median response that demonstrates disagreement or no opinion with the recommendation are subsequently rejected.

To balance the questionnaire, an equal number of "Agree" and "Disagree" answers were expected to show full support for all recommendations by the participants. In order to achieve this balance, we used a method of polarising, where a positively worded question becomes a negatively worded question (e.g. should/shouldn't), to ensure that an even mix of each is asked. Using this balancing method, however, means that for some questions it is not possible to assume that the recommendation has been supported, rather, it demonstrates that the polarised opposite of the recommendation is disagreed with. This is countered by creating two questionnaires. Each question is the polarised opposite (positive/negative) on the opposing questionnaire, resulting in the average of both standard and reversed questions being used to evaluate agreement for each recommendation. This allows us to avoid patterns which can be detected by participants and bias results.

[3] http://www.w3.org/WAI/older-users/

	Question	Control UI Median & (Q1 - Q3)	Modified UI Median & (Q1 - Q3)	Wilcoxon		
1.	I think that I would like to use this system frequently	Disagree (1 - 2)	Agree (1 - 3)	$Z = -2.592$,	$p = .010$*,	$r = -.367$
2.	I found the system unnecessarily complex	No Opinion (1 - 3)	Disagree (1 - 2.5)	$Z = -2.496$,	$p = .013$*,	$r = -.353$
3.	I thought the system was easy to use	Disagree (1 - 3)	Agree (1 - 3)	$Z = -2.464$,	$p = .014$*,	$r = -.348$
4.	I think that I would need the support of a technical person to be able to use this system	No Opinion (1 - 3)	No Opinion (1 - 3)	$Z = -1.518$,	$p = .129$,	$r = -.215$
5.	I found the various functions in this system were well integrated	No Opinion (1 - 2)	No Opinion (2 - 3)	$Z = -2.191$,	$p = .028$*,	$r = -.310$
6.	I thought there was too much inconsistency in this system	No Opinion (1.5 - 2)	No Opinion (1 - 2)	$Z = -1.058$,	$p = .290$,	$r = -.150$
7.	I would imagine that most people would learn to use this system very quickly	Agree (1.5 - 3)	Agree (3 - 3)	$Z = -2.359$,	$p = .018$*,	$r = -.334$
8.	I found the system very cumbersome to use	No Opinion (1 - 3)	Disagree (1 - 2)	$Z = -2.251$,	$p = .024$*,	$r = -.318$
9.	I felt very confident using the system	Disagree (1 - 2)	No Opinion (1 - 3)	$Z = -2.636$,	$p = .008$**,	$r = -.373$
10.	I needed to learn a lot of things before I could get going with this system	Agree (1.5 - 3)	Agree (1 - 3)	$Z = -1.155$,	$p = .248$,	$r = -.163$

* $p < .05$; ** $p < .01$; *** $p < .001$

Table 3. Table showing the median responses, and first (Q1) and third (Q3) numerical quartiles, to the individual Likert questions in the System Usability Scale for each UI version. Results from a Wilcoxon signed-rank test between the two UI versions per question are included. For Q1 and Q3, 0 = 'Strongly Disagree', 1 = 'Disagree', 2 = 'No Opinion', 3 = 'Agree', 4 = 'Strongly Agree'.

RESULTS

System Usability Scale Scores

This study generates two SUS scores [4] (one for each UI version) per participant. Using a Wilcoxon signed-rank test, we can show that there was a significant difference in the SUS scores for the Control UI (*Mdn* = 40) and the Modified UI (*Mdn* = 55); $Z = -3.056$, $p = .002$, $r = -.432$.

We can additionally look at the individual answers to gain insights into the different components of the questionnaire. Table 3 shows the median response to each question per UI version, as well as a Wilcoxon signed-rank test comparing the two UI versions for each question. Seven of the ten tests confirm a significant difference between the responses. Of those seven questions, five have a different median response for each system (questions 1, 2, 3, 8 and 9). The remaining two questions are significantly different on each UI version while having the same median response option (questions 5 and 7).

The individual Likert questions of the two SUS scales also allow for more specific comparisons into the different components of the SUS's usability model over just the score alone. For example, participants mostly agreed that they would like to use the Modified UI regularly, but disagreed with the same question regarding the Control UI. Similarly, participants generally agreed that the Modified UI was easy to use, but did not agree that the Control UI was.

UI Preference Per Task

While examining the participant responses to the Likert-based preference question for each task, we categorize answers into 3 categories: (1) Control UI is preferred ("greatly" or "slightly"), (2) Modified UI is preferred ("greatly" or "slightly") or (3) "No Opinion" is selected. We group the Likert points together to compare the three overall perspectives, while not limiting choice.

A Friedman test was used after the assumptions of a one-way repeated ANOVA were not met. The results of the Friedman test show that there was a statistically significant difference between the number of instances where participants preferred either the Control UI (*Mdn* = 1), the Modified UI (*Mdn* = 5) or "No Opinion" (*Mdn* = 4); $\chi^2(2, 25) = 24.344$, $p < .001$. Post-hoc analysis, using three Wilcoxon paired rank tests, was conducted with a Holm-Bonferroni correction applied. There were statistically significant differences between the Control UI and Modified UI categories, $Z = -4.053$, $p < .001$, $r = -.573$), between the Modified UI and "No Opinion" categories, $Z = -2.043$, $p = 0.041$, $r = -.289$, and between the Control UI and "No Opinion", $Z = -2.989$, $p = .003$, $r = -.423$).

The high frequency of "No Opinion" being selected may be partially explained by considering that not all methods of completing the tasks were significantly modified by the recommendations. This resulted in some tasks having the

	Task	CUI	MUI	Wilcoxon		
1	Leave a 'Post' on a contact's profile page.	22	20	$Z = -1.414$,	$p = .157$,	$r = -.200$
2	Change privacy settings.	16	24	$Z = -2.828$,	$p = .005$**,	$r = -.400$
3	Report a 'Status Update' from a contact.	5	11	$Z = -2.449$,	$p = .014$*,	$r = -.346$
4	Create a Status containing text.	24	23	$Z = -1.000$,	$p = .317$,	$r = -.141$
5	'Like' and comment on a contact's Status.	6	7	$Z = -1.000$,	$p = .317$,	$r = -.141$
6	Change how often the site emails the user.	8	22	$Z = -3.742$,	$p < .001$***,	$r = -.529$
7	Hide a Status from the 'News Feed'.	14	19	$Z = -1.890$,	$p = .059$,	$r = -.267$
8	Delete a Status created by the user.	22	24	$Z = -1.414$,	$p = .157$,	$r = -.200$
9	Delete a Post created by someone else on the user's profile.	20	22	$Z = -1.414$,	$p = .157$,	$r = -.200$
10	'Unfriend' a contact.	22	22	$Z = 0.0$,	$p > .999$,	$r = 0.0$
11	Deactivate the user's account.	7	8	$Z = -1.000$,	$p = .317$,	$r = -.141$

* $p < .05$; ** $p < .01$; *** $p < .001$

Table 4. A brief description of each task each participant attempted along with the number of participants who completed each task on the Control UI (CUI) and the Modified UI (MUI). Results from a Wilcoxon signed-rank test between the two UI versions are also included (N = 25).

same steps to completion on both versions of the interface. This does, however, raise interesting implications for the modifications which were only aesthetic (e.g. a reduction in advertisements). Such results suggest that these aesthetic alterations did not lead participants to prefer the Modified UI over the Control UI. Figure 3 shows the number of each Likert response selected on each task and which tasks had a high number of "No Opinion" responses.

Task Completion Rates

It is worth considering that neither interface is meant as a solution, only as a means for examining the guidelines. As a result, increasing task completion rates remain secondary to the main goals of the study. However, they are included for completeness and for further analysis of the findings.

Initially, we look at the number of tasks that each participant completes on each UI version. A significant Shapiro-Wilk test of normality confirmed that the assumptions of a paired t-test were not met. Thus, the Wilcoxon signed-rank test was used, which shows that a statistically significant difference

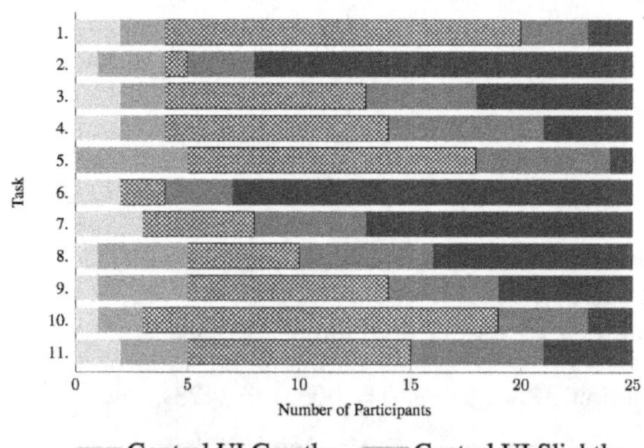

Figure 3. Bar chart showing UI preference responses for each task.

exists between the median number of tasks completed on the Control UI ($Mdn = 6$) and the Modified UI ($Mdn = 8$) across participants; $Z = -4.025$, $p < .001$, $r = -.569$.

This result gives us an idea of the number of successfully completed tasks on each UI version by participants, but we can also compare the number of successful task completions for the Control UI and the Modified UI on participants' first attempts at each task only, reducing the practice effect. Since half of the participants started each task on each version of the UI, the variables of the test cease to be paired.

A significant Shapiro-Wilk test of normality indicated that the data were not normally distributed, therefore a Mann-Whitney U test is used to show that there was a significant difference in the median number of tasks completed on the Control UI ($Mdn = 3$) and the Modified UI ($Mdn = 5$) on participants' first attempts at tasks; $U = 137.0$, $Z = -3.556$, $p < .001$, $r = -.503$.

Table 4 additionally shows how many participants completed each task on each UI version. Wilcoxon signed-rank tests are used to identify tasks where a significant difference occurred in the number of participants who were able to complete it. Three such tasks are statistically significant.

Accepted Recommendations

The data have been processed to take into account the two versions of the questionnaire and the reversed questions, providing a 0-4 value representing the degree of agreement participants had with, and subsequent validity of, each recommendation. Recommendations are classed as supported when the median response is 3 or above, which represents a median response of "Agree" or "Strongly Agree" on the Likert item. 27 recommendations are found to be supported, while 5 have been listed as "Rejected" due to a median response of "Strongly Disagree", "Disagree" or "No Opinion". The codes for these recommendations are listed on Table 5 and can be looked up on Table 1, where rejected recommendations are marked with an asterisk.

Accepted (SA)	Accepted (A)	Rejected
1.1 - 1.5 2.1 - 2.5 3.1 - 3.6	1.6 - 1.8 2.6 - 2.8 3.7 - 3.11	1.9 (NO) 2.9 - 2.11 (NO) 2.12 (D)

Table 5. Recommendations accepted and rejected by the evaluation. Codes can be looked up on Table 1. SA = 'Strongly Agree', A = 'Agree', NO = 'No Opinion', D = 'Disagree'. Those rejected should not be used.

DISCUSSION

This study investigated potential solutions to barriers faced by older adults when using SNSs and explored how these recommendations could be utilised by developers. This study should be viewed as a case study into the impact of the recommendations on a theoretical but representative SNS site. The study suggests that improvements can be made when taking the recommendations into consideration, at least in terms of perceived usability, task completion and user preference (for completing certain tasks).

The third subset of the recommendations (3.1 - 3.11) generalise beyond SNSs. A number have been identified as good design principles for older adults, such as in the WAI-AGE guidelines[4] or those by Kurniawan and Zaphiris [12]. While these recommendations may be generally applicable, they were identified as barriers to SNS usage, and are therefore included in Table 1.

Our contribution is firstly to identify these potential solutions as a collection and then to investigate the impact that they may have on a SNS. Other research in the literature corroborates some of our findings.

Considerations for Development

While the results suggest that the recommendations led to improvements in usability and task completion rates, such improvements depend on how these recommendations are applied to SNSs. Thus, an important aspect of what can be gained from this research is likely in the observations of how these improvements are made and the implications for the design of inclusive SNSs.

There were significant differences in the number of participants who completed a task for each UI version in 3 of the 11 tasks, as seen on Table 4. Two of these are related to changing settings. Observational notes from these tasks highlight that many participants who did not complete the task could not find out how to navigate to either the settings or the privacy page. Modifying the navigation panel in the top right to include text in addition to the white arrow of the drop down box led to participants discovering the privacy and settings pages. Using unambiguous text for buttons, rather than abstract icons or symbols (e.g. 'Your Settings' rather than a gear or arrow icon) can avoid this issue.

For task 2, participants who couldn't find the 'Settings' drop down box on the Control UI often then found a 'Privacy' link at the bottom of the page, which isn't always possible when sites utilise AJAX to generate new content when the bottom of the page is reached. While AJAX allows for a fluid experience, developers should be conscious of any text, link or information at the bottom of the page which will be difficult or unreachable because of this feature, and consider moving them to a static location on the page (e.g. a sidebar).

While task 3 (reporting content to an administrator) was statistically higher on the Modified UI, the completion rates for either UI were not encouraging. Our method of having the collapsed set of options appear when hovering over content did not go far enough to allow a majority of participants to complete the task. Observing the participants revealed that they simply did not know what to do, and it was not apparent that hovering the mouse over that content would uncover additional features, as was the case for both UI versions. Developers should therefore aim to reduce mouse-hover functionality for older adults, or leave clear indicators that functionality is there. An example may be an always-visible 'Delete' link within content, which expands into different options when the user hovers over the area.

Some tasks did not have a high completion rate on either system, such as reporting a status, deactivating the account and 'liking' and commenting on a contact's status update. For the latter, many participants had difficulty differentiating their profile from that of other people. Many created their own status as a reply, which wasn't linked to that of the original. Many participants also struggled due to the lack of a visible 'Submit' button when writing a comment and did not know that pressing the 'Enter' key on the keyboard was needed. Again, this assumption of prior knowledge made the task difficult for participants to complete.

The findings of this study suggest that careful design considerations can increase the usability and inclusivity of a SNS. Assumptions of prior knowledge, such as the meaning of icons, features which appear on mouse hover and enter-to-submit text boxes, should be removed or reconsidered. These assumptions are increasingly common on the Internet, and thus, these recommendations may generalise beyond SNSs. The Modified UI version was preferred more frequently than the Control UI. We believe that this demonstrates that common practices used on SNSs can be improved upon, leading to a more inclusive online environment. By investigating how we can improve these sites for older adults, we can provide an online environment where a wider range of people can feel comfortable communicating and sharing content with family and friends, with implications for social capital, loneliness and life satisfaction. Developers of such sites can consider and implement these recommendations as they feel appropriate.

Future Work

Future research which evaluates the recommendations on a wider range of sites, to varying degrees of application and with different age ranges of older adults will improve our understanding of the impact such measures can have. Due to the fast changing nature of SNSs, it is also likely that more barriers to SNS usage may present themselves in the future. Future iterations can expand these recommendations as SNSs evolve by using the methods outlined in this paper.

[4]http://www.w3.org/WAI/older-users/

CONCLUSION

While social networking sites (SNSs) have become increasingly popular, a digital divide has emerged between younger and older people regarding SNS use. For this study we identified barriers faced by older adults and defined novel solutions to these by exploring how recommendations could be developed for use in SNS design. We verified and evaluated these recommendations using a comparative evaluation with older participants, finding that an SNS version which utilised these recommendations received a higher usability score, had a higher task completion rating and was preferred more frequently than one that did not. Observational notes were used to outline key considerations for developers, and we have argued that utilising these recommendations can improve SNSs for a greater number of people. We have presented these findings and discussed the implications for developers of social networking sites.

ACKNOWLEDGMENTS

The authors wish to thank colleagues and reviewers for their feedback, and all participants of the study. They gratefully acknowledge support from RCUK Digital Economy Research Hub EP/G066019/1 "SiDE", a UK EPSRC doctoral training grant, and a Royal Society Wolfson Award to the third author.

REFERENCES

1. Blit-Cohen, E., and Litwin, H. Elder participation in cyberspace: A qualitative analysis of Israeli retirees. *J. of Aging Studies 18*, 4 (2004), 385 – 398.
2. Braun, V., and Clarke, V. Using thematic analysis in psychology. *Qualitative Research in Psychology 3*, 2 (2006), 77–101.
3. Brenner, J., and Smith, A. 72% of online adults are social networking site users. Tech. rep., Pew Internet & American Life Project, 2013.
4. Brooke, J. SUS: A quick and dirty usability scale. In *Usability evaluation in industry*. Taylor and Francis, London, 1996.
5. Burke, M., Marlow, C., and Lento, T. Social network activity and social well-being. In *Proc. CHI 2010*, ACM Press (2010), 1909–1912.
6. Chen, Y. Usability analysis on online social networks for the elderly. Tech. rep., Helsinki University of Technology, 2009.
7. Chou, W. H., Lai, Y.-T., and Liu, K.-H. User requirements of social media for the elderly: A case study in Taiwan. *Beh. & Inf. Tech. 32*, 9 (Sept. 2013), 920–937.
8. Cornejo, R., Favela, J., and Tentori, M. Ambient displays for integrating older adults into social networking sites. In *Collaboration and Technology*, vol. 6257 of *LNCS*. Springer, 2010, 321–336.
9. Gibson, L., Moncur, W., Forbes, P., Arnott, J., Martin, C., and Bhachu, A. S. Designing social networking sites for older adults. In *Proc. HCI 2010*, BCS (2010), 186–194.
10. Hoofnagle, C., King, J., Li, S., and Turow, J. How different are young adults from older adults when it comes to information privacy attitudes and policies? *UC Berkeley Center for Law and Technology* (2010).
11. Karahasanović, A., Brandtzæg, P. B., Heim, J., Lüders, M., Vermeir, L., Pierson, J., Lievens, B., Vanattenhoven, J., and Jans, G. Co-creation and user-generated content-elderly peoples user requirements. *Computers in Human Behavior 25*, 3 (2009), 655 – 678.
12. Kurniawan, S., and Zaphiris, P. Research-derived web design guidelines for older people. In *Proc. ASSETS 2005*, ACM Press (2005), 129–135.
13. Lehtinen, V., Näsänen, J., and Sarvas, R. A little silly and empty-headed: older adults' understandings of social networking sites. In *Proc. HCI 2009*, BCS (2009), 45–54.
14. Lewis, S., and Ariyachandra, T. Seniors and online social network use. In *Proc. CONISAR 2010* (2010).
15. Lipford, H. R., Besmer, A., and Watson, J. Understanding privacy settings in Facebook with an audience view. In *Proc. UPSEC 2008* (2008), 2:1–2:8.
16. Mikkola, K., and Halonen, R. "Nonsense?" - ICT perceived by the elderly. In *the European, Mediterranean & Middle Eastern Conference on Information Systems* (2011), 306–317.
17. Nyemba, E. S. F., Mukwasi, C. M., Mhakure, S., Mosiane, S., and Chigona, W. Golden baby boomers' perceptions of online social networking sites. *Int. J. Comp. Tech. App 2*, 3 (2011), 695–703.
18. Ofcom. Adults' media use and attitudes report 2013. Tech. rep., Ofcom, 2013.
19. Pullin, G., and Newell, A. Focussing on extra-ordinary users. In *Universal Access in HCI. Coping with Diversity*. Springer, 2007, 253–262.
20. Sundar, S. S., Oeldorf-Hirsch, A., Nussbaum, J., and Behr, R. Retirees on Facebook: can online social networking enhance their health and wellness? In *Proc. CHI EA 2011*, ACM Press (2011), 2287–2292.
21. Valenzuela, S., Park, N., and Kee, K. F. Is there social capital in a social network site?: Facebook use and college students' life satisfaction, trust, and participation. *JCMC 14*, 4 (2009), 875–901.
22. Watson, P., Hanson, V., Olivier, P., Tanaka, A., Li, F., Arnott, J., Gregor, P., and van Moorsel, A. Social inclusion through the digital economy. In *Digital Futures 2010* (2010).
23. Wherton, J., and Prendergast, D. The building bridges project: Involving older adults in the design of a communication technology to support peer-to-peer social engagement. In *HCI and Usability for e-Inclusion*, vol. 5889 of *LNCS*. Springer, 2009, 111–134.
24. Xie, B., Watkins, I., Golbeck, J., and Huang, M. Understanding and changing older adults' perceptions and learning of social media. *Educational Gerontology 38*, 4 (2012), 282–296.

Being Senior and ICT: A Study of Seniors Using ICT in China

Yuling Sun, Xianghua Ding, Silvia Lindtner, Tun Lu, Ning Gu

School of Computer Science
Fudan University
Shanghai 201203, China

Shanghai Key Laboratory of Data Science
Fudan University
Shanghai 201203, China

yulingsun.lv@gmail.com, dingx@fudan.edu.cn, lindtner@gmail.com, {lutun, ninggu}@fudan.edu.cn

ABSTRACT

System design for seniors often focuses on the decline of their biological capabilities and social connectedness. This approach has been challenged as too simplistic to capture what it really means to be senior. This paper presents a qualitative study of 17 seniors in urban China (age ranging from 50s to 70s), who have adopted and incorporated ICT into their daily lives. Findings from this study show that the ways in which seniors attend to ICT are not simply shaped by changes in health or other wellbeing, but also by their life attitudes, value systems, relationships to younger generations as well as historical specifics during their coming of age. This paper contributes by showing that 1) what it means to be senior is shaped from within a whole social ecology of past and current experiences, values and interactions; 2) senior identities are not fixed, but continuously negotiated, articulated and enacted through ICT; 3) social interaction and access of technologies are highly intertwined.

Key words

Seniors; elders; ICT; values; qualitative study; companionship; cross-generational communication.

ACM Classification Keywords

H.5.m. Information interfaces and presentation (e.g., HCI): Miscellaneous.

INTRODUCTION

"We are a group that is relatively old compared to you, but we don't refuse the young. Although we are traditional, we don't refuse innovation. Although we are quite experienced, we are still as curious as a child. Although we seem a bit conservative, we don't refuse anything new. We are a group similarly with blood and flesh, with delight, anger, sorrow and happiness, and with affection and desire. We love our country, dislike boasting and empty talk, and hate corruption… …People say that there is a generational gap between you and us, and that we don't have much to talk, but that is not just us who shall be responsible for that. It is because the Internet, the smart phone, and entertainments that have occupied most of the capacity of your brain, and have left little for us. We love radio, but nine out of ten are to sell medicine. We occasionally watch TV, but it is either wine selling or all sorts of talent shows for those who wish to become famous over night."

- A translated post from a Chinese online forum for retirees.[1]

In HCI fields, technology design for seniors is often based on the assumption that seniors need the help of technologies because they face new limitations due to their age such as memory problems, loss of physical abilities, reduction in social connectedness, and so on. Design for seniors in HCI is then motivated by the goal to compensate for these limitations [5, 31, 39]. This dominant conception of seniors, however, has been increasingly critiqued as being inaccurate and too simplistic [8, 18, 23]. Ito *et al.*, for instance, in their study of SeniorNet in United States, uncover a number ways in which the seniors are different from "stereotypes that characterize seniors as technophobic and technologically incompetent" [18]. Similarly, Lindley *et al.*, based on an extended literature review, note that the model of elders as a socially isolated group to be monitored and better connected via technology is often inconsistent with the insights gained from deploying technologies in real settings [23]. As Östlund insightfully put it, the dominant approach sees seniors first as "old" and only second as technology users [28].

As an alternative, a more human-centered approach and a view from seniors' perspective are called for to better design for seniors [11, 23, 28]. Following this call, we conducted a qualitative study with 17 seniors in urban China (with their age ranging from 51 to 73), who have adopted and used ICT (the internet penetration among seniors is only 5.9% in China [6, 41]). We started with generic and open research questions, *i.e.* what motivated their ICT use, how they experienced ICT, and what role

CHI 2014, April 26 - May 01 2014, Toronto, ON, Canada
Copyright 2014 ACM 978-1-4503-2473-1/14/04…$15.00.
http://dx.doi.org/10.1145/2556288.2557248

[1] http://bbs.ltxjob.com/

ICT played in their lives. From our engagement with the seniors and data analysis, a central research question emerged: what does it mean to be a senior and how is it expressed at the site of ICT?

Our findings highlight that the ways seniors adopt and use ICT is not simply shaped by their limitations due to age or health, but evolves within a whole social ecology of living including life attitudes and values, shaped by their economic and social environments as well as life experiences and upbringing. We show in this paper how China's historical events such as the Cultural Revolution and economic reformation shaped the coming of age of our study population, their values, belief systems and attitudes towards the world. This generation, born in the 40s, 50s, or 60s, is often called "the lost generation" [3], because of the hardship they experienced during the Cultural Revolution, the Movement of Chinese Educated Urban Youth to the Countryside in the 1960s and 70s as well as the challenge of layoffs, early retirement and reemployment due to the policy of reform and opening in the 1990s. We recruited several participants based on retirement, and the early retirement led us to cover a broader range of age compared to previous work and rendered more open the question of what it means to be a senior. We demonstrate how the seniors we worked with reflected on these life experiences as having shaped their attitudes towards life, and in turn their technology use and social interactions online.

The rest of the paper is organized as follows. After briefly reviewing the related work, we will describe our study methods and participants, and present our findings in details. We will end by discussing how being senior and their use of ICT are not simply shaped physiologically, but also shaped historically and socially.

RELATED WORK

While much work on technologies for the ageing population focuses on the decline and negative aspects of being senior, recently, alternative views and approaches have been explored. Rather than categorizing seniors as a homogeneous group, prior work highlights the heterogeneity of being old [7, 17]. They suggest, for instance, focusing on a specific practices amongst older people or their concerns and issues, rather than older people in general. Take as an example Gaver *et al.*'s design of the Prayer Companion focusing on nuns who are mostly in their 80s [14]. Similarly, Vines *et al.*'s "Cheque Mate" focuses on understanding the values and ethics of British in their eighties in regards to finances and technology [37].

Instead of seeing seniors as passively receiving care and support, there is also work that draws attention to their values and contributions [12, 39]. Lindley *et al.* note that elder people prefer to give than receive from younger people [23]. Ellis and Bruckman's "Designing Palaver Tree Online" supports seniors to contribute to the learning of cultural history for schoolchildren [12]. And relatedly, Waycott *et al.* explore ways to support seniors to produce media content, instead of passively consuming it [39].

At the same time, a view from seniors' perspective is also called for. Ito *et al.,* in their study of SeniorNet, make an attempt to look at how members of SeniorNet themselves address the question of what it means to be senior [18]. Lindley *et al.* call for "a focus on the ways in which *older people themselves* approach their relationships" [23] (original emphasis). Wallace *et al.*'s [38] and Lindsay *et al.*'s [25] work focuses on people living with dementia and treats them as centers of expertise and value in their own right. This work resonates well with the World Health Organization's call for a turn from designing for needs to designing for rights [40].

Relevant to our analysis here is the view that emphasizes the importance of context in shaping ageing [9, 16, 28], as noted in Durick *et al.*'s literature review [11]. Östlund reminds us that we shall not simply attribute lower adoption rate of ICT among seniors to their being technophobic or being incapable to learn, but shall also consider for other realities (e.g. lack of exposure to ICT due to retirement) in affecting their adoption [28]. Crowley argues that ageing is defined more by culture than by age [9]. Harvey and Thurnwald show that generational differences are shaped by their historical, social and cultural context [16]. For instance, improved life conditions and education evidenced a more active, healthier and productive life amongst their study population of elders in Australia in comparison to previous generations. That is, context is important not simply because it shapes people's actions and daily practices, but also because it shapes who they are, their values and lifestyles.

THE STUDY

To gather the data, we first conducted semi-structured interviews with 17 participants in total. The participants were recruited through two approaches: 7 from our own social network and 10 from an online forum dedicated to retirees, which we subsequently call the Retiree Forum. The first author, a native Mandarin speaker, contacted her classmates and friends to recruit their parents who used ICT. Seven were contacted, and all agreed to be interviewed. To avoid bias from our own social networks and also to learn more about online senior communities, we then sought for more participants from the Retiree Forum. We chose this forum because of our general interest in the so-called independent post-work [22] – and so an online retiree forum founded and managed by retirees was particularly apt. In addition, this particular Retiree Forum was on the top of the result list when searching for 退休在线社区 ("retiree online community") on Baidu. The first author registered on the forum and started by posting a self-introduction message on the forum. Her message got active responses from the members, and triggered social interactions, both online and offline. She also posted on the forum a recruitment message, which disclosed our intention of doing research about seniors and technologies, as well as her QQ information for contact. Nine responded either with their QQ information or added her contact to their QQ directly, and six of them agreed to be interviewed. Based on the impressions gained from observations and social interactions on the forum, we also actively reached out for more members who appeared active and interesting for interviews, and recruited the remaining four this way. Details about our participants are shown in Table 1. As shown in this table, participants recruited from the second approach had relatively more people with more years of retirement and experiences with ICT.

Of the 17 interviewees, 10 were male and 7 were female, with their age ranging from 50 to 73. All except two had already retired, and all had used ICT for more than one year. Except for the three who lived together with their unmarried children, the rest (14) lived alone with their partners (four of them had their children living abroad, and seven lived in the same city with their children and could see their children regularly, e.g. daily or weekly). Their occupations before retirement were varied, ranging from middle school teacher, journalist, army officer, company manager, engineers, to factory worker, and they had diverse education backgrounds, ranging from primary school to university education (2 primary school, 5 junior high school, 2 senior high school, 3 technical school, 3 junior college, 2 university). Most of them had enough retirement pensions to self-sustain and lead enjoyable lives, except for one who complained about being retired and his pension payment not having started yet. All of them lived in urban areas, either cities or towns.

In our interviews, we asked about details of how they had first started using ICT, and how specifically they used ICT on daily basis. When some interesting points came up, we followed up for more details and concrete examples. Interviews were conducted by the first author via phone, online chat, and in-person in seniors' homes, depending on their preferences. All interviews were conducted in Mandarin, audio recorded, and were later transcribed into Chinese.

Besides interviews, we also did participant observation on two online forums: the Retiree Forum and the Radio Forum[2] (an online forum dedicated to radio hobbyists and collectors, and most members were seniors). The Radio Forum was recommended by one of the managers of the Retiree Forum, as he was also actively managing the Radio Forum. By observing and engaging in interactions with the seniors on the forums from March to May 2013, we gained deeper insights into the values and interests of its members, which also shaped our subsequent interview questions. Overall, members were supportive of our research, and appreciated our interests in them as well as the energy we brought to the forums.

In addition, the first author was invited by one of the managers of the Radio Forum, and attended two of their offline gatherings. During the gatherings, we observed their use of ICT. We also conducted two focus groups (one focus group per gathering) with 27 seniors to discuss their adoption/use of ICT and the role of the forum in particular. The participants in the focus groups were all male, with their age ranging from 62 to 74. Most of them got to know each other from the Radio Forum, and through regular online and offline conversations they had become well acquainted. The focus group discussions, about 6 hours' long each, were also audio recorded and later transcribed into Chinese.

Taken together, our study focused on seniors who had already adopted ICT or online forums. As such, they only constitute a very small percentage of seniors living in China, as Internet and technology access among seniors is still low, especially in areas beyond the first tier cities [6].

Name \ Info	A	G	YR	YU	Education background	Previous job	Location
recruited from our own social circles							
Kanya	51	F	5	5	junior college	public sector employee	Jinan, Shandong
Zhou	50	F	0	6	technical school	accountant	Weihai, Shandong
Chenxiu	56	F	6	6	primary school	hotel manager	Weihai, Shandong
Liao	56	M	8	8	senior high school	company employee	Kunming, Yunnan
Wanghe	62	F	7	8	junior high school	company employee	Pudong, Shanghai
Zhangsu	58	F	3	6	technical school	teacher	Yangpu, Shanghai
Zhangxin	58	M	0	9	junior college	engineer	Weifang, Shandong
recruited from the forums							
Dong	62	M	1	15	junior high school	engineer	Changning, Shanghai
Yueru	59	M	10	12	university	engineer	Putuo, Shanghai
Moyan	73	M	2	2	junior college	journalist	Huangpu, Shanghai
Wan	69	M	8	8	senior high school	public sector employee	Changzhou, Jiangsu
Lulu	62	F	14	14	technical school	teacher	Xuhui, Shanghai
Qiang	62	M	2	12	junior high school	company HR	Pudong, Shanghai
Liulin	58	F	3	8	university	company manager	Haidian, Beijing
Quan	68	M	8	2	junior high school	company manager	Taiyuan, Shanxi
Yinfu	63	M	3	12	junior high school	company employee	Huangpu, Shanghai
David	66	M	14	12	primary school	company employee	Yangpu, Shanghai

Table 1: Study participants' information

* A, Age * G, Gender
* YR, Years after retirement
* YU, Years of ICT exerpiences

The fact that they had already adopted ICT means they could enjoy certain financial security and lifestyles, which

[2] http://bbs.newradios.net/

may have had shaped their self-perception, values, and attitudes toward the world as well.

We applied a grounded theory approach [35] for analysis. The first and the second author started coding and analysis while the data was being collected and also discussed with each other to ensure reliability. Through open and axial coding of the data, themes started to emerge. In this paper, we will use representative quotes, which were then translated into English for this paper to illustrate our points. All of the names used in this paper are pseudonyms.

FINDINGS

Our study participants represent a small percentage of the senior population in China, as the Internet penetration among seniors is still very low (only 5.9% in China [6, 41]). Nonetheless, for this particular population, ICT had become an integral component of their everyday lives, or as one study participant put it: "*older people can't live without the Internet anymore.*" All of them reported that they started off with the computer and the Internet everyday to learn what is new. On average, they spent about 7 hours a day online. They were exposed to computers in a variety of ways, either from work before retirement or friends and family members, and half of them started to learn to use computer after retirement. Except for four who had more formal trainings from work (3) or outside (1), most of them learned to use computer by themselves, with some help from family and friends.

Except for three, who had backgrounds in engineering disciplines or were computer enthusiasts, others reported difficulties to learn how to use computer. While declined age-related functions such as memory, vision, and others played a role, as found similarly in previous work [13, 42], we found typing represented even a bigger barrier for this particular group of people. Several of our informants, who were born in 50s or 60s and were interrupted for their formal education during the Cultural Revolution, reported that they had not had the chance to learn pinyin[3], the main computer input method for Chinese characters. Yet, most of them were motivated enough to overcome these difficulties, either to communicate with their children abroad (4) or to fulfill their work requirements (5).

Interestingly, for our study participants, ICT has found a place that was left empty for the absence of work. Wanghe considered using the computer was similar to work: *"It is just like others who do their work. The first thing we do when we open our eyes (in the morning) is to turn on the computer."* Kanya similarly compared computer to work: "*In the past it was work. After I retired, it was the computer.*" Liao described how he got emotionally attached to the computer after his retirement: "*In the past, when you went to work everyday, it was fine without a computer, because you were busy with your work. After you became free, there was a computer, and it became my intimate friend. I feel I have a deeper relationship with the computer than with my friends.*" With the exception of two, who consciously and actively controlled their time on the computer for health considerations, the rest of our participants reported that, the computer and the Internet had occupied all of their spare time. We now will discuss in more detail how they attended ICT and why in the sections below.

Being Old or Not: an Open Question

Lindley *et al.* point out that how to define "old age" is not as obvious it might seem [23]. They list multiple ways "old age" can be defined, *e.g.* as biological decline, or as the third-stage of life, or independent post-work [27]. In China, economical reforms as well as social changes over the past decades add another layer of complexity. For instance, many of our study participants were laid off or retired sooner than normally expected (the statutory retirement age is 55 for female and 60 for male in China). As a result, there is a large population who have already entered the stage of "independent post-work", but are still in their 50s, and still physically, mentally and socially active.

In our interviews, while the majority of our informants were quite comfortable identifying themselves as "old" by using words such as "we older people", several of them were more ambivalent. For example, Liao, 56, retired for 3 years, described himself as different from other seniors as he did not "admit the age", and considered learning and using ICT was a way to illustrate that:

"*They (other seniors) never want to accept (ICT), and always think that we have passed that anyway, that is for the young, the world also belongs to the young, and we only need to live well. That is their thought, but I am not like that. I want to learn more. I am still physically in a good condition, and want to learn more about new stuff and the world, because I do not admit the age. I do not look like a senior, from my appearance... The people around me, those who I know, when they see I am playing (computer), say I am very trendy, wearing headsets and listening to music. They said I am too trendy.*"

This way, adopting, choosing or refusing to use technologies became a way to resist or at least to slow down the process of getting "old." For some, this was accomplished by refusing technologies or services specifically labeled as for older people. For instance, Kanya, who was 51 but had retired for more than 5 years, was outspokenly against the idea of using an online space specifically designed for "old" people: "*this is not necessary. I am not old.*" We found that the seniors' self-perceptions might have less to do with age, but more with their attitudes and mental states. Zhangsu, 58, had retired

[3] The official phonetic system for transcribing the sound of Chinese characters into Latin script, which is the most common method of Chinese typing.

for 2 years and emphasized that she preferred to interact with younger people: *"The people in our circle all have similar ideas as mine. That is, we don't like to hang out with those who are older, thinking if we hang out with them then we would become older, so we prefer to hang out with the younger (generation).* " She was also one of the few informants who regularly used WeChat (Weixin, 微信), a popular Chinese social media application for mobile phones. She used WeChat mainly to interact with younger members of her extended family. For her, using technologies that young people were attracted to constituted a crucial way to feel young.

Ito *et al.* note that in the popular culture, ICT is usually represented as something new that belongs to the young [18]. They further suggest that this cultural imagination of ICT has become a barrier for seniors to use ICT in the first place. Our own findings suggest that the image of ICT being something for the young did not always lead to non-use, but in many cases was the very reason for use, especially for those who emphasized that they didn't think of themselves as "old."

"It was Blissful to be Steady": Values of Being Senior and Their Expression through ICT

While some of our study participants did not fully accept or struggle with the "senior" identity of being senior, others more strongly identified with it, and expressed the kinds of value and ethics that came associated with older age. This association with being senior in turn shaped ICT practice. For instance, the Retiree Forum was regulated by a series of forum rules as well by several senior volunteers, who guaranteed a level of courtesy and "cleanness", or being "clean" from flaming, insults, advertisement. Many members of the Retiree Forum reported that the cleanness was the main reason for them to join and continue to use the forum. One such participant, Dong, 62 years old, told us how they learned from their life experiences that a steady life was not something to be assumed but something to be appreciated. For him this was one of the main reasons why people his age tried to avoid quarrels online:

"Right. We will behave ourselves. That is part of being senior. He is not like an angry young man that will say anything he wants... That is the self-discipline of being senior, because their life experiences tell them that it is blissful to be steady ...We think it is not easy to have a steady life, right? We have children that have set up their own family and their own career. These are all not easy. ... If we can be steady and peaceful, actually it is a blessing already."

Some explicitly mentioned the Cultural Revolution and other historical events as having shaped their attitudes towards life, the world, and technology. During an offline gathering of the Radio Forum, one commented that harsh life experiences, in particular, shaped his generation's attitudes, practices, and values: "*We have lived for so many years, and experienced Cultural Revolution, going to the countryside, and so forth. We've experienced all these. Now life is much better, so it is easy for us to be satisfied and be happy."* Wan, 71 years old, expressed a similar attitude, and considered that being polite was a way to avoid conflicts and seek a more harmonious atmosphere.

Dong told us that this attitude of his generation also stemmed from their perceived responsibility towards the world. He believed that while younger people in China took it as their responsibility to change the world, seniors preferred steadiness. In other words, for many of our study participants, being senior meant a shift in responsibilities towards others. They also believed that while they could not change the world, they could change their own attitudes towards the world.

Importantly, this attitude towards harmonious living also shaped online behavior. For instance, many described the Retiree Forum as a happy place, and were reserved sharing sad or negative things. When someone posted photos or articles, replies were mostly non-substantial, but one or two lines of supportive and encouraging words. Many members described the content on the online forum as bland, as a side effect of this form of self-censorship online [26]. They told us that this was one common problem with seniors' online communities, *i.e.* providing "support" (pengchang, 捧场) but lacking discussion.

Our study participants also talked about safety, egalitarianism, and self-respect as important values that shaped their choice and use of technologies. For example, they considered the online forum as egalitarian and thus preferred using it over other social media such as Sina Weibo, which was described as a one-directional communication stream: "*someone well-known has an account, and many people follow him, and he does not follow back."* As such, the consistency and inconsistency between values expressed by the seniors we worked with and values inscribed in system design figure centrally in adoption and rejection of technologies. Lulu, one of our participants, when asked whether she had used the "shake" feature of WeChat (people can shake the cell phone, WeChat will offer a list of people who shake the phone at the same time, who can then be contacted), replied: "I *almost never use it. I don't think that is something for our age.*" That is, the WeChat "shake" feature, associated with risk taking and adventurous, was not something that aligned well with their values. Notably, here, Lulu only described the "shake" feature and not the entire WeChat platform as misaligned with her values. What this suggests for future system design is that features could be fine-tuned for different populations, while still allowing them to come together across the platform.

Situated Socialization with Peers: Quality Over Quantity

Previous studies show that one important reason for seniors to join online communities is for companionship [33, 34]. Companionship was also an important theme that our study participants pursued in their interactions. Prior work also notes that, for companionship, "having a few close friendships may be more important than having a large social network" [23]. This "quality over quantity" or "focus on enough, not more" attitude toward companionship also hold true in our study. What we found in addition was that the particular forms companionships took depended on their social, physical and cultural environments. Only one of our study participants seemed not very interested in using ICT to communicate with her peers. She lived in one of the traditional "work unit" (单位) residential spaces, where coworkers also share living space and often know each other for years. For her, engaging in regular contact and activities with her neighbors seemed sufficient for companionship. Others, however, did leverage social media for connections, but mostly with those who they already knew rather than making new friends. Zhangsu, for instance, was connected with her friends and family members through various social media such as WeChat and QQ. When asked whether she would use social media to make new friends, she answered: *"I've never thought of that. I don't even have enough time to play with my current friends and old colleagues."*

In some cases, people chose computer-mediated communications over offline face-to-face meetings to achieve a balance between obligations at home and interactions with others. This balance was especially important to those who took over the responsibility to take care of their grandchildren, a common practice we found in China. Wanghe's case is a telling example. She and her friends created a media space [10] of their own by keeping the video chat open on a daily basis. She told us that this way, she was able to simultaneously take care of family obligation and connect with their friends. For her, these online interactions felt more like "hanging out," remote presence being important than the actual content of the conversation:

"*When we say chatting, actually we don't have much to chat... We may speak one minute and be quiet the next. Sometimes, if there are other things coming up, we will just leave. Like this one (she pointed to the chat window for us while we were at her home and observed how she video chat with her friends), someone came to her home, so she is getting busy for that and going cooking now.*"

In addition to remote presence, what many enjoyed about the video chat was the fact that it did not require to use the Pinyin input system, which many of them had not learned coming of age during the Cultural Revolution. Our findings suggest that Media Space [10, 19] can extend beyond the immediate work and family settings.

While Wanghe or Zhangsu were able to connect to many of their friends online, others emphasized that only few of their elder peers used the Internet. Internet penetration amongst seniors in China is low in general, but especially amongst those living outside first tier cities such as Beijing and Shanghai [6]. Further, some participants who lived in big cities in China described to us that years of industrialization and commercialization had drastically changed communal life in the cities, accompanied by a decrease in interaction among neighbors. As such, the Internet provided a way to overcome such changes to social connectivity and meet new friends online [4]. However, even for them, the principle of "focusing on enough, not more" friends still holds. Liao, for instance, who couldn't find his friends online, met new friends using QQ and emphasized that one or two good friends would be good enough. Lulu, similarly, stressed that it was not necessary to reach out further, as she considered her life fulfilling with a small group of friends. Taken together, although the particular forms of seniors' socializations were varied broadly across our participants, "quality over quantity" as a central value in directing their socialization with peers was commonly shared.

Communication with Children: Distance Matters Differently

Our data suggests that "distance matters" differently [29] in the ways in which seniors maintained relationships with their children. Several of them expressed that they missed children who were abroad and sought regular interaction. For many this changed upon the return of their children, even if they ended up living in a remote town or city. Chenxiu, for instance, described this change when her child moved back to China: *"we used video (chat) often when he was abroad. I missed him very much, for example I worried whether he gained or lost weight, whether he was ok living there. Now I don't have that thought anymore. Now he is back every month."* Liulin, similarly, reported that the most frequent time when she used video chat with her daughter was when she lived in Japan, mostly because it was expensive to call and use text messages.

Technology use, here, was varied depending on the "type" of remoteness between elders and their children, *i.e.* international or within China. This suggests that the felt separation shaped interactions – international separation increasing interaction. Those whose children lived in the same city or in a city nearby were able to see their children face-to-face fairly regularly. However, this did not lead to a felt improvement of connectivity. Indeed, many of our study participants often complained that their children put less effort into staying in touch remotely, when they lived elsewhere in China. Chenxiu expressed this as: *"For the few days he is back, he doesn't stay at home, and he would go out with his classmates and friends, rather than be at home."* What this suggests is that being able to see each other regularly may actually lead to the reduction of more focused and meaningful cross-generational conversations, resonating with previous counter-intuitive hypothesis that by deploying technologies to monitor elders for reassurance, it might actually reduce the meaningful interactions across the generations [15].

Communication with Children: Asymmetric Relationships

What we observed across our study participants was a seeming "lack of interest" amongst our participants to interact with their children. When we asked whether they would miss and would like to interact with their children more, most of them firmly answered "No." This "lack of interest" attitude towards their children runs contrast to common perceptions that seniors are socially isolated and value connections with family [24], an assumption underlying much work of cross-generation communication design [32, 33]. We delved deeper and found that this seeming disinterest mostly stemmed from asymmetrical relationship between seniors and children. Lindley *et al.* observed that parents strive towards communicating with their children, but do not want to be invasive in their children's lives [23]. Our findings suggest that seniors want to communicate with their children but do not want to feel declined. Many of our study participants emphasized that they were often the ones initiating contact and putting efforts on sustaining communication. Zhou, 50, revealed: *"sigh...I do. I miss her, but she does not miss me... When I communicate with Ye (her daughter), and when I send short text messages, she just replies with one or two words. Very simple."* It was this feeling of being declined that led to their "lack of interest". They described to us that when responses from their children remained sparse, they also became less active in their efforts to stay in touch regularly. Liao explained why he did not want to call his son: *"Call him? Rarely. I don't want to call him. When you talk to him, we can't say much. He will always think we talk too much... he just says things carelessly, he seems not very interested in chatting with me..."* Wanghe expressed a similar attitude: *"Children nowadays are what they call 'independent,' and find there is nothing to talk about with us anymore. They will not talk to us, and are not willing to talk to us. Then, we just don't talk..."* Over time, our study participants became more and more hesitant to actively reach out to their children, especially when their attempts repeatedly did not receive a reciprocal response.

On the other hand, those who engaged in asynchronous communication had more satisfying experiences communicating with their children. Lulu, for instance, expressed she felt connected to her son by using lightweight and asynchronous interaction: *"My kid is a journalist now. I read his article everyday... If my kid is at work and is online, we may use QQ (to chat a bit), actually just some domestic trivia, not much. My kid also read my article."* Similarly, Zhangsu used WeChat to interact with her son studying in Italy, which allowed her to feel connected to his new lifestyle and whereabouts: *"wow, what he is like today, what clothes he wears, or his nearby computer desk, or what he eats for dinner."* Others reported that they regularly used Renren (a social media platform similar to Facebook) to follow their children's lives. Taken together, seniors who adopted lightweight and asynchronous media felt connected with their children, and also expressed satisfaction with the lightweight technology itself. Our findings here are, then, in contrast to previous work that shows a gap between seniors' preferences for focused and heavy-weighted communication and the preference for lightweight media interaction amongst younger generations [24].

Technology Set-up and Maintenance as a Site for Cross-generational Interconnectedness

While many of our study participants expressed that they felt their children to be missing from their day-to-day social lives, we also found that children played important roles in introducing ICT to the seniors' lives and helped them set up technologies in their homes. When asked how they obtained their first computer, laptop, iPad or smart phone, almost all answered it was from their children as gifts, or passed down from their children. This practice of technology gifting between generations relates to Oreglia et al.'s findings on gift giving in rural areas in China as a way for people to obtain their first mobile phones [30], Many of our participants reported that their children installed and set up Internet in their homes, and also created accounts for them in social media applications such as QQ, Renren, WeChat, and Weibo.

Take for instance Qiang describing his early experiences with the computer: *"I didn't know anything back then, and I had to rely on my child to install everything. I could only use what he had installed for me. If he did not install things for me, I would not be able to do anything."* While Qiang today told us that he was mostly self-reliant when it came to both technology use and set-up, many others such as Kanya remained reliant on her child for the use of computers: *"I don't (create an account, posting photos). I don't know how. It is my child who has registered and created these accounts for me. I just know how to use."* For many, installation and registration was only the first hurdle in adopting a new technology. They emphasized that it took even more effort to make these technologies actually work in practice. Their children remained central in also helping them set things up, and make it work. What it suggests is that introducing technologies and providing technical support can be a way of children to express care and connectedness.

DISCUSSION

In this paper, we have illustrated how seniors' self-perceptions, their attitudes towards life, relationship to their children, and upbringing together form a whole social ecology that shapes their adoption and use of ICT. By social ecology we refer to both their social lives, e.g. connectedness with peers and/or family members, and their values and attitudes towards life shared by many members of their generation. That is, ICT practice amongst our study participants evolved through this social ecology of their upbringing, values and social norms as well as negotiations with a younger generation.

In what follows, we provide an in-depth discussion of our three main findings, summarized again here: first, acting senior with ICT was not simply shaped by health concerns due to age or immediate access to technology alone, but also by their coming of age and particular historical periods our participants experienced; second, being senior was not a fixed identity, but something our participants continuously negotiated, articulated and enacted through ICT on daily basis; third, social interactions and technology practice were deeply intertwined.

Being Senior: a Historical Lens

We have shown in this paper how particular cultural processes and historical moments in China such as the Cultural Revolution have shaped our participants' attitudes towards technology and life writ large. As Harvey and Thurnwald argue, generations are shaped by their specific historical, social and cultural context [16]. In this paper, we have shown how historical events and changes in China over the last 60 years constituted one shaping element in our study participants lives, attitudes and ICT choices. In our conversations and interviews with them, many spoke about their coming of age and their experiences of hardship. They strongly believed that these experiences had impacted and shaped their current livelihood and relationship to others. Some of these experiences shaped their technology use more directly: for instance, many did not receive training in the Pinyin system when they were young and as such experienced difficulties in typing on the computer and mobile phones. As a consequence, many preferred video or voice chatting to texting. Historical aspects, however, also went deeper and shaped seniors' values and attitudes toward life. For instance, they emphasized that their upbringing made them appreciate steadiness and stability more, which in turn shaped online practice, *i.e.* on the online forums, many consciously avoided conflicts and tensions, and sought for more harmonious relationships with their peers.

What we would like to emphasize, here, is how a whole social ecology of our participants' *previous* and current experiences played a role in shaping how they acted with technology, and how they chose certain technologies over others. Or in other words, what it meant to be senior and how to act senior in China today was shaped by the historical, political, and economic processes central to their coming of age. By incorporating this historical lens, we build on prior work in HCI on "socio-technical systems" [21] and "situated actions" [36], emphasizing how social and technical processes are mutually constituent and cannot be understood independently or separately from actors' specific situatedness. While these concepts have found much resonance in HCI broadly, considering historical processes in research and design with elders is rare in HCI. We hope that this research provides a first-stepping stone in this direction.

Being Senior: Negotiating Senior Identities through ICT

Prior work has acknowledged the limits of the category "old" inherently associated with things such as mental and physical "decline" when it comes to understanding elders [14, 17]. Yet, relative little prior work has explored in-depth what it means to be senior, how it relates to past and present experiences and value systems. Durick *et al.,* based on an extensive literature review, dispel seven myths about ageing that have been embedded in system design work, including "the same", "socially isolated and lonely" and others, and suggest other alternative views such as "ageing people are diverse", "ageing people can and do have meaningful relationships" [11]. While these views are largely drawn from the fields of gerontology and gerontechnology, we argue that much can be gained by applying their overall idea to HCI research.

Our findings further show that being senior is not a stable identity, but continuously negotiated and enacted as part of daily life. Answering what it means to be a senior is an uneasy task [23], and perhaps a question even more complex for the senior population in China. We did not recruit study participants based on age, but based on life stage, i.e. either being parents of adult children or retired. By recruiting participants in this way, we already defined in some ways what we meant by "senior". Not all of our study participants, however, accepted this identity we had assigned to them. Some even outspokenly rejected technologies that were labeled or designed specifically for seniors. Others made an effort to use technologies and/or join online groups that were oriented towards younger people. These findings remind us that the question of how to design for and with senior should not always necessarily begin with a fixed notion of being senior, but with an exploration of who they want to and believe to be.

Our findings highlight that ICT was a site for them to express and reflect their value systems and life attitudes. Those who identified themselves strongly as seniors understood "being senior" as in line with the broader values they held, which in turn shaped ICT adoption and use. Many of our study participants believed that young people in China value adventure, serendipity, growth, learning, making changes, and quantity. In contrast, they valued safety, predictability, self-respect, egalitarianism, steadiness, quality, and others. They often refused technologies when the values embedded in their design appeared as misaligned with those of our participants. Our findings, then, support social gerontologist Stephen Katz's critique of common medicalised approaches to studying the human aging processes [20], and call for an alternative views of seniors by turning attention towards expressions of identity [2] and values [1].

Social Interaction and Access of ICT

Seniors are often perceived as suffering from social isolation and loneliness. In this sense, technology design in and beyond HCI is largely targeted at helping seniors better connect with family and peers. However, our findings show that achieving a sense of social connectedness is more complex. For example, cross-generational communications were not simply about bridging physical distance, but also about accommodating differences of infrastructures and expectations.

In addition, we've also shown that social interactions and their access of technologies are highly intertwined. As shown in this paper, younger family members often played important roles in helping seniors to adopt and use ICT, by introducing technologies into their lives, motivating them to learn, and providing technical support. Social pressure from their peers played a role as well. These social aspects of access to ICT are especially important for those who do not have genuine interest in technologies. We revealed how some of our study participants used ICT through *socially mediated interactions*, *i.e.* technology set up and configured by others. So even those seniors who were unable to fully grasp the functioning of their technologies were not excluded from the digital world. With their children, family members, and sometimes their friends, they were still able to access and benefit from ICT. To address this question of access, then, we recommend not only approaching it from a technical perspective, but also socially, for example, by enabling easier technical support between seniors and others.

CONCLUSION

In this paper, we reported findings from a study of seniors using ICT in China. In HCI and related fields, attempts have been made to go beyond seeing seniors as merely "old" or "limited" in system design. With a particular generation and population segment of seniors in China, we extend from this work, pointing to the importance of considering the historical processes that shape elders' upbringing, and the values that seniors hold, which in turn have shaped their technology practices. We have also shown how their ICT adoption and use was a site of continuous negotiation of senior identity and expression of senior values. That is, with ICT, seniors negotiated new models of value systems, connectivity, and friendship.

Finally, we would like to stress that our findings are rooted in a culturally specific site, which provided culturally specific insights into how being senior is enacted amongst a particular generation and demographic of elders in China. We cannot draw generalizing conclusions in terms of whether some of the values uncovered here apply to seniors elsewhere or to seniors from a different demographic. Indeed, some of our participants suggested we engage with other senior populations in China such as laid-off workers, street cleaners, and broadly members of the working class, in order to gain yet another perspective. A study of such different groups might bring forth other sets of values and ICT practices, constituting a rich space for future research.

ACKNOWLEDGMENTS

We thank the reviewers for their valuable comments and suggestions to improve the paper. The work is supported by the National Natural Science Foundation of China (NSFC) under Grants No.61332008, No. 61272533 & No. 61300201, Shanghai Science & Technology Committee Project under Grant No.11JC1400800 & No.13ZR1401900, and Fudan Young Teacher Initial Grant No. 20520131119. Silvia Lindtner is in part supported by the ISTC-Social (Intel Science and Technology Center for Social Computing at UC Irvine) and the US National Science Foundation under the award 1321065.

REFERENCES

1. Andrews, G.J., Kearns, R.A., Kontos, P. and Wilson, V. 'Their finest hour': Older people, oral histories, and the historical geography of social life. *Social \& Cultural Geography 7*, 02 (2006), 153-177.
2. Biggs, S. Beyond appearances: Perspectives on identity in later life and some implications for method. *The Journals of Gerontology Series B: Psychological Sciences and Social Sciences 60*, 3 (2005), S118-S128.
3. Bonnin, M. *The Lost Generation: The Rustification of China's Educated Youth (1968-1980)*. Chinese University Press, 2009.
4. Burmeister, O.K. What users of virtual social networks value about social interaction: The case of GreyPath. *Virtual Social Networks: Mediated, Massive and Multiplayer. Hampshire, UK: Palgrave* (2009).
5. Cesta, A. and Pecora, F. The robocare project: Intelligent systems for elder care. *AAAI Fall Symposium on Caring Machines: AI in Elder Care, USA* (2005).
6. CNNIC. Development Situation Statistics Report of Chinese Internet (2013).
7. Coleman, R. Designing for our future selves. *Universal Design Handbook* (2001), 4-1.
8. Coleman, R., Lebbon, C., Clarkson, J. and Keates, S. From margins to mainstream. *Inclusive Design, Design for the Whole Population* (2003), 1-25.
9. Crowley, J. Editorial. *International Social Science Journal 58*, 190 (2006), 539-543.
10. Dourish, P. Culture and control in a media space. *In Proc. ECSCW* (1993), 125-137.
11. Durick, J., Robertson, T., Brereton, M., Vetere, F. and Nansen, B. Dispelling ageing myths in technology design. *In Proc. OZCHI 2013*.

12. Ellis, J.B. and Bruckman, A.S. Designing palaver tree online: Supporting social roles in a community of oral history. *In Proc. CHI 2001*, 474-481.
13. Garattini, C., Wherton, J. and Prendergast, D. Linking the lonely: An exploration of a communication technology designed to support social interaction among older adults. *Universal Access in the Information Society 11*, 2 (2012), 211-222.
14. Gaver, W., Blythe, M., Boucher, A., Jarvis, N., Bowers, J. and Wright, P. The prayer companion: Openness and specificity, materiality and spirituality. *In Proc. CHI 2010*, 2055-2064.
15. Harley, D. and Fitzpatrick, G. YouTube and intergenerational communication: The case of Geriatric1927. *Universal Access in the Information Society 8*, 1 (2009), 5-20.
16. Harvey, P.W. and Thurnwald, I. Ageing well, ageing productively: The essential contribution of Australia's ageing population to the social and economic prosperity of the nation. *Health Sociology Review 18*, 4 (2009), 379-386.
17. Hernandez-Encuentra, E., Pousada, M. and Gomez-Zuniga, B. ICT and older people: Beyond usability. *Educational Gerontology 35*, 3 (2009), 226-245.
18. Ito, M., O'Day, V.L., Adler, A., Linde, C. and Mynatt, E.D. Making a place for seniors on the Net: SeniorNet, senior identity, and the digital divide. *ACM SIGCAS Computers and Society 31*, 3 (2001), 15-21.
19. Judge, T.K., Neustaedter, C. and Kurtz, A.F. The family window: The design and evaluation of a domestic media space. *In Proc. CHI 2010*, 2361-2370.
20. Katz, S. *Disciplining Old Age: The Formation of Gerontological Knowledge*. University of Virginia Press, 1996.
21. Kling, R., McKim, G., Fortuna, J. and King, A. Scientific collaboratories as socio-technical interaction networks: A theoretical approach. *ArXiv Preprint Cs/0005007* (2000).
22. Laslett, P. *Fresh Map of Life: The Emergence of the Third Age*. Harvard University Press, 1991.
23. Lindley, S.E., Harper, R. and Sellen, A. Designing for elders: Exploring the complexity of relationships in later life. *In Proc. BCS-HCI 2008*, 77-86.
24. Lindley, S.E., Harper, R. and Sellen, A. Desiring to be in touch in a changing communications landscape: Attitudes of older adults. *In Proc. CHI 2009*, 1693-1702.
25. Lindsay, M.E. Spirituality and personhood in dementia. *International Journal of Person Centered Medicine 1*, 2 (2011), 419-421.
26. Link, P. The anaconda in the chandelier: Chinese censorship today. *New York Rev. of Books* (2002).
27. Midwinter, E. How many people are there in the third age?. *Ageing and Society 25*, 1 (2005), 9-18.
28. Britt, Ö. Design paradigms and misunderstood technology: The case of older users. *Young Technologies in Old Hands - An International View on Senior Citizens' Utilization of ICT* (2005), 25-39.
29. Olson, G.M. and Olson, J.S. Distance matters. *Human-Computer Interaction 15*, 2 (2000), 139-178.
30. Oreglia, E. and Kaye, J. A gift from the city: Mobile phones in rural China. *In Proc. CSCW 2012*, 137-146.
31. Piper, A.M., Weibel, N. and Hollan, J. Audio-enhanced paper photos: Encouraging social interaction at age 105. *In Proc. CSCW 2013*, 215-224.
32. Plaisant, C., Clamage, A., Hutchinson, H.B., Bederson, B.B. and Druin, A. Shared family calendars: Promoting symmetry and accessibility. *ACM Transactions on Computer-Human Interaction (TOCHI) 13*, 3 (2006), 313-346.
33. Rodriguez, M.D., Gonzalez, V.M., Favela, J. and Santana, P.C. Home-based communication system for older adults and their remote family. *Computers in Human Behavior 25*, 3 (2009), 609-618.
34. Rook, K.S. Support, companionship, and control in older adults' social networks: Implications for well-being. *Handbook of Communication and Aging Research* (1995), 437-463.
35. Strauss, A.L. and Corbin, J. *Basics of Qualitative Research*. Sage publications Newbury Park, CA, 1990.
36. Suchman, L.A. *Plans and Situated Actions: The Problem of Human-Machine Communication*. Cambridge University Press, 1987.
37. Vines, J., Blythe, M., Lindsay, S., Dunphy, P., Monk, A. and Olivier, P. Questionable concepts: Critique as resource for designing with eighty somethings. *In Proc. CHI 2012*, 1169-1178.
38. Wallace, J., Wright, P.C., McCarthy, J., Green, D.P., Thomas, J. and Olivier, P. A design-led inquiry into personhood in dementia. *In Proc. CHI 2013*, 2617-2626.
39. Waycott, J., Vetere, F., Pedell, S., Kulik, L., Ozanne, E., Gruner, A. and Downs, J. Older adults as digital content producers. *In Proc. CHI 2013*, 39-48.
40. World Health Organization. Active ageing: A policy framework. *Geneva: World Health Organization* (2002), 1-60.
41. Wu, Y. China Aging Development Report, *China National Committee on Ageing* (2013).
42. Xie, B. Multimodal computer-mediated communication and social support among older Chinese internet users. *Journal of Computer-Mediated Communication 13*, 3 (2008), 728-750.

The Lonely Raccoon at the Ball: Designing for Intimacy, Sociability, and Selfhood

Jeffrey Bardzell
Indiana University
Bloomington, IN 47408
jbardzel@indiana.edu

Shaowen Bardzell
Indiana University
Bloomington, IN 47408
selu@indiana.edu

Guo Zhang
Indiana University
Bloomington, IN 47408
guozhang@indiana.edu

Tyler Pace
Indiana University
Bloomington, IN 47408
tympace@indiana.edu

ABSTRACT
Designing for sociable systems requires, among other abilities, a sensitivity to the meanings, structures, and nuances of technology-mediated experiences that are simultaneously felt by users to be intimate and also social. Such a sensitivity is not easily acquired, and design researchers have recommended the use of social theories to guide designers' readings of technology-mediated social experiences. We use philosopher Michel Foucault's theory of identity (and social power, discourse, sexuality, creativity, and style) known as "the care of the self," as a scaffold with which to produce a sensitive interpretation of the intimacy (and expert social creative) practices of adult users of the virtual world *Second Life* (*SL*). This reading sheds light on several skilled and creative intimacy practices in *SL*. It also offers a philosophically grounded hermeneutic strategy for designers interested in analyzing intimate experiences.

Author Keywords
HCI; design; intimacy; identity; sociability; sexuality; user experience; creativity; amateurs; making; maker culture

ACM Classification Keywords
H.5.m. Information interfaces and presentation (e.g., HCI): Miscellaneous

INTRODUCTION
The turn to experience in HCI research [33], which began over a decade ago, has led to a focus on social as well as intimate experiences. Often, these two are intertwined. For example, HCI studies have focused on communicating and supporting intimacy for couples in long-distance relationships [8,24], maintaining intimate relationships between family members in their domestic lives [23,44], creating experiences of relatedness [21], understanding the roles of interactive technologies on intimate relationships [44], and theorizing intimacy in virtual worlds [2,3,9,36,40]. Intimacy also emerges as a related topic in research on embodied interaction [26], identity and selfhood [30,46], domestic life [6], and human sexuality [1,7,10,19,25].

CHI 2014, April 26 - May 01 2014, Toronto, ON, Canada
Copyright is held by the owner/author(s). Publication rights licensed to ACM.
ACM 978-1-4503-2473-1/14/04 $15.00.
http://dx.doi.org/10.1145/2556288.2557127

This research suggests that intimacy is a phenomenon that is difficult to isolate from a host of other equally complex topics. Schiphorst et al. characterize social intimacy as "the interplay between people and a set of networked objects in a social or public space [that] can be used to create awareness between others, sensitivity and more vital connection between groups of people in a public space" [42, p.23]. Koefoed Hansen and Kozel write, "Acknowledging the sensory, affective, poetic and corporeal qualities of the moment of lived experience" has become the key to designing the next generation of technologies [26].

A challenge for designers is to develop the skills needed to insightfully interpret intimate social experiences. To improve these skills in design, Batterbee and Koskinen call for a "research paradigm" distinct from experimental studies, which would combine the following three elements: "a theoretical framework that sensitizes designers to how...social organization takes shape, and how it affects the ways in which people experience designs"; a means of observing interaction as it is experienced in socially meaningful ways; and a cogent "interpretative procedure for making sense of the data" [4, p.474]. "The most important thing," they add, "is that there be a sensitizing framework that helps designers in making sense of the intricacies of interaction and what it does to experience" [*ibid*]. Such research does not always yield easily packaged design implications, but instead it enriches the perspective from which design framings and concepts are generated.

In sum, designers have a need to understand experiences of social intimacy; such experience requires a trained "sensitivity" to perceive and understand the "intricacies" of technology-mediated intimate experiences as they are embedded in (and not abstracted from) deep issues of selfhood, embodiment, social power, pleasure, and emancipation; this activity is supported by the appropriation of a theoretical framework that sensitizes designers to social experience.

The present work fits within that paradigm to offer a "sensitive" analysis of technology mediated social intimacy. Specifically, we present a critical interpretation of an empirical study of how *Second Life* (*SL*) users characterize their online experiences of "intimacy" (as they themselves define and understand the term). The study is empirical, because the source material we work from is user accounts of intimate experiences. This study is critical in that it explicitly appropriates the identity theory of philosopher Michel Foucault to amplify our sensitivity to these users' responses. We appropriate Foucault's identity theory, in particular his "care of the self" as developed in [15,16] and other works, because it offers a system of concepts and a hermeneutic approach that helps render visible the diverse relationships among intimacy, sexuality, identity, and social power.

Briefly, Foucault argues that the self emerges as an emergent outcome of *subjectification*, which he characterizes as the dual processes of becoming *subjected to* regulatory systems, comprising institutions, body practices, and discursive frameworks, and so forth, as well becoming the *subject of* our individual responses to and creative stylizations of that subjection. A simple example of this is motherhood. Mothers are governed by laws, moral prescriptions, and social conventions not only to care for their children, but to do so in certain ways. At the same time, the mother's feelings of love for the child are usually experienced from within; they do not *feel* imposed on from the outside, and neither do laws or prescriptions for care typically interfere with the intimacy of that love (indeed, a Foucauldian perspective would argue that external forms of governance often *enhance* that felt intimacy, e.g., by rewarding the mother's child care labor with social praise). Obviously, the point is not to explore the labor politics of motherhood, but simply to point out that "mother" is both a public and a private designation and that the two aspects interrelate.

Our analysis of user accounts of intimate experiences in *SL*, guided by Foucault's "care of the self," helps us understand the nuances of the relations between designs and human experiences. Recent HCI research [e.g., 18,28,45] on collective creativity, craft, expert amateurs, machinimators, everyday design, and appropriation, for example, is about highly skilled users formed into social collectives and using open-ended technologies (or technological ecologies) in highly creative ways. *SL*, whose content is nearly all user-created, puts its users in this category. However, our research focus is on their social experiences, rather than their creativity practices narrowly construed. Our analysis reveals, then, not only the expected linkages among intimacy, selfhood, and the social, but also linkages between intimacy and skilled social and creative practices mediated by sociotechnical systems, specifically, avatar design, virtual confession, gender performance, and cybersex.

Another aspect of our contribution is that our respondents are older (avg age 42) and also more gender diverse than is typical for empirical studies of social technologies: 51.7% female; 46.4% male; and 1.9% transgender. At the time of the data collection, the median age of *SL* users was 37 and the gender split was nearly even. We argue that this study reveals the ways that the intimate, social, and identity-constructing habits of *mature adults* can be mediated and creatively fashioned in and through technological systems.

RESEARCH APPROACH

Study Site. We chose the virtual world of *SL* as our study site. Virtual environments have long been of interest for research on identity practices: [39] writes of creation of the cyber "I," "me," and digital "generalized other"; [34] analyzes the co-evolvement of avatars and ourselves, [5] studies the emergence of new forms of personal connection, and [9,12,31] explicate the evolving performances of gender, race, conflict, and the interplay of self and group. We chose *SL* in particular primarily on account of its culture of intimate interaction [2,9], its emphasis on skilled user-created content [3], its blurred boundaries between the real and the virtual [27], and emphasis on identity performance [32].

Data Collection. The main reason we focus our research specifically on intimacy is that it is deeply linked with physical and social behaviors, with attitudes, experiences, and other psychological phenomena, and it is an important locus of sociability. Not too surprisingly, the closely related topic of sexuality comes up much, both in our data and in diverse literatures about intimacy, so we want to take up this question head-on. Sexuality has been argued to be directly linked to identity by sociologists [17,20], psychologists [13,37], and philosophers [41]. Researchers have proposed sexuality as constituting identities that give sociopolitical meaning to the body [11], as the purpose of establishing a primary identity [29], as a major developmental issue during adolescence to construct the psychosocial identity and self-understanding [43,41], as a subjective impression of being part of the private self and distinct from the public one [37], as the embodiment of self-realization and the definition of oneself as well as the relation to others [14]. As philosopher Russon writes, "[s]exual experience is the experience of our embodiment as the locus of *intersubjective* contact and compulsion" [41, p.106].

We asked SL users to tell us about their experience of intimacy in SL. This method was based on psychology researchers Register and Henley's [38] phenomenological approach to intimacy. In the Register and Henley study, study participants were asked to

> *recall and describe a specific incident in which you experienced what you would call an "intimate experience."*

No additional information was given, including any definition of "intimacy," because the researchers wanted the subjects to tell them what they thought intimacy was. For Register and Henley, such a phenomenological approach to intimacy offered a means to solicit a "systematic, descriptive account of the most fundamental aspects of an experience" from study participants.

For this study, conducted in parallel with [36], we adapted Register and Henley's question to address the specificity of intimacy in a virtual world. Following Register and Henley, we did not offer any definition of "intimacy" and encouraged participants to recount and share as much detail as they feel comfortable. An emphasis on the words and descriptions provided by participants is at the foundation of the work presented in this paper. Our question was as follows:

> *Please recall and describe a specific incident in which you experienced what you could call an "intimate experience" in the virtual world you chose. This can be as short or as long of an experience as you would care to write about. For our purposes, it is not as important what you say, as that you say it clearly and **in as much detail as possible.** Please try to include as much of what you were aware of in the account as possible.*

We used a Web form to solicit their responses. We distributed the URL to 12 different channels, including popular forums, such as *SL*, *SL Universe*, and *MMO Champion* as well as numerous group lists and game research forums, such as *SLED* and *DiGRA*. The form was widely distributed across virtual worlds not just for the purpose of increasing participation but as an intentional strategy to incorporate the perspectives of participants of many different virtual worlds into our research on intimacy.

As of this writing, 211 *SL* players (109 reported females, 98 males, and 4 transgender) completed it. They provided their ages within ranges, as follows: 17 were aged 18-25, 80 were aged 26-41, and 114 were older than 42. Regarding virtual world experience, 73.9% of all participants (N=156) had used SL for at least 1 year, while only 13.3% (N=28) had used SL for less than 7 months (and another 27 had no response). We conclude that our sample was composed largely of serious, veteran users of *SL*. Seven participants said they had never had such intimate experiences in *SL*. Two participants skipped this question. In all valid responses (N = 202) analyzed for this study, the median word length was 85, with a max length of 4078 words.

Analytical Procedures. We conducted our analysis through a procedure known as *explication de texte*, or close reading, an analytical method originating in the humanities [35] and involving the careful examination of diction, rhetorical devices, style, and other formal and thematic elements in a text. Two of the three researchers involved in the data analysis have doctoral training in the humanities and are experienced with this analytical practice.

This phase followed a process. Initially all three researchers conducted their close readings independently of one another to identify her or his own set of findings and the corresponding examples. Based on what we were seeing, we agreed that Foucault's identity theory could be of service in unpacking the complexity of issues surrounding intimacy, for the reasons we summarized in the introduction. We individually returned to the data, focusing on participant statements in which they characterized their becoming *subjected to* external structures (e.g., *SL* as a platform, practices of cybersex, and practices of avatar, gender norms) and characterized themselves as the *subjects of* their own experiences and intentions. After independently returning to the data to read from this perspective, we collaborated to combine, refine, and distinguish among the preliminary findings before arriving at the most resonant ones, presented in the next section.

INTIMACY, SUBJECTIFICATION, AND SECOND LIFE

We present our findings by focusing on those aspects of the intimacy accounts that express different aspects of the system of concepts that comprise Foucault's "care of the self." Again, our research goal is to perceive design-mediated intimacy situated in its complex relationships with sexuality, selfhood, pleasure, and sociability, with the hope that this helps us to generate new design insights and more broadly contribute to designerly sensibilities. Our goal is *not* to empirically validate the "truth" of Foucault's theory. Nor is it to champion *SL*. Neither is it our goal to produce an account that faithfully represents participant self-perceptions; as Hebdige [22] explains and demonstrates in his seminal analysis of punk subcultures, such self-perceptions are often based in ideological or unconscious processes that are interpretable and important from a research standpoint but that are not conscious (or important) to participants themselves.

We organize our findings under two main headings:

- **Governance**: Governance characterizes that which individuals are *subjected to*: systems, institutions, practices, laws, technologies, norms, prohibitions, etc.
- **Care of the self**. Care of the self characterizes that which individuals are *subjects of*: their own experiences of, responses to, and choices about how they exist in relation to systems of governance.

Governance

Individuals are governed by external structures that enable and regulate their social and body habits, behaviors, knowledge practices, etc. Governance systems prescribe norms (e.g., of gender, hygiene, speaking, etc.), prohibitions, taboos, etc. Governance not only prescribes how we behave with others (e.g., laws against murder, turn-taking in conversations, standards of dress, etc.), but also how we govern ourselves, that is, how we form, maintain, and transform our own identities (e.g., confession to purify one's soul or *t'ai chi ch'uan* to improve the body).

SL both as software and as a user culture inherits many of these, often with modifications, and introduces its own; for example, bathing practices take on different forms in a world where bodies don't sweat or get dirty. *SL* is also (mostly) anonymous, so that behaviors in-world are not easily connected to a person's real-life identity, which makes many practices that are taboo the physical world—such as harassment and public sexual displays—safer to practice in *SL*. *SL* only minimally simulates physical world laws, such as gravity, and the aging, injury, or death of the body is not a part of the default system. *SL* offers a robust—and massively extensible—avatar design system, so norms in *SL*'s user culture about highly individuated and aesthetically appealing avatars constitutes a way that *SL* governs one's relationship with oneself. With that background, we turn to our reading of the governance data.

Anonymity, or, The Apparent Absence of Governance is Still Governance. One of the most basic issues of governance in *SL* is that participation is mostly anonymous. The system itself provides no indication of anyone's physical world identity, and in fact it is a violation of the Terms of Service to reveal someone's physical world identity against their will. Of course, individuals can and do reveal their identities in-world through a variety of means, but such individuals are in the minority. Thus the system itself and user culture agree: *SL* is primarily an anonymous world. The benefits of such a system are obvious: *SL* is a fantasy environment where users are liberated from the social constraints of everyday life in the physical world. Users can (and do) present and pass themselves off as a different gender, have sex in public, harass others, explore alternative and even extreme lifestyles, and even simulate illegal activities, such as simulated pedophilia (though Linden Labs, who run *SL*, attempted to put a stop that). Thus it may seem that anonymity provides liberation from governance.

Indeed, many participants suggested such a view, for example, participant 73 (female, 50-57), writes, "*We have never met in real life, do not know who we are in real life, and regret nothing about our virtual 'fling.'*" Because of the anonymity of her "fling," she views herself exempt from the traditional consequences of a fling (e.g., regret). She is not at all alone in this line of reasoning: 152 (male, 18-25) writes, "*Although my avatar maintains probably 5 primary relationships and a dozen or so secondary, there are no attachments. After all, its a game.*"

However, although many participants see anonymity as a form of liberation from physical world governance, it is evident that anonymity is in fact its *own* system of governance. Even in the two quotes just above, the participants view anonymity to grant them license to engage in traditionally prohibited behavior, and license-granting is a form of governance. Participant 100 (female, 34-41) expresses another sense in which anonymity is a form of governance:

> *I have shared things with a few close in-world friends that I have not shared with my RL friends, or even husband. Perhaps it is the element of anonymity that allows one to express some of ones deepest thoughts and emotions.*

Here, anonymity is a license to heighten intimacy through the practice of confession to reveal (and also to perform) one's "deepest thoughts and emotions." This participant's interlocutor becomes obligated to take on the role of the confessee, which, understood in its Christian, psychoanalytic, or friendship formulations, prescribes that the confessee acknowledge and accept the confessor's "deepest thoughts and emotions" and propose changes to attitude or behavior to guide or help the confessor improve her- or himself. Participant 46 (female, 42-49), a social scientist conducting research in *SL*, describes how participant confessions were sometimes *too* intimate for her; for example concerning the confessions of a recently divorced man, she writes:

> *For me, the discomfort was in the level of intimacy I encountered ... like I had landed right in the middle of this very intimate real life situation and not by choice. What's odd to me is that this person didn't consider or perhaps wasn't aware of the entry way into this (to me) very private situation that the technology enabled.*

Anonymity in *SL* seems to have two, and apparently contradictory, meanings: it liberates users from responsibility (it's "just a game") and/or it actually places users under new codes of social obligation (e.g., confessions).

Transgressions, or, The (In)scrutibility of Conflicting Codes. Just as in real-life, where the roles of a mother as a parent conflicts with her role as a caregiver on a school outing when her child picks a fight with another child, so systems of governance blend and clash in *SL* experiences. One example of this can be seen in the practice of exploring one's body as a sexual instrument, developing a repertoire of sexual skills and sensibilities, a practice that most people engage in adolescence and which many *SL* users do again to learn about the erotic possibilities of their avatars. Moreover, this seemingly private practice is nonetheless political, because it is often felt to be transgressive and because evidence of its existence is often met with various forms of censure (e.g., mores against masturbation, expressed as derision or spiritual threat). Participant 152 (male, 18-25) summarizes his practice of exploring his virtual body as a sexual instrument playing different repertoires, writing,

> *My avatar has had threesomes, foursomes, been bound and flogged (didn't like that too much), tried out most pose balls, been bit by vampires, killed by orcs, harassed by angry lesbians (don't ask), just about anything but gay sex.* [Note: pose balls are small balls containing canned animations available in the world; most player-created sexual animations are deployed in-world as poseballs.]

This quote amounts to a list of avatar sensual experimentations: group sex, animated sex, vampiric blending of sex and pain, death, sexual ostracization, etc. Interestingly, this list contains two items—being bound and flogged and gay sex—that the participant does not like. He is more comfortable with his avatar being violently killed or vampirically corrupted than with his avatar having sex with another male avatar or taking a submissive position in sex. It is hard to overlook the fact that both of these items are excluded from traditional heterosexual constructions of masculinity: the freedoms of *SL* do not liberate him from caring for his avatar's manhood in physical world ways.

Some transgressive explorations of the sexual potential of the avatar go much farther, for example, the practice of "yiffing," or "furry sex," which is the practice of cybersex while in the form of animal avatars. Yiffing gestures toward social taboos against bestiality and creates experiences that are, as one participant put it, "quite risqué," though no actual animals are involved. Participant 195 (female, 58-65) offered this account of her experience as a furry:

> *My avatar is a female raccoon and I wear a tux. It was a dj and ball gown affair. There was a white fox at the club - male. He clearly did not realize I was a female until I pointed this out to him. We got very friendly after that, exchanging flirtatious IMs.*

This participant mixed codes (a human *SL* user presenting as an animal, a female wearing a tux, an animal wearing formal human clothing, etc.) to the point that her sexual availability to the male fox was not even perceptible to him—he had to be told verbally. Thus, as a potential intimate partner, she was inscrutable.

A similar problem arises from how *SL* users perceive the virtual body. Participant 167 (male, 18-25) writes, "*The difference is that virtually, you're at a distance. You're getting to know someone's mind faster, but the kinetic/body stuff is totally missing.*" In contrast, participant 136 (female, 50-57) shares a cybersex chat transcript including the following lines, "*I like the feel of your touch too ... the smell of your hair, the warmth of your breath on my lips, the softness of your skin as I caress your shoulders and arms.*" For participant 167, there is a categorical distinction between his physical body and the avatar body he is controlling. In contrast, 136 writes as though she inhabits her avatar body—she makes no distinction between her physical body and her avatar's—and she expects her partner to do the same. These views are logically incommensurable, and yet they often co-exist within the same accounts.

One of the governing factors of *SL* is that it makes possible a highly open-ended practice of combining and recombining codes of governance, and this sometimes yields intimate practices that have no physical world analogues. Optimistically, such practices contain the potential for *SL* users to invent new ways of being, or of being intimate—a profoundly Foucauldian and arguably also a designerly goal. But such practices can also result in both repugnant behaviors (e.g., virtual pedophilia) and also inscrutable behaviors (such as the tux-wearing female raccoon ready for romance) which can lead to misunderstandings among users that sometimes lead to real—not simulated—emotional pain.

The Care of the Self

The concept of governance focuses on extant conventions, norms, prohibitions, regulating forces, and so on—all of which exist independently of the individual, and all of which the individual has to reckon with to such a fundamental degree that, according to Foucault, the self is heavily constituted by it. But such a view might seem to deny individuals any individualism or agency. However, Foucault's theory proposes a powerful counterweight to the pressures of governance, and that is the possibility of exerting agency via one's responses to governance, and, more powerfully, the possibility of creatively stylizing such responses to governance over time: Foucault refers to this countervailing practice as "the care of the self."

Foucault notes that individuals have many forms of agency, even from positions within systems of governance. One can choose to resist or reject governance (albeit often with difficult consequences). One can choose among prescribed alternatives; for example, individuals are supposed to take care of their bodies, but whether they do so through regular bathing, bodybuilding, dieting, yoga, going for walks (and so on) provides quite a bit of room for choice. One can also *stylize* one's participation in such systems, that is, engage in the contingencies of governance systems in a consistently patterned way. For example, the punk is a stylized self: she or he appropriates certain attitudes toward authority and hegemony (e.g., resistance, contempt), specific fashion practices (e.g., Mohawks, spiked leather clothing), media consumption practices (e.g., punk music)—all from within (in the case of 1970s punks in the UK) the position of a young member of the English working class subject to diverse socioeconomic constraints [22].

Because of the complexities surrounding the care of the self, we will focus on a smaller number of longer quotes, but we nonetheless want to stress that while these may be the best quotes to use from an analytic perspective, nonetheless their sentiments are typical of a great number of responses; we are not choosing complete outliers.

Governed Agents, or, How Submitting to the Law Brings Pleasure and Meaning. Many of us intuitively feel that power and governance constrains us, that it alienates us from our true selves. Foucault offers a much more nuanced picture that, while still allowing that power can and does alienate, suggests that power is more systemic, pervasive, and more productive than our intuitive sensibility allows. In the first quote we analyze in this section, participant 163 (female, 50-57) recounts her experience trying out the role of a sex slave in a virtual sadomasochistic community.

> *I discovered that I responded to a particular male avatar who was playing the role of a Gorean Master by becoming aroused by the idea of playing the part of his slave. After talking about it and learning more I acted out submitting and being "collared" by my Master. I used animations to make my avatar kneel and assume an arms raised submissive position. We roleplayed the words of my submission and his placing the collar on my neck without too much rehearsal in advance. He removed my clothing and told me I would remain naked until he allowed me clothing again as I had to learn to be accessible and unguarded all the time. He then locked me in a chastity belt... gave me one in inventory that I then had to wear... and gave me to understand that only he had the key and he*

> *would use me if and when he chose and not before he chose. The roleplay of being collared was one of the most intimate I have experienced.*

We will analyze this in some detail, but we want to call attention to three key features of this passage: it is framed in terms of knowledge, i.e., what she learned; it is about her voluntarily becoming a sex slave through roleplay; and this process was an intensely "intimate" experience. Stated in another way, being *subjected to* a governance structure (i.e., sexual slavery) has both epistemological and experiential consequences that she is the *subject of.* Epistemologically, she becomes the subject of new self-knowledge, specifically, about her own erotic capabilities as well as what it means to roleplay a sex slave. Experientially, she becomes the subject of a privately felt and very intense experience of intimacy.

The passage also bears a number of striking grammatical features. In the first half, she is the subject of all the verbs: "I discovered … responded … [was] becoming aroused … [was] talking and learning about [slavery] … acted out … used animations." It is hard to miss how active she is in doing what it takes to make this happen. But after the midpoint (hinging not coincidentally on a verb with two subjects: "We roleplayed"), her partner is the logical or grammatical subject of nearly all of the verbs: "He removed my clothing … told me … allowed me … I had to … He then locked … gave me … when he chose." After the line, "we roleplayed," she has become subjected to the governance system of the roleplay sex slave. Put another way, in the first half, she is not a slave at all (as her strong agency clearly demonstrates); in the second half she has entered into a new subject role, and this entry into subjecthood is emotionally powerful and authentic for her.

We see another striking difference between the two halves: in the first half, she and her avatar are distinct: "I acted out submitting … I used animations to make my avatar kneel." But after she enters the subject position of the slave, her body merges with her avatar: "his placing the collar on my neck … He removed my clothing … He then locked me in a chastity belt." This is evidence of her individual or felt subjectivity, which fluidly moves from the subject position of a virtual world user manipulating an avatar to the subject position of a sex slave, a movement facilitated by the highly individuated avatar design practices prevalent in SL's toolset and user culture. Interestingly, the more immersive position—the one that merges user and avatar into a single indivisible entity—is the one that emerges as a result of placing herself into an external system of governance.

Foucault claims that the care of the self requires the self-conscious knowledge of one's participation in various forms of external governance. Once aware that one is governed, one can decide what sort of governed subject one wants to be; lacking that awareness at all is to be in a powerless state of alienation. In this example, a woman in her 50s experimentally places herself in an extreme subject position—it is quite clear that this is an informed and self-conscious decision—and that doing so brings her feelings and experiences that she has never had before. If nothing else, this narrative complicates the emancipatory narratives found in much design research, not, obviously, because of the slavery (which is merely simulated in erotic roleplay sessions), but rather because emancipation is frequently framed in terms of liberation from governance; however, in this example emancipation is better characterized as voluntarily entering into a system of governance on one's own terms. The issue, then, isn't governance itself but rather how one has entered into it, and how participation is enacted and experienced by individuals subjected to it.

***Askēsis*, or, The Labored and Progressive Consideration of the Self**. One of the central tenets of Foucault's thought is his rejection of the notion of a pre-given, transcendent, "true" self. Again, our purpose is not to evaluate this notion as philosophy, but to consider pragmatically how it helps us think or what it helps us do. As design researchers, this idea appeals to us because it leaves plenty of room for individuals to change, to grow, and also for themselves to have a say in how they do that. Such moments of self-cultivation seem to be very powerful, and a design approach that seeks to facilitate them has a certain appeal. However, all of this is very abstract. What does it really look like, with actual people using an actual system? In this section, we present two such examples.

First is the example of "Z," a *SL* user going through a life transition as summarized by participant 144 (male, 50-57):

> *The most compelling example [of an intimacy experience] I can recall was when Z revealed to me that she is a transwoman going through her transition. Z had dropped hints that she was a lesbian, involved in a long-term RL relationship, but the revelation of her transgender status was a huge statement of trust in me. Clearly, Z had … been testing my tolerance for deviance from the norm and for discretion. I was rather speechless when Z told me; first by the revelation itself, and secondly by the level of trust implied. I have known Z [for 2 years]. During most of that time, I was totally unaware that her avatar's appearance w/respect to gender did not match her RL appearance. In another way, I am not surprised though, because her avatar matches who she IS inside. And who she is striving to become.*

In a culture where transgender is systemically considered a transgressive form of deviance (and harsh forms of repression remain politically sanctioned), Z's carefully managed identity performance reveals "the complex interrelationship between desire, sex, and power" [14, p.85]. Z is extremely skilled at using available choices to build up her confidence in the participant and to come out to him. She displays both the social skill to "drop hints" and to "test his tolerance for deviance … and for discretion" and also the SL skill to express "who she IS inside" and "who she is striving to become" through the design and performance of her avatar.

The intermingling of political power, self-expression, and the careful staging of "coming out" is perceived by the speaker as an enactment of trust and thus intimacy. It is possible in the physical world that Z cannot (or does not want to) "pass" as a woman, but she can in *SL* and does. Stated in more Foucauldian terms, Z's gender transition mediated through *SL*'s avatar design and performance tools helps her invent new ways of relating to others, and new ways of experiencing her gender, that are neither the same as nor superimposed on existing cultural practices. Her participation in *SL*—in which she presents herself publicly as female and only selectively as trans female—is a choice she has made within the contingency of her situation to work through her transition.

The final example we present is the account of participant 203 (male, 34-41), whose progressive consideration of himself was far less deliberate than Z's and much more dependent on a surprising situation he put himself in:

> *I was very curious about cybering. I hadn't ever done it and ... I decided to give it a shot. I logged in with a female avatar because I figured it would be easier to find a partner... The sex chat itself was also a great deal more pornographic than i expected. It was very much an aggressive male fantasy he was creating. I actually felt a little used and a little dirty (not in a good way).... [He] talked about how he was masturbating IRL which I hadn't expected and freaked me out a little. He offered to exchange pictures which freaked me out even more...On a different level, I was also thinking that maybe I was experiencing a sexual encounter from a female perspective and felt a little ashamed of my usual male sexuality, how maybe it is not as different from this guys as I wish it was. I also surprised at how I adopted (i guess?) a female perspective, tolerating things i didnt want to do in the face of his intensity, suffering a transition from his sexual partner to his sexual object. But to be fair it was also pleasant in a way to be wanted like that. The point I am making is that it was very intense, it felt a little out of control, and I had very mixed feelings about it.*

This account, as with the slave example, is framed by connecting a will to knowledge ("I was curious about cybering") to voluntary subjection to a system of governance ("I decided to give [cybersex] a shot"). However, with a casualness that would come back to bite him, he also chose to subject himself to the governing conditions of a female sex partner, "because I figured it would be easier to find a partner." He appears not to have anticipated the consequences of either of these voluntary self-subjections (i.e., to the discursive practice of cybersex or to doing so presenting as a female). The passage details his experiences of and reflections on the consequences of each of these choices.

The first of his voluntary subjections—to the discursive practice of cybersex—surprises him because he and his partner produced a discourse other than what he expected, and also because he had less control over it than he expected. He realizes that the discursive gender conventions of pornography, along with associated practices of masturbation, serve as source scripts for cybersex discourse, and he has become subjected to those scripts as well. These discoveries are all accompanied by very strong feelings: he expresses a sense of surprise, feeling unclean and even violated: instances include his partner's description of his physical world masturbation, the partner's offer to share real-life erotic photos, and (not included in this excerpt) the partner's unexpected and non-consensual switch to anal intercourse in the text chat.

The second of participant 203's voluntary subjections—to the governance of the female sex partner—also generates new knowledge, feelings, and reflections. No longer seeing a female avatar merely as a ticket to getting laid, he now perceives what it is like to play the role of the woman in the script of a pornographic male fantasy. It is such an alien experience for him—the lack of control, the sense of "tolerating things I didnt want to do," performing sex acts in the face of his partner's "intensity," being construed as another's "sexual object." All of these aspects of his experience he links together and speculates that it all adds up to having "a sexual encounter from a female perspective." But this is no abstract speculation, because he turns these discoveries reflexively back on himself: "I felt a little ashamed of my usual male sexuality, how maybe it is not as different from this guys as I wish it was." He begins to implicate himself in subjecting women to such a script.

In short, by subjecting himself to two systems of governance (those of cybersex and female sex partner), he discovered that he was a subject of a third system of governance—the misogynistic male fantasy—that he had not been so vividly aware of before. This discovery is "intense," "a little out of control," and the source of "mixed feelings" and yet also "pleasant in a way": it was a struggle, but perhaps ultimately a fulfilling one. Foucault characterizes such struggle as an *askēsis*, which is the notion that the assimilation of truth, which connects one to everyday life, leads to a progressive consideration of oneself and demands that one change oneself in response to it. The speaker of this passage, like Z, can be seen to be caught up in an *askēsis*, where new ways of being and relations to others are tried out as strategies of self-cultivation.

MOSTLY GRAMMATICAL AVATARS

What are designers or design researchers to make of all this? Batterbee and Koskinen write, "the purpose of paying attention to co-experience is not so much about saying what the future product or system should be like in its details. Rather, it is about providing a more sensitive description of the social phenomena to inform designing technology" [4, p.475]. In other words, the goal is not to produce implications for design but rather to enrich the perspective from which we design. We have sought, through such a sensitive description, to understand human experiences as they have (partly) been designed, where identity, sexuality, sociability, pleasure, politics, knowledge acquisition, self-care, and so forth are not analytically isolated from one another but rather viewed from within these entanglements.

The central idea involves an encounter between an individual who is feeling, intending, and performing on the one hand and systems of social governance, of which the software system is one, on the other. Governance structures are like a grammar—a generative rule system—that specifies what can and cannot be said, what should and should not be said. Yet people nonetheless actively use those grammars to create their own social meanings. Some performances merely haven't ever been done before, while others not only haven't been done before but also transgress or invent new grammars that hadn't existed before. For example, a user can design a unique avatar in *SL* without changing the grammar of avatars. But when a user figures out a way to create a "furry"—that is, to subvert the humanoid assumptions built into the avatar design system and disseminate a viable alternative—the system has been expanded to incorporate a whole new avatar design vocabulary.

Compared to most other virtual worlds, *SL*'s avatar design system is vastly more flexible, and that flexibility became a crucial part of its user culture, as witnessed by its thriving virtual fashion industry. Users with default avatars are instantly recognizable as "noobs," so the social pressure to become an "expert amateur" [28] at least of avatar design in this world is very high. Avatar design in *SL* seems to be a powerful example of what Foucault calls a "technology of the self," that is, a sanctioned set of tools offered by the system of governance (in this case *SL*) to its subjects for their own self-care. In other words, user's sense of self and their avatar design practices are intertwined, if not in a literal way (i.e., designing an avatar to look just like one's physical world body), then in a deeper sense, as 144 wrote of Z: "her avatar matches who she IS inside."

Individuals subjected to any grammar of governance can be understood as a "speaker," or an "avatar," within that governance, that is, as a personal manifestation within that system, which has certain agencies, constraints, rights, and responsibilities. In other words, not only do *SL* users have *SL* avatars, defined in the technical sense that the system provides, but they also have avatars defined in relation to each system of governance they are subjected to in-world. For example, users have avatars in the gender system of governance: one must be male, female, or (more recently: trans), but in a personally individuated way, not a generic way. Thus, Z, a physical world trans woman, presents in *SL* at times as a woman and at other times as a trans woman. Participant 203, a physical world male, presented as a female in *SL* in order to more easily find a cybersex partner. *SL* users subjected themselves to other systems of governance: to practices of group sex, sexual slavery, and yiffing and in each case they were present as avatars of those social governance systems. They also subjected themselves to systems of verbal practices, in particular anonymized confession (where they became avatar manifestations of the confessor or the confessee) and cybersex chat (where they became avatars of a loosely scripted collaborative verbal performance of cybersex). And, as we have seen, users combine, stylize, and perform these on the fly (e.g., the date-seeking, tux-wearing female raccoon at the ball).

This understanding of avatar is known in the philosophical literature as a *subject* because it is that which is *subjected to* a system of governance and the *subject of* the experiences, agencies, and performances of the individual inhabiting it. Many of these avatars or subjects that we've explored here are provisional roles that SL users inhabit for pleasure, to learn and to explore. In some cases, they do so as tourists (i.e., to visit someplace new with the intention of going back home as before), such as the user who said she feels no remorse about her fling. But others never "go back home"; that is, they have changed perceptions of themselves; for example, the male participant who presented in-world as a woman to make it easier to try out cybersex seems to have learned something surprising about himself that demanded his reflection and possible change.

Complicatedly, as our data revealed, the avatar is always already both part of the felt experience of selfhood and also a simulated and separate extension of that experienced self: participant 163 is a user making her *avatar* kneel and raise her arms, but later she *herself* is stripped and placed in a chastity belt. We saw this shift over and over again in the data. And this happened not just in the *SL* avatar in the software sense, but also in all of the avatars we have described. This ambiguity between the avatar as self and as not-self can be really powerful in supporting profoundly creative practices—i.e., those that lead to the invention of new ways of being and relating to others by creating sufficient cover for people to put themselves (and/or their avatars) in extreme situations with (sometimes) profound, moving, and even life-altering results, as in the case of the trans woman who, according to participant 144, both *already is* a woman and *is becoming* a woman. But the ambiguity can also lead to negative experiences, including intimacies forced on others (as we saw both with the social scientist as confessee and the cybersex explorer offered real-life pictures) as well as intimacies violated (e.g., when users relating to each other with one set of norms, say, the commitments implied in monogamy, suddenly switch to another, e.g., by saying that "it's just a game").

We want to stress once again that the majority of our participants were not impressionable teens, but people who have been married, raised children, worked as professionals for decades, etc. In other words, their creative intimate practices are mature, experienced, and above all *skilled. SL* as a system didn't "cause" these intimate practices ex nihilo. But neither were these practices (in their final specificity) "in" the users, as predefined needs, simply waiting for a system that could give them expression. Rather, *SL* provided a particular regulatory infrastructure (e.g., its powerful avatar design system) in which these individuals could emergently and reflexively deploy themselves as avatar-subjects in new—in many cases extreme—situations, to discover their own limits, to face their own (often taboo) desires, to progressively consider themselves, and to learn new ways of being and relating to others.

CONCLUSION

We have presented a critical and empirical study of intimacy in *SL*, having analyzed user accounts of their intimate experiences in relation to two high-level modes of subjectification, as theorized by the work of philosopher Michel Foucault: governance and the care of the self. This theory provided us with a conceptual scaffold to help us read this data "sensitively" [4], that is, to insightfully perceive technology-mediated intimacy without abstracting it away from the related concepts of selfhood, embodiment, sociability, politics, and creative self-expression.

As a research field, HCI is taking up notions of creative collectives, appropriation, the expert amateur, everyday design, craft, and cultures of making. As we have demonstrated, the intimate experiences that our participants reported unfolded *within* such practices: for example, designing a compelling *SL* avatar is the work (or craft) of an expert amateur, as are creative practices of virtual confession, gender performance, and cybersex. So intimacy is not a private feeling divorced from such practices but rather one that arises by engaging such practices in a socially connected way. In other words, designing to support social creativity and designing intimate social experiences are not separate problems or HCI specialties, but different faces of the same thing: social creative practices often unfold in intimate experiences; conversely, being intimate with others often demands skilled creativity (e.g., of self-presentation).

Our analysis adds to these discourses additional nuances surrounding the notion of pleasure, because what our participants characterized as pleasurable was often morally ambiguous, emotionally risky, and aesthetically dark. It also suggests additional nuances to design notions of emancipation (often raised in HCI discourses on or about democratization), mainly because our analysis frames emancipation as the stylized subjection to, and not as the release from, systems (or grammars) of governance. It has also demonstrated the inseparability of aesthetics and politics: aesthetic stylizations of the self often entail strong political positions and consequences; these issues cannot be treated as distinct.

The practical difficulty surrounding this work is that perceptive insights and understandings about such experiences demand skills and sensitivities that participants may not have and therefore may not be able to express. Worse, if Batterbee and Koskinen are correct, many designers may lack these skills and sensitivities, too. Our reading, informed by a decades-long engagement with Foucault's philosophy, is intended as a self-standing study about the ways that agency and constraint, intimacy and sociability, and governance and the self were experienced with and through social technologies and articulated by our participants. But we also hope that the analytical approach, both in its data collection strategy (based on the phenomenological intimacy research of Register & Henry) and its data analysis strategy (i.e., reading user accounts in relation to subjectivity, comprising systems of governance and practices of self care) serves as a practical resource that other designers can also adapt in their practice as a way of cultivating their sensitivities to the intricacies of technology-mediated social experiences.

ACKNOWLEDGMENTS

This research was funded by NSF IIS Creative IT (#1002772) and the Intel Science and Technology Center for Social Computing. We also thank Olav Bertelsen, Erik Stolterman, and our anonymous reviewers.

REFERENCES

1. Bardzell, J., & Bardzell, S. (2011). Pleasure is your birthright: Digitally enabled designer sex toys as a case of third-wave HCI. In *Proc CHI'11*. ACM, 257-266.
2. Bardzell, S., & Bardzell, J. (2007). Docile avatars: Aesthetics, experience, and sexual interaction in Second Life. In *Proc. BCS HCI'07*. British Computer Society.
3. Bardzell, S., & Odom, W. (2008). The experience of embodied space in virtual worlds: An ethnography of a Second Life community. *Space and Culture*, *11*(3), 239-259.
4. Batterbee, K. & Koskinen, I. Co-experience: Product experience as social interaction. In Schifferstein & Hekkert (eds.), *Product Experience*. Elsevier, 461-476.
5. Baym, N. (2010). *Personal connections in the digital age: Digital media and society*. Cambridge, UK: Polity.
6. Bell, G., Blythe, M., & Sengers, P. (2005). Making by making strange: Defamiliarization and the design of domestic technologies. *ACM Transactions on Computer-Human Interaction (TOCHI)*, *12*(2), 149-173.
7. Bertelsen, O. W., & Petersen, M. G. (2007). Erotic life as a new frontier in HCI. In *Proc. BCS HCI'07*. British Computer Society.
8. Bhandari, S., & Bardzell, S. (2008). Bridging gaps: Affective communication in long distance relationships. In *CHI'08 EA*. New York: ACM, 2763-2768.
9. Boellstorff, T. (2008). *Coming of age in second life: An anthropologist explores the virtually human.* Princeton: Princeton UP.
10. Brewer, J., Kaye, J. J., Williams, A., & Wyche, S. (2006). Sexual interactions: why we should talk about sex in HCI. In *CHI'06 EA*. New York, ACM, 1695-1698
11. Bucholtz, M., & Hall, K. (2004). Theorizing identity in language and sexuality research. *Language in Society*, *33*(4), 469-516.

12. Croon Fors, A. (2013). The ontology of the subject in digitalization. In R. Luppicini (Ed.), *Handbook of research on technoself: Identity in a technological society*. Hershey, PA: Information Science Reference, 45-63.
13. Eissler, K. R. (1958). Problems of identity. *Journal of the American Psychoanalytic Association*, *6*, 131-142.
14. Elliott, A. (2007). *Concepts of the Self*. Malden, MA: Polity.
15. Foucault, M. (1990). *The History of Sexuality*. Three vols. Trans. Robert Hurley. Vintage.
16. Foucault, M. (1989 [1984]). *Foucault Live*. S. Lotringer (Ed.). New York: Semiotext(e).
17. Giddens, A. (1992). *The transformation of intimacy: Sexuality, love, and eroticism in modem societies*. Stanford, CA: Stanford University Press.
18. Goodman, E., & Rosner, D. 2011. From garments to gardens: negotiating material relationships online and 'by hand'. *Proc. CHI'11*. New York: ACM, 2257-2266.
19. Goodman, E., & Vertesi, J. 2012. Design for X?: distribution choices and ethical design. In *CHI '12 EA*. New York: ACM, 81-90.
20. Hall, S. (1996). Who needs identity. *Questions of cultural identity*, *16*(2), 1-17.
21. Hassenzahl, M., Heidecker, S., Eckoldt, K., Diefenbach, S., & Hillmann, U. (2012). All You Need is Love: Current Strategies of Mediating Intimate Relationships through Technology. *ACM TOCHI 19*(4), Article 30.
22. Hebdige, D. (1979). *Subcultures: The Meaning of Style*. Routledge.
23. Howard, S., Vetere, F., Gibbs, M., Kjeldskov, J., Pedell, S., Mecoles, K., Bunyan, M., & Murphy, J. (2004). Mediating Intimacy: digital kisses and cut and paste hugs. In *Proc. CHI'04*. New York: ACM.
24. Kaye, J. J., Levitt, M. K., Nevins, J., Golden, J., & Schmidt, V. (2005). Communicating intimacy one bit at a time. In *Proc. CHI'05*. New York: ACM, 1529-1532.
25. Kannabiran, G., Bardzell, J., & Bardzell, S. (2011). How HCI talks about sexuality: discursive strategies, blind spots, and opportunities for future research. In *Proc. CHI'11*. New York: ACM, 695-704.
26. Koefoed Hansen, L., & Kozel, S. (2007). Embodied imagination: a hybrid method of designing for intimacy. *Digital Creativity*, *18*(4), 207-220.
27. Kolotkin, R., Williams, M., Lloyd, C., & Hallford, E. (2012). Does loving an avatar threaten real life marriage? *Journal of Virtual Worlds Research*, *5*(3).
28. Kuznetsov, S. and Paulos, E. Rise of the expert amateur: DIY projects, communities, and cultures. *Proc. of NordiCHI 2010,* ACM Press (2010), 295-304.
29. Lichtenstein, H. (1977). *The dilemma of human identity*. New York: Jason Aronson.
30. Light, A. (2011). HCI as heterodoxy: Technologies of identity and the queering of interaction with computers. *Interacting with Computers*, *23*(5), 430-438.
31. Nakamura, L. (2002). *Cybertypes: Race, Ethnicity, and Identity on the Internet*. Routledge.
32. Malaby, T. M. (2007). Contriving constraints (the gameness of Second Life and the persistence of scarcity). *Innovations: Technology, Governance, Globalization*, *2*(3), 62-67.
33. McCarthy, J., & Wright, P. (2004). *Technology as experience*. Cambridge, MA: The MIT Press.
34. Meadows, M. (2008). *I, avatar: The culture and consequences of having a second life*. Berkeley, CA: New Riders.
35. Ogden, C. K., & Richards, I. A. (1923). *The meaning of meaning*. New York: Mariner Books.
36. Pace, T. Bardzell, J., and Bardzell, S.. (2010). The rogue in the lovely black dress: Intimacy in World of Warcraft. *Proc. CHI'10*. New York: ACM, 233-242.
37. Person, E. S. (1980). Sexuality as the mainstay of identity: Psychoanalytic perspectives. *Signs*, *5*(4), 605-630.
38. Register, L. M., & Henley, T. B. (1992). The phenomenology of intimacy. *Journal of Social and Personal Relationships*, *9*(4), 467-481.
39. Robinson, L. (2007). The cyberself: The self-ing project goes online, symbolic interaction in the digital age. *New Media & Society*, *9*(1), 93–110.
40. Ross, M. W. (2005). Typing, doing, and being: Sexuality and the Internet. *Journal of sex research*, *42*(4), 342-352.
41. Russon, J. (2003). *Human experience: Philosophy, neurosis, and the elements of everyday life*. Albany: State University of New York Press.
42. Schiphorst, T., et al. (2007). PillowTalk: Can we afford intimacy? *Proc. TEI'07*. New York: ACM, 23-30.
43. Subrahmanyam, K., Greenfield, P. M., & Tynes, B. (2004). Constructing sexuality and identity in an online teen chat room. *Journal of Applied Developmental Psychology*, *25*(6), 651-666.
44. Vetere, F., Gibbs, M. R., Kjeldskov, J., Howard, S., Mueller, F. F., Pedell, S., Mecoles, K., & Bunyan, M. (2005). Mediating intimacy: designing technologies to support strong-tie relationships. In Proc. CHI'05. New York: ACM, 471-480.
45. Tanenbaum, J., Tanenbaum, K., Wakkary, R. Steampunk as design fiction. *Proc. of CHI 2012*, ACM Press (2012), 1583-1592.
46. Zimmerman, J. (2009). Designing for the self: making products that help people become the person they desire to be. In *Proc. CHI'09*. New York: ACM, 395-404.

Room for Interpretation: The Role of Self-Esteem and CMC in Romantic Couple Conflict

Lauren Scissors, Michael E. Roloff, Darren Gergle
Northwestern University
2240 Campus Drive, Evanston, IL 60208 USA
{l-scissors, m-roloff, dgergle}@northwestern.edu

ABSTRACT
This work explores the role of communication technologies during romantic couple conflict, and the impact that self-esteem has on behavior, preferences for communication channels, and attitudes about mediated communication during conflict. Results revealed that lower levels of self-esteem and communicating via text messaging (vs. face-to-face) were associated with increased distancing and perceived partner distancing behaviors. Lower levels of self-esteem and using mediated communication were also associated with a greater likelihood of thinking that a conflict had a negative impact on the relationship. Yet, there was no evidence to suggest that individuals with lower levels of self-esteem exhibited more negative behaviors and perceptions in text-based communication than in FtF communication. In addition, lower levels of self-esteem were associated with increased use of and preferences for text-based mediated communication over FtF communication during conflict. Overall, this study suggests that both self-esteem and communication channel impact the nature of romantic couple conflict.

Author Keywords
Self-esteem; conflict; computer-mediated communication (CMC); romantic couples; relationships; CSCW

ACM Classification Keywords
H.5.m. Information interfaces and presentation (e.g., HCI): Miscellaneous.

INTRODUCTION
Relationships can enrich our lives in many ways; however, they are not always rosy. Conflict is inevitable in romantic relationships, and how partners handle conflict can greatly impact relational outcomes (see [20] for a review) and mental and physical well-being [9]. Yet, the vast majority of our understanding of romantic couple conflict is based on conflicts that occur face-to-face (FtF).

Recent studies indicate, however, that couples use a host of communication technologies for managing conflicts (e.g., [5], [23]). Given the myriad differences between mediated and FtF communication, communication channel likely influences the nature of romantic couple conflict. In addition, it is important to remember that individuals utilize and experience communication channels in different ways. For instance, imagine that you texted your partner but your partner took a while to respond. You may conclude that there is a reasonable explanation for the delay, but another individual might immediately think the worst of their partner. This example highlights the fact that CMC can be more ambiguous than FtF communication since communicators are not co-located and certain nonverbal social cues like facial expressions, body language, and tone of voice are not typically transmitted (see [18] for a discussion). This ambiguity may be particularly salient for individuals who are prone to negative interpretations.

In fact, being biased toward negative interpretations of a partner's communication and behavior is a key attribute of individuals with low self-esteem (LSEs). Self-esteem is a trait that plays a significant role in romantic relationships, particularly in threatening contexts like conflict, with lower levels of self-esteem being associated with a number of harmful relational behaviors (e.g., [1], [14]). While LSEs' insecurities may cause them to prefer using technology during conflicts in order to distance themselves from potentially hurtful behavior, it may be that individuals' negative biases are actually *heightened* when communicating through technology, since there is more room for interpretation of a partner's behavior.

The goals of this paper are to understand how self-esteem and communication channel impact the nature of couple conflict. More specifically, we aim to investigate how self-esteem and communication channel impact one's behavior and perception of one's partner's behavior during conflict, perception of how the conflict impacts the relationship, and overall preferences and experiences during conflict with one's romantic partner. These investigations will increase our understanding of how technologies impact relational partners' abilities to communicate and carry out relationship work.

CHI 2014, April 26 - May 01 2014, Toronto, ON, Canada
Copyright 2014 ACM 978-1-4503-2473-1/14/04$15.00.
http://dx.doi.org/10.1145/2556288.2557177

RELATED WORK

Self-Esteem and Romantic Relationships

Previous research has demonstrated that LSEs tend to have trouble in their romantic relationships [15]. LSEs are biased toward negative interpretations of their partners' behavior and are sensitive to feelings of threat and rejection. A key component in how LSEs function in their close relationships has to do with how they interpret communication and behavior from their partners. Murray and colleagues found that LSEs "read too much into problems" with their partners, interpreting the problems as signs of fading feelings or commitment [16], p.256. Furthermore, LSEs over-interpret their dating partners' negative moods, internalizing responsibility and hurt feelings when the cause of the mood was actually ambiguous [1]. This line of work suggests that LSEs tend to overanalyze situations with their partners, and tend to believe the worst in ambiguous situations.

When faced with potential threats, LSEs distance themselves from or behave badly towards their partners in order to derogate the relationship and preserve their sense of self ([10],[14],[16]). In fact, LSEs' "oversensitivity to rejection manifests in defensive behaviors that ... undermine the well-being of the relationship" [10], p.232. These "distancing behaviors" (see [6]) can be harmful to relationships. Alternatively, individuals with high self-esteem (HSEs) tend to be less sensitive to relationship threats and actually draw closer to their partners in these situations [16]. The fact that they feel self-assured likely helps HSEs to diminish threats or signs of rejection in order to focus on the positive aspects of the relationship. It is unclear, however, how common these distancing behaviors are across different communication channels.

CMC, Relationships, and Conflict

As computer-mediated communication and other text-based technologies proliferated, scholars began to examine technology's role in couple conflict. A 2010 study found that nearly two-thirds of participants had used a mediated channel (e.g., text messaging, phone, instant messenger (IM), social network sites (SNS), email) during a conflict with their partner, with text messaging and phone being the most common [5]. Moreover, a 2013 market research report found that 30% of 16- to 24-year-olds and 12% of adults in the UK felt it was acceptable to have an argument via private text-based communications [17]. Another study demonstrated that, in some cases, individuals make more positive partner attributions when communicating about a conflict via CMC than when communicating FtF [24].

Yet, there are also drawbacks to using CMC during conflict. For instance, Burge and Tatar found that couples discussing a conflict via mediated communication (phone and IM) may experience significantly lower mood states than couples who communicated FtF [2]. Another study found that when individuals choose email (over FtF) to discuss a conflict, they perceive their partners and themselves as more avoidant [12]. In addition, Coyne and colleagues found that using text messaging to discuss serious issues or broach a potentially confrontational topic with one's partner was associated with increased levels of negative communication in the relationship overall [3]. Using CMC is typically thought of as a convenient way to avoid or ignore one's communication partner in face-threatening situations like conflict (e.g., [11],[18]), since lack of immediacy and reduced cues provide more opportunities for ambiguity. Studies have also found that relational tensions can arise about the use of technologies themselves (e.g., [26]). Scissors and Gergle, however, found that there were both benefits and drawbacks to using CMC during couple conflict [23]. They also found that while some individuals preferred to use CMC during conflict, others preferred FtF communication [23]. Yet, this study was based on interviews and did not systematically explore attitudes and behaviors in mediated couple conflict, nor did it uncover what personality variables might be associated with the variance in preferences for technology during conflict.

CMC, Relationships, and Self-Esteem

A handful of studies have investigated the connection between self-esteem and CMC in relationships. Ehrenberg and colleagues found that lower levels of self-esteem were associated with increased time spent using IM and stronger IM addictive tendencies, though these results were not detected for text messaging and talking on the phone [4]. In a 2004 study, Joinson found that, in hypothetical situations involving interpersonal risk or face-threat (e.g., asking for a pay raise, asking for a date), LSEs showed a stronger preference for email and weaker preference for FtF communication compared to HSEs [8]. Since LSEs are more sensitive to negative feedback, it may be that the separation CMC provides acts as a "buffer" [18] that makes LSEs feel more secure in threatening situations. In addition, the distance and visual anonymity that CMC provides likely makes it easier for LSEs to enact their self-protection strategies. Although these findings suggest that LSEs are drawn to mediated communication in risky interpersonal situations, the current work expands on Joinson's study by specifically looking at conflict and by exploring additional channels (IM, SNS and text messaging) along with the previously explored channels (FtF, email, and phone). We also analyze actual situations with relational partners, as opposed to hypothetical scenarios.

In another study of individuals in dating relationships, increased frequency of text messaging was associated with more positive relationships for highly avoidant participants but not for less avoidant participants [13]. (Avoidance is a dimension of attachment anxiety, a trait that plays a similar role to self-esteem in romantic relationships.) In addition, greater use of SNS was associated with increased levels of intimacy and support in relationships for anxiously attached participants but not for securely attached participants [13]. These findings suggest that the use of text-based communication may lead to positive relational outcomes for people who feel insecure in their relationships. This work, however, did not focus specifically on self-esteem or conflict. It may be that given the heightened emotional states, feelings of threat, and potential impact of a conflict on the relationship that these findings may be different in the context of conflict communication.

Theoretical Motivation

Since text-based communication does not require individuals to be co-present, it may be easier to disengage from conversation in text-based CMC than in FtF communication. The increased ambiguity of CMC may make individuals feel more distant from their partners, even if their partners are not purposefully avoiding them. This suggests that conflicts that occur in CMC may be experienced as more negative than conflicts that occur FtF.

Given that LSEs are prone to interpreting their partners' communication and behavior negatively in ambiguous contexts, it stands to reason that the more ambiguous the context, the more room for (mis)interpretation. And since text-based communication transmits fewer social cues (e.g., tone of voice, body language, facial expressions) that help individuals interpret communication, we argue that LSEs' biases will be heightened in CMC. In other words, the effects of self-esteem on various behaviors and interpretations should be stronger in CMC than FtF. In fact, Walther's Hyperpersonal model of communication posits that, in CMC, all individuals are prone to "making exaggerated attributions based on limited information" [19], p.216. Walther theorizes that individuals "decode text-based cues" and "encode relational messages" in the process of forming an impression of their communication partner and managing their relationship, and that they may do so in biased ways [25], p.67. Therefore, although mediated environments might lead LSEs to focus more strongly on the negative, the lack of nonverbal cues may help to further bolster HSEs' ability to ignore relationship threats and focus on their partners' past caring actions.

Research Questions and Hypotheses

Distancing Behaviors

Because LSEs are more likely to distance themselves from their partner under threat, and because mediated communication may make it easier to avoid communicating with one's partner, we predict:

H1a: Lower levels of self-esteem will be associated with increased distancing behaviors during conflict.

H1b: Distancing behaviors will be more likely to occur in text-based CMC than in FtF communication.

Theories of CMC suggest that mediated communication has more ambiguity than FtF communication, which may leave more room for interpretation, leading biases to be enhanced. Because these enhanced biases may then lead LSEs to draw away from their partners, we predict:

H1c: Lower levels of self-esteem will be more strongly associated with distancing behaviors in text-based CMC than in FtF communication.

Perceived Partner Distancing Behaviors

In addition to exploring participants' distancing behavior, we also examine the *perceptions* participants have of their *partners'* distancing behavior. Because LSEs are more likely to have negative interpretations of their partners' behavior, and because mediated communication makes it easier to avoid communicating with one's partner we predict:

H2a: Lower levels of self-esteem will be associated with a greater likelihood of perceiving partner distancing behaviors.

H2b: Partner distancing behaviors will be more likely to be perceived in text-based CMC than in FtF communication.

Because mediated communication has more room for interpretation than FtF communication, which may enhance biases, we predict:

H2c: Lower levels of self-esteem will be more strongly associated with perceiving partner distancing behaviors in text-based CMC than in FtF communication.

Perceived Impact of Conflict on Relationship

We also examine how conflicts impact participants' subsequent impressions of their relationships. Because LSEs are biased toward negative interpretations, we predict:

H3a: Lower levels of self-esteem will be associated with more negative assessments of the conflict's impact on the relationship.

Though previous research findings are mixed, because using CMC during conflict is associated with multiple negative outcomes (e.g., [2], [3], [12]), we predict:

H3b: Conflicts in mediated communication will be associated with more negative assessments of the conflict's impact on the relationship than will FtF conflicts.

Because LSE's negative interpretations may be stronger in more ambiguous communication channels, we predict:

H3c: Lower levels of self-esteem will be more strongly associated with negative assessments of the conflict's impact on the relationship for conflicts in mediated communication than for FtF conflicts.

Preferences and Overall Behavior

Lastly, we examine individuals' preferences for and use of CMC during conflict with their partners in general. Because LSEs tend to prefer CMC over FtF communication for a variety of reasons, we predict that:

H4a: Lower levels of self-esteem will be associated with stronger preferences for text-based CMC over FtF during conflict.

H4b: Lower levels of self-esteem will be associated with a greater likelihood of using text-based CMC over FtF during conflict.

METHOD

Participants

Participants (N = 182) were students and community members of a Midwestern, midsized university and were recruited via flyers and listservs. Some participants (26%) were from a student subject pool, for which they were required to participate in research for course credit; 74% were non-subject pool participants. Seventy-three percent of participants were female (27% male). Age ranged from 18 to 64, (M = 21.9).[1] Forty-nine percent of participants were Caucasian (6% African-American, 28% Asian/ Pacific Islander, 5% Hispanic/Latino (non-white), 10.4% Mixed Race/ Other; 2% missing). The majority (164) of participants' partners were of the opposite sex and 8 participants' partners were of the same sex. Individuals were prevented from participating if they had never been in a romantic relationship.

Eighty-six percent of participants reported on a current relationship and 14% reported on a past relationship. Thirty-one percent reported on a long-distance relationship and 69% reported on a non-long-distance relationship (1 missing). The majority (69%) of participants were "seriously dating" their partners (23% "casually dating", 3% "engaged", 4% "married"; 1% missing). In addition, 86% were not cohabitating with their partners and 14% of participants were cohabitating. Relationship length ranged from 1 to 360 months (30 years), (M= 19.4 months).

Procedure

Participants completed an online survey and were asked to report on a current romantic relationship. If they were not currently in a romantic relationship, they could report on a past romantic relationship. Upon completion, participants were either awarded course credit (if they participated as part of the subject pool) or a virtual $10 Amazon gift card.

Participants filled out a series of questions about themselves and their relationship. Then, participants were asked to describe the most recent conflict they had with their partner in which a communication technology such as texting, email, or IM was used to communicate in some capacity. Participants could report on a conflict where only one technology was used, where multiple technologies were used, or where technology and FtF communication were both used. If participants never engaged in a conflict where technology was used, they reported on the most recent conflict that occurred during FtF communication. They were then asked a series of questions about the conflict, including questions about which technologies were used and when, their behaviors and their partner's behaviors during the conflict, what channel was used during attempted conflict resolution, whether the conflict was resolved, and how they perceived the conflict impacted the nature of the relationship. Finally, participants filled out a series of questions about their attitudes and preferences regarding the use of CMC during conflict with their partner.

Measures

All items were scored on a scale of 1 (*strongly disagree*) to 7 (*strongly agree*) unless otherwise indicated.

Self-Esteem. Participants completed a 10-item version of the Rosenberg self-esteem scale [21], which included items like "On the whole, I am satisfied with myself" and "I take a positive attitude toward myself" (α = .86).

Relationship Satisfaction. Participants completed Rusbult et al.'s 10-item scale measuring relationship satisfaction [22], which included items like "My partner fulfills my needs for intimacy" and "I feel satisfied with our relationship" (α = .94).

Distancing Behaviors. Distancing can take many forms [6]. We were interested in two types of distancing behaviors salient in mediated communication: delaying and ignoring. We asked participants two yes/no questions for each communication channel that was used during the conflict: "When communicating via (channel) ..." "did you purposefully delay your responses?" and "did you purposefully ignore your partner?"

Perceived Partner Distancing Behaviors. Participants were asked two yes/no questions for each communication mode that was used during the conflict: "When communicating via X ..." "did you feel like your partner was purposefully delaying his/her responses?", and "did you feel like your partner was purposefully ignoring you?"

Perceived Impact of Conflict on Relationship. Participants completed a 3-item scale measuring the conflict's impact on relational quality [7]: "After this conflict, did your relationship become ..." "*more distant* (1) or *closer* (7)?", "*weaker* (1) or *stronger* (7)", and "*more sad* (1) or *happier* (7)?" (α = .97). They also completed a 4-item measure of the conflict's damage to the relationship: "The initial argument about this topic ..." "was very damaging to our relationship"; "was not at all damaging to our relationship" (reverse scored), "had a severely negative impact on our relationship", "had almost no negative impact on our relationship" (reverse scored), (α = .89).

[1] A few participants were much older than the rest of the sample. Excluding these participants from analyses did not alter any findings so they remained in the final data set.

Preferences and Overall Behavior. A series of questions was created to understand participants' preferences and behaviors during conflict with their partner overall, not just during the incident on which they mainly reported: "When having a conflict with my partner, I would rather communicate with my partner via mediated communication than in a FtF setting", "When having a conflict with my partner, I tend to avoid FtF communication in favor of communicating via mediated communication", "When trying to resolve a conflict with my partner, I tend to communicate FtF rather than through a mediated communication", "When trying to resolve a conflict with my partner, I prefer to communicate FtF rather than through a mediated communication", "When having a conflict with my partner, it is easier to say what I really feel via mediated communication than in a FtF setting", and "There are certain types of fights or conflicts that should never be discussed via mediated communication". (For each item, "mediated communication" was followed by "such as email, instant messenger, or text messaging").

Analysis

To test hypotheses about distancing and perceived partner distancing behaviors, we conducted four mixed effects logistic regression models, one for each of the four items measuring distancing and perceived partner distancing behaviors, with self-esteem and communication channel as the main independent variables. This approach allowed us to address the dichotomous nature of the distancing behavior variables. This approach also allowed us to account for the fact that some participants used multiple channels during a conflict and reported on distancing and perceived partner distancing behaviors in each channel that was used. To clarify, the "channel" variable does not represent individuals who *only* used FtF or *only* used a form of CMC, but rather individuals who used FtF or CMC *at some point* during the conflict episode.

To test hypotheses about the perceived impact of the conflict on the relationship, we conducted two standard OLS regression models, one for relational quality and one for damage to the relationship, with self-esteem, communication channel, and whether or not the conflict was resolved as the main independent variables.

To test hypotheses about preferences and overall behavior during conflict, we conducted six regression models, one for each of the items detailed in the Measures section, with self-esteem as the main independent variable. In all models, we included three control variables: relationship satisfaction, current/past relationship, and long-distance/non-long-distance relationship.

RESULTS

Use of Technology with Partner

When asked if they had ever used a technology with their partner, 85% had used email, 99% had talked on a cell phone, 98% had used text messaging, 89% had used an SNS, and 86.8% had used IM. Of those who used a given technology with their partner, text messaging was the most likely to be used "often" or "very often" (90%), followed by IM (65%), SNS (62%), cell phone (62%), and email (40%).

Use of Technology with Partner during Conflict

Using technology during conflict was fairly common. Participants were asked whether a communication channel was used during conflict in the past six months. FtF was the most likely channel to be used (82%), followed by text messaging (64%), cell phone (60%), IM (37%), SNS (29%), other/video chat (22%), and email (21%). Of individuals who used a channel, the following percent of participants used the channel "often" or "very often": FtF (61%), cell phone (49%), text messaging (47%), IM (29%), SNS (27%), and email (19%).

Participants also reported on a specific conflict incident. Of all specific conflict incidents, 63% of participants used FtF communication, 22% used IM, 13% used email, 15% used SNS, 40% used cell phone, 57% used text messaging, and 8% used another communication channel. Twenty-eight percent of reported conflicts used only one channel while 72% used two or more channels.[2]

Self-Esteem and Control Variables

Across participants, the mean self-esteem was 5.15 (SD = 0.95, range: 2.5 to 7) and the mean relationship satisfaction was 5.50 (SD = 1.22). There was a small but significant correlation between self-esteem and relationship satisfaction ($r = 0.22$, $p < .01$). People in current relationships had higher self-esteem than people in past relationships ($M = 5.21$, $SD = 0.91$; $M = 4.82$, $SD = 1.11$; $t(180) = -1.84$, $p < .05$). People in current relationships also had higher levels of relationship satisfaction than people in past relationships ($M = 5.64$, $SD = 1.11$; $M = 4.73$, $SD = 1.51$, $t(180) = -3.67$, $p < .01$). Participants in long-distance relationships did not differ in levels of self-esteem ($M = 5.02$, $SD = 0.92$; $M = 5.20$, $SD = 0.96$, $t(180) = 1.17$, $p = 0.88$) or relationship satisfaction ($M = 5.51$, $SD = 1.12$; $M = 5.49$, $SD = 1.27$, $t(180) = -.04$, $p = 0.47$) from non-long-distance couples. There was a small but significant correlation between age and self-esteem ($r = .16$, $p < .05$), and a one-way ANOVA revealed that men ($M = 5.19$, $SD = .87$) and women ($M = 5.12$, $SD = .97$) did not differ in their levels of self-esteem [$F(2, 179) = 1.64$, $p > .05$]. Age and gender were included in all of the following analyses but were not significant predictors of any outcome variables and are thus not discussed.

[2] Sixteen percent of participants reported on a conflict where FtF was the only channel used. Excluding these participants from analyses did not alter any findings so they remained in the final data set.

Distancing and Perceived Partner Distancing Behaviors

We asked participants who used a certain channel during the conflict whether they purposefully delayed their responses, purposefully ignored their partners, thought their partners purposefully delayed their responses, or thought their partners purposefully ignored them when communicating in that channel. Both purposefully delaying responses and ignoring one's partner were more common in mediated communication than in FtF communication, with IM, text messaging, and email being the most common channels in which participants delayed their responses and ignored their partners (see Figure 1). Delaying responses was almost twice as common in IM, text messaging, and email as it was in FtF communication and ignoring one's partner was more than twice as common in text messaging and email than it was FtF. Thinking one's partner delayed his/her responses or ignored him/her was also more common in several mediated communication channels than it was in FtF communication (see Figure 2).

Since FtF and text messaging were the two most commonly used channels during conflict (see Use of Technology with Partner During Conflict), we explored the role of text messaging vs. FtF ("channel") and self-esteem on distancing behavior. Results revealed that lower levels of self-esteem were associated with an increased likelihood of purposefully delaying one's responses (*odds ratio* = .69, $z = -2.29$, $p < .05$) and ignoring one's partner (*odds ratio* = .69, $z = -2.02$, $p < .05$) (H1a supported) (see Table 1).

There was also a main effect of communication channel, such that individuals were 2.81 times more likely to report purposefully delaying their responses ($z = 3.50$, $p < .01$) and 3.81 times as likely to report purposefully ignoring their partners in text messaging than in FtF communication ($z = 4.19$, $p < .01$) (H1b supported).

For perceived partner distancing behavior, participants were 3.38 times more likely to report that their partner purposefully delayed his/her responses in text messaging than in FtF ($z = 4.20$, $p < .01$) and 2.88 times more likely to report that their partner purposefully ignored them when communicating via text messaging than when communicating FtF ($z = 3.25$, $p < .01$) (H2b supported). Self-esteem was not significantly associated with thinking one's partner purposefully delayed his/her responses but was significantly associated with a greater likelihood of thinking one's partner purposefully ignored him/her (*odds ratio* = .47, $z = -3.45$, $p < .01$; H2a supported).

In all four models, none of the control variables (relationship satisfaction, current/past relationship, and long-distance/non-long-distance relationship) were significant predictors of the DVs. In addition, while we expected to find that self-esteem would have a greater influence on distancing and perceived distancing behaviors in text messaging than it would in FtF communication (H1c and H2c), we found no evidence to support these hypothesized interactions.

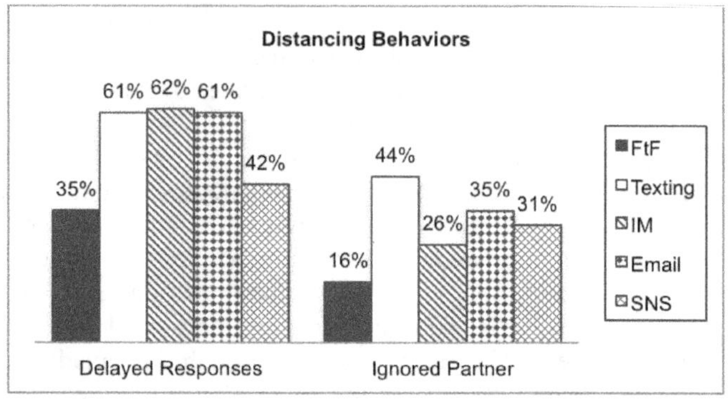

Figure 1. Percent of participants who exhibited distancing behaviors, by channel.

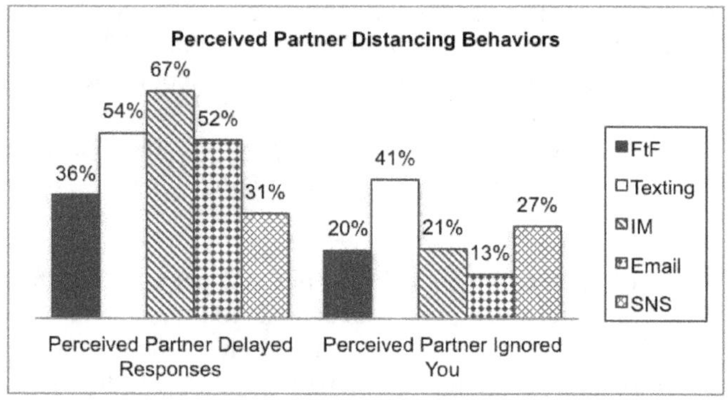

Figure 2. Percent of participants who perceived partner distancing behaviors, by channel.

	Delayed Responses	Ignored Partner	Perceived Partner Delayed Responses	Perceived Partner Ignored You
Variable	Odds ratio (z)			
Self-esteem	.69 (−2.29)*	.69 (−2.02)*	.79 (−1.41)	.47 (−3.45)**
Channel (text)	2.81 (3.50)**	3.81 (4.19)**	3.38 (4.20)**	2.88 (3.25)**

* = $p < .05$, ** = $p < .01$

Table 1. Self-esteem and channel predicting distancing and perceived partner distancing behavior.

Perceived Impact of Conflict on the Relationship

How are self-esteem and communication channel related to how participants view the impact of the conflict on the relationship? In these models, we operationalized channel as "resolution channel" (i.e., the communication channel that was used during the attempted resolution of the conflict), since the last channel used may be more likely to impact participants' impressions of the conflict. In addition, since all of the mediated channels represent a type of reduced-cues environment, we grouped text messaging, IM, email, SNS, phone, and other (video chat) into "mediated communication" for resolution channel, making resolution channel a binary variable comparing mediated to FtF communication. We also included participants' impressions

	Conflict's impact on Relational Quality	Conflict's Damage to Relationship
Variable	*b (SE)*	*b (SE)*
Self-esteem	0.04 (0.12)	−0.27* (0.12)
Resolution channel (FtF)	0.35** (0.13)	−0.02 (0.13)
Self-esteem × Resolution channel	0.15 (0.12)	−0.16 (0.12)
Relationship satisfaction	0.40** (0.09)	−0.41** (0.09)
Long-distance relationship	0.33* (0.13)	0.01 (0.14)
Current relationship	0.74** (0.16)	−0.35* (0.16)
Conflict resolved	0.57** (0.13)	−0.38** (0.13)
R-squared	0.47	0.35
Adj. R-squared	0.44	0.31
N	150	150

* = $p < .05$, ** = $p < .01$

Table 2. Self-esteem and channel predicting perceptions of the conflict's impact on the relationship overall.

of whether the conflict was resolved, reasoning that unresolved conflicts might have a more negative impact on the relationship than would resolved conflicts. We conducted two standard OLS regression models, one predicting the conflict's impact on relational quality and one predicting the conflict's damage to the relationship. Results revealed that conflicts where resolution was attempted FtF were more likely to be associated with a perceived increase in relational quality than conflicts where resolution was attempted in mediated communication (b = .35, t = 2.76, p < .01), supporting H3b (see Table 2). However, no relationship was detected between self-esteem and ratings of the conflict's impact on relational quality.

Resolution channel did not significantly impact perceptions that the conflict was damaging to the relationship. Lower levels of self-esteem, however, were associated with higher ratings of a conflict's perceived damage to the relationship (b = −.27, t = −2.20, p < .05), supporting H3a.

In both of these models, we found no evidence to support the hypothesized interactions of self-esteem × resolution channel. Higher relationship satisfaction, reporting on a current relationship (vs. past), and thinking the conflict was resolved were associated with higher ratings of the conflict's impact on relational quality and lower ratings of the conflict's damage to the relationship (see Table 2). In addition, participants reporting on a long-distance relationship reported higher ratings of the conflict's impact on relational quality.

Preferences and Overall Behavior during Conflict

When it comes to overall experiences with their romantic partners, self-esteem seems to influence both attitudes and behaviors regarding the use of different communication channels during conflict. Lower levels of self-esteem were associated with a *preference* for mediated over FtF communication during a conflict with their partner (supporting H4a), even when accounting for relationship satisfaction, distance, and recency of the relationship (see Table 3). In addition, when it comes to *behavior,* lower levels of self-esteem were associated with a greater likelihood of avoiding FtF communication in favor of communication via mediated communication during a conflict, supporting H4b. Relationship satisfaction was also a significant predictor of avoiding FtF during conflict, such that lower levels of relationship satisfaction were associated with a greater likelihood of avoiding FtF in favor of CMC.

We also looked at preferences and behavior for a specific stage of conflict: conflict resolution. For conflict resolution, higher levels of self-esteem were associated with a greater likelihood of *preferring* to communicate FtF over text-based communication, lending further support to H4a. Higher levels of relationship satisfaction were also associated with a greater likelihood of preferring to communicate FtF over mediated communication during conflict resolution (see Table 3). However, self-esteem was not significantly associated with *behavior* (a tendency to communicate via FtF over CMC) during conflict resolution. People in current relationships and people in non-long-distance relationships were more likely to tend to resolve conflicts FtF (vs. CMC) than people in past relationships, and people in long-distance relationships (see Table 3).

We asked two additional questions to further understand individuals' preferences and attitudes about using CMC during conflict with their partners (see Table 3). Individuals with lower levels of self-esteem were more likely to agree that it is easier to say what one really feels via text-based communication than FtF during conflict with one's partner. Higher levels of self-esteem were also associated with a greater likelihood of agreeing that "There are certain types of fights or conflicts that are better discussed via a mediated communication". Participants in non-long-distance relationships were also more likely to agree with this statement than those in long-distance relationships.

DISCUSSION

Results revealed that, in many cases, both communication channel and self-esteem were associated with behavior and communication technology preferences in the context of romantic couple conflict. When it comes to one's own behavior, lower levels of self-esteem were associated with increased distancing behaviors - purposefully delaying one's responses and ignoring one's partner. This verifies existing literature about self-esteem in romantic relationships. We also found that distancing behaviors were more common in text messaging than in FtF

	Conflict		Conflict Resolution		Attitudes about Conflict	
	Preference for text-based comm. over FtF during conflict	*Avoidance of* FtF in favor of text-based comm. during conflict	*Preference for* FtF over text-based comm. during conflict resolution	*Use of* FtF over text-based comm. during conflict resolution	"Easier to say what I really feel" via text-based comm. than FtF	"Certain types of fights or conflicts … should never be discussed" via text-based comm.
Variable	*b (SE)*	*b (SE)*	*b (SE)*	*b (SE)*	*b (SE)*	*b (SE)*
Self-esteem	−0.44** (0.14)	−0.50** (0.14)	0.23* (0.11)	0.14 (0.13)	−0.50** (0.15)	0.35** (0.12)
Relationship satisfaction	−0.03 (0.11)	−0.24* (0.11)	0.17* (0.09)	0.06 (0.10)	−0.18 (0.12)	−0.10 (0.10)
Long-distance relationship	0.15 (0.13)	0.05 (0.13)	−0.04 (0.11)	−0.35** (0.13)	0.12 (0.15)	−0.34** (0.12)
Current relationship	−0.06 (0.18)	0.03 (0.19)	0.26 (0.15)	0.65** (0.18)	0.27 (0.20)	0.30 (0.17)
R-squared	0.080	0.122	0.097	0.140	0.085	0.11
Adj. R-squared	0.058	0.102	0.076	0.114	0.064	0.09
N	175	176	175	174	176	177

* = $p < .05$, ** = $p < .01$

Table 3. Effect of self-esteem on preferences for text-based and FtF communication during conflict with partner.

communication. Yet, interestingly, we did not detect an interaction effect; lower levels of self-esteem were not more strongly associated with distancing behaviors in text messaging than they were in FtF communication. Given that text messaging is a more ambiguous channel than FtF, it is surprising that LSEs' interpretation biases are not heightened in text messaging.

In addition, lower levels of self-esteem were associated with an increase in perceiving that one's partner purposefully ignored them, though self-esteem was not associated with perceiving one's partner purposefully delayed his/her responses. Perceived partner distancing behaviors (both delaying and ignoring) were more common in text messaging than FtF. These are novel findings, suggesting that individuals are more likely to perceive distancing behavior from their partners in mediated communication vs. FtF communication.

Perceived distancing behavior may have been more common in text messaging than in FtF because it may be easier to delay one's responses or ignore one's partner via text (vs. FtF). And, if more partner distancing is exhibited, it makes sense that more partner distancing will be perceived. However, the current findings only reflect perceptions of partner distancing behavior and not the actual amount of partner distancing behavior that occurred. It could be that individuals perceive distancing behaviors when they do not actually occur, or fail to perceive distancing behaviors when they do actually occur. Therefore, it may be that the increased room for interpretation in text messaging, rather than actual partner behavior, is driving the results.

Taken together, results suggest that using text messaging during a conflict can be potentially harmful, as doing so is associated with increased distancing and some perceived partner distancing behaviors. Yet, using texting is no more harmful to LSEs than it is to HSEs. Or, put another way, using texting is not more helpful to HSEs than it is to LSEs when it comes to distancing behaviors.

When it comes to perceptions of how a conflict impacts one's relationship, findings were mixed, but self-esteem was associated with ratings of perceived increased relational quality (supporting H3a), and communication channel was associated with lower ratings of perceived relational damage (supporting H3b). It may be that the differences in immediacy and physical proximity between mediated and FtF communication are more closely related to perceptions of relational quality (e.g., closeness, strength) while the negative biases associated with lower levels of self-esteem are more closely related to perceptions of damage or harm. Yet, evidence does suggest that both self-esteem and channel are related to how one projects the effect of the conflict on the relationship.

Again, LSEs' perceptions of how the conflict impacted the relationship were not more negative in mediated communication than they were in FtF communication. It may be that self-esteem is a strong trait that manifests across communication channels. Or, it is possible that, while CMC provides more room for interpretation than FtF communication, it does not provide so much more room that LSEs' interpretations are further altered.

We also found that lower levels of self-esteem were significantly associated with *preferring* text-based mediated communication over FtF communication during both conflict and conflict resolution (H4a supported). But do LSEs report *using* mediated communication over FtF communication during conflict? Findings here are mixed, providing partial support for H4b. While lower levels of self-esteem were associated with greater likelihood of actually avoiding FtF in favor of CMC during conflict, self-esteem was not significantly associated with a greater likelihood of using mediated communication when trying to resolve a conflict with one's partner. While responses to these two items were significantly positively correlated ($r = .69$, $p < .0001$), it may be that even though LSEs prefer CMC, they may fight against those preferences and actually choose FtF communication for resolution, since individuals tend to feel that FtF is the most desired resolution channel [23]. Or it might be that their partners' prefer FtF communication and those partner preferences are driving what actually occurs during the conflict.

Although we have been discussing FtF as a better channel for conflict communication, lower levels of self-esteem were associated with agreeing that it is easier to say what one really feels via CMC than FtF during a conflict. That LSEs feel more comfortable expressing themselves through mediated communication is a clear benefit to using mediated communication during conflict, since withholding the expression of a conflict can be harmful in a relationship (see [20] for a discussion). Along these lines, LSEs also have a more accepting attitude about using CMC during conflict. So, instead of having a preference for CMC during conflict but feeling like it is inappropriate, it seems that LSEs prefer mediated communication and also feel that it is an acceptable form of communication.

LSEs might prefer mediated channels during a conflict for a number of other reasons. The increased distance and fewer cues might make LSEs feel safer from negative feedback. They might also feel they can dampen negative interpretations in CMC since they do not have to interact directly with their partners. Or, LSEs may subconsciously seek situations in which they have more room to convince themselves that their biases are true. HSEs are less likely to prefer CMC, perhaps because they do not have these self-protective motivations and thus less need for ambiguity.

Overall, findings suggest that individuals with lower levels of self-esteem have a preference for CMC in multiple aspects of conflict communication, whereas individuals with higher levels of self-esteem have a preference for FtF communication during conflict. These preferences seem to reflect the increased levels of comfort and/or control that CMC provides. In some cases, using CMC might be helpful for LSEs. For instance, LSEs find it easier to say what they really feel. Yet, contrary to predictions, using CMC was not more harmful for LSEs than it was for HSEs, suggesting that text-based CMC does not necessarily exacerbate the negative biases and tendencies that LSEs possess.

Limitations

There are several limitations to this work. First, the sample included undergraduate students and was a relatively young sample. Second, because of our study design, we are unable to comment on the causal nature of the relationships between self-esteem, communication channel, and the various dependent variables we explored in our models. Third, because individuals were reporting on past experiences with their partners, responses may be influenced by memory biases or by one's current mood toward one's partner. In addition, because participants reported on the most recent conflict where technology was used, the results on how often certain mediated channels were used are likely inflated, and should be interpreted within the constraints of the study design. Finally, it is important to note that this data reflects individuals' perceptions of partner behavior and of a conflict's impact on their relationship, rather than actual partner behavior or actual impact of a conflict on the relationship.

Implications for Design

The key insight for designers and users of interpersonal communication technologies is to consider the potential benefits and drawbacks of using text-based technologies during important or sensitive conversations. Although using text-based CMC is associated with more distancing and perceived distancing behaviors, it also allows individuals with lower levels of self-esteem to feel more comfortable saying what they really feel during conflict. Designers could incorporate features that minimize negative behaviors and encourage positive behaviors. Also, this work can provide insight into what types of individuals choose text-based CMC during interpersonal conflict with close relational partners, which can in turn inform how designers provide customization options for users.

CONCLUSION

This study demonstrates that both self-esteem and communication channel impact behaviors, perceived behaviors, and perceived relational consequences in romantic couple conflict. However, communication channel does not exacerbate biases stemming from individual difference variables, suggesting that, for individuals with lower levels of self-esteem, using text-based CMC during conflict is no better or worse than communicating FtF. Yet, individuals with lower levels of self-esteem do have a preference for CMC over FtF in multiple aspects of conflict communication. Overall, CMC does seem to provide room for negative interpretation during couple conflict.

ACKNOWLEDGMENTS

We thank the CollabLab and reviewers for their insightful feedback on this work. Funding was provided by National Science Foundation grant #0953943.

REFERENCES

1. Bellavia, G., & Murray, S. (2003). Did I do that? Self-esteem related differences in reactions to romantic partners' moods. *Personal Relationships, 10*, 77-95.
2. Burge, J., & Tatar, D. (2009). Affect and dyads: Conflict across different technological media. In S. Harrison (Ed.), *Media Space 20+ Years of Mediated Life* (pp. 123-144): Springer.
3. Coyne, S. M., Stockdale, L., Busby, D., Iverson, B., & Grant, D. M. (2011). "I luv u :)": A descriptive study of the media use of individuals in romantic relationships. *Family Relations, 60*, 150-162.
4. Ehrenberg, A., Juckes, S., White, K. M., & Walsh, S. P. (2008). Personality and self-esteem as predictors of young people's technology use. *CyberPsychology & Behavior, 11*(6), 739-741.
5. Frisby, B. N., & Westerman, D. (2010). Rational actors: Channel selection and rational choices in romantic conflict episodes. *Journal of Social and Personal Relationships, 27*(7), 970-981.
6. Hess, J. A. (2000). Maintaining nonvoluntary relationships with disliked partners: An investigation into the use of distancing behaviors. *Human Communication Research, 26*(3), 458-488.
7. Johnson, K. L., & Roloff, M. E. (2000). Correlates of the perceived resolvability and relational consequences of serial arguing in dating relationships: Argumentative features and the use of coping strategies. *Journal of Social and Personal Relationships, 17*(4-5), 676-686.
8. Joinson, A. N. (2004). Self-esteem, interpersonal risk, and preference for e-mail to face-to-face communication. *CyberPsych.ology & Behavior, 7*(4), 479-485.
9. Kiecolt-Glaser, J. K., & Newton, T. L. (2001). Marriage and health: His and hers. *Psychological Bulletin, 127*(4), 472-503.
10. Marigold, D. C., Holmes, J. G., & Ross, M. (2007). More than words: Reframing compliments from romantic partners fosters security in low self-esteem individuals. *Journal of Personality and Social Psychology, 92*(2), 232-248.
11. Merkle, E. R., & Richardson, R. A. (2000). Digital dating and virtual relating: Conceptualizing computer mediated romantic relationships. *Family Relations, 49*, 187-192.
12. Mitchell, M. M., Rankin, C. T., D'Urso, S. C., & Malone, P. (2002). The impact of intention to handle conflict face-to-face or via e-mail on perceived conflict resolution style. Paper presented at *ICA 2002*.
13. Morey, J. N., Gentzler, A. L., Creasy, B., Oberhauser, A. M., & Westerman, D. (2013). Young adults' use of communication technology within their romantic relationships and associations with attachment style. *Computers in Human Behavior, 29*, 1771-1778.
14. Murray, S. L., Bellavia, G., Rose, R., & Griffin, D. (2003). Once hurt, twice hurtful: How perceived regard regulates daily marital inter- action. *Journal of Personality and Social Psychology, 84*, 126-147.
15. Murray, S. L., Holmes, J. G., & Griffin, D. W. (2000). Self-esteem and the quest for felt security: How perceived regard regulates attachment processes. *J. of Personality and Social Psychology, 78*(3), 478-498.
16. Murray, S. L., Rose, P., Bellavia, G. M., Holmes, J. G., & Kusche, A. G. (2002). When rejection stings: How self-esteem constrains relationship-enhancement processes. *Interpersonal Relations and Group Processes, 83*(3), 556-573.
17. Ofcom (2013). Communications Market Report 2013. http://stakeholders.ofcom.org.uk/binaries/research/cmr/cmr13/2013_UK_CMR.pdf.
18. O'Sullivan, P. B. (2000). What you don't know won't hurt me: Impression management functions of communication channels in relationships. *Human Communication Research, 26*(3), 403-431.
19. Ramirez, A., Walther, J. B., Burgoon, J. K., & Sunnafrank, M. (2002). Information-seeking strategies, uncertainty, and computer-mediated communication: Toward a conceptual model. *Human Communication Research, 28*(2), 213-228.
20. Roloff, M., & Soule, K. (2002). Interpersonal Conflict: A review. In M. L. Knapp & J. A. Daly (Eds.), *Handbook of Interpersonal Communication, 3rd edition*. Thousand Oaks, CA: Sage.
21. Rosenberg, M. (1965). *Society and the adolescent self-image*. Princeton, NJ: Princeton University Press.
22. Rusbult, C. E., Martz, J. M., & Agnew, C. R. (1998). The investment model scale: Measuring commitment level, satisfaction level, quality of alternatives, and investment size. *Personal Relationships, 5*, 357-391.
23. Scissors, L. E., & Gergle, D. (2013). "Back and forth, back and forth": Channel switching in romantic couple conflict. *Proc. CSCW 2013*, 237-248.
24. Turner, M. M., D'Urso, S. C., Rankin, C. T., & Malone, P. C. (2003). Cognition during conflict: The impact of communication medium and perceived intentions on attributions. Paper presented at *ICA 2003*.
25. Walther, J. B. (1992). Interpersonal effects in computer-mediated interaction: A relational perspective. *Communication Research, 19*(1), 52-90.
26. Zhao, X., Sosik, V. S., & Cosley, D. (2012). It's complicated: How romantic partners use Facebook. *Proc. CHI 2012*, 771-780.

Exploring Affective Communication Through Variable-Friction Surface Haptics

Joe Mullenbach, Craig Shultz, J. Edward Colgate, Anne Marie Piper
Northwestern University
{mullenbach, craigdshultz}@u.northwestern.edu, {colgate, ampiper}@northwestern.edu

ABSTRACT
This paper explores the use of variable friction surface haptics enabled by the TPad Tablet to support affective communication between pairs of users. We introduce three haptic applications for the TPad Tablet (text messaging, image sharing, and virtual touch) and evaluate the applications with 24 users, including intimate couples and strangers. Participants used haptics to communicate literal texture, denote action within a scene, convey emotional information, highlight content, express and engage in physical playfulness, and to provide one's partner with an experience or sensation. We conclude that users readily associate haptics with emotional expression and that the intimacy of touch in the contexts we study is best suited for communications with close social partners.

Author Keywords
Surface Haptics; Touchscreen; Variable Friction; Tablet; Communication

ACM Classification Keywords
H.5.2. Information interfaces and presentation: Input devices and strategies, Haptic I/O

INTRODUCTION
Human touch conveys many social messages, including level of intimacy, hostility, and affiliation [9]. Physical touch is a crucial aspect of most human relationships [16]. While haptic interfaces have been shown to convey emotional information [3,8,33], the potential for surface haptic technologies to support person-to-person affective communication has yet to be explored. Different than vibration feedback that is common in mobile devices and force feedback that is common in graspable devices such as joysticks, surface haptic technologies provide force feedback directly to the fingertip in form factors that are increasingly appropriate for mobile devices [1,24,1]. This paper explores variable-friction technology for direct person-to-person communication and seeks insights into designing surface haptics for communication. While this technology has been used to improve navigation tasks on touch screens (e.g., [18]), the present study is the first known to explore haptic communication between two people using connected variable-friction tablet displays.

CHI 2014, April 26-May 1 2014, Toronto, Ontario, Canada.

ACM 978-1-4503-2473-1/14/04...$15.00.
http://dx.doi.org/10.1145/2556288.2557343

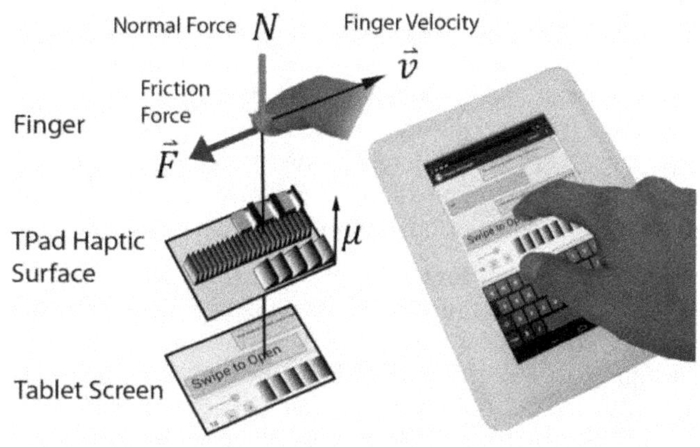

Figure 1: The TPad Tablet is a hand-held device with a variable-friction haptic surface. When the user swipes to open a text message, for example, the friction coefficient is varied, resulting in a pattern of forces felt by the fingertip.

Beyond application context, we also seek to explore how intimate communication, with its concerns of privacy, expression, and co-presence, might be better supported through touch. A brainstorming session of experts outside of the research team coupled with idea evaluation by the research team yielded three application ideas that were prototyped. These include *haptic text messaging* (Fig. 1) that enables users to embed haptic patterns within traditional text messages, *haptic image sharing* where users annotate and exchange images with a range of haptic textures, and *haptic virtual touch* where users move their fingers on their personal displays while seeing and feeling their partner's touch simultaneously.

The technology used in this study is a TPad Tablet (tactile pattern display) which is a self-contained, handheld device incorporating a haptic surface above a touchscreen tablet (Fig. 1) [24,25]. The feeling of a variable-friction TPad surface is not simply that of vibration. Rather, the coefficient of friction, and therefore the resistance force can be varied as the fingertip slides across the screen, creating perceptions of shape and texture. This means, for example, that the device can visually and haptically display a slider that resists and then releases as it unlocks, or a textured button that grabs the finger to confirm that it is currently selected [18,21,1].

We evaluated the three applications with 24 users, including couples in a long-term relationship and stranger pairs. We allowed for open-ended exploration of the applications so that users controlled the haptic experience. Observations and user feedback provided insights into expectations about with whom and under which circumstances communication involving surface haptics is appropriate and meaningful.

RELATED WORK

As is noted by Picard [28], there is a need for systems that better support person-to-person affective communication. We examine how applications might be designed with variable friction surface haptics to address this need, drawing from the literature on technology supported affective communication, person-to-person haptic interaction, and emotional information in haptics.

Technology for Affective Communication & Intimacy

This paper focuses on haptics for affective communication, and we consider intimacy to play an important role in this design space. While it is difficult to define intimacy, the literature describes intimate communications as information poor but rich in emotion and meaning, seemingly ambiguous (particularly to outsiders), involving a sense of presence in absence, often private and created in ways that can be hidden from others, and involving reciprocity [1,22,29]. Kieldskov et al. [15] used cultural probes to better understand how technology could support intimacy. They suggest that intimate acts require support for privacy, enable communication of emotion, particularly in unspoken ways, transmit a feeling of presence in absence, and play with ambiguity and incompleteness.

Mobile phones, through the use of voice, SMS, and e-mail, help people who are separated geographically establish a sense of awareness and connection, which may reduce loneliness [13]. A number of research prototypes explore supporting intimate connections through technology, and while space precludes a full treatment of this work, we mention several examples. One notable example is the Virtual Intimate Object [14], where couples may express intimacy in a rich manner through a simple and purposefully minimalistic interface. LumiTouch [8] involves digitally augmented picture frames that transmit touch from one frame to light in the other frame, providing an ambient display that communicates emotional content. Cubble [17], designed to support couples in long distance relationships, allows sharing of simple messages through color signals, vibrations, and thermal feedback. Cubble also involves touch and light-based interaction over mobile devices, which is similar to the haptic virtual touch application we present here as well as smartphone applications such as Pair and FeelMe. Unique to our haptic virtual touch application is an exploration of how to design the subtleties of joint touch through variable friction.

Person-to-Person Haptic Interaction

Much related work involves the development of haptic interfaces to support interaction between two people. InTouch [4] is an early haptic-only system that allows distributed users to interact with a set of rollers using their hands. This allows users to passively feel their partner's manipulation of the device, providing the sense of joint interaction with a shared physical object. Similarly, HandJive involves joysticks to support playful interaction among dyads [12]. Other haptic systems use stroking (e.g., [10]) or a hug (e.g., [23]) to support physical closeness. While most systems examine the haptic channel alone, ComTouch [7] explores verbal and haptic channels in combination by converting hand pressure on a handheld phone-like device into vibrational intensity between users in real-time.

Haptic Interaction and Emotional Information

Several studies have sought to understand whether specific emotions map to certain haptic patterns or textures. A notable example is work by Smith and MacLean [33], which examines how dyads (intimate pairs and strangers) communicate specific emotional states (angry, delighted, relaxed, unhappy) through a haptic interface of simple knobs. They focus on synchronous, bidirectional dyadic interaction and conclude that emotion can be communicated through their prototype interface. Other related work examines how well users are able to differentiate friction-based haptic stimuli and measures the emotional responses to such stimuli [32], suggesting that even simple haptic stimulation can carry emotional information. Our approach builds on these findings and explores emotional expression within the context of specific applications.

Considerable research also investigates the idea of haptic icons or hapticons [5,6,11,19,20,30], which are patterns of programmed force, friction, or vibration that can be used to communicate a basic idea similar to traditional graphical icons. Building on this research, we design and present users with haptic patterns as part of a text messaging application. In contrast to studies that distinguish unique tactile feelings and attempt to map emotions onto such patterns, Wang and Quek [35] argue that touch interaction needs to be coupled with other communication channels to clarify its meaning. They also suggest the use of touch as an immediate channel by not assigning any symbolic meaning to touch interactions. Our research also avoids assigning specific symbolic meanings or affective qualities to haptic interactions; instead, we seek to understand ambiguities in haptic interaction within the context of social relationships and established practices with social applications (e.g., text messaging). Furthermore, we explore whether such symbolic systems should be pre-determined or develop organically among people depending on their relationship.

SYSTEM IMPLEMENTATION

The devices used in this study are two internet-connected second-generation TPad Tablets as shown in Figure 1. Inside the device is a Google Nexus 7™ tablet, an

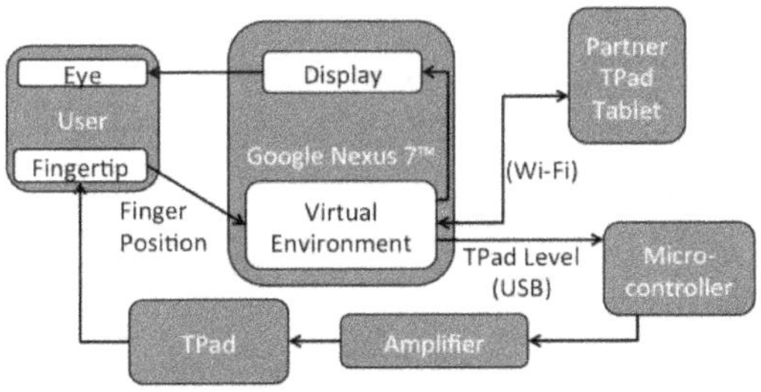

Figure 2: System diagram of TPad Tablet.

overlaying glass sheet with piezoelectric actuators (TPad), a printed circuit board, and a lithium polymer battery. A system diagram is shown in Figure 2. Finger position is sensed at approximately 60 Hz, and for the direct touch application, it is immediately sent via Wi-Fi to the partner tablet. Finger position is also used to update the virtual environment and generate friction-level commands. These are sent via USB at 1000Hz to a microcontroller which sends a pulse-width-modulated signal to actuate the piezos. Full instructions for building and programming an open-hardware TPad Tablet are available free for research and other non-commercial use at http://tpadtablet.org [24].

The friction reduction effect of the TPad haptic surface is generated through high frequency (~35 kHz) and low amplitude (~1 μm) out-of-plane oscillating motion. Higher amplitude oscillation corresponds to a lower value of friction coefficient μ, allowing modulation between low (full oscillation) and high (no oscillation) friction [1]. Referring to Figure 1, the resistance force F is modeled as equal to the normal force N times the coefficient of friction in the direction opposite to the finger velocity: $F = -N\mu \frac{\vec{v}}{|v|}$.

This effect is very distinct both physically and perceptually from vibratory actuation. When the fingertip passes over real-world textures and features, mechanoreceptors in the finger body and in the skin of the fingertip respond to vibration, force, and skin-stretch. While high-bandwidth vibration alone is sufficient to stimulate some textures, it cannot apply shear force to the finger or stretch the skin. With variable friction, controlled forces stretch the skin and react against the finger while retaining the ability to create vibration through amplitude modulation of friction level.

APPLICATION DESIGN

Brainstorming and Ideation

As part of our exploration, we first conducted a brainstorming session with nine experts in the fields of communication, design, and human-computer interaction around the themes of privacy, emotional expression, and co-presence in dyadic communication, all of which are central to technology designed for intimacy support [15]. The participants were given a brief overview and demonstration of the technology and were asked to first generate situations where the themes are important and then generate ideas of ways to use the technology to support them. The session was video recorded and moderated by two researchers, and all sketches were collected. Four

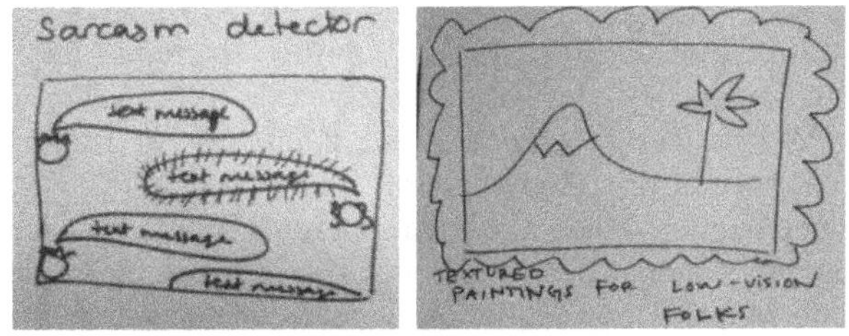

Figure 3: Sketches from brainstorming session describe using friction to indicate sarcasm within a text message (left) and enhance images for low-vision users (right).

researchers analyzed and discussed a total of 24 application ideas. Several ideas generated by participants included: using surface friction to indicate the tone of a news story, sarcasm within a text message, and important parts of a message; adding haptics to an image to support interaction with children, low-vision users, and artistic expression; and sharing and entering passwords haptically to enhance privacy. Example sketches generated during the brainstorming session are presented in Figure 3.

Applications

The research team rated ideas based on their relevance to affective communication, technical feasibility, amount of discussion and interest the idea generated during the brainstorming session, and relevance of surface haptics to the application idea. Similar ideas were grouped and merged together. Three final ideas were selected for prototyping and evaluation, each with a distinct use of surface haptic feedback across different modes of person-to-person communication.

Haptic Text Messaging

This application involves embedding haptic information within the context of mobile text messaging, similar to [27,30]. Users type a message as they would in a traditional text messaging application but also may choose to add one of 24 unique friction patterns (see Fig. 1). A visual representation of the friction pattern (white for low friction, black for high) is shown above the keyboard where users may touch to preview the feeling as well. After a message is sent, the recipient swipes across to open it and reveal the text, feeling the embedded tactile pattern as they move. The patterns were created as sets or families, inspired by past haptic communication studies [20,32] and mathematical

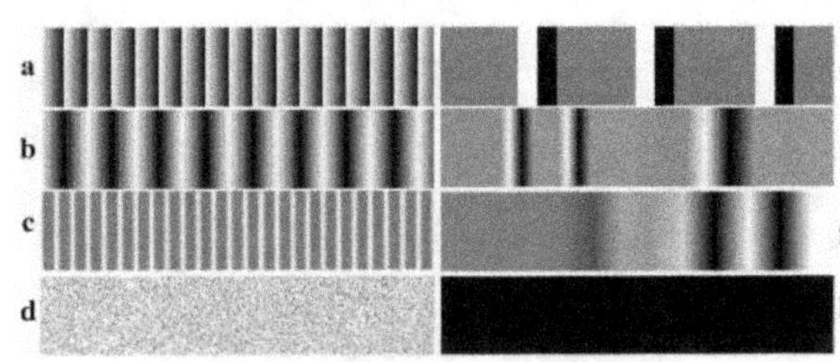

Figure 4: Representative haptic patterns in text messaging app: (a) sawtooth pattern, (b) triangle pattern, (c) low friction triangle, (d) white noise, (e) alternative direction, (f) rhythmic bumps, (g) crescendo, and (h) default blank pattern.

variation (see Fig 4). Within families, patterns vary by spatial frequency (4a, 4b, 4d), magnitude (4c), rhythm (4e, 4f), and increasing or decreasing magnitude or frequency across space (4g). These patterns are not meant to define a surface haptic vocabulary or complete set, nor is it tested as such, but are provided to gain insights, such as: What types of messages, if any, make sense to augment with haptics? Do users attempt to convey affect with haptics, and how do they interpret received haptic messages? Is a preset vocabulary wanted or needed?

Haptic Image Sharing

The second application enables users to "paint" friction patterns as an additional layer above an image. Users select an image from a collection of 10 photos, including works of art, landscapes, and animals. They then select from a palette of simple color-coded textures, painting them to a semi-transparent overlay on top of the image. The color hue corresponds to the waveform: red is a 100Hz square wave, yellow is a 70Hz sinusoid, green is a 30Hz sawtooth wave, blue is a 20Hz sinusoid, and cyan is a constant friction level. The value of the color corresponds to the magnitude of the effect, with five levels varying from full power to 20% of full power. Users may resize the brush stroke and apply an eraser to the image. Figure 5 illustrates the sequence of authoring a haptic image. This application allows us to pose questions about which types of photos and what elements within the photos are interesting to annotate with haptics. Do people annotate images based on a literal texture (e.g., rocks have a rough texture) or use texture in other ways relating to affective communication?

Haptic Virtual Touch

The third application examines expressivity in communication and co-presence by enabling remote users to draw on the TPad Tablet with their finger and feel a tactile pattern when their finger intersects with their partner's finger. When a user touches the screen, an image of a fingerprint appears on their screen and on their partner's screen (Fig. 6). Moving on the screen creates a colored trail that is visible on both screens. Users have access to sliders that adjust how quickly their trail fades and the diameter of the trail. Two methods of rendering haptic "touches" were explored: (1) a force-based physical rendering of a fingertip-shaped three-dimensional object, designed for realism, and (2) a texture-based target. For the 3D rendering, the fingertip was modeled as a 120x200 pixel hemispheroid (Fig. 7a1), and the resistance force was modeled as proportional to the instantaneous slope in the direction of travel (Fig. 7a2). In this way, as users move up the virtual slope (z increasing), they experience a resistance force. As they travel down the virtual slope, they experience a reduction in resistance. The second rendering of touch was texture-based, varying friction level as a 100 Hz sine wave that increases in magnitude as the radial distance, R, between the fingers decreases (Fig 7b). The maximum radius at which the effect is displayed, Rmax, was set to be proportional to the partner's radius.

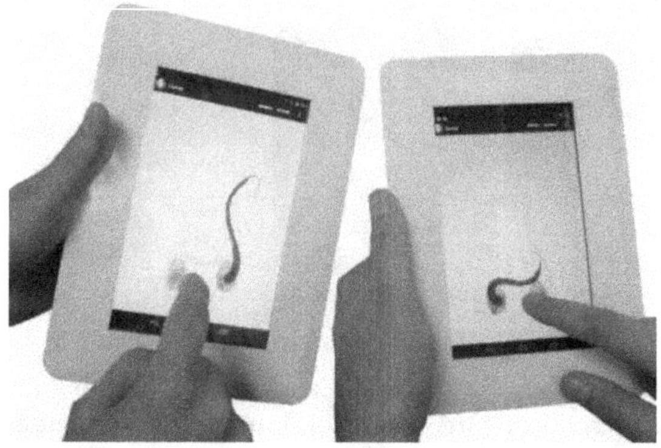

Figure 6: Haptic Virtual Touch allows users to see and feel where their partner is touching the screen. When users touch virtually, they feel a haptic rendering of their partner's finger.

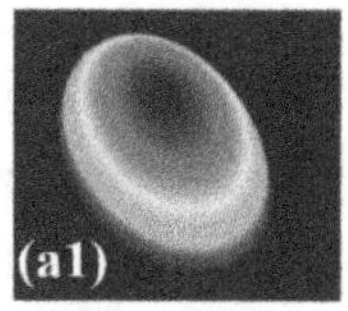

(a1)

(a2) $$TPaD\ Level = 0.5 - A * \frac{z - zlast}{mag(\Delta R)}$$

(b) $$TPaD\ Level = 0.5 + \frac{Rmax - R}{2 * Rmax} * \sin(2\pi * 100t)$$

Figure 7: a1, a2. Visual representation of 3D haptic rendering of fingertip and related function for TPad level approximating (a) directional derivative, (b) texture based touch rendering.

While related work investigates how haptic feedback may increase perceived virtual presence [31] and coordination in group work [6], our aim is to understand how familiar and unfamiliar pairs react to another person's touch as it is conveyed through surface haptics and whether this yields an interesting and intimate form of co-present touch [26]. We want to observe whether couples or strangers would engage in touching behavior across the TPads or whether they would try to avoid collisions. We also examine whether a more realistic rendering aids interaction and the sense of co-presence or connection with one's partner.

Figure 5: Haptic Image Sharing allows users to select an image to customize, select from a palette of friction patterns, draw a texture overlay in "edit" mode, and explore the image in "feel" mode.

EVALUATION

We conducted a laboratory study with 24 participants, including six participant pairs (n=12; 6 male; mean age=38.0, SD=10.9) who were in an intimate relationship (dating one year or more) and six pairs (n=12; 6 male; mean age=31.1, SD=8.2) who had not met prior to the study. We recruited male-female stranger pairs who were close in age but were unable to control for gender or age gaps in partner pairs. No participants had used a TPad prior to the study. Participant pairs used each application in the same laboratory space but were unable to see or hear each other during the task. While using each application, participants wore noise-reducing headphones to avoid hearing sounds created by the TPad or comments by their partner.

Participants first experienced a brief training period that introduced them to the TPad and different surface haptic textures. The order of applications was varied among participant pairs. When presented with an application, participants received brief instructions and a written prompt to guide their interaction. We crafted the prompts to be open-ended and flexible to accommodate diverse interests and relationships. After using each application, the pair individually filled out a questionnaire to evaluate that particular application's usability and appeal. Participants rated their agreement with statements on a five-point (zero neutral) Likert scale. At the end of the study, each pair sat face-to-face and discussed their experience with two researchers. The discussion sessions were video recorded, transcribed, and analyzed.

Results

We first describe the high-level themes that emerged from the laboratory study, and then we present application-specific results. Participants viewed surface haptics as a way of communicating emotional information. Within a messaging context, S5M (stranger pair 5, male) said, "The strongest ones [haptic patterns] definitely can convey emotion." S4M said of the haptic image application, "What I was trying to convey is the emotion behind that scene." Participants often associated the strongest haptic patterns with strong emotions such as anger, and we elaborate this point below. Only one participant (C2F2; couple pair 2, female) mentioned that, to her, haptics did not have an emotional connection. Rather, she viewed the interaction as increasing expression more broadly.

Surface haptics were not wanted in isolation; participants described haptics as another dimension for communication and indicated that haptics should be used as a supplement to voice, text, and image-based communication. By studying haptic interaction in context of specific applications and existing social relationships, we better understand how one might design affective haptic experiences. For example, C2F1 called the haptic feedback "weird, creepy, and unsettling" when she touched things and did not expect a texture or did not expect it to feel the way it did.

Participants described the applications as "playful" and "fun" and rated them correspondingly (see Fig. 8; no sig. differences between couples vs. strangers for these data, so we report overall means). C1M2 said his favorite part was "being synchronized with your partner, being able to play with each other..." His partner said, "The whole textural sense was very novel... Discovering the feedback and the touch was fun." S3F commented, "I just thought it was a fun way to communicate." C6M "had fun playing with the texture." Users were neutral about whether the applications helped them understand their partner better, likely resulting from the short time using the technology together. This result and the lower rating of text messaging for self-expression are likely due to users needing to develop a shared haptic language, which we describe below.

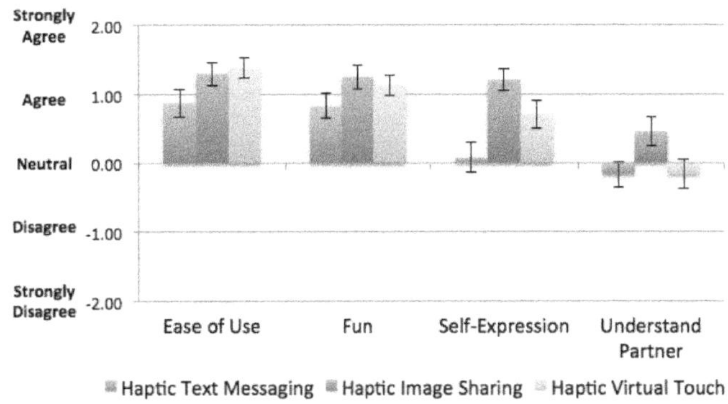

Figure 8: Likert ratings by app with mean and SE.

We analyzed Likert scale ratings for preferred communication partner across applications (Fig 9) using a mixed-effects statistical model to account for between and within-subject factors. The independent variables included were preferred communication partner, application, and the interaction between them. Because observations were not independent, subjects nested within partner type (couple/stranger) were modeled as a random effect. Participants viewed the applications to be most appropriate for interaction with a significant other or close friend (see Fig. 9), and this was significantly different from their preference for using applications with strangers and acquaintances ($F(3,253)=30.62$, $p< .0001$). To compare differences across levels we used Tukey's HSD, which revealed that ratings for spouse/sig. other and close friends were not different ($F(1,253)=0.30$, $p<0.59$), but ratings for close friends versus acquaintances and strangers versus acquaintances are both significant ($F(1,253)=12.8$, $p<0.0004$; $F(1,253)=18.8$, $p<0.0001$). C5M said, "Touching is like a personal thing, so this is not the kind of thing you

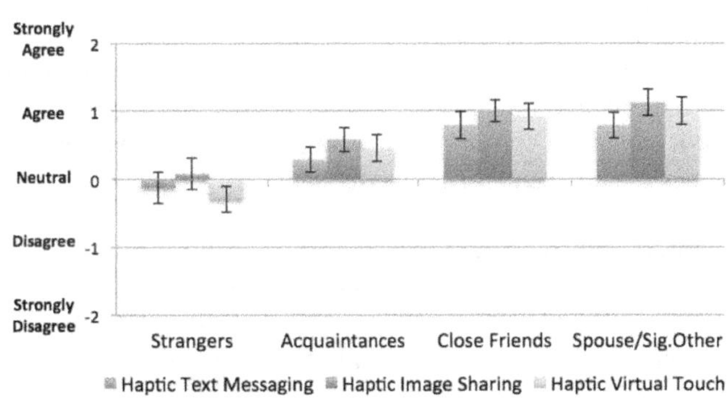

Figure 9: Mean Likert ratings with SE for preferred communication partner for each application.

would use with strangers." Additionally, during the discussions, half of participants (n=12) suggested using various applications with children. S2M explained, "Based on the fact that it's mostly touch, I would see myself using it more with a child because...you have more of an intimate feeling with a child as far as touch goes with hugs and kisses..." This finding supports the playful nature of interaction and the intimacy of haptics.

Haptic Text Messaging

On average participants previewed 11.5 (SD=6.4) different patterns and sent 6.8 (SD=2.5) different patterns to their partner. Users added a pattern to 66% (182/278) of messages they sent; however, follow-up discussion with participants indicated that they would send haptic patterns with messages less frequently if they were using this application outside of the lab. Two participants mentioned that it interrupted the conversation to send a texture with every message. We anticipate use in a field study to be less than that of emoticons, which were found in 4% of text messages [34].

Adding haptics to a message was viewed as only one aspect of a person's communication repertoire, and haptics were seen as a supplement to text, voice, and image-based communication. Users were able to send haptic messages without text, but only two of 278 messages were sent as a haptic pattern without text (see Fig 10, top). Furthermore, users thought that not all messages or words should have a texture or vibration pattern. For example, C3F said, "'Fun' could have a texture, but 'How was your day?' didn't seem to fit with a texture." Our application allowed users to apply a single texture to an entire message, but participants wanted to specify the texture of individual words.

We analyzed the content of participants' text messages and the haptic patterns they associated with various messages. Four primary uses of haptics in a text-messaging context emerged from our analysis of the logfiles and group discussion:

(1) Emotional expression. The majority of participants associated haptic patterns with emotional expression, and four participants compared the idea of haptic messaging to emoticons or emojis. Strong haptic patterns were often associated with anger. C5F said this application "would be great if you were fighting with someone," and that she would use it to "add a layer of expression." S5F said, "If you can't communicate what you're trying to say with words, it would be good to use a strong one to show anger." S5M explained that haptic messaging doesn't make sense "unless you can do something really intense." C3M explained that texture on words makes sense with "a strong emotion, anger... Dragging your finger across would take more effort." C4M said, "The problem with texting... there's implied tones...undertones that are part of the message..." and suggested haptics may help clarify this. S5M echoed this statement and said, "You'd be able to sense tone without using the cap locks button."

(2) Literal representation of texture. Participants applied texture to words in a literal sense. This was part of how participants shared a sensory experience with their partner (see Fig. 10, top). C2F1 explained, "In the context where I was experiencing something and I wanted to share with her multiple aspects of it, I would possibly use haptic feedback in that... 'Here's the sound. Here's what it looks like. Here's what it feels like.' To give her a rich experience." Another participant described using texture to communicate an experience of falling on ice.

(3) Highlighting content or messages. Participants applied haptics to highlight a particular message or content for the recipient. For example, S6M used contrasting haptic patterns to differentiate the punch line of a joke (Fig 10, center), and during the discussion he explained this was his intention. C1M1 wanted to use haptics to highlight important items on a shopping list, and C6M suggested using haptics for emphasis, as "an exclamation point." Five participants mentioned sending haptic messages as a surprise or on special occasions like a birthday [14].

(4) Physical playfulness. Both couples and strangers used haptics to be physically playful with their partner. C1M2 described adding rougher, higher friction patterns to impede his partner from opening the message, and his partner correctly interpreted this as a joke. Figure 10 illustrates a playful exchange between C3 where a series of static-like patterns became "boring" and they broke this trend by introducing a different texture (sawtooth wave) for fun. C2F1 said she would use haptics in a messaging context "to surprise somebody." S5M would use "an intense feeling where someone could get shocked, like a hand buzzer."

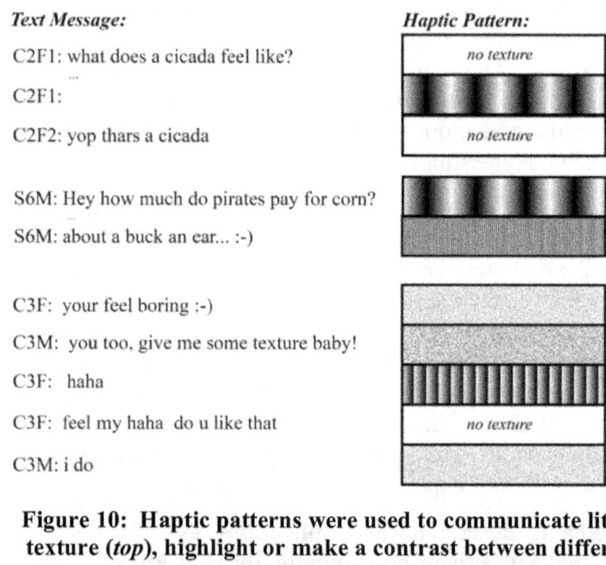

Figure 10: Haptic patterns were used to communicate literal texture (*top*), highlight or make a contrast between different messages such as a joke punch line (*center*), and as part of physical playfulness between pairs (*bottom*).

To understand the relationship between haptics and communicating affect, two researchers independently examined the corpus of text messages and extracted all messages (resolving any differences) that use text to explicitly indicate tone (i.e. with laughter "haha", exclamation points, smiley/frowning faces, and acronyms like "lol"). We found that 15% (42/278) of messages in the corpus included explicit tonal information. Of these messages, 79% (33/42) included a haptic pattern (compared to 66% of messages overall containing haptics), suggesting that users are slightly more inclined to add a haptic pattern when they explicitly indicate tone with textual information.

Overall, participants acknowledged that it would take time to learn to use haptic messaging in an everyday context, as they would need to learn or develop a "haptic vocabulary" and learn to weave it into conversation. Some users wanted a pre-defined vocabulary where others felt strongly it should develop organically between partners. C5M viewed the haptics as "a fancy emoticon" and acknowledged that it takes time to create shared meaning out of ambiguity: "People didn't use colons and parentheses like that [as a smiley face] 20 years ago to express feeling but now they do." Knowing one's partner is a critical piece of establishing this shared haptic language. C5F said, "I would only use [this application] with close friends or family, to add a layer of expressions to what I write." Thinking about learning a haptic vocabulary led participants to comment on exploiting touch for private communication. Two people described using haptics like a secret code to ensure onlookers did not view their message.

Haptic Image Sharing

Overall, the addition of haptics in an image editing and sharing context made sense to participants. When relating haptics to emotional expression, C2F2 said, "Words don't have a feeling but objects do." In general, participants responded favorably to this application and described it as a fun experience. C2F2 said, "I can see it being like a meme online... I can see it going viral." S4F said, "I think it was cool how it made the different images come alive, like the rocks 'cause you had feeling around the rocks. Then the water had this novel touch on it." We were surprised by the amount of thought many participants put into designing haptic images. We learned during the discussion that participants selected images they thought their partner would enjoy and/or images that had what they perceived to be varied or high contrasting textures. Participants selected images of a waterfall (n=6), a lion (n=4), sunset (n=3), field of flowers and mountains (n=3), puppy (n=2), cat (n=2), explosion (n=2), and impressionist painting (n=2). An image of rocks and an image of a still life painting were never selected. C5F said about selecting an image, "I thought it would have to be something I can imagine putting textures to… [It] would be too abstract for me to choose a painting…. Whereas with water, you can kind of feel, it's moist and soft." On average, participants added 4.7 different textures to their image (SD=2.09), with one participant adding nine different textures to a single image. Participants who selected a landscape-type image tended to add more textures (mean=5.5; SD=2.0) than participants who selected an image of an animal (mean=3.0; SD=1.1), indicating that images with greater variation in textures led participants to apply more varied haptic feelings.

Figure 11: Participants used haptics for literal texture (feeling of animal's tongue, fur), experiential/sensory information (intensity of an explosion), and hidden messages ("bliss" written over a waterfall). Color-coded textures are overlaid.

Analysis of the images participants selected and their application of texture revealed three primary uses of haptics in this context:

(1) Literal texture of an object or scene. As we observed in the text messaging application, participants applied various haptic patterns to convey the literal feeling of objects or a scene. For example, C2F1 selected an image of a dog (Fig. 11, left). She explained, "I made the nose and tongue...a color that kind of stuck to your fingers a little bit... Then I tried to pick one that gave a little bit of resistance and vibration for the fur of the body that was a little coarse..." As she described this during the discussion session, her partner said he noticed those differences in texture. Another participant (C3M) commented, "I liked the [texture] that I used for the water because it felt almost like your finger was wet when you tried to drag it across [the surface]."

(2) Texture as action or sensation. Participants also used haptics to create an interactive experience or tactile sensation based on the image content. C2F2 said, "The yellow color felt most like a waterfall..." She went on to explain that the yellow "rumbled" like a waterfall. Two other participants also used the yellow texture (70Hz sine wave) for the waterfall. S6F selected a cat photo and explained, "I was thinking of the feelings [textures] as the cat's purring, so I tried to map the intensity of the feeling to the places cats tend to like to be scratched." C4M selected an image of an explosion. He said, "I associated the explosion with the haptic… I figured there would be a concentrated center with a loud energy and then it would dissipate as it went out, so I really thought about painting that out with different sensory kinds of frequencies..."

(3) Hidden messages. Participants also applied haptics to an image in the form of a hidden message. For example, one participant drew a peace sign over a lion's face. Another wrote the word bliss in multiple layers over a waterfall (Fig. 11, right). When participants exchanged haptic images, we encouraged them to first explore the image in the haptic "feel" mode and then look at the visual of the haptic layer. Participants described exploring hidden messages as a game and tried to guess the message.

Participant couples reported feeling significantly more connected with their partners while using this application than strangers reported ($F(1,22)=7.40$, $p=.0125$); however, no differences in connectedness were found for haptic text messaging ($F(1,22)=0.24$, $p=.627$) or haptic virtual touch ($F(1,22)=0.303$, $p=.588$). We suspect that this difference is for two reasons. First, the task involved creating a haptic image for one's partner. This required thinking about what one's partner would enjoy and understand, which is a more difficult task for strangers than intimate couples. Second, as we found through our analysis, this application allowed for creative expression, providing opportunities for a person to demonstrate their understanding of their partner through the selection of an image and the way in which they add haptic patterns to it. We observed this connectedness between couples play out in interesting ways. For example, C1M2 said he "went with a Snoop Lion," which was an image of a lion with facial hair like the music artist. His partner laughed upon receiving this image and said, "Yeah, I got it completely." Other couples described selecting an image that they knew their partner would enjoy (e.g., a puppy dog or sunset). Relatedly, six participants mentioned using this application as a way to understand how other people think. C5M said, "It's a different vehicle for expressing feelings or sensations…meaning you want to attribute."

Haptic Virtual Touch

Overall, participants seemed to enjoy using this application. S5M said, "I thought it was fun. I liked it." C5F said, "It was playful, funny" to cross paths with her partner and that it "made me smile." We aimed to understand differences in interaction between pairs of couples and strangers, exploring whether a haptic virtual touch application might provide a sense of co-presence and intimacy between couples or possible discomfort between strangers [33].

Analysis of log files indicated how often and for how long participants touched virtually (Table 3). This data has high individual variation with no significant difference between couples and strangers. We highlight pairs who touched the most in Table 3 and understand their actions through observation and discussion data. Interestingly, most pairs turned this application into a game, and in some cases this lead to a high number of overlapping touches. C2F1 said, "We chased each other around for a while and touched finger tips a little bit. One of us would leave our finger still while the other would circle it." C6M told his partner, "I made a circle at one point, really fast, and I was wondering if you would do something inside it." S1F commented, "It was fun... It was like cat and mouse with your fingers." S6 mimicked each other's movements, and S6F said that they touched "most when playing hide-and-seek." In contrast, pairs with lower numbers of intersecting touches (C3, C4, S5) focused on turn taking, which requires consideration of protocols to manage transitions [6]. A couple participants wanted haptic virtual touch to be embedded within shared tasks (e.g., document editing) to be more meaningful.

	Times crossed	Time touching		Times crossed	Time touching
C1	22	0.77%	S1	**86**	**1.78%**
C2	**134**	**2.38%**	S2	35	0.81%
C3	2	0.06%	S3	19	0.41%
C4	10	0.10%	S4	27	0.41%
C5	34	0.59%	S5	9	0.07%
C6	**94**	**1.78%**	S6	**248**	**3.83%**
	49.3 (53.7)	*1.06 (0.94)*		*70.6 (90.9)*	*1.22 (1.41)*

Table 3: Number of times pair crossed finger paths and percent time spent touching partner virtually. Means (SD) reported.

While there was no difference in Likert ratings for whether this application made strangers vs. couples uncomfortable ($F(1,22)=0.712$, $p=.408$), several users described haptic virtual touch as an intimate experience that conveys a sense of touching one's partner. C5M said, "You're replicating the other person's moves, so you're kind of touching the other person," to which his wife replied, "which is nice because I know you, you're my spouse." His wife said she would not use it with a stranger because "it feels kind of intimate… You're kind of touching the other person…" Although, she said she might use the application with far away relatives because "it is a nice way to make contact." P1M explained "I could see this with a significant other… Though it's cyber it's a little closer to hand holding… I can see that almost in a way being 'footsies.'" S5M said he would use the application for "flirting." C2F2 explained, "It would be really creepy to do with a stranger, but then I could see it would really be a big thing to have total strangers connecting like that." In this sense, the intimacy of virtual touch may provide a novel social experience for strangers.

Other participants did not perceive the experience to be too intimate to perform with a stranger. When asked what she thought of the haptics when a finger overlap occurred, S5F said she "felt it but didn't really think of it." S3M said, "When my lines crisscrossed with hers, I felt her finger moving so that was kind of neat." His partner (S3F) responded, "That was kind of cool... Then we tried to do follow the leader." S6F said touching fingers was "a good sensation," and it "takes on different meanings when you're doing it with someone you don't know."

We also examined the subtleties in designing the haptic experience for a virtual touch application. For this application, we tested two variations of the haptics experienced when participants' fingers overlapped. Six participant pairs (three stranger pairs and three couples) received a 3D rendered version (Fig. 7a) of haptics and six participant pairs received a textured version (Fig. 7b), as described in the application section. Five of 12 people who used the 3D version said that they did not notice the haptics when their fingers intersected, indicating that the haptics were too subtle to feel or notice during the interaction. Two of the 12 participants who used the textured version said they did not notice the haptics. Furthermore, this application has a heavy visual component, and participant comments indicated that they focused on the visuals instead of the haptics. C4M said, "You're paying so much attention to what you're seeing that you don't notice the haptic[s]." The experience also varied by person with some people wanting stronger haptics and others calling the experience "sensory overload."

DISCUSSION

The present study provides insights into the use of surface haptics for communication, both in terms of designing better applications for affective communication as well as understanding haptic languages. Prior work indicates that haptics can convey emotional information [3,8,33], and we found that users associated haptics with emotional expression in multiple different contexts. Haptics are seen as only one facet of a communication experience, and users wanted texture to supplement existing forms of voice, text, and image-based communication. Past studies identified haptics as appropriate for interaction with close social partners [33], which we found as well, but this intimate and playful interaction may generalize to parent-child dyads.

For text-based communications, haptics provide another way of communicating affective information [27,30]. We observed the use of haptics for communicating emotion, conveying literal texture, highlighting information, and physical playfulness. Adding haptic patterns to individual words may be more meaningful than adding a pattern to an entire message, and we expect haptic messages would be used sparingly as a way of emphasizing or elaborating a particular communication. When defining a haptic language, users wanted established haptic mappings with flexibility to create an evolving haptic language unique to different social partners.

We found that adding haptics to an image sharing application engaged and made sense to users. Naturally, images that had a diversity of textures and action in the scene encouraged users to more fully exploit the palette of haptic textures as a way to make the image "come alive." Users explored and noted the differences between various intensities of a single texture and the contrasts between multiple textures. This use case is promising, and further exploration is needed into defining a range of textures that work well for various categories of pictures as well as how the application might engage other populations, such as children and visually impaired people.

The haptic virtual touch application was the most abstract and open-ended of the applications. Based on user feedback and log file data, users tended not to come in close proximity to each other for a large majority of the time. This application encouraged movement, and movement was indicated visually by a trail, which may have detracted from noticing the haptic experience of direct touch. One question we posed was whether the 3D rendering added realism and connection. Unfortunately, the 3D rendering was not noticed by almost half of participants, and we attribute this to both the rendering itself and the context in which it was presented. That is, the alternate "texture target" 100Hz sine wave went unnoticed by people as well. However, in the image sharing application, participants articulated subtle differences between haptic patterns, such as a 100Hz square wave or a 70Hz sine wave. In the real world, touch is complex. As variable friction technology improves, we plan to refine the design of virtual touch to enhance the feeling of co-presence.

Examining these use cases outside of the lab is critical. We speculate that virtually touching fingers as implemented here may be too ambiguous or simple without a larger context of a long-distance relationship or additional media (e.g., voice, video). While participants indicated that the applications enhanced self-expression (Fig 8), their ability to understand their partner was not enhanced, and we expect such understandings to develop over time. Future work should examine how haptic languages evolve "in the wild" and how tactile information may be used for emphasis, mimicry, and turn-taking (e.g.,[6]).

CONCLUSION

We presented the design and evaluation of three applications for affective communication involving variable friction surface haptics. Users readily related emotional expression and affect with haptic interaction in multiple contexts. We found that users perceive touch interaction through haptics most suitable for use with close social partners or even their children, although surface haptics present possibilities for new social interactions with strangers. Participants used haptics in varied ways to communicate literal texture, convey emotional information, highlight content, for physical playfulness, and to provide one's partner with an experience or sensation. The rich communication repertoire enabled by variable friction surface haptics makes it a promising platform for exploring affective computing.

ACKNOWLEDGEMENTS

We would like to thank Felix Hu, Ted Schwaba, and Darren Gergle for their help with the study and analysis, our study participants, and Michael Peshkin for continued support of the TPad Tablet Project. This work is supported by NSF (0964075), McCormick School of Engineering, and the Segal Design Institute.

REFERENCES

1. Bau, O., Poupyrev, I., Israr, A. & Harrison, C. TeslaTouch: electrovibration for touch surfaces. In *Proc of UIST 2010*, 283–292.
2. Battarbee, K., *et al.* Pools and satellites: intimacy in the city. In *Proc of DIS 2002*, 237–245.
3. Brave, S., & Dahley, A. inTouch: a medium for haptic interpersonal communication. In *Proc of CHI 1997 Extended Abstracts*, 363–364.
4. Brave, S., Ishii, H., & Dahley, A. Tangible interfaces for remote collaboration and communication. In *Proc of CSCW 1998*, 169–178.
5. Brown, L. M., Brewster, S. A., & Purchase, H. C. Multidimensional tactons for non-visual information presentation in mobile devices. In *Proc of HCI with mobile devices and services 2006,* 231–238.
6. Chan, A., MacLean, K., & McGrenere, J. (2008). Designing haptic icons to support collaborative turn-taking. *I. J. of Hum-Comp. Studies*, *66*(5), 333–355.
7. Chang, A., O'Modhrain, S., Jacob, R., Gunther, E., & Ishii, H. ComTouch: design of a vibrotactile communication device. In *Proc of DIS 2002,* 312–320.
8. Chang, A., Resner, B., Koerner, B., Wang, X., & Ishii, H. LumiTouch: an emotional communication device. In *Proc of CHI 2001 Extended Abstracts,* 313–314.
9. Collier, G. (1985). *Emotional Expression*. Lawrence Erlbaum Associates, Incorporated.
10. Eichhorn, E., Wettach, R., & Hornecker, E. A stroking device for spatially separated couples. In *Proc of HCI with mobile devices and services* 2008, 303–306.
11. Enriquez, M. J., & MacLean, K. E. The Hapticon Editor: A Tool in Support of Haptic Communication Research. In *Proc of HAPTICS 2003,* 356.
12. Fogg, B., Cutler, L. D., Arnold, P., & Eisbach, C. HandJive: a device for interpersonal haptic entertainment. In *Proc of CHI 1998,* 57–64.
13. Itō, M., Okabe, D., & Matsuda, M. (2005). Personal, portable, pedestrian: mobile phones in Japanese life. Cambridge, Mass.: MIT Press.
14. Kaye, J. "Jofish," Levitt, M. K., Nevins, J., Golden, J., & Schmidt, V. Communicating intimacy one bit at a time. In *Proc of CHI 2005 Ext. Abs.,* 1529–1532.
15. Kjeldskov, J., *et al.* (2007). Using Cultural Probes to Explore Mediated Intimacy. *Aust. Jour. Info. Sys.*, *11*(2).
16. Knapp, M. L., & Hall, J. A. (2010). *Nonverbal communication in human interaction.* Boston, MA: Wadsworth, Cengage Learning.
17. Kowalski, R., Loehmann, S., & Hausen, D. cubble: a multi-device hybrid approach supporting communication in long-distance relationships. In *Proc of TEI 2013,* 201–204.
18. Levesque, V., *et al.* Enhancing physicality in touch interaction with programmable friction. In *Proc of CHI 2011,* 2481–2490.
19. Luk, J., Pasquero, J., Little, S., MacLean, K., Levesque, V., & Hayward, V. A role for haptics in mobile interaction: initial design using a handheld tactile display prototype. In *Proc of CHI 2006,* 171–180.
20. Maclean, K., & Enriquez, M. (2003). Perceptual design of haptic icons. In *Proc of Eurohaptics*, 351–363.
21. Marchuk, N. D., Colgate, J. E., & Peshkin, M. A. Friction measurements on a Large Area TPaD. In *Proc of HAPTICS 2010,* 317–320.
22. Moss, B.F., & Schwebel, A.I. (1993). Defining Intimacy in Romantic Relationships. *Fam. Rel.*, *42*(1), 31–37.
23. Mueller, F. Vetere, F., Gibbs, M. R., Kjeldskov, J., Pedell, S., & Howard, S. (2005). Hug over a distance. In *Proc of CHI 2005 Ext. Abs.,* 1673–1676.
24. Mullenbach, J., Shultz, C., Piper, A.M., Peshkin, M., and Colgate, J.E. "TPad Fire: Surface Haptic Tablet", Proc of *HAID 2013.*
25. Mullenbach, J., Shultz, C., Piper, A.M., Peshkin, M., and Colgate, J.E. Surface Haptic Interactions with a TPad Tablet. In *Proc of UIST 2013 Ext. Abs*.
26. Nguyen, T., Heslin, R., & Nguyen, M. L. (1975). The Meanings of Touch: Sex Differences. *Journal of Communication*, *25*(3), 92–103.
27. Oakley, I. (n.d.). *Contact IM: Exploring Asynchronous Touch Over Distance*.
28. Picard, R. W. (2000). *Affective computing*. Cambridge, Mass.: MIT Press.
29. Register, L. M., & Henley, T. B. (1992). The Phenomenology of Intimacy. *Journal of Social and Personal Relationships*, *9*(4), 467–481.
30. Rovers, L., & Essen, H. V. (2004). Design and evaluation of hapticons for enriched instant messaging. In *Virtual Reality,* 177–191.
31. Sallnäs, E.-L., Rassmus-Gröhn, K., & Sjöström, C. (2000). Supporting presence in collaborative environments by haptic force feedback. *ACM ToCHI*, *7*(4), 461–476.
32. Salminen, K., *et al.* Emotional and behavioral responses to haptic stimulation. In *Proc of CHI 2008,* 1555–1562.
33. Smith, J., & MacLean, K. (2007). Communicating emotion through a haptic link: Design space and methodology. *Int. J. Hum.-Comp. Stud.*, *65*(4), 376–387.
34. Tossell, C. C., Kortum, P., Shepard, C., Barg-Walkow, L. H., Rahmati, A., & Zhong, L. (2012). A longitudinal study of emoticon use in text messaging from smartphones. *Comp. in Human Behav.*, *28*(2), 659–663.
35. Wang, R., & Quek, F. Touch & talk: contextualizing remote touch for affective interaction. In *Proc of TEI 2010* (pp. 13–20).

35. Winfield, L., Glassmire, J., Colgate, J. E., & Peshkin, M. (2007). T-PaD: Tactile Pattern Display through Variable Friction Reduction. In *Proc of EuroHaptics 2007,* 421–426.

Wrigglo: Shape-Changing Peripheral for Interpersonal Mobile Communication

Joohee Park, Young-Woo Park, Tek-Jin Nam
CIDR Lab, Department of Industrial Design, KAIST
291 Daehak-ro, Yuseong-gu, Daejeon 305-701, Republic of Korea
{joohee.a.park, pyw, tjnam}@kaist.ac.kr

ABSTRACT
We introduce Wrigglo, a shape-changing smart phone peripheral that allows pairs of users to share wriggling movements with one another. Attached to a smart phone, Wrigglo captures the sender's motions and activates the receiver's Wrigglo which repeats the motion simultaneously. The result of our in-lab use observation with twelve couples showed that Wrigglo supported emotional and functional roles of body gestures and postures, creating vocabularies related to the motion of specific body parts and, to some extent, reflected the connected user's presence through the device's movement. Through its peripheral anthropomorphization, Wrigglo can deliver new forms of telepresence by embodied posturing and gesturing in mobile communication.

Author Keywords
Shape-changing; mobile peripheral; remote communication;

ACM Classification Keywords
H.5.2 Information interfaces and presentation: User interfaces—Input devices and strategies, interaction styles.

INTRODUCTION
The development of shape-changing material has generated considerable recent research interest especially with regard to new interactive systems. It implies the possibilities of technology and, moreover, is influential in interactions between users and computers. Shape-changing devices enable users to communicate in affective and rich ways. Hemmert et al. [6] have demonstrated that shape-changing objects deliver their messages to users as a living object does. Shape-changing devices can also easily draw users' attention. Soft computing, especially using nitinol as an actuator, shows that shape-changing devices give users effective, subtle, and quiet notifications [5].

In particular, shape-changing mobile devices [5, 6] have been increasingly studied nowadays in HCI. These studies propose possible new experiences that shape-changing mobile devices can make, as they interact with users most frequently. But, they mostly focus on the transformation of the mobile phone itself, which requires more time before it can be applied to current phones. In addition, they rarely figured out how the devices were used with actual applications of smart phones. From the studies, we found that a shape-changing peripheral is needed to improve these issues. Previously, Yim and Shaw suggested Callo [15], a shape-changing peripheral for communications use, which is essential in a mobile device. However, its complex movement requires overloaded cognitive effort for control during synchronous communication. Similarly, there were cases that applied the haptic [1, 3] and visual [7] feedback to aid in verbal communication, and we discovered that transmitting a simple expression is adequate for manipulation during conversation. There remains a need for an investigation into how users apply simple shape changes of the peripherals in mobile communications.

We propose a novel mobile peripheral called Wrigglo (Figure 1) and discuss what purpose it can serve in communication from the result of user observations.

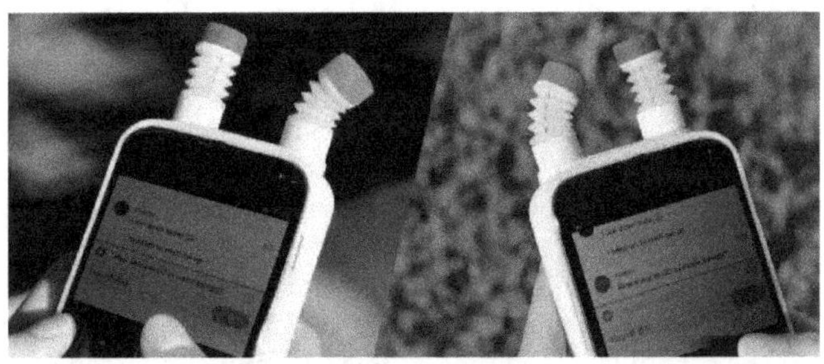

Figure 1. A set of systems: 4 Wrigglos and 2 phone cases.

WRIGGLO DESIGN
Wrigglo is an antennae-like attachment for mobile phone casings that supports pairwise non-verbal communication through real-time actuated coupling. To design it, we took the following into account:

- Portability: it should be lightweight and handheld.
- Simple & quiet motion: the motions should be easy to manipulate during conversation. Also, the actuated motion must be quiet so that it does not interrupt the user.
- Real-time responsiveness & transmission: User A's input should be delivered to User B's shape-changing movement device in real time.

CHI 2014, April 26 - May 01 2014, Toronto, ON, Canada
Copyright 2014 ACM 978-1-4503-2473-1/14/04...$15.00.
http://dx.doi.org/10.1145/2556288.2557166

The Wrigglo system consists of two Wrigglos (Figure 2, b) that change shape and are attached to a phone case controller (Figure 2, a). Each user puts two different color-coded Wrigglos in the top of the case: left for the connected user and right for the self. If the user manipulates the rear joystick (Figure 2, k) of the case, his/her Wrigglos in two sides simultaneously bend their bodies in the same direction (Figure 1). As the joystick is pulled to the right/left/top/bottom, the Wrigglos follow in the same direction. Also, if user touches the head of the Wrigglo, both Wrigglos shrink.

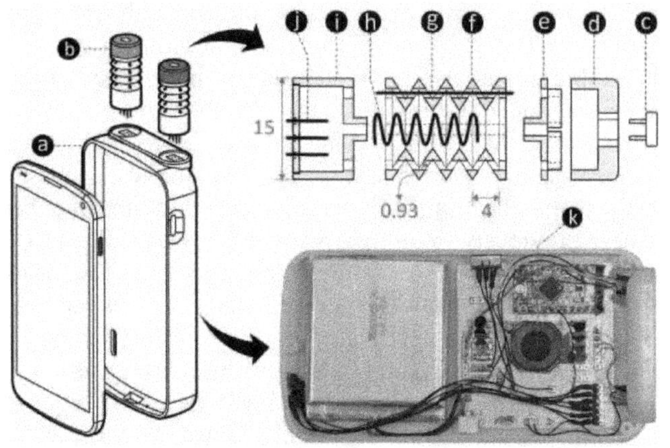

Figure 2. A detailed structure of Wrigglo (b) and the opened backside of a case controller (a) (unit: mm) (c) Photo cell, (d) Cap, (e, i) Holder, (f) Rubber bellows, (g) SMA, (h) Spring, (j) Connector pins, (k) Joystick

Implementation

We extended Walters and McGoran's 2-way bendable tentacle concept [13] into a 4-way bendable, collapsible, and touch-sensitive concept with a photocell (Figure 2, c), a bellow structure, and a spring pillar (h) inside. We concluded that SMA is an appropriate material for peripheral devices for mobile communication because it is light, flexible, thin, and quietly actuates an object [9]. We arranged 4 SMA coils (g) into the holes of the 3D-printed rubber-like bellows cover (f) so that contraction of the heated coil controls the orientation of bending movement. The maximum angle of bending is 45 degrees when the joystick input is applied for 470ms (9.2 mm contracted coil, 3.7V). If the adjacent coils are heated together, the body bends to the middle. If 4 coils are heated, it shrinks. To stretch the coils to their original length, we adjusted the shape of the bellows, the height unit of the bellows, the thickness of the bellows' cover, and one spring pillar. It turned out that Wrigglo has weaker restoring force but better flexibility when: (1) the bellows is cylindrical rather than rectangular, (2) the height unit is long, and (3) the thickness is thin. From 12 different prototypical shapes, we adopted the appropriate unit height (4mm) and thickness (0.93mm) with a cylindrical bellows. We reinforced the restoring force by mounting a spring pillar. With this balance, the bent Wrigglo was restored to its original position. This takes 2100ms without any control or 290ms by heating the opposite coil. The 3D printed phone case controller contains a rear thumb-size joystick and a custom Arduino board to drive the Wrigglos, powered by a 3.7v/2000mA Li-Po battery. The Arduino communicates with a Processing sketch that runs on the laptop and that also provides communication between the sender and the receiving system. A phone case controller adds 10mm to the grabbing point and 117g to a smartphone. Although the current system was implemented as a proof-of-concept version, a software application on a smartphone and the microcontroller-embedded case would make the prototype practically feasible.

USER STUDY

We conducted an exploratory study to investigate the value of Wrigglo in a mobile communication context. Specifically, our questions in the study were: (1) how do shape changes with the mobile peripheral improve communication between people? (2) how are shape changes perceived by participants? and (3) what kinds of shape-changing vocabularies are created?

Twelve female friend couples (aged 19–28, 1A&1B–12A&12B) participated. We recruited them because they were expected to chat in an expressive way [8, 14]. We introduced the device and gave a 5-minute overview of the study. Then, we gave a 10-minute training session before starting the session. We taught the dyads how to manipulate the Wrigglo and each participant sent the other Wrigglo signals by following the preset instructions. Then, each participant was led to one of two separate rooms and asked to have a 10-minute video call and participate in 10 minutes of instant messaging time. For both situations, we asked them to use Wrigglo during each dialogue. Since Wrigglo gives visual impressions, we selected a video call and instant messaging (IM) instead of an audio call as a mobile communication context. We used the Skype application as software, and videos were not recorded but the instant messages were saved on Skype. After two exploratory sessions, participants were debriefed for 20 minutes on the impressions when they used Wrigglo, what the role of the subtle wriggling motion was, and overall usability. The interview were recorded and transcribed afterward.

FINDINGS

Emotional and Functional Use in Conversation

We explored how participants utilized Wrigglos in texting and video calls. Eleven couples found uses for Wrigglo in conveying body gestures. First, they considered Wrigglo as an emotive tool to respond to the other or to gain sympathy. For instance, participant 9A stated that moving forward showed an "*interested*" attitude while backwards showed "*disagreeing.*" Couple4 won sympathy from her partner by venting frustration using shrinking Wrigglos. These results indicate that the Wrigglo's expressions mimicked the participants' body gestures: forward/backward and plumping down, that can be found in the existing work revealing the relationship between body action and emotion specific information [4].

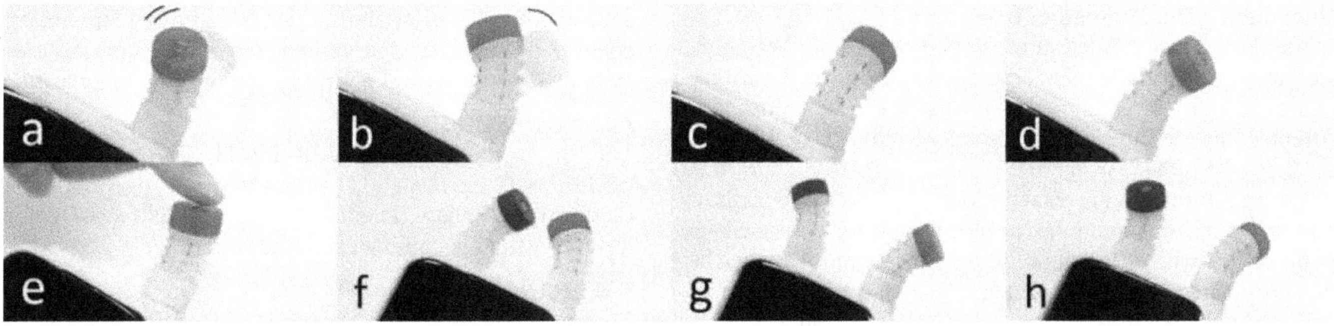

Figure 3: Expression of Wrigglo. (a) forward and backward (*Yes*), (b) side to side (*No*), (c) expansion (*So what?* or *I disagree.*), (d) forward (*Huh?* or *Pointing right*), (e) shrinking (*Overwhelmed* or *Doubtful*), (f) facing each other, (g) outwards, (h) crossing

were more frequently used for functional purposes. In the context of a video call, Couple12 signed *yes* and *no* to each other by using Wrigglo for secret dialogues. They said Wrigglos could replace speech so that no one else could hear the answer. Some participants created punctuation gestures to emphasize speech by bending Wrigglo with the stressed syllables. Besides the sign language and punctuation gestures, Couple2 bent the Wrigglo toward each other while asking, *"What about you?"* as if they were pointing. This action visualizes the content of speech. Similarly, Couple6 and Couple7 mentioned that they would bend the Wrigglo to the right before lunchtime while saying, *"Let's go get something to eat."* Also, in a messaging context, responding gestures such as *Yes* (nodding), *No* (wagging a head or finger), and *Okay* (making a ring) were commonly found. Seven couples mentioned that they expressed a nodding action by repeatedly bending Wrigglo forward to show they were listening instead of texting a response while the friend was continuing texting. These functional uses of Wrigglo are in line with speech-independent gestures and speech-related gestures [8], and envelope feedback [2].

Reflection of the Connected User in Wrigglo

Some researchers [10, 11] have proposed the concept of an interactive object reflecting a person, and we also found the possibility of reflecting the connected partner from the use observation. Half of all participants answered that Wrigglo seemed to reflect the connected user. The automatic movement controlled by the other user was the biggest contributor to this feeling. In texting, in particular, many participants sensed the telepresence of the other since they could not see their face. 1A said, *"Usually, you cannot see your friend's finger typing texts. But the moving Wrigglo looked like her finger's motion when I was waiting for her next messages. This gave me a feeling that I was with her."* In a video call, 12B reported that she regarded the moving Wrigglos as 12A's hand/arm gestures, which are usually not visible on the screen. As a second reason, some participants answered that touching the other's moving Wrigglo made them feel like they were touching each other. 6B stated that the haptic impression of the moving Wrigglo let her think she was close to 6A, whereas she did not feel anything about the standing Wrigglo.

On the contrary, the other half of the users did not agree that Wrigglo reflected the other user. They stated that 20 minutes was not enough to develop empathy with Wrigglo, but they suggested this could be improved by applying their partner's features to the Wrigglo's design.

Gesture and Posture Vocabulary Creation

As mentioned earlier, Wrigglo has a simple expression, unlike Callo and Cally [15]. In general, it appears that the simple motion mimics a gesture or posture of a different body part depending on situations or participants. Eleven couples developed the vocabulary considering Wrigglo as a stand-in for the head, torso, arm, wrist, or fingers.

When embodying head movement, which was the most common use, participants tended to map positive words (e.g., *yes*) into y-axis movement and negative words (e.g., *no* and *huh?*) into the x-axis. The torso gestures of the Wrigglo were associated with the contrast of expansion and shrinking. Four couples used shrinking motions to show they were *overwhelmed* or *doubtful*. Similarly, the torso posture of a shrunk Wrigglo meant the physical status of tiredness. While the shrinking motion was related to negative meanings, Couple10 mentioned that the expansion movement (bending backward) stood for positive words or phrases such as *"So what? (confident)."* By way of exception, one couple used the inward torso gesture to symbolize *"Hi (bowing),"* a common greeting in Asian culture.

However, two other couples visualized *"Hi (waving)"* by shaking the Wrigglo from side to side. There were also cases in which participants using Wrigglo's to represent fingers formed posture-related vocabularies such as pointing and mimicking emblems. 7B even imagined the future use of Wrigglo motion, saying, *"If I can control both left and right Wrigglos together, I would express a double quotation mark as like you bend two fingers to emphasize a word."*

Our finding related to vocabulary creation parallels with the result that the restricted expressions flexibly extended the variety of vocabularies [3, 7]. Here, we found that the Wrigglos' movement vocabularies naturally reflected different body parts depending on the context.

Unexpected Discoveries of Uses

In addition, we found unexpected uses of Wrigglo, suggesting new potentials. Three couples explored various expressions by creating joint postures of the Wrigglos. Couple6 depicted the heart symbol by bending one Wrigglo to face the other Wrigglo (Figure 3, f). Although the completed form did not exactly look like the symbol, they thought it did not matter because the posture was used in conjunction with a dialogue. Two other couples played a posture-related game by chance. One played a guessing game involving guessing the direction of the other's bent Wrigglo by chanting *"Cham, Cham, Cham!"* and, at the last syllable, both players bent their Wrigglos at random. These uses imply the potential of the medium to develop a bond of sympathy beyond a basic means, including turn-taking in mobile communication. Second, Wrigglo motion seems to be utilized as a form of customized and informative notification, like MorePhone [5]. 11A mentioned that the movement notification might imply her mood so that the connected user can react appropriately in conversation and liven up the mood.

DISCUSSION & IMPLICATIONS

Based on the results, we suggest the following implications for the development of actuating mobile peripherals. First, embodying the cues of the connected user may bring improved empathy because Wrigglo has anthropomorphic features. The characteristics of appearance (e.g., hairstyles, fashions) can be applied to the cap of Wrigglo like Lego's figures. The traits of personality can include one variable for motion (e.g., fast movement for a hot-tempered person). Second, if a movement is delivered in relative perspective (inward/ outward), rather than in an absolute way (left/ right), the joint gestures can be actively created. The asymmetry of representation control has led to the interaction between two Wrigglos. Third, the appropriate input interface should be taken into account. For instance, direct deformation of SMA [9] and preset motion may help users to use Wrigglo in highly cognitive load task. These issues must be taken into account to make Wrigglo more robust and cost-effective enough to be used in the real use.

CONCLUSION

We proposed the Wrigglo, a novel mobile shape-changing peripheral that can send 4-way bending, collapsing motion to a connected user not only with the joystick but also by touching the Wrigglo itself. The design of the Wrigglo contributed to develop the optimized structure of a shape-changing peripheral that is light, small, and silent. Our in-lab use observation with twelve couples uncovered how its shape-changing feature aided texting and video conversation. Wrigglo supported the emotional and functional roles of body gestures and postures; and, even with subtle movements, couples created vocabularies that considered Wrigglo as a specific part of the body. Additionally, the movement and design of Wrigglo seemed to reflect the connected users. Through the peripheral anthropomorphization and the asymmetry of representation control, Wrigglo can deliver new forms of telepresence and embodied posturing and gesturing in mobile communication.

ACKNOWLEDGEMENT

This research was supported by IT R&D program of MSIP/KEIT (2013, 10041313, UX-oriented Mobile SW Platform). We thank Daniel Saakes and Matthew Baldwin for their valuable comments on the paper.

REFERENCES

1. Brave, S., Ishii, H. and Dahley, A. (1998) Tangible interfaces for remote collaboration and communication. In *Proc. CSCW '98*, 169-178.
2. Cassell J. & Thorisson, K. R. (1999) The power of a nod and a glance: Envelope vs. emotional feedback in animated conversational agents, *Applied Artificial Intelligence* 13, 4-5, 519-538.
3. Chang, A., O'Modhrain, S., Jacob, R., Gunther, E., and Ishii, H. (2002) Comtouch: Design of a vibrotactile communication device. In *Proc. DIS 2002*, 312-320.
4. Dael, N., Mortillaro, M. & Scherer, K.R. (2012) Emotion Expression in Body Action and Posture. *Emotion* 12(5), 1085-1101.
5. Gomes, A., Nesbitt, A. & Vertegaal, R. (2013) MorePhone: a study of actuated shape deformations for flexible thin-film smartphone notifications. In *Proc. CHI'13*, 583-592.
6. Hemmert, F., Löwe, M., Wohlauf, A. & Joost, G. (2013) Animate Mobiles: Proxemically Reactive Posture Actuation as a Means of Relational Interaction with Mobile Phones. In *Proc. TEI'13*, 267-270.
7. Kaye, J. J. (2006) I just clicked to say I love you: rich evaluations of minimal communication. *Ext. Abs. CHI'06,* 363-368.
8. Knapp, M. L. & Hall, J. A. (1997) *Nonverbal Communication in Human Interaction.* Thomson Wadsworth Press, 6th Edit.
9. Nakagawa, Y., Kamimura, A. & Kawaguchi, Y. (2012) MimicTile: a variable stiffness deformable user interface for mobile devices. In *Proc. CHI'12*, 745-748.
10. Quintanilha, M. (2008) Buddy Wall: a tangible user interface for wireless remote communication. Ext. *Abs. CHI'08*, 3711-3716.
11. Raffle, H.,Wang, R., Seada, K. & Ishii, H. (2011) Communiclay: a modular system for tangible telekinetic communication. Ext. Abs. CHI'11, 233-242.
12. Rasmussen, R. K., Lehoux, N., Ocnarescu, I. & Krogh, P. G. (2012) I'll knock you when I'm ready...: reflecting on media richness beyond bandwidth and imitation. In *Proc. DIS'12*, 106-115.
13. Walters, P. & McGoran, D. (2011) Digital fabrication of smart structures and mechanism: Creative applications in art and design. In *Proc. IS&T '11*, 185-188.
14. Witmer, D. F. and Katzman, S. L., (1997) On-Line Smiles: Does Gender Make a Difference in the Use of Graphic Accents? Computer-Mediated Communication 2, 4.
15. Yim, J-D. & Shaw, C.D. (2011) Design Considerations of Expressive Bidirectional Telepresence Robots. *Ext. Abs. CHI'11*, 781-790.

Recreating Living Experiences from Past Memories through Virtual Worlds for People with Dementia

Panote Siriaraya
Faculty of Industrial Design Engineering, Delft University of Technology, Landbergstraat 15 2628 CE Delft, The Netherlands

Chee Siang Ang
School of Engineering and Digital Arts, University of Kent, CT2 7NT, United Kingdom

ABSTRACT
This paper describes a study aimed to understand the use of 3D virtual world (VW) technology to support life engagement for people with dementia in long-term care. Three versions of VW prototypes (reminiscence room, virtual tour and gardening) utilising gestured-base interaction were developed iteratively. These prototypes were tested with older residents (80+) with dementia in care homes and their caregivers. Data collection was based on observations of how the residents and care staff interacted collaboratively with the VW. We discussed in depth the use of VWs in stimulating past memories and how this technology could help enhance their sense of self through various means. We also highlighted key approaches in designing VWs to sustain attention, create *ludic experiences* and facilitate interaction for older people with dementia.

Author Keywords
3D virtual worlds; older people; care home; dementia; gesture-based interaction

ACM Classification Keywords
H.5.m. Information interfaces and presentation (e.g., HCI): Miscellaneous.

INTRODUCTION
The care of dementia is becoming a key agenda in health care research. A report published by the Health Economics Research Centre estimated that the cost of dementia in care and lost productivity in the UK could be as high as £23 billion [26]. Another report estimated the cost of care in the US to be $203 billion in 2013 [1]. Dementia not only affects those suffering from it but also incurs a personal cost to those taking care of them. Therefore, there is a strong interest in finding ways to assist the care of people with dementia. Increasingly, the CHI community is looking into ways to design technology to support specifically dementia care and more generally older people in care homes [35, 18, 17]. Virtual world (VW) technologies have great potentials in enhancing dementia care. The high fidelity imagery generated in VW could create "living experiences", experiences which are interactive, engaging and immersive for people with dementia. Reliving past experiences could help stimulate memories, provide positive emotions and enhance their sense of self. In line with the recent work in dementia within the CHI community, the aim of this study is to understand how 3D VWs can be designed to support life engagement for people with dementia in long-term care. More specifically, the objectives of this study are to:

- investigate how older people with dementia engage with virtual worlds and how they relate their selfhood and identity to the various aspects of virtual worlds.
- examine how virtual worlds can be designed to encourage sustained *ludic experiences* with residents.

CHI 2014, April 26 - May 01 2014, Toronto, ON, Canada

http://dx.doi.org/10.1145/2556288.2557035

Dementia and old age
Various declines in the physical and cognitive abilities are almost inevitable as we enter old age, and this could result in deterioration of quality of life [33]. Dementia is an increasingly common condition related to the decline of cognitive abilities. Dementia is not a single disease, but a set of symptoms which include losses of cognitive functions, declines in memory, attention as well as impairments in reasoning and planning abilities [37]. In some cases, those with dementia are also found to undergo changes in their personality and behaviour [7]. Alzheimer's disease is a common cause of dementia, resulting in a progressive deterioration in cognitive abilities, memory and mood changes [28]. Due to this variability of dementia, providing good care for people with dementia is not easy. They often have difficulties in communication, making interaction very challenging. Apart from cognitive declines due to dementia, many of them have impaired abilities in various daily activities such as problems with eating, and high level of incontinence. To further exacerbate the situation, they do not usually have the verbal ability to complain about their care. If they try to communication via their behaviour, it is often treated as a symptom to be suppressed [27].

In recent years, dementia care has gradually adopted a person-centred approach based on social interaction [14]. One such approach is known as Intensive Interaction (II).

Introduced by Ephraim [15], it is traditionally used with people with learning disabilities and autism. A main issue II aims to address is to promote social interaction for individuals with difficulty in communication. Caldwell, a practitioner and advocate of II, outlined some useful practical guides in [8]. The key technique involves using the client's own non-verbal body language to get in touch with them by understanding their noises, movements, gestures and rhythms. Virtual worlds are a way of helping patients use non-verbal body language to affect their environment that could complement traditional II and support reminiscence by transporting users back to familiar contexts

Technology in dementia care

Various technologies have been designed and proposed to assist the care of people with dementia. These include context-aware memory aids to provide useful reminders, and devices to help older people carry out everyday tasks such as hand washing (see a summary in [2]). A number of these technologies were targeted at residents in care homes. Examples include a photostroller device which displays a stream of pictures to provide ludic engagement [17] and a touch screen system to facilitate the creation of music [32]. Many of these devices were based on the idea of supporting reminiscence activities to a certain extent. Reminiscence therapy is described as an activity where older people are asked to recall memories of events and experience from their past. Often, visual and audio aids or other tangible artefacts such as photographs are used [39]. Such activities have been shown to improve cognitive functioning and morale [36]. Some technologies have been developed to facilitate reminiscence therapy. These include an interactive multimedia tool [18] and a networked system employing an IP videophone and a photo/video sharing system [23].

Virtual worlds and their potential in dementia care

One technology with potential benefits to people with dementia is the 3D virtual world (VW). The combination of interactivity and the ability to provide a high fidelity 3D visualisation of places and objects offers a unique experience for users that is difficult to achieve using traditional media. For instance, VWs could be used as aids in reminiscence activities, allowing users to interact with objects which are hard (or expensive) to obtain in the physical world (e.g. a retro car) or to provide an experience of a place which is no longer possible to access (such as a historic street from the past). The interactivity of the virtual environments could allow older people to not only be passive viewers of the objects and scenes, but also engage actively in a more playful and creative experience of reminiscence. There have been few studies looking into the use of VW technology in the care of older people with dementia in care homes. This technology has been used indirectly as visualisation tools to visualise the activities and locations of older people for caregivers and their family members [4]. It has also been used to provide relaxation to trigger positive emotions among older people [6] and to provide a representation of a place from the past (e.g. a bar) [18]. In this study, we examined in depth the idea of using VW to support life engagement for those with dementia in the long-term care. In this paper, we documented the key observations throughout our eight-month study, highlighting the design process and the relationship between selfhood and memories which emerged from their engagement with VW.

Our approach is different from previous work such as project CIRCA [18] in several ways. Firstly, we focus on creating a lively real time rendered 3D environment, instead of more "static" visualisation such as 360 Degree Panorama. This would potentially enhance the feeling of "presence", thus enhancing the benefit of use. Secondly, we make use of gesture-based technology (i.e. Kinect) to enhance the interaction and empower older people to interact with the system in a more natural manner. Thirdly, our design puts an emphasis on creating a virtual space for use in social interaction.

METHOD

Due to the difficulties in verbal communication for people with dementia, design studies involving older people with cognitive impairment are challenging [22]. Moreover, this user group tends to have little experience with technology. In order to overcome this, we used a mixed method in our study, involving observations, focus groups and interviews. Throughout the study, the virtual worlds design evolved iteratively based on the observations and feedback from the care staff. A series of facilitated sessions with different versions of the VW prototypes were carried out, during which the researchers observed and make detailed notes of the interaction and the personal conversation of residents and caregivers. A number of studies in care homes have also adopted similar approaches in their research [17,18].

Data collection & Analysis

The data collection was centred around the iterative development of a VW (see Table 1). A typical data collection session involved the carers (or activity facilitators) using the prototypes to engage the residents with virtual activities. The observation was carried out in a room designated for activity in the care homes. The groups ranged from five residents to sometimes just one resident. The residents were free to leave the room if they were no longer interested in the activity. The researchers were only there as external observers and to provide technical support. Detailed notes were taken during the observation. No voice or video recording devices were used due to ethical reasons. A total of 9 visits were made to 2 care homes and 8 observation sessions were carried out over the period of eight months, involving 6 carers/activities facilitators, 2 care home managers, and approximately 20 residents. After each visit where observation sessions were conducted, interviews were carried out with the care staff. The interviews were open-ended and involved discussing their opinions about the prototypes, suggesting ways to improve them and providing clarification on the observations. Additionally, two focus group sessions were carried out with the care staff and managers. The focus groups involved discussing the issues related to the prototypes design and identifying appropriate activity and content design (see table 1). The study was approved by the University Ethics Committee.

Data was analysed and categorised into themes using thematic analysis. The notes were read through by two researchers independently to gain an overall understanding. Patterns in the data were coded and the codes were refined into themes. Finally, to further refine and verify the themes, the two researchers critically discussed and reviewed each theme and underlying code together until they reached an agreement. Each theme highlights a key aspect of our observations on the recursive process used in the development of the prototypes and our interpretation of what was reflected when older people with dementia interacted with VWs.

Visit	Home	Participants
1	1	2 managers (initial discussion)
2	1	1 staff, 1 volunteer, 4 residents; 1 session with prototype version 1
3	1	1 staff, 1 volunteer, 4 residents; 1 session with version 1 and 2(river tour)
4	1	3 staff and 5 residents; 1 session with version 2 (river and park tour)
5	1	2 managers, 3 staff (further discussion)
6	1	4 staff (focus group)
7	1	3 staff (focus group)
8	2	3 staff and 4 residents; 3 sessions with version 3
9	2	3 staff and 5 residents; 2 sessions with version 3

Table 1: A summary of the visits with the care homes.

The care homes

Two care homes based in South East England participated in the study. The first one was a large care facility housing more than 100 residents. The second was a smaller care home with around 50 residents. The residents had a variety of declines in their cognitive and physical abilities. All of them had some forms of dementia. The residents were aged between 80 and 101 years old. To promote the well-being and life engagement of the resident, both care homes regularly organise activities, which include gardening activities and dancing. Occasional outings are also organised in which participants are taken to the beach, the bar or go shopping. Most of these activities require close supervision of the carers. This is especially true for outdoor activities, which according to the carers, typically involve one carer looking after no more than 3 residents.

Virtual world prototypes

Three versions of VW prototypes were developed in this study using Unity3D[1]. A main feature of the design we specified early on was to make interaction as simple as possible to enable a group of users to simultaneously interact with the VW. A number of studies have emphasised how older people prefer and benefit from interactive applications (in particular, video games) that could be enjoyed in a social setting [21]. Moving away from the traditional mouse and keyboard interface, we focused on gesture and touch-based interfaces. The Microsoft Kinect sensor[2] was used to detect the user's gestures and motions and the ZDK[3] (Zigfu development Kit) was used as a middleware to facilitate the development of the gesture controlled system through Unity3D. A projector was used to display the VW. Initially, we aimed to utilize the capacity of the Kinect in detecting full body interactions. However from the observation sessions, we found that the residents became physically exhausted. In addition, residents in wheelchairs were unable to participate. Hence, in the later designs, the Kinect was set to seated mode and only movements from the user's arms were used.

Version 1: Reminiscence Room Prototype

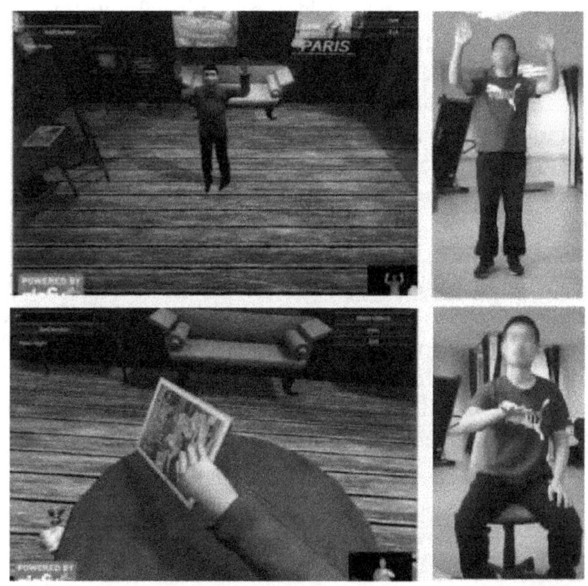

Figure 1: Virtual room prototypes. The top images depict the walking mode and the bottom images depict the seated mode. The images on the left depict what is shown in the VW and the images on the right depict the user (not actual participant).

The first prototype presented the user with an avatar placed in a virtual room with objects from the past (old posters, magazines, TVs, books). A radio was also included in the virtual room playing music of that period. Two modes of interaction were available. In the first mode (walking

[1] http://unity3d.com/

[2] http://www.microsoft.com/en-us/kinectforwindows/

[3] http://zigfu.com/en/zdk/unity3d/

mode), Kinect was used to map the users interaction to the avatars. More than 10 joints (e.g. Head, Torso, Waist, etc.) were detected and their movements mapped onto the avatar (see Figure 1). In the second mode (seated mode), the avatar was seated in front of a table with virtual objects (a book, a magazine, a radio and a lamp) placed in front of the user. In this mode, Kinect only detected the movements of the upper body (arms and upper torso) and the user would remain seated in the physical world. The user could pick up items on the table by moving their hands to touch the object. Each mode had a first and third person view.

Version 2: Virtual Tour Prototype

Figure 2: The river tour (left) and park tour (right).

The second version of the prototype was created based on the idea of users being taken along for a virtual tour through a pre-determined path. Two virtual worlds were created: the river tour and the park tour. In the river tour, the participant was taken through a virtual river trip. The environment was created to resemble a tropical forest, with vegetation, plants and animated animals (such as elephants, rhinoceros, etc.). The user would tour around the river by doing a "rowing" motion with their arms, which would propel the boat forward along the path. The park tour was created to depict the experience of walking through a park. Users would move their arms to simulate a "jogging" motion to move around the virtual park. In this prototype, various animals were programmed to respond to the user as they got close. For instance, rabbits would hop away from the user and humanoid characters would wave at the user as they "walked" closer. A screenshot is shown in Figure 2.

Version 3: Gardening Prototype

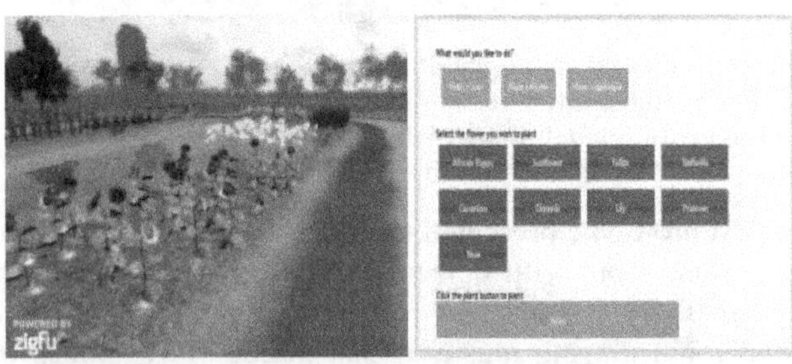

Figure 3: A screenshot of the virtual garden prototype (left) and the interface of the tablet controller (Right)

In this prototype, the participant would work together with the caregivers to design a virtual garden. 20 objects were available for selection including nine types of flowers, four types of trees and seven types of vegetables. An Android-based tablet computer was used to allow the caregiver/residents to select the vegetation to plant in the virtual garden (see Figure 3). The participant would "walk" to the empty plot using Kinect in a similar manner as prototype version 2. As they came close to an empty lot, a text would be displayed on the screen, asking the participant to select the plant. The user would then select the plant with the tablet computer and the plant would slowly pop up from the ground, followed by text feedback with a cheering sound effect as well as visual effects.

Version change	Design choices and changes in each iteration
1(virtual room)	Gesture-base technology instead of the traditional mouse and keyboard was adopted
1(virtual room) -> 2(river tour)	Interaction in version 1 was too complex, To reduce the complexity, the design approach for passive interaction is adopted. To include residents in wheelchairs, the prototype utilized interaction only from arm movements. Ambient sound effects (river flowing, bird sounds) were added to enhance engagement. This replaced the music from the radio in version 1 which drew their attention away from the VW.
2(river tour) -> 2(park tour)	As residents had trouble relating to unfamiliar content (animals and plants in the river tour etc.), this version focused on more common objects (e.g. flower and animals seen more in daily life). We adopted a design approach which mimics a "wonderland". This was aimed to better retain the attention of residents.
2(park tour)-> 3 (garden)	This prototype was designed to provide social interaction that allowed the resident and the care staff to design the garden together

Table 2: A summary of prototype iterations

FINDINGS

The findings are organised and presented to reflect three key aspects of the use of VW to support life engagement for people with dementia. The first theme relates to how the experiences as a result of their interaction with the VW stimulate past memories, helping to augment a sense of self. The second theme outlines the approaches employed to draw users' attention and create *ludic experiences*, a challenging task considering the cognitive impairments faced by people with dementia. The final theme involves addressing how interaction in VWs could be facilitated. Conventionally, many tasks required to interact with the VW (such as navigation, manipulation, etc.) are difficult to carry out especially for people with cognitive disabilities. We discussed in depth how we attempted to overcome these issues. Since the main form of data were observation notes, passages were quoted from our notes to provide illustration to the findings.

Augmenting the sense of self

The declines in cognition and memory among people with dementia have been argued to result in a "loss of self" [10]. The experiences and memories invoked by the VW could help augment the sense of self for older people with dementia. VWs allow the residents to temporarily step outside of their closed physical environment of long-term care facilities and transport them to a (albeit virtual) world of reminiscence. When the residents are institutionalised, their life is disrupted, the continuity broken [25]. VWs could provide a "memory sanctuary" to maintain this continuity of self. Three main aspects of reminiscence were observed in the study: i) reminiscence from the sense of place, ii) virtual object-based reminiscence, iii) reminiscence from the motion (gesture-based interactions).

Augmenting the sense of self through places

A quintessential feature of VW is its ability to simulate a variety of places; places no longer accessible to the residents in long-term care (these could be as simple as their own garden or kitchen, or holiday destinations) or places which have ceased to exist physically, but still linger in their memory (such as a historic street destroyed in the war). Place-based reminiscence is a particularly noteworthy example which was reflected in our observation. The ability to re-experience past places has been argued to help in the recovery of self [9]. An interesting observation from this study was how some interactions of the residents were in essence an attempt to connect the virtual place to self, actively creating meaning through conversation and interaction. In line with previous studies looking into selfhood and (physical) places [38], we observed how engaging with the virtual garden not only prompted the residents to tell stories about their own garden, but also personal stories about people and experiences related to their past. VWs not only allowed the resident to remember particular objects (flowers, trees, buildings etc.), but also triggered the overall feeling of "being in a garden."

Note: During the virtual garden design activity with the caregivers, the resident began by talking about plants he grew in his own garden when he was younger and gave detailed descriptions about his garden. He told us about the rail track [note that there was no rail track in our virtual garden] next to his garden and then moved on to telling stories about his family rail trips to Europe.

As previous studies have argued that meaningful places could play a role in the maintenance and construction of one's identity [34], the example here points to the potential of virtual places in augmenting the resident's sense of self. One limitation for those living with cognitive and physical disabilities is that much of their environment is confined to within the space of the care home [13]. Although the care homes we visited organise occasional trips, it might not be logistically feasible to frequently organise outdoor visits to certain places and for all the residents. Although photographs of past places could also invoke this type of reminiscence, a full interactive 3D environment (which allows one to see trees waving in the wind and hear the ambient sounds of birds singing and the wind blowing) could provide a platform to immerse the users and increase the perception of them being in the place.

Augmenting the sense of self through the virtual objects

Like most care homes, the two care homes we visited were filled with objects of the past: old radio, old furniture and dinnerware, etc. Perhaps the most common form of reminiscence activity practiced in care homes is based on objects and the two care homes actively engage their residents in such activity. Researchers have argued that physical day-to-day objects from everyday life have as much value in storing memories as photographs, helping to remind us of past experience and achievements [31]. Therefore, it is not surprisingly that in many occasions, the virtual objects in VW seemed to invoke reminiscence among the residents, prompting them to express a sense of self and remember stories from their past. Such instances were commonly observed (such instances were observed in 5 observation sessions.):

Note: In the virtual garden prototype, the resident mentioned how she wanted to grow a lily and then explained to us how she could never have one in her own garden as she is allergic to it.

VWs containing objects of personal relevance to the residents were much more successful in stimulating conversation and life engagement. In the virtual river tour prototype for instance, the discussion did not go beyond simply pointing out the names of the animals as for most residents, the objects had no relevance to their past (apart from one resident who used to live in South Africa). The virtual park and virtual garden prototypes contained objects commonly seen by the residents in their daily life and were more successful in engaging the residents.

Note: Since women live longer than men, it is not surprisingly that there are more female and male residents in the care homes. Whilst most female residents greatly enjoyed the garden prototype (7 residents) and the park prototype (3 out of the 4 who participated), two of the male residents who used the park prototype were completely switched off. The caregiver later told us about the fascination of one male resident in cars and tractors.

Augmenting the sense of self through motion

One unexpected observation in this study was how motions provided an opportunity for the augmentation of selfhood. Although the decision to use Kinect was originally made mainly to address the issue of "ease of use", mapping user motion to the avatars (in the reminiscence room prototype) prompted the residents to try to recreate past experiences through movements. A particularly memorable example was found in the following case.

Note: During the testing of the virtual room prototype, one participant (who was familiar with boxing) took a boxing stance and tried to make the avatar engage in boxing. He enjoyed watching the on screen avatar mimicking his movement.

Despite the virtual room offering no artefacts or stimulus related to boxing (the room contained only household objects from the past and no boxing gloves or other related apparatus), the resident devised and acted out an activity based on something that was more personally relevant to him. This aspect of interaction opens a new and unique way in which digital technology can engage with older people in augmenting their sense of self and reminiscence. Perhaps it is not only the visual and audio stimulus but also motions which could help older people recall their past memories.

Research has suggested that the ways in which we think is an extension of our existence as embodied minds [5]. The way we think is driven by our physical motions, which in turn drive the way that we think. For instance, a piano player is not normally able to write down the keys that they hit in a piece of music they know, but if they can sit at the piano and use their "muscle memory", they will remember the order of the keys. This is because their memory isn't a visual memory but is embodied within finger movements. Tapping into this fundamental human ability could enable people with dementia engage their memory more fully. Indeed, one technique used in reminiscence encourages older people to act out their past experiences, such as asking them to waiter or use props such as a washboard for someone who has worked in a cafe [20]. In the same vein, gesture sensors such as Kinect could be used to facilitate such actions and relate them to the virtual environment.

The suspension of disbelief: slipping into alternate reality

For VW to be effective, users should be able to suspend their disbelief and maintain the illusion that the alternative place simulated by the VW is believable. During the observations, we were pleasantly surprised by the ease in which the people with dementia suspended their disbelief and expressed a strong sense of "being inside" the VW:

Note: The activity coordinator asked what the resident had thought [about the garden]. She answered that it was wonderful and it looked like she was in a real garden.

Note: After the resident had finished planting the whole garden, she asked the activity coordinators where this garden was. She assumed that this garden was one existing in reality and this was a real-time visual display of an actual garden.

Some observations highlighted not only the perception of "being present" but also the feeling of actually carrying out the activity.

Note: In the river prototype, the resident grinned as she was moving her hands to row the boat enthusiastically, one made a comment of "I am rowing the boat!"

Overall, almost all residents were able to see the projected screen as a place they were situated in and perceive themselves as actually performing the activity. This was a surprising observation. The concept of presence has always been one of the key research topics in virtual world/reality studies. Although generally most users were able to suspend disbelief and "pretend" they were inside the virtual world, in one case, the resident mistook the virtual environment as being the "real world". Indeed, studies looking into the use of virtual reality and dementia found that despite having cognitive disabilities, users with dementia were able to perceive a sense of presence [16]. This would certainly calls for further studies investigating the sense of presence among people with dementia.

Designing sustained ludic experiences

A key challenge to design VW for people with dementia is to find ways to engage and entertain them. Cognitive impairments caused by dementia result in impairment to attention [29], making it difficult to design activities which sustian their attention for prolonged periods. In this section, we outline the approach we adopted to create and maintain *ludic experiences* for the residents.

The construction of "wonderland" effects

At first, the audio-visual design aspects of the VW did not seem to be an important factor to us. However after two sessions, we learnt the importance of this design issue. Our initial assumption was that VWs should look as realistic as possible, given the constraint of computing power and labour intensity. Our early prototypes attempted to depict the virtual environment as it is in the "physical world." It quickly transpired that realism alone is insufficient. In fact, it might even be less engaging for the residents. After a focus group session with the care staff, one method we devised and found particularly effective was to present the environment in a manner which mimics "a wonderland" from the children's stories. We created the virtual park and the virtual gardening prototypes to incorporate this idea. Designing for this effect involved modifications such as:

- Objects with bright and contrasting colours were used and image filters applied to further highlight and create a "glowing" effect on the objects.
- When providing feedback to users (such as when growing a plant), stimulating visual and sound effects were used. A text animation of "well done" whizzed in from the top of the screen, followed by clapping and cheering sounds.
- Colourful particle effects were used. Brightly coloured particles were programmed to spring from the ground as the plant was growing and firework particles were used to further draw the user's attention after the "well done" text animation was played (see Figure 4).

The main purpose of this design approach was to create an over-the-top experience. Use of bright colours, particles and sound effects proved successful to help draw in and sustain the attention of the residents:

Figure 4: A screenshot of the particle affects and bright growing colours used to create the "wonderland" feeling

Note: In the virtual park tour prototype, the bright flowers drew the attention of the residents, prompting them to try to figure out what type of flowers they were. In addition, some of the residents pointed to the screen and asked the others to look at the flower.

In addition to drawing in the attention of residents, contrasting and bright colours may also improve usability for older people in general [12]. Using bright and contrasting colours make the objects stand out and serve to draw in the viewer's attention [11]. This is similar to the designs of toys for young children which have used similar techniques to attract their attention [24].

We also made interesting observations regarding the use of sound and music. In the reminiscence room prototype, old music was initially included with the hope to engage the residents with the VW. We indeed observed the residents getting more lively and energetic. Some of them started dancing to the music. They were however engaged in the music and less so with the virtual room. Instantly, they were drawn out of the virtual environment, into the world of music. The use of ambient sounds (e.g. river flowing, birds chirping, etc.) however, seemed to have increased their engagement with the VW. For people with dementia in long-term care, their world is largely constrained within the care home environment. What for many of us are day-to-day activities, such as walking down a street on our own, taking a stroll in a park, gardening, are for some of them "extraordinary" things they can no longer do due to physical and cognitive decline. Often, these are fragment of memories remained in their mind. Thus, we believe that VWs provide a means for them to reconnect their experience to the "day-to-day" yet "extraordinary" worlds.

Inducing positivity

Engaging with virtual activities could also help induce a feeling of positivity. This point was frequently raised during the focus group discussions with the care staff. They emphasised that one beneficial aspect of VWs in care was to help restore the mood of the residents to a more positive state. It is because depression and rapid changes in mood and emotion are common problems associated with dementia [37]. An example is shown in the following case:

Note: Although the resident started his story with his garden and his happy time with his parents, the story took a turn when he begun talking about the death of his father after the war, and how this affected his life. He became teary and the care staff promptly drew him back to the virtual garden and stopped the negative emotion from escalating

Drawing his attention back to garden creation activity helped the resident to deal with his negative experiences in a more positive way.

User Interactions

We observed that rarely was meaningful interaction confined between the VW and the resident. Often, the interactions between the residents with each other and with the carers played a crucial role in forming their experience. Therefore, VW design needs to weave together these different types of interactions meaningfully to support the residents. In this section, we discuss our reflections with each type of user interaction.

Designing for passive interactivity

We learnt that a key challenge in designing interaction for people with dementia was in finding a balance between the complexity of the virtual activity and the simplicity of the user interaction. Increasing the level of user interaction provides more rooms for potential engagement, but could also increase the level of complexity and thus alienate less capable residents. An example could be observed with the reminiscence room prototype. Giving the participants full freedom to move around in the 3D room provided more avenues for interaction, but required a substantial level of effort to interact with the system. This often made residents with more severe cognitive disabilities confused:

Note: One participant was not able to identify from the third person view that they were controlling their avatar. As the camera in this prototype was linked to the avatar's movements, participants were confused and frightened of the lack of control they felt as they perceived the wall to move on its own.

Despite this, merely reducing the level of interaction could severely limit the activities available and result in a less interesting prototype. To solve this problem, we focused on creating experiences of "passive interactivity". Creating experiences of "passive interactivity" was aimed to increase the level of interactivity without increasing complexity to a large degree. Most commercial 3D VWs adopt a form of "active interaction", using the avatar as the base for interaction. For instance, if the user wants to interact with an object, they would navigate their avatar to the vicinity of the object to interact with it. This form of active interaction would be challenging with people with dementia [30].

Drawing from the lessons in early sessions, we revised our prototypes by including more "passive interactive" experiences. We found more successes when the objects were designed to "come" to the participants and "respond" to their interactions instead of needing the user to "go" to the objects. Previous technologies designed for dementia have adopted similar forms of interaction. For instance, in the design of an interactive photostroller, researchers devised a "tuner" to give participants the ability to select the category of the photos (a sense of control), while the photos would be showed in an automatic "drifting" motion (the pictures would in essence, be "presented" automatically to the users [17]). To a certain extent, we were creating an experience similar to a ride in an amusement park. The objects of interest were designed to interact with the participants as they drew closer. As Kinect ensured that participants were able to maintain a sense of control, participants were able to "interact" with the environment in a state of relative passivity.

To increase the range of interaction and activities for residents who had more severe cognitive disabilities, "passive interactivity" in the form of mediated interaction was achieved by including carers to help in the decision process. The virtual garden prototype for instance was designed around the idea of a collaborative activity between the carer and the resident. The carers helped older users make the decision of which plant to use, giving participants a level of control over the decision process whilst allowing residents to passively observe the results of their interactions. In a sense, the carers played the role of "game orchestrator", constructing narratives and helping direct and guide the experience of the residents [19].

The role of the carer

In our early prototypes (the reminiscence room and river tour prototypes), our design emphasis was focusing on designing the VWs to work with the residents with minimal support from care staff. This approached yielded limited success. We observed that some residents were able to interact with the prototype without help (rowing the boat in the river tour, some were able to interact with the avatar etc.), and they were able to recognise various objects and expressed interest in them. However it often required further prompting from the carers to stimulate more meaningful activities. For instance, the carers played a key role in stimulating storytelling, a core aspect in reminiscence activities. For residents with more severe levels of cognitive declines, carers also played a role in directing the attention of the residents. Facilitating a more meaningful interaction for these users often required additional guidance from staff the residents were familiar with and trusted. The virtual garden prototype in particular was designed around this idea, as a joint activity between the carers and residents. In this respect, we believe that VWs could be useful to foster relationship between care staff and the resident beyond basic-care interaction (such as feeding, washing, etc.). Engaging care staff and residents in playful social activities together could help enhance expressive relationships and trust.

Interaction between the residents

A key feature of VWs is the ability of the users interacting with each other. We were keen to explore this social aspect in the context of dementia care. Although the prototypes were helpful in supporting expressive and personal interactions between residents and care staff, we observed only few instances where meaningful social interactions occurred between the residents through the VW. In the focus group with the care staff, we explored this issue:

Note: the care staff thought that the residents might not benefit hugely from a group activity around virtual world in the virtual garden activity. He believed that it is because the residents need to cognitively process the information (remembering the flowers options, linking flower name with what it looks like, looking at the screen, and the tablet computer). In addition, in a group, they will have to process social information as well: deciding what to plant together. Some might be dominant, and argue, and some might just sit back. Cognitive and social skills will be competing for their mental capacity.

In hindsight, it was perhaps not surprising that the main meaningful social interactions were between the residents who were passively observing the activity and those who were using the prototype. For instance, in the virtual park and river tour prototypes, some residents observing the activity had as much fun being a passive observer as those who were using the prototype. In one case, a resident decided to join in only after having seen someone use the prototype. The VW setup in the care home (i.e. using a projector as display and Kinect as motion controller) in particular opened opportunities for such forms of interaction, as they allowed multiple residents to observe and interact with the system simultaneously. Some residents preferred to be a "passenger", passively observing the VW and talking to residents interacting with the prototype.

DISCUSSION

Through the study, we have explored in depth how VW technology was used by people with dementia and their caregivers in long-term care. Testing and revising a number of prototypes also gave insights related to design issues. Each prototype had different benefits for difference group of users and it could not be said that one is better than the other. We are also not advocating replacing physical activities with only virtual activities. Instead, we believe that VW can provide interactive experiences to promote a continuing selfhood which may have been lost due to dementia and/or moving to long-term care facilities. It can also provide stimulation and engagement to promote a feel good factor. Negative memories could be mitigated by playful design. VW could also be a "place" that allows staff and residents to foster personal relationship and trust, which may improve care. Although it appeared from the observation that VWs worked with many residents to a certain extent, there were incidents where they did not work well. We highlight some problems we encountered, which could direct future design and research work:

- Excessive physical motion: for some residents, continuous use of Kinect caused fatigue. In addition, many residents were confined to wheelchairs and this did not permit them to use the virtual room prototype (version 1). Although later versions utilised only hand movements, those who have difficulty moving their arms (such as those relying on Zimmer frames for movements) could still find their experience limited.
- Personally, irrelevant places, objects and activities: The virtual garden and park prototypes were especially successful among female residents but less so with the male residents who preferred other activities such as driving or sports. This underlines a key limitation of the wider use of VW in care home as creating different virtual environment is rather costly at the moment.
- In some cases, negative memories were triggered from the VW. This required the care staff to redirect their attention back to the positive aspect of the activity.
- Although some care staff was very keen to try the technology, others were less enthusiastic as the technology was perceived as adding extra workload to their already busy schedule.
- Most of the people with dementia were able to interact with the prototypes with relative ease. However, we observed a few cases (those with more severe cognitive declines) where the residents were unable to perform the simple tasks on touch screen or using gesture. In these cases, their visual audio capabilities have been significantly reduced and often the caregivers would guide them by physically touching them (especially their shoulders and hands) to get their attention.

Given these limitations and challenges, we envision at least two immediate ways future research could focus on. The first would be the use of intelligent avatars as social agents to facilitate these virtual activities, such as guiding the users through the VW and offering prompts to stimulate further conversation/storytelling. One key limitation of the current prototypes was the extensive involvement required from the care home staff. With the social agents, the role of the caregivers would be to oversee these virtual activities and intervene when unexpected problems arise. Prior studies have shown that such agents have been used successfully to converse or give instructions to older users [13]. The second research direction involves the use of tangible user interfaces, especially for those with more severe dementia. We often observed how important tactile interaction was in the interaction with VW. For instance, in the virtual gardening prototype, there was a tendency for the care staff to give the tablet to the residents, and physically guide them to click and select the flowers by touching their hands. These help them feel more empowered carrying out the activity. Therefore, future work could address this by designing a tangible/physical interface such as using replicas of the plants instead of a touch screen interface.

In summary, we hope that the outcomes from the study offer some insights into the design and use of VW technology for dementia care.

ACKNOWLEDGMENT

The project is funded by EPSRC (EP/J010766/1).

REFERENCES

1. Alzheimer's association. 2013 Alzheimer's disease facts and figures. Alzheimer's association (2013).
2. Bharucha, A. J., Anand, V., Forlizzi, J., & Dew, M. Intelligent assistive technology applications to dementia care: current capabilities, limitations, and future challenges. The American journal of geriatric psychiatry, 17, 2 (2009), 88-104.
3. Bickmore, T. W., Caruso, L., Clough-Gorr, K., & Heeren, T. 'It's just like you talk to a friend' relational agents for older adults. Interacting with Computers, 17,6 (2005), 711-735.
4. Boers, N. M., Chodos, D., Huang, J., Gburzynski, P., Nikolaidis, I., & Stroulia, E.. The Smart Condo: Visualizing independent living environments in a virtual world. Pervasive Computing Technologies for Healthcare, 2009. PervasiveHealth 2009. IEEE (2009), 1-8.
5. Borghi , A. M., & Cimatti, F. Embodied cognition and beyond: Acting and sensing the body. Neuropsychologia, 48, 3 (2010), 763–773.
6. Botella, C., Etchemendy, E., Cast, D., Baños, R. M., García-Palacios, A., Quero, S., et al. An e-Health System for the Elderly (Butler Project): A Pilot Study on Acceptance and Satisfaction. CyberPsychology & Behavior 12,3 (2009), 255-262.
7. Bózzola, F. C., Gorelick, P. B., & Freels, S. Personality changes in Alzheimer's disease. Archives of Neurology, 49,5 (1992), 486-491.
8. Caldwell, P. Finding You Finding Me: Using Intensive Interaction To Get In Touch With People Whose Severe Learning Disabilities Are Combined With Autistic Spectrum Disorder. Jessica Kingsley Pub : London (2006).
9. Chaudhury, H. Journey Back Home Recollecting Past Places by People with Dementia. Journal of Housing For the Elderly 16,1-2 (2008), 85-106.
10. Cohen, D., & Eisdorfer, C. the loss of self: A family resource for the care of Alzheimer's disease and related disorders. . Norton & Company, (2001).
11. Creusen, M. E., & Schoormans, J. P. The different roles of product appearance in consumer choice. J. of product innovation management 22,1(2005), 63-81.

12. Czaja, S. J., & Lee, C. C. Information technology and older adults. In A. Sears, & J. A. Jacko, HCI Handbook: Fundamentals, Evolving Technologies and Emerging Applications. New York: Lawrence Elbaum Associates. 2007, 777-792.
13. Dupuis, S. L., B. J., & Wiersma, E. Creating open environments in long-term care settings: an examination of influencing factors. Therapeutic Recreation Journal, 39,4 (2005), 277–298.
14. Edvardsson, D, Edvardsson, B & Sandman, PO Person-centred care of people with severe Alzheimer's disease: current status and ways forward. The Lancet Neurology. 7, 4 (2008), 362-367
15. Ephraim, G. A brief introduction to augmented mothering. Playtrack pamphlet, Harpebury Hospital School:Radlet Herts, (1986)
16. Flynn, D., van Schaik, P., Blackman, T., Femcott, C., Hobbs, B., & Calderon, C. Developing a virtual reality-based methodology for people with dementia: a feasibility study. CyberPsychology & Behavior 6, 6 (2003), 591-611.
17. Gaver, W., Boucher, A., Bowers, J., Blythe, M., Jarvis, N., Cameron, D., et al. The photostroller: supporting diverse care home residents in engaging with the world. Chi '11 Proceedings of the SIGCHI Conference on Human Factors in Computing Systems. ACM (2011), 1757-1766.
18. Gowans, G., Campbell, J., Alm, N., Dye, R., Astell, A., & Ellis, M. Designing a multimedia conversation aid for reminiscence therapy in dementia care environments. CHI '04 Extended Abstracts on Human Factors in Computing Systems. ACM (2004), 825-836.
19. Graham, T. N., Schumann, I., Patel, M., Bellay, Q., & Dachselt, R. Villains, architects and micro-managers: what tabula rasa teaches us about game orchestration. Proceedings of the SIGCHI Conference on Human Factors in Computing Systems. ACM (2013), 705-714.
20. Head, D. M., Portnoy, S., & Woods, R. T. The impact of reminiscence groups in two different settings. International Journal of Geriatric Psychiatry 5,5 (1990), 295-302.
21. Ijsselsteijn, W., Nap, H. H., de Kort, Y., & Poels, K.. Digital game design for elderly users. Future Play '07, Proceedings of the 2007 conference on Future Play. ACM(2007), 17-22 .
22. Jaffe, D. J. Problematizing meaning. In Qualitative methods in aging research. Thousand Oaks, CA: Sage Publications, 1994.
23. Kuwahara, N., Abe, S., Yasuda, K., & Kuwabara, K. Networked reminiscence therapy for individuals with dementia by using photo and video sharing. Proceedings of the 8th international ACM SIGACCESS conference on Computers and accessibility. ACM (2006), 125-132.
24. Light, J. C., Drager, K. D., & Nemser, J. G. Enhancing the Appeal of AAC Technologies for Young Children: Lessons from the Toy Manufacturers. Augmentative and Alternative Communication 20,3(2004), 137-149.
25. Lin, Y. C., Dai, Y. T., & Hwang, S. L. The Effect of Reminiscence on the Elderly Population: A systematic Review." Public Health Nursing. 20,4(2003), 297-306.
26. Luengo-Fernandez, R., Leal, J., & Gray, A. Dementia 2010: The economic burden of dementia and associated research funding in the United Kingdom. Cambridge: Alzheimer's Research Trust, 2010.
27. Marshall, M. The challenge of looking after people with dementia: Professional carers need higher expectations and better training and support. BMJ: British Medical Journal 323, 7310 (2001), 410-411
28. Mayeux, R. Early Alzheimer's Disease. New England Journal of Medicine, 362 (2010), 2194-2201.
29. McGuinness, B., Barrett, S. L., Craig, D., Lawson, J., & Passmore, P. A. Attention deficits in Alzheimer's disease and vascular dementia. Journal of Neurology, Neurosurgery and Psychiatry, 81,2 (2010), 157-159.
30. Moffat, S. D., Zonderman, A. B., & Resnick, S. M. Age differences in spatial memory in a virtual environment navigation task. . Neurobiology of aging, 22,5 (2001), 787-796.
31. Petrelli, D., & Whittaker, S. Family memories in the home: contrasting physical and digital mementos. Personal and Ubiquitous Computing 14,2(2010), 153-169.
32. Riley, P., Alm, N., & Newell, A. An interactive tool to promote musical creativity in people with dementia. Computers in Human Behavior 25,3 (2009), 599-608.
33. Rogers, W. A. Human factors, applied cognition, and aging. (2000).
34. Twigger-Ross, C. L., & Uzzell, D. L. Place and identity processes. Journal of Environmental Psychology 16,3 (1996), 205–220.
35. Wallace, J., Wright, P. C., McCarthy, J., Green, D. P., Thomas, J., & Olivier, P. A design-led inquiry into personhood in dementia. CHI '13 Proceedings of the SIGCHI Conference on Human Factors in Computing Systems . ACM (2013), 2617-2626.
36. Wang, J. J. Group reminiscence therapy for cognitive and affective function of demented elderly in Taiwan. International Journal of Geriatric Psychiatry 22,12 (2007), 1235-1240.
37. Whalley, L. Early Onset Dementia. In S. Hunter, Dementia: Challenges and new directions. Jessica Kingsley Publishers. 1997, 71-78.
38. Williams, A. Changing geographies of care: employing the concept of therapeutic landscapes as a framework in examining home space. Social Science & Medicine, 55,1 (2002), 141-154.
39. Woods, B., Spector, A. E., Jones, C. A., Orrell, M., & Davies, S. P. Reminiscence therapy for dementia. Cochrane Database Syst Rev 2 (2005).

Addressing the Subtleties in Dementia Care: Pre-study & Evaluation of a GPS Monitoring System

Lin Wan, Claudia Müller, Volker Wulf, David Randall
Institute for Information Systems, University of Siegen
Hölderlinstr. 3, 57076 Siegen, Germany
{lin.wan, claudia.mueller, volker.wulf, dave.randall}@uni-siegen.de

ABSTRACT
In this work we present a user-centered development process for a GPS-based monitoring system to be used in dementia care. Our research covers a full design process including a qualitative-empirical pre-study, the prototyping process and the investigation of long-term appropriation processes of the stable prototypes in three different practice environments. Specifically, we deal with the problem of 'wandering' by persons suffering from late-phase dementia. Although GPS tracking is not a novel technological objective, the usage of those systems in dementia care remains very low. The paper therefore takes a socio-technical stance on development and appropriation of GPS technology in dementia care and assesses the practical and ideological issues surrounding care to understand why. We additionally provide design research in two different settings, familial and institutional care, and report on the design of a GPS-based tracking system reflecting these considerations. What comes to the fore is the need for ICT to reflect complex organizational, ideological and practical issues that form part of a moral universe where sensitivity is crucial.

Author Keywords
Dementia, Privacy, Autonomy, GPS monitoring system, Evaluation.

ACM Classification Keywords
D.2.10 [**Design**]: *Methodologies.*
H.5.2. [**User Interfaces**]: *Theories and Methods, User-Centered Design.*
J.3. [**Computer and Society**]: *Computer-related health issues.*

INTRODUCTION
Recent research work on ICT for dementia care has demonstrated the deep embedding of technology in every-day practices which implicate the value judgments and attitudes when having to care for and take decisions for another person [9, 10, 31]. The literature demonstrates a picture of the dual nature of surveillance [12], which in the field of dementia care produces value conflicts of awareness against privacy and safety against autonomy [20, 21]. Other authors provide a more nuanced picture on the basis of qualitative research results, such as [9], who point at the multi-faceted nature of stakeholders' views on the dilemmas of GPS tracking of patients in professional dementia care. In the same vein, we demonstrate that different aspects of a GPS-based monitoring measure are linked to distinctive and heterogeneous values that range across settings and roles.

For late-phase dementia sufferers, a tracking system in theory gives a balance between preserving the autonomy and protecting the safety for them. However, in a first trial of global positioning system (GPS) technology to locate missing persons, Miskelly [23] (though validating the accuracy and performance of the system) found that 5 out of the 11 respondents dropped out of the test. This is a starting point of our study – a detailed investigation of the sociotechnical factors which make GPS deployment so problematic. As of today, even though there are commercial GPS tracking devices, they are seldom bought and used [31]. Our study shows that the take-up of such technologies in this complicated context has been underwhelming, both by familial carers and by institutions.

Brodaty et al. [5] show low take-up in general by caregivers of available services. Reasons, they suggested, were perceived lack of need and lack of knowledge of related services. Stigmatization was given as another reason for the caregivers' reluctance to use services. The low uptake of technological aids in dementia care points at the need to a better understanding of the social/socio-technical issues in technology usage in dementia care. The social, ethical and legal universe in which caregivers operate problematizes the deployment of such technologies in a variety of ways and this paper aims to detail this.

Here, we present a study of qualitative work which leads to designs of a tracking system for late-phase dementia care, including: 1.) the pre-phase of qualitative investigation into the practices of professional and familial caregivers of sufferers from dementia who wander, 2.) design and prototyping of the technology and 3.) an evaluation phase in which the appropriation and usage of the developed technologies in real environment is being observed over a long-term period.

CHI 2014, April 26 - May 01 2014, Toronto, ON, Canada
Copyright 2014 ACM 978-1-4503-2473-1/14/04...$15.00.
http://dx.doi.org/10.1145/2556288.2557307

Our contributions to the field include: 1.) a more fine-grained understanding of attitudes and practices in GPS-based wandering management in familial and institutional care. 2.) a better understanding of the sheer complexity of the different situations which occasion concern, the heterogeneous nature of organizational and family routines, and the nuances of moral/ideological commitments expressed by different parties, and 3.) Implications for successful assistive technology in such sensitive contexts which include but go beyond technology itself.

RELATED WORK

There is a general move in studies of healthcare technologies to move towards understanding of sociotechnical problems [4, 13, 18]. Themes in the area of home-based healthcare, for instance, evolve around the communication & cooperation needs of various stakeholders in chronic illness treatment [22, 27, 28, 30]. Research has demonstrated that values and attitudes of each stakeholder play an important role in appropriation and usage of ICT [6].

Other research stresses the social side of healthcare, e.g. research into support for social interaction and the sense of belonging for the elderly [15, 17, 36, 37]. Such work increasingly focuses on maintaining and boosting the participation and autonomy of older adults so that they can continue living, as much as possible, independently even in circumstances where older people are experiencing cognitive and/or physical decline. Research work in the context of cognitive issues has aimed at key problems such as the role of various stakeholders in the care process and has dealt with such issues as 'whereabouts' or 'biographical' awareness [1, 7, 26, 39] and monitoring [11, 24, 29].

The sociotechnical stance is all the more significant in the field of ICT for dementia care. Assistive GPS technology for healthcare, work on the living conditions of older adults with chronic diseases (e.g. dementia), and ICT support options point to the high degree of social embedding of e.g. location-based systems and how different strategies have been applied to minimize the tension between *privacy and awareness* and *safety and autonomy*, respectively [9, 16, 20, 21, 25, 31, 35]. This in turn has led some researchers to reflect on appropriate research methods, such as the testing of off-the-shelf technologies in real circumstances [10] and to a claim for more long-term evaluations of developed prototypes in general [13].

While some research alludes to the insufficient acceptance of tracking devices in dementia care [3], we do not fully understand why the take-up of such technology has been underwhelming. Our review of the literature found no example of previous work which compared different care settings and the moral and ideological world they inhabit. This study, instead, shows that the differences to be found in different contexts are sometimes striking, and have a direct impact on willingness to deploy technology.

Because of the richly situated, continuously evolving, and collaborative nature of healthcare, studies in the field of HCI or CSCW often are carried out with qualitative methods. In the case of dementia care – an example of the 'sensitive setting' that Crabtree et al. refer to – research into the problems of dementia sufferers and their families is particularly challenging. Crabtree et al. [8] reported on their experience of adapting cultural probes when developing computer support for former psychiatric patients living in residential care settings, for older members of the community, and for disabled people living at home. Underpinning such work is a concern for 'responsibility'-who is responsible for care and in what circumstances? Can sufferers be relied on to act responsibly in their own interests?

Some authors noted that when conducting Participatory Design workshops with both dementia patients and caregivers, it is important to prevent caregivers from becoming the dominant or only voice. Patients may be otherwise unheard [10]. Value sensitive design [14], as an information system design methodology, emphasizes how values play out in design, and how balancing competing values in various situations plays an important role. Robinson et al. [31] aim at supporting independent living and involving early-onset dementia patients in the design process. We, however, are dealing with late-stage dementia and frequently in an institutional care setting. The methodological challenges of the two are very different. In fact, we tried to involve the patients in our work but the methodological challenges proved to be insurmountable.

The issue of how to analyze the complex, detailed qualitative data from in-situ studies in healthcare is a further challenge. We align our methodological approach with the practice-oriented design research framework of Wulf et al. [40]. Under this framework we approach our research in three phases: 1. Pre-study: empirically analyzing actual practice in specific application context; 2. Development: designing ICT artifacts based on the findings of phase one; 3. Evaluation: examining the appropriation of the technical artifact over a significant period of time. Our work, then, focuses on presenting a whole design process that includes building, deploying and evaluating a system over a long period of time as recommended by Fitzpatrick and Ellingsen [13].

PRE-STUDY: EXPLORING THE FIELD

The aim of the pre-study was to gather data on how conflicting demands and values in dementia care are being dealt with in practice. To do this, we examined practices in domestic as well as in three different institutional care environments, relying mainly on interviews and participant observation for our data. Interviews were only loosely structured, reflecting our general, but initially unfocused, interest in attitudes to, and practices with, dementia care tools and resources.

The three different care environments in which we found interview partners were representative of: care homes, special dementia living groups, and institutional care facilities. In general, it should be pointed out, accessing 'users' in these circumstances is difficult. Our first attempts at user contact showed that many dementia-affected families feel reluctant to discuss this sensitive topic with unfamiliar people. It required, as is always the case in such sensitive settings, the development over time of trust in our motives and our ability to behave responsibly.

We conducted 21 semi-structured interviews, with 6 family caregivers (2 wives, 1 husband, 2 adult daughters, and 1 adult son of a dementia sufferer) and 15 professional caregivers (6 ward nurses and 9 managers) from stationary care facilities. Each interview lasted about 2 hours. All the interviews were audio recorded with user approval, and were transcribed and anonymized for data analysis. Besides interviews, we have held several meetings with an Alzheimer self-help organization. These meetings have been documented in field notes. Furthermore, we spent some days on participant observation in institutions and families (10 hours in care home and 10 hours in a dementia flat share). They were also documented in the form of field notes.

After we readied all the empirical data (interview transcripts, field notes), we started a collective and systematic coding process. As a team, we held data analysis workshops regularly to update the code system, cross-code each other's material, and group-discuss on unclear points. This has helped minimize diverse interpretations between individual team members.

PRE-STUDY: FINDINGS

Understanding the complexities of caregiving for persons with dementia in institutions

Patient admission: Bias in the bilateral selection

Taking care of a dementia patient at home is a demanding job for relatives, especially when the patient has a wandering tendency. The physical and mental strain can be overwhelming for family caregivers who often lack professional insight into care management. When they turn to stationary care institutions, patients and the care institutions can in theory choose each other freely and bilaterally. In reality, there is a strong biased power distribution in this bilateral selection. Notably, it is extremely difficult for families to find a suitable institution for the dementia patient with wandering tendencies.

The first issue families consider when prioritizing their choices is the distance of the institution from their home. Very soon they realize that very few of these institutions have a clear care concept for the 'wanderer'. Their initial choice pool, that is, rapidly diminishes.

One institution, for instance, noted that they would not accept wandering clients because *"we cannot take the responsibility for them"*. This was not, to be clear, because of legal ramifications, but because of a moral concern for the welfare of the wanderer in the absence of a reliable and practical monitoring solution. Another institution, in contrast, which did accept dementia patients with wandering tendency, claimed: *"we are an open house"*. They argued that the doors are open and the inhabitants can leave the house at will. Having said that, they applied a series of precautionary measures, such as heavy doors that are very difficult to open, hidden door knobs, hidden exits behind curtains, and so on. Again, measures of this kind were not universally accepted amongst professional caregivers. Some considered these measures to be a legitimate expediency, whilst others saw them as an affront to human dignity: as manipulative of a group who were not able to distinguish aspects of reality.

Prevention in practice: heterogeneity and controversy

The strategies that institutional care workers use on a daily basis when dealing with the wandering behaviors of dementia patients are highly heterogeneous and contextual. This is partially decided by the complex and volatile situations they face on a daily basis. Decision-making in such conditions is constantly mediated by legal, ethical, and moral trade-offs. In Germany, detailed legal standards have been institutionalized in such facilities to prevent abuses such as tying patients to beds or chairs. Professionals now routinely refer to 'freedom depriving measures' and told us about their concern that certain preventive actions may be deemed freedom depriving measures. The standards – although established some years ago – work more as a guideline rather than a solution (although some restrictions on freedom, such as locked bedroom doors, are clearly illegal). In the absence of an unambiguous definition, there is significant uncertainty and confusion, not to mention a variety of moral positions, on the part of professional caregivers and managers when making decisions.

From our samples, such preventive measures fall into 3 categories: 1). constructional measures, 2). technical support, and 3). human intervention.

Constructional measures include tricks such as heavy doors and camouflaged (or hidden) exit. Creating 'endless corridors' is another commonly used measure. In one dementia flat share we saw, the corridor was built in a circular form around a public area in the middle. This lets the patient take walks along the hallway, but never reach the exit. Such measures were controversial for care workers and, often, there were quite different perspectives on the acceptability of the measures on view. The 'constructional' principle was viewed by some as inhuman: *"This is awful to imagine: you are walking and walking and you never arrive. This can make you even more confused!"* (female relative).

The second category of preventive measures is using technology to monitor patient behavior. The following monitoring technologies have been (or partially) applied in our samples: video cameras, door safety systems, and sensor mats. The professional caregivers' attitudes towards monitoring technology are more consistent and are characterized as a general reluctance. Their reluctance stemmed from the following reasons: 1). fear that it might be categorized as a 'freedom depriving measure', 2). usability issues with the system, 3). distrust in the reliability of the system.

Thirdly, human intervention describes the way in which some caregivers developed measures to keep patients busy and distracted from the urge to wander. Activities such as reading, chatting with each other, eating together, and going for walks together are the most common ones. Keeping patients busy during the day also helps them sleep better at night, which reduces the danger of patients wandering off. Many caregivers told us that they have to constantly keep an eye on the patients' activities and assess the situation, because "*Most of the time we don't know whether they have a wandering tendency. Sometimes we can predict it based on the patient's behaviors*". This is especially challenging when they are undertaking care routines in patients' rooms. One solution is to put temporary barriers in the way. Commonly used barriers are e.g. the nursing cart or toilet chairs. The nurses told us this is a compromise, because normally they try to keep the hallway barrier-free so that the residents can walk safely but at the same time they have to monitor while coping with staff shortages.

Problems in finding and retrieving

Patients can, and do, wander. When a patient is presumed to be lost, members of the care staff will be organized to look for the lost one. The approach is normally ordered as follows: looking inside the building, calling the patient's relatives, looking outside, and finally calling the police. Interviewees told us that some patients have their favorite wandering routes. These routes can be the way home, or a personally favorite path. But there were still many practical problems in coordinating the search and finally bringing back the patient. How to bring the patient back to the institution is another challenge, especially when the patient doesn't recognize the care staff and is reluctant to return to the home with them. Some professionals reflected that they sometimes use 'white lies' to trick the found patients to come back with them, e.g. *"your daughter has just called"*. They mentioned that for each patient there are several 'key words' that typically work well. But these 'key words' are highly individual for each patient. And it requires deep understanding of the patient so that one can apply them appropriately in a challenging situation.

Attitudes towards GPS monitoring system

None of the institutions we interviewed used a GPS tracking system to monitor patients. Despite the fact that they have a need (care staff are over-burdened) the sheer heterogeneity of care concepts/practices makes commercial products unsatisfactory. Inappropriate merchandising of providers to technology non-savvy users is another reason given by caregivers for the reluctance to deal with the technology. Inconsistent attitudes inside institutions also inhibit unanimous acceptance of such technology. At the macro level, legal and ethical standards are vague and subjective, and guidelines are in short supply.

Understanding the complexities of caregiving for persons with dementia at home

Autonomy vs safety: Two entirely opposite cases

The analysis of the interviews with family carers - husbands, wives, sons and daughters - offers very different perspectives on the evaluation and discussion of the autonomy and freedom needs of the affected family member. The difference can be significant. In one case, where care took place in the home, a husband reported that he allowed very little freedom of movement to his wife. While in their home, he wouldn't allow her to be alone in another floor – for fear that she might hurt herself. Being a retired engineer, he developed coping mechanisms for their every-day life: he 'engineered' her eating-, sleeping- and bathroom times with medication. In his understanding autonomy was not a relevant issue to his wife as she was 'no more here' with her mind.

In contrast, the daughter of a woman with medium-stage dementia has built a social network to collaboratively take care of her mother, so that her mother can live independently in her home and conduct everyday tasks – even go to the city – on her own. For the daughter it is vital that her mother feels that she is autonomous – and she has adopted many measures to 'artificially' achieve this, such as: asking shop clerks and bank officers to give the mother what she wants, but up to a certain level. Sometimes the daughter 'shadows' her mother on her way to town. For the daughter, her mother's ability to maintain a public and independent 'face' is of primary importance.

For many of the relatives we interviewed, the classic value trade-off between safety and autonomy is of minor relevance in their decision-making, especially when the disease advances. Many relatives report primarily on the overwhelming burden of concern for the dementia suffering family member. So for them, keeping the loved ones safe is much more important than preserving their autonomy. As the disease progresses, the patient's mental existence is normally perceived as 'fading away', and autonomy becomes less and less important for them (this is not universal. It is a feature of such relationships that they engender a great deal of reflexive concern, contingently negotiated).

Impact of pre-existing family patterns on care concept

In the home context, families tailor care strategies to fit local conditions and needs. Each family has its own habitual familial pattern, such as structure, hierarchy, balancing between genders, and children/parent roles. Our empirical analysis indicates that pre-existing roles can have completely different effects on the care concept when dementia occurs. For example, in one case, a daughter and her mother who took care of the father who suffers from dementia at home reported that the father had always had a dominant role in the family and a strongly independent attitude. Even with the onset of dementia, he continued to assert this dominance. He still took long walks on his own, leaving his family in a self-confessed position of helplessness: *"We cannot hold him." (Mrs. C)*. This, we discovered, is quite common in situations where female relatives have to cope with male dementia sufferers. As an opposite example, in the case of the husband who 'engineered' the behavior of her wife, his pre-existing and continuing dominance in the family had actually 'helped' him manage his wife's life with less resistance.

Thus, dementia care is mediated by prior family patterns and the role expectations contained therein. How to design a universal technical support that will work in all familial situations is, unsurprisingly, challenging. Technology support in the family context needs somehow to balance the continuities and changes experienced by both patients and their caregivers.

Attitudes towards GPS monitoring system

Family caregivers tend to be more open about the possibilities of a GPS-based monitoring system. However, the degree to which such a system is required depends very much on the progression of the disease and the coping strategies adopted by caregivers.

As in the institutional context, the interviewed families have a need for technological support and are aware of its existence, but none has bought a commercial product. Some of our users made the frustration with their experience of searching for a GPS solution very clear, such as lack of reliable information channels about such products, or insufficient information provided by the product websites which in addition were perceived as addressing technological specialists only.

Design Implications

From the empirical results of the pre-study, we were able to summarize the following design implications. Clearly, heterogeneous assumptions demand flexible solutions. Tailorability here is of great importance. The system should provide as much flexibility as possible to allow for divergent attitudes, ethical/legal concerns, and care routines to find their footing in it:

- *Reliability*: reliability is an important requirement for all IT systems, but is critical in this context. Tolerance of system failure is very low, especially in the institutional context.
- *History of paths*: almost all caregivers, no matter whether professional or familial, told us that patients have their favorite wandering routes, and in large degree are predictable. Keeping a history of the wandering routes in system could help identify such favorite routes, giving a hint for the searching for patient. More importantly, provided with the history, caregivers might be able to identify the patients' motives behind the wandering and their reasons of choosing these routes.
- *High flexibility of system configuration*: the constant value trade-off between safety and autonomy requires the system to provide options for the user to tailor the system according to temporal and spatial evaluation of the situation. It should be possible, for instance, to set safety areas (also named as *digital fence*) on the map and prompt notification when the patient leaves those areas. The caregiver should be able to configure the tracker to either automatic update the positions or manually (pulling or polling mode). Also the position update interval should be adjustable. Information on the patient needs to be anonymized to meet the requirements of certain institutions.
- *Support for cooperative monitoring*: caregivers already cooperate with each other to manage the care work in practice and cooperation also happens between professional and familial caregivers. The system should therefore support communication, coordination, and negotiation between them.

For the mobile application we have the following design implications:

- *Elderly-friendly UI*: the design of the mobile application should supply simple design and straightforward user interaction. Many caregivers are themselves elderly and have difficulty in reading small screens and understanding smartphone operations.
- *Navigation function*: It is essential to provide a navigation function in the mobile application to locate the wandering patient and navigate the caregiver to it.
- *'Key words' and integrated contact lists*: the caregiver should be able to access some 'hint' information to help persuade the patient to come back, such as the 'key words' mentioned earlier. In addition a contact list should be added so that the caregiver can order help via the mobile if needed.

The design decision for the combination of a web portal and a mobile application allows a distribution of function. On one hand, this helps certain functions to excel on their most suitable screen size. The web portal is designed for the PC screen which provides enough space for location monitoring, system configuration, and jobs that are easier done with mouse and keyboard, such as drawing a safety area. The mobile application suits situations that require mobility, such as the navigation function in a patient searching. Having said that, flexibility of access turned out to be extremely important.

PROTOTYPE DEVELOPMENT

Actual development of the prototype was the responsibility of a software company who formed part of the project from the start. We conducted regular project meetings every 3-4 weeks with the developers from the company to transfer our results and design. As a research institute we also developed an iPhone application which was not envisioned in the draft of the project plan.

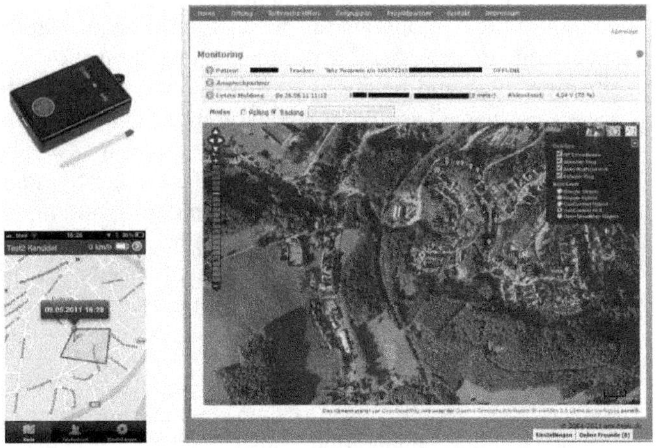

Figure 1. Screenshots of the prototype

The final prototype was a complete GPS-based location monitoring system to help caregivers better manage the wandering behavior of dementia patients. The system consists of GPS-trackers to be carried by the patients, a web portal for monitoring the actual position and adjusting settings (e.g. configuring trackers and defining safety areas on the map), and an iPhone App for mobile monitoring (see Fig. 1).

The prototype featured all of the above-mentioned features, save one: the cooperative monitoring feature. Given that we were partnered with a commercial organization, our design ideas had to be filtered through their interests and this is the main reason why the cooperative monitoring feature was not implemented. Nevertheless, we were able to refine our part (the iPhone App) in multiple design cycles based on several PD workshops together with the caregivers. We experienced, we should say, significant difficulties in working with commercial interests alongside our own research objectives. However, a detailed analysis of such organizational issues is not in the scope of this paper.

EVALUATION: LONG-TERM FIELD TEST

We rolled out the prototype in three different locations and tested it in real-life situations over a time span of three to five months. These included a family in which the husband is suffering from dementia (age 55), a care home with a focus on dementia care, and a special ward of a hospital.

Deploying the technology was anything but straightforward. Prior to the actual deployment, we conducted several semi-structured interviews in each setting in order to grab a detailed overview of their technology infrastructure and any specific conditions, so that we could make a customized deployment plan for each setting. In the institutions we had at least two on-site meetings to inform management and ward nurses about the evaluation plan. Prior to our visits, all evaluation partners had tried to get information on GPS support technology on the internet but all gave up due to the poor quality of provider websites in terms of understanding of the technical issues. The on-site visits were audio-recorded and field notes were taken.

Despite detailed preparation, we still faced unexpected difficulties during the technology installation in each location. We had to be very flexible and creative to fine-tune the prototype so that it could be integrated into daily practice. For example for the special ward in the hospital, we had to deliver an iPad with 3G connection to access the monitoring website because the Internet speed in that hospital was too slow to allow serious prototype testing.

We visited the family and the institutions regularly every 2-4 weeks and were 24/7 available by phone in case of questions and problems. We conducted altogether 12 on-site visits and 6 telephone interviews with interviews typically lasting 1,5-2 hours. All the interview sessions were audio recorded with consent and later transcribed. During the evaluation we kept close contact with our testers, and all the emails and phone calls were documented in field notes. Furthermore, we asked the testers to fill in a media diary of their daily experience with the system. The diaries also worked as a basis for discussion in the on-site interviews. The data analysis was approached in the same as in the pre-study. We started with an open code system and regularly held internal analysis workshops.

EVALUATION: FINDINGS

The settings: two institutions & a family

The prototype system was evaluated in three locations, chosen because they enabled 'real world' evaluation without endangering patients. A hospital ward, an elderly care home for dementia care and a family constituted such environments. We identified three scenarios of use where different experiences were reported.

House A: Dementia care home

House A is a dementia care institution in a rural area. The house is committed to new dementia care philosophies which include the idea of giving the residents as much space as possible to be mobile on their own. There is large protected area around the house in which they are allowed to walk freely. There is an alarm system attached to the main entrance, and patients with a special wristband passing through will trigger a phone call to the care staff. The manager is of the view that patients should be able to leave the area if they wish to, although care workers are less liberal in their views.

Three young male volunteers, to whom the head nurse had handed the devices, mainly tested the system. Interestingly, these young men were all IT-familiar but saw older professional caregivers as 'lay' users of such technology. The head nurse shared this view, saying: "*older persons [meaning her colleagues] could not use this system, because in this institution they have only low experiences with technology and computers*". She emphasized this with reference to her colleagues' general problems with care documentation work at the computer: *"my colleagues already have problems with simply clicking the right things in our records."*

House B: Hospital ward

House B is located in a big city and is a big hospital- and care complex. The ward in which we tested the system has a special focus on long-term care for persons with cranial-cerebral trauma and co-morbidities such as dementia. Here, location-tracking services were welcomed but worries were also raised because of the high mobility of the patient. In this case, a relatively young man, who used to be a marathon runner, suffered from severe dementia as consequence of a car accident. The ward is an 'open ward', which means that locking the doors is forbidden. This patient 'escapes' regularly and is very difficult to manage as a result of his level of physical fitness. A specific limitation of the tracker was its' low precision in indoor positioning, and this patient was often 'lost' in the house, e.g. he happened to be found in the basement, having spent hours in a disoriented state.

On the day we brought our prototype to the house, we noticed that the Internet connection in the hospital was too slow for a sensible field test. As an alternative, we bought an iPad with 3G data tariff so that the staff could use the iPad to access the web portal. Two days later when we visited the house again, they told us that *"the iPad is safely locked in the cabinet [so that nobody will steal it]"*. Because of the high mobility of patients and relatives in the hospital in general, they were extremely afraid of losing the costly device and it was initially locked away unused. We then bought a protection case and a lock for the iPad so it could be securely attached to a desk.

The staff then started to use the system. Several days later we received a phone call from our contact person – a nurse in the house – telling us that the patient was lost for 20 hours, and was found the next day 30 kilometers away from the house. She told us that before this accident happened, the patient was carrying the tracker 24 hours a day, and the battery life of the tracker was inadequate. She tried to charge the tracker in the meantime, and she had no idea how the patient went out without triggering an alarm, and *"in this form we cannot trust the system"*. After investigating the system together with the nurse, we found out that the battery died within the safety area, right before the patient left the house. What we learnt from this case is that the system should send a notification when the tracker battery is low. After discussion with the house, we deployed another tracker for the patient, so that they could simply exchange the trackers, always having one fully charged. Since then the system has been used 24 hours a day and our contact person in the ward has reported on several successful instances where the system has helped, and the staff have started to trust the system more and more. The relatives of the patient also started to trust the system and grew dependent on it.

Family C

Here, the sufferer is cared for at home by a spouse. He, a former doctor, lives with his wife and three children aged between 15 and 20. Mr. C. walks the dog several times a day on a short round in the near neighborhood. The routes he walks along are well known to the family, and are, according to his wife, 'routinized'. Before he leaves the house, he tells his wife or children where he intends to go. The relatives estimate roughly the time he should return. It has already happened several times that the man was not able to return home on his own. That's why a volunteer from a local charity organization now comes 3 times a week to take him and the dog for a long walk. Mr. C., however, very much dislikes the company of the volunteer, because he thinks he is still autonomous enough to walk on his own.

In our interviews with Mrs. C, she told us that the system is extremely helpful for her. She began, she said, to rely strongly on the technology after only a few weeks. She used the system not only at home, but also at work. She said that the system gives her peace of mind as she can see on the map that he is walking on the regular route. But she appropriated the system in a way that preserves as much privacy as possible for the husband. For example, she hadn't used the digital fence at all, as it feels too intrusive for her. And she slightly reduced the frequency of the tracker's position report. She didn't want to constantly track her husband, for her, having a look into the system and knowing that he is safe, is already a great relief.

Some general findings across cases

Some general issues in acceptance towards the trackers were also identified. Firstly, the size of tracker was seen as a problem by the interviewees. Although it is quite small (size of a match box), dementia sufferers often dislike devices attached to their body or clothes. Caregivers would prefer something very small, like a thin bracelet, or in the form of wristwatch or necklace which - as a known artifact to the sufferers - would be better accepted by them. Given the need for battery size, that is in current years difficult to realize.

Given the demand for autonomy, 'open house' philosophies mean that caregivers negotiate the freedoms of patients, where possible, to maximize them. 'Digital fences' are, in principle, extremely useful in this respect. Professional caregivers, however, suggested an additional structuring of the feature into three zones, a green one, a yellow (be alerted, person has left the safe area) one and a red one (act immediately, he/she is in danger). (Family carers, unlike those in institutional settings, scarcely used the digital fence function at all).

The system was viewed as extremely useful in the institutional context even when it could not locate accurately indoors, because it helped refine search strategies. Thus and for instance, in the case of the former marathon runner, although the system could not tell the exact position in the building, it nevertheless indicated that the patient was not outside, which greatly reduced the search area, and thus made the search more targeted.

A similar benefit of the technology was perceived by Mrs. C, who argued that because the system allowed her to retrace routes taken, she was able to get a better sense of why her husband deviated from his normal route, thus reduces anxiety. Decreasing cognitive capability has led to situations where the sufferer has been found on a highway (Autobahn) construction site, and unable to explain how he found himself there. As Mrs. C says: *"we do not know even today why he had gone to this Autobahn construction site ... Something must be happened that made him leave the normal route. It can drive you crazy that you do not know the reason why."* Now, with the technology, there is the option to at least to reflect on possible reasons for new path choices.

DISCUSSION & CONCLUSION

Overall, we are confident that our proposed solutions have a positive effect on the experiences of dementia sufferers, their families and professional caregivers. Having said that, the sheer complexity of the different situations which occasion concern, the heterogeneous nature of organizational and family routines, and the different moral/ideological commitments expressed by different parties underpin the need for solutions which are both very flexible and practical to implement. In the organizational context, it is clear that these complexities mean that support for collaborative searching and for the flexible definition of 'boundaries' needs to be better implemented. Professional management of issues of autonomy, privacy and safety are constantly negotiated and arranged in accordance with specific and local definitions of patient condition. Solutions must allow tailoring to meet these conditions. Tracker design, as one feature of this, is important. And variable shapes, due to the individual preferences and habits of the patient.

In addition, technical support must fit with the established routines of family and institutional life. Constant monitoring from fixed positions is extremely difficult in many care institutions where there is a constant level of demand on time and a need to be available in different locations. In family contexts, demands include the fact that carers themselves are sometimes elderly, or have other family or work commitments. Solutions, we suggest, are better fitted to selective management of situations rather than to constant monitoring for those reasons.

Nevertheless, it would be naive to imagine that technical solutions can solve all problems. As Rogers has argued:

"*While most projects are sensitive to the privacy and ethical problems surrounding the monitoring of people, they are not easy to solve and have ended up overwhelming UbiComp research. Indeed, much of the discussion about the human aspects in the field has been primarily about the trade-offs between security and privacy, convenience and privacy, and informedness and privacy. This focus has often been at the expense of other human concerns receiving less airing, such as how recording, tracking and re-representing movements and other information can be used to facilitate social and cognitive processes.*" [32]

Our long-term field test shows several impacts of the monitoring technology on the cooperative and social process of dementia care. For example, it allows the 'lines of conflict' to be renegotiated. Concerns such as awareness vs. privacy and safety vs. autonomy can be differently managed given location-awareness support. To a large degree, the management of these concerns is a function of varying institutional and familial arrangements. This is compounded by the evident fact that policy, especially in the institutional context, around 'freedom deprivation' is often ambiguous.

The constant renegotiation of care philosophies is a complicating factor. With Dahl et al [9, 10] we see that new care philosophies, such as Person Centered Care [19], are being used in many care institutions. However, the related practices are not clear-cut. Therefore we do – slightly different as [33] who promote Patient Centered Care as *"[...] appropriate for applying the norm of human-centered design"* – recommend to put a deeper look in how differently care theories are being worked out in situated practices.

Thus, autonomy is not a fixed metric. On the one hand, as indicated, this points at the need for flexibility in design technologies in its functionalities and settings. Just as importantly, however, it points to ethical issues in respect of how the researcher positions his/herself in these developing ideologies. If we support changing views of patient care in organizational settings, are we not bound to have a view of how patients are treated in family settings? Can we be comfortable supporting highly 'engineered' solutions like the one described above?

The cooperation with the software company in the consortium has been a further difficulty in conducting this research project. It was especially hard for us to transfer qualitative-empirical results and design suggestions to the company. This discrepancy in design philosophies brought some friction to the cooperation. It is our view that agile development processes are much more suitable for environments of this kind. The ability to customize artefacts as well as aesthetic aspects in products for the elderly, and especially in dementia care, has also been stressed elsewhere [2, 38] and our inability to customize the tracker to cope with 'indoor' situations limited perceived value.

In conclusion, we set out to contribute to a better understanding of the subtleties and complexities in familial and institutional dementia of sufferers with wandering tendencies. With a full description of a design case study (investigative pre-study, design & long-term evaluation) we have established, we feel, a fine-grained basis for understanding of how lines of conflicts may occur and how a suitably flexible GPS locating system can aid in their resolution. It is clear to us that technology does not provide a full assistive solution.

Besides technological features, a planned market roll-out requires detailed consideration of support for installation, education, legal matters, after-sales service (counseling, adaptation) and so on. The business model of such a product needs careful thought since service before-, at- and after-sale are at least as important as the technology itself. We believe that fixed contact persons with some knowledge of local conditions might better facilitate communication in this challenging context. Finally, the heterogeneity of caregiving contexts means assistive solutions must be very flexible and creative, adapting to differing users needs in each specific context. Caregivers in our study found these things in very short supply.

ACKNOWLEDGMENTS

Our thanks to the persons who unhesitatingly provided us with insights of their challenging every-day and working life and discussed their concerns, attitudes and ideas in regard of technical aids with us. Special thanks to the self-help organization "Alzheimer Selbsthilfe e.V. Köln".

REFERENCES

1. Abowd, G.D., Hayes, G.R., Kientz, J.A., Mamykina, L., and Mynatt, E.D. Challenges and Opportunities for Collaboration Technologies for Chronic Care Management. *The HumanComputer Interaction Consortium HCIC 2006*, (2006).
2. Angelini, L., Caon, M., Carrino, S., et al. Designing a desirable smart bracelet for older adults. In *Proc. UbiComp 2013 Adjunct*, ACM Press (2013), 425-434.
3. Astell, A. REAFF - A framework for developing technology to address the needs of people with dementia, In Proc. of First International Workshop on Reminiscence Systems, Cambridge, UK, 2009.
4. Ballegaard, S.A., Hansen, T.R., and Kyng, M. Healthcare in everyday life: designing healthcare services for daily life. In *Proc. CHI 2008*, ACM Press (2008), 1807-1816.
5. Brodaty, H., Thomson, C., Thompson, C., and Fine, M. Why caregivers of people with dementia and memory loss don't use services. *International journal of geriatric psychiatry 20*, 6 (2005), 537–546.
6. Christensen, L. and Grönvall, E. Challenges and Opportunities for Collaborative Technologies for Home Care Work. In *Proc. ECSCW 2011, 24-28 September 2011, Aarhus Denmark*. Springer London, (2011), 61–80.
7. Consolvo, S., Roessler, P., Shelton, B.E., LaMarca, A., Schilit, B., and Bly, S. Technology for care networks of elders. *IEEE Pervasive Computing 3*, 2 (2004), 22–29.
8. Crabtree A, Hemmings T, Rodden T, et al. Designing with care: Adapting cultural probes to inform design in sensitive settings. *Proceedings of the 2004 Australasian Conference on Computer-Human Interaction (OZCHI2004),* (2003), 4-13.
9. Dahl, Y. and Holbø, K. "There are no secrets here!": professional stakeholders' views on the use of GPS for tracking dementia patients. In *Proc. MobileHCI 2012*, ACM Press (2012), 133-142.
10. Dahl, Y. and Holbø, K. Value biases of sensor-based assistive technology: case study of a GPS tracking system used in dementia care. In *Proc. DIS 2012*, ACM Press (2012), 572-581.
11. Demiris, G. Independence and shared decision making: The role of smart home technology in empowering older adults. *Conference Proceedings of the International Conference of IEEE Engineering in Medicine and Biology Society 2009*, January (2009), 6432–6436.
12. Essén, A. The two facets of electronic care surveillance: an exploration of the views of older people who live with monitoring devices. *Social Science & Medicine (1982) 67*, 1 (2008), 128–136.
13. Fitzpatrick, G. and Ellingsen, G. A Review of 25 Years of CSCW Research in Healthcare: Contributions, Challenges and Future Agendas. *Computer Supported Cooperative Work (CSCW) 22*, 4-6 (2012), 609–665.
14. Friedman, B. Value-sensitive design. *interactions 3*, 6 (1996), 16–23.
15. Gaver, W., Wright, P., Boucher, A., et al. The photostroller: supporting diverse care home residents in engaging with the world. In *Proc. CHI 2011*, ACM Press (2011), 1757-1766.
16. Gowans, G., Campbell, J., Alm, N., Dye, R., Astell, A., and Ellis, M. Designing a multimedia conversation aid for reminiscence therapy in dementia care environments. *Ext. Abstracts CHI 2004*, ACM Press (2004), 825-836.
17. Judge, T.K., Neustaedter, C., and Kurtz, A.F. The family window: the design and evaluation of a domestic media space. In *Proc. CHI 2010*, ACM Press (2010), 2361-2370.
18. Kaplan, B. and Harris-Salamone, K.D. Health IT success and failure: recommendations from literature and an AMIA workshop. *Journal of the American Medical Informatics Association 16*, 3 (2009), 291–299.

19. Kitwood, T. Dementia reconsidered: the person comes first. Open University Press, 1997.
20. Landau, R., Auslander, G.K., Werner, S., Shoval, N., and Heinik, J. Families' and professional caregivers' views of using advanced technology to track people with dementia. *Qualitative health research 20*, 3 (2010), 409–419.
21. Landau, R., Werner, S., Auslander, G.K., Shoval, N., and Heinik, J. Attitudes of Family and Professional Care-Givers towards the Use of GPS for Tracking Patients with Dementia: An Exploratory Study. *British Journal of Social Work 39*, 4 (2009), 670–692.
22. Mamykina, L., Mynatt, E., Davidson, P., and Greenblatt, D. MAHI: investigation of social scaffolding for reflective thinking in diabetes management. In *Proc. CHI 2008*, ACM Press (2008), 477-486.
23. Miskelly, F. *Electronic tracking of patients with dementia and wandering using mobile phone technology*. Age and ageing, 2005, 43(5): 497-499.
24. Morris, M., Lundell, J., Dishman, E., and Needham, B. New perspectives on ubiquitous computing from ethnographic study of elders with cognitive decline. *UbiComp 2003: Ubiquitous Computing*. Springer Berlin Heidelberg, (2003), 227-242.
25. Müller, C., Wan, L., and Hrg, D. Dealing with wandering: a case study on caregivers' attitudes towards privacy and autonomy when reflecting the use of LBS. In *Proc. GROUP 2010*, ACM Press (2010), 75-84.
26. Mynatt, E.D., Rowan, J., Craighill, S., and Jacobs, A. Digital family portraits: supporting peace of mind for extended family members. In *Proc. CHI 2001*, ACM Press (2001), 333–340.
27. Palen, L. and Aaløkke, S. Of pill boxes and piano benches: "home-made" methods for managing medication. In *Proc. CSCW '06*, ACM Press (2006), 79-88.
28. Pang, C.E., Neustaedter, C., Riecke, B.E., Oduor, E., and Hillman, S. Technology preferences and routines for sharing health information during the treatment of a chronic illness. In *Proc. CHI 2013*, ACM Press (2013), 1759-1768.
29. Petrakou A. Exploring cooperation through a binder: a context for IT tools in elderly care at home. *ECSCW 2007*. Springer London, (2007), 271-290.
30. Pratt, W., Unruh, K., Civan, A., and Skeels, M. Personal health information management. *Communications of the ACM 49*, 1 (2006), 51-55.
31. Robinson, L., Brittain, K., Lindsay, S., Jackson, D., and Olivier, P. Keeping In Touch Everyday (KITE) project: developing assistive technologies with people with dementia and their carers to promote independence. *International psychogeriatrics IPA 21*, 3 (2009), 494–502.
32. Rogers, Y. Moving on From Weiser's Vision of Calm Computing: Engaging UbiComp Experiences. *UbiComp 2006 Ubiquitous Computing 4206*, 6 (2006), 404–421.
33. Sugihara, T., Fujinami, T., Phaal, R., and Ikawa, Y. A technology roadmap of assistive technologies for dementia care in Japan. *Dementia*, (2013).
34. Taylor, N., Cheverst, K., Wright, P., and Olivier, P. Leaving the wild: lessons from community technology handovers. In *Proc. CHI 2013*, ACM Press (2013), 1549-1558.
35. Tsai, J.Y., Kelley, P., Drielsma, P., Cranor, L.F., Hong, J., and Sadeh, N. Who's viewed you?: the impact of feedback in a mobile location-sharing application. In *Proc. CHI 2009*, ACM Press (2009), 2003-2012.
36. Uzor, S. and Baillie, L. Exploring & designing tools to enhance falls rehabilitation in the home. In *Proc. CHI 2013*, ACM Press (2013), 1233-1242.
37. Vines, J., Blythe, M., Lindsay, S., Dunphy, P., Monk, A., and Olivier, P. Questionable concepts: critique as resource for designing with eighty somethings. In *Proc. CHI 2012*, ACM Press (2012), 1169-1178.
38. Wallace, J., Thieme, A., Wood, G., Schofield, G., and Olivier, P. Enabling self, intimacy and a sense of home in dementia: an enquiry into design in a hospital setting. In *Proc. CHI 2012*, ACM Press (2012), 2629-2638.
39. Wittenberg-Lyles, E., Oliver, D.P., Demiris, G., and Baldwin, P. The ACTive Intervention in Hospice Interdisciplinary Team Meetings: Exploring Family Caregiver and Hospice Team Communication. *Journal of Computer-Mediated Communication 15*, 3 (2010), 465–481.
40. Wulf, V., Rohde, M., Pipek, V., and Stevens, G. Engaging with practices: design case studies as a research framework in CSCW. In *Proc. CSCW 2011*, ACM Press (2011), 505-512.

Sweet Home: Understanding Diabetes Management via a Chinese Online Community

Xiaomu Zhou, Si Sun
School of Communication and Information
Rutgers, The State University of New Jersey
{xmyzhou,sisun} @rutgers.edu

Jiang Yang
IBM, New York
yangjiang@us.ibm.com

ABSTRACT
China has overtaken India and the U.S. as host to the largest diabetic population in the world. Many problems exist in the Chinese healthcare system and very small number of diabetes patients receives treatment. Our paper reports on a case study through the lens of an online diabetes patient community, *Sweet Home*. We conducted participant observations, text analysis, and interviews, to understand the health management of patients at *Sweet Home*. Our findings reveal that patients' understanding of diabetes, their choice of treatments, their routine management, and their interactions with others (in the physical world) and among themselves (in the online world) are influenced by many factors: belief in traditional Chinese versus modern western medicine, cultural and social norms regarding social eating and drinking, conflicts over self-images, and responses to comments and pressures of coworkers. That is, social context may significantly affect patients' behaviors and each individual patient's actions may also help reshape the social context. We draw out implications for how our society as a whole may respond to these issues, from the perspective of public health, education, and information technology design.

Author Keywords
Diabetes; chronic disease management; Chinese table culture; Chinese medicine; social eating; online community

ACM Classification Keywords
H.5.m. Information interfaces and presentation (e.g., HCI): Miscellaneous.

INTRODUCTION
China has overtaken India and the U.S. as host to the largest diabetic population in the world. According to the report published in Journal of American Medical Association (September 4, 2013), this population (18 or older) reached 113.9 million (11.6% of the population), and the growth of this population is much faster than in the U.S. and other countries.

CHI 2014, April 26–May 1, 2014, Toronto, Ontario, Canada.

http://dx.doi.org/10.1145/2556288.2557344

There are many problems in the Chinese healthcare system. Its large populations, lack of medical resources, inadequacy of long-term health insurance, concerns with patient safety, and tension between patients and healthcare providers [27], among others [21], are all contributing factors to the failure of people to go see doctors unless the situation is acute and needs urgent care. As a result, many chronically ill patients largely rely on self-management without health professionals' guidance. In the context of diabetics, only 25.8% of the patient received treatment, and only 39.7% of these treated patients had adequate glycemic control [22].

Researchers in HCI have made significant efforts to understand diabetes patients and design tools to help them manage their health (e.g. [8, 12, 13, 14]). In this paper, we aim to study diabetic management in the context of a popular online Chinese diabetic community (bbs.tnbz.com), *Sweet Home*[1], aiming to explore how a specific social and cultural environment may influence individual diabetic management for these patients. Sweet Home was founded September 8, 2005, by a type II diabetes patient for nonprofit purposes focusing on diabetic education. The owner runs the forum as an administrator with a number of volunteer board masters, and the site is now supported by nonintrusive advertisements. The online discussion forum was not introduced until later, in 2009, and it has quickly become the largest of its kind in China. The forum has attracted close to 130,000 members (mostly patients, family caregivers, and doctors), and accumulated more than 3.2 million posts by September 2013.

Our case study investigates the patients at Sweet Home, and thus is not able to cover all perspectives of Chinese diabetic population. Our effort, however, choosing the largest diabetic online community in China, is an attempt to understand an intrinsically large population. Through analyzing their online discussion (based on their everyday

[1] This is a literal translation from the original Chinese characters for the title of the forum. The Chinese character for the concept of "home" is often used as a root character to form a more specific term for various social entities, such as clubs, communities, organizations, or the country.

experiences in self-management), we hope to understand the issues they face in reality and how they receive online support via a specific community. More specifically, we hope to gain insights from discovering: (1) how these patients understand their illness and treatments, particularly under the historical influence of traditional Chinese medicine; (2) how they manage their diet; (3) how they act at social events where eating often plays a big part of social life in Chinese context; 4) how the social interaction is like at Sweet Home and what it means as to support individual's diabetic management. As a first step to respond to the Chinese epidemic growth with as yet inadequate diabetic management in general, our goal is to explore how online social interaction may play a role in patients' experience of diabetic management, and how information technology may be better designed to provide more meaningful help.

In the rest of the paper, we first briefly review related work, including recent developments in patients' health management, use of social media, and Chinese users' online interactions. We then introduce the structure of Sweet Home and research methods. Next, we present findings focusing on three themes, i.e. understanding diabetes and choice of treatment (particularly under the influence of traditional Chinese medicine); disruptions of diabetic management (how social eating and table culture may disrupt diabetes patients' health management; and how they navigate between multiple identities online and offline in the social context around them. Then we will further unpack these issues and propose suggestions for the design to support public health education and social interactions for diabetes patients.

RELATED WORK

The complexity and chronic nature of diabetes has increasingly attracted the attention of the HCI/CSCW community, and more efforts have been put into understanding diabetes patients' health management before designing supporting technologies. For example, Mamykina and colleagues noted that diabetes patients learn from their past experiences by discerning patterns of successful management in their health records and evaluating them over long periods of time [13, 14]. However, this process presents various challenges (e.g. making an individualized care plan) for untrained patients, thus it is necessary to develop tools for monitoring and education to assist this process. Researchers also investigated patients' health information use for diabetes management and called for the incorporation of psychosocial activities in the design of supporting management technologies, and further advocated for considering contexts, such as location and mobile phone activities, when designing these technologies [2, 18].

Another research theme is the interaction between chronic patients through social media such as social networking sites and online communities. Diabetes may cause identity crises in patients, which may lead to health consequences such as patients' nonconformity to treatments; however, participating in social media and integrating social media in health management technologies can help diabetes patients construct and manage their identities, which is a more subtle aspect of health management [1, 12]. While studies have found that online platforms can support patients' informational and emotional needs, social media may present challenges for new patients in locating patient expertise and help for their health management, and commercial activities can further affect the effective use of social media [3, 6]. Effective communication through social media can be complicated by users' needs to balance information sharing with managing self-presentation, health professionals' involvement, and other factors [8].

Due to our interest in a Chinese patient population, we are inspired by earlier Chinese cultural studies. Research has found that Chinese interact differently compared to Americans in online social media. For example, they are generally less concerned with privacy violation [26] and more trusting [10]. Existing studies have also examined how group norms, social identity, and certain design features affect online interactions [25, 28]. Further, in contrast to the West, a culture with analytic and individualistic traits, Chinese culture is more defined by holistic cognition, high-context communication, and collective social orientation [11, 16]. These cultural traits have been interacting and co-evolving with people's preference and use of sociotechnical systems [23, 24].

These studies suggest that informational and social behaviors and issues in diabetic management can be very complex and diverse. A different cultural context might further introduce challenges in understanding diabetic patients' needs and designing social media tools to support their information seeking, sharing, and social interactions, which forms the core motivation for this study.

SWEET HOME: STRUCTURE AND METHODS

As did thousands of other grassroots online forum sites in China, Sweet Home (SH hereafter) adopted the open source BBS platform Discuz[2], which provides comprehensive forum features and requires minimal development cost. In the SH forum, five discussion zones are set by function: *Special Themes* (including sub-forums such as *Type I Diabetes, Diabetic Mothers,* and *Diet and Exercise*), *User Service* (including sub-forms about specific medical products and services), *Exchange* (supporting various online services in the form of sub-forums, e.g., archived educational resources, second-hand exchanges, and reports of untrustworthy information, products or advertisements), *Colorful Life* (including sub-forums to share stories, photos, and hobbies), and *Forum Affairs* (forum policy and administration issues, and announcements, etc.).

[2] www.discuz.net

Figure 1. Interface of the initial post of a typical thread at Sweet Home (with an overlay of some translations): the author announced that she starts to record her "fight" with diabetes with information about diet and exercise.

There are five major types of SH users, including one administrator (also the owner of the site), board masters (BMs), volunteers, regular registered users, and lurkers. The administrator is ultimately in charge of the forum, by assigning board masters (who usually have earned a good reputation), organizing community activities, and maintaining relationships with partners. BMs manage the designated boards by deleting and editing/noting posts, blocking post content, and banning user IDs due to the inaccuracy of the information, selling advertisements on the discussion board, or other unacceptable posts. Volunteers help organize community activities, collect and manage diabetes-related materials, help BMs on routine maintenance of specific boards, and answer fellow users' questions. Regular registered users can create threads, post comments, and rate others' posts.

With the goal of understanding diabetes management of online patients and their social interactions at Sweet Home, we conducted a qualitative research including participant observation, text analysis, and interview study. All researchers are native Chinese and have received or are pursuing a degree in the U.S. We read through approximately 1,300 threads between December 2012 and August 2013. While most of these threads have 20 to 30 comments, some of them have attracted many users and long conversations, accumulating thousands of replies.

We first used bottom-up and then top-down methods of directed data collection (a similar method in other online forum studies, e.g. [25].) At first, we were exploring all possible themes by reading all active threads across all sub-forums. This task was enormous; we quickly identified a few major themes similar to those discussed in previous studies (e.g. [12].) However, the very unique and prominent themes emerged around Chinese traditional medicine and 'forced' social eating that generated the most interesting topics, engaging discussions, and intense interactions on three sub-boards. Then we focused our inquiry, selection of reading, coding, and analysis on these two general themes, i.e., how the unique Chinese elements (traditional Chinese medicine and social eating) might influence patients' diabetic practice. We also looked at how specific Chinese social norms (e.g. *guanxi*[3]) influenced patients both in their understanding of the disease, their social interaction with people at SH and in their everyday environment, their adopting, changing, or maintaining routine diabetic management.

To facilitate interview recruitment, one author (non-diabetic) joined SH with an identity marked as a researcher (ID: Chronic Condition Research). We used the forum's private messaging to acquire consent from three largest sub-board masters, posted a recruiting message. To include experienced members, we further sent 97 private messages to users who contributed 1000+ posts and were active the week before recruiting began. 21 responded, including 20 patients and one doctor. The interviews were done via private chat at SH (an approach similar to [25]) along with follow-up emails for clarifications, resulting in about 3000 words average per transcript.

FINDINGS

Designed originally as an online educational platform for diabetes patients, SH eventually attracted patients, their family members, and even doctors to share information and experiences, and exchange social support, particularly after their implementation of the online discussion forum. From the perspective of information sharing, SH serves as a trusted information center for patients to compare hospitals, doctors, and diabetes medication and equipment products and sellers.

While we found similarities in the various themes diabetic patients often discussed and shared that earlier studies also found, such as sharing glucose values and other numbers and then problem-solving strategies, describing diet and recipes through storytelling, etc. [12], we were impressed by how much the unique Chinese elements can influence their understanding of the disease and choice of treatment, may cause disruption of routine management habits, and how the community members support one another on

[3] *guanxi*: "ties between an individual and others, fostered through exchanges of favors." [25, p46]

various issues they have dealt with as a result of being diabetic in the Chinese context. Our analysis, therefore, focuses on these unique perspectives.

Understanding Diabetes and Choice of Treatment

From our reading of new patients' posts, many of them joined the community after they were diagnosed with diabetes in a hospital. While we did not come across discussions of doubts about their diagnosis, we found many questions or arguments were made surrounding the choice of treatment and long-term management, particularly under the influence of traditional Chinese medicine, which often conflicts with treatments suggested in modern Western medicine.

For instance, in traditional Chinese medicine (TCM hereafter), a practice that dates back 5,000 years ago in ancient China, any medication is considered more or less toxic, and therefore that illness should be cured in a minimally invasive way and that patients' health can be gradually improved mainly by adjusting the patient's diet. In contrast, while Western medicine is usually considered by Chinese to be more powerful and convenient, it is also considered to have much stronger side effects, and herbal medicine is seen as less toxic [9]. This view was also reflected among SH members. A large majority of the threads sampled from a sub-forum board titled "Traditional Chinese Medicine for Health Enhancement" involve discussions or debates on the two treatment perspectives.

Although there were disagreements as to what specific medications to take and how to use them, most members generally agreed that the combination of the two would yield the best outcome. While they acknowledged the effectiveness of Western medicine to control blood glucose value in a timely fashion, they kept a long-term goal of not taking any medication and coming to rely simply on food adjustments based on the TCM principle. As a member explained:

> "Food treatment is fundamental. A diabetes patient would not be able to control her blood glucose if she does not control her diet and drink, or not check nutrition balance....... Also, Chinese herbals can adjust the body (*yin/yang* balance[4]) but is expensive and ineffective for glucose control. I am diabetic, and I own a diabetes food and equipment store where I sell Chinese herbals for glucose control. I have been observing and studying diabetes for 12 years, and I noticed that patients who try to control their glucose with only Chinese medicine all still have high glucose values. However, Chinese medicine is far more powerful in adjustments for mild conditions."

Indeed, many patients strongly believe in the food treatment. They explored a wide variety of food and beverages, sometimes along with Chinese medicine when needed. For example, some members recommended Tartary buckwheat as a major food source, as it was "known as the natural insulin". Members also shared recipes they created and considered good for controlling diabetes, such as a simple rice mixture of wheat, oat, buckwheat, and rice with a specific ratio, or a sophisticated meal comprised of more than twenty types of ingredients and food materials, which were all supposed to be good for diabetic patients.

Recipe sharing to help control diet is quite common at SH. However, when a recipe is claimed to be able to serve as well as medication, it may cause arguments, and many members will show skepticism. For instance, one member shared a folk prescription (i.e., unrecognized or not officially recorded in TCM), mixing soybeans, black beans, peanuts, pecans, and eggs as a substitute for a medication. Although most members do not believe in its power as a medication, they still consider it to be a good breakfast option.

We also found collaborative searching among established TCM medications for substitutes for sugar and other foods. Understandably, many diabetic patients still crave sweet foods, so sweet herbs such as licorice (a type of sweet herb commonly used in TCM for treating cough and other throat problems), chrysanthemum, and ageratum extractives were all brought up for debate.

While SH members generally embrace the fundamental principles of TCM (e.g., food adjustment, herbal medications, etc.) and are often inspired by TCM to try a new diet as part of routine self-management, other members may come forward to challenge TCM, believing that TCM is unscientific, dangerous, and should not be a part of any treatment. As one member commented:

> "Chinese medicine can at the most be considered as a culture, but should not be considered as a science, because we basically have no idea about its pathology and pharmacodynamics. First, Chinese medication can do nothing about the diseases that are commonly treated with western medicine, except for ailments like the cold, which will eventually recover on its own. Second, we do not know about the possible toxicity in these plants. Third, many Chinese medication for diabetes have included an unknown amount of cheap western medication which can run the danger of overdosing if the patient is also taking other western medication. Fourth, Chinese medicine has some placebo effects,...... a lot of Chinese feel obliged to believe in Chinese medicine because it is of historical value to our country."

---

[4] One of the fundamental TCM concepts is the balance between *yin* and *yang*, which represent the complementary characteristics of the human body or natural objects. The Chinese medication prescribed by TCM is often to adjust effects from a mixture of a wide range of plants, minerals, or even animal parts. When multiple herbs selected according to their natures are boiled together, they can adjust the human body to reach the balance between *yin* and *yang* [7].

Indeed, the conflict at SH is evident between the understanding of treatment from the perspective of modern Western medicine and the perspective of TCM. However, some members hold the very extreme belief that taking any medication (Western or TCM) is more harmful than the disease itself and choose to have no medication at all. For example, a user posted a link to an electronic book about diabetes medications, and commented:

> "… usually the medication instructions would mention that the side effects are unclear, which means that the side effects are not found … sometimes the side effects would be stronger than the healing effects. That's why I prefer to have no medication at all…"

Whether or not the patients agree with this comment, many of them seem to hold the long-term goal of taking no medication and controlling the condition only with diet and exercise.

Disruptions of Routine Diabetic Management

In China, it is common for people to have big meals together. It may be a working lunch or dinner with colleagues, a business negotiation, a gathering of family and friends (birthday celebration, house warming, wedding, celebration for newborns for their 100 days, traditional and national holidays throughout the year, etc.). This type of social event runs very long (many courses and much chatting). People involving themselves in these social events often expect a high quality and variety of food, and use the opportunity to bond and get to know each other better (e.g. in the context of business negotiations [15]). However, big meals in these social events present great challenges for diabetes patients. As one member said,

> "The Chinese food culture … is a great threat for diabetes patients' health. The fat in restaurant food is several times that of home cooking. Also, people keep on eating for hours at these gatherings. These [habits] greatly increase the difficulties for controlling blood glucose and blood fat levels."

Inseparable from food culture[5] is wine culture (i.e., the social norm related to alcohol drinking), which is also an important part of table culture in China. In social eating events, people are often pressed to drink as much as possible, and whether you comply or not is considered as evidence of your respect for the people (who can be your friends, boss, family members, etc.) This table cultural norm has put diabetes patients in a dilemma between being active socially and maintaining a routine healthy diet. As a patient commented, "when you give up drinking, you are also giving up your social life". Another member reported her excessive drinking at a gathering with colleagues:

> "Yesterday was our end-of-year dinner. I was drunk, and my blood glucose level is a tragedy… at 12.3 mmol/L [4.4-6.6 mmol/L for healthy people – authors note]…… I really don't want to drink anymore, but my bosses all drink hard liquor; even my colleagues who usually skip drinking all would hold up their cups (to please them). If you don't drink when others propose a toast to you, you would look distant and unsupportive. Once, there were several colleagues who were diabetics at the table. We asked about each other's blood glucose value and reminded each other, 'We seriously need to take care of ourselves.'"

Sometimes, the pressure of drinking not only affects patients socially and physically, but also emotionally and at career level. One member shared her huge frustration from her business duty:

> "…… because of my job, I cannot escape from the responsibility of accompanying my boss, and drinking has become an inevitable problem. I have always tried to avoid drinking with the reason that 'I inherently cannot drink', but my boss always pushes me saying 'Young people should drink more. You may not be able to drink a lot at first, but you will improve gradually if you keep on practicing'. Who would understand my pain?"

It is true that for many Chinese, if you do not drink alcohol up to your ultimate limit (which often involves rice fermented hard liquor, equivalent to vodka), you are not giving your friends "面子" (pronounced as '*mian zi*' meaning literally face, implying you do not respect the person, or involved parties do not get along very well.) An old popular saying "酒逢知己千杯少" (meaning when likely minds meet, they can never have enough cups of wine[6]) is often cited when trying to persuade people who show any hesitation to bottom-up the wine in their cups. As discussed at SH, this alcohol drinking culture has forced diabetic patients to drink the wine as a way to show respect to their friends or boss, although this means huge disruption of their diabetic management. Considering that social gatherings can be very frequent for Chinese, this disruption is a common problem to many diabetic patients in our study.

Regardless, SH members in fact actively seek and learn from one another how to cope with social eating norms. While patients at SH shared various strategies, some can be a significant change in their lifestyle and social network. For example, one member was concerned about the coming Chinese New Year, when extensive eating and drinking would be involved with all family members and friends for many rounds starting New Year evening until the 15th of the New Year. The specific strategies she received from her fellow patients at SH included giving up old connections and making new friends who would favor workouts during

[5] The word "culture" is used in this context to reflect a direct and literal translation from the Chinese characters to phrases used to describe social eating events.

[6] Chinese wine, i.e., hard liquor fermented from rice or other crops, is served in small cups.

holidays, or increasing the dosage of medications for just the holiday, or playing around by adding water to Chinese wine when nobody around the table was watching, or active vomiting after excessive eating and drinking.

As illustrated, coping with social events can be very challenging for diabetic patients under social or cultural norms in China. Patients may have to change their social life, or they face new health problems from the disruption of routine management. A diabetes specialist who served a board master at SH provided his understanding in this context during our interview:

> "Drinking and smoking are part of social life. The key [to both socializing and keeping healthy] is to know that we have a limit, but this is the hard part. [As doctors,] what we can do is to inform or persuade, but we cannot control our patients."

Community Support and Social Interactions

A community such as Sweet Home can be successful only if the underlying community culture and design encourage and motivate members to share information and learn from one another. The community as a whole provides emotional support when members bring up issues they have to deal with in their physical social settings. In this section, we report several observations that may shed light on our understanding of how social interaction works among members in this community.

Cheerful and being positive

Diabetes patients at SH refer to themselves and their fellow patients as "*tang ren*", meaning sugary or sweet man, if literally translated. The pronunciation and the characters of *tang ren* in Chinese read cheerful and sound sweet as a nickname to refer to diabetes patients. As well, SH members also created slang terms to describe their control of their conditions and management. For instance, "*luo ben*" (literally translated as running naked, or streaking, in English) was created to describe the status of solely relying on diet adjustment and not taking any medications to maintain their glucose value. Members used this slang for all related questions and discussion, such as, "When can I start running naked given my current status?", "Here is the data for my recent running naked, please comment."

Understandably, newly diagnosed diabetes patients are usually terrified by and pessimistic about their prospects. When these patients came across SH at this stage, they often started the topic with such comments as: "I was just diagnosed and I find no hope for my life", "I will be stuck with diabetes for the rest of my life and I cannot help crying". Such emotional posts seem to draw many more positive responses from experienced and long-term members, such as: "You can live to 90 years old with diabetes if you are careful enough with food and exercises". One initial sad post drew more than 50 responses from members using their own understanding of the disease, referring to the diagnosis of diabetes as "the right time to start a healthy lifestyle", or "Misfortune may be a blessing in disguise." (Note: an ancient Chinese idiom referring to the dialectics of loss and gain in one's life journey.)

These supportive interactions between experienced and new patients have helped new members go through the initial fear to become more positive, and have reinforced healthy community culture, as one patient mentioned in the interview:

> "We were inexperienced when we first came here [Sweet Home], and we were both frightened and baffled …… with the help and encouragement of fellow patients, I can control my blood glucose perfectly now, as well as give advice to new patients."

Trust and Privacy

SH members generally trust the community for getting the right advice and information. Members often ask their fellow patients for their experience before they take a new medication or adjust the dosage. This seems particularly important for the patients who live in a rural area where medical resources are limited. One of our interview participants made similar comments:

> "I came from a small town where doctors and nurses have limited knowledge. What I learned here is very useful, to such an extent that once I mentioned those diabetic problems I learned at SH, my doctor was surprised that I knew so much."

The doctor who serves as a board master at SH is also a source of trust. New posts often read, "I am lost. Dr. Board Master, or other friends, please help me out;" "Dr. Board Master, please help me regarding my mom's insulin". Indeed, many members expressed that they came to the SH community because there was a doctor who was very active serving as a board master, who was "very knowledgeable and considerate."

It is worth noting that the SH does not ban commercial ads. In fact, to help members communicate with product suppliers, the forum has a specific board for ads, and members can compare and exchange information about the products (e.g., monitoring equipment, insulin pump, and related consumer materials). This is considered by the members to help them "solve practical problems."

When asked about the reason for such a high level of trust, our interviewees explained that the community has strict controls for bad commercial behavior. Any user ID or IP address identified as trying to persuade patients to buy fake or less effective medication or medication for an inappropriate price will be banned permanently. In addition, many long-term members at SH have become diabetic experts themselves; new members trust their recommendation on the treatment, equipment, and testing materials. As a member explained in in the interview:

"An old saying goes 'prolonged illness makes a doctor out of a patient'. If one is experienced enough, she can tell the truth. It is easy to tell people who are here to share experiences from those who are trying to sell stuff - the latter will quickly give in if you keep on asking questions… There are just several brands of blood glucose meters and [insulin] pumps, and there are only limited choices for insulin and medication. You see people talk about these in the forum all the time, and you have a basic idea when people mention any of them."

This well regulated and trusted environment provides the basis for healthy online interactions. This leads to perhaps less concern about their personal information. For instance, many members use their real photos as their avatars at SH as encouraged by the community, and they share their real names and medical records (which often includes their full name, gender, age, the name of the workplace, dates of their tests, and all test data.) Our interviews also confirmed our observations.

Friendship and Community of Belonging

High level of trust and less concern about personal information sharing seems naturally to help establish friendship. When we asked some members why they would feel comfortable enough to share such personal information, the most frequent answer was that most members at SH are diabetes patients who share the same problems and concerns, and their ultimate goal is to control diabetes. An interviewee cited a line in Bai Ju-Yi's[7] poem *The Pipa Tune* "We are wretched drifters in this unfortunate world, and we treasure this encounter even though we are strangers."

Similarly, other members mentioned that they appreciated the ambiance in the forum:

"Indeed, I feel a part of my life is missing if I cannot visit here [Sweet Home] even for one day. The atmosphere here is so nice and I've made a lot of friends. Once in a while, I participate in offline gatherings with some of my online friends who live in the same city."

Another referred to the SH forum as her home:

"I have made a lot of good friends at Sweet Home, such as … [five names or IDs were mentioned; two served as board masters – authors note] A friend from Beijing even drove to our little town just to visit me."

It is perhaps an interesting contrast that while members can openly share their information at SH, they feel uncomfortable revealing their health conditions to people around them in real life. In one incident, a female member took a business trip to a beach with her colleagues, and only told them she had high uric acid to explain her strict diet. Unexpectedly, her colleagues gossiped about some acquaintances who died or went blind because of diabetes. The conversations deeply upset her but she had to hide her emotions to pretend she was normal. When she came back from the trip, she posted at SH about this incident. Many members comforted her, mentioning that that they had all experienced and already got used to similar situations. One member, in particular, expressed her anger toward these gossips, "I really want to beat them up. They do not know how much psychological pressure they are putting on us just by these casual talks."

Indeed, SH seems a real "sweet home" to many members, an online space where they can socialize, discuss all types of the issues they experience in everyday life, and develop a sense of belonging. As one member's first post commented: "I came across this forum, and really feel I belong here"; and another one, "Thanks for everyone's welcoming notes, I feel like I've finally found my home." The sense of belonging seems to grow even stronger as members spend more time at SH.

DISCUSSION AND IMPLICATIONS

Our findings reveal that patients' understanding of diabetes, their choice of treatments, their routine management, and their interactions with others (in the physical world) and among themselves (in the online world) are influenced by many factors: belief in traditional Chinese versus Western medicine, cultural and social norms regarding social eating and drinking, conflicts over self-images, and responses to comments and pressures of coworkers. In this section, we further unpack diverse issues in Chinese diabetic patients' health management. We hope to deepen understanding and draw out implications for how our society as a whole may respond to these issues from the perspective of public health, education, and information technology design.

Social Context and Individual Action

Human practices should be understood via the mutual constitution of social structure and human actions [4]. In the context of diabetes practice, there are many specific factors that Chinese diabetes patients need to take into account for their health management in their unique context. These factors can be cultural, social, economic, personal, circumstantial, and pragmatic, which are all embedded in a larger social structure. Patients' actions, e.g., their choice of treatment, their routine activities for diabetes management, their participation in social events, and how they interact with others (e.g. with coworkers offline, with online peer patients) also reshape the social context, which further influences how other patients perceive the issues of diabetic management and take informed actions. In our study, for instance, social pressure to drink in physical world leads patients to seek solace and corrective actions at SH; advice from fellow online SH patients leads them to water their wine and to take other actions offline.

Distinct from earlier studies on diabetes patients (e.g. [8, 12, 13, 14]), Chinese patients in our study often need to

[7] Bai Ju-Yi (772-846): one of the greatest Chinese poets in Tang Dynasty.

compare the treatments and routine management offered by Western modern medicine relative to alternatives from traditional Chinese medicine (TCM). Regardless of criticism of TCM (e.g., not being scientific, not being effective in severe conditions), most patients at SH indeed embrace the principles of TCM (e.g., food therapy, herbal remedies, and minimum to zero medications). Patients set goals based on their beliefs in TCM, e.g., stop taking any medications. However, this belief without considering individual context has consequences, as one member at SH points out based on her years of experience of selling herbal medications: many patients who only use herbal medication (even more expensive ones) are not able to control their glucose levels and TCM only works in mild cases.

Due to its 5000 years of history in China, the concept of TCM, including its ideas for health enhancement, has deep roots in daily Chinese life. Particularly in chronic situations, TCM has significant influence on people's choice when considering specific treatments. While modern medicine has proved to be more effective and powerful in general, TCM indeed works well in certain cases. At SH, patients with success stories use their own experience to advocate for TCM within the community, which may further influence people who also consider TCM treatments (as illustrated in our findings). In this case, TCM has been reinterpreted to be effective, which will draw new patients to consider TCM as an alternative, regardless of their individual condition. This is perhaps one of the reasons why we see constant debate on the choice between modern Western vs. traditional Chinese medicine treatments, not only at SH, but also in the larger context of Chinese society.

Indeed, at Sweet Home, even patients who suspect the toxicity of and have doubts about the effectiveness of Chinese herbal medicine in treating diabetes still believe that TCM herbal treatment is less toxic than western medication. They use Chinese herbals more or less in their treatment, whether as a supplement or as a critical treatment plan. Regardless, all of them strive to reach the level of "running naked", i.e., not taking any medication and only relying on diet adjustment and exercise. Scientific comparison of the effectiveness and toxicity of Western versus Chinese herbal medication is beyond the scope of this research. Rather, as a case study, we add to existing studies that have explored the cultural underpinnings and practices of TCM [9]. Indeed, discussions about this topic are also highly popular at Sweet Home.

Eating and drinking in a social context adds another layer of complexity in Chinese diabetes patients' management. Indeed, food is a big part of Chinese life, which is reflected in the variety of ingredients and food materials, cuisines, and well-established table culture. Much business negotiation and many deals cannot be made without the two parties meeting in restaurants [15]. As illustrated in our findings, excessive, prolonged meals and peer-pressured drinking cause disruptions in diabetic management, and these can be psychologically affecting as well. However, social eating and table culture are important elements in organizational and social life. Negotiating the presentation of self as a normal person to social groups [5], and of being diabetic, presents a huge challenge to patients' health management. It is understandable that many diabetes patients do not reveal their health condition to their friends and coworkers. As a result, in social gatherings, they are "forced" to eat and drink like a normal healthy person, just so they can still be seen as part of the social group, and they can show their respect and closeness to the people who propose a toast (as the table culture requires).

If social norms and table culture indeed have caused harm to patients' routine diabetic management, then the patients' actions responding to such social pressure present another side of the story. As illustrated, while some patients may choose to withdraw from existing social networks, many of them share their strategies about how to "cheat" (e.g., secretly watering hard liquor), or actively vomit after eating and drinking, or increase their medication for a short time. By responding with this type of action (i.e. putting on a social face, conforming to their coworkers and friends' expectation about their health) rather than directly addressing the issue in the social context, their "seemingly normal" participation at these social events may have just reinforced the table culture and social norms in China that extensive eating and drinking are expected, accepted, and appreciated in their social life. This is obviously not what they want. Still, huge social pressure may prevent patients from acting purely from the perspective of healthy diabetes management. As illustrated, some may have to change their job (e.g. the patient who has to frequently accompany her boss for business meals and excessive drinking).

Sweet Home as a Third Place

To study community building, Oldenburg used the term *Third Place* to refer to social settings distinct both from one's home (first place) and work environment (second place) [17]. According to Oldenburg:

> "Third places exist on neutral ground and serve to level their guests to a condition of social equality. Within these places, conversation is the primary activity and the major vehicle for the display and appreciation of human personality and individuality."

A third place is a physical entity (e.g. a bar or café) in Oldenburg's view, where people can get together for communication, joy, and to feel a sense of the place, "a home away from home". Researchers have also used the concept to interpret and understand online communities [19]. In the context of our study, Sweet Home appears to be a place for many Chinese diabetes patients to get together, exchange information, learn from experienced patients, and seek comfort and social support.

As described in our findings, patients come to SH to get a better understanding of what life would be once diagnosed to be diabetic. The welcoming and supportive community culture, abundant educational materials and insightful information for strategies to cope with the diseases, and all seem to be contributing factors for a community being successful. While we observed similar patterns regarding identity construction through an individual's storytelling [12], the more distinctive aspect of SH is its strong sense of shared group identity [5, 19] (e.g. "We are all diabetes patients here,") and the feeling of belonging and having found the right place (e.g. "I feel I belong here", "I feel like I've finally found my home.")

Indeed, many new patients received encouraging and cheering-up feedback from experienced members at Sweet Home. Through interactions with fellow patients, they gain a better understanding of the nature of their illness. They learn alternative treatments and other pragmatic details on how other patients define and deal with diabetes in everyday life. A better understanding of self as being diabetic (with the need to adjust individual lifestyle) and sharing of a group identity (people are socially equal and all diabetic at Sweet Home) help prepare patients to psychologically and emotionally accept their health condition and actively manage their illness [20].

The feeling of belonging and being at home may also explain why many patients at Sweet Home do not have significant privacy concerns (e.g. using real photos, detailed medical records uploaded for everyone to see, including full name, age, gender, employment organization, etc.), which in fact, have facilitated locating expertise (e.g. [3,8]). As patients noted, suffering the same diabetic health condition is the reason for them to trust one another. They have fewer concerns over disclosing personal information. A stronger motive is to establish online and offline friendships among diabetic patients. As illustrated, patients are unwilling to reveal their diabetic status in their physical social context, due to concerns of stigmatization. These patients are very clear about how to present themselves to different social groups, i.e., trustful and friendly at Sweet Home, but protective and cautious when interacting offline [5].

Public Health Awareness

The findings from our study imply an urgent need for the general public to gain a better understanding of diabetes as a chronic situation and education about its routine management. The stereotype for the Chinese population is that they maintain their body weight well, but research has shown that many people's blood glucose is prediabetic even they only minimally overweigh, which is very different from other ethnic groups [22]. As previously mentioned, China is currently the host to the largest diabetic population in the world with limited medical resources. In a cultural context that features such intensive social eating and drinking, it is crucially important to raise the society's awareness of diabetic health management and help patients successfully cope with their disease in social settings.

Therefore, the health administration system, social services and programs, and social media (e.g. Sweet Home), may need to work on increasing social awareness about the prevalence and the nature of diabetes, and the importance of its long-term health management. In particular, the Chinese diabetes patients (particularly in rural areas) are critically in need of more authentic and profound information and education about the difference between traditional Chinese and modern Western medicine, particularly in the context of treating diabetes. As illustrated in our findings, when a medical intervention is needed, Chinese patients often have to navigate their understanding between the two systems [7], which is affected by various conflicting information resources and dynamic social influences. Indeed, patients' decision-making takes place in its social context (their own value along with their observation of others, their belief in traditional Chinese medicine, their interactions with other patients, etc.). Furthermore, improving the whole society's awareness and understanding about diabetes can in turn help patients cope with social pressures and develop healthy practices.

Social Media as a Platform for Education

Our analysis illustrates a wide variety of interesting social patterns at SH that reflects the interaction between diabetes health management and its social and cultural context. These include how they build the forums, how they have developed unique jargons and norms, how they participate in extensive self-exposure in social sharing, and how they maintain social bonds with reciprocity. SH has been a successful example of how such grassroots online forums can play a crucial role in providing information and social supports for Chinese diabetes patients, given the fact that China lacks adequate official information/education providers, very few nonprofit organizations and social workers. The patients themselves have been able to adopt some open source BBS tools to establish this very popular and helpful online community, with almost zero cost at the beginning. This may suggest that it is probably more practical and cost-efficient for the stakeholders in the public health system to invest in and improve such social media tools, to better help the diabetes population. On the other side, developers may also look for such opportunities to design social media to help patient users suffering from other kinds of epidemic diseases.

Furthermore, for the aforementioned need to improve diabetes education and social awareness, it is important to explore other types of social media besides online forums for inexpensive and effective solutions to address specific diabetes population's social and informational needs. For example, a wiki-like site that can accumulate and compare articles, citations, and data between traditional Chinese and modern Western medicines may better serve as a collaborative construction space and provide structured and ever-evolving knowledge. In addition, Microblogging (*Weibo* in Chinese) and social instant messaging tool

(*Weixin* in Chinese) may be used to advocate social campaigns such as "understanding the diabetes diet" to alleviate the social pressure on eating and drinking.

CONCLUSION

We conducted participant observation, text analysis, and interviews to understand diabetes management through the lens of a Chinese online community called "Sweet Home." Findings from this study, limited to the patients who sought online support, might not generalize and we do not claim to understand all Chinese perspectives about diabetes management. Still, our findings provide several rich insights into how social context can significantly affect patients' routine management. Context includes the cultural value of and practical beliefs in traditional Chinese medicine, social eating and table culture, and online/offline social interactions. As well, we also show how an individual patient's actions choice of treatment and social participation can help reshape the social context.

While earlier studies of diabetes management in HCI focus on individual diet control, identity construction, and impression management, our study adds a rich empirical account of diabetic management for an online population situated in a unique social and cultural context. We provide a deep analysis of the complicated and cyclic relationship between individuals and social context, offline struggles and online support seeking. This leads us to recommend policy modifications to extend and raise public health awareness. Considering that diabetes patients are situated in their own social and cultural context, we also hope our study serves an example for understanding disease management in social and cultural settings more generally.

REFERENCES

1. Armstrong, N., Koteyko, N., & Powell, J., 'Issues of identity and authority in an online diabetes community'. *Health*, 16, 4(2011), 347–365.
2. Chen, Y. Take it personally. In *Proc.* DIS '10. ACM Press (2010), 252–261.
3. Civan, A. et. al . Bringing the Field into Focus: User-Centered Design of a Patient Expertise Locator. In *Proc.* CHI '2010, ACM Press (2010), 1675-1684.
4. Giddens, A. *New rules of sociological method: A positive critique of interpretative sociologies.* Stanford, CA: Stanford University Press, 1993.
5. Goffman, E. *The presentation of self in everyday life.* New York [N.Y.], Doubleday, 1990.
6. Greene, J.A. et. al. Online Social Networking by Patients with Diabetes. *Journal of General Internal Medicine*, 26, 3(2010), 287–292.
7. Hesketh, T., Zhu, W. X. Health in China. Traditional Chinese medicine: one country, two systems. *BMJ*, 315, 7100(1997), 115–117.
8. Huh, J., Patel, R., & Pratt, W. Tackling dilemmas in supporting "the whole person" in online patient communities, *In Proc.* CHI '2012, 923-926.
9. Lam, T. P. Strengths and weaknesses of traditional Chinese medicine and Western medicine in the eyes of some Hong Kong Chinese. *JECH*, 55, 10(2001), 762–765.
10. Liao, Q. et. al. Chinese online communities. In *Proc.* CHI '2010. ACM Press(2010), 2193-2202.
11. Markus, H.R., Kitayama, S. Culture and the self: Implications for cognition, emotion, and motivation. *Psychological Review,* 98, (1991), 224–253.
12. Mamykina, L. et.al. Constructing identities through storytelling in diabetes management. In *Proc.* CHI '2010. ACM Press, 1203-1212.
13. Mamykina, L. et. al. Investigation Of Social Scaffolding For Reflective Thinking In Diabetes Management. In *Proc.* CHI '2008. ACM Press (2008), 477-486.
14. Mamykina, L. et. al Investigating health management practices of individuals with diabetes. In *Proc.* CHI' 2006, ACM Press (2006), 927-936.
15. Newman, J. M. *Food Culture in China.* Westport, Conn: Greenwood Press, 2004.
16. Nisbett, R.E. et. al. Culture and systems of thought: Holistic vs. analytic cognition. *Psychological Review*, 108(2001), 291–310.
17. Oldenburg, Ray. *The Great Good Place.* New York: Marlowe & Company, 1991.
18. Preuveneers, D., & Berbers, Y. Mobile phones assisting with health self-care. In *Proc.* MobileHCI '2008. ACM Press (2008), 177-186.
19. Rheingold, Howard. *The Virtual Community: Homesteading on the Electronic Frontier.* New York: Harper Perennial, 1993.
20. Tilden, B. Identity and Adherence in a Diabetes Patient: Transformations in Psychotherapy. *Qualitative Health Research*, 15, 3(2005), 312–324.
21. Xinhua. Attack prompts concern over doctor-patient tensions in China. http://www.wantchinatimes.com/news-subclass- cnt.aspx?id= 20120328000110&cid=1103, retrieved on March 28, 2012
22. Xu, Y. et al. Prevalence and Control of Diabetes in Chinese Adults. *JAMA,* 310, 9(2013), 948-959.
23. Yang, J. et al. Activity Lifespan: In *Proc.* ICWSM, IAAA'2010, 186-193.
24. Yang, J. et. al. Collaborating Globally: Culture and Organizational Computer-Mediated Communication. In *Proc.* ICIS'2011, 2011, 1-20.
25. Yang, J., Ackerman, M. S., & Adamic, L. A. Virtual gifts and guanxi. In *Proc.* CSCW '2011, 45-54.
26. Zhao, C. et. al. How and to whom people share. In *Proc.* CSCW '2012, ACM Press (2012), 67-76.
27. Zheng, P. et. al. Public hospitals in China. *Journal of law and medicine*, 13, 4 (2006), 465–470.
28. Zhou, T. Understanding online community user participation: a social influence. *Internet Research*, 21, 1(2011), 67–81.

Investigating the Feasibility of Extracting Tool Demonstrations from In-Situ Video Content

Ben Lafreniere[*†], **Tovi Grossman**[*], **Justin Matejka**[*], **George Fitzmaurice**[*]

[*]Autodesk Research, Toronto, Ontario, Canada
{*tovi.grossman,justin.matejka,george.fitzmaurice*}@autodesk.com

[†]University of Waterloo, Ontario, Canada
bjlafren@cs.uwaterloo.ca

ABSTRACT

Short video demonstrations are effective resources for helping users to learn tools in feature-rich software. However manually creating demonstrations for the hundreds (or thousands) of individual features in these programs would be impractical. In this paper, we investigate the potential for identifying good tool demonstrations from within screen recordings of users performing real-world tasks. Using an instrumented image-editing application, we collected workflow video content and log data from actual end users. We then developed a heuristic for identifying demonstration clips, and had the quality of a sample set of clips evaluated by both domain experts and end users. This multi-step approach allowed us to characterize the quality of "naturally occurring" tool demonstrations, and to derive a list of good and bad features of these videos. Finally, we conducted an initial investigation into using machine learning techniques to distinguish between good and bad demonstrations.

Author Keywords

Help; learning; feature-rich software; video tooltips; toolclips; in-situ usage data.

ACM Classification Keywords

H.5.m. Information interfaces and presentation (e.g., HCI): Miscellaneous.

INTRODUCTION

Software applications for content design and creation can be difficult to learn and use [4, 14, 23]. One particular aspect of these programs that makes them difficult for users is their feature richness [21, 26]. These programs typically contain hundreds or even thousands of commands, each with their own particular usage dynamics, making it difficult to *understand* [14] how to use individual tools.

While many learning techniques have been proposed, recent work has found animated demonstrations to be quite useful in the context of graphical user interfaces [6, 15, 22]. In particular, ToolClips—short, 10–25 sec. video clips that demonstrate how to use a command or tool—have been shown to be a promising technique for communicating how to use tools in feature rich software [15].

Unfortunately video content is time consuming to author. As a result, it would be impractical for software vendors to provide video-based demonstrations for the entire set of a software's features. For example, Autodesk's AutoCAD includes ToolClips, but only for 35 of its 1000+ commands.

In contrast, free screen capture systems are making it easier for members of the public user community to record *in-situ* video content, while technologies such as Tutorial Builder [32], Pause-and-Play [30], Chronicle [16], and Waken [3] enable the tagging of workflows with command usage meta-data. This raises an interesting possibility: can short segments from collections of workflow videos be repurposed as contextual, tool-based demonstrations? Our key insight is that meta-data associated with videos (e.g. tool usage logs, or changes to canvas content), could be used to infer segments that could serve as good demonstration videos. This would allow software systems to provide an exhaustive collection of tool-based demonstration videos, without requiring the time-consuming and costly effort of manually creating demonstrations.

In this paper, we utilize a multi-stage methodology to answer the fundamental questions surrounding the feasibility of such an approach. Using an instrumented version of Pixlr, an online image-editing application, we collect workflow video content from end users, marked up with usage meta-data. We then extract candidate tool-based demonstrations, and have the quality of these videos assessed by both domain experts and end-users. This allows us to characterize the quality of "naturally occurring" tool use examples within in-situ video content, and derive a list of good and bad features for such videos. Finally, we investigate the potential of automatically distinguishing good and bad clips using machine learning techniques.

Our findings indicate that there is wide variation in the quality of clips extracted from in-situ video content, but high quality demonstration videos do occur. We also found that users evaluate the quality of such video clips based on a mix of technical aspects of the demonstration that can be detected programmatically, and subjective aspects, such as the nature of the image being edited. Finally, machine learning shows promise as a "first pass" method of filtering

CHI 2014, April 26 - May 01 2014, Toronto, ON, Canada

ACM 978-1-4503-2473-1/14/04...$15.00.
http://dx.doi.org/10.1145/2556288.2557142

clips, but may need to be supplemented with collaborative filtering or other techniques to create an effective contextual help system. We close by discussing design implications and future directions.

RELATED WORK

Software Learnability

Early HCI research recognized the challenge of providing effective help systems for software applications [4], and established the benefits of minimalist and task-centric help resources [5] and user-centered designs for help systems [20, 31]. Since the conception of on-line help, there have been explorations into many types of learning aids, such as interactive tutorials, contextual assistance [1, 10] and video demonstrations [2, 28, 29, 30]. Below we review the systems most relevant to our own work.

Video Demonstrations

Software video demonstrations were proposed in early work by Palmiter, Elkerton [28, 29], and Harrison [17], but it was unclear if this new help modality would actually be more effective than static help methods [13, 18].

More recently, studies have better identified when animated assistance can be beneficial. A study of ToolClips, short (10–25 sec.) in-context video demonstrations of tools, found that they significantly improve task-completion rates compared to traditional static online help [15]. ToolClips are particularly useful as they are accessed in the context of the software application, making them available on-demand. Similarly, the MixT multimedia tutorial system showed that short video demonstrations are useful for demonstrating individual tutorial steps involving dynamic actions [6]. Additional techniques have been developed to address some of the shortcomings of video-based assistance, such as Pause-and-Play [30], which automatically synchronizes playback of a video to a user's workflow.

A limitation of these techniques is that they require the video content to be explicitly authored or recorded for the purpose of the demonstration. In contrast, we explore the feasibility of generating such content automatically from in-situ workflow recordings.

Workflow Capture

A number of efforts have looked at the possibility of capturing users' workflows. Automatic Photo Manipulation Tutorials [13] and the MixT system [6] allow users to perform a workflow, and have that workflow converted into a tutorial. MixT produces multi-media tutorials that include short video clips of individual steps. However, in both cases, users need to explicitly choose to author a tutorial.

In contrast, systems like MeshFlow [8] and Chronicle [16] are used to continuously record a user's workflow *in-situ*, capturing meta-data, and in the case of Chronicle, a video screen capture as well. The authors of these systems envision that eventually such recording mechanisms could be running at all times, making such workflow histories available for any document. If this were to become a reality, there would be a potential of creating immense libraries of software workflow videos. In this paper, we look at how such libraries could be utilized as a source for video demonstrations.

Automatic Generation of Help Video Collections

Due to the time associated with authoring video, researchers have explored a number of strategies for expanding databases of video demonstration content.

The Ambient Help system [24] dynamically loads and displays potentially helpful video content. The system contains a large database of existing YouTube and professional tutorial videos, and attempts to retrieve sections of videos related to the user's current task. The Waken [3] system is able to recognize UI components and activities from screen capture videos with no prior knowledge of an application. Work on "learnersourcing" asks short questions of viewers of a video, and applies machine learning to the responses to automatically label the activities being performed in the video [19]. Community Enhanced Tutorials provide videos of individual tutorial steps, and the database of video demonstration increases by capturing the workflows of any user that completes the online tutorial [22].

The work above presents a number of plausible routes through which libraries of software workflow videos with meta-data might be created. However, it is unclear if segments of video content created during in-situ workflows could be reliably used within help components such as ToolClips, to assist end-users with learning the software.

METHODOLOGY

The goals of this paper are twofold: to characterize the quality of naturally occurring demonstrations in real-world usage data, and to produce a set of guidelines for what makes a good short video demonstration of a tool. To achieve these goals, we followed a five stage methodology. In this section we give an overview of each of the stages, which will be followed by a detailed section for each stage.

Data Collection: We started by collecting a corpus of real-world usage data from remote participants recruited online. Participants installed a custom screen recording utility and used an instrumented version of the Pixlr.com image editor to work on image editing tasks of their choice, and then submitted at least one hour of the workflow data to us.

Clip Segmentation: Next, we developed a method for selecting short video clips showing the use of individual commands. In total, we sampled a set of 277 clips for six commands, covering a range of different types of tools.

Internal Assessment: Three internal raters independently analyzed and rated the quality of the entire set of individual sample clips. This provided us with a sense of the distribution of quality that the sampling process would produce, as well as insights on the features and criteria that separate good and bad clips.

User Validation: To validate our internal ratings, 12 participants with experience using image editing software were recruited to rate a sampling of the clips. Participants were asked to think aloud as they rated the clips, to provide additional insights into their criteria for judging the clips.

Automatic Identification: Finally, we report on our initial efforts to use machine learning techniques as a method of automatically identifying good examples of tool demonstration videos from in-situ usage data.

The primary contributions of this paper are based on our methods and findings from the first four stages, which provide new data on the spectrum of quality of automatically extracted video demonstrations, and report on the features which high quality examples possess. The final stage serves as a secondary contribution, where we report on an initial attempt to automatically classify demonstration videos as good or bad.

DATA COLLECTION

In this section we describe our method for collecting in-situ workflow data. Our methods are guided by previous research that has captured usage logs of web browsing [27], software usage [21], and low-level input activities [9, 12].

In this work we do not consider recording or use of audio, because users would not typically narrate their workflows during in-situ use.

Task and Participants

To collect a corpus of real-world usage data, we recruited freelance graphic designers through online postings on oDesk and Reddit. Our ad asked participants to use an instrumented version of the web-based Pixlr image editor (www.pixlr.com/editor) for at least 1 hour, and submit the resulting usage data to us.

In a pre-screening process, we asked users to give us an idea of the types of jobs they would work on during the session. The intention here was to confirm that participants understood that they would need to choose their own work to do during the study. We did not screen users based on the tasks they proposed to perform during the study.

We hired a total of 21 participants, 17 from oDesk and 4 from Reddit. Contractors on oDesk were paid an average of \$23.92 and participants recruited on Reddit were given a \$25 Amazon.com gift card.

Screen Recording and Logging

Participants were asked to install a customized screen recording and logging utility on their computers. In addition to recording the screen, the utility hosted a local server on the participant's computer that received and recorded log events sent to it by the instrumented Pixlr editor (Figure 1).

Our goal was to be as exhaustive as possible with respect to the metadata which we collected. This would allow us to later investigate which, if any, features of the workflow would correlate to the quality of the demonstrations. The instrumented Pixlr editor gathered the following additional data, synchronized with the screen recording:

- Mouse movement and click logs
- Tool invocations (including start and end timestamps)
- Dialog open and close events
- All changes to the undo stack
- Document Snapshots after each change to the undo stack
- Changes to the selection state, and the selection region
- Changes to settings for the current tool
- Changes to the color palette

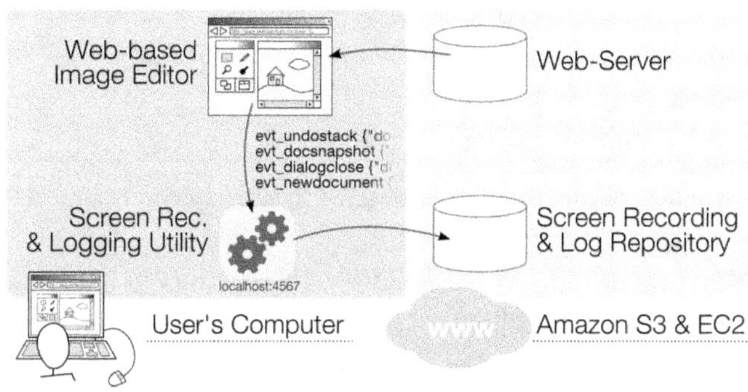

Figure 1. Architecture for remotely gathering synchronized screen recording and log data.

Collected Data

Across all participants, we gathered 25 hours, 23 minutes of usage data at an average cost of \$22.80 per hour. Our data set included 11,553 tool invocations of 93 unique tools. The distribution of tool invocations was very uneven and drops off exponentially when considering commands ordered by the number of invocations (Figure 2). For example, the ten most frequent commands make up 75% of command invocations. This exponential distribution of command invocations is consistent with previous research characterizing the frequency of tool use in feature-rich software [21].

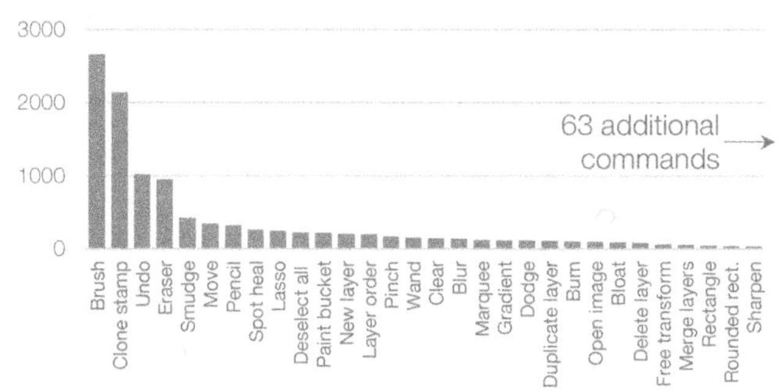

Figure 2. Invocation counts for the 30 most used tools.

CLIP SEGMENTATION

The next stage in the methodology was to create a set of candidate clips to serve as tool demonstration videos. This involved selecting a set of tools, and segmenting out clips of those tools.

Tool Selection

To focus our efforts we choose a set of six tools that were all invoked at least 20 times within the collected usage data.

The six tools we selected are shown in Table 1. These tools were chosen to get a perspective on a variety of different tool types, including direct manipulation tools which are primarily applied using brush strokes (DM-Brush), direct manipulation tools that are typically applied in one invocation that affects a large area (DM-Area), and dialog commands such as adjustments and filters (Dialog).

Tool Name	TYPE	TOTAL CLIPS	SAMPLE
Brush	DM-Brush	1311	60
Clone Stamp	DM-Brush	855	59
Fill	DM-Area	138	60
Gradient	DM-Area	80	46
Hue Saturation	Dialog	33	30
Levels	Dialog	22	22

Table 1. Summary of clips selected by our selection criteria.

Clip Segmentation

Next, we developed a method for segmenting out clips that demonstrate each of the six tools that we selected.

A naive method would be to simply cut the video up so that each clip shows a single tool invocation, with a short time before and after the invocation to provide some context on the operation being performed (Figure 3a). In a pilot implementation using this selection method, we found that direct manipulation tools were difficult to follow because users typically make a number of strokes in quick succession. This made for a large number of short and ineffective demonstration videos. As well, these clips seldom show the user selecting the tool from the toolbox, or making setting adjustments (e.g. setting the brush size before a stroke).

An alternative approach is to aggregate consecutive invocations of the same tool into a single clip, and adjust segmentation boundaries to include preceding operations such as selecting the tool [6] (Figure 3b). However, we found that aggregating all successive invocations of a tool resulted in clips that could be quite long. This makes them less appropriate for contextual videos, which should be in the range of 10–25 seconds [15].

Based on the above considerations, we developed a segmentation algorithm that balances clip time and includes tool selection and settings adjustments (Figure 3c).

For a given tool, we first find consecutive sequences where the tool is invoked. For each such sequence, we start by adding the first invocation to an empty segment *S*. Successive invocations of the tool are then appended to *S* if their starting timestamps are less than 5 seconds from start of the first invocation in *S* (this threshold was tuned through testing). When we reach an invocation that does not meet this criterion, segment *S* is reported and the current invocation is used to start a new segment. This process continues until the consecutive sequence of invocations is exhausted.

In addition, for modal tools, if the tool was selected less than 10 seconds before the first invocation in a segment, the segment boundary is adjusted to show the user selecting the tool. This 10 sec limit on pre-command time was chosen based on our log data, which showed that the median time between tool selection and first invocation is less than 10 seconds for all modal tools in Pixlr. Finally, a 2 second padding is added to the start and end of all sequences.

Though our algorithm is designed to keep demonstrations short it intentionally does not impose a hard limit on the duration of a segment, because our log data indicates that that the duration of an invocation for different tools can vary by orders of magnitude.

This algorithm generated a total of 2439 clips across our six selected tools. For each tool, we then randomly chose up to 30 clips with selection, and up to 30 clips without selection to be included in our quality assessments. A summary of the clip selection and sampling is provided in Table 1.

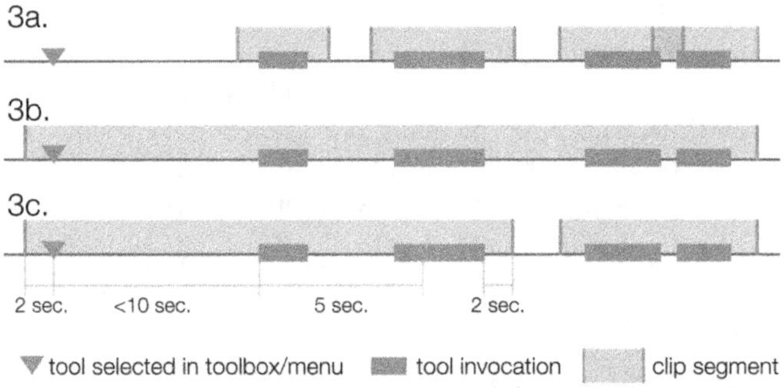

Figure 3. Three clip segmentation approaches. (a) Segment each invocation, (b) Include tool selection and merge contiguous invocations, (c) Our segmentation algorithm.

INTERNAL ASSESMENT OF CLIP QUALITY

While the clips generated by our selection algorithm may be of appropriate length, this alone is no guarantee that the content of the clips are appropriate for learning. In fact, we can imagine numerous reasons why clips might be of poor quality, including the author working too quickly, or making mistakes as they learn to use the software.

Method

To characterize the quality of naturally occurring tool use examples, three raters independently analyzed and rated the quality of each individual sample clip. All three of the raters were authors of this paper, and all had research experience in video-based help systems.

Each rater was instructed to view the 277 clips sampled in the previous section, and rate the quality of each on a seven-point scale for the question "*How good would this clip be for demonstrating how the [name] tool works to a novice user?*" (1=Very Poor, 7=Very Good). Each rater was also asked to record free-form notes on features of clips that influenced their ratings.

The order in which raters viewed the tools was fixed for all raters, and the order of clips within each group was randomized. It took each rater approximately 1.5 hours to rate the set of 277 clips. Once all clips were rated, the raters met to discuss clips with a large spread between the maximum and minimum ratings. Clips with a spread of 5, 4 and a selection of clips with spread 3 were discussed. In some cases, raters modified their ratings based on the discussion.

Results

For the purposes of calculating inter-rater reliability, we consider a rating of 5 or higher to indicate that a clip is "good", and compute Fleiss' Kappa on raters' assessments of clips as good or not. Before the meeting to discuss the clips, the inter-rater reliability was 0.49, and it increased to 0.57 after the meeting. Both of these values indicate moderate agreement between the raters.

We assigned each clip an overall score based on the median of its 3 ratings. The average score across all clips was 3.3 (SD 1.7). Figure 4 shows the distribution of clip scores.

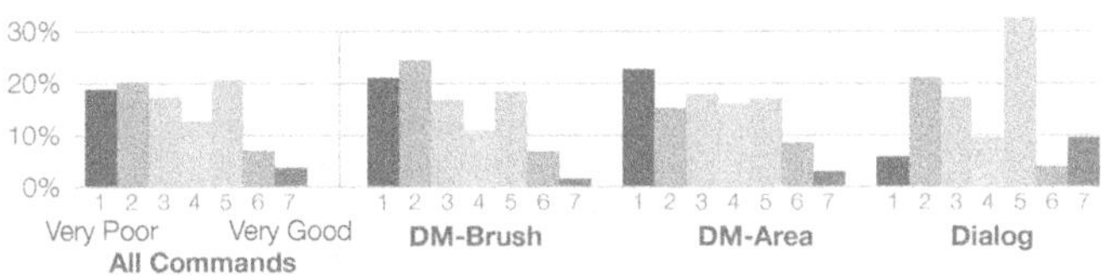

Figure 4. Distribution of median ratings for all six tools (left), and for each of the tool types (right).

We highlight two findings. First, while only 3.6% of the clips had a score of 7, almost a third of the clips (31%) had a score of 5 or greater. This suggests that good tool demonstrations do occur within in-situ workflow recordings.

Second, more than half (56.3%) of clips had a score of less than 4, which suggests that poor quality clips also occur in in-situ workflow recordings. This suggests that appropriate clip filtering mechanisms will also be required to identify good clips; an effective clip selection algorithm is not sufficient on its own.

We also examined the distribution of scores by tool type (Figure 4). Though the data is noisy, there appears to be a similarity between the distributions of scores for the two direct manipulation tool classes, with clips for the Dialog tools receiving relatively higher scores.

In addition to assessing the quality of clips, this phase of the methodology was used to obtain initial insights into the features that distinguish good and poor demonstrations. The first author of the paper used an open coding approach to analyze the list of features noted by the raters. The most commonly mentioned features were:

- Extent of change to the image in the clip
- How well the clip demonstrates the dynamics of the tool
- The pace of the clip, or how smoothly actions are performed
- Whether the clip shows tool settings being adjusted
- The presence of unrelated or distracting actions in the clip
- Qualities of the image being edited

In the next section we derive a more nuanced look at features impacting clip quality, based on the results of a think aloud protocol with users of image editing software.

USER VALIDATION

The results of our internal assessment indicate that:

1. *Good tool demonstration clips exist within in-situ workflow recordings.*
2. *The quality of naturally occurring tool demonstrations ranges widely.*

These findings represent the judgment of domain experts in the area of video-based help systems. However, a caveat to these results is that they are also the opinions of the authors of this paper, who are familiar with the goals of the project. Thus, we felt it necessary to obtain external validation for these findings from an unbiased group.

In this section, we report on a laboratory study we conducted with users of image editing software to validate the internal ratings, and to evaluate the quality of the clips as a help resource.

Method

We recruited 12 participants (5 male, 7 female), with a mean age of 27.5 (SD 7.2, min 20, max 46) via email and mailing list postings. Participants were screened to ensure they had some image editing experience by asking them to describe their experience using image editing software, and their familiarity with image editing concepts (e.g. selections, filters, and layers). Participants were given a $25 gift certificate for an online retailer for participating.

For each of the six tools from the previous section, we selected nine clips, three each with *Good*, *Neutral*, and *Poor* median ratings from the internal assessment. For the *Good* and *Poor* rating classes, we selected the top and bottom rated three clips respectively. The *Good* clips had an average score of 6.6 (SD 0.5) and the *Bad* clips had an average score of 1.4 (SD 1.0). For the *Neutral* clips, we selected the three clips with median ratings closest to 4 for each tool. These clips had an average score of 4.1 (SD 0.2).

For each of the six commands, the study included a *viewing stage*, in which participants viewed the nine clips for the command, followed by a *rating stage* where they viewed each clip again and rated their agreement to the statement *"This is a good video clip for demonstrating the [name] tool."* (1=Strongly Disagree, 7=Strongly Agree).

The order of each command block was counterbalanced across participants in a balanced Latin square design. Within each block, clip order was randomized but was consistent across the viewing and rating stage for each participant. We asked participants to "think aloud" about their rationale for rating each clip as they were rating. We intentionally did not specify to participants where the video clips came from, to avoid introducing a bias that might impact their ratings.

An experimenter was present to take notes, and the sessions were video recorded so they could be later reviewed. Occasionally, the experimenter would ask the participant for clarifications of their rationales, or remind the participant to state their rationale aloud while rating.

A qualitative coding scheme was developed using open coding to record the attributes of the video clips that were mentioned by participants. The experimenter additionally assigned each code an affect (positive or negative) depending on whether the participant cited an attribute as contributing positively or negatively to their rating of a clip.

Results – Ratings

The ratings assigned by participants, broken down by the category of each clip based on the expert ratings can be seen in Figure 5.

Participants assigned *Good* clips an average rating of 5.6 (SD 1.4), *Neutral* clips 4.9 (SD 1.7), and *Poor* clips 2.8 (SD 1.8). A one-way repeated measure ANOVA found a significant main effect of expert-rating category on average ratings ($F_{2,22}$=101.4, $p < .01$, η^2=0.72), and post-hoc analysis using paired t-tests with Bonferroni correction revealed significant differences between all pairs of expert-rating categories ($p < .01$ in all cases).

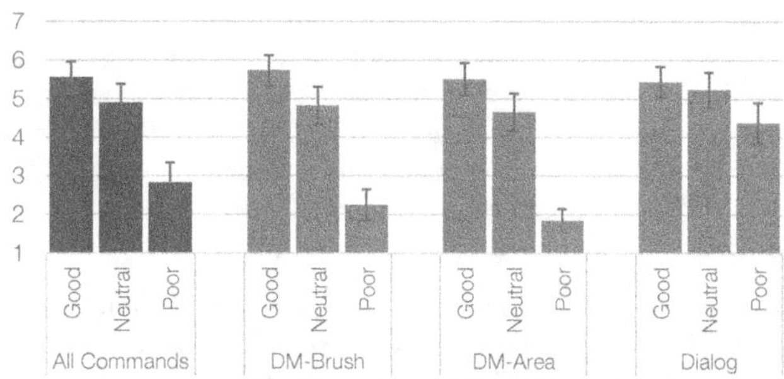

Figure 5. Average clip ratings for each of the expert-rating categories. Error bars show standard error.

These results provide evidence to validate that demonstrations of a wide range of different levels of quality occur in in-situ workflow recordings.

Examining the median ratings of clips by participants, we found that 3 clips (5.6% of those rated) were assigned a median rating of 7, and 15 clips (27.8%) were assigned a median rating of 6 or higher. This provides encouraging evidence that good quality clips do exist in in-situ workflow data, as these clips consistently received high ratings from a majority of the 12 study participants.

We also found evidence to suggest that tool type impacts the distribution of quality of demonstrations. As can be seen in Figure 5, the ratings for the *Poor* clips for Dialog tools is significantly higher than for the two DM- tool types (Welch's two-sample t-test, $t_{18.73} = 8.55$, $p < .01$, Cohen's d = 3.22). This is consistent with our observations from the internal assessment, and suggests that it may be easier to find good clips for dialog tools.

In summary, the quantitative results of our study validate our finding that tool demonstrations of a range of distinct levels of quality exist in in-situ workflows, including good demonstrations. In the next section we examine the attributes that participants used when evaluating demonstrations.

Results – Think Aloud Rationales

A summary of attributes cited by participants while thinking aloud is shown in Figure 6. The majority of attributes were mentioned with a particular affect (positive or negative), however some attributes were mentioned as both positives and negatives. These attributes are shown with both positive and negative bars in Figure 6.

In this section, we discuss some of the common themes that emerged from participants' stated rationales, with an eye toward how these features could be automatically detected.

Figure 6. Participants' rationales for their clip ratings. Blue bars on the right indicate attributes cited as positive. Red bars on the left indicate attributes cited as negative.

Change in the Image

The most often cited positive rationale was that the clip showed a clear change in the image. Likewise, the most often cited negative rationale was when the clip showed no change in the document, or only a subtle change. It is clear why this is an important feature: if no changes are visible, a user couldn't be expected to understand how the tool works.

We examined clips cited with these attributes to better understand the cause of this rating, and found a number of reasons why clips drawn from in-situ workflows might not show a large change in a document. First, users sometime make mistakes, such as performing an operation with the wrong layer selected, so a change made to the document is not visible. Second, users often make several experimental applications of a tool before settling on a final result, and some of these experimental applications have less than the intended effect. Third, this may be intentional; it's not always desirable to make a bold change to an image.

Fortunately, changes in an image are easy to detect algorithmically. We explicitly logged snapshots of users' documents before and after each operation, but it's conceivable that this data could be extracted from screen recording videos as well.

Unclear Intention

The second most common negative attribute was that the clip appeared to be incomplete, or the participant was not sure what the clip was trying to communicate.

We observed two frequent causes for this confusion. The first was when there was only a subtle or undetectable change shown in the clip, as discussed above. Second, some clips included actions unrelated to the tool being demonstrated, during the padding time at the start or end of the clip. For example, in one clip an author applies the Gradient tool to an image. After the tool is applied, but before the clip ends, the author is shown to adjust the Gradient tool's opacity setting and undo the Gradient they just created, presumably preparing to apply the Gradient tool again.

For users who are new to a tool, these extraneous actions can lead to an incorrect mental model of how a tool works. One participant misinterpreted the Gradient clip discussed above as demonstrating that a gradient can be adjusted after it's been applied, which is not true in Pixlr:

So this one, I think goes to show that you can also alter the opacity after you've applied the gradient. So, yeah, a good kind of indication of what you can do, that it's more versatile than just applying [the] gradient and then you're finished with it. (P10)

These observations suggest that we should refine our clip selection algorithm to crop out additional actions from the start and end of the clips. Another option would be to give the viewer the ability to access additional video around a clip on demand (e.g. a "Play next 30 seconds" button.)

Settings Adjustments

Participants frequently mentioned that showing adjustment of a tool's settings was positive, and conversely cited not showing setting adjustments as a negative.

This provides some validation of our clip selection heuristic for direct manipulation tools, which was designed to include the time between a tool's selection and its invocation, which is often spent adjusting the tool settings (e.g. selecting a brush to use.)

For Dialog commands, participants particularly cared about whether the *majority* of available settings were adjusted in a tool demonstration. For example, the Hue Saturation command in Pixlr includes three parameters (Hue, Saturation, and Lightness), and a Colorize option. Participants frequently cited showing the effect of multiple or all of these settings as a positive attribute.

Usage Scenarios

In some clips, the user had set up layers or selections before applying a command, but due to our segmentation heuristic, the setup operations were not shown in the clip. Some participants immediately recognized what was going on in these clips, and commented that they were useful to demonstrate the tool in a particular scenario. Other participants did not realize that setup operations had occurred, or cited these clips as problematic because novice users might not understand how to recreate the context shown in the clip.

This suggests that it may be beneficial to choose a variety of clips showing a tool used in different contexts. Some participants explicitly expressed a desire for variety:

I'd like to see an example where you have an extremely bright image, and you do the opposite, you darken the image. Because I think most of [the clips], they're darker and you lighten them. I'd like to see the opposite. (P3)

From a design perspective, this motivates the idea of providing a range of short demonstrations showing tools used in different contexts, or geared toward users with particular knowledge or expertise.

Difficult to Detect Features

While the features mentioned up to this point can be detected from video or log data, participants also mentioned a number of features of clips that are difficult to detect, or which have a subjective component to them.

Some participants expressed a preference for clips that showed a basic use of a tool, as in the following comment for a Levels clip that showed the tool on a document consisting of one solid color:

This one I really liked. I put [it] as my favorite [rates as 7/7], because it's very simple. It shows how [the tool] was selected, and shows exactly what's going on when you change each of the settings. (P11)

Other participants commented that this clip was too simple. On other clips, participants expressed a preference for demonstrations on realistic images, as in this comment:

I like this video because it shows how you actually use this. [...] It's something that people would actually use [the Clone Stamp tool for] in real life. (P12)

The aesthetic quality of the result in a demonstration was also mentioned by participants. For example, one clip clearly shows how the Clone tool operates, but several participants mentioned that the end result didn't look good:

It does kind of screw up the picture as it went on with the Clone brush... Which does happen when you use Clone brush a little too much. (P2)

Subjective or aesthetic features pose a challenge because different users will react to them in different ways, and they are difficult to detect algorithmically. However, these features were in the minority of those mentioned by participants. As well, it is possible that demonstrations of tools with imperfect results can still effectively communicate the dynamics of how a tool works. For example, P2 assigned the Clone tool clip discussed above a 6/7, suggesting that, for him, the imperfect end result did not significantly detract from the demonstration's value.

AUTOMATICALLY IDENTIFYING GOOD CLIPS

In the previous section we discussed some of the most commonly cited positive and negative features of clips. Next, we conduct an experiment to see if low-level features can be used to automatically distinguish good clips.

We processed the meta-data associated with 274 clips rated in our initial evaluation to add a set of automatically extractable features (Table 2). Many of these features were suggested by our qualitative findings, including features that quantify changes in the image, changes in settings, the pace and duration of the clip, and the presence of extraneous command invocations in the clip.

Image Features	% of Pixels Changed, Start Entropy, End Entropy, Entropy Change, Pixels in Viewport, Median Zoom Level, % of Image Selected, Entropy of Selection Mask.
Mouse Features	Idle Time, Mean Velocity, Mean Acceleration, Mouse-Down time, # of Clicks, Mouse Bound Area
Behavior Features	Command ID, Timestamp, Total Clip Duration, % Pre-Command Time, % Command Time, # of Command Invocations, # of Other Commands, # of Settings Changed

Table 2. Features used to train the SVM.

We assigned all clips with a median rating of 5 or higher from the initial evaluation a label as *Good*, and the remaining clips as *Poor*. We then trained a Support Vector Machine (SVM) classifier [7] to distinguish between *Good* and *Poor* clips. SVMs are a widely used supervised learning method for classification, supported by many machine learning libraries (we used the scikit-learn Python library).

The *Cost* and *Gamma* parameters of the SVM classifier were tuned using grid search, with the $F_{0.5}$ score as an objective function. This objective function was chosen to bias the classifier toward higher precision (fewer false positives) at the cost of lower recall (more false negatives), with the rationale that it is better to reject some good clips than to classify poor clips as good.

True +	37	*Accuracy*	77.4%
True −	175	*Precision*	0.71
False +	15	*Recall*	0.44
False −	47	*F_1 Score*	0.54

Table 3. Results of SVM classification of tool clips.

We evaluated our classifier using 10-fold cross validation. The results are shown in Table 3. The overall accuracy of our approach was 77.4%, with a precision of 0.71. As expected from our decision to bias toward higher precision, the recall (0.44) and F_1 score (0.54) were lower. In interpreting the results we note that only 31% of the original clips were *Good*, so a randomly selected sample of clips would have an expected precision of 0.31.

The average score for clips classified as *Good* (4.67, SD 1.7) was significantly higher than the average score for clips classified as *Poor* (2.98, SD 1.6) (Welch's t-test, $t_{74.91}$ = 6.68, p < .01, Cohen's *d*=1.05). This indicates that the classifier was generally successful in separating good and bad clips.

These results provide promising evidence that lower-level features of clips extracted from in-situ workflow data can be used to identify good demonstrations. However, the low recall and F_1 score indicate room for improvement.

It may be that additional training data, or more sophisticated machine learning techniques, could allow us to improve on these results. However, there is likely an upper limit on the accuracy that can be achieved by automatic methods; recall that we found only moderate agreement in our internal ratings, and subjective features played a role in evaluations of clip quality. Even so, the accuracies reported above make this approach suitable as a "first-pass" method of indicating potentially good clips in a large set produced by a selection heuristic. These could then be refined using other techniques, such as collaborative filtering, as we discuss in the next section.

DESIGN IMPLICATIONS

In this section, we discuss two main implications of our findings. First, we propose design guidelines for demonstration videos. Second, we present a design sketch of an interface for delivering automatically extracted video clips.

Design Guidelines for Demonstration videos

The input we elicited from study participants and domain experts provide us with a clear picture of the attributes of a good tool-based demonstration video. Despite the recent popularity of video-based assistance, we are unaware of any such existing set of attributes. Our insights can be distilled into the following five guidelines:

1. Be short and concise, 15–25 sec.
2. Show the tool making a clear change to the document.
3. Demonstrate how the various parameters or settings of the tool affect the dynamics of how the tool works.
4. Demonstrate an example that is representative of how the tool would typically be used.
5. Avoid including extraneous actions not directly related to the tool being demonstrated.

This set of guidelines for individual clips contains some tensions. For example, the Brush tool includes eight settings dictating the dimensions of the brush and the dynamics of how the brush affects the document; an example showing all of these would not be concise. As such, we can include a set of additional guidelines relating to multiple examples:

1. Provide multiple clips to demonstrate the range of settings for a given tool.
2. Provide clips tailored to a range of users with different backgrounds and knowledge of the system.

In the next section, we provide a mockup of what the interface for such a system might look like.

Delivery Interface

The results of our machine learning experiment suggest that the low-level features of demonstration clips could be used to filter out obviously poor clips. This smaller set of clips could be presented to the community of users with a voting mechanism for flagging good or poor clips (e.g. Figure 7). This would allow the community to refine the set of clips over time, and at the same time provide additional training data for machine learning algorithms.

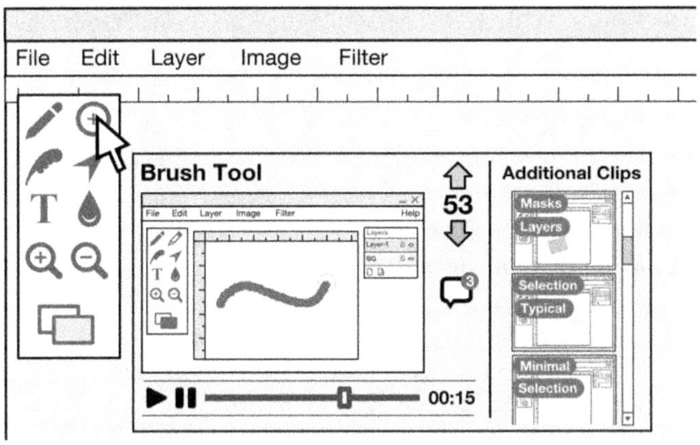

Figure 7. Design sketch showing how tool clips could be collaboratively filtered, and how multiple tool clips could be presented to users.

This approach would also allow the system to tailor the clips it presents to individual users, using techniques similar to those explored for command recommender systems [25]. The voting behavior of users could be combined with metrics on how long the voter has used the software, or the set of tools they use most frequently, to create models of which clips are good or bad for individual users. For example, if a user that has never used a tool before votes a clip up, this may indicate the clip is good for novice users of the tool.

This connects with another theme that emerged from our user evaluation, that it may be useful to make multiple clips available for each tool. These could show a tool used in different contexts, or for users with varying levels of expertise. Figure 7 demonstrates this idea as well, with an area where users can view additional clips for a given tool. Clips could be tagged with badges indicating fundamental skills (e.g. knowledge of Selections, Layers, or Masks) associated with each clip. This would help the user to select clips that fit their personal skill level and knowledge of these fundamental concepts. Similarly, clips could be tagged with the setting parameters that are adjusted in the clip, or grouped to show a complementary set of settings or adjustments that together give a full idea of how the tool operates.

DISCUSSION AND FUTURE WORK

Our initial assessment and validation study have shown that in-situ workflows include tool demonstrations of a range of levels of quality, including demonstrations that are suitable for use as help resources. Our investigation also revealed attributes that impact the quality of demonstrations, and proposed a set of corresponding guidelines for demonstration videos. Finally, we experimented with using machine learning to distinguish good demonstrations. In doing so, we've shown that low-level features extracted from log data can be used to identify potentially good clips from in-situ workflows. These results are encouraging, and we can envision several avenues for extending this work.

First, we could investigate the problem of identifying good demonstrations of higher-level tasks, which may involve use of multiple tools. This is a more challenging problem than automatically identifying tool demonstrations because it requires a model of the tools and procedures involved in higher-level tasks. However, recent work provides some potential sources for this information. Fourney et al. have presented a technique for identifying command-task relationships using web search query logs [11], and work on "learnersourcing" suggests the potential of crowdsourced tagging of activities in video clips [19]. Finally, our own work on Community Enhanced Tutorials has investigated a modified web tutorial design that could gather in-situ workflow recordings of individual tutorial steps [22].

Second, we could consider other sources of video content. In this work, we examined workflow data from in-situ use. It would be interesting to contrast our results with video data gathered from existing libraries of online video tutorials (e.g. on YouTube). These videos provide longer and more extensive instruction than the short demonstrations of tools that we seek to provide. However, it is possible that these videos include a higher occurrence of good quality demonstrations than in-situ workflow recordings, because they are created with the intent to communicate with an audience. They also typically include audio narration, which adds another dimension to the problem of clip segmentation. Some of the issues with segmenting clips with audio have been identified in past work on multimedia tutorials [6], but this a largely unexplored area.

Finally, the approach that we have presented could be generalized or repeated. A first step toward generalizing our results is to consider other feature-rich applications that include concepts such as modal tools (e.g. MS Office). The main challenge to extend our approach to a new application or domain is in identifying the features that indicate where to cut clips, and that impact the quality of demonstrations. It would be interesting to see if similar features to those we identified for image editing apply in other domains as well.

Extending our approach to drastically different domains, such as video lectures for online courses, is another possibility. For example, it would be interesting to investigate whether demonstrations of mathematical operations (e.g. matrix diagonalization) could be automatically identified.

Regarding the repeatability of this work, while we instrumented our test application directly, the log data we gather is standard (e.g. command timings, mouse movement), and could potentially be gathered using publicly-available accessibility APIs.

In conclusion, we feel that the automatic extraction of help resources from in-situ usage data has great potential, and the work presented here opens important opportunities for future efforts in this area.

REFERENCES

1. Ames, A.L. Just what they need, just when they need it: an introduction to embedded assistance. *ACM SIGDOC '01*, (2001), 111–115.
2. Baecker, R. Showing instead of telling. *ACM SIGDOC '02*, (2002), 10–16.
3. Banovic, N., Grossman, T., Matejka, J., and Fitzmaurice, G. Waken: reverse engineering usage information and interface structure from software videos. *ACM UIST '12*, (2012), 83–92.
4. Carroll, J.M. and Rosson, M.B. Paradox of the active user. In *Interfacing Thought: Cognitive Aspects of Human-Computer Interaction*. MIT Press, 1987, 80–111.
5. Carroll, J.M. *The Nurnberg funnel: designing minimalist instruction for practical computer skill*. MIT Press, 1990.
6. Chi, P.-Y., Ahn, S., Ren, A., Dontcheva, M., Li, W., and Hartmann, B. MixT: Automatic generation of step-by-step mixed media tutorials. *ACM UIST '12*, (2012), 93–102.
7. Cortes, C. and Vapnik, V. Support-vector networks. *Machine Learning 20*, 3 (1995), 273–297.
8. Denning, J.D., Kerr, W.B., and Pellacini, F. MeshFlow: Interactive visualization of mesh construction sequences. *ACM Trans. Graph. 30*, 4 (2011), 66:1–66:8.
9. Evans, A. and Wobbrock, J. Taming wild behavior: the input observer for obtaining text entry and mouse pointing measures from everyday computer use. *ACM CHI '12*, (2012), 1947–1956.
10. Farkas, D.K. The role of balloon help. *ACM SIGDOC Asterisk J. Comput. Doc. 17*, 2 (1993), 3–19.
11. Fourney, A., Mann, R., and Terry, M. Query-feature graphs: bridging user vocabulary and system functionality. *ACM UIST '11*, (2011), 207–216.
12. Gajos, K., Reinecke, K., and Herrmann, C. Accurate measurements of pointing performance from in situ observations. *ACM CHI '12*, (2012), 3157–3166.
13. Grabler, F., Agrawala, M., Li, W., Dontcheva, M., and Igarashi, T. Generating photo manipulation tutorials by demonstration. *ACM Trans. Graph. 28*, 3 (2009), 66:1–66:9.
14. Grossman, T., Fitzmaurice, G., and Attar, R. A survey of software learnability: metrics, methodologies and guidelines. *ACM CHI '09*, (2009), 649–658.
15. Grossman, T. and Fitzmaurice, G. ToolClips: An investigation of contextual video assistance for functionality understanding. *ACM CHI '10*, (2010), 1515–1524.
16. Grossman, T., Matejka, J., and Fitzmaurice, G. Chronicle: Capture, exploration, and playback of document workflow histories. *ACM UIST '10*, 143–152.
17. Harrison, S.M. A comparison of still, animated, or nonillustrated on-line help with written or spoken instructions in a graphical user interface. *ACM CHI '95*, (1995), 82–89.
18. Kelleher, C. and Pausch, R. Stencils-based tutorials: Design and evaluation. *ACM CHI '05*, (2005), 541–550.
19. Kim, J., Miller, R.C., and Gajos, K.Z. Learnersourcing subgoal labeling to support learning from how-to videos. *ACM CHI EA '13*, (2013), 685–690.
20. Knabe, K. Apple guide: a case study in user-aided design of online help. *ACM CHI '95*, (1995), 286–287.
21. Lafreniere, B., Bunt, A., Whissell, J., Clarke, C.L.A., and Terry, M. Characterizing large-scale use of a direct manipulation application in the wild. *GI '10*, (2010), 11–18.
22. Lafreniere, B., Grossman, T., and Fitzmaurice, G. Community enhanced tutorials: Improving tutorials with multiple demonstrations. *ACM CHI '13*, (2013), 1779–1788.
23. Lazar, J., Jones, A., and Shneiderman, B. Workplace user frustration with computers: an exploratory investigation of the causes and severity. *Behaviour and Information Technology 25*, 3 (2006), 239–251.
24. Matejka, J., Grossman, T., and Fitzmaurice, G. Ambient help. *ACM CHI '11*, (2011), 2751–2760.
25. Matejka, J., Li, W., Grossman, T., and Fitzmaurice, G. CommunityCommands: Command recommendations for software applications. *ACM UIST '09*, 193–202.
26. McGrenere, J. and Moore, G. Are we all in the same "bloat"? *GI '00*, (2000), 187–196.
27. Obendorf, H., Weinreich, H., Herder, E., and Mayer, M. Web page revisitation revisited: implications of a long-term click-stream study of browser usage. *ACM CHI '07*, (2007), 597–606.
28. Palmiter, S., Elkerton, J., and Baggett, P. Animated demonstrations vs written instructions for learning procedural tasks: a preliminary investigation. *Int. J. Man-Mach. Stud. 34*, 5 (1991), 687–701.
29. Palmiter, S. and Elkerton, J. Animated Demonstrations for Learning Procedural Computer-Based Tasks. *Human–Computer Interaction 8*, 3 (1993), 193–216.
30. Pongnumkul, S., Dontcheva, M., Li, W., et al. Pause-and-play: automatically linking screencast video tutorials with applications. *ACM UIST '11*, (2011), 135–144.
31. Sellen, A. and Nicol, A. Building user-centered on-line help. In R.M. Baecker, J. Grudin, W.A.S. Buxton and S. Greenberg, eds., *Human-Computer Interaction*. Morgan Kaufmann Publishers Inc., 1995, 718–723.
32. Adobe Labs Tutorial Builder. 2012. http://labs.adobe.com/technologies/tutorialbuilder/.

Crowdsourcing Step-by-Step Information Extraction to Enhance Existing How-to Videos

Juho Kim[1] **Phu Nguyen**[1] **Sarah Weir**[1] **Philip J. Guo**[2] **Robert C. Miller**[1] **Krzysztof Z. Gajos**[3]

[1]MIT CSAIL
Cambridge, MA USA
{juhokim, phun, sweir, rcm}@mit.edu

[2]University of Rochester
Rochester, NY USA
pg@cs.rochester.edu

[3]Harvard SEAS
Cambridge, MA USA
kgajos@eecs.harvard.edu

ABSTRACT
Millions of learners today use how-to videos to master new skills in a variety of domains. But browsing such videos is often tedious and inefficient because video player interfaces are not optimized for the unique step-by-step structure of such videos. This research aims to improve the learning experience of existing how-to videos with *step-by-step annotations*.

We first performed a formative study to verify that annotations are actually useful to learners. We created ToolScape, an interactive video player that displays step descriptions and intermediate result thumbnails in the video timeline. Learners in our study performed better and gained more self-efficacy using ToolScape versus a traditional video player.

To add the needed step annotations to existing how-to videos at scale, we introduce a novel crowdsourcing workflow. It extracts step-by-step structure from an existing video, including step times, descriptions, and before and after images. We introduce the Find-Verify-Expand design pattern for temporal and visual annotation, which applies clustering, text processing, and visual analysis algorithms to merge crowd output. The workflow does not rely on domain-specific customization, works on top of existing videos, and recruits untrained crowd workers. We evaluated the workflow with Mechanical Turk, using 75 cooking, makeup, and Photoshop videos on YouTube. Results show that our workflow can extract steps with a quality comparable to that of trained annotators across all three domains with 77% precision and 81% recall.

Author Keywords
Crowdsourcing; how-to videos; video annotation.

ACM Classification Keywords
H.5.2 User Interfaces: Graphical User Interfaces

INTRODUCTION
How-to videos on the web have enabled millions of learners to acquire new skills in procedural tasks such as folding origami, cooking, applying makeup, and using computer software. These videos have a unique step-by-step structure, which encourages learners to sequentially process and perform steps in the procedure [29]. While most text- and image-based tutorials (e.g., webpages) are naturally segmented into distinct steps, how-to video tutorials often contain a single continuous stream of demonstration. Because comprehensive and accurate step-by-step information about the procedure is often missing, accessing specific parts within a video becomes frustrating for learners. Prior research shows that higher interactivity with the instructional content aids learning [13, 28], and that the completeness and detail of step-by-step instructions are integral to task performance [11].

To better understand the role of step-by-step information in how-to videos, we ran a formative study where learners performed graphical design tasks with how-to videos. For this study, we designed ToolScape, an interactive how-to video player that adds step descriptions and intermediate result thumbnails to the video timeline. Learners using ToolScape showed a higher gain in self-efficacy and rated the quality of their own work higher, as compared to those using an ordinary video player. Moreover, external judges gave higher ratings to the designs produced by learners using ToolScape.

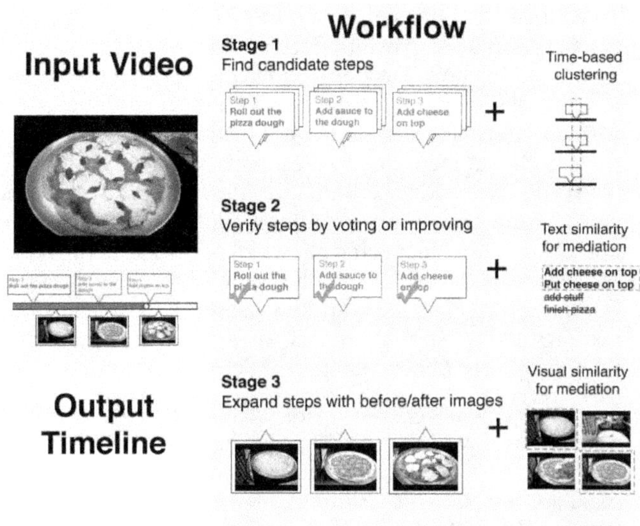

Figure 1. Our crowdsourcing workflow extracts step-by-step information from a how-to video with their descriptions and before/after images. It features the Find-Verify-Expand design pattern, time-based clustering, and text/visual analysis techniques. Extracted step information can be used to help learners navigate how-to videos with higher interactivity.

ACM 978-1-4503-2473-1/14/04..$15.00.
http://dx.doi.org/10.1145/2556288.2556986

Providing such navigation support for how-to videos requires extracting step-by-step information from them. One solution is to ask instructors to include this information at tutorial generation time, but this adds overhead for instructors and does not solve the problem for existing videos. Another approach uses automatic methods such as computer vision. Previous research [3, 26] has shown success in limited domains with extensive domain-specific customization. When working with "videos in the wild", however, vision-based algorithms often suffer from low-resolution frames and a lack of training data. A scalable solution applicable beyond limited task domains and presentation formats is not yet available.

To address the issues of high cost or limited scalability with existing methods, we introduce a crowdsourcing workflow for annotating how-to videos, which includes the Find-Verify-Expand design pattern shown in Figure 1. It collects step-by-step information from a how-to video in three stages: (1) find candidate steps with timestamps and text descriptions, (2) verify time and description for all steps, and (3) expand a verified step with before and after images. The workflow does not rely on domain-specific knowledge, works on top of existing videos, and recruits untrained, non-expert crowd workers. For quality control, the workflow uses time-based clustering, text processing, and visual analysis to merge results and deal with noisy and diverse output from crowd workers.

To validate the workflow with existing how-to videos, we asked crowd workers on Mechanical Turk to annotate 75 YouTube how-to videos spanning three domains: cooking, makeup, and graphics editing software. Results show that the crowd workflow can extract steps with 77% precision and 81% recall relative to trained annotators. Successfully extracted steps were on average 2.7 seconds away from ground truth steps, and external evaluators found 60% of before and after images to be accurately representing steps.

The contributions of this paper are as follows:

- A how-to video player interface and experimental results showing that increased interactivity in a video player improves learners' task performance and self-efficacy.
- A domain-independent crowd video annotation method and the Find-Verify-Expand design pattern for extracting step-by-step task information from existing how-to videos.
- A novel combination of time-based clustering, text processing, and visual analysis algorithms for merging crowd output consisting of time points, text labels, and images.
- Experimental results that validate the workflow, which fully extracted steps from 75 readily available videos on the web across three distinct domains with a quality comparable to that of trained annotators.

RELATED WORK

We review related work in crowdsourcing workflows, video annotation, and tutorials.

Crowdsourcing Workflows

Research on multi-stage crowd workflows inspired the design of our method. Soylent [5] has shown that splitting tasks into the Find-Fix-Verify stages improves the quality and accuracy of crowd workers' results. Other multi-stage crowdsourcing workflows were designed for nutrition information retrieval from food photos [24], activity recognition from streaming videos [21], and search engine answer generation [6]. These applications demonstrated that crowdsourcing can yield results comparable to those of experts at lower cost. Our work contributes to this line of research a novel domain, video annotation, by extending [18] and [23].

Video Annotation Methods

This work focuses on providing a scalable and generalizable video annotation solution without relying on trained annotators, experts, or video authors. Video annotation tools capture moments of interest and add labels to them. Many existing tools are designed for dedicated annotators or experts in limited context. Domain-specific plug-ins [8, 14, 15] automatically capture task information, but require direct access to internal application context (e.g., Photoshop plug-ins accessing operation history). But plug-ins do not exist for most procedural tasks outside of software applications (e.g., makeup), which limits the applicability of this method.

Crowdsourcing video annotation has recently gained interest as a cost-effective method without relying on experts while keeping humans in the loop. Existing systems were designed mostly to collect training data for object recognition [31], motion tracking [30], or behavior detection [25]. Rather than use crowdsourcing to support qualitative researchers, this work supports end users learning from videos. Adrenaline [4] uses crowdsourcing to find the best frame from a video in near real-time. While [4] and our work both aim to detect a time-specific event from a video stream, our work additionally labels the event and expands to capture surrounding context.

Interactive Tutorials

In designing user interfaces for instructional videos, higher interactivity with the content has been shown to aid learning [13, 28]. Tversky et al. [28] state that "stopping, starting and replaying an animation can allow reinspection", which in turn can mitigate challenges in perception and comprehension, and further facilitate learning. Semantic indices and random access have been shown to be valuable in video navigation [32, 22], and the lack of interactivity has been deemed a major problem with instructional videos [16]. This work introduces a user interface for giving learners more interactivity in video navigation, and a crowdsourcing method for acquiring metadata handles to create such an interface at scale.

Recent systems create interactive tutorials by either automatically generating them by demonstration [8, 14], connecting to examples [26], or enhancing the tutorial format with annotated information [8, 9, 18, 20]. Our crowdsourcing workflow can provide annotations required to create these interfaces and further enable new ways to learn from tutorials.

EFFICACY AND CHALLENGES OF VIDEO ANNOTATIONS

To motivate the design of our crowdsourcing workflow for how-to video annotations, we first performed a formative study to (1) verify that annotations are actually useful to

Figure 2. Progress in many how-to videos is visually trackable, as shown in screenshots from this Photoshop how-to video. Adding step annotations to videos enables learners to quickly scan through the procedure.

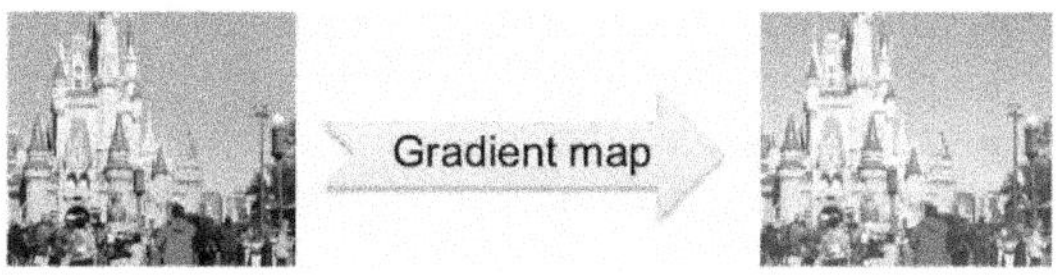

Figure 3. How-to videos often contain a series of task steps with visually distinct before and after states. Here the author applied the "Gradient map" tool in Photoshop to desaturate the image colors.

learners, and (2) reveal the challenges of manually annotating videos and show the need for a more scalable technique.

Annotations on How-To Videos

How-to videos often have a well-defined step-by-step structure [15]. A *step* refers to a low-level action in performing a procedural task. Literature on procedural tasks suggests that step-by-step instructions encourage learners to sequentially process and perform steps in the workflow [29] and improve task performance [11]. Annotations can make such structure more explicit. In this paper, we define *annotation* as the process of adding step-by-step information to a how-to video. In determining which information to annotate, we note two properties of procedural tasks. First, for many domains, task states are visually distinct in nature, so progress can be visually tracked by browsing through a video (Figure 2). Examples include food in cooking videos, a model's face in makeup videos, and an image being edited in Photoshop videos. Second, how-to videos contain a sequence of discrete steps that each advance the state of the task (Figure 3). Our annotation method uses these two properties to accurately capture a sequence of steps, extracting timestamps, textual descriptions, and before and after images for each step.

We manually created a corpus of annotations for 75 how-to videos in three procedural task domains: cooking, applying makeup, and using Photoshop. We used this corpus to create our interface in the formative study, and ground truth data for evaluating our crowdsourcing workflow. We collected videos from YouTube's top search results for "[domain] [task name]" (e.g., "cooking samosa", "Photoshop motion blur").

Annotation-Aware Video Player: ToolScape

To display step annotations, we created a prototype video player named ToolScape. ToolScape augments an ordinary web-based video player with a rich timeline containing links to each annotated step and its respective before and after thumbnail images (Figure 4). ToolScape is a Javascript library that manages a timestamped list of steps and before/after images, which can connect to any embedded video player with a "play from this time point" Javascript API call.

In the timeline, the top and bottom streams represent annotated steps and thumbnail images from the video, respectively (Figure 4(a), (c)). Clicking on a step or image moves the

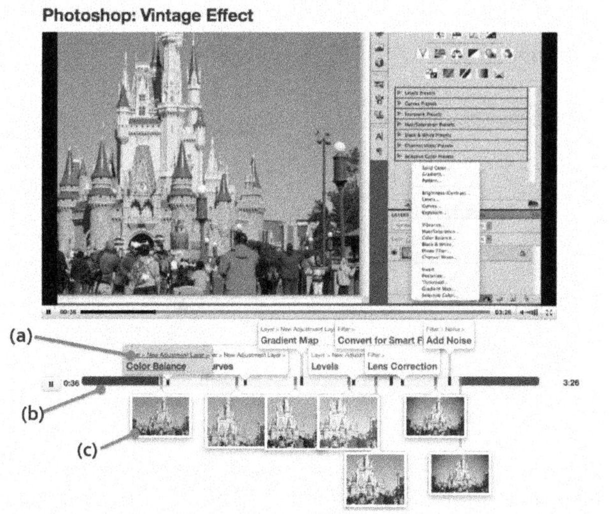

Figure 4. ToolScape augments a web-based video player with an interactive timeline. Annotations are shown above the timeline (a), screenshots of intermediate states are shown below the timeline (c), and the gray regions at both ends (b) show "dead times" with no meaningful progress (e.g., waiting for Photoshop to launch).

video player's slider to 5 seconds before the moment it occurred. The 5-second buffer, determined from pilot testing, helps learners catch up with the context preceding the indicated moment. Finally, ToolScape supports annotations of "dead times" at the beginning and end of videos (Figure 4(b)), which often contain introductory or concluding remarks. Pilot user observations showed that learners often skip to the main part of the tutorial. In our manually annotated video corpus, on average, 13.7% of time at the beginning and 9.9% at the end were "dead times" with no task progress.

Formative Study Design

To assess the effects of step annotations, we ran a formative study on novice Photoshop learners watching how-to videos on image manipulation tasks. We compared the experiences of learners using ToolScape and a baseline video player without the interactive timeline. We hypothesized that interacting with step annotations provided by ToolScape improves both task performance and learner satisfaction. Specifically:

H1 Learners complete design tasks with a higher self-efficacy gain when watching how-to videos with ToolScape.

H2 Learners' self-rating of the quality of their work is higher when watching with ToolScape.

H3 Learners' designs when watching with ToolScape are rated higher by external judges.

H4 Learners show higher satisfaction with ToolScape.

H5 Learners perceive design tasks to be easier when watching with ToolScape.

In addition to external ratings (H3), our measures of success include self-efficacy (H1) and self-rating (H2). In the context of how-to videos, these measures are more significant than

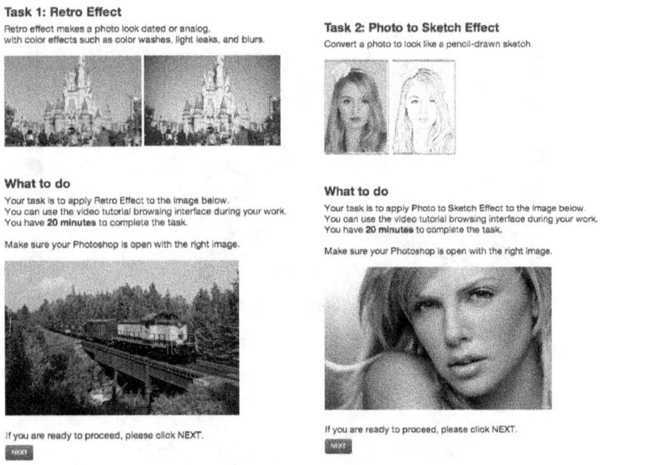

Figure 5. These task instructions are shown before the participant starts working on their image manipulation task. It includes a description of the effect to be implemented and a before-and-after example image pair.

just user preference. Educational psychology research shows that self-efficacy, or confidence in application of skills, is an effective predictor of motivation and learning [2, 33]. Positive self-rating has also been shown to accurately predict learning gains [27]. Finally, we chose not to count errors made in repeating tutorial steps as in [8], because our goal was to help users explore and learn new skills in open-ended design tasks.

Participants: We recruited twelve participants through university mailing lists and online community postings. Their mean age was 25.2 ($\sigma = 3.2$), with 8 males and 4 females. Most rated themselves as novice Photoshop users, but all had at least some experience with Photoshop. They received \$30 for up to two hours of participation, on either a Mac or PC.

Tasks and Procedures: Our study had 2 x 2 conditions: two tasks each using ToolScape and baseline video players. We used a within-subject design with interface, task, and order counterbalanced. Each participant performed two image manipulation tasks in Photoshop: applying retro effect and transforming a photo to look like a sketch. In both interface conditions, we provided participants with the same set of how-to videos; the interface was the only difference. In addition, we disallowed searching for other web tutorials to ensure that any effect found in the study comes from the interaction method, not the content.

After a tutorial task covering all features of the video player interface, we asked participants self-efficacy questions adapted from Dow et al. [10], whose study also measured participants' self-efficacy changes in a design task. The questions asked: On a scale of 1 (not confident at all) to 7 (very confident), how confident are you with...

- solving graphic design problems?
- understanding graphic design problems?
- applying design skills in practice?
- incorporating skills from video tutorials in your design?

Next, participants attempted two 20-minute image manipulation tasks in Photoshop, with instructions shown in Figure 5. Participants could freely browse and watch the 10 how-to videos we provided (with annotations in the ToolScape condition). After each task, we asked questions on task difficulty, self-rating, and interface satisfaction. We also asked the self-efficacy questions again to observe any difference, followed by a 15-minute open-ended interview.

Finally, we asked four external judges to evaluate the quality of all transformed images by ranking them, blind to user and condition. They ranked the images from best to worst, based on how well each participant accomplished the given task.

Formative Study Results

H1 (higher self-efficacy for ToolScape) is supported by our study. For the four self-efficacy questions, we take the mean of the 7-point Likert scale ratings as the self-efficacy score. The participants' mean initial score was 3.8; with the baseline video player, the score after the task was 3.9 (+0.1) whereas with ToolScape the score was 5.2 (+1.4), which meant that learners felt more confident in their graphical design skills after completing tasks with ToolScape. (For H1, H2, and H4, differences between interfaces were significant at $p<0.05$ using a Mann-Whitney U test.)

H2 (higher self-rating for ToolScape) is supported. Participants rated their own work quality higher when using ToolScape (mean rating of 5.3) versus baseline (mean of 3.5).

H3 (higher external judge rating for ToolScape) is supported. The overall ranking was computed by taking the mean of the four judges' ranks. The mean rankings (lower is better) for output images in the ToolScape and Baseline conditions were 5.7 and 7.3, respectively. A Wilcoxon Signed-rank test indicates a significant effect of interface ($W=317$, $Z=-2.79$, $p<0.01$, $r=0.29$). Furthermore, nine of the twelve participants produced higher-rated images with ToolScape. The ranking method yielded high inter-rater reliability (Krippendorff's alpha=0.753) for ordinal data.

H4 (higher satisfaction with ToolScape) is supported. Mean ratings for ToolScape and Baseline were 6.1 and 4.5, respectively.

H5 (easier task difficulty perception for ToolScape) is not supported: The mean ratings for ToolScape and Baseline were 4.0 and 3.7, respectively. Combined with H2 and H3, this might indicate that participants did not find the tasks easier yet still produced better designs with greater confidence.

In conclusion, ToolScape had a significant effect on learners' belief in their graphical design skills and output quality. They also produced better designs as rated by external judges. Note that participants were watching the same video content in both conditions. Thus, the video annotation browsing interface affected design outcomes. Participants especially enjoyed being able to freely navigate between steps within a video by clicking on annotations.

Lessons for Video Browsing Interfaces

The features of ToolScape that provided higher interactivity and non-sequential access were highly rated and frequently used. In participants' responses to the 7-point Likert scale questions on the usability of interface features, the time-marked image thumbnails (6.4) and step links (6.3) were among the highest rated, as well as the graying out of "dead times" with no workflow progress (6.5). Participants noted, "It was also easier to go back to parts I missed.", "I know what to expect to get to the final result.", and "It is great for skipping straight to relevant portions of the tutorial."

All participants frequently used the ability to click on time-line links to navigate directly to specific images and steps. They clicked the interactive timeline links 8.9 times on average (σ = 6.7) in a single task. We also analyzed the tracking log, which records an event when the user clicks on an interactive link or a pause button, or drags the play-head to another position. The learners watched videos less linearly with ToolScape: The ToolScape condition recorded 150 such events, versus only 96 in the Baseline condition. In ToolScape, 107 out of 150 events were interactive link clicks and 43 were pause button clicks or direct scrubbing on the player. These findings indicate that interactive links largely replaced the need for pause or scrubbing, and encouraged the stepwise navigation of the procedure.

Lessons for How-To Video Annotation

The study results suggest that annotated step information makes how-to videos much more effective for learners. However, the bottleneck is in obtaining the annotations. Here are some lessons from our experience annotating videos by hand:

- Extracting step information from how-to videos involves detecting timing, generating a natural language description of a step, and capturing before and after states.
- It often requires multi-pass watching, which adds to task complexity. Before knowing what each step is, the annotator cannot extract before and after thumbnail images. This experience supports a design choice to split the work into multiple stages so that in each stage, the annotator's attention is focused on a single, simple task.
- Hand annotation is time-consuming. Roughly three times the original video length was required by trained annotators to annotate each how-to video.
- Timing detection is difficult. Sometimes there is an interval between when a step is spoken and demonstrated. Also, if the goal is to find a starting time of a step, the annotator has to watch, verify, and scroll back to mark as a valid step.

These lessons informed the design of our crowdsourced how-to video annotation method, which we now present.

CROWDSOURCING WORKFLOW: FIND-VERIFY-EXPAND

Using lessons from our formative study, we designed a three-stage crowdsourcing workflow for annotating how-to videos with procedural steps, timings, textual descriptions, and before and after thumbnail images. This workflow works with any how-to video regardless of its domain, instructional style, and presentation. It also collects annotations with untrained crowd workers (e.g., workers on Mechanical Turk).

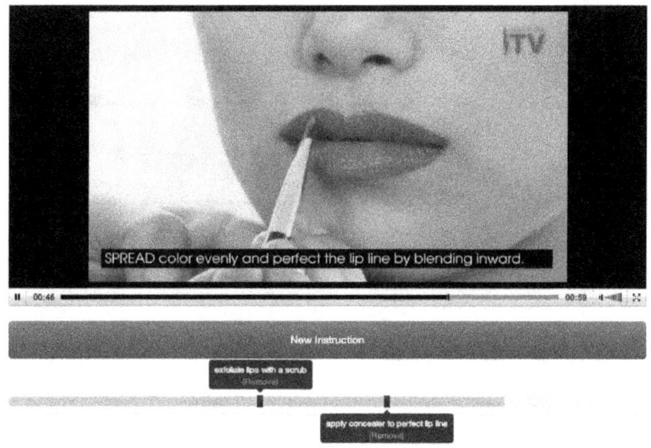

Figure 6. In the Find stage, the crowd worker adds new steps to the timeline by clicking on the "New Instruction" button.

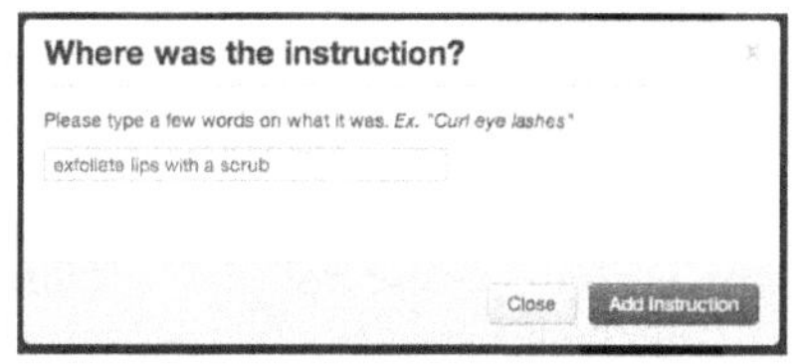

Figure 7. Upon clicking on the "New Instruction" button, a popup window asks the worker to describe what the step is about in free-form text.

Inspired by crowd design patterns that segment a bigger task into smaller micro-tasks [5], our workflow decomposes the annotation task into three stages and each video into shorter segments. This design addresses the task complexity and multi-pass overhead problems of manual annotation.

We developed a generalizable crowd workflow pattern called **Find-Verify-Expand** (Figure 1) for detecting temporal and visual state changes in videos, such as steps in a how-to video, highlights from a sports game, or suspicious incidents from a surveillance video. The unique *Expand* stage captures surrounding context and causal relationships (e.g., before/after images for a step in a how-to video) by expanding on the detected event (e.g., a step in a how-to video). To better handle crowd output coming from timing detection and image selection, we apply clustering algorithms and text and visual analysis techniques to intelligently merge results from workers.

Stage 1: FIND candidate steps

This crowd task collects timestamps and text descriptions for possible steps from a video segment. While watching the video, the worker adds a step by clicking on the "New Instruction" button every time the instructor demonstrates a step (Figure 6). Each time the worker clicks on the button, the task prompts the worker to describe the step in free-form text (Figure 7). The same segment is assigned to three workers, whose results get merged to create candidate steps.

Pre-processing: A video is segmented into one-minute chunks. We learned from pilot runs that longer video segments lead to lower annotation accuracy toward the end and slower responses on Mechanical Turk. However, a drawback in using segmented video is the possibility of missing steps

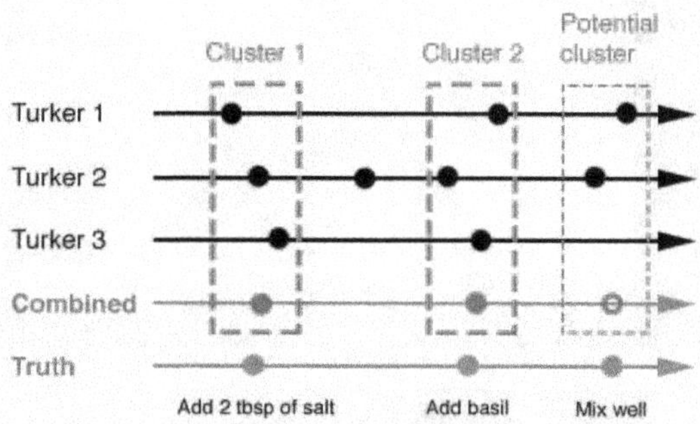

Figure 8. Our clustering algorithm groups adjacent time points into a candidate step. It further adds a potential cluster as a candidate, which might turn out to be a proper step once checked in the Verify stage. This inclusive strategy mitigates the effect of clustering errors.

near segment borders. We address this issue by including a five-second overlap between segments, and attaching the final segment to the prior one if it is shorter than 30 seconds.

Task Design: For quality control, the task first ensures that the user has audio by giving a test that asks the worker to type in a word spoken from an audio file. Our pilot runs showed that labeling accuracy drops significantly when the worker does not listen to audio. Secondly, we disable the Submit button until the video playhead reaches the end to ensure that the worker watches the entire segment. Finally, when the worker clicks on the "New Instruction" button, the video pauses and a dialog box pops up to ask what the step was. Our initial version simply added a tick on the timeline and continued playing without pausing or asking for a label. But this resulted in workers clicking too many times (as many as 100 for a 60-second chunk) without thinking. The prompt adds self-verification to the task, which encourages the worker to process the workflow by each step. The prompt also includes an example label to show the format and level of detail they are expected to provide (Figure 7).

Post-Processing: The workflow intelligently merges results from multiple workers to generate step candidates. To cluster nearby time points given by different workers into a single step, we use the DBSCAN clustering algorithm [12] with a timestamp difference as the distance metric. The clustering idea is shown in Clusters 1 and 2 in Figure 8. The algorithm takes ϵ as a parameter, which is defined by the maximum distance between two points that can be in a cluster relative to the distance between farthest points. We train ϵ once initially on a small set of pilot worker data and ground truth labels. Our tests show that the values between 0.05 and 0.1 yield high accuracy, regardless of domain or video. We configured the algorithm to require at least two labels in every cluster, similar to majority voting among the three workers who watched the segment. We considered other clustering algorithms such as K-Means, but many require the number of clusters as an input parameter. In video annotation, the number of steps is neither known a priori nor consistent across videos.

Depending on videos and parameters, the DBSCAN algorithm might over-generate (false positive) or under-generate

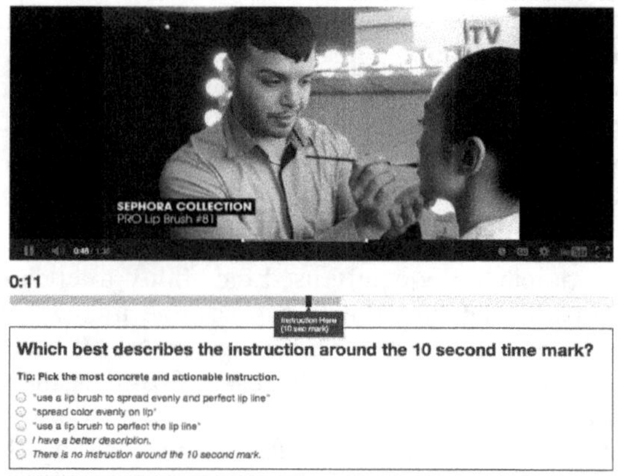

Figure 9. The Verify stage asks the worker to choose the best description of a candidate step. The options come from workers in the Find stage. Additional default options allow the worker to either suggest a better description or mark the step as invalid.

(false negative) clusters. We bias the algorithm to over-generate candidate steps ('potential cluster' in Figure 8) and aim for high recall over high precision, because the first stage is the only time the workflow generates new clusters. We improve the initial clusters in three ways, with the goal of higher recall than precision. First, we take into account the textual labels to complement timing information. The clustering initially relies on workers' time input, but using only time might result in incorrect clusters because steps are distributed unevenly time-wise. Sometimes there are steps every few seconds, and other times there might be no step for a minute. We run a string similarity algorithm between text labels in border points in clusters, to rearrange them to the closer cluster. Second, we break down clusters that are too large by disallowing multiple labels from one worker to be in a cluster. Finally, if there are multiple unclustered points within ϵ between clusters, we group them into a candidate cluster. For each cluster, we take a mean timestamp as the representative time to advance to the Verify stage.

Stage 2: VERIFY steps

Here the worker's verification task is to watch a 20-second clip that includes a candidate step and textual descriptions generated from the prior stage, and vote on the best description for the step (Figure 9). The workflow assigns three workers to each candidate step, whose votes are later merged.

Pre-processing: For each of the candidate steps from Stage 1, the workflow segments videos into 20-second clips around each step (10 seconds before and after).

Task Design: To prevent workers from selecting the first result without reviewing all options, we randomize the order of options presented each time. We also lowercase all labels to prevent capitalized descriptions from affecting the decision. Also, the Submit button becomes clickable only after the worker finishes watching the 20-second clip.

In addition to candidate text descriptions, two additional options are presented to workers: "I have a better description",

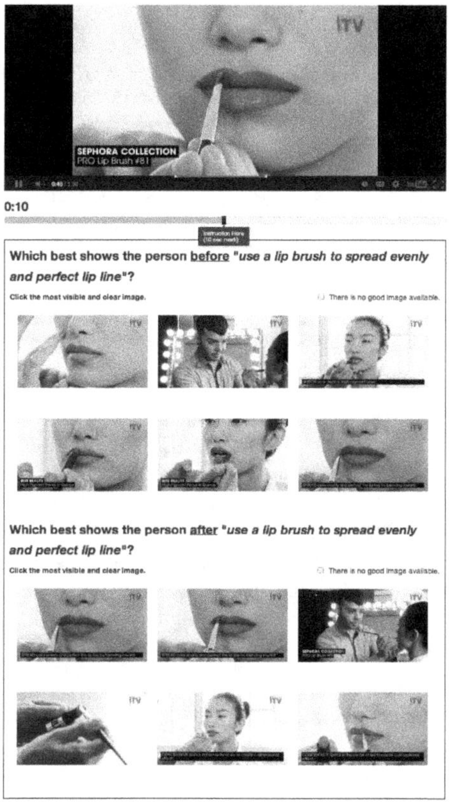

Figure 10. The Expand stage asks the worker to choose the best before and after images for a step. The worker visually reviews the thumbnail options and clicks on images to decide.

which improves the step label, and "There is no instruction", which filters out false positives from Stage 1.

Post-Processing: Two possible outputs of this stage are 1) finalizing the timestamp and description for a valid step, or 2) removing a false step. The workflow uses majority voting to make the final decision: If two or more workers agreed on a description, it becomes the final choice. If workers are split between three different options, it checks if some of the selected text descriptions are similar enough to be combined. We first remove stop words for more accurate comparisons, and then apply the Jaro-Winkler string matching algorithm [17]. If the similarity score is above a threshold we configured with initial data, we combine the two descriptions with a longer one. If not, it simply picks the longest one from the three. The decision to pick longer description for tie-breaking comes from a pilot observation that longer descriptions tend to be more concrete and actionable (e.g., "grate three cups of cheese" over "grate cheese").

Stage 3: EXPAND with before and after images for steps

This final stage collects the before and after images of a step, which visually summarize its effect. This stage captures surrounding context and causal relationships by expanding on what is already identified in Find and Verify. The worker's task here is to watch a 20-second video clip of a step, and select a thumbnail that best shows the work in progress (e.g., food, face, or Photoshop image) before and after the step (Figure 10). The workflow assigns three workers to each step.

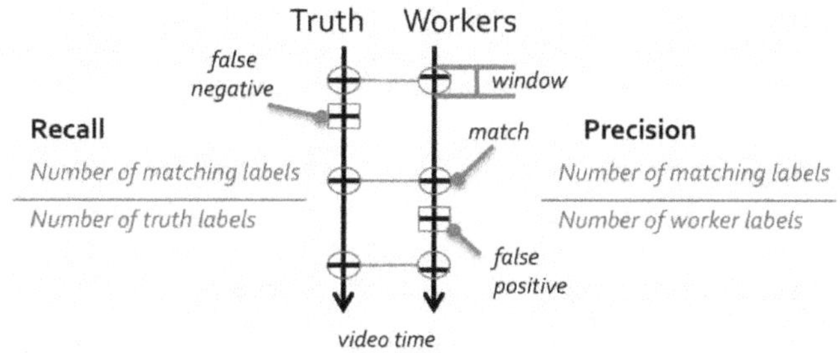

Figure 11. Our evaluation uses the Hungarian method to match extracted and ground truth steps with closest possible timestamp within a 10-second window size. Then we compute precision and recall, which indicate if our workflow over- or under-extracted steps from ground truth.

Pre-processing: This stage uses a 20-second video clip of a step verified in Stage 2, and uses its final text label to describe the step. It creates thumbnails at two-second intervals to present as options, 10 seconds before and after the step.

Task Design: Our initial design asked workers to click when they see good before and after images, but this resulted in low accuracy due to variable response time and the lack of visual verification. We then simplified the task to a multiple choice question. Selecting from static thumbnail images makes the task easier than picking a video frame.

Post-Processing: Similar to the Verify stage, we apply majority voting to determine the final before and after images. For merging and tie breaking, we use Manhattan distance, an image similarity metric that computes pixel differences between two images.

EVALUATION

We deployed our annotation workflow on Mechanical Turk and evaluated on:

- **Generalizability**: Does the workflow successfully generate labels for different types of how-to tasks in different domains with diverse video production styles?
- **Accuracy**: Do collected annotations include all steps in the original video, and avoid capturing too many (false positive) or too few (false negative)? How do textual descriptions generated by crowd workers compare to those generated by trained annotators?

Methodology

We used our workflow and Mechanical Turk to fully extract step information from the 75 how-to videos in our annotation corpus, with 25 videos each in cooking, makeup, and graphics editing software (Photoshop). We did not filter out videos based on use of subtitles, transitions, or audio, to see if our annotation workflow is agnostic to presentation styles. Out of 75 videos in our set, 7 did not have audio, and 27 contained text overlays. For each domain, we picked five tasks to cover diverse types of tasks: Cooking – pizza margherita, mac and cheese, guacamole, samosa, and bulgogi; Makeup – bronze look, reducing redness, smokey eyes, bright lips, and summer glow; Photoshop: motion blur, background removal, photo to sketch, retro effect, and lomo effect. The mean video length was 272 seconds, summing to over 5 hours of videos.

Results

Our evaluation focuses on comparing the quality of step information produced by our crowdsourcing workflow against ground truth annotations from our corpus.

The Turk crowd and trained annotators (two co-authors with educational video research experience) generated similar numbers of steps (Table 1). In Stage 1, 361 one-minute video segments were assigned to Turkers, who generated 3.7 candidate steps per segment, or 53.6 per video. Clustering reduced that to 16.7 steps per video. Stage 2 further removed over-generated steps, resulting in 15.7 per video, which is nearly equivalent to the ground truth of 15 steps per video.

Precision indicates how accurate extracted steps are compared to ground truth, while *recall* shows how comprehensively the workflow extracted ground truth steps (Figure 11). We present precision and recall results considering only the timing of steps (Stage 1), and both the timing and the textual description accuracy (Stage 2). For matching crowd-extracted steps to ground truth steps, we use the Hungarian method [19] whose cost matrix is filled with a time distance between steps.

Evaluating Stage 1: FIND

We consider only precision and recall of times in the Stage 1 evaluation because final textual descriptions are not yet determined. Detecting the exact timing of a step is not straightforward, because most steps take place over a time period, verbal and physical steps are commonly given with a time gap.

To more accurately account for the timing issue, we set a highest threshold in time difference that accepts a Turker-marked point as correct. We set the threshold to 10 seconds, which indicates that a step annotation more than 10 seconds off is discarded. This threshold was based on heuristics from step intervals in our corpus: We hand-annotated, on average, one step every 17.3 seconds in our video corpus (mean video length / number of steps in ground truth = 272/15.7), so a maximum 10-second difference seems reasonable.

The mean distance between ground truth steps and extracted steps (ones within 10 seconds of the ground truth) was only 2.7 seconds. This suggests that for matched steps, the time-based clustering successfully detected the timing information around this distance. When considering only time accuracy, our workflow shows 0.76 precision and 0.84 recall (Table 2).

Evaluating Stage 2: VERIFY

Here we combine the accuracy of both timing and text descriptions. Precision for this stage captures what fraction of steps identified by the workflow are both placed correctly on the time line and whose description reasonably matches the ground truth. The analysis shows 0.77 precision and 0.81 recall over all the videos (Table 2).

For text accuracy measurement, we use the string similarity algorithm to see if a suggested description is similar enough to a description from ground truth. We apply the same threshold as what we configured in the workflow for tie breaking in the Verify stage. The precision and recall both go down when the text similarity condition is added, but precision recovers from the post-processing of steps in this stage. Two enhancements contribute to this recovery: removing steps that workers indicated as "no instruction" from the task, and merging nearby steps that have identical descriptions.

By Turkers	After Stage1	After Stage2	Ground Truth
53.6	16.7	**15.7**	**15.0**

Table 1. The mean number of steps generated by the workflow in each stage. At the end the workflow extracted 15.7 steps per video, which is roughly equivalent to 15.0 from ground truth. Stage 1 clusters the original Turker time points, and Stage 2 merges or removes some.

Stage 1. Time only		Stage 2. Time + Text	
Precision	Recall	Precision	Recall
0.76	0.84	0.77	0.81

Table 2. When considering time information only, recall tends to be higher. When considering both time and text descriptions, incorrect text labels lower both precision and recall, but removing unnecessary steps in Stage 2 recovers precision.

In 76% of the steps, two or more Turkers agreed on a single description. For the rest, the tie breaking process determined the final description. For 13% of the steps, Turkers provided their own description.

Evaluating Stage 3: EXPAND

This evaluation should judge if crowd-selected before and after images correctly capture the effect of a step. Because this judgment is subjective, and there can be multiple correct before and after images for a step, we recruited six external human evaluators to visually verify the images. We assigned two evaluators to each domain based on their expertise and familiarity with the domain, and gave a one-hour training session on how to verify before and after images. For each workflow-generated step, we presented an extracted text description along with a before and after image pair. Their task was to make binary decisions (yes / no) on whether each image correctly represents the before or after state of the step.

We used Cohen's Kappa to measure inter-rater agreement. The values were 0.57, 0.46, 0.38, in cooking, makeup, and Photoshop, respectively, which show a moderate level of agreement [1]. Results show that on average, both raters marked 60% of before and after images as correct. At least one rater marked 81.3% as correct.

Cost, time, and tasks

We created a total of 8,355 HITs on Mechanical Turk for annotating 75 videos. With three workers on each task and a reward of $0.07, $0.03, and $0.05 for Find, Verify, and Expand, respectively, the average cost of a single video was $4.85, or $1.07 for each minute of a how-to video. The Expand stage was more costly ($2.35) than the first two; thus, time points and text descriptions can be acquired at $2.50 per video. The average task submission time was 183, 80, and 113 seconds for Find, Verify, and Expand, respectively.

Results summary

In summary, our workflow successfully extracted step information from 75 existing videos on the web, generalizing to three distinct domains. The extracted steps on average showed 77% precision and 81% recall against ground truth, and were 2.7 seconds away from ground truth. Human evaluators found 60% of before and after images to be accurate.

DISCUSSION AND LIMITATIONS

We now discuss qualitative findings from the experiment, which might have practical implications for future researchers designing crowd workflows.

Detecting precise timing of a step. We observed that Turkers add new steps with higher latency than trained annotators, resulting in Turker-labeled time points being slightly later than those by annotators for the same step. The trained annotators often rewinded a few seconds to mark the exact timing of a step after seeing the step, whereas most Turkers completed their tasks in a single pass. While this might be a limitation of the workflow, our results show that a reasonable window size mitigates such differences. We will explore time-shifting techniques to see if timing accuracy improves.

Handling domain and video differences. Extraction accuracy in our workflow was consistent across the three domains with different task properties. This finding validates our domain-agnostic approach based on the general properties of procedural tasks. Photoshop videos were often screencasts, whereas cooking and makeup videos were physical demonstrations. Cooking videos contained higher number and density of steps than makeup or Photoshop videos, while Photoshop and makeup videos often had longer steps that required fine-grained adjustments and tweaking. Also, some videos were studio-produced with multiple cameras and high-quality post-processing, while others were made at home with a webcam. Our workflow performed robustly despite the various differences in task properties and video presentation styles.

Extracting steps at different conceptual levels. Video instructors present steps at different conceptual levels, and this makes it difficult to keep consistent the level of detail in Turkers' step detection. In a makeup video, an instructor said "Now apply the bronzer to your face evenly", and shortly after applied the bronzer to her forehead, cheekbones, and jawline. While trained annotators captured this process as one step, our workflow produced four, including both the high-level instruction and the three detailed steps. Turkers generally captured steps at any level, but our current approach only constructs a linear list of steps, which sometimes led to redundancy. Previous research suggests that many procedural tasks contain a hierarchical solution structure [7], and we plan to extend this work to hierarchical annotation.

POSSIBLE APPLICATIONS AND GENERALIZATION

We list possible applications that leverage step information extracted from our workflow, and discuss ways to generalize the Find-Verify-Expand pattern beyond how-to videos.

Our scalable annotation workflow can enable a series of novel applications in addition to the ToolScape player. First, better video search can be made possible with finer-grained video indices and labels. For example, ingredient search for cooking or tool name search for Photoshop can show all videos and time points that cover a specific tutorial element. Furthermore, video players can present alternative examples to a current step. If a learner is watching how to apply the eyeliner, the interface can show just the snippets from other videos that include demonstrations of the eyeliner. This allows the learner to hop between different use cases and context for the step of interest, which can potentially improve learning outcomes.

We believe the Find-Verify-Expand pattern can generalize to annotating broader types of metadata beyond steps from how-to videos. For example, from a soccer video this pattern can extract goal moments with Find and Verify, and then use Expand to include a crucial pass that led to the goal, or a ceremony afterward. Generally, the pattern can extract metadata that is human-detectable but hard to completely automate. It is a scalable method for extracting time-sensitive metadata and annotating streaming data, which can be applied to video, audio, and time-series data.

CONCLUSION AND FUTURE WORK

This paper presents a scalable crowdsourcing workflow for annotating how-to videos. The Find-Verify-Expand pattern efficiently decomposes the complex annotation activity into micro-tasks. Step information extracted from the workflow can enable new ways to watch and learn from how-to videos. We also present ToolScape, an annotation-enabled video player supporting step-by-step interactivity, which is a potential client of this workflow. Our lab study shows the value of accessing and interacting with step-by-step information for how-to videos. Participants watching videos with ToolScape gained higher self-efficacy, rated their own work higher, and produced higher-rated designs.

Our future work will explore applying the workflow to additional procedural task domains such as origami, home DIY tasks, and Rubik's cube. We will also explore procedural tasks that require a conceptual understanding of the underlying concept, such as solving algorithm or physics problems.

Another direction for research is collecting task information using learners as crowd. We believe learners can potentially provide more advanced, higher-level, and richer information not possible with Turkers, if their learning interactions can naturally provide useful input to the system. Combining crowdsourcing with "learnersourcing" can extract rich annotations from existing resources while enhancing learning.

ACKNOWLEDGMENTS

The authors would like to thank the members of the UID Group at MIT CSAIL for their feedback. This work was funded in part by Quanta Computer. Juho Kim is supported by the Samsung Fellowship.

REFERENCES

1. Altman, D. G. *Practical statistics for medical research*, vol. 12. CRC Press, 1991.

2. Bandura, A. Self-efficacy: toward a unifying theory of behavioral change. *Psychological review 84*, 2 (1977), 191.

3. Banovic, N., Grossman, T., Matejka, J., and Fitzmaurice, G. Waken: Reverse engineering usage information and interface structure from software videos. In *UIST '12* (2012).

4. Bernstein, M. S., Brandt, J., Miller, R. C., and Karger, D. R. Crowds in two seconds: Enabling realtime crowd-powered interfaces. In *UIST '11*, ACM (2011).

5. Bernstein, M. S., Little, G., Miller, R. C., Hartmann, B., Ackerman, M. S., Karger, D. R., Crowell, D., and Panovich, K. Soylent: a word processor with a crowd inside. In *UIST '10* (2010), 313–322.

6. Bernstein, M. S., Teevan, J., Dumais, S., Liebling, D., and Horvitz, E. Direct answers for search queries in the long tail. In *CHI '12'* (2012), 237–246.

7. Catrambone, R. The subgoal learning model: Creating better examples so that students can solve novel problems. *Journal of Experimental Psychology: General 127*, 4 (1998), 355.

8. Chi, P.-Y., Ahn, S., Ren, A., Dontcheva, M., Li, W., and Hartmann, B. Mixt: Automatic generation of step-by-step mixed media tutorial. In *UIST '12* (2012).

9. Chi, P.-Y. P., Liu, J., Linder, J., Dontcheva, M., Li, W., and Hartmann, B. Democut: generating concise instructional videos for physical demonstrations. In *UIST '13*, ACM (2013).

10. Dow, S. P., Glassco, A., Kass, J., Schwarz, M., Schwartz, D. L., and Klemmer, S. R. Parallel prototyping leads to better design results, more divergence, and increased self-efficacy. *ACM Trans. Comput.-Hum. Interact. 17*, 4 (Dec. 2010), 18:1–18:24.

11. Eiriksdottir, E., and Catrambone, R. Procedural instructions, principles, and examples: how to structure instructions for procedural tasks to enhance performance, learning, and transfer. *Hum Factors 53*, 6 (2011), 749–70.

12. Ester, M., Kriegel, H.-P., Sander, J., and Xu, X. A density-based algorithm for discovering clusters in large spatial databases with noise. In *KDD*, vol. 96 (1996).

13. Ferguson, E. L., and Hegarty, M. Learning with real machines or diagrams: application of knowledge to real-world problems. *Cognition and Instruction 13*, 1 (1995), 129–160.

14. Grabler, F., Agrawala, M., Li, W., Dontcheva, M., and Igarashi, T. Generating photo manipulation tutorials by demonstration. In *SIGGRAPH '09* (2009), 1–9.

15. Grossman, T., Matejka, J., and Fitzmaurice, G. Chronicle: capture, exploration, and playback of document workflow histories. In *UIST '10* (2010).

16. Hadidi, R., and Sung, C.-H. Students' acceptance of web-based course offerings: an empirical assessment. *AMCIS 1998* (1998).

17. Jaro, M. A. Advances in record-linkage methodology as applied to matching the 1985 census of tampa, florida. *Journal of the American Statistical Association 84*, 406 (1989), 414–420.

18. Kim, J. Toolscape: enhancing the learning experience of how-to videos. In *CHI EA '13* (2013), 2707–2712.

19. Kuhn, H. W. The hungarian method for the assignment problem. *Naval research logistics quarterly 2*, 1-2 (1955), 83–97.

20. Lafreniere, B., Grossman, T., and Fitzmaurice, G. Community enhanced tutorials: improving tutorials with multiple demonstrations. In *CHI '13* (2013), 1779–1788.

21. Lasecki, W. S., Song, Y. C., Kautz, H., and Bigham, J. P. Real-time crowd labeling for deployable activity recognition. In *CSCW '13* (2013), 1203–1212.

22. Li, F. C., Gupta, A., Sanocki, E., He, L.-w., and Rui, Y. Browsing digital video. In *CHI '00*, ACM (2000).

23. Nguyen, P., Kim, J., and Miller, R. C. Generating annotations for how-to videos using crowdsourcing. In *CHI EA '13*, ACM (2013), 835–840.

24. Noronha, J., Hysen, E., Zhang, H., and Gajos, K. Z. Platemate: crowdsourcing nutritional analysis from food photographs. In *UIST '11* (2011), 1–12.

25. Park, S., Mohammadi, G., Artstein, R., and Morency, L.-P. Crowdsourcing micro-level multimedia annotations: The challenges of evaluation and interface. In *CrowdMM Workshop* (2012).

26. Pongnumkul, S., Dontcheva, M., Li, W., Wang, J., Bourdev, L., Avidan, S., and Cohen, M. Pause-and-play: Automatically linking screencast video tutorials with applications. In *UIST 2011* (2011).

27. Schunk, D. Goal setting and self-efficacy during self-regulated learning. *Educational psychologist 25*, 1 (1990), 71–86.

28. Tversky, B., Morrison, J. B., and Betrancourt, M. Animation: can it facilitate? *International journal of human-computer studies 57*, 4 (2002), 247–262.

29. van der Meij, H., Blijleven, P., and Jansen, L. What makes up a procedure? *Content & Complexity* (2003).

30. Vondrick, C., Ramanan, D., and Patterson, D. Efficiently scaling up video annotation with crowdsourced marketplaces. In *ECCV 2010*. Springer, 2010, 610–623.

31. Yuen, J., Russell, B., Liu, C., and Torralba, A. Labelme video: Building a video database with human annotations. In *ICCV 2009*, IEEE (2009), 1451–1458.

32. Zhang, D., Zhou, L., Briggs, R. O., and Jr., J. F. N. Instructional video in e-learning: Assessing the impact of interactive video on learning effectiveness. *Information & Management 43*, 1 (2006), 15 – 27.

33. Zimmerman, B. J., Bandura, A., and Martinez-Pons, M. Self-motivation for academic attainment: The role of self-efficacy beliefs and personal goal setting. *American Educational Research Journal 29*, 3 (1992), 663–676.

EverTutor: Automatically Creating Interactive Guided Tutorials on Smartphones by User Demonstration

Cheng-Yao Wang, Wei-Chen Chu, Hou-Ren Chen, Chun-Yen Hsu, Mike Y. Chen
Mobile and HCI Research Lab, National Taiwan University
{r00944052,r01922013,r01922002,b99204007,mikechen}@csie.ntu.edu.tw

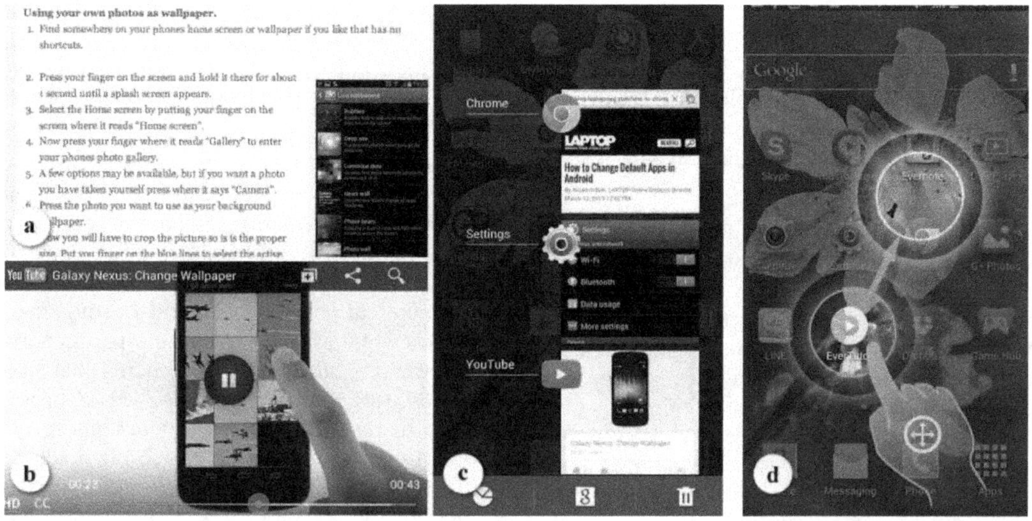

Figure 1. Common types of smartphone tutorials: (a) Static text and images, (b) Video, (c) EverTutor's interactive, step-by-step guided tutorial. Compared to EverTutor which overlays each step on top of the corresponding screen, static and video tutorials require users to constantly switch between the tutorial and the primary task, as shown in (d).

ABSTRACT
We present EverTutor, a system that automatically generates interactive tutorials on smartphone from user demonstration. For tutorial authors, it simplifies the tutorial creation. For tutorial users, it provides contextual step-by-step guidance and avoids the frequent context switching between tutorials and users' primary tasks. In order to generate the tutorials automatically, EverTutor records low-level touch events to detect gestures and identify on-screen targets. When a tutorial is browsed, the system uses vision-based techniques to locate the target regions and overlays the corresponding input prompt contextually. It also identifies the correctness of users' interaction to guide the users step by step. We conducted a 6-person user study for creating tutorials and a 12-person user study for browsing tutorials, and we compared EverTutor's interactive tutorials to static and video ones. Study results show that creating tutorials by EverTutor is simpler and faster than producing static and video tutorials. Also, when using the tutorials, the task completion time for interactive tutorials were 3-6 times faster than static and video tutorials regardless of age group. In terms of user preference, 83% of the users chose interactive type as the preferred tutorial type and rated it easiest to follow and easiest to understand.

CHI'14, April 26–May 1, 2014, Toronto, Canada.

http://dx.doi.org/10.1145/2556288.2557407

Author Keywords
Tutorials; Contextual help; Touchscreen gesture; Smartphone.

ACM Classification Keywords
H.5.2. Information Interfaces and Presentation (e.g. HCI): Graphical User Interfaces.

INTRODUCTION
Smartphones have become ubiquitous in our daily lives. For the times when users need help, they currently resort to finding tutorials that are static or video, and by asking friends to demonstrate how it is done. For static tutorials, text and images are arranged to describe the steps of operations required to accomplish a task. Video tutorials are screen recordings that show the process of performing a task (see Figure 1). Both of static and video tutorials frequently require users to switch between the tutorials and user contexts. In addition,

users often repeatedly pause and replay the videos. This out-of-context process indicates two usability problems: split attention and delayed practice [18].

Contextual interactive tutorials, such as the ones when an Android device is used for the very first time, address these usabilities problems, but they require significant programming skills and privileged access to system source code. Recent research on tutorial content have included contextual associations, such as Stencils-based tutorials [14], Graphstracts [13] and "Photo Manipulation Tutorials" [8]. However, these contextual tutorials are limited to particular applications and tasks and can't be viewed on smartphones. Vision-based analysis are applicable to any GUI regardless whether the source code and accessibility APIs are available [26]. However, users need to write Sikuli scripts [25] and take screenshots for each step; in addition, touchscreen gestures are not supported.

We present EverTutor, a system that automatically generates interactive step-by-step tutorials from user demonstration. EverTutor records low-level touch events, distinguishes different touchscreen gestures and extracts regional screenshot around event location to generate tutorials automatically. When a tutorial is browsed, the system uses vision-based techniques to locate the target interactive region in a given tutorial step. Besides, EverTutor identifies the correctness of the user's interaction and gives response, making the contextual help more interactive. Moreover, EverTutor even automatically injects scroll or swipe event to find the unseen interactive region for users.

We compare the interactive step-by step tutorials generated by EverTutor with static and video tutorials. To evaluate user experience, user preferences, the overall time of creating tutorials, and the task completion time, we conducted a 6-person user study for creating tutorials, and another 12-person user study for browsing tutorials. In the first study, we demonstrated that creating tutorials by EverTutor is simpler and faster than producing static and video tutorials. According to the second study, interactive tutorial is 3-6 times as fast as static and video tutorials. In addition, with interactive tutorials, older users can complete a task as fast or faster than younger users. When participants were asked to rate all the methods in terms of 1) easy to follow, 2) easy to understand, and 3) easy to remember, interactive tutorial is rated highest in easy to follow and easy to understand. In addition, 83% of the users chose interactive type as the preferred tutorial type.

In summary, the main contributions of this paper include:

- a tutorial system that simplifies the generation process of contextual tutorials across apps and supports general touchscreen gestures on Android smartphones.
- a general approach to automatically generating interactive step-by-step tutorials from demonstrations.
- presenting interactive step-by-step tutorials that help older users complete a task as fast as youngsters
- an evaluation of interactive step-by-step tutorials comparing with static and video tutorials on smartphone.

RELATED WORK

Capturing touchscreen events

Gomez et al. described RERAN that permits record-and- replay for the Android smartphone platform by capturing and replaying the low-level events triggered on the phone [6]. Henze et al. derived a compensation function that shifts the users' touches to reduce errors from the large amounts of touch events, which were collected from a published smartphone game in the Android Market [12]. Daryl et al. recorded user touch inputs and improved touch accuracy on mobile devices by learning user-specific touch input models [23]. In EverTutor, the system analyzes the recorded low-level touch events and regional screenshot around touch event location to generate interactive contextual tutorials automatically.

Generation of tutorials by user demonstrations

Most existing tutorial generation approaches trace user interactions by analyzing screencast video of the demonstration or the application. Grabler et al. presented a system that automatically creates tutorials from recorded demonstrations of application usage [8], and Berthouzoz et al. developed a framework, which learned the parameters for image editing operations and generated macros that take into account the context of the current image [3]. Chronicle captures video and history of graphical documents to create an interactive learning tool that offers video playback and visualization of user actions [10]. The MixT tutorial system [4] uses a command log, an input device log and screencapture video to generate mixed media tutorials that combine the strengths of static with video tutorial types. However, tutorials generated by above creation tools must be viewed outside the actual user interface.

Contextual Assistance

Contextual help has been proved effective for learning graphical user interfaces [14, 9, 2]. Unlike traditional help based on screenshots or screencasts, contextual help allows users to receive assistance in the actual interface they are interacting with. Researchers have explored a range of tutorial systems that are presented in the context of the application [14, 9, 5]. Stencils-based tutorials overlay step- by-step instructions on the interface and limit interaction to UI elements related to the current step [14]. Sketch-Sketch Revolution offers in-application tutorials that assist the user in completing drawing tasks, enabling the user to experience success while learning [5]. ToolClips provides users with short video clips and other rich help content next to toolbar buttons contextually [9]. However, these contextual tutorials are limited to specific applications or suited only for a single, specific task.

Yeh et al. developed a tool [26] that allows help designers to create contextual help across applications by taking screenshots and writing Sikuli script language [25]. When the help is presented to a user, the system uses computer vision method to locate the component on user's screen that matches the screenshot. Though we also use vision-based techniques to locate the target interactive region in a given tutorial step, with the recorded low-level touch events, EverTutor distinguishes different touchscreen gestures during the automatic generation process of tutorials. Also, when a tutorial is presented, EverTutor identifies the correctness of the user's interaction and gives response, making the contextual help more interactive. In addition, EverTutor even automatically injects scroll or swipe event to help the user find the interactive area which is unseen in current screen.

Evaluation of different tutorial types

Different findings on the effectiveness of media formats of software tutorials are shown. The work in the early 90's by Palmiter, Elkerton [19, 20], and Harrison [11] studied the effect of animated demonstrations on learning and instruction recall. More recently, Grabler et al. showed that automatically generated text and image tutorials outperformed video or book instructions on time and errors [13]. ToolClips short (1025 sec.) video demonstrations of features displayed as tooltips has been shown to result in significantly improved task-completion rates as compared to static text+image tooltips [9]. The MixT multimedia tutorial system reported that short, step-specific video demonstrations are useful for performing dynamic actions that are difficult to express via text or static images alone [4]. Pause-and-Play [21] improves a user's ability to follow video demonstrations by automatically pausing and resuming video to stay in sync with the user's progress. Lafreniere et al. designed FollowUs [16] that brought enhanced community features to the tutorial experience, including additional demonstrations of each tutorial step, and noted that the presence of multiple demonstrations helps users complete tasks with less frustration. Differently, we perform an evaluation of EverTutor to understand the user experience of browsing three tutorial types on smartphone and users' preferred type.

DESIGN GOALS

In this section, based on previous research and smartphone characteristics, we outline the design goals of our tutorial system, EverTutor.

Contextual

Although users can long press the home button or use other app-switching apps to switch back and forth between user context and tutorials, this process could cause delayed, disruptive, inconsistent, and obtrusive user experience [1, 15]. Therefore, our first goal is to make our tutorials contextual.

Touchscreen gestures support

Touchscreen is the factor that has changed the way people use mobile phones and tablets. When using smartphones, users perform many touchscreen gestures, such as scrolling through a web page, pinching to zoom in a photo, and dragging an app icon to home screen. As a result, one of our goals is to enable the 7 touchscreen gestures supported by Android to be contained in the tutorial [22].

Interactive

Inspired by Stencils-based tutorial [14] and Google SketchUp Training [7], we intend to design the tutorials that are aware of a user's interactions and able to respond. In addition, since the smartphone screen is too small to show directly the unseen targets in several situations, we expect EverTutor to automatically find the unseen target area for users, making our contextual help more interactive and improving users' learning experience.

Automatic generation from user demonstration

In order to simplify the generation process of contextual tutorials, we intend to allow users to create tutorials during their demonstration. Considering smartphones having so many apps and features, automatic generation could possibly meet smartphone users' increasing demand for tutorials.

Across apps and platforms

We expect our tutorial system to be suited for any task or any app on smartphone and hope our approach to be easily applied to any other touchscreen-based devices.

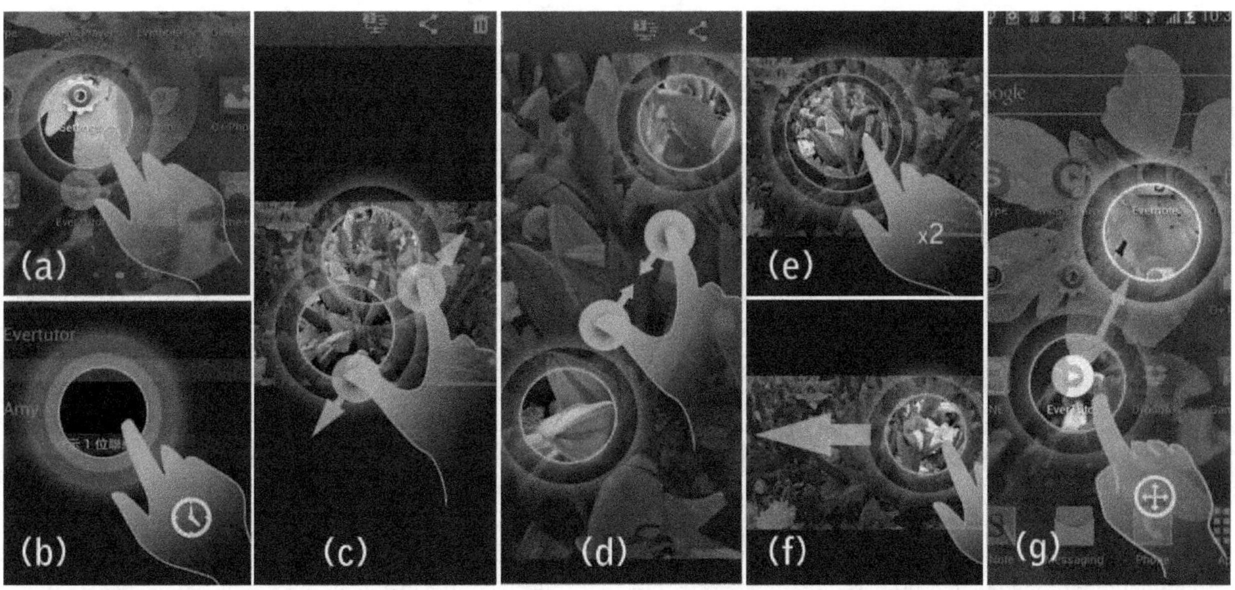

Figure 2. The overlays for touchscreen gestures in EverTutor. (a) Touch (b) Long press (c, d) Pinch open/close (e) Double touch (f) Swipe (g) Drag.

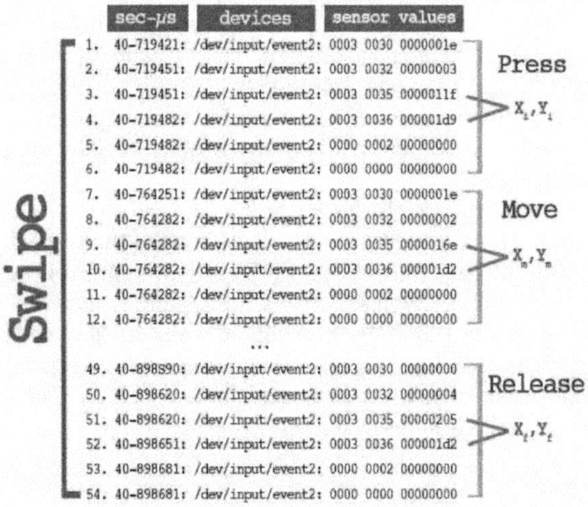

Figure 3. Series of events representing a swipe; X_i, Y_i are the initial coordinates, X_m, Y_m are the coordinates during moving (still holding down), and X_f , Y_f are the final coordinates.

SYSTEM IMPLEMENTATION

We developed EverTutor on a Samsung Note 2 smartphone with root access running Android 4.1.2.

Gesture Recognizer

The Android software stack consists of a custom Linux kernel and libraries, the Dalvik Virtual Machine (VM) and apps running on top of the VM. When a user interact with an Android app, the Android device's sensors generate and send events to the kernel via the /dev/input/event* device files. The standard, five-field format of every event is as follows: timestamp:, device:, type, code, value, and touchscreen gestures are encoded as a stream of touchscreen events in the same format, which could be displayed as the following example:

40-719451: /dev/input/event2: 0003 0035 0000011f.

The timestamp indicates that the event was generated 40 seconds and 719,451 microseconds since the system restart; "event2" is the input device which refers to the touchscreen on our device. The next three columns provide position information: 0035 represents the x position of the event and 0000011f (hex) corresponds to coordinate 287 (decimal) of the screen. However, this single event is not enough for reconstituting the high-level gesture. For instance, a single press usually involves roughly 18 touchscreen events, while a swipe usually involves roughly 50 touchscreen events. In Figure 3, we show a subset of events involved in a single typical gesture, swipe. We implemented a gesture recognizer to distinguish different gestures based on the default properties of a gesture defined by Android, for example, standard long press time is 500 ms.

Template Matching

We implemented template matching based on image pyramid (3 levels), where the results of each layer is used to define the region of interest for the next layer. To improve performance, we implemented it in C++ using the OpenCV library and used Android's Native Development Kit (NDK) to access the function via Java Native Interface (JNI).

Client-server Architecture

EverTutor is constructed under a client-server architecture. When a tutorial is created by EverTutor, all images are uploaded to Amazon S3 and a tutorial data is newed in the Database of Rails Server. When a user browses a tutorial, EverTutor downloads all necessary images from Amazon and accesses the step-by- step tutorial data from Rails Database, such as event type, touchscreen position, etc..

EVERTUTOR

Tutorial Format

In order to free users from switching back and forth between a tutorial and user context, we design the interactive and contextual guide that shows step-by-step instructions on the actual interface rather than in a separate viewer. Inspired by the "Cling" view from Launcher on Android Jelly Bean and Stencils-Based Tutorials [14], we put full-screen and transparent overlays containing cling holes upon the active application interface. In every step, the cling holes in the overlay layer draw the user's attention to the region they should interact with; Also, we add a finger image beside the cling hole to present the 7 core gestures supported by Android as shown in Figure 2. Hoping to direct users correctly, users can proceed to the next step only after interacting with the intended position by the expected gesture.

Generating tutorial with EverTutor

Record and distinguish touchscreen gesture

When creating tutorials with EverTutor, the user starts recording by performing a swipe gesture to select the start item in pie menu. System keeps reading the /dev/input/event* files, detecting the timestamp, position and event types to distinguish the used gesture. Meanwhile, system opens the framebuffer (/dev/graphics/fb0) to capture bitmap data representing the screenshot and extract the regional image around the touch event location (Figure 4). An Android toast message pops up when a tutorial step data is saved completely. Besides tutorial authors can perform mode switching by using a bezel swipe gesture to open a pie menu containing the mode choices.

Record Options

During the recording process, gestures other than scroll and swipe (e.g. tap, pinch) are regarded as separate steps, and we exclude scroll and swipe because the two gestures are possibly applied by the users for many times to find a specific target. On the other hand, when a tutorial is browsed, gestures of swipe and scroll recorded can be analyzed by EverTutor to find the interactive area unseen in the current screen for users.

Scroll/swipe mode

Some swipe and scroll gestures are used to extend the hidden interface; for instance, in Google Maps, place details, such as business information, can be accessed by swiping up on the

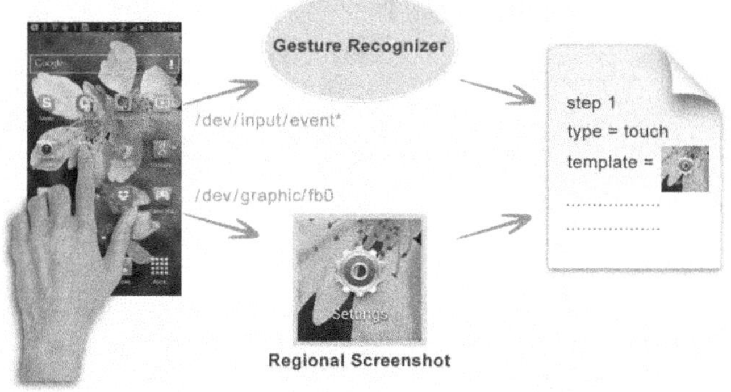

Figure 4. The workflow of generating tutorial with EverTutor.

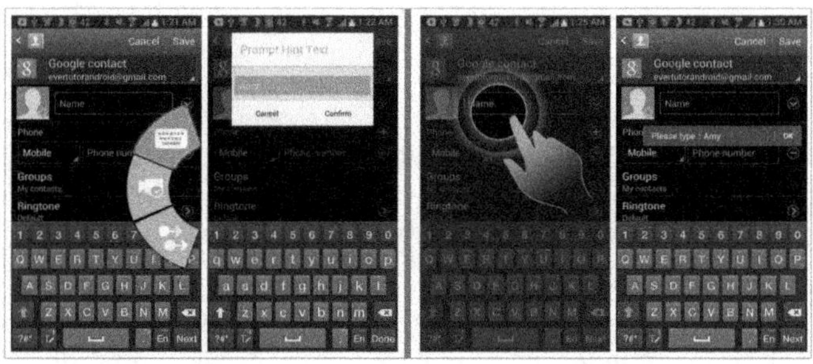

Figure 5. (Left) Switch to typing mode and set the prompt instructional text in dialog. (Right) The user inputs the texts by following the prompt instruction.

info sheet header. In the above situations, the tutorial author can switch to "scroll/swipe" mode to include the two gestures into dependent steps.

Typing mode

For steps containing typing, the user can select "typing" mode to stop capturing the sensitive information, such as username and password, and after finishing typing, the user can set the prompt text in pop up dialog for users browsing the tutorial afterward as shown in Figure 5(left).

Set title and review tutorial

After completing all steps, the tutorial author swipes to open the pie menu selecting "finish" icon, titles the tutorial and checks the screenshots for every step, and then the tutorial is finally inserted into database with all images uploaded to Amazon S3.

Browsing tutorials with EverTutor

EverTutor firstly downloads interactive region images of every tutorial step from Amazon S3 and the tutorial information from database, such as event type and event location of every step.

Finding the interactive region

When a user browses a tutorial, EverTutor continuously reads the screen framebuffer (/dev/graphics/fb0) and scans for regions that match the templates. Currently, it takes 0.1 0.3s to match a 240x240 pixel template image within a 1280x720 pixel image on a Samsung Note 2. If the matching is failed and the recorded operation consists of swipe or scroll gesture, system would inject swipe or scroll events to find the interactive area (Figure 6). For example, in the tutorial of "changing system font size to large," the system automatically scrolled up the list in "Settings" to find "Accessibility." If no templates are matched after auto-scrolling, the system will show the template image and prompt users to find the target.

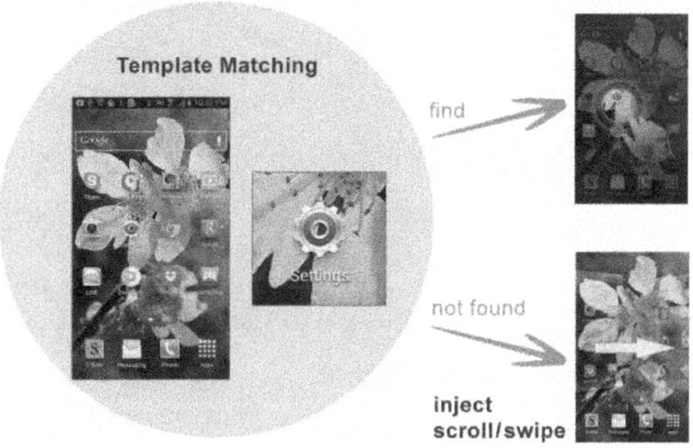

Figure 6. The workflow of browsing tutorials with EverTutor.

Showing the interactive step-by-step tutorial

After locating the interactive region, based on the type of touchscreen gestures in the given step, the system puts a full-screen and transparent overlay containing cling holes and a finger image upon the active application interface. When a typing action is asked in the step, the user can input the texts following the prompt hint as shown in Figure 5(right).

Identifying the correctness of the user's interaction

Aiming to direct users correctly, the system reads files in /dev/input/event* to obtain touch locations and identify the performed touchscreen gestures. Therefore, users can proceed to the next step only after interacting with the intended position by the expected gesture.

EVALUATION

Task and Tutorial Materials

We selected 9 smartphone tutorials of different tasks from courses held by Samsung and HTC as well as common questions on the telecommunications company websites. The tutorials were classified into three levels by the number of steps required to finish the task, including easy (4 steps), normal (8 steps) and hard (16 steps) as shown in Table 1. Because the original tutorials may not consist of the exact steps of the three predefined levels, we slightly modified them by adding or deleting a few steps. "Typing" steps were included in the hard level with typing characters limited to exactly 13 in each tutorial, and all characters were on the default keyboard. Touchscreen gestures contained by the 9 tutorials were as follows: touch, pinch, swipe, scroll and long press. We didn't present "drag" and "double touch" in our tutorials because drag (consisting of long press, move and lift) is more difficult and double touch is seldom used in smartphone operations.

At each level, 3 different tasks were designed; for each task, we created 3 types of tutorials, static, video, and interactive type (EverTutor), and made these 3 types present as equivalent the information as possible. Our video tutorials were

	Easy (4 steps)	Normal (8 steps)	Hard (16 steps containing entering 13 characters)
T1	Change system font size to large.	Check the battery level and adjust the screen brightness.	Create a new contact (name: Amy, phone number: 0923456789) and practice long press gesture to share.
T2	Enable WiFi hotspot to share the internet.	Set a repeating alarm on Tuesday and Thursday.	Use Evernote to add a note (enter "Evertutor hi.") including an image and a time reminder.
T3	Install Facebook app from Google play.	View photos with pinch and swipe gesture and add a photo to favorite.	Send an email to a@a.a (subject:hi, content:hihihi)

Table 1. The nine tasks users were asked to perform in user study, arranged by level.

recorded by Screencast Recorder app, with subtitles and red circles added to direct users. Though the default delay between each step was 2 seconds, participants were asked to view a video tutorial and optional adjust the playback speed during the practice session prior to the study tasks. Only 2 (older) participants slowed the speed down to 0.8x. Besides, we provided no vocal explanation in video tutorials to avoid situations when users only relied on auditory instructions rather than screen content. To generate our static tutorials, we extracted the frame of each step in the video tutorial and added texts for explanation. For interactive tutorials, we selected the tutorials that were created by users using EverTutor in user study 1.

User Study 1: Creating Tutorials

The goal of the study is to explore if the 3 tutorials of the same level have equivalent difficulty and understand the user experience of generating interactive tutorials by EverTutor as well as users' preferred types to create tutorials.

Participants

We recruited 6 app developers (4 male, 2 female), ranging in age from 20 to 26.

Procedure

We firstly familiarized participants with EverTutor operation, and then asked them to use EverTutor to create 9 designated interactive tutorials ordered by the level from easy to hard. Before making each tutorial, participants must understand every step of the task, and after performing it once, participants used EverTutor to complete the task and generate interactive tutorial simultaneously. After 9 tutorials were all created, we showed participants the generated tutorials and conducted a 15-minute interview. During the study, we used a camera to record user performance.

Quantitative Result

We calculated the difference in operation time for the 3 tutorials of the same level: the difference is less than 3s in 4-step level, 5s in 8-step and 7s in 16-step. The 3 tutorials not only consist of the same number of steps but also cost similar operation time, which proves that they can be grouped into the same difficulty level.

According to Figure 7, the average processing time of each step cost by EverTutor is 2.4s, and plus the time spent on typing the tutorial title and checking for correctness, the overall time is respectively 41.1s, 60.47s, and 128.87s for easy-level, normal-level, and hard-level task.

In Participants' estimate (see Figure 9), they would spend about 20 minutes on making a normal-level tutorial in static type and 40 minutes on a video tutorial of the same level, which obviously shows that creating tutorials by EverTutor is simpler and faster.

Qualitative Result

According to the questionnaire result as shown in Figure 9, all the participants preferred EverTutor to make interactive tutorials. Participant D6 commented, "As I demonstrate a smartphone feature to my parents, the tutorial is generated automatically by EverTutor, and they can browse the tutorial whenever they wants." However, four participants would like to make static or video tutorials as well. "Static tutorial could have more detailed instructions for each step and is suitable

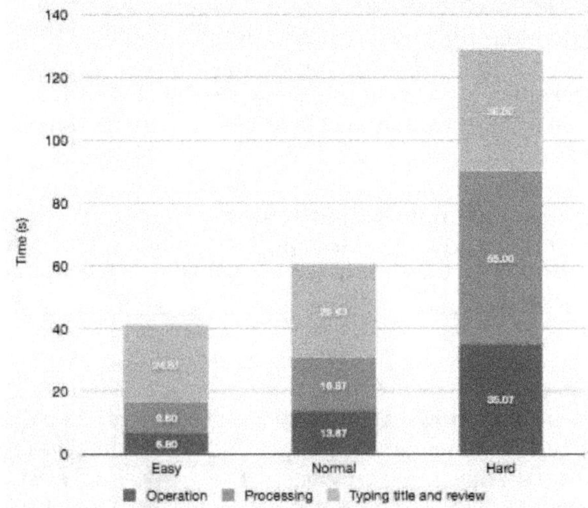

Figure 7. Operation time and overall time for creating tutorials with EverTutor.

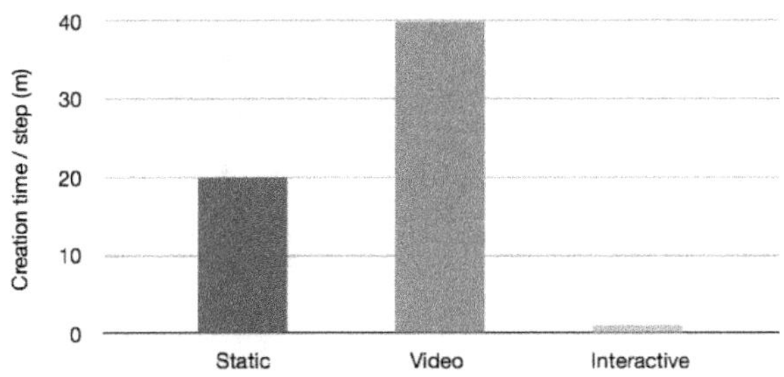

Figure 8. Overall time for creating tutorials.

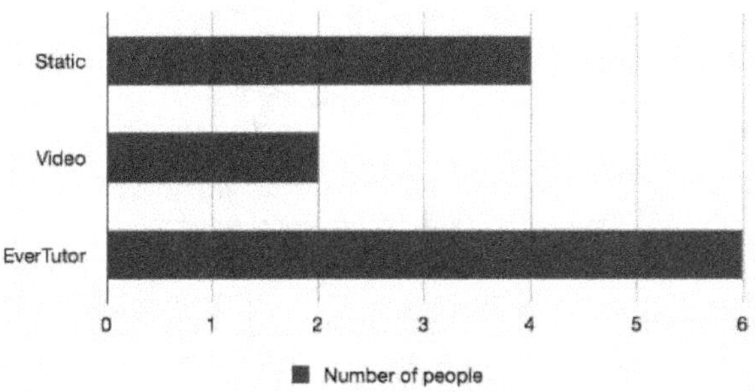

Figure 9. The tutorial types that tutorial authors prefer to create (multiple-selection question).

for the browse on the computer," said D1. D2 said that additional static and video tutorials could offer users more access to the tutorial.

User Study 2: Browsing Tutorials

The goal of this study is to understand the user experience of three types of tutorials (static, video, interactive) and users' preferred types.

Participants

12 Android Smartphone Beginners were recruited, including 6 older participants (3 female, 3 male) ranging in age from 48 to 58 (median 54.3) and 6 young participants (4 female, 2 male) ranging in age from 21 to 29 (median 24.2).

Procedure

We first familiarized participants with basic smartphone gestures and demonstrated three types of tutorials. In static type, using "Chrom" app as the browser, we informed users about the pinch gesture to zoom in the tutorial website and scroll gesture to roam the steps. For video type, we provided "DicePlayer" app, which can adjust the speed of video and taught them the essential operations to manipulate the movie player, including pausing, playing, resuming, forwarding, rewinding, and replaying. Also, participants learned how to switch between user context and the tutorial with home button. In interactive type, they ran through a completely interactive tutorial and got familiar with the indicated gestures. In the experiment, we prepared 3 home screens in launcher to display 41 app icons, referring to the average number of apps per smartphone [17]. In each task of static and video types, user must swipe across home screens to find the target app, but with EverTutor, the target was automatically pointed out.

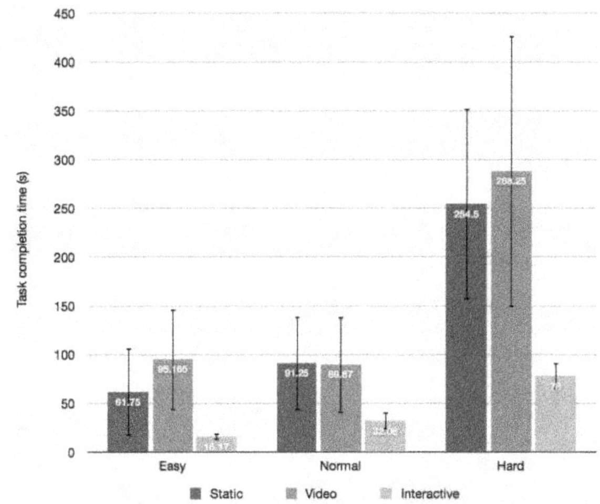

Figure 10. Task completion time with static, video and interactive tutorial.

Afterward, participants were asked to complete nine tasks with tutorials in the order of the difficulty level from easy to hard, and the sequence of tutorial types in each difficulty is counterbalanced. After the 9 tasks, participants filled out a questionnaire and had a 15-minute interview. During the experiment, we used a camera to record user performance.

Quantitative Result

Figure 10 shows the average completion time of 3 tutorial types in each level. There is a significant difference across three tutorial types in each level ($F_{easy}(2,33) = 10.09$, $P_{easy} < .001$, $F_{normal}(2,33) = 11.31$, $P_{normal} < .001$ and $F_{hard}(2,33) = 16.76$, $P_{hard} < .001$). Interactive tutorial is fastest and 3 times as fast as static and video tutorials in all levels .($p < 0.05$). On the other hands, static tutorial is slightly faster than video tutorial in "easy" and "hard" levels, yet there is no significant difference ($p > 0.05$). Besides, it tooks twice the time for older participants to complete the task with static and video tutorials than young participants. Surprisingly, with interactive tutorial, the completion time of older participants is equal to or even less than young participants' as shown in Figure 11.

Qualitative Result

Figure 12 shows the subjective ratings for all tutorial types regarding 1) Easy to Follow, 2) Easy to Understand, and 3) Easy to Remember. Participants rated interactive tutorial the highest in all categories, and a significant difference is shown in Easy to Follow and Easy to Understand ($F_{follow}(2,33) = 20.23$, $P_{follow} < .001$ and $F_{understand}(2,33) = 3.78$, $P_{uderstand} < .05$). One participant stated, "The interactive tutorial is intuitive and easily understood. I don't need a frequent switch between actual interface and the tutorial." Another participant reported, "Interactive tutorial is like a real person who teaches me step by step, and it can find the app for me automatically. It is really cool."

When asked about most preferred tutorial type, 83% of the users chose interactive type over the other types, as shown in Figure 13. The reason why the two users preferred static type

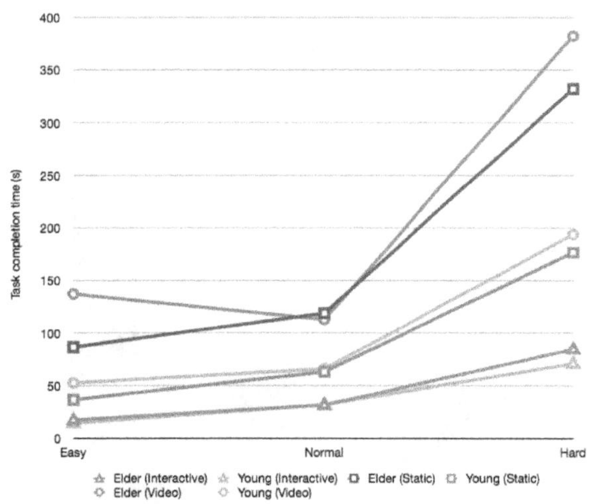

Figure 11. Task completion time of older and young participants with all tutorial types.

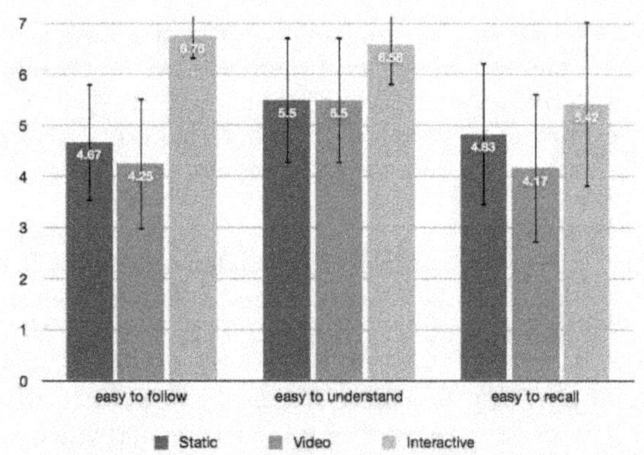

Figure 12. Subjective results comparing the interactive tutorials with static and video tutorials (7-Likert scale).

is that they could realize the relations among steps and jump to the critical step directly. Besides, the step-by-step interactive type is too intuitive for users to remember the whole tutorial.

DISCUSSION

Significant gain in performance

EverTutor's gain in performance is significantly greater than observed in Stencils[14] (3x faster vs 26% faster completion time compared to static tutorials). It's not only because context switching is much more difficult on smartphones, but also because EverTutor's interactive tutorial is significantly easier for users to understand and follow.

Differences between older and younger participants

Older participants had equal or faster completion time using interactive tutorials compared to younger participants, but spent at least 2 times longer than young participants when using static and video tutorials, which indicates that contextual tutorials are particularly well-suited for older users. One of our initial concerns with the interactive step-by-step tutorials

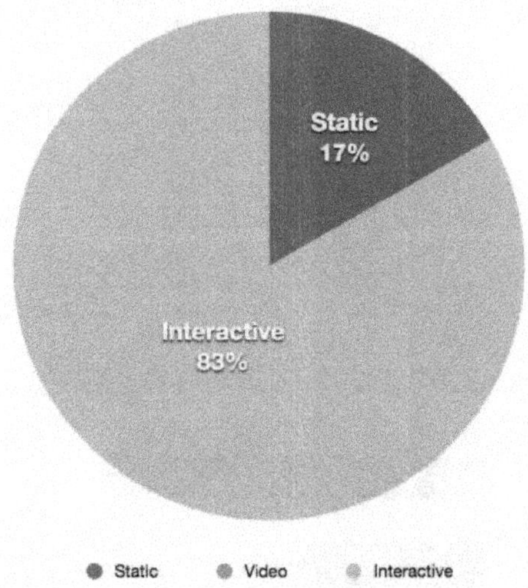

Figure 13. Users' preferred tutorial types.

was that users might follow tutorials quickly without remembering what they were learning. According to our questionnaire result in Figure 14, older participants rated interactive tutorials easiest to remember (6.0 vs 4.2 vs 3.8 on a 7-point scale) whereas younger participants rated static tutorial easiest to remember (5.5 vs 4.8 vs 4.5).

An older participant said, "Despite the detailed explanation of static tutorial, it's hard for me to remember the whole steps. In contrast, by using interactive tutorials, I can just memorize the interactive regions." According to another older user, though he couldn't memorize all the steps after following the interactive tutorial by one time, he could learn fast by repeating the tutorial for some more times, which was much easier than watching static or video types for several times. However, two younger participants preferred static type. A young user considered, "the relation among steps is clear in static tutorial, and I can understand the tutorial more; but I tend to forget what I've done after following interactive tutorials."

Automatic scrolling feature

10 of the 12 participants regarded the function of finding the unseen target region automatically very useful especially when users hoped to find an app icon on Launcher, but others commented that they wanted the system to just show the regional screenshot of target region and found the target by themselves.

Automation macro

During the interview, users suggested that EverTutor could generate a shortcut that automatically completed the task for users. However, since hands-on practice and exploration at the same time have been shown to be key ingredients of successful learning of an interface [24], the shortcut feature would be suited only for the simple functions that users had already learned.

LIMITATION AND FUTURE WORK

The current implementation of EverTutor has some limitations that should be discussed. EverTutor can't generate

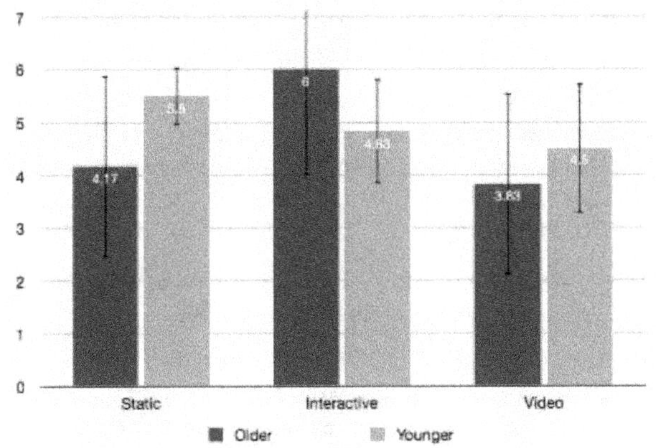

Figure 14. Subjective results in easy to remember catagory of older and younger participants.

tutorials containing motion gestures like throwing and continuous, complex operation, such as drawing and playing a game. A possible solution worth pursuing in the future is to record the whole low-level events and replay them when user browses the step. With the record-and-replay approach, EverTutor can also automatically make the user jump to a particular step by replaying the recorded events of previous steps.

Besides, our system, like any other vision-based techniques, suffers from the limitations like scale changes and theme variations. To alleviate the problem, EverTutor can record the information of system version, device name, and some details about the apps, such as package and activity names in each tutorial step, to assist users in finding tutorials generated from similar system environments. Users also mentioned that they preferred to add some instructional texts when making tutorial steps, which will be addressed in our future work.

CONCLUSION

In this paper, we present EverTutor that automatically generate interactive step-by-step tutorials on smartphone. EverTutor analyzes the recorded low-level touch events, distinguishes different touchscreen gestures and extracts regional screenshot around touch event location to generate step-by-step tutorials automatically. The system locates the target interactive regions of each step to overlay tutorial contextually. To make the tutorial more interactive, EverTutor is aware of the user's interaction and gives response. Besides, EverTutor automatically scrolls or swipes to help users find the unseen interactive region.

To compare interactive step-by step tutorials with static and video tutorials, we firstly conducted a 6-person user study for creating tutorials. The result shows that creating tutorials by EverTutor is simpler and faster than producing static and video ones. In the second 12-person user study for browsing tutorials, we demonstrated that interactive tutorial is fastest in task completion time and 3 times faster than static and video tutorials. Moreover, interactive tutorials even enable older users to complete a task faster than youngsters. To rate all the methods in terms of 1) easy to follow, 2) easy to understand and 3) easy to remember, interactive tutorial was highest rated in easy to follow and easy to understand. In addition, 83% of the users chose interactive type as the most preferred tutorial type.

ACKNOWLEDGMENTS

We gratefully acknowledge the helpful comments of the Associate Chairs and the anonymous reviewers. This paper was partially supported by National Science Council of Taiwan under 101-2628-E-002-030-MY2.

REFERENCES

1. Ames, A. L. Just what they need, just when they need it: An introduction to embedded assistance. In *Proc. ACM SIGDOC'01 (2001)*, 111–115.
2. Bergman, L., Castelli, V., Lau, T., and Oblinger, D. Docwizards: A system for authoring follow-me documentation wizards. In *Proc. ACM UIST'05 (2005)*, 191–200.
3. Berthouzoz, F., Li, W., Dontcheva, M., and Agrawala, M. A framework for content-adaptive photo manipulation macros: Application to face, landscape, and global manipulations. *ACM Trans. Graph (2011)*, 120:1–120:14.
4. Chi, P.-Y., Ahn, S., Ren, A., Dontcheva, M., Li, W., and Hartmann, B. Mixt: Automatic generation of step-by-step mixed media tutorials. In *Proc. ACM UIST'12 (2012)*, 93–102.
5. Fernquist, J., Grossman, T., and Fitzmaurice, G. Sketch-sketch revolution: An engaging tutorial system for guided sketching and application learning. In *Proc. ACM UIST'11 (2011)*, 373–382.
6. Gomez, L., Neamtiu, I., Azim, T., and Millstein, T. Reran: Timing- and touch-sensitive record and replay for android. In *Proc. ACM ICSE'13 (2013)*, 72–81.
7. Google SketchUp Training. `http://sketchup.google.com/intl/en/training/index.html`.
8. Grabler, F., Agrawala, M., Li, W., Dontcheva, M., and Igarashi, T. Generating photo manipulation tutorials by demonstration. In *Proc. ACM SIGGRAPH'09 (2009)*, 66:1–66:9.
9. Grossman, T., and Fitzmaurice, G. Toolclips: An investigation of contextual video assistance for functionality understanding. In *Proc. ACM CHI'10 (2010)*, 1515–1524.
10. Grossman, T., Matejka, J., and Fitzmaurice, G. Chronicle: Capture, exploration, and playback of document workflow histories. In *Proc. ACM UIST'10 (2010)*, 143–152.
11. Harrison, S. M. A comparison of still, animated, or nonillustrated on-line help with written or spoken instructions in a graphical user interface. In *Proc. ACM CHI'95 (1995)*, 82–89.
12. Henze, N., Rukzio, E., and Boll, S. 100,000,000 taps: Analysis and improvement of touch performance in the large. In *Proc. ACM MobileHCI'11 (2011)*, 133–142.

13. Huang, J., and Twidale, M. B. Graphstract: Minimal graphical help for computers. In *Proc. ACM UIST'07 (2007)*, 203–212.

14. Kelleher, C., and Pausch, R. Stencils-based tutorials: Design and evaluation. In *Proc. ACM CHI'05 (2005)*, 541–550.

15. Knabe, K. Apple guide: A case study in user-aided design of online help. In *Proc. ACM CHI'95 (1995)*, 286–287.

16. Lafreniere, B., Grossman, T., and Fitzmaurice, G. Community enhanced tutorials: Improving tutorials with multiple demonstrations. In *Proc. ACM CHI'13 (2013)*, 1779–1788.

17. Nielsen: Average Number of Apps per Smartphone. `http://www.nielsen.com/us/en/newswire.html`.

18. Palaigeorgiou, G., and Despotakis, T. Known and unknown weaknesses in software animated demonstrations (screen-casts): A study in self-paced learning settings.

19. Palmiter, S., E. J., and Baggett, P. Animated demonstrations vs written instructions for learning procedural tasks: a preliminary investigation. 687701.

20. Palmiter, S., and Elkerton, J. Animated demonstrations for learning procedural computer-based tasks. 193216.

21. Pongnumkul, S., Dontcheva, M., Li, W., Wang, J., Bourdev, L., Avidan, S., and Cohen, M. F. Pause-and-play: Automatically linking screencast video tutorials with applications. In *Proc. ACM UIST'11 (2011)*, 135–144.

22. Android core gesture set. `http://developer.android.com/design/patterns/gestures.html`.

23. Weir, D., Rogers, S., Murray-Smith, R., and Löchtefeld, M. A user-specific machine learning approach for improving touch accuracy on mobile devices. In *Proc. ACM UIST'12 (2012)*, 465–476.

24. Wiedenbeck, S., and Zila, P. L. Hands-on practice in learning to use software: A comparison of exercise, exploration, and combined formats. 169–196.

25. Yeh, T., Chang, T.-H., and Miller, R. C. Sikuli: Using gui screenshots for search and automation. In *Proc. ACM UIST'09 (2009)*, 183–192.

26. Yeh, T., Chang, T.-H., Xie, B., Walsh, G., Watkins, I., Wongsuphasawat, K., Huang, M., Davis, L. S., and Bederson, B. B. Creating contextual help for guis using screenshots. In *Proc. ACM UIST'11 (2011)*, 145–154.

TaggedComments: Promoting and Integrating User Comments in Online Application Tutorials

Andrea Bunt[1], Patrick Dubois[1], Ben Lafreniere[2], Michael Terry[2], David Cormack[1]

Department of Computer Science[1]
University of Manitoba,
Winnipeg, Manitoba, Canada
bunt@cs.umanitoba.ca, umdubo26@cc.umanitoba.ca

Cheriton School of Computer Science[2]
University of Waterloo
Waterloo, Ontario, Canada
{bjlafren, mterry} @cs.uwaterloo.ca

ABSTRACT

User comments posted to popular online tutorials constitute a rich additional source of information for readers, yet current designs for displaying user comments on tutorial webpages do little to support their use. Instead, comments are separated from the tutorial content they reference and tend to be ordered according to post date. We propose and evaluate the TaggedComments system, a new approach to displaying comments that users post to online tutorials. Using tags supplied by commenters, TaggedComments seeks to enhance the role of user comments by 1) improving their visibility, 2) allowing users to personalize their use of the comments according to their particular information needs, and 3) providing direct access to potentially helpful comments from the tutorial content. A laboratory evaluation with 16 participants shows that, in comparison to the standard comment layout, TaggedComments significantly improves users' subjective impressions of comment utility when interacting with Photoshop tutorials.

Author Keywords

Web-based Tutorials; Feature-Rich Software; Tagging

ACM Classification Keywords

H.5.m. Information interfaces and presentation (e.g., HCI): Miscellaneous.

INTRODUCTION

Feature-rich software can be difficult for users to learn and use [9]. While most applications include in-application help pages, users' help-seeking practices typically involve turning to their favourite search engines [5], where they are directed to a large array of web-based tutorials. Given the now important role of online tutorials, there has been strong interest within the research community in improving the experience of interacting with tutorials (e.g., [2,6,16]).

An element of online tutorial design that has received little attention is the comments section. A recent analysis found that user comments on popular text- and image-based tutorials constitute a rich and diverse source of information [15]. For example, readers thank the author, write content-specific questions, provide answers to other users' questions, offer tips, and make requests for help on tasks that are extensions of the given tutorial, or are only tangentially related. Despite the utility of these comments, current comment display interfaces place the comments at the bottom of the tutorial and order them chronologically, doing little to leverage their value. This design is problematic when the reader seeks information likely found in the comments, as the next example illustrates.

Consider a user attempting to solve a problem that a previous user has faced with the tutorial. To find relevant comments, she would need to scroll to the bottom of the tutorial, and read through the chronologically-ordered list of comments, sifting through dozens of unrelated comments (e.g., social comments, requests for help on other tasks). If she does manage to find a relevant comment, she would then need to re-locate her place in the tutorial content before continuing the tutorial. This added cognitive load would be on top of any created by trying to follow and learn from the original tutorial content.

We present an alternative design for tutorial comment sections of online text- and image-based tutorials that allows users to tag their comments, and optionally pin them to particular locations in the tutorial content. Based on this design, we illustrate how TaggedComments 1) allows for *personalized comment use* by allowing tutorial authors and users to filter the comments according to their information needs; 2) provides *tutorial help in context*, by integrating comments with the tutorial content they reference; and 3) *highlights community feedback* to aid in the tutorial selection process and to assist with community building.

We also describe the results of a laboratory evaluation examining TaggedComments' impact on users' experience completing a Photoshop tutorial. Our results show that users' perceptions of comment utility were significantly higher with TaggedComments than with the standard comment organization. Our results also suggest that TaggedComments helped create a sense of community surrounding the tutorial.

CHI 2014, April 26 - May 01 2014, Toronto, ON, Canada

ACM 978-1-4503-2473-1/14/04...$15.00.
http://dx.doi.org/10.1145/2556288.2557118

RELATED WORK

Our coverage of related work focuses on approaches to improving application tutorials, alternative forms of crowdsourced help for feature-rich software, and comment tagging in support of other types of complex tasks.

Enhancing Application Tutorials

Prior work on enhancing application tutorials falls into three primary areas: automatically generating tutorials, supporting tutorial selection, and supporting use of tutorials. We discuss each area in turn.

Automatic Generation

One line of work has looked to improve application tutorials by making it easier for authors to create them. Much of this work has focused on automatically generating tutorials based on workflow demonstrations. For example, Grabler *et al.*'s system automatically generates text- and image-based tutorials through a combination of image-recognition techniques and author demonstration [8], whereas MixT adds short video demonstrations to tutorial instructions [2]. Taking a different approach, Chronicle provides interactive, annotated document histories [10].

Supporting Tutorial Selection

Work on helping users select between tutorials has primarily focused on highlighting the application commands used in the tutorial. Delta supports tutorial selection by displaying the commands used for each workflow (and their order) [14]. Ekstrand *et al.* use knowledge of the user's command history to augment Google's search results with the icons for the commands referenced within each result page [5]. In contrast to these approaches, TaggedComments uses a summary of the community's response to a tutorial to help guide selection.

Supporting Tutorial Completion

Lastly, there have been a number of approaches to designing more effective and engaging tutorials. Stencil-based tutorials scaffold the user's progress through the tutorial by highlighting the commands required at each step [13]. Sketch-Sketch Revolution guides the user through a drawing tutorial, providing feedback and stroke guidance [6]. TApps use automation to reduce the effort involved in completing a tutorial, while still allowing the user to experiment with parameter settings [17]. Recent work has also proposed gamifying tutorials as a mean of increasing tutorial engagement [19].

There has been little work on enhancing tutorials using feedback from its user community. One exception is FollowUs, which captures video demonstrations from users and makes them available on a step-by-step basis [16]. An evaluation showed that users experienced less frustration with FollowUs than they did in a control condition where only the author's demonstration was available.

Crowdsourced Help for Feature-Rich Software

By integrating user comments with the tutorial content they reference, TaggedComments enables a form of crowdsourced help. In this sense, our work shares similarities with systems like IP-QAT [22] and LemonAid [3], which provide in-application assistance for use of software through integrated, crowdsourced Q&A. In contrast to this prior work, tutorials are typically multi-step documents describing complete and often complex workflows. As a result, most tutorial comments are targeted toward the *tutorial*, the workflow it describes, and the use of the software to accomplish that workflow, as opposed to use of the software in general. Tutorials also include multiple stakeholders and interested parties that must be addressed in any design: the readers and the tutorial author.

Tagged Contributions to Support Complex Tasks

While we are not aware of other systems that support tutorial comment tagging, our approach is motivated by prior work demonstrating the value of tagged contributions in support of other complex tasks. CommentSpace, a collaborative visual analytics tool, encourages users to tag their comments as hypotheses, questions or to-do items [23]. An evaluation showed that when using CommentSpace, users generated higher-quality responses for a data synthesis task than when they performed the task using untagged user comments. Similarly, PathFinder supports citizen science by allowing individuals to annotate findings and comments [20]. An evaluation of Pathfinder showed that the increased organization afforded by tagged comments had a number of positive subjective impacts on users' perceived utility of the system.

COMMENT-ENHANCED TUTORIALS

In this section we describe our design for the TaggedComments system (see Figure 1), which aims to enhance the role of user comments within a tutorial. In designing the system, our goals were as follows:

- *Comment visibility:* User comments contain a wealth of information, but are typically deemphasized at the end of the tutorial. Our goal was to promote comments, increasing their visibility to other tutorial followers.
- *Comment personalization:* Comments contain diverse types of information, from bug fixes to words of praise for the author. Our goal was to allow both tutorial authors and consumers to personalize their use of comments according to their information needs.
- *Comment/content integration:* Many posted comments pertain directly to content of the tutorial, for example by pointing out problems with the instructions, providing quality assurance (e.g., testing with multiple versions) or suggesting a solution to an error-prone instruction. We wanted to reduce the separation between comments and their target tutorial content.

To accomplish these goals, the system asks users to both tag their comments and, when appropriate, to "pin" their comments next to the tutorial content to which their comments refer. The next section describes how users tag and pin their comments, followed by an illustration of how TaggedComments leverages this information.

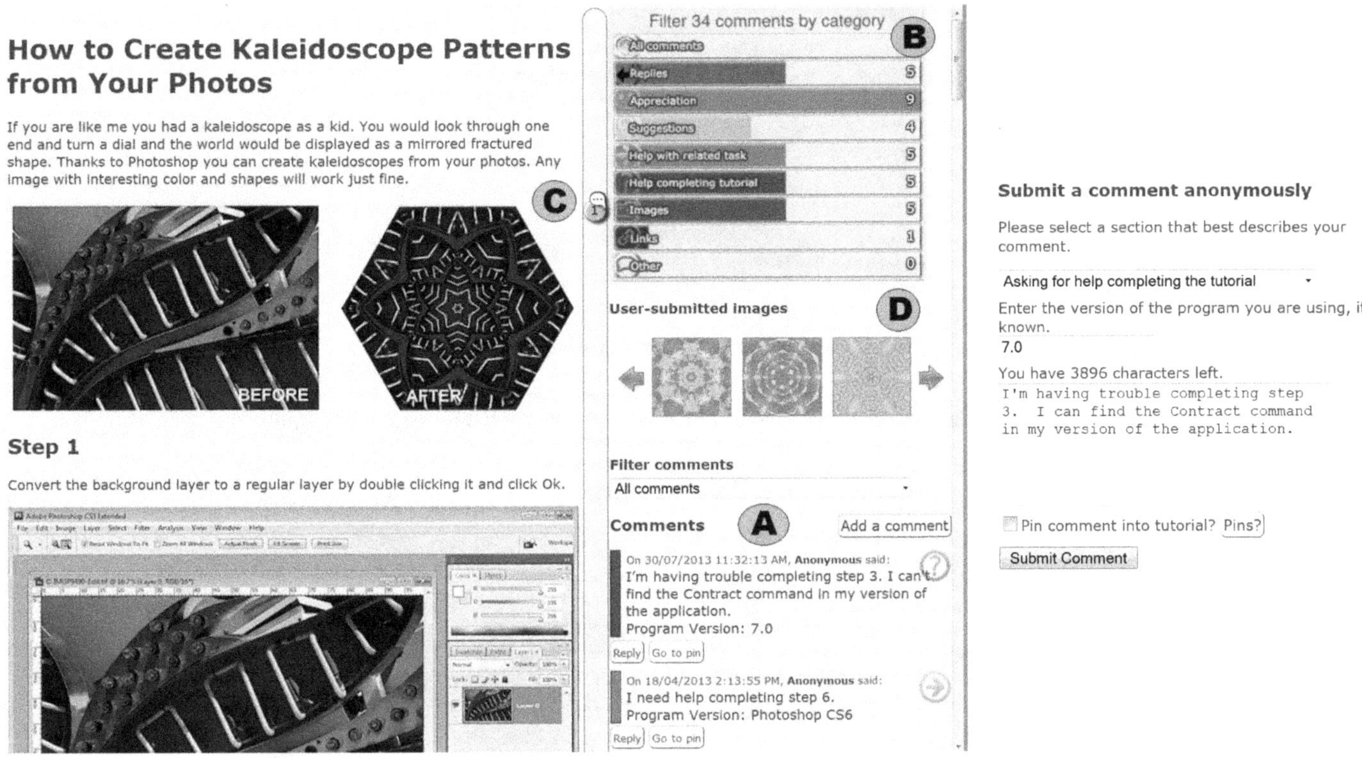

Figure 1: Left: The TaggedComments interface, consisting of: the comments section (A); a graph representation of community response (B); an area for users to "pin" comments to the tutorial content (C); an image carousel of user-submitted results (D). Tutorial source: http://digital-photography-school.com. Right: Submitting a comment.

Allowing Users to Tagging and Pinning Their Comments

TaggedComments augments the traditional tutorial comment posting interface with a request for information to categorize the comment. As shown in Figure 1(Right), when the user enters a comment, s/he is asked to categorize the comment using one of six pre-defined tags. These categories, based on Lafreniere *et al.*'s analysis of tutorial comments [15] and refined through pilot testing, are:

- *Appreciation:* praise or encouragement for the tutorial author.
- *Suggestion:* a suggestion or tip that may help with completing the tutorial.
- *Help completing the tutorial:* a request for help with some aspect of completing the tutorial.
- *Help with a related task:* a request for help with a task that goes beyond the focus of the tutorial.
- *Images*: a link to the results achieved by following the tutorial.
- *Link to related resource:* a link to resources that are helpful for completing the tutorial (e.g., brush sets).

We chose to focus on pre-defined tags for two reasons. First, prior work suggests that pre-defined tags offer a number of advantages over free-form tags (e.g., [1,7]). Second, using pre-defined tags allowed us to build dialogs into the system that prompt users for additional category-specific information to make the comments more valuable. For example, as shown in Figure 1(Right), when requesting help, the user is asked to specify which version of the application s/he is using. To accommodate emerging comment categories, users also have the option to enter their own free-form tags.

In addition to tagging their comments, users can choose to associate a comment with a position in the tutorial content by placing a "pin" on the vertical strip separating the tutorial content and the commenting interface (see Figure 1(C) and Figure 2(Right) for a closer view). Each pin displays the number of user comments associated with that location and a callout to help reinforce the association between the pin and the comments. We initially experimented with allowing users to pin the comments within the text itself (as opposed to alongside the content), but pilot testing revealed that readers had difficulty locating the pins with such tight embedding.

The addition of tags and pins to comments enables the system to highlight community feedback, support personalized comment use, and provide in-context community help. We describe each feature below.

Highlighting Community Feedback

To help users decide whether a tutorial is worth their time and effort, the system provides a succinct summary of community feedback based on the tags assigned by users. At the top of the TaggedComments sidebar on the tutorial page, feedback is displayed using a color-coded bar graph

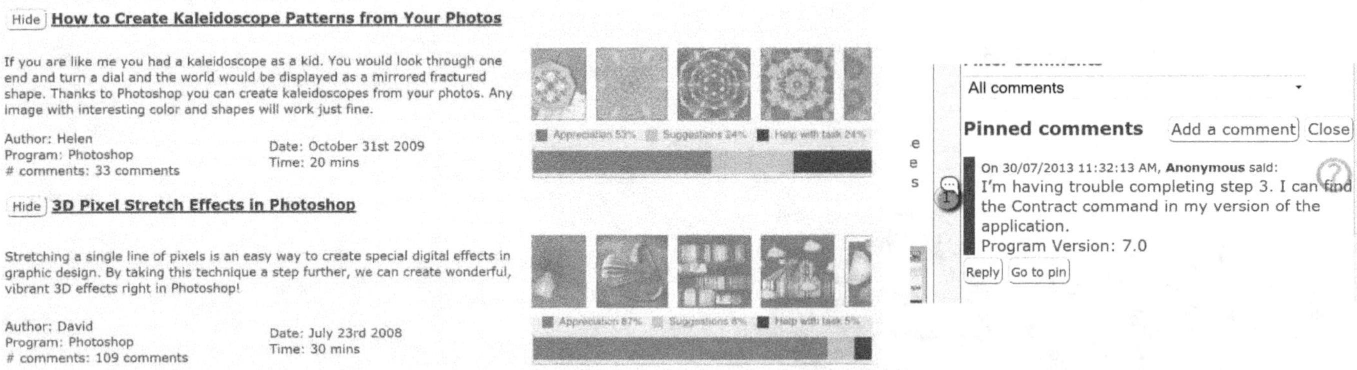

Figure 2: Left: Displaying comment prevalence for a set of tutorials. Right: Accessing a pinned comment.

depicting the prevalence of each comment type (Figure 1(B)). Below the graph, the system displays an image carousel of example images (or other content) that users have produced by following the tutorial (Figure 1(D)).

This information could also be embedded in search results, or a list of tutorials in a repository (Figure 2(Left)), to enable users to quickly evaluate a number of potential tutorials based on the percentage of appreciation comments, suggestions, and requests for help associated with each. This kind of summary mechanism captures community response to the tutorial and could complement command-oriented approaches (e.g., [14]) for helping users to select between tutorials.

In addition to guiding tutorial selection, highlighting community feedback reinforces the notion of the tutorial as a "community meeting place" [15] and may encourage users to post. There is also evidence that the act of tagging can encourage participation and create a greater sense of community [18].

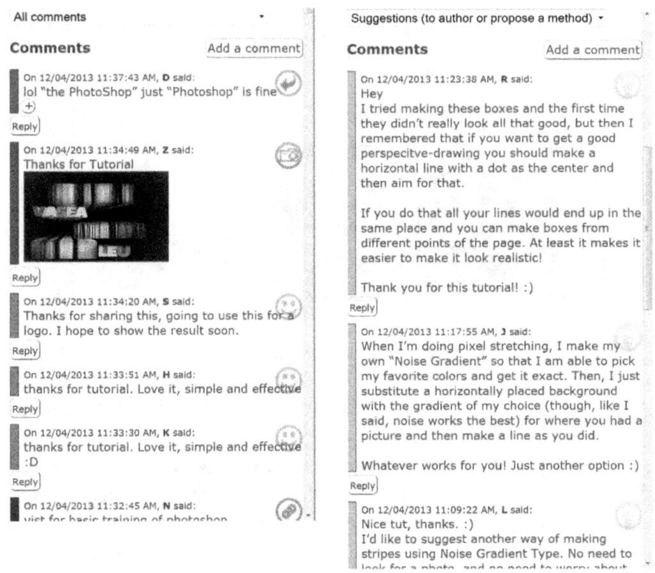

Figure 3: All comments colour-coded according to category (Right) and filtered to display only "Suggestions" (Left).

Personalized Comment Use

To enable users to personalize the comment display to their particular information needs, TaggedComments includes features to filter and organize comments. For example, a tutorial author might want to look only at requests for help when attempting to improve a tutorial, or requests for help on related tasks when planning to author a new tutorial. Tutorial readers, on the other hand, might wish to focus only on suggestions and tips. With TaggedComments, users can filter comments by clicking on the corresponding label in the bar graph or by selecting a category from the drop down menu. Figure 3 shows an example of both an original set of comments and those filtered according to the "Suggestions" tag. For this particular tutorial, tagged by us for illustration, there are 6 suggestion comments buried within 68 social comments. This is a typical ratio for tutorials with comments on the web [15].

In-Context Community Help

Finally, pinned comments enable users to view content-related comments in context, alongside the content they are referencing. For example, when in the process of performing a tutorial, users can view any difficulties other tutorial users have experienced at the current step, and any suggestions for overcoming difficulties. Clicking on a pin in the vertical strip next to the tutorial brings the user to the associated comment(s) as shown in Figure 2(Right). Users can also navigate to pins from the comments section using "Go to Pin" buttons (see the comment in Figure 2, Right).

STUDY

We conducted a laboratory study comparing TaggedComments to a control condition designed to emulate existing tutorial comment systems. The goal of our study was to see how users would react to TaggedComments' interface, and to understand how its features would change how users referred to comments while completing tutorials. We chose Adobe Photoshop, a feature-rich application with one of the widest showings of web-based tutorials, as our target application.

In the TaggedComments condition, participants completed a Photoshop tutorial with comments marked up and dis-

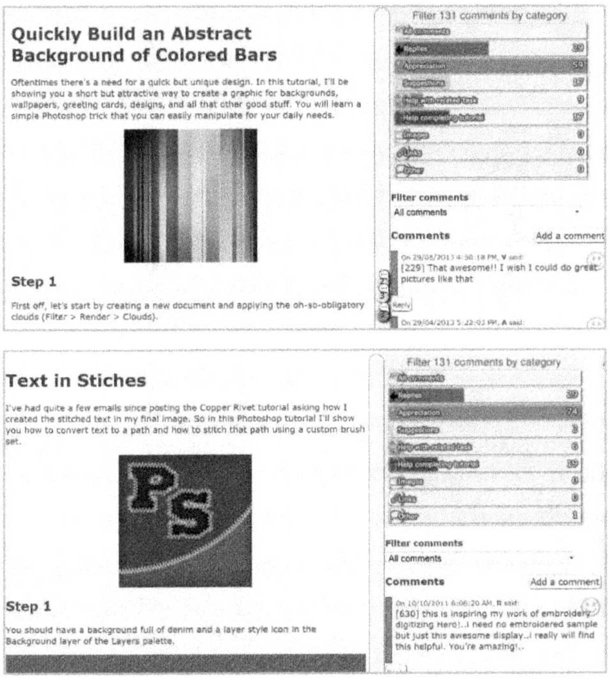

Figure 4: The two study tutorials displayed using the TaggedComments interface: the Background tutorial (Top) and the Stitches tutorial (Bottom).

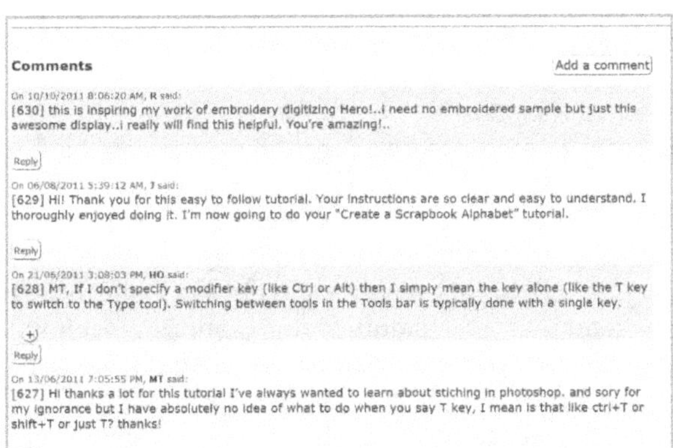

Figure 5: Default condition: Comments are at the bottom of the tutorial content and ordered reverse chronologically.

played using the system as described above (and shown in Figure 4). In the Default condition, participants completed a Photoshop tutorial with comments displayed below the tutorial content in reverse chronological order by posting date (Figure 5). This is the standard design for comment systems on web-based tutorials.

Participants

We recruited 16 volunteers (12 male, 4 female), ages 18-40 via signs posted around a university campus. Participants were pre-screened to ensure that they had some experience using Photoshop. Participants had a range of Photoshop experience levels; four participants indicating using the software multiple times per week, six used it weekly, five used it monthly, and one yearly. Participants were compensated with a $15 honorarium.

	Background	*Stitches*
Tutorial Source	psd.tutsplus.com	pshero.com
Original Steps	11	16
Original Comments	190	128
Experiment Steps	8	8
Experiment Comments	131 (41 content-specific)	131 (41 content-specific)

Table 1: Properties of the two study tutorials.

Tutorials

Our study followed a within-subjects design, with each participant attempting two different text- and image-based tutorials, one per condition. We chose a within-subjects design to elicit comparative statements and to account for individual variability (e.g., owing to Photoshop expertise). To increase external validity, we used tutorials from the web and the user comments already posted on them as a starting point for the tutorials used in the study.

In selecting tutorials from the web, we had three primary criteria. First, we wanted each tutorial to include a reasonable number of comments, some of which could be helpful in completing the tutorial. Second, we wanted two tutorials of similar length and complexity. Finally, we wanted tutorials for tasks likely to be achievable by participants with moderate levels of Photoshop expertise, to ensure access to a sufficiently wide participant pool.

The two tutorials selected are shown in Figure 4 and summaries of their characteristics are listed in Table 1. The *Background* task involved creating an abstract background and the *Stitches* task involved creating a stitches effect around the borders of text. As can be seen in Table 1, we modified the tutorials to balance their length, and to keep them feasible to complete within a 90-minute study session. These modifications consisted of removing steps from the beginning (i.e., providing the participant with a more advanced starting point) and end of the tutorials.

Both tutorials included two steps that were difficult to complete by following the instructions as written, but for which there was helpful advice contained in the user comments. For example, in Step 3 of the Background tutorial, the author suggests using Motion Blur to turn a noisy image into a series of crisp vertical bars. This effect, however, does not work properly with all canvas sizes (including the size that our participants started with). Below are two comments pertaining to this issue, a request for help and a reply with a suggestion:

> *Photoshop CS4 creates that stripe pattern, but there is always a strange cloud in the middle.*

If you get a blurry centre of the image apply the motion blur 4-6 more times. Then increase the contrast to 100% and you should get a decent result.

Following the tip suggested in the comment above would allow the user to complete Step 3 properly. Each tutorial included an additional step where comments could potentially be helpful (e.g., if users deviated from the author's recommend path) but were not as critical.

While we initially intended to use only original user comments, we found that there were more helpful comments on the Background tutorial than there were on the Stitches tutorial. To compensate, we created and added 15 content-specific comments (a mix of questions, comments and tips) to the Stitches tutorial, using similar terminology and commenting styles as the original comments. We then selectively removed non-content related comments from both tutorials to balance the number of comments on each tutorial and the percentage of comments pertaining to tutorial content. Finally, we manually added a tag to each comment, using the tagging scheme described earlier in the paper.

Procedure

After completing a demographics questionnaire, participants completed the two tutorials described Table 1, one with TaggedComments, and one with the Default interface. Interface and task order were fully counterbalanced across participants.

Prior to beginning each tutorial, participants were given a brief demonstration of the interface to be used in that condition. While completing the tutorial, we asked participants to write down the three-digit code that we assigned to each tutorial comment for any comment that they tried to use to help complete the tutorial. Participants were given 30 minutes to complete each tutorial.

After completing each tutorial, participants completed the NASA Task-Load Index (TLX), which measures perceived mental workload [11]. In addition to the six NASA TLX questions, we asked two questions to gauge participants perceptions of the comments in that condition (using the same 20-point scale as the TLX): 1) "Comment Helpfulness: How much did the comments help you complete the task?" and 2) "Ease of Finding Comments: How easy was it to find helpful comments?"

At the end of the session, participants completed a post-session questionnaire and participated in a short semi-structured interview. Each session lasted approximately 90 minutes.

Data were captured via log files, videotape and audiotape. The videotape and audiotape recordings were later coded and transcribed for analysis purposes.

The experiment was run on a desktop computer with 12 GB of RAM and a 21-inch monitor with 1920×1080 resolution. The TaggedComments interface was implemented using JavaScript.

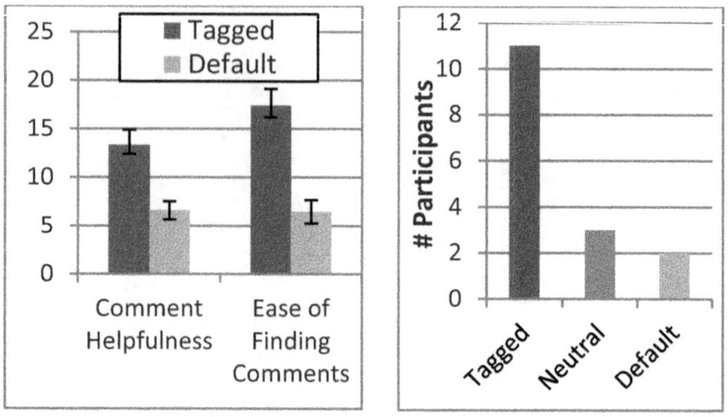

Figure 6: Left: Subjective impressions of comment utility measured after each condition (measured on a 20-point scale). Right: Participants' stated preference for the two interfaces.

Results

We analyzed quantitative data using a repeated-measures ANOVA with condition (TaggedComments vs. Default) as the within-subjects factor. We did not find significant effects or interactions for the order of the conditions or tasks, so we do not discuss these in our analysis below. In all figures, error bars show standard error.

We begin by describing the impact of the two interfaces on participants' subjective impressions of comment utility and their ability to find comments, followed by their impact on task performance and comment use.

Subjective Response

Responses to our questions regarding comment helpfulness, and participants' ability to find comments both clearly favoured TaggedComments (Figure 6, Left). On both measures, the mean values for TaggedComments were more than double those for Default, and both differences were found to be significant (Comment Helpfulness: TaggedComments 13.3, s.e. 1.6 vs. Default 6.6, s.e. 1.7, $F_{1,14} = 12.350$, $p = .003$, $\eta^2 = .469$; Ease of Finding Comments: TaggedComments 17.4, s.e. 0.9 vs. Default 6.5, s.e. 1.2, $F_{1,12} = 35.594$, $p < .001$, $\eta^2 = .656$).[1]

The majority of participants also expressed a preference for the TaggedComments system in a post-study questionnaire, with 11 participants preferring TaggedComments, 2 preferring the Default interface and 3 expressing no preference. This difference was found to be significant according a chi-squared test (χ^2=*9.125.0, p = .01)*.

Despite this clear difference in subjective preference, we did not find a difference in perceived mental workload as measured by the NASA TLX, either overall ($F_{1,15} = 0.224$, $p = .634$, $\eta^2 = .015$) or on any of the individual subscales.

[1] After not accessing comments, some participants responded "N/A" (1 for "Comment Helpfulness" and 3 for "Ease of Finding Comments").

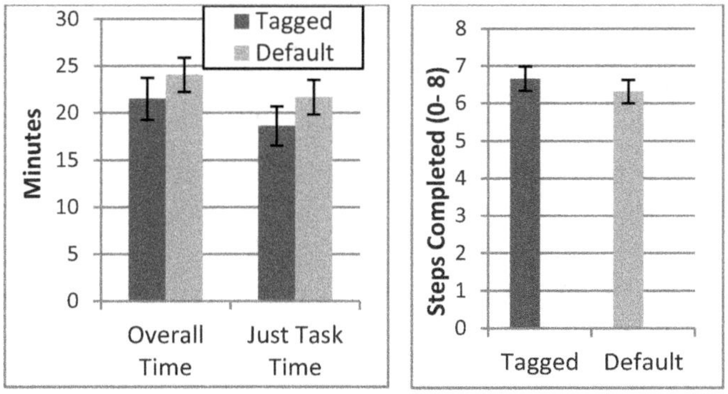

Figure 7: Left: Task time per condition overall and removing the time spent in the comments section. Right: The number of tutorial steps completed per condition.

	Tagged mean (s.e.)	**Default** mean (s.e.)	$F_{1,15}$	p	η^2
Visits	7.7 (1.5)	4.8 (1.7)	1.493	0.241	0.091
Time (min)	2:52 (0:32)	2:24 (0:34)	0.434	0.520	0.34
Read	10.4 (2.0)	5.8 (1.8)	2.586	0.129	0.147
Used	2.3 (0.4)	1.3 (0.4)	2.00	0.178	0.118

Table 2: Comment use by interface.

Task Performance

We analyzed three measures of task performance: overall time spent completing the tutorial, time spent on the tutorial not including time spent in the comments section, and task completeness. We determined time spent in the comment section from the video by using mouse position as a proxy for gaze, a technique validated in prior work [12].

Figure 7 (Left) displays the impact of condition on task time. On average, participants were faster overall with TaggedComments (21min 30s, s.e. 2min 14s) than with Default (24min 30s, s.e. 2min 5s), however, this difference was not significance ($F_{1,15}$ = 1.002, p = .333, η^2 = .063). Considering only time spent working in the tutorial, participants spent less time on average with TaggedComments (18min 40s, s.e. 1min 50) than with Default (21mins 40s, s.e. 1min 50s), but this difference also did not reach significance ($F_{1,15}$ = 1.957, p = .18, η^2 = .16). Participants completed roughly the same numbers of steps in each condition (Tagged: 6.7 steps, s.e. 0.3; Default: 6.3 steps, s.e. 0.3; $F_{1,15}$ = 1.634, p = .221, η^2 = .098).

The lack of significant performance differences between the two conditions indicates that, at a minimum, promoting user comments did not interfere with participants' abilities to complete the tutorials. Given the large variability in completion times, however, it is also possible that we might start to see impacts of TaggedComments on performance with a larger number of participants.

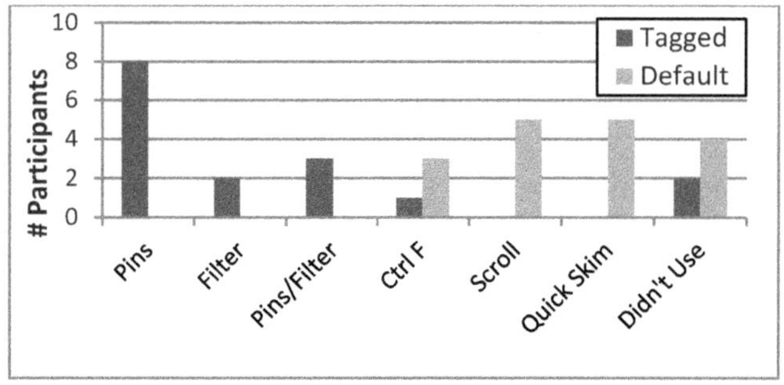

Figure 8: Strategies for finding relevant comments.

Comment Use

Using the video recordings and the log files, we analyzed the extent to which participants were relying on the comments in the two conditions and the strategies that they used to search through the comments.

Table 2 displays the following: the number of visits to the comment section (Visits), the total time spent in the comment section (Time), the number of comments participants appeared to read (Read), and the number of comments that participants attempted to apply to their task (Used). While there are no significant differences between the two conditions, the data suggest two possible trends. First, TaggedComments might have encouraged people to read through more comments than the Default interface. Second, participants might have tried to apply a larger number of comments to their task with TaggedComments than with Default. As with the impact of TaggedComments on task performance, further data would be needed to verify these trends.

Figure 8 summarizes the different strategies that participants used to find comments in the two interfaces. With TaggedComments, 14/16 participants visited the comments section. Participants' predominant strategy was to use the pins (8/14); however, filtering was also used (5/14). With the Default interface, only 7/16 participants made meaningful use of the comment section, with the remaining nine participants either not visiting the comments at all or scrolling through the comments quickly. The 7 participants who did look at the comments did so by either systematically scrolling through them or attempting to locate relevant comments using keyword search via Ctrl-F.

The above results suggest that a larger number of participants made a concerted effort to use comments as an information source when using TaggedComments than with the Default interface. That scrolling and quickly skimming comments were not used extensively also indicates that the features offered by TaggedComments provide participants with a viable alternative strategy for making use of comment data.

Participant Attitudes Towards TaggedComments

In the interviews, most participants expressed enthusiasm for the TaggedComments interface. For example, two participants suggested that they would like to see the TaggedComments interface more widely adopted:

> *I'd like to see that more often -- I like that. I've never really thought about the old way until seeing that and it's like yeah -- the old way could use some work. [P10]*

> *It seems really good. I would actually like to see that adopted more in tutorials. [P16]*

Conversely, with the default design, a number of participants felt that the comments were close to unusable, as the following quote illustrates:

> *In the [Default interface] the comments were almost useless. [...] I thought that going through the comments [with the Default interface] would consume too much time. I [would] try to do the instructions two or three times first. [P5]*

Comment/Integration: The above quotes were part of a larger theme of appreciation for the greater integration of comments and content that TaggedComments provides, which was seen to provide two complementary benefits. The first was the ability to retrieve relevant help in context:

> *With the pinned comments, it was not like I had to search through all of the comments, because I could just pick the comment [...] It was very useful for me. [P6]*

> *Because usually if you are looking through the comments for help you are going to be looking for a certain step, not generic -- you're not looking for the generic feedback, you are looking for one thing that someone is commenting on. [P10]*

Participants also liked being able to interact with the tutorial content and the comments simultaneously:

> *[I] liked that you could scroll in the comments without scrolling in the tutorial itself, so that you could see both at the same time, which was nice. [P11]*

> *I like how it is side-by-side with the tutorial so I don't have to be scrolling down, scrolling back up -- it gets annoying. [P15]*

Personalized Comment Use: Participants valued the ability to filter the information according to their needs either explicitly or using the colours (or icons) as visual guides. As expected given the experimental tasks, participants wanted to focus on the content-specific comments and to ignore social comments intended for the author of the tutorial:

> *I think that it's good that you differentiate 'appreciations' [from] 'how to do it'. In the [Default interface] there were too many comments about just appreciations, just thanking the author [...] You go through many comments thanking the author of tutorial and you cannot actually find the answer to what you are looking for [P2]*

> *The colour coding makes it easy to tell which ones are actually going to be useful. Like the little 'yay thumbs up' stuff -- much easier when you can just skip over that. [P16]*

Given that the percentage of appreciation comments in the tutorials we selected is representative of that in tutorials with comments on the web, this desire to isolate content-pertinent comments is likely to extend beyond these particular tutorials.

Visual Complexity: While most interview comments were in favour of the TaggedComments' design, two participants spoke to the additional visual complexity to the tutorial, though in both cases this was not cited as a major issue:

> *It is a little bit busier, so there's a lot more on your screen. [P10]*

> *It was a little distracting, but maybe not that much. [P14]*

It may be possible to adjust the design of the system to present relevant information more subtly; however, any design that promotes and integrates user comments will inevitably add some visual complexity.

Promoting a Sense of Community

To explore TaggedComments' potential role in promoting a sense of community surrounding the tutorial, we asked participants in the interviews to reflect on if and how the design might influence their willingness to post comments.

Participants spoke to two reasons for an increased willingness to contribute. The first was a desire to help others:

> *I think [I would post comments] because it would help others the way it helped me -- they would be able to learn the things they don't know and they won't have to use a lot of effort to learn that, it will be categorized and organized [P5]*

One participant also felt his posts would be more likely to be seen and responded to:

> *I would probably feel that the odds of my question getting answered relative to what I'm asking would be higher. With the other format, it lends itself more to people saying 'oh well you should read the question better'. Whereas this one, I feel like -- and it might just be my perception -- because it is linking much more closely and much more organized, if people were actually trying to help, they would be more directed to do so. [P16]*

In both cases, the manner in which TaggedComments' organizes contributions appears to be helping participants view user comments as a legitimate help resource, one that they are interested in contributing to.

Not all participants, however, felt that TaggedComments would encourage them to post comments. Two participants indicated that they often work with old tutorials and feel that there is little chance that their posts will be seen or responded to:

> *One of the big factors -- it is so silly -- but the comments are just so old. So of course there is nobody who is contributing anymore to the tutorial that's been there for 5 years on-line and nobody ever looks there or needs help anymore. [P11]*

> *Generally the tutorials that I'm looking at are years old so people don't really respond back. [P15]*

These comments show that users are picking up a sense of how active the user community around a tutorial is, and that this is influencing their choice of whether or not to contribute. This is encouraging for the general idea of improved systems for commenting and creating a sense of community around tutorials, and suggests that an indicator of the level of community activity around a tutorial might be a useful addition to TaggedComments' interface.

DISCUSSION

In our study, TaggedComments had a positive impact on users' subjective experience of interacting with tutorial comments. Participants found comments significantly more helpful and easier to find with the TaggedComments interface, and they expressed a strong preference for its design over the status quo. These positive subjective impacts are encouraging on a number of fronts. Our interview data suggests that improved perception of comment utility might increase community participation, which could improve the quality of community help over time. Designs that display community feedback in a more attractive, accessible manner could also make completing tutorials more compelling, motivating more users to expand their skill sets.

Impact on Performance

While our study results suggest that TaggedComments improved the subjective experience of completing tutorials, we did not find a significant improvement in task performance. We believe that there are several reasons why this may have been the case.

First, conducting our study on the granularity of entire tutorials allowed us to investigate participants' experience of using TaggedComments in a realistic setting, but it also introduced noise into our performance measures. For example, some participants had trouble completing tutorial steps leading up to those that were intended to be challenging, and for which useful comments existed. When participants did reach these steps, some proceeded with incorrect results or skipped over the step entirely. A more tightly controlled study could address these issues by asking participants to complete a series of individual tutorial steps presented in isolation. This would eliminate the impact of difficulties leading up to a step.

Second, not all participants had sufficient Photoshop skills to complete the tutorials. As a result, some participants were able to find a tip in the comments, but did not have the necessary skills to apply it successfully. While it is difficult to accurately gauge knowledge of complex software such as Photoshop, we could try using a pre-screening sample task in place of self-reports of expertise.

Finally, our study did not hide the fact that tutorial comments were potentially useful, and that comment use was a feature being studied. This allowed us to elicit comparisons of the two systems from participants, but it may have also diminished the effect of a feature of TaggedComments -- that it reveals to users that comments contain valuable information. We suspect that more participants would have disregarded comments entirely in the control condition were they not aware that we were interested in measuring their use. This could be tested using a between-subjects study design, where the role of comments is not revealed to participants.

Generalizability

While we evaluated TaggedComments as applied to Photoshop tutorials, there are a number of aspects of the design of the system and findings from the evaluation that are likely to generalize beyond this particular application. First, Photoshop tutorials follow a format that is typical of many text/image-based tutorials for software use (i.e., step-by-step instructions followed by comments). The one caveat is that TaggedComments' image-carousel feature would need to be modified to provide previews for other media, such as audio. If one considers *video-based* tutorials, the notions of promoting, personalizing and integrating comments are also applicable, and there are existing analogues to pinning comments for time-based media. For example, SoundCloud provides facilities for users to post comments at particular points of time for streaming audio files, with these comments visible within the timeline. Beyond tutorials, we also envision applications of TaggedComments to other forms of long-form authored content, such as blog posts and news articles.

Community Participation

An open question with respect to the TaggedComments' design is whether users would be willing to tag their comments. While only a deployment could provide a definitive answer, we believe there are reasons to be optimistic. Our interviews suggest that users see value in tagging both for their own benefit and that of the community, and there are precedents in online communities that people are willing to annotate their content if they see value in doing so (e.g. YouTube video posters tagging with keywords). Wikipedia and StackOverflow [21] provide two further examples of communities where users align with cultural norms surrounding contribution. One could also imagine designs that explicitly reward tagging, such as promoting only tagged comments (increasing the likelihood of them receiving a response), or delaying the appearance of non-tagged comments for a certain period of time. Finally, one could explore supplementing user-supplied tags with automatically generated ones, following work on automatically identifying recipe refinements within user comments [4].

Alternative Models of Community Refinement

In a sense, TaggedComments allows people to become co-authors of a tutorial after the fact, while leaving the original tutorial content unchanged. This represents an interesting alternative to community refinement via wiki-style interfaces, where content continually evolves. A system like TaggedComments preserves author control and recognition, while still enabling the community to tweak and improve the content. This is particularly important in tutorials for content-generation applications such as Photoshop, where authors often use tutorials as a platform to demonstrate their skills and abilities. TaggedComments allows individuals to contribute to improving a tutorial's content in an organized manner, while allowing the tutorial author to maintain control over his/her work.

SUMMARY AND FUTURE WORK

TaggedComments introduces a novel way of incorporating community feedback within a tutorial. In TaggedComments, user comments are highly visible, tightly integrated with the tutorial content, and personalizable to the individual needs of both tutorial followers and authors. Our study revealed that this design led to greater perceived comment utility and was preferred to the status quo. Many users also responded positively to the increased sense of community surrounding the tutorial.

As future work, we plan to evaluate TaggedComments' role in aiding tutorial selection, as well its impact on user commenting quality and quantity. We are also interested in understanding the utility of the design from the tutorial author's perspective, including whether or not it helps focus their efforts, and their attitudes towards this model of community refinement. Finally, we intend to investigate the generalizability of the design and findings to other types of tutorials and long-form content.

ACKNOWLEDGEMENTS

This work was supported by the GRAND Network Centre of Excellence and the Natural Sciences and Engineering Research Council (NSERC).

REFERENCES

1. Chi, E.H. and Mytkowicz, T. Understanding the efficiency of social tagging systems using information theory categories and subject descriptors. In *Proc. HT*, (2008), 81–88.
2. Chi, P.P., Ahn, S., Ren, A., Dontcheva, M., Li, W., and Hartmann, B. MixT: Automatic generation of step-by-step mixed media tutorials. In *Proc. UIST*, (2012), 93–102.
3. Chilana, P.K., Ko, A.J., and Wobbrock, J.O. LemonAid: Selection-based crowdsourced contextual help for Web applications. In *Proc. CHI*, (2012), 1549–1558.
4. Druck, G. and Pang, B. Spice it up? Mining refinements to online instructions from user generated content. In *Proc. ACL*, (2012), 545–553.
5. Ekstrand, M., Li, W., Grossman, T., Matejka, J., and Fitzmaurice, G. Searching for software learning resources using application context. In *Proc. UIST*, (2011), 195–204.
6. Fernquist, J., Grossman, T., and Fitzmaurice, G. Sketch-Sketch Revolution: An engaging tutorial system for guided sketching and application learning. In *Proc. UIST*, (2011), 373–382.
7. Golder, S.A. and Huberman, B.A. Usage patterns of collaborative tagging systems. *Journal of Information Science 32*, 2 (2006), 198–208.
8. Grabler, F., Agrawala, M., and Erato, J.S.T. Generating photo manipulation tutorials by demonstration. In *Proc. SIGGRAPH*, (2009), 1–9.
9. Grossman, T., Fitzmaurice, G., and Attar, R. A survey of software learnability: Metrics, methodologies and guidelines. In *Proc. CHI*, (2009), 649–658.
10. Grossman, T., Matejka, J., and Fitzmaurice, G. Chronicle: Capture, exploration, and playback of document workflow histories. In *Proc. CHI*, (2010), 143–152.
11. Hart, S.G., California, M.F., and Staveland, L.E. Development of NASA-TLX (Task Load Index): Results of empirical and theoretical research. In P. Hancock and N. Meshkati, eds., *Human Mental Workload*. 1988, 139–183.
12. Huang, J., White, R.W., and Dumais, S. No clicks, no problem: Using cursor movements to understand and improve search. In *Proc. CHI*, (2011), 1225–1234.
13. Kelleher, C. and Pausch, R. Stencils-based tutorials: Design and evaluation. In *Proc. CHI*, (2005), 541–550.
14. Kong, N., Grossman, T., Hartmann, B., Fitzmaurice, G., and Agrawala, M. Delta: A tool for representing and comparing workflows. In *Proc. CHI*, (2012), 1027–1036.
15. Lafreniere, B., Bunt, A., Lount, M., and Terry, M. Understanding the roles and uses of Web tutorials. In *Proc. ICWSM*, (2013), 303–310.
16. Lafreniere, B., Grossman, T., and Fitzmaurice, G. Community enhanced tutorials: Improving tutorials with multiple demonstrations. In *Proc. CHI*, (2013), 1779–1788.
17. Laput, G., Adar, E., Arbor, A., Dontcheva, M., and Li, W. Tutorial-based interfaces for Cloud-enabled applications. In *Proc. UIST*, (2012), 113–122.
18. Lee, K.J. What goes around comes around: An analysis of del.icio.us as social space. In *Proc. CSCW*, (2006), 191–194.
19. Li, W., Grossman, T., and Fitzmaurice, G. GamiCAD: A gamified tutorial system for first time AutoCAD users. In *Proc. UIST*, (2012), 103–112.
20. Luther, K., Counts, S., Stecher, K.B., Hoff, A., and Johns, P. Pathfinder: An online collaboration environment for citizen scientists. In *Proc. CHI*, (2009), 239–248.
21. Mamykina, L., Manoim, B., Mittal, M., Hripcsak, G., and Hartmann, B. Design lessons from the fastest Q&A site in the west. In *Proc. CHI*, (2011), 2857 – 2866.
22. Matejka, J., Grossman, T., and Fitzmaurice, G. IP-QAT: In-product questions, answers & tips. In *Proc. UIST*, (2011), 175–184.
23. Willett, W., Heer, J., Hellerstein, J.M., and Agrawala, M. CommentSpace: Structured support for collaborative visual analysis. In *Proc. CHI*, (2011), 3131–3140.

A Smartphone-based Sensing Platform to Model Aggressive Driving Behaviors

Jin-Hyuk Hong, Ben Margines, Anind K. Dey
Human-Computer Interaction Institute, Carnegie Mellon University
{hjinh7, benjamin.margines}@gmail.com, anind@cs.cmu.edu

ABSTRACT
Driving aggressively increases the risk of accidents. Assessing a person's driving style is a useful way to guide aggressive drivers toward having safer driving behaviors. A number of studies have investigated driving style, but they often rely on the use of self-reports or simulators, which are not suitable for the real-time, continuous, automated assessment and feedback on the road. In order to understand and model aggressive driving style, we construct an in-vehicle sensing platform that uses a smartphone instead of using heavyweight, expensive systems. Utilizing additional cheap sensors, our sensing platform can collect useful information about vehicle movement, maneuvering and steering wheel movement. We use this data and apply machine learning to build a driver model that evaluates drivers' driving styles based on a number of driving-related features. From a naturalistic data collection from 22 drivers for 3 weeks, we analyzed the characteristics of drivers who have an aggressive driving style. Our model classified those drivers with an accuracy of 90.5% (violation-class) and 81% (questionnaire-class). We describe how, in future work, our model can be used to provide real-time feedback to drivers using only their current smartphone.

Author Keywords
Driving assessment, smartphone, in-vehicle sensing platform

ACM Classification Keywords
H.5.m. Information interfaces and presentation (e.g., HCI): Miscellaneous.

INTRODUCTION
Driving is an integral part of many peoples' lives, as it allows them to travel faster and further to accomplish more. It even provides for an improved quality of life [29]. However, it also exposes individuals to the risk of being involved in harmful and even fatal accidents [5, 8]. Not only are these accidents injurious to the people involved, but also they are expensive: accident-related costs in 2011 in the US were estimated to be $299.5 billion [6]. Road traffic accidents are directly attributable to human behavior because they are related to vehicle control and sensitive to the complex driving environment (*e.g.*, weather, traffic) [7, 30]. Significant research has been performed to understand the relationship between human behavior and road safety, for example, asking which behavioral factors can indicate 'good' or 'bad' driving, or which behavioral factors might convey the risk that a driver poses to others [3,18].

Aggressive driving, a particular type of driving style, has long been studied due to its strong correlation with accidents and traffic safety hazards: by one estimate, it was influential in causing the majority of accidents in the United States from 2003 to 2007. [1]. This style of driving refers to a behavior that deliberately or likely increases the risk of collision and is motivated by impatience, annoyance, hostility and/or an attempt to save time [35]. A similar definition by the NHTSA refers to aggressive driving as that which "directly affects other road users by placing them in unnecessary danger" [9]. More specifically, it may involve a variety of behaviors such as excessive speeding, tailgating, weaving in and out of traffic, and improper lane changes [17, 35]. Aggressive driving is a major contributing factor to road accidents and is now perceived as being one of the most significant problems of modern day driving [33].

By understanding an individual's driving style and providing feedback, he or she may change driving styles to reduce aggressive driving. For example, a monitoring system may reduce aggressive driving through voluntary recommendations (*e.g.*, safety belt use [28]) or involuntary controls (*e.g.*, speed governor [15]). Drivers can also manage situational and environmental factors that may motivate or stimulate them to drive more aggressively. To support this feedback, we need an automated method for assessing driving style in real-time.

Many approaches have been used to understand and assess one's driving style, and in-vehicle sensing technology, which yields more objective measures of driving style, has shown its potential for real-time, continuous, automated assessment and feedback on the road [5, 18, 36]. From cameras to an OBD2 connector (on-board diagnostic system that collects variables from the car computer, such as engine RPM and vehicle speed), a number of in-vehicle sensing platforms have been developed to collect a variety of information on the driver, the vehicle and their driving environment [2, 14]. However, because the systems are

CHI 2014, April 26–May 1, 2014, Toronto, Ontario, Canada.

http://dx.doi.org/10.1145/2556288.2557321

typically cost thousands of dollars, most consumers are not able to afford to equip their cars, limiting the overall applicability to the general public. We are interested in a solution that is accessible to all drivers.

To meet this need, we propose to model aggressive driving by: 1) constructing a lightweight in-vehicle sensing platform based on drivers' own smartphones to provide an objective measurement of driving style, 2) using a machine learning (ML) technique with a number of driving-related features for an automated assessment of driving style, and 3) evaluating our approach with real-life daily driving data. In the future, such models can be used to identify aggressive driving in real time and to provide feedback to the driver to encourage a change in driving style.

Using our lightweight sensor platform, we collected naturalistic driving data from 22 participants for three weeks and were able to differentiate between aggressive and non-aggressive driving styles. To assess driving style, driver models are built using a machine learning technique and a number of sensor-based driving features. These models identify drivers who have an aggressive driving style with an accuracy of 90.5% (violation-class) and 81% (questionnaire-class). We discuss the limitations of our system, describe how it can support driving feedback, and identify opportunities for future work.

ASSESSMENT OF DRIVING STYLE

The ability to provide feedback to drivers about their driving style, especially if it is aggressive, can help drivers to become more aware of and improve their behavior. This would likely reduce the probability of poor driving outcomes. Because of this potential, a number of different assessment approaches have been investigated, including questionnaires [32], simulated driving environments [20], in-vehicle sensing technology [31], and expert-based examinations [26]. Figure 1 ranks these assessment methods along the dimensions of cost and how easily they can be applied to evaluations of real-world driving.

Relevant *questionnaires* have been created that ask about a driver's personality and driving styles to understand his risk of having an accident [4, 7, 33, 38]. The questionnaires are simple and inexpensive to administer. Those targeted toward assessing aggressive driving include the Aggressive Driving Behavior Scale [17], the Driving Vengeance Questionnaire [37], the Driving Anger Scale [11], and the Driving Anger Expression Inventory [12]. These questionnaires have allowed for great progress in studying driving style and driver aggression [10]. Of these, the most popular questionnaire is the Manchester Driving Behavior Questionnaire (DBQ). The DBQ was initially developed to investigate whether a questionnaire could distinguish between driving errors and driving violations; the authors that three factors could explain 33% of the variance in aggressive driving - violations, hazardous errors, and nonhazardous errors [32].

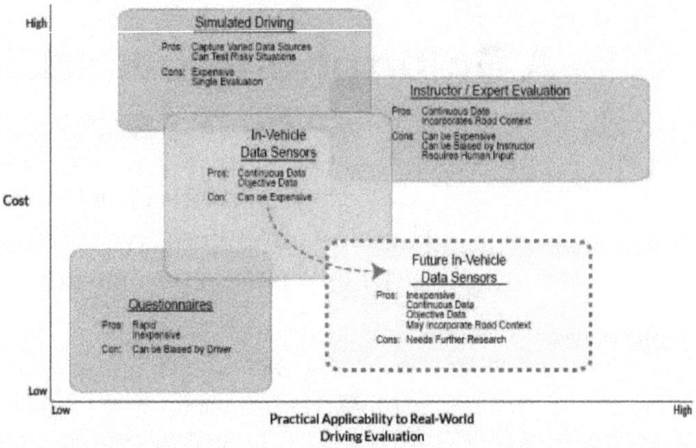

Figure 1. Ranking of existing assessment methods

Despite their clear benefits, questionnaires are not ideal when applied to the creation of an automated and objective assessment system. The very nature of the data collection method precludes real-time evaluation: it would be unsafe to ask drivers to take a questionnaire while driving. Furthermore, because questionnaires are answered *post hoc*, drivers need to rely on their memory, which can be flawed due to impression-management and self-deception. Consequently, self-reports may be biased and may not yield sufficient information to interpret vehicle driving, which is a complex task composed of continuous and reactive interactions between the driver, the vehicle and their environment [5, 34, 36, 40]. Taken together, another approach to studying driving style is required to obtain objective, real-time data.

An alternative approach for assessing driving style is to use a *simulated driving environment*. Here, a driver controls a vehicle in a virtual driving environment, providing a safe and somewhat naturalistic way to study driver behavior. One key benefit of simulators is that they can be manipulated to put the drivers in situations which could be unsafe in a real driving environment, *e.g.*, to simulate an accident or near-accident. Except for academic research or training purposes however, simulated driving environments are used less frequently to provide real-time driving feedback, as they can be quite expensive and risk misrepresenting reality.

In many countries, an *expert-based examination* is administered as an initial test to judge driving performance. Here, a certified driving expert evaluates and provides appropriate feedback in real time about a driver's skill and style. It has been widely adopted in road tests of driving ability. Because no other real-time alternatives exist, expert-based examination is used by default for licensing tests. However, providing this type of feedback to drivers is expensive, which is why it occurs only when someone is initially learning to drive, or when they explicitly pay an expert to help improve their driving.

Due to great advances in mobile sensing technology, *in-vehicle data recorders* have emerged as a powerful tool to collect data on driving styles [36]. These platforms now allow a wide range of information to be recorded to understand interaction between the driver, the vehicle and the environment [2]. Various sensing platforms have been exploited, from the OBD2 and radar to cameras or even smartphones [22, 39], to collect information and understand driving style [2, 18, 24]. For example, Boyce and Geller used a smart car equipped with four cameras to monitor the driver and the roadway environment of the vehicle, and an on-line computer to measure information like vehicle velocity, and investigated relationships between age, personality and driving style [5]. Miyajima *et al.* analyzed drivers' car-following and pedal operation patterns for driver identification [24]. Also, the 100-Car Naturalistic Driving Study used an in-vehicle data recorder, an accelerometer, multiple cameras, and GPS to capture information on driver performance and behavior in the moments leading up to a crash [27]. Malta *et al.* used the multimodal signals of brake pedal use and driver speech in addition to vehicle speed to detect incidents from a real-world driving database [23].

Despite the promise of such an approach, these in-vehicle sensing platforms tend to be too expensive for the average consumer to own. To solve this problem, some researchers have turned to smartphones as a sensor platform, which are quite powerful, widely available, and are often already owned by drivers [19, 22, 39]. Smartphone owners now almost always have the device in their possession, and it can be an accurate proxy to collect a variety of information about users [13], even while driving. Johnson and Trivedi tried to characterize driving style based on smartphone-based sensors including an accelerometer, gyroscope, magnetometer, GPS, and camera [19], while You *et al.* used dual-cameras on smartphones to detect dangerous driving behavior [39]. Johnson and Trivedi used dynamic time warping to detect the type of maneuvering based on the movement of a smartphone mounted on a car in a controlled experiment, while You *et al.* have only presented the idea of using the dual-camera without any experimental validation. Despite their issues, these studies have shown that a lightweight smartphone-based sensing platform can collect useful information related to driving style.

SENSOR-BASED EVALUATION OF DRIVING STYLE

Lightweight Sensing Platform using Android Phones

Our In-Vehicle SmartPhone Sensing Platform (IV-SP2) is depicted in Figure 2. It differs from other sensing platforms that rely on powerful but heavyweight computers and expensive sensors [2, 14]. The core part of our system is the driver's own Android smartphone mounted on the front dashboard, which not only collects the location and movement of the vehicle but also accesses data from two additional sensors. Current Android smartphones are equipped with many sensing and communication capabilities, including dual cameras (front and back), microphones, GPS, a 3D accelerometer, a 3D gyroscope, a 3D magnetometer, a proximity sensor, an illumination sensor and a barometer, and WiFi, 3G and Bluetooth. They are powerful and portable enough for data collection in vehicles, and can even connect to other sensors through Bluetooth. Our system exploits most of these sensing modalities, but we do not include cameras and microphones due to privacy concerns.

In addition to the Android smartphone, we include two other modules: a Bluetooth-based on-board diagnostic (OBD2) reader and an inertial measurement unit (IMU) to support more diverse sensing modalities related to driving style (Figure 2). The OBD2 reader is connected to the OBD2 port of a vehicle and reads a variety of information from the vehicle, such as vehicle speed, engine RPM, and throttle position. It can stream the captured data via Bluetooth to the smartphone. The IMU (in our case, a YEI 3-Space Sensor™ Bluetooth), attached to the upper back of the steering wheel (toward the dashboard) without impacting its operation, and it captures the wheel movement with an accelerometer, gyroscope and compass sensors. It is also communicates via Bluetooth and can download data in real time. In this study, we collect all available variables every half second; Table 1 summarizes what our data sensing platform collects.

Figure 2. Overview of the Android-based in-vehicle sensing platform

Source	Variables	Cost
Android	GPS (location, speed, bearing), 3D acceleration, orientation, compass, gyroscope, linear acceleration, gravity, rotation vector, illumination, air pressure	$0, already purchased
OBD2	Engine coolant temperature, engine load, engine RPM, throttle position, speed	$25
IMU	3D acceleration, gyroscope, compass	$15-300

Table 1: Smartphone and sensor variables and costs

Modeling Driving Style

To use this sensed data to assess driving style, there are a number of steps to perform: preprocessing the data, extracting features, and creating a model of driving style.

Preprocessing

Ideally, smartphones and IMUs mounted in different vehicles would have the same orientation that would not change over time. In practice, however, vehicles usually have different shapes of steering wheels and dashboards, and users may mount them at an arbitrary orientation. In order to build a general model of driving styles across a population, we convert sensory signals to have a consistent orientation across all vehicles. A virtual reorientation method [25] is used to re-calibrate the 3D measurements, by repeatedly adjusting the 3D orientation of the smartphone and IMU with respect to their orientation when the vehicle stops moving. Also, information from the OBD2 is normalized per vehicle by simply subtracting baseline readings (car not in motion) from the in-motion readings.

Feature Extraction

To objectively characterize driving style based on sensor data, we define a number of driving features from the set of three sensors that are used in building a machine learning (ML)-based model of driving style. Because naturalistic data collection does not force drivers to drive predefined routes, the features need to be independent of the context of any specific trip. For example, trips on highways and city roads are very different in their characteristics and a model built for one will not work well on the other. To address this, we instead define six specific driving situations, which we can use to compare a driver's driving style more independently of her own trips, including 1) START: for five seconds after a start, 2) STOP: for five seconds before a stop, 3) H-SPEED: while the vehicle is moving faster than 50 kph, 4) TURN: when the vehicle is turning (turn is detected based on z-axis acceleration of IMU) due to the road turning or a turn at an intersection, 5) B-TURN: for the five seconds just before the vehicle makes a turn, 6) A-TURN: for five seconds just after the vehicle makes a turn. In addition, we analyze certain driving features, such as maximum engine RPM and throttle position, across all driving trips.

To characterize one's driving style, we define the driving features based on the variables of the three sensors as shown in Table 2. The smartphone, mounted on the car, is used to detect speed (via GPS), speed change (acceleration), and the lateral and longitudinal acceleration of the car. The OBD2 reader, installed in the vehicle, records more fine-grained speed and also pulls some vehicle-specific data, such as engine RPM, accelerator (throttle) position, and the derivatives of those variables (note that we only use the three main variables (speed, engine RPM, and throttle position) out of a number of potential variables since they are commonly available from the vehicles of all drivers that participated in this study). From the IMU mounted on the steering wheel, we first detect turn events based on the change of z-axis acceleration, and identify three driving situations, including TURN, B-TURN, and A-TURN. IV-SP2 produces a sample composed of the driving features every half second.

Source	Features
Smartphone	Max/avg/std of speed, speed change, longitudinal/lateral acceleration
OBD2	Max/avg/std of speed, speed change, engine RPM, engine RPM change, throttle position, throttle position change
IMU	Used to detect turn events based on its z-axis acceleration change

Table 2: Features used in characterizing driving style

Aggressive Driving Style Ground Truth

Samples composed of the driving features defined in Table 2 are used to predict a driver's driving style by evaluating them for aggressiveness. To acquire the ground truth of whether a driver is aggressive, we use two methods: self-reports of accidents and ticket records, and a driving style questionnaire.

Measure 1: Driving violations

As one measure of aggressive driving style, a driver can be characterized by his record of driving violations. We characterize a driver as aggressive (violator) or not (non-violator) using the number of accidents or tickets from the past 3 years. This time frame ensures that there is sufficient time for any accidents and tickets to accumulate, but is short enough so as not to mischaracterize drivers who have changed their driving patterns. Compared to questionnaire responses, this measure is more objective and more directly represents the risk of poor or aggressive driving style (unless a driver misrepresents his driving record). However, it lacks the nuance of questionnaires because it does not distinguish between the causes of the accidents or tickets.

Measure 2: Questionnaire responses

To complement the driving outcome record, we characterize drivers' driving style differently based on the responses to the DBQ [32] and additional aggressive driving related questions [7, 16]; drivers who score high are characterized as relatively aggressive and the others as relatively calm. Incorporating the latter questions that cover similar, but non-overlapping behaviors of aggressive violations and ordinary violations [21], allows a clearer division into aggressive and calm groups by allowing aggressive drivers to accrue more points. Aggressive violations are when a driver inconveniences or acts vengefully toward another driver, *e.g.*, flashing his headlights for driving too slowly, which clearly falls under the common denotation for aggressive driving. Ordinary violations are when a driver violated highway laws and acted unsafely, but not aggressively towards another driver, *e.g.*, driving too quickly or not coming to a complete stop, also refers to unsafe driving practices which can be improved through feedback. Aggressive violations and ordinary violations are given the same weight and summed as a measure of driving aggressiveness.

Modeling Driving Style

To create a machine learning (ML)-based model of driving style, we build a feature vector using the variables in Table 2 and use it to predict the target driving style. From the extracted driving features on the 6 driving situations of each trip of a driver, we first produce a feature vector (called trip-profile). A new feature vector (called driver-profile) for each driver is constructed by summarizing a number of his trip-profiles obtained over 3 weeks. From the driver-profiles and ground truth of drivers, the ML-based driver model is built to evaluate a driver's aggressiveness. Given an input driver-profile feature vector, the driver model evaluates a driver's driving style: violator, non-violator, aggressive, or calm, from our two measures.

Before creating the model, all the continuous driving features are discretized into five states {very low, low, medium, high, very high} where the range of values in each state is chosen to make the number of samples equivalent across the states. Then to create the driver model, we select informative driving features based on their information gain and apply a probabilistic technique, a naive Bayes classifier (NB), to model the relationship between driving style and the selected driving features. NB is a simple probabilistic model based on Bayes' theorem and independence assumptions of features. Despite its use of over-simplified assumptions, it often exhibits good performance on many real-world problems and the resulting model can be easily interpreted and understood.

In modeling driving style from our driving features, one goal is to assess driving style with a set of affordable sensors. To this end, we create three models to predict driving styles using the driver-profiles.

- Model 1, Smartphone Only: This model does not require any installation of external sensors. It will capture only the general movement of a vehicle.
- Model 2, Smartphone and OBD2: This model only requires the simple and quick installation of an OBD2 reader. The OBD2 reader costs about $25. This model provides more accurate and detailed information about vehicle operation.
- Model 3, Smartphone, OBD2, and IMU: The sensors for this model cost more than the other models because of the IMU. However, a Nintendo Wii remote is a potential replacement for our IMU, and costs only $15 and provides 3D acceleration. (Note that our choice of IMU instead of the Wii remote is due to the usability of its programmatic interface and usability in a car.) This model additionally incorporates information about steering wheel control, when mounted on the steering wheel.

METHOD

We recruited 22 licensed drivers (11 males and 11 females) from a mid-sized city in the United States, ranging in age from 21 to 34 years (M = 26). A prescreening questionnaire was used to recruit a number of people in our target population: drivers who owned and used an Android smartphone and drove at least several hours per week. Participants were asked to drive their own vehicles, which we equipped with our sensing platform, and to use their usual daily driving routes plus a predesigned 10-minute driving course (once per week) to verify the proper operation of the sensing platform. As described earlier, all sensor data are collected and stored on their smartphone.

During their first visit to our lab, we installed an IMU and an OBD2 reader in their vehicles and a logging application on their smartphones, and provided brief instructions on how to use the system. Then, they were asked to list their driving violations for the past 3 years, and complete our driving behavior questionnaire. For each question, participants ranked the frequency of a driving behavior, on a six-point Likert-scale (ranging from 0=never, 5=nearly all the time). Participants were required to visit our lab each week for data downloading, and were compensated with $60 for completing 3 weeks of data collection. A total of 542 hours of driving data were collected from 1,017 trips.

RESULT & ANALYSIS

Questionnaire Analysis

According to the self-reports of accidents and speed violations, we divided participants into two groups: *violator* and *non-violator* (we will call this group division *violation-class*). As an additional measure of aggressive driving style based on the questionnaires, we also divided our participants into two groups: *relatively aggressive* and *relatively calm*. (Note that the term *relatively* indicates that our participants cover a subpopulation of drivers, the division is measured by looking at the *relative* interquartile ranges for aggressive versus calm drivers, and we will call this group division *questionnaire-class* and use *aggressive* and *calm* without mentioning the term *relatively* in the rest of the paper).

Figure 3 shows the basic distribution of our population in terms of their violation-class and questionnaire-class. Out of the 22 participants, 12 were characterized as *violators*; these drivers had an average of 2 accidents and tickets. 11 of the participants were characterized as *aggressive,* where they had an average score of 28.1% (σ=0.05) from the questionnaire, compared to *calm* drivers' scoring 16% (σ=0.05). While there was a significant participant overlap between *violators* and *aggressive* drivers (10 participants), the participants' questionnaire scores were not always correlated with their accident/ticket record. The correlation across all drivers is 0.26.

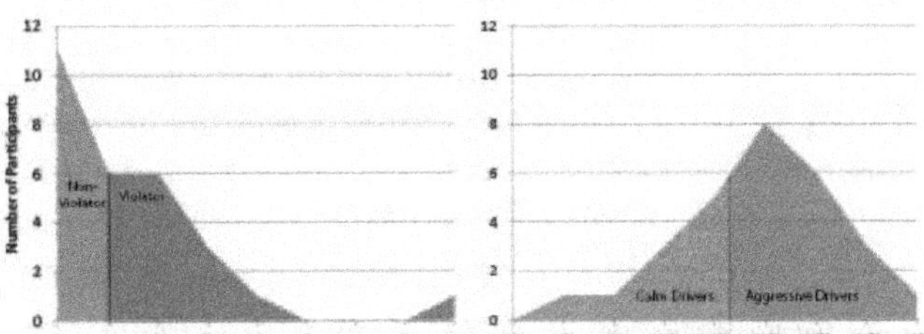

Figure 3. Distribution of Accident & Ticket Record and Questionnaire Responses

Sensor-based Driving Style Analysis

In order to have an understanding of the relationship between the sensor data and driving style, we first compared the driving features from drivers (10) who were classified as *aggressive violators* (*i.e.*, those who were classified as both *aggressive* and *violators*) versus *calm non-violators* (6). This allows the data to more clearly define aggressive driving style. The remaining 6 participants who were either *aggressive non-violators* or *calm violators* will be discussed later in this paper.

Classifying the sensor-based driving feature data as coming from *aggressive violators* or *calm non-violators* yields two findings. First, in line with intuition, the average *aggressive-violator* generally experiences higher g-forces (forces the body is subjected to during acceleration). Second, *aggressive violators* have larger within-person and between-people variation, which signifies that their individual driving style is more inconsistent.

Aggressive Drivers and Violators Have Higher G-Forces

Contrary to our intuition, both *aggressive violators* and *calm non-violators* have similar maximum speeds, as shown in Figure 4a; for naturalistic driving data, *speed* is not a good way to distinguish aggressive and calm drivers. However, its derivative, acceleration, proves to be. Aggressive violators have higher maximum acceleration and deceleration (derived from speed) throughout their trips in general and also in specific situations, such as during a turn (Figure 4b), when driving at high speed (Figure 4c), accelerating from a stopped position, and decelerating to stop their vehicles.

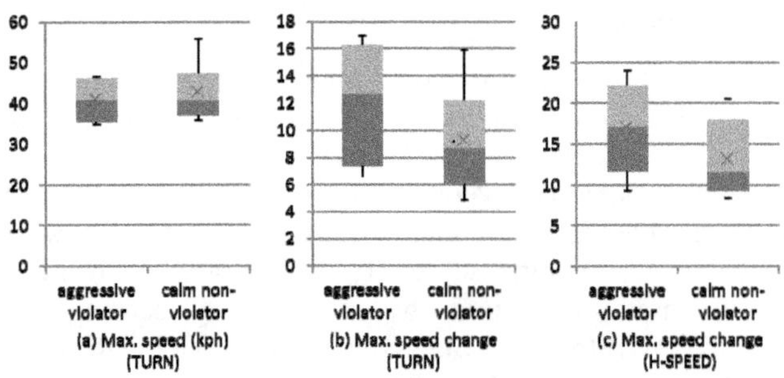

Figure 4. Driving feature distribution on aggressive driving style

Furthermore as shown in Figure 5, in the 5 seconds after an *aggressive violator* begins moving the car, the car has a higher maximum speed and engine RPM, but shows the same average speed and engine RPM as for a *calm non-violator*. Figure 5 implies that *aggressive violators* tend to wait longer to make a change to their speed, and then make a more forceful change. In contrast *calm non-violators* may respond sooner and make lower magnitude changes.

Many driving features extracted from our sensing platform more directly support the fact that *aggressive violators* have higher g-forces for both acceleration and deceleration, such as higher smartphone acceleration in the vehicle's longitudinal (y-axis) and lateral (x-axis) directions. For instance, the acceleration of the smartphone shows *aggressive violators* experience higher g-forces than *calm non-violators* when travelling at high speeds (>50 kph), which means the higher g-forces they experience are not limited to starting and stopping the vehicle, but also to highway travel (*e.g.*, a quick deceleration from 100kph to 60kph or weaving between lanes in high speed traffic with frequent lane changes). More concretely, when an *aggressive violator* accelerates from a stop, she has a maximum lateral acceleration of .38g versus .35g for *calm non-violators*, and a maximum longitudinal acceleration of .39g versus .31g for *calm non-violators*. These are the same g-forces that put strain on the vehicle and can be felt by passengers in the car.

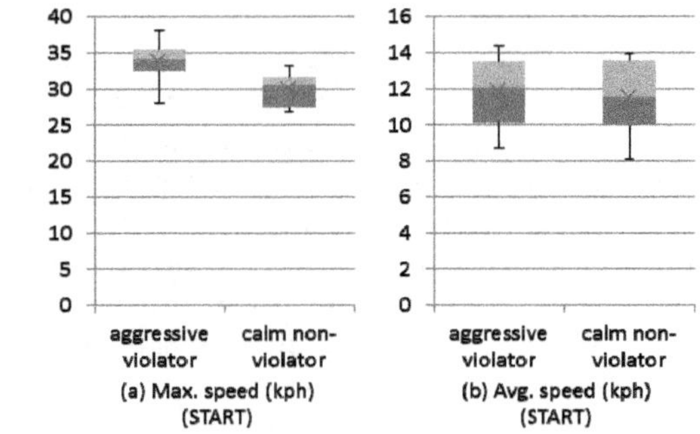

Figure 5. Speed comparison on START

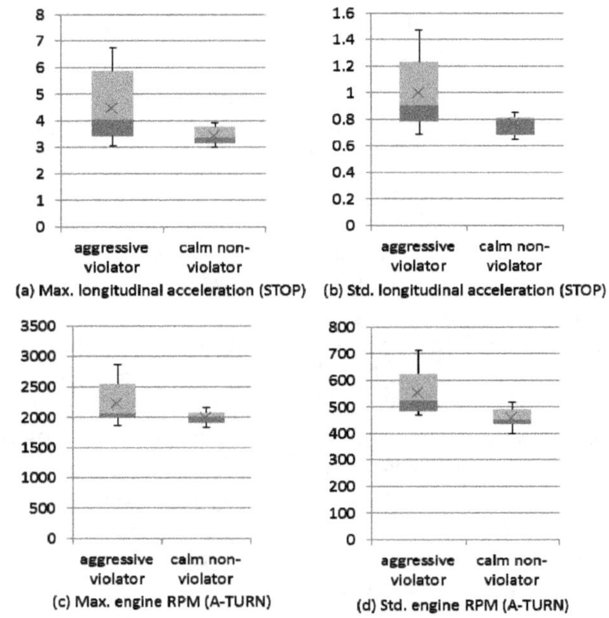

Figure 6. Consistency analysis of drivers

Aggressive Drivers and Violators Behave Less Consistently

Aggressive violators, in contrast to *calm non-violators*, have an inconsistent driving style, as evidenced by several driving features, such as the change of speed and the selection of engine RPMs or throttle positions in our driving situations, extracted from the sensor data. First, *aggressive violators* have lower levels of group consistency in general, meaning that drivers who are classified as aggressive by the questionnaire have a greater variation for many metrics than do drivers who are classified as *calm non-violators*. This is measured by looking at the relative interquartile ranges (IQR) for *aggressive violators* versus *calm non-violators*. *Aggressive violators* have a broader distribution of maximum longitudinal acceleration for the 5 seconds before the vehicle comes to a stop as shown in Figure 6. There is a similar result for the maximum engine

RPM for the 5 seconds after the vehicle makes a turn. This finding implies that one potential application of this research could be to identify a particular driver behavior as being aggressive or calm, and then provide feedback to the driver on the specific behavior that needs to be corrected. This finding also indicates that an *aggressive violator* driving style is characterized by multiple driving features. Because some *aggressive violators* have a lower maximum RPM and longitudinal acceleration than some *calm non-violators*, we must use a sophisticated model that incorporates a number of driving features.

Second, *aggressive violators* have lower levels of individual consistency in most of our driving features (as calculated from their average standard deviations over all of their trips), meaning that an average aggressive driver will be on the lower end of a variable for some trips, and on the higher end of that same spectrum on other trips. In contrast, an average *calm non-violator* will behave more similarly from trip to trip. For instance, as shown in Figure 6b, *calm non-violators* have a lower standard deviation of longitudinal g-forces when coming to a stop. This finding also holds when looking just at high-speed driving, after starting the car, and during a turn. Especially when drivers are travelling faster than 50 kph, the maximum, average and standard deviation of the lateral g-forces (measured by the x-axis acceleration of the smartphone) of *aggressive violators* is larger than those of *calm non-violators*. This indicates that an average aggressive driver subjects the car and its passengers to a larger variety of g-forces than do *calm non-violators*, who are more consistent.

Building a Machine Learning Model

From our feature analysis, we created two driver models that predict whether a driver has an aggressive driving style or not, one determined by the record of accidents and speeding tickets (*violator-class*), and another determined by the questionnaire responses (*questionnaire-class*). To model the relationship of driving features from the three data sources (smartphone, OBD2, and IMU) with each class, we perform feature selection using information gain and use a naïve Bayes classifier with 5-bin discretization, and we conduct leave-one subject-out cross validation for performance evaluation. Figure 7 shows the result.

IV-SP2-Based Model Accuracy

The average model accuracy with all three sensors was 90.5% (2 false negatives) when predicting the violation-class and 81% (2 false negatives & 2 false positives) when predicting the questionnaire-class. These are particularly high accuracies, compared with the baseline model (ZeroR, which always predicts the most frequent classification): 57% and 52.4% for violation-class and questionnaire-class, respectively. We also found that our driver model performed relatively well without using all the sensors in the IV-SP2 system. More specifically, when modeling the violation-class with just the smartphone and the OBD2 (without considering turn situations (B-TURN, TURN, and A-TURN, identified by steering wheel information, using the IMU), we achieved 81% accuracy. With only the smartphone (without utilizing car information, such as RPM and throttle position), we achieved 66.7% accuracy. Similarly, when predicting the questionnaire-class, the model is 76.2% accurate with the smartphone and OBD2 only, and 66.7% with just the smartphone.

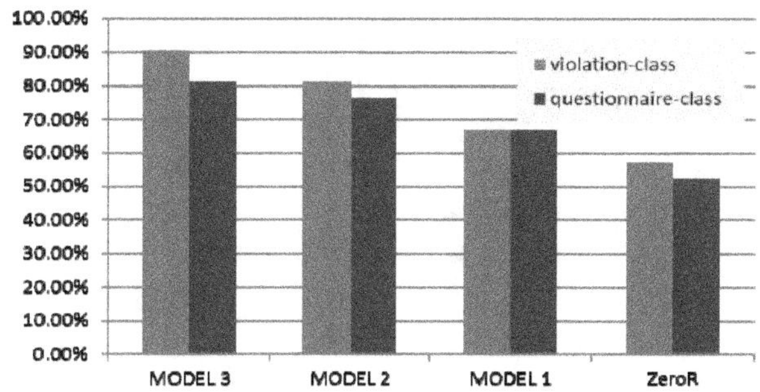

Figure 7. Prediction of aggressive driving style. Model 1 uses smartphone data only, Model 2 uses smartphone and OBD2 data, and Model 3 uses smartphone, OBD2 and IMU data.

Participant S18, a violator, provides an example of a misclassification when fewer sensors are used to predict driving style. When using the 3-sensor IV-SP2 system, S18 is classified correctly as a violator. However, with only the smartphone and OBD2 reader, he is classified incorrectly as a non-violator. This occurred because his general driving style is mild but he is very aggressive in his turning behavior, *e.g.*, he often accelerates more than an average violator while turning. As this behavior occurs frequently, the 3-sensor model correctly characterizes him as a violator. With our sensor-based driving feature data, we achieved higher model accuracy when predicting the violation-class as opposed to the questionnaire-class (90.5% *vs.* 81%).

DISCUSSION

In the discussion section, we will address issues on the applicability of our IV-SP2 and driver models in practice, limitations of using the driving questionnaire, and difficulty of conducting naturalistic driving data collection.

Applying IV-SP2 to Real-World Driving in Practice

Using our driving models, we can assess driving style at three different levels. First, our sensing platform can collect one's naturalistic driving data and, based on all trips taken, let the driver know whether she has an aggressive driving style which may lead to an increased risk of accidents. This level of assessment can be performed periodically to coach drivers "at risk" for aggressive driving styles, *e.g.*, re-training drivers who have at-fault accidents or who have received a number of speed tickets over some time period, or to monitor for a decrease in driver performance due to aging or cognitive disorder [3]. Second, the driver models can evaluate one's driving style on a particular trip. Due to a number of internal and external factors, *e.g.*, stress [4], heavy traffic and road construction, aggressiveness can increase, which may increase the risk of an accident.

Objective feedback about an elevated risk may encourage the driver to correct his or her driving. Figure 8 shows the evaluations of driving style for each trip for each participant. Drivers characterized as being aggressive have more aggressive trips in general, but are not aggressive on all trips. Likewise, a non-aggressive driver sometimes drives aggressively.

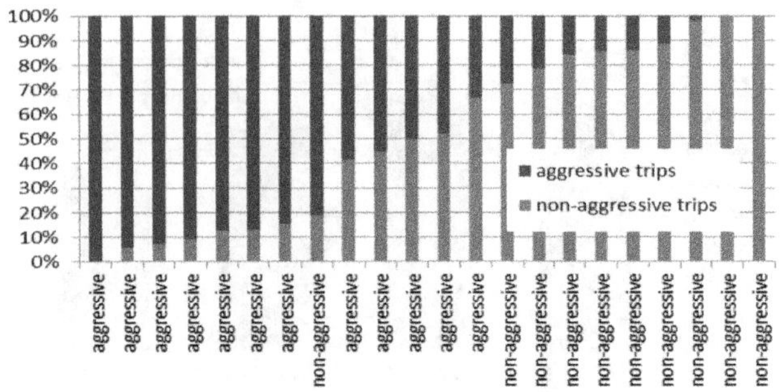

Figure 8. Assessment of individual trips

Third, our driver models can detect aggressive driving in specific situations and provide feedback on driving behaviors. A driver who has an aggressive driving style could get specific advice on how to change her driving style, *e.g.*, keeping a constant engine RPM when driving at a high speed instead of frequently changing speed. Also, if a driver turns very aggressively, the system can coach him to make a better/safer turn. By expanding this to a wider variety of driving situations, it is also possible to provide both more specific assessments and feedback.

Still, the way that characterizes driving styles has to be diversified to present a broader spectrum for understanding aggressive driving styles. For example, considering driving style as a continuous variable will better reflect reality and improve the capability of our system in practice.

Limitations of Questionnaire-Based Classification and its Impact on Our Model

While questionnaires can provide a cost effective and fast method for assessing driving style, they suffer from a few weaknesses when they are used as an initial starting point to build a driver model with machine learning.

Research suggests that behavioral questionnaires yield responses that are loosely correlated with real world poor driving outcomes [38]. Assuming that these responses are less accurate than self-reports of one's accident and ticket record, the driver model based on the questionnaire-class may have inherited the same limitation. Three findings point us in this direction.

First, one effect of this can be seen by cross referencing the responses from the questionnaire and the self-reported accident and ticket record. If the questionnaire responses were perfectly correlated with real-world poor driving outcomes, we would expect all aggressive drivers to be classified as violators, and calm drivers as non-violators. In fact, for 6 participants (24%), this relationship does not hold. These drivers could be referred to as "lucky" (2 participants classified as aggressive, but also as a non-violator) or "unlucky" (4 participants classified as calm, but also as a violator). Especially, being referred to as unlucky could be because they have been really unlucky, or because their poor driving is due to errors and lapses (which are not captured in our questionnaire), or because their responses on the questionnaires are not accurate.

Second, for the majority of driving features we examined, the distinction between violators and non-violators was much clearer than the distinction between aggressive and calm drivers. However, when comparing aggressive versus calm drivers, we cannot so easily find a distinction: the averages and IQRs are much more similar. Thus, when we group participants according to their more objective accident and ticket record, the distinction between groups is much clearer than when- we group them solely by their self-reported driving behavior.

Third, the sensor-based driver model did not predict the *questionnaire-class* as accurately as it did the *violation-class* (81% *vs* 90.5%). The misclassifications in the questionnaire-class model occurred for 3 drivers, which we believe occurred because these drivers were either lucky or unlucky. The misclassifications of the model may be due to the limitation of the more subjective questionnaire approach. Accidents and tickets are objective records of driving style or performance, as are the data from the IV-SP2 system. Future work in this line of research should investigate a more accurate ground truth that includes driver perception and verified accident and ticket data. In addition, further augmenting with range sensors and cameras will provide higher-fidelity ground truth and a validation study using multiple methods would greatly contribute to the field.

Difficulties of Naturalistic Data Collection

Recording naturalistic data provides a more objective view of driver behavior, but it still presents challenges with data processing, some of which were easily surmountable, while others require more work.

For example, because people generally drive on the same roads over a short period of time, the variety of road type data for each participant is not the same. While we attempted to control this by collecting data over 3 weeks, some calm drivers spent much of their time traveling faster on the highways, while some aggressive drivers spent a lot of their driving time sitting at red lights on city streets. Without controlling where our participants drove, as has been done in other studies, we could not use those variables that would be affected by this bias (*e.g.*, speed), when averaging across all driving behaviors. For the variables, we were able to find more distinction between aggressive and calm drivers only in specific driving situations (*e.g.*, high speed data, or at vehicle starts and stops).

Also, the fact that each participant is driving his or her own car and using his or her own smartphone creates an additional source of bias in the data that is difficult to control for. Some variables coming from the car, such as the engine load, are very sensitive to the type of car and transmission in the car. For these variables, we created new data features based on the difference and performed basic calibrations such as normalization and subtracting the baseline. Still, these calibrations are not ideal; further work is required to improve the quality of the sensor data and more reliably and accurately extract values of the variables.

Third, one limitation of the ML-based model which only uses the smartphone is that it uses the GPS data to determine speed. GPS sampling rates are not high enough to reliably determine speed with enough nuance; sampling rates were closer to 1/2 Hz as opposed to 4-5 Hz for the other sensors. Furthermore, the GPS data becomes inaccurate around large buildings and in tunnels; for this reason, even though the phone-only model achieves good accuracy, adding an OBD2 reader provides an alternate source of speed information.

Finally, the IV-SP2 is limited in its ability to detect the driver's road context, since it is optimized to capture information on how the driver is controlling the car. We suspect that variables such as the weather and traffic or even the body position of the driver, could improve the classification accuracy by allowing the model to understand some intentionality behind behaviors. As our system solely focuses on the driver's behavior, additional contextual information could improve the predictability of our model by allowing a more nuanced look at the causes and correlates of particular aggressive driving behaviors.

CONCLUSION

In this paper, we introduced the In-Vehicle Smartphone-based Sensing Platform (IV-SP2), which has the potential to provide real-time feedback to drivers using their own Android smartphone with relatively cheap sensors. With this sensing platform, we collected a variety of information from drivers' naturalistic driving, *e.g.*, speed, acceleration, deceleration, engine RPM, throttle position, and steering wheel movement, and built driver models to predict aggressive driving style. With naturalistic driving data collected from 22 drivers, we could identify aggressive driving (in an accuracy of 90% for violation-class and 81% for questionnaire-class). In the future, we aim to enhance IV-SP2 by introducing new driving situations and driving features to assess more diverse driving styles, and will develop and deploy an end-user application that provides three levels of feedback to improve driver's driving style.

REFERENCES

1. Aggressive driving: research update, *American Automobile Assoc. Foundation for Traffic Safety*, (2009).
2. Amditis, A., Pagle, K., Joshi, S., and Bekiaris, E. Driver-vehicle-environment monitoring for on-board driver support systems: lessons learned from design and implementation. *Applied Ergonomics 41*, 2 (2010), 225-235.
3. Barkley, R.A. and Cox, C. A review of driving risks and impairments associated with attention-deficit/hyperactivity disorder and the effects of stimulant medication on driving performance. *J. of Safety Research 38*, 1 (2007), 113–128.
4. Berdoulat, E., Vavassori, D., and Sastre, M. Driving anger, emotional and instrumental aggressiveness, and impulsiveness in the prediction of aggressive and transgressive driving. *Accident Analysis and Prevention 50*, (2013), 758-767.
5. Boyce, T.E. and Geller, E.S. An instrumented vehicle assessment of problem behavior and driving style: Do younger males really take more risks? *Accident Analysis and Prevention 34*, 1 (2002), 51-64.
6. Cambridge Systematics. 2011. Crashes vs Congestion: What's the Cost to Society? *American Automobile Association*, (November 2011). Retrieved Sept. 5, 2013,
7. Chilaoutakis, J.E., Demakakos, P., Tzamalouka, G., Bakou, V., Koumaki, M., and Darviri, C. Aggressive behavior while driving as predictor of self-reported car crashes. *J. of Safety Research 33*, 4 (2002), 431-443.
8. Coughlin, J.F., Reimer, B., and Mehler, B. Monitoring, managing, and motivating driver safety and well-being. *Pervasive Computing IEEE 10*, 3 (2011), 14-21.
9. Countermeasures that work: A highway safety countermeasure guide for state highway safety offices. *National Highway Traffic Safety Administration Fourth Edition*. (2009).
10. Dahlen, E.R., Edwards, B.D., Tubre, T., Zyphur, M.J., and Warren, C.R. Taking a look behind the wheel: An investigation into the personality predictors of aggressive driving. *Accident Analysis & Prevention 45*, (2012), 1-9.
11. Deffenbacher, J.L., Oetting, E.R., and Lynch, R.S. Development of a driving anger scale. *Psychological Reports 74,* 1 (1994), 83-91.
12. Deffenbacher, J.L., Oetting, E.R., and Swaim, R.C. The Driving Anger Expression Inventory: A measure of how people express their anger on the road. *Behavior Research and Therapy 40,* 6 (2002), 7-737.
13. Dey, A.K., Wac, K., Ferreira, D., Tassini, K., Hong, J.-H., and Ramos, J. Getting closer: an empirical investigation of the proximity of user to their smart phones. *Ubicomp'11*, (2011), 163-172.
14. Espinosa, F., Jimenez, J.A., Santiso, E., Gardel, A., Perez, D., Casanova, J. and Santos, C. Design and implementation of a portable electronic system for vehicle-driver-route activity measurement. *Measurement 44*, 2 (2011), 326-337.

15. Evans, L. 1991. Traffic Safety and the Driver. Van Nostrand, New York, NY.

16. Hennessey, D. and Weisenthal, D.L. Traffic congestion, driver stress, and driver aggression. *Aggressive Behavior 25,* 6 (1999). 409-423

17. Houston, J.M., Farris, P.B., and Norman, M. The aggressive driving behavior scale: developing a self-report measure of unsafe driving practices. *North American J. of Psychology 5*, 2 (2003), 269-278.

18. Jensen, M., Wagner, J., and Alexander, K. Analysis of in-vehicle driver behaviour data for improved safety. *Int. J. of Vehicle Safety 5*, 3 (2011), 197-212.

19. Johnson, D.A. and Trivedi, M.M. Driving style recognition using a smartphone as a sensor platform. In *Proc. 11th Int. Conf. Mobile and Ubiquitous Multimedia*, (2011), 1609-1615.

20. Kee, S., Shamsul, B, and Goh, Y Differences of drivers' driving performance in simulated driving. *Research J. of Applied Sciences 4,* 6 (2009), 230-237.

21. Lawton, R., Parker, D., Manstead, A.S.R., and Stradling, S.G. The role of affect in predicting social behaviors: the case of road traffic violations. *J. of Applied Social Psychology 27*, 14 (1997), 1258-1276.

22. Li, K., Lu, M., Lu, F., Lv, Q., Shang, L., and Maksimovic, D. Personalized driving behavior monitoring and analysis and emerging hybrid vehicles. *Pervasive* (*LNCS 7319*), (2012), 1-19.

23. Malta, L., Miyajima, C. and Takeda, K. A study of driver behavior under potential threats in vehicle traffic. *IEEE Transactions on Intelligent Transportation Systems 10*, 2 (2009), 201-210.

24. Miyajima, C., Nishiwaki, Y., Ozawa, K., Wakita, T., Itou, K.,Takeda, K., and Itakura, F. Driver modeling based on driving behavior and its evaluation in driver identification. *Proc. of the IEEE 95*, 2 (2007), 427-437.

25. Mohan, P., PadManabhan, V.N., and Ramjee, R. Nericell: rich monitoring of road and traffic conditions using mobile smartphones. *SenSys '08*, (2008), 323.

26. Mynttinen, S., Sundstrom, A., Vissers, J. Koivukoski, M., Hakuli, K., and Keskinen, E. Self-assessed driver competence among novice drivers – a comparison of driving test candidate assessments and examiner assessments in a Dutch and Finnish sample. *J. of Safety Research 40*, 4 (2009), 301-309.

27. Neale, V.L., Dingus, T.A., Klauer, S., Sudweeks, J. and Goodman, M. An overview of the 100-car naturalistic study and findings. *ESV Paper 05-0400*, (2005).

28. Nichols, J. New opportunities: Can behavior analysis help with traffic safety? Panel discussion (panel session). *24th Annual Convention of the Association for Behavior Analysis*, (1998).

29. Owsley, C. Driving mobility, older adults, and quality of life. *Gerontechnology 1*, 4 (2002), 220-230.

30. Özkan, T., Lajunen, T., Chliaoutakis, J.E., Parker, D., and Summala, H. Cross-cultural differences in driving behaviours: A comparison of six countries. *Transportation Research Part F: Traffic Psychology and Behaviour 9*, 3 (2006), 227–242.

31. Paefgen, J., Kehr, F., Zhi, Y., and Michaelles, F. Driving behavior analysis with smartphones: insights from a controlled field study. In *Proc. 11th Int. Conf. Mobile and Ubiquitous Multimedia*, (2012), 36.

32. Reason, J., Manstead, A., Stradling, S., Baxter, J., and Campbell, K. Errors and violations on the roads: a real distinction? *Ergonomics 33,* 10-11 (1990), 1315-1332.

33. Shinar, D. and Compton, R. Aggressive driving: an observational study of driver, vehicle, and situational variables, *Accident Analysis and Prevention 36*, 3 (2004), 429-437.

34. Sundström, A. Self-assessment of driving skill – A review from a measurement perspective. *Transportation Research Part F*, 11 (2008), 1-9.

35. Tasca, L. A review of the literature on aggressive driving research. *Aggressive Driving Issues Conf.*, (2000).

36. Toledo, T., Musicant, O., Lotan, T. In-vehicle data recorders for monitoring and feedback on drivers' behavior. *Transportation Research Part C 16*, 3 (2008), 320-331.

37. Wiesenthal, D.L., Hennessy, D., and Gibson, P.M. The Driving Vengeance Questionnaire (DVQ): The development of a scale to measure deviant drivers' attitudes. *Violence and Victims 15,* 2 (2000), 115-136.

38. Winter, J. and Dodou, D. The driver behavior questionnaire as a predictor of accidents: a meta-analysis. *J. of Safety Research 41*, 6 (2010), 463-470.

39. You, C.-W., Montes-de-Oca, M., Bao, T.J., Lane, N.D., Lu H., Cardone, G., Torresani, L., and Campbell, A.T. CarSafe: a driver safety app that detects dangerous driving behavior using dual-cameras on smartphones. *Ubicomp'12*, (2012), 671-672.

40. Zhang, Y., Lin, W.C., and Chin, Y.-K. A pattern-recognition approach for driving skill characterization. *IEEE Trans. on Intelligent Transportation Systems 11*, 4 (2010), 905-916.

Classifying Driver Workload Using Physiological and Driving Performance Data: Two Field Studies

Erin T. Solovey[12], Marin Zec[2], Enrique Abdon Garcia Perez[2], Bryan Reimer[2], Bruce Mehler[2]
[1]Drexel University
Philadelphia, PA
[2]MIT AgeLab
Cambridge, MA
erin@cs.drexel.edu, marin.zec@tum.de, engarpe@mit.edu, reimer@mit.edu, bmehler@mit.edu

ABSTRACT
Understanding the driver's cognitive load is important for evaluating in-vehicle user interfaces. This paper describes experiments to assess machine learning classification algorithms on their ability to automatically identify elevated cognitive workload levels in drivers, leading towards the development of robust tools for automobile user interface evaluation. We look at using both driver performance as well as physiological data. These measures can be collected in real-time and do not interfere with the primary task of driving the vehicle. We report classification accuracies of up to 90% for detecting elevated levels of cognitive load, and show that the inclusion of physiological data leads to higher classification accuracy than vehicle sensor data evaluated alone. Finally, we show results suggesting that models can be built to classify cognitive load across individuals, instead of building individual models for each person. By collecting data from drivers in two large field studies on the highway (20 drivers and 99 drivers), this work extends prior work and demonstrates feasibility and potential of such measures for HCI research in vehicles.

Author Keywords
Cognitive workload; driving; physiological computing; heart rate; skin conductance; machine learning.

ACM Classification Keywords
H.5.2. Information interfaces and presentation (e.g., HCI): User Interfaces.

INTRODUCTION
In 2011, the U.S. National Highway Traffic Safety Administration reported that 3,331 people were killed and an estimated 387,000 were injured on U.S. roadways in motor vehicle crashes involving distracted driving [26]. As a consequence, technology usage in the vehicle is a major safety concern. A casual observation of drivers suggests that they increasingly attend to mobile devices and interact with new technology built in their vehicles, creating distracted driving scenarios.

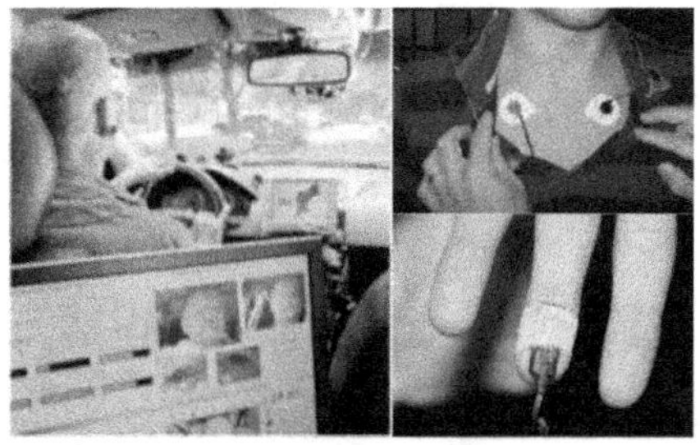

Figure 1. Recording of physiology during on-road driving. Electrocardiogram (top right) and skin conductance (bottom right) sensor placement are shown.

Driving itself is a dynamic, complex activity involving visual, cognitive and manual tasks: the driver has to form strategic goals, monitor the roadway environment and the vehicle systems, process information and make tactical action plans as well as execute control level activities [23]. Thus, the driving task imposes varying levels of workload on the driver. Understanding the workload induced during driving is important for preventing accidents and hazards on the road, and human factors researchers have studied driver workload in depth. It has been shown that operators perform better at intermediate levels of workload compared to extreme levels (i.e. too low or too high workload) [8]. The roots of this are in the Yerkes Dodson law of arousal [41] (inverted U) that suggests that during periods of underload, added workload may improve performance, while during heightened demand, higher workload may reduce performance. As they vie for driver attention, the workload imposed on the driver by in-vehicle user interfaces is constantly changing.

Advances in technology have led to a shift in the demands in many working environments from the largely physical to more supervisory oversight of automation, more cognitive demand, and increased frequency of vocal command interaction [34,42]. This development can be observed in the field of driving as well [16,37]. Modern cars provide driver support systems such as power steering, assistive cruise control and lane keeping assist, which decrease the physical

CHI 2014, April 26 - May 01, 2014, Toronto, ON, Canada.
Copyright 2014 ACM 978-1-4503-2473-1/14/04…$15.00.
http://dx.doi.org/10.1145/2556288.2557068

demands of driving. The next generations of automated vehicles will likely partially, if not completely, relieve the driver of safety critical control. However, the increasing level of automation is expected to place more variable demands on driver attention and cognitive activities. The complexity of in-vehicle interfaces will continue to increase at a rapid rate. Vehicles will likely contain more infotainment options, and proposed automated driving systems will demand new interfaces. In addition, the increased autonomy of the car may provide the driver with a sense that they have the capacity to undertake additional tasks while driving. Understanding how the evolving vehicle interface affects the driver's cognitive load is critical for optimizing the user experience and safety during system design and through adaptive interfaces. This work aims to explore automatic detection of driver cognitive workload through physiology and vehicle data.

Although mental workload is not directly observable [10], several measurement approaches to assessing mental workload are employed. Empirical measures are generally divided into three categories: subjective measures, performance measures and psychophysiological measures. Each method has advantages as well as disadvantages [19,43]. Subjective measures are cost-effective and suitable in prototype testing; however they suffer from time delay, subjective biases and are highly intrusive which ultimately makes them unsuitable for continuous workload assessment. Performance and psychophysiological measures can be measured non-intrusively and continuously throughout the tasks [19].

Recently, with sensing capabilities improving and costs decreasing, there has been a growing interest among automotive vendors in enabling their products to monitor and exploit driver and vehicle sensor data. Driving measures of speed, acceleration, location and inter-vehicle distance are more readily available for inferring the current situation. In addition, cameras and other sensors are increasingly able to measure driver data such as heart rate, gaze direction and other physiological measures. These vehicle and physiological measures provide the potential to monitor the dynamic state of the driver while actually driving and provide inputs to make adjustments in the characteristics of the vehicle or interfaces to improve performance [6].

Starting initially in a driving simulator [19] and moving to field studies [18,28,29], previous work demonstrated that vehicle sensor and physiological measures can both be collected in real-time and do not interfere with the primary task, making them potentially valuable for evaluating workload associated with automotive user interfaces. This work was largely based on normative assessment of group level data. While a simple threshold based assessment showed promise for detecting changes in cognitive load at the individual level [18], it remained to be shown how effectively this can be achieved using more advanced modeling.

This paper builds from this prior work with the goal of improving methods available for evaluating automotive user interfaces that may be used during driving tasks. It brings us closer to automatic cognitive workload classification and makes the following contributions. 1) We report machine learning classification results along with details of the techniques and parameters for recognizing elevated cognitive load, based on data from a moderately sized and a large on-road field study. 2) We compare the value of heart rate, skin conductance and driving data for classification. 3) We explore the differences between training classifiers within individuals and across individuals. By successfully training across individuals, we demonstrate the potential of building models that can generalize to work for new drivers.

RELATED WORK

The following sections provide background on peripheral physiological measures for workload detection in driving.

Cognitive Load and Heart Rate and Skin Conductance

Cardiovascular measures have been reported to be sensitive to mental workload changes (e.g. [5,12,25,38,39]). The heart is innervated by both parts of the autonomic nervous system: the sympathetic nervous system (SNS) and the parasympathetic nervous system (PNS). Heart rate (HR) and heart rate variability (HRV) are widely adopted mental workload measures because they are easy to use and provide fundamental information about the autonomic nervous system [3,25]. While the SNS activation promotes arousal (e.g. "flight-or-fight" response in emergency), the PNS is responsible for maintaining bodily functions and resting. Sympathetic activation increases heart rate while parasympathetic activation decreases heart rate.

Electrodermal activity (EDA) refers to the electrical activity from (eccrine) sweat glands and their associated dermal and epidermal tissues [4]. There are two types of sweat glands in the human skin: the eccrine and the apocrine. Though related, eccrine and apocrine sweat glands are distinct in size, structure, function, distribution and nervous control [31]. Eccrine sweat glands are under control of the SNS. Thus, physiological arousal affects the production of ionic sweat by eccrine sweat glands resulting in changes of electrical resistance and conductance at the surface of the skin. EDA has been used as a measure for psychophysiological arousal for more than a century (e.g. [28]). EDA measures such as skin conductance level (SCL) and skin conductance response (SCR) have been reported to be sensitive to arousal and mental workload in driving as well [14,36]. SCL represents the overall tonic conductance level and SCR captures momentary (phasic) changes in electrical conductivity. This paper explores HR and SCL.

Measuring Physiological Signals in the Car

Literature on measuring physiological signals in the car can be divided into simulator studies [13,18,19,24,36] and field studies [14,15,18,28,30,33,40]. The major advantage of simulator studies is their relative ease of controlling experimental variables and conditions. However, there are disadvantages compared to a field study as well, e.g. lower risk perception or simulator sickness. Since driver-vehicle interfaces eventually have to be effective and safe in real-world settings with dynamic environmental factors such as lighting or soundscape, this paper utilizes data from two field-studies to examine classification performance in a more realistic setting than a driving simulator. In addition, while most of these studies report significant normative differences in physiological signals during driving, this paper works to automatically detect these differences at an individual level using machine learning. Below, we discuss some related field studies.

De Waard et al. [40] studied 28 male participants driving an instrumented car on two different roads, each associated with a different demand level. The data suggests significant effects of road type on heart rate measures, but they did not look specifically at workload.

Healey et al. [14] used physiological data (EKG, EMG, EDA, and respiration) from nine drivers in three real-world settings: rest, highway and urban. Three drivers accomplished seven drives each. Another six drivers completed one single drive. The three driving conditions were low (rest), medium (highway) or high (city) stress, respectively. This was validated through questionnaires. Using a linear discriminant function, an overall accuracy of 97.4% was reported for stress level classification. However, the generalizability is limited since 21 of the 27 drive datasets are attributed to three drivers only (each one of these repeated the course on multiple days).

In a larger study of 49 professional drivers, Jahn et al. [15] found heart rate to be sensitive to workload manipulation in their driving study. However, they conclude that the heart rate changes they observed reflect emotional strain or physical workload from steering actions as well. According to the authors, heart rate proved to be a sensitive but not selective measure for workload. In contrast, [25] claims HRV to be a selective measure for mental load. (See [22] for discussion of HR vs. HRV in high workload detection.).

The European HASTE study [8] produced mixed results on the relative sensitivity of heart rate and skin conductance in response to the demands surrogate secondary tasks in a sample of 24 drivers in the field. In contrast, Collet et al. [5] collected heart rate and skin resistance (inverse of SCL) data in 10 drivers on a closed driving track and found that both measures increased during secondary tasks requiring their attention (a phone conversation, a radio broadcast with content they would be quizzed on, and a conversation).

Schneegaß, et al. [33] present a field study with ten participants in which they collected EKG, skin conductance, and skin temperature data while participants drove in road environments presumed to induce differing levels of demand. This preliminary report only considered the skin conductance and skin temperature data, and found skin conductance for the group varied significantly across the road types and to be the more sensitive measure.

The in-vehicle evaluation framework and two on-road field experiments described in this paper extend this previous work by collecting data from a significantly larger, gender-balanced group of drivers across different age groups and looks at on-road responses to secondary task demands.

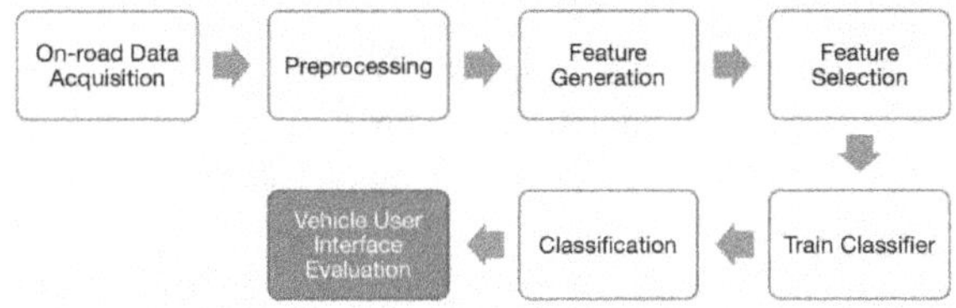

Figure 2. Steps required for on-road cognitive state classification for vehicle user interface evaluation.

CLASSIFYING DRIVER DATA FOR UI EVALUATION

The related work in this area has generated interest from automotive companies for utilizing physiological and vehicle sensor data in user interface evaluation. However, bringing this research into the in-vehicle user evaluation is still a challenge, as there are few standard methods in place for doing so. We detail our procedure and results as a step toward this. We employ machine learning techniques to learn a model for elevated workload based on physiological and vehicle data for automatic classification. This involves several steps as shown in Figure 2. We describe each of the steps in more detail below, along with the potential choices that need to be made to conduct on-road user evaluations using these methods. Research questions are highlighted.

First, there is a broad range of sensor technology available for *on-road data acquisition,* and more will be available in the future. In the studies described below, we investigate heart rate, skin conductance and vehicle telemetry because they have shown to be sensitive to changes in cognitive workload, and are relatively easy to measure during driving. We also assess their relative sensitivity to elevated cognitive demand to determine the most effective sensors. As additional sensors are shown to be indicative of cognitive workload in the future, they could be added to this framework. This leads to a research question addressed in this paper: *Can peripheral physiological and driver performance measures be used for accurate classification of elevated levels of driver workload for interface evaluation?*

Raw sensor data is often not suitable for direct analysis due to various forms of artifact and errors. Often, the first step in data *preprocessing* involves a manual or automated cleaning of the input signals. In addition, some useful data features cannot be directly measured but have to be computed first. The data pre-processing steps deal with such issues, but are often omitted in study descriptions. For each experiment below, we detail the pre-processing steps taken.

Feature generation and *feature selection* convert the preprocessed data into a set of values that could be used for learning a model for the various cognitive states. With sensor data, the recorded measurements form a time series that could be used directly as a set of features. Also, some features have to be extracted from raw data because they provide more information than the actual raw signal (e.g. heart rate is more informative than raw EKG). Other approaches aggregate the time series into summary functions such as the mean over a window. This reduces the dimensionality of the data. Previous work has shown that parameters such as window size can have an impact on classification results in EEG data [11]. Understanding how these factors influence classification of other physiological and vehicle data will be addressed in the experiments below in order to answer the question: *How is classification accuracy affected by feature generation and selection parameters?*

With a set of features, we can employ machine learning techniques to *train a classifier* for detecting the cognitive workload of the driver, based on data previously acquired. Supervised learning techniques were employed using the empirical data from the two field studies with labeled data (*elevated* and *normal* workload levels). Supervised learning algorithms generally consist of two phases: a *training* phase and a *classification* phase. In the learning phase, the algorithm builds a model on the basis of training data and their labels. The resulting model is used in the classification phase to predict labels (i.e. class membership) for unlabeled data. The training period could happen just prior to classification, or the classification models could be built earlier, based on historical data. The quality of the training data will impact the performance of the classifier. We look at answering: *How does training data within and across individuals impact automatic cognitive workload recognition?*

Numerous classification algorithms have emerged and we report results with five different classifiers. We aim to investigate: *How does classification algorithm impact the ability estimate elevated workload with physiological data?*

The final goal with the real-time classifier is to *evaluate in-vehicle interfaces and technology* using the automatic cognitive workload detection in combination with more traditional measures. Using this framework, we can identify moments of interest during task performance where cognitive workload is elevated. This can be analyzed to identify interface, driving, and environmental conditions that may have induced elevated cognitive load. The rest of the paper focuses on practical issues for using this in realistic settings.

EXPERIMENT FRAMEWORK

We conducted two experiments based on data collected in field studies to explore the practical considerations for automatic classification of cognitive load during actual on-road driving. In both field studies, participants drove on an interstate highway while vehicle performance and physiology data were recorded. In addition to the primary driving task, participants had to complete a cognitive demand task described below as a proxy for secondary tasks that cause elevated workload.

We describe our approach to classification and the various parameters that could affect the classification results. These include: machine learning algorithm, window size, overlap of windows and features used. In the first experiment with 20 subjects, we look at classifying individual driver's workload levels by building unique models for each person. In the second experiment with 99 subjects, we explore building classification models across individuals, reducing the need for training on each individual. Common elements of the field studies are detailed below.

Stimulus	9	3	7	1	8	0	2	4	6	5
Response	.	.	9	3	7	1	8	0	2	4

Table 1. Example task block of auditory stimuli and the appropriate verbal responses in a 2-back secondary task performed during on-road driving.

Secondary Task Procedure

In the two field studies, an auditory presentation - verbal response delayed digit recall task was employed to impose additional mental workload while driving. This "n-back" task is documented in detail in [21]. The single digits 0-9 were presented one at a time at 2.25 second intervals in a randomly ordered sequence. As each new item was presented, participants were required to say out loud the digit two items back in the current sequence. An example set of a 2-back task is shown in Table 1. (The 0-back where a participant simply repeats each number as it is presented and 1-back where the number one item back in the sequence have also been used and elicit lower levels of demand.) This secondary task requires auditory perception and cognitive processing involving working memory. This has been shown in previous work to increase cognitive demand [20,29] and is being utilized as a calibration task that provides drivers with a consistent, and validated, dose of high cognitive demand that has been used in prior studies.

Vehicle Equipment and Physiological Sensors

In both experiments, a vehicle was instrumented for time-synchronized data collection from embedded vehicle sensors, a MEDAC System/3 monitoring system (NeuroDyne Medical Corp., Cambridge, MA). Vehicle performance data were logged at 10 Hz and physiological data at 250 Hz. The first data set was collected in a 2010 Lincoln MKS and the second data set was collected in a 2004 Volvo XC90.

Electrocardiogram (EKG) recordings employed a modified lead II configuration: the negative lead was placed just under the right clavicle (collar bone), the ground lead just under the left clavicle (Figure 1), and the positive lead on the left side over the lower rib. The skin was cleaned with isopropyl alcohol and standard pre-gelled silver/silver chloride disposable electrodes (Vermed A10005, 7% chloride wet gel) were applied. Skin conductance was measured utilizing a constant current configuration and non-polarizing, low impedance gold plated electrodes that allow electrodermal recording without the use of conductive gel. Sensors were placed on the underside of the outer segments of the middle fingers of the non-dominant hand and secured with medical grade paper tape. The thin surface, low profile design of the electrodermal sensors minimize interference with a natural grip of the steering wheel associated with the use of more traditional cup style electrodes. Figure 1 shows one of the two sensors. Measures of driving speed, steering wheel position, and acceleration data were recorded directly from the controller area network (CAN) bus of the vehicle.

A research associate was seated in the rear of the vehicle and was responsible for providing driving directions, ensuring safe vehicle operation, that participants understood and followed instructions, recording telemetry was working properly and that the experiment proceeded according to a predefined script (Figure 1). The data acquisition system supported playing recorded audio and this ensured that primary instructions and tasks were presented consistently.

Data Preprocessing

A typical EKG waveform of a heartbeat consists of six components labeled P, Q, R, S, T and U. Each wave represents a specific stage in the underlying physiological process of a cardiac cycle. The most prominent pattern in the EKG waveform is the QRS segment since it usually contains a sharp spike in the signal (R-wave peak). However, EKG recordings often contain artifact (e.g. interference from skeletal muscle activity or electrical noise) and anomalies (e.g. as a result of heart conditions or equipment failures). We employed a QRS detection algorithm [2,7] to identify heart beats in the signal. The results of the heart beat detection were manually reviewed and edited. Heart rate (HR) and heart rate variability (HRV) have both been used successfully for assessing operator workload. However, prior work [22] found HR to be more robust than HRV during driving and a similar secondary task. This motivated our choice to use HR features instead of HRV features.

The skin conductance recordings were filtered using a wavelet transform to remove high frequency noise ([29]). Decomposition at level 4 using Coiflet wavelets with 5 vanishing moments showed best results during our exploratory analysis. Gross low frequency movement artifact was identified by manual inspection and removed.

Steering wheel reversal rates measure the frequency of steering wheel reversals exceeding a certain threshold angle (commonly referred to as gap). This reflects stability of control as distraction can cause quick large corrections. Steering wheel reversal rates were calculated using a 2nd order Butterworth filter as described in [27], and were provided as reversals per minute. Large reversals have gap size 3 and cut-off 0.6Hz whereas small reversals have gap size 0.1 and cut-off 2Hz. After preprocessing, signals were resampled to 10 Hz.

Feature Generation

In both experiments, similar feature generation methods were used for testing classification approaches. A labeled dataset was built from the synchronized sensor data. Data acquired during the cognitive demand task periods are labeled as *elevated* workload. A period is extracted from driving only periods and labeled *normal* workload.

To preserve information about the temporal dynamics, a sliding-window approach was used to aggregate attributes over specific time intervals (Figure 3). Each feature is computed using a fixed-length sliding window operator moving over the data. For each window, a set of features is computed. We take the mean, standard deviation, minimum, maximum and first derivative of the following measures: heart rate, skin conductance level (SCL), and vehicle velocity. In addition, we compute the number of small and large steering wheel reversals.

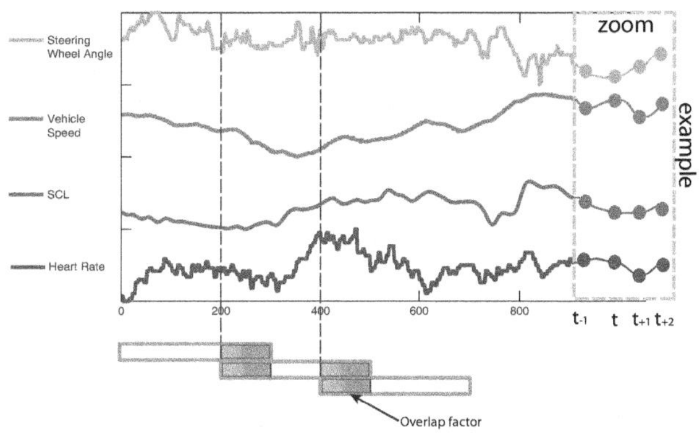

Figure 3. Sequential sensor data can be broken into fixed-length windows (green bars at bottom), which slide across the data. Within each window, we can calculate average, standard deviation, etc. The size of the window and the amount of overlap will affect the analysis.

Two parameters have to be specified to generate aggregate feature vectors: the window length and overlap factor. The window length determines the number of data points per signal to be considered for a single window. The overlap factor effectively determines the time offset between the first data points of two successive windows. While window length influences how much historical information is contained in a single window, the overlap factor influences how much historical information is shared among successive windows. In the results reported below, sliding windows of 10, 15, 20, 25, and 30 seconds are used with overlap percentages of 0%, 25%, 50%, and 75%.

Five feature based learning techniques are used in this analysis: decision trees, logistic regression, 1-nearest neighbor, multilayer perceptron, and naïve Bayes. These were chosen because they are simple learners, they generate explicit interpretable models and they can be implemented as incremental learners (i.e. they can adjust the existing model and do not have to relearn from scratch when confronted with new training data).

EXPERIMENT 1: AUTOMATIC CLASSIFICATION OF ELEVATED WORKLOAD IN INDIVIDUAL DRIVERS

In the first study, we collected data from 20 participants with the goal of examining the feasibility and practical considerations for automatic classification of elevated work-

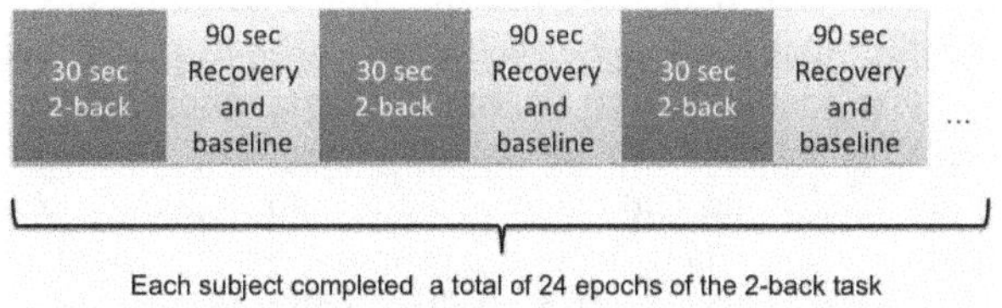

Figure 4. Experimental protocol for Experiment 1.

load, based on an individual's vehicle and physiological patterns. We wanted to look at building individual models to account for individual differences between drivers.

Participants

Twenty-six individuals driving more than three times a week and having a valid driver's license for at least three years were recruited. Participants had to report a driving record free of accidents for the past year. We collected reliable heart rate data from 20 participants (9 female, mean age of 23.9, standard deviation of 23.0). Due to recording issues, only 13 of the participants (7 female, mean age of 23.2, standard deviation of 2.6) had both reliable heart rate and skin conductance levels.

Procedure

Participants drove in urban traffic for approximately ten minutes before reaching an interstate highway. Subsequently, drivers were provided an additional twenty minutes of interstate driving to familiarize themselves with the vehicle and environment before a two minute single task driving reference period was established. Afterwards, subjects were presented 24 task periods consisting of the 2-back cognitive demand task described above, while they continued to drive on the highway. Each 30-second task period was followed by a ninety second recovery and baseline period (Figure 4). Throughout the study, heart rate, skin conductance level, speed, and steering wheel position were recorded.

Classification Approach

This section describes the signal processing, feature generation and classification approaches that we explored for automatic detection of elevated cognitive workload during the experiment.

We were interested in individual classification methods, and built separate datasets for each of the 13 participants and performed the classification within each set. For each dataset, we have 24 30-second examples of *elevated* cognitive load from the task periods, and 24 30-second examples of *normal* cognitive load extracted from the middle of the recovery and baseline periods when the participants were just driving. After the signal processing and feature generation steps described above, classification algorithms were run.

Ten-fold cross-validation was used for evaluating the approaches. To choose the window size and window overlap that yielded the highest classification accuracy, we performed an inner ten-fold cross-validation process within the training set. Our data was split first into a training and test set. Within that training set, the data was split into a training and validation set to choose the parameters that performed the best. The outer test set, thus, was not used in parameter selection and can provide an estimate of generalizability of the classification accuracy. In all iterations, when data was chosen for a training, validation or test set, the entire two-minute task period (including the n-back task and rest) was included. This is to ensure that data from a task period was not used for choosing parameters, or building the model as well as testing the accuracy of the method.

	All Features		Heart Rate	
	Mean	**S.D.**	**Mean**	**S.D.**
Decision Tree	75.0	10.8	72.8	12.8
Logistic Regression	75.5	10.9	73.9	11.3
Multilayer Perceptron	75.7	10.9	74.0	12.4
Naïve Bayes	75.0	12.5	74.1	11.8
Nearest Neighbor	69.4	11.6	71.5	10.3

Table 2. Mean and standard deviation for classification of *elevated* cognitive load from *normal* driving across 13 subjects using all features (20 subjects for heart rate only).

Classification Results

We report results as the average accuracy achieved from each of the datasets, using the nested cross-validation described above. The mean accuracy and standard deviation for each classifier are shown in Table 2. We looked at classification using *heart rate data* only for all 20 subjects and also ran the analysis using *all features* for the 13 subjects with complete data. For *all features*, a one-way analysis of variance shows that there is a significant difference in the accuracy of the five algorithms, ($p < 0.0001$). Tukey-Kramer post-hoc test showed that the nearest-neighbor classifier performed significantly worse than all four of the other algorithms. There were no additional significant results. For *heart rate only* (13 subjects), a one-way analysis of variance showed significant differences ($p < 0.0001$). Tukey-Kramer post-hoc test showed that the nearest-neighbor classifier performed significantly worse than logistic regression, multilayer perceptron and naïve Bayes, but not decision tree. There were no other significant results.

Discussion

The results of this experiment show that we could achieve reasonable classification accuracy, using simple features and classification methods. Even with only the heart rate data, the accuracy did not decrease by much, showing that this simple measure has promise for classifying cognitive workload for in-vehicle user interfaces. One thing to note is that the entire set of 24 trials translates to about 48 minutes of data. Thus, with 10-fold cross-validation, we were training on 90% of this data (or ~43 minutes). This makes sense for experiments and a proof-of-concept. However, this amount of training time for the classifier is not ideal for real-world evaluation. It is likely that future work would reduce this training time, and also improve the classification results. However, it still is not ideal to build individual models. Experiment 2 investigates classification across individuals that may reduce or eliminate this training time.

EXPERIMENT 2: ESTABLISHING METHODS ACROSS INDIVIDUALS

Experiment 2 moves toward having general classifiers that detect elevated cognitive workload without extensive training on individual drivers. We worked with data collected from 99 participants [20,29] with the goal of finding com-

Age group (years)	Mean (SD)	Females	Males
20-29	24.75 (2.81)	17	18
40-49	44.74 (3.01)	16	16
60-69	63.97 (3.02)	16	16

Table 3. Age and gender of participants in Experiment 2.

mon features and algorithms that reliably can classify cognitive load automatically across individuals.

Participants

Healthy individuals driving more than three times a week and having held a valid driver's license for at least three years were recruited. As in the previous study, participants had to report a driving record free of accidents for the past year. 146 individuals took active part in the driving portion of the study; however, 38 cases were excluded from the final dataset for reasons such as heavy traffic, poor weather conditions, or technical issues [20]. In addition, nine more subjects were removed from the dataset due to missing data or poor measurement quality in at least one signal domain. The dataset considered in this paper contains recordings from 99 subjects. Aiming for reliability in the real world, participants were balanced in age and gender (Table 3).

Procedure

Participants drove in urban traffic for approximately 10 minutes before reaching an interstate highway, on which they drove for 20 minutes to familiarize themselves with the vehicle and environment prior to a two minute single task driving period which established reference data. Afterwards, subjects were presented three task periods consisting of a series of four secondary task blocks each. In this study, there were periods of the 0-back, 1-back, and 2-back task described earlier. However, in this analysis, we focused on classifying the 2-back *elevated* periods from the single-task *normal* driving, as in Experiment 1. Future work will look at the other levels of demand. Each task period was followed by a two minute recovery period. The order of presentation of the three task difficulty levels was counterbalanced across participants. Figure 6 shows an overview of the experimental protocol.

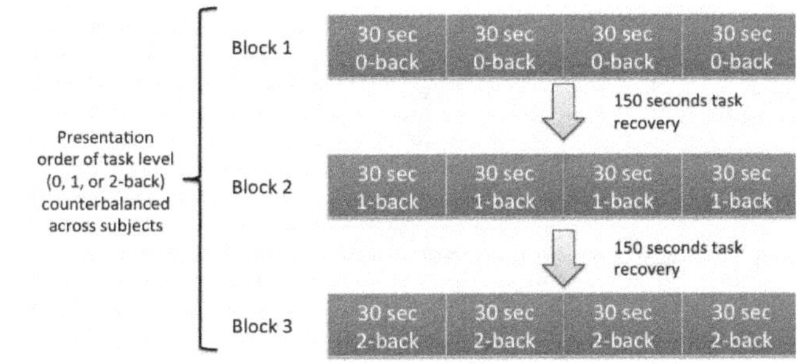

Figure 6. Procedure for Experiment 2.

Exploratory Analysis

The data shows that participants had a significant physiological response when presented and engaged in the secondary task. Figure 5 illustrates the value changes of heart rate during the experiment. Task periods are readily identifiable. Also, the counterbalanced presentation order can be recognized in each plot. The illustration support the hypothesis that cardiovascular measures are generally sensitive to changes in cognitive workload. We saw similar results looking at the skin conductance level and thus there is promise for classifiers that work across individuals.

Classification Approaches

For this experiment, we used similar processing and classification approaches as in the first experiment. However, the data set used included data from 99 participants, and classification was done across individuals. In addition, we have only the set of four consecutive 30-second *elevated* 2-back task periods per individual (24 trials in Experiment 1).

We were most interested in looking at high demand periods, and considered only the 2-back high demand periods and the single task driving periods. We looked at sliding windows of 10, 15, 20, 25, and 30 seconds and overlap factors of 0%, 25%, 50% and 75% to see the effects that these pre-processing parameters have on the classification accuracy. We were also interested in understanding the value of physiology features, driving features and their combination.

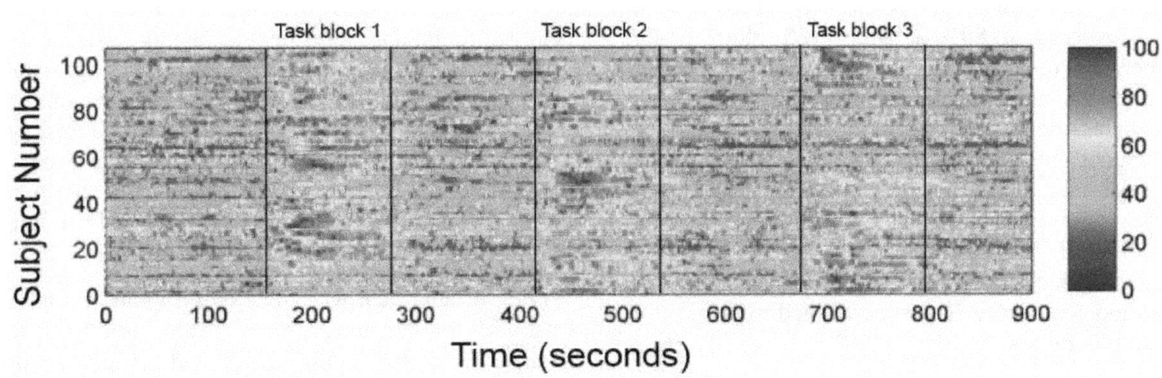

Figure 5. Heart rate change during experiment drive. Each row represents the change in heart rate of a single subject during experiment drive. Within three task block periods, subjects had to perform a secondary cognitive task (three levels of cognitive demand) in addition to the primary driving task. Red indicates maximum heart rate, blue color indicates minimum heart rate.

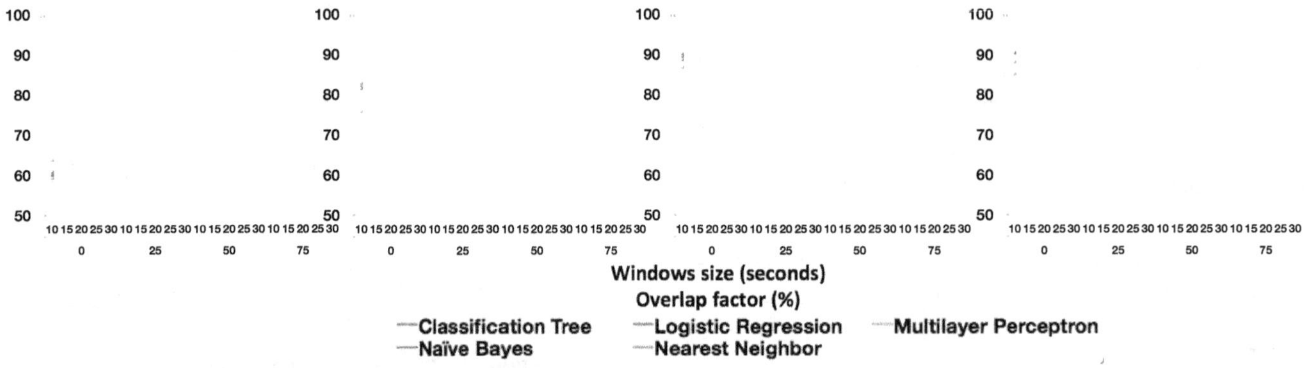

Figure 7. Classification accuracy using (from left to right) 1) driving features only 2) heart rate features only 3) all physiology features 4) physiology and driving features. Accuracy tends to increase with increased window size. The overlap factor had little influence. Nearest neighbor learning algorithm had the lowest classification accuracy, while the other algorithms had similar performance. The best performance was found in 3 and 4, indicating that HR was most sensitive to the cognitive load changes.

As in Experiment 1, ten-fold cross-validation was used for evaluating the approaches. However, we did not choose parameters using nested cross-validation. Instead, we report results from all choices of parameters as well as from five different classification algorithms for exploratory purposes. Folds were created based on individuals, so each fold held out 10% of the participants. Training and test sets never contained data from the same individual.

Classification Results

Our exploratory analysis resulted in a large amount of results (Figure 7). We highlight the main results that are significant for in-vehicle HCI research. Figure 7 shows the average accuracy for each combination of learning algorithm, sliding window size, overlap factor, and feature type.

Comparison of Physiological and Vehicle Features

The type of features had a clear effect on the classification results. When physiology features are ignored and classification algorithms are trained with features generated from *driving performance measures only*, we found the average classification accuracy to be 64% (1st plot in figure). We investigated using only *heart rate features* (mean, min, max, standard deviation, and first derivative), ignoring features extracted for electrodermal activity measures and driving data. With the exception of 1-Nearest Neighbor, all other learning techniques performed reasonably well, achieving an average of 80% accuracy (2nd plot). Using features generated from all available physiology data (heart rate and skin conductance level), logistic regression outperformed other classifiers achieving the highest performance with a 30 second sliding window. Multilayer perceptron and naïve Bayes had a significantly lower performance of 89% accuracy. The best classification performance using features from both physiology and driving performance data is similar to that using only physiology features. Logistic regression and naïve Bayes performed significantly better than all other classifiers.

Window size and window overlap

Figure 7 demonstrates the tradeoff that exists between window size and classification accuracy. Increasing the window size improved classification in all cases, except when the vehicle telemetry data was used by itself. This is important as the window sizes imply lag if the classification is operating in real time. As one might expect, the curves rise much more steeply as smaller window sizes increase to medium, and then seem to mostly plateau at the larger window sizes. It is interesting to note that the overlap factor doesn't have a significant impact on the classification accuracy.

Classification Algorithm

In the driving only analysis, the multilayer perceptron achieved the highest classification performance. In the analysis of the heart-rate data, the 1-nearest neighbor algorithm performed worse than the other algorithms. For most other analyses, the classifier choice did not make a large difference in the results, showing that feature generation and selection are key to accuracy in this domain.

DISCUSSION AND FUTURE WORK

Through the experiments described above, we examined several considerations for developing an automatic cognitive workload classifier for use in evaluating interfaces in real-world driving. We illustrate the impact that window size, classification algorithm, and training data set have on the robustness of the detection, and provide some guidance on the choice of these parameters. Similar to Grimes, et al. [11], we found a tradeoff between window size and classification accuracy. We did not find significant effects of window overlap. By using large datasets collected in real-world driving, we provide realistic estimates of the results of such systems. In experiment 1, we train models based on ~40 minutes of training data per individual. In experiment 2, we train models across individuals, using only 4 minutes of training data per person.

While our approach was successful in classifying cognitive load with high accuracy, there may be additional measures or algorithms that could also provide similar or improved results. In fact, it is likely that more sensitive driving performance measures, characterization of visual behavior and improved feature sets and algorithms will be developed in the future. In addition, there has been interest in classifying workload from brain data during driving (e.g. [17]). However, these would all fit in with the framework in Figure 2.

From the results of Experiment 2, it is apparent that classification power in this dataset is coming from physiology features, specifically from heart rate derived features. On the other hand, for this experiment only a handful of driving performance measures were used (velocity and both large and short steering wheel reversals); other metrics may prove valuable for classification.

In Experiment 1, we take into account individual differences by training a classifier for each individual. The approach employed in Experiment 2 however, makes the assumption, that the response to workload is somewhat consistent across all types of drivers. In other words, the models built using the proposed approach do compensate for different physiological or behavioral responses among drivers, but they assume that the structural response pattern is the same for all drivers. In the future, we could move closer to a deployable system where the algorithm is trained on a large dataset, and then is able to classify new system interactions among a different set of drivers when they enter the vehicle. In a hybrid approach, automatic recognition algorithms could be trained on large datasets. Then, a new driver may spend a short time providing additional training data that is specific to the individual. This could fine-tune the model to be customized for the individual that is driving.

While our paper provides comparative results of five classification algorithms, there are additional algorithms and approaches that may achieve higher performance. Future efforts may wish to consider additional modeling approaches. In addition, this work focused on classifying high demand periods from single-task driving. We plan to integrate the 0-back and 1-back data that we collected into our models to get a comprehensive model of physiological changes as demand levels change. Future investigation could also look at classification results when the models trained on the n-back task data are used to classify workload in other, more realistic tasks. It may be useful to compare physiological sensing with cognitive modeling tools such as Distract-R [32] that also can be used for in-vehicle interface evaluation. Finally, while we used a somewhat invasive medical grade EKG, measures of heart rate could be integrated in future cars using steering wheel, seat back, or other sensor sites to provide physiological measures in less invasively.

CONCLUSION

In this paper, we have shown that machine learning techniques can be applied to vehicle sensor data as well as driver physiological sensor data to provide recognition of elevated cognitive load periods. In addition, we report on the results of experiments to investigate specific parameters and approaches. This work was motivated by the need for additional methods for evaluating novel in-vehicle user interfaces to provide effective and safe experiences on the road. Poorly designed in-vehicle user interfaces can lead to distracted and potentially unsafe driving. Thus, the goal of this work was to evaluate the feasibility and practical considerations of physiological workload detection during natural driving, with a large, balanced group of drivers. We consider this to be a foundation for concrete applications such as in-vehicle user interface evaluation. Most previous work was either done in a simulator or with a small number of participants. In addition, the methods we described would apply to classifying workload in other contexts, such as game user experience evaluation or passive, adaptive user interfaces (similar to passive BCI work [1,9,35,44]), and our sample size is larger than most papers in those areas. This has implications for broader applications for real-time cognitive load assessment and evaluating user interface technology in the wild, beyond driver user interfaces.

ACKNOWLEDGMENTS

Acknowledgment is extended to NSF (NSF Grant#1136996 awarded to Computing Research Association for the CI Fellows Project) and US DOT's Region I New England University Transportation Center at MIT for support. EAGP acknowledges financial support from CONACYT-DAAD grant 308755. MZ was supported by a scholarship from the Max Weber-Program Bayern.

REFERENCES

1. Afergan, D., et al. Dynamic Difficulty Using Brain Metrics of Workload. *Proc. CHI,* (2014).
2. Afonso, V.X., Tompkins, W.J., Nguyen, T.Q., and Luo, S. Multirate processing of the ECG using filter banks. *Computers in Cardiology*, (1996), 245–248.
3. Backs, R.W.et al. Cardiac measures of driver workload during simulated driving with and without visual occlusion. *Human Factors 45*, 4, (2003), 525–38.
4. Christie, M.J. Electrodermal activity in the 1980s: a review. *J Royal Soc of Medicine 74*, 8 (1981), 616–22.
5. Collet, C., et al. Physiological and behavioural changes associated to the management of secondary tasks while driving. *Applied Ergonomics 40*, 6 (2009), 1041–6.
6. Coughlin, J.F., Reimer, B., and Mehler, B. Monitoring, managing, and motivating driver safety and well-being. *IEEE Pervasive Computing 10*, 3 (2011), 14–21.
7. Eldar, Y.C., Oppenheim, A.V. Filter bank interpolation and reconstruction from generalized and recurrent nonuniform samples. *IEEE ICASSP* (2000) 2–5.
8. Engström, J., Johansson, E., Östlund, J. Effects of visual and cognitive load in real and simulated motorway driving. *Transportation Research F*, 2 (2005), 97–120.
9. Girouard, A, Solovey, E.T., Jacob, R.J.K.. Designing a passive brain computer interface using real time classification of functional near–infrared spectroscopy. *IJAACS 6*, no. 1 (2013): 26-44.
10. Gopher, D. and Donchin, E. Workload: An examination of the concept. In K.R. Boof, L. Kaufman and J.P. Thomas, eds., *Handbook of Perception and Human Performance*. (1986), 41–1–41–49.
11. Grimes, D., Tan, D.S., Hudson, S.E., Shenoy, P., and Rao, R.P.N. Feasibility and Pragmatics of Classifying Working Memory Load with an Electroencephalograph. *Proc. CHI.* (2008), 835–844.

12. Haigney, D., Taylor, R., Westerman, S. Concurrent mobile (cellular) phone use and driving performance: task demand characteristics and compensatory processes. *Transportation Research F 3*, 3 (2000), 113–121.
13. Hajek, W., et al. Workload-adaptive cruise control – A new generation of advanced driver assistance systems. *Transportation Research Part F 20*, 0 (2013), 108–120.
14. Healey, J.A. and Picard, R.W. Detecting Stress During Real-World Driving Tasks Using Physiological Sensors. *IEEE Transactions on Intelligent Transportation Systems 6*, 2 (2005), 156–166.
15. Jahn, G., et al. Peripheral detection as a workload measure in driving: Effects of traffic complexity and route guidance system use in a driving study. *Transportation Research Part F 8*, 3 (2005), 255–275.
16. Just, M.A., Keller, T.A., and Cynkar, J. A decrease in brain activation associated with driving when listening to someone speak. *Brain research 1205*, (2008), 70–80.
17. Kohlmorgen, Jens, et al. Improving human performance in a real operating environment through real-time mental workload detection. *Toward Brain-Computer Interfacing* (2007), 409-422.
18. Liang, Y.L.Y., Reyes, M.L., and Lee, J.D. Real-Time Detection of Driver Cognitive Distraction Using Support Vector Machines. *IEEE Transactions on Intelligent Transportation Systems 8*, (2007), 340–350.
19. Mehler, B., et al. Impact of Incremental Increases in Cognitive Workload on Physiological Arousal and Performance in Young Adult Drivers. *Transportation Research 2138*, 12 (2009), 6–12.
20. Mehler, B., Reimer, B., and Coughlin, J.F. Sensitivity of Physiological Measures for Detecting Systematic Variations in Cognitive Demand From a Working Memory Task: An On-Road Study Across Three Age Groups. *Human Factors 54*, 3 (2012), 396–412.
21. Mehler, B., Reimer, B., Dusek, J. MIT AgeLab Delayed Digit Recall Task (n-back). (2011) http://agelab.mit.edu/mit-agelab-delayed-digit-recall-task-white-paper.
22. Mehler, B., Reimer, B., Wang, Y. A comparison of heart rate and heart rate variability indices in distinguishing single task driving and driving under secondary cognitive workload. *Proc Driving Symposium on Human Factors in Driver Assessment, Training & Vehicle Design*, (2011), 590–597.
23. Michon, J.A. A Critical View of Driver Behavior Models: What Do We Know, What Should We Do? *Human behavior and traffic safety*, (1985), 485–520.
24. Miyaji, M., Danno, M., Kawanaka, H., and Oguri, K. Driver's cognitive distraction detection using AdaBoost on pattern recognition basis. *ICVES*, (2008), 51–56.
25. Mulder, L.J.M. Measurement and analysis methods of heart rate and respiration for use in applied environments. *Biological Psychology 34*, 2-3 (1992), 205–236.
26. National Highway Traffic Safety Admin. *Traffic Safety Facts: Distracted Driving*. Washington, DC, (2011).
27. Östlund, J., et al. *Adaptive Integrated Driver-Vehicle Interface (AIDE): Driving performance assessment - methods and metrics*. Gothenburg, Sweden, (2005).
28. Peterson, F., Jung, C.G. Psycho-Physical Investigations with the Galvanometer and Pneumograph in Normal and Insane Individuals. *Brain 30*, 2 (1907), 153–218.
29. Reimer, B., Mehler, B., Wang, Y., and Coughlin, J.F. A Field Study on the Impact of Variations in Short-Term Memory Demands on Drivers' Visual Attention and Driving Performance Across Three Age Groups. *Human Factors 54*, 3 (2012), 454–468.
30. Reimer, B. and Mehler, B. The impact of cognitive workload on physiological arousal in young adult drivers: a field study and simulation validation. *Ergonomics 54*, (2011), 932–42.
31. Saga, K. Histochemical and immunohistochemical markers for human eccrine and apocrine sweat glands: an aid for histopathologic differentiation of sweat gland tumors. *J of Investigative Dermatology 6*, 1 (2001).
32. Salvucci, D.D., Zuber, M., Beregovaia, E., and Markley, D. Distract-R: rapid prototyping and evaluation of in-vehicle interfaces. *Proc. CHI.* (2005), 581–589.
33. Schneegaß, S., et al. A Data Set of Real World Driving to Assess Driver Workload. *Proc of Auto UI*, (2013).
34. Singleton, W.T. *The Mind at Work*. Cambridge University Press, (1989).
35. Solovey, E.T., et al., Brainput: Enhancing interactive system with streaming fNIRS brain input. *Proc. CHI.* (2012).
36. Son, J., Reimer, B., Mehler, B., et al. Age and cross-cultural comparison of drivers' cognitive workload and performance in simulated urban driving. *Internl J of Automotive Technology 11*, 4 (2010), 533–539.
37. Stanton, N., & Young, M. Vehicle automation and driving performance. *Ergonomics, 41*(7) (1998)1014-1028.
38. Szabo, A., et al. Mental challenge elicits "additional" increases in heart rate during low and moderate intensity cycling. *Intl J Psychophysiology 17*, 3 (1994), 197–204.
39. Veltman, J.A. and Gaillard, A.W. Physiological workload reactions to increasing levels of task difficulty. *Ergonomics 41*, 5 (1998), 656–69.
40. de Waard, et al. Effect of road layout and road environment on driving performance, drivers' physiology and road appreciation. *Ergonomics 38*, 7 (1995), 1395–407.
41. Yerkes, R. M., Dodson, J.D. "The relation of strength of stimulus to rapidity of habit-formation," *J of Comparative Neurology and Psychology 18*, (1908).
42. Young, M.S. Stanton, N.A. Malleable attentional resources theory: a new explanation for the effects of mental underload on performance. *Human Factors 44*, (2002), 365–375.
43. Young, M.S. and Stanton, N.A. Mental Workload. In N.A. Stanton, A. Hedge, K. Brookhuis, E. Salas and H. Hendrick, eds., *Handbook of Human Factors and Ergonomics Methods*. CNC Press, (2004), 1–9.
44. Zander T. O., Kothe C. Towards passive brain–computer interfaces: applying brain-computer interface technology to human–machine systems in general. *J. Neural Eng. 8*, (2011).

Evaluating Multimodal Driver Displays under Varying Situational Urgency

Ioannis Politis[1], Stephen Brewster[2]
Glasgow Interactive Systems Group
School of Computing Science
University of Glasgow
Glasgow, G12 8QQ, UK
[1]I.Politis.1@research.gla.ac.uk
[2]Stephen.Brewster@glasgow.ac.uk

Frank Pollick
School of Psychology
University of Glasgow
Glasgow G12 8QB, UK
Frank.Pollick@glasgow.ac.uk

ABSTRACT
Previous studies have investigated audio, visual and tactile driver warnings, indicating the importance of communicating the appropriate level of urgency to the drivers. However, these modalities have never been combined exhaustively and tested under conditions of varying situational urgency to assess their effectiveness both in the presence and absence of critical driving events. This paper describes an experiment evaluating all multimodal combinations of such warnings under two contexts of situational urgency: a lead car braking and not braking. The results showed that participants responded quicker to more urgent warnings, especially in the presence of a car braking. They also responded faster to the multimodal as opposed to unimodal signals. Driving behaviour improved in the presence of the warnings and the absence of a car braking. These results highlight the influence of urgency and number of modalities in warning design and indicate the utility of non-visual warnings in driving.

Author Keywords
Multimodal Interaction; Warnings; Audio; Visual; Tactile; Situational Urgency; Response Time; Lateral Deviation; Steering Angle; Simulator.

ACM Classification Keywords
H.5.2 [Information interfaces and presentation]: User Interfaces. -Auditory (non-speech) feedback; Haptic I/O.

INTRODUCTION
Multimodal displays are increasingly finding their way inside the car, making the driving experience more and more multisensory [13]. While this offers potential for designing a wealth of warnings for the driver, there is on-going research into which warnings offer the best results. Several combinations of audio, visual and tactile modalities have been utilized to design driver alerts [7,11,24,27,31]. However, there has been no exhaustive research on how all unimodal and multimodal combinations of these modalities perform when situational urgency is varied. Effective warnings need to aid rather than hinder the driving task when critical events arise, for example when a car in front brakes rapidly. Therefore, it is essential to compare drivers' performance when exposed to warnings both in the presence and the absence of such events to ensure their effectiveness in different driving settings. This has not been addressed before and is important so as to extend knowledge on multimodal warning design.

CHI 2014, April 26 - May 01 2014, Toronto, ON, Canada

http://dx.doi.org/10.1145/2556288.2556988

This paper presents an experiment where all combinations of audio, tactile and visual modalities were used to alert drivers in a simulated driving task (see Figure 1). The signals were designed across three different urgency levels, according to existing guidelines [9,10,24,28]. Situational urgency was varied by manipulating the behaviour of a simulated lead vehicle. The study aimed to reveal how participants would respond to the presentation of differently urgent signals in the presence or absence of a critical event and how driving behaviour would be influenced by the parallel presentation of such an event.

Figure 1. The setup of the experiment. Headphones, tactile belt and computer screen were used to deliver the multimodal signals.

In summary, the following guidelines can be derived from this work:

- Using bimodal and trimodal warnings rather than unimodal ones can cause faster reaction times to critical events;
- Using warnings of high designed urgency can speed up reactions critical situations;
- Using warnings of medium designed urgency can provide an overall alertness, as well as improved lane keeping and steering behavior when no critical event is present;
- Non-visual signals are more effective in visually demanding situations.

RELATED WORK

A number of studies indicate the usefulness of multimodal displays for providing information related to the driving task. Ablaßmeier *et al.* [1] used a head-up display (HUD) to provide such information and observed fewer glances and higher acceptance in comparison to a central information display. Ho & Spence [12] showed that responses to a critical event were more rapid when naturalistic audio cues (car horn sounds) come from the direction of the event (front or back) and when participants' attention was directed to the appropriate direction through a verbal cue. Further, according to Ho, Tan & Spence [14] vibrotactile cues presented from the same direction as an approaching threat (front or back) can decrease drivers' reaction times during a simulated driving task, compared to cues presented from the opposite direction.

Using bimodal signals, Ho, Reed & Spence [11] showed the potential of audiotactile presentation in front-to-rear-end collision warnings, using vibration on the torso and a car horn sound. These bimodal warnings led to lower reaction times in a simulated driving task compared to the unimodal variants. Using audio, tactile as well as visual modalities for alerting drivers, Scott & Gray [31] found that tactile warnings on the abdomen, simulating seat belt warnings, can induce quicker reactions in a critical driving situation compared to sounds and visual warnings on the dashboard. The signals used in their study were unimodal, so no modality combinations were used. Murata, Kanbayashi & Hayami [25] presented a study using some combinations of audio, tactile and visual modalities to alert drivers of an approaching hazard. The three modalities in isolation, as well as the combinations of audio + tactile, audio + visual and visual + tactile modalities were used (the trimodal combination was not used). Results showed that tactile and audio + tactile warnings produced the shortest reaction times to presented hazards. Oskarsson, Eriksson & Carlander [26] investigated the use of the trimodal combination when driving a simulated combat vehicle. The cues used were abstract sound and vibration patterns and a visual pointer to a virtual threat in the simulator. When responding to the stimuli by turning the vehicle as fast and as accurately as possible and firing at the target, it was found that the use of trimodal combinations of audio, visual and tactile cues improved performance compared to the unimodal presentation of the warnings. There was also no increase in mental workload when the trimodal displays were used.

The studies described above have investigated some of the unimodal and multimodal combinations of warnings. However, the urgency designed in the warnings was not varied. Additionally, not all combinations of the audio, visual or tactile modalities were used in warnings. In our study, all combinations of modalities are used in warnings designed to convey different urgency levels.

Warnings of Varying Urgency

In the aforementioned work, the signals were designed to convey a single level of urgency, usually related to critical events. However, in a real driving situation, alerts may not always refer to situations that are equally urgent. Kaufmann *et al.* [18] presented a set of guidelines for the use of audio, tactile and visual warnings along three priority levels. The authors defined high priority warnings as requiring immediate action, while medium required no immediate reaction and low priority ones bore no immediate relevance to the driving task. Audio and tactile modalities were demonstrated as suitable for high priority messages, visual and tactile for medium and audio and visual for low priority ones. The suggestions were based on measures of speed and steering performance of participants, while response times to the signals were not measured and modality combinations were not tested exhaustively.

Cao *et al.* [7] investigated the use of audio and tactile cues conveying four different levels of urgency. Number of pulses and inter-pulse-interval were manipulated for all cues to signify urgency. Additionally, pitch was manipulated for the audio cues and intensity for the tactile ones. The main task in this study was visual tracking with different levels of auditory distractions (namely radio, conversation and noise) but no driving task was simulated. A general trend of higher urgency = faster response was found, indicating that the designed urgency of the cues was successfully perceived. Vibration cues were also identified more accurately but sound cues more quickly. Finally, sound cues were reported as easier to distinguish by the participants.

Serrano *et al.* [32] tested a set of speech messages indicating either a hazardous or a non-hazardous situation. They presented these messages followed by pictures of either hazardous or non-hazardous road scenes, asking drivers to identify whether the scenes were hazardous or not by pressing a button. Reaction times of drivers to this identification task were shorter and responses more accurate when the speech messages were presented from the direction of the hazard (informative) as opposed to a random direction (non-informative). Reaction times were also shorter for informative messages, when the direction of the threat (left or right) was uttered in the message as opposed to not specified. In our study, all multimodal combinations of cues, rather than only audio, were presented from the direction of the hazard along with a simulated driving task, rather than a visual recognition task.

Lindgren *et al.* [21] investigated a set of integrated visual and auditory warnings for events in the driving task varying in criticality. Auditory warnings similar to commercially available ones for collision avoidance, lane departure and curve speed were provided with or without advisory warnings in a driving simulator. The advisory warnings were visual indicators, graphically showing the distance of the car to a vehicle in front, behind or relative to a curve. It was found that the presence of warnings did not influence the driving speed or how often drivers moved their gaze off the road. Additionally, participants drove with higher average lateral deviation from the centre of the lane when no warnings were present, indicating a lower level of vigilance. However, these driving metrics were averaged per condition (i.e. no warnings, auditory warnings only, auditory + advisory warnings) and not per warning used. In the present study, we examine lateral deviation in greater accuracy and present steering angle measurements for every multimodal warning rather than for a whole condition.

Using audio, visual and tactile modalities, Lewis *et al.* [20] observed quicker response times in bimodal cues compared to unimodal ones and in high urgency warnings compared to low urgency ones. Measures of response times were taken with a primary simulated driving task and under two conditions of memory load in a secondary memory task (high load and low load). Performance was especially improved in the low load task compared to the high one. Increasing the levels of urgency and the number of modalities used, Politis, Brewster & Pollick [27] evaluated all unimodal, bimodal and trimodal combinations of audio, visual and tactile warnings to alert drivers of events in three urgency levels. These were impending collision (high urgency), low fuel (medium urgency) and incoming message (low urgency). Participants were engaged in a simulated driving task and were asked to rate the stimuli in terms of urgency and annoyance, as well as recognise the level of urgency to which each signal belonged. It was found that participants recognised highly urgent signals most quickly, while increasing the number of modalities used in warnings (one, two or three) caused higher ratings of urgency and lower response times. Ratings of annoyance were also higher as more modalities were used, but the observed effect of annoyance was lower compared to urgency.

The above studies have investigated the effect of designed urgency in warnings in the audio, visual and tactile modalities. With the exception of [27], the warnings evaluated did not involve all the combinations of these modalities in different levels of urgency. Additionally, in [27] the response times were gathered during a cue recognition task involving button pressing, with limited ecological validity. In the study presented here, responses are gathered during a simulated braking event with higher realism. The scope of [27] is also extended by evaluating the multimodal warnings used in different contexts of situational urgency.

Guidelines for Warning Urgency Design

There have been numerous studies investigating how signal parameters of warnings relate to their perceived urgency. Edworthy, Loxley & Dennis [9] showed that higher fundamental frequency, higher speed and larger pitch range can increase the perceived urgency ratings of auditory warnings. Edworthy *et al.* [8] observed significantly lower response times for highly urgent warnings, compared to warnings designed to be of medium and low urgency levels. Marshall, Lee & Austria [24] demonstrated how parameters like higher pulse duration and lower interpulse interval increased ratings of urgency of audio alerts. Different sound cues were investigated in three driving contexts of varying urgency, namely impending collision, navigation and email messages. Baldwin [3] reported how stimulus intensity influenced the ratings of perceived urgency and response times in a simulated driving task.

Gonzalez *et al.* [10] found that fundamental frequency, pulse rate and intensity of warning sounds positively influenced the ratings of urgency and annoyance of participants. However, pulse rate was suggested as the most suitable for conveying events of varying urgency, since it did not elicit such high ratings of annoyance compared to the ratings of urgency. In this study no simulated driving task was present. Pratt *et al.* [28] reported a similar observation for the tactile modality, where pulse rate was found to positively influence the ratings of perceived urgency and to have less impact on the ratings of perceived annoyance. Extending the investigation to audio, tactile and visual modalities Baldwin *et al.* [2] and Lewis & Baldwin [19] initiated the creation of a crossmodal urgency scale. Pulse rate (flash rate for visual signals) was suggested as an effective parameter to vary urgency across these three modalities. Sound intensity and frequency were effective for audio signals, with word choice and colours for visual ones. In [2], Baldwin *et al.* mention that there is limited information regarding the impact of presenting warnings of multiple modalities to drivers in varying situational urgency contexts. This is addressed in our study by evaluating the cues under different simulated events, namely the front vehicle braking and not braking.

The Effect of Situational Urgency

As described earlier, there is interest in investigating how the modality combinations perform in situations of different urgency. This will provide insight into whether the response to the cues will be affected by events that occur when driving. In all the studies discussed above, participants' responses were acquired under situations of urgency that did not vary. Whether they were critical events, such as an impending collision or less critical, such as navigational instructions, all responses were measured only in the presence of these events and not in their absence. It is important to evaluate the cues under varying levels of situational urgency to understand how this affects their performance. For example, they may be effective in one setting but perform poorly in another. Serrano *et al.* [32] have partly addressed this by treating events like lane departure and increased speed when entering curves as differently urgent. However, they did not test all combinations of multimodal cues. Lindgren *et al.* [21] also used different urgency levels but their scenarios were only presented as pictures. They also only tested audio warnings. Therefore, as also acknowledged in [2], there remain many questions around the design of multimodal cues for creating messages of different urgency levels and their evaluation in a driving simulator. We address these questions in this paper.

SITUATIONAL URGENCY EXPERIMENT

A set of multimodal warnings was designed to represent three different levels of urgency and tested in a driving simulator. We tested them across three levels of situational urgency: a lead car braking and a warning presented, a lead car braking with no warning presented and just a warning presented. The goal was to investigate the effect of the situation simulated on observed driver responses. As described above, several studies have reported how designed urgency and modality affected response times, for example [8,11,27]. The influence of modalities used in warnings to lateral deviation and steering angle has also been shown in the past, for example in [21]. Therefore, it was hypothesized that in our study response times and driving behaviour would be influenced by the modalities used in the warnings, the level of designed urgency of the warnings, as well as the situational urgency of the simulated event.

Warning Design

The set of warnings used in this study were identical to those in [27]. As in [27], three Levels of Designed Urgency (LDU) were created to indicate conditions varying in importance. L_H (Level High) was designed to signify situations of high urgency, such as an impending collision, L_M (Level Medium) situations of medium urgency, such as low fuel and L_L (Level Low) situations of low urgency, such as an incoming message. All unimodal and multimodal combinations of the audio, visual and tactile modalities were used in the warnings: Audio (A), Visual (V), Tactile (T), Audio + Visual (AV), Audio + Tactile (AT), Tactile + Visual (TV), Audio + Tactile + Visual (ATV). The result was 21 different signals: 7 signals with the above modalities × 3 levels of designed urgency.

Pure tones, colours or vibrations were used in the warnings and were delivered repeatedly as pulses to the participants. Depending on the level of urgency, pulse rate varied, increasing as signals became more urgent, as in [2,19,27]. Independent of modality, warnings of the same urgency level had the same pulse rate. 8 pulses with 0.1 sec single pulse duration and 0.1 sec interpulse interval were used for L_H, 5 pulses with 0.17 sec single pulse duration and 0.17 sec interpulse interval for L_M and 2 pulses with 0.5 sec single pulse duration and 0.5 sec interpulse interval for L_L. All warnings lasted 1.5 sec each.

Auditory warnings were additionally varied in base frequency, as suggested in [2,9,19,24] (1000 Hz for L_H, 700 Hz for L_M and 400 Hz for L_L).Visual warnings were also varied in colour, in line with [2,27] (Red for L_H, Orange for L_M and Yellow for L_L [1]). A C2 Tactor from Engineering Acoustics[2] was used for the tactile stimuli, a common device in studies of tactile feedback, e.g. [15,16]. Tactile stimuli had a constant frequency of 250 Hz, the nominal centre frequency of the C2 - the frequency at which the skin is most sensitive. Stimulus intensity was kept constant in all modalities, to avoid discomfort, a common practice in studies of both Earcons and Tactons [15,16]. Simultaneous delivery of unimodal signals was used for multimodal ones, to create a synchronous effect of sound, vibration, visuals and their combinations.

Driving Metrics

In addition to measuring the response times of drivers to warnings, we also measured lateral deviation and variation of steering angle to give a complete picture of performance. Lower lateral deviation and variation of the steering angle indicate lower driver distraction [21,23]. As in [6,30], the Root Mean Square Error (RMSE) of the vehicle's lateral deviation and steering angle were used as metrics of driver distraction. The effect of presenting multimodal warnings in the presence and the absence of a critical event on these driving metrics has not been investigated in the past.

Experiment Design

A 7×3×3 within subjects design was used for this experiment, with Modality, LDU and Situational Urgency as the Independent Variables. Response Time (RT), RMSE of Lateral Deviation (LatDev) and RMSE of Steering Angle (SteAng) were Dependent Variables. Modality had 7 levels: A, T, V, AT, AV, TV, ATV. LDU had 3 levels: L_H (High Urgency), L_M (Medium Urgency) and L_L (Low Urgency). Situational urgency had 3 levels: Car Braking + No Warning Presented, No Car Braking + Warning Presented and Car Braking + Warning Presented. There were the following hypotheses:

- The observed values of RT will be affected by the Situational Urgency simulated (H_{1a}), the LDU of the warnings (H_{1b}) and the Modality of the warnings (H_{1c}).
- The observed values of LatDev will be affected by the Situational Urgency simulated (H_{2a}), the LDU of the warnings (H_{2b}) and the Modality of the warnings (H_{2c}).

---

[1] Red was *RGB*(255,0,0), Orange was *RGB*(255,127,0) and Yellow was *RGB*(255,255,0).

[2] http://www.atactech.com/PR_tactors.html

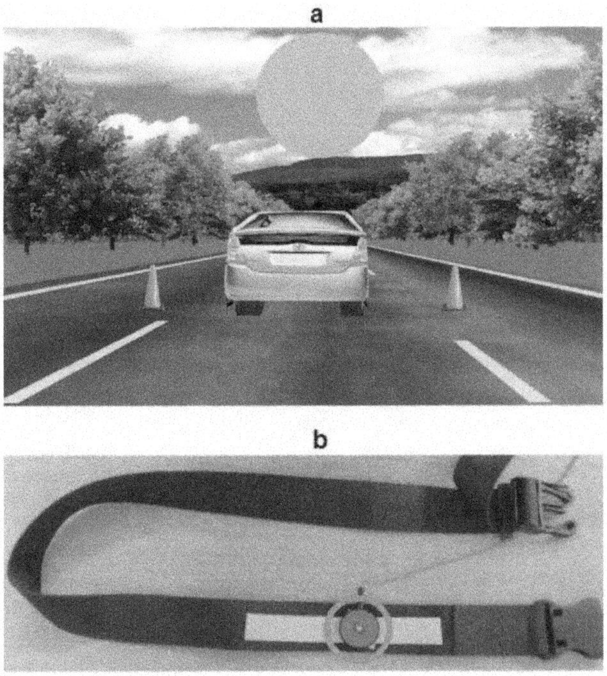

Figure 2. (a) A screen from the simulator software, depicting the front car braking and a visual stimulus of medium LDU presented. (b) The waist belt used to provide tactile stimuli, Tactor is highlighted.

- The observed values of SteAng will be affected by the Situational Urgency simulated (H_{3a}), the LDU of the warnings (H_{3b}) and the Modality of the warnings (H_{3c}).

Participants

Fifteen participants (10 female) aged between 19 and 28 years (*M* = 22.67, *SD* = 2.66) took part. They all held a valid driving license and had between 1.5 and 8 years of driving experience (*M* = 4.5, *SD* = 2.02). There were 14 university students and one journalist. They reported normal or corrected to normal vision and hearing and no injuries around the abdominal area where vibrations were delivered.

Equipment

The experiment took place in a usability lab, where participants sat on a chair in front of a desk with a 27-inch Dell 2709W monitor and a PC running the simulator software. In the software a three lane road in a rural area with a lead car was depicted, maintaining a steady speed (see Figure 2.a). This simulator has been used in several previous research studies, e.g. [6]. As in [6], safety cones were placed on either side of the central lane, to reinforce lane keeping. Participants used the Logitech G27[3] gaming wheel to steer the simulated vehicle and brake. Participants' inputs were logged with a frequency of 50 Hz. Sound was delivered through a set of Sennheiser HD 25-1 headphones. Tactile cues were delivered through a C2 Tactor attached to an adjustable waist belt. The belt was placed by the participants in the middle of the abdominal area and was designed to simulate a vibrating seat belt, similar to [27,31]. Visual cues were delivered through coloured circles that flashed in the top central area of the screen, and were sized 400×400 pixels (12×12 cm). The circles did not obstruct the lead car and were designed to simulate the feedback of a HUD. Figure 1 depicts the setup of the experiment, Figure 2.a a screen from the simulator with the car braking and a visual signal presented and Figure 2.b the waist belt and Tactor.

[3] http://gaming.logitech.com/en-gb/product/g27-racing-wheel

Procedure

Participants were welcomed and provided with a brief introduction. To cover any noise from the Tactor, car sound was heard through the headphones throughout the experiment. The car sound was an extract from a recording of a vehicle idling, retrieved from the Internet.

Before beginning the procedure, all 21 signals were played once to the participants, always in the following order: A → V → T → AV → AT → TV → ATV for L_H, then the same order for L_M and then for L_L. In two cases, sound and vibration were slightly adjusted to maintain comfortable intensities. No specific information about the levels of designed urgency was given to the participants. The only information provided was that the signals presented were not always designed to convey the same level of urgency. Next, participants were asked to drive with the simulator for 90 sec, to get accustomed to the experimental setup.

In the main part of the experiment, participants were presented with a driving scene, where they drove a simulated vehicle along a straight rural road and followed a car in front. Participants were able to steer the vehicle and brake, but did not use the accelerator pedal, since the controlled vehicle maintained a constant speed of about 80 mph. This speed was chosen so as to exceed the UK motorway speed limit (70 mph) and create a hazardous driving situation requiring the drivers' attention. The participants encountered three possible situations during one session. The first involved the front car braking and a warning presented at the same time (Car & Stimulus: CarStim). The second situation involved only the Car braking (Car) and the third only the warning presented (Stim). There were 21 trials for each of the CarStim, Car and Stim conditions (one for each type of multimodal warning). This resulted in 63 trials, which happened in a random order and were separated by a random interval of any integral value of 8 – 20 sec. These values were chosen to be similar to previous studies investigating a repeated occurrence of critical events in the driving task, such as [11,12,14,27] and gave the driver time to settle back into driving before receiving another warning.

Participants were asked to maintain a central position in the lane and press the brake whenever they saw the front car braking, or felt a stimulus presented or both of the above. Their RT was calculated from the onset of the stimulus and / or the start of the braking event of the lead car, until the participant first pressed the brake pedal. Their LatDev and SteAng were logged from 4 seconds to 1 second before any situation arose, forming their baseline value for driving performance. They were logged again for 3 seconds immediately after the event to assess the effects on driving. For both LatDev and SteAng, the RMSE values were then computed from the logged values. As a result, for each of the 63 trials of one condition, there was one value for each participant's RT, two values for their LatDev (baseline value and value after the situation arose) and two values for their SteAng (baseline value and value after the situation arose). Each participant repeated the above procedure twice during the course of a week. After the second session the experiment was concluded and participants were debriefed. The experiment lasted about 120 minutes (60 min per session) and participants received payment of £12.

RESULTS

Response Time

Data for response time were first analysed using a one-way ANOVA with Situational Urgency as a factor. There was a significant effect of situation on RT ($F(2,1883) = 48.56$, $p < 0.001$, $\omega = 0.20$). Planned contrasts revealed that situation CarStim induced significantly shorter RT compared to situations Car and Stim ($t(1883) = 9.85$, $p < 0.001$, $r = 0.22$), while situations Car and Stim did not differ. As a result H_{1a} was accepted. See Figure 3.a for the mean response times across situations.

Data for situations Stim and CarStim, where there was a signal present, were analysed using a three-way repeated measures ANOVA, with Situational Urgency, LDU and Modality as factors. Mauchly's test revealed that the assumption of sphericity had been violated for Modality, therefore degrees of freedom for Modality were corrected using Greenhouse–Geisser estimates.

There was a significant main effect of Situational Urgency ($F(1,27) = 59.34$, $p < 0.001$). Contrasts revealed, as expected, that situation CarStim induced quicker responses compared to Stim ($F(1,27) = 59.34$, $r = 0.83$, $p < 0.001$).

There was a significant main effect of LDU ($F(2,54) = 12.88$, $p < 0.001$). Contrasts revealed that warnings of L_H induced significantly quicker reactions compared to L_M ($F(1,27) = 10.36$, $r = 0.53$, $p < 0.05$), while the difference between levels medium and low did not reach significance ($F(1,27) = 3.865$, $p = 0.06$). Thus H_{1b} was accepted.

There was also a significant main effect of Modality ($F(4.12,111.16) = 23.39$, $p < 0.001$). Contrasts revealed that warnings of the AV, ATV, AT and TV modality all created quicker responses compared to A, V and T warnings ($F(1,27) = 28.18$, $r = 0.71$, $p < 0.001$) (see Figure 3.b), as a result H_{1c} was accepted.

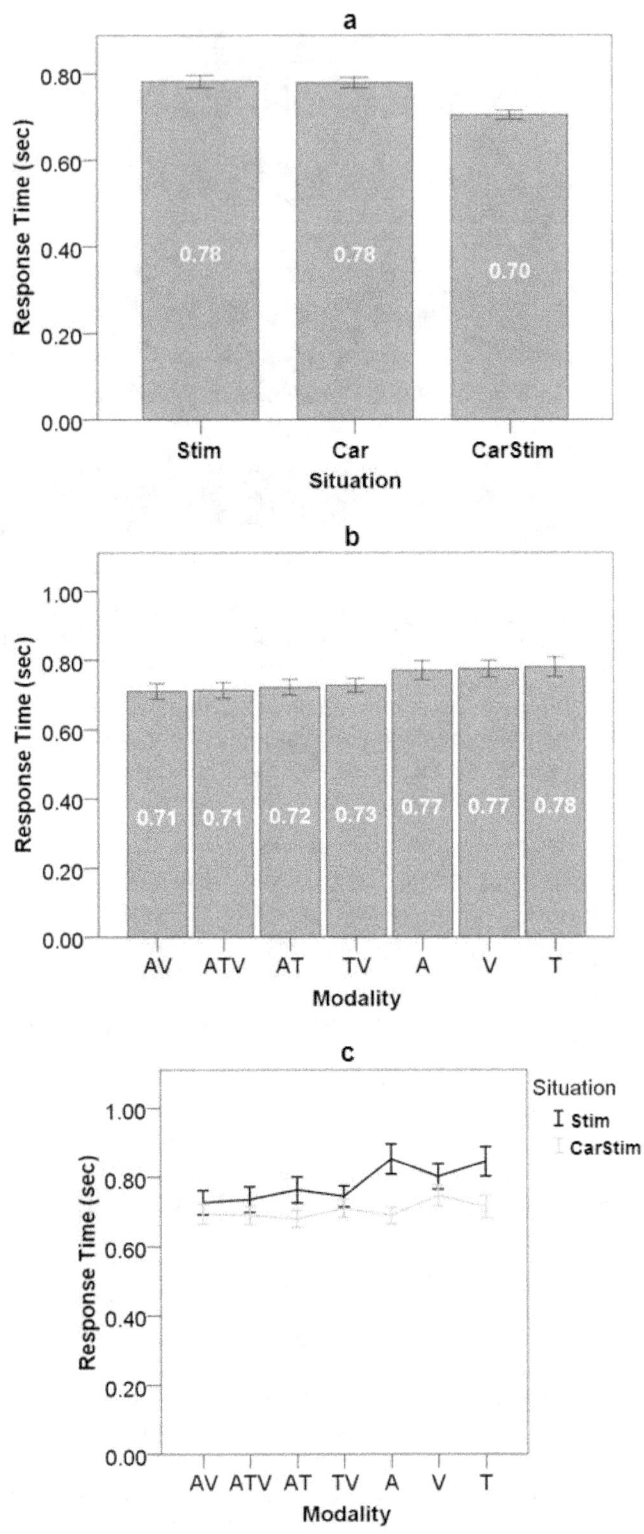

Figure 3. (a) The response times across situations. (b) The response times across modalities, sorted by their mean values. (c) The interaction between Situation and Modality with modalities sorted by their mean values. For all graphs, error bars represent 95% Confidence Intervals.

There was a significant interaction between Situation and Modality ($F(4.83,130.27) = 22.48$, $p < 0.001$). Contrasts revealed that while in situation Stim, ATV warnings created significantly quicker responses than AT ones, this effect was reversed for situation CarStim ($F(1,27) = 9.04$, $r = 0.50$, $p < 0.05$). Further, AT warnings created significantly slower responses compared to TV ones in situation Stim, but this effect was again reversed in situation CarStim ($F(1,27) = 7.43$, $r = 0.46$, $p < 0.05$). Finally, A warnings had significantly slower response times than V in situation Stim, but this effect was reversed in situation CarStim ($F(1,27) = 32.03$, $r = 0.74$, $p < 0.001$), see Figure 3.c.

These results indicate that Situational Urgency, LDU and Modality all influenced driver responses. They also show that warnings including visuals did not create as quick responses in situation CarStim.

Lateral Deviation

Data for LatDev were first analysed using a two-way repeated measures ANOVA, with Situation and Time as factors. Situation had three levels: Stim, Car and CarStim. Time had two levels: Before Situation (baseline data) and After Situation (data after the situation arose). Mauchly's test revealed that the assumption of sphericity had been violated for Situation, therefore degrees of freedom for Situation were corrected using Greenhouse–Geisser estimates. There was a significant main effect of Situation ($F(1.93,1215.88) = 59.17$, $p < 0.001$). Contrasts revealed that situation CarStim induced higher values of LatDev compared to Car ($F(1,629) = 81.04$, $r = 0.34$, $p < 0.001$), while values of LatDev did not differ among situations Stim and Car ($F(1,629) = 0.56$, $p = 0.81$). There was a significant main effect of Time ($F(1,629) = 258.22$, $p < 0.001$). Contrasts revealed that LatDev was significantly lower after any situation arose compared to before ($F(1,629) = 258.22$, $r = 0.54$, $p < 0.001$).

There was a significant interact between Situation and Time ($F(1.97,1240.66) = 64.74$, $p < 0.001$). Contrasts revealed that while in situation Car values of LatDev were lower after the event compared to before it, but there was no such difference for situation CarStim ($F(1,629) = 103.52$, $r = 0.38$, $p < 0.001$). As a result H_{2a} was accepted. See Figure 4.a for the interaction between Situation and Time for LatDev values. A separate four-way ANOVA test for situations Stim and CarStim (where warnings were present) with Situation, Time, LDU and Modality as factors showed no significant results, so H_{2b} and H_{2c} were rejected.

Steering Angle

Data for SteAng were first analysed using a two-way repeated measures ANOVA, with Situation and Time as factors as above. Mauchly's test revealed that the assumption of sphericity had been violated for Situation, therefore degrees of freedom for Situation were corrected using Greenhouse–Geisser estimates. There was a significant main effect of Situation ($F(1.98,1244.49) = 196.07$, $p < 0.001$). Contrasts revealed that situation CarStim induced higher values of SteAng compared to Car ($F(1,629) = 297.35$, $r = 0.57$, $p < 0.001$), while values of SteAng did not differ among situations Stim and Car ($F(1,629) = 0.68$, $p = 0.79$). There was a significant main effect of Time ($F(1,629) = 601.05$, $p < 0.001$). Contrasts revealed that SteAng was lower after any situation arose compared to before ($F(1,629) = 601.05$, $r = 0.70$, $p < 0.001$).

There was a significant interaction between Situation and Time ($F(1.93,1216.11) = 317.76$, $p < 0.001$). Contrasts revealed that while in situation Car values of SteAng were lower after the event compared to before it, this effect was reversed for situation CarStim ($F(1,629) = 421.21$, $r = 0.63$, $p < 0.001$). As a result H_{3a} was accepted. See Figure 4.b for the interaction between Situation and Time for SteAng.

A separate four-way ANOVA for situations Stim and CarStim (where warnings were present) with Situation, Time, LDU and Modality as factors showed a significant interaction between Situation and LDU ($F(1.93,55.99) = 4.94$, $p < 0.05$). Contrasts revealed that in situation CarStim the SteAng was significantly higher for L_L compared to L_M, which was not the case in situation S ($F(1,29) = 8.99$, $r = 0.49$, $p < 0.05$).

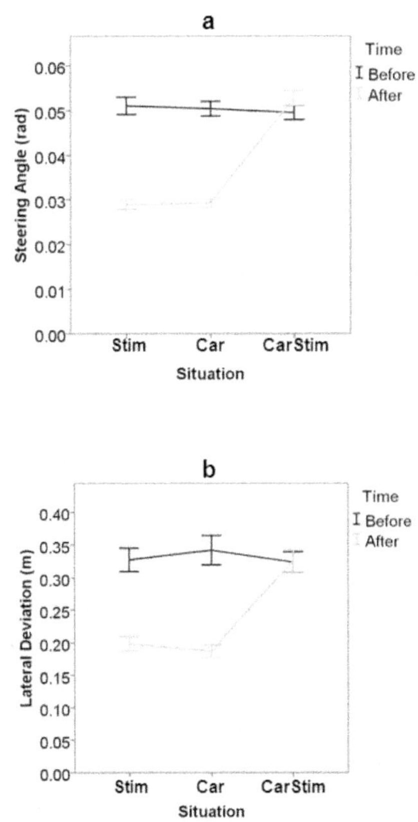

Figure 4. (a) The interaction between Situation and Time for Lateral Deviation. (b) The interaction between Situation and Time for Steering Angle.

No other significant findings related to LDU or Modality were present. As a result H_{3b} was accepted and H_{3c} was rejected.

Results for LatDev and SteAng both show a differential effect of Situation and Time in the driving metrics. While in situations Car and Stim the metrics improved after a situation arose, this was not the case for CarStim.

DISCUSSION

Response Times

The results for response times indicate a clear advantage of using warnings in synergy with a critical event in the driving task (H_{1a} was accepted). This result addresses the research space highlighted by [2,27], providing clear evidence that there is an effect of situational urgency in driver warnings. While there were no differences in terms of RT for the simple Car and Stim conditions, when these events occurred together in CarStim, there was a pronounced effect in how quickly people reacted. This also extends the results of Ho & Spence and Ho, Tan & Spence, where spatially predictive audio [12] and vibrotactile cues [14], meaning cues that correctly predicted the direction of an approaching threat, resulted in better reaction times compared to their non-predictive variants. A similar result was also found when combining multimodal audio and visual cues [22]. In the present study, it became clear that the advantages of providing combinations of audio, visual and tactile cues hold not only when they predict the direction but also the existence of a critical event.

In terms of the modalities used, there was an advantage of multimodal warnings over unimodal ones in terms of RT, since A, T and V warnings were all slower than AT, AV, TV and ATV ones (H_{1c} was accepted). This advantage of using more than one modality to alert drivers has been discussed in several previous studies [11,20,26]. However, never before has this effect been shown in all modality combinations and with a braking task, rather than just a button pressing task as in [27]. In the driving context, there seems to be an additive effect of conveying the same information across more than one sensory channel. Possible explanations of this effect will be attempted in future work, investigating the fit of human data to known models of multisensory perception, such as the Race Model [29]. As will be discussed later, this advantage in RT does not necessarily come with a similar advantage in other metrics, such as LatDev and SteAng. Even so, the benefit of using multimodal signals in the driving task, especially when signifying critical situations, is clear.

The level of designed urgency of warnings was another factor that influenced responses (H_{1b} was accepted). Warnings of high designed urgency elicited significantly quicker responses, even with no prior information related to the type or content of the message given to participants. When asked after each experimental session which properties of the signals in their opinion affected the perceived urgency of a stimulus, participants identified interpulse interval, colour and frequency in almost all cases. This result extends prior work like [2,20,27] by evaluating reaction time across unimodal, bimodal and trimodal combinations of warnings and in varying contexts of situational urgency. Guidelines related to fundamental frequency of sounds, colour for visuals and interpulse interval for all three modalities used [9,19,24] seem to apply uniformly in the driving task. These should be considered when designing driver displays, as the resulting warnings elicit quicker responses when designed to be highly urgent. This is an important conclusion especially as the cues used in this study provided no information on the event they signified. Future work will explore the influence of using richer multimodal cues than those used here and evaluate whether these benefits will hold also in that case. Previous studies such as [12,20] have looked at the efficacy of informative driver displays, but there is need to evaluate how such cues combine multimodally and what type of information is best delivered in which modality.

Finally, there was a significant decrease in performance when encountering warnings involving the visual modality in situation CarStim. None of the advantages of ATV warnings over AT ones, TV ones over AT ones and V warnings over A ones were present in situation CarStim. This indicates that the benefits of visual signals as driver displays can be limited when there is high visual load in the task at hand. The presentation of a car braking was visual and in combination with visual signals it seemed to damage rather than benefit the response times. A similar disadvantage of the visual modality was found in [25]. In [22], there was also an advantage of audio over visual displays when a visual indicator to a critical situation was provided. This result extends [27], where multimodal signals involving visuals created quicker responses, but in absence of any visually demanding events in the driving task. Horrey & Wickens [17] also found that response times to a critical event degraded when voice dialling was aided by a head-down display. Although we used no side task in our study, these results also suggest a cluttering of the visual modality during a visual critical event. As a guideline, visual warnings should be avoided in road events of high situational urgency, and signals involving audio or tactile modalities should be preferred, as they reduce the visual load of driving.

Lateral Deviation and Steering Angle

The results of LatDev and SteAng showed a differential effect of Situation on the driving metrics. Situations Stim and Car both led to improved lane keeping behaviour and to less variation in the steering angle (H_{2a} and H_{3a} were accepted). However, this effect was not present in situation CarStim. In terms of SteAng, values were significantly higher after situation CarStim arose. However, the disturbance to the driving behaviour reflected in SteAng was not high enough to also increase values of LatDev (see Figures 4.a and 4.b). In any case, for both LatDev and SteAng there was no improvement in situation CarStim.

This result can be accounted to the increased workload created by situation CarStim. The simultaneous onset of warnings and a critical event may have created a startle effect, similar to the one observed in [4], where participants' control over the simulated vehicle was poor when critical warnings were delivered. This also comes in line with some participants' comments, mentioning that situation CarStim was startling. Along with the observed increase of reaction times to signals including the visual modality, this observation provides evidence for how the increased amount of visual information can affect driving performance. Lindgren *et al.* [21] and Liu [23] also observed poorer lane keeping and steering behaviours when using visual as opposed to audio displays to aid non-critical tasks (list selection [21] and navigation [23]). Although no differences in terms of modalities were found in our study, the findings of Lindgren *et al.* and Liu also add to the argument that visual load is increased during driving. The addition of a critical visual event as CarStim in the present study could only have added to this load.

From the results of LatDev and SteAng several conclusions can be derived. When there is no critical situation demanding attention, multimodal warnings seem to improve drivers' alertness and lead to a better driving behaviour. The benefit of this effect disappears when there is a visual task demanding immediate action, such as situation CarStim. Although response times improve when a multimodal signal is presented in situation CarStim, lane keeping behaviour is neither improved nor worsened by the cues. Quicker reactions are essential in more critical situations, so the benefits of multimodal cues are valuable in this context. However, lane keeping performance is also essential when there is no imminent critical event, so the benefit of multimodal cues in this case is still present.

Finally, there was a marginally better performance in terms of SteAng for warnings at L_M and in situation CarStim (H_{3b} was accepted). It appears that warnings of L_M aided driving behaviour in terms of SteAng more than the ones of L_L or L_H. Combined with the result of intermediate response times achieved by these warnings, they seem a good option to facilitate overall alertness for drivers in situations that require quick but not immediate responses. Interestingly, these situations, for example low fuel, were the ones that these warnings were designed to address.

CONCLUSIONS

This study investigated the effects of varying situational urgency on the response times, lateral deviation and steering angle of participants in a simulated driving task. Three situations were simulated: a car braking without warnings, warnings without a car braking and both simultaneously. The results showed a clear reduction in response times to warnings when the critical event in the driving scene occurred at the same time as a warning. Quicker responses were observed when responding to bimodal and trimodal warnings compared to unimodal ones and to warnings of high urgency compared to medium and low urgency. Further, the use of visual warnings slowed responses in the critical situation, providing evidence of high load in the visual modality. This effect was also observed in lateral deviation and steering angle values, where the benefit in driving metrics when there were either warnings or a critical event, was not present when the event arose together with the warnings.

These results extend knowledge of in car warning design by identifying the effect of situational urgency on participant response times as well as driving metrics. They also verify the benefit of using multimodal displays of varying designed urgency to alert drivers in a context of varying situational urgency, a case not previously simulated. The evidence of high visual load during a critical event highlights the limitation of the visual modality when encountering critical events in the driving scene. A unique feature of this study is that it investigates the effect of multimodal displays on driving metrics in detail, evaluating driver responses to each combination of modality and situation. Assessing these metrics in such detail showed the differential effect of providing warnings to the lane keeping and steering behaviors. These results indicate the utility of multimodal driver displays when requiring immediate responses and the potential of non-visual warnings to decrease driving workload.

ACKNOWLEDGMENTS

The study was partly funded by Freescale Semiconductor Inc., Automotive Microcontroller Product Group.

REFERENCES

1. Ablaßmeier, M., Poitschke, T., Wallhoff, F., Bengler, K., and Rigoll, G. Eye gaze studies comparing head-up and head-down displays in vehicles. *IEEE International Conference on Multimedia and Expo*, IEEE (2007), 2250–2252.
2. Baldwin, C.L., Eisert, J.L., and Garcia, A. Multimodal urgency coding: auditory, visual, and tactile parameters and their impact on perceived urgency. *Work 41*, (2012), 3586–3591.
3. Baldwin, C.L. Verbal collision avoidance messages during simulated driving: perceived urgency, alerting effectiveness and annoyance. *Ergonomics 54*, 4 (2011), 328–337.
4. Bliss, J.P. and Acton, S.A. Alarm mistrust in automobiles: how collision alarm reliability affects driving. *Applied ergonomics 34*, 6 (2003), 499–509.
5. Brewster, S.A., Wright, P.C., and Edwards, A.D.N. An evaluation of earcons for use in auditory human-computer interfaces. *Proceedings INTER CHI'93*, ACM Press (1993), 222–227.
6. Brumby, D.P., Davies, S.C.E., Janssen, C.P., and Grace, J.J. Fast or Safe ? How Performance Objectives Determine Modality Output Choices While Interacting on the Move. *CHI 2011*, ACM (2011), 473–482.

7. Cao, Y., van der Sluis, F., Theune, M., op den Akker, R., and Nijholt, A. Evaluating informative auditory and tactile cues for in-vehicle information systems. *AutomotiveUI '10*, AutomotiveUI (2010), 102 – 109.

8. Edworthy, J., Hellier, E., Walters, K., Weedon, B., and Adams, A. The Relationship between Task Performance, Reaction Time, and Perceived Urgency in Nonverbal Auditory Warnings. *HFES Annual Meeting 44*, 22 (2000), 674–677.

9. Edworthy, J., Loxley, S., and Dennis, I. Improving auditory warning design: Relationship between warning sound parameters and perceived urgency. *Human Factors 33*, 2 (1991), 205 –231.

10. Gonzalez, C., Lewis, B.A., Roberts, D.M., Pratt, S.M., and Baldwin, C.L. Perceived Urgency and Annoyance of Auditory Alerts in a Driving Context. *HFES Annual Meeting 56*, 1 (2012), 1684–1687.

11. Ho, C., Reed, N., and Spence, C. Multisensory In-Car Warning Signals for Collision Avoidance. *Human Factors 49*, 6 (2007), 1107–1114.

12. Ho, C. and Spence, C. Assessing the effectiveness of various auditory cues in capturing a driver's visual attention. *Journal of experimental psychology. Applied 11*, 3 (2005), 157–74.

13. Ho, C. and Spence, C. *Multisensory Driver*. Ashgate, 2008.

14. Ho, C., Tan, H.Z., and Spence, C. Using spatial vibrotactile cues to direct visual attention in driving scenes. *Traffic Psychology and Behaviour 8*, 6 (2005), 397–412.

15. Hoggan, E., Raisamo, R., and Brewster, S.A. Mapping information to audio and tactile icons. *ICMI-MLMI '09*, (2009), 327 – 334.

16. Hoggan, E.E. and Brewster, S.A. Crossmodal icons for information display. *CHI EA '06*, ACM Press (2006), 857 – 862.

17. Horrey, W.J. and Wickens, C.D. Driving and Side Task Performance: The Effects of Display Clutter, Separation, and Modality. *Human Factors 46*, 4 (2004), 611–624.

18. Kaufmann, C., Ohg, F., Risser, R., Geven, A., and Sefelin, R. Effects of simultaneous multi-modal warnings and traffic information on driver behaviour. *Human Centred Design for Intelligent Transport Systems*, (2008), 33–42.

19. Lewis, B.A. and Baldwin, C.L. Equating Perceived Urgency Across Auditory, Visual, and Tactile Signals. *HFES Annual Meeting 56*, 1 (2012), 1307–1311.

20. Lewis, B.A., Penaranda, B.N., Roberts, D.M., and Baldwin, C.L. Effectiveness of Bimodal Versus Unimodal Alerts for Distracted Drivers. *Human Factors in Driver Assessment, Training and Vehicle Design*, (2013), 376–382.

21. Lindgren, A., Angelelli, A., Mendoza, P.A., and Chen, F. Driver behaviour when using an integrated advisory warning display for advanced driver assistance systems. *IET Intelligent Transport Systems 3*, 4 (2009), 390–399.

22. Liu, Y.-C. and Jhuang, J.-W. Effects of in-vehicle warning information displays with or without spatial compatibility on driving behaviors and response performance. *Applied ergonomics 43*, 4 (2012), 679–86.

23. Liu, Y.C. Comparative study of the effects of auditory, visual and multimodality displays on drivers' performance in advanced traveller information systems. *Ergonomics 44*, 4 (2001), 425–42.

24. Marshall, D.C., Lee, J.D., and Austria, P.A. Alerts for In-Vehicle Information Systems: Annoyance, Urgency, and Appropriateness. *Human Factors 49*, 1 (2007), 145–157.

25. Murata, A., Kanbayashi, M., and Hayami, T. Effectiveness of automotive warning system presented with multiple sensory modalities. *SICE Annual Conference*, IEEE Comput. Soc (2012), 920–925.

26. Oskarsson, P.A., Eriksson, L., and Carlander, O. Enhanced Perception and Performance by Multimodal Threat Cueing in Simulated Combat Vehicle. *Human Factors 54*, 1 (2011), 122–137.

27. Politis, I., Brewster, S., and Pollick, F. Evaluating Multimodal Driver Displays of Varying Urgency. *Automotive UI 2013*, ACM Press (2013).

28. Pratt, S.M., Lewis, B.A., Penaranda, B.N., Roberts, D.M., Gonzalez, C., and Baldwin, C.L. Perceived Urgency Scaling in Tactile Alerts. *HFES Annual Meeting 56*, 1 (2012), 1303–1306.

29. Raab, D.H. Statistical Facilitation of Simple Reaction Times. *Transactions of the New York Academy of Sciences 24*, 5 Series II (1962), 574 – 590.

30. Salvucci, D.D. Modeling driver behavior in a cognitive architecture. *Human factors 48*, 2 (2006), 362–380.

31. Scott, J.J. and Gray, R. A Comparison of Tactile, Visual, and Auditory Warnings for Rear-End Collision Prevention in Simulated Driving. *Human Factors 50*, 2 (2008), 264–275.

32. Serrano, J., Di Stasi, L.L., Megías, A., and Catena, A. Effect of directional speech warnings on road hazard detection. *Traffic injury prevention 12*, 6 (2011), 630–635.

Multi-Viewer Gesture-Based Interaction for Omni-Directional Video

Gustavo Rovelo[1,2], Davy Vanacken[1], Kris Luyten[1], Francisco Abad[3], Emilio Camahort[3]
[1]Hasselt University - tUL - iMinds, Expertise Centre for Digital Media
Wetenschapspark 2, 3590 Diepenbeek, Belgium
[2]Dpto. de Sistemas Informáticos y Computación.
[3]Inst. Universitario de Automática e Informática Industrial
Universitat Politècnica de València - Camino de Vera S/N, Valencia, Spain
{gustavo.roveloruiz, davy.vanacken, kris.luyten}@uhasselt.be, {fjabad, camahort}@dsic.upv.es

ABSTRACT
Omni-directional video (ODV) is a novel medium that offers viewers a 360° panoramic recording. This type of content will become more common within our living rooms in the near future, seeing that immersive displaying technologies such as 3D television are on the rise. However, little attention has been given to how to interact with ODV content. We present a gesture elicitation study in which we asked users to perform mid-air gestures that they consider to be appropriate for ODV interaction, both for individual as well as collocated settings. We are interested in the gesture variations and adaptations that come forth from individual and collocated usage. To this end, we gathered quantitative and qualitative data by means of observations, motion capture, questionnaires and interviews. This data resulted in a user-defined gesture set for ODV, alongside an in-depth analysis of the variation in gestures we observed during the study.

Author Keywords
Gesture Elicitation; User-Defined Gestures; Omni-Directional Video; Multi-User Interaction

ACM Classification Keywords
H.5.m. Information Interfaces and Presentation (e.g. HCI): Miscellaneous

General Terms
Human Factors; Design; Measurement.

INTRODUCTION
ODV is an emerging media format that offers viewers a 360° panoramic video (Figure 1). To create an immersive experience, ODV is typically shown in a CAVE-like setup, or a personal display (e.g. a head-mounted display) in combination with a tracking system to calculate the viewer's correct viewpoint. Recent efforts such as Microsoft's Illumiroom [15] provide interesting possibilities for ODV, as they show how a living room environment could be turned into a small CAVE-like theatre. Benko and Wilson [4] show different scenarios in which ODV can be used, as they describe a portable dome setup in which users can interact with applications such as a 360° video conferencing system, a multi-user game or an astronomical data visualization system.

Although capturing and rendering ODV have been widely investigated and optimized over time, little attention is given to interaction with ODV content. Interaction with ODV includes triggering typical control operations we know from regular video (e.g. play, pause, fast forward and go backward), but also includes changing viewpoint by means of typical spatial interactions such as zooming and panning. These spatial interactions are, however, somewhat constrained, since spatial manipulations are always relative to the original camera position that was used while recording the ODV.

Bleumers et al. [6] recently presented a number of interesting findings regarding users' expectations of ODV. Their research highlights the uncertainty among users about how to interact with ODV and puts forward mid-air gestural interfaces as a possible solution, although they did not explore such interfaces in their work. Mid-air gesturing has been used since the early nineties for controlling television sets [2, 8], and nowadays television sets with a built-in camera and simple gestural interface are commercially available.

We envision ODV content becoming more and more common in the future and accessible within the context of our living rooms. As a result, traditional television watching experiences will change, since multiple viewers no longer have the same region of focus (i.e. the television screen in front of them), but are able to watch video content in any direction. This change also implies that traditional interaction methods, such as a remote control or the current gesture-based TV interfaces, need to be re-evaluated.

Our aim is to understand which mid-air gestures are the most appropriate for interacting with ODV, not only when users are

CHI 2014, April 26 - May 01 2014, Toronto, ON, Canada

ACM 978-1-4503-2473-1/14/04...$15.00. http://dx.doi.org/10.1145/2556288.2557113

Figure 1. ODV workflow. From left to right, an omni-directional camera, the recording process during a concert, and projection of the resulting omni-directional video in a CAVE-like setup.

on their own, but also in a collocated scenario, in the presence of other viewers who might want to interact with the ODV. More specifically, we investigate which factors users take into account when eliciting gestures for the most frequent ODV control operations. For this purpose, we gather both qualitative and quantitative data through observations, motion capture, questionnaires and interviews.

The main contributions of this paper are: (1) a quantitative and qualitative study to capture user-defined gestures for ODV, (2) an analysis and classification of these gestures and (3) an analysis of the changes in gestures when used in two different configurations: single and collocated settings. Our results inform the design of gestures for future ODV systems and highlight the expected flexibility in tracking and recognizing these gestures when being used in collocated settings. Although our contributions are focused on designing appropriate gesture-based interactions for ODV, our findings can also be useful in other domains that require spatial or time-related operations (e.g. interacting with home cinema systems or controlling the viewpoint during predefined navigation sequences inside a virtual environment).

RELATED WORK

ODV and mid-air gestures are both very active and broad research areas. In this section, we describe the related work that is most relevant to the work presented in this paper.

User-Defined Gestures

In the areas of user-defined gestures and exploration of users' preferences, researchers often focus on finding the best set of gestures for specific tasks, such as grabbing and rearranging a set of objects [12], or pan-and-zoom operations [19]. Others analyse the gestures for a very specific action such as rotation [14], evaluate users' behaviour when interacting with zoomable video [1], study how users rate the appropriateness of the gestures they observe [7], or compare the acceptance level of different gesture sets (i.e. one set created by HCI experts and another by "inexperienced" users) [18].

To generate a set of user-defined gestures, Nielsen et al. [21] and Wobbrock et al. [27] propose similar elicitation approaches: define what operations have to be executed through gestures, ask participants to perform gestures for those operations, and finally extract the gesture set from the collected data. Wobbrock et al. also use Likert scales to gather qualitative feedback, while Nielsen et al. benchmark the set in a second round of trials. Nielsen's et al. methodology has for instance been applied to find gestures that can be used to interact with music players [11]. Another approach is proposed by Grandhi et al. [9], who ask a group of users to describe and mimic different daily tasks that can be extrapolated to human-computer interactions.

Interaction with Omni-Directional Video

Benko et al. [3, 5] describe the challenges of interactive curved and spherical displays, which we believe to be representative for CAVE-like ODV setups. These challenges include developing walk-up-and-use interaction techniques, creating a transparent environment where users can interact with the appropriate device for each task, and devising compelling applications for this type of device. Our focus lies on the challenge of designing appropriate interaction in the context of ODV.

Researchers already investigated several aspects of ODV interaction. Macq et al. [16] implement ODV navigation using the camera of a tablet PC as the orientation tracker and the screen as the display device (i.e. a peephole display). Neng and Chambel [20], on the other hand, describe the use of 360° "hypervideos", which provide extra information through embedded navigational links. These videos are watched over the Internet, on a regular computer screen. We are, however, specifically interested in mid-air gestural interfaces.

Bleumers et al. [6] describe user expectations on ODV, and how users think gestural interfaces would be appropriate for this new media format. Zoric et al. [28] present a user study in which they observed pairs of participants interacting with high definition panoramic TV through gestures. Their observations suggest that the design of multi-user gesture systems should allow for socially adapted gestures for controlling and navigating video content. However, Zoric et al. consider this study to be merely a first step in exploring how users interact with such content using a gesture-based system. We investigate this topic more in-depth.

STUDY ON ODV GESTURES

The aim of our study is to determine how users conceive gesture-based ODV interaction, when alone and when interacting with other participants in a collocated scenario. We not only look into interactions that map on control operations typically performed with video content, either on television or digital video players, but also on some control operations that are typical for spatial exploration. As a result, the control operations considered in this study are commands that manipulate time (i.e. play, pause, skip scene, fast forward and go backward) or space (i.e. panning and zooming).

Methodology

Since user-generated gesture sets tend to have a higher acceptance level among users [18], we adapted the gesture elicitation methodology of Nielsen et al. [21] to gather the gestures that participants consider most appropriate for the aforementioned control operations. The study consisted of two sessions: first, a participant was asked to perform the gestures alone, and in the second session, two participants had to perform the gestures in a collocated setting.

Participants were seated on a couch, inside a CAVE-like ODV setup, as seen in Figure 2. This kind of setup helps participants to explore the interaction possibilities, since it clearly reveals the spatial properties of the ODV content. It also prevents participants from being influenced by the form factor of the output device (e.g. when using a rectangular screen, participants are more likely to unnecessarily frame gestures within a rectangle in front of them). To evaluate the impact of the collocated setting, participants were seated reasonably close to each other during the second session (as it would happen in a living room, sitting next to each other on a couch). Participants were not forced to sit uncomfortably close to each other, however, and had sufficient space to sit without invading each other's personal space.

Figure 2. Participants performed the experiment while sitting on a couch inside a CAVE-like ODV setup.

The ODV did not respond to the gestures of the participants. Similar to Wobbrock et al. [27], we decided against a Wizard of Oz to avoid that participants constrain or adapt their gestures according to the feedback they receive (e.g. to compensate for a delay or mismatch). A Wizard of Oz approach would also be impractical in the collocated scenario, because providing feedback for each participant simultaneously would inevitably result in inconsistencies. Before the sessions, an observer explained the list of control operations by showing an actual ODV to the participants. During the sessions, however, only still images of an ODV were shown to avoid unnecessary distractions.

Participants were asked to perform one easy to repeat and easy to understand gesture for each operation. They were informed that they had complete freedom of action to devise a gesture or posture using hand(s) and/or finger(s), and that the same gesture could be repeated for more than one operation, if considered appropriate. Before the collocated session, the observer explained that they would be interacting with the ODV independently, but at the same time.

After the short explanation, the observer asked the participants to devise an appropriate gesture for each operation, one by one. The observer did not impose any time constraints. Participants simply had to signal when they were ready to perform a gesture, and next, the observer gave the go-ahead to execute the gesture. During the collocated session, both participants had to perform their gesture at the same time, so the observer waited to give the go-ahead until both participants were ready.

When both participants finished performing the gestures for all control operations during the collocated session, they were asked to swap positions on the couch and repeat the trial. In other words, participants performed gestures for each control operation three times in total: once alone, and twice when sitting next to another participant.

To control order effects, we divided the participants in two groups: each group received the control operations in a different order during the sessions. However, we did not simply randomize the order of the control operations, but decided to maintain a logical structure (e.g. by grouping related operations such as fast forward and go backward), to make it easier for the participants to devise gestures.

Personal information such as age, gender and experience was recorded before the first session. After completing both sessions, participants filled out a questionnaire regarding their experience and discussed their opinions with the observer.

Participants

Sixteen participants took part in our study: twelve male and four female, with ages ranging from 23 to 52 years old (average age 31.5). All of them are colleagues at our research centre. Two participants are left handed, two ambidextrous, and the others are right handed. Most participants are experienced touch screen users (twelve participants use them daily), but merely two participants play video games on consoles like the Nintendo Wii or Microsoft Xbox with Kinect more than once a month. Only two participants make regular use of gestures to interact with their PC, either by performing mouse gestures to control the web browser, or by using a multi-touch mouse. None of the participants have interacted

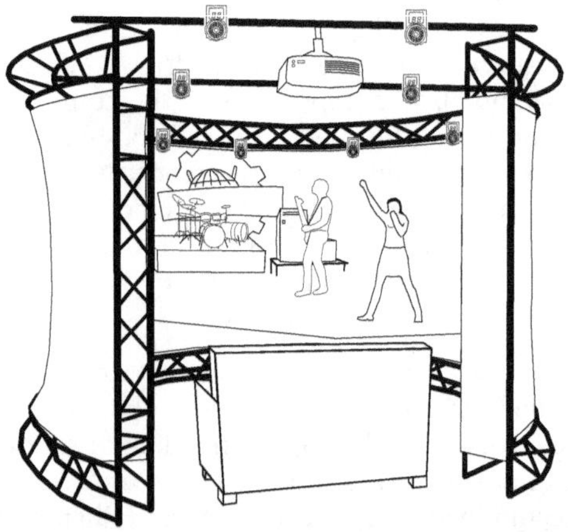

Figure 3. Motion capture setup for our study. An 8-camera OptiTrack system and a set of rigid body markers were used to track hand movements. The tracking system was set up in a 360° CAVE-like environment, with a couch in the centre of the tracking volume.

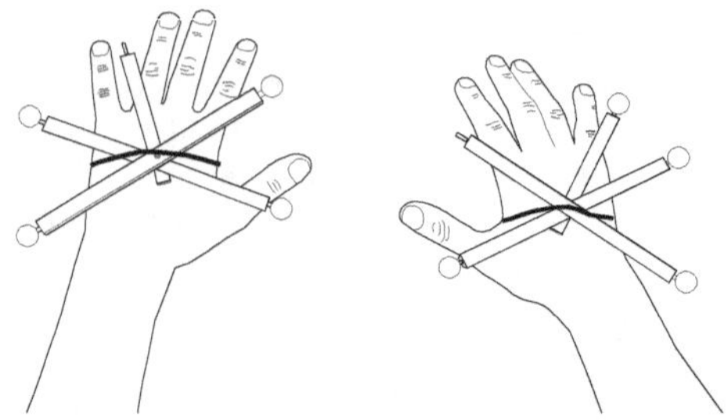

Figure 4. Rigid body markers composed of small IR reflective balls, used for motion capture. The markers are sufficiently large to ensure that they always exceed the size of the participant's hands.

with gesture-based TVs. Finally, twelve participants knew beforehand what ODV is, but only two of them had previously interacted with an ODV system.

For the collocated session of the study, we formed eight pairs according to the following criteria: four pairs with participants who are used to interact with each other and four pairs with participants who rarely interact with each other. We based our grouping criteria on the *"friendship ties"* described by Haythornthwaite and Wellman [10]:

Close friendship: people who work in the same office, usually have lunch together, and would go to the movie theatre together.

Working together: people who know each other, but rarely interact with each other in the work environment.

Apparatus

To gather data on the gestures that participants performed, we used motion capture, allowing us to measure the spacial dimensions of the gestures. For this purpose, we used eight OptiTrack V100:R2 cameras and the Natural Point Tracking Tools software (Figure 3). The OptiTrack cameras have a 640x480 pixels image resolution and a maximum capture frame rate of 100 fps. They are capable of tracking markers with sub-millimetre accuracy. We also used a normal video camera to record the sessions, to make classifying the different gesture easier during analysis.

To track participants, a rigid body marker composed of small IR reflective balls had to be attached to each hand. Before the actual study, we ran a pilot study for two purposes: (1) to verify whether the instructions and study design were clear and (2) to uncover limitations and issues with our apparatus. It allowed us to optimise the rigid body markers in order to avoid occlusion problems when participants turned their hands. We therefore built the markers with wooden sticks that exceed the size of the participant's hand (Figure 4). In this manner, only the hands' centres are tracked and not the small finger movements, but this suffices for our purposes, since we have complementary video recordings.

RESULTS

We analysed the video recordings of all the sessions, following the strategy proposed by Peltonen et al. [23]: first extracting the video segments with useful data and then extracting all the required information. For this purpose, we defined parameters to annotate the videos of each gesture according to the suggestions of Nielsen et al. [21]. The parameters we used are *hand usage (one or two hands)*, *trajectory of the movement* (*linear or circular*), *type of gesture* (*movement or steady posture*) and *granularity* (*fine-grained finger movements or coarser hand movements*). We also described all the gestures in natural language using these parameters, in such way that others would be able to understand and reproduce them.

The *Hand usage* column of Table 1 shows that participants had **no clear preference for using one or both hands for most gestures**. They did prefer to use one hand for performing a pause gesture and both hands for zooming (these differences are statistically significant, based on a non-parametric binomial test between the two possibilities). Furthermore, participants **preferred to use linear movements rather than circular movements**. As indicated in the *Trajectory* column of Table 1, the difference is statistically significant for all control operations. This confirms the findings previously reported for pan-and-zoom interaction with wall-sized displays [19]. People prefer linear movements when they are asked to devise easy to perform, easy to remember and easy to repeat gestures.

We classified all the gestures as either static (e.g. a steady hand posture that uses both index fingers to represent the typical pause symbol), or dynamic (e.g. performing a "push" gesture by moving a hand away from the body and back, with the palm outwards). Both examples are depicted in Figure 5. The *Gesture type* column of Table 1 shows a **clear preference for using dynamic movements rather than static hand postures to represent most control operations**. Pause and stop are control operations for which the participants' preference is less clear, but for the other operations, the differences are statistically significant. We believe that the number of participants using steady postures is higher for pause and stop, because they both implicitly denote turning the video into a standstill state. A number of participants used the same gesture with different speed/timing to represent different control operations. P15, for instance, explicitly mentioned that he did the same gesture for play and fast forward, moving his right

	Hand usage		Trajectory		Gesture type		Granularity	
Control operation	One	Two	Linear	Circular	Static	Dynamic	Fine	Coarse
Play	31	17	48	0	14	34	14	34
Pause	36	12	48	0	27	21	9	39
Stop	19	29	48	0	26	22	0	48
Skip scene	24	24	33	15	3	45	2	46
Fast forward	31	17	41	7	3	45	7	41
Go backward	29	19	39	9	6	42	9	39
Pan	18	30	46	2	1	47	4	44
Zoom	3	45	48	0	0	48	10	38

Table 1. The gesture elements that were used for analysis of the video recordings. The value in each cell represents the number of participants who used the element during the study (16 participants performed a gesture for each control operation three times, resulting in 48 samples per control operation in total). Coloured cells represent a statistically significant difference between levels (non-parametric binomial test, $\alpha = 0.05$)

hand to the right, but varying the time he kept pointing in that direction (he used more time for fast forward).

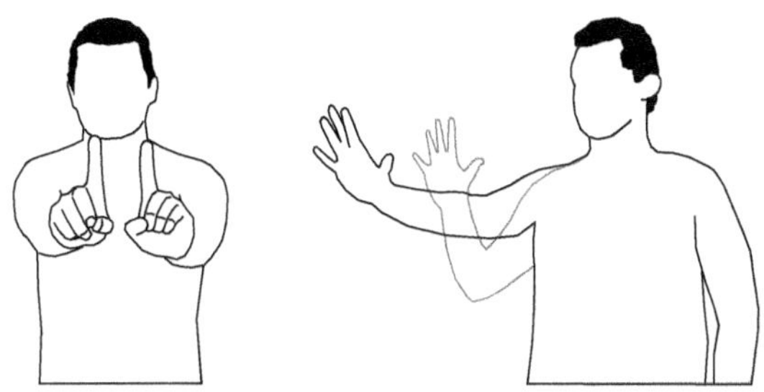

Figure 5. A steady hand posture and a dynamic hand movement to represent the pause operation. Grey lines represent early states of the gesture, black lines represent the final state.

We also found statistically significant differences comparing the usage of fingers (fine granularity) and whole hands (coarse granularity) to perform the gestures (*Granularity* column of Table 1). Participants **preferred to use coarser hand movements instead of fine-grained finger movements**, even though they were informed that they could use finger movements to represent the control operations.

As expected, participants extrapolated their knowledge from real-life devices and software applications (in this case, mostly video or DVD players), an observation that was also made by Henze et al. [11] in the context of gestures for music playback. This was especially true for play, pause, stop and zoom. Participants for instance tried to transform a symbolic representation into a gesture or posture, such as a triangle for play or a square for stop (e.g. P14 explicitly asked *"... do I have to do the square for stop?"*). Another form in which participants extrapolated their real-life knowledge is when they considered that play, pause and sometimes stop should be represented by the same gesture, as these control operations are often mapped to the same button on devices or in software applications (e.g. a lot of media players use the same button for play/pause and do not have a stop button). For zooming, twelve of the sixteen participants employed the typical spread-and-pinch gesture, even those participants who mentioned they are not frequent multi-touch users.

Collocated Interaction

We asked participants to choose one or several factors that influenced their decision on gestures when sitting next to another person. "Avoid invading the other participant's private space" and "Avoid colliding with the other participant's gestures" were chosen by seven out of the sixteen participants. "Avoid blocking the other participant's view of the video", however, only received two votes, one of which belongs to P14, who felt his field of view was blocked and reported collisions with his fellow participant while performing the gestures. We believe the fact that "Avoid blocking the other participant's view of the video" received few votes is due to the absence of a particular task to perform with the ODV. Participants did not need to be engaged with the content and thus did not consider blocking the other participant's view an important factor.

Analysis of our study notes and video recordings shows that participants of the four pairs of the *"close friendship"* category had no problems performing gestures side by side. One pair of participants even made jokes about synchronized dancing, because they performed nearly identical movements for some control operations. Participants who were part of a *"working together"* pair, on the other hand, were more uncomfortable and some of them expressed that feeling during an informal interview after the study. P5 reported, for instance, that *"It was not comfortable doing the gestures with the other participant."* and P16 reported that *"I felt limited by the presence of the other participant. She invaded my private space."*

By analysing the video recordings and motion capture data, we identified three interesting situations that resulted from the collocated interaction: participants adapted the size of their gesture, changed hands to perform the same gesture, and chose a completely different gesture for the same control operation. We discuss each of these gesture adaptations in the next sections.

Size Adjustment

A number of scripts were implemented to automatically analyse the motion capture data gathered by the OptiTrack system. We first measured the space participants can cover when they completely stretch their arms to the side, to the front and to the top. The areas created on each plane (*XY - frontal*, *XZ - top* and *YZ - lateral*) represent the maximum distances that a participant is able to reach. These areas were used to create baseline bounding boxes. Next, we decomposed the captured hand movements and determined the 2D bounding boxes that represent the areas covered by each gesture on the three planes. Finally, we calculated the ratios between the sizes of the bounding boxes for each gesture and the participant's baseline bounding boxes.

	Lateral adjustment (X)			Vertical adjustment (Y)			Depth adjustment (Z)		
Control operation	S vs A	S vs B	A vs B	S vs A	S vs B	A vs B	S vs A	S vs B	A vs B
Play	3	3	2	2	0	1	4	7	2
Pause	1	1	0	4	3	0	2	3	0
Stop	2	3	1	1	1	0	4	3	0
Skip scene	6	3	1	2	3	0	7	2	1
Fast forward	5	5	0	2	3	0	5	5	2
Go backward	4	5	1	4	3	1	5	6	3
Pan	8	4	1	1	2	0	7	5	3
Zoom	8	7	0	1	1	0	6	5	0

Table 2. Size adjustments. Values in each cell represent the number of participants adapting the size of the gesture by more than 10% between the specified sessions. Column names stand for S-Single participant session, A-First collocated trial, and B-Second collocated trial.

We used these ratios to detect changes in size of a gesture for each control operation across the sessions, to investigate if participants used this as a strategy to adapt gestures in the collocated setting. Table 2 presents the number of participants who reduced the size of their gestures by more than 10%, for each of the three axes. The size adjustment is especially noticeable for control operations that typically involved lateral movements (e.g. fast forward, go backward, pan, zoom), due to the presence of the other participant.

Analysis of the friendship ties revealed an expected trend: participants of *"working together"* pairs used the size adjustment strategy more often. They adjusted 42.2% of all the gestures performed during the sessions (for all the control operations and in any of the three movement directions), while participants of the *"close friendship"* pairs adjusted 17.2% of their gestures. We did not find a statistically significant correlation between friendship ties and size adjustments, which can probably be attributed to the limited number of pairs per friendship tie.

Figure 6. An example of how participants adapted the size of their gestures. P8 and P13 displaced their movements when doing the zoom gesture, after their hands collided during the first collocated trial.

As an example, we briefly discuss the gestures for the zoom operation of a *"working together"* pair. When P8 and P13 performed the zoom gestures for the first time, their hands collided. The second time, after switching positions, both participants adjusted their gesture by displacing the movements to the free space (Figure 6). While looking into another *"working together"* pair, P4 and P16, we clearly noticed both participants reducing the movement of their hands between the single and collocated session to represent the skip scene operation.

Gesture Mirroring

Analysis of the video recordings shows that participants also adapted their gestures by using a different hand to perform the same gesture. Table 3 depicts how many participants used gesture mirroring across the different sessions. In total, five participants adapted their gestures in this manner. Only one of those participants was ambidextrous, and four were part of a *"working together"* pair. In total, the *"working together"* pairs used gesture mirroring for 17.2% of the gestures performed during the sessions and the *"close friendship"* pairs for 4.17% of their gestures, but again, no statistically significant correlation was found between friendship ties and the adaptations.

Control operation	S vs A	S vs B	A vs B
Play	1	2	3
Pause	1	2	1
Stop	1	1	0
Skip scene	1	1	2
Fast forward	0	0	1
Go backward	1	1	0
Pan	2	1	3
Zoom	0	0	0

Table 3. Gesture mirroring. Values in each cell represent the number of participants who mirrored gestures between the specified sessions. Column names stand for S-Single session, A-First collocated trial, and B-Second collocated trial.

To illustrate the gesture mirroring strategy, we briefly discuss three examples. P8 used his left hand for the fast forward gesture when performing the gesture during the single session, but he used his right hand when sitting to the right of P13 (Figure 7). Similarly, P14 used his right hand when he was sitting to the right of P7 when doing the skip scene gesture, and then his left hand when he was sitting to the left of P7. Finally, P1 did the play gesture using her left hand when P10 was sitting at her right, and her right hand after exchanging positions on the couch.

Figure 7. An example of how participants mirrored gestures. P8 used a different hand to perform the same gesture when another participant was present.

Although only a limited number of participants adopted this mirroring strategy, it is still interesting to note that users will expect a gesture to be recognized by the system in both cases, whether they are using their left or right hand. The Microsoft Kinect development guidelines already suggest this strategy to create flexible gestural interfaces [17].

Choosing New Gestures

Table 4 depicts the number of participants who changed gestures across the sessions. Eleven participants changed at least one of their gestures. In total, 11.5% of the gestures performed by participants of a *"working together"* pair were changed across the sessions, and 9.38% in case of *"close friendship"* pairs. No statistically significant correlation was found between friendship ties and choosing new gestures.

The main reason for this behaviour is the extra time participants spent thinking about the gestures. P15, for example, mentioned that the second time he had to perform the gestures, he *"tried to put some logic"* in them, and P2 mentioned that he tried *"to do more energy efficient"* gestures.

Control operation	S vs A	S vs B	A vs B
Play	2	3	1
Pause	1	1	0
Stop	2	2	1
Skip scene	1	3	2
Fast forward	3	3	1
Go backward	4	3	1
Pan	3	2	1
Zoom	0	0	0

Table 4. Choosing new gestures. Values in each cell represent the number of participants who chose a new gesture between the specified sessions. Column names stand for S-Single session, A-First collocated trial, and B-Second collocated trial.

Most pairs (all the *"close friendship"* pairs and two of the *"working together"* pairs) discussed the reasons and implications of their gestures, with comments like *"your gesture is not energy efficient"* or *"your gesture is error prone"*. This interaction between participants sometimes resulted in them changing the gesture. For instance, P4 used both hands for panning when she represented the operation the first time. She completely stretched both arms to the front, making a clockwise circle with her right arm to pan right and a counter clockwise circle with her left arm to pan left. The second time, she used only one hand, copying the gesture of her fellow participant: moving her right hand, pointing with the index finger to the left and then to the right.

Agreement Level

We classified all the gestures for every control operation into groups of similar gestures, based on the parameters *hand usage (one or two hands)*, *trajectory of the movement* (*linear or circular*), and *type of the gesture* (*movement or steady posture*). In addition to these parameters, we considered the overall movement pattern of the gesture (e.g. the directions of the movements). We did not include *granularity* (*fine-grained finger movements or coarser hand movements*), so we classified a spread-and-pinch performed with two fingers or with both hands as similar gestures.

Next, we calculated the percentage of participants who used a particular type of gesture and the agreement level for each operation. For this purpose, we used the formula of Wobbrock et al. [26]:

$$A_i = \sum_{j=1}^{n} \left(\frac{G_{ij}}{G_i} \right)^2 \qquad (1)$$

A_i is the agreement level of the ith operation, G_i the total number of gestures performed for the ith operation and G_{ij} the number of elements in the jth group of gestures for the ith operation. Park and Hand [22] used this formula in a similar manner.

We illustrate the formula's usage by applying it to the gestures used for panning (Equation 2). We found three groups of similar gestures, with sizes 30, 2 and 16. As a result, the agreement level was 0.5036 for the panning operation.

$$A_{Panning} = \left(\frac{30}{48} \right)^2 + \left(\frac{2}{48} \right)^2 + \left(\frac{16}{48} \right)^2 = 0.5036 \qquad (2)$$

We also calculated the percentage of participants who chose a particular type of gesture, taking into account the 48 gestures performed for each operation. Table 5 depicts both these percentages and the agreement levels for the top-rated gesture for each operation.

DISCUSSION

We propose the user-defined gesture set described in Table 5. We believe these gesture will lead to a high acceptance level among users. Figure 8 gives a graphical representation of this gesture set. The different states of gestures that require movements are represented with different line colours: grey colours represent early states of a gesture and the black line the final state.

We considered the most repeated gestures across all the sessions to assemble our gesture set. In 62.5% of the cases, the difference between the most repeated gesture and the second most repeated gesture was very large. For the fast forward and go backward operations, however, the differences were small. There were six groups of similar gestures for the fast forward operation (representing 35.42%, 29.16%, 18.75%, 10.42%, 4.17% and 2.08% of the participants) and eight groups for the go backward operation (representing 41.67%, 33.33%, 8.33%, 6.26%, 4.17%, 2.08%, 2.08% and 2.08% of the participants). In case of the stop operation, performing the halt gesture with one hand was the most repeated one (performed by 33.33% of the participants), but as we already chose this gesture to represent the pause operation, we decided to use the second most repeated gesture: the halt gesture using both hands (performed by 22.92% of the participants).

We can observe in Figure 9 that the large variety of gestures to represent certain control operations sometimes causes low agreement levels, for instance for the play and skip scene operations. The zoom operation, on the other hand, was the one with the most consensus. This can be explained by the fact that participants regularly relied on existing mental models to devise gestures to represent control operations. The following three examples illustrate this behaviour:

Zoom and pan. Not surprisingly, the most repeated gesture for zoom was the widely used spread-and-pinch gesture, as indicated by the agreement level. For panning, "grabbing" the video and moving the hand was the most repeated gesture. Similar gestures have been proposed by Fikkert et al. [7] for zooming and by Stellmach et al. [24] for panning, in the context of large display control.

Play and pause. Some participants mentioned that video players use the same button to represent play and pause,

Control operation	Gesture	Rate (%)	Agreement level
Play	Push gesture, moving the hand with the palm outwards toward the front and back in a fluent movement.	35.41	0.18
Pause	Halt gesture, holding the arm completely stretched with the palm outwards for a few seconds.	41.67	0.22
Stop	Halt gesture, holding both arms completely stretched with the palm outwards for a few seconds.	22.92	0.21
Skip scene	Moving the hand from right to left or from left to right one time and returning to the starting position.	33.33	0.16
Fast forward	Left to right movement, holding the hand pointing to the right for a few seconds.	35.42	0.26
Go backward	Right to left movement, holding the hand pointing to the left for a few seconds.	41.67	0.30
Pan	Using one hand to "grab" the video and then move it from left to right or from right to left.	62.50	0.50
Zoom	Using the spread-and-pinch gesture, moving two hands apart (spread) and bringing them back together (pinch).	75.00	0.63

Table 5. Top-rated gestures for the eight control operations. The rate represents the % of participants who performed this type of gesture during the study. The agreement level gives an indication about the variety of gestures that were performed for an operation.

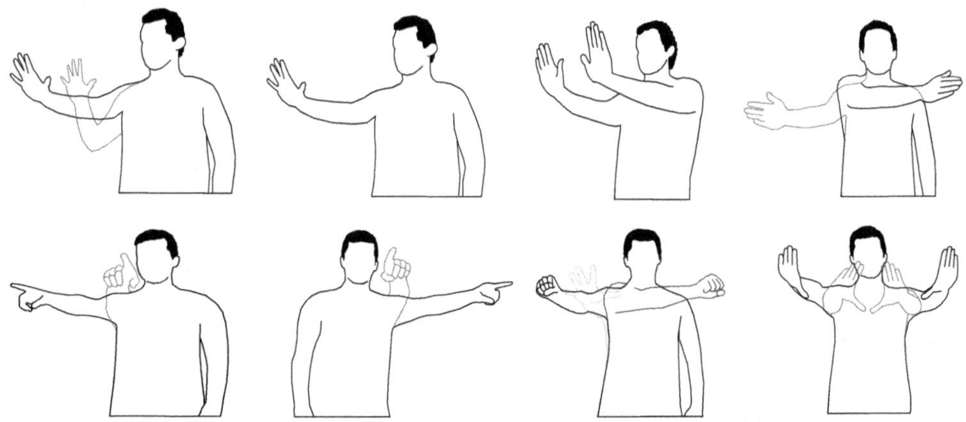

Figure 8. User-defined gesture set for ODV. From left to right and top to bottom: play, pause, stop, skip scene, fast forward, go backward, pan and zoom. Grey lines represent early states of the gesture, black lines represent the final state.

and thus they also used the same gesture for both control operations. This behaviour was also reported by Henze et al. [11] in the context of gestures for music playback. Overall, there was a great diversity in gestures to represent play and pause, leading to lower agreement levels.

Fast forward and go backward. Most media players and timelines associate "the future" with the right side (e.g. arrows pointing to the right in video players for fast forward), and "the past" with the left side. Participants in our study represented both control operations following this established mental model, which is consistent with the observations of Henze at al. [11].

Although we considered the most repeated gestures to assemble our gesture set, not all gestures are necessarily the most optimal solution. Participants sometimes changed their gesture to copy their fellow participant (imitative behaviour was also reported by Walter et al. [25], in the context of a public display game), so they considered their first gesture to be suboptimal. Eleven participants also chose a new gesture for at least one of the control operations, due to reasons such as wanting a more "energy efficient" gesture. This implies that using a gesture set over a prolonged period of time might lead to a different prioritisation of gestures. Our gesture set thus needs further validation and refinement before its actual implementation, and the next step is to benchmark the chosen gestures, as suggested in the methodology of Nielsen et al. [21]. Another component to consider before implementing the set, is how to discriminate between gestures and other movements, for instance by indicating the start of an interaction with a specific body pose [25].

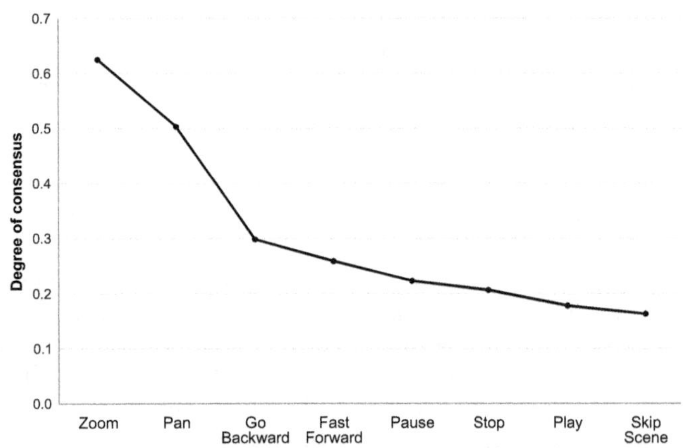

Figure 9. Gesture set agreement level in descending order.

We noticed that minimal friendship ties between participants had a negative effect on their experience. Participants of the *"working together"* category often felt uncomfortable performing gestures close to each other. This must be taken into consideration when designing a gestural interface: when users are likely to be unfamiliar with each other, less invasive gestures might need to be considered, while such gestures might be a source of fun for close friends.

We identified a number of gesture adaptations caused by the collocated setting: participants used a different hand to perform the same gesture, changed the size of the gesture, or performed the gesture more to the left or to the right to avoid colliding with their fellow participant. Participants expect their gestures to be recognized in all cases, regardless of the hand they use or the scale of their gesture. Therefore, the system has to be designed to recognize all (or at least the most common) forms of a gesture (e.g. recognize a spread-and-pinch gesture performed with two hands, but also one performed with two fingers). The need to support gesture variations was already observed in other contexts, such as multi-touch surfaces [13] and interactive public displays [25].

We only looked into which gestures participants found to be the most appropriate for every operation. We neither took into account the parameterization of control operations (e.g. how users express how many degrees to pan with their gesture), nor the focus point of those control operations (e.g. how users express on which area they want to zoom in). These factors also need to be investigated, because they can influence how gestures are scaled. When a single user performs a small panning gesture, for instance, it probably means that she wants to move only a little. In a collocated setting, on the other hand, the same small panning gesture might be the result of the presence of others. A gesture recognizer should take this into account by scaling the panning operation according to the situation. Care has to be taken, however, that this kind of adaptation does not confuse users. The system needs to provide sufficient feedback about the scale of control operations.

During our study, participants did not need to be engaged with the actual ODV content, nor did they have different points of focus, which is likely to happen in a CAVE-like setup. As a result, they rarely considered aspects such as blocking the other participant's view. Such aspects will become an important factor when participants do engage with the content, which might lead to additional adaptation strategies when performing gestures. However, participants not having different points of focus during the study does allow us to generalise our results beyond CAVE-like setups.

CONCLUSIONS

We presented the results of a gesture elicitation study that we carried out with the goal of understanding which mid-air gestures users consider to be the most appropriate for interacting with ODV. We not only considered interacting with ODV when users are on their own, but also when they are together with other viewers in a collocated setting. We gathered both quantitative and qualitative data by means of observations, motion capture, questionnaires and interviews. Based on an in-depth analysis of this data, we described a user-defined gesture set for ODV, and gesture variations and adaptations that came forth from individual and collocated usage.

The user-defined gesture set contains the most repeated gestures in our study. We observed a clear preference for using linear movements to represent easy to perform and easy to remember gestures. Participants also preferred to use dynamic movements rather than static hand postures to represent most control operations, and coarser hand movements instead of fine-grained finger movements. We also found that participants tried to extrapolate their knowledge from interaction with real-life devices or software applications.

Analysis of the collocated interactions revealed interesting behaviours that participants exhibited while devising and performing gestures. They adapted their gestures in several ways because of the presence of another participant. The most prominent adaptations were changing the size of the gesture and shifting the hand movements to the opposite side of where the other participant was sitting. Other gesture adaptations were using a different hand for the same gesture or devising a new gesture. These adaptation strategies highlight the importance of a good system design. The ODV system must be able to interpret the user's actions (e.g. adapting the scale of a gesture because of the proximity of another person versus adapting the scale to make smaller adjustments), give sufficient feedback about the scale, and provide sufficient flexibility to cope with different variations of gestures (e.g. a spread-and-pinch with both hands or two fingers).

By forming pairs of participants with different friendship ties, we observed that the level of comfort between participants was an important factor. Participants who are familiar with each other enjoyed the study and even started making jokes about a choreographed dance when they made similar gestures. Participants who are not used to close interaction were less comfortable and made comments such as *"I felt limited by the presence of the other participant. She invaded my private space."* The analysis revealed a trend showing that those participants also used the adaptation strategies more often. The effect of gestures on the level of comfort between users should be taken into account when deciding on a gesture set.

Although our findings are based on a gesture elicitation study regarding control operations for ODV in a CAVE-like setup, we believe the user-defined gesture set and user expectations can also be useful in other setups and domains that require spatial or time-related operations. Furthermore, this study is only a first step in the exploration of ODV gestures, with many interesting avenues for future research, such as studying collaborative tasks with users who each have different points of focus, or an in-depth analysis of the reasons for choosing a specific gesture, which might reveal certain cultural, educational or generational influences.

ACKNOWLEDGMENTS

We thank the participants of our study, Miguel Nacenta for feedback on early drafts, Raf Ramakers for his help with the OptiTrack system and Philippe Bekaert for the use of the ODV infrastructure. The iMinds ICON AIVIE project, with project support from IWT, is co-funded by iMinds, a research institute founded by the Flemish Government. This research was also partially supported by the National Council of Science and Technology of México as part of the Special Program of Science and Technology.

REFERENCES

1. Axel, C., Ravindra, G., and Tsang, O. W. Towards characterizing users' interaction with zoomable video. In *Proc. of the ACM Workshop on Social, Adaptive and Personalized Multimedia Interaction and Access*, SAPMIA (2010), 21–24.
2. Baudel, T., and Beaudouin-Lafon, M. Charade: remote control of objects using free-hand gestures. *Communications of the ACM 36*, 7 (1993), 28–35.

3. Benko, H. Beyond flat surface computing: challenges of depth-aware and curved interfaces. In *Proc. of the ACM Int. Conference on Multimedia*, MM (2009), 935–944.

4. Benko, H., and Wilson, A. D. Multi-point interactions with immersive omnidirectional visualizations in a dome. In *Proc. of the ACM Int. Conference on Interactive Tabletops and Surfaces*, ITS (2010), 19–28.

5. Benko, H., and Wilson, A. D. Pinch-the-sky dome: freehand multi-point interactions with immersive omni-directional data. In *CHI Extended Abstracts on Human Factors in Computing Systems* (2010), 3045–3050.

6. Bleumers, L., den Broeck, W. V., Lievens, B., and Pierson, J. Seeing the bigger picture: a user perspective on 360° TV. In *Proc. of the European Conference on Interactive TV and Video*, EuroiTV (2012), 115 – 124.

7. Fikkert, W., van der Vet, P., van der Veer, G., and Nijholt, A. Gestures for large display control. In *Proc. of the Int. Gesture Workshop*, GW (2010), 245–256.

8. Freeman, W. T., and Weissman, C. D. Television control by hand gestures. In *Proc. of the Int. Workshop on Automatic Face and Gesture Recognition*, FG (1995), 179–183.

9. Grandhi, S. A., Joue, G., and Mittelberg, I. Understanding naturalness and intuitiveness in gesture production: insights for touchless gestural interfaces. In *Proc. of the SIGCHI Conference on Human Factors in Computing Systems*, CHI (2011), 821–824.

10. Haythornthwaite, C., and Wellman, B. Work, friendship, and media use for information exchange in a networked organization. *Journal of the American Society for Information Science 49*, 12 (1998), 1101–1114.

11. Henze, N., Löcken, A., Boll, S., Hesselmann, T., and Pielot, M. Free-hand gestures for music playback: deriving gestures with a user-centred process. In *Proc. of the Int. Conference on Mobile and Ubiquitous Multimedia*, MUM (2010), 1–10.

12. Hespanhol, L., Tomitsch, M., Grace, K., Collins, A., and Kay, J. Investigating intuitiveness and effectiveness of gestures for free spatial interaction with large displays. In *Proc. of the Int. Symposium on Pervasive Displays*, PerDis (2012), 1–6.

13. Hinrichs, U., and Carpendale, S. Gestures in the wild: Studying multi-touch gesture sequences on interactive tabletop exhibits. In *Proc. of the SIGCHI Conference on Human Factors in Computing Systems*, CHI (2011), 3023–3032.

14. Hoggan, E., Williamson, J., Oulasvirta, A., Nacenta, M., Kristensson, P. O., and Lehtiö, A. Multi-touch rotation gestures: performance and ergonomics. In *Proc. of the SIGCHI Conference on Human Factors in Computing Systems*, CHI (2013), 3047–3050.

15. Jones, B., Benko, H., Ofek, E., and Wilson, A. IllumiRoom: peripheral projected illusions for interactive experiences. In *Proc. of the SIGCHI Conference on Human Factors in Computing Systems*, CHI (2013), 869–878.

16. Macq, J.-F., Verzijp, N., Aerts, M., Vandeputte, F., and Six, E. Demo: omnidirectional video navigation on a tablet pc using a camera-based orientation tracker. In *Proc. of the ACM/IEEE Int. Conference on Distributed Smart Cameras*, ICDSC (2011), 1–2.

17. Microsoft. Kinect for Windows Human Interface Guidelines v1.8.0 (2013). Retrieved Jan. 2014, from: msdn.microsoft.com/en-us/library/jj663791.aspx.

18. Morris, M. R., Wobbrock, J. O., and Wilson, A. D. Understanding users' preferences for surface gestures. In *Proc. of Graphics Interface*, GI (2010), 261–268.

19. Nancel, M., Wagner, J., Pietriga, E., Chapuis, O., and Mackay, W. Mid-air pan-and-zoom on wall-sized displays. In *Proc. of the SIGCHI Conference on Human Factors in Computing Systems*, CHI (2011), 177–186.

20. Neng, L. A. R., and Chambel, T. Get around 360° hypervideo. In *Proc. of the Int. Academic MindTrek Conference*, MindTrek (2010), 119–122.

21. Nielsen, M., Störring, M., Moeslund, T. B., and Granum, E. A procedure for developing intuitive and ergonomic gesture interfaces for HCI. *Gesture Based Communication in Human-Computer Interaction 2915* (2004), 409–420.

22. Park, W., and Han, S. H. Intuitive multi-touch gestures for mobile web browsers. *Interacting with Computers 25*, 5 (2013), 335–350.

23. Peltonen, P., Kurvinen, E., Salovaara, A., Jacucci, G., Ilmonen, T., Evans, J., Oulasvirta, A., and Saarikko, P. It's mine, don't touch!: interactions at a large multi-touch display in a city centre. In *Proc. of the SIGCHI Conference on Human Factors in Computing Systems*, CHI (2008), 1285–1294.

24. Stellmach, S., Jttner, M., Nywelt, C., Schneider, J., and Dachselt, R. Investigating freehand pan and zoom. In *Mensch & Computer* (2012), 303–312.

25. Walter, R., Bailly, G., and Müller, J. StrikeAPose: revealing mid-air gestures on public displays. In *Proc. of the SIGCHI Conference on Human Factors in Computing Systems*, CHI (2013), 841–850.

26. Wobbrock, J. O., Aung, H. H., Rothrock, B., and Myers, B. A. Maximizing the guessability of symbolic input. In *CHI Extended Abstracts on Human Factors in Computing Systems* (2005), 1869–1872.

27. Wobbrock, J. O., Morris, M. R., and Wilson, A. D. User-defined gestures for surface computing. In *Proc. of the SIGCHI Conference on Human Factors in Computing Systems*, CHI (2009), 1083–1092.

28. Zoric, G., Engström, A., Barkhuus, L., Hidalgo, J. R., and Kochale, A. Gesture interaction with rich TV content in the social setting. In *CHI workshop on Exploring and Enhancing the User Experience for TV*, TVUX (2013).

Making Big Gestures: Effects of Gesture Size on Observability and Identification for Co-Located Group Awareness

Adrian Reetz and Carl Gutwin
Department of Computer Science, University of Saskatchewan
110 Science Place, Saskatoon, Canada, S7N 5C9
adrian.reetz@usask.ca, gutwin@cs.usask.ca

ABSTRACT

Co-located work environments allow people to maintain awareness by observing others' actions (called *consequential communication*), but the computerization of many tasks has dramatically reduced the observability of work actions. The recent interest in gestural interaction techniques offers the possibility of recreating some of the noticeability of previous work actions, but little is known about the observability and identifiability of command gestures. To investigate these basic issues, we carried out a study that asked people to observe and identify different sizes and morphologies of gestures from different locations, while carrying out an attention-demanding primary task. We studied small (tablet sized), medium (monitor-sized), and large (full-arm) gestures. Our study showed that although size did have significant effects, as expected, even small gestures were highly noticeable (rates above 75%) and identifiable (rates above 69%). Our results provide empirical guidance about the ways that gesture size, morphology, and location affect observation, and show that gestural interaction has potential for improving group awareness in co-located environments.

Author Keywords

Gestures; consequential communication; group awareness

ACM Classification Keywords

H.5.2. Information interfaces and presentation (e.g., HCI): Interaction styles

INTRODUCTION

In 1993, Don Norman describes the usefulness of "big controls and big actions" for shared work:

> The critical thing about doing shared tasks is to keep everyone informed about the complete state of things [...] each pilot or member of the control team must be fully aware of the situation, of what has happened, what is planned. And here is where those big controls come in handy. When the captain reaches across the cockpit over to the first officer's side and lowers the landing-gear lever, the motion is obvious: the first officer can see it even without paying conscious attention. The motion not only controls the landing gear, but just as important, it acts as a natural communication between the two pilots, letting both know that the action has been done. [...] Automatically, naturally, without any need for talking. [25, p. 142]

CHI 2014, April 26–May 1, 2014, Toronto, Ontario, Canada.

ACM 978-1-4503-2473-1/14/04...$15.00..
http://dx.doi.org/10.1145/2556288.2557219

This kind of information flow, also called *consequential communication*, has been shown by several researchers to be an important part of the natural way in which people maintain awareness in a group [12, 30, 33]. However, consequential communication depends on large easily-observable actions and controls, which are no longer common in most workplaces. Instead, most tasks are now carried out on general-purpose computers with standard graphical user interfaces. On these computers, activities that once had characteristic actions and artifacts (e.g., getting a file from a cabinet, using a Rolodex to find a telephone number, drawing a diagram, or entering numbers in a ledger) now all look very similar to an observer—that is, they all look like a person sitting at a computer monitor and moving a mouse.

Researchers in distributed groupware have looked at the problem of reduced observability (since people's bodies are not visible in a distributed setting), and have proposed visualization techniques to make others' actions in a shared workspace more obvious [13]. However, these enhancements often work only when people are observing the same part of the shared workspace, and the techniques do not provide a solution in situations where people are carrying out loosely coupled work in a co-located setting.

A recent development, and one that could potentially improve observability, is the rise of *gestural* interaction techniques. Gestures are now common on touch-screen devices of all sizes, and larger gestures that involve full-body interaction have also been extensively studied (e.g., Kinect-based interaction, Virtual Shelves [19], Air Pointing [6], and Skinput [16]). Gestures and full-body interactions bring large easily-observable actions to general-purpose computers, and could thus be a solution to the problem of observability for collocated environments—they could be one way that designers help people maintain group awareness.

There is little information available, however, about whether gestural commands are in fact observable and interpretable, and what size of gesture is needed for an observer to notice the gesture while carrying out other tasks. That is, how should gestures be designed to make possible the kind of group awareness that Norman described?

We carried out an experiment to answer this question. We measured how well participants were able to observe and identify gestures of various sizes and morphologies from different locations in a co-located environment, while carrying out an attention-demanding primary task. We tested three gesture sizes: small gestures that took place on a tablet-sized device; medium gestures that occurred on a monitor-sized display; and large gestures that involved full-arm pointing to different locations in the room.

The study provided three main results:

- Gesture size did significantly affect both observation and identification. However, small gestures had surprisingly high rates of both observation (74%) and identification (69%). Medium and large gestures showed no differences for observation (82% vs. 83%), but large gestures were more accurately identified (92% for large vs. 83% for medium);
- Observation and identification were strongly affected by both location (both rates ranged from 65% to 91% by location) and gesture morphology (observation ranged from 59% to 99%, and surprisingly, the least-observed gesture was one of the large full-arm pointing gestures);
- Participants subjectively rated larger gestures as requiring significantly less effort than smaller gestures, and as being more observable and identifiable; people also strongly preferred the large gestures for the task of maintaining group awareness.

Our results suggest that gestural interaction techniques can provide the foundation for the consequential communication that underlies Norman's idea of 'big actions'—and that although gesture size does matter, even small gestures on small devices are surprisingly visible. We considered how smaller gestures could be so well observed; our analysis showed that even when command gestures are small, the preparatory and staging actions that precede them are often much more observable—for example, moving one's hand up to a mobile device is noticeable action that draws attention to the upcoming command gesture.

Our study provides empirical evidence about the benefits of gestural interfaces for collaborative activity, and is the first to analyze the specific effects of gesture size, morphology, and location on observability and identification. Our work indicates that designers could use gestural interaction techniques as a way to improve the natural communication and awareness that occur in co-located work environments.

RELATED WORK

Groups and Mixed-focus Collaboration

Groups are sets of two to five people who carry out tasks in medium-sized workspaces [14]. Whenever people engage in collaborative activities, they have to split their attention between their working task and awareness maintenance. Since these two tasks compete for people's attention, groupware designers try to minimize the cognitive load from awareness maintenance (see next section for examples) and find a balance between these two tasks [13]. When people work in a group, they often engage in mixed-focus collaboration, i.e. people shift frequently between loosely and tightly coupled activities during a work session [7]. Coupling refers to the degree with which people have to interact to progress with their work [29]. When people are loosely coupled, they have to interact less with each other to complete their task as when they are tightly coupled [29]. However, even during loosely coupled work, people still need to be aware of others' activities [26].

Group Awareness and Consequential Communication

Awareness is the perception and comprehension of the state of the environment [8, 14]. Group awareness, that is an understanding of the activities of others, provides context for people's activities and is critical to successful collaboration [7]. Two factors determine the level of group awareness: the actor's nimbus (the space in which actors make their activity available to others), and the observer's focus (the space which is covered by the observer's attention) [3]. When nimbus and focus overlap, observers go through a three-phase process to gain group awareness: perception of an action, comprehension of the situation, and projection of the future status [9]. There are several methods for creating group awareness in collocated environments [12]: direct communication, indirect productions, consequential communication, feedthrough, and environmental feedback.

Consequential communication occurs through visible or audible signs of interaction with a workspace [30]. The size of the actions necessary to operate controls makes actions public and creates situation awareness, which is important in many collaborative real-world tasks [30]. In HCI research, consequential communication is frequently mentioned as an awareness mechanism, and observational studies show that it is frequently used in real-world situations [18, 30]. However, it is rarely explored in controlled studies and occasionally considered to be of little importance [31]. This is in contrast to other fields, which showed that consequential communication plays a crucial role throughout life, for example, as facilitator for learning through observation and imitation [15, 28].

Gestures

In HCI, the term gesture is used for a wide variety of concept (see [5] for an overview). A classification that fits best within the scope of this work might be a combination of 2-D plane-based finger movements [1] and 3-D mid-air arm movements [6].

Initially, swipe gestures were used to move elements around a touch screen [20]. Researchers extended these simple gestures to include geometric forms, script, and multi-touch input [10, 17]. Next, researchers created technologies that enables the use of gestures on different surfaces, such as the human arm [16] and virtual space in front of the user [11, 21]. Two-D plane-based gestures have been investigated in great detail. Researches have evaluated, for example, learnability [23], ergonomics [24], and social aspects [27] of gestures (see [35] for a recent overview). Very few papers, however, have implicitly investigated gestures as a method for creating group awareness in co-located environments. Morris et al., for example, used collaborative gestures to create awareness in a co-located work environment [22].

Full 3-D input using arm gestures was first mentioned by Bolt [4] and explored by Baudel and Beaudouin-Lafon [2]. Unfortunately, most papers in this area focus on technical aspects, and only two articles explore human factors of full-arm gestures in HCI: Virtual Shelves [19] and Air Pointing [6]. Neither of these works have investigated the consequential communication aspect of full-arm gestures.

A STUDY OF GESTURE OBSERVABILITY

To determine how factors such as gesture size, morphology, and location affect people's ability to see and interpret these gestures, we carried out a controlled experiment. We picked these factors because they are of high importance for the observability of gestures [32]. We chose a dual-task study setup because it embodies the trade-off between primary working task and awareness-maintenance task. In our simulated collaborative scenario, the study participants (the *observer*) carried out an attention-demanding choice reaction task (word selection) as primary task in a room where another person (the *actor*, a confederate) executed various gestures. The observer's job was to maintain awareness of the actor, but without reducing their performance on their primary task. With our setup, the primary task required the majority of participants' attention. The task required foveal vision focus on the touch screen, thus forcing participants to temporarily dedicate their full attention. Furthermore, participants completed the primary task 2.5x as often as the actor performed gestures.

Study Methods

Participants and Apparatus

We recruited 18 participants from a local university, ages $19 - 45$ ($\bar{x} = 29$), 9 female, 9 male. These participants were all experienced with traditional computer systems (mean 35 hours / week), and were all familiar with gestures on touch-based devices such as mobile phones and tablets.

The study was carried out in a large laboratory (approximately $10\,m \times 10\,m$), in which we placed two moveable carts holding the study computers. The actor's cart held a 22″ monitor and remained stationary during the study. The observer's cart was moved to several different locations during the session (see Figure 2). It held a 7″ MiMo touch screen, on which the primary task was displayed, and on which the observer indicated their observations and identifications of the actor's gestures.

Study Conditions: Gesture Size, Morphology, and Location

We defined three gesture sizes: *small* touch-gestures performed on a 7″ hand-held tablet; *medium* hover-gestures performed approximately $1\,cm$ above a 22″ horizontal screen; and *large* full-arm pointing gestures.

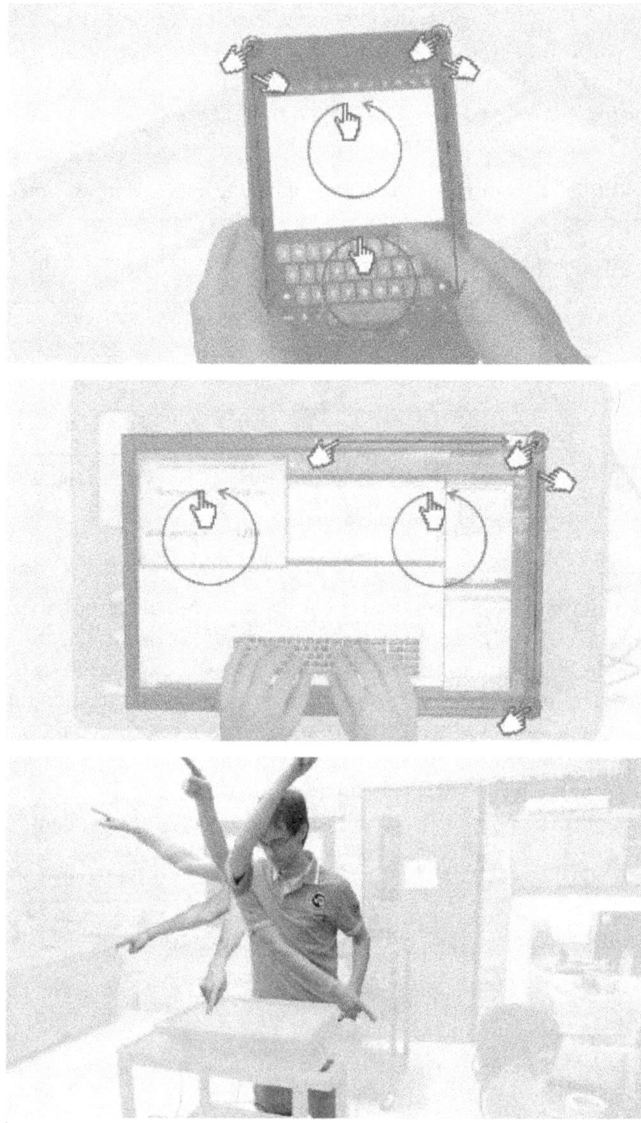

Figure 1: Overview of small gestures (top), medium gestures (center), and large gestures (bottom)

For each of the gesture sizes, we created 6 different gestures (see Figure 1 and Table 1). We chose a small gesture vocabulary in order to keep the recognition task simple, and to focus on our main interests of gesture observability and identifiability. For small and medium gestures, we chose two gesture types that can be found on most touch screens (tap and swipe) and one geometric gesture (circle). We based our large gestures on systems such as Virtual Shelves [19] or Air Pointing [6], which partition the space around the user into zones. For our system, we used six zones that were arranged in front of the actor (from $-90°$ to $+90°$ horizontally, and from $-45° - +45°$ vertically).

To gain quantifiable values for each of the gesture sizes, we measured magnitude and execution time of the actor's arm movement with an IR-based motion-tracking system. The actor performed each gesture 10 times while we captured his shoulder, elbow, wrist, and index finger movement.

Naturally, the index finger travelled the longest distance: $\bar{x} = 0.46\,m$ (small gestures), $\bar{x} = 0.94\,m$ (medium gestures), and $\bar{x} = 1.65\,m$ (large gestures). Small gestures were performed in $\bar{x} = 1.9\,s$, medium gestures in $\bar{x} = 2.3\,s$, and large gestures in $\bar{x} = 1.7\,s$.

Table 1: Gestures with mean magnitude and execution time

Small	Medium	Large
Tap: top left corner ($0.40\,m, 1.8\,s$)	Tap: top right corner ($0.77\,m, 1.7\,s$)	Point: left, high ($2.09\,m, 1.7\,s$)
Tap: top right corner ($0.30\,m, 1.6\,s$)	Tap: bottom right corner ($0.60\,m, 1.9\,s$)	Point: front, high ($1.55\,m, 1.7\,s$)
Circle: top half ($0.58\,m, 2.1\,s$)	Circle: left half ($1.10m\,, 2.6\,s$)	Point: right, high ($2.05\,m, 1.7s$)
Circle: bottom half ($0.50\,m, 2.0\,s$)	Circle: right half ($1.06\,m, 2.5\,s$)	Point: left, low ($1.16\,m, 1.7\,s$)
Swipe: left edge ($0.55\,m, 1.9\,s$)	Swipe: top edge ($1.03\,m, 2.3\,s$)	Point: front, low ($1.16\,m, 1.7\,s$)
Swipe: right edge ($0.44\,m, 1.9\,s$)	Swipe: left edge ($1.05\,m, 2.4\,s$)	Point: right, low ($1.88\,m, 1.6\,s$)

Participants observed the actor from seven different locations (L1–L7), comprising three positions arranged in a semicircle around the actor, and either two or three orientations at each position (facing the actor, or facing perpendicularly away). Figure 2 shows these locations. Six locations formed a symmetry: L1–L7, L2–L6, and L3–L5. The first two pairs, however, differ in a way that in L1 and L2 participants are behind the actor; in L6 and L7 they are in front.

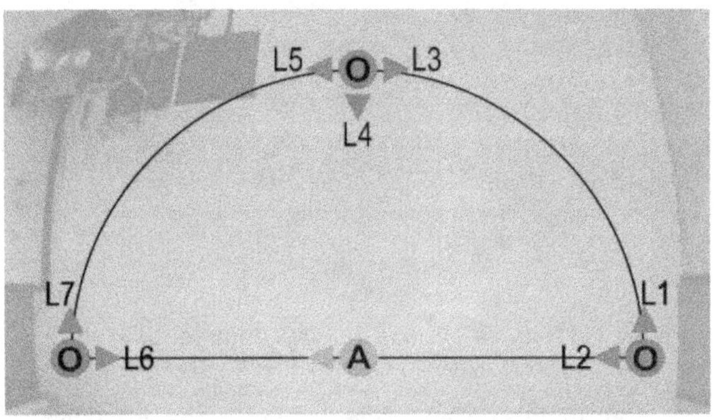

Figure 2: Observer locations (O) and actor location (A)

Observer's Primary Task

In order to simulate a realistic work environment, we created an attention-demanding primary task for the observer to perform during the experiment. The task involved repeatedly selecting one of four possible buttons indicated by a written message displayed on the observer's display (displayed on a 7" MiMo touch screen, see Figure 3). Participants were given a short period to complete the selection ($1.0\,s - 2.0\,s$, randomly chosen); if they did not finish their selection in time or made a wrong selection, the system would play a warning sound. After each correct selection, the system would wait $1.0\,s$ and then display another message.

Procedure

After completing a demographics survey and being introduced to the system, participants completed 12 training trials. Participants were then moved to the starting location and asked to start the primary task; they were instructed to maintain awareness of the actor's activities, and report any gestures they observed using their interface (see Figure 3).

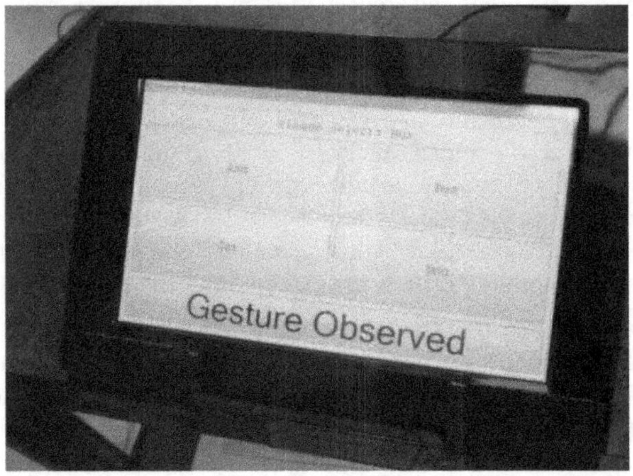

Figure 3: User interface for the primary working task

The actor then started performing typical tasks at his station, which acted as distractor tasks in between gestures that the observer had to report. The actor texted on the handheld tablet (small gestures); he typed using the on-screen keyboard on the horizontal screen (medium gestures); and he fidgeted and moved objects around at the cart (large gestures). Within these typical activities, the actor performed a total of 12 gestures (each gesture twice, randomized order) per location. The actor's UI indicated when to perform the next gestures; the interval was randomly chosen (from $1.5\,s$ to $6.0\,s$). When participants noticed a gesture, they could pause the primary working task, and specify the gesture they just observed from the UI.

Study Design and Hypotheses

The study used a 3×7 within-participants factorial design with factors *Gesture size* (small, medium, large) and *Location* (L1–L7, as shown in Figure 2). Order of gesture size was balanced using Latin square between participants; order of locations was randomized within gesture size.

The actor performed a total of $(12 + 12 \times 7) \times 3 = 288$ gestures per participant. The observer's system recorded all gesture observations and identifications, and tracked the participant's performance on the primary task. After the experiment, participants filled out a basic demographic questionnaire, one NASA TLX form per gesture size, and one ranking questionnaire.

We formulated four hypotheses for our study:

H1. Larger gestures will be observed at a higher rate than smaller gestures.

H2. Larger gestures will be identified more accurately than smaller gestures.

H3. Larger gesture size will reduce the negative effects of occlusion

H4. Facing the actor will have higher observation and identification rates.

Data Analysis

We performed a univariate ANOVA to investigate the effect of *Gesture Size* and *Location* on primary task performance measured as reaction rate. All post-hoc tests used Bonferroni corrections.

To determine the effect of factors *Gesture size* and *Location* on observation and identification rates, we analyzed the trials in a 3×7 repeated-measures ANOVA. We carried out separate analyses of our dependent measures by gesture morphology (since morphologies were not the same across sizes) with a 3×6 RM-ANOVA. All post-hoc tests used Bonferroni corrections. We evaluated the TLX data using a repeated-measures ANOVA, and we analyzed the rank data using a Friedman test for k related samples.

RESULTS

Primary Task Performance

We did not find effects of Gesture size ($F(2,216) = 1.1,\ p > .1$) and Location ($F(6,216) = 1.8,\ p > .1$) on primary task performance. We found, however, a significant effect of Participant x Gesture size for 8 participants ($F(34,216) = 4.3,\ p < .01$). When looking more closely at this finding, we saw that all affected participants performed significantly worse with the first gesture size they saw during the experiment. We concluded that the training phase was too short for them to achieve their highest level of proficiency. Since we counter-balanced the order of gesture sizes between participants and therefore controlled for this factor, we felt confident that primary task performance was independent from *Gesture size* and *Location*. As a result, we omitted it from all further analyses.

Observation Rate and Identification Rate

Observation rate is the number of gesture observations made by a participant divided by the number of gestures performed by the actor. Identification rate is the number of gestures correctly identified by a participant divided by the number of observations.

Sphericity was violated for observation rate by both Gesture size and Location (Mauchly's test: $p = .00$), and for identification rate by Location (Mauchly's test: $p < .01$). For these analyses, we use Greenhouse-Geisser corrections.

Effects of Gesture Size

On average, participants showed the highest observation (see Table 2 and Figure 4) and identification rates (see Table 3 and Figure 5) with large gestures, followed by medium and small gestures.

Observation Rate

ANOVA showed a significant effect of *Gesture size* on *Observation rate* ($F(1.1, 18.9) = 9.7,\ p < .01$). Followup analyses showed that medium and large gestures had a higher observation rate than small gestures ($p < .05$).

Identification Rate

ANOVA also showed a significant effect of *Gesture size* on *Identification rate* ($F(2,34) = 51.2,\ p = .00$). Follow-up analyses showed that all three gesture sizes were significantly different (p < .01).

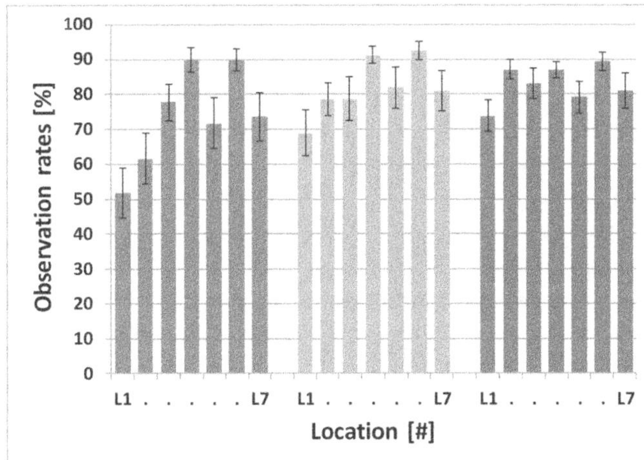

Figure 4: Observation rates per gesture size (small: blue / left; medium: green / center; large: red / right)

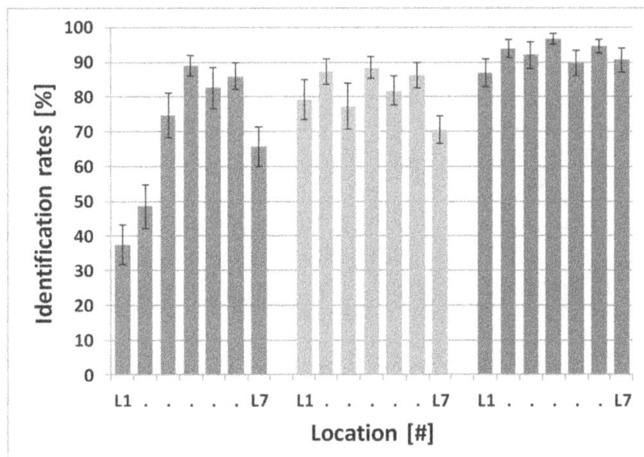

Figure 5: Identification rates per gesture size (small: blue / left; medium: green / center; large: red / right)

Table 2: Observation and identification rates [%]

Gesture size	Small	Medium	Large
Observation rate: Mean ± Std. err.	74 ± 5.0	82 ± 4.3	83 ± 3.0
Identification rate: Mean ± Std. err.	69 ± 3.8	82 ± 3.5	92 ± 2.0

Table 3: Observation and identification rates [%]

Location	L1	L2	L3	L4	L5	L6	L7
Observation rate: Mean ± Std. err.	65 ± 5.4	76 ± 4.2	80 ± 4.5	89 ± 2.1	78 ± 5.7	91 ± 2.5	79 ± 5.5
Identification rate: Mean ± Std. err.	68 ± 4.5	77 ± 3.4	91 ± 5.0	91 ± 1.8	85 ± 3.7	89 ± 2.5	76 ± 3.3

Effects of Location

Observation Rate

ANOVA showed a significant effect of *Location* on *Obser-*

vation rate ($F(2.4, 40.0) = 15.8$, $p = .00$). As shown in Table 1, the different locations were associated with a wide variety of observation rates: the highest at L6 and L4, and the lowest at L1 (see Figure 6 for a map of observation rates by location). Follow-up analyses showed that the observation rate at L1 was significantly worse than from all other locations ($p < .05$), and L6 had a higher observation rate than its symmetric counterpart L2 ($p < .01$).

Identification Rate

ANOVA also showed a significant effect of *Location* on *Identification rate* ($F(3.2, 53.7) = 13.4$, $p = .00$). As shown in Table 3 and Figure 7, participants had the highest identification rate from L4, followed by L6, and the worst observation rate from L1. The identification rate from L1 was significantly worse than from L3 through L6 (all $p < .05$), and L4 and L6 had significantly higher identification rates than L1, L2, and L7 (all $p < .01$)

Gesture Size x Location Interaction

Observation Rate

ANOVA showed a significant interaction between *Gesture size* and *Location* ($F(5.7, 97.4) = 4.1$, $p < .01$) for *Observation rate*. As shown in Figure 4, small gestures were significantly better observed from L4 and L6 (both $\bar{x} = 0.90$) than from L1 ($\bar{x} = 0.52$) and L2 ($\bar{x} = 0.62$) (all $p < .01$). Observation rate from L1 was significantly worse than from all other locations except L2 (all $p < .05$). As expected, mean differences were high between symmetric locations L1–L7 ($.22$) and L2–L6 ($.28$) and low between L3–L5 ($.06$) and L4–L6 ($.00$).

Medium gestures were best observed from L6 ($\bar{x} = 0.93$) and L4 ($\bar{x} = 0.91$) and worst observed from L1 ($\bar{x} = 0.69$). Observation rates from L1 were significantly worse than from L3 through L6 (all $p < .05$) and from L2 worse than from L6 and L4 (both $p < .05$). Compared to small gestures, observation rate in L2 improved close to average ($\bar{x} = 0.79$). As expected, mean differences became lower between symmetric locations L1–L7 ($.12$) and L2–L6 ($.14$) and stayed low between L3–L5 ($.03$) and L4–L6 ($.01$).

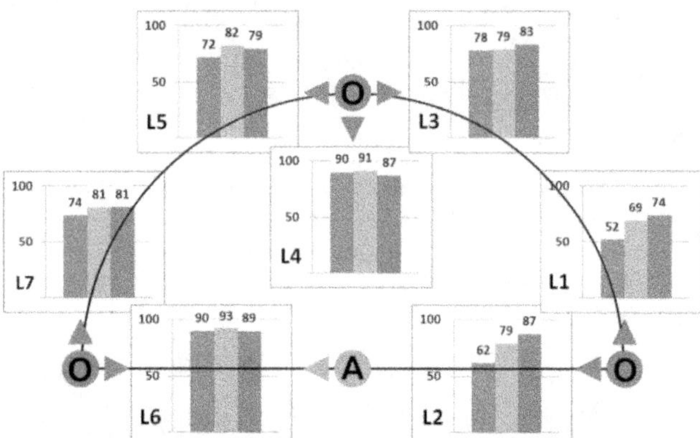

Figure 6: Observation rates per location (small: blue / left; medium: green / center; large: red / right)

Large gestures were best observed from L6 ($\bar{x} = 0.89$) and L2 and L4 (both $\bar{x} = 0.87$) and worst observed from L1 ($\bar{x} = 0.74$). The only significant difference appeared between L6 and L1 ($p < .05$). Overall, differences between symmetric locations are for amongst large gestures: L1–L7 ($.07$) and L2–L6 ($.02$), L3–L5 ($.04$) and L4–L6 ($.02$).

At L1 and L2, participants showed significantly lower observation rates with small gestures than with medium and large gestures (all $p < .05$).

Identification Rate

ANOVA also showed a significant *Gesture size* × *Location* interaction ($F(4.5, 76.7) = 12.5, p = .00$) for identification rate. As shown in Figure 5, small gestures were significantly better identified from L4 ($\bar{x} = 0.89$) and L6 ($\bar{x} = 0.86$) than from L1 ($\bar{x} = 0.37$), L2 ($\bar{x} = 0.49$), and L7 ($\bar{x} = 0.66$) (all $p = .00$). Identification rates from L1 and L2 were significantly worse than from all other locations (all $p < .05$). As expected, mean differences were high between symmetric locations L1–L7 ($.28$) and L2–L6 ($.37$) and low between L3–L5 ($.08$) and L4–L6 ($.03$).

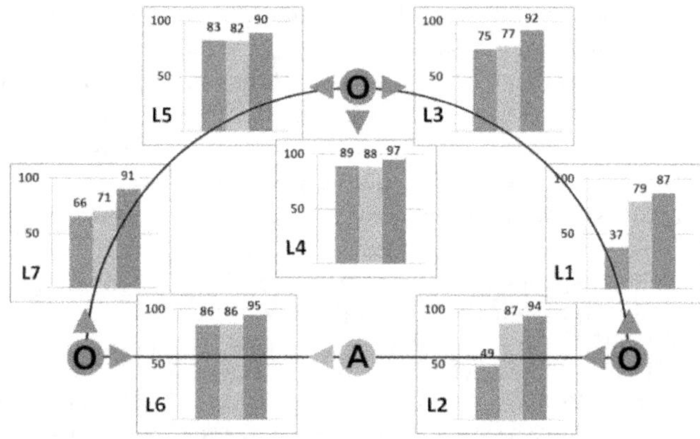

Figure 7: Identification rates per location (small: blue / left; medium: green / center; large: red / right)

Medium gestures were best identified from L4 ($\bar{x} = 0.88$) and L6 ($\bar{x} = 0.86$) and worst identified from L7 ($\bar{x} = 0.71$). Identification rate from L7 was significantly worse than from L2, L4, and L6 ($p < .05$). As expected, mean differences became low between symmetric locations L1–L7 ($.09$) and L2–L6 ($.01$) and stayed low between L3–L5 ($.05$) and L4–L6 ($.02$).

Large gestures were best identified from L4 ($\bar{x} = 0.97$), L6 ($\bar{x} = 0.95$) and L2 ($\bar{x} = 0.94$) and worst identified from L1 ($\bar{x} = 0.87$). There were no significant differences between locations. Overall, mean differences between symmetric locations are very similar with large gestures: L1–L7 ($.04$) and L2–L6 ($.01$), L3–L5 ($.03$) and L4–L6 ($.02$).

At L1 and L2, participants showed significantly lower identification rates with small gestures than with medium and large gestures (all four $p = .00$); at L3 and L7, participants showed significantly higher identification rates with large gestures than with small and medium gestures (all $p < .05$).

Effects of Gesture Morphology

We analyzed *Gesture morphology* separately within each gesture size (since they were different across sizes). Since sphericity was violated for all measures (Mauchly's test: all $p < .05$), we use Greenhouse-Geisser corrections.

For small gestures, ANOVA showed a significant effect of *Gesture morphology* on *Observation rate* ($F(3.6, 61.1) = 5.7$, $p < .01$) and on *Identification rate* ($F(3.0, 51.4) = 6.1$, $p < .01$); for medium gestures, ANOVA showed a significant effect of *Gesture morphology* on *Observation rate* ($F(3.5, 60.0) = 5.7$, $p < .01$) and on *Identification rate* ($F(2.7, 46.5) = 5.3$, $p < .01$); for large gestures, ANOVA showed a significant effect of *Gesture morphology* on *Observation rate* ($F(2.4, 61.0) = 17.1$, $p = .00$), but not *Identification rate*.

Observation Rate

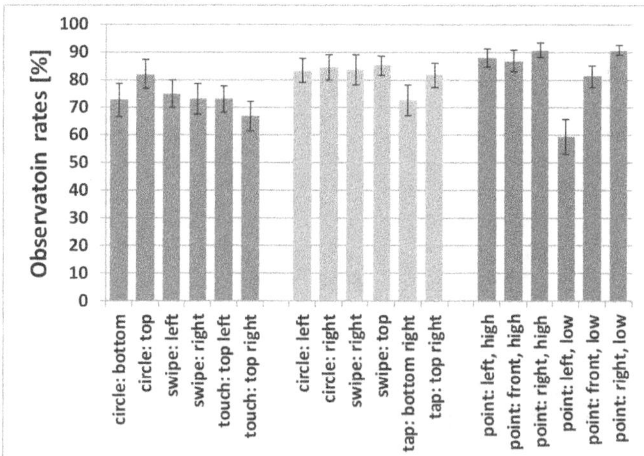

Figure 8: Observation rates per gestures (small: blue / left; medium: green / center; large: red / right)

Identification Rate

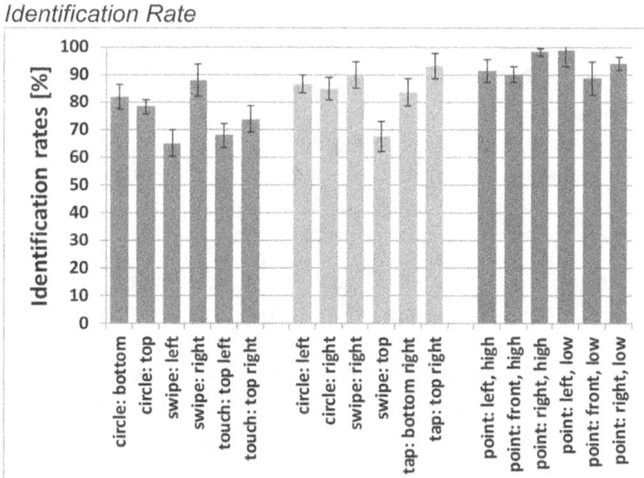

Figure 9: Identification rates per gestures (small: blue / left; medium: green / center; large: red / right)

We found that participants observed the small gesture *circle: top* significantly more often than the gestures *tap: top left*, *tap: top right*, and *circle: bottom* (all $p < .05$). For medium gestures, participants observed *tap: bottom right* significantly less often than the gestures *circle: left*, *circle: right*, *tap: top right*, and *swipe: top* (all $p < .05$). Among large gestures, *point: left, low* had a significantly lower observation rate than any other large gestures (all $p < .05$), and was the least-observed gesture at any size.

Participants showed a significantly higher identification rate for the small gesture *swipe: right* than for the gestures *swipe: left* and *tap: top right* (all $p < .05$). For medium gestures, participants identified *swipe: top* significantly less often than all gestures except *tap: bottom right* ($p < .05$). For large gestures, there were no significant differences.

Subjective Measures

Participants rated their experience using the NASA TLX questionnaire. Overall, participants felt that larger gestures were less effort and less frustration than smaller gestures.

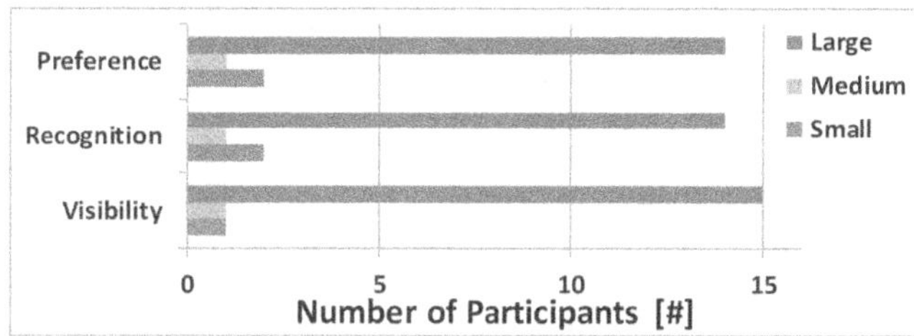

Figure 10: Participant preference rating

We found a significant difference in mental demand between all three gesture sizes (all $p < .01$). For physical demand and frustration, there were significant differences between large gestures and small and medium gestures (all $p < .05$). Finally, participants rated small gestures as more effortful than medium and large ones (both $p < .01$).

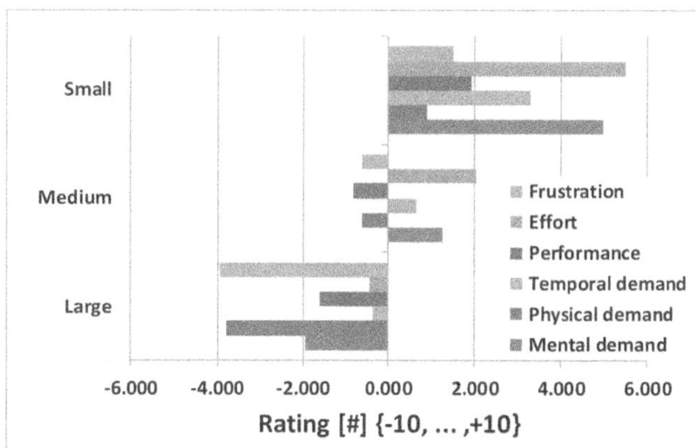

Figure 11: NASA TLX results

We also asked participants to rank the different gesture sizes in terms of perceived visibility, recognition accuracy, and their preference to work with (Figure 11). (We discarded the data from one participant because the questionnaire was not filled out correctly.) A significant majority of participants ranked large gestures most visible (15/17: $\chi^2(2, 17) = 21.5$, $p = .00$) and most recognizable (15/17: $\chi^2(2, 17) = 19.9$, $p = .00$). Overall, 14 of 17 participants preferred to work with large gestures over small and medium ones ($\chi^2(2,17) = 17.3, p = .00$).

DISCUSSION

In this discussion, we first explain how our results confirm our hypotheses and discuss some additional insights we gained from analyzing our results. Then, we come back to our premise and lay out how our findings support Norman's idea of "big controls and big actions". We describe some use cases, mention potential directions for future work, and address issues that come with the use of big gestures. Finally, we list the limitations of our work.

Hypotheses

We confirmed all of our hypotheses.

H1: Larger gestures lead to higher observation rates

As predicted, participants showed significantly higher observation rates with large and medium gestures than with small gestures, and higher observation rates with large gestures than with medium gestures. While this result is true on the (categorical) gesture-size scale (small—medium—large), we also found a similar pattern when looking at the (continuous) gesture magnitude. Figure 12 illustrates the logarithmic relationship between gesture magnitude and observation rate ($F(1,15) = 119.0, p = .00, R^2 = .89$). However, our regression analysis revealed that one large gesture ("point: left, low") was a residual outlier. For the curve fit, we removed this outlier (case-wise analysis with 3σ cutoff); we talk about this case later in the discussion.

We want to emphasize that the logarithmic relationship continues across different gesture sizes and morphologies (2D touch and hover gestures as well as 3D pointing gestures). This means we can generalize our findings to most gestures that fit our definition in the related work section.

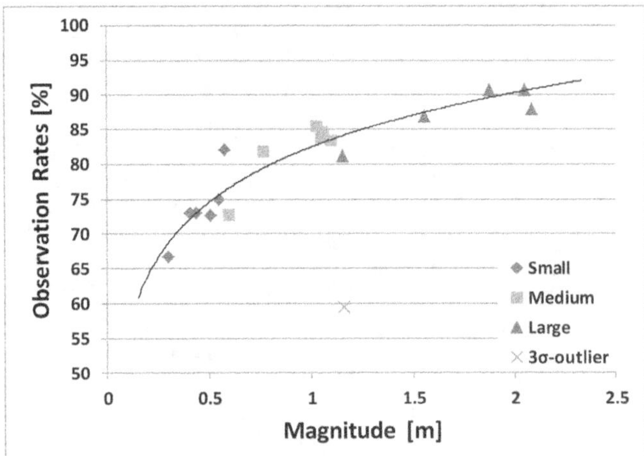

Figure 12: Observation rate per gesture magnitude

H2: Larger gestures lead to higher identification rates

Participants showed significantly better performance with large gestures than with medium and significantly better performance with medium than with small gestures. The overall identification rate of larger gestures is better than that of smaller gestures; even when observed, larger gestures are easier to identify than smaller gestures.

We found a logarithmic relationship between magnitude and identification rate, similar to the one between magnitude and observation rate ($F(1,15) = 19.3, p < .01, R^2 = .56$). Not surprisingly, the effect is smaller because there are other factors that affect identification rate. Again, our regression analysis revealed, that one gesture (medium size, "swipe top") was a residual outlier. For the curve fit, we removed this outlier (case-wise analysis with 2σ cutoff); we will come back to this particular case later in the discussion.

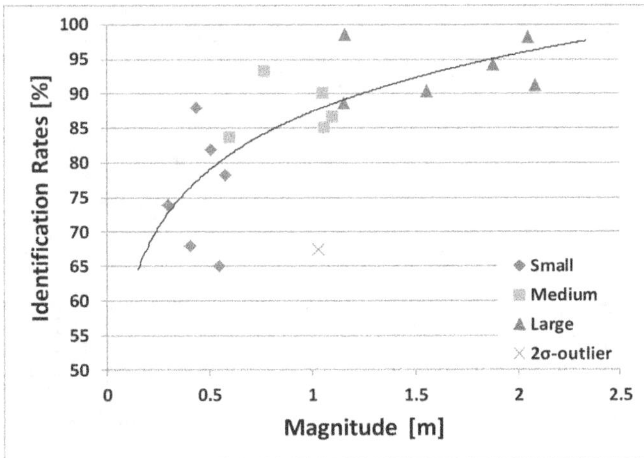

Figure 13: Identification rate per gesture magnitude

H3: Larger gestures are less affected by occlusion

In locations L1 and L2, gestures were occluded by the actor's body. A comparison of symmetrical pairs L1–L7 and L2–L6 therefore shows how much occlusion affected participants' observation rate. Our results showed that the mean differences in observation rate between L1 and L7 and between L2 and L6 decreased with increasing gesture size. This implies that small gestures suffer significantly from occlusion and that this effect diminishes with increased gesture size. With an unobstructed view to the actor, gesture size does not affect performance. However, in multi-display environments where people move around freely, it is likely that occlusion will occur; in this case, larger gestures can enable higher group awareness.

Identification rates of all gestures were affected in similar ways by occlusion than observation rate. For medium gestures, differences in identification rates between L1 and L7 and between L2 and L6 were smaller than these differences in observation rate. We suspect that the location of the gestures on the 22" screen were responsible for this effect: five out of six gestures were performed close to the right edge of the screen, so observers were able to catch a glimpse of these gestures around the right side of the actor's body.

H4: facing the actor leads to higher performance

In locations L2, L4, and L6, participants were facing the actor, in locations L1, L3, L5, and L7, they were perpendicularly seated to the actor. When pairwise comparing L1–

L2, L3–L4, L5–L4, and L6–L7, we found that participants performed on average better when facing the actor. However, most of these comparisons showed no significant difference. While these results might sound surprising, they are in accordance with theory. Vision research has shown that human response to rapidly moving targets is almost invariant with its location in the field of vision [34].

Additional Findings and Research Questions

Are all gestures of one size equally easy to observe?
For small gestures, we found that "circle: top" was the easiest gesture to observe, significantly easier than both "taps" and "circle bottom" (all $p < .05$). This was most likely because it had the longest execution time (2.1 s) and largest magnitude (0.58 m) among all small gestures.

For medium gestures, we found that "tap: bottom right" was significantly harder to observe than any other gesture except "swipe: right" (all $p < .05$). Contributing factors were its low execution time (second lowest in its category: 1.9 s) and its small magnitude (smallest in its category: 0.60 m).

For large gestures, we found that participants showed a significantly lower observation rate with "point: left, low" than with any other gesture (all $p < .05$). As before, we assume that mostly execution time (1.7s) and lack of magnitude (1.16 m) are responsible for this effect. In addition, the gesture was performed very close to the body, which made it more difficult to spot than other large gestures, which were all performed away from the actor's body.

Are all gestures of one size equally easy to identify?
For small and large gestures, we found no gesture that was consistently better or worse than the other ones.

For medium gestures, however, we found that participants performed significantly worse with "swipe: top" than with any other gesture except "tap: bottom right"(all $p < .05$). A detailed analysis showed that we can attribute more than half of the errors to confusing this gesture with the gesture "tap: top right". These two seemingly different gestures share a similar post-stroke hold and retraction phase. Apparently, participants oftentimes required the preparation and stroke phase of the actor's gesture to shift their attention from their primary working task to the perception phase of consequential communication. To make gestures more distinguishable, we therefore recommend avoiding gestures that end with similar strokes and the same post-stroke hold and retraction. For example, the small-gesture swipes were rarely confused with the small-gesture taps.

Are large gestures generally easy to observe and identify?
Ironically, the least likely observed gesture in our study was a large one. A good strategy to make large gestures visible is to make them lead away from the actor's body.

Did the labels "left" and "right" confuse participants?
All directions in gesture descriptions were meant to be relative to the actor. As a result, there was a danger that participants confused left and right and top and bottom when they were in front of the actor (e.g., his "left" became their "right"). We analyzed all errors in conditions L6 and L7; no participant systematically confused any of these labels.

"Big Controls and Big Actions"

Norman's original idea was that big controls and big actions create awareness. Our results showed that gestures, independently from their size, are indeed observable and can therefore improve group awareness: people know that *something* has happened. When looking at identification rate, we can also give an initial estimation for the next step toward group awareness, knowing *what exactly* has happened. Our results indicate that people can distinguish between at least six gestures. We also showed that identification rate depends on more factors than observation rate. A more thorough investigation of these factors could give us more insight about potential limitations, such as upper limits of an alphabet of discernible gesture, as well as guidelines for designing distinguishable gestures. Another important issue is finding gesture sets with different levels of observability, so that interaction designers can select a gesture that matches an action's desired publicity.

There are many cases in which people would want to make their actions public. Public gestures can be part of, for example, co-located multiplayer games where the group should be aware of certain actions. Another example are Scrum-teams where the team should know about the completion of a single Scrum-task. Likewise, there are many cases in which people want to keep actions private or do not want to distract others. As said before, our findings show that people can control the publicity or privacy of their actions through gesture size.

There are, however, some disadvantages to large gestures. For example, they require more physical effort, and there are some socio-cultural restrictions to the use of big gestures. Again, we assume that large gestures will mostly be used in group environments, where each member accepts and understand large gestures in the context of their work.

Limitations

There are a couple of limitations to our study. While we selected our gesture sizes to reflect a broad variety of gestural interfaces, we only used a typical set of gestures within each size and not a broad variety of all possible gestures. This allows us to only give an initial assessment and lower boundary about identification rates, leaving a more systematic approach to future work. Common contextual and semantic knowledge, for example, can increase identification rates. In addition, our study took place in a controlled laboratory environment. We are confident but cannot guarantee how much our findings apply to a real-world scenario.

CONCLUSION

In this paper, we demonstrated that gestural interaction techniques can be used for creating visible device interaction, thus laying the groundwork for providing consequential communication to co-located collaborators. We measured observation and identification rates of different gestures and showed that even small gestures are visible and could create consequential communication. However, larger gestures are more easily observable, mainly due to a reduced effect from occlusion. In addition, increasing size makes gestures more easily identifiable. Considering our findings, we encourage interaction designer to include gestural interfaces in their groupware applications, so that users can benefit from having consequential communication as an implicit method for gaining group awareness.

REFERENCES

1. Baecker, R., Grudin, J., Buxton, W., and Greenberg, S. Touch, gesture, and marking. In *HCI: Toward the Year 2000*. Morgan Kaufmann Publishers, 1995.
2. Baudel, T. and Beaudouin-Lafon, M. Charade: remote control of objects using free-hand gestures. *Communications of the ACM 36*, 7 (1993), 28–35.
3. Benford, S. and Fahlén, L. A spatial model of interaction in large virtual environments. *Proc. of ECSCW '93*, 109–124.
4. Bolt, R. Put-that-there: Voice and gesture at the graphics interface. *Proc. of GRAPH '80*, 262–270.
5. Cadoz, C. and Wanderley, M. Gesture: music. In *Trends in gestural control of music*. IRCAM, 2000.
6. Cockburn, A., Quinn, P., Gutwin, C., Ramos, G., and Looser, J. Air pointing: design and evaluation of spatial target acquisition with and without visual feedback. *IJHCS 69*, 6 (2011), 401–414.
7. Dourish, P. and Bellotti, V. Awareness and coordination in shared workspaces. *Proc. of CSCW '92*, 107–114.
8. Endsley, M. Design and evaluation for situation awareness enhancement. *Meeting of the Human Factors and Ergonomics Society 32*, 2 (1988), 97–101.
9. Endsley, M. Toward a theory of situation awareness in dynamic systems. *JHFES* 37, 1 (1995), 32–64.
10. Goldberg, D, Richardson, C. Touch-typing with a stylus. *Proc. of the CHI '93*, 80–87
11. Gustafson, S., Bierwirth, D., and Baudisch, P. Imaginary interfaces: spatial interaction with empty hands and without visual feedback. *Proc. of UIST '10*, 3–12.
12. Gutwin, C. and Greenberg, S. Workspace awareness for groupware. *Proc. of CHI '96*, 208–209.
13. Gutwin, C. and Greenberg, S. Design for individuals, design for groups: tradeoffs between power and workspace awareness. *Proc. of CSCW '98*, 207–216.
14. Gutwin, C. and Greenberg, S. A descriptive framework of workspace awareness for real-time groupware. *CSCW 11*, 3–4 (2002), 411–446.
15. Hanna, E. and Meltzoff, A. Peer imitation by toddlers in laboratory, home, and day-care contexts. *Developmental psychology 29*, 4 (1993), 701–710.
16. Harrison, C., Tan, D., and Morris, D. Skinput: appropriating the body as an input surface. *Proc. of CHI '10*, 453–462.
17. Hauptmann, A. Speech and gestures for graphic image manipulation. *Proc. of CHI '89*, 241–245
18. Heath, C. and Luff, P. Collaborative activity and technological design. Proc. of ECSCW '91, 65–80.
19. Li, F, Dearman, D., and Truong, K. Virtual shelves: interactions with orientation aware devices. *Proc. of UIST '09*, 125–128.
20. Minsky, R. Manipulating simulated objects with real-world gestures using a force and position sensitive screen. *Proc. of GRAPH '84*, 195–203.
21. Mistry, P, Maes, P., Chang L. Wear ur world: a wearable gestural interface. *EA of CHI '09*, 4111–4116.
22. Meredith, M., Huang, A., Paepcke, A., Winograd, T. Cooperative gestures: multi-user gestural interactions for co-located groupware. *Proc. of CHI '06*, 1201–1210
23. Nacenta, M., Kamber, Y., Qiang, Y., Kristensson, P. Memorability of pre-designed and user-defined gesture sets. *Proc. of CHI '13*, 1099–1108.
24. Nielsen, M., Störring, M., Moeslund, B., Granum, E. A procedure for developing intuitive and ergonomic gesture interfaces for HCI. *Proc. of GW '03*, 409-420.
25. Norman, D. *Things that make us smart*. Basic Books, 1993.
26. Olson, J. and Teasley, S. Groupware in the wild: lessons learned from a year of virtual collocation. *Proc. of CSCW '96*, 419–427.
27. Rico, J., Brewster S. Usable gestures for mobile interfaces: evaluating social acceptability. *Proc. of CHI '10*, 887–896.
28. Rogoff, B., Paradise, R., Arauz, R., Correa-Chavez, M. and Angelillo, C. Firsthand learning through intent participation. *Annu. Rev. Psychol. 54*, 1 (2003): 175–203.
29. Salvador, T., Scholtz, J., and Larson, J. The Denver model for groupware design. *ACM SIGCHI Bulletin 28*, 1 (1996), 52–58.
30. Segal, L. Actions speak louder than words: how pilots use nonverbal information for crew communications. *Proc. of HFES '94*, 21–40.
31. Storey, D., Čubranić, D., and German, D. On the use of visualization to support awareness of human activities in software development. *Proc. of SoftVis '05*, 193–202.
32. Streeck, J. Gesture as communication I: Its coordination with gaze and speech. *Communication Monographs 60*, 4 (1993), 275–299.
33. Tang, A., Neustaedter, C., and Greenberg, S. Videoarms: embodiments for mixed presence groupware. *Proc. of HCI '06*, 85–102.
34. Tynan, D., Sekuler, R. Motion processing in peripheral vision: Reaction time and perceived velocity. *Vision Research 22*, 1 (1982), 61–68.
35. Zhai, S., Kristensson, P., Appert, C., Andersen, T., Cao, X. Foundational issues in touch-screen stroke gesture design. In *FTHCI 5*, 2 (2012), 97–205.

A Chair as Ubiquitous Input Device: Exploring Semaphoric Chair Gestures for Focused and Peripheral Interaction

Kathrin Probst David Lindlbauer Michael Haller
Media Interaction Lab
University of Applied Sciences Upper Austria
mi-lab@fh-hagenberg.at

Bernhard Schwartz Andreas Schrempf
Department of Medical Engineering
University of Applied Sciences Upper Austria

ABSTRACT
During everyday office work we are used to controlling our computers with keyboard and mouse, while the majority of our body remains unchallenged and the physical workspace around us stays largely unattended. Addressing this untapped potential, we explore the concept of turning a flexible office chair into a ubiquitous input device. To facilitate daily desktop work, we propose the utilization of semaphoric chair gestures that can be assigned to specific application functionalities. The exploration of two usage scenarios in the context of focused and peripheral interaction demonstrates high potential of chair gestures as additional input modality for opportunistic, hands-free interaction.

Author Keywords
Input Technologies; Interactive Chair; Gestural Interaction;

ACM Classification Keywords
H.5.2 [Information Interfaces & Presentation]: User Interfaces – Input Devices and Strategies, Interaction Styles;

General Terms
Human Factors; Design; Measurement

INTRODUCTION
While working on a desktop computer, we are used to traditional mouse and keyboard input. We have learned how to handle these devices and utilize them as powerful tools for our daily computer-based activities. Their operation, however, involves making the same small repetitive movements with our hands over and over again, while the rest of our body remains largely unchallenged [15,29]. On the other hand, with computing interfaces becoming more and more ubiquitous, we see increasing numbers of input technologies making their way into the user interface that support free-form manipulation of digital objects through touch, speech, gaze, or body gestures [7,30].

CHI 2014, April 26 - May 01 2014, Toronto, ON, Canada
Copyright 2014 ACM 978-1-4503-2473-1/14/04...$15.00.
http://dx.doi.org/10.1145/2556288.2557146

Taking this evolution further, we believe that interaction through furniture has high potential to open a new input domain beyond the current mouse-and-keyboard paradigm. Thus, in a common desktop workplace for example, where we are surrounded by functional furniture of various kinds, we believe that these readily available elements (e.g., chair, desk) could actually become part of the computer interface.

The ubiquity of seated activities in our daily lives, for example, provides an excellent context for the development of alternative human-computer interfaces. Thus, we have only recently begun to explore the potential of chair-based interaction as novel input dimension for desktop interfaces [23]. Extending this concept in the present work, we explore the potential of gestural chair interaction during regular desktop activities. By tracking the movements of a seated person, specific gestures can be identified, and transformed into input commands (e.g., tilting left to show the previous webpage in a browser, or tilting right to play the next track in a playlist). This way, a chair becomes a ubiquitous input device providing us with the opportunity to use the movements of our body for operating a computer (see Figure 1).

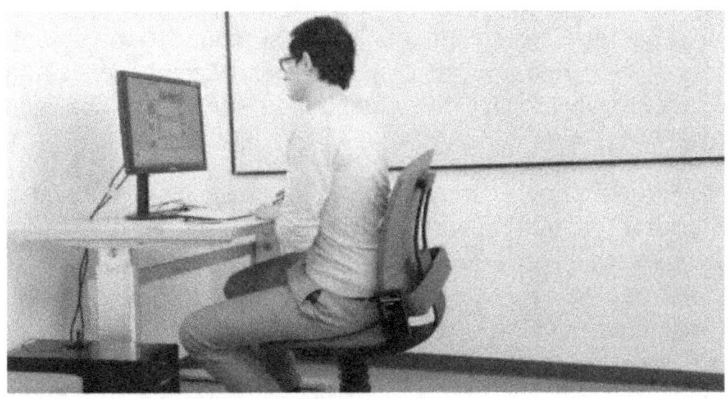

Figure 1. A user controlling a computer through the movements of his body, while sitting on a flexible office chair.

In this paper, we investigate the integration of gestural chair interaction into the desktop computing experience. We describe an iterative design process from the definition of a basic set of semaphoric chair gestures to their application for focused and peripheral interaction scenarios. The results of two explorative studies provide implications on the benefits and limitations of the proposed concept. User feedback and performance show high potential of chair gestures as additional input modality for ubiquitous, hands-free interaction with a desktop computer.

RELATED WORK

Following the trend of designing more natural ways of interaction with computer systems, several attempts have been made to develop technologies that extend interaction beyond long-established mouse-and-keyboard input. Along with that, we see more and more devices with embedded sensing and communication capabilities [30]. While early work in the field of smart office environments has demonstrated the ubiquitous integration of interactive technology [27], research interest has more recently also considered the extension of interaction into the periphery. The *Unadorned Desk* is an example for this kind of interaction, which used the physical space around a desktop computer as input canvas [12]. Similarly, our work adds to the research conducted within this field by proposing the utilization of a chair as ubiquitous input device.

Interactive chair interfaces have been used for unobtrusive measurement of body movements to infer a person's physical and emotional state [1,28,33], or support everyday activities [9]. Besides that, chairs have been used in computer-based scenarios, where body movements are sensed and interpreted as implicit input to a system. The *Internet Chair* for example, used orientation tracking to support social situation awareness through spatialized audio [6]. The *Chair Mouse* translated natural chair rotation into large-scale cursor movement for navigation on large displays [8]. Rather than exploiting existing user behavior, however, our work focuses on the encouragement of new interaction metaphors that are currently not possible with traditional input devices. Based on a similar concept, *ChairIO* introduced a gaming interface that allows users to navigate virtual environments by controlling a flexible chair with their body [3]. In contrast to this, we are interested in the application of input metaphors for more general scenarios beyond the gaming context, which have the potential to enrich and facilitate user interaction during everyday desktop work.

In particular, our work explores chair input in the context of gestural interaction, which has been proposed as alternative human-computer interface in the context of hand, finger, or full-body gestures (e.g., [17,24]). Integrating our physical body into interactions with digital interfaces [7], it has been shown that such gestural interfaces can potentially provide wide-reaching benefits over traditional input devices, including naturalness and expressiveness of interaction, learnability, directness of interaction, available degrees of freedom, and exploitation of existing dexterous skills [2,4]. Based on that, we have only recently come up with the idea of applying different gesture styles to flexible chairs [23], since we believe that many of the benefits seen in in other body-based gestural interfaces can transfer to the desktop environment. Building upon this work, we are further exploring the specific subset of *semaphoric* chair gestures, as they provide high flexibility for a variety of computer functionalities and have proven particularly beneficial for secondary task interactions [16].

CHAIR-BASED APPLICATION CONTROL

While chairs can be found everywhere, embedded into our daily lives, growing focus on the ergonomics of sitting [26] has evolved with the emergence of innovative products that provide increased freedom of movement and dynamic transition between postures (i.e., *active sitting*). Based on the inherent characteristics of such flexible chairs, we believe they can provide attractive features that recommend them as alternative input technology in a desktop environment. First of all, chair-based gestures can be used to expand the input bandwidth of desktop work. Relying on simple kinesthetic movement patterns of the lower body (e.g., swinging hips to the side), such semaphoric chair gestures can be mapped directly to specific input commands. This concept of *chair-based application control* can be integrated into a multitude of interactions that take place in the focus (e.g., browsing) or periphery of attention (e.g., music control).

While sitting in front of a computer, motion gestures on an interactive chair can potentially be detected anytime, providing *always-available* access to application functions without switching windows or losing visual focus on the current task. Rather than applying multiple clicks on the graphical user interface, interaction can be reduced to a simple one-step chair gesture. By using a chair as *hands-free* input device, users can be provided with a true additional input dimension, as their hands can remain on keyboard and mouse, or are available for other tasks (e.g., writing, making a phone call). Moreover, it can be operated *eyes-free* [22], as the input is based on motion-based input that provides functional feedback, but requires no attention to a visual interface. Finally, chair-based interaction can support *opportunistic physical activity* by leveraging our physical body as a means of interaction with the system. Resulting dynamic, complex movements (i.e., movements that involve multiple muscle groups) can help breaking up the physical monotony of daily desktop work, and smoothly integrate light physical activity into the work routine [15,18].

Design Approach

While chair gestures have many theoretical advantages, the goal of this work was to explore their feasibility as novel input technique for desktop computing. During an iterative participatory design process, we designed two application scenarios in the context of focused and peripheral interaction. First, to explore the design space of semaphoric chair gestures, we elicited user input on possible movements and suitable gestures. Next, to collect early user feedback on the concept of chair-based application control, we conducted a first experiment where participants used semaphoric chair gestures to control a web browser. Finally, to gain insights on the performance and user experience of chair gestures in comparison to more common input devices (touch, keyboard), we conducted a second experiment where we applied semaphoric chair gestures to a peripheral music control scenario.

INTERACTIVE CHAIR INTERFACE

For the demonstration of gestural interactions with a chair, we implemented an interactive chair interface that is based on a commercially available flexible chair (see Figure 2).

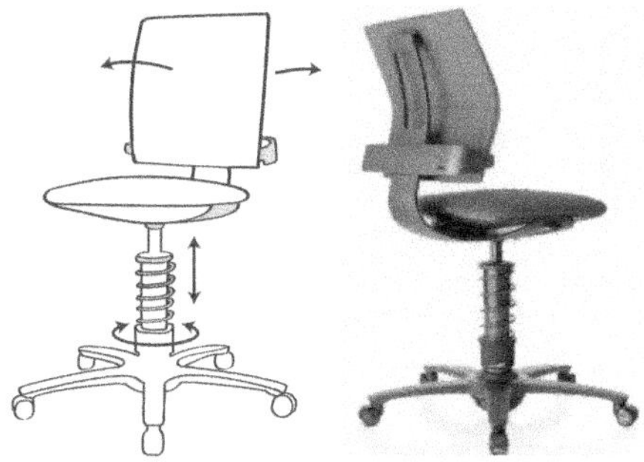

Figure 2. Horizontal and vertical degrees of freedom provided by the 3Dee™ flexible chair.

The 3Dee™ office chair incorporates an active suspension system that provides three degrees of freedom in horizontal and vertical direction. This provides users with dynamic operation through tilting, rotating, or bouncing movements. Adjustable features of the chair include height, horizontal flexibility, vertical flexibility (sensitivity of the suspension system), and tension of the backrest (lumbar support).

Figure 3. Smartphone sensor attached to the backrest of the 3Dee™ flexible chair.

To detect movements along any axis of the chair, we use a motion-sensing smartphone (Nokia Lumia 920) attached to the backrest of the chair (see Figure 3). To calculate the relative position of the sensor, accelerometer and gyroscope measurements (50 Hz sample rate) are transmitted via Bluetooth® to a desktop computer, where a custom background application processes the motion data to recognize the different chair gestures and invokes corresponding application-specific input commands via the *Microsoft UI Automation Framework* that provides programmatic access to interface elements in Windows applications.

DETERMINING A BASIC CHAIR GESTURE SET

To understand the design space of semaphoric chair gestures for interactive application control, we conducted a guessability-style user study [32] where we asked 10 unpaid participants (age 24–32) to demonstrate movements on a 3Dee™ office chair, which they would associate spontaneously with common web browser commands (i.e., *launch, quit, minimize, maximize, previous/next webpage, open/ close tab, previous/next tab, scroll up/down, zoom in/out, start page, reload, bookmark, search, print, save, options*).

Among the resulting 210 gestures observed, 54% included tilting, 19% rotating, and 17% bouncing movements. *Tilting* was performed by briefly swinging the hips to a specific direction along the left-right, front-back, or diagonal axis of the chair. *Rotating* involved swinging the chair counter-clockwise (left) or clockwise (right) by an angle of up to 90 degree, and some cases of full rotations by 360 degree. *Bouncing* was performed through a sweep downward movement to compress the elastic spring of the chair. Overall, the majority of proposed gestures consisted of unique, repeated, or combined execution of the above described movements. Few gestures included other metaphors like position changes (e.g., standing up), or symbolic motion patterns (e.g., circles, crosses, letters). Regarding the assignment of the gestures to specific browser commands, the majority of participants suggested simple tilting/rotating along the left-right axis to navigate between websites, or along the front-back axis to scroll content within a website. Bouncing was preferred for more specific functionalities such as launching/quitting the browser, bookmarking, or opening/closing tabs. Based on these results, we determined a set of seven basic chair gestures that most occurred during the initial study: *tilt left, tilt right, tilt forward, tilt backward, rotate right, rotate left*, and *bounce* (see Figure 4).

Gesture Recognition

To recognize the user-suggested chair gestures, we implemented a real-time gesture recognition algorithm that was trained with a sequence of sample measurements collected from participants in a follow-up session. The data samples were analyzed for characteristic patterns in the raw motion data (i.e., acceleration/velocity peaks), and served as a basis for the development of a threshold model algorithm that recognizes a gesture once the corresponding threshold values are exceeded. While this could also have been implemented with other algorithms, our primary focus in this early design stage was mainly on the interaction perspective.

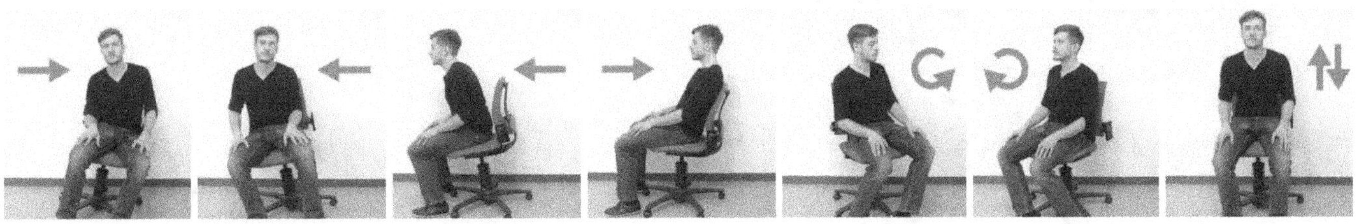

Figure 4: Basic set of *tilting* (left, right, forward, backward), *rotating* (left, right), and *bouncing* chair gestures.

FOCUSED CHAIR INTERACTION

During the next steps of the design process, our main goal was to collect initial user feedback on the idea of chair-based application control, and gain insights into user acceptance of gestural chair interaction in general. Therefore, we conducted a Wizard of Oz experiment that integrated semaphoric chair gestures into web browsing experience.

Experimental Design

12 unpaid participants (2 female; age 22-32) took part in the experiment. All participants were experienced users of web browsers, who usually invoked browser commands through mouse input or keyboard shortcuts.

During the experiment, participants performed a simple navigation task where they interacted with a web browser through chair, mouse, and keyboard input. The experimental task was a web search and planning scenario where participants were asked to plan for a city roundtrip. Thereby, they were given step-by-step instructions to search for basic facts, figures, images, and locations (e.g., researching facts about a city, browsing the top sights to visit, searching for images and locations). To simulate a casual web browsing scenario that supports opportunistic chair interaction, the task was designed to balance searching and reading activities with content navigation through mouse, keyboard, or chair input. Thereby, chair gestures were assigned to the following browser functionalities: *previous website* (tilt left), *next website* (tilt right), *previous tab* (tilt backward), *next tab* (tilt forward), and *start page* (bounce).

The experiment was conducted in a calm desktop environment on a workstation with a Windows PC and a 3Dee^{TM} flexible chair (see Figure 5). Application control was simulated to avoid any potential bias from recognition errors in this early design stage i.e., corresponding input commands being remotely invoked by the experimenter.

User feedback was collected through interviews and questionnaires, where participants rated their experience with the chair in the following areas: satisfaction, ease-of-use, learnability, and engagement. Task load ratings [10] were collected for physical, mental, and temporal demand.

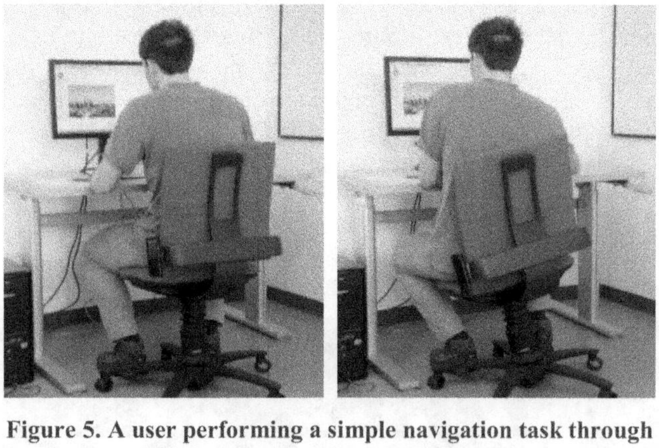

Figure 5. A user performing a simple navigation task through chair-based web browser control.

Results

Initial user feedback showed that participants were positive about the concept of chair-based application control in general (see Figure 6). On a five-point Likert scale (1 = very low, 5 = very high), participants rated the chair interaction as overall satisfying (*ME* = 4). Most participants agreed that the gestures were easy to use, and easy to learn (*ME* = 4). During the experiment participants did not experience any problems in operating the chair to issue browser commands, and strongly agreed that the body-based interaction supported engagement with the web browsing task (*ME* = 5). Most of them enjoyed the possibility of utilizing the flexible chair for invoking actions on the computer, and described the novel interaction technique as futuristic and playful. Eight participants mentioned, that the chair gestures added a welcome feeling of activity to the otherwise joyless ones of pointing and clicking. Overall, participants stated that they could imagine using the chair gestures in real-world situations, and largely agreed to the statement *"I would like to use the chair control as additional input modality during everyday computing activities."* (*ME* = 4).

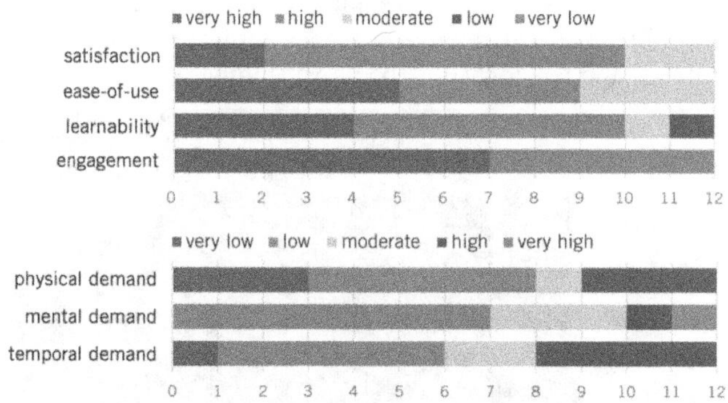

Figure 6: User experience (top) and task load (bottom) ratings for chair-based input in the experimental web browsing task.

Regarding the perceived task load, ratings were overall low for physical and temporal demand (*ME* = 2), and moderate for mental demand (*ME* = 3). During the experiment, participants were able to use the chair interface without considerable effects of mental or bodily fatigue. Yet, four participants mentioned they would not like to use the gestures too extensively in real-world situations (e.g., continuously leaning forward/backward during scrolling), as they thought this could be exhausting or annoying over time. Two other participants raised concerns on social acceptance of the chair gestures in real-world settings, as they might seem awkward to other people (e.g., within an office space). Besides that, a common problem was raised with the participants' varying ability to accommodate to the pre-defined gesture mapping. As reflected in the mental demand ratings, some participants pointed out that they did not feel confident with using front/back-tilting gestures to navigate among browser tabs. Therefore, gaining further understanding of people's mental models for gestural chair interaction, and addressing inconsistencies through user-defined gestures will be part of our future research.

Discussion

Summarizing, the initial feedback indicates that the chair-based gestures were overall easy to learn, and did not require excessive levels of physical or cognitive demand. While most participants were skeptical about the novel interaction technique in the beginning, they seemed to become more and more positive when they realized that the gestures actually invoked the desired actions in the web browser. This observation indicates that reliability and robustness must be considered critical factors for user acceptance of future gestural chair interfaces [21,24]. While it is worth to mention that user feedback regarding future use of the novel input technique might have been influenced by the good participant effect to some extent, the questionnaire ratings and additional comments still provide valuable insights for the further design process:

First of all, participants seemed to be concerned about accidentally triggering actions on the computer through naturally occurring movements or posture changes (e.g., fidgeting, stretching, slouching): "*I wonder how using such an intelligent chair would work out during everyday usage. So, for example, would it trigger actions on my computer when I'm leaning to the side to grab something out of a bottom drawer, or when I'm leaning back to stretch my arms?*" (P2). Indeed, since users are constantly moving while seated–especially on ergonomic, flexible chairs–a major challenge for chair-based interaction is how to effectively distinguish chair gestures from natural body movement that may occur unconsciously during regular work [21,24,31]. A common method to avoid such unintentional input is to let the user decide when input happens by providing mechanisms to toggle gesture recognition on demand. In the current system, we experimented with different methods of coupling chair-based interaction with other input modalities to enable/disable gesture recognition (e.g., pressing a modifier key on the keyboard, clicking an icon in the task bar). Further investigation of this kind of manual mode-switching (e.g., triggering touch-sensitive or proximity-aware areas within the workspace, activating a foot control near the resting place of the feet) will be part of our future research.

Moreover, some participants had reservations regarding the chair gestures becoming annoying or tiring when used over longer periods of time: "*You know, I would like to use the chair if I can use it in a way that somehow eases my work, and makes it less boring. Of course, I wouldn't want to swing around my hips all day long! (...) But a bit of movement from time to time would be nice I guess, especially if I can do something useful with it.*" (P9). As a matter of fact, since moving the whole body to perform gestures with an active chair involves more muscles than mouse or keyboard interaction, a certain level of fatigue may occur with frequent gestures over a long period of time [2,24,31]. Results of the initial evaluation show that participants were able to use the chair gestures without considerable effects of mental or bodily fatigue. However, it is worthwhile to carefully consider the trade-off between potentially positive (i.e., breaking up the monotony of the day, promoting activity) and negative effects (i.e., fatigue, distraction) of the proposed gestural chair interaction. Keeping this in mind, we think the chair gestures have to be designed as optional input modality that people can make use of on a rather occasional basis. To achieve that, gestures should be concise, quick to issue, and avoid movements that require high precision over extended periods of time.

Closely related to the above stated concerns, some participants mentioned that they would prefer chair gestures for usage scenarios where commands can be triggered on a rather occasional basis: "*I could imagine using the chair for rather small actions, which are not occurring too often. (...) Maybe to skip a song that I don't want to listen to.*" (P1). This statement is largely confirmed by participants' comments during the post-experiment interviews. When asked which other usage scenarios they could imagine for gestural chair interaction, seven participants suggested applications for common system-level functions such as task- or window management (e.g., tilting for task switching or window snapping; bouncing for application launching, start menu invocation, or screen locking), and five participants mentioned application-specific functions such as text editing or media control (e.g., tilting to navigate a document, or play the next song; bouncing to print a text, or pause the music).

Design Implications

Based on the insights gained in this first explorative experiment, we identified a number of implications for the design of gestural chair interaction:

- Chair gestures should serve as *opportunistic* input technique that users can smoothly integrate into their computing activities. Consequently, the body-based gestures are most likely suitable for casual, occasional usage in situations where it is desirable for a user to break up the monotony of continuous desktop work.
- Chair gestures could therefore serve as *additional* interaction technique rather than substitution for common input devices such as keyboard and mouse. Provided the hands-free operability, a true additional input dimension can be introduced. Along with that, however, it will be necessary to provide sufficient solutions that prevent accidental activation of the chair control through natural movements.
- Chair gestures should be utilized as *discrete* rather than continuous input to avoid effects of fatigue or annoyance during long-term usage. While discrete input has relatively few parameters to control, continuous input would require careful design considerations on the mapping to a control parameter (e.g., scrolling, zooming).
- Chair gestures are most suitable for *non-precise* interactions that take into account the imprecise nature of the seated body-movements in comparison to high-accuracy input from traditional pointing devices. If a task requires precise control (e.g., positioning, target acquisition), chair gestures might not be appropriate in most cases.

PERIPHERAL CHAIR INTERACTION

The results from the first experiment motivated us to consider the application of gestural chair interaction for computing activities where interaction is not the primary focus of a user's attention, but rather in the periphery [11]. Existing work in the emerging field of *peripheral interaction* has investigated the design of inattentive interaction techniques that can be easily performed in the periphery of attention, and demonstrated significant benefits for such secondary task interactions [13,14,16]. Karam et al. showed in a dual-task lab study that semaphoric hand gestures, in comparison to function keys, lead to significantly reduced task recovery time [16]. Hausen et al. extended these insights by comparing touch, freehand, and graspable interaction for peripheral music control [13,14]. Similarly, in the next step of the design process, we conducted an experiment to explore the potential of chair gestures for such peripheral interaction scenarios. With this experiment, we wanted to gain further insights into the applicability of chair gestures for peripheral interaction in terms of performance and user acceptance, and explore how it compares to common input techniques like keyboard and touch.

Experimental Design

15 paid volunteers (6 female; 20–51 years; all right-handed) participated in the experiment. All participants were experienced computer users, who listened to music while working at the computer on a moderately to highly frequent basis.

During the experiment, participants performed an attention-demanding primary task, while at the same time interacting with a music player in the periphery. The primary square-click task, adapted from previous studies [14,25], was based on a game-style system that dynamically displayed a square (150×150 pixels, approx. 4×4 cm) with a random single-digit label at a random screen location. To successfully resolve a square, participants had to click on it, and then type the corresponding number within a time limit (2 seconds). In the peripheral task, participants controlled music playback as indicated by random-interval (15–20 seconds) on-screen notifications. To simulate a realistic scenario where users control the music in a spontaneous manner, we instructed participants to focus on the primary task, and respond to notifications within a reasonable timeframe.

Building upon previous studies in the context of peripheral interaction [13,14,16], the experiment supported three interaction techniques (*chair, touch, keyboard),* assigned to frequently used music player commands that were mapped to the four canonical directions: left/right to play the *previous/next track*, and up/down to *increase/decrease volume*. To keep interaction consistent among all techniques, chair input was based on simple directional tilt gestures. Touch input was mapped to directional swipe gestures on a tablet, and keyboard input was invoked using the arrow keys[1].

[1] arrow keys were chosen rather than media keys, as these are oftentimes hard to locate for users due to varying keyboard layouts [13]

To provide input devices within easy reach, the arrangement on the desk surface was adjusted to participants individually. All participants used their dominant right hand for touch input (supported by recent findings on strong user preference for dominant-hand interaction in peripheral interaction scenarios [13]), while twelve participants (80%) used their non-dominant hand for keyboard input.

The experiment was conducted in a calm office workspace with a Windows PC, wired keyboard and mouse, wired headphones, a tablet device (Microsoft Surface Pro), and a 3Dee™ flexible chair (see Figure 7). A custom application displayed task instructions, processed the user input, and recorded performance measures in the background.

Figure 7. A participant performing the primary square-click and peripheral music control task during the experiment.

For each interaction technique, five blocks of four different music player commands occurred in randomized order. At the beginning of the experiment, participants completed a short primary task training to become accustomed to the square-click task. They were introduced to the music control for every technique in a peripheral task training with 20 randomized commands (provided a reference sheet with the corresponding directions). Thereafter, both tasks had to be carried out in parallel (without reference sheet) during a combined training, and during the experimental task. To avoid learning effects, the order of techniques was counterbalanced. After each task, participants completed a questionnaire asking for the perceived task load and user experience. In a final questionnaire, participants provided additional subjective feedback on the different input techniques.

Primary task performance and *peripheral task performance* were measured in terms of completion time (i.e., time taken to resolve a shape, or issue a music control command) and success rate (i.e., percentage of correctly resolved squares, or correctly issued commands). *Recovery time* was measured as the time taken from the end of interaction in the peripheral music control task to the resumption of the primary square-click task (i.e., first mouse click or key press). *User feedback* was collected through questionnaires and informal interviews, where participants were asked for quantitative (i.e., perceived task load and user experience) and qualitative (i.e., positive/negative aspects) feedback.

Results

Primary task performance was not significantly different among input techniques, showing similar results for completion times ($M = 1.37$ s, $SD = 0.18$), and success rates ($M = 92.56\%$, $SD = 4.30$). Peripheral interaction thus seemed to cause a similar degree of distraction on the primary task for all three input techniques. Six participants stated the chair gestures made them perceive the task less monotonously, whereas four others mentioned that the motor body movements somehow distracted them from the primary task.

Peripheral Task Performance (Figure 8) was significantly different among interaction techniques ($p < .001$). The time taken to leave the primary task and execute the peripheral music command was shortest with keyboard ($M = 1.83$ s, $SD = 0.53$), followed by touch ($M = 2.08$ s, $SD = 0.84$), and chair ($M = 2.83$ s, $SD = 1.17$). Looking at these times in detail, we found that the *input time* to execute a music control command (i.e., key pressed, touch down, chair motion above baseline level) was longest for chair interaction, as participants needed on average 1.28 s ($SD = 0.31$) to execute a chair gesture, while input time was only 0.11 s ($SD = 0.09$) for touch, and 0.10 s ($SD = 0.03$) for keyboard. The remaining *response time* was shortest with chair ($M = 1.55$ s), followed by keyboard ($M = 1.73$ s), and touch ($M = 1.97$ s). For touch and keyboard, this response time may be partially attributed to the *homing time* [5] needed for physical hand movements towards input devices[2]. In contrast to that, almost all participants positively mentioned the convenience of hands remaining on mouse and keyboard while performing gestures with the flexible office chair.

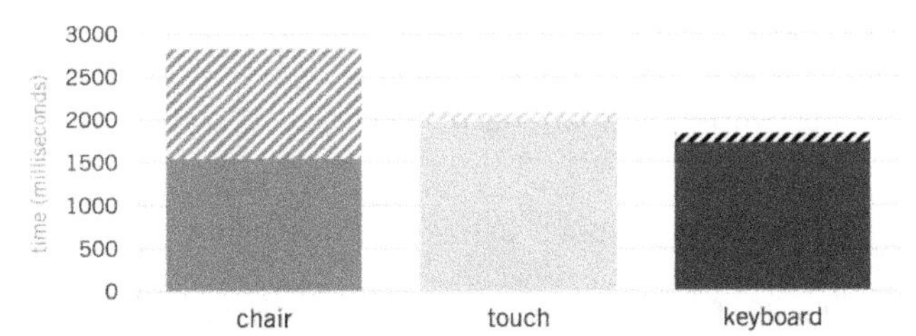

Figure 8. Peripheral task completion time including *input time* to execute a music control command (hatched), and remaining *response time* (solid).

Success rates in the peripheral task showed no significant difference in the number of incorrect commands issued with the three input techniques (chair 3.45%, touch 3.90%, keyboard 5.09%). Participants were equally successful in associating chair gestures, touch gestures, and arrow keys with the given music control commands. Recognition accuracy of gesture-based input was 93.83% ($SD = 6.74$) for chair and 97.00% ($SD = 4.14$) for touch, with most errors being attributable to imprecise user input (e.g., ambiguous direction of touch gestures, low acceleration of chair gestures).

[2] *homing time* could not be determined for the present experiment (since participants decided autonomously when to attend to the peripheral task)

While participants seemed to be equally successful in building cognitive models of the music control commands associated with the different input techniques, additional comments indicate that recognition issues in the gestural chair and touch conditions were perceived to influence task performance negatively to some extent.

Recovery Time (Figure 9) was significantly different among techniques ($p < .001$). The time taken to resume the primary task after executing the music control command was shortest for chair ($M = 0.39$ s, $SD = 0.32$), followed by keyboard ($M = 0.86$ s, $SD = 0.50$), and touch ($M = 0.93$ s, $SD = 0.47$). Participants stated that it was comfortable to keep visual focus on the primary task during chair and touch interaction. With keyboard in contrast, we observed most of them briefly turning focus off the screen to locate the arrow keys.

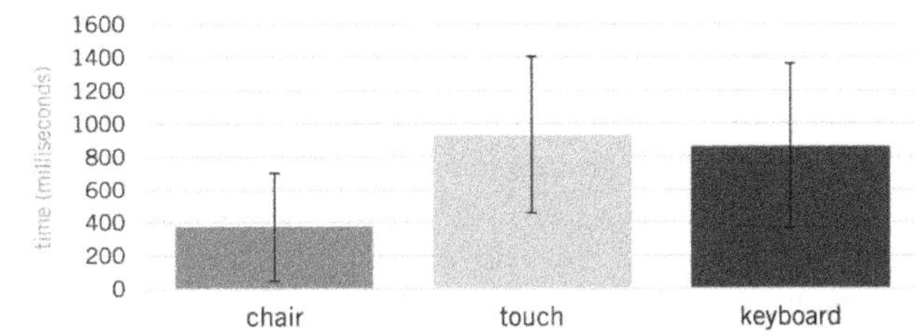

Figure 9. *Recovery Time* when participants switched back from the peripheral to the primary task.

User feedback was collected through questionnaires and post-experiment interviews. Similar to the first experiment, perceived task load and user experience were rated on 5-point Likert scales (1 = very low, 5 = very high). In addition, we asked participants for qualitative feedback on the most positive/negative aspects of each input technique.

User experience ratings (Figure 10, top) show overall moderate satisfaction ($ME = 3$) with peripheral chair interaction. It was easy to learn ($ME = 4$) and easy to use during the peripheral music control task ($ME = 4$). Although ratings were slightly higher for familiar touch and keyboard input, participants stated that it was easy to perform the directional tilt gestures with the chair. Nevertheless, it took a while for some of them to get used to the rather unconventional novel input technique, and gestures were not recognized correctly in a few cases. As reflected in the moderate satisfaction ratings, these factors might have influenced feedback negatively. On the other hand, similar to the first experiment, participants were positive about the playful aspect of the chair gestures, which resulted in higher engagement ratings ($ME = 4$) than for touch and keyboard interaction.

Task load ratings (Figure 10, bottom) for chair input were similar to touch and keyboard on all scales ($ME = 3$). In some rare cases participants experienced problems in linking the chair gestures to the given music control commands, and handling the egocentric mapping of the chair gestures along the front and back axis (i.e., forward/backward tilting). Yet, there was no considerable increase in overall cognitive and physical effort with the chair gestures.

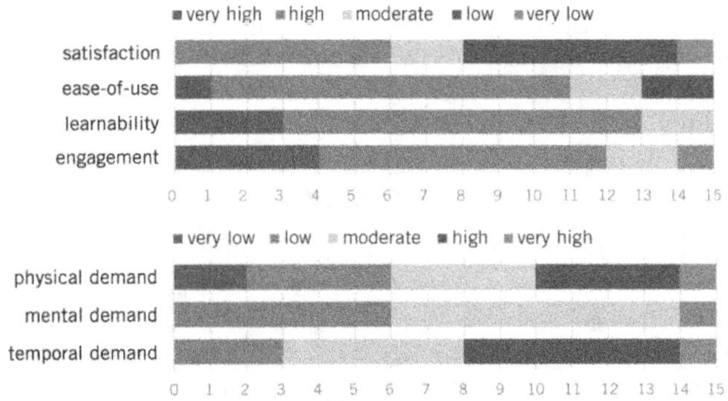

Figure 10: User experience (top) and task load (bottom) ratings for chair-based peripheral interaction.

Most commonly mentioned positive aspects of chair input were hands-free control (13), engagement (6), and activity promotion (6). On the negative side, comments referred to recognition issues (6), practical restrictions (5), and unconventionality of the interface (5). Example comments included "*no alternating between devices*", "*fun to control the PC through movement*", "*welcome change for the body*", "*could bring up the wrong action*", "*constrains natural movement*", and "*probably needs time to familiarize*" Most commonly mentioned positive aspects of touch and keyboard input were ease-of-use, and familiarity with the input technique, while negative aspects referred to the loss of focus during interaction, or physical restrictions: "*more used to controlling a computer with my hands*", "*additional device occupies valuable desk space*".

Discussion

Summarizing, the results of the second experiment largely confirm previous research demonstrating peripheral usage of touch- and keyboard-based interfaces [14,16], and show that chair gestures are another promising alternative to extend the design space for peripheral interaction. Regarding the recovery time needed to return to the primary task after a peripheral input command, they even outperformed touch and keyboard interaction. This supports previous findings indicating that semaphoric gestures can support secondary task interaction as target acquisition is less demanding for gestures than keyboard, visual focus remains on the primary task, and the threshold for recovering focus can be reduced significantly [16]. Besides that, chair gestures can potentially be detected anytime a user is sitting in front of the computer, thereby maintaining a persistent number of steps for completing a peripheral task, whereas traditional hand-mediated input may not be readily available in some situations [16]. This supports our assumptions that gestural interaction with chairs opens a broad design space for interaction with a desktop computer when the user's hands or eyes are be occupied with other tasks (e.g., during a mouse- or keyboard-heavy computing activity, holding a phone in one hand while taking notes with the other), or when quick access to specific application functionalities is required (e.g., issuing input commands, typing special characters, launching/opening applications or files).

In the present peripheral interaction scenario, no difference in primary task performance or perceived task load was found between the chair gestures and more familiar touch or keyboard input. Therefore, it appears that–despite the novelty of the chair-based input technique–no additional complexity was added to the primary task. Clearly, as people were much more familiar with the keyboard and touch interfaces, it seems natural that the chair interactions demanded more time and effort in the short term experiment. In the course of the experiment, however, we observed participants getting more and more confident with the chair control once they got used to performing the tilting gestures. This indicates promising potential for performance improvement with further practice, which should be evaluated in a future long-term field deployment. Despite the fact that execution of chair gestures required more time than the hand-mediated input techniques, reduced requirements on visual and motor channels (i.e., focus could remain on the primary task, hands could stay on primary input devices) allowed for short response and short recovery times. With digital information and communication technologies finding their ways into the work environment, people spend increasing time in managing various activities simultaneously. Therefore, being able to minimize recovery times with hands-free, eyes-free chair interaction can provide significant benefits for users by minimizing distraction, and supporting effortless transitions between primary and secondary tasks.

User feedback indicates that participants appreciated these above-mentioned attractive features recommending chair gestures for peripheral interaction scenarios. Similar to the first experiment, nevertheless, participants were slightly skeptical about the novel interaction technique, and raised practical concerns (i.e., unintentional activation of the gesture control through natural movements, fatigue during usage over longer periods of time, social acceptability).

Additionally, the present experiment added further insights regarding the gesture recognition, which was not sufficiently reliable for some participants during the experiment: "*When I used the chair to control the music player, there was a situation when nothing happened, although I had performed the tilt to the correct direction. When I repeated the movement with more power, it finally worked.*" (P15). One specific problem was that the force at which different users tilted the chair varied a lot. In some cases, gestures were at first not detected when the movements were performed with too little force. Furthermore, gestures as such did not provide immediate feedback confirming the input (in contrast to e.g. haptic feedback of a keystroke). This confused some participants, and in some rare cases led to unnecessary repetitions of gestures. Consequently, as our recognition was tuned to look for clear peaks in the motion data, any oscillation effects or additional accelerations disturbed the recognition. User feedback, however, points out the importance of reliable recognition and real-time response for successful adoption of chair-based interaction.

Closely related to that, some participants mentioned they would rather avoid chair gestures for critical interactions: "*I like the chair, but there's certain things I wouldn't want to use it for. Sending e-mails, for example. What if it is triggered somehow accidentally? Then the message is gone, and I cannot undo it anymore.*" (P10). Therefore, we think that chair gestures are most suitable for non-critical usage scenarios, where consequences of unintentional command activation are negligible. If making an error during a task presents any serious risks for users, chair input might not be appropriate in most cases. In addition, more research is needed to support mediation of ambiguous input [19], and provide easy ways of undoing falsely recognized gestures.

Clearly, there is a trade-off between sensitivity and robustness of the gesture recognition. In the current implementation of our gesture recognition algorithm, we tried to optimize the balance between high rates of recognized gestures and low rates of misclassified gestures with careful threshold selection. However, recognizing specific human movements and complex actions solely with the help of accelerometer and gyroscope represents a technical challenge. While the focus of the present work was on a gesture recognition that was practical to implement with minimal hardware requirements, we will continue exploring ways to increase the reliability of our system, including experiments with additional sensors (e.g., pressure, bending, proximity). Besides that, with constantly improving recognition algorithms and insights from machine learning, we are confident that with modern recognition approaches (e.g., DTW, HMM, SVM), we will be able to overcome these issues and provide a more robust gesture recognition.

Concerns regarding social acceptability go in line with existing research pointing out potential problems of gestures that are publicly visible (e.g., tilting the chair to the right) but the effects of the actions (e.g., playing the next song) remain hidden to others [20]. This issue, however, might be reduced in environments where flexible chairs are already established, as they afford sitting "in-motion" (e.g., tilting, bouncing) even without the goal of triggering specific actions. Therefore, we believe the benefits of flexible (interactive) chairs can outweigh or even eliminate potential social awkwardness. Also, enabling users to perform the gestures with more subtle movements may increase acceptance.

CONCLUSION & FUTURE WORK

In this paper, we presented the iterative design process of a novel input technique based on gestural interaction with a sensor-equipped flexible office chair. A basic set of semaphoric chair gestures was defined, which can be mapped to specific functions for controlling applications on a desktop computer. We explored the application of these chair gestures as additional input modality for focused interaction with a web browser, and peripheral interaction with a music player. Corresponding experimental results indicate overall positive user feedback, and comparable task performance as with more familiar keyboard or touch input.

The embodied aspects of chair-based input [7] seemed to facilitate interaction, which indicates high potential to enrich the computing experience and capture the interest of a larger audience. However, as with other gestural interfaces, there are some challenges when designing for chair-based gestural interaction [21,24,31], such as distinguishing between natural behavior and gestural input, revealing the gestural input scope, creating understandable metaphors for actions invoked by the gestural input, or providing reliable real-time system feedback [23]. Further, ergonomic aspects regarding the effects of physical body movements to perform gestures with a flexible chair will have to be taken into account for future design of gestures and applications.

Summarizing, as for any other input modality, there are always trade-offs: While input time and physical effort may be higher for chair gestures than traditional hand-mediated input devices, this must be balanced against the benefits of always-available, eyes-free, hands-free operation that an interactive chair can provide in a computing environment. Based on these unique features, chair gestures seem highly promising for opportunistic interaction in a desktop environment. Particularly suitable in the context of peripheral interaction, interactive chairs could therefore serve as platform for a whole range of applications that enable users to quickly issue commands to an application and rapidly return to their other ongoing activities. In addition, the introduction of technologies integrating the body into our interactions is a strategy with great potential to avoid physical inactivity [7]. Chair gestures are certainly not a panacea for every potential input problem faced by end users. Still, the gestures can serve a valuable purpose as alternative input modality in situations that afford eyes- or hands-free interaction, or when we simply want to break up the monotony of the mouse-and-keyboard desktop paradigm.

Future work will focus on solving practical challenges that arise with gestural chair interaction, including improvement of recognition robustness, further exploration of the gestural input scope, and definition of suitable applications that integrate chair gestures into the computing experience. Therefore, we will investigate the application of gestural chair input for other usage scenarios besides the proposed web browser and music player control (e.g., application launching, task management, notification handling). Finally, as for a novel input technique it is always the question of long-term acceptance and use, we plan to conduct a long-term in-situ deployment to further explore the integration of semaphoric chair gestures into the computing experience.

ACKNOWLEDGEMENTS

This research is supported by the Austrian Research Promotion Agency GmbH (FFG) within the Bridge project #2579-917 and the Singapore National Research Foundation under its International Research Center Keio-NUS CUTE Center @ Singapore Funding Initiative and administered by the IDM Program Office.

REFERENCES

1. Anttonen, J. and Surakka, V. Music, Heart Rate, and Emotions in the Context of Stimulating Technologies. *ACII 2007*, 290–301.
2. Baudel, T. and Beaudouin-Lafon, M. Charade: Remote Control of Objects Using Free-Hand Gestures. *Communications of the ACM 36*, 7 (1993), 28–35.
3. Beckhaus, S., Blom, K., and Haringer, M. ChairIO – The Chair-Based Interface. In *Concepts and Technologies for Pervasive Games*. 2007, 231–264.
4. Van Beurden, M., Ijsselsteijn, W., and De Kort, Y. User Experience of Gesture Based Interfaces: A Comparison with Traditional Interaction Methods on Pragmatic and Hedonic Qualities. *GW 2011*, 36–47.
5. Card, S., Moran, T., and Newel, A. The Keystroke-Level Model for User Performance Time with Interactive Systems. *Communications of the ACM 23*, 7 (1980), 396–410.
6. Cohen, M. The Internet Chair. *International Journal of Human Computer Interaction 15*, 2 (2003), 56–57.
7. Dourish, P. *Where The Action Is*. MIT Press, 2001.
8. Endert, A., Fiaux, P., Chung, H., Stewart, M., Andrews, C., and North, C. ChairMouse: Leveraging Natural Chair Rotation for Cursor Navigation on Large, High-Resolution Displays. *Ext. Abstracts CHI 2011*, 571–580.
9. Forlizzi, J., DiSalvo, C., Zimmerman, J., Mutlu, B., and Hurst, A. The SenseChair: The Lounge Chair as an Intelligent Assistive Device for Elders. *DUX 2005*, 31.
10. Hart, S. and Staveland, L. Development of NASA-TLX (Task Load Index): Results of Empirical and Theoretical Research. In *Human Mental Workload*. 1988, 139–183.
11. Hausen, D., Bakker, S., Van den Hoven, E., Butz, A., and Eggen, B. Peripheral Interaction: Embedding HCI in Everyday Life. *Workshop at INTERACT 2013*.
12. Hausen, D., Boring, S., and Greenberg, S. The Un-adorned Desk: Exploiting the Physical Space around a Display as an Input Canvas. *INTERACT 2013,* 140–158.
13. Hausen, D., Richter, H., Hemme, A., and Butz, A. Comparing Input Modalities for Peripheral Interaction: A Case Study on Peripheral Music Control. *INTERACT 2013*, 162–179.
14. Hausen, D. Comparing Modalities and Feedback for Peripheral Interaction. *Ext. Abstracts CHI 2013*, 1263–1268.
15. Healy, G., Lawler, S., Thorp, A., Neuhaus, M., Robson, E., Owen, N., and Dunstan, D. *Reducing Prolonged Sitting in the Workplace*. Human Factors and Ergonomics Society, 2012.
16. Karam, M. and schraefel, m.c. A Study on the Use of Semaphoric Gestures to Support Secondary Task Interactions. *Ext. Abstracts CHI 2005*, 1961–1964.
17. Karam, M. and schraefel, m.c. *A Taxonomy of Gestures in Human Computer Interaction*. 2005.
18. Levine, J. a. Non-Exercise Activity Thermogenesis (NEAT). *Best Practice & Research Clinical Endocrinology & Metabolism 16*, 4 (2002), 679–702.
19. Mankoff, J., Hudson, S., and Abowd, G. Interaction Techniques for Ambiguity Resolution in Recognition-based Interfaces. *UIST 2000*, 11–20.
20. Montero, C. and Marshall, M. Would You Do That? – Understanding Social Acceptance of Gestural Interfaces. *MobileHCI 2010*, 275–278.
21. Norman, D. Natural User Interfaces Are Not Natural. *Interactions 17*, 3 (2010), 6–10.
22. Oakley, I. and Park, J. Designing Eyes-Free Interaction. In *Haptic & Audio Interaction Design*. 2007, 121–132.
23. Probst, K., Lindlbauer, D., Greindl, P., Trapp, M., Haller, M., Schwartz, B., and Schrempf, A. Rotating, Tilting, Bouncing: Using an Interactive Chair to Promote Activity in Office Environments. *Ext. Abstracts CHI 2013*, 79–84.
24. Quek, F., McNeill, D., Bryll, R., and McCullough, K. Multimodal Human Discourse: Gesture and Speech. *Transactions on Computer-Human Interaction 9*, 3 (2002), 171–193.
25. Shen, X. An Evaluation Methodology for Ambient Displays. *Journal of Engineering, Computing and Architecture 1*, 2 (2007).
26. Springer, T. *The Future of Ergonomic Office Seating*. Knoll Workplace Research, 2010.
27. Streitz, N., Geißler, J., Holmer, T., Konomi, S., Müller-Tomfelde, C., Reischl, W., Rexroth, P., Seitz, P., and Steinmetz, R. i-LAND: An Interactive Landscape for Creativity and Innovation. *CHI 1999*, 120–127.
28. Tan, H., Slivovsky, L., and Pentland, A. A Sensing Chair Using Pressure Distribution Sensors. *Transactions on Mechatronics 6*, 3 (2001), 261–268.
29. Van Uffelen, J., Wong, J., Chau, J., van der Ploeg, H., Riphagen, I., Gilson, N., Burton, N., Healy, G., Thorp, A., Clark, B., Gardiner, P., Dunstan, D., Bauman, A., Owen, N., and Brown, W. Occupational Sitting and Health Risks: A Systematic Review. *American Journal of Preventive Medicine 39*, 4 (2010), 379–88.
30. Weiser, M. The Computer for the 21st Century. *Scientific American 265*, 3 (1991), 66–75.
31. Wexelblat, A. Research Challenges in Gesture: Open Issues and Unsolved Problems. *GW 1997*, 1–11.
32. Wobbrock, J., Aung, H., Rothrock, B., and Myers, B. Maximizing the Guessability of Symbolic Input. *Ext. Abstracts CHI 2005*, 1869–1872.
33. Zheng, Y. and Morell, J. A Vibrotactile Feedback App-roach to Posture Guidance. *HAPTIC 2010*, 351–358.

Exploring the Design Space of Gestural Interaction with Active Tokens through User-Defined Gestures

Consuelo Valdes[1], Diana Eastman[1], Casey Grote[1], Shantanu Thatte[3], Orit Shaer[1], Ali Mazalek[2], Brygg Ullmer[3,4], Miriam K. Konkel[5]

Dept. of Computer Science[1]
Wellesley College
Wellesley, MA, USA

Synaesthetic Media Lab[2]
Digital Media & GVU Center
Georgia Institute of Technology
Atlanta, GA, USA

School of EECS[3], Center for Computation and Technology[4], and Dept. of Biological Sciences[5]
Louisiana State University
Baton Rouge, LA, USA

oshaer@wellesley.edu, mazalek@gatech.edu, ullmer@lsu.edu, konkel@lsu.edu

ABSTRACT
Multi-touch and tangible interfaces provide unique opportunities for enhancing learning and discovery with big data. However, existing interaction techniques have limitations when manipulating large data sets. Our goal is to define novel interaction techniques for multi-touch and tangible interfaces, which support the construction of complex queries for big data. In this paper, we present results from a study, which investigates the use of gestural interaction with active tokens for manipulating large data sets. In particular, we studied user expectations of a hybrid tangible and gestural language engaging this space. Our main results include a vocabulary of user-defined gestures for interaction with active tokens, which extends beyond familiar multi-touch gestures; characterization of the design space of gestural interaction with active tokens; and insight into participants' mental models, including common metaphors. We also present implications for the design of multi-touch and tangible interfaces with active tokens.

Author Keywords
Gestures; tabletop; queries; multi-display environments; cross-device interaction; physical tokens.

ACM Classification Keywords
H.5.2 [Information Interfaces and Presentation]: User Interfaces---input devices and strategies, interaction styles

INTRODUCTION
Multi-touch and tangible interfaces are a growing area of human-computer interaction (HCI) research. Recent studies have focused on their use in entertainment, formal and informal learning environments, as well as collaborative search. Multi-touch and tangible interfaces provide form factors that foster collaboration through visibility of actions and egalitarian input [16, 23] and support distributed cognition by affording spreading, piling, and organizing information artifacts [3, 4]. Such affordances are well suited for sensemaking [37]. Research also indicates that tabletop interfaces support active reading [29] and promote reflection [44]. Considering these qualities of tabletop interaction, as well as other factors such as improving display quality, increasing availability, and falling prices of commercial hardware platforms, tabletop interfaces provide unique opportunities for learning and discovery with large and abstract data sets.

Figure 1: Horizontal experimental setup (left) - first generation Microsoft Surface and first generation Sifteo cubes. Vertical experimental setup (right) – second generation Microsoft Surface and first generation Sifteo cubes.

However, designing multi-touch and tangible interfaces that support learning and discovery in data-intense areas requires going beyond the application of existing interaction techniques [43]. While direct touch is currently a standard input method for multi-touch and tangible interfaces, in data-intense applications, representations are typically small [9]. Finger size and occlusion make it difficult to interact directly with small targets through touch [9, 54, 55]. Furthermore, in data-intense applications, WIMP-style control elements provided by various toolkits, such as scrollbars, sliders, and text fields, may often be either too small for effective and accurate touch interaction, consume expensive screen real-estate [5, 9], or lead to cognitive dissonance with the broader interaction paradigm.

CHI 2014, April 26 - May 01 2014, Toronto, ON, Canada

http://dx.doi.org/10.1145/2556288.2557373

Several studies have considered novel multi-touch interaction techniques for data driven multi-touch and tangible applications; e.g. [5, 9, 17, 55]. However, while providing advantage over touch interaction with WIMP-style controls, multi-touch gestures often suffer from low discoverability and lack of persistence [9]. In this paper, we investigate an alternative approach: exploring large data sets on multi-touch and tangible interfaces using tangible interaction with active tokens. Our goal is to identify novel interaction techniques for multi-touch and tangible interfaces, which support the construction of complex queries for large data sets.

Our work draws and expands on Tangible Query Interfaces (TQI) [50], which introduced tangible interaction techniques for querying large databases. TQI utilized systems of tokens embodying query parameters. These were manipulated, interpreted, and graphically augmented on a series of physical constraints. Technological advances and mass-market offerings such as Sifteo Cubes [1] have opened up the possibilities to revisit this approach and consider novel tangible and gesture-based interaction techniques for the manipulation of large data sets that use active tokens [60].

Active tokens are programmable physical objects with integrated display, sensing, or actuation technologies (e.g., [1, 6, 21, 24, 60]). Thus, they can be reconfigured over time, allowing users to dynamically modify their associations with datasets or controls. The use of active tokens could support the exploration of large data sets by expanding the design space of token and constraints interaction [42, 49], which leverages physical expression of digital syntax. Combining interactive multi-touch surfaces with active tokens could facilitate the presentation and manipulation of big data while preserving the benefits of tangible interaction [41] such as support for two-handed interaction, co-located collaboration, and strong affordances.

We focus on a sub-class of active tokens that can be manipulated using gestures independently from global constraints. Gestural interaction with active tokens blurs the boundaries between tangible and gestural interaction, between manipulations and gestures [20]; and fits within the area defined as "tangible gesture interaction" [52]. Active tokens also enable the expansion of tangible interaction with multi-touch and tangible interfaces beyond interaction on the surface into less explored areas such as tangible interaction *on-bezel* and *in-air,* hovering above or in front the surface.

While technological advances facilitate the recognition and tracking of on-surface, in-air, and on-bezel interactions with active tokens, the gesture language for such interactions has yet to be explored in a task–driven scenario. What kinds of gestures should be employed to manipulate and explore large data sets? What gestures might typically or best be performed on-surface, on-bezel, and in-air? In users' minds, what are the important characteristics of such gestures? Are there guessable gestures for navigating a data set and for constructing complex queries? How consistently do different users employ gestures for the same commands?

On the one hand, we regard the design of a hybrid tangible and gestural language as a highly complex task, which pushes the skills of even expert tangible and gestural interaction designers. On the other, gestural interaction with smart phones and tablets is now routine for many millions of people. To understand and respect the expectations of users, we see it important to explore a cross-section of users' first anticipations of new systems in this space.

In this paper, we present findings from a user study with 19 users. The study investigated user expectations of a hybrid tangible and gestural language for multi-touch and tangible interaction with active tokens. Our findings include a vocabulary of user-defined gestures for active tokens, and insights into the mental models and experiences that shape users' expectations. Based on our findings we characterize the design space of gestural interaction with active tokens and discuss implications for the design of multi-touch and tangible interfaces with active tokens.

RELATED WORK

We begin with a survey of existing work on multi-touch and tangible interfaces for data exploration.

Multi-touch and Tangible Interfaces for Big Data

With the increasing importance of and access to large data sets by diverse prospective users [31], several multi-touch and tangible interfaces have been created to support learning and understanding in data intense areas in informal and formal settings. For example, Block et al. created the DeepTree exhibit for science museums [5], a tabletop interactive visualization of the Tree of Life that facilitates collaborative exploration of phylogenetic data while offering guided discovery. Involve [15] is a precursor of DeepTree that utilized Vornoi maps to visualize phylogenetic data. Both applications allow users to zoom, pan, and find a particular element in a visualization of the Life on Earth database. Thudt et al. created the Bohemian Bookshelf [46], a multi-touch interface, which supports serendipitous discoveries in the context of digital book collections through five interlinked visualizations. These multi-touch interfaces support collaborative and playful interaction with large data sets, which is appropriate for informal learning settings, but limit exploration through designer-defined guided discovery scenarios and visual representations.

G-nome Surfer [45] and GreenTouch [51] are tabletop multi-touch applications for collaborative exploration of genomic and phenology databases. Both applications target college-level inquiry-based learning and support open-ended data investigation. However, their expressivity is limited as users cannot define and set query operators directly. Schkolne et al. [39] developed an immersive tangible interface for the design of DNA; the interface does not support search and comparison. Morris et al. [30] surveyed the design space of collaborative tabletop search applications, examining several dimensions including domain, collaboration style, and search input. While application domains for search interfaces varied from personal data to large databases, search input techniques have relied on touch, keyboard, and mouse input. Facet-Streams [19] is a recent tabletop search interface that explores the design space of tangible-tabletop interaction. The interface allows users to construct expressive queries using passive tokens that are augmented with content and functionality when placed upon the tabletop surface through the display of a surrounding circular menu. Similarly to the TQI [50], Facet-Streams utilizes passive tokens that could only be used on top of a tabletop interactive surface. While simplifying the construction of complex queries, this system also has some limitations such as physical clutter, separation of query formulation and result browsing, and lack of persistency for query parameters. Our focus is on the use of *active tokens* that, when combined with multi-touch and tangible interfaces, could be manipulated on-surface, on-bezel, and in-air. Such interaction remains unexplored within search interfaces.

Tangible Queries

Several tangible interfaces have explored the use of tokens for query formulation. Navigational Blocks [6] is an early tangible user interface for querying a database where each block represents one query parameter, its six faces represent the possible values. Depending on whether two parameter values would yield information, the blocks attract or repel each other, providing users with actuated feedback. The number of blocks and their fixed values limited the search space to a predefined number of queries. DataTiles [36] combines tiles – graspable windows for digital information – on top of a horizontal display. Each tile represents particular information or control (e.g. parameter, storage, portal). While DataTiles provides a highly expressive physical language, interaction is constrained to a horizontal surface.

Ullmer et al. [50] introduced two tangible interfaces for query formulation that use tokens to represent query parameters. One employed "parameter wheels" for fixed query parameters; the other, "parameter bars" that can be dynamically assigned to represent various parameters. In both interfaces, tokens can represent either discrete or continuous values, and are manipulated and interpreted on a series of physical constraints (e.g. racks). Such token and constraint interaction, while expressive, makes the tokens less portable and limits possibilities for collaboration. In later evolutions, cartouches [48] build on DataTiles and TQI toward generalizing representation of digital information across diverse systems. Examples include systems of tokens and constraints that could be combined with systems ranging from interactive walls to information kiosks. We extend this work by investigating the design space of active tokens, which as active physical objects could be manipulated using gestures independently from mechanical constraints.

While most tangible query interfaces utilize horizontal arrangements [6, 19, 36, 50], Stackables [21] explores the use of tangible objects that are arranged vertically. Each stackable token represents a query parameter; multiple tokens are stacked to express a query. Stackables utilize active tokens that could be reprogrammed and support interaction independently from global constraints. Multiple tokens can be combined with a logical AND or negation through vertical stacking. Interaction with a single stackable token is limited to using its sliders and button. Stackables provides a step in the direction of using active tokens for search. Our focus is on identifying possibilities for rich gestural interaction with active tokens combined with multi-touch and tangible interfaces. We seek to explore gestural interaction that extends beyond the surface into less explored areas such as on-bezel and in-air, hovering above or in front of the surface.

Active Token Interaction Languages

The use of active tokens has been explored in various contexts. For example, the Tangible Video Editor [60] employed active tokens to represent video clips. To guide users' interaction, video clip tokens were embedded in cases that resembled jigsaw puzzle pieces. Video clips were associated by connecting the puzzle pieces on a surface or in-air. However, while the affordances and physical constraints provided a clear association pattern, they also restricted the use of the active tokens. Siftables [24], a precursor of Sifteo Cubes [1], explored interaction gestures based on reality-based [18] metaphors such as grouping cubes to tag them with a common element; shaking to express yes or no; and "sugar pack snap" to clear cube contents. Sifteo [1] implements various gestures including shaking, flipping, tilting, neighboring, and touching. However, these gesture are expert-designed and were not evaluated with users. Six-Forty by Four-Eighty [7] is an art installation that uses a set of gestures for manipulating "tile" displays. SynFlo [59] is an interactive installation for introducing Synthetic Biology concepts to non-scientists. It utilizes Sifteo cubes to simulate a wet-lab bench and evoke gestures such as pouring and shaking. The installation incorporates a Microsoft PixelSense, which serves as a test bed for a virtual experiment.

Though these systems present explorations into the design space of gesture-based interaction with active tokens, they neither tackle the big data context nor evaluate the gesture set in a task-driven scenario

User-Elicitation Studies

User-elicitation studies are a specific type of participatory design methodology that involves end-users in the design of gesture-sets [12, 28, 54]. Such studies have been used to design gesture interfaces of various types including multi-touch gestures on small and large surfaces [2, 10, 11, 22, 25, 32, 57] and multi-modal interactions [28]. There is evidence that user-defined gesture sets are more complete than those defined solely by experts [2, 32, 35, 57].

In a user-elicitation study, users are shown referents (an action's effects) and are asked to demonstrate the interactions that result in a given referent [57]. In this work, we draw upon the user-elicitation methodology to identify user expectations and suggestions for active-token interaction with multi-touch and tangible interfaces for big data exploration. Our intention is not to present a complete user-defined gesture language, but rather to identify and understand user expectations when transitioning from familiar multi-touch interaction into a new space. We examine when users use on-bezel and in-air interactions, and how users associate active tokens with data displayed on top of multi-touch and tangible interfaces. We identify common gestures for search and query formulation tasks and discuss users' perceptions of the benefits and drawbacks of each.

ELICITING USER EXPECTATION THROUGH USER-DEFINED GESTURES

To explore user expectations of a hybrid tangible and gestural interaction language with active tokens, we designed a user elicitation study that prompts users to suggest gestures for various tasks within a particular task scenario (i.e. model world) of personal genomics. Personal genomics engages the study of individual (typically human) genomes.

We chose personal genomics as an application area for several reasons. First, user interfaces for personal genomics could prospectively benefit from the novel HCI techniques we investigate here [43]. Second, we were motivated by the increasing public interest and media coverage of personal genomics, broadening its relevance to both experts and lay people. Third, the genes chosen for the study task, BRCA1 and BRCA2, received extensive news coverage reflecting actress Jolie's medical decision around the time of the study. While personal genomics was chosen as a context for this study, the tasks investigated were selected from taxonomy of search interactions and could be generalized to various contexts. The chosen application area did not pose observed difficulties to our participants (college students). Participants typically did not have domain knowledge beyond general familiarity with basic genetic concepts.

Users where asked to perform eight distinct commands for exploring the human genome, with selection based on a taxonomy of search interactions [38]. Four of the commands were repeated throughout the task. These included select an item from a list; display information from the cube onto the surface; modify and define a range; associate information to a cube; create a query; zoom in; make a query more specific; replace part of a query, and create a compound query. Table 2 lists the eight commands for which participants were asked to choose a gesture. The order of the commands was determined by the task, which mirrors a real-world scenario of genomic investigation.

To avoid restricting users' gesture interactions, we presented users with a prompt asking them to perform a gesture for a particular command (e.g., select an item from a list). Only upon confirming the gesture, we displayed the effect of that command. To further avoid bias [10], no elements specific to a particular platform (e.g., Microsoft PixelSense or Sifteo) were presented.

The system did not recognize users' gestures, but did log sensor information, touch events, and neighboring events generated by the cubes. Participants used the think-aloud protocol. Video from these sessions was recorded. Participants also supplied subjective preference ratings. By using a think-aloud protocol, we obtained rich qualitative data that illuminates users' mental models. The logged data and questionnaires supplied quantitative measures regarding gesture performance, timing, and user preferences. The results provide a detailed description of user-defined gestures for the manipulation of large data sets, which combine active physical tokens with multi-touch interaction, and insight into the mental models accompanying them.

Study Design

We conducted a within-subjects design with 19 users. They were asked to complete a query-building task in two conditions: 1) using six active tokens combined with a vertical multi-touch interface; 2) using six active tokens combined with a horizontal multi-touch interface. The task was identical across both conditions, with the order of conditions counterbalanced to account for learning. A within-subjects design was employed to solicit gestures for both form factors (vertical and horizontal), and to explore the impact of a particular form factor on user-defined gestures. We decided to compare horizontal and vertical form factors. This was motivated by observations from pilot studies where we noticed that cubes tend to stay on the surface, occluding the workspace when a horizontal surface is used. Our goal was to test for differences between these two form factors.

Device	Mean (SD)
Smart phones	4.11 (0.83)
Tablets	3.44 (1.04)
Accelerometers	2.06 (1.21)
Sifteo cubes	1.11 (0.32)
Xbox Kinect	1.17 (0.71)

Table 1: Technology experience demographic questionnaire.

Experimental Task

To elicit task-driven gestures for querying large data sets using an interactive surface with active tokens, we created a casual genome browser application (see Figure 1). The application enables users to search the human genome for a particular gene and find related scientific publications; we prompted users to search for BRCA1 and BRCA2 genes.

The task began with the selection of a chromosome on a cube (i.e., active physical token). Results were displayed on the surface. Next, participants zoomed in to a gene of interest, and saved this back to a cube. The task was then repeated for another gene on another chromosome. Next, the participant was guided through a series of steps to formulate a publication query by retrieving publications on a particular gene, defining the publication date parameter, adding a Boolean operator and another gene to the query, and saving the results to a cube. Following the guided query formulation, participants were asked to formulate a new compound query on their own and save the results.

This task was designed to examine eight commands for the manipulation of large data sets and query formulation. We selected these commands based on existing taxonomies for search interactions [38]. Users manipulated both discrete and continuous query parameters. Table 2 shows the eight commands with corresponding user task description.

Procedure

Participants were greeted, briefed about the goal of the study, and given a standard consent form. Users were then introduced to the Sifteo cubes with the official demo video [1] followed by five minutes of "free-play." Our decision to expose users to the Sifteo instruction video resulted from our pilot study, which showed that Sifteo gestures suffered from low discoverability (partly attributable to limited public exposure, esp. outside of a gaming context). The video provides users with additional possibilities for action beyond gestures users are familiar with based on their experience using phone and tablet interfaces. Playing with Sifteo cubes prior to the experimental task allowed users to explore gesture possibilities independently of the task context.

Participants were introduced to and walked through the process using a simple demo task. Following introduction, the interactive surface and active physical tokens displayed still images, serving as a starting point for the task. Users were read a prompt describing a subtask (e.g. select chromosome 13 from the cube and display it on the surface) and asked to perform a gesture that would accomplish this subtask. Prompts were read from a standard script for consistency. Users were instructed to think aloud and confirm their gesture for each subtask verbally. The surface application did not respond in real-time to any touch or gesture, and the Sifteo application provided only basic visual feedback: offsetting the image depending on the tilt, rotating the image when a cube was rotated, and magnifying the image if the screen was clicked. Upon confirming their gesture, participants were shown two 5-point scales and asked to rate the gesture goodness and ease. The effect of the gesture would then be presented on both the surface and the Sifteo cubes: a still image illustrating the state of the application following the user's action.

The complete experimental task was comprised of 11 outlined sub-tasks that tested eight query commands. Upon completion of the experimental task, users were asked to repeat the task on a different condition. Condition order was counterbalanced to account for learning. For each session, log and video data were collected. An observer tracked the gestures generated by participants while a second observer transcribed user comments.

Participants

19 participants (15 female) ranging in age from 18 to 25 with an average age of 20, volunteered for the study. All participants were compensated for their time with a five-dollar gift card. Before the study, users completed a questionnaire about their exposure to multi-touch and gesture-based interfaces. Results are shown in Table 1.

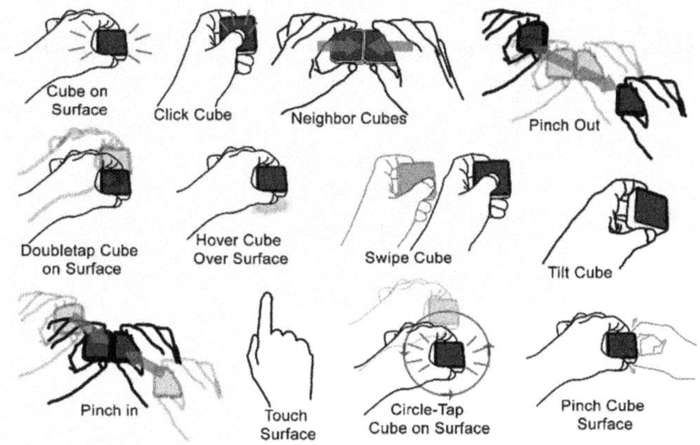

Figure 2: User-generated gesture vocabulary.

Apparatus

The study was conducted using six Sifteo Cubes that served as active physical tokens. A first generation Microsoft Surface measuring 30 inches at 1024 by 768 resolution was used as a horizontal surface. A Microsoft PixelSense measuring 40 inches at 1920 by 1080 resolution was used as a vertical surface. Our decision to use different platforms (Microsoft Surface vs. Pixelsense) was based on the availability and ease of setup of the devices. The surface interfaces were resized accordingly for each resolution to maintain a comparable user experience. We used Sifteo Cubes to accelerate realization of an initial prototype, as early commercial reprogrammable examples of active tokens. However, our results could be generalized to active tokens with similar functionality using other commercially available technologies (e.g. small Android devices or a future iOS iPod Nano). Figure 1 shows the experimental setup.

The Sifteo application gave users some feedback for interaction such as offsetting the image depending on the tilt, rotating the image if two are neighbored, or magnifying the image if the screen is clicked; but no menu structure was presented so as not to affect the users' mental model of information association on the cubes. It also collected accelerometer data, touch events, and neighboring events for gesture analysis. The Sifteo application was implemented using Sifteo 1.0 (written in C#); the surface application was identical for both conditions. It displayed still images as feedback for user gestures. It was built on the Surface 1.0 (for Horizontal condition) and Surface 2.0 SDK (for Vertical condition) and was written in C#.

DATA ANALYSIS AND RESULTS

In this section, we present qualitative and quantitative results from our gesture elicitation study.

User-Defined Gestures

Overall, 19 participants proposed a total of 560 gestures, for eight commands, of which 21 were distinct (considering distinctness on a per-command basis). Figure 2 and Table 2 show proposed gestures per command for each condition with a consensus threshold of two (i.e., with repetition by at least two participants).

Command	Gesture	H	V
Select an item from a list	Swipe cube screen	45%	40%
	Tilt cube	39%	40%
	Cube on Surface	5%	9%
Display information from the cube onto the surface	Cube on Surface	71%	72%
	GUI-WIMP	21%	17%
	Hover cube over surface	0%	4%
	Click cube	6%	3%
Modify and define a range	Cube on Surface	26%	29%
	Pinch 2 cubes out	9%	17%
	Tilt cube	3%	14%
	Pinch 2 cubes in	14%	0%
	Pinch on cube	9%	17%
	Touch surface	6%	9%
	Hover cube over surface	6%	9%
	Click cube	9%	6%
Associate information to a cube	Cube on Surface	35%	38%
	Click cube	28%	28%
	GUI-WIMP	7%	10%
	Double tap cube on surface	10%	7%
	Hover cube over surface	7%	6%
	Circle tap cube on surface	4%	4%
	Touch surface	3%	4%
Create a query	Cube on Surface	23%	33%
	Click cube	27%	22%
	GUI-WIMP	18%	6%
	Tilt cube	5%	17%
	Touch surface	9%	17%
Zoom in - make a query more specific	Cube on Surface	14%	31%
	Tilt cube	7%	19%
	Neighbor cubes	21%	13%
	Click cube	21%	13%
Shift - Replace part of a query	Neighbor cubes	43%	31%
	Cube on Surface	14%	38%
Create a compound query	Neighbor cubes	25%	29%
	Cube on Surface	25%	14%
	Click cube	25%	5%

Table 2: Gestures generated per command by condition: H (horizontal) and V (vertical). GUI-WIMP refers to gestures such as tapping a button or using a slider on the cube.

While Table 2 shows popular gestures, it is not conflict free. The same gestures were observed to be reused for similar commands. For example, conflicting gestures were suggested for "displaying information from a cube onto the surface" and "associating information to a cube".

Agreement Performance and Preference

We used the formula introduced by Wobbrock et al. [57] for calculating an agreement score for each of the eight commands listed in Table 2. We also calculated and compared the means of the goodness and ease scores obtained from user preference questionnaires. Table 3 shows agreement, goodness, and ease scores for each of the eight commands used in the elicitation study per condition. We did not find significant differences between conditions in terms of agreement, goodness, and ease of gestures. Overall, we found that when simple gestures were mapped to simple commands they had more agreement and higher goodness.

Commands	Agreement		Good Mean *SD*		Ease Mean *SD*	
	H	V	H	V	H	V
Select an item from a list	0.36	0.33	4.26 *1.05*	4.00 *1.00*	4.58 *0.84*	4.32 *1.11*
Display information from the cube onto the surface	0.54	0.56	4.47 *1.07*	4.16 *1.21*	4.63 *0.96*	4.37 *1.07*
Modify and define a range	0.12	0.16	4.00 *0.88*	3.55 *0.96*	4.13 *1.01*	3.97 *0.82*
Associate information to a cube	0.23	0.24	4.34 *1.05*	4.29 *1.10*	4.58 *1.04*	4.42 *1.02*
Create a query	0.18	0.21	4.37 *0.83*	3.53 *1.31*	4.37 *1.01*	3.89 *1.05*
Zoom in - make a query more specific	0.15	0.19	3.79 *0.98*	3.58 *1.35*	4.00 *0.88*	3.58 *1.22*
Shift - Replace part of a query	0.20	0.17	3.84 *1.12*	3.58 *1.31*	4.05 *1.03*	3.74 *0.87*
Create a compound query	0.17	0.17	3.53 *1.17*	3.58 *1.12*	3.79 *1.13*	3.47 *1.12*

Table 3: Gesture agreement, goodness, and ease by condition: H (horizontal) and V (vertical).

Gesture classification

In order to better understand the design space of active tokens with multi-touch and tangible interfaces, we manually classified each gesture along three dimensions: space, flow, and cardinality. While there are numerous gesture taxonomies in the literature, our focus is on characterizing dimensions that are mostly relevant for the manipulation of active physical tokens within multi-touch and tangible interfaces.

Interaction *space* describes where a gesture was performed: *on-surface* – upon the interactive workspace, *on-bezel* – in the area surrounding the interactive surface, or *in-air* – above or in-front the interactive surface. Some gestures have a hybrid interaction space; for example initiated in-air and concluded on-surface. The dimension of *flow* is adopted from [57]; within this dimension *discrete* refers to a gesture where a computationally mediated response is expected after the user acts, and *continuous* refers to a gesture where response is expected while the user acts. To accomplish more complex tasks, some gestures had combined flow; for example, one hand was sliding along the screen while another was clicking a cube screen.

Cardinality indicates the number of hands and tokens involved in a gesture. We regard *atomic* gestures as performed by one hand on a single token, and *compound* gestures as comprising a sequence of atomic gestures and involving one or two hands interacting with multiple tokens. Parallel gestures are bimanual and consist of two atomic gestures performed at the same time. Guiard's Kinematic Chain theory [13] provides a theoretical basis for the understanding and design of two-handed interactions, also several HCI studies have explored cooperation of the hands (e.g. Hinckley [14]). We intend to continue to explore the design space of two-handed interaction with active tokens and multi-touch interfaces.

Figure 3 shows percentage of gestures in each category per dimension.

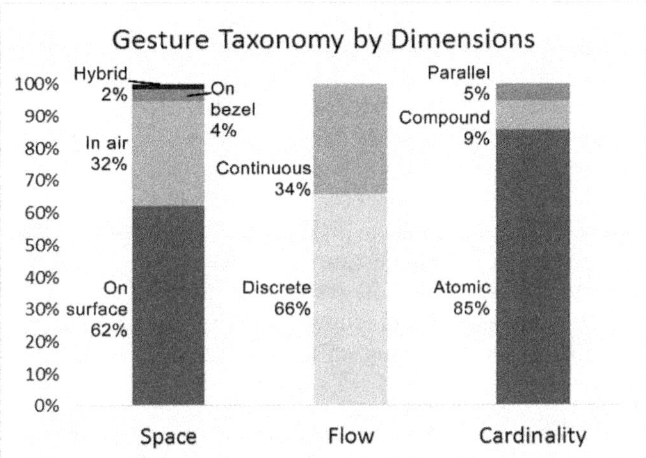

Figure 3: Gesture Taxonomy presented as percentage per dimension

Mental Model Observations

Common Metaphors – the 'think aloud' protocol provided us with insight into participants' mental models. We identified several common metaphors that were suggested by multiple participants. Users often used the active tokens (i.e. cubes) as containers, dragging information from the display surface into the cube, displaying information from the cube by placing it on the surface, or tilting the cube above the surface. Several users treated the cubes as physical knobs for information presented on the surface. For example, one user described: "put [the cube] on the BRCA1 gene and then rotate the cube to bring up different data sources…" Some participants used active tokens as tools for indirect touch, such as a pen or a marker; for example: "I will circle 2007 with the drawing edge of the cube." The use of naïve physics metaphors to describe the way the active tokens (i.e. cubes) operate was also common. For example, in the words of users: "Depending on [the angle of] the tilt, the speed will be faster or slower…"; "Tilt it again so that the lower number would gravitationally fall…"

Impact of Experience with Existing Interfaces – we observed that gestures suggested by users were heavily influenced by participants' experiences with traditional GUIs and with multi-touch interfaces. For example, one popular gesture was to swipe a finger on top of a cube's display, other common gestures included pinching-in and out with two fingers on the face of a cube. Users also suggested that a keypad or keyboard appear on the cube, as well as various buttons such as 'ok' and 'save.' One user described, "Instinctively, I just want to zoom in like that [pinches out] and it is probably because I have a Mac." Another user said, "Try to swipe the cube like on an iPad or on a phone." These observations are aligned with findings from previous studies indicating that users' creativity in suggesting gestures for new form-factors are impacted by their experiences with existing interface technologies [10, 28, 57].

Display orientation – while we did not find significant differences between horizontal and vertical conditions in terms of agreement, ease, and goodness (i.e. fit) (see Table 3), several users expressed strong preference toward the use of active tokens with a horizontal surface. Reasons include hand fatigue, effort, and persistence. For example, one user said, "I thought it was easier on the horizontal. I felt like with the vertical, I couldn't put the cubes down." Another user mentioned, "I like the table better than the PixelSense. It felt weird tapping a cube to an upright screen. You can drag things around and leave them there. More intuitive." A different user described, "The horizontal surface feels more personal, it's like you own space. When it moved to the vertical surface, I was more reluctant to use more than one cube at a time because that requires more effort ..."

Possibilities for action –The minimal visual feedback (and the absence of any other form of feedback) combined with the simple and clean design of the cubes provides only minimal real and perceived affordances. Several users commented on the difficulty of coming up with new ideas for interaction. In the words of one user, "It's hard to come up with a way to use this cube"; and in the words of another user, "I really wouldn't use these cubes at all. I don't find them intuitive." One explanation to these views is that the form of the Sifteo cubes did not provide users with sufficient clues regarding possibilities for action.

DISCUSSION

In this section, we describe the implications of our results for the design of multi-touch and tangible interfaces with active tokens. While we elicited user-defined gestures for active physical tokens within a particular model world of personal genomic investigation, the design considerations we discuss below could apply to many domains; For example, Twitter data mining, or the exploration of medical records. Following, we describe implications for design, which are based on our findings, and intended to inform expert designers in the creation of novel interactions combining active tokens with multi-touch and tangible interfaces.

Implications for design

Several implications for the design of novel interactions that combine active tokens with interactive surfaces have emerged based on our findings:

Interaction beyond the surface – roughly 30% of gestures in both conditions were performed in-air, around 5% of gestures performed on the bezel, while 2% were hybrid (e.g. initiated off the surface and concluded on-surface). This suggests interaction above, in-front, or next-to an interactive surface might profitably be considered by designers along multi-touch interaction. Designing interactions beyond the surface could help designers to overcome challenges common to data-intense multi-touch and tangible interfaces such as finger size, occlusion, and clutter. In our study, participants employed in-air and on-bezel gestures for selecting and setting query operators, modifying and defining ranges, and formulating queries.

Continuous interaction – roughly 40% of gestures operating active tokens were continuous. Among these, hovering above the surface, rotating a cube, and scrolling a cube were all common interactions. This suggests that users might value immediate response and continuous control over information. The use of parallel and compound gestures, combined with on-bezel and hybrid interactions (see Figure 3) suggests that system designers might also consider using active tokens in control panel-like structures (as in [47]). Such structures could enable users to gain fine control of the displayed information while avoiding occlusion and fat finger challenges.

Gesture reuse – we found that participants occasionally reused gestures for multiple commands. For example, the gesture of placing a cube on the surface was suggested for each of the commands; however, the target on the surface was different for each command. For example, placing a cube on a chromosome start region was suggested to bind modifying functionality to the cube. Alternately, placing a cube on the gene BRCA1 was suggested to cause the gene to be saved to that cube. Gesture reuse and consistency are important for increasing learnability and memorability. Multi-touch gestures often suffer from low memorability, which could be improved using active tokens combined with contextual constraints to disambiguate gestures. The notion of interpreting an action based on a combination of token and constraints is discussed in the TUI literature [42, 49] and should be applied when using active tokens with multi-touch and tangible interfaces.

Affordances, metaphors, and constraints – we observed that the design of the cubes combined with the lack of feedback in our study did not provide users with sufficient affordances. Affordances denote the possibilities for action; inviting and allowing specific actions [33, 53]. Norman distinguishes perceived affordances, which are only visually conveyed and rely on the interpretation of images, from real physical affordances [33]. The power of tangible interaction lies in providing both real and perceived affordances [41]. When integrating active physical tokens with multi-touch and tangible interfaces, designers should conduct a careful investigation of tokens' affordances, considering both perceived (i.e. visual) and physical affordances. Variations in size, shape, and material of a token as simple as a cube can affect the ways in which users handle it. We found that with the lack of sufficient affordance users' expectations were deeply influenced by traditional GUIs and multi-touch interfaces. For example, some users used the cubes as means for indirect touch. Users also suggested gestures that draw upon reality-based [18] metaphors such as naïve physics, containers, and knobs. Constraints (physical or digital), which restrict and provide context to possible actions, work in tandem with affordances [8]. Designers could employ both physical and digital constraints (e.g. visual targets) to guide users through sequences of action [8, 42, 49].

Limitations and Future Work

Our study has several limitations that point toward future work. First, we aimed to gain insight into users' behavior and preferences without the bias caused by computationally-mediated feedback. Hence, we removed the dialogue between the user and the system; instead creating a monologue, in which users' behavior is always accepted. This approach has several weaknesses; such as the absence of guiding cues, which makes it difficult for users to imagine possible gestures, and the lack of opportunities for users to reflect back on their gestures and change the interactions they proposed. In the words of one user: "It was really weird trying to build something from the ground up because I'm more used to relying on the feedback of whatever I'm interacting with to know what my next move is."

Also, the use of active physical tokens offers opportunities for supporting collaborative work with big data around an interactive surface or between distant surfaces; however, in this study we did not investigate a collaborative scenario. Rather, we focused on the engagement of a single user. It is possible that a collaborative scenario would highlight additional classes of gestures – e.g. proximal (but non-contiguous or coordinated across distant surfaces). These issues are worthy of investigation, but are beyond the scope of the current work. In the future, we intend to draw on our findings to design, implement, and evaluate a multi-touch and tangible interface for querying genomic data.

CONCLUSION

In this paper, we conducted a study with 19 users, which investigated gestural interaction with active-tokens. Our work provides four main contributions: 1) a vocabulary of user-defined gestures for interaction with active tokens; this gesture set extends familiar multi-touch gestures and includes gestures on-surface, in-air, and on-bezel; 2) characterization of the design space of gestural interaction with active tokens; 3) insight into participants' mental models including common metaphors, sources of influence, and a strong preference of horizontal (vs. vertical) surfaces; and 4) implications for the design of multi-touch and tangible interfaces with active tokens for exploring large data sets. We intend to apply our findings in the design of tangible interface for the exploration of large genomic data sets.

ACKNOWLEDGMENTS

We thank our study participants. This work has been partially funded by NSF grant nos. IIS-1017693, IIS-1320350, and CNS-1126739.

REFERENCES

1. (n.d.). Retrieved from Sifteo: https://www.sifteo.com/
2. Anthony, L., Brown, Q., Nias, J., Tate, B., & Mohan, S. (2012). Interaction and recognition challenges in interpreting children's touch and gesture input on mobile devices. In Proc.of the ITS, ACM.
3. Antle, A. N., & Wise, A. F. (2013). Getting down to details: Using theories of cognition and learning to inform tangible user interface design. Interacting with Computers, 25(1).
4. Antle, A. N., Droumeva, M., & Ha, D. (2009). Hands on what?: comparing children's mouse-based and tangible-based interaction. In Proc. of IDC, ACM.
5. Block, F., Horn, M. S., Phillips, B. C., Diamond, J., Evans, E. M., & Shen, C. (2012). The DeepTree Exhibit: Visualizing the tree of life to facilitate informal learning.Visualization and Computer Graphics, IEEE, 18(12).
6. Camarata, K., Do, E. Y. L., Johnson, B. R., & Gross, M. D. (2002). Navigational blocks: navigating information space with tangible media. In Proc. of IUI, ACM.
7. Coelho, M., Zigelbaum, J., & Kopin, J. (2011). Six-forty by four-eighty: the post-industrial design of computational materials. In Proc. of TEI. ACM.
8. Djajadiningrat, T., Overbeeke, K., & Wensveen, S. (2002). But how, Donald, tell us how?: on the creation of meaning in interaction design through feedforward and inherent feedback. In Proc. of DIS, ACM.
9. Drucker, S., Fisher, D., Sadana, R., Herron, J., & Schraefel, M. C. (2013). TouchVix: A Case Study Comparing Two Interfaces for Data Analytics on Tablets. In Proc. of CHI, ACM.
10. Epps, J., Lichman, S., & Wu, M. (2006). A study of hand shape use in tabletop gesture interaction. In Proc. of CHI extended abstracts, ACM.
11. Findlater, L., Lee, B., & Wobbrock, J. (2012). Beyond QWERTY: augmenting touch screen keyboards with multi-touch gestures for non-alphanumeric input. In Proc. of CHI, ACM.
12. Good, M. D., Whiteside, J. A., Wixon, D. R., & Jones, S. J. (1984). Building a user-derived interface. Communications of the ACM, 27(10), 1032-1043.
13. Guiard, Y. (1987). Asymmetric division of labor in human skilled bimanual action: The kinematic chain as a model. Journal of motor behavior, 19, 486-517.
14. Hinckley, K., Pausch, R., Proffitt, D., Patten, J., & Kassell, N. (1997). Cooperative bimanual action. In Proc. of CHI, ACM.
15. Horn, M. S., Tobiasz, M., & Shen, C. (2009). Visualizing biodiversity with voronoi treemaps. In Voronoi Diagrams, IEEE.
16. Hornecker, E., Marshall, P., Dalton, N. S., & Rogers, Y. (2008). Collaboration and interference: awareness with mice or touch input. In Proc. of CSCW, ACM.
17. Isenberg, P., Isenberg, T., Hesselmann, T., Lee, B., Von Zadow, U., & Tang, A. (2013). Data visualization on interactive surfaces: A research agenda. Computer Graphics and Applications, IEEE, 33(2), 16-24.
18. Jacob, R. J., Girouard, A., Hirshfield, L. M., Horn, M. S., Shaer, O., Solovey, E. T., & Zigelbaum, J. (2008). Reality-based interaction: a framework for post-WIMP interfaces. In Proc. of CHI, ACM.
19. Jetter, H. C., Gerken, J., Zöllner, M., Reiterer, H., & Milic-Frayling, N. (2011). Materializing the query with facet-streams: a hybrid surface for collaborative search on tabletops. In Proc. of CHI, ACM.
20. Jetter, H.-C., Reiterer, H., and Geyer, F. (2013). Blended Interaction: understanding natural human–computer interaction in post-WIMP interactive spaces. Personal and Ubiquitous Computing.
21. Klum, S., Isenberg, P., Langner, R., Fekete, J. D., & Dachselt, R. (2012). Stackables: combining tangibles for faceted browsing. In Proc. of AVI. ACM.
22. Lahey, B., Girouard, A., Burleson, W., Vertegaal, R., and Canada, K.L.(2011). PaperPhone : Understanding the Use of Bend Gestures in Mobile Devices with Flexible Electronic Paper Displays. In Proc. of CHI, ACM.
23. Marshall, P., Hornecker, E., Morris, R., Sheep Dalton, N., & Rogers, Y. (2008). When the fingers do the talking: A study of group participation with varying constraints to a tabletop interface. In Proc. of ITS, IEEE.
24. Merrill, D., Kalanithi, J., & Maes, P. (2007). Siftables: towards sensor network user interfaces. In Proc. of TEI, ACM.
25. Micire, M., Desai, M., Courtemanche, A., Tsui, K. M., & Yanco, H. A. (2009). Analysis of natural gestures for controlling robot teams on multi-touch tabletop surfaces. In Proc. of ITS, ACM.
26. Microsoft. (n.d.). Microsoft PixelSense. Retrieved from Microsoft PixelSense: http://www.microsoft.com/en-us/pixelsense/default.aspx
27. Microsoft Surface. (n.d.). Retrieved from www.microsoft.com/surface
28. Morris, M. R. (2012). Web on the wall: insights from a multimodal interaction elicitation study. In Proc. of ITS, ACM.

29. Morris, M. R., Brush, A. B., & Meyers, B. R. (2007). Reading revisited: Evaluating the usability of digital display surfaces for active reading tasks. In Proc. of ITS,2007, IEEE.

30. Morris, M. R., Fisher, D., & Wigdor, D. (2010). Search on surfaces: Exploring the potential of interactive tabletops for collaborative search tasks. Information processing & management, 46(6), 703-717.

31. Nature Specials: Big Data. (2013). Retrieved from Nature: http://www.nature.com/news/specials/bigdata/index.html

32. Nielsen, M., Störring, M., Moeslund, T. B., & Granum, E. (2004). A procedure for developing intuitive and ergonomic gesture interfaces for HCI. In Gesture-Based Communication in HCI. Springer Berlin Heidelberg.

33. Norman, D. A. (1999). Affordance, conventions, and design. Interactions, 6(3).

34. Patten, J., & Ishii, H. (2000). A comparison of spatial organization strategies in graphical and tangible user interfaces. In Proc. of DARE, ACM.

35. Pyryeskin, D., Hancock, M., & Hoey, J. (2012). Comparing elicited gestures to designer-created gestures for selection above a multi-touch surface. In Proc. of ITS, ACM.

36. Rekimoto, J., Ullmer, B., & Oba, H. (2001). DataTiles: a modular platform for mixed physical and graphical interactions. In Proc. of CHI, ACM.

37. Russell, D. M., Stefik, M. J., Pirolli, P., & Card, S. K. (1993). The cost structure of sensemaking. In Proc. of CHI, ACM.

38. Sacco, G. M., & Tzitzikas, Y. (2009). Dynamic taxonomies and faceted search (Vol. 25). Springer.

39. Schkolne, S., Ishii, H., Schroder, P. (2004). Immersive design of DNA molecules with a tangible interface. Visualization , IEEE, pp. 227- 234.

40. Seyed, T., Burns, C., Costa Sousa, M., Maurer, F., & Tang, A. (2012). Eliciting usable gestures for multi-display environments. In Proc. of ITS, ACM.

41. Shaer, O., & Hornecker, E. (2010). Tangible user interfaces: past, present, and future directions. Foundations and Trends in HCI, 3(1–2).

42. Shaer, O., Leland, N., Calvillo-Gamez, E. H., & Jacob, R. J. (2004). The TAC paradigm: specifying tangible user interfaces. Personal and Ubiquitous Computing, 8(5).

43. Shaer, O., Mazalek, A., Ullmer, B., & Konkel, M. (2013). From Big Data to Insights: Opportunities and Challenges for TEI in Genomics. In Proc. of TEI. ACM.

44. Shaer, O., Strait, M., Valdes, C., Feng, T., Lintz, M., & Wang, H. (2011). Enhancing genomic learning through tabletop interaction. In Proc. of CHI, ACM.

45. Shaer, O., Strait, M., Valdes, C., Wang, H., Feng, T., Lintz, M., ... & Liu, S. (2012). The design, development, and deployment of a tabletop interface for collaborative exploration of genomic data. International Journal of Human-Computer Studies, 70(10), 746-764.

46. Thudt, A., Hinrichs, U., & Carpendale, S. (2012). The bohemian bookshelf: supporting serendipitous book discoveries through information visualization. In Proc. of CHI, ACM.

47. Ullmer, B., Dell, C., Gill, C., Toole, C., Wiley, C., Dever, Z., . . . Parker, R. (2011). Casier: Structures for Composing Tangibles and Complementary Interactors for User Across Diverse Systems. In Proc of TEI, ACM.

48. Ullmer, B., Dever, Z., Sankaran, R., Toole, C., Freeman, C., Cassady, B., . . . Parker. (2009). Cartouche: conventions for tangibles bridging diverse interactive systems. In Proc of TEI, ACM.

49. Ullmer, B., Ishii, H., & Jacob, R. J. (2005). Token+ constraint systems for tangible interaction with digital information. ACM TOCHI, 12(1), 81-118.

50. Ullmer, B., Ishii, H., & Jacob, R. J. (2003). Tangible query interfaces: Physically constrained tokens for manipulating database queries. In Proc. of Interact.

51. Valdes, C., Ferreirae, M., Feng, T., Wang, H., Tempel, K., Liu, S., & Shaer, O. (2012). A collaborative environment for engaging novices in scientific inquiry. In Proc. of ITS, ACM.

52. van den Hoven, E., Mazalek, A. (2011). Grasping gestures: Gesturing with physical artifacts. AI EDAM 25(3).

53. Vermeulen, J., Luyten, K., van den Hoven, E., and Coninx, C. (2013). Crossing the bridge over Norman's gulf of execution: revealing feedforward's true identity. In Proc. Of CHI, ACM.

54. Vogel, D., & Baudisch, P. (2007). Shift: a technique for operating pen-based interfaces using touch. In Proc of CHI, ACM.

55. Voida, S., Tobiasz, M., Stromer, J., Isenberg, P., & Carpendale, S. (2009). Getting practical with interactive tabletop displays: designing for dense data, fat fingers, diverse interactions, and face-to-face collaboration. In Proc. of the ITS, ACM.

56. Weiser, M. (1999). The computer for the 21 st century. ACM SIGMOBILE, 3(3), 3-11.

57. Wobbrock, J. O., Morris, M. R., & Wilson, A. D. (2009). User-defined gestures for surface computing. In Proc. of CHI, ACM.

58. Wu, M., Shen, C., Ryall, K., Forlines, C., & Balakrishnan, R. (2006). Gesture registration, relaxation, and reuse for multi-point direct-touch surfaces. In Proc. of HIHCS,

59. Xu, W., Chang, K., Francisco, N., Valdes, C., Kincaid, R., & Shaer, O. (2013). From wet lab bench to tangible virtual experiment: SynFlo. In Proc. of TEI. ACM.

60. Zigelbaum, J., Horn, M. S., Shaer, O., & Jacob, R. J. (2007). The tangible video editor: collaborative video editing with active tokens. In Proc. of TEI, ACM.

Pervasive Information through Constant Personal Projection: The Ambient Mobile Pervasive Display (AMP-D)

Christian Winkler, Julian Seifert, David Dobbelstein, Enrico Rukzio
Ulm University, Ulm, Germany
{firstname.name}@uni-ulm.de

a) Vision b) Pervasive display c) Floor interaction d) Hand interaction

Figure 1. a). The vision: small wearable projectors reveal serendipitous information. b) A user discovers information with the AMP-D prototype. c) The user has received a text message and picks it up from the floor. d) The scrolling message text is read in the user's hand.

ABSTRACT
The vision of pervasive ambient information displays which show relevant information has not yet come true. One of the main reasons is the limited number of available displays in the environment which is a fundamental requirement of the original vision. We introduce the concept of an Ambient Mobile Pervasive Display (AMP-D) which is a wearable projector system that constantly projects an ambient information display in front of the user. The floor display provides serendipitous access to public and personal information. The display is combined with a projected display on the user's hand, forming a continuous interaction space that is controlled by hand gestures. The paper introduces this novel device concept, discusses its interaction design, and explores its advantages through various implemented application examples. Furthermore, we present the AMP-D prototype which illustrates the involved challenges concerning hardware, sensing, and visualization.

Author Keywords
Pervasive displays; Augmented reality; Personal projection

ACM Classification Keywords
H.5.2 [Information interfaces and presentation]: User Interfaces. - Graphical user interfaces.

INTRODUCTION
Today, we observe an ever increasing interest of mobile users towards pervasive information access and serendipitously discovering new information. This is currently achieved by means of smartphones and public displays in the environment. Public displays will likely never be widespread enough to fulfill this desire alone. Inversely, smartphones can only contribute to this vision when they are held in hand and are actively operated. This becomes a challenge especially when the user is on-the-go as the device distracts the user's focus and connection to the environment. The idea of wearing a location-aware pervasive display that alerts to new relevant information and provides quick access to deal with it, is very compelling. It could provide access to a great variety of information, ranging from *public* content (e.g. stationary pictures from Flickr) to *personalized* content (e.g. personalized advertisements in front of shopping windows (Figure 1a)), and *personal* content (e.g. notifications about new text messages). Previous works on mobile speech interfaces, head-mounted displays, public-display networks, and mobile projectors attended to this vision one way or the other. One crucial requirement for such a wearable pervasive display is that the display is always available. Another is that the display is located in the user's periphery and uses ambient presentation to minimize the risk of annoying users and distracting them from their primary tasks.

CHI 2014, April 26–May 1, 2014, Toronto, Ontario, Canada.

http://dx.doi.org/10.1145/2556288.2557365

In this paper we propose to use constant personal projection as a novel pervasive display. The Ambient Mobile Pervasive Display (AMP-D) integrates a wearable projected display that accompanies users on the floor in front of them with a projected hand display and a smartphone to a continuous interaction space. The floor display is a constant pervasive window into the user's digital world, lying in the user's visual periphery (see Figure 1a). As such it allows for subtle user alerts without occupying the user's hands or field of view (FOV). The hand display allows to deal with information instantly without having to reach to a physical device. The smartphone supports exploring and sharing content from and to the virtual world. Users interact with AMP-D entirely through hand gestures. For instance, when a new text message is received, a message notification box rolls into the user's view on the floor (Figure 1c). Users can then pick the box up and read the message instantly in their hand (Figure 1d). Optionally, they can answer the message using their smartphone.

In addition to the wearable multi-display, AMP-D uses a consistent information space for typical public and personal mobile content that augments users' virtual world through spatial augmented reality, giving users a natural means of discovering new information.

The contributions of this paper are the AMP-D concept of constant personal projection and its interaction techniques, its prototype implementation, and various implemented application examples that explore and highlight the applicability of AMP-D to typical mobile scenarios. Further, we contribute our lessons learned from the evolution of the prototype and a small user study.

RELATED WORK

Mobile Projection

The recent emergence of pico-projector technology allows for the integration of projectors into mobile and wearable devices [22].

Karitsuka et al. envisioned the concept of a wearable projector that provides an interactive display on any plain surface [11]. SixthSense [17] advances this concept and shows a pendant device and several context-aware application scenarios (e.g., recommendations projected on books or delays on flight tickets). Further, simple pointing interactions in mid-air between the projector and the projection are supported, which have been studied in greater detail by Winkler et al. [28]. OmniTouch [9] employs a shoulder-mounted projector and advances the interaction by using a depth camera to support multitouch interaction on planar surfaces within reach. The SLAMProjector of Molyneaux et al. [18] advances touch interaction even further to arbitrarily shaped surfaces and also supports geometrically correct projections on such. These works focus on a (touchable) display within reach, similar to the hand display of AMP-D. LightGuide [23] demonstrates navigational help on the user's hand. Different to these works, AMP-D also supports passive usage of projected augmentations and multiple projected displays.

Ota et al. explored different positions of the projector on the body in regard to wearability, and the viewability of a floor projection [19]. McFarlane et al. [15] also explored floor-projected support in the context of military tasks with varying interaction techniques. Both found out that the shoulder position is best suited for floor projections, especially if the keystone effect and swinging of the projection can be neglected (as in the world-fixed projection of AMP-D). These works use mobile floor projections, yet do not consider its ambient properties, nor do they support a world-fixed spatial augmented reality as does AMP-D.

The only works that consider combining a *distant* (floor) and a close display are the GuidingLight prototype by Chung et al. [4], and the steerable projection prototype by Cauchard et al. [3]. Although both show working application scenarios for each of these display locations, they do not define a continuous interaction space between the displays, and do not support interaction in both display configurations.

In contrast, AMP-D enables a mobile multi-display environment with floor and hand projection in a continuous interaction and information space. It further leverages the peripheral characteristics of the floor projection.

Smart spaces

In contrast to mobile setups, static projector setups, belonging to the field of smart spaces, have the advantage that the environment is known in advance or can be instrumented to be analyzable in real-time, e.g. by introducing cameras at known positions. For instance, the LightSpace [27] and Beamatron [26] by Wilson et al. implement a smart space through projection. By dynamically building a 3D model of the room and present actors by means of multiple depth cameras, the steerable projector system can augment any surface in the room with perspectively correct projections for one user. It thereby defines a continuous interaction space that, for instance, allows users to carry virtual objects in their hand. The concept of RoomProjector [18] uses spatially-aware handheld projectors to reveal parts of the 3D scenery instead of fixed projectors. Further, it supports geometrically corrected projections and interactions on arbitrary surfaces. WorldKit provides a method for dynamically creating projected interfaces in the environment [29].

AMP-D aims to bring the underlying concept to the mobile user on the go who has very different information interests (public or smartphone content) and options for interaction, which leads to new conceptual and technical challenges.

Mobile Peripheral and Head-Mounted Displays

Wearable augmented reality displays date back to the works of Feiner et al. [6, 7] who developed head-mounted see-through displays for spatial augmented reality. This display type constantly overlays the user's foveal view making it less suitable for everyday scenarios. Apart from that, head-mounted displays to date entail unsolved challenges such as perceptual issues (e.g. different focus planes and narrow FOV); security issues (e.g. they may distract from or obstruct an approaching danger), and social issues (e.g. collocutors having no means of knowing what I'm looking at).

A mobile *peripheral* display is the eye-q system [5] that uses a low-resolution LED display embedded in a pair of eyeglasses to provide a small set of notifications. An advanced display version is promised by Google Glass [8], whose display lies slightly to the top of the foveal field of view, also qualifying it for ambient display. Unfortunately, at the same time, its position and small size make it less suitable for complex visual output, augmented reality, or direct interaction.

Leung et al. [13] demonstrate a system that constantly projects a representation of the wearer's online social identity to the ceiling above. As its intended audience are spectators it is not designed to be interactive, though.

Discussion

Works on mobile displays so far dealt with close and distant displays separately whereas AMP-D presents a continuous interaction and information space between these display types. Similar continuous interaction spaces have only been presented in static smart-space setups. In this work, we aim to bring this compelling vision to the mobile user in everyday use cases. In these mobile scenarios, ambient display properties are much more important, which so far have been neglected in works on mobile wearable or handheld displays.

CONCEPT AND DESIGN OF AMP-D

The AMP-D is a wearable multi-display system that provides a pervasive window into the user's virtual world on the floor. Unlike smartphones which have to be taken out to be operated, the AMP-D display is constantly available. Therefore it is suited for ambient alerting to many kinds of public or personal information that is available via the user's connected smartphone. Among others, these information types include location-aware notifications, communication, reminders, and navigational instructions. Additionally, information is not only visualized, but can be handled through gestures in the user's hand which is used as on-demand secondary display.

We illustrate the concept of AMP-D by first discussing each of its basic concepts. Following on that we present various use-cases that highlight the applicability of AMP-D. All of these use cases have been implemented in the AMP-D prototype which is presented later.

Basic Concepts

Pervasive and Ambient Floor Display

To provide an always-available display, we think the floor is well suited since it is the only space that is always existent in our current life. Further, it "must" be looked at regularly, at least while moving which is a benefit for notifications that cannot be missed for too long. Besides, it is easy to glance at quickly. Thus AMP-D projects the permanently available display on the foor, yet content is only displayed when required. The floor display lies outside the foveal field of view (FOV) of the user, therefore it is qualified for peripheral display. Research on peripheral vision and cognitive psychology offers evidence that peripheral vision supports a separate cognitive channel, thereby reducing overall cognitive load [25]. More importantly, the effect of tunnel vision supports users in effectively blending out unnecessary information in the periphery when their cognitive load is high [5]. Inversely, when users' cognitive load is low, the display supports the serendipitous discovery of new information.

As the peripheral vision is much more sensitive to movement than to color or detail [5], we adapt the degree of animation on the display to the priority of the shown content and let the user's cognition outbalance load and priority. We have tested this with AMP-D in a pilot study and the effect can be described as similar to the sudden recognition of a nearby small animal such as a mouse on the ground that is only detected when it starts moving, even though it was present before.

Pousman et al. provide a thorough definition of key characteristics of ambient systems [20]. Based on this definition, to make AMP-D more environmentally appropriate, we "focus on tangible representations in the environment" [20] by refraining from including any typical GUI elements such as windows or buttons on the display. Instead, the projection only shows a projected window into the user's virtual world, i.e. invariably, all projected content is clearly located in the worldwide coordinate system. This concept builds on Spatial Augmented Reality (SAR) [2] and world-fixed presentation [6], as opposed to the standard display-fixed presentation. In the context of projections, it feels like uncovering the virtual world with a spotlight — or in case of AMP-D, a wearable lantern — which is why it is referred to as the spotlight metaphor [21]. The system tracks users' movement and orientation to provide the corresponding illusion (Figure 2).

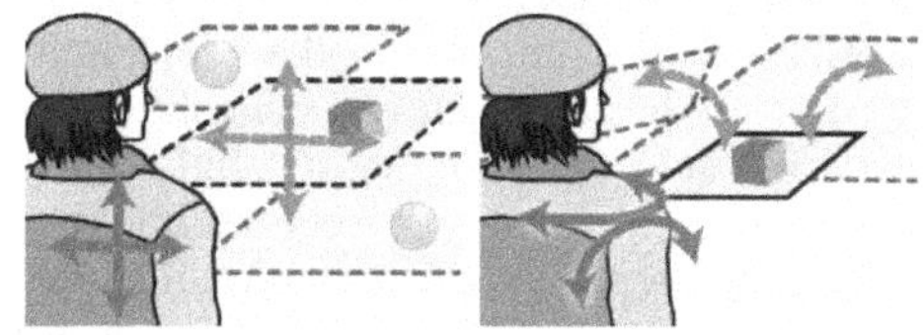

Figure 2. The virtual window follows the user's movement (left) and orientation (right).

As all content is only revealed on a fixed location on top of the real world, the projection blends with the environment, for the user as well as for spectators. The publicity of the projection might also lead to interesting new behaviors. For instance, seeing a person uncover public content such as a sign or advertisement with the projection may lead spectators to explore the item themselves with their own AMP-D (or similar AR) devices. Thus the public floor projection also provides a new way of blending real and virtual worlds between users and spectators.

Information Space: World Graffiti, Boxes, and Spheres

The virtual world of AMP-D consists of only two distinct types of visualizations: two-dimensional *World Graffiti* and two three-dimensional objects; *boxes* or *spheres* (Figure 3).

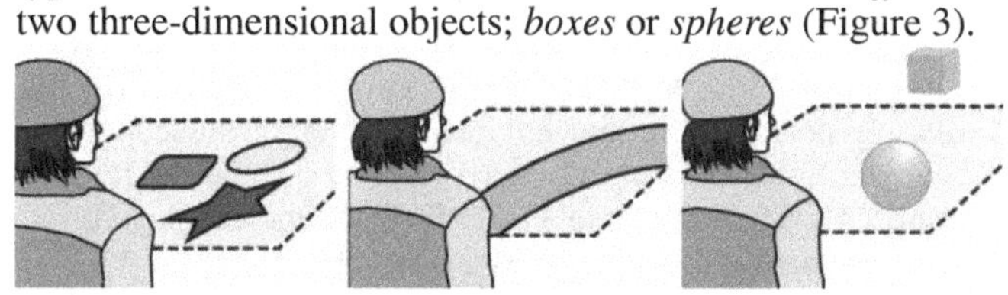

Figure 3. 2D World Graffiti (left), navigation paths (middle), and spheres and boxes as interactive elements (right)

The two-dimensional graffiti is a stationary texture on the ground, such as a navigation path or personalized advertisement. Its flatness indicates that it is not meant to be interacted with. In contrast, the three-dimensional box and sphere items indicate that they are supposed to be interacted with. We choose and limit the system to these two shapes, as it enforces consistency for the user who can approach items from arbitrary angles and they still look familiar. Of course, both visualizations can be combined to create interactive World Graffiti by placing virtual items on top of it.

Spheres are always rolling, accompanying the user wherever they go until they interact with it, or until the sphere is no longer required. For instance, an incoming phone call is represented as sphere item that accompanies the user until the call is taken, declined, or eventually missed. As opposed to spheres, boxes typically lie at static places. However if they are new and supposed to have an ambient alerting impact on the user (e.g. a notification), they roll into the user's field of view. If the user is currently moving, they further accompany the user for several seconds before coming to rest.

Boxes and spheres have defined content types which the user can quickly recognize from their different textures. Additionally, new boxes the user has not yet interacted with, carry a yellow border. In this manner, unlike with the use of ambient vibration alerts in smartphones, the user can quickly discern the type and novelty of new notifications by just glancing at the projection. To further interact with the box or sphere, users use their bare hands which are tracked by the system. By reaching out with their splayed hand towards the object, a green selection disk appears in the projection. It acts as hand extension that can be moved beneath the object of interest. The pre-selected item begins slightly bouncing. By closing their fingers, the user selects the object (picks it up) and the object performs a jump animation into the user's hand (see Figure 4). Initially we tried with a lot of different hand

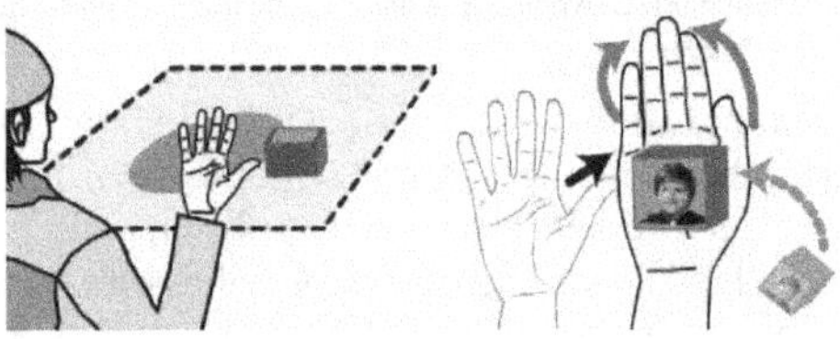

Figure 4. Object selection (left) and pick-up of objects by moving the fingers of the hand together (right).

gestures, especially for picking up objects and releasing them again. Up and down gestures come to mind quickly, but, as other gestures, do not work as they inhibit movement themselves. As the user is moving anyway, we found that gestures based on hand postures work best, followed after gestures that only inhibit horizontal movement.

Private Hand Display

Previous works [10, 9, 23] have demonstrated that various interactions can be performed in people's hands. The hand display perfectly fits our envisioned interaction scenarios, as many actions can be performed without a separate device. In contrast to the floor display, AMP-D's hand display supports two-dimensional, display-fixed content.

As soon as content has been picked up to the user's hand, the focus of the projection changes to follow the user's hand, showing a focused image within the hand's boundaries. Consequently, the floor projection becomes blurry. This provides the user with a very suitable means of knowing which interaction zone is currently active.

The hand provides a more private display than the public floor projection, comparable to a phone display. When picked up, many objects can disclose more sensitive information. Message boxes, for example, can show a picture of the sender of the message. Hand gestures allow the user to interact further with the content. By turning the hand 90 degrees towards the center of the body, the user switches to *reading mode*. The box held in the hand shrinks and a preview of the content is displayed. For instance, a text message or the subject of an email as scrolling text, or a preview of a picture can be displayed (see Figure 5).

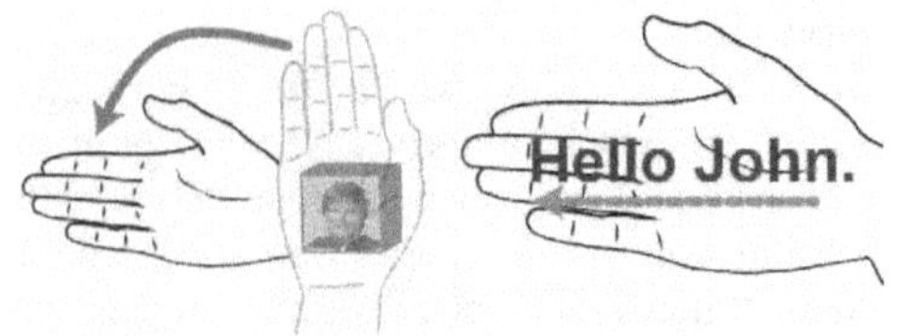

Figure 5. By turning the hand 90° degrees a preview (scrolling text, thumbnail, etc.) of the content in hand is displayed.

Furthermore, binary decisions (e.g. accept a call with or without loudspeakers activated) are supported. Users toggle between binary options by flipping their hands so that the thumb points inwards or outwards and select the option by performing a click gesture by briefly moving the thumb to the palm and back (see Figure 6).

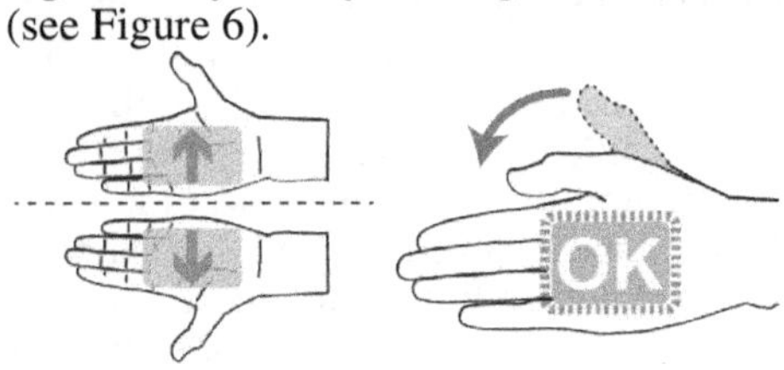

Figure 6. Binary decision gestures.

As long as the user holds the box in hand, it moves with them. This way, users can reposition any three-dimensional item in their virtual world. Finally, users have two options how to proceed with the object: By splaying out their fingers and/or moving their hand outside of the projected area, the item falls down back to the floor in front of them. Or, by performing a gesture as if to throw the item over one's own shoulder, the item is removed from the virtual world (see Figure 7). The meaning of these gestures depends on the content type (use case) and is explained later.

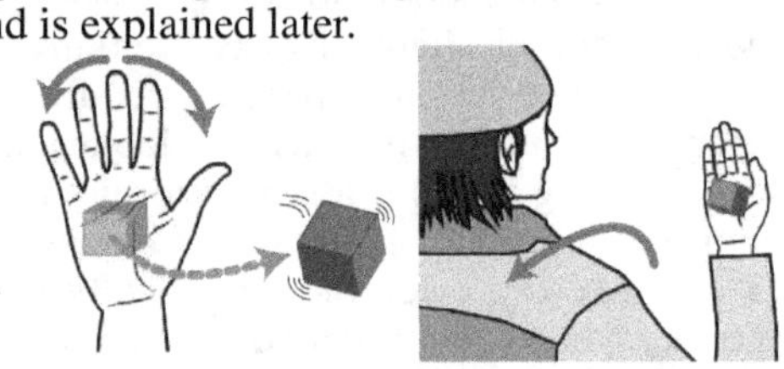

Figure 7. By unfolding the fingers the object falls back to the ground (for notifications this is equivalent to "snoozing" the alert). By throwing the object over the shoulder it is removed from the virtual world.

Continuous Interaction Space: Floor / Hand / Smartphone

In situations when the hand display is not sufficient to adequately deal with content (e.g. to answer a text message), interaction can continue on the smartphone. When a user picks up an object, the smartphone is notified of the selected item. For as long as the user holds the item in hand and a short grace period after that, the smartphone is automatically unlocked and presents the full representation (e.g. the full email view) either immediately, or as soon as it is taken out from where it was stowed (see Figure 8). When users are in a private environment or to support collaboration, they may also want to show full content representations on the large floor display. AMP-D could easily support this through an additional gesture. Also more complex interactions such as text-entry could be supported on the floor projection.

Another usage of the smartphone is to add content from the smartphone to the virtual world. Despite auto-generated items, the user may want to share content at specific locations. For a personal purpose, for example, a reminder such as "don't forget to put the bins out" can be placed on the threshold. Moreover, pictures, for instance, can be dropped to the world where they were taken to share them with friends or the public (explained in a moment). The smartphone provides an always available "share service" that allows supported content on the smartphone to be dropped into the environment as virtual boxes of the corresponding type (see Figure 8).

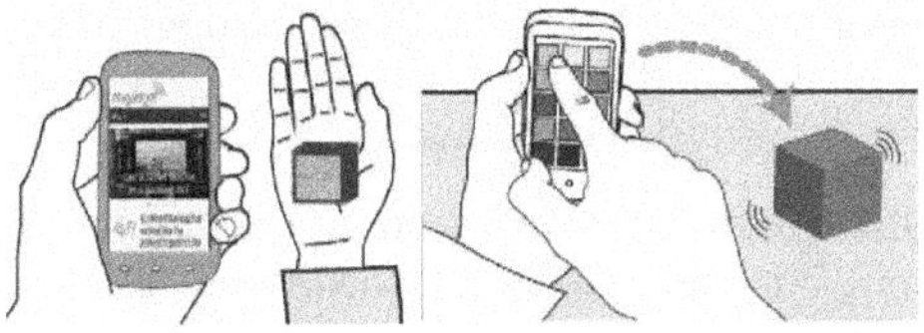

Figure 8. Content in hand can be continued exploring on the phone (left) and arbitrary content from the phone can be placed as box item in the virtual world (right).

Thus, the three interconnected displays form a continuous interaction space providing different levels of details to the user's requirements at that time.

Public Content And Collaboration

Besides personal content of the user, the constant availability of the projection invites friends, advertisers, or even the local administration to create public content in the virtual world similar to physical signs, banners, etc. The virtual content has the advantage that it is much cheaper to create and can be personalized for the user. Their disadvantage is that the projection is smaller than a person's physical FOV, therefore they may not reach the same audience. The intrinsic publicity of the projection also invites many co-located multi-user scenarios. For instance, co-located AMP-D users can overlap and "merge" their floor projections to drop content from the smartphone on one side, to then be picked up on the other side by the second user.

Privacy

When using AMP-D, users neither exclusively select the content to project, nor do they monitor the projection all the time as is the case with existing projected displays. Furthermore, the surrounding audience of the projection is rather random. Projected content may be appropriate in the current context, but not in another. Thus, users require effective means to protect sensitive information and ensure that only appropriate information is disclosed. A first means is already given through the concept of SAR. When a user wants to hide information on the floor display quickly and for a short moment only, a small movement or rotation along any axis is often enough to move the window in order to hide previously disclosed items. If this is not sufficient, AMP-D supports a simple horizontal swipe gesture in front of the projector to enable/disable the projection entirely (see Figure 9).

History and Overview

The SAR concept entails another advantage within the context of AMP-D. The implicit revealing or hiding of information using body motion can also be used to look up upcoming content or to revisit past content. For instance, when a user recognizes content on the floor projection too late, walking a few steps back or just turning around will bring the item back into the projected window. Similarly, when users share their foot trails as World Graffiti, they can revisit them later, e.g. to find their way back to their car. As opposed to that, for instance, tilting the projection far ahead during navigation tasks allows users to preview directions further ahead. Results from a study by Billinghurst et al. [2] indicate that people can easily navigate and relocate spatially augmented information as they are used to the interaction from real life. Therefore, the SAR concept should be able to provide a natural interaction with the information space of AMP-D.

Despite AMP-D's support in changing the FOV in all directions, no contemporary display technology can compete with the overview (FOV and resolution) of a person's real view into the distance. Thus, searching for virtual content on the ground can require significantly more effort than searching for real objects. Therefore, the system provides vertical swipe gestures to change between AMP-D's standard view and an elevated third-person perspective. This acts like a map on a scale of 1:10 to spot nearby objects of interest without having to actually go there or search for them (see Figure 9).

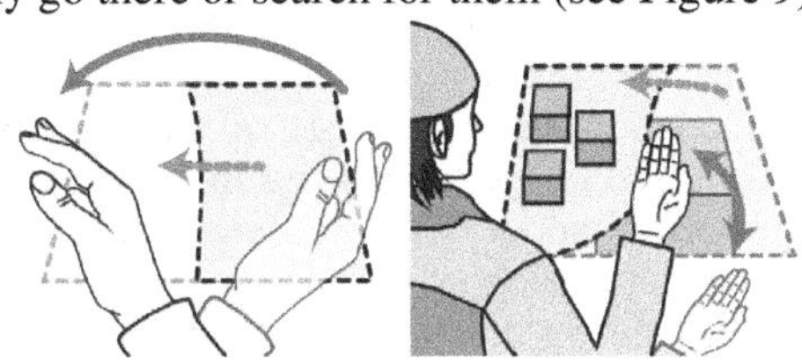

Figure 9. Enable/disable the projection entirely with a horizontal gesture (left). Change from a real to an elevated perspective to get an overview of content around (right).

AMP-D Use Cases

We understand AMP-D as a general mobile companion and the following implemented use cases (cf. video figure) highlight how AMP-D supports typical mobile scenarios.

Context- and Location Awareness

Context- and especially location-aware information such as friends being nearby, or interesting offers in the vicinity are increasingly available to users. With AMP-D being constantly active and capable of displaying visual context information, it is well-suited to provide such information to users on the go. People on a shopping stroll, for instance, see additional offers as World Graffiti and box items (textured with a t-shirt icon) on the ground in front of the shopping windows they pass. By picking up the box and reading its contents, a personalized advertisement appears in the user's hand (Figure 10a).

We also implemented the system to support persuasive hints. They have been shown to be able to motivate users to change their behavior in a positive way [24]. For instance, when users walk close to an elevator, the system reminds them of their activated fitness plan by showing a red line leading to the elevator and a green line leading to the staircase as World Graffiti beneath the users' feet (Figure 10b).

Data sharing

Data sharing via the smartphone is used to create new virtual items in the virtual world. Currently, we support two data sharing applications on the smartphone. The first allows the user to create note boxes with text content at world-fixed

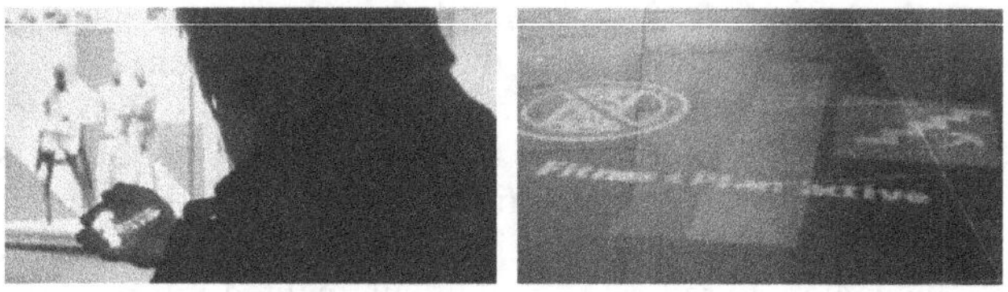

a) Personalized offers b) Persuasive Computing

Figure 10. Two location-aware use cases

positions. This can be used to place location-dependent reminders or messages for oneself, or, for example, a colleague or family member in the own environment who will literally stumble over the information (Figure 11a), and can read the contained message in their hand.

The second application supports the sharing of pictures from the smartphone's gallery. The boxes are created right in front of the user (Figure 11b) and are textured with the contained image (in a gray inset, identifying them as boxes of the type "picture"). Given the small size of the boxes, it is not possible to recognize the actual image on the floor projection, but it is already useful to distinguish between different items in a pile of pictures. Once users pick up an image box they are interested in, the image is revealed in the user's hand when entering reading mode. This presentation already delivers a much better impression of the picture than the floor projection. As with other content types, the picture can further be viewed on the phone.

Once boxes are created, they can also be easily repositioned by taking them by hand, moving with the box to the desired location, and releasing them again.

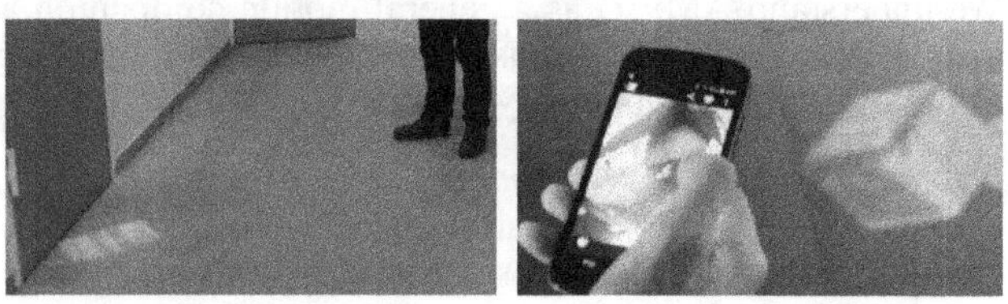

a) Note sharing b) Picture Sharing

Figure 11. a) A note is found in front of an office door ("Meet me at coffee place"). b) A picture box transfered from phone to virtual world.

Notifications: Communication, Reminders, News Feeds

The most frequent tasks performed on smartphones - especially while the user is on the go - are related to communication, and management of notifications. Calendar and task reminders, for instance, have become very popular on smartphones. The most important aspect is to actually read them, be reminded at regular intervals if the notification was missed in the first place, and perhaps perform some simple interaction such as snoozing or dismissing the notification. For the user on the go reading the notification on a smartphone often involves a significant overhead. The user must stop or at least slow down, take out the device, possibly unlock it, only to read a few words of text.

AMP-D uses its box items to visualize new notifications regarding text messages, emails, calendar reminders, and news feed updates. As described earlier, the user can quickly discern the type of the notification from their appearance prior to any interaction (see Figure 1c). When a message box is picked up, a picture of the sender is displayed on the upper face of the box. The first 160 characters of the item's content are displayed as scrolling text in the user's hand when turned to reading mode (see Figure 1d). Otherwise, only a teaser is displayed, or the subject in case of an email, and the whole message can then be read, for instance, on the smartphone. Similarly, news feed updates appear as feed boxes that show their source (publisher) as a texture on the box, reveal their subject in the user's hand, and can be continued to be read on the user's smartphone. They particularly demonstrate the usefulness of serendipitously stumbling over new information when the cognitive load is low.

The visualization of dynamic notifications using the world-fixed SAR concept is not straightforward as the information is time- and context-dependent instead of location-dependent. Our solution is to multiplex the information in the time and location domain. For instance, when users receive a new notification, it is created at the user's current location and rolled into their projected window. Shortly after the user passes by the notification without picking it up, it is removed from the old position and inserted in the same animated way at the user's current location. Once the notification box has been picked up, users decide whether they want to return the box to their world to either "snooze" the notification or dismiss it by throwing it over their shoulder. In the former case, the box will continue to regularly appear across the user's way but without any type of animation (these intervals can be defined on the corresponding smartphone app). In the latter case, the notification - not the content - is deleted.

Incoming calls, in contrast, are presented as a sphere that accompanies the user for the time of the call. It can be picked up to show the caller's picture - if available - as texture on the sphere and to reveal the name or phone number in the reading mode. In this scenario, taking out the smartphone after having picked up the sphere will automatically unlock the smartphone and accept the call; releasing it to the world will keep it ringing; and throwing the sphere over the shoulder will decline the call.

a) Path navigation b) Signs

Figure 12. Path navigation with additional turn-by-turn instructions and signs that help ahead-way planning

Navigation

AMP-D supports augmented reality navigation where the user follows a path as a virtual line overlaying the ground. The path approach fits the concept of World Graffiti on the floor display, since it gets by without time-based instructions the user could miss. Instead, whenever the user pays attention to the projected navigation, directions can be grasped at a glance (Figure 12a). Additionally, to provide the necessary context for users to plan their way upfront, turn-by-turn navigational instructions (e.g. turn left in 50 meters) and location-dependent help (e.g. take the stairs up, not down) are overlaid right next to the path similarly to road signs (Figure 12b).

PROTOTYPE

We implemented a prototype of the AMP-D concept in order to investigate the technical challenges involved in building such a system and explore possible interactions with aforementioned use cases.

Hardware design

Our AMP-D prototype (see Figure 13) consists of a procam (projector and camera) unit, a backpack, a laptop, and two batteries (one for the projector, one to increase battery time of the laptop). Part of the overall system is also a wirelessly connected Android smartphone running a corresponding service software.

The procam unit (Figure 13b) is attached to the backpack (Figure 13a) that positions it approximately 25cm to the side and 15cm to the top away from the user's eyes (no offset in the forward direction). We found this position to yield a good trade-off between the large size of the projection on the ground (appr. size 2m $\times$ 1.25m, 2 meters away) and the positioning of the hand in order for the user to comfortably reach into the projection for the selection of objects and the hand display.

On top of the projector sits an ASUS Xtion Pro Live depth and RGB camera (640 $\times$ 480px @ 30 FPS), which we chose for its very small size, low power consumption, and well-suited depth range (0.5m to 3.5m). Finally, an inertial measurement unit (IMU) by x-io technologies is part of the procam unit and delivers precise and robust 9DOF orientation and acceleration data of the user. The system is controlled by a Dell M11x laptop with i7 CPU, 1.7 GHz running Windows 7 and the prototype software that performs all computations at a frame rate of 60 Hz.

The projector and the IMU are powered by batteries and the rest of the components are powered by the laptop. The system's power lasts for 5 hours of continuous usage. The system can be worn to both sides, depending on the primary hand of the user, which should be on the same side as the projector to be within the projection path.

Software

The software components (except smartphone service software) are responsible for computing the graphics and physics of the 3D world augmentation, the user's movement, and the hand and gesture recognition. The software is written in C# and runs on the laptop.

3D World Augmentation

The virtual user and all projected content are modeled in a 3D scene using Microsoft's XNA, the JigLibX [14] physics engine, and a graphics framework [16]. The rendering of this scene delivers the 3D world augmentation to the projector.

The 3D scene includes World Graffiti as 2D floor textures, and 3D boxes and spheres. The skeleton of the virtual user, who moves through this world, consists of a lower and an upper body entity. The correct perspective projection is achieved by attaching the virtual camera to the user's torso entity with the exact offset that is has in reality. The engine will then compute the correct off-axis perspective homography that lets the projection appear as perceived through the user's virtual eyes. Moreover, it lets the virtual camera turn around the center of the user's body instead of turning around itself. In addition, the virtual field of view has to be inversely matched to the actual field of view provided by the projector. Currently, we do not account for lens distortion of the projector which would further improve registration accuracy.

As we use a fixed physical orientation for the projector (instead of adapting it to the user's height), we can calculate the user's height as required by the system automatically based on the floor distance we receive from the depth sensor. Thus the system does not require manual calibration. The accuracy of the optical illusion during tilting or rolling of the torso can be further improved, though, by providing the exact length of the torso to the system in order to accurately determine the center of the body.

Floor/Hand Tracking and Focus Adjustment

Floor and hand tracking is computed on the depth image from the camera. On every cycle, the algorithm first decides whether the user's hand is present in the depth image:

We use computer vision to recognize hand contour, finger gaps and tips, fingertip direction, the direction of the hand, and the centers of palm and hand (see Figure 13c left). The recognition builds on three-dimensional segmentation of hand-sized clusters and simple heuristics based on sizes, distances, and changes in the derivation of the contour. Our particular shoulder-worn setup allows some assumptions that further simplify the recognition procedure: valid hands must not be further away than 1.5m (depth culling); must not span a depth range larger than 0.5m; and the user's arm (the cluster) must always reach into the camera frame from the bottom and/or right edge (for right-handed users). The recognition is fast and accurate in various environments. When more than one finger is recognized, we detect the *unselected* state that allows the user to steer the green selection disk (cf. Figure 4) for object selection. When one or no fingers have been recognized, we detect the *selected* state. Further, we recognize the user's thumb and compute its relation to the center of the hand to distinguish between the two states of binary decisions. Comparing hand positions, hand directions, and finger counts over multiple frames allows us to recognize the remaining gestures such as *reading mode* (cf. Figure 5), click gesture, and the horizontal and vertical *swipe gestures* (cf. Figure 9).

When the user's hand is *not* detected, the surface in front of the user is analyzed to decide whether it is suitable for showing the floor projection. The depth image is sampled at several grid-based points across the image and first averaged individually for each row, then for the whole image. Based on the depth gradient from individual rows we can decide whether the projection falls on a floor-like (vertical), mostly

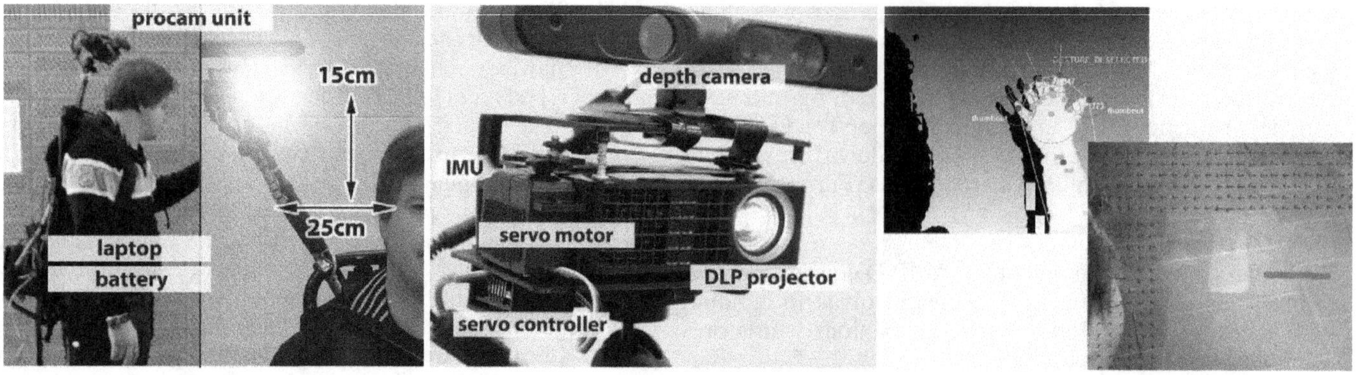

a) System setup b) Procam unit c) Software components

Figure 13. The AMP-D prototype. a) A backpack holds the procam unit, laptop, and battery (left). The procam unit appears as worn on the shoulder (right). b) Close-up of the procam unit. c) Software tracks hands for gesture-based interaction and computes optical flow to enhance step detection.

plain (depth deviation) surface. Additionally, based on the overall depth average, we can then adjust the projector's focus to show a sharp image on the floor.

Tracking of Orientation and Movement

In parallel, inertial sensor data is received from the IMU. It is used to compute the orientation of the user's torso in all three dimensions to adjust the virtual user and the attached virtual camera in the 3D world accordingly.

Additionally, we use the acceleration data from the IMU for step detection. As absolute positioning systems are not always available, particularly indoors, AMP-D needs a way of detecting the user's movement based on dead reckoning. Naturally, this will only work for a short time due to measurement errors and must be regularly corrected by reliable data from an absolute positioning system (e.g. GPS or indoor localization systems increasingly becoming deployed). For the sake of testing the AMP-D concept, we only require short movements for which the dead reckoning approach is sufficient. Algorithms for robust pedestrian navigation usually build on a technique known as zero-velocity-update that relies on data from an accelerometer attached to the user's foot (e.g. [12]). Following our initial vision of a palm-sized form factor of the system (Figure 1a), we want the system to get by without further user instrumentation. With the IMU unit attached to the procam unit, we cannot rely on the zero-velocity-update method. Instead, we detect steps by finding peaks of vertical and forward acceleration, which are homogeneous in human walking behavior. Step length is approximated based on the automatically calculated height of the user. With the IMU unit alone, we could not reliably detect the user's walking *direction*, though.

A working solution which increased the reliability of detecting the step direction was found in computing the optical flow of the camera's RGB image. More precisely, we calculate the optical flow in a 100 px wide border at the top and left side of the RGB image (for right-handed users) wherein the user does not interfere while interacting with the primary hand (see Figure 13c right). Optical flow towards the user indicates forward movement while optical flow away from the user indicates backward movement. Gyroscope data is used to counterbalance the effect on the optical flow generated by the up and down swings caused by the human gait.

Combining these approaches, our system can detect the user's forward and backward steps most of the time, although there is room for improvement. By decreasing the form factor of the prototype, for instance, the system can be brought closer to the user's body which will benefit a more accurate step detection. Nonetheless, a general problem with step detection based on inertial measurements would remain: as the algorithm cannot detect a step until it is close to being finished, a small computational delay is induced. This delay counteracts the optical illusion when walking starts or stops and sometimes leads users to walk one step further than they intended.

Smartphone Service

The Android smartphone is connected to the laptop via Wi-Fi and runs a background service which starts polling the phone's light sensor whenever the user takes a virtual box into their hand and stops soon after it was released again. Whenever the measured light significantly increases during this time interval, the service wakes the screen, disables the keyguard, and starts the corresponding activity showing the content related to the box. In addition, access to placing information in the world from the smartphone is provided through a notification service. By pulling down Android's notification center from the phone's status bar and selecting the AMP-D service, the user can create notes and select pictures from the gallery which are then dropped into the world.

Limitations and Improvements

For most indoor scenarios, the brightness of the displays of the present prototype are already sufficient. For most outdoor scenarios, only the hand display is sufficiently visible as it is very close to the projector and can be shielded against direct sunlight. To the floor projection these reasons do not apply, hence the prototype is currently limited to twilight conditions outdoors. As the brightness of pico-projectors increased fourfold between 2009 and 2011, we hope they will reach sufficient brightness for outdoor conditions in the future.

Another limitation is the current size of the system. With pico projectors advancing quickly, and as depth cameras of the size of a finger becoming available, the procam unit can likely be shrunken considerably in the near future. Additionally, the software should soon be able to run on an on-board system such as a Raspberry Pi. Power consumption will likely be the most challenging factor for a much smaller version. This could however be mitigated by intelligent power saving which reduces power consumption when no display surface is available.

Finally, the step detection needs to be further improved, e.g., by pointing a second camera towards the user's feet which can immediately decide whether the user starts moving, thereby eliminating the initial detection delay of the current system. Further, GPS can be used outdoors or geo-located image-based pose estimation indoors (cf. [1]) to correct step detection errors.

Preliminary Evaluation

While we are planning on conducting larger user studies using our prototype, in a first initial investigation we wanted to find out if the most important features of AMP-D work for untrained users. Thus we recruited 6 participants between 25 and 30 years (mean 27 years), to identify strengths and weaknesses of the concept or the current implementation. They have been smartphone users for 1.5 years on average (min 0.5, max 2 years) and all used their smartphones at least for messaging, web browsing, calendar, and traffic information. The study lasted between 45 and 60 minutes and was conducted in a public floor (12 x 7 meters) of our building with regular by-passers (to provide users experiencing their attitude towards public usage). First we asked participants (using 5-point Likert-scales from "strong agree" to "strong disagree") about their smartphone usage and all showed *strong agreement* that they receive regular updates (notifications) on their mobile phones. There was further *agreement* to check if notifications have been missed, also while on the go, by all participants. Finally, there was *strong agreement* by all participants that they usually react to new message immediately. These answers show that our participants were in the right target group addressed by AMP-D.

After that we had all participants try out all applications of the prototype. This includes: receiving boxes rolled into their view while walking looking straight ahead, picking up boxes, reading their contents, moving them, releasing and dismissing them. Further continuing reading the contents of a box on the phone as well as taking a picture with the phone and creating a reminder note on the phone and sharing both to the own virtual world. Finally, they also tried to follow a navigation path that led them a parkour around obstacles we had set up.

After having tried the AMP-D prototype, participants showed a generally very positive attitude towards the AMP-D. Again we asked using the same 5-point Likert scale. All participants at least *agreed* that they recognized new notification items on the floor without looking at them. Further, all but one assumed the system would not disturb but enrich their daily live if it was available at a smaller size. Further, all participants at least *agreed* that they think they could react to new information quicker using AMP-D versus a smartphone. Finally, all *agreed* that the prototype worked fine for them, that they enjoyed using it, and that they could handle its complexity. In contrast, users were split in their answers to our questions regarding social acceptance and price/performance ratio – considering AMP-D would double the costs of the smartphone – both resulting in overall *neutral* feedback.

In response to open ended questions participants criticized, for instance, physical fatigue caused by the high number of interactions tested in the user study. Two participants were concerned with performing large, eye-catching gestures in public space. We also received constructive comments regarding technical challenges like brightness, battery life, and size of the system. One participant, for instance, proposed to show and select between all objects in the vicinity along a virtual string in the hand when the floor display is not bright enough. On the other hand, participants suggested several further application scenarios, among those: using AMP-D for navigation and context-aware instructions for craftsmen on building sites; remotely placing reminder boxes for items to buy across the supermarket at the right locations (like a decentralized shopping list); similarly, using AMP-D as city tour guide with POIs realized as info boxes to stumble over interesting information while keeping connected to the primary interest, the environment.

Naturally, this evaluation is only a first step in evaluating the device. User studies with more users over longer periods and against ordinary smartphone usage, for instance, are required.

CONCLUSION & FUTURE WORK

In this paper we introduced the Ambient Mobile Pervasive Display (AMP-D). For the first time we propose constant personal projection and have shown a working implementation of it, solving technical and conceptual issues. Our prototype provides a wearable multi-display system that combines a pervasive ambient floor display, a private hand display, and a smartphone into a continuous interaction space for mobile everyday scenarios. This goes beyond previous works on wearable augmented reality or wearable multi-display environments as the interaction space between multiple mobile displays have not been considered, yet. We have demonstrated new interaction metaphors and use cases which highlight the applicability of AMP-D in mobile scenarios. Moreover, the presented applications are embedded into a consistent information space that uses spatial augmented reality together with World Graffiti and virtual items to cover a broad range of interaction scenarios. Our concept further presents a new approach to serendipitous access to digital information that can be applied to our physical world, thereby likely reducing the individual's effort to receive and deal with information. As such, it depicts a future direction towards the original vision of pervasive computing.

We contribute a realistic interaction concept and a complex prototype that demonstrates unique solutions to the specific challenges of the AMP-D concept: most noteworthy, automatically changing the projector's lens focus based on the user's zone of interaction, step detection fusing inertial and optical movement measurements, and tracking of novel hand gestures in a truly mobile environment. We have integrated these components to a standalone mobile system that does not require instrumentation of the environment or the user (despite wearing the system), and runs for several hours.

The positive results of our small evaluation call for larger user studies that assess how the display can blend into the fabric of everyday life. It would also be interesting to test AMP-D in public spaces, both to study the influence of AMP-D on spectators, and to see how well AMP-D performs in crowded places.

ACKNOWLEDGMENTS

This work has been conducted in the context of the DFG Emmy Noether research group *Mobile Interaction with Pervasive User Interfaces*. We thank Ken Pfeuffert for contributing to the gesture interface, and Florian Schaub and Markus Löchtefeld for very helpful discussions.

REFERENCES

1. Arth, C., Reitmayr, G., and Schmalstieg, D. Full 6dof pose estimation from geo-located images. In *Proc. of*, Computer Vision–ACCV 2012. Springer, 2013, 705–717.
2. Billinghurst, M., Bowskill, J., Dyer, N., and Morphett, J. Spatial information displays on a wearable computer. *IEEE Computer Graphics and Applications 18*, 6 (1998), 24–31.
3. Cauchard, J. R., Fraser, M., Han, T., and Subramanian, S. Steerable projection: exploring alignment in interactive mobile displays. *Personal Ubiquitous Comput. 16*, 1 (Jan. 2012), 27–37.
4. Chung, J., Kim, I.-J., and Schmandt, C. Guiding light: Navigation assistance system using projection based augmented reality. In *Proc. of*, ICCE '11 (Jan. 2011), 881 –882.
5. Costanza, E., Inverso, S. A., Pavlov, E., Allen, R., and Maes, P. eye-q: eyeglass peripheral display for subtle intimate notifications. In *Proc. of*, MobileHCI '06, ACM (2006), 211–218.
6. Feiner, S., MacIntyre, B., Haupt, M., and Solomon, E. Windows on the world: 2 d windows for 3 d augmented reality. In *Proc. of*, UIST '93, ACM (1993), 145–155.
7. Feiner, S., MacIntyre, B., Höllerer, T., and Webster, A. A touring machine: Prototyping 3D mobile augmented reality systems for exploring the urban environment. *Personal Technologies 1*, 4 (1997), 208–217.
8. Google Inc. Google glass - home. http://www.google.com/glass/start/. Accessed: 2013-03-21.
9. Harrison, C., Benko, H., and Wilson, A. D. OmniTouch: wearable multitouch interaction everywhere. In *Proc. of*, UIST '11, ACM (2011), 441–450.
10. Harrison, C., Tan, D., and Morris, D. Skinput: appropriating the body as an input surface. In *Proc. of*, CHI '10, ACM (2010), 453–462.
11. Karitsuka, T., and Sato, K. A wearable mixed reality with an on-board projector. In *Proc. of*, ISMAR '03, IEEE Computer Society (2003), 321–322.
12. Ladetto, Q., and Merminod, B. Digital magnetic compass and gyroscope integration for pedestrian navigation. In *9th International Conference on Integrated Navigation Systems, St. Petersburg* (2002), 111–120.
13. Leung, M., Tomitsch, M., and Vande Moere, A. Designing a personal visualization projection of online social identity. In *Extended Abstracts*, CHI EA '11, ACM (2011), 1843–1848.
14. Linneweber, T. JigLibX physics engine. http://jiglibx.codeplex.com/. 2013-03-27.
15. McFarlane, D. C., and Wilder, S. M. Interactive dirt: increasing mobile work performance with a wearable projector-camera system. In *Proc. of*, Ubicomp '09, ACM (2009), 205–214.
16. Microsoft. Quickstart game engine. http://quickstartengine.codeplex.com/, 2013. (Last Access: 2013/03/25).
17. Mistry, P., Maes, P., and Chang, L. WUW - wear ur world: a wearable gestural interface. In *Extended Abstracts*, CHI EA '09, ACM (2009), 4111–4116.
18. Molyneaux, D., Izadi, S., Kim, D., Hilliges, O., Hodges, S., Cao, X., Butler, A., and Gellersen, H. Interactive environment-aware handheld projectors for pervasive computing spaces. In *Proc. of*, Pervasive 2012, Springer (June 2012), 197–215.
19. Ota, S., Takegawa, Y., Terada, T., and Tsukamoto, M. A method for wearable projector selection that considers the viewability of projected images. *Computers in Entertainment (CIE) 8* (Dec. 2010), 17:1–17:16. ACM ID: 1902596.
20. Pousman, Z., and Stasko, J. A taxonomy of ambient information systems: Four patterns of design. In *Proc. of*, AVI '06, ACM (New York, NY, USA, 2006), 67–74.
21. Rapp, S. Spotlight navigation: a pioneering user interface for mobile projection. In *Ubiprojection Workshop at Pervasive '10* (2010).
22. Rukzio, E., Holleis, P., and Gellersen, H. Personal projectors for pervasive computing. *IEEE Pervasive Computing 11*, 2 (Feb. 2011), 30–37.
23. Sodhi, R., Benko, H., and Wilson, A. LightGuide: projected visualizations for hand movement guidance. In *Proc. of*, CHI '12, ACM (2012), 179–188.
24. Torning, K., and Oinas-Kukkonen, H. Persuasive system design: state of the art and future directions. In *Proc. of*, Persuasive '09, ACM (2009), 30:1 – 30:8.
25. Treisman, A. Preattentive processing in vision. *Computer Vision, Graphics, and Image Processing 31*, 2 (Aug. 1985), 156–177.
26. Wilson, A., Benko, H., Izadi, S., and Hilliges, O. Steerable augmented reality with the beamatron. In *Proc. of*, UIST '12, ACM (2012), 413–422.
27. Wilson, A. D., and Benko, H. Combining multiple depth cameras and projectors for interactions on, above and between surfaces. In *Proc. of*, UIST '10, ACM (2010), 273–282.
28. Winkler, C., Pfeuffer, K., and Rukzio, E. Investigating mid-air pointing interaction for projector phones. In *Proc. of*, ITS '12, ACM (New York, NY, USA, 2012), 85–94.
29. Xiao, R., Harrison, C., and Hudson, S. E. Worldkit: Rapid and easy creation of ad-hoc interactive applications on everyday surfaces. In *Proc. of*, CHI '13, ACM (New York, NY, USA, 2013), 879–888.

Bigger is not always better: Display Size, Performance, and Task Load during Peephole Map Navigation

Roman Rädle[1*], Hans-Christian Jetter[2*], Jens Müller[1], Harald Reiterer[1]
[1] Human-Computer Interaction Group, University of Konstanz, Germany
{Roman.Raedle,Simon.Butscher,Harald.Reiterer}@uni-konstanz.de
[2] Intel ICRI Cities, University College London, London, United Kingdom
h.jetter@ucl.ac.uk
[*] The first two authors contributed equally to this work.

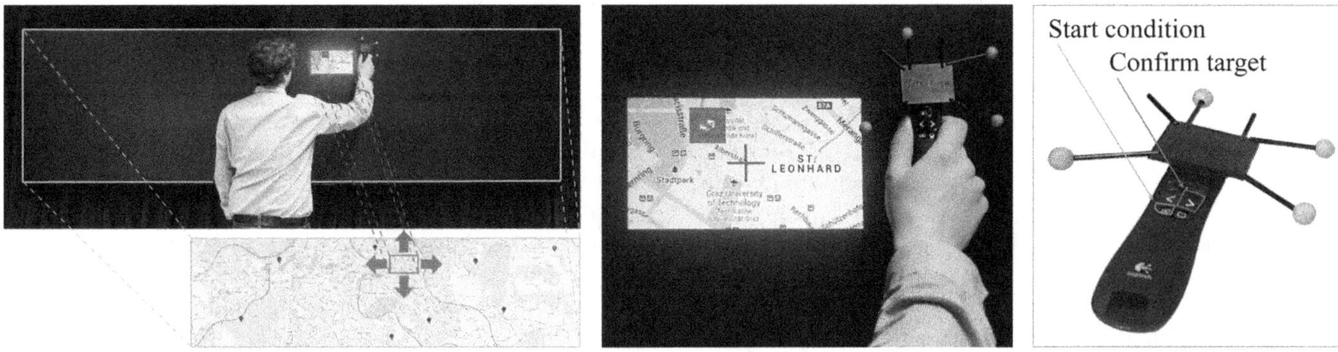

Figure 1. Dynamic peephole navigation of a map was simulated on a large vertical screen (left). The peephole was always displayed next to a handheld Presenter device (center) with buttons and a passive IR marker for 3D tracking (right).

ABSTRACT
Dynamic peephole navigation is an increasingly popular technique for navigating large information spaces such as maps. Users can view the map through handheld, spatially aware displays that serve as peepholes and navigate the map by moving these displays in physical space. We conducted a controlled experiment of peephole map navigation with 16 participants to better understand the effect of a peephole's size on users' map navigation behavior, navigation performance, and task load. Simulating different peephole sizes from 4″ (smartphone) up to 120″ (control condition), we confirmed that larger peepholes significantly improve learning speed, navigation speed, and reduce task load; however, this added benefit diminishes with growing sizes. Our data shows that a relatively small, tablet-sized peephole can serve as a "sweet spot" between peephole size and both user navigation performance and user task load.

CHI 2014, April 26 - May 01 2014, Toronto, ON, Canada

http://dx.doi.org/10.1145/2556288.2557071

Author Keywords
Peephole navigation; map navigation; display size; user study; navigation performance; experimentation

ACM Classification Keywords
H.5.2. User Interfaces: Input devices and strategies. Evaluation/methodology.

INTRODUCTION
Dynamic peephole navigation [11] is an increasingly popular technique for navigating large information spaces using small, spatially aware displays [4]. Typically, the display of a handheld computer [4,12,22,23], mobile phone [12,13,16,19], tablet [14], tangible display [21], or handheld projector [2,8,9,10,20] acts as a window or *peephole* to a much larger information space, such as a map [9,12,19,23]. Users can control the mobile display's content by physically moving it up, down, and sideways. By this, they can pan their view to move invisible off-screen content into the display and access the entire information space as if it was situated in physical space. This physical way of navigation provides users with more proprioceptive cues which are assumed to improve their orientation and understanding of the information space [4] and their spatial memory [9]. Ideally, peephole users are able to navigate quickly (short navigation time) and directly (short travelled path length) from their current location to any destination in the information space without an extensive task load, even if the location is off-screen or yet unknown.

We found that previous studies [9,13,14,19] have not sufficiently explored the peephole's size as an independent variable and how it affects navigation behavior, path lengths, navigation times, and user task load. This is surprising since it seems plausible that these aspects are all strongly dependent upon peephole size. A larger peephole reduces the need for slow physical panning and search in favor of a faster visual scanning of the display's content. It also allows for recognition rather than recall from spatial memory because it reveals more visual features that support user orientation all at once. However, a study of simulated tunnel-vision in front of large displays that included a task comparable to peephole navigation showed that the effect of a reduced peripheral vision and field of view is surprisingly small [1]. If this is also true for peepholes, it will open important design opportunities. In real-world systems, larger peepholes and displays increase cost, energy consumption, and weight, and the devices become more cumbersome. An alternative are small and lightweight handheld projectors which can produce a relatively large peephole. However, some practical problems (hand jittering, finding surfaces in the right size and lighting conditions for projection, privacy concerns when using projections in public spaces) come into play. Designers must make concessions due to these constraints. They want users to experience the benefits of larger peepholes while avoiding the many disadvantages that result from using and handling larger devices or mobile projections. Therefore answering the question of how small peepholes can become without overburdening their users during map navigation is of great practical relevance.

With this study, we wanted to find a good tradeoff, or "sweet spot", between peephole size and both user navigation performance and user task load. To do this, we conducted a controlled lab experiment during which 16 participants completed map navigation tasks on a large, vertical screen with physical navigation of simulated dynamic peepholes. The independent variable, peephole size, had 4 levels: smartphone, tablet, projector phone, and a control condition where the peephole was the size of the entire large, vertical screen. The dependent variables were travel path length, navigation time, and subjective workload. Results show that a relatively small, tablet-sized peephole can serve as the "sweet spot" mentioned above. In the following, we discuss related work, formulate our hypotheses, describe the experimental design, and report results before we conclude with a discussion of our findings.

RELATED WORK

Peephole navigation with handheld, spatially aware devices was originally conceived by Fitzmaurice et al. in 1993 [4]. It was then used in 2002 and 2003 for navigation and pen interaction in 3D [22] and 2D [23]. In 2004, Rapp et al. transferred this concept to handheld projectors for navigating the content of a general purpose UI (e.g., calendars, emails) [15]. From then on, many more peephole designs and systems were created, including augmented reality maps [6,12,19], peepholes using handheld projectors or projector phones [2,8,9,10,20], peephole navigation with smartphones, tablets, and tangible displays [6,13,14,21].

Comparative User Studies of Peephole Designs

Despite the popularity of peephole navigation, it took until 2006 for user studies to move beyond formative usability evaluations of individual systems and use controlled experiments to better understand the different design variants of peepholes more generally.

Mehra et al. [11] simulated a handheld peephole on a 15″ screen showing a 3.3″ peephole in two conditions: 1) *dynamic peephole navigation:* users move the peephole with the mouse across the screen to simulate physical navigation, 2) *static peephole navigation:* users use the mouse to scroll/pan the information space behind the peephole that always remains in the center of the screen to simulate virtual navigation. Results showed that dynamic peepholes improved users' speed and accuracy of discriminating lengths. Mehra et al. expect a substantial increase in users' situation-awareness and better estimation of spatial relationships when using handheld peepholes.

Rohs et al. used a phone as peephole for map navigation to compare virtual vs. physical navigation with and without visual context [19]. They found that physical navigation clearly outperforms virtual navigation with a joystick and that visual context (i.e. a map) behind the peephole does not substantially increase performance, potentially because of the costs of switching and refocusing between the two layers of information. These findings resonate with Henze & Boll who report that a simple off-screen visualization (i.e. arrow) can decrease the task completion time and that its effect is stronger than that of having visual context [6]. Rohs & Essl compared different peephole designs such as panning, zooming, and halo [16]. They report that the halo off-screen visualization is significantly faster and that only in complex situations zoom and halo show comparable performance, while the combination of halo and zooming is detrimental. In our study of peephole size, we therefore used only panning without zoom, no off-screen visualizations, and no visual context around the peephole to avoid confounding variables and to achieve better internal validity.

In 2013, three similar studies that compared physical vs. virtual touch-based peephole navigation were published: Kaufmann et al. conducted a study to find out if navigation performance and spatial memory performance during map navigation can be improved by using a projector phone with a peephole interface (54.7″) instead of a smartphone (4″) with a touchscreen. They report that users performed navigation in the zoomable map equally well, but that spatial memory performance was 41% better for projector phone users [9]. Rädle et al. compared physical vs. virtual navigation with a tablet (10.1″) in a zoomable landscape [14]. Opposed to Kaufmann et al., they report a significantly better navigation performance (47% decrease in path lengths and a 34% decrease in task time), but no significant effect on users' spatial memory. Finally, Pahud et al. show for a map navigation task with a smartphone as peephole (4.3″) that physical navigation is significantly slower than virtual navigation unless navigation happens between a few known targets [13]. In the light of these contradicting results and 20 years after Fitzmaurice [4], Pahud et al.'s concluding remark that, our understanding of the subtleties of peepholes is still not sufficient, appears particularly true. Therefore, we designed our research to explore these subtleties by isolating the peephole sizes from above studies (54.7″/4″, 10.1″ and 4.3″) in a controlled map navigation experiment to understand their effect on navigation behavior, navigation performance, and task load.

Fitts' Law Peephole Target Acquisition Models

Another stream of related research concerns formulating models of peephole target acquisition based on Fitts' law and validating them with one-directional [3,7,8] or multi-directional pointing [18] or AR tasks [17]. While this work is of fundamental importance, we believe that for understanding the subtleties of real-world map navigation with dynamic peepholes these models are only a first step. They accurately model a subtask of navigation, namely the time and precision of pointing at a distant target. However, real map navigation is far more complex than only one-directional pointing between two targets, since it is a multi-directional task that involves recalling multiple different (off-screen) locations from a mental representation of a 2D map and navigating between them. Such map navigation also involves initial phases of learning the yet unknown locations and spatial features or, at least, reactivating them from memory. All these aspects of map navigation are not part of Fitts' law models, because Fitts' law does not consider them. Fitts' law models cannot help with finding design tradeoffs for peephole size since they propose that pointing performance always gets better with growing peephole size and thus assume that "bigger is always better…" They do not take limiting factors or boundaries into account. For instance, upper boundaries like the users' maximum field of view or the aforementioned practicalities of using large displays or projections or lower boundaries like the higher mental and physical demand when using small or very small peepholes. This is why we chose an experimental approach to measure the "sweet spot" for map navigation instead of attempting to approximate it using existing predictive models.

FORMULATION OF HYPOTHESES

We entered our experiment with the following basic assumption about the nature of map navigation with peepholes: A typical map navigation activity can be separated into two phases, a *learning phase* and a *navigation phase*.

The *learning phase* only takes place if the content of the map is unknown to the user or the spatial relations within the map are only partially remembered and must be reactivated from the users' memory. This is the case when users navigate an unknown map or a map they have not seen or used recently, for example in typical augmented map scenarios for tourist or cultural heritage sites. During this phase, users first have to scan the entire map by physically moving the peephole to get an overview and to memorize positions, map features, and their spatial relations before they then can navigate efficiently. As discussed above, a larger display size should facilitate learning by revealing more content and visual features at a time and reducing the amount of slower physical panning in favor of more visual scanning. Therefore our hypotheses for the *learning phase* were that a larger peephole size decreases 1) the travelled path lengths and 2) the times for completing the navigation tasks.

In the *navigation phase*, a mental representation of the actual map is already present in the users' memory. This is either the case when a mental representation of a map remains in a user's memory after the *learning phase* is completed or when they are already familiar with the map. In the *navigation phase* users can, in principle, navigate toward destinations in the map efficiently, even if they are currently invisible. They do not have to scan large parts of the map anymore to find their destination but can rely on their spatial memory (and proprioceptive cues and motor memory from physical navigation) to reach their targets faster and with a shorter travelled distance. In comparison to the *learning phase*, the *navigation phase* more resembles a pointing task without exhaustive scanning or searching and thus is less affected by peephole size. However, based on Fitts' law models of peephole target acquisition [3,7,8,18], there still should be differences between the peephole sizes. Therefore our hypotheses for the *navigation phase* were that a larger peephole size decreases 1) the travelled path lengths and 2) the navigation times for completing the navigation tasks.

For the overall navigation task including both phases, we assumed that the cognitive load and the amount of physical panning increases with a smaller peephole size. Therefore, we hypothesized that the users' reported task load (based on the mental and physical demand items of NASA-TLX [5]) increases for smaller peepholes.

Finally, we predicted that the smaller the peephole, the greater the likelihood that users built an unreliable or incorrect mental spatial representation of the map and thus, when exposed to similar maps, they might not be able to recognize the one they navigated in the experiment. Therefore our final hypothesis is that the number of errors in a post-navigation map recognition task should increase for smaller peephole sizes.

EXPERIMENT

To better understand the role of peephole size during both phases of a map navigation task, we designed a controlled laboratory experiment with high internal validity. We isolated peephole size from other possible confounding variables, such as: existence of off-screen visualizations, design of navigation gestures, and ergonomic aspects or device-specific properties (weight of the device, readability from different viewing angles, resolution, or latency). The study was conducted as a 4×4 within-subjects design and systematically counterbalanced using a balanced Latin Square. The independent variable, peephole size (see Figure 2), had four within-subjects factors: control condition (S1), projector-sized peephole (S2), tablet-sized peephole (S3), and smartphone-sized peephole (S4). We used the four different maps A, B, C, D (Figure 4) to control for systemic errors and to avoid learning effects. The navigation path length, the navigation time, task load, and the post-navigation map recognition were the dependent variables.

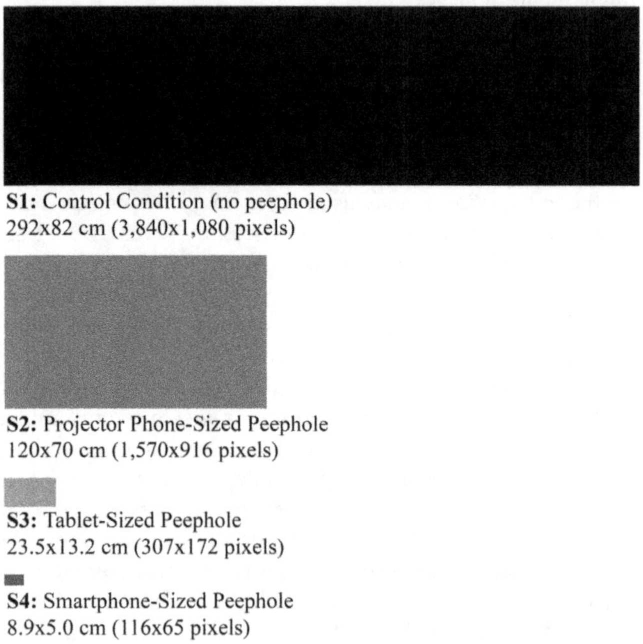

Figure 2. Overview of peephole sizes S1-S4 used as independent variable in the experiment.

In order to achieve a high degree of internal validity, we simulated the peepholes on a large display (rather than using the actual devices) so that the only variation from condition to condition was the peephole size itself. We initially discussed using different real-world devices instead of simulations, so that users would experience all device-specific properties such as different weight, resolution, or latency. However, we decided against this for following reason: Our overall goal is to understand the subtleties of peephole navigation as suggested by Pahud et al. [13] and the different factors that contribute to navigation performance. As a first step, in this study, we wanted to focus only on the effect of peephole size which arguably is the most important property and ideally arrive at generalizable results. Comparing devices would have led to recommending a certain device instead of a "sweet spot" peephole size without being able to isolate the role of peephole size from other device-specific properties (e.g. weight, resolution). We still would not truly understand the role of peephole size because other device properties such as weight and resolution would have come into play. Also, the recommendation would have been short-lived since such properties change with each new device generation.

Participants

16 participants (8 female, 8 male) were recruited to take part in the experiment. The mean age was 26.6 years (SD = 6.2, min = 19 years, max = 37 years) with a skewness of 0.64 (SE = 0.56) and kurtosis of -1.15 (SE = 1.10). One participant was left-handed. To get a realistic sample of participants, we excluded participants from the computer science department or with a background in computer science. 12 of the participants were students, 1 was a lecturer in linguistics, 2 were administrative staff, and 1 was a construction worker.

Apparatus

We used a large, vertical high resolution screen (size 292x82 cm, 120″ diagonal, 3,840x1,080 pixels resolution) to simulate peephole sizes of typical device displays at a constant resolution of 13.1 pixel/cm (or 33.5 ppi). This resolution was lower than that of actual mobile devices, but the display quality was more than sufficient for our purposes (Figure 3). The maps used in the experiment covered the entire screen, but users were only shown a rectangular section the size of the simulated peephole while the surrounding screen was black.

Participants used a wireless Logitech Professional Presenter R800 device (total weight 102 grams, Figure 1) to move the peephole on the screen. The Presenter was equipped with passive markers and continuously tracked in space using an OptiTrack 3D motion capturing system (18 cameras) with a tracking mean error of less than .5 mm and a tracking rate of 100 Hz. Participants held the Presenter in their preferred hand. A Kalman filter was used to reduce jittering caused by hand tremor and the noise or inaccuracies of the OptiTrack motion capturing system.

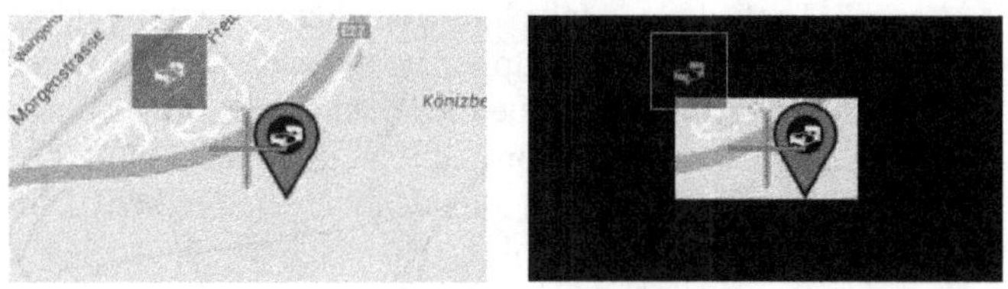

Figure 3. The tablet-sized peephole S3 with 307x172 pixels (left) and the smartphone-sized peephole S4 with 116x65 pixels (right). Note that the visual features and symbols stay recognizable and have sufficient detail.

During the experiment, the peephole travelled left or right of the Presenter (depending on handedness) to simulate physical navigation with a handheld dynamic peephole. By movement of their hands and lateral movement of their bodies, participants could move the rectangular peephole in the XY-plane of the display to view any location on the map, similar to the augmented maps in [6,19]. To minimize occlusion by hands, the anchor point was adjusted to right-

and left-handed users. The ratio between physical movement of the hand in control space and the peephole's XY-movement in display and map space was always 1:1. To constrain the distance between hand and screen to realistic holding and viewing of mobile devices, the peephole only appeared on the screen when the hand was within a range of 15 cm to the display. Except this, participants were free to choose their preferred head, body, and arm position during navigation and thereby set the optimal viewing distance to the display as it is the case when using an actual handheld device. However, they could not use rotation around the X-, Y-, or Z-axis as it is possible in AR see-through scenarios [12,17,22]. There was a red crosshair in the center of the peephole for selecting targets. We showed the target that the user searched for above and to the left of the crosshair.

Task Design

There was one condition for each peephole size. Due to the balanced Latin Square design, display sizes and maps were counterbalanced. Each map had 4 target pins that acted as navigation goals and 4 distractor pins. Maps were taken from Google Maps but were all unknown to the participants. All maps had similar visual features and complexity, such as a city with roads and a river (Figure 4).

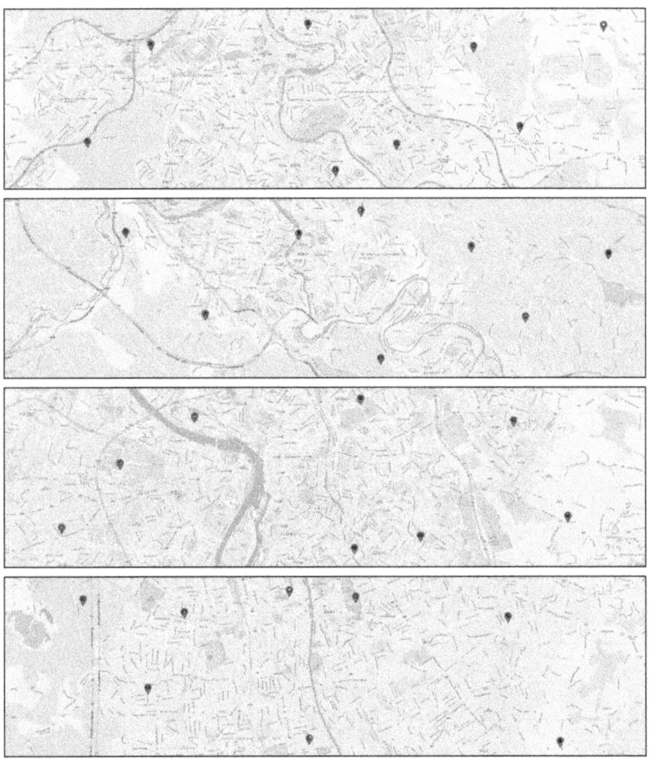

Figure 4. The four maps A-D used for the navigation tasks.

During the task, participants were asked to navigate with the peephole to a target pin in the map that shows a certain symbol, e.g., a bed (Figure 3). They were asked to navigate as quickly and as precisely as possible and to select the target with the peephole's crosshair by pressing the confirm button on the Presenter (Figure 1). The next target was presented to the participants if the correct target was selected. Otherwise the trial continued. The navigation path and time travelled between presenting the new symbol and its selection with the crosshair was recorded. The recording of a trial started immediately after completion of the previous trial and at the last position of the peephole. All targets were systematically placed on each map to ensure comparable target distances between the maps.

In each condition, participants had to navigate to 4 targets in the same order for 8 times (blocks). This added up to 16 participants × 4 conditions × 8 blocks × 4 targets = 2048 trials with 128 trials per participant.

After each condition participants reported their subjective workload ratings using the NASA-TLX questionnaire [5]. After this, they chose the map they navigated from a selection of three maps. Two maps served as distractors. The purpose of this task was to test if the participants could recognize the map they had just used based on the mental representation of the map that they created during the navigation tasks.

Procedure

Each participant was first asked to fill out a demographic questionnaire and was asked about their dominant hand. After this, participants were introduced to holding the Logitech Presenter device with their dominant hand, its two buttons, and how to move it with their hand. To avoid learning effects of handling the peephole during the actual data collection, they then could familiarize themselves with the task, the technique for moving the peephole, and the different peephole sizes during a training phase that lasted as long as they wanted.

After this preparation phase, the actual data collection started with the four conditions. After each condition they reported their task load using NASA-TLX and choose their map in the post-navigation map recognition task. The entire experiment lasted approximately 30 minutes per participant and each participant was rewarded with 8 Euros for their time.

RESULTS

For each peephole size, Figure 5 (top left) shows the mean path length that the participants travelled during each block. Path lengths were normalized by dividing them by the shortest possible path length, so that 1.0 is the minimum. Figure 5 (top right) shows the mean navigation time per block in milliseconds. Additional plots are provided for blocks 4-8 where the data points are too close together on the Y-axis to discriminate them.

Path length and movement time analyses were done using repeated measures ANOVAs (Greenhouse-Geisser corrections are marked as GGc) with post-hoc pairwise comparisons. Table 1 shows their p-values for the mean of each individual block, the mean of blocks 1-4 (B1-B4), the mean of blocks 5-8 (B5-B8), and the mean of blocks 1-8 (B1-B8). All post-hoc tests were Bonferroni corrected.

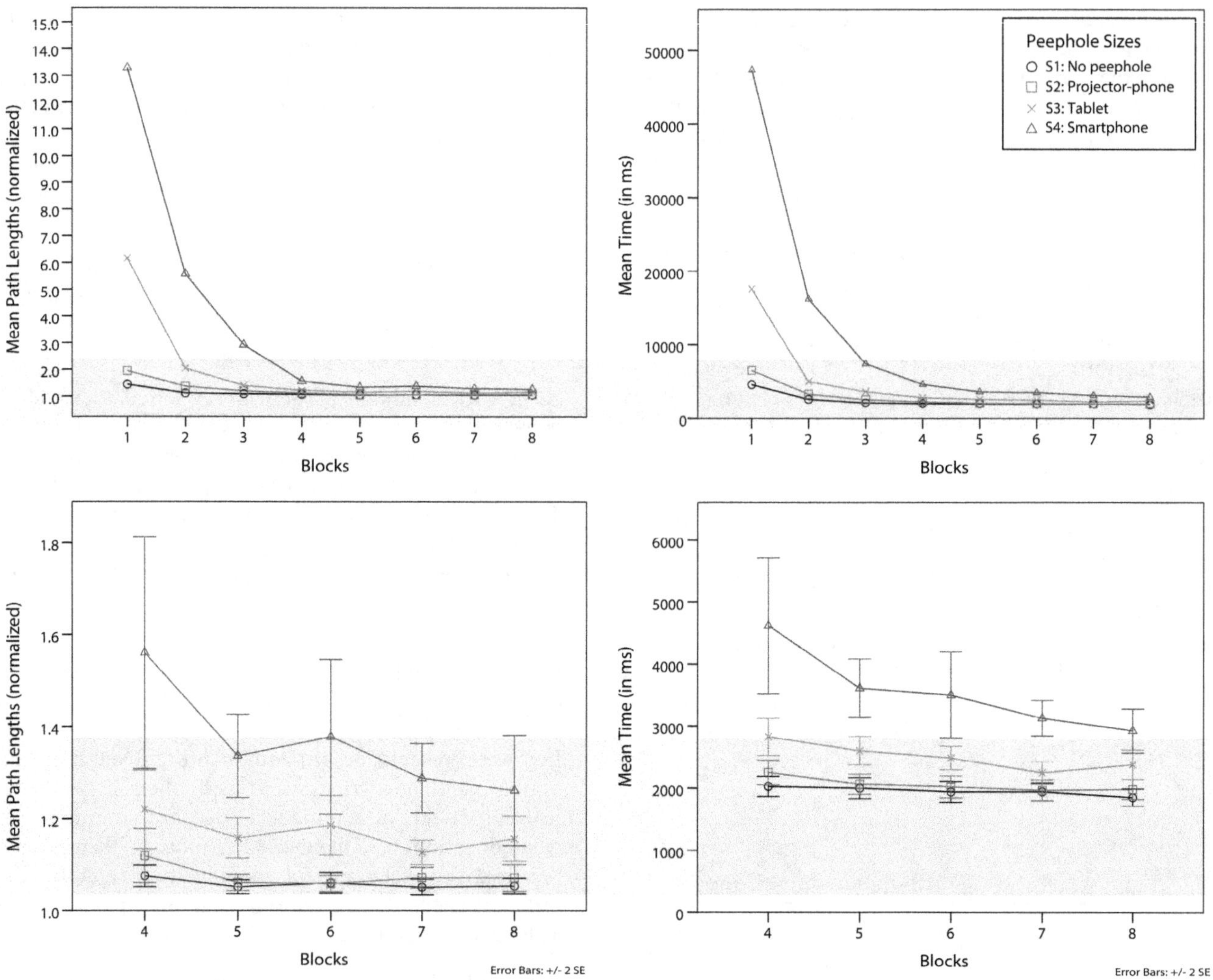

Figure 5. Plots of mean paths lengths and mean times.

		B1	B2	B3	B4	B5	B6	B7	B8	B1-B4	B5-B8	B1-B8
S1 vs. S2	Length	1.000	1.000	1.000	1.000	1.000	1.000	1.000	1.000	1.000	1.000	1.000
	Time	1.000	1.000	1.000	1.000	1.000	1.000	1.000	1.000	1.000	1.000	1.000
S1 vs. S3	Length	**.023***	1.000	1.000	.862	**.023***	.330	**.043***	.133	**.017***	**.000***	**.008***
	Time	.061	1.000	1.000	.279	**.001***	.178	.054	**.004***	**.014***	**.000***	**.036***
S1 vs. S4	Length	**.000***	**.000***	**.008***	**.000***	**.000***	**.000***	**.000***	**.000***	**.000***	**.000***	**.000***
	Time	**.000***	**.000***	**.000***	**.000***	**.000***	**.000***	**.000***	**.000***	**.000***	**.000***	**.000***
S2 vs. S3	Length	.057	1.000	1.000	1.000	**.049***	.310	.291	.340	.064	**.000***	**.038***
	Time	.168	1.000	1.000	.904	**.004***	.379	.095	.057	.078	**.000***	.146
S2 vs. S4	Length	**.000***	**.001***	**.015***	**.000***	**.000***	**.000***	**.000***	**.000***	**.000***	**.000***	**.000***
	Time	**.000***	**.000***	**.000***	**.000***	**.000***	**.000***	**.000***	**.000***	**.000***	**.000***	**.000***
S3 vs. S4	Length	**.000***	**.008***	**.045***	**.004***	**.000***	**.020***	**.000***	.119	**.000***	**.000***	**.000***
	Time	**.000***	**.000***	**.010***	**.000***	**.000***	**.000***	**.000***	**.002***	**.000***	**.000***	**.000***

Table 1. The *p*-values (* means significant) for pairwise comparisons of lengths and times.

Results NASA-TLX Task Load Index

The mean results of the NASA-TLX questionnaire about task load are S1: 13.07, S2: 18.49, S3: 25.51, and S4: 47.19 (scale from 0 to 100). An ANOVA with repeated measures revealed a statistically significant main effect of the subjective workload ratings on the peephole sizes, GGc: $F_{1.82,27.23} = 37.642$, $p < .001$, *partial* $\eta^2 = .715$. Pairwise comparisons (Bonferroni corrected) of subjective workload of peephole sizes revealed statistically significant differences between S1 vs. S3 ($p < .001$), S1 vs. S4 ($p < .001$), S2 vs. S4 ($p < .001$), and S3 vs. S4 ($p < .001$). All other comparisons were not significant. The individual subscales of NASA-TLX such as mental demand or physical demand are shown in Figure 6.

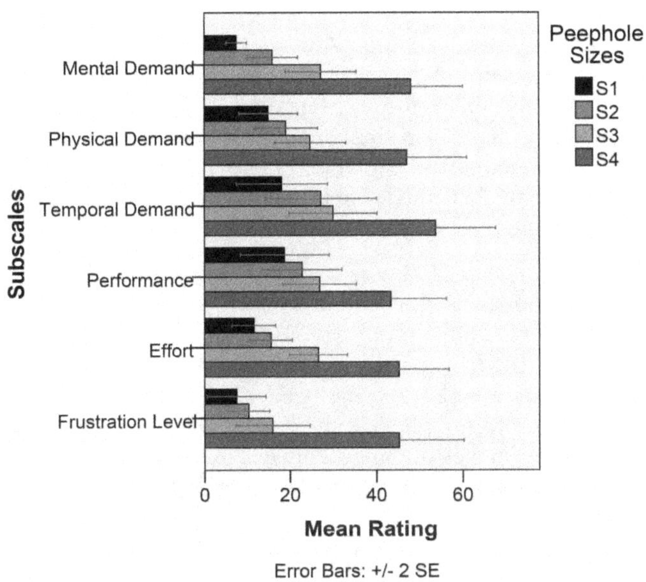

Figure 6. Subscales of the NASA-TLX questionnaire.

Results Map Recognition

The results of the map recognition task revealed the following error rates for each peephole size: S1: 5 errors (31.25%), S2: 4 errors (25%), S3: 4 errors (25%), and S4: 4 errors (25%). Since there are only marginal differences in the error rates for the different peephole sizes, we have not used the error rates in the further data analysis.

DISCUSSION

Resonating with our previous assumption about an initial *learning phase* followed by a *navigation phase*, the first blocks in Figure 5 (e.g. blocks 1-4) show very long path lengths and navigation times with great standard deviations. During these first blocks users still had to scan the information space to memorize locations and to build up a spatial mental representation of the map. This *learning phase* initially lead to a rapid fall of path lengths and times until the values stabilized and stayed roughly constant which indicates the beginning of the *navigation phase*. In the following, we discuss both phases in greater detail.

Evidence for a Learning Phase

Noticeable improvements in peephole navigation occurred during blocks 1-4. This can be explained by users' improving mental spatial representation of the map that they achieved by systematically scanning the map for targets with the peephole. The nature of this initial scanning process becomes evident when plotting peephole movements. Figure 7 shows two examples of such a scanning process by participant 1 for B1 to B4 using the tablet-sized peephole S3 (top) and the smartphone-sized peephole S4 (bottom). The blue dots show the movement of the peephole's anchor point on the screen. The red dots show the locations of the navigation targets. The figure illustrates characteristic scanning patterns with vertical scanning movements that are repeated horizontally or vice versa. They also visualize the potential benefit of a greater peephole size during this *learning phase*. Since a greater peephole reveals more visual information, it is possible to choose larger distances between the repeated movements, thus shortening the overall scanning path.

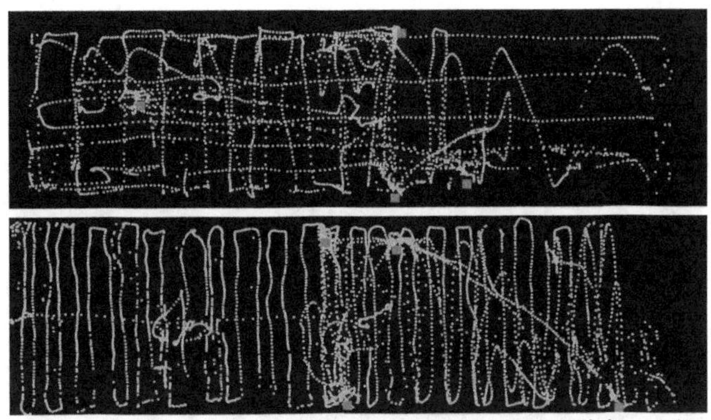

Figure 7. Example of peephole movement by participant 1 during B1 to B4 with S3 (top) and S4 (bottom).

A 4×4 (peephole size × repetition) ANOVA with repeated measures revealed a statistically significant main effect of peephole size in terms of travelled path lengths, GGc: $F_{1.12,16.82} = 26.79$, $p < .001$, *partial* $\eta^2 = .641$, as well as a significant effect of repetition, $F_{1.97,29.49} = 30.69$, $p < .001$, *partial* $\eta^2 = .672$. There was also an interaction between peephole size and repetition, GGc: $F_{2.39,35.91} = 13.69$, $p < .001$, *partial* $\eta^2 = .477$. This indicates that the effects of peephole size on path lengths and navigation time is depended on the number of repetitions. We consider this as evidence of a learning process during B1 to B4. This is further supported by the fact that the same interaction effect cannot be found in the assumed *navigation phase* during B5 to B8 as we discuss below.

Moreover, the results show that a larger peephole facilitates this learning process and leads to better initial performance. The initial performance in B1 for path length ($M_{S1} = 1.44$ with SE = .105, $M_{S2} = 1.94$ with SE = .152, $M_{S3} = 6.16$ with SE = .736, $M_{S4} = 13.29$ with SE = 2.096) shows significant differences between and the smartphone-sized peephole (S4) and all other peephole sizes (S1, S2, S3). Clearly, the smartphone-sized peephole was outperformed (Table 1, column B1). Interestingly, there are no significant differences for S1 vs. S2 and S2 vs. S3, a fact that we discuss below in a dedicated section on peephole sizes.

Looking at the entire learning phase B1-B4 reveals similar characteristics: The mean path lengths for B1-B4 (M_{S1} = 1.18 with SE = .031, M_{S2} = 1.41 with SE = .063, M_{S3} = 2.70 with SE = .240, M_{S4} = 5.84 with SE = .853) have significant differences between S1, S2, and S3 vs. the smartphone size S4, which is clearly outperformed again (Table 1, column B1-4). There are no significant differences for S1 vs. S2 and S2 vs. S3.

Evidence for a Navigation Phase

The different nature of the *navigation phase* compared to the *learning phase* becomes immediately visible when looking at the plots of peephole movement in Figure 8 that show the same tasks as Figure 7 but this time for B5 to B8. The navigation trajectories show direct navigation movements between the targets without scanning. This illustrates how participants successfully applied their mental spatial representation and proprioceptive cues of the physical peephole navigation to efficiently move between invisible but known targets without a need for scanning.

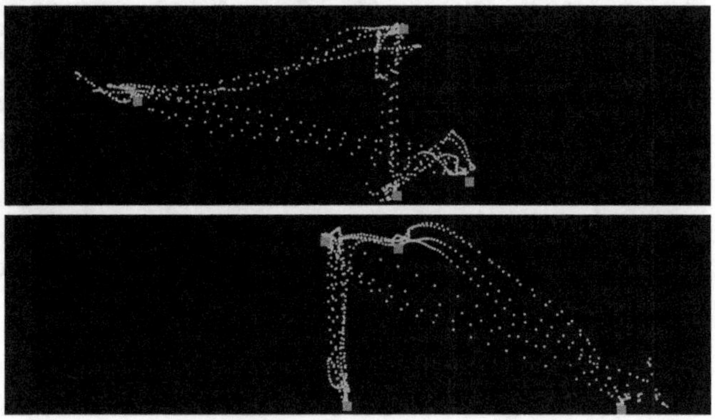

Figure 8. Example of peephole movement by participant 1 during B5 to B8 with S3 (top) and S4 (bottom).

As discussed, the navigation performance in terms of path lengths and navigation time substantially improved between B1 and B5. After this, as is visible in the plots of mean path lengths and mean time for B4-B8 in Figure 5, the navigation performance in B5, B6, B7, and B8 stayed almost constant, however at different levels depending on the peephole size. These results indicate gradual transition from the end of the *learning phase* to the beginning of the *navigation phase*.

A statistical indicator for the end of the learning phase and the beginning of the navigation phase is the absence of the interaction between peephole size and repetition that we witnessed for B1-B4: A 4×4 (peephole size × repetition) ANOVA with repeated measures on B5-B8 revealed a statistically significant main effect of peephole size on travelled path lengths, GGc: $F_{1.27,19.10}$ = 27.11, $p < .001$, *partial* η^2 = .644 but no difference for the repetition, $F_{1.88,28.21}$ = 1.87, p = .175, *partial* $\eta 2$ = .111. As stated above, there was no interaction between peephole size and repetition, GGc: $F_{3.47,51.98}$ = 1.04, p = .388, *partial* $\eta 2$ = .065. Also the small standard deviations in Figure 5 allow the conclusion that participants reached almost constant performance levels for the different peephole sizes.

A post-hoc pairwise comparison with Bonferroni corrections of peephole sizes for B5-B8 (Table 1) revealed statistically significant differences between peephole sizes S2 vs. S3, S2 vs. S4, and S3 vs. S4. However, it did not show a difference for the comparison of S1 vs. S2. The mean values for path lengths for B5-B8 are M_{S1}= 1.05 (SE = .006) for S1, M_{S2} = 1.07 (SE = .006) for S2, M_{S3} = 1.16 (SE = .017) for S3, and M_{S4} = 1.32 (SE = .043) for S4.

Peephole Sizes: Is Bigger Always Better?

Up to now, the results were largely reflecting our initial assumptions about the existence of a learning phase, a navigation phase, and the benefits of larger peepholes that we formulated above. However, there are some unexpected observations that shed light on the question, "Is bigger always better?"

Control Condition (S1) vs. Projector Phone-Size (S2)

Table 1 shows that for all blocks in B1-B8, each individual block, the learning phase (B1-B4), and navigation phase (B5-B8), there was no significant difference between control condition S1 and the peephole S2. This is clearly a case for projector phones since there were no significant differences in performance between S2 and a 120″ large screen without any peephole. Also the NASA-TLX questionnaires did not report a significantly different workload with S2 compared to S1. Therefore, when comparing S1 vs. S2, bigger is not better. To expand this conclusion, peephole sizes greater than a projector phone do not pay off in terms of navigation performance or task load when used in a map navigation scenario that is similar to our experiment.

However, in our study, S2's size of 54.7″ covers a greater field of view than might be typical in real-world uses of projector phones. Participants stood within a close range (approx. 40 cm) to the screen resulting in covering approx. 127° of the users' typical field of view. In [9], users stood at a distance of 200 cm, so that the projection covered approx. 33.4° of the users' field of view. Interestingly, in the light of this size of S2 in our study, it is therefore even more surprising that the tablet-sized peephole S3 achieved an almost comparable performance as we discuss in the following.

Projector Phone-Size (S2) vs. Tablet-Size (S3)

The comparison of the projector phone condition S2 vs. the tablet condition S3 in Table 1 reveals that there are no significant differences in both devices except for B5, B5-8 (*navigation phase*), and, as a result, also for the overall performance B1-B8. S2 outperforms S3 only during the *navigation phase*, but not during the *learning phase*. A comparison of the absolute differences in terms of path lengths and times during the navigation phase shows an 8.4% longer navigation path length and 419 ms longer navigation time per target.

While statistically significant, these differences have to be seen in relation to the afore-mentioned disadvantages and practicalities of mobile projections vs. tablets. In our interpretation, the only moderately increased performance during *navigation phase* cannot outweigh the many disadvantages of mobile projection and the many advantages of using off-the-shelf tablets. Furthermore, there are no significant differences between S2 and S3 in terms of the reported subjective workload. By this, we do not imply that a tablet-sized peephole should be considered as an equivalent to a projector-phone-sized peephole in every respect. However, designers of peephole navigation systems should carefully balance the specifics of both technologies. We therefore suggest for use cases that are similar to our experiment that a tablet-sized peephole is more suitable than a larger one.

Smartphone-Size (S4)

Our results clearly show that a peephole with the size of a smartphone is outperformed by all other peephole sizes. This is particularly interesting with respect to tablets which are natural competitors to smartphones in peephole navigation scenarios due to their great availability, popularity, price, and mobility. The tablet-size S3 outperforms S4 in blocks B1 to B7, during the learning phase B1-B4, the navigation phase B5-B8, and the overall performance B1-B8. This is also reflected in the report of subjective workload from the NASA-TLX questionnaires, which is 82% higher for S4 than for S3 and also higher in all subscales (MD = 72%, PD = 85%, TD = 76%, P = 53%, E = 69%, and F = 75%).

These findings about better navigation performance and less workload with S3 compared to S4 (13.8% in path lengths and 864 ms in time) could be helpful for revisiting the study of Pahud et al. [13]. Replacing the 4.3″ device in their study with a tablet should lead to better navigation performance and reduced task load in their physical navigation condition. This could possibly lead to different results for their comparison between virtual and physical navigation. These findings are also relevant for Kaufmann and Ahlström's study of spatial memory and map navigation performance with projector phones vs. a smartphone [9]. It would be interesting to see if the reported significant differences in spatial memory still exist when replacing the smartphone with a tablet-sized peephole.

Limitations of the Study

As this comparative study of the effect of peephole size on navigation performance is the first of its kind, it has some limitations that we are aware of and that could be addressed in future work.

First, controlling device-specific properties such as weight or resolution and only using peephole size as independent variable increases the internal validity but also decreases the external validity. It would be interesting to repeat the experiment using real-world physical devices to see if the same results can be replicated or if the differences in device-specific properties such as resolution, weight, or latency outweigh differences in peephole size.

Second, in future studies, the peephole size S2 in the projector phone condition should be reduced to reflect more realistic scenarios like in Kaufmann and Ahlström [9] where the peephole covers only a much smaller field of view. However, it is very likely that such an adjustment would have led to an even greater similarity between our conditions S2 and S3, thus further strengthening our recommendation of tablet-sized peepholes over projector phone-sized peepholes for many scenarios.

Third, compared to the size of S3 and S4, we used a large map and a large physical navigation space with a 1:1 control-display ratio. This could have penalized S3 and S4 and been in favor of S1 and S2. However, similar to [14], our intention was to employ frequent physical navigation and strong proprioceptive cues to support users' spatial memory. The absolute values for the NASA-TLX (all below 50 on a scale to 100) and the absence of significant differences between task loads of S2 vs. S3 reflect that the tasks were still solvable by the users even with a comparably small, tablet-sized display.

CONCLUSION

With this study of peephole map navigation, we wanted to find a "sweet spot" between peephole size and both user navigation performance and user task load. By simulating different peephole sizes from 4″ (smartphone size) up to 120″ (control condition), we found that a smartphone-sized peephole is outperformed by all other sizes and that larger peepholes significantly improve learning speed, navigation speed, and reduce task load. However, this added benefit diminishes with growing sizes, and peephole sizes greater than a projector phone do not pay off in terms of navigation performance or task load anymore. Our data shows that a relatively small, tablet-sized peephole can serve as a "sweet spot" in terms of both user navigation performance and user task load.

We have also shown that for understanding the subtleties of real-world map navigation with dynamic peepholes, existing models of peephole target acquisition based on Fitts' law [3,7,8,18] are only a first step. They were not intended to model different phases of map navigation such as a *learning phase* and a *navigation phase* whose existence we have shown using a statistical and visual analysis of the users' navigation paths in our study. By this, we have contributed to the better understanding of the subtleties of peephole navigation as motivated by Pahud et al. in [13].

ACKNOWLEDGMENTS
This work was partially supported by DFG Research Training Group GK-1042 and by the Ministry for Science, Research, and Art Baden-Wurttemberg under the project Blended Library.

REFERENCES
1. Ball, R. and North, C. The effects of peripheral vision and physical navigation on large scale visualization. *In Proc. of GI '08*, Canadian Information Processing Society (2008), 9–16.
2. Cao, X. and Balakrishnan, R. Interacting with dynamically defined information spaces using a handheld projector and a pen. *In Proc. of UIST '06*, ACM Press (2006), 225–234.
3. Cao, X., Li, J.J., and Balakrishnan, R. Peephole Pointing: Modeling Acquisition of Dynamically Revealed Targets. *In Proc. of CHI '08*, ACM Press (2008), 1699–1708.
4. Fitzmaurice, G.W. Situated information spaces and spatially aware palmtop computers. *Communications of the ACM 36*, 7 (1993), 39–49.
5. Hart, S. and Staveland, L. Development of NASA-TLX (Task Load Index): Results of empirical and theoretical research. *Human mental workload*, North Holland Press (1988).
6. Henze, N. and Boll, S. Evaluation of an off-screen visualization for magic lens and dynamic peephole interfaces. *In Proc. of MobileHCI '10*, ACM Press (2010), 191–194.
7. Huber, J., Steimle, J., and Mühlhäuser, M. A model of embodied dynamic peephole pointing for hidden targets. *In Proc. of BCS-HCI '11*, British Computer Society (2011), 315–320.
8. Kaufmann, B. and Ahlström, D. Revisiting Peephole Pointing: A Study of Target Acquisition with a Handheld Projector. *In Proc. of MobileHCI '12*, ACM Press (2012), 211–220.
9. Kaufmann, B. and Ahlström, D. Studying spatial memory and map navigation performance on projector phones with peephole interaction. *In Proc. of CHI '13*, ACM Press (2013), 3173–3176.
10. Löchtefeld, M., Gehring, S., and Krüger, A. Distributed User Interfaces for Projector Phones. In J.A. Gallud, R. Tesoriero and V.M.R. Penichet, eds., *Distributed User Interfaces: Designing Interfaces for the Distributed Ecosystem*. Springer London, London, 2011, 113–123.
11. Mehra, S., Werkhoven, P., and Worring, M. Navigating on Handheld Displays: Dynamic versus Static Peephole Navigation. *ACM Transactions on Computer-Human Interaction 13*, 4 (2006), 448–457.
12. Morrison, A., Oulasvirta, A., Peltonen, P., et al. Like bees around the hive: a comparative study of a mobile augmented reality map. *In Proc. of CHI '09*, ACM Press (2009), 1889–1898.
13. Pahud, M., Hinckley, K., Iqbal, S., Sellen, A., and Buxton, B. Toward Compound Navigation Tasks on Mobiles via Spatial Manipulation. *In Proc. of MobileHCI '13*, ACM Press (2013), 113–122.
14. Rädle, R., Jetter, H.-C., Butscher, S., and Reiterer, H. The effect of egocentric body movements on users' navigation performance and spatial memory in zoomable user interfaces. *In Proc. of ITS '13*, ACM Press (2013), 23–32.
15. Rapp, S., Michelitsch, G., Osen, M., et al. Spotlight Navigation: Interaction with a handheld projection device (Video paper). *In Proc. of Pervasive '04*, (2004).
16. Rohs, M. and Essl, G. Which one is better?: information navigation techniques for spatially aware handheld displays. *In Proc. of ICMI '06*, ACM Press (2006), 100–107.
17. Rohs, M., Oulasvirta, A., and Suomalainen, T. Interaction with magic lenses: real-world validation of a Fitts' Law model. *In Proc. of CHI '11*, ACM Press (2011), 2725–2728.
18. Rohs, M. and Oulasvirta, A. Target acquisition with camera phones when used as magic lenses. *Proceeding of the twenty-sixth annual CHI conference on Human factors in computing systems - CHI '08*, ACM Press (2008), 1409–1418.
19. Rohs, M., Schöning, J., Raubal, M., Essl, G., and Krüger, A. Map Navigation with Mobile Devices: Virtual versus Physical Movement with and without Visual Context Michael. *In Proc. of ICMI '07*, ACM Press (2007), 146–153.
20. Rukzio, E., Holleis, P., and Gellersen, H. Personal Projectors for Pervasive Computing. *IEEE Pervasive Computing 11*, 2 (2012), 30–37.
21. Spindler, M., Stellmach, S., and Dachselt, R. PaperLens: Advanced Magic Lens Interaction Above the Tabletop. *In Proc. of ITS '09*, ACM Press (2009), 69–76.
22. Tsang, M., Fitzmaurice, G.W., Kurtenbach, G., Khan, A., and Buxton, B. Boom Chameleon: Simultaneous capture of 3D viewpoint, voice and gesture annotations on a spatially-aware display. *In Proc. of UIST '02*, ACM Press (2002), 111–120.
23. Yee, K. Peephole displays: pen interaction on spatially aware handheld computers. *In Proc. of CHI '03*, ACM Press (2003), 1–8.

Mechanical Force Redistribution: Enabling Seamless, Large-Format, High-Accuracy Surface Interaction

Alex Grau, Charles Hendee, John-Ross Rizzo
Tactonic Technologies, LLC
{alexgrau, chendee, johnrossrizzo}@gmail.com

Ken Perlin
NYU Media Research Laboratory
perlin@cs.nyu.edu

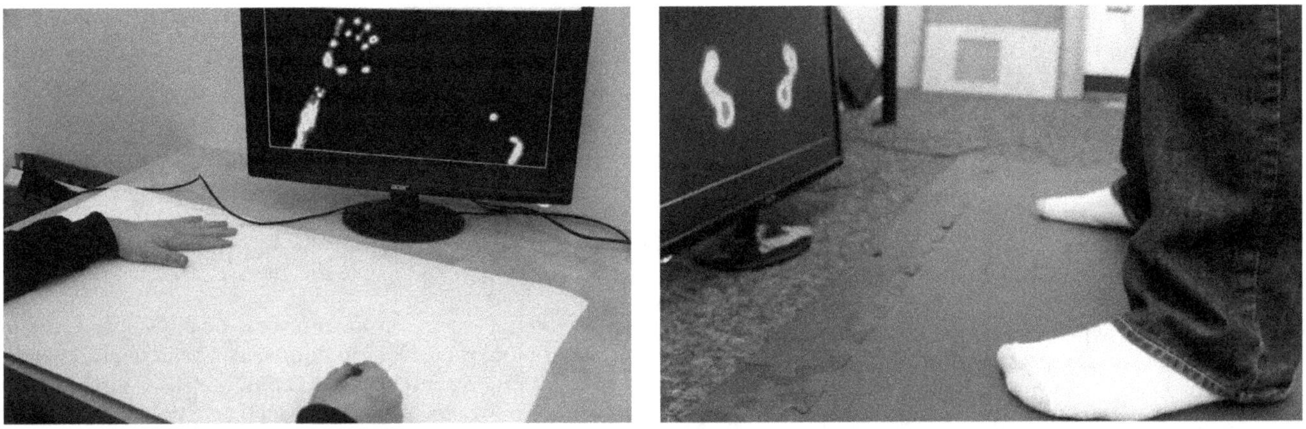

Figure 1. Mechanical Force Redistribution (MFR) (a) hand tiles and (b) floor tiles. MFR creates an anti-aliased image of all forces applied to a surface. In the visualization of the anti-aliased forces, a Gaussian blur is applied to demonstrate the high positional accuracy of an MFR tile.

ABSTRACT

We present Mechanical Force Redistribution (MFR): a method of sensing which creates an anti-aliased image of forces applied to a surface. This technique mechanically focuses the force from a surface onto adjacent discrete *forcels* (force sensing cells) by way of protrusions (small bumps or pegs), allowing for high-accuracy interpolation between adjacent discrete forcels. MFR works with any force transducing technique or material, including force variable resistive inks, piezoelectric materials and capacitive force plates. MFR sensors can be tiled such that the signal is continuous across contiguous tiles. By minimizing active materials and computational complexity, MFR makes large-format interactive walls, collaborative tabletops and high-resolution floor tiles possible and economically feasible.

ACM Classification Keywords

H.5.2 Information interfaces and presentation: Input devices and strategies

Author Keywords

Mechanical Force Redistribution; Input Device; Sensor; Pressure; Force; Large Format; Tabletop; Floors; Medical

CHI 2014, April 26–May 1, 2014, Toronto, Ontario, Canada.

ACM 978-1-4503-2473-1/14/04..$15.00.
http://dx.doi.org/10.1145/2556288.2557172

INTRODUCTION

Multi-touch sensors have become ubiquitous on small-format surface interaction devices such as smart phones and tablets. Recently, medium-format multi-touch has become more commonplace for larger capacitive and infrared touch screens [24, 14].

Large format surface interaction, on the other hand, still remains an expensive and fractured market. A variety of technologies exist for large-format interaction, each having its own strengths and weaknesses. None of these technologies, however, offer a seamless, high-accuracy, thin surface format for multi-touch human-computer interaction at arbitrarily large scales for tables, walls and floors.

We present a new method of sensing, Mechanical Force Redistribution (MFR), which creates an anti-aliased image of forces applied to a surface. We demonstrate MFR with two prototype sensors: a more traditional HCI wall/tabletop interaction sensor (hand based interaction) and a coarser resolution large format sensor for floor based interaction.

MFR contributes beyond previous work by providing a technology that is capable of inexpensively scaling-up (at a linear price curve relative to area), and of producing a seamless signal between contiguous sensor tiles to support arbitrarily large form factors. MFR tiles can be integrated with projectors to enable force sensitive electronic whiteboards, and with flexible OLEDs to enable durable displays with an opaque sensor. MFR tiles also represent an objective tool to be leveraged in the medical space as a sensing device for both clinical research and clinical testing.

MECHANICAL FORCE REDISTRIBUTION

Mechanical Force Redistribution (MFR) is a process by which forces applied to an outer surface are spread or distributed to protrusions (small bumps or pegs) in contact with discrete forcels (force sensing cells). The result is an anti-aliased image of pressure that can be used to perform highly accurate interactions with a low-density grid.

A key feature of MFR is that a signal is produced by the sensor even when the applied force lies completely between adjacent forcels. Applied force is redistributed as follows: (1) a small protrusion is positioned directly on top of each forcel, and (2) a semi-rigid sheet or piecewise rigid plate is placed atop these protrusions. This arrangement ensures that there is little signal lost relative to the forces applied to the surface of the sensor, and that the signal is continuous and smoothly interpolated even when forces are widely spaced.

Figure 3 shows mechanical force redistribution (shown here in one dimension, rather than two). Force imparted to the outermost layer is distributed to the protrusions and detected at each adjacent forcel. The proportion of the force imparted to each protrusion is dependent on the distance from each adjacent protrusion and is represented in the figure by the height of the corresponding black rectangle.

Figure 2 shows mechanical force redistribution over two dimensions, where the size of the black circles in the smaller image in the upper left-hand corner are proportional to the force being applied to the corresponding forcel. We can obtain, via bilinear interpolation of these four force values, the centroid and force of the contact applied to the sensors surface, whether the force is applied with a finger, stylus, foot or object.

Note that, while our prototype MFR sensors can be very sensitive (able to detect as little as two grams of force), they do require a non-zero force to be applied, and thus by definition are not a zero-touch technology.

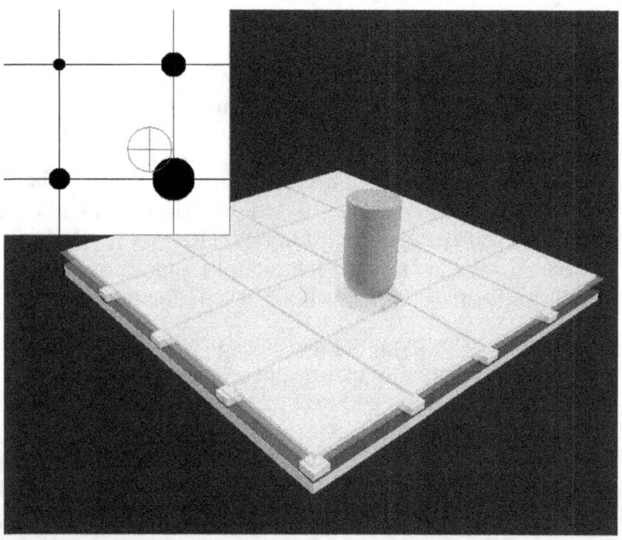

Figure 2. Mechanical Force Redistribution over two dimensions. The force imparted to each forcel decreases as distance from that forcel increases.

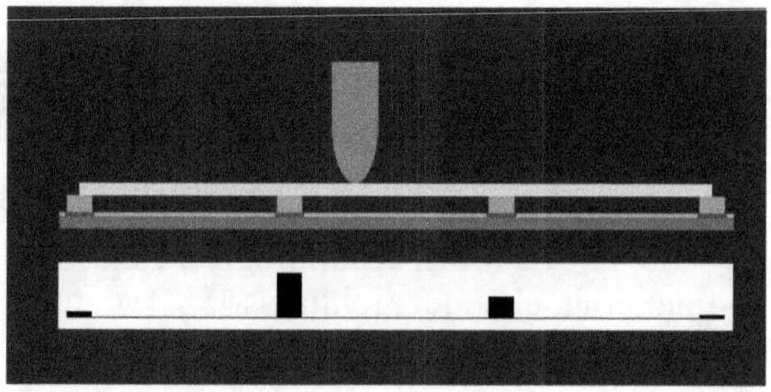

Figure 3. Mechanical Force Redistribution over one dimension.

RELATED WORK

Resistive

Resistive based force sensors have been in use for over thirty years [10, 13]. Four-wire resistive sensors were one of the earliest and most common uses of resistive sensing. These sensors, though common, generally detect only a single touch and are not durable.

In 1997, Paradiso et al. presented The Magic Carpet, a 60 square foot piezoelectric floor sensor paired with two doppler radar motion sensors [16]. The floor sensor utilizes a 16 x 32 grid of piezoelectric wires spaced at a 10 cm (4 inch) pitch to gain pressure/location data, while the Doppler radar estimates upper-body motion.

Z-Tiles, another project out of the MIT Media Lab, creates modular floor tiles that interlock to cover large areas[21]. Each tile contains 20 discrete hexagon-shaped force sensors with no interpolation.

The UnMousePad, which can also create a high-quality anti-aliased pressure image, utilizes Interpolated Force Sensitive Resistance (IFSR) [22]. The UnMousePad is made of two sheets of PET plastic with a flood coat of FSR ink printed over conductive trace wires. These sheets are brought into contact, forming a grid of intersecting trace wires. The flood coat of FSR allows for interpolation between the trace wires. However, UnMousePad sensors cannot seamlessly tile together without overlapping the sensor films. Also, the flood coat of FSR becomes cost prohibitive over large areas.

Synaptics ForcePad provides limited pressure sensing via bilinear interpolation of pressure sensed at each corner of a touch surface, but cannot distinguish the pressure of each finger touch and does not scale well to much larger sizes [23].

PyzoFlex is a pressure-sensing input device that is made from a ferroelectric material sensitive to pyroelectric and piezoelectric effects [20]. The discrete forcels demonstrated would work very well with MFR interpolation and would allow sensing between the large forcels.

Tekscan, a pressure imaging company, uses a high-density FSR grid to detect forces applied to the sensor [15]. Rangarajan et al. has done extensive research using FSR sensors from Tekscan. This research culminated in a 180-square-foot floor made from 96 sensors, called the AME floor [18]. The floor has a very high resolution and can maintain a frame rate of 43 frames-per-second despite its very high resolution. The

Sensor	Year	Sensor Type	Sensor Density (sensors/sq-in)	Signal Loss Gap (inch)	Point Tracking Resolution (dpi)	Interpolating	Pressure	Modular Tiles
MIT Magic Carpet	1997	Piezoeletric	0.06	4	N/A	No	Yes	No
Z-Tiles	2004	FSR	0.5	0	Low	No	Yes	Yes
SmartSkin	2002	Pro Cap	0.06	0	Low	Yes	No	No
Perceptive Pixel FTIR	2005	FTIR	645	0	Med	No	No[1]	No
UnMousePad/TouchCo	2009	IFSR	16	0	High	Yes	Yes	No
Multitoe, GravitySpace	2010	FTIR	645	0	Med	No	No[1]	No
AME Floor	2010	FSR	6.45	0.15	Low	No	Yes	Yes
PixelSense	2011	IR	740	0	Med	No	No	No
PyzoFlex	2012	Piezoelectric	2.8	0.2	N/A	No	Yes	No
MFR Hand Sensor	2013	FSR	16	0	High	Yes	Yes	Yes
MFR Foot Sensor	2013	FSR	1	0	High	Yes	Yes	Yes

Figure 4. A comparison of various surface interaction technologies. Note 1: While FTIR does not directly measure pressure, compliant surfaces can be used to approximate pressure.

sensors, however, have to overlap in order to prevent data loss on each edge, making installation difficult. Additionally, force data can be lost between adjoining forcels, even at this very high resolution. The overall cost for this system was quite prohibitive: each of its commercially available mats cost $600 or $333 per-square-foot for the sensor alone (i.e., control electronics not included) [18]. The first versions of the MRF floor tiles cost end users less than $250 per square foot, including housing and control electronics.

This highlights MFR's substantial price advantage: At large volumes MFR sensors would cost consumers on the order of $50 per square foot or less at a frame rate of over 400 fps.

Tekscan and PyzoFlex can approximate the continuous signal in MRF by making a finer pitched sensing grid and placing a sufficiently compliant material on the surface to spread the applied forces to sensing areas.

However, this interpolation method loses signal, as much of the force never makes its way to the sensors, especially when the force is applied by fine tipped styli. In addition, higher density sensors increase sensing and computation time, therefore reducing the maximum frame rate, assuming all other aspects of the system remain the same [18].

Capacitive

Most consumers are familiar with capacitive sensors, specifically projected capacitive, through their smart phones, tablets and laptop touch pads. Large format projected capacitive sensors, however, have been limited by the very high cost of scaling up this technology in area.

Perceptive Pixel, for instance, offers a 2 m (82 inch) projected capacitive touch screen [24]. Extending this as a single unit would be impractical for much larger areas, whereas if implemented as separate panels, touch interaction would not be seamless across units.

SmartSkin uses capacitive sensing in order to detect hand and finger gestures on and above a surface [19]. With their interactive tabletop capacitive sensing grid, which has a 10 cm pitch, they can interpolate between the signals and achieve 1cm accuracy (2.5 dpi).

Camera and Infrared

Camera and infrared systems have been the primary means of achieving large area sensors.

Han [12] used frustrated total internal reflection (FTIR) together with specialty compliant surfaces as the sensing element for large high-resolution Perceptive Pixel touch screens, and demonstrated possible interaction techniques [8]. The system, however, was bulky, heavy and required specialized installation.

As mentioned above, Perceptive Pixel switched its focus away from FTIR based sensors toward large format capacitive screens, which are flat and easily installed.

The Microsoft PixelSense, previously know as Surface, uses IR sensors to detect fingers, hands and objects on a touchscreen tabletop surface [9]. The screen, however, is designed to be a standalone unit. Now, with the Samsung PixelSense technology, multitouch is embedded into the display itself.

Due to its consumer level price and wide availability, the Microsoft Kinect has been both a commercial and academic success, making new forms of 3D and 2D interaction research possible. The Microsoft project LightSpace combines multiple depth cameras and projectors to allow interaction on and above a surface [25]. The gestures, however, are limited to low accuracy interactions due to the low resolution and low frame rate of the Kinect, as well as its inability to sense pressure.

Multi-toe [4] and GravitySpace [7] demonstrate possible user interfaces and uses of a high-resolution pressure-sensitive floor, through the use of an FTIR based floor sensor, which provides high resolution touch data in combination with low resolution optically sensed pressure sensing. Installation is expensive and requires an intensive set-up, which includes some relatively major reconstruction of the active sensing space and a 3.4 cm (1.34 inch) thick solid glass plate for mechanical support. In their discussion of future work, the authors of GravitySpace describe the need for a technology like the MFR sensing described in this paper: 'We expect sensing hardware of comparable size and resolution to soon be inexpensive and mass available, for example in the form of a large, thin, high-resolution pressure sensing foil.'

CONTRIBUTION

The primary contributions of this paper are to show the implementation of a method of sensing that is inherently inexpensive and scalable to arbitrary sizes, to delineate the advantages of pressure imaging sensors that can be scaled to large sizes, and to describe how the basic concept of MFR can be implemented to improve existing force sensing technologies.

MFR sensors provide several advantages over other interaction technologies. The following is a list of the benefits of the MFR technique that will be discussed later in depth.

- Continuous Signal: Due to its directed redistribution of applied force onto forcels, an MFR sensor contains no dead zones, even when forcels are spaced far apart.
- Seamless Tiling: MFR sensors can be tiled to cover arbitrarily large surfaces with a seamless signal, while maintaining accurate interpolation across contiguous tiles. In other surface sensor technologies a bezel or gap between sensors prevents continuous signal detection everywhere.
- Linear Cost by Area: Tiling removes the need for expensive large format touch panels, leading to a sensor cost that increases only linearly with area.
- Transducer Agnosticism: The MFR technique does not require a specific force sensing technology, technique, or material. For example, an MFR sensor can utilize Force Sensitive Resistive (FSR) ink, capacitive force sensing plates, or materials the exhibit piezoelectric properties.
- Design Flexibility: MFR sensors can be designed for a large variety of applications. The spacing between forcels can range from smaller than 1mm to larger than 100mm. Force detection can be tuned for specializing in finger/stylus sensing, foot sensing for gait disambiguation and tracking, or industrial sensing applications.
- Ease of Production: All of the layers used in an MFR sensor stack can be made using standard manufacturing techniques such as roll-to-roll screen printing, flexographic printing and injection molding [11]. The effort and investment required to move from prototype to mass production are relatively low, as standard equipment can be leveraged for low-cost manufacturing.
- Installation: MFR sensors are designed for mobility and rapid installation. Calibration upon installation is not required, and the tiles themselves are self-organizing. Tiles can be placed, mounted, or otherwise installed on any developable surface.
- No Occlusion: Unlike camera/vision based tracking systems, occlusion is not an issue. If a contact is applying force to the MFR sensor, then that contact will be detected.

MFR contributes beyond previous technologies (specifically the UnMousePad) in the following areas: sensitivity, tilability, linearity and price.

- Sensitivity: The mechanical focusing of force in MFR reduces the break force (minimum force required to produce signal), which is found in the UnMousePad and other flood-coat sensors. While the flood-coat sensors must overcome the break force over the entire area of a touch or object, MRF sensors focus the force of a touch onto a much smaller area, which greatly reduces the break force. Thus, MFR sensors can detect and track lighter touches and less dense objects.
- Tiling: While the UnMousePad can be tiled, this is done by overlapping multiple sensors, which is not a requirement for MFR sensors. Overlapping changes signal in overlapped areas and makes installation, repair, and replacement of modules difficult.
- Linearity: Due to the drone line construction of the UnMousePad, a pen tip between drone lines produces a weaker signal, therefore drawing a line across such sensors produces a small scallop effect, where force applied between the drones is lost to the substrate. With an MFR sensor, signal is continuous across its surface.
- Price: The UnMousePad and similar FSR based resistive sensors use large volumes of carbon based inks as their sensing areas and must be completely coated in these inks. As the required sensing area increases, the ink becomes cost prohibitive. Our MFR prototype sensors use very little FSR ink, minimizing material cost, which allows access to large area sensors for commercial and academic use. Where the UnMousePad requires 100% of the sensing area to be covered in FSR ink, the MFR floor sensors use about 5% of the sensing area. In addition to the reduced volume of FSR ink, the MFR require approximately 17% the conductive ink used for signal transmission, as MFR does not require the drone lines.

HARDWARE

An MFR sensor is made of several layers that, when combined into a single stack, create an anti-aliased image of pressure. The sensing array, protrusion layer, and redistribution layer make up the primary components of MFR and can also include a base substrate layer, touch layer, and/or housing.

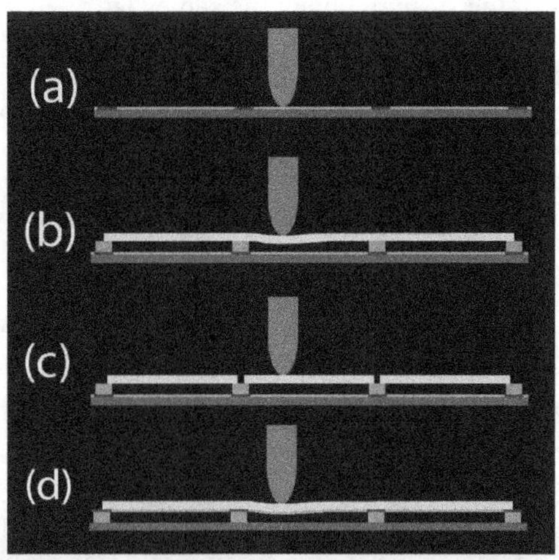

Figure 5. With (a) no protrusion or redistribution layer, signal is lost between forcels. With (b) semi-rigid redistribution layer, (c) piecewise rigid plate redistribution layer, or (d) semi-rigid redistribution layer with protrusions below the sensor film, force is sent to adjacent forcels.

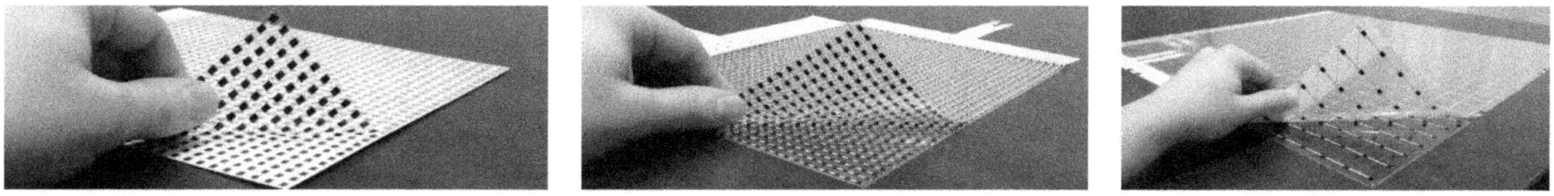

Figure 6. Sensing arrays for (a) a 0.2m by 0.2m pad, (b) an MFR hand tile, and (c) an MFR floor tile with FSR printed at the intersections.

Sensing Array

The sensing array is a grid of conductive electrodes with force sensing material located at each intersection. In our implementation, Force Sensitive Resistor (FSR) ink is printed on two sheets of mylar on top of printed silver traces at prescribed locations. These two sheets are brought into contact such that the FSR material on one sheet is facing the FSR on the other, forming a grid of forcels (Figure 6). While it is possible to deposit FSR over large areas, MFR sensors only need the FSR to cover the area under the base of each protrusion. Compared with the UnMousePad, this results in a significantly lower cost of materials. In the sensor in Figure 6 (a) FSR covers 14.5 percent of the area (2 mm by 3 mm pads), for our hand sensors (b), FSR covers 7.5 percent of the area (1.5 mm by 2 mm) and for our floor sensors (c), FSR covers 1.86 percent of the area (3 mm by 4 mm pads).

FSR ink is a variable resistive material in which electrical resistance decreases as greater force is applied. FSR inks are available in various formulations, each with a different force response curve. The FSR used for our hand tile sensors can detect forces between 2.5 g and 500 g, while the FSR formulation used for our larger floor sensors is tuned to respond to heavier forces (50g to 6kg). More information about the ink formulation can be found in the section called Force Response. Other force transducers, such as materials that exhibit piezoelectric properties and capacitive force sensors, can also be used in the sensing array [17].

If no other layers existed in the sensor, then force would only be detected at the forcels, not between them.

Protrusion Layer

The protrusion layer is made up of small bumps of material that are located at each forcel so that externally applied force is focused onto each forcel.

The protrusion layer can be above or below the sensing array, as seen in Figure 5, meaning the protrusion layer can be printed directly onto the outer sides of the sensing array sheet (Figure 7), merged with force redistribution layer (Figure 9), or made part of the base layer. In the case where the protrusions are merged with the base, the sensing array itself can act as the redistribution layer. Protrusions can be made of plastic, rubber, metal or any other rigid or semi-rigid material.

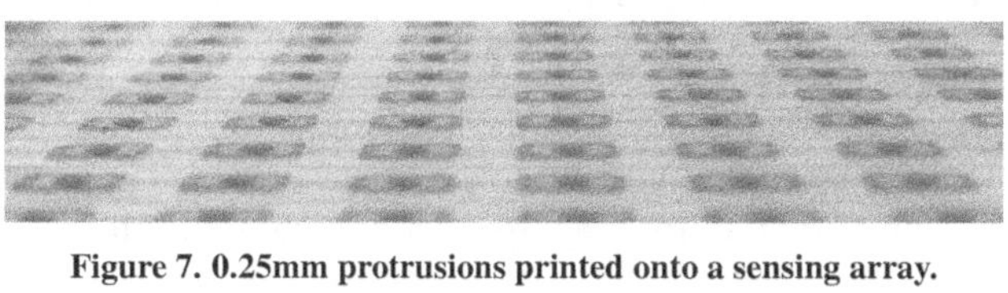

Figure 7. 0.25mm protrusions printed onto a sensing array.

For hand interaction sensors, we print 0.25mm (10mil) resin hemispherical dots directly onto the outer side of the sensing array sheet. For floor interaction and tracking sensors, we merge the protrusion layer with the redistribution layer via a 3D printed plastic part, which in mass production would be manufactured by injection molding.

Redistribution Layer

The redistribution layer distributes the force applied from the outer surface to adjacent protrusions. The redistribution layer can be made from either a semi-rigid sheet or a collection of piecewise rigid plates.

A semi-rigid sheet redistribution layer is chosen with a flexural modulus low enough that it distributes force to adjacent protrusions, yet high enough so that when forces are applied to the surface, the redistribution layer does not bend to touch the base layer [3]. If the flexural modulus were too high, then the force would be distributed evenly between all the forcels on the sensing array, thus the fidelity of the sensor would be lost. If the flexural modulus were too low, then the layer would touch the base and distribute little or no force to the protrusions (when not directly above them), and thus much of the force signal would be lost to the base substrate or surface. For hand based interaction MFR sensors, thin glass and plastics, such as polyester, have optimal properties as redistribution layers. For the MFR floor sensors, in which the forcel resolution is not as fine, materials with higher flexural moduli can be used.

To determine the minimum thickness of a material required, we use a flexural modulus equation where S is the spacing between traces (m), F is the maximum force desired for a point before some force can be lost to the base (N), D is the maximum deflection desired (m), E is the flexural modulus (Pa) and T is the optimal thickness of that material (m).

$$T > \sqrt[3]{\frac{(S^2 * F)}{8 * D * E}}$$

When working with our MFR hand tiles with 6.35 mm (0.25 inch) spacing, we want a 5N force to not flex beyond the height of the protrusions 0.25mm (10 mil) with a polyester paper with a flexural modulus of 2.75 GPa (2.75x10^9 Pa), which results in a thickness of at least 0.33mm (13 mil). With the same characteristics except with a thin glass redistribution layer (57 GPa), a thin glass at least 0.12 mm thick should be used.

The flexural modulus equation, however, only gives a lower-bound thickness. Often, thicker materials are used to give the appropriate durability and tactile experience. As a result, once the optimal material properties have been determined, we can use the following relative formula to adjust from old (A) to new (B) materials and trace spacings.

$$\frac{(E_A^{\frac{1}{3}} * T_A)}{(S_A^{\frac{2}{3}})} = \frac{(E_B^{\frac{1}{3}} * T_B)}{(S_B^{\frac{2}{3}})}$$

In addition to the flexural modulus, which is often not documented for a material, the Young's modulus of each material can be used in the relative formula due to a similar relationship of stress to strain. For instance, we obtain optimal mechanical interpolation with 0.375 mm (15 mil) polyester paper (with a Young's modulus of 4 GPa) for our hand tiles, which have 6.35 mm (0.25 inch) spacing. With this same 6.35 mm (0.25 inch) spacing, a thin glass with a Young's modulus of 73 GPa would produce an optimal signal at 0.142 mm (5.6 mil) thickness. We have tested 150 micron glass as the redistribution layer for the hand tiles, and have empirically confirmed that it provides a smooth interpolated signal.

When a collection of piecewise rigid plates is used as a redistribution layer, the corners of each plate are positioned so as to rest on a protrusion. Therefore, as a contact force moves along the plate, the force imparted to each forcel decreases as distance from that forcel increases. For manufacturing purposes, we merged the piecewise rigid plates with the protrusions to form a single 3D printed part.

Touch Layer

The touch layer is the outermost layer, upon which the user imparts the force. The touch layer is often merged with the redistribution layer in order to simplify the assembly process, but can be added as a separate material in order to provide a desired tactile sensation or aesthetic. For instance, users of an interactive whiteboard may prefer a continuous white matte surface for projection. In this instance, an opaque white polyester film can be placed over all the tiles to create the desired look and feel, without sacrificing interaction response. For floors, the touch layer can be carpet, rubber, linoleum or mosaic tiles.

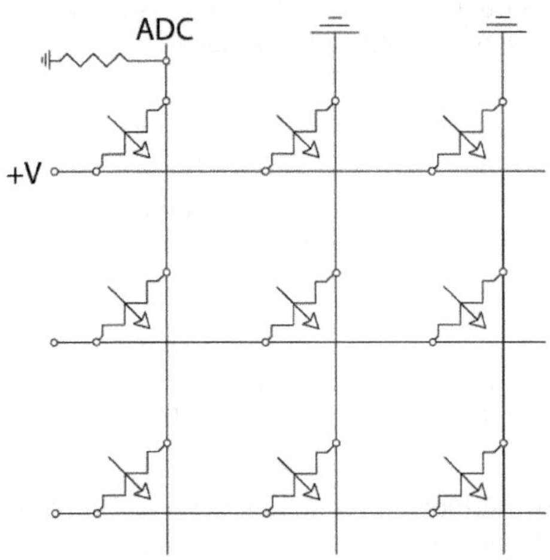

Figure 8. Circuit for scanning the top-left FSR forcel.

Figure 9. 3D printed piecewise rigid plates and protrusions.

Base Layer

The base layer is the substrate onto which the other layers of the sensor are adhered. The base layer is often a sheet of rigid material, but can also be flexible if the sensor is used to detect flexural forces or will be applied to a curved surface. The base layer can also be the table, wall or floor on which the sensor is placed. Our MFR sensor tiles use an acrylic substrate as the base layer.

Control Electronics

Currently the control electronics are mounted onto a PCB (printed circuit board), though, theoretically they could be mounted directly onto the sensing array film. We opted for a PCB so that we could use different formulations of the control electronics with the various sensors and vice versa. The primary control IC is a Microchip Technology, Inc. PIC24H microcontroller. We also used the Atmel ATxMega128A4u and ATSAM4LC4C to demonstrate that the sensors themselves are not dependent on a particular chipset.

Housing

The housing provides an enclosure for the printed circuit board (PCB) and allows for mechanical and electrical interconnection between tiles. In hand based interaction MFR tiles, we use a 3D printed part to mechanically interlock one tile to the next. A mezzanine connector is attached to this piece so that power, RS-485 communication and neighbor detection can all be passed from one tile to the next. For the floor / foot based interaction tiles, we separate the mechanical and electrical connections in order to prevent damage to the electrical connection from the higher forces. The physical connection is a 3D printed part and the electrical connection is a twisted pair jumper cable, which plugs into the main PCB.

CHARACTERISTICS

Scanning

Scanning techniques will vary depending on the force transducer used. The following is a description of how we scanned our FSR array. The sensing array is scanned one forcel at a time. Each output trace (e.g.,each row) is connected to a pin that either provides a positive supply voltage or can be set to high impedance. The input traces (e.g., the columns) are connected to pins that can direct to ground or to the Analog-Digital Converter (ADC) with a pull-down resistor to ground. Scanning begins by supplying one output trace with a positive voltage and reading into the ADC from one input trace. All other output traces will be set to high impedance and all other input traces will be disconnected from the ADC and set to ground. At this point, the ADC can determine the force value of the forcel located at the intersection between the corresponding output and the input traces, as seen in Figure 8. This process is repeated for every output and input trace combination until each MFR forcel has been visited. Once every forcel has been scanned, one anti-aliased force frame has been sensed and the frame data can be sent to the host computer. For our prototypes, we used the 12-bit ADC on our micrcontrollers. An external ADC can also be used to get faster and more accurate readings. Draining to ground on the input traces prevents false positives by shorting all the current down the input trace, which avoids the formation of alternate circuits to the ADC. This approach is similar to the UnMousePad but does not require draining on the output traces [22]. Our approach of draining to ground on the input traces can form alternate circuits to ground, which slightly lowers the detected voltage, but we have found the effects of this drain to be negligible for hand and foot interaction.

Communication

MFR tiles are wired together into inter-connected zones with one or more slave tiles and a master controller. The master controller can be located on a specified tile, called the master tile, or kept separate from the zone as a cable or box.

Our MFR tiles communicate with a single host computer over a 1Mbaud, full-duplex RS485 to USB bridge master controller. The host computer then communicates directly with each slave tile. In an alternate arrangement, a single master tile is connected to slave tiles and the master tile handles communication with the slave tiles and the host computer. When more than one zone is installed, the master tiles of each zone are networked to a host computer or server over an ethernet connection.

MFR hand tiles are connected via a series of flex cables and mezzanine connectors. For the MFR floor tiles, however, the distance between tiles becomes too long to use flex cables so twisted-pair jumper cables are used for communication.

Figure 10. Tracking touches on a 0.43 m by 0.84 m (17 inch by 33 inch) sensor made from six hand tiles.

Frame Rate

The maximum number of slaves per zone is dependent on the frame rate and resolution requirements for a particular application. With our MFR hand tiles, six slave tiles can be connected to one master tile to maintain 100 frames per second. With lower-resolution floor tiles, 14 floor tiles can be connected to one master tile to maintain 100 frames per second. The frame rate of a single MFR sensor tile is dependent on the number of microcontroller instructions per second (C), the ADC conversion time (T_{ADC}), the number of row (R) and column (C) traces, and communication time (T_{COM}). For a single tile, the frame rate equation is:

$$FPS = \frac{C_{IPS}}{(T_{ADC} * R * C)} + \frac{1}{T_{COM}}$$

For multiple tiles (N_T), optimal frame rate is achieved when the limiting factor is the communication time of all the tiles, not scanning time. In this case, by the time data is sent from the last tile, the first tile will be ready to send a new frame.

$$FPS = \frac{1}{T_{COM} * (N_T)}$$

Neighbor Detection

At startup, the tiles perform a depth first search (starting with the slave connected to the master controller or the master tile) to determine the topology of the tiles. Within the power and RS485 connection, there are an additional two wires that are used as flags for neighbor detection. One wire is connected to interrupt pins on each neighboring tile board and the other wire is connected to digital IO wires. Using these two pins, one tile can signal to its neighbor to report its direction relative to the previous tile. The neighboring tile is then given a temporary id number by the host or master and continues the depth first search until all the tiles have been reached.

Force Response

The force response of each MFR tile relies on the force transducer used at each forcel. For our MFR hand and floor tiles, we use two different formulations of FSR ink: a less resistive ink that detects lighter forces and a more resistive ink that detects heavier forces. The formulation of each ink determines the resistance as force is applied. A less resistive FSR formulation will quickly become less resistive as force is applied, which lowers the minimum force detection threshold. However, the less resistive ink approaches the minimum resistance of the ink quickly, which reduces the maximum force that can be detected. A more resistive ink formulation will slowly become less resistive, which increases the force detection threshold. Consequently, a more resistive ink will slowly approach the minimum resistance, which increases the maximum force force that can be detected. As stated in the sensing array section, the less resistive MFR hand tile ink can detect forces between 2.5 grams and 500 grams at each forcel. The more resistive MFR floor tiles can detect forces between 50 grams and 6 kg. The range of the force detection can be slightly widened by using alternate components and circuits but the resistance eventually gets too close to the vertical or horizontal resistance asymptote to distinguish signal from noise.

Tracking Resolution

There are two aspects to consider when discussing MFR resolution: touch tracking and touch disambiguation. Tracking resolution is the positional accuracy of a contact as it moves across the MFR sensor. To track a point, digital values from each forcel are converted to grams and the center of mass is equated from the active forcels to give the location and total force of the contact. We used a force gauge with 0.1 gram accuracy to determine the conversion equation for each forcel from ADC values to grams and the accuracy of the converted force values (Figures 11 and 12). The tracking accuracy (A_{Track}), therefore, can be determined with total force value (F) of a contact, the spacing between forcels (S), and the converted force accuracy (A_{Forcel}) of the sensor.

$$A_{Track} = \frac{A_{Forcel} * S}{F_{Total}}$$

For example, with 0.67 gram forcel accuracy, our MFR hand tiles should track a 20 gram contact with 0.21mm accuracy (121 DPI). We tested our hand tile tracking resolution with 20 gram point forces and tracked the point over straight and curved lines to determine the average accuracy of our hand tiles. The results yielded an average tracking resolution of 0.22mm (114 DPI). We conducted additional tests with 30 to 100 gram contacts to verify that the accuracy improved as greater forces were applied. The results were consistent with the equation above. With MFR floor tiles, the force conversion accuracy is poorer (4 gram accuracy) due to the more resistive FSR ink. Using more accurate ADCs, alternate scanning circuits, and less resistive FSR inks, we can improve the accuracy of gram conversion, which, in turn, improves the tracking resolution. Our future research will investigate each component to determine what alterations result in the best accuracy.

Disambiguation Resolution

Disambiguation resolution is the trace spacing required to distinguish two adjacent finger contacts. With the hand interaction sensors, there must be 6.35 mm (0.25 inch) between forcels to distinguish adjacent fingers. We ran an informal user study with a handful of colleagues to determine the comfortable distance between pressure peaks for adult users. The result was that a 6.35 mm (0.25 inch) trace spacing was sufficient to disambiguate between two adjacent fingers for all the adult participants. However, a 6.35mm (0.25 inch) forcel spacing may not be sufficient for children.

The large MFR sensors were designed for foot based interaction. Our goal with these sensors was to track people and objects over large areas. The primary features that we extract are foot shapes. Building upon previous work that had success with sparser sensing elements, 2.54 cm (1 inch) spacing was deemed sufficient for the foot sensors [21, 2].

Tile Size

The maximum size of each MFR tile is limited only by the manufacturing techniques available. Our hand sensors are 21.6 cm by 27.9cm (8.5 by 11 inches) and our floor sensors are 61cm by 61cm (24 by 24 inches) square, which neared the limit of the size that could be accommodated by the production equipment available to us. With different production equipment, sensor tiles could be made larger. A major factor in choosing the size of the tile is the processing available on the microcontroller and the resolution necessary for each tile. With our floor tiles, a 2.54 cm (1 inch) spacing means there are 576 forcels in a 24 by 24 grid. With the hand tiles, the 6.35 mm (0.25 inch) spacing means there are 1496 forcels in a 34 by 44 grid. As a result, even though a floor tile covers six times the area of a hand tile, the floor tile requires only a third of the scanning time.

Seamless Tiling

With MFR sensors, seamless pressure interpolation across tiles is possible by interlocking the redistribution layers from one tile to the next. With a semi-rigid mechanical layer, either one large touch layer is used to cover all the tiles, or else the mechanical layers are linked. With a collection of piecewise rigid plates, a row and column of plates hangs over one tile and reaches onto the next, continuing the force redistribution.

Thickness

The minimum thickness of the MFR sensor is dependent on the trace wire spacing and the technique used to spread the force. In our hand MFR sensors with 6.35mm (0.25 inch) trace wire spacing, 0.25 mm (10 mil) protrusions are printed on a 0.3 mm (12 mil) sensor with a 0.375 mm (15 mil) polyester paper as a redistribution layer, resulting in a total thickness of 0.925 mm (37 mil) for the three main layers. In our floor tiles, the sensor is 0.5 mm (20 mil) thick, and the redistribution and protrusion layers are merged into a single part that is 3.8 mm (0.150 inch) thick, bringing the total thickness to 4.3mm (170 mil).

APPLICATIONS

MFR sensors can be used in a variety of applications for use on tables, walls, floors and other large surfaces. Our initial research explored the opportunities available for MFR in interactive displays and medical floor tiles.

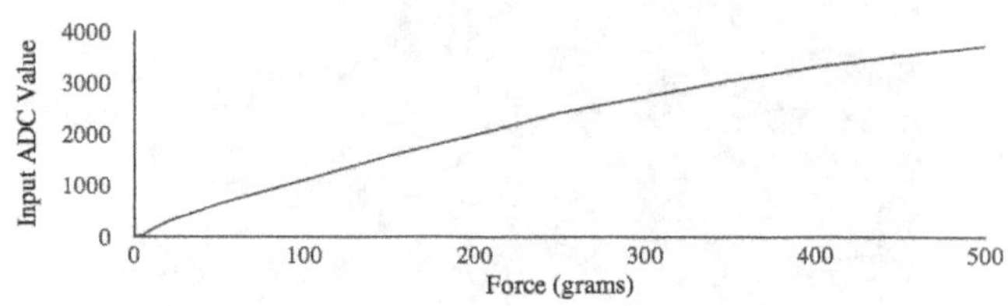

Figure 11. MFR hand tile force and ADC values. Forces between 2.5 grams and 500 grams were measured using a force gauge.

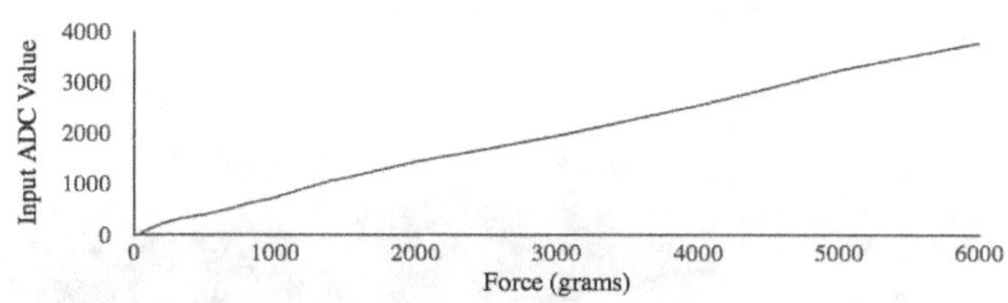

Figure 12. MFR floor tile force and ADC values. Forces between 50 grams and 6 kg were measured using a force gauge.

Figure 13. Multiple people on a 1.2m by 3.65m (48 inch by 144 inch) MFR floor made from twelve floor tiles with carpet.

Interactive Displays

MFR sensors can be made somewhat transparent, but the requisite materials for both sensing components and the mechanical interpolation layer are significantly higher in cost, particularly in larger form factors. For this reason, we have focused on display scenarios in which the display goes on top of an opaque sensor. Two display modalities in particular are a very good fit for MFR sensors: front projection and flexible Organic Light Emitting Diodes (OLEDs).

Front projection, in particular the use of an ultra short throw projector, such as the Ricoh WX4130N, is an attractive solution for very large form factors, such as when an MFR sensor array is used as the sensing component of an electronic whiteboard.

For non-flat interaction surfaces, such as an automobile dashboard control panel, OLEDs work well as a display that goes on top of the MFR sensor. Because OLEDs can be made flexible and relatively transparent to force, flexible OLEDs do not interfere with force input to an MFR sensor mounted behind the display.

Also, the combination of OLEDs and MFR sensors allows for a flexible, and therefore not fragile, hand-held interaction device. Such a device can be dropped from a significant height without suffering damage.

Medical Floor Tiles

Currently, floor pressure sensors as they are applied to the medical space are limited to low resolution load cells or very high resolution, expensive sensors [18, 21, 2], both requiring intensive installation processes. In contrast, MFR sensors are modular and can be integrated easily into single, large, highly accurate and reliable sensing areas, essential elements for clinical validation.

In fact, Richard Brand's criteria for biomechanical measures include the following nine characteristics: reproducible, stable, accurate, appropriately validated, capable of distinguishing normal and abnormal, must not alter the function it is measuring, reported in form analogous to accepted clinical concepts, cost-effective, and not observable by the skilled clinician [6]. The most obvious use case for MFR as it applies to a biomechanical measure is clinical gait analysis.

Reasons for performing clinical gait analysis as interpreted by Richard Baker are to distinguish diagnosis between disease entities, to determine severity, extent or nature of a disease or injury, monitoring progress in the presence or absence of intervention, and predicting the outcome of intervention or lack thereof [5]. Taken together, Brand's and Baker's criteria assist in judging the clinical practicality and utility of various tools in the clinician's armamentarium. While many conventional gait measures are described in the literature (examples including GaitRite, Protokinetics and Force Plates Bertec), none performs well on all of these indices. In preliminary investigation, MFR had proved to be a well-rounded candidate.

As the medical field responds to the increasing average life expectancy and the growth of the 50+ demographic, two areas that present vast emergence are the aging with vitality and the physical fitness domains [1]. The key to these areas of interest is personal engagement and biofeedback, a development apparent in the movement of telerehabilitation and virtual/augmented reality tools for rehabilitation training. MFR based interfaces can connect the client with the learning or relearning paradigm in real time, allowing users to participate in their own recovery, a dual purpose, client focused and clinician focused outcome measure, objectively analyzed and objectively participatory.

CONCLUSION

We have demonstrated how Mechanical Force Redistribution can be the underlying method of sensing for tables, walls, floors and other large area surfaces. Mechanical Force Redistribution offers a way to cost effectively offer high-accuracy, seamless anti-aliased force imaging across large-format surfaces.

For future work, we plan to produce MFR sensors based on piezoelectric and capacitive force plates sensing elements [17]. With these sensors we will be able to better determine which transducer gives the best signal for specific applications. Additionally, we will combine MFR sensors with other sensing technologies that detect hover. To this end we will compare projective capacitive sensors with pyro-electric sensors as alternate methods for adding zero-touch, hover states, and feature identification. We will also experiment with assembling control electronics directly onto the sensing film, as opposed to an external, rigid PCB [11]. In parallel to these efforts we will work toward a better understanding of interaction on floor based sensors with the goal of tracking and disambiguating multiple users simultaneously. Eventually we hope to build a model of intent and posture based on the data obtained from floor based pressure sensors.

Finally, we plan to use these sensors to develop and study new interaction techniques with the goal of adding pressure sensitivity to a variety of surfaces, allowing users to interact with their devices and environment as opposed to merely interacting on them.

ACKNOWLEDGMENTS

We thank Gerry Seidman, Michael Cole, Arti Karkar and Huapeng Su for their advice and support.

REFERENCES

1. AARP. Digital health insights report for the 50+ market. *Startup + Health* (2013).
2. Addlesee, M., Jones, A., Livesey, F., and Samaria, F. The orl active floor [sensor system]. *Personal Communications, IEEE 4*, 5 (1997), 35–41.
3. Ashby, M., and Johnson, K. *Materials and Design: The Art and Science of Material Selection in Product Design*. Elsevier Science, 2009.
4. Augsten, T., Kaefer, K., Meusel, R., Fetzer, C., Kanitz, D., Stoff, T., Becker, T., Holz, C., and Baudisch, P. Multitoe: high-precision interaction with back-projected floors based on high-resolution multi-touch input. In *Proceedings of the 23nd annual ACM symposium on User interface software and technology*, UIST '10, ACM (New York, NY, USA, 2010), 209–218.
5. Baker, R. Gait analysis methods in rehabilitation. *Journal of NeuroEngineering and Rehabilitation 3–4* (2006).
6. Brand, R. A. Can biomechanics contribute to clinical orthopaedic assessments. *Iowa Orthopaedic Journal 9:61–64* (1987).
7. Branzel, A., Holz, C., Hoffmann, D., Schmidt, D., Knaust, M., Luhne, P., Meusel, R., Richter, S., and Baudisch, P. Gravityspace: Tracking users and their poses in a smart room using a 2d pressure-sensing floor. In *CHI '13 Extended Abstracts on Human Factors in Computing Systems*, CHI '13 (2013).
8. Davidson, P. L., and Han, J. Y. Extending 2d object arrangement with pressure-sensitive layering cues. In *Proceedings of the 21st annual ACM symposium on User interface software and technology*, UIST '08, ACM (New York, NY, USA, 2008), 87–90.
9. Dietz, P., Raskar, R., Booth, S., van Baar, J., Wittenburg, K., and Knep, B. Multi-projectors and implicit interaction in persuasive public displays. In *Proceedings of the working conference on Advanced visual interfaces*, AVI '04, ACM (New York, NY, USA, 2004), 209–217.
10. Eventoff, F. Electronic pressure sensitive transducer apparatus. *US Patent No. 4314227* (1979).
11. Gong, N.-W., Hodges, S., and Paradiso, J. A. Leveraging conductive inkjet technology to build a scalable and versatile surface for ubiquitous sensing. In *Proceedings of the 13th international conference on Ubiquitous computing*, UbiComp '11, ACM (New York, NY, USA, 2011), 45–54.
12. Han, J. Y. Low-cost multi-touch sensing through frustrated total internal reflection. In *Proceedings of the 18th annual ACM symposium on User interface software and technology*, UIST '05, ACM (New York, NY, USA, 2005), 115–118.
13. Hillis, W. D. A high resolution imaging touch sensor. *International Journal of Robotics Research* (1982), 1, 2, 33–44.
14. Moeller, J., and Kerne, A. Zerotouch: an optical multi-touch and free-air interaction architecture. In *Proceedings of the 2012 ACM annual conference on Human Factors in Computing Systems*, CHI '12, ACM (New York, NY, USA, 2012), 2165–2174.
15. Papakostas, T., Lima, J., and Lowe, M. A large area force sensor for smart skin applications. In *Sensors, 2002. Proceedings of IEEE*, vol. 2 (2002), 1620–1624 vol.2.
16. Paradiso, J., Abler, C., Hsiao, K.-y., and Reynolds, M. The magic carpet: physical sensing for immersive environments. In *CHI '97 Extended Abstracts on Human Factors in Computing Systems*, CHI EA '97, ACM (New York, NY, USA, 1997), 277–278.
17. Puers, R. Capacitive sensors: when and how to use them. *Sensors and Actuators 37–38* (1993), 93–105.
18. Rangarajan, S., Kidane, A., Qian, G., Rajko, S., and Birchfield, D. The design of a pressure sensing floor for movement-based human computer interaction. In *Proceedings of the 2nd European conference on Smart sensing and context*, EuroSSC'07, Springer-Verlag (Berlin, Heidelberg, 2007), 46–61.
19. Rekimoto, J. Smartskin: an infrastructure for freehand manipulation on interactive surfaces. In *Proceedings of the SIGCHI Conference on Human Factors in Computing Systems*, CHI '02, ACM (New York, NY, USA, 2002), 113–120.
20. Rendl, C., Greindl, P., Haller, M., Zirkl, M., Stadlober, B., and Hartmann, P. Pyzoflex: printed piezoelectric pressure sensing foil. In *Proceedings of the 25th annual ACM symposium on User interface software and technology*, UIST '12, ACM (New York, NY, USA, 2012), 509–518.
21. Richardson, B., Leydon, K., Fernstrom, M., and Paradiso, J. A. Z-tiles: building blocks for modular, pressure-sensing floorspaces. In *CHI '04 Extended Abstracts on Human Factors in Computing Systems*, CHI EA '04, ACM (New York, NY, USA, 2004), 1529–1532.
22. Rosenberg, I., and Perlin, K. The unmousepad: an interpolating multi-touch force-sensing input pad. *ACM Trans. Graph. 28*, 3 (July 2009), 65:1–65:9.
23. Rottler, N., and Kemps, B. Synaptics forcepad technology chosen for prestigious uist contest. *Synaptics Press Release* (2012).
24. Slobodin, D. E., and Westhues, J. Projected capacitive touch sensing. *US Patent No. 20110096025* (2010).
25. Wilson, A. D., and Benko, H. Combining multiple depth cameras and projectors for interactions on, above and between surfaces. In *Proceedings of the 23nd annual ACM symposium on User interface software and technology*, UIST '10, ACM (New York, NY, USA, 2010), 273–282.

Effects of Display Size and Navigation Type on a Classification Task

Can Liu[1,2,3] Olivier Chapuis[1,2] Michel Beaudouin-Lafon[1,2] Eric Lecolinet[3] Wendy Mackay[2,1]

[1]Univ Paris-Sud & CNRS (LRI) F-91405 Orsay, France

[2]INRIA F-91405 Orsay, France

[3]Telecom ParisTech & CNRS (LTCI) F-75013 Paris, France

ABSTRACT

The advent of ultra-high resolution wall-size displays and their use for complex tasks require a more systematic analysis and deeper understanding of their advantages and drawbacks compared with desktop monitors. While previous work has mostly addressed search, visualization and sense-making tasks, we have designed an abstract classification task that involves explicit data manipulation. Based on our observations of real uses of a wall display, this task represents a large category of applications. We report on a controlled experiment that uses this task to compare physical navigation in front of a wall-size display with virtual navigation using pan-and-zoom on the desktop. Our main finding is a robust interaction effect between display type and task difficulty: while the desktop can be faster than the wall for simple tasks, the wall gains a sizable advantage as the task becomes more difficult. A follow-up study shows that other desktop techniques (overview+detail, lens) do not perform better than pan-and-zoom and are therefore slower than the wall for difficult tasks.

Author Keywords

Wall-size display; Classification task; Physical navigation; Pan-and-zoom; Lenses; Overview+detail

ACM Classification Keywords

H.5.2 [Information Interfaces and Presentation]: User Interfaces - Graphical user interfaces

INTRODUCTION

Wall-size displays are becoming more common, [5, 24] raising the question as to whether existing research findings on desktop-size displays still apply to this new environment. Revisiting this question is even more essential as the technology evolves. Projection-based systems with low pixel density (typically 30 dpi) can now be replaced by tiled displays with the same pixel density as desktop monitors, i.e. about 100 dpi. Overall resolution (number of pixels) is thus multiplied by a factor of 10. This increased density, in turn, affords physical navigation. Users simply approach the screen to see detail and step back for an overview, similar to the pan-and-zoom navigation available on a desktop display. This raises the question as to the relative trade-offs between physical navigation with a wall-size display versus virtual navigation on a desktop.

CHI 2014, April 26–May 1, 2014, Toronto, Ontario, Canada.
Copyright © 2014 ACM 978-1-4503-2473-1/14/04..$15.00.
http://dx.doi.org/10.1145/2556288.2557020

Most previous research has addressed search, visualization and sense-making tasks. However, our observations of actual users during prototyping and real-world tasks shows that they want to *reorganize* data displayed on the wall: users move items around and group them in a way that is meaningful to the task at hand. We are therefore interested in tasks that require explicit data manipulation. Such tasks can be conducted on a desktop computer with multi-scale navigation techniques such as interactive overviews, but the need to manipulate data, e.g. with pick-and-drop, increases the complexity of the interaction. We need to better understand the benefits and drawbacks of these differently sized displays in an interactive context to develop guidelines that better inform their design.

Our challenge is how to design an abstract task that operationalizes the critical aspects of data manipulation in order to conduct controlled experiments that compare task performance for both wall-size and desktop displays. To increase internal validity, the task should reduce the cognitive load associated with the decision-making process and focus on actual data manipulation. To increase external validity, it should feature the same typical interactions found in real-world tasks. Finally, experimenters should be able to vary, in a controlled way, the difficulty of the task.

The rest of this paper provides a more detailed motivation for our work, including specific observations of users that highlighted requirements and influenced the design of the abstract task. We review the related work and then describe our design of an abstract classification task that matches the above requirements. We report the results of two controlled experiments that use this task to compare physical navigation on a wall-size display to three forms of virtual navigation on a desktop monitor. We conclude with a discussion of the main result, which found a robust interaction effect between display type and task difficulty: Although the desktop is often faster for simple tasks, the wall-size display performs significantly better with increased task difficulty.

MOTIVATION

We conducted a series of participatory design workshops with users, mostly scientists, to observe how they interacted with their own data on our ultra-high resolution wall-size display, and we also used the wall for our own real-word tasks. We briefly describe four typical examples of use.

Application Examples

An early use of the wall involved two program committee chairs assigning 145 submitted papers to 13 associate chairs (ACs). We divided the wall into columns, one per AC, plus a scratch area for the papers left to be assigned. The committee

Figure 1. Scheduling a large conference on a wall-size display: Teams and individuals move close for detail or stand back for an overview.

chairs would pick one or more papers from the pile and assign it to an AC by moving it to the corresponding column, while taking conflicts of interest into account. During the process, undecided papers were left in the middle of the wall, to be assigned later. The piles of papers rising from the bottom created a sort of histogram, making it easy to determine the relative load for each AC. As the wall filled up, the chairs rearranged papers to optimize assignments and ensure each AC had a reasonable number of papers to review.

In another application, neuroanatomists wanted to display their collection of several hundred 3D brain scans. We prototyped an application that simultaneously displayed 64 high-resolution brain scans, each oriented in the same direction so that they could analyze the scans from the same angle. Since their goal was to compare, contrast and classify healthy and diseased brains, we provided the ability to rearrange the scans. They could drag and drop the brains into groups or place them side-by-side for easier comparison.

More recently, the wall display was used to schedule a large conference with almost 500 presentations in 200 sessions, organized into 13 parallel tracks over four days (Fig. 1). The scheduling task was highly constrained: related papers had to either be placed in the same session or else not in the same time slot, authors could not be in two places at once, "large draw" events had to be placed in large rooms, etc. Because of the high resolution of the wall, the complete program could be displayed, including titles, authors and a brief description. Various colors and labels served to visualize hard conflicts, softer constraints and inter-event affinities. The most common scheduling task consisted of identifying a misplaced or in-conflict presentation, finding a better slot, and moving it there[1]. Because the schedule was so heavily constrained, one move often triggered another and schedulers, often working in groups, had to juggle sequences of updates.

Finally, we are currently designing an application that lets users organize sequences of video clips on the wall. Each clip appears in one tile of the display. The user can play the clips, individually or in sequence, and reorganize them to try a different edit. A variant of this application lets users organize a deck of slides as if the wall were a giant light table.

Implications

These applications share three elements: A complex decision-making task that relies on the users' expertise as well as their ability to quickly access the full content of the wall; a structured display in which information is logically organized in a grid; and a need to manipulate data by moving items from one cell to another. These applications are also well-suited to collaborative work. Indeed, we observed a range of collaboration patterns, from independent, parallel work to pairs working closely together.

The above examples illustrate how benefits of wall-size displays extend beyond visualization of extremely large images to include tasks requiring human judgment and the active manipulation of large datasets[2]. Here, manipulating content is an integral part of the task, whether to better understand the data set, to form an opinion, or to enact a decision.

The size of the dataset is the primary reason why users want to move off the desktop onto a wall-size display[3]. Users can see all of it at once, yet access details simply by walking toward the wall. Users take better advantage of their spatial memory since it is coupled with their physical movement in space. In contrast, the virtual navigation imposed by a desktop interface can be disorienting, and the overhead of constantly navigating the data set, e.g. with pan-and-zoom, can distract users and increase their cognitive load. Even so, physical locomotion is more time-consuming and tiring than virtual navigation, and manipulating data with well-known devices and widgets may be more efficient than using mid-air techniques on a wall-size display [18]. Our goal is to delve deeper into the questions raised by our observations and systematically evaluate the advantages and disadvantages of manipulating data on ultra-high resolution wall-size displays.

RELATED WORK

Within the extensive body of literature on large displays, we focus on studies of the effects of display size on various tasks. We first consider studies conducted in desktop settings, then move on to those involving physical navigation and finally review relevant research in multiscale interfaces.

Large Displays in Desktop Settings

Previous work has demonstrated the benefits of larger displays for traditional desktop tasks. For instance, Czerwinski et al. [10] observe higher productivity and satisfaction with larger display surfaces when performing complex daily tasks. Bi and Balakrishnan [7] compare a large projected wall display with single and dual desktop monitors. Their results suggest that large displays facilitate tasks with multiple windows and rich information because they offer a more immersive experience, with enhanced peripheral awareness.

In sense-making tasks, high resolution displays not only display more information but also provide a virtual space where

[1]A separate application based on affinity matching [16] detected conflicts and suggested alternative moves.

[2]Relative to human cognitive skills, i.e. up to a few hundred items.

[3]The other (correlated) reason is to enable group work, but this is beyond the scope of this work.

meaning is encoded in the spatial relationship between data, documents, the display, and the user [1]. Similarly, increasing display size and resolution both improve user performance in rich-information environments [20].

Tan et al. [26] demonstrate that large projection displays support spatial orientation tasks better than desktop monitors, and argue that these more immersive environments encourage egocentric rotations, leading to improved performance. Similarly, Czerwinski et al. [11] found gender differences on the effect of the field of view in a spatial task.

Although these studies consistently show the benefits of larger displays, most were conducted in traditional desktop settings where users sit before a monitor, with limited or no physical locomotion.

Physical Navigation with Wall Displays

As display size and pixel density increase, standing and moving in front of large displays becomes necessary. Ball et al. [4] show that larger displays promote physical navigation and improve user performance for search, navigation and pattern-finding tasks. However, their tasks do not involve data manipulation, and they do not include a desktop condition for comparison. Ball and North [3] investigate the key advantages of large displays and find that physical navigation is more important than increasing the field of view. Yost et al. [27] show that user performance improves with larger displays despite the need for physical navigation.

Large displays also affects perception. For example, Endert et al. [12] demonstrate the impact of visual encodings on physical navigation on large displays and show that physical navigation improves user performance. Bezerianos and Isenberg [6] find that the perspective distortion that occurs when users do not look in front of them on the wall affects the accuracy of their judgments of relative size and orientation, and that physical movements rarely improve the situation. In summary, these studies show the benefits of physical navigation in some situations for certain tasks, none of which feature data manipulation.

Multiscale Interfaces and Display Size

Multiscale interfaces [9] were designed to visualize large quantities of data on displays that are too small. With few exceptions [18], multiscale interfaces have been deployed and studied on the desktop, presumably to obviate the need for large displays. However, the effect of display size on multiscale navigation has yet to be adequately investigated.

Guiard et al.'s [13] comparison of small-to-medium display sizes for a pan-and-zoom target acquisition task shows a minor performance improvement for the larger display. Jakobsen and Hornbæk [15] evaluate the usability of interactive visualization techniques (overview+detail, focus+context, pan-and-zoom) with three display sizes. Surprisingly, the large display is not always faster, and is sometimes slower than the medium display. The authors suggest that some techniques require increased target searching time on the large display.

These results suggest only a small or no benefit of large displays when using multiscale navigation techniques. However, these studies were conducted in desktop settings where users sit in front of the display, with tasks that involve only visualization or target acquisition.

Summary and Approach

Despite the growing literature examining the effects of display size and physical navigation, data manipulation tasks have been largely ignored. In fact, we know of no study of such tasks with very large displays where users were standing and moving in front of the display.

Our goal is to build upon previous work to improve our understanding of the trade-offs between wall-size displays and physical navigation on the one hand, and desktop monitors and virtual navigation on the other, for data manipulation tasks. We must identify which input techniques are most appropriate for each setting and construct an abstract data manipulation task that captures the essential elements of the real-world tasks we observed.

ABSTRACT CLASSIFICATION TASK

We chose a simple classification task in which users partition a set of items into classes depending upon their properties. On the desktop display, items from the same class are grouped together into containers, either freely, as when comparing brain scans, or constrained, as when assigning papers. The latter involves explicit containers (columns) to represent each class. The limited capacity of each container adds a constraint, turning this into a resource allocation task. Scheduling tasks are even more complex because they add more constraints, such as avoiding conflicts across parallel sessions.

We sought a middle ground between the simpler and more complex examples. Our task has more containers than classes. Users place like items into containers without letting the container overflow. For example, conference talks (items) must fit into sessions (containers) of limited capacity, but several sessions can have the same theme (class).

To classify the items, we need to know when two items are in the same class. In practice, such decisions are domain-specific, e.g., two conference papers on the same topic or two brains with similar features, and often require expert judgment or incur a heavy cognitive load. In order to properly control this aspect of the task, we needed to find a simple, easily tested relationship, that is well-known to participants. Our solution is to represent each class by a different letter.

We must also determine how much information to display about an item, so users can determine whether two items are in the same class. For example, the conference scheduling task displays the title, keywords and abstracts of the papers whereas the neuroanatomy application displays high-resolution images of the brain. Our experiment uses the simplest solution i.e. we operationalize information density by adjusting font size.

We control the complexity of our classification task via several parameters: number of items, number of classes, number of containers, and representation of the item, including the label font size. These factors define a rich yet easy-to-control design space for experimental tasks based on the abstract task.

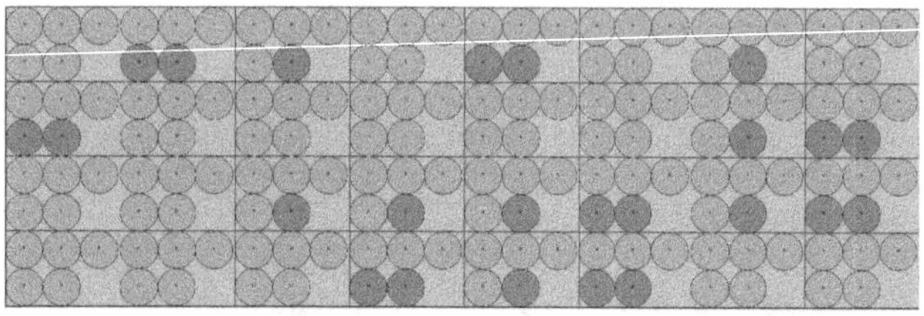

Figure 2. Display layout at the beginning of a trial (in the *Large-Easy* condition). Each cell has the size of one of the 30" monitors of the wall-size display and disks representing items have a diameter of about 20cm.

Experimental Task

For the experiment task, the number of items is set to 32 × 5 = 160, the number of containers is 32, and the maximum number of items in a container is 6. Containers are organized in a 8 × 4 matrix that matches the tiles on the wall. Items are depicted as discs whose diameter is such that 6 discs fill up one container (Fig. 2).

We control difficulty by setting the number of classes. We use two levels for the DIFFICULTY factor: *Easy* (2 classes labeled "C" and "D") and *Hard* (4 classes labeled "H", "K", "N" and "R"). These letters were chosen according to the BS 4274-1:2003 vision test standard [8] to guarantee equal legibility. Since the items display the name of their class, the similarity criterion is very simple: similar items have the same label.

Label size affects legibility at a distance and thus influences the level of physical or virtual navigation required to be able to read a label and make a decision. We use three levels for the LABELSIZE factor: *Small* is a standard computer font (12pt font, letter size about 1.8x2.3mm), *Medium* is twice the small size, *Large* is such that characters have the same size as the *Small* size when the whole scene is scaled down to the size of the desktop monitor used in the experiment (letter size about 15.5x20mm or 100pt).

Finally, we simplify the task by automatically coloring improperly classified items in red. More precisely, when a majority of the items in a container are of the same class, we color these green and the others red. This makes it easy to spot which items are left to be classified and also gives participants a clear goal: "Make everything green".

The task consists of moving disks between containers so that each container holds disks of the same class. Disks are moved with a pick-and-drop interaction: Clicking on a disk picks it up and attaches it to the cursor, a second click drops it into a container, unless the container is full, in which case the disk snaps back to its original container. On the desktop, participants can pan and zoom the scene in order to read the labels, find the target container, and identify which item to move. On the wall-size display, users stand or walk in front of the wall and use a tablet to control the cursor (Fig.3).

Since solving the task with a random configuration takes a long time, we generate initial configurations in which some items are already classified. This not only reduces the time needed to solve each task, but it also has ecological validity, since in the real-world tasks we observed, participants built upon an initial classification made by others or a computer had generated an initial pass for which some errors remain.

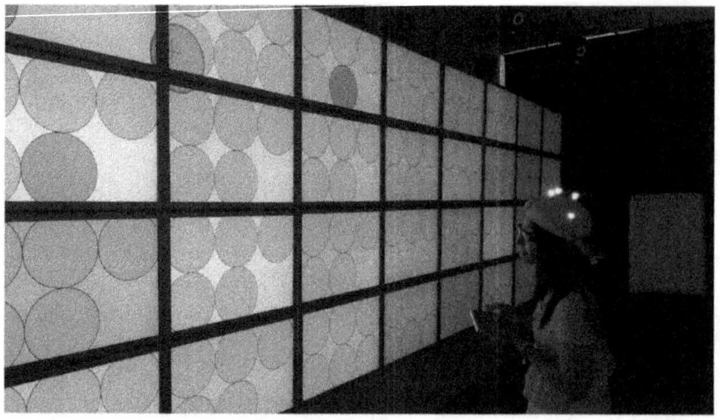

Figure 3. Wall condition: Using a trackpad to move a red disk into a container on the wall-size display.

Each task begins with a configuration of 24 incorrectly classified items (Fig. 2) that are evenly distributed across classes but randomly distributed among the containers: 8 containers hold 2 incorrect items and 8 other containers hold 1 incorrect item. To ensure that tasks are of equal difficulty, we generate random layouts and select those that satisfy the following constraint: The average distance[4] between a red disk (incorrectly classified item) and the closest suitable container is between 1.25 and 1.46 for *Easy* tasks and between 2.5 and 2.7 for *Hard* tasks.

We create one layout per LABELSIZE × DIFFICULTY condition. To minimize the effects of different layouts on performance, we create the layouts for the other conditions by permuting the labels and by applying horizontal, vertical or central symmetry. This results in structurally similar but visually different layouts, enabling us to create counter-balanced sets of tasks within and across participants.

EXPERIMENT 1: WALL VS. DESKTOP

Our goal is to investigate the trade-offs between physical and virtual navigation and how they affect task performance. We use the above classification task to compare the performance of a high-resolution wall display (condition *Wall*) with a desktop computer (condition *Desktop*). Based on our review of the literature and our experience using the wall-size display, we formulate three hypotheses:

- *Wall* performs better than *Desktop* for smaller labels;
- *Wall* performs better than *Desktop* for harder tasks;
- *Desktop* performs better than *Wall* for larger labels and simpler tasks.

Participants

We recruited 12 volunteers (5 female), aged 20 to 30, all with normal or corrected-to-normal vision. Seven use a trackpad daily; two had never used one.

Apparatus

In the *Wall* condition, we use a 5.5m × 1.8m wall-size display made of an 8×4 matrix of 30" LCD panels for a total resolution of 20480×6400 pixels (Fig. 3). A cluster of 16 Apple Mac Pro computers running Mac OS X communicate via a dedicated high-speed network and are controlled by a similar

[4]Euclidean distance between containers, where a unit is the size of a container (the distance between two adjacent containers is 1).

front-end computer. A VICON motion-capture system tracks the 3D positions of infrared retro-reflective markers attached to a hat worn by the participants with 1mm accuracy.

A 13×13cm Apple Magic Trackpad (weight 165g) controls the cursor of the front-end computer via Bluetooth. The computer displays a scaled-down image of the scene displayed on the wall and maps the cursor position to the wall cursor. Since the targets, i.e. the disks, are large, this technique provides sufficient precision for pointing. Users start and end the pick-and-drop actions by a simple tap on the trackpad.

For the *Desktop* condition, we use the same type of workstation and display as the wall (30" LCD panel, 2560×1600, 100 dpi). We use an Apple Mighty Mouse with default acceleration for input, with a wheel to control zooming. A pilot study suggested that this mouse was better suited to the *Desktop* than the Magic Trackpad used in the *Wall* condition.

The use of a different input device for the *Wall* and *Desktop* conditions is meant to maximize external validity. Since there is no standard input device for wall displays, we choose a trackpad based on previous work [17] and on our own experience and tests. For the desktop, we choose the most well-known input device, the mouse, to ensure that any results in which the wall outperforms the desktop cannot be attributed to an unusual or suboptimal desktop input device.

The experiment software is implemented using jBricks [22], a Java toolkit that supports applications running both on a cluster-driven wall display and on a regular desktop.

Procedure

The experiment is a [2×3×2] within-participants design with three factors:

- DISPLAY: display type, *Wall* or *Desktop*;
- LABELSIZE: label size, *Large*, *Medium* or *Small*;
- DIFFICULTY: number of classes, *Easy* (2 labels) or *Hard* (4 labels).

Prior to the study, participants take a vision and color-blindness test to ensure normal vision. Participants read a standard explanation of the task and perform an initial four-trial training session prior to each display condition. Participants are told to complete the tasks as quickly as possible but to avoid dropping items into the wrong containers, to discourage a trial-and-error strategy.

The experiment is split into two sessions, one per DISPLAY. Half the participants start with *Wall*, the other half with *Desktop*. The order of the DIFFICULTY and LABELSIZE conditions are counterbalanced across participants using Latin Squares. To minimize the potential order effect between DISPLAY conditions, we use the same sequence of trials and symmetric layouts for each participant between the *Wall* and *Desktop* conditions. The experiment lasts about one hour.

Data collection

We collected 288 measured trials (2 DISPLAY × 3 LABELSIZE × 2 DIFFICULTY × 2 replications x 12 participants). We measure Task Completion Time, *TCT*, and count the number of pick-and-drop actions to complete each trial. We also log kinematic data about cursor movements and user navigation, i.e. physical navigation using the tracking system for the *Wall* condition, panning and zooming for the *Desktop* condition. Participants fill out a questionnaire about their subjective work load at the end of each DISPLAY condition and another about their preferences at the end of the experiment.

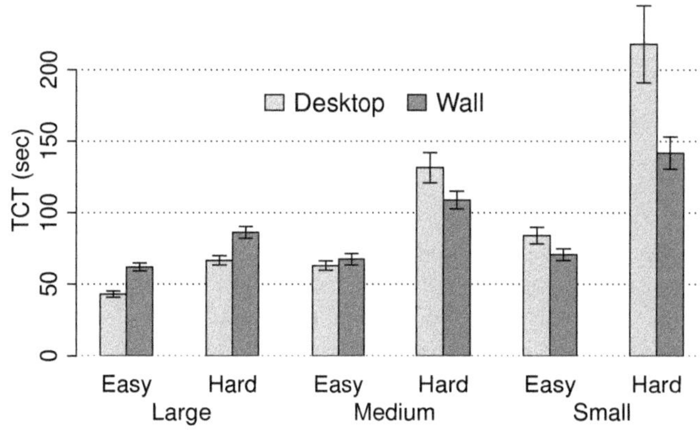

Effect	n,d	$F_{n,d}$	p	η^2_G
DISPLAY	1,11	6.95	0.0231	0.07
LABELSIZE	2,22	117	< 0.0001	0.62
DIFFICULTY	1,11	229	< 0.0001	0.68
DISPLAY×LABELSIZE	2,22	33.7	< 0.0001	0.29
DISPLAY×DIFFICULTY	1,11	28.4	0.0002	0.11
LABELSIZE×DIFFICULTY	2,22	62.9	< 0.0001	0.38
DISPLAY×LABELSIZE×DIFFICULTY	2,22	12.1	0.0003	0.09

Figure 4. Top: Task completion time (*TCT*) for each condition. Bottom: full factorial ANOVA with participant as random factor.

Results

Task Completion Time

An analysis of outliers showed that 95% percent of the trials were within 15% of the mean completion time per condition. Three trials were more than 20% slower. We kept all trials in the analyses below. The Shapiro-Wilk normality test showed evidence of non-normality only for the *Desktop-Large-Easy* condition, with two participants being very slow. This does not affect the results described below.

Fig. 4 highlights the differences between *Wall* and *Desktop* for task completion time[5]. It also displays the results of the full factorial ANOVA for the model *TCT* ~ DISPLAY×LABELSIZE×DIFFICULTY×Rand(Participant). All main and interaction effects are significant but with varying effect sizes[6]. While the effect sizes of DISPLAY and the triple interaction are moderate, others can be considered large.

Focusing our analysis on the effect of DISPLAY and given the significant interaction effects, we compare *TCT* for *Wall* and *Desktop* for all LABELSIZE×DIFFICULTY conditions with a t-test (Bonferroni correction, $n = 6$). We find that:

- For *Large* labels, *Desktop* is faster than *Wall* for both *Easy* ($p < 0.0001$, 30.5% faster) and *Hard* ($p = 0.0001$, 17.1% faster);

[5] All bargraphs display the average of all trials per condition, with the error bars showing the corresponding confidence intervals.

[6] The η^2_G statistic measures effect size. 0.02 is considered a small effect size, 0.13 medium and 0.26 large. However, Bakeman [2] recommends that each field develop their own guidelines.

- For *Medium* labels there is no significant difference for *Easy* ($p = 1$), but *Wall* is faster than *Desktop* for *Hard* ($p = 0.0222$, 22.7% faster);
- For *Small* labels, *Wall* is faster than *Desktop* for both *Easy* ($p = 0.0315$, 16.0% faster) and *Hard* ($p = 0.0059$, 34.9% faster).

As predicted, the desktop is faster for *Large* labels and the wall is faster for *Small* labels, in both DIFFICULTY conditions. However, we also see that the magnitude of the difference depends on DIFFICULTY. The wall shows a larger advantage for *Hard* tasks, while the desktop performs better for *Easy* tasks. In the *Medium* condition, the wall and desktop perform similarly in the *Easy* condition, but the wall is faster in the *Hard* condition.

We now turn our attention to DIFFICULTY and LABELSIZE and observe the expected effects (Fig. 4): *TCT* grows with higher DIFFICULTY and smaller LABELSIZE. The effect of smaller LABELSIZE is more important for the difficult task (hence the LABELSIZE×DIFFICULTY interaction). However, for the *Easy* task on the wall, the task completion times are very close across the three label sizes. To confirm this observation we compare *TCT* for the three LABELSIZE for all DISPLAY×DIFFICULTY conditions with a t-test (Bonferroni correction, $n = 12$). All differences are significant ($p < 0.005$) except for *Small* vs *Medium* and *Medium* vs *Large* in the *Wall-Easy* condition. This suggests that, for the wall, label size does not affect performance as much for easy tasks.

In contrast, the absolute difference between *Wall* and *Desktop* in the *Small-Hard* condition is large, with the wall being about 35% faster. This supports our hypothesis that complex tasks become intractable on the desktop but still manageable on the wall-size display.

Number of Pick-and-Drop Actions

All participants were able to solve the task in an almost optimal number of steps: while all configurations can be solved in 24 steps, participants performed 25.3±0.20 pick-and-drop actions on average, with no significant difference between *Wall* and *Desktop* overall. The only significant result is that participants performed more actions in the *Small-Hard* condition (27.0±1.43) than on any other LABELSIZE×DIFFICULTY conditions (24.91±0.15).

Movements of the Virtual Viewpoint and of the Participants

The wall and desktop displays have the same pixel density and render the exact same scene. Moreover, the maximum scale available when zooming in on the desktop displays the scene at the exact same size as on the wall. We can therefore compare the physical movements of participants in front of the wall with their virtual movements on the desktop.

For the wall, we compute the length of the participants' path from the tracking data. For the desktop, we compute two measures of the length of the movements of the viewpoint by considering the following two spaces. (i) *Scene space* is the space of the rendered scene at the maximum level of detail; panning movements are scaled by the current zoom factor in order to match the equivalent wall physical navigation. (ii) *Screen space* is the space of the desktop screen where panning movements are not scaled according to the zoom factor, in order to better match the mouse physical actions. Both measures are converted to centimeters for comparison.

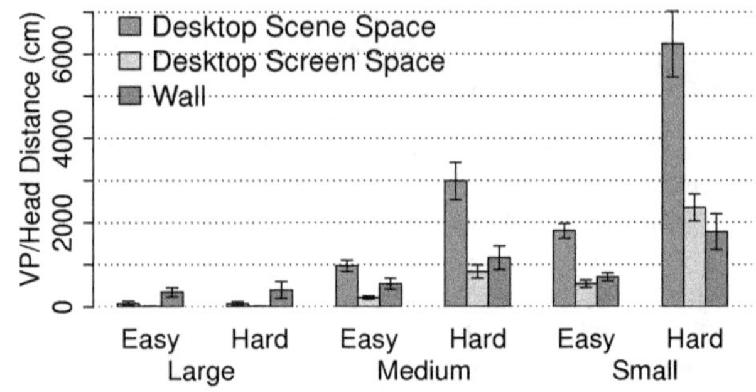

Figure 5. Average distance traveled by participants for each DISPLAY condition. (See the text for the definition of scene vs. screen space).

Fig. 5 shows the average distances covered by the participants according to these measures. Fig. 6 and 7 show the actual trajectories for one participant. With large labels, no navigation is needed to perform the task, and indeed almost no viewpoint movement occurs in the *Desktop* condition. However, most participants did move in front of the wall (about 482cm per trial on average), with no evidence that this depends upon DIFFICULTY. For the other conditions, the amount of movement increases significantly both with smaller LABELSIZE and higher DIFFICULTY. These differences correlate with the differences in task completion time. In particular, viewpoint movements increase sharply for *Small-Hard* (in scene space).

For *Small* and *Medium* sizes, in scene space, the length of the virtual navigation is longer than that of physical navigation (Fig. 5). This is not surprising, and can be attributed to the users' ability to move their head and eyes [4]. For example, the position of the head has very low variability in the y dimension, between 5.4±2.0cm for the *Medium-Easy* condition and 15±11cm for the *Small-Hard* condition, while the viewpoint has a larger amplitude (Fig. 7, bottom row): from 101±33cm for the *Medium-Easy* condition to 164±33cm for the *Small-Hard* condition.

However, the distance in *screen* space (Fig. 5) for the desktop is shorter or close to that of the wall. This indicates that virtual navigation competes with physical navigation in terms of distance covered in motor space, and therefore the difference in performance between *Wall* and *Desktop* for difficult tasks must have another explanation.

Physical vs Virtual Reach

To complement our analysis of participants' movements, we now look at their ability to interact with distant targets. Indeed, the larger size of the wall-size display enables users to reach targets at a distance without moving while on the desktop they must pan and/or zoom the scene. We did not use an eye-tracker to collect accurate data of where users were looking, however we can calculate the distance between the user and the target when they pick or drop an item. Below we report results at pick time. Results at drop time are similar.

For the *Wall* condition, Fig. 8 plots the cursor positions at pick time, relative to the orthogonal projection of the position of the head. For the *Desktop* condition, Fig. 9 plots the cur-

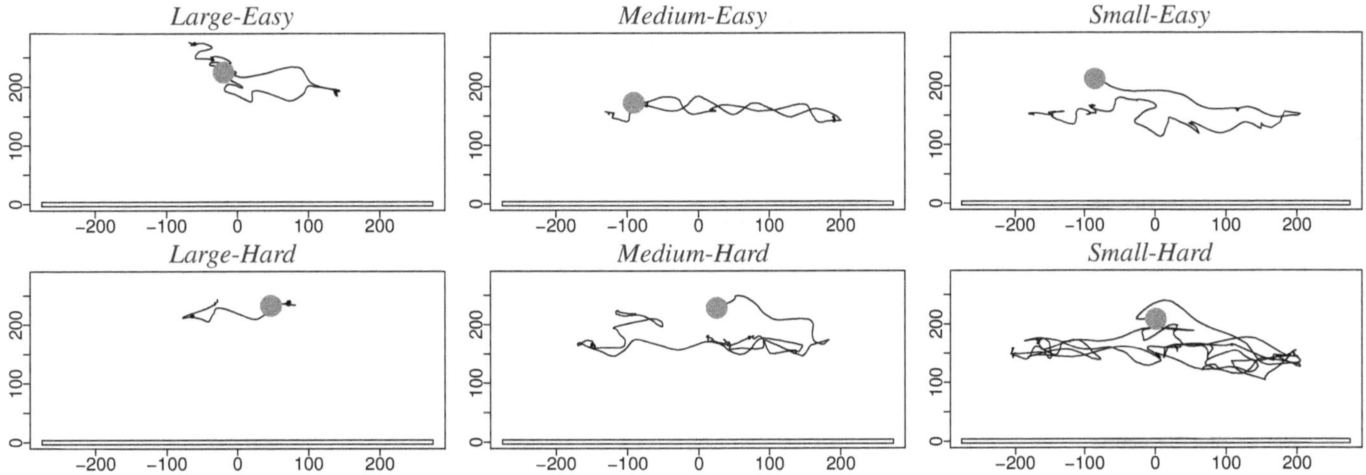

Figure 6. Movements of the head of participant P06 in front of the wall for the first measured block for each LABELSIZE×DIFFICULTY condition. This is a bird's eye view with the wall at the bottom of each graph. The axes represent the distance of the head to the wall in centimeters. These graphs are consistent with those reported in Ball et al. [4].

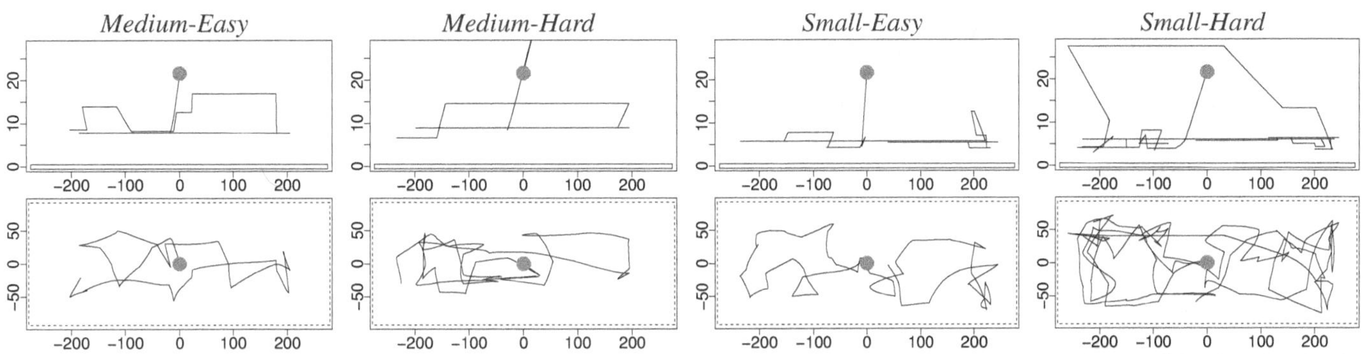

Figure 7. Movements of the viewpoint of participant P06 in scene space (*Desktop* condition). The top graphs plot the trajectory of the virtual navigation from a bird's eye view, as in the figure above (zoom factor is converted to a distance on the *y* axis). The bottom graphs plot the trajectory from a front view of the display (orthogonal projection of the viewpoint on the scene). All distances are in centimeters.

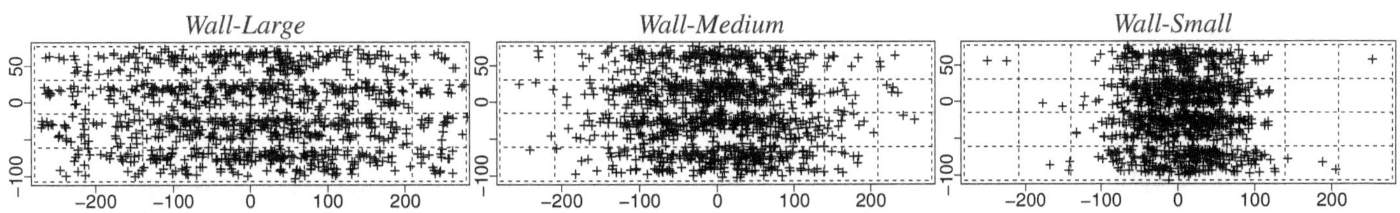

Figure 8. Positions of the cursor at pick time relative to the orthogonal projection of the head of the participants on the wall for each LABELSIZE condition (all participants, in centimeters). The dotted lines show the size of the wall for reference. The wall is at this position only when the user is in front of the center of the wall. Note that, in the *Large* condition, about 20 points are outside the wall boundaries and are thus not shown in the figure. These correspond to pick actions where the distance between the projection of the head and the cursor was greater than half the wall width, e.g. picking a disk on the left side of the wall while the user is on the right side.

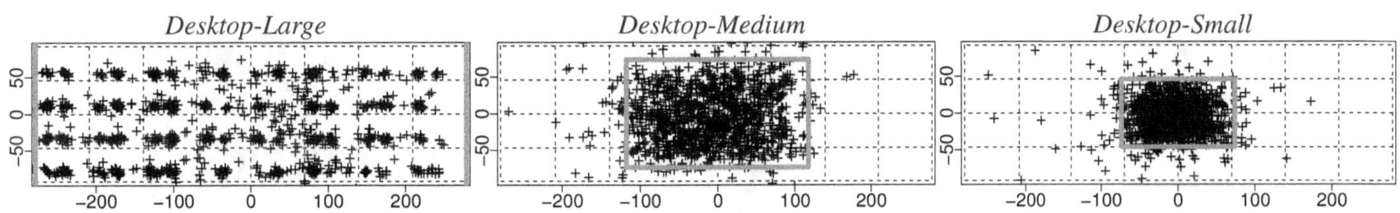

Figure 9. Positions of the cursor at pick time relatively to the position of the center of the view (translated to the origin of the graphs) for each LABELSIZE (all participants, in centimeters). The red rectangles show the average size of the scene that was displayed on the desktop at pick time. The dotted lines show the size of the scene and containers for reference. The scene is at this position only when the center of the view is at $(0, 0)$, which is almost always the case for *Large* since no panning is needed.

sor positions at pick time, relative to the center of the view. With *Medium* and *Small* labels, the points are more closely clustered for the desktop than for the wall, indicating that the participants' reach is larger on the wall. Indeed, while on the desktop users must bring the target into view with pan-and-zoom, they can act at a larger distance on the wall, reducing the need for navigation. On the other hand, with *Large* labels no navigation is needed for the *Desktop* nor the *Wall*. However the *Wall* requires more head movements, which might explain why the desktop is faster.

Fig. 9 also shows the average size of the area of the scene that was displayed on the desktop display. For *Small* labels, it is close to 4 containers (2×2). This explains the performance differences between *Easy* and *Hard* tasks for the *Desktop* condition. In the *Easy* condition, most misplaced items can be moved to an adjacent container while in the *Hard* condition, they often need to be moved to a container further away, requiring the participant to pan-and-zoom during the pick-and-drop action. With *Medium* labels, the average displayed size is about 9 containers (3×3), which reduces the chance that the destination of the move was out of sight, thus reducing virtual navigation. This is confirmed by the table below: the average number of pan and zoom actions during pick-and-drop more than doubles between the *Easy* and *Hard* conditions, albeit with large variability, probably due to different participant strategies.

	Easy-Medium	*Hard-Medium*	*Easy-Small*	*Hard-Small*
number of pan	14.4±5.2	42.5±18	30.6±11	97.8±29
number of pan in pick-drop	9.71±3.4	18.8±7.6	21.2±5.8	42.0±19
number of zoom	5.46±2.4	12.2±7.3	17.0±6.2	47.2±23
number of zoom in pick-drop	4.92±2.2	8.54±4.3	14.0±4.7	30.9±20

Angular Size of the Labels

In our design, LABELSIZE operationalizes information density: smaller text size forces participants to get closer to the display through either physical or virtual navigation in order to make an informed decision. We compute the angular sizes of labels when an item is picked, taking into account the perspective distortion due to the view angle of view. On the wall, we use the tracking data; on the desktop, we assume a 60cm distance between the participant's eyes and the display.

The table below shows the average angular width of the labels at pick time in arcminute for the *Medium* and *Small* labels:

DISPLAY	*Easy-Medium*	*Hard-Medium*	*Easy-Medium*	*Hard-Medium*
Wall	6.78 ± 0.37	6.74 ± 0.32	3.90 ± 0.16	4.20 ± 0.17
Desktop	5.78 ± 0.26	6.27 ± 0.25	4.22 ± 0.17	4.76 ± 0.24

These values are close to 5 arcminute, corresponding to 20/20 vision acuity. The differences between *Wall* and *Desktop* are small, suggesting that participants optimized their physical and virtual navigation according to their visual acuity.

Qualitative Results

At the end of each session (*Desktop* or *Wall*) we asked participants to rate their degree of fatigue, mental load and frustration while performing the task (Fig. 10). We use pairwise Wilcoxon rank sum tests with Bonferroni corrections to test

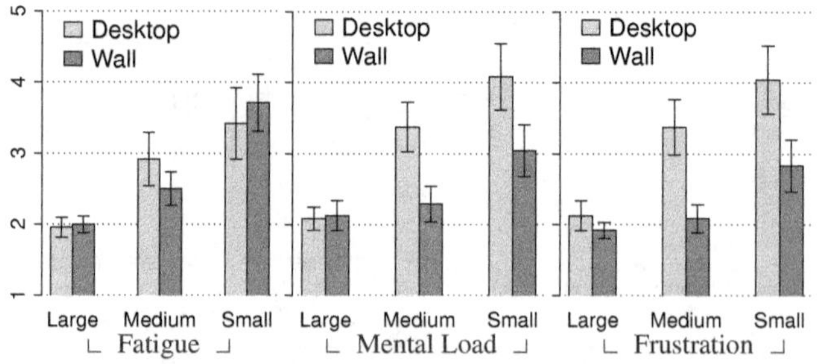

Figure 10. Physical fatigue, mental load and frustration on a five-point Likert item (1 is best, 5 is worst) for each LABELSIZE condition.

significant differences among DISPLAY×LABELSIZE conditions and focus on the differences between *Desktop* and *Wall*.

The results on fatigue are not significant ($p \geq 0.5$), in contrast to previous studies that found wall-size displays to be more tiring than desktop settings. Most participants found the small labels with four letters (hard task) tiring, in both conditions. One participant said: "*Desktop's repetitive work was somehow tiring. However the wall was very tiring after a while. If I could perform the wall task by resting my hands on a desk it would be ideal.*"

We find no significant differences for *Large* labels ($p \geq 0.9$) on mental load and frustration. However, for medium and large labels, the *Wall* causes significantly lower subjective mental load ($p = 0.0007$ for *Medium*, $p = 0.02$ for *Small*) and frustration ($p < 0.0001$ for *Medium*, $p = 0.01$ for *Small*). A few participants mentioned memory load: "*with the small labels, it was more difficult to get a mental map of the layout.*"

Fig. 11 summarizes participants preferences between the desktop and the wall. Except for *Large* labels, almost all participants preferred the wall. These results are stronger than the quantitative measure of performance, where the *Medium* label sizes performed about the same in both environments. This may be due to the novelty effect of using a wall-size display as well as other factors yet to be identified, including spatial memory.

11 out of 12 participants tried to remember the positions of the items and/or containers, and 7 of them commented that it was easier to remember the positions of the items when they were in front of the wall: "*...because I remembered the spatial location (in the room) of some particular rectangles*"; "*I have better vision with the wall. It was more fun standing up and walking. It was also easier to remember where to go because of the movement memory.*" This is consistent with the participants' description of their strategies: most participants

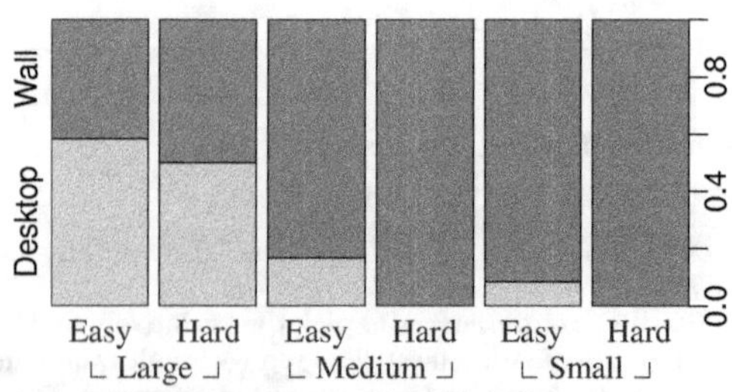

Figure 11. Proportion of the participants that preferred *Desktop* ( ) or *Wall* ( ) for all LABELSIZE×DIFFICULTY conditions.

tried to pick and drop locally in the easy conditions. In the hard conditions, they tried to remember the positions of the misplaced items and of the containers to reduce navigation.

Some participants explain the interaction effect between LABELSIZE and DISPLAY: *"The desktop with large labels is very fast, but exploring small and medium labels is painful"*; *"With the small and four letters in the wall, I didn't have to pan and zoom all the time, which was tiring. I just had to move a little bit, which was fine."* Other comments reflect the different sense of engagement between the desktop and the wall, e.g., *"For the desktop, I use the mouse [...] I feel I am under control. For the wall, I can move around, I feel I am a part of the interaction, and I feel I am controlling everything."*

In summary, these results show a robust interaction effect between display type and overall task difficulty (label size and number of classes), with the wall up to 35% faster in the hardest condition. This difference can be attributed to the ability to use more efficient strategies on the wall, as evidenced by the larger reach of users. Other factors are likely at work, though, such as a better use of spatial memory.

EXPERIMENT 2: THREE DESKTOP TECHNIQUES

Experiment 1 showed a strong performance advantage of physical navigation on a wall-size display when compared with pan-and-zoom navigation on a desktop interface for difficult classification tasks. Could these results be different with other types of virtual navigation? To test this hypothesis, we compared three desktop techniques in a second experiment: the baseline pan-and-zoom technique, an overview+detail technique and a focus+context technique [9].

Overview+detail adds a miniature view of the scene (the overview) displayed in a corner of the main view (the detail view). Many implementations let the user move the detail view by interacting with the overview, e.g. by dragging the rectangle that represents the detail view in the overview. The literature suggests that adding an overview to a pan-and-zoom interface increases user satisfaction [14, 19] and that an interactive overview can be very efficient for search tasks [21].

We tested an interactive overview but found that it slowed users down. The switching cost between views was too high when they performed pick-and-drop actions. This shows how a data manipulation task can affect the usability of a technique that has been tested only for search or visualization tasks. Instead, we chose to test a *PZ+OV* technique, which adds a passive overview in the lower-right corner of the screen, with a rectangle showing the current position of the detail view.

Lenses [25] are another way to combine focus and context in a single view. We implemented a fisheye lens that is permanently attached to the cursor and has the same radius as the disks. The entire scene is scaled down to fit the display and the lens has a magnifying factor of 6, making the small labels readable. To avoid occlusion during pick-and-drop, the disk being picked is attached to the bottom of the lens.

Method

We recruited 12 volunteers (6 female), aged 22 to 38, all with normal or corrected vision. Half had participated in Experiment 1. We use the same desktop apparatus as in Experiment 1, and the task is the same as in Experiment 1. Since we want to test whether desktop techniques can beat the wall-size display, we use a single task, corresponding to the *Small–Hard* condition of the first experiment. We also use the same initial configurations as in Experiment 1.

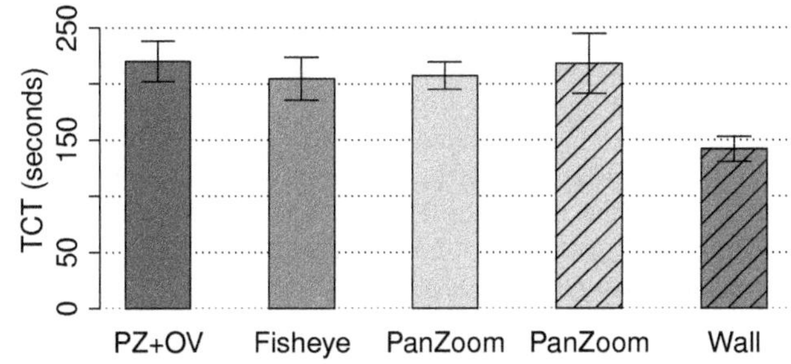

Figure 12. Task completion time (*TCT*) for the three techniques in Experiment 2. The hashed bars on the right show the results from the corresponding condition of Experiment 1.

The experiment is a within-subjects design with one factor (TECHNIQUE): *PanZoom*, *PZ+OV*, *Fisheye*. Trials are grouped by technique. The 6 possible orders are used once for each participant from Experiment 1 and once for each new participant. Participants start with a training trial with *PanZoom* to learn or recall the task. Then, they perform one training trial and two measured trails for each TECHNIQUE. At the end of the experiment, we ask participants for their preferences. The experiment lasts about 35 minutes. We collected the same data as in Experiment 1 for 72 trials: 3 TECHNIQUE x 2 REPLICATION x 12 participants.

Results

The analysis of variance reveals *no* significant effect of TECHNIQUE on task completion time *TCT*: $F_{2,22} = 0.68$, $p = 0.5149$, $\eta^2_G = 0.03$. Figure 12 shows that the three techniques are very close. The results from Experiment 1 show that none of these techniques comes close to the wall for this task.

Nine participants preferred the *Fisheye* technique, three preferred *PZ+OV*. Those who preferred the lens noted that they did not have to zoom and pan all the time. Although the lens was heavily preferred, some participants complained that it was hard to focus on the labels with the lens, despite the size of the lens being large enough to show a disk. This might be due to the high magnification factor we used, which made the lens more difficult to control, but this level of magnification was needed to make the labels readable.

Eight participants stated that the overview in *PZ+OV* was not very helpful while some mentioned that it helped them locate the red circles and empty slots. But they also said that they could do so by zooming out, so the overview was not needed.

In summary, this experiment confirmed that the wall-size display out performs the desktop for difficult data classification tasks. Although new techniques could be devised to improve the desktop condition, e.g., using multiple or adaptive lenses [23], we believe that they are unlikely to help the desktop beat the wall for complex data manipulation tasks.

CONCLUSION AND FUTURE WORK

This paper introduces a classification task that abstracts out a wide category of tasks that involve data manipulation and operationalizes two key factors: information density and task difficulty. This abstract task was informed by our observations of users of an ultra-high-resolution wall-size display, raising the question of the advantages of this type of display over a traditional desktop display.

We ran a controlled experiment comparing physical navigation in front of a wall-size display vs. virtual navigation on a desktop display for a data classification task. Our results show a robust interaction effect, such that the desktop is more efficient for easy tasks, but the wall is significantly more efficient (up to 35%) for difficult tasks. We tested three other desktop techniques with the difficult task in a follow-up experiment, but none could compete with the wall-size display.

This is but a first step in understanding the interaction environment provided by wall-size displays. Our next goal is to extend this research to collaborative work, where multiple users perform the classification task in various settings, e.g. a shared wall-size display vs. several desktop workstations working on a shared scene. A deeper understanding of spatial memory and of the respective advantages of physical and virtual navigation should also inform the design of new techniques for the wall and desktop environments that improve user performance and reduce fatigue and cognitive load.

ACKNOWLEDGEMENTS

This research was partially supported by Labex DigiCosme (project Idex Paris-Saclay ANR-11-IDEX-0003-02 operated by ANR as part of the program "Investissement d'Avenir").

REFERENCES

1. Andrews C., Endert A. & North C. Space to think: large high-resolution displays for sensemaking. *CHI '10*, ACM (2010).
2. Bakeman R. Recommended effect size statistics for repeated measures designs. *Behav. Res. Meth. 37*, 3 (2005).
3. Ball R. & North C. The effects of peripheral vision and physical navigation on large scale visualization. *GI '08*, CIPS (2008).
4. Ball R., North C. & Bowman D. A. Move to improve: promoting physical navigation to increase user performance with large displays. *CHI '07*, ACM (2007).
5. Beaudouin-Lafon M., Chapuis O., Eagan J., Gjerlufsen T., Huot S., Klokmose C., Mackay W., Nancel M., Pietriga E., Pillias C., Primet R. & Wagner J. Multi-surface interaction in the WILD room. *IEEE Computer 45*, 4 (2012).
6. Bezerianos A. & Isenberg P. Perception of visual variables on tiled wall-sized displays for information visualization applications. *IEEE TVCG 18*, 12 (2012).
7. Bi X. & Balakrishnan R. Comparing usage of a large high-resolution display to single or dual desktop displays for daily work. *CHI '09*, ACM (2009).
8. British Standards Institution. Test charts for clinical determination of distance visual acuity, 2003. London.
9. Cockburn A., Karlson A. & Bederson B. B. A review of overview+detail, zooming, and focus+context interfaces. *ACM CSUR 41*, 1 (2009).
10. Czerwinski M., Smith G., Regan T., Meyers B., Robertson G. & Starkweather G. Toward characterizing the productivity benefits of very large displays. *INTERACT '03*, IOS (2003).
11. Czerwinski M., Tan D. S. & Robertson G. G. Women take a wider view. *CHI '02*, ACM (2002).
12. Endert A., Andrews C., Lee Y. H. & North C. Visual encodings that support physical navigation on large displays. *GI '11*, CHCCS (2011).
13. Guiard Y., Beaudouin-Lafon M., Bastin J., Pasveer D. & Zhai S. View size and pointing difficulty in multi-scale navigation. *AVI '04*, ACM (2004).
14. Hornbæk K., Bederson B. B. & Plaisant C. Navigation patterns and usability of zoomable user interfaces with and without an overview. *ACM ToCHI 9*, 4 (2002).
15. Jakobsen R. M. & Hornbæk K. Sizing up visualizations: effects of display size in focus+context, overview+detail, and zooming interfaces. *CHI '11*, ACM (2011).
16. Kim J., Zhang H., André P., Chilton L. B., Mackay W., Beaudouin-Lafon M., Miller R. C. & Dow S. P. Cobi: A community-informed conference scheduling tool. *UIST '13*, ACM (2013).
17. Nancel M., Chapuis O., Pietriga E., Yang X.-D., Irani P. & Beaudouin-Lafon M. High-precision pointing on large wall displays using small handheld devices. *CHI '13*, ACM (2013).
18. Nancel M., Wagner J., Pietriga E., Chapuis O. & Mackay W. Mid-air pan-and-zoom on wall-sized displays. *CHI '11*, ACM (2011).
19. Nekrasovski D., Bodnar A., McGrenere J., Guimbretière F. & Munzner T. An evaluation of pan & zoom and rubber sheet navigation with and without an overview. *CHI '06*, ACM (2006).
20. Ni T., Bowman D. & Chen J. Increased display size and resolution improve task performance in information-rich virtual environments. *GI '06*, CIPS (2006).
21. Pietriga E., Appert C. & Beaudouin-Lafon M. Pointing and beyond: an operationalization and preliminary evaluation of multi-scale searching. *CHI '07*, ACM (2007).
22. Pietriga E., Huot S., Nancel M. & Primet R. Rapid development of user interfaces on cluster-driven wall displays with jbricks. *EICS '11*, ACM (2011).
23. Pindat C., Pietriga E., Chapuis O. & Puech C. Jellylens: Content-aware adaptive lenses. *UIST '12*, ACM (2012).
24. Rooney C., Endert A., Fekete J.-D., Hornbæk K. & North C. Powerwall: int. workshop on interactive, ultra-high-resolution displays. *CHI EA '13* (2013).
25. Sarkar M. & Brown M. H. Graphical fisheye views of graphs. *CHI '92*, ACM (1992).
26. Tan D. S., Gergle D., Scupelli P. & Pausch R. Physically large displays improve performance on spatial tasks. *ACM ToCHI 13*, 1 (2006).
27. Yost B., Haciahmetoglu Y. & North C. Beyond visual acuity: the perceptual scalability of information visualizations for large displays. *CHI '07*, ACM (2007).

Stewarding a Legacy: Responsibilities and Relationships in the Management of Post-mortem Data

Jed R. Brubaker, Lynn Dombrowski, Anita M. Gilbert, Nafiri Kusumakaulika, Gillian R. Hayes
Department of Informatics
University of California, Irvine
{jed.brubaker, ldombrow, gilbera1, nkusumak, hayesg}@uci.edu

ABSTRACT

This paper extends research on the giving and inheriting of digital artifacts by examining social network site accounts post-mortem. Given the important role that social network sites play in online bereavement practices, we conducted a series of in-depth qualitative interviews to explore issues around inheritance and post-mortem data management of Facebook accounts. We found that participants focused less on ownership of the data, and instead on the duties and potential conflicts associated with maintaining an account post-mortem. Subsequently, we argue for "stewardship" as an alternative to inheritance for framing post-mortem data management practices. Analysis of post-mortem data management activities highlights how stewards are accountable and responsible to the deceased and various survivors. However, weighing competing responsibilities is complicated by varied relationships with disparate survivors, as well as the inability to consult with the deceased. Based on our findings, we claim that post-mortem solutions need to account for the needs of stewards in addition to those of the deceased and survivors. We suggest that a model of stewardship better accounts for the interpersonal responsibilities that accompany online data than inheritance alone.

Author Keywords

Stewardship; digital legacy; inheritance; death; social network sites; Facebook; qualitative study

ACM Classification Keywords

H.5.3. [Information Interfaces and Presentation]: Group and Organization Interfaces; K.4.2 Computers and Society: Social Issues

INTRODUCTION

The growing centrality of online services has prompted questions and concerns surrounding post-mortem account and data management. Article headlines such as "What happens to your digital assets when you die?" [36] and "How to Manage Your Digital Afterlife" [2] frame these issues in individual terms, and stress the importance of including online accounts and data in one's living will and trust. In many cases, these conversations are timely and sensible. People already bequeath photo albums, why not digital photo albums?

CHI 2014, April 26 - May 01, 2014, Toronto, ON, Canada.

ACM 978-1-4503-2473-1/14/04...$15.00.
http://dx.doi.org/10.1145/2556288.2557059

Popular press, emerging tools and services, and current research frequently use the term "digital legacy" when referring to online data and its importance. Caring for one's digital legacy amounts to including overlooked digital assets in a will or living trust so they can be passed on like other forms of property. The term legacy is compelling – it speaks to the symbolic significance of these data in addition to their value. For example, two headings in a book entitled "Your Digital Afterlife", Carroll and Ramano [8] first argue, "Your content is a reflection of you" followed by "Your content is your legacy." In this swift move, one's data and one's social identity are collapsed into one.

Framing digital legacies in terms of inheritance privileges notions of ownership, however, digital legacies are more than just collections of digital assets. As has been noted elsewhere [17, 31], the process of bequeathing objects can act as more than a reflection of relationships, it can be constitutive of them. Additionally, inheritance as a model often presumes a defined heir, which is not necessarily the case with online accounts and data.

In this paper we present "stewardship" as an alternative model to inheritance when considering digital legacies. Focusing on Facebook accounts and their data, we discuss the needs of recipients of these accounts as a way of highlighting issues surrounding the stewardship of social network site (SNS) profiles. Grounded in the experiences of 20 interview participants, who reported at least one death of a friend with a Facebook profile within the last two years, we enumerate the various ways prospective stewards remain accountable to both the deceased and various survivors even in the face of limited knowledge about these people's interests and desires; the challenges that exist when trying to meet these obligations; and the role that future systems could play in the management of post-mortem data.

While social media accounts are frequently included in the list of data that comprises one's digital legacy (*e.g.*, [8]), the personal data associated with these accounts do more than provide an archived memorial. Social media profiles are sites of social interactions that continue on after the account holder has died, most notably through the memorial practices of survivors [5, 6, 7, 14, 16, 23, 29]. Thus, we considered the types of management that may accompany the ongoing use of these spaces.

Stewards act as mediators for the wishes of the deceased and their data, as well as moderators of the actions, needs, and requests of other survivors. As such, stewards are accountable to multiple parties—the deceased, surviving online friends, and friends and family who are not connected to the online social network—who all have varying claims to management of and interaction with the deceased's data and profile post-mortem. Based on their particular needs, we emphasize the importance of designing end-of-life planning tools in ways that incorporate stewards in the planning process, attend to their needs after the account owner's death, and support account owners to understand both that technological and social considerations relevant to digital data that may not be as familiar as traditional assets for inheritance.

LEGACY AND STEWARDSHIP

Engaging the connotations of "digital legacy" requires that we consider the use of the term "legacy" more broadly. There are two common understandings of the term: that which is bequeathed to another, an enduring representation of an individual after their death. Hunter & Rowles [18] provide a broader typology, noting that one's legacy is composed of a biological legacy, material legacy, and a legacy of values. Pertinent here are material legacies that can include heirlooms, possessions, and symbols.

Much of related HCI research has focused on material legacies, particularly the bequeathal of heirlooms and possessions (*e.g.*, [16, 25, 30, 31]). However, the third category, symbols, has been understudied in HCI to date. Symbolic legacies include "leaving social markers," such as a named building or endowing an academic chair that serve as "public legacies that might result in a form of symbolic immortality" [18]. In contrast to heirlooms and possessions that are amenable to ownership, symbolic legacies more commonly necessitate stewardship – someone to manage and maintain the marker on behalf of the deceased. The public nature of social media data and the broad set of stakeholders impacted by these data make analysis of them in symbolic terms appropriate.

Independent of the content of one's legacy, legacy crafting can be seen as a practice in which one engages, typically near the end of life, as in the Stage Theory Model of Adult Cognitive Development [35]. This understanding of legacy is as a curated self-presentation intended to endure after one's death. However, of course, people do not all die in old age or explicitly craft their legacies.

Stewardship involves taking on this responsibility of caring for and crafting a legacy on behalf of another. The etymology of the word "steward" can be traced back to "guardian", and starting in the late 14th century England and Scotland, was used as a title to refer to "one who manages affairs of an estate" [12]. Consistent with this definition, stewards do not necessarily own the things for which they are responsible. Instead, stewardship focuses upon carrying out responsibilities entrusted to the steward.

Stewardship has received the most significant treatment in the social sciences, particularly management and organizational science [27]. In particular, Stewardship Theory describes leaders who act in service of a collective, as opposed to in their own best interests [10]. Stewardship as a concept within technology, meanwhile, while not particularly new, is under-theorized. It is seen predominantly in security, data governance, and business information systems (*e.g.*, [11]) when describing a person who takes responsibility for existing data, or possible future data. For example, in large classification systems, it is a suggested practice to have a steward for each data node – someone who can speak on behalf of the data that exists or might exist in this node.

As the size and complexity of our personal data grow, it is not surprising to see similar needs emerge outside the traditional sphere of corporate and academic datasets. However, stewardship of SNS data can be distinguished from other types of stewardship based on the tight relationship between the data and identity of the individual who created it, an issue we explicitly address here.

RELATED WORK

Death and end-of-life issues have gained increased attention in HCI. Much of this work takes inspiration from Bell's call for the study of techno-spirituality [4], which consequentially includes practices surrounding death. Research focusing on end of life needs has been proposed as part of a broader lifespan-oriented approach to HCI [25]. Inheritance of technology is noted as a key area for further research, as well as the creation of and experiences surrounding legacies and monuments. The life record made available via Facebook profiles presents a particular challenge given the ad-hoc repurposing of these spaces for memorialization.

Inheritance and Bereavement

Among the various strategies users may prefer for the management of their online data post-mortem [38], strategies that enable inheritance are common. However, existing literature has documented substantial design challenges around inheritability, such as adequate planning for digital assets post-mortem or "the will-drafting problem" [24]. Meanwhile, Odom et al. [30] note potential tensions with the presence of uncurated social media data in family archives. One potential solution to these challenges could include "deep storage" and decay of digital artifacts [31]. However, decay is sometimes seen as antithetical to the nature of digital objects, which can always remain in their authentic condition [17]. A desire for authenticity may present some challenges when the data involved serves as a representation of the deceased, as is the case with a Facebook profile.

Concerns around inheritance necessarily extend to the needs of the bereaved. In particular, inheriting a physical object can be riddled with ambiguities when the recipient is uncertain of its meaning [31]. These ambiguities might be amplified in the case of SNS profiles where some individuals feel that profile ownership is retained by the deceased [6].

In an online support context, meanwhile, Masimmi highlights an important distinction between loss and grief when designing technologies to support the bereaved and cautions against approaches that may intermingle the two [26]. Loss includes the shock related to the initial loss, but the experience of grief is often ongoing. This distinction is pertinent when considering the specific practices in which a steward might engage, and their timing. Ideal solutions, however, remain unclear, and existing solutions take myriad approaches to meeting these needs.

Social Network Sites and Online Memorials

SNSs present additional challenges when considering inheritance and the needs of the bereaved [2, 5, 6, 16, 22, 26, 29]. As Facebook has matured, the number of profiles representing the deceased has grown [21]. The continued presence of SNS profiles, meanwhile, enables "post-mortem social networking" [6], practices which linguistically reflect the kinds of front-stage performances associated with funerals [14]. Likewise, post-mortem practices on Facebook, in particular, expand the site in which individuals experience and encounter death [5], which can result in over-exposure of the bereaved and trolling [23]. Finally, as younger generations are more likely to experience and engage in postmortem interactions [22], recommendations for existing and future services are important. A number of design considerations have been forwarded to address the evolving needs of survivors on SNS. Specifically, control over access to an account, the need for additional moderation tools, and means by which to communicate with the deceased's network [23, 29] speak to the kinds of stewardship practices we consider here.

Historically, many online services (including Facebook) deleted user accounts and content if and when they learned that the account owner had died. However, in late 2009, Facebook introduced their "Memorial Profile" feature – a state into which accounts are now placed when Facebook is notified of a death [13]. Anyone can notify Facebook that a user has died, and Facebook, after confirming the information, will change the account's state to "Memorialized." Memorializing a profile changes it in four significant ways: logging into the account is disabled; contact information (*e.g.*, street address) is removed; the profile becomes invisible to everyone except for the deceased's existing friends; and consequently, new friend requests can not be submitted or accepted.

Facebook's "Memorial Profile" does presents some challenges. Individuals report ambiguities around who has the right to tell Facebook that the account owner has died [5]. After the profile is memorialized, no one is allowed to login to the account, leaving Facebook in the position of stewarding the account and managing any potential issues with the profile or content posted to it. Circumstances could easily rise in which Facebook support staff may not be adequately responsive to the needs of survivors. Finally, by making the memorialized profile invisible and disabling the ability for individuals to connect with the deceased's profile, the profile's ability to serve as a memorial or long-term archive is severely limited [1].

Emerging Tools for Post-mortem Data Management

A handful of third-party tools also exist, most of which focus on sending messages post-mortem to loved ones. IfIDie [19], the most established service on Facebook, allows an account owner to create a message that will be posted to their profile after they die. Promotional materials suggest this message could include a piece of advice, a deep secret, or a set of final requests. Meanwhile, a newer service named Perpetu [33] allows individuals to automate a set of "final wishes" across a growing number of services. One might add a final post to one's Facebook Wall have photos emailed to a friend, delete Twitter posts, or set one's GitHub repositories to open-source. While these "wishes" are limited by the functionality of each service's API (*e.g.*, deleting Facebook statuses on Facebook is not an option), Perpetu will programmatically perform these wishes when a designated individual informs Perpetu of the user's death.

One major player, Google, has attempted to address issues related to post-mortem data access with their recently released "Inactive Account Manager" [28]. Instead of sharing data with "trusted contacts" when notified of a user's death, Google will automatically provide access when the account is deemed inactive for longer than the length chosen by the account owner.

The growing set of services allow account owners to prepare for their deaths, however, few of them are designed to facilitate the transfer of total ownership or control to another individual. This omission is undoubtedly impacted by the terms of use for each of these services; however, the importance of managing the deceased's account – in addition to accessing data – is important enough that legal efforts are underway throughout the United States to grant this right to next of kin [32]. While legal and policy issues around post-mortem data are evolving, this study reflects the perspective of would-be-inheritors and demonstrates that inheritance may not be the most appropriate model when designing future services or solutions.

STUDY DESIGN

In this exploratory qualitative study, we examined post-mortem data management on Facebook through both traditional interview questions and the use of design sketches for a potential application that could support the transfer of login credentials for a deceased Facebook user's account. We interviewed 20 participants (10 men, 10 women), age 20-50 (M=30.9; SD=10), from across the United States who reported having experienced the death of a Facebook friend within the previous two years. Interviews were conducted by three of the authors and ranged in length from 1-3 hours. Interviews were conducted primarily over video communication (*i.e.*, Skype or Google Hangouts), with the remainder conducted in-person (5) or over the phone (5). The majority of participants in our study described their relationship with the deceased as "close" or formerly close (as in the case of schoolmates who had grown apart), and while many participants reported experiencing multiple deaths of Facebook friends, the interview focused on the most recent.

The interview included two sections. During the beginning of the interview, we asked participants about their experiences with death and social media broadly, their relationship with the deceased, and about the specifics of their loss. During the second section, we provided participants with a set of sketches related to a fictional SNS application designed to transition data management permissions from the deceased's Facebook account to the participant. A variety of sketches depicting a message or notification to this effect were used to solicit perspectives on how such an exchange could or should be conducted. The interviewing researcher solicited feedback from the participant, sketch by sketch. In the case of remote participants, the sketches were shared via screen sharing or a digital packet sent in advance with instructions to not review the sketches but have them available during the interview. These sketches encouraged participants to "project" themselves into a realistic situation [37], an approach commonly used to discover a participant's perception of the world and how they behave in it [34]. This method proved particularly useful for discussing the sensitive topic of a recent death in a grounded way.

Participants were then provided with depictions of various current Facebook features and functionality (*e.g.*, edit photos) to prompt conversations around perceived norms of use under these circumstances. Specifics about possible practices and temporality were intentionally ambiguous, resulting in varied contextual narratives from participants. Our approach encouraged participants to think deeply about the use of familiar features under these conditions that they might otherwise consider inconsequential.

ANALYSIS

We performed analyses of the interviews using grounded methods. All interviews were transcribed, names were anonymized, and participants were assigned the participant numbers used in this paper. Three of the authors engaged in open-coding of the transcripts [9] focusing on participant practices and their decision making strategies. Individual practices were organized into preliminary categories, such as "preserving data", and contrasting data were noted as a way of identifying tensions across participants. All authors collaboratively refined these categories using the constant comparison method that "combines inductive category coding with a simultaneous comparison of all social incidents observed" [15]. Our final categories are presented as stewardship duties in our findings. Axial coding was then performed to determine how duties were prioritized, and under what circumstances. This analysis highlighted the primacy of interpersonal responsibilities in stewardship duties, and is presented in the second half of our findings.

FINDINGS

The role of a steward as seen in our data involves being responsible both for the deceased's account and the needs and interests of those connected to it. An understanding of the stewardship duties our participants described emerged from our analysis, and we refer to our participants as stewards throughout our findings for the sake of clarity.

Stewardship as defined here may align with concepts of ownership but is a distinctly different model than inheritance in its focus on *authorization* to perform *management* of data, alongside the *responsibility* to individuals connected to these data. *Authorization* refers to a steward's ability to access account functionality and perform particular actions. *Management*, made possible by the authorization a steward has been granted, involves the ability to make decisions about the account (*e.g.*, the addition or removal of data, friend requests, etc.) regardless of whether these activities are ever performed. Finally, *responsibility* refers to the obligations a steward has to other people connected to the deceased (online and off). In our study, participants described their sense of responsibility to multiple parties when controlling who has access to the deceased's profile, under what circumstances, as well as managing the influx of new data.

Personhood and interpersonal relationships are key to informing stewardship practices and defining the role of the steward. If *management* is understood as the practices of stewardship, and *authorization* as the technical capacity to perform them, then *responsibility* speaks to the interpersonal and symbolic relationships the steward has and maintains that motivate and inform his or her practices.

Across our findings, we demonstrate the impact of these three attributes across the four duties. We then describe ways in which conflicting needs might emerge when fulfilling these duties and challenges stewards may experience as they weigh their various responsibilities. We present a hierarchy of responsibilities to describe how stewards prioritize competing needs, and conclude our findings by demonstrating this hierarchy in relationship to an extreme act of stewardship: account deletion.

Assumed Duties of a Steward

Stewardship of post-mortem accounts involves four primary duties: honoring the last requests of the deceased, providing information surrounding the death, preserving the memory of the deceased, and facilitating memorial practices of survivors. These duties, coupled with strategies for balancing competing social responsibilities, influence how people make decisions about the accounts of the deceased.

Honoring the Last Requests of the Deceased

When presented with design sketches of a notification indicating that they had been selected to take over a friend's account, participants universally reported an expectation that a set of instructions or last requests would be provided. Anxiety about acting on behalf of someone who has died can lead to a desire that "last wishes" (P05) accompany any notification of stewardship.

I'm hoping it [the notification] is going to be followed by more details. "Please do not accept any more friend requests," "Please do not post as me," "Here's what I am comfortable with being there," "Take care of this," "Delete this"... I don't know. Some sort of instructions... (P04)

Assumptions about when they would receive such a request were split between participants: half suggesting in advance of the owner's death and half at the time of death. Pre-mortem notifications provide at least the option to speak to the owner and clarify any instructions:

If I did receive this [notification pre-mortem] without a conversation, I would make calls [to the account owner] asking, you know, "hey what's going on?" Kind of get a little bit more detail... (P01)

The ability for a steward to confirm the owner's wishes could also provide the opportunity to confirm the owner's choice of them as steward and clarify their rationale. Although participants all claimed they would accept the role of steward if no one else could, participants often questioned whether they would be the right person to steward the account regardless of the closeness of their relationship.

If for some reason I was the only person that Mara or Jean-Claude could find to take over their Facebook account and that was their wishes, then I would say yes and I would do what they asked. (P16)

I mean, you are not going to decline... (P10)

Given complex social situations, last requests often need clarification. The importance of discussing last requests pre-mortem is significant given that existing tools and services typically send messages, notifications, and provide access to data to the bereaved after the owner's death. Actions taken post-mortem foreclose the opportunity to clarify expectations, which, as others have noted, presents a challenge for the bereaved [24]. Indeed, most services activate some time after the owner's death (typically 1-3 months post-mortem), a design feature that presents challenges to the stewardship duty we discuss next.

Providing Information Surrounding the Death

Likely duties of the steward include posting informational and logistic details on the deceased's Wall, such as an obituary or funeral announcement. For example, P03 told us about the benefits of a family member who acted as a source of information on Facebook following the death of a high-school friend:

His timeline was filling... with lots of questions and people expressing grief and it was definitely in need for someone to come in and sort of manage the situation. It was almost like if everyone showed up at the church for a funeral and nothing was happening... I think it was very important for someone to come in and go "Thank you all for your kind messages. The family really appreciates it, I want to give you an update on what's happening..." And it really was purely informational... (P03)

In the absence of an individual to act as a central informational resource, information tends to emerge haphazardly on the deceased's profile or through other sources. Participants described distress at the absence of a clear indicator that the owner had indeed died. We frequently heard stories in which the profile was flooded with posts expressing shock and sorrow, but without anyone clearly sharing the news of the death. Typical of SNS-communication, friends post Wall content to communicate directly (though publicly) with the account owner, but rarely with others in the owner's social network. Based on our interviews, the designation of a steward appears to be one way to overcome this SNS-norm and provide an "official" source of information needed by the surviving community.

As stewards perform these informational tasks, identifying them and their role may be important. Participants provided a number of possibilities, such as an indicator next to any content they posted on the deceased's Wall, the ability to post content on behalf of the deceased, or as P16 explained, directly in their profile information:

I feel like its important... for the people to know that there was somebody who was [an] acting trustee... A message would come up "This account has now been given to the care of Sahar" or maybe I could write a message ... (P16)

Participants' desires were partially motivated by a wish to make others aware of them as a resource. However, such an indication would also serve to legitimatize their actions, particularly when their behavior differs from other survivors. Concerns over the legitimacy of their actions and how their actions impacted others were common throughout interviews.

Preserving the Memory of the Deceased

In absence of any clear directives, maintaining the status quo at the time of death was a common strategy described by participants to avoid disrespecting the wishes of the deceased. Participants often stated they would not alter account settings or existing content unless explicitly directed to do so in the owner's last requests. For most, the presence of profile content at the time of death represented at least an implicit acceptance by the deceased, and therefore should not be altered.

It's just sort of... weird. It would be like going into somebody's office and rearranging their stuff... like [how] you thought it should be [arranged], instead of how they had it already. (P13)

Participants commonly used place-based metaphors, such as the office above, to describe their inaction, overlooking, of course, that in the physical world inaction is almost never the answer. For example, after the mourning period, an office would be packed and made ready for a new inhabitant, a child's bedroom might eventually be turned into a home office, and so on. Stewards experience a tension between a desire to maintain the owner's content and the needs of new inhabitants of the owner's profile, raising questions about the length of time for which inaction is a viable strategy.

In some cases, stewards may feel that preserving an appropriate memory of a loved one mandates some content curation. Participants rationalized these changes in the name of creating a more accurate or appropriate representation of the deceased and an ideal memorial space for the bereaved. While in the minority, P14 explained that he would delete "the trivial stuff" to make the "page seem more humanized, more personal." In contrast, the majority of participants viewed any content removal as inauthentic representations of the person "even if... their entire Timeline was FarmVille notifications" (P13).

When stewards do make changes, the presumed intent of the deceased, as well as the expressiveness attributed to the data, help inform the steward's choices. In these cases, a helpful distinction can be made between factual and expressive data. Seven participants suggested they might change data they considered factual, such as removing a mailing address or adding a high school they imagined the deceased had "forgotten" to include on their profile. Expressive data, particularly status updates and photos, were approached much more cautiously. The lines between these types of data, however, can certainly blur:

Languages... maybe they fibbed a bit. I wouldn't go "They were wrong, they didn't know Arabic." If they thought they knew Arabic, they thought they knew Arabic. I wouldn't change that. (P14)

We see here a subtle distinction between information about the deceased and actions taken by the deceased. Preserving the memory of the deceased on SNSs is complicated, given that pre-mortem data about the deceased is typically available as a product of actions taken by the deceased.

Determining whether profile content was the result of the deceased's intentional actions was pertinent when considering changes to the data. To probe this issue, the screenshot of the Facebook Timeline in our sketch packet included a sensitive item: an indication that the owner had "Liked" a Facebook page titled "Having a fun day killing hookers and stealing cars, now time to play GTA [Grand Theft Auto]." When participants discussed this entry, they actively considered how best to manage it relative to a personal rubric in which they imagined both the circumstances under which this page was "Liked" (An accident? An avid gamer?), and how the deceased would have wanted them the participant to respond.

He's a jokester... and all of his friends could know that its a joke because he's a joker and you don't want to take that away so that people in a time of sorrow can have a little laugh... "He's dead but he still made me laugh." (P10)

In this case, P10's explanation reframes content that might offend some survivors into an item that might bring fellow survivors some relief from their grief.

Stewards also manage a plethora of different types of requests from friends, family, and other survivors. Participants almost always discussed requests in terms of conflicts – either between requests or with the status quo of the profile. While most participants talked about the potential difficulty of having to negotiate between conflicting requests, for P03, the ambiguities resulted in him erring on the side of inaction:

If I'm erasing all these pieces of Daniel that were real... just because they didn't fit into my way of viewing Daniel... I'm erasing pieces of him that are never coming back and what everybody is going to see is... my interpretation of Daniel. (P03)

Thus, even as stewards can play an important role in preserving the use of data, their actions can be a threat to the data itself. Even when well intended, changes to profile content about the deceased oblige us to ask: Whose version of the deceased?

In the absence of a steward, contrasting perspectives may result in the types of conflicts between survivors noted elsewhere [6, 23]. A steward – functionally acting as the deceased, while not actually the deceased – can moderate some of these issues, but must negotiate and reconcile their own understandings of the deceased with those of others. If stewards do act beyond the requests provided by the deceased, they must attempt to do so by balancing what they perceive as the deceased's intentions with the interests of those who are grieving – including themselves.

While the deceased's Facebook profile is filled with previous actions, the memory the steward seeks to preserve is one held by survivors. This requires stewards to decide between retaining the record of past actions of the deceased and actively managing the current needs of survivors. If stewards start making changes, they may be left having to account for the reasoning behind them. Even curation by the best-intended steward is selective and always represents some kind of loss. Others have already argued for the importance of technology to support "multiple representations in an archive" [30], but while the steward is technically empowered to make these representations, they may not know how to do this or for whom.

Facilitating Memorial Practices of Survivors

In addition to preserving a memory of the deceased, stewardship involves facilitating the practices of survivors as they mourn and memorialize the deceased. Participants provided diverse strategies for meeting survivors' needs, including non-action, changing privacy settings, encouraging the posting of memories and photos, and regular posting of memorial content. Participants consistently described a desire to facilitate memorializing practices, often drawing on experiences in their own lives:

Posting messages [on the deceased's Wall] seems to make some people feel better... I would want that to be available... (P16)

Participants focused on two types of content in particular: memories posted by other survivors to the deceased's Wall and photos of the deceased:

The things that I see on their walls are the absolute best... the little random memories. This is something that I started doing... inspired by these people [other survivors]... Just because my memories of somebody can be a lot different... and I like to see people share their memories of something that I may have forgotten. (P01)

The role of photography in how we represent and remember the dead [3] certainly extends to social media. The value participants placed on photos reflects their importance and confirms what others have documented [14, 22]:

I would want pictures... and nice memories... A space for their memories to be curated and maybe put some into an album of "Favorite moments" -- a place for other people to go to look at the good things... [they] did in their life. Kind of like a big scrapbook... for other people who also are fond of this person and remember the good stuff. (P16)

Stewards might also include the commemoration of important days and events from the deceased's life. This result complements other research that indicates an uptick in activity related to such events on deceased profiles [6].

Just as a social thing I would probably try to commemorate anniversaries, death,... the birthday. "Let's think about so-and-so on his birthday. Does anybody have a good story?" So try to make it like the community hang out... (P02)

Beyond common memorial events, some participants suggested that they might continue temporally-based social media practices in which the deceased engaged while alive. P13, for example, imagined she might continue to post "Throwback Thursdays":

It might be kind of cool... "Today, August 8th, back in '09 Mason was at the gym..." Because you can go back and see those posts, so it might be something to bring back... to share that again. This is what Mason liked to do...(P13)

In addition to fostering interaction, stewardship appears to involve meeting the unknown, but anticipated, needs of survivors. Issues around managing a safe space for grieving survivors frequently involved who was allowed to participate in the online memorial space. Most (but not all) participants described being ill-equipped to make decisions about new friend requests made to the deceased's account post-mortem and were skeptical of the motivations behind them. Otherwise, stewards leaned toward an inclusive approach provided individuals behaved in what participants felt was an appropriate manner:

Yeah, because it should function as kind of a safe space, like a memorial -- like going to somebody's grave, but on Facebook. If somebody is going to like deface it with graffiti then that's an issue, but if they're going to leave little flowers and notes and stuff, whatever. (P13)

As with the management of data posted by the deceased, data posted by survivors also creates some tensions. There is a tension between new data contributed by survivors and existing data – between preserving the deceased's profile and providing a space for memorialization – as well as between the potentially conflicting needs of survivors. However, a steward can speak to and negotiate with survivors, where no such option exists with the deceased.

Managing a defaced profile or a potential conflict between survivors on the Wall was often discussed as a hypothetical scenario. However, for a few, the importance of actively moderating the account was more prescient. P14 spoke to us about an auto-accident in high school, in which most in the car died as a result of an intoxicated driver. He shared the very real possibility of upsetting content:

Especially for Mason, if people started putting slander – "Oh, you were driving drunk and you were the reason my sister died"... I would block those people. I want it to be a peaceful account. He passed away. Let's keep it clean. His family is already hurting. They don't need to see those kinds of things... I'm not afraid to block people. (P14)

In these cases, to maintain a safe space for the bereaved [23], participants explained that they would prioritize the needs of those they perceive to be most close to the deceased. However, the priority given to various relationships deserves additional study.

Weighing Social Responsibilities

Approaching stewardship as a set of social responsibilities, there are questions around balancing the care of the deceased, survivors, and the data associated with the account. Participants described preserving the deceased's memory, often by maintaining as much of the deceased's profile data as possible and by executing any last requests. Acting as an information source and facilitating memorial practices, meanwhile, were important services a steward could provide to other survivors.

The duties outlined require that stewards balance two tensions: the needs of the deceased vs. survivors and preservation of existing data vs. facilitation of memorializing practices that result in new data. Often these tensions are aligned – for example, preservation of existing data frequently meets the needs of survivors. However, when these tensions are in conflict, stewards must prioritize needs. An analysis of how participants prioritized needs resulted in our development of a hierarchy of responsibility that describes how participants evaluated requests. In this section we start by describing the hierarchy and then we demonstrate how the hierarchy informed the ways participants approached the extreme scenario of deleting the deceased's account.

Hierarchy of Responsibility

When stewards are unable to resolve conflicting needs through alternative solutions, decisions may be informed by the identity of the requestor and their rationale for the request. Across our interviews a clear prioritization of needs was evident:

1. **Explicit requests from the deceased** serve as specific requests made in advance of death in anticipation of no longer being able to make requests.
2. **Needs of survivors** can be accommodated, provided they do not conflict with the wishes of the deceased or impact other survivors.
3. **Perceived wishes of the deceased** impact decisions that are made on behalf of the deceased, but for which there are no explicit instructions.

The priority the deceased holds in this hierarchy presents a problem given that they are not present to make their wishes known. Last requests are one way to make wishes explicit, but in the absence of tools designed to declare and share these requests for online accounts, explicit requests from the deceased rarely exist. Even when the deceased provided last requests, the requests imagined by interviewees lacked sufficient information or context to enable stewards to always understand the spirit or motivation behind them. Explicit instructions cannot cover all scenarios – many of which the deceased will have never experienced or anticipated. This results in stewards having to consider the perceived wishes of the deceased, wishes that cannot be verified.

Although perceived wishes are given least priority, they represent a means through which explicit requests of the deceased can be interpreted in ways that justify meeting the needs of survivors. For example, one can imagine a scenario in which the deceased's request to maintain the profile so that people have a place to convene is interpreted to also mean proactively supporting the bereaved. Conversely, perceived wishes of the deceased could be overruled by explicit requests of the deceased in unforeseen circumstances.

Throughout the hierarchy, but particularly when weighing needs of survivors, scope and severity of impact play a prominent role when considering content changes. For example, restricting an offensive commenter's access to the profile Wall may negatively impact one individual, while ensuring a "safe space" for everyone else. In contrast, a scenario in which a close family member requests the profile be deleted, despite the benefits it provides others, was deeply troubling for participants. Isolating content through separate spaces, such as a public memorial page and a private profile, can reduce conflicts between multiple requests. Likewise, reversible strategies, such as changing privacy settings instead of deleting content, preserves the ability to undo stewardship decisions at a later point.

Deleting an Account

To demonstrate use of the hierarchy and how survivors invoked the wishes of the deceased, we examine stewardship in relationship to one particular Facebook feature: account deletion. As an extreme act of stewardship, the prospect of deleting the deceased's account resulted in concerns that cut across the duties we have described. Participants' responses highlighted tensions between the privileging the profile as a site owned by the deceased and its new role as a memorial, and subsequently, tensions between the needs of the deceased and survivors.

Explicit requests from the deceased served as the most core obligation of stewardship. While participants typically had a strong preference for preserving content, the steward's role in executing last requests obligated most participants to delete the account if explicitly requested:

I think if Daniel had said... "I want you to maintain this account for a set amount of years" and if he had left instructions to delete the account after a certain amount of time, I would absolutely honor his wishes... It would be very difficult... [but] I would have *to do that. (P03)*

Likewise, if the owner had requested the account be kept active, participants indicated they would attempt to maintain the profile, even if others objected. Imagining a scenario in which the deceased's parents asked that their son's profile be deleted, P08 explained that he "would be clear with his parents that this was his last wish. And it would be this way in spite of their discomfort." However, requests from immediate family were particularly challenging given the potential depth of their grief. Continuing on, P08 explained:

For me the more difficult question is the opposite... if they [the parents] begged me to not delete it and he wanted it gone... I could see that their feeling on it might be something akin to me killing him all over again... killing off any remnant of their memory of him. (P08)

The responsibility a steward has to those grieving was a concern of participants, particularly for scenarios in which the steward cannot meet their needs. P08's comment speaks to the importance of developing additional tools (or making existing tools more readily apparent) that can provide stewards with alternative strategies for meeting divergent needs – in this case, perhaps an offline archive for the deceased's parents.

In very palpable ways, stewards bear responsibilities to those impacted by fulfilling requests of the deceased or other survivors. As such, deleting the profile becomes more fraught when it is an active site of memorialization for a grieving community. When we asked participants how the level of activity on the profile might impact their decisions, two common strategies were shared: alternative solutions that might decouple conflicting needs and explaining their actions (and the deceased's wishes) in a way that attempts to enroll others into the hierarchy. Both of these strategies were evident when P09 talked about how she might handle a request from the deceased to delete the account:

I mean I would delete the account. But maybe a different page can be made...? Yeah, I would send out some kind of message that just let people know that she requested it... that she told me that she wanted it to be deleted. (P09)

The challenge is that with the deceased unable to reiterate, clarify, or contextualize the meaning or importance of their request, survivors (including a steward) are left to interpret them on behalf of the deceased. The weighing of options, then, also becomes a process through which a steward must weigh the relative legitimacy of various interpretations of the deceased's intent. In more ambiguous scenarios, participants adopted the perspective of the deceased as a way of arriving at a rationale:

My goal would be to try to maintain the page at all cost, unless... I could not see hurting see my friend's mother. Because I would... go back and go "okay what would Daniel do? If something was hurting his mom would Daniel go 'look this is bigger than the both of us, you're just going to have to get over it'?" He would not do that... he probably would shut down the page. (P03)

In the most complex of scenarios, the steward is left weighing not only the explicit last requests of the deceased against the needs of survivors, but also the deceased's intent as projected by both the steward and the other survivors. This can be emotionally burdensome and may lead to questions about the legitimacy of their role as a steward.

CONCLUSION

Prevailing approaches to digital legacies adopt a model of inheritance for post-mortem data management. However, framing digital legacies in terms of inheritance reduces them to a collection of digital assets whose ownership can be transferred. In this study, we found that prospective inheritors of Facebook accounts did not talk in terms of inheritance or ownership, but instead as an undocumented role that we termed "stewardship." Notably, we argue that stewards are concerned with the relationships represented in and surrounding post-mortem data, rather than data alone. Subsequently, design efforts focused on the inheritance of data may be inadequate for the needs of stewards.

When using inheritance as a model, two positions are privileged: the deceased and the inheritor, the latter of which can be any survivor. Stewardship provides a model that allows us to account for alternatives to ownership and a new role that includes a small but important set of users. Stewardship allows us to consider needs particular to those who act as mediators of the deceased's data and moderators of the needs of various survivors. In the case of social network sites, the rich social interactions and public nature of profiles may ultimately limit the utility of inheritance. Stewardship, meanwhile, acknowledges profiles as active communal spaces with shifting needs by attending to the management of the profile space and multiple parties.

We have outlined duties and challenges that can accompany the stewardship of a deceased friend's Facebook account. Our analyses indicate that Facebook stewardship involves four types of duties that leave stewards weighing the needs of the deceased and various survivors. Enumerating specific design recommendations is beyond the scope of this initial study and requires future study. However, future research on the needs of stewards requires acknowledging the potential of stewardship in the design of systems that seek to attend to post-mortem issues.

The challenges associated with stewardship that we have presented here demonstrate the importance of both acknowledging stewardship in the design of systems that seek to support post-mortem data management as well as the need for tools to support stewardship duties. Most pertinent on Facebook is providing structure and support for the difficult and potentially emotionally taxing demands that a steward might face. In moments of conflict, stewards are placed in positions to have their judgment of and their relationship with the deceased challenged. This raises questions about the steward's own experience of mourning, and their ability to develop and maintain a "continuing bond" [20] with the deceased. When using stewardship as an approach, issues such as these are brought to the fore in ways unseen when designing for inheritance alone.

ACKNOWLEDGMENTS

We thank our participants for making this work possible, and Courtney Loder, Melissa Gregg, Sen Hirano, Steven Frost, Sara Bareilles, and members of LUCI for feedback and support. This work was supported in part by the Intel Science and Technology Center for Social Computing.

REFERENCES

1. Acker, A. and Brubaker, J. R. Death, Memorialization, and Social Media: A Platform Perspective for Personal Archives. *Archivaria 77,* (2014).
2. Arnold, C. How to Manage Your Digital Afterlife. *Scientific American Mind*, 2013. http://www.scientificamerican.com/article.cfm?id=how-to-manage-your-digital-afterlife.
3. Batchen, G. *Forget me not: Photography and remembrance*. Princeton Architectural Press, 2006.
4. Bell, G. No More SMS from Jesus : Ubicomp, Religion and Techno-spiritual Practices. *Ubicomp 2006*, Springer (2006), 141 – 158.

5. Brubaker, J.R., Hayes, G.R., and Dourish, P. Beyond the Grave: Facebook as a site for the expansion of death and mourning. *Information Society 29*, 3 (2013).
6. Brubaker, J.R. and Hayes, G.R. "We will never forget you [online]": An empirical investigation of post-mortem MySpace comments. *Proc. CSCW '11.*
7. Brubaker, J. R. and Vertesi, J. Death and the Social Network. Presented at the *CHI 2010 Workshop on HCI at the End of Life: Understanding Death, Dying, and the Digital.*
8. Carroll, E. and Romano, J. *Your Digital Afterlife: When Facebook, Flickr and Twitter are Your Estate, What's Your Legacy?* New Riders, 2010.
9. Corbin, J. and Strauss, A.L. *Basics of qualitative research.* Sage Newbury Park, CA, 2008.
10. Davis, J.H., Schoorman, F.D., and Donaldson, L. Toward a Stewardship Theory of Management. *The Academy of Management Review 22*, 1 (1997), 20–47.
11. English, L.P. *Improving Data Warehouse and Business Information Quality: Methods for Reducing Costs and Increasing Profits.* John Wiley & Sons, Inc, 1999.
12. etymonline. Steward. http://www.etymonline.com/index.php?term=steward.
13. Fletcher, D. What Happens to Your Facebook After You Die? *Time*, 2009. http://www.time.com/time/business/article/0,8599,1932803,00.html.
14. Getty, E., Cobb, J., Gabeler, M., Nelson, C., Weng, E., and Hancock, J.T. I Said Your Name in an Empty Room: Grieving and Continuing Bonds on Facebook. *Proc. CHI '11.*
15. Goetz, J.P. and LeCompte, M.D. Ethnographic Research and the Problem of Data Reduction. *Anthro & Education Quarterly 12*, 1 (1981), 51–70.
16. Graves, K. E. Social Networking Sites and Grief: An Exploratory Investigation of Potential Benefits. Dissertation at the University of Indiana at Pennsylvania. 2009.
17. Gulotta, R., Odom, W., Forlizzi, J., and Faste, H. Digital artifacts as legacy. *Proc. CHI '13.*
18. Hunter, E.G. and Rowles, G. Leaving a legacy: Toward a typology. *J. of Aging Studies 19*, 3 (2005), 327–347.
19. ifidie. http://ifidie.net/.
20. Klass, D., Silverman, P.R., and Nickman, S.L. *Continuing bonds: new understandings of grief.* Taylor & Francis, Philadelphia, 1996.
21. Lustig, N. 2.89m Facebook Users Will Die in 2012, 580,000 in the USA. *Nathan Lustig*, 2012. http://www.nathanlustig.com/2012/06/06/2-89m-facebook-users-will-die-in-2012-580000-in-the-usa/.
22. Maciel, C. and Pereira, V. C. The internet generation and its representations of death: considerations for posthumous interaction projects. *Proc. IHC '12.*
23. Marwick, A. and Ellison, N.B. "There Isn't Wifi in Heaven!" Negotiating Visibility on Facebook Memorial Pages. *J of Broad. &Elec Media 56*, 3 (2012), 378–400.
24. Massimi, M. and Baecker, R.M. A Death in the Family : Opportunities for Designing Technologies for the Bereaved. *Proc. CHI '10.*
25. Massimi, M. and Baecker, R.M. Dealing with death in design. *Proc. CHI '11.*
26. Massimi, M. Exploring remembrance and social support behavior in an online bereavement support group. *Proc. CSCW '13.*
27. Menyah, K. Stewardship Theory. In S. Idowu, N. Capaldi, L. Zu and A. Gupta, eds., *Encyclopedia of Corporate Social Responsibility.* Springer-Verlag, 2013.
28. Micklitz, S., Ortlieb, M., and Staddon, J. "I hereby leave my email to...": Data Usage Control and the Digital Estate. *2013 IEEE Security and Privacy Workshops.*
29. Mori, J., Gibbs, M., Arnold, M., Nansen, B., and Kohn, T. Design considerations for after death. *Proc. OzCHI '12.*
30. Odom, W., Banks, R., Kirk, D., Harper, R., Lindley, S., and Sellen, A. Technology heirlooms? *Proc. CHI '12.*
31. Odom, W., Harper, R., Sellen, A., Kirk, D., and Banks, R. Passing on & putting to rest. *Proc. CHI '10*
32. PBS Newshour. Law Lags Behind in Defining Posthumous Protocol for Online Accounts. 2013. http://www.pbs.org/newshour/bb/science/jan-june13/digitalassets_03-11.html.
33. perpetu. https://perpetu.co/.
34. Sampson, P. Qualitative research and motivation research. In R.M. Worchester and J. Downham, eds., *Consumer market research handbook.* Elsevier Science Ltd, 1986.
35. Schaie, K.W. and Willis, S.L. A stage theory model of adult cognitive development revisited. In M. Rubinstein, M. Moss and M.H. Kleban, eds., *The many dimension of aging.* Springer Publishing Company, New York, NY, 2000, 175–193.
36. Sweigman, B. What Happens to Your Digital Assets When You Die? *Huffington Post,* 2013. http://www.huffingtonpost.ca/brian-sweigman/digital-assets_b_2606822.html.
37. Webb, J. *Understanding and designing marketing research.* Academic Press Inc, London, 1992.
38. Zhang, M., Jennett, C., Malheiros, M., and Sasse, M. A. Data after death: User requirements and design challenges for SNSs and email providers. Presented at the *CHI 2012 Workshop Memento Mori: Technology Design for the End of Life.*

Captioned Photographs in Psychosocial Aged Care: Relationship Building and Boundary Work

Jenny Waycott[1] Hilary Davis[1] Frank Vetere[1] Amee Morgans[2] Alan Gruner[2] Elizabeth Ozanne[3] Lars Kulik[1]

[1] Department of Computing and Information Systems, The University of Melbourne, Australia, [jwaycott, davish, f.vetere, lkulik]@unimelb.edu.au

[2] Benetas Aged Care Services, Melbourne, Australia, [amee.morgans, agruner]@benetas.com.au

[3] Department of Social Work, The University of Melbourne, Australia, eao@unimelb.edu.au

ABSTRACT

In this paper we examine the use of a novel social technology to support the provision of formal aged care services to clients who live in their own homes. Social technologies offer enormous potential for enhancing aged care, but research on their use in aged care has largely focused on institutional or informal care settings, rather than formal care in the home. Meanwhile, technologies for aging in place typically focus on monitoring and security, rather than psychosocial support. We conducted a field study in which aged care managers used a photo and message-sharing tool to communicate with clients living in their own homes. Our findings demonstrate that visual and social forms of communication are valuable for supporting psychosocial care-giving, but there are barriers to effectively adopting new communication tools in this setting. Time constraints inhibited care managers' use of the technology, which was also influenced by their efforts to carefully maintain boundaries between their personal and professional lives.

Author Keywords

Aged care; social technologies; photo-sharing; iPad

ACM Classification Keywords

H.5.m. Information interfaces and presentation (e.g., HCI): Miscellaneous.

INTRODUCTION

In our aging society, independent living – or "aging in place" – is an important component of positive ageing. Many technologies have been created that aim to facilitate aging in place, including devices that remotely monitor older adults' movements and emergency alarms that can be worn on the body [e.g., 14, 19]. Existing telecare systems, however, primarily address the monitoring and security aspects of aged care, positioning older adults as the *subjects* of care, with little acknowledgement of the reciprocal relationship that develops between the care provider and the person being cared for. Psychosocial care, and those providing that care, are typically overlooked in the design of these technologies [18].

CHI 2014, April 26 - May 01 2014, Toronto, ON, Canada

http://dx.doi.org/10.1145/2556288.2557290

In this paper we examine how new social technologies can be utilized by aged care workers to support psychosocial care-giving and help build professional rapport between care providers and care recipients. We use the term *psychosocial care* to refer to care that attends to a person's social needs and emotional wellbeing. Social technologies offer numerous possibilities for enhancing this form of care, particularly when they incorporate visual and evocative forms of communication, such as captioned photographs.

We conducted a field study in which aged care managers used a novel photo and message-sharing tool to communicate with their clients. Analyses of the content that care managers created, and data from interviews conducted at the end of the study, illustrate how photo and message-sharing augmented the psychosocial aspects of care work but also created challenges. Our findings highlight the barriers faced by care managers in adopting the technology. It was challenging for care managers to integrate an additional form of communication into their busy work schedules, and they had to carefully negotiate social and personal communication in the context of their roles as professional caregivers. We conclude that social and visual forms of computer-mediated communication have the potential to enhance psychosocial aged care work but can also be problematic, making it necessary for care managers to engage in "boundary work" [15] in order to carefully define and maintain boundaries between their personal and professional lives.

TECHNOLOGY-SUPPORTED AGED CARE

The study reported in this paper focuses on the provision of government-funded aged care services that take place in the client's home, also known as community-based care. This form of care falls outside the realm of informal family-based care, institutional care, and health care, which together are the focus of much existing research on the design and use of technologies to support care work [e.g., 3, 4, 23]. There is a gap in this body of literature, with little attention given to the design of technologies to support the social aspects of community-based aged care work. Community-based care of older adults who live at home is becoming increasingly common [12]. While this care is often undertaken by family members, there are many organizations that provide care services in the home. Our research takes place in Australia, where older adults often receive support that is overseen by a care (or case) manager [13]. Care managers may come from a variety of professional backgrounds, including nursing, but in this role they are employed as aged care professionals, rather than nurses. The care manager's role involves assessing clients' support needs and organizing personal care services such as housecleaning, medical appointments, physical care, shopping, meal delivery, and transport [13, 27]. Care managers regularly visit clients at home. The relationship they develop with clients is the cornerstone of the care provision. Through detailed knowledge about the clients' home lives, care managers are able to identify the specific physical and social support that individual clients need [13].

Research in sociology has documented several challenges that occur when paid aged care work takes place in the client's home. One of the key challenges for aged care workers is negotiating boundaries between personal and professional roles, as caregivers attempt to provide personal care in a professional context [12, 20]. Of course, boundary-crossing between work and personal lives occurs in other settings too [15], and is especially challenging when new mobile and social technologies are introduced into the work and home environment [7]. Boundary negotiations also occur when new healthcare technologies are used in the home [1].

In addition, aged care workers must negotiate boundaries around their use of time, particularly regarding the provision of psychosocial care. Psychosocial care might include, for example, spending time in casual conversation with clients, or arranging for a socially isolated client to take part in organized group activities [e.g., 23]. Research suggests that many aged care workers consider spending time talking with clients to be an important component of good care, but are sometimes frustrated by professional expectations that prioritize task-oriented care and emotional detachment [9, 12, 20]. New communication technologies, such as social networking tools, could play a role in helping to overcome these challenges, providing opportunities for carers to interact with clients in an informal manner and augmenting the formal meetings that take place in the client's home. There have been studies in human-computer interaction that aimed to design technologies to support psychosocial care in institutional settings and with dementia patients [e.g., 6, 23, 26]. However, in community care settings, the focus has typically been on the use of telecare systems to provide security, rather than to support psychosocial care [14, 18].

In contrast, there is a growing body of research in HCI that has explored the use of social technologies to support informal care of older adults [e.g., 5] and, more broadly, to enhance intergenerational communications between older adults and remote family members [e.g., 10, 24]. There is a growing interest, too, in using photographs to foster communication with older adults, particularly in residential care settings [e.g., 6, 22, 26]. Photographs are emotional communications [11] and when combined with captions and text messages, they provide important opportunities for social engagement and self-expression [25]. In this study we explore the use of photo and message-sharing in a novel setting: formal care provision for older adults who live independently at home.

This paper focuses explicitly on care managers' experiences of using a novel tool to communicate with their clients. The older adults' perspective, albeit critical, is not the focus of this paper. Older adults' experiences of sharing captioned photographs have been discussed elsewhere [25]. The perspective of aged care workers, particularly professional care managers who provide psychosocial support for older adults living independently, has been largely overlooked in HCI research. The novelty of focusing on community care managers adds to the significance of our research.

THE FIELD STUDY

We conducted a qualitative field study over five months. Six care managers from an aged care organization, along with eight clients, were provided with an iPad to use during the study, which included a specially built iPad application. The application was developed for the purpose of this project, based on earlier research into older adults' social and communication needs [16]. We have described the application design and interface in earlier work [25].

Care Managers

The study was conducted in collaboration with a local aged care service provider. Care managers in the organization volunteered to take part and nominated clients from their case load who they believed would benefit from being part of the study because of a perceived need for increased social interaction. Clients with significant cognitive impairment or dementia were excluded. The clients (aged 67 – 93 years) all lived independently at home and received a community care package from the care provider [13]. This meant they had complex needs (e.g., frailty, ill health, limited mobility) and received assistance as required. Care managers oversaw clients' care and support provision. This involved developing a supportive relationship with the clients, telephoning regularly, conducting home visits every few weeks, and arranging additional support as required. In this organization, care managers would normally have a case load of 30 clients.

The pseudonyms used to identify the care managers are shown in Table 1. Care managers used the iPad application to communicate with the clients they had nominated to take part in the study (as listed in Table 1). This communication did not replace, but rather augmented, the face-to-face meetings and telephone contact that was a normal part of the care managers' role. Three care managers (Rebecca, Tonya, and Samantha) had only one client participating. Two other care managers (Sue and Mary) had nominated more than one client to participate. One care manager, Mary, resigned from the organization during the study and was replaced by Lucy.

Care manager	Client(s)
Sue	A (aged 93, male) B (aged 89, female) C (aged 86, male)
Mary Lucy	D (aged 71, female) E (aged 93, female)
Rebecca	F (aged 81, male)
Tonya	G (aged 82, female)
Samantha	H (aged 67, male)

Table 1: Care managers and their clients

Captioned Photographs and Messages

Aged care clients do not normally have access to existing social networking tools, and not all care managers own smartphones that can be used for multimedia messaging. Therefore, although there are existing social networking applications and mobile devices that enable users to share captioned photographs and messages, in this study we employed a purpose-built application.

The application featured a shared display showing user-created content moving down the iPad screen (see Figure 1). Content could take the form of: (a) a photograph on its own, (b) a photograph with a caption, or (c) a text message on its own. Content could not be saved on individual iPads, but was sent to a shared display, where it could be viewed by other users in the network. Users could also interact with the display by using the touch-screen interface to move objects around the screen. These interactions were visible to other users. Once connected, users could see each other's photographs and messages on the shared display. Each care manager was connected via this system to her own client (or clients), but not to other care managers or clients (see Table 1). For example, Sue's communications could be seen by Client A, B, and C. Clients were connected to each other, and could see all the photographs and messages that other clients created. In this paper, however, we focus on the interactions that occurred between care managers and their clients only.

Data Collection and Analysis

We utilized an ethnographic approach [8], which included close observation of participants' digital interactions, in-depth interviews, and focus group discussions. These methods are described further below.

Figure 1. Photo- and message-sharing display

Content created

The data for this study included all the content that care managers created and shared, which was stored on a server. While the clients also created photographs and messages, the purpose of this paper is to examine how care managers used the tool to communicate with clients. We therefore focus on the content that care managers created, only examining client's content when relevant to the analysis (e.g., when care managers responded to a specific photograph or message that a client created). Table 2, below, shows the total number of photographs and messages that care managers created during the field study. The number of contributions varied greatly, with one care manager (Rebecca) producing far more photographs and messages than others. Both Mary and Lucy were involved in the field study for a limited time and their input was therefore truncated.

Care manager	*Captioned photograph*	*Photograph (no caption)*	*Text only*	Total
Rebecca	43	3	46	92
Tonya	24	1	19	44
Samantha	12	0	11	23
Mary	3	4	7	14
Sue	5	0	7	12
Lucy	5	0	5	10
Total	92	8	95	195

Table 2: Content created by care managers

Focus group discussion

We held a focus group discussion with care managers after they had been using the technology for three months, at a morning tea event. During this event, each care manager was asked to describe how their use of the iPad application had impacted on their care management work. The group setting provided benefits that could not be realized through individual interviews, with care managers able to listen and respond to each others' reflections.

Interviews

We conducted individual interviews with care managers at the end of the study. These took place in the care managers' offices. We asked care managers to reflect on their experiences of using the application, any benefits the study appeared to provide for their clients, and the impact this form of communication had on their care work. In addition, we asked care managers to elaborate and reflect on some of the key points raised in the focus group discussion.

Data analysis

We used a grounded approach to conduct a thematic analysis of the data. That is, we did not apply an existing framework, but followed an iterative coding process [8]. We firstly examined the content that care managers created, and secondly the interview and focus group transcripts, to identify salient themes that emerged from each set of data. Two authors independently conducted a close examination of the data to identify core themes, which were assessed, refined, and finalized by the research team. This process was informed by our overall aim to understand how care managers utilized the technology to communicate with their clients.

CARE MANAGERS' COMMUNICATIONS WITH CLIENTS

In this section we describe findings from the analysis of the content that care managers created. The key themes we identified reflected four types of communication that the photographs and messages represented: a) encouragement; b) keeping in touch; c) responding to clients' personal interests; and d) sharing the care manager's world.

Encouragement

Throughout the field study, care managers gently encouraged their clients to use the technology by providing feedback, such as *"You're doing a really good job"* or *"great photo."* These messages often had more than one purpose. They let clients know their content had been delivered to the display, reassured clients they were using the technology correctly, and encouraged further use, e.g.: *"Hi, I got your message saying you are having a cup of tea! Well done! It worked!"* (Rebecca)

Humor and playfulness featured significantly in these messages. When a client sent a message asking if anyone had noticed her spelling mistake in a previous post, Mary replied: *"Hi, I didn't notice your error but... we all make misteaks! :)"* (sic). Mary's comment seeks to mitigate the client's embarrassment. In line with this lighthearted approach, care managers emphasized playfulness when encouraging their clients to interact with the system. Tonya sent a number of photographs with captions inviting her client to respond in game-like activities. She shared a photograph of a special lunch event with the caption *"Any guesses what this food is?"* and a photograph of a garden gnome (see Figure 2), which she captioned: *"This peaceful gnome is keeping us company in the office. Today we were trying to come up with a suitable name for him. Any suggestions?"* (Tonya)

These playful attempts to provoke response suggest that care managers viewed the technology, and the new form of communication it enabled, as a system that should be fun and enjoyable to all. The term "enjoy" appeared a number of times, e.g.: *"Hi! How are you enjoying it so far?"* and *"Hi, hope you are enjoying the project?"* (Sue). These encouraging messages can be viewed as a form of psychosocial care-giving and highlight the care managers' role as facilitators who gently support their clients to take part in social activities.

Figure 2. Playful encouragement: 'name the gnome'

Keeping in Touch

Care managers often used the technology to keep in touch with their clients. These messages typically involved "checking in" with clients (rather than "checking on" them) and often included an apology or an explanation for absence: *"Hi, I'm sorry that I have not checked in for a week. Have been busy trying to wrap things up before I go on leave."* (Samantha)

Checking in sometimes involved sending photographs of objects or scenes that might be considered mundane, e.g.: *"Hi, I am back at work after an unplanned week of sick leave. So here is a boring photo of my computer!"* (Rebecca). These photographs were not designed to stimulate a response from clients, but were used to let clients know that the care manager was thinking of them. The act of checking in is not simply an instrumental one. It is intrinsically linked with the care manager's desire to be assured of her clients' well-being. A lapse in interaction could mean the client was unwell, or required additional support using the technology. Thus Tonya's relief when her client who had been absent finally sent a photograph: *"Good morning. I am so happy to hear from you. I thought maybe something is not working. How is [your town] today, as beautiful as ever?" (Tonya)*

Care managers sent personal messages to check in with clients at times of specific concern. This study took place during the Australian summer, when temperatures can reach over 40 degrees Celsius (104F). This heat is problematic for older people and messages often contained advice to clients about staying well, e.g.: *"Hi, how was yr weekend? Keep cool.... Another hot day today" (Samantha)*. There were concerns about large bush or forest fires, particularly for clients who lived in rural areas, e.g.: *"Hello are you ok with the fire [in your area]?"* (*Tonya*). Rebecca sent a photograph and caption describing a friend's fire bunker, alluding to the danger of fires without specifically focusing on the client's own situation: *"Here's a photo of my friend's fire bunker at their property... Clever how they've planted vegies around it don't you think?"* (Rebecca). This ambiguity is reflected in another message that exhibits concern for the client, but segues into a more neutral concern about the garden: *"Good morning, be sure to keep cool today and drink plenty of water! I am worried about my newly planted lettuces and how they will hold up in the heat"* (Rebecca). This segue allows the sender to pull back from the advice-giving, paternal tone implicit in the early part of the message, and move onto a topic of common interest. This example illustrates how care managers were able to use this new form of communication to provide psychosocial care in subtle and non-intrusive ways.

"Keeping in touch" messages also included instrumental communication to organize care work and diarize appointments. The following message serves to check in with a client, inform him of a change in carer, wish him well, and remind him about a forthcoming appointment, all within a few short sentences: *"Just let you know that Sarah will be coming on Monday to help you as Anthony is still unwell. Have a great weekend! See you on Monday for the Christmas Lunch.!"* (Samantha). It is noteworthy that Samantha's communications primarily consisted of these instrumental communications. Samantha used the iPad to communicate with a bed-bound double-amputee who required substantial clinical care. There was clearly a place for new forms of communication to support Samantha's care management work, as we discuss later.

Responding to Clients' Personal Interests

The technology supported relationship-building by encouraging care managers to recognize and respond to their clients' personal interests. For instance, in response to a client who wrote several messages containing literary quotes, one care manager suggested: *"Perhaps we can develop our own iPad version of "Letters and Numbers"?!). Let's workshop it!"* (Mary). Here Mary playfully suggests they use the iPad to play a version of a popular Australian game show, which she knew would appeal to this client.

Another example from Mary illustrates that clients' contributions sometimes revealed new information, helping care managers develop a more holistic view of their clients' lives. A client shared a photograph of a flower, which she captioned: *"This is my 'Peace Lily', given to me by a friend when [my husband] died. [My friend], who was Librarian at the High School from which I retired as Principal, lives permanently now near Jerusalem."* This was clearly a very personal message, revealing much information about the client. Mary responded: *"I didn't know you were a school principal, now I'll have to behave or you might give me detention! The 'peace lily' is lovely, they should plant them throughout the world!!"* Mary acknowledges here that she has learned something new about her client's life, which may inform future interactions. Again, she has used humor, this time to lighten the response to a sensitive message.

Responses to clients' contributions provided insight into the rapport that existed between some clients and their care managers. In response to her client's photograph of a can of beer (captioned *"I'm just going to have one as per photo"*), Tonya sent a message that revealed an easy friendship: *"I guess you can be a bit naughty since you are not at work!"*

Knowing that gardening was a particular interest for her client, Rebecca initially shared photographs that showcased different parts of her garden (e.g., "*Here is a photo of my raspberry patch"*), which evolved into descriptions of her gardening activities (e.g., "*I did enjoy the day in my garden, pruning wisteria that is growing rampant at present"*). Eventually, Rebecca began using the technology to seek gardening advice, culminating in a lengthy exchange about garden ponds, e.g.: *"Your fish pond is lovely and clear – I can actually see the fish! Do you have a pump in yours or do the fish and plants keep it clean?"* This even led to a joint outing with her client to a garden centre. By responding to her client's personal interests, Rebecca has built common ground for ongoing conversation and rapport.

Figure 3. A shared interest: garden-themed images

Sharing of the Care Manager's World

While responding to the clients' personal interests helped care managers to view their clients as people, photographs illustrating the care manager's world similarly provided clients with a more holistic view of their care managers. This knowledge can help to build stronger client-care manager partnerships and enhance the clients' psychosocial care. However, there is a danger that personal disclosures might cross professional and personal boundaries, which the care managers carefully maintained, being mindful of the risk that lonely clients could become overly dependent on them for support.

The Workplace

The workplace was clearly considered an acceptable setting to photograph and describe. It featured in several early photographs the care managers shared. These photographs served to introduce clients to the care managers' world beyond the site of their regular home visits. For instance, Samantha showed an exterior view of her office building, with the caption *"This is our office at Western region."* Similarly, Tonya showed her desk at work, with the caption: *"This is where I work, right in the back of the office, so it is a little dark!"*(Figure 4). At first glance these photographs seem to represent mundane aspects of office life. They are significant, however, because they show aspects of the care managers' world that clients would not normally be privy to. Despite a professional relationship that can last for years, clients do not normally visit their care managers in the workplace. Furthermore, many clients are predominantly housebound; photographs illustrating settings other than the home provide clients with a window into a world they would not normally have access to.

The workplace is also a location where special events are recognized. This study took place over Christmas and many of the workplace photographs reflect this. Photographs showed Christmas trees and gifts in the office, and an otherwise ordinary photograph of the workplace became a celebratory message acknowledging the New Year: *"Happy new year to all from my office window."* (Sue). Representations of these celebratory events are physically located within the work environment but extend beyond it into other aspects of people's lives.

Figure 4. Care managers' workplaces: desk and office window

Home and Hobbies

Content from the care managers' home lives included photographs of pets, gardens and streetscapes (e.g., *"It looked better in real life, sunset in [my neighborhood]"* – Sue). Notably, no care managers sent photographs of family members. Instead, home life was represented in photographs that illustrated activities and hobbies. The inside of care managers' homes usually only appeared in Christmas-themed photographs, showing cards and decorations. Given the limited cultural diversity within this small client group, Christmas was a common event that pervaded the worlds of care manager and client, making it appropriate for care managers to share photographs of their domestic spaces. Few other photographs were taken inside the home. Those that were tended to reveal more personal content. Tonya, for instance, shared a photograph with the caption: *"My son's latest Lego creation"*. This was the only time that a care manager mentioned children.

Figure 5. Christmas-themed images from inside the home

Rebecca sent three photographs showing handmade quilts (see Figure 6). She included captions that described the personal meaning behind the quilts, e.g.: *"This is a hand stitched quilt I am working on. It has taken one year to hand sew the pieces together and now I am halfway through and quilting it."* In a sense, these captioned photographs represent carefully selected "gifts" from the care manger's personal life. Although Rebecca's client did not respond to this content, the photographs and captions appeared to be designed to provoke interest. As we saw above, personal hobbies, such as gardening can potentially reflect shared interests and help strengthen the client-carer relationship.

Figure 6. Hobbies: Images of home-made quilts

Holidays and Outings

Photographs and messages that represented holidays and outings were also common. These were taken outside the home and workplace, but still within the realm of care managers' personal lives. Sometimes care managers tried to provoke reminiscence by sharing photographs of recognizable landscapes, such as an historic building, captioned: *"Do you recognize this place?"(Tonya).*

Lucy, who joined the project near the end of the field study, took the iPad with her on several weekend outings and captured photographs of the scenery, using captions to provide context, e.g.: *"Lovely view of swan bay near [coastal town]. The black dots are swans*." Lucy's bay photograph provoked a response from a client who recognized the setting from previous holidays. Again, it is important to note that many clients were predominantly housebound and these photographs provided a means for care managers to bring the outside world to the clients. This could be seen as a form of psychosocial care, provoking reminiscence, shared interests, and storytelling.

Notably, care managers did not mention family members when describing their holidays and outings. In the following example, Rebecca tells a detailed story about a recent outing, in a caption that accompanied a photograph of a cruise boat: *"Here is a picture of the catamaran cruise boat I went on last Sunday. [...] It was amazing! I sat right at the front of the cruise boat with my legs dangling over the edge and during swells got my legs wet. It was a bit like a rollercoaster on the ocean! It was awesome! We had dolphins swimming alongside and in front of the cruiser putting on a show. It was fabulous to see large seal colonies out on the islands."*

Rebecca's enthusiasm for the outing is clear in the language she uses ("it was amazing!"). It is poignant that she wanted to share this experience with her client, in what appears to be another form of gift-giving. The description is designed to provoke positive feelings from the client, suggesting the care manager is making an attempt to attend to her client's psychosocial wellbeing. Despite the personal nature of the content, the absence of family members or people from this description suggests care has been taken to not make it too personal. As we discuss below, this was a deliberate strategy that Rebecca used as a form of boundary work.

INTERVIEW AND FOCUS GROUP FINDINGS

In this section we draw on the care managers' reflections about their use of the technology to consider how photo and message-sharing impacted on care managers' work and introduced new challenges. Our analysis of the interview and focus group discussions revealed three key themes: 1) Relationship building; 2) Boundary work; and 3) Time and technology. We discuss each of these below.

Relationship Building

A clear potential benefit of photo and message-sharing in this context is that it can help carers to build a supportive and holistic relationship with their clients. The content care managers created often spoke directly to clients or was created in response to clients' personal interests. During the interviews, care managers noted that they took their clients' interests into consideration when choosing photographs to share. The effect this had on relationship building depended partly on how well the clients and care managers already knew each other. For Lucy, who was developing a new relationship with the clients at the time of the study, it was difficult to know what she should photograph and share: *"I had only just met the clients so I didn't know what they would be interested in."* When one client responded to a photograph Lucy had shared, this seemed a promising start for their relationship. However, with that particular client Lucy believed *"it would be easy anyway, because she is such an easy-going person. But it's nice to get to know someone with photos. It could have been useful with other clients."* Similarly, for Tonya, photo and message-sharing did not appear to enhance the professional relationship she had with her client because this was already very strong: *"I think I've known her long enough. She knows that if she needs to talk she can [telephone me]."*

For others, however, photo and message-sharing clearly enhanced the client-carer partnership. This was particularly apparent for Rebecca and her client. Rebecca shared detailed and personal content that was designed to provoke interest and connect with her client. She commented during the interview that these mediated exchanges helped her to see her client as a whole person: *"I think it made me have a little less of a clinical sort of focus in my conversation during visits with him. You know, I saw him more as a person that's got other abilities, rather than as an aged client."* She noted that she chose gardening content because she knew this was of particular interest to him.

It was important that the technology supported direct communication between care managers and their clients. Samantha used the system primarily to support instrumental, rather than personal, communication. This had clear benefits for her relationship with her bed-bound client, as she no longer had to communicate via a third party: *"When we've got something like carers, a change of carers going in, instead of me telling her [daughter] to tell him [client], this is more direct."* However, Samantha was unable to keep using this form of communication because her client spent a lot of time in hospital and did not always have the iPad with him. Despite their limited use, Samantha could see possibilities of this technology for supporting psychosocial care: *"There are a lot of things that I want to encourage and motivate him (to do) on a daily basis."* Here, Samantha is alluding to the need to motivate a bed-bound client to maintain social activity and pursue personal interests, an aspect of care-giving that could be well-supported by new technologies.

Boundary Work

Describing the decisions they made when choosing content to share, care managers often spoke of the "boundary work" [15] they engaged in. That is, they had to carefully define and maintain the boundaries between their home and professional lives. Rebecca was particularly articulate about the challenges she faced in this regard. She may have experienced these challenges more acutely than other care managers, because of the amount and the nature of content she chose to share. Conversely, she also experienced the greatest benefit in terms of relationship building. Despite creating by far the most content, Rebecca said *"I struggled to come up with things to share so I didn't cross the boundary of 'case management professionalism' [...] I kept it to gardening, or general things. I kept family photos out."*

It is particularly important and yet problematic to maintain appropriate boundaries in the context of providing psychosocial care for lonely clients. As Rebecca stated: *"There's a real risk with some clients who are lonely, [of them] wanting you to fill that gap, and it's about balancing. ... You don't want them to rely on you"*. Photo-sharing in aged care work brings boundary negotiations to the surface. Care managers found it difficult to only choose content they felt was suitable in the context of their professional life, because they considered their work life to be too dull to photograph and share. However, the boundaries could become blurred when they were tempted to take photographs of their home life:

"I didn't know what to message. There's nothing interesting to photograph on a normal workday. I used it when I was out with my family. That's when there were interesting things to photograph. I always made sure it was in the back of the car when we went out. But I didn't want to take too many personal photographs – I didn't take any photos of my kids because that would have been too personal. I tried to keep it professional." (Lucy)

"I had it at home a few times but then I thought maybe that wouldn't be appropriate at home. Just the boundaries ... well I was probably over-cautious at times. And I think from [client's] perspective maybe it would have been more interesting to engage on a more personal level with me, but then I'm a paid worker and supposed to maintain professional boundaries, so that's what I tried to do." (Tonya).

Keeping family members absent from photographs was the main way that care managers maintained these boundaries. During the interview, Rebecca described her decision not to share photographs of her husband's woodwork, which would have aligned closely with her client's interests, who enjoyed making wooden toys for local schoolchildren: *"I could have taken photos of my husband's woodshed, because he [client] would have loved that, and the woodwork that my husband makes and sells at the market. There's a lot I could have shared, because he would have loved that but that's where I drew the line. Because I thought that's getting too personal."* Rebecca clearly felt that discussing a family member's hobby would have crossed professional boundaries. As noted above, however, she was happy to share information about her own hobbies.

Time and Technology

The issue of time as an area of conflict recurred throughout the conversations with care managers. Care managers expressed a feeling of guilt that they had not used the technology as much as they felt they should have. For those who did not use the technology extensively, time was consistently to blame, e.g.: *"I have such a busy schedule that I don't think I have actually maximized the [project]. I think it is more of the time factor for me."* (Samantha)

Even Rebecca, the most prolific content producer, felt the lack of time acutely: *"I actually have my iPad sitting on my desk every day. I put it there and look at it, I don't know how many times, and think 'I've got to do it, I've got to do it' but the next thing I know it's five o'clock and the day's gone."* Interestingly, this time pressure may have even contributed to Rebecca being so prolific: *"You just don't get time to even look at it. Most days were like that. And it was a [case of] 'Quick, take a photo or something, write something, and send it!'"* The immediacy of the technology is important here. The iPad could be positioned where it was always available and the application was designed to promote spontaneous communication. Photographs and messages could not be saved on the iPad to reconsider and revise before sending. Instead, content had to be sent to the shared display immediately, or otherwise lost.

The technology supported asynchronous communication, a clear point of difference between it and other forms of mediated communication, such as the telephone. Photo and message-sharing provided care managers with the opportunity to communicate with their clients at times when direct communication did not seem appropriate: *"With a phone call you never know whether you're not interrupting at the worst possible moment, whereas with this, you just leave them the time to respond when they feel like responding."* (Tonya) Similarly, for some care managers the iPad application provided clear time-saving benefits. On the telephone, care managers could get "caught" in lengthy conversations with clients. It was useful to use an indirect form of instrumental communication: *"I sent a client a message to remind him about the morning tea. It was a faster way of communicating. I could just tell him something. When I telephone him I sometimes get caught on the phone for a long time."* (Sue)

Social technologies can play a role in supporting care managers as they negotiate the temporal boundaries of their care work. However, while new technologies can be used to circumvent lengthy conversations, thus saving time, they also create tension. In this study, the technology was seen as valuable for augmenting psychosocial care. It was also, however, a source of guilt, serving as a reminder of the need to check in with clients, and introducing an additional form of communication that added to care managers' time pressure. This time pressure was a significant barrier that impeded care managers' use of the system.

DISCUSSION

Our findings demonstrate that social and visual forms of communication can be used to support the provision of community-based aged care services, but there are barriers that challenge their adoption and use. Researchers have previously identified the need for technologies in aged care to better respond to clients' social needs [4, 18]. However, there has been limited research on social technologies in formal aged care in the home. By demonstrating the potential for social and visual tools to enhance psychosocial care in this context, this study contributes to, and extends, research on technology-supported aging in place.

Photo and Message-sharing for Psychosocial Care

This study has shown that captioned photographs are visual and evocative forms of communication, well-suited to supporting psychosocial care. The key benefit of photo-sharing in aged care is that it helps to build the client and care manager [26]. This form of communication provided care managers with new opportunities to build rapport with their clients through shared interests, to communicate in creative and playful ways, and to keep in touch through casual communication. Previous research has similarly shown that photo-sharing can be valuable for relationship building in the workplace by creating a sense of community for geographically dispersed workers [21]. Photographs are highly personal forms of communication [7]. Studies have shown that photo-sharing has emotional significance in family settings and within intimate friendship groups [2, 11]. What happens when this highly personal communication medium is used in the context of professional care-giving? We found that care managers' photographs and messages were often personal, representing holidays, leisure activities, and hobbies. The captioned photographs presented clients with aspects of the care managers' worlds from beyond their usual relationship. While this clearly has the potential to strengthen the partnership, care managers found it challenging to share personal photographs and messages in the context of a professional relationship with clients. They ensured they did not create overly personal illustrations of their leisure activities by excluding family members from photographs. Given that family and friends often feature in leisure time, it appears that care managers were carefully crafting representations of their lives they considered to be suitable to share with clients. This finding highlights one of the significant challenges that can impede the use of social technologies in the context of providing professional care to older adults.

Barriers and Challenges

This study contributes insight into the challenges that occur when new social technologies are implemented into community-based aged care provision. These challenges can be seen most clearly in the boundary work that care managers engaged in [15]. This involved negotiating both temporal and spatial boundaries in order to effectively provide psychosocial care while also maintaining a clear distinction between "work" and "home". Maintaining this distinction was important for care managers to not only manage their workload, but also to ensure that their relationship with clients did not become too personal. Care managers were concerned that vulnerable clients could become overly dependent on them for support. Personal photographs may cause distress to clients. Although we did not examine clients' perspectives in this paper, the interviews we conducted with clients revealed they were all very positive about their care managers' use of the technology. Nevertheless, many clients lived alone, were widowed or single, and had limited mobility. For some people in this situation, photographs of outings, office life, and Christmas decorations may accentuate their feelings of loneliness and disconnection from the world.

In many ways the design of the technology contributed to the blurring of boundaries for care managers. The application was designed for use on an iPad, a mobile device that crosses spatial boundaries. The iPad accompanied care managers in both public and private spaces: in the back of the car while on family outings, in the office during the workday, and at home. While the iPad needed to be close by in case the opportunity arose to capture a photograph, this boundary crossing meant that the lines between work and home could easily become blurred.

As well as spatial boundaries between home and work, care managers had to negotiate temporal boundaries between "personal time" and "professional time." Time is an issue that receives much attention in the literature on computer-supported cooperative work, particularly regarding the use of mobile technologies in the workplace [e.g., 17]. While care managers in our study preferred to use the iPad application during the normal workday, time pressures and the banality of everyday work life made this difficult. This was a clear barrier to use. Care managers struggled to find objects or events in their work day they thought would be interesting to photograph and describe. For those who did not contribute much content, insufficient time was a significant impediment. The field study was a voluntary activity, on top of an already heavy workload. In addition, one care manager resigned from her job during the field study, which made it difficult for both her and her replacement to contribute substantially to the study because they were involved for a short period of time.

A clear limitation of the study, then, is that it was not fully integrated into care managers' work lives. A further limitation is the small number of participants. However, rather than generalizing from our data, the contribution of this research lies in the novel insights gleaned into the value and challenges of using social technologies to support formal psychosocial aged care for aging in place. We have presented data that highlights unique partnerships between clients and care managers and unique patterns of use, demonstrating the role the technology played in supporting individual relationships in home-based care.

CONCLUSION

In this paper we have demonstrated that photo and message-sharing can be valuable for augmenting psychosocial care-giving when used by community-based aged care managers to communicate with their clients. This study contributes to research on technology-supported aged care, demonstrating the possibilities that social technologies provide for supporting psychosocial care in the context of professional care in the home. Our findings suggest that novel technologies mediate caring in innovative ways, but also create tensions in boundary work, which must be carefully managed by professional care-givers to ensure boundaries between work life and home life are maintained.

ACKNOWLEDGEMENTS

We thank Kostas Kazakos for helpful feedback on an earlier draft of this paper and John Downs for technology development. This work was supported by Benetas, the Institute for a Broadband-Enabled Society, and the Australian Research Council (LP120100022). We thank the care managers and clients who participated in the project. This research was approved by the University of Melbourne's Human Research Ethics Committee.

REFERENCES

1. Aarhus, R. and Ballegaard, S. A. Negotiating boundaries: Managing disease at home. In Proc. *CHI 2010*, ACM Press (2010), 1223-1232.
2. Ames, M., Eckles, D., Naaman, M., Spasojevic, M. and Van House, N. Requirements for mobile photoware. *Pers. and Ubiq. Comp.*, *14* (2010), 95-109.
3. Ballegaard, S. A., Hansen, T. R. and Kyng, M. Healthcare in everyday life - Designing healthcare services for daily life. In *Proc. CHI 2008*, ACM Press (2008), 1807-1816.
4. Bratteteig, T. and Wagner, I. Moving healthcare to the home: The work to make homecare work. In *Proc. ECSCW 2013*, Springer-Verlag (2013).
5. Consolvo, S., Roessler, P., Shelton, B. E., LaMarca, A., Schilit, B. and Bly, S. Technology for care networks of elders. *IEEE Pervasive Computing*, *3*, 2 (2004), 22-29.
6. Gaver, W., Boucher, A., Bowers, J., Blythe, M., Jarvis, N., Cameron, D., Kerridge, T., Wilkie, A., Philliips, R. and Wright, P. The Photostroller: Supporting diverse care home residents in engaging with the world. In *Proc. CHI 2011*, ACM Press (2011), 1757-1766.
7. Graham, C., Laurier, E., O'Brien, V. and Rouncefield, M. New visual technologies: shifting boundaries, shared moments. *Visual Studies*, *26*, 2 (2011), 87-91.
8. Hammersley, M. and Atkinson, P. *Ethnography: Principles in Practice*. Routledge, 2007.
9. King, D. It's frustrating! Managing emotional dissonance in aged care work. *Aust. Journal of Social Issues*, *47*, 1 (2012), 51-70.
10. Lindley, S. E. Shades of lightweight: supporting cross-generational communication through home messaging. *Univ. Acc. in the Inf. Soc.*, *11*, 1 (2012), 31-43.
11. Lindley, S. E., Randall, D., Sharrock, W., Glancy, M., Smyth, N. and Harper, R. Narrative, memory and practice: Tensions and choices in the use of a digital artefact. In *Proc. HCI 2009*, BCS (2009).
12. Mears, J. Blurred boundaries: how paid careworkers and care managers negotiate work relationships. In *Paid Care in Australia: Politics, Profits, Practices*, Sydney University Press, Sydney, AUS (2009), 145-166.
13. Mears, J. and Garcia, E. *Transformations of Care: Living the Consequences of Changing Public Policies in Australia*. University of Western Sydney (2011)
14. Mort, M., Roberts, C. and Callen, B. Ageing with telecare: Care or coercion in austerity? *Sociology of Health & Illness*, *35*, 6 (2013), 799-812.
15. Nippert-Eng, C. E. *Home and Work: Negotiating Boundaries Through Everday Life*. The University of Chicago Press, Chicago, 1996.
16. Pedell, S., Vetere, F., Kulik, L., Ozanne, E. and Gruner, A. Social isolation of older people: the role of domestic technologies. In *Proc. OzCHI 2010*, ACM Press (2010), 167-170.
17. Perry, M., O'Hara, K., Sellen, A., Brown, B. and Harper, R. Dealing with mobility: Understanding access anytime, anywhere. *ACM Trans. Comput.-Hum. Interact.*, *8*, 4 (2001), 323-347.
18. Roberts, C. and Mort, M. Reshaping what counts as care: Older people, work and new technologies. *ALTER, Eur. Journ. of Dis. Res.*, *3* (2009), 138-158.
19. Rowan, J. and Mynatt, E. D. Digital family portrait field trial: support for aging in place. In *Proc. CHI 2005*, ACM Press (2005), 521-530.
20. Stone, D. Caring by the book. In *Care Work: Gender, Class, and the Welfare State*, Routledge, NY (2000).
21. Thom-Santelli, J. and Millen, D. R. Learning by seeing: Photo viewing in the workplace. In *Proc. CHI 2009*, ACM Press (2009), 2081-2090.
22. van Dijk, B., Dadlani, P., van Halteren, A. and Biemans, M. Life changes, connection stays: Photo sharing and social connectedness for people with special needs. In *Proc. ECCE*, ACM Press (2010), 135-142.
23. Vargheese, J. P. Persuasive dialogue for older adults: promoting and encouraging social interaction. In Ext. Abstracts *CHI 2013*, ACM Press (2013), 877-882.
24. Vetere, F., Davis, H., Gibbs, M. and Howard, S. The Magic Box and Collage: Responding to the challenge of distributed intergenerational play. *Int. J. Hum.-Comput. Stud.*, *67*, 2 (2009), 165-178.
25. Waycott, J., Vetere, F., Pedell, S., Kulik, L., Ozanne, E., Gruner, A. and Downs, J. Older adults as digital content producers. In *Proc. CHI 2013*, ACM (2013), 39-48.
26. Webster, G., Fels, D. I., Gowans, G., & Hanson, V. L. Portraits of individuals with dementia: Views of care managers. In *Proc. HCI 2011*, British Computer Society (2011), 331-340.
27. You, E. C., Dunt, D., Doyle, C., Hsueh, A. (2012). Effects of case management in community aged care on client and carer outcomes: a systematic review of randomized trials and comparative observational studies. *BMC Health Services Research, 12*, 395.

The Routines and Needs of Grandparents and Parents for Grandparent-Grandchild Conversations Over Distance

Azadeh Forghani and Carman Neustaedter
School of Interactive Arts and Technology, Simon Fraser University
250 – 13450 102nd Avenue, Surrey, BC, Canada
azadehf@sfu.ca, carman_neustaedter@sfu.ca

ABSTRACT

A variety of systems have been designed to support communication between distance-separated grandparents and grandchildren. Yet there are few studies of the actual conversational routines of these groups as well as the social challenges that might arise as a result of technology usage. To address this gap, we conducted an interview and diary study that explores the conversational practices of distance-separated grandparents and young grandchildren (aged 3-10) from the perspective of the grandparents and parents of the children. Our results describe the focus of grandparent-grandchild conversations. and show that grandparent-grandchild communication is not without its challenges: grandparents sometimes feel self-conscious, perceive that parents or children will be annoyed if they ask too many questions, and do not want to interfere too much in their grandchildren's lives. The implication is that designs should attempt to support the conversation routines and needs of grandparents and grandchildren while attempting to mitigate the social challenges.

Author Keywords

Grandparent and grandchild communication; family communication; design;

ACM Classification Keywords

H.5.3. Group and Organization Interfaces: Computer-supported cooperative work.

INTRODUCTION

The grandparent-grandchild bond is an important emotional relationship in a human's life, often considered to be very similar to the parent-child bond [31]. Both grandparents and grandchildren benefit from a strong relationship [31]. Yet, in reality, many grandparents and grandchildren face challenges in building and maintaining their relationship. This is often because of social challenges such as divorce, or poor relationships between parents and grandparents, yet it can also be caused by geographical separation [2,21].Technology such as the phone or video chat can help mitigate issues of distance-separation, yet they bring with them their own challenges, such as parental scaffolding and child engagement [2,26]. Time zones and busy schedules also add to the challenges [21] as does cultural differences and language barriers.

CHI 2014, April 26–May 1, 2014, Toronto, Ontario, Canada.

http://dx.doi.org/10.1145/2556288.2557255

There are several systems designed to support this demographic already where the focus is doing and sharing fun activities (e.g., [3,17,26]). While beneficial, these systems tend to not focus on direct conversation where grandparents and grandchildren might share their personal stories, achievements and experiences. We also see a gap in understanding how parents react to communication between grandparents and grandchildren and how they see such communication ideally working. Past research on grandparent-grandchild communication also does not focus on understanding social or cultural issues beyond scaffolding challenges for parents. Without this understanding, one may easily think that grandparent/child communication occurs with little social conflict.

Given this background, the goal of our research was to understand grandparent and grandchild communication over distance from the perspective of the grandparents and parents of the children. In particular, we were interested in families with children aged 3 to 10 years old and not yet at the pre-teen stage of life (where they want to talk less with grandparents [21]). We also wanted to understand the parent's role in facilitating this communication. For these reasons, we conducted a diary and interview study with grandparents or parents of children between the ages of 3 and 10. Both provided an understanding of how grandparents communicated with their grandchildren and how they engaged them for conversation. We also investigated what grandparents were already sharing or would like to share with their grandchildren as well as the challenges they faced in doing so.

Our results show that grandparents like to know nearly 'everything' about their grandchildren. Conversations focus on learning activities, unexpected happenings, storytelling (real life and fiction), sharing experiences, and cultural exchanges. Yet communication is not always an ideal situation. Grandparents face social challenges such as feeling self-conscious and overly inquisitive and often work hard to socially manage communication exchanges. Many parents desired additional social support from grandparents over distance. These findings show the value of conversational systems that focus on engaging children to share more details about their daily activities. They also suggest trying to mitigate the social pressures and challenges faced by grandparents and parents.

RELATED WORK

Studies of Family Communication

Family communication and the role of technology has been a widely studied topic in the fields of CSCW and HCI. In particular, there has been a large emphasis on how family members desire to connect with each other over distance to share stories about life, learn about the well-being of others, and coordinate times for visiting [22,23,27,28]. People prefer in-person communication, but when they cannot achieve this, they value synchronous systems like the phone or video chat to feel especially close to one another [5,14,15,16,23,28], and asynchronous systems to balance the time demands of communication [23,28].

More specifically focused on child-adult communication, Ballagas et al. [2] studied phone conversations between children and their remote family members. They found that children are easily distracted, not motivated to talk, and, depending on the age, have difficulties using the phone. They also show that phone conversations are not enough to build a close relationship with children. Other research has shown the value in adult-child conversations for healthy language development [33]; this motivated our own study.

There are also a number of studies of grandparent-grandchild relationships and communication. Geurts et al. [10] found that more frequent contact with a grandchild during childhood helped strengthen their relationship throughout life. Kenner et al. [18] showed that learning was enhanced for both grandparents and grandchildren when they jointly participated in activities. We also see that grandparent-grandchild relationships often depend on parents to help establish the relationship and subsequent communication [4]. Studies have shown conversations between grandparents and adult grandchildren (college students) tend to focus on education, family, friends, leisure and current events [20]. Evjemo et al. [8] found that grandparent-grandchild conversations were typically about the concurrent activities that kids were doing while on the phone. Yet phones did not suffice for sharing the activity.

Systems for Communication Over Distance

There have also been a variety of systems designed to support family communication over distance. First, several systems are targeted at the family as a whole in an effort to support a variety of relationships. Judge et al. [15,16] explored the effect of always-on video connections on creating stronger feelings of connection and togetherness between distance-separated family members. They found children liked such systems because they could easily show their grandparents objects and even participate in shared activities. Experience2Go [13] was designed for family members to share activities (e.g., school events, sports events, birthday parties) with remote loved ones such as grandparents regardless of where the activity happened. Other systems focus on child-child connections for school-aged children to support synchronous play dates over distance [17,32]. Here children can play together, show their toys and talk to each other [17,32]. We also see examples of asynchronous video communication systems for supporting intercultural communication between children [6] or connections amongst school friends [12]. Study results show the importance of allowing children to share objects, tell stories, and perform for friends [6,12].

Systems for Grandparents and Grandchildren

Several systems have also been proposed in order to engage children to stay in touch with their remote grandparents. First, some focus on supporting story telling. Family Story Play [24] is a tangible collaborative storytelling interface that uses a physical book coupled with video conferencing. A web-based version called Story Visit was also created [26] where grandparents and grandchildren can read an e-book together. People in Books [9] is a shared visual space for story reading, which immerses remote readers into online storybook illustrations, giving them an illusion that they are part of the magical world. Vutborg et. al. [30] proposed an asynchronous system that combines different components including collage and storytelling features where these components mediate play and oral storytelling.

Second, some systems focus on games and tangible objects to stimulate communication. Take Me With You [21] is a shared adventure game that promotes social interactions between remote grandparents and grandchildren along with physical movements in the real world reflecting an illusion of exploring a virtual world and doing shared activities together. Magic Box [29] is a physical box, which carries gifts, toys, photos, and any other special things between grandparents and grandchildren. Raffles et al. [25] developed a messaging system for preschoolers using a jack-in-the box toy with an embedded mobile phone.

Third, there also exist systems focused on grandparents who may face challenges in communicating because of their age, technical literacy, or illness [21].

Taken together, we see a variety of research on family communication and support for connecting grandparents and grandchildren. Yet we see little on how grandparents might converse with their grandchildren to learn about their life and how designs can support this aspect of relationship building. Several of the systems described above can facilitate and support conversation during other activities (e.g., play), however, we have yet to see studies focused on what that conversation might specifically be about, or how conversation happens (or could) without such activities. We also did not find any literature that describes the social or cultural challenges that exist as a result of grandparent-child communication over distance.

STUDY METHODOLOGY

We conducted a diary and interview study to explore grandparent-grandchild conversations over distance from the perspective of the grandparents and parents. Our goal was to reveal how grandparents and grandchildren conversed and what social challenges they faced from the adult perspective.

Participants

We recruited 20 participants through snowball sampling, emails to teachers and parents of a local elementary school, and ads on Facebook, Twitter, and CraigsList. Half of the participants were grandparents of children between 3 and 10 years old, while the other half were the parents of children in this age range. We recruited participants with diverse demographics and cultural backgrounds. Our study was largely focused in Vancouver, Canada but due to snowball sampling we had participants from several countries: 15 from Canada (although some migrated from countries, e.g., Italy, Albany, Iran, India, Ukraine, Brazil), 1 from the United States, 3 from Iran and 1 from Australia. All participants except two were female as women primarily contacted us about the study. However, this reflects past research that shows women are typically the most involved in family communication [11,23].

Some of our participants were living in different cities than their grandchildren and some were in different countries with different languages, cultures and time differences. We included participants with different family situations, such as single parents and step-grandparents. We also purposely recruited people with cultural differences in the family due to reasons such as marriage out of faith, or immigration to a new country. We wanted to investigate if this impacted the exchange of cultural knowledge between the grandparents and grandchildren. We did not include children as participants in our study because our focus was on an adult's perspective and topics related to such a perspective (e.g., family conflict, language, methods for engaging children). We suggest that future research explores children's needs as part of such communication.

Interview Method

We conducted semi-structured interviews with each participant individually. Interviews lasted between 45 and 60 minutes and occurred in person (at the participant's home or location of their choice), via Skype, or on the phone. Interviews contained questions in several categories:

1. **Background:** We asked about their cultural background and family situations, and reasons for distance-separation.

2. **Communication Patterns:** We asked participants to describe communication with their remote grandchildren or their children's communication with the remote grandparents. We focused on the methods, frequency, duration, and the existing and desired content of communication. We also asked several gender and age-specific questions for families who had both boys and girls.

3. **Communication Needs:** We also asked about communication needs that went beyond existing routines. This included questions about children's activities, daily routines, developmental stages, stories, and achievements. We asked those participants living in different countries with different cultures about concerns and issues that they might have faced due to cultural differences. On the parents side, we asked similar questions but from the parental perspective.

4. **Barriers and Conflicts:** We asked participants about communication challenges or issues. We specifically took a look at issues around speaking in different languages and living in different time zones. We wanted to explore how these issues influenced communication, if at all. Lastly, we asked about family conflicts that might occur as a result of communication either between parents and grandparents, parents and children or between siblings of the same family.

Online Diary

After our first two interviews with grandparents, we recognized that it was difficult for them to remember the specifics of how they communicated with their grandchildren, especially if the frequency of communication was low. For this reason, we asked our remaining 18 participants to keep an online diary of grandparent-grandchild communication over a period of three weeks before the interviews. An online form asked them about their recent communication, the content of the communication, and any issues or challenges they faced. Participants filled these in after communication episodes with their grandchildren or when they thought of things to note. We read all submitted diaries prior to the interview session and focused portions of the interview on getting more detailed information about communication episodes reported in the diaries. We found these participants were able to provide much more detailed responses during their interviews. However, we still used the data from our first two interviews in our analysis.

Data Collection and Analysis

We kept handwritten notes along with audio or video recordings for all interviews. Recordings were transcribed and then we performed an analysis using open, axial, and selective coding on our transcriptions and diary entries. The goal of our analysis was to document and understand the main themes in order to provide design implications for supporting this relationship. We did not find any gender differences aside from boys tending to talk about items normally associated with 'masculinity' (e.g., armies) and girls talking about more 'feminine' objects (e.g., Barbie).

We report on the most prominent findings focused on aspects of the communication routine and the use of technology and non-technology; conversational content during communication; and, social situations and challenges. Some of our results refer to a child's perspective, yet this is the interpretation through the grandparent or parent's eyes and not the actual child.

COMMUNICATION ROUTINES

Participants described a variety of communication routines with different technology preferences, methods for engaging children, and varied timing and frequency.

Technology and Non-Technology Preferences

Both the grandparents and parents in our study actively tried to build the relationship between the grandparents and grandchildren in a variety of ways. This included having phone calls, using video chat, exchanging email, and even sending post cards or other letters to the grandchildren. The most frequent mode of communication that we learned about was the use of phone calls between the grandparents and grandchildren. These calls were either deliberately targeted for the grandchildren, or were portions of calls between the parents and grandparents that then shifted focus to having the children converse.

Despite the prevalence of phone calls, 17 out of 20 participants actually preferred to use video chat instead because grandparents could actually see their grandchildren, their growth and looks, etc. and share the viewing of objects such as books and toys. Yet many grandparents in our study explained that they were not as familiar with video chat so it was often difficult to use it. Parents similarly described this as being an issue with the grandparents. As a result, video chat was most often used in situations when other family members were around to help set up a video chat session.

Communication Frequency and Timing

Our findings showed that grandparents typically tried to communicate with their grandchildren on a weekly basis, if possible, though many participants desired to talk with their grandchildren several times a week. Some grandparents only talked to their grandchildren once or twice a month. Weekends were the most popular time for communication because of busy work schedules during the week. Frequency was also dictated by the closeness between the parents and grandparents, as well as the occurrence of holidays, birthdays, and other special events or days. Those families that had relationship issues between the parents and grandparents caused grandparents and grandchildren to rarely communicate (once or twice a year). We found that children's communication with their remote grandparents usually depended on their parents' communication with the grandparents. Mother-daughter communication was typically more frequent, thus, children generally communicated more with their mother's parents. However, this was not the case in some divorced families when children stayed with their fathers. As one might expect, time zone differences made the communication between remote grandparents and grandchildren less frequent and often limited it to only weekends.

Regardless of the technology being used for grandparents and grandchildren to communicate, grandchildren did not want to be distracted while already playing or engaged in an activity. Communication that was a part of a routine (e.g., the same time each week) was more likely to be received well by grandchildren than a random phone call or video chat session that interrupted existing playtime. Children would routinely get bored after short durations of conversation with grandparents (e.g., 5 to 15 minutes) with video chat calls typically holding the child's attention longer. Some children would come and go from the room as parents conversed with grandparents where they would move into and out of the conversation.

We also found that the call duration of parents and grandparents often dictated how much time the grandparents talked with the grandchildren. Grandparents who talked more with the parents (their children) tended to talk longer with the grandchildren. This was because they had 'more to talk about.' Thus, parent-grandparent conversations can act as a catalyst for grandparent-grandchild conversations.

Engagement and Awareness

In order to engage grandchildren to talk, remote grandparents actively tried to learn about their interests and then focus on these during conversations. This may come from visits to see the child in person, or discussions with the child's parent or siblings. For example, P12's mother (the grandma) always learned a lot of information about her remote grandson from her. When the grandmother talked with her grandson, she already knew who his friends were, what activities they did together and, consequently, what to talk about. This allowed her to engage her grandson on the phone for a long time. Related to this, we also found that an awareness of a grandchild's life also helped grandparents to simply feel close to their grandchildren.

"Sometimes it is nice to know if the child is sick. Some kids like a phone call from Grandma when they do not feel well. Grandma would just like to say I love you! When their grandson or grand daughter are sick, it is important for the child to know Grandma and Grandpa care also." - P1, Grandmother, Diary

Grandparents also creatively did activities with their grandchildren over both the phone and video chat. For example, P2 whose grandson was interested in armies, camouflage, and going out hunting, made a blanket with camouflage to build a closer relationship with him. They spent large amounts of time talking about the blanket and making a story around it whenever they talked.

In addition to the above, grandparents also had particular topics or themes that they tried to focus conversations around in order to engage their grandchildren. We describe these in the next section.

CONVERSATIONAL CONTENT

All conversational content tended to favor recent activities as this was what the grandchildren would most often bring up. Children younger than five years tended to focus on describing the immediate or recent past (e.g., the past hour), even if the activities were short in duration and of everyday mundane things that might have little significance to the grandparents; prior research has also showed conversational focus on current activities [8]. Children older than five years discussed recent events but would go further back in time to talk about the current day or past week. Their descriptions were also of longer-term activities.

"My grandson told me that while they were at their farm, he was towed behind the tractor on ski and then he tried to drive the tractor." – P2, Grandparent, Grandchild Aged 6

Our analysis revealed that conversations between the grandparents and grandchildren focused around several main themes: learning, unexpected 'stuff,' storytelling, sharing experiences, and cultural exchanges. Some of the examples that we learned about fell into multiple categories; thus, they are not mutually exclusive groupings.

Learning Activities

We found that grandchildren often talked with their grandparents about what they learned, given the frequency of this activity at school, pre-school, through home activities with parents, or at extracurricular activities like sports. They liked to talk about or show their abilities, in particular, new ones, such as singing a song, reading a book, or showing their artwork and drawings.

"My daughter reads books for [her grandparents] in English although she knows that they cannot understand English at all but the way that the remote grandparents enjoy her reading encourages her to read for them." – P10, Parent, Children Aged 3 and 7

"We talk a lot about synchronized swimming when I talk with her because that's the focus of her life right now" – P7, Grandparent, Grandchildren Aged 4 & 6

"She had told me that she wanted to tell her grandmother that she had swam in the shallow end of the pool from one side to the other without help." - P18, Father, Diary

In many cases, video chat worked better for sharing learning activities because grandparents could actually see the child showing them the new skill or book they were reading. However, sports activities were routinely difficult to share over video chat because they occurred away from the home.

Unexpected 'Stuff'

Grandchildren also liked to follow and talk about unexpected happenings in their grandparents' lives. Thus, while children were keen to share everyday mundane things about their own life, their interest in their grandparents lives was more 'high level' where they talked about unexpected things. For example, one grandchild was surprised to learn that his grandparents lived in a different time zone (12 hours difference) and had different notions of day/night:

"My 6 year old grandson asks me whether it is day or night at my side and sometimes reminds me that he knows that although its night for him it is my daytime." – P4, Grandparent

P7 had a similar situation that revolved around different weather patterns. She lived in the same country as her grandchildren but with a different climate:

"They think it's very cool that we have snow and I think it's very cool that they don't." – P7, Grandparent Grandchildren Aged 4 & 6

Storytelling

As expected, children loved when grandparents told them stories. This included bedtime stories, fairy tales, and also real family stories. Grandchildren were also particularly interested in stories about their parents when they were kids, what it was like for the parent to be a child, or what the grandchildren were like when they were born.

Some grandparents were also very creative when telling stories to their grandchildren and would turn it in to an interactive game. For example:

"I'll start the story and then they continue it, and I'll continue it, that sort of thing, alternating. So, we make it up." – P7, Grandparent, Grandchildren Aged 4 & 6

Another grandparent leveraged artifacts from her travels to create special stories:

"One thing we do – my husband and I, often go on trips. one way we have communicated, and that has been quite fun, is to collect a number of postcards from everywhere we went, and then create a story and write one line of one sentence of the story on each of the postcards and mail it from a different city so that when we got home, they might have got 30 different postcards and a complete story. You know, that has been fun." – P2, Grandparent, Grandchild Aged 6, Step-grandchildren Aged 4,5, & 6

Sharing Experiences

Grandparents and grandchildren also shared their experiences with each other. This related to either grandparents or grandchildren talking about their travels to new places or talking about shared interests and passions, or the grandparent's occupation.

"Whenever I'm in exotic places, I send them post cards, ..., and they know that grandma travels, so when I go to visit, or sometimes they'd tell me... we talk about different places I've been, and they say, "grandma, have you been to blah, blah, blah?" – P5, Grandparent, Grandchildren 5 & 7

P13 described how her daughter (aged 8) had read a book about endangered animals and wanted to have a website created so she could write about it. Her 'granny' had a blog and so they had a long and interesting conversation where granny talked about blogs, webpages, and the difference between the two. They also talked about what kind of animals the granddaughter wanted to write about and how she was going to research and read about them for her blog.

Participants also described talking and reminding grandchildren about physical and shared experiences that they used to have with each other. For example, P2 used to make cookies and biscuits with her step-granddaughter (aged 5) whenever they visited each other and they usually talked about this when they were on the phone.

Cultural Exchange

Some grandparents and grandchildren also talked about big cultural events like Christmas, Thanksgiving, Easter, Halloween, and New Year celebrations. Both parents and grandparents liked the grandparents to talk about cultural events and heritage with remote grandchildren. This included simple conversations such as asking what gifts children received for a holiday, and also more detailed descriptions such as the meanings behind holidays. The extent to which this happened depended on the children's age, their interest, and family background. For example, grandparents that had different cultural backgrounds than their grandchildren sometimes talked about their own cultural celebrations.

"I think ritual and tradition also help to give people a sense of their place in the world and their history and their roots, a sense of belonging, and it's really important." – P6, Grandparent, Grandchild Aged 7 & 9

While beneficial for some, we elaborate on the challenges with cultural exchanges in subsequent sections.

SOCIAL SITUATIONS AND CHALLENGES

We also found additional social situations and challenges emerge as a result of communication between grandparents and grandchildren. These related to being recently separated by distance; parental support; self-consciousness and perceived annoyance; or, being of a different culture.

Becoming Separated by Distance

We found that communication between grandparents and grandchildren was often especially challenging right after separation. For example, several participants described how their grandchildren refused to talk on the phone or use video chat with the grandparents for the first few months after one of the parties moved away. This happened for all four families in our study where grandparents and grandchildren lived close by and then one party immigrated to a country far away. The grandchildren wondered why they had to move apart and felt resentment towards the situation. Once communication resumed, the grandchildren would remind the grandparents about emotional moments that they had with them to make sure that the remote grandparents still loved them despite the distance separation. For example, P3 said her grandson frequently asked her: *"Granny, did you remember that you used to tell me a story and I used to sleep in your arms when you were here? Would you do it again when you visit?"*

Parental Support

Our results also showed that some parents liked to have remote grandparents support them and become more involved in their children's activities from a parenting perspective. This most often occurred in households with single parents or parents with busy schedules, or when the grandparent's profession related to the support needed (e.g., a school teacher). For example, P10, who is a single mom and working full time said:

"I like my parents to read books for my children over Skype while they want to sleep or help my daughter in her math problems and homework." – P10, Parent, Children Aged 3 & 7

Grandparents also offered parental support for situations where they may know more about a topic than one of the parents. For example, one parent talked about how 'grandpa,' a dentist, was especially valuable to have talk to her son because of his occupational experience:

"Few months ago my son had some tooth problem and went to dentist. As my father is a dentist too, my son told the story for him and I asked my dad to remind hygienic routine to my son. My son enjoyed this practice and showed his teeth and the way he was brushing in a video chat to my dad. My father keeps looking at his teeth and pretends that he is checking up his teeth. My son encouraged taking care of his hygienic routine more." – P5, Parent, Child Aged 5

In addition, we also found that remote grandparents can become more involved in activities or topics where there is a lack of support or interest from the parents. For example, P2 described how she talked with her grandchildren about things that were not of interest to the children's parents:

"Animals. That's a huge, huge thing for one of [my step-grandchildren]. It might be more important to another if mom and dad were into animals, but they were not." – P2, Grandparent, Grandchildren Aged 6, Step-Grandchildren Aged 4, 5, & 6

While parental support by grandparents was certainly valuable, some grandparents described how they did not want to overstep their bounds and infringe on the parenting styles of their children.

"I deliberately behave like a grandparent, not like a parent. We would resist interfering with their discipline because it feels then like you're criticizing the parent." – P7, Grandparent, Grandchildren Aged 4 & 6

Similarly, some parents talked about how they did not want the grandparents to influence certain child behaviors.

"Some of the language from my father-in-law could be toned down. You can't just tell kids that 'if I were you, I'd just go and tell them I'm gonna kill you.' You can't say that in front of kids." – P13, Parent, Children Aged 5 & 8

Self-Consciousness and Perceived Annoyances

All grandparents in our study felt that being separated by distance from their grandchildren weakened their emotional bond with their grandchildren. This made some grandparents apprehensive or self-conscious when communicating with their grandchildren because they did not want to provide unneeded advice or annoy them by asking them about their unpleasant experiences.

For example, P2 described how she wanted to talk about her grandchildren's passions but this could easily change and she did not want to be embarrassed by asking about the wrong thing. She also did not know if her grandchildren were having bad experiences with their activities and did not want their short amount of conversational time to focus on negative thoughts:

"I would like to talk about whatever their passions are. One of them is hugely interested in animals; one is interested in language, stars, geography and history. One of them is going to a French and Russian school and not really enjoying it, so he doesn't want to talk about or talk in French at this stage. I'm just trying to build relationship with them wherever they are." – P2, Grandparent, Grandchild Aged 6, Step-Grandchildren Aged 4, 5 & 6

Similarly, P5 described wanting to know about a potentially unpleasant topic:

"You want to find out a little bit about the kind of people they are and also to watch their development... My grandson just last week was writing a test to get into a school in his area. So, I was very interested in how he did in the test. Was he anxious? Did he feel comfortable? And it will be interesting to see if the does get chosen." – P5, Grandparent, Grandchild Aged 7

Interestingly, we found out that while grandparents were interested to know about almost every detail of their grandchildren's lives, they did not want to bother them by asking 'too many' questions. Grandparents expressed a similar sentiment about asking parents too much information about their grandchildren. Thus, they perceived that the other parties might be annoyed with their questions. Because of this, nearly all of the grandparents we talked to did not push their grandchildren to talk about things. Instead, they preferred that their remote grandchildren directed the conversation and talked about what they wanted. This is surprising given the age and (lack of) conversational abilities of young children.

In cases where grandparents were part of divorced families or were step-grandparents, grandparents were additionally concerned about the focus of conversations with their grandchildren and 'saying the wrong thing'. This was despite having 'good' relationships with the parents and grandchildren. As one might imagine, situations like these were even worse when there *were* relationship issues between grandparents and either or both parents.

Cultural Differences

As mentioned, some grandparents really liked to share cultural knowledge with their grandchildren (e.g., traditional cultural holidays). This was especially the case for grandchildren who had moved away from one's native country (e.g., grandchildren living in Canada after moving from India). However, this also raised challenges. First, language was often an obvious barrier. Some grandchildren simply did not speak the same language as their grandparents, or their grandparents did not know how to say words associated with cultural events in the language that grandchildren understood. Second, in some cases, grandparents told us they would prefer not to overwhelm children with knowledge about their original roots because they felt that remote grandchildren had a lot of other things to deal with already. Instead, grandparents wanted to talk about the new culture of the grandchildren, despite a longing to share their native roots and traditions.

Exchanging cultural knowledge was also challenging when cultures clashed, such as when people were married 'out of faith' or with a person of another nationality or religion. For example, P5 described religious issues around holidays:

"I would like to talk more of our religious holidays but it's difficult because they celebrate more of the Christian, because of their father's family." – P5, Grandparent, Grandchildren Aged 5 & 7

Because of situations like these, many grandparents in our study simply tried to avoid such conflicting topics:

"I think you have to be very careful as a grandparent to recognize the boundaries, recognize the limits." – P7, Grandparent, Grandchildren Aged 4 & 6

On the other hand, parents' opinion about grandparents talking with the grandchildren about culture, religion, and heritage varied depending on personal attitudes, family backgrounds, or personal preferences. Several parents said that they did not like grandparents to talk about 'religious stuff' with their children, while others were okay with it.

DISCUSSION AND DESIGN IMPLICATIONS

We now summarize our results, compare them to the related work, and describe the implications for technology design.

Communication Routines

Our results described the communication routines of grandparents and grandchildren, which mostly focused on phone and video chat conversations. Previous work primarily focuses on understanding how children can be engaged through shared activities such as reading books or playing board games [3,26]. However, we have found that grandparents are also able to engage children with direct conversation. Thus, feelings of closeness and togetherness are also coming from shared awareness through conversation. For grandchildren, this comes from a high level understanding of major events in the grandparents' lives. For grandparents, this comes from low-level detailed knowledge about the grandchildren.

Overall, this suggests that, in addition to the systems we see in the related work that already focus on storytelling and activities, grandparents and grandchildren would also find value in systems focused on shared conversation. These systems should certainly be easy to use such that even grandparents and young grandchildren who have minimal knowledge of computers can use them without extra help. We also recognize that children have limited attention spans and may value conversing intermittently in more of an asynchronous manner; in general, grandparents like to 'talk more' and children like to 'talk less.' This suggests grandparent-grandchild conversations may best be supported through a mixture of asynchronous and synchronous technologies. If children are interested in talking for longer periods of time, they can use tools such as video chat. Yet those with more limited attention span in the current moment may benefit from the ability to record and send messages back and forth with grandparents. One may also consider video chat with multiple cameras or displays that allow children to migrate between rooms.

Conversational Content

Our results also showed that the content of conversations between grandparents and grandchildren is focused around new ideas and skills that children have learned, unexpected 'stuff' and interesting situations in both parties' lives, storytelling of both a fictional and real life nature, sharing experiences, and cultural exchanges. Each of these presents design opportunities for new communication technologies for grandparents and grandchildren where the majority are not described in the prior research. The related work has shown the large interest that children have in reading and listening to stories over distance [3,26]. We build on this understanding to show children would also love to hear stories about their parents when they were children or themselves when they were born. Thus, our work highlights the importance of personal stories, in addition to fictional stories from books.

This suggests that designers of communication technologies for grandparents and grandchildren could focus on enabling them with storytelling tools or features in an interactive and engaging way that can allow them to talk about their experiences such as traveling to new places with their remote grandchildren or telling them real stories where grandchildren or their parents are the main characters. This can even go beyond the idea of seeing 'talking heads' tell stories to incorporate real world visuals, pictures, and media that (e.g., [21]). This avenue may also allow grandparents to share cultural knowledge, if desired by the parents, where cultural stories could be embedded within communication technologies.

Beyond storytelling, we also see design opportunities for communication technologies to allow grandparents to support grandchildren in showing them the things they have learned to do, as well as the experiences they have in-the-moment (e.g., sports events [13]). This is a rich new area which has a high potential for technological improvement.

Social Situations and Challenges

Our results also described the social situations and challenges that can emerge for grandparent-grandchild communication over distance. These are not reported in the prior literature and present many interesting design challenges. Most importantly, they show that grandchild-grandparent communication is not always the ideal situation that much of the related work paints a picture of; conflict and difficult situations can easily emerge.

Becoming Separated by Distance

First, it can be especially challenging for grandparents and grandchildren to communicate when distance separation first arises. Thus, even the best-created design solutions (e.g., systems proposed in the related work [3,15,16,21,26]) may not be used by grandparents and grandchildren in real situations where separation has only recently occurred. Technology designs for cases of recent separation may best be focused on reminiscing about the mutual memories that grandparents and grandchildren hold. There may also be great value in using technology to show that grandparents still love their grandchildren (e.g., a huggable teddy or doll that 'transmits' such emotion). Then, when grandchildren are 'ready,' designs that allow them to share aspects of their new life with their grandparents may be beneficial.

Parental Support and Scaffolding

Second, we also found that some parents valued grandparents providing parental support during communication with their children. This was more desirable in divorced families where only one parent was taking care of the children, new immigrant families where parents were struggling with day-to-day responsibilities, or situations where parents did not have the necessary knowledge.

As a result, communication systems that allow grandparents to remotely help grandchildren with certain activities would be valuable for some people. Activities may include homework, extra-curricular planning, teaching a native language, or learning hygiene practices (e.g., brushing one's teeth). In such situations, careful and creative design is needed in order to provide a shared space for both parties to interact in where objects can be seen and gestured at. One must also consider real world privacy issues that might arise from the natural locations for such activities (e.g., a bathroom for teaching hygiene practices), as well as the social issues that could emerge where some parents may not want grandparents to 'interfere' past a certain threshold or introduce particular behaviors.

The related work has shown the need for parental scaffolding for grandparent-grandchild conversations over video chat because of technical challenges [**Error! Bookmark not defined.**,19]. Because of this, one may naively try to design video chat systems that removed the need for such scaffolding. However, this could easily create additional social tensions as some parents may, again, be concerned about grandparent interference in daily life, especially if they are not present during grandparent-child interactions. In turn, grandparents may be concerned about over-stepping their bounds if parents are not around. While cumbersome, parental scaffolding allows parents to observe grandparent and grandchild interactions to ensure they are desirable. Removing such scaffolding completely may introduce new problems. This suggests designs should attempt to mitigate parental scaffolding challenges, while still encouraging parental supervision during communication sessions.

Self-Consciousness and Perceived Annoyances

Third, despite being the older, experienced person in life, grandparents were sometimes self-conscious during conversations with their grandchildren. They did not always know what to talk about, did not want to make grandchildren upset, and did not want to feel like they knew little about their grandchild and exacerbate the feelings of a lack of connection. Moreover, even though they wanted to know lots of low level details about their grandchildren, they did not always want to ask because they perceived that the grandchildren or their parents may become easily annoyed. This is a social challenge that technology cannot solve alone. Yet one could think about focusing new designs on trying to foster confidence in grandparents by providing them with more information about their grandchildren without forcing them to ask or be told.

For example, one might imagine awareness systems, such as a shared family calendar, as providing an awareness of a grandchild's life to the grandparent. These systems can update grandparents in the background about topics that children are not interested in talking about. Designing applications that encourage children to provide information offline about their daily life, friends, and school activities in the form of paintings or other media could be also useful. This information could be used to increase the grandparent's true knowledge of the child and act as seeds for conversation. Grandparents may then feel more confident that they know information about their grandchildren, which could in turn reduce feelings of perceived annoyance since they may have to ask less in order to learn all of the details they are interested in knowing about their grandchildren.

Exchanging Cultural Information

Lastly, we learned that exchanging cultural information between grandparents and grandchildren was valued, yet it was sometimes difficult because of language barriers and other clashes of culture. This suggests design opportunities for cultural exchange between grandparents and grandchildren. Here it would be important that designers consider the effects of different languages on shared information and, possibly, even provide support for language learning for grandparents, grandchildren, or both. Designs could leverage existing storytelling systems (e.g., [3,24]) and couple them with stories focused on cultural knowledge exchange or the use of visual content as opposed to language-specific text. Of course, we also saw tensions about when and how to share cultural knowledge with children and this would need to be carefully thought through such that designs were targeted at appropriate ages.

Study Limitations

While valuable, our research also had several limitations. Our methods were largely retrospective and we did not observe any communication in practice because of concerns about behavior change during such observations. Results may have also been stronger if we had interviewed dyads of grandparents/parents. This would have allowed us to hear both sides of the story to understand social challenges, issues, conflicts, etc. Unfortunately we faced many real world challenges in finding study participants that fit our demographics. There were also sometimes language barriers which meant it would not have been possible to interview some dyads. We also suggest that future research explore children's perspectives on grandparent-grandchild communication to complement our study.

CONCLUSION

Our paper contributes a study of the routines and needs of grandparents and parents for grandparent-grandchild conversations over distance. Through a diary and interview study we found that distance-separated grandparents and grandchildren usually communicate around several main themes, including recent learning, unexpected 'stuff', storytelling, sharing experiences, and cultural exchange. Parents also desire parental support to varying degrees. While grandparent-grandchild communication is highly valued, it is not without its challenges. Both parents and grandparents must deal with social issues that arise from potential interference, a lack of truly knowing one's grandchild (leading to self-consciousness and feelings of perceived annoyance), and cultural differences. This suggests a new perspective for the design of grandparent-grandchild communication systems that attempt to balance the need for information exchange and support with solutions to the social issues being faced.

ACKNOWLEDGMENTS

We thank NSERC and the GRAND Network of Centres of Excellence DIGIKIDZ project for funding this research.

REFERENCES

1. Ames, M., Go, J., Kaye, J., and Spasojevic, M. Making love in the network closet: the benefits and work of family videochat. *Proc. CSCW 2010 , 145-154*
2. Ballagas, R., Kaye, J., Ames, M., Go, J., and Raffle, H. Family communication: phone conversations with children. *Proc. IDC 2009 , 321-324*
3. Ballagas, R., Raffle, H., Go, J., Revelle , J., Kaye, J., Ames, M., Horri, H., Mori, K., and Spasojevic, M., Story Time for the 21st Century. *IEEE Pervasive Computing*, 9(3), (2010), 28-36.
4. Becker, O. A., and Steinbach, A. (2012). Relations between Grandparents and Grandchildren in the Context of the Family System. *Comparative Population Studies*, *37*(3/4), (2012) 543-566
5. Cao, X., Sellen, A., Brush, A. J. B., Kirk, D., Edge, D., and Ding, X., Understanding family communication across time zones. *Proc. CSCW 2010, 155-158.*

6. Du, H., Inkpen, K., Chorianopoulos, K., Czerwinski, M., Johns, P., Hoff, A., Roseway, A., Morlidge, S., Tang, J., and Gross, T. VideoPal: Exploring Asynchronous Video-Messaging to Enable Cross-Cultural Friendships. *Proc. ECSCW 2011, 273-292.*
7. Druin A. "The Role of Children in the Design of New Technology" Behaviour and Information Technology, Vol. 21(1) , 1-25 (2002).
8. Evjemo, B., Svendsen, G. B., Rinde, E., and Johnsen, J. A. K. (2004, October). Supporting the distributed family: the need for a conversational context. *Proc Nordi CHI 2004, 309-312*
9. Follmer, S., Ballagas, R., Raffle, H., Spasojevic, M., and Ishii, H., People in books: using a FlashCam to become part of an interactive book for connected reading. *Proc. CSCW 2012* , 685–694.
10. Geurts, T., van Tilburg, T. G., and POORTMAN, A. R. The grandparent–grandchild relationship in childhood and adulthood: A matter of continuation?. *Personal Relationships*, *19*(2), (2010) 267-278.
11. Hutchinson, H., Mackay, W., Westerlund, B., Bederson, B., Druin, A., Plaisant, C., Beauduin, M., Conversy, S., Evans, H., Hansen, H., Roussel, N., Eiderback, B., Lindquist, S. and Sundbad, Y. Technology probes: inspiring design for and with families, *Proc. CHI,* ACM Press (2003), 17-24.
12. Inkpen, K., Du, H., Roseway, A., Hoff, A., Johns, P. Video kids: augmenting close friendships with asynchronous video conversations in videopal, *Proc. CHI,* ACM Press (2012).
13. Inkpen, K., Taylor, B., Junuzovic, S., Tang, J., and Venolia, G., Experiences2Go: Sharing Kids' Activities Outside the Home with Remote Family Members. CSCW 2013.
14. Judge, T., K., Neustaedter, C. Sharing conversation and sharing life: video conferencing in the home. *Proc. CHI 2010* , 655-658.
15. Judge, T., K., Neustaedter, C. The family window: the design and evaluation of a domestic media space. *Proc. CHI 2010* , 2361–2370.
16. Judge, T. Neustaedter, C., Harrison, S., and Blose, A., The Family Portals: Connecting Families Through a Multifamily Media Space. *Proc. CHI*, ACM Press (2011).
17. Junuzovic, S., Inkpen, K., Blank, T., and Gupta, A. IllumiShare: Sharing Any Surface, *Proc. CHI,* ACM Press (2012).
18. Kenner, C., Ruby, M., Jessel, J., Gregory, E., and Arju, T. Intergenerational learning between children and grandparents in East London. *Journal of Early Childhood Research, 5*(3), (2007) 219-243.
19. Kirk, D., Sellen, A., and Xianc, A., Home Video Communication: Mediating Closeness, *Proc. CSCW,* ACM Press (2010), 135-144.
20. Lin, M. C., Harwood, J., and Bonnesen, J. L. Conversation topics and communication satisfaction in grandparent-grandchild relationships. *Journal of Language and Social Psychology*, *21*(3), (2002).
21. Moffatt, K., David, J., and Baecker, R. M., Connecting Grandparents and Grandchildren. *Connecting Families*, C. Neustaedter, S. Harrison, and A. Sellen, Eds. *Springer (2013)*, 173–193.
22. Mynatt, E. D., Rowan, J., Craighill, S., & Jacobs, A. Digital family portraits. *Proc. CHI*, ACM Press (2001).
23. Neustaedter, C., Elliot, K. and Greenberg, S., Interpersonal awareness in the domestic realm. *Proc. OzCHI*, ACM Press (2006).
24. Raffle, H., Ballagas, R., Revelle, G., Horii, H., Follmer, S., Go, J., Reardon, E., Mori, K., Kaye, J., and Spasojevic, Family story play: reading with young children (and elmo) . *Proc. CHI 2010* , 1583–1592.
25. Raffle, H., Ballagas, R., Revelle, G., Mori, K., Horri, H., Paretti, C., Spasojevic, M. Pop goes the cell phone: *asynchronous messaging for preschoolers. Proc. IDC 2011, 99-108.*
26. Raffle, H., Revelle, G., Mori, K., Ballagas, R., Buza, K., Horii, H., Kaye, J., Cook, K., Freed, N., Go, J., and Spasojevic, M. Hello, is grandma there? let's read! StoryVisit: family video chat and connected e-books. *Proc. CHI 2011 , 1195-1204*
27. Romero, N., Markopoulos, P., Baren, J., Ruyter, B., Ijsselsteijn, W. and Farshchian, B. Connecting the family with awareness systems. *Personal Ubiquitous Computing*, *11* (4), (2007), 299-312.
28. Tee, K., Brush, A.J. and Inkpen, K. Exploring communication and sharing between extended families. *International Journal of Human-Computer Studies*, *67* (2), (2009), 128-138.
29. Vetere, F., Davis, H., Gibbs, M., and Howard, S. The Magic Box and Collage: Responding to the challenge of distributed intergenerational play. *International Journal of Human-Computer Studies*, 67(2), (2009).
30. Vutborg, R., Kjeldskov, J., Paay, J., Pedell, S., and Vetere, F. Supporting young children's communication with adult relatives across time zones. *Proc.OzCHI 2011, 291-300.*
31. Vutborg, R., Kjeldskov, J., Pedell, S., and Vetere, F. Family storytelling for grandparents and grandchildren living apart. *Proc. NordiCHI*, ACM Press (2010).
32. Yarosh, S., Inkpen, K. M., and Brush, A. J. B., Video playdate: toward free play across distance. *Proc CHI,* ACM Press (2010), *1251-1260.*
33. Zimmerman, F. J., Gilkerson, J., Richards, J. A., Christakis, D. A., Xu, D., Gray, S., and Yapanel, U. Teaching by listening: the importance of adult-child conversations to language development. *Pediatrics*, *124*(1), (2009), 342-349.

Growing Closer on Facebook: Changes in Tie Strength Through Social Network Site Use

Moira Burke
Facebook
mburke@fb.com

Robert Kraut
Human-Computer Interaction Institute
Carnegie Mellon University
robert.kraut@cs.cmu.edu

ABSTRACT

Scientists debate whether people grow closer to their friends through social networking sites like Facebook, whether those sites displace more meaningful interaction, or whether they simply reflect existing ties. Combining server log analysis and longitudinal surveys of 3,649 Facebook users reporting on relationships with 26,134 friends, we find that communication on the site is associated with changes in reported relationship closeness, over and above effects attributable to their face-to-face, phone, and email contact. Tie strength increases with both one-on-one communication, such as posts, comments, and messages, and through reading friends' broadcasted content, such as status updates and photos. The effect is greater for composed pieces, such as comments, posts, and messages than for "one-click" actions such as "likes." Facebook has a greater impact on non-family relationships and ties who do not frequently communicate via other channels.

Author Keywords

Tie strength; friendship; social relationships; relational closeness; families; social network sites; Facebook

ACM Classification Keywords

H.5.3 [Information Interfaces]: Group and Organization Interfaces - Collaborative computing, Web-based interaction, Computer-supported cooperative work.

INTRODUCTION

Social relationships are dynamic. Students make new friends in college, parents and teens negotiate the vagaries of adolescence, and coworkers depart for other companies. Communication drives the development and maintenance of relationships [10], at least off-line. Although social network sites (SNS) like Facebook and Google+ provide myriad ways to interact, their effect on relationships is ambiguous [24,28,36]. That people have very strong relationships online is not in dispute; 40% of SNS users have "friended" all of their closest offline confidants online [15], and tie strength can be inferred from site use [14,24]. But whether these sites simply reflect relationships maintained through other channels, displace more meaningful interactions, or enhance relationships is an open question.

The present study examines the connection between Facebook use and changes in relationship strength. It examines how the frequency of phone, email, and face-to-face conversations and different styles of Facebook communication for 26,134 pairs of friends predict changes in self-reported relationship strength month-to-month. People grow closer the more they communicate on Facebook, over and above communication via other channels. Exchanging substantive messages and comments with friends on Facebook and reading friends' news are associated with increases in tie strength, while exchanging less content-filled, "one-click" communicative acts, such as "likes," does not. The effect is stronger for non-family and for friends who rarely communicate via other media.

RELATIONSHIP FORMATION AND MAINTENANCE

Regular contact is at the heart of relationships with friends [1]. Communication jump starts relationships; People like each other better when they communicate more. And communication keeps them going; Duck describes "centripetal forces" acting on friendships that pull them apart without regular communication [10]. As a result, maintaining a portfolio of relationships requires sizable investment [18]. In particular, friendships are at greatest risk of failure when they are new. Each new relationship is a potential competitor for time invested in existing friends. Therefore, when two people first meet, they look for clues to evaluate whether the relationship's benefits will be worth its effort [2]. Because of competition with existing ties, many potential relationships never get started and others fail quickly.

While friendships require injections of communication to thrive, family relationships are generally more resilient and require less communication [1,29]. Kinship ties are resilient because of biological selection pressures to favor those who share a genetic line [29], early childhood experiences that foster strong attachments [4], and social institutions including marriage and child custody laws that support kinship. In contrast, friendship ties are more dependent on communication "because there are no institutional pressures for permanence" [25].

CHI 2014, April 26 - May 01 2014, Toronto, ON, Canada

http://dx.doi.org/10.1145/2556288.2557094

Social Technology and Relationships

Social network sites like Facebook change the economics of relationship initiation and decay, by making communication with specific others and broadcasts to whole networks more efficient. On Facebook, after a person initiates a friend request that is accepted by another, both parties receive regular updates about the other's social news. Without an explicit "unfriending," the connection and exchange of news persists [16].

Even though these sites make communication easier, some critics believe they foster superficial relationships. A common concern is that technology instills a false sense of connection [32], or that cognitive capacity and time limit the number and quality of relationships we can maintain, a constraint not mitigated by the Internet [28]. Moreover, early Internet research argued that people may have difficulty maintaining relationships online because computer-mediated communication is less rich [31], more effortful to produce, and more subject to misunderstanding than spoken conversation [23]. However, even if the early Internet was less effective in supporting social relationships than phone calls or in-person contact [22], the technology, norms, and Internet-using population have changed. With 72% of online adults in the US using social network sites, people now have a critical mass of close friends online [15]. People typically use the Internet to communicate with friends with whom they have existing off-line relationships, and do so using a variety of media [17].

Because people tend to communicate with the same partners both off-line and online [17,36], determining whether social network sites affect interpersonal relationships requires understanding how they fit into a broader ecology of communication. Though much research has established that people talk to friends over a variety of channels, we do not know whether SNS add anything over in-person conversation, phone calls, and email. Therefore, this study is guided by the following research question:

RQ1. Is communication between two people on Facebook associated with changes in tie strength beyond the effects of their communication by other channels, such as email, the phone, and in-person conversation?

Most previous work on this topic has been cross-sectional, simply measuring correlations between site use and tie strength, without being able to demonstrate causality. To overcome this problem, the present research uses longitudinal data, measuring both SNS use and tie strength at multiple points in time, to better infer causation from correlational data. Through these methods, the study then reveals the connection between Facebook use and *changes* in tie strength. While it is impossible to truly determine a causal relationship without random assignment—e.g., by randomly preventing some friends from communicating for a month—our method eliminates many confounds when inferring causation in observational studies.

CLASSES OF RELATIONAL COMMUNICATION

Online communication takes many forms, the details of which matter when considering its effect on relationships [6,12,35]. Most prior research on SNS has typically relied on self-report surveys, which tend to be inaccurate measures of interpersonal communication [3,19]. Furthermore, to reduce respondent burden these surveys generally fail to differentiate types of communication or partners, thus preventing researchers from conducting finer-grained analyses. The present study uses server data to avoid self-report biases and delve into specific types of communication and relationships.

Acts of communication can influence interpersonal ties though two routes. They deliver substantive content, such as self-disclosure, expression of support and simple small talk, which can directly influence tie strength. In addition, the mere act of communication independent of its content provides a symbolic message about the time and effort one person is willing to invest in another. On both of these dimensions, written exchanges targeted at specific partners are likely to have greater impact on relationship strength than untargeted broadcasts to a wider, undifferentiated circle of friends, passive monitoring of partners' broadcasts, and 'one-click' communication requiring little investment.

Directed, one-on-one communication

One-on-one communication strengthens relationships, both offline [4,10] and online (e.g., email and instant messenger) [17,33]. Similarly, Vitak [36] finds that geographically distant dyads or those for whom Facebook is their primary mode of communication report that Facebook has a positive impact on the closeness and stability of their relationship. One-on-one communication (hereafter "**directed communication**") is likely to strengthen relationships in part through self-disclosure and small-talk; revealing intimate thoughts and feelings increases liking [8]. And even small, seemingly trivial details, such as what someone had for lunch, "represents a form of communication that is critical to developing relationships," "a way of maintaining a sense of community or fellowship with others," a proving ground for both new and established relationships, and a prelude to deeper discussion [21] (p. 197-199). As Ellison and colleagues note, directed communication on Facebook also sustains relationships by signaling one person's level of caring about another. They term these exchanges "relationship maintenance behavior" that "signals attention and investment" in a friendship [12,36]. Writing on friends' walls or commenting on their photos is a form of social grooming that preserves connections between people [9]. Therefore, ties that exchange directed communication on Facebook should grow closer.

Different types of directed communication, both online and off, vary in the effort they demand and therefore their symbolic value. Consider the difference between a lengthy, handwritten letter and a postcard. Both provide information about the writer and indicate that the sender cares for the recipient, but the letter contains more content and took more effort. Social signaling theory suggests that because the lengthier message "costs more" recipients are more likely to use it as a reliable signal of relationship worth [30,37]. Ties should grow closer when they exchange more content-full and effortful forms of communication.

SNS communication can also be categorized in terms of the amount of content it contains and the effort required to produce it. **Composed communication**, such as private messages, wall posts, or comments, contain more content and require more effort to produce than **one-click interactions**, such as Facebook's "like" button or Google's "+1" button. The latter may reduce the cost associated with initiating or maintaining relationships because they require little premeditated thought. However, the fact that they require less effort may reduce their value in signaling relationship closeness. Beyond the signal conveyed by the differing degrees of effort, composed and one-click communication also vary in content. One-click actions are textless, and thus cannot possibly contain the kind of language associated with strong ties, such as self-disclosure or details of daily life. Therefore, composed communication is likely to bring ties closer together, one-click communication less so.

H1. Tie strength (a) increases with directed communication exchanges on SNS; (b) the is effect stronger for composed communication than one-click exchanges.

Broadcasts and Consumption

Friendships entail an obligation to keep up with each others' lives [1]. Learning the details of a tie's life, however, does not necessarily require direct communication. Broadcasted messages, such as holiday letters or Facebook status updates, distribute personal news to a wide audience of friends, family, and acquaintances.

Keeping up with a tie's life may be meaningful in its own right for the details learned, and it may make future one-on-one interactions more efficient or satisfying by filling in the news that occurred since the last interaction. Facebook aggregates news in a stream known as the News Feed, which contains ties' recent photos, status updates, and notifications of their activity, such as new friendships or their posts on other friends' walls. This kind of activity is comparable to small talk, quick bursts of information about friends' daily lives [21]. Much of these social streams is "me now"-focused content. [27,34], yet even these mundane details are commonly considered the building blocks of close relationships [11,21]. Therefore, passively consuming the details of ties' lives should be associated with increases in tie strength.

However, passive consumption is one-sided. Unlike in a bidirectional conversation, the recipients do not automatically indicate whether they have received a piece of news and can't easily engage in the back-channel communication that clarifies it. Therefore, the effect of directed communication, which notifies the recipient of the tie's interest and encourages responses, should be associated with greater increases in closeness than passive consumption.

H2. Tie strength (a) increases through passively consuming a tie's news on social network sites, but (b) the effect is weaker than receiving directed, composed communication from that tie.

Finally, broadcasting one's own news takes a one-size-fits-all approach that is inherently less intimate and requires less effort per-capita than writing an original letter or visiting each person in one's social circle. While these one-to-many missives may include self-disclosure—such as information about a family member's recent illness or feelings about a job—they are not focused at any particular recipient, and thus are less tailored to any given relationship and its history. Therefore, broadcasting may be less valuable for strengthening specific relationships than sending directed, composed communication.

H3. Tie strength (a) increases with broadcasting, but (b) less so than through sending directed, composed communication to that tie.

Interactions Between Tie Type and SNS Use

As previously reviewed, different kinds of ties are more or less susceptible to relationship decay [7,13], and so the link between SNS use and tie strength should differ by the type of relationship. Kin relationships have institutional support [25] and evolutionary pressure to persist [29], while non-kin relationships may need more regular interaction to survive. Similarly, ties who see each other frequently in person, or talk on the phone or email regularly may be less affected by their interactions on SNS. Indeed, Vitak found that ties for whom Facebook is their primary mode of communication report engaging in more relationship-maintenance behaviors on the site, and perceive Facebook as having a greater impact on their relationships [36]. However, for fledgling connections, social network sites may be more important. SNS provide the means and opportunity to communicate [17]; these ties may have no other ways of growing their relationships.

H4. Social network sites are more important among dyads at greater risk of relationship decay or among those that have few alternative communication mechanisms available, e.g., for non-kin ties, new relationships, and dyads not communicating over other channels.

METHODS

To analyze the relationship between SNS activity and changes in tie strength, we conducted a three-wave survey of Facebook users in June, July, and August 2011. The survey contained questions about their relationships with up to eight ties on Facebook. Survey responses were matched to the server logs of the participants' Facebook activity.

Participants

Participants (N = 11,701, 52% female, aged 13 – 90) were recruited through a combination of Facebook ads and email invitations. Recruiting was targeted at English-speaking users around the world who had been active on the site in the previous 30 days, stratified by gender and activity level (login days in the past month). Participants who completed at least two consecutive waves of the survey (n = 3,649) were included in analysis. Compared to a random sample of Facebook users at the time of the first wave, survey takers were 13.5 years older and 11% more likely to be female, had approximately 70 more friends than average, and had about twice the likelihood of logging in during the week prior to the survey (all $p < 0.001$).

Survey: Tie Strength, Communication Frequency, and Relationship Type

Respondents completed an online survey about their relationships with 26,134 Facebook friends. First, they were presented with a name generator question from [26]: "*Who are the people you feel closest to? This might include people you discuss important matters with, really enjoy socializing with, or anyone else you feel especially close to. Select up to 6 people. It's also okay to select no one.*" They chose up to 6 close friends (M = 4.4) from the widget commonly used for event invitations. The survey tool augmented this list with two or more randomly selected ties (totaling 8).

For each alter in random order, the system presented a set of questions (see [5], Appendix A for complete version), including:

1. *How close do you feel to [name]? (7 pts: Not at all close ... Somewhat close ... Extremely close)*
2. *Over the PAST MONTH, about how often have you and [name] talked in person? On the phone? Online/email (not Facebook)? (5 pts each: None ... Once ... Few times per month ... Few times per week ... Daily)*
3. *Which of the following describe your relationship with [name]? (Checkboxes: Friend, Professional colleague, Current romantic relationship, Former romantic relationship, Family member, We live together, Friend of a friend, Friend from long ago, Someone I recently met, I don't know who [name] is, None of the above.*
4. *Has Facebook affected your relationship with [name]? If so, please explain how. (Open-ended)*

Ties in the study were relatively strong (M = 4.7 out of 7, Median = 5.0, SD = 2.2) but represented a wide variety of tie strengths (Min = 1, Max = 7). Ties that participants selected via the name generator were very strong (M = 6.0), compared to the randomly selected ties (M = 2.9).

Behavioral Log Data

Site activity was collected for respondents and their ties beginning one month prior to the first survey through the date of the final survey, three months later. All data are anonymized counts. In the following sections, the term "ego" refers to the person who took the survey and "alter" refers to one of the people the respondent rated. Activity variables were divided into three categories (see Table 1): directed communication (by ego or alter), passive consumption of alter's news, and broadcasting (by ego or alter). Within each category variables are highly correlated with each other and so are collapsed into a single composite scale representing the entire category.

Directed communication consists of counts of targeted, one-on-one exchanges between ego and alter, such as wall posts, private messages, or comments. It only includes activity within the dyad, not with other ties. Directed communication is further separated into **one-click interactions**, when someone presses a single button ("like" or "poke"), and **composed interactions**, in which someone composes original text, such as a message or comment.

Broadcasting is the wider-audience posting a user performs, including photo uploads and status updates. This scale includes anything that is not targeted at a single friend. While some users have privacy settings enabled so that their broadcasts go to a limited number of Facebook friends, these actions are still counted as broadcasting to distinguish them from the single-friend focus of directed communication. Broadcasting by both ego and alter are included (separately) in models.

Passive consumption is comprised of viewing and reading other friends' broadcasted content, usually as feed stories, but also looking at a friend's profile and photos. This scale measures the extent to which a user consumes content, but does not communicate with the content owner about it.

Broadcasting and passive consumption are related but separate: A person may passively consume some, but not necessarily all of the content a friend broadcasts, depending on how often she logs in, how many other friends' stories are competing for space in her feed, and whether she visits her friend's profile to view older content.

Method of Analysis

To determine how site use relates to changes in tie strength, a multilevel linear model was created with ego's response to "*How close do you feel to [name]?*" as the dependent variable and communication measures as independent variables. The model includes a lagged dependent variable (reported tie strength last month) as a control. That is, the model predicts reported tie strength at time t as a linear combination of reported tie strength thirty days prior and communication activities during the intervening month, on Facebook and via other channels (email, face-to-face, or phone, as self-reported). Static data about the dyad (e.g., ages, sexes, whether they live in the same city) are included as controls (see Table 2). The model was grouped at the ego and alter levels to account for non-independence of the ego's responses, both about his or her alters and about the same alter on multiple occasions.

Facebook activity scales and items
Directed communication (by ego or alter)
(scale alphas: ego to alter = 0.66, alter to ego = 0.65)
Messages written to tie‡
Comments written on tie's content‡
Posts written on tie's wall‡
Likes†
Pokes†
Passive consumption by ego (scale alpha = 0.51)
Profile views
News Feed story clicks
Photo views
Broadcasting (by ego or alter)
(scale alphas: ego = 0.73, alter = 0.72)
Photos posted
Content posted to own wall
Status updates

‡ Composed communication
† One-click communication

Table 1. Classes of Facebook use. All activities are within dyads, e.g., "comments written" means comments written by ego to alter, or by alter to ego. All variables are log-transformed and standardized.

By including the lagged dependent variable, the model measures *changes* in tie strength associated with communication that took place in the month between surveys. Autoregressive lag models are common in econometrics and appropriate here, because the dependent variable is stationary and model residuals are not highly autocorrelated. Lagged independent variables (communication the previous month) are not included because they are highly collinear, and thus would produce biased estimates [20]. The three-wave design means that dyads are observed at least twice. This design produces measurements that are more robust to one-time, exogenous events such as holidays or birthdays, which may increase both Facebook activity and feelings of closeness.

RESULTS AND DISCUSSION

First we consider how Facebook use compares with other channels. Dyads who communicate regularly on Facebook also communicate over other channels: There is a modest positive correlation between directed communication on Facebook and on the phone (r = 0.26), online (outside of Facebook) (r = 0.26), and face-to-face (r = 0.24). Similar correlations are found between passive consumption on Facebook and communication via other channels.

Our main analysis examines how communication is associated with changes in tie strength month-to-month. Table 2 contains three sections: controls, including the lagged dependent variable (which together account for 85% of the variance), general communication variables (which increase R^2 to 86%), and Facebook communication variables (R^2 = 87%). Each section progressively improves the model (p < 0.001). Notice that the control portion

	Reported tie strength		
	Value	SE	p-value
(Intercept)	4.50	0.01	0.00***
Controls			
Reported tie strength last month	0.76	0.00	0.00***
Ego age (decades)	0.05	0.01	0.00***
Age difference (decades)	0.00	0.01	0.67
Ego is male†	0.04	0.01	0.00**
Same gender†	0.02	0.01	0.01**
Ego's friend count‡	0.00	0.03	0.99
Alter's friend count‡	-0.03	0.01	0.00***
Number of mutual friends	0.01	0.03	0.69
Is family†	0.27	0.01	0.00***
In a relationship together†	-0.13	0.03	0.00***
Same work†	-0.09	0.03	0.01*
Same school†	0.00	0.01	0.77
Same city†	-0.06	0.03	0.02*
General communication			
In-person contact	0.08	0.00	0.00***
Phone contact	0.10	0.01	0.00***
Online contact (not incl. Facebook)	0.11	0.00	0.00***
Facebook communication			
Directed communication			
Composed (alter to ego)	0.02	0.00	0.00***
Composed (ego to alter)	0.01	0.00	0.00**
One-click (alter to ego)	0.01	0.00	0.24
One-click (ego to alter)	0.00	0.00	0.95
Passive consumption by ego	0.02	0.00	0.00***
Broadcasting (by ego)	-0.02	0.01	0.03*
Broadcasting (by alter)	-0.03	0.01	0.00***

*** $p < 0.001$ ** $p < 0.01$ * $p < 0.05$ $R^2 = 0.87$

N=40,521 Egos=3,643 Alters=26,103
† Binary variable
‡ Continuous variable logged (base 2) and standardized
All continuous variables are centered at their means.

Table 2. Model of changes in ego-reported tie strength. Communicating on Facebook is related to changes in tie strength over and above changes attributable to other communication channels.

explains most of the variance (because tie strength does not change much month-to-month). With only 15% of the variance left to explain, the general communication variables explain 6.7% of this residual, and Facebook communication explains 7.1% of the remaining variance.

The intercept (4.50) in Table 2 represents the tie strength of the average dyad—one in which all continuous variables are at their means and all binary variables are zero. Therefore, the intercept represents a dyad where both the ego and alter are 43 years old, ego is female and alter is male, they have the average number of friends, are not family members, etc. Recall that tie strength is measured on a 7-point scale, so the closeness of the average dyad is above the midpoint of the scale. For every one-point increase in an independent variable, the estimated tie strength increases by the coefficient in the Value column. So, for every one point higher their tie strength was the previous month, their current tie strength is 0.76 points higher. (Tie strength one month correlates highly with tie strength the previous month, $r = 0.91$.) After accounting for this lagged dependent variable, all of the other coefficients represent the change in tie strength month-to-month associated with the other independent variables. A one-point increase in frequency of in-person contact (e.g., from a few times per month to a few times per week) is associated with a 0.08 point increase in tie strength. Phone and online contact (outside of Facebook) are also associated with increases in tie strength, consistent with previous research [17].

Directed Facebook Communication

Communication on Facebook was associated with increases in tie strength, beyond the effects of these other variables. H1a and b are confirmed: Directed communication was associated with significant increases in tie strength. However, the effect is only for composed communication (comments, messages, wall posts), not one-click communication ("likes" and "pokes"). A post-hoc test confirms that tie strength increases more with composed than one-click interactions ($\beta = 0.02, p < 0.001$). Notice this estimate is very conservative because the model also included communication initiated by ego, which may be a lead indicator of tie strength. When ego likes alter, ego is likely to comment and write more on alter's wall ($\beta = 0.01$, $p = 0.003$). Alter's communication toward ego seems to affect ego's reported closeness even when ego's communication toward alter is held constant.

The magnitude of these coefficients is smaller than the coefficients for non-Facebook communication (in-person, phone and other online). However, this comparison is misleading, because the coefficients for the non-Facebook communication measures are inflated from common-method biases. The non-Facebook communication measures are based on self-reports, which are generally inaccurate [3], while the measures of Facebook communication are based on more accurate server logs. When people report communication frequency with a partner, they compute this estimate based partly on their attachment to the partner, thus inflating the relationship between the two measures.

In their open-ended responses, respondents identified the connection between directed communication on Facebook and growing closer to ties.[1]

"Photos and comments and messaging allow us to be very close still even though we're 800 miles away."

"We got to 'know' each other through FB. We knew that both of us existed (she is daughter of my favorite cousin) but it was communication/comments/photos etc via FB that brought us little closer. we have never me personally but now we will. Thanks, in part, to fB."

In addition to offering a channel to share news, Facebook also allows the exchange of emotional support, which brings people closer:

"We have sent messages either on our wall posts or messages. I originally sent her a long supportive message regarding her struggles with her sick father and other issues. She was very grateful and over time we struck up a more meaningful relationship. We have given each other support via phone, email, fb, and have found that we have much in common and are working towards something longer term."

"facebook has given my granddaughter and myself the opportunity to talk about her fears of her mothers cancer privately she is only 13, and needs all the support I can give her only between her and I"

Moreover, they remarked on the lack of directed communication as a reason for concern:

"At least he could put in a comment or two making me realize that he's there."

In contrast, respondents rarely remarked on ties "liking" their content. The one exception mentioned a progression from "likes" to more content-filled interaction:

"my sister Theresa wasn't talking to me for 2 years...some falling out that was never forgiven...then one day she asked me to be her friend...slowly our conversation grew from her liking a few of my pics etc. to small comments to small messages and last week she messaged me to come and visit. So next week I will see her/speak with her for the first time in 2 years. I'm thankful for the non-threatening vibe of FB and hope we can communicate as easily in person...=)"

Overall, communication actions in which a tie takes the time to write a brief piece of text are linked with increases in tie strength, while one-click actions are not.

Passive Consumption and Broadcasting

We had predicted (H2a) that passive consumption—reading a tie's social news, looking at her photos and profile—would be associated with increases in tie strength. It is. When ego passively consumes news about alter, ego feels closer to alter, ($\beta = 0.02$, $p < 0.001$, Table 2). However, H2b is not confirmed: There is no difference between passively consuming a tie's news and receiving directed, composed communication from that tie ($\beta = 0.00, p = 0.99$). Reading and writing are both associated with increases in tie strength.

Why is passive consumption as effective as talking? Friends have an obligation to keep up with each others' lives [1],

[1] Quotes have been edited for length and names have been replaced, but are otherwise left as written.

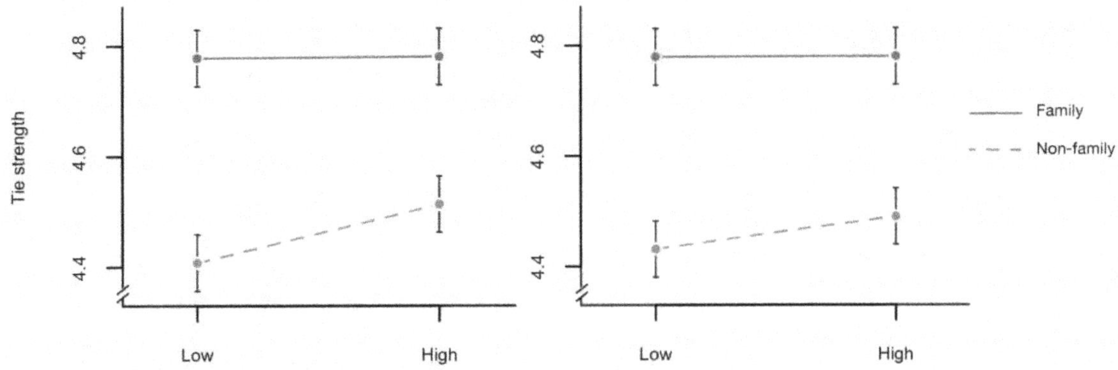

Figure 1. Different effects of Facebook on family and non-family relationships. For non-family members (dashed blue lines), increased Facebook use (directed communication or passive consumption) is associated with increases in tie strength. Neither activity significantly affects tie strength with family members (solid red lines).

and passive consumption allows friends and family members to keep up with small news and big events:

"With facebook we are able to keep up with what is going on with one another simply by reading the posts. It keeps us in touch without always having to talk."

"I get to see pictures and news of her children that have now graduated from college. I have known her and her family since her children were small. It's great to stay up on your friend's lives when you don't have time to see them."

What about broadcasting? After taking into account how much ego and alter directly communicated with each other, and how much content ego read about alter, ties appear to grow less close the more each one broadcasts content to a wider, undifferentiated circle. H3a is disconfirmed. Table 2 shows that as ego broadcasts more, she reports growing less close to any given alter; roughly one additional status update per month is associated with a 0.02 decline in tie strength ($p = 0.03$). Similarly, the more that alter broadcasts (but that ego does not necessarily read), ego reports growing less close ($\beta = -0.03$, $p < 0.001$). A post-hoc test confirms H3b: Receiving composed communication from alter is associated with greater increases in tie strength than alter's broadcasts, $\beta = 0.04$, $p < 0.001$, and ego's sending composed communication to alter is associated with greater increases in ego's reported tie strength with alter than ego's broadcasting, $\beta = 0.03$, $p = 0.005$ (all previous p's adjusted for multiple comparison). While broadcasting may be an efficient way to spread news to a large number of ties at once, merely having more information available about one's ties does not increase tie strength with any individual friend. The news must reach those ties (they need to consume it and/or directly talk with each other about it). Ego may see traces indicating the frequency of alter's broadcasts without actually reading all of those broadcasts; for example, you might not look at all of the photos in a friend's new photo album, but might see stories indicating that other friends commented on lots of photos within it. Facebook users may also hide a friend from their feed when they feel that friend's stories are too frequent, spammy, or political. In both of these cases, additional stories broadcast by alter but unseen by ego may account for ego's feelings of reduced closeness toward alter. The results speak to the importance of feed prioritization: Broadcasts have to make it in front of the right audience, or they have little value.

Facebook Communication with Different Kinds of Ties

Now we examine whether the effect size of Facebook communication differs by the type of tie. It does.

Family vs. non-family

Facebook communication is more strongly related to changes in tie strength for non-family than family (see Figure 1). A regression like that in Table 2 with an additional interaction term between directed communication and a binary variable representing family status bears this out.[2] Family members are less affected by directed communication (interaction: $\beta = -0.05$, SE = 0.01, $p < 0.001$) and passive consumption ($\beta = -0.03$, SE = 0.01, $p < 0.001$) than are non-family members; family status basically wipes out the gains from either activity. In Figure 1, the solid red line at the top represents family members, and the bottom dashed line represents non-family. The x-axis is split, showing directed communication one standard deviation below the mean and one standard deviation above the mean. Regardless of the amount of directed communication ego does with a family member, reported tie strength does not change. In contrast, tie strength increases with non-family members with directed communication (as shown by the upward slope of the dashed line).

Though neither directed communication nor passive consumption were associated with increases in tie strength

[2] See http://tinyurl.com/burkechi2014supp for these additional regressions omitted for space.

for family members (only non-family), respondents frequently remarked that Facebook allowed them to see other sides of their family, revealing personalities they do not get to see as a sibling or child.

"Yes, I get to see how she wants to present herself to her social world, which is different from how I get to interact with her in person as her cousin." "[My dad] is only on Facebook to see and share pictures of his grandkids, but it is interesting to read posts from his friends and see my dad as a social person rather than dad/grandpa."

"Josh is my son. I have been able to find out more about his friends and things he has been doing without having to feel like I am 'interogating or drilling' him about his personal life.."

These quotes center on passive consumption rather than directed communication—one's closest relationships may not require Facebook for one-on-one communication; they have other channels for that. Instead the site's value is in revealing the tie's wider interests and interactions with others, providing another lens on the family member's life.

Frequent versus infrequent contacts

As with kin, dyads who frequently communicate in person, on the phone, or over email do not report growing closer with increased Facebook communication. Frequent contacts—including ties who are in a romantic relationship, live together, or report talking a few times per week or more via the phone, email, or in person—are less affected by directed communication on Facebook ($\beta = -0.05$, $p < 0.001$) than infrequent contacts (everyone else). In contrast, passive consumption does not affect these two groups differently ($p = 0.29$). This confirms previous work based on self-reports of Facebook usage showing that SNS are more important for ties who do not have other regular means of communication [36].

The open-ended comments suggest that when dyads directly communicate on Facebook in addition to their regular face-to-face interaction, they use Facebook for photos, videos, and games:

"We see each other almost everyday so we do not use Facebook to chat or keep up to date, but we are able to share pictures of our adventures and it is an easy way to share links, websites, and videos."

Moreover, even though these strong ties use Facebook more for games and photos than for substantive communication, many respondents commented that they used Facebook for the next step in their relationship development after meeting their strong-tie partner for the first time. While Facebook may not be not important in maintaining a current relationship among strong ties, it seemed to have been important in achieving it in the first place.

"It's part of the reason we got together and ultimately got married. She found me on Facebook in college and sent a message, and we connected from there to begin our romantic relationship."

"Actually, it's how he got my phone number. We met through a friend and he didn't get my number, so he sent me a facebook message the next day. We now have been dating for over a year. But since then, no. We're not big on using FB to communicate."

"Charles and I were partners on many projects in college. We always meant to become better friends (e.g., 'We should go out to coffee sometime.' But, we never did. Ergo, we found each other on FB a few years later and started messaging each other. When I moved near him in recent years, we have become very close friends. It all started with Facebook."

New ties versus longstanding ties

Though respondents described using Facebook for the early steps in relationships, the quantitative data do not show different effects of Facebook use for new ties versus long-established ones. For ties the respondents marked as "someone I just met" (approximately 2% of ties, $n = 1480$), or for ties "friended" on Facebook in the last two months (approximately 9% of ties, $n = 7366$), the effect of directed communication on Facebook on tie strength is no different than for ties that have been connected longer ($p = 0.61$). Passive consumption also does not appear to affect new ties differently ($p = 0.31$). However, the present study does not include tie strength reports for extremely nascent ties—people with whom the respondents had not yet created a Facebook friendship. Therefore, it is possible that Facebook plays a role in uncertainty reduction with new ties, facilitating discreet lookups of each others' profiles and mutual friends, but this stage happens before one person initiates the friend request. After the tie is articulated on Facebook, use of the site is associated with increased tie strength, but the effects are no greater for new friends than more established ones.

CONCLUSION

This study examined the types of interaction on Facebook that are associated with changes in closeness over time. It demonstrates that social network sites like Facebook are a meaningful component in a portfolio of communication channels between friends.

This work demonstrates how social network sites fit into the ecology of communication media, showing changes in tie strength associated with Facebook use over and above the use of other channels. Table 3 summarizes the findings. Directed, composed communication is linked with increases in tie strength. So does passively reading a partner's posts. In contrast, both broadcasting by oneself and of one's partners is linked with declines in tie strength when those stories are not read. In this way, Facebook activity is both a reflection of tie strength as it is maintained elsewhere and a tool for nurturing relationships. Furthermore, the study unpacks different classes of communication common on

	Feature	Hypothesis	Confirmed
1a	Directed communication	Increases in tie strength	Y
b	Composed vs. one-click communication	Composed > one-click	Y
2a	Passive consumption	Increases in tie strength	Y
b	Passive consumption vs. receiving composed comm.	Passive < Receiving composed	N
3a	Broadcasting	Increases in tie strength	N
b	Broadcasting vs. sending composed communication	Broadcasting < Sending composed	Y
4	Kinship / frequent comm. elsewhere / longtime friend	SNS use less valuable for these relationships	Partial

Table 3. Summary of hypotheses and results

social network sites. We find that passive consumption—reading about ties without actually contacting them—is as strongly associated with growing closer to those ties as is directly receiving messages from them. Even though interpersonal communication literature indicates frequency of interaction and communication exchanges are the building blocks of relationships, the present study shows that two people may not have to synchronously interact or direct messages at each other to grow closer. Quietly taking in the mundane details of another's life also works.

Consistent with media multiplexity arguments that people use many channels to maintain relationships, this research suggests that Facebook supplements other channels. Communicating via Facebook is associated with changes in tie strength beyond communication in person, by phone or by email, although its influence is smaller for dyads that interact frequently via other media. Although family ties are less affected by Facebook activity than non-family, the qualitative data suggest that Facebook communication is valuable even for them. Siblings, children, and parents appreciate that the site reveals a different side of their kin. They see cousins talking candidly about politics, children interacting with peers, and grandparents as "social people" rather than simply fulfilling a grandparent role. Many parents valued learning about their teens' lives without intruding. Facebook can provide a different perspective on kin, even if it doesn't bring them closer.

Limitations and future work

The timeframe in the present study is short. Relationships take years to develop, and changes in tie strength may happen gradually over months or years, rather than the month-to-month window used here. However, despite the short window and the infrequent communication within dyads on Facebook, we do see substantive increases in tie strength, over and above those expected from numerous baselines, such as living together or talking on the phone. The sample is also biased toward strong ties, with more than half of the ties selected by participants as close friends. However, the sample includes a wide range of tie strengths and the sample size is much larger than previous survey-based studies, allowing in-depth examination of how Facebook affects different kinds of relationships.

Although we have suggested that the content of communication on Facebook drives some of the effects we observed, such as greater increases in tie strength for composed versus one-click communication, the research provides no direct evidence about communication content. A thorough, automated analysis of text exchanges may reveal linguistic markers of closeness missed in the present study. The relative impact of small talk is an open question in the literature, and the present study does not distinguish between chatty, mundane news, weightier disclosures and exchanges of support; it simply distinguishes between those directed at a specific tie or broadcast to all friends. Similarly, "composed" pieces differ in length and content, and it may be the case that shorter, more generic composed pieces (such as writing "happy birthday") are comparable to one-click actions: less powerful in eliciting feelings of closeness than longer, more meaningful messages.

Like all observational studies, this work is limited in its ability to infer causality. Participants were surveyed over time, but we cannot determine whether their communication patterns cause their relationships to grow closer, or if other underlying variables cause people to grow closer and to talk more. By unpacking different kinds of relationships, including kin and non-kin, frequent contacts and less frequent contacts, and new ties, as well as controlling for communication via other channels, we account for many other possible causal factors, but the study design cannot completely demonstrate causality.

Whether social technology brings us closer or provides a false sense of connection has been widely debated. The present study demonstrates that on average relationships improve when people use Facebook to communicate with each other.

ACKNOWLEDGMENTS

We thank Cameron Marlow for feedback. This project was supported by IIS-0808711 and IIS-0729286, and graduate research fellowships from the NSF and Google.

REFERENCES

1. Allan, G.A. *A sociology of friendship and kinship*. G. Allen & Unwin, 1979.
2. Berger, C.R. Beyond initial interaction: Uncertainty, understanding, and the development of interpersonal relationships. *Language and social psychology*, (1979), 122–144.
3. Bernard, H.R., Killworth, P., Kronenfeld, D., and Sailer,

L. The problem of informant accuracy: The validity of retrospective data. *Annual Review of Anthropology 13*, (1984), 495–517.

4. Berscheid, E. and Reis, H.T. Attraction and close relationships. *The handbook of social psychology 2*, (1998), 193–281.
5. Burke, M. *Reading, Writing, Relationships: The Impact of Social Network Sites on Relations and Well-Being.* Doctoral Dissertation. (2011). http://reports-archive.adm.cs.cmu.edu/anon/hcii/CMU-HCII-11-107.pdf.
6. Burke, M., Kraut, R.E., and Marlow, C. Social capital on Facebook: Differentiating uses and users. *Proceedings of the 29th international conference on human factors in computing systems (CHI '11)*, (2011), 571–580.
7. Burt, R. Decay functions. *Social Networks 22*, (2000), 1–28.
8. Collins, N.L. and Miller, L.C. Self-disclosure and liking: A meta-analytic review. *Psychological Bulletin 116*, 3 (1994), 457.
9. Donath, J. Signals in social supernets. *Journal of Computer-Mediated Communication 13*, 1 (2008), 231–251.
10. Duck, S. *Relating to others.* Dorsey Press, 1988.
11. Duck, S., Rutt, D.J., Hurst, M.H., and Strejc, H. Some evident truths about conversations in everyday relationships. *Human Communication Research 18*, 2 (1991), 228–267.
12. Ellison, N., Vitak, J., Grey, R., and Lampe, C. Cultivating Social Resources on Social Network Sites: Facebook Relationship Maintenance Behaviors and their Role in Social Capital Processes. *Journal of Computer-Mediated Communication*, (2014).
13. Fischer, C.S. *To dwell among friends: Personal networks in town and city.* University of Chicago Press, 1982.
14. Gilbert, E. and Karahalios, K. Predicting tie strength with social media. *Proc. 27th international conference on Human factors in computing systems (CHI '09)*, (2009), 211–220.
15. Hampton, K., Goulet, L.S., Rainie, L., and Purcell, K. *Social networking sites and our lives*. 2011.
16. Hampton, K.N., Lee, C.J., and Her, E.J. How new media affords network diversity: Direct and mediated access to social capital through participation in local social settings. *New Media & Society 13*, 7 (2011), 1031–1049.
17. Haythornthwaite, C. Strong, weak, and latent ties and the impact of new media. *The Information Society 18*, 5 (2002), 385–401.
18. Hill, R.A. and Dunbar, R.I.M. Social network size in humans. *Human Nature 14*, 1 (2003), 53–72.
19. Junco, R. Comparing actual and self-reported measures of Facebook use. *Computers in Human Behavior 29*, 3 (2013), 626–631.
20. Keele, L. and Kelly, N.J. Dynamic models for dynamic theories: The ins and outs of lagged dependent variables. *Political Analysis 14*, 2 (2006), 186.
21. Knapp, M.L. and Vangelisti, A.L. *Interpersonal communication and human relationships*. Allyn and Bacon Boston, 1992.
22. Kraut, R., Patterson, M., Lundmark, V., Kiesler, S., Mukophadhyay, T., and Scherlis, W. Internet paradox: A social technology that reduces social involvement and psychological well-being? *American Psychologist 53*, 9 (1998), 1017–1031.
23. Kruger, J., Epley, N., Parker, J., and Ng, Z.W. Egocentrism over e-mail: Can we communicate as well as we think?. *Journal of Personality and Social Psychology 89*, 6 (2005), 925.
24. Ledbetter, A.M., Mazer, J.P., DeGroot, J.M., Meyer, K.R., Yuping Mao, and Swafford, B. Attitudes Toward Online Social Connection and Self-Disclosure as Predictors of Facebook Communication and Relational Closeness. *Communication Research 38*, 1 (2011), 27–53.
25. Litwak, E. and Szelenyi, I. Primary group structures and their functions: Kin, neighbors, and friends. *American Sociological Review*, (1969).
26. Marin, A. and Hampton, K.N. Simplifying the Personal Network Name Generator. *Field Methods 19*, 2 (2007), 163–193.
27. Naaman, M., Boase, J., and Lai, C.H. Is it really about me?: message content in social awareness streams. *Proceedings of the 2010 ACM conference on Computer supported cooperative work*, (2010), 189–192.
28. Pollet, T.V., Roberts, S.G.B., and Dunbar, R.I.M. Use of Social Network Sites and Instant Messaging Does Not Lead to Increased Offline Social Network Size, or to Emotionally Closer Relationships with Offline Network Members. *Cyberpsychology, Behavior, and Social Networking 14*, 4 (2011), 253–258.
29. Roberts, S. and Dunbar, R.I.M. Communication in social networks: Effects of kinship, network size, and emotional closeness. *Personal Relationships*, (2010).
30. Spence, M. Job market signaling. *The quarterly journal of Economics 87*, 3 (1973), 355.
31. Sproull, L. and Kiesler, S. Reducing social context cues: Electronic mail in organizational communications. *Management science*, (1986), 1492–1512.
32. Turkle, S. *Alone together: Why we expect more from technology and less from each other*. Basic Books, 2011.
33. Valkenburg, P.M. and Peter, J. Preadolescents" and adolescents" online communication and their closeness to friends. *Developmental Psychology 43*, 2 (2007), 267.
34. van Grove, J. Twitter analysis: 40% of tweets are pointless babble. *Mashable*, 2009. http://mashable.com/2009/08/12/twitter-analysis/.
35. Vitak, J. Keeping connected in the Facebook age: The relationship between Facebook use, relationship maintenance strategies, and relational outcomes. (2012).
36. Vitak, J. Facebook Makes the Heart Grow Fonder: Relationship Maintenance Strategies Among Geographically Dispersed and Communication-Restricted Connections. (2014).
37. Zahavi, A. Mate selection--a selection for a handicap. *Journal of theoretical Biology 53*, 1 (1975), 205–214.

CHI 2014 Author Index

CHI 2014 Author Index

CHI 2014 Author Index

CHI 2014 Author Index

CHI 2014 Author Index

CHI 2014 Author Index

CHI 2014 Author Index

CHI 2014 Author Index

CHI 2014 Author Index

www.ingramcontent.com/pod-product-compliance
Lightning Source LLC
LaVergne TN
LVHW082343011026
849160LV00024B/1005